Small Business Sourcebook

ISSN 0883-3397

Small Business Sourcebook

Sourcebook

The Entrepreneur's Resource

THIRTIETH EDITION

Volume 2

Specific Small Business Profiles

(Entries 9231-18672)

Sonya D. Hill
Project Editor

GALE
CENGAGE Learning

Detroit • New York • San Francisco • New Haven, Conn • Waterville, Maine • London

Small Business Sourcebook, 30th edition

Project Editor: Sonya D. Hill

Editorial Support Services: Charles Beaumont

Composition and Electronic Prepress: Gary Leach

Manufacturing: Rita Wimberley

For product information and technology assistance, contact us at
Gale Customer Support, 1-800-877-4253.
For permission to use material from this text or product,
submit all requests online at **www.cengage.com/permissions.**
Further permissions questions can be emailed to
permissionrequest@cengage.com

While every effort has been made to ensure the reliability of the information presented in this publication, Gale, a part of Cengage Learning, does not guarantee the accuracy of the data contained herein. Gale accepts no payment for listing; and inclusion in the publication of any organization, agency, institution, publication, service, or individual does not imply endorsement of the editors or publisher. Errors brought to the attention of the publisher and verified to the satisfaction of the publisher will be corrected in future editions.

EDITORIAL DATA PRIVACY POLICY. Does this publication contain information about you as an individual? If so, for more information about our data privacy policies, please see our Privacy Statement at www.gale.cengage.com.

Gale
27500 Drake Rd.
Farmington Hills, MI, 48331-3535

ISBN-13: 978-1-4144-7957-6 (set)
ISBN-10: 1-4144-7957-3 (set)
ISBN-13: 978-1-4144-7958-3 (vol. 1)
ISBN-10: 1-4144-7958-1 (vol. 1)
ISBN-13: 978-1-4144-7959-0 (vol. 2)
ISBN-10: 1-4144-7959-X (vol. 2)
ISBN-13: 978-1-4144-7960-6 (vol. 3)
ISBN-10: 1-4144-7960-3 (vol. 3)
ISBN-13: 978-1-4144-7961-3 (vol. 4)
ISBN-10: 1-4144-7961-1 (vol. 4)
ISBN-13: 978-1-4144-7962-0 (vol. 5)
ISBN-10: 1-4144-7962-X (vol. 5)
ISBN-13: 978-1-4144-7963-7 (vol. 6)
ISBN-10: 1-4144-7963-8 (vol. 6)

ISSN 0883-3397

Printed in the United States of America
1 2 3 4 5   17 16 15 14 13

Contents

Volume 1

Introduction vii

User's Guide ix

Acknowledgments xv

List of Small Business Profiles xvii

Standard Industrial Classification (SIC) Codes for
   Profiled Small Businesses xxi

Licensing Assistance Programs xxxv

Guide to Publishers. xxxix

Glossary cxxv

Small Business Profiles 1

Provides start-up information, associations and other organizations, educational programs, directories of educational programs,
reference works, sources of supply, statistical sources, trade
periodicals, videocassettes/ audiocassettes, trade shows and
conventions, consultants, franchises and business opportunities,
computerized databases, computer systems/software, libraries,
and research centers.

Volume 2

Introduction. vii

User's Guide ix

Acknowledgments xv

List of Small Business Profiles xvii

Standard Industrial Classification (SIC) Codes for
   Profiled Small Businesses xxi

Small Business Profiles .601

Volume 3

Introduction. vii

User's Guide ix

Acknowledgments xv

List of Small Business Profiles xvii

Standard Industrial Classification (SIC) Codes for
   Profiled Small Businesses xxi

List of General Small Business Topics xxxv

Small Business Profiles .1205

General Small Business Topics 1380

Includes associations and other organizations, educational
programs, directories of educational programs, reference works,
sources of supply, statistical sources, trade periodicals,
videocassettes/audiocassettes, trade shows and conventions,
consultants, computerized databases, computer systems/
software, libraries, and research centers.

Volume 4

Introduction. vii

User's Guide ix

Acknowledgments xv

List of General Small Business Topics xvii

General Small Business Topics 1827

Volume 5

Introduction. vii

User's Guide ix

Acknowledgments xv

List of General Small Business Topics xvii

General Small Business Topics 2459

State Listings 2679

Offers sources of small business assistance by state, territory,
and Canadian province, including small business development
centers, small business assistance programs, SCORE offices,
better business bureaus, chambers of commerce, minority business assistance programs, financing and loan programs, procurement assistance programs, incubators/research and technol ogy
parks, educational programs, legislative assistance, small business development consultants, and publications

Volume 6

Introduction. vii

User's Guide ix

Acknowledgments xv

State Listings 3097

Federal Government Assistance 3344

Lists U.S. federal government agencies and offices,including
regional, branch, and district offices, which focus on small business issues, programs, assistance, and policy

Master Index 3439

The appeal of small business ownership remains perpetually entrenched in American culture as one of the most viable avenues for achieving the American Dream. To many entrepreneurs going into business for themselves represents financial independence, an increased sense of identity and self-worth, and the fulfillment of personal goals. Small business owners strive to make their mark in today's competitive marketplace by establishing healthy businesses that can, over time, become legacies handed down from one generation to the next. Entrepreneurs from each generation tackle the obstacles and adversities of the current business and economic climate to test their business savvy and generate opportunities. Today's entrepreneurs face many of the problems of their predecessors, as well as some distinctly new challenges.

With the rightsizing, downsizing, and reorganization of corporate America, many individuals have decided to confront the risks of developing and operating their own businesses. Small business ownership is rapidly becoming a viable alternative to what is perceived as an equally unstable corporate environment. These entrepreneurs, many of whom have firsthand experience with the problems and inefficiencies inherent in today's large corporations, seek to improve upon an archaic business model and to capitalize on their own ingenuity and strengths. Led by their zeal, many would-be entrepreneurs let their desire, drive, and determination overshadow the need for business knowledge and skill. Ironically, aids in obtaining these components of entrepreneurial success are widely available, easily accessible, and often free of charge.

Small Business Sourcebook (*SBS*) is a six-volume annotated guide to more than 21,310 listings of live and print sources of information designed to facilitate the start-up, development, and growth of specific small businesses, as well as over 26,280 similar listings on general small business topics. An additional 12,367 state-specific listings and over 2,220 U.S. federal government agencies and offices specializing in small business issues, programs, and assistance are also included. *SBS* covers 340 specific small business profiles and 99 general small business topics.

Features of This Edition

This edition of *Small Business Sourcebook* has been revised and updated, incorporating thousand of changes to names, addresses, contacts, and descriptions of listings from the previous edition.

Contents and Arrangement

The geographical scope of *SBS* encompasses the United States and Canada, with expanded coverage for resources pertaining to international trade and for resources that have a U.S. or Canadian distributor or contact. Internet sites that are maintained outside of the U.S. and Canada are also included if they contain relevant information for North American small businesses. Resources that do not relate specifically to small businesses are generally not included.

The information presented in *SBS* is grouped within four sections: Specific Small Business Profiles, General Small Business Topics, State Listings, and Federal Government Assistance. Detailed outlines of these sections may be found in the Users' Guide following this Introduction. Also included is a Master Index to Volumes 1 through 6.

Specific Small Business Profiles This section includes the following types of resources: start-up information, associations and other organizations, educational programs, directories of educational programs, reference works, sources of supply, statistical sources, trade periodicals, videocassettes/audiocassettes, trade shows and conventions, consultants, franchises and business opportunities, computerized databases, computer systems/software, Internet databases, libraries, and research centers-all arranged by business type. Entries range from Accounting Service to Word Processing Service, and include such businesses as Airbag Replacement Service Centers, Computer Consulting, Damage Restoration Service, and Web Site Design.

General Small Business Topics This section offers such resources as associations, books, periodicals, articles, pamphlets, educational programs, directories of educational programs, videocassettes/audiocassettes, trade shows and conventions, consultants, computerized databases, Internet databases, software, libraries, and research centers, arranged alphabetically by business topic.

State Listings Entries include government, academic, and commercial agencies and organizations, as well as select coverage of relevant state-specific publications; listings are arranged alphabetically by state, territory, and Canadian province. Some examples include small business development consultants, educational programs, financing and loan programs, better business bureaus, and chambers of commerce.

Federal Government Assistance Listings specializing in small business issues, programs, assistance, and policyare arranged alphabetically by U.S. government agency or office; regional or branch offices are listed alphabetically by state.

Master Index All entries in Volumes 1 through 6 are arranged in one alphabetic index for convenience.

Entries in *SBS* include (as appropriate andavailable):

- Organization, institution, or product name
- Contact information, including contact name, address and phone, toll-free, and fax numbers
- Author/editor, date(s), and frequency
- Availability, including price
- Brief description of purpose, services, or content
- Company and/or personal E-mail addresses
- Web site addresses

SBS also features the following:

Guide to Publishers—An alphabetic listing of 2,470 companies, associations, institutions, and individuals that publish the periodicals, directories, guidebooks, and other publications noted in the Small Business Profiles and General Topics sections. Users are provided with full contact information, including address, phone, fax,and e-mail and URL when available. The Guide to Publishers facilitates contact with publishers and provides a one- stop resource for valuable information.

Method of Compilation

SBS was compiled by consulting small business experts and entrepreneurs, as well as a variety of resources, including direct contact with the associations, organizations, and agencies through telephone surveys, Internet research, or through materials provided by those listees; government resources; and data obtained from other relevant Gale directories. *SBS* was reviewed by a team of small business advisors, all of whom have numerous years of expertise in small business counseling and identification of small business information resources. The last and perhaps most important resource we utilize is direct contact with our readers, who provide valuable comments and suggestions to improve our publication. *SBS* relies on these comprehensive market contacts to provide today's entrepreneurs with relevant, current, and accurate informationon all aspects of small business.

Available in Electronic Formats

Licensing. *Small Business Sourcebook* is available for licensing. The complete database is provided in a fielded format and is deliverable on such media as disk or CD-ROM. For more information, contact Gale's Business Development Group at1-800-877-GALE, or visit our website at www.gale.com/bizdev.

Comments and Suggestions Welcome

Associations, agencies, business firms, publishers, and other organizations that provide assistance and information to the small business community are encouraged to submit material about their programs, activities, services, or products. Comments and suggestions from users of this directory are also welcomed and appreciated. Please contact:

Project Editor
Small Business Sourcebook
Gale, Cengage Learning
27500 Drake Rd.
Farmington Hills, MI 48331-3535
Phone: (248) 699-4253
Fax: (248) 699-8070
E-mail: BusinessProductsgale.com
URL: www.gale.com

Small Business Sourcebook (*SBS*) provides information in a variety of forms and presentations for comprehensive coverage and ease of use. The directory contains four parts within two volumes:

- Specific Small Business Profiles

- General Small Business Topics

- State Listings

- Federal Government Assistance

Information on specific businesses is arranged by type of business; the many general topics that are of interest to the owners, operators, or managers of all small businesses are grouped in a separate section for added convenience. Users should consult the various sections to benefit fully from the information *SBS* offers. For example, an entrepreneur with a talent or interest in the culinary arts could peruse a number of specific small business profiles, such as Restaurant, Catering, Cooking School, Specialty Food/Wine Shop, Bakery/Doughnut Shop, Healthy Restaurant, or Candy/Chocolate Store. Secondly, the General Small Business Topics section could be consulted for any applicable subjects, such as Service Industry, Retailing, Franchising, and other relevant topics. Then, the appropriate state within the State Listings section would offer area programs and offices providing information and support to small businesses, including venture capital firms and small business development consultants. Finally, the Federal Government Assistance section could supply relevant government offices, such as procurement contacts.

Features Included in Volumes 1 through 3

List of Small Business Profiles. This list provides an alphabetic outline of the small businesses profiled, with cross-references for related profiles and for alternate names by which businesses may be identified. The page number for each profile is indicated.

Standard Industrial Classification (SIC) Codes for Profiled Small Businesses. This section lists four-digit SIC codes and corresponding classification descriptions for the small businesses profiled in this edition. The SIC system, which organizes businesses by type, is a product of the Statistical Policy Division of the U.S. Office of Management and Budget. Statistical data produced by government, public, and private organizations is usually categorized according to SIC codes, thereby facilitating the collection, comparison, and analysis of data as well as providing a uniform method for presenting statistical information. Hence, knowing the SIC code for a particular small business increases access and the use of a variety of statistical data from many sources.

Guide to Publishers. This resource lists alphabetically the companies, associations, institutions, and individuals that publish the periodicals, directories, guidebooks, and other publications noted in the "Small Business Profiles" and "General Topics" sections. Users are provided with full contact information, including address, phone, fax, and e-mail and URL when available. The "Guide" facilitates contact with publishers and provides a one-stop resource for valuable information.

Glossary of Small Business Terms. This glossary defines nearly 400 small business terms, including financial, governmental, insurance, procurement, technical, and general business definitions. Cross-references and acronyms are also provided.

Small Business Profiles A-Z. A total of 340 small businesses is represented in volumes 1 through 3. Profiles are listed alphabetically by business name. Entries within each profile are arranged alphabetically by resource type, within up to 17 subheadings. These subheadings are detailed below:

- *Start-up Information*—Includes periodical articles, books, manuals, book excerpts, kits, and other sources of information. Entries offer title; publisher; address; phone, fax, toll-free numbers; company e-mail and URL addresses; and a description. Bibliographic data is provided for cited periodical articles whenever possible.

- *Associations and Other Oganizations*—Includes trade and professional associations whose members gather and disseminate information of interest to small business owners. Entries offer the association's name; address; phone, toll-free and fax numbers; company e-mail address; contact name; purpose and objective; a description of membership; telecommunication services; and a listing of its publications, including publishing frequency.

- **Educational Programs**—Includes university and college programs, schools, training opportunities, association seminars, correspondence courses, and other educational programs.Entries offer name of program or institution, sponsor name, address, phone, toll-free and fax numbers, e-mail and URL addresses; and description of program.

- **Directories of Educational Programs**—Includes directories and other publications that list educational programs. Entries offer name of publication; publisher name, address, and phone, toll-free and fax numbers; editor; frequency or date of publication; price; and description of contents, including directory arrangement and indexes.

- **Reference Works**—Includes handbooks, manuals, textbooks, guides, directories, dictionaries, encyclopedias, and other published reference materials. Entries offer name of publication; publisher name, address, and phone, toll-free and fax numbers; e-mail and URL addresses; and, when available, name of author or editor, publication year or frequency, and price. A brief description is often featured.

- **Sources of Supply**—Includes buyer's guides,directories, special issues of periodicals, and other publications that list sources of equipment, supplies, and services related to the operation of the profiled small business. Entries offer publication name; publisher name, address, and phone, toll-free and fax numbers; e-mail and URL addresses; and, when available, editor's name, frequency or publication year, and price. A brief description of the publication, including directory arrangement and indexes, is often provided.

- **Statistical Sources**—Includes books, reports, pamphlets, and other sources of statistical data of interest to an owner, operator or manager of the profiled small business, such as wage, salary, and compensation data; financial and operating ratios; prices and costs; demographics; and other statistical information. Entries offer publication/data source name; publisher (if applicable); address; phone, toll-free and fax numbers of data source; publication date or frequency; and price. A brief description of the publication/data source is often provided.

- **Trade Periodicals**—Includes trade journals, newsletters, magazines, and other serials that offer information about the management and operation of the profiled small business. Such periodicals often contain industry news; trends and developments; reviews; articles about new equipment and supplies;

and other information related to business operations. Entries offer publication name; publisher name, address, phone, toll-free and fax numbers, and e-mail and URL addresses; editor name; publication frequency; andprice. A brief description of the publication's content is also included, when known.

- **Videocassettes/Audiocassettes**—Includes videocassettes, audiocassettes, and other audiovisual media offering information on the profiled small business. Entries offer program title; distributor name, address, phone, toll-free and fax numbers, and e-mail and URL addresses; description of program; release date; price; and format(s).

- **Trade Shows and Conventions**—Includes tradeshows, exhibitions, expositions, conventions, and other industry meetings that provide prospective and existing business owners with the opportunity to meet and exchange information with their peers, review commercial exhibits, establish business or sales contacts, and attend educational programs. Entries offer event name; sponsor or management company name, address, phone, toll-free and fax numbers, and e-mail and URL addresses; a description of the event, including audience, frequency, principal exhibits, and dates and locations of event for as many years ahead as provided by the event's sponsor.

- **Consultants**—Includes consultants and consulting organizations that provide services specifically related to the profiled small business. Entries offer individual consultant or consulting organization name, address, and phone, toll-free and fax numbers; company and individual e-mail addresses; and a brief description of consulting services. (For e-mail and URL addresses, see the Small Business Development Consultants subheadings in the State Listings section in Volume 2.)

- **Franchises and Business Opportunities**—Includes companies granting franchise licenses for enterprises falling within the scope of the profiled small business, as well as other non-franchised business opportunities that operate within a given network or system. Entries offer franchise name, address, phone, toll-free and fax numbers, and e-mail and URL addresses, as well as a description of the franchise or business opportunity, which has been expanded whenever possible to include the number of existing franchises, the founding date of the franchise, franchise fees, equity capital requirements, royalty fees, any managerial assistance offered, and available training.

- **Computerized Databases**—Includes diskettes, magnetic tapes, CD-ROMs, online systems, and other computer-readable databases. Entries offer database name; producer name, address, phone, toll-free and fax numbers, e-mail and URL addresses; description; and available format(s), including vendor name.

(Many university and public libraries offer online information retrieval services that provide searches of databases, including those listed in this category.)

- **Computer Systems/Software**—Includes softwareand computerized business systems designed to assist in the operation of the profiled small business. Entries offer name of the software or system; publisher name, address, phone, toll-free and fax-numbers; price; and description.

- **Libraries**—Includes libraries and special collections that contain material especially applicable to the profiled small business. Entries offer library or collection name; parent organization (where applicable); address; phone, toll-free and fax numbers; e-mail and URL addresses; contact name and title; scope of collection; and description of holdings, subscriptions, and services.

- **Research Centers**—Includes university-related and independently operated research institutes and information centers that generate, through their research programs, data related to the operation of the profiled small business. Also listed are associations and other business-related organizations that conduct research programs. Entries offer name of organization; address; phone, toll-free and fax numbers; company web site address; contact name and personale-mail; a description of principal fields of research or services; publications, including title and frequency; and related conferences.

Features Included in Volumes 2 through 6

General Small Business Topics. This section offers chapters on different topics in the operation of any small business, for example, venture capital and other funding, or compensation. Chapters are listed alphabetically by small business topic; entries within each chapter are arranged alphabetically, within up to 14 subheadings, by resource type:

- **Associations and Other Organizations**—Includes trade and professional associations that gather and disseminate information of interest to small business owners. Entries offer the association's name; address; phone, toll-free and fax numbers; organization e-mail and URL addresses; contact name;purpose and objectives; a description of membership; telecommunication services; and a listing of its publications, including publishing frequency.

- **Educational Programs**—Includes university and college programs, schools, training opportunities, association seminars, correspondence courses, and other educational programs. Entries offer name of program or institution, sponsor name, address, phone, toll-free and fax numbers, e-mail and URL addresses, and description of program.

- **Directories of Educational Programs**—Includes directories and other publications that list educational programs. Entries offer name of publication; publisher name, address, phone, toll-free and fax numbers, and e-mail and URL addresses; editor; frequency or date of publication; price; and description of contents, including arrangement and indexes.

- **Reference Works**—Includes articles, handbooks, manuals, textbooks, guides, directories, dictionaries, encyclopedias, and other published reference materials. Entries offertitle of article, including bibliographic information; name of publication; publisher name, address, phone, toll-free and fax numbers, and e-mail and URL addresses; and, when available, name of author oreditor, publication year or frequency, and price. A brief descriptionis often featured.

- **Sources of Supply**—Includes buyer's guides,directories, special issues of periodicals, and other publications that list sources of equipment, supplies, and services. Entries offer publication name; publisher name, address, phone, toll-free and fax numbers, and e-mail and URL addresses; editor's name, frequency or publication year, price, and a brief description of the publication, when available.

- **Statistical Sources**—Includes books, reports, pamphlets, and other sources of statistical data of interest to an owner, operator, or manager of a small business, such as wage, salary, and compensation data; financial and operating ratios; prices and costs; demographics; and other statistical information. Entries offer publication/data source name; publisher (if applicable); address; phone, toll-free and fax numbers of data source; publication date or frequency; and price. A brief description is often provided.

- **Trade Periodicals**—Includes journals, newsletters, magazines, and other serials. Entries offer name of publication; publisher name, address, phone, toll-free and fax numbers, and e-mail and URL addresses; and name of editor, frequency, and price.A brief description of the periodical's content is included when known.

- **Videocassettes/Audiocassettes**—Includes videocassettes, audiocassettes, and other audiovisual media. Entries offer program title; distributor name, address, phone, toll-free and fax numbers, and e-mail and URL addresses; price; description of program; release date; and format(s).

- **Trade Shows and Conventions**—Includes tradeshows, exhibitions, expositions, seminars, and conventions. Entries offer event name; sponsor or management company name, address, phone, toll-free and fax numbers, and e-mail and URL addresses; frequency of event; and dates and locations of the event for as many years ahead as known.

- **Consultants**—Includes consultants and consulting organizations. Entries offer individual consultant or-consulting organization name, address, and phone, toll-free and fax numbers; company and individual e-mail addresses; and a brief description of consulting services. (See also Consultants in the State Listings section.)

- **Computerized Databases**—Includes diskettes, CD-ROMs, magnetic tape, online systems and other computer-readable databases. Entries offer database name; producer, address, phone, toll-free and fax numbers, and e-mail and URL addresses; description; and available format(s), including vendor name. (Many university and public libraries offer online information retrieval services that provide searches of databases, including those listed in this category.)

- **Computer Systems/Software**—Includes software and computerized business systems. Entries offer name of the software or system; publisher name, address, phone, toll-free and fax numbers, and e-mail and URL addresses; price; and description.

- **Libraries**—Includes libraries and special collections that contain material applicable to the small business topic. Entries offer library or collection name, parent organization (where applicable), address, phone and fax numbers, e-mail and URL addresses, scope of collection, and description of holdings and services.

- **Research Centers**— Includes university-related and independently operated research institutes and information centers that generate, through their research programs, data related to specific small business topics. Entries offer name of organization, address, phone, toll-free and fax numbers, e-mail and URL addresses, a description of principal fields of research or services, and related conferences.

State Listings. This section lists various sources of information and assistance available within given states, territories, and Canadian provinces; entries include governmental, academic, and commercial agencies, and are arranged alphabetically within up to 15 subheadings by resource type:

- **Small Business Development Center Lead Office**— Includes the lead small business development center (SBDC) for each state.

- **Small Business Development Centers**—Includes any additional small business development centers (SBDC) in the state, territory, or province. SBDCs provide support services to small businesses, including individual counseling, seminars, conferences, and learning center activities.

- **Small Business Assistance Programs**—Includes state small business development offices and other programs offering assistance to small businesses.

- **SCORE Offices**—Includes SCORE office(s) for each state. The Service Corps of Retired Executives Association (SCORE), a volunteer program sponsored by the Small Business Administration, offers counseling, workshops, and seminars across the U.S. for small business entrepreneurs.

- **Better Business Bureaus**—Includes various better business bureaus within each state. By becoming a member of the local Better Business Bureau, a small business owner can increase the prestige and credibility of his or her business within the community, as well as make valuable business contacts.

- **Chambers of Commerce**—Includes various chambers of commerce within each state. Chambers of Commerce are valuable sources of small business advice and information; often, local chambers sponsor SCORE counseling several times per month for a small fee, seminars, conferences, and other workshops to its members. Also, by becoming a member of the local Chamber of Commerce, a small business owner can increase the prestige and credibility of his or herbusiness within the community, as well as make valuable business contacts.

- **Minority Business Assistance Programs**—Includes minority business development centers and other sources of assistance for minority-owned business.

- **Financing and Loan Programs**—Includes venture capital firms, small business investment companies (SBIC), minority enterprise small business investment companies (MESBIC), and other programs that provide funding to qualified small businesses.

- **Procurement Assistance Programs**—Includes state services such as counseling, set-asides, and sheltered-market bidding, which are designed to aid small businesses in bidding on government contracts.

- **Incubators/Research and Technology Parks**— Includes small business incubators, which provide newly established small business owners with work sites, business services, training, and consultation; also includes research and technology parks, which sponsor research and facilitate commercialization of new technologies.

- **Educational Programs**—Includes university and college programs, as well as those sponsored by other organizations that offer degree, nondegree, certificate, and correspondence programs in entrepreneurship and in small business development.

- **Legislative Assistance**—Includes committees, subcommittees, and joint committees of each state's senate and house of representatives that are concerned with small business issues and regulations.

- **Consultants**—Includes consultants and consulting firms offering expertise in small business development.

- **Publications**—Includes publications related to small business operations within the profiled state.

- **Publishers**—Includes publishers operating in or for the small business arena within the profiled state.

Federal Government Assistance. This section lists federal government agencies and offices, many with additional listings for specific offices, as well as regional or district branches. Main agencies or offices are listed alphabetically; regional, branch, ordistrict offices are listed after each main office or agency.

Master Index. This index provides an alphabetic listing of all entries contained in Volumes 1 throgh 6. Citations are referenced by their entry numbers. Publication titles are rendered in italics.

Acknowledgements

The editors would like to extend sincere thanks to the following members of the Small Business Sourcebook advisory board for their expert guidance, recommendations, and suggestions for the ongoing development of this title:

Susan C. Awe
Assistant Director,
William J. Parish Memorial Business Library

Jill Clever
Business Technology Specialist,
Toledo-Lucas County Public Library

Jules Matsoff
District Manager,
Service Corps of Retired Executives (SCORE) Milwaukee
Chapter

Ken MacKenzie
President,
Southeast Business Appraisal

The editors would also like to thank the individuals from associations and other organizations who provided information for the compilation of this directory.

This list is an outline of the 341 small businesses profiled in this edition of Small Business Sourcebook. The beginning page number of each profile is provided. For convenience, this index also provides cross-references to small businesses known by alternate names, businesses contained within other small business profiles, and synonymous or related businesses.

Abstracting and Indexing Service 1
Accounting Service 2
Adult Day Care Center 18
Advertising Service 22
Airbag Replacement/Service Centers . .40
Air Charter Service 42
Air-conditioning/Heating and Cooling
   Contractor. 46
Air Purification/Cleaning Service 55
Ambulance Service 57
Amusement Arcade 58
Amusement/Water Park. 60
Animal Breeder. 63
Animal Clinic 67
Antique Shop 72
Apartment Locating Service 75
Appliance Store 77
Appraisal Service 79
Aquarium Maintenance/Leasing
   Service 81
Archery/Target/Shooting Range 82
Architectural Restoration/Conservation .84
Art Gallery. 89
Art Supplies Store 93
Assisted Living Facilities 94
Association Management Service 97
Auctioneer/Broker 100
Auto Supply Store 103
Automobile Detailing/Painting Service .107
Automobile/Truck Leasing Service . . .109
Baby Store. 112
Bagel Shop 114
Bait and Tackle Shop. 116
Bakery/Doughnut Shop 119
Bar/Cocktail Lounge 125
Beauty Supply Center 129
Bed and Breakfast Operation. 131
Beekeeping 132
Beeper/Paging Service 134
Bicycle Shop 135
Billiards Hall. 137
Blacktop Surfacing Business 139
Blind Cleaning/Installation. 142
Body Care Shop 143
Book Publishing. 146
Bookbinder 156

Bookkeeping 158
Bookstore 164
Bottled Water Service 168
Bowling Alley 170
Brewery Operation 172
Bridal Shop/Bridal Consultant. 175
Building/Home Inspection Service . . .179
Building Maintenance/Custodial
   Service. 182
Bulletin Board Service 188
Business Broker Service 189
Business Consulting Service 192
Business Services Operation 214
Butcher Shop 220
Cable Network 222
Calligraphy Service. 226
Camera Shop 228
Campground Management 230
Candy/Chocolate Shop 233
Car Alarm and Stereo Store 236
Car Inspection Service. 237
Car Towing Service. 238
Car Wash 239
Career Counseling 241
Carpentry Service 246
Catering Service 249
CD-ROM Developer/Producer 252
Cellular Phone/Telephone Business . .261
Charter Boat Service. 271
Check Cashing Service 273
Children's Apparel Shop. 274
Children's Day Care Center. 277
Chimney Sweeping Business 285
Christmas Decoration Store. 286
Christmas Tree Farm 287
Clipping Service 289
Clothing Designer 291
Clothing Store. 297
Coffee Service 304
Coin/Stamp Dealer 306
Comedy Club 311
Comic Book/Collectibles Store 312
Commercial/Graphic Art Business . . .314
Commercial Mail Receiving Agency . .323
Compact Disc/Record Store 325
Computer Consulting. 326

Computer Data Storage Company . . .330
Computer Learning/Training Center . .334
Computer Maintenance and Repair
   Service. 338
Computer Programming and Data
   Processing Service. 341
Computer Store. 347
Computer System Integrators. 352
Computerized Billing Service 356
Computerized Matching Service 358
Concession Stand Business 359
Concierge/Virtual Assistant Service . .361
Consignment Shop. 362
Construction Company. 364
Consumer Electronics Store 394
Convenience Store. 398
Cooking School 401
Copy Shop 404
Cosmetics Business 406
Costume Shop 409
Craft Artisan. 411
Craft/Hobby Business 418
Create-Your-Own... Store 424
Credit Card Issuing Service. 425
Credit Repair Service 427
Credit Reporting and Collection
   Service. 430
Damage Restoration Service 435
Dance School 436
Delicatessen/Sandwich Shop 441
Desktop Publishing Company. 446
Dial-It Services 450
Disc Jockey Service 451
Domestic Help/Maid Service 452
Driving School 455
Drug Store/Pharmacy 457
Dry Cleaning Service/Coin-Operated
   Laundry 465
Editorial/Freelance Writing Business. .468
Electrical Contractor 474
Electrical Lighting Supply Store 478
Electronic/Online Publishing 480
Employee Leasing Service 481
Employment Agency 482
Engraving/Monogramming Service. . .487
Environmental Consultant 488

Environmental Store 508
Estate Planning. 522
Estate Sales Business 524
Executive Recruiting Agency 525
Fashion Accessories Business 527
Fax Service 531
Film and Video Production Operation .532
Financial Planning Service 540
Fish and Seafood Store 582
Fish Farm 584
Floor Covering/Restoration Business .588
Florist. 591
Food Delivery Service 594
Freight Forwarding Service 598
Fund-Raising Consultant 601
Funeral Service 607
Fur Farm 610
Fur Store 611
Furniture Restoration Service 612
Gambling Organization/Service. 614
Genealogy Service 617
Gift Basket Service. 626
Gift/Card Shop 628
Glass Repair and Replacement
    Service. 631
Golf Shop 633
Gourmet Coffee/Tea House 636
Greenhouse/Garden Center/Nursery Busi-
    ness 640
Greeting Card Publishing 648
Grocery Store 649
Gunsmith/Gun Shop 656
Hair Replacement/Electrolysis Clinic. .658
Hair Salon/Barber Shop 659
Handwriting Analysis Consultant 663
Hardware Store. 665
Hat Store 668
Hazardous Waste Disposal Business .669
Health Food Store 673
Healthy Restaurant. 677
Hearing Aid Testing and Fitting
    Service. 681
Herb Farm. 684
Home Accessory Store 687
Home Furnishings Store. 691
Home Health Care Service 695
Horse Riding Academy 701
Hotel/Motel/Resort Operations 705
Ice Cream/Frozen Yogurt Shop. 716
Image Consultant. 723
Import/Export Service 725
Incubator. 735
Information Broker 736
Insulation Contractor 739
Insurance Agency 740
Interior Design Service. 754
Internet/Online Service Provider 759
Investment/Securities Broker 776
Jewelry Store 831
Job Training/Retraining 835
Kiosk/Pushcart/Vendor Business 837
Landscape Equipment and Supplies. .839
Landscaping Service 841

Lawn Maintenance Service 848
Limousine Service 852
Lingerie Shop 854
Liquor Store 855
Literary Agency 858
Locksmith 859
Luggage and Leather Goods Busi-
    ness 861
Lumberyard 862
Machine Shop/Metalworking Shop . . .866
Mail Order Business 870
Management Consulting Service 872
Manufacturer's Representative 883
Marine Shop. 885
Market Research and Analysis 890
Martial Arts Studio 896
Masonry, Stonework, and Plastering
    Contractors 898
Massage Therapist 902
Mediation Service 904
Medical and Dental Instrument
    Manufacturing 906
Medical Claims Service 910
Medical Laboratory Service 911
Medical Supplies Store 915
Medical Transcription Service. 918
Messenger/Delivery/Subpoena
    Service 919
Miniature Golf Course Operation 920
Modeling School/Agency 921
Mortgage Broker 922
Motorcycle/Moped Store. 931
Movie Theatre Operation 933
Moving Service 936
Music School 937
Music Shop 945
Musical Instrument Repair/Piano Tuning
    Service. 949
Nail Salon 951
Nanny Service 952
New Age Services and Supplies 953
New and Used Car Dealer 955
Newsletter Publishing 964
Novelty Items Business 966
Nursing Home/Long-Term Care
    Center 968
Nutritional Consultant/Diet Planner. . .976
Office Design Service 983
Office Supply/Equipment Store 986
Online Store 988
Paint/Wall Covering Center 992
Painting Contractor 994
Party Entertainment Service 996
Party/Reunion Planning Service 998
Pawnbroker 1000
Payroll Preparation Service 1001
Periodical/Newspaper Publishing 1003
Personal Shopping Service 1011
Pest Control Service 1012
Pet Boarding/Grooming Service. 1015
Pet Cemetery 1017
Pet Obedience School 1018
Pet Shop 1020

Pet Sitting Service 1025
Photo Finishing Center. 1027
Photographer, Commercial 1028
Photographic Studio 1032
Physical Fitness Center 1035
Physical Therapy Clinic/Practice 1043
Pizzeria. 1048
Plant Leasing Service 1053
Plumbing Service 1054
Porcelain Refinishing Service 1060
Power Washing Service 1061
Prepaid Phone Card Business 1062
Print/Frame Shop 1063
Printing Business 1065
Private Investigation/Personal Security
    Service 1072
Private Label Product Manufacturer/
    Retailer. 1075
Professional Organizer 1076
Property Management 1078
Public Relations Consultant 1083
Public Warehousing/Ministorage Opera-
    tion 1087
Quick Oil Change Service 1090
Radio Station 1092
Radon Testing Service 1098
Real Estate Agency 1099
Real Estate Investment Service 1117
Recording Studio 1140
Recreational Vehicle Dealer 1143
Recycling Business 1145
Rental Service 1149
Restaurant 1155
Resume Service 1180
Roofing Contractor 1181
Satellite Dish Service 1183
Screen Printing Business 1185
Security Systems Service 1187
Seminar Planner/Lecturer 1195
Service Station/Auto Repair and Service
    Shop 1198
Sewer and Drain Cleaning Business .1205
Sewing Center. 1208
Shoe Repair Shop 1210
Shoe Store 1211
Sign Shop 1214
Silk Plant Shop 1216
Skating Rink Operation. 1217
Ski Shop 1218
Software Publishing. 1220
Solar Energy Design/Contracting Busi-
    ness. 1231
Specialized Staffing. 1236
Specialty Foods/Wine Shop 1240
Sporting Goods Store 1246
Sports Promotional Service 1252
Surveying Service. 1258
Swimming Pool/Hot Tub Business . . .1261
Tailor Shop 1263
Talent Agency 1264
Tanning Parlor/Sauna. 1265
Tattoo Parlor 1266
Tax Preparation Business 1267

Taxicab/Van Shuttle Service 1278
Taxidermy Service 1281
Teacher Supply Store. 1282
Telemarketing Service 1283
Telephone Answering Service 1285
Television/Radio Repair Service . . .1286
Television Station 1287
Temporary Employment Agency . . .1296
Tennis Court/Racquet Club Opera-
    tion 1298
Tire Dealer 1300
Tobacco Shop 1302

Tour Guide Operation/Adventure
    Service 1304
Toy Business 1310
Trade Show/Conference Management
    Service 1314
Translating/Interpreting Service 1323
Travel Agency 1326
Trucking Business. 1335
Tutoring Service 1340
Typesetting Business 1342
Typing/Stenographic Service 1345
Upholstery/Carpet Services 1346

Vending Machine Merchandising and
    Service Business 1348
Videocassette Rental Store 1350
Vision Center 1352
Voice Mail Service 1357
Water Conditioning Service 1359
Web Site Design 1363
Weight Reduction/Control Center. . .1375
Welcome Service 1377
Window Dressing Business 1378
Word Processing Service 1379

Standard Industrial Classification (SIC) Codes for Profiled Small Businesses

Included here are the four-digit SIC codes and corresponding classification descriptions for the businesses profiled in this edition. The SIC system, which organizes businesses by type, is a product of the Statistical Policy Division of the U.S. Office of Management and Budget. Statistical data produced by government, public, and private organizations usually are categorized according to SIC codes, thereby facilitating the collection, comparison, and analysis of data as well as providing a uniform method for presenting statistical information. Hence, knowing the SIC code for a particular small business increases the access to, and the use of, a variety of statistical data from many sources. The following SIC codes were obtained from the 1987 edition of the Standard Industrial Classification Manual, the most recent version available. (The term "nec" stands for "not elsewhere classified.")

Accounting Service

7291	Tax return preparation services
8721	Accounting, auditing, and bookkeeping services

Adult Day Care Center

8322	Individual and family social services (includes adult day carecenters)

Advertising Service

7311	Advertising agencies (includes advertising consultants)
7312	Outdoor advertising agencies
7313	Radio, television, and publishers' advertising representatives
7319	Advertising, nec
7331	Direct mail advertising services
8999	Services, nec (includes advertising copywriters)

Airbag Replacement Service Centers

7538	General automotive repair shops
7539	Automotive repair shops, nec

Air Charter Service

4512	Air transportation, scheduled (includes air cargo and passenger carriers)
4513	Air courier services
4522	Air transportation, nonscheduled (includes charter service)

Air-conditioning/Heating and Cooling Contractor

1711	Plumbing, heating, and air-conditioning contractors

Air Purification/Cleaning Service

7699	Repair shops and related services, nec (includes furnace cleaning service)

Ambulance Service

4119	Local passenger transportation, nec (includes ambulance service, road)
4522	Air transportation, nonscheduled (includes ambulance service, air)

Amusement Arcade

7993	Coin-operated amusement devices

Amusement/Water Park

7996	Amusement parks
7999	Amusement and recreation services, nec (includes waterslides and wave pools)

Animal Breeder

0279	Animal specialties, nec (includes kennels, breeding and raising own stock)
0752	Animal specialty services, except veterinary (includes breeding of animals other than farm animals)

Animal Clinic

0742	Veterinary service for animal specialties (includes animal hospitals for pets and other animals)

Antique Shop

5932	Used merchandise stores (includes retail antique stores)

7641	Reupholstery and furniture repair (includes antique furniture repair and restoration)
7699	Repair shops and related services, nec (includes antique repair and restoration, except furniture)

Apartment Locating Service

6531	Real Estate Agents and Managers

Appliance Store

5722	Household appliance stores

Appraisal Service

7389	Business services, nec (includes appraisers, except real estate)
6531	Real estate agents and managers (includes appraisers, realestate)

Aquarium Maintenance/Leasing Service

7359	Equipment rental and leasing, nec
8999	Services, nec

Archery/Target/Shooting Range

7999	Amusement and recreation services, nec (includes archery ranges, shooting galleries, shooting ranges, and trap-shooting facilities, except membership)

Architectural Restoration/Conservation

8712	Architectural Services

Art Gallery

5932	Used merchandise stores (includes retailers of art objects)

5999   Miscellaneous retail stores, nec (includes art dealers)

8412   Museums and art galleries (includes noncommercial art galleries)

Art Supplies Store

5999   Miscellaneous retail stores, nec (includes retail artists' supplies and materials stores)

Assisted Living Facilities

8051   Skilled nursing care facilities (includes extended care facilities and skilled nursing homes)

8052   Intermediate care facilities (includes intermediate care nursing homes)

8059   Nursing and personal care facilities, nec (includes rest homeswith health care)

Association Management Service

8611   Business associations

8621   Professional membership organizations

8631   Labor unions and similar labor organizations

8641   Civic, social, and fraternal associations

8699   Membership organizations, nec

8741   Management services (does not include operating staff)

Auctioneer

5154   Livestock (includes wholesale livestock auctioning)

5999   Miscellaneous retail stores, nec (includes retail general merchandise auction rooms)

7389   Business services, nec (includes auctioneering services)

Auto Supply Store

5531   Auto and home supply stores

Automobile Detailing/Painting Service

7532   Automotive paint shops

7542   Carwashes (includes detailing, cleaning and polishing, new autos on a contract or fee basis; washing and polishing, automotive; waxing and polishing, automotive)

Automobile/Truck Leasing Service

7513   Truck rental and leasing, without drivers

7514   Passenger car rental, without drivers

7515   Passenger car leasing, without drivers

Baby Store

5999   Miscellaneous retail stores, nec (includes retail baby)

Bagel Shop

2051   Bread and other bakery products, except cookies and crackers (includes bagels)

5461   Retail bakeries (includes retail bagel stores)

Bait and Tackle Shop

5941   Sporting goods stores and bicycle shops (includes bait and tackle shops and fishing equipment, retail)

Bakery/Doughnut Shop

5461   Retail bakeries

Bar/Cocktail Lounge

5813   Drinking places alcoholic beverages (includes bars, cocktail lounges, saloons, tap rooms, taverns, and like establishments)

Beauty Supply Center

5087   Service establishment equipment and supplies (includes wholesale barber shop and beauty parlor equipment and supplies)

Bed and Breakfast Operation

7011   Hotels and motels (includes bed and breakfast inns)

Beekeeping

0279   Animal specialties, nec (includes apiaries and bee farms)

Beeper/Paging Service

4812   Radiotelephone communications (includes beeper and paging services)

Bicycle Shop

5941   Sporting goods stores and bicycle shops

7699   Repair shops and related services, nec (includes bicycle repair shops)

Billiards Hall

7999   Amusement and recreation services, nec (includes billiard parlors)

Blacktop Surfacing Business

1771   Concrete work (includes blacktop work: private driveways and private parking areas contractors)

Blind Cleaning/Installation

2431   Millwork (includes wood blinds and shutters)

2591   Drapery hardware and window blinds and shades

Body Care Shop

5999   Miscellaneous retail stores, nec (includes cosmetics stores)

Book Publishing

2731   Books; publishing or publishing and printing

Bookbinder

2789   Bookbinding and related work

Bookkeeping

8721   Accounting, auditing, and bookkeeping services

Bookstore

5932   Used merchandise stores (includes used book retailers)

5942   Bookstores

Bottled Water Service

5149   Groceries and related products, nec (includes natural spring and mineral water bottling and distribution services)

5499   Miscellaneous food stores (includes mineral water, retail)

Bowling Alley

7933   Bowling centers

Brewery Operation

2082   Malt beverages

Bridal Shop/Bridal Consultant

5621   Women's clothing stores (includes retail bridal shops, exceptcustom designers)

Building/Home Inspection

7389   Business services, nec (includes safety inspection, except automotive)

Building Maintenance/Custodial Service

7349   Building cleaning and maintenance services, nec (includes interior building cleaning services, contract janitorial services, and like enterprises)

Bulletin Board Service

4822   Telegraph and other message communications (includes electronic mail services)

7379   Computer related services, nec

Business Broker Service

7389   Business services, nec (includes business brokers buying andselling business enterprises)

Business Consulting Service

8748   Business consulting services, nec

Business Services Operation

8744   Facilities support management services (includesbasemaintenance, providing personnel on continuing basis)

Butcher Shop

5423   Meat and fish (seafood) markets, including freezer provisioners

---

5499   Miscellaneous food stores (includes retail poultry dealers)

Cable Network

1623   Water, Sewer, Pipeline, and Communications and Power Line Construction (includes cable television line construction-contractors)

1731   Electrical Work (includes cable television hookup-contractors)

4841   Cable and Other Pay Television Services

Calligraphy Service

7389   Business services, nec (includes lettering services)

Camera Shop

5946   Camera and photographic supply stores

7699   Repair shops and related services, nec (includes camera repair shops)

Campground Management

7033   Recreational vehicle parks and campsites

Candy/Chocolate Shop

5441   Candy, nut, and confectionery stores

Car Alarm and Stereo Store

5531   Auto and home supply stores (includes automobile accessorydealers, retail)

5731   Radio, television, and consumer electronics stores (includesautomotive stereo equipment, retail)

Car Inspection Service

7549   Automotive services, except repair services and car washes(includes inspection service, automotive)

Car Towing Service

7549   Automotive services, except repair services and car washes(includes automotive towing and wrecker services)

Car Wash

7542   Car washes

Career Counseling

7389   Business services, nec (includes career counseling service)

Carpentry Service

1751   Carpentry work

Catering Service

5812   Eating places (includes caterers)

CD-ROM Developer/Producer

7372   Prepackaged software (includes pre-packaged computer software publishers)

7379   Computer related services, nec (includes database developers)

Cellular Phone/Telephone Business

4812   Radiotelephone communications

5999   Miscellaneous retail stores, nec (includes telephone stores, retail)

Charter Boat Service

4499   Water transportation service, nec (includes boat rental, commercial)

Check Cashing Service

6099   Functions related to depository banking, nec (includes check cashing agencies)

Children's Apparel Shop

5611   Men's and boys' clothing stores

5641   Children's and infants' wear stores

5651   Family clothing stores

5699   Miscellaneous apparel and accessory stores (includes children's wear)

5932   Used merchandise stores (includes retail second hand clothing stores)

Children's Day Care Center

8351   Child day care services

Chimney Sweeping Business

7349   Building cleaning and maintenance services, nec (includeschimney cleaning service)

Christmas Decoration Store

5999   Miscellaneous retail stores, nec

Christmas Tree Farm

0811   Timber tracts (includes Christmas tree growing)

Clipping Service

7389   Business services, nec (includes press clipping service)

Clothing Designer

2311   Men's and boys' suits, coats, and overcoats

2325   Men's and boys' separate trousers and slacks

2329   Men's and boys' clothing, nec

2331   Women's, misses', and juniors' blouses and shirts

2335   Women's, misses', and juniors' dresses

2337   Women's, misses', and juniors' suits, skirts, and coats

2361   Girls', children's, and infants' dresses, blouses, and shirts

Clothing Store

5611   Men's and boys' clothing and accessory stores

5621   Women's clothing stores

5632   Women's accessory and specialty stores

5641   Children's and infants' wear stores

5651   Family clothing stores

5699   Miscellaneous apparel and accessory stores

5932   Used merchandise stores (includes retail secondhand clothing stores)

Coffee Service

5149   Groceries and related products, nec (includes coffee, wholesale)

Coin/Stamp Dealer

5961   Catalog and mail order houses (includes retail mail order coinand stamp businesses)

5999   Miscellaneous retail stores, nec

Comedy Club

5813   Drinking placesMalcoholic beverages (includes nightclubs)

Comic Book/Collectibles Store

5999   Miscellaneous retail stores, nec

Commercial/Graphic Art Business

7336   Commercial art and graphic design

Commercial Mail Receiving Agency

7389   Business services, nec (includes post office contract stations)

Compact Disc/Record Store

5735   Recorded and prerecorded tape stores

Computer Consulting

7379   Computer related services, nec (includes computer consultants

Computer Data Storage Company

3572   Computer storage devices

Computer Learning/Training Center

8243   Data processing schools

Computer Maintenance and Repair Service

7378   Computer maintenance and repair

Computer Programming and Data Processing Service

7374   Computer processing and data preparation services

Computer Store

5734   Computer and computer software stores

Computer System Integrators

7371   Computer programming services

7373   Computer integrated systems design

7379   Computer related services, nec (includes computer consultants and database developers)

Computerized Billing Service

7374   Computer processing and data preparation and processing services

Computerized Matching Service

7299   Miscellaneous personal services, nec (includes dating services)

7375   Information retrieval services

Concession Stand Business

5812   Eating places (includes concession stands in airports and sports arenas, and refreshment stands)

7999   Amusement and recreation services, nec (concession operators andamusement concessions)

Consignment Shop

5932   Used merchandise stores (includes clothing stores, secondhand retail; furniture stores, secondhand retail; home furnishing stores, secondhand retail)

Construction Company

1521   General contractors—single family houses

1522   General contractors—residential buildings other than single-family

Consumer Electronics Store

5731   Radio, television, and consumer electronics stores

Convenience Store

5411   Grocery stores (includes retail convenience food stores)

Cooking School

8299   Schools and educational services, nec (includes cooking schools)

Copy Shop

7334   Photocopying and duplicating services

Cosmetics Business

2844   Perfumes, cosmetics, and other toilet preparations

5122   Drugs, drug proprietaries, and druggists' sundries (includes cosmetics—wholesale)

5963   Direct selling establishments (includes canvassers , headquarters for retail sale of merchandise, and direct selling organizations—retail)

5999   Miscellaneous retail stores, nec (includes cosmeticsstores—retail)

Costume Shop

7299   Miscellaneous personal services, nec (includes costume rental)

7922   Theatrical producers and miscellaneous theatrical services(includes theatrical costume design)

Craft Artisan

3269   Pottery products, nec (includes art and ornamental ware; pottery; ceramic articles for craft shops; cookware; crockery; china, earthenware and stoneware figures; kitchen articles; coarse earthenware; lamp bases; and vases)

Craft/Hobby Shop

5945   Hobby, toy, and game shops (includes retail hobby stores and craft kit and supply retailers)

5947   Gift, novelty, and souvenir shops pottery; ceramic articles for craft shops; cookware; crockery; china, earthenware and stoneware figures; kitchen articles; coarse earthenware; lamp bases; and vases)

Create Your Own...Store

3269   Pottery Products, nec

5947   Gift, Novelty, and Souvenir Shops

5999   Micellaneous Retail Stores, nec

Credit Card Issuing Service

6153   Short-Term Business Credit Institutions, Except Agricultural (includes credit card service, collection by central agency)

7389   Business Services, nec (includes credit card service collection by individual firms)

Credit Repair Service

7299   Miscellaneous personal services, nec (includes debt counseling and adjustment services)

Credit Reporting and Collection Service

7322   Adjustment and collection services

7323   Credit reporting services

Damage Restoration Service

1790   Special trade contractors, nec (includes cleaning building exteriors, dampproofing buildings, dewatering, fireproofing buildings, steam cleaning of building exteriors, and waterproofing)

Dance School

7911   Dance studios, schools, and halls

Delicatessen/Sandwich Shop

5812   Eating places (includes sandwich bars or shops and submarine sandwich shops)

Desktop Publishing Company

2711   Publishing, or publishing and printing newspapers

2721   Publishing, or publishing and printing periodicals

2731   Publishing, or publishing and printing books

2741   Miscellaneous publishing

Dial-it Services

4813   Telephone communications, except radio-telephone

Diaper Service

7219   Laundry and garment services, nec

Disc Jockey Service

8999   Services, nec

Domestic Help/Maid Service

7349   Building cleaning and maintenance services, nec (includes housekeeping and office cleaning services)

8811   Private households (includes private households employing cooks, maids, and other domestic help)

Driving School

8249   Vocational schools, nec (includes truck driving schools)

8299   Schools and educational services, nec (includes automobile driving instruction)

Drug Store/Pharmacy

5912   Drug stores and proprietary stores

Dry Cleaning Service/Coin-Operated Laundry

7215   Coin-operated laundries and dry cleaning services

7216   Dry cleaning plants, except rug cleaning

Editorial/Freelance Writing Business

8999   Services, nec (includes writing and ghostwriting services)

Electrical Contractor

1731   Electrical work (includes trade contractors engaged in on-site electrical work)

Electrical Lighting Supply Store

5719   Miscellaneous home furnishings stores (includes retail lamp and shade shops)

Employee Leasing Service

7363   Help supply services

Employment Agency

361   Employment agencies

Engraving/Monogramming Service

3479 Coating, engraving, and allied services, nec (includes jewelryand silverware engraving)

7389 Business services, nec (includes advertising embroidery services, embossing services, and identification engraving services)

Environmental Consultant

8748 Business consulting services, nec

Environmental Store

5999 Miscellaneous retail stores, nec

Estate Planning

8811 Private Households

Estate Sales Business

6530 Real estate agents and managers

Executive Recruiting Agency

7361 Employment agencies (includes executive placement)

Fashion Accessories Business

3961 Costume jewelry and costume novelties, except precious metal

5137 Women's, children's, and infants' clothing and accessories

5632 Women's accessory and specialty stores

Fax Service

4822 Telegraph and other message communications (includes facsimile transmission services)

Film and Video Production Operation

7812 Motion picture and videotape production services

Financial Planning Service

282 Investment Advice

Fish and Seafood Store

5421 Meat and fish (seafood) markets, including freezer provisioners

Fish Farm

0273 Animal aquaculture (includes fish farms except hatcheries)

Floor Covering/Restoration Business

5713 Floor covering stores—retail

Florist

5992 Florists

Food Delivery Service

5812 Eating places

5963 Direct selling establishments (includes door-to-door selling organizations and mobile lunch wagons)

5999 Miscellaneous retail stores, nec

Formalwear Rental Business

7299 Miscellaneous personal services, nec (includes tuxedo rental)

Freight Forwarding Service

4731 Arrangement of transportation of freight and cargo (includes freight forwarding services)

Fund Raising Consultant

7389 Business services, nec (includes fund raising on a contract or fee basis)

Funeral Service

7261 Funeral services and crematories

Fur Farm

0271 Fur-bearing animals and rabbits

Fur Store

5632 Women's accessory and specialty stores (includes fur shops and furriers)

Furniture Restoration Service

7641 Reupholstery and furniture repair

Gambling Organizations/Service

7011 Hotels and Motels (includes casino hotels)

7993 Coin-Operated Amusement Devices

7999 Amusement and Recreation Services, nec (includes gambling establishments not primarily operating coin-operated machines and lotteries, operation of)

9311 Public Finance Taxation, and Monetary Policy (includes gambling control boards-government and lottery control boards-government)

Genealogy Service

7299 Miscellaneous personal services, nec (includes genealogical investigation service)

Gift Basket Service

5961 Catalog and mail-order houses

Gift/Card Shop

5943 Stationery stores

5947 Gift, novelty, and souvenir shops (includes card shops)

Glass Repair and Replacement Service

1751 Carpentry work (includes prefabricated window and door installation)

7536 Automotive glass replacement shops

Golf Shop

5941 Sporting goods stores and bicycle shops (includes retail golf goods and equipment stores)

Gourmet Coffee/Tea House

5499 Miscellaneous food stores (includes coffee stores, retail)

5812 Eating places (includes coffee shops)

Greenhouse/Garden Center/Nursery Business

0181 Ornamental floricultural and nursery products (includes greenhouses for floral products, growing of nursery stock, growing of potted plants)

| 5261 | Retail nurseries, lawn and garden supply stores (includes nursery stock, seeds, and bulbs, retail) |

Greeting Card Publishing

| 2771 | Greeting card publishing and printing |
| 8999 | Services, nec (includes hand painting of greeting cards) |

Grocery Store

| 5411 | Grocery stores |

Gunsmith/Gun Shop

| 5941 | Sporting good stores and bicycle shops (includes firearms,retail) |
| 7699 | Repair shops and related services, nec (includes gunsmith shops) |

Hair Replacement/Electrolysis Clinic

| 7299 | Miscellaneous personal services, nec (includes depilatory salons, electrolysis, and hair weaving or replacement services) |

Hair Salon/Barber Shop

| 7231 | Beauty shops (includes beauty and barber shops combined) |
| 7241 | Barber shops |

Handwriting Analysis Consultant

| 7389 | Business services, nec (includes handwriting analysis) |

Hardware Store

| 5251 | Hardware stores |

Hat Store

| 5611 | Men's and boys' clothing and accessory stores (includes retail hat stores) |
| 5621 | Women's accessory and specialty stores (includes retail millinery stores) |

Hazardous Waste Disposal Business

| 4953 | Refuse systems (includes hazardous waste material disposal sites) |

Healthy Restaurants

| 5812 | Eating Places |

Health Food Store

| 5499 | Miscellaneous food stores (includes health food stores) |

Hearing Aid Testing and Fitting Service

| 5999 | Miscellaneous retail stores, nec (includes hearing aids, retail) |
| 8099 | Health and allied services, nec (includes hearing testing service) |

Herb Farm

0191	General farms, primarily crop
2833	Medical chemicals and botanical products (includes herb grinding, grading, and milling)
5499	Miscellaneous food stores (includes spice and herb stores)

Home Accessory Store

| 5714 | Drapery, curtain, and upholstery stores |
| 5719 | Miscellaneous home furnishings stores |

Home Furnishings Store

5712	Furniture stores
5719	Miscellaneous home furnishings stores
5932	Used merchandise stores (including antique and secondhand retail furniture stores)

Home Health Care Service

| 8082 | Home health care services |

Horse Riding Academy

| 752 | Animal specialty services, except veterinary (includes boarding and training horses) |

Hotel/Motel/Resort Operation

| 7011 | Hotels and motels (includes resort hotels) |

Housesitting Service

| 8999 | Services, nec |

Ice Cream/Frozen Yogurt Shop

| 5451 | Dairy products stores (includes retail packaged ice cream stores) |

| 5812 | Eating places (includes retail dairy bars) |
| 563 | Direct selling establishments (includes ice cream wagons) |

Image Consultant

| 8299 | Schools and educational services, nec (includes personal development schools) |
| 8743 | Public relations services |

Import/Export Service

| 4731 | Arrangement of the transportation of freight and cargo |

Incubator

| 7389 | Business services, nec |
| 8748 | Business consulting services, nec |

Information Broker

| 7375 | Information retrieval services |

Insulation Contractor

| 1742 | Plastering, dry wall, acoustical, and insulation work (includes insulation installation contractors) |

Insurance Agency

| 6411 | Insurance agents, brokers, and services |

Interior Design Service

| 7389 | Business services, nec (includes interior decoration consulting services and interior design services) |

Internet/Online Service Provider

| 4822 | Telegraph and other message communications (includes electronicmail services) |
| 7379 | Computer related services, nec |

Investment/Securities Broker

| 6211 | Security brokers, dealers, and flotation companies |

Jewelry Store

| 5632 | Women's accessory and specialty stores (includes costume jewelry stores) |

5944	Jewelry stores
7631	Watch, clock, and jewelry repair

Job Training/Retraining

8331	Job training and vocational rehabilitation services (includesjob training)

Kiosk/Pushcart/Vendor Business

5812	Eating places (includes box lunch stands, concession stands,food bars, hamburger and hot dog stands, ice cream stands, refreshment stands, and soft drink stands)

Landscaping Service

0781	Landscape counseling and planning services
0782	Lawn and garden services
0783	Ornamental shrub and tree services

Lawn Maintenance Service

0782	Lawn and garden services
0783	Ornamental shrub and tree services

Limousine Service

4119	Local passenger transportation, nec (includes hearse and limousine rental, with drivers)
7514	Passenger car rental (includes limo rental, w/o drivers)

Lingerie Shop

5632	Lingerie storesMretail

Liquor Store

5921	Liquor stores

Literary Agency

7389	Business services, nec (includes agents and brokers for authors and non-performing artists)

Locksmith

7699	Repair shops and related services, nec (includes locksmith shops and made-to order lock parts)

Luggage and Leather Goods Business

5948	Luggage and leather goods stores

Lumberyard

5211	Lumber and other building materials dealers

Machine Shop/Metalorking Shop

3541	Machine tools, metal cutting types
3542	Machine tools, metal forming types
3544	Special dies and tools, die sets, jigs and fixtures, and industrial molds
3545	Cutting tools, machine tool accessories, and machinists' precision measuring devices
3549	Metalworking machinery, nec

Mail Order Business

5961	Catalog and mail order houses

Management Consulting Service

8742	Management consulting services

Manufacturer's Representative

7389	Business services, nec

Marine Shop

5551	Boat dealers (includes retail marine supply dealers)

Market Research and Analysis

8732	Commercial, economic, sociological, and educational research
8742	Management consulting services

Martial Arts Studio

7999	Amusement and recreation services, nec (includes Judo and Karate instruction)

Masonry, Stonework, and Plastering Contractors

1741	Masonry, stone setting, and other stonework
1742	Plastering, dry wall, acoustical, and insulation work

Massage Therapist

7299	Massage parlor 8049 Offices and clinics of health practitioners,nec

Mediation Service

7389	Business services, nec (includes arbitration and conciliationservices)

Medical and Dental Instrument Manufacturing

3841	Surgical and medical instruments and apparatus
3843	Dental equipment and supplies

Medical Claims Service

6411	Insurance agents, brokers, and service (includes processing ofmedical claims on a contract or fee basis)

Medical Laboratory Service

8071	Medical laboratories

Medical Supplies Store

5047	Medical, dental, and hospital equipment and supplies

Medical Transcription Service

7374	Computer processing and data preparation and processing services

Messenger/Delivery/Subpoena Service

4215	Courier services, except by air (includes letter, mail, package,and parcel delivery services)
4822	Telegraph and other message communication (includes cablegrams, mailgrams, electronic mail, and other message services)
7389	Business services, nec (includes process serving services)

Miniature Golf Course Operation

7999	Amusement and recreation services, nec (includes miniature golf course operations)

Modeling School/Agency

7363	Help supply services (includes modeling services)

8299   Schools and educational services, nec (includes modeling schools)

Mortgage Broker

6162   Mortgage bankers and loan correspondents (includes mortgage brokers using own money)

6163   Loan brokers (includes mortgage brokers arranging for loans but using money of others)

6211   Security brokers, dealers, and flotation companies (includes buying and selling mortgages)

Motorcycle/Moped Store

5571   Motorcycle dealers

Movie Theatre Operation

7832   Motion picture theatres, except drive-ins

7833   Drive-in motion picture theatres

Moving Service

4212   Local trucking, without storage (includes furniture and other moving services)

4214   Local trucking, with storage (includes furniture and household goods moving services)

Music School

8299   Schools and educational services, nec (includes music schools)

Music Shop

5736   Musical instrument stores

5932   Used merchandise stores (includes retailers of secondhand musical instruments)

7699   Repair shops and related services, nec (includes musical instrument repair shops)

Musical Instrument Repair/Piano Tuning Service

7699   Repair shops and related services, nec (includes musical instrument repair shops and piano tuning and repair)

Nail Salon

7231   Beauty shops (includes manicure and pedicure salons)

Nanny Service

7299   Miscellaneous personal services, nec (includes babysitting bureaus)

New Age Services and Supplies

5999   Miscellaneous retail stores, nec

8999   Services, nec

New and Used Car Dealer

5511   Motor vehicle dealers (new and used)

5521   Motor vehicle dealers (used only)

Newsletter Publishing

2721   Periodicals; publishing or publishing and printing

2741   Miscellaneous publishing (includes business service newsletterspublishing and/or printing)

Novelty Items Business

2499   Wood products, nec (includes wood and wood fiber novelties)

2514   Metal household furniture (includes metal novelty furniture)

2679   Converted paper and paperboard products, nec (includes papernovelties)

3199   Leather goods, nec (includes leather novelties)

3229   Pressed and blown glass and glassware, nec (includes novelty glassware made in glassmaking plants)

3231   Glass products, made of purchased glass (includes glassnovelties)

3499   Fabricated metal products, nec (includes metal novelties and specialties, except advertising novelties)

3961   Costume jewelry and costume novelties, except precious metal andgems

3999   Manufacturing industries, nec (includes bone, beaded and shell novelties)

Nursing Home/Long-Term Care Center

8051   Skilled nursing care facilities

8052   Intermediate care facilities (includes intermediate care nursing homes)

8059   Nursing and personal care facilities, nec (includes convalescent homes, rest homes, and like facilities)

Nutritional Consultant/Diet Planner

7299   Miscellaneous personal services, nec (includes diet workshops)

8049   Offices and clinics of health practitioners, nec (includes offices of nutritionists and offices of dietitians)

Office Design Service

7389   Business services, nec (includes interior decorating and design services)

Office Supply/Equipment Store

5943   Stationery stores (includes retail office forms and supplies stores)

Online Store

5734   Computer and computer software stores

7375   Information retrieval services

Paint/Wall Covering Center

5231   Paint, glass, and wallpaper stores

Painting Contractors

1721   Painting and paperhanging contractors

Party Entertainment Services

7929   Bands, orchestras, actors, and other entertainers and entertainment groups

Party/Reunion Planning Service

7359   Equipment rental and leasing, nec (includes party supplies rental and leasing)

8999   Services, nec

Pawnbroker

5932   Used merchandise stores (includes pawnshops)

Payroll Preparation Service

8721   Accounting, auditing, and bookkeeping services (includes payrollaccounting service)

Periodical/Newspaper Publishing

2721   Periodicals; publishing or publishing and printing

Personal Shopping Service

7299   Miscellaneous personal services, nec (includes shopping servicesfor individuals)

Pest Control Service

0851   Forestry services (includes forest pest control)

7342   Disinfecting and pest control services

Pet Boarding/Grooming Service

0279   Animal specialties, nec (includes breeding kennels)

0752   Animal specialty services (includes boarding kennels, doggrooming services, and related services)

Pet Cemetery

0782   Lawn and garden services (includes independent cemetery upkeep services)

6531   Real estate agents and managers (includes cemetery management services)

6553   Cemetery subdividers and developers (includes animal cemetery operations)

Pet Obedience School

0752   Animal specialty services, except veterinary (includes training of pets and other animal specialties)

Pet Shop

5999   Miscellaneous retail stores, nec (includes pet shops)

Pet Sitting Service

0752   Animal specialty services, except veterinary

Photo Finishing Center

7384   Photo finishing laboratories

7819   Services allied to motion picture production (includes motion picture film processing)

Photographer, Commercial

7335   Commercial photography

Photographic Studio

7221   Photographic studios, portrait

Physical Fitness Center

7991   Physical fitness facilities

Physical Therapy Clinic/Practice

8049   Offices and clinics of health practitioners, nec (includes offices of physical therapists)

Pizzeria

5812   Eating places (includes pizza parlors and pizzerias)

Plant Leasing Service

7359   Equipment rental and leasing, nec (includes plants)

Plumbing Service

1711   Plumbing, heating, and air-conditioning contractors

Porcelain Refinishing Service

1799   Special trade contractors, nec

Power Washing Service

1799   Special trade contractors, nec (includes cleaning of building exteriors)

7349   Building cleaning and maintenance services, nec (includes cleaning of building interiors)

7542   Car washes (includes automotive washing and polishing)

Prepaid Phone Card Business

4812   Radiotelephone communications

4813   Telephone communications, except radiotelephone

Print/Frame Shop

7699   Repair shops and related services, nec (includes custom picture framing services)

Printing Business

2752   Commercial printing, lithographic

2754   Commercial printing, gravure

2759   Commercial printing, nec

2761   Manifold business form printers

Private Investigation/Personal Security Service

7381   Detective, guard, and armored car services

Private Label Product Manufacturer/Retailer

3999   Manufacturing industries, nec

5399   Miscellaneous general merchandise stores

5499   Miscellaneous food stores 5699 Miscellaneous apparel and accessory stores

5999   Miscellaneous retail stores, nec

Professional Organizer

7299   Miscellaneous personal services, nec

7389   Business services, nec

Property Management

6531   Real estate agents and managers

Public Relations Consultant

8743   Public relations services

Public Warehousing/Ministorage Operation

4221   Farm product warehousing and storage

4222   Refrigerated warehousing and storage

4225   General warehousing and storage

4226   Special warehousing and storage, nec (includes fur storage, household goods warehousing and storage, whiskey warehousing, and like enterprises)

Quick Oil Change Service

5541   Gasoline service stations (includes automobile servicestations—retail)

7538   General automotive repair shops

Radio Station

4832   Radio broadcasting stations

Radon Testing Service

1799   Special trade contractors, nec

8734   Testing laboratories

Real Estate Agency

6531   Real estate agents and managers

Real Estate Investment Service

6798   Real estate investment trusts

Recording Studio

7399   Business services, nec (includes recording studios operating on a contract or fee basis)

Recreational Vehicle Dealer

5561   Recreational vehicle dealers

Recycling Business

5093   Scrap and waste materials

Rental Service

7299   Miscellaneous personal services, nec (includes clothing rental)

7352   Medical equipment rental and leasing

7353   Heavy construction equipment and leasing

7359   Equipment rental and leasing, nec

7377   Computer rental and leasing

7999   Amusement and recreation services, nec (includes pleasure boat rental, canoe and rowboat rental, bicycle, motorcycle and moped rental, and sporting goods rental)

Restaurant

5812   Eating places (includes sit-down, carry-out, and fast food)

Resume Service

7338   Secretarial anc court reporting services (includes resumewriting services)

Roofing Contractor

1761   Roofing, siding, and sheet metal work

Satellite Dish Service

4841   Cable and other pay television services (includes directbroadcast satellite services and satellite master antenna systems services)

Screen Printing Business

2261   Finishers of broadwoven fabrics of cotton (includes printing andfinishing of cotton broadwoven fabrics)

2262   Finishers of broadwoven fabrics of manmade fiber and silk(includes printing manmade fiber and silk broadwoven fabrics)

2759   Commercial printing, nec (includes screen printing on glass, plastics, paper, and metal, including highway signs)

Security Systems Service

7382   Security systems services

Seminar Planner/Lecturer

8999   Services, nec (including lecturers)

Service Station/Auto Repair and Service Shop

5541   Gasoline service stations

7532   Top, body, and upholstery repair shops and paint shops

7533   Automotive exhaust system repair shops

7534   Tire retreading and repair shops

7536   Automotive glass replacement shops

7537   Automotive transmission repair shops

7538   General automotive repair shops

7539   Automotive repair shops, nec

Sewer and Drain Cleaning Business

7699   Repair shops and related services, nec (includes sewer cleaning and rodding and septic tank cleaning) Sewing Center 5722 Household appliance stores (includes retail sewing machine stores)

5949   Sewing, needlework, and piece goods stores

7699   Repair shops and related services, nec (includes sewing machine repair shops)

Shoe Repair Shop

7251   Shoe repair shops and shoe-shine parlors

Shoe Store

5661   Shoe stores

Sign Shop

3993   Signs and advertising specialties

7389   Business services, nec (includes sign painting shops)

Silk Plant Shop

5999   Miscellaneous retail stores, nec (includes artificial flowers—retail)

Skating Rink Operation

7999   Amusement and recreation services, nec (includes ice and rollerskating rink operations)

Ski Shop

5941   Sporting goods stores and bicycle shops

Software Publishing

7372   Packaged software

Solar Energy Design/Contracting Business

1711   Plumbing, heating, and air-conditioning contractors (includes solar heating apparatus contractors)

1742   Plastering, dry wall, acoustical, and insulation work (includes solar reflecting insulation film contractors)

Specialized Staffing

7361   Employment Agencies

7363   Help Supply Services

Specialty Foods/Wine Shop

5499   Miscellaneous food stores

5921   Liquor stores (includes packaged wine—retail)

Sports Promotional Services

7941   Professional Sports Clubs and Promoters

Sporting Goods Store

5941   Sporting goods stores and bicycle shops

Surveying Service

8713   Surveying services (includes surveying: land, water, and aerial)

Swimming Pool/Hot Tub Business

1799   Special trade contractors, nec (includes swimming pool construction contractors)

5999   Miscellaneous retail stores, nec (includes hot tubs, retail)

7389   Business services, nec (includes swimming pool cleaning and maintenance services)

7999   Amusement and recreation services, nec (includes swimming pooloperations)

Tailor Shop

5699   Miscellaneous apparel and accessory stores (includes customtailor shops) 7219 Laundry and garment services, nec (includes tailorshops, except custom or merchant tailors)

Talent Agency

7922   Theatrical producers and miscellaneous theatrical services (includes agents)

Tanning Parlor/Sauna

7299   Miscellaneous personal services (includes steam baths and tanning salons)

Tattoo Parlor

7299   Miscellaneous personal services, nec (includes tattoo parlors)

Tax Preparation Business

7291   Tax return preparation services

8721   Accounting, auditing, and bookkeeping services

Taxicab/Van Shuttle Service

4121   Taxicabs

Taxidermy Service

7699   Repair shops and related services, nec (includes taxidermy)

Teacher Supply Store

5999   Miscellaneous retail stores, nec

Telemarketing Service

7389   Business services, nec (includes telemarketing services operating on a contract or fee basis)

Telephone Answering Service

7389   Business services, nec (includes answering services)

Television/Radio Repair Service

7622   Radio and television repair shops

Television Station

4833   Television broadcasting stations

Temporary Employment Agency

7363   Help supply services (includes temporary help services

Tennis Court/Racquet Club Operation

7997   Membership sports and recreation clubs (includes racquetball and tennis clubs)

7999   Amusement and recreation services, nec (includes nonmembership racquetball and tennis court operations)

Tire Dealer

5531   Auto and home supply stores (includes retail tire dealers) 7534 Tire retreading and repair shops

Tobacco Shop

5993   Tobacco stores and stands

Tour Guide Operation/Adventure Service

4725   Tour operations

7999   Amusement and recreation services, nec (includes tour guides)

Toy Business

5945   Hobby, toy, and game shops

Trade Show/Conference Management Service

7389   Business services, nec (includes trade show arrangement)

Translating/Interpreting Service

7389   Business services, nec (includes translation service)

Travel Agency

4724   Travel agencies

Trucking Business

4212   Local trucking, without storage services

4213   Trucking, except local

4214   Local trucking, with storage services

Tutoring Service

8299   Schools and educational services, nec (includes tutoring services)

Typesetting Business

2791   Typesetting

Typing/Stenographic Service

7338   Secretarial and court reporting services (includes stenographic and typing services)

Upholstery/Carpet Services

1752   Floor laying and other floor work, nec (includes carpet laying and removing services)

5714   Drapery, curtain, and upholstery stores (includes upholstery materials stores)

7217   Carpet and upholstery cleaning

Vending Machine Merchandising and Service Business

5962   Automatic merchandising machine operators (includes retail sale of products through vending machines)

7359   Equipment rental and leasing services, nec (includes vending machine rental businesses)

Videocassette Rental Store

5735   Recorded and prerecorded tape stores (includes retail videotape stores)

7841   Videotape rental establishments

Vision Center

5995   Optical goods stores

Voice Mail Service

4813   Telephone communications, except radiotelephone (includes voice telephone communications)

Water Conditioning Service

7389   Business services, nec (includes water softener services)

Web Site Design

7371   Computer programming services (includes custom computer programsor systems software development and computer software systems analysis and design)

Weight Reduction/Control Center

7991   Physical fitness facilities (includes reducing facilities and slenderizing salons)

Welcome Service

7389   Business service, nec (includes welcoming service)

Window Dressing Business

3993   Signs and advertising specialties (includes advertising displays, except printed, and window and lobby cutouts and displays)

7319   Advertising, nec (includes display advertising services, exceptoutdoor)

Word Processing Service

7338   Secretarial and court reporting services (includes wordprocessing services)

ASSOCIATIONS AND OTHER ORGANIZATIONS

9231 ■ Association of Fund-Raising Distributors and Suppliers (AFRDS)
1100 Johnson Ferry Rd., Ste. 300
Atlanta, GA 30342
Ph: (404)252-3663
Fax: (404)252-0774
Co. E-mail: afrds@kellencompany.com
URL: http://www.afrds.org
Contact: Kurt Koehler, President
Description: Distributors, suppliers, and manufacturers of products sold to fundraising organizations. Seeks to enhance the image of the product fundraising industry. Works to establish a code of ethics; conducts public relations activities and seminars. **Founded:** 1992.

9232 ■ Association of Fundraising Professionals (AFP)
4300 Wilson Blvd., Ste. 300
Arlington, VA 22203
Ph: (703)684-0410
Free: 800-666-3863
Fax: (703)684-0540
Co. E-mail: afp@afpnet.org
URL: http://www.afpnet.org
Contact: Tom Clark, Chief Operating Officer
Description: Fundraising executives who work for non-profit and philanthropic organizations. Purposes are: to foster the development and growth of professional fundraising executives committed to the philanthropic process; to establish professional ethical standards and to require its members to adhere to those standards; to provide guidance and assistance to philanthropic institutions and agencies with fundraising programs; to offer continuing professional education and career enhancement services for philanthropic fundraising professionals. Maintains speakers' bureau. **Founded:** 1960. **Publications:** *NSFRE Directory* (Annual); *Advancing Philanthropy: Journal of the National Society of Fund Raising Executives* (Bimonthly). **Educational Activities:** International Conference on Fundraising (Annual); International Conference on Fund Raising (Annual). **Awards:** Abel Hanson Award; Outstanding Foundation Award; Award for Outstanding Philanthropist; Award for Outstanding Volunteer Fundraiser; Freeman Philanthropic Services Award for Outstanding Corporation; Community Counselling Service Award for Outstanding Fundraising Professional.

9233 ■ Association of Professional Researchers for Advancement (APRA)
401 N Michigan Ave., Ste. 2200
Chicago, IL 60611
Ph: (312)321-5196
Fax: (312)673-6966
Co. E-mail: info@aprahome.org
URL: http://www.aprahome.org
Contact: Michael Quevli, President
Description: Individuals involved in educational, medical, cultural, and religious organizations; fundraising consultants. Facilitates education and dis-semination of information about prospect research; encourages professional development and cooperative relationships among members. Prospect research is aimed at securing gifts, grants, and charitable donations for nonprofit organizations. **Founded:** 1987. **Publications:** *APRA Member Directory* (Annual); *Connections* (Quarterly). **Educational Activities:** Association of Professional Researchers for Advancement Conference (Annual). **Awards:** APRA Visionary Award (Annual); Distinguished Service Award (Annual); Researcher of the Year (Annual); APRA Foundation Margaret Fuhry Grant (Annual).

9234 ■ Giving Institute (GI)
303 W Madison St., Ste. 2650
Chicago, IL 60606
Ph: (312)981-6794
Co. E-mail: info@givinginstitute.org
URL: http://www.givinginstitute.org
Contact: Geoffrey E. Brown, Executive Director
Description: Represents fund-raising counseling firms engaged in consulting on the management and planning of campaigns for hospitals, universities, religious groups, community funds, arts organizations, social service groups and other nonprofit institutions. Conducts research in philanthropy. **Founded:** 1935.

9235 ■ Partnership for Philanthropic Planning—NCPG
233 McCrea St., Ste. 400
Indianapolis, IN 46225
Ph: (317)269-6274
Fax: (317)269-6276
Co. E-mail: info@pppnet.org
URL: http://www.pppnet.org
Contact: Tanya Howe Johnson, President
URL(s): www.ncpg.org. **Description:** Professional association of individuals from the fundraising, accounting, estate planning, insurance, and related fields. Members specialize in developing charitable gifts through bequests, trusts, annuities, life insurance, and real property. Provides education and networking opportunities. Conducts research. **Founded:** 1988. **Publications:** *The Journal of Gift Planning* (Quarterly); *Proceedings of the National Conference on Planned Giving* (Annual). **Educational Activities:** National Conference on Planned Giving (Annual); National Conference on Planned Giving (Annual). **Telecommunication Services:** ncpg@ncpg.org.

REFERENCE WORKS

9236 ■ "3CDC's Biggest Year" in Business Courier (Vol. 26, December 18, 2009, No. 34, pp. 1)
Pub: American City Business Journals, Inc.
Ed: Lucy May. **Description:** Cincinnati Center City Development Corporation (3CDC) will make 2010 its biggest year with nearly $164 million projects in the works. Historic tax credits and continued help from the city have allowed the private nonprofit organiza-tion to finance mega projects such as the $43 million renovation and expansion of Washington Park. Other projects that 3CDC will start or complete in 2010 are presented.

9237 ■ "$40M Fund Created for Big Energy Project" in Austin Business JournalInc. (Vol. 29, November 27, 2009, No. 38, pp. 1)
Pub: American City Business Journals
Ed: Christopher Calnan. **Description:** A group of Texas businessmen, called Republic Power Partners LP, is planning to raise $40 million in order to launch an alternative energy project. The 6,000-megawatt initiative would generate solar, biomass and wind power in West Texas and could cost as much as $10 billion.

9238 ■ "Alliance to End Hunger to Hold Press Conference on Fasting, Prayer and Budget Cuts" in Food & Beverage Close-Up (March 28, 2011)
Pub: Close-Up Media
Description: A coalition of religious and other leaders are launching a new campaign to protect programs for vulnerable people. Partners include: Alliance to End Hunger, American Jewish World Service, Bread for the World, Congressional Hunger Center, Feeding America, Food for the Hungry, Islamic Relief USA, Meals on Wheels Association of America, New Manna Inc., ONE, Society of Saint Andrews, Sojourners, and World Food Program USA.

9239 ■ American Association of Fund-Raising Counsel Membership Directory
Pub: American Association of Fund-Raising Counsel Inc.
URL(s): www.aafrc.org/. **Released:** Annual **Covers:** Member fund-raising consulting firms. **Entries include:** Company name, address, phone, fax, geographical area served, types of clients, description of services. **Database includes:** Fair Practice Code; section on selection of counsel; brief historical introduction of AAFRC. **Arrangement:** Alphabetical.

9240 ■ Annual Register of Grant Support: A Directory of Funding Sources, 45th Edition
Pub: National Register Publishing Co.
Contact: Charles Lillis, Manager
E-mail: charles.lillis@marquiswhoswho.com
URL(s): books.infotoday.com/directories/anreg.shtml. **Released:** Annual; 46th edition, 2013. **Price:** $289, Individuals. **Covers:** More than 3,100 current grant programs offered by government agencies, private foundations, educational and professional associations, corporations, unions, religious groups and other organizations; covers programs offering grants to individuals for study, travel, etc., as well as to nonprofit organizations. **Entries include:** Organization name, address, phone; major interests; program names and purposes; nature and amounts of support; eligibility requirements; application instructions; names of persons to whom inquiries are to be submitted. **Database includes:** Program planning and proposal writing. **Arrangement:** Classified by subject area or grant purpose (e.g., special populations,

humanities, international affairs, etc.). **Indexes:** Subject, organization and program, geographical, and individual name.

9241 ■ *"Bethesda Stepping Out" in Business Courier (Vol. 27, October 15, 2010, No. 24, pp. 1)*
Pub: Business Courier
Ed: James Ritchie. **Description:** Nonprofit organization Bethesda Inc. is planning to donate $5 million a year for the next three years to Greater Cincinnati health care reforms. Bethesda revealed that it announced its donations to pressure other organizations to help.

9242 ■ *"Big Shoes to Fill for New United Way Chairman" in Business Courier (Vol. 27, June 25, 2010, No. 8, pp. 4)*
Pub: Business Courier
Ed: Lucy May. **Description:** David Dougherty, chairman of the nonprofit United Way of Greater Cincinnati, explains how he can surpass the nonprofit's 2009 campaign kickoff that raised $62 million. For 2010, Dougherty has prepared a $2 million matching grant from a group of local individuals, corporations, and foundations. Dougherty also discusses what he learned from participating in the 2009 campaign.

9243 ■ *"Boring Bonds Gain Pizzazz as Investors Flock to Debt Issues" in Baltimore Business Journal (Vol. 28, June 11, 2010, No. 5, pp. 1)*
Pub: Baltimore Business Journal
Ed: Gary Haber. **Description:** Companies and nonprofit organizations have increased the pace of bond offerings in order to take advantage of the bonds' appeal among willing investors. Companies mostly issued corporate bonds to replace existing debt at lower interest rates and save them money from interest payments.

9244 ■ *"Bringing Charities More Bang for Their Buck" in Crain's Chicago Business (Vol. 34, May 23, 2011, No. 21, pp. 31)*
Pub: Crain Communications Inc.
Ed: Lisa Bertagnoli. **Description:** Marcy-Newberry Association connects charities with manufacturers in order to use excess items such as clothing, janitorial and office supplies.

9245 ■ *"Business Put Cash Behind Bernstein" in Baltimore Business Journal (Vol. 28, August 20, 2010, No. 15, pp. 1)*
Pub: Baltimore Business Journal
Ed: Scott Dance. **Description:** Baltimore, Maryland-based businesses have invested $40,000 to support lawyer Gregg L. Bernstein in the 2010 State Attorney election. The election campaign is being fueled by fear of a crime surge. Many businesses have been dealing with crimes such as muggings, shootings, and car break-ins.

9246 ■ *"Chemed's Vitas Aims to Acquire" in Business Courier (Vol. 27, July 9, 2010, No. 10, pp. 1)*
Pub: Business Courier
Ed: James Ritchie. **Description:** Chemed Corporation's Vitas Healthcare Corporation is looking for smaller nonprofit hospices as it looks to become more streamlined in a tougher reimbursement environment. CFO David Williams syas they want to acquire these hospices as fast as they can integrate them.

9247 ■ *"Coastal Luxury Management Reports Los Angeles Food and Wine Tickets On Sale" in Food & Beverage Close-Up (August 24, 2011)*
Pub: Close-Up Media
Description: Wolfgang Puck's Sunday Brunch and Charity Auction will raise money for Saint Vincent Meals on Wheels program.

9248 ■ *"Coming Up Short" in Boston Business Journal (Vol. 30, October 15, 2010, No. 36, pp. 1)*
Pub: Boston Business Journal
Ed: Tim McLaughlin, Mary Moore. **Description:** Boston, Massachusetts-based nonprofits have been profiting less from charity golf tournaments. Nonprof-

its have been collecting less than 50 cents on the dollar from such events. But nonprofits have been restructuring golf tournaments in order to boost profits.

9249 ■ *"Corporate Responsibility" in Professional Services Close-Up (July 2, 2010)*
Pub: Close-Up Media
Description: List of firms awarded the inaugural Best Corporate Citizens in Government Contracting by the Corporate Responsibility Magazine is presented. The list is based on the methodology of the Magazine's Best Corporate Citizen's List, with 324 data points of publicly-available information in seven categories which include: environment, climate change, human rights, philanthropy, employee relations, financial performance, and governance.

9250 ■ *"Courier 250 Companies Hope to Rebound From 2009" in Business Courier (Vol. 27, July 16, 2010, No. 11, pp. 1)*
Pub: Business Courier
Ed: Dan Monk, Jon Newberry. **Description:** Private companies that are featured in the Courier 250 publication have lost almost $4 billion in revenue, while combined sales dropped by 11 percent to 32 billion in 2009. Courier 250 is a guide to public companies, large nonprofits, private firms, and other related entities in Ohio's Cincinnati region.

9251 ■ *"Don't Cry For Me?' in Canadian Business (Vol. 83, July 20, 2010, No. 11-12, pp. 47)*
Pub: Rogers Media Ltd.
Ed: Joe Castaldo. **Description:** Canada's theaters are faced with low ticket sales, donations and endowments. The industry is producing popular works as a response to the situation.

9252 ■ *"Echo Vintage Clothing Fundraiser Set July 24" in Tri-City Herald (July 22, 2010)*
Pub: McClathcy-Tribune
Description: Bicentennial Echo Vintage Clothing Show and Tea was held July 24, 2010 at the Echo City Hall Ballroom in Echo, Oregon. The event is held every two years to fund project in Echo and to maintain the vintage clothing collection.

9253 ■ *"The Emerging Capital Market for Nonprofits" in Harvard Business Review (Vol. 88, October 2010, No. 10, pp. 110)*
Pub: Harvard Business School Publishing
Ed: Robert S. Kaplan, Allen S. Grossman. **Description:** Demonstration of how nonprofits can use intermediaries to grow their organizational structures, giving them improved scale and impact is offered. Some intermediaries play a mutual-fund role and conduct due diligence, while others act as venture capital funds and implement strategy.

9254 ■ *"Endowments for Colleges Hit Hard in '09" in Milwaukee Business Journal (Vol. 27, February 12, 2010, No. 20, pp. A1)*
Pub: American City Business Journals
Ed: Corrinne Hess. **Description:** Southeast Wisconsin college endowments declined by as much as 35 percent in 2009 due to the economic downturn. A list of 2009 endowments to colleges in southeast Wisconsin and their percent change from 2008 is presented.

9255 ■ *"Fight Ensues Over Irreplaceable Gowns" in Tampa Bay Business Journal (Vol. 30, January 15, 2010, No. 4, pp. 1)*
Pub: American City Business Journals
Ed: Janet Leiser. **Description:** People's Princess Charitable Foundation Inc. founder Maureen Rorech Dunkel has sought Chapter 11 bankruptcy protection before a state court decides on the fate of the five of 13 Princess Diana Gowns. Dunkel and the nonprofit were sued by Patricia Sullivan of HRH Venture LLC who claimed they defaulted on $1.5 million in loans.

9256 ■ *"FIS-Metavante Deal Paying Off for Many" in Business Journal-Milwaukee (Vol. 28, December 17, 2010, No. 11, pp. A1)*
Pub: Milwaukee Business Journal
Ed: Rich Kirchen. **Description:** Jacksonville, Florida-based Fidelity National Information Services Inc., also known as FIS, has remained committed to Milwaukee, Wisconsin more than a year after purchasing Meta-

vante Technologies Inc. FIS has transferred several operations into Metropolitan Milwaukee and has continued its contribution to charitable organizations in the area.

9257 ■ *"For Putting Down Roots in Business: Amy Norquist: Greensulate, New York City" in Inc. (Volume 32, December 2010, No. 10, pp. 106)*
Pub: Inc. Magazine
Ed: Christine Lagorio. **Description:** Profile of Amy Norquist who left her position at an environmental nonprofit organization to found Greensulate. Her firm insulates rooftops with lavender, native grasses and succulents called sedum in order to eliminate carbon from the atmosphere.

9258 ■ *"Freedom Center May have New Path" in Business Courier (Vol. 26, October 30, 2009, No. 27, pp. 1)*
Pub: American City Business Journals, Inc.
Ed: Dan Monk, Lucy May. **Description:** National Underground Railroad Freedom Center in Price Hill, Cincinnati is in negotiations with US Rep. John Conyers for its possible classification as an independent establishment within the US federal government. If this happens, funding for the museum might be possibly augmented and the rights to use national archives might be furnished.

9259 ■ *"Gallo Family Vineyards to Raise Funds for Meals On Wheels" in Food & Beverage Close-Up (November 4, 2011)*
Pub: Close-Up Media
Description: Gallo family is committed to raising funds for Meals On Wheels Association of America and hosts a fundraiser annually.

9260 ■ *"Generous Donations Fund Repairs for Benton Trail Kiosk" in Morning Sentinel (December 22, 2010)*
Pub: Morning Sentinel
Ed: Scott Monroe. **Description:** The new kiosk at the entrance to a trail off Benton Avenue was paid for through donations and community contributions after the original was destroyed by vandals. The new kiosk's material was donated by the Huhtamaki manufacturing firm.

9261 ■ *"GoodNews.com and the Little Cupcake Shoppe Support Calgary Food Bank With Unique $1.00 Deal" in Marketwire Canada (March 9, 2011)*
Pub: Marketwire Canada
Description: Socially-conscious group-buying Website, GoodNews.com has partnered with The Little Cupcake Shoppe in Calgary, to raise funds for the Inter-Faith Food Bank. The fundraiser will feature a half dozen, pre-packaged assorted miniature cupcakes for $1.00. The entire amount is donated to the Calgary Food Bank.

9262 ■ *"Katie's Cupcakes to Celebrate One-Year Anniversary" in Bellingham Business Journal (Vol. March 2010, pp. 3)*
Pub: Sound Publishing Inc.
Description: Katie Swanson, owner of Katie's Cupcakes, celebrated her firm's one-year anniversary with a fundraiser for the Whatcom Humane Society by offering free specialty cupcakes and other special events to the public. The specialty cupcakes will feature either a paw or bone and will be available throughout the month of March.

9263 ■ *"A Lifetime of Giving: Food Bank CEO Fights Hunger One Mouth At a Time" in Black Enterprise (Vol. 41, November 2010, No. 4, pp. 86)*
Pub: Earl G. Graves Publishing Co. Inc.
Ed: Tamara E. Holmes. **Description:** Profile of Valerie Traore, CEO of Food Bank of South Jersey. Traore stresses the importance of volunteerism that she learned from her grandparents. Hunger relief became her passion when she served as a temp office worker for the Maryland Food Bank in Baltimore. She earned her Bachelor's of Science in management and has dedicated herself to a career in nonprofit service.

9264 ▪ *"Meals on Wheels Filling 'Blizzard Bags"* in *Tulsa World (November 5, 2011)*
Pub: Tulsa World
Ed: Sara Plummer. **Description:** Cathy Perlingiere, director of volunteer services for Meals on Wheels of Metro Tulsa, Oklahoma reports that they do not deliver meals when the Tulsa Public Schools close because of weather so they try to prepare 'blizzard bags' with nonperishable food items to cover about three meals for when drivers cannot deliver.

9265 ▪ *"Mercy Parent Nets Almost $1B in 2011"* in *Sacramento Business Journal (Vol. 28, September 30, 2011, No. 31, pp. 1)*
Pub: Sacramento Business Journal
Ed: Kathy Robertson. **Description:** Catholic Healthcare West has reported almost $1 billion in profits for 2010. The company has reported a profit margin of 8.7 percent. It also absorbed more than $1 billion in costs from charity care and government programs.

9266 ▪ *National Guide to Funding in Arts and Culture*
Pub: Foundation Center
Contact: Bradford K. Smith, President
URL(s): foundationcenter.org/. **Released:** Biennial; latest edition 8th; May, 2004. **Price:** $75, Individuals. **Covers:** over 5,200 foundations and corporate direct giving programs in the U.S. that fund arts and culture-related projects and organizations in the U.S. **Entries include:** Company or organization name, address, phone, names and titles of key personnel, geographical area served, financial data, requirements for eligibility. **Arrangement:** Geographical by state, then alphabetical. **Indexes:** Organization or company name, subject, geographical, type of support, donor/officer/trustee name.

9267 ▪ *National Guide to Funding for the Environment and Animal Welfare*
Pub: Foundation Center
Contact: Bradford K. Smith, President
URL(s): foundationcenter.org. **Released:** Biennial; latest edition 7th; June, 2004. **Price:** $75, Individuals. **Covers:** Over 3,500 foundations and corporate direct giving programs that fund programs in conservation, ecological research, litigation, waste reduction, animal welfare, advocacy, and related projects; limited international coverage. **Entries include:** Organization or company name, address, phone, financial data, giving priorities, name and title of contact, names and titles of key personnel. **Arrangement:** Geographical. **Indexes:** Grantmaker name, subject, geographical, type of support given, donor/officer/trustee.

9268 ▪ *National Guide to Funding in Health*
Pub: Foundation Center
Contact: Bradford K. Smith, President
URL(s): www.foundationcenter.org. **Released:** Irregular; latest edition 9th; Published April, 2005. **Price:** $175, Individuals. **Covers:** Over 11,500 foundations and corporations in the U.S. That fund health-related projects and institutions. **Entries include:** Organization or company name, address, phone, financial data, giving priorities, applications procedures, name and title of contact, names and titles of key personnel. **Arrangement:** Geographical by state. **Indexes:** Grantmaker name, subject, geographical, donor/officer/trustee, type of support.

9269 ▪ *"A New Alliance For Global Change"* in *Harvard Business Review (Vol. 88, September 2010, No. 9, pp. 56)*
Pub: Harvard Business School Publishing
Ed: Bill Drayton, Valeria Budinich. **Description:** Collaboration between social organizations and for-profit firms through the development of hybrid value chains to target complex global issues is promoted. While social organizations offer links to communities and consumers, firms provide financing and scale expertise.

9270 ▪ *"Nonprofit to Grow"* in *Austin Business JournalInc. (Vol. 29, January 22, 2010, No. 46, pp. 1)*
Pub: American City Business Journals
Ed: Sandra Zaragoza. **Description:** Southwest Key Programs Inc. received a $2.1 million grant from the U.S. Economic Development Administration to help

finance the building of a $3.6 million 'Social Enterprise Complex'. The complex is expected to create at least 100 jobs in East Austin, Texas. Details of the plan for the complex are presented.

9271 ▪ *"Nonprofit Ready to Get More Girls into 'STEM' Jobs"* in *Austin Business JournalInc. (Vol. 29, December 25, 2009, No. 42, pp. 1)*
Pub: American City Business Journals
Ed: Sandra Zaragoza. **Description:** Girlstart has completed its $1.5 million capital campaign to buy the building it will care the Girlstart Tech Center. Girlstart is a nonprofit organization that prepares girls for science, technology, engineering and mathematics or STEM careers. Details of the program are highlighted.

9272 ▪ *"Nonprofits Find Plenty of Optimism for the Future"* in *Business Courier (Vol. 26, January 1, 2010, No. 37, pp. 1)*
Pub: American City Business Journals, Inc.
Ed: Lucy May. **Description:** Forecasts of various nonprofits in Cincinnati, Ohio such as the United Way of Greater Cincinnati, the Greater Cincinnati Foundation and The Fine Arts Fund for 2010 are presented.

9273 ▪ *"Nonprofits May Lose MBE Status in MD"* in *Boston Business Journal (Vol. 29, September 2, 2011, No. 17, pp. 1)*
Pub: American City Business Journals Inc.
Ed: Scott Dance. **Description:** A business group has been pushing to bar nonprofits from Maryland's Minority Business program. Nonprofits have been found to take a large portion of state contracts intended for women- and minority-owned businesses. The group is also crafting proposed legislation to remove nonprofits from the program.

9274 ▪ *"One Laptop Per Child Weighs Going For-Profit"* in *Boston Business Journal (Vol. 31, May 20, 2011, No. 17, pp. 1)*
Pub: Boston Business Journal
Ed: Mary Moore. **Description:** Nonprofit organization One Laptop Per Child is thinking of shifting into a for-profit structure in order to raise as much as $10 million in capital to achieve its goal of distributing more XO laptops to poor children worldwide. The organization has distributed 2 million computers since 2008 with Uruguay, Peru and Rwanda as its biggest markets.

9275 ▪ *"Paralysis Foundation has Big Plans"* in *Austin Business JournalInc. (Vol. 29, December 11, 2009, No. 40, pp. 1)*
Pub: American City Business Journals
Ed: Sandra Zaragoza. **Description:** Lone Star Paralysis Foundation revealed plans to launch a fundraising effort for the advancement of cures for spinal cord injuries via adult stem cells and also fund a new spinal injury rehabilitation center. Efforts to raise about $3 million will begin as soon as the adult stem cell research study by Dr. Wise Young receives Food and Drug Administration approval.

9276 ▪ *"Pet Food Bank 'Shares the Love"* in *Pet Product News (Vol. 64, December 2010, No. 12, pp. 6)*
Pub: BowTie Inc.
Description: Winston-Salem, North Carolina-based nonprofit Share the Love Pet Food Bank has donated 60,000 pounds of pet food since its establishment in 2009. It has been linking pet food manufacturers and rescue groups to supply unsold pet food to needy animals. The nonprofit intends to reach out to more animal welfare groups by building more warehouses.

9277 ▪ *"Points of Light Sells MissionFish to eBay"* in *Non-Profit Times (Vol. 25, May 15, 2011, No. 7, pp. May 15, 2011)*
Pub: NPT Publishing Group Inc.
Contact: John McIlquham, President
Description: eBay purchased MissionFish, a subsidiary of Points of Light Institute for $4.5 million. MissionFish allows eBay sellers to give proceeds from sales to their favorite nonprofit organization and helps nonprofits raise funds by selling on eBay.

9278 ▪ *"Preserving a Nonprofit's Mission"* in *Boston Business Journal (Vol. 31, June 17, 2011, No. 21, pp. 3)*
Pub: Boston Business Journal
Ed: Mary Moore. **Description:** Young Women's Christian Association Boston (YWCA) agreed to absorb the LeadBoston social issues and youth programs operated by the Boston Center for Community Justice. The BCCJ is scheduled to close after failing to stabilize its finances.

9279 ▪ *Profits for Non-Profits: Running a Successful Gift Shop*
Pub: Lulu.com
Ed: Nancy Kirk. **Released:** January 2005. **Price:** $19.95. **Description:** Guide for managing a non-profit gift shop in a hospital, zoo, museum or any other non-profit entity.

9280 ▪ *"Race-Week Schedule Filling Up With Galas, Nonprofit Fundraisers"* in *Boston Business Journal (Vol. 29, July 22, 2011, No. 11, pp. 1)*
Pub: American City Business Journals Inc.
Ed: Alexander Jackson. **Description:** Baltimore, Maryland-based businesses and nonprofit groups have been planning their own events to coincide with the Baltimore Grand Prix during the Labor Day weekend. They also plan to partner with others in hopes of drumming up new business, raising money or to peddle their brands.

9281 ▪ *"Rebels' Cause: Adult Stem Cell"* in *Austin Business Journal (Vol. 31, June 3, 2011, No. 13, pp. 1)*
Pub: American City Business Journals Inc.
Ed: Sandra Zaragoza. **Description:** MedRebels Foundation was launched in February 2011 with the goal of providing millions of dollars for research funding, education and advocacy for adult stem cell-focused medicine. The foundation, whose major contributor is SpineSmith LP, is a collaboration of other adult stem cell-related companies and nonprofit partners. It hopes to raise $200,000 by the end of 2011.

9282 ▪ *"Speak Better: Five Tips for Polished Presentations"* in *Women Entrepreneur (September 19, 2008)*
Pub: Entrepreneur Media Inc.
Ed: Suzannah Baum. **Description:** Successful entrepreneurs agree that exemplary public speaking skills are among the core techniques needed to propel their business forward. A well-delivered presentation can result in securing a new distribution channel, gaining new customers, locking into a new referral stream or receiving extra funding.

9283 ▪ *"Staples Advantage Receives NJPA National Contract for Janitorial Supplies"* in *Professional Services Close-Up (April 22, 2011)*
Pub: Close-Up Media
Description: Staples Advantage, the business-to-business division of Staples Inc. was awarded a contract for janitorial supplies to members of the National Joint Powers Alliance (NJPA). NJPA is a member-owned buying cooperative serving public and private schools, state and local governments, and nonprofit organizations.

9284 ▪ *"Tech Giving 2.0"* in *Boston Business Journal (Vol. 31, August 5, 2011, No. 28, pp. 1)*
Pub: Boston Business Journal
Ed: Mary Moore. **Description:** Entrepreneurs and venture capitalists in Boston have launched Technology Underwriting Greater Good, the tech industry's answer to the criticism that they are not charitable. The foundation finances nonprofits that aid young people through entrepreneurship, education and life experience. Other tech firms in Boston doing charitable works are discussed.

9285 ▪ *"Tech Tax Heroes Go from Political Neophytes to Savvy Fundraisers"* in *Baltimore Business Journal (Vol. 27,*

November 20, 2009, No. 28)
Pub: American City Business Journals
Ed: Scott Dance. **Description:** A group of computer services and information technology executives in Maryland have arranged a private dinner that will function as a fundraiser for Governor Martin O'Malley and Lieutenant Governor Anthony Brown. The event is seen as an effort to ensure the industry's involvement in the state after fighting for the repeal of the tech tax in 2007.

9286 ■ *"Tim Tebow Foundation to Hold Pink 'Cleats for a Cure' Auction" in Travel & Leisure Close-Up (October 20, 2011)*
Pub: Close-Up Media
Description: Tim Tebow Foundation partnered with XV Enterprises to hold the 'Cleats for a Cure' auction on eBay. Tebow is auctioning off a pair of pink cleans he wore during the Denver Broncos vs. Tennessee Titans game October 3, 2010. All funds will go toward finding a cure for breast cancer.

TRADE PERIODICALS

9287 ■ *The Chronicle of Philanthropy: The Newspaper of the Non-Profit World*
Pub: The Chronicle of Philanthropy
URL(s): philanthropy.com. **Released:** 24/yr. **Price:** $72, Individuals; $125, Two years; $72, Individuals online access only; $99.75, Canada; $72, Canada online access only; $135, Other countries; $72, Other countries online access only.

9288 ■ *Communication Briefings*
Pub: Briefings Publishing Group
Contact: Joe McGavin, Executive Editor
E-mail: jmcgavin@briefings.com
Ed: Nicole Behrens, Editor, nbehrens@briefings.com. **Released:** Monthly. **Price:** $169, individual. **Description:** Provides communication ideas and techniques for a wide variety of areas, including public relations, advertising, fund raising, speeches, media relations, human resources, and employee/manager relations. Carries interviews with top communicators, business leaders, university experts, and research specialists. Recurring features include news of research, book reviews, and abstracts of articles from national publications.

9289 ■ *Foundation News & Commentary*
Pub: Council on Foundations
Contact: Vikki N. Spruill, President
URL(s): www.foundationnews.org/. **Ed:** Paula Kelly. **Released:** Bimonthly

9290 ■ *The NonProfit Times: The Leading Business Publication For Nonprofit Management*
Pub: NPT Publishing Group Inc.
Contact: John McIlquham, President
URL(s): www.nptimes.com/. **Released:** 17/yr. **Price:** $49.95, Individuals print; $19.95, Individuals digital only; $59.95, Individuals digital & print.

TRADE SHOWS AND CONVENTIONS

9291 ■ International Conference on Fundraising
Association of Fundraising Professionals (AFP)
4300 Wilson Blvd., Ste. 300
Arlington, VA 22203
Ph: (703)684-0410
Free: 800-666-3863
Fax: (703)684-0540
Co. E-mail: afp@afpnet.org
URL: http://www.afpnet.org
Contact: Tom Clark, Chief Operating Officer
URL(s): www.afpnet.org. **Price:** $595, Pre-registered, members; $695, Onsite registered, members; $945, Pre-registered, non-members; $1250, Onsite registered, non-members. **Frequency:** Annual. **Audience:** Decision makers for development offices for nonprofits. **Principal Exhibits:** Fundraising tools. **Telecommunication Services:** conference@afpnet.org.

CONSULTANTS

9292 ■ Ashland Group L.P.
11550 Fuqua St., Ste. 560
Houston, TX 77034
Ph: (281)484-1700
Free: 800-684-2246
Fax: (281)484-1822
URL: http://www.ashlandgroup.com
Contact: Randy Casey, Managing Partner
E-mail: rcasey@ashlandgroup.com
Scope: Government and political affairs agency that specializes in government relations, advocacy communications, media relations, campaign management and government contract lobbying. Offers creative and innovative tax issues. **Founded:** 1990. **Publications:** "State Tax Guide," Jan, 2009; "State Tax Guide," Jan, 2007.

9293 ■ Democracy Data & Communications L.L.C.
44 Canal Center Plz., Ste. 200
Alexandria, VA 22314-1542
Ph: (703)684-9690
Fax: (703)683-9626
Contact: Jim Gianiny, President
Scope: Provides grassroots technology solutions and online database management. **Founded:** 1996.

9294 ■ Essex & Drake Fund Raising Counsel
1202 University Ave.
San Jose, CA 95126
Ph: (408)294-7779
Fax: (408)297-2722
Co. E-mail: contact@essexdrake.com
URL: http://www.essexdrake.com
Contact: Sharon Trenson Svensson, President
E-mail: sharon@essexdrake.com
Scope: Specializes in board development including governance issues, finding and putting new board members to work and moving the board to relevant action. Organizes fund raising campaigns including feasibility studies, major gift campaigns and strategy development. Offers training in board excellence and all areas of fund raising. **Founded:** 1982. **Publications:** "Fund raising for Non-Profits," Harper Collins. **Seminars:** Capital Campaigns that Really Work, 2012; Launching and Sustaining a Planned Giving Program in a Small Development Department, May, 2009; Web 2.0 for Nonprofits, San Francisco, Mar, 2009; Building and Sustaining a Board Driven Major Gifts Program, San Francisco; Marketing Your Organization for Fund raising Success; Strategies for a Successful Capital Campaign; Achieving Successful Online Fund raising; Identifying and Building Relationships with Major Donors; Best Practices in Managing a Capital, Endowment or Combination Campaign.

9295 ■ The Hathaway Group Inc.
1010 Pendleton St.
Alexandria, VA 22314-1837
Ph: (703)837-1818
Fax: (703)837-1822
Contact: Timothy Hathaway, President
E-mail: trh@thehathawaygroup.com
Scope: Political consultant whose services includes voter and databases, network design and administration, web site creation, maintenance and hosting, and fax broadcasting. **Founded:** 1997.

9296 ■ Jeffrey Lant Associates Inc.
50 Follen St., Ste. 507
Cambridge, MA 02138
Ph: (617)547-6372
Fax: (617)547-0061
URL: http://www.jeffreylant.com
Contact: Dr. Jeffrey L. Lant, President
E-mail: drjlant@worldprofit.com
Description: Description: Publishes technical assistance books for nonprofit organizations, consultants, independent professionals and small and home-based businesses. Offers audio cassettes, workshops and consultation services. Also publishes twice monthly Worlgram newsletter. Reaches market through commission representatives, direct mail, telephone sales and the Internet. Accepts unsolicited manuscripts. **Scope:** Sets up businesses online,

design websites and assists with marketing. **Founded:** 1979. **Publications:** "E-mail El Dorado," JLA Publications, 1998; "Web Wealth: How to Turn the World Wide Web Into a Cash Hose for Your Business. Whatever You're Selling," 1997; "Multi-Level Money," JLA Publications, 1994; "No More Cold Calls," JLA Publications, 1997; "Cash Copy"; "How to make at least $100000 a year"; "E-Money". **Seminars:** Business and personal development, including Establishing and Operating Your Successful Consulting Business; Successfully Promoting Your Small Business and Professional Practice; Succeeding in Your Mail Order Business; Successfully Raising Money for Your Nonprofit Organization from Foundations, Corporations and Individuals; Money Making Marketing: Finding the People Who Need What You're Selling and Making Sure They Buy It; Getting Corporations, Foundations, and Individuals to Give You the Money Your Nonprofit Organization Needs.

9297 ■ Matson & Associates (M&A)
7831 Western Ct. SE
Olympia, WA 98501-6839
Ph: (360)956-9694
Fax: (360)754-8114
Co. E-mail: support@olywa.net
URL: http://www.matsonassociates.com
Contact: Mike Matson, Owner
E-mail: mmatson@matsonassociates.com
Scope: Consulting in the areas of: strategic planning, issue management, needs analysis, political action, campaign consulting, campaign management, fund raising and custom-designed education and recruitment programs. **Founded:** 1985. **Seminars:** Politics. . .A Cost of Doing Business; Political Action Committee Development; Coalition Building; Keystone Conference; Activist/Advocate Training.

9298 ■ Maximum Response Marketing
PO Box 505, Sta. Central
Halifax, NS, Canada B3J 2R7
Ph: (902)444-9457
Fax: (902)444-9457
Co. E-mail: maxresponse@hotmail.com
Contact: Charles Salmon, President
E-mail: maxresponse@hotmail.com
Scope: Specialists in designing effective, results-driven, direct marketing programs that generate inquiries, orders or donations for business, consumer and not-for-profit. Services include campaign planning and implementation; project management; creative direction and package design; direct mail copywriting and copy editing; database analysis and segmentation; mailing list procurement and evaluation; developing privacy policies; print procurement and supplier liaison; email marketing strategy, copy and list; telemarketing, scripting and training. **Founded:** 1991. **Seminars:** Direct Mail Fundraising Communications and Fundraising, Mount Saint Vincent University, 2004; Federal Privacy Legislation, Atlantic Regional Meeting, United Way of Canada, 2003; DM Campaign Basics, United Way of Canada National Conference, 2002; Bayers Lake Business Seminar Service, 2002; Using DM to Group Your Business, Atlantic Regional Meeting, United Way of Canada, 2002; Tips, Tools and Techniques: DM Fundraising 101, Atlantic Philanthropy Conference, 1999; Direct Marketing Tips Tools and Techniques and A Strategic Approach to Direct Mail Creative, Dalhousie University; How to Use Direct Marketing to Build Your Business in the Export Marketplace, ACOA (Atlantic Canada Opportunities Agency)-Trade Outreach Sessions; How to Cultivate Your Customers Using Direct Marketing Tools, NS Dept. of Agriculture-Bi-Annual Conference.

9299 ■ Guy Rodgers & Associates Inc.
748 Montebello Cir.
Chesapeake, VA 23322-7257
Ph: (757)686-0088
Co. E-mail: graa@acninc.net
Contact: Guy Rodgers, Owner
E-mail: graa@pinn.net
Scope: Legislative and campaign consulting, grassroots and coalition development, fund raising, and political training. **Founded:** 1994.

9300 ▪ Stevens, Reed, Curcio and Potholm
201 N Union St., Ste. 200
Alexandria, VA 22314
Ph: (703)683-8326
Fax: (703)683-8826
Co. E-mail: pcurcio@srcpmedia.com
URL: http://www.srcpmedia.com
Contact: Betsy Vonderheid, Director
Scope: Republican media consulting firm that specializes in media production, public opinion research, direct mail design, opposition research and political strategy. **Founded:** 1993.

9301 ▪ Triad Strategies L.L.C.
116 Pine St.
Harrisburg, PA 17101
Ph: (717)238-2970
URL: http://www.triadstrategies.com
Contact: Roy J. Wells, President
E-mail: rwells@triadstrategies.com
Scope: Government relations firm. Services include legislative and regulatory monitoring, legislative and executive branch lobbying, independent and quasi-public agency lobbying, issue research, issue management, grassroots organizing, public relations, strategic planning, and network marketing. **Founded:** 2002.

FRANCHISES AND BUSINESS OPPORTUNITIES

9302 ▪ Heavenly Gold Card
Nova Media Inc.
1724 N State
Big Rapids, MI 49307-9073
Ph: (231)796-4637
Description: Fund raising for non profit organizations. **No. of Franchise Units:** 1. **Founded:** 1981.. **Franchised:** 1992. **Equity Capital Needed:** $100. **Franchise Fee:** $1,000. **Financial Assistance:** Yes. **Training:** Yes.

9303 ▪ Magis Fund Raising Specialists Services For Non-Profits
Magis Fund Raising Specialists
845 Heathermoor Ln.
Perrysburg, OH 43551
Ph: (419)874-4459
Fax: (419)874-4459
Description: Provides full-service fund raising, financial development, marketing and public relations services to non-profit organizations. Conducts major pledge campaigns for new facilities, increases annual giving by 20% or more, builds endowments of $1 million or more, conducts feasibility studies, fundraising audits, personnel searches, writes grant proposals, trains leadership, conducts seminars and workshops, strategic planning, video presentations and newsletters. is needed; business can be conducted from your home or added to an existing, already established office. **No. of Franchise Units:** 2. **No. of Company-Owned Units:** 2. **Founded:** 1989. **Franchised:** 1991. **Equity Capital Needed:** $100,000. **Franchise Fee:** $25,000. **Training:** 1 week of preliminary materials provided for at-home study. Second week at Magis' headquarters, where all systems are taught. Third week at your location. Ongoing contact by phone, fax and regular seminars.

COMPUTERIZED DATABASES

9304 ▪ *Foundation Directory Online*
79 5th Ave., 16th St.
New York 10003-3076
Ph: (212)620-4230
Free: 800-424-9836
Fax: (212)807-3677
Co. E-mail: feedback@foundationcenter.org
URL: http://foundationcenter.org/newyork
Contact: Bradford K. Smith, President
Availability: Online: ProQuest LLC - Dialog; ProQuest LLC - Dialog; Foundation Center. **Type:** Directory; Numeric.

LIBRARIES

9305 ▪ Brakeley Inc. - Library
86 Prospect St.
Stamford, CT 06901
Ph: (203)348-8100
Fax: (203)978-0114
Co. E-mail: info@brakeley.com
URL: http://www.brakeley.com/
Contact: George A. Brakeley, III
Scope: Fundraising, philanthropy. **Services:** Library open to the public with special permission. **Founded:** 1919. **Holdings:** 300 books; 30 VF drawers of clippings, pamphlets, foundation Annual reports; reports. **Subscriptions:** 10 journals and other serials.

9306 ▪ Council for Advancement and Support of Education Information Center
1307 New York Ave. NW, Ste. 1000
Washington, DC 20005-4701
Ph: (202)328-2273
Fax: (202)387-4973
Co. E-mail: infocenter@case.org
URL: http://www.case.org
Contact: Megan Galaida, Director
Scope: Alumni administration, educational fundraising, communications, marketing, institutional advancement. **Services:** Center not open to the public (open to CASE members by appointment). **Founded:** 1974. **Holdings:** Books; periodicals; reports; studies; speeches; surveys; college, university, and independent school publications and literature; CD-ROMs. **Subscriptions:** 40 journals and other serials. **Telecommunication Services:** memberservicecenter@case.org.

9307 ▪ Council on Foundations Resource Center
2121 Crystal Dr., Ste. 700
Arlington, VA 22202-3706
Ph: (703)879-0688
Free: 800-673-9036
Fax: (202)785-3926
URL: http://www.cof.org
Contact: Luis Maldonado, Director
Scope: Philanthropy, grantmaking, foundations, management. **Services:** Library not open to the public. **Founded:** 1949. **Holdings:** 5000 books; reports; articles; periodicals; archives; videotapes. **Subscriptions:** 10 journals and other serials; 3 newspapers.

9308 ▪ Foundation Center Cleveland Library
1422 Euclid Ave., Ste. 1600
Cleveland, OH 44115-2001
Ph: (216)861-1933
Fax: (216)861-1936
Co. E-mail: cgb@foundationcenter.org
URL: http://foundationcenter.org/cleveland
Contact: Cynthia Glunt Bailie, Director
Scope: Reports by and of foundations; government grants; corporate philanthropy; grantsmanship; proposal writing. **Services:** Interlibrary loan; copying; instructional sessions in the use of specialized materials on grants; library open to the public. **Founded:** 1977. **Holdings:** 1400 volumes; 500 pamphlets; 1000 current annual reports of foundations; clippings on philanthropic foundations. **Subscriptions:** 25 journals and other serials.

9309 ▪ Foundation Center, Washington, DC Library
1627 K St. NW, 3rd Fl.
Washington, DC 20006
Ph: (202)331-1400
Fax: (202)331-1739
Co. E-mail: dclibrary@foundationcenter.org
URL: http://foundationcenter.org/washington/
Contact: Jeff Carter, Executive Director
Scope: Private philanthropic giving, corporations, foundations. **Services:** Copying; Library open to the public. **Founded:** 1964. **Holdings:** 2500 volumes. **Subscriptions:** 50 journals and other serials. **Telecommunication Services:** pep@foundationcenter.org.

9310 ▪ Imagine Canada - John Hodgson Library
2 Carlton St., Ste. 600
Toronto, ON, Canada M5B 1J3
Ph: (416)597-2293, x-255
Free: 800-263-1176
Fax: (416)597-2294
Co. E-mail: library@imaginecanada.ca
URL: http://library.imaginecanada.ca/services
Contact: Kimberley Turner, Director, Library Services
Scope: Philanthropy, fundraising, marketing, voluntarism, management, government legislation. **Services:** Library not open to the public. **Founded:** 1981. **Holdings:** 7000 titles. **Subscriptions:** 5 journals and other serials; 1 newspaper. **Telecommunication Services:** info@imaginecanda.ca.

9311 ▪ State University of New York at Buffalo - University Development Library
3435 Main St.
Buffalo, NY 14214-3010
Ph: (716)829-2630
Fax: (716)829-2636
Co. E-mail: alkutner@buffalo.edu
URL: http://ublib.buffalo.edu/libraries/
Contact: Ann L. Kutner, Analyst
Scope: Fund raising, fund raising management. **Services:** Copying; Library open to the public. **Founded:** 1986. **Holdings:** 100 volumes. **Subscriptions:** 15 journals and other serials; 3 newspapers.

9312 ▪ Tucson Pima Public Library - Grants and Nonprofit Information Collection
101 N. Stone Ave.
Tucson, AZ 85701
Ph: (520)791-4010
Fax: (520)594-5621
URL: http://www.library.pima.gov
Contact: Nancy Ledeboer, Director, Library Services
Scope: Grants, foundations, corporate philanthropy, fundraising, nonprofit management, charities, government grants. **Services:** Copying; regular orientations to the Grants Collection; library open to the public. **Founded:** 1977. **Holdings:** 200 books; 50 reports. **Subscriptions:** 9 journals and other serials; 3 newspapers.

RESEARCH CENTERS

9313 ▪ Indiana University-Purdue University at Indianapolis - Center on Philanthropy
550 W N St., Ste. 301
Indianapolis, IN 46202-3491
Ph: (317)274-4200
Fax: (317)684-8900
Co. E-mail: rooney@iupui.edu
URL: http://www.philanthropy.iupui.edu
Contact: Patrick M. Rooney, Executive Director
Services: Research, surveys, project evaluation, etc. **Founded:** 1987. **Publications:** *Indiana Gives* (Quadrennial); *Million Dollar List* (Quarterly); *Occasional papers*; *Philanthropic Giving Index* (Semiannual); *Philanthropy Matters* (Semiannual). **Educational Activities:** Center on Philanthropy Conferences (Weekly), in cooperation with other academic institutions and nonprofit organizations; Fund Raising School (Weekly), providing training in ethical fund raising and management principles and practices to staff, board members, and other volunteers of the independent sector; Professional training, in grantmaking, nonprofit organizations, working with trustees and volunteers, and fundraising communications; Center on Philanthropy Seminars; Symposium on fundraising (Annual).

9314 ▪ New York University - National Center on Philanthropy and the Law (NCPL)
School of Law
139 MacDougal St., 1st Fl.
New York, NY 10012
Ph: (212)998-6168
Fax: (212)995-3149
Co. E-mail: ncpl.info@nyu.edu
URL: http://www1.law.nyu.edu/ncpl
Contact: Prof. Jill S. Manny, Executive Director
E-mail: jill.manny@nyu.edu
Founded: 1988. **Educational Activities:** NCPL Conferences and seminars; Courses on nonprofit law, tax aspects of charitable giving, and tax-exempt

organizations. **Awards:** NCPL Fellowships (Annual), to the Vera Institute of Justice and New York University Office of Legal Counsel. **Telecommunication Services:** hpd1@nyu.edu.

ASSOCIATIONS AND OTHER ORGANIZATIONS

9315 ■ American Board of Funeral Service Education (ABFSE)
3414 Ashland Ave., Ste. G
St. Joseph, MO 64506-1333
Ph: (816)233-3747
Fax: (816)233-3793
Co. E-mail: exdir@abfse.org
URL: http://www.abfse.org
Contact: Michael Smith, Executive Director
Description: Representatives from National Funeral Directors Association, International Conference of Funeral Service Examining Boards of the United States, the National Funeral Directors and Mortuaries Association and college program representatives and public members. Seeks to: formulate and enforce rules and regulations setting up standards concerning the schools and colleges teaching mortuary science; accredit schools and colleges of mortuary science. Sponsors the National Scholarship for Funeral Service program to provide capable young men and women studying in the field with financial assistance. Compiles statistics. **Founded:** 1946. **Publications:** *Directory of Accredited College Programs in Mortuary Science and Committees of the American Board of Funeral Service Education* (Semiannual). **Awards:** ABFSE National Scholarship Program; National Scholarship Program of the American Board of Funeral Service Education (Annual).

9316 ■ American Institute of Commemorative Art (AICA)
8015 Van Ness Way
Indianapolis, IN 46240
Ph: (317)731-6556
Fax: (317)731-6556
Co. E-mail: lelandb@monuments-aica.com
URL: http://www.monuments-aica.com
Contact: Jed Hendrickson, President
Description: Retailers of memorials and cemetery monuments with strong interest in commemorative design. **Scope:** cemetery memorials. **Founded:** 1951. **Subscriptions:** artwork. **Publications:** *Milestone* (Quarterly). **Awards:** Eugene H. Faehnle Award (Annual); Harold J. Schaller Award (Annual).

9317 ■ Casket and Funeral Supply Association of America (CFSA)
49 Sherwood Terr., Ste. Y
Lake Bluff, IL 60044-2231
Ph: (847)295-6630
Fax: (847)295-6647
Co. E-mail: brussell@cfsaa.org
URL: http://www.cfsaa.org
Contact: Kevin L. Thomson, President
Description: Manufacturers and distributors of burial caskets and other funeral supplies. **Founded:** 1913. **Publications:** *Casket & Funeral Supply Association of America Newsletter.*

9318 ■ Catholic Cemetery Conference (CCC)
1400 S Wolf Rd., Bldg. No. 3
Hillside, IL 60162-2197

Ph: (708)202-1242
Free: 888-850-8131
Fax: (708)202-1255
Co. E-mail: info@catholiccemeteryconference.org
URL: http://www.ntriplec.com
Contact: Carmen A. Colao, President
Description: Archdiocesan and diocesan directors of Catholic cemeteries; associate members are administrators of Catholic cemeteries. **Scope:** cemetery monuments, shrines. **Founded:** 1949. **Publications:** *Design and Construction Manual*; *Field Operation Manual*; *Mausoleum Maintenance Manual*; *National Catholic Cemetery Conference--Membership and Resource Directory* (Annual); *The Catholic Cemetery: A Vision for the Millennium.*

9319 ■ Cremation Association of North America (CANA)—Cremationist of North America
499 Northgate Pkwy.
Wheeling, IL 60090-2646
Ph: (312)245-1077
Fax: (312)321-4098
Co. E-mail: info@cremationassociation.org
URL: http://www.cremationassociation.org
Contact: Kevin Waterston, President
Description: Cemeteries, crematories, funeral directors, and manufacturers. Seeks to increase public awareness and knowledge of cremation and memorialization. Conducts research; compiles statistics. Holds certification programs and trade show. **Founded:** 1913. **Publications:** *Cremationist* (Quarterly); *Newsletter Update* (Bimonthly). **Educational Activities:** Cremation Association of North America Convention (Annual); Cremation Marketing (Annual); Cremation Association of North America Convention (Annual). **Telecommunication Services:** cana@smithbucklin.com.

9320 ■ Funeral Consumers Alliance
33 Patchen Rd.
South Burlington, VT 05403
Ph: (802)865-8300
Free: 800-765-0107
Fax: (802)865-2626
Co. E-mail: fca@funerals.org
URL: http://www.funerals.org/
Contact: Laurie Powsner, President
E-mail: lrpjak@verizon.net
Description: Promotes a consumer's right to choose a dignified, meaningful, affordable funeral. Provides educational material to the public and affiliates. Monitors the funeral and cemetery industry for consumers nationwide. Responds to consumer complaints. Maintains speakers' bureau. **Scope:** death, dying, grief, burials, cremation. **Subscriptions:** 50 books. **Publications:** *The FCA Newsletter*; *FCA Newsletter* (Quarterly); *Funeral Consumers Alliance* (Quarterly).

9321 ■ International Cemetery, Cremation and Funeral Association (ICCFA)
107 Carpenter Dr., Ste. 100
Sterling, VA 20164
Ph: (703)391-8400
Free: 800-645-7700

Fax: (703)391-8416
Co. E-mail: hq@iccfa.com
URL: http://www.iccfa.com
Contact: Nancy R. Lohman, President
URL(s): www.icfa.org/. **Description:** Owners and managers of cemeteries and funeral homes; related suppliers and professional service firms. **Founded:** 1887. **Publications:** *International Cemetery and Funeral Management* (10/year); *ICCFA Magazine*; *International Cemetery, Cremation & Funeral Association--Membership Directory and Buyers Guide* (Annual); *ICFA Buyer's Guide and Membership Directory* (Annual). **Educational Activities:** International Cemetery, Cremation & Funeral Association Annual Convention and Exposition (Annual). **Awards:** Keeping It Personal Awards (Annual). **Telecommunication Services:** gen4@icfa.org.

9322 ■ Jewish Funeral Directors of America (JFDA)
107 Carpenter Dr., Ste. 100
Sterling, VA 20164-4468
Free: 888-477-5567
Fax: (703)391-8416
Co. E-mail: jfdamer@aol.com
URL: http://www.jfda.org
Contact: Albert Bloomfield, President
Description: Predominantly serves members of the Jewish faith. Assists people of the Jewish faith arrange meaningful and affordable funerals in the Jewish tradition. **Founded:** 1932. **Publications:** *Jewish Funeral Director* (Annual); *How to Explain Death to Children* (3/year).

9323 ■ Monument Builders of North America (MBNA)
136 S Keowee St.
Dayton, OH 45402
Free: 800-233-4472
Fax: (937)222-5794
Co. E-mail: info@monumentbuilders.org
URL: http://www.monumentbuilders.org
Contact: Ron Bohman, President
Description: Monument retailers, manufacturers, and wholesalers; bronze manufacturers and suppliers. Provides sales, advertising, and management materials to members. Develops modern and religious memorial designs. Provides Affinity Programs such as discounts and low-cost credit card processing. Opposes "restrictive business practices and unfair competition". Compiles statistics; conducts specialized education and certification programs; maintains speakers' bureau. **Scope:** monument design and production. **Founded:** 1906. **Subscriptions:** 10 video recordings. **Publications:** *Monument Builders of North America--Membership Roster* (Annual); *Monument Builders News* (Monthly); *MB News* (Monthly). **Educational Activities:** Monument Industry Convention and Show (Annual). **Awards:** ASPIRE Awards (Annual).

9324 ■ National Concrete Burial Vault Association (NCBVA)
PO Box 917525
Longwood, FL 32791-7525
Ph: (407)788-1996

Free: 888-88N-CBVA
Fax: (407)774-6751
Co. E-mail: ncbva@ncbva.org
URL: http://ncbva.org
Contact: Hubert McQuestion, President
Description: Manufacturers of concrete burial vaults. Provides a unified voice for the concrete burial vault industry regardless of product affiliation, brand recognition or location. **Founded:** 1930.

9325 ■ National Funeral Directors Association (NFDA)
13625 Bishops Dr.
Brookfield, WI 53005-6607
Ph: (262)789-1880
Free: 800-228-6332
Fax: (262)789-6977
Co. E-mail: nfda@nfda.org
URL: http://www.nfda.org
Contact: Randall L. Earl, President
Description: Federation of state funeral directors' associations with individual membership of funeral directors. Seeks to enhance the funeral service profession and promote quality services to the consumers. Conducts professional education seminars and home study courses. Compiles statistics. **Scope:** dying, death, bereavement. **Founded:** 1882. **Subscriptions:** 1000 audio recordings books video recordings. **Publications:** National Funeral Directors Association--Directory of Members (Annual). **Awards:** Pursuit of Excellence (Annual); Pursuit of Excellence Award.

9326 ■ National Funeral Directors and Morticians Association (NFDMA)
6290 Shannon Pkwy.
Union City, GA 30291
Ph: (770)969-0064
Free: 800-434-0958
Fax: (770)969-0505
Co. E-mail: info@nfdma.com
URL: http://www.nfdma.com
Contact: Gregory T. Burrell, President
Description: State, district and local funeral directors and embalmers associations and their members. Promotes ethical practices; encourages just and uniform laws pertaining to funeral directing and embalming industry. **Scope:** training and development, industry updates, CEU credits. **Founded:** 1924. **Subscriptions:** periodicals. **Awards:** NFDM Scholarship (Annual).

9327 ■ Selected Independent Funeral Homes
500 Lake Cook Rd., Ste. 205
Deerfield, IL 60015
Ph: (847)236-9401
Free: 800-323-4219
Fax: (847)236-9968
Co. E-mail: info@selectedfuneralhomes.org
URL: http://www.selectedfuneralhomes.org
Contact: Thomas A. Broussard, President
Description: Funeral directors. Aims to study, develop, and establish a standard of service for the benefit of its consumers. Provides a continuing forum for the exchange, development and dissemination of knowledge and information beneficial to members and the public. **Founded:** 1917. **Publications:** Membership Roster (Quarterly).

REFERENCE WORKS

9328 ■ "Balancing Freedom of Speech with the Right To Privacy" in Pace Law Review (Fall 2007)
Pub: American Society on Aging
Contact: Robert Stein, President
Ed: Anna Zwierz Messa. **Description:** Information is offered to help authorities and funeral directors cope with protests occurring during a funeral.

9329 ■ "Cremation: Desecration, purification, or convenience?" in (Vol. 28, Summer 2004, No. 2, pp. 15-20)
Pub: American Society on Aging
Contact: Robert Stein, President
Ed: Michael C. Kearl. **Description:** The methods of disposing of the remains of the deceased is a problem all societies face. Different aspects of funeral

burials, including dropping into sea or converting to ashes by fire as well as new immortality-enhancing technologies are discussed.

9330 ■ Funeral Consumers Alliance
Pub: Funeral Consumers Alliance
Contact: Laurie Powsner, President
E-mail: lrpjak@verizon.net
URL(s): www.funerals.org. **Released:** Quarterly **Price:** Free. **Covers:** over 120 nonprofit funeral consumer groups that educate the public about affordable funeral options. Monitors funeral industry practices for consumers. **Entries include:** Name, address, phone, email address. **Arrangement:** Geographical.

9331 ■ "Funeral Directors Get Creative As Boomers Near Great Beyond" in Advertising Age (Vol. 79, October 13, 2008, No. 38, pp. 30)
Pub: Crain Communications, Inc.
Ed: Lenore Skenazy. **Description:** Despite the downturn in the economy, the funeral business is thriving due to the number of baby boomers who realize the importance of making preparations for their death. Marketers are getting creative in their approach and many companies have taken into consideration the need for a more environmental friendly way to dispose of bodies and thus have created innovative businesses that reflect this need.

9332 ■ Funeral Home & Cemetery Directory--Buyer's Guide
Pub: Nomis Publications Inc.
Contact: Lucille A. McGuire, President
URL(s): www.nomispublications.com/publications. aspx#TheBuyersGuide. **Released:** Annual; Latest edition 2011. **Price:** $30, Individuals. **Covers:** Over 2,000 suppliers to the funeral and cemetery industry. **Entries include:** Company name, address, phone, fax. **Arrangement:** Classified by product/service. **Indexes:** Product/service.

9333 ■ "Funeral Picketing Laws and Free Speech" in Kansas Law Review (Vol. 55, April 2007, No. 3, pp. 575-627)
Pub: American Society on Aging
Contact: Robert Stein, President
Ed: Stephen R. McAllister. **Description:** In-depth information covering laws governing protests and freedom of speech during funerals is presented.

9334 ■ "Funerals-R-Us: From Funeral Home to Mega-Industry" in (Vol. 28, Summer 2004, No. 2, pp. 11-14)
Pub: American Society on Aging
Contact: Robert Stein, President
Ed: Thomas Lynch. **Description:** Viewpoint from a funeral director as he looks at funerals and the sacred, secular, spiritual, emotional, social and practical duties and practices associated with funerals.

9335 ■ "A Grave Situation" in Chronicle of Higher Education (Vol. 54, November 30, 2007, No. 14)
Pub: Pace Law School
Ed: Don Troop. **Description:** W. Scott Walston has been selling funeral caskets with the University of Georgia's logo on them to graduates who pass away; however the University System of Georgia has a rule that forbids college logos on burial items.

9336 ■ NFDA Directory of Members and Transportation Guide
Contact: Kellie Schilling, Director, Business Development
URL(s): www.nfda.org/directory-of-members-a-transportation-guide.html. **Released:** Annual; Latest edition 2008-2009. **Price:** $35, Members print; $125, Nonmembers. **Covers:** 19,000 members of state funeral director associations affiliated with the National Funeral Directors Association. **Entries include:** Company name, address, phone, and principal executive. **Database includes:** Resource information. **Arrangement:** Geographical.

9337 ■ Purple Directory: National Listing of African-American Funeral Firms
Pub: Shugar's Publishing The Purple Directory
Contact: Jack Kynion, President
URL(s): www.purpledirectory.com. **Released:** Annual; Latest edition 10th, 2012-2013. **Price:** $40, Individuals inclusive of shipping and handling. **Cov-**

ers: Approximately 2,700 African-American funeral firms in the U.S. **Entries include:** Firm name, address, phone; some listings include fax and name and title of contact. **Database includes:** Information on literature dealing with death and dying. **Arrangement:** Geographical by state.

STATISTICAL SOURCES

9338 ■ RMA Annual Statement Studies
Pub: Risk Management Association
Contact: Kevin M. Blakey, President
Released: Annual. **Price:** $175.00 2006-07 edition, $105.00. **Description:** Contains composite balance sheets and income statements for more than 360 industries, including the accounting, auditing, and bookkeeping industries. Also contains five years of comparative historical data for discerning trends. Includes 16 commonly used ratios, computed for most of the size groupings for nearly every industry.

TRADE PERIODICALS

9339 ■ Casket & Funeral Supply Association of America Newsletter
Pub: Casket and Funeral Supply Association of America
Contact: Kevin L. Thomson, President
Ed: George W. Lemke, Editor, lemke@cfsaa.org. **Released:** Monthly. **Description:** Carries news items of interest to the funeral supply industry, including information on annual conventions, Federal Trade Commission regulations and other court rulings, and cost and pricing issues.

9340 ■ The Director: Official Publication of the National Funeral Directors Association
Contact: Edward J. Defort, President
URL(s): www.nfda.org/nfda-publications/the-director. html. **Ed:** Edward J. Defort. **Released:** Monthly **Price:** $50, Individuals; $65, Other countries including Canada.

9341 ■ The FCA Newsletter
Pub: Funeral Consumers Alliance
Contact: Laurie Powsner, President
E-mail: lrpjak@verizon.net
Ed: Lisa Carlson, Editor. **Released:** Quarterly. **Price:** $35, members. **Description:** Concerned with the funeral industry, activities of affiliates, and legislation related to consumer rights in making funeral arrangements. Includes articles and bibliographies pertaining to funerals, death, and dying.

9342 ■ NFDA Bulletin
Pub: National Funeral Directors Association
Ed: Renee L. Gryzkewicz, Editor, rgryzkewicz@nfda. org. **Released:** Monthly. **Price:** Included in membership. **Description:** Covers association activities and funeral business management topics. Reports on association news, government regulation, public relations issues, and local developments.

FRANCHISES AND BUSINESS OPPORTUNITIES

9343 ■ Select Community Funeral Homes Inc.
Select Management Partnerships
111 Paradise Row
Saint John, NB, Canada E2K 3H6
Ph: (506)632-1135
Free: 877-473-5328
Fax: (506)652-3251
Co. E-mail: info@selectFH.ca
URL: http://www.selectfunerals.com
Description: Offers management system for independent funeral homes. **No. of Company-Owned Units:** 6. **Founded:** 1872.. **Equity Capital Needed:** Varies, depending upon size of business. **Franchise Fee:** Varies. **Training:** Yes.

COMPUTER SYSTEMS/ SOFTWARE

9344 ■ Funeral Directors Management System
860 F Ave., Ste. 104
Plano, TX 75074

Ph: (866)230-0800
Free: 800-678-3367
Fax: (972)398-6454
Co. E-mail: info@aldorsolutions.com
URL: http://www.aldorsolutions.com
Price: Contact for pricing. **Description:** Available for IBM computers and compatibles. System stores funeral home information.

LIBRARIES

9345 ■ Center for Thanatology Research & Education, Inc. Library
391 Atlantic Ave.
Brooklyn, NY 11217-1701
Ph: (718)858-3026
Fax: (718)852-1846
Co. E-mail: thanatology@pipeline.com
URL: http://thanatology.org
Contact: Roberta Halporn, Director
Scope: Aging, dying, death, bereavement, gravestone studies. **Services:** Copying; Library open to the public by appointment. **Founded:** 1982. **Holdings:** 2945 books; 40 bound periodical volumes; 20 online databases; 1 CD-ROM; videotapes; audiocassettes; photographs; rubbings; archives. **Subscriptions:** 6 journals and other serials.

9346 ■ Funeral Consumers Alliance Library
33 Patchen Rd.
South Burlington, VT 05403
Ph: (802)865-8300
Free: 800-765-0107
Fax: (802)865-2626
Co. E-mail: info@funerals.org
URL: http://www.funerals.org/
Contact: Joshua Slocum, Executive Director
Scope: Death, dying, grief, burials, cremation, funeral law. **Services:** Library open to the public for reference use only. **Founded:** 1963. **Holdings:** 150 books. **Telecommunication Services:** fca@funerals.org.

9347 ■ National Funeral Directors Association - Howard C. Raether Library
13625 Bishop's Dr.
Brookfield, WI 53005-6607
Ph: (262)789-1880
Free: 800-228-6332
Fax: (262)789-6977
Co. E-mail: kwalczak@nfda.org
URL: http://www.nfda.org/about-nfda-/research-a-information/208.html
Contact: Kathie Walczak
Scope: Funeral service, mortuary management, death customs, burial, bereavement, embalming, mortuary science, restorative art. **Services:** Copying; performs searches on fee basis; library open to researchers by appointment. **Founded:** 1881. **Holdings:** 3100 books; 300 bound periodical volumes; 300 prints and pamphlets; reports; manuscripts; archives; microfilm. **Subscriptions:** 48 journals and other serials. **Telecommunication Services:** nfda@nfda.org.

9348 ■ Northampton Community College - Paul and Harriett Mack Library
3835 Green Pond Rd.
Bethlehem, PA 18020
Ph: (610)861-5358
Fax: (610)861-5373
Co. E-mail: ssander@northampton.edu
URL: http://www.northampton.edu/Library.htm
Contact: Sandra Sander, Director, Library Services
Scope: Nursing, dental auxiliaries, funeral service, veterinary technology. **Services:** Interlibrary loan; copying; center open to the public. **Founded:** 1967. **Holdings:** 65,341 books; periodicals; and AV titles. **Subscriptions:** 429 journals and other serials; 6 newspapers.

ASSOCIATIONS AND OTHER ORGANIZATIONS

9349 ■ Empress Chinchilla Breeders Cooperative (ECBC)
5525 Heidi St.
La Mesa, CA 91942-2411
Ph: (906)221-3819
Co. E-mail: empresschinchilla@gmail.com
URL: http://www.empresschinchilla.org
Contact: Mr. Gene Adcock, President
Description: Breeders of chinchillas for fur. Conducts research; supervises live animal and pelt shows. **Founded:** 1965.

9350 ■ Fur Council of Canada—Conseil Canadien de la Fourrure
1435 St. Alexandre, Ste. 1270
Montreal, QC, Canada H3A 2G4
Ph: (514)844-1945
Fax: (514)844-8593
Co. E-mail: info@furcouncil.com
URL: http://www.furcouncil.com/home.aspx
Description: Fur trappers and processors and distributors of fur and fur apparel. Promotes increased demand for fur and fur clothing. Represents members' commercial interests; conducts promotional activities. **Founded:** 1964.

9351 ■ Fur Information Council of America (FICA)
8424 A Santa Monica Blvd., No. 860
West Hollywood, CA 90069
Ph: (323)782-1700
Fax: (323)651-1417
Co. E-mail: info@fur.org
URL: http://www.fur.org
Contact: Keith Kaplan, Executive Director
Description: Fur retailers, manufacturers, and others involved in the fur industry. Aims to promote the fur industry and foster high standards, quality, and craftsmanship. Conducts public relations and advertising work. Committed to the wise use and humane care of animals; develops programs to ensure high standards for animal welfare in the fur industry; works with wildlife biologists to promote sound wildlife management. **Founded:** 1958. **Publications:** *American Fur Industry Fashion-Newsletter* (Annual); *Furs Naturally.* **Educational Activities:** Fur Information Council of America Show.

TRADE PERIODICALS

9352 ■ *Canadian Cooperative Wool Growers Magazine: Livestock Supply Catalogue*
Pub: Canadian Co-Operative Wool Growers Ltd.
URL(s): www.seregonmap.com/SCM/index.htm. **Released:** Annual

ASSOCIATIONS AND OTHER ORGANIZATIONS

9353 ■ Empress Chinchilla Breeders Cooperative (ECBC)
5525 Heidi St.
La Mesa, CA 91942-2411
Ph: (906)221-3819
Co. E-mail: empresschinchilla@gmail.com
URL: http://www.empresschinchilla.org
Contact: Mr. Gene Adcock, President

Description: Breeders of chinchillas for fur. Conducts research; supervises live animal and pelt shows. **Founded:** 1965.

9354 ■ Fur Council of Canada—Conseil Canadien de la Fourrure
1435 St. Alexandre, Ste. 1270
Montreal, QC, Canada H3A 2G4
Ph: (514)844-1945
Fax: (514)844-8593
Co. E-mail: info@furcouncil.com
URL: http://www.furcouncil.com/home.aspx

Description: Fur trappers and processors and distributors of fur and fur apparel. Promotes increased demand for fur and fur clothing. Represents members' commercial interests; conducts promotional activities. **Founded:** 1964.

9355 ■ Fur Information Council of America (FICA)
8424 A Santa Monica Blvd., No. 860
West Hollywood, CA 90069
Ph: (323)782-1700
Fax: (323)651-1417
Co. E-mail: info@fur.org
URL: http://www.fur.org
Contact: Keith Kaplan, Executive Director

Description: Fur retailers, manufacturers, and others involved in the fur industry. Aims to promote the fur industry and foster high standards, quality, and craftsmanship. Conducts public relations and advertising work. Committed to the wise use and humane care of animals; develops programs to ensure high standards for animal welfare in the fur industry; works with wildlife biologists to promote sound wildlife management. **Founded:** 1958. **Publications:** *American Fur Industry Fashion-Newsletter* (Annual); *Furs Naturally.* **Educational Activities:** Fur Information Council of America Show.

START-UP INFORMATION

9356 ■ *The 100 Best Businesses to Start When You Don't Want To Work Hard Anymore*
Pub: Career Press Inc.
Ed: Lisa Rogak. **Price:** $16.99. **Description:** Author helps burned-out workers envision a new future as a small business owner. Systems analysis, adventure travel outfitting, bookkeeping, food delivery, furniture making, and software development are among the industries examined.

ASSOCIATIONS AND OTHER ORGANIZATIONS

9357 ■ **American Society of Furniture Designers (ASFD)**
144 Woodland Dr.
New London, NC 28127
Ph: (910)576-1273
Fax: (910)576-1573
Co. E-mail: info@asfd.com
URL: http://www.asfd.com
Contact: Dudley Moore, President
Description: Represents professional furniture designers, teachers, students, corporate suppliers of products and services; others who supply products and services related to furniture design. Seeks to promote the profession of furniture design. Conducts and cooperates in educational courses and seminars for furniture designers and persons planning to enter the field. Maintains placement service. **Founded:** 1981. **Publications:** *American Society of Furniture Designers--Membership Directory* (Annual); *ASFD Official Directory* (Biennial). **Educational Activities:** American Society of Furniture Designers Meeting (Semiannual). **Awards:** David Kline Memorial Scholarship (Annual); Pinnacle Design Achievement Award (Annual); Pinnacle Design Achievement Awards.

REFERENCE WORKS

9358 ■ *American Society of Furniture Designers--Membership Directory*
Pub: American Society of Furniture Designers
Contact: Dudley Moore, President
URL(s): www.asfd.com. **Released:** Annual; January. **Price:** $75, Corporate membership representative; $225, Professional/International Professional membership; $140, Affiliate/Associate membership; $600, Corporate/International Corporate membership. **Covers:** Over 160 member furniture designers.

TRADE PERIODICALS

9359 ■ *Casual Living: The Voice of the Leisure Marketplace*
Pub: Sandow Media Corp.
URL(s): www.casualliving.com. **Released:** Monthly **Price:** $25.99, Individuals; $59, Canada and Mexico; $149.99, Other countries.

9360 ■ *Laminating Design and Technology: Materials Design and Technology for the Surfacing Industry*
Pub: Cygnus Business Media
Contact: Rich Reiff, President
URL(s): www.cygnusb2b.com/PropertyPub. cfm?PropertyID=i. **Ed:** Tim Fixmer. **Released:** Bimonthly **Price:** $48; $68, Individuals; $99, Canada and Mexico; $99, Other countries.

VIDEOCASSETTES/ AUDIOCASSETTES

9361 ■ *Refinishing Furniture with Bob Flexner*
Taunton Press Inc.
63 S Main St.
Newtown, CT 06470
Ph: (203)426-8171
Free: 800-477-8727
Fax: (203)426-3434
Co. E-mail: booksales@taunton.com
URL: http://www.taunton.com
Contact: John Lively, Chief Executive Officer
Released: 1989. **Price:** $29.95. **Description:** Viewers can make old furniture look like new with Bob's handy instructions. **Availability:** VHS.

9362 ■ *Repairing Furniture with Bob Flexner*
Taunton Press Inc.
63 S Main St.
Newtown, CT 06470
Ph: (203)426-8171
Free: 800-477-8727
Fax: (203)426-3434
Co. E-mail: booksales@taunton.com
URL: http://www.taunton.com
Contact: John Lively, Chief Executive Officer
Released: 1989. **Price:** $29.95. **Description:** Bob saves viewers money by showing them how to fix furniture instead of buying new stuff. **Availability:** VHS.

FRANCHISES AND BUSINESS OPPORTUNITIES

9363 ■ **Certirestore Certified Furniture Restoration**
612 2nd Ave. NW, Ste., J
West Fargo, ND 58078
Ph: (701)364-0660
Free: 888-50C-ERTI
Fax: (701)277-0534
Co. E-mail: brianmatson1703@msn.com
URL: http://www.certirestore.org
Description: Shop based, full service furniture restoration and repair franchise opportunity. We focus on providing professional furniture restoration to commercial clients, moving and insurance companies, restaurants, offices, churches, government and schools. Our staff has over 20 years of combined hands-on experience in the furniture restoration and repair industry. **No. of Franchise Units:** 28.

Founded: 1989.. **Franchised:** 2004. **Equity Capital Needed:** $62,980-$92,250. **Franchise Fee:** $37,500. **Royalty Fee:** 8%. **Financial Assistance:** Third party financng available. **Training:** Provides the tools, supplies, equipment, support and hands-on training. In their 11 day in-shop training class you will restore and repair several pieces of furniture, as well as marketing and business training.

9364 ■ **Furniture Medic of Canada**
ServiceMaster
5462 Timberlea Blvd.
Mississauga, ON, Canada L4W 2T7
Ph: (905)670-0000
Free: 800-263-5928
Fax: (905)670-0077
Co. E-mail: thould@smclean.com
URL: http://www.furnituremedic.com
Description: Provides furniture repair services and complete refinishing. **No. of Franchise Units:** 50. **No. of Company-Owned Units:** 8. **Founded:** 1993.. **Franchised:** 1993. **Equity Capital Needed:** $20,000-$50,000. **Franchise Fee:** $25,000 plus $17,200 equipment package available. **Training:** Yes.

9365 ■ **Furniture Medic, L.P.**
3839 Forest Hill-Irene Rd.
Memphis, TN 38125
Ph: (901)597-8600
Fax: (901)597-8663
URL: http://www.furnituremedicfranchise.com
Description: Onsite furniture repair and restoration of furniture, antiques, cabinetry, paneled walls etc. **No. of Franchise Units:** 300. **Founded:** 1992.. **Franchised:** 1993. **Equity Capital Needed:** $42,900, includes products and equipment. **Franchise Fee:** $29,900. **Financial Assistance:** Yes. **Training:** 5 week program, seminars, regional meetings, 24/7 technical assistance with key support in marketing, financial, customer acquisition and retention.

9366 ■ **Guardsman Furniturepro**
The Valspar Corp.
4999 36th St., SE
Grand Rapids, MI 49512
Free: 800-496-6377
Fax: (616)285-7882
Co. E-mail: furniturepro@valspar.com
URL: http://www.guardsmanfurniturepro.com
Description: Onsite, mobile, wood touch-up, repair service & refinishing industry. **No. of Franchise Units:** 123. **Founded:** 1806.. **Franchised:** 1994. **Equity Capital Needed:** $7,000 / discipline. **Franchise Fee:** $7,000. **Financial Assistance:** Yes. **Training:** All franchisee's receive complete technical and business training and provides quality onsite support.

9367 ■ **Leather Medic**
5565 Lee St., Ste. 1
Lehigh Acres, FL 33971
Free: 888-561-0423
Fax: (239)561-5715
Co. E-mail: klife@leathermedic.com
URL: http://www.leathermedic.com
Description: Repairing and refinishing leather furniture. **No. of Franchise Units:** 35. **No. of Company-Owned Units:** 1. **Founded:** 1988.. **Equity**

Capital Needed: $47,500. **Franchise Fee:** $47,500. **Financial Assistance:** Yes. **Training:** Offers 2 weeks of one-on-one training.

9368 ■ Weathersby Guild
PO Box 746
Lilburn, GA 30048-0746
Ph: (866)523-9929
URL: http://www.weathersbyguild.com
Description: On location mobile furniture repair service oriented to serving the household goods moving industry. The operation can be easily scaled to full-service. Store-front capability to include complete refinishing, upholstery and interior decorating. **No. of Franchise Units:** 11. **No. of Company-Owned Units:** 1. **Founded:** 1972.. **Franchised:** 2002. **Equity Capital Needed:** $60,000 minimum investment. **Franchise Fee:** $29,500. **Training:** The guild concept reflects our focus on skill level. Our twenty-one day training course is intensive and includes on-the-job training with a specialty in service to the moving van industry. Provides ongoing training and support.

COMPUTERIZED DATABASES

9369 ■ *Avery Index to Architectural Periodicals*
300 Avery
1172 Amsterdam Ave.
MC 0301
New York, NY 10027
Ph: (212)854-6199
Fax: (212)854-8904
Co. E-mail: avery@libraries.cul.columbia.edu
URL: http://library.columbia.edu/indiv/avery.html
Contact: Carole Ann Fabian, Director
Availability: Online: ProQuest LLC - CSA; EBSCO Publishing. **Type:** Bibliographic.

LIBRARIES

9370 ■ Art Institute of Portland Library
1122 NW Davis St.
Portland, OR 97209-2911

Ph: (503)382-4759
Free: 888-228-6528
Fax: (503)228-4227
URL: http://www.artinstitute.edu/portland/
Scope: Fashion and costume history, interior decoration, furniture history, world history, textiles, clothing and fashion industry, graphic design, multimedia, digital media production, media arts and animation, game art, advertising. **Services:** Copying; color copying; A/V viewing; Library open to professionals in the field. **Founded:** 1963. **Holdings:** 21,933 books; 900 videocassettes. **Subscriptions:** 204 journals and other serials; 3 newspapers.

9371 ■ Edward-Dean Museum & Gardens Art Reference Library
9401 Oak Glen Rd.
Cherry Valley, CA 92223
Ph: (951)845-2626
Co. E-mail: tomfreeman@rivcoeda.org
URL: http://www.edward-deanmuseum.org
Contact: Terri Bowen, Assistant Manager
Scope: Furniture, decorative arts, sculpture, architecture, costume design, history. **Services:** Library open to the public by special permission. **Founded:** 1964. **Holdings:** 2500 books.

9372 ■ Furniture Library Association Library
1009 N. Main St.
High Point, NC 27262
Ph: (336)883-4011
Fax: (336)883-6579
Co. E-mail: info@furniturelibrary.com
URL: http://www.furniturelibrary.com
Scope: Early architecture; design - interior, furniture, fabric; furniture styles, 1600 to present. **Services:** Photographing; library is open to the public. **Founded:** 1970. **Holdings:** 7000 books; bound periodical volumes, including over 100 years of furniture catalogs; Furniture World; trade journals. **Subscriptions:** 10 journals and other serials.

9373 ■ Grand Rapids Public Library - Furniture Design Collection
111 Library St., NE
Grand Rapids, MI 49503-3268

Ph: (616)988-5400
URL: http://www.grpl.org
Contact: Marcia Warner, Director
URL(s): newwww.grpl.org/furniture-collection. **Scope:** Furniture history and design - all periods and styles. **Services:** Copying; collection open to furniture designers and scholars by appointment only. **Founded:** 1913. **Holdings:** 4000 items. **Subscriptions:** 4 journals and other serials.

9374 ■ Harrington College of Design - Design Library
200 W. Madison St., 2nd Fl.
Chicago, IL 60606-3433
Ph: (312)697-3318
Free: 866-590-4423
Fax: (312)939-8005
Co. E-mail: elaine@interiordesign.edu
URL: http://www.harrington.edu
Contact: Elaine Lowenthal, Director, Library Services
Scope: Architecture, design, building materials, furniture, decorative arts, modern design. **Services:** Interlibrary loan; copying; library open to the public by appointment for reference use only and with referral from another library . **Founded:** 1974. **Holdings:** 22,000 books; 900 bound periodical volumes; 23,000 slides; 450 videotapes; 35,000 digital images. **Subscriptions:** 125 journals and other serials.

9375 ■ Kendall College of Art & Design Library
17 Fountain St. NW, 2nd Fl.
Grand Rapids, MI 49503-3002
Ph: (616)451-2787
Free: 800-676-2787
Fax: (616)451-9867
Co. E-mail: kcadlibrary@ferris.edu
URL: http://www.kcad.edu/facilities/library/
Contact: Michael J. Kruzich, Director, Library Services
Scope: Fine arts, applied arts, design. **Services:** Library open to the public. **Founded:** 1929. **Holdings:** 13,000 books; 1695 bound periodical volumes; 50,000 slides; 71 online databases. **Subscriptions:** 95 journals; 1 newspaper.

ASSOCIATIONS AND OTHER ORGANIZATIONS

9376 ■ American Gaming Association (AGA)
1299 Pennsylvania Ave. NW, Ste. 1175
Washington, DC 20004
Ph: (202)552-2675
Fax: (202)552-2676
Co. E-mail: info@americangaming.org
URL: http://www.americangaming.org
Contact: Richard Haddrill, Chairman
Description: Represents the commercial casino entertainment industry by addressing federal legislative and regulatory issues affecting its members and their employees and customers; provides leadership in addressing newly emerging national issues and in developing industrywide programs on critical issues; serves as the industry's national information clearinghouse which provides the media, elected officials, other decision makers and the public with timely and accurate gaming industry data. **Founded:** 1995. **Publications:** *Inside the AGA* (Bimonthly); *Responsible Gaming Quarterly* (Quarterly). **Educational Activities:** Global Gaming Expo (Annual). **Awards:** Gaming Voice Award (Annual).

9377 ■ Casino Chip and Gaming Token Collectors Club (CC&GTCC)
PO Box 691085
Houston, TX 77269-1085
Co. E-mail: president@ccgtcc.com
URL: http://www.ccgtcc.com
Contact: Doug Smith, President
Description: Member club of the American Numismatic Association. Collectors of casino gaming chips and tokens. Coordinates the exchange of information regarding gaming chips and tokens and the casinos where they are used. Conducts educational programs and competitions. **Founded:** 1988. **Publications:** *Casino Collectibles News* (Quarterly); *Club Directory* (Periodic). **Educational Activities:** Casino Collectibles Show and Convention (Annual). **Awards:** Best Article (Annual); Chip of the Year (Annual); Convention Chip Design Contest (Annual); Convention Design Contest (Annual); Token of the Year (Annual); Top Recruiter (Annual).

9378 ■ Gamblers Anonymous (GA)—Gamblers Anonymous Publishing Inc.Gamblers Anonymous International Service Office;
PO Box 17173
Los Angeles, CA 90017
Ph: (626)960-3500
Free: 888-424-3577
Fax: (626)960-3501
Co. E-mail: isomain@gamblersanonymous.org
URL: http://www.gamblersanonymous.org/ga
Contact: Karen K. Humphrey, President
Description: Men and women who have joined together in order to stop gambling and to help other compulsive gamblers do the same; is self-supporting, declines outside contributions, and neither opposes nor endorses outside causes. **Founded:** 1957.

9379 ■ National Association of Casino Party Operators (NACPO)
PO Box 5626
South San Francisco, CA 94083
Free: 888-922-0777
Co. E-mail: info@casinoparties.com
URL: http://www.nactpo.com
Contact: Mike Miller, Director
Description: Casino party operators, party planners, party rental shop owners, theme party and special events operators, and others involved in casino party rental business. Strives to strengthen the casino and theme party industry and advance the industry into more geographical markets. Promotes members' interests. **Founded:** 1992.

9380 ■ National Council on Problem Gambling (NCPG)
730 11th St. NW, Ste. 601
Washington, DC 20001
Ph: (202)547-9204
Free: 800-522-4700
Fax: (202)547-9206
Co. E-mail: ncpg@ncpgambling.org
URL: http://www.ncpgambling.org/i4a/pages/index.cfm?pageid=1
Contact: Don Feeney, President
Description: Professionals in health, education, and law; recovering gamblers; supportive citizens. Advocates for programs and services to assist problem gamblers and their families. Makes referrals for compulsive gamblers and their families; seeks to stimulate the concern of the medical profession, educators, legislators, and the criminal justice system. Conducts training programs for professionals and information programs to encourage business management, educators, and the public to become aware of and to understand compulsive gambling. Compiles statistics; maintains speakers' bureau. Administers national 24 hour toll-free helpline for individuals with gambling problems. **Founded:** 1972.

9381 ■ National Indian Gaming Association (NIGA)
224 2nd St. SE
Washington, DC 20003
Ph: (202)546-7711
Fax: (202)546-1755
Co. E-mail: estevens@indiangaming.org
URL: http://www.indiangaming.org
Contact: Mark Van Norman, Executive Director
E-mail: mvannorman@indiangaming.org
Description: Indian nations operating gambling establishments are members; tribes, organizations, and businesses supporting Indian gaming establishments are associate members. Works to protect and preserve the welfare of tribes seeking to achieve economic self-sufficiency through the operation of gaming establishments. Seeks to expand political self-determination of Indian nations. Cooperates with government agencies in the formulation and application of laws and regulations applicable to Indian gaming. Provides technical assistance and other support to tribal gaming establishments. Conducts educational programs. **Founded:** 1985. **Educational Ac-**
tivities: Election Meeting (Annual); Indian Gaming Trade Show & Convention (Annual). **Telecommunication Services:** questions@indiangaming.org.

9382 ■ North American Gaming Regulators Association (NAGRA)
1000 Westgate Dr., Ste. 252
St. Paul, MN 55114
Ph: (651)203-7244
Fax: (651)290-2266
Co. E-mail: ssyrenne@mgcc.mb.ca
URL: http://www.nagra.org
Contact: Simone Syrenne, President
Description: Domestic and foreign governmental agencies, bureaus, commissions, and Native American tribes and First Nations charged with the regulation and enforcement of any type of gambling. Works for the mutual exchange of regulatory techniques for training enforcement personnel; provides a medium for communication of common problems; offers resources to states enacting legislation; speaks on matters concerning non-profit and related gambling. **Founded:** 1984. **Publications:** *NAGRA News*; *Standards on Bingo*; *Standards on Pull-Tabs*.

REFERENCE WORKS

9383 ■ "AG Warns Slots MBE Plan Risky" in Boston Business Journal (Vol. 29, May 27, 2011, No. 3, pp. 1)
Pub: American City Business Journals Inc.
Ed: Scott Dance. **Description:** Attorney General Doug Gansler states that the law extending the minority business program on slots parlors contracting through 2018 could be open to lawsuits. He recommended that the state should conduct a study proving that minority- and women-owned businesses do not get a fair share in the gaming industry before it signs the bill to avoid lawsuits from majority-owned firms.

9384 ■ "Betting On Slots" in Baltimore Business Journal (Vol. 28, November 19, 2010, No. 28, pp. 1)
Pub: Baltimore Business Journal
Ed: Rachel Bernstein. **Description:** Penn National Gaming Company's Hollywood Casino in Perryville, Maryland has been betting on the slot machines to lure slot players to the region to boost the town's growth. The success of Maryland's first casino is expected to lead to the development of land in the area.

9385 ■ "Broadway Casino Climbing Hills to Get to Gambling" in Business Courier (Vol. 26, January 1, 2010, No. 37, pp. 1)
Pub: American City Business Journals, Inc.
Ed: Dan Monk. **Description:** Rock Ventures LLC, operators of the Broadway Commons Casino, needs approval from the Ohio General Assembly and the to-be-created Ohio Casino Control Commission to commence operations.

9386 ■ "Can Turfway Park Stay in the Race?" in Business Courier (Vol. 26, January 8, 2010,

No. 38, pp. 1)
Pub: American City Business Journals, Inc.
Ed: Jon Newberry. **Description:** Legalization of slot machine gambling in Kentucky could affect raceway Turfway Park and the state's thoroughbred industry. Thousands of farms and jobs in the industry could be lost if slot machine gambling is approved.

9387 ■ *Casino Gaming in the United States: A Research Guide*
Pub: Scarecrow Press Inc.
Contact: Patricia Zline, Manager
E-mail: pzline@rowman.com
URL(s): https://rowman.com/ISBN/978-0-8108-3230-5. **Price:** $95, Individuals Hardback; £59.95, Individuals Hardback. **Covers:** Bibliography of nearly 900 books, articles, periodicals, Internet sites and government publications from 1985-94 on casino gambling. Also includes state gambling agencies, associations, Indian gaming locations, consultants, and public gaming companies. **Entries include:** For publications--Publication title, subject, author, web site address where applicable. For organizations--Name, address, phone. **Indexes:** Subject, author.

9388 ■ *"Casino Minority Spend: $80 Million"* in Business Courier (Vol. 27, August 20, 2010, No. 16, pp. 1)
Pub: Business Courier
Ed: Lucy May. **Description:** Real estate developers are planning to invest $80 million to build the Harrah's casino project in Cincinnati, Ohio. Rock Ventures LLC is seeking a 20 percent inclusion rate in the project.

9389 ■ *"Casinos See College as Job Jackpot"* in The Business Journal-Serving Metropolitan Kansas City (Vol. 26, August 1, 2008, No. 47)
Pub: American City Business Journals, Inc.
Ed: Suzanna Stagemeyer. **Description:** Wyandotte County casino managers revealed plans to develop partnerships with Kansas City Kansas Community College. The planned partnership is expected to include curriculum development and degree programs that would help train employees for the planned casinos. Other views and information on the project are presented.

9390 ■ *"City Hopes Casino Will Be $333M Jackpot"* in Business First Buffalo (October 5, 2007, pp. 1)
Pub: American City Business Journals, Inc.
Ed: James Fink. **Description:** Construction of the $333 million Seneca Buffalo Creek Casino, which includes a hotel, spa and restaurants, is schedule to begin in October 2007. The 5,000 square-foot casino is expected to generate revenue and provide 1,000 jobs for the City of Buffalo, New York.

9391 ■ *"Contractors: Slots MBE Goal a Test"* in Baltimore Business Journal (Vol. 27, November 20, 2009, No. 28, pp. 1)
Pub: American City Business Journals
Ed: Scott Dance. **Description:** Slot machine manufacturers in Maryland have been searching minority business enterprises (MBEs) that will provide maintenance and delivery services to the machines. MBEs will also build the stands where the machines will be mounted.

9392 ■ *"Deal With Tribes Revives Revenue Stream"* in Crain's Detroit Business (Vol. 24, March 24, 2008, No. 12, pp. 6)
Pub: Crain Communications, Inc.
Ed: Amy Lane. **Description:** Michigan Bureau of State Lottery's 2003 launch of its Club Keno game caused the Little River Band of Ottawa Indians and the Little Traverse Bay Bands of Odawa Indians to halt payments of shared casino revenue with the state. The federal lawsuit that resulted has now been settled and tribal revenue-sharing will resume as well as $26 million in previous payments to the state of Michigan that the tribes had put into escrow.

9393 ■ *Double or Nothing: How Two Friends Risked It All to Buy One of Las Vegas' Legendary Casinos*
Pub: HarperBusiness
Ed: Tom Breitling, with Cal Fussman. **Released:** March 2008. **Price:** $24.95. **Description:** Founders of a successful Internet travel agency share their experience from startup to selling the company.

9394 ■ *"Fight Over Casino Funds Limits Kitty for MEDC"* in Crain's Detroit Business (Vol. 24, January 21, 2008, No. 3, pp. 3)
Pub: Crain Communications Inc. - Detroit
Ed: Amy Lane. **Description:** Michigan Economic Development Corporation is facing uncertainty due to a Michigan American Indian tribe from the southwestern portion of the state withholding its 8 percent casino revenue share.

9395 ■ *"For Yung, Lady Luck a Fickle Mistress"* in Business Courier (Vol. 24, November 30, 2008, No. 33, pp. 1)
Pub: American City Business Journals, Inc.
Ed: Dan Monk. **Description:** Bill Yung's Columbia Sussex Corp. won the bid for the parent company of Tropicana casinos in November 2006, and a year after, the company is facing regulatory and labor issues.

9396 ■ *"Giant Garages Could Rise Up Downtown"* in Business Courier (Vol. 27, October 22, 2010, No. 25, pp. 1)
Pub: Business Courier
Ed: Dan Monk. **Description:** More than 2,500 new parking spaces could rise up to the eastern edge of downtown Cincinnati, Ohio as public and private investors collect resources for new garage projects. These projects are expected to accommodate almost 1,500 monthly parkers who will lose access at Broadway Commons due to the construction of Harrah's casino.

9397 ■ *"Internet Cafe Logging in to Chardon Plaza?"* in News-Herald (July 16, 2011)
Pub: Journal Register Ohio
Ed: Betsy Scott. **Description:** Pearl's High Rollers Inc. applied for an Internet sweepstakes cafe license that would reside in a vacant space in Chardon Plaza. City officials have created regulations for such businesses and Pearl's applied for a license and is awaiting approval.

9398 ■ *"Internet Cafe Regulations Head to City Council Vote"* in Vindicator (April 13, 2011)
Pub: Vindicator
Ed: David Skolnick. **Description:** Youngstown City Council's safety committee agrees with proposed changes to the policy regulating Internet gaming cafes and sweepstakes businesses. The new amendments allow Internet cafe customers to buy Internet time and go to Websites and play sweepstakes games of change.

9399 ■ *"Internet Cafe 'Sweepstakes' Expanding in Arkansas"* in Arkansas Business (Vol. 28, September 5, 2011, No. 36, pp. 1)
Pub: Arkansas Business Publishing Group
Ed: Mark Friedman. **Description:** Despite the fact that video games resembling casino games in Lucky's Business Center in Little Rock, representatives of the Internet cafe insist they are not offering gambling but a type of sweepstakes promotion and that business model is thriving. Lucky's, Cancun Cyber Cafe & Business Center Inc., and Wild Rides Business Center & Internet Cafe has opened in the area in the last few weeks.

9400 ■ *"Lotteries Scratch Their Way to Billions"* in Saint Louis Business Journal (Vol. 31, August 19, 2011, No. 52, pp. 1)
Pub: Saint Louis Business Journal
Ed: Kelsey Volkmann. **Description:** Missouri Lottery reported $1 billion in sales in 2011. A six-fold increase in the lottery's advertising budget is seen to drive the revenue increase; a 4.5 percent rise in its scratch-off tickets and new sponsorships has also contributed to the development.

9401 ■ *"Maryland Ready to Defend Slots Minority Policy"* in Boston Business Journal (Vol. 29, July 8, 2011, No. 9, pp. 3)
Pub: American City Business Journals Inc.
Ed: Scott Dance. **Description:** The legality of Maryland's minority inclusion policy may be put under scrutiny once the lawsuit filed by rejected slots developer Baltimore City Entertainment Group on

July 5, 2011 is heard in court. The lawsuit aims to stop the bidding process on a proposed casino in Baltimore because the minority policy amounts to reverse discrimination.

9402 ■ *"Power Partnerships"* in Business Courier (Vol. 27, October 22, 2010, No. 25, pp. 1)
Pub: Business Courier
Ed: Lucy May. **Description:** The $400 million Harrah's casino and the $47 million redevelopment and expansion of Washington Park are project aimed at boosting the economy in downtown Cincinnati, Ohio. These projects will be done in cooperation with the National Association for the Advancement of Colored People. Insights into the role of minority-owned businesses in regional economic development are explored.

9403 ■ *"Silverdome Bidders Bring New Proposals"* in Crain's Detroit Business (Vol. 24, March 17, 2008, No. 11, pp. 23)
Pub: Crain Communications, Inc.
Ed: Daniel Duggan. **Description:** Discusses the seven plans which have been proposed as part of the third round of bidding for the Pontiac Silverdome; proposals range from Global Baseball Inc., a baseball league that would pit a team from every country against one another, to an Indian casino, a musical 'hall of fame', a convention center, a horse track, a hotel and an indoor water park.

9404 ■ *"Table Games Get a Leg Up"* in Philadelphia Business Journal (Vol. 28, January 15, 2010, No. 48, pp. 1)
Pub: American City Business Journals
Ed: Athena Merritt, Peter Van Allen. **Description:** Casino operators expect the addition of live table games such as poker and blackjack at existing and planned casinos in Philadelphia will generate 1,000 new jobs. Most of the jobs will be dealers and floor supervisors.

9405 ■ *"The Trader's Edge"* in Barron's (Vol. 88, March 31, 2008, No. 13, pp. 56)
Pub: Dow Jones & Company, Inc.
Ed: Dan McGuire. **Description:** There is a $3,000 a year annual limit to deducting investor's losses and normal investment expenses are purportedly deductible as miscellaneous expenses on Schedule A only to the extent that they exceed two percent of adjusted gross income. Professional gamblers who can use Schedule C are unable deduct a net gaming loss against income from any other sources.

9406 ■ *"Turfway Slowing its Gait"* in Business Courier (Vol. 26, November 6, 2009, No. 28, pp. 1)
Pub: American City Business Journals, Inc.
Ed: Jon Newberry. **Description:** Kentucky's Turfway Park will be decreasing its weekly race schedule from five days to three days in the first two months of 2010, and to four days in March 2010. The decision to make reductions in the schedule is attributed to the relocation of thoroughbred racing to states that allow casino gambling. As a result, Turfway Park's resources and purse money would be focused on less days.

9407 ■ *"Vegas in the D; Local Architects Collaborate On MGM Grand"* in Crain's Detroit Business (Vol. 23, October 1, 2007, No. 40, pp. 1)
Pub: Crain Communications Inc. - Detroit
Ed: Daniel Duggan. **Description:** Local Detroit architects, Smith Group and Hamilton Anderson Associates are among the contractors vying for subcontracted architecture, construction and consulting contracts for the new MGM Grand Detroit casino and hotel.

9408 ■ *"What Happens in Vegas Could Happen in Baltimore, Too"* in Boston Business Journal (Vol. 29, June 17, 2011, No. 6, pp. 1)
Pub: American City Business Journals Inc.
Ed: Daniel J. Sernovitz. **Description:** At least 36 companies expressed their interest in developing a casino in South Baltimore following the state commission's announcement for bids. Developers have

until July 28, 2011 to submit their proposals. Baltimore's strong economy is the major factor for the interest, yet the fact that blackjack and poker are outlawed in Maryland could be a drawback.

9409 ■ *Winner Takes All: Steve Wynn, Kirk Kerkorian, Gary Loveman, and the Race to Own Vegas*
Pub: Hyperion
Ed: Christina Binkley. **Released:** 2009. **Price:** $25.95. **Description:** The story of three men, Steve Wynn, Kirk Kerkorian, and Gary Loveman, each with different backgrounds are reinventing Las Vegas.

SOURCES OF SUPPLY

9410 ■ *American Casino Guide*
Casino Vacations
URL(s): www.americancasinoguide.com. **Ed:** Steve Bourie. **Released:** Annual; Latest edition 2013. **Price:** $18.95, Individuals plus shipping charges; $11.75, Individuals discounted price. **Covers:** more than 700 casino/resorts, riverboat casinos, and Indian casinos in the U.S. **Entries include:** Casino name, address, phone, toll-free number, room rates, dining information, games offered, features, web site addresses. **Database includes:** Maps, photos. **Arrangement:** Geographical. **Indexes:** Name.

TRADE PERIODICALS

9411 ■ *Anthony Curtis' Las Vegas Advisor*
Pub: Huntington Press
Contact: Anthony Curtis, Editor
Released: Monthly. **Price:** $50, U.S.; $60, Canada; $70, elsewhere. **Description:** Acts as a consumer's information source for Las Vegas visitors. Recurring features include letters to the editor, a calendar of events, book reviews, notices of publications available, and columns titled Couponomy, Top Ten Las Vegas Values, Dining, Entertainment News, Advance Planner, Letters & Tips, Gambling, Fast Track, Last Second Flash, Accommodations, Comp City, and Extra Stuff.

9412 ■ *Current Blackjack News*
Pub: Pi Yee Press
Ed: Stanford Wong, Editor, stanfwong@aol.com. **Released:** Monthly. **Price:** $129, individuals regular mail; $89 through email. **Description:** Features reviews of rule changes for the game of blackjack and reports on casinos in Nevada, Mississippi, Louisiana, Illinois, Iowa, New Jersey, New York, Connecticut, Minnesota, and other areas with legalized casino gambling. Announces new casino openings, as well as highlighting profitable opportunities to win at casinos.

9413 ■ *Las Vegas Insider*
Pub: Las Vegas Insider
Ed: Donald Currier, Editor. **Released:** Monthly. **Price:** $45, U.S. **Description:** Offers advice on low cost hotels, room bargains, food, gaming tips, and tourist information in Las Vegas, Reno, and Atlantic City. Recurring features include news of research, a calendar of events, job listings, book reviews, and notices of publications available.

9414 ■ *Lottery, Parimutuel & Casino Regulation*
Pub: Wakeman/Walworth Inc.
Ed: Keyes Walworth, Editor. **Released:** Weekly, 48/year. **Price:** $345, U.S. and Canada; $365, elsewhere; $620, two years U.S. and Canada;. **Description:** Covers state lottery regulations, prize structures, distribution of revenue, taxation and regulation of casinos, pari-mutuel gaming, horse racing, and other forms of gambling.

9415 ■ *Winning!*
Pub: NewsLinc
Contact: Steven M. Brown, Managing Editor
E-mail: sbrown@natcom.publications.com
Released: Monthly. **Price:** $21, individuals in the U.S. **Description:** Covers contests, sweepstakes, gambling, lotteries, and bingo.

TRADE SHOWS AND CONVENTIONS

9416 ■ North American Association of State and Provincial Lotteries Conference and Trade Show
North American Association of State and Provincial Lotteries
6 N. Broadway
Geneva, OH 44041
Ph: (440)466-5630
Fax: (440)466-5649
Co. E-mail: info@nasplhq.org
URL: http://www.naspl.org
URL(s): www.naspl.org. **Price:** $925, lottery vendor; $825, lottery/government employee. **Frequency:** Annual. **Audience:** Lottery industry professionals. **Principal Exhibits:** Lottery equipment, supplies, and services. **Telecommunication Services:** nasplhq@aol.com.

CONSULTANTS

9417 ■ Casino, Hotel & Resort Consultants L.L.C.
4825 Quality Ct., Ste. B
Las Vegas, NV 89103
Ph: (702)528-9537
Co. E-mail: info@hraba.com
URL: http://www.hraba.com
Contact: John S. Hraba, President
E-mail: jshraba@aol.com
Scope: Casino and hospitality industry consultants. Firm specializes in developing and implementing customized forecast and labor management control systems that deliver immediate, positive impact to the company's bottom line. Involved in production planning, employ surveys and communication, inventory management, business process reviews, audits, development and implementation of key management reports. **Founded:** 1989. **Seminars:** Payroll Cost Control; Effective Staff Scheduling. **Telecommunication Services:** john.hraba@hraba.com.

LIBRARIES

9418 ■ Atlantic City Free Public Library - Alfred M. Heston Collection
1 N. Tennessee Ave.
Atlantic City, NJ 08401
Ph: (609)345-2269
Fax: (609)345-5570
Co. E-mail: reflib@acfpl.org
URL: http://www.acfpl.org
Contact: Maureen Sherr Frank, Director
Scope: Local history, genealogy, Atlantic City government records. **Services:** Copying; collection open to the public two days a week (Wednesdays and Thursdays) and by appointment; limited remote reference help. **Founded:** 1901. **Holdings:** 5000 books; 200 bound periodical volumes; 30 online subscriptions; photographs; scrapbooks; oral histories. **Subscriptions:** 15 journals and other serials; 5 newspapers. **Telecommunication Services:** hperez@acfpl.org.

9419 ■ Loto-Quebec - Centre de Documentation
500 Sherbrooke St. W.
Montreal, QC, Canada H3A 3G6
Ph: (514)282-8000
Free: 866-611-5686
Fax: (514)873-8999
Co. E-mail: centred@loto-quebec.com
URL: http://lotoquebec.com/cms/corporatif/fr/la-societe/documentation/centre-de-documentation
Scope: Lotteries, casinos, horse racing, video games, sports betting. **Services:** Interlibrary loan; copying; center open to the public. **Founded:** 1978. **Holdings:** 5000 books; 215 annual reports; 3255 monographs; 27,000 bibiliographic records. **Subscriptions:** 180 journals and other serials.

9420 ■ University of Nevada, Las Vegas - Special Collections - Gaming Studies Collection
4505 Maryland Pkwy.
Box 457010
Las Vegas, NV 89154-7010
Ph: (702)895-2234
Fax: (702)895-2253
Co. E-mail: peter.michel@unlv.edu
URL: http://www.library.unlv.edu/speccol/
Contact: David G. Schwartz, Director
Scope: History and statistical basis of games and gambling; economics and regulation of the gaming industry; psychological, social, and political effects of gambling; history of specific hotel and casinos throughout the world; fiscal history of gaming; social and cultural realities of gaming. **Services:** Copying; collection open to the public. **Founded:** 1966. **Holdings:** Figures not available. **Telecommunication Services:** david.schwartz@unlv.edu.

9421 ■ Washoe County Law Library
Court House
75 Court St., Rm. 101
Box 30083
Reno, NV 89520-3083
Ph: (775)328-3250
Fax: (775)328-3441
Co. E-mail: lawlib@washoecounty.us
URL: http://www.washoecounty.us/lawlib
Contact: Howard Conyers, Director, Library Services
URL(s): www.washoecourts.com/index.cfm?page=lawlib. **Scope:** Nevada, California and Federal Law. **Services:** Interlibrary loan; copying; library open to the public. **Founded:** 1915. **Holdings:** 54,605 books; 4931 bound periodical volumes; 9214 volumes in microform; 52,000 microfiche. **Subscriptions:** 393 periodicals. **Telecommunication Services:** smarz@washoecounty.us.

RESEARCH CENTERS

9422 ■ McGill University - International Centre for Youth Gambling Problems and High-Risk Behaviors (YGI)—McGill University - Centre international d'étude sur le je et les comportements à risque chez les jeunes
Duggan House
3724 McTavish St.
Montreal, QC, Canada H3A 1Y2
Ph: (514)398-1391
Fax: (514)398-3401
Co. E-mail: jeffrey.derevensky@mcgill.ca
URL: http://www.youthgambling.com
Contact: Prof. Jeffrey L. Derevensky, Director
Founded: 2001. **Publications:** *Journal of Gambling Studies* (Monthly); *YGI Newsletter* (Quarterly). **Educational Activities:** YGI Conferences (5/year); YGI Training programs (5/year), for researchers, treatment providers and educators; YGI Workshops (Monthly). **Awards:** Award for graduate paper on gambling (Annual). **Telecommunication Services:** ygi@youthgambling.com.

9423 ■ Pennsylvania Family Institute (PFI)
23 N Front St.
Harrisburg, PA 17101-1606
Ph: (717)545-0600
Fax: (717)545-8107
Co. E-mail: mgeer@pafamily.org
URL: http://www.pafamily.org
Contact: Michael Geer, President
Services: Assists advocacy groups in planning seminars and conferences. **Founded:** 1989. **Publications:** *Pennsylvania Citizen Magazine Newsletter* (Monthly); *Pennsylvania Families & Schools* (Bimonthly); *PFI Research Reports*. **Educational Activities:** Physicians Resource Council meetings; CME seminars in Pennsylvania on life issues; sex education and other topics. **Telecommunication Services:** mail@pafamily.org.

ASSOCIATIONS AND OTHER ORGANIZATIONS

9424 ■ Board for Certification of Genealogists (BCG)
PO Box 14291
Washington, DC 20044
Co. E-mail: office@bcgcertification.org
URL: http://www.bcgcertification.org
Contact: Elissa Scalise Powell, President
Description: Works to formulate and administer standards of professional genealogical research. Grants certification in classifications of Certified Genealogists, Certified Genealogical Lecturers, and Certified Genealogical Instructors. Maintains free on-line roster of persons who have been certified. Investigates and offers resolutions for complaints against the work of certificants. **Founded:** 1964. **Publications:** *Onboard* (3/year); *BCG Application Guide*; *BCG Genealogical Standards Manual*.

9425 ■ Czechoslovak Genealogical Society International (CGSI)
PO Box 16225
St. Paul, MN 55116-0225
Ph: (651)964-2322
Co. E-mail: info@cgsi.org
URL: http://www.cgsi.org
Contact: Ginger Simek, President
Description: Individuals of Bohemian, Moravian, Silesian, Carpatho-Rusyn, Slovakian, German, or Jewish descent. Promotes research and interest in Czechoslovakian culture and genealogy. Provides a forum for information exchange; collects and disseminates research materials. **Founded:** 1988. **Publications:** *Czechoslovak Surname Index* (Annual); *Nase Rodina* (Quarterly). **Educational Activities:** Genealogical/Cultural Conference (Biennial).

9426 ■ Federation of Genealogical Societies (FGS)
PO Box 200940
Austin, TX 78720-0940
Free: 888-FGS-1500
Fax: (888)347-1350
Co. E-mail: office@fgs.org
URL: http://www.fgs.org
Contact: Patricia Farmer Oxley, President
Description: Genealogical societies, genealogical libraries, historical societies, family associations, and other organizations dealing with genealogy and family history. Aims to: stimulate the activities of state and local organizations interested in genealogy and family history; collect, preserve, and disseminate information with reference to genealogical and historical data; promote careful documentation and scholarly genealogical writing and publication; avoid duplication of effort; promote interest in genealogy and family history. Supports state organizations' efforts to promote legislation to open and protect the integrity of birth, death, and marriage records. Provides educational programs to further genealogical knowledge. Acts as collection agent for National Archives Gift Fund. **Founded:** 1976. **Publications:** *FGS Forum* (Quarterly). **Awards:** Award of Merit;

Certificate of Appreciation; Director's Award; Distinguished Service Award; David S. Vogels, Jr. Award; George E. Williams Award; President's Citation; Delegate Award; Distinguished Service Award; Rabbi Malcolm H. Stern Humanitarian Award.

9427 ■ Gottscheer Heritage and Genealogy Association (GHGA)
PO Box 725
Louisville, CO 80027-0725
Co. E-mail: anthro@privatei.com
URL: http://www.gottschee.org
Contact: Elizabeth Nick, President
Description: Descendants of the Gottschee Region of Slovenia, which was inhabited by German-speaking people from the 14th century until 1941, when they were relocated to Untersteiermark (lower Syria) and the Gottschee Region was transferred to Italian rule. Gottschee is now a part of Slovenia. Seeks to preserve the history of the Gottschee region and its German-speaking inhabitants. Conducts historical and genealogical research on the Gottschee Region and its German-speaking inhabitants; assists family historians and genealogists. Provides support to agencies maintaining historic properties in the Gottschee Region; organizes tours to view Gottschee historic sites. **Founded:** 1992. **Publications:** *The Gottschee Tree* (Quarterly); *The Gottscheer Connection* (3/year). **Educational Activities:** Gottscheer Heritage and Genealogy Association Meeting (Annual).

9428 ■ Groberg - Holbrook Genealogical Organization (GHGO)
1605 S Woodruff Ave.
Idaho Falls, ID 83404
Co. E-mail: mmpowell9@msn.com
URL: http://www.dvgroberg.com
Description: Members of the Groberg and Holbrook families; other interested individuals. Seeks to strengthen family ties and foster and encourage family genealogical research. Serves as a clearinghouse on the Groberg and Holbrook families and their histories; assists family historians and genealogists. **Founded:** 1985. **Telecommunication Services:** tom@govirtuoso.com.

9429 ■ Italian Genealogical Group (IGG)
PO Box 626
Bethpage, NY 11714-0626
Co. E-mail: info@italiangen.org
URL: http://www.italiangen.org
Description: Individuals of Italian descent. Promotes study of Italian family history and genealogy. Serves as a clearinghouse on Italian history, culture, and genealogy; sponsors educational and social programs. **Founded:** 1993. **Publications:** *Italian Genealogical Newsletter* (Monthly).

9430 ■ Lancaster Mennonite Historical Society (LMHS)
2215 Millstream Rd.
Lancaster, PA 17602-1499
Ph: (717)393-9745

Fax: (717)393-8751
Co. E-mail: lmhs@lmhs.org
URL: http://www.lmhs.org
Contact: Carolyn C. Wenger, Director
E-mail: cwenger@lmhs.org
Description: Individuals interested in the historical background, religious thought and expression, culture, and genealogy of Mennonite- and Amish-related groups originating in Pennsylvania. Sponsors field trips and exhibits. Maintains speakers' bureau, library, archives and museum. Conducts historical and genealogical seminars, research publications, and children's programs. Compiles statistics. **Founded:** 1958. **Publications:** *Pennsylvania Mennonite Heritage* (Quarterly); *Pennsylvania Mennonite Heritage* (Quarterly). **Educational Activities:** Genealogy Conference (Annual). **Awards:** Community Historians Award (Annual).

9431 ■ National Genealogical Society (NGS)
3108 Columbia Pike, Ste. 300
Arlington, VA 22204-4370
Ph: (703)525-0050
Free: 800-473-0060
Fax: (703)525-0052
Co. E-mail: ngs@ngsgenealogy.org
URL: http://www.ngsgenealogy.org
Contact: Janet A. Alpert, President
E-mail: alpert@ngsgenealogy.org
Description: Individuals, families, societies and organizations. Promotes genealogical research and education; stimulates and fosters preservation and publication of records of genealogical interest including national, state, county, township, city, town, church, cemetery, Bible, and family records. **Founded:** 1903. **Publications:** *NGS Newsmagazine*; *National Genealogical Society Quarterly: A Journal for Today's Family Historian* (Quarterly). **Educational Activities:** Conference in the States (Annual). **Awards:** Award of Merit; Rubincam Youth Award; Honorary Member (Individual); Honorary Member (Institutional); Fellow of the National Genealogical Society; Distinguished Service Award; Certificate of Appreciation; Newsletter Competition; Family History Writing Contest; National Genealogy Hall of Fame; Award of Distinction; Award of Distinction (Annual); Award of Merit (Annual); Distinguished Service Award (Annual); Family History Writing Award (Annual); Filby Award for Librarianship (Annual); Honorary Member (Annual); Rubincam Youth Award (Annual); Award for Excellence: Genealogy and Family History Book; Award for Excellence: Genealogical Methods and Sources.

9432 ■ National Public Records Research Association (NPRRA)
2501 Aerial Center Pkwy., Ste. 103
Morrisville, NC 27560
Ph: (919)459-2078
Fax: (919)459-2075
Co. E-mail: info@nprra.org
URL: http://www.nprra.org
Contact: Blair Wagner, President
Description: Companies that provide research and information from public records.

9433 ■ New Canaan Historical Society (NCHS)

13 Oenoke Ridge
New Canaan, CT 06840
Ph: (203)966-1776
Fax: (203)972-5917
Co. E-mail: newcanaan.historical@gmail.com
URL: http://www.nchistory.org
Contact: Susan Bishop, President
Description: Individuals interested in the history of New Canaan, CT. Seeks to "bring together and arrange the historical events of the town of New Canaan and the genealogies of the families who have lived in town". Sponsors research and educational programs; serves as a clearinghouse on the history of New Canaan, CT; maintains six historical structures; operates museums within these structures. **Scope:** New Canaan and New England history, genealogy of New Canaan families, colonial architecture. **Founded:** 1889. **Subscriptions:** 5000. **Publications:** *Tydings* (Quarterly). **Educational Activities:** Ice Cream Social (Annual); Ice Cream Social (Annual). **Telecommunication Services:** newcanaan. historical@snet.net.

REFERENCE WORKS

9434 ■ *Address Book for Germanic Genealogy*

Pub: Genealogical Publishing Company Inc.
Contact: Michael H. Tepper, Manager
URL(s): www.genealogical.com. **Ed:** Ernest Thode. **Released:** Irregular; Latest edition 6th. **Price:** $27, Individuals paperback. **Covers:** Over 2,700 sources useful for genealogical researchers with interest in Germany, Austria, Switzerland, and other German-speaking areas; includes about 275 European genealogical societies, 282 European governmental archives, 194 American societies, 380 European religious archives, 175 American religious archives, 770 European municipal archives, 254 genealogists, and numerous libraries, publishers, museums, organizations, etc. **Entries include:** Name of source, address, brief description. **Arrangement:** By type of resource.

9435 ■ *Biography and Genealogy Master Index: A Consolidated Index to Biographical Sketches in Current and Retrospective Biographical Dictionaries*

Pub: Cengage Learning Inc.
Contact: Ronald Dunn, President
URL(s): www.gale.cengage.com. **Released:** Annual; Latest edition 2011. **Price:** $611, Individuals volume 2. **Description:** BGMI and its updates provide consolidated indexes that indicate whether a biographical sketch being sought is contained in one or more of about 5,000 volumes and editions of more than 1,700 biographical dictionaries and who's who listing contemporary and historical personalities; the indexes contain more than 15 million citations. Publications indexed include "Who's Who in America," "American Men and Women of Science," "Standard & Poor's Register of Corporations, Directors, and Executives," and other standard biographical reference works. **Entries include:** Name, year of birth (and death, where applicable), code indicating publication in which biographical sketch appears, code indicating when a portrait is included. Available in an abridged version titled "Abridged Biography and Genealogy Master Index" (see separate entry). **Arrangement:** Alphabetical.

9436 ■ *Directory of Family Associations*

Pub: Genealogical Publishing Company Inc.
Contact: Michael H. Tepper, Manager
URL(s): www.genealogical.com. **Ed:** Elizabeth Petty Bentley, Deborah Ann Carl. **Released:** Irregular; Latest edition 4th, Published 2001. **Price:** $21, Individuals paperback. **Covers:** Over 6,000 organizations, each devoted to the study of a family name. **Entries include:** Family name, related family names, organization name, address, phone, contact name, publications. **Arrangement:** Alphabetical.

9437 ■ *Directory of Professional Genealogists*

Pub: Association of Professional Genealogists
Contact: Laura G. Prescott, President
URL(s): www.apgen.org/publications/index. html#Directory. **Ed:** Kathleen W. Hinckley. **Released:**

Biennial; latest edition 2004-2005. **Covers:** Member genealogists and related research services. **Entries include:** Genealogist's name or company name, address; telephone, fax, e-mail biography. **Arrangement:** Geographical. **Indexes:** Institutional members, geographical speciality, research speciality, related service, member residence by state.

9438 ■ *Dutch Genealogical Research*

Pub: Ye Olde Genealogie Shoppe
Contact: William Henry Sullivan, Jr., President
URL(s): www.yogs.com. **Released:** Irregular **Price:** $14, Individuals softbound. **Publication includes:** Lists of United States and Dutch vital statistics offices, periodical publishers, libraries, and genealogical societies of assistance in Dutch genealogical research. **Entries include:** Generally, listings show organization, agency, or other name, address.

9439 ■ *French and French-Canadian Family Research*

Pub: Ye Olde Genealogie Shoppe
Contact: William Henry Sullivan, Jr., President
URL(s): www.yogs.com. **Released:** Irregular **Price:** $10, Individuals softbound. **Publication includes:** List of French and French Canadian genealogical societies and provincial archives in French and French Canadian provinces. **Entries include:** Institution name, and address. **Arrangement:** Alphabetical. **Indexes:** Organization name.

9440 ■ *Genealogical Helper--Bureau of Missing Ancestors Section*

Pub: Everton Publishers
Contact: Bobbie Coray, Chief Executive Officer
URL(s): www.everton.com. **Price:** $12, Individuals online edition; $29, Individuals includes online edition; $53, Two years includes online edition. **Covers:** About 1,000 amateur and professional genealogists who are researching family names; listings are paid. **Entries include:** Researcher's name, address, status (whether amateur, family genealogist, or professional), county of residence of researcher, and information on families and surnames being researched. **Arrangement:** Alphabetical by researcher name. **Indexes:** Surname.

9441 ■ *Genealogical and Local History Books in Print*

Pub: Genealogical Publishing Company Inc.
Contact: Michael H. Tepper, Manager
URL(s): www.genealogical.com/index.php?main_ page=product_info&item_number=2169. **Ed:** Marian Hoffman. **Released:** Latest edition 5th. **Publication includes:** List of over 4,600 suppliers of genealogical books, microform, and computer software in four volumes. **Entries include:** Organization or personal name, address, name and title of contact, product. Principal content is a description of genealogical and local history books, reprints, microform collections, and specific surname publications, with ordering information. Titles of five separate volumes are: Family History Volume; General Reference Volume; World Resources Volume; U.S. Sources & Resources Volume: Alabama-New York; U.S. Sources & Resources Volume: North Carolina-Wyoming. **Arrangement:** Alphabetical, by publisher name.

9442 ■ *Genealogical Periodical Annual Index: Key to the Genealogical Literature*

Pub: Heritage Books Inc.
Contact: Craig R. Scott, President
E-mail: crscott@HeritageBooks.com
URL(s): www.heritagebooks.com. **Ed:** Laird C. Towle. **Released:** Annual; Latest edition Volume 41. **Price:** $23.50, Individuals. **Publication includes:** Contact information for about 330 periodicals published by genealogical societies and genealogists and used in indexing surnames, place names, and related topics for this book. **Entries include:** Name of publication, name of publisher, address, issues indexed, title abbreviation used in book. Publication mainly consists of an index containing 14,000 genealogical citations (surnames, place names, etc.). **Arrangement:** Alphabetical by title abbreviation.

9443 ■ *The Genealogist's Address Book*

Pub: Genealogical Publishing Company Inc.
Contact: Michael H. Tepper, Manager
URL(s): www.genealogical.com. **Ed:** Elizabeth Petty Bentley. **Released:** Biennial; latest edition 6th; Published 2009. **Price:** $69.95, Individuals Paper-

back. **Covers:** 27,000 archives, historical societies, libraries, and genealogical societies; religious and ethnic organizations, research centers, surname registries, hereditary societies, and other groups useful to persons doing genealogical research. **Entries include:** Name, address, phone, name and title of contact. **Arrangement:** Geographical.

9444 ■ *German Family Research Made Simple*

Pub: Ye Olde Genealogie Shoppe
Contact: William Henry Sullivan, Jr., President
URL(s): www.yogs.com. **Price:** $15, Individuals softbound. **Publication includes:** Lists with addresses of archives, periodicals, professional researchers, and publishers of maps likely to be helpful to genealogists; covers each state within Germany. **Entries include:** Name, address. **Arrangement:** Classified by type of source.

9445 ■ *Handbook of Genealogical Sources*

Pub: George K. Schweitzer
URL(s): www.gensources.com. **Released:** Irregular **Price:** $12, Individuals plus shipping and handling. **Covers:** About 750 libraries, repositories, archives, court houses, etc., with detailed instructions for obtaining genealogical information from them. **Entries include:** Source name, address, types of data available. **Arrangement:** Alphabetical.

9446 ■ *Handy Book for Genealogists*

Pub: Everton Publishers
Contact: Bobbie Coray, Chief Executive Officer
URL(s): www.everton.com. **Released:** Irregular; latest edition 11th; published 2005. **Price:** $50, Individuals; $60, Individuals with CD. **Publication includes:** List of associations, societies, libraries, archives, and other organizations and institutions that provide genealogical information. **Database includes:** Descriptions of records and histories of the counties and states of the United States, list of printed census records, etc.

9447 ■ *In Search of Your German Roots: A Complete Guide to Tracing Your Ancestors in the Germanic Areas of Europe*

Pub: Genealogical Publishing Company Inc.
Contact: Michael H. Tepper, Manager
URL(s): www.genealogical.comwww.genealogical. com/products/ In%20Search%20of%20Your%20German%20Roots/ 396.html. **Ed:** Angus Baxter. **Released:** Irregular; latest edition 4th; 2008. **Price:** $16.95, Individuals paperback; $19, Individuals. **Publication includes:** Lists of genealogical associations in Germany and German genealogical societies in the United States. **Entries include:** Association name and address, names and titles of key personnel, and description of services provided. Principal content of publication is researching techniques for genealogists. **Arrangement:** Alphabetical.

9448 ■ *"Interactive Stores a Big Part of Borders' Turnaround Plan" in Crain's Detroit Business (Vol. 24, February 18, 2008, No. 7, pp. 4)*

Pub: Crain Communications Inc. - Detroit
Description: Borders Group Inc. is using digital technology and interactive media as a part of the firm's turnaround plan. The digital store will allow shoppers to create CDs, download audio books, publish their own works, print photos and search family genealogy.

9449 ■ *International Vital Records Handbook*

Pub: Genealogical Publishing Company Inc.
Contact: Michael H. Tepper, Manager
URL(s): www.genealogical.com. **Ed:** Thomas Jay Kemp. **Released:** Triennial; latest edition 5th; 2009. **Price:** $54.50, Individuals paperback. **Covers:** vital records offices for 67 countries and territories in North America, the British Isles and other English-speaking countries, and Europe. **Entries include:** Office name, address, phone, application fees, method of payment, description of holdings, actual application forms to use in obtaining copies of records, and alternative record locations. **Arrangement:** Geographical.

9450 ■ *The Source: A Guidebook of American Genealogy*
Pub: Ancestry.com Inc.
Contact: Timothy P. Sullivan, President
URL(s): www.ancestry.com/search/db.aspx?d-bid=3259. **Ed:** Lou Szucs, Sandra Luebking. **Released:** Irregular **Publication includes:** Lists of federal archives, record centers, state archives, and historical societies, research libraries, heraldry and lineage societies, genealogy publications and publishers, sources of business records, and fraternal organizations. **Entries include:** Name of the genealogical source, location, contents of the record, means of access, use in research or family history. Main content of the publication is discussion of records useful for research in American genealogy, including Native Americans, Jewish Americans, and African Americans. **Database includes:** Bibliographies. **Arrangement:** Classified by type of source. **Indexes:** Subject.

9451 ■ *"Underworld Acquires Yukon Gold Property" in Canadian Corporate News (May 16, 2007)*
Pub: Comtex News Network Inc.
Description: Underworld Resources Inc., a well-structured junior exploration company, announced that it has secured an option to earn a 100 percent right, title, and interest in the 11,850 acre White and Black Fox gold Properties in Yukon Territory, Canada. The company will be exploring both vein hosted and sedimentary hosted gold targets.

TRADE PERIODICALS

9452 ■ *Ancestry*
Pub: Palm Beach County Genealogical Society
Contact: Carlos Ruth, President
URL(s): www.pbcgensoc.org/cpage.php?pt=46. **Released:** Quarterly **Price:** $20, Individuals volume.

9453 ■ *Family Findings*
Pub: White Publishing Co.
Ed: Richard Cochrane, Editor. **Released:** Quarterly. **Price:** $15, individuals; $4, single issue. **Description:** Consists of genealogical news.

9454 ■ *Genealogical Computing*
Pub: Ancestry.com Inc.
Contact: Timothy P. Sullivan, President
Ed: Elizabeth Kelley Kerstens, Editor. **Released:** Quarterly. **Price:** $25, U.S.; $30, Canada; $35, elsewhere. **Description:** Focuses on the uses of personal computers for genealogical records management. Reviews and discusses the applications of various computer software and offers how-to articles and tips from users. Recurring features include program directories, survey results, letters to the editor, and interest group directories.

9455 ■ *Genealogical Journal of Jefferson County, New York*
Pub: NewYorkAncestry.com
URL(s): www.newyorkancestry.com/scripts/J088.htm. **Ed:** Patricia R. James. **Released:** Quarterly **Price:** $20, Individuals plus postage.

9456 ■ *Heartlines*
Pub: Heart of America Genealogical Society
Contact: Marilyn R. Finke, President
Released: 4/year. **Description:** Supplies information on genealogical research resources, news of the Society and its library, news of other genealogical societies, and a list of library acquisitions.

9457 ■ *The Hoosier Genealogist*
Pub: Indiana Historical Society Press
Ed: M. Teresa Baer, Editor, tbaer@indianahistory.org. **Released:** Quarterly. **Price:** $40, members; $4, single issue. **Description:** Contains state and local historical and genealogical information.

9458 ■ *Hunterdon Historical Newsletter*
Pub: Hunterdon County Historical Society
Contact: Roxanne K. Carkhuff, Chairperson
Price: $15, individuals; $25, institutions. **Description:** Publishes local history and genealogy articles, as well as Society news. Recurring features include a collection, book reviews, and Notes and Queries, Acquisitions, and Family Associations.

9459 ■ *Immigration Digest*
Pub: Genealogical Institute
Contact: Arlene H. Eakle, President
E-mail: researchmyfamilytree@yahoo.com
Ed: Arlene H. Eakle, PhD, Editor, eakle@xmission.com. **Released:** 3/year. **Price:** $13.50, single issue plus $3 shipping. **Description:** Reports on new resources to link immigrant ancestors with their origins. Includes analytical reviews of source books and passenger lists.

9460 ■ *Irish Families*
Pub: Irish Genealogical Foundation
Contact: Michael C. O'Laughlin, President
E-mail: mike@irishroots.com
Released: 12/year. **Price:** $54 6/year; $104 12/year; Included in membership. **Description:** Promotes research on Irish heritage and genealogy. Recurring features include letters to the editor, news of members, a calendar of events, news of research, and notices of publications available.

9461 ■ *ISGS Newsletter*
Pub: Illinois State Genealogical Society
Ed: Karl Moore, Editor. **Released:** Bimonthly. **Price:** Included in membership. **Description:** Keeps members abreast of what is going on in Illinois and surrounding areas in genealogy. Recurring features include a question and answer column.

9462 ■ *Loyalist Gazette*
Pub: United Empire Loyalists' Association of Canada
URL(s): www.uelac.org/publications.php#gazette. **Ed:** Robert McBride. **Released:** Semiannual **Price:** $16, Individuals; $30, Two years; $43, Individuals three years; $23, Other countries.

9463 ■ *The Maple Leaflet*
Pub: French-Canadian Genealogical Society of Connecticut Inc.
Contact: Ivan N. Robinson, President
Ed: Ivan Robinson, Editor. **Released:** Quarterly, 2/year. **Price:** $20, members. **Description:** Contains articles on French-Canadian Genealogical Society of Connecticut's library events and new acquisitions.

9464 ■ *Missouri State Genealogical Association Journal*
Pub: Missouri State Genealogical Association
URL(s): www.mosga.org/journal.shtml. **Ed:** Carrie V. Tuck. **Released:** Quarterly

9465 ■ *National Genealogical Society Quarterly: A Journal for Today's Family Historian*
Pub: National Genealogical Society
Contact: Janet A. Alpert, President
E-mail: alpert@ngsgenealogy.org
URL(s): www.ngsgenealogy.org/cs/ngsq. **Ed:** Thomas W. Jones, Melinde Lutz Sanborn. **Released:** Quarterly **Price:** $12, Individuals printing.

9466 ■ *New England Connexion*
Pub: New England Connexion
Ed: Nancy H. Smit, Editor. **Released:** Quarterly. **Price:** $10, individuals. **Description:** Covers New England genealogy.

9467 ■ *New England Historical and Genealogical Register*
Pub: New England Historic Genealogical Society
Contact: Mr. D. Brenton Simons, President
URL(s): www.americanancestors.org/the-register. **Ed:** Henry B. Hoff. **Released:** Quarterly

9468 ■ *NGS Newsmagazine*
Pub: National Genealogical Society
Contact: Janet A. Alpert, President
E-mail: alpert@ngsgenealogy.org
Ed: Elizabeth Kelley Kerstens, Editor, henderson@ngsgenealogical.org. **Released:** 4/year. **Price:** Included in membership. **Description:** Features news of the Society and the genealogical community, articles on genealogical methods, sources, repositories, and members' queries. Recurring features include a calendar of events.

9469 ■ *Northern Arizona Genealogical Society Bulletin*
Pub: Northern Arizona Genealogical Society
Ed: Virginia Grundvig, Editor, chichicoivig@juno.com. **Released:** Quarterly. **Price:** $15. **Description:** Focuses on the Society's activities and provides genealogical information.

9470 ■ *Oklahoma Genealogical Society Quarterly*
Pub: Oklahoma Genealogical Society
Released: Quarterly. **Price:** $15, single issue; $18 family. **Description:** Features information pertaining to local genealogy and history.

9471 ■ *Oregon Genealogical Society Quarterly*
Pub: Oregon Genealogical Society Inc.
Ed: Nancy Hodgkinson, Editor, nlh43@aol.com. **Released:** Quarterly. **Price:** $25, individuals; $3, single issue. **Description:** Contains information on the Society's activities, Oregon history, and genealogical research.

9472 ■ *Polish Genealogical Society--Journal*
Pub: Polish Genealogical Society of America
Contact: Terry Carter, President
Ed: William F. Hoffman, Editor, wfhoffman@aol.com. **Released:** Quarterly. **Description:** Promotes research in Polish genealogies and heraldry. Carries information on research methodology, geographic locations, bibliographies, and selected histories. Recurring features include original material by professional genealogists and personal accounts by amateurs, letters to the editor, book reviews, news of research, an information-exchange section, and a question-and-answer column.

9473 ■ *Presidential Families Gazette*
Pub: Presidential Families of America
Contact: Dr. Lawrence Kent, Founder
Released: 3/year. **Price:** Included in membership. **Description:** Publishes general Society news and on subjects relating to Presidents of the U.S. and to their kin who are PFA members.

9474 ■ *Research News*
Pub: Genealogical Institute
Contact: Arlene H. Eakle, President
E-mail: researchmyfamilytree@yahoo.com
Ed: Arlene H. Eakle, PhD, Editor, eakle@xmission.com. **Released:** Monthly. **Price:** $5.50, single issue; $25 one volume. **Description:** Carries practical information on genealogical research. Identifies new research methods, tools, and publications. Recurring features include statistics, book reviews, and news of research. Recurring features include Back issues available.

9475 ■ *The Searcher*
Pub: Southern California Genealogical Society & Family Research Library
Released: Bimonthly. **Price:** Included in membership; $2.50, individuals. **Description:** Contains articles and news pertaining to genealogy and family research. Recurring features include feature articles, genealogical records; listings of the Society's library acquisitions; news of members; editorials; book reviews; a calendar of events; letters to the editor; notices of seminars, workshops, and conferences; and columns titled Periodical News and Queries.

9476 ■ *Voyageur Magazine: Northeast Wisconsin's Historical Review*
Pub: Voyageur Magazine
URL(s): www.uwgb.edu/voyageur/archive.html. **Ed:** Victoria Goff. **Released:** Semiannual; (June & Dec.). **Price:** $16, Individuals.

FRANCHISES AND BUSINESS OPPORTUNITIES

9477 ■ Swyrich Corporation
Hall of Names Marketing
830 Development Dr.
Kingston, ON, Canada K7M 5V7
Ph: (613)384-2257
Free: 800-265-7099

Fax: (613)384-0606

Description: offers history of names software. **No. of Franchise Units:** 350. **No. of Company-Owned Units:** 2. **Founded:** 1968.. **Franchised:** 1970. **Equity Capital Needed:** $7,500. **Franchise Fee:** $5,000. **Training:** Yes.

COMPUTERIZED DATABASES

9478 ■ *Anthropological Literature Database*
21 Divinity Ave.
Cambridge, MA 02138
Ph: (617)495-2253
Fax: (617)496-2741
Co. E-mail: tozref@fas.harvard.edu
URL: http://hcl.harvard.edu/libraries/tozzer
Availability: Online: Harvard University - Tozzer Library. **Type:** Bibliographic.

9479 ■ *Family Tree Maker®*
360 West 4800 North
Provo, UT 84604
Ph: (801)705-7000
Free: 800-262-3787
Fax: (801)705-7001
Co. E-mail: support@ancestry.com
URL: http://corporate.ancestry.com
Contact: Timothy P. Sullivan, President
Availability: CD-ROM: Ancestry.com Inc. **Type:** Directory.

9480 ■ *International Genealogical Index®*
(IGI)
35 NW Temple St., Ste. 344
Salt Lake City, UT 84150
Ph: (801)240-2584
Free: 866-406-1830
Fax: (801)240-1794
Co. E-mail: fhl@familysearch.org
URL: https://www.familysearch.org
Availability: Online: Church of Jesus Christ of Latter-Day Saints-FamilySearch International. **Type:** Directory.

LIBRARIES

9481 ■ Adams County Genealogical Society Library
PO Box 231
West Union, OH 45693-0231
Ph: (937)386-2309
Co. E-mail: acgs@bright.net
URL: http://www.adamshistory.org
Contact: Ethel Chambers, President
Scope: Genealogy, family histories, Adams County. **Services:** Copying; Library open to the public on a limited schedule. **Founded:** 1979. **Holdings:** 1200 books; 200 bound periodical volumes; 30 manuscripts; 50 archives; 100 reels of microfilm; 60 exchange newsletters.

9482 ■ American-Canadian Genealogical Society Library
4 Elm St.
Manchester, NH 03108-6478
Ph: (603)622-1554
Co. E-mail: acgs@acgs.org
URL: http://www.acgs.org/library/
Contact: Gerard Savard, Director
Scope: French-Canadian, American materials, genealogy, history. **Services:** Copying; library open to the public (fee). **Founded:** 1973. **Holdings:** 4500 books; 3000 bound periodical volumes; family histories, town histories; marriage repertories, Quebec and some U.S. - New England; archival resources; maps. **Subscriptions:** 41 journals and other serials.

9483 ■ American-French Genealogical Society Library
PO Box 830
Woonsocket, RI 02895-0870
Ph: (401)765-6141

Fax: (401)597-6290
Co. E-mail: database@afgs.org
URL: http://www.afgs.org
Contact: Janice Burkhart, President
Scope: French-American genealogy, vital records from Quebec and United States, family history and biography. **Services:** Library open to the public ($5 fee per visit for non-members). **Founded:** 1978. **Holdings:** 10,000 books; 1000 bound periodical volumes; microfilm; microfiche. **Subscriptions:** 114 journals and other serials.

9484 ■ Atchison County Kansas Genealogical Society - Collection
Atchison Public Library
401 Kansas
Atchison, KS 66002-0303
Ph: (913)367-1902
Fax: (913)367-2717
Co. E-mail: ackgs2@yahoo.com
URL: http://skyways.lib.ks.us/genweb/society/atchison/ackgs.htm
Contact: Myrna McConnaughey, President
URL(s): www.atchisonlibrary.org. **Scope:** Atchison County, Kansas, surrounding counties, Missouri, genealogy. **Services:** Library open to the public for reference use only. **Founded:** 1991. **Holdings:** 300 books; 10 bound periodical volumes; 34 reports; 30 microfiche; 400 reels of microfilm.

9485 ■ Barton County Historical Society
85 S. Hwy. 281
Great Bend, KS 67530-1091
Ph: (620)793-5125
Fax: (620)793-5125
Co. E-mail: bchsdirector@gmail.com
URL: http://bartoncountymuseum.org
Contact: Beverly Komarek, Executive Director
Scope: Barton County, Kansas, genealogy. **Services:** Copying; library open to the public with restrictions. **Founded:** 1970. **Holdings:** Reports; manuscripts; archives; photographs. **Subscriptions:** 1 journal; 1 newspaper.

9486 ■ Branches and Twigs Genealogical Society - Collection
Kingman Carnegie Library
455 N. Main
Kingman, KS 67068-1395
Ph: (316)532-3061
Fax: (316)532-2528
Co. E-mail: kingc1lb@websurf.net
URL: http://skyways.lib.ks.us/library/kingman/
Contact: Olive Ann McCormick, President
Scope: Genealogy. **Services:** Interlibrary loan; copying; SDI; library open to the public. **Founded:** 1913. **Holdings:** 312 books; 8000 microfiche; 210 reels of microfilm; manuscripts. **Subscriptions:** 3 journals and other serials; 2 newspapers. **Telecommunication Services:** graceg@kingmanlibrary.org.

9487 ■ Brigham Young University - Family History Library—BYU Family History Library.
2250 Harold B. Lee Library
Provo, UT 84602
Ph: (801)422-6200
Fax: (801)422-0466
Co. E-mail: howard_bybee@byu.edu
URL: http://www.lib.byu.edu/sites/familyhistory
Contact: Howard Bybee, Librarian, Historical Collections
Scope: Genealogy. **Services:** Scanning; copying; center open to the public. **Founded:** 1964. **Holdings:** 35,000 journals, serials, and newspapers on microfilm; maps; online databases; primary and secondary source material in microform. **Subscriptions:** 50 journals and other serials; 400 newspapers. **Telecommunication Services:** byufhl.coordinator@byu.edu.

9488 ■ British Columbia Genealogical Society Resource Centre
PO Box 88054
Richmond, BC, Canada V6X 3T6
Ph: (604)502-9119

Fax: (604)502-9119
Co. E-mail: bcgs@bcgs.ca
URL: http://www.bcgs.ca
Contact: Mrs. Betty Allen, Administrator
Scope: Genealogy, history. **Services:** Library open to the public on fee basis for non-members. **Founded:** 1971. **Holdings:** 6500 books; 250 bound periodical volumes; 200 reels of microfilm; 12,000 microfiche; Canadian census films; maps; 14,000 publication titles. **Subscriptions:** 275 journals and other serials.

9489 ■ Brooklyn Historical Society Library
4442 Ridge Rd.
Brooklyn, OH 44144-0422
Ph: (216)749-2804
Co. E-mail: groundhogsgarden@wowway.com
Contact: Barbara Stepic, President
Scope: Brooklyn history, area history. **Services:** Library open to the public with restrictions. **Founded:** 1973. **Holdings:** Reports; area yearbooks; photographs; records; newspaper clippings, 1930-1964; maps; local newspapers.

9490 ■ Brown County Genealogy Society Library
PO Box 83
Georgetown, OH 45121
Ph: (937)378-2582
Contact: Ann Kenney
Scope: Local history, genealogy. **Services:** Copying; Library open to the public. **Founded:** 1976. **Holdings:** 300 books; microfilm; reports; archives; microfiche. **Subscriptions:** 350 journals and other serials.

9491 ■ Chase County Historical Society - Museum and Library
301 Broadway
Cottonwood Falls, KS 66845
Ph: (316)273-8500
URL: http://skyways.lib.ks.us/genweb/society/cottonwd/
Contact: Pat Donelson, Curator
Scope: Chase County history, genealogy. **Services:** Copying; library open to the public. **Founded:** 1934. **Holdings:** 200 books; 85 reels of microfilm; Collectibles; pictures. **Subscriptions:** 1 newspaper.

9492 ■ Cherokee County Genealogical-Historical Society Library
100 S. Tennessee
Columbus, KS 66725-0033
Ph: (620)429-2992
Co. E-mail: cckghs@columbus-ks.com
URL: http://skyways.lib.ks.us/genweb/cherokee/society/cckghs.html
Contact: Marilyn Schmitt
Scope: Genealogy - Cherokee County, Kansas. **Services:** Genealogy research; copying; library open to the public. **Founded:** 1980. **Holdings:** 1100 books; 1000 reels of microfilm. **Subscriptions:** 22 journals and other serials.

9493 ■ Cherry County Historical Society
324 N, Main St.
Valentine, NE 69201
Ph: (402)376-2105
Co. E-mail: dtorg@threeriver.net
URL: http://www.rootsweb.com/~necherry/
Contact: Jan Howell, Curator
Scope: Genealogy. **Services:** Copying; open to public. **Founded:** 1934. **Holdings:** 300 books; 200 bound periodical volumes; 500 archival materials; 150 reels of microfilm; photographs; newspapers, 1887 to present. **Telecommunication Services:** mb29@inetnebr.com.

9494 ■ Church of Jesus Christ of Latter-Day Saints - Cleveland, Ohio Stake Family History Center
25000 Westwood Rd.
Westlake, OH 44145
Ph: (440)777-1518
URL: http://www.familysearch.org
Scope: Genealogy. **Services:** Access to the microfilm collection of the main center in Salt Lake City; center open to the public. **Founded:** 1966. **Holdings:** 265 reels of microfilm of U.S., British, Canadian collec-

tions; 112 reels of microfilm of non-English speaking countries (continental European, Afro-Asian, Latin American, Iberian Peninsula, Scandinavian Collections).

9495 ■ Church of Jesus Christ of Latter-day Saints - Valley Forge, Pennsylvania Stake - Family History Center
721 Paxon Hollow Rd.
Broomall, PA 19008
Ph: (610)356-8507
Contact: John Lee, Director
Scope: Genealogy. **Services:** Access to microfilm and microfiche records of the main library in Salt Lake City; center open to the public. **Founded:** 1973. **Holdings:** 1500 books; 42,000 microfiche; 1000 reels of microfilm.

9496 ■ Clarkesville-Habersham County Library
178 E. Green St.
Clarkesville, GA 30523
Ph: (706)754-4413
Fax: (706)754-3479
URL: http://www.habershamga.com/libraries.cfm
Scope: Genealogy, history. **Services:** Copying; library open to the public. **Founded:** 1940. **Holdings:** 40,000 items; 150 bound periodical volumes; 1000 CD-ROMs; 1000 videotapes; 300 audiocassettes. **Subscriptions:** 80 journals and other serials; 4 newspapers.

9497 ■ Collegiate Reformed Dutch Church Library
45 John St., Rm. 1000
New York, NY 10038-3706
Ph: (212)233-1960
Fax: (212)406-1856
Co. E-mail: rhollenga@collegiatechurch.org
URL: http://www.collegiatechurch.org
Contact: Maria Hollenga, Librarian
Scope: Genealogical data, 1633 to present. **Services:** Library not open to the public. **Founded:** 1633. **Holdings:** 45 books; archival materials; documents. **Subscriptions:** 20 journals and other serials.

9498 ■ Collin County Genealogical Society Library
PO Box 865052
Plano, TX 75086-5052
Ph: (972)769-4240
Co. E-mail: ccgs.members@gmail.com
URL: http://www.rootsweb.ancestry.com/~txcolcgs/
Scope: Collin County, Texas history and genealogy. **Services:** Library open to the public with restrictions. **Holdings:** Figures not available.

9499 ■ Connecticut Society of Genealogist Library
PO Box 435
Glastonbury, CT 06033-0435
Ph: (860)569-0002
Fax: (860)569-0339
Co. E-mail: csginc@csginc.org
URL: http://www.csginc.org
Contact: Stephanie Hyland, Office Manager
Scope: Genealogy. **Services:** Copying; Library open to the public. **Founded:** 1968. **Holdings:** Books; manuscripts; microfiche; CD-ROM.

9500 ■ Connecticut State Library - History and Genealogy Unit
231 Capitol Ave.
Hartford, CT 06106-1537
Ph: (860)757-6580
Fax: (860)757-6677
Co. E-mail: isref@cslib.org
URL: http://www.cslib.org/handg.htm
Contact: Richard C. Roberts, Director
Scope: Genealogy, state history. **Services:** Library open to the public. **Founded:** 1854. **Holdings:** Books; bound periodical volumes; manuscripts; archives; microfiche; microfilms; patents; reports. **Subscriptions:** 75 journals and other serials; 75 newspapers.

9501 ■ Croatian Genealogical & Heraldic Society Library
2527 San Carlos Ave.
San Carlos, CA 94070
Ph: (650)592-1190
Co. E-mail: croatians@aol.com
URL: http://www.croatians.com
Contact: Adam S. Eterovich, Director
URL(s): www.feefhs.org/. **Scope:** Genealogy, heraldry, census, Croatian history prior to 1900. **Services:** Copying; Library open to the public by appointment. **Founded:** 1974. **Holdings:** 2000 books; 20 bound periodical volumes; 20 drawers of index cards; 30 manuscripts. **Subscriptions:** 10 journals and other serials; 5 newspapers.

9502 ■ Darke County Historical Society Library—Darke County Genealogy Library.
205 N. Broadway St.
Greenville, OH 45331-0908
Ph: (937)548-5250
Fax: (937)548-7645
Co. E-mail: ahuffman@wesnet.com
URL: http://www.garstmuseum.org/
Contact: Alice Huffman, President
URL(s): www.garstmuseum.org. **Scope:** Genealogy, Darke County history. **Services:** Library open to the public for reference use only. **Founded:** 1984. **Holdings:** 1200 books; 20,000 microfiche; 5000 surname folders.

9503 ■ Decatur Genealogical Society Library
1255 W. South Side Dr.
Decatur, IL 62525-1548
Ph: (217)429-0135
Co. E-mail: decaturgensoc@att.net
URL: http://www.rootsweb.ancestry.com/~ildecgs/library.htm
Contact: Cheri Hunter, Librarian
Scope: Genealogy; Macon County history. **Services:** Copying; library open to the public for a nonimal fee. **Founded:** 1964. **Holdings:** 60,000 books; 16,000 bound periodical volumes; 5000 microfiche; census on microfilm; birth, marriage, court, and death and cemetery records; family histories; microfiche, microfilm. **Subscriptions:** 180 journals and other serials (some exchanges) and other serials.

9504 ■ Finney County Genealogical Society Library
403 S. 4th St.
Garden City, KS 67846-0592
Co. E-mail: myravgormley@yahoo.com
URL: http://www.rootsweb.ancestry.com/~ksfinney
Scope: Genealogy; local history. **Services:** Copying; library open to the public. **Founded:** 1967. **Holdings:** 1025 books; 427 periodical volumes; 500 reports; 1500 microfiche; 85 microfilm. **Subscriptions:** 14 journals and other serials.

9505 ■ Firelands Historical Society Library
9 Case Ave.
Norwalk, OH 44857-0572
Ph: (419)663-0392
Contact: Henry Timman, Librarian
Scope: Genealogy, local history. **Services:** Copying; Library open to the public. **Founded:** 1857. **Holdings:** 5000 books; 10,000 archival materials; 50 reels of microfilm; photographs; manuscripts.

9506 ■ Franklin Area Historical Society Library
302 Park Ave.
Franklin, OH 45005-3549
Ph: (937)746-8295
Contact: Harriet Foley, Librarian
Scope: Franklin history, Warren County history, military history. **Services:** Library open to the public by appointment (and Sunday afternoon, April to November). **Founded:** 1972. **Holdings:** 940 books; 24 bound periodical volumes; vertical files. **Subscriptions:** 1 newspapers.

9507 ■ French-Canadian Genealogical Society of Connecticut, Inc. - French-Canadian Genealogical Library
53 Tolland Green
Tolland, CT 06084-0928
Ph: (860)872-2597
Co. E-mail: ghoffman@fcgsc.org
URL: http://www.fcgsc.org/library-holdings.html
Contact: Ernest A. Laliberté, President
Scope: French-Canadian genealogy and history. **Services:** Copying; Library open to the public with restrictions. **Founded:** 1981. **Holdings:** 3000 books; 500 bound periodical volumes; 550 other cataloged items; 10,000 index cards on Acadians; index to 10,000 births, deaths, and marriages of Franco-Americans in Connecticut; 5000 index cards on Worcester County, Massachusetts, area; maps; periodicals. **Subscriptions:** 22 serial titles. **Telecommunication Services:** elaliberte@fcgsc.org.

9508 ■ James A. Garfield Historical Society Library
8107 Main St.
Garrettsville, OH 44231
Co. E-mail: garrettsvillehistory@gmail.com
URL: http://jamesagarfieldhistoricalsociety.com
Contact: Kit Semplak, President
Scope: Garrettsville history. **Services:** Library open to the public with restrictions. **Founded:** 1996.

9509 ■ German-Texan Heritage Society - Charles G. Trenckmann Memorial Library
507 E. 10th St.
Austin, TX 78768-4171
Ph: (512)482-0927
Free: 866-482-4847
Fax: (512)482-0636
Co. E-mail: info@germantexans.org
URL: http://www.germantexans.org/
Contact: Jean Warneke, Executive Director
Scope: German cultural heritage of Texas, German Texana, genealogy, Texas history, German history, German literature, travel to Germany. **Services:** Library open to the public for reference use only. **Founded:** 1978. **Holdings:** 472 pioneer books; 1150 research books; 50 manuscripts; 163 multimedia materials; 400 archival materials; microfiche. **Subscriptions:** 10 journals and other serials.

9510 ■ Godfrey Memorial Library
134 Newfield St.
Middletown, CT 06457-2534
Ph: (860)346-4375
Fax: (860)347-9874
Co. E-mail: library@godfrey.org
URL: http://www.godfrey.org
Contact: James Benn, Director
Scope: Genealogy, local history, biography. **Services:** Genealogical research; copying; Library open to the public. **Founded:** 1947. **Holdings:** 18,000 books; microfiche; microfilm. **Subscriptions:** 3 journals and other serials.

9511 ■ Greeley County Historical Society Library
PO Box 231
Tribune, KS 67879
Ph: (620)376-4996
Co. E-mail: greeley@pld.com
Contact: Nadine Cheney, Curator
Scope: Kansas history, genealogy, agriculture, poetry, diaries. **Services:** Copying; email; Library open to the public. **Founded:** 1975. **Holdings:** 500 books, maps, newspapers; telephone directories, soldier's enrollments, Civil War and obituaries; reports; manuscripts; patents; archives; microfilm. **Subscriptions:** 4 journals and other serials.

9512 ■ Guysborough Historical Society Archives
PO Box 232
Guysborough, NS, Canada B0H 1N0
Ph: (902)533-4008
Fax: (902)533-2258
Co. E-mail: guysborough.historical@ns.sympatico.ca
URL: http://www.guysboroughcountyheritage.ca
Contact: Mark Haynes, President
URL(s): www.guysboroughhistoricalsociety.ca. **Scope:** Local history, genealogy, historical research. **Services:** Copying; library open to members only. **Founded:** 1976. **Holdings:** Books; reports.

9513 ■ Hamilton City Library - Bluestem Genealogical Society Collection
21 E. Main St.
Hamilton, KS 66853
Ph: (770)678-3646
Fax: (770)78-3646
Co. E-mail: hclibrary66853@yahoo.com
URL: http://hamiltoncity.mykansaslibrary.org
Contact: Janice Ashley, Director
Scope: Genealogy - Greenwood County, Kansas, U.S. **Services:** Interlibrary loan; copying; library open to the public with restrictions. **Founded:** 1970. **Holdings:** 100 books; 100 bound periodical volumes; 21 reels of microfilm. **Subscriptions:** 50 journals and other serials.

9514 ■ Harper County Genealogical Society Library
c/o Harper Public Library
1002 Oak St.
Harper, KS 67058
Ph: (620)896-2959
Co. E-mail: harperlib@cyberlodge.com
URL: http://skyways.lib.ks.us/genweb/society/harper/
Contact: Tina Welch, Librarian
Scope: Harper County (Kansas) history; Kansas history; genealogy. **Services:** Library open to the public for reference use only. **Holdings:** 400 books; 1 microfiche; 11 reels of microfilm. **Telecommunication Services:** peterson@kanokla.net.

9515 ■ Haskell County Historical Society
Fairgrounds
Sublette, KS 67877
Ph: (316)675-8344
Co. E-mail: museum@pld.com
Scope: Local history. **Services:** Library open to the public for reference use only. **Founded:** 1983. **Holdings:** 59 reels of microfilm; 60 yearbooks. **Subscriptions:** 2 journals and other serials; 1 newspaper.

9516 ■ Heritage Commission Corporation Library
147 W. Mound St.
South Charleston, OH 45368
Ph: (937)462-7277
Contact: Janice Brubaker, Secretary
Scope: Local history, genealogy, D.T&I Railroad. **Services:** Interlibrary loan; library open to the public. **Founded:** 1980. **Holdings:** 100 books; 25 feet of archival material. **Subscriptions:** 10 journals and other serials.

9517 ■ HeritageQuest - Library
500 N. Marketplace Dr., Ste. 222
Centerville, UT 84014
Ph: (801)298-5358
Fax: (801)298-5468
Co. E-mail: custserv@heritagequest.com
URL: http://www.heritagequestonline.com
Contact: Carolyn Starke, Manager
URL(s): www.heritagequest.com. **Scope:** Genealogy. **Services:** Microfilming. **Founded:** 1983. **Holdings:** 250,000 reels of microfilm including census records, mortality schedules; ship passenger lists; military records, vital records, deeds, wills, tax lists, county and family histories; 250 CD-ROMs; books; indexes; digital CDs.

9518 ■ Houston Public Library - Clayton Library - Center for Genealogical Research
5300 Caroline St.
Houston, TX 77004-6896
Ph: (832)393-2600
URL: http://www2.houstonlibrary.org/clayton/
Contact: Susan Kaufman, Manager
Scope: Genealogy. **Services:** Copying; Center open to the public. **Founded:** 1921. **Holdings:** 100,000 books; 3000 bound periodical volumes; 70,000 reels of microfilm; 60,000 microfiche; VF material. **Subscriptions:** 285 journals and other serials.

9519 ■ Huguenot Society of America Library
General Society of Mechanics and Tradesmen Bldg., Ste. 510
20 W. 44th St.
New York, NY 10036
Ph: (212)755-0592

Fax: (212)317-0676
Co. E-mail: hugsoc@verizon.net
URL: http://www.huguenotsocietyofamerica.org
Scope: French Huguenot migration to America, Huguenot history in France and elsewhere, biography, genealogy. **Services:** Copying; library open on a limited schedule and by appointment. **Founded:** 1883. **Holdings:** 10,000 items; 30 manuscripts; 20 autograph letters.

9520 ■ Huguenot Society of South Carolina Library
138 Logan St.
Charleston, SC 29401
Ph: (843)723-3235
Fax: (843)853-8476
Co. E-mail: archivist@huguenotsociety.org
URL: http://www.huguenotsociety.org/library.htm
Contact: Karen King, Director
Scope: Genealogical data on Huguenots and allied families. **Services:** Library open to the public. **Founded:** 1885. **Holdings:** 4500 volumes; 16 VF drawers of genealogical data; microfilm; microfiche; CDs; 2200 vertical files. **Subscriptions:** 19 journals and other serials. **Telecommunication Services:** director@huguenotsociety.org.

9521 ■ Huxford Genealogical Society, Inc. - Huxford Library
20 S. College St.
Homerville, GA 31634
Ph: (912)487-2310
Fax: (912)487-3881
Co. E-mail: huxford@windstream.net
URL: http://www.huxford.com
Scope: Genealogy. **Services:** Copying; research library open to nonmembers on a fee basis. **Founded:** 1972. **Holdings:** 4000 volumes; 1300 family surname files; 79 boxes of magazines; 600 boxes of microfilm; reports; manuscripts; archives; Georgia Death Index; Florida Death Index. **Subscriptions:** 2000 journals and other serials. **Telecommunication Services:** huxford.spearlibrary@windstream.net.

9522 ■ Jackson County Public Library - Indiana & Jackson County History and Genealogy Collection
303 W. 2nd St.
Seymour, IN 47274
Ph: (812)522-3412
Fax: (812)522-5456
Co. E-mail: csellers@myjclibrary.org
URL: http://myjclibrary.org
Contact: Charlotte Sellers, Specialist
Scope: Indiana and Jackson County genealogy and history. **Services:** Library open to the public. **Founded:** 1905. **Holdings:** Books; maps; microfiche; microfilm; records; papers; pictures. **Subscriptions:** 2 journals and other serials.

9523 ■ Jewish Historical Society of New York, Inc. Library
8 W. 70th St.
New York, NY 10023
Ph: (212)415-5544
Co. E-mail: swsiegel@pipeline.com
Contact: Steven W. Siegel, President
Scope: American and New York Jewish history, Jewish genealogy. **Services:** Provides telephone and email reference service only. **Founded:** 1973. **Holdings:** Figures not available.

9524 ■ Kings County Museum Library
37 Cornwallis St.
Kentville, NS, Canada B4N 2E2
Ph: (902)678-6237
Fax: (902)678-2764
Co. E-mail: museum@okcm.ca
URL: http://www.okcm.ca
Contact: Bria Stokesbury, Curator
Scope: Genealogy, local history. **Services:** Copying; library open to the public for a fee. **Founded:** 1980. **Holdings:** 300 books; 2000 archival materials; 100 microfiche; 200 reels of microfilm; photographs. **Subscriptions:** 4 journals and other serials. **Telecommunication Services:** curator@okcm.ca; genealogy@okcm.ca.

9525 ■ Kittochtinny Historical Society Library
175 E. King St.
Chambersburg, PA 17201
Ph: (717)264-1667
Fax: (717)264-1451
Co. E-mail: history@pa.net
URL: http://pafch.tripod.com
Scope: History, genealogy. **Services:** Library open to the public on a limited schedule. **Founded:** 1898. **Holdings:** Books; manuscripts; newspapers (microfilm, hard copy); cemetery records; funeral directors' records; abstracts of wills; family files; historical files; historical photographs. **Subscriptions:** 3 journals and other serials. **Telecommunication Services:** jlhorst@innernet.net .

9526 ■ Lake Erie Islands Historical Society Library
25 Town Hall Pl.
Put-in-Bay, OH 43456
Ph: (419)285-2804
Fax: (419)285-3814
Co. E-mail: director@leihs.org
URL: http://www.leihs.org
Contact: Barb Cooper, Curator
Scope: Battle of Lake Erie, early trimotor aviation, Lake Erie western basin history, John Brown Jr., Put-in-Bay and Lake Erie steamships. **Services:** Copying; Library open to the public at librarian's discretion. **Founded:** 1986. **Holdings:** 800 books; reports; 3500 archival materials; genealogical files; manuscripts; microfilm. **Subscriptions:** 6 journals and other serials.

9527 ■ Leavenworth County Historical Society and Museum Library
1128 5th Ave.
Leavenworth, KS 66048
Ph: (913)682-7759
Fax: (913)682-7759
Co. E-mail: leavenworthhistory@sbcglobal.net
URL: http://www.leavenworthhistory.org/History.htm
Contact: Mark Bureman, Administrator
Scope: Leavenworth County history, genealogy. **Services:** Copying; Library open to the public. **Founded:** 1954. **Holdings:** 1000 books; 10,000 archival materials; microfilm; photographs. **Subscriptions:** 3 journals and other serials.

9528 ■ Library of Congress - Humanities and Social Sciences Division - Local History & Genealogy Reading Room
101 Independence Ave., SE
Thomas Jefferson Bldg., LJ G42
Washington, DC 20540-4660
Ph: (202)707-5537
Fax: (202)707-1957
URL: http://www.loc.gov/rr/genealogy
Contact: Judith P. Roach, Team Leader
Scope: U.S. local history; genealogy - International in scope. **Services:** Copying; section open to adults only. **Holdings:** Books; vertical files; manuscripts; microfilms; newspapers; photographs; maps.

9529 ■ Madison County Historical Society Library
260 E. High St.
London, OH 43140
Ph: (740)852-2977
Co. E-mail: lplgen@oplin.org
URL: http://hometown.aol.com/payne3467/mchs.html
Contact: Dorthy Richmond, Museum Director
URL(s): www.london.lib.oh.us/history.htm. **Scope:** Madison County history. **Services:** Library open to the public. **Founded:** 1980. **Holdings:** 2000 books.

9530 ■ Manitoba Genealogical Society Inc. - MGS Resource Center and Library
E-1045 St. James St.
Winnipeg, MB, Canada R3H 1B1
Ph: (204)783-9139
Fax: (204)783-0190
Co. E-mail: library@mbgenealogy.com
URL: http://www.mbgenealogy.com/index.php?page=library-resources
Contact: Mary Bole, Librarian
Scope: Large collection of Manitoba local history books; 1279 transcripts of Manitoba cemeteries; Anglican, Roman Catholic and United Church BMD

indexes; all Manitoba census returns; a good collections of Ontario, Saskatchewan and Great Britain material. **Services:** Library open to the public on Tuesday to Thursday (free to members but $5 per day for visitors). **Founded:** 1976. **Holdings:** 8000 volumes; genealogical resource periodicals; microfilm; microfiche; CD-ROMs, directories, telephone books. **Subscriptions:** 120 journals and other serials. **Telecommunication Services:** contact@mbgenealogy.com.

9531 ■ Marion Area Genealogical Society Library
169 E. Church St.
Marion, OH 43301-0844
Co. E-mail: marshall255@verizon.net
URL: http://www.rootsweb.com/~ohmags/
Contact: Maxine Marshall, Genealogist
Scope: Marion County history, Ohio history, genealogy, Marion city history. **Services:** Copying; Library open to the public. **Founded:** 1995. **Holdings:** 250 books; 100 bound periodical volumes; 50 reports.

9532 ■ McAllen Public Library - McAllen Genealogical Society Collection
Main Library, 1st Fl.
4001 N. 23rd St.
McAllen, TX 78504
Ph: (956)681-3000
Fax: (956)681-3009
Co. E-mail: genref@mcallen.net
URL: http://www.mcallenlibrary.net/resources/genealogy.aspx
Contact: Kate Horan, Director, Library Services
Scope: Genealogy. **Services:** Copying; Library open to the public. **Founded:** 1975. **Holdings:** 6500 books; 640 bound periodical volumes. **Subscriptions:** 20 journals and other serials.

9533 ■ Mennonite Historians of Eastern Pennsylvania - Mennonite Historical Library & Archives
Mennonite Heritage Center
565 Yoder Rd.
Harleysville, PA 19438-1020
Ph: (215)256-3020
Fax: (215)256-3023
Co. E-mail: alderferjoel@mhep.org
URL: http://www.mhep.org/index.php?id_pag=4
Contact: Joel D. Alderfer, Curator Librarian
Scope: History - Mennonite church, Anabaptist, local; genealogy; folklore; church music; Pennsylvania Germans; peace and non-resistance. **Services:** Copying; microfilm reader and printer; Library open to the public. **Founded:** 1967. **Holdings:** 12,000 books; 786 bound periodical volumes; 393 manuscript collections; 592 bound church bulletins; 236 reels of microfilm; 2075 audiocassettes; 3500 photographs; archival collections (668 linear shelf ft.); 61 videotapes; 650 flat file items (broadsides, posters, prints, and maps); 480 vertical and genealogical files; 130 transcripts (church and cemetery records, diaries, account books). **Subscriptions:** 130 journals and other serials; 30 newspapers. **Telecommunication Services:** library@mhep.org.

9534 ■ Milford Area Historical Society Library
Promont House
906 Main St.
Milford, OH 45150
Ph: (513)248-0324
Co. E-mail: library@milfordhistory.net
URL: http://www.milfordhistory.net/
Contact: Maxine Van Aken, Librarian
Scope: Local history, genealogy. **Services:** Copying; library open to the public. **Holdings:** 250 books; 30 bound periodical volumes; 150 archival items; 200 photographs. **Telecommunication Services:** damann@milfordhistory.net.

9535 ■ The Montgomery County Genealogy Society Library
PO Box 444
Coffeyville, KS 67337-0444
Ph: (620)251-1370

Fax: (316)251-1512
Co. E-mail: royd@hit.net
URL: http://www.rootsweb.com/~ksmontgo/
Contact: Carol Duvall, President
Scope: Genealogy. **Services:** Interlibrary loan; copying; Library open to the public. **Founded:** 1970. **Holdings:** Archival materials; newspapers and censuses; microfiche; reels of microfilm; obits (1975-1995). **Subscriptions:** 12 journals and other serials.

9536 ■ Montgomery's Inn Museum - Heritage Resource Centre
4709 Dundas St. W
Etobicoke, ON, Canada M9A 1A8
Ph: (416)394-8113
Fax: (416)394-6027
Co. E-mail: montinn@toronto.ca
URL: http://www.toronto.ca/culture/museums/montgomery.htm
Contact: Randall Reid, Program Manager
Scope: Decorative arts, local history, genealogy. **Services:** Library open to the public for reference use only. **Founded:** 1975. **Holdings:** 1000 books.

9537 ■ Napa Valley Genealogical & Biographical Society Library
1701 Menlo Ave.
Napa, CA 94558
Ph: (707)252-2252
Co. E-mail: nvgbs@earthlink.net
URL: http://www.napavalleygenealogy.org
Contact: Virginia Wakeman
Scope: Genealogy. **Services:** Copying; Library open to the public on fee basis. **Founded:** 1974. **Holdings:** 6000 books; Hartford Times; family and surname files, census microfilm.

9538 ■ National Society of the Sons of the American Revolution - Genealogy Library—SAR Library.
809 W. Main St.
Louisville, KY 40202-2619
Ph: (502)589-1776
Fax: (502)585-7674
Co. E-mail: library@sar.org
URL: http://library.sar.org
Contact: Robin Christian, Director, Library Services
Scope: American history and genealogy, Revolutionary War, Colonial America. **Services:** Copying; library open to the public on a fee basis. **Founded:** 1927. **Holdings:** 40,000 books; 2800 volumes periodicals; 15,000 microforms. **Subscriptions:** 11 journals and other serials. **Telecommunication Services:** rchristi@sar.org.

9539 ■ National Society of the Sons of Utah Pioneers Library
3301 E. 2920 S.
Salt Lake City, UT 84109
Ph: (801)484-4441
Free: 866-724-1847
Fax: (801)484-2067
Co. E-mail: sup1847@comcast.net
URL: http://www.sonsofutahpioneers.org/about/suplibrary/
Contact: Marilyn Johnson, Director, Library Services
Scope: Genealogy, pioneer history. **Services:** Library open to the public by appointment. **Founded:** 1981. **Holdings:** 5000 books; 5000 personal pioneer histories; articles; family histories; old photographs; genealogical histories; magazines; microfiche; films; manuscripts; archives; microfiche. **Subscriptions:** 10 journals and other serials.

9540 ■ Ness County Historical Society Library
113 S. Iowa St.
Ness City, KS 67560-1992
Ph: (785)798-3415
Fax: (785)798-2313
Co. E-mail: director@nesscitylibrary.org
URL: http://skyways.lib.ks.us/towns/NessCity/museum.html
Contact: Jean Schlegel, Director
URL(s): www.nesscitylibrary.org. **Scope:** History of Ness County, Kansas; antiques; cemetery information. **Services:** Interlibrary loan; copying; library open to the public. **Founded:** 1887. **Holdings:** 17,000

books; 100 bound periodical volumes; microfilm; artifacts. **Subscriptions:** 4 journals and other serials. **Telecommunication Services:** illdesk@nesscitylibrary.org.

9541 ■ New York Genealogical and Biographical Society Library
36 W. 44th St., 7th Fl.
New York, NY 10036-8105
Ph: (212)755-8532
Fax: (212)754-4218
Co. E-mail: library@nygbs.org
URL: http://www.newyorkfamilyhistory.org
Contact: Edward Smith, Director, Library Services
Scope: Genealogy, biography, U.S. and local history. **Services:** Copying by mail; library search services by mail; library open to the public with limitations (membership available to all). **Founded:** 1869. **Holdings:** 80,000 volumes; 4800 bound periodical volumes; 33,000 manuscripts; 14,000 reels of microfilm; 9000 microfiche; 250 CDs; 80 audiocassettes. **Subscriptions:** 1320 journals and other serials.

9542 ■ Norfolk Historical Society Archives—Norfolk Heritage Centre.
Norfolk Heritage Centre
109 Norfolk St., S.
Simcoe, ON, Canada N3Y 2W3
Ph: (519)426-1583
Fax: (519)426-1584
Co. E-mail: office@norfolklore.com
URL: http://www.norfolklore.com
Contact: Jo-Anne Barber, President
Scope: History - local, Ontario, United States, Europe; census; vital statistics; cemeteries; churches. **Services:** Microfilm loan services; copying; library open to non-members for a fee. **Founded:** 1900. **Holdings:** 4000 books; 3000 bound periodical volumes; 1000 microfiche; 2000 reels of microfilm; archives. **Telecommunication Services:** marketing@norfolklore.com; curator@norfolklore.com.

9543 ■ North York Central Library - Canadiana Department—Gladys Allison Canadiana Room.
5120 Yonge St.
Toronto, ON, Canada M2N 5N9
Ph: (416)395-5623
Co. E-mail: clca@torontopubliclibrary.ca
URL: http://www.torontopubliclibrary.ca
Contact: Greg Kelner, Manager
Scope: North York history, genealogy, local history of Ontario and historical Canadiana. **Services:** Copying; collection open to the public for reference use only. **Founded:** 1961. **Holdings:** Over 130,000 monographs; microfilm. **Subscriptions:** 100 journals and other serials.

9544 ■ Norwegian American Genealogical Center and Naeseth Library
415 W. Main St.
Madison, WI 53703-3116
Ph: (608)255-2224
Fax: (608)255-6842
Co. E-mail: genealogy@nagcnl.org
URL: http://www.nagcnl.org
Contact: Jeanne Wright, Executive Director
Scope: Norwegian-American genealogy and history. **Services:** Copying; library open to the public by appointment. **Founded:** 1975. **Holdings:** 3100 books; 3800 reels of microfilm; 60 notebooks. **Subscriptions:** 45 journals and other serials.

9545 ■ Norwegian-American Historical Association Archives
1510 St. Olaf Ave.
Rolvaag Library
St. Olaf College
Northfield, MN 55057-1097
Ph: (507)786-3229
Fax: (507)646-3734
Co. E-mail: sauve@stolaf.edu
URL: http://www.naha.stolaf.edu/archives/index.htm
Contact: Gary DeKrey, Archivist
Scope: Norwegian-American history, genealogy, and culture. **Services:** Interlibrary loan (through St. Olaf College Library; PALS); archives open to the public by appointment. **Founded:** 1925. **Holdings:** 8000

books; 1500 bound periodical volumes; newspapers; correspondence; diaries, scrapbooks; obituaries; photographs. **Subscriptions:** 15 journals and other serials. **Telecommunication Services:** naha@stolaf. edu.

9546 ■ Ohio Genealogical Society - Coshocton County Chapter Library
PO Box 128
Coshocton, OH 43812-0128
Ph: (740)622-4706
Fax: (740)545-6223
Co. E-mail: bjoans@tusco.net
URL: http://www.coshoctongenealogy.org
Contact: Joan Sheets, President
Scope: Genealogy. **Holdings:** Figures not available. **Telecommunication Services:** kwright88@roadrunner.com.

9547 ■ Ohio Genealogical Society - Perry County, Ohio Chapter Library
117 S. Jackson St.
New Lexington, OH 43764
Ph: (740)342-4194
Co. E-mail: mmarolt@pcdl.org
URL: http://perrycountychapterogs.org
Contact: Melissa Marolt, Director, Library Services
URL(s): www.pcdl.org. **Scope:** Genealogy. **Services:** Copying; genealogical searches. **Founded:** 1983. **Holdings:** 2000 books; 100 bound periodical volumes; 100 manuscripts; 100 microfiche; 43 microfilm. **Telecommunication Services:** perrycountychapterogs@yahoo.com.

9548 ■ Perry Historians Library—Harry W. Lenig Library.
763 Dix Hill Rd.
New Bloomfield, PA 17068
Ph: (717)582-4896
Co. E-mail: donna@theperryhistorians.org
URL: http://www.theperryhistorians.org
Contact: Donna Zinn
Scope: Genealogy, local history. **Services:** Copying; library open to the public on a limited schedule; provides genealogical and historical research services. **Founded:** 1976. **Holdings:** 5000 books; 500 reels of microfilm; 1000 land drafts; 4500 family surname files; 1 million index cards. **Subscriptions:** 9 journals and other serials. **Telecommunication Services:** staff@theperryhistorians.org.

9549 ■ Thomas Raddall Research Centre Archives
PO Box 1078
Liverpool, NS, Canada B0T 1K0
Ph: (902)354-4058
Fax: (902)354-2050
Co. E-mail: rafusela@gov.ns.ca
URL: http://www.raddallresearchcentre.com
Contact: Linda Rafuse, Director
Scope: Genealogy, local history, businesses, shipping. **Services:** Copying; library open to the public. **Founded:** 1932. **Holdings:** 100 books; 100 bound periodical volumes; 600 archival files; 2500 microfiche; 300 reels of microfilm. **Subscriptions:** 2 journals and other serials. **Telecommunication Services:** stittkim@gov.ns.ca.

9550 ■ W.A. Rankin Memorial Library
502 Indiana St.
Neodesha, KS 66757
Ph: (620)325-3275
Co. E-mail: rankin.library@neodesha.com
URL: http://www.rootsweb.ancestry.com/~kswarml
Contact: Mary Meckley, Director
URL(s): rankin.mykansaslibrary.org. **Scope:** Local history, family genealogies. **Services:** Interlibrary loan; copying; library open to the public. **Founded:** 1912. **Holdings:** 20,000 books; 200 reels of microfilm; DVDs; audiobooks. **Subscriptions:** 50 magazines; 5 newspapers. **Telecommunication Services:** neodeshalibrary@hotmail.com.

9551 ■ Rawlins County Genealogical Society Library
PO Box 405
Atwood, KS 67730-0405
Ph: (785)626-3805

Fax: (785)626-3805
Co. E-mail: atwoodli@ruraltel.net
URL: http://skyways.lib.ks.us/genweb/rawlins/rawgenesoc.html
Contact: Delores Luedke, Researcher
Scope: Genealogy. **Services:** Copying; library open to the public for reference use only. **Founded:** 1980. **Holdings:** Figures not available.

9552 ■ Frederic Remington Area Historical Society Library
PO Box 133
Whitewater, KS 67154
Ph: (316)799-2913
URL: http://skyways.lib.ks.us/towns/Brainerd
Contact: Melvin Epp, President
Scope: Local history, local family history. **Services:** Library open to the public with restrictions. **Founded:** 1978. **Holdings:** 75 books; 100 manuscripts; 15 archive volumes; 600 slides on CD; 101 reels of microfilm; 36 videotapes.

9553 ■ Rock Island County Illinois Genealogical Society - Library
822 11th Ave.
Moline, IL 61265-1221
Ph: (309)764-8590
Co. E-mail: ricigs@speedconnect.com
URL: http://www.rootsweb.ancestry.com/~ilbgsrim/index.html
Contact: Debra Van Sant, Librarian
Scope: Genealogy. **Services:** Library open to the public. **Founded:** 1972. **Holdings:** 2000 books, publications, documents, CDs, and maps. **Subscriptions:** 20 journals and other serials.

9554 ■ Ross County Genealogical Society Library
444 Douglas Ave.
Chillicothe, OH 45601-6352
Ph: (740)773-2715
Co. E-mail: rcgs@bright.net
URL: http://www.rosscountyhistorical.org/genealogy. html
URL(s): www.rootsweb.ancestry.com/~ohrcgs/. **Scope:** Genealogy. **Services:** Copying; library open to the public. **Founded:** 1973. **Holdings:** Books; microfiche; reels of microfilm.

9555 ■ Annie Halenbake Ross Library Special Collections
232 W. Main St.
Lock Haven, PA 17745
Ph: (570)748-3321
Fax: (570)748-1050
Co. E-mail: ross1@rosslibrary.org
URL: http://www.rosslibrary.org/
Contact: Diane L. Whitaker, Executive Director
Scope: Pennsylvania, genealogy. **Services:** Interlibrary loan; copying; Library open to the public. **Founded:** 1910. **Holdings:** 133,608 books; 85 bound periodical volumes; 833 reels of microfilm. **Subscriptions:** 115 journals and other serials; 10 newspapers.

9556 ■ Russell County Historical Society Library
331 Kansas St.
Russell, KS 67665
Ph: (785)483-3637
Co. E-mail: rchs@russellks.net
URL: http://www.rwisp.com/~rchs/
Contact: Pauline Bender
Scope: Genealogy; history - county and general. **Services:** Copying; Library open to the public. **Founded:** 1970. **Holdings:** 300 books; 750 archival items; 3000 microfiche. **Subscriptions:** 2 journals and other serials.

9557 ■ St. Clair Shores Public Library - Local History Center
22500 E. 11 Mile Rd.
St. Clair Shores, MI 48081
Ph: (586)771-9020

Fax: (810)771-8935
Co. E-mail: orlandor@libcoop.net
URL: http://www.scslibrary.org/
Contact: Rosemary Orlando, Director, Library Services
Scope: Michigan history and genealogy. **Services:** Library open to the public. **Founded:** 1939. **Holdings:** Books and periodicals; photographs.

9558 ■ St. Louis Genealogical Society Library
4 Sunnen Dr., Ste. 140
St. Louis, MO 63143
Ph: (314)647-8547
Fax: (314)647-8548
Co. E-mail: library@stlgs.org
URL: http://www.stlgs.org
Contact: Joyce Loving, Manager
Scope: Genealogy, family history. **Services:** Copying; limited genealogical research (fee based); library open to the public. **Founded:** 1968. **Holdings:** 20,000 items including books, journals, maps, and CDs. **Subscriptions:** 275 journals and other serials. **Telecommunication Services:** office@stlgs.org; scollections@slcl.org.

9559 ■ Scarborough Historical Society - Scarborough Archives
6282 Kingston Rd.
Scarborough, ON, Canada M1C 1K9
Ph: (416)396-6930
Fax: (416)282-9482
Co. E-mail: info@scarboroughhistorical.com
URL: http://www.scarboroughhistorical.com/
URL(s): scarboroughhistorical.ca/?page_id=55. **Scope:** History, genealogy. **Services:** Copying; microfilm/microfiche reading; archives open to the public by appointment. **Founded:** 1978. **Holdings:** 800 published volumes; 1000 aerial photos.

9560 ■ Shenandoah County Library - Local History and Genealogy Collection
514 Stoney Creek Blvd.
Edinburg, VA 22824
Ph: (540)984-8200
Fax: (540)984-8207
URL: http://www.shenandoah.co.lib.va.us
Contact: Sandy Whitesides, Director
Scope: Shenandoah County and the Shenandoah Valley history and genealogy; Civil War; Pennsylvania; Maryland; West Virginia; Virginia. **Services:** Copying; library open to the public. **Founded:** 1985. **Holdings:** Books; microforms; microfilm; records; photographs; letters; archival materials; Civil War materials. **Subscriptions:** 30 journals and other serials; 6 newspapers.

9561 ■ Societe de Genealogie de Quebec Library
C.P. 9066
Ste. Foy, QC, Canada G1V 4A8
Ph: (418)651-9127
Fax: (418)651-2643
Co. E-mail: sgq@total.net
URL: http://www.sgq.qc.ca
Contact: Mariette Parent, Librarian
Scope: Genealogy. **Services:** Copying; Library open to the public ($5 fee for non-members). **Founded:** 1961. **Holdings:** 10,000 books; microfiche; microfilm; archives. **Subscriptions:** 120 journals and other serials.

9562 ■ Southern Ohio Genealogical Society Reference Library
PO Box 414
Hillsboro, OH 45133
Co. E-mail: sogs414@sbcglobal.net
URL: http://www.sogs.info
Contact: Pat Young, Librarian
Scope: Genealogy, local history. **Services:** Library open to the public. **Founded:** 1978. **Holdings:** 1200 books; 250 bound periodical volumes; 100 family files; 85 family history files; 3700 burial records of veterans buried in Highland County, OH; 83 volumes of published family histories; 75 family history manuscripts; census maps; passenger and immigration records.

9563 ■ Stafford County Historical & Genealogical Society Library
100 N. Main St.
Stafford, KS 67578
Ph: (620)234-5664
Co. E-mail: staffordcountymuseum@earthlink.net
URL: http://home.earthlink.net/~mjhathaway61
Contact: Marion Hearn, President
Scope: Stafford County and Kansas history. **Services:** Library open to the public. **Founded:** 1976. **Holdings:** Stafford Courier and St; John News; 5000 books; 23 reels of microfilm; 20 manuscripts; 10 patents; 1000 archives folders; 29,000 Gray Studio glass plate negatives; CDs; photographs.

9564 ■ University of California, Berkeley - The Bancroft Library - The Magnes Collection of Jewish Art and Life - Western Jewish Americana Archives - Western Jewish History Center
2121 Allston Way
Berkeley, CA 94720-6300
Ph: (510)643-2526
Co. E-mail: wjhc@magnes.org
URL: http://www.magnes.org/collections/archives/western-jewish-americana
Contact: Aaron T. Kornblum, Archivist
Scope: The history and experiences of the Jewish community in the thirteen western United States, particularly relating to the San Francisco Bay Area. **Services:** Copying; Center open by appointment only. **Founded:** 1967. **Holdings:** 336 rolls of microfilm; 677 archival collections; 288 audio tapes (89 oral histories); books; vertical subject file; photographs. **Telecommunication Services:** akornblum@magnes.org.

9565 ■ Warren County Genealogical Society Library
406 Justice Dr.
Lebanon, OH 45036-0296
Ph: (513)695-1144
Co. E-mail: wcgs@co.warren.oh.us
URL: http://www.co.warren.oh.us/genealogy/index.htm
Contact: Dana Palmer, President
Scope: Genealogy. **Services:** Copying; research on Warren families for small fee; library open to the public. **Founded:** 1982. **Holdings:** 3000 volumes; microfiche; microfilm. **Subscriptions:** 70 journals and other serials.

9566 ■ Washington County Historical & Genealogical Society Library
216 Ballard St.
Washington, KS 66968
Ph: (785)325-2198
Fax: (785)325-2198
Co. E-mail: wchgs31@hotmail.com
URL: http://skyways.lib.ks.us/genweb/washingt/wchs.htm
Contact: Jack Barley, President
URL(s): skyways.lib.ks.us/orgs/wchgs. **Scope:** Washington County history, Washington County genealogy. **Services:** Copying; library open to the public. **Founded:** 1983. **Holdings:** Microfilm newspapers; books; manuscripts.

9567 ■ West Hants Historical Society - Genealogies Collections
281 King St.
Windsor, NS, Canada B0N 2T0
Ph: (902)798-4706
Fax: (902)798-8535
Co. E-mail: whhs@ns.aliantzinc.ca
URL: http://www.westhantshistoricalsociety.ca
Contact: Rev. David Curry, President
Scope: Genealogy, local history. **Services:** Copying; library open to the public on a limited schedule and by appointment. **Founded:** 1973. **Holdings:** 400 books; 12 reels of microfilm; maps; scrapbooks; photographs. **Subscriptions:** 2 journals and other serials.

9568 ■ Wichita Genealogical Society Library
PO Box 3705
Wichita, KS 67201-3705
Co. E-mail: wgs@wichitagensoc.org
URL: http://www.wichitagensoc.org
Contact: Sage Joyner, Liaison
Scope: Genealogy, local history. **Services:** Library open to the public. **Founded:** 1987. **Holdings:** Figures not available.

9569 ■ World Jewish Genealogy Organization Library
1605 48th St.
Brooklyn, NY 11219-0009
Ph: (718)435-4400
Fax: (718)633-7050
Contact: Rabbi N. Halberstam, Librarian
Scope: Judaica. **Services:** Library not open to the public. **Holdings:** 12,000 books.

RESEARCH CENTERS

9570 ■ College of Southern Maryland - Southern Maryland Studies Center (SMSC)
8730 Mitchell Rd.
La Plata, MD 20646-0910
Ph: (301)934-7606
Fax: (301)934-7699
Co. E-mail: smsc@csmd.edu
URL: http://www.csmd.edu/library/SMSC
Contact: Bradley Gottfried, President
Founded: 1976. **Telecommunication Services:** askme@csmd.edu.

9571 ■ Historic Annapolis Foundation Research Center
Shiplap House
18 Pinkney St.
Annapolis, MD 21401
Ph: (410)267-7619
Free: 800-603-4020
Fax: (410)267-1030
Co. E-mail: john.guild@annapolis.org
URL: http://www.annapolis.org
Contact: John Guild, President
Founded: 1952. **Publications:** *Historic Annapolis Foundation Journal* (Semiannual). **Awards:** Preservation Awards (Annual), given to individuals and organizations who have demonstrated best practices in preservation in the Greater Annapolis Community.

9572 ■ Samford University - Institute of Genealogy and Historical Research (IGHR)
Samford University Library
800 Lakeshore Dr.
Birmingham, AL 35229
Ph: (205)726-4447
Fax: (205)726-4009
Co. E-mail: ighr@samford.edu
URL: http://www4.samford.edu/schools/ighr
Contact: Della Holland Darby, Director
Founded: 1962.

9573 ■ Southwest Minnesota State University - Southwest Minnesota Historical Center
Social Science, Rm. 141
1501 State St.
Marshall, MN 56258
Ph: (507)537-7373
Fax: (507)537-6147
Co. E-mail: jlouwagie@southwestmsu.edu
URL: http://www.southwestmsu.edu/history_center/
Contact: Jan Louwagie, Coordinator
Founded: 1972. **Educational Activities:** Southwest Minnesota Historical Center Conferences; Speakers series.

9574 ■ Starsmore Center for Local History (SCLH)
Colorado Springs Pioneers Museum
215 S Tejon St.
Colorado Springs, CO 80903
Ph: (719)385-5990

Fax: (719)385-5645
Co. E-mail: lwitherow@springsgov.com
URL: http://www.springsgov.com/Page.aspx-?NavID=2547
Contact: Leah Davis Witherow, Archivist
Services: Consultation: for paper and photograph preservation. **Founded:** 1938. **Telecommunication Services:** sclh@springsgov.com.

9575 ■ Stearns History Museum
235 33rd Ave. S
Saint Cloud, MN 56301-3752
Ph: (320)253-8424
Free: 866-253-8424
Fax: (320)253-2172
Co. E-mail: jdecker@stearns.history.museum
URL: http://www.stearns.history.museum
Contact: Sarah Warmka, Archivist
E-mail: swarmka@stearns-museum.org
Founded: 1936. **Publications:** *Crossings Magazine* (Bimonthly). **Educational Activities:** Annual genealogical conference/workshop; Century Farms, first week in June; Spring bus tour, third Friday in May. **Telecommunication Services:** info@stearns.history.museum.

9576 ■ University of Moncton - Centre for Acadians Studies—University of Moncton - Centre d'Études Acadiennes
Moncton, NB, Canada E1A 3E9
Ph: (506)858-4085
Fax: (506)858-4530
Co. E-mail: isabelle.cormier@umoncton.ca
URL: http://www.umoncton.ca/etudeacadiennes/centre/cea.html
Contact: Isabelle Cormier, Director
Founded: 1968. **Publications:** *Contact-Acadie* (Annual).

9577 ■ University of Wisconsin—Eau Claire - Eau Claire Area Research Center
McIntyre Library
105 Garfield Ave.
Eau Claire, WI 54702
Ph: (715)836-2739
Fax: (715)836-2949
Co. E-mail: mcfarlcd@uwec.edu
URL: http://www.uwec.edu/library/archives/arc.htm
Founded: 1975. **Telecommunication Services:** library.archives@uwec.edu.

9578 ■ University of Wisconsin—Green Bay - Area Research Center
2420 Nicolet Dr.
Green Bay, WI 54311-7001
Ph: (920)465-2539
Fax: (920)465-2388
Co. E-mail: andersod@uwgb.edu
URL: http://www.uwgb.edu/library/spc/arc.asp
Founded: 1972.

9579 ■ University of Wisconsin—Parkside - Archives and Area Research Center
900 Wood Rd.
Kenosha, WI 53141-2000
Ph: (262)595-2345
Fax: (262)595-2545
Co. E-mail: nicholas.weber@uwp.edu
URL: http://www.uwp.edu/departments/library/archives
Contact: Nicholas Weber, Director
Founded: 1972. **Telecommunication Services:** archives@uwp.edu.

TRADE PERIODICALS

9580 ■ Gifts & Decorative Accessories
Pub: Sandow Media Corp.
URL(s): www.giftsanddec.com/. **Released:** Monthly
Price: $36, Individuals; $39, Canada; $135, Other
countries.

TRADE SHOWS AND CONVENTIONS

**9581 ■ Accent on Design - A Division of the
New York International Gift Fair**
George Little Management, LLC
1133 Westchester Ave., Ste. N136
White Plains, NY 10606
Ph: (914)421-3200
Free: 800-272-SHOW
Co. E-mail: cathy_steel@glmshows.com
URL: http://www.glmshows.com

URL(s): www.nyigf.com. **Frequency:** Annual. **Audience:** Buyers from specialty, department, and jewelry stores and; gift shops; interior designers; home products importers and distributors; mail order catalogs. **Principal Exhibits:** General giftware, tabletop and housewares, decorative and personal accessories, museum gifts, ethnic, traditional, country and contemporary design products, juvenile products, floral products and pet products. **Dates and Locations:** Jacob K. Javits Convention Center. **Telecommunication Services:** maureen_smith@glmshows.com.

9582 ■ Boston Gift Show
Urban Expositions
1395 S. Marietta Pkwy., Bldg. 400, Ste. 210
Marietta, GA 30067
Ph: (678)285-3976
Free: 800-318-2238

URL(s): www.bostongiftshow.com/. **Frequency:** Annual. **Audience:** Specialty and department store retailers, importer/export firms, distributors, gift shops, mail-order/catalog, houses and boutique. **Principal Exhibits:** Stationery, gourmet products and foods, toys, general gifts, floral items, decorative and personal accessories, souvenirs, jewelry, traditional and contemporary crafts, and tabletop items. Features Handmade and Made in New England sections. **Dates and Locations:** Bayside Expo Center.

9583 ■ California Gift Show
George Little Management, LLC
10130 Market St., Unit 9
Naples, FL 34112
Ph: (239)732-6642
Co. E-mail: customerservice@glmshows.com
URL: http://www.glmshows.com
Contact: Betty Wilson, Manager, Public Relations

URL(s): www.californiagiftshow.com. **Frequency:** and July. **Audience:** Retailers from qualified specialty, gallery, gift and department stores from 50 U.S. and 60 foreign countries. **Principal Exhibits:** The product categories are: child's play, fashion jewelry/accessories, fine gift, gardens, general gift, gourmet and

housewares, high design/contemporary handcrafted, home accents, international/multicultural, stationery, resort/souvenirs/novelty, pampered pets, body and soul, aromatherapy/personal care. **Dates and Locations:** , Convention Center.

9584 ■ Home Entertainment Show
Trigger Agency
3539 Clipper Mill Rd.
Baltimore, MD 21211
Free: 800-830-3976
Fax: (410)878-9911
Co. E-mail: info@triggeragency.com
URL: http://www.triggeragency.com/
Contact: Greg Nivens, President
E-mail: gnivens@triggeragency.com

URL(s): www.mooreamarketing.com. **Price:** $32, Pre-registered 3-day pass; $37, Onsite 3-day pass; $22, Pre-registered 1-day pass; $27, Onsite 1-day pass. **Frequency:** Biennial. **Audience:** Consumers, trade and press. **Principal Exhibits:** Home theater and high-fidelity audio equipment, supplies, and services. **Telecommunication Services:** gnivens@mooreamarketing.com.

9585 ■ Memphis Gift and Jewelry Show Fall
Helen Brett Enterprises, Inc.
5111 Academy Dr.
Lisle, IL 60532-2171
Ph: (630)241-9865
Fax: (630)241-9870
URL: http://www.gift2jewelry.com

URL(s): www.gift2jewelry.com. **Frequency:** Semiannual. **Audience:** Wholesale buyers. **Principal Exhibits:** Giftware and jewelry, apparel, home decor, novelties, silk flowers, fine/costume jewelry and accessories.

9586 ■ New Orleans Gift and Jewelry Show Spring
Helen Brett Enterprises, Inc.
5111 Academy Dr.
Lisle, IL 60532-2171
Ph: (630)241-9865
Fax: (630)241-9870
URL: http://www.gift2jewelry.com

URL(s): www.gift2jewelry.com. **Frequency:** Semiannual. **Audience:** Wholesale buyers. **Principal Exhibits:** Giftware and jewelry, apparel, home decor, rugs, silk plants, fine jewelry, costume jewelry, loose gemstones.

9587 ■ Pittsburgh Gift Show
Pittsburgh & Western New York Gift Shows
100 Bickford St.
Rochester, NY 14606-2298
Ph: (585)254-2580
Free: 800-997-GIFT
Fax: (585)458-1511
Co. E-mail: giftshows@coralproductions.com
URL: http://www.pittsburghgiftshow.com

URL(s): www.pittsburghgiftshow.com. **Price:** $100. **Frequency:** Twice a year. **Audience:** Gift retailers. **Principal Exhibits:** Gifts, decorative accessories,

jewelry, florals, stationery, crafts, and general and unique merchandise, collectibles. **Dates and Locations:** Expomart.

9588 ■ Washington Gift Show
George Little Management, LLC
1133 Westchester Ave., Ste. N136
White Plains, NY 10606
Ph: (914)421-3200
Free: 800-272-SHOW
Co. E-mail: cathy_steel@glmshows.com
URL: http://www.glmshows.com

URL(s): www.washingtongiftshow.com. **Frequency:** Semiannual. **Audience:** Specialty and department store retailers, importers, and distributors. **Principal Exhibits:** Gifts, stationery, gourmet products, floral industry products and services, decorative accessories, souvenirs, crafts, jewelry, personal accessories, china, glass, fine and fashion jewelry, collectibles, and related tabletop items. **Dates and Locations:** Capital Expo Center.

9589 ■ Western New York Gift Show
Pittsburgh & Western New York Gift Shows
100 Bickford St.
Rochester, NY 14606-2298
Ph: (585)254-2580
Free: 800-997-GIFT
Fax: (585)458-1511
Co. E-mail: giftshows@coralproductions.com
URL: http://www.pittsburghgiftshow.com

URL(s): www.westernnewyorkgiftshow.com. **Frequency:** Semiannual. **Audience:** Gift retailers. **Principal Exhibits:** Gifts, decorative accessories, jewelry, floral, stationery, crafts, and general merchandise. **Dates and Locations:** Dome Center Minett Hall. **Telecommunication Services:** giftshows@coralproductions.com.

FRANCHISES AND BUSINESS OPPORTUNITIES

9590 ■ Cookies in Bloom
7208 La Cosa Dr.
Dallas, TX 75248
Ph: (972)490-8644
Free: 800-222-3104
Fax: (972)490-8846
URL: http://www.cookiesinbloom.com

Description: Cookie gift business. **No. of Franchise Units:** 15. **Founded:** 1988.. **Franchised:** 1992. **Equity Capital Needed:** $85,000-$140,000. **Franchise Fee:** $19,500. **Royalty Fee:** 5%. **Training:** 10 days at headquarters, 5 days at franchisee's location, on-the-job training at corporate approved shop and ongoing support.

9591 ■ FruitFlowers/Incredibly Edible Delites
Incredible Franchise Corp.
3720 W Chester Pike
Newtown Sq., PA 19073

Ph: (610)353-8702
Fax: (610)353-8760
URL(s): www.fruitflowers.com. **Description:** Floral fruit and vegetable bouquets. **No. of Franchise**

Units: 25. **No. of Company-Owned Units:** 2. **Founded:** 1984.. **Franchised:** 1993. **Equity Capital Needed:** $250,000. **Franchise Fee:** $35,000. **Financial Assistance:** Yes. **Training:** Yes.

START-UP INFORMATION

9592 ■ *The Specialty Shop: How to Create Your Own Unique and Profitable Retail Business*
Pub: AMACOM
Ed: Dorothy Finell. **Released:** February 27, 2007. **Price:** $21.95. **Description:** Advise to start retail businesses, including bakeries, gift shops, toy stores, book shops, tea houses, clothing boutiques, and other unique stores.

ASSOCIATIONS AND OTHER ORGANIZATIONS

9593 ■ Gift Associates Interchange Network (GAIN)
c/o ABC-Amega, Inc.
1100 Main St.
Buffalo, NY 14209-2356
Ph: (716)887-9504
Free: 800-746-9428
Fax: (716)878-0479
Co. E-mail: rosanne.battaglia@abc-amega.com
URL: http://www.gaingroup.com
Contact: Rosanne Battaglia, Director, Member Services
Description: Represents manufacturers and importers of giftware, tabletop accessories, china, greeting cards, silk and floral products, book publishers, desk and wall calendar manufacturers. Collects, computes, and exchanges factual ledger information on mutual customers. Conducts seminars. **Founded:** 1974.

9594 ■ Souvenir Wholesale Distributors Association (SWDA)
2105 Laurel Bush Rd., Ste. 200
Bel Air, MD 21015
Ph: (443)640-1055
Fax: (443)640-1086
Co. E-mail: marci@kingmgmt.org
URL: http://www.souvenircentral.org
Contact: Marci L. Hickey, Executive Vice President
URL(s): www.postcardcentral.org. **Description:** Represents distributors and manufacturers of post cards, souvenirs, and novelty items. **Founded:** 1973. **Educational Activities:** PCSDA Annual Convention and Trade Show (Annual). **Awards:** Distributor of the Year (Annual); Industry Awards (Annual); Printer of the Year (Annual); Souvenir Supplier of the Year (Annual); Distributor of the Year; Postcard Awards; Printer of the Year; Souvenir Awards.

REFERENCE WORKS

9595 ■ *"Award Win Highlights Slingsby's Green Credentials" in Ecology,Environment & Conservation Business (August 20, 2011, pp. 3)*
Pub: HighBeam Research
Description: Slingsby, an industrial and commercial equipment supplier, was joint winner with Hallmark Cards of the Baildon Business in the Community's

Yorkshire and Humber Long Term Environmental Improvement Award. The firm cites its commitment to reducing environmental impact.

9596 ■ *"Doing Good: Cause and Effect" in Entrepreneur (Vol. 36, February 2008, No. 2, pp. 23)*
Pub: Entrepreneur Media Inc.
Description: Lisa Knoppe established Art for a Cause LLC that employs people with mental and physical disabilities. The company makes hand-painted tools and furniture to be sold at gift retailers and hardware stores.

9597 ■ *Gift and Decorative Accessories Center Association--Directory: The Center Directory*
Pub: Gift and Decorative Accessories Center Association
URL(s): www.giftsanddec.com. **Released:** Continuous **Price:** Free. **Covers:** About 60 individuals who are giftware manufacturers' representatives in New England; also lists their manufacturers and suppliers. **Entries include:** For representatives--Name, address, phone, e-mail, manufacturers and products represented. **Arrangement:** Alphabetical.

9598 ■ *Gift, Housewares & Home Textiles Buyers*
Pub: Briefings Media Group
Contact: Alan M. Douglas, President
E-mail: adouglas@douglaspublications.com
URL(s): www.douglaspublications.comwww.thesalesmansguide.com. **Released:** Annual; latest edition 2011-2012. **Price:** $329, Individuals directory price; $659, Individuals directory/CD combo. **Covers:** 12,700 buyers in the gift, housewares, and textiles industry throughout the United States, Puerto Rico, the Virgin Islands, and Canada. **Entries include:** Company name, address, phone, fax; e-mail; URL; names and titles of key personnel; financial data; branch/subsidiary names and addresses; products and/or services provided; price points; sales volume; type of stores; number of stores; divisions of parent companies; corporate buying offices. **Arrangement:** Geographical. **Indexes:** Store name, new listings, mail order, online retailer.

9599 ■ *Greeting Card Industry Directory*
Pub: Greeting Card Association
URL(s): www.greetingcard.org/publications.php. **Released:** Biennial; Latest edition 13th. **Price:** $75, Members; $150, Nonmembers plus shipping & handling charges. **Covers:** Over 3,000 greeting card publishers and suppliers in the United State and many foreign countries. **Entries include:** Company name, address, phone, e-mail, Internet, toll-free, fax numbers, key personnel, licensed properties, plant locations, description of products & services, distribution outlets and methods, geographic area covered, industry background, and related information. **Arrangement:** Alphabetical. **Indexes:** Product, geographical, brand name.

9600 ■ *"Halls Give Hospital Drive $11 Million Infusion" in The Business Journal-Serving*

Metropolitan Kansas City (Vol. 26, July 18, 2008)
Pub: American City Business Journals, Inc.
Ed: Rob Roberts. **Description:** Don Hall, chairman of Hallmark Cards Inc., and eight family members have announced that they will give $11 million to Children's Mercy Hospitals and Clinics for its $800 million expansion plan. Hall Family Foundation president Bill Hall that contributions such as that for Children's Mercy reflect the charitable interests of the foundation's board and founders. The possible impacts of the Hall's donation are analyzed.

9601 ■ *Profits for Non-Profits: Running a Successful Gift Shop*
Pub: Lulu.com
Ed: Nancy Kirk. **Released:** January 2005. **Price:** $19.95. **Description:** Guide for managing a non-profit gift shop in a hospital, zoo, museum or any other non-profit entity.

9602 ■ *Publishers Weekly--Calendar Roundup Issue*
Pub: Reed Business Information
Contact: Jeff Greisch, President
URL(s): www.bookwire.comwww.publishersweekly.com. **Released:** Annual; Latest edition 2010. **Publication includes:** Listing of more than 100 publishers of calendars and engagement books. **Entries include:** Publisher name, address, phone, brief descriptions of calendars being planned for the next year, with prices, discounts, etc. **Arrangement:** Alphabetical.

9603 ■ *"Retail Briefs - Dollar Store Opens in Long Leaf Mall" in Star-News (November 5, 2010)*
Pub: Star-News Media
Ed: Judy Royal. **Description:** Dollar Delight$ opened a new shop in Long Leaf Mall in Wilmington, North Carolina. The store will carry gift bags, balloons, party supplies, greeting cards, school supplies, health and beauty products, hardware, baby items, toys, Christmas goods, crafts, housewares and jewelry in its inventory.

9604 ■ *"Retail News: Children's Boutique Relocates to Conway" in Sun News (June 4, 2010)*
Pub: The Sun News
Description: Little Angel's Children's Boutique and Big Oak Frame Shop have moved to downtown locations in Conway, South Carolina. Little Angel's will sell children's clothing and accessories, shoes and gifts, while the frame shop will offer custom framing along with the sale of stationary, invitations and local prints.

9605 ■ *"Use Common Sense in Office Gift-Giving" in Women In Business (Vol. 61, October-November 2009, No. 5, pp. 32)*
Pub: American Business Women's Association
Ed: Maureen Sullivan. **Description:** Tips on office gift-giving during the Christmas season are discussed. Aside from ensuring appropriateness of the gift with respect to the recipient, a fixed giving budget

must be adhered to. Gifts that can be used by anyone may be selected and those with religious overtones must be avoided.

9606 ■ *"VISA: Canadians Spend $97 Million on Mom This Mother's Day"* **in** *Canadian Corporate News (May 16, 2007)*
Pub: Comtex News Network Inc.
Description: Visa Canada finds that Canadians are spending more on Mother's Day in recent years. Since 2002, sales of jewelry, flowers, and cards have climbed steadily in the week before Mother's Day weekend.

9607 ■ *"Worldwide Food Services (EREI) Tests Mini Dollar Store Program"* **in** *Internet Wire (August 6, 2009)*
Pub: Comtex News Network, Inc.
Description: Mini Dollar Stores and Eagle View LLC, wholly-owned subsidiaries of Worldwide Food Services, Inc., recently met with government officials and purchasing agents to lay out a test program which would distribute Mini Dollar Store items into VA hospital gift shops.

STATISTICAL SOURCES

9608 ■ *Greeting Cards - US*
Pub: MarketResearch.com
Released: 2008. **Price:** $3995.00. **Description:** The U.S. greeting card industry remains a mature and stable market with sales growth of 8.7% between 1999 and 2004.

9609 ■ *RMA Annual Statement Studies*
Pub: Risk Management Association
Contact: Kevin M. Blakey, President
Released: Annual. **Price:** $175.00 2006-07 edition, $105.00. **Description:** Contains composite balance sheets and income statements for more than 360 industries, including the accounting, auditing, and bookkeeping industries. Also contains five years of comparative historical data for discerning trends. Includes 16 commonly used ratios, computed for most of the size groupings for nearly every industry.

TRADE PERIODICALS

9610 ■ *Country Business: The Magazine for Today's Independent Gift Retailers*
Pub: Country Sampler Group
URL(s): www.country-business.com/. **Released:** Bimonthly

9611 ■ *Gifts & Decorative Accessories*
Pub: Sandow Media Corp.
URL(s): www.giftsanddec.com/. **Released:** Monthly **Price:** $36, Individuals; $39, Canada; $135, Other countries.

9612 ■ *Gifts & Tablewares*
Pub: Business Information Group
Contact: Bruce Creighton, President
URL(s): www.giftsandtablewares.ca/. **Ed:** Lori Smith. **Released:** 7/yr. **Price:** $43.95, Canada plus taxes; $49.95, Individuals in U.S.; $54.95, Other countries.

9613 ■ *Giftware News*
Pub: Talcott Communication Corp.
URL(s): www.giftwarenews.com. **Released:** Monthly **Price:** $43, Individuals; $59, Two years; $82, Individuals 3 years; $55, Canada; $196, Other countries.

9614 ■ *Party & Paper Retailer*
Pub: Great American Publishing Co.
URL(s): www.partypaper.com. **Released:** Monthly **Price:** $25, Individuals; $56, Canada; $100, Other countries.

TRADE SHOWS AND CONVENTIONS

9615 ■ Accent on Design - A Division of the New York International Gift Fair
George Little Management, LLC
1133 Westchester Ave., Ste. N136
White Plains, NY 10606
Ph: (914)421-3200

Free: 800-272-SHOW
Co. E-mail: cathy_steel@glmshows.com
URL: http://www.glmshows.com
URL(s): www.nyigf.com. **Frequency:** Annual. **Audience:** Buyers from specialty, department, and jewelry stores and; gift shops; interior designers; home products importers and distributors; mail order catalogs. **Principal Exhibits:** General giftware, tabletop and housewares, decorative and personal accessories, museum gifts, ethnic, traditional, country and contemporary design products, juvenile products, floral products and pet products. **Dates and Locations:** Jacob K. Javits Convention Center. **Telecommunication Services:** maureen_smith@glmshows.com.

9616 ■ Boston Gift Show
Urban Expositions
1395 S. Marietta Pkwy., Bldg. 400, Ste. 210
Marietta, GA 30067
Ph: (678)285-3976
Free: 800-318-2238
URL(s): www.bostongiftshow.com/. **Frequency:** Annual. **Audience:** Specialty and department store retailers, importer/export firms, distributors, gift shops, mail-order/catalog, houses and boutique. **Principal Exhibits:** Stationery, gourmet products and foods, toys, general gifts, floral items, decorative and personal accessories, souvenirs, jewelry, traditional and contemporary crafts, and tabletop items. Features Handmade and Made in New England sections. **Dates and Locations:** Bayside Expo Center.

9617 ■ California Gift Show
George Little Management, LLC
10130 Market St., Unit 9
Naples, FL 34112
Ph: (239)732-6642
Co. E-mail: customerservice@glmshows.com
URL: http://www.glmshows.com
Contact: Betty Wilson, Manager, Public Relations
URL(s): www.californiagiftshow.com. **Frequency:** and July. **Audience:** Retailers from qualified specialty, gallery, gift and department stores from 50 U.S. and 60 foreign countries. **Principal Exhibits:** The product categories are: child's play, fashion jewelry/accessories, fine gift, gardens, general gift, gourmet and housewares, high design/contemporary handcrafted, home accents, international/multicultural, stationery, resort/souvenirs/novelty, pampered pets, body and soul, aromatherapy/personal care. **Dates and Locations:** , Convention Center.

9618 ■ Charlotte Gift and Jewelry Show
Charlotte Gift and Jewelry Show
3710 Latrobe Dr., Ste. 110
Charlotte, NC 28211
Ph: (704)365-4152
Fax: (704)365-4154
Co. E-mail: michael@charlottegiftshow.com
URL: http://www.charlottegiftshow.com
URL(s): www.charlottegiftshow.com. **Frequency:** Quarterly. **Audience:** Trade buyers. **Principal Exhibits:** Gifts, housewares, jewelry, crafts, silk plants and flowers, tabletop, glassware, collectibles, accessories, home decorating accessories, basketry, and other related products. **Dates and Locations:** Merchandise Mart. **Telecommunication Services:** michael@charlottegiftshow.com.

9619 ■ Home Entertainment Show
Trigger Agency
3539 Clipper Mill Rd.
Baltimore, MD 21211
Free: 800-830-3976
Fax: (410)878-9911
Co. E-mail: info@triggeragency.com
URL: http://www.triggeragency.com/
Contact: Greg Nivens, President
E-mail: gnivens@triggeragency.com
URL(s): www.mooreamarketing.com. **Price:** $32, Pre-registered 3-day pass; $37, Onsite 3-day pass; $22, Pre-registered 1-day pass; $27, Onsite 1-day pass. **Frequency:** Biennial. **Audience:** Consumers, trade and press. **Principal Exhibits:** Home theater and high-fidelity audio equipment, supplies, and services. **Telecommunication Services:** gnivens@mooreamarketing.com.

9620 ■ Memphis Gift and Jewelry Show Fall
Helen Brett Enterprises, Inc.
5111 Academy Dr.
Lisle, IL 60532-2171
Ph: (630)241-9865
Fax: (630)241-9870
URL: http://www.gift2jewelry.com
URL(s): www.gift2jewelry.com. **Frequency:** Semiannual. **Audience:** Wholesale buyers. **Principal Exhibits:** Giftware and jewelry, apparel, home decor, novelties, silk flowers, fine/costume jewelry and accessories.

9621 ■ Montreal Spring Gift Show
dmg world media inc.
180 Duncan Mill Rd., Ste. 400
Toronto, ON, Canada M3B 1Z6
Ph: (416)385-1880
Free: 888-823-7469
Fax: (416)385-1855
Co. E-mail: corpinfo@ca.dmgworldmedia.com
URL: http://www.dmgworldmedia.com
URL(s): www.montrealgiftshow.com. **Frequency:** Annual. **Principal Exhibits:** Giftware and related items.

9622 ■ New Orleans Gift and Jewelry Show Spring
Helen Brett Enterprises, Inc.
5111 Academy Dr.
Lisle, IL 60532-2171
Ph: (630)241-9865
Fax: (630)241-9870
URL: http://www.gift2jewelry.com
URL(s): www.gift2jewelry.com. **Frequency:** Semiannual. **Audience:** Wholesale buyers. **Principal Exhibits:** Giftware and jewelry, apparel, home decor, rugs, silk plants, fine jewelry, costume jewelry, loose gemstones.

9623 ■ Offinger's Handcrafted Marketplace
Offinger Management Co.
1100-H Brandywine Blvd.
Zanesville, OH 43701-7303
Ph: (740)452-4541
Free: 888-878-6334
Fax: (740)452-2552
Co. E-mail: omc.info@offinger.com
URL: http://www.offinger.com
URL(s): www.offinger.com. **Frequency:** Quarterly. **Audience:** Trade professionals. **Principal Exhibits:** Gift decor and gift-related items, such as candles, gourmet food, framed prints, country, primitive, folk art products, floral, crafts, and jewelry. **Dates and Locations:** Veterans Memorial Building. **Telecommunication Services:** gift@offinger.com.

9624 ■ Pittsburgh Gift Show
Pittsburgh & Western New York Gift Shows
100 Bickford St.
Rochester, NY 14606-2298
Ph: (585)254-2580
Free: 800-997-GIFT
Fax: (585)458-1511
Co. E-mail: giftshows@coralproductions.com
URL: http://www.pittsburghgiftshow.com
URL(s): www.pittsburghgiftshow.com. **Price:** $100. **Frequency:** Twice a year. **Audience:** Gift retailers. **Principal Exhibits:** Gifts, decorative accessories, jewelry, florals, stationery, crafts, and general and unique merchandise, collectibles. **Dates and Locations:** Expomart.

9625 ■ Vancouver Fall Gift Show
dmg world media inc.
4601 CanadaWay, Ste. 402
Burnaby, BC, Canada V5G 4X7
Ph: (604)433-5121
Fax: (604)434-6853
URL: http://www.dmgworldmedia.com
URL(s): www.vancouvergiftshow.com. **Frequency:** Annual. **Audience:** Retail buyers from gift shops; drugstores; hardware and general stores; bed, bath and linen stores; and department stores. **Principal Exhibits:** Giftware, housewares, jewelry, leather goods, toys, and games. **Dates and Locations:** , B.C. Place Stadium.

9626 ■ Vancouver Spring Gift Show
dmg world media inc.
4601 CanadaWay, Ste. 402
Burnaby, BC, Canada V5G 4X7
Ph: (604)433-5121
Fax: (604)434-6853
URL: http://www.dmgworldmedia.com
URL(s): www.vancouvergiftshow.com. **Frequency:** Annual. **Audience:** Retail buyers from gift shops; drugstores; hardware and general stores; bed, bath, and linen stores; and department stores. **Principal Exhibits:** Bed, bath, and linen supplies; interior design supplies; jewelry and accessories; souvenirs, stationery, store fixtures, tabletop gourmet items, and toys and games. **Dates and Locations:** Place Stadium.

9627 ■ Washington Gift Show
George Little Management, LLC
1133 Westchester Ave., Ste. N136
White Plains, NY 10606
Ph: (914)421-3200
Free: 800-272-SHOW
Co. E-mail: cathy_steel@glmshows.com
URL: http://www.glmshows.com
URL(s): www.washingtongiftshow.com. **Frequency:** Semiannual. **Audience:** Specialty and department store retailers, importers, and distributors. **Principal Exhibits:** Gifts, stationery, gourmet products, floral industry products and services, decorative accessories, souvenirs, crafts, jewelry, personal accessories, china, glass, fine and fashion jewelry, collectibles, and related tabletop items. **Dates and Locations:** Capital Expo Center.

9628 ■ Western New York Gift Show
Pittsburgh & Western New York Gift Shows
100 Bickford St.
Rochester, NY 14606-2298
Ph: (585)254-2580
Free: 800-997-GIFT
Fax: (585)458-1511
Co. E-mail: giftshows@coralproductions.com
URL: http://www.pittsburghgiftshow.com
URL(s): www.westernnewyorkgiftshow.com. **Frequency:** Semiannual. **Audience:** Gift retailers. **Prin**cipal Exhibits: Gifts, decorative accessories, jewelry, floral, stationery, crafts, and general merchandise. **Dates and Locations:** Dome Center Minett Hall. **Telecommunication Services:** giftshows@coralproductions.com.

FRANCHISES AND BUSINESS OPPORTUNITIES

9629 ■ Hometown Threads
209 Hudson Trace
Augusta, GA 30907
Ph: (706)737-7687
Fax: (706)737-7690
Co. E-mail: info@hometownthreads.com
URL: http://www.hometownthreads.com
Description: Retail embroidery store located within Wal-Mart encourage shoppers to create and buy custom designed gifts and products. **No. of Franchise Units:** 44. **No. of Company-Owned Units:** 4. **Founded:** 1998.. **Franchised:** 2001. **Equity Capital Needed:** Total investment $165,000. **Franchise Fee:** $29,000. **Royalty Fee:** 6%. **Financial Assistance:** Third party financing available. **Training:** Offers 3 weeks training at headquarters, 2 weeks at franchisees location with ongoing support.

9630 ■ The Panhandler
Liv Canada Gift Group Inc.
294 Walker Dr., Unit 2
Brampton, ON, Canada L6T 4Z2
Ph: (905)790-9023
Free: 866-463-4124
Fax: (905)790-7059
Co. E-mail: franchises@franchisebancorp.com
URL: http://www.livcan.com
Description: Boutiques specializing in gift, home decor, and kitchen items. **No. of Franchise Units:** 25. **Founded:** 1970.. **Franchised:** 1970. **Equity Capital Needed:** $140,000-$180,000. **Franchise Fee:** $25,000. **Training:** Yes. s.

9631 ■ Party Land
5215 Militia Hill Rd.
Plymouth Meeting, PA 19462
Ph: (610)941-6200
Free: 800-778-9563
Fax: (610)941-6301
Co. E-mail: jbarry@partyland.com
URL: http://www.partyland.com
Description: Retail party supply stores. **No. of Franchise Units:** 43. **Founded:** 1986.. **Franchised:** 1988. **Equity Capital Needed:** $150,000 -$297,000. **Franchise Fee:** $35,000. **Royalty Fee:** 5%. **Training:** 1 week training.

LIBRARIES

9632 ■ Hallmark Cards, Inc. - Business Research Library
Mail Drop 216
Kansas City, MO 64141
Ph: (816)274-5111
Free: 800-425-5627
Fax: (816)274-5061
URL: http://www.hallmark.com
Contact: Isidro de la Herran, Librarian, Business
Scope: Marketing, business forecasting, demographics, operations research. **Services:** Library not open to the public. **Founded:** 1980. **Holdings:** 800 books. **Subscriptions:** 100 journals and other serials.

9633 ■ Hallmark Cards, Inc. - Creative Research Library
2501 McGee, No. 146
Kansas City, MO 64108
Ph: (816)274-5525
Free: 800-425-5627
Fax: (816)274-7245
Co. E-mail: hallmarkplus@hallmark.com
URL: http://www.hallmark.com
Contact: Mark Spencer, Manager
Scope: Fine art, lettering, advertising, graphic art, design, illustration, photography. **Services:** Library open to Hallmark employees only. **Founded:** 1930. **Holdings:** 18,000 books; 60 bound periodical volumes. **Subscriptions:** 150 journals and other serials; 3 newspapers.

ASSOCIATIONS AND OTHER ORGANIZATIONS

9634 ■ Independent Glass Association (IGA)
354 Westlind Rd.
Syracuse, NY 13219
Ph: (315)706-9172
Fax: (810)227-0443
Co. E-mail: info@iga.org
URL: http://www.iga.org
Contact: Alan Epley, President
Description: Helps automotive and architectural glass retailers compete with the national chains. Unites the efforts, interests and ideas of its members. Offers marketing, billing, and purchasing programs and promotes a high standard for consumer safety, quality, service and fair trade principles. Encourages a competitive, free market environment and the independence of each member. **Founded:** 1995. **Publications:** *Beacon Bulletin* (Weekly). **Educational Activities:** Independents' Days National Convention and Spring Glass Show (Annual).

9635 ■ International Window Film Association (IWFA)
PO Box 3871
Martinsville, VA 24115-3871
Ph: (276)666-4932
Fax: (276)666-4933
Co. E-mail: admin@iwfa.com
URL: http://www.iwfa.com/industry.htm
Contact: Darrell L. Smith, Executive Director
Description: Manufacturers, distributors, suppliers, and installers of solar control, safety and security film for windows in automobiles, houses, and commercial buildings. Acts as a forum for communication and works to increase professionalism in the window film industry. Maintains educational programs and speakers' bureau. **Scope:** business. **Founded:** 1990. **Subscriptions:** 100 audiovisuals. **Publications:** *Flat Glass Training Manual* (Annual).

9636 ■ National Glass Association (NGA)
1945 Old Gallows Rd., Ste. 750
Vienna, VA 22182
Ph: (703)442-4890
Free: 866-342-5642
Fax: (703)442-0630
Co. E-mail: pjames@glass.org
URL: http://www.glass.org
Contact: Chris Mammen, Chairman
URL(s): www.glass.org/gef.html. **Description:** Manufacturers, installers, retailers, distributors and fabricators of flat, architectural, automotive and specialty glass and metal products, mirrors, shower and patio doors, windows and tabletops. Provides informational, educational and technical services. **Founded:** 1948. **Publications:** *AutoGlass Installation Guide* (Annual); *Glass Magazine* (Monthly); *Window & Door Magazine* (Bimonthly); *National Glass Association Directory*; *Glass Magazine*; *Window & Door, Glass Magazine*; *Glass Magazine: The Voice of the Architectural Glass Industry*; *AutoGlass: Glass on the Move*; *Glass Magazine--Directory of Suppliers Section* (Monthly). **Educational Activities:** GlassBuild America: The

Glass, Window & Door Expo (Annual); National Auto Glass Conference and Expo (Annual); The NGA Show: America's Glass Expo (Annual); National Glass Association Glazing Executives Forum; National Auto Glass Conference & Expo (Annual). **Awards:** Community Service Award (Annual); Glass Professional of the Year (Annual); Glass Professional of the Year; Award for Community Service. **Telecommunication Services:** membership@glass.org; nga@glass.org; administration@glass.org.

REFERENCE WORKS

9637 ■ "On the Cutting Edge" in Inc. (November 2007, pp. 28)
Pub: Gruner & Jahr USA Publishing
Ed: Elaine Appleton Grant. **Description:** Information is provided about a Nashville-area glass and glazing company that is on the market for $8.2 million. The owner started the company from the back of his truck in 2990 with $2,200. The firm has $9 million worth of contracts signed through 2008. Statistical data included.

TRADE PERIODICALS

9638 ■ Architects' Guide to Glass, Metal & Glazing
Pub: Key Communications Inc.
Contact: Debra Levy, President
E-mail: deb@glass.com
URL(s): www.glassguides.com/. **Ed:** Tara Taffera, Megan Headley, Ellen Rogers, Charles Cumpston. **Released:** 6/yr. **Price:** $19, Individuals one day; $39, Individuals one month; $259, Individuals.

9639 ■ Glass Canada: The Magazine of the Canadian Glass Industry
Pub: Annex Publishing & Printing Inc.
URL(s): www.annexweb.com/www.glasscanadamag.com/. **Ed:** Patrick Flannery. **Released:** 6/yr. **Price:** $39, Individuals.

9640 ■ Glass Magazine: The Voice of the Architectural Glass Industry
Pub: National Glass Association
Contact: Chris Mammen, Chairman
URL(s): www.glassmagazine.net/. **Released:** 11/yr. **Price:** $34.95, U.S., Canada, and Mexico; $44.95, Other countries.

FRANCHISES AND BUSINESS OPPORTUNITIES

9641 ■ Apple Auto Glass Limited
7111 Kennedy Rd., Unit 4
Mississauga, ON, Canada L5S 0A4
Ph: (289)562-5633
Free: 800-267-6175
Fax: (289)562-5642
Co. E-mail: franchiseingappleautoglass@belron-canada.ca
URL: http://www.appleautoglass.com
Description: The franchise system specializes in auto glass repair and replacement, sunroofs, auto

upholstery and vehicle accessories. **No. of Franchise Units:** 118. **No. of Company-Owned Units:** 4. **Founded:** 1983.. **Equity Capital Needed:** $100,000-$300,000. **Franchise Fee:** $25,000. **Training:** Training provided as required.

9642 ■ Atlantic Windshield Repair, Inc.
PO Box 361153
Birmingham, AL 35236
Free: 877-230-4487
Co. E-mail: atlanticwindshieldrepair@hotmail.com
URL: http://www.atlanticwindshieldrepair.com
Description: Complete package, including art equipment, training and electronic filing with over 200 insurance companies. Check status of jobs and print reports directly from the website. Set-up multiple shops and multiple installers and have the ability to check their progress with just a click of the mouse. See instantly what jobs you have been paid for and any that are waiting to be paid, and reorder supplies using only your dealership number. **No. of Franchise Units:** 7. **No. of Company-Owned Units:** 2. **Founded:** 1997.. **Franchised:** 2003. **Equity Capital Needed:** $25,000-$45,000. **Franchise Fee:** $19,000. **Royalty Fee:** 6%. **Training:** An initial 3 day training course covering windshield repair, insurance filing, customer service and advanced techniques and procedures. Ongoing video training and call in support available.

9643 ■ Belron Canada Inc.
8288 Boul. PIE-IX
Montreal, QC, Canada H1Z 3T6
Ph: (514)593-3824
Fax: (514)593-7028
URL: http://www.belroncanada.com
Description: Provides services and solutions for auto glass repair and replacement. Operates under four retail banners - Apple Auto Glass, Speedy Glass, Lebeau Vitres d'autos, DURO vitres d'autos - and conducts its wholesale activities under the Vanfax and Technicentre Plus trade names. It also offers claims management services. **No. of Franchise Units:** 150. **No. of Company-Owned Units:** 211. **Founded:** 1965. **Franchised:** 1982. **Equity Capital Needed:** $40,000-$300,000. **Franchise Fee:** $25,000.

9644 ■ DURO vitres d'autos
9061 Boul Pie IX
Montreal, QC, Canada H1Z 3V6
Ph: (514)593-3876
Fax: (514)326-8118
URL: http://www.durovitresdautos.com
Description: Part of Belron Canada providing glass repair/replacement service that is fast and accessible. **No. of Franchise Units:** 53. **No. of Company-Owned Units:** 9. **Founded:** 1954.. **Franchised:** 1990. **Equity Capital Needed:** $30,000-$80,000. **Franchise Fee:** $10,000. **Training:** Yes.

9645 ■ Glass Doctor
The Dwyer Group
1020 N University Parks Dr.
Waco, TX 76707
Free: 800-298-9858

Fax: (800)378-9480

Description: Auto, commercial, and residential glass replacement. **No. of Franchise Units:** 190. **Founded:** 2004.. **Equity Capital Needed:** $114,000-$295,000. **Franchise Fee:** $28,000. **Financial Assistance:** Yes. **Training:** Yes.

9646 ■ Novus Glass / Novus Franchising Inc.
TCC International, Inc.
12800 Hwy. 13 S, Ste. 500
Savage, MN 55378
Free: 800-944-6811
Fax: (952)946-0481
Co. E-mail: jimo@novusglass.com
URL: http://www.novusglass.com

Description: The franchisee's offer customers a convenient, economical alternative to windshield replacement by repairing stone-damaged windshields. **No. of Franchise Units:** 2,000. **No. of Company-Owned Units:** 11. **Founded:** 1972.. **Franchised:** 1985. **Equity Capital Needed:** From $15,400-$222,000. **Franchise Fee:** $10,000. **Financial Assistance:** Yes. **Training:** Gives franchisee's the ongoing training and support needed to from their first day of training and throughout their career as a franchise owner. Offers complete technical and business training at the Minneapolis, MN headquarters. Offers one-on-one consultation with an 8-day program and teaches how to offer a full-service windshield repair franchise.

RESEARCH CENTERS

9647 ■ Alfred University - Center for Glass Research (CGR)
Binns-Merrill Hall
New York State College of Ceramics
Alfred, NY 14802
Ph: (607)871-2662
Fax: (607)871-2383
Co. E-mail: stevenshj@alfred.edu
URL: http://engineering.alfred.edu/research/cgr.cfm
Contact: Dr. Harrie J. Stevens, Director
Services: Glass information and research. **Founded:** 1985.

ASSOCIATIONS AND OTHER ORGANIZATIONS

9648 ■ American Junior Golf Association (AJGA)—Ajga
1980 Sports Club Dr.
Braselton, GA 30517
Ph: (770)868-4200
Free: 877-373-2542
Fax: (770)868-4211
Co. E-mail: ajga@ajga.org
URL: http://www.ajga.org
Contact: Stephen A. Hamblin, Executive Director
Description: Works for the overall growth and development of young men and women through competitive junior golf. Provides exposure vehicle for college scholarships. **Founded:** 1977. **Publications:** *Golfweek.* **Awards:** HP Scholastic All-American Team (Annual); Jerry Cole Sportsmanship Award (Annual); Polo Golf Junior All-American Teams (Annual); Polo Golf Players of the Year (Annual).

9649 ■ Association of Golf Merchandisers (AGM)
PO Box 7247
Phoenix, AZ 85011-7247
Ph: (602)604-8250
Fax: (602)604-8251
Co. E-mail: info@agmgolf.org
URL: http://www.agmgolf.org
Contact: Desane Blaney, Executive Director
Description: Golf buyers and vendors. Dedicated to maximizing members' learning and earning capabilities. Conducts continuing educational programs; provides networking opportunities, scholarships and a forum for communication; compiles statistics. **Founded:** 1989. **Publications:** *AGM Merchandise Manual.* **Awards:** AGM Scholarship Fund (Annual).

9650 ■ Golf Range Association of America (GRAA)
c/o Mr. Steve J. di Costanzo, Founder/Pres.
PO Box 240
Georgetown, CT 06829
Ph: (610)745-0862
Co. E-mail: rsummers@golfrange.org
URL: http://www.golfrange.org
Contact: Rick Summers, Chief Executive Officer
Description: Owners of golf driving ranges and other practice facilities; suppliers to the golf practice industry. Promotes growth and development of the golf industry. Gathers and disseminates information on economic and social trends affecting the golf industries; conducts educational programs. **Founded:** 1992. **Publications:** *Golf Range Development and Operations; Golf Range Magazine* (Bimonthly); *Profile of Golf Practice Facility Operations 2003.* **Educational Activities:** Golf Range Industry Conference & Exhibition (Semiannual). **Awards:** Top 50 Golf Range Instructors (Annual); Top 100 Ranges in America (Annual); Top Short Courses in America (Annual).

9651 ■ International Golf Federation (IGF)
PO Box 708
Far Hills, NJ 07931-0708

Ph: (908)234-2300
Fax: (908)234-2178
Co. E-mail: igfinfo@usga.org
URL: http://www.internationalgolffederation.org
Contact: James B. Hyler, Jr., Chairman
Description: Strives to encourage the international development of golf, and to foster friendship and sportsmanship among the peoples of the world through the conduct of the biennial Amateur Team Championships for the Eisenhower Trophy and the Espirito Santo Trophy. Promotes golf as an Olympic sport and acts as the Federation for golf in the Olympic games. **Founded:** 1958. **Publications:** *International Golf Federation--Record Book: World Amateur Team Championships* (Biennial). **Awards:** Eisenhower Trophy; Espirito Santo Trophy; Eisenhower Trophy (Biennial); Espirito Santo Trophy (Biennial).

9652 ■ Ladies Professional Golf Association (LPGA)
100 International Golf Dr.
Daytona Beach, FL 32124-1092
Ph: (386)274-6200
Fax: (386)274-1099
Co. E-mail: feedback@lpga.com
URL: http://www.lpga.com
Contact: Michael Whan, Commissioner
URL(s): www.lpga.com/default_new.aspx. **Description:** Represents and promotes women golfers, teachers and competitors. Compiles statistics on tournaments, money winnings, and scoring. **Founded:** 1950. **Publications:** *Ladies Professional Golf Association--Schedule Directory* (Annual); *Player Guide* (Annual); *Ladies Professional Golf Association--Schedule Directory* (Annual). **Awards:** Patty Berg Award; Coach of the Year; LPGA Hall of Fame; William and Mousie Powell Award; Professional of the Year; Teacher of the Year; Vare Trophy; Commissioner's Award; Ellen Griffin Rolex Award; Louise Suggs Rolex Rookie of the Year Award; Rolex Player of the Year Award.

9653 ■ National Golf Foundation (NGF)
1150 S US Hwy. 1, Ste. 401
Jupiter, FL 33477
Ph: (561)744-6006
Free: 888-275-4643
Fax: (561)744-6107
Co. E-mail: general@ngf.org
URL: http://www.ngf.org
Contact: Joseph F. Beditz, President
E-mail: jbeditz@ngf.org
Description: Golf-oriented businesses including: equipment and apparel companies; golf facilities; golf publications; golf course architects, developers and builders; companies offering specialized services to the golf industry; golf associations; teachers, coaches and instructors and other interested individuals. Serves as a market research and strategic planning organization for the golf industry and promotes public golf course development in the U.S. Provides information and consulting services for golf course planning, construction, and operation. Conducts golf course development and operations seminars including the National Institute of Golf Management. **Founded:**

1936. **Publications:** *NGF Membership Directory* (Quarterly); *The NGF's Golf Course Directory; The NGF's Media Directory; Golf Industry Report* (Quarterly); *Golf Industry Report* (Bimonthly); *Golf Course Directory; The NGF's Directory of Golf Retailers: Off-Course Golf Retail Stores in the U.S.; The NGF's Executive and Par-3 Golf Course Directory: A Viable Enterprise; The NGF's Golf Course Directory and Range Directory; The NGF's Golf Practice Range and Learning Center Directory; Directory of Golf: The People and Businesses in Golf* (Annual); *Golf Facilities in the U.S.* (Annual). **Educational Activities:** Golf course management schools. **Awards:** Graffis Award. **Telecommunication Services:** ngf@ngf.org; research@ngf.org.

9654 ■ Professional Golfers' Association of America (PGA)
100 Avenue of the Champions
Palm Beach Gardens, FL 33418-3653
Ph: (561)624-8400
Free: 800-474-2776
Fax: (561)624-8448
URL: http://www.pga.com
Contact: Allen Wronowski, President
Description: Recruits and trains men and women to manage a variety of golf businesses, including golf clubs, courses, and tournaments. Sponsors PGA Championship, PGA Seniors' Championship, Ryder Cup Matches, PGA Grand Slam of Golf, Club Professional Championship, PGA Foundation, and Senior Club Professional Championship; PGA Junior Championship; PGA Assistants Championship. Conducts Professional Golf Management; certifies college programs in golf management at 14 universities. Sponsors winter tournament program for club professionals including tournaments held in south Florida. Offers complementary employment services for PGA members and employers, owns and operates PGA Golf Club and PGA Learning Center. **Founded:** 1916. **Educational Activities:** PGA Merchandise Show (Annual). **Awards:** PGA Championship; Horton Smith Award; Teacher of the Year Award; Vardon Trophy; Ryder Cup; Club Professional of the Year (Annual); Junior Golf Leader Award; Merchandiser of the Year (Annual); Player of the Year (Annual); Teacher of the Year (Annual); Vardon Trophy; Bill Strausbaugh Club Relations Award.

9655 ■ United States Golf Association (USGA)
PO Box 708
Far Hills, NJ 07931
Ph: (908)234-2300
Free: 800-223-0041
Fax: (908)234-9687
Co. E-mail: membership@usga.org
URL: http://www.usga.org
Contact: James F. Vernon, President
Description: Regularly organized golf clubs and golf courses. Serves as governing body for golf in the United States. Turfgrass Visiting Service promotes scientific work in turf management. Provides data on rules, handicapping, amateur status, tournament procedure, turf maintenance, and golf balls and implements. Administers Golf House Museum, a col-

lection of memorabilia including clubs of champions, the Moon Club, and paintings, insignia, and portraits of USGA champions. Sponsors USGA Research and Educational Fund. Conducts 13 annual national championships and research programs; sponsors teams for international competitions. **Founded:** 1894. **Publications:** *Golf Journal* (9/year); *Golf Journal: Official Publication of the United States Golf Association.* **Awards:** United States Golf Association Fellowship Program; United States Golf Association Scholarship Program; Curtis Cup; Green Section Award; Bob Jones Award; Walker Cup; Joe Dey Award; U.S. Women's Open; U.S. Senior Open; U.S. Amateur Championship; Bob Jones Award; Golf House Book Award; USGA Green Selection Award; U.S. Women's Amateur Championship.

REFERENCE WORKS

9656 ■ *"Coming Up Short"* in *Boston Business Journal (Vol. 30, October 15, 2010, No. 36, pp. 1)*
Pub: Boston Business Journal
Ed: Tim McLaughlin, Mary Moore. **Description:** Boston, Massachusetts-based nonprofits have been profiting less from charity golf tournaments. Nonprofits have been collecting less than 50 cents on the dollar from such events. But nonprofits have been restructuring golf tournaments in order to boost profits.

9657 ■ *"Driving Passion"* in *Small Business Opportunities (Spring 2008)*
Pub: Harris Publications Inc.
Ed: Chuck Green. **Description:** Profile of Joe Assell, founder of Golftec, a company offering golf instruction that uses the latest technology with professional teachers.

9658 ■ *"Get on the Green"* in *Entrepreneur (Vol. 35, November 2007, No. 11, pp. 44)*
Pub: Entrepreneur Media Inc.
Ed: James Park. **Description:** Golf is a sport where business people are provided with a casual atmosphere where they can open a conversation regarding business topics. Details on how spending time on the course provides a good environment for business discussions.

9659 ■ *Golf Magazine--Golf Club Buyers' Guide Issue*
Pub: Time4 Media
Contact: Thomas Beusse, President
URL(s): www.golfonline.com. **Ed:** Rob Sauerhaft. **Released:** Annual; May. **Publication includes:** List of golf club manufacturers. **Entries include:** Company name, address, phone, description of product line, whether women's or left-handed models are available, type of shaft and club head, prices. Principal content of publication is feature articles on golf equipment, tips on improving readers' golf scores, and interviews with golfing personalities. **Database includes:** *"Club Test"* section, in which amateur golfers test and appraise golf equipment. **Arrangement:** Alphabetical.

9660 ■ *"Here's the Deal"* in *Crain's Cleveland Business (Vol. 30, June 15, 2009, No. 23, pp. 14)*
Pub: Crain Communications, Inc.
Description: Incentives being offered by hotels, restaurants, golf courses and major chains in order to promote bookings for meetings or conferences in the Cleveland area are listed.

9661 ■ *"Hit the Green"* in *Canadian Business (Vol. 79, August 14, 2006, No. 16-17, pp. 73)*
Pub: Rogers Media
Ed: Andrew Wahl. **Description:** Reorganization of the bankrupt 4everSports golf company in the United States is discussed.

9662 ■ *"Hitting the Green"* in *Canadian Business (Vol. 81, July 22, 2008, No. 12-13, pp. 34)*
Pub: Rogers Media Ltd.
Ed: Andy Holloway. **Description:** RBC is sponsoring the Canadian Open golf tournament, which is the second-oldest event in the PGA Tour. RBC is ex-

pected to receive television exposure on CBS and the Golf Channel. Additional information relating to the sponsorship is presented.

9663 ■ *"How Has City Golf Privatization Played?"* in *Business Courier (Vol. 27, September 10, 2010, No. 19, pp. 1)*
Pub: Business Courier
Ed: Dan Monk. **Description:** It was reported that private contractors are getting more revenue from fewer golfers on city-owned courses in Cincinnati, Ohio. In 1998, the city handed over seven municipal courses to private management. However, some believe that the city has escalated a price war among the region's golf courses.

9664 ■ *"Internal Auditor Wants Ethics Review of City's Casper Golf Contract"* in *Business Courier (Vol. 27, September 10, 2010, No. 19, pp. 1)*
Pub: Business Courier
Ed: Dan Monk. **Description:** Mark Ashworth, an internal auditor for Cincinnati, Ohio is pushing for an ethics review of management contract for seven city-owned golf courses. Ashworth wants the Ohio Ethics Commission to investigate family ties between a superintendent for the Cincinnati Recreation Commission and Billy Casper Golf.

9665 ■ *"Major Golf Retail Show in the Rough for 2010"* in *Orlando Business Journal (Vol. 26, January 15, 2010, No. 33, pp. 1)*
Pub: American City Business Journals
Ed: Anjali Fluker. **Description:** The 57th Annual PGA Merchandise Show in Orlando, Florida is projected to attract 39,000 attendees in 2010, compared with 41,000 in 2009. According to the Orange County Convention Center, economic benefits that could be obtained from the 2010 edition of the golf retail show might reach only $77 million, compared with $78 million generated last year.

9666 ■ *"Making the Cut; Osprey Takes Undervalued Courses to the Leader Board"* in *Crain's Detroit Business (Vol. 24, April 7, 2008, No. 14)*
Pub: Crain Communications, Inc.
Ed: Jason Deegan. **Description:** Profile of Osprey Management Co., a diverse real estate company that continues to expand its golf portfolio through the company's recreation division; although many developers are getting out of the field due to Michigan's sluggish golf industry, Osprey has found success by purchasing properties in turmoil for more affordable prices.

9667 ■ *"Members Make Sacrifices for a World-Class Course"* in *Crain's Detroit Business (Vol. 24, April 7, 2008, No. 14, pp. 21)*
Pub: Crain Communications, Inc.
Ed: Jason Deegan. **Description:** Rees Jones Inc. completed a $1.8 million redesign of the Oakland Hills Country Club golf course last year. By all indications, the redesign has been a success since it is among the handful of courses good enough to host future majors which is beneficial for the local economy.

9668 ■ *"Mixing Business and Pleasure On the Green"* in *Black Enterprise (Vol. 41, October 2010, No. 3, pp. 65)*
Pub: Earl G. Graves Publishing Co. Inc.
Ed: Annya M. Lott. **Description:** Glow Golf, sponsored by Glow Sports, will offer instruction to 150 female corporate executives and entrepreneurs to learn the fundamentals of the game of golf.

9669 ■ *"A New Way to Swing"* in *Canadian Business (Vol. 81, December 8, 2008, No. 21, pp. S8)*
Pub: Rogers Media Ltd.
Ed: Robert Thompson. **Description:** Golf developer Mike Keiser believes that remote is the new luxury, and finances golf projects in out-of-the-way locales in various countries. Keiser is currently developing Cabot Links in Canada, which is expected to open by 2011.

9670 ■ *"On the Green: Sheila Johnson Adds $35 Million Golf Resort To Her Expanding Portfolio"* in *Black Enterprise (January 2008)*
Pub: Earl G. Graves Publishing Co. Inc.
Ed: Donna M. Owens. **Description:** Profile of Sheila Johnson, CEO of Salamander Hospitality LLC, made history when she purchased the Innisbrook Resort and Golf Club, making her the first African American woman to own this type of property. The resort includes four championship golf courses, six swimming pools, four restaurants, eleven tennis courts, three conference halls, and a nature preserve.

9671 ■ *"PGA Tour: Course Management"* in *Retail Merchandiser (Vol. 51, September-October 2011, No. 5, pp. 38)*
Pub: Phoenix Media Corporation
Ed: Eric Slack. **Description:** PGA Tour must reach new customers and solidify relationships with its traditional base in order to continue its success. The PGA brand equity has translated into one of the largest retail licensing operations worldwide.

9672 ■ *"PGA Tourney Drives Area Economy, Image"* in *Crain's Detroit Business (Vol. 24, April 7, 2008, No. 14, pp. 22)*
Pub: Crain Communications, Inc.
Ed: Jason Deegan. **Description:** Discusses the major economic impact the 2008 PGA Championship will have when it visits the south course at Oakland Hills Country Club August 4-10.

9673 ■ *"Wild-Goose Chaser"* in *Entrepreneur (Vol. 37, September 2009, No. 9, pp. 96)*
Pub: Entrepreneur Media, Inc.
Ed: Jason Daley. **Description:** Geese Police owner David Marcks says he discovered that trained collies could chase geese off golf courses, which started his business. He gives new franchises two dogs to start their business. The company has fared well even during the economic crisis.

TRADE PERIODICALS

9674 ■ *Golf Digest*
Pub: Conde Nast Publications
Contact: David Carey, President
URL(s): www.golfdigest.com/. **Released:** 12/yr. **Price:** $12, Individuals; $20, Two years.

9675 ■ *Golf Magazine*
Pub: Time4 Media
Contact: Thomas Beusse, President
URL(s): www.golf.com/golf/. **Released:** Monthly **Price:** $20, Canada; $30, Two years.

9676 ■ *Mountainwest Golf*
Pub: Harris Publishing Inc.
URL(s): mountainwestgolf.com/. **Ed:** Steve Smeed. **Released:** Quarterly **Price:** $8.95, Individuals; $15.95, Two years; $21.95, Individuals 3 years; $28.95, Other countries; $55.95, Other countries 2 years; $81.95, Other countries 3 years; $23.95, Canada; $45.95, Canada 2 years; $66.95, Canada 3 years.

9677 ■ *Sporting Goods Dealer: The Voice of Team Dealers Since 1899*
Pub: Bill Communications Inc.
URL(s): www.sgdealer.com/sportinggoodsdealer/index.jsp. **Released:** Bimonthly

TRADE SHOWS AND CONVENTIONS

9678 ■ **Cincinnati Golf Show**
Hart Productions, Inc.
322 E. Main St.
Batavia, OH 45103
Ph: (513)797-7900
Free: 877-704-8190
Fax: (513)797-1013
URL: http://www.hartproductions.com
URL(s): www.hartproductions.com. **Price:** $11, Onsite; children ages 13 and under. **Frequency:** Annual. **Audience:** General public. **Principal Exhibits:** Golf equipment, apparel, and travel destinations. **Telecommunication Services:** chip@hartproductions.com.

9679 ■ FUN Expo
Reed Exhibitions North American Headquarters
383 Main Ave.
Norwalk, CT 06851
Ph: (203)840-4800
Fax: (203)840-5805
Co. E-mail: inquiry@reedexpo.com
URL: http://www.reedexpo.com
URL(s): www.funexpo.com. **Price:** $20, Pre-registered, members; $40, Pre-registered, non-members; $65, Onsite registered, members; $90, On-site registered, non-members. **Frequency:** Annual. **Principal Exhibits:** Amusement and recreation products for family and location based entertainment centers, small amusement parks and family oriented businesses such as bowling centers, skating rinks, sports parks, miniature golf courses, golf driving ranges, family restaurants, resorts and other entertainment/recreation businesses.

9680 ■ International Golf Course Conference and Show
Golf Course Superintendents Association of America
1421 Research Pk. Dr.
Lawrence, KS 66049-3859
Ph: (785)841-2240
Free: 800-472-7878
Fax: (785)832-3643
Co. E-mail: infobox@gcsaa.org
URL: http://www.gcsaa.org
URL(s): www.golfindustryshow.com. **Price:** $250, Members full conference pack; $350, Non-members full conference pack; $150, advance trade show only; $200, Onsite trade show only. **Frequency:** Annual. **Audience:** Golf course superintendents' owners, builders, architects, club managers and related turf professionals. **Principal Exhibits:** Equipment, supplies, and services for golf course and facility maintenance. **Telecommunication Services:** expomail@gcsaa.org.

9681 ■ PGA Merchandise Show
Professional Golfers' Association of America (PGA)
100 Avenue of the Champions
Palm Beach Gardens, FL 33418-3653
Ph: (561)624-8400
Free: 800-474-2776
Fax: (561)624-8448
URL: http://www.pga.com
Contact: Allen Wronowski, President
URL(s): www.pgashow.com/. **Frequency:** Annual. **Audience:** Golf professionals, retail buyers, club managers and superintendents. **Principal Exhibits:** Golf apparel, clubs, bags, balls, range equipment, club components, golf cars, golf shoes, and related equipment, supplies, and services.

CONSULTANTS

9682 ■ Jim Castello Marketing Communications Consultants
711 Red Wing Dr.
Lake Mary, FL 32746
Ph: (407)321-6322
Fax: (407)321-8460
Contact: James E. Castello, Jr., President
Scope: Consultant develops creative ideas and marketing strategies, including collateral programs, public relations, advertising, and brochures. Industries served: All golf related industry/business, golf manufacturers, golf resorts, golf residential developments, golf professionals, golf clothing, golf accessories, golf associations, and golf travel. **Founded:** 1989. **Seminars:** How To Seminar for Family Fun Center Entrepreneurs; How To Seminar for Creativity in Golf Marketing; The Golf Business on the Internet.

FRANCHISES AND BUSINESS OPPORTUNITIES

9683 ■ Golf USA, Inc.
7608 N Harvey Ave.
Oklahoma City, OK 73116
Ph: (405)751-0015
Fax: (405)755-0065
Description: Retail golf stores. **No. of Franchise Units:** 100. **No. of Company-Owned Units:** 2. **Founded:** 1987.. **Franchised:** 1989. **Equity Capital Needed:** $254,050-$449,200. **Franchise Fee:** $34,000-$44,000. **Training:** Yes.

COMPUTER SYSTEMS/ SOFTWARE

9684 ■ *Proshop Retail*
PO Box 87
Jenison, MI 49428-0087
Ph: (616)457-9581
Free: 800-833-0033
Fax: (616)457-6833
Co. E-mail: handisales@handicomp.com
URL: http://www.handicomp.com/
Price: Contact Handicomp for pricing. **Description:** Available for IBM and NCR Tower computers. System geared for the golf pro shop. Assists with inventory and accounting needs.

LIBRARIES

9685 ■ Canadian Golf Hall of Fame Library and Archives
1333 Dorval Dr.
Oakville, ON, Canada L6M 4X7
Ph: (905)849-9700
Free: 800-263-0009
Fax: (905)844-3366
Co. E-mail: khewson@golfcanada.ca
URL: http://www.golfcanada.ca/about-us/hall-of-fame/
Contact: Karen Hewson, Director
Scope: Golf. **Services:** Copying; photograph printing. **Founded:** 1975. **Holdings:** 3500 books; 200 bound periodical volumes; 10 manuscripts; 1000 lin. ft. archival materials; 100 microfiche; 50,000 images. **Subscriptions:** 10 journals and other serials. **Telecommunication Services:** ssnell@golfcanada.ca; info@golfcanada.ca.

9686 ■ United States Golf Association Library
77 Liberty Corner Rd.
Far Hills, NJ 07931
Ph: (908)234-2300, x1107
Fax: (908)470-5013
Co. E-mail: nstulack@usga.org
URL: http://www.usgamuseum.com/
Contact: Nancy Stulack, Librarian
Scope: Golf. **Services:** Library open to the public by appointment. **Founded:** 1938. **Holdings:** 25,000 books; 800 bound periodical volumes; 125 scrapbooks of newspaper clippings; archives; microfilm. **Subscriptions:** 20 journals and other serials. **Telecommunication Services:** museum@usga.org.

START-UP INFORMATION

9687 ■ *How to Open a Financially Successful Coffee, Espresso and Tea Shop*
Pub: Atlantic Publishing Company

Ed: Lora Arduser, Elizabeth Godsmark, Douglas R. Brown. **Released:** July 23, 2009. **Price:** $39.95. **Description:** Coffee is currently the largest food import in the U.S. Comprehensive and detailed information is offered for anyone interested in opening a coffee, espresso or tea shop.

9688 ■ *"It's Tea-Riffic! Natural Bottled Tea Satisfies Void In Beverage Market" in Small Business Opportunities (November 2007)*
Pub: Harris Publications Inc.

Description: Profile of Skae Beverage International LLC, offering franchise opportunities for its New Leaf all-natural tea beverage, available in eight flavors of green, white and blue tea.

9689 ■ *"Proven Success Pays Off" in Small Business Opportunities (January 2011)*
Pub: Harris Publications Inc.

Description: Industry pioneers of the fast-casual restaurant launch new venture with sales of $43 million. Profile of Newk's Express Cafe and its founders is included.

9690 ■ *The Specialty Shop: How to Create Your Own Unique and Profitable Retail Business*
Pub: AMACOM

Ed: Dorothy Finell. **Released:** February 27, 2007. **Price:** $21.95. **Description:** Advise to start retail businesses, including bakeries, gift shops, toy stores, book shops, tea houses, clothing boutiques, and other unique stores.

ASSOCIATIONS AND OTHER ORGANIZATIONS

9691 ■ **Coffee Association of Canada (CAC)**
885 Don Mills Rd., Ste. 301
Toronto, ON, Canada M3C 1V9
Ph: (416)510-8032
Fax: (416)510-8044
Co. E-mail: info@coffeeassoc.com
URL: http://www.coffeeassoc.com
Contact: Sandy McAlpine, President

Description: Coffee importers and processors. Seeks to make "the coffee beverage experience a more integral and meaningful part of Canadian lives." Serves as a clearinghouse on the coffee industry; represents members' interests in publicly addressing industry issues. **Founded:** 1991.

9692 ■ **National Coffee Association of U.S.A. (NCA)**
45 Broadway, Ste. 1140
New York, NY 10006
Ph: (212)766-4007

Fax: (212)766-5815
Co. E-mail: info@ncausa.org
URL: http://www.ncausa.org
Contact: Robert F. Nelson, President
E-mail: rfnelson@ncausa.org

URL(s): www.coffeescience.org. **Description:** Green coffee importers, jobbers, brokers, and agents; instant coffee and liquid extract processors; roasters and allied coffee industries; exporters; retailers. Promotes sound business relations and mutual understanding among members of the trade, and to increase coffee consumption. Collects and publishes consumer, market and technical information on the coffee industry. **Scope:** coffee, caffeine. **Founded:** 1911. **Subscriptions:** 600. **Publications:** *CoffeeTrax* (Quarterly); *National Coffee Drinking Trends* (Annual); *US Coffee Industry Review 2005*; *National Coffee Association of U.S.A.--Membership Directory* (Annual). **Educational Activities:** National Coffee Association of U.S.A. Annual Convention (Annual).

9693 ■ **Specialty Coffee Association of America (SCAA)**
330 Golden Shore, No. 50
Long Beach, CA 90802
Ph: (562)624-4100
Fax: (562)624-4101
Co. E-mail: info@scaa.org
URL: http://www.scaa.org
Contact: Max Quirin, President

Description: Coffee roasters, green coffee brokers, retailers, distributors, and others involved in the gourmet coffee industry. Provides business, professional, promotional, and educational assistance in the areas of cultivation, processing, preparation, and marketing of specialty coffee; increase consumer awareness, understanding, and consumption of specialty coffee. Provides a forum for discussion of the purpose and unified character of the industry and represents members in national and regional coffee concerns. Distributes posters, surveys, articles, and other promotional information; develops coffee education curricula for culinary school programs. Maintains reference materials. Sponsors tastings of specialty coffees. **Scope:** coffee. **Founded:** 1982. **Subscriptions:** 1 books. **Publications:** *Specialty Coffee Association of America--Member Directory*. **Educational Activities:** SCAA Exposition (Annual); SCAA Planning Meeting; SCAA Symposium (Annual); SCAA Leadership Summit. **Awards:** SCAA Achievement Awards (Annual); SCAA Sustainability Award (Annual); SCAA Best New Product (Annual); Achievement Awards (Annual); TOPS (Annual); Mose Drachman Sales and Service Award (Annual).

9694 ■ **Tea Association of the U.S.A. (TA)**
362 5th Ave., Ste. 801
New York, NY 10001
Ph: (212)986-9415
Fax: (212)697-8658
Co. E-mail: info@teausa.com
URL: http://teausa.org
Contact: Joseph P. Simrany, President

Description: Packers, importers, brokers, agents, and other firms dedicated to the interests and growth

of the U.S. tea industry. **Scope:** tea. **Founded:** 1899. **Subscriptions:** 200 books periodicals.

9695 ■ **Tea Council of the United States of America (TC)**
362 5th Ave., Ste. 801
New York, NY 10001
Ph: (212)986-9415
Fax: (212)697-8658
Co. E-mail: info@teausa.com
URL: http://www.teausa.com
Contact: Joseph P. Simrany, President

Description: Represents companies and countries trading tea in the U.S. Works to increase tea consumption. **Scope:** tea. **Founded:** 1950. **Subscriptions:** 200 books periodicals. **Publications:** *Tea World* (Annual); *TeaBits* (Quarterly). **Educational Activities:** World Tea Forum (Annual); World Tea Forum (Annual).

REFERENCE WORKS

9696 ■ *Beans: Four Principles for Running a Business in Good Times or Bad*
Pub: John Wiley & Sons, Incorporated

Ed: Leslie Yerkes, Charles Decker, Bob Nelson. **Released:** June 2003. **Price:** $19.95. **Description:** Profile of Monorail Espresso, the popular Seattle coffee company that has become prosperous by intentionally staying small and building a strong customer service program.

9697 ■ *"Blue Tractor Barbeque and Brewery, Cafe Havana" in Crain's Detroit Business (Vol. 23, October 1, 2007, No. 40, pp. 15)*
Pub: Crain Communications Inc. - Detroit

Ed: Daniel Duggan. **Description:** Two restaurants are converted from a Buddhist Temple to become the most unique spaces in Ann Arbor, Michigan.

9698 ■ *"Brewed to Succeed; Mokarbia Perks Up Sales for King Coffee" in Crain's Detroit Business (Vol. 24, March 17, 2008, No. 11, pp. 3)*
Pub: Crain Communications, Inc.

Ed: Brent Snavely. **Description:** Profile of King Coffee Tea Services, Royal Oak-based company, whose distributing deal with Mokarabia coffee has generated an increase in sales.

9699 ■ *"Brewing a Love-Haiti Relationship" in The Business Journal - Serving Phoenix and the Valley of the Sun (Vol. 28, July 4, 2008, No. 44)*
Pub: American City Business Journals, Inc.

Ed: Yvonne Zusel. **Description:** Jean and Alicia Marseille have ventured into a coffee distribution company called Ka Bel LLC which markets Marabou brand of coffee imported from Haiti. Part of the proceeds of the business is donated to entrepreneurs from Jean's country, Haiti. Details of the Marseille's startup business and personal mission to help are discussed.

9700 ■ *"City Board Tweaks Internet Cafe Ordinance"* in Ocala Star-Banner (July 19, 2011)

Pub: Ocala Star-Banner

Ed: Susan Latham Carr. **Description:** Ocala Planning and Zoning Commission revised the proposed draft of the Internet Cafe ordinance by eliminating the cap on the number of locations allowed, but keeping fees and number of devices the same.

9701 ■ *"Dunnellon Welcomes Internet Cafe Jobs"* in Ocala Star-Banner (August 18, 2011)

Pub: Ocala Star-Banner

Ed: Fred Hiers. **Description:** Despite the fact that a few Internet cafes offering patrons to win cash and are facing legal challenges, the city's planning commission would welcome the cafes in order to provide more jobs for its residents.

9702 ■ *"Fair Exchange"* in Food and Drink (Winter 2010, pp. 84)

Pub: Schofield Media Group

Ed: Don Mardak. **Description:** Bartering can assist firms in the food and beverage industry to attract new customers, maximize resources, and reduce cash expenses.

9703 ■ *"Internet Cafe Logging in to Chardon Plaza?"* in News-Herald (July 16, 2011)

Pub: Journal Register Ohio

Ed: Betsy Scott. **Description:** Pearl's High Rollers Inc. applied for an Internet sweepstakes cafe license that would reside in a vacant space in Chardon Plaza. City officials have created regulations for such businesses and Pearl's applied for a license and is awaiting approval.

9704 ■ *"Internet Cafe 'Sweepstakes' Expanding in Arkansas"* in Arkansas Business (Vol. 28, September 5, 2011, No. 36, pp. 1)

Pub: Arkansas Business Publishing Group

Ed: Mark Friedman. **Description:** Despite the fact that video games resembling casino games in Lucky's Business Center in Little Rock, representatives of the Internet cafe insist they are not offering gambling but a type of sweepstakes promotion and that business model is thriving. Lucky's, Cancun Cyber Cafe & Business Center Inc., and Wild Rides Business Center & Internet Cafe has opened in the area in the last few weeks.

9705 ■ *"Lombard Leaves Starbucks"* in Black Enterprise (Vol. 38, July 2008, No. 12, pp. 28)

Pub: Earl G. Graves Publishing Co. Inc.

Ed: Tamara E. Holmes. **Description:** Ken Lombard stepped down from his position as head of Starbuck's entertainment division; the company is restructuring its entertainment unit in an attempt to revitalize sales and reduce costs.

9706 ■ *"Lux Coffees, Breads Push Chains to React"* in Advertising Age (Vol. 77, June 26, 2006, No. 26, pp. S14)

Pub: Crain Communications, Inc.

Ed: Kate MacArthur. **Description:** Fast-food giants such as McDonald's, Burger King, Dunkin' Donuts and Subway have adjusted their menus in order to become more competitive with gourmet coffee shops and bakeries like Panera Bread and Starbucks which have taken a large share in the market. Statistical data included.

9707 ■ *Nirvana in a Cup: The Founding of Oregon Chai*

Pub: Moby Press

Ed: Tedde McMillen; Heather Hale. **Released:** July 2006. **Price:** $12.99. **Description:** Profile of a mother-daughter team who founded Oregon Chai, a tea company.

9708 ■ *"Show Me the Love"* in Canadian Business (Vol. 79, November 6, 2006, No. 22, pp. 77)

Pub: Rogers Media

Ed: Jeannette Hanna. **Description:** The strategies to improve brand image with relation to success of Tim Horton's brand are presented.

9709 ■ *"South Park Draws Brewers, Vintners"* in Puget Sound Business Journal (Vol. 29, August 29, 2008, No. 19, pp. 1)

Pub: American City Business Journals

Ed: Heidi Dietrich. **Description:** Craft breweries and wineries are moving into Seattle, Washington's South Park neighborhood due to the area's low rents, convenience, and ample equipment space. These industries bring a more upscale flavor to the heavily industrial area and the tastings and festivals draw people from throughout the Seattle region.

9710 ■ *"Starbucks Drive-Throughs: Can the Cafe Keep Its Cool?"* in Globe & Mail (January 6, 2006, pp. B7)

Pub: CTVglobemedia Publishing Inc.

Ed: Steven Gray. **Description:** The feasibility of Starbucks Corp.'s plans to introduce drive-through cafes is discussed.

9711 ■ *The Starbucks Experience*

Pub: McGraw-Hill

Ed: Joseph A. Michelli. **Released:** September 14, 2006. **Price:** $24.95. **Description:** Boardroom strategies, employee motivation tips, community involvement, and customer satisfaction are issues addressed, using Starbucks as a model.

9712 ■ *The Starbucks Experience: 5 Principles for Turing Ordinary into Extraordinary*

Pub: McGraw-Hill

Ed: Joseph A. Michelli. **Released:** November 2006.

9713 ■ *"Starbucks' Wheel Strategy"* in Puget Sound Business Journal (Vol. 29, October 3, 2008, No. 24, pp. 1)

Pub: American City Business Journals

Ed: Greg Lamm. **Description:** Starbuck Corporation has placed drive-through windows in nearly 50 percent of its locations. Dorothy Kim, executive vice president of global strategy, revealed that the firm's transformation strategy includes the addition of even more drive-through windows since people want the car-friendly conveniences.

9714 ■ *"Sun Capital Partners Affiliate Acquires Timothy's Coffees"* in Miami Daily Business Review (March 26, 2008)

Pub: ALM Media Inc.

Description: An affiliate of Sun Capital Partners acquired Timothy's Coffees of the World. Timothy's operates and franchises 166 stores offering coffees, muffins, and Michel's Baguette products.

9715 ■ *"This CEO's Mom Taught Him Everything He Needs to Know"* in Globe & Mail (February 19, 2007, pp. B9)

Pub: CTVglobemedia Publishing Inc.

Ed: Gordon Pitts. **Description:** Interview with Paul House, chairman and chief executive officer of Tim Hortons Inc., who shares a few things about his entrepreneurial life and career.

9716 ■ *"Top Coffee Has Concord Ties"* in Charlotte Observer (February 7, 2007)

Pub: Knight-Ridder/Tribune Business News

Ed: Adam Bell. **Description:** McDonald's highly rated premium coffee is supplied by Concord's S&D Coffee, one of three McDonald's coffee suppliers. The blend outranked Starbucks and Dunkin' Donuts coffee by Consumer Reports.

9717 ■ *"Verizon Small Business Awards Give Companies a Technology Edge"* in Hispanic Business (July-August 2009, pp. 32)

Pub: Hispanic Business

Ed: Patricia Marroquin. **Description:** Verizon Wireless awards grants to twenty-four companies in California. The winning businesses ranged from barbershop to coffee shop, tattoo parlor to florist.

9718 ■ *"Waste Not"* in Entrepreneur (Vol. 36, April 2008, No. 4, pp. 21)

Pub: Entrepreneur Media, Inc.

Ed: JJ Ramberg. **Description:** RecycleBank is a company that provides homes with carts in which recyclables are thrown. An identification chip measures the amount of recyclables and converts them into points, which can be redeemed in stores, such as

Starbucks and Whole Foods. RecycleBank earns revenue from cities that save landfill waste spending with the use of the program.

9719 ■ *"'We Had to Won the Mistakes"* in Harvard Business Review (Vol. 88, July-August 2010, No. 7-8, pp. 108)

Pub: Harvard Business School Publishing

Ed: Adi Ignatius. **Description:** Interview with Howard Schultz, CEO of Starbucks, covers topics that include investment in retraining, the impact of competition, premium quality, authenticity, customer services, strategy development, work-and-life issues, and international presence.

9720 ■ *"While Competitors Shut Doors, Subway Is Still Growing"* in Advertising Age (Vol. 79, July 21, 2008, No. 28, pp. 4)

Pub: Crain Communications, Inc.

Ed: Emily Bryson York. **Description:** Subway, the largest fast-food chain, with 22,000 U.S. locations, is adding 800 this year, despite the economic downturn that has caused competitors such as Starbucks to close stores and McDonald's to focus its expansion abroad.

STATISTICAL SOURCES

9721 ■ *Standard & Poor's Industry Surveys*

Pub: Standard & Poor's Corp.

Released: Annual. **Price:** $3633.00. **Description:** Two-volume book that examines the prospects for specific industries, including trucking. Also provides analyses of trends and problems, statistical tables and charts, and comparative company analyses.

TRADE PERIODICALS

9722 ■ *Fresh from the Roaster*

Pub: Green Mountain Coffee

Released: Quarterly. **Price:** Free. **Description:** Offers information about coffee roasting, brewing, and drinking. Recurring features include a letter from the president, financial update, and a recipe.

9723 ■ *Tea and Coffee Trade Journal*

Pub: Lockwood Publications Inc.

Contact: Robert M. Lockwood, President

E-mail: robertlockwoodsr@lockwoodpublications.com

URL(s): www.teaandcoffee.net. **Released:** Monthly **Price:** $49, Individuals; $74, Two years; $129, Other countries airmail; $89, Other countries surface mail; $199, Two years airmail; $139, Two years surface mail.

FRANCHISES AND BUSINESS OPPORTUNITIES

9724 ■ **Barnie's Coffee & Tea Co., Inc.**

2126 W Landstreet Rd., Ste. 300

Orlando, FL 32809-7902

Ph: (407)854-6600

Free: 800-456-1416

Fax: (407)854-6666

Description: Gourmet coffee and tea. **No. of Franchise Units:** 23. **No. of Company-Owned Units:** 14. **Founded:** 1980.. **Franchised:** 1981. **Equity Capital Needed:** $222,000-$414,000 total investment. **Franchise Fee:** $25,000. **Royalty Fee:** 7%. **Training:** Yes.

9725 ■ **The Bearclaw Coffee Company**

780 Taylor St.

Chelsea, MI 48118

Ph: (734)395-3864

Fax: (734)433-0009

Description: Coffee and espresso drinks. **No. of Franchise Units:** 20. **No. of Company-Owned Units:** 5. **Founded:** 2002. **Franchised:** 2003. **Equity Capital Needed:** $73,700-$293,000. **Franchise Fee:** $24,500. **Royalty Fee:** 6%. **Financial Assistance:** Third party financing available. **Training:** Provides 1 week at headquarters, at franchisee's location with ongoing support.

9726 ■ Cafe Ala Carte
Cafe Ala Carte Corp.
19512 S Coquina Way
Weston, FL 33332
Ph: (949)349-1030
Fax: (954)349-3100
Description: Carts serving coffee and espresso drinks. **No. of Franchise Units:** 2. **No. of Company-Owned Units:** 13. **Founded:** 1996.. **Franchised:** 2000. **Equity Capital Needed:** $56,200-$80,800 total investment. **Franchise Fee:** $25,000. **Royalty Fee:** 8-5%. **Training:** Provides 1 week at headquarters, 1 week in Fort Lauderdale, FL with ongoing support.

9727 ■ Cafe Depot/Coffee Depot
2464 Jean-Talon E
Montreal, QC, Canada H2E 1W2
Ph: (514)281-2067
Fax: (514)281-6405
Co. E-mail: info@cafedepot.ca
URL: http://www.cafedepot.ca
Description: We specialize in coffees from all over the world serving delicious sandwiches and desserts in a warm friendly atmosphere. **No. of Franchise Units:** 82. **No. of Company-Owned Units:** 6. **Founded:** 1994.. **Franchised:** 1994. **Equity Capital Needed:** $100,000 start-up capital required; $250,000 investment required. **Franchise Fee:** $25,000, includes training. **Training:** Yes.

9728 ■ Caffino Inc.
4070 Nelson Ave., Ste. G
Concord, CA 94520-5714
Ph: (925)363-3200
Fax: (925)246-9985
Co. E-mail: info@caffino.com
URL: http://www.caffino.com
Contact: Dennis Miller, President
Description: Coffee. **No. of Franchise Units:** 19. **No. of Company-Owned Units:** 8. **Founded:** 1993. **Franchised:** 2002. **Equity Capital Needed:** $212,900-$373,000. **Franchise Fee:** $10,000. **Royalty Fee:** 8%. **Training:** Provides 3 weeks training at headquarters. ers.

9729 ■ Coffee Beanery
Coffee Beanery, Ltd.
3429 Pierson Pl.
Flushing 48433
Ph: (810)733-1020
Free: 888-385-2326
Fax: (810)733-1536
Co. E-mail: stacyp@beanerysupport.com
URL: http://www.coffeebeanery.com
Description: The Coffee Beanery retails whole bean coffees and beverages, espresso and cappuccino in a variety of styles in carts, kiosks, in-line mall stores and street front cafes. **No. of Franchise Units:** 93. **No. of Company-Owned Units:** 2. **Founded:** 1976.. **Franchised:** 1985. **Equity Capital Needed:** $74,250-$545,000. **Franchise Fee:** $27,500. **Training:** 4 weeks training at corporate headquarters plus 1 week orientation including customer service, merchandising, marketing & daily operations. Additional onsite training, site selection assistance, lease negotiation, layout & construction supervision, and on-going support via 800 line, Internet, fax, enewsletter, & field support.

9730 ■ Coffee News
Coffee News USA, Inc.
120 Linden St.
Bangor, ME 04402-8444
Ph: (207)941-0860
Fax: (207)941-1050
Co. E-mail: bill@coffeenews.com
URL: http://www.coffeenewsusa.com
Description: Weekly publication for distribution in coffee shops and restaurants. **No. of Franchise Units:** 1,005. **Founded:** 1988. **Franchised:** 1995. **Equity Capital Needed:** $6,000 per franchise, plus a one-time training fee of $2,500 for first franchise. **Franchise Fee:** $8,500. **Training:** Quarterly training sessions, open to all franchisees and personal mentor program.

9731 ■ Coffee Time Donuts Inc.
77 Progress Ave.
Toronto, ON, Canada M1P 2Y7

Ph: (416)288-8515
Fax: (416)288-8895
Co. E-mail: franchising@coffeetime.ca
URL: http://www.coffeetime.ca
Description: The menu includes donuts, muffins, croissants, pastries and gourmet blend coffee, soups, chili, salads, sandwiches and various hot and cold beverages. store, serving customers in a warm and efficient manner and fostering good employee relationships. **No. of Franchise Units:** 184. **No. of Company-Owned Units:** 16. **Founded:** 1982.. **Franchised:** 1986. **Equity Capital Needed:** $100,000-$360,000. **Training:** Yes.

9732 ■ Country Style
2 E Beaver Creek Rd., Bldg. 1
Richmond Hill, ON, Canada L4B 2N3
Ph: (905)762-4670
Free: 800-563-6688
Fax: (905)764-1601
URL: http://www.countrystyle.com
Description: The franchise is a pioneer in country style coffee. **No. of Franchise Units:** 419. **No. of Company-Owned Units:** 3. **Founded:** 1962.. **Franchised:** 1963. **Equity Capital Needed:** $100,000. **Franchise Fee:** $35,000. **Training:** Provides 4 weeks initial training.

9733 ■ Coyote Canyon - A Steak Buffet
Stockade Franchising, LP
2908 N Plum St.
Hutchinson, KS 67502-8400
Ph: (620)669-9372
Fax: (620)669-0531
Description: One low price all you can eat steak buffet. **No. of Franchise Units:** 7. **Founded:** 1999.. **Franchised:** 1999. **Equity Capital Needed:** $1,000,000 net worth; $250,000 liquid assets. **Franchise Fee:** $20,000. **Training:** Yes.

9734 ■ Dazbog Coffee
1090 Yuma St.
Denver, CO 80204
Ph: (303)892-9999
Free: 888-9DA-ZBOG
Fax: (303)893-9999
Co. E-mail: coffee@DAZBOG.com
URL: http://www.dazbog.com
Description: Coffee. **No. of Franchise Units:** 5. **No. of Company-Owned Units:** 4. **Founded:** 1996.. **Franchised:** 2006. **Equity Capital Needed:** $187,300-$376,800. **Franchise Fee:** $25,000. **Royalty Fee:** 6%.

9735 ■ Dunn Bros Coffee
111 3rd Ave. S, Ste. 220
Minneapolis, MN 55401
Ph: (612)877-3603
Fax: (612)334-9749
Description: Coffeehouse. **No. of Franchise Units:** 79. **No. of Company-Owned Units:** 3. **Founded:** 1987.. **Franchised:** 1994. **Equity Capital Needed:** $139,000-$429,400. **Franchise Fee:** $24,000-$32,000. **Royalty Fee:** 5%. **Financial Assistance:** Limited third party financing available. **Training:** Offers 2 1/2 weeks at headquarters and ongoing support.

9736 ■ Ellianos Coffee Co.
PO Box 1208
Lake City, FL 32056
Ph: (386)755-5828
Fax: (386)758-2999
URL: http://www.ellianos.com
Description: Drive-thru coffee shop. **No. of Franchise Units:** 7. **Founded:** 2002.. **Franchised:** 2003. **Equity Capital Needed:** $167,300-$292,500. **Franchise Fee:** $20,000. **Royalty Fee:** 5%. **Training:** Offers 1-2 weeks at headquarters, 3 days onsite with ongoing support.

9737 ■ Gloria Jean's Coffees USA—Gloria Jean's
17691 Mitchell N
Irvine, CA 92614
Free: 877-320-5282

Fax: (949)752-5282
Co. E-mail: customerservice@gloriajeans.com
URL: http://www.gloriajeanscoffees.com
Contact: Robert Rodriguez, President
URL(s): www.gloriajeans.com. **Description:** Retail gourmet coffee franchisor offering coffee, teas, and accessories. **Founded:** 1979. **Financial Assistance:** No. **Training:** Yes. **Telecommunication Services:** franchiseinfo@gloriajeans.com; nromero@gloriajeans.com.

9738 ■ Good Earth Coffee House & Bakery
4020 7 St., SE
Calgary, AB, Canada T2G 2Y8
Ph: (403)294-9330
Free: 888-294-9330
Fax: (403)294-9329
Co. E-mail: franchise@goodearthcafes.com
URL: http://www.goodearthcafes.com
Description: An innovative coffeehouse and fresh food concept with 15 years of success. We began with a passion for excellent coffee and wholesome, healthful food. While our company has grown, we have stayed true to our original purpose "to be a coffeehouse with good food." Join our team and prosper with purpose. **No. of Franchise Units:** 40. **Founded:** 1991.. **Franchised:** 2005. **Equity Capital Needed:** $150,000-$250,000. **Franchise Fee:** $35,000. **Training:** Provides 6 weeks training.

9739 ■ A Grande Finale Franchise LLC
995 Ash St.
Broomfield, CO 80020
Ph: (720)849-2432
Fax: (303)410-9568
Description: Desserts, coffee, and tea. **No. of Company-Owned Units:** 2. **Founded:** 1999.. **Franchised:** 2007. **Equity Capital Needed:** $125,900-$237,800. **Franchise Fee:** $35,000-$60,000. **Royalty Fee:** 5-6%.

9740 ■ The Human Bean Drive Thru
545 Rossanley Dr., Ste. A
Medford, OR 97501
Ph: (541)608-0564
Free: 888-262-2215
Fax: (541)608-3757
URL: http://www.thehumanbean.com
Description: Specialty coffee. **No. of Franchise Units:** 34. **No. of Company-Owned Units:** 15. **Founded:** 1998. **Franchised:** 2002. **Equity Capital Needed:** $155,300-$619,800. **Franchise Fee:** $20,000. **Royalty Fee:** None. **Financial Assistance:** Third party financing available. **Training:** Offers 3 weeks training at headquarters and at franchisee's location at time of opening and ongoing support.

9741 ■ It's A Grind Coffee House
Praise IAG Franchisor, LLC
Description: Provides help in establishing and running a coffee house. **No. of Franchise Units:** 50. **No. of Company-Owned Units:** 2. **Founded:** 1995.. **Franchised:** 2001. **Equity Capital Needed:** $450,000 net worth; $200,000 liquidity. **Franchise Fee:** $32,500. **Training:** Yes.

9742 ■ Kelly's Coffee & Fudge Factory
PO Box 21538
Bakersfield, CA 93390
Ph: (661)663-8416
Fax: (661)664-4785
Description: Coffee and fudge retail store. **No. of Franchise Units:** 42. **Founded:** 1983.. **Franchised:** 2005. **Equity Capital Needed:** $350,000. **Franchise Fee:** $20,000. **Training:** Yes.

9743 ■ Lox of Bagels
11801 Prestwick Rd., Ste. 301
Potomac, MD 20854
Ph: (301)299-8523
Description: Bagels and gourmet coffee. **No. of Franchise Units:** 12. **Founded:** 1983.. **Franchised:** 1998. **Equity Capital Needed:** $50,000 in equity with typical cost of $150,000-$200,000 per unit. **Franchise Fee:** $9,500. **Training:** Yes.

9744 ■ Melt Inc.
31556 Loma Linda Rd.
Temecula, CA 92592
Ph: (310)601-7907

Fax: (310)601-7906
Co. E-mail: info@meltgelato.com
URL: http://www.meltgelato.com
Description: Gelato, Italian coffee, and crepes. **No. of Franchise Units:** 8. **No. of Company-Owned Units:** 2. **Founded:** 2003. **Franchised:** 2005. **Equity Capital Needed:** $200,000-$400,000 (Express/kiosk option available). **Franchise Fee:** $25,000. **Royalty Fee:** 6%. **Financial Assistance:** Limited third party financing available. **Training:** Includes 6 days training at headquarters, 4 days at franchisee's location and ongoing support. **Telecommunication Services:** brandonbarwin@meltgelato.com.

9745 ■ Mocha Delites Inc.

PO Box 674228
Marietta, GA 30006-0071
Free: 800-539-9532
Fax: (888)453-1172
URL: http://www.mochadelites.com
Description: Coffeehouse. **No. of Franchise Units:** 41. **No. of Company-Owned Units:** 3. **Founded:** 2000.. **Franchised:** 2001. **Equity Capital Needed:** $53,500-$232,500. **Franchise Fee:** $22,500. **Royalty Fee:** 5%. **Financial Assistance:** Limited third party financing available. **Training:** 1 week at corporate headquarters, 1 week of onsite with ongoing support.

9746 ■ Mountain Mudd Espresso

Cafe International LLC
2120 3rd Ave., N
Billings, MT 59101
Free: 800-218-6833
Fax: (406)256-5397
Co. E-mail: info@mountainmudd.com
URL: http://www.mountainmudd.com
Contact: Brenda Burkhantsmeier, President
E-mail: blair@mountainmudd.com
Description: Specialty coffee. **No. of Franchise Units:** 5. **No. of Company-Owned Units:** 12. **Founded:** 1994. **Franchised:** 2007. **Equity Capital Needed:** $22,500-$266,000 total investment. **Franchise Fee:** $5,000-$10,000. **Royalty Fee:** 4%. **Financial Assistance:** Limited in-house and third party financing available. **Training:** Provides 5 days training at headquarters and ongoing at franchisee's location.

9747 ■ PJ's Coffee of New Orleans

Raving Brands
109 New Camellia Blvd., Ste. 201
Covington, LA 70433
Ph: (404)351-3500
URL: http://www.pjscoffee.com
Description: Founded in New Orleans, PJ's has been brewing its distinguished brand of signature roasts for over 25 years. Our beans are hand-selected, hand-roasted and brewed to perfection. PJ's also offers a variety of gourmet pastries and deserts. **No. of Franchise Units:** 107. **No. of**

Company-Owned Units: 1. **Founded:** 1978.. **Franchised:** 1989. **Equity Capital Needed:** $400,000 net worth; $100,000 liquid assets. **Franchise Fee:** $25,000. **Training:** Raving Brands University classroom and onsite training provided. From register operation to food preparation, from hiring staff to accounting procedures, you'll improve your management skills, setup your back office and develop an airtight sales and marketing plan.

9748 ■ The Second Cup Ltd.

6303 Airport Rd.
Mississauga, ON, Canada L4V 1R8
Ph: (905)362-1818
Free: 800-569-6318
Fax: (905)362-1121
Co. E-mail: franchising@secondcup.com
URL: http://www.secondcup.com
Description: Retails specialty coffee. **No. of Franchise Units:** 360. **No. of Company-Owned Units:** 7. **Founded:** 1975.. **Franchised:** 1980. **Equity Capital Needed:** $350,000 minimum net worth requirement; $120,000 start-up capital required. **Franchise Fee:** $40,000. **Training:** Provides 6 weeks training.

9749 ■ Tapioca Express Inc.

1908 Central Ave.
South El Monte, CA 91733
Ph: (626)453-0777
Free: 888-887-1616
Fax: (626)453-0778
Co. E-mail: franchise@tapiocaexpress.com
URL: http://www.tapiocaexpress.com
Contact: Wayne Lin, Owner
Description: Tapioca and milk tea beverages. **No. of Franchise Units:** 50. **Founded:** 1999. **Franchised:** 2000. **Equity Capital Needed:** $136,000-$402,000. **Franchise Fee:** $15,000. **Royalty Fee:** 2.5%. **Training:** Offers 8 days at company store and ongoing support.

9750 ■ Tealuxe, A Tea Bar & Cafe

Tealuxe, Inc.
201 Newtown Rd.
Plainview, NY 11803
Free: 888-TEA-LUXE
URL: http://www.tealuxe.com
Description: A tea bar and cafe. **No. of Company-Owned Units:** 3. **Founded:** 1996.. **Franchised:** 2003. **Equity Capital Needed:** $150,000-$250,000. **Franchise Fee:** $25,000. **Training:** Yes.

9751 ■ Tim Hortons Inc.

874 Sinclair Rd.
Oakville, ON, Canada L6K 2Y1
Ph: (905)845-6511
Free: 888-601-1616

Fax: (905)845-0265
Co. E-mail: investor_relations@timhortons.com
URL: http://www.timhortons.com
Contact: Donald B. Schroeder, President
Description: Offers the highest quality fresh baked goods to enjoy with our famous premium blend Tim Hortons Coffee. **No. of Franchise Units:** 3,300. **No. of Company-Owned Units:** 18. **Founded:** 1964. **Franchised:** 1964. **Equity Capital Needed:** $203,000. **Franchise Fee:** $50,000. **Training:** Yes. **Telecommunication Services:** franchise_requests@timhortons.com.

9752 ■ Timothy's World Coffee

Threecaf Brands Canada Inc.
7880 Keele St., Ste. 101
Vaughan, ON, Canada L4K 4G7
Ph: (905)482-7300
Free: 877-434-3223
Fax: (905)482-7330
Co. E-mail: franchise@timothys.com
URL: http://www.timothys.com
Description: Specializes in a variety of whole bean and freshly brewed specialty coffees, pastries, light sandwiches and coffee accessories. Offers good quality control in the selection, capping and roasting of coffee beans. **No. of Franchise Units:** 75. **No. of Company-Owned Units:** 11. **Founded:** 1975.. **Franchised:** 1979. **Equity Capital Needed:** $300,000-$450,000. **Franchise Fee:** $25,000 plus applicable taxes. **Training:** Offers 3 week training program.

9753 ■ Van Houtte

8300 19th Ave.
Montreal, QC, Canada H1Z 4J8
Ph: (514)789-4611
Free: 877-593-7722
Fax: (514)593-9582
Co. E-mail: clmonette@vanhoutte.com
URL: http://www.vanhoutte.com
Description: Cafe offering coffee and espresso drinks, tea, soups and sandwiches. **No. of Franchise Units:** 70. **Founded:** 1919.. **Franchised:** 1983. **Equity Capital Needed:** $150,000 minimum investment required; $150,000 minimum start-up capital required. **Franchise Fee:** $40,000.

LIBRARIES

9754 ■ Unilever Bestfoods - Library/Information Center

800 Sylvan Ave.
Englewood Cliffs, NJ 07632
Ph: (201)894-7532
Fax: (201)894-7532
Contact: Beth Currie, Manager
Scope: Tea, food technology. **Services:** Interlibrary loan; Library not open to the public. **Founded:** 1942. **Holdings:** 10,000 books; 300 bound periodical volumes; U.S. chemical patents (1970 to 1993, on microfilm; 1994 to present, on CD-ROM). **Subscriptions:** 250 journals and other serials.

START-UP INFORMATION

9755 ■ *How to Open and Operate a Financially Successful Landscaping, Nursery or Lawn Service Business: With Companion CD-ROM*
Pub: Atlantic Publishing Company
Ed: Lynn Wasnak. **Released:** June 1, 2009. **Price:** $39.95. **Description:** Guide provides understanding of the basic concepts of starting and running a service business, focusing on the operation of a small nursery, landscaping, or lawn service or combining the three operations. It also offers tips for running the business from the home.

ASSOCIATIONS AND OTHER ORGANIZATIONS

9756 ■ **American Horticultural Society**
7931 East Blvd. Dr.
Alexandria, VA 22308-1300
Ph: (703)768-5700
Free: 800-777-7931
Fax: (703)768-7533
Co. E-mail: editor@ahs.org
URL: http://www.ahs.org
Contact: Henry Rissetto, Chairman
Description: Represents amateur and professional gardeners. Aims to educate and inspire people of all ages to become successful and environmentally responsible gardeners by advancing the art and science of horticulture. Operates free seed exchange and gardeners' information service for members. Offers internships and children's services. **Publications:** *The American Gardener: The Magazine of the American Horticultural Society* (Bimonthly); *The American Gardener* (Bimonthly); *North American Horticulture: A Reference Guide* (Irregular); *AHS A-Z Encyclopedia of Garden Plants*; *AHS Encyclopedia of Plants and Flowers*; *AHS Great Plant Guide.* **Educational Activities:** Great American Gardeners (Annual); National Children and Youth Gardening Symposium (Annual). **Awards:** Great American Gardeners Awards (Annual); Liberty Hyde Bailey Medal; Paul Ecke Jr. Commercial Award; G. B. Gunlogson Medal; B.Y. Morrison Communication Award; Horticultural Therapy Award; Landscape Design Award; Meritorious Service Award; Frances Jones Poetker Award; Professional Award; H. Marc Cathey Award; Catherine H. Sweeney Award; Teaching Award; Urban Beautification Award; Luther Burbank Award; Jane L. Taylor Award.

9757 ■ **American Hydrangea Society (AHS)**
PO Box 53234
Atlanta, GA 30355
Co. E-mail: pearlworks@hotmail.com
URL: http://www.americanhydrangeasociety.org
Contact: Sandy Jones, President
Description: Represents growers and other individuals with an interest in the genus Hydrangea. Promotes the study of the cultivation of Hydrangea and related

plant species. Conducts educational programs and serves as a clearinghouse on Hydrangea. Hosts members only garden tour each June. **Founded:** 1994.

9758 ■ **American Nursery and Landscape Association (ANLA)**
1200 G St. NW, Ste. 800
Washington, DC 20005
Ph: (202)789-2900
Fax: (202)789-1893
Co. E-mail: info@anla.org
URL: http://www.anla.org
Contact: Robert S. Lyons, President
Description: Vertical organization of wholesale growers; landscape firms; garden centers; mail order nurseries; suppliers. Promotes the industry and its products. Offers management and consulting services and public relations programs. Provides government representation and bank card plan for members. Maintains hall of fame. **Founded:** 1876. **Publications:** *American Nursery & Landscape Association-- Member Directory: Who's Who in the Nursery Industry* (Annual).

9759 ■ **American Seed Trade Association (ASTA)**
1701 Duke St., Ste. 675
Alexandria, VA 22314
Ph: (703)837-8140
Fax: (703)837-9365
Co. E-mail: info@amseed.org
URL: http://www.amseed.com
Contact: Andrew W. LaVigne, President
Description: Breeders, growers, assemblers, conditioners, wholesalers, and retailers of grain, grass, vegetable, flower, and other seed for planting purposes. **Founded:** 1883. **Publications:** *Corn and Sorghum Proceedings* (Annual); *Soybean Seed Proceedings* (Annual).

9760 ■ **Canadian Nursery Landscape Association (CNLA)—Association Candienne des Pepinieristes et des Paysagistes**
RR No. 4, Sta. Main
7856 5th Line S
Milton, ON, Canada L9T 2X8
Ph: (905)875-1399
Free: 888-446-3499
Fax: (905)875-1840
Co. E-mail: info@canadanursery.com
URL: http://www.canadanursery.com
Contact: Victor Santacruz, Executive Director
Description: Growers, retail garden centers, lawn care and gardening services, sod growers, landscape, construction, and maintenance contractors, and other horticultural industries. Promotes expansion of the nursery and related industries. Devises standards and develops and administers tests to ensure competence in nursery production, garden supply retailing, landscape contracting, and construction and maintenance. Makes available support and services to members including discount insurance policies and merchant credit cards, educational programs, and representation before government agencies. Sponsors research; compiles statistics. **Founded:** 1922.

Publications: *CNLA Newsbrief* (Bimonthly). **Awards:** Honourary Life Member (Periodic); President's Award (Periodic). **Telecommunication Services:** victor@canadanursery.com.

9761 ■ *CNLA Newsbrief*
RR No. 4, Sta. Main
7856 5th Line S
Milton, ON, Canada L9T 2X8
Ph: (905)875-1399
Free: 888-446-3499
Fax: (905)875-1840
Co. E-mail: info@canadanursery.com
URL: http://www.canadanursery.com
Contact: Victor Santacruz, Executive Director
Released: Bimonthly

9762 ■ **Flowers Canada (FC)**
99 5th Ave., Ste. 305
Ottawa, ON, Canada K1S 5P5
Free: 800-447-5147
Fax: (866)671-8091
Co. E-mail: flowers@flowerscanada.org
URL: http://flowerscanada.ca
Contact: James Fuller, Chairman
Description: Retail florists, distributors, and greenhouse operators. Promotes growth and development in the domestic floriculture industry. Provides technical and promotional services to floral retailers, producers, and distributors; sponsors continuing professional development and educational programs for members. Represents members' interests before government agencies; serves as a liaison between members and related trade organizations. Makes available discount credit card, insurance, automotive fleet, lodging, and other business services to members. **Founded:** 1897. **Subscriptions:** reports photographs. **Publications:** *News Vine* (Bimonthly). **Awards:** Flowers Canada Friend of Floriculture (Periodic); Walter Good Award (Annual).

9763 ■ **Hobby Greenhouse Association (HGA)**
c/o HGA Publications Office
80 Deaconess Rd., Ste. 443
Concord, MA 01742
Co. E-mail: tomsherron@msn.com
URL: http://www.hobbygreenhouse.org
Contact: Tom Karasek, President
Description: Greenhouse owners and those who grow plants indoors with lights; windowsill and porch gardeners. Promotes the hobby of greenhouse and indoor gardening. Provides information on plants and diseases, propagation of seeds, insect control, and greenhouse building and maintenance. **Founded:** 1976. **Publications:** *HGA News* (Quarterly); *Hobby Greenhouse* (Quarterly); *Directory of Manufacturers of Residential Greenhouses and Distributors of Imported Greenhouses* (Annual). **Educational Activities:** Hobby Greenhouse Association Convention (Biennial).

9764 ■ **National Gardening Association (NGA)**
1100 Dorset St.
South Burlington, VT 05403

Ph: (802)863-5251
Free: 800-538-7476
Fax: (802)864-6889
Co. E-mail: customerservice@garden.org
URL: http://www.garden.org
Contact: Mike Metallo, President
E-mail: mikem@garden.org
URL(s): www.kidsgardening.org, www.nationalgardenmonth.org. **Description:** Serves as a clearing-house for home, community and educational gardening information. Conduct programs providing technical assistance, materials, and grants to children's gardens nationwide. Sponsor events forums and programs to raise the awareness for the benefits of gardening. Constituents include home gardeners, community garden groups, nursing and rehabilitation homes, schools, youth clubs, camps, educators and parents. Aims to promote home, school and community gardening as a means to renew and sustain the essential connection between people, plants and the environment. Promotes environmental responsibility, advance multi-disciplinary learning and scientific literacy, and create partnerships that restore and enhance communities. **Founded:** 1973. **Publications:** *Environmental Survey* (Triennial); *Gardening with Kids* (3/year); *Growing Ideas* (Quarterly); *National Gardening Survey* (Annual); *What Gardeners Think* (Triennial); *Gardener's Dictionary*; *National Gardening: For the Food and Flower Gardening Enthusiast* (Bimonthly); *Growing Ventures*; *Math in the Garden*. **Awards:** Dutch Bulb Awards (Annual); Healthy Sprouts Award (Annual); Youth Garden Grant (Annual). **Telecommunication Services:** membership@garden.org.

9765 ■ *News Vine*
99 5th Ave., Ste. 305
Ottawa, ON, Canada K1S 5P5
Free: 800-447-5147
Fax: (866)671-8091
Co. E-mail: flowers@flowerscanada.org
URL: http://flowerscanada.ca
Contact: James Fuller, Chairman
Released: Bimonthly

9766 ■ North American Flowerbulb Wholesalers Association (NAFWA)
c/o Marlboro Bulb Company
2424 Hwy. 72/221 E
Greenwood, SC 29649
Ph: (864)229-1618
Fax: (864)229-5719
Co. E-mail: nafwa1@aol.com
URL: http://www.nafwa.com
Contact: Thijs Leenders, President
Description: Wholesalers and dealers of flower bulbs and related floricultural commodities. **Founded:** 1983. **Awards:** Karl Schroff Memorial Scholarship (Annual).

9767 ■ Nursery and Landscape Association Executives of North America (NLAE)
2130 Stella Ct.
Columbus, OH 43215
Ph: (614)487-1117
Fax: (614)487-1216
Co. E-mail: nlae@ofa.org
URL: http://www.nlae.org
Contact: Michael V. Geary, Executive Director
Description: Professional society of executives of state, national, regional, and provincial nursery trade associations. **Founded:** 1947.

9768 ■ Ornamental Concrete Producers Association (OCPA)
759 Phelps Johnson Rd.
Leitchfield, KY 42754
Ph: (270)879-6319
Fax: (270)879-0399
Co. E-mail: ocpa@windstream.net
URL: http://www.ocpainfo.com
Contact: Donna Dunkelberger, Executive Director
Description: Producers of ornamental concrete products. Seeks to advance the ornamental concrete and related industries. Conducts educational programs; sponsors competitions; holds mold auctions. **Scope:** ornamental concrete. **Founded:** 1991. **Subscriptions:** video recordings.

DIRECTORIES OF EDUCATIONAL PROGRAMS

9769 ■ *Directory of Private Accredited Career Schools and Colleges of Technology*
Pub: Accrediting Commission of Career Schools and Colleges of Technology
Contact: Michale S. McComis, Executive Director
Released: On web page. **Price:** Free. **Description:** Covers 3900 accredited post-secondary programs that provide training programs in business, trade, and technical fields, including various small business endeavors. Entries offer school name, address, phone, description of courses, job placement assistance, and requirements for admission. Arrangement is alphabetical.

REFERENCE WORKS

9770 ■ *"Active Sales" in Green Industry Pro* (Vol. 23, September 2011)
Pub: Cygnus Business Media
Ed: Gregg Wartgow. **Description:** Craig den Hartog, owner of Emerald Magic Lawn Care located in Holtsville, New York, describes the various marketing tactics he has developed to increase sales in the current economic environment. Statistical data included.

9771 ■ *"All the Trimmings" in Green Industry Pro* (Vol. 23, March 2011, No. 3, pp. 29)
Pub: Cygnus Business Media
Ed: Gregg Wartgow. **Description:** When choosing lawn mowing equipment, it is advised to purchase commercial-grade 21-inch walk mowers rather than less expensive consumer-grade mowers. John Deere is reentering the commercial 21-inch walk behind mower market after a five-year hiatus.

9772 ■ *Andersen Horticultural Library's Source List of Plants and Seeds*
Pub: Andersen Horticultural Library
URL(s): www.arboretum.umn.edu. **Ed:** Richard T. Isaacson. **Released:** Irregular; latest edition 6th, 2004. **Price:** $39.95, Individuals postpaid. **Covers:** More than 600 nurseries that offer over 70,000 different plants. **Entries include:** Company name, address, phone. **Arrangement:** Alphabetical. **Indexes:** Product code, geographical.

9773 ■ *"Be Innovative In Other Ways" in Green Industry Pro* (Vol. 23, March 2011, No. 3, pp. 4)
Pub: Cygnus Business Media
Ed: Rod Dickens. **Description:** Emphasis is put on the importance of putting the customer first in order to successfully market any product or service. Six marketing ideas are presented to promote a landscaping business.

9774 ■ *"Customer Retention is Proportionate to Employee Retention" in Green Industry Pro* (Vol. 23, September 2011)
Pub: Cygnus Business Media
Description: Presented in a question-answer format, information is provided to help retain customers as well as keeping workers happy.

9775 ■ *"Customized Before Custom Was Cool" in Green Industry Pro* (July 2011)
Pub: Cygnus Business Media
Ed: Gregg Wartgow. **Description:** Profile of Turf Care Enterprises and owner Kevin Vogeler, who discusses his desire to use more natural programs using little or no chemicals in 1986. At that time, that sector represented 20 percent of his business, today it shares 80 percent.

9776 ■ *"Deep in the Heart of Drought" in Green Industry Pro* (Vol. 23, October 2011)
Pub: Cygnus Business Media
Ed: Gregg Wartgow. **Description:** Challenges faced by landscape contractors during the recent drought in Texas are explored. Despite these challenges, opportunity for contractors providing irrigation services has risen.

9777 ■ *"Dozens 'Come Alive' in Downtown Chicago" in Green Industry Pro* (July 2011)
Pub: Cygnus Business Media
Ed: Gregg Wartgow. **Description:** Highlights from the Come Alive Outside training event held in Chicago, Illinois July 14-15, 2011 are shared. Nearly 80 people representing 38 landscape companies attended the event that helps contractors review their services and find ways to sell them in new and various ways.

9778 ■ *"Finding a Way to Continue Growing" in Green Industry Pro* (Vol. 23, March 2011, No. 3, pp. 31)
Pub: Cygnus Business Media
Description: Profile of Brett Lemcke, VP of R.M. Landscape located in Rochester, New York. Lemcke tells how his Landscape Industry Certified credentials helped him to grow his business and beat out his competition.

9779 ■ *"Five Distinct Divisions, One Collective Focus" in Green Industry Pro* (Vol. 23, October 2011)
Pub: Cygnus Business Media
Ed: Gregg Wartgow. **Description:** Profile of ACLS Inc., an amalgamation of All Commercial Landscape Service (commercial maintenance), All Custom Landscape Service (design/build), Fresno Tree Service, Certified Water Consulting (irrigation), and Tractor Service (disking and flailing services on everything from one-acre lots to hundreds of acres of open land). The firm discusses its rebranding effort in order to increase sales.

9780 ■ *"Forward Motion" in Green Industry Pro* (July 2011)
Pub: Cygnus Business Media
Ed: Gregg Wartgow. **Description:** Several landscape contractors have joined this publication's Working Smarter Training Challenge over the last year. This process is helping them develop ways to improve work processes, boost morale, drive out waste, reduce costs, improve customer service, and be more competitive.

9781 ■ *"Gain the 'Come Alive Outside' Selling Edge" in Green Industry Pro* (July 2011)
Pub: Cygnus Business Media
Ed: Jim Paluch. **Description:** Marketing the 'Come Alive Outside' slogan can help landscapers to increase their market share by identifying and applying these elements to each customer as well as their workers.

9782 ■ *Garden Seed Inventory: 6th Edition*
Pub: Seed Savers Exchange
Contact: Tom Wahlberg, Manager
E-mail: tom@seedsavers.org
URL(s): www.seedsavers.org. **Ed:** Arllys Adelmann, Kent Whealy. **Released:** Irregular; latest edition 2005. **Price:** $26, Individuals softcover (current edition). **Publication includes:** List of 255 mail-order companies supplying non-hybrid vegetable seeds; coverage includes the U.S. and Canada. **Entries include:** Company name, address, and description, type of seeds offered. Principal content is an inventory of 255 mail-order seed catalogs and descriptions of the 8,494 non-hybrid seed varieties they offer. Detailed descriptions are compiled from the catalogs. **Arrangement:** Classified by varieties of seeds offered.

9783 ■ *"The Green Industry Jobs Gap" in Green Industry Pro* (Vol. 23, October 2011)
Pub: Cygnus Business Media
Ed: Gregg Wartgow. **Description:** According to the U.S. Bureau of Labor Statistics, the landscaping industry employs over 829,000 workers. According to another private study, the industry would employ more if they were able to find more people interested in performing the required work.

9784 ■ *"Hey, You Can't Do That" in Green Industry Pro* (Vol. 23, September 2011)
Pub: Cygnus Business Media
Ed: Rod Dickens. **Description:** Manufacturers of landscape equipment are making better use of energy resources, such as the use of fuel-injection

systems instead of carburetors, lightweight materials, better lubricants, advanced battery technology, and innovative engine designs.

9785 ■ "How to Dominate in Residential Maintenance" in Green Industry Pro (Vol. 23, October 2011)
Pub: Cygnus Business Media
Ed: Gregg Wartgow. **Description:** Lawn care services were ranked among the most expendable consumer expenditures, according to the National Retail Federation data accumulated in early 2011. This makes it critical for any landscape firm to target sales efforts toward higher-income households and higher-value homes.

9786 ■ "How To Turn Your Efforts Into Results" in Green Industry Pro (Vol. 23, September 2011)
Pub: Cygnus Business Media
Ed: Bob Coulter. **Description:** Working Smarter Training Challenge teaches that leaders are able to carry out solutions directly into their organization, develop skills and drive business results in key areas by creating a culture of energized workers who are able to take ownership of their performance as well as the performance of the company as a whole.

9787 ■ "KC Sewer Solutions May Overflow With Green Ideas" in The Business Journal-Serving Metropolitan Kansas City (August 22, 2008)
Pub: American City Business Journals, Inc.
Ed: Suzanna Stagemeyer. **Description:** Adding green solutions such as small, dispersed basins to catch runoffs and the use of deep rooted natural plants to fix the sewer system of Kansas could probably justify the $2.3 billion worth of funds needed for the project. The city has been ordered by the EPA and the Missouri Department of Natural Resources to fix their sewer systems that are overwhelmed by significant rains.

9788 ■ "Labor of Love" in Green Industry Pro (Vol. 23, March 2011, No. 3, pp. 14)
Pub: Cygnus Business Media
Ed: Gregg Wartgow. **Description:** Profile of CLS Landscape Management in Chino, California and its owner who started the company when he was 21 years old. Kevin Davis built his landscape firm into a $20 million a year business without using any dedicated salesperson.

9789 ■ "The Price of Profitability" in Green Industry Pro (Vol. 23, March 2011, No. 3, pp. 18)
Pub: Cygnus Business Media
Ed: Tony Bass. **Description:** Profit Builder Process is used to help landscaping companies be more competitive. Landscape contractors report pricing among their largest challenges and although the economy is improving, homeowners are paying closer attention to quality and service.

9790 ■ "Rediscovering the Land of Opportunity" in Green Industry Pro (July 2011)
Pub: Cygnus Business Media
Ed: Gregg Wartgow. **Description:** Landscape contractors need to discover new strategies that will generate leads and convert those leads into sales.

9791 ■ "Take Control of Your Company's Finances" in Green Industry Pro (Vol. 23, March 2011, No. 3, pp. 24)
Pub: Cygnus Business Media
Ed: Gregg Wartgow. **Description:** Understanding that when certain leading indicators that affect the outcome of certain lagging indicators are aligned, companies will be able to take control of their firm's finances. Ways to improve the processes that drive financial performance for landscape firms are outlined.

9792 ■ "Take This Job and Love It" in Green Industry Pro (Vol. 23, October 2011)
Pub: Cygnus Business Media
Ed: Gregg Wartgow. **Description:** Details of the lawsuit filed by the Professional Landcare Network (PLANET) against the U.S. Department of Labor are

explained. Challenges faced by landscape firms because of employment costs are outlined. Statistical data included.

9793 ■ "Time to Fight Back" in Green Industry Pro (Vol. 23, March 2011, No. 3, pp. 8)
Pub: Cygnus Business Media
Ed: Rod Dickens. **Description:** Lawn care operators in the United States must learn from Canada that a shift to socialism will impact their industry in a negative way. Government regulation over the application of control products regarding environmental health in Canada has been a death sentence for small lawn care businesses.

9794 ■ "Tough Climate for Nurseries" in Crain's Cleveland Business (Vol. 30, June 29, 2009, No. 25, pp. 1)
Pub: Crain Communications, Inc.
Ed: Stan Bullard. **Description:** After 81 years in the business, Sunnybrook Farms & Nursery is closing its doors. The owner sites the bad economy along with cold weather the reason for lack of sales. Other nursery owners discuss the bad economy and weather conditions and how they are affecting their business.

9795 ■ "Way More Than Mowing" in Green Industry Pro (Vol. 23, September 2011)
Pub: Cygnus Business Media
Ed: Rod Dickens. **Description:** Shipp Shape Lawn Services located in Sylvester, Georgia now offers aeration, fertilizing and weed control, mulching, yard renovation, flowerbed maintenance, landscaping, as well as irrigation repairs and installation in order to diversify the business and stay competitive.

STATISTICAL SOURCES

9796 ■ The Market for Lawn, Garden, & Snow Equipment
Pub: Business Trend Analysts, Inc.
Released: 2004-2005. **Price:** $2195.00. **Description:** An in-depth industry report tracking market size and growth for residential and commercial mowers, edgers and trimmers, shredders and grinders, yard vacs and blowers, garden tractors, snowthrowers, chain saws, commercial grounds care equipment, lawn and more.

9797 ■ RMA Annual Statement Studies
Pub: Risk Management Association
Contact: Kevin M. Blakey, President
Released: Annual. **Price:** $175.00 2006-07 edition, $105.00. **Description:** Contains composite balance sheets and income statements for more than 360 industries, including the accounting, auditing, and bookkeeping industries. Also contains five years of comparative historical data for discerning trends. Includes 16 commonly used ratios, computed for most of the size groupings for nearly every industry.

9798 ■ The U.S. Lawn and Garden Market, 5th Edition
Pub: MarketResearch.com
Released: 2003. **Price:** $2250.00. **Description:** The information in The U.S. Lawn and Garden Market is based on both primary and secondary research. Primary research involved on-site examination of the retail milieu, interviews with marketing, public relations and industry analysts within the lawn and garden market and consultants to the industry.

TRADE PERIODICALS

9799 ■ The American Gardener: The Magazine of the American Horticultural Society
Pub: American Horticultural Society
Contact: Henry Rissetto, Chairman
URL(s): www.ahs.org/publications/the_american_gardener/index.htm. **Ed:** David J. Ellis. **Released:** Bimonthly **Price:** $10, Individuals.

9800 ■ American Nurseryman: Covering Commercial Horticulture Since 1904
Pub: American Nurseryman Publishing Co.
URL(s): www.amerinursery.com/. **Released:** Semimonthly **Price:** $48, Individuals; $80, Other countries; $84, Canada.

9801 ■ The Avant Gardener
Pub: Horticultural Data Processors
Ed: Thomas Powell, Editor. **Released:** Monthly. **Price:** $24 year. **Description:** Contains information on such subjects as indoor and outdoor plants, edible plants, new products, methods of cultivation, breeding and growing techniques, pest control, fertilizers, and landscaping. Recurring features include several special issues per year on specific topics.

9802 ■ Baer's Garden Newsletter
Pub: John Baer's Sons
Ed: Gerald S. Lestz, Editor. **Released:** Quarterly. **Price:** Free. **Description:** Presents news for gardeners--new developments in flowers and gardens, information on where to send for gardening catalogs, and articles on such topics as public gardens and gardening with children. Includes news of research, book reviews, and notices of publications available.

9803 ■ California Garden
Pub: San Diego Floral Association
Contact: Barbara Clark, President
URL(s): www.sdfloral.org/magazine.htm. **Released:** Bimonthly

9804 ■ Chicago Home and Garden
Pub: Chicago Home & Garden
URL(s): www.chicagohomemag.com/. **Ed:** Jan Parr. **Released:** Quarterly **Price:** $9.95, Individuals; $25, Canada; $35, Other countries.

9805 ■ Country Home
Pub: Meredith Corp.
URL(s): www.countryhome.com. **Released:** Monthly; 10/yr. **Price:** $4.95, Individuals newsstand; $21.97, Two years.

9806 ■ FloraCulture International Magazine
Pub: Ball Publishing
Contact: Anissa Lobrillo, Director
URL(s): www.floracultureinternational.com/. **Ed:** Ron van del Ploeg. **Released:** Bimonthly **Price:** €75, Individuals; €142.50, Other countries.

9807 ■ Garden Center Products & Supplies: Professional Purchasing Guide for Garden Centers
Pub: G.I.E. Media Inc.
Contact: Chris Foster, President
URL(s): www.gardencentermagazine.com. **Released:** Monthly

9808 ■ Green Profit Magazine
Pub: Ball Publishing
Contact: Anissa Lobrillo, Director
URL(s): www.ballpublishing.com/GreenProfit/CoverStory.aspx?articleid=18051. **Ed:** Chris Beytes. **Released:** 9/yr.

9809 ■ Greenhouse Management and Production
Pub: G.I.E. Media Inc.
Contact: Chris Foster, President
URL(s): www.greenhousemanagementonline.com/. **Ed:** David Kuack. **Released:** Monthly

9810 ■ Horticulture: The Art and Science of Smart Gardening
Pub: FW Publications
Contact: Sara Domville, President
E-mail: sara.domville@fwpubs.com
URL(s): www.hortmag.com. **Released:** 8/yr. **Price:** $19.95, Individuals; $39.95, Canada; $39.95, Other countries.

9811 ■ HortIdeas
Pub: Greg and Pat Williams
Ed: Greg Williams, Editor, gwill@mis.net. **Released:** Monthly. **Price:** $25, individuals; $32, Canada and Mexico; $30, elsewhere by surface mail;. **Description:** Reviews the latest research on vegetable, fruit, and flower gardening. Provides practical information

and tips on growing techniques, tools, plant varieties, and resources in abstract form with full references to original sources. Recurring features include book reviews. Remarks: Also available via e-mail.

9812 ■ Landscape Trades: Canada's Premier Horticultural Trade Publication

Pub: Landscape Ontario Horticultural Trades Association

URL(s): www.landscapetrades.com. Ed: Robert El-lidge. Released: 9/yr (not published Feb., Aug., and Dec.). Price: $43.58, Individuals; $78.74, Two years; $110.24, Individuals 3 years.

9813 ■ Missouri Botanical Garden Annals

Pub: Missouri Botanical Garden Press
Contact: Victoria Hollowell, Editor
E-mail: victoria.hollowell@mobot.org
URL(s): www.mbgpress.org. Ed: Victoria C. Hollowell. Released: Quarterly; March, June, September, December. Price: $180, Individuals; $190, Canada and Mexico; $215, Other countries.

9814 ■ New Horizons

Pub: Horticultural Research Institute
Contact: William D. Wells, Jr., President
Released: 2/year. Price: Included in membership. Description: Explores research of the science and art of nursery, retail garden center, and landscape plant production, marketing, and care.

9815 ■ Nursery News

Pub: Cenflo Inc.
URL(s): www.cenflo.com/nurserynews.html. Released: Monthly Price: $20, Individuals; $36, Two years; $125, Other countries.

9816 ■ Organic Gardening

Pub: Rodale Inc.
Contact: Maria Rodale, Chief Executive Officer
URL(s): www.organicgardening.com. Released: Bimonthly Price: $23.94, Two years plus free delivery.

9817 ■ Ornamental Outlook: Growing the Florida Landscape

Pub: Meister Publishing Co.
Contact: Gary T. Fitzgerald, Chief Executive Officer
E-mail: gtfitzgerald@meistermedia.com
URL(s): www.ornamentaloutlook.com/. Released: Monthly

9818 ■ Plants & Gardens News

Pub: Brooklyn Botanic Garden
Ed: Niall Dunne, Editor, nialldunne@bbg.org. Released: Quarterly. Price: Included in membership. Description: Discusses gardening, planting tips, news of gardening products, sources for new seeds and plants, and book reviews. Recurring features include plant profile, news of research, and fun for kids.

9819 ■ Tree City USA Bulletin

Pub: Arbor Day Foundation
Contact: John Rosenow, President
Ed: James R. Fazio, Editor. Released: Bimonthly. Price: $3, single issue; $15 membership subscription. Description: Provides tree planting and care instructions and information.

9820 ■ Tri-Ology

Pub: Florida Department of Agriculture and Consumer Services, Division of Plant Industry
URL(s): doacs.state.fl.us/pi/enpp/triology.html. Released: Monthly

9821 ■ Yard and Garden: Market Insights for Equipment Dealers

Pub: Cygnus Business Media
Contact: Rich Reiff, President
URL(s): www.cygnusb2b.com/PropertyPub.cfm?PropertyID=564www.greenindustrypros.com/magazine/yg/issue/2012/aug. Released: 8/yr.

VIDEOCASSETTES/AUDIOCASSETTES

9822 ■ Foliage Plant Production

CEV Multimedia
1020 SE Loop 289
Lubbock, TX 79404

Ph: (806)745-8820
Free: 877-610-5017
Fax: (800)243-6398
Co. E-mail: cev@cevmultimedia.com
URL: http://www.cevmultimedia.com
Contact: Jeff Lansdell, President
Released: 19??. Price: $95.00. Description: Presents techniques for producing foliage plants in the greenhouse, covering propagation, equipment, facilities, tip cuttings, leaf-stem bud cuttings, seed, direct stick usage, light intensity, watering, and fertilization. Part of the "Greenhouse Production Series.". Availability: VHS.

9823 ■ Training Greenhouse Workers to Handle Pesticides Safely

CEV Multimedia
1020 SE Loop 289
Lubbock, TX 79404
Ph: (806)745-8820
Free: 877-610-5017
Fax: (800)243-6398
Co. E-mail: cev@cevmultimedia.com
URL: http://www.cevmultimedia.com
Contact: Jeff Lansdell, President
Released: 1986. Price: $95.00. Description: Features the key points of applicator training such as pesticide types, toxicology, pesticide regulation, safety equipment, protective clothing, and first-aid procedures. Availability: VHS.

TRADE SHOWS AND CONVENTIONS

9824 ■ Birmingham Home and Garden Show

Home And Garden Show TV
PO Box 430
Pinson, AL 35126-0430
Ph: (205)680-0234
Free: 800-226-3976
Fax: (205)680-0615
Co. E-mail: sales@homeandgardenshow.tv
URL(s): www.homeshowbirmingham.com. Price: $9; $8, for senior citizens; free for children below 12 years. Frequency: Annual. Audience: General public. Principal Exhibits: Home and garden products and services. Dates and Locations: , Jefferson Civic Center.

9825 ■ Buffalo Home and Garden Show

First Niagara Bank
6950 S Transit Rd.
Lockport, NY 14095-0514
Ph: (716)625-7526
Free: 800-421-0004
Fax: (716)625-8681
URL: http://www.firstniagara.com
URL(s): www.buffalohomeshow.com. Price: $10, On-site adult rate; $7, Non-members buy online; $3, Non-members children 6-12 years old; $X, children 5 years and under. Frequency: Annual. Audience: General public. Principal Exhibits: Everything for your home and garden. Windows, doors, siding, sheds, gazebo's, lawn equipment, swimming pools, spas, mirrors, kitchen cabinets, bathroom products, closet organizers, security, playground equipment, electronics, furniture, fireplaces and any other product related to building, remodeling, decorating and landscaping. Dates and Locations: Buffalo Convention Center.

9826 ■ Builders St. Charles Home Show

Home Builders Association of Greater St. Louis
10104 Old Olive St. Rd.
St. Louis, MO 63141
Ph: (314)994-7700
Fax: (314)432-7185
URL: http://www.stlhba.com
Contact: Patrick Sullivan, Executive Vice President
E-mail: sullivap@hbastl.com
URL(s): www.stlhomeshow.com/stcharles. Price: $9, Onsite adults; $4, children 6-12; children 5 and under free. Frequency: Annual. Audience: General public and construction industry. Principal Exhibits: Home remodeling equipment and supplies, lawn and garden

equipment, swimming pools, home furnishings, model homes and kitchen and bath. Dates and Locations: , America's Center & Edward Jones Dome.

9827 ■ Cincinnati Home and Garden Show

Hart Productions, Inc.
322 E. Main St.
Batavia, OH 45103
Ph: (513)797-7900
Free: 877-704-8190
Fax: (513)797-1013
URL: http://www.hartproductions.com
URL(s): www.hartproductions.com. Price: $12, Non-members adults; children ages 13 and under. Frequency: Annual. Audience: General public. Principal Exhibits: Home and garden products and services. Dates and Locations: , Convention Center. Telecommunication Services: chip@hartproductions.com.

9828 ■ Farwest Nursery Show

Oregon Association of Nurseries
29751 S.W. Town Center Loop W
Wilsonville, OR 97070
Ph: (503)682-5089
Free: 800-342-6401
Fax: (503)682-5099
Co. E-mail: info@oan.org
URL: http://www.oan.org
Contact: Kristin Van Hoose, President
E-mail: kristin@amethyst-hill.com
URL(s): www.farwestshow.com. Price: Pre-registered free before early bird date; $10, Pre-registered late registration. Frequency: Annual. Audience: Wholesale nursery growers, garden centers, and landscapers. Principal Exhibits: Nursery stock, equipment, machinery, chemicals, and miscellaneous supplies and services for the wholesale and retail green industry. Dates and Locations: , Convention Center.

9829 ■ Minneapolis Home & Garden Show

dmg world media inc.
Northcliffe House
2 Derry St.
London W8 5TT, United Kingdom
Ph: 44 20 79386000
URL: http://www.dmgevents.com
URL(s): www.homeandgardenshow.com/MHGS/EventsHome.aspx. Frequency: Annual. Audience: General public. Principal Exhibits: Home and garden products and services. Telecommunication Services: info@homeandgardenshow.com.

9830 ■ Nursery/Landscape Expo

Texas Nursery & Landscape Association
7730 S. IH-35
Austin, TX 78745-6698
Ph: (512)280-5182
Free: 800-880-0343
Fax: (512)280-3012
Co. E-mail: info@tnlaonline.org
URL: http://www.txnla.org
URL(s): www.txnla.org. Frequency: Annual. Audience: Nursery, landscape and related trades professionals. Principal Exhibits: Plant materials including foliage, bedding plants, trees, palms; allied products including machinery, equipment and supplies for horticulture and landscape industry. Dates and Locations: , Convention Center.

9831 ■ Spokane Home and Garden Show

Creighton and Associates, Inc.
611 E Broward Blvd., Ste. 207
Fort Lauderdale, FL 33301
Contact: Sharon Panther, President
URL(s): www.spokanehomeandgardenshow.com/. Frequency: Annual. Audience: General public. Principal Exhibits: Products and services for the home and garden. Broad spectrum home improvement show. Dates and Locations: , Convention Center.

9832 ■ Spring Home & Patio Show

Industrial Expositions, Inc.
1675 Larimer St., No. 700
Denver, CO 80248-0084
Ph: (303)892-6800
Free: 800-457-2434

Fax: (303)892-6322
Co. E-mail: info@iei-expos.com
URL: http://www.iei-expos.com/
URL(s): www.agievents.com. **Frequency:** Annual.
Audience: General public. **Principal Exhibits:**
Garden and home improvement equipment, interior
designs, landscaping techniques and supplies, and
patios and patio furniture and supplies. **Dates and
Locations:** National Western Complex. **Telecom-
munication Services:** jsibert@affinitygroup.com.

9833 ■ Tacoma Home and Garden Show
O'Loughlin Trade Shows
PO Box 110849
Tacoma, WA 98411
Ph: (253)756-2121
Fax: (253)756-6898
Co. E-mail: infotac@otshows.com
URL: http://www.otshows.com/contact/tacoma/
URL(s): www.otshows.com/ths/. **Price:** $10, adults;
$8, seniors; children 16 and under free. **Frequency:**
Annual. **Audience:** General public. **Principal Exhib-
its:** Home and garden equipment, supplies, and
services; related products. **Dates and Locations:** ,
Tacoma Dome.

9834 ■ The World's Showcase of Horticulture
Southern Nursery Association
894 Liberty Farm Rd.
Oak Grove, GA 22443-5200
Ph: (804)224-9352
Co. E-mail: mail@sna.org
URL: http://www.sna.org
Contact: Danny Summers, Executive Vice President
E-mail: danny@mail.sna.org
URL(s): www.sna.org. **Frequency:** Annual. **Audi-
ence:** Wholesale and retail nursery professionals and
landscapers. **Principal Exhibits:** Nursery products,
including plants, chemicals, machinery and equip-
ment, soil and soil supplements, and plant contain-
ers. **Dates and Locations:** , Georgia World Congress
Center. **Telecommunication Services:** mail@sna.
org.

CONSULTANTS

9835 ■ Jobs In Horticulture Inc.
57 Rosedown Blvd.
Debary, FL 32713
Ph: (386)753-0996
Free: 800-428-2474
Fax: (386)753-0997
Co. E-mail: info@hortjobs.com
URL: http://www.hortjobs.com
Contact: David Shaw, Director
Scope: Career consulting and career services with
emphasis on horticulture. **Founded:** 1993.

FRANCHISES AND BUSINESS OPPORTUNITIES

9836 ■ Grower Direct Fresh Cut Flowers Inc.
9613-41 Ave., Ste. 201
Edmonton, AB, Canada T6E 5X7
Ph: (780)436-7774
Fax: (780)436-3336
Co. E-mail: franchises@grower.com
URL: http://www.growerdirect.com
Description: Supplies top quality, fresh cut flowers
and marketing expertise to its retail outlets. **No. of
Franchise Units:** 41. **No. of Company-Owned
Units:** 1. **Founded:** 1991.. **Franchised:** 1993. **Equity
Capital Needed:** $55,000-$75,000. **Franchise Fee:**
$15,000. **Training:** Provides 10 days training.

COMPUTERIZED DATABASES

9837 ■ Alaska AVHRR Data
47914 252nd St.
Sioux Falls, SD 57198-0001
Ph: (605)594-6151
Free: 800-252-4547

Fax: (605)594-6589
Co. E-mail: custserv@usgs.gov
URL: http://edc.usgs.gov
Availability: CD-ROM: U.S. Geological Survey -
Earth Resources Observation and Science Center.
Type: Image.

**9838 ■ Southwest Exotic Plant Mapping
Program (SWEMP)**
2255 N Gemini Dr.
Flagstaff, AZ 86001
Ph: (928)556-7000
Co. E-mail: webmaster@flagmail.wr.usgs.gov
URL: http://arizona.usgs.gov/Flagstaff
Availability: Online: United States Geological Survey
- Flagstaff Science Campus. **Type:** Image; Time
Series.

COMPUTER SYSTEMS/ SOFTWARE

**9839 ■ Advance Grower Solutions / Nursery/
Greenhouse Accounting Software**
4900 SW Griffith Dr., Ste. 248
Beaverton, OR 97005
Ph: (503)646-5581
Free: 800-367-7082
Fax: (503)646-0622
Co. E-mail: rickg@adgrower.com
URL: http://www.advgrower.com/
Price: Prices vary depending on modules needed.
Description: Available for IBM computers and
compatibles. System provides accounting and report
capabilities for nursery and landscaping businesses.

LIBRARIES

**9840 ■ American Horticultural Society
Library**
7931 E. Boulevard Dr.
Alexandria, VA 22308
Ph: (703)768-5700
Free: 800-777-7931
Fax: (703)768-8700
Co. E-mail: tunderwood@ahs.org
URL: http://www.ahs.org/
Contact: Tom Underwood, Executive Officer
Scope: Horticulture. **Services:** Copying; Library open
to the public by appointment. **Holdings:** 5000 books.

**9841 ■ Atlanta Botanical Garden - Sheffield
Botanical Library**
1345 Piedmont Ave., NE
Atlanta, GA 30309
Ph: (404)591-1546
Fax: (404)876-7472
Co. E-mail: lschwarz@atlantabotanicalgarden.org
URL: http://www.atlantabotanicalgarden.org
Contact: LuAnne Schwarz, Librarian
Scope: Botany, horticulture, gardening. **Services:**
Copying; Library open to the public for reference use
only. **Founded:** 1986. **Holdings:** 8000 books; 125
unbound periodical titles; society newsletters. **Sub-
scriptions:** 125 journals and other serials.

**9842 ■ Bartlett Arboretum and Gardens -
Horticulture Resource Library**
151 Brookdale Rd.
Stamford, CT 06903-4199
Ph: (203)322-6971
Fax: (203)595-9168
Co. E-mail: horticulture@bartlettarboretum.org
URL: http://www.bartlettarboretum.org
Contact: Eric C. Morgan, Curator Director, Education
Scope: Horticulture, plant science, botany, arboricul-
ture. **Services:** Library open to the public. **Founded:**
1965. **Holdings:** 2500 books; 1000 bound periodical
volumes; 30 VF drawers. **Subscriptions:** 25 journals
and other serials.

**9843 ■ Berkshire Botanical Garden -
Horticulture Library**
5 W. Stockbridge Rd.
Stockbridge, MA 01262
Ph: (413)298-3926

Fax: (413)298-4897
Co. E-mail: info@berkshirebotanical.org
URL: http://www.berkshirebotanical.org
Contact: Molly Boxer, Executive Director
Scope: Horticulture. **Services:** Library open to the
public by appointment. **Founded:** 1934. **Holdings:**
900 books. **Subscriptions:** 20 journals and other
serials.

**9844 ■ Birmingham Botanical Gardens -
Library**
2612 Lane Park Rd.
Birmingham, AL 35223
Ph: (205)414-3920
Fax: (205)414-3922
Co. E-mail: hopel@bham.lib.al.us
URL: http://www.bbgardens.org/library.php
Contact: Hope Long, Director, Library Services
Scope: Horticulture, botany, floriculture, gardens and
gardening, landscaping, flower arranging and children's books, organic gardening, insects, animals,
nature crafts. **Services:** Copying; printing (black and
white, color); faxing; free wifi and internet access;
Library open to the public. **Founded:** 1971. **Holdings:** 6000 circulating books; 870 reference books;
450 children's books; 100 CD-ROMs; DVDs. **Subscriptions:** 60 journals and other serials. **Telecommunication Services:** thelibrary@bbgardens.org.

9845 ■ Brookgreen Gardens Library
PO Box 3368
Pawleys Island, SC 29585-3368
Ph: (843)235-6000
Free: 800-849-1931
Fax: (843)235-6003
Co. E-mail: info@brookgreen.org
URL: http://www.brookgreen.org
Contact: Robin Salmon
Scope: Sculpture, South Carolina history. **Services:**
Library not open to the public. **Founded:** 1931. **Hold-
ings:** 2000 books; 2000 newspaper clippings; 15,000
slides; 2000 photographs.

9846 ■ Brooklyn Botanic Garden Library
1000 Washington Ave.
Brooklyn, NY 11225-1099
Ph: (718)623-7200
Co. E-mail: library@bbg.org
URL: http://www.bbg.org/research/library
Contact: Pat Jonas, Director, Library Services
Scope: Horticulture, botany. **Services:** Interlibrary
loan; copying. **Founded:** 1911. **Holdings:** 60,000
volumes; 28,000 (3500 titles) bound periodical
volumes; 5120 pamphlets; manuscripts; archives.
Subscriptions: 350 journals and other serials.

**9847 ■ Cheekwood Botanical Gardens
Library**
1200 Forrest Park Dr.
Nashville, TN 37205
Ph: (615)356-8000
Co. E-mail: info@cheekwood.org
URL: http://www.cheekwood.org
Scope: Horticulture, landscape architecture, plant
science, ecology, wildflowers, garden design, botanical art, orchids, herbs, natural history. **Services:**
Interlibrary loan; copying; Library open to the public
with restrictions. **Founded:** 1971. **Holdings:** 4750
books; 260 bound periodical volumes; 72 slide
programs; 147 videocassettes; flower and seed
catalogs. **Subscriptions:** 108 journals and other serials.

**9848 ■ Chicago Park District - Garfield Park
Conservatory**
300 N. Central Park Ave.
Chicago, IL 60624-1945
Ph: (312)746-5100
Fax: (773)638-1777
URL: http://www.garfield-conservatory.org/
Contact: Mary Eysenbach, Director
Scope: Horticulture. **Services:** Library not open to
the public. **Founded:** 1907. **Holdings:** 600 books.
Subscriptions: 2 journals and other serials.

**9849 ■ Cleveland Botanical Garden - Eleanor
Squire Library**
11030 East Blvd.
Cleveland, OH 44106

Ph: (216)721-1600
Fax: (216)721-2056
Co. E-mail: info@cbgarden.org
URL: http://www.cbgarden.org/Learn/Library.html
Contact: Gary Esmonde, Librarian
Scope: Gardening, horticulture, landscape architecture, herbs, flower arranging, botany. **Services:** Library open to the public with paid admission (members may borrow); rare books open to the public by appointment for review, research, and study. **Founded:** 1930. **Holdings:** 17,000 volumes; seed and nursery catalogs; slides; botanical prints; 1000 rare books. **Subscriptions:** 50 journals and other serials. **Telecommunication Services:** gesmonde@cbgarden.org.

9850 ■ Cornell University - Bailey Hortorium Library
430 Mann Library Bldg.
Ithaca, NY 14853
Ph: (607)255-0455
Fax: (607)256-5407
Co. E-mail: pf13@cornell.edu
URL: http://www.plantbio.cornell.edu/hortorium/
bhortlibr.cfm
Contact: Dr. William Crepet, Department Chairman
Scope: Taxonomic botany and horticulture. **Services:** Interlibrary loan; Library open to the public. **Founded:** 1935. **Holdings:** 30,000 books; 20,000 reprints on taxonomic botany and allied subjects; 1500 reprints on paleobotany; 8000 photographs of type specimens and other important specimens in European herbaria. **Subscriptions:** 260 journals and other serials. **Telecommunication Services:** wlc1@cornell.edu.

9851 ■ Cylburn Arboretum Association Library
4915 Greenspring Ave.
Baltimore, MD 21209
Ph: (410)367-2217
Fax: (410)367-7112
Co. E-mail: info@cylburnassociation.org
URL: http://www.cylburnassociation.org/
Scope: Horticulture, gardening, wild flowers, trees, shrubs. **Services:** Copying; library open to the public by appointment on a limited schedule. **Founded:** 1960. **Holdings:** 1600 books; 2 VF drawers of clippings and pamphlets; seed catalogs. **Subscriptions:** 2 journals and other serials.

9852 ■ Dawes Arboretum Library
7770 Jacksontown Rd., SE
Newark, OH 43056
Ph: (740)323-2355
Free: 800-44-DAWES
Fax: (740)323-4058
Co. E-mail: information@dawesarb.org
URL: http://www.dawesarb.org
Contact: Beth Spieles, Specialist, Education
Scope: Horticulture, botany, ecology, nature, forestry, gardening. **Services:** Copying; printing; Internet access; library open to the public for reference use only. **Founded:** 1929. **Holdings:** 1400 books. **Subscriptions:** 50 journals and other serials.

9853 ■ Denver Botanic Gardens - Helen Fowler Library
1007 York St.
Denver, CO 80206-3799
Ph: (720)865-3570
Fax: (720)865-3723
Co. E-mail: library@botanicgardens.org
URL: http://www.botanicgardens.org/content/helen-fowler-library
Contact: Colleen Nunn, Librarian
Scope: Horticulture, botany. **Services:** Interlibrary loan; copying; library open to the public (only members may borrow). **Founded:** 1948. **Holdings:** 30,000 books; 400 bound periodical volumes; 8000 pamphlets; 300 brochures describing botanic gardens; 1000 slides; 150 index seminum lists. **Subscriptions:** 431 journals and other serials.

9854 ■ Detroit Garden Center Library
Moross House, 2nd Fl.
1900 E. Jefferson, Ste. 227
Detroit, MI 48207
Ph: (313)259-6363

Fax: (313)259-0107
Co. E-mail: information@detroitgardencenter.org
URL: http://www.detroitgardencenter.org
Contact: Beverly Donaldson, Librarian
Scope: Horticulture, floral culture. **Services:** Library open to the public for research. **Founded:** 1932. **Holdings:** 5000 books. **Subscriptions:** 10 journals and other serials.

9855 ■ Harvard University - Botany Libraries
22 Divinity Ave.
Cambridge, MA 02138
Ph: (617)495-2366
Fax: (617)495-8654
Co. E-mail: botref@oeb.harvard.edu
URL: http://www.huh.harvard.edu/libraries/
Contact: Judith A. Warnement, Director
Scope: Systematic botany and horticulture. **Services:** Copying; Library open to the public for reference use only. **Founded:** 1864. **Holdings:** 286,000 volumes and pamphlets; archives; manuscripts; microfiche; portraits; photographs. **Subscriptions:** 1500 journals and other serials. **Telecommunication Services:** warnemen@oeb.harvard.edu.

9856 ■ Holden Arboretum - Warren H. Corning Library
9500 Sperry Rd.
Kirtland, OH 44094
Ph: (440)946-4400
Fax: (440)256-5836
Co. E-mail: holden@holdenarb.org
URL: http://www.holdenarb.org/resources/Libraryat-TheHoldenArboretum.asp
Contact: Susan Swisher, Librarian
Scope: Horticulture, botany, environmental education, natural history, conservation. **Services:** Copying; library open to the public for reference use only. **Founded:** 1963. **Holdings:** 9500 books and pamphlets; 10 VF drawers; 10,000 slides; 100 videocassettes. **Subscriptions:** 125 journals and other serials.

9857 ■ L.A. County Arboretum and Botanic Garden - Plant Science Library
301 N. Baldwin Ave.
Arcadia, CA 91007-2697
Ph: (626)821-3213
Fax: (626)445-1217
Co. E-mail: susan.eubank@arboretum.org
URL: http://www.arboretum.org/index.php/explore/library/
Contact: Susan Eubank, Librarian
Scope: Botany, horticulture. **Services:** Interlibrary loan; copying; circulating to Arboretum Foundation members; library open to the public. **Founded:** 1948. **Holdings:** 28,000 volumes; microfiche; maps. **Subscriptions:** 100 journals and other serials.

9858 ■ Lenhardt Library of the Chicago Botanic Garden—June Price Reedy Horticultural Library.
1000 Lake Cook Rd.
Glencoe, IL 60022
Ph: (847)835-8201
Co. E-mail: library@chicagobotanic.org
URL: http://www.chicagobotanic.org/library/index.html
Contact: Leora Siegel, Director
Scope: Horticulture, botany, gardening, plant conservation, landscape design, garden design, Midwest ecology, botanical illustration, phytopathology, horticultural therapy. **Services:** Interlibrary loan; copying; library open to the public. **Founded:** 1951. **Holdings:** 28,000 books; 600 videos and DVDs; 10,000 slides; 1000 nursery catalogs. **Subscriptions:** 1000 journals and other serials. **Telecommunication Services:** lsiegel@chicagobotanic.org.

9859 ■ Longwood Gardens, Inc. Library
1001 Longwood Rd.
Kennett Square, PA 19348-0501
Ph: (610)388-1000
Fax: (610)388-2078
Co. E-mail: library@longwoodgardens.org
URL: http://www.longwoodgardens.org/LibraryandArchives.html
Scope: Botany, horticulture, allied sciences. **Services:** Interlibrary loan; copying; Library open to the public with restrictions. **Founded:** 1961. **Holdings:**

31,000 volumes; 57 lin.ft. hanging shelves; 36 lin.ft. plant materials; 18 lin.ft. Foundations organizations, bibliographies; 9 lin.ft. of high school, university, and colleges records; 15 botanical gardens; 12 geographical; 1751 volumes of microforms; archives. **Subscriptions:** 300 journals and other serials.

9860 ■ Massachusetts Horticultural Society Library
Elm Bank Horticulture Ctr.
900 Washington St.
Wellesley, MA 02482-5725
Ph: (617)933-4910
Fax: (617)262-8780
Co. E-mail: library@masshort.org
URL: http://www.masshort.org
Contact: Maureen Horn, Librarian
Scope: Ornamental horticulture, garden history, landscape design, pomology, early agriculture, floras of the world. **Services:** Interlibrary loan; copying; library open to the public for reference use only. **Founded:** 1829. **Holdings:** 31,000 books; 24 VF drawers of pamphlets and clippings; 4000 documents; archives. **Subscriptions:** 50 journals and other serials. **Telecommunication Services:** mhorn@masshort.org.

9861 ■ Memphis Botanic Garden Foundation, Inc. - Goldsmith Civic Garden Center - Sybile Malloy Memorial Library
750 Cherry Rd.
Memphis, TN 38117
Ph: (901)685-1566
Fax: (901)682-1561
Co. E-mail: jim.duncan@memphistn.gov
URL: http://www.memphisbotanicgarden.com
Contact: Jim Duncan, Executive Director
Scope: Horticulture, gardening, landscape design, flower arranging, environmental science, botany, agriculture. **Services:** Copying; Library open to the public for reference use only. **Founded:** 1964. **Holdings:** 2150 books; 10 bound periodical volumes; 200 horticultural magazines and pamphlets. **Subscriptions:** 15 journals and other serials.

9862 ■ Missouri Botanical Garden Library
4Fl. 4500 Shaw Blvd.
St. Louis, MO 63110
Ph: (314)577-5155
Free: 800-642-8842
Fax: (314)577-0840
Co. E-mail: doug.holland@mobot.org
URL: http://www.mobot.org/mobot/molib/
Contact: Douglas Holland, Director, Library Services
Scope: Plant taxonomy and floristic, horticulture, botanical history and exploration. **Services:** Interlibrary loan; copying; Library open to the public by appointment. **Founded:** 1859. **Holdings:** 62,300 monographs; 66,000 bound periodical volumes; 100,000 pamphlets; 35,000 slides; 7000 vegetation and topographic maps; 220,000 archival items; 3059 historic manuscripts; 40,000 microfiche of herbaria; 7000 art works; 1300 vertical files. **Subscriptions:** 2000 journals and other serials. **Telecommunication Services:** linda.oestry@mobot.org.

9863 ■ Morton Arboretum - Sterling Morton Library
4100 Illinois Rte. 53
Lisle, IL 60532-1288
Ph: (630)719-2430
Fax: (630)719-7956
Co. E-mail: library@mortonarb.org
URL: http://www.mortonarb.org/sterling-morton-library.html
Contact: Rita Hassert, Manager, Collections
Scope: Botany, horticulture, dendrology, botanical art and illustration, arboriculture, landscape architecture, natural history, ecology and the environment. **Services:** Interlibrary loan; copying; SDI; library open to the public. **Founded:** 1922. **Holdings:** 28,000 volumes; 1000 nursery and seed catalogs. **Subscriptions:** 800 journals and other serials.

9864 ■ National Gardening Association Library
1100 Dorset St.
South Burlington, VT 05403-8000
Ph: (802)863-5251

Fax: (802)864-6889
Co. E-mail: sarahp@garden.org
URL: http://www.garden.org
URL(s): www.kidsgardening.com. **Scope:** Gardening - vegetable, fruit, ornamental; plant and soil science, flowers, herbs. **Services:** Library not open to the public. **Founded:** 1979. **Holdings:** 7500 books. **Subscriptions:** 40 journals and other serials.

9865 ■ New York Botanical Garden - LuEsther T. Mertz Library
200th St. & Kazimiroff Blvd.
Bronx, NY 10458-5126
Ph: (718)817-8728
Fax: (718)817-8956
Co. E-mail: libref@nybg.org
URL: http://www.nybg.org/library/
Contact: Susan Fraser, Director
Scope: Systematic and Floristic botany, gardening, horticulture, plant ecology, landscape design. **Services:** Interlibrary loan; copying; Library open to the public. **Founded:** 1896. **Holdings:** 260,000 volumes; 12,000 serial titles; 371 lin.ft. of nursery catalogs and seed lists; 675 lin.ft. of scientific reprints and pamphlets; 184 lin.ft. microforms; 100,000 photographs and slides; 3000 artifacts; 4800 lin.ft. of archival materials. **Subscriptions:** 711 journals and other serials.

9866 ■ Norfolk Botanical Garden Society - Frederic Heutte Memorial Library
6700 Azalea Garden Rd.
Norfolk, VA 23518-5337
Ph: (757)441-5830
Co. E-mail: library@nbgs.org
URL: http://www.norfolkbotanicalgarden.org
Contact: Marcia Oubre, Librarian
Scope: Horticulture and allied subjects. **Services:** Library open to the public for reference use only. **Founded:** 1962. **Holdings:** 3500 books.

9867 ■ Pennsylvania Horticultural Society - McLean Library
100 N. 20th St., 5th Fl.
Philadelphia, PA 19103-1455
Ph: (215)988-8800
Fax: (215)988-8810
Co. E-mail: wiredgardener@pennhort.org
URL: http://www.pennsylvaniahorticulturalsociety.org
Contact: Janet Evans, Director, Library Services
Scope: Ornamental horticulture, botany, landscape design, garden history. **Services:** Interlibrary loan; photocopying; Garden Q&A (telephone plant information service); Library open to the public for reference use only (borrowing privileges for members and PHS staff). **Founded:** 1827. **Holdings:** 15,000 books; 4000 bound periodical volumes; 1000 slides; 250 videotapes on gardening. **Subscriptions:** 100 journals and other serials. **Telecommunication Services:** mcleanlibrary@pennhort.org.

9868 ■ Planting Fields Arboretum - The Garden Library
PO Box 58
Oyster Bay, NY 11771
Ph: (516)922-8631
Fax: (516)922-8610
Co. E-mail: pfalib@prodigy.net
URL: http://www.plantingfields.org
Contact: Rosemarie Papayanopulos, Librarian
Scope: Horticulture, botany. **Services:** Library open to the public for browsing and reference use only (members of Planting Fields Foundation and Arboretum staff, as well as members of garden societies that meet on the grounds, have borrowing privileges). **Founded:** 1975. **Holdings:** 8000 books. **Subscriptions:** 150 journals and other serials. **Telecommunication Services:** henry.joyce@plantingfields.org.

9869 ■ Rancho Santa Ana Botanic Garden Library
1500 N. College Ave.
Claremont, CA 91711-3157
Ph: (909)625-8767

Fax: (909)626-7670
Co. E-mail: info@rsabg.org
URL: http://www.rsabg.org
Contact: Harvey Brenneise, Librarian
Scope: Botany, horticulture, drought tolerant plants, ethnobotany of California Indians, evolutionary biology. **Services:** Copying; library open to the public by appointment. **Founded:** 1927. **Holdings:** 50,000 volumes; 28,360 reprints; 2000 maps; nursery catalogs. **Subscriptions:** 750 journals and other serials.

9870 ■ Rochester Civic Garden Center Horticultural Library
5 Castle Park
Rochester, NY 14620
Ph: (585)473-5130
Fax: (716)473-8136
Co. E-mail: gardencenter@frontiernet.net
URL: http://www.rcgc.org/Library
Contact: Christine Froehlich, Executive Director
Scope: Horticulture, landscaping, plant identification, garden history, nature study, flower arrangement. **Services:** Interlibrary loan; Library open to the public for reference use only. **Founded:** 1945. **Holdings:** 4000 books; 875 bound periodical volumes; 12 VF drawers of clippings; pamphlets. **Subscriptions:** 34 journals and other serials. **Telecommunication Services:** rcgclib@frontiernet.net; rcgccf@frontiernet.net.

9871 ■ Rodale Press Library
33 E. Minor St.
Emmaus, PA 18098
Ph: (610)967-8729
Fax: (610)967-7708
URL: http://www.rodale.com
Scope: Health, gardening, sports. **Services:** Library open to the public by appointment. **Founded:** 1967. **Holdings:** 40,000 books. **Subscriptions:** 1500 journals and other serials.

9872 ■ San Francisco Botanical Garden at Strybing Arboretum - Helen Crocker Russell Library of Horticulture
Golden Gate Park
1199 9th Ave.
San Francisco, CA 94122-2370
Ph: (415)661-1316
Fax: (415)661-3539
Co. E-mail: bpitschel@sfbotanicalgarden.org
URL: http://www.sfbotanicalgarden.org/library/index.html
Contact: Brandy Kuhl, Librarian
Scope: Horticulture, plant propagation, landscape gardening, flora of Mediterranean climates, plant hunting, history of gardening, children and gardens, ethnobotany, botanical illustration, garden design, biology. **Services:** Copying; slide duplication; Library open to the public. **Founded:** 1972. **Holdings:** 27,000 books, including 300 rare volumes; 2500 bound periodical volumes; 1 shelf of William Hammond Hall Archives; 3000 slide transparencies of plants (accessible through online catalog); 26 VF drawers of brochures and pamphlets; 3000 old and current nursery catalogs. **Subscriptions:** 450 journals and other serials. **Telecommunication Services:** library@sfbotanicalgarden.org.

9873 ■ Santa Barbara Botanic Garden - Blaksley Library
1212 Mission Canyon Rd.
Santa Barbara, CA 93105
Ph: (805)682-4726, x-107
Fax: (805)563-0352
Co. E-mail: jariel@sbbg.org
URL: http://www.sbbg.org/index.cfm?fuseaction=collections.library
Contact: Joan Ariel, Director, Library Services
Scope: Botany; floras of Western North America and Mediterranean climates; California horticulture; California offshore islands; cactus and succulents. **Services:** Copying; library open to the public by appointment. **Founded:** 1942. **Holdings:** 15,000 books; 2800 bound volumes; 700 maps; 20,000 plant images. **Subscriptions:** 200 journals and other serials. **Telecommunication Services:** info@sbbg.org.

9874 ■ State Botanical Garden of Georgia Library
Callaway Bldg.
University of Georgia
2450 S. Milledge Ave.
Athens, GA 30605
Ph: (706)542-1244
Co. E-mail: garden@uga.edu
URL: http://www.botgarden.uga.edu
Scope: Plants, gardening, horticulture, botany, conservation, ethnobotany, landscape design, floral crafts. **Services:** Library open to the public for reference use only. **Founded:** 1975. **Holdings:** 2000 books; 85 videotapes; CD-ROMs; archives; manuscripts. **Subscriptions:** 14 journals and other serials.

9875 ■ Texas Discovery Gardens Horticulture Library
3601 Martin Luther King Jr. Blvd.
Dallas, TX 75210
Ph: (214)428-7476
Fax: (214)428-5338
Co. E-mail: tdg@texasdiscoverygardens.org
URL: http://texasdiscoverygardens.org
Contact: Melissa Martin, Executive Director
Scope: General horticulture. **Services:** Library accessible on a restricted basis only. **Founded:** 1941. **Holdings:** 1000 bound periodical volumes. **Subscriptions:** 4 journals and other serials. **Telecommunication Services:** mmartin@texasdiscoverygardens.org.

9876 ■ U.S. National Arboretum Library
3501 New York Ave., NE
Washington, DC 20002-1958
Ph: (202)245-2726
Fax: (202)245-4575
Co. E-mail: everlyr@ars.usda.gov
URL: http://www.usna.usda.gov/
Contact: Robin Everly, Librarian
Scope: Botany, taxonomy, floristics, horticulture, gardening, plant genetics and breeding. **Services:** Interlibrary loan (through National Agricultural Library only); Library open to the public by appointment for onsite research only. **Founded:** 1966. **Holdings:** 10,000 books; 500 periodical titles. **Subscriptions:** 165 journals and other serials.

9877 ■ University of Alberta - Devonian Botanic Garden Library
Edmonton, AB, Canada T6G 2E1
Ph: (770)987-3054, x2240
Fax: (780)987-4141
Co. E-mail: rbelland@ualberta.ca
URL: http://www.devonian.ualberta.ca
Contact: Rene Belland, Curator
Scope: Horticulture, botany, gardening, landscape design, natural history, plant diversity, conservation. **Services:** Library open to the public with restrictions. **Founded:** 1971. **Holdings:** 1000 books; reports; manuscripts; archives. **Subscriptions:** 6 journals and other serials.

9878 ■ University of California, Berkeley - Botanical Garden - Myrtle R. Wolf Botanical & Horticultural Library
200 Centennial Dr., No. 5045
Berkeley, CA 94720-5045
Ph: (510)643-8040
Fax: (510)642-5045
Co. E-mail: hforbes@berkeley.edu
URL: http://botanicalgarden.berkeley.edu/
Contact: Holly Forbes, Curator
Scope: Horticulture, floras, plant taxonomy, botanical gardens. **Services:** Library open to the public for reference use only. **Founded:** 1890. **Holdings:** 3000 books; 30 feet of other cataloged items. **Subscriptions:** 20 journals and other serials.

9879 ■ University of California, Davis - Arboretum Library
1 Shield Ave.
Davis, CA 95616
Ph: (530)752-4880

Fax: (530)752-5796
Co. E-mail: arboretum@ucdavis.edu
URL: http://arboretum.ucdavis.edu
Contact: Mia Ingolia, Curator

Scope: Botany, horticulture, gardening, ecology. **Services:** Library open to the public for reference use only. **Founded:** 1975. **Holdings:** 1500 books; 86 bound periodical volumes; unbound periodicals; vertical files. **Subscriptions:** 14 journals and other serials.

9880 ■ University of Michigan - Matthaei Botanical Gardens Library
1800 N. Dixboro Rd.
Ann Arbor, MI 48105-9406
Ph: (734)763-0645
Fax: (734)998-6205
Co. E-mail: bgrese@umich.edu
URL: http://www.lsa.umich.edu/mbg
Contact: Robert Grese, Director

URL(s): library.mbgna.umich.edu. **Scope:** Botany, horticulture, natural history of plants, ecology of plants. **Services:** Library not open to the public. **Holdings:** 2500 books. **Subscriptions:** 7 journals and other serials.

9881 ■ University of Minnesota - Minnesota Landscape Arboretum - Andersen Horticultural Library
Leon C. Snyder Bldg., Main Fl.
3675 Arboretum Dr.
Chaska, MN 55318-9613
Ph: (952)443-1405
Fax: (612)443-2521
Co. E-mail: hortlib@umn.edu
URL: http://www.arboretum.umn.edu/library.aspx
Contact: Katherine Allen, Librarian

Scope: Horticulture, botany, natural sciences, landscape architecture. **Services:** Collection is noncirculating; Library open to the public. **Founded:** 1973. **Holdings:** 100,000 volumes; 12 AV programs; 9 feet of manuscripts; 1388 microforms; 350 periodicals. **Subscriptions:** 300 journals and other serials.

9882 ■ University of Pennsylvania - Morris Arboretum Library
100 E. Northwestern Ave.
Philadelphia, PA 19118
Ph: (215)247-5777

Fax: (215)248-4439
Co. E-mail: info@morrisarboretum.org
URL: http://www.business-services.upenn.edu/
  arboretum/
Contact: Timothy Block, Director

Scope: Ornamental horticulture, garden history (especially Victorian period), floristic botany, urban forestry and silviculture, plant exploration. **Services:** Interlibrary loan; copying; reference services; library open to the public. **Founded:** 1932. **Holdings:** 4000 books; 2000 bound periodical volumes. **Subscriptions:** 100 journals and other serials.

9883 ■ University of Washington Botanic Gardens - Elisabeth C. Miller Horticulture Library
3501 NE 41 St.
Box 354115
Seattle, WA 98105-5699
Ph: (206)543-0415
Fax: (206)897-1435
Co. E-mail: mferg@uw.edu
URL: http://depts.washington.edu/hortlib/index.shtml
Contact: Martha Ferguson, Specialist

Scope: Horticulture, gardening, urban forestry, botanical gardens. **Services:** Copying; library open to the public. **Founded:** 1985. **Holdings:** 15000 books; 1000 bound periodical volumes; archives. **Subscriptions:** 300 serials. **Telecommunication Services:** uwbg@uw.edu; hortlib@uw.edu.

9884 ■ Worcester County Horticultural Society Library
11 French Dr.
Boylston, MA 01505-0598
Ph: (508)869-6111, x-116
Fax: (508)869-0314
Co. E-mail: librarian@towerhillbg.org
URL: http://www.towerhillbg.org
Contact: Kathy Bell, Librarian

Scope: Agriculture, botany, conservation, gardening, fruit culture, general horticulture, landscape design. **Services:** Copying; library open to the public for reference use only. **Founded:** 1842. **Holdings:** 8000 books; 1000 bound periodical volumes; 200 seed, tool, plant, and equipment catalogs; 14,500 slides. **Subscriptions:** 22 journals and other serials; 40 newsletters.

RESEARCH CENTERS

9885 ■ Auburn University - Alabama Agricultural Experiment Station - Ornamental

Horticulture Research Center
411 N McGregor Ave.
Mobile, AL 36689
Ph: (251)342-2366
Fax: (251)342-1022
Co. E-mail: olivejw@auburn.edu
URL: http://www.aaes.auburn.edu/researchcenters/
  ohrc
Contact: John W. Olive, Director
Founded: 1952. **Educational Activities:** Horticulture Field Day (Semiannual).

9886 ■ Horticultural Research Institute (HRI)
1200 G St. NW, Ste. 800
Washington, DC 20005
Ph: (202)789-2900
Fax: (888)761-7883
Co. E-mail: tjodon@hriresearch.org
URL: http://www.hriresearch.org
Contact: William D. Wells, Jr., President

Description: Nursery firms; nursery supply companies; state and regional nurserymen's associations. Conducts nursery industry research in areas of management, marketing, production, integrated pest management, water use, and a continuing study of the industry scope. Administered by the staff of the American Nursery and Landscape Association. **Founded:** 1962. **Publications:** New Horizons; Peer-Reviewed Journal of Environmental Horticulture (Quarterly); New Horizons (Semiannual); Journal of Environmental Horticulture (Quarterly); New Horizons. **Educational Activities:** Horticultural Research Institute Convention (Annual). **Awards:** HRI Research Grants (Annual); Carville M. Akehurst Memorial Scholarship (Annual); Spring Meadow Nursery Scholarship; Usrey Family Scholarship; Timothy Bigelow and Palmer W. Bigelow, Jr. Scholarship. **Telecommunication Services:** tjodon@anla.org; mteffeau@anla.org.

9887 ■ Ohio State University - Agricultural Technical Institute (ATI)
1328 Dover Rd.
Wooster, OH 44691-4000
Ph: (330)287-1331
Free: 800-647-8283
Fax: (330)262-7634
Co. E-mail: nameth.2@osu.edu
URL: http://ati.osu.edu
Contact: Prof. Stephen Nameth, Director
Services: Telephone reference service. **Founded:** 1972. **Educational Activities:** Continuous education and distance learning. **Telecommunication Services:** ati@osu.edu.

ASSOCIATIONS AND OTHER ORGANIZATIONS

9888 ■ **Souvenir Wholesale Distributors Association (SWDA)**
2105 Laurel Bush Rd., Ste. 200
Bel Air, MD 21015
Ph: (443)640-1055
Fax: (443)640-1086
Co. E-mail: marci@kingmgmt.org
URL: http://www.souvenircentral.org
Contact: Marci L. Hickey, Executive Vice President
URL(s): www.postcardcentral.org. **Description:** Represents distributors and manufacturers of post cards, souvenirs, and novelty items. **Founded:** 1973. **Educational Activities:** PCSDA Annual Convention and Trade Show (Annual). **Awards:** Distributor of the Year (Annual); Industry Awards (Annual); Printer of the Year (Annual); Souvenir Supplier of the Year (Annual); Distributor of the Year; Postcard Awards; Printer of the Year; Souvenir Awards.

REFERENCE WORKS

9889 ■ *"Award Win Highlights Slingsby's Green Credentials" in Ecology,Environment & Conservation Business (August 20, 2011, pp. 3)*
Pub: HighBeam Research
Description: Slingsby, an industrial and commercial equipment supplier, was joint winner with Hallmark Cards of the Baildon Business in the Community's Yorkshire and Humber Long Term Environmental Improvement Award. The firm cites its commitment to reducing environmental impact.

9890 ■ *Greeting Card Industry Directory*
Pub: Greeting Card Association
URL(s): www.greetingcard.org/publications.php. **Released:** Biennial; Latest edition 13th. **Price:** $75, Members; $150, Nonmembers plus shipping & handling charges. **Covers:** Over 3,000 greeting card publishers and suppliers in the United State and many foreign countries. **Entries include:** Company name, address, phone, e-mail, Internet, toll-free, fax numbers, key personnel, licensed properties, plant locations, description of products & services, distribu-tion outlets and methods, geographic area covered, industry background, and related information. **Arrangement:** Alphabetical. **Indexes:** Product, geographical, brand name.

9891 ■ *"Halls Give Hospital Drive $11 Million Infusion" in The Business Journal-Serving Metropolitan Kansas City (Vol. 26, July 18, 2008)*
Pub: American City Business Journals, Inc.
Ed: Rob Roberts. **Description:** Don Hall, chairman of Hallmark Cards Inc., and eight family members have announced that they will give $11 million to Children's Mercy Hospitals and Clinics for its $800 million expansion plan. Hall Family Foundation president Bill Hall that contributions such as that for Children's Mercy reflect the charitable interests of the foundation's board and founders. The possible impacts of the Hall's donation are analyzed.

9892 ■ *"Search and Discover New Opportunities" in DM News (Vol. 31, December 14, 2009, No. 29, pp. 13)*
Pub: Haymarket Media, Inc.
Ed: Chantal Tode. **Description:** Although other digital strategies are gaining traction in Internet marketing, search marketing continues to dominate this advertising forum. Companies like American Greetings, which markets e-card brands online, are utilizing social networking sites and affiliates to generate a higher demand for their products.

STATISTICAL SOURCES

9893 ■ *Greeting Cards - US*
Pub: MarketResearch.com
Released: 2008. **Price:** $3995.00. **Description:** The U.S. greeting card industry remains a mature and stable market with sales growth of 8.7% between 1999 and 2004.

TRADE SHOWS AND CONVENTIONS

9894 ■ **National Stationery Show**
Greeting Card Association
1133 Westchester Ave., Ste. N136
White Plains, NY 10604-3547
Ph: (914)421-3331
Fax: (914)948-1484
Co. E-mail: info@greetingcard.org
URL: http://www.greetingcard.org
Contact: Jack Withiam, Executive Vice President
E-mail: jwithiam@gcamail.org
URL(s): www.nationalstationeryshow.com. **Frequency:** Annual. **Audience:** Retail buyers, including: representatives from specialty, department, chain, independent retail, catalog publishers, card and gift shops. **Principal Exhibits:** Greeting cards, social stationery, and related products such as calendars, desk accessories, small leather goods, photo frames, party goods, home office products, prints and posters, postcards, note paper, games, toys, balloons, and wedding, back-to-school, and holiday supplies. **Dates and Locations:** , Jacob K. Javits Convention Center.

LIBRARIES

9895 ■ **American Life Foundation - Prang-Mark Society - Library**
1601 Sheridan Ln.
Norristown, PA 19403-3336
Ph: (610)539-3010
Contact: John Crosby Freeman, Coordinator
Scope: Printing, early greeting cards, tradecards. **Services:** Library open to the public by appointment only (June 1 through September 1). **Holdings:** 7000 books.

9896 ■ **Hallmark Cards, Inc. - Creative Research Library**
2501 McGee, No. 146
Kansas City, MO 64108
Ph: (816)274-5525
Free: 800-425-5627
Fax: (816)274-7245
Co. E-mail: hallmarkplus@hallmark.com
URL: http://www.hallmark.com
Contact: Mark Spencer, Manager
Scope: Fine art, lettering, advertising, graphic art, design, illustration, photography. **Services:** Library open to Hallmark employees only. **Founded:** 1930. **Holdings:** 18,000 books; 60 bound periodical volumes. **Subscriptions:** 150 journals and other serials; 3 newspapers.

START-UP INFORMATION

9897 ■ *"Local Flavor" in Entrepreneur (Vol. 35, November 2007, No. 11, pp. 110)*
Pub: Entrepreneur Media Inc.
Ed: Nichole L. Torres. **Description:** Local food products are growing in the market today as consumers are becoming interested in where their food comes; you can start a business by investigating the kinds of foods popular in your region.

ASSOCIATIONS AND OTHER ORGANIZATIONS

9898 ■ **Canadian Federation of Independent Grocers (CFIG)—Federation Canadienne des Epiciers Independants**
2235 Sheppard Ave. E, Ste. 902
Willowdale, ON, Canada M2J 5B5
Ph: (416)492-2311
Free: 800-661-2344
Fax: (416)492-2347
Co. E-mail: info@cfig.ca
URL: http://www.cfig.ca
Contact: John F.T. Scott, President
Description: Independent retail grocers. Promotes growth and development of members' businesses. Represents the commercial and regulatory interests of independent grocers; conducts promotional activities. **Founded:** 1962. **Awards:** Canadian Master Merchandiser Awards (Annual); Canadian Master Merchandiser Awards.

9899 ■ **Food Industry Association Executives (FIAE)**
5657 W 10770 N
Highland, UT 84003
Ph: (801)599-1095
Fax: (815)550-1731
Co. E-mail: jolsen@fiae.net
URL: http://www.fiae.net
Contact: Joe Williams, Chairman
Description: Professional executives of local, state, and national retail grocers associations. **Founded:** 1927.

9900 ■ **Food Institute (FI)**
10 Mountainview Rd., Ste. S125
Upper Saddle River, NJ 07458
Ph: (201)791-5570
Free: 800-966-5225
Fax: (201)791-5222
Co. E-mail: questions@foodinstitute.com
URL: http://www.foodinstitute.com
Contact: Brian Todd, President
E-mail: bTodd@foodinstitute.com
Description: Growers, food processors, importers, exporters, brokers, wholesalers, supermarket chains, independent retailers, food industry suppliers, food service distributors, advertising and banking executives, and government officials. Strives to provide food industry-related information to its members. **Scope:** food industry. **Founded:** 1928. **Publications:** *Food Institute Report* (Weekly); *OSHA Manual*; *Regu-*

latory Directory (Periodic); *Today in Food*; *Food Business Mergers & Acquisitions* (Annual); *The Food Institute Report* (Weekly); *Food Institute Report* (Weekly); *The Food Institute Report*; *Almanac of the Canning, Freezing, Preserving Industries* (Annual); *The Food Institute Report*; *Get It Out, Get It Right, Get It Over! Avoiding Food Product Recalls*; *2008 Edition of Food Business Mergers and Acquisitions* (Annual). **Telecommunication Services:** info@foodinstitute.com; memberservices@foodinstitute.com; ads@foodinstitute.com; foodl@foodinstitute.com.

9901 ■ **Food Marketing Institute (FMI)**
2345 Crystal Dr.Ste. 800
Arlington, VA 22202
Ph: (202)452-8444
Fax: (202)429-4519
Co. E-mail: fmi@fmi.org
URL: http://www.fmi.org
Contact: Leslie G. Sarasin, President
Description: Grocery retailers and wholesalers. Maintains liaison with government and consumers. Conducts 30 educational conferences and seminars per year. Conducts research programs; compiles statistics. **Founded:** 1977. **Publications:** *Facts About Supermarket Development* (Annual); *Food Marketing Industry Speaks* (Annual); *FMI Annual Financial Review*; *Food Retailing Industry Speaks*; *Operating Results of Independent Supermarkets*; *Advantage* (Monthly); *FMI Newsletter*; *Food Storage Information*; *FMI News: Aisle by Aisle* (Monthly); *Information Systems Directory* (Biennial). **Educational Activities:** Trade workshops and seminars, about thirty per year; FMI Annual Convention; GEO India (Biennial); MARKETECHNICS (Annual); Productivity Convention & Expo; Supermarket Industry Convention and Educational Exposition (Annual). **Awards:** William H. Albers Industry Relations Award; Esther Peterson Consumer Service Award; Sidney R. Rabb Award.

9902 ■ **Grocery Manufacturers Association (GMA)**
1305 I St. NW, Ste. 300
Washington, DC 20005
Ph: (202)639-5900
Fax: (202)639-5932
Co. E-mail: info@gmaonline.org
URL: http://www.gmaonline.org
Contact: Mr. Gary M. Rodkin, Chairman
Description: Global manufacturers of food and nonfood products sold in the United States. **Founded:** 1908. **Publications:** *GMA Executive Update* (Weekly); *GMA State Legislative Report* (Weekly); *GMA Washington Report* (Monthly). **Educational Activities:** Executive Conference (Annual).

9903 ■ **International Council of Grocery Manufacturer Associations (ICGMA)**
1350 I St. NW, Ste. 300
Washington, DC 20005
Ph: (202)639-5900
Fax: (202)637-0958
Co. E-mail: info@icgma.com
URL: http://www.icgma.com
Contact: Pam Bailey, President
Description: Grocery manufacturers' associations of Australia, Austria, Belgium, Brazil, Canada, Denmark,

France, Germany, Italy, Japan, Mexico, New Zealand, South Africa, Switzerland, the United Kingdom, the United States, and Venezuela. Promotes high standards in the manufacture and distribution of grocery products. Coordinates activities of grocery manufacturers worldwide. **Founded:** 1982.

9904 ■ **National Frozen and Refrigerated Foods Association (NFRA)**
PO Box 6069
Harrisburg, PA 17112
Ph: (717)657-8601
Fax: (717)657-9862
Co. E-mail: info@nfraweb.org
URL: http://www.nfraweb.org
Contact: John Larsen, Chairman
Description: Comprised of over 400 member companies representing all segments of the frozen and refrigerated dairy foods industry. Promotes the sales and consumption of frozen and refrigerated foods through education, training, research, sales planning and menu development and provides a forum for industry dialogue. Sponsors National Frozen Food Month, in March; June Dairy Month; June and July Ice Cream and Novelties Promotion; Frozen and Refrigerated Foods Festival, in October; and Bring Us To Your Table! Freezer Favorites. **Founded:** 1945. **Publications:** *NFRA Update* (Monthly); *Year End Report* (Annual); *Frozen Food Book of Knowledge*. **Educational Activities:** Retail Executive Conference (Annual). **Awards:** Golden Penguin Award (Annual); Golden Penguin Awards.

9905 ■ **National Grocers Association (NGA)**
1005 N Glebe Rd., Ste. 250
Arlington, VA 22201-5758
Ph: (703)516-0700
Fax: (703)812-1821
Co. E-mail: info@nationalgrocers.org
URL: http://www.nationalgrocers.org
Contact: Thomas K. Zaucha, President
Description: Independent food retailers; wholesale food distributors servicing 29,000 food stores. Promotes industry interests and works to advance understanding, trade and cooperation among all sectors of the food industry. Represents members' interests before the government. Aids in the development of programs designed to improve the productivity and efficiency of the food distribution industry. Offers services in areas such as store planning and engineering, personnel selection and training, operations and advertising. Sponsors seminars and in-house training. Maintains liaison with Women Grocers of America, which serves as an advisory arm. **Founded:** 1980. **Publications:** *Congressional or Regulatory Update* (Periodic). **Educational Activities:** Supermarket Synergy Showcase (Annual); NGA Show (Annual); America's Supermarket Showcase (Annual). **Awards:** Clarence G. Adamy Great American Award; Spirit of America Award. **Telecommunication Services:** feedback@nationalgrocers.org.

9906 ■ **Women Grocers of America (WGA)**
1005 N Glebe Rd., Ste. 250
Arlington, VA 22201-5758

Ph: (703)516-0700
Fax: (703)516-0115
Co. E-mail: kcomley@nationalgrocers.org
URL: http://www.nationalgrocers.org/WGA/WGA.html
Contact: Joseph Sheridan, Chairman
Description: Serves as an information and advisory arm to the National Grocers Association. Supports and encourages the education of students pursuing grocery industry-related careers in the independent segment of the industry through its scholarship program. Encourages all segments of the food industry to promote breast cancer awareness and prevention. Participates in and supports the programs offered by the National Grocers Association. **Founded:** 1983. **Awards:** Mary Macey Scholarship (Annual); Woman of the Year (Annual).

DIRECTORIES OF EDUCATIONAL PROGRAMS

9907 ■ *Major Food & Drink Companies of the World*
Pub: Graham & Whiteside
URL(s): www.gale.cengage.com. **Ed:** Heather Brewin, Sandra James, Helen Porter, Chris Tapster. **Released:** Annual; Latest edition 16th; Published May, 2012. **Price:** $1460, Individuals. **Covers:** Over 9,200 worldwide companies involved in the food and drink industry. **Entries include:** Company name, address, phone and names and titles of key personnel. **Availability:** Online: Cengage Learning Inc. **Type:** Directory.

REFERENCE WORKS

9908 ■ *"AdvacePierre Heats Up" in Business Courier (Vol. 27, October 29, 2010, No. 26, pp. 1)*
Pub: Business Courier
Ed: John Newberry. **Description:** Bill Toler, chief executive officer of AdvancePierre Foods, is aiming for more growth and more jobs. The company was formed after the merger of Pierre Foods with two Oklahoma-based food processing companies. Toler wants to expand production and is set to start adding employees in the next 6-12 months.

9909 ■ *"Bagging Profits; High-End Grocers Expand Despite Stale Economy" in Crain's Detroit Business (Vol. 24, March 24, 2008, No. 12, pp. 1)*
Pub: Crain Communications, Inc.
Ed: Nancy Kaffer. **Description:** Discusses the expansion plans of several high-end grocery stores in the Detroit area and the reasons why, despite the poor economy, these gourmet grocers are doing well. Statistical data included.

9910 ■ *"Baking Up Bigger Lance" in Charlotte Business Journal (Vol. 25, December 3, 2010, No. 37, pp. 1)*
Pub: Charlotte Business Journal
Ed: Ken Elkins. **Description:** Events that led to the merger between Charlotte, North Carolina-based snack food manufacturer Lance Inc. and Pennsylvania-based pretzel maker Snyder's of Hanover Inc. are discussed. The merger is expected to help Lance in posting a 70 percent increase in revenue, which reached $900 million in 2009. How the merger would affect Snyder's of Hanover is also described.

9911 ■ *"Bankruptcies" in Crain's Detroit Business (Vol. 24, October 6, 2008, No. 40, pp. 26)*
Pub: Crain Communications, Inc.
Description: Current businesses that have filed for Chapter 7 or 11 protection in U.S. Bankruptcy Court include an auto dealership, a gun range and a grocery service.

9912 ■ *"Battered Loblaw Makes Deep Job Cuts" in Globe & Mail (January 23, 2007)*
Pub: CTVglobemedia Publishing Inc.
Description: Loblaw Companies Ltd., supermarket giant, is eliminating up to 1,000 administrative jobs and shifting more buying responsibilities to its suppliers. The grocer will also introduce a national inventory strategy called 'category management'.

9913 ■ *"Beer Sales 'Foament' a Dispute" in Philadelphia Business Journal (Vol. 28, October 9, 2009, No. 34, pp. 1)*
Pub: American City Business Journals
Ed: Peter van Allen. **Description:** Malt Beverages Distributors Association of Pennsylvania filed a case against the Liquor Control Board (LCB) at the Pennsylvania Supreme Court in order to further restrict store sales. The dispute stems from the supermarket chains circumventing the liquor law with the blessings of LCB.

9914 ■ *"Bertha's Birth Stirs Juice" in Barron's (Vol. 88, July 14, 2008, No. 28, pp. M11)*
Pub: Dow Jones & Co., Inc.
Ed: Tom Sellen. **Description:** Price of frozen concentrated orange juice, which has risen to four-month highs of $1.3620 in July 2008 is due, in part, to the hurricane season that has come earlier than normal in the far eastern Atlantic thereby possibly harming the 2008-2009 Florida orange crop. Future tropical-storm development will affect the prices of this commodity.

9915 ■ *"Better Made's Better Idea: Diversify Despite Rising Costs" in Crain's Detroit Business (Vol. 24, September 22, 2008, No. 38, pp. 18)*
Pub: Crain Communications Inc.
Ed: Nathan Skid. **Description:** Better Made Snack Foods Inc. is planning to expand its product lines and market reach as well as boost manufacturing capability during a time in which the company is being buffeted by rising commodity and fuel costs. The company feels that diversification is the key to maintain sales and growth.

9916 ■ *"Businessman Legend Passes: Charles H. James II Credited With Transforming Family Business" in Black Enterprise (December 2007)*
Pub: Earl G. Graves Publishing Co. Inc.
Ed: Tara C. Walker. **Description:** Profile of Charles H. James II, president and chairman of The James Corporation, a family-owned multigenerational food distribution company that started as a produce firm.

9917 ■ *"Cheese Spread Whips Up a Brand New Bowl" in Brandweek (Vol. 49, April 21, 2008, No. 16, pp. 17)*
Pub: VNU Business Media, Inc.
Ed: Mike Beirne. **Description:** Mrs. Kinser's Pimento Cheese Spread is launching a new container for its product in order to attempt stronger brand marketing with a better bowl in order to win over the heads of households as young as in their 30s. The company also intends to begin distribution in Texas and the West Coast. Mrs. Kinser's is hoping that the new packaging will provide a more distinct branding and will help consumers distinguish what flavor they are buying.

9918 ■ *"Coca-Cola Bottler Up for Sale: CEO J. Bruce Llewellyn Seeks Retirement" in Black Enterprise (Vol. 37, December 2006, No. 5, pp. 31)*
Pub: Earl G. Graves Publishing Co. Inc.
Ed: Marcia A. Wade. **Description:** J. Bruce Llewellyn of Brucephil Inc., the parent company of the Philadelphia Coca-Cola Bottling Co. has agreed to sell its remaining shares to Coca-Cola Co., which previously owned 31 percent of Philly Coke. Analysts believe that Coca-Cola will eventually sell its shares to another bottler.

9919 ■ *"Condensed Capitalism" in Human Resource Management (Vol. 49, September-October 2010, No. 5, pp. 965-968)*
Pub: John Wiley
Ed: Matthew M. Bodah. **Description:** Review of the book, 'Condensed Capitalism: Campbell Soup and the Pursuit of Cheap Production in the Twentieth Century'.

9920 ■ *Directory of Foodservice Distributors*
Pub: Chain Store Guide
Contact: Lisa Patterson, President
URL(s): www.chainstoreguide.com. **Released:** Annual; Latest edition 2012. **Price:** $425, Individuals Directory; $495, Individuals online lite; $1175,

Individuals online pro; $1475, Individuals online pro plus. **Covers:** About 4,700 companies in the United States and Canada with at least $500,000 in sales to foodservice companies. Included companies must distribute more than one product line and obtain no more than 95% of its total sales volume from self-manufactured merchandise. **Entries include:** Company name, address, phone and fax numbers, e-mail and web addresses; Internet order processing indicator and sales percentage; total sales; foodservice and wholesale sales; product lines; total units served; foodservice accounts served; trading areas; distribution center locations; markets served; buying/marketing group name and location; subsidiaries names and locations; divisional, regional and branch office locations; year founded; public company indicator; key personnel with titles; 21,700 foodservice distribution contacts; 9,642 Name, address, phone, fax. **Arrangement:** Geographical. **Indexes:** Product lines, alphabetical, exclusions.

9921 ■ *Directory of Supermarket, Grocery & Convenience Store Chains*
Pub: Chain Store Guide
Contact: Lisa Patterson, President
URL(s): www.chainstoreguide.com. **Released:** Annual; Latest edition 2011. **Price:** $425, Individuals Directory; $495, Individuals Online lite; $1175, Individuals Online pro; $1475, Individuals online pro plus. **Covers:** Over 3,269 supermarket, grocery, and convenience store chains operating 71,000 stores in the United States and Canada. **Entries include:** For supermarkets/groceries--company name, address, phone, fax, e-mail and web address; total annual sales; grocery sales; Internet order processing indicator; total units; number of units by type; number of units by trade name; number of units franchised to and from; total selling square feet; prototype sizes; average number of checkouts; projected number of units by specialty department; primary wholesaler type, name and location; parent company name and location; subsidiary name and location; divisional and branch office locations; warehouse locations; year founded; public company indicator; key personnel with titles. For convenience stores--company name, address, phone and fax numbers, web and e-mail addresses; total annual sales; convenience store sales; gasoline sales percentage; Internet order processing indicator; total units; number of units by trade name; number of units franchised to and from; total selling square footage; prototype sizes; average number of checkouts; projected number of openings and remodeling; packaged liquor indicators; trading areas; distribution center locations; number of units by specialty department; primary wholesaler type, name and location; parent company, subsidiary, warehouse, divisional and branch office names and locations; year founded; public company indicator; key personnel with titles. **Arrangement:** Geographical with sections for supermarkets and convenience stores. **Indexes:** Top 200 chains, trading area, alphabetical, exclusions.

9922 ■ *"Eagle's Wine Kiosk Is Area's 1st" in Pittsburgh Post-Gazette (October 28, 2010)*
Pub: Pittsburgh-Post Gazette
Ed: Bob Batz Jr. **Description:** Giant Eagle Market District store at Settlers Ridge opened the first self-serve wine kiosk in Western Pennsylvania. The kiosk will have a built-in breathalyzer panel to ensure safety.

9923 ■ *"Egg Fight: The Yolk's on the Short" in Barron's (Vol. 88, July 7, 2008, No. 27, pp. 20)*
Pub: Dow Jones & Co., Inc.
Ed: Christopher C. Williams. **Description:** Shares of Cal-Maine Foods, the largest egg producer and distributor in the US, are due for a huge rise because of the increase in egg prices. Short sellers, however, continue betting that the stock, priced at $31.84 each, will eventually go down.

9924 ■ *"The End of the Line for Line Extensions?" in Advertising Age (Vol. 79, July 7, 2008, No. 26, pp. 3)*
Pub: Crain Communications, Inc.
Description: After years of double-digit growth, some of the most heavily extended personal-care products have slowed substantially or even declined in the

U.S. Unilever's Dove and P&G's Pantene and Olay are two such brands that have been affected. Statistical data included.

9925 ■ *Ethnic Solidarity for Economic Survival: Korean Greengrocers in New York City*
Pub: Russell Sage Foundation Publications
Ed: Pyong Gap Min. **Released:** August 2008. **Price:** $32.50. **Description:** Investigations into the entrepreneurial traditions of Korean immigrant families in New York City running ethnic businesses, particularly small grocery stores and produce markets. Social, cultural and economic issues facing these retailers are discussed.

9926 ■ *"Fast Fact: Quality of Foods, Cost Top Factors in Determining Where to Grocery Shop" in Marketing to Women (Vol. 22, August 2009)*
Pub: EPM Communications Inc.
Contact: Ira Mayer, President
E-mail: imayer@epmcom.com
Description: Efficient check-outs, customer service and a wide variety of products were all less important to female shoppers than the quality of food and value, which were seen as the ultimate factors in a woman's decision as to which grocery store they decide to frequent.

9927 ■ *"Floral-Design Kiosk Business in Colorado Springs Blossoming" in Colorado Springs Business Journal (September 24, 2010)*
Pub: Dolan Media Newswires
Ed: Monica Mendoza. **Description:** Profile of Shellie Greto and her mother Jackie Martin who started a wholesale flower business in their garage. The do-it-yourself floral arrangement firm started a kiosk business in supermarkets called Complete Design.

9928 ■ *"Food Fight" in Canadian Business (Vol. 79, November 6, 2006, No. 22, pp. 18)*
Pub: Rogers Media
Ed: Zena Olijnyk. **Description:** The war between Canadian grocers and Wal-Mart due to its plans for opening new stores is analyzed.

9929 ■ *"Fresh Direct's Crisis" in Crain's New York Business (Vol. 24, January 14, 2008, No. 2, pp. 3)*
Pub: Crain Communications, Inc.
Ed: Lisa Fickenscher. **Description:** Freshdirect, an Internet grocery delivery service, finds itself under siege from federal immigration authorities, customers and labor organizations due to its employment practice of hiring illegals. At stake is the grocer's reputation as well as its ambitious growth plans, including an initial public offering of its stock.

9930 ■ *"Frosted Flakes Goes For Gold" in Marketing to Women (Vol. 21, April 2008, No. 4, pp. 3)*
Pub: EPM Communications Inc.
Contact: Ira Mayer, President
E-mail: imayer@epmcom.com
Description: Kellogg is appealing to health-conscious moms with its new product Frosted Flakes Gold.

9931 ■ *"GM's Decision to Boot Dealer Prompts Sale" in Baltimore Business Journal (Vol. 27, November 6, 2009, No. 26, pp. 1)*
Pub: American City Business Journals
Ed: Daniel J. Sernovitz. **Description:** General Motors Corporation's (GM) decision to strip Baltimore's Anderson Automotive Group Inc. of its GM franchise has prompted the owner, Bruce Mortimer, to close the automotive dealership and sell the land to a developer. The new project could make way for new homes, a shopping center and supermarket.

9932 ■ *"Good Things Happen When We Buy Local" in Crain's Detroit Business (Vol. 24, October 6, 2008, No. 40, pp. 7)*
Pub: Crain Communications, Inc.
Description: Michigan is facing incredibly difficult economic times. One way in which each one of us can help the state and the businesses located here is by purchasing our goods and services from local vendors. The state Agriculture Department projected that if Michigan households earmarked $10 per week in their grocery purchases to made-in-Michigan products, this would generate $30 million a week in economic impact.

9933 ■ *"Green and Clean" in Retail Merchandiser (Vol. 51, July-August 2011, No. 4, pp. 56)*
Pub: Phoenix Media Corporation
Description: Green Valley Grocery partnered with Paragon Solutions consulting firm to make their stores environmentally green.

9934 ■ *"The Harris Teeter Grocery Chain Has Started a New Ice Cream Club for Shoppers" in Ice Cream Reporter (Vol. 21, July 20, 2008)*
Pub: Ice Cream Reporter
Description: Store loyalty cards are being issued to Harris Teeter customers to purchase any variety of Ben & Jerry's, Haagen-Dazs, Dove, Starbucks, Ciao Bella, Clemmy's, Purely Decadent, So Delicious, Harris Teeter Naturals, HT Traders, Hunter Farms or Denali Ice Cream. One point is earned for every dollar spent, 30 total points earns a $5 electronic coupon towards the next purchase.

9935 ■ *"Health Care Leads Sectors Attracting Capital" in Hispanic Business (March 2008, pp. 14-16, 18)*
Pub: Hispanic Business
Ed: Scott Williams. **Description:** U. S. Hispanic healthcare, media, and food were the key industries in the U.S. gaining investors in 2007.

9936 ■ *"Health Care Leads Sectors Attracting Capital" in Hispanic Business (Vol. 30, March 2008, No. 3, pp. 14)*
Pub: Hispanic Business
Ed: Scott Williams. **Description:** Discusses the capital gains of Hispanic-owned companies and other Hispanic leaders in the investment and retail fields in the year 2007. Sectors like health care, media, food and technology saw a healthy flow of capital due to successful mergers, acquisitions and increased private equity investments.

9937 ■ *"High Growth Reported for the Natural Supermarket Pet Department Close-Up" in Canadian Corporate News (October 20, 2008)*
Pub: Comtex News Network Inc.
Description: Leading natural supermarket chains have been outperforming mainstream grocers by carrying natural and organic pet products. Statistical data included.

9938 ■ *"Hometown Value" in Retail Merchandiser (Vol. 51, July-August 2011, No. 4, pp. 50)*
Pub: Phoenix Media Corporation
Ed: Todd Vowell. **Description:** Profile of family-owned Vowell's Marketplace located in Noxapater, Mississippi. The 10-store chain caters to its Southern roots and is run by the third generation of the Vowell family.

9939 ■ *"Hopes Grow for Milk Price Increase From Tesco" in Farmer's Weekly (March 28, 2008, No. 320)*
Pub: Reed Business Information
Contact: Jeff Greisch, President
Description: Farmers will see an increase in the price supermarket Tesco will pay for their milk.

9940 ■ *"Impulse Buys Find Their Way Into Grocery Cart" in Marketing to Women (Vol. 23, November 2010, No. 11, pp. 6)*
Pub: EPM Communications Inc.
Contact: Ira Mayer, President
E-mail: imayer@epmcom.com
Description: Impulse purchases are made by 90 percent of grocery shoppers according to a recent study. The number of items shoppers buy impulsively during a typical trip to the grocery store in 2010 are outlined.

9941 ■ *"In the Wake of Pet-Food Crisis, Iams Sales Plummet Nearly 17 Percent" in Advertising Age (Vol. 78, May 14, 2007, No. 18, pp. 3)*
Pub: Crain Communications, Inc.
Ed: Jack Neff. **Description:** Although the massive U.S. pet-food recall impacted more than 100 brands, Procter & Gamble Co.'s Iams lost more sales and market share than any other industry player. According to Information Resources Inc. data, the brand's sales dropped 16.5 percent in the eight-week period ended April 22. Many analysts feel that the company could have handled the crisis in a better manner.

9942 ■ *"Industry Vet To Spread Glory's Word" in Business First-Columbus (November 9, 2007, pp. A1)*
Pub: American City Business Journals, Inc.
Ed: Dan Eaton. **Description:** Glory Foods, Inc. chose Jacqueline Neal as its new president in October 2007. Neal has eleven years experience in brand management and has worked with food industry leaders such as Mars Inc., Kraft Foods Inc., and Nabisco Holdings Corporation. Neil's plans for the company are presented.

9943 ■ *"J&J Snack Rakes in Sales" in Philadelphia Business Journal (Vol. 28, September 25, 2009, No. 32, pp. 1)*
Pub: American City Business Journals
Ed: Peter van Allen. **Description:** Analysts expect J&J Snack Foods Corporation to boost earnings by 48 percent for fiscal year ending September 2009. Stable commodity prices have benefited the company.

9944 ■ *"Kroger Forges Ahead with Fuel Centers" in Business Courier (Vol. 26, December 25, 2009, No. 35, pp. 1)*
Pub: American City Business Journals, Inc.
Ed: Jon Newberry. **Description:** Cincinnati-based grocery chain Kroger Company plans to construct more fuel centers near supermarkets and food stores despite declining profit margins in gasoline sales. Statistical data included.

9945 ■ *"Kroger Girds for Invasion of U.K. Chain" in Business Courier (Vol. 24, November 2, 2008, No. 29, pp. 1)*
Pub: American City Business Journals, Inc.
Ed: Jon Newberry. **Description:** Tesco PLC will be opening its first Fresh & Easy Neighborhood Markets in Southern California. The company has committed $500 million per year to get a share of the $500 billion US food retailing market and will be opening more stores in quick succession. Tesco's arrival can be difficult for Kroger because Kroger had obtained much of its success by using Tesco's UK model.

9946 ■ *"Lafley Gives Look At His Game Plan" in Business Courier (Vol. 24, March 21, 2008, No. 50, pp. 1)*
Pub: American City Business Journals, Inc.
Ed: Lisa Biank Fasig. **Description:** Overview of A.G. Lafley's book entitled 'The Game-Changer', is presented. Lafley, Procter & Gamble Co.'s chief executive officer, documented his philosophy and strategy in his book. His work also includes Procter & Gamble's hands-on initiatives such as mock-up grocery stores and personal interviews with homeowners.

9947 ■ *"Landlord Puts 7 Tops Locations On Market" in Business First Buffalo (November 16, 2007, pp. 1)*
Pub: American City Business Journals, Inc.
Ed: James Fink. **Description:** New York-based Benesen Capital Partners LLC has put its 388,000-square-foot property up for sale. Seven Tops Grocery Markets have two to nine years remaining on their lease contracts.

9948 ■ *"LCB Puts a Cork in Kiosk Wine Sales" in Times Leader (December 22, 2010)*
Pub: Wilkes-Barre Publishing Company
Ed: Andrew M. Seder. **Description:** The Pennsylvania Liquor Control Board closed down thirty Pronto Wine Kiosks located in supermarkets throughout the state. The Board cited mechanical and technological issues such as products not dispensing.

9949 ■ "Li'l Guy Rolls Up Into Bigger Company" in The Business Journal-Serving Metropolitan Kansas City (Vol. 26, September 12, 2008)
Pub: American City Business Journals, Inc.

Ed: Suzanna Stagemeyer. **Description:** Li'l Guy Foods, a Mexican food company in Kansas City, Missouri, has merged with Tortilla King Inc. Li'l Guy's revenue in 2007 was $3.3 million, while a newspaper report said that Tortilla King's revenue in 2001 was $7.5 million. Growth opportunities for the combined companies and Li'l Guy's testing of the Wichita market are discussed.

9950 ■ "A Local Affair: Decisions for Tops Again Being Made at Amherst HQ" in Business First Buffalo (December 7, 2007, pp. 3)
Pub: American City Business Journals, Inc.

Ed: James Fink. **Description:** Tops Market LLC merged with Morgan Stanley Private Equity and names its new CEO, Frank Curci. The company headquarters moved to its new location in Amherst, New York.

9951 ■ "Lords Should Get Real About Food" in Farmer's Weekly (March 28, 2008, No. 320)
Pub: Reed Business Information
Contact: Jeff Greisch, President

Description: Discusses the reasons why farming needs subsidies and suggests that the House of Lords should look at the way that grocery stores are operating.

9952 ■ "Market Share" in Business Journal-Milwaukee (Vol. 28, December 3, 2010, No. 9, pp. A1)
Pub: Milwaukee Business Journal

Ed: Stacy Vogel Davis. **Description:** Roundy's Supermarkets' market share has decreased with the expansion of low-price grocery chains in Milwaukee, Wisconsin. Wal-Mart stores Inc., Aldi Inc., and Target Corporation have all opened new stores in the area.

9953 ■ "Marketer Bets Big on U.S.'s Growing Canine Obsession" in Advertising Age (Vol. 79, April 14, 2008, No. 15, pp. 14)
Pub: Crain Communications, Inc.

Ed: Emily Bryson York. **Description:** Overview of FreshPet, a New Jersey company that began marketing two brands of refrigerated dog food-Deli Fresh and FreshPet Select-which are made from fresh ingredients such as beef, rice and carrots. The company projects continued success due to the amount of money consumers spend on their pets as well as fears derived from the 2007 recalls that inspired consumers to look for smaller, independent manufacturers that are less likely to source ingredients from China.

9954 ■ "Moms Give More Thought to Nutrition" in Marketing to Women (Vol. 21, February 2008, No. 2, pp. 8)
Pub: EPM Communications Inc.
Contact: Ira Mayer, President
E-mail: imayer@epmcom.com

Description: Moms are thinking more about nutritional issues than they did in the past and spending more time reading labels in the grocery store. 74 percent of moms consider the nutritional content of foods purchased for their children more now than they did two years ago.

9955 ■ "Moms Rely on Coupons, Specials to Lower Grocery Bills" in Marketing to Women (Vol. 23, November 2010, No. 11, pp. 8)
Pub: EPM Communications Inc.
Contact: Ira Mayer, President
E-mail: imayer@epmcom.com

Description: Eighty-four percent of moms surveyed reported using coupons when grocery shopping in order to lower costs. They are also purchasing less snack foods, fewer brand name items, alcoholic beverages, organic items, meat and fresh fruits and vegetables.

9956 ■ National Frozen and Refrigerated Foods Association--Membership Directory
Pub: National Frozen & Refrigerated Foods Association Inc.
Contact: H. V. Shaw, Jr., President
URL(s): www.nfraweb.org. **Released:** Annual; Latest edition 2009. **Price:** $25. **Covers:** 800 member companies worldwide, including distributors, manufacturers, sales agents, logistics providers, suppliers, retailers, and food service operators. **Entries include:** Company name, address, phone, names of executives, products or services, trade and brand names. **Arrangement:** Geographical within membership category; supplier members and manufacturer members listed in product classifications. **Indexes:** Company name.

9957 ■ "Need Fiber in Your Diet? Pour Some Milk" in Globe & Mail (April 10, 2007, pp. B7)
Pub: CTVglobemedia Publishing Inc.

Ed: William Illsey Atkinson. **Description:** The growing market and demand for functional foods and neutraceuticals in Canada is discussed. The research being conducted by University of Manitoba's Richardson Centre for Functional Foods and Nutraceuticals to explore new health compounds in food is highlighted.

9958 ■ "Need Grub? Start Texting at Kroger" in Business Courier (Vol. 24, December 21, 2008, No. 36, pp. 1)
Pub: American City Business Journals, Inc.

Ed: Laura Baverman. **Description:** Discusses the University of Cincinnati which is teaming up to release a technology platform called Macopay that would link a cell phone to a bank account and allow a person to make payments at participating retailers by sending a text message. Details with regard to the new service and its growth potential are discussed.

9959 ■ "Neighbors Rally for Dollar Store" in Chattanooga Times/Free Press (August 4, 2010)
Pub: Chattanooga Times/Free Press

Description: Neighbors are rallying to keep the Family Dollar Store in their city open. The proposed new store would expand the grocery portion of its retail discount shop.

9960 ■ "New Stores, New Headquarters in Schenectady for Golub Corporation" in Business Review, Albany New York (November 23, 2007)
Pub: American City Business Journals, Inc.

Ed: Michael DeMasi. **Description:** Details of Golub Corporation's expansion plan are presented. The supermarket chain, which has 116 stores in six northeastern states, plans to open thirty more stores within the next three or four years. The company will also build 524,000 square feet of warehouse space which will help in supplying new stores. Its corporate headquarters will also move to a vacant lot in Schenectady, New York.

9961 ■ "A Nice Consistency" in Inc. (Vol. 31, January-February 2009, No. 1, pp. 94)
Pub: Mansueto Ventures LLC

Ed: Jason Del Rey. **Description:** PJ Madison spent almost a quarter of its revenue promoting its latest product, organic ice cream. The Texas-based firm saw sales increase dramatically.

9962 ■ "P&G's Iams Finds Itself in a Pet-Food Dogfight" in Advertising Age (Vol. 78, March 5, 2007, No. 10, pp. 6)
Pub: Crain Communications, Inc.

Ed: Jack Neff. **Description:** Proctor & Gamble Co.'s Iams has been slow to embrace the trend toward foods for pets that appear fit for human consumption. Competitors such as Nestle Purina have made big gains with its colorful premium Beneful brand and dry nuggets that look like chunks of vegetables and meat. Statistical data included.

9963 ■ "Patience May Pay Off" in Barron's (Vol. 89, July 13, 2009, No. 28, pp. 30)
Pub: Dow Jones & Co., Inc.

Ed: Johanna Bennett. **Description:** New CEO Craig Herkert can turn around Supervalu and their shares could double to $30 in three years from June 2009

according to one investment officer. Herkert knows how to run a lean and tight operation since he has worked for Albertsons and Wal-Mart in the past.

9964 ■ "Phillips Edison Launches $1.8B Retail REIT" in Business Courier (Vol. 27, October 15, 2010, No. 24, pp. 1)
Pub: Business Courier

Ed: Dan Monk. **Description:** Retail center operator Phillips Edison & Company is organizing a real estate investment trust (REIT) to raise $1.8 billion to finance the planned purchase of 150 grocery-centered shopping centers around the U.S. The offering would be Phillips largest. Phillips Edison employesss 174 workers and operates 250 shopping centers nationwide.

9965 ■ "Procter & Gamble Boosts Bet on Exclusive Brands" in Business Courier (Vol. 27, July 9, 2010, No. 10, pp. 1)
Pub: Business Courier

Ed: Jon Newberry. **Description:** Procter & Gamble is creating more special versions of its brands such as Pringles and Pampers exclusively for retail partners such as Tesco in the U.K. The greater push towards this direction is seen as a way to regain market share.

9966 ■ Progressive Grocer's Marketing Guidebook: The Comprehensive Source for Grocery, Drug and Mass Merchant Insights
Pub: Trade Dimensions
Contact: Lynda Gutierrez, Director
URL(s): www.tradedimensions.com. **Released:** Annual; Latest edition 2011. **Covers:** Over 1,000 U.S. and Canadian supermarket chains, large independents and wholesalers; also includes 350 specialty distributors include smaller food wholesalers, food brokers, non-food distributors, and candy/tobacco/media distributors and over 15,000 key executives and buyers. **Entries include:** For retailers and wholesalers--Company name, address, phone, email and websites, number of stores operated or served, areas of operation, major grocery supplier, three-year financial summary, buying policies, private label information, lists of executives, buyers, and merchandisers. For specialty distributors--Name, address, phone, list of key personnel including buyers' categories, list of items handled, URL. **Arrangement:** Alphabetical by hierarchy, geographical by eight regions and 50 market areas. **Indexes:** Grocery related organizations, chain and wholesalers, state index, store operating name/parent company reference.

9967 ■ "Putting 'Great' Back Into A&P" in Crain's New York Business (Vol. 24, January 7, 2008, No. 1, pp. 3)
Pub: Crain Communications, Inc.

Description: After five straight years ending in 2005, A&P Grocery lost revenue; due to a sweeping plan to freshen up its supermarkets the company returned to growth mode and was able to acquire longtime competitor Pathmark Stores.

9968 ■ "Ralcorp Investigated for Rejecting ConAgra Bid" in Saint Louis Business Journal (Vol. 32, September 16, 2011, No. 3, pp. 1)
Pub: Saint Louis Business Journal

Ed: Evan Binns. **Description:** New York-based Levi & Korsinsky started investigating Ralcorp Holidngs Inc. after it rejected ConAgra Foods Inc.'s third and latest takeover bid of $5.17 billion. The investigation would determine whether Ralcorp's directors had acted on behalf of shareholders' best interest.

9969 ■ "Restaurants Slammed by Economy" in Business Courier (Vol. 24, April 4, 2008, No. 52, pp. 1)
Pub: American City Business Journals, Inc.

Ed: Lisa Biank Fasig. **Description:** Restaurants in Cincinnati are closing some of their stores due to growing costs of fuel, eggs and meat. The establishments are also affected by lower consumer spending that was brought on by unemployment, higher grocery prices and foreclosures. The economic problems in Cincinnati are also compared to those in other cities.

9970 ■ *"Roundy' Pushing Chicago Expansion"* in *Milwaukee Business Journal (Vol. 27, February 12, 2010, No. 20, pp. A1)*

Pub: American City Business Journals

Ed: Rich Kirchen. **Description:** Roundy Supermarkets Inc. is expanding in Chicago, Illinois as the Milwaukee-based company is set to open one store in downtown Chicago and another in the Arlington suburb. The store openings have been pushed back to spring and early summer in 2010 due to the economic downturn.

9971 ■ *"Safeway"* in *Ice Cream Reporter (Vol. 23, September 20, 2010, No. 10, pp. 8)*

Pub: Ice Cream Reporter

Description: Safeway supermarkets have upsized their private label ice cream to a full half gallon, thus reversing the trend where most brands were shrinking their containers.

9972 ■ *"Silver Springs Creamery Opens Retail"* in *Bellingham Business Journal (Vol. March 2010, pp. 3)*

Pub: Sound Publishing Inc.

Description: Eric Sundstrom, owner of Silver Springs Creamery, announced the opening of its on-site retail store that will sell the farm's goat and cow cheese, yogurt, ice cream and flesh milk.

9973 ■ *"Similac Introduces New Packaging"* in *Marketing to Women (Vol. 21, February 2008, No. 2, pp. 3)*

Pub: EPM Communications Inc.

Contact: Ira Mayer, President

E-mail: imayer@epmcom.com

Description: Baby formula brand Similac introduces a new ready to feed packaging which requires no mixing, measuring or preparation.

9974 ■ *"Small Fish, Big Box Stores"* in *Hawaii Business (Vol. 53, November 2007, No. 5, pp. 55)*

Pub: Hawaii Business Publishing

Ed: Jolyn Okimoto Rosa. **Description:** Ohana Seafoods can be found at big-box stores such as Costco, Marukai and Don Quijote. Owner Jeffrey Yee spends his weekend at a farmers market to have direct contact with his customers and get feedback right away. Ohana offers ready-to cook fish products, sauces and fish.

9975 ■ *"Still Stretching"* in *Business Courier (Vol. 24, December 28, 2008, No. 37, pp. 1)*

Pub: American City Business Journals, Inc.

Ed: Lucy May. **Description:** Minority-owned businesses have experienced growth in 2007 as Cincinnati and Hamilton County used a workforce development and economic inclusion policy. Kroger Co., for example, has been inducted to the Billion Dollar Roundtable in 2007 for attaining $1 billion in annual spending with suppliers that are minority- owned. The need for more progress within the minority-owned enterprises is discussed.

9976 ■ *"Stone to Run Hickory Farmer's Market"* in *Charlotte Observer (January 31, 2007)*

Pub: Knight-Ridder/Tribune Business News

Ed: Jen Aronoff. **Description:** Betty Stone has been hired to manage the Downtown Hickory Farmers Market. The market will run from May 5 through October 6, 2007.

9977 ■ *"Substantial Deal Expected to Create Jobs, Help Industrial Market"* in *Tampa Bay Business Journal (Vol. 30, January 8, 2010, No. 3)*

Pub: American City Business Journals

Ed: Janet Leiser. **Description:** Food distribution firm Gordon Food Service (GFS) is on the brink of purchasing Albertson's million-square-foot warehouse along with 158 acres of space. The deal between GFS and Albertson's could expand GFS' presence in west Central Florida. A history of GFS' growth is included.

9978 ■ *"Super Success"* in *Small Business Opportunities (November 2008)*

Pub: Entrepreneur Press

Contact: Perlman Neil, President

Description: Profile of PromoWorks LLC, a company founded by Michael Kent, that distributes samples of food at grocery stores for clients like Kraft Foods, Inc. and Kellogg Co. and also handles the logistics, provides the employees and tracks the products' sales.

9979 ■ *"A Switch in the Kitchen"* in *Barron's (Vol. 88, March 24, 2008, No. 12, pp. 17)*

Pub: Dow Jones & Company, Inc.

Description: Men are doing more kitchen duties, with 18 percent of meals at home being made by men in 2007 compared to 11 percent four years previously. Young wives, however, choose to forgo work and stay at home.

9980 ■ *"They Like It Cold"* in *Business Journal Portland (Vol. 27, October 15, 2010, No. 33, pp. 1)*

Pub: Portland Business Journal

Ed: Erik Siemers. **Description:** Ajinomoto Frozen Foods USA Inc. has been investing in its Portland, Oregon facility. The company has completed a new rice production line. It has also spent $1.2 million on a new packaging technology.

9981 ■ *"Top 50 Exporters"* in *Hispanic Business (Vol. 30, July-August 2008, No. 7-8, pp. 42)*

Pub: Hispanic Business, Inc.

Ed: Hildy Medina. **Description:** Increases in exports revenues reported by food exporters and green companies in a time of economic slowdown in the U.S are described. Food exporters have benefited from the growth of high-volume grocery stores in underdeveloped countries and the German governments' promotion of solar energy has benefited the U.S. solar heating equipment and solar panel manufactures.

9982 ■ *"Trading Down at the Supermarket"* in *Barron's (Vol. 88, July 14, 2008, No. 28, pp. 36)*

Pub: Dow Jones & Co., Inc.

Ed: Alexander Eule. **Description:** Shares of Ralcorp Holdings are cheap at around $49.95 after slipping 20 percent prior to their acquisition of Post cereals from Kraft. Some analysts believe its shares could climb over 60 percent to $80 as value-seeking consumers buy more private label products.

9983 ■ *"V&J Scores Partnership with Shaq"* in *Business Journal-Milwaukee (Vol. 25, October 12, 2007, No. 2, pp. A1)*

Pub: American City Business Journals, Inc.

Ed: Rich Kirchen. **Description:** O'Neal Franchise Group has agreed to a partnership with V&J Foods of Milwaukee to handle Auntie Anne's shops in New York, South Africa, Michigan, and the Caribbean. V&J O'Neal Enterprises will open six Auntie Anne's soft pretzel shops in Detroit towards the end of 2007. Planned international ventures of the partnership are presented.

9984 ■ *"'Wal-Mart Effect' Feeds Grocer Price Wars"* in *Globe & Mail (March 15, 2007, pp. B14)*

Pub: CTVglobemedia Publishing Inc.

Ed: Marina Strauss. **Description:** The decrease in profit reports by Canadian grocery giants amidst high expansion plans by Wal-Mart Stores Inc. are discussed. This industry is witnessing the most severe pricing competitions in recent times.

9985 ■ *"Wary Investors Turn to a Different Market for Strong Returns"* in *Boston Business Journal (Vol. 29, September 2, 2011, No. 17, pp. 1)*

Pub: American City Business Journals Inc.

Ed: Daniel J. Sernovitz. **Description:** Maryland-based investors have been choosing to put their money in the supermarket business. Retail property sales have increased during the second quarter of 2011.

9986 ■ *"Waugh Chapel to Expand"* in *Baltimore Business Journal (Vol. 28, August 27, 2010, No. 16, pp. 1)*

Pub: Baltimore Business Journal

Ed: Daniel J. Sernovitz. **Description:** Developer Greenberg Gibbons Corporation has broken ground on a $275 million, 1.2 million-square-foot addition to its Village at the Waugh Chapel mixed-use complex. Aside from creating 2,600 permanent jobs, the addition, named Village South, is expected to lure Target and Wegmans Food Markets to Crofton, Maryland. Funding for this project is discussed.

9987 ■ *"Wegmans Uses Database for Recall"* in *Supermarket News (Vol. 56, September 22, 2008, No. 38)*

Pub: Penton Business Media, Inc.

Ed: Carol Angrisani. **Description:** Wegmans used data obtained through its loyalty card that, in turn, sent automated telephone calls to every customer who had purchased tainted pet food when Mars Petcare recalled dog food products.

9988 ■ *"Welch's Uses Taste Strips in Ads"* in *Marketing to Women (Vol. 21, April 2008, No. 4, pp. 3)*

Pub: EPM Communications Inc.

Contact: Ira Mayer, President

E-mail: imayer@epmcom.com

Description: Welch's is positioning its 139-year-old brand in a new and inventive way with a new marketing campaign in which print ads will feature a tamper-evident flavor pouch that contains a dissolving taste strip flavored with Welch's grape juice.

9989 ■ *"What's New"* in *Crain's Cleveland Business (Vol. 30, June 29, 2009, No. 25, pp. 19)*

Pub: Crain Communications, Inc.

Description: More Than Gourmet, located in Akron, Ohio has introduced a new line of ready-to-use sauces, packed in 11-ounce containers that hold three-five servings.

STATISTICAL SOURCES

9990 ■ *Grocery Industry Market Share Report*

Pub: Chain Store Guide Information Services

Ed: Compiled by Chain Store Guide staff. **Released:** 2008. **Price:** $195.00 (PDF or Excel File). The Grocery Industry Market Share Report is a.

9991 ■ *The Market for Value-Added Fresh Produce*

Pub: MarketResearch.com

Released: 1999. **Price:** $2750.00. **Description:** This Packaged Facts report discusses how precuts (those popular bags of shredded lettuce), as well as organics, have rocketed at double-digit rates to the $9.7 billion mark at retail.

9992 ■ *RMA Annual Statement Studies*

Pub: Risk Management Association

Contact: Kevin M. Blakey, President

Released: Annual. **Price:** $175.00 2006-07 edition, $105.00. **Description:** Contains composite balance sheets and income statements for more than 360 industries, including the accounting, auditing, and bookkeeping industries. Also contains five years of comparative historical data for discerning trends. Includes 16 commonly used ratios, computed for most of the size groupings for nearly every industry.

9993 ■ *Standard & Poor's Industry Surveys*

Pub: Standard & Poor's Corp.

Released: Annual. **Price:** $3633.00. **Description:** Two-volume book that examines the prospects for specific industries, including trucking. Also provides analyses of trends and problems, statistical tables and charts, and comparative company analyses.

9994 ■ *The U.S. Kids' Foods Market*

Pub: MarketResearch.com

Released: 1999. **Price:** $2750.00. **Description:** Analyzes the market for children's prepared foods, concentrating on cereals, lunch foods and snacks, beverages, meals and entrees, and ice cream and frozen novelties. Offers sales data; gives insight into marketing; highlights the demographic forces driving the market; profiles major players; and provides market forecasts.

TRADE PERIODICALS

9995 ■ *Canadian Grocer: The Voice of Grocer Industry in Canada*
Pub: Rogers Media Publishing
URL(s): www.canadiangrocer.com/. **Released:** 10/yr. **Price:** $89, Individuals plus applicable taxes.

9996 ■ *The Food & Beverage International*
Pub: Journal Publications Inc.
URL(s): www.fbworld.com. **Released:** Bimonthly

9997 ■ *The Food & Beverage Journal*
Pub: Journal Publications Inc.
URL(s): www.fbworld.com. **Ed:** Ellen Walsh, Jason Barlow. **Released:** Bimonthly **Price:** $30, Individuals; $40, Two years.

9998 ■ *The Food Industry Advisor*
Pub: GC Publishing Company Inc.
URL(s): www.gccomm.net/foodindustryadvisor/index. asp. **Released:** Monthly **Price:** $48, Individuals.

9999 ■ *The Food Institute Report*
Pub: Food Institute
Contact: Brian Todd, President
E-mail: bTodd@foodinstitute.com
Released: Weekly. **Description:** Reports on developments in the food industry, including new products, the food service industry, mergers and acquisitions, current legislation and regulations, judicial decisions, and financial and marketing information.

10000 ■ *Food Trade News*
Pub: Best-Met Publishing Company Inc.
Contact: Beth Pripstein, Office Manager, Finance
URL(s): www.best-met.com. **Released:** Monthly **Price:** $69, Individuals.

10001 ■ *Grocery Headquarters*
Pub: Macfadden Communications Group L.L.C.
URL(s): www.groceryheadquarters.com. **Ed:** Tom Weir. **Released:** Monthly

10002 ■ *IGA Grocergram*
Pub: Pace Communications Inc.
URL(s): www.iga.com/igagrocergram.aspx. **Released:** Monthly

10003 ■ *Iowa Grocer*
Pub: Iowa Grocery Industry Association
Contact: Michelle Hurd, Director
URL(s): www.iowagrocers.com/igia-magazine.cfm. **Released:** Bimonthly

10004 ■ *The Packer: The Business Newspaper of the Produce Industry*
Contact: Shannon Shuman, Publisher
E-mail: sshuman@thepacker.com
URL(s): www.thepacker.comwww.vancepublishing. com. **Ed:** Greg Johnson. **Released:** Weekly **Price:** $99, Individuals; $139, Other countries.

10005 ■ *Progressive Grocer: The Industry's Source for News Analysis and Marketing Tactics*
Pub: Nielsen Co.
Contact: Greg Farrar, President
URL(s): www.progressivegrocer.com/progressivegrocer/index.jsp. **Released:** 13/yr.

10006 ■ *Shelby Report of the Southeast*
Pub: Shelby Publishing Company Inc.
Contact: Bob Reeves, Manager
URL(s): www.shelbypublishing.com. **Released:** Monthly **Price:** $36, Individuals; $60, Two years; $75, Individuals 3 years.

10007 ■ *Shelby Report of the Southwest*
Pub: Shelby Publishing Company Inc.
Contact: Bob Reeves, Manager
URL(s): www.shelbypublishing.com/index. php?option=com_content&task=view&id=2 2&Itemid=43. **Ed:** Lorrie Griffith. **Released:** Monthly **Price:** $36, Individuals; $60, Two years.

VIDEOCASSETTES/ AUDIOCASSETTES

10008 ■ *Successful Food Demonstration & Sampling*
International Dairy-Deli-Bakery Association (IDDBA)
PO Box 5528
Madison, WI 53705-0528
Ph: (608)310-5000
Fax: (608)238-6330
Co. E-mail: iddba@iddba.org
URL: http://www.iddba.org
Contact: Steve Beekhuizen, President
Released: 19??. **Price:** $100.00. **Description:** Presents ways supermarket dairy, deli, bakery and food-service employees can sell more through food demonstrations and sampling. **Availability:** VHS.

TRADE SHOWS AND CONVENTIONS

10009 ■ Connecticut Food Association Convention
Connecticut Food Association
195 Farmington Ave., Ste. 200
Farmington, CT 06032
Ph: (860)677-8097
Fax: (860)677-8418
Co. E-mail: ctfood@ctfoodassociation.org
URL: http://www.ctfoodassociation.org/
URL(s): www.ctfoodassociation.org/. **Frequency:** Annual. **Audience:** Trade professionals. **Principal Exhibits:** Wholesale and retail food industry equipment, supplies, and services. **Telecommunication Services:** info@ctfood.org.

10010 ■ Food & Fuel Expo
Tennessee Grocers Association
1838 Elm Hill Pike., Ste. 136
Nashville, TN 37210-3726
Ph: (615)889-0136
Free: 800-238-8742
Fax: (615)889-2877
URL: http://www.tngrocer.org
Contact: Jarron Springer, President
E-mail: jbspringer@tngrocer.org
Price: $200, Pre-registered, non-members; $200, Pre-registered, non-members; $200, Pre-registered, non-members. **Frequency:** Annual. **Audience:** Food wholesalers, retail grocers, and retail industry personnel. **Principal Exhibits:** Food products and equipment, supplies, and services. **Telecommunication Services:** jspringer@tngrocer.org.

10011 ■ Michigan Grocers Association Annual Convention and Trade Show
Michigan Grocers Association (MGA)
221 N Walnut St.
Lansing, MI 48933-1121
Ph: (517)372-6800
Free: 800-947-6237
Fax: (517)372-3002
Co. E-mail: contact@michigangrocers.org
URL: http://www.michigangrocers.org/
Contact: Linda Gobler, Chief Executive Officer
E-mail: linda@michigangrocers.org
URL(s): www.michigangrocers.org. **Frequency:** Annual. **Principal Exhibits:** Equipment, supplies, and services for wholesale and retail grocers and suppliers.

10012 ■ Missouri Grocers Association Annual Convention and Trade Show
Missouri Grocers' Association
315 N Ken Ave.
Springfield, MO 65802
Ph: (417)831-6667
Fax: (417)831-3907
URL: http://www.missourigrocers.com
Contact: Linda Ryan, President
URL(s): www.missourigrocers.com. **Frequency:** Annual. **Audience:** Owner and operators; independent retailers. **Principal Exhibits:** Grocery equipment, supplies, and services.

10013 ■ NFRA Convention
American Frozen Food Institute
2000 Corporate Ridge Rd., Ste. 1000
McLean, VA 22102
Ph: (703)821-0770
Fax: (703)821-1350
Co. E-mail: info@affi.com
URL: http://www.affi.com
URL(s): www.nfraweb.org. **Audience:** Frozen food buyers, brokers, manufacturers, suppliers, distributors, and warehouse personnel. **Principal Exhibits:** Manufacturers showcasing and sampling their products; a reception.

10014 ■ Western Food Industry Expo
Arizona Food Marketing Alliance (AFMA)
120 E Pierce St.
Phoenix, AZ 85004
Ph: (602)252-9761
Fax: (602)252-9021
Co. E-mail: tmccabe@afmaaz.org
URL: http://www.afmaaz.org
Contact: Tim McCabe, President
E-mail: tmccabe@afmaaz.org
URL(s): www.foodexpowest.com. **Frequency:** Annual. **Audience:** Trade buyers, retail operators, convenience store franchises, independent store owners, wholesalers, distributors, manufacturers, and marketing agencies. **Principal Exhibits:** Grocery store equipment, supplies, and services, including frozen foods, meats, poultry, store supplies, health and beauty aids, bakery products, beer, and wine. **Dates and Locations:** , Civic Plaza.

CONSULTANTS

10015 ■ Maine Coalition For Safe Kids Inc.
304 Hancock Pl., Ste. 3G
Bangor, ME 04402
Ph: (207)973-5788
Free: 800-706-7233
Fax: (207)778-5097
Co. E-mail: safekids@somtel.com
Contact: Retha Bobb, President
Scope: Consultants to management in food marketing, offering market development services, consumer research, trade research, preparation of training manuals, training workshops for sales supervisors and store supervisors, and sales promotion services. Serves government also. Provides injury safety solutions to the children. **Founded:** 1959. **Seminars:** Supermarket Supervision; Home Health Care Product Retailing; Marketing to Aging Americans; Childhood Injury Prevention.

10016 ■ R.D. Network Inc.
PO Box 375
Lafayette Hill, PA 19444
Ph: (215)482-4461
Free: 877-482-4991
Fax: (215)836-0378
Co. E-mail: info@rdnetwork.com
URL: http://www.rdnetwork.com
Contact: Leslie Grant, Owner
Scope: Dietitians, diet technicians, and certified dietary managers available nationwide and worldwide through an international registry for consulting positions to wellness and employee education programs, drug or alcohol rehabilitation, hospital, LTC, nutrition and labeling communications, nutrition consultation, weight control classes, healthcare staff supplementation, media and program development, and all nutrition and food-related needs. Expert witness and speakers bureau also available. Industries served: healthcare, food industry, food service, restaurateurs, supermarkets, pharmaceutical companies, home health agencies, insurance companies, HMOs, and government agencies. **Founded:** 1983. **Seminars:** Labour/Staffing; Outsourcing; Healthy Dining Etiquette for Executives and Sales Staff Diet and Wellness; Cardiovascular Nutrition; Starting a Nutrition Consulting Practice; AIDS and Diet Therapy; Nutrition Care for Your Parents in Their Elder Years; Increase Your Energy-Increase Your Sales.

10017 ■ Thole Associates—Thole Enterprises
1400 Shadwell Cir.
Lake Mary, FL 32746-4344

Ph: (407)333-2174
Fax: (407)333-2174
Contact: Jerome L. Thole, President
Scope: Consulting organization specializing in food and drug store merchandising and operations. In addition to serving retailers, the firm provides consulting service to wholesalers and manufacturers as well. Areas of expertise include store operations, store conditions, operating cost control, customer service training, research, and budget control and scheduling. Industries served: retail food supermarket and drug companies. **Founded:** 1988. **Seminars:** How to Improve Customer Service-Without Sacrificing Productivity; Customer Satisfaction-Develop a Strategy for Success; How to Control Expense in Tough Economic Times.

FRANCHISES AND BUSINESS OPPORTUNITIES

10018 ■ The Honeybaked Ham Co. and Cafe
The HBH Franchise Co. LLC
3875 Mansell Rd.
Alpharetta, GA 30022
Ph: (678)966-3254
Free: 866-968-7424
Fax: (678)966-3134
URL: http://www.honeybakedonline.com
Description: Specialty retailer of high quality spiral-sliced hams and turkeys. **No. of Franchise Units:**

183. **No. of Company-Owned Units:** 280. **Founded:** 1957.. **Franchised:** 1998. **Equity Capital Needed:** $350,000 net worth with $100,000 available as equity contribution. **Franchise Fee:** $30,000. **Training:** Comprehensive 14 day program at corporate training store.

COMPUTERIZED DATABASES

10019 ■ *Consumer Buying Power™*
770 Broadway
New York, NY 10003-9595
URL: http://www.claritas.com/sitereports/default.jsp
Availability: Online: The Nielsen Co. - Nielsen SiteReports. **Type:** Statistical.

LIBRARIES

10020 ■ American Institute of Food Distribution, Inc. - Information and Research Center—The Food Institute.
1 Broadway Plaza, 2nd Fl.
Elmwood Park, NJ 07407
Ph: (201)791-5570
Fax: (201)791-5222
Co. E-mail: jkastrinsky@foodinstitute.com
URL: http://www.foodinstitute.com/
Contact: Brian Todd, President
Scope: Food industry. **Services:** Center open to the public on fee basis. **Founded:** 1928. **Subscriptions:**

400 journals and other serials. **Publications:** *Food Business Mergers and Acquisitions.* **Telecommunication Services:** food1@foodinstitute.com.

10021 ■ National Grocers Co. Ltd. - ISD Technical Library
6 Monogram Pl.
Weston, ON, Canada M9R 4C4
Ph: (416)246-7665
Fax: (416)246-7875
Contact: Fran Markland, Librarian
Scope: Grocery business. **Services:** Library not open to the public. **Founded:** 1988. **Holdings:** Figures not available.

RESEARCH CENTERS

10022 ■ St. Joseph's University - Academy of Food Marketing
150 Mandeville Hall
5600 City Ave.
Philadelphia, PA 19131
Ph: (610)660-1600
Fax: (610)660-1604
Co. E-mail: rhiggins@sju.edu
URL: http://www.sju.edu/academics/hsb/foodmarketing/academy
Contact: Robert R. Higgins, Executive Director
Founded: 1960. **Educational Activities:** Industry seminars.

ASSOCIATIONS AND OTHER ORGANIZATIONS

10023 ■ **American Custom Gunmakers Guild (ACGG)**
22 Vista View Ln.
Cody, WY 82414-9606
Ph: (307)587-4297
Fax: (307)587-4297
Co. E-mail: acgg@acgg.org
URL: http://www.acgg.org
Contact: Jan Billeb, Executive Director
Description: Seeks to preserve and promote the art of fine custom gun making. **Founded:** 1983. **Publications:** *Directory of Custom Gun making Services* (Biennial); *Directory of Regular Members* (Biennial); *Gunmaker* (Quarterly); *Directory of Custom Gunmaking Services* (Biennial); *Realizing Your Dream: A Client's Guide to Building a Custom Gun.* **Educational Activities:** Firearms Engravers and Gunmakers Exhibition (Annual). **Awards:** Gunsmithing Student Grant-in-Aid (Annual).

10024 ■ **Sporting Arms and Ammunitions Manufacturers Institute (SAAMI)**
11 Mile Hill Rd.
Newtown, CT 06470-2359
Ph: (203)426-4358
Fax: (203)426-3592
Co. E-mail: rpatterson@saami.org
URL: http://www.saami.org
Description: Producers of firearms, ammunition, and propellants. Promotes and facilitates voluntary compliance with industry performance standards for sporting ammunitions. **Founded:** 1926.

DIRECTORIES OF EDUCATIONAL PROGRAMS

10025 ■ *Directory of Private Accredited Career Schools and Colleges of Technology*
Pub: Accrediting Commission of Career Schools and Colleges of Technology
Contact: Michale S. McComis, Executive Director
Released: On web page. **Price:** Free. **Description:** Covers 3900 accredited post-secondary programs that provide training programs in business, trade, and technical fields, including various small business endeavors. Entries offer school name, address, phone, description of courses, job placement assistance, and requirements for admission. Arrangement is alphabetical.

REFERENCE WORKS

10026 ■ *"Bankruptcies" in Crain's Detroit Business (Vol. 24, October 6, 2008, No. 40, pp. 26)*
Pub: Crain Communications, Inc.
Description: Current businesses that have filed for Chapter 7 or 11 protection in U.S. Bankruptcy Court include an auto dealership, a gun range and a grocery service.

10027 ■ *"EOTech Product Improves Holographic Gun Sights" in Crain's Detroit Business (Vol. 24, February 4, 2008, No. 5, pp. 9)*
Pub: Crain Communications Inc. - Detroit
Description: L-3 Communications EOTech Inc. procured new business contracts to fulfill military and law enforcement's demand for improved holographic sites used on handheld weapons.

10028 ■ *"Fire Destroys Surplus Store, Sets Off Live Rounds Near Jacksonville NAS" in Florida Times-Union (December 5, 2010)*
Pub: Florida Times-Union
Ed: John Leacock. **Description:** Fire which caused numerous explosions at a military surplus store near Jacksonville Naval Air Station is under investigation. Heat and flames ignited lighter fluid and set off live rounds of ammunition sold in the store.

10029 ■ *Lethal Logic: Exploding the Myths that Paralyze American Gun Policy*
Pub: Potomac Books
Ed: Dennis A. Henigen. **Released:** 2009. **Price:** $29.95. **Description:** Marketing tactics being used by gun manufacturers regarding possible new gun control laws are examined.

10030 ■ *The World Directory of Custom Bullet Makers*
Pub: Corbin Manufacturing & Supply Inc.
Contact: David R. Corbin, Chief Executive Officer
E-mail: dave@corbins.com
URL(s): www.corbins.com. **Released:** Annual; August. **Price:** $24.50, print; $9.50, e-book. **Covers:** 300 manufacturers of custom projectiles for small arms (to 20 mm). **Entries include:** Company name, address, phone, telex, names and titles of key personnel, subsidiary and branch names and locations, description of products and services provided, including specific calibers of bullets produced. **Arrangement:** Alphabetical. **Indexes:** Product/service, geographical.

TRADE PERIODICALS

10031 ■ *Gun Digest*
Pub: Krause Publications Inc.
Contact: Roger Case, President
URL(s): www.gundigest.com. **Ed:** Andy Belmas. **Released:** 26/yr. **Price:** $171.98, Other countries; $37.98, Individuals; C$113.98, Individuals.

10032 ■ *Gun & Knife Show Calendar*
Pub: Krause Publications Inc.
Contact: Roger Case, President
URL(s): www.ccgdata.com/0862-4.html. **Released:** Quarterly **Price:** $15.95, Individuals; $31.90, Two years; $47.85, Individuals 3 years.

10033 ■ *The Gun Report*
Pub: World Wide Gun Report Inc.
URL(s): www.thegunreport.com/. **Released:** Monthly **Price:** $35, Individuals; $45, Other countries.

10034 ■ *Rifle: The Sporting Firearms Journal*
Pub: Wolfe Publishing Co.
Contact: Mark Harris, President
URL(s): www.riflemagazine.com. **Released:** Bimonthly **Price:** $19.97, Individuals; $51, Individuals combo; $11.99, Individuals military; $19.97, Individuals online.

10035 ■ *Shooting Industry*
Pub: Publishers Development Corp.
URL(s): www.shootingindustry.com. **Ed:** Russ Thurman. **Released:** Monthly **Price:** $45, Other countries.

10036 ■ *Shotgun News: The World's Largest Gun Sales Publication*
Pub: PRIMEDIA Los Angeles
URL(s): shotgunnews.com/. **Ed:** Robert W. Hunnicutt. **Released:** 3/month. **Price:** $16.99, Individuals; $28.99, Individuals 36 issues; $54.99, Individuals 72 issues; $23.49, Canada; $41.99, Canada 36 issues; $80.99, Canada 72 issues; $24.49, Other countries; $43.99, Other countries 36 issues; $84.99, Other countries 72 issues.

VIDEOCASSETTES/ AUDIOCASSETTES

10037 ■ *Choose Your Weapon*
Gun Video
4585 Murphy Canyon Rd.
San Diego, CA 92123
Ph: (858)569-4000
Free: 800-942-8273
Fax: (858)569-0505
Co. E-mail: info2@gunvideo.com
URL: http://www.gunvideo.com
Released: 1991. **Price:** $49.95. **Description:** A comprehensive look at gun types, operation, safety and usage. **Availability:** VHS.

10038 ■ *Gun Safety*
Tapeworm Video Distributors
25876 The Old Road #141
Stevenson Ranch, CA 91381
Ph: (661)257-4904
Fax: (661)257-4820
Co. E-mail: sales@tapeworm.com
URL: http://www.tapeworm.com
Released: 19??. **Price:** $14.95. **Description:** Professional firearms instructor Dan West presents the five basic safety rules of gun safety. **Availability:** VHS.

10039 ■ *Handgun Fundamentals*
RMI Media
1365 N. Winchester St.
Olathe, KS 66061-5880
Ph: (913)768-1696
Free: 800-745-5480
Fax: (800)755-6910
Co. E-mail: actmedia@act.org
URL: http://www.actmedia.com
Released: 1987. **Description:** Expert Jeff Cooper presents a guide to handgun use and safety, including grip and stance, sighting, target shooting, rapid fire, and gun care. **Availability:** VHS; 3/4 U.

TRADE SHOWS AND CONVENTIONS

10040 ■ The Shooting, Hunting, and Outdoor Trade Show (SHOT SHOW)
Reed Exhibitions Contemporary Forums
6377 Clark Ave., Ste. 200
Dublin, CA 94568
Ph: (925)828-7100
Fax: (800)329-9923
Co. E-mail: info@cforums.com
URL: http://www.contemporaryforums.com
URL(s): www.shotshow.org. **Audience:** Federally licensed firearms dealers and legitimate sporting goods dealers. **Principal Exhibits:** Shooting and hunting equipment and products; sports accessories, clothing, and supplies. **Telecommunication Services:** nbogdanski@reedexpo.com.

LIBRARIES

10041 ■ Brady Center to Prevent Gun Violence Library
1225 Eye St. NW, Ste. 1100
Washington, DC 20005
Ph: (202)289-7319
Fax: (202)408-1851
URL: http://www.bradycenter.org
Scope: Handgun violence, firearms litigation, accidental shootings, Second Amendment, gun control, children and guns, violence prevention. **Services:** Copying; SDI; library open to the public by appointment. **Founded:** 1983. **Holdings:** 1000 articles; 8 VF; books; videotapes. **Subscriptions:** 10 journals and other serials.

10042 ■ J.M. Davis Arms & Historical Museum - Charles R. Suydam Library
330 N. J.M. Davis Blvd.
Claremore, OK 74017
Ph: (918)341-5707
Fax: (918)341-5771
Co. E-mail: info@thegunmuseum.com
URL: http://www.thegunmuseum.com
Scope: Firearms, edged weapons, American Indian artifacts, steins, musical instruments. **Services:** Copying; Library open to the public. **Founded:** 1969. **Holdings:** 3300 volumes; 30 bound periodical volumes; old gun catalogs; pins, buttons, and badges. **Subscriptions:** 15 journals and other serials.

10043 ■ Francis Marion University - James A. Rogers Library - Special Collections
PO Box 100547
Florence, SC 29502-0547
Ph: (843)661-1300
Co. E-mail: jdurant@fmarion.edu
URL: http://www.fmarion.edu/rogerslibrary/specialcollectionsandarchives
Contact: Joyce M. Durant, Dean, Library Services
Scope: Firearms; Americana. **Services:** Interlibrary loan; copying; library open to the public with restric-

tions on borrowing. **Founded:** 1970. **Holdings:** 10,000 books; 30 manuscripts. **Subscriptions:** 978 journals and other serials; 28 newspapers.

10044 ■ National Rifle Association of America - National Firearms Museum Library
NRA Headquarters Bldg., 2nd Fl.
11250 Waples Mill Rd.
Fairfax, VA 22030-7400
Ph: (703)267-1603
Fax: (703)267-3913
Co. E-mail: nfmstaff@nrahq.org
URL: http://www.nramuseum.org/the-museum/store-library.aspx
Contact: Doug Wicklund, Curator
Scope: Firearms, arms technology, cartridges/reloading, military history. **Services:** Library open to the public by appointment. **Founded:** 1871. **Holdings:** 3500 books; 300 video tapes. **Subscriptions:** 125 journals and other serials.

10045 ■ National Rifle Association of America - NRA-ILA Library
11250 Waples Mill Rd.
Fairfax, VA 22030-7400
Free: 800-392-8683
Fax: (703)267-3957
URL: http://www.nraila.org
Contact: Richard Wahl
Scope: Firearms and hunting; criminal justice; natural resources; legislative issues. **Services:** Library not open to the public. **Founded:** 1976. **Holdings:** 2300 books; 750 lin.ft. of vertical file materials. **Subscriptions:** 70 journals and other serials; 7 newspapers.

10046 ■ Ontario Ministry of Community Safety and Correctional Services - Centre of Forensic Sciences
George Drew Bldg.
25 Grosvenor St.
Toronto, ON, Canada M7A 2G8
Ph: (416)314-3200
URL: http://www.mcscs.jus.gov.on.ca/english/default.html
Contact: Eva Gulbinowicz, Librarian
Scope: Forensic science, toxicology, biology, chemistry, engineering, firearms, photography, questioned documents. **Services:** Interlibrary loan; copying (limited); library open to criminal justice and medical professionals by telephone appointment. **Founded:** 1967. **Holdings:** 20,000 books; 4000 bound periodical volumes; 1000 reports; 13,000 reprints; 2500 government documents and pamphlets; 15,000 slides. **Subscriptions:** 300 journals and other serials; 2 newspapers.

10047 ■ Royal Canadian Artillery Museum Library—RCA Museum - Library.
Canadian Forces Base Shilo
Shilo, MB, Canada R0K 2A0

Ph: (204)765-3000
Co. E-mail: stag@mts.net
URL: http://www.rcamuseum.com/
Contact: R.A. Sanderson, Director
Scope: Military history; artillery - ordnance, carriages, ammunition, technical data, small arms, vehicles. **Services:** Copying; scanning; reference; library open to the public by appointment for research. **Founded:** 1956. **Holdings:** 13,000 books; 13,000 bound periodical volumes; 428 maps; 81 boxes of documents; 118 videotapes; pamphlets. **Subscriptions:** 14 journals and other serials; 5 newspapers.

10048 ■ Second Amendment Foundation Library
James Madison Bldg.
12500 NE 10th Pl.
Bellevue, WA 98005
Ph: (425)454-7012
Free: 800-426-4302
Fax: (425)451-3959
URL: http://www.saf.org
Scope: Second amendment, gun rights. **Services:** Library not open to the public. **Founded:** 1974. **Holdings:** 200 books; 30 reports. **Subscriptions:** 2 journals and other serials; 2 newspapers.

10049 ■ Shooting Federation of Prince Edward Island Library
PO Box 1900
Charlottetown, PE, Canada C1A 7N9
Ph: (902)892-2938
Fax: (902)628-1714
Co. E-mail: deighanj@isn.net
Contact: James Deighan, Editor
Scope: Fire arms - rules, regulations. **Services:** Library not open to the public. **Founded:** 1973. **Holdings:** 100 books; 200 bound periodical volumes. **Subscriptions:** 9 journals and other serials; 11 newspapers.

10050 ■ U.S. Bureau of Alcohol, Tobacco and Firearms - National Laboratory Center Library
6000 Ammendale Rd.
Beltsville, MD 20705-1250
Ph: (202)648-6074
Fax: (301)315-0519
Co. E-mail: susan.barned@atf.gov
URL: http://www.atf.gov/
Contact: Sue Wright, Librarian
URL(s): www.atf.gov/contact/service-centers/. **Scope:** Alcohol, analytical techniques, forensic sciences, firearms, tobacco, explosives. **Services:** Library not open to the public. **Founded:** 1972. **Holdings:** 5700 books; 4000 bound periodical volumes; 200 total journal titles; government documents; archives. **Subscriptions:** 42 journals and other serials. **Telecommunication Services:** susan.barned@usdoj.gov.

ASSOCIATIONS AND OTHER ORGANIZATIONS

10051 ■ American Electrology Association (AEA)
6 Market Pl., Ste. 1
Essex Junction, VT 05452
Ph: (802)879-1898
Co. E-mail: infoaea@electrology.com
URL: http://www.electrology.com
Contact: Sharon Ortiz, President
Description: Electrologists united for education, professional advancement, and protection of public welfare. Promotes uniform legislative standards throughout the states. Coordinates efforts of affiliated associations in dealing with problems of national scope. Sponsors the International Board of Electrologist Certification and Council on Accreditation of Electrology Schools/Programs. Maintains referral, reference, advisory, and consulting services. **Founded:** 1958. **Publications:** *Journal of the American Electrology Association* (Semiannual).

10052 ■ American Hair Loss Council (AHLC)
30 S Main St.
Shenandoah, PA 17976-2331
Co. E-mail: info@ahlc.org
URL: http://www.ahlc.org
Contact: Betty Budgen, Director, Member Services
Description: Dermatologists, plastic surgeons, cosmetologists, barbers, and interested others. Provides nonbiased information regarding treatments for hair loss in both men and women. Facilitates communication and information exchange between professionals in different areas of specialization. Conducts educational programs; compiles statistics. **Founded:** 1985. **Publications:** *AHLC News* (Quarterly). **Educational Activities:** American Hair Loss Council Symposium (Annual). **Awards:** Volunteer of the Year and The Community Service Award (Annual).

10053 ■ Society for Clinical and Medical Hair Removal (SCMHR)
2424 American Ln.
Madison, WI 53704-3102
Ph: (608)443-2470
Fax: (608)443-2474
Co. E-mail: homeoffice@scmhr.org
URL: http://www.scmhr.org
Contact: Nedra D. Lockhart, President
Description: Professional society of electrologists (persons engaged in the removal of superfluous hair by galvanic blend or short wave methods for cosmetic and medical purposes). Conducts continuing education and leadership development seminars. **Founded:** 1985. **Publications:** *SCME Directory of Membership* (Annual). **Awards:** Dr. Bordier Award (Annual).

DIRECTORIES OF EDUCATIONAL PROGRAMS

10054 ■ *Directory of Private Accredited Career Schools and Colleges of Technology*
Pub: Accrediting Commission of Career Schools and Colleges of Technology
Contact: Michale S. McComis, Executive Director
Released: On web page. **Price:** Free. **Description:** Covers 3900 accredited post-secondary programs that provide training programs in business, trade, and technical fields, including various small business endeavors. Entries offer school name, address, phone, description of courses, job placement assistance, and requirements for admission. Arrangement is alphabetical.

REFERENCE WORKS

10055 ■ *"Every Little Bit Helps" in Black Enterprise (Vol. 38, November 2007, No. 4, pp. 102)*
Pub: Earl G. Graves Publishing Co. Inc.
Ed: Tennille M. Robinson. **Description:** After a career in the cosmetics industry, Tricialee Riley is marketing and advertising her new venture, the Polish Bar, a salon offering manicures, pedicures, makeup application, and waxing.

10056 ■ *"Secret Ingredient" in Entrepreneur (Vol. 35, November 2007, No. 11, pp. 172)*
Pub: Entrepreneur Media Inc.
Ed: Sara Wilson. **Description:** Ojon Corporation in Burlington, Ontario, Canada has developed a natural hair- and skin-care line from ojon oil. The oil, which has very good restorative effects on hair, is extracted from nuts found in ojon trees in the rainforests of Honduras. Details on how Ojon Corporation started and its growing venture in the market are outlined.

FRANCHISES AND BUSINESS OPPORTUNITIES

10057 ■ Women's Health Boutique
Women's Health Boutique Franchise System, Inc.
12715 Telge Rd.
Cypress, TX 77429
Free: 888-708-9982
Fax: (281)256-4100
Co. E-mail: w-h-bsales@w-h-b.com
URL: http://www.w-h-b.com
Description: Products and services related to pre and postnatal care, post-mastectomy, compression therapy, hair loss, incontinence, and skin care. **No. of Franchise Units:** 13. **Founded:** 1991.. **Franchised:** 1994. **Equity Capital Needed:** $49,000 minimum start-up cash. **Training:** Yes.

ASSOCIATIONS AND OTHER ORGANIZATIONS

10058 ■ Allied Beauty Association (ABA)
145 Traders Blvd. E, Units 26 and 27
Mississauga, ON, Canada L4Z 3L3
Ph: (905)568-0158
Free: 800-268-6644
Fax: (905)568-1581
Co. E-mail: abashows@abacanada.com
URL: http://www.abacanada.com
Contact: Marc E. Speir, Executive Director
Description: Individuals and corporations engaged in the beauty industries. Promotes growth and development of members' businesses. Represents members' interests, conducts public relations campaigns and serves as a clearinghouse on the Canadian beauty industries. **Scope:** AIDS, HIV. **Founded:** 1934. **Subscriptions:** archival material books clippings monographs periodicals video recordings. **Publications:** *Riben Nehrah Quarterly* (Quarterly).

10059 ■ American Association of Cosmetology Schools (AACS)
9927 E Bell Rd., Ste. 110
Scottsdale, AZ 85260
Ph: (480)281-0431
Free: 800-831-1086
Fax: (480)905-0993
Co. E-mail: jim@beautyschools.org
URL: http://www.beautyschools.org
Contact: Jim Cox, Executive Director
E-mail: jim@beautyschools.org
Description: Owners and teachers in cosmetology schools. **Founded:** 1924. **Publications:** *CEA Update* (Quarterly); *Salon City Star*; *Skin Inc.*. **Educational Activities:** Spring Management (Annual); American Association of Cosmetology Schools Annual Conference - AACS Annual Convention & Expo (Annual). **Awards:** Educator of the Year (Annual). **Telecommunication Services:** dilsah@beautyschools.org.

10060 ■ American Health and Beauty Aids Institute (AHBAI)
PO Box 19510
Chicago, IL 60619-0510
Ph: (708)633-6328
Fax: (708)633-6329
Co. E-mail: ahbai1@sbcglobal.net
URL: http://www.ahbai.org
Contact: Clyde Hammond, Chairman
Description: Minority-owned companies engaged in manufacturing and marketing health and beauty aids for the black consumer. Represents the interests of members and the industry before local, state, and federal governmental agencies. Assists with business development and economic progress within the minority community by providing informational and educational resources. Maintains speakers' bureau. Conducts annual Proud Lady Beauty Show. **Founded:** 1981. **Awards:** Fred Luster, Sr. Education Foundation Cosmetology Scholarship (Annual); Fred Luster, Sr. Education Foundation Scholarship Fund (Annual).

10061 ■ Intercoiffure America
c/o Maryanne McCormack, Membership Chair
1303 Campbell Rd.
Houston, TX 77055
Ph: (713)984-8800
Free: 800-442-3007
Fax: (713)935-4409
Co. E-mail: info@intercoiffure.com
URL: http://www.intercoiffure.us
Contact: Lois Christie, President
Description: Owners of beauty salons in the United States and Canada who meet the ethical standards set down by Intercoiffure. Seeks to make the women of America the best in hair fashion. **Founded:** 1915. **Educational Activities:** Intercoiffure America Show (Semiannual).

10062 ■ National Accrediting Commission of Cosmetology Arts and Sciences (NACCAS)
4401 Ford Ave., Ste. 1300
Alexandria, VA 22302
Ph: (703)600-7600
Fax: (703)379-2200
Co. E-mail: amirando@naccas.org
URL: http://www.naccas.org
Contact: Tony Mirando, Executive Director
Description: Accrediting body for schools of cosmetology; presently there are 1030 accredited schools. Objectives are to: raise standards of cosmetology schools throughout the country; encourage use of modern educational methods and techniques; stimulate self-improvement by the schools. Sponsors standards and professional team training workshops. **Founded:** 1981. **Publications:** *Directory of Accredited Cosmetology Schools* (Annual); *Directory of Accredited Cosmetology Schools* (Annual); *NACCAS Review* (3/year).

10063 ■ National Association of Barber Boards of America (NABBA)
2703 Pine St.
Arkadelphia, AR 71923
Ph: (501)682-2806
Fax: (501)682-5073
Co. E-mail: nabba@att.net
URL: http://www.nationalbarberboards.com
Contact: Charles Kirkpatrick, Executive Director
Description: Represents state boards of barber examiners. Promotes the exchange of information among state barber boards and state agencies that examine, license, and regulate the barber industry. Improves standards and procedures for examining barbers and regulates the barber industry. Furthers continuing education and development of curricula for educating barbers. Devises procedures for ensuring that consumers are informed and protected. Maintains library. **Founded:** 1935. **Awards:** Conference Attendance (Annual).

10064 ■ National Beauty Culturists' League (NBCL)
25 Logan Cir. NW
Washington, DC 20005-3725
Ph: (202)332-2695

Fax: (202)332-0940
Co. E-mail: nbcl@bellsouth.net
URL: http://www.nbcl.org
Contact: Dr. Katie B. Catalon, President
Description: Beauticians, cosmetologists, and beauty products manufacturers. Encourages standardized, scientific, and approved methods of hair, scalp, and skin treatments. Offers scholarships and plans to establish a research center. Sponsors: National Institute of Cosmetology, a training course in operating and designing and business techniques. Maintains hall of fame; conducts research program. **Founded:** 1919. **Educational Activities:** National Beauty Culturists' League Annual Trade Show (Annual).

10065 ■ National - Interstate Council of State Boards of Cosmetology (NIC)
7622 Briarwood Cir.
Little Rock, AR 72205
Ph: (501)227-8262
Fax: (501)227-8212
Co. E-mail: dnorton@nictesting.org
URL: http://www.nictesting.org
Contact: Kay Kendrick, President
Description: Persons commissioned by 50 state governments as administrators of cosmetology laws and examiners of applicants for licenses to practice cosmetology. **Founded:** 1956. **Educational Activities:** National - Interstate Council of State Boards of Cosmetology Seminar (Annual).

10066 ■ Professional Beauty Association (PBA) - National Cosmetology Association
15825 N 71st St., Ste. 100
Scottsdale, AZ 85254
Ph: (480)281-0424
Free: 800-468-2274
Fax: (480)905-0708
Co. E-mail: info@probeauty.org
URL: http://www.probeauty.org
Contact: Max Wexler, Chairman
Description: Manufacturers and manufacturers' representatives of beauty and barber products, cosmetics, equipment, and supplies used in or resold by beauty salons or barbershops. Promotes the beauty industry; works to ensure product safety; disseminates information. Holds educational seminars; organizes charity events. **Founded:** 1985. **Publications:** *PBA Progress* (3/year). **Educational Activities:** Cosmoprof North America; Cosmoprof North America; International Salon & Spa Expo (Annual); Pro Termal (Annual); Professional Beauty Africa (Annual). **Awards:** Sally Beauty Scholarships for High School Graduates.

10067 ■ *Riben Nehrah Quarterly*
145 Traders Blvd. E, Units 26 and 27
Mississauga, ON, Canada L4Z 3L3
Ph: (905)568-0158
Free: 800-268-6644
Fax: (905)568-1581
Co. E-mail: abashows@abacanada.com
URL: http://www.abacanada.com
Contact: Marc E. Speir, Executive Director
Released: Quarterly

DIRECTORIES OF EDUCATIONAL PROGRAMS

10068 ■ *Directory of Private Accredited Career Schools and Colleges of Technology*
Pub: Accrediting Commission of Career Schools and Colleges of Technology
Contact: Michale S. McComis, Executive Director
Released: On web page. **Price:** Free. **Description:** Covers 3900 accredited post-secondary programs that provide training programs in business, trade, and technical fields, including various small business endeavors. Entries offer school name, address, phone, description of courses, job placement assistance, and requirements for admission. Arrangement is alphabetical.

REFERENCE WORKS

10069 ■ *"Because He Is Still Growing: Horst Rechelbacher: Intelligent Nutrients Minneapolis" in Inc. (Volume 32, December 2010, No. 10)*
Pub: Inc. Magazine
Ed: Mike Hoffman. **Description:** Horst Rechelbacher, founder of hair care company Aveda, and after selling Aveda to Estee Lauder, he is expanding into a nutraceuticals company offering hair care products that are organically grown.

10070 ■ *Doing Business with Beauty: Black Women, Hair Salons, and the Racial Enclave Economy*
Pub: Rowman & Littlefield Publishers Inc.
Contact: Jason Aronson, President
Ed: Adia Harvey Wingfield. **Released:** June 28, 2008. **Price:** $19.95. **Description:** Factors that draw black women into the hair industry are examined. Interviews with hair salon owners explore aspects of owning a salon, owner-employee relationships, and the black female owner's struggle for autonomy and success in entrepreneurship.

10071 ■ *Enterprising Women in Urban Zimbabwe: Gender, Microbusiness, and Globalization*
Pub: Indiana University Press
Contact: Janet Rabinowitch, Director
E-mail: jrabinow@indiana.edu
Ed: Mary Johnson Osirim. **Released:** April 1, 2009. **Price:** $39.95. **Description:** An investigation into the business and personal experiences of women entrepreneurs in the microenterprise sector in Zimbabwe. Many of these women work as market traders, crocheters, seamstresses, and hairdressers.

10072 ■ *"Secret Ingredient" in Entrepreneur (Vol. 35, November 2007, No. 11, pp. 172)*
Pub: Entrepreneur Media Inc.
Ed: Sara Wilson. **Description:** Ojon Corporation in Burlington, Ontario, Canada has developed a natural hair- and skin-care line from ojon oil. The oil, which has very good restorative effects on hair, is extracted from nuts found in ojon trees in the rainforests of Honduras. Details on how Ojon Corporation started and its growing venture in the market are outlined.

10073 ■ *"Verizon Small Business Awards Give Companies a Technology Edge" in Hispanic Business (July-August 2009, pp. 32)*
Pub: Hispanic Business
Ed: Patricia Marroquin. **Description:** Verizon Wireless awards grants to twenty-four companies in California. The winning businesses ranged from barbershop to coffee shop, tattoo parlor to florist.

10074 ■ *"V's Barbershop Opening in Bakerview Square in May" in Bellingham Business Journal (Vol. March 2010, pp. 2)*
Pub: Sound Publishing Inc.
Description: Upscale barbershop franchise catering to men, V's Barbershop, will open a new location in Bakerview Square (its first in Washington) in 2010. The new location will include six chairs and will appear like an old-time barbershop with a contemporary flavor featuring real barber chairs, flat-screen TVs, and hot lather shaves using a straight-edge razor.

10075 ■ *"What Moms Want" in Marketing to Women (Vol. 21, February 2008, No. 2, pp. 6)*
Pub: EPM Communications Inc.
Contact: Ira Mayer, President
E-mail: imayer@epmcom.com
Description: According to a survey conducted by Eureka's Spa, moms would rather have an experience gift than flowers or chocolate. The top five dream gifts include a spa day, a weekend getaway, maid service, a bathroom makeover or a getaway weekend with girlfriends.

STATISTICAL SOURCES

10076 ■ *RMA Annual Statement Studies*
Pub: Risk Management Association
Contact: Kevin M. Blakey, President
Released: Annual. **Price:** $175.00 2006-07 edition, $105.00. **Description:** Contains composite balance sheets and income statements for more than 360 industries, including the accounting, auditing, and bookkeeping industries. Also contains five years of comparative historical data for discerning trends. Includes 16 commonly used ratios, computed for most of the size groupings for nearly every industry.

TRADE PERIODICALS

10077 ■ *The Beauty Industry Report*
Pub: The Beauty Industry Report
Contact: Mike Nave, Editor
E-mail: mikenave@aol.com
Released: Monthly. **Price:** $96, individuals. **Description:** Dedicated to the professional beauty salon and store industry. Recurring features include columns titled Guest Column.

10078 ■ *Haircut and Style*
Pub: Harris Publications Inc.
URL(s): www.style-stars.com/prizes-2006.html. **Released:** Quarterly **Price:** $3, Single issue.

10079 ■ *Modern Salon*
Contact: Michele Musgrove, Associate Publisher
E-mail: mmusgrove@vancepublishing.com
URL(s): www.modernsalon.com/. **Released:** Monthly

10080 ■ *Salon Today Magazine*
Contact: Stacey Soble, Editor-in-Chief
E-mail: ssoble@vancepublishing.com
URL(s): www.salontoday.com/. **Released:** Monthly **Price:** $45, Individuals; $63, Other countries; $75, Two years; $111, Two years other countries.

VIDEOCASSETTES/ AUDIOCASSETTES

10081 ■ *Haircutting Basics*
Instructional Video
2219 C St.
Lincoln, NE 68502
Ph: (402)475-6570
Free: 800-228-0164
Fax: (402)475-6500
Co. E-mail: feedback@insvideo.com
URL: http://www.insvideo.com
Released: 19??. **Price:** $29.95. **Description:** Teaches haircutting basics, including how to cut an outline, a one-level bob, a bi-leveled with bobbed back, long-layered, and a wedge. Available only in the U.S. **Availability:** VHS.

10082 ■ *Haircutting with Clippers—Basic Techniques*
Instructional Video
2219 C St.
Lincoln, NE 68502
Ph: (402)475-6570
Free: 800-228-0164
Fax: (402)475-6500
Co. E-mail: feedback@insvideo.com
URL: http://www.insvideo.com
Released: 19??. **Price:** $24.95. **Description:** Teaches basic haircutting techniques using clippers, including the clipper over skin, fingers, and comb techniques, how to trim and shape beards, mustaches, and sideburns, how to taper men's hair, cut-

ting the design line, cutting layers, the bob haircut, and the modern flattop. Available only in the U.S. **Availability:** VHS.

10083 ■ *My First Haircut*
Tapeworm Video Distributors
25876 The Old Road #141
Stevenson Ranch, CA 91381
Ph: (661)257-4904
Fax: (661)257-4820
Co. E-mail: sales@tapeworm.com
URL: http://www.tapeworm.com
Released: 1996. **Price:** $9.95. **Description:** Video footage of children getting their haircut helps prepare toddlers for their first haircut. **Availability:** VHS.

TRADE SHOWS AND CONVENTIONS

10084 ■ *Beauty Fair*
The Finnish Fair Corp.
PO Box 21
FIN-00521 Helsinki, Finland
Ph: 358 40 4503250
Fax: 358 9 142358
Co. E-mail: info@finnexpo.fi
URL: http://web.finnexpo.fi/en/Yritys/finnishfair/
Pages/default.aspx
URL(s): www.finnexpo.fi. **Frequency:** Annual. **Audience:** General public. **Principal Exhibits:** Beauty and fashion, cosmetics and services; hair products and services; clothing, showes, bags, accessories, jewelry, education, and publications.

10085 ■ *National Beauty Show - HAIRWORLD*
National Cosmetology Association
15825 N. 71st St., Ste. 100
Scottsdale, AZ 85254
Ph: (480)281-0424
Free: 800-468-2274
Fax: (480)905-0708
Co. E-mail: info@probeauty.org
URL: http://www.probeauty.org/nca/
Frequency: Annual. **Audience:** Salon owners and cosmetologists. **Principal Exhibits:** Hair products, cosmetics, and jewelry.

FRANCHISES AND BUSINESS OPPORTUNITIES

10086 ■ *Cartoon Cuts*
5501 NW 21st Ave., Ste. 410
Ft. Lauderdale, FL 33309
Ph: (954)653-2887
Free: 800-701-2887
Fax: (954)653-9074
Description: Hair salons for children. **No. of Company-Owned Units:** 19. **Founded:** 1991. **Franchised:** 2001. **Equity Capital Needed:** $97,000-$216,000. **Franchise Fee:** $25,000. **Training:** Yes.

10087 ■ *Chatters Salon*
271 Burnt Park Dr.
Red Deer County, AB, Canada T4S 2L4
Ph: (403)342-5055
Free: 888-944-5055
Fax: (403)347-7759
Co. E-mail: franchise@chatters.ca
URL: http://www.chatters.ca
Description: Hair salon and beauty supply full salon services with extensive retail component. **No. of Franchise Units:** 68. **No. of Company-Owned Units:** 22. **Founded:** 1988.. **Franchised:** 1991. **Equity Capital Needed:** $400,000-$700,000. **Franchise Fee:** $40,000.

10088 ■ *City Looks*
Charleswood Centre
3900 Grant Ave., Ste. 11
Winnipeg, MB, Canada R3R 3C2
Ph: (204)896-3177
URL(s): www.citylooks.ca. **Description:** City Looks caters to women looking for an exceptional hair care experience. Located primarily in shopping malls and strip centers. City Looks is backed by the strength and support of Regis Corporation. **No. of Franchise Units:** 19. **No. of Company-Owned Units:** 2. Fran-

chised: 1968. **Equity Capital Needed:** $150,000 liquid assets; $400,000 net worth. **Franchise Fee:** $22,500 1st salon, each additional $12,500. **Training:** Provides training and ongoing support.

10089 ■ Cookie Cutters Haircuts for Kids
CC Franchising
212 W 10th St., Ste. F-185
Indianapolis, IN 46202
Ph: (317)334-1680
Fax: (888)430-6378
Description: Children's interactive hair care. **No. of Franchise Units:** 40. **Founded:** 1993.. **Franchised:** 1995. **Equity Capital Needed:** $200,000 net worth. **Franchise Fee:** $25,000. **Training:** Yes.

10090 ■ Cost Cutters Family Hair Care
The Barbers, A Div. of Regis Corp.
7201 Metro Blvd.
Minneapolis, MN 55439
Free: 888-888-7008
Fax: (952)947-7900
Co. E-mail: franchiseleads@regiscorp.com
URL: http://www.costcutters.com
Description: A value priced, full-service salon concept that provides low-cost, no-frills hair services for the family. The franchisor created Cost Cutters to meet the demand for providing the public with quality hair services and products at a moderate price. **No. of Franchise Units:** 447. **No. of Company-Owned Units:** 364. **Founded:** 1963.. **Franchised:** 1982. **Equity Capital Needed:** $300,000 net worth; $100,000 liquid. **Franchise Fee:** $22,500 1st, $12,500 additional. **Financial Assistance:** Yes. **Training:** 1 week onsite training with ongoing support.

10091 ■ Fantastic Sams
50 Dunham Rd.
Beverly, MA 01915
Ph: (978)232-5600
Fax: (888)315-4437
Description: Full service family hair salons. **No. of Franchise Units:** 1,216. **Founded:** 1974.. **Franchised:** 1976. **Equity Capital Needed:** $115,000-$228,600. **Franchise Fee:** $30,000. **Training:** Yes.

10092 ■ First Choice Haircutters
Regis Corp.
6465 Millcreek Dr., Ste. 210
Mississauga, ON, Canada L5N 5R6
Free: 800-617-3961
Fax: (905)567-7000
Co. E-mail: franchiseleads@regiscorp.com
URL: http://www.firstchoice.com
Description: Value-priced family hair care centers. High-volume, low-cost, a la carte hair care for men, women and children. **No. of Franchise Units:** 189. **No. of Company-Owned Units:** 260. **Founded:** 1980.. **Franchised:** 1982. **Equity Capital Needed:** $300,000 net worth; $100,000 liquid. **Franchise Fee:** $22,500/1st, $12,500 each additional. **Financial Assistance:** 30-V, FRA handbook. **Training:** Provides 1 week managerial and technical training, 1 week onsite training with support in all areas including real estate, grand opening, staffing, marketing and ongoing support.

10093 ■ Great Clips, Inc.
Great Clips, Inc.
7700 France Ave. 425
Minneapolis, MN 55435
Free: 800-947-1143
Fax: (952)844-3443
Co. E-mail: franchise@greatclips.com
URL: http://www.greatclips.com
Description: High-volume, quality hair salons that specialize in cuts and perms for the entire family. Unique and attractive decor and quality advertising. Emphasis on strong, hands-on support to franchisee's. Definite opportunity for growth in a fast-growing industry. directors. **No. of Franchise Units:** 2,650. **Founded:** 1982.. **Franchised:** 1983. **Equity Capital Needed:** $300,000 net worth; $50,000 liquid. **Franchise Fee:** $25,000. **Financial Assistance:** Yes. **Training:** Training begins with New Franchisee Orientation & Training. This 5 day session covers all aspects of the Great Clips operating systems. All style and employee training is provided through our field staff and our area training centers.

10094 ■ Lemon Tree Family Hair Salon
Lemon Tree Development, LLC
400 Jericho Tpk., Ste. 326
Jericho, NY 11753
Ph: (516)605-2080
Fax: (516)605-2078
Co. E-mail: info@lemontree.com
URL: http://www.lemontree.com
Description: Offers franchises for unisex hair care services. **No. of Franchise Units:** 45. **Founded:** 1976.. **Franchised:** 1976. **Equity Capital Needed:** $55,100-$87,700. **Franchise Fee:** $9,000. **Training:** Includes 1 week of training at corporate headquarters and a company representative spends 1 week at salon grand opening.

10095 ■ Magicuts
6465 Millcreek Dr., Ste. 210
Mississauga, ON, Canada L5N 5R6
Ph: (905)363-4105
Fax: (952)995-3403
Co. E-mail: franchiseleads@regiscorp.com
URL: http://www.regisfranchise.com
Description: Full service hair salons with professional services and products at affordable prices. **No. of Franchise Units:** 84. **No. of Company-Owned Units:** 131. **Founded:** 1981.. **Franchised:** 1982. **Equity Capital Needed:** $100,000 liquid assets; $300,000 net worth. **Franchise Fee:** $22,500 first salon; $12,500 each additional. **Training:** Full training and support.

10096 ■ Pro-Cuts
Regis Corp.
7201 Metro Blvd.
Minneapolis, MN 55439
Ph: (952)947-7777
Fax: (952)947-7600
Co. E-mail: info@regiscorp.com
URL: http://www.regiscorp.com
Description: Family hair care centers, providing quality haircuts for a low price. Also carrying a line of private-label, high-quality, hair care products exclusive to Pro-Cuts. **No. of Franchise Units:** 165. **Founded:** 1982.. **Franchised:** 1984. **Equity Capital Needed:** $300,000 net worth; $100,000 liquid assets. **Franchise Fee:** $22,500. **Financial Assistance:** Yes. **Training:** Provides 1 week managerial and technical training, 1 week onsite, support in real estate, grand opening and ongoing support.

10097 ■ Regal Nails, Salon & Spa
Regal Nails, Salon & Spa LLC
5150 Florida Blvd.
Baton Rouge, LA 70806
Free: 888-414-6245
Fax: (800)422-4608
Co. E-mail: book@regalnails.com
URL: http://www.regalnails.com
Description: Nail salon. **Founded:** 2006..

10098 ■ Roosters Men's Grooming Centers
Roosters MGC Intl., LLC
5523 East Nine Mile Rd.
Warren, MI 48091
Ph: (763)201-1470
Free: 866-642-2625
Fax: (586)619-2167
Co. E-mail: joe@roostermgc.com
URL: http://www.roostersmgc.com
Description: Men beauty salons supply cosmetic products and specialist in tanning. **No. of Franchise Units:** 50. **No. of Company-Owned Units:** 1. **Founded:** 1999.. **Franchised:** 2002. **Equity Capital Needed:** $100,000-$250,000. **Franchise Fee:** $35,000-$73,000. **Training:** Yes.

10099 ■ Snip N' Clip Haircut Shops
11427 Strang Line Rd.
Lenexa, KS 66215
Ph: (913)345-0077
Free: 800-622-6804
Fax: (913)345-1554
Co. E-mail: info@snipnclip.net
URL: http://www.snipnclip.com
Description: Family hair salons. **No. of Franchise Units:** 23. **No. of Company-Owned Units:** 40. **Founded:** 1976.. **Franchised:** 1986. **Equity Capital**

Needed: $75,100-$88,950, includes of $15,000 franchise fee & turn-key package. **Franchise Fee:** $15,000. **Training:** Onsite training.

10100 ■ Sport Clips
Sport Clips, Inc.
PMB 266
Georgetown, TX 78627-3000
Ph: (512)869-1201
Free: 800-872-4247
Fax: (512)868-4699
Co. E-mail: Sara.Clements@sportsclips.com
URL: http://www.sportclips.com
Description: Men's hair care centers with sports theme. **No. of Franchise Units:** 850. **No. of Company-Owned Units:** 21. **Founded:** 1993. **Franchised:** 1995. **Equity Capital Needed:** $100,000. **Franchise Fee:** $25,000-$49,500. **Training:** Initial and ongoing technical and management training by Sport Clips area Coaches.

10101 ■ Supercuts
Regis Corp.
7201 Metro Blvd.
Edina, MN 55439
Free: 888-888-7008
Fax: (952)947-7900
Co. E-mail: franchiseleads@regiscorp.com
URL: http://www.supercuts.com
Description: Franchisee offering haircutting services for men, women, and children. **No. of Franchise Units:** 1,035. **No. of Company-Owned Units:** 1,097. **Founded:** 1976.. **Franchised:** 1976. **Equity Capital Needed:** $300,000 net worth; $100,000 liquid. **Franchise Fee:** $22,500/1st ; $12,500 each additional. **Financial Assistance:** Yes. **Training:** Provides 1 week managerial and technical training, 1 week onsite training. Support in all areas including real estate, grand opening, staffing, marketing, and ongoing support.

10102 ■ Supercuts
Regis Corp.
6465 Millcreek Dr. Ste. 210
Mississauga, ON, Canada L5N 5R6
Ph: (905)363-4105
Fax: (952)995-3403
Co. E-mail: franchiseleads@regiscorp.com
URL: http://www.regisfranchise.com
Description: The franchise offers affordable hair care. **No. of Franchise Units:** 15. **No. of Company-Owned Units:** 37. **Founded:** 1975.. **Franchised:** 1978. **Equity Capital Needed:** $100,000 liquid assets; $300,000 net worth. **Franchise Fee:** $22,500 first salon; $12,500 each additional. **Training:** Initial and ongoing support.

10103 ■ Trade Secrets
Trade Secrets / Glamour Secrets
101 Jevlan Dr.
Woodbridge, ON, Canada L4L 8C2
Ph: (905)264-2799
Free: 888-264-7444
Fax: (905)264-2779
Co. E-mail: franchising@tradesecrets.ca
URL: http://www.tradesecrets.ca
Description: Trade Secrets provides full service salon and branded products for sale. **No. of Franchise Units:** 44. **No. of Company-Owned Units:** 21. **Founded:** 1989.. **Franchised:** 1990. **Equity Capital Needed:** $80,000-$325,000 invermment requied. **Franchise Fee:** $20,000. **Training:** Offers 3 weeks training in a corporate store.

10104 ■ Treehouse Cuts Salon
8800 Kelly Dr.
Yorktown, IN 47396-0231
Free: 888-928-TREE
Fax: (219)271-9646
Description: Family haircare salon. **No. of Franchise Units:** 7. **No. of Company-Owned Units:** 6. **Founded:** 1996.. **Franchised:** 1999. **Equity Capital Needed:** $75,000-$220,000. **Franchise Fee:** $22,500. **Training:** Yes.

10105 ■ The Yellow Balloon
12448 Ventura Blvd.
Studio City, CA 91604

Ph: (818)760-7141
URL: http://www.theyellowballoon.com
Description: Hair salons for children. **Founded:** 1983.. **Franchised:** 2000. **Equity Capital Needed:** $55,000-$103,500. **Franchise Fee:** $25,000. **Royalty Fee:** 4%. **Financial Assistance:** In-house financial assistance available for franchise fee. **Training:** Provides 7 days at corporate headquarters.

COMPUTER SYSTEMS/ SOFTWARE

10106 ■ *Hairshaping*
13064 Indian Rocks Rd.
Largo, FL 33774
Ph: (727)593-2700
Free: 800-255-9085
Fax: (727)595-2685
Co. E-mail: info@philliproy.com
URL: http://www.philliproy.com
Price: $145.00. **Description:** Available for PC computers.

10107 ■ *Salon 2.0 - Salon and Spa Managment Software*
1386 Newton Ave., SW
Atlanta, GA 30316
Ph: (404)835-7157
Free: 800-927-0260
Co. E-mail: info@grantparksoftware.com
URL: http://www.grantparksoftware.com
Price: $199. **Description:** Software program designed for small salons. Contains all the features of E-Z Way Salon Software (Basic). Advanced functions include an accounting module and a payroll system; an appointment book for viewing and printing appointments; sales history analysis; product recommendations; and referral tracking.

LIBRARIES

10108 ■ Aesthetics International Association Library
310 E. Interstate 30, Ste. B107
Garland, TX 75043

Ph: (469)429-9300
Free: 877-968-7539
Fax: (972)226-2339
URL: http://www.aestheticsassociation.com
Contact: Melissa Lawrence
Scope: Skin care, makeup, body therapy, spa treatments, permanent cosmetics, paramedical cosmetics; aromatherapy; business; reference. **Services:** Library not open to the public. **Founded:** 1978. **Holdings:** 250 volumes; 50 audio/visual programs.

10109 ■ Clairol Research Library
1 Blachley Rd.
Stamford, CT 06922
Free: 800-252-4765
URL: http://www.clairol.com
Scope: Chemistry and technology of cosmetics, hair dyes and dyeing, personal care. **Services:** Library open to the public with restrictions. **Holdings:** 10,000 books; 6000 bound periodical volumes; 30 titles on microfilm. **Subscriptions:** 350 journals and other serials.

ASSOCIATIONS AND OTHER ORGANIZATIONS

10110 ■ American Association of Handwriting Analysts (AAHA)
4143 Lorna Ct. SE
Lacey, WA 98503
Ph: (360)455-4551
Free: 800-826-7774
Co. E-mail: aahatreasjane@aol.com
URL: http://aahahandwriting.com
Contact: Jane O'Brien, Treasurer
Description: Persons who have completed recognized courses in handwriting analysis, passed examinations by a committee of the Association, and displayed proficiency in the science of analyzing character from handwriting are certified members; individuals who have passed an exam on the guiding principles of graphology are associate members. Those who are interested in graphology are affiliate members. Serves as a forum for the exchange of information on graphology and research in the field. Promotes professionalism in the "science of analyzing character through examination of all forms of writing." Seeks public recognition of handwriting analysis as an important aid in the solution of problems involving personality and identification of signatures or writing. Promotes research in handwriting analysis. **Scope:** handwriting analysis; psychology in English, German and French. **Founded:** 1962. **Subscriptions:** 750 articles books. **Awards:** Honorary Membership; Honorary Membership.

10111 ■ American Handwriting Analysis Foundation (AHAF)
PO Box 460385
Escondido, CA 92046-0385
Ph: (315)720-9296
Free: 800-826-7774
Co. E-mail: ahafpresident@gmail.com
URL: http://www.ahafhandwriting.org
Contact: Debra Peddy, President
Description: Individuals interested in handwriting analysis. Seeks to advance graphology (the art and science of determining qualities of the personality from the script) as a helping profession; provide certification program for members; establish a code of ethics; foster research in handwriting analysis and cooperation among all handwriting analysts and handwriting societies. Maintains research and educational programs. Maintains speakers' bureau. Disseminates resource information. **Scope:** handwriting analysis, questioned document work, psychology. **Founded:** 1967. **Subscriptions:** 800 books monographs periodicals. **Publications:** *AHAF Journal* (Bimonthly); *Manual for Graphological Researchers*; *Guide to Self-Published Papers, 1978-1988* (Annual); *International Bibliography of Graphological Journal Articles, 1968-1988*; *Recommended Reading Dossier*; *Write Learning*; *Standard Terms for Handwriting Analysts: English Terms, Document Examination Terms, Health Terms, International Terms*. **Awards:** Flandrin/Michon Life Achievement Award; President's Award; Honorary Membership Award (Periodic); Michael-Flandrin Award.

10112 ■ Association of Forensic Document Examiners (AFDE)
5432 E Karen Dr.
Scottsdale, AZ 85254-8205
Co. E-mail: journal.jfde@gmail.com
URL: http://www.afde.org
Contact: Emily J. Will, President
Description: Represents forensic document examiners and students of document examination. Sponsors annual continuing education conferences and offers a certification program. **Scope:** forensic analysis, handwriting identification, question documents. **Founded:** 1986. **Publications:** *Journal of Forensic Document Examination* (Annual). **Educational Activities:** Continuing Education (Annual).

10113 ■ International Graphoanalysis Society (IGAS)—International Grapho-Analysis Society Inc.
842 5th Ave.
New Kensington, PA 15068
Ph: (724)472-9701
Fax: (509)271-1149
Co. E-mail: greg@igas.com
URL: http://www.igas.com
Contact: Greg Greco, President
E-mail: greg@igas.com
Description: Represents handwriting analysts and identification experts. Maintains hall of fame and speakers' bureau. Compiles statistics; conducts research programs, specialized education, and placement service. **Scope:** psychology and identification. **Founded:** 1929. **Subscriptions:** 500. **Publications:** *Journal of Graphoanalysis.*

10114 ■ National Society for Graphology (NSG)
250 W 57th St., Ste. 1228A
New York, NY 10107-1221
Ph: (212)265-1148
Co. E-mail: irenicnyc@aol.com
URL: http://www.handwriting.org/nsg/nsgmain.html
Description: Professionally certified graphologists and individuals interested in Gestalt graphology. (Graphology is the study of handwriting for purposes of character analysis.) Promotes the study of graphology. Encourages individuals to train in graphology and seek professional status within the organization. **Scope:** graphology, psychology. **Founded:** 1972. **Subscriptions:** 400 books clippings monographs periodicals.

TRADE PERIODICALS

10115 ■ *Journal of Graphoanalysis*
Pub: International Graphoanalysis Society
Contact: Greg Greco, President
E-mail: greg@igas.com
URL(s): www.igas.com.

CONSULTANTS

10116 ■ All Handwriting Services L.L.C.
PO Box 204
Bountiful, UT 84011
Ph: (801)915-7715
Fax: (801)294-3201
Co. E-mail: allhandwriting@hotmail.com
URL: http://allhandwritingservicesllc.com
Contact: Linda L. Cropp, Principal
E-mail: allhandwriting@hotmail.com
Scope: Offers questioned document examination, letters of opinion, testimony, forgery detection, anonymous letters, psychological profiles, jury selection, behavior profiling for personnel selection and promotions, vocation selection, business compatibility reports, and litigation support. Qualified for district and federal courts. Industries served include legal, law enforcement, retail, manufacturing, business, and personnel departments. **Founded:** 1987. **Seminars:** Basics of Handwriting Analysis; Know Yourself and Others Through Handwriting Analysis; The Troubled Teen; Introduction to Handwriting Analysis; Preemployment Screening and Handwriting Analysis; How to Hire a Document Examiner: Credentials, Expertise, Certifications, Fees; When to Hire document Examiner; Detect Violence in the Workplace Through Handwriting Analysis; The Dishonest/Abusive Personality.

COMPUTER SYSTEMS/ SOFTWARE

10117 ■ *Handwriting Analyst*
3800 Golf Rd., Ste. 100
Rolling Meadows, IL 60008
Ph: (630)467-7000
Free: 800-323-9540
Fax: (630)467-7192
Co. E-mail: rpcsupport@hmco.com
URL: http://www.riverpub.com
Contact: Van Mabie, Director
E-mail: van.mabie@hmhpub.com
Price: $79.95, plus shipping. **Description:** Available for Apple Macintosh, Apple II, and IBM computers. System analyzes handwriting to describe personalities.

LIBRARIES

10118 ■ American Association of Handwriting Analysts Library
4143 Lorna Ct., SE
Lacey, WI 98503
URL: http://aahahandwriting.com
Scope: Handwriting analysis. **Services:** Library not open to the public. **Founded:** 1964. **Holdings:** 860 volumes.

10119 ■ Handwriting Analysis Research Library—HARL.
PO Box 104
Greenfield, MA 01342-0104
Ph: (413)774-4667
URL: http://handwritinganalysisresearchlibrary.org
Scope: Graphology, handwriting, analysis, penmanship, questioned documents. **Services:** Interlibrary loan; copying; Library open to the public for reference use only. **Founded:** 1949. **Holdings:** 174

bound periodical volumes; 791 research reports; 68,471 manuscripts, clippings, photocopies; 901 translated items; 4891 abstracts; archival records of 17 defunct handwriting analysis organizations (closed reserve); 126 reports; 377 manuscripts; 14 archives; 41 notebooks; 3 CD-ROMs. **Subscriptions:** 16 journals and other serials.

ASSOCIATIONS AND OTHER ORGANIZATIONS

10120 ■ American Hardware Manufacturers Association (AHMA)
801 N Plaza Dr.
Schaumburg, IL 60173
Ph: (847)605-1025
Fax: (847)605-1030
Co. E-mail: info@ahma.org
URL: http://www.ahma.org
Contact: Donald D. Dray, President
Description: Represents the hardware, home improvement, lawn and garden, paint and decorating, and related industries. **Founded:** 1901. **Publications:** *AHMA Eagle* (Bimonthly); *AHMA Employee Relations Report* (Monthly); *AHMA Issue Briefing* (Monthly); *AHMA Washington Report* (Monthly); *The Hard Fax International* (Biweekly). **Educational Activities:** AHMA Hardware Show (Annual); Executive Conference for the Home Improvement Industry (Annual).

10121 ■ Builders Hardware Manufacturers Association (BHMA)
355 Lexington Ave., 15th Fl.
New York, NY 10017
Ph: (212)297-2122
Fax: (212)370-9047
Co. E-mail: bhma@kellencompany.com
URL: http://www.buildershardware.com
Contact: Peter Rush., Executive Director
Description: Manufacturers of builders' hardware, both contract and stock. Provides statistical services; maintains standardization program; sponsors certification programs for locks, latches, door closers and cabinet hardware. Maintains 12 product sections. **Founded:** 1925.

10122 ■ Canadian Institute of Plumbing and Heating
295 West Mall, Ste. 330
Toronto, ON, Canada M9C 4Z4
Ph: (416)695-0447
Fax: (416)695-0450
Co. E-mail: rcp@ciph.com
URL: http://www.ciph.com
Contact: Ralph Suppa, President
Description: Manufacturers, distributors and wholesalers of plumbing and heating equipment and supplies. Promotes advancement of members' businesses; seeks to improve plumbing and heating practice and technology. Serves as a clearinghouse on the plumbing and heating industries; represents members' interests before government agencies; assists in the formation of industry standards; encourages increased use of hydronic heating systems. Sponsors educational and training programs for members; compiles industry statistics. **Publications:** *Canadian Institute of Plumbing and Heating Pipeline* (Quarterly). **Educational Activities:** Harnessing the Tides of Change.

10123 ■ *Canadian Institute of Plumbing and Heating Pipeline*
295 West Mall, Ste. 330
Toronto, ON, Canada M9C 4Z4
Ph: (416)695-0447
Fax: (416)695-0450
Co. E-mail: rcp@ciph.com
URL: http://www.ciph.com
Contact: Ralph Suppa, President
Released: Quarterly

10124 ■ *Directory of Ontario Lumber and Building Materials, Hardware and Home Improvement Retailers*
5155 Spectrum Way, Unit 27
Mississauga, ON, Canada L4W 5A1
Ph: (905)625-1084
Free: 888-365-2626
Fax: (905)625-3006
Co. E-mail: dwcampbell@lbmao.on.ca
URL: http://www.lbmao.on.ca
Contact: David W. Campbell, President
Released: Annual

10125 ■ Lumber and Building Materials Association of Ontario (LBMAO)
5155 Spectrum Way, Unit 27
Mississauga, ON, Canada L4W 5A1
Ph: (905)625-1084
Free: 888-365-2626
Fax: (905)625-3006
Co. E-mail: dwcampbell@lbmao.on.ca
URL: http://www.lbmao.on.ca
Contact: David W. Campbell, President
Description: Retailers of building supplies. Seeks to advance the lumber and building supplies industries. Facilitates communication and cooperation among members; represents members' interests before labor and industrial organizations, government agencies, and the public. **Founded:** 1917. **Publications:** *Reporter* (Bimonthly); *Directory of Ontario Lumber and Building Materials, Hardware and Home Improvement Retailers* (Annual); *Directory of Ontario Lumber & Building Materials Retailers--Buyers' Guide & Product Directory* (Annual).

10126 ■ National Lumber and Building Material Dealers Association (NLBMDA)
2025 M St. NW, Ste. 800
Washington, DC 20036-3309
Ph: (202)367-1169
Free: 800-634-8645
Fax: (202)367-2169
Co. E-mail: info@dealer.org
URL: http://www.dealer.org
Contact: Cally Fromme, Chairman of the Board
Description: Represents more than 8,000 lumber and building material companies with over 400,000 employees, 20 state and regional associations and the industry's leading manufacturers and service providers. **Founded:** 1917. **Publications:** *Building Material Dealer*; *NLBMDA Advocate* (Monthly); *Nuts & Bolts*; *ProSales* (Monthly); *Cost of Doing Business* (Annual); *Forklift and You*; *Risk Management Best Practices*; *Your National Perspective* (Quarterly).

Educational Activities: Industry Summit (Annual); Legislative Conference (Annual). **Awards:** Grassroots Award (Annual); Safety Award (Annual); Excellence in Human Resources (Annual); Member of Congress Award (Annual). **Telecommunication Services:** nlbmda@dealer.org.

10127 ■ North American Retail Hardware Association (NRHA)
6325 Digital Way, Ste. 300
Indianapolis, IN 46278-1787
Ph: (317)275-9400
Free: 800-772-4424
Fax: (317)275-9403
Co. E-mail: pfbowman@nrha.org
URL: http://www.nrha.org
Contact: Mike O'Hara, President
Description: Represents independent family-owned hardware/home improvement retailers. Sponsors correspondence courses in hardware and building materials retailing; conducts annual cost-of-doing-business study. **Founded:** 1900. **Publications:** *National Retail Hardware Association Management Report: Cost of Doing Business Study*; *Hardware Retailing: Serving Hardware, Home Center, Building Material Retailers* (Monthly); *Buyer's Book*. **Awards:** Young Retailer of the Year (Annual).

10128 ■ *Reporter*
5155 Spectrum Way, Unit 27
Mississauga, ON, Canada L4W 5A1
Ph: (905)625-1084
Free: 888-365-2626
Fax: (905)625-3006
Co. E-mail: dwcampbell@lbmao.on.ca
URL: http://www.lbmao.on.ca
Contact: David W. Campbell, President
Released: Bimonthly **Price:** included in membership dues.

REFERENCE WORKS

10129 ■ *"Code Name: Investors: Go From Golden Idea to Agent of Invention" in Black Enterprise (Vol. 41, November 2010, No. 4, pp. 78)*
Pub: Earl G. Graves Publishing Co. Inc.
Ed: Renita Burns. **Description:** Profile of Andre Woolery, inventor of a magnetic wristband that holds small nails, screws, drill bits, and small tools, allowing handymen to keep essential tools at hand while working.

10130 ■ *Directory of Home Center Operators & Hardware Chains*
Pub: Chain Store Guide
Contact: Lisa Patterson, President
URL(s): www.chainstoreguide.com. **Released:** Annual; Latest edition 2012. **Price:** $395, Individuals Directory; $445, Individuals online lite; $1075, Individuals online pro; $1375, Individuals online pro plus. **Covers:** 4,500 U.S. and Canadian companies which operate home centers, home center warehouses, lumber and building material outlets, specialty paint and home decorating stores, and kitchen

and bath centers. Concentrates on companies with a minimum annual sales of one million dollars. **Entries include:** Company name, address, phone, fax, 6,100 personnel e-mail address, web site, Internet order processing indicator, listing type, product lines, total sales, sales percentage per customer type, total selling square footage, total stores, units by type of store operated, units made by trade name, trading areas, projected openings and remodeling, distribution center locations, buying and/or marketing group name and location, number of nurseries operated, average number of check-outs, year founded, public company indicator, parent and subsidiary company information, division and branch office locations, key personnel, and number of locations by city. **Arrangement:** Geographical. **Indexes:** Product line, alphabetical, exclusions, state.

10131 ■ *"Doing Good: Cause and Effect" in Entrepreneur (Vol. 36, February 2008, No. 2, pp. 23)*
Pub: Entrepreneur Media Inc.
Description: Lisa Knoppe established Art for a Cause LLC that employs people with mental and physical disabilities. The company makes hand-painted tools and furniture to be sold at gift retailers and hardware stores.

10132 ■ *"The Final Piece; Lowe's to Fill Last Big Parcel Near Great Lakes Crossing" in Crain's Detroit Business (March 10, 2008)*
Pub: Crain Communications, Inc.
Ed: Daniel Duggan. **Description:** Silverman Development Co. is developing a Lowe's home-improvement store on the last major retail parcel near the intersection of I-75 and Joslyn Road, an area which was once desolate but is now home to several restaurants and other retail facilities.

10133 ■ *"High Hopes: Ralph Mitchell's Picks Have Growth Potential" in Black Enterprise (Vol. 37, February 2007, No. 7, pp. 42)*
Pub: Earl G. Graves Publishing Co. Inc.
Ed: Carolyn M. Brown. **Description:** Ralph Mitchell, president and senior financial advisor of Braintree-Carthage Financial Group, offers three recommendations: Toll Brothers, Home Depot, and Lowe's.

10134 ■ *"Home Improvement Marketers Target Women With New Products, New Campaigns and Plenty of Pink" in Marketing to Women (March 2008)*
Pub: EPM Communications Inc.
Contact: Ira Mayer, President
E-mail: imayer@epmcom.com
Description: From creating tools that fit a woman's ergonomics to designs that fit a woman's fashion sense, home improvement is finding new ways in which to market to women.

10135 ■ *"The Main Event" in Canadian Business (Vol. 80, November 19, 2007, No. 23, pp. 28)*
Pub: Rogers Media
Ed: Zena Olijnyk. **Description:** U.S.-based Lowe's Companies, Inc. will be opening three stores in Canada in December 2007 and another three in 2008. The housing market crisis in the U.S. is the reason behind the home improvement store's Canadian expansion. The impacts of the expansion on Canadian home care stores and on the market competition are evaluated.

10136 ■ *"Milwaukee Rolls Out Major Line Expansion" in Contractor (Vol. 56, July 2009, No. 7, pp. 3)*
Pub: Penton Media, Inc.
Ed: Robert P. Mader. **Description:** Milwaukee Electric Tool Corp. introduced a new line of products that include corded tools and cordless tools, measurement instruments, and tool accessories. The products include four new Deep Cut Band Saws and the M12 Cordless 3/8-inch Impact Wrench.

10137 ■ *"Most Popular Tools? The Survey Says" in Contractor (Vol. 57, February 2010, No. 2, pp. 1)*
Pub: Penton Media, Inc.
Ed: Robert P. Mader. **Description:** According to a survey of individuals in the field, mechanical contractors are purchasing more of their tools at home

centers and they are also increasingly working in the service, repair, and retrofit markets. The survey also found that the reciprocating saw is the most used corded power tool. Additional purchasing habits of mechanical contractors are listed.

10138 ■ *"Profit Strong Rona to Maintain Acquisition Strategy" in Globe & Mail (February 22, 2007, pp. B14)*
Pub: CTVglobemedia Publishing Inc.
Description: Canada-based Rona Inc., home improvement retailer that reported record annual profit in 2006, will continue its strategy of acquisitions. The company has reported profits of $190.6 million in 2006.

10139 ■ *"Retail Briefs - Dollar Store Opens in Long Leaf Mall" in Star-News (November 5, 2010)*
Pub: Star-News Media
Ed: Judy Royal. **Description:** Dollar Delight$ opened a new shop in Long Leaf Mall in Wilmington, North Carolina. The store will carry gift bags, balloons, party supplies, greeting cards, school supplies, health and beauty products, hardware, baby items, toys, Christmas goods, crafts, housewares and jewelry in its inventory.

STATISTICAL SOURCES

10140 ■ *The Home Improvement Market*
Pub: MarketResearch.com
Released: 1999. **Price:** $2750.00. **Description:** This study analyzes the growing market for do-it-yourself (DIY) home improvement in the United States.

10141 ■ *RMA Annual Statement Studies*
Pub: Risk Management Association
Contact: Kevin M. Blakey, President
Released: Annual. **Price:** $175.00 2006-07 edition, $105.00. **Description:** Contains composite balance sheets and income statements for more than 360 industries, including the accounting, auditing, and bookkeeping industries. Also contains five years of comparative historical data for discerning trends. Includes 16 commonly used ratios, computed for most of the size groupings for nearly every industry.

10142 ■ *Standard & Poor's Industry Surveys*
Pub: Standard & Poor's Corp.
Released: Annual. **Price:** $3633.00. **Description:** Two-volume book that examines the prospects for specific industries, including trucking. Also provides analyses of trends and problems, statistical tables and charts, and comparative company analyses.

TRADE PERIODICALS

10143 ■ *Building Products Digest*
Pub: Cutler Publishing Inc.
URL(s): www.building-products.com/BPDSiteMap.aspx. **Released:** Monthly **Price:** $24, Individuals; $39, Two years.

10144 ■ *Hardware Merchandising: Solutions for home improvement retailers*
Pub: Rogers Media Publishing
URL(s): www.hardwaremagazine.ca/. **Ed:** Lori Smith. **Released:** Monthly **Price:** C$99, Canada 2 years; plus applicable taxes; C$60, Canada plus applicable taxes; C$85, U.S.

10145 ■ *Home Channel News*
Contact: Jeff Arlen, Publisher
E-mail: jarlen@homechannelnews.com
URL(s): www.homechannelnews.com. **Released:** 16/yr. **Price:** $189, Individuals.

10146 ■ *Home Improvement Retailing*
Pub: Powershift Communications Inc.
URL(s): www.hirmagazine.com/. **Released:** Bi-monthly **Price:** $76, Individuals; $110, Canada plus applicable taxes.

TRADE SHOWS AND CONVENTIONS

10147 ■ Door and Hardware Institute Annual Convention and Exposition
Door and Hardware Institute
14150 Newbrook Dr., Ste. 200
Chantilly, VA 20151-2223

Ph: (703)222-2010
Fax: (703)222-2410
URL: http://www.dhi.org
URL(s): www.dhi.org/INDUSTRY/events/annual/index.php. **Frequency:** Annual. **Audience:** Industry distributors, sales representatives, and manufacturers; engineers; and facility administrators. **Principal Exhibits:** Doors, hardware, and specialty building products. **Telecommunication Services:** steveh@ptd.net.

10148 ■ H2X Canada Hardware & Home Improvement Expo & Conference
Messe Frankfurt Inc.
1600 Parkwood Cir., Ste. 515
Atlanta, GA 30339
Ph: (770)984-8016
Fax: (770)984-8023
Co. E-mail: info@usa.messefrankfurt.com
URL: http://www.usa.messefrankfurt.com
URL(s): meesefrankfurt.com/shows/northamerica/h2x/index.htm. **Frequency:** Annual. **Audience:** Volume buyers, including retailers and manufacturers' representatives. **Principal Exhibits:** Hardware, housewares, giftware, paint, wallcovering, and products for leisure living, and home improvement. **Dates and Locations:** , Coliseum Exhbition Place.

10149 ■ Northwestern Building Products Expo
Northwestern Lumber Association
5905 Golden Valley Rd., Ste. 110
Minneapolis, MN 55422
Ph: (763)544-6822
Free: 888-544-6822
Fax: (763)595-4060
Co. E-mail: nlassn@nlassn.org
URL: http://www.nlassn.org
Contact: Paula Siewert, President
E-mail: psiewert@nlassn.org
Frequency: Annual. **Audience:** Retail lumber and building material dealers. **Principal Exhibits:** Any product or service that is ultimately sold or used by retail lumber and building material dealers. **Dates and Locations:** , Convention Center.

10150 ■ Wisconsin Manufacturing & Technology Show
Expo Productions Inc.
510 Hartbrook Dr.
Hartland, WI 53029
Ph: (262)367-5500
Free: 800-367-5520
Fax: (262)367-9956
Co. E-mail: expo@execpc.com
URL: http://www.expoproductionsinc.com
URL(s): www.expoproductionsinc.com/tool_home.htm. **Price:** $5. **Frequency:** Biennial. **Audience:** Purchasing agents, presidents and CEOs of companies, and plant engineers. **Principal Exhibits:** Metal working machinery and related manufacturing equipment, supplies, and services machine tools. **Telecommunication Services:** jill@epishows.com.

FRANCHISES AND BUSINESS OPPORTUNITIES

10151 ■ Atlantic Mower Parts
Atlantic Mower Part Supplies Inc.
13421 SW 14 Pl.
Ft. Lauderdale, FL 33325
Ph: (954)474-4942
Fax: (954)475-0414
Description: Hardware Stores. **No. of Franchise Units:** 12. **No. of Company-Owned Units:** 1. **Founded:** 1978.. **Franchised:** 1988. **Equity Capital Needed:** $45,000. **Franchise Fee:** $15,900. **Training:** Yes.

10152 ■ Matco Tools
Danaher Corp.
4403 Allen Rd.
Stow, OH 44224
Ph: (330)929-4949
Free: 800-368-6651

Fax: (330)926-5325
Co. E-mail: matcofh@franchisehub.com
URL: http://www.matcotools.com

Description: Matco Tools is a provider of precision mechanics hand tools, service equipment, and diagnostic computers that are distributed through franchised mobile tool distributors. From well-stocked Matco Tools trucks, Matco Distributors provide weekly service to customers at their place of employment. **No. of Franchise Units:** 1,450. **Founded:** 1979.. **Franchised:** 1993. **Equity Capital Needed:** $25,000-$30,000 start-up cash; $82,800-$216,800 total investment. **Franchise Fee:** None. **Financial Assistance:** Yes. **Training:** All new Matco Distributors are required to attend and successfully complete the Matco Tools New Distributor Training Program. This training is presented in a 6 day classroom training in Stow, OH, and a 3 week on truck training with a designated trainer.

10153 ■ Snap-On Inc.—Sun ElectricSnap-on Tools Company LLC;
2801 80th St.
Kenosha, WI 53141
Ph: (262)656-5200
Free: 877-4SN-APON
Fax: (262)656-5577
Co. E-mail: sales@snapon.com
URL: http://www.snapon.com
Contact: Donald E. Broman, President

Description: Develops, produces & markets professional equipment & tools. **No. of Franchise Units:** 4,520. **No. of Company-Owned Units:** 248. **Founded:** 1920. **Franchised:** 1991. **Equity Capital Needed:** Low cost start-up programs. **Franchise Fee:** $7,500-$15,000. **Financial Assistance:** A variety of financing options are available through Snap-on Credit LLC, an affiliate of Snap-on, or through other third-party resources. **Training:** Provides 3 weeks training at franchisees location, 1 week each at branch and regional centers and ongoing support.

10154 ■ Woodcraft Franchise, LLC
SBR, Inc.
1177 Rosemar Rd.
Parkersburg, WV 26105
Ph: (304)422-5412
Fax: (304)485-1939
Co. E-mail: woodcraftfranchise@woodcraft.com
URL: http://www.woodcraft.com

Description: Specialty retail store. **No. of Franchise Units:** 88. **No. of Company-Owned Units:** 4. **Founded:** 1928.. **Franchised:** 1997. **Equity Capital Needed:** $150,000 liquid capital; $503,300-$650,300 total investment. **Franchise Fee:** $50,000. **Training:** Yes.

REFERENCE WORKS

10155 ■ *Hat Life Directory*
Pub: Mint Publishing
Contact: Johanna O'Kelley, Director
E-mail: Johanna.okelley@sierraclub.org
URL(s): https://www.hatlife.com/order.php. **Released:** Annual; Latest edition 2010. **Price:** $84, Individuals directory: U.S. orders only; $94, Individuals directory: includes international delivery. **Covers:** About 1,000 hat manufacturers, wholesalers, renovators, and importers of men's headwear, plus trade suppliers listed (SIC 2253, 2352, 5036); includes about 120 Canadian manufacturers. **Entries include:** Company name, address, phone, fax, trade and brand names. **Arrangement:** Classified by product.

VIDEOCASSETTES/ AUDIOCASSETTES

10156 ■ *Accessory Allure*
Cambridge Educational
c/o Films Media Group
132 West 31st Street, 17th Floor
Ste. 124
New York, NY 10001
Free: 800-257-5126
Fax: (609)671-0266
Co. E-mail: custserve@films.com
URL: http://www.cambridgeol.com
Released: 1987. **Price:** $29.95. **Description:** This video shows viewers how to make the most of their wardrobe by using scarves, earrings, hats, and other accessories. **Availability:** VHS.

CONSULTANTS

10157 ■ **Contex Analytical Inc.—Textile Consultatnt Associates**
2032 Lurting Ave.
Bronx, NY 10461-1314
Ph: (718)829-0080
Fax: (718)829-0080
Co. E-mail: teachtex@earthlink.net
Contact: Robert J. Beaulieu, President
Scope: Provider of professional consulting services to the apparel textile trades. These services include: textile and sewn products design engineering, textile and sewn products defect analysis, market research, and expert witness. Industries served: textile, apparel and other sewn products manufacturers; retail stores, government agencies, law firms, and insurance. **Founded:** 1987.

LIBRARIES

10158 ■ **Fashion Institute of Design & Merchandising - Cyril Magnin Resource and Research Center**
55 Stockton St., 5th Fl.
San Francisco, CA 94108-5829
Ph: (415)675-5200
Free: 800-422-3436
Fax: (415)296-7299
URL: http://fidm.edu
Contact: Jim Glenny, Director, Library Services
Scope: Fashion design and merchandising, interior design, apparel manufacturing, advertising, merchandising, marketing. **Services:** Center not open to the public. **Founded:** 1977. **Holdings:** 4000 books; 800 AV programs; 1000 newspaper clipping files; 4000 videos, DVDs, and slides. **Subscriptions:** 200 journals and other serials.

10159 ■ **Fashion Institute of Design & Merchandising - Orange County Library**
17590 Gillette Ave.
Irvine, CA 92614-5610
Ph: (949)851-6200
Free: 888-974-3436
Fax: (949)851-6808
URL: http://fidm.com
Scope: Apparel manufacturing management, cosmetics and fragrance merchandising, fashion design, interior design, merchandise marketing, textile design, visual presentation and space design. **Services:** Copying; library open to the public by appointment. **Founded:** 1980. **Holdings:** 3000 books; 130 bound periodical volumes; 40 pamphlet headings; 475 videotapes; 135 slide sets; 300 retail catalogs; 100 Annual reports; 50 CD-ROMs. **Subscriptions:** 80 journals and other serials; 8 newspapers.

10160 ■ **Fashion Institute of Technology - Gladys Marcus Library**
7th Ave. at 27th St.
E-Bldg. E502
New York, NY 10001-5992
Ph: (212)217-4340
Fax: (212)217-4371
Co. E-mail: greta_earnest@fitnyc.edu
URL: http://www.fitnyc.edu/library.asp
Contact: Prof. N.J. Wolfe, Director, Library Services
Scope: Costume, fashion, interior design, management engineering technology, fashion buying and merchandising, textiles, toy design, packaging design, advertising. **Services:** Interlibrary loan; copying; library open to the public for reference use only by appointment. **Founded:** 1944. **Holdings:** 130,260 books; 113,265 nonprint units; 20,637 bound periodical volumes; 125,000 fashion slides; 4712 reels of microfilm; 438 CD-ROM serials and digital monographs. **Subscriptions:** 4000 journals and other serials. **Telecommunication Services:** nj_wolfe@fitnyc.edu.

ASSOCIATIONS AND OTHER ORGANIZATIONS

10161 ■ Council on Safe Transportation of Hazardous Articles (COSTHA)
7803 Hill House Ct.
Fairfax Station, VA 22039-2043
Ph: (703)451-4031
Fax: (703)451-4207
Co. E-mail: mail@costha.com
URL: http://www.costha.com
Contact: Robert Heinrich, President
Description: Participates in international harmonization efforts. Promotes regulatory compliance and safety in the hazardous materials transportation industry. Promotes the growth and development of its members as Hazardous Materials Professionals. **Founded:** 1972. **Publications:** *COSTHA Quarterly* (Quarterly).

10162 ■ Dangerous Goods Advisory Council (DGAC)—Hazardous Materials Advisory Council
1100 H St. NW, Ste. 740
Washington, DC 20005-5484
Ph: (202)289-4550
Fax: (202)289-4074
Co. E-mail: info@dgac.org
URL: http://www.dgac.org
Contact: Rebecca Cernick, Chairwoman
Description: Represents shippers, carriers, and container manufacturers of hazardous materials, substances, and wastes, shipper and carrier associations. Works to promote safe transportation of these materials; provides assistance in answering regulatory questions, guidance to appropriate governmental resources, and advice in establishing corporate compliance and safety programs. Conducts seminars on domestic and international hazardous materials packaging and transporting; sponsors educational programs. Provides training courses. **Founded:** 1978. **Awards:** George L. Wilson Memorial Award (Annual).

10163 ■ National Solid Wastes Management Association (NSWMA)
4301 Connecticut Ave. NW, Ste. 300
Washington, DC 20008
Ph: (202)244-4700
Free: 800-424-2869
Fax: (202)966-4824
Co. E-mail: bparker@nswma.org
URL: http://www.nswma.org
Contact: Bruce J. Parker, President
Description: Commercial firms that collect and dispose solid wastes. Acts as a forum for the discussion of specific aspects of hazardous waste transport. Promotes professionalism in the industry to minimize the risks to public health and safety. Aids in the development of industry laws and regulations. Fosters public understanding of waste transport and disposal through educational programs. Urges members to: comply with federal liability insurance requirements; employ drivers who have completed a comprehensive training program and obtained their Department of Transportation commercial vehicle operator's license and medical evaluation certificate; set limits on drivers' hours of service; and maintain transport vehicles in accordance with federal motor carrier safety regulations. **Founded:** 1962. **Publications:** *Legal Bulletin* (Quarterly); *Waste Industry News* (Quarterly); *National Solid Wastes Management Association: Member Companies*; *Manual of Recommended Safety Practices*; *Directory of Chemical Waste Transporters* (Biennial). **Educational Activities:** WasteExpo (Annual). **Awards:** Distinguished Service Awards (Annual); Member of the Year (Annual); Special Governors Awards (Annual). **Telecommunication Services:** jleca@envasns.org.

10164 ■ Waste Equipment Technology Association (WASTEC)
4301 Connecticut Ave. NW, Ste. 300
Washington, DC 20008-2304
Ph: (202)244-4700
Free: 800-424-2869
Fax: (202)966-4824
Co. E-mail: jbradley@wastec.org
URL: http://www.wastec.org
Contact: Bruce Parker, President
URL(s): www.environmentalistseveryday.org. **Description:** Manufacturers, designers, and distributors of waste collection, treatment, and storage equipment; waste handling consultants. Promotes effective processing of solid and hazardous wastes and more extensive use of recycling. Represents members' interests; conducts research and educational programs; maintains hall of fame; compiles statistics. **Founded:** 1972. **Publications:** *Waste Industry News* (Monthly); *Products and Services Directory* (Annual); *WASTEC E-News* (8/year); *WASTEC's Equipment Technology News* (Quarterly); *Recycling Times: The Newspaper For Recycling and Waste Professionals* (Biweekly); *WASTEC Product and Service Directory* (Annual); *Listing of Rated Stationary Compactors* (3/year); *Waste Age: The Authoritative Voice of Waste Systems and Technology* (Monthly); *Directory of Waste Equipment Manufacturers & Distributors* (Annual); *Waste Age--Waste Industry Buyer Guide* (Annual). **Educational Activities:** Waste Equipment Technology Association Roundtable (Annual); Waste Expo (Annual); Waste Expo (Annual). **Awards:** Distinguished Service (Annual); Employee of the Year (Annual); Member of the Year (Annual); Distinguished Service Award; Employee of the Year Awards; Member of the Year; Environmental Industry Associations Hall of Fame Award (Annual); Environmental Industry Associations' Hall of Fame Award. **Telecommunication Services:** membership@envasns.org.

DIRECTORIES OF EDUCATIONAL PROGRAMS

10165 ■ Habitats and Ecosystems: An Encyclopedia of Endangered America
Pub: ABC-Clio Inc.
Contact: Ron Boehm, President
E-mail: rboehm@abc-clio.com
URL(s): www.abc-clio.com. **Released:** Published December 1999. **Price:** $75, Individuals print; £51.

95, Individuals. **Covers:** A listing of more than 1,400 of the most hazardous pollution sites since 1980. **Entries include:** Location. **Database includes:** Maps. **Arrangement:** Geographical by state.

REFERENCE WORKS

10166 ■ Hazardous Waste Consultant--Directory of Commercial Hazardous Waste Management Facilities Issue
URL(s): www.info.sciencedirect.com. **Released:** Semiannual **Publication includes:** List of 170 licensed commercial facilities that treat and/or dispose of hazardous waste in North America. **Entries include:** Facility name, address, phone, contact name, type of waste handled, methods of on-site treatment and/or disposal, Environmental Protection Agency permit status and identification number, restrictions, description of other services. **Arrangement:** Geographical. **Indexes:** Organization name.

10167 ■ "Uranium Energy Corp Provides an Update on Its Goliad Operations" in Canadian Corporate News (May 16, 2007)
Pub: Comtex News Network Inc.
Description: Complaints against Uranium Energy Corp. and its Goliad Project in South Texas have been dismissed. The Railroad Commission of Texas (RRC), the regulatory authority which oversees mineral exploration in Texas, concluded that Uranium Energy Corp.'s drilling activities on the Goliad Project have not contaminated certain water wells or the related aquifier.

10168 ■ WASTEC Product and Service Directory
Pub: Waste Equipment Technology Association
Contact: Bruce Parker, President
URL(s): www.wastec.org. **Released:** Annual **Covers:** About 250 member consultants, manufacturers, and distributors of waste handling, collection, and processing equipment; coverage includes Canada. **Entries include:** Company name, address, phone, e-mail, URL, products, contact name. **Arrangement:** Alphabetical, product category. **Indexes:** Product.

STATISTICAL SOURCES

10169 ■ Market for Medical Waste Management
Pub: Theta Corp. Reports
Released: 1995. **Price:** $1625.00. **Description:** examines the handling of medical waste, and provides a comprehensive analysis of 5 market segments: disposable products, hazardous waste, infectious waste, pathological waste, and sharps.

TRADE PERIODICALS

10170 ■ Chemical Week Price Report
Pub: Chemical Week Associates
Contact: Lynn Tattum, Group Vice President
Ed: David Hunter, Editor. **Released:** Weekly. **Price:** $675, U.S.; $750, elsewhere. **Description:** Covers

weekly market trends concerning chemicals, and reports on price developments.

10171 ■ *Environmental Engineering Science*
Pub: Mary Ann Liebert Inc. Publishers
URL(s): www.liebertpub.com/publication.aspx?pub_id=15. **Ed:** Julia Stegemann. **Released:** Monthly **Price:** $909, Individuals online only; $1984, Institutions online only.

10172 ■ *Waste Age: The Business Magazine for Waste Management Professionals*
Pub: Primedia Business
URL(s): www.wasteage.com. **Ed:** Stephen Ursery. **Released:** Monthly **Price:** Free.

VIDEOCASSETTES/ AUDIOCASSETTES

10173 ■ *The Global Dumping Ground: International Traffic in Hazardous Waste*
The Video Project
PO Box 411376
San Francisco, CA 94141-1376
Free: 800-4-PLANET
Fax: (888)562-9012
Co. E-mail: support@videoproject.com
URL: http://www.videoproject.com
Released: 1990. **Price:** $99.95. **Description:** PBS Frontline report examines of the problem of exporting hazardous waste to countries with less-stringent regulations on disposal. **Availability:** VHS; 3/4 U; Special order formats.

10174 ■ *Handling Hazardous Waste*
Learning Communications L.L.C.
5520 Trabuco Rd.
Irvine, CA 92620-5705
Free: 800-622-3610
Fax: (949)727-4323
Co. E-mail: sales@learncom.com
URL: http://www.learncom.com
Contact: Lloyd W. Singer, President
Released: 1991. **Price:** $175.00. **Description:** A seven-module program designed to train workers how to deal effectively with hazardous waste. **Availability:** VHS; 3/4 U.

10175 ■ *Hazard Management Safety Series*
Gulf Publishing Co.
2 Greenway Plz., Ste. 1020
Houston, TX 77046-0208
Ph: (713)529-4301
Free: 800-231-6275
Fax: (713)520-4433
Co. E-mail: advertising@gulfpub.com
URL: http://www.gulfpub.com
Contact: John Royall, President
Released: 1991. **Price:** $375.00. **Description:** A four-tape series covering the safe management of hazardous materials, sites, and procedures. A workbook is included. **Availability:** VHS; 3/4 U.

10176 ■ *Hazardous Waste*
Emergency Film Group
Detrick Lawrence Corp.
Edgartown, MA 02539
Ph: (508)627-8844
Free: 800-842-0999
Fax: (508)627-8863
Co. E-mail: info@efilmgroup.com
URL: http://www.efilmgroup.com
Released: 1989. **Price:** $330.00. **Description:** Find out the proper way to deal with hazardous waste. **Availability:** VHS; 3/4 U.

10177 ■ *The New Superfund—What It Is, How It Does—A Series*
National Audiovisual Center
5301 Shawnee Rd.
Alexandria, VA 22312
Ph: (703)605-6000
Free: 800-553-6847

Fax: (703)321-8547
Co. E-mail: customerservice@ntis.gov
URL: http://www.ntis.gov/products/nac.aspx
Released: 1987. **Price:** $585.00. **Description:** The Environmental Protection Agency's new cleanup process is profiled in extensive detail. **Availability:** VHS; 3/4 U.

TRADE SHOWS AND CONVENTIONS

10178 ■ Expo Yate Mundial - Mexico Boat Show
E.J. Krause & Associates, Inc.
6550 Rock Spring Dr., Ste. 500
Bethesda, MD 20817
Ph: (301)493-5500
Fax: (301)493-5705
Co. E-mail: info@ejkrause.com
URL: http://www.ejkrause.com
Contact: Sharon Deutch, Director
E-mail: deutch@ejkrause.com
URL(s): www.ejkrause.com. **Frequency:** Annual. **Audience:** Public. **Principal Exhibits:** Powerboats, sailboats, sports and fishing equipment, marinas and resorts, financial and insurance, clothing, jewelry and lifestyle.

CONSULTANTS

10179 ■ American Waste Processing Ltd.—American Resource Recovery Ltd.American Waste Industries Inc.;
2100 W Madison St.
Maywood, IL 60153-1744
Ph: (708)681-3999
Free: 800-841-6900
Fax: (708)681-5583
Co. E-mail: american@american-waste.com
Contact: William J. Vajdik, President
Scope: Consultants in hazardous waste management, treatment and disposal. Particular expertise in environmental audits, plant closures, treatment of waste on and off site, waste disposal, transportation, remedial action, complete clean up services and underground tank removal to include cleaning, excavating and disposal. **Founded:** 1972.

10180 ■ Analytical Consulting Services
2278 Woodsfield Ln. NE
Marietta, GA 30062
Ph: (770)565-0078
Fax: (770)565-0078
URL: http://www.analytical-consultants.com
Contact: Richard H. Belote, Owner
E-mail: rbelote@analytical-consultants.com
Scope: Provider of training and consulting services in accident or incident investigations, root cause analysis of complex problems, system safety, team membership and leadership, risk analysis, structured problem solving, nuclear safety assessment, and management oversight and risk tree analysis. Industries served: industries that deal with highly hazardous chemicals, substances or have substantial risk to their employees; emphasis on nuclear, petrochemical, government (OSHA), and military (ship and aircraft maintenance and overhaul). **Founded:** 1991. **Seminars:** Accident Investigation Workshop; Root Cause Analysis; Team Effectiveness Training; Process Safety Management; Occupational Accident Investigations; Incident/Accident Investigations (Nuclear industry); Root Cause Analysis of Operating Events (Nuclear industry); Report Writing and Oral Briefings; Advanced Techniques Upgrade for Basic Level Graduates; Process Safety Management Overview; OSHA 102 - Basic Accident Investigation (link to OSHA); OSHA 202 - Advanced Accident Investigation (link to OSHA); OSHA 141Legal Aspects of Inspection (link to OSHA); Occupational Accident Investigations; Occurrence Reporting (Department of Energy and Contractors).

10181 ■ Baxter & Woodman Inc.—Baxter Woodman Consulting Engineers
8678 Ridgefield Rd.
Crystal Lake, IL 60012
Ph: (815)459-1260

Fax: (815)455-0450
Co. E-mail: info@baxterwoodman.com
URL: http://www.baxterwoodman.com
Contact: Darrel R. Gav, President
Scope: Provides municipalities, sanitary districts, and counties in Illinois and Wisconsin consulting engineering services specializing in water and wastewater treatment, wells, water mains, sanitary and storm sewers, flood control, roads, intersections, downtown transportation, UST remediation, GIS, SCADA systems, and general municipal engineering. **Founded:** 1946.

10182 ■ CH2M Hill Companies Ltd.—CH2M Hill
9191 S Jamaica St.
Englewood, CO 80112
Ph: (303)771-0900
Free: 888-242-6445
Fax: (720)286-9250
Co. E-mail: info@ch2m.com
URL: http://www.ch2mhill.com
Contact: Jacqueline Rast, President
URL(s): www.ch2m.com. **Scope:** International consulting firm of engineers, planners, economists and scientists in many technical fields. Services include general civil engineering; structural engineering; municipal and industrial waste water, solid waste and water resources management; construction management; toxic and hazardous waste management; irrigation; transportation; and environmental studies. Serves private industries as well as government agencies. **Founded:** 1946. **Seminars:** Intranet Services.

10183 ■ Dangerous Goods Council Inc. (DGC)
1040 Detwiler Dr.
York, PA 17404
Ph: (717)848-8840
Fax: (717)848-8841
Co. E-mail: hazmat@hazshipper.com
URL: http://www.hazshipper.com
Contact: Neil Wrobleski, President
Scope: Offers a wide range of hazardous materials transportation regulatory compliance training programs. Provides awareness training, initial and recurrent training, and safety training. Materials used include: CFR 49, iCAO/IATA, HM 181, and emergency response guidebook. Firm gives seminars and in-house consultation. Training is accomplished through lecture, work projects, question-and-answer sessions and testing. These courses are designed to meet the training requirements of United States Department of Transportation Docket HM 126F. Also provides safety audits that comply with all OSHA, Dot, and FAA regulations. Industries served: manufacturing, industrial, and transportation. **Founded:** 1990. **Publications:** "PHMSA-02-11989 (HM-224C) and PHMSA-04-19886 (HM-224E): Hazardous Materials; Transportation of Lithium Batteries," 2008; "Hazardous Materials Regulations: Transportation of Compressed Oxygen, Other Oxidizing Gases and Chemical Oxygen Generators on Aircraft; correction," 2007; "Hazardous Materials: Security Requirements for Offerors and Transporters of Hazardous Materials," 2003. **Seminars:** Initial and recurrent training for dangerous goods; Awareness/familiarization training for dangerous goods; Safety training for dangerous goods, Hazmat Training. **Special Services:** HazShipper™.

10184 ■ Global Secure Training—Haztrain Inc.
10485 Theodore Green Blvd.
White Plains, MD 20695
Ph: (301)932-0994
Free: 800-258-7501
Fax: (301)934-9584
Co. E-mail: traininginfo@globalsecurecorp.com
Contact: Timothy J. Czysz, President
Scope: Consultants in hazardous waste management. Specialists in the development of site specific, employee hazardous waste training to most major industries dealing with hazardous waste, specifically the automobile and transportation industries. Industries served: Auto, manufacturing, and government agencies. **Founded:** 1983.

10185 ■ Kimmel & Associates Inc.

25 Page Ave.
Asheville, NC 28801
Ph: (828)251-9900
Fax: (828)251-9955
Co. E-mail: kimmel@kimmel.com
URL: http://www.kimmel.com
Contact: Joseph Kimmel, President
E-mail: kimmel@kimmel.com
Scope: Offers executive search and personnel consulting, management practices consultation, and merger and acquisition consultation. Industries served: general contracting, construction engineering, specialty contracting, environmental engineering firms, waste management, recycling, remedial or hazardous waste contractors, engineering consulting firms, and government agencies. **Founded:** 1981. **Publications:** "GRAY POWER can give you an EDGE," ENR magazine; "A Guide to Hiring Forwarder Talent," CNS Focus Magazine, 2004.

10186 ■ MVTL Laboratories Inc.

1126 N Front St.
New Ulm, MN 56073
Ph: (507)354-8517
Free: 800-782-3557
Fax: (507)359-2890
Co. E-mail: crc@mtvl.com
URL: http://www.mvtl.com
Contact: Jerry Balbach, President
E-mail: jbalbach@mvtl.com
Scope: Environmental consultants offering analytical consulting and field services in the following areas: air, water and wastewater, ground water, solid and hazardous waste, industrial hygiene and transportation and disposal of hazardous waste. **Founded:** 1951. **Publications:** "What You Need to Know About Salmonella," 2007; "The What, Where, Why of Nataymcin," Apr, 2007; "Why Gluten Testing is needed," Apr, 2007; "Sulfates in Your Well," 2007; "What Is Your Well Water Telling You". **Seminars:** Soil Seminar, 2008.

10187 ■ OMI Government Relations Inc.—Organization Management Inc.

915 L St., Ste. 1110
Sacramento, CA 95814-2724
Ph: (916)447-4113
Co. E-mail: burnsdc@aol.com
Contact: Donald Burns, President
E-mail: burnsdc@aol.com
Scope: Offers governmental affairs consulting services to trade and professional associations and corporations. Also offers general consulting services to nonprofit corporations. Industries served: radioactive waste disposal, toxic waste management, timber, consumer information and credit reporting, construction, electronics, multi housing, laundry, manufacturing, retailing, pharmaceuticals, and government agencies. **Founded:** 1969.

10188 ■ Michael Senew & Associates

6320 Capital Blvd., Ste. 116
Raleigh, NC 27616
Ph: (919)872-6601
Fax: (919)872-6626
Co. E-mail: msenew@martiniprint.com
URL: http://martiniprint.com
Contact: Michael Senew, President
E-mail: msenew@aol.com
Scope: A registered professional engineer and consultant specializing in manpower development and training. Publishes environmental, health safety, quality assurance, and human resource training materials as well as other short-run publications. On a consultant basis, will assist in the development of instructional programs and will provide complete editing, writing, graphic and printing support. Industries served: Environmental, safety, hazardous materials, educational, trainers and curriculum developers, and government agencies worldwide. **Founded:** 1970. **Publications:** "OSHA Regulations"; "Basic Industrial Processes"; "Hazard Communications"; "Worker Right-to-Know"; "DOT Regulations"; "EPA Regulations"; "Incident Management"; "Recovery Incineration and Disposal". **Seminars:** Brown fields awareness worker and implementation strategies; Environmental training, and safety training.

10189 ■ Smyth Fivenson Co.

8513 Irvington Ave.
Bethesda, MD 20817-3815
Ph: (301)493-6600
Fax: (301)530-7557
URL: http://www.smythfivenson.com
Contact: A. Jack Smyth, President
E-mail: jsmyth@smythfivenson.com
Scope: A Human Resources consulting firm providing services to two business areas, both nationally. First, provides temporary human resource professionals to all industries. Second, Smyth Fivenson Co. performs recruiting and placement services for the environmental industry. **Founded:** 1982.

LIBRARIES

10190 ■ Air & Waste Management Association Collection

1 Gateway Ctr., 3rd Fl.
420 Ft. Duquesne Blvd.
Pittsburgh, PA 15222-1435
Ph: (412)232-3444
Free: 800-270-3444
Fax: (412)232-3450
Co. E-mail: info@awma.org
URL: http://www.awma.org/Public
Contact: Nancy Bernheisel, Coordinator
Scope: Air pollution, hazardous waste management. **Services:** Copying; library open to members of the association and students. **Founded:** 1907. **Holdings:** 200 books. **Subscriptions:** 1 journal. **Telecommunication Services:** nbernheisel@awma.org; support@awma.org.

10191 ■ Brown & Caldwell Library

201 N. Civic Dr.
Walnut Creek, CA 94596
Ph: (925)937-9010
Free: 800-727-2224
Fax: (925)937-9026
Co. E-mail: info@brwncald.com
URL: http://www.brownandcaldwell.com
Scope: Environmental engineering, water and wastewater treatment, civil engineering. **Services:** Library open to the public by appointment. **Founded:** 1972. **Holdings:** 4000 books; 100 bound periodical volumes; 8000 reports; 400 microfiche; 400 reels of microfilm; 700 vendor catalogs. **Subscriptions:** 100 journals and other serials.

10192 ■ Brown University - Center for Environmental Studies

135 Angell St.
Box 1943
Providence, RI 02912
Ph: (401)863-3449
Fax: (401)863-3503
Co. E-mail: timmons@brown.edu
URL: http://envstudies.brown.edu
Contact: J. Timmons Roberts, Director
Scope: Environmental issues. **Services:** Library open to the public for reference use only. **Holdings:** 500 books; 200 reports. **Subscriptions:** 7 journals and other serials.

10193 ■ California Department of Conservation - Division of Recycling - Resource Center

801 K St.
MS-18-58
Sacramento, CA 95814-3530
Ph: (916)323-3836
Free: 800-RECYCLE
Fax: (916)324-1224
Co. E-mail: doriis@calrecycle.ca.gov
URL: http://www.consrv.ca.gov
Contact: Patti Holmes, Director, Library Services
URL(s): www.calrecycle.ca.gov/BevContainer/DORIIS/. **Scope:** Recycling, waste reduction, resource conservation. **Services:** Copying; library open to the public with restrictions. **Founded:** 1989. **Holdings:** 300 books; 400 reports; 277 videocassettes. **Subscriptions:** 93 journals and other serials.

10194 ■ CH2M Hill, Inc. Technical Library

3011 SW Williston Rd.
Gainesville, FL 32614-7009

Ph: (352)335-7991
Free: 888-242-6445
Fax: (352)335-2959
URL: http://www.ch2m.com/corporate/default_north_america.asp
Scope: Water supply, wastewater treatment and disposal, domestic and industrial waste treatment, solid and hazardous wastes disposal, environmental sciences, construction management, transportation. **Services:** Center not open to the public. **Founded:** 1968. **Holdings:** 6500 books; 243 bound periodical volumes; 3000 engineering reports; 2800 specifications; 500 reels of microfilm; 5500 microfiche; AV equipment; maps. **Subscriptions:** 150 journals and other serials.

10195 ■ Environmental Hazards Management Institute Library

10 Newmarket Rd.
Durham, NH 03824-2808
Ph: (603)868-1496
Free: 800-558-EHMI
Fax: (603)868-1547
URL: http://www.ehmi.org
Scope: Environmental health and safety, toxicology, mold prevention, public health and the environment, waste minimization, disaster prevention and homeland security, education. **Services:** Library open to the public. **Founded:** 1979. **Holdings:** 3000 books; 2000 bound periodical volumes; 300 reports; 60 manuscripts.

10196 ■ Long Island Lighting Company Resource Center

131 Hoffman Ln.
Central Islip, NY 11722
Ph: (516)436-4003
Fax: (516)436-4036
Contact: Carolyn Jaskot, Specialist
Scope: Energy, electricity, public utilities, business management. **Services:** Library not open to the public. **Founded:** 1986. **Holdings:** 1570 books; 100 periodical titles; videocassettes; audiocassettes. **Subscriptions:** 30 journals and other serials; 2 newspapers.

10197 ■ Metcalf & Eddy, Inc. - Harry L. Kinsel Library

701 Edgewater Dr.
Wakefield, MA 01880-5371
Ph: (781)246-5200
Fax: (781)245-6293
Co. E-mail: richard_mansfield@metcalfeddy.com
URL: http://www.aecom.com
Contact: Richard Mansfield, Librarian
Scope: Environment, hazardous waste, drinking water, wastewater/sewage, civil engineering. **Services:** Interlibrary loan; Library open to the public by appointment. **Founded:** 1912. **Holdings:** 6000 books; 658 bound periodical volumes. **Subscriptions:** 234 journals and other serials; 3 newspapers. **Telecommunication Services:** me.info@m-e.aecom.com.

10198 ■ Pennsylvania Environmental Council Library

1315 Walnut St., Ste. 532
Philadelphia, PA 19107
Ph: (215)545-4570
Free: 800-322-9214
Fax: (215)545-4594
URL: http://www.pecpa.org
Contact: Paul King, President
Scope: Solid waste and energy issues, water issues, air pollution, transportation, growth management, land use, industrial sites reuse, mediation, population. **Services:** Copying; faxing; library open to the public by appointment. **Founded:** 1970. **Holdings:** 400 books; 100 reports; 40 videotapes; 10 slide shows. **Subscriptions:** 200 journals and other serials.

10199 ■ U.S. Environmental Protection Agency Headquarters Library

Mailcode 3404T
Washington, DC 20460-0001
Ph: (202)566-0556

Fax: (202)260-5153
Co. E-mail: hqchemlibraries@epa.gov
URL: http://www.epa.gov/libraries/hqrepository.html
Scope: Water - pollution, quality, supply; air pollution; noise abatement; radiation; hazardous wastes; solid waste management; resource recovery; pesticides; chemistry and toxicology; social, economic, legislative, legal, administrative, and management aspects of environmental policy. **Services:** Interlibrary loan; SDI; library open to the public with restrictions. **Founded:** 1971. **Holdings:** 16,000 books; 7000 hardcopy documents and technical reports; 400,000 documents and reports from the EPA and its predecessor agencies on microfiche; newspapers, abstracts and indexes, periodicals on microfilm. **Subscriptions:** 20 journals and other serials.

RESEARCH CENTERS

10200 ■ Environmental Hazards Management Institute (EHMI)
10 Newmarket Rd.
Durham, NH 03824
Ph: (603)868-1496
Free: 800-558-3464
Fax: (603)868-1547
Co. E-mail: aborner@ehmi.org
URL: http://www.ehmi.org
Contact: Alan John Borner, Chief Executive Officer

Services: Compost Education Wheel; Household Hazardous Waste Wheel; Kidswheel: on hazardous household products; Water Sense Wheel: interactive tools that educate workers, community leaders, and homeowners. **Founded:** 1976. **Publications:** *EHMI. University Blogs* (Daily). **Educational Activities:** Educational bookcovers; Mold Wheel; Seminars, training. **Awards:** EHMI Awards for Leadership. **Telecommunication Services:** info@ehmi.org.

10201 ■ The Nature Conservancy - Ohio Chapter
6375 Riverside Dr., Ste. 100
Dublin, OH 43017
Ph: (614)717-2770
Free: 877-TNC-OHIO
Fax: (614)717-2777
Co. E-mail: ohio@tnc.org
URL: http://www.nature.org/ourinitiatives/regions/northamerica/unitedstates/ohio
Contact: Josh Knights, Executive Director

Services: Research use of preserves. **Founded:** 1958. **Publications:** *Nature Conservancy Magazine* (Quarterly); *Ohio Chapter Newsletter* (Semiannual). **Educational Activities:** Field trips and special

events (Monthly), throughout the state; Prescribed burn and land management training (Occasionally); Annual Membership meeting; Volunteer Award Dinner (Annual).

10202 ■ University of Alabama - Environmental Institute
103 Bevill Research Bldg.
Tuscaloosa, AL 35487-0205
Ph: (205)348-1677
Co. E-mail: rpitt@eng.ua.edu
URL: http://ei.ua.edu
Contact: Prof. Robert Pitt, Director

Services: environmental science information; Information Resource Service: for government agencies and legislative committees; Waste reduction and pollution prevention technical support: to Alabama businesses and industry. **Founded:** 1984. **Publications:** *NIGEC-Southeast Regional Center Annual Report* (Annual). **Educational Activities:** Environmental Institute Seminars and conferences, to promote dialogue and information exchange on waste management and global environmental change issues; Environmental Institute Symposium, on Global Climate Change Research.

10203 ■ University of Florida - Hinkley Center for Solid and Hazardous Waste Management (FCSHWM)
4635 NW 53rd Ave., Ste. 205
Gainesville, FL 32653
Ph: (352)392-6264
Fax: (352)846-0183
Co. E-mail: jschert@ufl.edu
URL: http://www.hinkleycenter.com
Contact: John D. Schert, Director

Services: Information dissemination, publications listing. **Founded:** 1988. **Publications:** *Annual Research Booklet*; *FCSHWM Newsletter* (Quarterly). **Educational Activities:** Exhibits at workshops and conferences; Research symposium (Annual); FCSHWM Seminars. **Awards:** FCSHWM Grants (Annual), to state universities and colleges in the amount of $350,000.

10204 ■ University of Iowa - Center for Health Effects of Environmental Contamination (CHEEC)
Bioventures Ctr., W140
2500 Crosspark Rd.
Coralville, IA 52241
Ph: (319)335-4550
Fax: (319)335-4077
Co. E-mail: gene-parkin@uiowa.edu
URL: http://www.cheec.uiowa.edu
Contact: Prof. Gene Parkin, Director

Services: Develops and maintains environmental databases: that can be accessed by state agencies;

Engineering, health, and laboratory consultations; Health assessments: at hazardous waste disposal sites; Responds to public inquiries: regarding health effects of exposure to environmental contaminants. **Founded:** 1988. **Publications:** *CHEEC Annual Report*; *CHEEC Newsletter*; *CHEEC Technical Report*. **Educational Activities:** Educational seminars and conferences, on the causes and prevention of environmentally-induced disease. **Awards:** Oversees the CHEEC Seed Grant Program, for pilot studies on exposure and risk assessment. **Telecommunication Services:** cheec@uiowa.edu.

10205 ■ University of Northern Iowa - Iowa Waste Reduction Center (IWRC)
BCS Bldg., Ste. 113
Cedar Falls, IA 50614-0185
Ph: (319)273-8905
Free: 800-422-3109
Fax: (319)273-6582
Co. E-mail: john.konefes@uni.edu
URL: http://www.iwrc.org
Contact: John Konefes, Director

Services: Consulting for the Iowa Automobile Dealers Service and painting technicians; Maintains mobile exhibits that travel to small companies and rural areas. **Founded:** 1987. **Publications:** *The Closed Loop* (Quarterly); *Point Source Newsletter*. **Educational Activities:** Air permitting workshops and proper spray application technique training; Workshops in hazardous waste, laboratory and photoprocessing waste management, and solid waste management. **Awards:** IWRC Paid internships, for MIS, environmental science, biology, chemistry, economics, etc students.

10206 ■ Western Region Hazardous Substance Research Center (WRHSRC)
204 Apperson Hall
Oregon State University
Corvallis, OR 97331-2302
Ph: (541)737-2751
Fax: (541)737-3099
Co. E-mail: lewis.semprini@oregonstate.edu
URL: http://wrhsrc.oregonstate.edu
Contact: Dr. Lewis Semprini, Director

Services: On-line searchable publications database; Technical assistance: regarding brownfields; Technical outreach services: for communities. **Founded:** 1989. **Publications:** *WRHSRC Annual report*; *WRHSRC Journal articles*. **Educational Activities:** Research meeting (Annual). **Telecommunication Services:** wrhsrc@engr.orst.edu.

START-UP INFORMATION

10207 ■ *"Organic Chain Scouting Tri-State Sites, Including Kenwood"* in *Business Courier (Vol. 27, December 3, 2010, No. 31, pp. 1)*

Pub: Business Courier

Ed: Tom Demeropolis. **Description:** Asheville, North Carolina-based Earth Fare has been planning to add a total of six stores in 2011, including the potential opening of more than one store in the Greater Cincinnati area market. Earth Fare has not named specific locations but Kenwood area was reportedly being considered for its first location. Insights on growing trends toward health food stores are also given.

10208 ■ *"Vitamins to Spice Up Food"* in *Philadelphia Business Journal (Vol. 28, October 2, 2009, No. 33, pp. 1)*

Pub: American City Business Journals

Ed: John George. **Description:** VitaminSpice, a start-up company established by Ed Bukstel, makes a line of spice and vitamin blends that come in seasoning form. The form of the blends could facilitate easier ingestion of vitamins into people's diets. A reverse merger that will allow a publicly-traded company status for VitaminSpice will be accomplished by early October 2009.

ASSOCIATIONS AND OTHER ORGANIZATIONS

10209 ■ **Canadian Health Food Association (CHFA)—Association Canadienne des Aliements de Sante**
235 Yorkland Blvd., Ste. 302
Toronto, ON, Canada M2J 4Y8
Ph: (416)497-6939
Free: 800-661-4510
Fax: (416)497-3214
Co. E-mail: info@chfa.ca
URL: http://www.chfa.ca
Contact: Matthew James, Chairman
Description: Represents producers and distributors of health foods. Seeks to advance the health food industries. Facilitates communication and cooperation among members; represents the commercial and regulatory interests of the health food industries; sponsors educational and promotional programs. **Founded:** 1964. **Publications:** *The Natural Voice* (5/year).

10210 ■ **Health Information Resource Center (HIRC)**
1850 W Winchester Rd., Ste. 213
Libertyville, IL 60048
Ph: (847)816-8660
Free: 800-828-8225
Fax: (847)816-8662
Co. E-mail: info@healthprograms.com
URL: http://www.healthawards.com
Contact: Patricia Henze, Executive Director
URL(s): www.health.gov, www.fitnessday.com. **Description:** Clearinghouse for consumer health information. Provides information and referral services to many organizations that use or produce consumer health information materials. Conducts market research. **Scope:** consumer health. **Founded:** 1993. **Subscriptions:** articles audiovisuals books clippings monographs periodicals. **Publications:** *Health and Medical Media: The Comprehensive Sourcebook of Media Contacts for Healthcare Professionals* (Biennial); *Health and Medical Media* (Annual); *The Health Events Calendar* (Annual). **Awards:** National Health Information Awards (Annual); WWW Health Awards (Semiannual). **Telecommunication Services:** maturemkt@aol.com.

10211 ■ **National Association for the Specialty Food Trade (NASFT)**
136 Madison Ave., 12th Fl.
New York, NY 10016
Ph: (212)482-6440
Free: 800-627-3869
Fax: (212)482-6459
Co. E-mail: customerservice@nasft.org
URL: http://www.specialtyfood.com
Contact: Dennis Deschaine, Chairman

Description: Represents manufacturers, distributors, processors, importers, retailers, and brokers of specialty and gourmet foods. Aims to foster trade, commerce and interest in the specialty food industry. **Founded:** 1952. **Publications:** *Specialty Food Magazine* (10/year). **Awards:** Sofi Awards (Annual).

10212 ■ **Natural Products Association (NPA)**
1773 T St. NW
Washington, DC 20009
Ph: (202)223-0101
Free: 800-966-6632
Fax: (202)223-0250
Co. E-mail: natural@npainfo.org
URL: http://www.npainfo.org
Contact: Jeff Wright, President

Description: Represents retailers, wholesalers, brokers, distributors and manufacturers of natural, nutritional, dietetic foods, supplements, services and natural body and home care products. **Founded:** 1936. **Educational Activities:** Natural Products Day (Annual). **Awards:** Rachel Carson Environmental Award (Annual); Socially Responsible Retailer Award (Annual); Statesman/Stateswoman Award (Annual); Burton Kallman Scientific Award (Annual); Natural Products Association Clinician Award (Annual); Natural Products Association Industry Champion Award (Annual); Presidents Award (Annual).

10213 ■ *The Natural Voice*
235 Yorkland Blvd., Ste. 302
Toronto, ON, Canada M2J 4Y8
Ph: (416)497-6939
Free: 800-661-4510
Fax: (416)497-3214
Co. E-mail: info@chfa.ca
URL: http://www.chfa.ca
Contact: Matthew James, Chairman

Released: 5/year

REFERENCE WORKS

10214 ■ *"Bagging Profits; High-End Grocers Expand Despite Stale Economy"* in *Crain's Detroit Business (Vol. 24, March 24, 2008, No. 12, pp. 1)*

Pub: Crain Communications, Inc.

Ed: Nancy Kaffer. **Description:** Discusses the expansion plans of several high-end grocery stores in the Detroit area and the reasons why, despite the poor economy, these gourmet grocers are doing well. Statistical data included.

10215 ■ *"Ben & Jerry's Changing Some 'All Natural' Labels"* in *Ice Cream Reporter (Vol. 23, October 20, 2010, No. 11, pp. 1)*

Pub: Ice Cream Reporter

Description: Following criticism from the Center for Science in the Public Interest, Ben & Jerry's will omit the term 'All Natural' from its labeling, however the firm reports it will continue to use the most natural ingredients they can find for its products.

10216 ■ *"Beverage Brand Vies To Be the Latest Purple Prince"* in *Brandweek (Vol. 49, April 21, 2008, No. 16, pp. 20)*

Pub: VNU Business Media, Inc.

Ed: Becky Ebenkamp. **Description:** Profile on the new beverage product Purple and its founder, Ted Farnsworth; Purple is a drink that blends seven antioxidant-rich juices to create what Mr. Farnsworth calls a 'Cascade Effect' that boosts antioxidants' effectiveness. Mr. Farnsworth is marketing the brand's Oxygen Radical Absorbance Capability (ORAC) which is a value of 7,600 compared with orange juice's 1,200.

10217 ■ *"Canine Cuisine: Tips for a Healthful Diet"* in *Seattle Times (September 13, 2008, pp. D9)*

Pub: Associated Press

Description: The American Kennel Club recommends feeding dogs food with balanced essential nutrients, including proteins, carbohydrates, fats, vitamins, minerals, and water; types of food, feeding practices and what not to feed a dog is discussed.

10218 ■ *"Careers in Organic Food Preparation"* in *Occupational Outlook Quarterly (Vol. 54, Fall 2010, No. 3, pp. 3)*

Pub: U.S. Bureau of Labor Statistics

Ed: Adam Bibler. **Description:** Organic methods of food production, including methods that combine science with traditional farming practices, are outlined. Facts regarding careers in organic food preparation are presented.

10219 ■ *"Drink Up"* in *Black Enterprise (Vol. 38, March 2008, No. 8, pp. 50)*

Pub: Earl G. Graves Publishing Co. Inc.

Ed: Tennille H. Robinson. **Description:** Advice is given to an individual seeking to start a natural juice small business, along with information for finding a bottling company.

10220 ■ *"Earth Angels" in Playthings (Vol. 106, September 1, 2008, No. 8, pp. 10)*
Pub: Reed Business Information
Contact: Jeff Greisch, President
Ed: Karyn M. Peterson. **Description:** ImagiPlay toy company has partnered with Whole Foods Market to distribute the company's wooden playthings across the country. The company's Earth-friendly business model is outlined.

10221 ■ *"Effort Is Growing to Offer Healthier Choices in Vending Machines" in Philadelphia Inquirer (July 29, 2011)*
Pub: Philadelphia Media Network Inc.
Ed: Don Sapatkin. **Description:** Since Boston's mayor announced a ban on the sale of all sugar sweetened beverages on city properties, it seems more cities, states, hospitals, businesses, and even park systems are following suit. Thus, vending machines are beginning to offer healthier snacks and drinks to consumers.

10222 ■ *"Essentially Organic Vending Takes Healthy Snacks to Ohio High School" in Entertainment Close-Up (September 13, 2011)*
Pub: Close-Up Media
Description: Essentially Organic Vending is offering students a healthy alternative for their snacking. The vending machines will be stocked with nutritious energy options.

10223 ■ *"Hain Celestial Acquires Greek Gods Yogurt" in Ice Cream Reporter (Vol. 23, July 20, 2010, No. 8, pp. 1)*
Pub: Ice Cream Reporter
Description: Hain Celestial Group acquired The Greek Gods LLC. Hain Celestial is a natural and organic products company and Greek Gods makes all natural, Greek-style yogurt and ice cream.

10224 ■ *"Half Empty or Half Full" in Crain's Chicago Business (Vol. 31, March 24, 2008, No. 12, pp. 4)*
Pub: Crain Communications, Inc.
Ed: Meghan Streit. **Description:** Lifeway Foods Inc., the health food company which manufactures a yogurt-like drink called kefir, is being negatively affected by the soaring price of milk; however, the fact that probiotics are picking up in the market may mean that Lifeway stands a good chance of bouncing back and the company's lower share price could be an opportunity for long-term investors who have a tolerance for risk.

10225 ■ *"Healthy Fast Food Acquires Rights to U-Swirl Yogurt" in Ice Cream Reporter (Vol. 21, October 20, 2008, No. 11, pp. 5)*
Pub: Ice Cream Reporter
Description: Healthy Fast Food Inc. will acquire worldwide rights to U-Swirl Frozen Yogurt; the firm will use the new acquisition to create a yogurt superstore in a cafe setting concept for its operations.

10226 ■ *"High Growth Reported for the Natural Supermarket Pet Department Close-Up" in Canadian Corporate News (October 20, 2008)*
Pub: Comtex News Network Inc.
Description: Leading natural supermarket chains have been outperforming mainstream grocers by carrying natural and organic pet products. Statistical data included.

10227 ■ *"His Way" in Inc. (February 2008, pp. 90-97)*
Pub: Gruner & Jahr USA Publishing
Ed: Stephanie Clifford. **Description:** Profile of Chris Reed, founder of a natural soda company, who undertook an initial public offering (IPO). Reed discusses the challenges he faced mediating with the Securities Exchange Commission regarding his firm's IPO.

10228 ■ *"In the Raw: Karyn Calabrese Brings Healthy Dining to a New Sophisticated Level" in Black Enterprise (Vol. 41, September 2010)*
Pub: Earl G. Graves Publishing Co. Inc.
Ed: Sonia Alleyne. **Description:** Profile of Karyn Calabrese whose businesses are based in Chicago, Illinois. Calabrese has launched a complete line of

products (vitamins and beauty items), services (spa, chiropractic, and acupuncture treatments), and restaurants to bring health dining and lifestyles to a better level.

10229 ■ *"Loseley Dairy Ice Cream" in Ice Cream Reporter (Vol. 23, November 20, 2010, No. 12, pp. 8)*
Pub: Ice Cream Reporter
Description: Neil Burchell has been named managing director of Loseley Dairy Ice Cream, one of the UK's largest independent producers. Burchell, with over 30 years experience in the food industry, was recently managing director of Rachel's, the leading organic dairy foods company in the UK, where he is credited with driving a sixfold increase in sales.

10230 ■ *"Medicine Men" in Canadian Business (Vol. 80, February 12, 2007, No. 4, pp. 19)*
Pub: Rogers Media
Ed: Joe Castaldo. **Description:** The effort of HPI Health Products' owners Dong Pedersen and Kent Pedersen to popularize their pain reliever product 'Lakota' is discussed.

10231 ■ *"Moms Give More Thought to Nutrition" in Marketing to Women (Vol. 21, February 2008, No. 2, pp. 8)*
Pub: EPM Communications Inc.
Contact: Ira Mayer, President
E-mail: imayer@epmcom.com
Description: Moms are thinking more about nutritional issues than they did in the past and spending more time reading labels in the grocery store. 74 percent of moms consider the nutritional content of foods purchased for their children more now than they did two years ago.

10232 ■ *"Need Fiber in Your Diet? Pour Some Milk" in Globe & Mail (April 10, 2007, pp. B7)*
Pub: CTVglobemedia Publishing Inc.
Ed: William Illsey Atkinson. **Description:** The growing market and demand for functional foods and neutraceuticals in Canada is discussed. The research being conducted by University of Manitoba's Richardson Centre for Functional Foods and Nutraceuticals to explore new health compounds in food is highlighted.

10233 ■ *"Net Profits: Get a Social Life" in Entrepreneur (Vol. 35, October 2007, No. 10, pp. 140)*
Pub: Entrepreneur Media Inc.
Ed: Amanda C. Kooser. **Description:** Social networking sites such as Facebook and MySpace have millions of users, a sign that social networking is a growing industry. One way to enter this industry is target marketing, like Med3Q, a site for health-conscious individuals had done. How Med3q is earning through online advertising and sponsors is explained.

10234 ■ *"New Recipes Added to IAMS Naturals Pet Food Line" in MMR (Vol. 28, August 1, 2011, No. 11, pp. 17)*
Pub: Racher Press Inc.
Description: Procter & Gamble Company's IAMS brand has created a new pet food line called IAMS Naturals for pet owners wishing to feed their pets natural, wholesome food. IAMS Sensitive Naturals has ocean fish and its first ingredient for dogs with sensitivities. IAMS Simple & Natural features chicken with no fillers.

10235 ■ *"New Zealand Natural Ice Cream is Opening a Second U.S. Scoop Shop" in Ice Cream Reporter (Vol. 21, October 20, 2008, No. 11, pp. 7)*
Pub: Ice Cream Reporter
Description: New Zealand Natural Ice Cream is opening a second store in California. The company is a market leader in New Zealand and has gained distribution through 300 outlets in California.

10236 ■ *"A Nice Consistency" in Inc. (Vol. 31, January-February 2009, No. 1, pp. 94)*
Pub: Mansueto Ventures LLC
Ed: Jason Del Rey. **Description:** PJ Madison spent almost a quarter of its revenue promoting its latest product, organic ice cream. The Texas-based firm saw sales increase dramatically.

10237 ■ *"Organic Dairy Farmers Wanted" in Canadian Business (Vol. 80, April 23, 2007, No. 9, pp. 11)*
Pub: Rogers Media
Ed: Wendy Glauser. **Description:** The growth of the Harmony Organic due to demand for organic dairy products is presented.

10238 ■ *"Organic Dog Treats" in Veterinary Economics (Vol. 49, November 2008, No. 11, pp. 52)*
Pub: Advanstar Communications Inc.
Contact: Mr. Joseph Loggia, Chief Executive Officer
E-mail: jloggia@advanstar.com
Description: Wet Noses all-natural dog treats come in six flavors: dogranola, pumpkin, sweet potato curry, apples and carrots, cheddar, and peanut butter and molasses. The treats are made without animal by-products, added chemicals, preservatives, corn, soy or wheat.

10239 ■ *"Perry's Goes Organic" in Ice Cream Reporter (Vol. 22, December 20, 2008, No. 1, pp. 1)*
Pub: Ice Cream Reporter
Description: Family-owned Perry's Ice Cream is starting a new line of organic ice cream in both vanilla and chocolate flavors. All Perry's products are made with milk and cream from local dairy farmers.

10240 ■ *"R&R Launches Upscale Spoony's and Low Fat Dragon's Den" in Ice Cream Reporter (Vol. 23, August 20, 2010, No. 9, pp. 3)*
Pub: Ice Cream Reporter
Description: European ice cream manufacturer R&R has acquired French ice cream maker Rolland and will position itself as an upscale challenger to brands like Ben & Jerry's.

10241 ■ *"A Recipe for Change" in Canadian Business (Vol. 80, October 22, 2007, No. 21, pp. 25)*
Pub: Rogers Media
Ed: Erin Pooley. **Description:** Market conditions have changed and customers around the world are demanding low-fat alternatives. Labor costs have risen and so did the price of foodstuffs. The impacts of this on fast food restaurants as well as the measures they have taken to cope with the new demands are discussed.

10242 ■ *"Red Mango Set to Grow in Florida" in Ice Cream Reporter (Vol. 23, September 20, 2010, No. 10, pp. 2)*
Pub: Ice Cream Reporter
Description: Red Mango will add 12 new locations throughout Florida. The stores offer healthy, nutritious frozen yogurt, smoothies and parfaits.

10243 ■ *"Secaucus-Based Freshpet is Barking Up the Right Tree" in Record (September 8, 2011)*
Pub: North Jersey Media Group
Ed: Rebecca Olles. **Description:** Freshpet produces a variety of nutritious, refrigerated pet foods and treats for cats and dogs. The firm introduced five new recipes and treats to its grain-free line called Vital line. The Vital line mimics the ancestral diets of dogs and cats.

10244 ■ *"Sodexo Updates Healthy Vending Program" in Entertainment Close-Up (September 25, 2011)*
Pub: Close-Up Media
Description: Sodexo launched its Your Health Your Way On-the-Go program for its vending machines across the nation.

10245 ■ *"A Switch in the Kitchen" in Barron's (Vol. 88, March 24, 2008, No. 12, pp. 17)*
Pub: Dow Jones & Company, Inc.
Description: Men are doing more kitchen duties, with 18 percent of meals at home being made by men in 2007 compared to 11 percent four years previously. Young wives, however, choose to forgo work and stay at home.

10246 ■ *"Tapping the 'Well' in Wellness" in Pet Product News (Vol. 64, November 2010, No. 11, pp. 1)*

Pub: BowTie Inc.

Ed: Wendy-Bedwell Wilson. **Description:** Healthy food and treats are among the leading wellness products being sought by customers from specialty retailers to keep their pets healthy. With this demand for pet wellness products, retailers suggest making sure that staff know key ingredients to emphasize to customers. Other insights into this trend and ways to engage customers are discussed.

10247 ■ *"Waste Not" in Entrepreneur (Vol. 36, April 2008, No. 4, pp. 21)*

Pub: Entrepreneur Media, Inc.

Ed: JJ Ramberg. **Description:** RecycleBank is a company that provides homes with carts in which recyclables are thrown. An identification chip measures the amount of recyclables and converts them into points, which can be redeemed in stores, such as Starbucks and Whole Foods. RecycleBank earns revenue from cities that save landfill waste spending with the use of the program.

10248 ■ *"Yogun Fruz Adds First Location in Southern New York State" in Ice Cream Reporter (Vol. 23, September 20, 2010, No. 10, pp. 2)*

Pub: Ice Cream Reporter

Description: Yogen Fruz signed a master franchise agreement to expand into the southern counties of New York State. The firm offers a healthy and beneficial option to fast food and typical dessert choices.

STATISTICAL SOURCES

10249 ■ *The Organic Food and Beverage Market*

Pub: Rector Press, Ltd.

Contact: Lewis Sckolnick, President

Released: 2009. **Price:** Contact Rector Press.

10250 ■ *Outlook For The Health and Natural Food Market*

Pub: Business Trend Analysts, Inc.

Released: 2005-2006. **Price:** $3795.00. **Description:** Covers the U.S. market for health and natural foods. Offers historical, current, and projected sales data; consumer demographics; strategies for advertising and promotion; product mix; distribution methods and patterns; and profiles of large industry competitors.

10251 ■ *RMA Annual Statement Studies*

Pub: Risk Management Association

Contact: Kevin M. Blakey, President

Released: Annual. **Price:** $175.00 2006-07 edition, $105.00. **Description:** Contains composite balance sheets and income statements for more than 360 industries, including the accounting, auditing, and bookkeeping industries. Also contains five years of comparative historical data for discerning trends. Includes 16 commonly used ratios, computed for most of the size groupings for nearly every industry.

TRADE PERIODICALS

10252 ■ *Natural Foods Merchandiser: News, Trends and Ideas for the Business of Natural Products/A Penton Publication*

Contact: Carlotta Mast, Editor-in-Chief

E-mail: anna.soref@penton.com

URL(s): www.naturalfoodsmerchandiser.com/ASP/home.asp. **Released:** Monthly **Price:** Free.

10253 ■ *No Salt Week-The Newsletter*

Pub: Prosperity & Profits Unlimited, Distribution Services

Ed: A. Doyle, Editor. **Released:** Annual. **Price:** $2, U.S.; $3, Canada; $4, elsewhere. **Description:** Presents possibilities for herb and spice blends that contain no added salt. Also contains ideas for cooking and much more.

10254 ■ *Nutrition Action Healthletter*

Pub: Center for Science in the Public Interest

Ed: Stephen Schmidt, Editor. **Released:** 10/year. **Description:** Covers food and nutrition, the food industry, and relevant government regulations and legislation. Focuses on the connections among diet, lifestyle, and disease. Includes nutritional comparisons of food products, reader questions and answers, and health-promoting recipies.

10255 ■ *The Tan Sheet*

Pub: F-D-C Reports Inc.

Contact: Jaimie Kelley, Managing Editor

Ed: Christopher Walker, Editor. **Released:** Weekly, 50/year. **Price:** $2,020, U.S. print and web. **Description:** Provides 'in-depth coverage of nonprescription pharmaceuticals and dietary supplement/nutritionals.' Topics include congressional hearings and legislation, business and marketing news, FDA recalls and seizures, regular listing of product trademarks, and activities of FTC, CPSC, and FDA.

10256 ■ *Whole Foods: Informing and Educating Natural Products Retailers on Dietary Supplements, Herbs, HBC, Homeopathy, Foods*

Pub: WFC Inc.

URL(s): www.wholefoodsmagazineonline.com. **Ed:** Kaylynn Chiarello-Ebner. **Released:** Monthly; 2 in May. **Price:** $70, Individuals; $80, Two years in U.S.; $80, Canada and Mexico; $195, Other countries.

FRANCHISES AND BUSINESS OPPORTUNITIES

10257 ■ *Berrybrook Farm Franchising Inc.*

1257 East Blvd.

Charlotte, NC 28203

Ph: (704)334-6528

Fax: (704)334-2299

Description: Natural foods, supplements, health and beauty aids and juice bar deli. **No. of Franchise Units:** 1. **Founded:** 1972.. **Franchised:** 2005. **Equity Capital Needed:** $95,000-$175,000. **Franchise Fee:** $25,000. **Royalty Fee:** 5%. **Training:** Provides 16 days at headquarters, 14 days onsite with ongoing support.

10258 ■ *Booster Juice*

8915-51 Ave., Ste. 205

Edmonton, AB, Canada T6E 5J3

Ph: (780)440-6770

Fax: (416)621-3968

Co. E-mail: franchise@boosterjuice.com

URL: http://www.boosterjuice.com

Description: Serves fresh juice and sells a health food concept. **No. of Franchise Units:** 273. **No. of Company-Owned Units:** 2. **Founded:** 1999.. **Franchised:** 1999. **Equity Capital Needed:** $235,000-$265,000 turn-key, $85,000-$95,000 start-up capital required. **Franchise Fee:** $20,000. **Training:** Training includes 2 weeks at head office and ongoing support.

10259 ■ *Sangster's Health Centres*

2218 Hanselman Ave.

Saskatoon, SK, Canada S7L 6A4

Ph: (306)653-4481

Fax: (306)653-4688

Description: Retail sale of vitamins, herbs, natural cosmetics, natural foods, body building and supplies, specializing in their own name-brand products and also national company brands. **No. of Franchise Units:** 36. **No. of Company-Owned Units:** 5. **Founded:** 1971.. **Franchised:** 1978. **Equity Capital Needed:** $30,000 minimum. **Franchise Fee:** $25,000. **Training:** Yes.

10260 ■ *Smoothie King Franchises, Inc.*

121 Park Pl.

Covington, LA 70433

Ph: (985)635-6973

Fax: (985)635-6987

Description: Smoothie King centers offer guests the industry's first, original nutritional fruit and function based fresh-blended smoothies. Each "Lifestyle Center" also offers healthy retail product solutions, including sports beverages, energy bars, healthy

snacks, vitamin supplements, herbs, minerals and other sports nutrition products. **No. of Franchise Units:** 618. **No. of Company-Owned Units:** 1. **Founded:** 1973.. **Franchised:** 1989. **Equity Capital Needed:** $75,000. **Franchise Fee:** $25,000. **Financial Assistance:** Yes. **Training:** Provides 1 day pre-opening (orientation), 14 days management training at Corporate store, 8 days store opening (14 days before open & 4 days after opening) onsite. Assistance in real estate, design and construction.

10261 ■ *Uncle Louie G, Inc.*

101M Ellis Rd.

Staten Island, NY 10307

Ph: (718)966-3763

Fax: (718)966-3764

Description: Handmade in state of the art factory. **No. of Franchise Units:** 51. **No. of Company-Owned Units:** 3. **Founded:** 1998.. **Franchised:** 1999. **Equity Capital Needed:** $30,000-$75,000 costs to open. **Franchise Fee:** $7,500. **Financial Assistance:** Yes. **Training:** Yes.

COMPUTERIZED DATABASES

10262 ■ *Consumer Buying Power™*

770 Broadway

New York, NY 10003-9595

URL: http://www.claritas.com/sitereports/default.jsp

Availability: Online: The Nielsen Co. - Nielsen SiteReports. **Type:** Statistical.

LIBRARIES

10263 ■ *American Dietetic Association - Knowledge Center*

120 S. Riverside Plaza, Ste. 20000

Chicago, IL 60606-6995

Ph: (312)877-1600, x4864

Free: 800-877-1600

Fax: (312)899-4739

Co. E-mail: knowledge@eatright.org

URL: http://www.eatright.org/

Scope: Nutrition, dietetics, food service. **Services:** Interlibrary loan; copying; Library open to the public by appointment. **Founded:** 1990. **Holdings:** 3000 books. **Subscriptions:** 60 journals and other serials; 4 newspapers.

10264 ■ *Geisinger Medical Center - Community Health Library*

100 N. Academy Ave.

Danville, PA 17822-4401

Ph: (570)271-5638

Fax: (570)271-5635

Co. E-mail: chrl@geisinger.edu

URL: http://www.geisinger.edu

Contact: Patricia A Ulmer, Librarian

Scope: General medicine, nutrition, alternative and complementary medicine, pediatrics, cancer, AIDS. **Services:** Interlibrary loan. **Founded:** 1996. **Holdings:** 860 books; 200 audio/visual materials. **Subscriptions:** 14 journals and other serials.

10265 ■ *Lemmen-Holton Cancer Pavilion Library*

145 Michigan, NE

Grand Rapids, MI 49503

Ph: (616)486-5700

URL: http://www.spectrumhealth.org/lhcp

Scope: Cancer. **Services:** Library open to the public. **Holdings:** Pamphlets.

10266 ■ *New York Public Library - Mid-Manhattan Library - General Reference and Advisory Services/Health Information Center*

455 5th Ave. at 40th St.

New York, NY 10016

Ph: (212)340-0863

URL: http://www.nypl.org/locations/mid-manhattan-library

Contact: Theresa Myrhol, Librarian

URL(s): legacy.www.nypl.org/branch/collections/hic.html. **Scope:** Consumer, health medicine, nursing, allied health. **Services:** Copying; Library open to the public. **Founded:** 1996. **Holdings:** 22,000 books and videocassettes; 4 VF of pamphlets. **Subscriptions:** 278 journals and other serials.

10267 ■ Price-Pottenger Nutrition Foundation Library—Health and Healing Wisdom; PPNF.
7890 Broadway
Lemon Grove, CA 91945
Ph: (619)462-7600
Free: 800-366-3748
Fax: (619)433-3136
Co. E-mail: info@ppnf.org
URL: http://www.ppnf.org
Contact: Edward Bennett, President
Scope: Nutrition, preventative medicine, health, natural farming and gardening, pesticides, fluoride, mercury, dental health, natural farming and gardening, natural pet care, traditional/historic diets, primitive diets, holistic medicine. **Services:** Copying; library open to members only for reference use. **Founded:** 1952. **Holdings:** Journals and other serials; 10,000 volumes; 18,000 film positives; 6000 glass lantern slides; scientific reprints; video and audio tapes; reports; archives. **Telecommunication Services:** jack@ppnf.org; joan@ppnf.org.

10268 ■ U.S.D.A. National Agricultural Library - Food and Nutrition Information Center
10301 Baltimore Ave., Rm. 108
Beltsville, MD 20705-2351
Ph: (301)504-5414
Fax: (301)504-6409
Co. E-mail: shirley.evans@ars.usda.gov
URL: http://fnic.nal.usda.gov
Contact: Shirley King Evans
Scope: Human nutrition education, nutrition resources for USDA food and nutrition programs. **Ser**vices: Interlibrary loan; Center open to the public with restricted lending. **Founded:** 1971. **Holdings:** 50,000 books; VF drawers. **Subscriptions:** 200 journals and other serials.

10269 ■ Voice for Animals Library
PO Box 120095
San Antonio, TX 78212
Ph: (210)737-3138
Co. E-mail: voice@voiceforanimals.org
URL: http://www.voiceforanimals.org/
Scope: Animal rights; vegetarianism. **Services:** Library not open to the public. **Founded:** 1987. **Holdings:** 200 books; newsletters; videocassettes.

START-UP INFORMATION

10270 ■ *"Ahead of the Pack" in Small Business Opportunities (Fall 2010)*
Pub: Harris Publications Inc.
Description: Profile of an organic fast-food business that is carving out a niche that is gaining favor. Elevation Burger is a unique concept offering healthier burgers in sustainable buildings.

10271 ■ *"Organic Chain Scouting Tri-State Sites, Including Kenwood" in Business Courier (Vol. 27, December 3, 2010, No. 31, pp. 1)*
Pub: Business Courier
Ed: Tom Demeropolis. **Description:** Asheville, North Carolina-based Earth Fare has been planning to add a total of six stores in 2011, including the potential opening of more than one store in the Greater Cincinnati area market. Earth Fare has not named specific locations but Kenwood area was reportedly being considered for its first location. Insights on growing trends toward health food stores are also given.

10272 ■ *"Vitamins to Spice Up Food" in Philadelphia Business Journal (Vol. 28, October 2, 2009, No. 33, pp. 1)*
Pub: American City Business Journals
Ed: John George. **Description:** VitaminSpice, a startup company established by Ed Bukstel, makes a line of spice and vitamin blends that come in seasoning form. The form of the blends could facilitate easier ingestion of vitamins into people's diets. A reverse merger that will allow a publicly-traded company status for VitaminSpice will be accomplished by early October 2009.

ASSOCIATIONS AND OTHER ORGANIZATIONS

10273 ■ *Canadian Foodservice Industry Operations Report*
316 Bloor St. W
Toronto, ON, Canada M5S 1W5
Ph: (416)923-8416
Free: 800-387-5649
Fax: (416)923-1450
Co. E-mail: info@crfa.ca
URL: http://www.crfa.ca
Contact: Garth Whyte, President
Released: Biennial

10274 ■ **Canadian Health Food Association (CHFA)—Association Canadienne des Aliements de Sante**
235 Yorkland Blvd., Ste. 302
Toronto, ON, Canada M2J 4Y8
Ph: (416)497-6939
Free: 800-661-4510
Fax: (416)497-3214
Co. E-mail: info@chfa.ca
URL: http://www.chfa.ca
Contact: Matthew James, Chairman
Description: Represents producers and distributors of health foods. Seeks to advance the health food industries. Facilitates communication and coopera-tion among members; represents the commercial and regulatory interests of the health food industries; sponsors educational and promotional programs. **Founded:** 1964. **Publications:** *The Natural Voice* (5/year).

10275 ■ **Canadian Restaurant and Foodservices Association (CRFA)—Association Canadienne des Restaurateurs et des Services Alimentaires**
316 Bloor St. W
Toronto, ON, Canada M5S 1W5
Ph: (416)923-8416
Free: 800-387-5649
Fax: (416)923-1450
Co. E-mail: info@crfa.ca
URL: http://www.crfa.ca
Contact: Garth Whyte, President

Description: Restaurant and food service corporations, hotels, caterers, and food service suppliers and educators. Seeks to create a favorable business environment for members. Represents members' interests before government; conducts trade research. Makes available group buying programs and other services to members; owns and operates three industry trade shows. **Scope:** hospitality industries. **Founded:** 1944. **Subscriptions:** books periodicals. **Publications:** *Foodservice Facts* (Annual); *Legislation Guide* (Quarterly); *Canadian Foodservice Industry Operations Report* (Biennial); *CRFA National Hospitality News.* **Educational Activities:** Canadian Food and Beverage Show (Annual); ApEx; Canadian International Food and Beverage Show (Annual).

10276 ■ *Foodservice Facts*
316 Bloor St. W
Toronto, ON, Canada M5S 1W5
Ph: (416)923-8416
Free: 800-387-5649
Fax: (416)923-1450
Co. E-mail: info@crfa.ca
URL: http://www.crfa.ca
Contact: Garth Whyte, President
Released: Annual

10277 ■ *Legislation Guide*
316 Bloor St. W
Toronto, ON, Canada M5S 1W5
Ph: (416)923-8416
Free: 800-387-5649
Fax: (416)923-1450
Co. E-mail: info@crfa.ca
URL: http://www.crfa.ca
Contact: Garth Whyte, President
Released: Quarterly

10278 ■ **National Restaurant Association**
2055 L St. NW
Washington, DC 20036
Ph: (202)331-5900
Free: 800-424-5156
Fax: (202)331-2429
Co. E-mail: info@restaurant.org
URL: http://www.restaurant.org
Contact: Dawn Sweeney, President
E-mail: dsweeney@restaurant.org
Description: Represents restaurants, cafeterias, clubs, contract foodservice management, drive-ins, caterers, institutional food services and other members of the foodservice industry; also represents establishments belonging to non-affiliated state and local restaurant associations in governmental affairs. Supports foodservice education and research in several educational institutions. Is affiliated with the Educational Foundation of the National Restaurant Association to provide training and education for operators, food and equipment manufacturers, distributors and educators. Has 300,000 member locations. **Scope:** restaurant management, cookery, menus. **Founded:** 1919. **Subscriptions:** 5000 periodicals. **Publications:** *National Restaurant Association--Washington Report* (Semimonthly); *Restaurant Industry Operations Report*; *Restaurants USA: The Monthly Magazine of the National Restaurant Assn* (Monthly); *Who's Who in the Foodservice Industry*; *Restaurant Information Abstracts* (Biweekly). **Awards:** Restaurant Good Neighbor Award (Annual); Hennessy Awards.

10279 ■ *The Natural Voice*
235 Yorkland Blvd., Ste. 302
Toronto, ON, Canada M2J 4Y8
Ph: (416)497-6939
Free: 800-661-4510
Fax: (416)497-3214
Co. E-mail: info@chfa.ca
URL: http://www.chfa.ca
Contact: Matthew James, Chairman
Released: 5/year

REFERENCE WORKS

10280 ■ *"Beverage Brand Vies To Be the Latest Purple Prince" in Brandweek (Vol. 49, April 21, 2008, No. 16, pp. 20)*
Pub: VNU Business Media, Inc.
Ed: Becky Ebenkamp. **Description:** Profile on the new beverage product Purple and its founder, Ted Farnsworth; Purple is a drink that blends seven antioxidant-rich juices to create what Mr. Farnsworth calls a 'Cascade Effect' that boosts antioxidants' effectiveness. Mr. Farnsworth is marketing the brand's Oxygen Radical Absorbance Capability (ORAC) which is a value of 7,600 compared with orange juice's 1,200.

10281 ■ *"Careers in Organic Food Preparation" in Occupational Outlook Quarterly (Vol. 54, Fall 2010, No. 3, pp. 3)*
Pub: U.S. Bureau of Labor Statistics
Ed: Adam Bibler. **Description:** Organic methods of food production, including methods that combine science with traditional farming practices, are outlined. Facts regarding careers in organic food preparation are presented.

10282 ■ *Directory of High Volume Independent Restaurants*
Pub: Chain Store Guide
Contact: Lisa Patterson, President
URL(s): www.chainstoreguide.com. **Released:** Annual; Latest edition 2010. **Price:** $1375, Individuals online pro plus; $1075, Individuals online pro; $445, Individuals online lite. **Covers:** Approximately 4,200 independently owned restaurants with annual sales of at least $1 million. **Entries include:** Company name, address, phone and fax numbers, e-mail and web addresses; total annual sales; average check amount; type of food service; menu type; alcohol types served; catering services indicator; food wholesaler name and location; year founded; key personnel with titles. **Arrangement:** Geographical. **Indexes:** Alphabetical, exclusions.

10283 ■ *"Drink Up" in Black Enterprise (Vol. 38, March 2008, No. 8, pp. 50)*
Pub: Earl G. Graves Publishing Co. Inc.
Ed: Tennille H. Robinson. **Description:** Advice is given to an individual seeking to start a natural juice small business, along with information for finding a bottling company.

10284 ■ *"Effort Is Growing to Offer Healthier Choices in Vending Machines" in Philadelphia Inquirer (July 29, 2011)*
Pub: Philadelphia Media Network Inc.
Ed: Don Sapatkin. **Description:** Since Boston's mayor announced a ban on the sale of all sugar sweetened beverages on city properties, it seems more cities, states, hospitals, businesses, and even park systems are following suit. Thus, vending machines are beginning to offer healthier snacks and drinks to consumers.

10285 ■ *"Essentially Organic Vending Takes Healthy Snacks to Ohio High School" in Entertainment Close-Up (September 13, 2011)*
Pub: Close-Up Media
Description: Essentially Organic Vending is offering students a healthy alternative for their snacking. The vending machines will be stocked with nutritious energy options.

10286 ■ *"Hain Celestial Acquires Greek Gods Yogurt" in Ice Cream Reporter (Vol. 23, July 20, 2010, No. 8, pp. 1)*
Pub: Ice Cream Reporter
Description: Hain Celestial Group acquired The Greek Gods LLC. Hain Celestial is a natural and organic products company and Greek Gods makes all natural, Greek-style yogurt and ice cream.

10287 ■ *"Healthy Fast Food Acquires Rights to U-Swirl Yogurt" in Ice Cream Reporter (Vol. 21, October 20, 2008, No. 11, pp. 5)*
Pub: Ice Cream Reporter
Description: Healthy Fast Food Inc. will acquire worldwide rights to U-Swirl Frozen Yogurt; the firm will use the new acquisition to create a yogurt superstore in a cafe setting concept for its operations.

10288 ■ *"In the Raw: Karyn Calabrese Brings Healthy Dining to a New Sophisticated Level" in Black Enterprise (Vol. 41, September 2010)*
Pub: Earl G. Graves Publishing Co. Inc.
Ed: Sonia Alleyne. **Description:** Profile of Karyn Calabrese whose businesses are based in Chicago, Illinois. Calabrese has launched a complete line of products (vitamins and beauty items), services (spa, chiropractic, and acupuncture treatments), and restaurants to bring health dining and lifestyles to a better level.

10289 ■ *"New Zealand Natural Ice Cream is Opening a Second U.S. Scoop Shop" in Ice Cream Reporter (Vol. 21, October 20, 2008, No. 11, pp. 7)*
Pub: Ice Cream Reporter
Description: New Zealand Natural Ice Cream is opening a second store in California. The company is a market leader in New Zealand and has gained distribution through 300 outlets in California.

10290 ■ *"Organic Dairy Farmers Wanted" in Canadian Business (Vol. 80, April 23, 2007, No. 9, pp. 11)*
Pub: Rogers Media
Ed: Wendy Glauser. **Description:** The growth of the Harmony Organic due to demand for organic dairy products is presented.

10291 ■ *"R&R Launches Upscale Spoony's and Low Fat Dragon's Den" in Ice Cream Reporter (Vol. 23, August 20, 2010, No. 9, pp. 3)*
Pub: Ice Cream Reporter
Description: European ice cream manufacturer R&R has acquired French ice cream maker Rolland and will position itself as an upscale challenger to brands like Ben & Jerry's.

10292 ■ *"A Recipe for Change" in Canadian Business (Vol. 80, October 22, 2007, No. 21, pp. 25)*
Pub: Rogers Media
Ed: Erin Pooley. **Description:** Market conditions have changed and customers around the world are demanding low-fat alternatives. Labor costs have risen and so did the price of foodstuffs. The impacts of this on fast food restaurants as well as the measures they have taken to cope with the new demands are discussed.

10293 ■ *"Red Mango Set to Grow in Florida" in Ice Cream Reporter (Vol. 23, September 20, 2010, No. 10, pp. 2)*
Pub: Ice Cream Reporter
Description: Red Mango will add 12 new locations throughout Florida. The stores offer healthy, nutritious frozen yogurt, smoothies and parfaits.

10294 ■ *"Sodexo Updates Healthy Vending Program" in Entertainment Close-Up (September 25, 2011)*
Pub: Close-Up Media
Description: Sodexo launched its Your Health Your Way On-the-Go program for its vending machines across the nation.

10295 ■ *"Turmoil Means Changes For Retailers" in The Business Journal-Serving Metropolitan Kansas City (Vol. 27, October 10, 2008, No. 4)*
Pub: American City Business Journals, Inc.
Ed: Suzanna Stagemeyer. **Description:** Impacts of the financial crisis on Kansas Metropolitan Area retailers are varied. Rob Dalzell, for instance, found it difficult to secure a loan for his new self-serve yogurt store Yummo. The trends in retailing in the area are examined further as well as ways in which local businesses are changing in an attempt to stay solvent during the economic downturn.

10296 ■ *"Yogun Fruz Adds First Location in Southern New York State" in Ice Cream Reporter (Vol. 23, September 20, 2010, No. 10, pp. 2)*
Pub: Ice Cream Reporter
Description: Yogen Fruz signed a master franchise agreement to expand into the southern counties of New York State. The firm offers a healthy and beneficial option to fast food and typical dessert choices.

TRADE PERIODICALS

10297 ■ *Chef: The Food Magazine for Professionals*
Pub: Talcott Communication Corp.
URL(s): www.chefmagazine.com. **Released:** 11/yr. **Price:** $32, Individuals; $47, Two years; $64, Individuals 3 years; $43, Canada; $96, Other countries.

10298 ■ *ConcepTrac*
Pub: Technomic Information Services
Ed: Eric Giandelone, Editor, egiandelone@technomic.com. **Released:** Monthly. **Price:** $395, individuals. **Description:** Provides news on chain restaurant development. Includes information on decor, atmosphere, service styles, cooking preparation methods, and unit economics.

10299 ■ *Cooking for Profit*
Pub: CP Publishing Inc.
Contact: Craig Culver, President
URL(s): www.cookingforprofit.com/home.html. **Released:** Monthly **Price:** $30, Individuals; $55, Two years; $52, Canada; $98, Canada 2 years; $85, Other countries; $160, Other countries 2 years.

10300 ■ *Foodservice and Hospitality Magazine: Canada's Hospitality Business Magazine*
Pub: Kostuch Publications Ltd.
URL(s): www.foodserviceworld.com/foodservice-and-hospitality-mag.html. **Ed:** Rosanna Caira. **Released:** Monthly **Price:** $55, Canada; $80, Individuals U.S.; $100, Other countries.

10301 ■ *No Salt Week-The Newsletter*
Pub: Prosperity & Profits Unlimited, Distribution Services
Ed: A. Doyle, Editor. **Released:** Annual. **Price:** $2, U.S.; $3, Canada; $4, elsewhere. **Description:** Presents possibilities for herb and spice blends that contain no added salt. Also contains ideas for cooking and much more.

10302 ■ *Restaurant Hospitality: Ideas for Full Service Restaurants*
Pub: Penton Media Inc.
URL(s): restaurant-hospitality.comwww.penton.com. **Released:** Monthly **Price:** Free.

10303 ■ *Sunbelt Foodservice*
Pub: Shelby Publishing Company Inc.
Contact: Bob Reeves, Manager
URL(s): www.shelbypublishing.com/index.php?option=com_content&task=view&id=24&Itemid=45. **Ed:** Lorrie Griffith. **Released:** Monthly **Price:** $36, Individuals; $60, Two years.

10304 ■ *Vegetarian Journal*
Pub: The Vegetarian Resource Group
Contact: Charles Stahler, Director
E-mail: charles@vrg.org
Ed: Charles Stahler, Editor. **Released:** Quarterly. **Price:** $20, members; $32, Canada and Mexico; $42, elsewhere. **Description:** Focuses on the ethical and nutritional aspects of vegetarianism, as well as health, ecology, animal rights, and world hunger. Recurring features include product reviews, recipes, a calendar of events, and reviews of scientific and informational articles.

10305 ■ *Vegetarian Journal's Foodservice Update*
Pub: The Vegetarian Resource Group
Contact: Charles Stahler, Director
E-mail: charles@vrg.org
Ed: Nancy Berkoff, R.D., Editor. **Released:** Quarterly. **Price:** $20, U.S. **Description:** Provides information about serving vegetarian meals in institutions. Includes advice and recipes.

VIDEOCASSETTES/ AUDIOCASSETTES

10306 ■ *Healthy Habits Video Series*
Cambridge Educational
c/o Films Media Group
132 West 31st Street, 17th Floor
Ste. 124
New York, NY 10001
Free: 800-257-5126
Fax: (609)671-0266
Co. E-mail: custserve@films.com
URL: http://www.cambridgeol.com
Released: 19??. **Price:** $139.95. **Description:** Five-part series offering educational information and health tips on the importance of proper nutrition. Discusses such topics as cooking, cholesterol, good and bad foods, vitamins, and food allergies. **Availability:** VHS.

TRADE SHOWS AND CONVENTIONS

10307 ■ ApEx
Canadian Restaurant and Foodservices Association (CRFA)
316 Bloor St. W
Toronto, ON, Canada M5S 1W5
Ph: (416)923-8416
Free: 800-387-5649
Fax: (416)923-1450
Co. E-mail: info@crfa.ca
URL: http://www.crfa.ca
Contact: Garth Whyte, President
URL(s): www.crfa.ca/tradeshows/apex. **Audience:** Trade. **Principal Exhibits:** Products and services for the restaurant and hospitality industry, as well as institutions, convenience stores, delis and bakeries. **Telecommunication Services:** escanlan@crfa.ca.

10308 ■ International Restaurant & Foodservice Show of New York
Reed Exhibitions North American Headquarters
383 Main Ave.
Norwalk, CT 06851
Ph: (203)840-4800
Fax: (203)840-5805
Co. E-mail: inquiry@reedexpo.com
URL: http://www.reedexpo.com
URL(s): www.internationalrestaurantny.com/. **Frequency:** Annual. **Principal Exhibits:** Equipment, supplies, and services for the food products, foodservice, restaurant, and institutional food service industries. **Dates and Locations:** , Jacob K. Javits Convention Center.

10309 ■ Michigan Restaurant Show
Michigan Restaurant Association (MRA)
c/o Robert A. Gifford, Pres./CEO
225 W Washtenaw St.
Lansing, MI 48933-1506
Ph: (517)482-5244
Free: 800-968-9668
Fax: (517)482-7663
Co. E-mail: rgifford@mramail.org
URL: http://www.michiganrestaurant.org
Contact: Robert A. Gifford, President
URL(s): www.michiganrestaurant.org. **Price:** $5, Pre-registered restaurant non-member (per attendee). **Frequency:** Annual. **Audience:** Food service industry professionals. **Principal Exhibits:** Equipment, supplies, and services for the food service industry.

10310 ■ Natural Products Expo East
Delicious Living
New Hope Natural Media
1401 Pearl St.
Boulder, CO 80302
Ph: (303)939-8440
Fax: (303)998-9020
Co. E-mail: info@newhope.com
URL: http://www.deliciouslivingmag.com
URL(s): www.expoeast.com. **Frequency:** Annual. **Audience:** Retailers, wholesalers, distributors, and brokers from the natural products industry. **Principal Exhibits:** Natural, organic and environmentally sound products, including: alternative health care, vegetarian and allergy-free personal care recycled/recyclable products, biodegradable products, and organic meats. **Dates and Locations:** , Convention Center. **Telecommunication Services:** tradeshows@newhope.com.

10311 ■ West Ex: The Rocky Mountain Regional Hospitality Exposition
Colorado Restaurant Association
430 E. 7th Ave.
Denver, CO 80203
Ph: (303)830-2972
Free: 800-522-2972
Fax: (303)830-2973
Co. E-mail: info@coloradorestaurant.com
URL: http://www.coloradorestaurant.com
Contact: Pete Meersman, President
E-mail: meersman@coloradorestaurant.com
URL(s): www.coloradorestaurant.com. **Frequency:** Annual. **Audience:** Food service and restaurant industry personnel. **Principal Exhibits:** Food service and lodging products, equipment, and services.

10312 ■ Western Food Service & Hospitality Expo Los Angeles
California Restaurant Association
621 Capitol Mall, Ste. 2000
Sacramento, CA 95814
Ph: (916)447-5793
Free: 800-765-4842
Fax: (916)447-6182
Co. E-mail: membership@calrest.org
URL: http://www.calrest.org
URL(s): www.westernfoodexpo.com. **Audience:** Food service hospitality and lodging industry professionals. **Principal Exhibits:** Food, equipment, supplies, and services for food service and lodging industries.

CONSULTANTS

10313 ■ Birchfield Jacobs Foodsystems Inc.
519 N Charles St., Ste. 350A
Baltimore, MD 21201-5022
Ph: (410)528-8700
Fax: (410)528-6060
URL: http://www.birchfieldjacobs.com
Contact: Robert Jacobs, Owner Principal
E-mail: rjacobs@birchfieldJacobs.com
Scope: Food facilities design consultants for colleges; universities; schools; healthcare facilities; government; military; correctional; country clubs and restaurants. Services include facilities design; feasibility studies; operations analysis and master planning. **Founded:** 1979.

10314 ■ GEC Consultants Inc.
4604 Birchwood Ave.
Skokie, IL 60076-3835
Ph: (847)674-6310
Fax: (847)674-3946
Co. E-mail: experts@gecconsultants.com
URL: http://www.gecconsultants.com
Contact: Lloyd M. Gordon, President
E-mail: legal@gecconsultants.com
Scope: Consulting in all areas of bar and restaurant operations. Restaurant manager development appraises existing locations or sites. Studies the feasibility of projects. Develop new concepts. Assist in expanding, existing food operations, marketing, expert witness (legal) for hospitality/restaurant industry. **Founded:** 1963. **Publications:** "How You Can Fight Back to Minimize This Recession!"; "New Thoughts On Leases"; "The Use of Job Analysis to Actually Reduce Payroll Costs"; "Do You Need a Feasibility Study?"; "Combat Negative Hospitality"; "How To Run A Successful Night club"; "Are Capitalists In Your Cabinet?"; "Marketing For The 21st Century"; "Profitability In The Banquet Industry"; "Starting a Restaurant, Bar or Catering Business"; "How To Find And Retain Suitable Employees"; "26 Things To Do To Plan A Restaurant"; "Wall Fabric or Paint: Decor Magic It's Your Call"; "The Art of Cafe Ambiance"; "Why You Need A Consultant". **Telecommunication Services:** legal@gecconsultants.com.

10315 ■ L G Anthony Associates
40 Wellington Blvd.
Reading, PA 19610
Ph: (610)670-0477
Contact: Louis G. Anthony, Owner
Scope: Provides food service facility planning, layout and design, including equipment selection and specification. Also offers management systems and operations analysis, such as the development of operating policies and procedures. Firm can design menu planning and recipe development, food selection and specification, work simplification, service, and quality control around current concepts in the field. Industries served: hospital, nursing home, restaurant, group homes; commercial and institutional food service industries. **Founded:** 1986. **Seminars:** Food Service Sanitation; Menu Planning; Work Simplification; Quality Control in Food Service.

10316 ■ Linda Lipsky Restaurant Consultants Inc.
216 Foxcroft Rd.
Broomall, PA 19008-2039
Ph: (610)325-3663
Free: 877-425-3663
Fax: (610)325-3329
Co. E-mail: lipsky@restaurantconsult.com
URL: http://www.restaurantconsult.com
Contact: Linda J. Lipsky, President
E-mail: lipsky@restaurantconsult.com
Scope: Provider of marketing and survey solutions. It offers management training and evaluation programs, recipe documentation, cost analysis, and bridge management services. **Founded:** 1988. **Seminars:** Designing Menus for Maximum Sales and Profits; How to Maximize Your Check Average; Going Beyond Your Customer's Expectations; Seeing Your Restaurant Through a Customer's Eyes; Making the Best First and Last Impression; Basic Training in Kitchen Management Techniques; Basic Training in Bar Management Techniques; Make Every Labor Dollar Count; Back to Basics/More Than Shift Management; Conducting Your Own In-House Inspection; Basics of Sanitation Training for Kitchen Employees; Basics of Sanitation Training for Dining Room Employees.

FRANCHISES AND BUSINESS OPPORTUNITIES

10317 ■ Evos
609 S Howard Ave.
Tampa, FL 33606
Ph: (813)258-3867
Free: 877-888-3867
Fax: (813)514-4713
URL: http://www.evos.com
Description: Healthy fast food. **No. of Franchise Units:** 5. **No. of Company-Owned Units:** 3. **Founded:** 1999.. **Franchised:** 2006. **Equity Capital Needed:** $350,000-$440,000. **Franchise Fee:** $35,000. **Royalty Fee:** 5.5%. **Financial Assistance:** Limited third party financing available. **Training:** Provides 4-6 weeks training at headquarters and ongoing support.

10318 ■ Ho-Lee-Chow
GCF Food Services Inc.
5415 Dundas St. W, Ste. 110
Toronto, ON, Canada M9B 1B5
Ph: (416)778-8028
Fax: (416)778-6818
Co. E-mail: holeechow@holeechow.com
URL: http://www.holeechow.com
Description: Quick-food service industry catering fresh, attractive, delicious and healthful, low in additives and free of MSG, Chinese food with a quality product and impeccable standards of preparation and delivery. **No. of Franchise Units:** 18. **No. of Company-Owned Units:** 3. **Founded:** 1989.. **Franchised:** 1989. **Equity Capital Needed:** $175,000. **Franchise Fee:** Included in turn-key package. **Training:** Offers 4-6 weeks and ongoing support provided.

10319 ■ Indigos Fruit Smoothies
Indigos Franchising, Inc.
21551 Arbor Way
Boca Raton, FL 33433
Ph: (407)383-3872
Description: Retail smoothie/juice bar & healthy restaurant. **No. of Franchise Units:** 9. **Founded:** 2004.. **Franchised:** 2004. **Equity Capital Needed:** $89,800-$272,000. **Franchise Fee:** $25,000. **Royalty Fee:** 6%. **Financial Assistance:** Limited third party financing available. **Training:** Includes 6 days training at headquarters, 7 days at franchisee's location and ongoing support.

10320 ■ Pockets Restaurant
1001 Green Bay Rd., Ste. 237
Winnetka, IL 60093
Ph: (847)242-0738
Fax: (847)242-0739
Description: Fast food; healthy choices. **No. of Franchise Units:** 2. **No. of Company-Owned Units:** 10. **Founded:** 1989.. **Franchised:** 2007. **Equity Capital Needed:** $150,000 in liquid assets; $300,000 net worth. **Franchise Fee:** $25,000-$30,000. **Training:** Yes.

10321 ■ Subway
Doctor's Associates Inc.
Franchise Sales Dept.
325 Bic Dr.
Milford, CT 06460
Ph: (203)877-4281
Free: 800-888-4848
Fax: (203)783-7325
Co. E-mail: franchise@subway.com
URL: http://www.subway.com
Description: Submarine sandwich category with fresh, great tasting, made-for-you sandwiches and salads, many of which have 6 grams of fat or less. Offering a healthful alternative to fatty fast food has made Subway a popular destination for health-conscious consumers. **No. of Franchise Units:** 33,000. **No. of Company-Owned Units:** 1. **Founded:** 1974.. **Franchised:** 1974. **Equity Capital Needed:** $114,800-$258,300 total investment. **Franchise Fee:** $15,000. **Financial Assistance:** 30-V, FRA handbook. **Training:** Provides training and assistance to franchisee's in all areas of business operation.

10322 ■ Vitality Juice, Java & Smoothie Bar
790 Florida St., Ste. 1
Mandeville, LA 70448
Ph: (985)674-6898
Fax: (985)674-4464
Description: Smoothies, juices, coffee and vitamins. **No. of Franchise Units:** 4. **No. of Company-Owned Units:** 2. **Founded:** 2004.. **Franchised:** 2005. **Equity Capital Needed:** $128,000-$393,500. **Franchise Fee:** $15,000-$35,000. **Royalty Fee:** 5%. **Training:** Offers 2 weeks training at headquarters, 1 week on-site and ongoing as needed at any location.

COMPUTERIZED DATABASES

10323 ■ *Food Code - Recommendations of the United States Public Health Service Food and Drug Administration*
10903 New Hampshire Ave.
Silver Spring, MD 20993-0002
Free: 888-INFO-FDA
URL: http://www.fda.gov
Availability: CD-ROM: U.S. Department of Commerce - Technology Administration - National Technical Information Service. **Type:** Full-text.

LIBRARIES

10324 ■ American Dietetic Association - Knowledge Center
120 S. Riverside Plaza, Ste. 20000
Chicago, IL 60606-6995
Ph: (312)877-1600, x4864
Free: 800-877-1600
Fax: (312)899-4739
Co. E-mail: knowledge@eatright.org
URL: http://www.eatright.org/
Scope: Nutrition, dietetics, food service. **Services:** Interlibrary loan; copying; Library open to the public by appointment. **Founded:** 1990. **Holdings:** 3000 books. **Subscriptions:** 60 journals and other serials; 4 newspapers.

10325 ■ California Culinary Academy Library
350 Rhode Island St.
San Francisco, CA 94103
Ph: (415)771-3500
Free: 888-897-3222
Co. E-mail: bgk@baychef.com
URL: http://www.chefs.edu/San-Francisco
Scope: Culinary arts, nutrition, restaurant and hospitality industry. **Services:** Library open to the public by special appointment only. **Founded:** 1989. **Holdings:** 3500 books. **Subscriptions:** 90 journals and other serials.

10326 ■ City College of San Francisco - Department - Culinary Arts and Hospitality Studies Alice Statler Library
50 Phelan Ave.
Statler Wing, Rm. 10
San Francisco, CA 94112
Ph: (415)239-3460
Co. E-mail: aniosi@ccsf.edu
URL: http://www.ccsf.edu/NEW/en/library/about-library/library-locations/statler.html
Contact: Andrea Niosi, Librarian
Scope: Public hospitality industries - hotels, motels, restaurants, catering services, cookery and nutrition; tourism; beverages. **Services:** Copying; Wi-Fi; library open to the public for reference use only. **Founded:** 1964. **Holdings:** 10,000 books; 3500 pamphlets; 900 menus; videotapes; archives. **Subscriptions:** 80 journals and other serials. **Telecommunication Services:** astatler@ccsf.edu.

10327 ■ Geisinger Medical Center - Community Health Library
100 N. Academy Ave.
Danville, PA 17822-4401
Ph: (570)271-5638
Fax: (570)271-5635
Co. E-mail: chrl@geisinger.edu
URL: http://www.geisinger.edu
Contact: Patricia A Ulmer, Librarian
Scope: General medicine, nutrition, alternative and complementary medicine, pediatrics, cancer, AIDS. **Services:** Interlibrary loan. **Holdings:** 860 books; 200 audio/visual materials. **Subscriptions:** 14 journals and other serials.

10328 ■ Lemmen-Holton Cancer Pavilion Library
145 Michigan, NE
Grand Rapids, MI 49503
Ph: (616)486-5700
URL: http://www.spectrumhealth.org/lhcp
Scope: Cancer. **Services:** Library open to the public. **Holdings:** Pamphlets.

10329 ■ New York Public Library - Mid-Manhattan Library - General Reference and Advisory Services/Health Information Center
455 5th Ave. at 40th St.
New York, NY 10016
Ph: (212)340-0863
URL: http://www.nypl.org/locations/mid-manhattan-library
Contact: Theresa Myrhol, Librarian
URL(s): legacy.www.nypl.org/branch/collections/hic.html. **Scope:** Consumer, health medicine, nursing, allied health. **Services:** Copying; Library open to the public. **Founded:** 1996. **Holdings:** 22,000 books and videocassettes; 4 VF of pamphlets. **Subscriptions:** 278 journals and other serials.

10330 ■ Voice for Animals Library
PO Box 120095
San Antonio, TX 78212
Ph: (210)737-3138
Co. E-mail: voice@voiceforanimals.org
URL: http://www.voiceforanimals.org/
Scope: Animal rights; vegetarianism. **Services:** Library not open to the public. **Founded:** 1987. **Holdings:** 200 books; newsletters; videocassettes.

ASSOCIATIONS AND OTHER ORGANIZATIONS

10331 ■ Academy of Doctors of Audiology (ADA)
3493 Lansdowne Dr., Ste. 2
Lexington, KY 40517-1147
Ph: (859)271-0607
Free: 866-493-5544
Fax: (859)977-7441
Co. E-mail: info@audiologist.org
URL: http://www.audiologist.org
Contact: Stephanie Czuhajewski, Executive Director
Description: Individuals with graduate degrees in audiology who dispense hearing aids as part of a rehabilitative practice. Fosters and supports professional dispensing of hearing aids by qualified audiologists; encourages audiology training programs to include pertinent aspects of hearing aid dispensing in their curriculums; conducts seminars on the business aspects of the hearing aid industry. **Founded:** 1977. **Publications:** *ADA Membership Directory* (Annual); *Academy of Doctors of Audiology--Membership Directory* (Annual). **Awards:** Joel Wernick Award (Annual).

10332 ■ American Auditory Society (AAS)
19 Mantua Rd.
Mount Royal, NJ 08061
Ph: (856)423-3118
Free: 800-638-6423
Fax: (856)423-3420
Co. E-mail: aas@talley.com
URL: http://www.amauditorysoc.org
Contact: Timothy D. Trine, President
Description: Audiologists, otolaryngologists, scientists, hearing aid industry professionals, and educators of hearing impaired people; individuals involved in industries serving hearing impaired people, including the amplification systems industry. Works to increase knowledge and understanding of: the ear, hearing, and balance; disorders of the ear, hearing, and balance; prevention of these disorders; habilitation and rehabilitation of individuals with hearing and balance dysfunction. **Founded:** 1974. **Publications:** *The Bulletin of the American Auditory Society* (3/ year); *Ear and Hearing* (Bimonthly). **Educational Activities:** Scientific Meeting (Annual); American Auditory Society Annual Meeting (Annual). **Awards:** Carhart Memorial Lecturer (Annual); Lifetime Achievement Award (Periodic).

10333 ■ HEAR Center (HEAR)
301 E Del Mar Blvd.
Pasadena, CA 91101
Ph: (626)796-2016
Fax: (626)796-2320
Co. E-mail: info@hearcenter.org
URL: http://www.hearcenter.org
Contact: Lawrence Wilson, President
URL(s): hearcenter.org. **Description:** Auditory and verbal program designed to help hearing-impaired children, infants, and adults lead normal and productive lives. Seeks to develop auditory techniques to aid people who have communication problems due to deafness; primary objectives include early identification of hearing loss in infants and children and early amplification. Operates a program involving: binaural hearing aids where appropriate; continuous exposure to sound; development of auditory perception; wide-range amplification; environmental stimulation. Provides services in: diagnosis and audiological evaluation; hearing aid evaluation and trial use; development of listening skills and articulation; speech therapy; hearing aid dispensing; parent counseling. **Founded:** 1954. **Publications:** *HEAR Center Proceedings* (Periodic); *The Listener* (Quarterly); *The Listener*; *Hear: A Four Letter Word.* **Awards:** Glen H. Bollinger Humanitarian Award (Periodic). **Telecommunication Services:** ellensimon@hearcenter.org.

10334 ■ Hearing Industries Association (HIA)
1444 I St. NW, Ste. 700
Washington, DC 20005
Ph: (202)449-1090
Fax: (202)216-9646
Co. E-mail: mjones@bostrom.com
URL: http://www.hearing.org
Contact: Carole M. Rogin, Executive Director
Description: Companies engaged in the manufacture and/or sale of electronic hearing aids, their component parts, and related products and services on a national basis. Cooperates in and contributes toward efforts to promote the number of hearing aid users; collects trade statistics; conducts market research activities, investigations, and studies in connection with hearing and hearing aids. **Founded:** 1957.

10335 ■ International Hearing Society
16880 Middlebelt Rd., Ste. 4
Livonia, MI 48154
Ph: (734)522-7200
Free: 800-521-5247
Fax: (734)522-0200
URL: http://www.ihsinfo.org
Contact: Kathleen Mennillo, Executive Director
URL(s): ihsinfo.org/. **Description:** Hearing aid specialists who test hearing for the selection, adaptation, fitting, adjusting, servicing, and sale of hearing aids. Members counsel the hearing impaired and instruct them in care and use of hearing aids. Activities include: administration of a qualification program for screening persons designated as Hearing Instrument Specialists; administration of a consumer information program; publication of information and research concerning hearing health care; establishment of standards of education, equipment, and techniques in the fitting of hearing aids; cooperation with other professional organizations engaged in hearing health care; cooperation and consultation with government officials and agencies in the development of policies and legislation. Accredits seminars and workshops for the education of hearing aid specialists. Maintains the International Institute for Hearing Instruments Studies as the educational arm of the society. **Founded:** 1951. **Publications:** *The Hearing Professional: Official Journal of the International Hearing Society* (Bimonthly); *International Hearing Aid Society* (Annual); *The Hearing Professional* (Quarterly); *International Hearing Society--Directory of Members* (Annual).

REFERENCE WORKS

10336 ■ *Academy of Doctors of Audiology--Membership Directory*
Pub: Academy of Doctors of Audiology
Contact: Stephanie Czuhajewski, Executive Director
URL(s): www.audiologist.org/. **Released:** Annual **Covers:** Nearly 250 member audiologists. **Entries include:** Name, address, phone.

10337 ■ *Hearing Journal--Hearing Health Industry World Directory Issue*
Pub: Lippincott Williams & Wilkins
Contact: Rich Wohl, Executive Vice President
URL(s): www.thehearingjournal.comwww.audiology-online.com/thehearingjournal/. **Released:** Annual; latest edition 2005, Published with December issue of HJ. **Price:** $124, Individuals in U.S.; $151, Institutions in U.S.; $232, Individuals international; $278, Institutions international. **Covers:** Manufacturers and suppliers of hearing aids, earmolds, audiometers, testing equipment, calibrators, and accessory items; hearing aid repair laboratories; services; related publishers, trade associations, organizations; international coverage. **Entries include:** Company name, address, phone, names and titles of executives, whether manufacturer or distributor, trade and brand names, list of products or services provided. **Arrangement:** Alphabetical. **Indexes:** Product (Trade name).

10338 ■ *International Hearing Society--Directory of Members*
Pub: International Hearing Society
Contact: Kathleen Mennillo, Executive Director
URL(s): www.ihsinfo.org. **Released:** Annual; spring. **Price:** Free. **Covers:** 5,400 hearing instrument specialists and board certificants. **Entries include:** Individual name, address, phone. **Database includes:** List of board certified hearing instrument dispensers and hearing aid manufacturers and suppliers. **Arrangement:** Geographical, alphabetical.

TRADE PERIODICALS

10339 ■ *The Hearing Professional: Official Journal of the International Hearing Society*
Pub: International Hearing Society
Contact: Kathleen Mennillo, Executive Director
URL(s): ihsinfo.org/IhsV2/hearing_professional. **Ed:** Kara Nacarato. **Released:** Bimonthly **Price:** $35, Individuals U.S.; $45, Elsewhere.

10340 ■ *The League Letter*
Pub: Center for Hearing and Communication
Contact: Laurie Hanin, Executive Director
Price: Included in membership. **Description:** Reports on news and events of the The League for the Hard of Hearing. Recurring features include a calendar of events. Remarks: TTY available at (917)305-7999.

10341 ■ *Volta Voices*
Pub: The Alexander Graham Bell Association for the Deaf and Hard of Hearing
Contact: Kathleen S. Treni, President
URL(s): nc.agbell.org/netcommunity/page.aspx-?pid=256. **Released:** Bimonthly **Price:** $7.50, Single issue.

VIDEOCASSETTES/ AUDIOCASSETTES

10342 ■ *Extra Sense-Assistive Listening Devices for the Hearing Impaired*
House Ear Institute (HEI)
2100 W 3rd St.
Los Angeles, CA 90057
Ph: (213)483-4431
Free: 800-388-8612
Fax: (213)483-8789
Co. E-mail: info@hei.org
URL: http://www.hei.org
Contact: James D. Boswell, Chief Executive Officer
Released: 1985. **Price:** $30.00. **Description:** Nanette Fabray demonstrates "listening devices" which are used to help people with hearing impairments. **Availability:** VHS; 3/4 U.

10343 ■ *Hearing Aids in Children and Adults*
House Ear Institute (HEI)
2100 W 3rd St.
Los Angeles, CA 90057
Ph: (213)483-4431
Free: 800-388-8612
Fax: (213)483-8789
Co. E-mail: info@hei.org
URL: http://www.hei.org
Contact: James D. Boswell, Chief Executive Officer
Released: 1985. **Price:** $30.00. **Description:** An explanation of how hearing aids work and what type is best for each kind of patient. **Availability:** VHS; 3/4 U.

FRANCHISES AND BUSINESS OPPORTUNITIES

10344 ■ Miracle Ear
Amplifon
5000 Cheshire Lane N
Plymouth, MN 55446
Free: 800-234-7714
Fax: (763)268-4253
Co. E-mail: cejohns@miracle-ear.com
URL: http://www.miracle-ear.com
Description: Manufacturer and retail sales of hearing aids. **No. of Franchise Units:** 916. **No. of Company-Owned Units:** 187. **Founded:** 1948.. **Franchised:** 1983. **Equity Capital Needed:** $112,500-$570,000; minimum $25,000 cash. **Franchise Fee:** $30,000. **Training:** Yes.

COMPUTERIZED DATABASES

10345 ■ *Health Devices® Alerts*
5200 Butler Pke.
Plymouth Meeting, PA 19462-1298
Ph: (610)825-6000
Fax: (610)834-1275
Co. E-mail: info@ecri.org
URL: http://www.ecri.org
Contact: Jeffrey C. Lerner, President
Availability: Online: ProQuest LLC - Dialog; German Institute of Medical Documentation and Information; ECRI Institute. **Type:** Bibliographic; Full-text.

10346 ■ *Health Devices International Sourcebase*
5200 Butler Pke.
Plymouth Meeting, PA 19462-1298
Ph: (610)825-6000
Fax: (610)834-1275
Co. E-mail: info@ecri.org
URL: http://www.ecri.org
Contact: Jeffrey C. Lerner, President
Availability: Online: ProQuest LLC - Dialog; German Institute of Medical Documentation and Information; ECRI Institute. **Type:** Directory.

LIBRARIES

10347 ■ Atlanta-Fulton Public Library - Learning and Career Center
One Margaret Mitchell Sq., 4th Fl.
Atlanta, GA 30303

Ph: (404)730-1700
Co. E-mail: librarycomments@fultoncountyga.gov
URL: http://www.afpls.org
Contact: Dr. Rick Wright
Scope: Literacy program, visually impaired assistance, hearing impaired assistance, test preparation materials. **Services:** Interlibrary loan; copying; free Wi-Fi; library open to the public. **Founded:** 1902. **Subscriptions:** 10 journals and other serials.

10348 ■ Berks Deaf & Hard of Hearing Services Library
2045 Centre Ave.
Reading, PA 19605
Ph: (610)685-4520
Fax: (610)685-4526
Co. E-mail: lfisher@bdhhs.org
URL: http://www.bdhhs.org
Contact: Kandy Reyes, Executive Director
Scope: Deafness and hard of hearing. **Services:** Center open to the public. **Founded:** 1972. **Holdings:** 480 books; videotapes; patents; archives. **Subscriptions:** 4 journals and other serials; 2 newspapers. **Telecommunication Services:** bdhhs@bdhhs. org.

10349 ■ Central Institute for the Deaf - Speech, Hearing and Education Library
825 S. Taylor Ave.
St. Louis, MO 63110
Ph: (314)977-0132
Free: 877-444-4574
Fax: (314)977-0023
Co. E-mail: mgremp@cid.edu
URL: http://pacs.wustl.edu/pacs/pacsweb.nsf/CI-D?Open
Contact: Michelle Gremp, Coordinator, Education Resources
URL(s): www.cid.edu/home.aspx. **Scope:** Audiology, early childhood education, behavioral sciences, speech pathology, physiology, otolaryngology, education of the deaf, noise control, electro-acoustics, digital instrumentation, aural rehabilitation, neurophysiology. **Services:** Copying; Library open to the public for reference use only. **Founded:** 1929. **Holdings:** 5000 books; 1195 bound periodical volumes; 150 dissertations; 30 videotapes. **Subscriptions:** 70 journals and other serials. **Telecommunication Services:** aosman@cid.edu.

10350 ■ New York Public Library - Mid-Manhattan Library - Accessibility Services
455 5th Ave. at 40th St., 2nd Fl.
New York, NY 10016
Ph: (212)340-0843
Co. E-mail: mmprojac@nypl.org
URL: http://legacy.www.nypl.org/branch/central/mml/pa
Contact: Theresa Myrhol, Librarian
Scope: The disabled - vision impaired, hearing impaired, learning and mobility impaired. **Services:** Special equipment, including Kurzweil Personal Reader, available for use by appointment; TTY on circulation; Library open to the public. **Founded:** 1979. **Holdings:** 300 books; 7 VF drawers of pamphlets material concerning the disabled; zoom text (XTRA 7.0). **Subscriptions:** 20 journals and other serials.

10351 ■ Oregon Health & Science University - Oregon Hearing Research Center
3181 SW Sam Jackson Park Rd.
Portland, OR 97239-3098
Ph: (503)494-8032
Fax: (503)494-5656
Co. E-mail: ohrc@ohsu.edu
URL: http://www.ohsu.edu/xd/health/services/ent/research/ohrc-research/index.cfm
Contact: Rachel Dresbeck, PhD, Director
Scope: Auditory science, hearing, tinnitus. **Services:** Library open to members of academic community only. **Founded:** 1966. **Holdings:** 200 books; 500 bound periodical volumes. **Subscriptions:** 10 journals and other serials.

RESEARCH CENTERS

10352 ■ House Ear Institute (HEI)
2100 W 3rd St.
Los Angeles, CA 90057
Ph: (213)483-4431
Free: 800-388-8612
Fax: (213)483-8789
Co. E-mail: info@hei.org
URL: http://www.hei.org
Contact: James D. Boswell, Chief Executive Officer
Services: Safety Patrol, Bridging the Gap, Family Camp; Workshops for the Hearing Impaired; Young Adult Work Program. **Founded:** 1946. **Publications:** *House Calls Magazine; Progress report; The Review.* **Educational Activities:** Conference of Auditory Prostheses; Hearst Laboratory Internships for undergraduates; International Skullbase Congress; Meniere's Conference; Rupley Fellowships for graduate students; Seminars on Primary Care in Otology; Skullbase surgical dissection courses; Temporal Bone Surgical Dissection Courses (Monthly); IHCON International Hearing Aid Research Conference. **Awards:** Quota Scholarships for graduate student research.

10353 ■ Houston Ear Research Foundation (HERF)
7737 SW Fwy., Ste. 630
Houston, TX 77074
Ph: (713)771-9966
Free: 800-843-0807
Fax: (713)771-0546
Co. E-mail: jgilden@houstoncochlear.org
URL: http://houstoncochlear.org/
Contact: Jan Gilden, Executive Director
Founded: 1983. **Publications:** *HERF Newsletter* (Annual). **Educational Activities:** Cochlear implant candidacy testing, provide all testing and counseling to determine if adult/child is cochlear implant candidates; Aural rehabilitation therapy for adult and children cochlear implant recipients; Initial stimulation/reprogramming/follow-up testing/troubleshooting of cochlear implant, provide all initial hook up, follow-up reprogramming and testing with cochlear implant. **Telecommunication Services:** info@houstoncochlear.org.

10354 ■ University of Michigan - Kresge Hearing Research Institute (KHRI)
Medical Science II, Rm. 4605
1150 W Medical Ctr. Dr.
Ann Arbor, MI 48109-5616
Ph: (734)764-8110
Fax: (734)764-0014
Co. E-mail: schacht@umich.edu
URL: http://www.khri.med.umich.edu
Contact: Prof. Jochen Schacht, Director
Founded: 1963. **Educational Activities:** KHRI Seminars (Weekly).

10355 ■ University of Michigan - Kresge Hearing Research Institute - Auditory Anatomy Laboratory
1150 W Medical Ctr. Dr.
Ann Arbor, MI 48109-5616
Ph: (734)763-0060
Fax: (734)764-0014
Co. E-mail: shuler@umich.edu
URL: http://www2.khri.med.umich.edu/research/altschuler_lab
Contact: Prof. Richard A. Altschuler, Director
Founded: 1985. **Educational Activities:** Demonstrations and visitor participation programs.

10356 ■ University of Oklahoma - Keys Speech and Hearing Center
1200 N Stonewall
Oklahoma City, OK 73117
Ph: (405)271-4214
Fax: (405)271-3360
Co. E-mail: stephen-painton@ouhsc.edu
URL: http://www.ah.ouhsc.edu
Founded: 1947. **Awards:** Master's and doctoral stipends.

10357 ■ University of Tulsa - Mary K. Chapman Center for Communicative Disorders
800 Tucker Dr.
Tulsa, OK 74104
Ph: (918)631-2504

Fax: (918)631-3668
Co. E-mail: paula_cadogan@utulsa.edu
URL: http://www.cas.utulsa.edu/commdis/
Contact: Paula Cadogan, Chairperson
Services: Speech, language, and clinical hearing assessments. **Founded:** 1947. **Educational Activities:** Graduate training; Route 66 Annual Conference, on communication disorders. **Awards:** Hearst Foundation Grants; Rumley Foundation Grants.

ASSOCIATIONS AND OTHER ORGANIZATIONS

10358 ■ American Herb Association (AHA)
PO Box 1673
Nevada City, CA 95959
Ph: (530)265-9552
URL: http://www.ahaherb.com
Contact: Robert Brucia, Director
Description: Enthusiasts and specialists of medicinal herbs and herbal products. Seeks to increase knowledge and provide up-to-date scientific and experiential information on herbs. Offers a network to exchange data and resources among members nationwide. Maintains herb garden. **Scope:** herb gardening, botany, botanical art, medicinal herbs. **Founded:** 1981. **Subscriptions:** 1000. **Publications:** *Directory of Herbal Education* (Biennial); *Directory of Mail-Order Medicinal Herb Products*; *American Herb Association - Quarterly Newsletter*; *Directory of Mail Order Medicinal Herbs* (Biennial).

10359 ■ American Herbal Products Association (AHPA)
8630 Fenton St., Ste. 918
Silver Spring, MD 20910-5606
Ph: (301)588-1171
Fax: (301)588-1174
Co. E-mail: ahpa@ahpa.org
URL: http://www.ahpa.org
Contact: Katie Huggins, Chairman
Description: Represents growers, brokers, manufacturers, distributors, retailers, importers and related consultants of herbal products such as bulk ingredients, teas, dietary supplements, and body care products. Seeks to effectively deal with common interests and industry-related problems by acquiring, affecting and disseminating business and regulatory information. Represents industry to legislators, regulating agencies and media. Conducts trade promotion and research activities; compiles statistics. Publishes resource documents and provides educational programs. Maintains New Dietary Ingredient Database, based on FDA dockets, other databases under development. **Founded:** 1982. **Publications:** *Botanical Safety Handbook*; *Herbs of Commerce*; *St. John's Wart, Ephedra, Echinacea or Saw Palmetto*. **Awards:** AHPA Herbal Hero Award (Annual); AHPA Herbal Industry Leader Award (Annual); AHPA Herbal Insight Award (Annual); Herbal Hero Award; Herbal Industry Leader Award; Herbal Insight Award.

10360 ■ Herb Growing and Marketing Network (HGMN)
PO Box 245
Silver Spring, PA 17575-0245
Ph: (717)393-3295
Fax: (717)393-9261
Co. E-mail: herbworld@aol.com
URL: http://www.herbworld.com
Contact: Maureen Rogers, Director
Description: Herb retailers, wholesalers, and growers; manufacturers of related products; serious hobbyists. Provides information on all segments of the herb industry with an emphasis on marketing and locating wholesale sources. **Scope:** herbs, gardening, and business. **Founded:** 1990. **Subscriptions:** 3000; 3000. **Publications:** *The Herbal Green Pages* (Annual); *Proceedings from 1st Annual Conference*; *Proceedings from 2nd Annual Conference*; *Starting an Herb Business*; *Herbal Green Pages* (Annual); *Proceedings from 5th Annual Conference*; *Proceedings from 4th Annual Conference*; *Proceedings from 3rd Annual Conference*.

10361 ■ Herb Research Foundation (HRF)
5589 Arapahoe Ave., Ste. 205
Boulder, CO 80303
Ph: (303)449-2265
Fax: (303)449-7849
Co. E-mail: info@herbs.org
URL: http://www.herbs.org
Contact: Robert S. McCaleb, President
Description: Professionals in the health food industry, plant research scientists, herbal medicine practitioners and their patients, pharmacologists, herbal manufacturers and trade organizations, ethnobotanists, and interested consumers; scientists and students in the fields of pharmacognosy, botany, ethnobotany, and medicine. Encourages and supports research on the chemistry, pharmacology, and use of herbal folk medicines, teas, and other botanical products; provides a forum for discussion and cooperation among herbalists, physicians, health food advocates, and scientists. Works to form a liaison between the U.S. herbal movement and the worldwide scientific community. Disseminates research information on botanicals and serves as a source of information for the public and press on medicinal plants. Provides botanical literature research service. **Scope:** medical plants, pharmacognosy, pharmacology, botany, herbs, herbal medicine. **Founded:** 1983. **Subscriptions:** 250000 papers reports. **Publications:** *Herbal Research News* (Quarterly); *HRF HerbalGram* (Quarterly); *HRF Herbs Companion* (Bimonthly).

10362 ■ Herb Society of America (HSA)
9019 Kirtland Chardon Rd.
Kirtland, OH 44094
Ph: (440)256-0514
Fax: (440)256-0541
Co. E-mail: herbs@herbsociety.org
URL: http://www.herbsociety.org
Contact: Ms. Katrinka Morgan, Executive Director
URL(s): herbsociety.org. **Description:** Represents scientists, educators, and others interested in botanical and horticultural research on herbs and the culinary, economic, decorative, fragrant, and historic use of herbs. Maintains herb gardens in arboreta and other public sites. Establishes and maintains gardens for the blind. Planned and funded the National Herb Garden, which was donated to the National Arboretum in Washington, DC. Promotes the knowledge, use and delight of herbs through educational programs, research, and sharing the experience of its members with the community. **Scope:** botany, horticulture, herbs, folklore, gardening. **Founded:** 1933. **Subscriptions:** 3000 audiovisuals books periodicals. **Publications:** *Herbarist*; *The Beginners Herb Garden* (Semiannual); *The Herb Society of America Newsletter* (Quarterly); *The Herbarist* (Annual); *Herb Society of America--Membership Directory and By-laws* (Biennial); *The Herb Society of America New Encyclopedia of Herbs and Their Uses*. **Educational Activities:** Educational Conference (Annual). **Awards:** The Nancy Putnam Howard Award for Horticulture (Annual); Certificate of Achievement; Certificate of Appreciation; Herb Society of America Research Grant; Nashville Unit Scholarships; Pennsylvania Heartland Unit Scholarships; South Texas Unit Scholarships; Western Reserve Herb Society Scholarships; Francis Sylvia Zverina Scholarships; The Helen de Conway Little Medal of Honor (Annual); Helen de Conway Little Medal of Honor; Nancy Putnam Howard Award for Excellence in Horticulture. **Telecommunication Services:** herb@herbsociety.org.

10363 ■ International Herb Association (IHA)
PO Box 5667
Jacksonville, FL 32247-5667
Ph: (904)614-7745
Fax: (904)399-3241
URL: http://www.iherb.org
Contact: Matthias Reisen, President
URL(s): iherb.org. **Description:** Herb professionals. Works to unite members for growth through promotion and education. Offers help with business concerns such as the packaging and labeling of herbal products, budgets and projections, computerized business problem solving, and retail display and design. Maintains speakers' bureau. **Founded:** 1985. **Publications:** *IHA Newsletter* (Quarterly); *IHA Membership Directory* (Annual); *Herb of the Year* (Annual). **Awards:** Professional Award (Annual); Service Award (Annual).

REFERENCE WORKS

10364 ■ "Because He Is Still Growing: Horst Rechelbacher: Intelligent Nutrients Minneapolis" in Inc. (Volume 32, December 2010, No. 10)
Pub: Inc. Magazine
Ed: Mike Hoffman. **Description:** Horst Rechelbacher, founder of hair care company Aveda, and after selling Aveda to Estee Lauder, he is expanding into a nutraceuticals company offering hair care products that are organically grown.

10365 ■ Herb Society of America--Membership Directory and By-laws
Pub: Herb Society of America
Contact: Ms. Katrinka Morgan, Executive Director
URL(s): www.herbsociety.org/member-directory.html. **Released:** Biennial; odd years. **Covers:** 3,000 scientists, educators, and others interested in botanical and horticultural research on herbs and the culinary, economic, decorative, fragrant, and historic use of herbs. **Entries include:** Name, address, unit or region. **Arrangement:** By unit or region.

10366 ■ Herbal Green Pages
Pub: Herb Growing and Marketing Network
Contact: Maureen Rogers, Director
URL(s): www.herbworld.com/green_pages.htm. **Ed:** Maureen Rogers. **Released:** Annual; August. **Covers:** Over 6,000 companies and individuals involved

in herb growing, marketing, and related areas. **Entries include:** Name, address, phone, contact, products or services, nature of business (wholesale, retail, etc.), catalog availability. **Arrangement:** Alphabetical. **Indexes:** Product, service, contact person, geographical.

TRADE PERIODICALS

10367 ■ *Kitchen Gardener: Growing and Cooking Great Food*
Pub: Taunton Press Inc.
Contact: John Lively, Chief Executive Officer
URL(s): www.tauntonstore.com/kitchen-gardener-back-issues.html. **Released:** Bimonthly **Price:** $4.95, Individuals back issue.

10368 ■ *No Salt Week-The Newsletter*
Pub: Prosperity & Profits Unlimited, Distribution Services
Ed: A. Doyle, Editor. **Released:** Annual. **Price:** $2, U.S.; $3, Canada; $4, elsewhere. **Description:** Presents possibilities for herb and spice blends that contain no added salt. Also contains ideas for cooking and much more.

LIBRARIES

10369 ■ **Abbey of Regina Laudis, Order of St. Benedict - Our Lady of the Rock Monastery - Priory Library**
PO Box 425
Shaw Island, WA 98286
Ph: (360)468-2321
Co. E-mail: mhildegard@rockisland.com
URL: http://www.ourladyoftherock.com
Contact: Mother Therese Critchley, Leader
Scope: Scripture, theology, patristics, musicology, ecclesiastical history, art, Japanese history and literature, oriental studies. **Services:** Library not open to the public. **Founded:** 1977. **Holdings:** 4000 books. **Subscriptions:** 12 journals and other serials.

10370 ■ **American Herb Association - Library**
PO Box 1673
Nevada City, CA 95959
Ph: (530)265-9552
URL: http://www.ahaherb.com
Contact: Kathi Keville, Director
Scope: Herbs, herbal products, antique herbs, flora. **Services:** Library not open to the public. **Founded:** 1981. **Holdings:** 1000 volumes. **Subscriptions:** 60 journals and other serials.

10371 ■ **Carnegie-Mellon University - Hunt Institute for Botanical Documentation Library**
5000 Forbes Ave.
Pittsburgh, PA 15213-3890
Ph: (412)268-2434
Fax: (412)268-5677
Co. E-mail: dwbrown@andrew.cmu.edu
URL: http://huntbot.andrew.cmu.edu
Contact: Charlotte A. Tancin, Librarian
Scope: Botanical history; plant taxonomy, including 15th- to 17th-century herbals; extensive collection of 18th- and 19th-century color plate works, floras, monographic works, and other works on natural history, plant exploration and introduction. **Services:** Interlibrary loan (limited); copying; Library open to the public for reference use only. **Founded:** 1961. **Holdings:** 30,150 books; 29,000 portraits; 29,270 watercolors, drawings and prints; 2000 autograph letters and manuscripts. **Subscriptions:** 275 journals and other serials. **Telecommunication Services:** ctancin@cmu.edu.

10372 ■ **Cleveland Botanical Garden - Eleanor Squire Library**
11030 East Blvd.
Cleveland, OH 44106
Ph: (216)721-1600
Fax: (216)721-2056
Co. E-mail: info@cbgarden.org
URL: http://www.cbgarden.org/Learn/Library.html
Contact: Gary Esmonde, Librarian
Scope: Gardening, horticulture, landscape architecture, herbs, flower arranging, botany. **Services:** Library open to the public with paid admission

(members may borrow); rare books open to the public by appointment for review, research, and study. **Founded:** 1930. **Holdings:** 17,000 volumes; seed and nursery catalogs; slides; botanical prints; 1000 rare books. **Subscriptions:** 50 journals and other serials. **Telecommunication Services:** gesmonde@cbgarden.org.

10373 ■ **Dittrick Medical History Center**
Allen Memorial Medical Library
11000 Euclid Ave.
Cleveland, OH 44106-1714
Ph: (216)368-3648
Fax: (216)368-0165
Co. E-mail: laura.travis@case.edu
URL: http://www.cwru.edu/artsci/dittrick/museum
Contact: James M. Edmonson, Curator
Scope: History of medicine. **Services:** Copying; photographic services; Library open to the public. **Founded:** 1894. **Holdings:** 35,000 books; 75,000 artifacts, Archives, and Image collections. **Telecommunication Services:** james.edmonson@case.edu.

10374 ■ **Florida State University - Special Collections**
Robert Manning Strozier Library
116 Honors Way
Tallahassee, FL 32306-2047
Ph: (850)644-3271
Fax: (850)644-1221
Co. E-mail: spc@reserves.lib.fsu.edu
URL: http://www.lib.fsu.edu/specialcollections
Contact: William Modrow
Scope: Florida, Florida State University, early Americana, Confederate imprints, book arts, herbals, poetry, Napoleon, North Florida/South Georgia area business. **Services:** Collections open to the public. **Founded:** 1953. **Telecommunication Services:** wmodrow@fsu.edu.

10375 ■ **Horticultural Society of New York Library**
148 W. 37th St., 13th Fl.
New York, NY 10018-6976
Ph: (212)757-0915, x-100
Fax: (212)246-1207
Co. E-mail: kpowis@hsny.org
URL: http://www.hsny.org
Contact: Katherine Powis, Librarian
Scope: Gardening; garden design and garden history; horticulture; landscape design; botanical illustration; flower arrangement. **Services:** Library open to the public for reference use only. **Founded:** 1922. **Holdings:** 6000 books; 3500 bound periodical volumes; 75 lin.ft. of institutional archives. **Subscriptions:** 120 journals and other serials. **Telecommunication Services:** library@thehort.org.

10376 ■ **Idaho State University - Idaho Museum of Natural History - Stirton-Kelson Library**
Bldg. 12, Rm. 205C
921 S. 8th Ave.
ISU Mail Stop 8096
Pocatello, ID 83209-0001
Ph: (208)282-5417
Fax: (208)282-5893
Co. E-mail: maschner@isu.edu
URL: http://imnh.isu.edu/Collections/Library.htm
Contact: Dr. Herbert Maschner, Director
Scope: Paleontology, anthropology, biology, geology, herpetology, botany, natural history. **Services:** Interlibrary loan; Library open to University community and museum researchers. **Founded:** 1960. **Holdings:** 900 books; 2150 bound periodical volumes; 24,000 reprints; 1500 journals/government documents.

10377 ■ **Kingwood Center Library**
900 Park Ave., W.
Mansfield, OH 44906
Ph: (419)522-0211, x-108
Co. E-mail: cgleaves@kingwoodcenter.org
URL: http://www.kingwoodcenter.org/cms/index.php/education/library
Contact: Chuck Gleaves, Director
Scope: Horticulture, natural history. **Services:** Interlibrary loan; copying; library open by appointment to members and researchers. **Founded:** 1953.

Holdings: 8000 books; 500 bound periodical volumes; 12 VF drawers of pamphlets, pictures, clippings; 600 current seed and nursery catalogs. **Subscriptions:** 100 journals and other serials. **Telecommunication Services:** bcollins@kingwoodcenter.org.

10378 ■ **Miami University - Walter Havighurst Special Collections Library**
321 King Library
Oxford, OH 45056
Ph: (513)529-3323
Fax: (513)529-1719
Co. E-mail: tullykk@muohio.edu
URL: http://www.lib.muohio.edu
Contact: Kimberly Tulley, Librarian, Special Collections
URL(s): spec.lib.muohio.edu. **Scope:** Early children's literature books, book arts, James T. Farrel, Percy MacKaye, George Orwell, William Dean Howells, William H. McGuffey, William Faulkner, Rodolfo Usigli, Hamlin Garland. **Services:** Library open to the public for reference use only with identification. **Founded:** 1973. **Holdings:** 65,000 books; 2330 bound periodical volumes; literary annuals and gift books. **Subscriptions:** 13 journals and other serials.

10379 ■ **New York Public Library - The Research Libraries - Humanities and Social Sciences Library - Arents Tobacco Collection**
Brooke Russell Astor Reading Room, 3rd Fl., Rm. 328
5th Ave. and 42nd St.
New York, NY 10018-2788
Ph: (212)642-0110
Fax: (212)302-4815
Co. E-mail: rarebook@nypl.org
URL: http://www.nypl.org/locations/schwarzman/arents-collection
Contact: Sarah Augusta Dickson, Curator
Scope: Tobacco, herbals, history, medicine, law, manufacture, marketing; smoking and health. **Services:** Open to qualified researchers by card of admission secured in Special Collections Office. **Founded:** 1944. **Holdings:** 13,000 books and manuscripts; 150,000 cards and pieces of ephemera. **Subscriptions:** 10 journals and other serials.

10380 ■ **Pennsylvania Horticultural Society - McLean Library**
100 N. 20th St., 5th Fl.
Philadelphia, PA 19103-1455
Ph: (215)988-8800
Fax: (215)988-8810
Co. E-mail: wiredgardener@pennhort.org
URL: http://www.pennsylvaniahorticulturalsociety.org
Contact: Janet Evans, Director, Library Services
Scope: Ornamental horticulture, botany, landscape design, garden history. **Services:** Interlibrary loan; photocopying; Garden Q&A (telephone plant information service); Library open to the public for reference use only (borrowing privileges for members and PHS staff). **Founded:** 1827. **Holdings:** 15,000 books; 4000 bound periodical volumes; 1000 slides; 250 videotapes on gardening. **Subscriptions:** 100 journals and other serials. **Telecommunication Services:** mcleanlibrary@pennhort.org.

RESEARCH CENTERS

10381 ■ **Alberta Agriculture and Rural Development - Crop Diversification Centre South (CDCS)**
301 Horticultural Station Rd. E
Brooks, AB, Canada T1R 1E6
Ph: (403)362-1350
Fax: (403)362-1306
Co. E-mail: shelley.barkley@gov.ab.ca
URL: http://www1.agric.gov.ab.ca/$department/deptdocs.nsf/all/opp4386
Services: Extension for agricultural industries. **Founded:** 1935. **Educational Activities:** Grower meetings and seminars.

10382 ■ **Herb Research Foundation (HRF)**
5589 Arapahoe Ave., Ste. 205
Boulder, CO 80303
Ph: (303)449-2265

Fax: (303)449-7849
Co. E-mail: info@herbs.org
URL: http://www.herbs.org
Contact: Robert S. McCaleb, President
Services: Research services. **Founded:** 1983. **Publications:** *Herb Research News* (Quarterly); *HerbalGram*; *Herbs for Health*; *Information Services Catalog*; *HRF Reports*. **Educational Activities:** Literature research on many aspects of herb use (Periodic); Technical information, on medicinal plants and professional literature searching and review. **Telecommunication Services:** rmccaleb@herbs.org.

10383 ■ Rodale Institute
611 Siegfriedale Rd.
Kutztown, PA 19530-9320
Ph: (610)683-1400
Fax: (610)683-8548
Co. E-mail: info@rodaleinst.org
URL: http://www.rodaleinstitute.org
Contact: Mark Smallwood, Executive Director
Founded: 1947. **Publications:** *Rodale Institute Brochures*; *Rodale Institute Fact sheets*; *Rodale Institute Pamphlets*; *Rodale Institute Technical Reports*. **Edu**-

cational Activities: Rodale Institute Field Days, open to farmers, researchers, and students; Rodale Institute Internship program; Rodale Institute Workshops. **Awards:** Rodale Institute Paid Internships (Annual).

ASSOCIATIONS AND OTHER ORGANIZATIONS

10384 ■ Cookware Manufacturers Association (CMA)
PO Box 531335
Birmingham, AL 35253-1335
Ph: (205)592-0389
Fax: (205)599-5598
Co. E-mail: hrushing@usit.net
URL: http://www.cookware.org
Contact: Hugh J. Rushing, Executive Vice President
Description: Represents manufacturers of cooking utensils and cooking accessories. Compiles statistics. **Scope:** cookware brand name history. **Founded:** 1922. **Subscriptions:** archival material business records.

10385 ■ Home Fashion Products Association (HFPA)
355 Lexington Ave., Ste. 1500
New York, NY 10017-6603
Ph: (212)297-2122
Fax: (212)370-9047
Co. E-mail: contactus@hfpaonline.org
URL: http://www.homefashionproducts.com
Contact: Katie Goshgarian, Executive Director
Description: Manufacturers of curtains, draperies, bedding, rugs and related products. Sponsors annual scholarship for students attending accredited schools in home textiles. **Founded:** 1968. **Awards:** Scholarship (Annual).

10386 ■ International Housewares Association (IHA)
6400 Shafer Ct., Ste. 650
Rosemont, IL 60018
Ph: (847)292-4200
Fax: (847)292-4211
Co. E-mail: showteam@housewares.org
URL: http://www.housewares.org
Contact: Phil J. Brandl, President
E-mail: pbrandl@housewares.org
Description: Manufacturers and distributors of housewares and small appliances. Conducts annual market research survey of the housewares industry. Manages the international housewares show. **Founded:** 1939. **Publications:** *IHA Membership Directory* (Annual); *BusinessWatch* (Monthly); *Housewares MarketWatch* (Quarterly); *IHA Reports* (Bimonthly); *January Exhibitors Directory* (Annual); *NHMA Reports Newsletter* (Bimonthly); *NHMA Export Interest Directory; Exhibitors' Directory to the International Housewares Exposition* (Annual). **Educational Activities:** International Housewares Association Show (Annual); International Home & Housewares Show (Annual). **Awards:** National Student Design Competition Award (Annual). **Telecommunication Services:** pbrandl@housewares.org.

REFERENCE WORKS

10387 ■ *American Edged Products Manufacturers Association--Annual*

Membership Directory
Pub: American Edged Products Manufacturers Association
Contact: Bob Clemence, President
URL(s): www.aepma.org. **Released:** Annual; September. **Price:** Free. **Covers:** Approximately 35 member manufacturers and suppliers of knives, scissors, and edged hand tools. **Entries include:** Company name, address, phone, names and titles of key personnel, number of employees, products provided, year founded. **Arrangement:** Alphabetical. **Indexes:** Company name and personnel listing.

10388 ■ *"Bedding a Leader in Kohl's Q1 Gains"* in Home Textiles Today (Vol. 31, May 24, 2011, No. 13, pp. 1)
Pub: Reed Business Information
Contact: Jeff Greisch, President
Description: Kohl's credited home furnishings, particularly bedding, as the leading source of its first-quarter sales and profit gains in 2011. Statistical data included.

10389 ■ *"Bon-Ton Halves Q1 Losses, Show Operating Profit"* in Home Textiles Today (Vol. 31, May 24, 2011, No. 13, pp. 7)
Pub: Reed Business Information
Contact: Jeff Greisch, President
Ed: James Mammarella. **Description:** Bon-Ton Stores reported progress in its multi-year push to profitability, with soft home sales leading the way. Statistical data included.

10390 ■ *"CGG Home Fashions to Show Hand-Loomed Textiles"* in Home Textiles Today (Vol. 31, May 24, 2011, No. 13, pp. 4)
Pub: Reed Business Information
Contact: Jeff Greisch, President
Description: CGG Home Fashions introduced textiles made from natural fibers and vegetable dyes for upscale industry use at the HD Expo in Las Vegas, Nevada.

10391 ■ *"Colores Origenes: Martha Kruse"* in Advertising Age (Vol. 77, November 13, 2006, No. 46, pp. S12)
Pub: Crain Communications, Inc.
Ed: Laurel Wentz. **Description:** Home Depot has created a range of Latin paint colors called Colores Origenes; the new line was originally intended to launch only at locations with heavily Hispanic patrons but the company decided to make the line available at all of their stores.

10392 ■ *"A Counter Offer"* in Inc. (February 2008, pp.)
Pub: Gruner & Jahr USA Publishing
Ed: Elaine Appleton Grant. **Description:** Online retailer offering a line of kitchen and home products has upgraded its Website in order to make the business more attractive to possible buyers of the company. The firm is asking $9.9 million and reported gross revenue of $12.7 in 2007. The owner suggests that a buyer add product lines geared towards more rooms of the home than currently offer on the retail site.

10393 ■ *"Doing Good: Cause and Effect"* in Entrepreneur (Vol. 36, February 2008, No. 2, pp. 23)
Pub: Entrepreneur Media Inc.
Description: Lisa Knoppe established Art for a Cause LLC that employs people with mental and physical disabilities. The company makes hand-painted tools and furniture to be sold at gift retailers and hardware stores.

10394 ■ *"Dreamy Fortune: Pillow Biz Dreams of Sales Reaching $10 Million a Year"* in Small Business Opportunities (Spring 2008)
Pub: Harris Publications Inc.
Ed: Stan Roberts. **Description:** Profile of Michale Lezberg, owner of a pillow factory. Lezberg shares insight into building his firm to a multi-million dollar a year business.

10395 ■ *"Entrepreneur Says Spirituality Has Been a Key to Her Success"* in Business First Columbus (Vol. 25, October 17, 2008, No. 8, pp. 1)
Pub: American City Business Journals
Ed: Scott Rawdon. **Description:** Profile of Carolyn Williams Francis, CEO of Williams Interior Designs Inc. She outlines her mantra for success in her furniture design business, but emphasizes that faith has taken her business to greater heights.

10396 ■ *"Furniture Chain Moving to Harford"* in Baltimore Business Journal (Vol. 27, January 22, 2010, No. 38, pp. 1)
Pub: American City Business Journals
Ed: David J. Sernovitz. **Description:** Manchester, Connecticut-based Bob's Discount Furniture signed a lease for 672,000 square feet of space in Harford County, Maryland. The site will become the discount furniture retailer's distribution center in mid-Atlantic US. As many as 200 jobs could be generated when the center opens.

10397 ■ *"Home Helps Push Macy's to First-Quarter Profit"* in Home Textiles Today (Vol. 31, May 24, 2011, No. 13, pp. 2)
Pub: Reed Business Information
Contact: Jeff Greisch, President
Description: Macy's Inc. reported home goods as one of the three strong performing categories for first quarter 2011. Home goods sales, both big and small ticket items, have improved significantly for the retailer.

10398 ■ *"Home Shows Signs of Life at Target"* in Home Textiles Today (Vol. 31, May 24, 2011, No. 13, pp. 1)
Pub: Reed Business Information
Contact: Jeff Greisch, President
Description: Retailer, Target, is experience a boost in sales for apparel and products for the home.

10399 ■ *"Home Sits Out Q1 Surge at JCP"* in Home Textiles Today (Vol. 31, May 24, 2011,

No. 13, pp. 1)
Pub: Reed Business Information
Contact: Jeff Greisch, President
Ed: James Mammarella. **Description:** JCPenney chairman and CEO, Mike Ullman, reported sales gains for first quarter 2011 in all products except home goods.

10400 ■ *"Home Source Debuts Diesel Home Collection"* in *Home Textiles Today (Vol. 31, May 24, 2011, No. 13, pp. 1)*
Pub: Reed Business Information
Contact: Jeff Greisch, President
Ed: Carole Sloan. **Description:** Home Source is highlighting the debut collection of bed and bath products made by Diesel. These items interpret the jeans culture into home furnishings.

10401 ■ *"Just Add Water and Lily Pads"* in *Crain's Chicago Business (Vol. 31, April 28, 2008, No. 17, pp. 50)*
Pub: Crain Communications, Inc.
Ed: Phuong Ly. **Description:** Aquascape Inc., a major manufacturer of pond-building supplies, is using the recent drought in the South which hurt its business significantly to create a new product: an upscale, decorative version of the rain barrel which will collect rainwater to circulate through a pond or a fountain.

10402 ■ *LDB Interior Textiles Annual Buyers' Guide*
Pub: E.W. Williams Publications Co.
Contact: Andrew Williams, President
E-mail: awilliams@ewwpi.com
URL(s): www.ldbinteriortextiles.com/pdf/buyers-guide2010.pdf. **Released:** Annual; Latest edition 2010. **Covers:** Over 3,000 manufacturers, importers, and suppliers of home fashions products and services, decorative fabric converters, and alternative window coverings; fabricators; manufacturer's representatives; and others allied to the home fashions trade. **Entries include:** For manufacturers, importers, converters, fabricators, and suppliers--Company name, address, phone, fax, contact, product line. For manufacturer's representatives--Name, address, phone, contact, lines carried. For others--Name, address, phone, fax. **Arrangement:** Classified by product/service. **Indexes:** Product.

10403 ■ *"Liora Manne to Debut Fabric Line"* in *Home Textiles Today (Vol. 31, May 24, 2011, No. 13, pp. 4)*
Pub: Reed Business Information
Contact: Jeff Greisch, President
Description: Textile and product designer Liora Manne will debut her new decorative fabric collection at the Showtime in High Point, North Carolina in June 2011. More than 22 fabric patterns and solid colors using Manne's patented Lamontage textile design process will be featured and can be used for indoor/outdoor decorative fabrics, furniture, decorative pillows, upholstery and more.

10404 ■ *Martha, Inc.*
Pub: John Wiley and Sons, Inc.
Ed: Christopher Byron. **Released:** 2002. **Price:** $28.00. **Description:** Profile of Martha Stewart's rise from working class to a billionaire businesswoman is presented. The book covers Stewart's power struggles and personal conflicts as well as her triumphs.

10405 ■ *"New Kittinger Showroom Twice the Size of the Last One"* in *Business First Buffalo (December 7, 2007, pp. 4)*
Pub: American City Business Journals, Inc.
Ed: Tracey Drury. **Description:** Kittinger Furniture Company, an upscale furniture maker, has opened a 6,000 square foot retail outlet at the Transit Road, New York. The company's moved to attract suburban and affluent customers for its high-end furniture products.

10406 ■ *"New Year's Resolutions: How Three Companies Came Up With Their 2008 Growth Strategies"* in *Inc. (January 2008, pp. 47-49)*
Pub: Gruner & Jahr USA Publishing
Ed: Martha C. White. **Description:** Three companies share 2008 growth strategies; companies include a candle company, a voice mail and text messaging marketer, and hotel supplier of soap and shampoo.

10407 ■ *"P/Kaufmann Sells Bennettsville"* in *Home Textiles Today (Vol. 31, May 24, 2011, No. 13, pp. 6)*
Pub: Reed Business Information
Contact: Jeff Greisch, President
Description: Decorative Screen Printers purchased the printing and finishing facility of P/Kaufmann in Bennettsville, South Carolina. However, the firm will continue its focus on its core business, a vat printing facility for home furnishings fabrics.

10408 ■ *The Pampered Chef*
Pub: Doubleday Broadway Publishing Group
Ed: Doris Christopher. **Description:** The Pampered Chef has been selling high quality kitchen tools through in-home cooking demonstration for twenty-five years. CEO and founder explains how she turned her one woman company into a a business with sales approaching $1 billion. Christopher shares her story by providing the foundation, strategies for entrepreneurs, setting priorities, knowing when to expand and when to slow growth, and dealing with adversity.

10409 ■ *"Peking Launches Trina Turk Bedding Collection"* in *Home Textiles Today (Vol. 31, May 24, 2011, No. 13, pp. 4)*
Pub: Reed Business Information
Contact: Jeff Greisch, President
Description: Peking Handicraft is launching designer Trina Turk's bedding collection of four beds that reflect her approach to contemporary fabric design using color and prints with strong graphic effects.

10410 ■ *"Procter Gambles on Wallpaper; Putting Paint On a Roll"* in *Advertising Age (Vol. 77, September 18, 2006, No. 38, pp. 4)*
Pub: Crain Communications, Inc.
Ed: Jack Neff. **Description:** Procter & Gamble Co. has launched a new line of textured paints that are already applied to a wallpaper-like roll that can be hung without paste or wallpaper tools.

10411 ■ *"Ross Stores Reports Spectacular First Quarter"* in *Home Textiles Today (Vol. 31, May 24, 2011, No. 13, pp. 2)*
Pub: Reed Business Information
Contact: Jeff Greisch, President
Ed: James Mammarella. **Description:** Retailer Ross Stores reported strong sales and profit gains for first quarter 2011, with their home department helping to lead the way.

10412 ■ *"Sales at Furniture Showrooms Sink"* in *Puget Sound Business Journal (Vol. 29, October 10, 2008, No. 25, pp. 1)*
Pub: American City Business Journals
Ed: Greg Lamm. **Description:** Furniture showrooms are seeing a drop in sales due to the bad economy. Buyer demand has also fallen because of the slumping real estate market.

10413 ■ *"Shaw Joins Green Institute Launch"* in *Home Textiles Today (Vol. 31, May 24, 2011, No. 13, pp. 4)*
Pub: Reed Business Information
Contact: Jeff Greisch, President
Description: Shaw Industries Group joined the Green Products Innovation Institute, the first nonprofit institute of its kind in America. The institute promotes the concepts of reverse engineering, elimination of waste, safe chemistries, and closed loop technical nutrients.

10414 ■ *"Sheets Makers Optimistic Amid Price, Delivery Issues"* in *Home Textiles Today (Vol. 31, May 24, 2011, No. 13, pp. 8)*
Pub: Reed Business Information
Contact: Jeff Greisch, President
Ed: Jill Rowen. **Description:** Retail sales of sheets and pillowcases dropped 4.7 percent in volume in 2009. Retailers pulled back inventory significantly in 2010. Statistical data included.

10415 ■ *"Sunbrella Engages Consumers Via Social Media"* in *Home Textiles Today (Vol. 31, May 24, 2011, No. 13, pp. 4)*
Pub: Reed Business Information
Contact: Jeff Greisch, President
Description: Performance fabric brand Sunbrella is marketing to social media, such as Facebook and Twitter, in order to boost consumer interest and retailer support.

10416 ■ *"Williams-Sonoma Beats Expectations in Q1"* in *Home Textiles Today (Vol. 31, May 24, 2011, No. 13, pp. 2)*
Pub: Reed Business Information
Contact: Jeff Greisch, President
Description: Both retail nameplates, Williams-Sonoma and Pottery Barn reported gains in 2011's first quarter, accredited to the way shoppers responded to new opening price point programs for several of its brands.

SOURCES OF SUPPLY

10417 ■ *Casual Living--Casual Outdoor Furniture and Accessory Directory Issue*
Reed Business Information
Contact: Jeff Greisch, President
URL(s): www.reedbusiness.com. **Released:** Annual; Latest edition 2008. **Price:** $22.99, Individuals; C$55.99, Canada; $55.99, Other countries; $138.99, Individuals air delivery; $10, Individuals single copy; $15, Other countries single copy other. **Publication includes:** List of manufacturers, manufacturers' representatives, and suppliers of outdoor furniture, wicker and rattan furniture, and backyard accessories, such as barbecue grills, picnic accessories, outdoor lighting, cushions and pads, patio umbrellas, vinyl refinishing and maintenance products. **Entries include:** Name of firm, address, phone, products. **Arrangement:** Alphabetical. **Indexes:** Organization name.

10418 ■ *Dallas Market Center--Permanent Directory*
Dallas Market Center Co.
URL(s): www.dallasmarketcenter.com. **Released:** Semiannual; January and June. **Covers:** Representatives of manufacturers, importers, and wholesale distributors of residential and contract furniture, home furnishings, floor coverings, gifts and decorative accessories, jewelry, lamps, and lighting products. **Entries include:** Firm name, mart address, phone. **Arrangement:** Classified by product/service. **Indexes:** Company name, product/service.

10419 ■ *Gifts & Tablewares--Directory Issue*
Business Information Group
Contact: Bruce Creighton, President
URL(s): www.gifts-and-tablewares.comwww.businessinformationgroup.ca. **Released:** Annual; Latest edition 2010. **Price:** C$46.95, Individuals; $52.95, Individuals; $57.95, Other countries. **Publication includes:** List of approximately 1,000 manufacturers and suppliers of gift, home decor, stationery, and tableware items in Canada. **Entries include:** Company name, address, phone, fax, name, address, and phone of branches and showrooms; description of products and services; email and web sites. **Database includes:** Calendar of Canadian, American, European, and Asian trade shows. **Arrangement:** Alphabetical. **Indexes:** Product, brand name.

10420 ■ *Merchandise Mart Buyers Guide*
Hoyt Publishing
Contact: Peter Hoyt, President
E-mail: peter_hoyt@hoytpub.com
URL(s): www.hoytpub.com. **Ed:** Jennifer Woolford. **Released:** Semiannual; June and December. **Price:** $5. **Covers:** About 3,000 representatives of manufacturers, importers, and wholesale distributors of residential and contract furniture, home furnishings, floor coverings, gifts and accessories, lamps and lighting products, domestics, and small appliances. **Entries include:** Firm name, mart address; alphabetical listings include phone. **Arrangement:** Alphabetical by company.

STATISTICAL SOURCES

10421 ■ *Tabletop Market*
Pub: Rector Press, Ltd.
Contact: Lewis Sckolnick, President
Released: 2009. **Price:** Contact Rector Press. **Description:** Profiles the tabletop market, covering dinnerware, glassware, and flatware. Includes projections to the year 2000. Provides information on pric-

ing, factors affecting demand, design trends, foreign trade, and distribution channels. Also contains profiles of leading marketers.

10422 ■ The U.S. Tabletop Market
MarketResearch.com
Released: 2000. **Price:** $1375.00. **Description:** This report explores the question of whether the situation may be changing as tabletop marketers embrace the trend toward more casual living. The report estimates industry sales over the last five years and gives projections through 2004 based on close consideration of all relevant data and trends. growth with projections to 1996, the bridal market, market breakouts, leading marketers, consumer advertising and promotion, advertising expenditures and positioning, distribution, retail, pricing, and purchasing habits and attitudes. Also contains tables, charts, and examples of trade and consumer advertising.

TRADE PERIODICALS

10423 ■ Casual Living: The Voice of the Leisure Marketplace
Pub: Sandow Media Corp.
URL(s): www.casualliving.com. **Released:** Monthly **Price:** $25.99, Individuals; $59, Canada and Mexico; $149.99, Other countries.

10424 ■ The duPont Registry: A Buyer's Gallery of Fine Boats
Pub: duPont Publishing Inc.
Contact: Steve Chapman, Chief Executive Officer
URL(s): www.dupontregistry.com/boats/. **Released:** Monthly **Price:** $15.95, Individuals; $25.95, Canada; $45.95, Other countries.

10425 ■ Gifts & Decorative Accessories
Pub: Sandow Media Corp.
URL(s): www.giftsanddec.com/. **Released:** Monthly **Price:** $36, Individuals; $39, Canada; $135, Other countries.

10426 ■ Gifts & Tablewares
Pub: Business Information Group
Contact: Bruce Creighton, President
URL(s): www.giftsandtablewares.ca/. **Ed:** Lori Smith. **Released:** 7/yr. **Price:** $43.95, Canada plus taxes; $49.95, Individuals in U.S.; $54.95, Other countries.

10427 ■ Home Improvement Retailing
Pub: Powershift Communications Inc.
URL(s): www.hirmagazine.com/. **Released:** Bimonthly **Price:** $76, Individuals; $110, Canada plus applicable taxes.

10428 ■ LDB Interior Textiles
Pub: E.W. Williams Publications Co.
Contact: Andrew Williams, President
E-mail: awilliams@ewwpi.com
URL(s): www.ldbinteriortextiles.com. **Released:** Monthly **Price:** $72, Individuals; $125, Canada; $150, Elsewhere airmail; $100, Two years; $7, Single issue; $12, Single issue, Canada; $18, Single issue elsewhere.

VIDEOCASSETTES/ AUDIOCASSETTES

10429 ■ Home Decorating Combo
Nancy's Notions Ltd.
333 Beichl Ave.
P.O. Box 683
Beaver Dam, WI 53916-0683
Ph: (920)887-7321
Free: 800-725-0361
Fax: (800)255-8119
Co. E-mail: customerservice@nancysnotions.com
URL: http://www.nancysnotions.com
Released: 1987. **Description:** This video contains two programs on fabric-based home decoration: "Window Treatments" and "Instant Decorating." **Availability:** VHS.

10430 ■ Home Improvement: Decorating
S.I. Video Sales Group
PO Box 63745
Philadelphia, PA 19147

Ph: (267)519-2222
Co. E-mail: stann@sivideo.com
URL: http://www.sivideo.com
Released: 19??. **Price:** $12.95. **Description:** Discusses basic decorating and design concepts to consider in making your house feel like a home. Also explains how to make the right choice in carpets for each room. **Availability:** VHS.

10431 ■ Home Improvement: Interior Projects
S.I. Video Sales Group
PO Box 63745
Philadelphia, PA 19147
Ph: (267)519-2222
Co. E-mail: stann@sivideo.com
URL: http://www.sivideo.com
Released: 19??. **Price:** $12.95. **Description:** Learn how to install wall shelving and kitchen counter tops, repair holes and cracks in walls and ceilings, remove wallpaper, and more. **Availability:** VHS.

10432 ■ Home Improvement Videos
Baker & Taylor Inc.
2550 W. Tyvola Rd., Ste. 300
Charlotte, NC 28217
Ph: (704)998-3100
Free: 800-775-1800
Co. E-mail: btinfo@btol.com
URL: http://www.btol.com
Released: 1986. **Price:** $19.95. **Description:** This is a series of in-depth home improvement instructions. Videos are available individually and a booklet comes with each one. **Availability:** VHS.

TRADE SHOWS AND CONVENTIONS

10433 ■ Accent on Design - A Division of the New York International Gift Fair
George Little Management, LLC
1133 Westchester Ave., Ste. N136
White Plains, NY 10606
Ph: (914)421-3200
Free: 800-272-SHOW
Co. E-mail: cathy_steel@glmshows.com
URL: http://www.glmshows.com
URL(s): www.nyigf.com. **Frequency:** Annual. **Audience:** Buyers from specialty, department, and jewelry stores and; gift shops; interior designers; home products importers and distributors; mail order catalogs. **Principal Exhibits:** General giftware, tabletop and housewares, decorative and personal accessories, museum gifts, ethnic, traditional, country and contemporary design products, juvenile products, floral products and pet products. **Dates and Locations:** Jacob K. Javits Convention Center. **Telecommunication Services:** maureen_smith@glmshows.com.

10434 ■ Accent on Design - A Division of the San Francisco International Gift Fair
George Little Management, LLC
1133 Westchester Ave., Ste. N136
White Plains, NY 10606
Ph: (914)421-3200
Free: 800-272-SHOW
Co. E-mail: cathy_steel@glmshows.com
URL: http://www.glmshows.com
URL(s): www.weshows.com. **Frequency:** Semiannual. **Audience:** Specialty, department, stationery, jewelry, and juvenile stores, gift and gourmet shops, interior designers, importers/distributors of home products, museums. **Principal Exhibits:** Decorative accessories, lighting and home furnishings, housewares, stationery, tabletop, gourmet and general gift merchandise. **Dates and Locations:** Moscone Convention Center. **Telecommunication Services:** showinfo@weshows.com.

10435 ■ Charlotte Gift and Jewelry Show
Charlotte Gift and Jewelry Show
3710 Latrobe Dr., Ste. 110
Charlotte, NC 28211
Ph: (704)365-4152

Fax: (704)365-4154
Co. E-mail: michael@charlottegiftshow.com
URL: http://www.charlottegiftshow.com
URL(s): www.charlottegiftshow.com. **Frequency:** Quarterly. **Audience:** Trade buyers. **Principal Exhibits:** Gifts, housewares, jewelry, crafts, silk plants and flowers, tabletop, glassware, collectibles, accessories, home decorating accessories, basketry, and other related products. **Dates and Locations:** Merchandise Mart. **Telecommunication Services:** michael@charlottegiftshow.com.

10436 ■ H2X Canada Hardware & Home Improvement Expo & Conference
Messe Frankfurt Inc.
1600 Parkwood Cir., Ste. 515
Atlanta, GA 30339
Ph: (770)984-8016
Fax: (770)984-8023
Co. E-mail: info@usa.messefrankfurt.com
URL: http://www.usa.messefrankfurt.com
URL(s): meesefrankfurt.com/shows/northamerica/ h2x/index.htm. **Frequency:** Annual. **Audience:** Volume buyers, including retailers and manufacturers' representatives. **Principal Exhibits:** Hardware, housewares, giftware, paint, wallcovering, and products for leisure living, and home improvement. **Dates and Locations:** , Coliseum Exhbition Place.

10437 ■ International Bedding Exposition
International Sleep Products Association
501 Wythe St.
Alexandria, VA 22314-1917
Ph: (703)683-8371
Fax: (703)683-4503
Co. E-mail: info@sleepproducts.org
URL: http://www.sleepproducts.org
Contact: Ryan Trainer, President
E-mail: rtrainer@sleepproducts.org
URL(s): www.sleepproducts.org. **Price:** $50, Preregistered, members; $55, Onsite registered, members; $100, Pre-registered, non-members; $105, Onsite registered, non-members. **Frequency:** Biennial. **Audience:** Bedding manufacturers, suppliers, and trade professionals. **Principal Exhibits:** Manufacturing supplies related to mattresses, including machinery, textiles foam, inner springs, fiber, hard goods, and soft goods. **Telecommunication Services:** kbellias@sleepproducts.org.

10438 ■ International Fancy Food and Confection Show/Winter
National Association for the Specialty Food Trade Inc.
8 W 40th St., 4th Fl.
New York, NY 10018-3901
Ph: (212)921-1690
Fax: (212)921-1898
URL(s): www.specialtyfood.com. **Frequency:** Annual. **Audience:** Retailers, brokers, importers, buyers, chefs, caterers and related personnel. **Principal Exhibits:** Pates, cheeses, specialty meats and seafood, condiments, sauces, mustards, vinegars, chocolates, fine candies, biscuits, cookies, cakes, jams, jellies, preserves, coffees, teas, fruits, nuts, special beverages, beer, wine, ice creams, desserts, and cooking accessories. **Dates and Locations:** , Moscone Convention Center.

10439 ■ Supermarket Promotion Show
Association of Retail Marketing Services
10 Drs. James Parker Blvd., Ste. 103
Red Bank, NJ 07701-1500
Ph: (732)842-5070
Fax: (732)219-1938
Co. E-mail: info@goarms.com
URL: http://www.goarms.com
Contact: Michael Levine, President
Price: $Free. **Frequency:** Annual. **Audience:** Buyers of retail, consumer incentives. **Principal Exhibits:** Dinnerware, glassware, housewares, books, videos, games, sweepstakes, dolls, and plush toys suppliers. **Dates and Locations:** , Ramada Congress Hotel. **Telecommunication Services:** info@goarms.com.

CONSULTANTS

10440 ■ KV Marketing Inc.
12 Huntsville Rd.
Katonah, NY 10536-2002
Ph: (914)232-7566
Fax: (914)232-7848
Co. E-mail: pci19@optonline.net
URL: http://www.p-c-i.org
Contact: Katherine L. Vockins, Executive Director
Scope: Provider of international marketing expertise including market research and analysis, new product development, marketing plans, and general management assistance to both nonprofits and the commercial sectors. **Founded:** 1979. **Publications:** "Analysis of US market-opportunities for pygeum," Oct, 2000.

FRANCHISES AND BUSINESS OPPORTUNITIES

10441 ■ Miracle Method Bath And Kitchen Restoration
5020 Mark Dabling Blvd.
Colorado Springs, CO 80918

Free: 800-444-8827
Fax: (719)594-9282
Co. E-mail: sales@miraclemethod.com
URL: http://www.miraclemethod.com
Description: Bath and kitchen refinishing business. **No. of Franchise Units:** 125. **Founded:** 1977.. **Franchised:** 1979. **Equity Capital Needed:** $85,000-$123,000. **Franchise Fee:** $35,000. **Financial Assistance:** Yes. **Training:** Includes 10 days training.

10442 ■ The Panhandler
Liv Canada Gift Group Inc.
294 Walker Dr., Unit 2
Brampton, ON, Canada L6T 4Z2
Ph: (905)790-9023
Free: 866-463-4124
Fax: (905)790-7059
Co. E-mail: franchises@franchisebancorp.com
URL: http://www.livcan.com
Description: Boutiques specializing in gift, home decor, and kitchen items. **No. of Franchise Units:** 25. **Founded:** 1970.. **Franchised:** 1970. **Equity Capital Needed:** $140,000-$180,000. **Franchise Fee:** $25,000. **Training:** Yes. s.

10443 ■ Pot Pourri Accent
216 Migneron
St. Laurent, QC, Canada H4T 1Y7

Ph: (514)341-4000
Fax: (514)341-4241
Co. E-mail: info@potpourri.ca
URL: http://www.potpourri.ca
Description: The franchise specializes in retailing of kitchen items and decorations. **No. of Franchise Units:** 30. **No. of Company-Owned Units:** 4. **Founded:** 1990.. **Franchised:** 1990. **Equity Capital Needed:** $50,000-$100,000. **Franchise Fee:** $20,000-$30,000. **Training:** Yes.

10444 ■ Rafters Home Store
Franchise Bancorp Inc.
294 Walker Dr., Unit 2
Brampton, ON, Canada L6T 4Z2
Ph: (905)790-9023
Free: 866-463-4124
Fax: (905)790-7059
Co. E-mail: franchises@franchisebancorp.com
URL: http://www.livcan.com
Description: The franchise offers house ware and kitchen items. **No. of Franchise Units:** 6. **Founded:** 1975.. **Franchised:** 1975. **Equity Capital Needed:** $200,000-$350,000. **Franchise Fee:** $25,000. **Training:** Yes.

ASSOCIATIONS AND OTHER ORGANIZATIONS

10445 ■ American Home Furnishings Alliance (AHFA)
317 W High Ave., 10th Fl.
High Point, NC 27260
Ph: (336)884-5000
Fax: (336)884-5303
Co. E-mail: acounts@ahfa.us
URL: http://www.ahfa.us
Contact: Andy Counts, Chief Executive Officer
Description: Furniture manufacturers seeking to provide a unified voice for the furniture industry and to aid in the development of industry personnel. Provides: market research data; industrial relations services; costs and operating statistics; transportation information; general management and information services. Compiles statistics; develops quarterly Econometric Forecast. **Founded:** 1984. **Publications:** *Furniture Executive* (Monthly); *Human Resources Close-Up* (Monthly); *Suppliers on Demand*.

10446 ■ High Point Market Authority
164 S Main St., Ste. 700
High Point, NC 27260
Ph: (336)869-1000
Free: 800-874-6492
Co. E-mail: bcasey@highpointmarket.org
URL: http://www.highpointmarket.org
Contact: Tom Conley, President
Description: Furniture manufacturers and exhibition buildings working to create a cooperative business environment. **Educational Activities:** High Point Market Authority Meeting (Semiannual).

10447 ■ Home Furnishings Independents Association (HFIA)
PO Box 420807
Dallas, TX 75342
Ph: (214)741-7632
Free: 800-942-4663
Fax: (214)742-9103
Co. E-mail: info@hfia.com
URL: http://www.hfia.com
Contact: Mary Frye, President
E-mail: mary@hfia.com
Description: Retailers and suppliers of home furnishings organized to protect and advance industry and member interests and increase profitability. Conducts educational seminars; makes discount bank card and group health and life insurance programs available to members. **Scope:** home furnishing industry. **Founded:** 1923. **Subscriptions:** books periodicals.

10448 ■ International Furniture Rental Association (IFRA)
c/o Alston & Bird LLP
950 F St., NW, 10th Fl.
Washington, DC 20004
Ph: (202)239-3818

Fax: (202)654-4818
Co. E-mail: info@ifra.org
URL: http://www.ifra.org
Contact: Bill Anaya, Executive Director
Description: Companies whose major business is the leasing and rental of home furnishings and accessories; suppliers of products and services to these companies are associate members. Dedicated in upholding ethical standards of the furniture rental industry and providing quality products and service. Conducts industry exposition and statistical surveys. Promotes industry through nationwide consumer education program. Works to safeguard against adverse legislation and regulation. **Founded:** 1967. **Publications:** *Furniture Rental Association of America--Newsletter* (Bimonthly).

10449 ■ International Furniture Transportation and Logistics Council (IFTLC)
282 N Ridge Rd.
Brooklyn, MI 49230-9047
Ph: (517)467-9355
Co. E-mail: russ111@comcast.net
URL: http://www.iftlc.org
Description: Represents and promotes furniture transportation logistics professionals. **Scope:** transportation and law. **Founded:** 1926. **Subscriptions:** 500 articles books periodicals. **Educational Activities:** International Conference of Furniture Transportation and Logistics Managers (Annual).

10450 ■ International Home Furnishings Representatives Association (IHFRA)
PO Box 670
High Point, NC 27261
Ph: (336)889-3920
Fax: (336)802-1959
Co. E-mail: info@ihfra.org
URL: http://www.ihfra.org
Contact: Michael Root, President
Description: Local affiliated organizations of approximately 2,000 home furnishings representatives. Provides services to affiliates and individual members, including information exchange, listing manufacturers seeking representatives in all territories and representatives seeking manufacturers' lines in specific territories. Conducts certified home furnishings educational program. **Founded:** 1934.

10451 ■ Kitchen Cabinet Manufacturers Association (KCMA)
1899 Preston White Dr.
Reston, VA 20191-5435
Ph: (703)264-1690
Fax: (703)620-6530
Co. E-mail: info@kcma.org
URL: http://www.kcma.org
Contact: Greg Stoner, President
Description: Serves as a national trade association representing cabinet and countertop manufacturers and suppliers to the industry. Promotes the cabinet manufacturing industry, develops standards for the industry, administers a testing and certification program, conducts education programs and meetings, provides management information and industry data, and engages in activities on behalf of members

on legislative and regulatory issues. **Founded:** 1955. **Publications:** *Kitchen Cabinet Manufacturers Association Income & Expense Report*; *Cabinet News* (Bimonthly); *Directory of Certified Cabinet Manufacturers* (Annual). **Telecommunication Services:** dtitus@kcma.org.

10452 ■ National Home Furnishings Association (NHFA)
3910 Tinsley Dr., Ste. 101
High Point, NC 27265-3610
Ph: (336)886-6100
Free: 800-888-9590
Fax: (336)801-6102
Co. E-mail: info@nhfa.org
URL: http://www.nhfa.org
Contact: Sharron Bradley, Executive Director
Description: Provides business services to help retailers of home furnishings grow their businesses. Provides educational programs for retail sales managers and trainers, for middle management, for owners and executives, and for family businesses. **Founded:** 1920. **Publications:** *Home Furnishings Retailer* (8/year). **Educational Activities:** All Industry Convention (Annual). **Awards:** Retailer of the Year (Annual); Willis Award of Merit.

10453 ■ National Kitchen and Bath Association (NKBA)
687 Willow Grove St.
Hackettstown, NJ 07840
Ph: (908)852-0033
Free: 800-843-6522
Fax: (908)852-1695
Co. E-mail: feedback@nkba.org
URL: http://www.nkba.org
Contact: Bill Darcy, Chief Executive Officer
Description: Manufacturers and firms engaged in retail kitchen sales; manufacturers' representatives and wholesale distributors; utilities, publications and other firms supplying products or services to the kitchen and bathroom industry. Protects and promotes the interest and welfare of members by fostering a better business climate in the industry. Awards titles of Certified Kitchen Designer and Certified Bathroom Designer to individuals with proven knowledge, ability and experience in the design, planning, and installation supervision of residential kitchens. Conducts kitchen and bathroom training schools throughout the country. Sponsors business management and consumer awareness programs. Maintains speakers' bureau and Hall of Fame. **Founded:** 1963. **Publications:** *National Kitchen & Bath Association--Directory of Accredited Members* (Annual). **Educational Activities:** National Design Competition (Annual). **Telecommunication Services:** feeback@nkba.org.

10454 ■ Summer and Casual Furniture Manufacturers Association (SCFMA)
317 W High Ave.
High Point, NC 27260
Ph: (336)884-5000
Fax: (336)884-5303
Co. E-mail: jlogan@ahfa.us
URL: http://www.ahfa.us/divisions/scfma.asp
Contact: Joseph P. Logan, Executive Director
Description: A division of American Home Furnishings Alliance. Manufacturers of household summer

and casual furniture. Compiles trade statistics; provides legislative, technical, management, and marketing services. Conducts technical and marketing research. **Founded:** 1959. **Awards:** Apollo Award (Annual); Design Excellence Award (Annual); Lifetime Achievement Award (Annual).

10455 ▪ Upholstered Furniture Action Council (UFAC)
PO Box 2436
High Point, NC 27261
Ph: (336)885-5065
Fax: (336)885-5072
Co. E-mail: info@ufac.org
URL: http://www.ufac.org
Contact: Joseph Ziolkowski, Director
Description: Conducts research and disseminates information regarding the development and adoption of voluntary guidelines for production of more cigarette-resistant upholstered furniture; educates the public in the safe use of smoking materials. Maintains speakers' bureau; compiles statistics. **Founded:** 1978. **Publications:** *UFAC: Action Guide* (Annual); *Upholstered Furniture Action Council--Directory of Materials Suppliers* (Annual).

REFERENCE WORKS

10456 ▪ *"Bedding a Leader in Kohl's Q1 Gains"* in Home Textiles Today (Vol. 31, May 24, 2011, No. 13, pp. 1)
Pub: Reed Business Information
Contact: Jeff Greisch, President
Description: Kohl's credited home furnishings, particularly bedding, as the leading source of its first-quarter sales and profit gains in 2011. Statistical data included.

10457 ▪ *"Bon-Ton Halves Q1 Losses, Show Operating Profit"* in Home Textiles Today (Vol. 31, May 24, 2011, No. 13, pp. 7)
Pub: Reed Business Information
Contact: Jeff Greisch, President
Ed: James Mammarella. **Description:** Bon-Ton Stores reported progress in its multi-year push to profitability, with soft home sales leading the way. Statistical data included.

10458 ▪ *"CGG Home Fashions to Show Hand-Loomed Textiles"* in Home Textiles Today (Vol. 31, May 24, 2011, No. 13, pp. 4)
Pub: Reed Business Information
Contact: Jeff Greisch, President
Description: CGG Home Fashions introduced textiles made from natural fibers and vegetable dyes for upscale industry use at the HD Expo in Las Vegas, Nevada.

10459 ▪ *"Colores Origenes: Martha Kruse"* in Advertising Age (Vol. 77, November 13, 2006, No. 46, pp. S12)
Pub: Crain Communications, Inc.
Ed: Laurel Wentz. **Description:** Home Depot has created a range of Latin paint colors called Colores Origenes; the new line was originally intended to launch only at locations with heavily Hispanic patrons but the company decided to make the line available at all of their stores.

10460 ▪ *"A Counter Offer"* in Inc. (February 2008, pp.)
Pub: Gruner & Jahr USA Publishing
Ed: Elaine Appleton Grant. **Description:** Online retailer offering a line of kitchen and home products has upgraded its Website in order to make the business more attractive to possible buyers of the company. The firm is asking $9.9 million and reported gross revenue of $12.7 in 2007. The owner suggests that a buyer add product lines geared towards more rooms of the home than currently offer on the retail site.

10461 ▪ *Directory of Home Furnishings Retailers*
Pub: Chain Store Guide
Contact: Lisa Patterson, President
URL(s): www.chainstoreguide.com. **Released:** Annual; Published March, 2007. **Price:** $275, Individuals online lite; $875, Individuals online pro; $1175,

Individuals online pro plus. **Covers:** 2,900 U.S. and Canadian companies operating 8,300 executives and buyers. Also covers 1,000 wholesale companies. **Entries include:** Company name; physical address; mailing address; main phone number; main fax number; 1,430 executive e-mail and web addresses; total sales; industry sales; Internet order processing; Internet sales percentage; total units; units by trade name; total selling square footage; average number of checkouts; projected openings and remodeling; product lines; furniture styles; furniture price lines; trading areas; distribution center locations; services provided; products rented; private label credit card indicator; gallery names; primary wholesaler's name and location; parent company name and location; public company indicator; year founded; subsidiaries names and location; divisional office locations; key personnel with titles; store locations with addresses and manager's names. Wholesale listings also include import and export indicators. **Arrangement:** Geographical. **Indexes:** Alphabetical, product line, specialty, exclusions.

10462 ▪ *"Doing Good: Cause and Effect"* in Entrepreneur (Vol. 36, February 2008, No. 2, pp. 23)
Pub: Entrepreneur Media Inc.
Description: Lisa Knoppe established Art for a Cause LLC that employs people with mental and physical disabilities. The company makes hand-painted tools and furniture to be sold at gift retailers and hardware stores.

10463 ▪ *"Dreamy Fortune: Pillow Biz Dreams of Sales Reaching $10 Million a Year"* in Small Business Opportunities (Spring 2008)
Pub: Harris Publications Inc.
Ed: Stan Roberts. **Description:** Profile of Michale Lezberg, owner of a pillow factory. Lezberg shares insight into building his firm to a multi-million dollar a year business.

10464 ▪ *"Entrepreneur Says Spirituality Has Been a Key to Her Success"* in Business First Columbus (Vol. 25, October 17, 2008, No. 8, pp. 1)
Pub: American City Business Journals
Ed: Scott Rawdon. **Description:** Profile of Carolyn Williams Francis, CEO of Williams Interior Designs Inc. She outlines her mantra for success in her furniture design business, but emphasizes that faith has taken her business to greater heights.

10465 ▪ *"Forget Your Pants, Calvin Klein Wants Into Your Bedroom"* in Globe & Mail (March 31, 2007, pp. B4)
Pub: CTVglobemedia Publishing Inc.
Ed: Barrie McKenna. **Description:** The plans of Phillips-Van Heusen Corp. to open more Calvin Klein stores for selling the new ranges of clothing, personal care products, luggage and mattresses are discussed.

10466 ▪ *"Furniture Chain Moving to Harford"* in Baltimore Business Journal (Vol. 27, January 22, 2010, No. 38, pp. 1)
Pub: American City Business Journals
Ed: David J. Sernovitz. **Description:** Manchester, Connecticut-based Bob's Discount Furniture signed a lease for 672,000 square feet of space in Harford County, Maryland. The site will become the discount furniture retailer's distribution center in mid-Atlantic US. As many as 200 jobs could be generated when the center opens.

10467 ▪ *"The Furniture Company Wanted to Sell Him Its Buildings-And Close Down. Should He Buy the Company, Too?"* in Inc. (November 2007)
Pub: Gruner & Jahr USA Publishing
Ed: Alex Salkever. **Description:** Rick Detkowski, real estate investor, discusses his decision to purchase the furniture company housed in the buildings he was interested in buying. The property would have cost him between $500,000 to $1 million, he was able to purchase the property and business with its entire inventory of furniture, vehicles, and machinery for $1.8 million.

10468 ▪ *"Furniture Making May Come Back--Literally"* in Business North Carolina (Vol. 28, March 2008, No. 3, pp. 32)
Pub: Business North Carolina
Description: Due to the weak U.S. dollar and the fact that lumber processors never left the country, foreign furniture manufacturers are becoming interested in moving manufacturing plants to the U.S.

10469 ▪ *Gift, Housewares & Home Textiles Buyers*
Pub: Briefings Media Group
Contact: Alan M. Douglas, President
E-mail: adouglas@douglaspublications.com
URL(s): www.douglaspublications.comwww.thesalesmansguide.com. **Released:** Annual; latest edition 2011-2012. **Price:** $329, Individuals directory price; $659, Individuals directory/CD combo. **Covers:** 12,700 buyers in the gift, housewares, and textiles industry throughout the United States, Puerto Rico, the Virgin Islands, and Canada. **Entries include:** Company name, address, phone, fax; e-mail; URL; names and titles of key personnel; financial data; branch/subsidiary names and addresses; products and/or services provided; price points; sales volume; type of stores; number of stores; divisions of parent companies; corporate buying offices. **Arrangement:** Geographical. **Indexes:** Store name, new listings, mail order, online retailer.

10470 ▪ *"Home Helps Push Macy's to First-Quarter Profit"* in Home Textiles Today (Vol. 31, May 24, 2011, No. 13, pp. 2)
Pub: Reed Business Information
Contact: Jeff Greisch, President
Description: Macy's Inc. reported home goods as one of the three strong performing categories for first quarter 2011. Home goods sales, both big and small ticket items, have improved significantly for the retailer.

10471 ▪ *"Home Shows Signs of Life at Target"* in Home Textiles Today (Vol. 31, May 24, 2011, No. 13, pp. 1)
Pub: Reed Business Information
Contact: Jeff Greisch, President
Description: Retailer, Target, is experience a boost in sales for apparel and products for the home.

10472 ▪ *"Home Sits Out Q1 Surge at JCP"* in Home Textiles Today (Vol. 31, May 24, 2011, No. 13, pp. 1)
Pub: Reed Business Information
Contact: Jeff Greisch, President
Ed: James Mammarella. **Description:** JCPenney chairman and CEO, Mike Ullman, reported sales gains for first quarter 2011 in all products except home goods.

10473 ▪ *"Home Source Debuts Diesel Home Collection"* in Home Textiles Today (Vol. 31, May 24, 2011, No. 13, pp. 1)
Pub: Reed Business Information
Contact: Jeff Greisch, President
Ed: Carole Sloan. **Description:** Home Source is highlighting the debut collection of bed and bath products made by Diesel. These items interpret the jeans culture into home furnishings.

10474 ▪ *"Liora Manne to Debut Fabric Line"* in Home Textiles Today (Vol. 31, May 24, 2011, No. 13, pp. 4)
Pub: Reed Business Information
Contact: Jeff Greisch, President
Description: Textile and product designer Liora Manne will debut her new decorative fabric collection at the Showtime in High Point, North Carolina in June 2011. More than 22 fabric patterns and solid colors using Manne's patented Lamontage textile design process will be featured and can be used for indoor/outdoor decorative fabrics, furniture, decorative pillows, upholstery and more.

10475 ▪ *Market Resource Guide*
Pub: International Home Furnishings Center
Contact: Tom Mitchell, President
URL(s): www.ihfc.com/ContentItemDetail.aspx?ContentID=199. **Released:** Semiannual; Latest edition 2011. **Price:** $25, Individuals market resource guide

& add $40 for shipments. **Publication includes:** List of 80,000 manufacturers and distributors in the furniture industry who exhibit at the International Home Furnishings Market. **Entries include:** Company name, address, phone; showroom name and location, president, vice president, dir. of marketing. **Arrangement:** Alphabetical.

10476 ■ "Martha Stewart Launches Macys Line" in Marketing to Women (Vol. 21, March 2008, No. 3, pp. 5)
Pub: EPM Communications Inc.
Contact: Ira Mayer, President
E-mail: imayer@epmcom.com
Description: Martha Stewart launches an exclusive line of home decor called Wedgwood as part of her relationship with Macy's stores.

10477 ■ "New Kittinger Showroom Twice the Size of the Last One" in Business First Buffalo (December 7, 2007, pp. 4)
Pub: American City Business Journals, Inc.
Ed: Tracey Drury. **Description:** Kittinger Furniture Company, an upscale furniture maker, has opened a 6,000 square foot retail outlet at the Transit Road, New York. The company's moved to attract suburban and affluent customers for its high-end furniture products.

10478 ■ "P/Kaufmann Sells Bennettsville" in Home Textiles Today (Vol. 31, May 24, 2011, No. 13, pp. 6)
Pub: Reed Business Information
Contact: Jeff Greisch, President
Description: Decorative Screen Printers purchased the printing and finishing facility of P/Kaufmann in Bennettsville, South Carolina. However, the firm will continue its focus on its core business, a vat printing facility for home furnishings fabrics.

10479 ■ "Peking Launches Trina Turk Bedding Collection" in Home Textiles Today (Vol. 31, May 24, 2011, No. 13, pp. 4)
Pub: Reed Business Information
Contact: Jeff Greisch, President
Description: Peking Handicraft is launching designer Trina Turk's bedding collection of four beds that reflect her approach to contemporary fabric design using color and prints with strong graphic effects.

10480 ■ "Procter Gambles on Wallpaper; Putting Paint On a Roll" in Advertising Age (Vol. 77, September 18, 2006, No. 38, pp. 4)
Pub: Crain Communications, Inc.
Ed: Jack Neff. **Description:** Procter & Gamble Co. has launched a new line of textured paints that are already applied to a wallpaper-like roll that can be hung without paste or wallpaper tools.

10481 ■ "Ross Stores Reports Spectacular First Quarter" in Home Textiles Today (Vol. 31, May 24, 2011, No. 13, pp. 2)
Pub: Reed Business Information
Contact: Jeff Greisch, President
Ed: James Mammarella. **Description:** Retailer Ross Stores reported strong sales and profit gains for first quarter 2011, with their home department helping to lead the way.

10482 ■ "Sales at Furniture Showrooms Sink" in Puget Sound Business Journal (Vol. 29, October 10, 2008, No. 25, pp. 1)
Pub: American City Business Journals
Ed: Greg Lamm. **Description:** Furniture showrooms are seeing a drop in sales due to the bad economy. Buyer demand has also fallen because of the slumping real estate market.

10483 ■ "Shaw Joins Green Institute Launch" in Home Textiles Today (Vol. 31, May 24, 2011, No. 13, pp. 4)
Pub: Reed Business Information
Contact: Jeff Greisch, President
Description: Shaw Industries Group joined the Green Products Innovation Institute, the first nonprofit institute of its kind in America. The institute promotes the concepts of reverse engineering, elimination of waste, safe chemistries, and closed loop technical nutrients.

10484 ■ "Sheets Makers Optimistic Amid Price, Delivery Issues" in Home Textiles Today (Vol. 31, May 24, 2011, No. 13, pp. 8)
Pub: Reed Business Information
Contact: Jeff Greisch, President
Ed: Jill Rowen. **Description:** Retail sales of sheets and pillowcases dropped 4.7 percent in volume in 2009. Retailers pulled back inventory significantly in 2010. Statistical data included.

10485 ■ "Sunbrella Engages Consumers Via Social Media" in Home Textiles Today (Vol. 31, May 24, 2011, No. 13, pp. 4)
Pub: Reed Business Information
Contact: Jeff Greisch, President
Description: Performance fabric brand Sunbrella is marketing to social media, such as Facebook and Twitter, in order to boost consumer interest and retailer support.

10486 ■ Too Good to be Threw: The Complete Operations Manual for Resale and Consignment Shops
Pub: Katydid Press
Price: $69.95. **Description:** Revised edition covers all the information needfed to start and run a buy-outright or consignment shop, covering anything from clothing to furniture resale.

10487 ■ "Williams-Sonoma Beats Expectations in Q1" in Home Textiles Today (Vol. 31, May 24, 2011, No. 13, pp. 2)
Pub: Reed Business Information
Contact: Jeff Greisch, President
Description: Both retail nameplates, Williams-Sonoma and Pottery Barn reported gains in 2011's first quarter, accredited to the way shoppers responded to new opening price point programs for several of its brands.

10488 ■ "Women Take Care of a Home's Inside, Men Work on the Outside" in Marketing to Women (Vol. 23, November 2010, No. 11, pp. 2)
Pub: EPM Communications Inc.
Contact: Ira Mayer, President
E-mail: imayer@epmcom.com
Description: Women spend more time doing housework, caring for children, and talking on the telephone; while men's time is spent working, participating in sports, watching TV, and lawn maintenance.

STATISTICAL SOURCES

10489 ■ RMA Annual Statement Studies
Pub: Risk Management Association
Contact: Kevin M. Blakey, President
Released: Annual. **Price:** $175.00 2006-07 edition, $105.00. **Description:** Contains composite balance sheets and income statements for more than 360 industries, including the accounting, auditing, and bookkeeping industries. Also contains five years of comparative historical data for discerning trends. Includes 16 commonly used ratios, computed for most of the size groupings for nearly every industry.

10490 ■ Standard & Poor's Industry Surveys
Pub: Standard & Poor's Corp.
Released: Annual. **Price:** $3633.00. **Description:** Two-volume book that examines the prospects for specific industries, including trucking. Also provides analyses of trends and problems, statistical tables and charts, and comparative company analyses.

TRADE PERIODICALS

10491 ■ Casual Living: The Voice of the Leisure Marketplace
Pub: Sandow Media Corp.
URL(s): www.casualliving.com. **Released:** Monthly
Price: $25.99, Individuals; $59, Canada and Mexico; $149.99, Other countries.

10492 ■ The duPont Registry: A Buyer's Gallery of Fine Boats
Pub: duPont Publishing Inc.
Contact: Steve Chapman, Chief Executive Officer
URL(s): www.dupontregistry.com/boats/. **Released:** Monthly **Price:** $15.95, Individuals; $25.95, Canada; $45.95, Other countries.

10493 ■ The Furniture Executive
Pub: American Home Furnishings Alliance
Contact: Andy Counts, Chief Executive Officer
E-mail: acounts@ahfa.us
Ed: Pat Bowling, Editor, pbowling@afma4u.org. **Released:** Monthly. **Price:** Included in membership. **Description:** Reports on the activities of the American Furniture Manufacturers Association and on issues impacting the industry.

10494 ■ Furniture Today: The Weekly Business Newspaper of the Furniture Industry
Pub: Reed Business Information
Contact: Jeff Greisch, President
URL(s): www.furnituretoday.com/. **Released:** 50/yr. **Price:** $127.48, U.S. and Canada; $244.49, Other countries.

10495 ■ Furniture Transporter
Pub: Bohman Industrial Traffic Consultants Inc.
Ed: Ray Bohman, Jr., Editor. **Released:** Monthly.
Description: Reports important news and developments in shipping, packaging, and transporting that affect the furniture and allied products industries.

10496 ■ Furniture World Magazine: Furniture Buyer & Decorator
Pub: Towse Publishing Co.
URL(s): www.furninfo.com. **Released:** Semiannual **Price:** $19, Individuals; $29, Canada; $89, Other countries; $39, three years.

10497 ■ Home Furnishings Retailer
Pub: Home Furnishings Retailer
Contact: Carolyn McManus, Publisher
URL(s): nhfa-retailer.epubxpress.com/. **Ed:** Mary Wynn Ryan. **Released:** 11/yr. **Price:** $60, Individuals; $80, Canada; $120, Other countries.

10498 ■ Home Improvement Retailing
Pub: Powershift Communications Inc.
URL(s): www.hirmagazine.com/. **Released:** Bimonthly **Price:** $76, Individuals; $110, Canada plus applicable taxes.

10499 ■ Laminating Design and Technology: Materials Design and Technology for the Surfacing Industry
Pub: Cygnus Business Media
Contact: Rich Reiff, President
URL(s): www.cygnusb2b.com/PropertyPub. cfm?PropertyID=i. **Ed:** Tim Fixmer. **Released:** Bimonthly **Price:** $48; $68, Individuals; $99, Canada and Mexico; $99, Other countries.

TRADE SHOWS AND CONVENTIONS

10500 ■ Fort Lauderdale Furniture and Accessory Market
Karel Exposition Management Co.
3590 Mystic Pointe Dr.
Aventura, FL 33180
Ph: (305)792-9990
Fax: (305)792-9898
Co. E-mail: info@kemexpo.com
URL: http://www.kemexpo.com
URL(s): www.kemexpo.com. **Frequency:** Annual. **Audience:** Furniture trade. **Principal Exhibits:** Furniture. **Telecommunication Services:** info@kemexpo.com.

10501 ■ Fort Lauderdale Home Design & Remodeling Show
Home Show Management
1450 Madruga Ave., Ste. 301
Coral Gables, FL 33146
Ph: (305)667-9299
Free: 800-353-EXPO
Fax: (305)667-3266
Co. E-mail: info@homeshows.net
URL: http://www.homeshows.net
URL(s): www.homeshows.net. **Frequency:** Annual. **Audience:** Designers, decorators, builders, developers, contractors, and consumers. **Principal Exhibits:** Architecture, interior design, furnishings, home

improvement, and remodeling equipment, supplies, and services. **Dates and Locations:** , Broward County Convention Center.

10502 ■ International Contemporary Furniture Fair (ICFF)
Abitare
Via Ventura, 5
20134 Milan, Italy
Ph: 39 2 210581
Fax: 39 2 21058271
Co. E-mail: redazione@abitare.rcs.it
URL: http://www.abitare.it
URL(s): www.icff.com. **Price:** $25, Onsite. **Frequency:** Annual. **Audience:** Retailers, architects, interior designers, and manufacturers. **Principal Exhibits:** Contemporary furniture, lighting, wall coverings, floor coverings, textiles, and decorative accessories for the residential, home office, and contract markets. **Dates and Locations:** , Jacob K. Javits Convention Center.

10503 ■ The Miami Home Design & Remodeling Show
Home Show Management
1450 Madruga Ave., Ste. 301
Coral Gables, FL 33146
Ph: (305)667-9299
Free: 800-353-EXPO
Fax: (305)667-3266
Co. E-mail: info@homeshows.net
URL: http://www.homeshows.net
URL(s): www.homeshows.net. **Price:** $8, Onsite. **Frequency:** Annual. **Audience:** Designers, decorators, builders, developers, contractors, and consumers. **Principal Exhibits:** Architecture, interior design, furnishings, home improvements, and remodeling equipment, supplies, and services.

10504 ■ Toronto International Home Furnishings Market
Quebec Furniture Manufacturers Association, Inc.
101-1111 St.-Urbain St.
Montreal, QC, Canada H2Z 1Y6
Ph: (514)866-3631
Free: 800-361-6681
Fax: (514)871-9900
Co. E-mail: info@qfma.com
URL: http://www.qfma.com
URL(s): www.tchfm.com. **Frequency:** Annual. **Audience:** Trade only; retailers, designers, architects, and decorators. **Principal Exhibits:** Furniture, lamps, and accessories. **Dates and Locations:** , International Center of Commerce. **Telecommunication Services:** info@tchfm.com.

CONSULTANTS

10505 ■ KV Marketing Inc.
12 Huntsville Rd.
Katonah, NY 10536-2002
Ph: (914)232-7566
Fax: (914)232-7848
Co. E-mail: pci19@optonline.net
URL: http://www.p-c-i.org
Contact: Katherine L. Vockins, Executive Director
Scope: Provider of international marketing expertise including market research and analysis, new product development, marketing plans, and general management assistance to both nonprofits and the commercial sectors. **Founded:** 1979. **Publications:** "Analysis of US market-opportunities for pygeum," Oct, 2000.

10506 ■ Riedel Marketing Group (RMG)
5327 E Pinchot Ave.
Phoenix, AZ 85018-2963
Ph: (602)840-4948
Fax: (602)840-4928
Co. E-mail: ajr@4rmg.com
URL: http://www.4rmg.com
Contact: Timothy D. Riedel, President
Scope: The house wares and food service industry strategic marketing planning experts. Help manufacturers of house wares and food products solve marketing problems and identify and exploit marketing opportunities. Provides a full-range of strategic marketing planning services including development of marketing strategy, development of fact-based sales presentations, category management, definition of market opportunities and new product development exclusively to the house wares and food service industries. **Founded:** 1991. **Publications:** "Your Key Consumer: Her Take on the International Home & Housewares Show," Mar, 2008; "What's Hot, What's Not: The Consumer Speaks," Mar, 2006; "HIPsters SPEAK: What We Love to Buy and Why," Apr, 2005; "Influentials: Who They Are and Why You Should Care," Jun, 2004; "The Seven Secrets to Selling More Housewares," Jan, 2003. **Seminars:** Consumers Speak: What We Love to Buy and Why, What Do Those Consumers Think; The Seven Secrets to Selling More House wares. **Special Services:** Home Trend Influentials Panel.

FRANCHISES AND BUSINESS OPPORTUNITIES

10507 ■ Bath Fitter
Bath Fitter Franchising, Inc.
102 Evergreen Dr.
Springfield, TN 37172
Ph: (800)437-7471
Fax: (800)254-0024
URL: http://www.bathfitter.com
Description: Sales and installation of custom-molded acrylic bathtub liners, made-to-measure acrylic bath walls, shower bases, shower walls and related accessories. **No. of Franchise Units:** 146. **No. of Company-Owned Units:** 40. **Founded:** 1984.. **Franchised:** 1992. **Equity Capital Needed:** $300,000. **Franchise Fee:** $40,000. **Training:** Provides 3 weeks at headquarters and 2 weeks at franchisees location with ongoing support.

10508 ■ Children's Lighthouse Franchise Co.
101 S Jennings Ave., Ste. 209
Fort Worth, TX 76104
Ph: (888)338-4466
Fax: (817)338-2716
Co. E-mail: info@ChildrensLighthouse.com
URL: http://childrenslighthouse.com
Description: Childcare franchise. **No. of Franchise Units:** 24. **No. of Company-Owned Units:** 8. **Founded:** 1997.. **Franchised:** 1999. **Equity Capital Needed:** $501,500-$3,351,000 total investment. **Franchise Fee:** $60,000. **Royalty Fee:** 7%. **Financial Assistance:** Third party financing available. **Training:** Available at headquarters for 4 weeks, 4 weeks at franchisee's location, unlimited training for the first year and unlimited support.

10509 ■ More Space Place
More Space Place, Inc.
5040 140th Ave. N
Clearwater, FL 33760
Free: 888-731-3051
Fax: (727)524-6382
Description: Storage units and furniture designed to provide maximum space utilization. **No. of Franchise Units:** 42. **No. of Company-Owned Units:** 5. **Founded:** 1985.. **Franchised:** 1993. **Equity Capital Needed:** $40,000-$65,000 cash, $133,000-$203,000 total investment. **Franchise Fee:** $22,000-$29,500. **Training:** Yes.

10510 ■ Verlo Mattress Factory Stores
VyMaC Corporation Co.
201 N Main St., Ste. 5
Fort Atkinson, WI 53538
Ph: (920)568-3100
Free: 800-229-8957
Fax: (920)568-3140
Description: Factory direct mattress manufacturer. **No. of Franchise Units:** 40. **Founded:** 1958.. **Franchised:** 1980. **Equity Capital Needed:** $375,000 net worth; minimum $75,000 liquid. **Franchise Fee:** $50,000. **Training:** Yes.

START-UP INFORMATION

10511 ■ *"Caring Concern" in Small Business Opportunities (September 2010)*
Pub: Harris Publications Inc.
Description: Profile of Joshua Hoffman, founder and CEO of HomeWell Senior Care, Inc., provider of non-medical live-in and hourly personal care, companionship and homemaker services for seniors so they can remain in their own homes.

10512 ■ *"Home: Where the Money Is!" in Small Business Opportunities (May 2008)*
Pub: Harris Publications Inc.
Description: Profile of ComForcare, a franchise company that serves the senior population in America; a franchise can be started with one owner and add and build a team as it grows.

10513 ■ *"This Biz Is Booming" in Small Business Opportunities (Winter 2010)*
Pub: Harris Publications Inc.
Description: Non-medical home care is a $52 billion industry. Advice to start a non-medical home care business is provided, focusing on franchise FirstLight HomeCare, but showing that independent home care agencies are also successful.

ASSOCIATIONS AND OTHER ORGANIZATIONS

10514 ■ American Association for Homecare (AAHomecare)
2011 Crystal Dr., Ste. 725
Arlington, VA 22202
Ph: (703)836-6263
Fax: (703)836-6730
Co. E-mail: info@aahomecare.org
URL: http://www.aahomecare.org
Contact: Joel D. Marx, Chairman
Description: Represents all elements of home care; dedicated to advancing value and practice of quality healthcare services at home. **Founded:** 2000. **Publications:** *AAHomecare Update* (Weekly); *HME Answer Book* (Quarterly). **Awards:** Industry Achievement Awards (Annual).

10515 ■ American Hospital Association (AHA)
155 N Wacker Dr.
Chicago, IL 60606
Ph: (312)422-3000
Free: 800-242-2626
Fax: (312)422-4796
Co. E-mail: rich@aha.org
URL: http://www.aha.org
Contact: Richard Umbdenstock, President
E-mail: rwade@aha.org
URL(s): www.aha.org/research/rc/index.shtml, americanhospitalassociation.com, www.aha.org/aha/. **Description:** Represents health care provider organizations. Seeks to advance the health of individuals and communities. Leads, represents, and serves health care provider organizations that are accountable to the community and committed to health improvement. **Scope:** Administration, planning, and financing of healthcare facilities; administrative aspects of medical, nursing, paramedical, and prepayment fields. **Services:** Interlibrary loan (fee); copying; center open to the public for reference use only (access fee for non-members). **Founded:** 1898. **Holdings:** Advocacy reports, news articles, regulatory information, products and services.; 66,000 volumes. **Subscriptions:** ; 100 journals and other serials. **Publications:** *Coding Clinic for ICD-9-CM*; *Healthcare QuickDisc*; *Guide to the Health Care Field* (Annual); *Hospital Statistics* (Annual); *Hospitals and Health Networks* (Monthly); *American Hospital Association--Ambulatory Outreach*; *AHA News Now* (Daily); *AHA Guide to the Health Care Field* (Annual); *AHA Integrated Delivery Network Directory: U.S. Health Care Systems, Networks, and Alliances*; *AHA Directory of Health Care Professionals*; *Directory of Planning and Design Professionals for Health Facilities* (Annual); *American Hospital Association--Guide to the Health Care Field* (Annual). **Awards:** Hospital Awards for Volunteer Excellence; Award of Honor; Distinguished Service Award; Honorary Life Membership; Justin Ford Kimball Innovators Award; Board of Trustees Award; Federal Health Care Executive Special Achievement Award. **Telecommunication Services:** rwade@aha.org; storeservice@aha.org; hbaumann@aha.org; rc@aha.org.

10516 ■ Canadian Association of Nurses in Oncology (CANO)—Association canadienne des infirmieres en oncologie
375 W 5th Ave., Ste. 201
Vancouver, BC, Canada V5Y 1J6
Ph: (604)874-4322
Fax: (604)874-4378
Co. E-mail: cano@malachite-mgmt.com
URL: http://www.cano-acio.ca
Contact: Brenda Sabo, President
Description: Registered nurses in independent practice. Promotes improved public access to health care; seeks to increase the role of nurses in the delivery of health care services. Develops business and practice guidelines for members. Provides support and assistance to members; conducts educational programs to raise public awareness of nursing and other health care services; sponsors business and continuing professional development courses for members. Conducts lobbying activities; undertakes research projects; compiles statistics. **Scope:** nursing, business. **Founded:** 1984. **Subscriptions:** books business records. **Publications:** *Canadian Oncology Nursing Journal*.

10517 ■ Canadian Home Care Association (CHCA)—Association Canadienne de Soins et Services a Domicile
10 Kingsbridge Garden Cir., Ste. 704
Mississauga, ON, Canada L5R 3K6
Ph: (905)361-3277
Fax: (905)361-3274
Co. E-mail: chca@cdnhomecare.ca
URL: http://www.cdnhomecare.ca
Contact: John Schram, President
Description: Providers of home health care services. Promotes excellence in the practice of home care.

Represents members' interests before medical organizations, government agencies, and the public. Conducts continuing professional development courses for home care personnel. Sponsors promotional programs. **Founded:** 1990. **Publications:** *Cnez Nous, At Home* (Quarterly).

10518 ■ Canadian Nurses Foundation (CNF)—Fondation des Infirmieres et Infirmiers du Canada
50 Driveway
Ottawa, ON, Canada K2P 1E2
Ph: (613)237-2133
Free: 800-361-8404
Fax: (613)237-3520
Co. E-mail: info@cnf-fiic.ca
URL: http://www.cnf-fiic.ca
Contact: Helene Sabourin, Executive Director
Description: Promotes health and patient care in Canada. Fosters excellence in nursing through nursing research grants, scholarships, and specialty certification. **Founded:** 1962.

10519 ■ *Canadian Oncology Nursing Journal*
375 W 5th Ave., Ste. 201
Vancouver, BC, Canada V5Y 1J6
Ph: (604)874-4322
Fax: (604)874-4378
Co. E-mail: cano@malachite-mgmt.com
URL: http://www.cano-acio.ca
Contact: Brenda Sabo, President

10520 ■ Canadian Society of Gastroenterology Nurses and Associates (CSGNA)—Societe Canadienne des Infirmieres et Infirmiers en Gastoenterologie et Travailleurs Associes
c/o Palma Colacino
No. 224 - 1540 Cornwall Rd.
Oakville, ON, Canada L6J 7W5
Ph: (905)829-8794
Free: 866-544-8794
Fax: (905)829-0242
Co. E-mail: csgnaexecutiveassistant@csgna.com
URL: http://www.csgna.com
Contact: Joanne Glen, President
Description: Gastroenterology nurses, medical technicians, and sales representatives of medical equipment and pharmaceutical manufacturers. Promotes excellence in the teaching and practice of gastroenterological nursing. Facilitates communication among members; produces patient education materials. Conducts continuing professional education programs; maintains speakers' bureau. **Scope:** gastroenterology, endoscopy, specialized testing. **Founded:** 1984. **Subscriptions:** audio recordings books video recordings. **Awards:** CSGNA (Annual).

10521 ■ *Cnez Nous, At Home*
10 Kingsbridge Garden Cir., Ste. 704
Mississauga, ON, Canada L5R 3K6
Ph: (905)361-3277

Fax: (905)361-3274
Co. E-mail: chca@cdnhomecare.ca
URL: http://www.cdnhomecare.ca
Contact: John Schram, President
Released: Quarterly

10522 ■ *Foundation Focus*
Released: Semiannual **Price:** included in membership dues.

10523 ■ National Association for Home Care and Hospice (NAHC)
228 7th St. SE
Washington, DC 20003
Ph: (202)547-7424
Fax: (202)547-3540
Co. E-mail: exec@nahc.org
URL: http://www.nahc.org
Contact: Andrea Devoti, Chairperson
Description: Represents providers of home health care, hospice, and homemaker-home health aide services; interested individuals and organizations. Develops and promotes high standards of patient care in home care services. Seeks to affect legislative and regulatory processes concerning home care services; gathers and disseminates home care industry data; develops public relations strategies; works to increase political visibility of home care services. Provides legal and accounting consulting services; conducts market research and compiles statistics. Sponsors educational programs for organizations and individuals concerned with home care services. **Founded:** 1982. **Publications:** *NAHC Caring* (Monthly); *Hospice Forum* (Biweekly); *NAHC Report* (Weekly); *NAHC Report*; *NAHC National Home Care and Hospice Directory* (Annual). **Educational Activities:** Homemaker-Home Health Aide Conference (Annual).

10524 ■ National Health Council (NHC)
1730 M St. NW, Ste. 500
Washington, DC 20036
Ph: (202)785-3910
Fax: (202)785-5923
Co. E-mail: info@nhcouncil.org
URL: http://www.nationalhealthcouncil.org
Contact: Myrl Weinberg, President
Description: National association of voluntary and professional societies in the health field; national organizations and business groups with strong health interests. Seeks to improve the health of patients, particularly those with chronic diseases, through conferences, publications, policy briefings and special projects. Distributes printed material on health careers and related subjects. Promotes standardization of financial reporting for voluntary health groups. **Founded:** 1920. **Publications:** *Council Currents* (Bimonthly); *Directory of Health Groups in Washington*; *National Health Council--Listing of Member Organizations*; *Health Groups in Washington: A Directory* (Biennial); *Guide to America's Voluntary Health Agencies*; *300 Ways to Put Your Talent to Work in the Health Field* (Irregular); *Congress and Health: An Introduction to the Legislative Process and Its Key Participants* (Biennial); *Standards of Accounting and Reporting for Voluntary Health and Welfare Organizations*; *300 Ways to Put Your Talent to Work in the Health Field*.

10525 ■ National League for Nursing (NLN)
61 Broadway, 33rd Fl.
New York, NY 10006
Ph: (212)363-5555
Free: 800-669-1656
Fax: (212)812-0391
Co. E-mail: generalinfo@nln.org
URL: http://www.nln.org
Contact: Judith A. Halstead, President
Description: Champions the pursuit of quality nursing education. A professional association of nursing faculty, education agencies, health care agencies, allied/public agencies, and public members whose mission is to advance quality nursing education that prepares the nursing workforce to meet the needs of diverse populations in an ever-changing health care environment. Serves as the primary source of information about every type of nursing education program, from the LVN and LPN to the EdD and PhD. There are 20 affiliated constituent leagues that

provide a local forum for members. The National League for Nursing Accrediting Commission is an independent corporate affiliate of the NLN, responsible for providing accreditation services to all levels of nursing education. **Founded:** 1893. **Publications:** *Nursing Education Perspectives* (Bimonthly); *Nursing Education Perspectives* (Bimonthly); *Professional Development Bulletin* (Biweekly); *Directory of Accredited Nursing Programs*; *State-Approved Schools of Nursing: R.N.* (Annual); *State-Approved Schools of Nursing: L.P.N./L.V.N.* (Annual); *Scholarships and Loans for Nursing Education* (Annual); *Education for Nursing: The Diploma Way*; *Baccalaureate Education in Nursing: Key to a Professional Career in Nursing*; *Nursing Data Review* (Annual); *State Approved Schools of Nursing - RN* (Annual); *Undergraduate & Graduate Nursing Programs, 2nd Ed.*. **Awards:** Award for Outstanding Leadership in Workforce Development (Annual); NLN Award for Excellence in Teaching (Annual); NLN Award for Public Service (Annual); NLN Award for Excellence in Nursing Education Research (Annual); NLN Award for Outstanding Leadership in Nursing Education (Annual).

REFERENCE WORKS

10526 ■ *"Advancing the Ball" in Inside Healthcare (Vol. 6, December 2010, No. 7, pp. 31)*
Pub: RedCoat Publishing Inc.
Ed: Michelle McNickle. **Description:** Profile of Medicalodges an elder-care specialty company that provides both patient care and technology development. President and CEO of the firm believes that hiring good employees is key to growth for any small business.

10527 ■ *"Breaking the Mold" in Entrepreneur (Vol. 37, September 2009, No. 9, pp. 87)*
Pub: Entrepreneur Media, Inc.
Ed: Tracy Stapp. **Description:** Profiles of top franchise businesses in the United States are presented. Hey Buddy! Pet Supply Vending Co. offers pet supply vending machines. Home Health Mates, on the other hand, provides professional medical care at home.

10528 ■ *Case Management Resource Guide*
Pub: Phillips Business Information Inc. Access Intelligence L.L.C.
Contact: Heather Farley, President
E-mail: hfarley@accessintel.com
URL(s): www.cmrg.com. **Released:** Annual; latest edition 2005-2006. **Price:** $60, Individuals for additional copy, per volume. **Entries include:** Facility name, address, phone names and titles of key personnel; number of employees, geographical area served, type of service or programs provided branch office or parent organization name and phone, and credentials. **Database covers:** In four regional volumes, lists 110,000 health care facilities and support services, including homecare, rehabilitation, psychiatric, and addiction treatment program; hospices, adult day care, and burn and cancer centers. **Arrangement:** Classified by service provided and location. **Indexes:** Company name, advertiser.

10529 ■ *"Chemed's Vitas Aims to Acquire" in Business Courier (Vol. 27, July 9, 2010, No. 10, pp. 1)*
Pub: Business Courier
Ed: James Ritchie. **Description:** Chemed Corporation's Vitas Healthcare Corporation is looking for smaller nonprofit hospices as it looks to become more streamlined in a tougher reimbursement environment. CFO David Williams syas they want to acquire these hospices as fast as they can integrate them.

10530 ■ *"Connecting the Dots Between Wellness and Elder Care" in Benefits and Compensation Digest (Vol. 47, August 2010, No. 8, pp. 18)*
Pub: International Foundation of Employee Benefit Plans
Contact: Richard Lyall, President
Ed: Sandra Timmermann. **Description:** Employees caring for aged and infirm parents deal with time and financial issues and other stresses. The connection

between health status of caregivers and employers' health care costs could be aided by linking programs and benefits with wellness and caregiving.

10531 ■ *"Elder Care Costs Surge" in National Underwriter Life & Health (Vol. 114, November 8, 2020, No. 21, pp. 25)*
Pub: Summit Business Media
Ed: Trevor Thomas. **Description:** Nursing home and assisted living rates rose from 2009 to 2010, according to MetLife Mature Market Institute. Statistical data included.

10532 ■ *"Elder Care, Rx Drugs Reforms Top Zoeller's Agenda" in Times (December 21, 2010)*
Pub: The Times
Ed: Sarah Tompkins. **Description:** Indiana Attorney General Greg Zoeller is hoping to develop a program in the state that will help regulate care for the elderly; freeze medical licenses for doctors involved in criminal investigations; address illegal drug use; and to establish a program to help individuals dispose of old prescription medications easily at pharmacies.

10533 ■ *"Elder-Care Seminar to Teach Ways to Avoid Falls" in Virginian-Pilot (November 25, 2010)*
Pub: Virginian-Pilot
Ed: Amy Jeter. **Description:** ResCare HomeCare, a home health services firm, offers free seminars on helping to make residences safer for seniors prone to falling.

10534 ■ *"EVMS Gets Grant to Train Providers for Elder Care" in Virginian-Pilot (October 29, 2010)*
Pub: Virginian-Pilot
Ed: Elizabeth Simpson. **Description:** Eastern Virginia Medical School received a federal grant to train health providers in elder care. Details of the program are provided.

10535 ■ *"Face Issues if Elder Care, Unemployment Collide" in Atlanta Journal-Constitution (December 26, 2010, pp. G1)*
Pub: Atlanta Journal-Constitution
Ed: Amy Lindgren. **Description:** More issues arise during holiday for families with older members requiring care, including the issue of employment for those doing the caregiving.

10536 ■ *"GeckoSystems Reduces Sensor Fusion Costs Due to Elder Care Robot Trials" in Internet Wire (December 14, 2010)*
Pub: Comtex
Description: GeckoSystems International Corporation has been able to reduce the cost of its sensor fusion system while maintaining reliability and performance. The firm's ongoing first in-home elder care robot trials have sparked interest regarding its business model, technologies available for licensing, and joint domestic and international ventures.

10537 ■ *Healthcare Standards Directory*
Pub: ECRI Institute
Contact: Jeffrey C. Lerner, President
URL(s): https://www.ecri.org/Pages/default.aspx. **Released:** Annual; Latest edition 2009. **Price:** $650, Individuals plus shipping and handling charges. **Covers:** Over 40,000 standards, guidelines, laws, and regulations from over 1,200 organizations. **Entries include:** In 'Organizations and Their Standards' section--Organization name, address, phone, standards or guidelines, year of issue, price, catalog number, author, bibliographic information. **Database includes:** "Laws, Legislation, & Regulation--Federal" section, includes laws and regulations issued by the federal government; and "Laws, Legislation & Regulation--State" section, includes state government information. **Indexes:** Keyword.

10538 ■ *Medical and Health Information Directory: A Guide to Organizations, Agencies, Institutions, Programs, Publications, Services, and Other Resources*

Concerned with Clinical Medicine. . .
Pub: Cengage Learning Inc.
Contact: Ronald Dunn, President
URL(s): www.gale.cengage.com. **Released:** Annual; Latest edition April 2011. **Price:** $1190, Individuals set; $501, Individuals per volume. **Covers:** In volume 1, more than 33,000 medical and health oriented associations, organizations, institutions, and government agencies, including health maintenance organizations (HMOs), preferred provider organizations (PPOs), insurance companies, pharmaceutical companies, research centers, and medical and allied health schools. In Volume 2, over 20,000 medical book publishers; medical periodicals, directories, audiovisual producers and services, medical libraries and information centers, electronic resources, and health-related internet search engines. In Volume 3, more than 40,500 clinics, treatment centers, care programs, and counseling/diagnostic services for 34 subject areas. **Entries include:** Institution, service, or firm name, address, phone, fax, email and URL; many include names of key personnel and, when pertinent, descriptive annotation. Volume 3 was formerly listed separately as Health Services Directory. **Arrangement:** Classified by organization activity, service, etc. **Indexes:** Each volume has a complete alphabetical name and keyword index.

10539 ■ *"New Elder Care Center to Focus on Residents with Failing Memories" in Tulsa World (November 30, 2010)*
Pub: World Publishing
Ed: Robert Evatt. **Description:** People with Alzheimer's disease and other mental disorders require specialized care. Constant Care Management Company runs 'memory care' centers designed for the elderly with such conditions.

10540 ■ *"Q&A With Devin Ringling: Franchise's Services Go Beyond Elder Care" in Gazette (October 2, 2010)*
Pub: The Gazette
Ed: Bill Radford. **Description:** Profile of franchise, Interim HealthCare, in Colorado Springs, Colorado; the company offers home care services that include wound care and specialized feedings to shopping and light housekeeping. It also runs a medical staffing company that provides nurses, therapists and other health care workers to hospitals, prisons, schools and other facilities.

10541 ■ *"Taking the Right Road" in Entrepreneur (Vol. 37, October 2009, No. 10, pp. 104)*
Pub: Entrepreneur Media, Inc.
Ed: Jason Daley. **Description:** Joe Grubb's franchise of BrightStar Healthcare, a home health care provider, in Knoxville, Tennessee has grown into a $1 million business. Grubb, a former sales agent, experienced slow growth for his franchise and had to deal with cash flow issues during its first few months.

10542 ■ *"VPA to Pay $9.5 Million to Settle Whistle-Blower Lawsuits" in Crain's Detroit Business (Vol. 26, January 11, 2010, No. 2, pp. 13)*
Pub: Crain Communications Inc.
Ed: Jay Greene. **Description:** According to Terrence Berg, first assistant with the U.S. Attorney's Office in Detroit, Voluntary Physicians Association, a local home health care company, has agreed to pay $9.5 million to settle four whistle-blower lawsuits; the agreement settles allegations that VPA submitted claims to TriCare, the Michigan Medicaid program and Medicare for unnecessary home visits, tests and procedures.

STATISTICAL SOURCES

10543 ■ *RMA Annual Statement Studies*
Pub: Risk Management Association
Contact: Kevin M. Blakey, President
Released: Annual. **Price:** $175.00 2006-07 edition, $105.00. **Description:** Contains composite balance sheets and income statements for more than 360 industries, including the accounting, auditing, and bookkeeping industries. Also contains five years of comparative historical data for discerning trends. Includes 16 commonly used ratios, computed for most of the size groupings for nearly every industry.

TRADE PERIODICALS

10544 ■ *Abbeyfield Houses Society of Canada Newsletter*
Pub: Abbeyfield Houses Society of Canada
Ed: Robert McMullan, Editor. **Released:** Quarterly. **Description:** Reports on news of Abbeyfield Houses Society of Canada, a provider of care and companionship for the elderly. Also features articles related to aging, housing, and lifestyle in Canada and internationally. Recurring features include letters to the editor, and columns titled News of Local Societies and Bits 'n Bites.

10545 ■ *Adult Day Services Letter*
Pub: Health Resources Publishing
Contact: Beth-Ann Kerber, Managing Editor
Released: Monthly. **Price:** $97, individuals. **Description:** Provides crucial management information and serves as a link between adult day programs across the country.

10546 ■ *American Hospital Association--Ambulatory Outreach*
Pub: American Hospital Association
Contact: Richard Umbdenstock, President
E-mail: rwade@aha.org
Ed: Glen Brown, Editor, gbrownl@aha.org. **Released:** Quarterly. **Price:** $85, members; $99, nonmembers. **Description:** Analyzes the factors influencing market supply, demand, and competition. Recurring features include statistics, details on the latest accreditation standards, reviews of current literature, education and technical assistance updates, news of research, and resources.

10547 ■ *Care Management Journals: "Journal of Case Management" and "The Journal of Long Term Home Health Care"*
Pub: Springer Publishing Co.
Contact: Ursula Springer, President
URL(s): www.springerpub.com/product/15210987#. UB8RbPbiZIR. **Ed:** F. Russell Kellogg, Joan Quinn. **Released:** Quarterly **Price:** $110, Individuals print or online; $165, Individuals print & online; $289, Individuals print or online; $240, Institutions print & online.

10548 ■ *Caring*
Pub: National Association for Home Care
URL(s): digitalcaringmagazine.nahc.org/(S(-z2s0am55ixcqduyi2dajoo55))/default .aspx?bhcp=1. **Released:** Monthly

10549 ■ *Caring People*
Pub: National Association for Home Care
URL(s): www.nahc.org/CARINGMAGAZINE/. **Ed:** Val Halamandaris. **Released:** Monthly

10550 ■ *Home Health Care Management and Practice*
Pub: SAGE Publications USA
Contact: Blaise R. Simqu, President
URL(s): www.sagepub.com/journalsProdDesc. nav?prodId=Journal201504. **Ed:** Barbara Stover Gingerich. **Released:** Bimonthly **Price:** $555, Institutions print & e-access; $611, Institutions current volume print & all online content; $500, Institutions e-access; $556, Institutions all online content; $500, Institutions content through 1998; $544, Institutions print only; $170, Individuals print only; $100, Institutions single print; $37, Individuals single print.

10551 ■ *Home Health Care Services Quarterly*
Pub: Routledge Journals Taylor & Francis Group
URL(s): www.tandf.co.uk/journals/WHHC. **Ed:** Maria Aranda. **Released:** Quarterly **Price:** $125, Individuals online; $134, Individuals print & online.

10552 ■ *Home Health Line*
Pub: United Comunications Group
Contact: Jason Huffman, Publisher
E-mail: jhuffman@decisionhealth.com
Released: Weekly, 48/yr. **Price:** $497. **Description:** Reports on Medicare, Medicaid, and other federal and managed care coverage and payment for home health care, including home health agencies, hospice care, home medical equipment, home infusion therapy, and the home care industry as a business.

10553 ■ *Home Healthcare Nurse: The Journal for the Home Care and Hospice Professional*
Pub: Lippincott Williams & Wilkins
Contact: Rich Wohl, Executive Vice President
URL(s): journals.lww.com/homehealthcarenurseonline/pages/default.aspxwww.lww.com/product/?0884-741X. **Ed:** Carolyn J. Humphrey, Tina M. Marrelli. **Released:** 10/yr. **Price:** $65, Individuals; $354, Institutions; $162, Other countries; $510, Institutions, other countries; $42, Individuals in-training.

10554 ■ *Homecare Administrative HORIZONS*
Pub: Beacon Health Corp.
Contact: Diane J. Omdahl, Editor-in-Chief
Released: Monthly. **Price:** $347, individuals. **Description:** Provides homecare agency management information on all kinds of business and personnel topics. Incorporates comprehensive how-to information, current regulatory requirements, and documentation strategies. Runs a series of articles, including how to move into managed care, how to manage and measure outcomes, how to survive scrutiny by medicare's fraud squad, strengthening agency/physician relationships, and personnel issues. Recurring features include columns titled Peaks & Valleys, Fine-tuning the Fundamentals, Clearing the Fog, and Higher Ground.

10555 ■ *Homecare DIRECTION*
Pub: Beacon Health Corp.
Contact: Diane J. Omdahl, Editor-in-Chief
Released: Monthly. **Price:** $337. **Description:** Delivers timely regulatory information with how-to elements to apply to everyday care delivery. Equips agency patient care personnel with knowledge they need to deliver quality care and comply with medicare certification and reimbursement requirements. Offers valuable tips on interpreting medicare rules to justify care; how to create policies that reduce survey surprises, and documentation tips and examples. Recurring features include columns titled Documenting with Impact, Survey Sense, Looking for Direction, and From the Lamp Room.

10556 ■ *HomeCare Magazine: For Business Leaders in Home Medical Equipment*
Pub: Penton Media Inc.
Contact: John French, President
URL(s): homecaremag.com/www.penton.com/ Market/HealthCare.aspx. **Released:** Monthly **Price:** Free in US; $135, Canada; $150, Two years Canada; $250, Other countries; $250, Two years other countries.

10557 ■ *Hospital Home Health*
Pub: American Health Consultants
Contact: Donald R. Johnson, Publisher
Released: Monthly. **Price:** $499, individuals $349/year, U.S.; $399 elsewhere. **Description:** Provides clinical, legal, and management information pertinent to hospital-based home health agencies. Also monitors government regulation and profiles successful or unique programs.

10558 ■ *Modern Healthcare: The Weekly Healthcare Business News Magazine*
Pub: Crain Communications Inc.
URL(s): www.modernhealthcare.com. **Ed:** David Burda. **Released:** Weekly **Price:** $164, Individuals; $255, Canada; $218, Other countries.

10559 ■ *NAHC Report*
Pub: National Association for Home Care and Hospice
Contact: Andrea Devoti, Chairperson
Released: Weekly. **Price:** $325. **Description:** Reports on legislative, regulatory, judicial affairs, and research developments in the home care industry.

VIDEOCASSETTES/ AUDIOCASSETTES

10560 ■ *The Business of Caring*
Victoria International Corp.
1 Harts Cove, PO Box 14
New Castle, NH 03854

Ph: (603)436-1067
Fax: (603)433-4204
URL: http://www.victoriainternationalcorp.com
Released: 1987. **Description:** A series of programs for nursing professionals about patient care, consideration and relation to the family. Each program has nine episodes. **Availability:** VHS; 3/4 U.

10561 ■ *Home Health Nursing: Nursing Diagnosis in the Home Health Setting*
AJN Video Library/Lippincott Williams & Wilkins
American Journal of Nursing
345 Hudson St., 16th Fl.
New York, NY 10014
Ph: (212)886-1200
Free: 800-256-4045
Fax: (212)886-1276
Co. E-mail: info@nursingcenter.com
URL: http://www.nursingcenter.com
Released: 19??. **Price:** $195.00. **Description:** Features actual home health nurse visiting a patient to provide an overview of the entire nursing process, including information on patient assessment, patient history, goal setting, physical assessment, teaching the caregiver, and environmental assessment. Also furnishes a look at nursing diagnoses, including alteration in comfort, knowledge deficit and self-care deficit. **Availability:** VHS.

10562 ■ *Home Visits: The Nursing Bag*
AJN Video Library/Lippincott Williams & Wilkins
American Journal of Nursing
345 Hudson St., 16th Fl.
New York, NY 10014
Ph: (212)886-1200
Free: 800-256-4045
Fax: (212)886-1276
Co. E-mail: info@nursingcenter.com
URL: http://www.nursingcenter.com
Released: 19??. **Price:** $195.00. **Description:** Provides instructional material for nursing students and home health providers on proper use of the nursing bag, including information on safety precautions, universal precautions when dealing with blood and body fluids, and supplies and equipment commonly found in the nursing bag. Also contains general guidelines for the care of the nursing bag, protection against loss or theft, and the history of the bag. **Availability:** VHS.

10563 ■ *Lazaris: Forgiving Yourself*
Tapeworm Video Distributors
25876 The Old Road #141
Stevenson Ranch, CA 91381
Ph: (661)257-4904
Fax: (661)257-4820
Co. E-mail: sales@tapeworm.com
URL: http://www.tapeworm.com
Released: 1985. **Price:** $29.95. **Description:** Insights of Lazaris, a non-physical entity that channels his message of love and fulfillment through Jach Pursel. **Availability:** VHS.

TRADE SHOWS AND CONVENTIONS

10564 ■ NAHC's Annual Meeting and Home Care and Hospice Expo
National Association for Home Care
228 7th St. S.E.
Washington, DC 20003
Ph: (202)547-7424
Fax: (202)547-3540
URL: http://www.nahc.org
Contact: Val J. Halamandaris, President
URL(s): www.nahc.org. **Frequency:** Annual. **Audience:** Home health professionals, hospital administrators, healthcare suppliers, consultants, and certified public accountants. **Principal Exhibits:** General home health products, emergency response systems, computers, uniforms, publications, surgical and medical supplies, pharmaceuticals, durable and home medical equipment. **Telecommunication Services:** expo@nahc.org.

CONSULTANTS

10565 ■ Linda Berkowitz
1938 Soule Rd.
Clearwater, FL 33759
Ph: (727)726-7442
Fax: (727)785-7656
Co. E-mail: magicrb1216@yahoo.com
Contact: Linda Berkowitz, Manager
Scope: Consultant in health care and employee and systems management.

10566 ■ R.D. Network Inc.
PO Box 375
Lafayette Hill, PA 19444
Ph: (215)482-4461
Free: 877-482-4991
Fax: (215)836-0378
Co. E-mail: info@rdnetwork.com
URL: http://www.rdnetwork.com
Contact: Leslie Grant, Owner
Scope: Dietitians, diet technicians, and certified dietary managers available nationwide and worldwide through an international registry for consulting positions to wellness and employee education programs, drug or alcohol rehabilitation, hospital, LTC, nutrition and labeling communications, nutrition consultation, weight control classes, healthcare staff supplementation, media and program development, and all nutrition and food-related needs. Expert witness and speakers bureau also available. Industries served: healthcare, food industry, food service, restaurateurs, supermarkets, pharmaceutical companies, home health agencies, insurance companies, HMOs, and government agencies. **Founded:** 1983. **Seminars:** Labour/Staffing; Outsourcing; Healthy Dining Etiquette for Executives and Sales Staff Diet and Wellness; Cardiovascular Nutrition; Starting a Nutrition Consulting Practice; AIDS and Diet Therapy; Nutrition Care for Your Parents in Their Elder Years; Increase Your Energy-Increase Your Sales.

10567 ■ Carol K. Revilock
1004 Tuxedo Ave.
Parma, OH 44134-1726
Contact: Duane M. Revilock, Principal
Scope: Offers health care consulting services, specializes in the following areas: home health care, geriatrics, non-profit organizations and staff development. **Founded:** 1984.

10568 ■ United American Healthcare Corp.
303 E Wacker Dr., Ste. 1200
Chicago, IL 60601-5214
Ph: (313)393-4571
Fax: (313)393-3394
URL: http://www.uahc.com
Contact: John Fife, President
Scope: Provides services to the health care industry, including information systems, claims processing, and strategic planning. Also provides contract manufacturing services to the medical device industry. **Founded:** 1983.

FRANCHISES AND BUSINESS OPPORTUNITIES

10569 ■ Accessible Home Health Care
210 N University Dr., Ste. 806
Coral Springs, FL 33071
Ph: (954)341-5600
Fax: (954)757-3009
Description: Home health-care services. **No. of Franchise Units:** 102. **No. of Company-Owned Units:** 1. **Founded:** 2001.. **Franchised:** 2006. **Equity Capital Needed:** $55,000-$95,000. **Franchise Fee:** $39,500. **Royalty Fee:** 5%. **Financial Assistance:** Yes. **Training:** Provides 1 week training at headquarters, 2 days at franchisee's location and ongoing support.

10570 ■ AtWork HelpingHands Services
3215 John Sevier Hwy.
Knoxville, TN 37920
Ph: (865)609-6911
Free: 800-383-0804

Fax: (865)573-1171
Co. E-mail: info@atwork.com
URL: http://www.atworkfranchise.com
Description: Customized staffing services. **No. of Franchise Units:** 37. **No. of Company-Owned Units:** 12. **Founded:** 1990.. **Franchised:** 1992. **Equity Capital Needed:** $77,495-$121,495. **Franchise Fee:** $24,995. **Royalty Fee:** 6%. **Financial Assistance:** Limited in-house financing available. **Training:** Offers 5 days training at headquarters, 3-5 days at franchisee's location, meetings 2 days, and ongoing support.

10571 ■ A Better Solution, Inc.
PO Box 653
Venice, FL 34284
Ph: (941)416-2540
Co. E-mail: absifranchise@earthlink.net
URL: http://www.abettersolutionusa.com
Description: A non-medical solution for our everyday needs. You will offer a staff of caring, experienced, dependable caregivers able to assist clients of all ages with non-medical needs. homemaking, companionship, transportation, meal planning, etc. **No. of Franchise Units:** 3. **Founded:** 1998.. **Franchised:** 2003. **Equity Capital Needed:** $35,000-$65,000. **Franchise Fee:** $19,700. **Training:** 2 week training and on the job, in your live office location. Your comprehensive FL training class covers marketing and sales, recruitment, operations, scheduling, payroll, and client relations. Full ongoing support includes phone, onsite visits and website support.

10572 ■ BrightStar Healthcare
BrightStar Franchising, LLC
Description: Medical/non-medical home care and medical staffing. **No. of Franchise Units:** 234. **No. of Company-Owned Units:** 2. **Founded:** 2002.. **Franchised:** 2005. **Equity Capital Needed:** $95,998-$162,102. **Franchise Fee:** $47,500. **Royalty Fee:** 5-6%. **Financial Assistance:** Third party financing available. **Training:** Provides 10 days at headquarters, 10 days onsite with ongoing support.

10573 ■ Comfort Keepers
CK Franchising, Inc.
6640 Poe Ave., Ste. 200
Dayton, OH 45414
Ph: (937)665-1320
Free: 888-329-1368
Fax: (937)264-3103
Co. E-mail: LarryFrance@comfortkeepers.com
URL: http://www.comfortkeepersfranchise.com
Description: Non-medical in-homecare for elderly people, new mothers, and those needing assistance. **No. of Franchise Units:** 658. **Founded:** 1998.. **Franchised:** 1999. **Equity Capital Needed:** $61,450-$88,500. **Franchise Fee:** $42,000. **Training:** Franchisee's complete a comprehensive training curriculum with ongoing support.

10574 ■ Comfort Keepers, Canada
245 Fairview Mall Dr., Ste. 505
Toronto, ON, Canada M2J 4T1
Ph: (604)941-4361
Free: 866-363-0072
Fax: (416)498-7155
Co. E-mail: campaign8405755@mail.emaximation.com
URL: http://www.comfortkeepers.ca
Description: Provides non-medical in-home care for the elderly and others who need assistance with daily living activities. Comfort Keepers believes and practices the philosophy of "Thinking Outside The Box." Our marketing and advertising methods are extremely proprietary and unlike anything else on the market. We have become one of the fastest growing new franchises in North America, as recognized by INC., Successful Franchises, Entrepreneur, Fortune, HGTV, and over 100 major newspapers. This is a business of caring - you can find businesses that are personally rewarding and you can find businesses that are financially rewarding, but it is not every day you can be in a business that can be both!. **No. of Franchise Units:** 45. **No. of Company-Owned Units:** 1. **Founded:** 1998.. **Franchised:** 1999. **Equity Capital Needed:** $88,000-110,000. **Franchise Fee:** $39,500. **Training:** Offers extensive training.

10575 ■ GEM Health Care Services
383 Parkdale Ave., Ste. 304
Ottawa, ON, Canada K1Y 4R4
Ph: (416)997-4242
Free: 877-761-4361
Fax: (613)761-7738
URL: http://www.gemhealthcare.com
Description: Health care agency. **No. of Franchise Units:** 2. **No. of Company-Owned Units:** 1. **Founded:** 1994.. **Franchised:** 2006. **Equity Capital Needed:** $97,500-$137,000. **Franchise Fee:** $37,500. **Training:** Provides 3 weeks training.

10576 ■ Home Care Assistance
HCAFranchise Corp.
148 Hawthorne Ave.
Palo Alto, CA 94301
Ph: (800)536-2973
Fax: (650)462-6907
Co. E-mail: jj@homecareassistance.com
URL: http://www.hcafranchise.com
Description: Home Care Assistance offers 'Assisted Living at Home' to seniors. We focus on 24/7 live-in service and offer exclusive 'We Will Be There' guarantee. Business model makes use of strong consumer advertising. Looking for franchisees with good business background. Serious business people wanting substantial business opportunity. **No. of Franchise Units:** 42. **No. of Company-Owned Units:** 4. **Founded:** 2002. **Franchised:** 2004. **Equity Capital Needed:** $75,000-$150,000. **Franchise Fee:** $24,950. **Training:** 1 week at national training headquarters, and ongoing by phone and email.

10577 ■ Home Helpers
10700 Montgomery Rd., Ste. 300
Cincinnati, OH 45242
Free: 866-708-8921
Fax: (513)563-2691
Co. E-mail: inquiry@homehelpers.cc
URL: http://www.homehelpers.cc
Description: Non-medical, in-home companion care for the elderly, new mothers, and those recuperating from illness. **No. of Franchise Units:** 658. **Founded:** 1997.. **Franchised:** 1997. **Equity Capital Needed:** $47,200-$86,400 total investment. **Franchise Fee:** $36,900. **Financial Assistance:** Yes. **Training:** Yes.

10578 ■ Nurse Next Door Senior Care Services
5511 West Blvd., Ste. 320
Vancouver, BC, Canada V3M 3W6
Ph: (877)330-1819
Fax: (604)228-4359
URL: http://www.nursenextdoor.c0m
Description: Home health care for seniors. **No. of Franchise Units:** 54. **No. of Company-Owned Units:** 1. **Founded:** 2001.. **Franchised:** 2007. **Equity Capital Needed:** $114,000-$138,000. **Franchise Fee:** $40,000. **Training:** 1 week training and ongoing support.

10579 ■ Retire-At-Home Services
1704 Carling Ave., Ste. 100
Ottawa, ON, Canada K2A 1C7
Free: 877-444-9001
Fax: (877)444-9002
Co. E-mail: franchiseinfo@retireathome.com
URL: http://www.retireathomefranchise.com
Description: In home healthcare for seniors. **No. of Franchise Units:** 25. **No. of Company-Owned Units:** 1. **Founded:** 1994.. **Franchised:** 2007. **Equity Capital Needed:** $59,500-$69,500. **Franchise Fee:** $35,000. **Training:** Provides 7 days training.

10580 ■ Right at Home
Right At Home, Inc.
6464 Center St., Ste. 150
Omaha, NE 68106
Ph: (402)697-7537
Fax: (402)697-0289
Co. E-mail: info@rightathome.org
URL: http://www.rightathome.net
Description: In home, senior care and supplemental staffing for the healthcare industry. **No. of Franchise Units:** 224. **Founded:** 1995.. **Franchised:** 2000. **Equity Capital Needed:** $100,000-$200,000 net worth. **Franchise Fee:** $41,500. **Training:** A comprehensive program of pre-training, 2 week initial training

program, and follow up onsite training visit. Full ongoing support includes telephone, onsite visits and web site support.

10581 ■ Stay At Home
The Arden Group
9821 Cogdill Rd., Ste. 1
Knoxville, TN 37932
Ph: (865)692-1101
Free: 877-261-0793
Co. E-mail: info@StayHomeWeb.com
URL: http://www.StayHomeWeb.com
Description: With over two decades of experience in non-medical in-home care, our founders led the way in establishing the industry, launching & successfully operating several home healthcare companies. The key to our success lies in genuine compassion for patients & commitment to uncompromising dependability, both for patients & franchise owners. Our training programs ensure owners are well prepared to capitalize on one of the country's fastest growing demographics. **No. of Franchise Units:** 10. **Franchised:** 2007. **Equity Capital Needed:** $49,900-$69,900. **Franchise Fee:** $35,900. **Training:** Our Quick Start, Immersion & Continuing Education programs are quick, easy & through. Each of our key business processessales, advertising, patient care, staffing, payroll, etc. is clearly documented using our easy to follow Stay At Home Process Maps.

10582 ■ Synergy Homecare
Synergy Homecare Franchising, LLC
1757 E Baseline Rd., Bldg. 6, Ste. 124
Gilbert, AZ 85234
Ph: (480)659-7771
Fax: (480)659-7713
Co. E-mail: info@synergyhealthcare.com
URL: http://www.synergyhealthcare.com
Description: Non-medical homecare services. **No. of Franchise Units:** 80. **Founded:** 2000.. **Franchised:** 2005. **Equity Capital Needed:** $49,240-$99,540. **Franchise Fee:** $35,000. **Training:** Yes.

10583 ■ Tender Loving Care
Staff Builders, Inc.
PO Box 90002
Baton Rouge, LA 70879
Ph: (516)327-3361
Free: 800-444-4633
Fax: (516)358-3678
Description: Home health care. **No. of Franchise Units:** 248. **No. of Company-Owned Units:** 32. **Founded:** 1961.. **Franchised:** 1987. **Equity Capital Needed:** $125,000-$135,000, includes franchise and working capital. **Franchise Fee:** $$29,500. **Training:** Yes.

10584 ■ Touching Hearts At Home
Touching Hearts, Inc.
2314 University Ave. W, Ste. 14
St. Paul, MN 55114
Ph: (651)236-8447
Free: 877-870-8750
Fax: (651)452-7829
Co. E-mail: contact@touchinghearts.com
URL: http://www.touchinghearts.com
Description: Help seniors and people with disabilities remain independent by providing non-medical in-home care. Each franchise offers companionship, light housekeeping, laundry, meal preparation, transportation, and much more through a staff of dependable kind caregivers. **No. of Franchise Units:** 27. **No. of Company-Owned Units:** 1. **Founded:** 1998.. **Franchised:** 2007. **Equity Capital Needed:** Initial start-up $47,000-$67,000+. **Franchise Fee:** $34,500. **Training:** Comprehensive 5 day training gives you the knowledge, skills and tools required to run a successful franchise. Outstanding ongoing support is provided through toll free number assistance, email, internal website discussion forum, HQ support staff, and regional and national seminars.

10585 ■ Visiting Angels
Living Assistance Services, Inc.
28 W Eagle Rd., Ste. 201
Havertown, PA 19083
Ph: (610)924-9663

Fax: (610)924-9690
Description: Non-medical senior homecare. **No. of Franchise Units:** 435. **Founded:** 1992.. **Franchised:** 1998. **Equity Capital Needed:** $58,285-$95,035. **Franchise Fee:** $31,950-$54,950. **Royalty Fee:** 2-3. 5%. **Financial Assistance:** Limited third party financing available. **Training:** Offers 5.5 days training at headquarters, 5 plus regional refresher meetings per month, monthly webinars, annual conference and ongoing support.

10586 ■ We Care Health Services Inc.
151 Bloor St. W, Ste. 602
Toronto, ON, Canada M5S 1S4
Ph: (416)922-7601
Free: 800-316-2212
Fax: (416)922-6280
Co. E-mail: larry_smith@wecare.ca
URL: http://www.wecare.ca
Description: Offers homecare services. **No. of Franchise Units:** 20. **No. of Company-Owned Units:** 28. **Founded:** 1984.. **Equity Capital Needed:** $125,000-$150,000 investment required; $75,000-$90,000 start-up capital required. **Franchise Fee:** $40,000. **Training:** Offers 2 weeks training.

COMPUTERIZED DATABASES

10587 ■ *Health and Medical Care Archive (HMCA)*
PO Box 1248
Ann Arbor, MI 48106-1248
Ph: (734)615-8400
Fax: (734)647-8200
Co. E-mail: netmail@icpsr.umich.edu
URL: http://www.icpsr.umich.edu
Contact: George Alter, Director
Availability: Online: Inter-University Consortium for Political and Social Research. CD-ROM: Inter-University Consortium for Political and Social Research. **Type:** Full-text.

10588 ■ *Home Healthcare Agency & Chains Directory*
25 Vintinner Rd.
Campton, NH 03223
Ph: (603)726-4800
Free: 800-729-2600
Fax: (603)726-4840
Co. E-mail: info@firstmark.com
URL: http://www.firstmark.com
Contact: Michael H. Pomerantz, President
Availability: CD-ROM: F1RSTMARK Inc. **Type:** Directory.

10589 ■ *KINETIDEX® System*
777 E Eisenhower Pky.
Ann Arbor, MI 48108
Co. E-mail: info@truvenhealth.com
URL: http://www.truvenhealth.com
Availability: Online: Truven Health Analytics Inc. **Type:** Full-text; Numeric.

LIBRARIES

10590 ■ Boone Hospital Center Medical Library
1600 E. Broadway
Columbia, MO 65201
Ph: (573)815-3504
Fax: (573)815-2629
URL: http://www.boone.org
Contact: Judy Feintuch, Librarian, Medical Science
Scope: Medicine, nursing. **Services:** Interlibrary loan; copying; document delivery; library not open to the public. **Holdings:** 2500 books. **Subscriptions:** 225 journals and other serials.

10591 ■ El Camino Hospital - Health Library and Resource Center
Main Bldg., 1st Fl.
2500 Grant Rd.
Mountain View, CA 94040
Ph: (650)940-7210

Fax: (650)940-7174
Co. E-mail: healthlib@elcaminohospital.org
URL: http://www.elcaminohospital.org/Patient_
  Services/Health_Library
Contact: Jack Black, Librarian, Medical Science
Scope: Medicine, nursing, healthcare administration,
caregiving, elder care. **Services:** Interlibrary loan;
copying; library open to the public. **Founded:** 1986.
Holdings: 5500 books and videotapes. **Subscrip-
tions:** 150 journals and other serials; 3 newspapers.

**10592 ■ Virginia Commonwealth University -
Virginia Center on Aging - Information**
Resources Center
730 E. Broad St.
Theatre Row Building
Richmond, VA 23219
Ph: (804)828-1525
Fax: (804)828-7905
Co. E-mail: eansello@vcu.edu
URL: http://www.sahp.vcu.edu/vcoa
Contact: Dr. Edward F. Ansello, Director
Scope: Gerontology, mental health, sociology and
the politics of aging, geriatrics, family relationships,
long-term care, lifelong learning. **Services:** Library
open to the public with restrictions (audio/visual
materials available to Virginia residents only).
Founded: 1978. **Holdings:** 1500 books; 4 archives;
120 AV items. **Subscriptions:** 6 journals and other
serials.

START-UP INFORMATION

10593 ■ *Starting and Running Your Own Horse Business*
Pub: Storey Publishing, LLC
Ed: Mary Ashby McDonald. **Released:** November 1, 2009. **Price:** $19.95. **Description:** Insight into starting and running a successful equestrian business is given. The book covers safety, tips for operating a riding school or horse camp, strategies for launching a carriage business, along with tax and insurance advice.

ASSOCIATIONS AND OTHER ORGANIZATIONS

10594 ■ American Association for Horsemanship Safety (AAHS)
4125 Fish Creek Rd.
Estes Park, CO 80517
Ph: (512)488-2220
Free: 866-485-6800
Fax: (512)488-2319
Co. E-mail: mail@horsemanshipsafety.com
URL: http://www.horsemanshipsafety.com
Contact: Jan Dawson, President
URL(s): horsemanshipsafety.com. **Description:** Promotes safe horsemanship skills through training and education. Offers systematic approach to teaching horsemanship safety. Provides information to the general public about safe horsemanship practices. **Founded:** 1995. **Publications:** *Caution: Horses* (Quarterly).

10595 ■ American Driving Society (ADS)
PO Box 278
Cross Plains, WI 53528
Ph: (608)237-7382
Fax: (608)237-6468
Co. E-mail: info@americandrivingsociety.org
URL: http://www.americandrivingsociety.org
Contact: John Freiburger, President
E-mail: frei@chorus.net
Description: Persons interested in the sport of driving horses and carriages. Promotes horse and pony driving both competitively and for pleasure; creates and maintains public interest in driving events; organizes or facilitates the organization of driving events; establishes a list of qualified judges. Sponsors educational programs, judge's clinics, and a junior judging program; recognizes driving competitions. Maintains speakers' bureau. **Founded:** 1974. **Publications:** *American Driving Society--Handbook* (Biennial); *The Wheelhorse*; *The Whip Magazine* (Quarterly).

10596 ■ American Horse Council (AHC)
1616 H St. NW, 7th Fl.
Washington, DC 20006
Ph: (202)296-4031
Fax: (202)296-1970
Co. E-mail: ahc@horsecouncil.org
URL: http://www.horsecouncil.org
Contact: James J. Hickey, Jr., President
E-mail: ahc@horsecouncil.org
Description: Equine breed registries, horse-related organizations, and commercial businesses; individuals with commercial interest in the equine industry; those who have a recreational and pleasure interest in the horse industry. Represents the horse industry before congress and federal agencies. Promotes equitable taxation and legislation; maintains liaison with government agencies and advises members of current national developments affecting the equine industry. Provides advisory, consulting, and referral services; offers tax and information service. Sponsors public affairs program on the contributions of the horse industry to the American economy and quality of life. Compiles statistics. **Founded:** 1969. **Publications:** *Horse Industry Directory* (Annual); *AHC Business Quarterly* (Quarterly).

10597 ■ American Horse Publications (AHP)
49 Spinnaker Cir.
South Daytona, FL 32119
Ph: (386)760-7743
Fax: (386)760-7728
Co. E-mail: ahorsepubs@aol.com
URL: http://www.americanhorsepubs.org
Contact: Cheryl Erpelding, President
Description: Members are horse-oriented publications, professionals and businesses. Aims to improve the horse publication field and network within the equine publishing industry. **Founded:** 1970. **Publications:** *Communique: Horse Industry Directory.* **Awards:** AHP Champion Award (Annual); Equine Industry Vision Award (Annual).

10598 ■ American Youth Horse Council (AYHC)
577 N Boyero Ave.
Pueblo West, CO 81007
Ph: (719)594-9778
Free: 800-TRY-AYHC
Fax: (775)256-0382
Co. E-mail: info@ayhc.com
URL: http://www.ayhc.com
Contact: Jill Montgomery, Executive Director
Description: Works as the umbrella organization providing resources and leadership to the youth horse industry. Promotes the youth horse industry and responsible equine management practices. Provides a forum for information exchange within the horse industry. Conducts educational forums for youth leaders. Establishes youth conference guidelines. **Founded:** 1968. **Publications:** *Safety Manual; Horse Industry Handbook: A Guide to Equine Care and Management; Youth Leaders Manual.* **Awards:** Distinguished Service Award (Annual); Leader of the Year (Annual); National Youth Horse Leader of the Year (Annual); Regional Youth Leader Symposium Grant (Annual).

10599 ■ Canadian Long Distance Riding Association (CaLDRA)
c/o Marion Shearer, Sec.-Treas.
48 Long Stan Rd.
Whitchurch-Stouffville, ON, Canada L4A 1P5
Ph: (905)640-7915
Co. E-mail: secretary@caldra.net
URL: http://www.caldra.net
Contact: Kelli Hayhurst, President
Description: Long distance horseback riding enthusiasts. Promotes increased participation in long distance horseback riding and other equestrian events. Serves as a clearinghouse on long distance horseback riding; sponsors educational and recreational programs. **Founded:** 1983.

10600 ■ Canadian Therapeutic Riding Association (CanTRA)—Association Canadienne d'Equitation Therapeutique
5420 Hwy. 6 N, Ste. 11, R.R. No. 5
Guelph, ON, Canada N1H 6J2
Ph: (519)767-0700
Fax: (519)767-0435
Co. E-mail: ctra@golden.net
URL: http://www.cantra.ca
Contact: Donna Naylor, Executive Director
Description: Therapists with an interest in the use of equestrian activities to promote health and fitness. Seeks to advance the practice of therapeutic riding; promotes ongoing professional development of members. Serves as a clearinghouse on therapeutic horseback riding; sponsors research and educational programs. **Founded:** 1980.

10601 ■ CHA - Certified Horsemanship Association
4037 Iron Works Pkwy., Ste. 180
Lexington, KY 40511
Ph: (859)259-3399
Free: 800-399-0138
Fax: (859)255-0726
Co. E-mail: office@cha-ahse.org
URL: http://www.cha-ahse.org
Contact: Brent Morgan, President
Description: Certifies riding instructors and trail guides, accredits equine facilities, maintains an active database of instructors and stables for the general public on the website. **Founded:** 1967. **Publications:** *CHA Composite Horsemanship Manual; Riding Instructors Manual; Ready to Ride; Standards for Group Riding Programs.* **Awards:** Partnership in Safety Award (Annual).

10602 ■ Equine Canada (EC)—Canada Hippique
2685, Queensview Dr., Ste. 100
Ottawa, ON, Canada K2B 8K2
Ph: (613)248-3433
Free: 866-282-8395
Fax: (613)248-3484
Co. E-mail: inquires@equinecanada.ca
URL: http://www.equinecanada.ca
Contact: Mike Gallagher, President
Description: Participants in equestrian events; admirers of horses. Promotes increased interest and participation in equestrian sports. Sponsors competitions; compiles statistics. **Founded:** 1977. **Telecommunication Services:** mike4755@nb.sympatico.ca.

10603 ■ Gladstone Equestrian Association (GEA)
PO Box 469
Gladstone, NJ 07934
Ph: (908)453-3332

Fax: (908)453-3332
Co. E-mail: gladstoneeq@gladstonedriving.org
URL: http://www.gladstonedriving.org
Description: Individuals with an interest in carriage driving and other equestrian events and activities. Seeks to increase interest and participation in carriage driving and related sports. Sponsors competitions. **Founded:** 1985. **Educational Activities:** Gladstone Driving Event (Annual).

10604 ■ InterCollegiate Horse Show Association (IHSA)
8125 Verbeck Dr.
Manlius, NY 13104
Co. E-mail: glihsa@aol.com
URL: http://www.ihsainc.com
Contact: Robert Cacchione, Executive Director
Description: Colleges and universities; individuals. Promotes the education of students in horsemanship and sportsmanship. Provides a basis of competition for intercollegiate riders from beginning through advanced levels. Sponsors clinics, seminars, and other horse-oriented activities. **Founded:** 1967. **Publications:** *Regional Directory* (Annual). **Educational Activities:** National Champion Horse Show (Annual). **Awards:** Grand Champion National Trophy (Annual); Intercollegiate Equestrian Foundation (Annual); Senior Athletic Academic Achievement (Annual); Senior Athletic Academic Special (Annual).

10605 ■ International Gay Rodeo Association (IGRA)
PO Box 460504
Aurora, CO 80046-0504
Co. E-mail: askigra@igra.com
URL: http://www.igra.com
Contact: Tommy Channel, Administrative Assistant
Description: Gay rodeo associations in the United States and Canada. Promotes public interest in rodeo events and seeks to increase participation in rodeo by gay people. Facilitates communication and cooperation among members; sponsors competitions. **Founded:** 1985. **Publications:** *Safety Video*; *2005 Rodeo Resource Guidebook*.

10606 ■ International Jumper Futurity (IJF)
PO Box 1445
Georgetown, KY 40324
Ph: (502)535-6787
Fax: (502)535-4412
Co. E-mail: yjcoffice@youngjumpers.com
URL: http://youngjumpers.com/yjcblog/
Description: Owners, breeders, and trainers of sport horses. Promotes interest and participation in show jumping and other equestrian events; seeks to improve sport horse bloodlines. Serves as a clearinghouse on North American sport horses; recognizes outstanding equestrian riders, trainers, and breeders. **Founded:** 1989.

10607 ■ National Association of Competitive Mounted Orienteering (NACMO)
c/o Alison Bennett, Pres.
4309 Laura St. NW
Comstock Park, MI 49321
Ph: (616)784-1645
Co. E-mail: alisonannebennett@gmail.com
URL: http://www.nacmo.org
Contact: Alison Bennett, President
Description: Horse enthusiasts with a special interest in wilderness-type riding. Promotes horseback riding and fellowship among members. Fosters regulation of the sport through a uniform rules system. Offers competitive and noncompetitive mounted orienteering activities. (Mounted orienteering combines horseback riding with map reading and direction-finding.) Provides assistance to members wishing to manage a ride, and informs members of ride dates and locations. Responds to discrepancies and complaints reported by members. Emphasizes competition through orientation skills as opposed to the speed of individual horses. Conducts charitable program. Compiles statistics. **Founded:** 1981. **Publications:** *Meadow Muffin Reports* (5/year); *NACMO How to Ride the Sport*. **Educational Activities:** National Association of Competitive Mounted Orienteering Banquet (Annual). **Awards:** Rider Awards; Horse Awards; Horse Award (Annual); National Award (Annual); National Team (Annual); Ride Manager (An-

nual); Rider Award; State Award (Annual); National High Point Awards; Ride Manager Awards; State Awards and National Awards; High Point of the Year (Annual); National Junior Rider Award; National Short Course Individual Award Male; National Short Course Team Award; National Single Rider Female Award (Annual); National Single Rider Male Award (Annual).

10608 ■ North American Horsemen's Association (NAHA)
PO Box 223
Paynesville, MN 56362
Ph: (320)243-7250
Free: 800-328-8894
Fax: (320)243-7224
Co. E-mail: ark@lakedalelink.net
URL: http://www.arkagency-naha.com
Contact: Linda L. Liestman, President
Description: Represents individual horse owners and clubs. Promotes interests of members. Encourages equine safety. Maintains a reference library of books, periodicals, and clippings on equine law and safety in business issues. Gathers statistics, conducts research, maintains hall of fame, and provides educational programs. **Founded:** 1986. **Publications:** *Risk Reduction Program Catalog* (Semiannual); *Yearbook of News* (Annual). **Awards:** Artist of Distinction (Annual); Horseman of Distinction (Annual); Horsewoman of Distinction (Annual); Safety Award Program (Annual).

10609 ■ United Professional Horsemen's Association (UPHA)
4059 Iron Works Pkwy., Ste. 2
Lexington, KY 40511
Ph: (859)231-5070
Fax: (859)255-2774
Co. E-mail: uphakgr@aol.com
URL: http://www.uphaonline.com
Contact: Bret Day, President
Description: Professional horse trainers involved in the show horse industry; horse owners and breeders. Seeks to educate the public about show horses and improve the industry. Sponsors classics for Three- and Four-Year Olds. Maintains hall of fame. **Founded:** 1968.

10610 ■ United States Dressage Federation (USDF)
4051 Iron Works Pkwy.
Lexington, KY 40511
Ph: (859)971-2277
Fax: (859)971-7722
Co. E-mail: usdressage@usdf.org
URL: http://www.usdf.org
Contact: George Williams, President
E-mail: president@usdf.org
Description: Members of local dressage organizations and other interested individuals. Promotes and encourages a high standard of accomplishment in dressage throughout the U.S., primarily through educational programs, and to improve understanding of dressage through educational clinics, forums, and seminars. (In dressage, a horse is trained to execute intricate and highly refined steps and maneuvers. Ideally, the signals from rider to horse are not visible to the spectator.) Certifies dressage instructors. **Founded:** 1973. **Publications:** *USDF Connection* (Monthly); *USDF Directory* (Annual); *USDF Dressage Directory--Instructors, Licensed Officials, and Dressage Tests* (Biennial); *United States Dressage Federation--Calendar of Competitions* (Annual). **Awards:** Horse of the Year Awards; Junior/Young Rider Awards; Musical Freestyle Rider Awards; Rider Award Program; Vintage Cup Awards; Adequan/USDF All-Breed Awards; Adequan/USDF All-Breeds Dressage Sport Horse Breeding Awards; USDF/Dover Saddlery Adult Amateur Medal. **Telecommunication Services:** president@usdf.org.

10611 ■ United States Equestrian Federation (USEF)
4047 Iron Works Pkwy.
Lexington, KY 40511-8483
Ph: (859)258-2472

Fax: (859)231-6662
Co. E-mail: lrawls@usef.org
URL: http://www.usef.org
Contact: John Long, Chief Executive Officer
Description: Individuals and horse shows. Promotes interest in equestrian sports; establishes and enforces rules governing equestrian competitions; maintains records and sanctions dates for competitions. Administers drugs and medication testing program and research. Provides general and specific assistance on equestrian sports in the U.S. as well as referrals. Conducts educational programs for licensed officials throughout the year. Licenses judges and stewards. National Federation of Equestrian Sports for the U.S. National Governing Body for Equestrian Sports (USOC). **Founded:** 1917. **Publications:** *Rule Book* (Biennial). **Awards:** Horse of the Year (Annual); Media Awards (Annual).

10612 ■ United States Eventing Association (USEA)
525 Old Waterford Rd. NW
Leesburg, VA 20176
Ph: (703)779-0440
Fax: (703)779-0550
Co. E-mail: nancy@useventing.com
URL: http://www.useventing.com
Contact: Nancy Knight, Director, Education
Description: Horsemen and others supporting the objectives of the USCTA. Formulates, distributes, and explains standards, rules, and regulations for the proper conduct of combined training instruction and equestrian combined training competitions. (A combined training competition is composed of two or all three of the following equestrian activities: dressage, cross-country, and show jumping; when all three activities are included the competition is called a horse trial or event.) Sponsors clinics. Assists to provide training opportunities for potential Olympic games competitors. Approves competitions; compiles records and statistics. **Founded:** 1959. **Publications:** *USCTA News* (Bimonthly). **Awards:** Courtney C. Reeves Memorial Trophy (Annual); High Score Award (Annual).

10613 ■ United States Pony Clubs (USPC)
4041 Iron Works Pkwy.
Lexington, KY 40511-8483
Ph: (859)254-7669
Fax: (859)233-4652
Co. E-mail: ceo@ponyclub.org
URL: http://www.ponyclub.org
Contact: Dan Murphy, President
Description: Provides education in riding, mounted sports, horse management, and the care of horses and ponies. Grants certificates of proficiency. Promotes responsibility, moral judgment, leadership, and self-confidence in youth. Sponsors local, regional, and national competitions. Cooperates with the British Horse Society - Pony Club. Offers educational programs. Maintains 20 committees. **Founded:** 1954. **Publications:** *Pony Club News* (Quarterly); *USPC Handbook and Rules for Eventing Competition*. **Educational Activities:** United States Pony Clubs Festival (Triennial). **Awards:** Founders Award (Annual).

DIRECTORIES OF EDUCATIONAL PROGRAMS

10614 ■ *Directory of Private Accredited Career Schools and Colleges of Technology*
Pub: Accrediting Commission of Career Schools and Colleges of Technology
Contact: Michale S. McComis, Executive Director
Released: On web page. **Price:** Free. **Description:** Covers 3900 accredited post-secondary programs that provide training programs in business, trade, and technical fields, including various small business endeavors. Entries offer school name, address, phone, description of courses, job placement assistance, and requirements for admission. Arrangement is alphabetical.

REFERENCE WORKS

10615 ■ *ARICP Directory of Certified Riding Instructors*
Pub: American Riding Instructors Association
Contact: Charlotte Kneeland, Editor
URL(s): www.riding-instructor.com/certification/www.riding-instructor.com. **Released:** Quarterly **Covers:**

Horseback riding instructors who have passed written, practical and oral examinations to earn ARICP certification. **Arrangement:** Geographical.

10616 ■ *"Can Turfway Park Stay in the Race?" in Business Courier (Vol. 26, January 8, 2010, No. 38, pp. 1)*
Pub: American City Business Journals, Inc.
Ed: Jon Newberry. **Description:** Legalization of slot machine gambling in Kentucky could affect raceway Turfway Park and the state's thoroughbred industry. Thousands of farms and jobs in the industry could be lost if slot machine gambling is approved.

10617 ■ *Horse Industry Directory*
Pub: American Horse Council
Contact: James J. Hickey, Jr., President
E-mail: ahc@horsecouncil.org
URL(s): www.horsecouncil.org. **Released:** Annual; Latest edition 2011. **Price:** $25, Individuals; Free for certain levels of membership. **Covers:** Organizations concerned with all aspects of the horse industry, including breed registries, racing and showing organizations, transportation and sales companies, and rodeo/trail organizations and equine publications. **Entries include:** Organization name, address, phone, names and titles of key personnel, e-mail & Internet addresses. **Database includes:** List of state horse specialists, state veterinarians, and state departments of agriculture. **Arrangement:** Classified by service. **Indexes:** Organization name.

10618 ■ *"Northwest Washington Fair Building Larger Horse Arena" in Bellingham Business Journal (Vol. March 2010, pp. 6)*
Pub: Sound Publishing Inc.
Description: Northwest Washington Fair is building a new equestrian arena that will provide larger show space for the horse community. The existing arena will function as a warm-up arena when hosting large shows.

10619 ■ *"Turfway Slowing its Gait" in Business Courier (Vol. 26, November 6, 2009, No. 28, pp. 1)*
Pub: American City Business Journals, Inc.
Ed: Jon Newberry. **Description:** Kentucky's Turfway Park will be decreasing its weekly race schedule from five days to three days in the first two months of 2010, and to four days in March 2010. The decision to make reductions in the schedule is attributed to the relocation of thoroughbred racing to states that allow casino gambling. As a result, Turfway Park's resources and purse money would be focused on less days.

TRADE PERIODICALS

10620 ■ *Saddle & Bridle Magazine: Oldest Name In Show Horse Magazines*
Pub: Saddle & Bridle Inc.
URL(s): www.saddleandbridle.com. **Ed:** Jeffrey Thompson. **Released:** Monthly **Price:** $79, Individuals; $119, Two years; $179, Individuals three years; $79, Other countries.

VIDEOCASSETTES/ AUDIOCASSETTES

10621 ■ *Horsemanship, Vol. 1-3*
ESPN Inc.
ESPN Plz.
Bristol, CT 06010
Ph: (860)766-2000
Free: 888-549-3776
Fax: (860)766-2213
Co. E-mail: espnpr@espn.com
URL: http://espn.go.com
Contact: Steven M. Bornstein, President
Released: 1995. **Price:** $29.95. **Description:** A fundamental training program for the novice viewer in horse riding and racing techniques, as well as care and grooming. Three volumes. **Availability:** VHS.

LIBRARIES

10622 ■ **American Mustang and Burro Association, Inc. - Library**
PO Box 608
Greenwood, DE 19950
Co. E-mail: in2horses4@yahoo.com
URL: http://www.ambainc.net
Contact: George W. Berrier, Jr., Chief Executive Officer
Scope: Wild horses and burros - history, care, general information, fiction. **Services:** Copying;

library open to the public. **Founded:** 1983. **Holdings:** Books; newspaper and magazine article files; artwork; sculpture.

10623 ■ **American Saddlebred Museum - Library**
4083 Iron Works Pkwy.
Lexington, KY 40511
Ph: (859)259-2746, x-312
Fax: (859)255-4909
Co. E-mail: museum@asbmuseum.org
URL: http://www.asbmuseum.org
Contact: Tolley Graves, Executive Director
Scope: Saddlebred history, Saddlebred bloodlines, training, riding, driving, art. **Services:** Library not open to the public (museum members only). **Founded:** 1962. **Holdings:** 2400 volumes. **Subscriptions:** 4 journals and other serials.

10624 ■ **American Suffolk Horse Association Library**
4240 Goehring Rd.
Ledbetter, TX 78946-5004
Ph: (979)249-5795
Co. E-mail: suffolks@cvtx.com
URL: http://www.suffolkpunch.com
Contact: Don Evia, President
Scope: Suffolk horses. **Holdings:** 30 books. **Telecommunication Services:** rread@cvtx.com.

10625 ■ **Arabian Horse Owners Foundation - W.R. Brown Memorial Library**
4101 N. Bear Canyon Rd.
Tucson, AZ 85749
Ph: (520)760-0682
Free: 800-892-0682
Co. E-mail: info@ahof.org
URL: http://www.arabianhorseowners.org/
Contact: Howard F. Shenk, Executive Director
Scope: Arabian horses - history, breeding, use; horses in general - use, care, training, literature, history. **Services:** Copying; library open to the public by appointment. **Founded:** 1957. **Holdings:** 1200 books; 20 bound periodical volumes; films; photographs; Arabian show and sale programs. **Subscriptions:** 5 journals and other serials.

10626 ■ **Arabian Horse Trust Library**
12000 Zuni St.
Westminster, CO 80234
Contact: Linda Gruver
Scope: Arabian horses - breeding, history, bloodlines; horsemanship. **Services:** Copying; video viewing room; library open to the public. **Founded:** 1974. **Holdings:** 1500 books; 160 bound periodical volumes; 18,000 horse photographs. **Subscriptions:** 43 journals and other serials.

10627 ■ **Bay Meadows Racetrack - William P. Kyne Memorial Thoroughbred Racing Library**
PO Box 5050
San Mateo, CA 94402
Ph: (650)574-7223
Fax: (415)573-4670
URL: http://www.baymeadows.com/index.php
Contact: Rusty Mathieson, Assistant Librarian
Scope: Thoroughbred horses - racing, breeding, training, diseases, history; personalities in racing. **Services:** Copying; library open to the public for reference use only. **Founded:** 1973. **Holdings:** 1681 books; 157 bound periodical volumes; photographs; national and International racing programs.

10628 ■ **Bloodstock Research Information Services, Inc. Library**
801 Corporate Dr., 3rd Fl.
Lexington, KY 40544-4097
Ph: (859)223-4444
Free: 800-354-9206
Fax: (859)223-7024
Co. E-mail: brisinfo@brisnet.com
URL: http://www.brisnet.com
Scope: Thoroughbred horses, horse breeding, horse racing, horse and farm management. **Services:** Library not open to the public. **Founded:** 1972. **Holdings:** 1000 bound volumes. **Subscriptions:** 20 journals and other serials. **Telecommunication Services:** bristech@brisnet.com.

10629 ■ **California State Polytechnic University - W.K. Kellogg Arabian Horse Library**
3801 W. Temple Ave.
Pomona, CA 91768-4080
Ph: (909)869-3092
Fax: (909)869-2129
Co. E-mail: kestaab@csupomona.edu
URL: http://www.csupomona.edu/~library/wkkahl
Contact: Katherine Staab, Curator
Scope: Arabian horses - history, breeding, use, pedigrees, literature. **Services:** Photocopying; Library open to the public for reference use only. **Founded:** 1975. **Holdings:** 9500 books; 760 bound periodical volumes; 5 VF drawers of club newsletters; 2 VF drawers of farm brochures; 124 videotapes; photographs; show programs; auction catalogs; films; negatives; manuscripts; prints; paintings; bronzes. **Subscriptions:** 50 journals and other serials. **Telecommunication Services:** kestaab@csupomona. edu.

10630 ■ **Camelot Therapeutic Horsemanship - Camelot Library**
23623 N. Scottsdale Rd., Ste. D3
PMB 259
Scottsdale, AZ 85255-3471
Ph: (480)515-1542
Fax: (480)515-1542
Co. E-mail: info@camelot-th.org
URL: http://www.camelotaz.org/
Scope: Equines, therapeutic horsemanship, domestic animals, therapeutic use of animals, nature, chivalry, King Arthur. **Services:** Interlibrary loan; copying; library open to the public by appointment. **Founded:** 1985. **Holdings:** 300 books.

10631 ■ **Harness Racing Museum & Hall of Fame - Peter D. Haughton Memorial Library**
240 Main St.
Goshen, NY 10924
Ph: (845)294-6330
Fax: (845)294-3463
Co. E-mail: director@harnessmuseum.com
URL: http://harnessmuseum.com
Contact: Gail Cunard, Director
Scope: History of Standardbred horses, history of harness racing, training horses, horses in literature, veterinary medicine. **Services:** Library open to members. **Founded:** 1951. **Holdings:** 8061 archival items; 389 books; 1165 bound periodical volumes; 4706 unbound periodicals, pamphlets, and other materials; 2431 videos; 5305 photographs; 1006 programs, newspapers, and other print and manuscript materials. **Subscriptions:** 10 journals and other serials; 5 newspapers. **Telecommunication Services:** hrmdir@frontiernet.net.

10632 ■ **Keeneland Association Library**
Keeneland Race Course
4201 Versailles Rd.
Box 1690
Lexington, KY 40588-1690
Ph: (859)254-3412
Free: 800-456-3412
Fax: (859)255-2484
Co. E-mail: library@keeneland.com
URL: http://www.keeneland.com
Contact: Bill Thomason, President
Scope: Thoroughbred horse racing and breeding, horse sports. **Services:** Library open to the public for reference use only on limited schedule. **Founded:** 1939. **Holdings:** 10,000 books; 1000 bound periodical volumes; 1500 videocassettes; 225,000 photo negatives; 3000 files containing newspaper clippings; pamphlet file. **Subscriptions:** 35 journals and other serials.

10633 ■ **Palomino Horse Breeders of America Library**
15253 E. Skelly Dr.
Tulsa, OK 74116-2620
Ph: (918)438-1234

Fax: (918)438-1232
Co. E-mail: yellahrses@palominohba.com
URL: http://www.palominohba.com
Contact: Terri Green, General Manager
Scope: Horses and equine-related activities, the Palomino horse. **Services:** Library not open to the public. **Founded:** 1941.

10634 ■ University of Kentucky - Gluck Equine Research Center - John A. Morris Memorial Library
Gluck Equine Research Center, 2nd Fl.
1400 Nicholasville Rd.
Lexington, KY 40546-0099
Ph: (859)257-4757 x81147
Fax: (859)257-8542
Co. E-mail: ghale@email.uky.edu
URL: http://www.ca.uky.edu/gluck/ServLibrary.asp
Contact: Gracie Hale, Librarian
Scope: Equine veterinary medicine, horses and horse care. **Services:** Document delivery; SDI; Library open to the public for reference use only. **Founded:** 1987. **Holdings:** 300 books; 250 bound periodical volumes; 25 videotapes. **Subscriptions:** 20 journals and other serials. **Telecommunication Services:** eceber2@uky.edu.

10635 ■ University of Minnesota, Crookston Library
160 Kiehle Bldg.
2900 University Ave.
Crookston, MN 56716
Ph: (218)281-8399

Fax: (218)281-8080
Co. E-mail: willi099@umn.edu
URL: http://www1.crk.umn.edu/library
Contact: Owen E. Williams, Director, Library Services
Scope: Agriculture, horsemanship, business, foods, hospitality, hotel management. **Services:** Interlibrary loan; copying; wireless Internet; scanning; computer access for research; document delivery; library open to public. **Founded:** 1966. **Holdings:** 32,265 books; 135 periodicals on microfilm; 1900 AV programs. **Subscriptions:** 766 journals and other serials; 55 newspapers. **Telecommunication Services:** umclib@umn.edu.

RESEARCH CENTERS

10636 ■ Grayson-Jockey Club Research Foundation
821 Corporate Dr.
Lexington, KY 40503
Ph: (859)224-2850
Fax: (859)224-2853
Co. E-mail: ebowen@jockeyclub.com
URL: http://www.grayson-jockeyclub.org/
Contact: Edward L. Bowen, President
Founded: 1940. **Telecommunication Services:** contactus@grayson-jockeyclub.org.

10637 ■ Michigan State University - Michigan State University Horse Teaching and Research Center (HTRC)
1290 Anthony
East Lansing, MI 48824

Ph: (517)355-8391
Co. E-mail: shelle@msu.edu
URL: http://www.msuarabians.com
Contact: Prof. John Shelle, Coordinator

10638 ■ University of Florida - Horse Research Center
2655 NW 100th St.
Ocala, FL 34475
Ph: (352)622-7084
Co. E-mail: esc@ifas.ufl.edu
URL: http://www.animal.ufl.edu/extension/equine/esc.shtml
Contact: Chris Cooper, Coordinator Farm Manager
Founded: 1973. **Educational Activities:** FFA, 4-H, generation connection and other mentoring organizations (Annual), events include land judging competitions and tours.

10639 ■ University of Kentucky - Horse Research Farm
900 W.P. Garrigus Bldg.
Department of Animal & Food Sciences
Lexington, KY 40546-0215
Ph: (859)257-2686
Fax: (859)257-2538
Co. E-mail: rharmon@uky.edu
URL: http://www.uky.edu/Ag/AnimalSciences/equine/horsefarm.html
Contact: Robert J. Harmon, Chairperson
Founded: 1967. **Awards:** Horse Research Farm Graduate research assistantships.

START-UP INFORMATION

10640 ■ *"Do Your Homework" in Black Enterprise (Vol. 38, November 2007, No. 4, pp. 114)*
Pub: Earl G. Graves Publishing Co. Inc.
Ed: Tennille M. Robinson. **Description:** Preschool teacher seeks advice for starting a hotel resort and day spa.

ASSOCIATIONS AND OTHER ORGANIZATIONS

10641 ■ **American Hotel and Lodging Association (American Hotel & Motel Association)**
1201 New York Ave. NW, Ste. 600
Washington, DC 20005-3931
Ph: (202)289-3100
Free: 800-752-4567
Fax: (202)289-3199
Co. E-mail: informationcenter@ahla.com
URL: http://www.ahla.com
Contact: Joseph A. McInerney, President
E-mail: joe@ahla.com
Description: Represents state lodging associations throughout the United States with some 13,000 property members worldwide, representing more than 1.7 million guest rooms. Provides its members with assistance in operations, education and communications and lobbies on Capitol Hill to provide a business climate in which the industry can continue to prosper. Individual state associations provide representation at the state level and offer many additional cost-saving benefits. **Scope:** lodging, hospitality, travel, tourism. **Founded:** 1910. **Subscriptions:** 5000 articles periodicals. **Publications:** *Construction & Modernization Report* (Monthly); *Lodging Magazine* (Monthly); *AH&LA Register* (10/year); *Lodging News* (Biweekly); *Who's Who in the Lodging Industry* (Annual). **Educational Activities:** American Hotel and Motel Association Annual Conference and Leadership Forum (Annual); IH/M & RS - International Hotel/Motel & Restaurant Show (Annual). **Awards:** Stars of the Industry Awards (Annual). **Telecommunication Services:** info@ahla.com.

10642 ■ **American Hotel and Lodging Educational Foundation (AH&LEF)**
1201 New York Ave. NW, No. 600
Washington, DC 20005-3931
Ph: (202)289-3100
Fax: (202)289-3199
Co. E-mail: cboatman@ahlef.org
URL: http://www.ahlef.org
Contact: Christa Boatman, Manager
Description: Provides financial support that enhances the stability, prosperity, and growth of the lodging industry through educational and research programs. **Founded:** 2002. **Publications:** *Lodging* (Monthly). **Awards:** American Express Scholarship (Annual); Ecolab Scholarship Program (Annual); Lodging Management Program Scholarships (LMP); Pepsi Scholarships; American Express Scholarship;

Ecolab Scholarship; Arthur J. Packard Memorial Scholarship (Annual); Rama Scholarship for the American Dream (Annual); The American Automobile Association Five Diamond Hospitality Scholarships (AAA); American Express Professional Development Scholarships; The American Express Scholarship Competition; The Hyatt Hotels Fund For Minority Lodging Management Students; The Steve Hymans Extended Stay Scholarship Program; The Arthur J. Packard Memorial Scholarship Competition; Rama Scholarships for the American Dream; Arthur J. Packard Memorial Scholarship; Rama Scholarships for the American Dream.

10643 ■ **Asian American Hotel Owners Association (AAHOA)**
7000 Peachtree Dunwoody Rd. NE, Bldg. 7
Atlanta, GA 30328
Ph: (404)816-5759
Free: 888-692-2462
Fax: (404)816-6260
Co. E-mail: info@aahoa.com
URL: http://www.aahoa.com
Contact: Alkesh R. Patel, Chairman
Description: Serves as advocacy, educational, and professional development group for Asian-American hotel owners. **Founded:** 1989.

10644 ■ **Canadian Resort Development Association (CRDA)**
147 Liberty St.
Toronto, ON, Canada M6K 3G3
Ph: (416)960-4930
Free: 800-646-9205
Fax: (416)533-0591
Co. E-mail: crda@rogers.com
URL: http://www.crda.com
Contact: Jon Zwickel, President
Description: Owners and operators of resorts. Promotes Canada as a vacation destination; seeks to improve the quality of accommodation and service at Canadian resorts. Interacts with provincial and federal governments regarding legislation affecting the resort industries; facilitates exchange of information among members; represents members' interests; conducts research and educational programs. **Scope:** resort development, timesharing. **Founded:** 1980. **Subscriptions:** artwork business records clippings periodicals. **Publications:** *Resort Report* (Semiannual); *Consumers' Guide to Timesharing and Resort Report* (Semiannual). **Educational Activities:** Canadian Resort Development Association Seminar (Semiannual).

10645 ■ **CDS International (CDS)**
440 Park Ave. S
New York, NY 10016
Ph: (212)497-3500
Fax: (212)497-3535
Co. E-mail: info@cdsintl.org
URL: http://culturalvistas.org
Contact: Howard A. Rollins, Chairman
Description: Committed to the advancement of international career training opportunities customized to provide individuals with in-depth practical knowledge of other nations' business practices, cultures,

and political traditions. Helps strengthen global cooperation and understanding amongst individuals, businesses, organizations and communities. Annually serves approximately 1,700 individuals from the United States, Germany, Japan, and almost 60 other nations around the globe in a wide variety of internship, fact-finding, and work-study programs. Provides opportunities for individuals to enhance their professional abilities cross-culturally in order to obtain and maintain the skills necessary for successful careers in global economy. Promotes international exchange to help strengthen cooperation between different cultures and nations. **Founded:** 1968.

10646 ■ *Consumers' Guide to Timesharing and Resort Report*
147 Liberty St.
Toronto, ON, Canada M6K 3G3
Ph: (416)960-4930
Free: 800-646-9205
Fax: (416)533-0591
Co. E-mail: crda@rogers.com
URL: http://www.crda.com
Contact: Jon Zwickel, President
Released: Semiannual

10647 ■ **Green Hotels Association**
PO Box 420212
Houston, TX 77242-0212
Ph: (713)789-8889
Fax: (713)789-9786
Co. E-mail: green@greenhotels.com
URL: http://greenhotels.com
Contact: Patricia Griffin, President
Description: Hotels, motels, inns, bed and breakfasts, and all other lodging establishments with an interest in protecting the environment. Encourages, promotes and supports ecological consciousness in the hospitality industry. **Founded:** 1993. **Publications:** *Greening Newsletter* (Bimonthly); *Membership Conservation Guidelines and Ideas* (Quadrennial).

10648 ■ **Hospitality Financial and Technology Professionals (HFTP)**
11709 Boulder Ln., Ste. 110
Austin, TX 78726
Ph: (512)249-5333
Free: 800-646-4387
Fax: (512)249-1533
Co. E-mail: membership@hftp.org
URL: http://www.hftp.org
Contact: Lisa Funk, President
Description: Accountants, financial officers and MIS managers in 50 countries working in hotels, resorts, casinos, restaurants, and clubs. Develops uniform system of accounts. Conducts education, training, and certification programs; offers placement service; maintains hall of fame. **Founded:** 1952. **Publications:** *The Bottomline* (7/year); *Bottomline*. **Awards:** Chapter Choice Award (Annual); Paragon Award (Annual); Technology Award of Merit (Quinquenial); International Hospitality Technology Hall of Fame (Annual). **Telecommunication Services:** hftp@hftp.org.

10649 ■ Hospitality Sales and Marketing Association International (HSMAI)
1760 Old Meadow Rd., Ste. 500
McLean, VA 22102
Ph: (703)506-3280
Free: 877-643-3511
Fax: (703)506-3266
Co. E-mail: info@hsmai.org
URL: http://www.hsmai.org
Contact: Robert A. Gilbert, President
E-mail: bgilbert@hsmai.org

Description: Description: Publishes on hospitality sales and marketing. Also publishes quarterly journal. Reaches market through direct mail. Accepts unsolicited manuscripts. **Scope:** sales, marketing, hospitality, travel, tourism. **Founded:** 1927. **Publications:** HSMAI Marketing Review (Quarterly); HSMAI Update (Bimonthly); H.S.M.A.I. Marketing Review: An Educational Magazine for Congregational Leaders (Quarterly). **Educational Activities:** HSMAI Affordable Meetings Exposition and Conference (Annual); HSMAI - Affordable Meetings West (Annual); Affordable Meetings Mid-America (Annual); Affordable Meetings West (Annual). **Awards:** Adrian Awards; Adrian Awards Competition (Annual). **Telecommunication Services:** bgilbert@hsmai.org.

10650 ■ Hotel Brokers International (HBI)
1420 NW Vivion Rd., Ste. 111
Kansas City, MO 64118
Ph: (816)505-4315
Fax: (816)505-4319
Co. E-mail: info@hbihotels.com
URL: http://www.hbihotels.com
Contact: Charles H. Fritsch, President

Description: Real estate brokers specializing in sales of and investments in hotel and motel properties. Members cooperate in the interchange of listings and data by computer, so the buying public will have information concerning all hotels available through the members of the association. Maintains speakers' bureau. **Founded:** 1959. **Publications:** TransActions Recap (Annual). **Awards:** Broker of the Year (Annual).

10651 ■ Hotel Electronic Distribution Network Association (HEDNA)
750 National Press Bldg.
529 14th St. NW
Washington, DC 20045
Ph: (202)204-8400
Fax: (703)223-9741
Co. E-mail: info@hedna.org
URL: http://www.hedna.org
Contact: Reed Hitchcock, Executive Director

Description: Hotel distribution industry. Strives to increase hotel industry revenues and profitability from electronic distribution channels such as the Internet. **Founded:** 1991.

10652 ■ IHG Owners Association
3 Ravinia Dr., Ste. 100
Atlanta, GA 30346
Ph: (770)604-5555
Free: 877-500-4244
Fax: (770)604-5684
Co. E-mail: eva.ferguson@owners.org
URL: http://www.owners.org
Contact: Eva Ferguson, President

Description: Holiday Inn hotel owners and franchisees. Serves as liaison among members through owner committees. Sponsors programs in government relations and financial review; reviews corporate programs. Operates employment resume service. **Founded:** 1956.

10653 ■ International Council on Hotel, Restaurant, and Institutional Education (CHRIE)
2810 N Parham Rd., Ste. 230
Richmond, VA 23294
Ph: (804)346-4800

Fax: (804)346-5009
Co. E-mail: publications@chrie.org
URL: http://www.chrie.org
Contact: Susan Fournier, President
E-mail: susan.fournier@ritz.edu

Description: Schools and colleges offering specialized education and training in hospitals, recreation, tourism and hotel, restaurant, and institutional administration; individuals, executives, and students. Provides networking opportunities and professional development. **Founded:** 1946. **Publications:** A Guide to College Programs in Hospitality, Tourism, & Culinary Arts (Biennial); Guide to Hospitality Education (Semiannual); Hosteur Magazine (Biennial); The Journal of Hospitality and Tourism Education (Quarterly); The Journal of Hospitality and Tourism Research (3/year); Membership Directory and Research Guide (Annual); Journal of Hospitality & Tourism Research (Quarterly); Council on Hotel, Restaurant and Institutional Education--Member Directory and Resource Guide (Biennial). **Awards:** Chef Herman Breithaupt Award; Stevenson W. Fletcher Achievement Award; Industry Recognition Award; W. Bradford Wiley Memorial Best Research Paper of the Year Award; Howard B. Meek Award; John Wiley and Sons Lifetime Research Achievement Award; John Wiley and Sons Award for Innovation in Teaching. **Telecommunication Services:** kmccarty@chrie.org.

10654 ■ Resort Hotel Association (RHA)
2100 E Cary St., Ste. 3
Richmond, VA 23223
Ph: (804)525-2020
Fax: (804)525-2021
Co. E-mail: info@rhainsure.com
URL: http://www.resorthotelinsurance.com
Contact: Brooks W. Chase, President

Description: Represents resort and hotel owners. Develops and administers products and services customized for the hospitality industry. Offers both liability and property insurance programs. **Founded:** 1987. **Publications:** Resort Hotel Association Newsletter (Quarterly). **Telecommunication Services:** brooks@rhainsure.com.

10655 ■ Resort Report
147 Liberty St.
Toronto, ON, Canada M6K 3G3
Ph: (416)960-4930
Free: 800-646-9205
Fax: (416)533-0591
Co. E-mail: crda@rogers.com
URL: http://www.crda.com
Contact: Jon Zwickel, President
Released: Semiannual

10656 ■ Unite Here
275 7th Ave.
New York, NY 10001-6708
Ph: (212)265-7000
Co. E-mail: ccarrera@unitehere.org
URL: http://www.unitehere.org
Contact: John W. Wilhelm, President

Description: AFL-CIO. Helps improve working conditions, wages, and benefits across the U.S. and Canada. Organizes the unorganized in the industry. Works with employers to resolve issues in the workplace and in the relevant industry. **Founded:** 1891. **Publications:** Catering Industry Employee (Monthly).

DIRECTORIES OF EDUCATIONAL PROGRAMS

10657 ■ Directory of Private Accredited Career Schools and Colleges of Technology
Pub: Accrediting Commission of Career Schools and Colleges of Technology
Contact: Michale S. McComis, Executive Director
Released: On web page. **Price:** Free. **Description:** Covers 3900 accredited post-secondary programs that provide training programs in business, trade, and technical fields, including various small business endeavors. Entries offer school name, address, phone, description of courses, job placement assistance, and requirements for admission. Arrangement is alphabetical.

REFERENCE WORKS

10658 ■ "$50 Million Project for West Chester" in Business Courier (Vol. 24, December 14, 2008, No. 35, pp. 1)
Pub: American City Business Journals, Inc.
Ed: Laura Baverman. **Description:** Commercial developer Scott Street Partners is planning to invest $50 million for the development of a site south of the Streets of West Chester retail center. The 31-acre project will generate 1,200 jobs, and will bring in offices, restaurants and a hotel. The development plans and the features of the site are discussed as well.

10659 ■ "$100 Million Complex To Be Built..On a Bridge" in Business Courier (Vol. 27, November 12, 2010, No. 28, pp. 1)
Pub: Business Courier
Ed: Lucy May. **Description:** A development firm closed a deal with the Newport Southbank Bridge Company for a $100M entertainment complex that will be built on tope of the Purple People Bridge. The proposed project will cover 150,000 square feet with attractions such as restaurants, a boutique hotel, and pubs.

10660 ■ "2010 Book of Lists" in Austin Business JournalInc. (Vol. 29, December 25, 2009, No. 42, pp. 1)
Pub: American City Business Journals
Description: Rankings of companies and organizations within the business services, finance, healthcare, hospitality and travel, insurance, marketing and media, professional services, real estate, education and technology industries in Austin, Texas are presented. Rankings are based on sales, business size, and other statistics.

10661 ■ "2010 Book of Lists" in Business Courier (Vol. 26, December 26, 2009, No. 36, pp. 1)
Pub: American City Business Journals, Inc.
Description: Rankings of companies and organizations within the business services, education, finance, health care, hospitality and tourism, real estate, and technology industries in the Cincinnati, Ohio-Northern Kentucky area are presented. Rankings are based on sales, business size, or other statistics.

10662 ■ "2010 Book of Lists" in Tampa Bay Business Journal (Vol. 30, December 22, 2009, No. 53, pp. 1)
Pub: American City Business Journals
Description: Rankings of companies and organizations within the human resources, banking and finance, business services, healthcare, real estate, technology, hospitality and travel, and education industries in the Greater Tampa Bay area are presented. Rankings are based on sales, business size, and more.

10663 ■ "Atlific Adds Management of 4 Hotels to Its Portfolio in Fort McMurray" in Canadian Corporate News (May 16, 2007)
Pub: Comtex News Network Inc.
Description: Atlific Hotels & Resorts took over management for Merit Inn & Suites, The Merit Hotel, The Nomad Hotel and The Nomad Suites in Fort McMurray. The company feels that they will be able to increase the hotels' abilities to promote their services through their vast network of sales personnel and marketing and e-commerce team.

10664 ■ "Benchmark Makes Granduca Entrance" in Houston Business Journal (Vol. 40, January 8, 2010, No. 35, pp. 2)
Pub: American City Business Journals
Ed: Jennifer Dawson. **Description:** Houston, Texas-based Interfin Company, owner of the Hotel Granduca, has tapped the services of Benchmark Hospitality International to manage the property. The hiring of Benchmark is part of Interfin's efforts to develop Granduca hotels in other markets. Statistical data included.

10665 ■ "Big Spenders" in Hawaii Business (Vol. 53, November 2007, No. 5, pp. 28)
Pub: Hawaii Business Publishing
Ed: Cathy S. Cruz-George. **Description:** Blackstone Group announced its acquisition of Hilton Hotels

Corp. valued at $26 billion in July 2007, one of the largest buyouts in the history of hotels. Blackstone now becomes the second most powerful landowners in Hawaii.

10666 ■ *"Book of Lists 2010" in Philadelphia Business Journal (Vol. 28, December 25, 2009, No. 45, pp. 1)*
Pub: American City Business Journals
Description: Rankings of companies and organizations within the banking, biotechnology, economic development, healthcare, hospitality, law and accounting, marketing and media, real estate, and technology industries in the Philadelphia, Pennsylvania area are presented. Rankings are based on sales, business size, and more.

10667 ■ *"Building Targeted for Marriott in Violation" in Business Journal-Milwaukee (Vol. 28, December 24, 2010, No. 12, pp. A1)*
Pub: Milwaukee Business Journal
Ed: Sean Ryan. **Description:** Milwaukee, Wisconsin's Department of Neighborhood Services has ordered structural improvements and safeguards for the Pioneer Building after three violations from structural failures were found. Pioneer was among the five buildings wanted by Jackson Street Management LLC to demolish for the new Marriott Hotel.

10668 ■ *"Business Start-Up a Learning Experience for Young Bellingham Entrepreneur" in Bellingham Herald (July 18, 2010)*
Pub: Bellingham Herald
Ed: Dave Gallagher. **Description:** Profile of 21-year-old entrepreneur, Chase Larabee, who developed an online program that helps airport fixed-based operators handle refueling, hotel and transportation reservations and other requests from private airplane pilots.

10669 ■ *Buying and Running a Guesthouse or Small Hotel*
Pub: Hot To Books Ltd.
Ed: Dan Marshall. **Released:** December 2007. **Price:** $30.00. **Description:** Teaches how to build and enjoy a lifestyle while running a guesthouse or small hotel.

10670 ■ *"City Eyeing Tax Breaks for Arena" in Boston Business Journal (Vol. 29, June 3, 2011, No. 4, pp. 1)*
Pub: American City Business Journals Inc.
Ed: Daniel J. Sernovitz. **Description:** Baltimore City is opting to give millions of dollars in tax breaks and construction loans to a group of private investors led by William Hackerman who is proposing to build a new arena and hotel at the Baltimore Convention Center. The project will cost $500 million with the state putting up another $400 million for the center's expansion.

10671 ■ *"City Hopes Casino Will Be $333M Jackpot" in Business First Buffalo (October 5, 2007, pp. 1)*
Pub: American City Business Journals, Inc.
Ed: James Fink. **Description:** Construction of the $333 million Seneca Buffalo Creek Casino, which includes a hotel, spa and restaurants, is schedule to begin in October 2007. The 5,000 square-foot casino is expected to generate revenue and provide 1,000 jobs for the City of Buffalo, New York.

10672 ■ *"City Wooing Red Roof Inn for Return of Corporate HQ" in Business First-Columbus (October 19, 2007, pp. A1)*
Pub: American City Business Journals, Inc.
Description: Department of Development of Columbus, Ohio offered Red Roof Inns Inc. a four-year, 40 percent jobs growth initiative to entice the company to move its corporate headquarters into the city from Dallas, Texas. The Watermark Island office building off Dublin Road and Grandview Avenue will be the headquarters of the company if it accepts the offer.

10673 ■ *"City's Hilton Hotel Still Losing Money" in Baltimore Business Journal (Vol. 28, October 15, 2010, No. 23, pp. 1)*
Pub: Baltimore Business Journal
Ed: Danile J. Sernovitz. **Description:** Baltimore, Maryland-owned Hilton Baltimore Convention Center Hotel has been expected by Baltimore Hotel Corpora-

tion to wrap up 2010 with a $9.8 million deficit after completing its first year in operation in the red. The forecast would mark the controversial project's third-straight year of losses.

10674 ■ *"Click Here to Book" in Caterer & Hotelkeeper (October 28, 2011, No. 288)*
Pub: Reed Reference Publishing
Ed: Ross Bentley. **Description:** Customers expectations are determined by the quality of a Website when booking hotel rooms.

10675 ■ *"Clock Ticks On Columbia Sussex Debt" in Business Courier (Vol. 27, July 30, 2010, No. 13, pp. 1)*
Pub: Business Courier
Ed: Dan Monk. **Description:** Cincinnati, Ohio-based Columbia Sussex Corporation has made plans to restructure a $1 billion loan bundle that was scheduled to mature in October 2010. The privately held hotel has strived in a weak hotel market to keep pace with its $3 billion debt load.

10676 ■ *"Commercial Builders Take It on the Chin" in Crain's Chicago Business (Vol. 31, April 28, 2008, No. 17, pp. 16)*
Pub: Crain Communications, Inc.
Ed: Alby Gallun. **Description:** Although the health care development sector has seen growth, the rest of Chicago's local commercial building industry has seen steep declines in the first quarter of this year. According to McGraw-Hill Construction, Chicago-area non-residential construction starts totaled $731 million in the quarter, a 60 percent drop from the year-earlier period. Volume in the retail, office and hotel markets fell by nearly 70 percent.

10677 ■ *"Corporex Checks Into Hotel Niche" in Business Courier (Vol. 24, October 12, 2008, No. 26, pp. 1)*
Pub: American City Business Journals, Inc.
Ed: Laura Baverman. **Description:** Corporex Companies Inc. is investing $900 million on select-service hotels ranging from $12 million to $20 million each, with eight hotels under construction and nine sites under contract.

10678 ■ *"Corus Eases Off Ailing Condo Market; Office Developers Get Majority of 1Q Loans" in Crain's Chicago Business (April 28, 2008)*
Pub: Crain Communications, Inc.
Ed: H. Lee Murphy. **Description:** Corus Bankshares Inc., a specialist in lending for the condominium high-rise construction market, is diversifying its portfolio by making loans to office developers and expects to be investing in hotels through the rest of the year. Corus' $7.57 billion loan portfolio is also discussed in detail as well as the company's earnings and share price. Statistical data included.

10679 ■ *Council on Hotel, Restaurant and Institutional Education--Member Directory and Resource Guide*
Pub: International Council on Hotel, Restaurant, and Institutional Education
Contact: Susan Fournier, President
E-mail: susan.fournier@ritz.edu
URL(s): www.chrie.org. **Released:** Biennial; March of even years. **Covers:** Over 2,000 educational programs and institutions in the hotel, restaurant, and tourism industries. **Entries include:** Name, address, phone, fax. **Arrangement:** Alphabetical. **Indexes:** Geographical, membership category.

10680 ■ *"A Crystal Ball" in Business Journal Portland (Vol. 27, December 31, 2010, No. 44, pp. 1)*
Pub: Portland Business Journal
Ed: Wendy Culverwell. **Description:** McMenamins Pubs and Breweries has resumed construction of its Crystal Hotel project. The company has been working to convert a former bath house into a 51-room hotel. The hotel is expected to open in 2011.

10681 ■ *"Deals Still Get Done at Drake's Coq d'Or" in Crain's Chicago Business (Vol. 31, November 17, 2008, No. 46, pp. 35)*
Pub: Crain Communications, Inc.
Ed: Shia Kapos. **Description:** Chicago's infamous Coq d'Or, a restaurant and lounge located at the Drake Hotel, is still a favorite establishment for noted

executives but the eatery is now trying to cater to younger professionals through marketing and offering new beverages that appeal to that demographic. Many find it the perfect environment in which to close deals, relax or network.

10682 ■ *"The Debt Mountain in Mid-Collapse" in Canadian Business (Vol. 83, October 12, 2010, No. 17, pp. 28)*
Pub: Rogers Media Ltd.
Ed: Michael McCullough. **Description:** A growing real estate market has made Intrawest ULC's Whistler-Blackcomb resort a model for a booming industry for years. However, resorts are now required to manage themselves better because of the recession. Some mountains are also trimming the cost of labor and cutting peripheral services.

10683 ■ *"DePaul To Train Hotel Leaders" in Chicago Tribune (September 22, 2008)*
Pub: McClatchy-Tribune Information Services
Ed: Kathy Bergen. **Description:** With help from a $7.5 million grant from the Conrad N. Hilton Foundation, DePaul University will dramatically expand its role as a training ground for the tourism-industry with the opening of a School of Hospitality.

10684 ■ *"Developers Await Hotel" in The Business Journal-Portland (Vol. 25, July 11, 2008, No. 18, pp. 1)*
Pub: American City Business Journals, Inc.
Ed: Wendy Culverwell. **Description:** Developers are eager to start the construction of a new hotel at the Oregon Convention Center in Portland, Oregon as hey say that the project will help boost the convention center neighborhood. The project, called The Westin Portland at the Convention Center, is partly handled by Ashforth Pacific Inc.

10685 ■ *"Discover the Wedding Location of Your Dreams" in Benzinga.com (December 24, 2011)*
Pub: Benzinga.com
Ed: Benzinga Staff. **Description:** Ritz Carlton Hotel Company helps couples choose from their 70 wedding locations worldwide with wedding advisors to assist in planning.

10686 ■ *"Doubletree Finds a Niche for Giving Back" in Hotel and Motel Management (Vol. 225, July 2010, No. 8, pp. 6)*
Pub: Questex Media Group Inc.
Ed: Paul J. Heney. **Description:** Profile of Doubletree Hotel's community outreach programs that help employee volunteers work to educate children and the public about issues important to the environment.

10687 ■ *"Embassy Suites Signs On: Dulski Building Developer Lands Anchor Tenant" in Business First Buffalo (October 26, 2007, pp. 1)*
Pub: American City Business Journals, Inc.
Ed: James Fink. **Description:** Embassy Suites will open a 150-room hotel at the former Dulski Federal Office Building in Buffalo, New York. Bringing in Embassy Suite to the building is hoped to increase the interest of tenants at the building which is being renovated by Uniland Development Company and Acquest Development Company.

10688 ■ *Exceptional Service, Exceptional Profit: The Secrets of Building a Five-Star Customer Service Organization*
Pub: AMACOM
Ed: Leonard Inghilleri, Micah Solomon. **Released:** April 1, 2010. **Price:** $21.95. **Description:** Team of insiders share exclusive knowledge of the loyalty-building techniques pioneered by the world's most successful service leaders, including brick-and-mortar stars such as The Ritz-Carlton and Lexus and online success stories such as Netflix and CD Baby.

10689 ■ *"F1 Makes Room(s) for Aspiring Entrepreneur" in Austin Business Journal (Vol. 31, July 1, 2011, No. 17, pp. 1)*
Pub: American City Business Journals Inc.
Ed: Vicky Garza. **Description:** Formula One fan and graphic designer Danielle Crespo cashes in on the June 17, 2012 racing event in Austin, Texas via host-

ing a Website that allows users to book hotel rooms. She invested less than $100 and long hours on this enterprise which now has 74,000-plus visitors.

10690 ■ *"Finding Room for Financing"* in *The Business Journal-Serving Metropolitan Kansas City (Vol. 26, August 1, 2008, No. 47, pp. 1)*

Pub: American City Business Journals, Inc.

Ed: Rob Roberts. **Description:** Kansas City officials are expecting to receive financing recommendations for a new 1,000-room convention headquarters hotel. The $300-million project could be financed either through private ownership with public subsidies, or through public ownership with tax-exempt bond financing. Other views and information on the project and its expected economic impact, are presented.

10691 ■ *"Founding Family Acquires Airport Marriott"* in *Crain's Cleveland Business (Vol. 28, November 5, 2007, No. 44, pp. 3)*

Pub: Crain Communications, Inc.

Ed: Stan Bullard. **Description:** Big River Real Estate LLC, part of the Marriott family's investment fund, is the new owner of the Cleveland Airport Marriott; renovations estimated at about $11 million will ensure that the hotel meets Marriott's standards.

10692 ■ *"A Gambling Man: Career Transitions that Put a Vegas Hotshot on Top"* in *Black Enterprise (Vol. 37, October 2006, No. 3, pp. 89)*

Pub: Earl G. Graves Publishing Co. Inc.

Ed: Laura Egodigwe. **Description:** Interview with Lorenzo Creighton, president and chief operating officer of MGM Mirage's New York-New York Hotel and Casino. Creighton talks about his history and the challenges he faced since he didn't come from the casino industry.

10693 ■ *"Grand Bohemian Hotel in Orlando, Fla. Takes Lead in Wedding Planning"* in *Benzinga.com (August 4, 2011)*

Pub: Benzinga.com

Ed: Benzinga Staff. **Description:** MAD-Marketing launched a newly-designed Website for the Grand Bohemian Hotel in Orlando, Florida. The site features the hotel's wedding vanity site to help target prospective couples planning their weddings.

10694 ■ *Heads in Beds*

Pub: Prentice Hall PTR

Ed: Ivo Raza. **Released:** May 28, 2004. **Description:** Advice is given to help build brands, generate sales and grow profits through marketing for any hospitality or tourism business.

10695 ■ *"Here's the Deal"* in *Crain's Cleveland Business (Vol. 30, June 15, 2009, No. 23, pp. 14)*

Pub: Crain Communications, Inc.

Description: Incentives being offered by hotels, restaurants, golf courses and major chains in order to promote bookings for meetings or conferences in the Cleveland area are listed.

10696 ■ *"Higher Thread Count for Metropole"* in *Business Courier (Vol. 26, September 25, 2009, No. 22, pp. 1)*

Pub: American City Business Journals, Inc.

Ed: Lisa Biank Fasig, Lucy May. **Description:** Cincinnati Center City Development Corporation is under contract to buy the 225-unit apartment building called Metropole Apartments and 21c Museum Hotel is the lead candidate for the space. Advocates of some residents of the low-income rental complex complain that this move could leave them homeless.

10697 ■ *"Host Your Dream Wedding at the Minneapolis Marriott Southwest"* in *Benzinga.com (June 6, 2011)*

Pub: Benzinga.com

Ed: Benzinga Staff. **Description:** Minneapolis Marriott Southwest is helping engaged couples plan their wedding destination at their property. Details of wedding reception options are outlined.

10698 ■ *"Hotel Confidential"* in *Canadian Business (Vol. 80, Winter 2007, No. 24, pp. 91)*

Pub: Rogers Media

Ed: Erik Heinrich. **Description:** Celebrities such as Jason Priestley, Clint Eastwood, and Francis Ford Coppola have made investment in the hospitality industry. Investing in the hospitality industry has proved to be an excellent long-term investment and the venture also has a vanity aspect to it.

10699 ■ *"Hotel Tax Eyed For Waukesha"* in *The Business Journal-Milwaukee (Vol. 25, August 29, 2008, No. 49, pp. A1)*

Pub: American City Business Journals, Inc.

Ed: Rich Kirchen. **Description:** Midwest Airlines Center chairman Frank Gimbel wants Waukesha County to help in the funding of the $200-million expansion of the convention center through a hotel room tax. The Waukesha hotel industry is expected to oppose the new room tax. Other views and information on the planned new room tax in Waukesha are presented.

10700 ■ *Hotel & Travel Index*

Pub: Northstar Travel Media L.L.C.

Contact: Thomas Kemp, Chief Executive Officer

E-mail: tkemp@ntmllc.com

URL(s): hotelandtravelindex.travelweekly.com. **Released:** Quarterly; late February, May, August, November. **Price:** Free per copy. **Covers:** over 110,000 hotels, resorts, inns, and guest houses, worldwide; hotel representatives and reservations services. **Entries include:** All entries show company name, address, phone; hotel listings show rates, manager's name, hotel representative, telex, toll-free number, fax, automated CRT access codes, travel agency commission, and corporate rate. **Arrangement:** Geographical, alphabetical.

10701 ■ *"Hotel Woes Reflect Area Struggle"* in *Business Journal Serving Greater Tampa Bay (Vol. 30, December 3, 2010, No. 50, pp. 1)*

Pub: Tampa Bay Business Journal

Ed: Mark Holan. **Description:** Quality Inn and Suites in East Tampa, Florida has struggled against the sluggish economy but remained open to guests despite facing a foreclosure. The hotel project is the center of East Tampa's redevelopment plans and public officials defend the $650,000 investment in public amenities near the building.

10702 ■ *"Hotels Get a Fill-Up"* in *Crain's Detroit Business (Vol. 25, June 1, 2009, No. 22, pp. 1)*

Pub: Crain Communications Inc. - Detroit

Ed: Daniel Duggan. **Description:** Hot Rod Power Tour will have a $1 million economic impact on the area when it arrives in June 2009; the tour will bring 3,500 out-of-state custom vehicles to the event, whose owners will be needing hotel rooms.

10703 ■ *"Hotels' Healthy Finish in '07"* in *Crain's Chicago Business (Vol. 31, March 24, 2008, No. 12, pp. 16)*

Pub: Crain Communications, Inc.

Ed: Alby Gallun. **Description:** Chicago's hotel market saw mostly rising occupancies and room rates in the fourth quarter of 2007, reflecting continued strong demand from leisure and business travelers; however, due to the current state of the economy hoteliers face an increasingly uncertain outlook.

10704 ■ *"Hotels Seeking Room Downtown"* in *Crain's New York Business (Vol. 24, January 14, 2008, No. 2, pp. 32)*

Pub: Crain Communications, Inc.

Ed: Laura Koss-Feder. **Description:** In a rush to expand capacity in New York City, particularly lower Manhattan, the hotel industry plans to more than double the existing rooms in the area.

10705 ■ *"How He Thinks"* in *Canadian Business (Vol. 80, Winter 2007, No. 24, pp. 78)*

Pub: Rogers Media

Ed: Roger Martin. **Description:** Isadore Sharp sought to combine the best of the small hotel with the best of the large hotel so that he could provide his guests with the sense of intimacy and personalized service while also bringing a wide array of amenities. Sharp decreed that there would be no customer service department at his hotel but every member of the staff are in charge of customer service.

10706 ■ *How to Open a Financially Successful Bed & Breakfast or Small Hotel*

Pub: Atlantic Publishing Company

Ed: Lora Arduser; Douglas R. Brow. **Released:** May 1, 2004. **Price:** $39.95. **Description:** Handbook with CD ROM demonstrates ways to set up, operate and manage a financially successful bed-and-breakfast or small hotel.

10707 ■ *How to Open and Operate a Bed & Breakfast, 8th Edition*

Pub: Globe Pequot Press

Ed: Jan Stankus. **Released:** January 1, 2007 (paperback). **Price:** $18.95 (paperback). **Description:** Handbook outlines how to set up and run a bed and breakfast, whether using a spare room of a home or a small inn.

10708 ■ *How to Start and Operate Your Own Bed-and-Breakfast: Down-To-Earth Advice from an Award-Winning B&B Owner*

Pub: Owl Books

Ed: Martha W. Murphy. **Released:** May 15, 1994. **Price:** $18.00. **Description:** Bed and breakfast owner shares tip for running a successful business.

10709 ■ *"The Idea That Saved My Company"* in *Inc. (October 2007, pp. 42)*

Pub: Gruner & Jahr USA Publishing

Description: Profile of Chip Conley, founder of seventeen boutique hotels in the San Francisco, California Bay Area. Conley learned to overcome depression and regain his entrepreneurial inspiration, which in turn saved his company. Abraham Maslow, author of 'Toward of Psychology of Being' promoted Conley to write his own book, 'Peak: How Great Companies Get Their Mojo From Maslow'.

10710 ■ *"Increased Competition Prompts Detroit Hotels to Make Upgrades"* in *Crain's Detroit Business (Vol. 24, March 31, 2008, No. 13, pp. 1)*

Pub: Crain Communications, Inc.

Ed: Daniel Duggan. **Description:** Five Detroit hotels have recently undergone upgrades or are preparing for major construction projects due to a more competitive hospitality market in the city.

10711 ■ *"Inland Snaps Up Rival REITs"* in *Crain's Chicago Business (Vol. 31, November 17, 2008, No. 46, pp. 3)*

Pub: Crain Communications, Inc.

Ed: Alby Gallun. **Description:** Discusses Inland American Real Estate Trust Inc., a real estate investment trust that is napping up depressed shares of publicly traded competitors, a possible first step toward taking over these companies; however, with hotel and retail properties accounting for approximately 70 percent of its portfolio, the company could soon face its own difficulties.

10712 ■ *"Inn at Saratoga Owners Buy Caribbean Hotel"* in *Business Review, Albany New York (Vol. 34, November 2, 2007, No. 31, pp. 3)*

Pub: American City Business Journals, Inc.

Ed: Robin K. Cooper. **Description:** Bob Israel, owner of the Inn at Saratoga in Saratoga Springs, New York, made a $3 million to $4 million acquisition of the 22-room Mafolie Hotel and Restaurant in the Island of St. Thomas in the Caribbean. This is Israel's first real estate venture out of Saratoga Springs.

10713 ■ *INNside Scoop: Everything You Ever Wanted to Know About Bed & Breakfast Inns*

Pub: The B&B and Country Inn Marketplace

Ed: Maxine Pinson. **Released:** December 2002. **Description:** Guide for running a successful bread and breakfast inn.

10714 ■ *"Kent Officials Seek Further KSU, City Unity" in Crain's Cleveland Business (Vol. 28, December 3, 2007, No. 48, pp. 3)*

Pub: Crain Communications, Inc.

Ed: Jay Miller. **Description:** Kent State University and Portage County are searching for a developer who will use a three-acre parcel to bring new life to the city's sagging downtown and create an area that will better link the town and the Kent State campus. The project will include a hotel and conference center as well as retail and restaurant space.

10715 ■ *"The Lap of Eco-Luxury" in Entrepreneur (Vol. 37, August 2009, No. 8, pp. 38)*

Pub: Entrepreneur Media, Inc.

Ed: Dina Mishev. **Description:** Founder Rob DesLauriers of the Terra Resort Group says that the natural world has taken very good care of him and that he wants to do his part to take care of it. The mattresses that their hotel uses are made from recycled steel springs and their TVs are Energy Star-approved. Their linens are made from organically grown cottons and their walls use by-products from coal burning.

10716 ■ *"Laterooms and Octopus Travel Top Greenlight's Integrated Search Report for the Hotel Sector" in Internet Wire (October 23, 2009)*

Pub: Comtex News Network, Inc.

Description: According to a research report conducted by Greenlight, the UK's leading independent Internet search marketing agency, the most visible hotel websites in natural search during June 2009 are premierinn.com, booking.com and laterooms. com; OctopusTravel.com generated the greatest share of the paid search section with 21 percent visibility. The report is focused on the hotel sector and covers the second quarter of 2009. Statistical data included.

10717 ■ *"Latest Falls, Ontario Hotel Will Be 25-Story Westin" in Business First Buffalo (October 19, 2007, pp. 1)*

Pub: American City Business Journals, Inc.

Ed: James Fink. **Description:** Niagara Falls, Ontario-based Canadian Niagara Hotels has announced the construction of a Westin Hotel on Robinson Street that is 25-stories high and has 518 suites starting in 2008. The scope of the $120 million construction project is expected to be completed in 2010.

10718 ■ *"Leave It Behind; Novel Packing Strategy" in Crain's Chicago Business (Vol. 31, April 21, 2008, No. 16, pp. 32)*

Pub: Crain Communications, Inc.

Ed: Sarah A. Klein. **Description:** Patrick Brady who investigates possible violations of the Foreign Corrupt Practices Act has a novel approach when traveling to frequent destinations which allows him to travel with only a carry-on piece of luggage: he leaves suits at dry cleaners in the places he visits most often and since he mainly stays at the same hotels, he also leaves sets of workout clothes and running shoes with hotel staff.

10719 ■ *"Legacy Hotels Looks for a Buyer" in Globe & Mail (March 2, 2007, pp. B3)*

Pub: CTVglobemedia Publishing Inc.

Ed: Elizabeth Church. **Description:** Legacy Hotels Real Estate Investment Trust, which has a portfolio of 25 properties, plans to sell its businesses. The shares of the real estate investment trust climbed $13.21, as the sales news was delivered.

10720 ■ *"Like a Business Militia" in Crain's Detroit Business (Vol. 25,*

Pub: Crain Communications Inc. - Detroit

Ed: Daniel Duggan. **Description:** Hotel executives are forming hotel committees and associations in Southeastern Michigan in the hopes of drawing more visitors to the region. Meetings are encouraging the use of promoting specific regions in ways that will secure multi-hotel events.

10721 ■ *"Local Hotels Brace for Downturn" in Crain's Chicago Business (Vol. 31, March 31,*

2008, No. 13, pp. 3)

Pub: Crain Communications, Inc.

Ed: Bob Tita. **Description:** Chicago hotels are seeing a noticeable drop in business-related guests so far this year due to a slumping national economy, tighter corporate expense budgets and higher airfares.

10722 ■ *Lodging Magazine*

Pub: American Hotel and Lodging Association

Contact: Joseph A. McInerney, President

E-mail: joe@ahla.com

URL(s): www.lodgingmagazine.comwww.ahla.com, www.lodgingmagazine.com/ME2/Default.asp. **Ed:** Len Vermillion, Philip Hayward. **Released:** Monthly; September. **Price:** Free for lodging. **Publication includes:** List of about 4,000 suppliers to the hotel industry. **Entries include:** Company name, address, phone, name of principal executive, list of products or services. **Arrangement:** Classified by product or service. **Indexes:** Alphabetical listing, categorical listings.

10723 ■ *"Loop Hotel Plan Locks Up Funding" in Crain's Chicago Business (Vol. 31, March 24, 2008, No. 12, pp. 2)*

Pub: Crain Communications, Inc.

Ed: Eddie Baeb. **Description:** Signaling further expansion in the downtown hotel market, the secured $395 million in financing will fund a 610-room luxury hotel operated by J.W. Marriott, a more upscale brand in the Marriott line.

10724 ■ *"Luxe Hotels on a Budget" in Inc. (Volume 32, December 2010, No. 10, pp. 60)*

Pub: Inc. Magazine

Ed: Adam Baer. **Description:** Off & Away Website allows users to vie for discounted hotel rooms at more than 100 luxury properties. To compete, uses buy $1 bids and each time an individual bids the price of the room goes up by 10 cents.

10725 ■ *"Marriott Checks Out Hotel Prospect" in The Business Journal-Serving Metropolitan Kansas City (Vol. 27, November 14, 2008, No. 10)*

Pub: American City Business Journals, Inc.

Description: Marriott International Inc. is planning to operate a hotel in Kansas City, Missouri and may take over the Kansas City Marriot Downtown although other hotel operators are interested in bidding on the project.

10726 ■ *"Memphis Marriott Downtown Offers Wedding Reception Discounts to Soon-To-Be Newlyweds" in Benzinga.com (June 23, 2011)*

Pub: Benzinga.com

Ed: Benzinga Staff. **Description:** Memphis Marriott Downtown in Memphis, Tennessee is offering wedding reception discounts to couples planning their weddings.

10727 ■ *"More Details Emerge on Maersk Plan" in Charlotte Business Journal (Vol. 25, August 13, 2010, No. 21, pp. 1)*

Pub: Charlotte Business Journal

Ed: Will Boye. **Description:** Children Klen Properties has announced the details of its redevelopment plan for a property in Charlotte, North Carolina. The plan includes office and retail space and residential units. The construction of a hotel has also been proposed.

10728 ■ *"New Year's Resolutions: How Three Companies Came Up With Their 2008 Growth Strategies" in Inc. (January 2008, pp. 47-49)*

Pub: Gruner & Jahr USA Publishing

Ed: Martha C. White. **Description:** Three companies share 2008 growth strategies; companies include a candle company, a voice mail and text messaging marketer, and hotel supplier of soap and shampoo.

10729 ■ *"No Rooms for the Inn In This High-Rise" in Chicago Tribune (October 4, 2008)*

Pub: McClatchy-Tribune Information Services

Ed: Ameet Sachdev; Jim Kirk. **Description:** Construction has stalled for several hotel expansion projects due to the economy which has caused a decline in occupancy and little growth in average daily

room rates in downtown Chicago because consumers and businesses are becoming more cautious in the amount of money they spend on travel.

10730 ■ *"Not Enough Room" in Austin Business JournalInc. (Vol. 29, November 13, 2009, No. 36, pp. A1)*

Pub: American City Business Journals

Ed: Jacob Dirr. **Description:** Hotel and convention business in downtown Austin, Texas lost nearly $5.3 million when Dell Inc. relocated its annual convention to Las Vegas. However, lack of capital caused the postponement of various hotel projects which need to be finished in order to attract well-attended conventions. Makeover projects on Austin's Waller Creek and Sixth Street are discussed.

10731 ■ *"O'Loughlin Cuts $6 Million for Chesterfield Doubletree" in Saint Louis Business Journal (Vol. 32, September 2, 2011, No. 1, pp. 1)*

Pub: Saint Louis Business Journal

Ed: Angela Mueller. **Description:** Lodging Hospitality Management (LHM) acquired the Doubletree Hotel and Conference Center in Chesterfield, Missouri and added it as the 18th hotel in its portfolio. LHM chairman and CEO Bob O'Loughlin plans to invest nearly $15 million in the hotel, including $9 for renovation.

10732 ■ *"On the Green: Sheila Johnson Adds $35 Million Golf Resort To Her Expanding Portfolio" in Black Enterprise (January 2008)*

Pub: Earl G. Graves Publishing Co. Inc.

Ed: Donna M. Owens. **Description:** Profile of Sheila Johnson, CEO of Salamander Hospitality LLC, made history when she purchased the Innisbrook Resort and Golf Club, making her the first African American woman to own this type of property. The resort includes four championship golf courses, six swimming pools, four restaurants, eleven tennis courts, three conference halls, and a nature preserve.

10733 ■ *"Out With the Old? City Officials Investigating Options for New Hopkins Hotel" in Crain's Cleveland Business (October 22, 2007)*

Pub: Crain Communications, Inc.

Ed: Jay Miller. **Description:** Cleveland officials have begun talks that could lead to a new hotel which would replace the aging, nine-story Sheraton Cleveland Hopkins Hotel at Cleveland Hopkins International Airport.

10734 ■ *"Plan Your Next Event at Newport News Marriott at City Center" in Benzinga.com (July 29, 2011)*

Pub: Benzinga.com

Ed: Benzinga Staff. **Description:** Newport News Marriott at City Center is promoting itself as the premier venue for business meetings, conventions and weddings.

10735 ■ *"Plan Your Wedding with Cleveland Airport Marriott's Certified Event Planners" in Benzinga.com (February 2, 2011)*

Pub: Benzinga.com

Ed: Benzinga Staff. **Description:** Cleveland's Airport Marriott makes wedding planning easy with its venue spaces and a full team of wedding planners.

10736 ■ *"Plans for $160M Condo Resort in Wisconsin Dells Moves Forward" in Commercial Property News (March 18, 2008)*

Pub: Nielsen Company

Description: Plans for the Grand Cambrian Resort in the Wisconsin Dells is discussed. The luxury condominium resort will include condos, townhomes, and condo-hotel style residences, two water parts, meeting space and indoor entertainment space, as well as a spa, four restaurants and retail offerings.

10737 ■ *"Portland's Hilton For Sale" in Business Journal Portland (Vol. 27, October 22, 2010, No. 34, pp. 1)*

Pub: Portland Business Journal

Ed: Wendy Culverwell. **Description:** Hilton Portland & Executive Tower, Portland's biggest hotel, is being sold by Cornerstone Real Estate Advisers LLC. Cornerstone hopes to close the deal for the 782-room complex by the end of 2010. Cornerstone contracted Jones Lang LaSalle to manage the sale, but terms to the deal are not available.

10738 ■ *"Pre-Certified LEED Hotel Prototype Reduces Energy Use, Conserves Water" in Contractor (Vol. 57, January 2010, No. 1, pp. 3)*
Pub: Penton Media, Inc.
Ed: Candace Roulo. **Description:** Marriott International Inc.'s LEED pre-certified prototype hotel will reduce a hotel's energy and water consumption by 25 percent and save owners approximately $100,000. Their Courtyard Settler's Ridge in Pittsburgh will be the first hotel built based on the prototype.

10739 ■ *"'Pre-Sale' for Planned Could Mich Tower" in Crain's Chicago Business (Vol. 31, March 24, 2008, No. 12, pp. 14)*
Pub: Crain Communications, Inc.
Ed: Eddie Baeb. **Description:** Condominium developer William Warman is planning to build a mixed-use tower at 300 North Michigan Avenue which would include a hotel, retail space, apartments and a parking garage. Mr. Warman is looking for investors to buy part or all of the space in order to make it easier to land financing.

10740 ■ *"Prominent Hispanic Businessman Signs with Choice Hotels" in Hispanic Business (March 2008, pp. 36)*
Pub: Hispanic Business
Ed: Melinda Burns. **Description:** Profile of John C. Lopez, who has signed an agreement with Choice Hotels International to build five new Cambria Suites in the U.S.; cost of the project will total $14 million.

10741 ■ *"Prominent Hispanic Businessman Signs With Choice Hotels" in Hispanic Business (Vol. 30, March 2008, No. 3, pp. 36)*
Pub: Hispanic Business
Ed: Melinda Burns. **Description:** Chairman of the board of Lopez Food Inc., John C. Lopez signs the agreement with Choice Hotels International to build five new Cambria suites in the USA. This is his first hotel venture and also the first Hispanic franchisee to enter into business with Choice Hotels.

10742 ■ *"Real Opportunities: Don't Let Mortgage Mayhem Steer You Away From Sound Investments" in Black Enterprise (December 2007)*
Pub: Earl G. Graves Publishing Co. Inc.
Ed: James A. Anderson. **Description:** Real estate investment trusts (REITs) that operate office buildings, industrial parks, shopping malls, hotels, hospitals, or other commercial properties may be a sound investment, despite the mortgage crisis facing the U.S. financial sector.

10743 ■ *Resort and Commercial Recreation--Membership Directory*
Pub: Resort and Commercial Recreation Association
Contact: Kari Bowman, President
E-mail: kari.bowman@rcra.org
URL(s): www.rcra.org. **Released:** Annual; April. **Covers:** Approximately 600 professionals, educators, and students in the field of commercial recreation and leisure services. **Entries include:** personal name, address, phone, corporate or university affiliation, and title, e-mail. **Arrangement:** Geographical.

10744 ■ *"Restoring Grandeur" in Business Courier (Vol. 26, December 4, 2009, No. 32, pp. 1)*
Pub: American City Business Journals, Inc.
Ed: Dan Monk. **Description:** Eagle Realty Group intends to spend more than $10 to restore the historic 12-story Phelps apartment building in Lytle Park in Cincinnati. Its president, Mario San Marco, expressed the need to invest in the building in order to maintain operations. The building could be restored into a hotel catering to executives and consultants.

10745 ■ *"Revelations Derek Johnstone, Head Chef, Greywalls Hotel and Chez Roux" in Caterer & Hotelkeeper (October 28, 2011, No. 288)*
Pub: Reed Reference Publishing
Description: Profile of Derek Johnstone, head chef at Greywalls Hotel and Chez Roux and his love for catering.

10746 ■ *"Rise in Occupancy Rate Fuels Area Hotel Building Boom" in Crain's Detroit Business (Vol. 24, March 10, 2008, No. 10, pp. 14)*
Pub: Crain Communications, Inc.
Ed: Jonathan Eppley. **Description:** Due to a rise in the region's yearly occupancy rate, a number of new hotel construction and renovation projects are slated for the Detroit area.

10747 ■ *"Ritz Kapalua Sells 93 Suites for $176M to Fund Renovation" in Commercial Property News (March 17, 2008)*
Pub: Nielsen Company
Description: Ritz-Carlton, Kapalua in Lahaina, Hawaii sold ninety-three of its units in order to fund renovations of 463 rooms and suites along with construction of a new spa and fitness center, new and expanded restaurants and pools and an environmental education center for children.

10748 ■ *"Sales Gave W&S Record '07" in Business Courier (Vol. 24, March 14, 2008, No. 49, pp. 1)*
Pub: American City Business Journals, Inc.
Ed: Jon Newberry. **Description:** Western & Southern Financial Group was able to achieve a record $365 million in net income thanks in large part to the double-digit increases in profits by its W&S Agency Group field offices and non-insurance businesses. The sale of their Integrated Investment Services Subsidiary and shares in several Marriot hotels also added to the record profit.

10749 ■ *"Silverdome Bidders Bring New Proposals" in Crain's Detroit Business (Vol. 24, March 17, 2008, No. 11, pp. 23)*
Pub: Crain Communications, Inc.
Ed: Daniel Duggan. **Description:** Discusses the seven plans which have been proposed as part of the third round of bidding for the Pontiac Silverdome; proposals range from Global Baseball Inc., a baseball league that would pit a team from every country against one another, to an Indian casino, a musical 'hall of fame', a convention center, a horse track, a hotel and an indoor water park.

10750 ■ *So, You Want to Be an Innkeeper*
Pub: Chronicle Books LLC
Ed: JoAnn M. Bell; Susan Brown, Mary Davies; Pat Hardy. **Released:** March 2004. **Description:** Provides information for aspiring innkeepers, includes information on cottages, luxury properties, and spa services.

10751 ■ *"Son of Sandman: Can Tom Gaglardi Really Outdo His Old Man?" in Canadian Business (Vol. 80, Winter 2007, No. 24, pp. 106)*
Pub: Rogers Media
Ed: Calvin Leung. **Description:** Bob Gagliardi of Northland Properties started to learn about his family's business by working at a construction site at one of the high-rise buildings in downtown Vancouver. Gagliardi wants to expand their Moxie's restaurant chain and increase the market share of their Sandman hotel by 2018.

10752 ■ *Start and Run a Profitable Bed and Breakfast*
Pub: Self-Counsel Press Inc.
Ed: Monica Taylor, Richard Taylor. **Released:** October 1999. **Description:** Information for starting and running a successful bed and breakfast is presented.

10753 ■ *"Survey Says Commercial Real Estate Headed for Turbulence" in Commercial Property News (March 17, 2008)*
Pub: Nielsen Company
Description: Commercial real estate sector is declining due to the sluggish U.S. economy. According to a recent survey, national office, retail and hospitality markets are also on the decline.

10754 ■ *"Tom Gaglardi" in Canadian Business (Vol. 82, April 27, 2009, No. 7, pp. 56)*
Pub: Rogers Media
Ed: Calvin Leung. **Description:** Northland Properties Corporation president Tom Gaglardi believes that their business model of keeping much of operations

in-house allows the firm to crate assets at a lesser price while commanding higher margins than their competitors. He believes that it is an ideal time to invest in the hospitality industry because of opportunities to purchase hospitality properties at low prices.

10755 ■ *"Tourism Bureau Seeks Hotel Tax Hike" in Baltimore Business Journal (Vol. 27, December 18, 2009, No. 32, pp. 1)*
Pub: American City Business Journals
Ed: Rachel Bernstein. **Description:** Baltimore, Maryland's tourism agency, Visit Baltimore, has proposed a new hotel tax that could produce $2 million annually for its marketing budget, fund improvements to the city's 30-year-old convention center and help it compete for World Cup soccer games. Baltimore hotel leaders discuss the new tax.

10756 ■ *"Tourism Push Rising in Fall" in Philadelphia Business Journal (Vol. 30, August 26, 2011, No. 28, pp. 1)*
Pub: American City Business Journals Inc.
Ed: Peter Van Allen. **Description:** Philadelphia is offering events for tourists this fall despite massive cuts for tourism promotion. Governor Tim Corbet slashed $5.5 million in funding for the state's tourism-promotion agencies which received $32 million in 2009. The agencies were forced to cooperate and fend for themselves using the hotel taxes that sustain them.

10757 ■ *"Travel Tears" in Crain's Chicago Business (Vol. 31, November 17, 2008, No. 46, pp. 3)*
Pub: Crain Communications, Inc.
Ed: Bob Tita. **Description:** Hotels, restaurants and conventions are seeing a decline in profits due to corporate travel cutbacks and the sagging economy. City and state revenues derived from taxes on tourism-related industries are also suffering.

10758 ■ *"Unfilled Hotels Go All Out for Business Meetings" in Crain's Detroit Business (Vol. 25, June 8, 2009, No. 23, pp. 9)*
Pub: Crain Communications Inc. - Detroit
Ed: Daniel Duggan. **Description:** Hotels in Michigan are offering discounts to companies holding business meetings at their properties. Details of competition and plans are included.

10759 ■ *"'Unknown' Muted Grand Prix Impact" in Boston Business Journal (Vol. 29, September 9, 2011, No. 18, pp. 3)*
Pub: American City Business Journals Inc.
Ed: Alexander Jackson. **Description:** Baltimore Grand Prix caught restaurateurs, hoteliers and street vendors in Baltimore, Maryland unprepared for the thousands of race fans who attended the inaugural event over Labor Day weekend. The race popularity is relatively unknown to them and some felt they were not able to make as much money as they had hoped.

10760 ■ *Upstart Guide to Owning and Managing a Bed and Breakfast*
Pub: Kaplan Publishing
Ed: Lisa Angowski Rogak. **Released:** November 1, 1994. **Description:** Guide for running a profitable bed and breakfast.

10761 ■ *"Vegas in the D; Local Architects Collaborate On MGM Grand" in Crain's Detroit Business (Vol. 23, October 1, 2007, No. 40, pp. 1)*
Pub: Crain Communications Inc. - Detroit
Ed: Daniel Duggan. **Description:** Local Detroit architects, Smith Group and Hamilton Anderson Associates are among the contractors vying for subcontracted architecture, construction and consulting contracts for the new MGM Grand Detroit casino and hotel.

10762 ■ *"Vernon Revamp" in Business Courier (Vol. 26, October 9, 2009, No. 24, pp. 1)*
Pub: American City Business Journals, Inc.
Ed: Dan Monk. **Description:** Al Neyer Inc. will redevelop the Vernon Manor Hotel as an office building for the Cincinnati Children's Hospital Medical Center. The project will cost $35 million and would

generate a new investment vehicle for black investors who plan to raise $2.7 million in private offerings to claim majority ownership of the property after its renovations.

10763 ■ "Wal-Mart Doesn't Sell Council' in The Business Journal-Serving Metropolitan Kansas City (Vol. 26, July 4, 2008, No. 43, pp. 1)
Pub: American City Business Journals, Inc.
Ed: Steve Vockrodt. **Description:** Wal-Mart Stores Inc. announced that it will move the location of its annual convention from Kansas City, Missouri to Orlando, Florida. The change of venue came after Rick Hughes, Kansas City Convention and Visitors Association president rejected Wal-Mart's proposal to subsidize a new hotel in the downtown area that is needed for the event.

STATISTICAL SOURCES

10764 ■ RMA Annual Statement Studies
Pub: Risk Management Association
Contact: Kevin M. Blakey, President
Released: Annual. **Price:** $175.00 2006-07 edition, $105.00. **Description:** Contains composite balance sheets and income statements for more than 360 industries, including the accounting, auditing, and bookkeeping industries. Also contains five years of comparative historical data for discerning trends. Includes 16 commonly used ratios, computed for most of the size groupings for nearly every industry.

10765 ■ Standard & Poor's Industry Surveys
Pub: Standard & Poor's Corp.
Released: Annual. **Price:** $3633.00. **Description:** Two-volume book that examines the prospects for specific industries, including trucking. Also provides analyses of trends and problems, statistical tables and charts, and comparative company analyses.

TRADE PERIODICALS

10766 ■ Cornell Hoospitality Quarterly
Pub: Cornell University School of Hotel Administration
URL(s): cqx.sagepub.com. **Ed:** J. Bruce Tracey. **Released:** Quarterly **Price:** £311, Institutions combined print and electronic access; £305, Institutions print only; £98, Individuals print & online; £32, Single issue.

10767 ■ FIU Hospitality Review
Pub: Florida International University School of Hospitality Management
URL(s): www2.fiu.edu/~review/FIUREV.html. **Ed:** Prof. William G. O'Brien, Rocco M. Angelo. **Released:** Biennial **Price:** $40, Individuals; $60, Individuals libraries; $80, Elsewhere.

10768 ■ Hospitality Design
Pub: Nielsen Co.
Contact: Greg Farrar, President
URL(s): www.hdmag.com. **Released:** 10/yr. **Price:** $79, Individuals; $94, Canada; $139, Other countries by airmail.

10769 ■ Hospitality Law
Pub: LRP Publications
Released: Monthly. **Price:** $217 plus $22 s/h. **Description:** Discusses legal issues pertaining to the hospitality industry, using actual cases as illustration. Offers articles on liability, contract law, tax codes, and legal trends relevant to the lodging industry. Recurring features include interviews, book reviews, notices of publications available, and columns titled Trends and Observations, Test Your Knowledge, Security, Legal Briefs, Legal Basics, and Employee Management.

10770 ■ Hotel Business
Pub: ICD Publications
URL(s): www.hotelbusiness.com/hb/main.asp. **Ed:** Dennis Nessler. **Released:** Biweekly **Price:** $260, Individuals domestic; $315, Canada and Mexico; $695, Other countries; $395, Individuals digital.

10771 ■ Hotel & Motel Management
Contact: Jason Q. Freed, Senior Editor
E-mail: jfreed@questex.com
URL(s): www.hotelmanagement.net/hotel-management/hotel-management-archive. **Released:** 21/yr. **Price:** $58.85, Individuals; $81.40, Canada and Mexico; $143, Other countries; $75, Individuals additional airmail shipping.

10772 ■ Hotelier
Pub: Kostuch Publications Ltd.
URL(s): www.hoteliermagazine.com/. **Ed:** Rosanna Caira. **Released:** 8/yr. **Price:** $25, Canada; $30, Individuals U.S.; $40, Other countries.

10773 ■ HOTELS: The Magazine of the Worldwide Hotel Industry
Pub: Marketing & Technology Group Inc.
Contact: Mark Lefens, President
E-mail: mlefens@meatingplace.com
URL(s): www.hotelsmag.com/. **Released:** Monthly **Price:** Free.

10774 ■ Journal of Hospitality Marketing & Management
Pub: Routledge Journals Taylor & Francis Group
URL(s): www.tandf.co.uk/journals/titles/19368623.asp. **Released:** 8/yr. **Price:** $841, Institutions print + online; $757, Institutions online; $172, Individuals online; $191, Individuals print + online.

10775 ■ Lodging Magazine
Pub: American Hotel and Lodging Association
Contact: Joseph A. McInerney, President
E-mail: joe@ahla.com
URL(s): www.lodgingmagazine.comwww.ahla.com, www.lodgingmagazine.com/ME2/Default.asp. **Ed:** Len Vermillion, Philip Hayward. **Released:** Monthly; September. **Price:** Free for lodging. **Publication includes:** List of about 4,000 suppliers to the hotel industry. **Entries include:** Company name, address, phone, name of principal executive, list of products or services. **Arrangement:** Classified by product or service. **Indexes:** Alphabetical listing, categorical listings.

10776 ■ Los Cabos Magazine
Pub: Promociones Tyson S.A. de C.V. Tyson Promotions
URL(s): www.loscabosmagazine.com/. **Released:** Quarterly **Price:** $28.95, Individuals.

10777 ■ Newsline
Pub: Ontario Accommodation Association
Ed: Bruce M. Gravel, Editor. **Released:** Quarterly. **Price:** Included in membership. **Description:** Provides news of Association activities, government lobbying and regulatory changes.

VIDEOCASSETTES/ AUDIOCASSETTES

10778 ■ Inside Business Today
GPN Educational Media
1550 Executive Drive
Elgin, IL 60123
Ph: (402)472-2007
Free: 800-228-4630
Fax: (800)306-2330
Co. E-mail: askgpn@smarterville.com
URL: http://www.shopgpn.com
Released: 1989. **Description:** Leaders in business and industry tell their success stories in this extensive series. **Availability:** VHS; 3/4 U.

TRADE SHOWS AND CONVENTIONS

10779 ■ Annual Hotel, Motel, and Restaurant Supply Show of the Southeast
Leisure Time Unlimited, Inc.
708 Main St.
Myrtle Beach, SC 29577
Ph: (843)448-9483
Free: 800-261-5591

Fax: (843)626-1513
Co. E-mail: ltushows@sc.rr.com
URL: http://www.leisuretimeunlimited.com/
Contact: Brooke P. Baker, Show Manager
E-mail: dickensshow@sc.rr.com
URL(s): www.hmrsss.com. **Frequency:** Annual. **Audience:** Hospitality industry, managers, and buyers. **Principal Exhibits:** Carpeting, furniture, coffee makers, produce companies, wine and beer and food companies, and services to motels, hotels, and restaurants. **Dates and Locations:** , Convention Center. **Telecommunication Services:** hmrss@sc.rr.com.

10780 ■ ApEx
Canadian Restaurant and Foodservices Association (CRFA)
316 Bloor St. W
Toronto, ON, Canada M5S 1W5
Ph: (416)923-8416
Free: 800-387-5649
Fax: (416)923-1450
Co. E-mail: info@crfa.ca
URL: http://www.crfa.ca
Contact: Garth Whyte, President
URL(s): www.crfa.ca/tradeshows/apex. **Audience:** Trade. **Principal Exhibits:** Products and services for the restaurant and hospitality industry, as well as institutions, convenience stores, delis and bakeries. **Telecommunication Services:** escanlan@crfa.ca.

10781 ■ Arkansas Hospitality Association Convention & Exhibition
Arkansas Hospitality Association
603 S. Pulaski, PO Box 3866
Little Rock, AR 72203-3866
Ph: (501)376-2323
Free: 800-472-5022
Fax: (501)376-6517
Co. E-mail: aha@arhospitality.org
URL: http://www.arhospitality.org
Contact: Montine McNulty, Executive Director
E-mail: montine@arhospitality.org
URL(s): www.arhospitality.org/events/trade-show/. **Frequency:** Semiannual. **Audience:** Restaurant owners, motel and hotel owners and operators, and resort and recreational attraction trade professionals. **Principal Exhibits:** Food products, furniture, fixtures for hotels and restaurants, and telephones. **Telecommunication Services:** holly@arhospitality.org.

10782 ■ CENTREX Hotel & Restaurant Tradeshow
Manitoba Hotel Association
1534 Gamble Pl., Ste. 200
Winnipeg, MB, Canada R3T 1N6
Ph: (204)942-0671
Free: 888-859-9976
Fax: (204)942-6719
Co. E-mail: jbaker@manitobahotelassociation.ca
URL: http://www.manitobahotelassociation.ca
URL(s): www.centrex.ca. **Price:** $10, Onsite registered, members; $5, Pre-registered, non-members; $10, Onsite registered, non-members. **Frequency:** Annual. **Audience:** Representatives from hotels, restaurants, motels, bars, cabarets. **Principal Exhibits:** Hotel and restaurant food equipment, supplies, and services. **Dates and Locations:** , Convention Centre.

10783 ■ Florida International Restaurant & Hotel Expo
Florida International Medical Expo Inc.
3348 17th St.
Sarasota, FL 34235
Ph: (941)366-2554
Fax: (941)366-9861
Co. E-mail: info@fimeshow.com
URL: http://www.fimeshow.com
Frequency: Annual. **Audience:** Restaurant managers and owner/operators; hotel and motel managers and food service managers; and related food service professionals. **Principal Exhibits:** Restaurant, hotel, motel, leisure, hospitality, and bakery industries equipment, supplies, and services, including foods and beverages, furniture, paper goods and disposables, chemicals, computers, amenities, advertising,

and trade publications. **Dates and Locations:** , Coconut Grove Convention Center. **Telecommunication Services:** fimee@aol.com.

10784 ■ HSMAI - Affordable Meetings West
Hospitality Sales and Marketing Association International (HSMAI)
1760 Old Meadow Rd., Ste. 500
McLean, VA 22102
Ph: (703)506-3280
Free: 877-643-3511
Fax: (703)506-3266
Co. E-mail: info@hsmai.org
URL: http://www.hsmai.org
Contact: Robert A. Gilbert, President
E-mail: bgilbert@hsmai.org
URL(s): events.jspargo.com/AMW09/public/enter.
aspx. **Frequency:** Annual. **Audience:** Trade professionals. **Principal Exhibits:** Equipment, supplies, and services for the hospitality and marketing industry. **Telecommunication Services:** affordable-meetings@jspargo.com.

10785 ■ IH/M & RS - International Hotel/Motel & Restaurant Show
American Hotel and Lodging Association (American Hotel & Motel Association)
1201 New York Ave. NW, Ste. 600
Washington, DC 20005-3931
Ph: (202)289-3100
Free: 800-752-4567
Fax: (202)289-3199
Co. E-mail: informationcenter@ahla.com
URL: http://www.ahla.com
Contact: Joseph A. McInerney, President
E-mail: joe@ahla.com
URL(s): www.ihmrs.com. **Frequency:** Annual. **Audience:** Representatives from mass feeding, lodging, and healthcare industries. **Principal Exhibits:** Products and services for lodging and food serving properties, including: technology, uniforms, linens and bedding, tabletop accessories, guest amenities and services, food and beverages, cleaning maintenance, food service equipment and supplies, franchising information, finance and management furnishings and fixtures, fitness equipment, and leisure and entertainment services. **Dates and Locations:** , Jacob K. Javits Convention Center. **Telecommunication Services:** ihmrs@glmshows.com.

10786 ■ National Restaurant Association Restaurant and Hotel-Motel Show
National Restaurant Association Convention Office
2055 L St., NW
Washington, DC 20036
Ph: (202)331-5900
URL: http://www.restaurant.org
Contact: Sally Smith, Chairman of the Board
URL(s): show.restaurant.org/NRA11/public/content.
aspx?id=813. **Frequency:** Annual. **Audience:** Restaurant operators and owners, hotel and motel managers, food service managers, purchasing agents, and related food service professionals. **Principal Exhibits:** Food service equipment, supplies, and services and food and beverage products for the hospitality industry. Includes international cuisine pavilion. **Dates and Locations:** , McCormick Place.

10787 ■ Ocean City Hotel, Motel, and Restaurant Association Spring Trade Exposition
Ocean City Hotel, Motel, and Restaurant Association
PO Box 340
Ocean City, MD 21843
Free: 800-626-2326
Co. E-mail: inquire@ocvisitor.com
URL: http://www.ocvisitor.com
URL(s): www.ocvisitor.com. **Price:** $10, Onsite. **Frequency:** Annual. **Audience:** Trade and buyers. **Principal Exhibits:** Food products, restaurant equipment, bedding, laundry supplies, televisions (commercial), media, and any trade related items. **Dates and Locations:** , Convention Center.

10788 ■ West Ex: The Rocky Mountain Regional Hospitality Exposition
Colorado Restaurant Association
430 E. 7th Ave.
Denver, CO 80203

Ph: (303)830-2972
Free: 800-522-2972
Fax: (303)830-2973
Co. E-mail: info@coloradorestaurant.com
URL: http://www.coloradorestaurant.com
Contact: Pete Meersman, President
E-mail: meersman@coloradorestaurant.com
URL(s): www.coloradorestaurant.com. **Frequency:** Annual. **Audience:** Food service and restaurant industry personnel. **Principal Exhibits:** Food service and lodging products, equipment, and services.

CONSULTANTS

10789 ■ Certified Housekeeping Consultants
115-01 Lefferts Blvd.
Jamaica, NY 11420-2488
Ph: (718)848-0200
Fax: (718)848-0203
Co. E-mail: finehousekeeping@att.net
Contact: Alfred Fine, President
Scope: Housekeeping consulting services specializing in housekeeping operations, planning cost reduction, training linen inventory laundry, employee scheduling and budgeting. Serves the hotel, motel, and assisted living industries.

10790 ■ Cini-Little International Inc.
20251 Century Blvd., Ste. 375
Germantown, MD 20874
Ph: (301)528-9700
Fax: (301)528-9711
Co. E-mail: info@cinilittle.com
URL: http://www.cinilittle.com
Contact: James H. Little, Chief Executive Officer
E-mail: jlittle@cinilittle.com
Scope: Offers a full range of independent management and design consulting services in all aspects of food service to industries such as hospitality, business, and health care. Services include feasibility studies and or operations analyses, food service programs and concepts, operational training programs and manuals, food service contractor selection, contract documents, review of contractor submittal and site inspections. Offers consulting in materials management, materials handling, vertical horizontal transport elevator escalator moving sidewalks to all segments of the construction, hospitality, health-care and related industries. **Founded:** 1968.

10791 ■ Clevenger Associates
11803 101st Avenue Ct. E, Ste. 203
Puyallup, WA 98373-3473
Ph: (253)841-7811
Fax: (253)841-7435
Co. E-mail: info@clevengerassoc.com
URL: http://www.clevengerassoc.com
Contact: Anthony A. Clevenger, President
E-mail: tony@clevengerassoc.com
Scope: Offers food service and laundry/valet design and consulting. Will design new and remodeled space; specify equipment, and follow-up to ensure quality and likeness to specifications. Industries served: hotels, restaurants, clubhouses, health care, educational, institutional corrections, convention centers, business and industry. **Founded:** 1974.

10792 ■ Health Fitness Dynamics Inc.—HFD Spa
1012 N Ocean Blvd., Ste. 103
Pompano Beach, FL 33062
Ph: (954)942-0049
Fax: (954)941-0854
Co. E-mail: hfd@hfdspa.com
URL: http://www.hfdspa.com
Contact: Patricia A. Monteson, Owner Founder
E-mail: pattymonteson@hfdspa.com
Scope: Offers spa consulting services in the following areas: program development, facility planning, feasibility and market studies, staffing requirements, product and equipment selection, coordinating of support departments, systems of operation, personnel, and on-going management. Industries served: hospitality, hotels and resorts, and health spas. **Founded:** 1983. **Publications:** "Spa News & Views: If The Spa Will Not Help Sell Rooms, Do Not Add A Spa," Spa Management, Mar, 2006; "Thinking of Jumping on the Spa Bandwagon Look Before You Leap"; "Spa

Savvy-Best Practices for Hiring, Training & Retaining Your Staff". **Seminars:** Management Workshop; Managing a Revenue Generating Spa within a Resort; The Health Spa - Another Marketable and Complementary Dimension of a Resort; Planning and Managing a Health Spa in a Resort.

10793 ■ Hostline
School of Hotel Administration Library
Cornell University
Ithaca, NY 14853-6902
Ph: (607)255-9393
Fax: (607)255-0021
Co. E-mail: hostline@cornell.edu
URL: http://www.nestlelib.cornell.edu/hostline
Contact: Mihoko Hosoi, Manager
Scope: Provider of reference service for the hospitality industry in the areas such as hotel management, franchising and management contracts, tourism and travel, and food and beverage management. **Telecommunication Services:** hotelref@cornell.edu.

10794 ■ Isaksen Foodservice Consultants Inc.
11228 Georgia Ave.
Silver Spring, MD 20902-2712
Ph: (301)933-2100
Fax: (301)933-2101
Co. E-mail: isaksen@erols.com
Contact: Ron Isaksen, Manager
Scope: Consultants to architects, developers, and owners regarding layout and design of food service equipment for health care, elder care, country clubs, bakeries, hotels, hospitals, restaurants, nursing homes, schools, prisons and other institutions, as well as government agencies. Also space planning, lighting and acoustic design, laundry layout and design and food service area construction and installation supervision services. **Founded:** 1982. **Publications:** "Contemporary Long Term Care," Oct, 1997; "Pantries Take on Non-Institutional Look"; "Hospitality Profiles," Nov, 1994; "Interview: Ron Isak sen of Isak sen Food services Strategies"; "Food service Equipment and Supplies Specialist," Sep, 1991; "Winning Kitchens Show Their Metal"; "Food service Equipment and Supplies Specialist," Jun, 1991; "Isak sen, Others Devote Time to Charity," Restaurants and Institutions, Feb, 1991; "Nothing Fishy About Proper Seafood Refrigeration," Food service Equipment and Supplies Specialist, Oct, 1990; "Seven Great Kitchen Design Ideas". **Seminars:** Recipe for Success: New Concepts in Nutrition for the Aging; Integration of Food Delivery Systems with Decentralized Cluster Concepts.

10795 ■ Nisonger Associates Inc.
202 Elm St.
Milford, OH 45150-1185
Ph: (513)248-1441
Fax: (513)248-1445
Co. E-mail: info@nisongerassoc.com
URL: http://www.nisongerassoc.com
Contact: Harry T. Nisonger, Principal
E-mail: nisongerai@aol.com
Scope: Food service consultants offering management and design services to the food service, lodging, health care, and leisure time industries, as well as to schools, private clubs and other institutions, and government agencies. Not only will the firm evaluate and prescribe, but it will take the project through the implementation process. Services include financial planning, menu development, facilities design, operations assessment, programming, systems studies, corporate valuations, contract and lease negotiations, consumer surveys, market and feasibility studies, prototype planning, and expert witness services. Construction division formed to provide clients with design or build services for fast track projects with cost efficiencies. **Founded:** 1980.

10796 ■ Tarbutton Associates Inc.
1072 Laskin Rd.
Virginia Beach, VA 23451-6364
Ph: (757)422-2020
Contact: Kenton L. Tarbutton, President
Scope: A consulting firm specializing in franchise consulting worldwide for expert witness court and legislative testimony as well as the sale or acquisition of franchising parent companies. **Founded:** 1962.

Publications: "Franchising: The How-To Book," Prentice-Hall Inc. **Seminars:** 21st Century Management Techniques; Developing Your Business for Franchising; Developing People into Producers; The Franchising Possibilities.

FRANCHISES AND BUSINESS OPPORTUNITIES

10797 ■ Aloha Hotels and Resorts
PO Box 3347
Princeville, HI 96722
Ph: (808)826-6244
URL: http://www.franchisedirectory.ca
Description: Provides independent Inn, Hotel and Resort owners with the ability to obtain new sources of revenue. Membership in the Aloha Hotels and Resort chain brings a wide variety of benefits to the property owner. Aloha Hotel and Resort president has over 25 years of enhancing financial performance for 3 major hotel and resort chains. **Equity Capital Needed:** $1,000-$200,000 total investment; $1,000-$200,000 required cash liquidity. **Training:** Provides training an support programs. There is one assigned management team member to your property that is available to answer any questions and take you through the steps to become an Aloha Hotel and Resort member. There are many training and support areas that are included in your membership.

10798 ■ Baymont Inn & Suites
Baymont Franchise Systems
22 Sylvan Way
Parsippany, NJ 07054
Free: 800-758-8999
Fax: (973)753-8724
Description: Hotel chain. **No. of Franchise Units:** 256. **Founded:** 1974. **Franchised:** 1987. **Equity Capital Needed:** $179,370-$5,787,700 total investment. **Franchise Fee:** $26,000-$27,000. **Royalty Fee:** 5%. **Financial Assistance:** Limited in-house and third party financing available. **Training:** Provides 5 days at headquarters, 2 days at franchisee's location, regional workshops 1-3 days, customized property training with ongoing support.

10799 ■ Choice Hotels Canada Inc.
5090 Explorer Dr., Ste. 500
Mississauga, ON, Canada L4W 4T9
Ph: (905)206-7316
Fax: (905)206-7318
Co. E-mail: franchising@choicehotels.ca
URL: http://www.choicehotels.ca
Description: Hotel chain in which applicants must have their own hotel asset or be prepared to buy or build. Choice provides marketing, reservation, sales and purchasing support. **No. of Franchise Units:** 303. **Franchised:** 1993. **Equity Capital Needed:** $1,000,000 plus start-up capital required; $3,000,000 plus total investment. **Franchise Fee:** $25,000-$5,000. **Training:** Yes.

10800 ■ Choice Hotels International
10750 Columbia Pike
Silver Spring, MD 20901
Free: 800-547-0007
Description: Hotel/motel franchise. Economy to mid-price to up-scale. **No. of Franchise Units:** 5,024. **No. of Company-Owned Units:** 3. **Founded:** 1939.. **Franchised:** 1972. **Equity Capital Needed:** $89,000-$14,636,550. **Franchise Fee:** $10,000-$60,000. **Royalty Fee:** Varies. **Financial Assistance:** Third party financing available. **Training:** Provides 1 week at headquarters and ongoing regional training.

10801 ■ Country Inns & Suites by Carlson
PO Box 59159
Minneapolis, MN 55459-8205
Ph: (763)212-2525
Free: 800-336-3301
Description: Mid-priced lodging. **No. of Franchise Units:** 442. **No. of Company-Owned Units:** 8. **Founded:** 1987.. **Franchised:** 1987. **Equity Capital Needed:** $4,600,420-$7,114,620. **Franchise Fee:** $45,000. **Royalty Fee:** 4.5%. **Training:** Provides 1 week training at headquarters, 1 week onsite and ongoing support.

10802 ■ Days Inn Worldwide, Inc.
Wyndham Hotel Group
22 Sylvan Way
Parsippany, NJ 07054
Free: 888-222-7484
Description: Days Inn Worldwide is the licensor of Days Inn guest lodging facilities. **No. of Franchise Units:** 1,624. **Founded:** 1970.. **Franchised:** 1972. **Equity Capital Needed:** $187,370-$6,992,935 total investment. **Franchise Fee:** $36,000-$37,500. **Royalty Fee:** 5.5%. **Financial Assistance:** Limited in-house and third party financing available. **Training:** Available 5 days at headquarters, 2 days at franchisee's location, and 1-3 day workshops with ongoing support.

10803 ■ Howard Johnson
Wyndham Hotel Group
22 Sylvan Way
Parsippany, NJ 07054
Free: 888-222-7484
Description: Licensor of Howard Johnson guest lodging facilities. **No. of Franchise Units:** 500+. **Founded:** 1954.. **Franchised:** 1954. **Equity Capital Needed:** Varies depending upon project. **Franchise Fee:** $10,000 minimum; $100/room. **Training:** Yes.

10804 ■ Howard Johnson Canada Franchise Systems Limited
2904 South Sheridan Way, Ste. 101
Oakville, ON, Canada L6J 7L7
Ph: (905)829-4002
Free: 800-249-4656
Fax: (905)390-2977
URL: http://www.howardjohnson.ca
Description: Master franchisor in Canada for Howard Johnson Plaza Hotels, Hotels, Inns and Express Inns. Howard Johnson is recognized as the leading mid-market brand for leisure and business travel. Services include advertising/marketing, asset management services, franchise services and support, Preferred Alliance Group purchasing services, operations consulting and support, and quality assurance, training. **No. of Franchise Units:** 67. **Founded:** 1972.. **Franchised:** 1991. **Equity Capital Needed:** $350,000. **Franchise Fee:** $35,000 or $350,000/room. **Training:** Yes.

10805 ■ Knights Inn
Wyndham Hotel Group
22 Sylvan Way
Parsippany, NJ 07054
Ph: (888)222-7484
Free: 888-222-7484
Description: Budget lodging. **No. of Franchise Units:** 353. **Founded:** 1972.. **Franchised:** 1991. **Equity Capital Needed:** $119,200-$6,948,400. **Franchise Fee:** $7,000. **Royalty Fee:** Varies. **Training:** Provides 5 days training at headquarters, 2 days at franchisee's location, regional workshops, property training and ongoing support.

10806 ■ Knights Inn Canada Franchise Systems Limited
2904 South Sheridan Way, Ste 101
Oakville, ON, Canada L6J 7L7
Ph: (905)829-4002
Free: 800-248-4656
Fax: (905)829-4716
URL: http://www.knightsinn.ca
Description: Budget lodging brand appealing to value conscious frequent business and leisure/family travel. **No. of Franchise Units:** 24. **Founded:** 1999.. **Franchised:** 2000. **Equity Capital Needed:** $250,000. **Franchise Fee:** $5,000. **Training:** Provides training and ongoing support.

10807 ■ La Quinta Canada Inc.
Franchise Div.
135 Queens Plate Dr., Ste. 410
TOR, ON, Canada M9W 6V1
Free: 800-248-4656
Co. E-mail: info@CanadianFranchiseDirectory.ca
URL: http://www.canadianfranchisedirectory.ca
Description: La Quinta brand is a high quality mid-priced, limited service product which appeals to both the business and leisure traveler and is franchised under two tiers: La Quinta Inn- A mid market, limited service property with the business and leisure traveler

in mind - comfortable guest rooms with coffee maker, dataport phones, meeting facilities, swimming pool, complimentary continental breakfast. La Quinta Inn & Suites- All the benefits of a La Quinta Inn plus - two room suites with microwave, refrigerator, extra dataports, fitness center, guest laundry and more. La Quinta properties are multi level configurations with a minimum of 100 to 150 units per location. **Equity Capital Needed:** $750,000-$1,500,000 total investment; $500,000 required cash liquidity. **Franchise Fee:** $500,000. **Training:** Services include Marketing/ Advertising services, operational and revenue management support, asset management services, franchise services and support, AFM Preferred Alliance purchasing services, operations consulting and support, quality assurance, and training.

10808 ■ Mainstay Suites
Choice Hotels International
10750 Columbia Pike
Silver Spring, MD 20901
Free: 800-547-0007
Fax: (301)592-6205
Description: Mid-priced extended-stay hotel. **No. of Franchise Units:** 40. **No. of Company-Owned Units:** 3. **Founded:** 1996.. **Franchised:** 1996. **Equity Capital Needed:** $300/room; $30,000 minimum. **Franchise Fee:** 4.5% GRR. **Training:** Yes.

10809 ■ Microtel Inn & Suites
Wyndham Hotel Group
22 Sylvan Way
Parsippany, NJ 07054
Free: 888-222-7484
Description: Budget sector hotel chain. **No. of Franchise Units:** 220. **Founded:** 1987.. **Franchised:** 1987. **Equity Capital Needed:** $250,000-$600,000. **Franchise Fee:** $35,000. **Training:** Yes.

10810 ■ Motel 6
IBL, LTD
4001 International Pky.
Carrollton, TX 75007
Ph: (972)360-2547
Free: 888-842-2942
Fax: (972)360-5567
Description: Budget lodging. **No. of Franchise Units:** 406. **No. of Company-Owned Units:** 605. **Founded:** 1962.. **Franchised:** 1996. **Equity Capital Needed:** $2,094,000-$2,909,900. **Franchise Fee:** $25,000-$35,000. **Royalty Fee:** 5%. **Training:** Offers 1 week at headquarters and training available at franchisees location, annual convention with ongoing support.

10811 ■ Motel6Canada
77 Bloor St. W, Ste. 2000
Toronto, ON, Canada M5S 1M2
Ph: (416)966-8387
Fax: (416)923-5424
Co. E-mail: motel6@realstarhospitality.ca
URL: http://www.motel6.com
Description: Establishing franchised and corporate properties in all major cities across the country in the economypriced segment of the market. Providing franchisees with extensive and dedicated franchise services, national sales & marketing, training and purchasing power. **No. of Franchise Units:** 16. **No. of Company-Owned Units:** 1. **Founded:** 2003.. **Franchised:** 2003. **Franchise Fee:** $40,000. **Training:** Assistance with opening and ongoing support.

10812 ■ Ramada Worldwide
Wyndham Hotel Group
22 Sylvan Way
Parsippany, NJ 07054
Free: 888-222-7484
Fax: (993)496-5351
Description: Ramada Franchise Systems is licensor of Ramada guest lodging facilities. **No. of Franchise Units:** 965. **Founded:** 1954.. **Franchised:** 1954. **Equity Capital Needed:** Varies depending on project. **Franchise Fee:** $35,000; $350/room. **Training:** Yes.

10813 ■ Realstar Hospitality
77 Bloor St. W, Ste. 2000
Toronto, ON, Canada M5S 1M2
Ph: (416)966-8387

Fax: (416)923-5424
URL: http://www.realstargroup.com
Description: The master franchisor for Days Inn, Motel 6, Studio 6 and Novotel in Canada. Establishing franchised and corporate hotels across the country in the limited and full service sectors. Providing franchisees with extensive and dedicated franchise services, national sales & marketing, training and purchasing power.

10814 ■ Red Roof Inn
Accor North America
4001 International Pky.
Carrolton, TX 75007
Ph: (972)360-2547
Free: 888-842-2942
Fax: (972)360-5567
Description: Economy lodging. **No. of Franchise Units:** 95. **No. of Company-Owned Units:** 240. **Founded:** 1972.. **Franchised:** 1996. **Equity Capital Needed:** $100,000-$500,000; $3,500,000 total investment. **Franchise Fee:** $30,000. **Training:** Yes.

10815 ■ The Residence Inn by Marriott
The Plamondon Cos.
321 Ballenger Ctr. Dr., Ste. 201
Fredrick, MD 21703
Ph: (301)380-5237
Description: Extended-stay hotels. **No. of Franchise Units:** 106. **No. of Company-Owned Units:** 60. **Founded:** 1976.. **Equity Capital Needed:** $5,000,000, not including land. **Franchise Fee:** $400 per suite. **Training:** Yes.

10816 ■ Rodeway Inn
Choice Hotels Intl.
10750 Columbia Pike
Silver Spring, MD 20901
Free: 800-547-0007
Fax: (301)592-6205
Co. E-mail: franchise_sales@choicehotels.com
Description: Hotels. **No. of Franchise Units:** 146. **Founded:** 1964.. **Franchised:** 1964. **Equity Capital Needed:** $125/room; $10,000 minimum. **Franchise Fee:** 3.5% GRR. **Royalty Fee:** $31 per room/month. **Training:** Yes.

10817 ■ Scottish Inns, Red Carpet Inns, Master Hosts Inns
Hospitality International, Inc.
1726 Montreal Cir.
Tucker, GA 30084
Ph: (770)270-1180
Free: 800-247-4677
Fax: (800)813-6322
Description: Budget motels. Limited amenity lodging. **No. of Franchise Units:** 259. **Founded:** 1982.. **Franchised:** 1982. **Equity Capital Needed:** Varies. **Franchise Fee:** $5,000-$12,500. **Training:** Yes.

10818 ■ Sleep Inn
Choice Hotels International
10750 Columbia Pike
Silver Spring, MD 20901
Free: 800-547-0007
Fax: (301)592-6205
Co. E-mail: franchise_info@choicehotels.com
Description: Motel with state-of-the-art guestrooms. **No. of Franchise Units:** 307. **Founded:** 1988.. **Franchised:** 1988. **Equity Capital Needed:** $300/room; $40,000 minimum. **Franchise Fee:** 4.5% GRR. **Training:** Yes.

10819 ■ Studio 6
Accor North America
4001 International Pky.
Carrollton, TX 75007
Ph: (972)360-2547
Free: 888-842-2942
Fax: (972)360-5567
Description: Provider of lodging services. **No. of Franchise Units:** 7. **No. of Company-Owned Units:** 34. **Founded:** 1998.. **Franchised:** 1999. **Equity Capital Needed:** $100,000-$500,000; $3,500,000 total investment. **Franchise Fee:** $25,000. **Training:** Training and support provided.

10820 ■ Studio6Canada
77 Bloor St., W, Ste. 2000
Toronto, ON, Canada M5S 1M2
Ph: (416)966-8387
Fax: (416)923-5424
Co. E-mail: Studio6@realstarhospitality.com
URL: http://www.staystudio6.com
Description: Economy extended stay lodging and short term housing sector. Provides franchisees with extensive and dedicated franchise services, national sales and marketing, and purchasing power. **No. of Company-Owned Units:** 1. **Founded:** 2003.. **Franchised:** 2003. **Franchise Fee:** $40,000. **Training:** Yes.

10821 ■ Super 8 Motels, Inc.
Wyndham Hotel Group
22 Sylvan Way
Parsippany, NJ 07054
Ph: (888)222-7484
Free: 888-222-7484
Description: Economy motels. **No. of Franchise Units:** 1,980. **Founded:** 1974.. **Franchised:** 1976. **Equity Capital Needed:** Varies depending on project. **Franchise Fee:** $20,000. **Training:** Offers 5 days at headquarters, 2 days at franchisees location, regional workshops, and customized property training 1-3 days.

10822 ■ Travelodge Hotels
Cendant Corp.
22 Sylvan Way
Parsippany, NJ 07054
Ph: (888)223-4675
Free: 800-758-8999
Fax: (973)753-8724
Description: Hotels and motels. **No. of Franchise Units:** 433. **Founded:** 1939.. **Franchised:** 1966. **Equity Capital Needed:** $186,370-$6,788,300. **Franchise Fee:** $36,000. **Royalty Fee:** 4.5%. **Training:** Available at headquarters for 5 days, 2 days at franchisee's location, regional workshops and customized property training 1-3 days.

10823 ■ Value Place
Value Place Franchise Services LLC
8621 E 21st St. N, Ste. 250
Wichita, KS 67206
Ph: (316)630-5505
Fax: (316)631-1333
Description: Hotels/motels franchisor. **No. of Franchise Units:** 175. **No. of Company-Owned Units:** 43. **Founded:** 2003.. **Franchised:** 2004. **Equity Capital Needed:** $500,000 liquid; $1,000,000 or greater net worth. **Franchise Fee:** $49,600. **Training:** Yes.

10824 ■ Yogi Bear's Jellystone Park Camp-Resorts
Leisure Systems, Inc.
50 W TechneCenter Dr., Ste. G
Milford, OH 45150
Ph: (513)831-2100
Free: 800-626-3720
Fax: (513)576-8670
URL: http://www.jellystonefranchise.com
Description: Leisure Systems, Inc. holds an exclusive license to franchise Yogi Bear's Jellystone Park Camp/Resorts in the US and Canada. Presently, there are 70 units in the U.S. and 3 in Canada. **No. of Franchise Units:** 71. **Founded:** 1969.. **Franchised:** 1970. **Equity Capital Needed:** $25,000+. **Franchise Fee:** $20,000. **Financial Assistance:** Yes. **Training:** Franchisee's are required to attend a 5 day training program held at the home office in Cincinnati, OH. Additional onsite training is also conducted for a period of 2-3 days.

COMPUTER SYSTEMS/ SOFTWARE

10825 ■ *Resort Data Processing*
PO Box 1170
Vail, CO 81658
Ph: (970)845-1140

Fax: (970)845-0150
Co. E-mail: info@resortdata.com
URL: http://www.resortdata.com
Price: Contact Resort Data for pricing. **Description:** Available for IBM computers and compatibles. System designed for hotels with less than 74 rooms. Options include a package with full accounts payable, general ledger, and financial reporting.

LIBRARIES

10826 ■ American Hotel & Lodging Association Information Center
1201 New York Ave. N.W., Ste. 600
Houston, TX 77204-3028
Ph: (202)289-3100
Free: 888-743-2515
Fax: (202)289-3199
Co. E-mail: informationcenter@ahla.com
URL: http://www.ahla.com
Contact: Lydia Westbrook, Director, Research
Scope: Hotels and restaurants; travel and tourism. **Services:** Library open to the public with restrictions by appointment only. **Founded:** 1988. **Holdings:** 2500 volumes; microfilms; archives. **Subscriptions:** 100 journals and other serials.

10827 ■ California Culinary Academy Library
350 Rhode Island St.
San Francisco, CA 94103
Ph: (415)771-3500
Free: 888-897-3222
Co. E-mail: bgk@baychef.com
URL: http://www.chefs.edu/San-Francisco
Scope: Culinary arts, nutrition, restaurant and hospitality industry. **Services:** Library open to the public by special appointment only. **Founded:** 1989. **Holdings:** 3500 books. **Subscriptions:** 90 journals and other serials.

10828 ■ City College of San Francisco - Department - Culinary Arts and Hospitality Studies Alice Statler Library
50 Phelan Ave.
Statler Wing, Rm. 10
San Francisco, CA 94112
Ph: (415)239-3460
Co. E-mail: aniosi@ccsf.edu
URL: http://www.ccsf.edu/NEW/en/library/about-library/library-locations/statler.html
Contact: Andrea Niosi, Librarian
Scope: Public hospitality industries - hotels, motels, restaurants, catering services, cookery and nutrition; tourism; beverages. **Services:** Copying; Wi-Fi; library open to the public for reference use only. **Founded:** 1964. **Holdings:** 10,000 books; 3500 pamphlets; 900 menus; videotapes; archives. **Subscriptions:** 80 journals and other serials. **Telecommunication Services:** astatler@ccsf.edu.

10829 ■ Colorado Mountain College - Alpine Campus Library
1330 Bob Adams Dr.
Steamboat Springs, CO 80487-5027
Ph: (970)870-4445
Co. E-mail: kwilliams@coloradomtn.edu
URL: http://library.coloradomtn.edu/steamboat
Contact: Kevin Williams, Director, Library Services
Scope: Small business, hotel and restaurant management, health and fitness, U.S. history and literature, American music, skiing. **Services:** Interlibrary loan; library open to the public; copying. **Founded:** 1982. **Holdings:** 30,000 books; 580 CDs; maps; state documents; CD-ROMs. **Subscriptions:** 225 journals and other serials; 15 newspapers.

10830 ■ Cornell University - The Nestle Library
G80 Statler Hall
School of Hotel Administration
Ithaca, NY 14853-6901
Ph: (607)255-3673

Fax: (607)255-0021
Co. E-mail: hotelref@cornell.edu
URL: http://www.hotelschool.cornell.edu/research/
library/
Contact: Donald Schnedeker, Director
Scope: Hotel, motel, and restaurant management, administration, accounting, quantity cookery, food facilities engineering, sanitation, advertising, sales promotion, public relations, marketing, hospitality law, franchising, real estate, tourist industry, resort development. **Services:** Interlibrary loan; Library open to the public by appointment on a fee basis. **Founded:** 1922. **Holdings:** 37,000 volumes; 17,000 microforms; 500 computer files; 1000 reels of microfilm; 16,500 microfiche; 1500 videos. **Subscriptions:** 500 serials; 12 newspapers. **Telecommunication Services:** dws2@cornell.edu.

10831 ■ Hospitality Sales and Marketing Association International - Research Library
1760 Old Meadow Rd., Ste. 500
McLean, VA 22102
Ph: (703)506-3280
Fax: (703)506-3266
Co. E-mail: bgilbert@hsmai.org
URL: http://www.hsmai.org
Contact: Robert A. Gilbert, President
Scope: Hotels, hospitality, travel and tourism, promotion, merchandising, public relations, marketing, direct mail, publicity, advertising, sales education, revenue management, internet marketing, distribution and channel management, travel and tourism. **Services:** Library open to members by appointment. **Founded:** 1927. **Holdings:** 200 volumes. **Subscriptions:** 22 journals and other serials. **Telecommunication Services:** info@hsmai.org.

10832 ■ Johnson & Wales University - Harborside Culinary Library
321 Harborside Blvd.
Providence, RI 02905

Ph: (401)598-1282
Co. E-mail: bjanson@jwu.edu
URL: http://www.jwu.edu
Contact: Barbara Janson, Librarian
Scope: Cookbooks, food service, menu planning, nutrition, professional management, catering and banquets, household manuals, canning, preserving and freezing, hotel and motel management. **Services:** Copying; Library open to the public. **Founded:** 1979. **Holdings:** 10,000 books; 700 menus. **Subscriptions:** 100 journals and other serials.

10833 ■ Oregon Lodging Association - Materials Library
8565 SW Salish Ln., Ste. 120
Wilsonville, OR 97070-9675
Ph: (503)682-4422
Free: 800-462-0619
Fax: (503)682-4455
Co. E-mail: info@oregonrla.org
URL: http://www.oregonrla.org
Contact: Steve McCoid, President
Scope: Hospitality. **Services:** Library open to lodging members. **Holdings:** 57 books; 86 videocassettes. **Subscriptions:** 1 journal. **Telecommunication Services:** smccoid@oregonrla.org.

10834 ■ PKF Consulting Library
50 California St., 19th Fl.
San Francisco, CA 94111
Ph: (415)788-3102
Fax: (415)433-7844
Co. E-mail: thomas.callahan@pkfc.com
URL: http://www.pkfc.com/
Contact: Thomas E. Callahan
Scope: Hotel operations, travel, tourism. **Services:** Library not open to the public. **Founded:** 1935. **Subscriptions:** 15 journals and other serials; 4 newspapers.

10835 ■ Paul Smith's College of Arts and Sciences - Joan Weill Adirondack Library
Rte. 86 and 30
Paul Smiths, NY 12970-0265
Ph: (518)327-6313
Free: 800-421-2605
Fax: (518)327-6016
Co. E-mail: library@paulsmiths.edu
URL: http://www.paulsmiths.edu/library
Contact: Neil Surprenant, Director, Library Services
Scope: Hotel and restaurant management, chef training, culinary arts, forestry, urban tree management, environmental science, forest recreation, surveying, ecotourism, natural resources management, fisheries management, business management. **Services:** Interlibrary loan; copying; library open to the public with restrictions. **Founded:** 1946. **Holdings:** 54,000 books; pamphlets. **Subscriptions:** 504 journals and other serials; 7 newspapers. **Telecommunication Services:** nsurprenant@paulsmiths.edu.

10836 ■ South College Library
3904 Lonas Dr.
Knoxville, TN 37909
Ph: (865)251-1800
Fax: (865)637-0127
Co. E-mail: mmchugh@southcollegetn.edu
URL: http://www.southcollegetn.edu/library/
Contact: Mel McHugh, Librarian
Scope: Business, physical therapy, occupational therapy, administration, medical administration, legal administration, small business, secretarial science, paralegal, hotel and restaurant management. **Services:** Interlibrary loan; copying; printing; SDI; library open to South College staff and students. **Holdings:** 6700 books; 10 VF drawers; 214 volumes on microfilm; 1 cabinet of microfiche. **Subscriptions:** 106 journals and other serials. **Telecommunication Services:** scref@southcollegetn.edu.

START-UP INFORMATION

10837 ■ *"Lee's Launches With Focus on Liqueur-based Ice Creams" in Ice Cream Reporter (Vol. 23, August 20, 2010, No. 9, pp. 6)*
Pub: Ice Cream Reporter
Description: Lee's Cream Liqueur Ice Cream Parlors launched their grand opening in Old Town Scottsdale in July, featuring premium liqueurs to create adult-only ice creams that can be served on their own or blended into exotic drinks.

10838 ■ *"Young Entrepreneur's Business Plan? An Ice Cream Boat? Really Floats: Maine at Work" in Portland Press Herald (August 9, 2010)*
Pub: Portland Press Herald
Ed: Ray Routhier. **Description:** Profile of Jake Viola, founder of and ice cream boat located near Portland, Maine. Viola is a sophomore at Yale University and sells ice cream from his pontoon boat on Little Sebago lake.

ASSOCIATIONS AND OTHER ORGANIZATIONS

10839 ■ **Allied Purchasing**
1334 18th St. SW
Mason City, IA 50401-5602
Ph: (641)423-1824
Free: 800-247-5956
Fax: (800)635-3775
Co. E-mail: dennis@alliedpurchasing.com
URL: http://www.alliedpurchasing.com
Contact: Brian Janssen, President
Description: Represents dairies, ice cream plants and soft drink bottlers. Collaborates to obtain group purchasing rates on equipment, ingredients, services, and supplies. **Founded:** 1937.

10840 ■ **Dairy Management, Inc. (DMI)**
10255 W Higgins Rd., Ste. 900
Rosemont, IL 60018-5616
Ph: (312)240-2880
Free: 800-853-2479
Co. E-mail: marykateg@rosedmi.com
URL: http://www.dairyinfo.com
Contact: Gregory D. Miller, Executive Vice President, Research
Description: Operates under the auspices of the United Dairy Industry Association. Milk producers, milk dealers, and manufacturers of butter, cheese, ice cream, dairy equipment, and supplies. Conducts programs of nutrition research and nutrition education in the use of milk and its products. **Founded:** 1915. **Publications:** *Dairy Council Digest* (Bimonthly). **Telecommunication Services:** ndc@dairyinfo.com.

10841 ■ **Food Processing Suppliers Association (FPSA)**
1451 Dolley Madison Blvd., Ste. 101
McLean, VA 22101-3847

Ph: (703)761-2600
Fax: (703)761-4334
Co. E-mail: info@fpsa.org
URL: http://www.fpsa.org
Contact: Jeff Dahl, Chairman
Description: Manufacturers and distributors of dairy and food processing and packaging equipment, machinery, ingredients, and supplies. Provides marketing and technical services to member firms. Compiles market statistics. **Founded:** 1911. **Publications:** *IAFIS--Reporter* (Monthly); *IAFIS--Directory of Membership Products and Services* (Biennial). **Educational Activities:** Process Expo (Annual). **Awards:** Food Engineering Award; Career Development Scholarships; Career Development Scholarship (Annual).

10842 ■ **National Ice Cream Retailers Association (NICRA)**
1028 W Devon Ave.
Elk Grove Village, IL 60007
Ph: (847)301-7500
Free: 866-303-6960
Fax: (847)301-8402
Co. E-mail: info@nicra.org
URL: http://www.nicra.org
Contact: Dan Messer, President
Description: Represents frozen dessert retailers that operate ice cream and frozen yogurt dipping stores or parlors. Provides free and frank exchange of information among members so that all may improve their operations, increase profits and prosper. **Founded:** 1933. **Publications:** *NICRA Bulletin* (Monthly); *NICRA Yearbook* (Annual). **Awards:** Bryce Thomson Scholarship Fund (Annual); Forrest Mock Person of the Year (Annual); Promotion of the Year (Annual).

REFERENCE WORKS

10843 ■ *"7-Eleven Considers Private Label Ice Cream" in Ice Cream Reporter (Vol. 22, December 20, 2008, No. 1, pp. 1)*
Pub: Ice Cream Reporter
Description: 7-Eleven is considering the introduction of a private label of snack foods, including ice cream desserts.

10844 ■ *"Allied Brands Loses Baskin-Robbins Franchise Down Under" in Ice Cream Reporter (Vol. 23, November 20, 2010, No. 12, pp. 2)*
Pub: Ice Cream Reporter
Description: Dunkin Brands, worldwide franchisor of Baskin-Robbins, terminated the master franchise agreement for Australia held by the food marketer Allied Brands Services.

10845 ■ *"Also Active in the Fight Against Cancer is Dreyer's Grand Ice Cream" in Ice Cream Reporter (Vol. 23, October 20, 2010, No. 11, pp. 8)*
Pub: Ice Cream Reporter
Description: Dreyer's Grand Ice Cream partnered with Experience Project's BroadCause.com to raise awareness around pediatric cancer research.

10846 ■ *"B. Jannetta" in Ice Cream Reporter (Vol. 21, August 20, 2008, No. 9, pp. 8)*
Pub: Ice Cream Reporter
Description: B. Jannetta ice cream parlor, run by Owen and Nicola Hazel, is celebrating its 100th Anniversary. The ice cream parlor is believed to be the oldest business still operating in its original shop in Saint Andrews. Owen and Nicola are the fourth generation to run the shop since Hazel's grandfather founded the business in 1908.

10847 ■ *"Baskin-Robbins" in Ice Cream Reporter (Vol. 23, November 20, 2010, No. 12, pp. 7)*
Pub: Ice Cream Reporter
Description: Baskin-Robbins is reintroducing its popular Turkey Ice Cream Cake for the holiday.

10848 ■ *"Baskin-Robbins" in Ice Cream Reporter (Vol. 23, September 20, 2010, No. 10, pp. 6)*
Pub: Ice Cream Reporter
Description: Baskin-Robbins will feature an old favorite called Quarterback Crunch as its September Flavor of the Month. The item was created in 1978 and features vanilla ice cream with chocolate covered rice crunchies and a carmel ribbon.

10849 ■ *"Baskin-Robbins Expanding in China and U.S." in Ice Cream Reporter (Vol. 21, August 20, 2008, No. 9, pp. 1)*
Pub: Ice Cream Reporter
Description: Baskin-Robbins will open its first store in Shanghai, China along with plans for 100 more shops in that country. They will also be expanding their market in the Dallas/Fort Worth, Texas area as well as Greater Cincinnati/Northern Kentucky regions.

10850 ■ *"Baskin-Robbins Expanding to South Texas" in Ice Cream Reporter (Vol. 23, July 20, 2010, No. 8, pp. 4)*
Pub: Ice Cream Reporter
Description: Baskin-Robbins will develop six new shops in south Texas after signing agreements with two franchisees.

10851 ■ *"Baskin-Robbins: New in U.S., Old in Japan" in Ice Cream Reporter (Vol. 23, August 20, 2010, No. 9, pp. 2)*
Pub: Ice Cream Reporter
Description: Baskin-Robbins is celebrating its first franchise in Japan.

10852 ■ *"Baskin-Robbins Reopens in New Orleans" in Ice Cream Reporter (Vol. 23, September 20, 2010, No. 10, pp. 3)*
Pub: Ice Cream Reporter
Description: Baskin-Robbins will open its first shop in New Orleans, Louisiana after Hurricane Katrina in 2005. The shop stands in the exact location of a Baskin-Robbins shop destroyed by Katrina.

10853 ■ *"Baskin-Robbins Tests New Upscale Concept" in Ice Cream Reporter (Vol. 21,*

September 20, 2008, No. 10, pp. 1)
Pub: Ice Cream Reporter
Description: Baskin-Robbins is opening its new upscale store, Cafe 31 in an effort to invigorate its brand. The shop will serve fondues, cakes and other treats prepared by an in-store chef.

10854 ■ *"Ben & Jerry" in Ice Cream Reporter (Vol. 21, August 20, 2008, No. 9, pp. 7)*
Pub: Ice Cream Reporter
Description: Ben & Jerry's created a limited-batch ice cream to honor singer Elton John when he performed in Vermont. The treat was called 'Goodbye Yellow Brick Road' and featured chocolate ice cream, peanut butter cookie dough, butter brickle, and white chocolate chunks.

10855 ■ *"Ben & Jerry's Changing Some 'All Natural' Labels" in Ice Cream Reporter (Vol. 23, October 20, 2010, No. 11, pp. 1)*
Pub: Ice Cream Reporter
Description: Following criticism from the Center for Science in the Public Interest, Ben & Jerry's will omit the term 'All Natural' from its labeling, however the firm reports it will continue to use the most natural ingredients they can find for its products.

10856 ■ *"Ben & Jerry's Introduces 'Green' Freezer" in Ice Cream Reporter (Vol. 21, October 20, 2008, No. 11, pp. 1)*
Pub: Ice Cream Reporter
Description: Ben & Jerry's describes its latest concept as a cleaner, greener freezer. The hydrocarbon-based freezer provides great environmental benefits by minimizing the freezer's impact on global warming.

10857 ■ *"Blue Bell Breaks Ground in South Carolina" in Ice Cream Reporter (Vol. 23, August 20, 2010, No. 9, pp. 3)*
Pub: Ice Cream Reporter
Description: Texas-based Blue Bell Creameries will open a new 2,000 square foot transfer facility in North Charleston, South Carolina. The facility will expand Blue Bell's distribution efforts in the state.

10858 ■ *"Blue Bell Touts Non-Shrinkage" in Ice Cream Reporter (Vol. 21, July 20, 2008, No. 8, pp. 1)*
Pub: Ice Cream Reporter
Description: Blue Bell Ice Cream is promoting its decision to keep their ice cream products in a full half-gallon container rather than downsizing the package. Thirty-second television ads contrast the move by other ice cream makers to offer less for the same money.

10859 ■ *"Boston Globe" in Ice Cream Reporter (Vol. 21, August 20, 2008, No. 9, pp. 7)*
Pub: Ice Cream Reporter
Description: Boston City Council approved an ordinance that will limit when ice cream vendors can announce their presence with music over loud speakers. The rules are simple: when the wheels stop moving, the jingles stop playing.

10860 ■ *"Carvel" in Ice Cream Reporter (Vol. 23, September 20, 2010, No. 10, pp. 7)*
Pub: Ice Cream Reporter
Description: Pamela Carvel, niece of Carvel founding soft serve has been barred from bringing any more lawsuits against her uncle's estate.

10861 ■ *"Carvel Offers Franchisee Discount" in Ice Cream Reporter (Vol. 21, August 20, 2008, No. 9, pp. 2)*
Pub: Ice Cream Reporter
Description: Carvel Ice Cream is offering new franchise opportunities in Florida, New Jersey, and New York. The company will offer incentive for new franchise owners.

10862 ■ *"Cold Stone Creamery" in Ice Cream Reporter (Vol. 22, January 20, 2009, No. 2, pp. 8)*
Pub: Ice Cream Reporter
Description: Franchise News reports that Cold Stone Creamery is looking for master franchisees to support its expansion into the North German market. The report notes that following its successful launch in Denmark, the firm is also preparing for expansion into France.

10863 ■ *"Cold Stone Creamery" in Ice Cream Reporter (Vol. 23, November 20, 2010, No. 12, pp. 6)*
Pub: Ice Cream Reporter
Description: Doug Ducey, former CEO of Cold Stone Creamery, was elected to the post of Arizona State Treasurer. Ducey was responsible for the firm's expansion to major brand status.

10864 ■ *"Cold Stone Creamery Offers New Eight-Layer Ice Cream Cakes" in Ice Cream Reporter (Vol. 23, October 20, 2010, No. 11, pp. 2)*
Pub: Ice Cream Reporter
Description: Cold Stone Creamery is introducing a new line of eight-layer ice cream cakes, which are crafted with three layers of cream, three layers of cake and two mid-layers of mix-ins and finished with frosting and a creative design.

10865 ■ *"Cold Stone in Licensing Agreement with Turin Chocolates" in Ice Cream Reporter (Vol. 22, December 20, 2008, No. 1, pp. 2)*
Pub: Ice Cream Reporter
Description: Cold Stone Creamery and Turin Chocolatier are teaming up to offer a new line of chocolate truffles under the Cold Stone label. The treats will feature four the most popular Cold Stone flavors: Coffee Lovers Only, Chocolate Devotion, Our Strawberry Blonde, and Peanut Butter Cup Perfection.

10866 ■ *"CoolBrands" in Canadian Business (Vol. 83, September 14, 2010, No. 15, pp. 25)*
Pub: Rogers Media Ltd.
Ed: Joe Castaldo. **Description:** CoolBrands International Inc.'s merger with Swisher International Inc., a US hygiene products and services company, has formally erased the last traces of the former ice cream company. CoolBrands began as a frozen yogurt stand in 1986 and flourished across the world. How the string of acquisitions and poor corporate governance led to its demise are cited.

10867 ■ *"Dairy Queen Aims to Blitz Blizzberry" in Ice Cream Reporter (Vol. 23, August 20, 2010, No. 9, pp. 1)*
Pub: Ice Cream Reporter
Description: International Diary Queens has filed a lawsuit to stop Yogubliz Inc. from using Blizzberry and Blizz Frozen Yogurt as the name of its shops because the name is so close to Dairy Queen's Blizzard frozen dessert.

10868 ■ *"Dairy Queen Ends Effort Against Yogubliz" in Ice Cream Reporter (Vol. 23, November 20, 2010, No. 12, pp. 1)*
Pub: Ice Cream Reporter
Description: Dairy Queen has stopped demands that Yogubliz Inc. change its Blizzberry and Blizz Frozen Yogurt shops because they sound too much like Dairy Queen's Blizzard frozen dessert treat. Dairy Queen feared consumers would confuse the two brands.

10869 ■ *"Dean Foods" in Ice Cream Reporter (Vol. 23, November 20, 2010, No. 12, pp. 8)*
Pub: Ice Cream Reporter
Description: The impact of higher commodity prices can be seen in the recent news from Dean Foods, the largest U.S. dairy company, which reported that rising butterfat and other dairy commodity costs have led to lower-than-expected quarterly profits after it cut prices to compete with private-label brands.

10870 ■ *"Dean Foods" in Ice Cream Reporter (Vol. 23, September 20, 2010, No. 10, pp. 8)*
Pub: Ice Cream Reporter
Description: Dean Foods promoted Joseph Scalzo to President and Chief Operating Officer to oversee the firm's operational turnaround and near-term strategic initiatives as well as business units. Key functions will include worldwide supply chain and research and development.

10871 ■ *"Denali Asks Consumers to Name Next Moose Tracks Flavor" in Ice Cream Reporter (Vol. 23, August 20, 2010, No. 9, pp. 4)*
Pub: Ice Cream Reporter
Description: Denali Flavors based in Michigan is inviting consumer to name its newest Moose Tracks version of ice cream flavors.

10872 ■ *"Department of Agriculture" in Ice Cream Reporter (Vol. 23, November 20, 2010, No. 12, pp. 8)*
Pub: Ice Cream Reporter
Description: Department of Agriculture notes that food price inflation for 2010 will be at its lowest since 1992.

10873 ■ *"Dreyer's Grand Ice Cream" in Ice Cream Reporter (Vol. 23, September 20, 2010, No. 10, pp. 8)*
Pub: Ice Cream Reporter
Description: Dreyer's Grand Ice Cream will add one hundred new manufacturing jobs at its plant in Laurel, Maryland and another 65 new hires before the end of 2010 and another 35 in 2011.

10874 ■ *"Emack & Bolio" in Ice Cream Reporter (Vol. 23, October 20, 2010, No. 11, pp. 8)*
Pub: Ice Cream Reporter
Description: Emack & Bolio's is engaging in scent marketing using various odors to help boost sales by attracting consumers with scents appropriate to their products.

10875 ■ *"Fieldbrook Foods Acquired By Private Equity Firm" in Ice Cream Reporter (Vol. 23, October 20, 2010, No. 11, pp. 1)*
Pub: Ice Cream Reporter
Description: Fieldbrook Foods Corporation, manufacturer of frozen novelty and ice cream products was acquired by Chicago-based private equity firm Arbor Investments. Arbor partnered with Herman 'Bing' Graffunder, a long-term dairy industry partner, in its acquisition of Fieldbrook.

10876 ■ *"First Airport Location for Paciugo Gelato" in Ice Cream Reporter (Vol. 23, October 20, 2010, No. 11, pp. 2)*
Pub: Ice Cream Reporter
Description: Paciugo Gelato and Caffee has partnered with airport concessions developer Airmail to open a shop in the Cleveland Hopkins International Airport. The firm will create a wide variety of choices for travelers.

10877 ■ *"Fraser and Neave Acquires King's Creameries" in Ice Cream Reporter (Vol. 23, November 20, 2010, No. 12, pp. 1)*
Pub: Ice Cream Reporter
Description: Fraser and Neave Ltd., a Singapore-based consumer products marketer, has entered a conditional agreement to acquire all outstanding shares of King's Creameries, the leading manufacturer and distributor of frozen desserts.

10878 ■ *"Friendly" in Ice Cream Reporter (Vol. 21, August 20, 2008, No. 9, pp. 8)*
Pub: Ice Cream Reporter
Description: Advertising Age presented Friendly's with the award, 'Ad of the Day' for its television commercial depicting a Norman Rockwell-esque family transported to a psychedelic wonderland.

10879 ■ *"Friendly Ice Cream Corporation" in Ice Cream Reporter (Vol. 23, August 20, 2010, No. 9, pp. 8)*
Pub: Ice Cream Reporter
Description: Friendly Ice Cream Corporation appointed Andrea M. McKenna as vice president of marketing and chief marketing officer.

10880 ■ *"Frozen Dessert Year in Review.." in Ice Cream Reporter (Vol. 22, January 20, 2009, No. 2, pp. 1)*
Pub: Ice Cream Reporter
Description: Falling economy caused the closing of several ice cream plants across the U.S. in 2008. Top stories of interest to the industry are presented.

10881 ■ *"Frozen Yogurt Market Heats Up Again" in Houston Business Journal (Vol. 40, November 27, 2009, No. 29, pp. 1)*
Pub: American City Business Journals
Ed: Allison Wollam. **Description:** Frozen yogurt stores are being reestablished or expanding in new sites throughout Houston, Texas due to presumed oversupply of ice cream stores in the market. Among

these stores are Berripop, BlueBerryHill, Fruituzy, and Tasti D-Lite. Suggestions for these stores to focus on frozen yogurts in order to distinguish them from stores offering other products such as specialty drink items and sandwiches are outlined.

10882 ■ *"Gifford's Tops in Chocolate"* in Ice Cream Reporter (Vol. 21, August 20, 2008, No. 9, pp. 3)
Pub: Ice Cream Reporter
Description: Gifford's Ice Cream was presented with two major awards at the World Dairy Expo: 'World's Best Chocolate Ice Cream' and 'Worlds Best Vanilla Ice Cream'. Entries are judged on flavor, body and texture, color and appearance, melting quality, and quality assurance.

10883 ■ *"Gillette Creamery"* in Ice Cream Reporter (Vol. 23, September 20, 2010, No. 10, pp. 8)
Pub: Ice Cream Reporter
Description: Gillette family of Gillette Creamery in Ellenville have been Entrepreneurs of the Year in Ulster County, New York. Gillette is the largest supplier of ice cream products in Eastern New York.

10884 ■ *"Golden Spoon Accelerates Expansion Here and Abroad"* in Ice Cream Reporter (Vol. 22, December 20, 2008, No. 1, pp. 2)
Pub: Ice Cream Reporter
Description: Golden Spoon frozen yogurt franchise chain is developing 35 more locations in the Phoenix, Arizona area along with plans to open a store in Japan.

10885 ■ *"Haagen-Dazs Recruits Shop Owners through Facebook"* in Ice Cream Reporter (Vol. 23, November 20, 2010, No. 12, pp. 1)
Pub: Ice Cream Reporter
Description: Haagen-Dazs Shoppe Company is using Facebook, the leading social media, to recruit new franchises.

10886 ■ *"Hain Celestial Acquires Greek Gods Yogurt"* in Ice Cream Reporter (Vol. 23, July 20, 2010, No. 8, pp. 1)
Pub: Ice Cream Reporter
Description: Hain Celestial Group acquired The Greek Gods LLC. Hain Celestial is a natural and organic products company and Greek Gods makes all natural, Greek-style yogurt and ice cream.

10887 ■ *"The Harris Teeter Grocery Chain Has Started a New Ice Cream Club for Shoppers"* in Ice Cream Reporter (Vol. 21, July 20, 2008)
Pub: Ice Cream Reporter
Description: Store loyalty cards are being issued to Harris Teeter customers to purchase any variety of Ben & Jerry's, Haagen-Dazs, Dove, Starbucks, Ciao Bella, Clemmy's, Purely Decadent, So Delicious, Harris Teeter Naturals, HT Traders, Hunter Farms or Denali Ice Cream. One point is earned for every dollar spent, 30 total points earns a $5 electronic coupon towards the next purchase.

10888 ■ *"Healthy Fast Food Acquires Rights to U-Swirl Yogurt"* in Ice Cream Reporter (Vol. 21, October 20, 2008, No. 11, pp. 5)
Pub: Ice Cream Reporter
Description: Healthy Fast Food Inc. will acquire worldwide rights to U-Swirl Frozen Yogurt; the firm will use the new acquisition to create a yogurt superstore in a cafe setting concept for its operations.

10889 ■ *"Herrell's Launches New Corporate Identity at Fancy Food Show"* in Ice Cream Reporter (Vol. 23, July 20, 2010, No. 8, pp. 3)
Pub: Ice Cream Reporter
Description: Herrell's ice cream introduced a new corporate branding at the Summer 2010 Fancy Food Show last summer. Slightly Mad Communications advertising agency developed the new brand to reflect the era of the early 1970s.

10890 ■ *"In Addition, Pinkberry Reports It Is Opening a New Shop in Sunnyvale, CA"* in Ice Cream Reporter (Vol. 23, October 20, 2010)
Pub: Ice Cream Reporter
Description: Pinkberry opened a new shop in Sunnyvale, California, its fourth opening in the South Bay and its 101st location worldwide.

10891 ■ *"International Dairy Queen"* in Ice Cream Reporter (Vol. 23, October 20, 2010, No. 11, pp. 7)
Pub: Ice Cream Reporter
Description: International Dairy Queen will open more than 100 new outlets in China in 2011, adding to the current level of more than 300 outlets in that country.

10892 ■ *"Kosher Ice Cream Features Traditional Jewish Ingredients"* in Ice Cream Reporter (Vol. 23, August 20, 2010, No. 9, pp. 5)
Pub: Ice Cream Reporter
Description: Chozen Ice Cream is offering traditional Jewish dessert and snack foods using tradition Jewish ingredients to name items: regelach, coconut-almond macaroon, and chocolate matzo.

10893 ■ *"Looking To Hire Young? Be Careful"* in Boston Business Journal (Vol. 30, November 19, 2010, No. 43, pp. 1)
Pub: Boston Business Journal
Ed: Lisa van der Pool. **Description:** The Massachusetts Commission Against Discrimination (MCAD) has been using undercover job applicants to expose discrimination. Cabot's Ice Cream and Restaurant has been accused of denying older workers equal employment opportunities. MCAD has discovered unfair hiring practices such as hiring high school and college students.

10894 ■ *"Loseley Dairy Ice Cream"* in Ice Cream Reporter (Vol. 23, November 20, 2010, No. 12, pp. 8)
Pub: Ice Cream Reporter
Description: Neil Burchell has been named managing director of Loseley Dairy Ice Cream, one of the UK's largest independent producers. Burchell, with over 30 years experience in the food industry, was recently managing director of Rachel's, the leading organic dairy foods company in the UK, where he is credited with driving a sixfold increase in sales.

10895 ■ *"MaggieMoo's Ice Cream and Treatery"* in Ice Cream Reporter (Vol. 23, September 20, 2010, No. 10, pp. 7)
Pub: Ice Cream Reporter
Description: MaggieMoo's Ice Cream and Treatery has launched a new Website where visitors can learn about the brands newest ice cream innovations.

10896 ■ *"Marble Slab Creamery"* in Ice Cream Reporter (Vol. 23, November 20, 2010, No. 12, pp. 7)
Pub: Ice Cream Reporter
Description: Marble Slab Creamery is promoting its company by offering a New Year's Eve Sweepstakes.

10897 ■ *"Menchie's Tops Restaurant Business' Future 50 List"* in Ice Cream Reporter (Vol. 23, August 20, 2010, No. 9, pp. 4)
Pub: Ice Cream Reporter
Description: Menchie's, frozen yogurt shop, announced it placed first in the Restaurant Business Magazine's Future 50, ranking the franchise the fastest-growing in the food industry.

10898 ■ *"Mini Melts"* in Ice Cream Reporter (Vol. 23, August 20, 2010, No. 9, pp. 8)
Pub: Ice Cream Reporter
Description: Mini Melts appointed David S. Tade to position of director of sales USA in order to cultivate existing distributors and add new partners to its distribution network.

10899 ■ *"Mini Melts Offers 'Win an Ice Cream Business' Contest"* in Ice Cream Reporter (Vol. 23, October 20, 2010, No. 11, pp. 3)
Pub: Ice Cream Reporter
Description: Mini Melts USA launched a promotional program offering contestants the opportunity to win a Mini Melts ice cream business. The business is not a franchise and there are not royalty fees.

10900 ■ *"MooBella Adds Two Airports"* in Ice Cream Reporter (Vol. 23, November 20, 2010, No. 12, pp. 5)
Pub: Ice Cream Reporter
Description: MooBella Inc. has placed MooBella Ice Creamery machines in New England's Logan International Airport in Boston and in New Hampshire's Manchester-Boston Regional Airport.

10901 ■ *"New CEO For Friendly's"* in Ice Cream Reporter (Vol. 23, September 20, 2010, No. 10, pp. 1)
Pub: Ice Cream Reporter
Description: Friendly Ice Cream Corporation named Harsha V. Agadi as new chief executive officer. Agadi has 24 years experience in food service, most recently serving as CEO of Church's Chicken.

10902 ■ *"New Zealand Natural Co-Branding with Mrs. Fields"* in Ice Cream Reporter (Vol. 23, November 20, 2010, No. 12, pp. 2)
Pub: Ice Cream Reporter
Description: Mrs. Fields has partnered with a New Zealand firm to co-brand ice cream and cookies in Australian markets.

10903 ■ *"New Zealand Natural Ice Cream is Opening a Second U.S. Scoop Shop"* in Ice Cream Reporter (Vol. 21, October 20, 2008, No. 11, pp. 7)
Pub: Ice Cream Reporter
Description: New Zealand Natural Ice Cream is opening a second store in California. The company is a market leader in New Zealand and has gained distribution through 300 outlets in California.

10904 ■ *"NexCen Brands Sells Chains and Will Liquidate"* in Ice Cream Reporter (Vol. 23, August 20, 2010, No. 9, pp. 1)
Pub: Ice Cream Reporter
Description: NexCen Brands is closing the sale of its franchise businesses, which include the frozen dessert chains MaggieMoo's and Marbel Slab Creamery, to Global Franchise Group.

10905 ■ *"A Nice Consistency"* in Inc. (Vol. 31, January-February 2009, No. 1, pp. 94)
Pub: Mansueto Ventures LLC
Ed: Jason Del Rey. **Description:** PJ Madison spent almost a quarter of its revenue promoting its latest product, organic ice cream. The Texas-based firm saw sales increase dramatically.

10906 ■ *"Oberweis Tests Home Ice Cream Delivery"* in Ice Cream Reporter (Vol. 21, November 20, 2008, No. 12, pp. 1)
Pub: Ice Cream Reporter
Description: Oberwies Dairy launched its Treat Delivery Program in the Saint Louis area. The program allows customers to order milkshakes, ice cream cones, sundaes and scoops of ice cream and they are delivered to their home or office. Oberweis is a fourth generation family run business.

10907 ■ *"Other First Place Winners From the Expo"* in Ice Cream Reporter (Vol. 23, September 20, 2010, No. 10, pp. 8)
Pub: Ice Cream Reporter
Description: Sassy Cow Creamery, Columbus, Wisconsin; Stewarts, Saratoga Springs, New York; Purity Dairies, Nashville, Tennessee; Kemps, Cedarburg, Wisconsin, and Kelly Country Creamery also won first place awards for various categories at the 2010 World Dairy Expo.

10908 ■ *"Penny Chapman"* in Canadian Business (Vol. 79, July 17, 2006, No. 14-15, pp. 75)
Pub: Rogers Media
Ed: Erin Pooley. **Description:** Interview with Penny Chapman, president of Chapman's Ice Cream, who speaks about her journey from rags to riches.

10909 ■ *"Perry's Goes Organic" in Ice Cream Reporter (Vol. 22, December 20, 2008, No. 1, pp. 1)*
Pub: Ice Cream Reporter
Description: Family-owned Perry's Ice Cream is starting a new line of organic ice cream in both vanilla and chocolate flavors. All Perry's products are made with milk and cream from local dairy farmers.

10910 ■ *"Pierre's Ice Cream" in Ice Cream Reporter (Vol. 23, October 20, 2010, No. 11, pp. 8)*
Pub: Ice Cream Reporter
Description: Pierre's Ice Cream has started work on its new $8 million manufacturing facility in Cleveland, Ohio.

10911 ■ *"Pinkberry" in Ice Cream Reporter (Vol. 23, October 20, 2010, No. 11, pp. 6)*
Pub: Ice Cream Reporter
Description: Pinkberry introduced its new Fresh Fruit Bowl, a made-to-order dessert with fresh cut fruit and topped with signature P:inkberry Swirly Whip whipped cream.

10912 ■ *"Private Label Manufacturers Association" in Ice Cream Reporter (Vol. 23, July 20, 2010, No. 8, pp. 7)*
Pub: Ice Cream Reporter
Description: Branded frozen dessert manufacturers sold more frozen desserts in terms of sales volume and revenue and market share in 2009. Statistical details included.

10913 ■ *"R&R Ice Cream" in Ice Cream Reporter (Vol. 23, November 20, 2010, No. 12, pp. 8)*
Pub: Ice Cream Reporter
Description: R&R Ice Cream, the United Kingdom's largest ice cream manufacturer, has completed a private offering of senior secured notes that has raised 298 million (pounds sterling) to fund expansion and acquisitions.

10914 ■ *"R&R Launches Upscale Spoony's and Low Fat Dragon's Den" in Ice Cream Reporter (Vol. 23, August 20, 2010, No. 9, pp. 3)*
Pub: Ice Cream Reporter
Description: European ice cream manufacturer R&R has acquired French ice cream maker Rolland and will position itself as an upscale challenger to brands like Ben & Jerry's.

10915 ■ *"Red Mango Set to Grow in Florida" in Ice Cream Reporter (Vol. 23, September 20, 2010, No. 10, pp. 2)*
Pub: Ice Cream Reporter
Description: Red Mango will add 12 new locations throughout Florida. The stores offer healthy, nutritious frozen yogurt, smoothies and parfaits.

10916 ■ *"Safeway" in Ice Cream Reporter (Vol. 23, September 20, 2010, No. 10, pp. 8)*
Pub: Ice Cream Reporter
Description: Safeway supermarkets have upsized their private label ice cream to a full half gallon, thus reversing the trend where most brands were shrinking their containers.

10917 ■ *"SBA Lauds Anchorage DQ Franchise" in Alaska Business Monthly (Vol. 27, October 2011, No. 10, pp. 9)*
Pub: Alaska Business Publishing Company
Ed: Nancy Pounds. **Description:** US Small Business Administration (SBA) honored Greg Todd, operator of four DQ Grill and Chill eateries in Anchorage, Alaska. The firm has created 100 jobs since receiving SBA assistance.

10918 ■ *"Silver Springs Creamery Opens Retail" in Bellingham Business Journal (Vol. March 2010, pp. 3)*
Pub: Sound Publishing Inc.
Description: Eric Sundstrom, owner of Silver Springs Creamery, announced the opening of its on-site retail store that will sell the farm's goat and cow cheese, yogurt, ice cream and flesh milk.

10919 ■ *"Styles" in Ice Cream Reporter (Vol. 21, July 20, 2008, No. 8, pp. 6)*
Pub: Ice Cream Reporter
Description: British ice cream maker Styles is using sheep's milk in its new frozen dessert, Slim Ewe Iced Dessert. The products has all the natural taste, texture and health advantages of sheep's milk with less than 2.5 grams of fat and under 75 calories per serving.

10920 ■ *"Target Gets Exclusive with Ben & Jerry's" in Ice Cream Reporter (Vol. 23, July 20, 2010, No. 8, pp. 1)*
Pub: Ice Cream Reporter
Description: Target Corporation will launch two new Ben & Jerry's ice cream flavors at its retail stores in 49 states. The new ice cream flavors will be available in mini cups and pints and are called Berry Voluntary and Brownie Chew Gooder.

10921 ■ *"Tastee-Freez Celebrates 60th Anniversary" in Ice Cream Reporter (Vol. 23, July 20, 2010, No. 8, pp. 2)*
Pub: Ice Cream Reporter
Description: Tastee-Freez founders, Leo Moranz (inventor) and Harry Axene, an inventor partnered to market the soft-serve pump and freezer for serving frozen treats back in 1950.

10922 ■ *"Tasti D-Lite Has Franchise Agreement for Australia" in Ice Cream Reporter (Vol. 23, November 20, 2010, No. 12, pp. 3)*
Pub: Ice Cream Reporter
Description: Tasti D-Lite signed an international master franchise agreement with Friezer Australia Pty. Ltd. and will open 30 units throughout Australia over the next five years.

10923 ■ *"Thai Ice Cream Cremo Expanding to Middle East" in Ice Cream Reporter (Vol. 23, September 20, 2010, No. 10, pp. 3)*
Pub: Ice Cream Reporter
Description: Thai-based frozen dessert manufacturer Chomthana, maker of Cremo brand ice cream, is expanding into the Middle East.

10924 ■ *"To Help Maintain an Adequate Blood Supply During the Summer Months" in Ice Cream Reporter (Vol. 21, August 20, 2008, No. 9, pp. 8)*
Pub: Ice Cream Reporter
Description: Friendly's and the American Red Cross have partnered to offer blood donors a coupon for one free carton of Friendly's ice cream in order to maintain an adequate supply during summer months.

10925 ■ *"Tofutti Brands" in Ice Cream Reporter (Vol. 23, September 20, 2010, No. 10, pp. 6)*
Pub: Ice Cream Reporter
Description: Tofutti Brands announced net sales at $4.5 million for second quarter 2010.

10926 ■ *"U-Swirl Added to SBA's Franchise Registry" in Ice Cream Reporter (Vol. 23, September 20, 2010, No. 10, pp. 1)*
Pub: Ice Cream Reporter
Description: Healthy Fast Food Inc., parent to the U-SWIRL Frozen Yogurt cafe chain announced that the U.S. Small Business Administration listed U-SWIRL Frozen Yogurt on its official franchise registry. This move will allow U-SWIRL the benefits of a streamlined review process for SBA financing.

10927 ■ *"U-Swirl To Open in Salt Lake City Metro Market" in Ice Cream Reporter (Vol. 23, November 20, 2010, No. 12, pp. 4)*
Pub: Ice Cream Reporter
Description: Healthy Fast Food Inc., parent company to U-SWIRL International Inc., the owner and franchisor of U-SWIRL Frozen Yogurt cafes signed a franchising area development agreement for the Salt Lake City metropolitan area with Regents Management and will open 5 cafes over a five year period.

10928 ■ *"Unilever Acquiring Danish Operations of Diplom-Is Ice Cream" in Ice Cream Reporter (Vol. 23, August 20, 2010, No. 9, pp. 1)*
Pub: Ice Cream Reporter
Description: Unilever will acquire Danish operations of the ice cream company Diplom-Is from Norwegian dairy group Tine.

10929 ■ *"Unilever Acquiring EVGA's Ice Cream Brands in Greece" in Ice Cream Reporter (Vol. 23, October 20, 2010, No. 11, pp. 1)*
Pub: Ice Cream Reporter
Description: Unilever will acquire the ice cream brands and distribution network of the Greek frozen dessert manufacturer EVGA.

10930 ■ *"Unilever to Sustainably Source All Paper and Board Packaging" in Ice Cream Reporter (Vol. 23, July 20, 2010, No. 8, pp. 1)*
Pub: Ice Cream Reporter
Description: Unilever, a leader in the frozen dessert market, has developed a new sustainable paper and board packaging sourcing policy that will reduce environmental impact by working with suppliers to source 75 percent of paper and board packaging from sustainably managed forests or from recycled material. Unilever is parent company to Breyers, Haagen-Dazs, Klondike, Popsicle and other ice cream brands.

10931 ■ *"Velvet Ice Cream" in Ice Cream Reporter (Vol. 21, July 20, 2008, No. 8, pp. 7)*
Pub: Ice Cream Reporter
Description: Velvet Ice Cream is adding a $7 surcharge on deliveries of its products in order to offset rising fuel costs.

10932 ■ *"Velvet Ice Cream" in Ice Cream Reporter (Vol. 23, November 20, 2010, No. 12, pp. 7)*
Pub: Ice Cream Reporter
Description: Velvet Ice Cream will open its Ye Olde Mill for private corporate parties around the holidays. Their facility can accommodate groups ranging from 30 to 125 individuals. The historic site houses the company headquarters, an ice cream museum, and a restaurant.

10933 ■ *"Wells' Is Title Sponsor for Volleyball Championship" in Ice Cream Reporter (Vol. 22, August 20, 2008, No. 9, pp. 4)*
Pub: Ice Cream Reporter
Description: Wells' Dairy was chosen to sponsor the 29th Annual National Association of Intercollegiate Athletics (NAIA) Volleyball National Championship to be held in Sioux City, Iowa. Blue Bunny will sponsor the 2008 NAIA Women's Volleyball National Championship, also a Wells' brand.

10934 ■ *"YoCream" in Ice Cream Reporter (Vol. 23, September 20, 2010, No. 10, pp. 6)*
Pub: Ice Cream Reporter
Description: YoCream reported a sales increase for third quarter 2010 at 15.6 percent and net income increasing 25 percent to $2,141,000 for that quarter.

10935 ■ *"Yogun Fruz Adds First Location in Southern New York State" in Ice Cream Reporter (Vol. 23, September 20, 2010, No. 10, pp. 2)*
Pub: Ice Cream Reporter
Description: Yogen Fruz signed a master franchise agreement to expand into the southern counties of New York State. The firm offers a healthy and beneficial option to fast food and typical dessert choices.

10936 ■ *"Yogurtini" in Ice Cream Reporter (Vol. 23, September 20, 2010, No. 10, pp. 7)*
Pub: Ice Cream Reporter
Description: Self-serve frozen yogurt chain, Yogurtini has opened its second store in Kansas City, Missouri.

TRADE PERIODICALS

10937 ■ *IDDBA Legis-Letter*
Pub: International Dairy-Deli-Bakery Association
Contact: Steve Beekhuizen, President
Ed: Carol L. Christison, Editor, cchristison@iddba.org. **Price:** Included in membership. **Description:**

Reports on legislative activity concerning the super-market dairy-deli-bakery industry.

10938 ■ The National Dipper: The Magazine for Frozen Dessert Retailers
Pub: The National Dipper
URL(s): www.nationaldipper.com. **Ed:** Lynda Utter-back. **Released:** 6/yr.

10939 ■ WrapUp
Pub: International Dairy-Deli-Bakery Association
Contact: Steve Beekhuizen, President
Ed: Carol L Christison, Editor, cchristison@iddba.org. **Released:** Quarterly. **Price:** Included in membership. **Description:** Reports on news, activities, and topics of interest to the Association.

VIDEOCASSETTES/ AUDIOCASSETTES

10940 ■ Ice Cream and Economics: Ben and Jerry's Homemade
Ambrose Video Publishing, Inc.
145 W. 45th St., Ste. 1115
New York, NY 10036
Ph: (212)768-7373
Free: 800-526-4663
Fax: (212)768-9282
Co. E-mail: customerservice@ambrosevideo.com
URL: http://www.ambrosevideo.com
Released: 1989. **Price:** $69.95. **Description:** The story of the two men who started the successful ice cream company, Ben and Jerry's. **Availability:** VHS.

FRANCHISES AND BUSINESS OPPORTUNITIES

10941 ■ Abbott's Frozen Custard Inc.
4791 Lake Ave.
Rochester, NY 14612-2154
Ph: (585)865-7400
Fax: (585)865-6034
Co. E-mail: sales@abbottscustard.com
URL: http://www.abbottscustard.com
Contact: Robert Amico, Chief Executive Officer
Description: Frozen custard. **No. of Franchise Units:** 20. **No. of Company-Owned Units:** 5. **Founded:** 1902. **Franchised:** 1977. **Equity Capital Needed:** $120,000-$126,800. **Franchise Fee:** $19,000. **Royalty Fee:** $2.20/gallon. **Training:** Offers 1 week at headquarters and 1 week at franchisee's location with ongoing support.

10942 ■ All American Ice Cream & Frozen Yogurt Shops
The All American Frozen Yogurt Co.
1201 SW 12th Ave., Ste. 415
Portland, OR 97205
Ph: (503)224-6199
Free: 800-311-3930
Fax: (503)224-5042
Co. E-mail: franchise@allamericanrestaurants.com
URL: http://www.allamericanrestaurants.com
Description: Retail shop selling frozen yogurt and ice cream. Majority of shops are in enclosed shopping centers. Upscale design. **No. of Franchise Units:** 29. **Founded:** 1986. **Franchised:** 1987. **Equity Capital Needed:** $35,000-$50,000. **Franchise Fee:** $6,000-$25,000. **Financial Assistance:** Yes. **Training:** Yes.

10943 ■ Andrew Smash
Smash International, Inc.
PO Box 12233
Eugene, OR 97440
Ph: (541)465-9088
Fax: (541)465-9088
Description: Meatless burger and smoothie restaurant. **No. of Company-Owned Units:** 1. **Founded:** 1995.. **Franchised:** 1998. **Equity Capital Needed:** $100,000-$175,000. **Franchise Fee:** $10,000-$20,000. **Training:** Yes.

10944 ■ Angels Ice Cream and Hot Dog Franchise
Angels Franchising, Inc.
37252 Hwy. 26
Seaside, OR 97138
Ph: (503)717-9560
Fax: (503)717-9558
Description: Ice cream and hot dog restaurant. **No. of Franchise Units:** 40. **Founded:** 1999.. **Franchised:** 2003. **Equity Capital Needed:** $50,000. **Franchise Fee:** $14,900-$19,900. **Financial Assistance:** Yes. **Training:** Yes.

10945 ■ Applegate Inc.
616 Grove St.
Upper Montclair, NJ 07043
Ph: (973)744-7000
Free: 800-784-3848
Fax: (973)744-0334
Co. E-mail: info@applegatefarm.com
URL: http://www.applegatefarm.com
Contact: Stephen Mcdonnell, Chief Executive Officer
Description: Ice cream. **Founded:** 1848.. **Training:** Offers 2 weeks training at headquarters, 1 week on-site and ongoing support. **Telecommunication Services:** Julie.Kupst@applegatefarms.com.

10946 ■ Bahama Buck's Original Shaved Ice Co.
Bahama Buck's Franchise Corp.
5123 69th St.
Lubbock, TX 79424
Ph: (806)771-2189
Fax: (806)771-2190
Description: Bahama Buck's serves gourmet shaved ice in over 70 different flavors and combinations. They also serve serve fresh-squeezed lemonades, limeades and many $155,000. **No. of Franchise Units:** 20. **No. of Company-Owned Units:** 3. **Founded:** 1989.. **Franchised:** 1993. **Equity Capital Needed:** $163,422-$463,884. **Franchise Fee:** $29,500. **Royalty Fee:** 6%. **Training:** Provides 5 days training at headquarters and 5 days onsite.

10947 ■ Baskin-Robbins Ice Cream
Baskin-Robbins USA, Co.
130 Royall St.
Canton, MA 02021
Free: 800-777-9983
Fax: (781)737-4000
Description: Operates retail specialty ice cream and yogurt stores. **No. of Franchise Units:** 3,456. **No. of Company-Owned Units:** 4. **Founded:** 1945.. **Equity Capital Needed:** $600,000 liquid assets; $1,200,000 net worth. **Franchise Fee:** $30,000. **Financial Assistance:** Yes. **Training:** Yes.

10948 ■ Ben and Jerry's
Ben and Jerry's Homemade, Inc.
30 Community Dr.
S Burlington, VT 05403
Ph: (802)846-1500
Fax: (802)846-1538
Description: Franchised ice cream parlors. **No. of Franchise Units:** 286. **No. of Company-Owned Units:** 7. **Founded:** 1978.. **Franchised:** 1981. **Equity Capital Needed:** $148,800-$451,800. **Franchise Fee:** $37,000. **Royalty Fee:** 3%. **Training:** Training includes 8 days at headquarters and 3-5 days onsite.

10949 ■ Blue Sky Creamery
Blue Sky Creamery, Inc.
Description: Franchisees use our patented Nitro Freeze technology to manufacture premium brand ice cream products. Franchisees operating Factory Stores manufacture and distribute our products within the exclusive territory to grocery stores, convenience stores, third party distributors, and to other franchisees operating Blue Sky Creamery Ice Cream Cafes. **No. of Franchise Units:** 4. **No. of Company-Owned Units:** 2. **Founded:** 2005. **Equity Capital Needed:** $35,000-$95,000 liquid; $300,000 minimum net worth. **Franchise Fee:** $25,000-$35,000. **Training:** Training program covering unit operations, accounting, food safety, manufacturing, marketing and advertising at headquarters with additional onsite, start-up and ongoing support.

10950 ■ Breeze Freeze
13340 Merriman Rd.
Livonia, MI 48150
Free: 866-472-6482
Fax: (734)414-6537
Description: Frozen fruit drinks. **No. of Franchise Units:** 31. **No. of Company-Owned Units:** 303. **Founded:** 2001.. **Franchised:** 2004. **Equity Capital Needed:** $9,200-$94,300, express/kiosk option available. **Franchise Fee:** $5,000/$40,000. **Royalty Fee:** None. **Training:** Offers 1-3 days at headquarters, 1-2 days at franchisees location with ongoing support.

10951 ■ Bruster's Real Ice Cream Inc.
1005 S Bee St.
Pittsburgh, PA 15220-3406
Ph: (412)919-2100
Fax: (412)937-9209
URL: http://www.brustersicecream.com
Contact: Jim Sahene, Chief Executive Officer
Description: "Homemade" ice cream and yogurt shop. **No. of Franchise Units:** 227. **No. of Company-Owned Units:** 3. **Founded:** 1989. **Franchised:** 1993. **Equity Capital Needed:** $50,000 minimum liquidity. **Franchise Fee:** $20,000. **Training:** Yes.

10952 ■ Carvel Ice Cream
Focus Brands, Inc.
200 Glenridge Point Pky., Ste. 200
Atlanta, GA 30342
Ph: (404)255-3250
Fax: (404)255-4978
URL: http://www.carvel.com
Description: Custom ice cream desserts and novelties. **No. of Franchise Units:** 449. **No. of Company-Owned Units:** 15. **Founded:** 1934.. **Franchised:** 1947. **Equity Capital Needed:** $100,000 liquid cash; $300,000 net worth. **Franchise Fee:** $30,000. **Training:** 2 week ice cream training school; access to the Carvel Development Network (real estate brokers, architects, lenders, contractors, etc.); Design & construction support & assistance; Grand opening support and toll-free hotline available.

10953 ■ Chocolate Chocolate Chocolate Co.
Abels Chocolates Inc.
Description: Fine chocolates made fresh daily. **No. of Franchise Units:** 11. **Founded:** 1981.. **Franchised:** 2003. **Equity Capital Needed:** $185,000. **Franchise Fee:** $20,000. **Training:** Yes.

10954 ■ Cold Stone Creamery
9311 E Via De Ventura
Scottsdale, AZ 85258
Ph: (866)452-4252
Fax: (480)362-4310
Co. E-mail: franchise@coldstonecreamery.com
URL: http://www.coldstonecreamery.com
Description: Ice cream and desserts. **No. of Franchise Units:** 1,500. **No. of Company-Owned Units:** 34. **Founded:** 1988.. **Franchised:** 1995. **Equity Capital Needed:** $286,075-$474,325 traditional. **Franchise Fee:** $42,000 traditional. **Training:** 10 day training program at headquarters; ongoing support.

10955 ■ Culvers Frozen Custard
Culver Franchising System, Inc.
1240 Water St.
Prairie du Sac, WI 53578
Ph: (608)644-2130
Fax: (608)644-2626
Description: Frozen custard and butter burgers. **No. of Franchise Units:** 447. **No. of Company-Owned Units:** 9. **Founded:** 1984.. **Franchised:** 1990. **Equity Capital Needed:** $350,000-$600,000. **Franchise Fee:** $55,000. **Training:** Yes.

10956 ■ Dairy Queen Canada Inc.
5045 S Service Rd., Unit 3000
Box 430
Burlington, ON, Canada L7R 3Y3
Ph: (905)637-4741
Fax: (905)681-3623
URL: http://www.dairyqueen.com
Description: Dairy Queen is on the move with a new look, a new menu, and a new attitude. We are a Berkshire Hathaway Company with more than 60 years of franchising. We offer a full line of hamburgers,

sandwiches, and of course the traditional soft serve treats. **No. of Franchise Units:** 588. **No. of Operating Units:** 5,117. **Founded:** 1940.. **Equity Capital Needed:** $300,000 plus. **Franchise Fee:** $30,000-$45,000. **Training:** Yes.

10957 ▪ Dippin' Dots Franchising Inc.

1640 McCracken Blvd., Ste. 100
Paducah, KY 42001
Ph: (270)575-6990
Fax: (270)575-6997
URL: http://www.dippindots.com

Description: The franchise is a homemade ice cream shop including specialist ice cream, frozen yogurt and ices. **No. of Franchise Units:** 441. **No. of Company-Owned Units:** 1. **Founded:** 1988.. **Franchised:** 2000. **Equity Capital Needed:** $80,428-$235,250. **Franchise Fee:** $12,500. **Royalty Fee:** 4%. **Training:** Provides 3 days of training at corporate headquarters and 2 days onsite.

10958 ▪ FreshBerry Natural Frozen Yogurt

8801 S Yale, Ste. 400
Tulsa, OK 74137
Ph: (918)488-9727
Fax: (918)497-1916
Co. E-mail: contact@freshberry.net
URL: http://www.freshberry.net

Description: Natural frozen yogurt, smoothies, and yogurt popsicles. **No. of Franchise Units:** 21. **Founded:** 2007.. **Franchised:** 2007. **Equity Capital Needed:** $170,750-$392,200. **Franchise Fee:** $25,000. **Royalty Fee:** 6%. **Financial Assistance:** Limited third party financing available. **Training:** Step-by-step method for developing your own business. The Freshberry Management Training program is a 12 day comprehensive management course, covering every aspect of ownership and management. Ongoing support focuses on communication with daily email communications from operations and marketing at corporate headquarters, and 7 day a week phone support. **Telecommunication Services:** franchise@freshberry.net.

10959 ▪ Fuzziwig's Candy Factory

Fuzziwig's Candy Factory Inc.
656 Main Ave.
Durango, CO 81301
Ph: (970)247-2770
Free: 877-247-2770
Fax: (970)247-2735
Co. E-mail: info@fuzziwigs.com
URL: http://www.fuzziwigs.com

Description: Offers franchise in ice cream, candy and related business. **No. of Franchise Units:** 54. **No. of Company-Owned Units:** 12. **Founded:** 1995.. **Franchised:** 2002. **Equity Capital Needed:** Start-up cash $50,000-$75,000; Total investment $150,300-$284,250, includes franchise fee. **Franchise Fee:** $30,000. **Training:** Training provided at one of three locations, choose the one nearest to you. Training covers: merchandising, marketing, customer service, inventory and cost control, record keeping, pre-opening training, ongoing support, regional and national meetings, web site support with current trends in the business.

10960 ▪ Gelato Amare/ Jazzy Juices

11504 Hyde Pl.
Raleigh, NC 27614
Ph: (919)847-4435

Description: Serves Italian-style super-premium, low-fat, low-calorie ice cream made right in the store, with several flavors. Lactose-free. Also features all-natural, sugar-free frozen yogurt, espresso, cappuccino, cookies, light soups, salads and sandwiches. **No. of Franchise Units:** 2. **Founded:** 1983.. **Franchised:** 1986. **Equity Capital Needed:** $75,000-$250,000. **Franchise Fee:** $18,900. **Training:** Yes.

10961 ▪ Haagen-Dazs Shops

The Haagen-Dazs Shoppe Co, Inc.
500 S Washington Ave., Ste. 2040
Minneapolis, MN 55415
Ph: (612)337-3314
Free: 800-793-6872

Fax: (612)337-3301
Co. E-mail: development@haagendazsshoppecompany.com
URL: http://www.haagen-dazs.com

Description: Retail super-premium ice cream shops. **No. of Franchise Units:** 253. **Founded:** 1961.. **Franchised:** 1977. **Equity Capital Needed:** $80,000 liquid; $200,000 net worth. **Franchise Fee:** $30,000. **Training:** 2 weeks of comprehensive training in operations, management and customer service at corporate training facility.

10962 ▪ Happy & Healthy Products Inc.

1600 S Dixie Hwy., Ste. 200
Boca Raton, FL 33432
Ph: (561)367-0739
Free: 800-426-0084
Fax: (561)368-5267
Co. E-mail: behappy@fruitfull.com
URL: http://www.fruitfull.com
Contact: Linda Kerr Kamm, President

Description: 100% natural frozen fruit bars. **No. of Franchise Units:** 56. **Founded:** 1991. **Franchised:** 1993. **Equity Capital Needed:** $35,000-$85,000. **Franchise Fee:** $23,000. **Training:** Yes. **Telecommunication Services:** franchiseinfo@fruitfull.com.

10963 ▪ Happy Joes, Inc.

2705 Happy Joe Dr.
Bettendorf, IA 52722
Ph: (319)332-8811

Description: Family style pizza and ice cream parlor. **No. of Franchise Units:** 58. **No. of Company-Owned Units:** 1. **Founded:** 1972.. **Franchised:** 1973. **Equity Capital Needed:** $79,700-$1,019,000, depending on full-service or delivery only. **Franchise Fee:** $1,500-$20,000. **Training:** Yes.

10964 ▪ Hogi Yogi

Hogi Yogi Franchise Corp.
375 W 200 S, Ste. 300
Salt Lake City, UT 84101
Ph: (801)222-9004

Description: Sandwiches, frozen yogurt, and fruit smoothies. **No. of Franchise Units:** 82. **No. of Company-Owned Units:** 4. **Founded:** 1989.. **Franchised:** 1992. **Equity Capital Needed:** Approximately $150,000. **Franchise Fee:** $15,000. **Training:** Yes.

10965 ▪ Juice Heaven

Juice Heaven Franchise Corp.
17834 Burbank Blvd., Ste. 229
Encino, CA 91316
Ph: (818)668-8488
Fax: (818)668-8489

Description: Franchise of beverages and fruit juice businesses. **No. of Franchise Units:** 2. **Founded:** 1999.. **Franchised:** 2002. **Equity Capital Needed:** $88,500-$187,500. **Franchise Fee:** $20,000. **Training:** Yes.

10966 ▪ Juice It Up!

17915 Sky Park Cir., Ste. J
Irvine, CA 92614
Ph: (949)475-0146
Fax: (949)475-0137
Co. E-mail: lidiad@juiceitup.com
URL: http://www.juiceitup.com

Description: The franchise offers ice cream, yogurt, smoothies, candy and beverages services. **No. of Franchise Units:** 90. **No. of Company-Owned Units:** 5. **Founded:** 1995.. **Franchised:** 1999. **Equity Capital Needed:** Net worth of $300,000 with $75,000 liquid. **Franchise Fee:** $25,000. **Training:** Provides extensive training.

10967 ▪ Juiceblendz International

2893 Executive Dr., Ste. 202
Weston, FL 33331
Ph: (866)525-3639

Description: Juice. **No. of Franchise Units:** 5. **No. of Company-Owned Units:** 1. **Founded:** 2005.. **Franchised:** 1005. **Equity Capital Needed:** $125,000 liquid; $350,000 net worth. **Franchise Fee:** $50,000. **Training:** Yes.

10968 ▪ Kohr Bros. Frozen Custard & Smoothie Station

Kohr Bros. Franchise Systems, Inc.
2151 Richmond Rd., Ste. 200
Charlottesville, VA 22911
Ph: (434)975-1500
Fax: (434)975-1505
Co. E-mail: dennispoletti@kohrbros.com
URL: http://www.kohrbros.com

Description: Frozen custard and related products. **No. of Franchise Units:** 37. **No. of Company-Owned Units:** 11. **Founded:** 1919.. **Franchised:** 1994. **Equity Capital Needed:** $250,000 liquid, $500,000 net worth, multiple units only. **Franchise Fee:** $27,500. **Training:** Yes.

10969 ▪ La Paletera Franchise Systems, Inc.

3000 Weslayan Dr., Ste. 120
Houston, TX 77027
Ph: (713)622-9500
Fax: (713)621-8200

Description: La Paletera is a food centre, which provides ice cream, yogurt, smoothies, fruit bars, candy and beverages. **No. of Franchise Units:** 30. **No. of Company-Owned Units:** 1. **Founded:** 1997.. **Franchised:** 2003. **Equity Capital Needed:** $45,000-$60,000. **Franchise Fee:** $28,000. **Financial Assistance:** Yes. **Training:** Yes.

10970 ▪ La Paloma Gelateria & Cafe

1357 St. Clair Ave. W
Toronto, ON, Canada M6E 1C5
Ph: (416)656-2340
Fax: (416)656-8602
Co. E-mail: info@lapaloma.ca
URL: http://www.lapaloma.ca

Description: Established in 1967, La Paloma is the most authentic Italian dessert experience. Over 40 years developing countless proprietary recipes, La Paloma is now franchising. 'The ART of Italian Artisan Ice Cream'. Our turnkey 'Gelato Cafe' concept features over 40 flavours in-store to offer a taste of Italy that is unequalled. **No. of Franchise Units:** 2. **No. of Company-Owned Units:** 2. **Founded:** 1967.. **Franchised:** 2004. **Equity Capital Needed:** $250,000-$550,000. **Franchise Fee:** $25,000. **Training:** 2 weeks pre-opening at corporate head office.

10971 ▪ MaggieMoo's Ice Cream & Treatery

Global Franchise Group
1346 Oakbrook Dr., Ste. 170
Norcross, GA 30093
Ph: (880)524-6444
Fax: (770)514-4903
URL: http://www.theathletesfoot.com

Description: Unique & exciting retail shop, featuring homemade, super-premium ice cream, non-fat ice cream, sorbet, smoothies, custom-made cakes, homemade fudge, plus a line of specialty merchandise. We make our ice cream fresh in the store & serve it in fresh-baked waffle cones. Featuring over 40 mix-ins and folded in on a frozen granite slab to create 1,000s of great combos. Association with a marketable spokes character MAGGIEMOO-in a fun, contemporary store design. **No. of Franchise Units:** 144. **Founded:** 1989.. **Franchised:** 1997. **Equity Capital Needed:** $250,000 net worth; $85,000 liquid. **Franchise Fee:** $25,000 first store. **Training:** Franchisees receive 14 day training program with ongoing field support provided continuously throughout.

10972 ▪ Marble Slab Creamery

734-42nd Ave. SE, 2nd Fl.
Calgary, AB, Canada T2G 5N9
Ph: (403)287-7633
Free: 888-337-7522
Fax: (403)283-7698
Co. E-mail: franchiseinfo@marbleslab.ca
URL: http://www.marbleslab.com

Description: Homemade ice cream, combined with your choice of "mixins" - nuts, cookies, candies & fresh fruit - then piled high on a freshly baked waffle cone. Founded in 1983, Marble Slab Creamery is the innovator of the "frozen slab" concept and is best known for its superpremium, homemade ice cream. Stores also offer a wide variety of alternate desserts including frozen yogurt and made-from-scratch brownies. **No. of Franchise Units:** 76. **No. of Company-Owned Units:** 2. **Founded:** 2004.. **Fran-**

chised: 1986. **Equity Capital Needed:** $300,000 investment required; $80,000-$100,000 start-up capital required. **Franchise Fee:** $25,000. **Training:** 11-day extensive interactive training provided.

10973 ■ Marble Slab Creamery Inc.
Global Franchise Group
1346 Oakbrook Dr., Ste. 170
Norcross, GA 30093
Ph: (880)524-6444
Fax: (770)514-4903
URL: http://www.theathletesfoot.com
Contact: Chris Dull, Chief Executive Officer
Description: Marble Slab Creamery is a unique concept where ice cream is actually made fresh daily at each store. Customers can create their own ice cream fantasies by combining any flavor of superpremium ice cream with 'mixins' such as fresh fruit, candy, cookies or nuts. The ice cream & mixins are then folded together on a frozen marble slab & served on a freshly baked waffle cone. Other products include non-fat yogurt, ice cream pies/cakes, specialty coffees & bakery items. **No. of Franchise Units:** 360. **Founded:** 1983. **Franchised:** 1984. **Equity Capital Needed:** $250,000 net worth, $85,000 liquid. **Franchise Fee:** $25,000. **Financial Assistance:** No. **Managerial Assistance:** Maintains an ongoing business relationship with its franchisees, with assistance available in all phases of store operations. A complete operations manual is provided to all franchisees. Company field personnel visit stores on a regular basis to insure consistency of operations. **Training:** Marble Slab Creamery offers assistance in site selection, lease negotiation, architectural layout and construction supervision. There is a required 10 day training program in Houston, Texas, store opening assistance, continued field supervision, and advertising/public relations assistance.

10974 ■ Maui Wowi Hawaiian Coffees & Smoothies
Maui Wowi Franchising, Inc.
5445 DTC Pky., Ste. 1050
Greenwood Village, CO 80111
Ph: (303)781-7800
Free: 888-862-8555
Fax: (303)781-2438
Description: Hawaiian coffee & smoothie franchise. **No. of Franchise Units:** 550. **Founded:** 1982.. **Franchised:** 1997. **Equity Capital Needed:** $150,000 net worth; $70,000 needed. **Franchise Fee:** $36,500 std/$59,500 empire. **Financial Assistance:** Yes. **Training:** Yes.

10975 ■ Mini Melts
www.minimelts.com
245 Asylum St.
Norwich, CT 06360
Ph: (860)889-7300
Fax: (860)887-1033
Description: Mini Melts ice cream product. **No. of Franchise Units:** 2,000+. **Founded:** 1996.. **Franchised:** 1997. **Equity Capital Needed:** $25,000-$1,000,000. **Franchise Fee:** $12,500-$200,000. **Training:** Yes.

10976 ■ Mister Softee, Inc.
Mr. Softee Inc.
901 E Clements Bridge Rd.
Runnemede, NJ 08078
Ph: (856)939-4103
Fax: (856)939-0490
URL: http://www.mistersoftee.com
Description: Retails soft ice cream from vehicles. **No. of Franchise Units:** 600. **Founded:** 1956.. **Franchised:** 1956. **Equity Capital Needed:** $35,000. **Franchise Fee:** $5,000. **Financial Assistance:** Yes. **Training:** Yes.

10977 ■ Paciugo Gelato
Paciugo Franchising, LP
1215 Viceroy Dr.
Dallas, TX 75247
Ph: (214)654-9501

Fax: (214)654-9509
Description: Italian gelato. **No. of Franchise Units:** 43. **No. of Company-Owned Units:** 1. **Founded:** 2000.. **Franchised:** 2004. **Equity Capital Needed:** Total unit cost $195,100-$442,800. **Franchise Fee:** $30,000. **Training:** Yes.

10978 ■ Planet Smoothie
Petrus Brands
1425 Ellsworth Industrial Blvd. NW, Ste. 38
Atlanta, GA 30318
Ph: (404)856-4320
Fax: (404)856-4334
Description: Smoothie franchise with nutritional products. **No. of Franchise Units:** 124. **No. of Company-Owned Units:** 1. **Founded:** 1995. **Franchised:** 1995. **Equity Capital Needed:** $250,000 net worth; $80,000 liquid. **Franchise Fee:** $25,000. **Training:** Raving Brands University classroom and onsite training provided. From register to food preparation, from hiring staff to accounting procedures, you'll improve your management skills, setup your back office and develop an airtight sales and marketing plan.

10979 ■ Rita's Italian Ice
Rita's Water Ice Franchise Co., LLC
1210 Northbrook Dr., Ste. 310
Trevose, PA 19053
Ph: (800)677-7482
Description: Italian ice, custard, and gelatin. **No. of Franchise Units:** 600. **Founded:** 1984. **Franchised:** 1989. **Equity Capital Needed:** $100,000 liquid; $300,000 net worth. **Franchise Fee:** $25,000. **Financial Assistance:** Yes. **Training:** Training is divided into two phases, with 6 days at a corporate training center and 2 days at the franchisee's location for the grand opening. Training covers production, quality control, advertising concepts and strategies and general business practices.

10980 ■ Shake's Frozen Custard
PO Box 8700
Fayetteville, AR 72703
Ph: (479)587-9115
Fax: (479)587-0780
Co. E-mail: info@shakesfrozencustard.com
URL: http://www.shakesfrozencustard.com
Description: Frozen custard. **No. of Franchise Units:** 44. **No. of Company-Owned Units:** 3. **Founded:** 1991.. **Franchised:** 1998. **Equity Capital Needed:** $100,000 liquid; $500,000 net worth. **Franchise Fee:** $30,000. **Training:** 2 weeks at headquarters, 1 week at franchisee's location and ongoing support.

10981 ■ Smoothie King Franchises, Inc.
121 Park Pl.
Covington, LA 70433
Ph: (985)635-6973
Fax: (985)635-6987
Description: Smoothie King centers offer guests the industry's first, original nutritional fruit and function based fresh-blended smoothies. Each "Lifestyle Center" also offers healthy retail product solutions, including sports beverages, energy bars, healthy snacks, vitamin supplements, herbs, minerals and other sports nutrition products. **No. of Franchise Units:** 618. **No. of Company-Owned Units:** 1. **Founded:** 1973.. **Franchised:** 1989. **Equity Capital Needed:** $75,000. **Franchise Fee:** $25,000. **Financial Assistance:** Yes. **Training:** Provides 1 day pre-opening (orientation), 14 days management training at Corporate store, 8 days store opening (14 days before open & 4 days after opening) onsite. Assistance in real estate, design and construction.

10982 ■ Son's
319 W State St.
Quarryville, PA 17566
Ph: (717)786-5665
Fax: (717)786-5645
Description: Gourmet Italian ice, ice cream, and sandwiches. **No. of Franchise Units:** 2. **No. of Company-Owned Units:** 1. **Founded:** 2003.. **Franchised:** 2004. **Equity Capital Needed:** $200,000-$350,000. **Franchise Fee:** $35,000. **Training:** Yes.

10983 ■ Surf City Squeeze
Kahala Corp.
9311 E Via De Ventura
Scottsdale, AZ 85258
Ph: (480)362-4800
Free: 800-438-2590
Fax: (480)362-4812
Description: The franchise caters ice cream, yogurt, smoothies, candy and beverages. **No. of Franchise Units:** 122. **No. of Company-Owned Units:** 3. **Founded:** 1988.. **Franchised:** 1994. **Equity Capital Needed:** $70,150-$392,250. **Franchise Fee:** $30,000. **Royalty Fee:** 6%. **Financial Assistance:** Limited third party financing available. **Training:** Provides 1 week training at headquarters, 2 weeks at franchisee's location, and ongoing support.

10984 ■ TCBY
Mrs. Fields Famous Brands
1141 West 2400 South
Salt Lake City, UT 84121
Ph: (303)573-4800
Free: 800-348-6311
Fax: (435)752-9216
Co. E-mail: tlynch@mrsfields.com
URL: http://www.mrsfieldsfranchise.com
Description: yogurt treats. **No. of Franchise Units:** 500. **No. of Company-Owned Units:** 2. **Founded:** 1981.. **Franchised:** 1982. **Equity Capital Needed:** $191,300-$356,600 estimated initial investment. **Franchise Fee:** $25,000. **Training:** Yes.

10985 ■ Tropical Smoothie Cafe
Tropical Smoothie Franchise Development Corp.
12598 US Hwy. 98 W, Ste. 200
Destin, FL 32550
Free: 888-292-2522
Fax: (850)269-9845
Co. E-mail: scole@tropicalsmoothie.com
URL: http://www.tropicalsmoothie.com
Description: Offers nutritional smoothies. **No. of Franchise Units:** 305. **No. of Company-Owned Units:** 1. **Founded:** 1997.. **Franchised:** 1997. **Equity Capital Needed:** $164,500-$398,000. **Franchise Fee:** $25,000. **Training:** Comprehensive training on operations, marketing & management of your business.

10986 ■ Wienerschnitzel/Tastee-Freez
Galardi Group, Inc.
7700 Irvine Center Dr., Ste. 550
Irvine, CA 92618
Ph: (949)892-2619
Free: 800-764-9353
Fax: (949)892-2615
Co. E-mail: KPeters@GalardiGroup.com
URL: http://www.tastee-freez.com
Description: Fast food, including soft-serve ice cream and desserts. Plans available for free-standing building/food court/seasonal stores considered. **No. of Franchise Units:** 370. **Founded:** 1950.. **Franchised:** 1950. **Equity Capital Needed:** $150,000-$250,000 liquid; $1,200,000 total investment. **Franchise Fee:** $32,000. **Financial Assistance:** Yes. **Training:** Consists of 2 weeks at the corporate office - total operation and business training given.

10987 ■ Yogen Fruz
210 Shields Ct.
Markham, ON, Canada L3R 8V2
Ph: (905)479-8762
Fax: (905)479-5235
URL: http://www.yogenfruz.com
Description: Frozen yogurt and frozen dairy-related treats. **No. of Franchise Units:** 66. **No. of Company-Owned Units:** 4. **Founded:** 1986.. **Franchised:** 1987. **Equity Capital Needed:** $135,679-$472,179. **Franchise Fee:** $25,000. **Royalty Fee:** 3%. **Financial Assistance:** Limited third party financing available. **Training:** Offers 1 week at headquarters and 1 week onsite.

ASSOCIATIONS AND OTHER ORGANIZATIONS

10988 ■ **Association of Image Consultants International (AICI)**
1255 SW Prairie Trl. Pkwy.
Ankeny, IA 50023-7068
Ph: (515)282-5500
Fax: (515)243-2049
Co. E-mail: staff@aici.org
URL: http://www.aici.org
Contact: Kimberly Law, President
Description: Personal color, style, wardrobe, and image planning consultants. Promotes quality service for clients; aids in establishing working relations between retail stores and consultants; assists community colleges in offering accredited image consulting programs; maintains standards of professionalism for members in the image consulting industry. Provides continuing education and training; maintains speakers' bureau. **Scope:** A non profit professional association of men and women specializing in visual appearance, and verbal and non-verbal communication. Members counsel both individual and corporate clients on appearance, behavior and communication skills to help achieve their specific goals with authenticity, credibility and confidence. **Founded:** 1990. **Educational Activities:** Association of Image Consultants Annual Convention and Exhibitor Showcase (Annual). **Awards:** Image Makers Merit for Industry Excellence Award (Annual). **Telecommunication Services:** info@aici.org.

REFERENCE WORKS

10989 ■ *"1914 Proved to Be Key Year for Chevy"* in *Automotive News (Vol. 86, October 31, 2011, No. 6488, pp. S18)*
Pub: Crain Communications Inc.

Ed: Jamie Lareau. **Description:** Chevy Bow Tie emblem was born in 1914, creating the brand's image that has carried through to current days.

10990 ■ *"Another California Firm On Way"* in *Austin Business Journal (Vol. 31, May 6, 2011, No. 9, pp. 1)*
Pub: American City Business Journals Inc.

Ed: Christopher Calnan. **Description:** Main Street Hub Inc. is planning to build a facility in Austin, Texas. The company helps businesses manage their online reputations. Main Street has selected Aquila Commercial LLC as its real estate broker.

10991 ■ *Birthing the Elephant: The Woman's Go-for-It! Guide to Overcoming the Big Challenges of Launching a Business*
Pub: Celestial Arts Publishing Co.

Contact: Patricia Kelly, Manager

Ed: Karin Abarbanel; Bruce Freeman. **Released:** March 2008. **Price:** $15.95. **Description:** Advice for women entrepreneurs is given. The book explores the emotional challenges faced by women starting businesses, along with advice for reshaping image. This handbook helps women survive and succeed in business.

10992 ■ *"Brand Imaging"* in *Small Business Opportunities (November 2010)*
Pub: Harris Publications Inc.

Ed: Karen Harnesk. **Description:** Design and branding pro shares strategies and tips to help guide any small business' image development.

10993 ■ *"The Buck Stops Here"* in *Canadian Business (Vol. 81, November 10, 2008, No. 19, pp. 25)*
Pub: Rogers Media Ltd.

Ed: Sarka Halas. **Description:** Reputation strategist Leslie Gaines-Ross says that minimizing the damage followed by the identification of what went wrong are the first steps that companies need to take when trying to salvage their reputation. Gaines-Ross states that it is up to the CEO to ensure the company's speedy recovery and they need to be at the forefront of the process.

10994 ■ *"Deskside Story: As the Latest Buzzword Suggests, PR Firms Are Happy To Drop By"* in *Inc. (December 2007, pp. 70, 73)*
Pub: Gruner & Jahr USA Publishing

Ed: Nitasha Tiku. **Description:** Setting up a meeting between a company's CEO and a journalist is known as deskside and is becoming popular again whereby a publicist offers clients deskside visits, briefings and alerts to help promote public relations for a company.

10995 ■ *"Empowered"* in *Harvard Business Review (Vol. 88, July-August 2010, No. 7-8, pp. 94)*
Pub: Harvard Business School Publishing

Ed: Josh Bernoff, Ted Schadler. **Description:** HERO concept (highly empowered and resourceful operative) which builds a connection between employees, managers, and IT is outlined. The resultant additional experience and knowledge gained by employees improves customer relationship management.

10996 ■ *"Hopkins' Security, Reputation Face Challenges in Wake of Slaying"* in *Baltimore Business Journal (Vol. 28, August 6, 2010, No. 13)*
Pub: Baltimore Business Journal

Ed: Gary Haber. **Description:** The slaying of Johns Hopkins University researcher Stephen Pitcairn has not tarnished the reputation of the elite school in Baltimore, Maryland among students. Maintaining Hopkins' reputation is important since it is Baltimore's largest employer with nearly 32,000 workers. Insights on the impact of the slaying among the Hopkins' community are also given.

10997 ■ *If You Have to Cry, Go Outside: And Other Things Your Mother Never Told You*
Pub: HarperOne

Ed: Kelly Cutrone. **Released:** February 2, 2010. **Price:** $22.99. **Description:** Women's mentor advises on how to make it in one of the most competitive industries in the world, fashion. She has kicked people out of fashion shows, forced some of reality television's shiny start to fire their friends, and built her own company which is one of the most powerful public relations firms in the fashion business.

10998 ■ *"Increasing Building Work at Ryan Cos."* in *Crain's Chicago Business (Vol. 34, May 23, 2011, No. 21, pp. 6)*
Pub: Crain Communications Inc.

Ed: Eddie Baeb. **Description:** Profile of Tim Hennelly, who is working to make Ryan Company known as a pure builder rather than a developer-builder.

10999 ■ *"It's Time to Take Full Responsibility"* in *Harvard Business Review (Vol. 88, October 2010, No. 10, pp. 42)*
Pub: Harvard Business School Publishing

Ed: Rosabeth Moss Kanter. **Description:** A case for corporate responsibility is cited, focusing on long-term impact and the effects of public accountability.

11000 ■ *"Let Your Stuff Tell a Story: How to Edit Your Accessories to Showcase Your Personality"* in *Charlotte Observer (February 8, 2007)*
Pub: Knight-Ridder/Tribune Business News

Ed: Nancy Brachey. **Description:** Tips to accessorize any home or office are presented; eliminating clutter is stressed.

11001 ■ *Media, Organizations and Identity*
Pub: Palgrave Macmillan

Ed: Lilie Chouliaraki, Mette Morsing. **Released:** January 19, 2010. **Price:** $90.00. **Description:** The mass media, press and television are essential in the formation of corporate identity and the promotion of business image and reputation. This book offers a new perspective into the interrelationships between media and organizations over three dimensions: media as business, media in business and business in the media.

11002 ■ *"Optima Public Relations Gains Partners"* in *Alaska Business Monthly (Vol. 27, October 2011, No. 10, pp. 10)*
Pub: Alaska Business Publishing Company

Ed: Nancy Pounds. **Description:** OPrima Public Relations has partnered with Gogerty Marriott of Seattle and Seattle Design Group.

11003 ■ *"Reputation Warfare"* in *Harvard Business Review (Vol. 88, December 2010, No. 12, pp. 70)*
Pub: Harvard Business School Publishing

Ed: Leslie Gaines-Ross. **Description:** Steps are presented for addressing attacks on corporate public image. These include responding promptly, avoiding disproportionate displays of force, empowering employees to present the firm's position, and stockpiling credentials to bolster credence.

11004 ■ *Sarbanes-Oxley for Dummies, 2nd Ed.*
Pub: John Wiley and Sons, Inc.

Ed: Jill Gilbert Welytok. **Released:** February 2008. **Price:** $21.99. **Description:** Provides the latest Sarbanes-Oxley (SOX) legislation with procedures to safely and effectively reduce compliance costs. Topics include way to: establish SOX standards for IT professionals, minimize compliances costs for every aspect of a business, survive a Section 404 audit, avoid litigation under SOX, anticipate future rules and trends, create a post-SOX paper trail, increase a company's standing and reputation, work with SOX in a small business, meet new SOX standards, build a board that can't be bought, and to comply with all SOX management mandates.

11005 ■ "Timberland's CEO On Standing Up to 65,000 Angry Activists" in Harvard Business Review (Vol. 88, September 2010, No. 9, pp. 39)

Pub: Harvard Business School Publishing

Ed: Jeff Swartz. **Description:** Timberland Company avoided a potential boycott by taking a two-way approach. It addressed a supplier issue that posed a threat to the environment, and launched an email campaign to keep Greenpeace activists informed of the development of a new supplier agreement.

11006 ■ "To Be Seen Is to Be Successful" in Pet Product News (Vol. 64, December 2010, No. 12, pp. 12)

Pub: BowTie Inc.

Ed: David Arvin. **Description:** Guidelines on how pet business retailers can boost customer visibility are described considering that complacency could hamper retailers' efforts to effectively market their businesses. To enhance customer base and stand out from competing businesses, being different, strategic, creative, and differentiated is emphasized.

11007 ■ "Toss the Gum Before You Speak" in Agency Sales Magazine (Vol. 39, July 2009, No. 7, pp. 34)

Pub: MANA

Ed: Stephen D. Boyd. **Description:** When preparing to present to a prospective principal, a salesperson should anticipate the speaking situation and find out in advance the program events that occur around their speech. They should also practice their material in front of a friend or colleague.

11008 ■ "Vanity Plates" in Canadian Business (Vol. 82, April 27, 2009, No. 7, pp. 26)

Pub: Rogers Media

Ed: Andy Holloway. **Description:** Politicians in the U.S. called for the review of firms that availed of the bailout money but are under deals for naming rights of sports stadiums. Angus Reid's Corporate Reputation and Sponsorship Index found for example, that there is little correlation between sponsoring arenas on having a better brand image. It is suggested that firms who enter these deals build closer to people's homes.

11009 ■ "Voice: Rebuilding Trust" in Business Strategy Review (Vol. 21, Summer 2010, No. 2, pp. 79)

Pub: Wiley-Blackwell

Ed: David De Cremer. **Description:** The financial world's attempts to rebuild trust are charted. Three steps to jump-start that process are outlined.

11010 ■ "We Had to Won the Mistakes" in Harvard Business Review (Vol. 88,

July-August 2010, No. 7-8, pp. 108)

Pub: Harvard Business School Publishing

Ed: Adi Ignatius. **Description:** Interview with Howard Schultz, CEO of Starbucks, covers topics that include investment in retraining, the impact of competition, premium quality, authenticity, customer services, strategy development, work-and-life issues, and international presence.

11011 ■ When the Headline Is You: An Insider's Guide to Handling the Media

Pub: Jossey-Bass

Ed: Jeff Ansell, Jeff Lesson. **Price:** $29.95. **Description:** How-to guide for executives and other professionals whose high-visibility requires frequent interviews with the media. Tested techniques, tools, and insights for how to respond to all types of media in tough situation are provided. The books also reveals the lessons learned and the pitfalls to avoid by referencing actual news stores from around the world and provides exercises for readers who wish to sharpen their media-handling skills.

VIDEOCASSETTES/ AUDIOCASSETTES

11012 ■ Building a Profitable Consulting Practice Series

Instructional Video
2219 C St.
Lincoln, NE 68502
Ph: (402)475-6570
Free: 800-228-0164
Fax: (402)475-6500
Co. E-mail: feedback@insvideo.com
URL: http://www.insvideo.com
Released: 19??. **Description:** Two-part business educational series by Howard Shenson offers tips on how to build a profitable consulting practice. Covers consulting opportunities, market strategies, proposal writing, contracting strategies, fee setting, disclosure, and collection techniques. **Availability:** VHS.

11013 ■ The Professional Image

Thomson South-Western
5191 Natorp Blvd.
Mason, OH 45040
Ph: (513)229-1020
Free: 800-543-0487
Released: 1985. **Description:** An instructional program for the business-person in how to choose the right sartorial look for success in the jobplace. **Availability:** VHS; 3/4 U; Q.

CONSULTANTS

11014 ■ Bixler Consulting Group (BCG)

200 Galleria Pky., Ste. 850
Atlanta, GA 30339
Ph: (770)953-1653
Fax: (770)953-4560
Co. E-mail: info@bixlerconsulting.com
URL: http://www.bixlerconsulting.com
Contact: Susan Bixler, President
E-mail: sbixler@bixlerconsulting.com
Scope: Offers executive coaching, leadership workshops, career transitioning programs to enable individuals and organizations to excel in a highly

competitive, transforming marketplace. Target audience: mid-level to senior level leaders. Serves private industries as well as government agencies. **Founded:** 1980. **Publications:** "Professional Presence"; "Take Action!"; "The Professional Image"; "5 Steps to Professional Presence"; "Remaining professional can be more important than the latest fashion"; "Body language can speak volumes during interview," Feb, 2003; "Gift-giving takes careful thought - Don't turn gesture into a faux pas," Dec, 2002; "Role Models," Apr, 2002; "Laugh break can benefit all As seen in The Atlanta Journal-Constitution," Apr, 2002; "E-mail Etiquette," Sep, 2002; "Gaining Co-Workers' Respect," Jan, 2000; "Are You Ignoring Your Rising Stars?". **Seminars:** Team Building Workshop; Professional Presence Workshop; The Business Case for Leadership Workshops; The 360-Degree Feedback Workshop. **Special Services:** 360-Degree Feedback Report.

11015 ■ Lisa Cunningham & Associates

905 W End Ave., Ste. 64
New York, NY 10025-3530
Ph: (212)662-7783
Free: 800-662-7784
Fax: (212)662-7782
Contact: Lisa A. Cunningham, President

Scope: Image consulting firm providing unique indepth professional image management solutions for corporations, retail businesses, and individuals. **Founded:** 1986. **Seminars:** Color Facts for Business Men and Women; Principles of Business Clothing Selection; Basic Grooming (for Hospitality Industries); Proper Fit and Business Do's and Dont's; Building Business Wardrobes; Business Casual Dress; Customer Service; Nonverbal Communications. Executive coachings: Offer high-level executives intensive coachings in one-on-one settings on Facial/Body Language; Vocal Intonation; Communications Styles; and Appearance, Grooming, and Wardrobe.

11016 ■ The Rothschild Image

13900 Tahiti Way, Ste. 308
Marina del Rey, CA 90292
Ph: (310)574-6018
Co. E-mail: info@rothschildimage.com
URL: http://www.rothschildimage.com
Contact: Ashley Rothschild, President
E-mail: ashley@rothschildimage.com

Scope: Image consultant offering advice through group exercises, lectures, wardrobe, and hair and makeup makeovers on how to discover the key components of a winning image. Specializes in designing the images of power brokers, politicians, and entrepreneurs, as well as clients at the start of their careers. **Publications:** "Is There an O'Neal Family Curse? - ABC News," Feb, 2007; "Can an Image Consultant Help You Dress for Success? - Wall Street Journal," Feb, 2006; "Reality Check - Paris Hilton & Amber Moore," Jan, 2004; "Britney's Mystery Man - Britney Spears," Dec, 2003; "People who need to redo their image," Jun, 2003; "Reshaping an Image," Jun, 2003; "Dress to Impress the World International Business Fashion," Apr, 2003. **Seminars:** S.T. A.R.POWER: A Professional Image Consultant Training Program; Learn How to Have More Success, Power and Romance in Your Life.

START-UP INFORMATION

11017 ■ *"Savvy Solutions" in Black Enterprise (Vol. 41, September 2010, No. 2, pp. 46)*
Pub: Earl G. Graves Publishing Co. Inc.
Ed: Tennille M. Robinson. **Description:** Insight is given to help start an import and export business.

ASSOCIATIONS AND OTHER ORGANIZATIONS

11018 ■ **American Association of Exporters and Importers (AAEI)**
1050 17th St. NW, Ste. 810
Washington, DC 20036
Ph: (202)857-8009
Fax: (202)857-7843
Co. E-mail: hq@aaei.org
URL: http://www.aaei.org
Contact: Steve Johnsen, Chairman
Description: Exporters and importers of goods, products, and raw materials; wholesalers and retailers; customs brokers and forwarders; banks; insurance underwriters; steamship companies; customs attorneys and others engaged directly or indirectly in dealing with exports and imports. Seeks fair and equitable conditions for world trade. Anticipates problems of interpretation of laws and regulations affecting members' businesses; gathers and disseminates data on world trade; supports and creates legislation promoting balanced international trade; works for fair administration of policy. Maintains liaison with government committees, agencies, and other trade policy groups. Testifies for exporters and importers before government and other official bodies. Studies problems concerning export and import; offers advice and support to members facing problems in their businesses; conducts forums and workshops on timely topics and developments; holds exporting and importing seminars. Operates extensive library of research information and government data, and records legal precedents. **Founded:** 1921. **Publications:** *International Trade Alert* (Weekly). **Awards:** Lifetime Achievement (Annual); Trade Warrior (Annual).

11019 ■ **Council for International Tax Education (CITE)**
PO Box 1012
White Plains, NY 10602
Ph: (914)328-5656
Free: 800-207-4432
Fax: (914)328-5757
Co. E-mail: info@citeusa.org
URL: http://www.citeusa.org
Contact: Diane Pastore, Executive Director
Description: Corporations, professional firms, and individual tax advisors. Works to maximize members' understanding of U.S. tax incentives and other offshore benefits available to exporters. Conducts educational programs for companies that generate tax incentives for the export of U.S. goods. Holds seminars on international tax, export and cross-

border lease finance, and incentives offered companies that set up manufacturing or operating sites abroad. **Founded:** 1982. **Educational Activities:** CITE Conference.

11020 ■ **Foreign Credit Insurance Association (FCIA)**
125 Park Ave., 14th Fl.
New York, NY 10017
Ph: (212)885-1500
Fax: (212)885-1535
Co. E-mail: service@fcia.com
URL: http://www.fcia.com
Description: Represents marine, property, and casualty insurance companies. Insures companies against the risks of nonpayment by buyers for commercial and/or political reasons. Facilitates the financing of term credit sales, thus providing companies with support to meet competitive terms of payment offered by others. **Founded:** 1991.

11021 ■ **Joint Industry Group (JIG)**
111 Rockville Pike, Ste. 410
Rockville, MD 20850
Ph: (202)466-5490
Fax: (202)559-0131
Co. E-mail: jig@moinc.com
URL: http://www.jig.org
Contact: Megan Giblin, Chairperson
Description: Trade associations and business and professional firms engaged in international trade. Seeks to influence administration of customs and related trade laws to facilitate trade and encourage compliance. **Founded:** 1976. **Awards:** Excellence in Government Award (Annual).

11022 ■ **National Association of Export Companies (NEXCO)**
Grand Central Station
New York, NY 10163
Free: 877-291-4901
Fax: (646)349-9628
Co. E-mail: director@nexco.org
URL: http://www.nexco.org
Contact: Barney Lehrer, President
Description: Established independent international trade firms, bilateral chambers of commerce, banks, law firms, accounting firms, trade associations, insurance companies, and product/service providers; export trading companies; export management companies. Promotes expansion of U.S. trade. Promotes the participation of members in international trade. Conducts educational programs. **Founded:** 1963.

11023 ■ **National Foreign Trade Council (NFTC)**
1625 K St. NW, Ste. 200
Washington, DC 20006
Ph: (202)887-0278
Fax: (202)452-8160
Co. E-mail: nftcinformation@nftc.org
URL: http://www.nftc.org
Contact: William A. Reinsch, President
Description: Manufacturers, exporters, importers, foreign investors, banks, transportation lines, and insurance, communication, law, accounting, service,

and publishing firms. Works to promote and protect American foreign trade and investment. Areas of concern include the removal of arbitrary barriers to expansion of international trade and investment; a greater awareness by the government that this expansion is essential to the economic growth of the U.S.; the formation of a cohesive, consistent international economic policy. **Scope:** trade, human resources, general business in over 150 countries. **Founded:** 1914. **Awards:** NFTC Trade Award (Annual).

11024 ■ **Small Business Exporters Association of the United States (SBEA)**
1156 15th St. NW, Ste. 1100
Washington, DC 20005
Ph: (202)659-9320
Free: 800-345-6728
Fax: (202)872-8543
Co. E-mail: info@sbea.org
URL: http://www.sbea.org
Contact: James Morrison, President
Description: Exporters with fewer than 500 employees, banks, insurance underwriters, carriers, custom brokers, trade associations, trade clubs, researchers, students, and individuals employed by federal or state agencies. Promotes interests of small and mid-size export companies. Informs public and governmental agencies of small business concerns and issues. Disseminates information to members on legislation that influences small export companies. Offers information on marketplace opportunities. Conducts educational and research programs. Operates extensive, interactive website. **Founded:** 1937. **Awards:** Export Enhancement Awards (Annual).

11025 ■ **U.S.-China Business Council (USCBC)**
1818 N St. NW, Ste. 200
Washington, DC 20036-2470
Ph: (202)429-0340
Fax: (202)775-2476
Co. E-mail: info@uschina.org
URL: http://www.uschina.org
Contact: Muhtar Kent, Chairman of the Board
Description: Represents American companies trading with and investing in the People's Republic of China (PRC). Established to facilitate the development of U.S.-China business relations. Provides representation, practical assistance, and up-to-date information to members. Provides business advisory services and sponsors briefings on China trade and investment subjects for member firms. Maintains offices in Washington, DC, in Beijing, and Shanghai. **Founded:** 1973. **Publications:** *China Business Review* (Bimonthly); *China Market Intelligence* (Weekly).

11026 ■ **United States Council for International Business (USCIB)**
1212 Avenue of the Americas
New York, NY 10036
Ph: (212)354-4480
Fax: (212)575-0327
Co. E-mail: info@uscib.org
URL: http://www.uscib.org
Contact: Mr. Peter M. Robinson, President
Description: Serves as the U.S. National Committee of the International Chamber of Commerce. Enables

multinational enterprises to operate effectively by representing their interests to intergovernmental and governmental bodies and by keeping enterprises advised of international developments having a major impact on their operations. Serves as: U.S. representative to the International Organization of Employers; national affiliate to the U.S.A. Business and Industry Advisory Committee to the BIAC. Operates ATA Carnet export service, which enables goods to be shipped overseas duty-free for demonstration and exhibition. Sponsors seminars and luncheon briefings. **Founded:** 1945. **Publications:** *United States Council Foundation: Occasional Paper.* **Awards:** International Leadership Award; International Leadership Award (Annual). **Telecommunication Services:** membership@uscib.org; probinson@uscib.org.

11027 ■ World Trade Centers Association (WTCA)
420 Lexington Ave., Ste. 518
New York, NY 10170
Ph: (212)432-2626
Free: 800-937-8886
Fax: (212)488-0064
Co. E-mail: wtca@wtca.org
URL: http://www.wtcaonline.com/cms_wtca
Contact: Guy F. Tozzoli, President
E-mail: gtozzoli@wtca.org
URL(s): iserve.wtca.org/. **Description:** Regular members are organizations involved in the development or operation of a World Trade Center (WTC). Affiliate members are Chambers of Commerce, clubs, exhibit facilities or other international trade related organizations. Encourages expansion of world trade and international business relationships. **Founded:** 1970. **Publications:** *WTCA News* (Monthly); *WTCA Services Directory* (Annual); *World Trade Centers Association--Membership Directory* (Annual). **Educational Activities:** World Trade Centers Association Spring Meeting (Annual).

EDUCATIONAL PROGRAMS

11028 ■ Import/Export Procedures and Documentation (Onsite)
Seminar Information Service, Inc.
20 Executive Park, Ste. 120
Irvine, CA 92614
Ph: (949)261-9104
Free: 877-SEM-INFO
Fax: (949)261-1963
Co. E-mail: info@seminarinformation.com
URL: http://www.seminarinformation.com
Price: $2,195.00. **Description:** Obtain the skills necessary to deal with banks, freight forwarders, customs brokers, and foreign customers, as well as how to mark merchandise, use forms, licenses, and insurance documents for profitable and error-free passage. **Dates and Locations:** New York, NY.

DIRECTORIES OF EDUCATIONAL PROGRAMS

11029 ■ *AAPEX Export Interest Directory: 2008*
Pub: Motor and Equipment Manufacturers Association
Contact: Robert E. McKenna, President
URL(s): www.oac-intl.orgwww.mema.org. **Released:** Latest edition 2008. **Price:** Free to MEMA/OESA members. **Description:** Lists U.S. companies that are interested in overseas markets, and exhibited at AAPEX 2008.

11030 ■ *Directory of Private Accredited Career Schools and Colleges of Technology*
Pub: Accrediting Commission of Career Schools and Colleges of Technology
Contact: Michale S. McComis, Executive Director
Released: On web page. **Price:** Free. **Description:** Covers 3900 accredited post-secondary programs that provide training programs in business, trade, and technical fields, including various small business endeavors. Entries offer school name, address, phone, description of courses, job placement assistance, and requirements for admission. Arrangement is alphabetical.

11031 ■ *International Directory of Importers--Food and Beverage*
Pub: International Directory of Importers
Contact: Esther Camacho, Manager
URL(s): www.importersnet.com/. **Released:** Annual; latest edition 2009. **Price:** $320, Individuals print; $320, Individuals CD-ROM; $370, Individuals print and CD-ROM. **Covers:** 7,200 major food and beverage importers around the world. **Entries include:** Company name, address, phone, fax, email addresses when available, importing manager, year established. **Indexes:** Geographical by country, company, and by commodity.

11032 ■ *International Directory of Importers - Sporting Goods and Toys*
Pub: International Directory of Importers
Contact: Esther Camacho, Manager
URL(s): www.importersnet.com/. **Released:** Annual; latest edition 2009. **Price:** $295, Individuals print; $295, Individuals CD-ROM; $345, Individuals print and CD-ROM. **Covers:** 5,000 worldwide manufacturers, and importers trading sporting goods, toys, and commodities. **Entries include:** Company name, address, phone, fax, email addresses when available, importing manager, year established. **Arrangement:** Alphabetical. **Indexes:** Alphabetical By country/company and by commodity.

REFERENCE WORKS

11033 ■ *"Abroad, Not Overboard" in Entrepreneur (Vol. 36, April 2008, No. 4, pp. 68)*
Pub: Entrepreneur Media, Inc.
Ed: Crystal Detamore-Rodman. **Description:** Export-Import Bank is an agency created by the U.S. government to help exporters get credit insurance and capital loans by providing them with loan guarantees. The bank, being criticized as supporting more the bigger exporters, has allotted to smaller businesses a bigger portion of the annual credit being approved.

11034 ■ *"Advances in Pump Technology - Part Two" in Contractor (Vol. 57, February 2010, No. 2, pp. 22)*
Pub: Penton Media, Inc.
Ed: Mark Eatherton. **Description:** Chinese and Japanese companies have come up with refrigerant based heat pump products that are air based which will significantly lower the installed cost of heat pump based systems. Some of these newer models have variable speed, soft start compressors and have the ability to perform high-efficiency heat pump operation on a modulating basis.

11035 ■ *"Africa Rising" in Harvard Business Review (Vol. 86, September 2008, No. 9, pp. 36)*
Pub: Harvard Business School Press
Ed: John T. Landry. **Description:** Review of the book entitled, 'Africa Rising: How 900 Million African Consumers Offer More Than You Think' provides advice for marketing to those on the African continent.

11036 ■ *"Ag Officials Employ Preventive Pest Control" in Yakima Herald-Republic (June 24, 2011)*
Pub: Yakima Herald-Republic
Ed: Ross Courtney. **Description:** Washington State Department of Agriculture is placing vineyard traps for the European grapevine moth, an invasive species whose larvae eat grape buds and fruit clusters, thus exposing the vines to diseases that could destroy them.

11037 ■ *"Airing It Out" in The Business Journal-Serving Greater Tampa Bay (Vol. 28, July 11, 2008, No. 29, pp. 1)*
Pub: American City Business Journals, Inc.
Ed: Jane Meinhardt. **Description:** Flanders Corp. is planning to expand its business in Europe and Southeast Asia. The St. Petersburg, Florida-based company has about 2,800 employees and manufactures air filtration products for industrial and residential applications.

11038 ■ *"All About The Benjamins" in Canadian Business (Vol. 81, September 29, 2008, No. 16, pp. 92)*
Pub: Rogers Media Ltd.
Ed: David Baines. **Description:** Discusses real estate developer Royal Indian Raj International Corp., a company that planned to build a $3 billion 'smart city' near the Bangalore airport; to this day nothing has ever been built. The company was incorporated in 1999 by Manoj C. Benjamin one investor, Bill Zack, has been sued by the developer for libel due to his website that calls the company a scam. Benjamin has had a previous case of fraud issued against him as well as a string of liabilities and lawsuits.

11039 ■ *"All For One, None for All?" in Canadian Business (Vol. 83, October 12, 2010, No. 17, pp. 60)*
Pub: Rogers Media Ltd.
Ed: Michael McCullogh. **Description:** The effect of the growth of Canada's overseas provincial trade offices on Canadian trade is discussed. Economic development commissions in the country have devised a single 'Consider Canada' campaign to pitch foreign investors. It is hoped that large cities will gain from banding together rather than competing against one another.

11040 ■ *"An Amazing Race" in Canadian Business (Vol. 81, March 3, 2008, No. 3, pp. 25)*
Pub: Rogers Media
Ed: Rachel Pulfer. **Description:** U.S. presidential candidates Barack Obama and Hilary Clinton lead the Democratic Part primaries while John McCain is a frontrunner at the Republican Party. These leading candidates have different plans for the U.S. economy which will affect Canada's own economy particularly concerning trade policies. The presidential candidates' proposals and the impacts of U.S. economic downturn on Canada are examined.

11041 ■ *"Ampm Focus Has BP Working Overtime; New Convenience-Store Brand Comes to Chicago" in Crain's Chicago Business (April 28, 2008)*
Pub: Crain Communications, Inc.
Ed: John T. Slania. **Description:** Britian's oil giant BP PLC is opening its ampm convenience stores in the Chicago market and has already begun converting most of its 78 Chicago-area gas stations to ampms. The company has also started to franchise the stores to independent operators. BP is promoting the brand with both traditional and unconventional marketing techniques such s real or simulated 3D snacks embedded in bus shelter ads and an in-store Guitar Hero contest featuring finalists from a recent contest at the House of Blues.

11042 ■ *"And The Winner Is.." in Canadian Business (Vol. 81, March 3, 2008, No. 3, pp. 21)*
Pub: Rogers Media
Ed: Joe Castaldo. **Description:** Thirty out of 141 Canadian chief executive officers think that Hilary Clinton would be best for U.S.-Canada relations if elected as U.S. president. Findings also revealed that 60 respondents believe that presidential candidate John McCain would be best on handling issues of international military-security. Views on the candidates' performance and their ability to deal with the declining U.S. economy as well as international trade issues are also given.

11043 ■ *"Arizona Firms In Chicago Go For Gold With '08 Games" in The Business Journal - Serving Phoenix and the Valley of the Sun (Vol. 28, August 8, 2008, No. 49, pp. 1)*
Pub: American City Business Journals, Inc.
Ed: Patrick O'Grady. **Description:** More than 20 U.S. athletes will wear Arizona-based eSoles LLC's custom-made insoles to increase their performance at the 2008 Beijing Olympics making eSoles one of the beneficiaries of the commercialization of the games. Translation software maker Auralog Inc saw a 60 percent jump in sales from its Mandarin Chinese language applications.

11044 ■ *"A Baby Step to the South"* in *Canadian Business (Vol. 81, July 22, 2008, No. 12-13, pp. 21)*

Pub: Rogers Media Ltd.

Ed: Jane Bao. **Description:** Canada's free trade agreement (FTA) with Colombia is seen as Canada's re-engagement with Latin America. Some politicians believe that the FTA is more of a political agreement than a trade agreement with Colombia. Key information on Canada's trade agreements, as well as trade with Colombia and Latin American countries, is presented.

11045 ■ *Bad Samaritans: The Myth of Free Trade and the Secret History of Capitalism*

Pub: Bloomsbury USA

Ed: Ha-Joon Chang. **Released:** 2009. **Price:** $26.95. **Description:** Economist challenges open-market proponents and believes that free trade would do more harm than good.

11046 ■ *"The Believer"* in *Inc. (December 2007, pp. 130-138)*

Pub: Gruner & Jahr USA Publishing

Ed: Leigh Buchanan. **Description:** Profile of Selena Cuffe, wine importer and socially conscious woman entrepreneur, who is focusing her talents on helping South Africa get wine products to America.

11047 ■ *Benchmarking the Canadian Business Presence in East Asia*

Pub: University of Toronto Press Inc.

Ed: A.E. Safarian; Wendy Dobson. **Released:** October 27, 1995. **Price:** $19.00. **Description:** Covers Canadian trade with East Asian economies.

11048 ■ *"Betting On Volatile Materials"* in *Barron's (Vol. 88, July 14, 2008, No. 28, pp. M11)*

Pub: Dow Jones & Co., Inc.

Ed: John Marshall. **Description:** Economic slowdowns in the U.S., Europe and China could cause sharp short-term declines in the materials sector. The S&P Materials sector is vulnerable to shifts in the flow of funds. Statistical data included.

11049 ■ *"Beware this Chinese Export"* in *Barron's (Vol. 90, August 30, 2010, No. 35, pp. 21)*

Pub: Barron's Editorial & Corporate Headquarters

Ed: Bill Alpert, Leslie P. Norton. **Description:** A look at 158 China reverse-merger stocks in the U.S. reveal that the median underperformed the index of U.S. listed Chinese companies by 75 percent in their first three years. These reverse merger stocks also lagged the Russell 2000 index of small cap stocks by 66 percent.

11050 ■ *"Bottler Will Regain Its Pop"* in *Barron's (Vol. 88, March 17, 2008, No. 11, pp. 56)*

Pub: Dow Jones & Company, Inc.

Ed: Alexander Eule. **Description:** Discusses he 30 percent drop in the share price of PepsiAmericas Inc. from their 2007 high which presents an opportunity to buy into the company's dependable U.S. market and fast growing Eastern European business. The bottler's Eastern European operating profits in 2007 grew to $101 million from $21 million in 2006.

11051 ■ *"Bottom-Fishing and Speed-Dating in India"* in *Barron's (Vol. 88, March 24, 2008, No. 12, pp. M12)*

Pub: Dow Jones & Company, Inc.

Ed: Elliot Wilson. **Description:** Indian stocks have fallen hard in 2008, with Mumbai's Sensex 30 down 30 percent from its January 2008 peak of 21,000 to 14,995 in March. The India Private Equity Fair 2008 attracted 140 of the world's largest private equity firms and about 24 of India's fastest-growing corporations. Statistical data included.

11052 ■ *"Bountiful Barrels: Where to Find $140 Trillion"* in *Barron's (Vol. 88, July 14, 2008, No. 28, pp. 40)*

Pub: Dow Jones & Co., Inc.

Ed: Andrew Bary. **Description:** Surge in oil prices has caused a large transfer of wealth to oil-producing countries thereby reshaping the global economy. Oil reserves of oil exporting countries are now valued at

$140 trillion. Economist Stephen Jen believes that this wealth will be transformed into paper assets as these countries invest in global stocks and bonds.

11053 ■ *"Brazil's New King of Food"* in *Barron's (Vol. 89, July 13, 2009, No. 28, pp. 28)*

Pub: Dow Jones & Co., Inc.

Ed: Kenneth Rapoza. **Description:** Perdigao and Sadia's merger has resulted in the creation of Brasil Foods and the shares of Brasil Foods provides a play on both Brazil's newly energized consumer economy and its role as a major commodities exporter. Brasil Foods shares could climb as much as 36 percent.

11054 ■ *"Brewing a Love-Haiti Relationship"* in *The Business Journal - Serving Phoenix and the Valley of the Sun (Vol. 28, July 4, 2008, No. 44)*

Pub: American City Business Journals, Inc.

Ed: Yvonne Zusel. **Description:** Jean and Alicia Marseille have ventured into a coffee distribution company called Ka Bel LLC which markets Marabou brand of coffee imported from Haiti. Part of the proceeds of the business is donated to entrepreneurs from Jean's country, Haiti. Details of the Marseille's startup business and personal mission to help are discussed.

11055 ■ *"Brewing National Success"* in *Hawaii Business (Vol. 53, November 2007, No. 5, pp. 46)*

Pub: Hawaii Business Publishing

Ed: Alex Salkever. **Description:** Kona Brewing Co. (KBC) is already selling its brews in four cities in Florida and 17 other states and Japan as well. KBC is currently forming a deal with Red Hook to produce Longboard Lager and other KBC brews at Red Hooks' brewery in New Hampshire. KBC's chief executive officer Mattson Davis shares KBC's practices for success.

11056 ■ *Building Wealth in China: 36 True Stories of Chinese Millionaires and How They Made Their Fortunes*

Pub: Crown Business Books

Ed: Ling, Zhu. **Released:** April 27, 2010. **Price:** $15.00. **Description:** Thirty-six of China's most successful and innovative entrepreneurs discuss valuable lessons for growing a business in China.

11057 ■ *"Calendar"* in *Crain's Detroit Business (Vol. 26, January 11, 2010, No. 2, pp. 16)*

Pub: Crain Communications Inc.

Description: Listing of events includes seminars sponsored by the Detroit Economic Club as well as conferences dealing with globalization and graphic design.

11058 ■ *"Calendar"* in *Crain's Detroit Business (Vol. 26, January 18, 2010, No. 3, pp. 16)*

Pub: Crain Communications Inc.

Description: Listing of events includes seminars sponsored by the Detroit Economic Club as well as conferences dealing with globalization and marketing.

11059 ■ *"Cambodia Calls"* in *Barron's (Vol. 89, July 27, 2009, No. 30, pp. M7)*

Pub: Dow Jones & Co., Inc.

Ed: Leslie P. Norton. **Description:** Interest in frontier markets could jump if enthusiasm about growth in the developed world gathers steam. Cambodia is the latest market to get attention where a handful of investors are trying to set up funds. One investor believes that Cambodia is back open for business but others are still cautious about investing in the country.

11060 ■ *"Can a Brazilian SUV Take On the Jeep Wrangler?"* in *Business Week (September 22, 2008, No. 4100, pp. 50)*

Pub: McGraw-Hill Companies, Inc.

Ed: Helen Walters. **Description:** Profile of the Brazilian company TAC as well as the flourishing Brazilian car market; TAC has launched a new urban vehicle, the Stark, which has won prizes for innovation; the company uses local technology and manufacturing expertise.

11061 ■ *Canada Business and Investment Opportunities Yearbook*

Pub: USA International Business Publications

Released: March 20, 2009. **Price:** $149.95. **Description:** Yearbook contains basic information on export-import, investment and business opportunities in Canada.

11062 ■ *Canada Investment and Business Guide*

Pub: USA International Business Publications

Released: March 20, 2009. **Price:** $149.95. **Description:** Guide for conducting investment, export-import activity in Canada; includes strategic and business information, contacts regulations and more.

11063 ■ *"Canada, Not China, Is Partner In Our Economic Prosperity"* in *Crain's Chicago Business (Vol. 31, April 14, 2008, No. 15, pp. 14)*

Pub: Crain Communications, Inc.

Ed: Paul O'Connor. **Description:** In 2005 more than $500 billion in two-way trade crossed the friendly border between the Great Lakes states and Canadian provinces and for decades Canada is every Great Lakes State's number one and growing export market.

11064 ■ *"CBC Chief: Future is Now"* in *Business Courier (Vol. 27, August 13, 2010, No. 15, pp. 1)*

Pub: Business Courier

Ed: Lucy May. **Description:** Tom Williams, chairman of the Cincinnati Business Committee (CBC), maintains that politicians and business leaders must cooperate to ensure the competitiveness of the city for the 21st Century. Under Williams' leadership, the CBC has put emphasis on initiatives related to government efficiency, economic development, and public education. Williams' views on a proposed inland port are given.

11065 ■ *"Cemex Paves a Global Road to Solid Growth"* in *Barron's (Vol. 88, March 10, 2008, No. 10, pp. 24)*

Pub: Dow Jones & Company, Inc.

Ed: Sandra Ward. **Description:** Shares of Cemex are expected to perform well with the company's expected strong performance despite fears of a US recession. The company has a diverse geographical reach and benefits from a strong worldwide demand for cement.

11066 ■ *"Cents and Sensibility"* in *Playthings (Vol. 107, January 1, 2009, No. 1, pp. 19)*

Pub: Reed Business Information

Contact: Jeff Greisch, President

Ed: Pamela Brill. **Description:** Recent concerns over safety, phthalate and lead paint and other toxic materials, as well as consumers going green, are issues discussed by toy manufacturers. Doll manufacturers also face increase labor and material costs and are working to design dolls that girls will love.

11067 ■ *"Champion Enterprises Buys UK Company"* in *Crain's Detroit Business (Vol. 24, March 17, 2008, No. 11, pp. 4)*

Pub: Crain Communications, Inc.

Ed: Daniel Duggan. **Description:** With the acquisition of ModularUK Building Systems Ltd., a steel-frame modular manufacturer, Champion Enterprises has continued its expansion outside the United States.

11068 ■ *"Charlotte Pipe Launches Satirical Campaign"* in *Contractor (Vol. 57, January 2010, No. 1, pp. 6)*

Pub: Penton Media, Inc.

Description: Charlotte Pipe and Foundry Co. launched an advertising campaign that uses social media and humor to make a point about how it can be nearly impossible to determine if imported cast iron pipes and fittings meet the same quality standards as what is made in the U.S. The campaign features 'pipe whisperers' and also spoofs pipe sniffing dogs.

11069 ■ *"China Trade Deficit Costs California Jobs"* in *Sacramento Business Journal* (Vol. 25, August 8, 2008, No. 23, pp. 1)

Pub: American City Business Journals, Inc.

Ed: Melanie Turner. **Description:** California topped the ranking of states with job losses because of the rising trade deficit with China, losing 325,800 jobs between 2001-2007. The U.S. has lost 2.3 million workers within the period. Other views and information on the job loses because of the trade deficit with China, are presented.

11070 ■ *"China Vs. the World: Whose Technology Is It?"* in *Harvard Business Review* (Vol. 88, December 2010, No. 12, pp. 94)

Pub: Harvard Business School Publishing

Ed: Thomas M Hout, Pankaj Ghemawat. **Description:** Examination of the regulation the Chinese government is implementing that require foreign corporations wishing to do business in the country to give up their new technologies. These regulations avoid World Trade Organization technology transfer provisions and complicate the convergence of socialism and capitalism.

11071 ■ *"Chinese Fund Loans $33.5 Million to Prestolite"* in *Crain's Detroit Business* (Vol. 26, January 18, 2010, No. 3, pp. 1)

Pub: Crain Communications Inc.

Ed: Ryan Beene. **Description:** Prestolite Electric Inc., a distributor of alternators and starter motors for commercial and heavy-duty vehicles, looked to China for fresh capital in order to fund new product launches.

11072 ■ *"City Slickers"* in *Canadian Business* (Vol. 81, March 31, 2008, No. 5, pp. 36)

Pub: Rogers Media

Ed: Joe Castaldo. **Description:** Richard Florida believes that the creative class drives the economy and the prosperity of countries depends on attracting and retaining these people. Florida has brought attention to developing livable and economically vibrant cities thanks in part to his promotional skills. However, he has also drawn critics who see his data on his theories as flimsy and inadequate.

11073 ■ *"Closed Minds and Open Skies"* in *Barron's* (Vol. 88, March 10, 2008, No. 10, pp. 50)

Pub: Dow Jones & Company, Inc.

Ed: Thomas Donlan. **Description:** American politicians have closed minds when it comes to fair trade. The American government must not interfere with the country's manufacturing industries or worry about outsourcing defense contracts to European aerospace company Airbus.

11074 ■ *"Coming: Cheaper Oil and a Stronger Buck"* in *Barron's* (Vol. 88, March 24, 2008, No. 12, pp. 53)

Pub: Dow Jones & Company, Inc.

Ed: Lawrence C. Strauss. **Description:** Carl C. Weinberg, the chief economist of High Frequency Economics, forecasts that Chinese economic growth will slow down and that oil prices will drop to $80 a barrel in 2008. He also believes that the US dollar will start rising the moment the Federal Reserve stops cutting interest rates.

11075 ■ *"Compelling Opportunities"* in *Barron's* (Vol. 88, March 10, 2008, No. 10, pp. 39)

Pub: Dow Jones & Company, Inc.

Ed: Neil A. Martin. **Description:** Michael L. Reynal, portfolio manager of Principal International Emerging Markets Fund, is bullish on the growth prospects of stocks in emerging markets. He is investing big on energy, steel, and transportation companies.

11076 ■ *"Coping With a Shrinking Planet"* in *Agency Sales Magazine* (Vol. 39, December 2009, No. 11, pp. 46)

Pub: MANA

Ed: Mark Young. **Description:** China and India are forcing big changes in the world and are posing a huge threat to U.S. manufacturers and their sales representatives. Reps may want to consider expand-

ing into these territories. Helping sell American products out of the country presents an opportunity for economic expansion.

11077 ■ *"Cost Remains Top Factor In Considering Green Technology"* in *Canadian Sailings* (June 30, 2008)

Pub: UBM Global Trade

Contact: Leonard J. Corallo, President

Ed: Julie Gedeon. **Description:** Improving its environmental performance remains a priority in the shipping industry; however, testing new technologies can prove difficult due to the harsh conditions that ships endure as well as installation which usually requires a dry dock.

11078 ■ *"CPR-CN Deal to Ease Vancouver Logjam"* in *Globe & Mail* (January 27, 2006, pp. B4)

Pub: CTVglobemedia Publishing Inc.

Ed: Brent Jang. **Description:** In a bid to lessen West coast port grid lock Canadian Pacific Railway Ltd and Canadian National Railway Co. has agreed to share tracks in the Vancouver region. This will allow the trains to operate more efficiently from the Vancouver Port.

11079 ■ *Currency Internationalization: Global Experiences and Implications for the Renminbi*

Pub: Palgrave Macmillan

Ed: Wensheng Peng, Chang Shu. **Released:** January 5, 2010. **Price:** $100.00. **Description:** A collection of academic studies relating to the potential internationalization of China's remninbi. It also discusses the increasing use of China's remninbi currency in international trade and finance.

11080 ■ *D & B Principal International Businesses: The World Marketing Directory*

Pub: Dun and Bradstreet Corp.

Contact: David J. Emery, President

URL(s): dnb.com.au/Sales_and_Marketing/International_business_directories/Principal_International_Business_Directory. **Released:** Annual **Price:** $595, commercial & library price. **Covers:** approximately 55,000 leading businesses in all lines, outside of the U.S., in 143 countries. **Entries include:** Company name, address, phone, fax, D&B number, telex, up to six Standard Industrial Classification (SIC) code, line of business, sales volume (in U.S. currency), number of employees, parent company and location, executive name and title, year established, and import/export designation. **Arrangement:** Geographical. **Indexes:** Geographical, cross-referenced alphabetical, industry classification.

11081 ■ *"Dollar Doldrums; How American Companies are Beating the Currency Crunch"* in *Inc.* (March 2008, pp. 45-46)

Pub: Gruner & Jahr USA Publishing

Ed: Sarah Goldstein. **Description:** Despite the low American dollar, some exporters are seeing a growth in their businesses, while other have had to relocate operations and switch to U.S. supplier. Four business owners tell how they are dealing with the current economic conditions.

11082 ■ *"Don't Try This Offshore"* in *Harvard Business Review* (Vol. 86, September 2008, No. 9, pp. 39)

Pub: Harvard Business School Press

Description: Fictitious outsourcing scenario is presented, with contributors offering advice. The suggestions address the ease or complexity of offshoring business creativity, along with challenges and benefits.

11083 ■ *"Down the Tracks, a Whistle Is a Blowin"* in *Barron's* (Vol. 89, July 27, 2009, No. 30, pp. 36)

Pub: Dow Jones & Co., Inc.

Ed: Jim McTague. **Description:** Higher numbers of freight-rail carloads are a sign that the economy is improving and it is no stretch to imagine that this is aided by the American Recovery and Reinvestment Act. It is also predicted that 2009 municipal bond is-

suance will be above $373 billion with at least $55 billion of it made up of Buy America Bonds that are subsidized by the federal government.

11084 ■ *"Dragon, but.."* in *Canadian Business* (Vol. 81, December 8, 2008, No. 21, pp. 45)

Pub: Rogers Media Ltd.

Ed: Matthew McLearn. **Description:** The greatest challenge in smooth trade relations between China and Canada is believed to be lukewarm relations with China over human rights issues. Australia on the other hand, has attracted huge Chinese outward direct investments because of strong trade relations.

11085 ■ *"Dreaming in Macau"* in *Canadian Business* (Vol. 81, December 8, 2008, No. 21, pp. 65)

Pub: Rogers Media Ltd.

Ed: Joe Chidley. **Description:** Key information, as well as views on the economic aspects of Macau are presented. Macau was once monopolized by Stanley Ho's Sociedad de Turismo e Diversoes de Macau, but the government transformed the area into a leisure-and-entertainment spot. Details about Cirque de Soleil are also presented.

11086 ■ *"EBay Finally Gaining Traction in China"* in *San Jose Mercury News* (October 26, 2011)

Pub: San Jose Mercury News

Ed: John Boudreau. **Description:** eBay has developed a new strategy in China that allows exporters of every type of merchandise to sell directly to eBays 97 million overseas users.

11087 ■ *Effect of the Overvalued Dollar on Small Exporters: Congressional Hearing*

Pub: DIANE Publishing Company

Ed: Donald Manzullo. **Released:** September 2002. **Price:** $30.00. **Description:** Congressional hearing: Witnesses: Dr. Lawrence Chimerine, Economist; Tony Raimondo, President and CEO, Behlen Manufacturing Company; Robert J. Weskamp, President, WesTech, Inc.; Wayne Dollar, President, Georgia Farm Bureau; and Vargese George, President and CEO, Westex International, Inc. Appendix includes correspondence sent to committee on the overvalued dollar.

11088 ■ *"European Stocks on Deck"* in *Barron's* (Vol. 89, July 27, 2009, No. 30, pp. M7)

Pub: Dow Jones & Co., Inc.

Ed: Vito J. Racanelli. **Description:** European stocks are cheap and these trade at a discount to U.S. equities rarely seen in the past 40 years. This represents an opportunity for Americans and trends show that Europe's stocks outperform when there is a discrepancy between the price to earnings ratio in European stocks versus U.S. stocks and when sentiment on European equities are downbeat.

11089 ■ *"Europe's Meltdown"* in *Canadian Business* (Vol. 83, June 15, 2010, No. 10, pp. 76)

Pub: Rogers Media Ltd.

Ed: Bryan Borzykowski. **Description:** As European countries such as Greece, Spain, and Portugal struggle with debt problems, it is worth noting that its equities trade at a 30 percent discount to the U.S. and that a 10 percent drop in the Euro translates to a 10 percent rise in profitability for exporters. Investors may also want to focus on business-to-business operations rather than consumer-focused ones.

11090 ■ *"Event Stresses Cross-Border Cooperation"* in *Crain's Detroit Business* (Vol. 24, March 31, 2008, No. 13, pp. 5)

Pub: Crain Communications, Inc.

Ed: Chad Halcom. **Description:** According to John Austin, a senior fellow of The Brookings Institution, open immigration policies, better transportation and trade across the border and a cleanup of the Great Lakes will bring economic resurgence to Midwestern states and Canadian provinces with manufacturing economies.

11091 ■ *"Export Initiative Launched" in Philadelphia Business Journal (Vol. 28, December 11, 2009, No. 43, pp. 1)*
Pub: American City Business Journals
Ed: Athena D. Merritt. **Description:** The first initiative that came out of the partnership between the Export-Import Bank of the US, the city of Philadelphia, and the World Trade Center of Greater Philadelphia is presented. A series of export finance workshops have featured Ex-Im Bank resources that can provide Philadelphia businesses with working capital, insurance protection and buyer financing.

11092 ■ *"Export Opportunity" in Business Journal-Portland (Vol. 24, October 12, 2007, No. 33, pp. 1)*
Pub: American City Business Journals, Inc.
Ed: Matthew Kish. **Description:** U.S. dollar is weak, hitting an all-time low against the Euro, while the Canadian dollar is also performing well it hit parity for the first time after more than thirty years. The weak U.S. dollar is making companies that sell overseas benefit as it makes their goods cheaper to buy.

11093 ■ *Export Sales and Marketing Manual*
Pub: Export Institute
Contact: Mr. John R. Jagoe, Director
URL(s): www.exportusa.comwww.exportinstitute.com/agora.cgi?page=products01.htm, www.exportinstitute.com. **Released:** Annual; Latest edition 24th; 2011. **Price:** $295, Individuals print or CD; $395, Other countries print & CD. **Publication includes:** List of approximately 4,000 international trade contacts, including World Trade Centers, U.S. Department of Commerce Trade Specialists and Country Desk Officers, State International Trade offices, small business development centers, U.S. Customs services, U.S. Port Authorities, U.S. embassies, foreign trade associations in the U.S., and chambers of commerce in foreign countries, and foreign embassies and chambers of commerce in the U.S. **Entries include:** Name, address, phone, fax, name and title of contact, geographical area served, products covered, description of services, and 1,200 internet addresses of export-related sites. Principal content of publication is a step-by-step program showing U.S. companies and entrepreneurs how to begin exporting or increase their existing overseas sales. **Arrangement:** Classified by product/service and export marketing functions. **Indexes:** General, international trade or export/import. Worksheets, graphs, flow charts, pricing and budgeting formats, international price quotations, export contracts, international shipping documents, samples of international correspondence, glossaries, index and illustrations.

11094 ■ *Exporters' Encyclopedia*
Pub: Dun and Bradstreet Corp.
Contact: David J. Emery, President
URL(s): www.dnb.com. **Released:** Annual; August; biweekly updates. **Publication includes:** List of United States and foreign government agencies, international trade associations, and firms specializing in international business and trade research; covers about 220 countries. **Entries include:** Country profile, communications, key contacts, trade regulations, documentation, marketing data, transportation, business travel. Principal content of publication is analysis of 220 export markets. **Arrangement:** Geographical.

11095 ■ *"Fair Play? China Cheats, Carney Talks and Rankin Walks; Here's the Latest" in Canadian Business (Vol. 81, March 17, 2008, No. 4)*
Pub: Rogers Media
Description: Discusses the World Trade Organization which says that China is breaking trade rules by taxing imports of auto parts at the same rate as foreign-made finished cars. Mark Carney first speech as the governor of the Bank of Canada made economists suspect a rate cut on overnight loans. Andre Rankin was ordered by the Ontario Securities Commission to pay $250,000 in investigation costs.

11096 ■ *"Fed May Ban Amphibian Trade" in Pet Product News (Vol. 64, November 2010,* No. 11, pp. 13)
Pub: BowTie Inc.
Description: U.S. Fish and Wildlife Service is seeking public input on a petition submitted by the conservation activist group Defenders of Wildlife. The petition involves possible classification of chytrid fungus-infected amphibians and amphibian eggs as 'injurious wildlife' under the Lacey Act. Interstate trading or importation of injurious wildlife into the U.S. is not allowed.

11097 ■ *"Fight Against Fake" in The Business Journal-Portland (Vol. 25, July 18, 2008, No. 19, pp. 1)*
Pub: American City Business Journals, Inc.
Ed: Erik Siemers. **Description:** Companies, such as Columbia Sportswear Co. and Nike Inc., are fighting the counterfeiting of their sportswear and footwear products through the legal process of coordinating with law enforcement agencies to raid factories. Most of the counterfeiting factories are in China and India. Other details on the issue are discussed.

11098 ■ *"Finding A Higher Gear" in Harvard Business Review (Vol. 86, July-August 2008, No. 8, pp. 68)*
Pub: Harvard Business School Press
Ed: Thomas A. Stewart; Anand P. Raman. **Description:** Anand G. Mahindra, the chief executive officer of Mahindra and Mahindra Ltd., discusses how his company fosters innovation, drawn from customer centricity, and how this will grow the company beyond India's domestic market.

11099 ■ *"Fries With That?" in Canadian Business (Vol. 81, September 29, 2008, No. 16, pp. 33)*
Pub: Rogers Media Ltd.
Ed: Calvin Leung. **Description:** Profile of Toronto-based New York Fries, which has four stores in South Korea, is planning to expand further as well as into Hong Kong and Macau; the company also has a licensee in the United Arab Emirates whom is also planning to expand.

11100 ■ *Fugitive Denim: A Moving Story of People and Pants in the Borderless World of Global Trade*
Pub: W.W. Norton & Company
Ed: Rachel Snyder. **Released:** April 2009. **Price:** $16.95. **Description:** In-depth study of the global production and processes of how jeans are designed, sewn, and transported as well as how the cotton for denim is grown, regulated, purchased and processed.

11101 ■ *"Getting Rid of Global Glitches: Choosing Software For Trade Compliance" in Black Enterprise (Vol. 41, September 2010, No. 2, pp. 48)*
Pub: Earl G. Graves Publishing Co. Inc.
Ed: Marcia Wade Talbert. **Description:** Compliance software for trading with foreign companies must be compatible with the U.S. Census Bureau's Automated Export System (www.aesdirect.gov). It has to be current with regulatory requirements for any country in the world. Whether owners handle their own compliance or hire a logistics company, they need to be familiar with this software in order to access reports and improve transparency and efficiency of theft supply chain.

11102 ■ *"Global Market Could Be Silver Lining" in Hispanic Business (January-February 2008, pp. 14, 16, 18)*
Pub: Hispanic Business
Description: Economic slowdown in the U.S. is expected to continue through 2008. However, the export sector should hold steady during the same period.

11103 ■ *"Going the Distance" in Hispanic Business (July-August 2007, pp. 38-40, 42-43)*
Pub: Hispanic Business
Ed: Keith Rosenblum. **Description:** Top Hispanic export companies are discussed; charts with exporters by sector as well as a complete listing that includes company name, CEO, number of employees, revenue information, export sales, growth, products and services and destinations are included.

11104 ■ *"The Great Cleanup" in Canadian Business (Vol. 81, April 14, 2008, No. 6, pp. 50)*
Pub: Rogers Media
Ed: Graham Silnicki. **Description:** China's rectification program includes the licensing of 100 percent of food producers and monitoring of 100 percent of raw materials for exports between August and December, 2007. There is a lot of money to be made for those who are willing to help China win its quality battle. PharmEng International Inc. is one of the companies that helps Chinese companies meet international quality standards.

11105 ■ *"Grin and Bear It" in Canadian Business (Vol. 81, March 3, 2008, No. 3, pp. 53)*
Pub: Rogers Media
Ed: Jeff Sanford. **Description:** Discusses the United States economic downturn, caused by the credit market crisis, which is expected to affect the Canadian economy, as Canada depend on the U.S. for 80 percent of its exports. Economist David Rosenberg thinks that in 2008, housing prices will decline by 15 percent and gross domestic product growth will slow to 0.8 percent. Other forecasts for Canadian economy are given.

11106 ■ *"Headwinds From the New Sod Slow Aer Lingus" in Barron's (Vol. 88, March 10, 2008, No. 10, pp. M6)*
Pub: Dow Jones & Company, Inc.
Ed: Sean Walters; Arindam Nag. **Description:** Aer Lingus faces a drop in its share prices with a falling US market, higher jet fuel prices, and lower long-haul passenger load factors. British media companies Johnston Press and Yell Group are suffering from weaker ad revenue and heavier debt payments due to the credit crunch.

11107 ■ *"Hot For All The Wrong Reasons" in Canadian Business (Vol. 81, March 31, 2008, No. 5, pp. 19)*
Pub: Rogers Media
Ed: Andrea Jezovit. **Description:** Soaring platinum prices are due to South Africa's platinum mining industry's safety issues and power supply disruptions that exacerbate the metal's supply problems. South Africa supplies 80 percent of the world's platinum. South Africa's power utility has said that it cannot guarantee the industry's power needs until 2013.

11108 ■ *"How Bad Is It?" in Hawaii Business (Vol. 54, July 2008, No. 1, pp. 35)*
Pub: Hawaii Business Publishing
Ed: Jolyn Okimoto Rosa. **Description:** Donald G. Horner, chief executive officer of First Hawaiian Bank, says that the current Hawaiian economic situation is a cyclical slowdown. Maurice Kaya, an energy consultant, says the slowdown is due to overdependence on imported fuels. Other local leaders, such as Constance H. Lau, also discuss their view on the current economic situation in Hawaii.

11109 ■ *"How Exports Could Save America" in Barron's (Vol. 89, July 20, 2009, No. 29, pp. 15)*
Pub: Dow Jones & Co., Inc.
Ed: Jonathan R. Laing. **Description:** Increase in US exports should help drive up the nation's economic growth, according to Wells Capital Management strategist Jim Paulsen. He believes US gross domestic product could grow by 3-3.5 percent annually starting in 2010 due to a more favorable trade balance.

11110 ■ *"How High Can Soybeans Fly?" in Barron's (Vol. 88, March 10, 2008, No. 10, pp. M14)*
Pub: Dow Jones & Company, Inc.
Ed: Kenneth Rapoza. **Description:** Prices of soybeans have risen to $14.0875 a bushel, up 8.3 percent for the week. Increased demand, such as in China and in other developing economies, and the investment-driven commodities boom are boosting prices.

11111 ■ *"How to Secure U.S. Jobs" in Gallup Management Journal (October 27, 2011)*
Pub: Gallup
Ed: Jim Clifton. **Description:** If America doubled its number of engaged customers globally, it could triple

exports, which would create more good jobs and put the US economy back on track.

11112 ■ *"How Two Flourishing Exporters Did It"* in *Hispanic Business (Vol. 30, July-August 2008, No. 7-8, pp. 46)*
Pub: Hispanic Business, Inc.

Ed: Richard Kaplan. **Description:** Vigorous growth in export revenues posted by two Hispanic-owned export companies Compasa LLC and Ametza LLC is discussed; both firms have benefited from their closer locations to major Mexican markets, superior quality of their products, market knowledge and the relationships of trust developed with key business partners.

11113 ■ *"Ill Winds; Cuba's Economy"* in *The Economist (Vol. 390, January 3, 2009, No. 8612, pp. 20)*
Pub: The Economist Newspaper Inc.

Description: Cuba's long-term economic prospects remain poor with the economy forecasted to grow only 4.3 percent for the year, about half of the original forecast, due in part to Hurricane Gustav which caused $10 billion in damage and disrupted the food-supply network and devastated farms across the region; President Raul Castro made raising agricultural production a national priority and the rise in global commodity prices hit the country hard. The only bright spot has been the rise in tourism which is up 9.3 percent over 2007.

11114 ■ *"Immigration Issues Frustrate Owners From Overseas"* in *The Business Journal-Serving Greater Tampa Bay (Vol. 28, August 15, 2008)*
Pub: American City Business Journals, Inc.

Ed: Margie Manning. **Description:** Investors who availed the E-2 visa program believe that the tightened restrictions on the visa program has trapped them in the United States. The E-2 investor visa program was designed to attract investors into the U.S., but restrictions were tightened after the September 11, 2001 attacks. Other views and information on E-2 and its impact on investors are presented.

11115 ■ *Import/Export for Dummies*
Pub: John Wiley and Sons, Inc.

Ed: John J. Capela. **Released:** June 2008. **Price:** $19.99. **Description:** Provides entrepreneurs and small- to medium-size businesses with information required to start exporting products globally and importing goods to the U.S. Topics covered include the ins and outs of developing or expanding operations to gain market share, with details on the top ten countries in which America trades, from Canada to Germany to China.

11116 ■ *Importers Manual USA: The Single Source Reference Encyclopedia for Importing to the United States*
Pub: World Trade Press
Contact: Roy Hinkelman, Manager
E-mail: roy@worldtradepress.com

URL(s): store.worldtradepress.com/Importers_ Manual_USA.php. **Released:** Biennial; latest edition 4, 2003. **Price:** $145, Individuals Hardcover; $108.75, Individuals Sale Price. **Publication includes:** Lists of trade fairs, embassies, chambers of commerce, banks, and other sources of information on various aspects of international trade. **Entries include:** Source name, address, phone, telex, description. Principal content of publication is information on importing to the U.S. , including coverage of U.S. Customs, banking, laws, shipping, and insurance. **Indexes:** Product/service, geographical, source name.

11117 ■ *"Importers Share Safety Liability"* in *Feedstuffs (Vol. 80, January 21, 2008, No. 3, pp. 19)*
Pub: Miller Publishing Company, Inc.

Description: Pet food and toys containing lead paint are among products from China being recalled due to safety concerns. American Society for Quality's list of measures that outsourcing companies can take to help ensure safer products being imported to the U.S.

11118 ■ *"In China, Railways to Riches"* in *Barron's (Vol. 88, July 7, 2008, No. 27, pp. M9)*
Pub: Dow Jones & Co., Inc.

Ed: Assif Shameen. **Description:** Shares of Chinese railway companies look to benefit from multimillion-dollar investments aimed at upgrading the Chinese railway network. Investment in the sector is expected to reach $210 billion for the 2006-2010 period.

11119 ■ *"In India, A Gold-Price Threat?"* in *Barron's (Vol. 88, June 30, 2008, No. 26, pp. M12)*
Pub: Dow Jones & Co., Inc.

Ed: Melanie Burton. **Description:** Gold purchases in India are falling as record prices take its toll on demand. Gold imports to India fell by 52 percent in May 2008 from the previous year and local prices are higher by one-third from the previous year to 12,540 rupees for 10 grams.

11120 ■ *"Is the Sun Setting on Oil Sector's Heydey?"* in *Globe & Mail (January 25, 2007, pp. B3)*
Pub: CTVglobemedia Publishing Inc.

Ed: Shawn McCarthy. **Description:** The effects of fuel efficiency management policies of the United States on Canadian petroleum industry are discussed. Canada is the largest exporter of crude oil to America after the Middle East.

11121 ■ *"Is 'Tsunami' of Freight in our Future?"* in *Business Courier (Vol. 26, November 27, 2009, No. 31, pp. 1)*
Pub: American City Business Journals, Inc.

Ed: Dan Monk. **Description:** Freight companies are planning for cargo-container shipping facilities on the riverfront of Cincinnati in light of the completion of $5 billion Panama Canal expansion in 2015. The city's capability to utilize the growth in freight has been under investigation by authorities.

11122 ■ *"It's Time To Swim"* in *Canadian Business (Vol. 81, March 3, 2008, No. 3, pp. 37)*
Pub: Rogers Media

Ed: Megan Harman. **Description:** Canadian manufacturers should consider Asian markets such as India and the United Arab Emirates as the U.S. economic downturn continues. Canada's shortage in skilled labor is also expected to negatively affect manufacturing industries. Ontario's plans to assist manufacturers are also presented.

11123 ■ *"Jobs, Export Surge Confirm Recovery"* in *Globe & Mail (March 10, 2007, pp. B5)*
Pub: CTVglobemedia Publishing Inc.

Ed: Heather Scoffield. **Description:** The increase in the number of jobs and exports that is forecast to reverse the slowdown in the Canadian economy is discussed.

11124 ■ *"Keeping Railcars 'Busy At All Times' At TTX"* in *Crain's Chicago Business (Vol. 31, April 28, 2008, No. 17, pp. 6)*
Pub: Crain Communications, Inc.

Ed: Bob Tita. **Description:** Profile of the president of Chicago railcar pool operator TTX Co. and his business plan for the company which includes improving fleet management and car purchasing through better use of data on railroad demand.

11125 ■ *Leonard's Guide--International Air Cargo Directory*
Pub: G.R. Leonard & Co.
Contact: David Ercolani, Manager

URL(s): www.leonardsguide.com. **Released:** Latest edition 2011-2012. **Price:** $175, Individuals print. **Covers:** Companies providing air cargo service from North America to international and domestic destinations.

11126 ■ *"Lightening the Load"* in *Crain's Cleveland Business (Vol. 28, October 8, 2007, No. 40, pp. 3)*
Pub: Crain Communications, Inc.

Ed: Jay Miller. **Description:** Companies reliant on barge deliveries are running well below capacity due to both the building up of silt at the bottom of the

Cuyahoga River as well as the lower water levels which are causing a number of problems for the barges and big boats that deliver goods to the region.

11127 ■ *"Li'l Guy Rolls Up Into Bigger Company"* in *The Business Journal-Serving Metropolitan Kansas City (Vol. 26, September 12, 2008)*
Pub: American City Business Journals, Inc.

Ed: Suzanna Stagemeyer. **Description:** Li'l Guy Foods, a Mexican food company in Kansas City, Missouri, has merged with Tortilla King Inc. Li'l Guy's revenue in 2007 was $3.3 million, while a newspaper report said that Tortilla King's revenue in 2001 was $7.5 million. Growth opportunities for the combined companies and Li'l Guy's testing of the Wichita market are discussed.

11128 ■ *"Madeleine Paquin"* in *Canadian Business (Vol. 81, March 3, 2008, No. 3, pp. 92)*
Pub: Rogers Media

Ed: Regan Ray. **Description:** Madeleine Paquin, chief executive officer and president of Logistec Corp., talks about how she balanced her career and her life as a mother to two girls. Paquin thinks that working mothers need to focus on some things instead of trying to do everything. Her career in the marine cargo handling industry is also discussed.

11129 ■ *"Making Factory Tours Count"* in *Playthings (Vol. 107, January 1, 2009, No. 1, pp. 14)*
Pub: Reed Business Information
Contact: Jeff Greisch, President

Ed: Malcolm Denniss. **Description:** The importance of touring an overseas toy supplier's manufacturing facility is stressed. Strategies for general factory visits are outlined in order to determine safety-related quality assurance issues in production.

11130 ■ *Managing Economies, Trade and International Business*
Pub: Palgrave Macmillan

Ed: Aidan O'Connor. **Released:** January 19, 2010. **Price:** $90.00. **Description:** An in-depth look at the areas that affect and influence international business, exploring specific issues businesses face in terms of economic development, trade law, and international marketing and management.

11131 ■ *"Marine Act Amendments Gain Parliamentary Approval"* in *Canadian Sailings (July 7, 2008)*
Pub: UBM Global Trade
Contact: Leonard J. Corallo, President

Ed: Alex Binkley. **Description:** Changes to the Canada Marine Act provides better borrowing deals as well as an ability to tap into federal infrastructure funding for environmental protection measures, security improvements and other site enhancements.

11132 ■ *"Market Watch"* in *Barron's (Vol. 88, March 24, 2008, No. 12, pp. M18)*
Pub: Dow Jones & Company, Inc.

Ed: Ashraf Laidi; Marc Pado; David Kotok. **Description:** Latest measures implemented by the Federal Reserve to address the credit crisis did not benefit the US dollar, with the Japanese yen and the euro recouping earlier losses against the dollar. Goldman Sachs reported earnings of $3.23 per share, claiming a stronger liquidity position. The US markets bottomed early on 22 January 2007, according to evidence.

11133 ■ *"Melamine Analytical Methods Released"* in *Feedstuffs (Vol. 80, October 6, 2008, No. 41, pp. 2)*
Pub: Miller Publishing Company

Description: Romer Labs has released new validations for its AgraQuant Melamine enzyme-linked immunosorbent assay. The test kit screens for melamine in feed and diary products, including pet foods, milk and milk powder. Melamine by itself is nontoxic in low doses, but when combined with cyanuric acid it can cause fatal kidney stones. The Chinese dairy industry is in the midst of a huge melamine crisis; melamine-contaminated dairy and food products from China have been found in more than 20 countries.

11134 ■ *"Miami's 'Big Wheels' Keep Latin America Rolling"* in *Hispanic Business* *(July-August 2007, pp. 46-47)*

Pub: Hispanic Business

Ed: Frank Nelson. **Description:** Four top Hispanic owned exporters of tires are discussed. All four companies are based in Miami, Florida.

11135 ■ *"Minimizing Import Risks"* in *Canadian Sailings (July 7, 2008)*

Pub: UBM Global Trade

Contact: Leonard J. Corallo, President

Ed: Jack Kohane. **Description:** New food and product safety laws may be enacted by Canada's Parliament; importers, retailers and manufacturers could face huge fines if the new laws are passed.

11136 ■ *"Mission to China"* in *Canadian Business (Vol. 81, December 8, 2008, No. 21, pp. 28)*

Pub: Rogers Media Ltd.

Ed: Andrew Wahl. **Description:** Canada China Business Council and the Council of the Federation visited China for a three-city trade mission. The trade mission aims to re-establish the strong relationship between China and Canada.

11137 ■ *"Montreal Port Head Lands CP Ships Deal"* in *Globe & Mail (January 5, 2006, pp. B4)*

Pub: CTVglobemedia Publishing Inc.

Description: The opinions of president Dominic Taddeo, on the positive impact of TUI AG's acquisition of CP Ships Ltd. on operations at Port of Montreal, are presented.

11138 ■ *"The Mood of a Nation"* in *Canadian Business (Vol. 81, April 14, 2008, No. 6, pp. 56)*

Pub: Rogers Media

Ed: Joe Castaldo. **Description:** Independent Fish Harvesters Inc. processes more kilograms a year and has had to hire more workers but its managers worry about how a slowdown in the U.S. economy will affect his business. A planned shopping complex in Mirabel Quebec, the manufacturing industry in Kitchener, Ontario, and a cattle farming business in Sarnia, Ontario are discussed to provide a snapshot of the challenges that business in Canada are facing as recession looms.

11139 ■ *"More Pain"* in *Canadian Business (Vol. 81, December 24, 2007, No. 1, pp. 12)*

Pub: Rogers Media

Ed: Lauren McKeon. **Description:** Manufacturing sector in Canada is sinking with a forecast by as much as 23 percent for 2008, which can be offset as manufacturers say they plan to increase productivity by 25 percent. Details on the sector's competitiveness, workforce, importing of machinery from the U.S. and financial needs for research and development are examined.

11140 ■ *"Mover and Sheika"* in *Conde Nast Portfolio (Vol. 2, June 2008, No. 6, pp. 104)*

Pub: Conde Nast Publications

Contact: David Carey, President

Ed: John Arlidge. **Description:** Profile of Princess Sheika Lubna who is the first female foreign trade minister in the Middle East, the United Arab Emirates biggest business envoy, paving the way for billions in new investment, and also a manufacturer of her own perfume line.

11141 ■ *"No Shortage of Challenges for Cross-Border Trade"* in *Canadian Sailings (June 30, 2008)*

Pub: UBM Global Trade

Contact: Leonard J. Corallo, President

Ed: Kathlyn Horibe. **Description:** Pros and cons of the North American Free Trade Agreement are examined. The agreement between the U.S. and Canada concerning trade was an essential step toward securing economic growth for Canadian citizens. Two-way trade between the counties has tripled since the agreement and accounts for 7.1 million American and 3 million Canadian jobs.

11142 ■ *Official Export Guide*

Pub: UBM Global Trade

Contact: Leonard J. Corallo, President

URL(s): www.cbizmedia.comwww.officialexportguide. com. **Released:** Annual; January; inter-edition supplements. **Price:** $449.50, sale price; $899, regular price. **Covers:** Customs officials, port authorities, embassies and consulates, chambers of commerce, foreign trade zones, and other organizations and agencies involved in international trade; prospective foreign buyers; related trade services. **Entries** include: Generally, organization or company name, address, phone, phone, telex, fax, names and titles of key personnel. **Database includes:** For each country, description of seaport, airport, and trade zone facilities, documentary requirements, trade, and discussion of export prospects; Export Administration Regulations. **Arrangement:** Geographical, then classified by service.

11143 ■ *"On the Itinerary: Your Future"* in *Entrepreneur (Vol. 37, October 2009, No. 10, pp. 92)*

Pub: Entrepreneur Media, Inc.

Ed: Joel Holland. **Description:** Josh Hackler's Spanish Vines imports and distributes wines from Spain while using Spanish culture to help market the wines. The business was hatched after Hackler signed up for a study-abroad program in Spain.

11144 ■ *"Online Fortunes"* in *Small Business Opportunities (Fall 2008)*

Pub: Entrepreneur Media Inc.

Description: Fifty hot, e-commerce enterprises for the aspiring entrepreneur to consider are featured; virtual assistants, marketing services, party planning, travel services, researching, web design and development, importing as well as creating an online store are among the businesses featured.

11145 ■ *"OPEC Exposed"* in *Hawaii Business (Vol. 54, September 2008, No. 3, pp. 2)*

Pub: Hawaii Business Publishing

Ed: Serena Lim. **Description:** Organization of the Petroleum Exporting Countries (OPEC) has said that their effort in developing an alternative energy source has driven prices up. The biofuel sector is criticizing the statement, saying that a research study found that biofuels push petroleum prices down by 15 percent. Details on the effect of rising petroleum prices are discussed.

11146 ■ *"Open Skies: Opportunity, Challenge for Airlines"* in *Crain's Chicago Business (April 21, 2008)*

Pub: Crain Communications, Inc.

Ed: Paul Merrion. **Description:** Discusses the new aviation agreement between Europe and the United States known as Open Skies; the pact creates opportunities for U.S. carriers to fly to new destinations in Europe from more U.S. cities; it also allows carriers to fly between European cities, something they have not been able to do until now.

11147 ■ *"Parent Firm's Global Reach, Stricter Air Quality Rules Have Stock Smiling"* in *Crain's Cleveland Business (October 15, 2007)*

Pub: Crain Communications, Inc.

Ed: David Bennett. **Description:** Since Stock Equipment Co., a firm that makes industrial pollution control equipment, was acquired by Schenck Process Group, a diversified global manufacturer based in Germany, the company's orders from abroad have been on the rise. The purchase has opened the doors to regions such as Eastern and Central Europe, Latin America and Australia.

11148 ■ *"Paying for the Recession: Rebalancing Economic Growth"* in *Montana Business Quarterly (Vol. 49, Spring 2011, No. 1, pp. 2)*

Pub: Bureau of Business & Economic Research

Ed: Patrick M. Barkey. **Description:** Four key issues required to address in order to rebalance economic growth in America are examined. They include: savings rates, global trade imbalances, government budgets and most importantly, housing price correction.

11149 ■ *"Port Metro Vancouver Unveiled"* in *Canadian Sailings (July 7, 2008)*

Pub: UBM Global Trade

Contact: Leonard J. Corallo, President

Description: Vancouver Fraser Port Authority is marketing the port as Port Metro Vancouver; Along with the new name the port has announced additional strategies for continued growth and launched a new logo.

11150 ■ *"Procter & Gamble Boosts Bet on Exclusive Brands"* in *Business Courier (Vol. 27, July 9, 2010, No. 10, pp. 1)*

Pub: Business Courier

Ed: Jon Newberry. **Description:** Procter & Gamble is creating more special versions of its brands such as Pringles and Pampers exclusively for retail partners such as Tesco in the U.K. The greater push towards this direction is seen as a way to regain market share.

11151 ■ *"Pulque with Flavor"* in *Canadian Business (Vol. , pp.)*

Pub: Rogers Media Ltd.

Ed: Augusta Dwyer. **Description:** Mexico-based Pulque Poliqhui, which has exported 20,000 bottles of Pulque into Canada in March 2008, plans to distribute in Ontario and Quebec. Pulque Poliqhui is introducing Cool Passion, a fruit-flavored version of pulque in Canada.

11152 ■ *"Q&A Interview With Perrin Beatty"* in *Canadian Business (Vol. 80, October 8, 2007, No. 20, pp. 13)*

Pub: Rogers Media

Description: Perrin Beatty, president and chief executive officer of the Canadian Chamber of Commerce, talks about his move from the Canadian Manufacturers and Exporters to his current organization. He also discusses the state of Canada's economy, as well as the need for leadership.

11153 ■ *"Recalls Cause Consumers to Put More Stock in Online Reviews"* in *Crain's Cleveland Business (Vol. 28, November 12, 2007, No. 45)*

Pub: Crain Communications, Inc.

Ed: Jack Neff. **Description:** Due to the string of product recalls over the last year, consumers are looking at online product reviews to help them make purchasing decisions which could reshape marketing for a wide range of products.

11154 ■ *"Religious Revival"* in *Canadian Business (Vol. 81, December 8, 2008, No. 21, pp. 57)*

Pub: Rogers Media Ltd.

Ed: Paul Webster. **Description:** Canada-based lawyer Cyndee Todgham Cherniak believes that Canadians wishing to do business in China should have professional competence, as well as cultural and spiritual sensitivity. Chinese government officials also acknowledge the role of religion in China's economy.

11155 ■ *"Reportlinker Adds Report: Social Networks: Five Consumer Trends for 2009"* in *Wireless News (October 23, 2009)*

Pub: Close-Up Media

Description: 'Social Networks: Five Consumer Trends for 2009,' a new market research report by Reportlinker.com found that in the countries of Italy and Spain lag behind their European neighbors in Internet development. Since large numbers of consumers in these two countries remain offline, only a minimal portion of total advertising spending goes into Internet marketing, and those advertising campaigns are directed at the relatively young, affluent users. Statistical data included.

11156 ■ *"Reps Continue to Move to International Trade"* in *Agency Sales Magazine (Vol. 39, September-October 2009, No. 9, pp. 24)*

Pub: MANA

Ed: Jack Foster. **Description:** Sales representatives should get involved and look into international trade if they want to be successful in the future. The weak

U.S. dollar, labor costs, and the low cost of transportation are factors that drive the trend towards international trade.

11157 ■ *"Research and Markets Adds Report: Asian - Internet Market" in Health and Beauty Close-Up (January 19, 2010)*
Pub: Close-Up Media
Description: Overview of Research and Markets new report regarding Internet marketing and e-commerce in the Asian region; statistical data included.

11158 ■ *"Riding the Export Wave: How To Find a Good Distributor Overseas" in Inc. (January 2008, pp. 49)*
Pub: Gruner & Jahr USA Publishing
Ed: Sarah Goldstein. **Description:** Small companies should contact the U.S. embassy in foreign companies in order to connect with the U.S. Commercial Service's Gold Key program that is designed to work with small and midsize exporters.

11159 ■ *"Rising in the East; Research and Development" in The Economist (Vol. 390, January 3, 2009, No. 8612, pp. 47)*
Pub: The Economist Newspaper Inc.
Description: Impressive growth of the technological research and development in Asian countries is discussed. Statistical data included.

11160 ■ *"Rough Trade" in Canadian Business (Vol. 79, September 11, 2006, No. 18, pp. 31)*
Pub: Rogers Media
Ed: Christina Campbell. **Description:** The divergence between trade policy agreements entered into by Chile and the Canadian government are highlighted. Canada-Chile Free Trade Agreement and the myth around the big benefits to be reaped by bilateral trade policy agreements are discussed.

11161 ■ *"Russian Renaissance" in Chicago Tribune (September 22, 2008)*
Pub: McClatchy-Tribune Information Services
Ed: Alex Rodriguez. **Description:** Winemakers from Russia are returning to the craft and quality of winemaking now that they are free from Soviet restraints.

11162 ■ *"Saudi Overtures" in The Business Journal-Portland (Vol. 25, August 15, 2008, No. 23, pp. 1)*
Pub: American City Business Journals, Inc.
Ed: Aliza Earnshaw. **Description:** Saudi Arabia's huge revenue from oil is creating opportunities for Oregon companies as the country develops new cities, industrial zones, and tourism centers. Oregon exported only $46.8 million worth of goods to Saudi Arabia in 2007 but the kingdom is interested in green building materials and methods, renewable energy and water quality control, and nanotechnology all of which Oregon has expertise in.

11163 ■ *"Sedo Keeps Trucking in Good Times and Bad" in Crain's Chicago Business (Vol. 31, April 28, 2008, No. 17, pp. 35)*
Pub: Crain Communications, Inc.
Ed: Samantha Stainburn. **Description:** Discusses Seko Worldwide Inc., an Itasca-based freight forwarder, and its complicated road to growth and expansion on a global scale.

11164 ■ *"Shaky on Free Trade" in Canadian Business (Vol. 81, December 24, 2007, No. 1, pp. 29)*
Pub: Rogers Media
Ed: Rachel Pulfer. **Description:** Rhetoric at the U.S. presidential elections seems to be pointing toward a weaker free trade consensus, with Democratic candidates being against the renewal of free trade deals, while Republican candidates seem to be for free trade.

11165 ■ *"Shopped Out; Retailing Gloom" in The Economist (Vol. 390, January 3, 2009, No. 8612, pp. 26)*
Pub: The Economist Newspaper Inc.
Description: Economic volatility in the retail sector is having an impact on a number of countries around the globe. Europe is experiencing hard economic times as well and unless businesses have a strong business plan banks feel unable to lend the money

necessary to tide the retailers over. The falling pound has increased the cost of imported goods and small to midsize retail chains may not be able to weather such an unforgiving economic climate.

11166 ■ *"Sign of Progress" in Playthings (Vol. 106, October 1, 2008, No. 9, pp. 4)*
Pub: Reed Business Information
Contact: Jeff Greisch, President
Ed: Cliff Annicelli. **Description:** The ramifications of the toy recalls in 2007 are discussed. Mandates for lead-free toys and other safety issues are having an impact on the American toy industry.

11167 ■ *"Slimmed-Down Supplier TI Automotive Relaunches" in Crain's Detroit Business (Vol. 26, January 11, 2010, No. 2, pp. 14)*
Pub: Crain Communications Inc.
Ed: Robert Sherefkin. **Description:** TI Automotive Ltd., one of the world's largest suppliers of fuel storage and delivery systems, has reorganized the company by splitting it into five global divisions and is relaunching its brand which is now more focused on new technology.

11168 ■ *"Some Relief Possible Following Painful Week" in Barron's (Vol. 88, July 14, 2008, No. 28, pp. M3)*
Pub: Dow Jones & Co., Inc.
Ed: Kopin Tan. **Description:** Dow Chemical is offering a 74 percent premium to acquire Rohm & Haas' coatings and electronics materials operations. Frontline amassed a 5.6 percent stake in rival Overseas Shipholding Group and a merger between the two would create a giant global fleet with pricing power. Highlights of the U.S. stock market during the week that ended in July 11, 2008 are discussed. Statistical data included.

11169 ■ *A Splendid Exchange: How Trade Shaped the World*
Pub: Atlantic Monthly Press
Ed: William J. Bernstein. **Released:** 2009. **Price:** $30.00. **Description:** Chronicle of how commerce defined cultures and shaped history.

11170 ■ *"The Superpower Dilemma" in Canadian Business (Vol. 83, August 17, 2010, No. 13-14, pp. 42)*
Pub: Rogers Media Ltd.
Description: Canada has been an energy superpower partly because it controls the energy source and the production means, particularly of fossil fuels. However, Canada's status as superpower could diminish if it replaces petroleum exports with renewable technology for using sources of energy available globally.

11171 ■ *"Supply Chain Visibility A Two-Way Street" in Canadian Sailings (July 7, 2008)*
Pub: UBM Global Trade
Contact: Leonard J. Corallo, President
Ed: Jack Kohane. **Description:** Canada is experiencing unprecedented market pressures due to globalization. Competition from foreign countries, demand for better and faster service from customers and shorter innovation cycles are some of the problems the country is facing regarding trade and the importing and exporting industry.

11172 ■ *"Tales of the City" in Canadian Business (Vol. 81, December 8, 2008, No. 21, pp. 37)*
Pub: Rogers Media Ltd.
Ed: Joe Chidley. **Description:** Key information on doing business in Hong Kong are shared by an entrepreneur, a consultant, an exporter, and a financier who were from Canada. Hong Kong hosts about 3,900 regional headquarters or offices of international companies.

11173 ■ *"The Three Amigos" in Canadian Business (Vol. 81, March 17, 2008, No. 4, pp. 19)*
Pub: Rogers Media
Ed: Rachel Pulfer. **Description:** Mexican president Felipe Calderon said that Mexico exported 30 percent more to Europe and 25 percent more to other countries in Latin America in 2006 in light of the

downturn in the U.S. economy. Calderon made this announcement in a speech at Harvard University while protestors marched outside protesting against NAFTA.

11174 ■ *"Tied to Home: Female Owned Businesses Export Less, And It's Not Just Because They're Smaller" in Canadian Business (April 14, 2008)*
Pub: Rogers Media
Ed: Lauren McKeon. **Description:** Only 12 percent of small and midsized enterprises that are run by women export their products and services. Government agencies can be more proactive in promoting the benefits of exporting by including women in case studies and recruiting women as mentors. Exporting provides great growth potential especially for the service sector where women have an advantage.

11175 ■ *"Timken's Bearings Rolling in China, India" in Crain's Cleveland Business (Vol. 28, October 29, 2007, No. 43, pp. 14)*
Pub: Crain Communications, Inc.
Ed: David Bennett. **Description:** Canton-based Timken Co., a manufacturer of bearings and specialty metals, is seeing growing demand for its line of tapered roller bearings, which allow rail users to carry heavy car loads. The company is finding significant growth in China and India due to their rapidly growing rail markets.

11176 ■ *"To Keep Freight Rolling, Springfield Must Grease the Hub" in Crain's Chicago Business (Vol. 31, April 21, 2008, No. 16, pp. 22)*
Pub: Crain Communications, Inc.
Ed: Paul O'Connor. **Description:** Discusses the importance of upgrading Chicago's continental-hub freight rail system which is integral to moving international products as well as domestic ones. Global tonnage is expected to double by 2020 and unless more money is designated to upgrade the infrastructure the local and national economy will suffer.

11177 ■ *"Too Much Precaution About Biotech Corn" in Barron's (Vol. 88, March 17, 2008, No. 11, pp. 54)*
Pub: Dow Jones & Company, Inc.
Ed: Mark I. Schwartz. **Description:** In the U.S., 90 percent of cultivated soybeans are biotech varietals as well as 60 percent of the corn. Farmers have significantly reduced their reliance on pesticides in the growing of biotech corn. Biotech cotton cultivation has brought hundreds of millions of dollars in net financial gains to farmers. The European Union has precluded the cultivation or sale of biotech crops within its border.

11178 ■ *"Top 50 Exporters" in Hispanic Business (Vol. 30, July-August 2008, No. 7-8, pp. 42)*
Pub: Hispanic Business, Inc.
Ed: Hildy Medina. **Description:** Increases in exports revenues reported by food exporters and green companies in a time of economic slowdown in the U.S are described. Food exporters have benefited from the growth of high-volume grocery stores in underdeveloped countries and the German governments' promotion of solar energy has benefited the U.S. solar heating equipment and solar panel manufactures.

11179 ■ *"Top Private Companies" in Baltimore Business Journal (Vol. 28, August 27, 2010, No. 16, pp. 1)*
Pub: Baltimore Business Journal
Ed: Gary Haber. **Description:** The combined revenue of the 100 largest private firms in Maryland's Baltimore region dropped from about $22.7 billion in 2008 to $21 billion in 2009, an annual decrease of more than 7 percent. To survive the recession's impact, these firms resorted to strategies such as government contracting and overseas expansion. How these strategies affected the revenue of some firms is described.

11180 ■ *Trade with Italy*
Pub: Italy-America Chamber of Commerce
Contact: Alberto Comini, President
URL(s): www.italchambers.org. Released: Biennial; Latest edition 2009. Price: $150. Covers: more than 6,600 importers and exporters to and from the United States. Entries include: Company name, address, phone, fax, name and title of contact, products or services; importer listings show brand names and firms represented; listings for U.S. companies in Italy show address and name of Italian representative. Database includes: Business rules, taxation, tariffs, etc. Arrangement: Classified by activity. Indexes: Commodity, brand name, exporter name.

11181 ■ *"Trade Winds" in Canadian Sailings (June 30, 2008)*
Pub: UBM Global Trade
Contact: Leonard J. Corallo, President
Ed: Peter Malkovsky. Description: Trade between Canada and the United States is discussed as well as legislation concerning foreign trade and the future of this trade relationship.

11182 ■ *"Transborder Short-Sea Shipping: Hurdles Remain" in Canadian Sailings (June 30, 2008)*
Pub: UBM Global Trade
Contact: Leonard J. Corallo, President
Ed: Kathlyn Horibe. Description: Legislation that would exempt non-bulk commercial cargo by water in the Great Lakes region from U.S. taxation is discussed.

11183 ■ *"The Transparent Supply Chain" in Harvard Business Review (Vol. 88, October 2010, No. 10, pp. 76)*
Pub: Harvard Business School Publishing
Ed: Steve New. Description: Examination of the use of new technologies to create a transparent supply chain, such as next-generation 2D bar codes in clothing labels that can provide data on a garment's provenance.

11184 ■ *"Tweaking On-Board Activities, Equipment Saves Fuel, Reduces CO2" in Canadian Sailings (June 30, 2008)*
Pub: UBM Global Trade
Contact: Leonard J. Corallo, President
Description: Optimizing ship activities and equipment uses less fuel and therefore reduces greenhouse gas emissions. Ways in which companies are implementing research and development techniques in order to monitor ship performance and analyze data in an attempt to become more efficient are examined.

11185 ■ *"Uncle Volodya's Flagging Christmas Spirit; Russia" in The Economist (Vol. 390, January 3, 2009, No. 8612, pp. 22)*
Pub: The Economist Newspaper Inc.
Description: Overview of Russia's struggling economy as well as unpopular government decisions such as raising import duties on used foreign vehicles so as to protect Russian carmakers.

11186 ■ *Understanding Exporting in the Small and Micro Enterprise*
Pub: Nova Science Publishers, Inc.
Ed: Densil A. Williams. Released: April 1, 2009. Price: $79.00. Description: An examination into the reasons why some small and micro locally-owned businesses choose to sell a portion of their goods abroad while others facing similar market conditions remain focused on the domestic market.

11187 ■ *"U.S. Targets China's Exported Paper" in Globe & Mail (March 31, 2007, pp. B5)*
Pub: CTVglobemedia Publishing Inc.
Ed: Barrie McKenna. Description: The prospects of the rise in duties on goods imported into the United States, due to the levy of duties on imports of Chinese paper, are discussed.

11188 ■ *"Up On The Farm" in Canadian Business (Vol. 81, March 31, 2008, No. 5, pp. 23)*
Pub: Rogers Media
Ed: John Gray. Description: Agricultural products have outperformed both energy and metal and even the prospect of a global economic slowdown does not seem to hinder its prospects. The Organization for Economic Cooperation and Development sees prices above historic equilibrium levels during the next ten years given that fuel and fertilizers remain high and greater demand from India and China remain steady.

11189 ■ *"Venture Gap" in Canadian Business (Vol. 81, March 17, 2008, No. 4, pp. 82)*
Pub: Rogers Media
Ed: Joe Castaldo. Description: Money raised by Canadian venture capitalist firms has been declining since 2001. A strong venture capital market is important if Canada is to build innovative companies. Fixing Canada's tax policy on foreign investments is a start in reviving the industry.

11190 ■ *"Wake-Up Call" in Canadian Business (Vol. 80, October 8, 2007, No. 20, pp. 58)*
Pub: Rogers Media
Ed: Andrea Mandel-Campbell. Description: The need for Canadian companies to develop global marketing strategies is discussed. Thomas Caldwell, chairman of Caldwell Securities, believes the country's average performance in global markets should be a cause for alarm. The factors affecting the country's current economic state is also presented.

11191 ■ *"We May Finally Find the Silver Lining" in Crain's Detroit Business (Vol. 24, April 7, 2008, No. 14, pp. 8)*
Pub: Crain Communications, Inc.
Description: Discusses a possible economic turnaround for Michigan which could be brought forth with such things as the new film initiative incentives which may make filming in the state more appealing than filming in Canada due to the weakened state of the dollar and more exportation from Michigan companies.

11192 ■ *"Wegmans Uses Database for Recall" in Supermarket News (Vol. 56, September 22, 2008, No. 38)*
Pub: Penton Business Media, Inc.
Ed: Carol Angrisani. Description: Wegmans used data obtained through its loyalty card that, in turn, sent automated telephone calls to every customer who had purchased tainted pet food when Mars Petcare recalled dog food products.

11193 ■ *What Has EX-IM Bank Done for Small Business Lately?: Congressional Hearing*
Pub: DIANE Publishing Company
Ed: Donald A. Manzullo. Description: Covers Congressional hearing: Witnesses: Philip Merrill, President and CEO, Export Import Bank of the U.S.; Victoria Hadfield, President, Semiconductor Equipment and Materials International (SEMI), North America; and Michael Vaden, President and CEO, Rutland Plastic Technologies, Inc. Attachments: April 1, 2005, letter to Chairman Philip Merrill from Semiconductor Manufacturing International Corporation (SMIC); Attachment A - Chronology of SMIC Transaction; Attachment B-Appendices; Appendix A: March 21, 2005, letter from EX-IM Chairman Philip Merrill to Congressman Donald A. Manzullo from the State of Illinois; and Appendix B: Congressional letter written on SMIC and equipment suppliers behest. Includes charts and tables.

11194 ■ *"What'll You Have Tonight?" in Barron's (Vol. 88, July 4, 2008, No. 28, pp. 22)*
Pub: Dow Jones & Co., Inc.
Ed: Neil A. Martin. Description: Shares of Diageo could rise by 30 percent a year from June 2008 after it slipped due to U.S. sales worries. The company also benefits from the trend toward more premium alcoholic beverage brands worldwide especially in emerging markets.

11195 ■ *"Who Produces for Whom in the World Economy?" in Canadian Journal of Economics (Vol. 44, November 2011, No. 4, pp. 1403)*
Pub: Blackwell Publishers Ltd.
Ed: Guillaume Daudin, Christine Rifflart, Danielle Schweisguth. Description: For two decades, the share of trade in inputs, also called vertical trade, has been dramatically increasing. In reallocating trade flows to their original input-producing industries and countries, the article suggests a new measure of international trade: 'value-added trade' and makes it possible to answer the question, 'who produces for whom?'.

11196 ■ *"Why Change?" in Canadian Business (Vol. 80, October 8, 2007, No. 20, pp. 9)*
Pub: Rogers Media
Ed: Joe Chidley. Description: The need for economic change in Canada is discussed. Despite the country's economic growth and low unemployment rate, economic reform is needed in order to maximize its economic potential in the future. Other reasons for the need to further develop its economy, such as the rise of manufacturing and service industries in Asia and the emergence of regional trade pacts in South America are also tackled.

11197 ■ *"Why You Aren't Buying Venezuelan Chocolate." in Harvard Business Review (Vol. 88, December 2010, No. 12, pp. 25)*
Pub: Harvard Business School Publishing
Ed: Rohit Deshpande. Description: The concept of provenance paradox is defined as the preconceived notions consumers have about the country of origin of a given product, which can pose significant difficulties for emerging markets. Five strategies are presented for combating this problem, including building on historic events that have informed cultural perspectives.

11198 ■ *"Winning Gold" in The Business Journal-Milwaukee (Vol. 25, August 8, 2008, No. 46, pp. A1)*
Pub: American City Business Journals, Inc.
Ed: Rich Rovito. Description: Johnson Controls Inc. of Milwaukee, Wisconsin is taking part in the 2008 Beijing Olympics with the installation of its sustainable control equipment and technology that monitor over 58,000 points in 18 Olympic venues. Details of Johnson Controls' green products and sustainable operations in China are discussed.

11199 ■ *"With Whom Do You Trade? Defensive Innovation and the Skill-Bias" in Canadian Journal of Electronics (Vol. 43, November 2010)*
Pub: Journal of the Canadian Economics Association
Ed: Pushan Dutt, Daniel Traca. Description: Examination into whether increased trade with ineffective protection of intellectual property has contributed to the skill-deepening of the 1980s. An index of effective protection of intellectual property at the country level, combining data on protection of patents and rule of law are presented. An industry-specific version of this index is given using as weights each country's trade share in the total trade of the industry. A decline is seen in this trade-weighted index, owing to a rise in trade with countries with low effective protection of intellectual property, which explains 29 percent of the rise within-industry skill-intensity.

11200 ■ *Your Guide to Canadian Export Financing: Successful Techniques for Financing Your Exports from Canada*
Pub: Productive Publications
Ed: Iain Williamson. Released: December 31, 2000. Description: Canadian export financing is covered.

TRADE PERIODICALS

11201 ■ *Bacard's Global Investor*
Pub: Ferney Scribes Inc.
Ed: Andre Bacard, Editor. Released: Monthly. Price: $129, U.S.. Description: Provides monthly updates of select no-load global and international funds, model portfolios, foreign market graphs, monthly analysis and current recommendations. Recurring features include news of research and a column titled Mutual Fund in the Spotlight.

11202 ■ *CUBANEWS*
Pub: Target Research
Ed: Larry Luxner, Editor. Released: Monthly. Price: $429, individuals; $199 academic institutions. De-

scription: Covers business and economic issues involving Cuba, including an economic overview, monthly developments, and industrial analysis.

11203 ■ *Export Finance Letter Quarterly / Export Finance Guide News*
Pub: International Business Affairs Corp.
Contact: Richard Barovick, Editor
E-mail: editor@exportsourcebook.com
Released: Quarterly. **Price:** $156, individuals. **Description:** Provides news and information on exporting.

11204 ■ *The Export Practitioner*
Pub: Gilston-Kalin Communications, LLC
Ed: Sam Gilston, Editor. **Released:** Monthly. **Price:** $499.00, individuals 499/year; $998.00, two years for print edition. **Description:** Focuses on regulatory policy and legal trends regarding export of products and services. Covers planning strategies for marketability.

11205 ■ *ImportCar: The Complete Import Service Magazine*
Pub: Babcox
URL(s): www.import-car.comwww.babcox.com/site/our-brands/importcar. **Ed:** Mary DellaValle. **Released:** Monthly **Price:** Free.

11206 ■ *International Trade Reporter*
Pub: Bureau of National Affairs Inc.
Contact: Linda G. Botsford, Managing Editor
Released: Weekly. **Price:** $1,159. **Description:** Covers current international trade policies of the U.S. and of major U.S. trading partners. Topics include bilateral negotiations, customs, export/import policy, foreign investment, standards, taxation, and other related issues. Recurring features include a calendar of events, reports of meetings, and notices of publications available.

11207 ■ *Ottawa Letter*
Pub: CCH Canadian Ltd.
Contact: Ian Rhind, President
Released: Biweekly. **Price:** $920. **Description:** Reports on current events and topics of Canada, such as free trade, human rights, employment, and defense. Also provides statistics, lending, and foreign exchange rates.

COMPUTERIZED DATABASES

11208 ■ *International Trade Reporter™*
1801 S Bell St.
Arlington, VA 22202
Free: 800-372-1033
Co. E-mail: customercare@bna.com
URL: http://www.bna.com
Availability: Online: Bloomberg LP-Bloomberg BNA; Thomson Reuters - Westlaw. **Type:** Full-text.

11209 ■ *U.S. Exports of Merchandise*
4600 Silver Hill Rd.
Washington, DC 20233
Ph: (301)763-4636
Free: 800-923-8282
Co. E-mail: comments@census.gov
URL: http://www.census.gov/foreign-trade
Availability: CD-ROM: U.S. Census Bureau. **Type:** Statistical.

LIBRARIES

11210 ■ The Economist Intelligence Unit Information Center
111 W. 57th St.
New York, NY 10019
Ph: (212)554-0600
Fax: (212)586-1181
Co. E-mail: newyork@eiu.com
URL: http://www.eiu.com
Contact: Beth Kilmer
Scope: Foreign investment, International trade, economics, finance, forecasting, critical issues monitoring. **Services:** Interlibrary loan; copying. **Founded:** 1957. **Holdings:** Economist Intelligence Unit publications (complete set); corporate directories; databases for the United Nations, the World Bank, and major regional economic organizations. **Subscriptions:** 7 newspapers.

11211 ■ Export-Import Bank of the United States Library
811 Vermont Ave., NW
Washington, DC 20571
Ph: (202)565-3946
Free: 800-565-3946
Fax: (202)565-3985
Co. E-mail: research@exim.gov
URL: http://www.exim.gov/about/links.cfm
Contact: Peggy Braly, Analyst
Scope: Export finance, world economics, U.S. and foreign business, trade statistics, International banking, insurance, law, country risk. **Services:** Interlibrary loan; SDI; daily news briefing; weekly and monthly subject briefings; Library open to the public for reference use only with prior appointment. **Founded:** 1934. **Holdings:** 15,000 books and pamphlets; 20,000 documents; 300 lin.ft. of archives. **Subscriptions:** 250 journals and other serials; 10 newspapers. **Telecommunication Services:** eugene.ferguson@exim.gov.

11212 ■ U.S. International Trade Commission - National Library of International Trade
500 E St., SW
USITC Bldg., 3rd Fl.
Washington, DC 20436
Ph: (202)205-2630
Fax: (202)205-2316
URL: http://www.usitc.gov/press_room/usitc_services.htm
Contact: Elizabeth A. Root, Section Chief
Scope: U.S. trade policy, International trade, foreign trade statistics, tariffs. **Services:** Interlibrary loan except for legislative histories and archival copies of ITC publications; copying; Library open to the public. **Founded:** 1917. **Holdings:** 100,000 volumes. **Subscriptions:** 2500 journals and other serials.

RESEARCH CENTERS

11213 ■ The Heritage Foundation - Asian Studies Center (ASC)
214 Massachusetts Ave. NE
Washington, DC 20002-4999
Ph: (202)546-4400
Fax: (202)546-8328
Co. E-mail: info@heritage.org
URL: http://www.heritage.org/about/staff/departments/asian-studies-center
Contact: Walter Lohman, Director
Services: Expert testimony: before Congress and party platform committees. **Founded:** 1983. **Publications:** *Asian Studies Center Backgrounders*; *Executive Memoranda Series*; *U.S. and Asia Statistical Handbook*. **Educational Activities:** Heritage Lectures and seminars; Public diplomacy engagements, in the United States and throughout Asia. **Awards:** ASC Paid internships. **Telecommunication Services:** staff@heritage.org.

ASSOCIATIONS AND OTHER ORGANIZATIONS

11214 ■ **National Business Incubation Association (NBIA)**
20 E Circle Dr., No. 37198
Athens, OH 45701-3571
Ph: (740)593-4331
Fax: (740)593-1996
Co. E-mail: info@nbia.org
URL: http://www.nbia.org
Contact: David Monkman, President
Description: Incubator developers and managers; corporate joint venture partners, venture capital investors; economic development professionals. (Incubators are business assistance programs providing business consulting services and financing assistance to start-up and fledgling companies.) Helps newly formed businesses to succeed. Educates businesses and investors on incubator benefits; offers specialized training in incubator formation and management. Conducts research and referral services; compiles statistics; maintains speakers' bureau; publishes information relevant to business incubation and growing companies. **Scope:** business incubation, entrepreneurship. **Founded:** 1985. **Publications:** *NBIA Insights* (Monthly); *NBIA Memberabilia* (Biweekly); *NBIA Review* (Bimonthly); *NBIA Business Incubation Industry Directory* (Annual); *Business Incubators of North America* (Biennial). **Educational Activities:** International Conference on Business Incubation (Annual). **Awards:** Incubator Innovation Award; Incubator of the Year; Outstanding Incubator Client Award; Outstanding Incubator Graduate Award; Incubator Innovation Award (Annual); Incubator of the Year (Annual); Outstanding Incubator Client (Annual); Outstanding Incubator Graduate (Annual).

REFERENCE WORKS

11215 ■ *"Funding Drought Stalls Biotech Incubators" in Saint Louis Business Journal (Vol. 31, July 29, 2011, No. 49, pp. 1)*
Pub: Saint Louis Business Journal
Ed: Angela Mueller. **Description:** Economic slowdown took its toll on cash-strapped startups that fill incubators such as the Bio-Research and Development Growth (BRDG) Park in Creve Coeur, Missouri and the Center for Emerging Technologies in Midtown St. Louis. BRDG put a hold on construction of of its two buildings.

11216 ■ *"Start-Up Pointers" in Inside Business (Vol. 13, September-October 2011, No. 5, pp. Y3)*
Pub: Great Lakes Publishing Co.
Description: Four tips to help entrepreneurs with startup firms are provided by Youngstown Business Incubator.

TRADE PERIODICALS

11217 ■ *Entrepreneur Magazine*
Pub: Entrepreneur Press
Contact: Perlman Neil, President
URL(s): www.entrepreneur.com/magazine/entrepreneur/index.html. **Released:** Monthly **Price:** $11.97, Individuals.

11218 ■ *Entrepreneurship Theory and Practice*
Pub: Baylor University Dept. of Management
URL(s): www.baylor.edu/business/etp/www.wiley.com/bw/subs.asp?ref=1042-2587. **Ed:** Barbara Bird. **Released:** Bimonthly **Price:** $602, Institutions Americas, print & online; £464, Institutions UK, print & online; $908, Institutions, other countries print & online; €589, Institutions Europe; print & online; $133, Individuals Americas, print & online; £126, Institutions U.K, print & online; €126, Individuals Europe (non-Euro zone) print & online; €188, Individuals Europe (Euro zone) print & online; $523, Institutions Americas, online only.

11219 ■ *Minority Business Entrepreneur*
Pub: Minority Business Entrepreneur
Contact: Anthony Robinson, President
URL(s): www.mbemag.com/. **Released:** Bimonthly **Price:** $18, Individuals print only; $30, Two years print only.

11220 ■ *Small Business Opportunities: Money Making Ideas for Entrepreneurs*
Pub: Harris Publications Inc.
URL(s): www.sbomag.com/. **Ed:** Susan Rakowski. **Released:** Bimonthly; (plus 4 special editions). **Price:** $14.97, U.S. and Canada; $29.94, Other countries.

ASSOCIATIONS AND OTHER ORGANIZATIONS

11221 ■ American Library Association (ALA)
50 E Huron St.
Chicago, IL 60611
Ph: (312)944-6780
Free: 800-545-2433
Fax: (312)280-5014
Co. E-mail: kfiels@ala.org
URL: http://www.ala.org
Contact: Keith Fiels, Executive Director
E-mail: kfiels@ala.org
URL(s): www.alastore.ala.org, www.booklistonline.com. **Description:** Librarians, libraries, trustees, friends of libraries, and others interested in the responsibilities of libraries in the educational, social, and cultural needs of society. Promotes and improves library service and librarianship. Establishes standards of service, support, education, and welfare for libraries and library personnel; promotes the adoption of such standards in libraries of all kinds; safeguards the professional status of librarians; encourages the recruiting of competent personnel for professional careers in librarianship; promotes popular understanding and public acceptance of the value of library service and librarianship. Works in liaison with federal agencies to initiate the enactment and administration of legislation that will extend library services. Offers placement services. **Scope:** library science, American Library Association. **Founded:** 1876. **Subscriptions:** 10000 archival material audio recordings books periodicals photographs video recordings. **Publications:** *American Libraries*; *Booklist: Includes Reference Books Bulletin*; *Library Technology Reports* (Bimonthly); *American Libraries* (Bimonthly); *Booklist* (Biweekly); *Public Libraries* (Bimonthly); *Booklist Online*; *American Libraries Online*; *Choice Magazine: Current Reviews for Academic Libraries*; *Networking CD-ROMs*; *Special Collections in Children's Literature*; *Book Links: Connecting Books, Libraries and Classrooms*; *Library Leadership & Management* (Quarterly); *Video for Libraries*; *Grapevine*; *Documents to the People (DttP)*; *Choice: Current Reviews for Academic Libraries* (Monthly); *Preservation Education Directory* (Irregular); *Reference Books Bulletin: A Compilation of Evaluations*; *Booklist*; *Great Library Promotion Ideas*; *Magazines for Children: A Guide for Parents, Teachers, and Librarians*; *Directory of Test Collections in Academic, Professional, and Research Libraries*; *Marketing to Libraries Through Library Associations* (Annual); *Library Technology Reports: Expert Guides to Library Systems and Services*; *Directory of Historical Textbook and Curriculum Collections*; *Journal of Youth Services in Libraries* (Quarterly); *Library Resources & Technical Services: The Official Journal of the Association of Library Collections & Technical Services* (Quarterly); *Children and Libraries: The Journal of the Association for Library Service to Children*; *One Hundred and One Software Packages to Use in Your Library*; *American Library Association--Handbook of Organization and Membership Directory* (Annual); *Reference and User Services Quarterly: The Official Journal of the Reference and User Services Association of the American Library Association* (Quarterly); *The Big Book of Library Grant Money*; *Directory of Ethnic and Multicultural Publishers, Distributors and Resource Organizations*; *Booklist/Reference Books Bulletin--Biographical Reference Sources*; *Librarian Career Resource Network*; *Genealogical Research and Resources: A Guide for Library Use*; *Technology Electronic Reviews* (Irregular); *American Library Association Guide to Information Access*; *FISCAL Directory of Fee-Based Research & Information Services* (Annual); *Minorities and Women: A List of Major Organizations in Librarianship* (Annual); *ALA Handbook of Organization and Membership Directory* (Annual); *Guide to Employment Sources in the Library and Information Professions*; *Pre- and Post-Retirement Tips for Librarians*. **Educational Activities:** American Library Association Annual Conference (Annual); American Library Association Mid-Winter Meeting (Annual). **Awards:** Caldecott Medal (Annual); Michael L. Printz Award (Annual); Newbery Medal (Annual); Theodor Seuss Geisel Award (Annual); Marshall Cavendish Scholarships; David H. Clift Scholarships; Christopher Hoy/ERT Scholarships; Equality Award; Beta Phi Mu Award; Melvil Dewey Medal; Scholastic Library Publishing Award; Joseph W. Lippincott Award; EBSCO ALA Conference Sponsorship; Mary V. Gaver Scholarship; Schneider Family Book Award; Gale Cengage Learning Financial Development Award; H.W. Wilson Library Staff Development Grant; ALA/Information Today Inc. Library of the Future Award; W.Y. Boyd Literary Award for Excellence in Military Fiction; Marshall Cavendish Excellence in Library Programming Award; Elizabeth Futas Catalyst for Change Award; Paul Howard Award for Courage; Tom and Roberta Drewes Scholarship; Loleta D. Fyan Public Library Research Grant; Ken Haycock Award for Promoting Librarianship; Sullivan Award for Public Library Administrators Supporting Services to Children. **Telecommunication Services:** ala@ala.org; acrl@ala.org; editionsmarketing@ala.org.

11222 ■ American Society for Information Science and Technology (ASIS&T)
1320 Fenwick Ln., Ste. 510
Silver Spring, MD 20910
Ph: (301)495-0900
Fax: (301)495-0810
Co. E-mail: asis@asis.org
URL: http://www.asis.org
Contact: Diane Sonnenwald, President
Description: Information specialists, scientists, librarians, administrators, social scientists, and others interested in the use, organization, storage, retrieval, evaluation, and dissemination of recorded specialized information. Seeks to improve the information transfer process through research, development, application, and education. Provides a forum for the discussion, publication, and critical analysis of work dealing with the theory, practice, research, and development of elements involved in communication of information. Members are engaged in a variety of activities and specialties including classification and coding systems, automatic and associative indexing, machine translation of languages, special librarianship and library systems analysis, and copyright issues. Sponsors National Auxiliary Publications Service, which provides reproduction services and a central depository for all types of information. Maintains placement service. Sponsors numerous special interest groups. Conducts continuing education programs and professional development workshops. **Founded:** 1937. **Publications:** *Handbook and Directory* (Annual); *Journal of the American Society for Information Science and Technology* (Monthly). **Educational Activities:** American Society for Information Science and Technology Meeting (Annual); American Society for Information Science and Technology Meeting (Annual). **Awards:** Award of Merit; Special Award; Chapter of the Year (Annual); Special Award (Periodic); Award for Research in Information Science; Best Information Science Book Award; John Wiley and Sons Best JASIST Paper Award; Chapter Publication of the Year Award; Pratt-Severn Best Student Research Paper Award; Chapter of the Year Award; Watson Davis Award; Thomson Reuters Outstanding Information Science Teacher Award; SIG of the Year Award; Student Chapter of the Year Award; SIG Publication of the Year Award; James M. Cretsos Leadership Award; SIG Member of the Year Award; Chapter Event of the Year Award; Chapter Member of the Year Award; ASIST Award for Research in Information Science (Annual); Chapter Event of the Year Award; Chapter member of the Year (Annual); Chapter Publication of the Year (Annual); Student Chapter-of-the-Year (Annual).

11223 ■ ARMA International - Canadian Region
PO Box 6000
Fredericton, NB, Canada E3B 5H1
Ph: (506)453-5618
Co. E-mail: bernita.cogswell@gnb.ca
URL: http://www.arma.org
Contact: Bernita Cogswell, Regional Manager
URL(s): www.armacanada.org. **Description:** Information management professionals. Promotes professional advancement of members and seeks to insure adherence to high standards of ethics and practice within the field of information management. Represents members' interests, conducts continuing professional development programs and serves as a clearinghouse on information management. **Awards:** Canadian Region Member Recognition Award (Annual); Roger Richard Memorial Award.

11224 ■ Canadian Association for Information Science (CAIS)—L'Association canadienne des sciences de l'information
c/o Nadia Caidi, Pres.
Toronto, ON, Canada M5S 1C7
Ph: (416)978-4664
Co. E-mail: siobhan.stevenson@utoronto.ca
URL: http://www.cais-acsi.ca
Contact: Nadia Caidi, President
Description: Institutions and individuals interested in the various aspects of information science, including information production, storage, and dissemination. Serves as a forum for dialogue and exchange of ideas concerned with the theory and practice of all factors involved in the communication of information.

Founded: 1970. **Publications:** *Canadian Journal of Information and Library Science* (Quarterly). **Tele-communication Services:** nadia.caidi@utoronto.ca.

11225 ■ *Canadian Journal of Information and Library Science*
c/o Nadia Caidi, Pres.
Toronto, ON, Canada M5S 1C7
Ph: (416)978-4664
Co. E-mail: siobhan.stevenson@utoronto.ca
URL: http://www.cais-acsi.ca
Contact: Nadia Caidi, President

Released: Quarterly **Price:** C$95, for delivery in Canada; C$110, for delivery in other countries; C$30, /copy.

11226 ■ **Information Technology Association of Canada (ITAC)—Association Canadienne de la Technologie de l'Information (ACTI)**
5090 Explorer Dr., Ste. 801
Mississauga, ON, Canada L4W 4T9
Ph: (905)602-8345
Fax: (905)602-8346
Co. E-mail: kgupta@itac.ca
URL: http://www.itac.ca
Contact: Karna Gupta, President

Description: Corporations producing information technologies and related components. Promotes growth and development in the domestic information technology industry. Represents members' interests; conducts research; maintains advocacy programs. Operates hall of fame; compiles statistics. **Scope:** information technologies. **Founded:** 1984. **Subscriptions:** archival material books clippings periodicals. **Educational Activities:** Executive Forum on Micro-electronics (Annual). **Awards:** Canadian Information Productivity Awards.

11227 ■ **National Federation of Advanced Information Services (NFAIS)**
1518 Walnut St., Ste. 1004
Philadelphia, PA 19102-3403
Ph: (215)893-1561
Fax: (215)893-1564
Co. E-mail: blawlor@nfais.org
URL: http://www.nfais.org
Contact: Terence Ford, President

URL(s): www.asidic.org. **Description:** Represents major abstracting and indexing service organizations, online vendors, CD-ROM vendors, and related organizations. Aims to improve the extent and quality of the documentation and use of the world's literature through research programs, publications, and seminars. Works to develop communications, cooperation, and coordination among all segments of the information processing and dissemination community, including primary publishers, libraries, commercial and industrial abstracting and indexing services, data analysis centers, information dissemination centers, and people teaching or undertaking research in the abstracting and indexing field. Serves as a communication forum for its members through meetings, workshops, committee activities, and formal publications. Provides programs that are designed to: facilitate communication among members; conduct research projects useful to the abstracting and indexing community; provide educational programs for the information-science community; act as a collective voice for member services. Compiles statistics. **Scope:** Information science. **Founded:** 1958. **Publications:** *National Federation of Abstracting and Information Services--Membership Directory* (Annual); *Guide to Database Distribution*; *NFAIS Newsletter* (Bimonthly); *National Federation of Abstracting and Information Services--Directory of Consultants and Contractors.* **Awards:** Miles Conrad Award/Lecture; Ann Marie Cunningham Memorial Award (Annual); Miles Conrad Memorial Lecturer Award (Annual). **Telecommunication Services:** nfais@nfais.org; jilloneill@nfais.org; info@asidic.org.

11228 ■ **Special Libraries Association (SLA)**
331 S Patrick St.
Alexandria, VA 22314-3501
Ph: (703)647-4900

Fax: (703)647-4901
Co. E-mail: janice@sla.org
URL: http://www.sla.org
Contact: Janice R. Lachance, Chief Executive Officer
E-mail: janice@sla.org

Description: International association of information professionals who work in specialized information environments such as business, research, government, universities, newspapers, museums, and institutions. Seeks to advance the leadership role of information professionals through learning, networking and advocacy. Offers consulting services to organizations that wish to establish or expand a library or information services. Conducts strategic learning and development courses, public relations, and government relations programs. Provides employment services. Operates knowledge exchange on topics pertaining to the development and management of special libraries. **Founded:** 1909. **Publications:** *Information Outlook* (8/year); *SLA Connections* (Monthly); *SpeciaList* (Monthly); *Information Outlook* (Monthly); *Information Outlook* (Monthly); *Directory of Catalogers in the Special Libraries Association; Who's Who in Special Libraries* (Annual). **Educational Activities:** Winter Education Conference (Annual); Special Libraries Association Information Revolution (Annual). **Awards:** Diversity Leadership Development Program Award (Annual); Factiva Leadership Award (Annual); Honorary Member Award (Annual); John Cotton Dana Award (Annual); President's Award; Professional Award; SLA Scholarship (Annual); Steven I. Goldspeil Memorial Research Fund (Annual); Fellow of the Special Libraries Association; Hall of Fame; Honorary Member; John Cotton Dana Award; Professional Award; H. W. Wilson Company Award; Affirmative Action Scholarships; Mary Adeline Conner Professional Development Scholarships; Institute for Scientific Information Scholarships (ISI); Plenum Scholarships; Special Libraries Association Scholarships (SLA); J.J. Keller Innovations in Technology Award. **Telecommunication Services:** sla@sla.org.

REFERENCE WORKS

11229 ■ *Conquering Information Chaos in the Growing Business: IBM Solutions for Managing Information in an On Demand World*
Pub: Maximum Press

Ed: Jim Hoskins. **Released:** April 2005. **Price:** $29.95. **Description:** Information management is critical to any business.

11230 ■ *Contingency Planning and Disaster Recovery: A Small Business Guide*
Pub: John Wiley & Sons, Incorporated

Ed: Donna R. Childs, Stefan Dietrich. **Released:** October 2002. **Description:** Four keys issues to help a business plan for disasters include: preparation, response, recovery, and sample IT solutions in order to secure property and confidential data files and covers the six types of disasters: human errors, equipment failures, third-party failures, environmental hazards, fires and other structural catastrophes, and terrorism and sabotage.

11231 ■ *Directory of Libraries in Canada*
Pub: Grey House Publishing Canada Inc.
Contact: Dick Gottlieb, President

URL(s): www.greyhouse.ca/library.htm. **Released:** Annual; Latest edition 2011. **Price:** $275, Individuals Hardcover. **Covers:** Over 6,700 libraries, library associations, library schools and technician programs, archives, periodicals, provincial library agencies, government libraries, regional systems, and library services suppliers (wholesalers, binders, subscription agencies, etc.) in Canada. **Entries include:** Library or firm name, address, phone, fax, TDD, e-mail; names and titles of key personnel and contact, description of collection, services offered to the public; budget range; computers and automated systems in use; publications and url addresses. **Arrangement:** Library schools are geographical; other lists are alphabetical. **Indexes:** Geographical, subject, personal name.

11232 ■ *International Literary Market Place: The Directory of the International Book Publishing Industry*
Pub: Information Today Inc.
Contact: Thomas H. Hogan, President
E-mail: ctuthill@infotoday.com

URL(s): www.literarymarketplace.combooks.infotoday.com. **Released:** Annual; Latest edition 2012. **Price:** $289, Individuals softbound; $260.10, Individuals first time standing order. **Covers:** Over 10,500 publishers in over 180 countries outside the United States and Canada, and about 1,499 trade and professional organizations related to publishing abroad; includes major printers, binders, typesetters, book manufacturers, book dealers, libraries, literary agencies, translators, book clubs, reference books and journals, periodicals, prizes, and international reference section. **Entries include:** For publishers--Name, address, phone, fax, telex, names and titles of key personnel, branches, type of publications, subjects, ISBN prefix. Listings for others include similar information but less detail. **Arrangement:** Classified by business activities, then geographical. **Indexes:** Company name, subject, type of publication.

TRADE PERIODICALS

11233 ■ *The DATA BASE for Advances in Information Systems*
Pub: Association for Computing Machinery
Contact: Dr. Dorothy Liedner, Editor
E-mail: d.leidner@tcu.edu

Released: Quarterly. **Price:** $20, Included in membership; $14, students; $38, nonmembers. **Description:** Presents articles on practical research relating to business uses of information systems.

11234 ■ *Data Base Alert*
Pub: Access Intelligence L.L.C.
Contact: Donald Pazour, President

Ed: Judy Duke, Editor. **Released:** Monthly. **Description:** Provides updates on publicly available online services. Contains a listing of distributors of new or revised data bases with data bases listed alphabetically under the appropriate distributor along with information about pricing, updates, and number of records. Remarks: Newsletter is part of DataBase Directory Service, which includes an annual directory and supplement.

11235 ■ *Dat@Line*
Pub: Dun and Bradstreet Corp.
Contact: David J. Emery, President

Ed: Jean Fitzgerald, Editor, fitzjean@mail.dnb.com. **Released:** 4/year. **Price:** Free. **Description:** Informs online users of database contents and applications. Also provides general information on Dun & Bradstreet. Recurring features include new product announcements, a calendar of training sessions and trade shows, and a page highlighting unique online database applications at a particular company or organization. Also includes columns titled Q&A Corner and Tips and Techniques.

11236 ■ *FEDLINK Technical Notes*
Pub: Federal Library and Information Network
Contact: Susan M. Tarr, Executive Director

Released: Monthly. **Price:** Included in membership. **Description:** Carries technical information about the Federal Library and Information Center Committee and its network component FEDLINK, its programs and services, and items of interest to those in library science and information fields.

11237 ■ *The Information Advisor*
Pub: Find/SVP

Ed: Robert I. Berkman, Editor, rberkman@javanet.com. **Released:** Monthly, plus Quarterly Knowledge Management Supplement. **Price:** $165, U.S.; $175, Canada and foreign. **Description:** Supplies business data users information on comparing and evaluating competing information sources. Provides comparison charts, reviews, advice on data reliability, and quality for both online and print business information produced in the U.S., Europe, Asia, and Latin America.

11238 ■ *Information Management*
Pub: Idea Group Publishing
Ed: Mehdi Khosrowpour, D.B.A., Editor. **Released:** Semiannual, 2/year. **Price:** $40, U.S.; $60, individuals only in USA; $46, Canada. **Description:** Follows trends and issues in the field of information technology and information resources technology. Strives to 'enhance the overall knowledge and understanding of effective information resources management in the 1990s and beyond.' Recurring features include interviews, news of research, a calendar of events, book reviews, news of product releases, and columns titled Technology Talk, An Information Management Tool, and End User Attitudes.

11239 ■ *Information Standards Quarterly*
Pub: National Information Standards Organization
Contact: Todd Carpenter, Executive Director
Released: Quarterly. **Price:** $130, U.S.; $165, elsewhere. **Description:** NISO's newsletter, Information Standards Quarterly (ISQ), features timely standards-related news, information about implementation of standards, and updates on standards-in-development. The January issue features an annual "State of the Standards" which reports on the status of each standard in NISO's program.

11240 ■ *Information Today*
Pub: Information Today Inc.
Contact: Thomas H. Hogan, President
E-mail: ctuthill@infotoday.com
URL(s): www.infotoday.com/IT/default.asp. **Released:** 11/yr. **Price:** $89.95, Individuals; $118, Canada and Mexico; $169, Two years; $129, Other countries.

11241 ■ *Journal of the American Society for Information Science and Technology: The Official Journal of the American Society for Information Science*
Pub: John Wiley & Sons Inc.
Contact: Stephen M. Smith, President
URL(s): onlinelibrary.wiley.com/journal/10.1002/(-ISSN)1532-2890. **Released:** Monthly **Price:** $2620, Institutions print only; $2760, Institutions, Canada and Mexico print only; $2879, Institutions, other countries print only.

11242 ■ *LIMS/Letter*
Pub: LIMS/Letter
Ed: Helen Gillespie, Editor. **Released:** Quarterly. **Price:** $139, U.S.; $144, Canada and Mexico; $159, elsewhere; $399, institutions. **Description:** Provides information for Laboratory Information Management Systems (LIMS) professionals. Recurring features include interviews, case studies, invited articles, trends, and a calendar of events.

11243 ■ *Ottawa Letter*
Pub: CCH Canadian Ltd.
Contact: Ian Rhind, President
Released: Biweekly. **Price:** $920. **Description:** Reports on current events and topics of Canada, such as free trade, human rights, employment, and defense. Also provides statistics, lending, and foreign exchange rates.

11244 ■ *Third Indicator*
Pub: Bibliographic Center for Research, Rocky Mountain Region Inc.
Ed: Cheryl Burkert, Editor, cburkert@bcr.org. **Released:** Bimonthly. **Price:** $30, individuals Free to BCR/OCLC libraries; $30/year to others; $6. **Descrip-**tion: Provides articles and information concerning the Online Computer Library Center (OCLC) and library automation.

TRADE SHOWS AND CONVENTIONS

11245 ■ **Special Libraries Association Information Revolution**
Special Libraries Association (SLA)
331 S Patrick St.
Alexandria, VA 22314-3501
Ph: (703)647-4900
Fax: (703)647-4901
Co. E-mail: janice@sla.org
URL: http://www.sla.org
Contact: Janice R. Lachance, Chief Executive Officer
E-mail: janice@sla.org
Frequency: Annual. **Audience:** Information managers and librarians. **Principal Exhibits:** Library equipment, supplies, and services, including computers and software, Database information.

CONSULTANTS

11246 ■ **A. Davis Grant & Co.**
295 Pierson Ave.
Edison, NJ 08837-3118
Ph: (732)463-1414
Fax: (732)494-3626
Co. E-mail: info@adg.net
URL: http://www.adg.net
Contact: Allan D. Grossman, Senior Partner
E-mail: allan@adg.net
Scope: Executive search firm dealing exclusively in the field of information systems and technology. **Founded:** 1985.

COMPUTERIZED DATABASES

11247 ■ **DIALOG Bluesheets™**
2250 Perimeter Park Dr., Ste. 300
Morrisville, NC 27560
Ph: (919)804-6400
Free: 800-334-2564
Fax: (919)804-6410
Co. E-mail: contact@dialog.com
URL: http://www.dialog.com
Availability: Online: ProQuest LLC - Dialog; ProQuest LLC - Dialog. CD-ROM: ProQuest LLC - Dialog. **Type:** Directory; Numeric.

11248 ■ **Information Today**
143 Old Marlton Pke.
Medford, NJ 08055
Ph: (609)654-6266
Free: 800-300-9868
Fax: (609)654-4309
Co. E-mail: custserv@infotoday.com
URL: http://www.infotoday.com
Availability: Online: Information Today Inc. **Type:** Full-text.

11249 ■ **Library Literature & Information Science Full Text™**
10 Estes St.
Ipswich, MA 01938-2106

Ph: (978)356-6500
Free: 800-653-2726
Fax: (978)356-6565
Co. E-mail: information@ebscohost.com
URL: http://www.ebscohost.com
Contact: Tim Collins, President
E-mail: tcollins@ebscohost.com
Availability: Online: EBSCO Publishing. **Type:** Bibliographic; Full-text.

LIBRARIES

11250 ■ **Seek Information Service Library**
2318 Bancroft Ave., Ste. B
Los Angeles, CA 90039
Ph: (323)660-0091
Free: 800-722-SEEK
Fax: (323)660-0678
URL: http://www.seekinfo.com
Scope: Information retrieval. **Services:** Copying; SDI; library not open to the public. **Founded:** 1976. **Holdings:** Figures not available.

11251 ■ **UMI InfoStore**
789 E. Eisenhower Pkwy.
Ann Arbor, MI 48106-1346
Ph: (734)761-4700
Free: 800-521-0600
Fax: (415)433-0100
Co. E-mail: info@proquest.com
URL: http://il.proquest.com/en-US/products/brands
Contact: Elyse Eisner, Product Manager
Scope: Information services, document retrieval, translation. **Services:** Library not open to the public. **Founded:** 1979. **Holdings:** Figures not available. **Subscriptions:** 15,000 journals and other serials.

11252 ■ **University of California, Los Angeles - Department of Education & Information Studies - Multimedia & Information Technology Lab**
102A GSE & IS Bldg.
Box 951520
Los Angeles, CA 90095-1520
Ph: (310)206-9263
Fax: (310)206-4460
Co. E-mail: kbotello@ucla.edu
URL: http://is.gseis.ucla.edu/resources/MIT_lab/lab/
Contact: Keri Botello, Director
Scope: Librarianship, information access, information Organization, information science, information retrieval systems, informatics, online searching, bibliography, history of printing, archives, preservation. **Services:** Library open to the public for reference use only. **Founded:** 1960. **Holdings:** 4000 books; 400 bound periodical volumes; 100 reports. **Subscriptions:** 55 journals and other serials. **Telecommunication Services:** jmscott@ucla.edu.

RESEARCH CENTERS

11253 ■ **Stanford University - Center for Information Technology (CIT)**
Computer Science Department
Stanford, CA 94305
Ph: (650)723-0934
Fax: (650)725-7411
Co. E-mail: genesereth@stanford.edu
URL: http://logic.stanford.edu/cit/cit.html

ASSOCIATIONS AND OTHER ORGANIZATIONS

11254 ■ EIFS Industry Members Association (EIMA)
513 W Broad St., Ste. 210
Falls Church, VA 22046-3257
Free: 800-294-3462
Fax: (703)538-1736
Co. E-mail: eifsinfo@eima.com
URL: http://www.eima.com
Contact: Buck Buchanan, President
Description: Represents the exterior insulation and finish systems industry. Aims to improve the exterior insulation industry and to widen the use of its products through collective action. Conducts educational and research programs. **Founded:** 1981. **Publications:** *EIFS Briefs* (Bimonthly). **Awards:** Excellence in EIFS Construction (Annual); Excellence in EIFS Construction.

11255 ■ Insulation Contractors Association of America (ICAA)
1321 Duke St., Ste. 303
Alexandria, VA 22314
Ph: (703)739-0356
Fax: (703)739-0412
Co. E-mail: icaa2008@insulate.org
URL: http://www.insulate.org
Contact: Kevin Kinzler, President
Description: Residential and commercial insulation contractors; manufacturing and supplier associates. Seeks to develop industry standards; promotes energy conservation in old and new buildings through proper specifications and applications of insulation; represents interests of the industry at all government levels; promotes exchange of information among insulation contractors. Sponsors seminars, field surveys, and research. **Founded:** 1977. **Publications:** *Insulation Contractors Association of America--Bulletin* (Periodic); *Insulation Contractors Report* (Bimonthly); *Insulation Industry Buyer's Guide* (Annual); *Insulation Industry Buyer's Guide* (Annual). **Educational Activities:** Insulation Contractors Association of America Convention and Trade Show (Annual). **Telecommunication Services:** icaa@insulate.org.

11256 ■ National Insulation Association (NIA)
12100 Sunset Hills Rd., Ste. 330
Reston, VA 20190
Ph: (703)464-6422
Fax: (703)464-5896
Co. E-mail: mjones@insulation.org
URL: http://www.insulation.org
Contact: Alec Rexroat, President
Description: Insulation contractors, distributors, and manufacturers. **Founded:** 1953. **Publications:** *National Insulation Association--Membership Directory and Resource Guide* (Annual); *Insulation Outlook* (Monthly); *Insulation Outlook* (Monthly); *National Industries and Commercial Standards Manual*; *NIA News* (Monthly); *Safety Handbook*; *Insulation Outlook: Business Solutions for Expanding or Relocating Companies*; *Asbestos Abatement Industry Directory*. **Educational Activities:** National Insulation Association Annual Convention (Annual); National Insulation Association Convention (Annual).

11257 ■ North American Insulation Manufacturers Association (NAIMA)
44 Canal Center Plz., Ste. 310
Alexandria, VA 22314
Ph: (703)684-0084
Fax: (703)684-0427
URL: http://www.naima.org
Contact: Jeff Templeton, Chairman of the Board
Description: Manufacturers of fiberglass, rock wool, and slag wool insulation products. Promotes energy efficiency and environmental preservation through the use of fiberglass, rock wool, and slag wool insulation products. Encourages safe production and use of insulation materials. **Founded:** 1933. **Awards:** I.Q. Award (Annual).

REFERENCE WORKS

11258 ■ *National Insulation Association--Membership Directory and Resource Guide*
Pub: National Insulation Association
Contact: Alec Rexroat, President
URL(s): www.insulation.org. **Released:** Annual; fall. **Covers:** About 600 member manufacturers, distributors, and contractors involved in the commercial and industrial insulation and asbestos abatement industries. **Entries include:** Company name, address, phone, names and titles of key personnel, subsidiary and branch names and locations, products and services. **Arrangement:** Alphabetical by company, classified by, product/service. **Indexes:** Product/service, subject, geographical.

TRADE PERIODICALS

11259 ■ *Roofing Contractor*
Pub: BNP Media
Contact: Al Reser, President
URL(s): www.roofingcontractor.com/. **Released:** Monthly **Price:** $25, Free to qualified subscribers; $5, Individuals; $5, Single issue.

START-UP INFORMATION

11260 ■ *"Docs Prop Up Health Insurer" in Business First-Columbus (December 14, 2007, pp. A1)*
Pub: American City Business Journals, Inc.
Ed: Carrie Ghose. **Description:** Doctors and executives supporting Physicians Assurance Corporation, a startup health insurer in Central Ohio, were required to raise $2.5 million before they could apply for a license from the state Department of Insurance. The company, which hopes to acquire its license by January 2007, will focus on doctor's offices and businesses with two to ninety-nine employees.

11261 ■ *"Startup Makes Attempt to 'Reform' Health Insurance" in Austin Business JournalInc. (Vol. 29, January 15, 2010, No. 45, pp. 1)*
Pub: American City Business Journals
Ed: Sandra Zaragoza. **Description:** Health insurance provider ETMG LLC of Austin, Texas plans to act as a managing general agent and a third-party administrator that can facilitate customized plans for small businesses and sole proprietors. According to CEO Mark Adams, profitability is expected for ETMG, which have also clinched $1.5 million worth of investments. Entities that have agreed to do business with ETMG are presented.

ASSOCIATIONS AND OTHER ORGANIZATIONS

11262 ■ **American Association of Insurance Management Consultants (AAIMCo)**
Texas Insurance Consulting
8980 Lakes at 610 Dr., Ste. 100
Houston, TX 77054
Ph: (713)664-6424
Co. E-mail: thomas.braniff@aaimco.com
URL: http://www.aaimco.com
Contact: Mr. Thomas M. Braniff, President
Description: Consists of individuals who devote a substantial portion of their services to insurance consulting, risk management activities, legal representation relating to insurance issues; as well as education and professional development training, employment consulting, and other technical and management advice to the insurance industry. Advises and assists the insurance industry and seeks to achieve professional recognition for insurance management consultants. Mediates the exchange of ideas; sets standards of service and performance; maintains a code of ethics; offers a referral service and a series of educational conferences and seminars. Operates speakers' bureau; offers placement services; compiles statistics. **Founded:** 1978.

11263 ■ **American Association of Insurance Services (AAIS)**
1745 S Naperville Rd.
Wheaton, IL 60189-8132
Ph: (630)681-8347
Free: 800-564-AAIS

Fax: (630)681-8356
Co. E-mail: info@aaisonline.com
URL: http://www.aaisonline.com
Contact: Edmund Kelly, President
Description: Property and casualty insurance companies; mutual, stock, and reciprocal companies. Develops loss costs, rules, forms, and statistical services for property and casualty insurance. Licensed in all states, the District of Columbia, and the Commonwealth of Puerto Rico. **Founded:** 1975. **Publications:** *AAIS Viewpoint.*

11264 ■ **American Association of Managing General Agents (AAMGA)**
610 Freedom Business Ctr., Ste. 100
King of Prussia, PA 19406
Ph: (610)992-0022
Fax: (610)992-0021
Co. E-mail: bernie@aamga.org
URL: http://www.aamga.org
Contact: Bernd G. Heinze, Executive Director
Description: Managing general agents of insurance companies. Conducts specialized education programs; compiles statistics. **Founded:** 1926. **Publications:** *Communique* (Quarterly). **Educational Activities:** Automation and Technology Management (Annual). **Awards:** Achievement Award.

11265 ■ **American Council of Life Insurers (ACLI)**
101 Constitution Ave. NW, Ste. 700
Washington, DC 20001-2133
Ph: (202)624-2000
Free: 877-674-4659
Co. E-mail: webadmin@acli.com
URL: http://www.acli.com
Contact: Dirk Kempthorne, President
Description: Represents the interests of legal reserve life insurance companies in legislative, regulatory and judicial matters at the federal, state and municipal levels of government and at the NAIC. Member companies hold majority of the life insurance in force in the United States. **Scope:** disability insurance, annuities, financial services, pension, retirement, insurance laws and regulations. **Founded:** 1976. **Subscriptions:** books papers periodicals. **Publications:** *Investment Bulletins* (Quarterly); *Life Insurance Fact Book* (Annual).

11266 ■ **American Institute for CPCU (AICPCU)**
720 Providence Rd., Ste. 100
Malvern, PA 19355-3433
Ph: (610)644-2100
Free: 800-644-2101
Fax: (610)640-9576
Co. E-mail: customerservice@cpcuiia.org
URL: http://www.aicpcu.org
Contact: Peter L. Miller, President
Description: Determines qualifications for professional certification of insurance personnel; conducts examinations and awards designation of Chartered Property Casualty Underwriter (CPCU). **Scope:** insurance, business, law, finance, risk management, economics. **Founded:** 1942. **Subscriptions:** 9000 periodicals. **Publications:** *CPCU/IIA Catalogue* (An-

nual); *Malvern Examiner* (Annual). **Educational Activities:** Conferment Ceremony (Annual); CPCU Conferment Ceremony (Annual). **Awards:** Awards for Academic Excellence (Annual); Distinguished Graduate Awards (Annual). **Telecommunication Services:** cserv@cpcuiia.org; customerservice@TheInstitutes.org.

11267 ■ **American Insurance Association (AIA)**
2101 L St. NW, Ste. 400
Washington, DC 20037
Ph: (202)828-7100
Fax: (202)293-1219
Co. E-mail: info@aiadc.org
URL: http://www.aiadc.org/aiapub
Contact: Leigh Ann Pusey, President
Description: Represents companies providing property and casualty insurance and suretyship. Monitors and reports on economic, political, and social trends; serves as a clearinghouse for ideas, advice, and technical information. Represents members' interests before state and federal legislative and regulatory bodies; coordinates members' litigation. **Scope:** property/causality law, legislation, theory, general law, legal and insurance treatises, all state codes and regulations. **Founded:** 1964. **Subscriptions:** 30000 archival material books clippings monographs papers periodicals. **Publications:** *Automobile Insurance Laws*; *Claims Administration Digest*; *Guide to Campaign Laws*; *State Rating Guide*; *Summary of States Regulations and Laws Affecting General Contractors*; *Termination and Renewal of Property/Casualty Insurance Policies.*

11268 ■ **American Risk and Insurance Association (ARIA)**
716 Providence Rd.
Malvern, PA 19355-3402
Ph: (610)640-1997
Fax: (610)725-1007
Co. E-mail: aria@theinstitutes.org
URL: http://www.aria.org
Contact: Mr. Anthony Biacchi, Executive Director
Description: Comprises of academics, individual insurance industry representatives, students, and retirees. Works to emphasize research relevant to the operational concerns and functions of insurance professionals. **Founded:** 1932. **Publications:** *The Journal of Risk and Insurance* (Quarterly); *Journal of Risk and Insurance* (Quarterly); *Risk Management and Insurance Review* (Semiannual). **Educational Activities:** American Risk and Insurance Association Conference (Annual). **Awards:** Kulp-Wright Book Award; Robert I. Mehr Award; Robert C. Witt Award; Casualty Actuarial Society Research Award (Annual); Early Career Scholarly Achievement Award (Annual); Excellence in Teaching Award (Annual); Hagen Family Foundation Travel Award (Annual); Hedges Undergraduate Student Award (Annual); Kulp-Wright Book Award (Annual); Presidents' Award (Annual); RMIR Feature Article Award (Annual); RMIR Perspectives Article Award (Annual); Robert C. Witt Award (Annual); Robert I. Mehr Award (Annual); Les B.

Strickler Innovation in Instruction Award; Les B. Strickler Innovation in Instruction Award (Annual). **Telecommunication Services:** aria@cpcuiia.org.

11269 ■ Canadian Association of Mutual Insurance Companies (CAMIC)—Association Canadienne des Compagnies d'Assurance Mutuelles (ACCAM)

311 Ave. McArthur, Ste. 205
Ottawa, ON, Canada K1L 6P1
Ph: (613)789-6851
Fax: (613)789-7665
Co. E-mail: nlafreniere@camic.ca
URL: http://www.camic.ca
Contact: Normand Lafreniere, President

Description: Mutual insurance companies. Seeks to advance the insurance industry. Facilitates communication and cooperation among members; represents members' commercial interests before government agencies and the public.

11270 ■ Canadian Board of Marine Underwriters (CBMU)

2233 Argentia Rd., Ste. 100
Mississauga, ON, Canada L5N 2X7
Ph: (905)826-4768
Fax: (905)826-4873
Co. E-mail: cbmu@cbmu.com
URL: http://www.cbmu.com/HOME/default.asp
Contact: Brent Chorney, President

Description: Marine underwriters. Promotes professional development of members; seeks to advance the practice of marine insurance underwriting. Serves as a forum for the exchange of information among members; conducts continuing professional education courses. **Founded:** 1917. **Publications:** *The Log* (Biennial).

11271 ■ *Canadian Independent Adjuster*

Centennial Ctre.
Etobicoke, ON, Canada M9C 5K6
Ph: (416)621-6222
Free: 877-255-5589
Fax: (416)621-7776
Co. E-mail: info@ciaa-adjusters.ca
URL: http://www.ciaa-adjusters.ca
Contact: Greg G. Merrithew, President
Released: Bimonthly

11272 ■ Canadian Independent Adjusters' Association (CIAA)—L'Association Canadienne des Experts Independants - Association Canadienne Des Experts Independants

Centennial Ctre.
Etobicoke, ON, Canada M9C 5K6
Ph: (416)621-6222
Free: 877-255-5589
Fax: (416)621-7776
Co. E-mail: info@ciaa-adjusters.ca
URL: http://www.ciaa-adjusters.ca
Contact: Greg G. Merrithew, President

Description: Independent insurance adjusters. Represents the collective interests of independent adjusters to government, industry and the public on a provincial, regional and national level. Promotes continuing professional development of members; encourages adherence to high standards of ethics and practice in the industry. Conducts educational programs. **Scope:** insurance claims, adjustment of claims. **Founded:** 1953. **Subscriptions:** books periodicals. **Publications:** *Canadian Independent Adjuster* (Bimonthly); *Canadian Independent Adjusters' Claims Manual* (Annual); *Claims Manual*. **Awards:** Canadian Insurance Claims Education Benevolent Foundation (Annual); CIAA Prize (Annual); CIAA Prize; Canadian Insurance Claims Education Benevolent Foundation Award.

11273 ■ *Canadian Independent Adjusters' Claims Manual*

Centennial Ctre.
Etobicoke, ON, Canada M9C 5K6
Ph: (416)621-6222
Free: 877-255-5589

Fax: (416)621-7776
Co. E-mail: info@ciaa-adjusters.ca
URL: http://www.ciaa-adjusters.ca
Contact: Greg G. Merrithew, President
Released: Annual

11274 ■ Canadian Life and Health Insurance Association (CLHIA)—Association Canadienne des Compagnies d'Assurances de Personnes

1 Queen St. E, Ste. 1700
Toronto, ON, Canada M5C 2X9
Ph: (416)777-2221
Free: 800-268-8099
Fax: (416)777-1895
URL: http://www.clhia.ca
Contact: Leslie Herr, Chairman

Description: Life and health insurance companies. Seeks to advance the insurance industry; promotes adherence to high standards of ethics and practice among members. Serves as a forum for the exchange of information among members; represents the collective interests of the life and health insurance industries. **Scope:** insurance, tax, law. **Founded:** 1894. **Subscriptions:** 2000 books periodicals. **Publications:** *Policyholder Tax Manual*.

11275 ■ Conference of Consulting Actuaries (CCA)

3880 Salem Lake Dr., Ste. H
Long Grove, IL 60047-5292
Ph: (847)719-6500
Fax: (847)719-6506
Co. E-mail: conference@ccactuaries.org
URL: http://www.ccactuaries.org
Contact: Dale H. Yamamoto, President

Description: Full-time consulting actuaries or governmental actuaries. Develops and maintains structure and programs to reinforce, enhance, or add to members' knowledge and skills; this includes continuing education, through diverse delivery methods, for all practice areas and for consulting and business skills. **Founded:** 1950. **Publications:** *The Proceedings* (Annual). **Awards:** John Hanson Memorial Prize (Annual); Lifetime Achievement Award (Annual); Most Valuable Volunteer Award (Annual); Wynn Kent Public Communication Award (Annual); John Hanson Memorial Prize; Lifetime Achievement Award; Most Valuable Volunteer Award; Wynn Kent Public Communications Award.

11276 ■ Consumer Credit Industry Association (CCIA)

6300 Powers Ferry Rd., Ste. 600-286
Atlanta, GA 30339
Ph: (678)858-4001
Co. E-mail: sjcipinko@cciaonline.com
URL: http://www.cciaonline.com
Contact: Scott J. Cipinko, Executive Vice President

Description: Insurance companies underwriting consumer credit insurance in areas of life insurance, accident and health insurance, and property insurance. **Founded:** 1951. **Publications:** *Consumer Credit Insurance Association--Digest Bulletin* (Periodic); *Consumer Credit Insurance Association--Information Bulletin* (Periodic); *Consumer Credit Insurance Association--Legislative Bulletin* (Periodic); *Consumer Credit Insurance Association--Annual Meeting Proceedings* (Annual). **Educational Activities:** Consumer Credit Industry Association Meeting (Annual). **Awards:** Arthur J. Morris Award; Arthur J. Morris Award (Periodic).

11277 ■ Council of Insurance Agents and Brokers

701 Pennsylvania Ave. NW, Ste. 750
Washington, DC 20004-2608
Ph: (202)783-4400
Fax: (202)783-4410
Co. E-mail: ciab@ciab.com
URL: http://www.ciab.com
Contact: Ken A. Crerar, President

Description: Represents the interests of the leading commercial property and casualty insurance agencies and brokerage firms in the U.S. and around the

world. **Scope:** insurance/risk management. **Founded:** 1913. **Subscriptions:** periodicals. **Publications:** *Leader's Edge* (Bimonthly); *For Your Benefit* (Monthly).

11278 ■ CPCU Society

720 Providence Rd.
Malvern, PA 19355-0709
Free: 800-932-2728
Fax: (610)251-2780
Co. E-mail: membercenter@cpcusociety.org
URL: http://www.cpcusociety.org
Contact: Steve McElhiney, President

Description: Serves as a professional society of individuals who have passed national examinations of the American Institute for Chartered Property Casualty Underwriters, have 3 years of work experience, have agreed to be bound by a code of ethics, and have been awarded the CPCU designation. Promotes education, research, social responsibility, and professionalism in the field. Holds seminars, symposia, and workshops. **Publications:** *CPCU News* (5/year); *CPCU Yearbook* (Annual); *CPCU Journal* (Quarterly). **Awards:** Circle of Excellence Recognition Program (Annual).

11279 ■ *Facts of the General Insurance Industry of Canada*

PO Box 121
Toronto, ON, Canada M5G 2C8
Ph: (416)362-2031
Free: 800-387-2880
Fax: (416)644-4961
Co. E-mail: memberservices@ibc.ca
URL: http://www.ibc.ca
Contact: Don Forgeron, President
Released: Periodic

11280 ■ GAMA International

2901 Telestar Ct., Ste. 140
Falls Church, VA 22042-1205
Ph: (571)499-4300
Free: 800-345-2687
Fax: (571)499-4302
Co. E-mail: gamamail@gamaweb.com
URL: http://www.gamaweb.com
Contact: Jeffrey R. Hughes, Chief Executive Officer

Description: Provides world-class education and training resources for individuals, companies and organizations involved with the recruitment and development of field managers, representatives and staff in the life insurance and financial services industry; advocates of the value-added role of field management and representatives in the ethical distribution of life insurance and financial products and services industry. **Founded:** 1951. **Publications:** *GAMA International Journal* (Bimonthly). **Awards:** Career Development Award (Annual); International Management Award (Annual); Master Agency Award (Annual); Recruiting Specialist Award (Annual). **Telecommunication Services:** gamamail@gama.naifa. org.

11281 ■ *IBC Between the Lines*

PO Box 121
Toronto, ON, Canada M5G 2C8
Ph: (416)362-2031
Free: 800-387-2880
Fax: (416)644-4961
Co. E-mail: memberservices@ibc.ca
URL: http://www.ibc.ca
Contact: Don Forgeron, President
Released: Periodic

11282 ■ *The Independent*

306-30 Eglinton Ave. W
Mississauga, ON, Canada L5R 3E7
Ph: (905)279-2727
Free: 800-654-3333
Fax: (905)276-7295
Co. E-mail: admin@ifbc.ca
URL: http://www.ifbc.ca
Contact: John Dargie, President
Released: Quarterly **Price:** free for members.

11283 ■ Independent Financial Brokers of Canada (IFB)—Courtiers Indenpendants en Securite Financiere (CISF)
306-30 Eglinton Ave. W
Mississauga, ON, Canada L5R 3E7
Ph: (905)279-2727
Free: 800-654-3333
Fax: (905)276-7295
Co. E-mail: admin@ifbc.ca
URL: http://www.ifbc.ca
Contact: John Dargie, President
Description: Represents members' interests. Conducts educational programs. **Founded:** 1987. **Publications:** The Independent (Quarterly). **Educational Activities:** Educational Summit (Semiannual).

11284 ■ Independent Insurance Agents and Brokers of America (IIABA)
127 S Peyton St.
Alexandria, VA 22314
Free: 800-221-7917
Fax: (703)683-7556
Co. E-mail: info@iiaba.org
URL: http://www.iiaba.net
Contact: Robert A. Rusbuldt, Chief Executive Officer
Description: Sales agencies handling property, fire, casualty, and surety insurance. Organizes technical and sales courses for new and established agents. Sponsors Independent Insurance Agent Junior Classic Golf Tournament. **Founded:** 1896. **Publications:** Independent Agent (Monthly); Insurance News and Views (Weekly). **Awards:** Maurice G. Herndon National Legislative Award; L. P. McCord National Education Award; Sidney O. Smith National Award; Woodworth Memorial Award; Outstanding Young Agents Committee Award; Dach Award for InVEST Agent of the Year; Bernard J. Burns Award.

11285 ■ Insurance Brokers Association of Canada (IBAC)—Association des courtiers d'assurances du Canada
18 King St. E, Ste. 1210
Toronto, ON, Canada M5C 1C4
Ph: (416)367-1831
Fax: (416)367-3687
Co. E-mail: ibac@ibac.ca
URL: http://www.ibac.ca
Contact: Dan Danyluk, Chief Executive Officer
Description: Insurance brokers. Promotes advancement of the insurance brokerage industry. Represents members' interests. Conducts educational and training programs for members' staff. **Founded:** 1921. **Telecommunication Services:** ddanyluk@ibac.ca.

11286 ■ Insurance Bureau of Canada (IBC)—Bureau D'Assurance du Canada
PO Box 121
Toronto, ON, Canada M5G 2C8
Ph: (416)362-2031
Free: 800-387-2880
Fax: (416)644-4961
Co. E-mail: memberservices@ibc.ca
URL: http://www.ibc.ca
Contact: Don Forgeron, President
Description: Trade association of the private property and casualty insurance industry. Works with members to improve communication with the public, government, news media, and other industry associations. Identifies and monitors legal and policy issues affecting the industry; conducts public opinion research; campaigns on a range of issues in order to reduce losses and increase public understanding of P&C insurance; promotes safety on the road, at work and at home. Gathers statistical data on insurance loss experience. **Scope:** property insurance, casualty insurance, insurance law, vehicle safety. **Founded:** 1964. **Subscriptions:** 7000 archival material books business records periodicals video recordings. **Publications:** Facts of the General Insurance Industry of Canada (Periodic); Perspective: Financial Affairs, Regulatory Affairs (Quarterly); IBC Between the Lines (Periodic).

11287 ■ Insurance Consumer Affairs Exchange (ICAE)
PO Box 746
Lake Zurich, IL 60047

Ph: (847)991-8454
Co. E-mail: nbrebner@icae.com
URL: http://icae.com
Contact: Nancy Brebner, Executive Director
Description: Voluntary, professional group of consumer affairs specialists from insurance companies, insurance regulators, and consumer information centers. Provides opportunities to exchange ideas for improving communication between insurers, consumers, and regulators. **Founded:** 1976. **Publications:** ICAE Catalyst (Semiannual); ICAE Resource Manual. **Educational Activities:** Winds of Change: Steering Customer Relations (Annual).

11288 ■ Insurance Information Institute (III)
110 William St.
New York, NY 10038
Ph: (212)346-5500
Free: 800-331-9146
Fax: (212)791-1807
Co. E-mail: members@iii.org
URL: http://www.iii.org
Contact: Dr. Robert P. Hartwig, President
Description: Property and casualty insurance companies. Provides information and educational services to mass media, educational institutions, trade associations, businesses, government agencies, and the public. **Scope:** property and casualty insurance and related topics. **Founded:** 1959. **Holdings:** The computer-readable I.I.I. Insurance Daily is updated daily; the I.I.I. Insurance Issues Update is updated monthly; and the I.I.I. Data Base contains some 85,000 records dating from 1984 to the present and is updated weekly with approximately 150 records. **Subscriptions:** 1400 books periodicals. **Publications:** Property-Casualty Insurance Facts; Insurance Information Institute Online; I.I.I. Data Base Search; I.I.I. Insurance Daily; Insurance Handbook for Reporters. **Educational Activities:** Property/Casualty Insurance Joint Industry Forum (Annual). **Telecommunication Services:** publications@iii.org; info@iii.org; consumer@iii.org.

11289 ■ Insurance Institute of America (IIA)
720 Providence Rd., Ste. 100
Malvern, PA 19355-3433
Free: 800-644-2101
Fax: (610)640-9576
Co. E-mail: customerservice@theinstitutes.org
URL: http://www.aicpcu.org
Description: Sponsors educational programs for property and liability insurance personnel. Conducts exams and awards certificates and diplomas. **Scope:** ethics, general insurance management, risk management, general property and liability insurance, information resources, insurer operations, insurer finances, public policy, quality improvement, regulation. **Founded:** 1909. **Subscriptions:** 9500 periodicals. **Publications:** Succeed (Annual). **Awards:** Award for Academic Excellence and Distinguished Graduate Award (Annual).

11290 ■ Insurance Marketing and Communications Association (IMCA)
4916 Point Fosdick Dr. NW, No. 180
Gig Harbor, WA 98335
Ph: (206)219-9811
Fax: (866)210-2481
Co. E-mail: info@imcanet.com
URL: http://www.imcanet.com
Contact: Linda J. Collins, President
Description: Advertising, marketing, public relations, and sales promotion executives of property and casualty insurance companies. Provides members with a forum for enhancing their knowledge of marketing and communications techniques and strategies, so that they can attain the highest standards of professional excellence in serving the information needs of their policyholders, employees, producers and the general public. **Founded:** 1923. **Publications:** UPDATE (Quarterly). **Awards:** Golden Torch Award (Annual); Sammy Award (Annual); Showcase Awards (Annual); Golden Torch Award.

11291 ■ The Log
2233 Argentia Rd., Ste. 100
Mississauga, ON, Canada L5N 2X7
Ph: (905)826-4768

Fax: (905)826-4873
Co. E-mail: cbmu@cbmu.com
URL: http://www.cbmu.com/HOME/default.asp
Contact: Brent Chorney, President
Released: Biennial

11292 ■ National Association of Health Underwriters (NAHU)
1212 New York Ave. NW, Ste. 1100
Washington, DC 20005
Ph: (202)552-5060
Fax: (202)747-6820
Co. E-mail: info@nahu.org
URL: http://www.nahu.org
Contact: Janet Trautwein, Chief Executive Officer
Description: Insurance agents and brokers engaged in the promotion, sale, and administration of disability income and health insurance. Sponsors advanced health insurance underwriting and research seminars. Testifies before federal and state committees on pending health insurance legislation. Sponsors Leading Producers Roundtable Awards for leading salesmen. Maintains a speakers' bureau and a political action committee. **Founded:** 1930. **Publications:** Health Insurance Underwriter (Monthly); The Health Insurance Underwriter (Monthly). **Educational Activities:** Capital Conference (Annual); National Association of Health Underwriters Convention (Annual); Capitol Conference (Annual). **Awards:** Harold R. Gordon Memorial Award (Annual); Leading Producers' Round Table (Annual); Harold R. Gordon Memorial Award; Leading Producer Round Table Awards (LPRT).

11293 ■ National Association of Insurance and Financial Advisors (NAIFA)
2901 Telestar Ct.
Falls Church, VA 22042-1205
Ph: (703)770-8100
Free: 877-866-2432
Fax: (703)770-8212
Co. E-mail: membersupport@naifa.org
URL: http://www.naifa.org
Contact: Robert A. Miller, President
Description: Federation of states and local associations representing 75,000 financial planners, life insurance agents, general agents, and managers; associate members are independent insurance agents, general managers of life companies and other life and health insurance professionals. Supports and maintains the highest principles and standards of life and health insurance. Promotes high ethical standards. Informs the public, render community service, and promotes public goodwill. Sponsors public service programs. Offers educational programs. **Scope:** life and health insurance. **Founded:** 1890. **Subscriptions:** archival material books periodicals. **Publications:** Advisor Today (Monthly). **Awards:** Manager's Membership Award (Annual); National Multiline Sales Award (Annual); National Quality Award (Annual); National Sales Achievement Award (Annual); Jack E. Bobo Award of Excellence (Annual); John Newton Russell Memorial Award (Annual).

11294 ■ National Association of Insurance Women International (NAIW)
9343 E 95th Ct. S
Tulsa, OK 74133
Ph: (918)294-3700
Free: 800-766-6249
Fax: (918)294-3711
Co. E-mail: joinnaiw@naiw.org
URL: http://www.naiw.org
Contact: Linda Wilson, President
Description: Insurance industry professionals. Promotes continuing education and networking for the professional advancement of its members. Offers education programs, meetings, services, and leadership opportunities. Provides a forum to learn about other disciplines in the insurance industry. **Founded:** 1940. **Publications:** Today's Insurance Professionals (Quarterly). **Educational Activities:** Annual NAIW Convention - National Association of Insurance Women International (Annual). **Awards:** Certified Professional Insurance Woman/Man; Diversified Advanced Education.

11295 ■ National Association of Professional Insurance Agents (PIA)—PIA National
400 N Washington St.
Alexandria, VA 22314
Ph: (703)836-9340
Fax: (703)836-1279
Co. E-mail: web@pianet.org
URL: http://www.pianet.com
Contact: Thomas C. Adderhold, President
Description: Represents independent agents in all 50 states, Puerto Rico and the District of Columbia. Represents members' interests in government and industry; provides educational programs; compiles statistics; conducts research programs; develops products/services unique to independent agencies; provides information and networking opportunities. **Founded:** 1931. **Publications:** *PIA Connection* (Monthly); *Professional Agent* (Monthly); *Consumer Brochures for Your Clients.* **Awards:** Agent of the Year (Annual); Agent of the Year (Annual); Company Award of Excellence (Annual); Professional Agent of the Year; CSR of the Year (Annual); Company Representative of the Year (Annual); Company Award of Excellence; National Company Representative of the Year. **Telecommunication Services:** piaweb@pianet.org.

11296 ■ Perspective: Financial Affairs, Regulatory Affairs
PO Box 121
Toronto, ON, Canada M5G 2C8
Ph: (416)362-2031
Free: 800-387-2880
Fax: (416)644-4961
Co. E-mail: memberservices@ibc.ca
URL: http://www.ibc.ca
Contact: Don Forgeron, President
Released: Quarterly

11297 ■ Physician Insurers Association of America (PIAA)
2275 Research Blvd., Ste. 250
Rockville, MD 20850
Ph: (301)947-9000
Fax: (301)947-9090
Co. E-mail: batchinson@piaa.us
URL: http://www.piaa.us
Contact: Brian Atchinson, President
Description: Physician liability insurance companies, including domestic physician and dental liability insurers, international affiliates, and reinsurers. Seeks to further the best interests of member companies in areas related to physician liability insurance. Focuses on the availability and affordability of professional liability insurance and the effective delivery of quality healthcare. Conducts research and educational programs; monitors and advocates for legislation. **Scope:** member companies, annual reports, insurance filings. **Founded:** 1977. **Subscriptions:** archival material business records. **Publications:** *The Physician Insurer* (Quarterly); *PIAA Membership Directory* (Annual); *Research Notes* (Quarterly); *Physician Insurers Association of America--Membership Directory* (Annual). **Educational Activities:** Physician Insurers Association of America Meeting (Annual); Physician Insurers Association of America Workshop (Periodic); Physician Insurers Association of America Annual Meeting (Annual). **Awards:** Peter Sweetland Award of Excellence (Annual). **Telecommunication Services:** wchao@piaa.us.

11298 ■ Policyholder Tax Manual
1 Queen St. E, Ste. 1700
Toronto, ON, Canada M5C 2X9
Ph: (416)777-2221
Free: 800-268-8099
Fax: (416)777-1895
URL: http://www.clhia.ca
Contact: Leslie Herr, Chairman
Price: C$100, for members; C$250, for nonmembers.

11299 ■ Property Casualty Insurers Association of America (PCI)
2600 S River Rd.
Des Plaines, IL 60018-3286
Ph: (847)297-7800

Fax: (847)297-5064
Co. E-mail: jeffrey.brewer@pciaa.net
URL: http://www.pciaa.net
Contact: David A. Sampson, President
Description: Independent property and casualty insurance companies. Provides advocacy and technical information. Maintains 32 committees, including political action. Conducts educational programs; compiles statistics. **Scope:** law, insurance. **Founded:** 2004. **Subscriptions:** audiovisuals books business records periodicals. **Publications:** *Individual State Profile* (Annual); *Legislative Reporter* (Biweekly); *State Insurance Department Directory* (Annual).

11300 ■ Risk and Insurance Management Society (RIMS)
1065 Ave. of the Americas, 13th Fl.
New York, NY 10018
Ph: (212)286-9292
Co. E-mail: membership@rims.org
URL: http://www.rims.org
Contact: Deborah Luthi, President
Description: Business association serving corporate risk and insurance managers. Dedicated to advancing the practice of risk management, a discipline that protects physical, financial, and human resources. **Founded:** 1950. **Publications:** *Annual Risk Management Buyers Guide* (Annual); *Compensation and Benefits Survey*; *RIMSCANADA* (Quarterly); *RIMSCOPE* (Monthly); *Risk Management* (Monthly). **Awards:** Arthur Quern Quality Award (Annual); Chapter Recognition Award (Annual); Harry & Dorothy Goodell Award (Annual); Richard W. Bland Memorial Award (Annual); Arthur Quern Quality Award; Fred H. Bossons Award; The Cristy Award; Ron Judd Heart of RIMS Award (Annual).

11301 ■ Society of Financial Service Professionals (SFSP)
19 Campus Blvd., Ste. 100
Newtown Square, PA 19073-3239
Ph: (610)526-2500
Free: 800-392-6900
Fax: (610)527-1499
Co. E-mail: info@financialpro.org
URL: http://www.financialpro.org
Contact: Richard M. Weber, Chairman
Description: Represents the interests of financial advisers. Fosters the development of professional responsibility. Assists clients to achieve personal and business-related financial goals. Offers educational programs, online professional resources and networking opportunities. **Founded:** 1928. **Publications:** *Journal of Financial Service Professionals* (Bimonthly). **Educational Activities:** Financial Service Forum (Annual). **Awards:** American Business Ethics Award (Annual); Kenneth Black, Jr. Journal Author Awards (Annual).

11302 ■ Society of Insurance Financial Management (SIFM)
PO Box 9001
Mount Vernon, NY 10552
Ph: (914)966-3180
Fax: (914)966-3264
Co. E-mail: sifm@cinn.com
URL: http://www.sifm.org
Contact: Edward J. Majkowski, President
Description: Represents insurance company officers and employees in financial management departments. Provides a timely forum for discussing current insurance industry issues relating to financial accounting and reporting, reinsurance, taxation, regulatory developments and other relevant topics. **Founded:** 1959.

REFERENCE WORKS

11303 ■ "2010 Book of Lists" in Austin Business JournalInc. (Vol. 29, December 25, 2009, No. 42, pp. 1)
Pub: American City Business Journals
Description: Rankings of companies and organizations within the business services, finance, healthcare, hospitality and travel, insurance, marketing and media, professional services, real estate, education

and technology industries in Austin, Texas are presented. Rankings are based on sales, business size, and other statistics.

11304 ■ "Abroad, Not Overboard" in Entrepreneur (Vol. 36, April 2008, No. 4, pp. 68)
Pub: Entrepreneur Media, Inc.
Ed: Crystal Detamore-Rodman. **Description:** Export-Import Bank is an agency created by the U.S. government to help exporters get credit insurance and capital loans by providing them with loan guarantees. The bank, being criticized as supporting more the bigger exporters, has allotted to smaller businesses a bigger portion of the annual credit being approved.

11305 ■ "All-Star Advice 2010" in Black Enterprise (Vol. 41, October 2010, No. 3, pp. 97)
Pub: Earl G. Graves Publishing Co. Inc.
Ed: Renita Burns, Sheiresa Ngo, Marcia Wade Talbert. **Description:** Financial experts share tips on real estate, investing, taxes, insurance and debt management.

11306 ■ "The Annual Entitlement Lecture: Trustees of Medicare and Social Security Issue Another Dismal Report" in Barron's (March 31, 2008)
Pub: Dow Jones & Company, Inc.
Ed: Thomas G. Donlan. **Description:** Expenditures on Medicare hospital insurance and the revenues available to pay for it have led to a gap of capital valued at $38.6 trillion. Slashing the benefits or raising taxes will not solve the gap which exists unless the government saves the money and invests it in private markets.

11307 ■ "Anthem Leading the Way in Social Tech Revolution" in Inside Business (Vol. 13, September-October 2011, No. 5, pp. 1B3)
Pub: Great Lakes Publishing Co.
Ed: Ryan Clark. **Description:** Anthem Blue Cross and Blue Shield is leading the way in social technology. The firm's social media initiatives to promote itself are outlined.

11308 ■ "An Apple a Day" in Entrepreneur (Vol. 36, February 2008, No. 2, pp. 19)
Pub: Entrepreneur Media Inc.
Ed: Mark Henricks. **Description:** Businesses are handling rising health coverage costs by providing employees with wellness programs, which include smoking-cessation programs, consumer-directed plans for savings on premiums, and limited medical care plans. Details on the growing trend regarding employee health coverage are discussed.

11309 ■ "Are Prepaid Legal Services Worthwhile?" in Contractor (Vol. 56, December 2009, No. 12, pp. 31)
Pub: Penton Media, Inc.
Ed: Susan Linden McGreevy. **Description:** Companies' provision of legal insurance as an employee benefit in the United States is discussed. Stoppage of premium payment halts employee coverage. It also does not cover all kinds of personal issues.

11310 ■ "Are You Overinsured? Some Policies May Not Offer Much Additional Benefit" in Black Enterprise (Vol. 38, March 2008, No. 8, pp. 126)
Pub: Earl G. Graves Publishing Co. Inc.
Ed: Tamara E. Holmes. **Description:** Travel insurance, identity-theft insurance, specific disease or health condition insurance policies are described. Advice is given to help determine if you are overinsured.

11311 ■ "Baldwin Connelly Partnership Splits" in Business Journal Serving Greater Tampa Bay (Vol. 30, November 19, 2010, No. 48, pp. 1)
Pub: Tampa Bay Business Journal
Ed: Alexis Muellner. **Description:** The fast-growing insurance brokerage Baldwin Connelly is now breaking up after five years. Two different entrepreneurial visions have developed within the organization and

founders Lowry Baldwin and John Connell will not take separate tracks. Staffing levels in the firm are expected to remain the same.

11312 ■ "Bank Forces Brooke Founder To Sell His Holdings" in The Business Journal-Serving Metropolitan Kansas City (October 10, 2008)

Pub: American City Business Journals, Inc.

Ed: James Dornbrook. **Description:** Robert Orr who is the founder of Brooke Corp., a franchise of insurance agencies, says that he was forced to sell virtually all of his stocks in the company by creditors. First United Bank held the founder's stock as collateral for two loans worth $5 million and $7.9 million, which were declared in default in September 2008. Details of the selling of the company's stocks are provided.

11313 ■ "Bankruptcy Claims Brooke, Gives Franchisees Hope" in The Business Journal-Serving Metropolitan Kansas City (October 31, 2008)

Pub: American City Business Journals, Inc.

Ed: James Dornbrook; Steve Vockrodt. **Description:** Insurer Brooke Corp. was required to file for Chapter 11 bankruptcy for a deal to sell all of its assets to businessmen Terry Nelson and Lysle Davidson. The new Brooke plans to share contingency fees with franchisees. The impacts of the bankruptcy case on Brooke franchisees are discussed.

11314 ■ Best's Key Rating Guide

Pub: A.M. Best Company Inc.

Contact: James Peavy, President

URL(s): www.ambest.com/sales/krg/. **Released:** Annual; Latest edition 2010. **Price:** $180, Individuals regular service; shipping/handling (16.95); $800, Individuals full service; online; $900, Individuals full service; print/online. **Covers:** Financial and operating characteristics on over 3,400 major property/casualty insurance companies, over 1,650 major life and health insurance companies. **Entries include:** Company name, city, state, phone, officers' names and titles, date founded, principal lines of business, capitalization, states in which licensed, Best's ratings for previous five years, other key financial ratios and tests. **Arrangement:** Alphabetical.

11315 ■ "Bills Raise Blues Debate; An Unfair Edge or Level Playing Field?" in Crain's Detroit Business (Vol. 24, January 21, 2008, No. 3)

Pub: Crain Communications Inc. - Detroit

Ed: Sherri Begin. **Description:** Changes in Michigan state law would change the way health insurance can be sold to individuals. Michigan Blue Cross Blue Shield is working to keep its tax-exempt status while staying competitive against for-profit insurers and nonprofit HMOs.

11316 ■ "Blue Cross Confronts Baby Blues" in Marketing to Women (Vol. 21, March 2008, No. 3, pp. 3)

Pub: EPM Communications Inc.

Contact: Ira Mayer, President

E-mail: imayer@epmcom.com

Description: Blue Cross of California has launched a Maternity Depression Program aimed at educating mothers suffering from postpartum depression.

11317 ■ "Blue Cross to Put Kiosk in Mall" in News & Observer (November 9, 2010)

Pub: News & Observer

Ed: Alan M. Wolf. **Description:** Blue Cross and Blue Shield of North Carolina has placed a kiosk in Durham's Streets of Southpoint in order to market its health insurance.

11318 ■ "Brooke Agents Claim Mistreatment" in The Business Journal-Serving Metropolitan Kansas City (Vol. 27, October 24, 2008, No. 7, pp. 1)

Pub: American City Business Journals, Inc.

Ed: James Dornbrook. **Description:** Franchisees of Brooke Corp., an insurance franchise, face uncertainty as their bills remain unpaid and banks threaten

to destroy their credit. The company bundled and sold franchisee loans to different banks, but the credit crunch left the company with massive debts and legal disputes.

11319 ■ Business Insurance--Agent/Broker Profiles Issue

Pub: Business Insurance

URL(s): www.businessinsurance.com. **Ed:** Regis J. Coccia. **Released:** Annual; Latest edition 2008. **Publication includes:** List of top 10 insurance agents/brokers worldwide specializing in commercial insurance. **Entries include:** Firm name, address, phone, fax, branch office locations, year established, names of subsidiaries, gross revenues, premium volume, number of employees, principal officers, percent of revenue generated by commercial retail brokerage, acquisitions. **Arrangement:** Alphabetical by company. **Indexes:** Geographical.

11320 ■ "Businesses Balk at 1099 Provision in Health Reform Law" in Baltimore Business Journal (Vol. 28, August 13, 2010, No. 14, pp. 1)

Pub: Baltimore Business Journal

Ed: Scott Dance. **Description:** Small business advocates and accountants have criticized the Internal Revenue Service Form 1099 provision in the health care reform law as not worth the cost of time and money. Critics believe the policy would create a deluge of the documents that is too much for the companies or the IRS to handle. Details of the provision are also discussed.

11321 ■ "Businesses Keep a Watchful Eye on Worker's Comp" in The Business Journal-Serving Greater Tampa Bay (September 5, 2008)

Pub: American City Business Journals, Inc.

Ed: Jane Meinhardt. **Description:** Pending a ruling from the Florida Supreme Court that could uphold the 2003 changes on workers' compensation law, the outcome would include restrictions on claimant attorneys' fees and allow the competitive workers' compensation insurance rates to remain low. However, insurance rates are expected to go up if the court overturns the changes.

11322 ■ "Cerner Works the Business Circuit" in Business Journal-Serving Metropolitan Kansas City (Vol. 26, October 5, 2007, No. 4, pp. 1)

Pub: American City Business Journals, Inc.

Ed: Rob Roberts. **Description:** Cerner Corporation is embracing the coming of the electronic medical record exchange by creating a regional health information organization (RHIO) called the CareEntrust. The RHIO convinced health insurers to share claims data with patients and clinicians. At the Center Health Conference, held October 7 to 10, Cerner will demonstrate the software it developed for CareEntrust to the 40,000 healthcare and information technology professionals.

11323 ■ "Changes Sought to Health Law" in Baltimore Business Journal (Vol. 28, July 30, 2010, No. 12, pp. 1)

Pub: Baltimore Business Journal

Ed: Kent Hoover. **Description:** Business groups that opposed health care reform are working to undo parts of the new laws even before they go into effect. Business groups are gaining support for one legislative fix, which is repealing the law's provision that requires all businesses to file 1099 forms with the IRS any time they pay more than $600 a year to another business.

11324 ■ "CNinsure Offers Safety in Numbers" in Barron's (Vol. 90, September 13, 2010, No. 37, pp. 29)

Pub: Barron's Editorial & Corporate Headquarters

Ed: Teresa Rivas. **Description:** China's insurance holding company CNinsure has a long growth future due to the nascent insurance market in the country. It has also been diversifying its offerings and it has a broad network in the nation. The shares of the company are trading cheaply at nearly 14 times its 2011 earnings, and is considered a good point for investors.

11325 ■ "Connecting the Dots Between Wellness and Elder Care" in Benefits and Compensation Digest (Vol. 47, August 2010, No. 8, pp. 18)

Pub: International Foundation of Employee Benefit Plans

Contact: Richard Lyall, President

Ed: Sandra Timmermann. **Description:** Employees caring for aged and infirm parents deal with time and financial issues and other stresses. The connection between health status of caregivers and employers' health care costs could be aided by linking programs and benefits with wellness and caregiving.

11326 ■ "Consulting Firm Goes Shopping" in Crain's Chicago Business (Vol. 31, April 28, 2008, No. 17, pp. 45)

Pub: Crain Communications, Inc.

Ed: Phuong Ly. **Description:** Clark & Wamberg LLC was created last year after the merger of Clark Inc. to a Dutch insurance conglomerate. Clark Inc. was a life insurance and benefits consultancy which had been on a downslide, returning just 5.6 percent a year to shareholders. In contrast Clark & Wamberg posted first-year revenue of $106.8 million, fueled by business from its executive compensation and health care clients.

11327 ■ "Continuously Monitoring Workers' Comp Can Limit Costs" in Crain's Cleveland Business (Vol. 28, October 8, 2007, No. 40, pp. 21)

Pub: Crain Communications, Inc.

Ed: Michael Lagnoni. **Description:** When operating without a plan for managing its workers' compensation program, a company risks losing money. For most companies workers' compensation insurance premiums are often reduced to an annual budget entry but employers who are actively involved in the management of their programs are more likely to experience reductions in premiums and limit indirect costs associated with claims.

11328 ■ "Controversial Bill Could Raise Rates for Homeowners" in Orlando Business Journal (Vol. 26, January 22, 2010, No. 34, pp. 1)

Pub: American City Business Journals

Ed: Oscar Pedro Musibay; Christopher Boyd. **Description:** Florida Senate Bill 876 and its companion House Bill 447 are pushing for the deregulation of rates in the state's home insurance market. The bill is being opposed by consumer advocates as it could mean higher rates for homeowner insurance policies.

11329 ■ "Cost of Md. Health Plan Not Known" in Baltimore Business Journal (Vol. 28, September 3, 2010, No. 17, pp. 1)

Pub: Baltimore Business Journal

Ed: Emily Mullin. **Description:** United States health reform is seen to result in increased health insurance prices in Maryland. However, health care reform advocates claim a new marketplace and increased competition will help keep costs down.

11330 ■ "Courting Canadian Customers Confounds Car Dealers" in Business First Buffalo (November 9, 2007, pp. 1)

Pub: American City Business Journals, Inc.

Ed: James Fink. **Description:** Strength of the Canadian dollar has led to an influx of potential customers for the Western New York automobile industry, but franchising restrictions and licensing as well as insurance issues have limited the potential of having larger sales figures. Border and trade issues that affect the car industry in WNY are also discussed.

11331 ■ "CreFirst To Reward Doctors for Reducing Costs, Improving Care" in Baltimore Business Journal (Vol. 28, June 4, 2010, No. 4, pp. 1)

Pub: Baltimore Business Journal

Ed: Scott Graham. **Description:** CareFirst Blue Cross Blue Shield plans to introduce a program that dangles big financial rewards to physicians who change the way they deliver primary care by improving the health of their sickest patients while reducing costs. The company will soon begin recruiting primary care physicians in Maryland, Washington DC, and Northern Virginia.

11332 ■ *"Crop Insurance Harvest Prices in 2011" in Farm Industry News (November 9, 2011)*
Pub: Penton Business Media Inc.
Ed: Gary Schnitkey. **Description:** Risk Management Agency (RMA) reported harvest prices for corn and soybean grown in the Midwest with corn at $6.32 per bushel, 31 cents higher than the project $6.01; soybeans were at $12.14 per bushel, down $1.35 from the projected price of $13.49.

11333 ■ *"Cutting Health Care Costs: the 3-Legged Stool" in HR Specialist (Vol. 8, September 2010, No. 9, pp. 1)*
Pub: Capitol Information Group Inc.
Description: Employer spending on health insurance benefits to employees is investigated.

11334 ■ *"Diana Bonta: Keeping People Healthy and Thriving" in Hispanic Business (Vol. 30, April 2008, No. 4, pp. 30)*
Pub: Hispanic Business
Ed: Leanndra Martinez. **Description:** Diana Bonta serves as vice president of public affairs for Kaiser Permanente and is a strong advocate for health reform and improving access to health care. In order to better serve the underinsured and uninsured, she directs Kaiser's Community Benefit division that devoted $369 million last year to this cause.

11335 ■ *Dictionary of Real Estate Terms*
Pub: Barron's Educational Series Inc.
Contact: Alex Holtz, President
E-mail: aholtz@berronseduc.com
Ed: Jack P. Friedman, Jack C. Harris, J. Bruce Lindeman. **Released:** October 2008. **Price:** $13.99. **Description:** More than 2,500 real estate terms relating to mortgages and financing, brokerage law, architecture, rentals and leases, property insurance, and more.

11336 ■ *"Discovery Communications" in Workforce Management (Vol. 88, December 14, 2009, No. 13, pp. 17)*
Pub: Crain Communications Inc.
Ed: Jeremy Smerd. **Description:** Discovery Communications provides its employees a wealth of free health services via a comprehensive work-site medical clinic that is available to its employees and their dependents. Overview of the company's innovative approach to healthcare is presented.??.

11337 ■ *"Doctors Eye Rating Plan With Caution" in The Business Journal-Portland (Vol. 25, July 4, 2008, No. 17, pp. 1)*
Pub: American City Business Journals, Inc.
Ed: Robin J. Moody. **Description:** Doctors in Portland, Oregon are wary of a new Providence Health Plan system that rates their performance on patients with certain medical conditions. The system is expected to discourage wasteful procedures, thereby, saving employers' money. Other mechanics of the rating system are also discussed.

11338 ■ *"Doctors, Health Insurers Squabble Over Who Sends Patients the Bill" in Baltimore Business Journal (Vol. 27, February 6, 2010)*
Pub: American City Business Journals
Ed: Scott Graham. **Description:** Issue of allowing patients to send reimbursement checks to physicians who are not part of their health insurer's provider network is being debated in Maryland. Details on the proposed Maryland bill and the arguments presented by doctors and insurers are outlined.

11339 ■ *"Doctor's Orders" in Canadian Business (Vol. 79, November 20, 2006, No. 23, pp. 73)*
Pub: Rogers Media
Ed: Jeff Sanford. **Description:** George Cohon, the founder of McDonald's in Canada and Russia, speaks about the Canadian market and the experience of starting McDonald's in Canada.

11340 ■ *"Doctors Warn of Problems" in Austin Business JournalInc. (Vol. 29, December 4, 2009, No. 39, pp. 1)*
Pub: American City Business Journals
Ed: Sandra Zaragoza. **Description:** Texas physicians have voiced their concern regarding the potential cuts in Medicare reimbursement rates due to the 21 percent cut imposed by Centers for Medicare and Medicaid at the start of 2010. Experts believe the large cuts would result in the closure of some physician practices. Details of the Texas Medical Association's stand on the health reform bill are examined.

11341 ■ *"Doing Without" in Baltimore Business Journal (Vol. 28, June 11, 2010, No. 5, pp. 1)*
Pub: Baltimore Business Journal
Ed: Scott Graham. **Description:** Maryland Health Care Commission report figures have shown only 47,661 small businesses provided some level of health coverage to 381,517 employees in 2009. These numbers are down from 51,283 employers who offered benefits to 407,983 employees in 2008 to highlight a disturbing trend in Maryland's small-group insurance market. Reasons for the drop are discussed.

11342 ■ *"E-Medical Records Save Money, Time in Ann Arbor" in Crain's Detroit Business (Vol. 24, January 21, 2008, No. 3, pp. 6)*
Pub: Crain Communications Inc. - Detroit
Ed: Jay Greene. **Description:** Ann Arbor Area Health Information Exchange is improving patient outcomes by sharing clinical and administrative data in electronic medical record systems.

11343 ■ *"Elder Care Costs Surge" in National Underwriter Life & Health (Vol. 114, November 8, 2020, No. 21, pp. 25)*
Pub: Summit Business Media
Ed: Trevor Thomas. **Description:** Nursing home and assisted living rates rose from 2009 to 2010, according to MetLife Mature Market Institute. Statistical data included.

11344 ■ *"Employer Jobless Tax Could Rise" in Sacramento Business Journal (Vol. 28, May 27, 2011, No. 13, pp. 1)*
Pub: Sacramento Business Journal
Ed: Kathy Robertson. **Description:** The government of California is facing an estimated $16 billion deficit in its unemployment insurance fund. Unemployment insurance spending has exceeded employer contributions to the fund. Statistics on unemployment insurance is included.

11345 ■ *"Employers Tied in Knots" in Sacramento Business Journal (Vol. 25, August 15, 2008, No. 24, pp. 1)*
Pub: American City Business Journals, Inc.
Ed: Kathy Robertson. **Description:** Conflicting laws on same sex marriage have been posing problems for companies, and insurers in California. The court ruling that allowed gay marriages has created differences between state and federal laws. Federal laws on same-sex spouse taxation are also seen to complicate the issue.

11346 ■ *"Employers Waking Up to Effects of Workers' Sleep Problems" in Crain's Cleveland Business (Vol. 28, December 3, 2007, No. 48, pp. 18)*
Pub: Crain Communications, Inc.
Ed: Jennifer Keirn. **Description:** Employers are beginning to realize that poor sleep quality can impact their bottom lines with higher health care costs and more lost-time accidents. The National Institutes of Health estimates that sleep deprivation, sleep disorders and excessive daytime sleepiness add about $15 billion to our national health care bill and cost employers $50 billion in lost productivity.

11347 ■ *"Experts Take the Temp of Obama Plan" in The Business Journal-Serving Metropolitan Kansas City (Vol. 27, November 14, 2008, No. 10)*
Pub: American City Business Journals, Inc.
Ed: Rob Roberts. **Description:** Kansas City, Missouri-based employee benefits experts say president-elect Barack Obama's health care reform plan is on track. Insurance for children and capitalization for health information technology are seen as priority areas. The plan is aimed at reducing the number of uninsured people in the United States.

11348 ■ *"Export Initiative Launched" in Philadelphia Business Journal (Vol. 28, December 11, 2009, No. 43, pp. 1)*
Pub: American City Business Journals
Ed: Athena D. Merritt. **Description:** The first initiative that came out of the partnership between the Export-Import Bank of the US, the city of Philadelphia, and the World Trade Center of Greater Philadelphia is presented. A series of export finance workshops have featured Ex-Im Bank resources that can provide Philadelphia businesses with working capital, insurance protection and buyer financing.

11349 ■ *"Firms Sue Doracon to Recoup More Than $1M in Unpaid Bills" in Baltimore Business Journal (Vol. 28, July 9, 2010, No. 9, pp. 1)*
Pub: Baltimore Business Journal
Ed: Scott Dance. **Description:** Concrete supplier Paul J. Rach Inc., Selective Insurance Company, and equipment leasing firm Colonial Pacific Leasing Corporation intend to sue Baltimore, Maryland-based Doracon Contracting Inc. for $1 million in unpaid bills. Doracon owed Colonial Pacific $794,000 and the equipment is still in Doracon's possession. Selective Insurance and Paul J. Rach respectively seek $132,000 and $88,000.

11350 ■ *"For All It's Worth" in Entrepreneur (Vol. 36, April 2008, No. 4, pp. 46)*
Pub: Entrepreneur Media, Inc.
Ed: Farnoosh Torabi. **Description:** Discusses the federal estate tax system requires that 45 percent of the money beyond $2 million be given to the government. Ways on how to minimize the effects of estate tax on assets include: creating bypass trusts for married couples; setting up an irrevocable life insurance trust to avoid taxation of estate for insurance benefactors; and having annual gift tax exclusion.

11351 ■ *"Generational Savvy" in Hawaii Business (Vol. 54, August 2008, No. 2, pp. 135)*
Pub: Hawaii Business Publishing
Ed: Jolyn Okimoto Rosa. **Description:** Lawrence Takeo Kagawa founded Security Insurance Agency, later renamed Occidental Underwriters of Hawaii Ltd., in 1933 to provide insurance to Asian-Americans in Hawaii at lower premiums. Details on the company's history, growth investment products and Transamerica Life products and 75 years of family-run business are discussed.

11352 ■ *Green Your Small Business: Profitable Ways to Become an Ecopreneur*
Pub: McGraw-Hill
Ed: Scott Cooney. **Released:** November 7, 2008. **Price:** $19.95 paperback. **Description:** Advice and guidance is given to help any entrepreneur start, build or grow a green business, focusing on green business basics, market research and financing, as well as handling legal and insurance issues.

11353 ■ *"Greenberg Sues U.S. Over AIG Rescue" in Wall Street Journal Eastern Edition (November 22 , 2011, pp. C3)*
Pub: Dow Jones & Company Inc.
Ed: Liam Pleven, Serena Ng. **Description:** Former Chief Executive Officer of American International Group Inc., Maurice R. 'Hank' Greenberg, has filed a lawsuit against the United States and the Federal Reserve Bank of New York on behalf of shareholders and his company, Starr International Company Inc., claiming that the government was wrong in taking control of the insurance giant and used it to move tens of millions of dollars to the trading partners of AIG.

11354 ■ "Harleysville Eyes Growth After Nationwide Deal' in Philadelphia Business Journal (Vol. 30, October 7, 2011, No. 34, pp. 1)

Pub: American City Business Journals Inc.

Ed: Jeff Blumenthal. Description: Harleysville Group announced growth plans after the company was sold to Columbus, Ohio-based Nationwide Mutual Insurance Company for about $1.63 billion. Nationwide gained an independent agency platform in 32 states with the Harleysville deal.

11355 ■ "Health Alliance Could Sell Group" in Business Courier (Vol. 27, June 18, 2010, No. 7, pp. 1)

Pub: Business Courier

Ed: James Ritchie. Description: Health Alliance could sell the 31-doctor Greater Cincinnati Associated Physicians Group. The group has seen several members withdraw ever since the group filed a complaint asking to be released from services to Health Alliance.

11356 ■ "Health Care Braces for Federal Cuts" in Boston Business Journal (Vol. 29, August 19, 2011, No. 15, pp. 1)

Pub: American City Business Journals Inc.

Ed: Scott Dance. Description: The healthcare industry in Baltimore is expecting negative effects from the federal debt ceiling on Medicare and Medicaid spending. Medicare funds are expected to be slashed and could impact hospitals and doctors.

11357 ■ "Health Care of the Future" in Business Journal Serving Greater Tampa Bay (Vol. 30, November 19, 2010, No. 48, pp. 1)

Pub: Tampa Bay Business Journal

Ed: Margie Manning. Description: Information about accountable care organizations (ACO), which are integrated care systems with doctors and hospitals working closely together to handle patient care, is provided. The Patient Protection and Affordable Care Act paved the way for ACOs as Medicare demonstration projects.

11358 ■ "Health Centers Plan Expansion" in Crain's Detroit Business (Vol. 25, June 15, 2009, No. 24, pp. 3)

Pub: Crain Communications Inc. - Detroit

Ed: Jay Greene. Description: Detroit has five federally qualified health centers that plan to receive over $3 million in federal stimulus money that will be used to expand projects that will care for uninsured patients.

11359 ■ "Health Insurance Dilemmas" in Hispanic Business (January-February 2008, pp. 58)

Pub: Hispanic Business

Ed: Anna Davison. Description: Small business owners discussed the challenges they face providing health insurance to employees.

11360 ■ "Health IT Regulations Generate Static Among Providers" in Philadelphia Business Journal (Vol. 28, January 29, 2010, No. 50, pp. 1)

Pub: American City Business Journals

Ed: John George. Description: US Centers for Medicaid and Medicare Services and the Office of the National Coordinator for Health Information Technology have proposed rules regarding the meaningful use of electronic health records. The rules must be complied with by hospitals and physicians to qualify for federal stimulus funds.

11361 ■ "Health Reform Could Expand HSA-Based Plans" in Workforce Management (Vol. 88, December 14, 2009, No. 13, pp. 6)

Pub: Crain Communications Inc.

Ed: Jeremy Smerd. Description: HSA-qualified plans are the cheapest insurance plans on the market as they have a higher deductible but cost less upfront. If health care reform passes, HSA-qualified plans should benefit greatly.

11362 ■ "Health Reform How-To" in Business Courier (Vol. 26, December 11, 2009, No. 33, pp. 1)

Pub: American City Business Journals, Inc.

Ed: James Ritchie. Description: Greater Cincinnati health care leaders shared views about the health care reform bill. Respondents included the Cincinnati Visiting Nurse's Wallen Falberg, healthcare consultant Hirsch Cohen, Greater Cincinnati Health Council's Coleen O'Toole, Employer Health Care Alliance's Sharron DiMario, Legal Aid Society of Greater Cincinnati's Col Owens, Christ Hospital's Susan Croushore, and Humana of Ohio's Tim Cappel.

11363 ■ "Healthcare: How To Get a Better Deal' in Inc. (November 2007, pp. 34)

Pub: Gruner & Jahr USA Publishing

Ed: Sarah Goldstein. Description: Things to consider when choosing an insurance carrier for your employees are explored.

11364 ■ "Here's How Buffett Spent 2007' in Barron's (Vol. 88, March 10, 2008, No. 10, pp. 48)

Pub: Dow Jones & Company, Inc.

Ed: Andrew Bary. Description: Earnings of Berkshire Hathaway may decline in 2008 due to a tighter insurance market, but its portfolio is expected to continue growing. Warren Buffett purchased $19.1 billion worth of stocks in 2007.

11365 ■ "Home Sweet Home" in Canadian Business (Vol. 79, October 9, 2006, No. 20, pp. 22)

Pub: Rogers Media

Ed: Peter Shawn Taylor. Description: Changes being made in the management of mortgage insurance business in Canada are critically analyzed.

11366 ■ "Hospital Fighting for Its Life; Board of St. Anthony Scrambles to Stem Losses" in Crain's Chicago Business (April 28, 2008)

Pub: Crain Communications, Inc.

Ed: Mike Colias. Description: Chicago's Catholic health chain was looking to sell the money-losing hospital St. Anthony Hospital on the West Side but with the financial picture improving and no merger offers in the works the investment bank hired to shop the hospital is hoping to operate the 111-year-old facility as an independent entity. St. Anthony serves as a 'safety net' for the region since an increasing number of its patients are uninsured or on public aid, which pays far less than commercial insurers.

11367 ■ "Hospitals See Major Shift To Outpatient Care" in The Business Journal-Milwaukee (Vol. 25, September 12, 2008, No. 51, pp. A1)

Pub: American City Business Journals, Inc.

Ed: Corrinne Hess. Description: Statistics show that the revenue of Wisconsin hospitals from outpatient medical care is about to surpass revenue from hospital patients who stay overnight. This revenue increase is attributed to new technology and less-invasive surgery. Trends show that the shift toward outpatient care actually started in the late 1980s and early 1990s.

11368 ■ "How to Maximize Your Investment Income" in Contractor (Vol. 56, December 2009, No. 12, pp. 33)

Pub: Penton Media, Inc.

Ed: Irv Blackman. Description: Private placement life insurance (PPLI) can minimize taxes and protect assets. PPLI is a form of variable universal insurance that is offered privately. Risk of insurance company illiquidity is avoided as investments are placed in separate accounts.

11369 ■ "How to Start a Home-Based Senior Care Business: Check-in-Care, Transportation Services, Shopping and Cooking

Pub: Globe Pequot Press

Ed: James L. Ferry. Released: January 1, 2010. Price: $18.95. Description: Information is provided to start a home-based senior care business.

11370 ■ "How a Unique Culture Proposition Became a USP' in Business Strategy Review (Vol. 21, Spring 2010, No. 1, pp. 52)

Pub: Wiley-Blackwell

Ed: Adam Kingl. Description: How can you transform the way you do things into a compelling sales proposition? Zurich Insurance has created a Unique Culture Proposition which may be its Unique Selling Point.

11371 ■ "Humana: Take Pay Cut or Get Out' in Business Courier (Vol. 24, February 1, 2008, No. 43, pp. 1)

Pub: American City Business Journals, Inc.

Ed: James Ritchie. Description: Insurer Humana Inc. is removing some surgery centers from its network for refusing to welcome the new payment system. Evendale Surgery Center and the Surgery Center of Cincinnati will be removed from the network because they resist the newly imposed lower rates. Speculations over Humana's decision are discussed.

11372 ■ "IBC Reverses Member Slide" in Philadelphia Business Journal (Vol. 30, September 23, 2011, No. 32, pp. 1)

Pub: American City Business Journals Inc.

Ed: John George. Description: Health insurer Independence Blue Cross (IBC) added more than 40,000 members across all product lines since the start of 2011. It has 2.2 million members in Pennsylvania's Philadelphia region and 3.1 million members across the U.S. Services and other growth-related plans of IBC are covered.

11373 ■ "Impressive Numbers: Companies Experience Substantial Increases in Dollars, Employment' in Hispanic Business (July-August 2007)

Pub: Hispanic Business

Ed: Derek Reveron. Description: Profiles of five fastest growing Hispanic companies reporting increases in revenue and employment include Brightstar, distributor of wireless products; Greenway Ford Inc., a car dealership; Fred Loya Insurance, auto insurance carrier; and Group O, packaging company; and Diverse Staffing, Inc., an employment and staffing firm.

11374 ■ "Injured Workers Caught in the Middle" in Sacramento Business Journal (Vol. 28, June 10, 2011, No. 15, pp. 1)

Pub: Sacramento Business Journal

Ed: Kelly Johnson. Description: A bill that would extend the cap on disability payments to nearly five years is in the works, but employers and insurance companies fear it would increase their costs. Proponents of the bill say, however, that it would correct unfairness suffered by the employees. Features of the bill are discussed as well as its effects on both parties and the State of California.

11375 ■ "Insurance Firm Consolidates Offices; Integro Finds the Right Price Downtown" in Crain's New York Business (January 14, 2008)

Pub: Crain Communications, Inc.

Description: Integro insurance brokers is relocating its headquarters to 1 State Street Plaza, where it will consolidate its operations in March. The firm feels that the upscale design will provide an appropriate setting for entertaining clients and an engaging work environment for employees.

11376 ■ "Insurance: Marathon Effort' in Canadian Business (Vol. 80, January 29, 2007, No. 3, pp. 11)

Pub: Rogers Media

Ed: Jeff Sanford. Description: The efforts of the insurance firm ING Canada Inc. to manage its relations with its customers are described. The enhancement of the insurance services provided by the company is discussed.

11377 ■ "An Insurance Roll-Up In Danger of Unraveling" in Barron's (Vol. 88, March 17, 2008, No. 11, pp. 51)

Pub: Dow Jones & Company, Inc.

Ed: Bill Alpert. Description: Shares of National Financial Partners have fallen below their initial offering price as sputtering sales and management turnover leave many investors wondering. One of the company's star brokers is being sued for their 'life settlement' contracts while another broker is being pursued by the IRS for unpaid taxes.

11378 ■ *"Insuraprise Growing Fast" in Austin Business Journal (Vol. 31, April 22, 2011, No. 7, pp. 1)*
Pub: American City Business Journals Inc.
Ed: Sandra Zaragoza. **Description:** Austin, Texas-based Insuraprise Inc. is finalizing the purchase of a 24,000-square-foot office at 12116 Jekel Circle. The firm, with 23 salespeople and sales that are growing nearly 300 percent over the past 18 months, will now have room to grow. Insuraprise plans to hire 35 new salespersons for its call center.

11379 ■ *"Insurer Buys Foundation's Uptown HQ" in Charlotte Business Journal (Vol. 25, December 17, 2010, No. 39, pp. 1)*
Pub: Charlotte Business Journal
Ed: Will Boye. **Description:** Charlotte, North Carolina-based Synergy Coverage Solutions has purchased the three-story building owned by Foundations For the Carolinas for slightly more than $3 million. Synergy plans to relocate its operation in the uptown building by August 2011.

11380 ■ *"Insurers No Longer Paying Premium for Advertising" in Brandweek (Vol. 49, April 21, 2008, No. 16, pp. SR3)*
Pub: VNU Business Media, Inc.
Ed: Eric Newman. **Description:** Insurance companies are cutting their advertising budgets after years of accelerated double-digit growth in spending due to the economic downturn, five years of record-breaking ad spend and a need to cut expenditures as claims costs rise and a competitive market keeps premiums in place. Statistical data included.

11381 ■ *"Insurers Warn Brokers" in Sacramento Business Journal (Vol. 25, August 22, 2008, No. 25, pp. 1)*
Pub: American City Business Journals, Inc.
Ed: Kathy Robertson. **Description:** Sacramento, California-based health plans have warned insurance brokers not to combine two different kinds of insurance products or they will be stricken from the sales network. The health plans also asked employers to promise not to combine plans with self-insurance. Such schemes are seen to destroy lower-premium health products.

11382 ■ *"Internet Marketing 2.0: Closing the Online Chat Gap" in Agent's Sales Journal (November 2009, pp. 14)*
Pub: Summit Business Media
Ed: Jeff Denenholz. **Description:** Advice regarding the implementation of an Internet marketing strategy for insurance agencies includes how and why to incorporate a chat feature in which a sales agent can communicate in real-time with potential or existing customers. It is important to understand if appropriate response mechanisms are in place to convert leads into actual sales.

11383 ■ *"Is Hawaii Ready for Universal Health Care?" in Hawaii Business (Vol. 53, February 2008, No. 8, pp. 26)*
Pub: Hawaii Business Publishing
Description: Representative Lyn Finnegan does not believe that a universal health is good for Hawaii as health insurance for everyone will be difficult to achieve. Representative John M. Mizuno says that House Bill 1008 introduced in the state was a landmark for Hawaii as it will provide the people with health care insurance. Other details about their opinion on the topic are presented.

11384 ■ *"Is There a Doctor In the House?" in Black Enterprise (Vol. 41, December 2010, No. 5, pp. 42)*
Pub: Earl G. Graves Publishing Co. Inc.
Ed: Renita Burns. **Description:** Health insurance premiums have increased between 15 percent and 20 percent for small business owners, making it one of the most expensive costs. Ways to evaluate a health plan's costs and effectiveness are examined.

11385 ■ *"The Keeper of Records" in Black Enterprise (Vol. 41, December 2010, No. 5, pp. 54)*
Pub: Earl G. Graves Publishing Co. Inc.
Ed: Denise Campbell. **Description:** Medical billing and coding, submission of claims to health insurance companies and Medicare or Medicaid for payment is one of the fastest growing disciplines in healthcare.

11386 ■ *King of Capital*
Pub: John Wiley and Sons, Inc.
Ed: Amey Stone; Mike Brewster. **Released:** 2004. **Price:** $16.95. **Description:** Biography of Sandy Weill describes how he became a billionaire business giant by creating successful companies from smaller, sometimes failing firms; creating successful new products where none previously existed; and making deals no one thought possible. He is also responsible for changing the landscape of the banking industry and insurance business when he created Citigroup in 1998, the world's largest financial services firm.

11387 ■ *"Labor Pains" in Canadian Business (Vol. 79, August 14, 2006, No. 16-17, pp. 80)*
Pub: Rogers Media
Description: Canada's employment insurance is analyzed in view of the growing shortage of labor.

11388 ■ *"Law Allows Captive Insurance Companies to Form in State" in Crain's Detroit Business (Vol. 24, March 31, 2008, No. 13, pp. 29)*
Pub: Crain Communications, Inc.
Description: Discusses new legislation allowing the formation of captive insurance companies in the state of Michigan; these companies are subsidiaries of non-insurers that are formed primarily to insure some or all of the risks of its parent company.

11389 ■ *"Leave Policies: How to Avoid Leave-Related Lawsuits" in Employee Benefit News (Vol. 25, December 1, 2011, No. 15, pp. 12)*
Pub: SourceMedia Inc.
Ed: John F. Galvin. **Description:** Tips for employers when adding disability and maternity leave benefits to workers are outlined, with focus on ways to avoid leave-related lawsuits.

11390 ■ *"Lifetime Planning with a Twist" in Contractor (Vol. 56, July 2009, No. 7, pp. 40)*
Pub: Penton Media, Inc.
Ed: Irv Blackman. **Description:** Private Placement Life Insurance lets wealthy investors make their investment gains tax-free and can be set up so investors can make tax-free loans from the policy. This can be used on a younger member of the family as a wealth-building strategy if the investor is uninsurable.

11391 ■ *"Local Hospitals Wage Wars on 'Bounce-Backs" in Business Courier (Vol. 27, July 30, 2010, No. 13, pp. 1)*
Pub: Business Courier
Ed: James Ritchie. **Description:** Health care organizations in Greater Cincinnati area have tried a number of care and follow up programs, primarily focused on congestive heart failure to prevent readmissions to hospitals. Hospital administrators have made the averting of bounce-backs a priority due to new federal government plans on reimbursement.

11392 ■ *"Luster Lost" in Saint Louis Business Journal (Vol. 32, September 16, 2011, No. 3, pp. 1)*
Pub: Saint Louis Business Journal
Ed: E.B. Solomont. **Description:** Express Cripts shares have plunged 22.71 percent since late July amid regulatory concerns, as the luster of the second-largest deal announced for 2011 wore off. Express Scripts has become the largest pharmacy benefit manager in the country after the $29 billion deal to take rival Medco Health Solutions.

11393 ■ *Managing Health Benefits in Small and Mid-Sized Organizations*
Pub: Amacom
Ed: Patricia Halo. **Released:** July 1999. **Description:** Comprehensive guide for developing health care plans for companies employing between 50 and 5,000 employees in order to provide employees with better health care at lower prices.

11394 ■ *"Markel American Insurance Company Announces Wedding and Special Event Insurance for Consumers" in Benzinga.com (February 16, 2011)*
Pub: Benzinga.com
Ed: Benzinga Staff. **Description:** Markel American Insurance Company, headquartered in Waukesha, Wisconsin has launched its new special event insurance and wedding insurance to protect both liabilities and cancellations associated with these events.

11395 ■ *"Maryland Hospitals Cope with Rare Drop in Patient Admissions" in Boston Business Journal (Vol. 29, September 23, 2011, No. 20, pp. 1)*
Pub: American City Business Journals Inc.
Ed: Scott Dance. **Description:** Admissions to Maryland hospitals have dropped to less than 700,000 in fiscal year 2010 and initial figures for fiscal 2011 show in-patient admissions are now nearing 660,000. The decline can be partly attributed to new ways health insurers are paying hospitals for care and to the financial reward hospitals get for cutting back on admissions.

11396 ■ *"The Massachusetts Mess: Good Health Care Is Expensive" in Barron's (Vol. 89, July 27, 2009, No. 30, pp. 39)*
Pub: Dow Jones & Co., Inc.
Ed: Thomas G. Donlan. **Description:** Massachusetts' mandatory health insurance has produced the highest rate of insurance coverage among the states but the state is now unable to afford its dream of universal coverage just three years after they enacted it. This supposed model for federal health-care reform is turning out to be a joke.

11397 ■ *"Meadowbrook CEO Sees 20 Percent Growth With New Acquisition" in Crain's Detroit Business (Vol. 24, March 10, 2008, No. 10, pp. 4)*
Pub: Crain Communications, Inc.
Ed: Jay Greene. **Description:** Discusses the major turnaround of Meadowbrook Insurance Group after Robert Cubbin became CEO and implemented a new business strategy.

11398 ■ *"Meadowbrook To Acquire ProCentury in $272.6 Million Deal" in Crain's Detroit Business (Vol. 24, February 25, 2008, No. 8, pp. 4)*
Pub: Crain Communications Inc. - Detroit
Description: Meadowbrook Insurance Group, based in Southfield, Michigan reports its proposed acquisition of ProCentury Corporation based in Columbus, Ohio. Meadowbrook provides risk-management to agencies, professional and trade associations and small-to-midsize businesses.

11399 ■ *"Medicaid Insurers See Growth in Small Business Market" in Boston Business Journal (Vol. 31, July 15, 2011, No. 25, pp. 1)*
Pub: Boston Business Journal
Ed: Julie M. Donnelly. **Description:** BMC HealthNet Plan announced plans to launch small business products to serve small businesses that are priced out of rising premium rates at large Massachusetts insurers. BMC joined competitors CeltiCare Health Plan and Neighborhood Health Plan in augmenting its core business.

11400 ■ *"Medicare Plans Step Up Battle for Subscribers" in Sacramento Business Journal (Vol. 28, October 21, 2011, No. 34, pp. 1)*
Pub: Sacramento Business Journal
Ed: Kathy Robertson. **Description:** California's market for health plans have become increasingly competitive as more than 313,000 seniors try to figure out the best plans to meet their needs for 2012. Health plans are rated on Medicare materials to help consumers distinguish among the Medicare health maintenance organizations (HMOs).

11401 ■ *"The Moody Blues" in Entrepreneur (Vol. 36, April 2008, No. 4, pp. 87)*
Pub: Entrepreneur Media, Inc.
Ed: Mark Henricks. **Description:** Depression among employees can affect their productivity and cost the company. Businesses with a workforce that is likely

to have depression should inform their employees about the health benefits covered by insurance. Other details on how to address depression concerns among employees are discussed.

11402 ■ "More Businesses Will Shift Health Costs to Workers" in Business Review, Albany New York (Vol. 34, November 16, 2007, No. 33, pp. 1)

Pub: American City Business Journals, Inc.

Ed: Barbara Pinckney. **Description:** Survey conducted by consulting firm Benetech Inc. showed that sixty percent of employers are planning to increase payroll deductions to pay for health insurance premiums. More than ninety percent of the employers prefer HMO plans, followed by Preferred Provider Organizations. Other details of the survey are discussed.

11403 ■ "More Small Businesses Willing to Fund Employees' Benefits" in Baltimore Business Journal (Vol. 28, June 18, 2010, No. 6, pp. 1)

Pub: Baltimore Business Journal

Ed: Scott Graham. **Description:** An increasing number of small businesses in Maryland are tapping into potentially cheaper self-funded health plans instead of providing fully insured benefits to employees through traditional health plans. Self-funded health plans charge employers for health care up to a specified level. Economic implications of self-funded plans to small businesses are discussed.

11404 ■ "Most States Have High-Risk Health Insurance Pools" in Crain's Detroit Business (Vol. 24, March 24, 2008, No. 12, pp. 31)

Pub: Crain Communications, Inc.

Ed: Jay Greene. **Description:** High-risk health insurance pools, designed to cover individuals with medical conditions that essentially make them otherwise uninsurable, are being debated by the Senate Health Policy Committee; the pool concept is supported by Blue Cross Blue Shield of Michigan and contested by a number of consumer groups and competing health insurers.

11405 ■ "Nationwide Bank Ready for December Conversion" in Business First-Columbus (October 12, 2007, pp. A1)

Pub: American City Business Journals, Inc.

Ed: Adrian Burns. **Description:** Nationwide Bank will increase marketing to its customers, including the 45,000 that came from the acquisition of Nationwide Federal Credit Union in December 2006. Upgrading its online banking system and Website will bring the company and its services closer to clients. The influence of the insurance industry on the bank's marketing strategy is also examined.

11406 ■ "New Database Brings Doctors Out of the Dark" in Business Courier (Vol. 26, October 23, 2009, No. 26, pp. 1)

Pub: American City Business Journals, Inc.

Ed: James Ritchie. **Description:** A database created by managed care consulting firm Praesentia allows doctors in Cincinnati to compare average reimbursements from health insurance companies to doctors in different areas. Specialist doctors in the city are paid an average of $172.25 for every office consultation.

11407 ■ "New Health Law, Lack of Docs Collide on Cape Cod" in Boston Business Journal (Vol. 27, October 12, 2007, No. 37, pp. 1)

Pub: American City Business Journals Inc.

Ed: Mark Hollmer. **Description:** There is a shortage of primary care providers at Outer Cape Health Services in Massachusetts, with the isolation of the area and as physicians look for higher paying careers in specialty positions. The Commonwealth Health Insurance Connector Authority is pushing for a new health insurance law and is working with Cape Cod Chamber of Commerce to conduct outreach programs.

11408 ■ "North American Pet Health Insurance Market Poised for Growth" in Pet

Product News (Vol. 64, December 2010, No. 12, pp. 4)

Pub: BowTie Inc.

Ed: David Lummis. **Description:** The pet health insurance market is expected to further grow after posting about $350 million in sales in 2009, a gain of more than $40 million. Pet insurance firms have offered strategies such as product humanization in response to this growth forecast. Meanwhile, pet insurance shoppers have been provided more by insurance firms with wider choices.

11409 ■ "Norvax University Health Insurance Sales Training and Online Marketing Conference" in Internet Wire (January 27, 2010)

Pub: Comtex News Network, Inc.

Description: Overview of the Norvax University Marketing and Sales Success Conference Tour which includes insurance sales training seminars, proven and innovative online marketing techniques and a host of additional information and networking opportunities.

11410 ■ "Now the Real Work Begins" in Baltimore Business Journal (Vol. 28, October 15, 2010, No. 23, pp. 1)

Pub: Baltimore Business Journal

Ed: Emily Mullin. **Description:** The Henry J. Kaiser Family Foundation's survey shows nearly 53 percent of Americans remain confused about health care reform and it was up to the states to educate the people. However, Maryland is still trying to figure out how to conduct the campaign without guidance or funding from the Federal government.

11411 ■ "Open Enrollment: Staying Healthy During Enrollment Season" in Employee Benefit News (Vol. 25, November 1, 2011, No. 14, pp. 41)

Pub: SourceMedia Inc.

Ed: Shana Sweeney. **Description:** Tips for staying healthy during your benefit open enrollment period are outlined.

11412 ■ "Passing It On: Using Life Insurance as an Estate Planning Tool" in Inc. (October 2007, pp. 47-49)

Pub: Gruner & Jahr USA Publishing

Ed: Elaine Appleton Grant. **Description:** Permanent life insurance policies can be used to cover estate taxes for heirs inheriting large estates, while allowing them time to sell any small business. Six tips are included to assist in choosing the right policy.

11413 ■ "Patients to Elect to Cut Care" in The Business Journal-Serving Metropolitan Kansas City (Vol. 27, November 21, 2008, No. 11, pp. 1)

Pub: American City Business Journals, Inc.

Ed: Rob Roberts. **Description:** Patients in Kansas City, Missouri are cutting down on health care services due to the economic crisis. A decline in diagnostic procedures has been observed at Northland Cardiology. Elective reconstructive procedures have also been reduced by 25 percent. Additional information and statistics regarding the healthcare sector is included.

11414 ■ "Patricia Hemingway Hall; President, Chief Operating Officer, Health Care Service Corp." in Crain's Chicago Business (May 5, 2008)

Pub: Crain Communications, Inc.

Ed: Mike Colias. **Description:** Profile of Patricia Hemingway Hall who is the president and chief operating officer of Health Care Service Corp., a new strategy launched by Blue Cross & Blue Shield of Illinois; the new endeavor will emphasize wellness rather than just treatment across its four health plans.

11415 ■ "PCH Gets Trauma Center Status" in The Business Journal - Serving Phoenix and the Valley of the Sun (Vol. 28, July 11, 2008, No. 45)

Pub: American City Business Journals, Inc.

Ed: Angela Gonzales. **Description:** Phoenix Children's Hospital has been allowed by the Arizona Department of Health Services to launch the state's first trauma center for children. The trauma center is expected to cost the hospital $7 million a year.

11416 ■ "The People Puzzle; Re-Training America's Workers" in The Economist (Vol. 390, January 3, 2009, No. 8612, pp. 32)

Pub: The Economist Newspaper Inc.

Description: With thousands of workers losing their jobs, America is now facing the task of getting them back to work. With an overall unemployment rate of 6.7 percent, the federal government has three main ways for leading workers back to employment: training them for new jobs, providing unemployment insurance in order to replace lost wages during the period of job-hunting; and matching employers who desire a skill with workers who have that skill. Specialized staffing agencies provide employers and potential employees with the help necessary to find a job in some of the more niche markets.

11417 ■ "Planning a Wedding Fit for a Royal? Read This First, Urge Legal and General" in Benzinga.com (April 21, 2011)

Pub: Benzinga.com

Ed: Benzinga Staff. **Description:** When planning a wedding, the author suggests checking life insurance to be sure you are covered for any situations that may arise.

11418 ■ "Prescription for Health: Choosing the Best Healthcare Plan" in Black Enterprise (Vol. 38, July 2008, No. 12, pp. 48)

Pub: Earl G. Graves Publishing Co. Inc.

Ed: Tamara E. Holmes. **Description:** According to a survey of small-business owners conducted by SurePayroll Inc., 20 percent of respondents have had a prospective employee refuse a job offer because healthcare benefits did not come with it. Cost is not the only reason many small-business owners do not offer these benefits. Guidelines to help take some of the confusion out of the guesswork that comes with trying to find the proper fit concerning healthcare benefits are outlined.

11419 ■ "The Price of Citizenship" in Canadian Business (Vol. 79, August 14, 2006, No. 16-17, pp. 13)

Pub: Rogers Media

Ed: Jack Mintz. **Description:** Safety and insurance benefits provided by the Canadian government to Canadian passport holders returning from Lebanon, is discussed.

11420 ■ "Public Health Care Funding and the Montana Economy" in Montana Business Quarterly (Vol. 49, Spring 2011, No. 1, pp. 23)

Pub: Bureau of Business & Economic Research

Ed: Gregg Davis. **Description:** Montana has more baby boomers and veterans per capita than any other state in the nation. The role of public health in the state is a crucial part of the state's economy.

11421 ■ "Recovery on Tap for 2010?" in Orlando Business Journal (Vol. 26, January 1, 2010, No. 31, pp. 1)

Pub: American City Business Journals

Ed: Melanie Stawicki Azam, Richard Bilbao, Christopher Boyd, Anjali Fluker. **Description:** Economic forecasts for Central Florida's leading business sectors in 2010 are presented. These sectors include housing, film and TV, sports business, law, restaurants, aviation, tourism and hospitality, banking and finance, commercial real estate, retail, health care, insurance, higher education, and manufacturing. According to some local executives, Central Florida's economy will slowly recover in 2010.

11422 ■ "Rich or Poor, Hospitals Must Work Together" in Crain's Chicago Business (Vol. 31, April 28, 2008, No. 17, pp. 22)

Pub: Crain Communications, Inc.

Description: Chicago=area safety-net hospitals that serve the poor, uninsured and underinsured are struggling to stay open while wealthier areas compete to build advanced facilities for the expensive surgical procedures their privately insured patients can afford. If these safety-net hospitals close, their patients, many of them in ambulances, will show up at the remaining hospitals resulting in a strain that will test the ability of hospitals across the region to care for all of their patients. Hospitals need to address the threats to the local health care system before it slips into crisis since the current every-hospital-for-itself approach that pays off big for some will eventually will make losers of everyone.

11423 ■ *"RPA Preps for Building Radiant Conference, Show" in Contractor (Vol. 57, January 2010, No. 1, pp. 5)*
Pub: Penton Media, Inc.
Description: Radiant Panel Association is accepting registrations for its Building Radiant 2010 Conference and Trade Show. The conference will discuss radiant heating as well as insurance and other legal matters for mechanical contractors.

11424 ■ *"A Safety Net in Need of Repair" in The Economist (Vol. 390, January 3, 2009, No. 8612, pp. 33)*
Pub: The Economist Newspaper Inc.
Description: America's unemployment-insurance scheme is outdated and skimpy compared to other industrialized countries despite the fact that Americans tend to work harder at returning to the job market; the benefits are lower and available for a smaller amount of time and less unemployed workers are even able to collect these benefits. Statistical data included.

11425 ■ *"Sluggish Market Gives Hospitals the Financial Chills" in The Business Journal-Serving Greater Tampa Bay (Vol. 28, August 1, 2008)*
Pub: American City Business Journals, Inc.
Ed: Margie Manning. **Description:** Operating margins for hospitals in the Tampa Bay, Florida area have been reduced from 2 percent in 2006 to 0.8 percent in 2007 due to a weaker US economy. Total margins, on the other hand, rose from 2.9 percent to 3.3 percent in the same period.

11426 ■ *"Small Biz Owners Are Tapping Into Health Savings Plans" in Small Business Opportunities (Fall 2007)*
Pub: Harris Publications Inc.
Ed: Michael L. Corne. **Description:** Health savings accounts were developed by Golden Rule, a United Healthcare company. Today, more than 40 percent of the company's customers are covered by health savings account plans.

11427 ■ *Small Business Access and Alternatives to Health Care: Congressional Hearing*
Pub: DIANE Publishing Company
Ed: Donald A. Manzullo. **Released:** July 2006. **Price:** $35.00. **Description:** Congressional hearings regarding the health care crisis facing America's small businesses is discussed.

11428 ■ *"Small Businesses Changing Their Health Plan Preferences" in Boston Business Journal (Vol. 29, June 24, 2011, No. 7, pp. 1)*
Pub: American City Business Journals Inc.
Ed: Scott Dance. **Description:** Small businesses in Maryland are shifting from traditional health plans to the consumer-oriented health savings accounts or HSAs. Health insurance industry experts say the change is indicative of the insurance buyers' desire to be more thrifty and discerning in their health care purchases.

11429 ■ *"Small, But Mighty" in Employee Benefit News (Vol. 25, November 1, 2011, No. 14, pp. 32)*
Pub: SourceMedia Inc.
Ed: Andrea Davis. **Description:** Three consulting firms are facing the challenge of helping clients understand the new health care reform in a tight economy.

11430 ■ *"The Smell of Fear: Is a Bottom Near?" in Barron's (Vol. 88, March 17, 2008, No. 11, pp. M3)*
Pub: Dow Jones & Company, Inc.
Ed: Kopin Tan. **Description:** Liquidity problems at Bear Stearns frightened investors in markets around the world due to the fear of the prospects of a big bank's failure. Shares of health maintenance organizations got battered led by WellPoint, and Humana

but longer-term investors who could weather short-term volatility may find value here. The value of J. Crew shares is also discussed.

11431 ■ *Starting and Running Your Own Horse Business*
Pub: Storey Publishing, LLC
Ed: Mary Ashby McDonald. **Released:** November 1, 2009. **Price:** $19.95. **Description:** Insight into starting and running a successful equestrian business is given. The book covers safety, tips for operating a riding school or horse camp, strategies for launching a carriage business, along with tax and insurance advice.

11432 ■ *"Steeling for Battle" in Crain's Chicago Business (Vol. 31, April 21, 2008, No. 16, pp. 3)*
Pub: Crain Communications, Inc.
Ed: Bob Tita. **Description:** Discusses contract negotiations between the United Steelworkers union and ArcelorMittal USA Inc., the nation's largest steelmaker, and U.S. Steel Corp., the third-largest; the union sees these negotiations as the best chance in two decades to regain lost ground but industry experts predict the companies will try to reduce benefits, demand a separate, lower wage scale for new hires and look for relief from the rising costs for retirees' health insurance coverage.

11433 ■ *"Struggling States Slashing Health Care For Poor" in Chicago Tribune (January 15, 2009)*
Pub: McClatchy-Tribune Information Services
Ed: Noam N. Levey. **Description:** Health officials warn that even the huge federal rescue plan may not be enough to restore health services being eliminated due to the economic crisis.

11434 ■ *"Survivorship Policies: Planning a Policy for Two" in Employee Benefit News (Vol. 25, November 1, 2011, No. 14, pp. 20)*
Pub: SourceMedia Inc.
Ed: Marli D. Riggs. **Description:** Survivorship insurance is becoming an added benefit high net worth individuals and executives should consider when evaluating life insurance policies.

11435 ■ *"Sutter, CHW Reject Blue Cross Deal" in Sacramento Business Journal (Vol. 25, August 15, 2008, No. 24, pp. 1)*
Pub: American City Business Journals, Inc.
Ed: Kathy Robertson. **Description:** California-based Sutter Health and Catholic Healthcare West have rejected the $11.8 million class action settlement in connection with contract rescissions between California hospitals and Anthem Blue Cross. Blue Cross can halt the settlement if not enough hospitals accept it. The deal covers all hospitals that owe money due to rescinded Blue Cross coverage.

11436 ■ *"Symbility Solutions Joins Motion Computing Partner Program" in Canadian Corporate News (May 14, 2007)*
Pub: Comtex News Network Inc.
Description: Symbility Solutions Inc., a wholly owned subsidiary of Automated Benefits Corp., announced an agreement with Alliance Partner of Motion Computing, a leader in wireless communications and mobile computing, in which both companies will invest in a sales and marketing strategy that focuses specifically on the insurance market.

11437 ■ *"Taking Full Advantage: What You Need To Know During Open-Enrollment Season" in Black Enterprise (Vol. 38, November 2007, No. 4)*
Pub: Earl G. Graves Publishing Co. Inc.
Ed: Donald Jay Korn. **Description:** Employees can change or enroll in new insurance benefits during the fall season. It is important to assess each plan offered and to determine your deductible. Statistical data included.

11438 ■ *"Tenacious Trailblazer" in Hispanic Business (Vol. 30, April 2008, No. 4, pp. 26)*
Pub: Hispanic Business
Ed: Melinda Burns. **Description:** Dr. Sandra Hernandez has been named as Hispanic Business Woman of the Year for her pioneering work in health care

reform. Dr. Hernandez is the first Hispanic and the first woman to serve as public health director for the city and county of San Francisco.

11439 ■ *"Thousands Balk at Health Law Sign-Up Mandate" in Boston Business Journal (Vol. 27, November 9, 2007, No. 41, pp. 1)*
Pub: American City Business Journals Inc.
Ed: Mark Hollmer. **Description:** About 100,000 Massachusetts residents have not signed up for insurance plans created as part of the state's health care reform law. Insurers have underestimated the number of new customers signing up for insurance and come close to risking penalties if they do not get insurance by the end of 2007. The Commonwealth Health Insurance Connector Authority's deadline to buy insurance before penalties kick in is November 15, 2007.

11440 ■ *"Top 50 In Total Revenue" in Canadian Business (Vol. 81, Summer 2008, No. 9, pp. 119)*
Pub: Rogers Media Ltd.
Description: Table showing the top 50 Canadian companies in terms of total revenue is presented. Manulife Financial Corp. topped the list with revenue of 34.5 billion. The financial services firm is the 6th largest provider of life insurance in the world and the second largest in North America.

11441 ■ *"United Insurance To Grow St. Pete's Corporate Base" in The Business Journal-Serving Greater Tampa Bay (August 29, 2008)*
Pub: American City Business Journals, Inc.
Ed: Margie Manning. **Description:** United Insurance Holdings LC is on its way to becoming a public company by agreeing in a reverse merger with FMG Acquisition Corp. The $104.3 million agreement will provide the company's St. Petersburg operations the opportunity to grow. The other impacts of the proposed reverse merger are examined.

11442 ■ *"UnitedHealthcare Resists Prognosis" in The Business Journal-Serving Metropolitan Kansas City (Vol. 26, August 29, 2008, No. 51)*
Pub: American City Business Journals, Inc.
Ed: Rob Roberts. **Description:** Saint Luke's Hospital Systems terminated UnitedHealthcare from its insurance provider network on July 25, 2008. Negotiators with both parties have stopped speaking, and employees under UnitedHealthcare plans will have to pay higher bills unless Saint Luke's reconsiders its decision. The parties' previous negotiations are discussed.

11443 ■ *"VPA to Pay $9.5 Million to Settle Whistle-Blower Lawsuits" in Crain's Detroit Business (Vol. 26, January 11, 2010, No. 2, pp. 13)*
Pub: Crain Communications Inc.
Ed: Jay Greene. **Description:** According to Terrence Berg, first assistant with the U.S. Attorney's Office in Detroit, Voluntary Physicians Association, a local home health care company, has agreed to pay $9.5 million to settle four whistle-blower lawsuits; the agreement settles allegations that VPA submitted claims to TriCare, the Michigan Medicaid program and Medicare for unnecessary home visits, tests and procedures.

11444 ■ *"W&S to Trim Rich Retirement Plan" in Business Courier (Vol. 27, October 15, 2010, No. 24, pp. 1)*
Pub: Business Courier
Ed: Dan Monk. **Description:** Insurance firm Western & Southern Financial Group announced that it will reduce the pension benefits of its 4,000 associates by more than 30 percent starting January 1, 2011. The move is expected to reduce annual retirement payments by several thousand dollars per associate. Western is a Fortune 500 company and has $34 billion in total assets.

11445 ■ *"We Have a Budget, Too" in Entrepreneur (Vol. 37, October 2009, No. 10, pp. 89)*
Pub: Entrepreneur Media, Inc.
Ed: Craig Matsuda. **Description:** One human resources executive at a financial services company claims that health care issues are as costly and ir-

ritating for companies as they are for the employees. Health care vendors and insurers try as much as possible to maximize profits, while companies exert much effort to maximize benefits for their workers.

11446 ■ "Week on the Web" in Crain's Detroit Business (Vol. 25, June 22, 2009, No. 25, pp. 19)

Pub: Crain Communications Inc. - Detroit

Description: Blue Cross Blue Shield of Michigan, in a class-action lawsuit, will pay about 100 families whose children were either denied coverage for autism treatment or paid for treatment out of pocket. The settlement is worth about $ million.

11447 ■ "What Choice Did I Have?" in Entrepreneur (Vol. 37, October 2009, No. 10, pp. 88)

Pub: Entrepreneur Media, Inc.

Ed: Craig Matsuda. **Description:** Profile of a worker at a financial services company who acquired first hand knowledge concerning the relationship between health insurance costs and coverage. The worker's son got severely ill, forcing the worker to spend above what is covered by health insurance.

11448 ■ "Work At It!" in Hawaii Business (Vol. 53, October 2007, No. 4, pp. 44)

Pub: Hawaii Business Publishing

Ed: Cathy S. Cruz-George. **Description:** Employers in Hawaii are mitigating the effects of rising healthcare costs by giving their employees health insurance and offering wellness programs. Employer-based health insurance has increases by 87 percent in the United States over the 2000-2006 period. Wellness programs that address different aspects of employees' health, such as food consumption, drug compliance and smoking habits, are discussed.

11449 ■ "The Worst-Run Industry in Canada: Health Care" in Canadian Business (Vol. 83, October 12, 2010, No. 17, pp. 39)

Pub: Rogers Media Ltd.

Ed: Rachel Mendleson. **Description:** Most Canadians believe that the problem of the country's health care system is rooted in insufficient funding, demographic overload, or corporate profiteering. However, health economists and policy analysts think the real issues is mismanagement, as the pervasive inefficiency is affecting the system's structure.

11450 ■ "Year-End Tax Tips" in Hawaii Business (Vol. 53, December 2007, No. 6, pp. 136)

Pub: Hawaii Business Publishing

Ed: Kathleen Bryan. **Description:** Tax planning tips for the end of 2007, in relation to the tax breaks that are scheduled to expire, are presented. Among the tax breaks that will be expiring at the 2007 year-end are sales tax deduction in the state and local level, premiums on mortgage insurance, and deduction on tuition. The impacts of these changes are discussed.

11451 ■ "Young Adults Choose to go Without Health Insurance" in Business Review, Albany New York (Vol. 34, November 30, 2007, No. 35, pp. 1)

Pub: American City Business Journals, Inc.

Ed: Barbara Pinckney. **Description:** U.S. Census Bureau revealed that in 2006, 19 million people between the ages of 18 and 34 were without health insurance, or 40 percent of the uninsured individuals in the country. College graduation usually means the end of health coverage, since most fresh graduates opt to not get any health insurance plan. Solutions to this growing issue are also addressed.

STATISTICAL SOURCES

11452 ■ RMA Annual Statement Studies

Pub: Risk Management Association

Contact: Kevin M. Blakey, President

Released: Annual. **Price:** $175.00 2006-07 edition, $105.00. **Description:** Contains composite balance sheets and income statements for more than 360 industries, including the accounting, auditing, and bookkeeping industries. Also contains five years of

comparative historical data for discerning trends. Includes 16 commonly used ratios, computed for most of the size groupings for nearly every industry.

11453 ■ Standard & Poor's Industry Surveys

Pub: Standard & Poor's Corp.

Released: Annual. **Price:** $3633.00. **Description:** Two-volume book that examines the prospects for specific industries, including trucking. Also provides analyses of trends and problems, statistical tables and charts, and comparative company analyses.

TRADE PERIODICALS

11454 ■ AAIS Viewpoint

Pub: American Association of Insurance Services

Contact: Edmund Kelly, President

Released: Quarterly, 4/Year (Mid-Feb., May, Aug., and Nov.). **Price:** Included in membership. **Description:** Contains news of current insurance issues, AAIS activities, insurance legislation, and other subjects of interest.

11455 ■ Barger & Wolen Newsletter

Pub: Barger & Wolen

Contact: Larry Golub, Managing Editor

Released: Quarterly. **Price:** Free. **Description:** Discusses current events in the legal field relating to insurance. Carries decision briefs.

11456 ■ Best's Review

Pub: A.M. Best Company Inc.

Contact: James Peavy, President

URL(s): www.ambest.com/sales/newsoverview. asp#brwww.ambest.com/review/default.asp. **Ed:** Lynna Goch. **Released:** Monthly **Price:** $50, Individuals.

11457 ■ BestWeek Life/Health Edition

Pub: A.M. Best Company Inc.

Contact: James Peavy, President

Ed: Brendan Noonan, Editor. **Released:** Weekly. **Description:** Contains annotated news articles and staff-written perspectives on current events in the life/health insurance industry. Reports on legislative developments, new products, and corporate changes. Recurring features include news of industry meetings and comparative operating results.

11458 ■ BestWeek Property/Casualty Editions

Pub: A.M. Best Company Inc.

Contact: James Peavy, President

Ed: Brendan Noonan, Editor. **Released:** Weekly. **Description:** Contains articles and staff-written perspectives on current events in the property/casualty and life/health insurance industries, statistical studies and special reports by A.M Best financial analysts. Reports on legislative developments, industry meetings, new products, and corporate changes. Recurring features include comparative operating results and news of industry regulation.

11459 ■ Business Insurance

Pub: Crain Communications Inc.

URL(s): www.businessinsurance.com. **Released:** Weekly **Price:** $399, Individuals print; $149, Individuals print & digital; $69, Individuals digital edition.

11460 ■ Healthcare Corporate Finance News

Pub: Irving Levin Associates Inc.

Contact: Stephen M. Monroe, Managing Editor

Ed: Gretchen S. Swanson, Editor. **Released:** Monthly. **Price:** $495. **Description:** Reports on the growth strategies of managed care providers, hospitals, drug companies, medical device manufacturers, and other healthcare organizations. Also reports on the latest deals in the healthcare sector, and how healthcare companies are doing on Wall Street.

11461 ■ Insurance Daily

Pub: SNL Financial L.C.

Contact: Reid Nagle, Publisher

Ed: Will Retzer, Editor. **Released:** Daily. **Description:** Provides information on the insurance industry. Features news releases, filings, and news on top-performing stocks, insider trades, ownership filings, and legislative issues.

11462 ■ Insurance Forum

Pub: Insurance Forum Inc.

Contact: Ann I. Belth, Business Manager

Ed: Joseph M. Belth, Editor. **Released:** Monthly. **Price:** $90 plus 6% sales tax. **Description:** Provides analyses and information on the insurance business.

11463 ■ Insurance Industry Litigation Reporter

Pub: Thomson West

Contact: Kathryn M. Downing, President

Ed: Jason Schossler, Editor. **Released:** Monthly. **Price:** $2683.56, individuals. **Description:** 'Follows insurance disputes involving triggers of coverage, occurrence, exclusions, foreseeability, duty to defend, bad faith allegations and emerging judicial theories of recovery such as risk contribution, emotional distress and enhanced risk of future injury.' Reprints complete texts of key decisions and pleadings.

11464 ■ Insurance Institute of Southern Alberta Newsletter

Pub: Insurance Institute of Southern Alberta

Released: 5/year. **Price:** Included in membership. **Description:** Covers insurance education.

11465 ■ The Insurance Journal of the West

Pub: Wells Publishing Inc.

URL(s): www.insurancejournal.com. **Released:** Semimonthly **Price:** $195, Individuals; $295, Other countries; $295, Two years; $495, Other countries 2 years.

11466 ■ The Insurance M&A Newsletter

Pub: SNL Financial L.C.

Ed: John Racine, Editor. **Released:** Biweekly. **Price:** $998, individuals. **Description:** Features articles and financial information on insurance mergers and acquisitions activity. Covers insurance companies, insurance brokers and agencies, managed care companies, and hospital administrators.

11467 ■ Insurance Weekly

Pub: SNL Financial L.C.

Ed: Mike Deane, Editor. **Released:** Weekly. **Description:** Summarizes events, market activity, and regulatory filings affecting insurance companies and insurance brokers.

11468 ■ The John Liner Letter

Pub: Standard Publishing Corp.

Contact: John Cross, President

Ed: Robert Montgomery, Editor. **Released:** Monthly. **Price:** $262, U.S.; $340.60, elsewhere. **Description:** Provides risk management and technical insurance advice for business firms, such as broadening coverage, cutting costs, and anticipating special insurance problems.

11469 ■ Journal of Financial Service Professionals

Contact: Kenn Beam Tacchino, Editor

URL(s): www.financialpro.org/sfsp_store/moreinfo. cfm?Product_ID=98&CFID=968& CFTOKEN=52077187. **Ed:** Kenn Beam Tacchino. **Released:** Bimonthly **Price:** $108, Other countries; $90, Individuals; $115, Institutions; $133, Institutions, other countries.

11470 ■ Journal of Insurance Regulation

Pub: National Association of Insurance Commissioners

Contact: Kevin M. McCarty, President

URL(s): www.naic.org/store_jir.htm. **Ed:** Lars Powell. **Released:** Quarterly **Price:** $70, Individuals; $85, Other countries.

11471 ■ Personal Perspective

Pub: Insurance Marketing and Management Services

Contact: George Nordhaus, Publisher

Ed: Pamela Grieman, Editor. **Released:** 4/year. **Description:** Provides a resource for insurance agents to explain homeowners, auto, personal property, health, and life coverages and related issues to clients. Recurring features include news of research and a column titled Short Shots.

11472 ■ Reinsurance News
Pub: Society of Actuaries
Ed: Bernard Goebel, Editor, goebelb@towers.com.
Released: 3-4/year. **Price:** Included in membership;
$25, nonmembers U.S. **Description:** Encourages the
professional development of Society members in the
field of reinsurance. Recurring features include letters to the editor, news of research, news of educational opportunities, and a calendar of events.

11473 ■ The Risk Report
Pub: International Risk Management Institute Inc.
Contact: Jack P. Gibson, President
Released: Monthly. **Price:** $199, individuals. **De-
scription:** Deals with risk management and commercial insurance. Monitors trends in loss exposures,
insurance pricing, and coverage. Suggests techniques for reducing insurance costs, and provides
detailed policy analyses.

11474 ■ Small Talk
Pub: Society of Actuaries
Contact: Terry M. Long, Chairperson
E-mail: tlong@lewisellis.com
Ed: James R. Thompson, FSA, Editor, jimthomp-
son@ameritech.net. **Released:** 2-3/year. **Price:**
Included in membership; $10, nonmembers U.S. **De-
scription:** The purpose of the Smaller Insurance
Company newsletter shall be to encourage and
facilitate the professional development of its members
through activities such as meetings, seminars, and
the generation and dissemination of literature pertaining to the unique problems that face actuaries
employed by smaller life insurance companies. The
Section focuses on methods, techniques and solutions that do not require the more extensive actuarial
resources available to large companies, and provides
a forum where professionals working in a smaller
company environment can discuss their special
concerns. The Section newsletter is small talk.

**11475 ■ Society of Financial Service
Professionals--Society Page**
Pub: Society of Financial Service Professionals
Ed: Maryanne Mennite, Editor. **Released:** Quarterly.
Price: Included in membership. **Description:** Reports
Society and member news, notices of the Society's
upcoming conferences and seminars, and continuing
education information.

11476 ■ Today's Insurance Professionals
Pub: National Association of Insurance Women
International
Contact: Linda Wilson, President
URL(s): www.naiw.org/?page=todays_mag_full. **Ed:**
Melissa Cobbs. **Released:** Quarterly **Price:** $15,
Individuals; $5, Single issue; $15, /year for nonmem-
bers in U.S.; $25, /year for nonmembers outside U.S.

VIDEOCASSETTES/
AUDIOCASSETTES

**11477 ■ Business Insurance: A Sales Skills
Introduction**
Custom Communications
1661 Greenview Dr. SW
Rochester, MN 55902-4215
Ph: (507)288-5522
Free: 800-274-8258
Fax: (507)287-0757
Co. E-mail: info@custom-alarm.com
URL: http://www.custom-alarm.com
Released: 19??. **Description:** Designed to develop
the vital sales skills an agent needs to make a smooth
transition into the lucrative area of business insur-
ance. **Availability:** VHS; 3/4 U.

11478 ■ Going Bare: Crisis in Insurance
New Jersey Network (NJN)
25 S Stockton St.
Trenton, NJ 08625-0777
Ph: (609)777-5273
Free: 800-792-8645

Fax: (609)643-4004
Co. E-mail: productioncenter@njn.org
URL: http://www.njn.net
Contact: Janice Selinger, Director
Released: 1988. **Description:** Examines the history
of the insurance industry, price wars between insurance companies, and small businesses who are
without liability insurance because of extremely high
premiums. **Availability:** VHS; 3/4 U.

TRADE SHOWS AND
CONVENTIONS

**11479 ■ Annual NAIW Convention - National
Association of Insurance Women
International**
National Association of Insurance Women
International (NAIW)
9343 E 95th Ct. S
Tulsa, OK 74133
Ph: (918)294-3700
Free: 800-766-6249
Fax: (918)294-3711
Co. E-mail: joinnaiw@naiw.org
URL: http://www.naiw.org
Contact: Linda Wilson, President
URL(s): www.naiw.org. **Frequency:** Annual. **Princi-
pal Exhibits:** Equipment, supplies, and services for
insurance industry professionals.

11480 ■ CPCU Conferment Ceremony
American Institute for CPCU (AICPCU)
720 Providence Rd., Ste. 100
Malvern, PA 19355-3433
Ph: (610)644-2100
Free: 800-644-2101
Fax: (610)640-9576
Co. E-mail: customerservice@cpcuiia.org
URL: http://www.aicpcu.org
Contact: Peter L. Miller, President
URL(s): www.aicpcu.org. **Frequency:** Annual. **Princi-
pal Exhibits:** Exhibits for insurance personnel and
Chartered Property Casualty Underwriters (CPCUs).

CONSULTANTS

11481 ■ Financial Computer Support Inc.
14 Commerce Dr.
Oakland, MD 21550-3940
Ph: (301)334-1800
Fax: (301)334-1896
Co. E-mail: sales@fcsi.com
URL: http://www.fcsi.com
Contact: David Huxford, Jr., President
Scope: Independent user group which provides
computer and administrative support for financial
planners, money managers, and insurance agents.
Serves finance and insurance industries. **Founded:**
1981. **Publications:** "Check Out Carmen Petote,"
Jul, 2006; "Control the Information Flow with Rep
Level Access," Feb, 2005.

11482 ■ Forensic Accident Investigations Inc.
6971 N Federal Hwy., Ste. 405
Boca Palm Professional Plz.
Boca Raton, FL 33487
Ph: (561)703-3881
Fax: (561)995-7168
Co. E-mail: rmcelroy@forensicaccident.com
URL: http://www.forensicaccident.com
Contact: Robert C. McElroy, President
E-mail: rmcelroy@forensicaccident.com
Scope: Accident reconstruction/investigation, product
failure and liability analysis, industrial standard and
safety research, regulatory compliance, design/
maintenance defects, mechanical inspections, preservation of evidence pertaining to collisions/insurance
fraud, documentation/determinations regarding oc-
cupant restraint function/usage, mechanical systems
failure/evaluation. Biomechanical analysis and
research, perception/reaction and time-distance
analysis, human factors, crash worthiness evaluations, 2-D and 3-D computer simulation and/or animation. **Founded:** 1986. **Seminars:** Bicycle Pedestrian
Collision Investigation, North Florida, Jan, 2005;
Safety Wins Defensive Driving Training, Homestead,

Nov, 2004; Human Factors in Traffic Crash Recon-
struction, North Florida, Nov, 2004; Collision Recon-
struction Technology and Application, Burlington, Aug,
2003; Intelligent Vehicle Initiative, On board Safety
Technology Workshop, Washington, Aug, 2003;
Contemporary Accident Reconstruction; Accident
Reconstruction; Accident Investigation, Reconstruc-
tion, Interpretation and the Law; Commercial Vehicle
Collision Investigation; Accident Reconstruction and
Event Data Recorders; EDR User Perspectives on
Parameters and Data Accessibility: Independent
Investigator Consultant Accident Reconstruction;
Retread Procedures for Commercial Tires; EDR
Transportation Event Data Recorders. **Special Ser-
vices:** PC-Crash and PC-Rect Simulation; AI Tools:
SLAM, Linear Momentum, Equations; SAE Data-
bases: MOVE, Stapp, Accident Reconstruction;
CAD:Designer, AutoSketch; PageMaker, MGI Video-
Wave, NHTSA Database Research, Autotrack Data-
base Research; VDO Accident Data Recorder; North
American Crash Analysis Center.

11483 ■ LIMRA International
300 Day Hill Rd.
Windsor, CT 06095
Ph: (860)688-3358
Free: 800-235-4672
Fax: (860)298-9555
Co. E-mail: webmaster@limra.com
URL: http://www.limra.com
Contact: Robert A. Kerzner, President
Description: Life insurance and financial services
companies. Conducts market, consumer, economic,
financial, and human resources research; monitors
industry distribution systems and product and service
developments. Provides executive and field management development schools and seminars. Offers human resource development consulting services,
including needs analysis and program design, evaluation, and implementation. **Scope:** A research and
management consulting organization specializing in
insurance marketing. Company research services apply scientific techniques to the areas of performance
appraisal, manpower utilization, employee and
consumer opinion sampling, and market analysis.
Management consultation services include strategic
planning, field cost controls and a computer modeling
service. Also offers financial services consulting
including defining distribution strategy, developing a
distribution channel, organizational development and
operations consulting. **Founded:** 1916. **Subscriptions:** 6000 archival material books periodicals. **Publications:** "28 Ways to Improve Your Sales Performance"; "Advanced Selection Interview Guide"; "LIM-
RA's Market Facts"; "Looking Ahead"; "Cross Selling".
Educational Activities: LIMRA International Conference (Annual). **Seminars:** Compensation and Motivation Plans that Deliver Results, Bangkok, Aug, 2009;
Sales Compensation Seminar, Simsbury, May, 2009;
Growth by Design; Strategic Marketing Review. **Telecommunication Services:** customer.service@limra.
com. **Special Services:** Career Profile.

**11484 ■ National Insurance Professionals
Corp. (NIPC)**
1040 NE Hostmark St., Ste. 200
Poulsbo, WA 98370-7454
Ph: (360)697-3611
Free: 800-275-6472
Fax: (360)697-3688
Co. E-mail: kathy_schufreider@rpsvcs.com
URL: http://www.nipc.com
Contact: Bill Reese, President
Scope: Program administrators for alternative
specialty markets. Includes social service agencies
and bicycle tour operators. Provides retail and
wholesale insurance brokers access to specialty
insurance carriers. **Founded:** 1976.

11485 ■ R.D. Network Inc.
PO Box 375
Lafayette Hill, PA 19444
Ph: (215)482-4461
Free: 877-482-4991
Fax: (215)836-0378
Co. E-mail: info@rdnetwork.com
URL: http://www.rdnetwork.com
Contact: Leslie Grant, Owner
Scope: Dietitians, diet technicians, and certified
dietary managers available nationwide and worldwide

through an international registry for consulting positions to wellness and employee education programs, drug or alcohol rehabilitation, hospital, LTC, nutrition and labeling communications, nutrition consultation, weight control classes, healthcare staff supplementation, media and program development, and all nutrition and food-related needs. Expert witness and speakers bureau also available. Industries served: healthcare, food industry, food service, restaurateurs, supermarkets, pharmaceutical companies, home health agencies, insurance companies, HMOs, and government agencies. **Founded:** 1983. **Seminars:** Labour/Staffing; Outsourcing; Healthy Dining Etiquette for Executives and Sales Staff Diet and Wellness; Cardiovascular Nutrition; Starting a Nutrition Consulting Practice; AIDS and Diet Therapy; Nutrition Care for Your Parents in Their Elder Years; Increase Your Energy-Increase Your Sales.

11486 ■ Strack Vaughan L.L.C.
4833 Rugby Ave., Ste. 201
Bethesda, MD 20814-3035
Ph: (301)654-7778
Fax: (301)951-0063
Contact: Steven G. Strack, Principal
Scope: Business and financial planning consultants providing services in mergers and acquisitions, strategic planning, and tax planning. Serves insurance agencies and the graphic arts industry. **Founded:** 1950.

FRANCHISES AND BUSINESS OPPORTUNITIES

11487 ■ Paul Davis Systems Canada, Ltd.
38 Crockford Blvd.
Scarborough, ON, Canada M1R 3C2
Ph: (416)299-8890
Free: 800-661-5975
Fax: (416)299-8510
URL: http://www.pds.ca
Description: Insurance claims and qualified restoration contractor across Canada and the U.S. **No. of Franchise Units:** 58. **Founded:** 1985.. **Franchised:** 1986. **Equity Capital Needed:** $100,000 investment required; $100,000 start-up capital required. **Franchise Fee:** $25,000-$45,000. **Training:** Provides 4 weeks training.

COMPUTERIZED DATABASES

11488 ■ Best's Statement File - Property/Casualty - United States
1 Ambest Rd.
Oldwick, NJ 08858-7000
Ph: (908)439-2200
Fax: (908)439-3296
Co. E-mail: customer_service@ambest.com
URL: http://www.ambest.com
Contact: James Peavy, President
Availability: CD-ROM: A.M. Best Company Inc.
Type: Numeric; Directory.

11489 ■ National Underwriter Life & Health
475 Park Ave. S, 6th Fl.
New York, NY 10016
Ph: (212)557-7480
Free: 800-543-0874
Fax: (212)557-7654
URL: http://www.summitbusinessmedia.com
Availability: Online: LexisNexis Group; Summit Business Media-National Underwriter Co. **Type:** Full-text.

11490 ■ National Underwriter Property & Casualty
475 Park Ave. S, 6th Fl.
New York, NY 10016
Ph: (212)557-7480
Free: 800-543-0874
Fax: (212)557-7654
URL: http://www.summitbusinessmedia.com
Availability: Online: LexisNexis Group; Summit Business Media-National Underwriter Co. **Type:** Full-text.

11491 ■ Sage Property & Casualty
11724 NE 195th St.
Bothell, WA 98011

Ph: (425)402-1000
Free: 800-444-4813
Fax: (425)402-9569
Co. E-mail: information@vertafore.com
URL: http://www.vertafore.com
Contact: Euan C. Menzies, President
Availability: Online: Vertafore Inc. **Type:** Full-text.

COMPUTER SYSTEMS/ SOFTWARE

11492 ■ Agency Accounting
681 S Parker St., Ste. 260
Orange, CA 92868
Ph: (714)836-0671
Fax: (714)836-0737
URL: http://www.itc-systems.com
Price: $20,000 Windows based licensing fee and maintenance and $600 per month. **Description:** Available for Windows 95, 98 NT and MICRO-based operating systems. System provides general agents with accounting and policy maintenance capabilities.

11493 ■ Agency Information Management System
433 Kitty Hawk, Ste. 211
Universal City, TX 78148
Ph: (800)456-7595
Free: 800-876-1466
Fax: (210)658-2220
URL: http://www.irsaims.com
Description: Windows 95/98 based agency management system. Combining the standard navigational tools and conventions of the windows operating system with an SQL data base, MARS offers complete customer and financial management yet is simple to use.

LIBRARIES

11494 ■ American Institute for Chartered Property Casualty Underwriters - Insurance Institute of America - Nancy W. Spellman Memorial Library
720 Providence Rd., Ste. 100
Malvern, PA 19355-3433
Ph: (610)644-2101
Fax: (610)640-9576
Co. E-mail: irc@cpcuiia.org
URL: http://www.aicpcu.org/
Contact: Adam Carmichael, Director
Scope: Insurance, risk management, economics, management, accounting, continuing education. **Services:** Copying; Library open to the public. **Founded:** 1978. **Holdings:** 9000 books. **Subscriptions:** 150 journals and other serials.

11495 ■ American Insurance Association Law Library
2101 L St. NW, Ste. 400
Washington, DC 20037
Ph: (202)828-7100
Fax: (202)293-1219
Co. E-mail: info@aiadc.org
URL: http://www.aiadc.org
Scope: Property and casualty insurance, law, healthcare policy. **Services:** Copying; Library open to the public by appointment. **Founded:** 1964. **Holdings:** 30,000 volumes; 215 VF drawers; reports; archives; proceedings. **Subscriptions:** 130 journals and other serials; 11 newspapers.

11496 ■ Buset & Partners Library
1121 Barton St.
Thunder Bay, ON, Canada P7B 5N3
Ph: (807)623-2500
Free: 866-532-8738
Fax: (807)622-7808
Co. E-mail: cenns@buset-partners.com
URL: http://www.buset-partners.com
Contact: Carolyn Enns, Librarian
Scope: Law - real estate, labor, corporate, commercial, family, personal injury, insurance; civil litigation, wills and estates, employment, municipal, environmental. **Services:** Library not open to the public. **Holdings:** 2100 books; 1 bound periodical

volumes. **Subscriptions:** 7 journals and other serials; 3 newspapers. **Telecommunication Services:** law@buset-partners.com.

11497 ■ Colonial Life & Accident Insurance Company - Archives and Library
1200 Colonial Life Blvd.
Columbia, SC 29202
Ph: (803)798-7000
Free: 800-325-4368
Fax: (803)731-2618
URL: http://www.coloniallife.com/
Scope: Insurance - life, health; employee benefits. **Holdings:** Figures not available.

11498 ■ Erie Insurance Group Corporate Library
100 Erie Insurance Pl.
Erie, PA 16530
Ph: (814)451-5000
URL: http://www.erieinsurance.com/
Scope: Insurance; management; law. **Services:** Interlibrary loan; copying; SDI; Library open to the public by appointment. **Founded:** 1975. **Holdings:** 1200 books; 1000 archival materials. **Subscriptions:** 150 journals and other serials; 10 newspapers.

11499 ■ Golden Rule Insurance Co. Library
7440 Woodland Dr.
Indianapolis, IN 46278
Ph: (317)715-7111
URL: http://www.goldenrule.com
Contact: Ellen Laden, Director, Public Relations
Scope: Insurance. **Services:** Library not open to the public. **Founded:** 1991. **Holdings:** 400 books; 500 reports; archives; videos. **Subscriptions:** 50 journals and other serials; 7 newspapers.

11500 ■ Hartford Conservatory - Carolyn B. Taylor Library
834 Asylum Ave.
Hartford, CT 06105
Ph: (860)246-2588
Fax: (860)249-6330
Co. E-mail: mhuntington@hartfordconservatory.org
URL: http://www.hartfordconservatory.org
Contact: Marilynn Huntington
Scope: Music (classical and jazz), dance, theater. **Services:** Interlibrary loan; Library open to the public for reference use only. **Founded:** 1890. **Holdings:** 1600 books and bound periodical volumes; 5114 music scores; 400 pieces of sheet music; 4800 sound recordings; 130 compact discs. **Subscriptions:** 10 journals and other serials.

11501 ■ Insurance Information Institute Library
110 William St.
New York, NY 10038
Ph: (212)346-5500
URL: http://www.iii.org
Contact: Shorna Lewis
Scope: Property and casualty insurance and allied subjects. **Services:** Library open to the public by appointment only. **Founded:** 1959. **Holdings:** 2000 books. **Subscriptions:** 75 journals and other serials.

11502 ■ Insurance Institute of Ontario Library
18 King St. E., 16th Fl.
Toronto, ON, Canada M5C 1C4
Ph: (416)362-8586
Fax: (416)362-8081
Co. E-mail: iiomail@insuranceinstitute.ca
URL: http://www.insuranceinstitute.ca
Contact: Peter Hohman, General Manager
Scope: Property and casualty insurance. **Services:** Library open to members. **Holdings:** 250 books; 12 serials; 6 other cataloged items. **Subscriptions:** 29 journals and other serials.

11503 ■ LeBoeuf, Lamb, Greene & MacRae Law Library
1 Riverfront Plaza
Newark, NJ 07102-5490
Ph: (973)643-8000

Fax: (973)643-6111
Co. E-mail: spierson@llgm.com
URL: http://www.llgm.com/Home.aspx
Contact: Stephanie Fox Pierson, Manager
Scope: Law - insurance, public utilities, corporate.
Services: Library not open to the public. **Founded:**
1984. **Holdings:** 3000 books. **Subscriptions:** 20
journals and other serials; 8 newspapers.

11504 ■ LIMRA International - InfoCenter
300 Day Hill Rd.
Windsor, CT 06095
Ph: (860)688-3358
Free: 800-235-4672
Fax: (860)298-9555
Co. E-mail: infocenter@limra.com
URL: http://www.limra.com
Contact: James Kerley, President
Scope: Life insurance, financial services, industrial
psychology, statistical methods. **Services:** Interlibrary
loan; Library open to members and to others upon
application. **Founded:** 1926. **Holdings:** 6000 books;
150 VF drawers of clippings, pamphlets, 26,000
documents. **Subscriptions:** 300 journals and other
serials.

**11505 ■ Manulife Financial - Canadian
Division Law Library**
500 King St., N.
Waterloo, ON, Canada N2J 4C6
Ph: (519)747-7000
Fax: (519)747-6325
Co. E-mail: tina_pedersen@manulife.com
Contact: Tina Pedersen, Specialist
Scope: Canadian insurance law. **Services:** Library
not open to the public. **Founded:** 1986. **Holdings:**
800 books; 1000 bound periodical volumes; 10
reports; CD-ROMs. **Subscriptions:** 70 journals and
other serials.

**11506 ■ McKenna Long & Aldridge LLP Law
Library**
1900 K St. NW, Lower Level
Washington, DC 20006-1108
Ph: (202)496-7500
Fax: (202)496-7756
Co. E-mail: tpapson@mckennalong.com
URL: http://www.mckennalong.com
Scope: Law - government contracts, environmental,
litigation, food and drug, International, health care,
labor, insurance, energy. **Services:** Interlibrary loan;
Library not open to the public. **Founded:** 1940. **Hold-
ings:** 15,000 books; 5000 bound periodical volumes.
Subscriptions: 400 journals and other serials.

**11507 ■ Metropolitan Life Insurance
Company - Corporate Information Center &
Library**
200 Park Ave.
New York, NY 10166
Free: 877-638-2862
Fax: (212)689-0926
Co. E-mail: metro_njsbc@metlife.com
URL: http://www.metlife.com/
Scope: Insurance, management. **Services:** Interli-
brary loan; archives open to researchers by appoint-
ment. **Founded:** 1909. **Holdings:** 65,000 volumes.
Subscriptions: 47 journals and other serials; 3
newspapers.

**11508 ■ National Association of Insurance
Commissioners - NAIC Support and Services
Office - Research Library**
2301 McGee, Ste. 800
Kansas City, MO 64108-2662

Ph: (816)842-3600
Fax: (816)783-8269
Co. E-mail: reslib@naic.org
URL: http://www.naic.org
Contact: Sandra Hollis, Director, Library Services
Scope: Insurance - regulation, law, business. **Ser-
vices:** Library not open to the public. **Founded:**
1970. **Holdings:** 13,000 volumes; reports; microfiche
and microfilm. **Subscriptions:** 160 journals and other
serials.

11509 ■ Parker, Smith & Feek, Inc. Library
2233 112th Ave., NE
Bellevue, WA 98004
Ph: (425)709-3600
Free: 800-457-0220
Fax: (425)709-7460
URL: http://www.psfinc.com/risk-management-center
Contact: Sherri L. Monteith, Specialist
Scope: Insurance. **Services:** Library open to clients.
Founded: 1985. **Holdings:** 100 books; 400 reports.
Subscriptions: 125 journals and other serials; 7
newspapers.

**11510 ■ Property Casualty Insurers
Association of America Library**
8700 W. Bryn Mawr Ave., Ste. 1200S
Chicago, IL 60631-3512
Ph: (847)297-7800
Fax: (847)297-5064
URL: http://www.pciaa.net/web/sitehome.nsf/main
Scope: Insurance, law. **Services:** Interlibrary loan.
Holdings: 4000 books. **Subscriptions:** 250 journals
and other serials; 6 newspapers.

11511 ■ Protape, Inc. Library
1540 Broadway
New York, NY 10036
Contact: Richard Sobelsohn
Scope: Accounting, law, real estate, English, math,
insurance, travel, taxation, stock broker, medical billing, claims adjusting, private investigation, paralegal.
Services: Library not open to the public. **Founded:**
1970. **Holdings:** 25,000 books; 250 bound periodical
volumes. **Subscriptions:** 65 journals and other serials; 20 newspapers.

**11512 ■ Ropers Majeski Kohn & Bentley
Library**
1001 Marshall St., Ste. 500
Redwood City, CA 94063
Ph: (650)364-8200
Fax: (650)367-0997
Co. E-mail: ccallahan@rmkb.com
URL: http://www.rmkb.com
Contact: Carmen Callahan, Administrator
Scope: Law - California, federal, insurance; civil
litigation; legal reference. **Services:** Library not open
to the public. **Founded:** 1954. **Holdings:** 4000
books; 400 bound periodical volumes; 175 reports;
1000 archival items; CD-ROMs. **Subscriptions:** 9
journals and other serials; 5 newspapers.

**11513 ■ Society of Insurance Research
Library**
631 Eastpointe Dr.
Shelbyville, IN 46176
Ph: (317)398-3684
Co. E-mail: sir.mail@comcast.net
URL: http://www.sirnet.org
Contact: Ed Budd, Executive Director
Scope: Insurance research. **Services:** Library open
to members only. **Founded:** 1970.

**11514 ■ Swidler Berlin Shereff Friedman, LLP
Library**
2020 K St., NW
Washington, DC 20006-1806
Ph: (202)373-6000
Fax: (202)373-6001
URL: http://www.bingham.com/Default.aspx
Scope: Law - communications, insurance, energy,
bankruptcy, the environment, government affairs,
antitrust, litigation, corporate, intellectual property.
Services: Library not open to the public. **Founded:**
1982. **Holdings:** 1800 volumes.

**11515 ■ XL Global Services Corporate
Library**
70 Seaview Ave.
Stamford, CT 06902-6036
Ph: (203)964-5216
Fax: (203)964-0763
Co. E-mail: diane.fischer@xlgroup.com
Contact: Diane Fischer, Manager, Information
Services
Scope: Reinsurance, insurance. **Services:** Interli-
brary loan; Library not open to the public. **Founded:**
1985. **Holdings:** 200 books. **Subscriptions:** 200
journals and other serials; 3 newspapers.

RESEARCH CENTERS

11516 ■ Insurance Research Council (IRC)
718 Providence Rd.
Malvern, PA 19355
Ph: (610)644-2212
Fax: (610)640-5388
Co. E-mail: corum@cpcuiia.org
URL: http://www.ircweb.org
Contact: David Corum, Vice President
Founded: 1977. **Publications:** *Auto Injury Study* (5/
year); *Public Attitude Monitor* (Annual). **Telecom-
munication Services:** irc@cpcuiia.org.

11517 ■ Society of Insurance Research (SIR)
631 Eastpointe Dr.
Shelbyville, IN 46176
Ph: (317)398-3684
Fax: (317)642-0535
Co. E-mail: sir.mail@comcast.net
URL: http://www.sirnet.org
Contact: Ed Budd, Executive Director
Description: Represents individuals or companies
interested or actively involved in insurance research
and planning. Stimulates insurance research through
the interchange of ideas on research methodology
and developments in technology. **Scope:** insurance
research. **Founded:** 1970. **Subscriptions:** 40 ar-
ticles. **Publications:** *SIR News* (Quarterly); *S.I.R.
News*; *Society of Insurance Research--Membership
Directory*. **Educational Activities:** SIR Conference
(Annual); SIR Workshops (Annual); Summer Workshop Series (Annual).

**11518 ■ University of Georgia - Center for
Insurance Education and Research**
206 Brooks Hall
Terry College of Business
Athens, GA 30602-6255
Ph: (706)542-4290
Fax: (706)542-4295
Co. E-mail: rhoyt@terry.uga.edu
URL: http://www.terry.uga.edu/insurance
Contact: Dr. Robert E. Hoyt, Director
Founded: 1981. **Educational Activities:** Insurance
Managers Seminar (Annual). **Awards:** Center for
Insurance Education and Research Research grants
(Periodic).

START-UP INFORMATION

11519 ■ *"Five Low-Cost Home Based Startups" in Women Entrepreneur (December 16, 2008)*
Pub: Entrepreneur Media Inc.
Ed: Lesley Spencer Pyle. **Description:** During tough economic times, small businesses have an advantage over large companies because they can adjust to economic conditions more easily and without having to go through corporate red tape that can slow the implementation process. A budding entrepreneur may find success by taking inventory of his or her skills, experience, expertise and passions and utilizing those qualities to start a business. Five low-cost home-based startups are profiled. These include starting an online store, a virtual assistant service, web designer, sales representative and a home staging counselor.

11520 ■ *How to Open and Operate a Financially Successful Redesign, Redecorating, and Home Staging Business: With Companion CD-ROM*
Pub: Atlantic Publishing Group, Inc.
Ed: Mary Larsen; Teri B. Clark. **Released:** January 2008. **Price:** $39.95 paperback. **Description:** Questions are asked to help individuals determine if they should launch their own redesign or real estate staging firm.

11521 ■ *How to Start a Home-Based Interior Design Business*
Pub: Globe Pequot Press
Ed: Nita Phillips. **Released:** January 2006.

11522 ■ *Interior Design Business*
Pub: Globe Pequot Press
Ed: Suzanne DeWalt; Nita B. Phillips. **Released:** January 2006. **Price:** $18.95. **Description:** Tips for starting and running a home-based interior design business are given.

11523 ■ *"No Place Like Home" in Small Business Opportunities (Winter 2010)*
Pub: Harris Publications Inc.
Description: Five reasons to start a home-staging business in any economy are listed. Home staging is listed as the top emerging career on Website, Careerbuilder.com.

ASSOCIATIONS AND OTHER ORGANIZATIONS

11524 ■ **American Floorcovering Alliance (AFA)**
210 W Cuyler St.
Dalton, GA 30720
Ph: (706)278-4101
Free: 800-288-4101
Fax: (706)278-5323
Co. E-mail: afa@americanfloor.org
URL: http://www.americanfloor.org
Contact: Wanda J. Ellis, Executive Director
URL(s): www.floor-tek.com. **Description:** Floorcovering manufacturers and companies providing ser-

vices or supplies to the floor covering industry. Promotes the floor covering industry. Provides insurance programs for members. **Founded:** 1979. **Publications:** *Floor Covering Weekly* (Weekly); *Floor Focus* (Monthly); *Floor Tek Source Guide* (Biennial); *Industry Profile* (Quarterly); *Floor Tek Source Guide* (Biennial). **Educational Activities:** Floor-Tek (Biennial).

11525 ■ **Association of University Interior Designers (AUID)**
c/o Carlos Lugo
Ohio State University
Office of Student Life
Facility Management and Logistics
1800 Cannon Dr., Ste. 710
Columbus, OH 43210
URL: http://www.auid.org
Contact: Julie Lenczycki, President
Description: In-house interior designers associated with universities. Serves as an educational forum to share ideas and concerns of interior design relating to universities and colleges. **Founded:** 1979. **Awards:** Scholarship Award (Annual).

11526 ■ **Council for Interior Design Accreditation (CIDA)**
206 Grandville Ave., Ste. 350
Grand Rapids, MI 49503
Ph: (616)458-0400
Fax: (616)458-0460
Co. E-mail: info@accredit-id.org
URL: http://www.accredit-id.org
Contact: Holly Mattson, Executive Director
E-mail: holly@accredit-id.org
Description: Formed by Interior Design Educators Council and American Society of Interior Designers. Administers voluntary plan for the special accreditation of interior design education programs offered at institutions of higher learning throughout the U.S. and its possessions and Canada; emphasizes the use of accreditation procedures to assure that the purposes and accomplishments of programs of interior design education meet the needs of society, students, and the interior design profession; recognized by the Council for Higher Education Accreditation as a national accrediting agency for programs in interior design in schools throughout the country. **Founded:** 1970. **Publications:** *Directory of Interior Design Programs Accredited by FIDER* (Semiannual).

11527 ■ **Home Fashion Products Association (HFPA)**
355 Lexington Ave., Ste. 1500
New York, NY 10017-6603
Ph: (212)297-2122
Fax: (212)370-9047
Co. E-mail: contactus@hfpaonline.org
URL: http://www.homefashionproducts.com
Contact: Katie Goshgarian, Executive Director
Description: Manufacturers of curtains, draperies, bedding, rugs and related products. Sponsors annual scholarship for students attending accredited schools in home textiles. **Founded:** 1968. **Awards:** Scholarship (Annual).

11528 ■ **Interior Design Society (IDS)**
164 S Main St., Fl. 8
High Point, NC 27260
Ph: (336)884-4437
Free: 888-884-4469
Fax: (336)885-3291
Co. E-mail: idsbenefits@interiordesignsociety.org
URL: http://www.interiordesignsociety.org
Contact: Anna Mavrakis, Chairman of the Board
URL(s): ids.membershipsoftware.org/index.asp. **Description:** Represents independent designers and decorators, retail designers and sales people, design-oriented firms, and manufacturers. Grants accreditation and recognition to qualified residential interior designers and retail home furnishing stores. Conducts educational seminars in design, sales training, and marketing. Offers products and publications for designers and a correspondence course for home furnishing sales people. **Founded:** 1973. **Publications:** *Design for Success* (Monthly); *Portfolio* (Quarterly); *Residential Interior Design Books and Designer Tools*. **Educational Activities:** Regional Chapter & National Events (Monthly).

11529 ■ **International Association of Lighting Designers (IALD)**
440 N Wells St., Ste. 210
Chicago, IL 60654
Ph: (312)527-3677
Fax: (312)527-3680
Co. E-mail: iald@iald.org
URL: http://www.iald.org
Contact: Kevin Theobald, President
Description: Represents professionals, educators, students, and others working in the field of lighting design worldwide. Promotes the benefits of quality lighting design and emphasizes the potential impact of lighting on architectural design and environmental quality. Furthers professional standards of lighting designers and seeks to increase their function in the interior design industry. Sponsors national awards program, summer intern program for qualified college students interested in lighting design as a profession, and career development lectures and seminars. **Scope:** lighting. **Founded:** 1969. **Subscriptions:** periodicals. **Publications:** *e-Reflections* (Monthly); *International Association of Lighting Designers--Membership Directory* (Annual); *Why Hire an IALD Lighting Designer*. **Educational Activities:** Lightfair International (Annual). **Awards:** IALD Award (Annual); IALD Scholarship (Annual); Lighting Design Awards; IALD Education Trust Scholarship Program.

11530 ■ **International Furnishings and Design Association (IFDA)**
610 Freedom Business Ctr. Dr., Ste. 110
King of Prussia, PA 19406
Ph: (610)535-6422
Fax: (610)535-6423
Co. E-mail: info@ifda.com
URL: http://www.ifda.com
Contact: Martha Heinze, Executive Director
Description: Represents individuals engaged in design, production, distribution, education, promotion and editorial phases of the interior furnishings

industry and related fields. Founded IFDA Educational Foundation in 1968. Conducts charitable programs; maintains speakers' bureau. **Founded:** 1947. **Publications:** *IFDA Directory* (Annual); *IFDA Network* (Quarterly). **Awards:** Fellow Recognition Award; Honorary Recognition Award; Trailblazer Award; IFDA Fellow (Annual); National Honorary Recognition Award (Annual); Trailblazer Award (Annual); International Furnishings and Design Association Educational Foundation Student Scholarships; International Furnishings and Design Association Part-time Student Scholarships; Charles D. Mayo Student Scholarships.

11531 ■ International Interior Design Association (IIDA)

222 Merchandise Mart, Ste. 567
Chicago, IL 60654
Ph: (312)467-1950
Free: 888-799-4432
Fax: (312)467-0779
Co. E-mail: iidahq@iida.org
URL: http://www.iida.org
Contact: Peter Conant, President

Description: Represents professional interior designers, including designers of commercial, healthcare, hospitality, government, retail, residential facilities; educators; researchers; representatives of allied manufacturing sources. Conducts research, student programs and continuing education programs for members. Has developed a code of ethics for the professional design membership. **Founded:** 1994. **Publications:** *GRAction*.

11532 ■ National Council for Interior Design Qualification (NCIDQ)

1602 L St. NW, Ste. 200
Washington, DC 20036-2581
Ph: (202)721-0220
Fax: (202)721-0221
Co. E-mail: inquiries@ncidq.org
URL: http://www.ncidq.org
Contact: Mary Jane Grigsby, President

Description: Independent organization of state and provincial regulatory bodies. Provides the public with the means to identify those interior designers who have demonstrated the minimum level of competence needed to practice in this profession. Provides a professional examination in interior design. Endeavors to maintain the most advanced examining procedures, and to update continually the examination to reflect expanding professional knowledge and design development techniques to protect the health, safety and welfare of the public. Seeks acceptance of the NCIDQ examination as a universal standard by which to measure the competency of interior designers practicing as professionals. **Scope:** interior design. **Founded:** 1972. **Publications:** *QLetter* (Semiannual); *The Mark of a Professional; Continuing Education.* **Awards:** Louis S. Tregre Award (Annual); Louis S. Tregre Award.

11533 ■ National Kitchen and Bath Association (NKBA)

687 Willow Grove St.
Hackettstown, NJ 07840
Ph: (908)852-0033
Free: 800-843-6522
Fax: (908)852-1695
Co. E-mail: feedback@nkba.org
URL: http://www.nkba.org
Contact: Bill Darcy, Chief Executive Officer

Description: Manufacturers and firms engaged in retail kitchen sales; manufacturers' representatives and wholesale distributors; utilities, publications and other firms supplying products or services to the kitchen and bathroom industry. Protects and promotes the interest and welfare of members by fostering a better business climate in the industry. Awards titles of Certified Kitchen Designer and Certified Bathroom Designer to individuals with proven knowledge, ability and experience in the design, planning, and installation supervision of residential kitchens. Conducts kitchen and bathroom training schools throughout the country. Sponsors business management and consumer awareness programs. Maintains speakers' bureau and Hall of Fame. **Founded:** 1963. **Publications:** *National Kitchen & Bath Association--Directory*

of Accredited Members (Annual). **Educational Activities:** National Design Competition (Annual). **Telecommunication Services:** feeback@nkba.org.

11534 ■ Organization of Black Designers (OBD)

300 M St. SW, Ste. N110
Washington, DC 20024
Ph: (202)659-3918
Co. E-mail: info@obd.org
URL: http://www.obd.org
Contact: David H. Rice, Chairman Founder

Description: African American designers holding college degrees who are practicing graphic advertising, industrial, fashion, textile, and interior design. Provides forum for discussion and educational programs, business, career and economic development. Sponsors competitions and speakers' bureau. **Scope:** design issues that impact black design professionals. **Founded:** 1994. **Subscriptions:** archival material articles. **Publications:** *DesigNation* (Biennial); *OBData.* **Educational Activities:** DesigNation (Annual). **Awards:** OBD Design Award (Annual); OBD Scholarship (Annual).

11535 ■ Paint and Decorating Retailers Association (PDRA)

1401 Triad Center Dr.
St. Peters, MO 63376-7353
Ph: (636)326-2636
Free: 800-737-0107
Fax: (636)229-4750
Co. E-mail: info@pdra.org
URL: http://www.pdra.org
Contact: Jeff Baggaley, President

Description: Serves as a trade association of locally-owned paint and decorating stores in the U.S., Canada and around the world. Offers professional advice, personal service and quality products for every paint, wall covering, window treatment and floor covering project. **Founded:** 1947. **Publications:** *Paint and Decorating Retailer; Paint & Decorating Retailer Magazine* (Monthly); *PDRA Decorating Registry* (Annual); *PDRA Gold Book* (Annual); *PDRA Paint and Decorating Retailer* (Monthly); *Gold Book* (Annual); *Decorating Registry* (Annual); *Decorating Retailer--Directory of the Wallcoverings Industry Issue* (Annual); *Gold Book: Directory of the Wallcovering Industry* (Annual). **Educational Activities:** Paint and Decorating Show (Annual). **Telecommunication Services:** dan@lloydspaint.com.

11536 ■ Painting and Decorating Contractors of America (PDCA)

1801 Park 270 Dr.
St. Louis, MO 63146-4020
Ph: (314)514-7322
Free: 800-332-7322
Fax: (314)890-2068
Co. E-mail: rbright@pdca.org
URL: http://www.pdca.org
Contact: Dave Ayala, President

Description: Painting and wall covering contractors. Operates educational and charitable programs. Compiles statistics. **Founded:** 1884. **Publications:** *Hazardous Waste Handbook; Painting and Wallcovering Contractor* (Bimonthly); *PDCA Directory* (Annual); *Painting and Wallcovering Contractor--PDCA Roster* (Annual). **Awards:** Humanitarian Award; Safety Awards (Annual); A.E. Robert Friedman Scholarships (Annual); "Picture It Painted Professionally" Awards; Al Quilici Outstanding Member Award; L.E. Travis, Jr. PDCA Craftsman of the Year Award (Annual); Picture It Painted Professionally Award (Annual). **Telecommunication Services:** rgreene@pdca.org; emcdermott@pdca.org.

11537 ■ Window Covering Manufacturers Association (WCMA)

355 Lexington Ave., 15th Fl.
New York, NY 10017
Ph: (212)297-2122
URL: http://www.wcmanet.org
Contact: Ralph Vasami, Executive Director

Description: Represents corporations engaged in the manufacture or assembly of Venetian blinds, vertical blinds, pleated shades, or their components. Promotes the use, utility, image, and attractiveness

of the products and services offered by the window covering industry. **Founded:** 1979. **Awards:** Product Innovation Awards (Annual).

DIRECTORIES OF EDUCATIONAL PROGRAMS

11538 ■ *Directory of Private Accredited Career Schools and Colleges of Technology*

Pub: Accrediting Commission of Career Schools and Colleges of Technology
Contact: Michale S. McComis, Executive Director

Released: On web page. **Price:** Free. **Description:** Covers 3900 accredited post-secondary programs that provide training programs in business, trade, and technical fields, including various small business endeavors. Entries offer school name, address, phone, description of courses, job placement assistance, and requirements for admission. Arrangement is alphabetical.

REFERENCE WORKS

11539 ■ *"Colores Origenes: Martha Kruse" in Advertising Age (Vol. 77, November 13, 2006, No. 46, pp. S12)*

Pub: Crain Communications, Inc.

Ed: Laurel Wentz. **Description:** Home Depot has created a range of Latin paint colors called Colores Origenes; the new line was originally intended to launch only at locations with heavily Hispanic patrons but the company decided to make the line available at all of their stores.

11540 ■ *"Entrepreneur Says Spirituality Has Been a Key to Her Success" in Business First Columbus (Vol. 25, October 17, 2008, No. 8, pp. 1)*

Pub: American City Business Journals

Ed: Scott Rawdon. **Description:** Profile of Carolyn Williams Francis, CEO of Williams Interior Designs Inc. She outlines her mantra for success in her furniture design business, but emphasizes that faith has taken her business to greater heights.

11541 ■ *"First the Merger: Then, The Culture Clash. How To Fix the Little Things That Can Tear a Company Apart" in Inc. (January 2008)*

Pub: Gruner & Jahr USA Publishing

Ed: Elaine Appleton Grant. **Description:** Ways three CEOs handled the culture classes that followed after company mergers; companies profiled include Fuel Outdoor, an outdoor advertising company; Nelson, an interior design and architecture firm; and Beber Silverstein, an ad agency.

11542 ■ *Floor Covering Weekly--Annual Product Source Guide*

Pub: FCW
Contact: Thomas Young, Manager, Production
E-mail: tdyoung@hearst.com

URL(s): floorcoveringweekly.com. **Ed:** Santiago Montero. **Released:** Annual; Latest edition 2011. **Price:** $66, Canada; $61, Individuals; $101, Two years; $184, Out of country. **Publication includes:** Lists of manufacturers and importers of carpet, rugs, carpet cushion, fiber, resilient wood, and ceramic floor coverings; separate listing of distributors by state, retail groups and associations. **Entries include:** For manufacturers--Company name, address, phone, regional sales offices, names and titles of key personnel, local distributors, products. For distributors-- Company name, address, phone, manufacturers represented. **Arrangement:** Alphabetical. **Indexes:** Geographical by distributor.

11543 ■ *Home Staging for Dummies*

Pub: John Wiley and Sons, Inc.

Ed: Christine Rae; Janice Saunders Maresh. **Released:** May 2008. **Price:** $19.99. **Description:** Guide shows how to make improvements room by room in order to generate a higher profit on home sales. The book offers tips to clear clutter and show the home's best features, inspire curb appeal, and how to depersonalize and neutralize every room.

11544 ■ *"How to Declutter Your Life Closet Cleanup: Putting a Lid on Clutter"* in Atlanta Journal-Constitution (May 1, 2011)
Pub: Atlanta Journal-Constitution
Ed: Felicia Feaster. **Description:** The annual Closets and Home Organization Convention and Expo spotlights new products and services designed to help people get organized at home or the workplace. The organization sector is holding steady despite the recession and is expected to expand into garage organization.

11545 ■ *"Inside the Googleplex"* in Canadian Business (Vol. 79, November 6, 2006, No. 22, pp. 59)
Pub: Rogers Media
Ed: Christina Campbell. **Description:** The views of Clive Wilkinson, a designer, on relationship between interior design and employee's productivity are presented.

11546 ■ *"Intel Joins Movement to Turn Cube Farms Into Wide-Open Spaces"* in Sacramento Business Journal (Vol. 28, May 27, 2011, No. 13, pp. 1)
Pub: Sacramento Business Journal
Ed: Melanie Turner. **Description:** Intel Corporation has remodeled its facility in Folsom, California. The renovation has required some workers to give up their cubicles. Comments from executives are included.

11547 ■ *Interior Design--Buyers Guide Issue*
Pub: Cahners Publishing Co.
URL(s): www.interiordesign.net. **Released:** Monthly; except April. **Price:** $64.95, Individuals 12 issues, annual rate for subscribers; C$87, Individuals 12 issues, annual rate for subscribers; $87, Individuals Other country. **Publication includes:** Lists of 4,000 manufacturers and suppliers of furniture, furnishings, and services to contract and residential designers; trade buildings and marts; trade associations; carpet guide. **Entries include:** Company name, address, phone, fax. **Arrangement:** Alphabetical. **Indexes:** Keyword, product, geographical. Calendar of industry events; reference book index.

11548 ■ *"Let Your Stuff Tell a Story: How to Edit Your Accessories to Showcase Your Personality"* in Charlotte Observer (February 8, 2007)
Pub: Knight-Ridder/Tribune Business News
Ed: Nancy Brachey. **Description:** Tips to accessorize any home or office are presented; eliminating clutter is stressed.

11549 ■ *"Make a Resolution: ADA Training"* in HRMagazine (Vol. 54, January 2009, No. 1, pp. 81)
Pub: Society for Human Resource Management
Contact: Henry G. Jackson, President
E-mail: hjackson@shrm.org
Ed: Victoria Zellers. **Description:** Americans with Disabilities Act (ADA) Amendments Act took effect January 1, 2009. The ADA Amendments Act means that more applicants and employees are eligible for reasonable accommodations and that employers need to develop a new ADA compliance strategy.

11550 ■ *"Monday Organizer: Clean and De-Clutter in 15 Minutes"* in Tulsa World (June 13, 2011)
Pub: McClatchy Company
Ed: Kim Brown. **Description:** New weekly series highlights practical tips and helpful ideas to simply life by taking 15 minutes to de-clutter your home or office. Paper clutter can be eliminated in 15 minutes by gathering up newspapers and magazines to recycle; sort mail as soon as you receive it and throw away any junk mail at that time. If watching TV, use commercial time to accomplish small tasks.

11551 ■ *Peggy's Corner: The Art of Staging*
Pub: Eaton-Moghannam Publishing
Ed: Peggy Selinger-Eaton; Gayla Moghannam. **Released:** June 2005. **Description:** Techniques to enhance the value of any home are given. Seven principles of staging a home for sale include making a great first impression, maximizing space and eliminating clutter, using lighting for open spacious feeling, de-emphasize flaws, make the home appealing to buyers with varied tastes, creating warmth, and modernizing the home.

11552 ■ *"Procter Gambles on Wallpaper; Putting Paint On a Roll"* in Advertising Age (Vol. 77, September 18, 2006, No. 38, pp. 4)
Pub: Crain Communications, Inc.
Ed: Jack Neff. **Description:** Procter & Gamble Co. has launched a new line of textured paints that are already applied to a wallpaper-like roll that can be hung without paste or wallpaper tools.

11553 ■ *"Staging a Martini-and-GQ Lifestyle; Faux Possessions Play to Buyer's Aspirations"* in Crain's Chicago Business (April 21, 2008)
Pub: Crain Communications, Inc.
Ed: Kevin Davis. **Description:** Due to the competition of the slumping housing market, home stagers are becoming more prominent and are using creative ways to make an impression beyond de-cluttering, painting and cleaning by using accents such as casually placed magazines, candles and table settings.

TRADE PERIODICALS

11554 ■ *Architectural Digest*
Pub: Conde Nast Publications
Contact: David Carey, President
URL(s): www.architecturaldigest.com. **Released:** Monthly **Price:** $24.99, Individuals; $44.99, Two years.

11555 ■ *ARIDO*
Pub: Association of Registered Interior Designers of Ontario
Ed: Lori Theoret, Editor, ltheoret@arido.on.ca. **Released:** 6/yr. **Price:** Included in membership. **Description:** Covers issues affecting the interior design profession. Contains information on association news as well as design resources. Recurring features include letters to the editor, research news, a calendar of events, technical and business articles, and columns titled Viewpoint and Announcements. Available via fax only.

11556 ■ *Award Magazine: Architecture, Construction, Interior Design*
Pub: Canada Wide Magazines & Communications Ltd.
URL(s): www.canadawide.com/canada-wide/our-products/2007/10/23/award-magazin e. **Ed:** Kim Mah, David Jordan, Tracy Tjaden, Shannon Miller. **Released:** Bimonthly **Price:** $22.34, Individuals plus HST.

11557 ■ *CAUS News*
Pub: Color Association of the United States
Released: Bimonthly. **Price:** Included in membership. **Description:** Explores aspects of color design, discussing applications to a wide variety of fields, including fashion, textiles, interior decorating, environmental construction, marketing, and advertising. Contains news of research, book reviews, and editorials. Recurring features include letters to the editor, news of members, and a calendar of events.

11558 ■ *Chicago Home and Garden*
Pub: Chicago Home & Garden
URL(s): www.chicagohomemag.com/. **Ed:** Jan Parr. **Released:** Quarterly **Price:** $9.95, Individuals; $25, Canada; $35, Other countries.

11559 ■ *Contract: Inspiring Commercial Design Solutions*
Contact: Sheila Kim, Managing Editor
E-mail: skim@contractdesign.com
URL(s): www.contractmagazine.com/. **Released:** Monthly

11560 ■ *Country Home*
Pub: Meredith Corp.
URL(s): www.countryhome.com. **Released:** Monthly; 10/yr. **Price:** $4.95, Individuals newstand; $21.97, Two years.

11561 ■ *Country Sampler*
Pub: Country Sampler Group
URL(s): www.sampler.com. **Ed:** Donna Marcel. **Released:** Bimonthly **Price:** $19.96, U.S.; $29.96, Canada; $49.96, Other countries.

11562 ■ *Hospitality Design*
Pub: Nielsen Co.
Contact: Greg Farrar, President
URL(s): www.hdmag.com. **Released:** 10/yr. **Price:** $79, Individuals; $94, Canada; $139, Other countries by airmail.

11563 ■ *House Beautiful*
Pub: Hachette Filipacchi Media U.S. Inc.
Contact: David Carey, President
URL(s): www.housebeautiful.comwww.hearst.com/magazines/house-beautiful.php. **Price:** $15, Individuals; $25, Two years.

11564 ■ *Interior Design*
Pub: Reed Business Information
Contact: Jeff Greisch, President
URL(s): www.interiordesign.net/. **Released:** 15/yr. **Price:** $59.95, Individuals; $87, Canada; $187, Other countries.

11565 ■ *LDB Interior Textiles*
Pub: E.W. Williams Publications Co.
Contact: Andrew Williams, President
E-mail: awilliams@ewwpi.com
URL(s): www.ldbinteriortextiles.com. **Released:** Monthly **Price:** $72, Individuals; $125, Canada; $150, Elsewhere airmail; $100, Two years; $7, Single issue; $12, Single issue, Canada; $18, Single issue elsewhere.

11566 ■ *Metropolitan Home*
Contact: Deborah Burns, Publisher
URL(s): www.hfmus.com/hfmus/our_brands/metropolitan_home. **Released:** 10/yr. **Price:** $16, Two years; $10, Individuals; $22, Canada; $29, Other countries.

11567 ■ *Old-House Interiors*
Pub: Gloucester Publishers
URL(s): www.oldhouseinteriors.com. **Released:** Bimonthly **Price:** $24, Individuals; $32, Canada; $38, Other countries; $42, Two years; $58, Canada 2 years; $70, Other countries 2 years.

VIDEOCASSETTES/ AUDIOCASSETTES

11568 ■ *The Art of Interior Decorating*
Cambridge Educational
c/o Films Media Group
132 West 31st Street, 17th Floor
Ste. 124
New York, NY 10001
Free: 800-257-5126
Fax: (609)671-0266
Co. E-mail: custserve@films.com
URL: http://www.cambridgeol.com
Released: 1988. **Price:** $49.95. **Description:** Learn professional techniques for decorating a room or a whole house. Discusses colors, style, furniture, and accessories. A workbook is included. **Availability:** VHS.

11569 ■ *Feng Shui Today*
Tapeworm Video Distributors
25876 The Old Road #141
Stevenson Ranch, CA 91381
Ph: (661)257-4904
Fax: (661)257-4820
Co. E-mail: sales@tapeworm.com
URL: http://www.tapeworm.com
Released: 19??. **Price:** $19.95. **Description:** Interior designer Jami Lin presents Feng Shui an interior decorating style with spirit. **Availability:** VHS.

TRADE SHOWS AND CONVENTIONS

11570 ■ Accent on Design - A Division of the New York International Gift Fair
George Little Management, LLC
1133 Westchester Ave., Ste. N136
White Plains, NY 10606
Ph: (914)421-3200
Free: 800-272-SHOW
Co. E-mail: cathy_steel@glmshows.com
URL: http://www.glmshows.com
URL(s): www.nyigf.com. **Frequency:** Annual. **Audience:** Buyers from specialty, department, and jewelry stores and; gift shops; interior designers; home products importers and distributors; mail order catalogs. **Principal Exhibits:** General giftware, tabletop and housewares, decorative and personal accessories, museum gifts, ethnic, traditional, country and contemporary design products, juvenile products, floral products and pet products. **Dates and Locations:** Jacob K. Javits Convention Center. **Telecommunication Services:** maureen_smith@glmshows.com.

11571 ■ Accent on Design - A Division of the San Francisco International Gift Fair
George Little Management, LLC
1133 Westchester Ave., Ste. N136
White Plains, NY 10606
Ph: (914)421-3200
Free: 800-272-SHOW
Co. E-mail: cathy_steel@glmshows.com
URL: http://www.glmshows.com
URL(s): www.weshows.com. **Frequency:** Semiannual. **Audience:** Specialty, department, stationery, jewelry, and juvenile stores, gift and gourmet shops, interior designers, importers/distributors of home products, museums. **Principal Exhibits:** Decorative accessories, lighting and home furnishings, housewares, stationery, tabletop, gourmet and general gift merchandise. **Dates and Locations:** Moscone Convention Center. **Telecommunication Services:** showinfo@weshows.com.

11572 ■ Chicago Design Show
Merchandise Mart Properties Inc.
222 Merchandise Mart, Ste. 470
Chicago, IL 60654
Ph: (312)527-4141
Free: 800-677-6278
URL: http://www.merchandisemart.com
URL(s): www.merchandisemart.com. **Frequency:** Annual. **Audience:** Interior design trade professionals and consumers. **Principal Exhibits:** Contemporary design in furniture, fashion, food.

11573 ■ Fort Lauderdale Home Design & Remodeling Show
Home Show Management
1450 Madruga Ave., Ste. 301
Coral Gables, FL 33146
Ph: (305)667-9299
Free: 800-353-EXPO
Fax: (305)667-3266
Co. E-mail: info@homeshows.net
URL: http://www.homeshows.net
URL(s): www.homeshows.net. **Frequency:** Annual. **Audience:** Designers, decorators, builders, developers, contractors, and consumers. **Principal Exhibits:** Architecture, interior design, furnishings, home improvement, and remodeling equipment, supplies, and services. **Dates and Locations:** , Broward County Convention Center.

11574 ■ The Miami Home Design & Remodeling Show
Home Show Management
1450 Madruga Ave., Ste. 301
Coral Gables, FL 33146
Ph: (305)667-9299
Free: 800-353-EXPO

Fax: (305)667-3266
Co. E-mail: info@homeshows.net
URL: http://www.homeshows.net
URL(s): www.homeshows.net. **Price:** $8, Onsite. **Frequency:** Annual. **Audience:** Designers, decorators, builders, developers, contractors, and consumers. **Principal Exhibits:** Architecture, interior design, furnishings, home improvements, and remodeling equipment, supplies, and services.

CONSULTANTS

11575 ■ A.P. Designs
33 Merrall Dr., Ste. 1
Lawrence, NY 11559
Ph: (516)239-2931
Fax: (516)239-2932
Contact: Ann Pollack, President
Scope: Provider of interior design business services. Industries served: All industries and individuals requiring interior design services. **Founded:** 1975.

11576 ■ Chambers Ltd.
1800 Washington Blvd., Ste. 111
Baltimore, MD 21230
Ph: (410)727-4535
Fax: (410)727-6982
Co. E-mail: rsnellinger@chambersusa.com
URL: http://www.chambersusa.com
Contact: Richard A. Snellinger, President
E-mail: rsnellinger@chambersusa.com
Scope: Performs architecture, interior design, planning and consulting work for the club, residential, commercial, banking, industrial, hotel, health care, restaurant, governmental and educational communities. **Founded:** 1899.

11577 ■ Ogden Roemer Wilkerson Architecture
2950 E Barnett Rd.
Medford, OR 97504
Ph: (541)779-5237
Fax: (541)772-8472
Co. E-mail: office@orwarch.com
URL: http://www.orwarchitecture.com
Contact: Warren Barnhart, Manager
Scope: Consultants active in architecture interior design, planning, as well as city, urban and site and master planning. Specific expertise in schools, hospitals, assisted living facilities and historic building evaluation. **Founded:** 1968. **Seminars:** City Of Medford, Mar, 2010.

FRANCHISES AND BUSINESS OPPORTUNITIES

11578 ■ Deck the Walls
Franchise Concepts, Inc.
101 S Hanley Rd., No. 1280
St. Louis, MO 63105
Free: 800-543-3325
Co. E-mail: franinfo@FClbiz.com
URL: http://www.deckthewalls.com
Description: Art and custom framing retail stores located in regional malls. **No. of Franchise Units:** 49. **Founded:** 1979.. **Franchised:** 1981. **Equity Capital Needed:** $250,000. **Franchise Fee:** $30,000. **Training:** Classroom and in-store training prepare franchisees for all aspects of business, including custom framing. Support includes: site, lease, construction aid; national buying power; vendor network and national marketing.

11579 ■ Decor & You, Inc.
900 Main St. S, Bldg. 2
Southbury, CT 06488
Ph: (203)264-2131
Fax: (203)264-5095
Co. E-mail: info@decorandyou.com
URL: http://www.decorandyou.com
Description: State of the art computerized sampling and personalized services from professionally trained interior decorators. **No. of Franchise Units:** 70. **Founded:** 1994.. **Franchised:** 1998. **Equity Capital Needed:** $54,100-$61,800 total investment. **Franchise Fee:** $25,000. **Training:** 4 phase training program for all franchisees. All aspects of the

decorating business are covered, including color and design, trends, product knowledge, client development, follow-up skills, advertising and virtual decorating through computer graphics.

COMPUTER SYSTEMS/ SOFTWARE

11580 ■ *Design Your Own Home*
PO Box 23333
Eugene, OR 97402
Ph: (541)431-0592
Free: 800-451-4871
Fax: (541)431-0592
Co. E-mail: sales@theliquidateher.com
URL: http://www.theliquidateher.com
Description: Offers several design programs, including Architecture, Interiors, Landscape, and Libraries. Provides methods for determining structural details and drawing floor plans.

11581 ■ *Microspot Interiors*
418 S Military Tr.
Deerfield Beach, FL 33441
Ph: (561)395-9996
Free: 800-622-7568
Fax: (561)395-9941
Co. E-mail: sales@microspot.com
URL: http://www.macroenter.com
Price: $229.00. **Description:** Available for Apple Macintosh and Macintosh Plus computers. System provides an interior design program. Formerly Microspot Interiors.

LIBRARIES

11582 ■ American Intercontinental University Library
231 N. Martingale Rd., 6th Fl.
Schaumburg, IL 60173
Ph: (847)851-5000
Free: 877-701-3800
Fax: (866)647-9403
URL: http://www.aiuniv.edu
Scope: Fashion, busines, commercial art, costume history, interior design, information technology, criminal justice, media production. **Services:** Library not open to the public. **Founded:** 1982. **Holdings:** 25,000 books; 225 bound periodical volumes; 25,000 microfiche; fashion clipping file. **Subscriptions:** 200 journals and other serials; 15 newspapers.

11583 ■ City College of City University of New York - Art Visual Resources Library
Compton-Goethals, Rm. 245A
160 Convent Ave.
New York, NY 10031
Ph: (212)650-7175
Fax: (212)650-7604
Co. E-mail: artimage@ccny.cuny.edu
URL: http://www.ccny.cuny.edu/library/art_resources/index.cfm
Contact: Ching-Jung Chen, Curator
Scope: Art, architecture, design. **Services:** Library not open to the public. **Holdings:** 100,000 slides. **Telecommunication Services:** cchen@ccny.cuny.edu.

11584 ■ Conde Nast Publications Library and Information Services
4 Times Sq.
New York, NY 10036
Ph: (212)286-2860
Co. E-mail: communications@condenast.com
URL: http://www.condenastdigital.com
Contact: Sarah Chubb, President
Scope: Fashion, houses, gardens, home furnishings, interior design, health, personalities, photographs. **Services:** Library not open to public. **Founded:** 1935. **Holdings:** 7000 volumes. **Subscriptions:** 200 journals and other serials; 4 newspapers.

11585 ■ Craigdarroch Castle
1050 Joan Crescent
Victoria, BC, Canada V8S 3L5
Ph: (250)592-5323

Fax: (250)592-1099
Co. E-mail: info@thecastle.ca
URL: http://www.thecastle.ca
Contact: Bruce Davies, Curator
Scope: Nineteenth Century European and North American domestic material. **Services:** Library open by appointment to serious researchers only. **Founded:** 1959. **Holdings:** Photographs; documents; memorabilia; graphic materials; moving images; sound recordings; textual records.

11586 ■ CUH2A, Inc. Library
1000 Lenox Drive
Lawrenceville, NJ 08540-6298
Ph: (609)452-1212
Fax: (609)719-7700
Co. E-mail: smoss@cuh2a.com
URL: http://www.cuh2a.com
Contact: Susan Moss, Manager, Information
  Services
Scope: Architecture, engineering, graphic arts, interior design. **Services:** Interlibrary loan; copying; SDI; Library open to the public for reference use only. **Founded:** 1981. **Holdings:** 2500 books. **Subscriptions:** 124 journals and other serials; 2 newspapers.

11587 ■ Leo A. Daly Company Library
1357 Kapiolani Blvd., Ste. 1230
Honolulu, HI 96814-4537
Ph: (808)521-8889
Fax: (808)521-3757
Co. E-mail: info@leoadaly.com
URL: http://www.leoadaly.com
Contact: Donna L. Ching, Director, Business
  Development
Scope: Structural engineering, precast and prestressed concrete, architecture, planning, interior design. **Services:** Reference services for librarians and qualified researchers; library not open to the public. **Founded:** 1960. **Holdings:** 2500 books; 33 bound periodical volumes; 46 VF drawers of clippings, archives, photographs, manufacturers' literature; slides; maps. **Subscriptions:** 75 journals and other serials; 6 newspapers.

11588 ■ Fashion Institute of Technology - Gladys Marcus Library
7th Ave. at 27th St.
E-Bldg. E502
New York, NY 10001-5992
Ph: (212)217-4340
Fax: (212)217-4371
Co. E-mail: greta_earnest@fitnyc.edu
URL: http://www.fitnyc.edu/library.asp
Contact: Prof. N.J. Wolfe, Director, Library Services
Scope: Costume, fashion, interior design, management engineering technology, fashion buying and merchandising, textiles, toy design, packaging design, advertising. **Services:** Interlibrary loan; copying; library open to the public for reference use only by appointment. **Founded:** 1944. **Holdings:** 130,260

books; 113,265 nonprint units; 20,637 bound periodical volumes; 125,000 fashion slides; 4712 reels of microfilm; 438 CD-ROM serials and digital monographs. **Subscriptions:** 4000 journals and other serials. **Telecommunication Services:** nj_wolfe@fitnyc. edu.

11589 ■ Furniture Library Association Library
1009 N. Main St.
High Point, NC 27262
Ph: (336)883-4011
Fax: (336)883-6579
Co. E-mail: info@furniturelibrary.com
URL: http://www.furniturelibrary.com
Scope: Early architecture; design - interior, furniture, fabric; furniture styles, 1600 to present. **Services:** Photographing; library is open to the public. **Founded:** 1970. **Holdings:** 7000 books; bound periodical volumes, including over 100 years of furniture catalogs; Furniture World; trade journals. **Subscriptions:** 10 journals and other serials.

11590 ■ Harrington College of Design - Design Library
200 W. Madison St., 2nd Fl.
Chicago, IL 60606-3433
Ph: (312)697-3318
Free: 866-590-4423
Fax: (312)939-8005
Co. E-mail: elaine@interiordesign.edu
URL: http://www.harrington.edu
Contact: Elaine Lowenthal, Director, Library Services
Scope: Architecture, design, building materials, furniture, decorative arts, modern design. **Services:** Interlibrary loan; copying; library open to the public by appointment for reference use only and with referral from another library . **Founded:** 1974. **Holdings:** 22,000 books; 900 bound periodical volumes; 23,000 slides; 450 videotapes; 35,000 digital images. **Subscriptions:** 125 journals and other serials.

11591 ■ Hillwood Museum & Gardens - Art Research Library
4155 Linnean Ave., NW
Washington, DC 20008
Ph: (202)243-3953
Fax: (202)966-7846
Co. E-mail: plynagh@hillwoodmuseum.org
URL: http://www.hillwoodmuseum.org/research-
  resources/art-research-library
Contact: Pat Lynagh, Assistant Librarian
Scope: Art - decorative, French, Russian; Russian imperial history; interior design. **Services:** Copying; library open to the public by appointment. **Founded:** 1960. **Holdings:** 30,000 volumes; 16,000 auction catalogs; pamphlets. **Subscriptions:** 30 journals and other serials.

11592 ■ Illinois Institute of Art/Schaumburg - Learning Resource Center
1000 N. Plaza Dr., Ste. 100
Schaumburg, IL 60173-4913

Ph: (847)619-3450
Free: 800-314-3450
Fax: (847)619-3064
URL: http://www.artinstitutes.edu/schaumburg/
Scope: Graphic design, interior design, applied art and design, furniture history. **Services:** Interlibrary loan. **Founded:** 1985. **Holdings:** Books; slides; periodicals; videotapes; DVDs; CD-ROMs. **Subscriptions:** 175 journals and other serials.

11593 ■ University of Nevada, Las Vegas - Architecture Studies Library
Box 454049
4505 Maryland Pkwy.
Las Vegas, NV 89154-4049
Ph: (702)895-1959
Fax: (702)895-1975
Co. E-mail: caroline.smith@unlv.edu
URL: http://www.library.unlv.edu/arch/index.html
Contact: Caroline Smith, Director
Scope: Architecture - history, design, theory, and criticism; landscape architecture; interior design; construction; urban planning. **Services:** Interlibrary loan; copying; scanners; Library open to the public. **Founded:** 1997. **Holdings:** 25,000 volumes; 600 videos/DVDs; archives; microfiche and microfilm. **Subscriptions:** 150 journals and other serials.

11594 ■ Watkins College of Art, Design, & Film Library
2298 Rosa L. Parks Blvd.
Nashville, TN 37228
Ph: (615)277-7427
Fax: (615)383-4849
Co. E-mail: library@watkins.edu
URL: http://www.watkins.edu/library
Contact: Lisa Williams, Director, Library Services
Scope: Film, fine arts, interior design, graphic design, photography. **Services:** Interlibrary loan; Library open to the public for reference use only. **Holdings:** 11,600 books; 1200 videotapes and films. **Subscriptions:** 50 journals and other serials; 11 newspapers. **Telecommunication Services:** lwilliams@watkins.edu.

11595 ■ Woodbury University Library
7500 Glenoaks Blvd.
Burbank, CA 91504-1052
Ph: (818)252-5201
Fax: (818)767-4534
Co. E-mail: jennifer.rosenfeld@woodbury.edu
URL: http://library.woodbury.edu
Contact: Nedra Peterson, Director
Scope: Business and management, International business, art, architecture, interior design, fashion marketing and design, psychology, animation. **Services:** Interlibrary loan; copying; Library open to the public for reference use only. **Founded:** 1884. **Holdings:** 65,000 books; 3070 bound periodical volumes; 17,401 slides; 2000 DVD/VHS. **Subscriptions:** 300 journals and other serials; 5 newspapers. **Telecommunication Services:** nedra.peterson@woodbury. edu.

START-UP INFORMATION

11596 ■ *101 Internet Businesses You Can Start from Home: How to Choose and Build Your Own Successful E-Business*
Pub: Maximum Press
Ed: Susan Sweeney. **Released:** June 2006. **Price:** $29.95. **Description:** Guide for starting and growing an Internet business; information for developing a business plan, risk levels, and promotional techniques are included.

11597 ■ *How to Start an Internet Sales Business*
Pub: Lulu.com
Ed: Dan Davis. **Released:** August 2005. **Price:** $19.95. **Description:** Small business guide for launching an Internet sales company. Topics include business structure, licenses, and taxes.

11598 ■ *"Online Fortunes" in Small Business Opportunities (Fall 2008)*
Pub: Entrepreneur Media Inc.
Description: Fifty hot, e-commerce enterprises for the aspiring entrepreneur to consider are featured; virtual assistants, marketing services, party planning, travel services, researching, web design and development, importing as well as creating an online store are among the businesses featured.

11599 ■ *Start Your Own Net Services Business*
Pub: Entrepreneur Press
Contact: Perlman Neil, President
Released: February 1, 2009. **Price:** $17.95. **Description:** Web design, search engine marketing, new-media online, and blogging, are currently the four most popular web services available. This book provides information to start a net service business.

11600 ■ *Starting an Ebay Business for Canadians for Dummies*
Pub: John Wiley & Sons, Incorporated
Ed: Marsha Collier; Bill Summers. **Released:** February 2007. **Price:** $35.99. **Description:** Tips for turning a hobby into a successful online eBay company.

11601 ■ *Starting a Yahoo! Business for Dummies*
Pub: John Wiley & Sons, Incorporated
Ed: Rob Snell. **Released:** June 2006. **Price:** $24.99. **Description:** Rob Snell offers advice for turning on-line browsers into buyers, increase online traffic, and build an online store from scratch.

11602 ■ *Starting a Yahoo! Business For Dummies*
Pub: John Wiley & Sons, Incorporated
Ed: Rob Snell. **Released:** May 27, 2006. **Price:** $24.99. **Description:** Advice helps turn Web browsers into buyers, boost online traffic, and information to launch a profitable online business.

11603 ■ *"Startup Aims to Cut Out Coupon Clipping" in The Business Journal-Serving Metropolitan Kansas City (Vol. 26, August 15,*

2008, No. 49)
Pub: American City Business Journals, Inc.
Ed: Suzanna Stagemeyer. **Description:** TDP Inc., who started operations 18 months ago, aims to transform stale coupon promotions using technology by digitizing the entire coupon process. The process is expected to enable consumers to hunt coupons online where they will be automatically linked to loyalty cards. Other views and information on TDP and its services are presented.

ASSOCIATIONS AND OTHER ORGANIZATIONS

11604 ■ **Internet Society (ISOC)—ISOC**
1775 Wiehle Ave., Ste. 201
Reston, VA 20190-5158
Ph: (703)439-2120
Fax: (703)326-9881
Co. E-mail: isoc@isoc.org
URL: http://www.isoc.org
Contact: Lynn St. Amour, President
URL(s): www.isoc.org/isoc/contact.shtml. **Description:** Technologists, developers, educators, researchers, government representatives, and business people. Seeks to ensure global cooperation and coordination for the Internet and related internetworking technologies and applications. Supports the development and dissemination of standards for the Internet. Promotes the growth of Internet architecture and Internet-related education and research. Encourages assistance to technologically developing countries in implementing local Internet infrastructures. **Founded:** 1992. **Publications:** *ISOC Forum* (Monthly); *IETF Journal; ISP Column.* **Educational Activities:** Internet Society Conference (Annual); Symposium on Network and Distributed System Security (Annual). **Awards:** Internet Society Fellowships to the IETF; Jonathan B. Postel Memorial Service Award (Annual).

11605 ■ **World Organization of Webmasters (WOW)**
PO Box 1743
Folsom, CA 95630
Ph: (916)989-2933
Fax: (916)987-3022
Co. E-mail: info@joinwow.org
URL: http://webprofessionals.org
Contact: Bill Cullifer, Executive Director
Description: Individuals who create, manage, market, or maintain websites. Seeks to advance the profession of website creation and management; promotes the online industries. Represents members' interests; facilitates communication and cooperation among members. **Founded:** 1996. **Awards:** Web Professional Awards (Annual).

DIRECTORIES OF EDUCATIONAL PROGRAMS

11606 ■ *Internet Industry Almanac: The Complete Guide to the Ever-Changing*

Internet Industry
Pub: Computer Industry Almanac Inc.
Contact: Dr. Egil Juliussen, President
E-mail: ej@c-i-a.com
URL(s): www.c-i-a.com. **Price:** $50, Individuals paperback; $60, Individuals hardcover. **Publication includes:** Lists of Internet companies; Internet publications; Internet research and testing companies; Internet conferences; Internet people; Internet resource directory; Internet publishers; Internet associations and organizations; and Internet conference companies. Principal content of publication is information about the Internet industry, including a definition of the Internet, employment data, Internet humor, salary information, Internet market forecasts, and technology forecasts. **Arrangement:** By industry.

REFERENCE WORKS

11607 ■ *10 Steps to Successful Social Networking for Business*
Pub: ASTD
Contact: Tony Bingham, President
E-mail: tbingham@astd.org
Ed: Darin Hartley. **Released:** July 1, 2010. **Price:** $19.95. **Description:** Designed for today's fast-paced, need-it-yesterday business environment and for the thousands of workers who find themselves faced with new assignments, responsibilities, and requirements and too little time to learn what they must know.

11608 ■ *"The 40-Year-Old Intern" in Entrepreneur (Vol. 37, October 2009, No. 10, pp. 90)*
Pub: Entrepreneur Media, Inc.
Ed: Kristin Ladd. **Description:** Brian Kurth's VocationVacation is an internship program aimed at helping people experience their dream job. The website, launched in January 2004, matches people with businesses that allow them to experience their fantasy jobs.

11609 ■ *"529.com Wins Outstanding Achievement in Web Development" in Investment Weekly (November 14, 2009, pp. 152)*
Pub: Investment Weekly News
Description: Web Marketing Association's 2009 WebAward for Financial Services Standard of Excellence and Investment Standard of Excellence was won by 529.com, the website from Upromise Investments, Inc., the leading administrator of 529 college savings plans.

11610 ■ *"Aiming at a Moving Web Target" in Entrepreneur (Vol. 37, August 2009, No. 8, pp. 30)*
Pub: Entrepreneur Media, Inc.
Ed: Dan O'Shea. **Description:** Rapidly increasing numbers of businesspeople are web surfing on mobile phones. To make a website that is accessible to people on the move, the main page should be light

on images and graphics and the most important information should be put near the top. A more intensive route is to create a separate mobile-specific website.

11611 ■ *"Airlines Mount PR Push to Win Public Support Against Big Oil" in Advertising Age (Vol. 79, July 14, 2008, No. 7, pp. 1)*

Pub: Crain Communications, Inc.

Ed: Michael Bush. **Description:** Top airline executives from competing companies have banded together in a public relations plan in which they are sending e-mails to their frequent fliers asking for aid in lobbying legislators to put a restriction on oil speculation.

11612 ■ *"All About The Benjamins" in Canadian Business (Vol. 81, September 29, 2008, No. 16, pp. 92)*

Pub: Rogers Media Ltd.

Ed: David Baines. **Description:** Discusses real estate developer Royal Indian Raj International Corp., a company that planned to build a $3 billion 'smart city' near the Bangalore airport; to this day nothing has ever been built. The company was incorporated in 1999 by Manoj C. Benjamin one investor, Bill Zack, has been sued by the developer for libel due to his website that calls the company a scam. Benjamin has had a previous case of fraud issued against him as well as a string of liabilities and lawsuits.

11613 ■ *"All Those Applications, and Phone Users Just Want to Talk" in Advertising Age (Vol. 79, August 11, 2008, No. 31, pp. 18)*

Pub: Crain Communications, Inc.

Ed: Mike Vorhaus. **Description:** Although consumers are slowly coming to text messaging and other data applications, a majority of those Americans surveyed stated that they simply want to use their cell phones to talk and do not care about other activities. Statistical data included.

11614 ■ *"Analyzing the Analytics" in Entrepreneur (Vol. 37, October 2009, No. 10, pp. 42)*

Pub: Entrepreneur Media, Inc.

Ed: Mikal E. Belicove. **Description:** Startups can maximize Web analytics by using them to monitor traffic sources and identify obstacles to converting them into targeted behaviors . Startups should set trackable Web site goals and continuously track traffic and conversion rates.

11615 ■ *"Anything Could Happen" in Inc. (March 2008, pp. 116-123)*

Pub: Gruner & Jahr USA Publishing

Ed: Max Chafkin. **Description:** Profile of Evan Williams, founder of Blogger and Twitter, a new type of technology idea; Williams answers ten questions and share insight into growing both of his companies.

11616 ■ *"Apparel Apparatchic at Kmart" in Barron's (Vol. 88, March 17, 2008, No. 11, pp. 16)*

Pub: Dow Jones & Company, Inc.

Description: Kmart began a nationwide search for women to represent the company in a national advertising campaign. Contestants need to upload their photos to Kmart's website and winners will be chosen by a panel of celebrity judges. The contest aims to reverse preconceived negative notions about the store's quality and service.

11617 ■ *"Apps For Anybody With an Idea" in Advertising Age (Vol. 79, October 20, 2008, No. 39, pp. 29)*

Pub: Crain Communications, Inc.

Ed: Beth Snyder Bulik. **Description:** Apple's new online App Store is open to anyone with an idea and the ability to write code and many of these developers are not only finding a sense of community through this venue but are also making money since the sales are split with Apple, 30/70 in the developer's favor.

11618 ■ *"Are Offline Pushes Important to E-Commerce?" in DM News (Vol. 31,*

September 14, 2009, No. 23, pp. 10)

Pub: Haymarket Media, Inc.

Description: With the importance of Internet marketing and the popularity of ecommerce increasing experts debate the relevance of more traditional channels of advertising.

11619 ■ *"Attention, Please" in Entrepreneur (Vol. 36, April 2008, No. 4, pp. 52)*

Pub: Entrepreneur Media, Inc.

Ed: Andrea Cooper. **Description:** Gurbaksh Chahal created his own company ClickAgents at the age of 16, and sold it two years later for $40 million to ValueClick. He then founded BlueLithium, an online advertising network on behavioral targeting, which Yahoo! Inc. bought in 2007 for $300 million. Chahal, now 25, talks about his next plans and describes how BlueLithium caught Yahoo's attention.

11620 ■ *"Attorney Internet Marketing Services Launched by SEO Advantage at SEOLegal.com" in Internet Wire (October 5, 2009)*

Pub: Comtex News Network, Inc.

Description: SEO Advantage, an Internet marketing and website designer firm, has extended its services to the legal industry.

11621 ■ *"Attract More Online Customers: Make Your Website Work Harder for You" in Black Enterprise (Vol. 37, November 2006, No. 4, pp. 66)*

Pub: Earl G. Graves Publishing Co. Inc.

Description: Having an impressive presence on the Internet has become crucial. Detailed advice on making your website serve your business in the best way possible is included.

11622 ■ *"Auto Show Taps Moms" in Marketing to Women (Vol. 21, April 2008, No. 4, pp. 3)*

Pub: EPM Communications Inc.

Contact: Ira Mayer, President

E-mail: imayer@epmcom.com

Description: Teamed with Mother Proof, an online site which features automotive content aimed at moms, the Chicago Auto Show will present a full day of programming with the emphasis on mom.

11623 ■ *"avVaa World Health Care Products Rolls Out Internet Marketing Program" in Health and Beauty Close-Up (September 18, 2009)*

Pub: Close-Up Media

Description: avVaa World Health Care Products, Inc., a biotechnology company, manufacturer and distributor of nationally branded therapeutic, natural health care and skin products, has signed an agreement with Online Performance Marketing to launch of an Internet marketing campaign in order to broaden its presence online. The impact of advertising on the Internet to generate an increase in sales is explored.

11624 ■ *"The Bankrate Double Pay" in Barron's (Vol. 88, March 24, 2008, No. 12, pp. 27)*

Pub: Dow Jones & Company, Inc.

Ed: Neil A. Martin. **Description:** Shares of Bankrate may rise as much as 25 percent from their level of $45.08 a share due to a strong cash flow and balance sheet. The company's Internet business remains strong despite weakness in the online advertising industry and is a potential takeover target.

11625 ■ *"Banks Fall Short in Online Services for Savvy Traders" in Barron's (Vol. 88, March 17, 2008, No. 11, pp. 35)*

Pub: Dow Jones & Company, Inc.

Ed: Theresa W. Carey. **Description:** Banc of America Investment Services, WellsTrade, and ShareBuilder are at the bottom of the list of online brokerages because they offer less trading technologies and product range. Financial shoppers miss out on a lot of customized tools and analytics when using these services.

11626 ■ *"BayTSP, NTT Data Corp. Enter Into Reseller Pact to Market Online IP Monitoring" in Professional Services Close-Up (Sept. 11, 2009)*

Pub: Close-Up Media

Description: Due to incredible interest from distributors and content owners across Asia, NTT Data Corp. will resell BayTSP's online intellectual property monitoring, enforcement, business intelligence and monetization services in Japan.

11627 ■ *"Be Wary of Legal Advice on Internet, Lawyers Warn" in Crain's Detroit Business (Vol. 24, September 22, 2008, No. 38, pp. 16)*

Pub: Crain Communications Inc.

Ed: Harriet Tramer. **Description:** While some lawyers feel that the proliferation of legal information on the Internet can point people in the right direction, others maintain that it simply results in giving false hope, may bring about confusion or worse yet, it sometimes makes their jobs even harder.

11628 ■ *"Being all a-Twitter" in Canadian Business (Vol. 81, December 8, 2008, No. 21, pp. 22)*

Pub: Rogers Media Ltd.

Ed: Andrew Wahl. **Description:** Marketing experts suggest that advertising strategies have to change along with new online social media. Companies are advised to find ways to incorporate social software because workers and customers are expected to continue its use.

11629 ■ *"Blacks Go Broadband: High Speed Internet Adoption Grows Among African Americans" in Black Enterprise (Vol. 38, February 2008)*

Pub: Earl G. Graves Publishing Co. Inc.

Ed: Cliff Hocker. **Description:** Number of black households using broadband Internet services tripled since 2005 according to a survey conducted by Pew Internet and American Life Project.

11630 ■ *"Blockbuster Launches Internet Movie Downloads to Compete Against Netflix, Others" in Chicago Tribune (December 3, 2008)*

Pub: McClatchy-Tribune Information Services

Ed: Eric Benderoff. **Description:** Blockbuster Inc., the DVD rental giant, has launched a new service that delivers movies to their customer's homes via the Internet in an attempt to compete against Netflix and other competitors.

11631 ■ *"Blog Buzz Heralds Arrival of IPhone 2.0" in Advertising Age (Vol. 79, June 9, 2008, No. 40, pp. 8)*

Pub: Crain Communications, Inc.

Ed: Abbey Klaasen. **Description:** Predictions concerning the next version of the iPhone include a global-positioning-system technology as well as a configuration to run on a faster, 3G network.

11632 ■ *"Boom has Tech Grads Mulling Their Options" in Globe & Mail (March 14, 2006, pp. B1)*

Pub: CTVglobemedia Publishing Inc.

Ed: Grant Robertson. **Description:** Internet giant Google Inc. has stepped up its efforts to hire the talented people, in Canada, at Waterloo University in southern Ontario, to expand its operations. The details of the job market and increasing salaries are analyzed.

11633 ■ *"Borders Previews New Web Site" in Crain's Detroit Business (Vol. 23, October 8, 2007, No. 41, pp. 4)*

Pub: Crain Communications Inc. - Detroit

Ed: Sheena Harrison. **Description:** Borders Group Inc. previewed its new Website that allows customers to buy items that include the Magic Shelf, a virtual bookcase that displays available recommended books, movies and music.

11634 ■ *"Bottoms Up!" in Entrepreneur (Vol. 36, April 2008, No. 4, pp. 128)*

Pub: Entrepreneur Media, Inc.

Ed: Amanda C. Kooser. **Description:** Jill Bernheimer launched her online alcohol business Domaine547 in 2007, and encountered challenges as legal issues over the licensing and launching of the business took about seven months to finish. Domain547 features blog and forum areas. Marketing strategy that connects to the social community is one of the ways to reach out to customers.

11635 ■ *"Branding Your Way" in Canadian Business (Vol. 80, February 12, 2007, No. 4, pp. 31)*
Pub: Rogers Media

Ed: Erin Pooley. **Description:** The trend in involving consumers in brand marketing by seeking their views through contests or inviting them to produce and submit commercials through Internet is discussed.

11636 ■ *"Break Up the Gang?" in Canadian Business (Vol. 81, November 10, 2008, No. 19, pp. 24)*
Pub: Rogers Media Ltd.

Ed: Andrew Wahl. **Description:** Nortel Networks Corporation announced they will their Metro Ethernet Network division, suggesting desperation on the part of the company. Some analysts suggest the division is promising, if still unprofitable.

11637 ■ *"Brite-Strike Tactical Launches New Internet Marketing Initiatives" in Internet Wire (September 15, 2009)*
Pub: Comtex News Network, Inc.

Description: Brite-Strike Tactical Illumination Products, Inc. has enlisted the expertise of Internet marketing guru Thomas J. McCarthy to help revamp the company's Internet campaign. An outline of the Internet marketing strategy is provided.

11638 ■ *"Broadband Reaches Access Limits in Europe" in Information Today (Vol. 26, February 2009, No. 2, pp. 22)*
Pub: Information Today, Inc.

Ed: Jim Ashling. **Description:** Eurostat (the Statistical Office of the European communities) reports results from is survey regarding Internet use by businesses throughout its 27-member states. Iceland, Finland and the Netherlands provide the most access at broadband speeds, followed by Belgium, Spain and France.

11639 ■ *"BusinessOnLine Launches a New Web-Based Search Engine Optimization Tool" in Internet Wire (October 19, 2009)*
Pub: Comtex News Network, Inc.

Description: First Link Checker, a complimentary new search engine optimization tool that helps site owners optimize their on-page links by understanding which of those links are actually being counted in Google's relevancy algorithm, was developed by BusinessOnLine, a rapidly growing Internet marketing agency. This tool will make it easy for the average web master to ensure that their internal link structure is optimized.

11640 ■ *"Campaigner Survey: 46 Percent of Small Businesses Use Email Marketing" in Wireless News (November 21, 2009)*
Pub: Close-Up Media

Description: Almost half (46 percent) of small businesses surveyed by Campaigner's 2009 State of Small Business Online Marketing, say that they rely on email marketing to help them find new customers, keep existing ones and grow their businesses. The survey also found that 36 percent of small businesses plan to begin using email marketing over the next year. The trend to utilize Internet marketing tools is allowing small businesses to grow faster and generate higher revenues than those that are not using these mediums.

11641 ■ *"Canadians Keep Memories in 'Inboxes' Instead of Shoe Boxes; MSN Canada" in Canadian Corporate News (May 14, 2007)*
Pub: Comtex News Network Inc.

Description: According to an MSN Canada online poll, 76 percent of Canadians are creating 'virtual shoeboxes' with their email inboxes and archiving important messages, photos, and documents.

11642 ■ *"CarTango Lauches Site for Women" in Marketing to Women (Vol. 21, April 2008, No. 4, pp. 5)*
Pub: EPM Communications Inc.
Contact: Ira Mayer, President
E-mail: imayer@epmcom.com

Description: CarTango.com is an Internet site that seeks to overcome what women say are dismissive or pushy salespeople by allowing the shoppers the chance to decide what they want before inviting dealers to compete for their business.

11643 ■ *"Cell Phone the Ticket on American Airlines" in Chicago Tribune (November 14, 2008)*
Pub: McClatchy-Tribune Information Services

Ed: Julie Johnsson. **Description:** American Airlines is testing a new mobile boarding pass at O'Hare International Airport. Travelers on American can board flights and get through security checkpoints by flashing a bar code on their phones. Passengers must have an Internet-enabled mobile device and an active e-mail address in order to utilize this service.

11644 ■ *"Charlotte Pipe Launches Satirical Campaign" in Contractor (Vol. 57, January 2010, No. 1, pp. 6)*
Pub: Penton Media, Inc.

Description: Charlotte Pipe and Foundry Co. launched an advertising campaign that uses social media and humor to make a point about how it can be nearly impossible to determine if imported cast iron pipes and fittings meet the same quality standards as what is made in the U.S. The campaign features 'pipe whisperers' and also spoofs pipe sniffing dogs.

11645 ■ *"Chris Curtis Preaches the Gospel of Internet Success" in Black Enterprise (Vol. 38, March 2008, No. 8, pp. 56)*
Pub: Earl G. Graves Publishing Co. Inc.

Ed: Anthony Calypso. **Description:** Profile of the Web Business Ownership Series, a collection of 20 free seminars that help small businesses learn about the Web development process.

11646 ■ *Cisco Network Design Solutions for Small-Medium Businesses*
Pub: Cisco Press

Ed: Peter Rybaczyk. **Released:** August 2004. **Price:** $55.00. **Description:** Solutions for computer networking professionals using computer networks within a small to medium-sized business. Topics cover not only core networking issues and solutions, but security, IP telephony, unified communications, customer relations management, wireless LANs, and more.

11647 ■ *"A Class Act" in Hawaii Business (Vol. 53, March 2008, No. 9, pp. 25)*
Pub: Hawaii Business Publishing

Ed: Cathy S. Cruz-George. **Description:** UBoost is a startup company that offers online content for the educational magazine 'Weekly Reader'. The website features quizzes and allows users to accumulate points and redeem rewards afterward. Other details about the company are discussed.

11648 ■ *"ClickFuel Launches New Products to Help Small and Mid-Sized Businesses Bolster Their Brand Online" in Internet Wire (Dec. 3,2009)*
Pub: Comtex News Network, Inc.

Description: Boostability, a provider of Enterprise Search Engine Optimization (SEO) software technology, has partnered with ClickFuel, a firm that designs, tracks and manages Internet marketing campaigns in order to leverage Boostability's technology in order to deliver comprehensive SEO solutions to small and mid-size businesses; three new products will also become available for these business clients to help them manage all facets of their online presence.

11649 ■ *"ClickFuel Launches New Products to Help Small and Mid-Sized Businesses Bolster Their Brand Online" in Internet Wire*

(Dec. 3, 2009)
Pub: Comtex News Network, Inc.

Description: Boostability, a provider of Enterprise Search Engine Optimization (SEO) software technology, has partnered with ClickFuel, a firm that designs, tracks and manages Internet marketing campaigns in order to leverage Boostability's technology in order to deliver comprehensive SEO solutions to small and mid-size businesses; three new products will also become available for these business clients to help them manage all facets of their online presence.

11650 ■ *"ClickFuel Unveils Internet Marketing Tools for Small Businesses" in Internet Wire (October 19, 2009)*
Pub: Comtex News Network, Inc.

Description: ClickFuel, a firm that manages, designs and tracks marketing campaigns has unveiled a full software suite of affordable services and technology solutions designed to empower small business owners and help them promote and grow their businesses through targeted Internet marketing campaigns.

11651 ■ *Clicking Through: A Survival Guide for Bringing Your Company Online*
Pub: Bloomberg Press

Ed: Jonathan I. Ezor. **Released:** October 1999. **Description:** Summary of legal compliance issues faced by small companies doing business on the Internet, including copyright and patent laws.

11652 ■ *"CN to Webcast 2007 Analyst Meeting in Toronto May 23-24" in Canadian Corporate News (May 16, 2007)*
Pub: Comtex News Network Inc.

Description: Canadian National Railway Company (CN) broadcast its analyst meeting in Toronto with a webcast which focused on CN's opportunities, strategies, and financial outlook through the year 2010.

11653 ■ *"Comcast Launches New Home Security Service, Developed in Portland" in The Oregonian (June 7, 2011)*
Pub: McClatchy-Tribune Regional News

Ed: Mike Rogoway. **Description:** Comcast introduced its new high-end home security system that provides 24-hour monitoring and control of homes and utilities, along with Web and mobile access.

11654 ■ *The Complete Guide to Google Adwords: Secrets, Techniques, and Strategies You Can Learn to Make Millions*
Pub: Atlantic Publishing Company

Released: December 1, 2010. **Price:** $24.95. **Description:** Google AdWords, when it launched in 2002 signaled a fundamental shift in what the Internet was for so many individuals and companies. Learning and understanding how Google AdWords operates and how it can be optimized for maximum exposure, boosting click through rates, conversions, placement, and selection of the right keywords, can be the key to a successful online business.

11655 ■ *"Connections: United We Gab" in Entrepreneur (Vol. 35, October 2007, No. 10, pp. 60)*
Pub: Entrepreneur Media Inc.

Ed: Mike Hogan. **Description:** T-Mobile and AT&T introduced dual-mode service to consumers, helping them to switch between cellular and Wi-Fi networks easily. These services, such as Hotspot@Home, reduces the cost of long distance calls by routing them over the Internet with the use of WiFi. Benefits of dual mode service, such as lower hardware price and better call coverage are given.

11656 ■ *"Contec Innovations Inc.: MovieSet.com First to Mobilize Content Using BUZmob" in Canadian Corporate News (May 16, 2007)*
Pub: Comtex News Network Inc.

Description: Contec Innovations Inc., a provider of mobile infrastructure software, announced that MovieSet.com is the first Internet portal to mobilize their content using BUZmob, the company's new mobile publishing service that allows content publishers to enable mobile access to their feed-based content on any mobile device or network in real-time.

11657 ■ *"Conversations with Customers"* in *Business Journal Serving Greater Tampa Bay (Vol. 31, December 31, 2010, No. 1, pp. 1)*
Pub: Tampa Bay Business Journal
Description: Tampa Bay, Florida-based businesses have been using social media to interact with customers. Forty percent of businesses have been found to have at least one social media platform to reach customers and prospects.

11658 ■ *"Coping with the Web"* in *Agency Sales Magazine (Vol. 39, December 2009, No. 11, pp. 52)*
Pub: MANA
Ed: Karen Saunders. **Description:** When branding your company on the Internet, strategy should first be discussed with the website designer and the target and niche audience should also be defined. Describing 'what' and 'how' the product or service is offering is also important. In addition, perception, the logo, and the tag line are some elements that are needed to create a brand.

11659 ■ *"Cox Opens Norfolk Mall Kiosk; Wireless Service Not Ready"* in *Virginian-Pilot (September 20, 2010)*
Pub: Virginian-Pilot
Ed: Carolyn Shapiro. **Description:** Cox Communications opened a kiosk at MacArthur Center that will sell wireless telephone devices and plans.

11660 ■ *"Cross Atlantic Commodities Launches National Internet Marketing Programs"* in *Manufacturing Close-Up (September 8, 2009)*
Pub: Close-Up Media
Description: Profile of the Internet campaign recently launched by Cross Atlantic Commodities, Inc., a manufacturer of specialty beauty and health products.

11661 ■ *Crossing the Chasm: Marketing and Selling Disruptive Products to Mainstream Customers*
Pub: HarperInformation
Ed: Geoffrey A. Moore. **Released:** September 2002. **Price:** $17.95. **Description:** A guide for marketing in high-technology industries, focusing on the Internet.

11662 ■ *"Cyber Thanksgiving Online Shopping a Growing Tradition"* in *Marketing Weekly News (December 12, 2009, pp. 137)*
Pub: Investment Weekly News
Description: According to e-commerce analysts, Thanksgiving day is becoming increasingly important to retailers in terms of online sales. Internet marketers are realizing that consumers are already searching for Black Friday sales and if they find deals on the products they are looking for, they are highly likely to make their purchase on Thanksgiving day instead of waiting.

11663 ■ *"Datran Media Executives to Lead Industry Debates Across Q1 Conferences"* in *Internet Wire (January 22, 2010)*
Pub: Comtex News Network, Inc.
Description: Datran Media, an industry-leading digital marketing technology company, will be sending members of its management team to several conferences in the early part of the first quarter of 2010; discussions will include Internet marketing innovations, e-commerce and media distribution.

11664 ■ *Design and Launch Your eCommerce Business in a Week*
Pub: Entrepreneur Press
Contact: Perlman Neil, President
Ed: Jason R. Rich. **Released:** July 2008. **Price:** $17.95. **Description:** Guide to help anyone start an online business in one week; included tips for Website design.

11665 ■ *"Designing Events Updates Online Suite"* in *Wireless News (October 25, 2009)*
Pub: Close-Up Media
Description: Designing Events, an outsourcing and consulting firm for conferences and meetings, announced the release of an update to its Designing Events Online suite of web-based management and marketing tools; features include enhanced versions of online registration and collaboration, content management, session development, social media and conference websites.

11666 ■ *Designing Websites for Every Audience*
Pub: F & W Publications, Incorporated
Ed: Ilise Benun. **Released:** January 2003. **Description:** Twenty-five case studies targeting six difference audiences are used to help a business design, or make over, a Website.

11667 ■ *Digital Divide: Civic Engagement, Information Poverty, and the Internet Worldwide*
Pub: Cambridge University Press
Contact: Richard Ziemacki, President
E-mail: rziemacki@cambridge.org
Ed: Pippa Norris. **Released:** January 22, 2010. **Price:** $28.99. **Description:** The expansive growth of the Internet is intensifying existing inequalities between the information rich and poor. The book examines the evidence for access and use of the Internet in 179 countries and discusses the global divide that is evident between industrialized and developing societies.

11668 ■ *"Diving Into Internet Marketing"* in *American Agent and Broker (Vol. 81, December 2009, No. 12, pp. 24)*
Pub: Summit Business Media
Ed: Steve Anderson. **Description:** Internet marketing is becoming an essential tool for most businesses; advice is provided regarding the social networking opportunities available for marketing one's product or service on the Internet.

11669 ■ *"Do-It-Yourself Portfolio Management"* in *Barron's (Vol. 89, July 13, 2009, No. 28, pp. 25)*
Pub: Dow Jones & Co., Inc.
Ed: Mike Hogan. **Description:** Services of several portfolio management web sites are presented. These web sites include MarketRiders E.Adviser, TD Ameritrade and E.

11670 ■ *"Don't' Hate the Cable Guy"* in *Saint Louis Business Journal (Vol. 31, August 5, 2011, No. 50, pp. 1)*
Pub: Saint Louis Business Journal
Ed: Angela Mueller. **Description:** Charter Communications named John Birrer as senior vice president of customer experience. The company experienced problems with its customer services.

11671 ■ *Double or Nothing: How Two Friends Risked It All to Buy One of Las Vegas' Legendary Casinos*
Pub: HarperBusiness
Ed: Tom Breitling, with Cal Fussman. **Released:** March 2008. **Price:** $24.95. **Description:** Founders of a successful Internet travel agency share their experience from startup to selling the company.

11672 ■ *"Drive Traffic To Your Blog"* in *Women Entrepreneur (January 13, 2009)*
Pub: Entrepreneur Media Inc.
Ed: Lesley Spencer Pyle. **Description:** Internet social networking has become a vital component to marketing one's business. Tips are provided on how to establish a blog that will attract attention to one's business and keep one's customers coming back for more.

11673 ■ *"The Easy Route"* in *Entrepreneur (Vol. 36, April 2008, No. 4, pp. 60)*
Pub: Entrepreneur Media, Inc.
Ed: Amanda C. Kooser. **Description:** Buyer's guide of wireless office routers is presented. All products included in the list use the latest draft-n technology. Price and availability of the products are provided.

11674 ■ *EBay Income: How ANYONE of Any Age, Location, and/or Background Can Build a Highly Profitable Online Business with eBay*
Pub: Atlantic Publishing Company
Released: December 1, 2010. **Price:** $24.95. **Description:** A complete overview of eBay is given and guides any small company through the entire process of creating the auction and auction strategies, photography, writing copy, text and formatting, multiple sales, programming tricks, PayPal, accounting, creating marketing, merchandising, managing email lists, advertising plans, taxes and sales tax, best time to list items and for how long, sniping programs, international customers, opening a storefront, electronic commerce, buy-it now pricing, keywords, Google marketing and eBay secrets.

11675 ■ *Electronic Commerce*
Pub: Course Technology
Ed: Gary Schneider, Bryant Chrzan, Charles McCormick. **Released:** May 1, 2010. **Price:** $117.95. **Description:** E-commerce can open the door to more opportunities than ever before for small business. Packed with real-world examples and cases, the book delivers comprehensive coverage of emerging online technologies and trends and their influence on the electronic marketplace. It details how the landscape of online commerce is evolving, reflecting changes in the economy and how business and society are responding to those changes. Balancing technological issues with the strategic business aspects of successful e-commerce, the new edition includes expanded coverage of international issues, social networking, mobile commerce, Web 2.0 technologies, and updates on spam, phishing, and identity theft.

11676 ■ *Electronic Commerce: Technical, Business, and Legal Issues*
Pub: Prentice Hall PTR
Ed: Oktay Dogramaci; Aryya Gangopadhyay; Yelena Yesha; Nabil R. Adam. **Released:** August 1998. **Description:** Provides insight into the goals of using the Internet to grow a business in the areas of networking and telecommunication, security, and storage and retrieval; business areas such as marketing, procurement and purchasing, billing and payment, and supply chain management; and legal aspects such as privacy, intellectual property, taxation, contractual and legal settlements.

11677 ■ *Emerging Business Online: Global Markets and the Power of B2B Internet Marketing*
Pub: FT Press
Ed: Lara Fawzy, Lucas Dworski. **Released:** October 1, 2010. **Price:** $49.99. **Description:** An introduction into ebocube (emerging business online), a comprehensive proven business model for Internet B2B marketing in emerging markets.

11678 ■ *"Empowered"* in *Harvard Business Review (Vol. 88, July-August 2010, No. 7-8, pp. 94)*
Pub: Harvard Business School Publishing
Ed: Josh Bernoff, Ted Schadler. **Description:** HERO concept (highly empowered and resourceful operative) which builds a connection between employees, managers, and IT is outlined. The resultant additional experience and knowledge gained by employees improves customer relationship management.

11679 ■ *"Endeca Gears Up for Likely IPO Bid"* in *Boston Business Journal (Vol. 31, July 1, 2011, No. 23, pp. 1)*
Pub: Boston Business Journal
Ed: Kyle Alspach. **Description:** Endeca Inc. is readying itself for its plans to register as a public company. The search engine technology leader is enjoying continued growth with revenue up by 30 percent in 2010 while its expansion trend makes it an unlikely candidate for an acquisition.

11680 ■ *"Entrepreneur Column"* in *Entrepreneur (September 24, 2009)*
Pub: Entrepreneur Media, Inc.
Ed: Allen Moon. **Description:** In an attempt to compete with Google, Microsoft and Yahoo have entered a partnership to merge their search services; advice on the best ways to get noticed on this new search engine entitled Bing, is provided.

11681 ■ *The Facebook Effect: The Inside Story of the Company That Is Connecting the World*
Pub: Simon & Shuster
Ed: David Kirkpatrick. **Released:** June 8, 2010. **Price:** $26.00. **Description:** There's never been a Website like Facebook: more than 350 million people

have accounts, and if the growth rate continues, by 2013 every Internet user worldwide will have his or her own page. No one's had more access to the inner workings of the phenomenon than Kirkpatrick, a senior tech writer at Fortune magazine. Written with the full cooperation of founder Mark Zuckerberg, the book follows the company from its genesis in a Harvard dorm room through its successes over Friendster and MySpace, the expansion of the user base, and Zuckerberg's refusal to sell.

11682 ■ *"Fast Fact: Women's Online Habits"* in Marketing to Women (Vol. 22, July 2009, No. 7, pp. 1)
Pub: EPM Communications Inc.
Contact: Ira Mayer, President
E-mail: imayer@epmcom.com
Description: Lists the Internet habits of women. Statistical data included.

11683 ■ *"Fast Revival Unlikely For Indian 'Net Stocks"* in Barron's (Vol. 88, July 7, 2008, No. 27, pp. 12)
Pub: Dow Jones & Co., Inc.
Ed: Leslie P. Norton. **Description:** Shares of Indian Internet companies Rediff.com and Sify are not likely to stage a rebound due to weak financial results. Rediff.com shares have declined 39.2 percent in 2008, while Sify shares are down 35.8 percent.

11684 ■ *"Financo Panel Lauds Product, Online Marketing"* in Home Textiles Today (Vol. 31, January 25, 2010, No. 3, pp. 1)
Pub: Reed Business Information, Inc.
Ed: James Mammarella. **Description:** Overview of the Financo Annual Merchandising Industry Chief Executives Event during which there was much discussion on the merits of e-commerce, online marketing as well as the traditional methods of brand recognition and retailing.

11685 ■ *"Fitter from Twitter"* in Boston Business Journal (Vol. 30, December 17, 2010, No. 47, pp. 1)
Pub: Boston Business Journal
Ed: Lisa van der Pool. **Description:** Small businesses are increasing their use of the Twitter microblogging platform to attract and retain customers. Lisa Johnson, who owns Modern Pilates studios, managed to raise awareness of her personal brand nationally through the social media platform.

11686 ■ *"Five Low-Cost Home Based Startups"* in Women Entrepreneur (December 16, 2008)
Pub: Entrepreneur Media Inc.
Ed: Lesley Spencer Pyle. **Description:** During tough economic times, small businesses have an advantage over large companies because they can adjust to economic conditions more easily and without having to go through corporate red tape that can slow the implementation process. A budding entrepreneur may find success by taking inventory of his or her skills, experience, expertise and passions and utilizing those qualities to start a business. Five low-cost home-based startups are profiled. These include starting an online store, a virtual assistant service, web designer, sales representative and a home staging counselor.

11687 ■ *"Fly Phishing"* in Canadian Business (Vol. 80, October 22, 2007, No. 21, pp. 42)
Pub: Rogers Media
Ed: Andy Holloway. **Description:** Symantec Corporation's report shows consumers and companies have effectively installed network defenses that prevent unwanted access. Phishing packages are readily available and are widely used. Other details of the Internet Security Threat Report are presented.

11688 ■ *"The Folly of Google's Latest Gambit"* in Barron's (Vol. 89, July 13, 2009, No. 28, pp. 23)
Pub: Dow Jones & Co., Inc.
Ed: Eric J. Savitz. **Description:** Google will enter the operating systems business with the introduction of the Google Chrome OS but its success is dubious because the project is still a year or so away while Microsoft will release an updated version of Windows

by then; another problem is that Google already has another OS called Android which will overlap with the Chrome OS's market.

11689 ■ *"For MySpace, A Redesign to Entice Generation Y"* in The New York Times (October 27, 2010, pp. B3)
Pub: The New York Times Company
Ed: Miguel Helft. **Description:** MySpace is redesigning its Website in order to attract individuals from the Generation Y group.

11690 ■ *"ForeSee Finds Satisfaction On Web Sites, Bottom Line"* in Crain's Detroit Business (Vol. 24, February 25, 2008, No. 8, pp. 3)
Pub: Crain Communications Inc. - Detroit
Ed: Tom Henderson. **Description:** Ann Arbor-based ForeSee Results Inc. evaluates user satisfaction on Web sites. The company expects to see an increase of 40 percent in revenue for 2008 with plans to expand to London, Germany, Italy and France by the end of 2009.

11691 ■ *"Forsys Metals Corporation Goes "Live" With Q4's On-Demand Disclosure Management Software"* in Canadian Corporate News (May 16, 2007)
Pub: Comtex News Network Inc.
Description: Forsys Metals Corp. selected Q4 Web Systems to automate its corporate website disclosure with Q4's software platform which also automates and simplifies many of the administrative tasks that Forsys was doing manually, allowing them to focus their internal resources on the business.

11692 ■ *"The Fort"* in Hawaii Business (Vol. 53, November 2007, No. 5, pp. 19)
Pub: Hawaii Business Publishing
Ed: Jason Ubay. **Description:** DRFortress' flagship data center The Fort located at Honolulu's Airport Industrial Park provides companies a place to store their servers in an ultra-secure environment. Anything stored in here that requires power has a back up and in case of an outage generators can supply power up to 80 hrs. The Fort caters to major carriers and Internet service providers.

11693 ■ *"Fresh Direct's Crisis"* in Crain's New York Business (Vol. 24, January 14, 2008, No. 2, pp. 3)
Pub: Crain Communications, Inc.
Ed: Lisa Fickenscher. **Description:** Freshdirect, an Internet grocery delivery service, finds itself under siege from federal immigration authorities, customers and labor organizations due to its employment practice of hiring illegals. At stake is the grocer's reputation as well as its ambitious growth plans, including an initial public offering of its stock.

11694 ■ *"The Frugal Billionaire"* in Canadian Business (Vol. 79, Winter 2006, No. 24, pp. 63)
Pub: Rogers Media
Ed: Joe Castaldo. **Description:** The achievements of David Cheriton are described, along with his investments in various firms, including Google Inc.

11695 ■ *"Funbrain Launches Preschool Content"* in Marketing to Women (Vol. 21, March 2008, No. 3, pp. 3)
Pub: EPM Communications Inc.
Contact: Ira Mayer, President
E-mail: imayer@epmcom.com
Description: Funbrain.com launches The Moms and Kids Playground, a section of the website devoted to activities and games for moms and kids aged 2 to 6; content aims at building early computer skills and to teach basic concepts such as counting and colors.

11696 ■ *"Generation Y Chooses the Mobile Web"* in PR Newswire (November 24, 2010)
Pub: PR Newswire Association LLC
Description: Generation Y individuals between the ages of 18 - 27 use their mobile phones to browse the Internet more often than a desktop or laptop computer, according to a survey conducted by Opera, a Web browser company.

11697 ■ *"Get Online or Be Left Behind"* in Women In Business (Vol. 61, August-September 2009, No. 4, pp. 33)
Pub: American Business Women's Association
Ed: Diane Stafford. **Description:** Technology's significance for the connectivity purposes among business people is discussed. Details on the use of wireless tools and online social media to boost technology IQ are presented.

11698 ■ *"Get Them Talking"* in Entrepreneur (Vol. 36, February 2008, No. 2, pp. 50)
Pub: Entrepreneur Media Inc.
Ed: Heather Clancy. **Description:** Yelp.com is an Internet search site that presents businesses across the U.S., sorted according to the number of customer reviews they have received. One to five stars are used by the reviewers, or yelpers, to rate businesses. Details on how the International Orange day spa benefited from Yelp are discussed.

11699 ■ *"Giants Now Admit They Roam Planet Earth; Time To Buy?"* in Barron's (Vol. 88, March 31, 2008, No. 13, pp. 39)
Pub: Dow Jones & Company, Inc.
Ed: Eric J. Savitz. **Description:** Oracle's third-quarter results showed that top-line growth fell short of expectations but the company is expected to fare better than most applications companies in the downturn. Google had a flat growth in the number of people who click their online ads. The time for investors in the tech sector with a long-term horizon has arrived.

11700 ■ *"Go Beyond Local Search With Hyper-Local"* in Women Entrepreneur (October 30, 2008)
Pub: Entrepreneur Media Inc.
Ed: Lena West. **Description:** According to Forrester Research, as much as $500 billion in local spending in 2007 was influenced by the Internet and industry analysts report that consumers spend approximately 80 percent of their income within 50 miles of their home. Discussion of ways in which to capitalize on the hyper-local trend that is being driven by greater Internet connectivity and use of the web to find information is provided.

11701 ■ *"Google Edges into Wireless E-Mail"* in Globe & Mail (February 19, 2007, pp. B5)
Pub: CTVglobemedia Publishing Inc.
Ed: Simon Avery. **Description:** Google Inc. has introduced a free mobile e-mail service in Canada. The mobile users can read, send, and search messages using the new software.

11702 ■ *"Google, MySpace Deal Hits Snag"* in Globe & Mail (February 7, 2007, pp. B11)
Pub: CTVglobemedia Publishing Inc.
Ed: Julia Angwin; Kevin J. Delaney. **Description:** MySpace's intention to partner with eBay which is delaying the finalization of its $900 million online advertising deal signed with Google Inc. is discussed.

11703 ■ *"Google Places a Call to Bargain Hunters"* in Advertising Age (Vol. 79, September 29, 2008, No. 36, pp. 13)
Pub: Crain Communications, Inc.
Ed: Abbey Klaassen. **Description:** Google highlighted application developers who have created tools for its Android mobile phone in the device's unveiling; applications such as ShopSavvy and CompareEverywhere help shoppers to find bargains by allowing them to compare prices in their local areas and across the web.

11704 ■ *The Google Story: Inside the Hottest Business, Media, and Technology Success of Our Time*
Pub: Random Housing Publishing Group
Ed: David A. Vise; Mark Malseed. **Price:** $26.00.

11705 ■ *"Google's Next Stop: Below 350?"* in Barron's (Vol. 88, March 10, 2008, No. 10, pp. 17)
Pub: Dow Jones & Company, Inc.
Ed: Jacqueline Doherty. **Description:** Share prices of Google Inc. are expected to drop from their level of $433 each to below $350 per share. The company

is expected to miss its earnings forecast for the first quarter of 2008, and its continued aggressive spending on non-core areas will eventually bring down earnings.

11706 ■ *"Googly Eyed" in Entrepreneur (Vol. 36, February 2008, No. 2, pp. 48)*
Pub: Entrepreneur Media Inc.
Ed: Mike Hogan. **Description:** Linux has developed desktops that boot into the Google toolbar and applications. These desktops include: Zonbu, Everex gPCTC2502, and Asus Eee PC 4G mini laptop. Details on the applications of these desktops are discussed.

11707 ■ *"Graceful Landing" in Entrepreneur (Vol. 37, November 2009, No. 11, pp. 59)*
Pub: Entrepreneur Media, Inc.
Ed: Mikal E. Belicove. **Description:** Successful marketers regularly use Website landing pages to capture qualified leads and make sales. It is believed that an effective landing page devoted to a single product or service offering can significantly boost leads and conversion rates. Organizations can create a top-notch landing page by anticipating customer expectations and focusing on a clear call to action.

11708 ■ *Groundswell: Winning in a World Transformed by Social Technologies*
Pub: Harvard Business School Press
Ed: Charlene Li; Josh Bernoff. **Released:** April 21, 2008. **Price:** $29.95. **Description:** Individuals are using online social technologies such as blogs, social networking sites, YouTube, and podcasts to discuss products and companies, write their own news, and find their own deals. When consumers you've never met are rating your company's products in public forums with which you have no experience or influence, your company is vulnerable. This book teaches the tools and data necessary to turn this treat into an opportunity.

11709 ■ *Grown Up Digital: How the Net Generation Is Changing Your World*
Pub: The McGraw-Hill Companies
Ed: Don Tapscott. **Released:** 2009. **Price:** $27.95. **Description:** As baby boomers retire, business needs to understand what makes the Internet work for business.

11710 ■ *"Growth of Free Dailies Dropping" in Globe & Mail (March 24, 2007, pp. B7)*
Pub: CTVglobemedia Publishing Inc.
Ed: Grant Robertson. **Description:** The decrease in the readership of free newspapers in Canada, in view of growing preference for online news, is discussed.

11711 ■ *"A Hacker in India Hijacked His Website Design and Was Making Good Money Selling It" in Inc. (December 2007, pp. 77-78, 80)*
Pub: Gruner & Jahr USA Publishing
Ed: Darren Dahl. **Description:** John Anton, owner of an online custom T-shirt business and how a company in India was selling software Website templates identical to his firm's Website.

11712 ■ *"Happy Blogging" in Black Enterprise (Vol. 38, January 2008, No. 6, pp. 47)*
Pub: Earl G. Graves Publishing Co. Inc.
Ed: Sonya A. Donaldson. **Description:** Individual seeks advice for setting up a Website and starting a blog; Squarespace and Weebly both offer Web design.

11713 ■ *"Harlequin Leads the Way" in Marketing to Women (Vol. 22, July 2009, No. 7, pp. 1)*
Pub: EPM Communications Inc.
Contact: Ira Mayer, President
E-mail: imayer@epmcom.com
Description: Although the publishing industry has been slow to embrace new media options, the Internet is now a primary source for reaching women readers. Harlequin has been eager to court their female consumers over the Internet and often uses women bloggers in their campaigns strategies.

11714 ■ *"Harley-Davidson Moves to Unconventional Marketing Plan" in Business Journal-Milwaukee (Vol. 28, November 26, 2010, No. 8, pp. A1)*
Pub: Milwaukee Business Journal
Ed: Rich Rovito. **Description:** Harley Davidson Inc. hired Boulder, Colorado-based Victors & Spoils, an agency that specializes in crowdsourcing, to implement a new creative marketing model. Under the plan, Harley Davidson will draw on the ideas of its brand enthusiasts to help guide the brand's marketing direction.

11715 ■ *"Harnessing the Wisdom of Crowds" in Entrepreneur (Vol. 37, September 2009, No. 9, pp. 74)*
Pub: Entrepreneur Media, Inc.
Ed: Mark Henricks. **Description:** Online customer service business Get Satisfaction has registered growth. The business enables customers to search for answers to common product questions. Customers use the service to post questions, complaints, and even product ideas.

11716 ■ *"Has Microsoft Found a Way to Get at Yahoo?" in Advertising Age (Vol. 79, July 7, 2008, No. 26, pp. 4)*
Pub: Crain Communications, Inc.
Ed: Abbey Klaassen. **Description:** Microsoft's attempt to acquire Yahoo's search business is discussed as is Yahoo's plans for the future at a time when the company's shares have fallen dangerously low.

11717 ■ *"HBC Enlists IBM to Help Dress Up Its On-Line Shopping" in Globe & Mail (February 7, 2006, pp. B3)*
Pub: CTVglobemedia Publishing Inc.
Ed: Simon Avery. **Description:** The details of management contract between Hudson's Bay Co. and International Business Machines Corp. are presented.

11718 ■ *"Help for Job Seekers" in Crain's Detroit Business (Vol. 26, January 18, 2010, No. 3, pp. 14)*
Pub: Crain Communications Inc.
Description: CareerWorks is aimed at helping those who are in career transition or are looking for new jobs; this weekly collection of news, advertising and information includes weekly stories, events and the highlighting of a person who has successfully made the transition from one profession to another. On the Website, readers are welcome to post an anonymous resume in order to attract employers.

11719 ■ *"A Home's Identity in Black and White" in Crain's Chicago Business (Vol. 31, April 21, 2008, No. 16, pp. 35)*
Pub: Crain Communications, Inc.
Ed: Lisa Bertagnoli. **Description:** Real estate agents are finding that showing customers a written floor plan is a trend that is growing since many buyers feel that Online virtual tours distort a room. Although floor plans cost up to $500 to have drawn up, they clearly show potential buyers the exact dimensions of rooms and how they connect.

11720 ■ *"Hoover's Mobile, MobileSP Now Available" in Information Today (Vol. 26, February 2009, No. 2, pp. 29)*
Pub: Information Today, Inc.
Description: Hoover's Inc. introduced its Hoover's Mobile for iPhone, BlackBerry and Windows Mobile smartphones along with Hoover's MobileSP for Blackberry and Windows Mobile. Both products allow users to access customer, prospect, and partner information; analyze competitors; prepare for meetings; and find new opportunities. In addition, MobileSP adds one-click calling to executives, GPS-enabled location searches, advanced search and list building, and a custom call queue and a 'save to contacts' capabilities.

11721 ■ *"How to Boost Your Super Bowl ROI" in Advertising Age (Vol. 80, December 7, 2009, No. 41, pp. 3)*
Pub: Crain's Communications
Ed: Abbey Klaassen. **Description:** Internet marketing is essential, even for the corporations that can afford to spend $3 million on a 30-second Super Bowl

spot; last year, Super Bowl advertising reached an online viewership of 99.5 million while 98.7 million people watched the game on television validating the idea that public relations must go farther than a mere television ad campaign. Social media provides businesses with a longer shelf life for their ad campaigns. Advice is also given regarding ways in which to strategize a smart and well-thought plan for utilizing the online marketing options currently available.

11722 ■ *How to Get Rich on the Internet*
Pub: Morgan James Publishing, LLC
Ed: Ted Ciuba. **Released:** August 2004. **Price:** $19.95. **Description:** Interviews with successful Internet entrepreneurs provide insight into marketing products and services online using minimal investment. The importance of a sound marketing ad campaign using the Internet is discussed; maintaining a database and Website will automatically carry out business transactions daily. Suggestions for various types of businesses to run online are given.

11723 ■ *How to Make Money with Social Media: Using New and Emerging Media to Grow Your Business*
Pub: FT Press
Ed: Jamie Turner; Reshma Shah. **Released:** October 1, 2010. **Price:** $24.99. **Description:** Marketers, executives, entrepreneurs are shown more effective ways to utilize Internet social media to make money. This guide brings together both practical strategies and proven execution techniques for driving maximum value from social media marketing.

11724 ■ *"How to Make Your Website Really Sell" in Entrepreneur (Vol. 37, September 2009, No. 9, pp. 79)*
Pub: Entrepreneur Media, Inc.
Ed: David Port. **Description:** Advice on how to succeed in Internet marketing is presented. Offering visitors purchase incentives on the home page is encouraged. Delivery of customized landing pages and content is also recommended.

11725 ■ *"How Marketers Can Tap the Web" in Sales and Marketing Management (November 12, 2009)*
Pub: Nielsen Business Media, Inc.
Description: Internet marketing strategies require careful planning and tools in order to track success. Businesses are utilizing this trend to attract new clients as well as keep customers they already have satisfied. Advice on website development and design is provided.

11726 ■ *"How Not to Build a Website" in Women Entrepreneur (December 24, 2008)*
Pub: Entrepreneur Media Inc.
Ed: Erica Ruback; Joanie Reisen. **Description:** Tips for producing a unique and functional Website are given as well as a number of lessons a pair of entrepreneurs learned while trying to launch their networking website, MomSpace.com.

11727 ■ *How to Open and Operate a Financially Successful Bookstore on Amazon and Other Web Sites: With Companion CD-ROM*
Pub: Atlantic Publishing Company
Released: December 1, 2010. **Price:** $39.95. **Description:** This book was written for every used book aficionado and bookstore owner who currently wants to take advantage of the massive collection of online resources available to start and run your own online bookstore business.

11728 ■ *"How to Ramp Up Marketing in a Downturn" in Entrepreneur (Vol. 37, July 2009, No. 7, pp. 55)*
Pub: Entrepreneur Media, Inc.
Ed: Jeff Wuorio. **Description:** How businesses can save money while boosting their marketing efforts during a down economy is discussed. Using price-driven marketing, online social networks, and cause-driven marketing are among the suggested ways companies can attract more customers. Guarantees and warrantees, as well as contests, can also be used as marketing tools.

11729 ■ *How to Use the Internet to Advertise, Promote, and Market Your Business or Web Site: With Little or No Money*
Pub: Atlantic Publishing Company
Released: December 1, 2010. **Price:** $24.95. **Description:** Information is given to help build, promote, and make money from your Website or brick and mortar store using the Internet, with minimal costs.

11730 ■ *"Hunter and the Hunted" in Canadian Business (Vol. 81, Summer 2008, No. 9, pp. 12)*
Pub: Rogers Media Ltd.
Ed: Thomas Watson. **Description:** Brian Hunter, a partner in oil and gas engineering firm Montane Resources, invested his life savings in Vancouver-based Canacord Capital Corp. Details of the asset-backed commercial paper fiasco and Hunter's use of Facebook to encourage other investors to participate in his claim against the mortgage company are presented.

11731 ■ *"iControl Networks Powers Comcast's XFINITY (Reg) Home Security Service" in Benzinga.com (June 9, 2011)*
Pub: Benzinga.com
Ed: Benzinga Staff. **Description:** Comcast's XFINITY Home Security Service is powered by iControl Networks' OpenHome (TM) software platform. The service provides intrusion and fire protection along with interactive features such as home monitoring, home management, and energy management services with Web and mobile access.

11732 ■ *I'm on LinkedIn - Now What? (Second Edition): A Guide to Getting the Most Out of LinkedIn*
Pub: Happy About
Ed: Diane Danielson. **Released:** January 7, 2009. **Price:** $19.95. **Description:** Designed to help get the most out of LinkedIn, the popular business networking site and follows the first edition and includes the latest and great approaches using LinkedIn. With over 32 million members there is a lot of potential to find and develop relationships to help in your business and personal life, but many professionals find themselves wondering what to do once they sign up. This book explains the different benefits of the system and recommends best practices (including LinkedIn Groups) so that you get the most out of LinkedIn.

11733 ■ *"Image Conscious" in Canadian Business (Vol. 81, March 17, 2008, No. 4, pp. 36)*
Pub: Rogers Media
Ed: Andrew Wahl. **Description:** Idee Inc. is testing an Internet search engine for images that does not rely on tags but compares its visual data to a database of other images. The company was founded and managed by Leila Boujnane as an off-shoot of their risk-management software firm. Their software has already been used by image companies to track copyrighted images and to find images within their own archives.

11734 ■ *"Impressive Numbers: Companies Experience Substantial Increases in Dollars, Employment" in Hispanic Business (July-August 2007)*
Pub: Hispanic Business
Ed: Derek Reveron. **Description:** Profiles of five fastest growing Hispanic companies reporting increases in revenue and employment include Brightstar, distributor of wireless products; Greenway Ford Inc., a car dealership; Fred Loya Insurance, auto insurance carrier; and Group O, packaging company; and Diverse Staffing, Inc., an employment and staffing firm.

11735 ■ *"In Print and Online" in Marketing to Women (Vol. 22, August 2009, No. 8, pp. 3)*
Pub: EPM Communications Inc.
Contact: Ira Mayer, President
E-mail: imayer@epmcom.com
Description: Seventeen magazine is unifying its print and Online editions with complementary content, a strategy that seems to be working as every aspect of Seventeen drives the reader to another component.

11736 ■ *Information Technology for the Small Business: How to Make IT Work For Your Company*
Pub: TAB Computer Systems, Incorporated
Ed: T.J. Benoit. **Released:** June 2006. **Price:** $17.95. **Description:** Basics of information technology to help small companies maximize benefits are covered. Topics include pitfalls to avoid, email and Internet use, data backup, recovery and overall IT organization.

11737 ■ *"Ingrian and Channel Management International Sign Distribution Agreement" in Canadian Corporate News (May 16, 2007)*
Pub: Comtex News Network Inc.
Description: Channel Management International (CMI), a Canadian channel management and distribution company, and Ingrian Networks, Inc., the leading provider of data privacy solutions, announced a Canadian distribution agreement to resell Ingrian encryption solutions to the Canadian market.

11738 ■ *"Inside Intel's Effectiveness System for Web Marketing" in Advertising Age (Vol. 81, January 25, 2010, No. 4, pp. 4)*
Pub: Crain's Communications
Ed: Beth Snyder Bulik. **Description:** Overview of Intel's internally developed program called Value Point System in which the company is using in order to evaluate and measure online marketing effectiveness.

11739 ■ *"Inside an Online Bazaar" in Entrepreneur (Vol. 37, September 2009, No. 9, pp. 38)*
Pub: Entrepreneur Media Inc.
Ed: Kara Ohngren. **Description:** Etsy.com is a website that provides a marketplace for handmade products. The site has attracted more than 250,000 sellers since its launch in 2005. Site features and services are also supplied.

11740 ■ *"Internet Marketing 2.0: Closing the Online Chat Gap" in Agent's Sales Journal (November 2009, pp. 14)*
Pub: Summit Business Media
Ed: Jeff Denenholz. **Description:** Advice regarding the implementation of an Internet marketing strategy for insurance agencies includes how and why to incorporate a chat feature in which a sales agent can communicate in real-time with potential or existing customers. It is important to understand if appropriate response mechanisms are in place to convert leads into actual sales.

11741 ■ *"Internet Marketing Agency .Com Marketing Wins National Awards for Web Design and SEO" in Marketing Weekly News (Jan. 2, 2010)*
Pub: Investment Weekly News
Description: Internet marketing agency .Com Marketing has won two bronze awards for its exceptional quality web services; the company is a full-service interactive marketing and advertising agency that specializes in a variety of online services including web design, social media marketing and press releases.

11742 ■ *"Internet Marketing Agency .Com Marketing Wins National Awards for Web Design and SEO" in Marketing Weekly News (January 2, 2010)*
Pub: Investment Weekly News
Description: Internet marketing agency .Com Marketing has won two bronze awards for its exceptional quality web services; the company is a full-service interactive marketing and advertising agency that specializes in a variety of online services including web design, social media marketing and press releases.

11743 ■ *"Internet Marketing and Social Media Knowledge Vital for SMBs" in Internet Wire (November 24, 2009)*
Pub: Comtex News Network, Inc.
Description: Small and medium-size businesses must learn to market themselves over the Internet in order to succeed and grow in today's marketplace. Web Marketing Today offers the largest source of the

most important information concerning doing business on the Internet including e-commerce, email marketing and social networking opportunities.

11744 ■ *"Internet and Mobile Media" in MarketingMagazine (Vol. 115, September 27, 2010, No. 13, pp. 60)*
Pub: Rogers Publishing Ltd.
Description: Market data covering the Internet and mobile media in Canada is given.

11745 ■ *"Into the Groove: Fine-Tune Your Biz By Getting Into the Good Habit Groove" in Small Business Opportunities (Spring 2008)*
Pub: Harris Publications Inc.
Description: Profile of Ty Freyvogel and his consulting firm Freyvogel Communications. Freyvogel serves the telecommunications need of Fortune 500 and mid-sized businesses.

11746 ■ *"Into the Light: Making Our Way Through the Economic Tunnel" in Agency Sales Magazine (Vol. 39, August 2009, No. 8, pp. 26)*
Pub: MANA
Ed: Michael Dotson. **Description:** Ways in which to avoid business stagnation brought about by the economic downturn, is presented. Being different, being a puzzle solver, and knowing the competition are among the things marketing personnel should do in order to wade through the economic downturn. Marketing via direct mail and the Internet also recommended.

11747 ■ *"Intrepid Souls: Meet a Few Who've Made the Big Leap" in Crain's Chicago Business (Vol. 31, November 10, 2008, No. 45, pp. 26)*
Pub: Crain Communications, Inc.
Ed: Meredith Landry. **Description:** Advice is given from entrepreneurs who have launched businesses in the last year despite the economic crisis. Among the types of businesses featured are a cooking school, a child day-care center, a children's clothing store and an Internet-based company.

11748 ■ *"Israeli Spam Law May Have Global Impact" in Information Today (Vol. 26, February 2009, No. 2, pp. 28)*
Pub: Information Today, Inc.
Ed: David Mirchin. **Description:** Israels new law, called Amendment 40 of the Communications Law, will regulate commercial solicitations including those sent without permission via email, fax, automatic phone dialing systems, or short messaging technologies.

11749 ■ *"It Was a Very Good Year..To Be Ted Rogers" in Canadian Business (Vol. 80, Winter 2007, No. 24, pp. 121)*
Pub: Rogers Media
Ed: Andrew Wahl. **Description:** Ted Rogers had a banner year in 2007 as Rogers Communications Inc. (RCI) took in huge profits from its phone and wireless business and his personal wealth grew sixty-seven percent to $7.6 billion. Rogers has record of betting on technologies that get the best returns relative to the investment in the marketplace such as its use of the GSM network and its cable hybrid fiber coaxial network.

11750 ■ *"It's a New Game: Killerspin Pushes Table Tennis to Extreme Heights" in Black Enterprise (Vol. 37, October 2006, No. 3, pp. 73)*
Pub: Earl G. Graves Publishing Co. Inc.
Ed: Bridget McCrea. **Description:** Profile of Robert Blackwell and his company Killerspin L.L.C., which is popularizing the sport of table tennis. Killerspin has hit $1 million in revenues due to product sales primarily generated through the company's website, magazines, DVDs, and event ticket sales.

11751 ■ *"It's Not About the G1; Google Just Wants You to Use the Mobile Web" in Advertising Age (Vol. 79, September 29, 2008,*

No. 36, pp. 32)
Pub: Crain Communications, Inc.
Ed: Abbey Klaassen. Description: Google's Android is the first serious competitor to Apple's iPhone; the company says that its goal is to simplify the mobile market and get wireless subscribers to use the mobile Internet and purchase smartphones.

11752 ■ "Jay Berkowitz to Present Making Social Media Money Seminar at Affiliate Summit West" in Entertainment Close-Up (January 15, 2010)
Pub: Close-Up Media
Description: Highlights of Jay Berkowitz's conference, 'Making Social Media Make Money' include ways in which to develop Internet marketing strategies that will maximize Website traffic and convert that traffic to sales.

11753 ■ "Johnny Royal of Luthier Society Unveils Archimedes 1.0 Trailer" in Internet Wire (October 22, 2009)
Pub: Comtex News Network, Inc.
Description: Luthier Society, a social media and viral branding agency, has released the first viral video for the company's ROI weighted-value software platform named Archimedes 1.0; users of the software will be able to determine the depth of their outreach efforts, saturation rate, value of their Internet presence and the geo-spatial location of their audience; this will give a true, monetized value for ROI (Return on Investment) in social media marketing.

11754 ■ "Johnson Publishing Expands: Moving Into Television and Internet To Extend Brand" in Black Enterprise (October 2007)
Pub: Earl G. Graves Publishing Co. Inc.
Ed: Tamara E. Holmes. Description: Johnson Publishing Company has followed the lives of black families in both Ebony and Jet magazines. The media firm has expanded its coverage by developing entertainment content for television, the Internet and other digital arenas.

11755 ■ "Johnson's Taps Online Animation" in Marketing to Women (Vol. 21, April 2008, No. 4, pp. 3)
Pub: EPM Communications Inc.
Contact: Ira Mayer, President
E-mail: imayer@epmcom.com
Description: Johnson's has launched a new integrated campaign for its baby lotion in an effort to appeal to the growing number of moms online.

11756 ■ "JumpTV to Hold Conference Call to Discuss Q1 Results and Annual General Meeting" in Canadian Corporate News (May 16, 2007)
Pub: Comtex News Network Inc.
Description: Profile of JumpTv, the world's leading broadcaster of ethnic television over the Internet, and the results of a conference that discussed their first quarter 2007 financial report as well as the company's business goals. Statistical data included.

11757 ■ "Kawasaki's New Top Gun" in Brandweek (Vol. 49, April 21, 2008, No. 16, pp. 18)
Pub: VNU Business Media, Inc.
Description: Discusses Kawasaki's marketing plan which included designing an online brochure in which visitors could create a video by building their own test track on a grid and then selecting visual special effects and musical overlay. This engaging and innovative marketing technique generated more than 166,000 unique users within the first three months of being launched.

11758 ■ "Keeping Up With the Joneses: Outfitting Your Company With Up-To-Date Technology is Vital" in Black Enterprise (November 2007)
Pub: Earl G. Graves Publishing Co. Inc.
Ed: Sonya A. Donaldson. Description: Small businesses, whether home-based or not, need to keep up with new technological developments including hardware, software, and the Internet.

11759 ■ "Kid-Friendly Business Sources" in Black Enterprise (Vol. 37, January 2007, No. 6, pp. 40)
Pub: Earl G. Graves Publishing Co. Inc.
Ed: Carolyn M. Brown. Description: Financial or business camps are a great way to encourage a child who interested in starting his or her own business. A number of these camps are available each year including Kidpreneurs Conference and Bull and Bear Investment Camp. Other resources are available online. Resources included.

11760 ■ "Kids, Computers and the Social Networking Evolution" in Canadian Business (Vol. 81, October 27, 2008, No. 18, pp. 93)
Pub: Rogers Media Ltd.
Ed: Penny Milton. Description: Social networking was found to help educate students in countries like the U.S., Canada and Mexico. Schools that embrace social networking teach students how to use computers safely and responsibly in order to counter threats to children on the Internet.

11761 ■ "Kuno Creative to Present B2B Social Media Campaign Webinar" in Entertainment Close-Up (August 25, 2011)
Pub: Close-Up Media
Description: Kuno Creative, an inbound marketing agency, will host Three Steps of a Successful B2B Social Media Campaign. The firm is a provider of Website development, branding, marketing strategy, public relations, Internet marketing, and inbound marketing.

11762 ■ "Last Founder Standing" in Conde Nast Portfolio (Vol. 2, June 2008, No. 6, pp. 124)
Pub: Conde Nast Publications
Contact: David Carey, President
Ed: Kevin Maney. Description: Interview with Amazon CEO Jeff Bezos in which he discusses the economy, the company's new distribution center and the hiring of employees for it, e-books, and the overall vision for the future of the firm.

11763 ■ "Laterooms and Octopus Travel Top Greenlight's Integrated Search Report for the Hotel Sector" in Internet Wire (October 23, 2009)
Pub: Comtex News Network, Inc.
Description: According to a research report conducted by Greenlight, the UK's leading independent Internet search marketing agency, the most visible hotel websites in natural search during June 2009 are premierinn.com, booking.com and laterooms.com; OctopusTravel.com generated the greatest share of the paid search section with 21 percent visibility. The report is focused on the hotel sector and covers the second quarter of 2009. Statistical data included.

11764 ■ "Lavante, Inc. Joins Intersynthesis, Holistic Internet Marketing Company" in Internet Wire (November 5, 2009)
Pub: Comtex News Network, Inc.
Description: Lavante, Inc., the leading provider of on-demand vendor information and profit recovery audit solutions for Fortune 1000 companies has chosen Intersynthesis, a new holistic Internet marketing firm, as a provider of pay for performance services. Lavante believes that Intersynthesis' expertise and knowledge combined with their ability to develop integrated strategies, will help them fuel more growth.

11765 ■ "Leading Ohio Internet Marketing Firm Announces Growth in September" in Marketing Weekly News (September 26, 2009, pp. 24)
Pub: Investment Weekly News
Description: Despite a poor economy, Webbed Marketing, a leading social media marketing and search engine optimization firm in the Midwest, has added five additional professionals to its fast-growing team. The company continues to win new business, provide more services and hire talented employees.

11766 ■ "Legal Aid: Sample Legal Documents can Lower Your Attorney Fees" in Black Enterprise (Vol. 37, October 2006, No. 3, pp. 210)
Pub: Earl G. Graves Publishing Co. Inc.
Ed: Tamara E. Holmes. Description: FreeLegalForms.net provides thousands of free legal forms. These forms are not a substitute for consultation with an attorney but the sample documents can help save you time and money.

11767 ■ "Legislating the Cloud" in Information Today (Vol. 28, October 2011, No. 9, pp. 1)
Pub: Information Today, Inc.
Description: Internet and telecommunications industry leaders are asking for legislation to address the emerging market in cloud computing. Existing communications laws do not adequately govern the modern Internet.

11768 ■ "Let the Online Games Begin" in Canadian Business (Vol. 80, January 29, 2007, No. 3, pp. 23)
Pub: Rogers Media
Ed: Andy Holloway. Description: The trends pertaining to the promotion of the products and services of different Canadian companies on the internet are discussed.

11769 ■ "Make It Easy" in Entrepreneur (Vol. 36, May 2008, No. 5, pp. 49)
Pub: Entrepreneur Media, Inc.
Ed: Mike Hogan. Description: Zoho has a Planner that keep contacts, notes and reminders and a DB & Reports feature for reports, data analysis and pricing comparisons. WebEx WebOffice Workgroup supports document management and templates for contacts lists, time sheets and sales tracking. Other online data manages are presented.

11770 ■ "Making It Click" in Barron's (Vol. 88, March 17, 2008, No. 11, pp. 31)
Pub: Dow Jones & Company, Inc.
Ed: Theresa W. Carey. Description: Listing of 23 online brokers that are evaluated based on their trade experience, usability, range of offerings, research amenities, customer service and access, and costs. TradeStation Securities takes the top spot followed by thinkorswim by just a fraction.

11771 ■ "Managing the Facebookers; Business" in The Economist (Vol. 390, January 3, 2009, No. 8612, pp. 10)
Pub: Economist Newspaper Ltd.
Description: According to a report from PricewaterhouseCoopers, a business consultancy, workers from Generation Y, also known as the Net Generation, are more difficult to recruit and integrate into companies that practice traditional business acumen. 61 percent of chief executive managers say that they have trouble with younger employees who tend to be more narcissistic and more interested in personal fulfillment with a need for frequent feedback and an over-precise set of objectives on the path to promotion which can be hard for managers who are used to a different relationship with their subordinates. Older bosses should prepare to make some concessions to their younger talent since some of the issues that make them happy include cheaper online ways to communicate and additional coaching, both of which are good for business.

11772 ■ "Mapping the Social Internet" in Harvard Business Review (Vol. 88, July-August 2010, No. 7-8, pp. 32)
Pub: Harvard Business School Publishing
Description: Chart compares and contrasts online social networks in selected countries.

11773 ■ "Marketing Management Analytics Announces MMA Digital" in Internet Wire (January 26, 2010)
Pub: Comtex News Network, Inc.
Description: Innovator and pioneer in marketing effectiveness, Marketing Management Analytics, is offering a new service called MMA Digital; using this service companies will be able to more accurately

measure the effects of digital media alongside other marketing tools in order to better understand and leverage the drivers of online marketing success.

11774 ■ *"A Matter of Online Trust" in Entrepreneur (Vol. 37, August 2009, No. 8, pp. 35)*
Pub: Entrepreneur Media, Inc.
Ed: Mikal E. Belicove. **Description:** Startup websites should make their potential customers feel confident to do business with them. To build customer's trust, the website should have an attractive and professional design, clear and simple navigation, error-free copy, and physical address, telephone number, and e-mail address.

11775 ■ *"McD's Warms Up For Olympics Performance" in Advertising Age (Vol. 79, July 7, 2008, No. 26, pp. 8)*
Pub: Crain Communications, Inc.
Description: Overview of McDonald's marketing plans for the company's sponsorship of the Olympics which includes a website, an alternate-reality game, names featured on U.S. athletes and on-the-ground activities.

11776 ■ *"Microsoft's Big Gamble" in Canadian Business (Vol. 81, March 3, 2008, No. 3, pp. 13)*
Pub: Rogers Media
Ed: Andrew Wahl. **Description:** Microsoft Corp. is taking a big risk in buying Yahoo, as it is expected to pay more than $31 a share to finalize the acquisition. The deal would be seven and a half times bigger than any other that Microsoft has entered before, an execution of such deal is also anticipated to become a challenge for Microsoft. Recommendations on how Microsoft should handle the integration of the two businesses are given.

11777 ■ *"Milk Producers Target Moms" in Marketing to Women (Vol. 21, January 2008, No. 1, pp. 3)*
Pub: EPM Communications Inc.
Contact: Ira Mayer, President
E-mail: imayer@epmcom.com
Description: In an attempt to encourage moms to serve milk with meals, the American Dairy Association partners with the New York State Dietetic Association to promote milk via a new logo, website and contest.

11778 ■ *Million Dollar Website: Simple Steps to Help You Compete with the Big Boys-Even on a Small Business Budget*
Pub: Prentice Hall Press
Ed: Lori Culwell. **Released:** May 9, 2010. **Price:** $19. 95. **Description:** Resource for any small business owner wishing to build a successful Website in order to compete with big box stores.

11779 ■ *"Mobile: Juanes Fans Sing for Sprint" in Advertising Age (Vol. 79, November 3, 2008, No. 41, pp. 22)*
Pub: Crain Communications, Inc.
Ed: Laurel Wentz. **Description:** Marketers are appealing to the Hispanic market since they are more prone to use their cell phones to respond to contests, download videos, ringtones, or other data activity. Sprint recently sponsored a contest inviting people to sing like Colombian megastar Juanes; the participants filmed and sent their videos using their cell phones rather than laptops or camcorders illustrating the Hispanic overindex on mobile-phone technology. The contest generated hundreds of thousands of dollars in additional fee revenue, as monthly downloads increased 63 percent.

11780 ■ *"Mobility: So Happy Together" in Entrepreneur (Vol. 35, October 2007, No. 10, pp. 64)*
Pub: Entrepreneur Media Inc.
Ed: Heather Clancy. **Description:** Joshua Burnett, CEO and founder of 9ci, uses index cards to keep track of what he needs to do despite the fact that he has a notebook computer, cell phone and PDA. Kim Hahn, a media entrepreneur, prefers jotting her ideas down in a spiral notebook, has a team that would organize her records for her, and a personal assistant

that would keep track of changes to her schedule. Reasons why these entrepreneurs use old-fashioned methods along with new technology are given.

11781 ■ *"Moosylvania Releases Latest XL Marketing Trends Report" in Wireless News (October 6, 2009)*
Pub: Close-Up Media
Description: Moosylvania, a digital promotion and branding agency that also has an on-site research facility, has released its 2nd XL Marketing Trends Report which focuses on digital video; the study defines the top digital video trends marketers must focus on now and well into the future and notes that in 2010, Mobile Web Devices, such as smart phones will outnumber computers in this country. Statistical data included.

11782 ■ *"More Leading Retailers Using Omniture Conversion Solutions to Boost Sales and Ecommerce Performance" in Internet Wire (Sept. 22,2009)*
Pub: Comtex News Network, Inc.
Description: Many retailers are utilizing Omniture conversion solutions to improve the performance of their ecommerce businesses; recent enhancements to Omniture Merchandising and Omniture Recommendations help clients drive increased conversion to their Internet ventures.

11783 ■ *"More Leading Retailers Using Omniture Conversion Solutions to Boost Sales and Ecommerce Performance" in Internet Wire (Sept. 22,2009)*
Pub: Comtex News Network, Inc.
Description: Many retailers are utilizing Omniture conversion solutions to improve the performance of their ecommerce businesses; recent enhancements to Omniture Merchandising and Omniture Recommendations help clients drive increased conversion to their Internet ventures.

11784 ■ *"Most Viewed Stories, Videos on farmindustrynews.com in 2010" in Farm Industry News (January 4, 2011)*
Pub: Penton Business Media Inc.
Description: The top ten most popularly viewed stories and videos presented on farmindustrynews. com Website are listed.

11785 ■ *"Moving Pitchers" in Entrepreneur (Vol. 37, December 2009, No. 12, pp. 46)*
Pub: Entrepreneur Media, Inc.
Ed: Gwen Moran. **Description:** Online videos have become accessible for business development and marketing due to the decline in production costs and the growth in viewership. Research company comScore reveals that 153 million Internet users in the U.S. watched an online video in August 2009. The benefits of using online videos to further market one's company are explained.

11786 ■ *"Navigate to Better Direct Response Messaging Through Search Marketing" in DM News (Vol. 32, January 18, 2010, No. 2, pp. 26)*
Pub: Haymarket Media, Inc.
Ed: Mark Simon. **Description:** Important lessons to apply when utilizing Internet marketing schemes include telling your customers you have what they want to buy, provide them with discounts or ways to save additional money and drive them to a customized destination like an Online store.

11787 ■ *"The Neighborhood Watch" in Hawaii Business (Vol. 53, March 2008, No. 9, pp. 36)*
Pub: Hawaii Business Publishing
Ed: David K. Choo. **Description:** OahuRe.com offers information on Hawaii real estate market, with spreadsheets and comparative market analysis page, which shows properties that are active, sold, or in escrow. Other details about OahuRe.com are discussed. A list of other top real estate websites in Hawaii and in the U.S. in general is provided.

11788 ■ *"Net Connections" in Black Enterprise (Vol. 38, July 2008, No. 12, pp. 28)*
Pub: Earl G. Graves Publishing Co. Inc.
Ed: Anthony S. Calypso. **Description:** Marketers are making strategic partnerships with online social networks in an attempt to gain further market reach.

The value of these networks appears to be on the rise forcing media companies to recalculate their strategies for delivering products to customers.

11789 ■ *"Netflix Gets No Respect" in Barron's (Vol. 89, July 27, 2009, No. 30, pp. 26)*
Pub: Dow Jones & Co., Inc.
Ed: Tiernan Ray. **Description:** Netflix met expectations when they announced their second quarter sales but their shares still fell by almost 10 percent. Analysts say their entry into the 'streaming video' business is a mixed bag since customers are increasingly buying the cheaper monthly plan and this is dragging the economics of the business.

11790 ■ *"A Network of One: Local Writer Adds Web Interviews to Creative Output" in La Crosse Tribune (September 14, 2009)*
Pub: La Crosse Tribune
Ed: Geri Parlin. **Description:** Profile of Andrew Revels, a freelance and aspiring writer, who has created a website in order to help gain attention for his own writing as well as for other local artists, musicians and comedians. His latest endeavor includes interviewing local talent and broadcasting the interviews on his site each week.

11791 ■ *"Networking Web Sites: a Two-Edged Sword" in Contractor (Vol. 56, October 2009, No. 10, pp. 52)*
Pub: Penton Media, Inc.
Ed: H. Kent Craig. **Description:** People need to be careful about the information that they share on social networking Web sites. They should realize that future bosses, coworkers, and those that might want to hire them might read those information. Posting on these sites can cost career opportunities and respect.

11792 ■ *"The New Guard" in Entrepreneur (Vol. 36, February 2008, No. 2, pp. 46)*
Pub: Entrepreneur Media Inc.
Ed: Amanda C. Kooser. **Description:** A natural language search engine is being developed by Powerset for better online searching. Zannel Inc. offers Instant Media Messaging platform, which allows for social networking using phones. Ning is an online platform that allows users to customize and control their social networks.

11793 ■ *"New IPhone Also Brings New Way of Mobile Marketing" in Advertising Age (Vol. 79, June 16, 2008, No. 24, pp. 23)*
Pub: Crain Communications, Inc.
Ed: Abbey Klaasen. **Description:** Currently there are two kinds of applications for the iPhone and other mobile devices: native applications that allow for richer experiences and take advantage of features that are built into a phone and web applications, those that allow access to the web through specific platforms. Marketers are interested in creating useful experiences for customers and opening up the platforms which will allow them to do this.

11794 ■ *"New Recession-Proof Internet Marketing Package Allows Businesses to Ramp Up Web Traffic and Profits" in PR Newswire (Jan. 25, 2010)*
Pub: PR Newswire Association, LLC
Description: Profile of Reel Web Design, a leading marketing firm in New York City that caters to small to medium sized businesses with smaller budgets that need substantial return on investment; Reel Web Design offers video production and submission, web design and maintenance and press release writing among additional services.

11795 ■ *"New Recession-Proof Internet Marketing Package Allows Businesses to Ramp Up Web Traffic and Profits" in PR Newswire (Jan. 25, 2010)*
Pub: PR Newswire Association, LLC
Description: Profile of Reel Web Design, a leading marketing firm in New York City that caters to small to medium sized businesses with smaller budgets that need substantial return on investment; Reel Web Design offers video production and submission, web design and maintenance and press release writing among additional services.

11796 ■ "New Sony HD Ads Tout Digital" in Brandweek (Vol. 49, April 21, 2008, No. 16, pp. 5)
Pub: VNU Business Media, Inc.
Description: Looking to promote Sony Electronics' digital imaging products, the company has launched another campaign effort known as HDNA, a play on the words high-definition and DNA; originally Sony focused the HDNA campaign on their televisions, the new ads will include still and video cameras as well and marketing efforts will consist of advertising in print, Online, television spots and publicity at various venues across the country.

11797 ■ "New TurnHere Survey Reveals Online Video Trends" in Internet Wire (October 22, 2009)
Pub: Comtex News Network, Inc.
Description: TurnHere, Inc., the leading online video marketing services company, released the findings of its recent survey regarding current and future trends in online video among marketing agencies and brand recognition; the report found that online video has and will continue to play a prominent role in the realm of marketing edging out both search and email marketing campaigns. Additional highlights and statistical data included.

11798 ■ "A New Way to Tell When to Fold" in Barron's (Vol. 88, July 7, 2008, No. 27, pp. 27)
Pub: Dow Jones & Co., Inc.
Ed: Theresa W. Carey. **Description:** Overview of the Online trading company SmartStops, a firm that aims to tell investors when to sell the shares of a particular company. The company's Web site categorizes stocks as moving up, down, or sideways, and calculates exit points for individual stocks based on an overall market trend.

11799 ■ "New Ways to Catch a Thief" in Barron's (Vol. 88, March 10, 2008, No. 10, pp. 37)
Pub: Dow Jones & Company, Inc.
Ed: Theresa W. Carey. **Description:** Online brokerage firms employ different methods to protect the accounts of their customers from theft. These methods include secure Internet connections, momentary passwords, and proprietary algorithms.

11800 ■ "Nine Sectors to Watch: Telecom" in Canadian Business (Vol. 81, December 24, 2007, No. 1, pp. 44)
Pub: Rogers Media
Ed: Andrew Wahl. **Description:** Forecasts on the Canadian telecommunications industry for 2008 are presented. Details on consumer spending growth, the popularity of broadband, and activities in the wireless sector are also discussed.

11801 ■ "Nobody Knows What To Do" in Barron's (Vol. 88, March 17, 2008, No. 11, pp. 40)
Pub: Dow Jones & Company, Inc.
Ed: Mark Veverka. **Description:** Attendees of the South by Southwest Interactive conference failed to get an insight on how to make money on the Web from former Walt Disney CEO Michael Eisner when Eisner said there's no proven business model for financing projects. Eisner said he finances his projects with the help of his connections to get product-placement deals.

11802 ■ "Norvax University Health Insurance Sales Training and Online Marketing Conference" in Internet Wire (January 27, 2010)
Pub: Comtex News Network, Inc.
Description: Overview of the Norvax University Marketing and Sales Success Conference Tour which includes insurance sales training seminars, proven and innovative online marketing techniques and a host of additional information and networking opportunities.

11803 ■ "Note to Marketers: A Viral Video Has a Life of Its Own" in Advertising Age (Vol. 80, October 5, 2009, No. 33, pp. 29)
Pub: Crain's Communications
Ed: Ken Wheaton. **Description:** Internet marketers do not decide whether or not an online video goes viral. It is the audience that decides what online

videos to spread and such fare is usually passed around due to its content being downright witty or creative or so laughably bad that the audience wants to share it.

11804 ■ "Nothing Plus Nothing" in Entrepreneur (Vol. 37, October 2009, No. 10, pp. 25)
Pub: Entrepreneur Media, Inc.
Ed: Joe Robinson. **Description:** Jason Fried and David Heinemeier Hansson of Web application firm 37signals believe that free Web services will never become profitable in the long term. They believe that Web service providers should charge a fair price on such services.

11805 ■ "Nowspeed and OneSource to Conduct Webinar" in Internet Wire (December 14, 2009)
Pub: Comtex News Network, Inc.
Description: OneSource, a leading provider of global business information, and Nowspeed, an Internet marketing agency, will conduct a webinar titled 'How to Develop Social Media Content That Gets Results' in order to provide marketers insight into how to develop and optimize effective social media content to get consumer results that translate into purchases and lead generation.

11806 ■ "Nowspeed's David Reske to Speak at SolidWorks World 2010 in Anaheim" in Internet Wire (January 7, 2010)
Pub: Comtex News Network, Inc.
Description: David Reske, managing director at Nowspeed, an Internet marketing agency based in the Boston area, will be presenting at SolidWorks World 2010; the convention's presentation will focus on proven methodologies, practical tips and real-world case studies in order to help attendees leverage the powerful Internet marketing innovations that are proving effective for businesses.

11807 ■ "Obama Plan May Boost Maryland Cyber Security" in Boston Business Journal (Vol. 29, May 20, 2011, No. 2, pp. 1)
Pub: American City Business Journals Inc.
Ed: Scott Dance. **Description:** May 12, 2011 outline of the cyber security policies of President Obama may improve the cyber security industry in Maryland as the state is home to large defense and intelligence activities. Details of the proposed policies are discusses as well as their advantages to companies that deal in developing cyber security plans for other companies.

11808 ■ "Office Retooled" in Canadian Business (Vol. 80, March 26, 2007, No. 7, pp. 67)
Pub: Rogers Media
Ed: Andrew Wahl. **Description:** The merits and demerits of using new Google Apps Premier Edition are presented.

11809 ■ "Oh, Behave!" in Entrepreneur (Vol. 36, April 2008, No. 4, pp. 87)
Pub: Entrepreneur Media, Inc.
Ed: Gwen Moran. **Description:** Online social networks can pose awkward situations for users. These include instances such as getting a link request from someone you do not know, having a contact post embarrassing information on your site, and a contact asking you to be refer him to one of your business contacts. Tips on how to deal with these situations are discussed.

11810 ■ "Omniture's Next Version of SearchCenter Delivers Landing Page Optimization" in Internet Wire (September 24, 2009)
Pub: Comtex News Network, Inc.
Description: Omniture, Inc., a leading provider of online business optimization software, has announced a new release of Omniture SearchCenter; this latest version will allow search engine marketers to test landing pages across campaigns and ad groups.

11811 ■ "On Target" in Canadian Business (Vol. 81, July 22, 2008, No. 12-13, pp. 45)
Pub: Rogers Media Ltd.
Ed: Calvin Leung. **Description:** Companies such as LavalifePRIME, a dating website devoted to singles 45 and older, discuss the value of marketing and services aimed at Canada's older consumers. One-third of Canada's 33 million people are 50-plus, controlling 77 percent of the countries wealth.

11812 ■ "Online Marketing and Promotion of Canadian Films via Social Media Tools" in CNW Group (January 27, 2010)
Pub: Comtex News Network, Inc.
Description: Telefilm Canada announced the launch of a pilot initiative aimed at encouraging the integration of online marketing and the use of social media tools into means of distribution ahead of a films' theatrical release. During this pilot phase Web-Cine 360 will target French-language feature films.

11813 ■ "Online Postings Really Influence Older Women" in Marketing to Women (Vol. 22, July 2009, No. 7, pp. 8)
Pub: EPM Communications Inc.
Contact: Ira Mayer, President
E-mail: imayer@epmcom.com
Description: Women over the age of 55 are more likely to be swayed to purchase a product by referrals from others, including Online postings by strangers. Another key influence is associated with the brand's ability to address their lifestyle needs.

11814 ■ "Online Self-Publishing Services" in Black Enterprise (Vol. 37, November 2006, No. 4, pp. 90)
Pub: Earl G. Graves Publishing Co. Inc.
Description: Profiles of five online self-publishing services.

11815 ■ "Orbitz Adds Parent Panel" in Marketing to Women (Vol. 21, March 2008, No. 3, pp. 5)
Pub: EPM Communications Inc.
Contact: Ira Mayer, President
E-mail: imayer@epmcom.com
Description: Orbitz introduces the Orbitz Parent Panel in an attempt to better connect with traveling families.

11816 ■ "Ordering Pizza Hut From Your Facebook Page?" in Advertising Age (Vol. 79, November 10, 2008, No. 42, pp. 50)
Pub: Crain Communications, Inc.
Ed: Emily Bryson York. **Description:** Fast-food chains are experimenting with delivery/takeout services via social networks such as Facebook and iPhone applications. This also allows the chains to build valuable databases of their customers.

11817 ■ "Our Gadget of the Week" in Barron's (Vol. 88, March 24, 2008, No. 12, pp. 47)
Pub: Dow Jones & Company, Inc.
Ed: Tiernan Ray. **Description:** Review of the $299 Apple Time Capsule, which is a 500-megabyte hard disk drive and a Wi-Fi router, rolled into one device. The device allows users to create backup files without the need for sophisticated file management software.

11818 ■ "Our Gadget of the Week: Mostly, I Liked It" in Barron's (Vol. 88, July 14, 2008, No. 28, pp. 31)
Pub: Dow Jones & Co., Inc.
Ed: Jay Palmer. **Description:** Review of the Apple iPhone 3G, which costs $199, has better audio and is slightly thicker than its predecessor; using the 3G wireless connection makes going online faster but drains the battery faster too.

11819 ■ "Our World with Black Enterprise" in Black Enterprise (Vol. 37, February 2007, No. 7, pp. 145)
Pub: Earl G. Graves Publishing Co. Inc.
Description: Our World with Black Enterprise is a television broadcast that features roundtable discussions and interviews with important African American figures.

11820 ∎ *Overcoming Barriers to Entrepreneurship in the United States*
Pub: Lexington Books
Ed: Diana Furchtgott-Roth. **Released:** March 28, 2008. **Price:** $24.95. **Description:** Real and perceived barriers to the founding and running of small businesses in America are discussed. Each chapter outlines how policy and economic environments can hinder business owners and offers tips to overcome these obstacles. Starting with venture capital access in Silicon Valley during the Internet bubble, the book goes on to question the link between personal wealth and entrepreneurship, examines how federal tax rates affect small business creation and destruction, explains the low rate of self-employment among Mexican immigrants, and suggests ways pension coverage can be increased in small businesses.

11821 ∎ *"Pagetender LLC Releases Website Design Package for HubSpot Users" in Internet Wire (September 30, 2009)*
Pub: Comtex News Network, Inc.
Description: Profile of Pagetender LLC, a Certified HubSpot partner, who announced a Website Design Package marketed specifically for HubSpot Owner and Marketer users. This packaged was developed for small to medium sized businesses that want a website designed or their current site redesigned on HubSpot's Content Management System. Companies that would like a more robust site have the option of adding Flash development, ecommerce and photo galleries.

11822 ∎ *"Partnering for Success" in Art Business News (Vol. 36, October 2009, No. 10, pp. 4)*
Pub: Summit Business Media
Ed: Jennifer Dulin Wiley. **Description:** In such a volatile economy many savvy artists and gallery owners are turning to out-of-the-box partnerships for continued success; these partnerships are also pervading the Internet, especially with such social media networks as Facebook and Twitter where artists and businesses can develop a loyal following.

11823 ∎ *"Paterson Plots Comeback With Internet IPO" in Globe & Mail (February 20, 2006, pp. B1)*
Pub: CTVglobemedia Publishing Inc.
Ed: Grant Robertson. **Description:** The initial public offering plans of chief executive officer Scott Paterson of JumpTV.com are presented.

11824 ∎ *"People; E-Commerce, Online Games, Mobile Apps" in Advertising Age (Vol. 80, October 19, 2009, No. 35, pp. 14)*
Pub: Crain's Communications
Ed: Nat Ives. **Description:** Profile of People Magazine and the ways in which the publisher is moving its magazine forward by exploring new concepts in a time of declining newsstand sales and advertising pages; among the strategies are e-commerce such as the brand People Style Watch in which consumers are able highlight clothing and jewelry and then connect to retailers' sites and a channel on Taxi TV, the network of video-touch screens in New Your City taxis.

11825 ∎ *"People; E-Commerce, Online Games, Mobile Apps: This Isn't Your Mom's People" in Advertising Age (Vol. 80, October 19, 2009, No. 35)*
Pub: Crain's Communications
Ed: Nat Ives. **Description:** Profile of People Magazine and the ways in which the publisher is moving its magazine forward by exploring new concepts in a time of declining newsstand sales and advertising pages; among the strategies are e-commerce such as the brand People Style Watch in which consumers are able highlight clothing and jewelry and then connect to retailers' sites and a channel on Taxi TV, the network of video-touch screens in New Your City taxis.

11826 ∎ *"Pet-Food Crisis a Boon to Organic Players" in Advertising Age (Vol. 78, April 9, 2007, No. 15, pp. 3)*
Pub: Crain Communications, Inc.
Ed: Jack Neff. **Description:** In the wake of the pet-food recall crisis, the natural-and-organic segment of the market is gaining recognition and sales; one such

manufacturer, Blue Buffalo, has not only seen huge sale increases but also has witnessed a 50-60 percent increase in traffic to the brand's website which has led to the decision to move up the timetable for the brand's first national ad campaign.

11827 ∎ *"Philanthropy Good For Business" in Crain's Detroit Business (Vol. 24, February 18, 2008, No. 7, pp. 14)*
Pub: Crain Communications Inc. - Detroit
Ed: Sheena Harrison. **Description:** Profile of Burce McCully, founder of Dynamic Edge Inc., and his views on philanthropy as a key to any small company's success. The Ann Arbor, Michigan information technology firm has volunteered and raised funds for many causes since 1999 when the company was founded.

11828 ∎ *Planet Google: One Company's Audacious Plan to Organize Everything We Know*
Pub: Free Press
Ed: Randall Stross. **Released:** 2009. **Price:** $26.00. **Description:** The book examines Google, the leader in Internet search engines.

11829 ∎ *"Planning Your Next Move in Ad Land" in Advertising Age (Vol. 81, January 4, 2009, No. 1, pp. 1)*
Pub: Crain's Communications
Description: Overview of the challenges that ad agencies face today and will face in the years to come; highlights include problems occurring in various industries, Internet marketing innovations and the social media landscape.

11830 ∎ *"PMA Launches Online Education Program" in Contractor (Vol. 56, October 2009, No. 10, pp. 8)*
Pub: Penton Media, Inc.
Description: Plumbing & Mechanical Association of Georgia launched an online program that covers technical and business management that will help contractors run their businesses. Future courses will include math for plumbers, graywater systems, and recession-proofing your business.

11831 ∎ *"PopCap Games Achieves Significant Increase in Return on Ad Spend With Omniture SearchCenter" in Internet Wire (September 15, 2009)*
Pub: Comtex News Network, Inc.
Description: PopCap Games, a leading computer games provider, is using Omniture SearchCenter together with Omniture SiteCatalyst to increase revenue from its search engine marketing campaign. Omniture, Inc. is a leading provider of Internet business optimization software.

11832 ∎ *"Pro Teams Shift Ad Budgets; Naming Rights Deals Near $1 Billion" in Brandweek (Vol. 49, April 21, 2008, No. 16, pp. 18)*
Pub: VNU Business Media, Inc.
Ed: Barry Janoff. **Description:** More and more professional sports marketers are spending less of their advertising budgets on traditional media outlets such as television, print and radio; the growing trend in sports marketing is in utilizing new media venues such as the Internet in which innovative means are used to encourage interaction with fans.

11833 ∎ *"Promote Your Business Through New Media" in Business Week (November 5, 2009)*
Pub: McGraw-Hill Companies
Ed: Karen E. Klein. **Description:** Traditional public relations strategies are becoming more and more outdated due to the rapid shift in Internet marketing opportunities. Ideas for marketing your company online are presented.

11834 ∎ *"Punta Gorda Interested in Wi-Fi Internet" in Charlotte Observer (February 1, 2007)*
Pub: Knight-Ridder/Tribune Business News
Ed: Steve Reilly. **Description:** Punta Gorda officials are developing plans to provide free wireless Internet services to businesses and residents.

11835 ∎ *"Q&A Patrick Pichette" in Canadian Business (Vol. 81, October 13, 2008, No. 17, pp. 6)*
Pub: Rogers Media Ltd.
Ed: Andrew Wahl. **Description:** Patrick Pichette finds challenge in taking over the finances of an Internet company that has a market cap of about $140 billion. He feels, however, that serving as Google's chief financial officer is nothing compared to running Bell Canada Enterprises (BCE). Pichette's other views on Google and BCE are presented.

11836 ∎ *"Quantivo Empowers Online Media Companies to Immediately Expand Audiences and Grow Online Profits" in Internet Wire (Nov. 18, 2009)*
Pub: Comtex News Network, Inc.
Description: Quantivo, the leader in on-demand Behavioral Analytics, has launched a new solution that includes 22 of the most critical Internet audience behavior insights as out-of-the-box reports; Internet marketers need to understand their audience, what they want and how often to offer it to them in order to gain successful branding and campaigns online.

11837 ∎ *"The Question: Who Do You Think Is the Most Genuine?" in Advertising Age (Vol. 79, July 7, 2008, No. 26, pp. 4)*
Pub: Crain Communications, Inc.
Ed: Ken Wheaton. **Description:** According to a survey conducted by Harris Interactive Reputation Quotient, Johnson & Johnson was deemed the most genuine brand. Google came in second followed by UPS.

11838 ∎ *"Quickoffice's MobileFiles Pro App Enables Excel Editing On-the-Go" in Information Today (Vol. 26, February 2009, No. 2, pp. 31)*
Pub: Information Today, Inc.
Description: Quickoffice Inc. introduced MobileFiles Pro, which features editable Microsoft Office functionality for the iPone and iPod touch. The application allows users to edit and save Microsoft Excel files in .xls format, transfer files to and from PC and Mac desktops via Wi-Fi, and access and synchronize with Apple MobileMe accounts.

11839 ∎ *"Recalls Cause Consumers to Put More Stock in Online Reviews" in Crain's Cleveland Business (Vol. 28, November 12, 2007, No. 45)*
Pub: Crain Communications, Inc.
Ed: Jack Neff. **Description:** Due to the string of product recalls over the last year, consumers are looking at online product reviews to help them make purchasing decisions which could reshape marketing for a wide range of products.

11840 ∎ *"Reply! Grows at Unprecedented Rate, Rips Beta Off Its Marketplace" in Marketing Weekly News (September 19, 2009, pp. 149)*
Pub: Investment Weekly News
Description: Profile of Reply.com, a leader in locally-targeted Internet marketing, announced significant growth in terms of revenue, enhanced features and services and new categories since launching its beta Reply! Marketplace platform. Even in the face of an economic downturn, the company has posted over 50 percent revenue growth in the Real Estate and Automotive categories.

11841 ∎ *"Reportlinker Adds Report: Social Networks: Five Consumer Trends for 2009" in Wireless News (October 23, 2009)*
Pub: Close-Up Media
Description: 'Social Networks: Five Consumer Trends for 2009,' a new market research report by Reportlinker.com found that in the countries of Italy and Spain lag behind their European neighbors in Internet development. Since large numbers of consumers in these two countries remain offline, only a minimal portion of total advertising spending goes into Internet marketing, and those advertising campaigns are directed at the relatively young, affluent users. Statistical data included.

11842 ■ "Reportlinker.com Adds Report: GeoWeb and Local Internet Markets: 2008 Edition" in Entertainment Close-Up (September 11, 2009)
Pub: Close-Up Media
Description: Reportlinker.com is adding a new market research report that is available in its catalogue: GeoWeb and Local Internet Markets - 2008 Edition; highlights include the outlook for consumer mapping services and an examination of monetizing services and an analysis the development outlook for geospacial Internet market, also referred to as the Geoweb.

11843 ■ "Research and Markets Adds Report: Asian - Internet Market" in Health and Beauty Close-Up (January 19, 2010)
Pub: Close-Up Media
Description: Overview of Research and Markets new report regarding Internet marketing and e-commerce in the Asian region; statistical data included.

11844 ■ "Research and Markets Adds Report: Cyprus: Convergence, Broadband and Internet Market" in Wireless News (September 4, 2009)
Pub: Close-Up Media
Description: Overview of a new report by Research and Markets entitled, 'Cyprus Convergence, Broadband and Internet Market - Overview, Statistics and Forecasts.' Highlights include information regarding broadband accounts which now account for the majority of household Internet connections.

11845 ■ "Research and Markets Adds Report: Ghana: Convergence, Broadband and Internet Market" in Wireless News (September 4, 2009)
Pub: Close-Up Media
Description: Overview of a new report by Research and Markets entitled, 'Ghana Convergence, Broadband and Internet Market - Overview, Statistics and Forecasts.' Ghana was among the first countries in Africa connected to the Internet and to introduce ADSL broadband services; however, only 30 of the 140 licensed ISP's are operational making the sector highly competitive.

11846 ■ "Research and Markets Adds Report: The U.S. Mobile Web Market" in Entertainment Close-Up (December 10, 2009)
Pub: Close-Up Media
Description: Highlights of the new Research and Markets report 'The U.S. Mobile Web Market: Taking Advantage of the iPhone Phenomenon' include: mobile Internet marketing strategies; the growth of mobile web usage; the growth of revenue in the mobile web market; and a look at Internet business communications, social media and networking.

11847 ■ "Research and Markets Adds Report: USA - Internet Market - Analysis, Statistics and Forecasts" in Wireless News (January 15, 2010)
Pub: Close-Up Media
Description: According to Research and Markets new report concerning the United State's Internet market, e-commerce and Online advertising are expected to recover strongly in 2010.

11848 ■ "Research Reports: How Analysts Size Up Companies" in Barron's (Vol. 88, March 17, 2008, No. 11, pp. M13)
Pub: Dow Jones & Company, Inc.
Ed: Anita Peltonen. **Description:** Shares of Applied Industrial Technologies are ranked Market Perform while the shares of Google get a buy rating. Salix Pharmaceuticals gets a Sell/Above-Average risk rating. The shares of Dune Energy, Franklin Resources, Internet Brands, Piper Jaffray, and Texas Instruments are also rated.

11849 ■ "Resource Line" in Black Enterprise (Vol. 37, January 2007, No. 6, pp. 6)
Pub: Earl G. Graves Publishing Co. Inc.
Description: Interactive Media Editor, Philana Patterson, writes a column for blackenterprise.com that offers advice and provides resources for entrepreneurs, corporate executives, business owners, and budding investors.

11850 ■ "The Right Time for REITs" in Barron's (Vol. 88, July 14, 2008, No. 28, pp. 32)
Pub: Dow Jones & Co., Inc.
Ed: Mike Hogan. **Description:** Discusses the downturn in U.S. real estate investment trusts so these are worth considering for investment. Several Websites that are useful for learning about real estate investment trusts for investment purposes are presented.

11851 ■ "Ring Ka-Ching" in Canadian Business (Vol. 79, November 6, 2006, No. 22, pp. 106)
Pub: Rogers Media
Description: A brief profile of Jajah including its web activated telephone services is presented.

11852 ■ "Rise Interactive, Internet Marketing Agency, Now Offers Custom Google Analytics Installation" in Internet Wire (September 29, 2009)
Pub: Comtex News Network, Inc.
Description: In order to optimize a client's return of investment, Rise Interactive, a full-service Internet marketing agency, now offers custom Google Analytics installation to its customers; the installation process includes identifying an Internet marketing campaign's unique key performance indicators, translating them to actions one will perform o n a website and configuring the analytical tool to ensure the customized advertising campaign goals are set and properly tracked.

11853 ■ "Rise Interactive, Internet Marketing Agency, Now Offers Social Media Training and Advisory Services" in Internet Wire (Nov. 4, 2009)
Pub: Comtex News Network, Inc.
Description: Profile of Rise Interactive, a full-service Internet marketing agency which has recently added social media to its list of offerings; the agency touts that its newest service gives their clients the power to have ongoing communication with current and potential customers on the sites they are most actively visiting.

11854 ■ "Ritchie Bros. Breaks Record for Internet Sales at Fort Worth Site During Multi-Million Dollar Unreserved Auction" in Canadian Corporate News
Pub: Comtex News Network Inc.
Description: Ritchie Bros. Auctioneers, the world's largest auctioneer of trucks and industrial equipment, conducted a large unreserved auction at its permanent auction facility in Fort Worth, Texas, in which the company broke the record for Internet sales with bidders using the company's online bidding service, rbauctionBid-Live. Internet bidders purchased more than 440 lots in the auction.

11855 ■ "ROIonline Announces Streaming Video Products" in Marketing Weekly News (December 5, 2009, pp. 155)
Pub: Investment Weekly News
Description: ROIonline LLC, an Internet marketing firm serving business-to-business and the industrial marketplace, has added streaming video options to the Internet solutions it offers its clients; due to the huge increase of broadband connections, videos are now commonplace on the Internet and can often convey a company's message in a must more efficient, concise and effective way that will engage a website's visitor thus delivering a high return on a company's investment.

11856 ■ "The Rypple Effect; Performance Management" in The Economist (Vol. 390, January 3, 2009, No. 8612, pp. 48)
Pub: The Economist Newspaper Inc.
Description: New companies such as Rypple, a new, web-based service, claim that they can satisfy the Net Generation's need for frequent assessments while easing the burden this creates for management.

11857 ■ "Save the Date" in Mergers & Acquisitions: The Dealmaker's Journal (March 1, 2008)
Pub: SourceMedia, Inc.
Description: Listing of conferences and forums that deal with business and investing, particularly with mergers and acquisitions. Includes dates, locations and Internet addresses.

11858 ■ The Savvy Gal's Guide to Online Networking
Pub: Booklocker.com Inc.
Ed: Diane K. Daneilson, Lindsey Pollak. **Released:** August 10, 2007. **Price:** $14.95. **Description:** It is a truth universally acknowledged that a woman in search of a fabulous career must be in want of networking opportunities. Or so Jane Austen would say if she were writing, or more likely, blogging today. So begins the must-read guide to networking in the 21st Century. Authors and networking experts share the nuts, bolts and savvy secrets that businesswomen need in order to use technology to build professional relationships.

11859 ■ "Say Goodbye to Voicemail" in Agency Sales Magazine (Vol. 39, November 2009, No. 10, pp. 3)
Pub: MANA
Description: Salespeople should think twice before leaving a voicemail. The emerging modern etiquette is to send a text message or to e-mail the customer or client. Communication suggestions for both salespeople and their principals are presented.

11860 ■ "Scitable Puts Nature Education on the Map" in Information Today (Vol. 26, February 2009, No. 2, pp. 29)
Pub: Information Today, Inc.
Description: Nature Education, a division of the Nature Publishing Group, released its first product, Scitable, a free online resource for undergraduate biology students and educators. The service includes over 180 overviews of key genetics concepts as well as social networking features, including groups and functionality, that lets students work with classmates and others. Teachers can use the service to set up public or private groups for students.

11861 ■ "Search and Discover New Opportunities" in DM News (Vol. 31, December 14, 2009, No. 29, pp. 13)
Pub: Haymarket Media, Inc.
Ed: Chantal Tode. **Description:** Although other digital strategies are gaining traction in Internet marketing, search marketing continues to dominate this advertising forum. Companies like American Greetings, which markets e-card brands online, are utilizing social networking sites and affiliates to generate a higher demand for their products.

11862 ■ The Search: How Google and Its Rival Rewrote the Rules of Business and Transformed Our Culture
Pub: Penguin Group Incorporated
Ed: John Battelle. **Released:** October 3, 2006. **Price:** $14.95. **Description:** Provides a history of Internet search technology.

11863 ■ The SEO Manifesto: A Practical and Ethical Guide to Internet Marketing and Search Engine Optimization
Pub: Cape Project Management Inc.
Ed: Dan Tousignant, Pamela Gobiel. **Released:** December 5, 2011. **Price:** $14.99. **Description:** Comprehensive guide for each phase of launching an online business; chapters include checklists, process descriptions, and examples.

11864 ■ "Shaw, Telus Take Up Battle Positions" in Globe & Mail (January 1, 2006, pp. B1)
Pub: CTVglobemedia Publishing Inc.
Ed: Catherine McKLean. **Description:** The competition between Shaw Communications Inc. and Telus Corp. over voice over Internet protocol offer for customers is presented.

11865 ■ "Sherwin-Williams Workers Forgo Travel for Virtual Trade Show" in Crain's Cleveland Business (Vol. 28, October 15,

2007, No. 41)
Pub: Crain Communications, Inc.

Ed: John Booth. **Description:** Overview of Cyber-Coating 2007, a cutting-edge virtual three-dimensional trade show that exhibitors such as Sherwin-Williams Co.'s Chemical Coatings Division will take part in by chatting verbally or via text messages in order to exchange information and listen to pitches just like they would on an actual trade show floor.

11866 ■ *"Shipping 2.0" in Entrepreneur (Vol. 36, April 2008, No. 4, pp. 54)*
Pub: Entrepreneur Media, Inc.

Ed: Heather Clancy. **Description:** Doggypads.com contacted with Web 2.0 service provider Shipwire to handle its warehouse concerns. The service works by paying a rent to Shipwire and they will store the client's items. The client's customers can continue to order from the client's website and Shipwire will take care of delivery. Doggypads was able to save up on costs by using Shipwire.

11867 ■ *"Shoestring-Budget Marketing" in Women Entrepreneur (January 5, 2009)*
Pub: Entrepreneur Media Inc.

Ed: Maria Falconer. **Description:** Pay-per-click search engine advertising is the traditional type of e-marketing that may not only be too expensive for certain kinds of businesses but also may not attract the quality customer base a business looking to grow needs to find. Social networking websites have become a mandatory marketing tool for business owners who want to see growth in their sales; tips are provided for utilizing these networking websites in order to gain more visibility on the Internet which can, in turn, lead to the more sales.

11868 ■ *"Show and Tell" in Entrepreneur (Vol. 36, May 2008, No. 5, pp. 54)*
Pub: Entrepreneur Media, Inc.

Ed: Heather Clancy. **Description:** FreshStart Telephone uses recorded video testimonials of customers, by using Pure Digital Flip Video that downloads content directly to the computer, and uploads it in the company's website to promote their wireless phone service.

11869 ■ *"Silverpop Recognized for Email Marketing Innovations by Econsultancy" in Marketing Weekly News (January 23, 2010, pp. 124)*
Pub: Investment Weekly News

Description: Econsultancy, a respected source of insight and advice on digital marketing and e-commerce, recognized Silverpop, the world's only provider of both marketing automation solutions and email marketing specifically tailored to the unique needs of B2C and B2B marketers at Econsultancy's 2009 Innovation Awards.

11870 ■ *SMEs and New Technologies: Learning E-Business and Development*
Pub: Palgrave Macmillan

Ed: Banji Oyelaran-Oyeyinka; Kaushalesh Lal. **Released:** October 2006. **Price:** $85.00. **Description:** Adoption and learning of new information technologies in developing nations is covered. New technologies are opening opportunities for small companies in these countries.

11871 ■ *"Social Media: Communicate the Important Stuff" in Agency Sales Magazine (Vol. 39, November 2009, No. 10, pp. 52)*
Pub: MANA

Ed: Jack Foster. **Description:** Social media such as Twitter or Facebook allows businesses to communicate with their customers over great distances but this technology can take away from the personal touch. For those that want to implement these tools in their marketing plans, they should first find out which social media networks their target audience use and give their customers reasons to become fans.

11872 ■ *"Social Media, E-Mail Remain Challenging for Employees" in Workforce*

Management (Vol. 88, December 14, 2009, No. 13, pp. 4)
Pub: Crain Communications Inc.

Ed: Ed Frauenheim. **Description:** Examining the impact of Internet social networking and the workplace; due to the power of these new technologies, it is important that companies begin to set clear policies regarding Internet use and employee privacy.

11873 ■ *"Social Networkers for Hire" in Black Enterprise (Vol. 40, December 2009, No. 5, pp. 56)*
Pub: Earl G. Graves Publishing Co., Inc.

Ed: Brittany Hutson. **Description:** Companies are utilizing social networking sites in order to market their brand and personally connect with consumers and are increasingly looking to social media specialists to help with this task. Aliya S. King is one such web strategist, working for ICED Media by managing their Twitter, Facebook, YouTube and Flickr accounts for one of their publicly traded restaurant clients.

11874 ■ *"Social Networking Site for Moms" in Marketing to Women (Vol. 21, March 2008, No. 3, pp. 3)*
Pub: EPM Communications Inc.
Contact: Ira Mayer, President
E-mail: imayer@epmcom.com

Description: The Cradle is a social networking site devoted to pregnancy and new parenthood.

11875 ■ *"The Solution" in Entrepreneur (Vol. 37, October 2009, No. 10, pp. 71)*
Pub: Entrepreneur Media, Inc.

Ed: Jennifer Wang. **Description:** Ford's 2010 Transit Connect is a compact commercial van developed specifically for small business owners. The compact van offers an integrated in-dash computer system providing a cellular broadband connection.

11876 ■ *"A Sports Extravaganza - To Go" in Canadian Business (Vol. 79, June 19, 2006, No. 13, pp. 21)*
Pub: Rogers Media

Ed: Andy Holloway. **Description:** Television broadcasting industry in Canada utilizing advanced technologies like mobile television and internet protocol television in broadcasting major sports events. Large number of new technologies are being invented to support increasing demand.

11877 ■ *"State Efforts to Boost Contract Efficiency Hurt Smaller Firms" in Boston Business Journal (Vol. 27, November 9, 2007, No. 41, pp. 1)*
Pub: American City Business Journals Inc.

Ed: Lisa van der Pool. **Description:** Massachusetts Operational Services Division, which provides statewide telecommunications and data infrastructure contracts, announced that it is cutting the list of companies on the new contract from twelve to six. The cost-cutting efforts began in 2005, after a review by an independent consultant advised the state to adopt strategies that would save millions of dollars.

11878 ■ *"Sticking to Stories; Havey Ovshinksy Changes Method, Keeps the Mission" in Crain's Detroit Business (Vol. 24, March 31, 2008)*
Pub: Crain Communications, Inc.

Ed: Daniel Duggan. **Description:** Profile of Harvey Ovshinsky, an award-winning documentary filmmaker who has reinvented his work with corporations who want to market themselves with the transition to digital media. His company, HKO Media, takes Ovshinsky's art of storytelling and enhances it through multimedia operations on the Internet through a joint venture with a man he once mentored, Bob Kernen.

11879 ■ *"Stimulating Fare at the SBA" in Barron's (Vol. 89, July 20, 2009, No. 29, pp. 12)*
Pub: Dow Jones & Co., Inc.

Ed: Jim McTague. **Description:** Internet access at the Small Business Administration slowed down on 7 July 2009, apparently caused by employees streaming videos of the Michael Jackson tribute. The agency claims that the event did not disrupt its operations.

11880 ■ *"Stretch Your Advertising Dollars" in Women Entrepreneur (January 27, 2009)*
Pub: Entrepreneur Media Inc.

Ed: Rosalind Resnick. **Description:** During such poor economic times, most businesses are having to cut their advertising budgets; tips for targeting your advertising dollars toward the customer base most likely to buy your product are given.

11881 ■ *"Study: New Moms Build A Lot of Brand Buzz" in Brandweek (Vol. 49, April 21, 2008, No. 16, pp. 7)*
Pub: VNU Business Media, Inc.

Description: According to a new survey which sampled 1,721 pregnant women and new moms, this demographic is having 109 word-of-mouth conversations per week concerning products, services and brands. Two-thirds of these conversations directly involve brand recommendations. The Internet is driving these word-of-mouth, or W-O-M, conversations among this segment, beating out magazines, television and other forms of media.

11882 ■ *"Success Products" in Black Enterprise (Vol. 37, February 2007, No. 7, pp. 135)*
Pub: Earl G. Graves Publishing Co. Inc.

Ed: Tanisha A. Sykes. **Description:** Using innovative resources that are already at your fingertips instead of trying to reach out to companies first is a great way to discover whether you have a viable idea or product. Be motivated to start an e-newsletter letting people know about your products and attend conferences like The Motivation Show, the world's largest exhibition of motivational products and services related to performance in business.

11883 ■ *Success Secrets of Social Media Marketing Superstars*
Pub: Entrepreneur Press
Contact: Perlman Neil, President

Ed: Mitch Meyerson. **Released:** June 1, 2010. **Price:** $21.95. **Description:** Provides access to the playbooks of social media marketers who reveal their most valuable strategies and tactics for standing out in the new online media environment.

11884 ■ *"Tale of the Tape: IPhone Vs. G1" in Advertising Age (Vol. 79, October 27, 2008, No. 40, pp. 6)*
Pub: Crain Communications, Inc.

Ed: Rita Chang. **Description:** T-Mobile's G1 has been positioned as the first serious competitor to Apple's iPhone. G1 is the first mobile phone to run on the Google-backed, open-source platform Android.

11885 ■ *"A Taxing Proposition" in Black Enterprise (Vol. 37, January 2007, No. 6, pp. 6)*
Pub: Earl G. Graves Publishing Co. Inc.

Description: Learn how to avoid tax problems on Black Enterprise's website, blackenterprise.com.

11886 ■ *"Tee Off Online" in Black Enterprise (Vol. 37, January 2007, No. 6, pp. 52)*
Pub: Earl G. Graves Publishing Co. Inc.

Ed: James C. Johnson. **Description:** The E-Com Resource Center is one of many resources that are available for those interested in starting an e-commerce business. One of the first steps is to create a business plan, of which there are free samples available at BPlans.com.

11887 ■ *"Texas Fold 'Em" in Canadian Business (Vol. 79, October 9, 2006, No. 20, pp. 44)*
Pub: Rogers Media

Ed: John Gray. **Description:** New policies of the United States law makers for the online casino industries that could force many of them out of business are discussed.

11888 ■ *"Things Really Clicking for Macy's Online" in Business Courier (Vol. 24, November 30, 2008, No. 33, pp. 1)*
Pub: American City Business Journals, Inc.

Ed: Lisa Biank Fasig. **Description:** Retailer Macy's online division Macys.com are projecting sales at $1billion in 2007, compared to $620 million in 2006. Macy's new online features and products and the growth of online retail sector are also discussed.

11889 ■ "Thomas Industrial Network Unveils Custom SPEC" in Entertainment Close-Up (March 3, 2011)
Pub: Close-Up Media

Description: Thomas Industrial Network assists custom manufacturers and industrial service providers a complete online program called Custom SPEC which includes Website development and Internet exposure.

11890 ■ "Tim Armstrong" in Canadian Business (Vol. 81, July 21, 2008, No. 11, pp. 10)
Pub: Rogers Media Ltd.

Ed: Calvin Leung. **Description:** Interview with Tim Armstrong who is the president of advertising and commerce department of Google Inc. for North America; the information technology company executive talked about the emerging trends and changes to YouTube made by the company since its acquisition in 2006.

11891 ■ "Time for a Little Pruning" in Barron's (Vol. 89, July 6, 2009, No. 27, pp. 13)
Pub: Dow Jones & Co., Inc.

Ed: Dimitra DeFotis. **Description:** Investors are advised to avoid the shares of Whole Foods, American Tower, T. Rowe Price, Iron Mountain, Intuitive Surgical, Salesforce.com, and Juniper Networks due to their high price to earnings ratios. The shares of Amazon.com, Broadcom, and Expeditors International of Washington remain attractive to investors despite their high price to earnings ratios due to their strong growth.

11892 ■ "To Blog, Or Not To Blog" in Canadian Business (Vol. 80, December 25, 2006, No. 1, pp. 15)
Pub: Rogers Media

Ed: Andy Holloway. **Description:** The growing use of weblogs for internet marketing by business enterprises is discussed.

11893 ■ "The Top Mistakes of Social Media Marketing" in Agency Sales Magazine (Vol. 39, November 2009, No. 9, pp. 42)
Pub: MANA

Ed: Pam Lontos; Maurice Ramirez. **Description:** One common mistake in social media marketing is having more than one image on the Internet because this ruins a business' credibility. Marketers need to put out messages that are useful to their readers and to keep messages consistent.

11894 ■ "Traits that Makes Blogs Attractive to Book Publishers" in Marketing to Women (Vol. 22, July 2009, No. 7, pp. 1)
Pub: EPM Communications Inc.
Contact: Ira Mayer, President
E-mail: imayer@epmcom.com

Description: Book publishers are finding a beneficial relationship between themselves and women bloggers on the Internet. A high visitor count, frequent updates and active readership are criteria for identifying the blogs with the most clout and therefore providing the greatest benefit to publishers.

11895 ■ "Transform Your Life" in Black Enterprise (Vol. 37, January 2007, No. 6, pp. 14)
Pub: Earl G. Graves Publishing Co. Inc.

Description: Through the magazine, television and radio programs, events, and the website, the various platforms of Black Enterprise will provide the tools necessary to achieve success in business ventures, career aspirations, and personal goals.

11896 ■ Twitterville: How Businesses Can Thrive in the New Global Neighborhoods
Pub: Portfolio Hardcover

Ed: Shel Israel. **Price:** $23.95. **Description:** Twitter is the most rapidly adopted communication tool in history, going from zero to ten million users in just over two years. On Twitter, word can spread faster than wildfire. Companies no longer have the option of ignoring the conversation. Unlike other hot social media spaces, Twitterville is dominated by professionals, not students. And despite its size, it still feels like a small town. Twitter allows people to interact much the way they do face-to-face, honestly and authentically.

11897 ■ "Two Field Service Management Solutions" in Contractor (Vol. 56, November 2009, No. 11, pp. 37)
Pub: Penton Media, Inc.

Ed: William Feldman; Patti Feldman. **Description:** Bella Solutions Field Service Software v. 4.2 is a web based solution for HVAC service contractors that enables scheduling of emergency, one-time, multivisit or periodically recurring jobs with drag and drop appointments. VaZing is another web based solution that costs $99 per month for contractors. It can handle line-item discounting and invoices aside from scheduling.

11898 ■ "Unlimited Priorities Strengthens Executive Team" in Entertainment Close-Up (November 1, 2011)
Pub: Close-Up Media

Description: Founder and president of Unlimited Priorities Corporation, Iris L. Hanney, added two executive level professionals to her team. The new employees will help increase the firm's capabilities in social media and information technology.

11899 ■ "Up To Code? Website Eases Compliance Burden for Entrepreneurs" in Black Enterprise (Vol. 38, March 2008, No. 8, pp. 48)
Pub: Earl G. Graves Publishing Co. Inc.

Ed: Robin White-Goode. **Description:** Business.gov is a presidential E-government project created to help small businesses easily find, understand, and comply with laws and regulations pertaining to a particular industry.

11900 ■ "Use Social Media to Enhance Brand, Business" in Contractor (Vol. 56, December 2009, No. 12, pp. 14)
Pub: Penton Media, Inc.

Ed: Elton Rivas. **Description:** Advice on how plumbing contractors should use online social networks to increase sales is presented including such issues as clearly defining goals and target audience. An additional advantage to this medium is that advertisements can easily be shared with other users.

11901 ■ "Utah Technology Council: Social Media Is Here to Stay; Embrace It" in Wireless News (December 14, 2009)
Pub: Close-Up Media

Description: Social media outlets such as Facebook and Twitter are blurring the lines between advertising, public relations, branding and marketing; businesses must stop thinking in terms of traditional marketing versus Internet marketing if they want to succeed in today's marketing climate.

11902 ■ "Verizon's Big Gamble Comes Down to the Wire" in Globe & Mail (February 3, 2007, pp. B1)
Pub: CTVglobemedia Publishing Inc.

Ed: Catherine McLean. **Description:** The launch of a new broadband service by Verizon Communications Inc. based on fibre optic cable technology is discussed. The company has spent $23 billion for introducing the new service.

11903 ■ "A View to a Killer Business Model" in Black Enterprise (Vol. 40, December 2009, No. 5, pp. 50)
Pub: Earl G. Graves Publishing Co., Inc.

Ed: Sonya A. Donaldson. **Description:** Profile of Gen2Media Corp., a production, technology and Internet marketing firm based in Florida with offices in New York; Gen2Media is utilizing the advances in technology to now include video in its online marketing offerings.

11904 ■ "The Virtual Office" in Canadian Business (Vol. 80, April 9, 2007, No. 8, pp. 64)
Pub: Rogers Media

Ed: Andrew Wahl. **Description:** The business operation of Eloqua which runs all its IT systems using its own online software is discussed.

11905 ■ "Virtus.com Wins 'Best of Industry' WebAward for Excellence in Financial Services" in Investment Weekly News (October 24, 2009)
Pub: Investment Weekly News

Description: Web Marketing Association honored Virtus.com, the Website of Virtus Investment Partners, Inc., for Outstanding Achievement in Web Development and Acsys Interactive was awarded the Financial Services Standard of Excellence Award for developing the site. The site was part of a rebranding effort and is a one-stop portal for both financial advisors and their investors.

11906 ■ "Virtus.com Wins 'Best of Industry' WebAward for Excellence in Financial Services" in Investment Weekly News (Oct. 24, 2009, pp. 227)
Pub: Investment Weekly News

Description: Web Marketing Association honored Virtus.com, the Website of Virtus Investment Partners, Inc., for Outstanding Achievement in Web Development and Acsys Interactive was awarded the Financial Services Standard of Excellence Award for developing the site. The site was part of a rebranding effort and is a one-stop portal for both financial advisors and their investors.

11907 ■ "Vistaprint Survey Indicates that Online Marketing Taking Hold Among Small Businesses" in Internet Wire (December 10, 2009)
Pub: Comtex News Network, Inc.

Description: According to a comprehensive survey from Vistaprint N.V., small businesses are very likely to increase their use of Internet marketing strategies such as paid and organic search, email marketing, social media networking and custom websites over the next year. Trends continue to show that more small businesses are indeed adapting to the changing marketplace and are more willing to diversify their marketing strategies than ever before.

11908 ■ "Vonage V-Phone: Use Your Laptop to Make Calls Via the Internet" in Black Enterprise (Vol. 37, January 2007, No. 6, pp. 52)
Pub: Earl G. Graves Publishing Co. Inc.

Ed: James C. Johnson. **Description:** Overview of the Vonage V-Phone, which is small flash drive device that lets you make phone calls through a high-speed Internet connection and plugs into any computer's USB port. Business travels may find this product to be a wonderful solution as it includes 250MB of memory and can store files, digital photos, MP3s, and more.

11909 ■ "Web-Based Marketing Excites, Challenges Small Business Use" in Colorado Springs Business Journal (January 20, 2010)
Pub: Dolan Media Co.

Ed: Becky Hurley. **Description:** Business-to-business and consumer-direct firms alike are using the fast-changing Web technologies to increase sales, leads and track consumer behavior but once a company commits to an Online marketing plan, experts believe, they must be prepared to consistently tweak and overhaul content and distribution vehicles in order to keep up.

11910 ■ "Web-Based Solutions Streamline Operations" in Contractor (Vol. 56, December 2009, No. 12, pp. 28)
Pub: Penton Media, Inc.

Ed: William Feldman; Patti Feldman. **Description:** Sage Project Lifecycle Management is a Web-based service platform for plumbing and HVAC contractors. It enables effective workflow and document management. Projectmates, on the other hand, is a Web-based enterprise-wide solution for managing both commercial plumbing and HVAC projects.

11911 ■ "Web Biz Brulant Surfing for Acquisition Candidates" in Crain's Cleveland Business (Vol. 28, December 3, 2007, No. 48, pp. 6)
Pub: Crain Communications, Inc.

Ed: Chuck Soder. **Description:** Brulant Inc., a provider of web development and marketing services, is looking to acquire other companies after growing for five years straight. The company is one of the largest technology firms in Northeast Ohio.

11912 ■ *"The Web Gets Real" in Canadian Business (Vol. 79, July 17, 2006, No. 14-15, pp. 19)*

Pub: Rogers Media

Ed: Andrew Wahl. **Description:** Ron Lake's efforts of bringing the virtual and physical worlds more closely together by using Geographic Markup Language (GML) are presented.

11913 ■ *"Web Sight: Do You See What I See?" in Entrepreneur (Vol. 35, October 2007, No. 10, pp. 58)*

Pub: Entrepreneur Media Inc.

Ed: Heather Clancy. **Description:** Owners of Trunkt, a boutique in New York that showcases independent designs, have created a new style of Website called Trunkt.org. The Website allows buyers to select the products they want to see and designers can choose anytime which of their items will be displayed on the site. An explanation of the strategy that helped bring Trunkt closer to its clients is presented.

11914 ■ *"Web Site Focuses on Helping People Find Jobs, Internships with Area Businesses" in Crain's Detroit Business (Vol. 26, Jan. 4, 2010)*

Pub: Crain Communications Inc.

Ed: Dustin Walsh. **Description:** DetroitIntern.com, LLC is helping metro Detroit college students and young professionals find career-advancing internships or jobs with local businesses.

11915 ■ *"Web Traffic Numbers Facing Scrutiny" in Boston Business Journal (Vol. 27, November 2, 2007, No. 40, pp. 1)*

Pub: American City Business Journals Inc.

Ed: Jesse Noyes. **Description:** Interactive Advertising Bureau (IAB) held a summit meeting with major industry players in an effort to create more transparent standards for measuring Internet traffic. The terms at issue were registered users, unique visitors, time spent and retention.

11916 ■ *"Webadvertising" in MarketingMagazine (Vol. 115, September 27, 2010, No. 13, pp. 70)*

Pub: Rogers Publishing Ltd.

Description: Website advertising in Canada is examined.

11917 ■ *"Website Backup Made Simple" in Inc. (Vol. 33, September 2011, No. 7, pp. 52)*

Pub: Inc. Magazine

Ed: John Brandon. **Description:** Tools to back up content on a Website are profiled. Vaultpress works only with sites that run on the WordPress publishing platform and CodeGuard works with a variety of publishing platforms and hosting services.

11918 ■ *"Website Triples Traffic in Three Weeks Using Press Releases" in PR Newswire (January 5, 2010)*

Pub: PR Newswire Association, LLC

Description: Irbtrax, an Internet marketing firm, concluded a comprehensive study revealing that online press release submission services offer measurable Website traffic-building results.

11919 ■ *"Website for Women 50 Launches" in Marketing to Women (Vol. 21, April 2008, No. 4, pp. 5)*

Pub: EPM Communications Inc.

Contact: Ira Mayer, President

E-mail: imayer@epmcom.com

Description: Vibrantnation.com is an online community targeting women over age 50; members can share recommendations on a variety of topics such as vacation spots, retailers and financial issues.

11920 ■ *"Wendy Turner; Vice-President and General Manager, Vocalo.org" in Crain's Chicago Business (Vol. 31, May 5, 2008, No. 18, pp. 22)*

Pub: Crain Communications, Inc.

Ed: Kevin McKeough. **Description:** Profile of Wendy Turner who is a leader at Vocalo, a combination of talk radio and Web site, where listeners can set up profile pages similar to those on Facebook.

11921 ■ *"What You Look Like Online" in Black Enterprise (Vol. 37, January 2007, No. 6, pp. 56)*

Pub: Earl G. Graves Publishing Co. Inc.

Ed: Marcia A. Reed-Woodard. **Description:** Of 100 executive recruiters 77 percent stated that they use search engines to check the backgrounds of potential job candidates, according to a survey conducted by ExecuNet. Of those surveyed 35 percent stated that they eliminate potential candidates based on information they find online so it is important to create a positive Web presence which highlights professional image qualities.

11922 ■ *"What's In Your Toolbox" in Women In Business (Vol. 61, August-September 2009, No. 4, pp. 7)*

Pub: American Business Women's Association

Ed: Mimi Kopulos. **Description:** Business owners are increasingly turning to using social networking websites, such as Facebook, LinkedIn and Twitter, to promote their companies. The number of adult social media users has increased from 8 percent in 2005 to 35 percent in 2009.

11923 ■ *"Why-Max?" in Canadian Business (Vol. 81, July 22, 2008, No. 12-13, pp. 19)*

Pub: Rogers Media Ltd.

Ed: Andrew Wahl. **Description:** Nascent technology known as LTE (Long Term Evolution) is expected to challenge Intel's WiMax wireless technology as the wireless broadband standard. LTE , which is believed to be at least two years behind WiMax in development, is likely to be supported by wireless and mobile-phone carriers. Views and information on WiMax and LTE are presented.

11924 ■ *"Why Some Get Shaften By Google Pricing" in Advertising Age (Vol. 79, July 14, 2008, No. 7, pp. 3)*

Pub: Crain Communications, Inc.

Ed: Abbey Klaassen. **Description:** Google's search advertising is discussed as well as the company's pricing structure for these ads.

11925 ■ *"Why Women Blog and What They Read" in Marketing to Women (Vol. 22, July 2009, No. 7, pp. 8)*

Pub: EPM Communications Inc.

Contact: Ira Mayer, President

E-mail: imayer@epmcom.com

Description: Listing of topics that are visited the most by female Internet users. Statistical data included.

11926 ■ *"Wi-Fi Finds Its Way Despite Nixed Plan for Free System" in Crain's Cleveland Business (Vol. 28, November 12, 2007, No. 45, pp. 3)*

Pub: Crain Communications, Inc.

Ed: Jay Miller. **Description:** Discusses the issues facing Cleveland and Northeast Ohio concerning their proposal to offer citizens wireless Internet services for free or a small fee.

11927 ■ *"Wi-Fi On Steroids: Will WiMAX Provide the Juice For Souped-Up Connections?" in Black Enterprise (November 2007)*

Pub: Earl G. Graves Publishing Co. Inc.

Ed: Fiona Haley. **Description:** WiMAX, Worldwide Interoperability for Microwave Access in the U.S. WiMax is technology that moves data and connects faster and at greater distances than before.

11928 ■ *Wikinomics: How Mass Collaboration Changes Everything*

Pub: Penguin Group Incorporated

Ed: Don Tapscott; Anthony D. Williams. **Released:** April 2008. **Price:** $27.95. **Description:** Research and information about the every changing world of the Internet is provided to help small businesses.

11929 ■ *"Will the Force Be With Salesforce?" in Barron's (Vol. 88, March 24, 2008, No. 12, pp. 20)*

Pub: Dow Jones & Company, Inc.

Ed: Mark Veverka. **Description:** Shares of Salesforce.com are likely to drop from the $44.83-a-share level in the face of a deteriorating economy and

financial sector and thus lower demand for business software. The company is unlikely to deliver on its ambitious earnings forecasts for 2008 especially with strengthening competition from Oracle.

11930 ■ *Winner Take All: How Competitiveness Shapes the Fate of Nations*

Pub: Basic Books

Ed: Richard J. Elkus Jr. **Released:** 2009. **Price:** $27.00. **Description:** American government and misguided business practices has allowed the U.S. to fall behind other countries in various market sectors such as cameras and televisions, as well as information technologies. It will take a national strategy to for America to regain its lead in crucial industries.

11931 ■ *"Wireless: Full Service" in Entrepreneur (Vol. 35, October 2007, No. 10, pp. 60)*

Pub: Entrepreneur Media Inc.

Ed: Amanda C. Kooser. **Description:** Palm Foleo, the $599 smart phone enables users to access and compose email, browse the Internet, view documents and play Powerpoint files. It weighs 2.5 pounds and has a 10-inch screen. Other features, such as built-in WiFi are described.

11932 ■ *"Wireless Provider's Star Grows $283 Million Brighter" in Hispanic Business (July-August 2007, pp. 60)*

Pub: Hispanic Business

Description: Profile of Brightstar Corporation, the world's largest wireless phone distribution and supply chain reported record growth in 2007.

11933 ■ *"Women Clicking to Earn Virtual Dollars" in Sales and Marketing Management (November 11, 2009)*

Pub: Nielsen Business Media, Inc.

Ed: Stacy Straczynski. **Description:** According to a new report from Internet marketing firm Q Interactive, women are increasingly playing social media games where they are able to click on an ad or sign up for a promotion to earn virtual currency. Research is showing that this kind of marketing may be a potent tool, especially for e-commerce and online stores.

11934 ■ *"Words at Work" in Information Today (Vol. 26, February 2009, No. 2, pp. 25)*

Pub: Information Today, Inc.

Description: Current new buzzwords include the following: digital amnesia, or overload by availability, speed and volume of digital information; maternal profiling, a form a discrimination against women; recipe malpractice, a reminder that just because you can turn on a stove it doesn't make you a chef; ringxiety, the act when everyone reaches for their cell phone when one rings; verbing, the practice of turning good nouns into verbs.

11935 ■ *"WordStream Announces a Pair of Firsts for SEO and PPC Keyword Research Tools" in Internet Wire (November 10, 2009)*

Pub: Comtex News Network, Inc.

Description: WordSteam, Inc., a provider of pay-per-click (PPC) and search engine optimization (SEO) solutions for continuously expanding and optimizing search marketing efforts has released two new features in their flagship Keyword Management solution; these tools will allow marketers to analyze data from paid search, organic search and estimated totals from keyword suggestion tools side-by-side.

11936 ■ *"Work Smarter" in Entrepreneur (Vol. 36, April 2008, No. 4, pp. 70)*

Pub: Entrepreneur Media, Inc.

Ed: Amanda C. Kooser. **Description:** Online applications that address a business' particular needs are presented. These web applications offer email services, collaboration services of sharing and editing documents and presentations, and tie-ups with online social networking sites. Details on various web applications are provided.

11937 ■ *"Xtium Has Its Head in the Clouds" in Philadelphia Business Journal (Vol. 30, September 23, 2011, No. 32, pp. 1)*

Pub: American City Business Journals Inc.

Ed: Peter Key. **Description:** Philadelphia-based cloud computing firm Xtium LLC received an $11.5 million first-round investment from Boston-

Massachusetts-based OpenView Venture Partners. Catering to midsize businesses and unit of bigger firms, Xtium offers disaster-recovery, hosting, and managed-information-technology-infrastructure services.

11938 ■ *"The Yahoo Family Tree" in Conde Nast Portfolio (Vol. 2, June 2008, No. 6, pp. 34)*

Pub: Conde Nast Publications

Contact: David Carey, President

Ed: Blaise Zerega. **Description:** Yahoo, founded in 1994 by Stanford students Jerry Yang and David Filo, is still an Internet powerhouse. The company's history is also outlined as well as the reasons in which Microsoft desperately wants to acquire the firm.

11939 ■ *"Yahoo! - Microsoft Pact: Alive Again?" in Barron's (Vol. 89, July 27, 2009, No. 30, pp. 8)*

Pub: Dow Jones & Co., Inc.

Ed: Mark Veverka. **Description:** Yahoo! reported higher than expected earnings in the second quarter of 2009 under CEO Carol Bartz who has yet to articulate her long-term vision and strategy for turning around the company. The media reported that Yahoo! and Microsoft are discussing an advertising-search partnership which should benefit both companies.

11940 ■ *"You Are What They Click" in Entrepreneur (Vol. 37, July 2009, No. 7, pp. 43)*

Pub: Entrepreneur Media, Inc.

Ed: Mikal Belicove. **Description:** Hiring the right website design firm is the first stage in building an online business, and this involves various factors such as price, technical expertise, and talent. Writing a request for proposal (RFP) detailing the website's details, which include purpose, budget and audience, is the first step the process. Other tips in finding the right web designer are given.

11941 ■ *"Your Annual Business Tune-Up" in Business Week (December 28, 2006)*

Pub: McGraw-Hill Companies

Ed: Karen E. Klein. **Description:** Interview with entrepreneurial expert, Ty Freyvogel, founder of EntrpreneursLab.com. Freyvogel gives tips on how a thorough review of existing systems, vendors, customers, and employees could help keep an entrepreneur's business not only safe but highly successful in the upcoming year.

11942 ■ *"Zen and the Art of Twitter Maintenance" in Agency Sales Magazine (Vol. 39, September-October 2009, No. 9, pp. 48)*

Pub: MANA

Ed: Terry Brock. **Description:** Online social networks such as Twitter, LinkedIn, and Facebook should be used to stay in touch with business relationships, especially customers. There should be a focus on making customers happy and building the bottom-line when using these tools.

11943 ■ *"Zeon Solutions Teams with Endeca for SaaS Version of Endeca InFront" in Entertainment Close-Up (October 25, 2011)*

Pub: Close-Up Media

Description: Zeon Solutions, an enterprise e-commerce and Website development firm announced a special licensing partnership with Endeca Technologies. Endeca is an information management software company that provides small and mid-size retailers with high-performance Customer Experience Management technology.

TRADE PERIODICALS

11944 ■ *Association for Computing Machinery*

Pub: Special Interest Group on Data Communication

Ed: Martha Steenstrup, Editor. **Released:** Quarterly. **Price:** $50. **Description:** Serves as a forum for computing professionals in the data communications field. Focuses on network architecture, including the Internet, network protocols, and distributed systems.

11945 ■ *Data Base Alert*

Pub: Access Intelligence L.L.C.

Contact: Donald Pazour, President

Ed: Judy Duke, Editor. **Released:** Monthly. **Description:** Provides updates on publicly available online services. Contains a listing of distributors of new or revised data bases with data bases listed alphabetically under the appropriate distributor along with information about pricing, updates, and number of records. Remarks: Newsletter is part of DataBase Directory Service, which includes an annual directory and supplement.

11946 ■ *Information Today*

Pub: Information Today Inc.

Contact: Thomas H. Hogan, President

E-mail: ctuthill@infotoday.com

URL(s): www.infotoday.com/IT/default.asp. **Released:** 11/yr. **Price:** $89.95, Individuals; $118, Canada and Mexico; $169, Two years; $129, Other countries.

11947 ■ *Internet Marketing Report*

Pub: Progressive Business Publications

Ed: Alan Field, Editor. **Released:** Semimonthly. **Price:** $299, individuals. **Description:** Communicates the latest news and trends in website marketing. g.

11948 ■ *Internet Telephone / Green Data Centers*

Pub: Information Gatekeepers Inc.

Contact: Paul Polishuk, President

E-mail: ppolishuk@igigroup.com

Ed: Tony Carmona, Editor. **Released:** Monthly. **Price:** $695, U.S. and Canada; $745, elsewhere. **Description:** Provides marketing and technology information on new developments in the internet telephone industry on a worldwide basis.

11949 ■ *ISP Business / IPTB*

Pub: Information Gatekeepers Inc.

Contact: Paul Polishuk, President

E-mail: ppolishuk@igigroup.com

Ed: Rebecca Jackson, Editor. **Released:** Monthly. **Price:** $695, U.S. and Canada; $745, elsewhere. **Description:** Covers news of the business aspects of Internet service providers worldwide. Includes information on finances, marketing, mergers and acquisitions, joint ventures, technologies, customer billing and service, new products, and international developments.

11950 ■ *Larry Chase's Web Digest for Marketers (WDFM)*

Pub: Chase Online Marketing Strategies,Inc

Contact: Larry Chase, Executive Editor

E-mail: a@wdfm.com

Ed: Mary Gillen, Editor. **Released:** Weekly. **Price:** Free. **Description:** Delivers 15 short reviews of business-related websites every issue. Remarks: America Online, Inc.

11951 ■ *Medicine on the Net*

Pub: COR Healthcare Resources

Ed: Bridget Meaney, Editor. **Released:** Monthly. **Price:** $147, U.S. and Canada; $159, elsewhere. **Description:** Spotlights developing issues in the use of the Internet by medical professionals. Recurring features include letters to the editor, interviews, news of research, and book reviews.

11952 ■ *Online: The Leading Magazine for Information Professionals*

Pub: Online, A Division of Information Today Inc.

URL(s): www.infotoday.com/online/default.shtml. **Ed:** Marydee Ojala. **Released:** Bimonthly **Price:** $124.95, Individuals; $235, Two years; $141, Canada and Mexico; $167, Other countries.

11953 ■ *Worldgram Newsletter*

Pub: Worldprofit Inc.

Ed: Dr. Jeffrey Lant, Editor, drjlant@worldprofit.com. **Released:** Bimonthly. **Price:** Free. **Description:** Internet newsletter with a marketing focus for businesses. Also offers tips on how to profit from the World Wide Web.

CONSULTANTS

11954 ■ Construction Computing Solutions Inc.—CCS Inc.

40 Orchard Ct.

Brick, NJ 08724-4396

Ph: (732)899-4319

Fax: (732)899-1921

Co. E-mail: constructioncomputing@comcast.net

URL: http://www.ccspcs.com

Contact: Gerry Bierbrauer, President

E-mail: gerryb@ccswebservices.com

Scope: Links home and small business customers, contractors and engineers with their PC system's hardware and software to achieve the maximum productivity that the hardware and software allow. Offers individual and network PC consulting services for home users, small (0-10 user) to medium (10-50 user) businesses, and construction and engineering companies in the tri-state area in the following general areas: Evaluation of computer needs, hardware, software and training, sales and installation of hardware and software as needed, sales, set up and training on construction specific software, training for and/or administration of software and network functions, internet sales, set up, access, email, and web pages. **Founded:** 1997.

11955 ■ Law Offices of Robert J. Keller P.C.

Farragut Sta.

Washington, DC 20033-3428

Ph: (202)223-2100

Fax: (202)223-2121

Co. E-mail: rjk@telcomlaw.com

URL: http://www.telcomlaw.com

Contact: Robert J. Keller, Chief Executive Officer

E-mail: rjk@telcomlaw.com

Scope: Specializes in telecommunications law, policy, and regulation, with particular emphasis on wireless telecommunications, new and emerging technologies, transactions involving FCC-regulated entities and licensees, and the special legal and regulatory issues relating to toll free telephone numbers. Experience in representing clients before the Federal Communications Commission, federal courts, and state and federal regulatory agencies. **Founded:** 1994.

FRANCHISES AND BUSINESS OPPORTUNITIES

11956 ■ Auction it Today Inc.

5424 E Grand River Ave., Ste. 101

Howell, MI 48843

Ph: (810)225-0555

Free: 866-216-3666

Fax: (810)225-8231

Co. E-mail: franchise@auction-itTODAY.com

URL: http://www.auction-itToday.com

Description: Takes the hassles out of selling on eBay. Handle the entire eBay selling process for individuals, businesses, charities, estates etc. Sell everything from small antiques and collectibles to heavy equipment and real estate. **No. of Franchise Units:** 105. **No. of Company-Owned Units:** 1. **Founded:** 2004.. **Franchised:** 2005. **Equity Capital Needed:** $19,000-$105,000. **Franchise Fee:** $14,000-$22,000. **Royalty Fee:** Varies. **Training:** Provides training, marketing, merchandising, and sales program with hands on experience in one of our stores, with ongoing phone and email support.

11957 ■ Instantfx Web Services

Expetec Corp.

12 2nd Ave., SW

Aberdeen, SD 57401

Free: 888-297-2292

Fax: (605)225-5176

Description: Web design and hosting services. **No. of Franchise Units:** 70. **Founded:** 1992.. **Franchised:** 2004. **Equity Capital Needed:** $13,300-$16,200, total investment. **Franchise Fee:** $12,500. **Training:** Yes.

11958 ■ Pak Mail

7173 S Havan St., Ste. 600

Centennial, CO 80112

Ph: (800)833-2821
Fax: (800)336-7363
Co. E-mail: sales@pakmail.org
URL: http://www.pakmail.com
Description: One-stop shop offers the customer a convenient location to send packages, make copies, send or receive a fax or rent a private mailbox. **No. of Franchise Units:** 500. **Founded:** 1983.. **Franchised:** 1984. **Equity Capital Needed:** $130,000-$164,300 total investment. **Franchise Fee:** $29,950. **Financial Assistance:** Yes. **Training:** Provides training, education & ongoing support to build your business.

11959 ■ The Utility Company Ltd.
One Hines Rd., Ste. 301
Kanata, ON, Canada K2K 3C7
Ph: (613)591-9800
Fax: (613)591-3966
URL: http://www.theutilitycompany.com
Description: Supplier of information technology delivered as a utility service to small and medium businesses, providing the required hardware, software and service for a monthly fee per user. Our Connected Office service suite empowers people to operate, communicate and manage their business more effectively. **No. of Franchise Units:** 52. **No. of Company-Owned Units:** 2. **Founded:** 2006.. **Franchised:** 2006. **Equity Capital Needed:** $45,119-$70,357 investment required; $45,119 start-up capital required. **Franchise Fee:** $39,000. **Training:** Yes.

11960 ■ WSI Internet
1660 Tech Ave., Unit 2
Mississauga, ON, Canada L4W 5S9
Ph: (905)678-7588
Free: 888-678-7588
Fax: (905)678-7242
Co. E-mail: wsileads@wsiworld.com
URL: http://www.wsicorporate.com
Description: Provides full service internet solutions. Helps operate internet consultancy franchise. **No. of Franchise Units:** 80. **Founded:** 1995.. **Franchised:** 1996. **Equity Capital Needed:** $49,700. **Franchise Fee:** $60,000. **Training:** Yes.

LIBRARIES

11961 ■ Gartner IRC
56 Top Gallant Rd.
Stamford, CT 06904

Ph: (203)964-0096
Fax: (203)316-6480
Co. E-mail: inquiry@gartner.com
URL: http://www.gartner.com
Contact: Karen Laughlin
Scope: Information technology, computers, system design, telecommunications. **Services:** SDI; center not open to the public (client research only). **Founded:** 1979. **Holdings:** 3000 items. **Subscriptions:** 1200 journals and other serials. **Telecommunication Services:** info@amstock.com.

11962 ■ International Data Corp. - IDC Library
2131 Landings Dr.
Mountain View, CA 94043
Ph: (650)962-6481
Fax: (650)691-0518
Co. E-mail: slake@idc.com
URL: http://www.idc.com
Contact: Sara Lake, Director, Library Services
Scope: Information technology. **Services:** Center not open to the public. **Founded:** 1990. **Holdings:** 350 books; 250 subject files. **Subscriptions:** 70 journals and other serials.

11963 ■ LexisNexis Technical Library
9595 Springboro Pike
Miamisburg, OH 45342
Ph: (937)865-6800
Fax: (937)865-1655
Co. E-mail: technical.library@lexisnexis.com
Contact: Patricia J. Carter, Manager
Scope: Online industry. **Services:** Interlibrary loan; Library not open to the public. **Founded:** 1992. **Holdings:** 6000 volumes. **Subscriptions:** 100 journals and other serials; 2 newspapers.

11964 ■ Queens Borough Public Library - Information Services Division
89-11 Merrick Blvd.
Jamaica, NY 11432
Ph: (718)990-0778
Fax: (718)658-8342
Co. E-mail: thomas.w.galante@queenslibrary.org
URL: http://www.queenslibrary.org
Contact: Thomas W. Galante, Chief Executive Officer
Scope: General. **Services:** Interlibrary loan; copying; email reference; faxing to New York State residents;

Library open to the public. **Holdings:** 1000 volumes; partial depository for federal government documents; state and city documents.

11965 ■ University of Michigan - Information and Library Studies Library
Hatcher Graduate Library, Rm. 209
Ann Arbor, MI 48109-1205
Ph: (734)764-1313
Co. E-mail: shevonad@umich.edu
URL: http://www.lib.umich.edu
Contact: Donna Hayward, Associate Director
URL(s): guides.lib.umich.edu/infostudies. **Scope:** Library science, history of libraries, history of publishing, history of bookselling, history of the book, bibliography, children's literature, online information services, information technology, storage and retrieval, micrographics, human computer interaction, archives and records management, information policy, information economics. **Services:** Interlibrary loan; Library open to the public. **Holdings:** 63,259 books; 701 dissertations; 453 reels of microfilm; 7020 sheets of microfiche; 20 AV programs; 22 CD-ROMs; 30,000 monographs; 400 serials; 300 periodicals. **Subscriptions:** 589 journals and other serials. **Telecommunication Services:** dlhodge@umich.edu.

RESEARCH CENTERS

11966 ■ Pennsylvania State University at Harrisburg - Pennsylvania State Data Center (PaSDC)
777 W Harrisburg Pke.
Middletown, PA 17057-4898
Ph: (717)948-6336
Fax: (717)948-6754
Co. E-mail: pasdc@psu.edu
URL: http://pasdc.hbg.psu.edu
Contact: Sue Copella, Director
Services: Demographic and socioeconomic data: via telephone requests. **Founded:** 1981. **Publications:** *Estimates* (Annual); *State Abstract*; *County Data Books*. **Educational Activities:** PaSDC Conference (Annual); Regional workshops, on census basics, CD-ROMS, on-line systems, and GIS; PASDC User Conference. **Telecommunication Services:** sdc3@psu.edu.

ASSOCIATIONS AND OTHER ORGANIZATIONS

11967 ■ Canadian Securities Institute (CSI)—Institut Canadien des Valeurs Mobilieres
200 Wellington St. W, 15th Fl.
Toronto, ON, Canada M5V 3C7
Ph: (416)364-9130
Free: 866-866-2601
Fax: (416)359-0486
Co. E-mail: customer_support@csi.ca
URL: http://www.csi.ca
Contact: Roberta Wilton, President
Description: Stock exchanges, brokers, and other investment professionals. Promotes increased public understanding of securities investment. Serves as a network linking members; sponsors educational programs. **Founded:** 1970.

11968 ■ Canadian ShareOwners Association
4 King St. W, Ste. 806
Toronto, ON, Canada M5H 1B6
Ph: (416)595-9600
Free: 800-268-6881
Fax: (416)595-0400
Co. E-mail: customercare@shareowner.com
URL: http://www.shareowner.com/index.html
Contact: John T. Bart, President
Description: Investors in securities. Promotes successful investment by independent investors. Conducts educational programs; sponsors research. **Publications:** *ShareOwner* (Bimonthly).

11969 ■ CFA Institute
560 Ray C. Hunt Dr.
Charlottesville, VA 22903-2981
Ph: (434)951-5499
Free: 800-247-8132
Fax: (434)951-5262
Co. E-mail: info@cfainstitute.org
URL: http://www.cfainstitute.org
Contact: Daniel S. Meader, Chairman
Description: Security and financial analyst association whose members are practicing investment analysts. Includes private, voluntary self-regulation program in which members are enrolled. Internationally renowned for its rigorous Chartered Financial Analyst curriculum and examination program, which has more than 86,000 candidates from 143 countries enrolled for exams. In addition, it is internationally recognized for its investment performance standards, which investment firms use to document and report investment results, as well as for its Code of Ethics and Standards of Professional Conduct. **Founded:** 1990. **Publications:** *AIMR Exchange* (Bimonthly); *AIMR Membership Directory* (Annual); *Financial Analysts Journal* (Bimonthly). **Awards:** Alfred C. Morley Distinguished Service Award; Graham and Dodd Award; Nicholas Molodovsky Award; Special Service Award; Award for Professional Excellence; C. Stewart Sheppard Award; James R. Vertin Award; Society Leader Award (Annual); Daniel J. Forrestal III Leader-

ship Award for Professional Ethics and Standards of Investment Practice; Thomas L. Hansberger Leadership in Global Investing Award.

11970 ■ Investment Adviser Association (IAA)
1050 17th St. NW, Ste. 725
Washington, DC 20036-5514
Ph: (202)293-4222
Fax: (202)293-4223
Co. E-mail: info@investmentadviser.org
URL: http://www.investmentadviser.org
Contact: Vivian Pan, President
Description: Federally registered investment adviser firms. Represents the interests of the investment management profession before legislative and regulatory bodies. **Founded:** 1937. **Publications:** *Directory of Member Firms* (Annual); *Investment Counsel Association of America--Directory of Member Firms* (Annual).

11971 ■ Investment Management Consultants Association (IMCA)
5619 DTC Pkwy., Ste. 500
Greenwood Village, CO 80111
Ph: (303)770-3377
Fax: (303)770-1812
Co. E-mail: imca@imca.org
URL: http://www.imca.org
Contact: Sean Walters, Chief Executive Officer
Description: Consultants, money managers, and others in the investment management consultant business. Seeks to increase public awareness of investment management consultants, provide educational programs to members, and encourage high business standards. Operates consulting industry certification program. Maintains a legislative network with state and federal legislative information affecting the industry. **Founded:** 1985. **Publications:** *Essentials of Investment Consulting*; *The Facts About Investing*; *The Monitor* (Bimonthly); *Wealth Management Course*; *The Journal of Investment Consulting* (Semiannual). **Educational Activities:** Investment Management Consultants Association Conference (Annual); Fall Investment Management Expo (Annual); Regional Consultants Conferences (Quarterly). **Awards:** IMCA Journalism Award (Annual); The Richard J. Davis Ethics Award (Annual); Stephen L. Kessler Writing Award (Annual).

11972 ■ National Investment Company Service Association (NICSA)
8400 Westpark Dr., 2nd Fl.
McLean, VA 22102
Ph: (508)485-1500
Fax: (508)485-1560
Co. E-mail: info@nicsa.org
URL: http://www.nicsa.org
Contact: Theresa Hamacher, President
Description: Mutual fund investment managers, distributors, custodians, transfer agents, accounting and legal firms, broker/dealers, and general providers of services and products to the mutual fund industry. Seeks to address future service needs and trends by providing a forum on operational and technological developments. **Founded:** 1962. **Publi-**

cations: *NICSA News* (Quarterly). **Awards:** Lifetime Achievement Award; PricewaterhouseCoopers Award (Annual); Robert L. Gould Award (Annual); NICSA/William T. Blackwell Scholarship (Annual); William T. Blackwell Scholarship Fund.

11973 ■ National Investor Relations Institute (NIRI)
225 Reinekers Ln., Ste. 560
Alexandria, VA 22314
Ph: (703)562-7700
Fax: (703)562-7701
Co. E-mail: info@niri.org
URL: http://www.niri.org
Contact: Jeffrey D. Morgan, President
Description: Executives engaged in investor relations. Identifies the role of the investor relations practitioner; protects a free and open market with equity and access to investors of all kinds; improves communication between corporate management and shareholders, present and future. Holds professional development seminars and conducts research programs. Maintains placement service and speakers' bureau; compiles statistics. **Founded:** 1969. **Publications:** *Investor Relations Weekly* (Weekly); *IR Update* (Monthly); *Roster* (Annual); *Standards of Practice for Investor Relations* (Periodic). **Educational Activities:** National Investor Relations Institute Conference (Annual).

11974 ■ National Society of Compliance Professionals (NSCP)
22 Kent Rd.
Cornwall Bridge, CT 06754
Ph: (860)672-0843
Fax: (860)672-3005
Co. E-mail: info@nscp.org
URL: http://www.nscp.org
Contact: Joan Hinchman, Executive Director
Description: Professionals in brokerage houses, investment advisers, accounting and law firms, and banks, who are responsible for compliance with government and other regulations. Provides access to accounting and legal expertise. Provides a forum for exchange between members. Monitors new state and federal laws and regulations. Offers interpretive and practical assistance in compliance matters. Conducts educational programs. **Founded:** 1987. **Publications:** *NSCP Currents* (Bimonthly); *NSCP Hotline Memo* (Monthly). **Educational Activities:** National Membership Meeting (Annual).

11975 ■ New York Society of Security Analysts
1540 Broadway, Ste. 1010
New York, NY 10036-2714
Ph: (212)541-4530
Free: 800-248-0108
Fax: (212)541-4677
Co. E-mail: ageffen@nyssa.org
URL: http://www.nyssa.org
Contact: Amy Geffen, President
Description: Security analysts and portfolio managers employed primarily in New York by brokerage houses, banks, insurance companies, mutual funds and other financial institutions. Conducts educational

forums on topics relating to the securities markets. Maintains placement service. **Scope:** corporate meetings, other investment topics. **Subscriptions:** audio recordings video recordings. **Publications:** *NYSSA News* (Monthly); *Corporate Governance Handbook.* **Telecommunication Services:** staff@nyssa.org.

11976 ■ North American Securities Administrators Association (NASAA)
750 1st St. NE, Ste. 1140
Washington, DC 20002-8034
Ph: (202)737-0900
Fax: (202)783-3571
Co. E-mail: ri@nasaa.org
URL: http://www.nasaa.org
Contact: Jack Herstein, President

Description: Represents the interests of the state, provincial and territorial securities administrators in the U.S., Canada, Mexico and Puerto Rico. Provides support to its members in government relations and with federal regulators, industry SROs and other groups. **Founded:** 1919. **Publications:** *NASAA Insight* (Quarterly). **Educational Activities:** Public Policy Spring Conference (Annual).

11977 ■ Securities Industry and Financial Markets Association (SIFMA)
120 Broadway, 35th Fl.
New York, NY 10271-0080
Ph: (212)313-1200
Fax: (212)313-1301
Co. E-mail: inquiry@sifma.org
URL: http://www.sifma.org
Contact: T. Timothy Ryan, Jr., President
E-mail: rkruszewski@sifma.org

URL(s): sifma.org, www.bondmarket.com, www.smgww.org. **Description:** Represents more than 650 member firms of all sizes, in all financial markets in the U.S. and around the world. Enhances the public's trust and confidence in the markets, delivering an efficient, enhanced member network of access and forward-looking services, as well as premiere educational resources for the professionals in the industry and the investors whom they serve. Maintains offices in New York City and Washington, DC. **Founded:** 1972. **Holdings:** The PSA databases in form in computer-readable form. **Publications:** *Securities Industry Association--Yearbook*; *Securities Industry Trends* (Quarterly); *Securities Industry Yearbook* (Annual); *Securities Industry Association--Directory and Guide* (Annual); *Securities Industry Association--Foreign Activity Report* (Quarterly); *Securities Industry Databank*; *Operation Update* (Quarterly); *Securities Industry Data Bank.* **Educational Activities:** Compliance and Legal Seminar (Annual); Internet Conference (Annual); Small Firms Conference (Annual); The Bond Market Association - Fixed Income Summit Expo on E-Commerce & Technology (Annual). **Telecommunication Services:** sifee@sia.com; info@sia.com; info@smg2000.org; info@sifma.org.

11978 ■ Security Traders Association (STA)
80 Broad St., 5th Fl.
New York, NY 10004-2257
Ph: (203)202-7680
Fax: (203)202-7681
Co. E-mail: sta@securitytraders.org
URL: http://www.securitytraders.org
Contact: Jennifer Green Setzenfand, Chairperson

Description: Brokers and dealers handling listed and OTC securities, stocks and bonds, and all securities. Conducts educational programs. Promotes the interests of members throughout the global financial markets. Provides representation of these interests in the legislative, regulatory and technological processes. Fosters goodwill and high standards of integrity in accord with the association's founding principle. **Founded:** 1934.

11979 ■ ShareOwner
4 King St. W, Ste. 806
Toronto, ON, Canada M5H 1B6
Ph: (416)595-9600
Free: 800-268-6881

Fax: (416)595-0400
Co. E-mail: customercare@shareowner.com
URL: http://www.shareowner.com/index.html
Contact: John T. Bart, President
URL(s): www.shareowner.com/index.html. **Released:** Bimonthly **Price:** C$149, Individuals.

11980 ■ Stable Value Investment Association (SVIA)
1025 Connecticut Ave. NW, Ste. 1000
Washington, DC 20036
Ph: (202)580-7620
Fax: (202)580-7621
Co. E-mail: info@stablevalue.org
URL: http://stablevalue.org
Contact: Marc Magnoli, Chairman

Description: Pension plan sponsors, investment managers, banks, life insurance companies and consultants. Promotes retirement savings and educates individuals on the role that stable value funds can play in achieving a financially secure retirement. **Scope:** stable-value asset management. **Founded:** 1990. **Subscriptions:** archival material articles clippings monographs periodicals.

REFERENCE WORKS

11981 ■ "3Par: Storing Up Value" in Barron's (Vol. 90, August 30, 2010, No. 35, pp. 30)
Pub: Barron's Editorial & Corporate Headquarters
Ed: Mark Veverka. **Description:** Dell and Hewlett Packard are both bidding for data storage company 3Par. The acquisition would help Dell and Hewlett Packard provide customers with a one-stop shop as customers move to a private cloud in the Internet.

11982 ■ "13D Filings" in Barron's (Vol. 88, March 24, 2008, No. 12, pp. M13)
Pub: Dow Jones & Company, Inc.
Description: HealthCor Management called as problematic the plan of Magellan Health Services to use its high cash balances for acquisitions. Carlson Capital discussed with Energy Partners possible changes in the latter's board. Investor Carl Icahn suggested that Enzon Pharmaceuticals consider selling itself or divest some of its assets.

11983 ■ "13D Filings" in Barron's (Vol. 88, March 10, 2008, No. 10, pp. M11)
Pub: Dow Jones & Company, Inc.
Description: Barington Capital and Clinton Group sent a letter to Dillard's demanding a list of the company's stockholders. Elliott Associates announced that it is prepared to take over Packeteer for $5.50 a share. Strongbow capital suggested a change in leadership in Duckwall-ALCO Stores.

11984 ■ "13D Filings: Investors Report to the SEC" in Barron's (Vol. 88, March 31, 2008, No. 13, pp. M10)
Pub: Dow Jones & Company, Inc.
Description: Obrem Capital Management wants Micrel to rescind Micrel's shareholder-rights plan and to boost its board to six members from five. Patricia L. Childress plans to nominate herself to the board of Sierra Bancorp, and Luther King Capital Management may consider a competing acquisition proposal for Industrial Distribution Group.

11985 ■ "13D Filings: Investors Report to the SEC" in Barron's (Vol. 88, March 17, 2008, No. 11, pp. M11)
Pub: Dow Jones & Company, Inc.
Description: Nanes Delorme wants Vaalco Energy to keep an investment bank to start an open-bid process to sell the company. West Creek Capital plans to nominate two directors at the 2008 annual meeting of the Capital Senior Living just as ValueVest Management wants to nominate the same number of people at Ampex's annual meeting.

11986 ■ "13D Filings: Investors Report to the SEC" in Barron's (Vol. 88, July 4, 2008, No. 28, pp. M10)
Pub: Dow Jones & Co., Inc.
Description: Robino Stortini Holdings will seek control of Investors Capital Holdings either alone or with members of the company's management. Discovery Group I will withhold its votes at the nomina-

tion of directors for TESSCO Technologies while JMB Capital Partners Master Fund plans to nominate a slate of candidates to the board of Maguire Properties.

11987 ■ "13D Filings: Investors Report to the SEC" in Barron's (Vol. 89, July 13, 2009, No. 28, pp. M9)
Pub: Dow Jones & Co., Inc.
Description: Bulldog Investors wants Hicks Acquisition Co. to liquidate and return money to shareholders and they believe that the acquisition of Graham Packaging by Hicks will not be completed in a timely manner. Discovery Group raised their holdings to 5.2 percent of Nobel Learning Communities.

11988 ■ "13D Filings: Investors Report to the SEC" in Barron's (Vol. 89, July 27, 2009, No. 30, pp. M14)
Pub: Dow Jones & Co., Inc.
Description: Duquesne Capital Management is opposed to Alpha Natural Resources' proposed merger with Foundation Coal Holdings since it is against the long-term interest of shareholders. Lime Rock Partners increased their holdings of Tesco to 5,234,516 shares while Nova A/S increased their holdings of BioMimetic Therapeutics to 3,729,065 shares.

11989 ■ "A 16-Year Housing Slump? It Could Happen" in Barron's (Vol. 88, March 17, 2008, No. 11, pp. 27)
Pub: Dow Jones & Company, Inc.
Ed: Gene Epstein. **Description:** Housing remains a good protection against inflation but over very long periods. Inflation-adjusted stock prices did even better but have greater volatility. Commodities, on the other hand, underperformed both housing and stocks as inflation hedges. House prices tend to rise faster than the consumer price index is because land is inherently limited.

11990 ■ "$50 Million Project for West Chester" in Business Courier (Vol. 24, December 14, 2008, No. 35, pp. 1)
Pub: American City Business Journals, Inc.
Ed: Laura Baverman. **Description:** Commercial developer Scott Street Partners is planning to invest $50 million for the development of a site south of the Streets of West Chester retail center. The 31-acre project will generate 1,200 jobs, and will bring in offices, restaurants and a hotel. The development plans and the features of the site are discussed as well.

11991 ■ "75 Most Powerful Blacks on Wall Street" in Black Enterprise (Vol. 37, October 2006, No. 3, pp. 136)
Pub: Earl G. Graves Publishing Co. Inc.
Ed: Carolyn M. Brown. **Description:** Profiles of seventy-five African American top executives. The listing is a compilation of the brightest and best venture capitalists, asset managers, CEOs, traders, and investment bankers.

11992 ■ "The 100 Most Bullish Stocks" in Canadian Business (Vol. 81, Summer 2008, No. 9, pp. 81)
Pub: Rogers Media Ltd.
Ed: Megan Harman; Lauren McKeon. **Description:** 100 of the most bullish stocks are taken from the list of the 500 best-performing stocks. The idea is to narrow the list help investors in their investment decisions since it is difficult to choose from a large list. Analysts rate the companies with 5 being the most bullish and 1 the least. Other details of the roster are presented.

11993 ■ "401(k) Keys to Stable Value" in Barron's (Vol. 88, March 10, 2008, No. 10, pp. 40)
Pub: Dow Jones & Company, Inc.
Ed: Tom Sullivan. **Description:** Stable-value funds offer investors stability in a period of volatility in financial markets, attracting $888 million in funds. The Securities and Exchange Commission approved the launch of actively managed exchange-traded funds.

11994 ■ "529.com Wins Outstanding Achievement in Web Development" in Investment Weekly (November 14, 2009, pp. 152)

Pub: Investment Weekly News

Description: Web Marketing Association's 2009 WebAward for Financial Services Standard of Excellence and Investment Standard of Excellence was won by 529.com, the website from Upromise Investments, Inc., the leading administrator of 529 college savings plans.

11995 ■ "2008: Year of the Rat Race" in Mergers & Acquisitions: The Dealmaker's Journal (March 1, 2008)

Pub: SourceMedia, Inc.

Ed: Danelle Fugazy. **Description:** Although China still presents opportunities to Western investors, many are discovering that much more research needs to be done concerning doing business in that country before investing there becomes truly mainstream. According to one source, there are at least 300,000 small state-owned enterprises in China and millions of middle-market privately owned companies; the Chinese stock market can only handle about 50 to 70 IPOs a year and lists about 1,500 companies at a time.

11996 ■ "2010 Book of Lists" in Austin Business JournalInc. (Vol. 29, December 25, 2009, No. 42, pp. 1)

Pub: American City Business Journals

Description: Rankings of companies and organizations within the business services, finance, healthcare, hospitality and travel, insurance, marketing and media, professional services, real estate, education and technology industries in Austin, Texas are presented. Rankings are based on sales, business size, and other statistics.

11997 ■ "2010 Book of Lists" in Business Courier (Vol. 26, December 26, 2009, No. 36, pp. 1)

Pub: American City Business Journals, Inc.

Description: Rankings of companies and organizations within the business services, education, finance, health care, hospitality and tourism, real estate, and technology industries in the Cincinnati, Ohio-Northern Kentucky area are presented. Rankings are based on sales, business size, or other statistics.

11998 ■ "2010 Book of Lists" in Tampa Bay Business Journal (Vol. 30, December 22, 2009, No. 53, pp. 1)

Pub: American City Business Journals

Description: Rankings of companies and organizations within the human resources, banking and finance, business services, healthcare, real estate, technology, hospitality and travel, and education industries in the Greater Tampa Bay area are presented. Rankings are based on sales, business size, and more.

11999 ■ "ABM Janitorial Services Receives Service Excellence Award from Jones Lang LaSalle" in Investment Weekly News (July 16, 2011, pp. 75)

Pub: NewsRX

Description: ABM Janitorial Services was awarded the 2010 Jones Lang LaSalle Distinction award in the category of Service Excellence. LaSalle is a leading financial and professional services firm that specializes in real estate services and investment management. The program recognizes supplier partners who play a vital role in LaSalle's aim to provide the highest quality of services, value and innovation to clients.

12000 ■ "ACE Agrees to Pay Out $266 Million to Investors" in Globe & Mail (February 17, 2006, pp. B1)

Pub: CTVglobemedia Publishing Inc.

Ed: Brent Jang. **Description:** Canada-based commercial aviation firm ACE Aviation Holdings has agreed to pay 266 million dollars to its investors after filing a bankruptcy one year ago. Complete details of this pay off are discussed.

12001 ■ "ACE Back in Unfriendly Skies" in Globe & Mail (February 14, 2006, pp. B17)

Pub: CTVglobemedia Publishing Inc.

Ed: Brent Jang. **Description:** ACE Aviation Holdings Inc. reported $258 million profit for 2005. The opinions of analysts on the share price of the company for 2006 are presented.

12002 ■ "Achieve Tampa Bay Thrown a Lifeline in Proposed Merger" in Tampa Bay Business Journal (Vol. 30, January 22, 2010, No. 5, pp. 1)

Pub: American City Business Journals

Ed: Margie Manning. **Description:** Mental Health Care Inc. proposed a merger with Achieve Tampa Bay Inc. The former proposes to administer the latter's operations and take over its assets while paying its debts.

12003 ■ "AdvacePierre Heats Up" in Business Courier (Vol. 27, October 29, 2010, No. 26, pp. 1)

Pub: Business Courier

Ed: John Newberry. **Description:** Bill Toler, chief executive officer of AdvancePierre Foods, is aiming for more growth and more jobs. The company was formed after the merger of Pierre Foods with two Oklahoma-based food processing companies. Toler wants to expand production and is set to start adding employees in the next 6-12 months.

12004 ■ "Advertising May Take a Big Hit in Southwest/AirTran Merger" in Baltimore Business Journal (Vol. 28, October 1, 2010, No. 21, pp. 1)

Pub: Baltimore Business Journal

Ed: Gary Haber. **Description:** Advertising on television stations and the publishing industry in Baltimore could drop as a result of the merger between rival discount airlines Southwest Airlines and AirTran Airways. Southwest is among the top advertisers in the U.S., spending $126 million in 2009. No local jobs are expected to be affected because neither airline uses a local advertising firm.

12005 ■ "After Price Cuts, Competition GPS Makers Lose Direction" in Brandweek (Vol. 49, April 21, 2008, No. 16, pp. 16)

Pub: VNU Business Media, Inc.

Ed: Steve Miller. **Description:** Garmin and TomTom, two of the leaders in portable navigation devices, have seen lowering revenues due to dramatic price cuts and unexpected competition from the broadening availability of personal navigation on mobile phones. TomTom has trimmed its sales outlook for its first quarter while Garmin's stock dropped 40 percent since February.

12006 ■ "Ag Firms Harvest Revenue Growth" in The Business Journal-Serving Metropolitan Kansas City (Vol. 26, July 18, 2008, No. 45, pp. 1)

Pub: American City Business Journals, Inc.

Ed: Steve Vockrodt. **Description:** Five of the biggest agricultural companies in the Kansas City area, except one, reported multibillion-dollar revenue increases in 2007. The companies, which include Lansing Trade Group, posted a combined $9.5 billion revenue growth. The factors that affected the revenue increase in the area's agricultural companies, such as prices and high demand, are also examined.

12007 ■ "Aggenix Completes Merger with German Giant" in Houston Business Journal (Vol. 40, December 25, 2009, No. 33, pp. 2)

Pub: American City Business Journals

Ed: Mary Ann Azevedo. **Description:** Agennix Inc. has completed its transformation into a German company after Germany-based GPC Biotech merged into the former publicly traded Agennix AG. One quarter of Agennix's 60 employees will remain in Houston. Details on Agennix's drug trials are examined.

12008 ■ "AIC To Buy $350M of Real Estate" in Austin Business JournalInc. (Vol. 28, November 14, 2008, No. 35, pp. 1)

Pub: American City Business Journals

Ed: Kate Harrington. **Description:** Austin-based AIC Ventures LP is planning to buy $350 million worth of commercial real estate. The company's move will double its acquisitions. It is also planning to acquire 30 assets for its eight fun in 2009 from middle-market companies.

12009 ■ "AIG Fixed; Is Michigan Next?' in Crain's Detroit Business (Vol. 24, September 22, 2008, No. 38, pp. 1)

Pub: Crain Communications Inc.

Ed: Jay Greene. **Description:** Michigan's economic future is examined as is the mortgage buyout plan and American International Group Inc.'s takeover by the U.S. government.

12010 ■ "Air Canada Boss Gains $3.5 Million in Options" in Globe & Mail (January 19, 2007, pp. B5)

Pub: CTVglobemedia Publishing Inc.

Ed: Brent Jang. **Description:** Air Canada chairman Robert Milton's sale of 200,000 shares in stock options is discussed.

12011 ■ "Alberta's Runaway Train" in Canadian Business (Vol. 80, December 25, 2006, No. 1, pp. 17)

Pub: Rogers Media

Ed: Andrew Nikiforuk. **Description:** The high revenue brought about by the growth in the number of oil sand plants in Canada and the simultaneous burden on infrastructure and housing is discussed.

12012 ■ "Algoma Resolves Hedge Fund Fight" in Globe & Mail (March 8, 2006, pp. B1)

Pub: CTVglobemedia Publishing Inc.

Ed: Greg Keenan. **Description:** Algoma Steel Inc. has ended a dispute with Paulson and Co., a New York hedge fund, by offering to pay $200 million special dividend, appointing new directors, and continue to go for a sale.

12013 ■ "Algoma Shares Soar on Growing Sale Rumors" in Globe & Mail (February 13, 2007, pp. B1)

Pub: CTVglobemedia Publishing Inc.

Ed: Andrew Willis; Greg Keenan. **Description:** The stock prices of Algoma Steel Inc. have touched record high of $40 on the Toronto Stock Exchange. The growing rumors about the possible takeover bid is the major reason for the stock price growth.

12014 ■ "All About The Benjamins" in Canadian Business (Vol. 81, September 29, 2008, No. 16, pp. 92)

Pub: Rogers Media Ltd.

Ed: David Baines. **Description:** Discusses real estate developer Royal Indian Raj International Corp., a company that planned to build a $3 billion 'smart city' near the Bangalore airport; to this day nothing has ever been built. The company was incorporated in 1999 by Manoj C. Benjamin one investor, Bill Zack, has been sued by the developer for libel due to his website that calls the company a scam. Benjamin has had a previous case of fraud issued against him as well as a string of liabilities and lawsuits.

12015 ■ "All Eyes On Iris" in Canadian Business (Vol. 81, July 22, 2008, No. 12-13, pp. 20)

Pub: Rogers Media Ltd.

Ed: Jack Mintz. **Description:** Provincial governments in Canada are believed to be awaiting Alberta Finance Minister Iris Evans' financial and investment policies as well as Evans' development of a new saving strategy. Alberta is the only Canadian province that is in position to invest in sovereign wealth funds after it eliminated its debt in 2005.

12016 ■ All the Money in the World: How the Forbes 400 Make - and Spend - Their Fortunes

Pub: AMACOM

Ed: Peter W. Bernstein; Annalyn Swan. **Released:** September 2007. **Description:** A fascinating and historical breakdown of the 400 richest Americans according to Forbes magazine. The book examines how the list's members actually make and spend their money. Illustrating the text with charts and informational sidebars, readers are given the opportunity to look at both production and consumption and insights in social and historical context.

12017 ■ *"All Revved Up"* in *Barron's (Vol. 90, September 13, 2010, No. 37, pp. 18)*
Pub: Barron's Editorial & Corporate Headquarters
Ed: Christopher C. Williams. **Description:** Shares of Advance Auto Parts has returned 55 percent in a span of three years and the stock could still reach the mid-60s by 2011 from its price of 46.07 in the second week of September 2010. The shares are trading at just 13 times the 2011 earnings.

12018 ■ *"All-Star Advice 2010"* in *Black Enterprise (Vol. 41, October 2010, No. 3, pp. 97)*
Pub: Earl G. Graves Publishing Co. Inc.
Ed: Renita Burns, Sheiresa Ngo, Marcia Wade Talbert. **Description:** Financial experts share tips on real estate, investing, taxes, insurance and debt management.

12019 ■ *"Alto Ventures Retains Investor Relations Professional"* in *Canadian Corporate News (May 16, 2007)*
Pub: Comtex News Network Inc.
Description: Alto Ventures Ltd., a gold exploration and development company with a portfolio of eleven properties in the Canadian Shield, announced that it has engaged the consulting services of Mark Prosser in order to focus on increasing investor awareness and exposure to the investment community through the dissemination of corporate information to a network of North American and European institutions, retail brokerage firms, and private investors.

12020 ■ *"Amit Wadhwaney"* in *Canadian Business (Vol. 80, March 12, 2007, No. 6, pp. 22)*
Pub: Rogers Media
Ed: Rachel Pulfer. **Description:** Manager of Third Avenue International Value Fund, Amit Wadhwaney, shares his views on buying Canadian agricultural and forestry stocks.

12021 ■ *"Analysts: More Mergers for the Region's Hospitals"* in *Boston Business Journal (Vol. 30, October 15, 2010, No. 36, pp. 1)*
Pub: Boston Business Journal
Ed: Julie M. Donnelly. **Description:** A number of hospitals in Boston, Massachusetts are engaging in mergers and acquisitions. Caritas Christi Health Care is set to be purchased by Cerberus Capital Management. The U.S. healthcare reform law is seen to drive the development.

12022 ■ *"Analysts Not Fazed By Constellation's Halt to New Nuclear Plants"* in *Baltimore Business Journal (Vol. 28, October 22, 2010, No. 24)*
Pub: Baltimore Business Journal
Ed: Scott Dance. **Description:** Wall Street analysts believe that Constellation Energy Group Inc.'s decision to pull out of the nuclear construction business would not change their outlook on the company. New nuclear power had been one of Constellation's long-term goals, but the company pulled the plug on the project. It is believed that most investors were not expecting any payoff from the venture.

12023 ■ *"And In This Briefcase"* in *Mergers & Acquisitions: The Dealmaker's Journal (March 1, 2008)*
Pub: SourceMedia, Inc.
Description: ACG San Diego decided to address the impact the changes in the economy will have on potential private equity transactions as well as what criteria private equity firms are looking for when assessing a company. At the opening of the chapter's 2008 breakfast meeting, real-world case studies were utilized with the audiences' participation in order to assess pre-deal risk scenarios.

12024 ■ *"The Annual Entitlement Lecture: Trustees of Medicare and Social Security Issue Another Dismal Report"* in *Barron's (March 31, 2008)*
Pub: Dow Jones & Company, Inc.
Ed: Thomas G. Donlan. **Description:** Expenditures on Medicare hospital insurance and the revenues available to pay for it have led to a gap of capital valued at $38.6 trillion. Slashing the benefits or raising taxes will not solve the gap which exists unless the government saves the money and invests it in private markets.

12025 ■ *"Another Man's Pain"* in *Canadian Business (Vol. 80, October 22, 2007, No. 21, pp. 33)*
Pub: Rogers Media
Ed: Andy Holloway. **Description:** U.S. financial collapse can have a positive impact on Canadian investors. Graphs on the total number of home foreclosures in the U.S. from January to August 2007, as well as foreclosure market by type, are presented.

12026 ■ *"Apartment Market Down, Not Out"* in *Crain's Detroit Business (Vol. 24, October 6, 2008, No. 40, pp. 9)*
Pub: Crain Communications, Inc.
Ed: Daniel Duggan. **Description:** Detroit's apartment market is considered to have some of the strongest fundamentals of any apartment market in the country with relatively low vacancy rates and a relatively low supply of new units compared with demand. Investors continue to show interest in the buildings but the national lending market is making it difficult to invest in the city.

12027 ■ *"Apartment Tower in River North Fetches More Than $90 Million"* in *Crain's Chicago Business (Vol. 34, October 24, 2011, No. 42, pp. 17)*
Pub: Crain Communications Inc.
Ed: Alby Gallun. **Description:** Apartment tower in River North was sold for over $90 million to a Texas pension fund adviser. Details are included.

12028 ■ *Are the Rich Necessary? Great Economic Arguments and How They Reflect Our Personal Values*
Pub: Axios Press
Contact: Stephanie Bosserman, President
Ed: Hunter Lewis. **Released:** 2007. **Price:** $20.00. **Description:** Investment advisor argues whether today's economic system promotes greed. Each chapter of the book poses a question and then he answers.

12029 ■ *"Are We There Yet?"* in *Business Courier (Vol. 24, April 4, 2008, No. 52, pp. 1)*
Pub: American City Business Journals, Inc.
Ed: Lucy May; Dan Monk. **Description:** Groundbreaking for The Banks project happened in April 2, 2008, however, the future of the development remains uncertain due to some unresolved issues such as financing. Developers Harold A. Dawson Co. and Carter still have to pass final financing documents to Hamilton County and Cincinnati. The issue of financial commitment for the central riverfront project is examined.

12030 ■ *"Are You Ready for Dow 20,000?"* in *Barron's (Vol. 88, March 24, 2008, No. 12, pp. 26)*
Pub: Dow Jones & Company, Inc.
Ed: Jonathan R. Laing. **Description:** Stock strategist James Finucane forecasts that the Dow Jones Industrial Average will rise from its 12,361 level to as high as 20,000 from 2008 to 2009. He believes that stock liquidation and a buildup of cash provide the perfect conditions for a huge rally.

12031 ■ *"Are You Ready To Do It Yourself? Discipline and Self-Study Can Help You Profit From Online Trading"* in *Black Enterprise (Feb. 2008)*
Pub: Earl G. Graves Publishing Co. Inc.
Ed: Steve Garmhausen. **Description:** Steps to help individuals invest in stocks online is given by an expert broker. Discount brokerage houses can save money for online investors.

12032 ■ *"As Capital Gains Tax Hike Looms, Merger Activity Percolates"* in *Baltimore Business Journal (Vol. 28, August 27, 2010, No. 16, pp. 1)*
Pub: Baltimore Business Journal
Ed: Scott Dance. **Description:** Concerns for higher capital gains taxes in 2011 have been provoking buyers and sellers to engage in mergers and acquisitions activity, which is expected to gain momentum before the end of 2010. Companies that had saved cash during the recession have been taking advantage of the buyer's market. Other trends in local and national mergers and acquisitions activity are presented.

12033 ■ *"Asia Breathes a Sigh of Relief"* in *Business Week (September 22, 2008, No. 4100, pp. 32)*
Pub: McGraw-Hill Companies, Inc.
Ed: Bruce Einhorn; Theo Francis; Chi-Chu Tschang; Moon Ihlwan; Hiroko Tashiro. **Description:** Foreign bankers, such as those in Asia, that had been investing heavily in the United States began to worry as the housing crisis deepened and the impact on Freddie Mac and Fannie Mae became increasingly clear. Due to the government bailout, however, central banks will most likely continue to buy American debt.

12034 ■ *"The Asian Decade"* in *Hawaii Business (Vol. 53, January 2008, No. 7, pp. 19)*
Pub: Hawaii Business Publishing
Ed: Cathy S. Cruz-George. **Description:** Chaney Brooks, a Hawaiian real estate company, has affiliated with commercial real estate network NAI Global. The NAI partnership will improve Hawaii's international business, particularly its Asian investments. Hawaii's diverse workforce is evaluated, with regards to being an asset for international businesses.

12035 ■ *Association for Investment Management & Research--Membership Directory*
Pub: CFA Institute
Contact: John D. Rogers, President
E-mail: john.rogers@cfainstitute.org
URL(s): www.cfainstitute.org. **Released:** Annual; January. **Price:** $150, per year. **Covers:** 38,000 security and financial analysts who are practicing investment analysis. **Entries include:** Name, firm affiliation and address, phone, fax, e-mail. **Arrangement:** Alphabetical.

12036 ■ *"ATS Secures Investment From Goldman Sachs"* in *The Business Journal - Serving Phoenix and the Valley of the Sun (Vol. 29, September 26, 2008, No. 4, pp. 1)*
Pub: American City Business Journals, Inc.
Ed: Patrick O'Grady. **Description:** Goldman Sachs made an investment to American Traffic Solutions Inc. (ATS) which will allow it to gain two seats on the board of the red-light and speed cameras maker. The investment will help ATS maintain its rapid growth which is at 83 percent over the past 18 months leading up to September 2008.

12037 ■ *"Attorney Guides Biotech Company in $6 Million Initial Public Offering"* in *Miami Daily Business Review (March 26, 2008)*
Pub: ALM Media Inc.
Description: In order to raise capital to engage in a full-scale trial of MyoCell to receive clinical approval, Bioheart Inc., launched an initial public offering. Bioheart researches and develops cell therapies to treat heart damage.

12038 ■ *"Au Revoir Or Goodbye?"* in *Barron's (Vol. 88, July 14, 2008, No. 28, pp. 5)*
Pub: Dow Jones & Co., Inc.
Ed: Alan Abelson. **Description:** Former Senator Phil Gramm's opinion that the U.S. is a 'nation of whiners' as they moan about recession is another example of the disconnection between Washington and Wall Street on one hand and the real world on the other. It would be a catastrophe for most of the world if Fannie Mae and Freddie Mac were to go under and take their trillions of mortgage debt with them.

12039 ■ "Auction-Rate Cash Frees Up" in The Business Journal-Portland (Vol. 25, August 15, 2008, No. 23, pp. 1)
Pub: American City Business Journals, Inc.
Ed: Aliza Earnshaw. Description: FEI Co. and Radi-Sys Corp. have received notices that UBS AG will buy back the auction-rate securities that were sold to them in around two years from 2008. FEI had $110.1 million invested in auction-rate securities while Radi-Sys holds $62.8 million of these securities.

12040 ■ "Austin Ventures: Is It a VC Firm?" in Austin Business Journal (Vol. 31, June 17, 2011, No. 15, pp. 1)
Pub: American City Business Journals Inc.
Ed: Christopher Calnan. Description: Investment firm Austin Ventures could lose its classification as a venture capital firm under a new definition of venture capital by the Securities and Exchange Commission. The reclassification could result in additional expenses for Austin Ventures, which has two-thirds of its investments in growth equity transactions.

12041 ■ "Auto Supplier Stock Battered In Wake Of Wall Street Woes" in Crain's Detroit Business (Vol. 24, September 29, 2008, No. 39, pp. 4)
Pub: Crain Communications Inc.
Ed: Ryan Beene. Description: Due to the volatility of the stock market and public perception of the $700 billion banking bailout, auto suppliers are now facing a dramatic drop in their shares. Statistical data included.

12042 ■ "Awaiting a Call from Deutsche Telekom" in Barron's (Vol. 90, September 6, 2010, No. 36, pp. M5)
Pub: Barron's Editorial & Corporate Headquarters
Ed: Vito J. Racanelli. Description: Deutsche Tele-kom's (DT) T-Mobile USA Unit has settled in the number four position in the market and the parent company will need to decide if it will hold onto the company in the next 12-18 months from September 2010. T-Mobile's rivals will make critical improve-ments during this time and DT has the option to upgrade T-Mobile at the cost of improvements to its other units.

12043 ■ "BABs in Bond Land" in Barron's (Vol. 89, July 6, 2009, No. 27, pp. 14)
Pub: Dow Jones & Co., Inc.
Ed: Jim McTague. Description: American Recovery and Reinvestment Act has created taxable Build America Bonds (BAB) to finance new construction projects. The issuance of the two varieties of taxable BABs is expected to benefit the municipal bond market.

12044 ■ "Back in the Race" in Barron's (Vol. 88, March 17, 2008, No. 11, pp. 43)
Pub: Dow Jones & Company, Inc.
Ed: Leslie P. Norton. Description: Katherine Scha-piro was able to get Sentinel International Equity's Morningstar classification to blended fund from a value fund rating after joining Sentinel from her former jobs at Strong Overseas Fund. Schapiro aims to benefit from the global rebalancing as the U.S.'s share of the world economy shrinks.

12045 ■ "Back Talk with Chris Gardner" in Black Enterprise (Vol. 37, January 2007, No. 6, pp. 112)
Pub: Earl G. Graves Publishing Co. Inc.
Ed: Kenneth Meeks. Description: Profile of with Chris Gardner and his Chicago company, Gardner Rich L.L.C., a multimillion-dollar investment firm. Dur-ing an interview, Gardner discusses his rise from homelessness. His story became a book, The Pursuit of Happyness and was recently released as a film starring Will Smith.

12046 ■ "Back on Track-Or Off the Rails?" in Business Week (September 22, 2008, No. 4100, pp. 22)
Pub: McGraw-Hill Companies, Inc.
Ed: Peter Coy; Tara Kalwarski. Description: Dis-cusses the possible scenarios the American economy may undergo due to the takeover of Fannie Mae and Freddie Mac. Statistical data included.

12047 ■ "Bad-Loan Bug Bites Mid-Tier Banks; More Pain, Tighter Lending Standards Ahead, CEOs Say" in Crain's Chicago Business (May 5, 2008)
Pub: Crain Communications, Inc.
Ed: Steve Daniels. Description: Mid-sized com-mercial banks form the bedrock of Chicago's financial-services industry and they are now feeling the results of the credit crisis that has engulfed the nation's largest banks and brokerages. Commercial borrowers are seeing tighter terms on loans and higher interest rates while bank investors are unable to forecast lenders' earnings performance from quarter to quarter. Statistical data included.

12048 ■ "Bad Loans Start Piling Up" in Crain's New York Business (Vol. 24, January 7, 2008, No. 1, pp. 2)
Pub: Crain Communications, Inc.
Ed: Tom Fredrickson. Description: Problems in the subprime mortgage industry have extended to other lending activities as evidenced by bank charge-offs on bad commercial and industrial loans which have more than doubled in the third quarter.

12049 ■ Bad Money
Pub: Viking Press/Penguin Group
Ed: Kevin Phillips. Released: April 15, 2008. De-scription: How the financial sector has hijacked the American economy, aided by Washington's ruinous faith in the efficiency of markets.

12050 ■ "Bad Paper" in Canadian Business (Vol. 80, November 19, 2007, No. 23, pp. 34)
Pub: Rogers Media
Ed: Al Rosen. Description: The Canadian govern-ment froze the market for non-bank asset-backed commercial paper (ABCP) August 2007, which means holders will be unable to withdraw investments. The crisis and value of ABCP are discussed.

12051 ■ "Bailout Forgets the 'Little Guys'" in The Business Journal-Milwaukee (Vol. 25, September 26, 2008, No. 53, pp. A1)
Pub: American City Business Journals, Inc.
Ed: Rich Kirchen. Description: Community Bankers of Wisconsin and the Wisconsin Bankers Association are urging members to approach congressional representatives and remind them to include local banks in building the $700 billion bailout plan. WBA president and CEO Kurt Bauer thinks that it is only fair to include smaller institutions in the bailout. The initial bailout plan and its benefit for the smaller banks are examined.

12052 ■ "Bailout May Force Cutbacks, Job Losses" in The Business Journal - Serving Phoenix and the Valley of the Sun (Vol. 29, September 26, 2008, No. 4, pp. 1)
Pub: American City Business Journals, Inc.
Ed: Mike Sunnucks. Description: Economists say the proposed $700 billion bank bailout could affect Arizona businesses as banks could be forced to reduce the amount and number of loans it has thereby forcing businesses to shrink capital expendi-tures and then jobs. However, the plan could also stimulate the economy by taking bad loans off banks balance sheets according to another economist.

12053 ■ "Baking Up Bigger Lance" in Charlotte Business Journal (Vol. 25, December 3, 2010, No. 37, pp. 1)
Pub: Charlotte Business Journal
Ed: Ken Elkins. Description: Events that led to the merger between Charlotte, North Carolina-based snack food manufacturer Lance Inc. and Pennsylvania-based pretzel maker Snyder's of Ha-nover Inc. are discussed. The merger is expected to help Lance in posting a 70 percent increase in revenue, which reached $900 million in 2009. How the merger would affect Snyder's of Hanover is also described.

12054 ■ "Bank Bullish on Austin" in Austin Business JournalInc. (Vol. 29, November 13, 2009, No. 36, pp. A1)
Pub: American City Business Journals
Ed: Kate Harrington. Description: American Bank's presence in Austin, Texas has been boosted by new management and a new 20,000 square foot building.

This community bank intends to focus on building relationship with commercial banking customers. American Bank also plans to extend investment bank-ing, treasury management, and commercial lending services.

12055 ■ "Bank Forces Brooke Founder To Sell His Holdings" in The Business Journal-Serving Metropolitan Kansas City (October 10, 2008)
Pub: American City Business Journals, Inc.
Ed: James Dornbrook. Description: Robert Orr who is the founder of Brooke Corp., a franchise of insur-ance agencies, says that he was forced to sell virtu-ally all of his stocks in the company by creditors. First United Bank held the founder's stock as collateral for two loans worth $5 million and $7.9 million, which were declared in default in September 2008. Details of the selling of the company's stocks are provided.

12056 ■ "Bank Sticks to Rate Rise Script but 'Modest' is the Salient Word" in Globe & Mail (January 25, 2006, pp. B5)
Pub: CTVglobemedia Publishing Inc.
Ed: Heather Scoffield. Description: The reasons behind the decision of Bank of Canada to increase interest rate, which is posted at 3.5 percent, are presented.

12057 ■ "Banking Bailout: Boost or Bust?" in Crain's Detroit Business (Vol. 24, September 29, 2008, No. 39, pp. 1)
Pub: Crain Communications Inc.
Ed: Amy Lane. Description: Economic insiders discuss the banking bailout and how it might impact the state of Michigan.

12058 ■ "A Banking Play Without Banking Plagues" in Barron's (Vol. 88, March 31, 2008, No. 13, pp. 26)
Pub: Dow Jones & Company, Inc.
Ed: Jack Willoughby. Description: Fiserv's shares have been dragged down by about 20 percent which presents an appealing entry point since the shares could rise by 30 percent or more by 2009. The company enables banks to post and open new checks and keeps track of loans which are not discretionary processes of banks.

12059 ■ "The Bankrate Double Pay" in Barron's (Vol. 88, March 24, 2008, No. 12, pp. 27)
Pub: Dow Jones & Company, Inc.
Ed: Neil A. Martin. Description: Shares of Bankrate may rise as much as 25 percent from their level of $45.08 a share due to a strong cash flow and bal-ance sheet. The company's Internet business remains strong despite weakness in the online advertising industry and is a potential takeover target.

12060 ■ "Bankruptcies Shoot Up 68 Percent" in Sacramento Business Journal (Vol. 25, July 18, 2008, No. 20, pp. 1)
Pub: American City Business Journals, Inc.
Ed: Kathy Robertson. Description: Personal bank-ruptcy in the Sacramento area rose by 88 percent for the first half of 2008 while business bankruptcies rose by 50 percent for the same period. The numbers of consumer bankruptcy reflects the effect of high debt, rising mortgage costs, and declining home values on U.S. households.

12061 ■ "Bankruptcy Blowback" in Business Week (September 22, 2008, No. 4100, pp. 36)
Pub: McGraw-Hill Companies, Inc.
Ed: Jessica Silver-Greenberg. Description: Changes to bankruptcy laws which were enacted in 2005 after banks and other financial institutions lobbied hard for them are now suffering the consequences of the laws which force more troubled borrowers to let their homes go into foreclosure; lenders suffer financially every time they have to take on a foreclosure and the laws in which they lobbied so hard to see enacted are now becoming a problem for these lending institu-tions. Details of the changes in the laws are outlined as are the affects on the consumer, the economy and the lenders.

12062 ■ *"Banks Fall Short in Online Services for Savvy Traders" in Barron's (Vol. 88, March 17, 2008, No. 11, pp. 35)*
Pub: Dow Jones & Company, Inc.
Ed: Theresa W. Carey. **Description:** Banc of America Investment Services, WellsTrade, and ShareBuilder are at the bottom of the list of online brokerages because they offer less trading technologies and product range. Financial shoppers miss out on a lot of customized tools and analytics when using these services.

12063 ■ *"Banks Fret About Gist Of Bailout" in The Business Journal-Serving Metropolitan Kansas City (Vol. 27, September 26, 2008, No. 2)*
Pub: American City Business Journals, Inc.
Ed: James Dornbrook. **Description:** Banks from the Kansas City area hope that the proposed $700 billion bailout will not send the wrong message. UMB Financial Corp. chairman says that he hopes that the bailout would benefit companies that were more risk restrained and punish those that took outsized risk. Other bank executives' perceptions on the planned bailout are given.

12064 ■ *"Banks Seeing Demand for Home Equity Loans Slowing" in Crain's Cleveland Business (Vol. 28, December 3, 2007, No. 48, pp. 1)*
Pub: Crain Communications, Inc.
Ed: Shawn A. Turner. **Description:** Discusses the reasons for the decline in demand for home equity loans and lines of credit. Statistical data included.

12065 ■ *"Barbarians Set Bar Low With Lowly Canadian Telco" in Globe & Mail (March 31, 2007, pp. B1)*
Pub: CTVglobemedia Publishing Inc.
Ed: Derek DeCloet. **Description:** The efforts of the private equity fund Kohlberg, Kravis, Roberts and Co. to acquire the Canadian telecommunications firm BCE are described.

12066 ■ *"Bargain Hunting In Vietnam" in Barron's (Vol. 88, July 14, 2008, No. 28, pp. M6)*
Pub: Dow Jones & Co., Inc.
Ed: Elliot Wilson. **Description:** Vietnam's economy grew by just 6.5 percent for the first half of 2008 and its balance of payments ballooned to $14.4 billion. The falling stock prices in the country is a boon for bargain hunters and investing in the numerous domestic funds is one way of investing in the country. Some shares that investors are taking an interest in are also discussed.

12067 ■ *"Barron's Lipper Fund Listings" in Barron's (Vol. 89, July 13, 2009, No. 28, pp. 19)*
Pub: Dow Jones & Co., Inc.
Description: Statistical tables are presented which show the assets and return of mutual funds up to a ten year period. The listing covers funds with at least $200 million in assets.

12068 ■ *"BASF Launches $4.9 Billion Bid for Rival Engelhard" in Globe & Mail (January 4, 2006, pp. B7)*
Pub: CTVglobemedia Publishing Inc.
Ed: Mike Esterl; Steve Levine. **Description:** The plans of BASF AG, to acquire Engelhard Corp. for $4.9 billion, are presented.

12069 ■ *"Battered U.S. Auto Makers in Grip of Deeper Sales Slump" in Globe & Mail (April 4, 2007, pp. B1)*
Pub: CTVglobemedia Publishing Inc.
Ed: Greg Keenan. **Description:** The fall in Canadian sales and market share of Ford Motor Co., General Motors Corp. and Chrysler Group is discussed.

12070 ■ *"Battle of the Titans" in Canadian Business (Vol. 81, March 17, 2008, No. 4, pp. 15)*
Pub: Rogers Media
Ed: Rachel Pulfer. **Description:** Regulatory authorities in Canada gave Thomson Corp and Reuters Group PLC the permission to go ahead with their merger. The merged companies could eclipse Bloomberg LP's market share of 33 percent. Authorities also required Thomson and Reuters to sell some of their databases to competitors.

12071 ■ *"BCE's Aliant Trust Spinoff Valued at About $8.5 Billion" in Globe & Mail (March 8, 2006, pp. B1)*
Pub: CTVglobemedia Publishing Inc.
Ed: Catherine McLean. **Description:** The details pertaining to the spinoff of Aliant Inc.'s landline business into an income trust by BCE Inc. are presented. The trust is valued at $8.5 billion.

12072 ■ *"BDC Launches New Online Business Advice Centre" in Internet Wire (July 13, 2010)*
Pub: Comtex
Description: The Business Development Bank of Canada (BDC) offers entrepreneurs the chance to use their new online BDC Advice Centre in order to seek advice regarding the challenges of entrepreneurship. Free online business tools and information to help both startups and established firms are also provided.

12073 ■ *"The Bear Arrives - With Bargain Hunters" in Barron's (Vol. 88, July 7, 2008, No. 27, pp. M3)*
Pub: Dow Jones & Co., Inc.
Ed: Kopin Tan. **Description:** US stock markets have dropped 20 percent below their highs, entering the bear market at the end of June 2008. It was also the worst performance of the stock markets during June. Wine maker Constellation Brands, however, reported a 50 percent rise in net income for the first quarter of 2008.

12074 ■ *"Bear Market Tough On Investors" in The Business Journal-Milwaukee (Vol. 25, July 4, 2008, No. 41, pp. A1)*
Pub: American City Business Journals, Inc.
Ed: Rich Kirchen. **Description:** Public companies and their investors in the Milwaukee area suffered as the bear market took hold of the Wisconsin stock market. There were 18 stocks out of the 36 publicly traded stocks that have fallen into the bear market, meaning a 20 percent decline from the market peak in the fall of 2007. The impacts of the bear market on investors are evaluated.

12075 ■ *"The Bear's Back" in Barron's (Vol. 88, July 7, 2008, No. 27, pp. 17)*
Pub: Dow Jones & Co., Inc.
Ed: Randall W. Forsyth; Vito Racanelli. **Description:** US stock markets have formally entered the bear market after the Dow Jones Industrial Average dropped 20 percent from its high as of June 2008. Investors remain uncertain as to how long the bear market will persist, especially with the US economy on the edge of recession.

12076 ■ *"The Beauty of Banking's Big Ugly" in Barron's (Vol. 89, July 27, 2009, No. 30, pp. 31)*
Pub: Dow Jones & Co., Inc.
Ed: Andrew Bary. **Description:** Appeal of the shares of Citigroup comes from its sharp discount to its tangible book value and the company's positive attributes include a strong capital position, high loan-loss reserves, and their appealing global-consumer. The shares have the potential to generate nice profits and decent stock gains as the economy turns.

12077 ■ *"Beer Stocks Rally on Anheuser, InBev Report" in Globe & Mail (February 16, 2007, pp. B3)*
Pub: CTVglobemedia Publishing Inc.
Ed: Keith McArthur. **Description:** The stock prices of beer manufacturing industries have increased considerably after impressive profit reports from Anheuser Busch Cos Inc. and InBev SA. Complete analysis in this context is presented.

12078 ■ *"Behind the Numbers: When It Comes to Earnings, Look for Quality, Not Just Quantity" in Black Enterprise (July 2008, pp. 35)*
Pub: Earl G. Graves Publishing Co. Inc.
Ed: Chris Keenan. **Description:** It is important for investors to examine the quality of a company's earnings rather than fixate on the quantity of those earnings. Advice is given regarding issues investors can look at when trying to determine the potential growth of a firm.

12079 ■ *"Being Big By Design" in Canadian Business (Vol. 82, April 27, 2009, No. 7, pp. 39)*
Pub: Rogers Media
Ed: Andrew Wahl. **Description:** Gennum expects that its planned acquisition of Tundra Semiconductor will expand its market presence and leverage its research and development better than working alone. The proposed friendly acquisition could challenge Zarlink Semiconductor as the largest Canadian semiconductor firm in terms of revenue. The merger could expand Gennum's addressable market to about $2 billion.

12080 ■ *"Beltway Monitor" in Mergers & Acquisitions: The Dealmaker's Journal (March 1, 2008)*
Pub: SourceMedia, Inc.
Description: Discusses in detail The Foreign Investment and National Security Act of 2007 which was put into legislation due to the initially approved acquisition of certain U.S. ports by Dubai Ports World which set off a firestorm of controversy.

12081 ■ *"Bertha's Birth Stirs Juice" in Barron's (Vol. 88, July 14, 2008, No. 28, pp. M11)*
Pub: Dow Jones & Co., Inc.
Ed: Tom Sellen. **Description:** Price of frozen concentrated orange juice, which has risen to four-month highs of $1.3620 in July 2008 is due, in part, to the hurricane season that has come earlier than normal in the far eastern Atlantic thereby possibly harming the 2008-2009 Florida orange crop. Future tropical-storm development will affect the prices of this commodity.

12082 ■ *"Best Cash Flow Generators" in Canadian Business (Vol. 81, Summer 2008, No. 9, pp. 73)*
Pub: Rogers Media Ltd.
Ed: Calvin Leung. **Description:** Table showing the five-year annualized growth rate and one-year stock performance of companies that have grown their cash flow per share at an annualized rate of 15 percent or more over the past five years. Analysts project that the cash flow trend will continue. Other details of the stock performance index are presented.

12083 ■ *"Best Cash Flow Generators" in Canadian Business (Vol. 82, Summer 2009, No. 8, pp. 40)*
Pub: Rogers Media
Ed: Calvin Leung. **Description:** Agrium Inc. and FirstService Corporation are in the list of firms that are found to have the potential to be the best cash flow generators in Canada. The list also includes WestJet Airlines Ltd., which accounts for 385 flights each day. More than 80 percent of analysts rate the airline stocks a Buy.

12084 ■ *"Best Defensive Stocks" in Canadian Business (Vol. 81, Summer 2008, No. 9, pp. 67)*
Pub: Rogers Media Ltd.
Ed: Calvin Leung. **Description:** Stocks of the companies presented have market capitalization of greater than $1 billion and dividend gains of at least 2 percent. A table showing the average one-year total return of the stocks is provided.

12085 ■ *"The Best Five-Month Run Since 1938" in Barron's (Vol. 89, August 3, 2009, No. 31, pp. M3)*
Pub: Dow Jones & Co., Inc.
Ed: Kopin Tan. **Description:** US stock markets ended July 2009 registering the highest five-month rise since 1938. The shares of Cablevision could rise as the company simplifies its structure and spins off

its Madison Square Garden unit. The shares of Potash Corp. could fall as the company faces lower earnings due to falling potash purchases.

12086 ■ *"Best Growth Stocks"* in *Canadian Business (Vol. 81, Summer 2008, No. 9, pp. 61)*
Pub: Rogers Media Ltd.
Ed: Calvin Leung. **Description:** Table showing the one-year performance of growth stocks is presented. Edmonton-based Stantec Inc. expects to advance its sales and profits by 15 percent to 20 percent per year through tapping international markets and acquisitions. Analysts forecast a 17.1 percent growth rate annually over the next 3 to 5 years.

12087 ■ *"Best Growth Stocks"* in *Canadian Business (Vol. 82, Summer 2009, No. 8, pp. 28)*
Pub: Rogers Media
Ed: Calvin Leung. **Description:** Canadian stocks that are considered as the best growth stocks, and whose price-earnings ratio is less than their earnings growth rate, are suggested. Suggestions include pharmaceutical firm Paladin Labs, which was found to have 13 consecutive years of revenue growth. Paladin Labs acquires or licenses niche drugs and markets them in Canada.

12088 ■ *"Best Income Trust"* in *Canadian Business (Vol. 81, Summer 2008, No. 9, pp. 69)*
Pub: Rogers Media Ltd.
Ed: Calvin Leung. **Description:** Table showing five-year annualized growth rate and one-year stock performance of real estate investment trusts firms in Canada is presented. Calgary-based Boardwalk REIT is projected to grow the fastest among North American REITs over the next two years. Other details on the stock performance analysis are presented.

12089 ■ *"Best Income Trusts"* in *Canadian Business (Vol. 82, Summer 2009, No. 8, pp. 36)*
Pub: Rogers Media
Ed: Calvin Leung. **Description:** Boardwalk REIT and Can. Apartment Properties REIT are among the income trusts in Canada that are found to have the potential as a good investment. Suggested income trusts also include the Yellow Pages Income Fund, which recently reported a 19.4 percent yield. The income trusts however, are expected to be affected by the Conservatives' tax that will take effect in 2011.

12090 ■ *"Best Managed Companies"* in *Canadian Business (Vol. 81, Summer 2008, No. 9, pp. 71)*
Pub: Rogers Media Ltd.
Ed: Calvin Leung. **Description:** Table showing the five-year annualized growth rate and one-year stock performance of companies that have grown their cash flow per share at an annualized rate of 15 percent or more over the past five years. Analysts project that the cash flow trend will continue. Other details of the stock performance index are presented.

12091 ■ *"Best Managed Companies (Canada)"* in *Canadian Business (Vol. 82, Summer 2009, No. 8, pp. 38)*
Pub: Rogers Media
Ed: Calvin Leung. **Description:** Agrium Inc. and Barrick Gold Corporation are among those that are found to be the best managed companies in Canada. Best managed companies also include software firm Open Text Corporation, which has grown annual sales by 75 percent and annual profits by 160 percent since 1995. Open Text markets software that allow firms to manage word-based data, and has 46,000 customers in 114 countries.

12092 ■ *"Best Turnaround Stocks"* in *Canadian Business (Vol. 81, Summer 2008, No. 9, pp. 65)*
Pub: Rogers Media Ltd.
Ed: Calvin Leung. **Description:** Share prices of Sierra Wireless Inc. and EXFO Electro Optical Engineering Inc. have fallen over the past year but have good chance at a rebound considering that the

companies have free cash flow and no long-term debt. One-year stock performance analysis of the two companies is presented.

12093 ■ *"Best Turnaround Stocks"* in *Canadian Business (Vol. 82, Summer 2009, No. 8, pp. 32)*
Pub: Rogers Media
Ed: Calvin Leung. **Description:** Canadian companies that are believed to have the potential for the best turnaround stocks are presented. Suggested stocks include those of Migao Corporation, which is rated by most research firms as a Buy. Migao produces potash-based fertilizers for the Chinese market.

12094 ■ *"Best Value Stocks"* in *Canadian Business (Vol. 81, Summer 2008, No. 9, pp. 63)*
Pub: Rogers Media Ltd.
Ed: Calvin Leung. **Description:** Table showing the one-year performance of bargain or best-value stocks is presented. These stocks are undervalued compared to their North American peers, but it is projected that their five-year average return on equity is greater.

12095 ■ *"Best Value Stocks"* in *Canadian Business (Vol. 82, Summer 2009, No. 8, pp. 30)*
Pub: Rogers Media
Ed: Calvin Leung. **Description:** Canadian companies that are believed to have the best value stocks are suggested. Suggestions include publishing firm Glacier Media, which has reported a four-fold growth in sales in the last three years. While publishers like Glacier Media face challenges such as declining circulation, the firm's industry diversification is expected to help it weather the economic downturn.

12096 ■ *"Bet on China"* in *Canadian Business (Vol. 80, November 5, 2007, No. 22, pp. 30)*
Pub: Rogers Media
Ed: Thomas Watson. **Description:** Former U.S. Federal Reserve Board head, Alan Greenspan, warns that contraction will happen in the Chinese market. However, the economic success of China does not seem to be at the point of ending, as the country remains the largest market for mobile telecommunications. Forecasts for Chinese trading and investments are provided.

12097 ■ *"Bet on the Subcontinent"* in *Canadian Business (Vol. 81, April 14, 2008, No. 6, pp. 27)*
Pub: Rogers Media
Ed: Calvin Leung. **Description:** Morgan Stanley Capital International India Index is down 28 percent for the first half of 2008 but this index rebounded 6 percent in 2002 then skyrocketed 65 percent in 2003. The economic reforms in the 1990's have created a growing middle class and households that can afford discretionary items will grow from eight million to 94 million by 2025. India's equity market could outperform developed markets if its economy grows at its current rate.

12098 ■ *"Betting Big, Winning Big"* in *Barron's (Vol. 88, March 17, 2008, No. 11, pp. 49)*
Pub: Dow Jones & Company, Inc.
Ed: Lawrence C. Strauss. **Description:** Bruce Berkowitz explains that the reason that his portfolio is concentrated is because getting more positions makes the portfolio more average compared to putting the money into your 10th or 20th-best idea. Berkowitz' picks include Berkshire Hathaway, Well-Care Health Plus, Sears Holdings, and Mohawk Industries.

12099 ■ *"Betting on a Happy Ending"* in *Barron's (Vol. 88, July 7, 2008, No. 27, pp. 14)*
Pub: Dow Jones & Co., Inc.
Ed: Dimitra DeFotis. **Description:** Shares of Time Warner, priced at $14.69 each, appear under-priced as financial analysts discount the value of the company. The company should be worth more than $20 a share as the company is spinning off Time Warner Cable.

12100 ■ *"Betting On Volatile Materials"* in *Barron's (Vol. 88, July 14, 2008, No. 28, pp. M11)*
Pub: Dow Jones & Co., Inc.
Ed: John Marshall. **Description:** Economic slowdowns in the U.S., Europe and China could cause sharp short-term declines in the materials sector. The S&P Materials sector is vulnerable to shifts in the flow of funds. Statistical data included.

12101 ■ *"Beware this Chinese Export"* in *Barron's (Vol. 90, August 30, 2010, No. 35, pp. 21)*
Pub: Barron's Editorial & Corporate Headquarters
Ed: Bill Alpert, Leslie P. Norton. **Description:** A look at 158 China reverse-merger stocks in the U.S. reveal that the median underperformed the index of U.S. listed Chinese companies by 75 percent in their first three years. These reverse merger stocks also lagged the Russell 2000 index of small cap stocks by 66 percent.

12102 ■ *"Beware the Ides of March"* in *Canadian Business (Vol. 81, April 14, 2008, No. 6, pp. 13)*
Pub: Rogers Media
Ed: Jeff Sanford. **Description:** Financial troubles of Bear Stearns in March, 2008 was part of the credit crunch that started in the summer of 2007 in the U.S. when subprime mortgages that were written for people who could barely afford the payments started defaulting. The bankruptcy protection given to 20 asset backed commercial paper trusts is being fought by the investors in these securities who could stand to lose 40 percent of their money under the agreement.

12103 ■ *"Beware of Rotting Money"* in *Barron's (Vol. 89, July 13, 2009, No. 28, pp. 31)*
Pub: Dow Jones & Co., Inc.
Ed: Thomas G. Donlan. **Description:** Inflation can take hold of a country and do it great harm; it is caused by people, most particularly central bankers in charge of the world's reserve currency. Arrogant economists pushed the belief that the government can engineer the economy and it is argued that there is trouble ahead when the government tries to control the economy.

12104 ■ *"Beyond Microsoft and Yahoo!: Some M&A Prospects"* in *Barron's (Vol. 88, March 17, 2008, No. 11, pp. 39)*
Pub: Dow Jones & Company, Inc.
Ed: Eric J. Savitz. **Description:** Weak quarterly earnings report for Yahoo! could pressure the company's board to cut a deal with Microsoft. Electronic Arts is expected to win its hostile $26-a-share bid for Take-Two Interactive Software. Potential targets and buyers for mergers and acquisitions are mentioned.

12105 ■ *"The Big 50"* in *Canadian Business (Vol. 81, Summer 2008, No. 9, pp. 125)*
Pub: Rogers Media Ltd.
Description: Large publicly held corporations are ranked based on market capitalization and stock performance. Potash Corp. of Saskatchewan topped the roster with 169.3 percent of return and even surpassing its 2007 result of 107 percent. A table showing the 2008 rankings of the companies is presented.

12106 ■ *"Big Gains Brewing at Anheuser-Busch InBev"* in *Barron's (Vol. 90, August 30, 2010, No. 35, pp. 34)*
Pub: Barron's Editorial & Corporate Headquarters
Ed: Christopher C. Williams. **Description:** Anheuser-Busch InBev is realizing cost synergies and it posted better than expected returns two years after the merger that formed the company. One analyst believes its American depositary receipt could be worth as much as 72 in a year.

12107 ■ *"Big Losses Mount for Hospitals"* in *Baltimore Business Journal (Vol. 27, October 23, 2009, No. 24, pp. 1)*
Pub: American City Business Journals
Ed: Scott Graham. **Description:** Reported losses by nine of the 22 hospitals in the Greater Baltimore area during fiscal 2009 have proven that the health care

industry is not immune to the recession. The rising costs of doing business and losses in the stock market have strongly affected the financial status of hospitals.

12108 ■ *The Big Rich: The Rise and Fall of the Greatest Texas Oil Fortunes*
Pub: Penguin Group USA Inc.

Ed: Bryan Burrough. **Released:** 2009. **Price:** $29.95. **Description:** The story of the great 20th Century oil-men offers lessons on the value of confidence, grit and guile.

12109 ■ *"Big Sell-Off At Sunwest"* in The Business Journal-Portland *(Vol. 25, July 25, 2008, No. 20, pp. 1)*
Pub: American City Business Journals, Inc.

Ed: Robin J. Moody. **Description:** Oregon's largest operator of assisted living facilities Sunwest Management Inc. is expected to sell 132 of its properties. The planned sale, which is believed to be worth more than $1 billion, will help Sunwest pay creditors and investors. Other views and information on the planned sale, as well as on Sunwest's services which include adult day care, are presented.

12110 ■ *"Big Trouble at Sony Ericsson"* in Barron's *(Vol. 88, March 24, 2008, No. 12, pp. M9)*
Pub: Dow Jones & Company, Inc.

Ed: Angelo Franchini. **Description:** Sony Ericsson is facing trouble as it warned that its sales and net income before taxes will fall by nearly half for the first quarter of 2008. The joint venture of Sony and Ericsson has a global mobile phone market share of nine percent as of 2007, fourth largest in the world.

12111 ■ *"Biotechs Are Using Back Door to Go Public"* in Boston Business Journal *(Vol. 31, May 27, 2011, No. 18, pp. 1)*
Pub: Boston Business Journal

Ed: Julie M. Donnelly. **Description:** Members of Massachusetts' biotechnology sector have been engaging in reverse mergers as an alternative to initial public offerings. Reverse mergers provide access to institutional investors and hedge funds.

12112 ■ *"Biovail Hits SAC With $4.6 Billion Suit"* in Globe & Mail *(February 23, 2006, pp. B1)*
Pub: CTVglobemedia Publishing Inc.

Ed: Shawn McCarthy. **Description:** The details of Biovail Corp.'s securities fraud case against SAC Management LLC are presented.

12113 ■ *"Black Diamond Holdings Corp. Receives SEC Approval"* in Canadian Corporate News *(May 16, 2007)*
Pub: Comtex News Network Inc.

Description: Black Diamond Holdings, Corp., a British Columbia domiciled company and its two wholly owned subsidiaries are engaged in the bottling, importation, distribution, marketing, and brand creation of premium spirits and wines to worldwide consumers, announced that it has completed the SEC review process and has applied to list for trading in the United States on the OTC.BB.

12114 ■ *"Blackstone Set to Sell Stake"* in Globe & Mail *(March 17, 2007, pp. B6)*
Pub: CTVglobemedia Publishing Inc.

Ed: Tennille Tracy. **Description:** The plan of Blackstone Group to sell 10 percent of its stake to raise $4 billion and its proposal to go for initial public offering is discussed.

12115 ■ *"Blackstone's Outlook Still Tough"* in Barron's *(Vol. 88, March 17, 2008, No. 11, pp. 19)*
Pub: Dow Jones & Company, Inc.

Ed: Andrew Bary. **Description:** Earnings for the Blackstone Group may not recover soon since the company's specialty in big leveraged buyouts is floundering and may not recover until 2009. The company earns lucrative incentive fees on its funds but those fees went negative in the fourth quarter of 2007 and there could be more fee reversals in the future.

12116 ■ *"A Bleak Earnings View"* in Barron's *(Vol. 88, March 10, 2008, No. 10, pp. 15)*
Pub: Dow Jones & Company, Inc.

Description: Analysts expect consumer discretionary profits in the S&P 500 to drop 8.4 percent in the first quarter of 2008. A less confident consumer is expected to pull profits down, putting forecasts of earnings growth in the S&P 500 at risk. Statistical data included.

12117 ■ *"Bloody Monday for Bear?"* in Barron's *(Vol. 88, March 17, 2008, No. 11, pp. M14)*
Pub: Dow Jones & Company, Inc.

Ed: Steven M. Sears. **Description:** Shares of Bear Stearns could slip further at the start of the trading week unless the company is bought out or bolstered by some other development over the weekend. Prices of the company's shares in the options market suggests about a 30 percent chance that the stock falls below $20 before March expirations expire.

12118 ■ *"Blue-Collar Broker"* in Boston Business Journal *(Vol. 31, July 15, 2011, No. 25, pp. 1)*
Pub: Boston Business Journal

Ed: Tim McLaughlin. **Description:** Richard F. Connolly Jr. was ranked 91st in Barron's latest annual ranking of top financial advisers and his team at Morgan Stanley Smith Barney oversee an estimated $3.7 billion in assets. However, anyone who knew him knows that he's just a blue-collar broker from Woburn who loves golf.

12119 ■ *"BMW Makes Bet on Carbon Maker"* in Wall Street Journal Eastern Edition *(November 19 , 2011, pp. B3)*
Pub: Dow Jones & Company, Inc.

Ed: Christoph Rauwald. **Description:** Eight months ago, Volkswagen AG acquired a 10 percent holding in carbon-fiber maker SGL Carbon SE. Its rival BMW AG is catching up by acquiring 15.2 percent stake in SGL as it seeks alliances like the rest of the industry in order to share industrial costs of new product development.

12120 ■ *"BMW Revs Up for a Rebound"* in Barron's *(Vol. 89, July 13, 2009, No. 28, pp. M7)*
Pub: Dow Jones & Co., Inc.

Ed: Jonathan Buck. **Description:** Investors may like BMW's stocks because the company has maintained its balance sheet strength and has an impressive production line of new models that should boost sales in the next few years. The company's sales are also gaining traction, although their vehicle delivery was down 1.7 percent year on year on June 2009, this was still the best monthly sales figure for 2009.

12121 ■ *"Boar Market: Penny-Wise Consumers Favoring Pork"* in Crain's Chicago Business *(Vol. 31, April 14, 2008, No. 15, pp. 4)*
Pub: Crain Communications, Inc.

Ed: Bruce Blythe. **Description:** Interview with Alan Cole who is the president of Cedar Hill Associates Inc. and who discusses ways in which his company is taking advantage of the record highs of oil and natural gas as well as his overall outlook on the market.

12122 ■ *"Board This Powertrain"* in Barron's *(Vol. 89, July 27, 2009, No. 30, pp. 30)*
Pub: Dow Jones & Co., Inc.

Ed: Naureen S. Malik. **Description:** Siemens' American Depositary Receipts have risen 60 percent from their March 2009 low and they should continue heading higher. The company has solid earnings and revenue growth since they lead in growing markets such as alternative energy and health-care infrastructure. Their shares also look cheap at 1.9 times book value.

12123 ■ *"Boeing Earns Its Wings With Strong Quarter"* in Crain's Chicago Business *(Vol. 31, April 28, 2008, No. 17, pp. 4)*
Pub: Crain Communications, Inc.

Ed: Daniel Rome Levine. **Description:** Interview with Michael A. Crowe, the senior managing director at Mesirow Financial Investment Management, who discusses highlights from the earnings season so far, his outlook for the economy and the stock market as well as what his company is purchasing. Mr. Crowe also recommends shares of five companies.

12124 ■ *"BofA May Part With U.S. Trust"* in Boston Business Journal *(Vol. 31, May 20, 2011, No. 17, pp. 1)*
Pub: Boston Business Journal

Ed: Tim McLaughlin. **Description:** Bank of America Corporation is willing to sell its U.S. Trust private banking division to improve its capital ratio. The unit remains to be the corporation's core asset and posted $696 million revenue in the first quarter 2010 in contract with Merrill Lynch Global Wealth Management's $3.5 billion. Analysts say that U.S. Trust would fetch more than $3 billion.

12125 ■ *"BofA Will Reach the Top with Countrywide Deal"* in Business North Carolina *(Vol. 28, March 2008, No. 3, pp. 36)*
Pub: Business North Carolina

Description: Bank of America, headquartered in Charlotte, North Carolina, will add Countrywide to its let of credits. Countrywide is the largest U.S. mortgage lender. Statistical data included.

12126 ■ *Bonds - the Other Market*
Pub: AuthorHouse

Ed: George L. Fulton. **Released:** March 16, 2005. **Price:** $15.50. **Description:** Professional bond broker provides fundamental information to help investors choose the bond market an alternative to the stock market. The book describes the various types of bonds available, including treasury bonds, issued by the U.S. Government; municipal bonds, issued by a municipal authority of a local or state government; and corporate bonds, issued by corporations. Risk vs. reward in bond investing is also covered.

12127 ■ *"Bonds v. Stocks: Who's Right About Recession?"* in Barron's *(Vol. 90, August 23, 2010, No. 34, pp. M3)*
Pub: Barron's Editorial & Corporate Headquarters

Ed: Kopin Tan. **Description:** The future of treasury securities and stocks should the U.S. enter or avoid a recession are discussed. The back to school business climate and BHP Billiton's bid for Potash Corporation of Saskatchewan are also discussed.

12128 ■ *"Book of Lists 2010"* in Philadelphia Business Journal *(Vol. 28, December 25, 2009, No. 45, pp. 1)*
Pub: American City Business Journals

Description: Rankings of companies and organizations within the banking, biotechnology, economic development, healthcare, hospitality, law and accounting, marketing and media, real estate, and technology industries in the Philadelphia, Pennsylvania area are presented. Rankings are based on sales, business size, and more.

12129 ■ *"The Book On Indigo"* in Canadian Business *(Vol. 81, July 22, 2008, No. 12-13, pp. 29)*
Pub: Rogers Media Ltd.

Ed: Thomas Watson. **Description:** Indigo Books & Music Inc. reported record sales of $922 million resulting in a record net profit of $52.8 million for the 2008 fiscal year ended March 29, 2008. Earnings per share were $2.13, greater than Standard & Poor's expected $1.70 per share. Additional information concerning Indigo Books is presented.

12130 ■ *"Boring Bonds Gain Pizzazz as Investors Flock to Debt Issues"* in Baltimore Business Journal *(Vol. 28, June 11, 2010, No. 5, pp. 1)*
Pub: Baltimore Business Journal

Ed: Gary Haber. **Description:** Companies and nonprofit organizations have increased the pace of bond offerings in order to take advantage of the bonds' appeal among willing investors. Companies mostly issued corporate bonds to replace existing debt at lower interest rates and save them money from interest payments.

12131 ■ *"Boston Hedge Fund Pours Money Into Real Estate Projects"* in *Charlotte Business Journal (Vol. 25, December 3, 2010, No. 37, pp. 1)*
Pub: Charlotte Business Journal
Ed: Will Boye. **Description:** Boston-based hedge fund Baupost Group has been financing real estate project in Charlotte, North Carolina including more than 80 acres just north of uptown. Aside from purchasing the $23.8 million note for the Rosewood Condominiums from Regions Financial Corporation, the Baupost Group is also negotiating with Regions to buy the $93.9 million debt of the EipCentre real estate project.

12132 ■ *"Bottler Will Regain Its Pop"* in *Barron's (Vol. 88, March 17, 2008, No. 11, pp. 56)*
Pub: Dow Jones & Company, Inc.
Ed: Alexander Eule. **Description:** Discusses he 30 percent drop in the share price of PepsiAmericas Inc. from their 2007 high which presents an opportunity to buy into the company's dependable U.S. market and fast growing Eastern European business. The bottler's Eastern European operating profits in 2007 grew to $101 million from $21 million in 2006.

12133 ■ *"Bottom-Fishing and Speed-Dating in India"* in *Barron's (Vol. 88, March 24, 2008, No. 12, pp. M12)*
Pub: Dow Jones & Company, Inc.
Ed: Elliot Wilson. **Description:** Indian stocks have fallen hard in 2008, with Mumbai's Sensex 30 down 30 percent from its January 2008 peak of 21,000 to 14,995 in March. The India Private Equity Fair 2008 attracted 140 of the world's largest private equity firms and about 24 of India's fastest-growing corporations. Statistical data included.

12134 ■ *"Bountiful Barrels: Where to Find $140 Trillion"* in *Barron's (Vol. 88, July 14, 2008, No. 28, pp. 40)*
Pub: Dow Jones & Co., Inc.
Ed: Andrew Bary. **Description:** Surge in oil prices has caused a large transfer of wealth to oil-producing countries thereby reshaping the global economy. Oil reserves of oil exporting countries are now valued at $140 trillion. Economist Stephen Jen believes that this wealth will be transformed into paper assets as these countries invest in global stocks and bonds.

12135 ■ *"Bracing for a Bear of a Week"* in *Barron's (Vol. 88, March 17, 2008, No. 11, pp. 24)*
Pub: Dow Jones & Company, Inc.
Ed: Jacqueline Doherty. **Description:** JPMorgan Chase and the Federal Reserve Bank of New York's opening of a line of credit to Bear Stearns cut the stock price of Bear Stearns by 47 percent to 30 followed by speculation of an imminent sale. JP Morgan may be the only potential buyer for the firm and some investors say Bears could be sold at $20 to $30. Bears prime assets include its enormous asset base worth $395 billion.

12136 ■ *"Brazil's New King of Food"* in *Barron's (Vol. 89, July 13, 2009, No. 28, pp. 28)*
Pub: Dow Jones & Co., Inc.
Ed: Kenneth Rapoza. **Description:** Perdigao and Sadia's merger has resulted in the creation of Brasil Foods and the shares of Brasil Foods provides a play on both Brazil's newly energized consumer economy and its role as a major commodities exporter. Brasil Foods shares could climb as much as 36 percent.

12137 ■ *"Brief: US-Business/eBay Earnings Rise 31 Per Cent"* in *Denver Post (July 21, 2011)*
Pub: The Denver Post
Ed: Andy Goldberg. **Description:** eBay's strong performance in second quarter 2011 is being attributed to Paypal online payments division. eBay's online auction sites reported gross merchandise volume up 34 percent. Statistical data included.

12138 ■ *"Briefly"* in *Crain's Detroit Business (Vol. 25, June 15, 2009, No. 24, pp. 18)*
Pub: Crain Communications Inc. - Detroit
Ed: Tom Henderson, Jay Greene. **Description:** Details of the merger between PI= anning Alterna-

tives Ltd. and Oakland Wealth Management are highlighted. The two investment advisory firms will have a combined staff of 12 and will maintain two offices.

12139 ■ *"Bristol-Myers Close to Settling Lawsuit"* in *Globe & Mail (January 23, 2006, pp. B6)*
Pub: CTVglobemedia Publishing Inc.
Ed: Barbara Martinez. **Description:** The details of shareholder case against Bristol-Myers Squibb Co. are presented. The dispute is over the company's claim on the efficiency of Vanlev drug.

12140 ■ *"Brooke Agents Claim Mistreatment"* in *The Business Journal-Serving Metropolitan Kansas City (Vol. 27, October 24, 2008, No. 7, pp. 1)*
Pub: American City Business Journals, Inc.
Ed: James Dornbrook. **Description:** Franchisees of Brooke Corp., an insurance franchise, face uncertainty as their bills remain unpaid and banks threaten to destroy their credit. The company bundled and sold franchisee loans to different banks, but the credit crunch left the company with massive debts and legal disputes.

12141 ■ *"Builders, Unions Aim to Cut Costs; Pushing Changes to Regain Share of Residential Market; Seek Council's Help"* in *Crain's New York Business*
Pub: Crain Communications, Inc.
Ed: Erik Engquist. **Description:** Union contractors and workers are worried about a decline in their market share for housing so they intend to ask the City Council to impose new safety and benefit standards on all contractors to avoid being undercut by nonunion competitors.

12142 ■ *"Building Confidence"* in *Black Enterprise (Vol. 38, January 2008, No. 6, pp. 50)*
Pub: Earl G. Graves Publishing Co. Inc.
Ed: Marcia A. Reed-Woodard. **Description:** Patriot Management in Chicago offers courses at its Investment Management Training Academy for the institutional asset management and investment sector. Classes are designed to help build investor confidence amid the scandals that hit the financial, investment and asset management industry.

12143 ■ *"Building Portfolios for a World of 2.5 Percent Gains"* in *Barron's (Vol. 88, July 7, 2008, No. 27, pp. L9)*
Pub: Dow Jones & Co., Inc.
Ed: Karen Hube. **Description:** Interview with Harold Evenski whom is a financial planner running a fee-only planning practice; he continues to caution investors against pursuing short-term gains and focusing on long-term trends. He advises investors against investing in commodity and real estate stocks and is concerned about the possible effects of high inflation.

12144 ■ *"Burned Investors Fire Back"* in *Canadian Business (Vol. 80, April 23, 2007, No. 9, pp. 12)*
Pub: Rogers Media
Ed: Geoff Kirbyson; Dan Lett. **Description:** The details of the oppression remedy suit filed by investors on Maple Leaf Distillers Inc. and Protos International are presented.

12145 ■ *"Business Through Hollywood's Lens"* in *Harvard Business Review (Vol. 88, October 2010, No. 10, pp. 146)*
Pub: Harvard Business School Publishing
Ed: Batia Wiesnefeld, Gino Cattani. **Description:** The authors contend that businesses are likely to be portrayed as villains in movies because corruption has higher entertainment draw. However, movies also depict popular opinion, which encourages businesses to be accountable and to help build communities.

12146 ■ *"C.A. Bancorp Inc. (TSX:BKP) Announces First Quarter 2007 Financial Results"* in *Canadian Corporate News (May 16, 2007)*
Pub: Comtex News Network Inc.
Description: Financial report for the first quarter of 2007 for C.A. Bancorp Inc., a publicly traded Canadian merchant bank and asset manager providing

investors access to a range of private equity and alternative asset class investment opportunities. Statistical data and highlights included.

12147 ■ *"Calming Customers"* in *The Business Journal-Portland (Vol. 25, August 29, 2008, No. 25, pp. 1)*
Pub: American City Business Journals, Inc.
Ed: Kirsten Grind; Rob Smith. **Description:** Credit unions and banks in the Portland area are reaching out to clients in an effort to reassure them on the security of their money and the firms' financial stability. Roy Whitehead of Washington Federal Savings, for instance, wrote 41,000 customers of the bank to reassure them. The strategies of different banks and credit unions to answer their client's worries are discussed.

12148 ■ *"Cambodia Calls"* in *Barron's (Vol. 89, July 27, 2009, No. 30, pp. M7)*
Pub: Dow Jones & Co., Inc.
Ed: Leslie P. Norton. **Description:** Interest in frontier markets could jump if enthusiasm about growth in the developed world gathers steam. Cambodia is the latest market to get attention where a handful of investors are trying to set up funds. One investor believes that Cambodia is back open for business but others are still cautious about investing in the country.

12149 ■ *Canada Business and Investment Opportunities Yearbook*
Pub: USA International Business Publications
Released: March 20, 2009. **Price:** $149.95. **Description:** Yearbook contains basic information on export-import, investment and business opportunities in Canada.

12150 ■ *Canada Investment and Business Guide*
Pub: USA International Business Publications
Released: March 20, 2009. **Price:** $149.95. **Description:** Guide for conducting investment, export-import activity in Canada; includes strategic and business information, contacts regulations and more.

12151 ■ *"Canadian Banks Too Timid in China, Beijing Tells Flaherty"* in *Globe & Mail (January 22, 2007, pp. B1)*
Pub: CTVglobemedia Publishing Inc.
Ed: Steven Chase. **Description:** The article discusses Canadian banks' investments on China according to the views of federal Finance Minister Jim Flaherty.

12152 ■ *Canadian Multinationals and International Finance*
Pub: International Specialized Books Services
Ed: Greg Marchildon. **Released:** October 1, 1992. **Price:** $190.00. **Description:** Seven stories that explore the role of Canadian multinational enterprise in world finance, trade and direct investment.

12153 ■ *"Canadian Satellite Investors Scoop Up Stratos"* in *Globe & Mail (March 20, 2007, pp. B4)*
Pub: CTVglobemedia Publishing Inc.
Ed: Simon Avery. **Description:** The proposed acquisition of Stratos Global Corp. by CIP Canada Investment Inc. for $229 million is discussed.

12154 ■ *"The Canadians Are Coming!"* in *Canadian Business (Vol. 80, October 22, 2007, No. 21, pp. 15)*
Pub: Rogers Media
Ed: Rachel Pulfer. **Description:** Toronto-Dominion Bank declared its acquisition of the New Jersey-based Commerce Bancorp for C$8.5 billion. Royal Bank of Canada has scooped up Trinidad-based Financial Group for C$2.2 billion. Details of the foreign acquisitions, as well as the impact of high Canadian dollars on the mergers are discussed.

12155 ■ *"Candidates Won't Bash Fed; Rate Cuts Bash Savers"* in *Barron's (Vol. 88, March 24, 2008, No. 12, pp. 31)*
Pub: Dow Jones & Company, Inc.
Ed: Jim McTague. **Description:** Candidates in the 2008 US presidential election, like the current administration, do not and will not bash the Federal

Reserve. The Federal Reserve's aggressive interest rate cuts hurt the incomes of people depending on their savings accounts.

12156 ■ *"Capital Position" in Business Journal-Milwaukee (Vol. 28, December 24, 2010, No. 12, pp. A1)*

Pub: Milwaukee Business Journal

Ed: Rich Kirchen. **Description:** Canada-based BMO Financial Group has purchased Marshall and Isley Corporation (M and I), which dominated lending among Wisconsin businesses for decades. The sale of M and I will enable other banks to recruit M and I's customers but BMO Financial remains a stronger competitor since it possesses a more potent capital position.

12157 ■ *"Capturing Generation Y: Ready, Set, Transform" in Credit Union Times (Vol. 21, July 14, 2010, No. 27, pp. 20)*

Pub: Summit Business Media

Ed: Senthil Kumar. **Description:** The financial services sector recognizes that Generation Y will have a definite impact on the way business is conducted in the future. The mindset of Generation Y is social and companies need to use networking tools such as Facebook in order to reach this demographic.

12158 ■ *"The Case of the Deflated IPO" in Boston Business Journal (Vol. 29, June 24, 2011, No. 7, pp. 1)*

Pub: American City Business Journals Inc.

Ed: Scott Dance. **Description:** IPO market is on the rebound from the recession but for some companies in Maryland, the time is not yet ripe to go public. One of the companies that chooses to wait for better timing is SafeNet Inc. and it is eyeing some possible acquisitions while doing so.

12159 ■ *"Cash Flow Myths" in Canadian Business (Vol. 80, March 12, 2007, No. 6, pp. 25)*

Pub: Rogers Media

Ed: Al Rosen. **Description:** Expert advice to Canadian investors about understanding the cash flow statements of companies before investing money is presented.

12160 ■ *"Catch the Wind to Hold Investor Update Conference Call on October 18, 2011" in CNW Group (October 4, 2011)*

Pub: CNW Group

Contact: Carolyn McGill-Davidson, President

Description: Catch the Wind Ltd., providers of laser-based wind sensor products and technology, held a conference call for analysts and institutional investors. The high-growth technology firm is headquartered in Manassas, Virginia.

12161 ■ *"Cemex Paves a Global Road to Solid Growth" in Barron's (Vol. 88, March 10, 2008, No. 10, pp. 24)*

Pub: Dow Jones & Company, Inc.

Ed: Sandra Ward. **Description:** Shares of Cemex are expected to perform well with the company's expected strong performance despite fears of a US recession. The company has a diverse geographical reach and benefits from a strong worldwide demand for cement.

12162 ■ *"Centrue Sets Down New Roots in St. Louis; Bank Looks to Expand in Exurbs of Chicago" in Crain's Chicago Business (May 5, 2008)*

Pub: Crain Communications, Inc.

Ed: H. Lee Murphy. **Description:** Centrue Financial Corp. has moved its headquarters from Ottawa to suburban St. Louis in search of higher-growth markets. The banks acquisitions and expansion plans are also discussed.

12163 ■ *"CEO Pay: The Details" in Crain's Detroit Business (Vol. 25, June 22, 2009, No. 25, pp.)*

Pub: Crain Communications Inc. - Detroit

Description: Total compensation packages for CEOs at area companies our outlined. These packages include salary, bonuses, stock awards, and options.

12164 ■ *"CEOs Gone Wild" in Canadian Business (Vol. 79, August 14, 2006, No. 16-17, pp. 15)*

Pub: Rogers Media

Ed: Thomas Watson. **Description:** Stock investment decisions of chief executive officers of metal companies in Canada, are discussed.

12165 ■ *"Certified Financial Planner Board of Standards Reacts to Jobs Program" in Professional Services Close-Up (September 14, 2011)*

Pub: Close-Up Media Inc.

Description: Certified Financial Planner Board of Standards Consumer Advocate, Eleanor Blayney, believe that people should be looking inward at their own ability to change their employment future. She shares tips for the job market to help out.

12166 ■ *"CGB Purchases Illinois Grain-Fertilizer Firm" in Farm Industry News (December 2, 2011)*

Pub: Penton Business Media Inc.

Description: CGB Enterprises Inc. bought Twomey Company's grain and fertilizer assets. The purchase includes eight locations and a barge loading terminal near Gladstone, Illinois and storage capacity of 51 million bushels and 18,000 tons of liquid fertilizer.

12167 ■ *"Chain of Blame: How Wall Street Caused the Mortgage and Credit Crisis*

Pub: John Wiley & Sons, Inc.

Ed: Paul Muolo, Mathew Padilla. **Released:** 2009. **Price:** $27.95. **Description:** The book describes how risky loans given irresponsibly put big investment banks at the center of the subprime crisis.

12168 ■ *"Challenges Await Quad in Going Public" in Milwaukee Business Journal (Vol. 27, January 29, 2010, No. 18, pp. A1)*

Pub: American City Business Journals

Ed: Rich Rovito. **Description:** Sussex, Wisconsin-based Quad/Graphics Inc.'s impending acquisition of rival Canadian World Color Press Inc. will transform it into a publicly held entity for the first time. Quad has operated as a private company for nearly 40 years and will need to adjust to changes, such as the way management shares information with Quad/Graphics' employees. Details of the merger are included.

12169 ■ *"Change of Plans" in Entrepreneur (Vol. 35, November 2007, No. 11, pp. 74)*

Pub: Entrepreneur Media Inc.

Ed: C.J. Prince. **Description:** Companies should provide 401K plans that meet employee needs and demographics, with new technology allowing providers to lower their own costs. Details on finding a plans that appeal to employees are examined.

12170 ■ *The Changing Geography of Banking and Finance*

Pub: Springer Publishing Company

Ed: Pietro Alessandrini, Michele Fratianni, Alberto Zazzaro. **Released:** May 1, 2009. **Price:** $139.00. **Description:** The two contrasting trends that have emerged from the integration and consolidation processes of the banking industry in both Europe and the United States in the 1990s is examined.

12171 ■ *"Chemed's Vitas Aims to Acquire" in Business Courier (Vol. 27, July 9, 2010, No. 10, pp. 1)*

Pub: Business Courier

Ed: James Ritchie. **Description:** Chemed Corporation's Vitas Healthcare Corporation is looking for smaller nonprofit hospices as it looks to become more streamlined in a tougher reimbursement environment. CFO David Williams syas they want to acquire these hospices as fast as they can integrate them.

12172 ■ *"Chuck's Big Chance" in Barron's (Vol. 89, July 13, 2009, No. 28, pp. L3)*

Pub: Dow Jones & Co., Inc.

Ed: Leslie P. Norton. **Description:** Charles Schwab is cutting prices and rolling out new products to lure customers and the company is well positioned to benefit from Wall Street's misery. Their shares are trading at just 17 times earnings, which should be at least at a multiple of 20.

12173 ■ *"CIBC Spends $1.1 Billion on Caribbean Expansion" in Globe & Mail (March 14, 2006, pp. B1)*

Pub: CTVglobemedia Publishing Inc.

Ed: Sinclair Stewart. **Description:** Canadian Imperial Bank of Commerce (CIBC), the fifth-largest bank of Canada, is planning to spend $1.1billion to buy major share of Barbados-based First Caribbean International Bank. The details of the acquisition plan are presented.

12174 ■ *"Citadel Hires Three Lehman Execs" in Chicago Tribune (October 2, 2008)*

Pub: McClatchy-Tribune Information Services

Ed: James P. Miller. **Description:** Citadel Investment Group LLC, Chicago hedge-fund operator, has hired three former senior executives of bankrupt investment banker Lehman Brothers Holding Inc. Citadel believes that the company's hiring spree will help them to further expand the firm's capabilities in the global fixed income business.

12175 ■ *"Citi Ruling Could Chill SEC, Street Legal Pacts" in Wall Street Journal Eastern Edition (November 29, 2011, pp. C1)*

Pub: Dow Jones & Company Inc. Enterprise Media Group

Contact: Clare Hart, President

Ed: Jean Eaglesham, Chad Bray. **Description:** A $285 million settlement was reached between the Securities and Exchange Commission and Citigroup Inc. over allegations the bank misled investors over a mortgage-bond deal. Now, Judge Jed S. Rakoff has ruled against the settlement, a decision that will affect the future of such attempts to prosecute Wall Street fraud. Rakoff said that the settlement was 'neither fair, nor reasonable, nor adequate, nor in the public interest.'.

12176 ■ *"Citigroup Moves to Buy Japan's Nikko" in Globe & Mail (March 7, 2007, pp. B12)*

Pub: CTVglobemedia Publishing Inc.

Ed: Jonathan Soble; Dan Wilchins. **Description:** Citigroup Inc. offered $10.8 billion to acquire troubled Nikko Cordial Corp., Japan's largest securities firm.

12177 ■ *"Clash of the Titans" in Canadian Business (Vol. 80, March 12, 2007, No. 6, pp. 27)*

Pub: Rogers Media

Ed: Andrew Wahl. **Description:** The frequent allegations of Google Inc. and Microsoft Corp. against each other over copyright and other legal issues, with a view to taking away other's market share, is discussed.

12178 ■ *"A Click In the Right Direction: Website Teaches Youth Financial Literacy" in Black Enterprise (Vol. 38, December 2007, No. 5)*

Pub: Earl G. Graves Publishing Co. Inc.

Ed: Nicole Norfleet. **Description:** Profile of Donald Lee Robinson who launched SkillsThatClick, a Website that teaches young individuals ages 12 to 15 about money management. Robinson shares how he used his Navy career as a model for designing the site.

12179 ■ *"Climbing the Wall of Worry, Two Steps at a Time" in Barron's (Vol. 89, July 13, 2009, No. 28, pp. L16)*

Pub: Dow Jones & Co., Inc.

Ed: Brian Blackstone. **Description:** Statistical table that shows the performance of different mutual funds for the second quarter of 2009 is presented. The data shows that on average, the 8,272 diversified equity funds gained 17 percent for this quarter.

12180 ■ *"Cloudy Future for VMware?" in Barron's (Vol. 90, September 13, 2010, No. 37, pp. 21)*

Pub: Barron's Editorial & Corporate Headquarters

Ed: Jonathan R. Laing. **Description:** VMWare dominated the virtualization market for years, but it may be ending as it faces more competition from rivals that offer cloud computing services. The company's stocks are also expensive and are vulnerable to the smallest mishap.

12181 ■ "CMO Nicholson Exits Pepsi as Share Declines" in Advertising Age (Vol. 79, July 7, 2008, No. 26, pp. 4)

Pub: Crain Communications, Inc.

Ed: Natalie Zmuda. Description: Cie Nicholson, the chief marketing officer at Pepsi-Cola UK, is leaving the company at a time when its market share is down; the brand, which was known for its dynamic marketing, has diverted much of its attention from its core brands and shifted attention to the ailing Gatorade brand as well as Sobe Life Water and Amp.

12182 ■ "CN 'Extremely Optimistic' After Record Profit" in Globe & Mail (January 24, 2007, pp. B3)

Pub: CTVglobemedia Publishing Inc.

Ed: Brent Jang. Description: The increase in Canadian National Railway Co.'s profits to $2.1 billion despite a harsh winter is discussed.

12183 ■ "CN to Webcast 2007 Analyst Meeting in Toronto May 23-24" in Canadian Corporate News (May 16, 2007)

Pub: Comtex News Network Inc.

Description: Canadian National Railway Company (CN) broadcast its analyst meeting in Toronto with a webcast which focused on CN's opportunities, strategies, and financial outlook through the year 2010.

12184 ■ "CNinsure Offers Safety in Numbers" in Barron's (Vol. 90, September 13, 2010, No. 37, pp. 29)

Pub: Barron's Editorial & Corporate Headquarters

Ed: Teresa Rivas. Description: China's insurance holding company CNinsure has a long growth future due to the nascent insurance market in the country. It has also been diversifying its offerings and it has a broad network in the nation. The shares of the company are trading cheaply at nearly 14 times its 2011 earnings, and is considered a good point for investors.

12185 ■ "Coca-Cola Looks Ready to Pause" in Barron's (Vol. 88, March 10, 2008, No. 10, pp. 18)

Pub: Dow Jones & Company, Inc.

Ed: Michael Santoli. Description: Shares of Coca-Cola are expected to turn sideways or experience a slight drop from $59.50 each to the mid-50 level. The company has seen its shares jump 40 percent since 2006, when it was in a series of measures to improve profitability.

12186 ■ "Cogeco Profit Jumps 47 Percent in First Quarter" in Globe & Mail (January 13, 2006, pp. B3)

Pub: CTVglobemedia Publishing Inc.

Ed: Catherine McLean. Description: The reasons behind 47 percent increase in first quarter 2006 profits for Cogeco Inc. are presented.

12187 ■ "Coherent Laying Off 144 As It Prepares To Shut Auburn Plant" in Sacramento Business Journal (Vol. 25, August 1, 2008, No. 22, pp. 1)

Pub: American City Business Journals, Inc.

Ed: Melanie Turner. Description: Sacramento, California-based Coherent Inc. is planning to lay off 144 workers at its Auburn facility. Coherent has been cutting payroll and its real estate holdings. Statistics on the company's earnings are also provided.

12188 ■ A Colossal Failure of Common Sense: The Inside Story of the Collapse of Lehman Brothers

Pub: Crown Business

Ed: Lawrence G. McDonald, Patrick Robinson. Released: 2009. Price: $27.00. Description: Former employee of Lehman Brothers details the failure of leadership that led to the demise of the company.

12189 ■ "Columbia's JPB Raising $175M to Acquire Companies, Real Estate" in Boston Business Journal (Vol. 29, May 27, 2011, No. 3, pp. 1)

Pub: American City Business Journals Inc.

Ed: Gary Haber. Description: JPB Enterprises is preparing to raise $175 million in its goal of acquiring companies and real estate that are major names in America. The $75 million will be raised for a buyout fund that will target wide range of industries while the $100 million will be used for land investment projects in the Florida Panhandle. Baltimore firms are expected to benefit from this deal.

12190 ■ "Coming: Cheaper Oil and a Stronger Buck" in Barron's (Vol. 88, March 24, 2008, No. 12, pp. 53)

Pub: Dow Jones & Company, Inc.

Ed: Lawrence C. Strauss. Description: Carl C. Weinberg, the chief economist of High Frequency Economics, forecasts that Chinese economic growth will slow down and that oil prices will drop to $80 a barrel in 2008. He also believes that the US dollar will start rising the moment the Federal Reserve stops cutting interest rates.

12191 ■ "Coming Soon: Bailouts of Fannie and Freddie" in Barron's (Vol. 88, July 14, 2008, No. 28, pp. 14)

Pub: Dow Jones & Co., Inc.

Ed: Jonathan R. Laing. Description: Assurances from the government that Fannie Mae and Freddie Mac are adequately capitalized and able to carry on their duties as guarantors or owners of over $5 trillion of U.S. home mortgages are designed to keep both entities afloat until they attempt to raise $10 billion in new equity. The government would assume any losses in a bailout and owners of the banks' papers would profit as yields drop.

12192 ■ "Commodities: Who's Behind the Boom?" in Barron's (Vol. 88, March 31, 2008, No. 13, pp. 3)

Pub: Dow Jones & Company, Inc.

Ed: Gene Epstein. Description: Proliferation of mutual funds and exchange traded funds tied to commodities indexes has helped speculative buying reach unusual levels. Index funds are estimated to account for 40 percent of all bullish bets on commodities. Commodities could drop by 30 percent as speculators retreat. Statistical data included.

12193 ■ "Commodity Speculation: Over the Top?" in Barron's (Vol. 89, July 13, 2009, No. 28, pp. 22)

Pub: Dow Jones & Co., Inc.

Ed: Gene Epstein. Description: Commodity Futures Trading Commission is planning to impose position limits on speculators of oil and other commodities as energy costs rebound from their lows. These regulations make much sense and these position limits would greatly diminish the cash commitment of the commodity index traders if these were imposed on speculators and swaps dealers properly.

12194 ■ "Compelling Opportunities" in Barron's (Vol. 88, March 10, 2008, No. 10, pp. 39)

Pub: Dow Jones & Company, Inc.

Ed: Neil A. Martin. Description: Michael L. Reynal, portfolio manager of Principal International Emerging Markets Fund, is bullish on the growth prospects of stocks in emerging markets. He is investing big on energy, steel, and transportation companies.

12195 ■ "Competition At Last?" in Canadian Business (Vol. 81, July 22, 2008, No. 12-13, pp. 7)

Pub: Rogers Media Ltd.

Description: Competition Policy Review Panel's 'Compete to Win' report revealed that Canada is being 'hollowed-out' by foreign acquisitions. The panel investigated competition and foreign investment policies in Canada. Key information on the report, as well as views on the Investment Canada Act and the Competition Act, is presented.

12196 ■ "Competition To Provide Liquidity on the New York Stock Exchange" in Business Horizons (November-December 2007, pp. 513)

Pub: Elsevier Technology Publications

Ed: Robert Battalio, Robert Jennings. Description: Provision of liquidity at the New York Stock Exchange is studied. On-floor traders enjoy some advantages in providing liquidity compared to off-floor traders.

The NYSE is justified in implementing measures designed to level the playing field between on- and off-floor traders.

12197 ■ "Competitors Line Up to Save Failing Banks" in The Business Journal - Serving Phoenix and the Valley of the Sun (Vol. 28, July 25, 2008, No. 47, pp. 1)

Pub: American City Business Journals, Inc.

Ed: Chris Casacchia. Description: Financial institutions in Arizona are positioning themselves as possible buyers in the event of failure of one of their competitors. These banks have already approached the Federal Deposit Insurance Corp. about their ability to take over their more troubled competitors.

12198 ■ "Comtech's Winning Streak" in Crain's New York Business (Vol. 24, January 7, 2008, No. 1, pp. 3)

Pub: Crain Communications, Inc.

Description: Comtech Telecommunications Corp., a designer and manufacturer of equipment that helps military track troops and vehicles on the field, has been one of the stock market's biggest winners over the past decade. Statistical data included.

12199 ■ "Connect the Thoughts" in Canadian Business (Vol. 81, October 27, 2008, No. 18, pp. 8)

Pub: Rogers Media Ltd.

Ed: Jeff Sanford. Description: Thomas Homer-Dixon believes the financial crisis that hit Wall Street is a systemic crisis and may result in the reconfiguration of financial markets in ways that people may never understand. He also thinks the U.S. may borrow against its assets, making it a weaker nation.

12200 ■ "Conquering Your Fear of Fees" in Entrepreneur (Vol. 37, October 2009, No. 10, pp. 86)

Pub: Entrepreneur Media, Inc.

Ed: Rosalind Resnick. Description: Entrepreneurs should study money management charges carefully before investing. They should understand how different forms of investments work and how much money managers and mutual funds charge for their services.

12201 ■ "Consumers Finding It Harder to Get and Keep Credit" in Chicago Tribune (January 10, 2009)

Pub: McClatchy-Tribune Information Services

Ed: Susan Chandler. Description: Five tips to maintain a good credit rating in these economic times are outlined and discussed.

12202 ■ "Conversation Starters for the Holiday" in Barron's (Vol. 89, July 6, 2009, No. 27, pp. 7)

Pub: Dow Jones & Co., Inc.

Ed: Michael Santoli. Description: Investors are concerned that the US will experience high inflation due to low interest rates and improved money supply. US consumer spending has increased to 70 percent of gross domestic product, brought by health-care spending increases, while savings rates have risen to 6.9 percent.

12203 ■ "A Conversation With Money Manager William Vellon" in Crain's Chicago Business (Vol. 31, November 17, 2008, No. 46, pp. 4)

Pub: Crain Communications, Inc.

Ed: Mike Colias. Description: Interview with William Vellon, the executive vice-president of Kingsbury Capital Investment Advisors; Vellon discusses ways in which the government can help the financial sector, his client base and bargains that investors should consider.

12204 ■ "A Conversation With; Ron Gatner, Jones Lang LaSalle" in Crain's Detroit Business (Vol. 24, October 6, 2008, No. 40, pp. 9)

Pub: Crain Communications, Inc.

Description: Interview with Ron Gatner who is a corporate real estate adviser with the real estate company Jones Lang LaSalle as well as the company's executive vice president and part of the tenant advisory team; Gatner speaks about the impact that the Wall Street crisis is having on the commercial real estate market in Detroit.

12205 ■ *"Cool on Chicago Office Properties"* in Crain's Chicago Business (Vol. 31, March 31, 2008, No. 13, pp. 16)
Pub: Crain Communications, Inc.
Ed: Eddie Baeb. **Description:** Investors predict values on Chicago office buildings to drop 1.3 percent over the next year.

12206 ■ *"CoolBrands"* in Canadian Business (Vol. 83, September 14, 2010, No. 15, pp. 25)
Pub: Rogers Media Ltd.
Ed: Joe Castaldo. **Description:** CoolBrands International Inc.'s merger with Swisher International Inc., a US hygiene products and services company, has formally erased the last traces of the former ice cream company. CoolBrands began as a frozen yogurt stand in 1986 and flourished across the world. How the string of acquisitions and poor corporate governance led to its demise are cited.

12207 ■ *"Copper Giant to Spin Off Silver Assets"* in Globe & Mail (February 27, 2006, pp. B1)
Pub: CTVglobemedia Publishing Inc.
Ed: Sinclair Stewart; Andrew Willis. **Description:** The reasons behind the sale of silver mining assets by Codelco are presented.

12208 ■ *"Copper, Zinc Prices Hammered"* in Globe & Mail (February 3, 2007, pp. B7)
Pub: CTVglobemedia Publishing Inc.
Ed: John Partridge. **Description:** The decline in the global prices of copper and zinc metals in January 2007 is discussed. Copper prices fell by 12 percent while zinc prices dropped by 6.3 percent.

12209 ■ *"Copy Karachi?"* in Barron's (Vol. 88, June 30, 2008, No. 26, pp. 5)
Pub: Dow Jones & Co., Inc.
Ed: Randall W. Forsyth. **Description:** Karachi bourse had a historic 8.6 percent one-day gain because the bourse banned short-selling for a month and announced a 30 billion rupee fund to stabilize the market. The shares of General Motors are trading within the same values that it had in 1974. The reasons for this decline are discussed.

12210 ■ *"Copycat"* in Canadian Business (Vol. 79, October 23, 2006, No. 21, pp. 53)
Pub: Rogers Media
Ed: Andrew Wahl. **Description:** The conversion of BCE Inc. into an income trust for tax advantages, soon after the transition of its business rival Telus Corp. into an income trust, is discussed.

12211 ■ *"Corn May Get Shucked By Soy"* in Barron's (Vol. 88, March 31, 2008, No. 13, pp. M12)
Pub: Dow Jones & Company, Inc.
Ed: Angie Pointer. **Description:** Acreage allotted to soybeans could jump by 12 percent from 2007's 63.6 million as the price for soybeans reaches record highs. Corn acreage could drop by 6.7 percent as other crops expand and higher fertilizer prices shift farmers away from corn.

12212 ■ *"Corporate Elite Show Resilience"* in The Business Journal-Serving Greater Tampa Bay (Vol. 28, August 1, 2008, No. 32, pp. 1)
Pub: American City Business Journals, Inc.
Ed: Margie Manning; Alexis Muellner. **Description:** Stocks of the largest public companies in Tampa Bay, Florida, outperformed the S&P 500 index by 28 percent in the first half of 2008. The escalation is attributed to the growth orientation of the companies in the area and the lack of exposure to the real estate and financial services sectors.

12213 ■ *"Corporex Checks Into Hotel Niche"* in Business Courier (Vol. 24, October 12, 2008, No. 26, pp. 1)
Pub: American City Business Journals, Inc.
Ed: Laura Baverman. **Description:** Corporex Companies Inc. is investing $900 million on select-service hotels ranging from $12 million to $20 million each, with eight hotels under construction and nine sites under contract.

12214 ■ *"Corus Eases Off Ailing Condo Market; Office Developers Get Majority of 1Q Loans"* in Crain's Chicago Business (April 28, 2008)
Pub: Crain Communications, Inc.
Ed: H. Lee Murphy. **Description:** Corus Bankshares Inc., a specialist in lending for the condominium high-rise construction market, is diversifying its portfolio by making loans to office developers and expects to be investing in hotels through the rest of the year. Corus' $7.57 billion loan portfolio is also discussed in detail as well as the company's earnings and share price. Statistical data included.

12215 ■ *"Cost Cuts Lead Dealers to Record Profits"* in Globe & Mail (March 24, 2006, pp. B3)
Pub: CTVglobemedia Publishing Inc.
Ed: Omar El Akkad. **Description:** The reasons behind posting of $4.3 billion profit by Canadian securities sector, for 2005, are presented.

12216 ■ *"Countdown"* in Canadian Business (Vol. 81, March 3, 2008, No. 3, pp. 27)
Pub: Rogers Media
Ed: Al Rosen. **Description:** According to a recent poll only 42 percent of portfolio managers in Canada are aware that the country is planning to adopt the International Financial Reporting Standards beginning 2011. The shift to the new standards will have significant impacts on investment values and will be the biggest revolution in Canadian financial reporting. The effects of the transition on portfolio managers and investors are analyzed.

12217 ■ *"CPI, Coal Lead Local Stock Decline"* in Saint Louis Business Journal (Vol. 32, October 14, 2011, No. 7, pp. 1)
Pub: Saint Louis Business Journal
Ed: Greg Edwards. **Description:** Coal companies and CPI Corporation were among those whose stocks have declined in St. Louis, Missouri. The stocks of local firms have plunged by 28 percent during the first nine months of 2011.

12218 ■ *"CPI Corporation Acquires Assets of Bella Pictures"* in Benzinga.com (January 28, 2011)
Pub: Benzinga.com
Ed: Benzinga Staff. **Description:** CPI Corporation acquired assets of Bella Pictures Inc., a leading provider of branded wedding photography services. Details of the acquisition are explained.

12219 ■ *"Crain's Picks Top '08 Stocks"* in Crain's New York Business (Vol. 24, January 7, 2008, No. 1, pp. 3)
Pub: Crain Communications, Inc.
Ed: Aaron Elstein. **Description:** Listing of five stocks that Crain's believes can deliver solid gains for shareholders.

12220 ■ *Crash Proof 2.0: How to Profit From the Economic Collapse*
Pub: John Wiley & Sons, Inc.
Ed: Peter D. Schiff. **Released:** September 22, 2009. **Price:** $27.95. **Description:** Factors that will affect financial stability in the coming years are explained. A three step plan to battle the current economic downturn is also included.

12221 ■ *Creating Capitalism Joint-Stock Enterprise in British Politics and Culture, 1800-1870*
Pub: Royal Historical Society
Ed: James Taylor. **Released:** October 2006. **Price:** $80.00. **Description:** The growth of joint-stock business in Victorian Britain is discussed, particularly the resistance to it.

12222 ■ *"The Credit Crisis Continues"* in Barron's (Vol. 88, March 10, 2008, No. 10, pp. M12)
Pub: Dow Jones & Company, Inc.
Ed: Randall W. Forsyth. **Description:** Short-term Treasury yields dropped to new cyclical lows in early March 2008, with the yield for the two-year Treasury

note falling to 1.532 percent. Spreads of the mortgage-backed securities of Fannie Mae and Freddie Mac rose on suspicion of collapses in financing.

12223 ■ *"Credit Crisis Puts Market in Unprecedented Territory"* in Crain's New York Business (Vol. 24, January 7, 2008, No. 1, pp. 14)
Pub: Crain Communications, Inc.
Ed: Aaron Elstein. **Description:** Banks are being forced to take enormous losses due to investors who are refusing to buy anything linked to subprime mortgages and associated securities.

12224 ■ *"Credit-Market Crisis Batters Origen Financial's Bottom Line"* in Crain's Detroit Business (Vol. 24, March 31, 2008, No. 13, pp. 4)
Pub: Crain Communications, Inc.
Description: Overview of the effect the credit-market crisis has had on Origen Financial Inc., a company that underwrites and services loans for manufactured housing. CEO Ronald Klein didn't think Origen would be affected by the collapse due to its sound operations but the company's share price dropped considerably causing its auditors to warn that the company's existence could be in jeopardy.

12225 ■ *"Credit Unions Cast Wary Eye at Paulson Plan, But Not Panicking Yet"* in The Business Review Albany (Vol. 35, April 11, 2008, No. 1)
Pub: The Business Review
Ed: Barbara Pinckney. **Description:** Credit unions are suspicious of US Treasury Secretary Henry Paulson's plan to establish a single federally insured depository institution charter for all institutions covered by federal deposit insurance. The charter would replace national banks, federal savings associations, and federal credit union charters.

12226 ■ *"Crime and Punishment"* in Canadian Business (Vol. 81, December 24, 2007, No. 1, pp. 21)
Pub: Rogers Media
Ed: Joe Castaldo. **Description:** Cmpass Inc.'s survey of 137 Canadian chief executive officers showed that they want tougher imposition of sentences on white-collar criminals, as they believe that the weak enforcement of securities laws gives an impression that Canada is a country where it is easy to get away with fraud.

12227 ■ *Currency Internationalization: Global Experiences and Implications for the Renminbi*
Pub: Palgrave Macmillan
Ed: Wensheng Peng, Chang Shu. **Released:** January 5, 2010. **Price:** $100.00. **Description:** A collection of academic studies relating to the potential internationalization of China's renmnibi. It also discusses the increasing use of China's remnnibi currency in international trade and finance.

12228 ■ *"Customers Turned Off? Not at Best Buy"* in Barron's (Vol. 88, March 24, 2008, No. 12, pp. 29)
Pub: Dow Jones & Company, Inc.
Ed: Sandra Ward. **Description:** Shares of Best Buy, trading at $42.41 each, are expected to rise to an average of $52 a share due to the company's solid fundamentals. The company's shares have fallen 20 percent from their 52-week high and are attractive given the company's bright prospects in the video game sector and high-definition video.

12229 ■ *"CVRD Inco Strike Shuts Sudbury Mines"* in Globe & Mail (April 2, 2007, pp. B1)
Pub: CTVglobemedia Publishing Inc.
Ed: Andy Hoffman. **Description:** The closure of nickel mining operations at the Sudbury mines due to the strike by employees of CVRD Inco Ltd. is described. The prospects of a rise in the prices of nickel are discussed, besides the production of metals in Canada.

12230 ■ *"Cyclicals, Your Day Is Coming"* in Barron's (Vol. 89, July 27, 2009, No. 30, pp. 24)
Pub: Dow Jones & Co., Inc.
Ed: Dimitra DeFotis. **Description:** Cyclical stocks are likely to be big winners when the economy

improves and 13 stocks that have improving earnings, decent balance sheets, and dividends are presented. These candidates include U.S. Steel, Alcoa, Allegheny Tech, Dow Chemical, and Nucor.

12231 ■ *"Danaher to Acquire Tectronix" in Canadian Electronics (Vol. 22, November-December 2007, No. 7, pp. 1)*
Pub: CLB Media Inc.
Description: Leading supplier of measurement, test and monitoring equipment Tektronix will be acquired by Danaher Corporation for $2.8 billion. Tektronix products are expected to complement Danaher's test equipment sector. The impacts of the deal on Tektronix shareholders and Danaher's operations are discussed.

12232 ■ *"Dancing With Giants: Acquisition and Survival of the Family Firm" in Family Business Review (Vol. 19, December 2006, No. 4, pp. 289)*
Pub: Family Firm Institute
Contact: Judy L. Green, President
Ed: Adam Steen, Lawrence S. Welch. **Description:** Responses of family firms to mergers and acquisitions are analyzed taking the example of the takeover of an Australian wine producer and family firm.

12233 ■ *"Darkness Falling.." in Barron's (Vol. 89, July 20, 2009, No. 29, pp. 13)*
Pub: Dow Jones & Co., Inc.
Description: Newsletter writer Arch Crawford believes that market indicators signal a possible downturn in US stock markets. High risk areas also include China and Japan .

12234 ■ *"Data Dispel Some Notions About Value of Stock Buybacks" in Crain's Cleveland Business (Vol. 28, November 19, 2007, No. 46, pp. 9)*
Pub: Crain Communications, Inc.
Ed: Megan Johnston. **Description:** According to new research on buybacks and their benefits, companies engaged in stock buybacks frequently do not enjoy a nice boost in their share prices despite the conventional wisdom that states that investors like stock buybacks.

12235 ■ *Data Driven Investing: Professional Edition*
Pub: Data Driven Publishing, LLC
Ed: Mitchell R. Hardy; Bill Matson. **Released:** 2004. **Description:** Investment concepts and trading techniques are explored in a simple and practical way. The book covers the unreliability of financial markets due to malpractices, appalling analysis, insider training and more. Information is based on data and common sense and easy to use for beginner as well as professional.

12236 ■ *"Dating Games" in Canadian Business (Vol. 79, September 25, 2006, No. 19, pp. 23)*
Pub: Rogers Media
Ed: John Gray. **Description:** Increasing stock option scandals in Canada and American companies is discussed.

12237 ■ *"David Azrieli" in Canadian Business (Vol. 82, April 27, 2009, No. 7, pp. 54)*
Pub: Rogers Media
Ed: Alex Mlynek. **Description:** David Azrieli wants to take advantage of opportunities, revealing that he has increased his portfolio nearly every recession. Azrieli has recently purchased properties of General Electric near the Toronto airport for about $100 million. He believes the economy will rebound in the second half of 2009.

12238 ■ *"A Day Late and a Dollar Short" in Indoor Comfort Marketing (Vol. 70, March 2011, No. 3, pp. 30)*
Pub: Industry Publications Inc.
Ed: Philip J. Baratz. **Description:** A discussion involving futures options and fuel oil prices is presented.

12239 ■ *"Deal Braces Cramer for Growth Run" in The Business Journal-Serving Metropolitan Kansas City (Vol. 26, July 4,*

2008, No. 43, pp. 1)
Pub: American City Business Journals, Inc.
Ed: James Dornbook. **Description:** Gardner, Kansas-based Cramer Products Inc. bought 100 percent of the stocks of Louisville, Kentucky-based Active Ankle Inc. from 26 private investors increasing its revenue by 20 percent. The latter is the second largest vendor of Cramer. Other details of the merger are presented.

12240 ■ *"Deal or No Deal?" in Canadian Business (Vol. 80, January 15, 2007, No. 2, pp. 38)*
Pub: Rogers Media
Ed: Andrew Wahl; Zena Olijnkyk; Jeff Sanford; Erin Pooley. **Description:** The trends in the stock prices of companies like Loblaw Companies Ltd., Domtar Inc. and Biovail Corp., from January 2006 to January 2007, are analyzed.

12241 ■ *"The Deal - Rhymes With Steal - Of A Lifetime" in Barron's (Vol. 88, March 24, 2008, No. 12, pp. 24)*
Pub: Dow Jones & Company, Inc.
Ed: Andrew Bary. **Description:** JPMorgan Chase's impending acquisition of Bear Stearns for $2.50 a share is a huge steal for the former. JPMorgan is set to acquire a company with a potential annual earnings of $1 billion while the Federal Reserve funds Bear's illiquid assets by providing $30 billion in nonrecourse loans.

12242 ■ *"Dean Foods" in Ice Cream Reporter (Vol. 23, November 20, 2010, No. 12, pp. 8)*
Pub: Ice Cream Reporter
Description: The impact of higher commodity prices can be seen in the recent news from Dean Foods, the largest U.S. dairy company, which reported that rising butterfat and other dairy commodity costs have led to lower-than-expected quarterly profits after it cut prices to compete with private-label brands.

12243 ■ *"Death Spiral" in Business Journal Serving Greater Tampa Bay (Vol. 30, October 29, 2010, No. 45, pp. 1)*
Pub: Tampa Bay Business Journal
Ed: Margie Manning. **Description:** Bay Cities Bank has started working on the loan portfolio of its acquisition, Progress Bank of Florida. Regulators closed Progress Bank in October 2010 after capital collapsed due to charge-offs and increases in the provision for future loan losses.

12244 ■ *"Debutante NYSE Soars 20 Percent" in Globe & Mail (March 9, 2006, pp. B1)*
Pub: CTVglobemedia Publishing Inc.
Ed: John Partridge. **Description:** The debutant share trading of NYSE Group Inc. is discussed. The prices rose by 20 percent before closing.

12245 ■ *"Decision CEO Cool to Acquisitions" in Globe & Mail (April 19, 2007, pp. B6)*
Pub: CTVglobemedia Publishing Inc.
Ed: Andy Hoffman. **Description:** The increase in the shares of Denison Mines Corp. due to hike in Uranium prices is discussed.

12246 ■ *"Decline in Assets Is Costly for Advisers" in The Business Journal-Serving Metropolitan Kansas City (Vol. 27, October 24, 2008)*
Pub: American City Business Journals, Inc.
Ed: James Dornbrook. **Description:** Financial advisers in the Kansas City, Missouri area are forced to cut costs as their assets have decreased sharply due to the huge drop in stock prices. American Century Investments was forced to diversify into foreign assets and cut 90 jobs as its assets dropped to $84 billion. Diversification has softened the impact of the steep decline in stock prices for Waddell & Reed Financial Inc.

12247 ■ *A Demon of Our Own Design: Markets, Hedge Funds, and the Perils of Financial Innovation*
Pub: John Wiley and Sons, Inc.
Ed: Richard Bookstaber. **Released:** December 2008. **Price:** $16.95 paperback. **Description:** Longtime hedge-fund manager offers his take on a market and investment system that he believes is needlessly

complex owing to investment banks, hedge funds, innovation, regulation, and safeguards and further compounded by investor and market instabilities. These complexities could create a large-scale disaster.

12248 ■ *"Detecting Crookery" in Canadian Business (Vol. 80, February 12, 2007, No. 4, pp. 23)*
Pub: Rogers Media
Ed: Al Rosen. **Description:** Expert advice to Canadian investors on proper financial reporting is presented and ways to protect their investments are discussed.

12249 ■ *"Deutsche Bank Joins the Club" in Barron's (Vol. 88, March 31, 2008, No. 13, pp. M6)*
Pub: Dow Jones & Company, Inc.
Ed: Arindam Nag. **Description:** Deutsche Bank's tangible leverage has worsened sharply in the past year from 2.1 percent to 2.3 percent during 2002-2006 to only 1.6 percent. The bank has also been accumulating a lot of illiquid assets and its Level-3 assets are three times its tangible equity.

12250 ■ *The Dhandho Investor: The Low Risk Value Method to High Returns*
Pub: John Wiley and Sons Inc.
Ed: Mohnish Pabrai. **Released:** April 2007. **Price:** $27.95. **Description:** Value investing is described using the Dhandho capital allocation framework for successfully investing in the stock market.

12251 ■ *"Diana Sands; Vice-President of Investor Relations, Boeing Co." in Crain's Chicago Business (Vol. 31, May 5, 2008, No. 18, pp. 32)*
Pub: Crain Communications, Inc.
Ed: John Rosenthal. **Description:** Profile of Diana Sands who is the vice-president of investor relations at Boeing Co. which entails explaining the company's performance to securities analysts and institutional investors.

12252 ■ *"Diary of a Short-Seller" in Conde Nast Portfolio (Vol. 2, June 2008, No. 6, pp. 44)*
Pub: Conde Nast Publications
Contact: David Carey, President
Ed: Jesse Eisinger. **Description:** Profile of David Einhorn who is a fund manager that spoke out against finance company Allied Capital whose stock fell nearly 20 percent the day after Einhorn's critique; Einhorn subsequently had to contend with attacks against his credibility as well as investigations by the S.E.C.; Einhorn's experience illuminates our current economic crisis.

12253 ■ *"Diaz Announces Financial and Operating Results for the First Three Months of 2007" in Canadian Corporate News (May 16, 2007)*
Pub: Comtex News Network Inc.
Description: Diaz Resources Ltd., an oil and gas exploration and production company, announced its financial results during the first quarter of 2007 which were hampered by lower gas prices and declining production volumes but anticipates the financial results should steadily improve in the second quarter of 2007.

12254 ■ *"Dick Haskayne" in Canadian Business (Vol. 81, March 31, 2008, No. 5, pp. 72)*
Pub: Rogers Media
Ed: Andy Holloway. **Description:** Dick Haskayne says that he learned a lot about business from his dad who ran a butcher shop where they had to make a decision on buying cattle and getting credit. Haskayne says that family, friends, finances, career, health, and infrastructure are benchmarks that have to be balanced.

12255 ■ *Dictionary of Finance, Investment and Banking*
Pub: Palgrave Macmillan
Ed: Erik Banks. **Released:** 2010. **Price:** $42.95. **Description:** Comprehensive dictionary covering terms used in finance, investment and banking sectors.

12256 ■ *"A Different Kind of Waiting List"* in *Canadian Business (Vol. 80, April 9, 2007, No. 8, pp. 17)*
Pub: Rogers Media
Ed: Erin Pooley. **Description:** The adverse impact on drug companies' profitability due to regulatory delays in approving drugs is discussed.

12257 ■ *"Different This Time?"* in *Canadian Business (Vol. 81, April 14, 2008, No. 6, pp. 38)*
Pub: Rogers Media
Ed: Matthew McClearn. **Description:** Irving Fisher believed that the low interest rates of the 1920's spurred investors to borrow and use the money to speculate with the proceeds thereby increasing the debt to unmanageable levels prior to the stock market crash in Oct. 29, 1929. The U.S. economic conditions in 1929 and U.S. economic conditions in 2008 are discussed.

12258 ■ *"Digging Deep for Gold"* in *Barron's (Vol. 88, March 24, 2008, No. 12, pp. 49)*
Pub: Dow Jones & Company, Inc.
Ed: Suzanne McGee. **Description:** David Iben, manager of the Nuveen Tradewinds Value Opportunities Fund, looks for value in companies and industries where the consensus of analysts is negative. He started investing in gold stocks well before gold prices started to rise.

12259 ■ *The Directory of Venture Capital and Private Equity Firms: 2009*
Pub: Grey House Publishing
Contact: Richard Gottlieb, President
E-mail: rhg2@greyhouse.com
Ed: Laura Mars-Proietti. **Released:** April 1, 2009. **Price:** $450.00. **Description:** Updated and expanded edition that includes new entries offering access to more than 3,500 domestic and international venture capital and private equity firms; detailed contact information and extensive data on investments and funds is included.

12260 ■ *"Disappearing Act"* in *Globe & Mail (April 21, 2007, pp. B1)*
Pub: CTVglobemedia Publishing Inc.
Ed: David Parkinson. **Description:** The effects of the buyout of BCE Inc. on the trends of stock prices at the Toronto Stock Exchange are described.

12261 ■ *"Discount Beers Take Fizz Out Of Molson"* in *Globe & Mail (February 10, 2006, pp. B3)*
Pub: CTVglobemedia Publishing Inc.
Ed: Omar El Akkad. **Description:** The reasons behind the decline in profits by 60 percent for Molson Coors Brewing Co., during fourth quarter 2005, are presented.

12262 ■ *"Diversity Stock Indexes"* in *Hispanic Business (September 2007, pp. 28)*
Pub: Hispanic Business
Description: Presentation of the Hispanic Business Stock Index shows the current value of fifteen Hispanic companies through August 2007.

12263 ■ *"DiversityStockIndexes"* in *Hispanic Business (October 2007, pp. 68)*
Pub: Hispanic Business
Description: Two proprietary stock indexes of interest to Hispanic businesses are presented.

12264 ■ *"Dividing to Conquer"* in *Barron's (Vol. 88, March 31, 2008, No. 13, pp. 22)*
Pub: Dow Jones & Company, Inc.
Ed: Andrew Bary. **Description:** Altria's spin off of Philip Morris International could unlock substantial value for both domestic and international cigarette concerns. The strong brands and ample payouts from both companies will most likely impress investors.

12265 ■ *"Do-It-Yourself Portfolio Management"* in *Barron's (Vol. 89, July 13, 2009, No. 28, pp. 25)*
Pub: Dow Jones & Co., Inc.
Ed: Mike Hogan. **Description:** Services of several portfolio management web sites are presented. These web sites include MarketRiders E.Adviser, TD Ameritrade and E.

12266 ■ *"Do the Math"* in *Canadian Business (Vol. 79, October 9, 2006, No. 20, pp. 17)*
Pub: Rogers Media
Ed: Al Rosen. **Description:** Faulty practices followed by regulators in Canadian stock market are discussed. The need for authorities to protect investors against these frauds are emphasized.

12267 ■ *"Doctor's Orders"* in *Canadian Business (Vol. 79, November 20, 2006, No. 23, pp. 73)*
Pub: Rogers Media
Ed: Jeff Sanford. **Description:** George Cohon, the founder of McDonald's in Canada and Russia, speaks about the Canadian market and the experience of starting McDonald's in Canada.

12268 ■ *"DoEs and DonEts"* in *Canadian Business (Vol. 79, July 17, 2006, No. 14-15, pp. 29)*
Pub: Rogers Media
Ed: Andy Holloway; Erin Pooley; Thomas Watson. **Description:** Strategic tips for planning systematic investments, in order to make life more enjoyable after retirement, are elucidated.

12269 ■ *"Dofasco Quarterly Profit Plunges on Lower Steel Prices, Rising Costs"* in *Globe & Mail (February 4, 2006, pp. B3)*
Pub: CTVglobemedia Publishing Inc.
Ed: Shirley Won. **Description:** Dofasco Inc. posted 71% decline in profits for fourth quarter 2005. The revenue drop is attributed to fall in steel prices.

12270 ■ *"Dofasco Warms to New Thyssen Bid"* in *Globe & Mail (January 4, 2006, pp. B1)*
Pub: CTVglobemedia Publishing Inc.
Ed: Greg Keenan. **Description:** The details on ThyssenKrupp AG's bid for Dofasco Inc., at $63 a share, are presented.

12271 ■ *"The Dogs of TSX"* in *Canadian Business (Vol. 81, Summer 2008, No. 9, pp. 77)*
Pub: Rogers Media Ltd.
Ed: Calvin Leung. **Description:** Table showing the one-year stock performance of the ten highest dividend-yielding stocks on the S&P/TSX 60 Composite Index is presented. This technique is similar to the 'Dogs of the Dow' approach. The idea in this investment strategy is to buy equal amounts of stocks from these companies and selling them a year later, and then repeat the process.

12272 ■ *"The Dogs of the TSX"* in *Canadian Business (Vol. 82, Summer 2009, No. 8, pp. 42)*
Pub: Rogers Media
Ed: Calvin Leung. **Description:** David Stanley revealed in an analysis of the ten companies on the S&P/TSX 60 index with the highest dividend yields, known as the Dogs of TSX, the dogs delivered an annual return of 13 percent between 1987 to 2005. The Dogs is a stock-picking method that involves buying the ten companies on the S&P/TSX 60 index with the highest dividend yields, and then selling them a year later.

12273 ■ *"The Dominance of Doubt"* in *Barron's (Vol. 89, July 13, 2009, No. 28, pp. M3)*
Pub: Dow Jones & Co., Inc.
Description: Five straight down days leading up to July 10, 2009 in the U.S. stock market reminds one strategist of 1982 when there was a feeling that things could never be the same again. One analyst is bullish on the stocks of Apple Inc. and sees the stocks rising to at least 180 in 12 months. The prospects of the shares of GM and Ford are also discussed.

12274 ■ *"Don't Bet Against The House"* in *Barron's (Vol. 88, July 14, 2008, No. 28, pp. 20)*
Pub: Dow Jones & Co., Inc.
Ed: Sandra Ward. **Description:** Shares of Nasdaq OMX have lost more than 50 percent of their value from November 2007 to July 2008 but the value of these shares could climb 50 percent on the strength

of world security exchanges. Only 15 percent of the company's revenues come from the U.S. and the shares are trading at 12.5 times the amount expected for 2008.

12275 ■ *"Don't Count Your Millions Yet"* in *Business Courier (Vol. 24, January 11, 2008, No. 40, pp. 1)*
Pub: American City Business Journals, Inc.
Ed: Steve Watkins. **Description:** Merger and acquisition deals have been difficult to complete since 2007 largely due to a weaker economy and the credit crunch. Buyers have become more cautious because of the state of the economy and capital has become tougher to obtain because of the credit market crisis. The trends in mergers and acquisitions are analyzed further.

12276 ■ *"Don't Expect Quick Fix"* in *The Business Journal-Serving Metropolitan Kansas City (Vol. 27, October 3, 2008, No. 3, pp. 1)*
Pub: American City Business Journals, Inc.
Ed: James Dornbrook. **Description:** United States governmental entities cannot provide a quick fix solution to the current financial crisis. The economy requires a systemic change in the way people think about credit. The financial services industry should also focus on core lending principles.

12277 ■ *"Don't Get Lulled by the Calm"* in *Barron's (Vol. 89, July 27, 2009, No. 30, pp. M13)*
Pub: Dow Jones & Co., Inc.
Ed: Steven M. Sears. **Description:** Options traders expect volatility to return in the fall of 2009 and to bring correlation with it. September and October are typically the most volatile months and the trick is to survive earnings season.

12278 ■ *"Don't' Hang Up On FairPoint"* in *Barron's (Vol. 88, July 7, 2008, No. 27, pp. M5)*
Pub: Dow Jones & Co., Inc.
Ed: Fleming Meeks. **Description:** Shares of FairPoint Communications, priced at $6.63 each, are undervalued and should be worth over $12 each. The company increased its size by more than five times by acquiring Verizon's local telephone operations in Vermont, New Hampshire, and Maine, but must switch customers in those areas into their system by the end of September 2007.

12279 ■ *"Dow Jones Gives Apple-Loving Sales Professionals a Boost"* in *Information Today (Vol. 26, February 2009, No. 2, pp. 30)*
Pub: Information Today, Inc.
Description: Dow Jones Sales Triggers for iPhone and iPod program helps sales professionals stay current to prospects and customers in their fields by providing real-time news on business changes, including management moves, mergers, and new investments. The application presents events that trigger best opportunities and allows users to look up companies and executives to retrieve information.

12280 ■ *"Downtown Bank Got High Marks for Irwin Purchase, Is Looking For More"* in *Business Courier (Vol. 27, September 3, 2010, No. 18, pp. 1)*
Pub: Business Courier
Ed: Steve Watkins. **Description:** First Financial Bancorp is looking to acquire more troubled banks following its purchase of Irwin Union Bank. The bank has reported a $383 million bargain purchase gain during the third quarter of 2009.

12281 ■ *"Downtown Retail Site Sold to ATCO"* in *Austin Business JournalInc. (Vol. 29, November 20, 2009, No. 37, pp. 1)*
Pub: American City Business Journals
Ed: Kate Harrington. **Description:** New York-based real estate company ATCO Advisory Services purchased a 13,700 square foot retail space in Austin, Texas from 360 Condominiums. The selection of the retail space, named the Shops at 360 has been attributed to the local tenant mix and its location in downtown Austin. Meanwhile, ATCO may continue investing in the area in the near future.

12282 ■ "Drilling Deep and Flying High" in Barron's (Vol. 88, June 30, 2008, No. 26, pp. 34)
Pub: Dow Jones & Co., Inc.
Ed: Kenneth Rapoza. **Description:** Shares of Petrobras could rise another 25 percent if the three deepwater wells that the company has found proves as lucrative as some expect. Petrobras will become an oil giant if the reserves are proven.

12283 ■ "Drug-Maker Plans IPO" in Business Courier (Vol. 24, November 23, 2008, No. 32, pp. 1)
Pub: American City Business Journals, Inc.
Ed: James Ritchie; Steve Watkins. **Description:** Xanodyne Pharmaceuticals Inc. filed plans with the Securities and Exchange Commission on November 9, 2007 for an initial public offering. The company, with annual sales of $75 million, had lost $222 million since it was founded in 2001.

12284 ■ "Drug, Seed Firms Offer Antidote For Inflation" in Crain's Chicago Business (Vol. 31, April 21, 2008, No. 16, pp. 4)
Pub: Crain Communications, Inc.
Ed: Daniel Rome Levine. **Description:** Interview with Jerrold Senser, the CEO of Institutional Capital LLC in Chicago, in which he discusses the ways that the company is adjusting to the economic slowdown and rising inflation, his favorite firms for investment and his prediction of an economic turnaround; he also recommends five companies he feels are worth investing in.

12285 ■ "Drug Trial Halt at YM Sets Stage for Selloff" in Globe & Mail (January 31, 2007, pp. B3)
Pub: CTVglobemedia Publishing Inc.
Ed: Leonard Zehr. **Description:** The decision of YM Biosciences Inc. to stop its trial of cancer drug tesmilifene and stocks following government concern over the safety of the drug is discussed.

12286 ■ "Dueling Visions" in Barron's (Vol. 89, July 27, 2009, No. 30, pp. 13)
Pub: Dow Jones & Co., Inc.
Ed: Michael Santoli. **Description:** Goldman Sachs' market strategists believe the stock market has entered a 'sustained-rally' mode while Morgan Stanley's strategist believes this is a 'rally to sell into'. What is not known in the stock market is how much of a 'V'-shaped recovery in earning the market rebound has already priced in.

12287 ■ "Dynamic Duo" in Barron's (Vol. 88, March 10, 2008, No. 10, pp. 45)
Pub: Dow Jones & Company, Inc.
Ed: Shirley A. Lazo. **Description:** General Dynamics, the world's sixth-largest military contractor, raised its dividend payout by 20.7 percent from 29 cents to 35 cents a share. Steel Dynamics, producer of structural steel and steel bar products, declared a 2-for-1 stock split and raised its quarterly dividend by 33 percent to a split-adjusted 10 cents a share.

12288 ■ "easyhome Ltd. Discovers Employee Fraud at an Easyfinancial Kiosk Company" in Internet Wire (October 14, 2010)
Pub: Comtex
Description: Canada's leading merchandise leasing company and provider of financial services, easyhome Ltd., reported employee fraud totaling $3.4 million that was perpetrated against the firm's easyfinancial services business.

12289 ■ "eBay Business Looking Up" in Zacks (July 26, 2011)
Pub: Comtex News Network Inc.
Ed: Sejuti Banerjea. **Description:** eBay reported solid revenue growth for 2011 second quarter, keeping in line with the Zacks Consensus Estimate, and third quarter earnings are expected to be higher. eBay's new strategy is to direct traffic to bigger sellers with improved customer service, making this good for eBay businesses.

12290 ■ "eBay Inc. Completes Acquisition of Zong" in Benzinga.com (October 29, 2011)
Pub: Benzinga.com
Ed: Benzinga Staff. **Description:** eBay Inc. acquired Zong, a provider of payments through mobile carrier billing. Terms of the agreement are outlined.

12291 ■ "Economic Distance and the Survival of Foreign Direct Investments" in Academy of Management Journal (Vol. 50, No. 5, October 2007)
Pub: Academy of Management
Contact: Ming-Jer Chen, President
Ed: Eric W.K. Tsang, Paul S.L. Yip. **Description:** Study was undertaken to assess the relationship between economic disparities of various countries and foreign direct investments, focusing on Singapore. Results revealed that economic distance has a definite impact on foreign direct investment hazard rates.

12292 ■ "Economic Prognosis" in Barron's (Vol. 89, July 13, 2009, No. 28, pp. 11)
Pub: Dow Jones & Co., Inc.
Ed: Karen Hube. **Description:** Loomis Sayles Bond Fund manager Dan Fuss believes that the economy is bottoming and that recovery will be long and drawn out. Fuss guesses that the next peak in 10-year Treasury yields will be about 6.25% in around 4 and a half or five years ahead of 2009.

12293 ■ "An Educated Play on China" in Barron's (Vol. 88, June 30, 2008, No. 26, pp. M6)
Pub: Dow Jones & Co., Inc.
Ed: Mohammed Hadi. **Description:** New Oriental Education & Technology Group sells English-language courses to an increasingly competitive Chinese workforce that values education. The shares in this company have been weighed down by worries on the impact of the Beijing Olympics on enrollment and the Sichuan earthquake. These shares could be a great way to get exposure to the long-term growth in China.

12294 ■ "Effect of Oil Prices on the Economy" in Canadian Business (Vol. 81, September 15, 2008, No. 14-15, pp. 5)
Pub: Rogers Media Ltd.
Ed: Joe Chidley. **Description:** Rise of oil prices above $100 in February 2008 and $140 in July signals the birth of a 'new economy' according to commentators; this shift is causing uneasiness from oil industry professionals who are unsure of how this trend could be sustained. Oil dropped below $120 in August, which could slow down global economic growth followed by oil demand, then oil prices.

12295 ■ "Egg Fight: The Yolk's on the Short" in Barron's (Vol. 88, July 7, 2008, No. 27, pp. 20)
Pub: Dow Jones & Co., Inc.
Ed: Christopher C. Williams. **Description:** Shares of Cal-Maine Foods, the largest egg producer and distributor in the US, are due for a huge rise because of the increase in egg prices. Short sellers, however, continue betting that the stock, priced at $31.84 each, will eventually go down.

12296 ■ "The Emerging Capital Market for Nonprofits" in Harvard Business Review (Vol. 88, October 2010, No. 10, pp. 110)
Pub: Harvard Business School Publishing
Ed: Robert S. Kaplan, Allen S. Grossman. **Description:** Demonstration of how nonprofits can use intermediaries to grow their organizational structures, giving them improved scale and impact is offered. Some intermediaries play a mutual-fund role and conduct due diligence, while others act as venture capital funds and implement strategy.

12297 ■ "The Emperor Strikes Back" in Canadian Business (Vol. 80, March 26, 2007, No. 7, pp. 48)
Pub: Rogers Media
Ed: Rachel Pulfer. **Description:** The financial performance of Fairfax Financial Holdings Ltd. in 2006 is presented. The efforts of chief executive Prem Watsa to lead the company towards growth track are also presented.

12298 ■ "Empire of the Sun" in Canadian Business (Vol. 82, April 27, 2009, No. 7, pp. 42)
Pub: Rogers Media
Ed: Jeff Sanford. **Description:** Suncor Energy Inc. and Petro-Canada announced on March 23, 2009 plans for a merger. The $19 billion merger will result in Suncor keeping their brand name and 60 percent of the company while Pe= tro-Canada will hold 40 percent. The new Suncor now has 7.5 billion barrels of proved and probable reserves of oil and could account for as much as 25 percent of North American production by 2025.

12299 ■ "EnCana Axes Spending on Gas Wells" in Globe & Mail (February 16, 2006, pp. B1)
Pub: CTVglobemedia Publishing Inc.
Ed: Dave Ebner. **Description:** The reasons behind EnCana Corp.'s cost spending measures by $300 million on natural gas wells are presented. The company projects 2 percent cut in gas and oil sales for 2006.

12300 ■ "End of the Beginning" in Canadian Business (Vol. 81, November 10, 2008, No. 19, pp. 17)
Pub: Rogers Media Ltd.
Ed: David Wolf. **Description:** The freeze in the money markets and historic decline in equity markets around the world finally forced governments into aggressive coordinated action. The asset price inflation brought on by cheap credit will now work in reverse and the tightening of credit will be difficult economically. Canada is exposed to the fallout everywhere, given that the U.S. the U.K. and Japan buy 30 percent of Canada's output.

12301 ■ "End of an Era" in Barron's (Vol. 88, July 7, 2008, No. 27, pp. 3)
Pub: Dow Jones & Co., Inc.
Ed: Alan Abelson. **Description:** June 2008 was a very bad month for US stocks, with investors losing as much as 41.9 percent in the first half of 2008 signaling an end to the financial environment that prevailed around the world since the 1980's. The US job market lost 62,000 jobs in June 2008.

12302 ■ "The End of the Line for Line Extensions?' in Advertising Age (Vol. 79, July 7, 2008, No. 26, pp. 3)
Pub: Crain Communications, Inc.
Description: After years of double-digit growth, some of the most heavily extended personal-care products have slowed substantially or even declined in the U.S. Unilever's Dove and P&G's Pantene and Olay are two such brands that have been affected. Statistical data included.

12303 ■ "Endeca Gears Up for Likely IPO Bid" in Boston Business Journal (Vol. 31, July 1, 2011, No. 23, pp. 1)
Pub: Boston Business Journal
Ed: Kyle Alspach. **Description:** Endeca Inc. is readying itself for its plans to register as a public company. The search engine technology leader is enjoying continued growth with revenue up by 30 percent in 2010 while its expansion trend makes it an unlikely candidate for an acquisition.

12304 ■ "Energy Firms Face Stricter Definitions" in Globe & Mail (March 26, 2007, pp. B3)
Pub: CTVglobemedia Publishing Inc.
Ed: David Ebner. **Description:** The Alberta Securities Commission has imposed strict securities regulations on oil and gas industries. Energy industries will have to submit revenue details to stake holders.

12305 ■ "Energy, MLPs: Pipeline to Profits" in Barron's (Vol. 89, July 27, 2009, No. 30, pp. 9)
Pub: Dow Jones & Co., Inc.
Ed: Dimitra DeFotis. **Description:** Energy master limited partnership stocks are range-bound in the next few months from July 2009 but there are there are some opportunities that remain. These include Energy Transfer Equity, Enterprise GP holdings, NuStar GP Holdings, and Plains All American Pipeline.

12306 ■ *"Energy Slide Slows Fourth Quarter Profits"* in Globe & Mail (April 13, 2007, pp. B9)

Pub: CTVglobemedia Publishing Inc.

Ed: Angela Barnes. **Description:** The decrease in the fourth quarter profits of several companies across various industries in Canada, including mining and manufacturing, due to global decrease in oil prices, is discussed.

12307 ■ *"Engine of Growth: U.S. Industry Funk hasn't Hurt Cummins or Its Investors"* in Barron's (Vol. 88, July 14, 2008, No. 28, pp. 43)

Pub: Dow Jones & Co., Inc.

Ed: Shirley A. Lazo. **Description:** Engine maker Cummins increased its quarterly common dividend by 40 percent to 17.5 cents per share from 12.5 cents. CVS Caremark's dividend saw a hike of 18.4 percent from 9.5 cents to 11.25 cents per share while its competitor Walgreen is continuing its 75th straight year of dividend distribution and its 33rd straight year of dividend hikes.

12308 ■ *"An Equity Fund of Their Own"* in Entrepreneur (Vol. 35, October 2007, No. 10, pp. 68)

Pub: Entrepreneur Media Inc.

Ed: Lee Gimpel. **Description:** About 100 new private equity funds have formed since 2002, proof that private equity investing is becoming popular among companies. There is also an increase in competition to close deals owing to the large number of investors that companies can choose; advantages of smaller funds over the larger one is explained.

12309 ■ *"Essential Releases Record First Quarter Results"* in Canadian Corporate News (May 14, 2007)

Pub: Comtex News Network Inc.

Description: The first quarter of 2007 saw record financial performance despite numerous challenges for Essential Energy Services Trust. Statistical data included.

12310 ■ *"ETF Score Card"* in Barron's (Vol. 89, July 13, 2009, No. 28, pp. 51)

Pub: Dow Jones & Co., Inc.

Description: Statistical table is presented which shows the net assets of various exchange-traded funds is presented. The table also shows the total return of these funds up to a three-year time period.

12311 ■ *"European Stocks on Deck"* in Barron's (Vol. 89, July 27, 2009, No. 30, pp. M7)

Pub: Dow Jones & Co., Inc.

Ed: Vito J. Racanelli. **Description:** European stocks are cheap and these trade at a discount to U.S. equities rarely seen in the past 40 years. This represents an opportunity for Americans and trends show that Europe's stocks outperform when there is a discrepancy between the price to earnings ratio in European stocks versus U.S. stocks and when sentiment on European equities are downbeat.

12312 ■ *"Europe's Meltdown"* in Canadian Business (Vol. 83, June 15, 2010, No. 10, pp. 76)

Pub: Rogers Media Ltd.

Ed: Bryan Borzykowski. **Description:** As European countries such as Greece, Spain, and Portugal struggle with debt problems, it is worth noting that its equities trade at a 30 percent discount to the U.S. and that a 10 percent drop in the Euro translates to a 10 percent rise in profitability for exporters. Investors may also want to focus on business-to-business operations rather than consumer-focused ones.

12313 ■ *"Even Gold Gets Tarnished When Everyone Wants Cash"* in Globe & Mail (February 28, 2007, pp. B1)

Pub: CTVglobemedia Publishing Inc.

Ed: John Partridge. **Description:** The impact of fall in Chinese equities on the United States stock market and metal prices, including gold, is discussed.

12314 ■ *"Everyone Out of the Pool"* in Barron's (Vol. 89, July 20, 2009, No. 29, pp. 18)

Pub: Dow Jones & Co., Inc.

Ed: Sandra Ward. **Description:** Shares of Pool Corp. could drop as continued weakness in the housing market weakens the market for swimming pool equipment. The company's shares are trading at $18.29, about 20 times projected 2009 earnings of $0.91 a share.

12315 ■ *"The Evolution of Corporate Social Responsibility"* in Business Horizons (November-December 2007, pp. 449)

Pub: Elsevier Technology Publications

Ed: Philip L. Cochran. **Description:** Corporate social responsibility is now perceived as vital in enhancing the profitability of businesses while improving their reputation. It has changed business practices such as philanthropy, investment, and entrepreneurship.

12316 ■ *"Expect a Rally as Waders Dive In"* in Barron's (Vol. 89, July 20, 2009, No. 29, pp. 11)

Pub: Dow Jones & Co., Inc.

Ed: Vito J. Racanelli. **Description:** US stock markets may experience a rally in the autumn of 2009 as skeptical investors start to return to the market. The Standard & Poor's Index may jump to the 1025-1050 point levels during this rally.

12317 ■ *"Experts: Market Shaky But Resilient"* in The Business Journal-Serving Metropolitan Kansas City (Vol. 27, September 19, 2008, No. 1)

Pub: American City Business Journals, Inc.

Ed: Steve Vockrodt. **Description:** Investment advisers believe that the local investors in Kansas City who have a long-term approach towards their portfolios may come out even or even experience gains despite the Wall Street financial crisis. The impacts of the crisis are expected to take time to reach the area of Kansas City. The potential impacts of the Wall Street meltdown are examined further.

12318 ■ *Facing Financial Dysfunction*

Pub: Infinity Publishing

Ed: Bert Whitehead. **Released:** April 2004. **Description:** Handbook to help individuals manage their finances, investments, taxes and retirement.

12319 ■ *"Fairfax Announces Acquisition of William Ashley"* in Benzinga.com (August 16, 2011)

Pub: Benzinga.com

Ed: Benzinga Staff. **Description:** Fairfax Financial Holdings Limited acquired the family-owned William Ashley China company, leader within the dinnerware and wedding registry industries and was the first company in North America to introduce a computerized wedding registry system.

12320 ■ *"Falling Local Executive Pay Could Suggest a Trend"* in Tampa Bay Business Journal (Vol. 30, January 15, 2010, No. 4, pp. 1)

Pub: American City Business Journals

Ed: Margie Manning. **Description:** Tampa Bay, Florida-based Raymond James Financial Inc. and MarineMax Inc.'s proxy statements have shown the decreasing compensation of the companies' highest paid executives. The falling trend in executive compensation was a result of intensified shareholder scrutiny and the economy.

12321 ■ *"Falling Markets' Nastiest Habits"* in Barron's (Vol. 88, July 7, 2008, No. 27, pp. 7)

Pub: Dow Jones & Co., Inc.

Ed: Michael Santoli. **Description:** US market conditions reflect a bear market, with the S&P 500 index falling 20 percent below its recent high as of June 2008. The bear market is expected to persist in the immediate future, although bear market rallies are likely to occur.

12322 ■ *"Falling Share Prices Will Convince Big Oil Producers to Pay Up to Drill"* in Globe

& Mail (April 21, 2007, pp. B1)

Pub: CTVglobemedia Publishing Inc.

Ed: Boyd Erman. **Description:** The effect of the increase in operational costs and the decline in share prices, on the exploration of petroleum deposits in Canada, is described.

12323 ■ *A Family Matter: A Guide to Operating Your Personal Estate*

Pub: Brown Books Publishing Group

Ed: William A. Verkest. **Released:** May 2003. **Price:** $22.95. **Description:** Guidebook to financial management of personal assets is presented. Important documents must be maintained in a safe, secure place for family members or attorneys to access when necessary. The author suggests that a personal diary be kept with important information regarding records of investment accounts and financial summaries for every year in order to calculate taxes and manage financial matters more efficiently.

12324 ■ *"Family Matters: Founding Family Firms and Corporate Political Activity"* in Business and Society (December 2007, pp. 395-428)

Pub: SAGE Publications USA

Contact: Blaise R. Simqu, President

Ed: Michael Hadani. **Description:** The impact of publicly traded family founding firms and their inclination for corporate political activity is examined. Publicly traded family founding firms are more predisposed to engage in corporate political activity when the founder is in an executive position. Details of these findings are reported.

12325 ■ *"Fannie and Freddie: How They'll Change"* in Business Week (September 22, 2008, No. 4100, pp. 30)

Pub: McGraw-Hill Companies, Inc.

Ed: Jane Sasseen. **Description:** Three possible outcomes of the fate of struggling mortgage giants Freddie Mac and Fannie Mae after the government bailout are outlined.

12326 ■ *"Fast Revival Unlikely For Indian 'Net Stocks"* in Barron's (Vol. 88, July 7, 2008, No. 27, pp. 12)

Pub: Dow Jones & Co., Inc.

Ed: Leslie P. Norton. **Description:** Shares of Indian Internet companies Rediff.com and Sify are not likely to stage a rebound due to weak financial results. Rediff.com shares have declined 39.2 percent in 2008, while Sify shares are down 35.8 percent.

12327 ■ *"February Hot for Mutual Fund Sales"* in Globe & Mail (March 3, 2006, pp. B10)

Pub: CTVglobemedia Publishing Inc.

Ed: Keith Damsell. **Description:** The details on Canadian mutual fund sector, which posted $4.7 billion for February 2005, are presented.

12328 ■ *"The Fed Still Has Ammunition"* in Barron's (Vol. 90, August 30, 2010, No. 35, pp. M9)

Pub: Barron's Editorial & Corporate Headquarters

Ed: Randall W. Forsyth. **Description:** Federal Reserve chairman Ben Bernanke said the agency still has tools to combat deflation and a second downturn but these strategies are not needed at this time. The prospects of the Federal Open Market Committee's purchasing of treasuries are also discussed.

12329 ■ *"Fed Tackles Bear of a Crisis"* in Barron's (Vol. 88, March 17, 2008, No. 11, pp. M10)

Pub: Dow Jones & Company, Inc.

Ed: Randall W. Forsyth. **Description:** Emergency funding package for Bear Stearns from the Federal Reserve Bank of New York through JPMorgan Chase is one of the steps taken by the central bank shore up bank liquidity. Prior to the emergency funding, the central bank announced the Term Securities Lending Facility to allow dealers to borrow easily saleable Treasuries in exchange for less-liquid issues.

12330 ■ *"Federal Bailout, Three Years Later"* in Business Owner (Vol. 35, September-October 2011, No. 5, pp. 6)
Pub: DL Perkins Company

Description: State of the economy and small business sector three years after the government stimulus and bailout programs were instituted.

12331 ■ *"Fees Come Down; Markets Come Down More"* in Barron's (Vol. 89, July 13, 2009, No. 28, pp. L8)
Pub: Dow Jones & Co., Inc.

Ed: J.R. Brandstrader. **Description:** Investors spent less on mutual fund fees in 2009 than they did in the last 25 years. These fees include administration, accounting, and legal expense. Despite the popularity of money market funds which has contributed to this decline, the short-term yields of these funds fell in the last year.

12332 ■ *"Fertilizer for Growth"* in Canadian Business (Vol. 83, September 14, 2010, No. 15, pp. 76)
Pub: Rogers Media Ltd.

Ed: Bryan Borzykowski. **Description:** Australian-based BHP Billiton launches a C$38.5 billion hostile takeover bid for Saskatchewan-based Potash Corporation and some investors immediately bought Potash stock at C$130. However, Potash has resisted BHP's offer and announced a plan to try to stop the deal.

12333 ■ *"A Few Points of Contention"* in Barron's (Vol. 88, July 14, 2008, No. 28, pp. 3)
Pub: Dow Jones & Co., Inc.

Ed: Michael Santoli. **Description:** Headline inflation tends to revert to the lower core inflation, which excludes food and energy in its calculation over long periods. Prominent private equity figures believe that regulators should allow more than the de facto 10 percent to 25 percent limit of commercial banks to hasten the refunding of the financial sector.

12334 ■ *"Fieldbrook Foods Acquired By Private Equity Firm"* in Ice Cream Reporter (Vol. 23, October 20, 2010, No. 11, pp. 1)
Pub: Ice Cream Reporter

Description: Fieldbrook Foods Corporation, manufacturer of frozen novelty and ice cream products was acquired by Chicago-based private equity firm Arbor Investments. Arbor partnered with Herman 'Bing' Graffunder, a long-term dairy industry partner, in its acquisition of Fieldbrook.

12335 ■ *"Fifth Third CEO Kabat: A World of Difference"* in Business Courier (Vol. 26, January 1, 2010, No. 37, pp. 1)
Pub: American City Business Journals, Inc.

Ed: Steve Watkins. **Description:** CEO Kevin Kabat of Cincinnati-based Fifth Third Bancorp believes that the bank's assets of $111 billion and stock value of more than $10 indicate the recovery from the low stock prices posted in February 2009. He attributes the recovery from the federal government's stress test finding in May 2009 that Fifth Third needs to generate $1.1 billion.

12336 ■ *"Fifth Third Spinoff"* in Business Courier (Vol. 27, July 16, 2010, No. 11, pp. 1)
Pub: Business Courier

Ed: Dan Monk, Steve Watkins. **Description:** Electronic-funds transfer company Fifth Third Solutions (FTPS), a spinoff of Fifth Third Bancorp, is seeking as much as 200,000 square feet of new office space in Ohio. The bank's sale of 51 percent ownership stake to Boston-based Advent International Corporation has paved the way for the growth of FTPS. How real estate brokers' plans have responded to FTPS' growth mode is discussed.

12337 ■ *"The File On..Skoda Minotti"* in Crain's Cleveland Business (Vol. 28, October 8, 2007, No. 40, pp. 26)
Pub: Crain Communications, Inc.

Ed: Kimberly Bonvissuto. **Description:** Overview of Skoda Minotti, the accounting and financial services firm located in Mayfield Village; the company has 140 employees and an expanded slate of services.

12338 ■ *"The Final Say"* in Hispanic Business (Vol. 30, March 2008, No. 3, pp. 52)
Pub: Hispanic Business

Ed: Hildy Medina. **Description:** Vice-Chairwoman of the pensions and investments committee and Illinois State Senator Iris Martinez is the first Hispanic woman to be elected Senator and is advocating for pension funds to include Hispanic money managers and minority- and female-owned businesses in the investment plans.

12339 ■ *"Finalist: BlackEagle Partners L.L.C."* in Crain's Detroit Business (Vol. 24, March 24, 2008, No. 12, pp. 12)
Pub: Crain Communications, Inc.

Ed: Brent Snavely. **Description:** Overview of private-equity firm, BlackEagle Partners L.L.C., an upstart that acquired Rockford Products Corp. in order to improve the performance of the company who does business with several major tier-one automotive suppliers; Rockford manufactures highly engineered chassis and suspension components for automakers and the automotive aftermarket.

12340 ■ *"Finally, Justice"* in Canadian Business (Vol. 82, April 27, 2009, No. 7, pp. 12)
Pub: Rogers Media

Ed: John Gray. **Description:** Former investment adviser Alex Winch feels that he was vindicated with the Canadian Court's ruling that Livent Inc. founders Garth Drabinsky and Myron Gottlieb were guilty of fraud. Drabinsky filed a libel case on Winch over Winch's letter that complained over Livent's accounting procedures. Winch also criticized the inconsistent accounting during Drabinsky's term as chief executive of another firm.

12341 ■ *"The Finance Function In A Global Corporation"* in Harvard Business Review (Vol. 86, July-August 2008, No. 8, pp. 108)
Pub: Harvard Business School Press

Ed: Mihir A. Desai. **Description:** Designing and implementing a successful finance function in a global setting is discussed. Additional topics include the internal capital market, managing risk and budgeting capital internationally.

12342 ■ *"Financial Education: Boomer's Spending Hurts Retirement"* in Employee Benefit News (Vol. 25, November 1, 2011, No. 14, pp. 18)
Pub: SourceMedia Inc.

Ed: Ann Marsh. **Description:** Financial planners and employers need to educate clients and employees about retirement planning. Boomers are spending money that should be saved for their retirement.

12343 ■ *Financing Growth: Strategies, Capital Structure, and M and A Transactions*
Pub: John Wiley and Sons, Inc.

Ed: Kenneth H. Marks, Larry E. Robbins, Gonzalo Fernandez, John P. Funkhouser, D.L. Williams. **Released:** September 1, 2009. **Price:** $95.00. **Description:** Guide for emerging growth and middle market companies includes information to help understand and apply the basics of corporate finance using empirical data and actual company cases to illustrate capital structures and financing approaches.

12344 ■ *Financing Your Small Business*
Pub: Barron's Educational Series Inc.
Contact: Alex Holtz, President
E-mail: aholtz@berronseduc.com

Ed: Robert Walter. **Released:** December 2003. **Description:** Tips for raising venture capital, dealing with bank officials, and initiating public offerings of stock shares for small business.

12345 ■ *"Finding Good Bets Down on the Farm"* in Crain's Chicago Business (Vol. 31, March 24, 2008, No. 12, pp. 4)
Pub: Crain Communications, Inc.

Ed: Daniel Rome Levine. **Description:** Interview with money manager Jeff James, the portfolio manager for Driehaus Capital Management LLC, who discusses the Federal Reserve and recommends several companies in which to make investments.

12346 ■ *"Finding the Voice of the Marketplace"* in Mergers & Acquisitions: The Dealmaker's Journal (March 1, 2008)
Pub: SourceMedia, Inc.

Description: Companies oftentimes are unable to achieve their strategic goals through acquisition due, in part, to not understanding the target's market and its position in the marketplace.

12347 ■ *"Finger-Pointing Time"* in Barron's (Vol. 88, March 10, 2008, No. 10, pp. 9)
Pub: Dow Jones & Company, Inc.

Ed: Michael Santoli. **Description:** Discusses who is to blame for the financial crisis brought about by the credit crunch in the United States; the country's financial markets will eventually digest this crisis but will bottom out first before the situation improves.

12348 ■ *"First Financial Aiming for Banking Big Leagues"* in Business Courier (Vol. 26, December 4, 2009, No. 32, pp. 1)
Pub: American City Business Journals, Inc.

Ed: Steve Watkins. **Description:** First Financial Bancorp could dominate the community banking market of Greater Cincinnati after buying failed banks with the supervision of the FDIC. Details of the transactions are presented.

12349 ■ *"First the Merger: Then, The Culture Clash. How To Fix the Little Things That Can Tear a Company Apart"* in Inc. (January 2008)
Pub: Gruner & Jahr USA Publishing

Ed: Elaine Appleton Grant. **Description:** Ways three CEOs handled the culture classes that followed after company mergers; companies profiled include Fuel Outdoor, an outdoor advertising company; Nelson, an interior design and architecture firm; and Beber Silverstein, an ad agency.

12350 ■ *"First U.S. :M-Press Tiger with Inline Screen Printing"* in American Printer (Vol. 128, June 1, 2011, No. 6)
Pub: Penton Media Inc.

Description: Graphic Tech located in California bought :M-Press Tiger, the first in North America with an inline screen printing unit.

12351 ■ *"FIS-Metavante Deal Paying Off for Many"* in Business Journal-Milwaukee (Vol. 28, December 17, 2010, No. 11, pp. A1)
Pub: Milwaukee Business Journal

Ed: Rich Kirchen. **Description:** Jacksonville, Florida-based Fidelity National Information Services Inc., also known as FIS, has remained committed to Milwaukee, Wisconsin more than a year after purchasing Metavante Technologies Inc. FIS has transferred several operations into Metropolitan Milwaukee and has continued its contribution to charitable organizations in the area.

12352 ■ *The Flaw of Averages: Why We Underestimate Risk in the Face of Uncertainty*
Pub: John Wiley & Sons, Inc.

Ed: Sam L. Savage. **Released:** June 3, 2009. **Price:** $22.95. **Description:** Personal and business plans are based on uncertainties on a daily basis. The common avoidable mistake individuals make in assessing risk in the face of uncertainty is defined. The explains why plans based on average assumptions are wrong, on average, in areas as diverse as finance, healthcare, accounting, the war on terror, and climate change.

12353 ■ *"A Flawed Yardstick for Banks"* in Barron's (Vol. 88, July 14, 2008, No. 28, pp. M6)
Pub: Dow Jones & Co., Inc.

Ed: Arindam Nag. **Description:** Return on equity is no longer the best measure for investors to judge banks by in a post-subprime-crises world. Investors should consider the proportion of a bank's total assets that are considered risky and look out for any write-downs of goodwill when judging a bank's financial health.

12354 ■ *"Florida's Housing Gloom May Add To Woes of National City"* in Crain's Cleveland Business (Vol. 28, October 29,*

2007, No. 43, pp. 1)
Pub: Crain Communications, Inc.
Ed: Shawn A. Turner. **Description:** Already suffering by bad loans in the troubled mortgage market, National City Corp. is attempting to diversify its geographic presence beyond the slow-growth industrial Midwest by acquiring two Florida firms. Analysts worry that the acquisitions may end up making National City vulnerable to a takeover if the housing slump continues and credit quality becomes more of an issue for the bank.

12355 ■ *"Flying High?" in Canadian Business (Vol. 80, April 9, 2007, No. 8, pp. 42)*
Pub: Rogers Media
Ed: Thomas Watson. **Description:** The increase in Bombardier Inc.'s income by 30 percent to $112 million and increase in its share prices are discussed. The caution of analysts about its accounting methods that may adversely hit the company in future, too is discussed.

12356 ■ *Fooling Some of the People All of the Time*
Pub: John Wiley & Sons, Inc.
Ed: David Einhorn. **Released:** March 10, 2010. **Price:** $29.95. **Description:** A chronicle of the ongoing saga between author, David Einhorn's hedge fund, Greenlight Capital, and Allied Capital, a leader in the private finance industry.

12357 ■ *Fool's Gold: How the Bold Dream of a Small Tribe at J.P. Morgan Was Corrupted by Wall Street Greed*
Pub: Free Press
Ed: Gillian Tett. **Released:** 2009. **Price:** $26.00. **Description:** An explanation of how swaps and CDOs, which were invented by J.P. Morgan, ended up creating more risk not controlling it.

12358 ■ *"For Baxter, A Lingering PR Problem; Ongoing Focus On Heparin Deaths Ups Heat On CEO" in Crain's Chicago Business (April 21, 2008)*
Pub: Crain Communications, Inc.
Ed: Mike Colias. **Description:** Baxter International Inc.'s recall of the blood-thinning medication heparin has exposed the company to costly litigation and put the perils of overseas drug manufacturing in the spotlight. Wall Street investors predict that an indefinite halt in production of the drug should not hurt the company's bottom line since heparin represents a tiny sliver of the business. Since Baxter began recalling the drug in January its shares have continued to outpace most other medical stocks.

12359 ■ *"For Buffet Fans, the Price Is Right" in Barron's (Vol. 89, July 13, 2009, No. 28, pp. 17)*
Pub: Dow Jones & Co., Inc.
Ed: Andrew Bary. **Description:** Shares of Warren Buffett's Berkshire Hathaway have fallen to $85,000 and these are cheap since they are trading at just 1.2 times estimated book value and are well below its peak of $149,000. One fan of the stock expects it to top $110,000 in the next year from June 2009.

12360 ■ *"For Gilead, Growth Beyond AIDS" in Barron's (Vol. 88, June 30, 2008, No. 26, pp. 18)*
Pub: Dow Jones & Co., Inc.
Ed: Jay Palmer. **Description:** First-quarter 2008 revenue for Gilead Sciences grew by 22 percent and an earnings gain of 19 percent thanks to their HIV-treatment drugs that comprised over two-thirds of the company's sales in 2007. An analyst has a 12-month target from June, 2008 of 65 per share. The factors behind the company's prospects are also discussed.

12361 ■ *"For Kenwood, Cavalry Could Be Close" in Business Courier (Vol. 26, October 2, 2009, No. 23, pp. 1)*
Pub: American City Business Journals, Inc.
Ed: Dan Monk. **Description:** New York-based Black-Rock Inc. is believed to be participating in the settlement liens at Kenwood Towne Place, a mixed-use development site in Cincinnati, Ohio. BlackRock may play a key role as an advisor or investor representative to an unnamed investors.

12362 ■ *"For Sale: Old Florida Panache" in The Business Journal-Serving Greater Tampa Bay (Vol. 28, July 4, 2008, No. 28, pp. 1)*
Pub: American City Business Journals, Inc.
Ed: Jane Meinhardt. **Description:** Linger Lodge, owned by real estate investor and developer Martin Kaplan and Senator Michael Bennett, is now on the market for a sealed bid process facilitated by Levin & Associates. The business partners bought the riverfront property for about $3 million in 2005. Other details on the sale of the property are presented.

12363 ■ *"Ford Canada's Edsel of a Year: Revenue Plummets 24 Percent in '05" in Globe & Mail (February 2, 2006, pp. B1)*
Pub: CTVglobemedia Publishing Inc.
Ed: Greg Keenan. **Description:** Ford Motor Company of Canada Ltd. posted 24% decline in revenues for 2005. The drop in earnings is attributed to plant shutdown in Oaksville, Canada.

12364 ■ *"Foreign (In)Direct Investment and Corporate Taxation" in Canadian Journal of Economics (Vol. 44, November 2011, No. 4, pp. 1497)*
Pub: Blackwell Publishers Ltd.
Ed: Georg Wamser. **Description:** Foreign investments of multinational firms are often complex in that they involve conduit entities. In particular, a multinational can pursue either a direct or an indirect investment strategy, where the latter involves an intermediate corporate entity and is associated with enhanced opportunities for international tax planning. As a consequence, in the case of indirect investments, the role of corporate taxation in destination countries may change. An investigation into the effects of corporation taxation on foreign investment decisions of German multinationals, taking explicitly into account that firms choose in a first stage the investment regime, (direct vs. indirect) is provided.

12365 ■ *"Former Mayor Driving $500 Million Real Estate Equity Fund" in The Business Journal - Serving Phoenix and the Valley of the Sun (Vol. 28, August 15, 2008, No. 50, pp. 1)*
Pub: American City Business Journals, Inc.
Ed: Jan Buchholz. **Description:** Paul John, the former mayor of Phoenix, is establishing a $500 million real estate asset management fund. The fund is dubbed Southwest Next Capital Management and has attracted three local partners, namely Joseph Meyer, Jay Michalowski, and James Mullany, who all have background in finance and construction.

12366 ■ *"The Four Cheapest Plays in Emerging Markets" in Barron's (Vol. 89, July 27, 2009, No. 30, pp. 34)*
Pub: Dow Jones & Co., Inc.
Ed: Lawrence C. Strauss. **Description:** Portfolio manager Arjun Divecha of the GMO Emerging Markets III Fund says that the main thing in investing in emerging markets is getting the country right since getting it wrong makes it harder to add value. Divecha says that the four countries that they are positive on are Turkey, Russia, South Korea, and Thailand.

12367 ■ *"Franchising Lures Boomers" in Business Journal-Portland (Vol. 24, November 9, 2007, No. 36, pp. 1)*
Pub: American City Business Journals, Inc.
Ed: Wendy Culverwell. **Description:** Popularity of franchising has increased, and investors belonging to the baby boom generation contribute largely to this growth. The number of aging baby boomers is also increasing, particularly in Oregon, which means further growth of franchises can be expected. Reasons why franchising is a good investment for aging baby boomers are given.

12368 ■ *"Francois Joly" in Canadian Business (Vol. 79, September 11, 2006, No. 18, pp. 146)*
Pub: Rogers Media
Ed: Andy Holloway. **Description:** President and chief operating officer of Desjardins Financial Security, Francois Joly speaks about his interests and emphasizes the need to be passionate about work.

12369 ■ *"Fraser and Neave Acquires King's Creameries" in Ice Cream Reporter (Vol. 23, November 20, 2010, No. 12, pp. 1)*
Pub: Ice Cream Reporter
Description: Fraser and Neave Ltd., a Singapore-based consumer products marketer, has entered a conditional agreement to acquire all outstanding shares of King's Creameries, the leading manufacturer and distributor of frozen desserts.

12370 ■ *"Fraud Alleged at Norshield; Investors Out $215 Million" in Globe & Mail (March 8, 2007, pp. B1)*
Pub: CTVglobemedia Publishing Inc.
Ed: Paul Waldie. **Description:** The investigation of the diversion of $215 million in investors' money by the management of Norshield Asset Management (Canada) Ltd. is described.

12371 ■ *"Freak Weather Dampens Intrawest Forecast" in Globe & Mail (February 8, 2006, pp. B3)*
Pub: CTVglobemedia Publishing Inc.
Ed: Peter Kennedy. **Description:** Intrawest Corp. dropped its earnings forecast by 7 percent. The impact of weather on earnings is discussed.

12372 ■ *"Friends With Money" in Canadian Business (Vol. 81, Summer 2008, No. 9, pp. 22)*
Pub: Rogers Media Ltd.
Description: Two of the most well connected managers in Canadian capital markets Rob Farquharson and Brian Gibson will launch Panoply Capital Asset Management in June. The investment management company aims to raise a billion dollars from institutions and high-net worth individuals.

12373 ■ *"From Buyout to Busted" in Business Week (September 22, 2008, No. 4100, pp. 18)*
Pub: McGraw-Hill Companies, Inc.
Ed: Emily Thornton; Deborah Stead. **Description:** Bankruptcy filings by private equity-backed companies are at a record high with 134 American firms taken private (or invested in) by buyout firms that have filed for protection this year under Chapter 11; this is 91 percent higher than the previous year, which had set a record when 70 of such companies filed for protection under Chapter 11.

12374 ■ *"From Fastenal, a Boost" in Barron's (Vol. 89, July 20, 2009, No. 29, pp. M13)*
Pub: Dow Jones & Co., Inc.
Ed: Shirley A. Lazo. **Description:** Fastenal increased its semi-annual common payout from $0.35 to $0.37 a share. Core Laboratories declared a special dividend of $0.75 a share along with its quarterly payout of $0.10. Ryder System and Landstar System raised their payouts to $0.23 and $0.045 a share respectively.

12375 ■ *"The Frugal Billionaire" in Canadian Business (Vol. 79, Winter 2006, No. 24, pp. 63)*
Pub: Rogers Media
Ed: Joe Castaldo. **Description:** The achievements of David Cheriton are described, along with his investments in various firms, including Google Inc.

12376 ■ *"Full-Court Press for Apple" in Barron's (Vol. 88, March 24, 2008, No. 12, pp. 47)*
Pub: Dow Jones & Company, Inc.
Ed: Mark Veverka. **Description:** Apple Inc. is facing more intellectual property lawsuits in 2008, with 30 patent lawsuits filed compared to 15 in 2007 and nine in 2006. The lawsuits, which involve products such as the iPod and the iPhone, present some concern for Apple's shareholders.

12377 ■ *"Funds "Friend" Facebook" in Barron's (Vol. 89, July 27, 2009, No. 30, pp. 30)*
Pub: Dow Jones & Co., Inc.
Ed: Leslie P. Norton. **Description:** Mutual-fund companies are the latest entrants to the 'social media' space and several companies have already set up Facebook and Twitter pages. The use of this

technology pose special challenges for compliance and regulators especially since the Financial Industry Regulatory Authority reminds companies that advertising, sales and literature are governed by regulations.

12378 ■ "The Future of Private Equity" in Canadian Business (Vol. 80, March 26, 2007, No. 7, pp. 19)
Pub: Rogers Media
Ed: Jack Mintz. Description: The impact growing Canadian economy and competition in global business on the performance of private equity funds is analyzed.

12379 ■ "Future's Brighter for Financial Stocks" in Barron's (Vol. 89, July 20, 2009, No. 29, pp. 14)
Pub: Dow Jones & Co., Inc.
Ed: Jacqueline Doherty. Description: Shares of US financial companies are projected to rise as their earnings start to normalize. Earnings of these companies have been hurt by credit losses but have been bolstered by one-time gains.

12380 ■ "Futures Shock for the CME" in Crain's Chicago Business (Vol. 31, November 10, 2008, No. 45, pp. 8)
Pub: Crain Communications, Inc.
Ed: Ann Saphir. Description: Chicago-based CME Group Inc., the largest futures exchange operator in the U.S., is facing a potentially radically altered regulatory landscape as Congress weighs sweeping reform of financial oversight. The possible merger of the CFTC and the Securities and Exchange Commission are among CME's concerns. Other details of possible regulatory measures are provided.

12381 ■ "Futures of the Street" in Barron's (Vol. 88, June 30, 2008, No. 26, pp. 27)
Pub: Dow Jones & Co., Inc.
Ed: Michael Santoli. Description: Prospects of the securities industry in terms of jobs and profit sources are discussed. Suggestions on what the industry needs with regards to its use of capital are also discussed.

12382 ■ "Gas Glut Pummels Prices" in Barron's (Vol. 89, July 27, 2009, No. 30, pp. M8)
Pub: Dow Jones & Co., Inc.
Ed: Christine Buurma. Description: Natural gas-futures prices have fallen 73 percent and the glut of output from onshore gas fields and the weak demand signals that a rebound is not near. An analyst expects U.S. production to show increasingly steep declines but the oversupply situation is not good for prices.

12383 ■ "Gateway Delays Start" in The Business Journal-Serving Metropolitan Kansas City (Vol. 27, October 31, 2008, No. 8, pp. 1)
Pub: American City Business Journals, Inc.
Ed: Rob Roberts. Description: Economic problems caused, in part, by the Wall Street crisis has resulted in the setback of a proposed mixed-use redevelopment project, The Gateway. The $307 million project, which includes the Kansas Aquarium, will be delayed due to financing problems. Details of the project are given.

12384 ■ "GE Looking to Extend Hot Streak" in Business Courier (Vol. 24, January 25, 2008, No. 42, pp. 1)
Pub: American City Business Journals, Inc.
Ed: John Newberry. Description: GE Aviation has enjoyed strong revenues and sales due to increase aircraft engine orders. It has an engine backlog order of $19 million as of the end of 2007. Data on the aviation company's revenues, operating profit and total engine orders for the year 2004 to 2007 are presented.

12385 ■ "GeckoSystems Reduces Sensor Fusion Costs Due to Elder Care Robot Trials" in Internet Wire (December 14, 2010)
Pub: Comtex
Description: GeckoSystems International Corporation has been able to reduce the cost of its sensor fusion system while maintaining reliability and perfor-

mance. The firm's ongoing first in-home elder care robot trials have sparked interest regarding its business model, technologies available for licensing, and joint domestic and international ventures.

12386 ■ "General Motors Can't Kick Incentives-But They Work" in Advertising Age (Vol. 79, July 7, 2008, No. 26, pp. 3)
Pub: Crain Communications, Inc.
Ed: Jean Halliday. Description: General Motors Corp. was able to maintain their market share just as Toyota Motor Corp. was beginning to pass the manufacturer; GM lured in customers with a sales incentive that they heavily advertised and subsequently helped build demand; investors, however, were not impressed and GM shares were hammered to their lowest point in 50 years after analysts speculated the company might go bankrupt.

12387 ■ "Generation Y - An Opportunity for a Fresh Financial Start" in (September 11, 2010, pp. 241)
Pub: VerticalNews
Description: Eleanor Blayney, the consumer advocate for the Certified Financial Planner Board of Standards, offers a financial strategy for Generation Y individuals starting their financial planning. The first segment of the non-profit's Lifelong Financial Strategies initiative is called 'Starting Out', and focuses on ways Generation Y people can avoid pitfalls of earlier generations by making smart financial decisions.

12388 ■ "Genzyme: Underrated Oversold" in Barron's (Vol. 88, March 24, 2008, No. 12, pp. 58)
Pub: Dow Jones & Company, Inc.
Ed: Johanna Bennett. Description: Shares of bio-technology company Genzyme appear oversold and underrated at their $71.86 level. The company's finances are on a solid foundation, with revenues over $3.8 billion in 2007 and forecasts of $4.5-4.7 billion in revenue for 2008.

12389 ■ "Get It While Its Hot" in Canadian Business (Vol. 80, January 15, 2007, No. 2, pp. 49)
Pub: Rogers Media
Ed: John Gray. Description: The rise in the demand for processed uranium and increase in the number of investors interested to invest in metal industries is discussed.

12390 ■ "Get Off The Rollercoaster" in Michigan Vue (Vol. 13, July-August 2008, No. 4, pp. 19)
Pub: Entrepreneur Media Inc.
Ed: Donald N. Hobley Jr. Description: Benefits of creating and implementing a solid financial plan during these rocky economic times are examined. Things to keep in mind before meeting with a financial planner include risk assessment, investment goals, the length of time required to meet those goals and the amount of money one has available to invest.

12391 ■ "Getting In on the Ground Floor" in Barron's (Vol. 89, July 27, 2009, No. 30, pp. 32)
Pub: Dow Jones & Co., Inc.
Ed: Jacqueline Doherty. Description: Shares of Ava-lonBay Communities have fallen 61 percent in the past two and a half years to July 2009 but at $56, the stock is trading near the asset value. The shares could rise as the economy improves and if the recovery takes longer, investors will be rewarded with a yield of 3.5 percent.

12392 ■ "Getting More Out of Retirement" in Agency Sales Magazine (Vol. 39, November 2009, No. 10, pp. 48)
Pub: MANA
Ed: Joshua D. Mosshart. Description: Overview of the Tax Increase Prevention and Reconciliation Act, which lets employees convert to a Roth IRA in 2010. The benefits of conversion depend on age and wealth and it is best to consult a tax advisor to determine the best strategy for retirement planners.

12393 ■ "Giant Garages Could Rise Up Downtown" in Business Courier (Vol. 27, October 22, 2010, No. 25, pp. 1)
Pub: Business Courier
Ed: Dan Monk. Description: More than 2,500 new parking spaces could rise up to the eastern edge of downtown Cincinnati, Ohio as public and private investors collect resources for new garage projects. These projects are expected to accommodate almost 1,500 monthly parkers who will lose access at Broadway Commons due to the construction of Harrah's casino.

12394 ■ "Giants Now Admit They Roam Planet Earth; Time To Buy?" in Barron's (Vol. 88, March 31, 2008, No. 13, pp. 39)
Pub: Dow Jones & Company, Inc.
Ed: Eric J. Savitz. Description: Oracle's third-quarter results showed that top-line growth fell short of expectations but the company is expected to fare better than most applications companies in the downturn. Google had a flat growth in the number of people who click their online ads. The time for investors in the tech sector with a long-term horizon has arrived.

12395 ■ "Give Me Liberty With DirecTV" in Barron's (Vol. 89, July 13, 2009, No. 28, pp. M5)
Pub: Dow Jones & Co., Inc.
Ed: Fleming Meeks. Description: Shares of Liberty Entertainment look cheap at $25.14 and the same goes for DirecTV at $23.19. A merger between the two companies was announced and the deal will likely close by September 2009. Barclays Capital has a target of $30 for Liberty Media and $32 for DirecTV.

12396 ■ "Global Good Time" in Canadian Business (Vol. 80, January 15, 2007, No. 2, pp. 53)
Pub: Rogers Media
Ed: Thomas Watson. Description: Speculations on the stock prices of global emerging markets for 2007 are presented.

12397 ■ "Global Steel Makers Circle Stelco" in Globe & Mail (April 19, 2007, pp. B3)
Pub: CTVglobemedia Publishing Inc.
Ed: Greg Keenan. Description: The details of the take over bids offered to Stelco Inc. are presented. Due to these bids the shares of Stelco Inc rose up to 70 percent.

12398 ■ "Gold Handshake" in Canadian Business (Vol. 79, September 11, 2006, No. 18, pp. 25)
Pub: Rogers Media
Ed: John Gray. Description: Goldcorp Inc.'s company's planned takeover of Glamis Gold Ltd. is discussed. Implications of the merger on its investors are presented.

12399 ■ "Gold Still Has That Glitter" in Barron's (Vol. 89, July 20, 2009, No. 29, pp. M8)
Pub: Dow Jones & Co., Inc.
Ed: Allen Sykora. Description: Gold prices appear to be ready for an increase starting in the fall of 2009 due to an increase in demand. The price of the August 2009 gold contract fell to as low as $904.08 an ounce before recovering to $937.50.

12400 ■ "A Golden Retirement?" in Canadian Business (Vol. 81, December 8, 2008, No. 21, pp. 7)
Pub: Rogers Media Ltd.
Ed: Paul Webster. Description: Canada Pension Plan Investment Board (CPPIB) is believed to have suffered heavy losses in global stock markets. CPPIB has moved aggressively into stock markets after independent managers started handling the funds in 2000.

12401 ■ "Goldeye Completes Private Placement" in Canadian Corporate News (May 16, 2007)
Pub: Comtex News Network Inc.
Description: Goldeye, a Canadian mineral exploration company acquiring, exploring, and advancing properties in Chile and Canada, announced that it

has completed a partially brokered private placement for gross proceeds of $1,232,660 which will be used to finance exploration on Goldeye's mineral properties in Chile and for administrative expenses, and working capital.

12402 ■ "A Good Book Is Worth a Thousand Blogs" in Barron's (Vol. 88, July 14, 2008, No. 28, pp. 42)
Pub: Dow Jones & Co., Inc.
Ed: Gene Epstein. **Description:** Nine summer book suggestions on economics are presented. The list includes 'The Revolution' by Ron Paul, 'The Forgotten Man' by Amity Shales, 'The Commitments of Traders Bible' by Stephen Briese, and 'Economic Facts and Fallacies' by Thomas Sowell.

12403 ■ "Good Going, Partners: Energy-Asset Firms Do Their Parents Proud" in Barron's (Vol. 89, July 27, 2009, No. 30, pp. M8)
Pub: Dow Jones & Co., Inc.
Ed: Shirley A. Lazo. **Description:** Four master limited partnerships boosted their dividends. Sunoco Logistics raised theirs by 11.2 percent, El Paso Pipeline by 12 percent, Holly Energy upped their dividends by a penny, and Western Gas hiked their dividend to 31 cents per unit.

12404 ■ "A Good Sign for Commercial Real Estate" in Austin Business Journallnc. (Vol. 29, December 18, 2009, No. 41, pp. 1)
Pub: American City Business Journals
Ed: Kate Harrington. **Description:** Factors that could contribute to the reemergence of the commercial mortgage-backed securities market in Texas are discussed. These securities can potentially boost the commercial real estate market statewide as well as nationwide. Commercial mortgage-backed securities origination in 2009 is worth less that $1 billion, compared with $238 billion in 2008.

12405 ■ "A Good Step, But There's a Long Way to Go" in Business Week (September 22, 2008, No. 4100, pp. 10)
Pub: McGraw-Hill Companies, Inc.
Ed: James C. Cooper. **Description:** Despite the historic action by the U.S. government to nationalize the mortgage giants Freddie Mac and Fannie Mae, rising unemployment rates may prove to be an even bigger roadblock to bringing back the economy from its downward spiral. The takeover is meant to restore confidence in the credit markets and help with the mortgage crisis but the rising rate in unemployment may make many households unable to take advantage of any benefits which arise from the bailout. Statistical data included.

12406 ■ "Good Things Happen When We Buy Local" in Crain's Detroit Business (Vol. 24, October 6, 2008, No. 40, pp. 7)
Pub: Crain Communications, Inc.
Description: Michigan is facing incredibly difficult economic times. One way in which each one of us can help the state and the businesses located here is by purchasing our goods and services from local vendors. The state Agriculture Department projected that if Michigan households earmarked $10 per week in their grocery purchases to made-in-Michigan products, this would generate $30 million a week in economic impact.

12407 ■ "Goodwill Haunts Local Companies; Bad Buyouts During Boom Times Producing Big Writedowns" in Crain's Chicago Business (Apr. 28, 2008)
Pub: Crain Communications, Inc.
Ed: Ann Saphir. **Description:** Many companies are having to face the reality that they overpaid for acquisitions made in better economic times; investors often dismiss such one-time charges as mere accounting adjustments but writeoffs related to past acquisitions can signal future problems because the writeoffs mean the expected profits that justified the purchase have not materialized. Writeoffs are particularly worrisome for firms with a lot of debt and whose banks require them to have enough assets to back up their borrowings.

12408 ■ "Google's Next Stop: Below 350?" in Barron's (Vol. 88, March 10, 2008, No. 10, pp. 17)
Pub: Dow Jones & Company, Inc.
Ed: Jacqueline Doherty. **Description:** Share prices of Google Inc. are expected to drop from their level of $433 each to below $350 per share. The company is expected to miss its earnings forecast for the first quarter of 2008, and its continued aggressive spending on non-core areas will eventually bring down earnings.

12409 ■ "Government Intervention" in Canadian Business (Vol. 79, November 6, 2006, No. 22, pp. 116)
Pub: Rogers Media
Description: The effects of income trust tax on economic conditions and investment of Canada are presented.

12410 ■ "Graduates to the TSX in 2008" in Canadian Business (Vol. 81, Summer 2008, No. 9, pp. 79)
Pub: Rogers Media Ltd.
Ed: Calvin Leung. **Description:** Table showing the market capitalization and stock performance of the companies that jumped to the TSX Venture Exchange is presented. The 17 companies that made the leap to the list will have an easier time raising capital, although leeway must be made in investing since they are still new businesses.

12411 ■ "The Great Deleveraging" in Canadian Business (Vol. 81, October 13, 2008, No. 17, pp. 45)
Pub: Rogers Media Ltd.
Ed: Jeff Sanford. **Description:** 'Hell Week' of financial crisis on Wall Street is believed to have started with the downgrade of AIG Inc.'s credit rating. AIG is a major player in the credit derivatives market, and its bankruptcy would have affected firms on Wall Street.

12412 ■ "The Great Fall" in Barron's (Vol. 88, March 10, 2008, No. 10, pp. 5)
Pub: Dow Jones & Company, Inc.
Ed: Alan Abelson. **Description:** Discusses the US economy is considered to be in a recession, with the effects of the credit crisis expected to intensify as a result. Inflation is estimated at 4.3 percent in January 2008, while 63,000 jobs were lost in February 2008.

12413 ■ "The Great Moderation" in Canadian Business (Vol. 80, February 12, 2007, No. 4, pp. 25)
Pub: Rogers Media
Ed: David Wolf. **Description:** Caution over the changes to stock inventory levels and their adverse impact on the Canadian economy is discussed.

12414 ■ "Great Stocks Cheap" in Canadian Business (Vol. 80, January 15, 2007, No. 2, pp. 31)
Pub: Rogers Media
Ed: Calvin Leung. **Description:** The stock performance of top 10 international companies like Furgo, Moody's Investor Service, Adidas Group and Nestle is analyzed.

12415 ■ "Green Assets Powering Boralex Shares" in Globe & Mail (March 30, 2007, pp. B10)
Pub: CTVglobemedia Publishing Inc.
Ed: Richard Blackwell. **Description:** The impact of econ-friendly power plant portfolio on the stock performance of Kingsey Falls-based Boralex Inc. is analyzed.

12416 ■ "The Green Trap" in Canadian Business (Vol. 80, April 9, 2007, No. 8, pp. 19)
Pub: Rogers Media
Ed: Al Rosen. **Description:** Expert advice to companies on investing in environmental-friendly measures is presented.

12417 ■ "Greenberg Sues U.S. Over AIG Rescue" in Wall Street Journal Eastern Edition (November 22 , 2011, pp. C3)
Pub: Dow Jones & Company Inc.
Ed: Liam Pleven, Serena Ng. **Description:** Former Chief Executive Officer of American International Group Inc., Maurice R. 'Hank' Greenberg, has filed a lawsuit against the United States and the Federal Reserve Bank of New York on behalf of shareholders and his company, Starr International Company Inc., claiming that the government was wrong in taking control of the insurance giant and used it to move tens of millions of dollars to the trading partners of AIG.

12418 ■ "Greener Pastures" in Canadian Business (Vol. 80, February 12, 2007, No. 4, pp. 69)
Pub: Rogers Media
Ed: Thomas Watson. **Description:** The effort of venture capitalists, including chief executive officer of Fun Technologies Lorne Abony, in successful running of several ventures in diverse fields is discussed.

12419 ■ "A Greenish Light for Financial-Sector Funds" in Barron's (Vol. 88, March 24, 2008, No. 12, pp. 52)
Pub: Dow Jones & Company, Inc.
Ed: Tom Sullivan. **Description:** Financial sector funds have lost value in 2008 through 17 March, and investors are advised to reduce investments in the financial sector. Exchange-traded funds present a good way to own financial stocks.

12420 ■ "Greg Stringham" in Canadian Business (Vol. 81, March 3, 2008, No. 3, pp. 8)
Pub: Rogers Media
Ed: Michelle Magnan. **Description:** Canadian Association of Petroleum Producers' Greg Stringham thinks that the new royalty plan will result in companies pulling out their investments for Alberta's conventional oil and gas sector. Stringham adds that Alberta is losing its competitive advantage and companies must study their cost profiles to retrieve that advantage. The effects of the royalty system on Alberta's economy are examined further.

12421 ■ "A Gripping Read: Bargains & Noble" in Barron's (Vol. 88, March 17, 2008, No. 11, pp. 20)
Pub: Dow Jones & Company, Inc.
Ed: Jonathan R. Laing. **Description:** Barnes & Noble's earnings forecast for the fiscal year ending in January, 2008 to be $1.70 to $1.90 per share which is way lower than the $2.12 analyst consensus. The company also said that sales at stores one-year old or older dropped 0.5 percent in the fourth quarter. However, the shares are now cheap at 4.9 times enterprise value with some analysts putting a price target of 41 per share.

12422 ■ "Grote Company Puts Final Wrap on Sandwich-Making Line" in Business First-Columbus (October 26, 2007, pp. A1)
Pub: American City Business Journals, Inc.
Ed: Dan Eaton. **Description:** Grote Company acquired Oxfordshire, England-based Advanced Food Technology Ltd., giving the Ohio-based food cutting equipment company a manufacturing base in Europe. This is the company's second deal in four months. Details on Grote Company's plan to tap into the prepared fresh sandwich market are discussed.

12423 ■ Grow Your Money: 101 Easy Tips to Plan, Save and Invest
Pub: HarperBusiness
Ed: Jonathan D. Pond. **Released:** December 2007. **Price:** $26.95. **Description:** In what should be required reading for anyone entering the work world, the author offers helpful investment and financial definitions, debt-management strategies, retirement and home ownerships considerations and more.

12424 ■ "Growing Subscriber Base Fuels Roger's Rosy Outlook for 2007" in Globe & Mail (February 16, 2007, pp. B3)
Pub: CTVglobemedia Publishing Inc.
Ed: Catherine McLean. **Description:** Canada-based Rogers Communications Inc. has projected increased profits for the 2007 fiscal year. The company has increased its market share by 14 percent with fourth quarter revenues of $176 million.

12425 ■ "Growth Back on CIBC's Agenda" in Globe & Mail (March 3, 2006, pp. B1)
Pub: CTVglobemedia Publishing Inc.
Ed: Sinclair Stewart. **Description:** The details on business growth of Canadian Imperial Bank of Com-

merce, which posted $547 million profit for first quarter 2006, are presented.

12426 ■ "Hain Celestial Acquires Greek Gods Yogurt" in Ice Cream Reporter (Vol. 23, July 20, 2010, No. 8, pp. 1)
Pub: Ice Cream Reporter
Description: Hain Celestial Group acquired The Greek Gods LLC. Hain Celestial is a natural and organic products company and Greek Gods makes all natural, Greek-style yogurt and ice cream.

12427 ■ "Half Empty or Half Full" in Crain's Chicago Business (Vol. 31, March 24, 2008, No. 12, pp. 4)
Pub: Crain Communications, Inc.
Ed: Meghan Streit. **Description:** Lifeway Foods Inc., the health food company which manufactures a yogurt-like drink called kefir, is being negatively affected by the soaring price of milk; however, the fact that probiotics are picking up in the market may mean that Lifeway stands a good chance of bouncing back and the company's lower share price could be an opportunity for long-term investors who have a tolerance for risk.

12428 ■ "Handleman Liquidation Leaves Questions For Shareholders" in Crain's Detroit Business (Vol. 24, October 6, 2008, No. 40, pp. 4)
Pub: Crain Communications, Inc.
Ed: Nancy Kaffer. **Description:** Discusses Handleman Co., a Troy-based music distribution company, and their plan of liquidation and dissolution as well as how shareholders will be affected by the company's plan. Handleman filed its plan to liquidate and dissolve assets with the Securities and Exchange Commission in mid-August, following several quarters of dismal earnings.

12429 ■ "Hank and Ben: Hedgies' BFFs" in Barron's (Vol. 88, March 31, 2008, No. 13, pp. 50)
Pub: Dow Jones & Company, Inc.
Ed: Tom Sullivan. **Description:** David Ballin of Alternative Investment Solutions says that everything in the financial markets is tainted and beaten-up which presents an extraordinary opportunity for hedge funds as long as they back up their decisions with sharp and intensive research. He adds that money managers should short suspect stocks and go long on undeservedly battered stocks in the same sector.

12430 ■ "Hank Paulson On the Housing Bailout and What's Ahead" in Business Week (September 22, 2008, No. 4100, pp. 19)
Pub: McGraw-Hill Companies, Inc.
Ed: Maria Bartiromo. **Description:** Interview with Treasury Secretary Henry Paulson in which he discusses the bailout of Fannie Mae and Freddie Mac as well as the potential impact on the American economy and foreign interests and investments in the country. Paulson has faith that the government's actions will help to stabilize the housing market.

12431 ■ "Happy New Year, Celestica?" in Canadian Business (Vol. 80, January 15, 2007, No. 2, pp. 25)
Pub: Rogers Media
Ed: Andrew Wahl. **Description:** Speculations on the performance of the electronics manufacturing company Celestica Inc. in 2007, which has been labelled as a 'sick' company in recent times, are presented.

12432 ■ "A Harbinger?" in The Business Journal-Milwaukee (Vol. 25, August 29, 2008, No. 49, pp. A1)
Pub: American City Business Journals, Inc.
Ed: Rich Kirchen. **Description:** Stock prices of Marshall & Ilsley Corp. (M&I) and MGIC Investment Corp. are expected to rebound after insiders were reported to have bought stocks of the companies. M&I director David Lubar bought $4.3 million, while MGIC CEO and chairman Curt Culver bought 20,000 stocks of MGIC. Other views and information on the insiders' purchase of stocks are presented.

12433 ■ "Harleysville Eyes Growth After Nationwide Deal" in Philadelphia Business Journal (Vol. 30, October 7, 2011, No. 34, pp. 1)
Pub: American City Business Journals Inc.
Ed: Jeff Blumenthal. **Description:** Harleysville Group announced growth plans after the company was sold to Columbus, Ohio-based Nationwide Mutual Insurance Company for about $1.63 billion. Nationwide gained an independent agency platform in 32 states with the Harleysville deal.

12434 ■ "Hartco Income Fund Announces the Completion of the CompuSmart Strategic Review" in Canadian Corporate News (May 14, 2007)
Pub: Comtex News Network Inc.
Description: Hartco Income Fund announced that it has completed the process of exploring strategic options for CompuSmart and found that it should implement a plan to sell select stores and assets while consolidating remaining CompuSmart locations over the next sixty days.

12435 ■ "Has Microsoft Found a Way to Get at Yahoo?" in Advertising Age (Vol. 79, July 7, 2008, No. 26, pp. 4)
Pub: Crain Communications, Inc.
Ed: Abbey Klaassen. **Description:** Microsoft's attempt to acquire Yahoo's search business is discussed as is Yahoo's plans for the future at a time when the company's shares have fallen dangerously low.

12436 ■ "Hastily Enacted Regulation Will Not Cure Economic Crisis" in Crain's Chicago Business (Vol. 31, May 5, 2008, No. 18, pp. 18)
Pub: Crain Communications, Inc.
Ed: Stephen P. D'Arcy. **Description:** Policymakers are looking for ways to respond to what is possibly the greatest financial crisis of a generation due to the collapse of the housing market, the credit crisis and the volatility of Wall Street.

12437 ■ "Have High-Tech Tax Credits Helped or Hurt Hawaii?" in Hawaii Business (Vol. 53, December 2007, No. 6, pp. 28)
Pub: Hawaii Business Publishing
Description: Presents the opinons of Channel Capital LLC's Walter R. Roth and Hawaii Venture Capital Association's Bill Spencer concerning the impacts of tax credits. Roth thinks that Act 221 appeals to investors who can earn despite business failure while Spencer thinks that the legislation promotes investments in innovative technology firms. The need to support tax credits is also discussed.

12438 ■ "Have I Got a Deal For You" in Canadian Business (Vol. 83, October 12, 2010, No. 17, pp. 65)
Pub: Rogers Media Ltd.
Ed: Bryan Borzykowski. **Description:** U.S. automobile market currently has more than three players, providing investors with a number of investment options. The sector is still mired in uncertainty, but people believe that these companies can only grow from this point forward. However, investors should use due diligence before jumping into the market.

12439 ■ "Hawaii's Identity Crisis" in Hawaii Business (Vol. 53, November 2007, No. 5, pp. 10)
Pub: Hawaii Business Publishing
Ed: Kelli Abe Trifonovitch. **Description:** Some Hawaiians have shown that the Superferry controversy makes it seem to the rest of the world as if they do not know what they are doing, and intensifies several issues regarding the stability of investing in Hawaii. With or without the Superferry, there is still no evidence that investors are afraid to put their money in Hawaii.

12440 ■ "Hawaii's Top Twenty Financial Advisors" in Hawaii Business (Vol. 53, February 2008, No. 8, pp. 32)
Pub: Hawaii Business Publishing
Description: Listing of Hawaii's top 20 financial advisors is presented. Details on the methodology used to create the rankings are discussed.

12441 ■ "HB Diversity Stock Index" in Hispanic Business (March 2008, pp. 10)
Pub: Hispanic Business
Description: Presentation of the Hispanic Business Diversity Stock Index as of February 1, 2008, which includes 54 publicly traded companies. Statistical data included.

12442 ■ "HBDiversity Stock Index" in Hispanic Business (July-August 2007, pp. 58)
Pub: Hispanic Business
Description: Listing of 43 Hispanic companies, their stock symbol, value and change over a six month period, January 3, 2007 through July 6, 2007.

12443 ■ "HBDiversityStockIndex" in Hispanic Business (January-February 2008, pp. 10)
Pub: Hispanic Business
Description: Presentation of the Hispanic Business Diversity Stock Index for 2007, which includes 54 publicly traded companies.

12444 ■ "HBDiversityStockIndex" in Hispanic Business (October 2009, pp. 1)
Pub: Hispanic Business
Description: Data covering the Hispanic Business Diversity Stock Index is highlighted. The HBDSI was up 0.12 percent through September 3, 2009. Statistical data included.

12445 ■ "Headwinds From the New Sod Slow Aer Lingus" in Barron's (Vol. 88, March 10, 2008, No. 10, pp. M6)
Pub: Dow Jones & Company, Inc.
Ed: Sean Walters; Arindam Nag. **Description:** Aer Lingus faces a drop in its share prices with a falling US market, higher jet fuel prices, and lower long-haul passenger load factors. British media companies Johnston Press and Yell Group are suffering from weaker ad revenue and heavier debt payments due to the credit crunch.

12446 ■ "Health Care Leads Sectors Attracting Capital" in Hispanic Business (March 2008, pp. 14-16, 18)
Pub: Hispanic Business
Ed: Scott Williams. **Description:** U. S. Hispanic healthcare, media, and food were the key industries in the U.S. gaining investors in 2007.

12447 ■ "Health Care Leads Sectors Attracting Capital" in Hispanic Business (Vol. 30, March 2008, No. 3, pp. 14)
Pub: Hispanic Business
Ed: Scott Williams. **Description:** Discusses the capital gains of Hispanic-owned companies and other Hispanic leaders in the investment and retail fields in the year 2007. Sectors like health care, media, food and technology saw a healthy flow of capital due to successful mergers, acquisitions and increased private equity investments.

12448 ■ "HealthTronics Eager to Buy" in Austin Business JournalInc. (Vol. 28, September 12, 2008, No. 26, pp. 1)
Pub: American City Business Journals
Ed: Laura Hipp. **Description:** HealthTronics Inc., an Austin, Texas urology equipment company has repeated its offer to buy Endocare Inc., an Irvine, California tumor technology firm for $26.9 million. The proposal has been revised to allow Endocare shareholders to choose between HealthTronics cash or shares. Endocare has not commented on the offer.

12449 ■ "Heart Test No Boom for BG Medical" in Boston Business Journal (Vol. 31, June 17, 2011, No. 21, pp. 1)
Pub: Boston Business Journal
Ed: Julie M. Donnelly. **Description:** The Galectin-3 test failed to boost stock prices of its manufacturer, BG Medicine, which has fallen to $6.06/share. The company hopes that its revenue will be boosted by widespread adoption of an automated and faster version of the test, which diagnoses for heart failure.

12450 ■ "The Heat Is On" in Crain's Chicago Business (Vol. 31, April 28, 2008, No. 17, pp. 4)
Pub: Crain Communications, Inc.
Ed: Steve Daniels. **Description:** Discusses Nicor Inc., a natural-gas utility serving 2 million customers in Chicago's suburbs, and its potential acquirers;

shares of the company have dropped 17 percent this year making Nicor the second-worst among 31 utilities in an index tracked by Standrd & Poor's. Statistical data included.

12451 ■ *"Heat's On, but Glacier Not Retreating" in Globe & Mail (January 26, 2006, pp. B3)*
Pub: CTVglobemedia Publishing Inc.
Ed: Grant Robertson. **Description:** The details on Glacier Ventures International Corp., which acquired Hollinger International Inc.'s assets, are presented.

12452 ■ *"Hedge-Fund Titan Cohen Plans Bid for Dodgers" in Wall Street Journal Eastern Edition (November 25 , 2011, pp. C3)*
Pub: Dow Jones & Company Inc. Enterprise Media Group
Contact: Clare Hart, President
Ed: Matthew Futterman, Gregory Zuckerman. **Description:** Steven A. Cohen, the founder and head of hedge-fund SAC Capital Advisors LLC is looking to make an offer at the bankruptcy auction for the financially-troubled Los Angeles Dodgers baseball team.

12453 ■ *"Hello, 9000! The Dow's Run Is Far From Over" in Barron's (Vol. 89, July 27, 2009, No. 30, pp. 20)*
Pub: Dow Jones & Co., Inc.
Ed: Andrew Bary. **Description:** Another 10 percent gain is possible for the rest of 2009 as the Dow Jones Industrial Average moved above 9000 level for the week ending July 24, 2009. Blue chip stocks could do well in the next 10 years.

12454 ■ *"Here are the Stocks of the Decade" in Business Courier (Vol. 26, December 18, 2009, No. 34, pp. 1)*
Pub: American City Business Journals, Inc.
Ed: Steve Watkins. **Description:** Listing of companies with stocks that made big gains since December 1999 to November 30, 2009 is presented.

12455 ■ *"Here's How Buffett Spent 2007" in Barron's (Vol. 88, March 10, 2008, No. 10, pp. 48)*
Pub: Dow Jones & Company, Inc.
Ed: Andrew Bary. **Description:** Earnings of Berkshire Hathaway may decline in 2008 due to a tighter insurance market, but its portfolio is expected to continue growing. Warren Buffett purchased $19.1 billion worth of stocks in 2007.

12456 ■ *"The Hidden Tax" in Canadian Business (Vol. 81, April 14, 2008, No. 6, pp. 28)*
Pub: Rogers Media
Ed: Al Rosen. **Description:** Accounting fraud could take out a sizable sum from one's retirement fund when computed over a long period of time. The much bigger tax on savings is the collective impact of the smaller losses that do not attract the attention they deserve. Ensuring that investors are not unnecessarily taxed 2 percent of their total investments every year outweighs the benefit of a 2 percent reduction in personal tax rates.

12457 ■ *"H.I.G. Capital Announces Acquisition of Next Generation Vending" in Benzinga.com (October 29, 2011)*
Pub: Benzinga.com
Ed: Benzinga Staff. **Description:** H.I.G. Capital LLC, a leader in global private investments, acquired Next Generation Vending and Food Service Inc. Next Generation is a provider of vending services for corporate and institutional clients in Northeastern United States.

12458 ■ *"High Hopes: Ralph Mitchell's Picks Have Growth Potential" in Black Enterprise (Vol. 37, February 2007, No. 7, pp. 42)*
Pub: Earl G. Graves Publishing Co. Inc.
Ed: Carolyn M. Brown. **Description:** Ralph Mitchell, president and senior financial advisor of Braintree-Carthage Financial Group, offers three recommendations: Toll Brothers, Home Depot, and Lowe's.

12459 ■ *"High Marks; Parker Hannifin's Stock Lauded by Wall Street Journal" in Crain's Cleveland Business (Vol. 28, November 5, 2007, No. 44)*
Pub: Crain Communications, Inc.
Description: According to The Wall Street Journal, Parker Hannifin Corp., a manufacturer of motion and control equipment, is one of eight stocks that are attractively priced and continuously showing growth.

12460 ■ *"High-Yield Turns Into Road Kill" in Barron's (Vol. 88, July 7, 2008, No. 27, pp. M7)*
Pub: Dow Jones & Co., Inc.
Ed: Emily Barrett. **Description:** High-yield bonds have returned to the brink of collapse after profits have recovered from the shock brought about by the collapse of Bear Stearns. The high-yield bond market could decline again due to weakness in the automotive sector, particularly in Ford and General Motors.

12461 ■ *"Higher Freight Rates Keep CPR Rolling in Profit" in Globe & Mail (February 1, 2006, pp. B3)*
Pub: CTVglobemedia Publishing Inc.
Ed: Brent Jang. **Description:** Canadian Pacific Railway Ltd. posted $135.4 million in revenues for fourth quarter 2005. The company's earnings projections for 2006 and workforce reduction plans are presented.

12462 ■ *"The Hired Guns" in Business Courier (Vol. 26, November 13, 2009, No. 29, pp. 1)*
Pub: American City Business Journals, Inc.
Ed: Lisa Biank Fasig. **Description:** YourForce has nearly 6,000 retired scientists and researchers who work together in helping Procter & Gamble (P&G) and other companies in addressing various project needs. Operating as an online innovation community, YourEncore is a result of P&G's Connect Develop program.

12463 ■ *"His Way" in Inc. (February 2008, pp. 90-97)*
Pub: Gruner & Jahr USA Publishing
Ed: Stephanie Clifford. **Description:** Profile of Chris Reed, founder of a natural soda company, who undertook an initial public offering (IPO). Reed discusses the challenges he faced mediating with the Securities Exchange Commission regarding his firm's IPO.

12464 ■ *"Hispantelligence Report" in Hispanic Business (January-February 2008, pp. 8)*
Pub: Hispanic Business
Description: Presentation of the Hispanic Business Stock Index shows the current value of fifteen Hispanic companies through December 2007. Forecasts showing increased growth for Hispanic-owned companies are also included.

12465 ■ *"Hispantelligence Report" in Hispanic Business (July-August 2007, pp. 18)*
Pub: Hispanic Business
Description: Presentation of the Hispanic Business Stock Index shows the current value of fifteen Hispanic companies from January 3 through July 6, 2007. Results of a survey covering Hispanic household spending on new automobiles are also included. Statistical data included.

12466 ■ *"Hispantelligence Report" in Hispanic Business (March 2008, pp. 8)*
Pub: Hispanic Business
Description: Listing of the Hispanic Business Stock Index covering Hispanic owned businesses; stock symbol, previous 30-day, year-to-date and one year performance is presented.

12467 ■ *"Hispantelligence Report" in Hispanic Business (July-August 2009, pp. 8)*
Pub: Hispanic Business
Description: After forty years, Hispanic-owned businesses have grown to more than three million, according to a U.S. Census report. The Hispanic business stock index is also presented. Statistical data included.

12468 ■ *"A History of Neglect" in Canadian Business (Vol. 79, September 11, 2006, No. 18, pp. 21)*
Pub: Rogers Media
Ed: Al Rosen. **Description:** Faulty practices being followed by auditors and regulators of Canada are discussed. The need for appropriate steps to protect investors against these frauds are emphasized.

12469 ■ *"Hit the Books" in Black Enterprise (Vol. 38, July 2008, No. 12, pp. 42)*
Pub: Earl G. Graves Publishing Co. Inc.
Ed: Mellody Hobson. **Description:** Four books that deal with investing are discussed as is the idea that reading even 15 minutes a day from one of these books will give you tools that far exceed what you can learn from magazines and the business section of your daily newspaper.

12470 ■ *"Hits and Misses" in Canadian Business (Vol. 80, December 25, 2006, No. 1, pp. 69)*
Pub: Rogers Media
Ed: Calvin Leung. **Description:** The performance of stocks of several Canadian companies is discussed.

12471 ■ *"Hitting Bottom?" in Barron's (Vol. 88, March 24, 2008, No. 12, pp. 21)*
Pub: Dow Jones & Company, Inc.
Ed: Jacqueline Doherty. **Description:** Brokerage houses and banks may stabilize in 2008 as a result of regulatory responses brought about by the near-collapse of Bear Stearns. Some of their shares may rise by as much as 20 percent from 2008 to 2009.

12472 ■ *"Hold the IPhone" in Canadian Business (Vol. 80, January 15, 2007, No. 2, pp. 22)*
Pub: Rogers Media
Ed: Andrew Wahl. **Description:** The rise in the price of shares of Apple Inc. after the introduction of its new product, the iPhone, is discussed.

12473 ■ *"Hold Your Nose, Say 'Da'" in Canadian Business (Vol. 79, September 11, 2006, No. 18, pp. 151)*
Pub: Rogers Media
Ed: Thomas Watson. **Description:** The changing business environment and investment opportunities in Russia despite its instable democracy are discussed. Russia's potential and its ability to attract productive investment are presented.

12474 ■ *"Hollinger Shares Plummet on Reports" in Globe & Mail (March 10, 2007, pp. B5)*
Pub: CTVglobemedia Publishing Inc.
Ed: Richard Blackwell. **Description:** The fall in the share prices of Hollinger Inc. to 49 percent soon after the company filed its annual statements is discussed.

12475 ■ *"A Home of Her Own" in Hawaii Business (Vol. 53, October 2007, No. 4, pp. 51)*
Pub: Hawaii Business Publishing
Ed: Maria Torres-Kitamura. **Description:** It was observed that the number of single women in Hawaii purchasing their own home has increased, as that in the whole United States where the percentage has increased from 14 percent in 1995 to 22 percent in 2006. However, First Hawaiian Bank's Wendy Lum thinks that the trend will not continue in Hawaii due to lending restrictions. The factors that women consider in buying a home of their own are presented.

12476 ■ *"Home Sweet Home?" in Canadian Business (Vol. 79, September 11, 2006, No. 18, pp. 17)*
Pub: Rogers Media
Ed: David Wolf. **Description:** Fading attractiveness of the Canadian stock market for its domestic investors is discussed. Changing investor's trends toward cross-border investments are presented.

12477 ■ *"Homebuilders Continue to be Our Nemesis" in Contractor (Vol. 56, July 2009, No. 7, pp. 50)*
Pub: Penton Media, Inc.
Ed: Bob Mader. **Description:** Homebuilders rank high on the greed scale along with Wall Street brokers. There is this one instance when a builder

gave copies of another contractor's quotes that have just been blackened out and another instance when one builder let other bidders visit a site while the current mechanical contractor is working.

12478 ■ "Honesty Doesn't Pay" in Canadian Business (Vol. 79, Winter 2006, No. 24, pp. 28)
Pub: Rogers Media
Ed: Al Rosen. **Description:** The effects of the outlook of financial analysts and investment bankers, on their career prospects, are described.

12479 ■ "Hong Kong's Boom in IPO" in Barron's (Vol. 89, July 13, 2009, No. 28, pp. M7)
Pub: Dow Jones & Co., Inc.
Ed: Nick Lord. **Description:** Hong Kong's IPO (initial public offering) market is booming with 13 Chinese IPOs already on the market for the year as July 2009. One of them is Bawang International which raised $214 million after generating $9 billion in order which makes it 42 times oversubscribed.

12480 ■ "Hospital Revenue Healthier in 2009" in Orlando Business Journal (Vol. 26, February 5, 2010, No. 36, pp. 1)
Pub: American City Business Journals
Ed: Melanie Stawicki Azam. **Description:** Orlando Health, Health Central and Adventist Health System are Florida-based hospital systems that generated the most profits in 2009. Orlando Health had the highest profit in 2009 at $73.3 million, contrary to about $31 million in losses in 2008. The increased profits are attributed to stock market recovery, cost-cutting initiatives, and rising patient volumes.

12481 ■ "Hot For All The Wrong Reasons" in Canadian Business (Vol. 81, March 31, 2008, No. 5, pp. 19)
Pub: Rogers Media
Ed: Andrea Jezovit. **Description:** Soaring platinum prices are due to South Africa's platinum mining industry's safety issues and power supply disruptions that exacerbate the metal's supply problems. South Africa supplies 80 percent of the world's platinum. South Africa's power utility has said that it cannot guarantee the industry's power needs until 2013.

12482 ■ "Hotel Confidential" in Canadian Business (Vol. 80, Winter 2007, No. 24, pp. 91)
Pub: Rogers Media
Ed: Erik Heinrich. **Description:** Celebrities such as Jason Priestley, Clint Eastwood, and Francis Ford Coppola have made investment in the hospitality industry. Investing in the hospitality industry has proved to be an excellent long-term investment and the venture also has a vanity aspect to it.

12483 ■ House of Cards
Pub: Doubleday, a Division of Random House
Ed: William D. Cohan. **Released:** March 10, 2009. **Price:** $27.95. **Description:** The fall of Bear Stearns and the beginning of the Wall Street Collapse.

12484 ■ House of Cards: A Tale of Hubris and Wretched Excess on Wall Street
Pub: Anchor Press
Ed: William D. Cohan. **Released:** February 9, 2010. **Price:** $16.95. **Description:** A historical account of the events leading up to the Bear Stearns implosion.

12485 ■ "How to Avoid the Three Big Mistakes" in Barron's (Vol. 88, March 10, 2008, No. 10, pp. 30)
Pub: Dow Jones & Company, Inc.
Ed: Karen Hube. **Description:** Investors, particularly those having retirement investments, are advised to diversify their investments, refrain from market timing, and minimize payments to maximize investment gains. An investor committing these mistakes could lose as much as $375,000 dollars over ten years.

12486 ■ "How to Beat the Pros" in Canadian Business (Vol. 81, Summer 2008, No. 9, pp. 59)
Pub: Rogers Media Ltd.
Ed: Calvin Leung. **Description:** Table showing the results of the Investor 500 beat the S&P/TSX composite index is presented. The average total return, best performing stocks and total return of the 2007 stock screen are provided.

12487 ■ How Come That Idiot's Rich and I'm Not?
Pub: Crown Publishing/Random House
Ed: Robert Shemin. **Released:** April 2009. **Price:** $13.95. **Description:** The book shows the average person not only how to get rich, but to create, connect and contribute greatly.

12488 ■ "How CoolBrand's Thrills Turned to Chills" in Globe & Mail (January 25, 2007, pp. B1)
Pub: CTVglobemedia Publishing Inc.
Ed: Keith McArthur. **Description:** The key reasons behind the sudden share price fall of ice cream giant CoolBrands International Inc. are discussed.

12489 ■ "How to Deal" in Canadian Business (Vol. 81, November 10, 2008, No. 19, pp. 36)
Pub: Rogers Media Ltd.
Ed: Calvin Leung. **Description:** The Great Depression, Japan's Lost Decade, and the Swedish Banking Crisis is compared to the 2008 financial crisis in the U.S. The chances for recession in the U.S. are discussed along with investment strategies to survive.

12490 ■ "How Foreigners Could Disrupt U.S. Markets" in Barron's (Vol. 90, September 13, 2010, No. 37, pp. 30)
Pub: Barron's Editorial & Corporate Headquarters
Ed: Jim McTague. **Description:** An informal meeting by the House Homeland Security Panel concluded that U.S. stock exchanges and related trading routes can be the subject of attacks from rogue overseas traders. A drop in funding for the U.S. Department of Defense is discussed.

12491 ■ "How High Can Soybeans Fly?" in Barron's (Vol. 88, March 10, 2008, No. 10, pp. M14)
Pub: Dow Jones & Company, Inc.
Ed: Kenneth Rapoza. **Description:** Prices of soybeans have risen to $14.0875 a bushel, up 8.3 percent for the week. Increased demand, such as in China and in other developing economies, and the investment-driven commodities boom are boosting prices.

12492 ■ "How Interest Rate Changes Affect You" in Agency Sales Magazine (Vol. 39, September-October 2009, No. 9, pp. 50)
Pub: MANA
Ed: Lee Eisinberg. **Description:** Falling interest rates make the prices of previously issued bonds rise and new issues are offered at lower rates. For stock investors, rising interest rates can have a positive or negative effect. Terminologies related to investing are explained.

12493 ■ "How Investors React When Women Join Boards" in Harvard Business Review (Vol. 88, July-August 2010, No. 7-8, pp. 24)
Pub: Harvard Business School Publishing
Ed: Andrew O'Connell. **Description:** Research reveals a cognitive bias in blockholders regarding the presence of women on boards of directors despite evidence showing that diversity improves results.

12494 ■ How to Make Money in Stocks: A Winning System in Good Times and Bad
Pub: The McGraw-Hill Companies
Ed: William J. O'Neil. **Released:** June 12. 2009. **Price:** $16.95. **Description:** The bestselling guide to buying stocks, from the founder of Investor's Business Daily. The technique is based on a study of the greatest stock market winners dating back to 1953 and includes a seven-step process for minimizing risk, maximizing return, and finding stocks that are ready to perform.

12495 ■ "How to Maximize Your Investment Income" in Contractor (Vol. 56, December 2009, No. 12, pp. 33)
Pub: Penton Media, Inc.
Ed: Irv Blackman. **Description:** Private placement life insurance (PPLI) can minimize taxes and protect assets. PPLI is a form of variable universal insurance that is offered privately. Risk of insurance company illiquidity is avoided as investments are placed in separate accounts.

12496 ■ "How Not to Raise Bank Capital" in Barron's (Vol. 88, June 30, 2008, No. 26, pp. M6)
Pub: Dow Jones & Co., Inc.
Ed: Sean Walters. **Description:** French bank Natixis wants to raise 1 billion euros from cash provided by their two major owners. Natixis will reimburse Banque Populaire and Caisses d'Epargne with hybrid securities so this move will not benefit Natixis' core Tier 1 ratio. This has also given the impression that the company is afraid of a full rights issue which could shake investors' faith in the bank.

12497 ■ "How Our Picks Beat The Bear" in Barron's (Vol. 88, July 14, 2008, No. 28, pp. 18)
Pub: Dow Jones & Co., Inc.
Ed: Andrew Bary. **Description:** Performance of the stocks that Barron's covered in the first half of 2008 is discussed; some of the worst picks and most rewarding pans have been in the financial sector while the best plays were in the energy, materials, and the transportation sectors.

12498 ■ "How to Play the Tech Mergers" in Barron's (Vol. 90, August 30, 2010, No. 35, pp. 18)
Pub: Barron's Editorial & Corporate Headquarters
Ed: Tiernan Ray. **Description:** The intense bidding by Hewlett-Packard and Dell for 3Par was foreseen in a previous Barron's cover story and 3Par's stock has nearly tripled since reported. Other possible acquisition targets in the tech industry include Brocade Communication Systems, NetApp, Xyratex, and Isilon Systems.

12499 ■ How to Protect and Manage Your 401K: Shield, Save, and Grow Your Money, Guard Against Corporate Corruption, Do What It Takes to Protect Your Future
Pub: Career Press, Incorporated
Ed: Elizabeth Opalka. **Released:** May 2003. **Description:** Ways to protect and manage 401(K) investments.

12500 ■ "How Sweet It Will Be" in Barron's (Vol. 89, July 13, 2009, No. 28, pp. M13)
Pub: Dow Jones & Co., Inc.
Ed: Debbie Carlson. **Description:** Raw sugar experienced a rally in the first half of 2009 and the long term outlook for sugar prices is still good. However, there is a likely near-term correction due to the onset of Brazilian harvest that could be 20.7 percent higher for 2009 as compared to the previous year and October contracts could fall to 15.61 cents per pound.

12501 ■ "HSBC Canada Posts 8.8 Percent Profit Gain in 2006" in Globe & Mail (February 20, 2007, pp. B14)
Pub: CTVglobemedia Publishing Inc.
Ed: Andrew Willis. **Description:** HSBC Bank Canada reported profits of $497 million in 2006. The financial results of the company for 2006 are presented.

12502 ■ "The Human Element" in Canadian Business (Vol. 80, April 23, 2007, No. 9, pp. 78)
Pub: Rogers Media
Ed: Jeff Sanford. **Description:** The effects of human resource programs on stocks and investor relations are presented.

12503 ■ "Huntington's Future At a Crossroads" in Crain's Cleveland Business (Vol. 30, June 22, 2009, No. 24, pp. 1)
Pub: Crain Communications, Inc.
Ed: Arielle Kass. **Description:** Despite Huntington Bancshares plans to expand in the Cleveland, Ohio area, experts wonder if the bank will be able to take advantage of the area's growth in the long run. Statistical data included.

12504 ■ "Ian Gordon" in Canadian Business (Vol. 81, Summer 2008, No. 9, pp. 10)
Pub: Rogers Media Ltd.
Ed: Matthew McClearn. **Description:** Bolder Investment Partners' Ian Gordon discussed the economic theory promulgated by Russian economist Nikolai Kondratieff. The cycle begins with a rising economy

then followed by deflationary depression. Details of his views on the Kondratieff cycle and its application to the current economy are presented.

12505 ■ *"Identity Crisis: The Battle For Your Data"* in *Canadian Business (Vol. 81, March 17, 2008, No. 4, pp. 12)*
Pub: Rogers Media
Description: Nigel Brown explains that businesses must protect their data through encryption and tightening up access to data. Brown also points out that banks and merchants bear most of the costs for identity fraud and leaves individuals with a lot of pain and heartache in clearing their name.

12506 ■ *"If You Go Into the Market Today.."* in *Canadian Business (Vol. 82, Summer 2009, No. 8, pp. 18)*
Pub: Rogers Media
Ed: Jeff Sanford. **Description:** Opinions of experts and personalities who are known to have bear attitudes towards the economy were presented in the event 'A Night with the Bears' in Toronto in April 2009. Known bears that served as resource persons in the event were Nouriel Roubini, Eric Sprott, Ian Gordon, and Meredith Whitney. The bears were observed to have differences regarding consumer debt.

12507 ■ *"An Ill Wind: Icelandic Bank Failures Chill Atlantic Canada"* in *Canadian Business (Vol. 81, November 10, 2008, No. 19, pp. 10)*
Pub: Rogers Media Ltd.
Ed: Charles Mandel. **Description:** Bank failures in Iceland have put a stop to flights ferrying Icelanders to Newfoundland to purchase Christmas gifts, thereby threatening Newfoundland's tourism industry. The credit of Newfoundland's fisheries is also being squeezed since most of Atlantic Canadian seafood processors hold lines of credit from Icelandic banks.

12508 ■ *"Ill Winds; Cuba's Economy"* in *The Economist (Vol. 390, January 3, 2009, No. 8612, pp. 20)*
Pub: The Economist Newspaper Inc.
Description: Cuba's long-term economic prospects remain poor with the economy forecasted to grow only 4.3 percent for the year, about half of the original forecast, due in part to Hurricane Gustav which caused $10 billion in damage and disrupted the food-supply network and devastated farms across the region; President Raul Castro made raising agricultural production a national priority and the rise in global commodity prices hit the country hard. The only bright spot has been the rise in tourism which is up 9.3 percent over 2007.

12509 ■ *"Immigrants Trapped in Forex Mess"* in *Boston Business Journal (Vol. 27, October 5, 2007, No. 36, pp. 1)*
Pub: American City Business Journals Inc.
Ed: Jackie Noblett. **Description:** U. S. Commodity Futures Trading Commission and Swiss Federal Banking Commission are jointly working on the case of Tradex Swiss AG. Investors have filed lawsuits to recover their money. Details of the illegal operation of the Forex company are discussed.

12510 ■ *"Immigration Issues Frustrate Owners From Overseas"* in *The Business Journal-Serving Greater Tampa Bay (Vol. 28, August 15, 2008)*
Pub: American City Business Journals, Inc.
Ed: Margie Manning. **Description:** Investors who availed the E-2 visa program believe that the tightened restrictions on the visa program has trapped them in the United States. The E-2 investor visa program was designed to attract investors into the U.S., but restrictions were tightened after the September 11, 2001 attacks. Other views and information on E-2 and its impact on investors are presented.

12511 ■ *"The Impact of Acquisitions On the Productivity of Inventors at Semiconductor Firms"* in *Academy of Management Journal (October 2007)*
Pub: Academy of Management
Contact: Ming-Jer Chen, President
Ed: Rahul Kapoor, Kwanghui Lim. **Description:** Study examined the relation between knowledge-based and incentive-based outlook in explaining the

impact of acquisitions on the productivity of inventors at acquired semiconductor firms. Results showed a definite relation between the two perspectives.

12512 ■ *"The Impact of Brand Quality on Shareholder Wealth"* in *Journal of Marketing (Vol. 75, September 2011, No. 5, pp. 88)*
Pub: American Marketing Association
Ed: Sundar G. Bharardwaj, Kapil R. Tuli, Andre Bonfrer. **Description:** The effects of brand quality on idiosyncratic risk, systematic risk, and stock returns are investigated. Findings reveal that unexpected changes in brand quality negatively associated with idiosyncratic risk changes and positively related to stock returns. However, unexpected changes in brand quality will reduce shareholder wealth due to positive relationship with changes n systematic risk.

12513 ■ *"Imports Frothing Up Beer Market"* in *Globe & Mail (February 16, 2006, pp. B4)*
Pub: CTVglobemedia Publishing Inc.
Ed: Andy Hoffman. **Description:** The reasons behind the rise in market share of beer imports, in Canada, are presented.

12514 ■ *"In the Bag?"* in *Canadian Business (Vol. 81, March 3, 2008, No. 3, pp. 57)*
Pub: Rogers Media
Ed: Calvin Leung. **Description:** American stocks are beginning to appear cheap amidst the threat of a worldwide economic slowdown, United States economic crisis and declining stock portfolios. Investors looking for bargain stocks should study the shares of Apple and Oshkosh Corp. Evaluation of other cheap-looking stocks such as the shares of Coach and 3M is also given.

12515 ■ *"In China, Railways to Riches"* in *Barron's (Vol. 88, July 7, 2008, No. 27, pp. M9)*
Pub: Dow Jones & Co., Inc.
Ed: Assif Shameen. **Description:** Shares of Chinese railway companies look to benefit from multimillion-dollar investments aimed at upgrading the Chinese railway network. Investment in the sector is expected to reach $210 billion for the 2006-2010 period.

12516 ■ *"In India, A Gold-Price Threat?"* in *Barron's (Vol. 88, June 30, 2008, No. 26, pp. M12)*
Pub: Dow Jones & Co., Inc.
Ed: Melanie Burton. **Description:** Gold purchases in India are falling as record prices take its toll on demand. Gold imports to India fell by 52 percent in May 2008 from the previous year and local prices are higher by one-third from the previous year to 12,540 rupees for 10 grams.

12517 ■ *"In Praise of How Not to Invest"* in *Barron's (Vol. 89, July 13, 2009, No. 28, pp. 11)*
Pub: Dow Jones & Co., Inc.
Ed: Vito J. Racanelli. **Description:** One research study found that the shares of companies that have growing market shares and expanding asset bases underperform. This is contrary to the widely held premise that stock prices for these companies rise. It is argued that this result is caused by these companies' tendency to sacrifice profitability to grab market share and this is reflected in their stock prices.

12518 ■ *"In the Public Eye"* in *Entrepreneur (Vol. 35, November 2007, No. 11, pp. 75)*
Pub: Entrepreneur Media Inc.
Ed: David Worrell. **Description:** The market for initial public offerings (IPOs) was booming in 2007 and strong fundamentals for companies that would like to go public are needed. The basics that companies should review before planning an IPO are outlined.

12519 ■ *"In Sickness and In Wealth Management"* in *Hispanic Business (Vol. 30, March 2008, No. 3, pp. 28)*
Pub: Hispanic Business
Ed: Rick Munarriz. **Description:** Discusses the investment and wealth management firms owned and operated by Hispanics. There are only a handful of these firms owned by Hispanics, as most of them prefer capital preservation by investing in hard assets like cash and real estate than in capital appreciation.

12520 ■ *"In Sickness and in Wealth Management"* in *Hispanic Business (March 2008, pp. 28, 30)*
Pub: Hispanic Business
Ed: Rick Munarriz. **Description:** Financial advice is offered by experts, Myrna Rivera and Samuel Ramirez Jr., with an overview of Hispanic-owned investment firms.

12521 ■ *"In Surging Oil Industry, Good Fortune Comes In Stages"* in *Barron's (Vol. 88, July 7, 2008, No. 27, pp. 12)*
Pub: Dow Jones & Co., Inc.
Ed: Sandra Ward. **Description:** Shares of US land oil and gas driller Helmerich and Payne, priced at $69 each, are estimated to be at peak levels. The shares are trading at 17 times 2008 earnings and could be in for some profit taking.

12522 ■ *"In the Wake of Pet-Food Crisis, Iams Sales Plummet Nearly 17 Percent"* in *Advertising Age (Vol. 78, May 14, 2007, No. 18, pp. 3)*
Pub: Crain Communications, Inc.
Ed: Jack Neff. **Description:** Although the massive U.S. pet-food recall impacted more than 100 brands, Procter & Gamble Co.'s Iams lost more sales and market share than any other industry player. According to Information Resources Inc. data, the brand's sales dropped 16.5 percent in the eight-week period ended April 22. Many analysts feel that the company could have handled the crisis in a better manner.

12523 ■ *"In With the Good"* in *Canadian Business (Vol. 80, November 5, 2007, No. 22, pp. 22)*
Pub: Rogers Media
Ed: Jack Mintz. **Description:** Restriction on foreign direct investment in Canada is unlikely to materialize despite Minister of Industry Jim Prentice's opinion that new rules be set in Ottawa regarding foreign state-owned businesses. Reasons why governments would not unreasonably regulate foreign investments are investigated.

12524 ■ *"Inflation Woes: Secure Your Portfolio Against Rising Prices"* in *Black Enterprise (Vol. 37, January 2007, No. 6, pp. 40)*
Pub: Earl G. Graves Publishing Co. Inc.
Ed: Donald Jay Korn. **Description:** Inflation has a huge impact on investing and it is important to take the steady increase on cost into account when looking at your financial goals and investing in your future. Statistical data included.

12525 ■ *"Inland Snaps Up Rival REITs"* in *Crain's Chicago Business (Vol. 31, November 17, 2008, No. 46, pp. 3)*
Pub: Crain Communications, Inc.
Ed: Alby Gallun. **Description:** Discusses Inland American Real Estate Trust Inc., a real estate investment trust that is napping up depressed shares of publicly traded competitors, a possible first step toward taking over these companies; however, with hotel and retail properties accounting for approximately 70 percent of its portfolio, the company could soon face its own difficulties.

12526 ■ *"Inmet Selling Nunavut Mining Properties"* in *Globe & Mail (February 15, 2006, pp. B6)*
Pub: CTVglobemedia Publishing Inc.
Ed: Allan Robinson. **Description:** The details on Wolfden Resources Inc.'s acquisition of mining assets of Inmet Mining Corp. are presented.

12527 ■ *"Insider"* in *Canadian Business (Vol. 81, March 31, 2008, No. 5, pp. 76)*
Pub: Rogers Media
Ed: John Gray. **Description:** Discusses a comparison of an average Canadian family's finances in 1990 with the data from 2007. The average family in 2007 has over $80,000 in debt compared to just under $52,000 in 1990. However, Canadians have also been accumulating solid assets such as homes and stocks. This means that Canadian debt load has fallen from 22 percent in 1990 to 20 percent in 2007 when taken as a percentage of total net worth.

12528 ■ "Insider" in Canadian Business (Vol. 81, March 3, 2008, No. 3, pp. 96)
Pub: Rogers Media
Description: History of gold usage and gold trading is presented in a timeline. Gold was a symbol of power and wealth in 2500 B.C., and in 1500 B.C., it became the first currency to be recognized internationally. Other remarkable events in the gold industry and laws that covered gold are discussed.

12529 ■ "An Insurance Roll-Up In Danger of Unraveling" in Barron's (Vol. 88, March 17, 2008, No. 11, pp. 51)
Pub: Dow Jones & Company, Inc.
Ed: Bill Alpert. **Description:** Shares of National Financial Partners have fallen below their initial offering price as sputtering sales and management turnover leave many investors wondering. One of the company's star brokers is being sued for their 'life settlement' contracts while another broker is being pursued by the IRS for unpaid taxes.

12530 ■ "Intangible Assets" in Canadian Business (Vol. 79, July 17, 2006, No. 14-15, pp. 17)
Pub: Rogers Media
Ed: Al Rosen. **Description:** Need for investors to check the actual worth of a company and not to get carried away by the inflated claims made by the company is emphasized.

12531 ■ "International ETFs: Your Passport to the World" in Barron's (Vol. 89, July 13, 2009, No. 28, pp. L10)
Pub: Dow Jones & Co., Inc.
Ed: John Hintze. **Description:** International exchange traded funds give investors more choices in terms of investment plays and there are 174 U.S. ETF listings worth $141 billion as of July 2009. Suggestions on how to invest in these funds based on one's conviction on how the global economy will unfold are presented.

12532 ■ "International Nickel Ventures Corporation Reports Results for the First Quarter 2007" in Canadian Corporate News (May 16, 2007)
Pub: Comtex News Network Inc.
Description: Profile of International Nickel Ventures Corporation (INV) including its financial report for the first quarter of fiscal 2007, its partnership and possible acquisition of Teck Cominco Limited, and its plans for the future. Statistical data included.

12533 ■ The Internationalization of Asset Ownership in Europe
Pub: Cambridge University Press
Contact: Richard Ziemacki, President
E-mail: rziemacki@cambridge.org
Ed: Harry Huizinga, Lars Jonung. **Released:** November 2005. **Price:** $112.00. **Description:** Ten financial experts provide analysis of the growth and the implications of foreign ownership in Europe's financial markets.

12534 ■ "Investment Bank Predicts Shakeup in Farm Equipment Industry" in Farm Industry News (November 16, 2011)
Pub: Penton Business Media Inc.
Ed: Jodie Wehrspann. **Description:** Farming can expect to see more mergers and acquisitions in the agricultural equipment industry, as it appears to be in the early stages of growth over the next few years.

12535 ■ Investment Counsel Association of America--Directory of Member Firms
Pub: Investment Adviser Association
Contact: Vivian Pan, President
URL(s): www.investmentadviser.org. **Released:** Annual Price: Free. **Covers:** over 300 member investment counseling firms. **Entries include:** Name and address of firm; contact, number of clients, assets under management, staff, type of account, minimum account and fee.

12536 ■ "Investment Firms Unite: Coalition Fights New Tax Law" in Black Enterprise (Vol. 38, December 2007, No. 5, pp. 52)
Pub: Earl G. Graves Publishing Co. Inc.
Ed: Joyce Jones. **Description:** Minorities working in private equity, real estate and investment management firms have united to form the Access to Capital

Coalition to oppose legislation that they feel would adversely affect their ability to attract investments and executives. Details of the group are included.

12537 ■ "Investment Manager Disciplined" in Sacramento Business Journal (Vol. 25, July 4, 2008, No. 18, pp. 1)
Pub: American City Business Journals, Inc.
Ed: Mark Anderson. **Description:** Community Capital Management's David A. Zwick is permanently barred by the Securities and Exchange Commission (SEC) from associating with any broker or dealer, after investigations revealed that he took part in paying kickbacks to a bond trader. Other views and information on Community Capital, and on the SEC investigation on Zwick, are presented.

12538 ■ "Investors Finding Bay Area Deals" in Tampa Bay Business Journal (Vol. 29, November 6, 2009, No. 46, pp. 1)
Pub: American City Business Journals
Ed: Margie Manning. **Description:** Private equity investors have found dozens of privately held companies in Tampa Bay area in Florida in which to invest $84 million fresh equity. Revenue generation, growth, solid management teams are some of the factors found by the investors on these companies which span a range of sizes and industries.

12539 ■ "An Investor's Guide to This Year's Inc. 500" in Inc. (October 2007, pp. 34)
Pub: Gruner & Jahr USA Publishing
Description: Three investment firms specializing in growth companies provide insight into today's market.

12540 ■ "Investors Lost Patience A Long Time Ago" in Globe & Mail (January 21, 2006, pp. B5)
Pub: CTVglobemedia Publishing Inc.
Ed: Konrad Yakabuski. **Description:** The financial impasse at Quebecor World Inc., under chief executive officer Pierre Karl Peladeau, is discussed.

12541 ■ "Investors Shrug Off the Turmoil" in Globe & Mail (March 1, 2007, pp. B1)
Pub: CTVglobemedia Publishing Inc.
Ed: Geoffrey York. **Description:** The decision of Chinese investors to continue to buy stocks despite the decade's biggest market crash is discussed. The rise in the stock price indexes of China is described.

12542 ■ "Investors Sue Jackson Properties for Fraud, Breach of Contract" in The Business Journal - Serving Phoenix and the Valley of the Sun (Vol. 28, July 18, 2008, No. 46, pp. 1)
Pub: American City Business Journals, Inc.
Ed: Jan Buchholz. **Description:** Investors sued Jackson Properties EVB Inc. and Jackson Properties EVB LLC for fraud and breach of contract over a botched housing development deal. The investors also filed a complaint before the Arizona Corporation Commission. The investors stand to lose $8 million from the halted development deal.

12543 ■ "Is this a Buying Opportunity?" in Canadian Business (Vol. 82, April 27, 2009, No. 7, pp. 46)
Pub: Rogers Media
Ed: Andy Holloway. **Description:** Home prices in Canada are down by as much as 14.2 percent in 2009 compared to prices in 2008, making homes more affordable now. Some housing experts believe that homes are still good investments as prices of rent and properties always recover. Meanwhile, a survey found that Canadians under 35 plan to buy a home within two years.

12544 ■ "Is the VIX in Denial?" in Barron's (Vol. 88, July 7, 2008, No. 27, pp. M12)
Pub: Dow Jones & Co., Inc.
Ed: Lawrence McMillan. **Description:** Volatility Index (VIX) of the Chicago Board Options Exchange did not rise significantly despite the drop in the US stock markets, rising to near 25. This market decline, however, will eventually result in investor panic and the rise of the VIX.

12545 ■ "It Could Be Worse" in Barron's (Vol. 89, July 27, 2009, No. 30, pp. 5)
Pub: Dow Jones & Co., Inc.
Ed: Alan Abelson. **Description:** Media sources are being fooled by corporate America who is peddling an economic recovery rather than reality as shown by the report of a rise in existing home sales which boosted the stock market even if it was a seasonal phenomenon. The phrase 'things could be worse' sums up the reigning investment philosophy in the U.S. and this has been stirring up the market.

12546 ■ "It Takes More Than One" in Black Enterprise (Vol. 38, July 2008, No. 12, pp. 38)
Pub: Earl G. Graves Publishing Co. Inc.
Ed: James A. Anderson. **Description:** Interview with Eric Small, the CEO of SBK-Brooks Investment Corp., whom discusses the importance of versatility when trying to find the best investment choices; the primary factors investors should be mindful of; his current stock picks; and recommendations for investing in an uncertain and volatile market.

12547 ■ "Itochu Joins KKR in Samson Buyout" in Wall Street Journal Eastern Edition (November 25 , 2011, pp. B7)
Pub: Dow Jones & Company Inc. Enterprise Media Group
Contact: Clare Hart, President
Description: Samson Investment Company is the target of a $7.2 billion leveraged buyout by a consortium led by US investment firm Kohlberg Kravis Roberts & Company and Tokyo-based Itochu Corporation, part of the consortium is coming in on the deal for a 25 percent holding, for which it will pay $1.04 billion.

12548 ■ "It's Good to be Goldman" in Barron's (Vol. 89, July 20, 2009, No. 29, pp. 5)
Pub: Dow Jones & Co., Inc.
Ed: Randall W. Forsyth. **Description:** Profits of Goldman Sachs rose to $3.44 billion in the second quarter of 2009, aided by federal financial stimulus programs. CIT Group is facing bankruptcy and may need up to $6 billion to survive. The federal economic stimulus programs are benefiting Wall Street more than the US economy itself.

12549 ■ "It's Time to Wise Up: Income Trusts" in Canadian Business (Vol. 79, November 6, 2006, No. 22, pp. 24)
Pub: Rogers Media
Ed: Mark Rosen. **Description:** The effects bogus financial reporting of income trusts on investors are analyzed.

12550 ■ "Ivernia Mine Closing Could Boost Lead" in Globe & Mail (April 4, 2007, pp. B5)
Pub: CTVglobemedia Publishing Inc.
Ed: Andy Hoffman. **Description:** The closing of Ivernia Inc.'s mine in view of government investigation into alleged lead contamination at the port of Esperance is discussed. The likely increase in the price of lead is also discussed.

12551 ■ "Jamieson Eyes $175 Million Trust IPO" in Globe & Mail (March 7, 2006, pp. B1)
Pub: CTVglobemedia Publishing Inc.
Ed: Sinclair Stewart; Leonard Zehr. **Description:** The reasons behind $175 million initial public offering plans of Jamieson Laboratories Ltd. are presented.

12552 ■ "Jean Coutu Resuscitates Bottom Line" in Globe & Mail (January 11, 2006, pp. B5)
Pub: CTVglobemedia Publishing Inc.
Ed: Bertrand Marotte. **Description:** The details on Jean Coutu Group (PJC) Inc., which posted $30.8 million profits for second quarter 2005, are presented.

12553 ■ "Jet Sales Put Bombardier Back in Black" in Globe & Mail (March 30, 2006, pp. B1)
Pub: CTVglobemedia Publishing Inc.
Ed: Bertrand Morotte. **Description:** The details on Bombardier Inc., which posted 20 percent rise in shares following $86 million profit for fourth quarter 2005, are presented.

12554 ■ *"Judge Gives RIM One Last Chance"* in Globe & Mail (February 25, 2006, pp. B5)
Pub: CTVglobemedia Publishing Inc.

Ed: Barrie McKenna; Paul Waldie. **Description:** United States District Court Judge James Spencer offers more time for Research In Motion Ltd. (RIM) to settle the patent infringement dispute with NTP Inc. RIM's shares increase by 6.2 percent following the decision.

12555 ■ *"The Judgment Deficit"* in Harvard Business Review (Vol. 88, September 2010, No. 9, pp. 44)
Pub: Harvard Business School Publishing

Ed: Amar Bhide. **Description:** The importance of individual, decentralized initiative and judgment in the capitalist system is outlined. While financial models have their use, they cannot always account appropriately for the inherent uncertainty in economic decision making.

12556 ■ *"Juiced on Energy"* in Barron's (Vol. 88, July 14, 2008, No. 28, pp. 33)
Pub: Dow Jones & Co., Inc.

Ed: Leslie P. Norton. **Description:** Brad Evans and his team at Heartland Value Plus were able to outperform their peers by significantly under-committing to financials and overexposing themselves with energy stocks. Brad Evans believes that there is a lot of value left in energy stocks such as natural gas.

12557 ■ *"Julie Holzrichter; Managing Director of Operations, CME Group Inc."* in Crain's Chicago Business (Vol. 31, May 5, 2008, No. 18)
Pub: Crain Communications, Inc.

Ed: Ann Saphir. **Description:** Profile of Julie Holzrichter who works as the managing director of operations for CME Group Inc. and is known as a decisive leader able to intercept and solve problems.

12558 ■ *"Just Hang Up"* in Barron's (Vol. 88, March 10, 2008, No. 10, pp. 45)
Pub: Dow Jones & Company, Inc.

Ed: Tiernan Ray. **Description:** Sprint's shares are expected to continue falling while the company attempts to attract subscribers by cutting prices, cutting earnings in the process. The company faces tougher competition from better-financed AT&T and Verizon Communications.

12559 ■ *"KC Presents Healthy Market for Medical REIT"* in Business Journal-Serving Metropolitan Kansas City (Vol. 26, November 30, 2007)
Pub: American City Business Journals, Inc.

Ed: Rob Roberts. **Description:** Medical Properties Trust, the only real estate investment trust that specializes in buying hospitals, is planning to invest in Kansas City due to its fast growing hospital market. The company owns 29 properties nationwide and is still planning to increase its portfolio.

12560 ■ *"Keeping the Faith in Fuel-Tech"* in Barron's (Vol. 88, March 24, 2008, No. 12, pp. 20)
Pub: Dow Jones & Company, Inc.

Ed: Christopher C. Williams. **Description:** Shares of air pollution control company Fuel-Tech remain on track to reach $40 each from their $19 level due to a continued influx of contracts. The stock has suffered from lower-than-expected quarterly earnings and tougher competition but stand to benefit from increased orders.

12561 ■ *"Kid Rock"* in Canadian Business (Vol. 81, Summer 2008, No. 9, pp. 54)
Pub: Rogers Media Ltd.

Ed: John Gray. **Description:** Damien Reynolds is the founder, chairman and chief executive officer of Vancouver-based Longview Capital Partners. The investment bank, founded in 2005, is one of the fastest-growing companies in British Columbia. The recent economic downturn has battered the stocks of the company and its portfolio of junior miners.

12562 ■ *King of Capital*
Pub: John Wiley and Sons, Inc.

Ed: Amey Stone; Mike Brewster. **Released:** 2004. **Price:** $16.95. **Description:** Biography of Sandy Weill describes how he became a billionaire business giant by creating successful companies from smaller, sometimes failing firms; creating successful new products where none previously existed; and making deals no one thought possible. He is also responsible for changing the landscape of the banking industry and insurance business when he created Citigroup in 1998, the world's largest financial services firm.

12563 ■ *"The King of Kincardine"* in Canadian Business (Vol. 79, October 9, 2006, No. 20, pp. 101)
Pub: Rogers Media

Ed: Paul Webster. **Description:** Motives of Duncan Hawthorne, president and chief executive officer of Bruce Power Ltd., behind investing in nuclear power plant in Ontario, Canada through private financing are discussed.

12564 ■ *"Land on Boardwalk"* in Canadian Business (Vol. 82, April 27, 2009, No. 7, pp. 19)
Pub: Rogers Media

Ed: Calvin Leung. **Description:** Boardwalk REIT remains as one of the most attractive real estate investment trusts in Canada, with 73 percent of analysts rating the firm a Buy. Analyst Neil Downey believes that good management, as well as a good business model, makes Boardwalk a good investment. Downey is concerned however, that a worsening of Alberta's economy could significantly impact Boardwalk.

12565 ■ *"The Last Ingredient?"* in Canadian Business (Vol. 81, October 13, 2008, No. 17, pp. 88)
Pub: Rogers Media Ltd.

Ed: Rachel Pulfer. **Description:** Views and information on Cookie Jar Group's plan to acquire rights for Strawberry Shortcake and the Care Bears are discussed. The move would make Cookie Jar a major player in the global children's entertainment market. Cookie Jar chief executive, Michael Hirsh is believed to be securing funds for the planned $195 million acquisition.

12566 ■ *"The Latin Beat Goes On"* in Barron's (Vol. 88, July 7, 2008, No. 27, pp. L5)
Pub: Dow Jones & Co., Inc.

Ed: Tom Sullivan. **Description:** Latin American stocks have outperformed other regional markets due to rising commodities prices and favorable economic climate. Countries such as Brazil, Mexico, Chile, and Peru provide investment opportunities, while Argentina and Venezuela are tougher places to invest.

12567 ■ *"Laugh or Cry?"* in Barron's (Vol. 88, March 24, 2008, No. 12, pp. 7)
Pub: Dow Jones & Company, Inc.

Ed: Alan Abelson. **Description:** Discusses the American economy which is just starting to feel the effect of the credit and housing crises. JPMorgan Chase purchased Bear Stearns for $2 a share, much lower than its share price of $60, while quasi-government entities Fannie Mae and Freddie Mac are starting to run into trouble.

12568 ■ *"Leaders and Lagards"* in Barron's (Vol. 89, July 13, 2009, No. 28, pp. 14)
Pub: Dow Jones & Co., Inc.

Ed: J.R. Brandstrader. **Description:** Statistical table that shows the returns of different mutual funds in different categories that include U.S. stock funds, sector funds, world equity funds, and mixed equity funds is presented. The data presented is for the second quarter of 2009.

12569 ■ *"Leaders and Lagards"* in Barron's (Vol. 89, July 13, 2009, No. 28, pp. 14)
Pub: Dow Jones & Co., Inc.

Ed: J.R. Brandstrader. **Description:** Statistical table that shows the returns of different mutual funds in different categories that include U.S. stock funds, sector funds, world equity funds, and mixed equity funds is presented. The data presented is for the second quarter of 2009.

12570 ■ *"Leaders Weigh In On Fannie Mae, Freddie Mac Failure, Fed Bailout"* in The Business Journal - Serving Phoenix and the Valley of the Sun (Vol. 28, September 12, 2008, No. 53, pp. 1)
Pub: American City Business Journals, Inc.

Ed: Chris Casacchia; Mike Sunnucks; Jan Buchholz. **Description:** Fannie Mae and Freddie Mac's federal takeover was a move to help stabilize the financial market and it helped bring down interest rates in the past week. Local executives from Arizona's Phoenix area share their thoughts on the immediate effect of the takeover and its upside and downside.

12571 ■ *"Lean on Me"* in Entrepreneur (Vol. 36, February 2008, No. 2, pp. 40)
Pub: Entrepreneur Media Inc.

Ed: Farnoosh Torabi. **Description:** Investing in tax liens is booming with the growth in the number of homeowners missing property tax payments. Details on how to bid for and when to redeem tax liens are outlined.

12572 ■ *"Leasing Midway; Look for Higher Parking Fees, More Retail Under Private Airport Operator"* in Crain's Chicago Business (May 5, 2008)
Pub: Crain Communications, Inc.

Ed: Paul Merrion. **Description:** According to experts, bids for the first privatization of a major U.S. airport could run as high as $3.5 billion. Information-gathering and negotiations will soon get under way with some or all of the six major international investor groups that recently expressed interest in running Midway.

12573 ■ *"Legg's Compensation Committee Chair Defends CEO Fetting's Pay"* in Boston Business Journal (Vol. 29, July 22, 2011, No. 11, pp. 1)
Pub: American City Business Journals Inc.

Ed: Gary Haber. **Description:** Legg Mason Inc. CEO Mark R. Fetting has been awarded $5.9 million pay package and he expects to receive questions regarding it in the coming shareholders meeting. However, Baltimore, Maryland-based RKTL Associates chairman emeritus Harold R. Adams believes Fetting has done a tremendous job in bringing Legg's through a tough market.

12574 ■ *"Lehman's Hail Mary Pass"* in Business Week (September 22, 2008, No. 4100, pp. 28)
Pub: McGraw-Hill Companies, Inc.

Ed: Matthew Goldstein; David Henry; Ben Levison. **Description:** Overview of Lehman Brothers' CEO Richard Fuld's plan to keep the firm afloat and end the stock's plunge downward; Fuld's strategy calls for selling off a piece of the firm's investment management business.

12575 ■ *"Lenders"* in The Business Journal - Serving Phoenix and the Valley of the Sun (Vol. 28, July 25, 2008, No. 47, pp. 1)
Pub: American City Business Journals, Inc.

Ed: Jan Buchholz. **Description:** Private equity lender Investor Mortgage Holdings Inc. has continued growing despite the crisis surrounding the real estate and financial industries and has accumulated a $700 million loan portfolio. Private lending has become increasingly important in financing real estate deals as commercial credit has dried up.

12576 ■ *"Lenders Capitalize on a Thinning Bulge Bracket"* in Mergers & Acquisitions: The Dealmaker's Journal (March 1, 2008)
Pub: SourceMedia, Inc.

Description: Regardless of what the economic markets look like, private equity firms will continue to invest capital and mid-market finance firms are becoming very attractive acquisition opportunities since not as much capital is needed to buy them.

12577 ■ *"Lending Idea Gets Mixed Review"* in Tampa Bay Business Journal (Vol. 29, October 30, 2009, No. 45, pp. 1)
Pub: American City Business Journals

Ed: Kent Hoover, Margie Manning. **Description:** Tampa Bay area, Florida's community banks have expressed disapproval to the proposal of President

Obama to increase lending to small business, wherein the government will provide cheap capital through US Treasury Troubled Asset Relief Program (TARP). The banks were hesitant on the plan because of the strings attached to TARP.

12578 ■ "Less Malaise in Malaysia" in Barron's (Vol. 88, March 17, 2008, No. 11, pp. M12)
Pub: Dow Jones & Company, Inc.

Ed: Assif Shameen. **Description:** Shares of Malaysia's Bursa have been in freefall while the Malaysia government prolongs its pitch to sell a 10 percent stake of the exchange to NYSE Euronext. Asian bourses had produced very good returns for five years and charge some of the highest fees for exchanges. A key growth driver for Asian bourses could be the derivatives markets and exchange-traded funds.

12579 ■ "Let Us Count the Ways" in Barron's (Vol. 88, July 7, 2008, No. 27, pp. M10)
Pub: Dow Jones & Co., Inc.

Ed: Bennet Sedacca. **Description:** Investors are advised to remain cautious after the drop in stock prices in June 2008. The stock markets remain in the downtrend after reaching a peak in October 2007 and are on the verge of a collapse.

12580 ■ Let's Buy a Company: How to Accelerate Growth Through Acquisitions
Pub: Career Press, Incorporated

Ed: H. Lee Rust. **Released:** January 2006. **Price:** $18.99 (US), $25.95 (Canadian). **Description:** Advice for negotiating terms and pricing as well as other aspects of mergers and acquisitions in small companies.

12581 ■ "Lifebank Grants Stock Options" in Canadian Corporate News (May 16, 2007)
Pub: Comtex News Network Inc.

Description: Lifebank, a biomedical service company that provides processing cryogenic storage of umbilical cord blood stem cells, announced that, under its stock option plan, it has granted incentive stock options to directors, officers, and consultants of the company.

12582 ■ "A Lifetime of Making Deals" in Crain's Detroit Business (Vol. 24, March 24, 2008, No. 12, pp. 11)
Pub: Crain Communications, Inc.

Ed: Tom Henderson. **Description:** Profile of Walter 'Bud' Aspatore who received Crain's Lifetime Achievement Award for mergers and acquisitions; Aspatore is chairman and co-founder of Amherst Partners L.L.C., an investment banking firm that does evaluations and financings, specializes in turnarounds and advises private and public companies on mergers and acquisitions.

12583 ■ "Lifetime Planning with a Twist" in Contractor (Vol. 56, July 2009, No. 7, pp. 40)
Pub: Penton Media, Inc.

Ed: Irv Blackman. **Description:** Private Placement Life Insurance lets wealthy investors make their investment gains tax-free and can be set up so investors can make tax-free loans from the policy. This can be used on a younger member of the family as a wealth-building strategy if the investor is uninsurable.

12584 ■ "A Limited Sphere of Influence" in Mergers & Acquisitions: The Dealmaker's Journal (March 1, 2008)
Pub: SourceMedia, Inc.

Ed: Ken MacFadyen. **Description:** Changes to the interest rate has had little impact on the mergers and acquisitions market since the federal funds rate does not link directly to the liquidity available to the M&A market; lenders are looking at cash flows and are likely to remain cautious due to other factors impacting the market.

12585 ■ "Listen to Bond Market on Tembec" in Globe & Mail (January 25, 2006, pp. B1)
Pub: CTVglobemedia Publishing Inc.

Ed: Derek DeCloet. **Description:** The feasibility of Tembec Inc.'s restructuring efforts is discussed.

12586 ■ "Listen Up: There's a Revolution in the Cubicle" in Barron's (Vol. 89, July 27, 2009, No. 30, pp. 18)
Pub: Dow Jones & Co., Inc.

Ed: Jay Palmer. **Description:** Plantronics will be among the first beneficiaries when the unified communications revolution arrives in the office. Plantronics' shares could rise to around 30 in 2009 from the 20s as of July 2009. Unified communications could create a huge new multimillion-dollar market for Plantronics.

12587 ■ "The Little Biotech that Could" in Barron's (Vol. 89, July 27, 2009, No. 30, pp. 19)
Pub: Dow Jones & Co., Inc.

Ed: Christopher C. Williams. **Description:** OSI Pharmaceuticals' shares is a compelling investment bet among small biotech firms due to its Tarceva anticancer drug which has a 23 percent market share as well as their strong balance sheet. OSI is planning to expand the use of Tarceva which could re-ignite sales and one analyst expects the shares to trade in the 40s one year from July 2009.

12588 ■ "A Load of Bull?" in Canadian Business (Vol. 82, Summer 2009, No. 8, pp. 12)
Pub: Rogers Media

Ed: Joe Castaldo. **Description:** Some experts and analysts believe that the improvement of some economic indicators in Canada suggest an economic recovery. A survey of Russell Investment in March 2009 found that 60 percent of investment managers are bullish on Canadian stocks. Some experts like Mike Zyblock, however, remain cautious on the economy.

12589 ■ "Loblaw Posts 40 Percent Profit Drop as it Scrambles to Lower Costs" in Globe & Mail (February 9, 2006, pp. B1)
Pub: CTVglobemedia Publishing Inc.

Ed: Marina Strauss. **Description:** The reasons behind 40 percent decline in profits for Lobalaw Companies Ltd., for fourth quarter 2005, are presented.

12590 ■ "A Local Affair: Decisions for Tops Again Being Made at Amherst HQ" in Business First Buffalo (December 7, 2007, pp. 3)
Pub: American City Business Journals, Inc.

Ed: James Fink. **Description:** Tops Market LLC merged with Morgan Stanley Private Equity and names its new CEO, Frank Curci. The company headquarters moved to its new location in Amherst, New York.

12591 ■ "Local Firms Will Feel Impact Of Wall St. Woes" in The Business Journal-Milwaukee (Vol. 25, September 19, 2008, No. 52, pp. A1)
Pub: American City Business Journals, Inc.

Ed: Rich Kirchen. **Description:** Wall Street's crisis is expected to affect businesses in Wisconsin, in terms of decreased demand for services and products and increased financing costs. Businesses in Milwaukee area may face higher interest rates and tougher loan standards. The potential impacts of the Wall Street crisis on local businesses are examined further.

12592 ■ "Local TV Hits Media Radar Screen" in Business Courier (Vol. 27, July 2, 2010, No. 9, pp. 1)
Pub: Business Courier

Ed: Dan Monk. **Description:** Fort Wright, Kentucky-based broadcasting company Local TV LLC has acquired 18 television stations since its founding in 2007, potentially boosting its chances of becoming a media empire. In the last twelve months that ended in March 2010, Local TV LLC has posted total revenues of $415 million. How Local TV LLC has entered into cost-sharing deals with other stations is also discussed.

12593 ■ "Locally Based Stocks Escape Worst of Market's Turmoil" in Crain's Detroit

Business (Vol. 24, September 22, 2008, No. 38, pp. 4)
Pub: Crain Communications Inc.

Ed: Daniel Duggan. **Description:** Locally-based companies did not take as big a hit as might be expected with the shock to the financial markets last week; this is due mainly to the fact that the region does not have heavy exposure to energy or capital markets.

12594 ■ "Long - And Leery" in Barron's (Vol. 88, March 31, 2008, No. 13, pp. 47)
Pub: Dow Jones & Company, Inc.

Ed: Jack Willoughby. **Description:** Tom Claugus' Bay Resource Partners hedge fund has returned 20 percent annually since it started in 1993. Claugus says that he is as aggressively long as he has ever been despite the dangers of the U.S. market. Claugus' stock picks include Canadian Natural Resources, NII Holdings, and Discover Financial.

12595 ■ "A Look Ahead Into 2007" in Canadian Business (Vol. 80, December 25, 2006, No. 1, pp. 40)
Pub: Rogers Media

Description: The 2007 forecasts for various industrial sectors like telecom, information technology, manufacturing, retail, financial and energy among others is discussed.

12596 ■ "Looking For Financing?" in Hispanic Business (Vol. 30, July-August 2008, No. 7-8, pp. 16)
Pub: Hispanic Business, Inc.

Ed: Frank Nelson. **Description:** Investment firms want to know about businesses that need funding for either expansion or acquisition; companies fitting this profile are interviewed and their perceptions are discussed. Investment firms need businesses to be realistic in their expectations and business plans which show spending of funds and expected benefits, long term goals, track record and strong management teams.

12597 ■ "Looking For Good Buys" in Black Enterprise (Vol. 38, November 2007, No. 4, pp. 39)
Pub: Earl G. Graves Publishing Co. Inc.

Ed: Steve Garmhausen. **Description:** Lower interest rates mean consumers generally have more money to spend, which could spur economic growth in the retail sector of the U.S.

12598 ■ "Loonie Tunes: When Will the Dollar Rise Again?" in Canadian Business (Vol. 81, November 10, 2008, No. 19, pp. 62)
Pub: Rogers Media Ltd.

Ed: Joe Castaldo. **Description:** The Canadian dollar has weakened against the U.S. Dollar as the U.S. financial crisis rocked global markets. A currency strategist says that the strength of the U.S. dollar is not based on people's optimism on the U.S. economy but on a structural demand where U.S. non-financial corporations have been repatriating greenbacks from foreign subsidiaries.

12599 ■ "Lotus Starts Slowly, Dodges Subprime Woes" in Crain's Detroit Business (Vol. 24, April 14, 2008, No. 15, pp. 3)
Pub: Crain Communications, Inc.

Ed: Tom Henderson. **Description:** Discusses Lotus Bancorp Inc. and their business plan, which although is not right on target due to the subprime mortgage meltdown, is in a much better position than its competitors due to the quality of their loans.

12600 ■ "Lower Prices No Shoo-In as Telcos Near Deregulation" in Globe & Mail (March 28, 2007, pp. B1)
Pub: CTVglobemedia Publishing Inc.

Ed: Catherine McLean. **Description:** The fall in market share and low quality of service among other issues that may disallow telecommunication industries in Canada from setting their phone rates is discussed.

12601 ■ *"Loyalty Pays" in Entrepreneur (Vol. 36, February 2008, No. 2, pp. 63)*

Pub: Entrepreneur Media Inc.

Ed: David Worrell. **Description:** Michael Vadini, chief executive officer of Titan Technology Partners looks after his stockholders and investors by making sure that they are protected from risk. Having been affected by the downturn in the technology industry between 2001 and 2004, Vadini granted his investors a liquidity preference. Details regarding his actions to retain investor loyalty are discussed.

12602 ■ *"Lundin Deal Leaves Nickel Market Thin" in Globe & Mail (April 5, 2007, pp. B4)*

Pub: CTVglobemedia Publishing Inc.

Ed: Andy Hoffman. **Description:** The likely acquisition of Rio Narcea Gold Mines Ltd. by Lundin Mining Corp. and the decreasing number of nickel mining companies on the list of Toronto Stock Exchange are discussed.

12603 ■ *"Luster Lost" in Saint Louis Business Journal (Vol. 32, September 16, 2011, No. 3, pp. 1)*

Pub: Saint Louis Business Journal

Ed: E.B. Solomont. **Description:** Express Cripts shares have plunged 22.71 percent since late July amid regulatory concerns, as the luster of the second-largest deal announced for 2011 wore off. Express Scripts has become the largest pharmacy benefit manager in the country after the $29 billion deal to take rival Medco Health Solutions.

12604 ■ *"Lux Coffees, Breads Push Chains to React" in Advertising Age (Vol. 77, June 26, 2006, No. 26, pp. S14)*

Pub: Crain Communications, Inc.

Ed: Kate MacArthur. **Description:** Fast-food giants such as McDonald's, Burger King, Dunkin' Donuts and Subway have adjusted their menus in order to become more competitive with gourmet coffee shops and bakeries like Panera Bread and Starbucks which have taken a large share in the market. Statistical data included.

12605 ■ *"Magna Banks on Big Cash Hoard" in Globe & Mail (March 1, 2006, pp. B3)*

Pub: CTVglobemedia Publishing Inc.

Ed: Greg Keenan. **Description:** The details on Magna International Inc., which posted decline in profits at $639 million for 2005, are presented.

12606 ■ *"Magna Shares Sink on Tepid Outlook" in Globe & Mail (January 13, 2006, pp. B1)*

Pub: CTVglobemedia Publishing Inc.

Ed: Greg Keenan. **Description:** The impact of Magna International Inc.'s sales projection for 2006, on its shares, is discussed.

12607 ■ *"Making It Click" in Barron's (Vol. 88, March 17, 2008, No. 11, pp. 31)*

Pub: Dow Jones & Company, Inc.

Ed: Theresa W. Carey. **Description:** Listing of 23 online brokers that are evaluated based on their trade experience, usability, range of offerings, research amenities, customer service and access, and costs. TradeStation Securities takes the top spot followed by thinkorswim by just a fraction.

12608 ■ *"M&I Execs May Get Golden Parachutes" in Business Journal-Milwaukee (Vol. 28, December 31, 2010, No. 14, pp. A3)*

Pub: Milwaukee Business Journal

Ed: Rich Kirchen. **Description:** Marshall and Isley Corporation's top executives have a chance to receive golden-parachute payments it its buyer, BMO Financial Group, repays the Troubled Asset Relief Program (TARP) loan on behalf of the company. One TARP rule prevents golden-parachute payments to them and the next five most highly paid employees of TARP recipients.

12609 ■ *"M&T On the March?" in Baltimore Business Journal (Vol. 28, November 12, 2010, No. 27, pp. 1)*

Pub: Baltimore Business Journal

Ed: Gary Haber. **Description:** Information on the growth of M&T Bank, as well as its expansion plans are presented. M&T recently acquired Wilmington

Trust and took over $500 million in deposits from the failed K Bank. Analysts believe that M&T would continue its expansion through Washington DC and Richmond, Virginia, especially after a bank executive acknowledged that the markets in those areas are attractive.

12610 ■ *"Many Roads Lead to Value" in Barron's (Vol. 88, March 10, 2008, No. 10, pp. 46)*

Pub: Dow Jones & Company, Inc.

Ed: Lawrence C. Strauss. **Description:** David J. Williams, lead manager of Excelsior Value & Restructuring Fund, invests in struggling companies and those companies whose turnarounds show promise. Morgan Stanley, Lehman Brothers, and Petroleo Brasileiro are some of the companies he holds shares in, while he has unloaded shares of Citigroup, Freddie Mac, and Sallie Mae.

12611 ■ *"Market Recoups Its Losses - And Its Optimism" in Barron's (Vol. 89, July 20, 2009, No. 29, pp. M3)*

Pub: Dow Jones & Co., Inc.

Ed: Kopin Tan. **Description:** US stock markets gained heavily in the third week of July 2009, rising by about 7 percent during the week. The shares of human resource management companies could be overpriced as they are trading at very high price-earnings multiples. Baxter International faces a class-action suit due to its alleged conspiracy with CSL to fix blood-plasma product prices.

12612 ■ *"Market Volatility and Your Retirement" in Agency Sales Magazine (Vol. 39, August 2009, No. 8, pp. 48)*

Pub: MANA

Ed: Joshua D. Mosshart. **Description:** Strategies for retirees in managing investments amid market volatility are presented. Retirees should keep their withdrawal assumptions conservative, maintain sensible asset allocation, review and rebalance their portfolio and allow a financial professional to guide them. Insights on market volatility are also given.

12613 ■ *"Market Watch" in Barron's (Vol. 88, March 24, 2008, No. 12, pp. M18)*

Pub: Dow Jones & Company, Inc.

Ed: Ashraf Laidi; Marc Pado; David Kotok. **Description:** Latest measures implemented by the Federal Reserve to address the credit crisis did not benefit the US dollar, with the Japanese yen and the euro recouping earlier losses against the dollar. Goldman Sachs reported earnings of $3.23 per share, claiming a stronger liquidity position. The US markets bottomed early on 22 January 2007, according to evidence.

12614 ■ *"Market Watch" in Barron's (Vol. 89, July 20, 2009, No. 29, pp. M10)*

Pub: Dow Jones & Co., Inc.

Ed: Peter Greene; Michael Darda; Ian Wyatt; Stephanie Pomboy. **Description:** Concerns about a possible increase in US inflation rates are overblown as the country remains in a deflationary environment. Goldman Sachs's second quarter 2009 earnings have already been priced in as its shares rose. Germany's plans of a possible dollar bond sale are in anticipation of a rise in the euro's value.

12615 ■ *"Market Watch: A Sampling of Advisory Opinion" in Barron's (Vol. 88, March 17, 2008, No. 11, pp. M10)*

Pub: Dow Jones & Company, Inc.

Ed: Paul Schatz; William Gibson; Michael Darda. **Description:** S&P 500 bank stocks were down 46 percent from their 2007 peak while the peak to through fall in 1989-1990 was just over 50 percent. This suggests that the bottom on the bank stocks could be near. The Federal Reserve Board announced they will lend up to $200 billion to primary lenders in exchange other securities.

12616 ■ *"Markets Defy the Doomsayers" in Barron's (Vol. 88, March 24, 2008, No. 12, pp. M5)*

Pub: Dow Jones & Company, Inc.

Ed: Leslie P. Norton. **Description:** US stock markets registered strong gains, with the Dow Jones Industrial Average rising 3.43 percent on the week to close at

12,361.32, in a rally that may be seen as short-covering. Shares of Hansen Natural are poised for further drops with a slowdown in the energy drink market.

12617 ■ *"Markets in Disarray..Fundamentals Still Strong?" in Hispanic Business (October 2007, pp. 14, 16, 18)*

Pub: Hispanic Business

Ed: Dr. Juan B. Solana. **Description:** Quarterly economic forecast is presented, covering credit, interest rates, home prices, stock market, and what lies ahead.

12618 ■ *"The Market's (Very) Tender Spring Shoots" in Barron's (Vol. 88, March 31, 2008, No. 13, pp. M3)*

Pub: Dow Jones & Company, Inc.

Ed: Kopin Tan. **Description:** Expansion in price-earnings multiples and a lower credit-default risk index has encouraged fans of the spring-awakening theory. Shares of industrial truckers have gone up 32 percent in 2008 and some shares are pushing five-year highs brought on by higher efficiency and earnings from more load carried. The prospects of the shares of Foot Locker are also discussed.

12619 ■ *The Match King: Ivar Kreuger, the Financial Genius Behind a Century of Wall Street Scandals*

Pub: Basic Books

Ed: Frank Portnoy. **Released:** 2009. **Price:** $26.95. **Description:** Ivar Kreuger, the so-called Match King, used a pyramid scheme to become the financier to European leaders.

12620 ■ *"Meadowbrook CEO Sees 20 Percent Growth With New Acquisition" in Crain's Detroit Business (Vol. 24, March 10, 2008, No. 10, pp. 4)*

Pub: Crain Communications, Inc.

Ed: Jay Greene. **Description:** Discusses the major turnaround of Meadowbrook Insurance Group after Robert Cubbin became CEO and implemented a new business strategy.

12621 ■ *"Meadowbrook To Acquire ProCentury in $272.6 Million Deal" in Crain's Detroit Business (Vol. 24, February 25, 2008, No. 8, pp. 4)*

Pub: Crain Communications Inc. - Detroit

Description: Meadowbrook Insurance Group, based in Southfield, Michigan reports its proposed acquisition of ProCentury Corporation based in Columbus, Ohio. Meadowbrook provides risk-management to agencies, professional and trade associations and small-to-midsize businesses.

12622 ■ *"Media Industry Collection Agency Completes Acquisition" in Collections & Credit Risk (Vol. 15, December 1, 2010, No. 11, pp. 22)*

Pub: SourceMedia Inc.

Description: Media Receivable Management Inc. (MRM) will take over the collection operations at Borden, Jones & Mitchell, in Miami, Florida. MRM clients are basically magazine and electronic media publishers.

12623 ■ *"The Medium 150" in Canadian Business (Vol. 81, Summer 2008, No. 9, pp. 129)*

Pub: Rogers Media Ltd.

Description: Medium-sized companies are ranked based on market capitalization and stock performance. Timminico Ltd. topped the roster with 1,294.2 percent returns, while Petrominerales Ltd. ranked second with 325.4 percent. A table showing the 2008 rankings of the companies is presented.

12624 ■ *Medium Sized Firms and Economics Growth*

Pub: Nova Science Publishers, Incorporated

Ed: Janez Prasniker. **Released:** April 2005. **Price:** $130.00. **Description:** Medium sized companies should have a more definitive presence in modern microeconomic theory, the theory of entrepreneurship, and the theory of financial markets.

12625 ■ *"Meet the Gatekeepers"* in Crain's Chicago Business (Vol. 30, February 2007, No. 6, pp. 40)
Pub: Crain Communications, Inc.
Ed: Kate Ryan. **Description:** Recruiters at big investment banking firms agree that the way to get your foot in the door requires common sense issues such as not answering your phone in the middle of an interview, proofreading your cover letter, and research. Interviews with three top executives give more insight and advice.

12626 ■ *"Merger Brings New Force to Hispanic Marketing Industry"* in Hispanic Business (July-August 2007, pp. 60)
Pub: Hispanic Business
Description: Merger between Latin Force LLC, a marketing strategy firm and Geoscape International Inc., a consumer intelligence and data analytics company is discussed.

12627 ■ *Mergers and Acquisitions from A to Z*
Pub: Amacom
Ed: Andrew J. Sherman, Milledge A. Hart. **Released:** January 2006. **Price:** $35.00. **Description:** Guide for the entire process of mergers and acquisitions, including taxes, accounting, laws, and projected financial gain.

12628 ■ *"Mettle Detector"* in Canadian Business (Vol. 79, July 17, 2006, No. 14-15, pp. 63)
Pub: Rogers Media
Ed: Calvin Leung. **Description:** The difficulties faced in completing the Certified Financial Analyst course, and the rewards one can expect after its completion, are discussed.

12629 ■ *"MF Global Moved Clients' Funds to BNY Mellon"* in Wall Street Journal Eastern Edition (November 19 , 2011, pp. B2)
Pub: Dow Jones & Company Inc.
Ed: Aaron Lucchetti. **Description:** Since the collapse of securities brokerage MF Global Holdings Ltd., one question has remained: where did the hundreds of millions of dollars in customers' accounts go? It has been revealed that MF Global moved those millions from its own brokerage unit to Bank of New York Mellon Corporation in August of this year, just two months before filing for bankruptcy protection.

12630 ■ *"MFS Survey: Generation X/Y Perplexed and Conservative about Future Investing"* in Wireless News (November 16, 2010)
Pub: Close-Up Media Inc.
Description: Generation X and Y tend to have a conservative approach to investing according to a survey conducted by MFS Investment Management. Statistical data included.

12631 ■ *"Micro-Cap Companies"* in Canadian Business (Vol. 81, Summer 2008, No. 9, pp. 157)
Pub: Rogers Media Ltd.
Description: Micro-cap companies have lower than $221 million in terms of market capitalization. Burnaby, British Columbia-based Fancamp Exploration Ltd. topped the roster with 1,116.7 percent in return. A table showing the 2008 rankings of the companies is presented.

12632 ■ *"Microsoft Goes Macrosoft"* in Barron's (Vol. 89, July 27, 2009, No. 30, pp. 25)
Pub: Dow Jones & Co., Inc.
Ed: Mark Veverka. **Description:** Microsoft reported a weak quarter on the heels of a tech rally which suggests the economy has not turned around. Marc Andreesen describes his new venture-capital fund as focused on 'classic tech' and that historical reference places him in the annals of the last millennium.

12633 ■ *"Microsoft's Big Gamble"* in Canadian Business (Vol. 81, March 3, 2008, No. 3, pp. 13)
Pub: Rogers Media
Ed: Andrew Wahl. **Description:** Microsoft Corp. is taking a big risk in buying Yahoo, as it is expected to pay more than $31 a share to finalize the acquisition.

The deal would be seven and a half times bigger than any other that Microsoft has entered before, an execution of such deal is also anticipated to become a challenge for Microsoft. Recommendations on how Microsoft should handle the integration of the two businesses are given.

12634 ■ *"Millions Needed To Finish First Place"* in The Business Journal-Milwaukee (Vol. 25, August 15, 2008, No. 47, pp. A1)
Pub: American City Business Journals, Inc.
Ed: Rich Kirchen. **Description:** First Place on the River condominium project in Milwaukee, Wisconsin, needs $18.2 million before it can be completed. A total of $6.8 million have already been spent since the project went into receivership on 31 January 2008.

12635 ■ *"Mine Woes Could Rouse Zinc"* in Barron's (Vol. 88, July 7, 2008, No. 27, pp. M12)
Pub: Dow Jones & Co., Inc.
Ed: Andrea Hotter. **Description:** Prices of zinc could increase due to supply problems in producing countries such as Australia and China. London Metal Exchange prices for the metal have dropped about 36 percent in 2008.

12636 ■ *"Mining Executive Telfer Pocketed Millions"* in Globe & Mail (April 5, 2007, pp. B4)
Pub: CTVglobemedia Publishing Inc.
Ed: Andy Hoffman. **Description:** The issue of huge compensation for former executive of both Goldcorp Inc. and UrAsia Energy Ltd., Ian Telfer, for his efficient management of stock options is discussed.

12637 ■ *"Mining Goldman for Insight"* in Barron's (Vol. 89, July 20, 2009, No. 29, pp. M8)
Pub: Dow Jones & Co., Inc.
Ed: Steven M. Sears. **Description:** Methods of investing in options for companies with earnings estimates from Goldman Sachs are discussed. These methods take advantage of increased volatility generated by earnings revisions.

12638 ■ *"Minor-League Baseball's Sliders Plan Stock Offering"* in Crain's Detroit Business (Vol. 25, June 15, 2009, No. 24, pp. 3)
Pub: Crain Communications Inc. - Detroit
Ed: Bill Shea. **Description:** New minor-league baseball team is raising funds to build a new stadium in Waterford Township, Michigan because banks are unwilling to provide loans for the project. Owners of the Midwest Sliders in Ypsilanti, Michigan are waiting for the federal Securities and Exchange Commission to approve a Regulation A public offering.

12639 ■ *"Misguided"* in Canadian Business (Vol. 81, July 22, 2008, No. 12-13, pp. 30)
Pub: Rogers Media Ltd.
Ed: Al Rosen. **Description:** Canada's securities regulations are discussed; differing views on using principles-based and rules-based securities regulations are also presented.

12640 ■ *"Misplaced Trust"* in Canadian Business (Vol. 79, October 23, 2006, No. 21, pp. 65)
Pub: Rogers Media
Ed: John Gray. **Description:** The reasons for the drop in the share prices of the income trusts of Retrocom Investment Management Inc. are analyzed.

12641 ■ *"Missing MF Global Funds Could Top $1.2 Billion"* in Wall Street Journal Eastern Edition (November 22 , 2011, pp. A1)
Pub: Dow Jones & Company Inc.
Ed: Aaron Lucchetti, Dan Strumpf. **Description:** As the investigation into the collapse of securities brokerage MF Global Holdings Ltd. continues, the question of what happened to customers' funds has to be answered. Now, it is believed that the actual amount of missing funds is much more than the $600 million originally thought, and could be well over $1.2 billion.

12642 ■ *"A Mixed-Bag Quarter"* in Barron's (Vol. 88, July 7, 2008, No. 27, pp. 19)
Pub: Dow Jones & Co., Inc.
Ed: Shirley A. Lazo. **Description:** Seven component companies of the Dow Jones Industrial Average increased their dividend payouts in the second quarter of 2008 despite the weak performance of the index. Five companies in the Dow Jones Transportation index and three in the Dow Jones Utilities also increased their dividends.

12643 ■ *"Modern-Day Midas Hasn't Lost Touch"* in Globe & Mail (January 19, 2006, pp. B4)
Pub: CTVglobemedia Publishing Inc.
Ed: Shirley Won. **Description:** The investment plans of chief executive officer Rob McEwen of U.S. Gold Corp. are presented.

12644 ■ *"Molson Coors Ends Ill-Fated Foray Into Brazil"* in Globe & Mail (January 17, 2006, pp. B1)
Pub: CTVglobemedia Publishing Inc.
Ed: Andy Hoffman. **Description:** The details of loss incurred by Molson Coors Brewing Co., from the sale of Cervejarias Kaiser SA to Fomento Economico Mexicano S.A. de C.V., are presented.

12645 ■ *"Molycorp Funds Wind Energy Technology Company"* in Manufacturing Close-Up (September 19, 2011)
Pub: Close-Up Media
Description: Molycorp Inc., producer of rare earth oxides (REO) and a REO producer outside of China, announced it will invest in Boulder Wind Power, which has designed a rare earth magnet powered wind turbine generator. This new generator can produce electricity as low as $0.04 per Kilowatt Hour. Boulder Wind Power's patented wind turbine technology allows for use of rare earth permanent magnets that do not require dysprosium, which is relatively scarce.

12646 ■ *"Moms Mull Money"* in Marketing to Women (Vol. 21, February 2008, No. 2, pp. 6)
Pub: EPM Communications Inc.
Contact: Ira Mayer, President
E-mail: imayer@epmcom.com
Description: According to a survey by Countrywide Bank, women, especially mothers, are more concerned about their financial fitness than men.

12647 ■ *"Money Man"* in Canadian Business (Vol. 80, January 15, 2007, No. 2, pp. 67)
Pub: Rogers Media
Ed: Jeff Sanford. **Description:** A profile of Donald A. Guloien, chief investment officer of Manulife Financial and chief executive officer of Global Investment Management, is presented.

12648 ■ *"Monsanto Acquires Targeted-Pest Control Technology Start-Up; Terms Not Disclosed"* in Benzinga.com (, 2011)
Pub: Benzinga.com
Ed: Benzinga Staff. **Description:** Monsanto Company acquired Beelogics, a firm that researches and develops biological tools that control pests and diseases. Research includes a product that will help protect bee health.

12649 ■ *"Montreal Exchange Buoyed by U.S. Takeover Moves"* in Globe & Mail (March 16, 2007, pp. B1)
Pub: CTVglobemedia Publishing Inc.
Ed: Sinclair Stewart. **Description:** The rise in the share prices of Montreal Exchange due to the derivatives exchange's bid to acquire the Chicago Board of Trade is discussed. The trends pertaining to the consolidation of global stock markets are described.

12650 ■ *"Moody and Paranoid"* in Barron's (Vol. 88, March 10, 2008, No. 10, pp. M14)
Pub: Dow Jones & Company, Inc.
Ed: Steven M. Sears. **Description:** Discusses the options market which remains liquid but is cautious of possible failures, especially for financial companies. Investors are in absolute fear when trading with options involving the financial sector.

12651 ■ *"More Gains in the Pipeline"* in *Barron's (Vol. 89, August 3, 2009, No. 31, pp. M5)*

Pub: Dow Jones & Co., Inc.

Ed: Fleming Meeks. **Description:** Shares of El Paso Corp. could recover as the company concludes a deal with a private-equity group to fund pipeline construction. The company's shares are trading at $10.06 and could move up to $12 as bad news has already been priced into the stock.

12652 ■ *"More Jobs Moving Out of City"* in *Business Courier (Vol. 24, March 14, 2008, No. 49, pp. 1)*

Pub: American City Business Journals, Inc.

Ed: Steve Watkins; Laura Baverman. **Description:** UBS Financial Services Inc. is moving Gradison to Kenwood Town Place in Sycamore Township a year after UBS acquired Gradison. The township does not have a tax on earnings so the move will save Gradison's employees the 2.1 percent Cincinnati tax.

12653 ■ *"More Questions Face Huntington"* in *Business First-Columbus (December 7, 2007, pp. A3)*

Pub: American City Business Journals, Inc.

Ed: Adrian Burns. **Description:** Marty Adams' abrupt resignation has lead to speculation that he was dismissed by the bank in relation to the unexpected run-in with the subprime mortgage fiasco. Analysis predict Columbus-based Huntington Bancshares Inc. might be targeted for acquisition. Details on the company's revenues and shares of stock prices are presented.

12654 ■ *"Mortgage Mess Continues To Trigger Bids To Ease Crisis"* in *Business First-Columbus (December 14, 2007, pp. A1)*

Pub: American City Business Journals, Inc.

Ed: Adrian Burns. **Description:** Measures to prevent foreclosures in Ohio are presented. On December 6, 2007, the Bush Administration started a national incentive that will establish a streamlined process for modifying loans. Some have questioned the proposal, since it is expected the plan will only help about 90,000 of the 1.8 million borrowers. According to Ohio Treasurer, Richard Cordray, one of the state's objectives is to calm the markets on Wall Street.

12655 ■ *"Mortgage Mess: How To Determine Your Exposure To the Subprime Crisis"* in *Black Enterprise (Vol. 38, November 2007, No. 4, pp. 46)*

Pub: Earl G. Graves Publishing Co. Inc.

Ed: Ilana Polyak. **Description:** Stocks and mutual funds have experienced declines because of the subprime crisis. Morningstar's Website can help investors research firms in which they have invested; if a fund is named high yield or high income or in the financial services sector, investments will have greater exposure to the mess.

12656 ■ *"Mortgage Securities Drop Hits Home"* in *The Business Journal-Serving Metropolitan Kansas City (Vol. 27, October 17, 2008, No. 5)*

Pub: American City Business Journals, Inc.

Ed: Rob Roberts. **Description:** Sale of commercial mortgage-backed securities (CMBS) in Kansas City, Missouri have declined. The area may avoid layoffs if the United States government succeeds in stabilizing the economy. Major CMBS players in the area include Midland Loan Services Inc. and KeyBank Real Estate Capital.

12657 ■ *"A Motorola Spinoff Is No Panacea"* in *Barron's (Vol. 88, March 31, 2008, No. 13, pp. 19)*

Pub: Dow Jones & Company, Inc.

Ed: Mark Veverka. **Description:** Motorola's plan to try and spinoff their handset division is bereft of details as to how or specifically when in 2009 the spinoff would occur. There's no reason to buy the shares since there's a lot of execution risk to the plan. Motorola needs to hire a proven cellphone executive and develop a compelling new cellphone platform.

12658 ■ *"Move Marks KKR's Latest Push into Retail"* in *Globe & Mail (March 13, 2007, pp. B17)*

Pub: CTVglobemedia Publishing Inc.

Ed: Heather Burke. **Description:** Investment giant Kohlberg Kravis Roberts and Co. has finalized a deal to acquire retail store chain Dollar General Corp. for an estimated 6.9 billion dollars. The company will be entering lucrative retail market by this acquisition.

12659 ■ *"Mover and Sheika"* in *Conde Nast Portfolio (Vol. 2, June 2008, No. 6, pp. 104)*

Pub: Conde Nast Publications

Contact: David Carey, President

Ed: John Arlidge. **Description:** Profile of Princess Sheika Lubna who is the first female foreign trade minister in the Middle East, the United Arab Emirates biggest business envoy, paving the way for billions in new investment, and also a manufacturer of her own perfume line.

12660 ■ *"'Mr. CEO, Please Do Elaborate On Your Firm's Metrics"* in *Business Courier (Vol. 24, February 29, 2008, No. 47, pp. 1)*

Pub: American City Business Journals, Inc.

Ed: Jon Newberry. **Description:** Discusses a rogue caller who goes by the name of Joe Herrick, Steven Nissan and Joe Harris has joined in over a dozen conference calls, asking chief executive officers on their plans and commenting on the companies' operations. The mystery caller attempts to pass himself off as a financial analyst. Transcripts of some conference calls, in which the rogue caller is involved, are provided.

12661 ■ *"Mr. Deeds"* in *Canadian Business (Vol. 81, March 31, 2008, No. 5, pp. 24)*

Pub: Rogers Media

Ed: Thomas Watson. **Description:** Ron Sandler has the right experience to save Northern Rock PLC get through its liquidity problems. Sandler is known for saving Lloyd's of London in the mid-90's and he is not afraid to make enemies. Ron Sandler's assignment to help Northern Rock comes at a time when the health of the U.K. housing is not great.

12662 ■ *"MTI Faces Touch Choices"* in *The Business Review Albany (Vol. 35, April 4, 2008, No. 53, pp. 1)*

Pub: The Business Review

Ed: Richard A. D'Errico. **Description:** Mechanical Technology Inc.'s auditor, PricewaterhouseCoopers LLP is concerned about the company's limited current cash and its $105 million accumulated deficit. MTI has already sold 1.45 million of its PlugPower Inc. shares, but still considers to sell more of the Plug stock. The problems at MTI and the difficult decisions it has to face to solve them are examined.

12663 ■ *"Muddy Portfolio Raises a Question: Just What Is National City Worth?"* in *Crain's Detroit Business (Vol. 24, April 7, 2008, No. 14)*

Pub: Crain Communications, Inc.

Ed: Jay Miller. **Description:** National City Bank is looking at strategies to help it deal with its credit and loan problems which are reflected in its falling stock price. One possible solution is a merger with another bank, however most national banks are facing their own home-loan portfolio issues and may be unable to tackle another company's unresolved problems. Statistical data included.

12664 ■ *"The Murky Tale of a Failed Fund"* in *Globe & Mail (January 3, 2006, pp. B1)*

Pub: CTVglobemedia Publishing Inc.

Ed: Bertrand Marotte. **Description:** The opinions of chief executive officer John Xanthoudakis of Norshield Financial Group, on controversy surrounding the company's handling of investors' money, are presented.

12665 ■ *"Mutual Fund Sales of $23.4 Billion Best Since 2001"* in *Globe & Mail (January 5, 2006, pp. B3)*

Pub: CTVglobemedia Publishing Inc.

Ed: Omar El Akkad. **Description:** The details on $23.4 billion net sales of mutual fund sector, in Canada, are presented.

12666 ■ *"Myths of Deleveraging"* in *Barron's (Vol. 90, August 23, 2010, No. 34, pp. M14)*

Pub: Barron's Editorial & Corporate Headquarters

Ed: Gene Epstein. **Description:** The opposite is true against reports about deleveraging or the decrease in credit since inflation-adjusted-investment factories and equipment rose 7.8 percent in the first quarter of 2010. On consumer deleveraging, sales of homes through credit is weak but there is a trend towards more realistic homeownership and consumer spending on durable goods rose 8.8 percent.

12667 ■ *"Naked Investing"* in *Canadian Business (Vol. 80, January 15, 2007, No. 2, pp. 27)*

Pub: Rogers Media

Ed: Al Rosen. **Description:** The need for Canadian investors to learn important facts about income trusts before investing in them is discussed.

12668 ■ *"Nancy Hughes Anthony"* in *Canadian Business (Vol. 81, October 13, 2008, No. 17, pp. 104)*

Pub: Rogers Media Ltd.

Ed: Andy Holloway. **Description:** Profile of Nancy Hughes Anthony, who believes her experience operating large enterprises as a public servant helped her earn positions that ultimately brought her to her current position as chief executive and president of the Canadian Bankers Association. She also thinks there should be more public-private sector coordination within industries.

12669 ■ *"Nanoready?"* in *Entrepreneur (Vol. 36, May 2008, No. 5, pp. 20)*

Pub: Entrepreneur Media, Inc.

Ed: Andrea Cooper. **Description:** Experts predict that the medicine and energy sectors are among those that will see nanotechnology innovations in the coming years, and that nanotechnology will produce significant commercial value in new products. Some entrepreneurs are investing in nanotech and are partnering with universities. Details on nanotech funding concerns are discussed.

12670 ■ *"Nautilus Fights For Its Life"* in *Business Journal-Portland (Vol. 24, November 23, 2007, No. 38, pp. 1)*

Pub: American City Business Journals, Inc.

Ed: Matthew Kish. **Description:** Shareholders meeting will determine whether four members at Nautilus Inc. will be ousted and control given to New York firm Sherborne Investors LP. The decision on December 18, 2007 is crucial since the investor's record is varied. For some it has significantly increased shares, while others have ended in near-bankruptcy stages.

12671 ■ *"Need Grub? Start Texting at Kroger"* in *Business Courier (Vol. 24, December 21, 2008, No. 36, pp. 1)*

Pub: American City Business Journals, Inc.

Ed: Laura Baverman. **Description:** Discusses the University of Cincinnati which is teaming up to release a technology platform called Macopay that would link a cell phone to a bank account and allow a person to make payments at participating retailers by sending a text message. Details with regard to the new service and its growth potential are discussed.

12672 ■ *"Needed: A Strategy; Banking In China"* in *The Economist (Vol. 390, January 3, 2009, No. 8612, pp. 54)*

Pub: The Economist Newspaper Inc.

Description: International banks are competing for a role in China but are finding obstacles in their paths such as a reduction in the credit their operations may receive from Chinese banks and the role they can play in the public capital markets which remain limited.

12673 ■ *Nelson Information's Directory of Investment Research*

Pub: Nelson Information

Contact: Mary Pinto, Manager

URL(s): www.nelsoninformation.com. **Released:** Annual; December. **Price:** $750, Individuals print. **Covers:** Over 7,000 firms; 14,000 public companies; and

9,000 analysts. **Entries include:** Name, address, phone, fax, names and titles of key personnel, five-year operating summary, description of business.

12674 ■ Nerds on Wall Street: Math, Machines and Wired Markets
Pub: John Wiley & Sons, Inc.

Ed: David J. Leinweber. **Released:** May 27, 2009. **Price:** $39.95. **Description:** The history of technology and how it will transform investing and trading on Wall Street is outlined.

12675 ■ "Nestle Acquires Waggin' Train Dog Treat Company" in Pet Product News (Vol. 64, November 2010, No. 11, pp. 7)
Pub: BowTie Inc.

Description: Vevey, Switzerland-based Nestle has acquired South Carolina-based dog treat firm Waggin' Train LLC from private equity firm VMG Partners in September 2010. Waggin' Train LLC, which will be operated as a wholly owned subsidiary, is expected to fill a gap in Nestle's dog treat product portfolio.

12676 ■ "Netflix Gets No Respect" in Barron's (Vol. 89, July 27, 2009, No. 30, pp. 26)
Pub: Dow Jones & Co., Inc.

Ed: Tiernan Ray. **Description:** Netflix met expectations when they announced their second quarter sales but their shares still fell by almost 10 percent. Analysts say their entry into the 'streaming video' business is a mixed bag since customers are increasingly buying the cheaper monthly plan and this is dragging the economics of the business.

12677 ■ "The New Arsenal of Risk Management" in Harvard Business Review (Vol. 86, September 2008, No. 9, pp. 92)
Pub: Harvard Business School Press

Ed: Kevin Bueler; Andrew Freeman; Ron Hulme. **Description:** Goldman Sachs Group Inc. is used to illustrate methods for successful risk management. The investment bank's business principles, partnerships, and oversight practices are discussed.

12678 ■ "New Century's Fall Has a New Culprit" in Barron's (Vol. 88, March 31, 2008, No. 13, pp. 20)
Pub: Dow Jones & Company, Inc.

Ed: Jonathan R. Laing. **Description:** Court examiner Michael Missal reports that New Century Financial's auditor contributed to New Century's demise by its negligence in permitting improper and imprudent practices related to New Century's accounting processes. New Century's bankruptcy filing is considered the start of the subprime-mortgage crisis.

12679 ■ "New Drug Could Revitalize Amgen" in Barron's (Vol. 88, July 7, 2008, No. 27, pp. 23)
Pub: Dow Jones & Co., Inc.

Ed: Johanna Bennett. **Description:** Shares of the biotechnology company Amgen could receive a boost from the release of the anti-osteoporosis drug denosumab. The shares, priced at $48.84 each, are trading at 11 times expected earnings for 2008 and could also be boosted by cost cutting measures.

12680 ■ "A New Kid on the Block" in Barron's (Vol. 88, March 17, 2008, No. 11, pp. 58)
Pub: Dow Jones & Company, Inc.

Ed: Thomas G. Donlan. **Description:** Discusses the Federal Reserve which has offered to lend $100 billion in cash to banks and $200 billion in Treasuries to Wall Street investment banks that have problems with liquidity. The reluctance of the banks to lend money to meet a margin call on securities that could still depreciate is the reason why the agency is going into the direct loan business.

12681 ■ "New Law Lets Shareholders Play Hardball With Firms" in Globe & Mail (January 2, 2006, pp. B1)
Pub: CTVglobemedia Publishing Inc.

Ed: Janet McFarland. **Description:** Business lawyer Wes Voorheis discusses about the launching of Bill 198 by plaintiffs' lawyers on behalf of ordinary retail investors.

12682 ■ "New Money" in Entrepreneur (Vol. 36, February 2008, No. 2, pp. 62)
Pub: Entrepreneur Media Inc.

Ed: C.J. Prince. **Description:** Tips on how to handle business finance, with regard to the tightened credit standards imposed by leading institutions, are provided. These include: selling receivables, margining blue chips, and selling purchase orders.

12683 ■ "The New Nimble" in Barron's (Vol. 90, August 30, 2010, No. 35, pp. S12)
Pub: Barron's Editorial & Corporate Headquarters

Ed: Suzanne McGee. **Description:** Financial advisors are making investments based on short-lived market trends due to the uncertainty in the long-term market. This strategy can be demanding and advisors should only try it if they are confident about their skill in spotting short-term trends.

12684 ■ "The New Risk Tolerance" in Entrepreneur (Vol. 37, September 2009, No. 9, pp. 66)
Pub: Entrepreneur Media, Inc.

Ed: Rosalind Resnick. **Description:** Offers advice on where to invest personal money in the United States. One could lose money from investing in gold and treasuries. High-quality corporate bonds and Treasury Inflation-Protected Securities are seen as ideal investments.

12685 ■ "New Thinking for a New Financial Order" in Harvard Business Review (Vol. 86, September 2008, No. 9, pp. 26)
Pub: Harvard Business School Press

Ed: Diana Farell. **Description:** Factors driving the current global economy are analyzed with a focus on the influence of new public and private sectors and the impact of unregulated markets.

12686 ■ "A New Way to Tell When to Fold" in Barron's (Vol. 88, July 7, 2008, No. 27, pp. 27)
Pub: Dow Jones & Co., Inc.

Ed: Theresa W. Carey. **Description:** Overview of the Online trading company SmartStops, a firm that aims to tell investors when to sell the shares of a particular company. The company's Web site categorizes stocks as moving up, down, or sideways, and calculates exit points for individual stocks based on an overall market trend.

12687 ■ "New Ways to Catch a Thief" in Barron's (Vol. 88, March 10, 2008, No. 10, pp. 37)
Pub: Dow Jones & Company, Inc.

Ed: Theresa W. Carey. **Description:** Online brokerage firms employ different methods to protect the accounts of their customers from theft. These methods include secure Internet connections, momentary passwords, and proprietary algorithms.

12688 ■ "The Next Government Bailout?" in Barron's (Vol. 88, March 10, 2008, No. 10, pp. 21)
Pub: Dow Jones & Company, Inc.

Ed: Jonathan Laing. **Description:** Fannie Mae may need a government bailout as it faces huge hits brought about by the effects of the housing crisis. The shares of the government-sponsored enterprise have dropped 65 percent since the housing crisis began.

12689 ■ "Nightmare on Wall Street" in Canadian Business (Vol. 80, November 19, 2007, No. 23, pp. 33)
Pub: Rogers Media

Ed: Thomas Watson. **Description:** Merrill Lynch Stanley O'Neal resigned after the company experienced a $2.2 billion loss in third quarter 2007. Citigroup's Charles Prince will also be leaving due to the crisis involving subprime mortgages and collaterized debt obligations. Forecasts for the stock market are supplied.

12690 ■ "Nightmare on Wall Street" in Canadian Business (Vol. 81, October 13, 2008, No. 17, pp. 9)
Pub: Rogers Media Ltd.

Ed: Rachel Pulfer. **Description:** Information on events that happened on Wall Street on the week that started September 15, 2008, as well on its effect on financial markets around the world, are presented. Lehman Brothers filed for bankruptcy on September 15, 2008 after negotiations with Barclays Group and Bank of America failed. Details on AIG and Morgan Stanley are also presented.

12691 ■ "Nine Sectors to Watch: Energy" in Canadian Business (Vol. 81, December 24, 2007, No. 1, pp. 54)
Pub: Rogers Media

Ed: Jeff Sanford. **Description:** One of the concerns in the petroleum industry is the fear of decline in production in many oilfields, as analysts predict the world will be pumping 17 percent less by 2025. Details on the continuing rise in demand and increase in prices are discussed.

12692 ■ "Nine Sectors to Watch: Gold" in Canadian Business (Vol. 81, December 24, 2007, No. 1, pp. 53)
Pub: Rogers Media

Ed: John Gray. **Description:** Turmoil in the financial markets, triggered by the meltdown in subprime mortgages, has pushed the price of gold to more than $840 an ounce in November 2007. Details on investor interest in gold and prediction on price trends in trade are discussed.

12693 ■ "No Surprises" in Canadian Business (Vol. 79, September 25, 2006, No. 19, pp. 49)
Pub: Rogers Media

Ed: Jeff Sanford. **Description:** The increasing income trust sector in Canada is discussed.

12694 ■ "Nonprofit NAIC Acquires Software Developer as For-Profit Arm" in Crain's Detroit Business (Vol. 25, June 22, 2009, No. 25, pp. 10)
Pub: Crain Communications Inc. - Detroit

Ed: Sherri Begin Welch. **Description:** Details of National Association of Investors Corporation's acquisition of a Massachusetts investment software developer in order to offer more products to investment clubs and individual investors nationwide.

12695 ■ "Nortel Outlook Shows Recovery Won't Come Quickly" in Globe & Mail (March 20, 2007, pp. B4)
Pub: CTVglobemedia Publishing Inc.

Ed: Catherine McLean. **Description:** The forecast about the unlikely recovery of Nortel Networks Corp. from decrease in its share prices is discussed.

12696 ■ "Nortel Plays Big to Settle Lawsuits" in Globe & Mail (February 9, 2006, pp. B1)
Pub: CTVglobemedia Publishing Inc.

Ed: Catherine McLean. **Description:** The details on Nortel Networks Corp.'s settlement of cases with shareholders are presented.

12697 ■ "Northern Overexposure" in Canadian Business (Vol. 79, August 14, 2006, No. 16-17, pp. 36)
Pub: Rogers Media

Description: Fall in revenue from foreign film productions in Canada due to its overexposure, and incentives offered by other nations to foreign film productions, are discussed.

12698 ■ "Not In My Backyard" in Entrepreneur (Vol. 36, May 2008, No. 5, pp. 42)
Pub: Entrepreneur Media, Inc.

Ed: Farnoosh Torabi. **Description:** More investors are turning to overseas real estate investments as the U.S. market sees a slowdown. Analysts say that risk-averse investors opt for funds with record of strong returns and U.S. real estate investment trusts that partner with foreign businesses for transparency purposes. Other details about foreign real estate investments are discussed.

12699 ■ "A Novel Fix for the Credit Mess" in Barron's (Vol. 88, March 31, 2008, No. 13, pp. 10)
Pub: Dow Jones & Company, Inc.

Ed: Michael Santoli. **Description:** Due to the common bank-leverage factor of 10, the $250 billion of lost bank capital would have supported $2.5 trillion in lending capacity. Jeffrey Lewis suggests onerous regulations on bank-holding companies that own 10 to 25 percent, as they are partly to blame. Statistical data included.

12700 ■ *"Now in Play, Score Keeps Head Up and Stick on Ice" in Globe & Mail (January 20, 2007, pp. B5)*
Pub: CTVglobemedia Publishing Inc.
Ed: Grant Robertson. **Description:** The hike in the shares of Score Media Inc. due to its new services is presented.

12701 ■ *"Now That's Rich" in Canadian Business (Vol. 80, February 12, 2007, No. 4, pp. 92)*
Pub: Rogers Media
Ed: Thomas Watson. **Description:** The effort of chief executive officer of Stelco Inc. Rodney Mott in resolving the issue of financial loss of the company by taking up backdating options for share price is discussed.

12702 ■ *"Now You See It.." in Canadian Business (Vol. 81, November 10, 2008, No. 19, pp. 20)*
Pub: Rogers Media Ltd.
Ed: Sharda Prashad. **Description:** Total return swaps were offered by Deutsche Bank AG and UBS AG to foreign investors for them to avoid paying taxes on the proceeds of their shares of Fording Canadian Coal Trust when Teck Cominco offered to buy the company. This means that the Canadian government is losing tax revenue from foreigners and it is argued that a simpler tax system would avoid this practice.

12703 ■ *"NStar Feels the Heat" in Cape Cod Times (September 30, 2011)*
Pub: Cape Cod Media Group
Ed: Patrick Cassidy. **Description:** Massachusetts energy officials wish to delay a merger between NStar and Northeast Utilities until it is clear how the partnership would meet the state's green energy goals. Governor Deval Patrick supports the proposed Nantucket Sound wind farm.

12704 ■ *"Nuclear Plans May Stall on Uranium Shortage" in Globe & Mail (March 22, 2007, pp. B4)*
Pub: CTVglobemedia Publishing Inc.
Ed: Shawn McCarthy. **Description:** The poor investments in uranium production and enrichment despite growing demand for it for nuclear energy is discussed.

12705 ■ *"Number of Mechanic's Liens Triple Since 2005" in The Business Journal - Serving Phoenix and the Valley of the Sun (Vol. 28, August 22, 2008, No. 51, pp. 1)*
Pub: American City Business Journals, Inc.
Ed: Jan Buchholtz. **Description:** Experts are blaming the mortgage and banking industries for the tripling of mechanic's liens that were filed in Arizona from 2005 through August 6, 2008. The rise in mechanic's liens is believed to indicate stress in the real estate community. Other views and information on the rise of mechanic's liens filed in Arizona are presented.

12706 ■ *"The Numbers Speak For Themselves" in Barron's (Vol. 88, July 14, 2008, No. 28, pp. 16)*
Pub: Dow Jones & Co., Inc.
Ed: Bill Alpert. **Description:** Discusses quant fund managers versus traditional long-short equity funds after quants outperformed traditional funds in the year 2000. Causes for the underperformance are outlined and statistical data is included.

12707 ■ *"Nvidia Shares Clobbered After Gloomy Warning" in Barron's (Vol. 88, July 7, 2008, No. 27, pp. 25)*
Pub: Dow Jones & Co., Inc.
Ed: Eric J. Savitz. **Description:** Shares of graphics chip manufacturer Nvidia suffered a 30 percent drop in its share price after the company warned that revenue and gross margin forecasts for the quarter ending July 27, 2008 will be below expectations. Stan Glasgow, chief operating officer of Sony Electronics, believes the US economic slowdown will not affect demand for the company's products. Statistical data included.

12708 ■ *"Nvidia's Picture Brighter Than Stock Price Indicates" in Barron's (Vol. 88, March 24, 2008, No. 12, pp. 46)*
Pub: Dow Jones & Company, Inc.
Ed: Eric J. Savitz. **Description:** Shares of graphics chip maker Nvidia, priced at $18.52 each, do not indicate the company's strong position in the graphics chip market. The company's shares have dropped due to fears of slower demand for PCs, but the company is not as exposed to broader economic forces.

12709 ■ *"N.Y. Investors Reject AnorMed Board Proposal" in Globe & Mail (February 21, 2006, pp. B11)*
Pub: CTVglobemedia Publishing Inc.
Ed: Leonard Zehr. **Description:** The reasons behind the denial of investors over the restructuring plans of AnorMed are presented.

12710 ■ *"Nymex Dissidents Rattle Sabers" in Crain's Chicago Business (Vol. 31, April 21, 2008, No. 16, pp. 2)*
Pub: Crain Communications, Inc.
Ed: Ann Saphir. **Description:** Two groups of New York Mercantile Exchange members say they have more than enough votes to stop CME Group Inc.'s $10 billion deal to acquire the oil and metals exchange and they are threatening a proxy fight if the Chicago exchange doesn't raise its offer.

12711 ■ *"OccuLogix Shares Plummet 65 Percent" in Globe & Mail (February 4, 2006, pp. B5)*
Pub: CTVglobemedia Publishing Inc.
Ed: Leonard Zehr. **Description:** The shares of Occu-Logix drop by 65% in Canada. The decline in share price is attributed to failure of blood filtering system.

12712 ■ *"October 2009: Recovery Plods Along" in Hispanic Business (October 2009, pp. 10-11)*
Pub: Hispanic Business
Ed: Dr. Juan Solana. **Description:** Economist reports on a possible economic recovery which will not be allowed to rely on a strong domestic demand in order to sustain it. Consumers, looking to counterbalance years of leverage financing based on unrealistic, ever-increasing home and portfolio valuations, are saving rather than spending money.

12713 ■ *"Off the RIM" in Canadian Business (Vol. 80, January 15, 2007, No. 2, pp. 7)*
Pub: Rogers Media
Ed: John Gray. **Description:** The reasons for the rise and fall in stock prices of the software company, Research In Motion Ltd., from September 2006 to January 2007, are analyzed.

12714 ■ *"Office Market May Turn Down" in Crain's New York Business (Vol. 24, January 14, 2008, No. 2, pp. 26)*
Pub: Crain Communications, Inc.
Description: Although still dominated by Wall Street, the downturn in the economy is raising fears that the continuing fallout from the subprime mortgage crisis could result in layoffs that will derail the office market.

12715 ■ *"Oil Patch Expects Richer Shell Offer" in Globe & Mail (January 3, 2006, pp. B1)*
Pub: CTVglobemedia Publishing Inc.
Ed: Andrew Willis; Patrick Brethour. **Description:** The concerns investors over the feasibility of Royal Dutch Shell PLC's acquisition of Shell Canada Ltd., for $7.6 billion, are presented. Shell Canada Ltd. reports rise in shares by ten percent.

12716 ■ *"Oil Picks and Pans" in Canadian Business (Vol. 79, August 14, 2006, No. 16-17, pp. 67)*
Pub: Rogers Media
Ed: Graham Scott. **Description:** A survey on investments in Canadian energy companies and the inflation caused by oil price hike, are discussed.

12717 ■ *"The Oilman" in Canadian Business (Vol. 79, Winter 2006, No. 24, pp. 64)*
Pub: Rogers Media
Ed: Michelle Magnan. **Description:** The achievements of David Werklund, the chairman of the CCS Income Trust, are described.

12718 ■ *"Oil's Going Down, Down, Down" in Canadian Business (Vol. 79, October 9, 2006, No. 20, pp. 148)*
Pub: Rogers Media
Ed: Ian McGugan. **Description:** Strategies for investors to benefit from the fall in global crude oil prices are discussed.

12719 ■ *"Ok, So Now What?" in Canadian Business (Vol. 79, November 6, 2006, No. 22, pp. 113)*
Pub: Rogers Media
Ed: Calvin Leung. **Description:** Details of healthy income-generating corporations, such as Cedar Fair L.P., are presented.

12720 ■ *"The Old Railway is on a Roll" in Globe & Mail (January 26, 2006, pp. B1)*
Pub: CTVglobemedia Publishing Inc.
Description: The reasons behind 5 percent rise in shares for Canadian National Railway Co. are presented.

12721 ■ *"Olympus is Urged to Revise Board" in Wall Street Journal Eastern Edition (November 28, 2011, pp. B3)*
Pub: Dow Jones & Company Inc. Enterprise Media Group
Contact: Clare Hart, President
Ed: Phred Dvorak. **Description:** Koji Miyata, once a director on the board of troubled Japanese photographic equipment company, is urging the company to reorganize its board, saying the present group should resign their board seats but keep their management positions. The company has come under scrutiny for its accounting practices and costly acquisitions.

12722 ■ *"On tap: More Could Get MEGA Credits; Need to Look Outside State May Be Cut" in Crain's Detroit Business (April 7, 2008)*
Pub: Crain Communications, Inc.
Ed: Amy Lane. **Description:** In order to qualify for Michigan Economic Growth Authority tax credits Michigan businesses may no longer have to shop outside the state due to a new bill which has already passed the state Senate and will move on to the House; the bill, along with further changes to the MEGA program, is designed to provide incentives for investments that would add relevance and make Michigan more competitive.

12723 ■ *"On the Trail of the Bear" in Canadian Business (Vol. 81, March 17, 2008, No. 4, pp. 28)*
Pub: Rogers Media
Ed: Thomas Watson. **Description:** Discusses the conservative rule of thumb which is to invest in equity markets when a five to ten percent market rally is sustained for more than a few months. Bear markets on the S&P 500 bear markets in the 20th century only lasts over a year based on average. It is also good to remember that bear markets are followed by bulls that exceed the previous market highs.

12724 ■ *"One-Time Area Trust Executive Finds Trouble in N.H." in The Business Journal-Serving Metropolitan Kansas City (September 12, 2008)*
Pub: American City Business Journals, Inc.
Ed: Steve Vockrodt. **Description:** About 200 investors, some from Missouri's Kansas City area, claim that they had conducted business with Noble Trust Co. The trust company was placed under New Hampshire Banking Department's conservatorship after $15 million was discovered to be missing from its account. It is alleged that the money was lost in a Colorado Ponzi scheme.

12725 ■ *"Online Forex Broker Tadawul FX Intros Arabic Website"* in *Entertainment Close-Up (June 23, 2011)*
Pub: Close-Up Media
Description: Online forex broker, Tadawul FX, launched its Arabic language Website, noting that the Middle East is a key market for the investment firm.

12726 ■ *"Open the Telecom Market"* in *Canadian Business (Vol. 80, April 23, 2007, No. 9, pp. 80)*
Pub: Rogers Media
Description: The effects of federal telecommunication law on foreign investments in telecommunication industry are presented.

12727 ■ *"Operation Fusion"* in *Black Enterprise (Vol. 38, November 2007, No. 4, pp. 30)*
Pub: Earl G. Graves Publishing Co. Inc.
Ed: Tara C. Walker. **Description:** Entrepreneur Albert H. Frazier tells how he combined three separate acquisitions in order to create Goods Movement Inc.:-W&H Systems Inc., a systems integrator and material handler supplier and North American Conveyor Inc. which fabricates and installs conveyor and sort equipment systems for the U.S. Postal Service and Total Transportation Services, a third-party logistics provider.

12728 ■ *"Opportunity Now Lies at Short End of the Market"* in *Barron's (Vol. 88, June 30, 2008, No. 26, pp. M9)*
Pub: Dow Jones & Co., Inc.
Ed: Michael S. Derby. **Description:** Renewed credit concerns and the lesser chance of a Federal Reserve interest rate hike boosted the bond market. Some portfolio managers are more bullish on short-dated securities as they expect the market to adjust to a more appropriate outlook.

12729 ■ *"An Opportunity for Patience"* in *Barron's (Vol. 88, June 30, 2008, No. 26, pp. M5)*
Pub: Dow Jones & Co., Inc.
Ed: Fleming Meeks. **Description:** Shares of Louisiana-Pacific are near their 52-week low at $8.95 per share making them look like a better buy than they were at $11.51 in May, 2008. The company is a to player in a cyclical business and its balance sheet is sound compared to its peers with net debt at just $84 million or 20 percent of total capital.

12730 ■ *"Optimize.ca Supplies Free Online Financial Advice"* in *Entertainment Close-Up (October 9, 2010)*
Pub: Close-Up Media Inc.
Description: Optimize.ca provides free online financial advice, focusing on instant savings for their mutual funds and other banking products while improving rates of return and overall financial health.

12731 ■ *"Oracle: No Profit of Doom"* in *Barron's (Vol. 88, March 31, 2008, No. 13, pp. 40)*
Pub: Dow Jones & Company, Inc.
Ed: Mark Veverka. **Description:** Oracle's revenues grew by 21 percent but fell short of expectation and their profits came in at the low-end of expectations. The company's shares dropped 8 percent but investors are advised to pay more attention to the company's earnings expansion rather than revenue growth in a slow economy. Nokia's Rick Simonson points out that their markets in Asia and particularly India is growing so they are not as affected by the U.S. economic conditions.

12732 ■ *"The Oracle's Endgame; Wrigley Investment Isn't What Many Call a Classic Buffett Play"* in *Crain's Chicago Business (May 5, 2008)*
Pub: Crain Communications, Inc.
Ed: Ann Saphir. **Description:** Discusses Warren Buffett's deal with Mars Inc. to buy Wm. Wrigley Jr. Co., a move which would make Mr. Buffett a minority shareholder in a privately held company, a departure from his typical investment strategy. Mr. Buffett's Berkshire Hathaway Inc. agreed to provide $4.4 bil-

lion to help finance the $23 billion deal to pay another $2.1 billion for an equity stake in the company once it became a subsidiary of Mars.

12733 ■ *"OSC Eyes New Tack on Litigation"* in *Globe & Mail (April 9, 2007, pp. B1)*
Pub: CTVglobemedia Publishing Inc.
Ed: Janet McFarland. **Description:** The efforts of the Ontario Securities Commission to set up a tribunal for the investigation and control of securities fraud are described. The rate of the conviction of corporate officials in cases heard by the courts is discussed.

12734 ■ *"Ottawa Attacks!"* in *Canadian Business (Vol. 79, November 6, 2006, No. 22, pp. 21)*
Pub: Rogers Media
Ed: Jeff Sanford. **Description:** The effects of new tax policy developed by Jim Flaherty, Finance Minister of Canada, on income trusts are presented.

12735 ■ *"Our Rich Past: a Guide to Some of Canada's Historic Fortunes"* in *Canadian Business (Vol. 80, Winter 2007, No. 24, pp. 131)*
Pub: Rogers Media
Ed: Graham F. Scott. **Description:** Donald Alexander Smith rose through the ranks at Hudson's Bay Company to become the company's principal shareholder. John Wilson McConnell started his career at the Standard Chemical Company but later shifted to selling stocks and receiving equity stocks in return for his endorsement. Bud McDougald is well known for his deal making skills before he died in 1978.

12736 ■ *"Out of Fashion"* in *Barron's (Vol. 88, March 17, 2008, No. 11, pp. 48)*
Pub: Dow Jones & Company, Inc.
Ed: Robin Goldwyn Blumenthal. **Description:** Shares of Perry Ellis International and G-III Apparel Group have taken some beating in the market despite good growth earnings prospects. Perry Ellis sees earnings growth of 8 to 11 percent for fiscal 2009, while G-III Apparel expects earnings growth of 25 percent.

12737 ■ *"Over A Barrel"* in *Canadian Business (Vol. 81, July 21, 2008, No. 11, pp. 13)*
Pub: Rogers Media Ltd.
Ed: Thomas Watson. **Description:** Analysts predict that the skyrocketing price of fuel will cause a crackdown in the market as purported in the peak oil theory. It is forecasted that the price of oil will reach $200 per barrel. Details of the effect of the increasing oil prices on the market are presented.

12738 ■ *"Over a Barrel"* in *Canadian Business (Vol. 80, February 12, 2007, No. 4, pp. 52)*
Pub: Rogers Media
Ed: Andrew Nikoforuk. **Description:** The potential of tar sands of Alberta in becoming the largest source of oil in the world and huge investments of Canadian companies to mine for the oil there are discussed.

12739 ■ *"Owner of IT Firm MK2 Tying Future to Software"* in *Crain's Cleveland Business (Vol. 30, June 15, 2009, No. 23, pp. 3)*
Pub: Crain Communications, Inc.
Ed: Chuck Soder. **Description:** Donald Kasper, owner of MK2 Technologies LLC of Cleveland, Ohio discusses his recent acquisition of a portion of ProSource Solution. The move will help expand the two companies' custom software development plans.

12740 ■ *"Packaging Firm Wraps Up Remake; Overseas Plants Help Firm Fatten Margins"* in *Crain's New York Business (January 7, 2008)*
Pub: Crain Communications, Inc.
Description: Sealed Air Corp., a packaging manufacturer, has seen its share price fall nearly 20 percent over the past two years, making it one of the worst performers in the packaging sector.

12741 ■ *"Pain Ahead as Profit Pressure Increases"* in *Crain's Chicago Business (Vol. 31, May 5, 2008, No. 18, pp. 4)*
Pub: Crain Communications, Inc.
Ed: Daniel Rome Levine. **Description:** Interview with David Klaskin, the chairman and chief investment officer at Oak Ridge Investments LLC, who discusses

the outlook for the economy and corporate earnings, particularly in the housing and auto industries, the impact of economic stimulus checks, the weakness of the dollar and recommendations of stocks that individual investors may find helpful.

12742 ■ *"P&G's Iams Finds Itself in a Pet-Food Dogfight"* in *Advertising Age (Vol. 78, March 5, 2007, No. 10, pp. 6)*
Pub: Crain Communications, Inc.
Ed: Jack Neff. **Description:** Proctor & Gamble Co.'s Iams has been slow to embrace the trend toward foods for pets that appear fit for human consumption. Competitors such as Nestle Purina have made big gains with its colorful premium Beneful brand and dry nuggets that look like chunks of vegetables and meat. Statistical data included.

12743 ■ *Panic! The Story of Modern Financial Insanity*
Pub: W.W. Norton & Company
Ed: Michael Lewis. **Released:** 2009. **Price:** $27.95.
Description: Two decades of stock market crashes are outlined.

12744 ■ *Paper Fortunes: Modern Wall Street: Where It's Been and Where It's Going*
Pub: St. Martin's Press LLC
Ed: Roy C. Smith. **Released:** 2010. **Price:** $35.00.
Description: Comprehensive history of Wall Street and lessons learned with insight into ways Wall Street will reinvent itself in this new economy.

12745 ■ *Partnership: Small Business Start-Up Kit*
Pub: Nova Publishing Company
Ed: Daniel Sitarz. **Released:** November 2005. **Price:** $29.95. **Description:** Guidebook detailing partnership law by state covering the formation and use of partnerships as a business form. Information on filing requirements, property laws, legal liability, standards, and the new Revised Uniform Partnership Act is covered.

12746 ■ *The Partnership: The Making of Goldman Sachs*
Pub: Penguin Group USA Inc.
Ed: Charles D. Ellis. **Released:** 2009. **Price:** $37.95.
Description: The history of Goldman Sachs is presented, along with a chronicle of Wall Street.

12747 ■ *"Patchy Oil Profits"* in *Canadian Business (Vol. 80, February 12, 2007, No. 4, pp. 89)*
Pub: Rogers Media
Ed: Michelle Magnan. **Description:** The fall in fourth-quarter earnings of several oil and gas companies in Canada, in view of rise in their expenditure, is discussed.

12748 ■ *"Paterson Plots Comeback With Internet IPO"* in *Globe & Mail (February 20, 2006, pp. B1)*
Pub: CTVglobemedia Publishing Inc.
Ed: Grant Robertson. **Description:** The initial public offering plans of chief executive officer Scott Paterson of JumpTV.com are presented.

12749 ■ *"Patience May Pay Off"* in *Barron's (Vol. 89, July 13, 2009, No. 28, pp. 30)*
Pub: Dow Jones & Co., Inc.
Ed: Johanna Bennett. **Description:** New CEO Craig Herkert can turn around Supervalu and their shares could double to $30 in three years from June 2009 according to one investment officer. Herkert knows how to run a lean and tight operation since he has worked for Albertsons and Wal-Mart in the past.

12750 ■ *"PC Connection Acquires Cloud Software Provider"* in *New Hampshire Business Review (Vol. 33, March 25, 2011, No. 6, pp. 8)*
Pub: Business Publications Inc.
Description: Merrimack-based PC Connection Inc. acquired ValCom Technology, a provider of cloud-based IT service management software. Details of the deal are included.

12751 ■ *"Peak Performer" in Canadian Business (Vol. 81, October 13, 2008, No. 17, pp. 30)*
Pub: Rogers Media Ltd.
Ed: Andrea Jezovit. **Description:** Jerry Del Missier's promotion as president of Barclays Capital (BarCap) has made him the likely successor to BarCap chief executive Bob Diamond. Diamond believes the technology Jerry Del Missier built on BarCap is producing record performance for the company. Public opinion on Jerry Del Missier, as well as his views, is discussed.

12752 ■ *"Penny Chief Shops For Shares" in Barron's (Vol. 88, July 7, 2008, No. 27, pp. 29)*
Pub: Dow Jones & Co., Inc.
Ed: Teresa Rivas. **Description:** Myron Ullman III, chairman and chief executive officer of J.C. Penney, purchased $1 million worth of shares of the company. He now owns 393,140 shares of the company and an additional 1,282 on his 401(k) plan.

12753 ■ *"A Perfect Predator: Brookfield Asset Management Isn't Brash" in Canadian Business (Vol. 83, July 20, 2010, No. 11-12, pp. 50)*
Pub: Rogers Media Ltd.
Ed: Joanna Pachner. **Description:** Brookfield Asset Management CEO Bruce Flatt manages $108 billion worth of real estate and the company has become one of the world's biggest prime real estate owners since he became leader. Flatt says their goal is to earn a 12-15 percent compound annual return per share and that they would shrink in size if it meant reaching that goal.

12754 ■ *"The Perks of Going Public" in Austin Business Journal (Vol. 31, July 15, 2011, No. 19, pp. A17)*
Pub: American City Business Journals Inc.
Ed: Christopher Calnan. **Description:** HomeAway Inc. launched a $216 million initial public offering. Austin Ventures has generated more than $32 million from the IPO.

12755 ■ *"Pet Food Insider Sold Shares Before Recall" in Globe & Mail (April 10, 2007, pp. B1)*
Pub: CTVglobemedia Publishing Inc.
Ed: Keith McArthur. **Description:** The issue related the selling of share units by Mark Weins, chief financial officer of pet food firm Menu Foods Income Fund, just before the recall of contaminated pet food is discussed.

12756 ■ *"Peter Bynoe Trades Up" in Black Enterprise (Vol. 38, July 2008, No. 12, pp. 30)*
Pub: Earl G. Graves Publishing Co. Inc.
Ed: Alexis McCombs. **Description:** Chicago-based Loop Capital Markets L.L.C. has named Peter Bynoe managing director of corporate finance. Bynoe was previously a senior partner at the law firm DLA Piper U.S. L.L.P., where he worked on stadium deals.

12757 ■ *"PetSmart: A Barking Buy" in Barron's (Vol. 89, July 6, 2009, No. 27, pp. 15)*
Pub: Dow Jones & Co., Inc.
Ed: Jay Palmer. **Description:** Shares of PetSmart could climb from $21.70 to about $28 due to the company's improving profits, cash flow, and product portfolio. The company's shares are trading at 14 times projected 2010 earnings of $1.64 a share.

12758 ■ *"Phillips Edison Launches $1.8B Retail REIT" in Business Courier (Vol. 27, October 15, 2010, No. 24, pp. 1)*
Pub: Business Courier
Ed: Dan Monk. **Description:** Retail center operator Phillips Edison & Company is organizing a real estate investment trust (REIT) to raise $1.8 billion to finance the planned purchase of 150 grocery-centered shopping centers around the U.S. The offering would be Phillips largest. Phillips Edison employeesss 174 workers and operates 250 shopping centers nationwide.

12759 ■ *"Phoenix Company Realizing Dream of Global Growth" in The Business Journal - Serving Phoenix and the Valley of the Sun*

(Vol. 28, July 18, 2008, No. 46, pp. 1)
Pub: American City Business Journals, Inc.
Ed: Chris Casaccia. **Description:** Phoenix, Arizona-based lubricant maker DreamBrands Inc. is realizing global growth. The company, which has been generating interest from institutional investors, is seeking a second round of funding. Details of the company's products and marketing plans are also discussed.

12760 ■ *"Picking a 529 College Savings Plan" in Black Enterprise (Vol. 37, February 2007, No. 7, pp. 46)*
Pub: Earl G. Graves Publishing Co. Inc.
Ed: Carolyn M. Brown. **Description:** Advice is given to help choose the right college savings plan.

12761 ■ *"Place Restrictions on Your Stock Shares" in Business Owner (Vol. 35, July-August 2011, No. 4, pp. 14)*
Pub: DL Perkins Company
Description: It is critical for any small business owner to be certain that the buyer or recipient of any part of the company represents that the stock is being acquired or given for investment purposes only.

12762 ■ *"A Place in the Sun" in Canadian Business (Vol. 81, July 22, 2008, No. 12-13, pp. 56)*
Pub: Rogers Media Ltd.
Description: Experts believe that it is the best time for Canadians to own a retirement home in the U.S., where real estate prices are up to 50 percent below their peak. Other views concerning the economic conditions occurring in the United States, as well as on the implications for Canadians planning to invest in the country are presented.

12763 ■ *"Planning Ahead: Steven Taylor Mulls a Second Career After Retirement" in Black Enterprise (Vol. 37, November 2006, No. 4, pp. 82)*
Pub: Earl G. Graves Publishing Co. Inc.
Ed: Sheryl Nance Nash. **Description:** Many workers are unprepared for retirement. Profile of Steven Taylor, a soon to retire dietary correctional officer who looked to Walt Clark, president of Clark Capital Financial in Maryland, to assess his retirement goals. Detailed advice and statistical data included.

12764 ■ *"Playing Citigroup's Woes" in Barron's (Vol. 88, March 31, 2008, No. 13, pp. M7)*
Pub: Dow Jones & Company, Inc.
Ed: Steven M. Sears. **Description:** Citigroup's first-quarter earnings estimate was slashed to a $1.15-per-share-loss from 28 cents. A strategist recommends buying the company's shares at Sept. 20, 2008 put and selling a Sept. 17.50 put with a maximum profit of $166 if the shares is at or below $17.50 at expiration.

12765 ■ *"Playing Defense" in Crain's Chicago Business (Vol. 31, November 10, 2008, No. 45, pp. 4)*
Pub: Crain Communications, Inc.
Ed: Monee Fields-White. **Description:** Chicago's money managers are increasingly investing in local companies such as Caterpillar Inc., a maker of construction and mining equipment, Kraft Foods Inc. and Baxter International Inc., a manufacturer of medical products, in an attempt to bolster their portfolios. These companies have a history of surviving tough economic times.

12766 ■ *"PNC Begins Search for New Local HQ" in Baltimore Business Journal (Vol. 28, June 4, 2010, No. 4, pp. 1)*
Pub: Baltimore Business Journal
Ed: Daniel J. Sernovitz. **Description:** PNC Financial Services Group Inc. is searching for a new headquarters building in Greater Baltimore, Maryland. The company is seeking about 150,000 square feet for its regional operations. However, PNC could also end up moving out of Baltimore for space in the surrounding suburbs.

12767 ■ *"Point, Click, Buy" in Barron's (Vol. 90, September 6, 2010, No. 36, pp. 11)*
Pub: Barron's Editorial & Corporate Headquarters
Ed: Vito J. Racanelli. **Description:** Non-travel online retail sales from January to July 2010 increased nine percent which indicates that online shopping for the coming holidays will be good. Online sales are outpacing traditional shopping, but pricing is still critical.

12768 ■ *"Polite Conversation" in Mergers & Acquisitions: The Dealmaker's Journal (March 1, 2008)*
Pub: SourceMedia, Inc.
Description: In January, industry leaders and dealmakers met at Davos to discuss topics ranging from the possibility of a recession to what lies ahead in the deal market.

12769 ■ *"Portfolio: Written in the Polls" in Entrepreneur (Vol. 35, October 2007, No. 10, pp. 74)*
Pub: Entrepreneur Media Inc.
Ed: Scott Bernard Nelson. **Description:** Ibbotsen Associates looked at trends in the U.S. presidential elections to see if the election has something to do with stock market behavior. It was found that election years beat non-election years in the stock market by nearly three percentage points each year. Details of the presidential elections' impact on the stock market are given.

12770 ■ *"Powder River Reports First Quarter Revenues Over 5 Million" in Canadian Corporate News (May 16, 2007)*
Pub: Comtex News Network Inc.
Description: Financial report for Powder River Basin Gas Corp., a revenue generating producer, marketer, and acquirer of crude oil and natural gas properties. Statistical data included.

12771 ■ *"The Power of Alumni Networks" in Harvard Business Review (Vol. 88, October 2010, No. 10, pp. 34)*
Pub: Harvard Business School Publishing
Ed: Lauren H. Cohen, Christopher J. Malloy. **Description:** Research indicates that members of alumni associations tend to invest in similar ways; implications for the mutual funds sector are discussed.

12772 ■ *"Power In the Boardroom" in Black Enterprise (Vol. 38, February 2008, No. 7, pp. 112)*
Pub: Earl G. Graves Publishing Co. Inc.
Ed: Derek T. Dingle. **Description:** Comprehensive list of Black corporate directors for 250 of the largest companies in the U.S.; these leaders play a critical role in business development.

12773 ■ *"The Power of Innovation" in Canadian Business (Vol. 81, March 17, 2008, No. 4, pp. 57)*
Pub: Rogers Media
Ed: Andrew Wahl. **Description:** Canada ranks badly in terms innovation yardsticks that directly translate to economic growth such as business R&D as a percentage of GDP and R&D per capita. Canada's reliance on natural resources does not provide incentives to innovate unlike smaller countries with little natural resources. Canada could spur innovation through regulations that encourage industrial research.

12774 ■ *"Power Partnerships" in Business Courier (Vol. 27, October 22, 2010, No. 25, pp. 1)*
Pub: Business Courier
Ed: Lucy May. **Description:** The $400 million Harrah's casino and the $47 million redevelopment and expansion of Washington Park are project aimed at boosting the economy in downtown Cincinnati, Ohio. These projects will be done in cooperation with the National Association for the Advancement of Colored People. Insights into the role of minority-owned businesses in regional economic development are explored.

12775 ■ *PPC's Guide to Choosing Retirement Plans for Small Businesses*
Pub: Practitioners Publishing Company
Released: June 2004. **Price:** $119.00. **Description:** Guide to evaluate and select retirement plans for small business.

12776 ■ *"Pre-Deal Trades More Common in Canada, Study Finds" in Globe & Mail (March 23, 2007, pp. B5)*
Pub: CTVglobemedia Publishing Inc.
Ed: John Kipphoff; Joe Schneider. **Description:** The results of the study conducted by Measuredmarkets Inc. to examine the impact of merger activity on insider trading of the companies are presented.

12777 ■ *"A Precious Resource: Investing In the Fate of Fresh Water" in Black Enterprise (Vol. 38, February 2008, No. 7, pp. 44)*
Pub: Earl G. Graves Publishing Co. Inc.
Ed: Charles Keenan. **Description:** Despite rising oil prices, water may become the most precious commodity in years to come because the world's supply of drinkable water is dwindling.

12778 ■ *Principles of Private Firm Valuation*
Pub: John Wiley & Sons, Incorporated
Ed: Stanley J. Feldman. **Released:** April 2005. **Price:** $85.00. **Description:** Tools and techniques to correctly perform private firm valuation, including value and how to measure it, valuing control, determining the size of the marketability discount, creating transparency and the implications for value, the value of tax pass-through entities versus a C corporation, etc.

12779 ■ *"Private Equity Firm Links First Arizona Deal" in Business Journal-Serving Phoenix and the Valley of the Sun (November 2, 2007)*
Pub: American City Business Journals, Inc.
Ed: Chris Cassacchia. **Description:** Pacific Investment Partners and Your Source Financial launched a $10 million fund and signed their first deal. The two companies acquires a minority stake in Dreambrands Inc. for $3 million. Dreambrands is using the capital to market its personal lubricant product Carrageenana.

12780 ■ *"Private Equity Firms Focus on Failing Banks" in Baltimore Business Journal (Vol. 28, July 16, 2010, No. 10, pp. 1)*
Pub: Baltimore Business Journal
Ed: Gary Haber. **Description:** Four deals in which assets of failed banks were acquired by private equity firms have been approved by the Federal Deposit Insurance Corporation in the past couple of years. Bay Bank FSK, for example, purchased Bay National Bank's assets in July 2010. Forecasts on more private equity acquisitions in the community banking industry are given.

12781 ■ *"Private Equity Firms Shopping Valley For Deals" in The Business Journal - Serving Phoenix and the Valley of the Sun (Vol. 29, September 19, 2008, No. 3, pp. 1)*
Pub: American City Business Journals, Inc.
Ed: Mike Sunnucks. **Description:** Private equity firms from California, Boston, New York, and overseas are expected to invest in growth-oriented real estate markets that include Phoenix. Real estate experts revealed that privately held investment and acquisition firms are looking to invest in real estate markets hit by the housing crisis. Views and information on private equity firms' real estate investments are presented.

12782 ■ *"Private Pitfalls" in Canadian Business (Vol. 80, October 22, 2007, No. 21, pp. 34)*
Pub: Rogers Media
Ed: Al Rosen. **Description:** Guidelines on how minority shareholders can avoid drawbacks at the time of purchase, during ownership, and when selling shares are discussed; contractual protection, sales taxation and share price are also presented. Investment in a private company entails knowing the party you are buying share from.

12783 ■ *"Private TV Industry's Profit Climbs Four Percent" in Globe & Mail (March 29, 2006, pp. B6)*
Pub: CTVglobemedia Publishing Inc.
Ed: Simon Tuck. **Description:** The private television industry in Canada is experiencing 4 percent increase in its profits, i.e. $242.2 millions. The revenues of CTV contributed more to this increase in profits.

12784 ■ *"Profico Takes Itself Off the Market" in Globe & Mail (March 14, 2006, pp. B1)*
Pub: CTVglobemedia Publishing Inc.
Ed: Deborah Yedlin; Dave Ebner. **Description:** Profico Energy Management Ltd., Canada's largest junior energy explorer, has backed off its potential acquisition plans. The decreased prices of the natural gas are the main reasons that caused Profico to back off from the acquisition plan.

12785 ■ *"Profit Predictions Look Too Plump" in Barron's (Vol. 88, March 31, 2008, No. 13, pp. 37)*
Pub: Dow Jones & Company, Inc.
Ed: Johanna Bennett. **Description:** Full-year forecast points to a 14 percent gain for 2008 but the second-half profit increases would have to grow at a fast rate and peak at 61 percent in the fourth quarter to achieve this. Trends in the U.S. economic conditions are also discussed.

12786 ■ *"Proof That Good Entrepreneurs Can Make Bad Investors" in Inc. (October 2007, pp. 77-78)*
Pub: Gruner & Jahr USA Publishing
Ed: Norm Brodsky. **Description:** Information for small business owners is offered to help decide which investments are right for them.

12787 ■ *"A Property Rights Analysis of Newly Private Firms" in Business Ethics Quarterly (Vol. 21, July 2011, No. 3, pp. 445)*
Pub: Society for Business Ethics
Ed: Marguerite Schneider, Alix Valenti. **Description:** A key factor in the decision to convert a publicly owned company to private status is the expectation that value will be create, providing the firm with rent. These rents have implications regarding the property rights of the firm's capital-contributing constituencies. The article identifies and analyzes the types of rent associated with the newly private firm. Compared to public firms, going private allows owners the potential to partition part of the residual risk to bond holders and employees, rendering them to be co-residual risk bearers with owners.

12788 ■ *PRWT Service Acquires Pharmaceutical Plant: Firm Wins Multimillion-Dollar Contract with Merck" in Black Enterprise (March 2008)*
Pub: Earl G. Graves Publishing Co. Inc.
Ed: Tamara E. Holmes. **Description:** PRWT Services Inc. expanded through its acquisition of a chemical manufacturing plant in New Jersey. The Whitehouse Station, part of Merck & Co. Inc. produces active pharmaceutical ingredients for antibiotics, making PRWT the first minority-owned company in the U.S. to manufacture active pharmaceutical ingredients.

12789 ■ *"Public Opinion" in Entrepreneur (Vol. 36, April 2008, No. 4, pp. 28)*
Pub: Entrepreneur Media, Inc.
Ed: Aliza Sherman. **Description:** According to a 2007 report from Group and Organization Management, women in top positions can lead publicly traded companies to stock price and earnings growth. Some women business owners say that going public has provided them with the capital to grow. Details on the potential of women-managed publicly traded companies are discussed.

12790 ■ *"Pulte May Be Bouncing Back From Stock-Price Doldrums" in Crain's Detroit Business (Vol. 23, October 8, 2007, No. 41, pp. 4)*
Pub: Crain Communications Inc. - Detroit
Ed: Daniel Duggan. **Description:** Pulte Homes saw a jump in its stocks due to Citigroup's analysts rating Pulte and other builders higher due to strong balance sheets.

12791 ■ *The Pursuit of Happyness*
Pub: HarperCollins Publishers Inc.
Ed: Chris Gardner. **Released:** May 2006. **Price:** $25.95. **Description:** Rags-to-riches saga of a homeless father who raised and cared for his son on the streets of San Francisco and worked to become a powerful leader on Wall Street.

12792 ■ *"Put It on MasterCard" in Barron's (Vol. 89, July 27, 2009, No. 30, pp. 16)*
Pub: Dow Jones & Co., Inc.
Ed: Bill Alpert. **Description:** Shares of MasterCard trade at a discount at just 15 times its anticipated earnings and some believe that these shares may be a better play in an economic recovery. The prospects of these shares are compared with those of Visa.

12793 ■ *"Putting SogoTrade Through Its Paces" in Barron's (Vol. 89, July 27, 2009, No. 30, pp. 27)*
Pub: Dow Jones & Co., Inc.
Ed: Theresa W. Carey. **Description:** SogoTrade options platform streams options quotes in real time and lets users place a trade in several ways. The site also features notable security tactics and is a reasonable choice for bargain-seekers. OptionsXpress' Xtend platform lets users place trades and get real time quotes.

12794 ■ *"Putting the World at Your Fingertips" in Barron's (Vol. 88, July 7, 2008, No. 27, pp. L13)*
Pub: Dow Jones & Co., Inc.
Ed: Neil A. Martin. **Description:** Currency-traded exchange funds allow investors to diversify their assets and take advantage of investment opportunities such as speculation and hedging. Investors can use these funds to build positions in favor of or against the US dollar.

12795 ■ *"Q&A: David Labistour" in Canadian Business (Vol. 81, March 17, 2008, No. 4, pp. 10)*
Pub: Rogers Media
Ed: Lauren McKeon. **Description:** David Labistour says that the difference between being a co-op retailer and a corporate-owned retailer in the case of Mountain Equipment Co-op (MEC) is that the company is owned by their customers and not by shareholders. Labistour also says that MEC works with their factories to ensure that these maintain ethical standards in the manufacturing process.

12796 ■ *"Qualcomm Could Win Big as the IPhone 3G Calls" in Barron's (Vol. 88, July 4, 2008, No. 28, pp. 30)*
Pub: Dow Jones & Co., Inc.
Ed: Eric J. Savitz. **Description:** Apple iPhone 3G's introduction could widen the smartphone market thereby benefiting handset chipmaker Qualcomm in the process. Qualcomm Senior V.P., Bill Davidson sees huge potential for his company's future beyond phones with their Snapdragon processor. The prospects of Sun Microsystems' shares are also discussed.

12797 ■ *"Quality at Bargain Prices" in Black Enterprise (Vol. 41, December 2010, No. 5, pp. 30)*
Pub: Earl G. Graves Publishing Co. Inc.
Ed: James A. Anderson. **Description:** Monica L. Walker, CEO of Holland Capital Management, suggests investors to watch prevailing trends in the financial market and to focus on using bottom-up analysis to identify companies meeting their investment criteria.

12798 ■ *The Quants*
Pub: Crown Business Books
Ed: Scott Patterson. **Released:** January 25, 2011. **Price:** $16.00. **Description:** The story of four rich and powerful men, along with Jim Simons, the founder of the most successful hedge fund in history and how they felt and what they thought in the days and weeks during the crash of Wall Street.

12799 ■ *"Quarreling Parties Keep Schenectady Redevelopment Plan In Limbo" in The Business Review Albany (Vol. 35, April*

4, 2008, No. 53)
Pub: The Business Review

Ed: Michael DeMasi. **Description:** First National Bank of Scotia chairman Louis H. Buhrmaster opposes the Erie Boulevard design project. as it could negatively affect access to the bank. Buhrmaster, aslo a vice president for Schenectady Industrial Corp, prohibits environmental assessment at the former American Locomotive property. The issues affecting the progress of the planned redevelopment at Schenectady are analyzed.

12800 ▪ *"Quebecor World Cuts Dividend" in Globe & Mail (January 20, 2006, pp. B1)*
Pub: CTVglobemedia Publishing Inc.

Description: The reasons behind the decrease in dividend by Quebecor World Inc., and its impact on investors, are discussed.

12801 ▪ *"A Questionable Chemical Romance" in Barron's (Vol. 88, July 14, 2008, No. 28, pp. 28)*
Pub: Dow Jones & Co., Inc.

Ed: Andrew Bary. **Description:** Dow Chemical paid $78-a-share for the surprise takeover of Rohm & Haas. The acquisition is reducing Dow Chemical's financial flexibility at a time when chemical companies are being affected by high costs and a weak U.S. economy.

12802 ▪ *"Quick Earnings Revival Unlikely" in Barron's (Vol. 88, June 30, 2008, No. 26, pp. 31)*
Pub: Dow Jones & Co., Inc.

Ed: Johanna Bennett. **Description:** Analysts are pushing back their prediction of a U.S. economy turnaround to 2009. A recession in the first half of 2008 may not have happened but unemployment is rising and house prices continue to fall.

12803 ▪ *Raising Capital*
Pub: Greenwood Publishing Group, Inc.

Ed: David Nour. **Released:** March 1, 2009. **Price:** $39.95. **Description:** An overview to help entrepreneurs find capital for starting and maintaining a small business is presented. The author shows how to develop long-term relationships with financial partners and ways to attract financing to fund the startup and growth phases of any business. Entrepreneurs tell how they raised money from friends, family, angel investors, banks and venture capitalists and private equity firms.

12804 ▪ *"Raising Money: the Bond that Lasts" in Entrepreneur (Vol. 35, October 2007, No. 10, pp. 73)*
Pub: Entrepreneur Media Inc.

Ed: Crystal Detamore-Rodman. **Description:** Tax-exempt bonds can be the solution to long-term financing needs of entrepreneurs. However, high initial costs may discourage some entrepreneurs to apply for these bonds, with transactions usually costing $3 mor more. How tax-exempt bonds work, and how rules vary with different states are discussed.

12805 ▪ *"Ralcorp Investigated for Rejecting ConAgra Bid" in Saint Louis Business Journal (Vol. 32, September 16, 2011, No. 3, pp. 1)*
Pub: Saint Louis Business Journal

Ed: Evan Binns. **Description:** New York-based Levi & Korsinsky started investigating Ralcorp Holidngs Inc. after it rejected ConAgra Foods Inc.'s third and latest takeover bid of $5.17 billion. The investigation would determine whether Ralcorp's directors had acted on behalf of shareholders' best interest.

12806 ▪ *"R&R Ice Cream" in Ice Cream Reporter (Vol. 23, November 20, 2010, No. 12, pp. 8)*
Pub: Ice Cream Reporter

Description: R&R Ice Cream, the United Kingdom's largest ice cream manufacturer, has completed a private offering of senior secured notes that has raised 298 million (pounds sterling) to fund expansion and acquisitions.

12807 ▪ *"R&R Launches Upscale Spoony's and Low Fat Dragon's Den" in Ice Cream Reporter (Vol. 23, August 20, 2010, No. 9, pp. 3)*
Pub: Ice Cream Reporter

Description: European ice cream manufacturer R&R has acquired French ice cream maker Rolland and will position itself as an upscale challenger to brands like Ben & Jerry's.

12808 ▪ *"Raptor Opens Consultancy" in Austin Business Journal (Vol. 31, July 8, 2011, No. 18, pp. 1)*
Pub: American City Business Journals Inc.

Ed: Christopher Calnan. **Description:** Boston hedge fund operator Raptor Group launched Raptor Accelerator, a consulting business providing sales and advisory services to early-stage companies in Central Texas. Aside from getting involved with the startups in which the Raptor Group invests, Raptor Accelerator will target firms operating in the sports, media, entertainment, and content technology sectors.

12809 ▪ *"Ratio-Cination" in Canadian Business (Vol. 79, October 23, 2006, No. 21, pp. 164)*
Pub: Rogers Media

Ed: Ian McGugan. **Description:** Tips for investors, on how to make market observations before selecting companies for purchasing stocks, are presented.

12810 ▪ *"The RBC Dynasty Continues" in Globe & Mail (January 30, 2006, pp. B1)*
Pub: CTVglobemedia Publishing Inc.

Ed: Gordon Pitts. **Description:** The details on business growth of Royal Bank of Canada, under chief executive officer Gordon Nixon, are presented.

12811 ▪ *"RBC's Hot Foreign Operations Contribute to Record Profit" in Globe & Mail (March 3, 2007, pp. B3)*
Pub: CTVglobemedia Publishing Inc.

Ed: Andrew Willis. **Description:** Royal Bank of Canada posted 27.6 percent growth in the final quarter of 2006. The bank posted $1.49 billion in profits.

12812 ▪ *"Ready for the Back Burner" in Barron's (Vol. 88, March 17, 2008, No. 11, pp. 47)*
Pub: Dow Jones & Company, Inc.

Ed: Vito J. Racanelli. **Description:** McDonald's has promised to return $15 billion to $17 billion to shareholders in 2007-2009 but headwinds are rising for the company. December, 2007 same-store sales were flat and the company's traffic growth in the U.S. is slowing. Its shares are likely to trade in tandem with the market until recession fears recede.

12813 ▪ *"Ready for a Rally?' in The Economist (Vol. 390, January 3, 2009, No. 8612, pp. 54)*
Pub: The Economist Newspaper Inc.

Description: Analysts predict that the recession could end by 2010. The current economic crisis is presented in detail.

12814 ▪ *"Real Estate's New Reality" in Entrepreneur (Vol. 37, July 2009, No. 7, pp. 32)*
Pub: Entrepreneur Media, Inc.

Ed: Rosalind Resnick. **Description:** Investing in real estate is still an advisable move, as long as investors are prepared to hold on to the property and there is a rent roll to provide a decent return on investment. Among the key considerations when investing in real estate is the property's expenses and cash flow. Other suggestions for future real estate investors are given.

12815 ▪ *"Real Opportunities: Don't Let Mortgage Mayhem Steer You Away From Sound Investments" in Black Enterprise (December 2007)*
Pub: Earl G. Graves Publishing Co. Inc.

Ed: James A. Anderson. **Description:** Real estate investment trusts (REITs) that operate office buildings, industrial parks, shopping malls, hotels, hospi-

tals, or other commercial properties may be a sound investment, despite the mortgage crisis facing the U.S. financial sector.

12816 ▪ *"Recent Deals Signal an M&A Resurgence" in Austin Business JournalInc. (Vol. 29, January 22, 2010, No. 46, pp. 1)*
Pub: American City Business Journals

Ed: Jacob Dirr. **Description:** The acquisition of at least six Austin, Texas technology companies reflects the growing acquisition activity in the US. Corporations have bought 86 companies and spent $7.3 billion during the fourth quarter of 2009. Insights into the impact of the acquisition activity to Austin's entrepreneurial energy are also given.

12817 ▪ *"Recession Fears Power Gold" in Barron's (Vol. 88, March 17, 2008, No. 11, pp. M14)*
Pub: Dow Jones & Company, Inc.

Ed: Melanie Burton. **Description:** Gold prices have been more attractive as the U.S. dollar weakens and the Dow Jones Industrial Average has slipped almost 10 percent in 2008. The rate cuts from the Federal Reserve Board has also spurred inflation fears adding upward pressure to the price of the metal.

12818 ▪ *"Recession Management" in Canadian Business (Vol. 81, March 3, 2008, No. 3, pp. 62)*
Pub: Rogers Media

Ed: Joe Castaldo. **Description:** Some companies such as Capital One Financial Corp. are managing their finances as if a recession has already taken place to prepare themselves for the looming economic downturn. Intel Corp., meanwhile shows how increasing its investments during a recession could be advantageous. Tips on how companies can survive a recession are provided.

12819 ▪ *"Recovery on Tap for 2010?' in Orlando Business Journal (Vol. 26, January 1, 2010, No. 31, pp. 1)*
Pub: American City Business Journals

Ed: Melanie Stawicki Azam, Richard Bilbao, Christopher Boyd, Anjali Fluker. **Description:** Economic forecasts for Central Florida's leading business sectors in 2010 are presented. These sectors include housing, film and TV, sports business, law, restaurants, aviation, tourism and hospitality, banking and finance, commercial real estate, retail, health care, insurance, higher education, and manufacturing. According to some local executives, Central Florida's economy will slowly recover in 2010.

12820 ▪ *"Red October" in Canadian Business (Vol. 81, December 8, 2008, No. 21, pp. 61)*
Pub: Rogers Media Ltd.

Ed: Mitch Moxley. **Description:** Analysts predict that Chinese stock market traders practice prudence amidst the challenging financial conditions in stock markets. The Chinese stock markets imploded in the last 12 months, losing two-thirds of its value.

12821 ▪ *"Reduce the Risk of Failed Financial Judgments" in Harvard Business Review (Vol. 86, July-August 2008, No. 8, pp. 24)*
Pub: Harvard Business School Press

Ed: Robert G. Eccles; Edward J. Fiedl. **Description:** Utilization of business consultants, evaluators, appraisers, and actuaries to decrease financial management risks is discussed.

12822 ▪ *"Regarding Warren" in Canadian Business (Vol. 80, November 5, 2007, No. 22, pp. 29)*
Pub: Rogers Media

Ed: Jeff Sanford. **Description:** Berkshire Hathaway's Warren Buffet believes that investing in energy shares is profitable, however, he warns investors about volatility in prices. Buffet, the second richest man in the world, forecasts that the value of the Canadian dollar will continue to rise. Buffet's investments are also discussed.

12823 ▪ *"Regent's Signal, Once Powerful, Fading From Local Scene" in Business Courier (Vol. 27, June 4, 2010, No. 5, pp. 1)*
Pub: Business Courier

Ed: Dan Monk. **Description:** Los Angeles, California-based Oaktree Capital Management bought former Regent Communications Inc. from Chapter 11 bankruptcy and transformed it into Townsquare Media Inc., a privately held firm. Regent's corporate presence has faded fast in Cincinnati, Ohio as its operations wind down. Insights on Regent's failed business model are also given.

12824 ■ *"The REIT Stuff" in Canadian Business (Vol. 80, March 26, 2007, No. 7, pp. 72)*
Pub: Rogers Media
Description: The stock performance of various real estate investment trusts in Canada is analyzed.

12825 ■ *"REIT's Decry Foreign Limits on Investment" in Globe & Mail (March 29, 2007, pp. B4)*
Pub: CTVglobemedia Publishing Inc.
Ed: Elizabeth Church. **Description:** The planned legislation by Canadian government for regulation foreign investments by real estate investment trusts is discussed.

12826 ■ *"Reports of Banks' Revival were Greatly Exaggerated" in Barron's (Vol. 88, July 7, 2008, No. 27, pp. L14)*
Pub: Dow Jones & Co., Inc.
Ed: Jack Willoughby. **Description:** Performance of mutual funds improved for the second quarter of 2008 compared to the previous quarter, registering an average gain of 0.13 percent; funds focusing on natural resources rose the highest, their value rising by an average of 24.50 percent.

12827 ■ *"A Research Firm With More Than One Foe" in Globe & Mail (February 24, 2006, pp. B1)*
Pub: CTVglobemedia Publishing Inc.
Ed: Shawn McCarthy. **Description:** The details of Biovail Corp.'s securities fraud case against Gradient Analytics Inc. are presented.

12828 ■ *"Research Reports" in Barron's (Vol. 88, March 24, 2008, No. 12, pp. M10)*
Pub: Dow Jones & Company, Inc.
Description: Investors are recommending purchasing shares of Ampco Pittsburgh due to an expected surge in earnings. Deteriorating credit quality presents problems for the shares of BankAtlantic Bancorp, whose price targets have been lowered from $7 to $5 each. Shares of Helicos Biosciences are expected to move sideways from their $6 level. Statistical data included.

12829 ■ *"Research Reports" in Barron's (Vol. 88, March 10, 2008, No. 10, pp. M13)*
Pub: Dow Jones & Company, Inc.
Description: Research reports on different company stocks by investment analysts are given. Shares of Cal Dive are rated Outperform by analysts, citing the shares' continued attractiveness and the company's acquisition of Horizon. Analysts recommend buying the shares of California Water Service Group.

12830 ■ *"Research Reports" in Barron's (Vol. 89, July 20, 2009, No. 29, pp. M12)*
Pub: Dow Jones & Co., Inc.
Description: Shares of Bank of the Ozarks, Broadpoint Gleacher Securities Group, Halozyme Therapeutics, and Take Two Interactive are rated as Buy. The shares of Fluor and PetMed Express are rated as Outperform, while those of Humana and Janus Capital Group are rated as Hold and Underweight respectively.

12831 ■ *"Research Reports: How Analysts Size Up Companies" in Barron's (Vol. 88, March 31, 2008, No. 13, pp. M13)*
Pub: Dow Jones & Company, Inc.
Ed: Anita Peltonen. **Description:** Sirius Satellite's shares are ranked Outperform as it awaits approval from the Federal Communications Commission in its merger with XM. TiVo's shares are ranked Avoid as the company is in a sector that's being commoditized. Verizon Communications' rising dividend yield earns it a Focus List ranking. The shares of Bear Stearns, Churchill Downs, Corning, and Deerfield Triarc Capital are also reviewed. Statistical data included.

12832 ■ *"Research Reports: How Analysts Size Up Companies" in Barron's (Vol. 88, March 17, 2008, No. 11, pp. M13)*
Pub: Dow Jones & Company, Inc.
Ed: Anita Peltonen. **Description:** Shares of Applied Industrial Technologies are ranked Market Perform while the shares of Google get a buy rating. Salix Pharmaceuticals gets a Sell/Above-Average risk rating. The shares of Dune Energy, Franklin Resources, Internet Brands, Piper Jaffray, and Texas Instruments are also rated.

12833 ■ *"Research Reports: How Analysts Size Up Companies" in Barron's (Vol. 88, June 30, 2008, No. 26, pp. M11)*
Pub: Dow Jones & Co., Inc.
Ed: Anita Peltonen. **Description:** Shares of Developers Diversified Realty Corp. get a 'Long-Term Buy' rating while the shares of HealthSouth Corp. and Onyx Pharmaceutical get a rating of 'Underperform' and a 'Buy' rating respectively. The shares of American Capital Agency, American Public Education, Bankrate, and Werner Enterprises are also ranked.

12834 ■ *"Research Reports: How Analysts Size Up Companies" in Barron's (Vol. 88, July 14, 2008, No. 28, pp. M13)*
Pub: Dow Jones & Co., Inc.
Ed: Anita Peltonen. **Description:** Shares of Bankrate and AutoZone both get a 'Buy' rating from analysts while Zions Bancorporation's shares are downgraded from 'Outperform' to 'Neutral'. The shares of Jet Blue Airline and Deckers Outdoor, a manufacturer of innovative footwear, are also rated and discussed. Statistical data included.

12835 ■ *"Research Reports: How Analysts Size Up Companies" in Barron's (Vol. 89, July 13, 2009, No. 28, pp. M11)*
Pub: Dow Jones & Co., Inc.
Description: Shares of Alaska Air Group get a 'Hold' rating while the shares of Art Technology Group and Cathay General Bancorp both get a 'Buy' rating. The shares of HCC Insurance Holdings, HMS Holdings, H&R Block, Intel, McDonald's, People's United Financial, Pride International, Sino Forest, and Virgin Media are also given ratings.

12836 ■ *"Research Reports: How Analysts Size Up Companies" in Barron's (Vol. 89, July 27, 2009, No. 30, pp. M12)*
Pub: Dow Jones & Co., Inc.
Ed: Anita Peltonen. **Description:** Shares of Allscripts-Misys gets an 'Outperform' rating while the shares of M&T Bank and Precision Castparts get a 'Sell' and 'Hold' rating respectively. The shares of Supervalu, Syniverse Holdings, Valley National Bancorp, Volterra, and Wesco are also rated.

12837 ■ *"Research Reports: How Analysts Size Up Companies" in Barron's (Vol. 90, August 23, 2010, No. 34, pp. M13)*
Pub: Barron's Editorial & Corporate Headquarters
Description: Shares of Sirius XM Radio, Target and Deere and Company received an eBuyE rating, while shares of Research in Motion got an eNeutralE rating.

12838 ■ *"Retail Woes: The Shoe Doesn't Fit for Gerald Loftin's Stock Picks" in Black Enterprise (Vol. 38, July 2008, No. 12, pp. 40)*
Pub: Earl G. Graves Publishing Co. Inc.
Ed: Steve Garmhausen. **Description:** Each of the three stocks that Gerald Loftin picked in May 2007 have lost money; DSW, the designer shoe retailer, fell by 63.7 percent; paint and coatings retailer Sherwin-Williams Co. fell by 7.2 percent; and Verizon Communications Inc. fell by 1.4 percent. Statistical data included.

12839 ■ *Retire Dollar Smart*
Pub: Trafford Publishing
Ed: Jim Miller. **Released:** July 2006. **Price:** $25.99. **Description:** The difference between savings and investments and their importance is examined, along with four rules for converting good investments into even greater ones. Contingency plans for healthcare costs as well as ways to manage taxes on investments are discussed. Five methods to control the

costs of investing and saving include the use of smart strategies; getting independent, accurate, complete information; investing passively; asking for a discount; and taking off your blinders. Ten steps for designing a foolproof retirement investment portfolio are also provided.

12840 ■ *"Return to Wealth; Bank Strategy" in The Economist (Vol. 390, January 3, 2009, No. 8612, pp. 56)*
Pub: The Economist Newspaper Inc.
Description: UBS' strategy to survive these trying economic times is presented. Statistical data included. UBS has a stronger balance-sheet than most of its investment-banking peers and has reduced its portfolio.

12841 ■ *Rich Dad, Poor Dad*
Pub: Warner Books Inc.
Ed: Robert Kiyosaki with Sharon Lechter. **Price:** $16.95. **Description:** What the wealthy teach their children about money that others do not.

12842 ■ *Rich Dad, Poor Dad: What the Rich Teach Their Kids About Money-That the Poor and Middle Class Do Not!*
Pub: Time Warner Paperbacks
Ed: Robert T. Kiyosaki; Sharon L. Lechter. **Released:** December 5, 2002. **Price:** $16.95. **Description:** Personal finance expert shares his economic perspective through exposure to a pair of disparate influences: his own highly education but fiscally unstable father and the multimillionaire eighth-grade dropout father of his closest friend.

12843 ■ *Rich Dad's Increase Your Financial IQ: Get Smarter with Your Money*
Pub: Business Plus
Ed: Robert T. Kiyosaki. **Released:** $16.99. **Price:** March 26, 2008. **Description:** Author describes his five key principles of financial knowledge to help readers build wealth.

12844 ■ *"The Right Time for REITs" in Barron's (Vol. 88, July 14, 2008, No. 28, pp. 32)*
Pub: Dow Jones & Co., Inc.
Ed: Mike Hogan. **Description:** Discusses the downturn in U.S. real estate investment trusts so these are worth considering for investment. Several Websites that are useful for learning about real estate investment trusts for investment purposes are presented.

12845 ■ *"RIM's Options Story Under Fire" in Globe & Mail (March 16, 2007, pp. B1)*
Pub: CTVglobemedia Publishing Inc.
Ed: Janet McFarland. **Description:** The investigation of the backdating of options by Research In Motion Ltd. is discussed. The analysis of the backdating of company's options issues by Professor Erik Lie from the University of Iowa is presented.

12846 ■ *"Risk Management Starts at the Top" in Business Strategy Review (Vol. 21, Spring 2010, No. 1, pp. 18)*
Pub: Wiley-Blackwell
Ed: Paul Strebel, Hongze Lu. **Description:** Authors question why, at the end of 2008, Citigroup, Merrill Lynch and UBS had well over $40 billion in sub-prime write-downs and credit losses, while some of their competitors were much less exposed. Their research into the situation revealed correlations of great import to today's firms.

12847 ■ *"Rob McEwen" in Canadian Business (Vol. 80, Winter 2007, No. 24, pp. 138)*
Pub: Rogers Media
Ed: John Gray. **Description:** Rob McEwen's interest in gold started with his father who was in the investment industry and was always talking about the value of gold. McEwen believes that there is a lot of room to innovate in mining and that Canada should be a leader in this field.

12848 ■ *"Rock Festival: High Spirited Conventioneers Celebrate Their Good Fortune" in Canadian Business (Vol. 81,*

March 31, 2008, No. 5)
Pub: Rogers Media
Ed: Jeff Sanford. **Description:** Soaring prices of commodities in the mining industry have been very good for the attendees of the 76th annual conference of the Prospectors & Developers Association of Canada. A speaker at the conference expects commodity prices to come off a bit but not fall dramatically as it did in the 1980's.

12849 ■ *"Rogue's Gallery" in Canadian Business (Vol. 81, November 10, 2008, No. 19, pp. 44)*
Pub: Rogers Media Ltd.
Ed: Rachel Pulfer. **Description:** Laissez-faire capitalism or poor oversight of Fannie Mae and Freddie Mac are causes for the financial crisis in the U.S., depending or Democrat or Republican viewpoint. Events leading up to the 2008 financial crisis are covered.

12850 ■ *"Roundtable - The Auto Sector Shifts Gears" in Mergers & Acquisitions: The Dealmaker's Journal (March 1, 2008)*
Pub: SourceMedia, Inc.
Description: Industry professionals discuss the current state of the automotive sector as well as what they predict for the future of the industry; also provides information for investors about opportunities in the sector.

12851 ■ *"RS Information Systems Signs Buyout Deal" in Black Enterprise (February 2008)*
Pub: Earl G. Graves Publishing Co. Inc.
Ed: Alan Hughes. **Description:** Details of the RS Information Systems buyout by Wyle, a privately held provider of high-tech aerospace engineering, testing, and research services.

12852 ■ *"Ryder's Shock Absorbers Are In Place" in Barron's (Vol. 88, March 24, 2008, No. 12, pp. 19)*
Pub: Dow Jones & Company, Inc.
Ed: Christopher C. Williams. **Description:** Shares of Ryder System Inc. are expected to continue rising on the back of rising earnings, forecast at $5.20 a share for 2009. The shares of the truck freight company hit a 52-week high of $62.27 each and may reach $70 a share.

12853 ■ *"SABMiller Deal Hit by Tax Ruling" in Wall Street Journal Eastern Edition (November 21, 2011, pp. B9)*
Pub: Dow Jones & Company Inc.
Ed: David Fickling, Simon Zekaria. **Description:** SABMiller PLC, the giant brewer in the United Kingdom, is acquiring Australian beer icon Foster's Group Ltd. for US$9.9 billion, but will have to come up with another A$582 million following a tax ruling by the Australian Taxation Office in order that shareholders of Foster's don't lose.

12854 ■ *Safety Net*
Pub: Crown Business Books
Ed: James Glassman. **Released:** February 22, 2011. **Price:** $23.00. **Description:** Ways to build a financial investment strategy that protects you, while ensuring growth in a strong financial future are presented.

12855 ■ *"St. Elizabeth Fights for Share at St. Lukes" in Business Courier (Vol. 27, November 12, 2010, No. 28, pp. 1)*
Pub: Business Courier
Ed: James Ritchie. **Description:** Key information on how St. Elizabeth Healthcare helps partner St. Luke's Hospitals increase market share in the healthcare industry are presented. Some of St. Luke's hospitals, such as the St. Elizabeth Fort Thomas in Kentucky, are struggling with low occupancy rates, prompting St. Elizabeth to invest about $24 million to help St. Luke's increase its market share.

12856 ■ *"Sales Gave W&S Record '07" in Business Courier (Vol. 24, March 14, 2008, No. 49, pp. 1)*
Pub: American City Business Journals, Inc.
Ed: Jon Newberry. **Description:** Western & Southern Financial Group was able to achieve a record $365 million in net income thanks in large part to the

double-digit increases in profits by its W&S Agency Group field offices and non-insurance businesses. The sale of their Integrated Investment Services Subsidiary and shares in several Marriot hotels also added to the record profit.

12857 ■ *"Sales of Pension Income Targeted by Senator" in Wall Street Journal Eastern Edition (November 21, 2011, pp. C7)*
Pub: Dow Jones & Company Inc.
Ed: Leslie Scism. **Description:** Senator Tom Harkin is concerned about a widening business in which retirees and veterans sell pension income to investors in the secondary market. The business provides major profits for middlemen. Harkin wants those who are considering such a sale to have adequate information provided and knowledge in order to avoid unscrupulous dealings.

12858 ■ *"Samll Fortunes" in Business Courier (Vol. 27, July 23, 2010, No. 12, pp. 1)*
Pub: Business Courier
Ed: Steve Watkins. **Description:** Small banks in Cincinnati, Ohio have been faring well despite the economic crisis, a survey has revealed. Sixty percent of local small banks have capital levels above 15.8 percent median. But regulators are seen to close more banks in 2010 than since the financial crises began.

12859 ■ *"Satellite Down, Stock Up: Raytheon Is On Target With Ten Percent Dividend Increase" in Barron's (Vol. 88, March 31, 2008, No. 13)*
Pub: Dow Jones & Company, Inc.
Ed: Shirley A. Lazo. **Description:** Raytheon hiked their quarterly dividend to 28 cents per share from 25.5 cents. Aircastle slashed their quarterly common dividend by 64 percent for them to retain additional capital that can be used to increase their liquidity position.

12860 ■ *"Save the Date" in Mergers & Acquisitions: The Dealmaker's Journal (March 1, 2008)*
Pub: SourceMedia, Inc.
Description: Listing of conferences and forums that deal with business and investing, particularly with mergers and acquisitions. Includes dates, locations and Internet addresses.

12861 ■ *"A Say on Pay" in Canadian Business (Vol. 82, April 27, 2009, No. 7, pp. 14)*
Pub: Rogers Media
Ed: Joe Castaldo. **Description:** A COMPAS Inc. survey of 134 Canadian chief executive officers found that 44 percent agree that CEO compensation should be subject to a non-binding vote. The respondents were also divided on whether to allow shareholders to exercise retroactive clawbacks on executive compensation if firm performance turns out to be worse than projected.

12862 ■ *Schaum's Outline Financial Management, Third Edition*
Pub: McGraw-Hill
Ed: Jae K. Shim; Joel G. Siegel. **Released:** May 2007. **Price:** $22.95 (CND). **Description:** Rules and regulations governing corporate finance, including the Sarbanes-Oxley Act are discussed.

12863 ■ *"Schwab: Lower Returns Ahead" in Barron's (Vol. 89, July 13, 2009, No. 28, pp. L4)*
Pub: Dow Jones & Co., Inc.
Ed: Leslie P. Norton. **Description:** Charles Schwab says that 8 percent to 10 percent equity-market returns are not realistic these days and that 4 percent to 5 percent are more realistic in the next four to five years from 2009. Schwab expects inflation to be close to 10 percent per annum in a couple of years.

12864 ■ *"Score One for 'Barron's'" in Barron's (Vol. 89, July 13, 2009, No. 28, pp. 14)*
Pub: Dow Jones & Co., Inc.
Ed: Andrew Bary. **Description:** 57 companies that were bullishly covered on 'Barron's' for the first half of 2009 were up an average of 20.4 percent com-

pared to the 10.2 percent gain in the relevant market indexes. The bearish stock picks by 'Barron's' were down 3.4 percent compared to a 6.4 percent for the benchmarks.

12865 ■ *"Scotiabank Targets More Baby Boomers" in Globe & Mail (March 4, 2006, pp. B5)*
Pub: CTVglobemedia Publishing Inc.
Ed: Elizabeth Church. **Description:** Bank of Nova Scotia posted $844 million profit for first quarter 2006. The plans of the bank to achieve baby boomer client base are presented.

12866 ■ *"Scottsdale Bank Plans 4Q Opening" in The Business Journal - Serving Phoenix and the Valley of the Sun (Vol. 28, August 15, 2008, No. 50)*
Pub: American City Business Journals, Inc.
Ed: Chris Casacchia. **Description:** Arizona's Department of Financial Institutions has approved Scottsdale Business Bank, a community bank which plans to open in the fourth quarter of 2008. The bank, which is to be located near McCormick Ranch in Scottsdale, Arizona, will cater to small business owners in the professional sector, such as accountants and doctors.

12867 ■ *"Screening for the Best Stock Screens" in Barron's (Vol. 90, September 13, 2010, No. 37, pp. 36)*
Pub: Barron's Editorial & Corporate Headquarters
Ed: Mike Hogan. **Description:** Pros and cons of the new and revised stock screening tools from Zack, Finviz.com, and GuruFocus are discussed. FinVix.com is more capable for screening through stocks and the service is free.

12868 ■ *"Sears' Lampert Solid in Game of Valuation Chicken" in Globe & Mail (February 25, 2006, pp. B2)*
Pub: CTVglobemedia Publishing Inc.
Ed: Eric Reguly. **Description:** The feasibility of share value of Sears Canada Inc., following Sears Holdings Corp.'s acquisition, is discussed.

12869 ■ *"SEC Doesn't Buy Biovail's Claims" in Barron's (Vol. 88, March 31, 2008, No. 13, pp. 20)*
Pub: Dow Jones & Company, Inc.
Ed: Bill Alpert. **Description:** Overstatement of earnings and chronic fraudulent conduct has led the SEC to file a stock fraud suit against Biovail, Eugene Melnyk and three others present or former employees of Biovail. Melnyk had the firm file suit in 2006 that blames short-sellers and stock researchers for the company's drop in share price.

12870 ■ *"SEC Report On Rating Agencies Falls Short" in Barron's (Vol. 88, July 14, 2008, No. 28, pp. 35)*
Pub: Dow Jones & Co., Inc.
Ed: Jack Willoughby. **Description:** The Securities and Exchange Commissions report on credit-rating firms should have drawn attention to the slipshod practices in the offerings of collateralized debt obligations. The report fell short of prescribing correctives for the flawed system of these agencies' relationship with their clients.

12871 ■ *The Secret of Exiting Your Business Under Your Terms!*
Pub: Outskirts Press, Incorporated
Ed: Gene H. Irwin. **Released:** August 2005. **Price:** $29.95. **Description:** Topics include how to sell a business for the highest value, tax laws governing the sale of a business, finding the right buyer, mergers and acquisitions, negotiating the sale, and using a limited auction to increase future value of a business.

12872 ■ *"A Security Risk?" in Canadian Business (Vol. 80, October 22, 2007, No. 21, pp. 36)*
Pub: Rogers Media
Ed: Joe Castaldo. **Description:** Garda World Security Corporation declared a C$1.5 million loss in the second quarter of 2007. The company's securities have been falling since June and hit a 52-week low

of $15.90 in September. Details of the physical and cash-handling firm's strategy to integrate its acquisitions are discussed.

12873 ■ *"Selling Michigan; R&D Pushed as Reason For Chinese To Locate In State"* in *Crain's Detroit Business (Vol. 24, January 14, 2008)*

Pub: Crain Communications Inc. - Detroit

Ed: Marti Benedetti. **Description:** Southeast Michigan Economic Development organizations are working to develop relationships with Chinese manufacturers so they will locate their automotive research and development operations in the state.

12874 ■ *"Selling Pressures Rise in China"* in *Barron's (Vol. 88, March 10, 2008, No. 10, pp. M9)*

Pub: Dow Jones & Company, Inc.

Ed: Mohammed Hadi. **Description:** There are about 1.6 trillion yuan worth of shares up for sale in Chinese stock markets in 2008, adding to the selling pressures in these markets. The Chinese government has imposed restrictions to prevent a rapid rise in selling stocks.

12875 ■ *"Sense of Discovery"* in *Business Journal Portland (Vol. 27, November 19, 2010, No. 38, pp. 1)*

Pub: Portland Business Journal

Ed: Erik Siemers. **Description:** Tigard, Oregon-based Exterro Inc. CEO Bobby Balachandran announced plans to go public without the help of an institutional investor. Balachandran believes Exterro could grow to a $100 million legal compliance software company in the span of three years. Insights on Exterro's growth as market leader in the $1 billion legal governance software market are also given.

12876 ■ *"Sentiment Split on Financials"* in *Barron's (Vol. 88, March 24, 2008, No. 12, pp. M14)*

Pub: Dow Jones & Company, Inc.

Ed: Steven M. Sears. **Description:** Experts in the financial sector are split as to whether or not the worst of the financial crisis brought on by the credit crunch is over. Some options traders are trading on are defensive puts, expecting the worst, while investors buying calls are considered as bullish.

12877 ■ *"Serious Signal Flashing?"* in *Barron's (Vol. 88, July 7, 2008, No. 27, pp. 11)*

Pub: Dow Jones & Co., Inc.

Description: Discusses the Hindenburg Omen, named after the airship disaster of May 1937, which is considered a predictor of market crashes and has appeared twice in June 2008. There is a 25 percent probability that the US stock market will suffer a crash in the July-October 2008 period.

12878 ■ *"Seven Ways to Fail Big"* in *Harvard Business Review (Vol. 86, September 2008, No. 9, pp. 82)*

Pub: Harvard Business School Press

Ed: Paul B. Carroll; Chunka Mui. **Description:** Seven factors involved in business failures are identified, and ways to avoid them are described. These factors include flawed financial engineering, hurrying into consolidation, and investing in technology that is not a good fit.

12879 ■ *"A Shallow Pool"* in *Canadian Business (Vol. 81, Summer 2008, No. 9, pp. 44)*

Pub: Rogers Media Ltd.

Ed: Joe Castaldo. **Description:** Bank of Canada projected in its 'Monetary Policy Report' a growth rate of 1.4 percent in 2008 and does not expect the economy to fully recover until mid-2010. The Canadian stock market has been recovering although slowly with just a 1.6 percent gain by April 30. Other details on the Canadian equity market are presented.

12880 ■ *"Shanghai Butterfly"* in *Canadian Business (Vol. 80, March 12, 2007, No. 6, pp. 69)*

Pub: Rogers Media

Ed: Thomas Watson. **Description:** The volatile nature of Shanghai stock markets and its impact on investors and the economy is discussed.

12881 ■ *"Shipwreck Floats Nickel's Boat"* in *Globe & Mail (January 24, 2007, pp. B1)*

Pub: CTVglobemedia Publishing Inc.

Ed: John Partridge. **Description:** The rise in the price of nickel to $38,300 a tonne following a shipwreck in which 1,000 tonnes of the metal was lost is discussed.

12882 ■ *"Shopped Out; Retailing Gloom"* in *The Economist (Vol. 390, January 3, 2009, No. 8612, pp. 26)*

Pub: The Economist Newspaper Inc.

Description: Economic volatility in the retail sector is having an impact on a number of countries around the globe. Europe is experiencing hard economic times as well and unless businesses have a strong business plan banks feel unable to lend the money necessary to tide the retailers over. The falling pound has increased the cost of imported goods and small to midsize retail chains may not be able to weather such an unforgiving economic climate.

12883 ■ *"Shoppes of Kenwood Files Chap. 11"* in *Business Courier (Vol. 26, December 18, 2009, No. 34, pp. 1)*

Pub: American City Business Journals, Inc.

Ed: Jon Newberry. **Description:** Shoppes of Kenwood filed for Chapter 11 reorganization in US Bankruptcy Court just as the property was scheduled to be offered at a sheriff's auction. Details of the filing are included.

12884 ■ *"Shorts Story"* in *Barron's (Vol. 89, July 6, 2009, No. 27, pp. 16)*

Pub: Dow Jones & Co., Inc.

Ed: Gene Epstein. **Description:** Shares of Compass Minerals, J2 Global Communications, K12, Middleby, and Pactiv should be shorted by investors. These companies suffer from weaknesses in their business models, making them vulnerable to a share price decline.

12885 ■ *"Shorts Story"* in *Barron's (Vol. 89, July 6, 2009, No. 27, pp. 16)*

Pub: Dow Jones & Co., Inc.

Ed: Gene Epstein. **Description:** Shares of Compass Minerals, J2 Global Communications, K12, Middleby, and Pactiv should be shorted by investors. These companies suffer from weaknesses in their business models, making them vulnerable to a share price decline.

12886 ■ *"Should the Fed Regulate Wall Street?"* in *Barron's (Vol. 88, March 24, 2008, No. 12, pp. M15)*

Pub: Dow Jones & Company, Inc.

Ed: Randall W. Forsyth. **Description:** Greater regulation of the financial sector by the Federal Reserve is essential for it to survive the crisis it is experiencing. The resulting regulation could be in complete contrast with the deregulation the sector previously experienced.

12887 ■ *"Should I or Shouldn't I?"* in *Indoor Comfort Marketing (Vol. 70, February 2011, No. 2, pp. 30)*

Pub: Industry Publications Inc.

Ed: Philip J. Baratz. **Description:** Investment tips are shared for investing in futures options.

12888 ■ *"Silver Standard Reports First Quarter 2007 Results"* in *Canadian Corporate News (May 14, 2007)*

Pub: Comtex News Network Inc.

Description: Silver Standard Resources Inc. reports a first quarter loss of $1.6 million compared with the first quarter of 2006 in which the loss was $1.1 million. Statistical data included.

12889 ■ *"A Simple Old Reg that Needs Dusting Off"* in *Barron's (Vol. 88, June 30, 2008, No. 26, pp. 35)*

Pub: Dow Jones & Co., Inc.

Ed: Gene Epstein. **Description:** Senator Joe Lieberman has a point when he accused speculators of inflating the prices of food and fuel futures but introducing legislation to address speculation has an alternative. The senator's committee should instead

demand that the Commodity Futures Trading Commission enforce position limits on the maximum number of contracts in a given market per speculative entity.

12890 ■ *"Six Great Stock Funds for the Long Haul"* in *Barron's (Vol. 89, July 13, 2009, No. 28, pp. L5)*

Pub: Dow Jones & Co., Inc.

Ed: Lawrence C. Strauss; Tom Sullivan. **Description:** Six mutual funds that have solid long-term performance, transparency, savvy stock picking, and discipline are presented. The managers of these funds are also evaluated. These funds include the T. Rowe Price Emerging Market Stock Fund, Fairholme, and Dodge & Cox Stock.

12891 ■ *"Six Things You Can Do To Ride Out A Turbulent Market"* in *Hispanic Business (Vol. 30, March 2008, No. 3, pp. 20)*

Pub: Hispanic Business

Ed: Hildy Medina; Michael Bowker. **Description:** Top financial experts' views on managing investment portfolios during turbulent periods in the stock market are reported. Experts prefer investing in health care, short term investments, international bonds and preferred stocks or just maintain cash until such times as the market settles.

12892 ■ *"Six Things You Can Do To Ride Out a Turbulent Market"* in *Hispanic Business (March 2008, pp. 20-21)*

Pub: Hispanic Business

Ed: Hildy Medina, Michael Bowker. **Description:** Experts in the financial industry suggest shifting portfolios; investing in cash; thinking long-term for market investments; investing in foreign bonds, covered calls and preferred stocks; and to rebalance a portfolio in order to survive the downturn in the stock market.

12893 ■ *"Skinner's No Drive-Thru CEO"* in *Crain's Chicago Business (Vol. 31, April 28, 2008, No. 17, pp. 1)*

Pub: Crain Communications, Inc.

Ed: David Sterrett. **Description:** Profile of James Skinner who was named CEO for McDonald's Corp. in November 2004 and has proved to be a successful leader despite the number of investors who doubted him when he came to the position. Mr. Skinner has overseen three years of unprecedented sales growth and launched the biggest menu expansion in 30 years.

12894 ■ *"Skype Ltd. Acquired GroupMe"* in *Information Today (Vol. 28, October 2011, No. 9, pp. 12)*

Pub: Information Today, Inc.

Description: Skype Ltd. acquired GroupMe, a group messaging company that allows users to form impromptu groups where they can text message, share data, and make conference calls for free and is supported on Android, iPhone, BlackBerry, and Windows phones.

12895 ■ *"The Skype's the Limit"* in *Canadian Business (Vol. 80, February 12, 2007, No. 4, pp. 70)*

Pub: Rogers Media

Ed: Gerry Blackwell. **Description:** The increase in the market share of Skype Technologies S.A.'s Internet phone service to 171 million users is discussed.

12896 ■ *"Sleeman Cuts Again as Cheap Suds Bite"* in *Globe & Mail (March 3, 2006, pp. B3)*

Pub: CTVglobemedia Publishing Inc.

Ed: Andy Hoffman. **Description:** The details on 5 percent employee reduction at Sleeman Breweries Ltd., which posted 86 percent decline in profits for fourth quarter 2005, are presented.

12897 ■ *"A Slice of Danish; Fixing Finance"* in *The Economist (Vol. 390, January 3, 2009, No. 8612, pp. 55)*

Pub: The Economist Newspaper Inc.

Description: Denmark's mortgage-holders and the county's lending system is presented.

12898 ■ *"Slow but Steady into the Future"* in *Barron's (Vol. 88, July 7, 2008, No. 27, pp. M)*
Pub: Dow Jones & Co., Inc.
Ed: Mark Veverka. **Description:** Investors are advised to maintain their watch on the shares of business software company NetSuite. The company's chief executive officer, Zach Nelson, claims that the company has a 10-year lead on its competitors with the development of software-as-a service.

12899 ■ *"The Small 300"* in *Canadian Business (Vol. 81, Summer 2008, No. 9, pp. 137)*
Pub: Rogers Media Ltd.
Description: Small cap-companies are ranked based on market capitalization and stock performance. Calgary-based Grande Cache Coal Corp. topped the roster with 1,000 percent of return resulting from strong sales. A table showing the 2008 rankings of the companies is presented.

12900 ■ *"Small is Bountiful for Intuit"* in *Barron's (Vol. 90, September 13, 2010, No. 37, pp. 22)*
Pub: Barron's Editorial & Corporate Headquarters
Ed: Mark Veverka. **Description:** Finance software maker Intuit wants to tap the underserved small business market. One analyst sees Intuit's shares rising 25 percent to 55 percent in the next 12 months from September 2010.

12901 ■ *"Small Firms Punch Ticket for Growth"* in *Houston Business Journal (Vol. 40, January 29, 2010, No. 38, pp. 1)*
Pub: American City Business Journals
Ed: Allison Wollam. **Description:** Independent ticket agencies anticipate growth as American and Canadian authorities approved a merger between Ticketmaster and concert promoter Live Nation. Expansion of service offerings and acquisition of venues have also been done by independent ticket agencies in light of the merger. Details of the merger are included.

12902 ■ *"Smart Investor's Shopping List: Coke, Walgreen, Drill Bits; A Conversation with Money Manager Paula Dorion-Gray"* in *Crain's Chicago Business*
Pub: Crain Communications, Inc.
Ed: Bruce Blythe. **Description:** Interview with Paula Dorion-Gray, president of Dorion-Gray Retirement Planning Inc., discusses the state of the investing environment, favored industries, industries to avoid, and her approach towards investing.

12903 ■ *"Smart Medicine"* in *Canadian Business (Vol. 80, February 26, 2007, No. 5, pp. 73)*
Pub: Rogers Media
Ed: Zena Olijnyk. **Description:** The stock price stability and future earnings prospects of Canadian biotechnology firm YM Biosciences are analyzed.

12904 ■ *"The Smell of Fear: Is a Bottom Near?"* in *Barron's (Vol. 88, March 17, 2008, No. 11, pp. M3)*
Pub: Dow Jones & Company, Inc.
Ed: Kopin Tan. **Description:** Liquidity problems at Bear Stearns frightened investors in markets around the world due to the fear of the prospects of a big bank's failure. Shares of health maintenance organizations got battered led by WellPoint, and Humana but longer-term investors who could weather short-term volatility may find value here. The value of J. Crew shares is also discussed.

12905 ■ *The Snowball: Warren Buffett and the Business of Life*
Pub: Bantam Books
Ed: Alice Schroeder. **Released:** 2009. **Price:** $35.00. **Description:** The first authorized biography of Warren Buffett provides deep and timely insight into the psyche of the billionaire investor.

12906 ■ *"A Socko Payout Menu: Rural Phone Carrier Plots to Supercharge Its Shares"* in *Barron's (Vol. 88, June 30, 2008, No. 26, pp. M5)*
Pub: Dow Jones & Co., Inc.
Ed: Shirley A. Lazo. **Description:** CenturyTel boosted its quarterly common payout to 70 cents from 6.75 cents per share due to its strong cash flows and solid balance sheet. Eastman Kodak's plan for a buyback will be partially funded by its $581 million tax refund. CME Group will buyback stocks through 2009 worth $1.1 billion.

12907 ■ *"Software's Last Hurrah"* in *Canadian Business (Vol. 81, December 24, 2007, No. 1, pp. 27)*
Pub: Rogers Media
Ed: Andrew Wahl. **Description:** Canada's software industry could be facing a challenge with IBM's acquisition of Cognos, which was the country's last major independent business intelligence company and was also IBM's largest acquisition ever. Next in line to Cognos in terms of prominence is Open Text Corporation, which could also be a possible candidate for acquisition, as analysts predict.

12908 ■ *"Solace for the Freshly Flaherty'd"* in *Canadian Business (Vol. 79, November 6, 2006, No. 22, pp. 114)*
Pub: Rogers Media
Ed: Ian McGugan. **Description:** Tips to manage investments with relation to cash distribution tax on income trusts are presented.

12909 ■ *"Somanetics to Buy Back Up to $15 Million of Common Shares"* in *Crain's Detroit Business (Vol. 24, April 7, 2008, No. 14, pp. 4)*
Pub: Crain Communications, Inc.
Ed: Tom Henderson. **Description:** Somanetics Corp., a company that manufactures and markets noninvasive devices for monitoring blood oxygen levels in the brain and elsewhere in the body during surgery, plans to buy back up to $15 million worth of its common shares. Statistical data included on the company's current and past earnings and stock prices as well as its plans to increase revenue.

12910 ■ *"Some Big Biotechs Buying Own Stock"* in *Boston Business Journal (Vol. 30, November 5, 2010, No. 41, pp. 1)*
Pub: Boston Business Journal
Ed: Julie M. Donnelly. **Description:** Biotechnology companies such as Biogen Idec and Genzyme Corporation are conducting stock buybacks as they look to invest their cash holdings. Other analysts see the buybacks as reluctance in committing to longer-term investments.

12911 ■ *"Some Relief Possible Following Painful Week"* in *Barron's (Vol. 88, July 14, 2008, No. 28, pp. M3)*
Pub: Dow Jones & Co., Inc.
Ed: Kopin Tan. **Description:** Dow Chemical is offering a 74 percent premium to acquire Rohm & Haas' coatings and electronics materials operations. Frontline amassed a 5.6 percent stake in rival Overseas Shipholding Group and a merger between the two would create a giant global fleet with pricing power. Highlights of the U.S. stock market during the week that ended in July 11, 2008 are discussed. Statistical data included.

12912 ■ *"Something to Like"* in *Canadian Business (Vol. 81, April 14, 2008, No. 6, pp. 22)*
Pub: Rogers Media
Ed: Jack Mintz. **Description:** Jim Flaherty's policy on tax-free savings account (TFSA) will allow Canadians to accumulate wealth at a much faster rate and these accounts could be especially good for people who are subject to high effective taxes on savings. Investors should put their money into a Registered Retirement Savings Plan (RRSP) when it comes to risky investments but the TFSA is better than an RRSP if investors expect very high taxes on withdrawals from their RRSP.

12913 ■ *"S.O.S. Sorting Out Subprime"* in *Black Enterprise (Vol. 38, November 2007, No. 4, pp. 76)*
Pub: Earl G. Graves Publishing Co. Inc.
Ed: Trevor Delaney. **Description:** Subprime distress in the housing market is discussed and the impact it has put on investors.

12914 ■ *"The Spark's Back in Sanyo"* in *Barron's (Vol. 88, March 31, 2008, No. 13, pp. M9)*
Pub: Dow Jones & Company, Inc.
Ed: Jay Alabaster. **Description:** Things are looking up for Sanyo Electric after its string of calamities that range from major losses brought on by earthquake damage to its semiconductor operations and its near collapse and bailout. The company looks poised for a rebound as they are on track for their first net profit since 2003 and could beat its earnings forecast for 2008.

12915 ■ *"Spectre of Iran War Spooks Oil Markets"* in *Globe & Mail (March 28, 2007, pp. B1)*
Pub: CTVglobemedia Publishing Inc.
Ed: Shawn McCarthy. **Description:** The increase in the price of crude oil by $5 a barrel to reach $68 in the United States following speculation over war against Iran, is discussed.

12916 ■ *"Spotlight on Pensions"* in *Business Horizons (Vol. 51, March-April 2008, No. 2, pp. 105)*
Pub: Elsevier Advanced Technology Publications
Ed: Laureen A. Maines. **Description:** Perceptions of pension burden and risk among financial statement users is likely to increase with changes in pension accounting. These perceptions might affect decisions on pension commitments and investments.

12917 ■ *"Spread Your Wings"* in *Canadian Business (Vol. 81, March 17, 2008, No. 4, pp. 31)*
Pub: Rogers Media
Ed: Megan Harman. **Description:** Financing from angel investors is one avenue that should be explored by startups. Angel investors are typically affluent individuals who invest their own money. Angel investors usually want at least 10 times their initial investment within eight years but they benefit the businesses through their help in decision-making and the industry expertise they provide.

12918 ■ *"Sprint Tries to Wring Out Positives"* in *The Business Journal-Serving Metropolitan Kansas City (Vol. 26, August 8, 2008, No. 48)*
Pub: American City Business Journals, Inc.
Ed: Suzanna Stagemeyer. **Description:** Sprint Nextel Corp. reported that 901,000 subscribers left the company in the quarter ending June 30, 2008; fewer than the nearly 1.1 million it lost in the previous quarter. Customer turnover also dropped to just less than 2 percent, compared to 2.45 percent in the first quarter of 2008.

12919 ■ *"Stand-Up Guy"* in *Barron's (Vol. 88, July 7, 2008, No. 27, pp. L11)*
Pub: Dow Jones & Co., Inc.
Ed: Suzanne McGee. **Description:** James O'Shaughnessy, a mutual fund manager with O'Shaughnessy Asset Management, is bullish on both financial and energy stocks. He was formerly involved with Bear Stearns until he left the firm in March 2008.

12920 ■ *"State of Play"* in *Canadian Business (Vol. 79, June 19, 2006, No. 13, pp. 25)*
Pub: Rogers Media
Ed: Andrew Wahl; Zena Olijnyk; Jeff Sanford. **Description:** Top 100 information technology companies in Canada are ranked by their market capitalization as of June 1. The statistics that show the revenues of these companies are also presented.

12921 ■ *"State Shock Prices Take Large Tumble"* in *The Business Journal-Milwaukee (Vol. 25, September 12, 2008, No. 51, pp. A1)*
Pub: American City Business Journals, Inc.
Ed: Rich Rovito. **Description:** Weak economic times have caused the stocks of most publicly traded companies in Wisconsin to dip in 2008. Companies that appeared on the worst performing stocks list also experienced drops in share price to as much as 70 percent. Information about the companies that experienced increases in stock prices is also presented. Statistical data included.

12922 ■ *"Stay Calm, Bernanke Urges Markets"* in Globe & Mail (March 1, 2007, pp. B1)

Pub: CTVglobemedia Publishing Inc.

Ed: Brian McKenna. **Description:** The views of Ben Bernanke, the chief of the United States Federal Reserve Board, on the future trends of the United States' economy are presented. The effect of the global stock market trends on the American stock markets is discussed.

12923 ■ *"Stelco Investors Told Their Stock Now Worthless"* in Globe & Mail (January 23, 2006, pp. B4)

Pub: CTVglobemedia Publishing Inc.

Ed: Greg Keenan. **Description:** The reasons behind Ontario Superior Court's approval of Stelco Inc.'s restructuring proposal are presented.

12924 ■ *"The Stem Cell Revolution"* in Canadian Business (Vol. 79, November 20, 2006, No. 23, pp. 31)

Pub: Rogers Media

Ed: Erin Pooley. **Description:** The commercial prospects and the future of stem cell therapeutics are presented. The use of stem cell therapy to heal the chronic conditions of patients is also discussed.

12925 ■ *"STMicroelectronics"* in Canadian Electronics (Vol. 23, February 2008, No. 1, pp. 1)

Pub: CLB Media Inc.

Description: STMicroelectronics, a semiconductor maker, revealed that it plans to acquire Genesis Microchip Inc. Genesis develops image and video processing systems. It was reported that the acquisition has been approved by Genesis' Board of Directors. It is expected that Genesis will enhance STMicroelectronics' technological capabilities.

12926 ■ *"Stock Analysts' Pans"* in Canadian Business (Vol. 81, Summer 2008, No. 9, pp. 75)

Pub: Rogers Media Ltd.

Ed: Calvin Leung. **Description:** Table showing the one-year stock performance of companies that are least loved by analysts and are rated either to be a Hold or Sell. These companies should not be included in the investment portfolio, at least in the short term.

12927 ■ *"Stock Car Racing"* in Canadian Business (Vol. 81, September 15, 2008, No. 14-15, pp. 29)

Pub: Rogers Media Ltd.

Ed: Thomas Watson. **Description:** Some analysts predict a Chapter 11-style tune-up making GM and Ford a speculative turnaround stock. However, the price of oil could make or break the shares of the Big Three U.S. automobile manufacturers and if oil goes up too high then a speculative stock to watch is an electric car company called Zenn Motor Co.

12928 ■ *"Stock Delisting Could Hamper First Mariner"* in Boston Business Journal (Vol. 29, July 29, 2011, No. 12, pp. 1)

Pub: American City Business Journals Inc.

Ed: Gary Haber. **Description:** Possible delisting of First Mariner Bancorp from the Nasdaq stock exchange could adversely impact the bank's ability to attract institutional investors. Some institutions limit their investments to companies trading on the Nasdaq.

12929 ■ *"Stockgroup Completes US $4.5 Million Financing"* in Canadian Corporate News (May 16, 2007)

Pub: Comtex News Network Inc.

Description: Stockgroup, a financial media company focused on collaborative technologies and user-generated content, will use the proceeds of the private placement for acquisitions and general working capital.

12930 ■ *"Street Beaters: How the Top Stock Earners on Our List Pulled It Off"* in Canadian Business (Vol. 80, Winter 2007, No. 24, pp. 135)

Pub: Rogers Media

Ed: Jeff Sanford. **Description:** Shares of Research in Motion Ltd. jumped 163 percent in 2007 after setting their patent dispute. ShawCor Ltd.'s stocks rose 99.6 percent while Onex Corporation's shares reached a high of $41.25 in 2007 from its $25 average in 2006.

12931 ■ *Street Fighters: The Last 72 Hours of Bears Stearns, the Toughest Firm on Wall Street*

Pub: Portfolio

Ed: Kate Kelly. **Released:** 2009. **Price:** $25.95. **Description:** An account of the investment bank, Bears Stearns fight for survival is documented.

12932 ■ *"Stressed Out: 7 Banks Rated 'At Riks'"* in Saint Louis Business Journal (Vol. 32, September 16, 2011, No. 3, pp. 1)

Pub: Saint Louis Business Journal

Ed: Greg Edwards. **Description:** St. Louis, Missouri has seven banks that are well above the 100 percent level that is considered 'at risk' based on a risk measurement called the Texas ratio. The banks are the Sun Security bank, 1st Advantage Bank, Superior Bank, Truman Bank, Reliance Bank, St. Louis Bank and Meramec Valley Bank.

12933 ■ *"Stretch Your Last Dollar Or Invest It?"* in Business Owner (Vol. 35, November-December 2011, No. 6, pp. 4)

Pub: DL Perkins Company

Description: Should small business owners cut expenses or invest in a downturned economy? Difficult times can be an opportunity to build a business brad.

12934 ■ *"Struggling Community Banks Find Little Help In Wall Street Bailout"* in Crain's Detroit Business (Vol. 24, September 29, 2008)

Pub: Crain Communications Inc.

Ed: Tom Henderson. **Description:** Both public and private Michigan bands have been hit hard by poorly performing loan portfolios and although their problems were not caused by high-risk securities but by a longtime statewide recession and a housing slump, these community banks have little hope of seeing any of the bailout money that has been allotted for the larger institutions.

12935 ■ *"Stymiest's RBC Compensation Triggers Shareholder Outrage"* in Gl obe & Mail (January 28, 2006, pp. B3)

Pub: CTVglobemedia Publishing Inc.

Ed: Sinclair Stewart. **Description:** The concerns of shareholders over the issue of Royal Bank of Canada's $6.6 million pay package for chief executive officer Barbara Stymiest, in 2004, are presented.

12936 ■ *"Subprime Hits Huntington"* in Business First-Columbus (November 23, 2007, pp. A1)

Pub: American City Business Journals, Inc.

Ed: Adrian Burns. **Description:** Huntington Bancshares Inc. picked up a $1.5 billion exposure to the country's subprime mortgage mess. It caused the bank to set aside $450 million to cover increases in loan losses. When Huntington acquired Sky Financial, it absorbed a 17-year relationship Sky had with Franklin Credit Corporation, which is a subprime lender and servicer.

12937 ■ *The Subprime Solution: How Today's Global Financial Crisis Happened, and What to Do About It*

Pub: Princeton University Press

Ed: Robert J. Shiller. **Released:** 2009. **Price:** $16.95. **Description:** Yale economist discusses the worldwide financial crisis and offers plans to reform the system.

12938 ■ *"Sudbury Waits With Future Up in the Air"* in Globe & Mail (February 22, 2006, pp. B1)

Pub: CTVglobemedia Publishing Inc.

Ed: Wendy Stueck. **Description:** The takeover of Falconbridge Ltd., by Inco Ltd Sudbury, is in the process with uncertainty. The transaction has been a long overdue.

12939 ■ *"Suiting Up; Yes, You're Smart, But Can You Look the Part"* in Crain's Chicago Business (Vol. 30, February 2007, No. 6, pp. 39)

Pub: Crain Communications, Inc.

Ed: Kate Ryan. **Description:** For investment bankers, fashion is a must. Advice for men and women included.

12940 ■ *"The Suits Look Better Than the Shares"* in Barron's (Vol. 88, March 31, 2008, No. 13, pp. 25)

Pub: Dow Jones & Company, Inc.

Ed: Bill Alpert. **Description:** Jos. A. Bank's inventory has increased sharply raising questions about the company's growth prospects. The company's shares have already dropped significantly from 46 to 23 and could still continue its slide. The company is also battling a class action suit where plaintiffs allege that the Bank inventories were bloated.

12941 ■ *"Sullivan Led Bucyrus through Unforgettable Year"* in Business Journal-Milwaukee (Vol. 28, December 17, 2010, No. 11, pp. A1)

Pub: Milwaukee Business Journal

Ed: Rich Rovito. **Description:** Bucyrus International's president and CEO, Tim Sullivan, was chosen as Milwaukee, Wisconsin's Executive of the Year for 2010. Sullivan led Bucyrus through a year of dramatic change which started with the acquisition of the mining business of Terex Corporation and culminating with a deal to sell Caterpillar Inc.

12942 ■ *"Summit, Lions Gate are in Talks to Merge Studios"* in Wall Street Journal Eastern Edition (November 29, 2011, pp. B2)

Pub: Dow Jones & Company Inc. Enterprise Media Group

Contact: Clare Hart, President

Ed: Erica Orden, Michelle Kung. **Description:** Movie studio Summit Entertainment LLC is in talks with television producer Lions Gate Entertainment Corporation about a possible merger. Previous talks have taken place, but no deal was ever reached. Such a deal would create a large, independent studio able to compete in the market with the big Hollywood giants.

12943 ■ *"Sun Capital Partners Affiliate Acquires Timothy's Coffees"* in Miami Daily Business Review (March 26, 2008)

Pub: ALM Media Inc.

Description: An affiliate of Sun Capital Partners acquired Timothy's Coffees of the World. Timothy's operates and franchises 166 stores offering coffees, muffins, and Michel's Baguette products.

12944 ■ *"Surprise Package"* in Business Courier (Vol. 27, June 25, 2010, No. 8, pp. 1)

Pub: Business Courier

Ed: Dan Monk, Jon Newberry, Steve Watkins. **Description:** More than 60 percent of the chief executive officers (CEOs) in Greater Cincinnati's 35 public companies took a salary cut in 2009, but stock grants resulted in large paper gains for the CEOs. The salary cuts show efforts of boards of directors to observe austerity. Statistics on increased values of stock awards for CEOs, median pay for CEOs, and median shareholder return are also presented.

12945 ■ *"A Survival Guide for Crazy Times"* in Canadian Business (Vol. 81, March 3, 2008, No. 3, pp. 61)

Pub: Rogers Media

Ed: David Wolf. **Description:** Investors should ensure that their portfolios are positioned defensively more than the average as the U.S. and Canadian markets face turbulent times. They should not assume that U.S. residential property is a good place to invest only because prices have dropped and the Canadian dollar is showing strength. Other tips that investors can use during unstable periods are supplied.

12946 ■ *"Surviving the Storm"* in Canadian Business (Vol. 81, July 22, 2008, No. 12-13, pp. 50)

Pub: Rogers Media Ltd.

Ed: Jeff Sanford. **Description:** Investment adviser Harry Dent and finance professor Paul Marsh discuss their views and forecasts on the United States' economic condition. Dent believes advisors should concentrate on wealth preservation rather than on returns. Other views regarding U.S. economic conditions are also presented.

12947 ■ *"Sweet Harmony" in Canadian Business (Vol. 82, April 27, 2009, No. 7, pp. 6)*
Pub: Rogers Media
Description: Canada will harmonize its 5 percent federal goods and services tax wit the 8 percent provincial sales tax effective July 1, 2010. Meanwhile, provinces like Ontario and Quebec have switched the sales taxes that are charged in new investments into a value-added tax. The conversion has led to an 11 percent increase in investments in Quebec and the three other provinces that made the conversion.

12948 ■ *"Sweet Spot" in Canadian Business (Vol. 79, November 20, 2006, No. 23, pp. 25)*
Pub: Rogers Media
Ed: John Gray. **Description:** The plans of Kinross Gold Corp., to acquire the stake of Bema Gold Corp., are discussed. Under the terms of the deal Kinross is offering Bema stockholders 0.441 of a Kinross share for each of Bema shares.

12949 ■ *"A Swifter, Better Marketplace" in Barron's (Vol. 89, July 13, 2009, No. 28, pp. M13)*
Pub: Dow Jones & Co., Inc.
Ed: Eric W. Noll. **Description:** Listed-derivatives market is moving towards greater trading through computerized systems with an emphasis on speed and innovation. The market for listed options is also being changed by new techniques from other markets such as algorithmic trading, dark pools, and new-order priority systems.

12950 ■ *"Swinging For the Fences" in Academy of Management Journal (October 2007, pp. 1055)*
Pub: Academy of Management
Contact: Ming-Jer Chen, President
Ed: William Gerard Sanders, Donald C. Hambrick. **Description:** Study examines managerial risk-taking vis-a-vis stock options of the company; results reveal that stock options instigate CEOs to take unwise risks that could bring huge losses to the company.

12951 ■ *"Sykes Group Targets GunnAllen" in The Business Journal-Serving Greater Tampa Bay (Vol. 28, September 5, 2008, No. 37, pp. 1)*
Pub: American City Business Journals, Inc.
Ed: Margie Manning. **Description:** GAH Holdings LLC. a newly formed investment company by John H. Sykes of Sykes Enterprises Inc., will add capital to Tampa Bay Area investment banking firm GunnAllen Holdings Inc. The capital infusion is to aid GunnAllen Holdings in expanding and diversifying as GAH becomes its largest shareholder.

12952 ■ *"Sykes Shift from GunnAllen to New Venture" in Tampa Bay Business Journal (Vol. 30, December 18, 2009, No. 52, pp. 1)*
Pub: American City Business Journals
Ed: Margie Manning. **Description:** Tampa, Florida's entrepreneur John H. Sykes acquired Pointe Capital Inc., a GunnAllen Holdings Inc. subsidiary, through his JHS Capital Holdings Inc. and changed the name to JHS Capital Advisors Inc. Sykes will become president and CEO of JHS Capital Advisors and will relocate its corporate headquarters to Tampa, Florida.

12953 ■ *"Take a Flyer on Choice" in Canadian Business (Vol. 79, October 23, 2006, No. 21, pp. 163)*
Pub: Rogers Media
Description: The variations in the stock market prices of companies like Nike Inc. and Black & Decker Corp. from October 2005-06 are discussed.

12954 ■ *"Take It to the Bank" in Barron's (Vol. 89, July 13, 2009, No. 28, pp. 20)*
Pub: Dow Jones & Co., Inc.
Ed: Jim McTague. **Description:** Banks are one of the safest place to put one's principal due to the temporary increase in the Federal Deposit Insurance Corp.'s insurance of bank accounts up to $250,000 and also because of the Cdars (Certificates of Deposit Registry Service) program which spreads the deposit to several banks thereby making the account covered as if the money was deposited at multiple banks.

12955 ■ *"Take the Wheel: the Pension Protection Act Doesn't Mean You Can Sit Back and Relax" in Black Enterprise (October 2007)*
Pub: Earl G. Graves Publishing Co. Inc.
Ed: Mellody Hobson. **Description:** Pension Protection Act provides multiple benefits and tax advantages for retirement, however the investment options and contribution rates are very conservative.

12956 ■ *"Takeover Frenzy Stokes Steel Stocks" in Globe & Mail (February 7, 2006, pp. B1)*
Pub: CTVglobemedia Publishing Inc.
Description: The impact of merger speculations, on shares of steel companies such as Ipsco Inc., is discussed.

12957 ■ *"Taking Collections" in Investment Dealers' Digest (Vol. 75, October 9, 2009, No. 38, pp. 19)*
Pub: SourceMedia, Inc.
Ed: Aleksandrs Rozens. **Description:** Although the nation's debt-collection industry has grown with increased reliance by consumers on credit, valuations of these firms have lessened due to the economy which has hurt some of the success of these firms in obtaining the debt back from consumers who are experiencing trying economic times.

12958 ■ *"Taking the Over-the-Counter Route to US" in Barron's (Vol. 88, July 7, 2008, No. 27, pp. 24)*
Pub: Dow Jones & Co., Inc.
Ed: Eric Uhlfelder. **Description:** Many multinational companies have left the New York Stock Exchange and allowed their shares to trade over-the-counter. The companies have taken advantage of a 2007 SEC rule allowing publicly listed foreign companies to change trading venues if less than 5 percent of global trading volume in the past 12 months occurred in the US.

12959 ■ *"Taking a Pounding; Recession Fears Weigh Down Steakhouse Operator Morton's" in Crain's Chicago Business (March 31, 2008)*
Pub: Crain Communications, Inc.
Ed: Monee Fields-White. **Description:** Morton's Restaurant Group Inc. has seen a 50 percent drop in shares in the past six months due to the economy and cutbacks in corporate expense accounts; business customers provide the restaurant about 80 percent of its revenue.

12960 ■ *"Tanganyika Announces First Quarter 2007 Results" in Canadian Corporate News (May 14, 2007)*
Pub: Comtex News Network Inc.
Description: Tanganyika Oil Company Ltd., announced the interim operating and financial results for the first quarter ending March 31, 2007. Statistical data included.

12961 ■ *"Tao of Downfall" in International Journal of Entrepreneurship and Small Business (Vol. 11, August 31, 2010, No. 2, pp. 121)*
Pub: Publishers Communication Group
Ed: Wenxian Zhang, Ilan Alon. **Description:** Through historical reviews and case studies, this research seeks to understand why some initially successful entrepreneurs failed in the economic boom of past decades. Among various factors contributing to their downfall are a unique political and business environment, fragile financial systems, traditional cultural influences and personal characteristics.

12962 ■ *"Tax Credit Crunch" in Miami Daily Business Review (March 26, 2008)*
Pub: ALM Media Inc.
Ed: Paula Iuspa-Abbott. **Description:** Uncertainty is growing over the future of the low-income housing project in South Florida and the tax credit program that helps fuel the projects.

12963 ■ *"The Tech 100" in Canadian Business (Vol. 81, July 21, 2008, No. 11, pp. 48)*
Pub: Rogers Media Ltd.
Ed: Calvin Leung. **Description:** Absolute Software Corp. Day4 Energy Inc., Sandvine Corp., Norsat International Inc. and Call Genie Inc. are the five technology firms included in the annual ranking of top companies in Canada by market capitalization. The services and the one-year total return potential of the companies are presented.

12964 ■ *"Tech Godfather Steve Walker Winding Down Howard Venture Fund" in Baltimore Business Journal (Vol. 27, December 11, 2009, No. 31)*
Pub: American City Business Journals
Ed: Scott Dance. **Description:** Steve Walker, president of venture capital fund firm Walker Ventures, will be closing the Howard County, Maryland-based firm as the economic situation is finding it difficult to recover investor's money. According to Walker, the economy also constrained investors from financing venture funds. Despite the closure, Walker will continue his work in the local angel investing community.

12965 ■ *"Tech Investing: March's Long Road" in Canadian Business (Vol. 80, January 29, 2007, No. 3, pp. 67)*
Pub: Rogers Media
Ed: Calvin Leung. **Description:** The efforts of March Networks, a manufacturer of digital surveillance equipment, from the decline in the price of its shares at the beginning of the year 2007 are described.

12966 ■ *"Tech's Payout Problem" in Barron's (Vol. 90, September 13, 2010, No. 37, pp. 19)*
Pub: Barron's Editorial & Corporate Headquarters
Ed: Andrew Bary. **Description:** Big tech companies have the potential to be good dividend payers, but instead just hoard their cash for acquisitions and share buybacks. If these companies offered more dividends, they could boost their shares and attract more income-oriented investors.

12967 ■ *"Tektronix Buys Arbor Networks for Security Business" in eWeek (August 9, 2010)*
Pub: Ziff Davis Enterprise
Description: Tektronix Communications, provider of communications test and network intelligence solutions will acquire Arbor Networks. The deal will help Tektronix build a brand in security. Details of the transaction are included.

12968 ■ *"TerraVest Income Fund Releases 2007 First Quarter Financial Results" in Canadian Corporate News (May 14, 2007)*
Pub: Comtex News Network Inc.
Description: Overview of TerraVest Income Fund's financial results for the quarter ended March 31, 2007 in which the net earnings increased 36.7 percent to $3.7 million from the 2006 first quarter. Statistical data included.

12969 ■ *"That's About It for Quantitative Easing" in Barron's (Vol. 89, July 20, 2009, No. 29, pp. M11)*
Pub: Dow Jones & Co., Inc.
Ed: Brian Blackstone. **Description:** US Federal Reserve appears to have decided to halt quantitative easing, causing bond prices to drop and yields to rise. The yield for the 1-year Treasury bond rose more than 0.3 percentage point to about 3.65 percent.

12970 ■ *"Theme Park Sale has Vendor Upside" in Tampa Bay Business Journal (Vol. 29, October 23, 2009, No. 44, pp. 1)*
Pub: American City Business Journals
Ed: Margie Manning. **Description:** Private equity firm The Blackstone Group has concluded its $2.7 billion purchase of Busch Entertainment Corporation. Aside from enhanced business opportunities in Florida's Tampa Bay area, new attractions might be built in the Busch Gardens and Adventure Island properties that will be acquired by Blackstone. Blackstone's other plans are also discussed.

12971 ■ "There's More Upside in Germany" in Barron's (Vol. 90, September 6, 2010, No. 36, pp. M7)

Pub: Barron's Editorial & Corporate Headquarters

Ed: Jonathan Buck. **Description:** Germany's stocks have gone up since the beginning of 2010, and investors can still benefit. These stocks will benefit from Germany's stellar economic performance and the relative weakness of the Euro. The prospects of the shares of Daimler and Hochtief are discussed.

12972 ■ "TheStree.com: Study Abroad" in Entrepreneur (Vol. 35, October 2007, No. 10, pp. 44)

Pub: Entrepreneur Media Inc.

Ed: Farnoosh Torabi. **Description:** Businessmen who wish to pursue foreign investments should study the country in which they will operate. Some investors do their research by completely exposing themselves to their prospective country, while others prefer studying the market home-based. Details of how investors pick their country and the different ways of investing in foreign land are presented.

12973 ■ "They Have Issues: New Black-Owned Investment Bank Nets $90 Million In Managed Issues" in Black Enterprise (Vol. 38, March 2008)

Pub: Earl G. Graves Publishing Co. Inc.

Ed: Marcia A. Wade. **Description:** Castle Oak Securities LP has co-managed multiple deals for more than 35 blue-chip clients. Their first deal earned $300 million for General Electric Capital Corporation and Castle Oak has since co-managed nine more deals with GE Capital, seven for Citigroup, six for American Express, and three for Goldman Sachs.

12974 ■ "They're Hopping Mad" in Canadian Business (Vol. 80, October 22, 2007, No. 21, pp. 20)

Pub: Rogers Media

Description: Alberta Review Panel is calling for a 20 percent increase in oil and gas development taxes. SABMiller and Molson Coors Brewing Company combined its U.S. and Puerto Rican operations, though the deal is still subject to regulatory approvals. Montreal Exchange Inc. filed for approval of the trade of Montreal Climate Exchange futures contracts.

12975 ■ "They've Fallen, But They Can Get Up" in Barron's (Vol. 88, March 10, 2008, No. 10, pp. 43)

Pub: Dow Jones & Company, Inc.

Ed: Kopin Tan. **Description:** Shares of senior housing companies present buying opportunities to investors because of their low prices. Companies such as Brookdale Senior Living are not as dependent on housing prices but have suffered declines in share prices.

12976 ■ "Things Will Improve, or Not: a Chartered Financial Analyst Explains It All" in Canadian Business (Vol. 81, November 10, 2008)

Pub: Rogers Media Ltd.

Description: Myles Zyblock expects the global economic slowdown to deepen over the next six to nine months. Zyblock addressed the Toronto CFA Society at their annual dinner in October 2008. He stressed a tight correlation between the credit ratio and asset prices and predicts the S&P 500 to be up by 11 percent by October 2009.

12977 ■ This Is Not Your Parents' Retirement: A Revolutionary Guide for a Revolutionary Generation

Pub: Entrepreneur Press

Ed: Patrick P. Astre. **Released:** July 2005. **Price:** $19.95 (US), $26.95 (Canadian). **Description:** Mutual funds, stocks, bonds, insurance products, and tax strategies for retirement planning.

12978 ■ "Time to Change Direction" in Canadian Business (Vol. 79, October 23, 2006, No. 21, pp. 21)

Pub: Rogers Media

Ed: Jack Mintz. **Description:** The decision of BCE Inc. to get converted into an income trust is discussed. The economic factors responsible for the conversion of firms to income trusts are analyzed.

12979 ■ "Time to Engage Europe" in Canadian Business (Vol. 79, June 19, 2006, No. 13, pp. 19)

Pub: Rogers Media

Ed: Jack Mintz. **Description:** European and Canadian governments improved their trade and investment relations with the March 18, 2004 frame work to develop a Trade and Investment Enhancement Agreement. Still there is lot of opportunities to solve tax and trade issues.

12980 ■ "Time to Leave the Party?" in Barron's (Vol. 88, March 24, 2008, No. 12, pp. M16)

Pub: Dow Jones & Company, Inc.

Ed: Andrea Hotter. **Description:** Prices of commodities such as gold, copper, crude oil, sugar, cocoa, and wheat have fallen from their all-time highs set in the middle of March 2008. Analysts, however, caution that this decline in prices may be temporary, and that a banking crisis may trigger new price rises in commodities.

12981 ■ "Time for a Little Pruning" in Barron's (Vol. 89, July 6, 2009, No. 27, pp. 13)

Pub: Dow Jones & Co., Inc.

Ed: Dimitra DeFotis. **Description:** Investors are advised to avoid the shares of Whole Foods, American Tower, T. Rowe Price, Iron Mountain, Intuitive Surgical, Salesforce.com, and Juniper Networks due to their high price to earnings ratios. The shares of Amazon.com, Broadcom, and Expeditors International of Washington remain attractive to investors despite their high price to earnings ratios due to their strong growth.

12982 ■ "A Timely Boon for Small Investors" in Barron's (Vol. 88, March 24, 2008, No. 12, pp. 48)

Pub: Dow Jones & Company, Inc.

Ed: Theresa W. Carey. **Description:** Nasdaq Data Store's new program called Market Replay allows investors to accurately track stock price movements. The replay can be as long as a day of market time and allows investors to determine whether they executed stock trades at the best possible price.

12983 ■ "Tiptoeing Beyond Treasuries" in Barron's (Vol. 88, March 31, 2008, No. 13, pp. M6)

Pub: Dow Jones & Company, Inc.

Ed: Michael S. Derby. **Description:** Risk-free assets like treasuries are still a good place for cash even if market conditions have calmed down and Treasury yields are low. Investors looking for yield and safety might want to consider Treasury inflation-indexed securities that are attractive given new inflation pressures.

12984 ■ "To Give and Receive: How to Pass On 401k Assets and Manage an Inheritance" in Black Enterprise (Vol. 38, October 2007, No. 3)

Pub: Earl G. Graves Publishing Co. Inc.

Ed: Steven Garmhausen. **Description:** Without proper planning, heirs could pay large tax bills to the government unless assets are managed properly. A common error is to avoid updating account records to reflect the names of designated beneficiaries.

12985 ■ "To Sell or Not To Sell" in Inc. (December 2007, pp. 80)

Pub: Gruner & Jahr USA Publishing

Ed: Patrick J. Sauer. **Description:** Owner of a private equity discusses the challenges he faces when deciding to sell his family's business.

12986 ■ "To Thine Own Self" in Entrepreneur (Vol. 35, November 2007, No. 11, pp. 50)

Pub: Entrepreneur Media Inc.

Ed: Torabi Farnoosh. **Description:** Self-directed individual retirement account (IRA) provides more investment options as payoff from this can be higher than an average mutual fund. Details on how to manage self-directed IRAs are discussed.

12987 ■ "Tofutti Brands" in Ice Cream Reporter (Vol. 23, September 20, 2010, No. 10, pp. 6)

Pub: Ice Cream Reporter

Description: Tofutti Brands announced net sales at $4.5 million for second quarter 2010.

12988 ■ "A Tonic for Irrationality" in Barron's (Vol. 89, July 13, 2009, No. 28, pp. 12)

Pub: Dow Jones & Co., Inc.

Description: Financial-personality assessment being introduced by Barclays Wealth, measures six personality aspects related to financial behavior through a profile that measures such traits including risk tolerance, composure and perceived financial expertise. The profile helps the company create a portfolio that are structured to meet their client's personality needs.

12989 ■ "Too Much Precaution About Biotech Corn" in Barron's (Vol. 88, March 17, 2008, No. 11, pp. 54)

Pub: Dow Jones & Company, Inc.

Ed: Mark I. Schwartz. **Description:** In the U.S., 90 percent of cultivated soybeans are biotech varietals as well as 60 percent of the corn. Farmers have significantly reduced their reliance on pesticides in the growing of biotech corn. Biotech cotton cultivation has brought hundreds of millions of dollars in net financial gains to farmers. The European Union has precluded the cultivation or sale of biotech crops within its border.

12990 ■ "Too Much too Soon" in Barron's (Vol. 89, July 27, 2009, No. 30, pp. 33)

Pub: Dow Jones & Co., Inc.

Ed: Leslie P. Norton. **Description:** Shares of hhgregg have risen 85 percent in the year leading up to July 2009 and analysts believe the stock could hit 25. However, their 113 outlets are concentrated in states where unemployment is above 10 percent and expanding into areas already overstored. Competition is also rife and credit availability is still tight.

12991 ■ "Tool-o-Rama" in Barron's (Vol. 90, September 6, 2010, No. 36)

Pub: Barron's Editorial & Corporate Headquarters

Description: New trading tool features from several online brokers are discussed. The new features from Fidelity, ChoiceTrade, JunoTrade and TradeKing are examined. Investors can now screen exchanged traded funds in the same way as stocks with Fidelity, while ChoiceTrade can run in any browser without the need to install additional plug-ins.

12992 ■ "Top 10 Retirement Mistakes and How to Avoid Them" in Canadian Business (Vol. 83, July 20, 2010, No. 11-12, pp. 39)

Pub: Rogers Media Ltd.

Ed: Jacqueline Nelson, Angelina Chapin. **Description:** Some of the top retirement mistakes is relying on selling one's house to find a retirement. Other mistakes are paying too much for investments and planning to work in retirement since no one can be sure that they will be healthy enough to accomplish this. Suggestions to avoid these pitfalls are discussed.

12993 ■ "Top 50 By 1-Year Return" in Canadian Business (Vol. 81, Summer 2008, No. 9, pp. 121)

Pub: Rogers Media Ltd.

Description: Table showing the top 50 Canadian companies ranked in terms of one-year return is presented. Toronto, Canada-based Timminco Ltd. topped the roster with a 1,294.2 percent in one-year return. However, the share prices of the company were affected by the recent controversy in its silicon purification process.

12994 ■ "Top 50 By 5-Year Return" in Canadian Business (Vol. 81, Summer 2008, No. 9, pp. 123)

Pub: Rogers Media Ltd.

Description: Table showing the rankings of the top 50 Canadian companies in terms of five-year return is presented. Silver Wheaton Corp. topped the roster with a 178.5 percent in five-year return. The company's share prices have skyrocketed despite increasing silver prices.

12995 ■ *"Top 50 in the Capital Market" in Canadian Business (Vol. 81, Summer 2008, No. 9, pp. 117)*

Pub: Rogers Media Ltd.

Description: Research in Motion Ltd. topped the list of companies in Canada in terms of market capitalization. The company's share prices surge to 119.8 percent in the year ended April 4. A table showing the top 50 Canadian companies in terms of market capitalization is presented.

12996 ■ *"Top 50 In Profits" in Canadian Business (Vol. 81, Summer 2008, No. 9, pp. 116)*

Pub: Rogers Media Ltd.

Description: Royal Bank of Canada topped the Investor 500 by profits list despite the slower economic growth in Canada and the U.S. The bank was in the runner-up position in the 2007. RBC's growth strategy is through hefty acquisitions in the U.S. A table ranking the top 50 companies in Canada in terms of profits is presented.

12997 ■ *"Top 50 In Total Revenue" in Canadian Business (Vol. 81, Summer 2008, No. 9, pp. 119)*

Pub: Rogers Media Ltd.

Description: Table showing the top 50 Canadian companies in terms of total revenue is presented. Manulife Financial Corp. topped the list with revenue of 34.5 billion. The financial services firm is the 6th largest provider of life insurance in the world and the second largest in North America.

12998 ■ *"Top Law Firms Join Forces" in Business Journal Portland (Vol. 27, December 3, 2010, No. 40, pp. 1)*

Pub: Portland Business Journal

Ed: Andy Giegerich. **Description:** Law Firms Powell PC and Roberts Kaplan LLP will forge a collaboration, whereby 17 Roberts Kaplan attorneys will join the Portland, Oregon-based office of Lane Powell. The partnership is expected to strengthen the law firms' grip on Portland's banking clients.

12999 ■ *"A Torch in the Darkness" in Canadian Business (Vol. 83, August 17, 2010, No. 13-14, pp. 66)*

Pub: Rogers Media Ltd.

Ed: Joe Castaldo. **Description:** Research In Motion (RIM) unveiled the BlackBerry Touch, featuring a touch screen as well as a physical keyboard, in an attempt to repel competitors and expand share in the consumer smart phone market. RIM shares have fallen 43 percent from its peak in 2009.

13000 ■ *"Tory or Liberal, Blue or Red, the Impact of the Election is All in Your Head" in Globe & Mail (January 14, 2006, pp. B19)*

Pub: CTVglobemedia Publishing Inc.

Ed: Derek DeCloet. **Description:** The effect of the outcome of 2006 Canadian federal elections on stock markets is discussed.

13001 ■ *"Toy Story" in Forbes (Vol. 180, October 15, 2007, No. 8, pp. 102)*

Pub: Forbes Inc.

Description: Three voluntary recalls of Chinese-made toys were announced by American toymakers, sending Mattel stocks plummeting.

13002 ■ *"Toyota Marks Record Profit Sales" in Globe & Mail (February 7, 2007, pp. B10)*

Pub: CTVglobemedia Publishing Inc.

Ed: Martin Fackler. **Description:** The record quarterly sales and earnings reported by Japanese automaker Toyota Motor Corp. are discussed. The company sold 2.16 million vehicles during the quarter while registering 426.8 billion yen in profits.

13003 ■ *"The Trader's Edge" in Barron's (Vol. 88, March 31, 2008, No. 13, pp. 56)*

Pub: Dow Jones & Company, Inc.

Ed: Dan McGuire. **Description:** There is a $3,000 a year annual limit to deducting investor's losses and normal investment expenses are purportedly deductible as miscellaneous expenses on Schedule A only to the extent that they exceed two percent of adjusted

gross income. Professional gamblers who can use Schedule C are unable deduct a net gaming loss against income from any other sources.

13004 ■ *"Trading Down at the Supermarket" in Barron's (Vol. 88, July 14, 2008, No. 28, pp. 36)*

Pub: Dow Jones & Co., Inc.

Ed: Alexander Eule. **Description:** Shares of Ralcorp Holdings are cheap at around $49.95 after slipping 20 percent prior to their acquisition of Post cereals from Kraft. Some analysts believe its shares could climb over 60 percent to $80 as value-seeking consumers buy more private label products.

13005 ■ *"Transcontinental to Exchange Assets with Quad/Graphics" in American Printer (Vol. 128, August 1, 2011, No. 8)*

Pub: Penton Media Inc.

Description: Transcontinental Inc. and Quad/Graphics Inc. entered into an agreement where Transcontinental will indirectly acquire all shares of Quad Graphics Canada Inc.

13006 ■ *"Treasuries Buffeted by Stocks" in Barron's (Vol. 89, July 27, 2009, No. 30, pp. M9)*

Pub: Dow Jones & Co., Inc.

Ed: Randall W. Forsyth. **Description:** Warren Buffett favors equities over long-term government bonds or stocks even with the Dow index at an eight-month high. The 10-year Treasury was up two basis points to 3.67 percent as of July 24, 2009. Corporate bond issuance hit a record $1.79 trillion for the first half of 2009.

13007 ■ *"Treasuries Rally Despite Huge Supply" in Barron's (Vol. 89, July 13, 2009, No. 28, pp. M10)*

Pub: Dow Jones & Co., Inc.

Ed: Randall W. Forsyth. **Description:** Prices of U.S. Treasuries were sent higher and their yields lower despite four auctions of coupon securities because of the strong appetite for government securities around the world. The reopening of the 10-year note in the week ending July 10, 2009 drew the strongest bidding since 1995.

13008 ■ *"A Trend Is His Friend" in Barron's (Vol. 89, July 27, 2009, No. 30, pp. 28)*

Pub: Dow Jones & Co., Inc.

Ed: Eric Uhlfelder. **Description:** Global Diversified Program fund under Quality Capital Management is managed through a trading system called the Advanced Resource Allocator which rebalances short-term tactical moves to gather quick profits. CEO Aref Karim's allocations are based on risk and he says their sentiments toward the market conditions are agnostic.

13009 ■ *"The Trials of Brian Hunter" in Canadian Business (Vol. 81, March 3, 2008, No. 3, pp. 64)*

Pub: Rogers Media

Ed: Thomas Watson. **Description:** Brian Hunter was a considered a brilliant trader in Wall Street before he was blamed for the fall of the Amaranth hedge fund. Some people blame Hunter for placing bets based on unpredictable weather when he was a trader for Amaranth Advisors LLC. The accusation against Hunter that he conspired to manipulate natural gas prices is also discussed.

13010 ■ *The Trillion Dollar Meltdown: Easy Money, High Rollers, and the Great Credit Crash*

Pub: Public Affairs

Ed: Charles R. Morris. **Released:** 2009. **Price:** $22.95. **Description:** Former banker believes that Wall Street and the financial community have too much power in America. He estimates that writedowns and defaults of residential mortgages, commercial mortgages, junk bonds, leveraged loans, credit cards, and complex securitized bonds could reach $1 trillion.

13011 ■ *"Trilogy Metals Inc.: Private Placement" in Canadian Corporate News (May 16, 2007)*

Pub: Comtex News Network Inc.

Description: Trilogy Metals Inc. announces a private placement of 10,000,000 units at $0.08 per unit in an

effort to raise total gross proceeds of $800,000 which will be allocated to working capital, new acquisitions, and to service existing debt.

13012 ■ *"Trust Buyouts Not My Fault, Flaherty Says" in Globe & Mail (April 3, 2007, pp. B1)*

Pub: CTVglobemedia Publishing Inc.

Ed: Tara Perkins; Doug Saunders; Steven Chase. **Description:** The causes of the acquisition of Canadian firms by foreign investors are discussed by the Canadian Finance Minister Jim Flaherty.

13013 ■ *"Trust Distrust" in Canadian Business (Vol. 79, July 17, 2006, No. 14-15, pp. 61)*

Pub: Rogers Media

Ed: John Gray. **Description:** The need to frame better trust deeds in order to protect the investor's money as well as their returns is examined.

13014 ■ *"TUSK Announces 2007 First Quarter Results" in Canadian Corporate News (May 14, 2007)*

Pub: Comtex News Network Inc.

Description: TUSK Energy Corp. announced its financial and operating results for the first quarter ending March 31, 2007.

13015 ■ *"TV Revenue Slide Hits CanWest Profit" in Globe & Mail (January 13, 2006, pp. B3)*

Pub: CTVglobemedia Publishing Inc.

Ed: Grant Robertson. **Description:** CanWest Global Communications Corp. posted drop in profits by 14 percent for first quarter 2006. The downward trend in profits is attributed to low television revenues.

13016 ■ *"UBS Buys Out Canadian Partner" in Globe & Mail (January 20, 2006, pp. B1)*

Pub: CTVglobemedia Publishing Inc.

Ed: Andrew Willis. **Description:** The details on UBS AG's acquisition of UBS Securities Canada Inc. are presented.

13017 ■ *Ultimate Startup Directory: Expert Advice and 1,500 Great Startup Ideas*

Pub: Entrepreneur Press

Ed: James Stephenson. **Released:** February 2007. **Price:** $30.95 (CND). **Description:** Startup opportunities in over 30 industries are given, along with information on investment, earning potential, skills, legal requirements and more.

13018 ■ *"Understanding the Economy: People Worry That a Recession Is Coming" in Inc. (December 2007, pp. 103-104)*

Pub: Gruner & Jahr USA Publishing

Ed: Joseph H. Ellis. **Description:** It is suggested that by the time a recession arrives, the worst economic damage has already occurred.

13019 ■ *"Understanding the Fed" in Black Enterprise (Vol. 38, December 2007, No. 5, pp. 66)*

Pub: Earl G. Graves Publishing Co. Inc.

Ed: Steve Garmhausen. **Description:** The Federal Reserve System along with twelve regional banks regulates the value of money through the law of supply and demand. The Feds increase or decrease the supply of dollars in circulation which makes them cheap or expensive.

13020 ■ *"An Unfair Knock on Nokia" in Barron's (Vol. 88, March 10, 2008, No. 10, pp. 36)*

Pub: Dow Jones & Company, Inc.

Ed: Mark Veverka. **Description:** Discusses the decision by the brokerage house Exane to recommend a Sell on Nokia shares, presumably due to higher inventories, which is unfounded. The news that the company's inventories are rising is not an indicator of falling demand for its products. The company is also benefiting from solid management and rising market share.

13021 ■ *"Unify Corp. Back in the Black, Poised to Grow"* in *Sacramento Business Journal (Vol. 25, August 29, 2008, No. 26, pp. 1)*

Pub: American City Business Journals, Inc.

Ed: Melanie Turner. **Description:** It was reported that Unify Corp. returned to profitability in the fiscal year ended April 30, 2008 with a net income of $1.6 million, under the guidance of Todd Wille. Wille, who took over as the company's chief executive officer in October 2000, was named as Turnaround CEO of the Year in June 2008 for his efforts.

13022 ■ *"Unilever Acquiring Danish Operations of Diplom-Is Ice Cream"* in *Ice Cream Reporter (Vol. 23, August 20, 2010, No. 9, pp. 1)*

Pub: Ice Cream Reporter

Description: Unilever will acquire Danish operations of the ice cream company Diplom-Is from Norwegian dairy group Tine.

13023 ■ *"Unilever Acquiring EVGA's Ice Cream Brands in Greece"* in *Ice Cream Reporter (Vol. 23, October 20, 2010, No. 11, pp. 1)*

Pub: Ice Cream Reporter

Description: Unilever will acquire the ice cream brands and distribution network of the Greek frozen dessert manufacturer EVGA.

13024 ■ *"U.S. Economy's Underlying Strengths Limit Recession Threat"* in *Hispanic Business (Vol. 30, April 2008, No. 4, pp. 14)*

Pub: Hispanic Business

Ed: Dr. Juan B. Solana. **Description:** Large and small businesses as well as consumers and policy-makers are attempting to identify the areas of risk and loss created by the economic crisis; analysts are now estimating that U.S. mortgage losses could reach the $380 to $400 billion mark. Also discusses the falling of wages and the rising of unemployment. Statistical data included.

13025 ■ *"Universal Energy Group Releases March 31, 2007 Financial Statements"* in *Canadian Corporate News (May 14, 2007)*

Pub: Comtex News Network Inc.

Description: Universal Energy Group Ltd., a company that sells electricity and natural gas to small to mid-size commercial and small industrial customers as well as residential customers, announced the release of its March 31, 2007 financial statements. Management's analysis and discussion of the company's financial condition and results of operations are listed. Statistical data included.

13026 ■ *"Unpleasant Surprise"* in *Barron's (Vol. 88, March 24, 2008, No. 12, pp. 60)*

Pub: Dow Jones & Company, Inc.

Ed: Shirley A. Lazo. **Description:** Discusses the $175 million that footwear company Genesco received in a settlement with Finish Line and UBS is considered as a stock distribution and is taxable as dividend income. Railroad company CSX raised its quarterly common payout from 15 cents to 18 cents.

13027 ■ *"The Upside of Fear and Loathing"* in *Barron's (Vol. 88, March 24, 2008, No. 12, pp. 11)*

Pub: Dow Jones & Company, Inc.

Ed: Michael Santoli. **Description:** Fear and risk aversion prevalent among investors may actually serve to cushion the decline and spark a rally in US stock prices. Surveys of investors indicate rising levels of anxiety and bearishness, indicating a possible positive turnaround.

13028 ■ *"US Airways Stock Up 5 Percent on Day Merger Try Ends"* in *Charlotte Observer (February 1, 2007)*

Pub: Knight-Ridder/Tribune Business News

Ed: Steve Harrison. **Description:** US Airways stock rose 5 percent on the day Doug Parker, CEO, cancelled his offer to purchase Delta Air Lines.

13029 ■ *"USAmeriBank Deals for Growth"* in *The Business Journal-Serving Greater Tampa Bay (Vol. 28, September 26, 2008, No. 40, pp. 1)*

Pub: American City Business Journals, Inc.

Ed: Margie Manning. **Description:** It is believed that the pending $14.9 million purchase of Liberty Bank by USAmeriBank could be at the forefront of a trend. Executives of both companies expect the deal to close by the end of 2008. USAmeriBank will have $430 million in assets and five offices in Pinellas, Florida once the deal is completed.

13030 ■ *Using Other People's Money To Get Rich: Secrets, Techniques, and Strategies Investors Use Every Day Using OPM*

Pub: Atlantic Publishing Company

Ed: Eric J. Leech. **Released:** December 2009. **Price:** $24.95 paperback. **Description:** Discussion showing individuals how to invest using other people's money.

13031 ■ *"Valener Announces that Gaz Metro has Achieved a Key Step in Acquiring CVPS"* in *CNW Group (September 30, 2011)*

Pub: CNW Group

Contact: Carolyn McGill-Davidson, President

Description: Valener Inc., which owns about 29 percent of Gaz Metro Ltd. Partnership, announced that Gaz Metro welcomes the sale of Central Vermont Public Service Corporation (CVPS). Valener owns an indirect interest of 24.5 percent in the wind power projects jointly developed by Beaupre Eole General Partnership and Boralex Inc. on private lands in Quebec. Details of the deal are included.

13032 ■ *"Valenti: Roots of Financial Crisis Go Back to 1998"* in *Crain's Detroit Business (Vol. 24, October 6, 2008, No. 40, pp. 25)*

Pub: Crain Communications, Inc.

Ed: Tom Henderson; Nathan Skid. **Description:** Interview with Sam Valenti III who is the chairman and CEO of Valenti Capital L.L.C., a wealth-management firm; Valenti discusses in detail the history that led up to the current economic crisis as well as his prediction for the future of the country.

13033 ■ *"V&J Scores Partnership with Shaq"* in *Business Journal-Milwaukee (Vol. 25, October 12, 2007, No. 2, pp. A1)*

Pub: American City Business Journals, Inc.

Ed: Rich Kirchen. **Description:** O'Neal Franchise Group has agreed to a partnership with V&J Foods of Milwaukee to handle Auntie Anne's shops in New York, South Africa, Michigan, and the Caribbean. V&J O'Neal Enterprises will open six Auntie Anne's soft pretzel shops in Detroit towards the end of 2007. Planned international ventures of the partnership are presented.

13034 ■ *"Venture Gap"* in *Canadian Business (Vol. 81, March 17, 2008, No. 4, pp. 82)*

Pub: Rogers Media

Ed: Joe Castaldo. **Description:** Money raised by Canadian venture capitalist firms has been declining since 2001. A strong venture capital market is important if Canada is to build innovative companies. Fixing Canada's tax policy on foreign investments is a start in reviving the industry.

13035 ■ *"Virtus.com Wins 'Best of Industry' WebAward for Excellence in Financial Services"* in *Investment Weekly News (October 24, 2009)*

Pub: Investment Weekly News

Description: Web Marketing Association honored Virtus.com, the Website of Virtus Investment Partners, Inc., for Outstanding Achievement in Web Development and Acsys Interactive was awarded the Financial Services Standard of Excellence Award for developing the site. The site was part of a rebranding effort and is a one-stop portal for both financial advisors and their investors.

13036 ■ *"Virtus.com Wins 'Best of Industry' WebAward for Excellence in Financial Services"* in *Investment Weekly News (Oct.*

24, 2009, pp. 227)

Pub: Investment Weekly News

Description: Web Marketing Association honored Virtus.com, the Website of Virtus Investment Partners, Inc., for Outstanding Achievement in Web Development and Acsys Interactive was awarded the Financial Services Standard of Excellence Award for developing the site. The site was part of a rebranding effort and is a one-stop portal for both financial advisors and their investors.

13037 ■ *"Vista-Based NCV Bought by Canteen Vending"* in *North County Times (October 18, 2011)*

Pub: Lee Enterprises Inc.

Ed: Pat Maio. **Description:** Details of North Carolina-based Canteen Vending Services' acquisition of NCV Refreshment Services, are given.

13038 ■ *"Vital Signs: The Big Picture"* in *Canadian Business (Vol. 81, Summer 2008, No. 9, pp. 153)*

Pub: Rogers Media Ltd.

Description: Results of the Investor 500 showing percentage of companies with positive returns, most actively traded companies over the past six months and market capitalization by industry are presented. Stock performance and revenues of publicly held corporations in Canada are also provided.

13039 ■ *"Vitamins to Spice Up Food"* in *Philadelphia Business Journal (Vol. 28, October 2, 2009, No. 33, pp. 1)*

Pub: American City Business Journals

Ed: John George. **Description:** VitaminSpice, a startup company established by Ed Bukstel, makes a line of spice and vitamin blends that come in seasoning form. The form of the blends could facilitate easier ingestion of vitamins into people's diets. A reverse merger that will allow a publicly-traded company status for VitaminSpice will be accomplished by early October 2009.

13040 ■ *"Vive La Resistance: Competing Logics and the Consolidation of U.S. Community Banking"* in *Academy of Management Journal (August 2007)*

Pub: Academy of Management

Contact: Ming-Jer Chen, President

Ed: Christopher Marquis, Michael Lounsbury. **Description:** Ways in which competing logics facilitate resistance to institutional change is presented, highlighting on banking professionals' resistance to large, national banks acquisitions of smaller, local banks.

13041 ■ *"Voice: Rebuilding Trust"* in *Business Strategy Review (Vol. 21, Summer 2010, No. 2, pp. 79)*

Pub: Blackwell Publishers Ltd.

Ed: David De Cremer. **Description:** An examination of the financial sector's attempt to rebuild trust is given. Three steps to jump start the process are explored.

13042 ■ *"Voice: Rebuilding Trust"* in *Business Strategy Review (Vol. 21, Summer 2010, No. 2, pp. 79)*

Pub: Wiley-Blackwell

Ed: David De Cremer. **Description:** The financial world's attempts to rebuild trust are charted. Three steps to jump-start that process are outlined.

13043 ■ *"Wachovia Gears Up for Major Arizona Expansion"* in *Business Journal-Serving Phoenix and the Valley of the Sun (Vol. 5, October 5, 2007)*

Pub: American City Business Journals, Inc.

Ed: Chris Casacchia. **Description:** Wachovia, America's fourth-largest bank is finalizing a deal to build its Arizona headquarters in downtown Phoenix. The bank plans to add an additional 100 employees by June 2008 and double its financial network to 30 offices in four years. Wachovia will also convert fifteen World Savings Bank branches it acquired in 2006 through Golden West Financial Corporation.

13044 ■ *"Wait for the Call' in Canadian Business (Vol. 80, April 9, 2007, No. 8, pp. 74)*
Pub: Rogers Media
Ed: Andrew Wahl. **Description:** The effort of chief executive of BCE Inc. Michael Sabia to deal with rumors about the company's private equity deal with Kohlberg Kravis Roberts & Co. is discussed.

13045 ■ *"Wait a Minute!' in Entrepreneur (Vol. 37, September 2009, No. 9, pp. 76)*
Pub: Entrepreneur Media, Inc.
Ed: Jennifer Wang. **Description:** Advice on how entrepreneurs in the United States should secure funding in view of the economic crisis is presented. Enough interest should be stimulated so as to secure a follow-up meeting. Investors should be asked questions that would encourage them to tell stories related to the downturn.

13046 ■ *"Walk This Way' in Barron's (Vol. 90, August 23, 2010, No. 34, pp. 13)*
Pub: Barron's Editorial & Corporate Headquarters
Ed: Christopher C. Williams. **Description:** Crocs and Skechers are selling very popular shoes and sales show no signs of winding down. The shares of both companies are attractively prices.

13047 ■ *"Wall Street Is No Friend to Radical Innovation" in Harvard Business Review (Vol. 88, July-August 2010, No. 7-8, pp. 28)*
Pub: Harvard Business School Publishing
Ed: Julia Kirby. **Description:** Research indicates that investors are skittish about backing a business that proposes significant changes to its product or service status quo.

13048 ■ *"W&S to Trim Rich Retirement Plan" in Business Courier (Vol. 27, October 15, 2010, No. 24, pp. 1)*
Pub: Business Courier
Ed: Dan Monk. **Description:** Insurance firm Western & Southern Financial Group announced that it will reduce the pension benefits of its 4,000 associates by more than 30 percent starting January 1, 2011. The move is expected to reduce annual retirement payments by several thousand dollars per associate. Western is a Fortune 500 company and has $34 billion in total assets.

13049 ■ *"Want People to Save? Force Them" in Harvard Business Review (Vol. 88, September 2010, No. 9, pp. 36)*
Pub: Harvard Business School Publishing
Ed: Dan Ariely. **Description:** Contrasts in U.S. attitudes towards savings and government regulation with those of Chile, where all employees are required to save 11 percent of their salary in a retirement account, are highlighted.

13050 ■ *"Want Some of This?' in Canadian Business (Vol. 80, April 9, 2007, No. 8, pp. 71)*
Pub: Rogers Media
Ed: Jeff Sanford. **Description:** The economic impact of growing private equity in Canada is discussed.

13051 ■ *"Water Works Spinoff Could Make Big Splash" in Business Courier (Vol. 24, October 19, 2008, No. 27, pp. 1)*
Pub: American City Business Journals, Inc.
Ed: Dan Monk. **Description:** Cincinnati, Ohio city manager Milton Dohoney proposed to spin off the city-owned Greater Cincinnati Water Works into a regionally focused water district that could allow the city to receive millions of dollars in annual dividends. A feasibility study is to be conducted by a team of outside consultants and city staffers and is expected to be finished by summer of 2008.

13052 ■ *"The Way to the Market's Heart?' in Canadian Business (Vol. 80, March 26, 2007, No. 7, pp. 74)*
Pub: Rogers Media
Ed: Erin Pooley. **Description:** The financial and stock performance of Canadian biotechnology companies Medicure Inc. and Angiotech Pharmaceuticals Inc. are analyzed.

13053 ■ *"The Wealth Portfolio" in Canadian Business (Vol. 79, Winter 2006, No. 24, pp. 146)*
Pub: Rogers Media
Ed: Jeff Sanford. **Description:** The trends pertaining to the pricing of shares of public enterprises, at the Montreal stock exchange, are described.

13054 ■ *"Website for Women 50 Launches" in Marketing to Women (Vol. 21, April 2008, No. 4, pp. 5)*
Pub: EPM Communications Inc.
Contact: Ira Mayer, President
E-mail: imayer@epmcom.com
Description: Vibrantnation.com is an online community targeting women over age 50; members can share recommendations on a variety of topics such as vacation spots, retailers and financial issues.

13055 ■ *"A Week of the Worst Kind of Selling" in Barron's (Vol. 88, June 30, 2008, No. 26, pp. M3)*
Pub: Dow Jones & Co., Inc.
Ed: Kopin Tan. **Description:** In the week that ended in June 27, 2008 the selloff in the U.S. stock market was brought on by mounting bank losses and the spread of economic slowdown on top of high oil prices. The 31 percent decrease in the share price of Ingersoll-Rand since October 2007 may have factored in most of its risks. The company has completed its acquisition of Trane to morph into a refrigeration-equipment company.

13056 ■ *A Weekend with Warren Buffett: And Other Shareholder Meeting Adventures*
Pub: Basic Books/Perseus Books Group
Ed: Randy Cepuch. **Released:** February 23, 2007. **Price:** $23.95. **Description:** Financial writer and personal investor relates his experiences attending various shareholder meetings, reviewing each meeting and grading its educational value. The book is essential for those hoping to learn more about the way companies invest and do business.

13057 ■ *"Welcome to the Neighborhood' in Hawaii Business (Vol. 53, October 2007, No. 4, pp. 48)*
Pub: Hawaii Business Publishing
Ed: Jolyn Okimoto Rosa. **Description:** Finance Factors is planning to build branches in Manoa, and Liliha, as part of its strategy to position itself in high-yield areas. The company chose Manoa and Liliha due to the sites' rich deposits. Its strategy with regards to the branches' location and to the building design is discussed.

13058 ■ *"Wells Fargo Will Soon Lead Local Banks in Deposits" in Austin Business JournalInc. (Vol. 28, December 5, 2008, No. 38, pp. A1)*
Pub: American City Business Journals
Ed: Christopher Calnan. **Description:** Acquisition of Wachovia Corporation by Wells Fargo and Company will leave the latter as the top bank for deposits in Austin, Texas. The merged bank will have deposits of more than $ billion, more than the $3.9 billion deposits Bank of America maintains in the area.

13059 ■ *"Welsh Meat Sales on the Rise" in Farmer's Weekly (March 28, 2008, No. 320)*
Pub: Reed Business Information
Contact: Jeff Greisch, President
Description: Due, in part, to marketing efforts, retail sales of Welsh lamb and beef rose significantly in the first two months of 2008.

13060 ■ *"Wenzel Downhole Tools Ltd. Announces First Quarter Results for 2007' in Canadian Corporate News (May 14, 2007)*
Pub: Comtex News Network Inc.
Description: Wenzel Downhole Tools Ltd., a manufacturer, renter, and seller of drilling tools used in gas and oil exploration, announced its financial results for the first quarter ended March 31, 2007 which includes achieved revenues of $14.5 million. Statistical data included.

13061 ■ *"Weyerhaeuser's REIT Decision Shouldn't Scare Investors Away" in Barron's (Vol. 88, June 30, 2008, No. 26, pp. 18)*
Pub: Dow Jones & Co., Inc.
Ed: Christopher Williams. **Description:** Weyerhaeuser Co.'s management said that a conversion to a real estate investment trust was not likely in 2009 since the move is not tax-efficient as of the moment and would overload its non-timber assets with debt. The company's shares have fallen by 19.5 percent. However, the company remains an asset-rich outfit and its activist shareholder is pushing for change.

13062 ■ *"What Enforcement?' in Canadian Business (Vol. 81, December 24, 2007, No. 1, pp. 26)*
Pub: Rogers Media
Ed: Al Rosen. **Description:** Securities enforcement in Canada needs to be improved in order to tackle white collar crimes that influence investors' opinion of the country. There have been high-profile cases where investigations have not been initiated. Details on the responsibilities of the securities commissions and the need for enforcement mandate in a separate agency are discussed.

13063 ■ *"What Ever Happened to TGIF?' in Barron's (Vol. 88, March 10, 2008, No. 10, pp. M3)*
Pub: Dow Jones & Company, Inc.
Ed: Kopin Tan. **Description:** US stock markets fell in early March 2008 to their lowest level in 18 months, venturing close to entering a bear market phase. The S&P 500 has dropped an average of 0.78 percent on Fridays for 2008.

13064 ■ *"What Has Sergey Wrought?' in Barron's (Vol. 89, July 13, 2009, No. 28, pp. 8)*
Pub: Dow Jones & Co., Inc.
Ed: Alan Abelson. **Description:** Sergey Aleynikov is a computer expert that once worked for Goldman Sachs but he was arrested after he left the company and charged with theft for bringing with him the code for the company's proprietary software for high-frequency trading. The stock market has been down for four straight weeks as of July 13, 2009 which reflects the reality of how the economy is still struggling.

13065 ■ *"What Recovery?' in Canadian Business (Vol. 82, April 27, 2009, No. 7, pp. 18)*
Pub: Rogers Media
Ed: Rachel Pulfer. **Description:** U.S. markets have rallied on the end of March 2009 but experts and analysts believe that it could be short-lived. Market rallies were found to be common during recessions and are not indicative of economic recovery. Meanwhile, it is believed that employment will be a key factor that will determine the U.S. economic recovery.

13066 ■ *"What'll You Have Tonight?' in Barron's (Vol. 88, July 4, 2008, No. 28, pp. 22)*
Pub: Dow Jones & Co., Inc.
Ed: Neil A. Martin. **Description:** Shares of Diageo could rise by 30 percent a year from June 2008 after it slipped due to U.S. sales worries. The company also benefits from the trend toward more premium alcoholic beverage brands worldwide especially in emerging markets.

13067 ■ *"What's In a Name?' in Barron's (Vol. 88, March 17, 2008, No. 11, pp. 7)*
Pub: Dow Jones & Company, Inc.
Ed: Alan Abelson. **Description:** Eliot Spitzer's resignation incidentally caused the stock market to go up by 400 points. The Federal Reserve Board's new Term Securities Lending Facility provides liquidity to the big lenders by funneling $200 billion in the form of 28-day loans of Treasuries. The analysis of Paul Brodsky and Lee Quaintance of QB Partners on the demand for commodities is also discussed.

13068 ■ *"What's More Important: Stag or Inflation?' in Barron's (Vol. 88, July 14, 2008, No. 28, pp. M8)*
Pub: Dow Jones & Co., Inc.
Ed: Randall W. Forsyth. **Description:** Economists are divided on which part of stagflation, an economic situation in which inflation and economic stagnation

occur simultaneously and remain unchecked for a period of time, is more important. Some economists say that the Federal government is focusing on controlling inflation while others see the central bank as extending its liquidity facilities to the financial sector.

13069 ■ *"When to Roll Over"* in *Black Enterprise (Vol. 37, November 2006, No. 4, pp. 50)*
Pub: Earl G. Graves Publishing Co. Inc.
Ed: Carolyn M. Brown. **Description:** Being proactive and rolling over your funds if you own stock of your former employee will give you more control over your money, especially if the company merges or is sold.

13070 ■ *"Where Are the Vultures?"* in *Mergers & Acquisitions: The Dealmaker's Journal (March 1, 2008)*
Pub: SourceMedia, Inc.
Ed: Ken MacFadyen. **Description:** Although the real estate market is distressed, not many acquisitions are being made by distress private equity investors; this is due, in part, to the difficulty in assessing real estate industry firms since it is a sector which is so localized.

13071 ■ *"Where the Money Is"* in *Conde Nast Portfolio (Vol. 2, June 2008, No. 6, pp. 113)*
Pub: Conde Nast Publications
Contact: David Carey, President
Description: Revenue generated from treatments for common brain disorders that are currently on the market are listed.

13072 ■ *"Where Oil-Rich Nations Are Placing Their Bets"* in *Harvard Business Review (Vol. 86, September 2008, No. 9, pp. 119)*
Pub: Harvard Business School Press
Ed: Rawi Abdelal; Ayesha Khan; Tarun Khanna. **Description:** Investment strategies of the Gulf Cooperation Council nations are examined in addition to how these have impacted the global economy and capitalism.

13073 ■ *"Where to Stash Your Cash"* in *Barron's (Vol. 88, March 17, 2008, No. 11, pp. 41)*
Pub: Dow Jones & Company, Inc.
Ed: Mike Hogan. **Description:** Investors are putting their money in money-market mutual funds seeking fractionally better yields and a safe haven from the uncertainties that was brought about by subprime lending. These funds, however, are hovering near 3.20 percent which is less than the 4 percent inflation rate.

13074 ■ *"Where To Look for Income"* in *Women In Business (Vol. 63, Summer 2011, No. 2, pp. 50)*
Pub: American Business Women's Association
Ed: William J. Lynott. **Description:** Advice on ways to invest in the US market are presented, with information on Certificates of Deposit and Money Markets included.

13075 ■ *"Whiplashed? That's a Bullish Sign"* in *Barron's (Vol. 88, March 31, 2008, No. 13, pp. 34)*
Pub: Dow Jones & Company, Inc.
Ed: Richard W. Arms. **Description:** Huge volatility often occurs just ahead of a substantial rally, according to an analysis of the volatility in the Dow Jones Index since 2000. The Average Percentage Change based on a 10-day moving average of volatility is a way to measure the level of fear in the market and reveals when buying or selling have been overdone.

13076 ■ *"Whistling Past the Graveyard?"* in *Barron's (Vol. 88, March 17, 2008, No. 11, pp. 15)*
Pub: Dow Jones & Company, Inc.
Ed: Michael Santoli. **Description:** Discusses the Federal Reserve's move to provide $200 billion to the system which can be seen as an effort to avoid the liquidity problems that Bear Stearns suffered. The Federal Reserve's move seems to frighten investors rather than reassure them.

13077 ■ *"Who Gets the Last Laugh?"* in *Barron's (Vol. 88, March 31, 2008, No. 13, pp. 17)*
Pub: Dow Jones & Company, Inc.
Ed: Leslie P. Norton. **Description:** Nord/LB will take a charge of 82.5 million euros to cover potential losses apparently related to Vatas' refusal to take the shares of Remote MDx Inc. after buying the shares. Remote MDx's main product is an ankle bracelet to monitor criminals; the firm has lost over half of its market cap due to the Nord/LB troubles and questions about its revenues.

13078 ■ *"Why Intel Should Dump Its Flash-Memory Business"* in *Barron's (Vol. 88, March 10, 2008, No. 10, pp. 35)*
Pub: Dow Jones & Company, Inc.
Ed: Eric J. Savitz. **Description:** Intel Corp. must sell its NAND flash-memory business as soon as it possibly can to the highest bidder to focus on its PC processor business and take advantage of other business opportunities. Apple should consider a buyback of 10 percent of the company's shares to lift its stock.

13079 ■ *"Why It Pays to be in the Boardroom"* in *Globe & Mail (January 16, 2006, pp. B1)*
Pub: CTVglobemedia Publishing Inc.
Ed: Janet McFarland. **Description:** The reasons behind higher stock compensation for board directors, in Canada, are presented. The survey is conducted by Patrick O'Callaghan & Associates and Korn/Ferry International.

13080 ■ *"Why the Rally Should Keep Rolling..for Now"* in *Barron's (Vol. 89, July 27, 2009, No. 30, pp. M3)*
Pub: Dow Jones & Co., Inc.
Ed: Kopin Tan. **Description:** Stocks rallied for the second straight week as of July 24, 2009 and more companies reported better than expected earnings but the caveat is that companies are beating estimates chiefly by slashing expenses and firing workers. The regulatory risks faced by CME Group and the IntercontinentalExchange are discussed as well as the shares of KKR Private Equity Investors LP.

13081 ■ *"Why the Rout in Financials Isn't Over"* in *Barron's (Vol. 88, June 30, 2008, No. 26, pp. 23)*
Pub: Dow Jones & Co., Inc.
Ed: Robin Goldwyn Blumenthal. **Description:** Top market technician Louise Yamada warns that the retreat in the shares of financial services is not yet over based on her analysis of stock charts. Yamada's analysis of the charts of Citigroup, Fifth Third Bancorp and Merrill Lynch are discussed together with the graphs for these shares. Statistical data included.

13082 ■ *"Why WestJet's Culture Guru Chooses to Fly Under the Radar"* in *Globe & Mail (January 22, 2007, pp. B1)*
Pub: CTVglobemedia Publishing Inc.
Ed: Brent Jang. **Description:** The views of co-founder Donald Bell of WestJet Airlines Ltd. on company's shares and services are presented.

13083 ■ *"Wielding a Big Ax"* in *Barron's (Vol. 89, July 13, 2009, No. 28, pp. 26)*
Pub: Dow Jones & Co., Inc.
Ed: Shirley A. Lazo. **Description:** Weyerhaeuser cut their quarterly common payout by 80 percent from 25 cents to a nickel a share which they say will help them preserve their long-term value and improve their performance. Paccar also cut their quarterly dividend by half to nine cents a share. Walgreen however, boosted their quarterly dividend by 22.2 percent to 13.75 cents a share.

13084 ■ *"The Wild West"* in *Canadian Business (Vol. 80, January 15, 2007, No. 2, pp. 57)*
Pub: Rogers Media
Ed: David Baines. **Description:** The impact of the introduction of regulations by the British Columbia Securities Commission on trading of securities by investors is discussed.

13085 ■ *"Will the Force Be With Salesforce?"* in *Barron's (Vol. 88, March 24, 2008, No. 12, pp. 20)*
Pub: Dow Jones & Company, Inc.
Ed: Mark Veverka. **Description:** Shares of Salesforce.com are likely to drop from the $44.83-a-share level in the face of a deteriorating economy and financial sector and thus lower demand for business software. The company is unlikely to deliver on its ambitious earnings forecasts for 2008 especially with strengthening competition from Oracle.

13086 ■ *"Wind Point Partners Closes Southfield HQ"* in *Crain's Detroit Business (Vol. 26, January 18, 2010, No. 3, pp. 18)*
Pub: Crain Communications Inc.
Ed: Tom Henderson. **Description:** Wind Point Partners, a private-equity firm that expanded its headquarters to Southfield in 1997, has closed down its Michigan operations opting to move its headquarters back to Illinois.

13087 ■ *Wine Investment for Portfolio Diversification: How Investing in Wine Can Yield Greater Returns than Stocks and Bonds*
Pub: Wine Appreciation Guild
Contact: Donna Bottrell, President
E-mail: donna@wineappreciation.com
Ed: Mahesh Kumar. **Released:** October 2005. **Price:** $45.00. **Description:** Analysis of the performance of investments in fine wines, particularly Bordeaux, is presented. History verifies that wine has traditionally been a sound investment offering a higher expected return over the market relative to its overall contribution of risk. Wine can be used as an effective means of diversifying one's portfolio.

13088 ■ *"With the Indian Market, You Take the Good With the Bad"* in *Globe & Mail (March 23, 2007, pp. B11)*
Pub: CTVglobemedia Publishing Inc.
Ed: David Parkinson. **Description:** The performance of Bombay Stock Exchange in the month of February 2007 is analyzed. The impact of growing economy on the stock market performance is also analyzed.

13089 ■ *"With Mine Approval, Crystallex's Value as Target Seen on Rise"* in *Globe & Mail (March 28, 2006, pp. B3)*
Pub: CTVglobemedia Publishing Inc.
Ed: Wendy Stueck. **Description:** Crystallex International Corp. obtains Venezuelan Ministry of Basic Industry and Mining's authorization on Las Cristinas mining project. The impact of the approval, which posted rise in shares by 21 percent for the company, is discussed.

13090 ■ *"Wobbling Economy"* in *The Business Journal-Serving Metropolitan Kansas City (Vol. 27, September 26, 2008, No. 2, pp. 1)*
Pub: American City Business Journals, Inc.
Ed: Rob Roberts. **Description:** Real estate developers in Kansas City Metropolitan Area are worried of the possible impacts of the crisis at Wall Street. They expect tightening of the credit market, which will result in difficulty of financing their projects. The potential effects of the Wall Street crisis are examined further.

13091 ■ *"Woes Portend Consumer Shift"* in *The Business Journal-Serving Metropolitan Kansas City (Vol. 27, September 26, 2008, No. 2, pp. 1)*
Pub: American City Business Journals, Inc.
Ed: Suzanna Stagemeyer. **Description:** Black Bamboo owner Tim Butt believes that prolonged tightening of the credit market will result in consumer spending becoming more cash-driven that credit card driven. The financial crisis has already constricted spending among consumers. Forecasts for the US economy are provided.

13092 ■ *The Working Man and Woman's Guide to Becoming a Millionaire*
Pub: Prentiss Publishing
Ed: Al Herron. **Released:** November 2006. **Description:** President and CEO of a Century 21 office in Dallas, Texas shares insight into financial security and commitment to community.

13093 ■ *"A World of Opportunity: Foreign Markets Offer Diversity to Keen Investors"* in *Canadian Business (Vol. 81, Summer 2008, No. 9)*
Pub: Rogers Media Ltd.

Ed: Andrew Wahl. **Description:** International Monetary Fund projected in its 'World Economy Outlook' that there is a 25 percent chance that a global recession will occur in 2008 and 2009. Global growth rate is forecasted at 3.7 percent in 2008. Inflation in Asia emerging markets and forecasts on stock price indexes are presented.

13094 ■ *"World's Best CEOs"* in *Barron's (Vol. 88, March 24, 2008, No. 12, pp. 33)*
Pub: Dow Jones & Company, Inc.

Ed: Andrew Bary. **Description:** Listing of the 30 best chief executive officers worldwide which was compiled through interviews with investors and analysts, analysis of financial and stock market performance, and leadership and industry stature.

13095 ■ *"The Worst Lies Ahead for Wall Street; More Losses Certain"* in *Crain's New York Business (Vol. 24, January 21, 2008, No. 3, pp. 1)*
Pub: Crain Communications, Inc.

Ed: Aaron Elstein. **Description:** Due to the weakening economy, many financial institutions will face further massive losses forcing them to borrow more at higher interest rates and dragging down their earnings for years to come. The effects on commercial real estate and credit card loans are also discussed as well as the trend to investing in Asia and the Middle East.

13096 ■ *"Xstrata's Takeover Bid Comes Up Short in Shareholder's Eyes"* in *Globe & Mail (March 27, 2007, pp. B16)*
Pub: CTVglobemedia Publishing Inc.

Ed: Andy Hoffman. **Description:** The share holders of LionOre Mining International have expressed dissatisfaction over $4.6 billion take over by Xstrata PLC. Share holders are demanding more prices for share value.

13097 ■ *"Yahoo! - Microsoft Pact: Alive Again?"* in *Barron's (Vol. 89, July 27, 2009, No. 30, pp. 8)*
Pub: Dow Jones & Co., Inc.

Ed: Mark Veverka. **Description:** Yahoo! reported higher than expected earnings in the second quarter of 2009 under CEO Carol Bartz who has yet to articulate her long-term vision and strategy for turning around the company. The media reported that Yahoo! and Microsoft are discussing an advertising-search partnership which should benefit both companies.

13098 ■ *"YoCream"* in *Ice Cream Reporter (Vol. 23, September 20, 2010, No. 10, pp. 6)*
Pub: Ice Cream Reporter

Description: YoCream reported a sales increase for third quarter 2010 at 15.6 percent and net income increasing 25 percent to $2,141,000 for that quarter.

13099 ■ *"You Won't Go Broke Filling Up On These Stocks"* in *Barron's (Vol. 88, July 14, 2008, No. 28, pp. 38)*
Pub: Dow Jones & Co., Inc.

Ed: Assif Shameen. **Description:** Due to high economic growth, pro-business policies and a consumption boom, the Middle East is a good place to look for equities. The best ways in which to gain exposure to this market include investing in the real estate industry and telecommunications markets as well as large banks that serve corporations and consumers.

13100 ■ *Young Bucks: How to Raise a Future Millionaire*
Pub: Thomas Nelson Inc.

Ed: Troy Dunn. **Released:** November 2007. **Price:** $17.99. **Description:** Advice is given to parents to teach their children how to save money, invest wisely and even start their own business.

13101 ■ *"Young People Speak Out On Credit Union Board Involvement"* in *Credit Union Times (Vol. 21, July 14, 2010, No. 27, pp. 20)*
Pub: Summit Business Media

Ed: Myriam Di Giovanni. **Description:** Results of a Credit Union Times survey of Generation Y individuals about serving on Credit Union boards across the country are examined.

13102 ■ *"Your 2010 Windfall"* in *Small Business Opportunities (July 2010)*
Pub: Harris Publications Inc.

Description: Make this a year of fiscal health and wealth. A survey says most will strive to save this year.

13103 ■ *"Your Exposure to Bear Stearns"* in *Barron's (Vol. 88, March 17, 2008, No. 11, pp. 45)*
Pub: Dow Jones & Company, Inc.

Ed: Tom Sullivan; Jack Willoughby. **Description:** Bear Stearns makes up 5.5 percent of Pioneer Independence's portfolio, 1.4 percent of Vanguard Windsor II's portfolio, 1.2 percent of Legg Mason Value Trust, about 1 percent of Van Kampen Equity & Income, and 0.79 percent of Putnam Fund for Growth & Income. Ginnie Mae securities are now trading at 1.78 percentage points over treasuries due to the mortgage crises.

13104 ■ *"Your Startup may be Worth Less than You Think"* in *Entrepreneur (Vol. 37, October 2009, No. 10, pp. 96)*
Pub: Entrepreneur Media, Inc.

Ed: Asheesh Advani. **Description:** Valuations of startups at the idea stage are dropping due to the effects of the recession. This drop is due to the decreasing availability of investment capital, the reduction in portfolio values of investors, and the increase in early stage startups.

13105 ■ *"Zell Takes a Gamble on Tribune"* in *Globe & Mail (April 3, 2007, pp. B1)*
Pub: CTVglobemedia Publishing Inc.

Ed: Sinclair Stewart. **Description:** The purchase of the majority share in Tribune Co. by Samuel Zell is described. Samuel Zell's plans to keep the company's assets intact are discussed.

13106 ■ *"Zucker Closes Deal on HBC With Sweeter Takeover Offer"* in *Globe & Mail (January 27, 2006, pp. B1)*
Pub: CTVglobemedia Publishing Inc.

Ed: Marina Strauss; Sinclair Stewart; Jacquie McNish. **Description:** Jerry Zucker, vice-president of InterTech Group Inc., has finalized a deal to buy retail store Hudson Bay Co, for 1.1 billion dollars. The shares will be purchased at a rate of 15.25 dollars per share in an all cash transaction. Complete details of the buyout are discussed.

13107 ■ *"Zucker's HBC Shakeup Imminent"* in *Globe & Mail (February 20, 2006, pp. B3)*
Pub: CTVglobemedia Publishing Inc.

Ed: Marina Strauss. **Description:** The plans of investor Jerry Zucker to revamp Hudson's Bay Co., upon its acquisition, are presented.

TRADE PERIODICALS

13108 ■ *Bacard's Global Investor*
Pub: Ferney Scribes Inc.

Ed: Andre Bacard, Editor. **Released:** Monthly. **Price:** $129, U.S.. **Description:** Provides monthly updates of select no-load global and international funds, model portfolios, foreign market graphs, monthly analysis and current recommendations. Recurring features include news of research and a column titled Mutual Fund in the Spotlight.

13109 ■ *Banking & Financial Services Policy Report: A Journal on Trends in Regulation and Supervision*
Pub: Aspen Publishers Inc.

Contact: Mark Dorman, President

URL(s): www.aspenpublishers.com/Product. asp?catalog_name=Aspen&category_name =&product_id=SS0730689X. **Released:** 12/yr. **Price:** $790, Individuals with free standard shipping on U.S prepaid orders.

13110 ■ *Barron's: The Dow Jones Business and Financial Weekly*
Pub: Dow Jones & Company Inc.

URL(s): online.barrons.com/public/mainwww.dow-jones.com. **Ed:** Edwin A. Finn, Jr. **Released:** Weekly (Mon.) **Price:** $149, Individuals print & online; $99, Individuals print only; $79, Individuals online only.

13111 ■ *Bernie Shaeffer's Option Advisor*
Pub: Schaeffer's Investment Research Inc.

Contact: Bernie Schaeffer, Senior Editor

E-mail: bschaeffer@sir-inc.com

Released: Monthly, 12/year. **Price:** $149, U.S. $149/year, U.S.; $225, Canada; $225, Canada. **Description:** Makes both aggressive and conservative recommendations on listed stock options for the individual investor. Reports on news pertinent to the options market including new options listings, and suggested brokerage firms. Remarks: Subscription includes a telephone hotline service and approximately six special bulletins per year.

13112 ■ *Bert Dohmen's Wellington Letter*
Pub: Dohmen Capital Research Institute

Ed: Bert Dohmen-Ramirez, Editor. **Released:** Monthly. **Price:** $350, U.S.; $385, elsewhere. **Description:** Provides a comprehensive monthly analysis of the major U.S. and world investments.

13113 ■ *The Bowser Directory of Small Stocks*
Pub: R. Max Bowser

Ed: Cindy Bowser, Editor. **Released:** Monthly. **Price:** $89, U.S. and Canada; $138, elsewhere. **Description:** Provides extensive information on stocks valued at $3/share or less.

13114 ■ *Chartcraft Weekly Service*
Pub: Chartcraft Inc.

Ed: Michael Burke, Editor. **Released:** Weekly. **Price:** $256. **Description:** Offers recommendations to investors in New York and American Stock Exchange securities, including buy and sell signals and relative strength. Discusses industry groups and option indexes. Lists more than 1,400 stocks and includes point and figure of each stock covered.

13115 ■ *The COINfidential Report*
Pub: Bale Publications

Ed: Don Bale, Jr., Editor. **Released:** Bimonthly, except July and August. **Price:** $19.95, individuals; $99 lifetime subscription. **Description:** Features coin, stock and bullion market forecasts and analyses, plus inside information and best coin and stock bets. Recurring features include interviews, book reviews, and notices of publications available.

13116 ■ *Consensus, National Futures & Financial Weekly*
Pub: Consensus Inc.

Ed: Robert E. Salva, Editor, rsalva@aol.com. **Released:** Weekly. **Price:** $365, U.S.; $395, Canada; $595, elsewhere; $295 online. **Description:** Presents market letters, special reports, and buy/sell advice from over 100 sources. Covers all stock and financial markets, metals, agricultural markets, livestock, grains, and oilseeds. Recurring features include graphic CONSENSUS Index of Bullish Market Opinion, CONSENSUS review of major indexes, Commitments of Traders reports, Futures Market Trading Facts, and a calendar of events.

13117 ■ *Conversion Watch*
Pub: SNL Financial L.C.

Released: Irregular. **Price:** $1200, per year. **Description:** Informs readers by fax whenever new activity is announced. Provides all relevant data on conversion related filings and important conversion dates. Recurring features include news of research and a calendar of events.

13118 ■ *Fitch Insights*
Pub: Fitch IPCA Inc.

Contact: Stephen W. Joynt, Chief Executive Officer

Released: Monthly. **Description:** Provides ratings actions, comments, criteria, and surveillance via fax. Includes explanations of ratings decisions as well as Fitch's views on market actions and events.

13119 ■ Ford Investment Management Report
Pub: Ford Investor Services Inc.
Ed: David C. Morse, Editor. **Released:** Monthly.
Price: $288. **Description:** Summarizes financial and
market data for 2,680 common stocks in the Ford
Data Base to provide investment managers with
information for selection. Includes news of research,
investment reviews, and special study reports covering research projects.

13120 ■ FXC Newsletter
Pub: FXC Investors Corp.
Ed: Francis Curzio, Editor. **Released:** Semimonthly.
Price: $119 one year, online; $129 one year, print;
$210 two years, online; $230. **Description:** Reports
on the securities of companies that have the potential
for extreme capital appreciation. Offers news of
research for investors with risk capital, conservative
and speculative investment recommendations, and
performance reports.

**13121 ■ Global Investment Magazine: The
Journal of Money Management, Trading and
Global Asset Services**
Pub: Investment Media Inc.
URL(s): www.globalinv.com. **Ed:** Michael Herton. **Re-
leased:** Biweekly **Price:** $995, Individuals; $1075,
Other countries.

13122 ■ The Grandich Letter
Pub: Grandich Publications
Ed: Peter Grandich, Editor, peter@grandich.com. **Released:** Bimonthly. **Price:** $99. **Description:** Covers
markets in banking and finance, commodities, bonds,
currencies, energy, estate planning, business,
futures, economics, metals, insurance, medical
research, new issues, oil, gas, mining, options, penny
stocks, precious metals, real estate, securities, taxes
and tax shelters, technology, and treasury bills.

13123 ■ Hulbert Financial Digest
Pub: Hulbert Financial Digest
Contact: John Kimble, Analyst
Ed: Mark Hulbert, Editor. **Released:** Monthly. **Price:**
$135 $59/intro year; $37.50/five month trial; $59
introductory price. **Description:** Provides performance ratings on more than 400 portfolios recommended by more than 145 financial newsletters,
calculated on the basis of model portfolios constructed according to each newsletter's advice.
Includes a timing scoreboard, analysis of newsletter
performance, list of mutual funds most frequently
recommended for sale or purchase, a stock market
sentiment index, and a question and answer section.

13124 ■ Investor, U.S.A.
Pub: Seahorse Financial Advisers Inc.
Ed: Edvard Jorgensen, Editor, edvard@seahorsead-
visers.com. **Released:** Monthly. **Description:** Discusses investment from a global perspective. Recurring features include portfolio updates and columns
titled Market Performances, Timing Indicators, and
Investment Strategy.

13125 ■ Investors Intelligence
Pub: Chartcraft Inc.
Ed: Michael Burke, Editor. **Released:** Biweekly.
Price: $184. **Description:** Serves as a comprehen-
sive and authoritative Stock Market Advisory Service
dedicated to bringing the investor facts, original
projections, and a cross section of the recommendations of other leading Services.

**13126 ■ John Bollinger's Capital Growth
Letter**
Pub: Bollinger Capital Management Inc.
Ed: John Bollinger, Editor. **Released:** Monthly. **Price:**
$300 $225/year; $300, two years. **Description:**
Provides investors with specific investment advice on
stocks, bonds, precious metals, oil, and the dollar.
Contains in-depth analysis, charts, and forecasts,
with investment recommendations based on a techni-
cally driven Asset Allocation model developed by
John Bollinger.

13127 ■ The Journal of Investing
Pub: Aspen Publishers Inc.
Contact: Mark Dorman, President
URL(s): www.iijournals.com/JOI/Default.asp. **Re-
leased:** Quarterly **Price:** $756, Institutions; $1285,
Institutions 2 years.

13128 ■ The Konlin Letter
Pub: Kon-Lin Research & Analysis Corp.
Ed: Konrad Kuhn, Editor. **Released:** Monthly. **Price:**
$95, individuals $95/year. **Description:** Provides
investment advice on stocks under $10, especially
Emerging Growth and Special Situations stock poised
for Explosive Price Appreciation Potential. Makes
specific buy and sell recommendations and monitors
a broad range of technical indicators for the best possible market timing advice.

13129 ■ The Lancz Letter
Pub: Alan B. Lancz and Associates Inc.
Contact: Alan B. Lancz, President
Ed: Alan B. Lancz, Editor. **Released:** 15-17/year.
Price: $250, U.S.; $275, Canada E-mail; $300,
elsewhere domestic prices by. **Description:** Gives
current advice on stocks, bonds, precious metals,
currencies and other related investment vehicles.
Analyzes interest rate and general investment trends
and suggests investments for both aggressive and
conservative investors. Recurring features include
portfolio performance statistics and columns titled
Investor's Corner and New Recommendations.
Remarks: Subscription includes occasional special
issues.

13130 ■ Louis Navellier's Emerging Growth
Pub: Navellier-MPT Review Inc.
Ed: Louis G. Navellier, Editor. **Released:** Monthly.
Price: $995 $995/year; $1795, two years online. **De-
scription:** Provides extensive quantitative analysis
on nearly 400 stocks and the market environment.
Offers 15 model portfolios.

13131 ■ Lovejoy's MarketBrief Hotline
Pub: Lovejoy Corp.
Ed: David Luciano, Editor. **Released:** Monthly. **Price:**
$195. **Description:** Gives fundamental, technical,
and psychological investment analysis of stocks,
mutual funds, and industries transformed into ratings
(Buy, Sell & Hold). Provides timing strategy for stock,
bond, and gold markets. Recurring features include
letters to the editor. Remarks: Available through
email.

13132 ■ MMA Cycles Report
Pub: Merriman Market Analyst
Ed: Raymond A. Merriman, Editor. **Released:** 17/
year. **Price:** $249, U.S.; $249, other countries plus
10% for postal delivery. **Description:** Presents summaries and strategies on the stock market, precious
metals, T-bonds, currencies, and grains.

13133 ■ Money Fund Report
Pub: iMoneyNet Inc.
Contact: Peter Crane, Managing Editor
E-mail: pcrane@imoneynet.com
Ed: Connie Bugbee, Editor, cbugbee@imoneynet.
com. **Released:** Weekly. **Price:** $2,695, individuals.
Description: Publishes weekly data on more than
1,600 taxable and tax-free money market mutual
funds. Provides summary of money fund activity,
including average 7-day, 30-day, 7-day compound
yields, assets, and average maturities. Includes 13-
week trend analysis, industry commentary, and fund
profiles.

13134 ■ The Moneychanger
Pub: Little Mountain Corp.
Contact: Franklin Sanders, Editor
Ed: Franklin Sanders, Editor. **Released:** Monthly.
Price: $95, individuals. **Description:** Makes invest-
ment recommendations congruent with the editors'
attempts to help Christians prosper with their principles intact in an age of monetary and moral chaos.
Focuses on the gold and silver markets. Recurring
features include interviews and columns titled Current Market Projections and Unforgettable (quotes
and commentary).

13135 ■ The MoneyLetter
Pub: MPL Communications Inc.
Contact: Barrie Martland, President
E-mail: bmartland@mplcomm.com
Released: Semimonthly. **Description:** Designed to
offer financial planning advice and investment and
tax-planning strategies to a broad range of investors.
Recommends specific stocks, bonds, mutual funds,
and occasional esoteric investments. Provides

specific columns aimed at particular types of investors: conservative, growth-oriented, 'value' investors,
and the smaller investor. Also offers items on tax-
saving strategies, portfolio management, real estate
investment, and stock market trends. Recurring
features include letters to the editor and updates on
previous recommendations. Remarks: Toll-free
telephone number in the U.S. is 800-222-4863.

13136 ■ NYSE Weekly Stock Buys
Pub: Elton Stephens Investments
Ed: Elton Stephens, Editor. **Released:** Weekly. **Description:** Identifies stocks with increases in dividends, earnings, and price appreciation.

13137 ■ The Option Strategist
Pub: McMillan Analysis Corp.
Ed: Lawrence G. McMillan, Editor. **Released:** 24/
year. **Price:** $295, individuals $250/year. **Description:** Discusses options on stocks, indices, and
futures. Includes investment recommendations and
educational articles.

**13138 ■ The Review of Securities &
Commodities Regulation**
Pub: Standard & Poor's
Contact: Deven Sharma, President
URL(s): rscrpubs.com. **Ed:** Michael O. Finkelstein.
Released: Semimonthly **Price:** $1197, Individuals.

13139 ■ Sadoff Investment Management
Pub: Bryan Sadoff
Ed: Ronald Sadoff, Editor. **Released:** 12/year. **Description:** Provides stock and bond market summaries and trends, advice on when and how to invest
for optimum growth and minimal risk. Interprets
losses or gains in the stock market as resulting from
the changes in four environments: monetary, psychological, technical, and the economic/business cycle.
Recurring features include a model portfolio.

13140 ■ The Secured Lender
Pub: Commercial Finance Association
Contact: John Fox, Chairman
URL(s): https://www.cfa.com/eweb/DynamicPage.
aspx?Site=CFA&WebKey=9c5cb84b-bcdb-4a5
c-b1cb-41a20eb09478. **Released:** Bimonthly **Price:**
$35, Members domestic; $65, Nonmembers domestic; $62, Two years members; $105, Two years 2mbs.

13141 ■ SNL Financial Services Daily
Pub: SNL Financial L.C.
Contact: John W. Milligan, Editor-in-Chief
E-mail: jmilligan@snl.com
Released: Daily. **Description:** Summarizes by email
or fax daily news headlines on finance companies,
mortgage banks, investment advisors, and brokers/
dealers, plus dividend and earnings announcements,
stock highlights and index values, registration statements, and ownership filings.

13142 ■ Special Investment Situations
Pub: George W. Southerland
Ed: George W. Southerland, Editor. **Released:**
Monthly. **Description:** Provides stock market investment recommendations. Focuses on companies that
offer the prospect of a substantial capital gain in a
relatively short time with comparatively small risk.
Includes a description of the company, pertinent
financial data, and factors influencing the recom-
mendation. Also updates previous recommendations.

13143 ■ Standard & Poor's The Outlook
Pub: Standard & Poor's
Released: 48/year. **Description:** Supplies investment advice, recommending specific stocks and
reviewing past recommendations and carries company profiles. Recurring features include columns
titled In the Limelight, 5-Star Stock of the Month,
Stocks for Total Return, and Statistical Highlights.

13144 ■ Stock Market Focus
Pub: Ned Davis Research Inc.
Ed: Tim Hayes, Editor, tim@ndr.com. **Released:**
Semimonthly. **Description:** Advises on timing model
readings and offers strategy for market timing. Covers technical analysis of the stock market and
monetary conditions. Includes charts.

13145 ■ Timer Digest
Pub: James H. Schmidt
Ed: James H. Schmidt, Editor. **Released:** 18/year.
Price: $175, individuals; $175, individuals Internet only; $225, individuals. **Description:** Compiles and ranks the performance of intermediate and long-term stock market, gold, and bond timing signals by monitoring advisory services. Includes articles on mutual fund switch programs, fidelity sector funds, Dow Jones Industrials, and profiles of investment advisors of 80 services. Remarks: Subscription includes a telephone hotline service.It monitors over 100 of the nations leading market timing models, ranking the top stock, bond, and gold timers according to the performance of their recommendations over the previous 52.

13146 ■ Vickers Weekly Insider Report
Pub: Vickers Stock Research Corp.
Ed: Richard Cuneo, Editor, rcuneo@argusmail.com.
Released: Weekly. **Price:** $176, individuals. **Description:** Reports on stock insider transactions and maintains portfolios based on insider buy signals-96 up 68%.

13147 ■ The Wall Street Digest
Pub: Donald H. Rowe The Wall Street Digest
Contact: Donald H. Rowe, Editor
Released: Monthly. **Price:** $99, individuals $150/year; $175, two years. **Description:** Covers major investment areas, including stocks and bonds; foreign currencies; gold, silver, and other precious metals; real estate; tax shelters; and estate planning. Recurring features include a digest of the month's best investment and financial seminars, newsletter reviews, and statistics.

13148 ■ Washington Weekly
Pub: Securities Industry and Financial Markets Association
Ed: Peter Roberson, Editor, proberson@bondmarkets.com. **Released:** Weekly, during Congressional sessions. **Price:** Included in membership. **Description:** Provides information on legislative activity relating to the municipal, corporate, and government securities and asset-backed securities markets. Analyzes taxes, budget, and banking issues.

13149 ■ Whisper on Wall Street
Pub: George Brooks
Ed: George Brooks, Editor. **Released:** 5-8/year. **Description:** Covers investments on all exchanges as well as emerging companies, promising speculations, and special situations.

13150 ■ The Yamamoto Forecast
Pub: The Yamamoto Forecast
Ed: Irwin T. Yamamoto, Editor. **Released:** Monthly. **Description:** Analyzes and reports on undervalued stocks, selling at bargain prices and ready to emerge, market timing and economy.

VIDEOCASSETTES/ AUDIOCASSETTES

13151 ■ Ask for the Order. . .and Get It!
Dartnell Corp.
2222 Sedwick Dr.
Durham, NC 34112
Ph: (239)417-2079
Free: 800-223-8720
Fax: (800)508-2592
Co. E-mail: customerservice@dartnellcorp.com
URL: http://www.dartnellcorp.com
Contact: Kenneth F. Kahn, Publisher
Released: 1972. **Description:** Hammers home a key principle of salesmanship—to get an order you must ask for it; from the "Tough-Minded Salesmanship" series. **Availability:** VHS; 3/4 U; Special order formats.

13152 ■ Bonds: Types, Terminology & Principles
Instructional Video
2219 C St.
Lincoln, NE 68502
Ph: (402)475-6570
Free: 800-228-0164

Fax: (402)475-6500
Co. E-mail: feedback@insvideo.com
URL: http://www.insvideo.com
Released: 19??. **Price:** $29.95. **Description:** Provides information on bonds, including the different types available, terminology, basic market principles, and how to be a knowledgeable creditor. **Availability:** VHS.

13153 ■ The Cold Call
Video Arts, Inc.
c/o Aim Learning Group
8238-40 Lehigh
Morton Grove, IL 60053-2615
Free: 877-444-2230
Fax: (416)252-2155
Co. E-mail: service@aimlearninggroup.com
URL: http://www.aimlearninggroup.com
Released: 1976. **Price:** $695.00. **Description:** This program demonstrates the specific skills and disciplines of telephone selling, and the dangers of ignoring them. **Availability:** VHS; 8 mm; 3/4 U; Special order formats.

13154 ■ The Competitive Edge
Film Library/National Safety Council California Chapter
4553 Glencoe Ave., Ste. 150
Marina Del Rey, CA 90292
Ph: (310)827-9781
Free: 800-421-9585
Fax: (310)827-9861
Co. E-mail: California@nsc.org
URL: http://www.nsc.org/nsc_near_you/FindYourLocalChapter/Pages/California.aspx
Released: 1989. **Description:** This program emphasizes finding out your customer's most immediate concern, and selling to that concern. **Availability:** VHS; 3/4 U.

13155 ■ Financial Business Services
Morris Video
12881 Knott St.
Garden Grove, CA 92841
Ph: (310)533-4800
Fax: (310)320-3171
Released: 1983. **Price:** $24.95. **Description:** Money management careers are explored, including investment counselers, securities brokers, trust officers and mortgage underwriters. **Availability:** VHS.

13156 ■ A Happy Beginning
Resources for Education & Management, Inc.
1804 Montreal Ct., Ste. A
Tucker, GA 30084
Released: 1971. **Description:** An examination of closing the sale, asking for the order, and answering the customer's objections. How to become a confident sale closer. **Availability:** VHS; 3/4 U.

13157 ■ How to Close the Sale
Dartnell Corp.
2222 Sedwick Dr.
Durham, NC 34112
Ph: (239)417-2079
Free: 800-223-8720
Fax: (800)508-2592
Co. E-mail: customerservice@dartnellcorp.com
URL: http://www.dartnellcorp.com
Contact: Kenneth F. Kahn, Publisher
Released: 1981. **Description:** This program shows salespeople how to ask for the order, and how to get it. **Availability:** VHS; 3/4 U; Special order formats.

13158 ■ How to Take the Butt Out of a Sales Rebuttal
Dartnell Corp.
2222 Sedwick Dr.
Durham, NC 34112
Ph: (239)417-2079
Free: 800-223-8720
Fax: (800)508-2592
Co. E-mail: customerservice@dartnellcorp.com
URL: http://www.dartnellcorp.com
Contact: Kenneth F. Kahn, Publisher
Released: 1967. **Description:** A look at how to cope with the difficult problem of rebutting a customer's objection-without being objectionable. **Availability:** VHS; 3/4 U; Special order formats.

13159 ■ Investing for Women by Women
Tapeworm Video Distributors
25876 The Old Road #141
Stevenson Ranch, CA 91381
Ph: (661)257-4904
Fax: (661)257-4820
Co. E-mail: sales@tapeworm.com
URL: http://www.tapeworm.com
Released: 1996. **Price:** $34.95. **Description:** Discusses stock market investing and retirement planning options for women. **Availability:** VHS.

13160 ■ Joy of Stocks: The Forbes Guide to the Stock Market
MGM Home Entertainment
2500 Broadway
Santa Monica, CA 90404-6061
Ph: (310)449-3000
Fax: (310)449-3100
URL: http://www.mgmhomevideo.com
Released: 1983. **Description:** This introductory video to the stock market is divided into ten instructional segments. **Availability:** VHS.

13161 ■ Knowing the Prospect
Resources for Education & Management, Inc.
1804 Montreal Ct., Ste. A
Tucker, GA 30084
Released: 1971. **Description:** Shows the relationship of product or service benefits to the sales prospect's personal goals, and illustrates the value of knowing a prospect's needs. Ignores the fast-talking sales pitch. **Availability:** VHS; 3/4 U.

13162 ■ Louis Rukeyser's Wall Street Investment Seminar
PBS Home Video
Catalog Fulfillment Center
Charlotte, NC 28275-1089
Ph: (800)531-4727
Free: 800-645-4PBS
Co. E-mail: info@pbs.org
URL: http://www.pbs.org
Released: 1986. **Description:** This seminar on value investment, market strategy, and mutual fund investing features the latest moneymaking ideas for individual investors. Also included are presentations by 12 of the nation's leading stock market professionals. **Availability:** VHS; 3/4 U.

13163 ■ Making It Live
Resources for Education & Management, Inc.
1804 Montreal Ct., Ste. A
Tucker, GA 30084
Released: 1971. **Description:** This tape demonstrates a key to sales success-knowing your product or service and telling your story with enthusiasm and conviction. **Availability:** VHS; 3/4 U.

13164 ■ More Awkward Customers
Video Arts, Inc.
c/o Aim Learning Group
8238-40 Lehigh
Morton Grove, IL 60053-2615
Free: 877-444-2230
Fax: (416)252-2155
Co. E-mail: service@aimlearninggroup.com
URL: http://www.aimlearninggroup.com
Released: 1973. **Description:** This program shows the importance of knowing your stock and services so that you can deal professionally with awkward customers. **Availability:** 3/4 U.

13165 ■ Mutual Funds, Options, Commodities, & Collectibles
Instructional Video
2219 C St.
Lincoln, NE 68502
Ph: (402)475-6570
Free: 800-228-0164
Fax: (402)475-6500
Co. E-mail: feedback@insvideo.com
URL: http://www.insvideo.com
Released: 19??. **Price:** $24.95. **Description:** Seminar-style program features six experts as they discuss what every investor needs to know about mutual funds, options, and commodities. **Availability:** VHS.

13166 ■ *Nightly Business Report: How Wall Street Works—The NBR Guide to Investing in the Financial Markets*
PBS Home Video
Catalog Fulfillment Center
Charlotte, NC 28275-1089
Ph: (800)531-4727
Free: 800-645-4PBS
Co. E-mail: info@pbs.org
URL: http://www.pbs.org
Released: 1990. **Price:** $19.95. **Description:** A thorough, basic look at the workings and terminology of the stock market. Includes much background information on getting started in the investment world. **Availability:** VHS; 3/4 U.

13167 ■ *Overcoming Objections*
Film Library/National Safety Council California Chapter
4553 Glencoe Ave., Ste. 150
Marina Del Rey, CA 90292
Ph: (310)827-9781
Free: 800-421-9585
Fax: (310)827-9861
Co. E-mail: California@nsc.org
URL: http://www.nsc.org/nsc_near_you/FindYourLocalChapter/Pages/California.aspx
Released: 198?. **Description:** This film emphasizes the importance of understanding the customer's point of view. **Availability:** VHS; 3/4 U.

13168 ■ *Prescription for Complaints*
Video Arts, Inc.
c/o Aim Learning Group
8238-40 Lehigh
Morton Grove, IL 60053-2615
Free: 877-444-2230
Fax: (416)252-2155
Co. E-mail: service@aimlearninggroup.com
URL: http://www.aimlearninggroup.com
Released: 1975. **Price:** $695.00. **Description:** This program shows a six-step, objective method for dealing with customer complaints. **Availability:** VHS; 8 mm; 3/4 U; Special order formats.

13169 ■ *Presenting the Story*
Resources for Education & Management, Inc.
1804 Montreal Ct., Ste. A
Tucker, GA 30084
Released: 1971. **Description:** How a salesman can best communicate benefits to a customer. Emphasis is on preparation of the story and practice. **Availability:** VHS; 3/4 U.

13170 ■ *Self-Motivation in Selling*
Learning Communications L.L.C.
5520 Trabuco Rd.
Irvine, CA 92620-5705
Free: 800-622-3610
Fax: (949)727-4323
Co. E-mail: sales@learncom.com
URL: http://www.learncom.com
Contact: Lloyd W. Singer, President
Released: 1979. **Description:** A look at how to avoid sales slumps and maintain peak performances. Four untitled programs cover frustrations and turndowns, seeking feedback, how to keep personal problems from affecting performance, and how sales managers can keep their people motivated. **Availability:** VHS; 3/4 U.

13171 ■ *So You Want to Be a Success at Selling?*
Video Arts, Inc.
c/o Aim Learning Group
8238-40 Lehigh
Morton Grove, IL 60053-2615
Free: 877-444-2230
Fax: (416)252-2155
Co. E-mail: service@aimlearninggroup.com
URL: http://www.aimlearninggroup.com
Released: 1982. **Price:** $790.00. **Description:** Four videos that describe the fundamental skills of selling, from the initial research to the close. Part 1 focuses on the preparation, including client research and product knowledge. Part 2 looks at the skills and techniques of sales presentation. Part 3 shows how to deal with problem clients. Part 4 demonstrates the

tactics for successfully closing a sale. Also available as a complete seminar kit. **Availability:** VHS; 8 mm; 3/4 U; Special order formats.

13172 ■ *The Stock Market*
Silver Mine Video Inc.
31316 Via Colinas, Ste. 104
Westlake Village, CA 91362-6715
Ph: (818)707-0300
Fax: (818)707-1606
Co. E-mail: quksil@aol.com
URL: http://www.quicksilverrecords.zoomshare.com
Contact: Howard L. Silver, President
Released: 1984. **Price:** $29.95. **Description:** An introduction to the world of investments, featuring a history of the stock market, and defining commonly used financial terms. **Availability:** VHS.

13173 ■ *Wall Street Week: An Investment Primer*
PBS Home Video
Catalog Fulfillment Center
Charlotte, NC 28275-1089
Ph: (800)531-4727
Free: 800-645-4PBS
Co. E-mail: info@pbs.org
URL: http://www.pbs.org
Released: 1987. **Description:** A two-part investment introduction from the popular financial TV program with Louis Rukeyser, dealing with stocks, bonds, futures, commodities, options and more. **Availability:** VHS; 3/4 U.

13174 ■ *When You're Turned Down—Turn On!*
Dartnell Corp.
2222 Sedwick Dr.
Durham, NC 34112
Ph: (239)417-2079
Free: 800-223-8720
Fax: (800)508-2592
Co. E-mail: customerservice@dartnellcorp.com
URL: http://www.dartnellcorp.com
Contact: Kenneth F. Kahn, Publisher
Released: 1977. **Description:** Examines the question: When is a turndown a true rejection and when is it just a disguised objection?; from the "Tough—Minded Salesmanship" series. **Availability:** VHS; 3/4 U; Special order formats.

13175 ■ *Your Money Series*
Cambridge Educational
c/o Films Media Group
132 West 31st Street, 17th Floor
Ste. 124
New York, NY 10001
Free: 800-257-5126
Fax: (609)671-0266
Co. E-mail: custserve@films.com
URL: http://www.cambridgeol.com
Released: 1987. **Price:** $99.80. **Description:** Roma Sim, a board member of the National Association of Securities School, shows people how they can make their money grow. **Availability:** VHS.

TRADE SHOWS AND CONVENTIONS

13176 ■ **The Bond Market Association - Fixed Income Summit Expo on E-Commerce & Technology**
Flagg Management, Inc.
353 Lexington Ave.
New York, NY 10016
Ph: (212)286-0333
Fax: (212)286-0086
Co. E-mail: flaggmgmt@msn.com
URL: http://www.flaggmgmt.com
URL(s): www.sifma.org. **Frequency:** Annual. **Audience:** Bond Market Association members, government bond officers, fixed income brokers and dealers. **Principal Exhibits:** Online services, Internet systems, fixed-income trading and executions systems, real-time systems, Internet and other new products and solutions; online trading and execution

systems; bond market services; online research and global markets information. **Telecommunication Services:** sweiss@bondmarkets.com.

13177 ■ **Futures and Options Expo**
Futures Industry Association (FIA)
2001 Pennsylvania Ave. NW, Ste. 600
Washington, DC 20006
Ph: (202)466-5460
Fax: (202)296-3184
Co. E-mail: info@futuresindustry.org
URL: http://www.futuresindustry.org
Contact: Michael C. Dawley, Chairman
URL(s): www.futuresindustry.org. **Price:** $800, Members full, early bird; $950, Non-members full, early bird. **Frequency:** Annual. **Audience:** Futures commission merchants, futures exchanges, clearing houses, brokers, commodity trading advisors, banks, and money managers. **Principal Exhibits:** Equipment, supplies, and services for the futures, options and derivatives industries. **Dates and Locations:** , Hyatt Regency. **Telecommunication Services:** tvitale-chan@futuresindustry.org.

CONSULTANTS

13178 ■ **Bedford Associates Inc.**
211 Greenwood Ave., 2-2
Bethel, CT 06801
Ph: (203)846-0230
Fax: (203)846-1487
Co. E-mail: nick.kroot@bedford.com
URL: http://www.bedford.com
Contact: Jose Badia, Principal
E-mail: jose.badia@bedford.com
Scope: Offers expertise in the areas of computer information systems design and management. Services include airline systems consulting; transaction processing facility (TPF) and airline control system (ALCS) services; system development and maintenance; step by step (SST) and C-view sales, support and maintenance; supplemental staffing (either on site or remotely); web development services. **Founded:** 1980. **Publications:** *Advanced Telecommunications Abuse Control System (ATACS)*.

13179 ■ **De Bellas & Co.**
7700 Irvine Center Dr., Ste. 800
Irvine, CA 92618
Ph: (949)859-3332
Fax: (949)859-9333
Co. E-mail: info@debellas.com
URL: http://www.debellas.com
Contact: Alfred F. de, Jr., President
E-mail: adebellas@debellas.com
Scope: Provides merger, acquisition and financial advisory services to staffing and information technology services businesses and professional employer service organizations. **Founded:** 1983. **Publications:** "Tools to Take Advantage of the Current IT Staffing M and A Market," 2005; "Healthcare Staffing: Buy, Sell or Build," 2005.

13180 ■ **Financial Computer Support Inc.**
14 Commerce Dr.
Oakland, MD 21550-3940
Ph: (301)334-1800
Fax: (301)334-1896
Co. E-mail: sales@fcsi.com
URL: http://www.fcsi.com
Contact: David Huxford, Jr., President
Scope: Independent user group which provides computer and administrative support for financial planners, money managers, and insurance agents. Serves finance and insurance industries. **Founded:** 1981. **Publications:** "Check Out Carmen Petote," Jul, 2006; "Control the Information Flow with Rep Level Access," Feb, 2005.

13181 ■ **Green Rhino Pixelbooks—The Investor Intelligence Group**
96 10th St.
Garden City, NY 11530
Ph: (516)248-1871

Fax: (516)248-6642
URL: http://greenrhinopixelbooks.com
Contact: John Rhein, Owner
Scope: Provider of expertise in investor relations, publishing, venture capital and lecturer. **Founded:** 1981.

13182 ■ Integrated Business Information Systems Ltd.
22 Colonial Pl.
New Haven, CT 06515
Ph: (203)397-1523
Fax: (203)397-1523
Contact: Dr. Michael L. Schneider, President
E-mail: mischni@idt.net
Scope: Provider of financial and marketing software applications, design and development for PC LAN, Wang VS and IBM AS or 400 computers. Offers sales and support for several software products from other vendors, including Tele-magic, Real world, Lotus Notes and Power Builder. Industries served: Finance, marketing, investment, airlines, insurance and reinsurance worldwide. **Founded:** 1994. **Publications:** "Future Scope".

13183 ■ International Institute of Trading Mastery Inc. (IITM)—Van Tharp Institute
102-A Commonwealth Ct.
Cary, NC 27511
Ph: (919)466-0043
Free: 800-385-4486
Fax: (919)466-0408
Co. E-mail: info@iitm.com
URL: http://www.iitm.com
Contact: Dr. Van K. Tharp, President
Scope: Teaches individual investors and traders the mental skills to become more successful. Trains traders to overcome fears and perform more consistently. Provides private counseling to CTAs, traders, brokers and floor traders worldwide. **Founded:** 1982. **Publications:** "New Series Research on New Ways to Manage Your Portfolio," Jun, 2010; "Gold Trend The Pause That Refreshes," Jun, 2010; "At the Half-way Mark: A Project Marathon Update," Jun, 2010; "Traders and Mistakes Part 3 Rule Based Discretionary Traders," Jun, 2010; "What Can You Do When the Markets Go Wild," May, 2010; "While Everyone Was Nervous, One Great Trader Took 100R from the Market Last Week," May, 2010; "Risk Calculation or Profit Factor," Apr, 2010; "Insidious Stress," Mar, 2010; "Should I Change My Figures For My Specific Market," Mar, 2010; "Volatility Highs and Lows," Jan, 2010; "Cause and Effect: Thinking Differently for Traders," Jan, 2010; "The Peak Performance Course for Investors and Traders"; "Trade Your Way to Financial Freedom"; "Financial Freedom Through Electronic Day Trading"; "Safe Strategies for Financial Freedom"; "Another Structural Change in the Market". **Seminars:** Peak Performance 101 Trading Course, Embassy Suites, Apr, 2007; Blue print for Trading Success, Embassy Suites, Apr, 2007; Highly Effective ETF and Mutual Fund Techniques, Crab tree Marriott, Mar, 2007; Professional E-Mini Futures Tactics, Crab tree Marriott, Mar, 2007; How To Design A Winning Trading System That Fits You; Infinite Wealth Workshop; Simulate Your Trading System and Position Sizing, Stock Market, Options, Electronic Day Trading; How to Develop a Winning Trading System That Fits You. **Telecommunication Services:** info@vantharp.com; suggestions@vantharp.com.com.

13184 ■ Kauffman & Drebing Registered Investment Advisors
230 S Broad St., 5th Fl.
Philadelphia, PA 19102
Ph: (215)546-8016
Contact: Neil B. Kauffman, President
Scope: Offers objective personal financial planning. Also conducts seminars on personal financial planning and provides investment management consulting for institutions. **Founded:** 1982.

13185 ■ Paul J. Litteau Consulting Services
516 S Kennicott Ave.
Arlington Heights, IL 60005
Ph: (847)255-4275

Fax: (847)255-1334
Contact: Paul J. Litteau, Owner
Scope: Securities consultancy whose clients include domestic and foreign governmental bodies, securities broker-dealers and related financial services organizations. Specializes in the areas of registration, administration, operations, regulatory reporting, training, and regulatory compliance. Also serves attorneys and other parties, including government agencies in securities-related litigation and arbitration particularly in regard to liability and damages in the U.S. **Founded:** 1982.

13186 ■ Scan Management Inc.
320 Spangler School Rd.
Gettysburg, PA 17325-8639
Ph: (717)359-7473
Fax: (717)359-7082
Co. E-mail: scanmngt@supernet.com
Contact: Budd Hallberg, President
E-mail: scanmngt@supernet.com
Scope: Consultants to the futures and securities industry. Provides services to institutions and corporations involved in using the futures market as a risk management tool. Conduct compliance audits - hedging and reporting audits and due diligence audits on use of derivative products. Clients include professional, corporate and institutional organizations in both the public and private sector, as well as government agencies. Also provides expert witness testimony. **Founded:** 1985.

13187 ■ SS & C Technologies
33 W Monroe, Ste. 420
Chicago, IL 60603-2401
Ph: (312)443-7501
Free: 800-234-0556
Fax: (312)443-7509
Co. E-mail: solution@sscinc.com
URL: http://www.ssctech.com
Contact: Normand A. Boulanger, President
Scope: Software development, consulting service, and turnkey systems provides servicing the investment/private wealth management, the financial/accounting services, and other markets requiring technical systems integration solutions. **Founded:** 1986. **Special Services:** Sun Solaris/MS NT Server Platforms. Software partners with Lotus Notes; Microsoft; Sybase; Ardent (Universe); and others.

13188 ■ Towneley Capital Management Inc.—Towneley Capital Management
23197 La Cadena Dr., Ste. 103
Laguna Hills, CA 92653-1484
Free: 800-545-4442
Fax: (949)837-3604
Co. E-mail: Gretchen@towneley.com
URL: http://www.towneley.com
Contact: Tracy Thatcher Kuntz, President
Scope: Offers investment counseling and mutual fund management services. Industries served: All. **Founded:** 1971. **Publications:** "Stock Market Extremes and Portfolio Performance"; "Keeping Finances Secure".

13189 ■ VRTRADER.com
PO Box 1451
Sedona, AZ 86339
Ph: (928)282-1275
Fax: (480)607-5243
Co. E-mail: mark.vrtrader@gmail.com
URL: http://www.vrtrader.com
Contact: Mark Leibovit, Principal
E-mail: mark@vrsurvey.com
Scope: Offers individual stock selection and overall market timing services. Offers stock pick telephone hotline service and online e-mail service. **Founded:** 1979. **Telecommunication Services:** customerservice@vrtrader.com.

FRANCHISES AND BUSINESS OPPORTUNITIES

13190 ■ High Touch - High Tech
PO Box 8495
Asheville, NC 28814
Ph: (800)444-4968

Fax: (828)684-3194
Description: Mobile hands-on science experiments for children. **No. of Franchise Units:** 145. **No. of Company-Owned Units:** 14. **Founded:** 1990.. **Franchised:** 1993. **Equity Capital Needed:** $59,875-$63,600. **Franchise Fee:** $35,000. **Royalty Fee:** 7%. **Financial Assistance:** Financial assistance for franchise fee available. **Training:** Provides 5 day training at regional programming office.

COMPUTERIZED DATABASES

13191 ■ *ABA Banking Journal*
345 Hudson St., 12th Fl.
New York, NY 10014
Ph: (212)620-7200
Free: 800-895-4389
URL: http://www.simmonsboardman.com
Contact: Arthur J. McGinnis, Jr., President
E-mail: amcginnis@sbpub.com
Availability: Online: LexisNexis Group; Simmons-Boardman Publishing Corp.; Intuit Inc. - Intuit Financial Services. **Type:** Full-text.

13192 ■ *American Banker Financial Publications*
1 State St. Plz., 27th Fl.
New York, NY 10004
Ph: (212)803-8200
Free: 800-221-1809
Fax: (212)843-9600
Co. E-mail: custserv@AmericanBanker.com
URL: http://www.americanbanker.com
Availability: Online: ProQuest LLC - Dialog. **Type:** Full-text.

13193 ■ *Banking Information Source™*
789 E Eisenhower Pkwy.
Ann Arbor, MI 48106-1346
Ph: (734)761-4700
Free: 800-521-0600
Co. E-mail: info@il.proquest.com
URL: http://www.il.proquest.com
Contact: Matt Dunie, President
Availability: Online: ProQuest Co.; ProQuest LLC - Dialog; ProQuest LLC - Dialog; LexisNexis Group. **Type:** Bibliographic; Full-text.

13194 ■ *Barron's Online*
1 World Financial Ctr.
200 Liberty St.
New York, NY 10281
Ph: (212)416-2000
Fax: (212)416-4348
Co. E-mail: info@dowjones.com
URL: http://www.dowjones.com
Availability: Online: Dow Jones & Company Inc. **Type:** Full-text; Numeric; Statistical.

13195 ■ *Best's Statement File - Property/ Casualty - United States*
1 Ambest Rd.
Oldwick, NJ 08858-7000
Ph: (908)439-2200
Fax: (908)439-3296
Co. E-mail: customer_service@ambest.com
URL: http://www.ambest.com
Contact: James Peavy, President
Availability: CD-ROM: A.M. Best Company Inc. **Type:** Numeric; Directory.

13196 ■ *BlockDATA®*
3 Times Sq.
New York, NY 10036
Ph: (646)223-4000
Co. E-mail: salesinquires@thomsonreuters.com
URL: http://thomsonreuters.com/products_services/financial
Availability: Online: Thomson Reuters - Financial Unit. **Type:** Full-text; Numeric.

13197 ■ *The Bond Buyer Online*
1 State St. Plz., 27th Fl.
New York, NY 10004
Ph: (212)803-8200

Free: 800-221-1809
Co. E-mail: custserv@sourcemedia.com
URL: http://www.sourcemedia.com
Availability: Online: ProQuest LLC - Dialog; Pro-Quest LLC - Dialog; Investcorp International Inc. - SourceMedia Inc. **Type:** Directory; Full-text.

13198 ■ Business Wire
44 Montgomery St., 39th Fl.
San Francisco, CA 94104
Ph: (415)986-4422
Free: 800-227-0845
Fax: (415)788-5335
Co. E-mail: SF_sales_group@bizwire.com
URL: http://www.businesswire.com
Availability: Online: ProQuest LLC - Dialog; Dow Jones & Company Inc.; Mzinga Inc.; LexisNexis Group; Bloomberg L.P. **Type:** Full-text.

13199 ■ CANNEX
1200 Bay St., Ste. 1001
Toronto, ON, Canada M5R 2A5
Ph: (416)926-0882
Free: 800-387-1269
Fax: (416)926-0706
Co. E-mail: cannex@cannex.com
URL: http://www.cannex.com
Availability: Online: CANNEX Financial Exchanges Ltd. **Type:** Numeric.

13200 ■ Capital Stock
60 E 42nd St.
New York, NY 10165
Ph: (212)986-9300
Fax: (212)986-5857
Co. E-mail: data@haver.com
URL: http://www.haver.com
Availability: Online: Haver Analytics - HaverSelect. **Type:** Time Series.

13201 ■ CNQ Market Data Feed
Exchange Twr., 3rd Fl.
130 King St. W
Toronto, ON, Canada M5X 1J2
Ph: (416)947-4670
Free: 888-873-8392
Fax: (416)947-4662
Co. E-mail: info@tsx.com
URL: http://www.tmx.com
Availability: Online: TMX Group Inc. **Type:** Numeric.

13202 ■ Dial-Data™
95 Rockwell Pl.
Brooklyn, NY 11217
Ph: (718)522-7373
Free: 800-367-5968
Co. E-mail: info@trackdata.com
URL: http://www.trackdata.com
Availability: Online: Track Data Corp. **Type:** Numeric.

13203 ■ Dialog Finance and Banking Newsletters
2250 Perimeter Park Dr., Ste. 300
Morrisville, NC 27560
Ph: (919)804-6400
Free: 800-334-2564
Fax: (919)804-6410
Co. E-mail: contact@dialog.com
URL: http://www.dialog.com
Availability: Online: ProQuest LLC - Dialog. **Type:** Full-text.

13204 ■ Dividend Record
55 Water St.
New York, NY 10041
Ph: (212)438-2000
Free: 800-523-4534
Fax: (212)438-7375
Co. E-mail: questions@standardandpoors.com
URL: http://www.standardandpoors.com
Availability: Online: The McGraw-Hill Cos., Inc.-Standard & Poor's Financial Services LLC. **Type:** Numeric.

13205 ■ EDR Sanborn® Maps
440 Wheelers Farms Rd.
Milford, CT 06461
Ph: (203)783-0300

Free: 800-352-0050
Fax: (203)231-6802
Co. E-mail: jhan@edrnet.com
URL: http://www.edrnet.com
Availability: Online: Environmental Data Resources Inc. **Type:** Image.

13206 ■ EIU ViewsWire
26 Red Lion Sq.
London WC1R 4HQ, United Kingdom
Ph: 20 7576 8181
Fax: 20 7576 8476
Co. E-mail: london@eiu.com
URL: http://www.eiu.com
Availability: Online: LexisNexis Group; Financial Times Ltd.; The Economist Group - Economist Intelligence Unit Ltd. **Type:** Full-text; Numeric.

13207 ■ Extel Financial Cards from Primark
3 Times Sq.
New York, NY 10036
Ph: (646)223-4000
Co. E-mail: salesinquires@thomsonreuters.com
URL: http://thomsonreuters.com/products_services/financial
Availability: Online: ProQuest LLC - Dialog. **Type:** Directory; Full-text; Numeric.

13208 ■ Ford Equity Research Databases
11722 Sorrento Valley Rd., Ste. I
San Diego, CA 92121
Ph: (858)755-1327
Free: 800-842-0207
Fax: (858)455-6316
Co. E-mail: info@fordequity.com
URL: http://www.fordequity.com
Type: Numeric.

13209 ■ IGM CorporateWatch
Graybar Bldg., Ste. 616
420 Lexington Ave.
New York, NY 10170
Ph: (212)509-5802
Fax: (212)949-4189
Co. E-mail: sales@informagm.com
URL: http://www.informagm.com/gml
Availability: Online: informa global markets. **Type:** Full-text; Numeric.

13210 ■ MarketScope®
55 Water St.
New York, NY 10041
Ph: (212)438-2000
Free: 800-523-4534
Fax: (212)438-7375
Co. E-mail: questions@standardandpoors.com
URL: http://www.standardandpoors.com
Availability: Online: The McGraw-Hill Cos., Inc.-Standard & Poor's Financial Services LLC. **Type:** Numeric; Full-text.

13211 ■ Mergers Unleashed People Database
1 State St. Plz., 27th Fl.
New York, NY 10004
Ph: (212)803-8200
Free: 800-221-1809
Co. E-mail: custserv@sourcemedia.com
URL: http://www.sourcemedia.com
Availability: Online: Investcorp International Inc. - SourceMedia Inc. **Type:** Directory.

13212 ■ Municipal Futures Data-Line®
22 Thomson Pl.
Boston, MA 02210
Ph: (617)856-2900
Free: 800-367-8215
Fax: (617)856-5610
Co. E-mail: clientservice@tm3.com
URL: http://www.tm3.com
Availability: Online: Thomson Reuters - Municipal Market Monitor. **Type:** Full-text; Numeric.

13213 ■ Municipal Market Data-Line®
22 Thomson Pl.
Boston, MA 02210
Ph: (617)856-2900
Free: 800-367-8215

Fax: (617)856-5610
Co. E-mail: clientservice@tm3.com
URL: http://www.tm3.com
Availability: Online: Thomson Reuters - Municipal Market Monitor. **Type:** Full-text; Numeric.

13214 ■ Mutual Fund Activity
60 E 42nd St.
New York, NY 10165
Ph: (212)986-9300
Fax: (212)986-5857
Co. E-mail: data@haver.com
URL: http://www.haver.com
Availability: Online: Haver Analytics - HaverSelect. **Type:** Time Series.

13215 ■ opTrack™ Service
95 Rockwell Pl.
Brooklyn, NY 11217
Ph: (718)522-7373
Free: 800-367-5968
Co. E-mail: info@trackdata.com
URL: http://www.trackdata.com
Availability: Online: Track Data Corp. **Type:** Full-text.

13216 ■ Pink Sheets
304 Hudson St., 2nd Fl.
New York, NY 10013
Ph: (212)896-4400
Fax: (212)868-3848
Co. E-mail: info@otcmarkets.com
URL: http://www.otcmarkets.com
Availability: Online: Solera Holdings Inc. - Audatex North America Inc.; Bloomberg L.P.; OTC Markets Group Inc. **Type:** Full-text; Numeric.

13217 ■ Quarterly Financial Report (QFR)
60 E 42nd St.
New York, NY 10165
Ph: (212)986-9300
Fax: (212)986-5857
Co. E-mail: data@haver.com
URL: http://www.haver.com
Availability: Online: Haver Analytics - HaverSelect. **Type:** Time Series.

13218 ■ Securities Law Daily™
1801 S Bell St.
Arlington, VA 22202
Free: 800-372-1033
Co. E-mail: customercare@bna.com
URL: http://www.bna.com
Availability: Online: Bloomberg LP-Bloomberg BNA; Thomson Reuters - Westlaw. **Type:** Full-text.

13219 ■ Securities Regulation & Law Report™
1801 S Bell St.
Arlington, VA 22202
Free: 800-372-1033
Co. E-mail: customercare@bna.com
URL: http://www.bna.com
Availability: Online: LexisNexis Group; Bloomberg LP-Bloomberg BNA; Thomson Reuters - Westlaw. **Type:** Full-text.

13220 ■ SNL Financial Banks & Thrifts Module
One SNL Plz.
Charlottesville, VA 22902
Ph: (434)977-1600
Fax: (434)977-4466
Co. E-mail: support@snl.com
URL: http://www.snl.com
Availability: Online: SNL Financial LC. **Type:** Full-text; Directory; Numeric; Statistical.

13221 ■ SNL Financial North American Real Estate Module
One SNL Plz.
Charlottesville, VA 22902
Ph: (434)977-1600
Fax: (434)977-4466
Co. E-mail: support@snl.com
URL: http://www.snl.com
Availability: Online: SNL Financial LC. **Type:** Directory; Numeric; Statistical.

13222 ■ *Trendvest Ratings*
923 First Colonial Rd., No. 1805
Virginia Beach, VA 23454
Ph: (757)412-4301
Fax: (757)412-4302
Co. E-mail: editor@trendvest.com
URL: http://www.trendvest.com
Availability: Online: Trendvest Management Inc.
Type: Full-text; Numeric.

13223 ■ *U.S. Weekly Statistics*
60 E 42nd St.
New York, NY 10165
Ph: (212)986-9300
Fax: (212)986-5857
Co. E-mail: data@haver.com
URL: http://www.haver.com
Availability: Online: Haver Analytics - HaverSelect.
Type: Statistical; Numeric.

13224 ■ *Value Line DataFile*
220 E 42nd St.
New York, NY 10017-5806
Ph: (212)907-1500
Free: 800-654-0508
Fax: (212)818-9747
Co. E-mail: vlcr@valueline.com
URL: http://www.valueline.com
Contact: Howard A. Brecher, President
Availability: Online: FactSet Research Systems Inc.;
Citigroup Inc. - Institutional Clients Group - Global
Markets. **Type:** Time Series; Numeric.

13225 ■ *Value Line Electronic Convertibles*
220 E 42nd St.
New York, NY 10017-5806
Ph: (212)907-1500
Free: 800-654-0508
Fax: (212)818-9747
Co. E-mail: vlcr@valueline.com
URL: http://www.valueline.com
Contact: Howard A. Brecher, President
Availability: Online: Value Line Inc. **Type:** Numeric.

**13226 ■ *Value Line Estimates and
Projections File***
220 E 42nd St.
New York, NY 10017-5806
Ph: (212)907-1500
Free: 800-654-0508
Fax: (212)818-9747
Co. E-mail: vlcr@valueline.com
URL: http://www.valueline.com
Contact: Howard A. Brecher, President
Availability: Online: FactSet Research Systems Inc.;
GIT Satellite LLC. **Type:** Numeric.

LIBRARIES

**13227 ■ Alberta Securities Commission
Library**
250-5th St. SW, Ste. 600
Calgary, AB, Canada T2P 0R4
Ph: (403)297-6454
Free: 877-355-0585
Fax: (403)297-6156
Co. E-mail: inquiries@asc.ca
URL: http://www.albertasecurities.com
Contact: Yanming Fei, Librarian
Scope: Securities legislation, corporate law. **Services:** Library not open to the public. **Holdings:**
Figures not available.

**13228 ■ AllianceBernstein - Information
Resources—Bernstein Global Wealth
Management.**
1345 Ave. of the Americans
New York, NY 10105
Ph: (212)756-4400
URL: http://www.alliancebernstein.com
Scope: Investments - finance and corporation. **Services:** Interlibrary loan; library open to SLA members
only. **Founded:** 1967. **Holdings:** Business directories, research materials, and newspapers. **Subscriptions:** 10 journals and other serials; 3 newspapers.

13229 ■ Ballard Spahr LLP Library
1735 Market St.
Philadelphia, PA 19103
Ph: (215)865-8500
Co. E-mail: proctor@ballardspahr.com
URL: http://www.ballardspahr.com/
Contact: David J. Proctor, Director
Scope: Law; public utilities, taxation; municipal
bonds; real estate. **Services:** Interlibrary loan; library
not open to the public. **Holdings:** 10,000 volumes.

13230 ■ BMO Nesbitt Burns Library
1 First Canadian Place, 3rd Fl.
Toronto, ON, Canada M5X 1H3
Ph: (416)359-4587
Co. E-mail: library@bmonb.com
URL: http://www.bmo.com/nesbittburns
Contact: Dani Breen, Manager
Scope: Investment. **Services:** Library not open to
the public. **Founded:** 1960. **Holdings:** 200 books;
1000 reports; 32 online databases. **Subscriptions:**
200 journals and other serials, 6 newspapers. **Telecommunication Services:** contact@bmonb.com.

**13231 ■ CMA Ontario - Member Services
Centre**
70 University Ave., Ste. 101
Toronto, ON, Canada M5J 2M4
Ph: (416)204-3142
Fax: (416)977-1365
Co. E-mail: msc@cma-ontario.org
Contact: Patricia Black, Manager, Member Services
Scope: Accounting, management, finance, strategy,
taxation, investments. **Services:** Copying; SDI;
Library not open to the public. **Founded:** 1990. **Holdings:** 2069 books; 267 videocassettes; 184 audiocassettes; 6 videodiscs. **Subscriptions:** 53 journals
and other serials; 2 newspapers.

13232 ■ Compass Lexecon Library
332 S. Michigan Ave., Ste. 1300
Chicago, IL 60604
Ph: (312)322-0845
Fax: (312)322-0881
Co. E-mail: cgriffin@lexecon.com
Contact: Christine Griffin, Office Manager
Scope: Economics, securities, finance, government,
business, reference. **Services:** Library not open to
the public. **Subscriptions:** 54 journals and other serials; 5 newspapers.

13233 ■ Dechert LLP Library
1775 I St., NW
Washington, DC 20006-2401
Ph: (202)261-7909
Fax: (202)261-3333
Co. E-mail: david.lang@dechert.com
Contact: David W. Lang, Librarian
Scope: Law - antitrust, investment and securities,
litigation. **Services:** Interlibrary loan; Library not open
to the public. **Founded:** 1969. **Holdings:** 6000
volumes. **Subscriptions:** 50 journals and other serials; 6 newspapers.

13234 ■ Fenwick & West LLP Law Library
Silicon Valley Center
801 California St.
Mountain View, CA 94041-2008
Ph: (650)988-8500
Fax: (650)938-5200
Co. E-mail: library@fenwick.com
URL: http://www.fenwick.com
Contact: Sharon McNally Lahey, Director, Library
Services
Scope: Securities, corporate, employment, International taxation, intellectual property, litigation. **Services:** Interlibrary loan; copying; Library not open to
the public. **Founded:** 1973. **Holdings:** 2500 books.
Subscriptions: 86 journals and other serials; 2
newspapers.

**13235 ■ Fidelity Management & Research
Company - Fixed Income Research Center**
82 Devonshire St., I39A
Boston, MA 02109
Ph: (603)791-7750

Fax: (617)476-9818
URL: http://fixedincome.fidelity.com/ftgw/fi/FILanding
Contact: Susan L. Johnson, Director
Scope: Investments and securities, economics and
business conditions. **Services:** Center not open to
the public. **Founded:** 1985.

13236 ■ Fulbright & Jaworski L.L.P. Library
801 Pennsylvania Ave., NW
Washington, DC 20004-2604
Ph: (202)662-4601
Fax: (202)662-4643
Co. E-mail: jweiss@fulbright.com
URL: http://www.fulbright.com
Contact: Judith M. Weiss, Librarian
Scope: Law - antitrust, bankruptcy, criminal, investment and securities, labor, patents. **Services:**
Interlibrary loan; library not open to the public. **Holdings:** 23,000 volumes; microforms; CD-ROMs. **Subscriptions:** 1200 journals and other serials.

**13237 ■ General Electric Company - G.E.
Asset Management Information Center**
3003 Summer St.
Stamford, CT 06904
Ph: (203)326-2404
Fax: (203)326-4026
Co. E-mail: mildred.lorenti@corporate.ge.com
Contact: Mildred Lorenti
Scope: Business, investment, finance. **Services:**
Center not open to the public. **Holdings:** 1300 books.
Subscriptions: 150 journals and other serials; 10
newspapers.

**13238 ■ Gibson, Dunn & Crutcher Research
& Information Management Department**
200 Park Ave.
New York, NY 10166-0193
Ph: (212)351-4005
Fax: (212)351-6262
Co. E-mail: sraber@gibsondunn.com
Contact: Steven Raber
Scope: Securities, corporate, litigation. **Services:**
Interlibrary loan; copying; Library not open to the
public. **Founded:** 1988. **Subscriptions:** 250 journals
and other serials; 20 newspapers.

13239 ■ Huddleston, Bolen LLP Law Library
611 3rd Ave.
Huntington, WV 25701
Ph: (304)529-6181
Fax: (304)522-4312
URL: http://www.huddlestonbolen.com/
Scope: Taxation/estate, corporate/securities/banking,
federal litigation, labor. **Services:** Library not open to
the public. **Holdings:** 35,000 books.

**13240 ■ Investment Company Institute
Library**
1401 H St. NW, Ste. 1200
Washington, DC 20005
Ph: (202)326-5800
URL: http://www.ici.org
Contact: Gregory E. Johnson, Chairman
Scope: Mutual funds; state, federal and International
mutual fund regulations; mutual fund legislation;
mutual fund research; "back office" operations;
marketing. **Services:** Library not open to the public.
Founded: 1940. **Holdings:** 500 books; 400 government documents; 150 other cataloged items; ICI
historical data and publications. **Subscriptions:** 225
journals and other serials; 10 newspapers.

**13241 ■ Ontario Teachers' Pension Plan
Board - Knowledge Centre**
5650 Yonge St.
North York, ON, Canada M2M 4H5
Ph: (416)228-5900
Fax: (416)730-5374
Co. E-mail: inquiry@otpp.com
URL: http://www.otpp.com/wps/wcm/connect/otpp_
en/home
Scope: Pension management, investment, economics, finance. **Services:** Library not open to the public.
Founded: 1995. **Holdings:** 900 books. **Subscriptions:** 30 journals and other serials.

13242 ■ Power Budd LLP Law Library
First Canadian Place, Ste. 7210
Toronto, ON, Canada M5X 1C7
Ph: (416)642-8580
Fax: (416)640-2777
Co. E-mail: lrhodes@powerbudd.com
Contact: Lesley Rhodes, Librarian
Scope: Energy, environmental and corporate law.
Services: Library not open to the public. **Holdings:**
Figures not available.

13243 ■ RCM Capital Management LLC - Research Library
555 Mission St., Ste. 1700
San Francisco, CA 94105
Ph: (415)954-5400
Free: 800-716-853
Fax: (415)954-8200
URL: http://www.rcm.com
Contact: Biff Moshe
Scope: Investment. **Services:** Interlibrary loan;
library not open to the public. **Founded:** 1976. **Holdings:** 230 books. **Subscriptions:** 400 journals and
other serials; 10 newspapers.

13244 ■ Scudder, Stevens & Clark Library
2 International Pl., Fl. 12
Boston, MA 02110-4103
Ph: (617)295-2282
Fax: (617)443-7063
Scope: Investments. **Services:** Interlibrary loan;
Library not open to the public. **Holdings:** 1750
volumes; 135 drawers of 10K reports, clippings, and
pamphlets; microfilm. **Subscriptions:** 200 journals
and other serials.

13245 ■ Stearns Weaver Miller Weissler Alhadeff & Sitterson Library
150 W. Flagler St., Ste. 2200
Miami, FL 33130
Ph: (305)789-3200
Fax: (305)789-3395
URL: http://www.stearnsweaver.com
Contact: Jeanne S. Korman, Director, Library
  Services
Scope: Law - Florida, securities, banking, labor and
immigration, corporate, litigation, land use, municipal
law. **Services:** Interlibrary loan; copying; library not
open to the public. **Founded:** 1976. **Holdings:**

20,000 books. **Subscriptions:** 200 journals and other
serials; 10 newspapers.

RESEARCH CENTERS

13246 ■ New York University - Glucksman Institute
Stern School of Business

44 W 4th St.
New York, NY 10012
Ph: (212)998-0700
Fax: (212)995-4220
Co. E-mail: wsilber@stern.nyu.edu
URL: http://w4.stern.nyu.edu/glucksman
Contact: Prof. William L. Silber, Director

ASSOCIATIONS AND OTHER ORGANIZATIONS

13247 ■ Accredited Gemologists Association (AGA)
3315 Juanita St.
San Diego, CA 92105
Ph: (619)501-5444
Co. E-mail: 5444@accreditedgemologists.org
URL: http://accreditedgemologists.org
Contact: Donna Hawrelko, President
Description: Gemologists. Promotes the advancement of the science of gemology. Conducts research and educational programs. **Founded:** 1974. **Publications:** *Certified Gemological Lab Directory* (Annual). **Awards:** Antonio C. Bonnano Award (Annual).

13248 ■ American Gem Trade Association (AGTA)
3030 LBJ Fwy., Ste. 840
Dallas, TX 75234
Ph: (214)742-4367
Free: 800-972-1162
Fax: (214)742-7334
Co. E-mail: info@agta.org
URL: http://www.agta.org
Contact: Ruben Bindra, President
Description: Represents suppliers of natural colored gemstones; retail jewelers and jewelry manufacturers. Promotes natural colored gemstones; encourages high ethical standards among members and within the industry. Seeks to establish closer communication within the industry; works to protect consumers from fraud and to create a greater awareness of natural colored gemstones. Conducts seminars; maintains speakers' bureau. **Founded:** 1981. **Publications:** *American Gem Trade Association Newsletter* (Quarterly); *AGTA Source Directory* (Biennial). **Educational Activities:** Design Competition (Annual); Gem Fair (Annual). **Awards:** Spectrum Awards Design Competition; Cutting Edge Gemstone Competition; Cutting Edge Awards (Annual); Spectrum Awards (Annual).

13249 ■ American Hatpin Society
c/o Cathy Miller, VP
2505 Indian Creek Rd.
Diamond Bar, CA 91765-3307
Ph: (909)861-4267
Co. E-mail: info@americanhatpinsociety.com
URL: http://www.americanhatpinsociety.com
Contact: Jodi Lenocker, President
Description: Collectors of hatpins. Promotes collection, preservation, and restoration of hatpins and related fashion accessories. Serves as a clearinghouse on hatpins and their history; facilitates exchange of information among members; conducts educational programs. **Founded:** 1989. **Publications:** *American Hatpin Society Newsletter*.

13250 ■ *At a Glance*
27 Queen St. E, Ste. 600
Toronto, ON, Canada M5C 2M6
Ph: (416)368-7616
Free: 800-580-0942

Fax: (416)368-1986
Co. E-mail: cja@canadianjewellers.com
URL: http://www.canadianjewellers.com
Contact: Kim Markwart, Chairman

13251 ■ *Be a Professional Gemmologist*

13252 ■ Canadian Gemmological Association
1301, 55 Queen St. E
Toronto, ON, Canada M5C 1R6
Ph: (647)466-2436
Fax: (416)366-6519
Co. E-mail: info@canadiangemmological.com
URL: http://www.canadiangemmological.com
Contact: Duncan Parker, President
Description: Jewelers and gemmologists. Promotes excellence in the practice of gemmology. Conducts continuing professional development programs for members; sponsors educational courses; sets and maintains standards of practice and competence for gemmologists. **Scope:** gemmology, geology, jewelry. **Subscriptions:** books clippings periodicals. **Publications:** *Canadian Gemmologist* (Quarterly); *Canadian Professional Gemmology Course*; *Canadian Gemmologist* (Quarterly).

13253 ■ *Canadian Gemmologist*
1301, 55 Queen St. E
Toronto, ON, Canada M5C 1R6
Ph: (647)466-2436
Fax: (416)366-6519
Co. E-mail: info@canadiangemmological.com
URL: http://www.canadiangemmological.com
Contact: Duncan Parker, President
Released: Quarterly **Price:** $45, /year, in U.S. and overseas.

13254 ■ Canadian Institute of Gemmology (CIG)
c/o Pacific School of Jewellery Arts
PO Box 57010
Vancouver, BC, Canada V5K 5G6
Ph: (604)530-8569
Free: 800-924-2211
Co. E-mail: info@cigem.ca
URL: http://www.cigem.ca
Description: Gemmologists and others with an interest in gemmology and gemmology training. Conducts educational programs in gem appreciation, gemology, gem identification, diamond grading and jewelry history and design; gathers and disseminates information to trade bodies and the public. **Scope:** gemmology, jewelry. **Founded:** 1983. **Subscriptions:** 150. **Publications:** *Gemmology Canada* (Quarterly). **Educational Activities:** Gem Forum Conference (Semiannual).

13255 ■ Canadian Jewellers Association (CJA)
27 Queen St. E, Ste. 600
Toronto, ON, Canada M5C 2M6
Ph: (416)368-7616
Free: 800-580-0942

Fax: (416)368-1986
Co. E-mail: cja@canadianjewellers.com
URL: http://www.canadianjewellers.com
Contact: Kim Markwart, Chairman
Description: National trade association for the jewelry industry in Canada, with both retail and supply members. Offers educational courses, information on Kimberley Process, Canadian Diamond Code of Conduct and source for Canadian diamond suppliers. **Founded:** 1918. **Subscriptions:** archival material books periodicals video recordings. **Publications:** *At a Glance*. **Educational Activities:** Jewellery World Expo (Annual).

13256 ■ *Canadian Professional Gemmology Course*
1301, 55 Queen St. E
Toronto, ON, Canada M5C 1R6
Ph: (647)466-2436
Fax: (416)366-6519
Co. E-mail: info@canadiangemmological.com
URL: http://www.canadiangemmological.com
Contact: Duncan Parker, President

13257 ■ Diamond Council of America (DCA)
3212 W End Ave., Ste. 202
Nashville, TN 37203
Ph: (615)385-5301
Free: 877-283-5669
Fax: (615)385-4955
URL: http://www.diamondcouncil.org
Contact: Peter Engel, Chairman
Description: Retail jewelry firms and suppliers of gemstones. Firms operating approximately 4900 retail jewelry stores; associated manufacturers and importers. Offers courses in "gemology" and "diamontology" to employees of member firms; bestows titles of Certified Diamontologist and Guild Gemologist upon those completing courses and examinations. Supplies members with advertising and educational materials, sales tools, displays, ad copy, radio and television scripts, and merchandise plans. **Scope:** gemstones, minerals, diamonds, jewelry. **Founded:** 1944. **Publications:** *Diamond Council of America--Directory* (Annual).

13258 ■ *Gemmology Canada*
c/o Pacific School of Jewellery Arts
PO Box 57010
Vancouver, BC, Canada V5K 5G6
Ph: (604)530-8569
Free: 800-924-2211
Co. E-mail: info@cigem.ca
URL: http://www.cigem.ca
Released: Quarterly **Price:** free.

13259 ■ Indian Diamond and Colorstone Association (IDCA)
56 W 45th St., Ste. No. 705
New York, NY 10036
Ph: (212)921-4488

Fax: (212)769-7935
Co. E-mail: office@idcany.org
URL: http://www.idcany.org
Contact: Nimish Mehta, President
Description: Diamond and colorstone dealers of Indian descent and others who work with diamonds and gemstones from India. Promotes the growth and awareness of the Indian gem industry in the U.S. **Founded:** 1984. **Publications:** *IDCA By-Laws Directory* (Annual); *IDCA Pocket Directory* (Periodic). **Awards:** Manufacturer of the Year (Annual); Retailer of the Year (Annual).

13260 ■ Jewelers of America (JA)
52 Vanderbilt Ave., 19th Fl.
New York, NY 10017-3827
Ph: (646)658-0246
Free: 800-223-0673
Fax: (646)658-0256
Co. E-mail: info@jewelers.org
URL: http://www.jewelers.org
Contact: Georgie Gleim, Chairman
Description: Retailers of jewelry, watches, silver, and allied merchandise. Conducts surveys and compiles statistics. Conducts educational programs. Provides information to consumers. **Founded:** 1957. **Awards:** Affiliate Design Competition (Annual); GIA Scholarship (Annual).

13261 ■ Jewelers' Security Alliance (JSA)
6 E 45th St.
New York, NY 10017
Ph: (212)687-0328
Free: 800-537-0067
Fax: (212)808-9168
Co. E-mail: jsa2@jewelerssecurity.org
URL: http://www.jewelerssecurity.org
Contact: John J. Kennedy, President
Description: Advocates for crime prevention in the jewelry industry. Provides crime information and assistance to the jewelry industry and law enforcement. **Founded:** 1883. **Publications:** *JSA Manual of Jewelry Security* (Biennial); *Annual Report on Crime Against the Jewelry Industry in U.S.* (Annual). **Educational Activities:** Security Seminar and Expo for Retail Jewelry Chains (Annual). **Awards:** Gold and Silver Shield Awards (Annual).

13262 ■ Jewelers Vigilance Committee (JVC)
25 W 45th St., Ste. 1406
New York, NY 10036
Ph: (212)997-2002
Fax: (212)997-9148
Co. E-mail: clg@jvclegal.org
URL: http://www.jvclegal.org
Contact: Cecilia L. Gardner, President
Description: Represents manufacturers, importers, wholesalers, and retailers. Combats deceptive trade practices and misleading advertising. Aims to develop and maintain high trade standards. Provides advice on markings and assists in prosecution of violations of marking, advertising, and related jewelry industry laws. **Founded:** 1917. **Publications:** *JVC Manufacturers' Legal Handbook.*

13263 ■ Jewellers Vigilance Canada (JVC)
27 Queen St. E, Ste. 600
Toronto, ON, Canada M5C 2M6
Ph: (416)368-4840
Free: 800-636-9536
Fax: (416)368-5552
Co. E-mail: info@jewellersvigilance.ca
URL: http://www.jewellersvigilance.ca
Contact: Phyllis Richard, Executive Director
Description: Strives to promote ethical practices within the jewelry industry. Offers educational programs and handles complaints from consumers. **Founded:** 1987. **Publications:** *Jewellers Vigilance Canada Action Update* (Quarterly).

13264 ■ Jewellers Vigilance Canada Action Update
27 Queen St. E, Ste. 600
Toronto, ON, Canada M5C 2M6
Ph: (416)368-4840
Free: 800-636-9536

Fax: (416)368-5552
Co. E-mail: info@jewellersvigilance.ca
URL: http://www.jewellersvigilance.ca
Contact: Phyllis Richard, Executive Director
Released: Quarterly

13265 ■ Jewelry Information Center (JIC)
52 Vanderbilt Ave., 19th Fl.
New York, NY 10017
Ph: (646)658-0246
Free: 800-223-0673
Fax: (646)658-0256
Co. E-mail: info@jic.org
URL: http://www.jic.org
Contact: David Bouffard, Chairman
Description: Represents retailers, wholesalers, and manufacturers of fine jewelry products. Conducts industry-wide promotional and educational programs; sponsors marketing seminars and consumer-oriented programs on radio, television, and print media. **Scope:** fine jewelry, history, design, manufacturing info. **Founded:** 1946. **Subscriptions:** 100. **Publications:** *LINK* (3/year). **Awards:** JIC's Gem Award (Annual).

13266 ■ Manufacturing Jewelers and Suppliers of America (MJSA)
57 John L. Dietsch Sq.
Attleboro Falls, MA 02763
Ph: (401)274-3840
Free: 800-444-6572
Fax: (401)274-0265
Co. E-mail: info@mjsa.org
URL: http://www.mjsa.org
Contact: Dave Meleski, Chairman
Description: Represents American manufacturers and suppliers within the jewelry industry. Seeks to foster long-term stability and prosperity of the jewelry industry. Provides leadership in government affairs and industry education. **Founded:** 1903. **Publications:** *Buyers Guide* (Biennial); *MJSA Journal* (Monthly). **Awards:** American Vision Award (Annual); Education Foundation Scholarship Award (Annual).

13267 ■ National Association of Jewelry Appraisers (NAJA)
PO Box 18
Rego Park, NY 11374-0018
Ph: (718)896-1536
Fax: (718)997-9057
Co. E-mail: office@najaappraisers.com
URL: http://www.najaappraisers.com
Contact: Ms. Gail Brett Levine, Executive Director
Description: Gem and jewelry appraisers, jewelers, importers, brokers, manufacturers, gemological students, and others professionally interested in jewelry appraisal. Seeks to recognize and make available to the public the services of highly qualified, experienced, independent, and reliable jewelry appraisers. Conducts seminars on jewelry appraisal techniques, methods, and pricing for members and the public. Supports legislation to establish minimum standards of competency and licensing of jewelry appraisers; maintains code of professional ethics. Operates appraiser referral program; sponsors ongoing public relations campaign. Offers equipment discounts, new appraisal forms, travel discounts, insurance, and professional aids for members only. Compiles statistics. **Founded:** 1981. **Publications:** *National Association of Jewelry Appraisers Membership Directory* (Annual); *The Jewelry Appraiser*.

13268 ■ Women's Jewelry Association (WJA)
52 Vanderbilt Ave., 19th Fl.
New York, NY 10017-3827
Ph: (212)687-2722
Fax: (646)355-0219
Co. E-mail: info@womensjewelry.org
URL: http://wjamarion.memberlodge.com
Contact: Kendra Bridel Weinman, President
Description: Represents those involved in jewelry design, manufacture, retail, and advertising. Aims to: enhance the status of women in the jewelry industry; make known the contribution of women to the industry; provide a network for women involved with fine jewelry. Maintains hall of fame. **Founded:** 1983. **Publications:** *Women's Jewelry Association-- Membership Directory*; *Jewelry Association Newsletter* (Semiannual). **Awards:** Women's Jewelry As-

sociation Member Grants; Awards for Excellence (Annual); Grant Program (Annual); Scholarship Program (Annual).

DIRECTORIES OF EDUCATIONAL PROGRAMS

13269 ■ *Directory of Private Accredited Career Schools and Colleges of Technology*
Pub: Accrediting Commission of Career Schools and Colleges of Technology
Contact: Michale S. McComis, Executive Director
Released: On web page. **Price:** Free. **Description:** Covers 3900 accredited post-secondary programs that provide training programs in business, trade, and technical fields, including various small business endeavors. Entries offer school name, address, phone, description of courses, job placement assistance, and requirements for admission. Arrangement is alphabetical.

REFERENCE WORKS

13270 ■ *"Former Apprentice Candidate Launches Jewelry Line" in Black Enterprise (Vol. 37, October 2006, No. 3, pp. 36)*
Pub: Earl G. Graves Publishing Co. Inc.
Ed: Philana Patterson. **Description:** Star of the second season of NBC's The Apprentice, Stacie J, has launched a line of jewelry and accessories which will be sold at Claire's stores nationwide.

13271 ■ *Gems & Jewelry Appraising: Techniques of Professional Practice*
Pub: GemStone Press
Ed: Anna M. Miller; Gail Brett Levine. **Released:** August 28, 2008. **Price:** $39.99 paperback. **Description:** Comprehensive book for practicing appraisers, would-be appraisers; provides extension information about the profession.

13272 ■ *"Gold Still Has That Glitter" in Barron's (Vol. 89, July 20, 2009, No. 29, pp. M8)*
Pub: Dow Jones & Co., Inc.
Ed: Allen Sykora. **Description:** Gold prices appear to be ready for an increase starting in the fall of 2009 due to an increase in demand. The price of the August 2009 gold contract fell to as low as $904.08 an ounce before recovering to $937.50.

13273 ■ *"High-End Jeweler Loses Street Sparkle" in Houston Business Journal (Vol. 40, November 27, 2009, No. 29, pp. 1)*
Pub: American City Business Journals
Ed: Allison Wollam. **Description:** High-end jeweler Bailey Banks & Biddle's 7,000 square foot prototype store in Houston, Texas' CityCentre will be ceasing operations despite its parent company's filing for Chapter 11 protection from creditors. According to the bankruptcy filing, parent company Finlay Enterprises Inc. of New York intends to auction off its business and assets. Finlay has 67 Bailey Banks locations throughout the US.

13274 ■ *Lapidary Journal--Annual Buyers' Directory Issue*
Pub: Lapidary Journal
Contact: Sean Holzman, Manager
URL(s): www.jewelrymakingdaily.com/blogs/jewelryartistmagazine/default.aspx. **Ed:** Merle White. **Released:** Annual; latest edition 2012. **Price:** $29.95, Individuals. **Publication includes:** List of 4,000 suppliers and retailers of gem-cutting and jewelry making and mineral collecting equipment, beads, fossils, minerals, and gems; gem and mineral clubs, bead societies, museums, schools, and shops. **Entries include:** Company or organization name, address, phone. **Arrangement:** Classified by product and service. **Indexes:** Product/service, geographical, alphabetical by dealers.

13275 ■ *"Midas Touch" in Entrepreneur (Vol. 36, April 2008, No. 4, pp. 160)*
Pub: Entrepreneur Media, Inc.
Ed: Sara Wilson. **Description:** Lana Fertelmeister is a model-turned-jewelry designer. Her company, Lana Jewelry, designs fine jewelry for women. Her jewelry

line is available in more than 100 stores worldwide and has been worn by celebrities like Cameron Diaz and Sandra Bullock.

13276 ■ *"Modern Bride Unveiled Exclusively at JCPenney" in Benzinga.com (February 3, 2011)*
Pub: Benzinga.com
Ed: Benzinga Staff. **Description:** JCPenney created its new Modern Bride concept in its bridal find jewelry departments. The new shopping experience is a collaboration between the retailer and Conde Nast catering to the bridal customer.

13277 ■ *"Retail Briefs - Dollar Store Opens in Long Leaf Mall" in Star-News (November 5, 2010)*
Pub: Star-News Media
Ed: Judy Royal. **Description:** Dollar Delight$ opened a new shop in Long Leaf Mall in Wilmington, North Carolina. The store will carry gift bags, balloons, party supplies, greeting cards, school supplies, health and beauty products, hardware, baby items, toys, Christmas goods, crafts, housewares and jewelry in its inventory.

13278 ■ *"Shop Around" in Houston Chronicle (December 7, 2010, pp. 3)*
Pub: Houston Chronicle
Ed: Tara Dooley. **Description:** Profile of Diana Candida and Maria Martinez who partnered to open Beatniks, a shop carrying vintage clothing, art from various artists, dance shoes, and jewelry.

13279 ■ *"The Silvery Moon Moves to Larger Space" in Bellingham Business Journal (Vol. March 2010, pp. 5)*
Pub: Sound Publishing Inc.
Description: Jewelry store, the Silvery Moon, moved to a larger location in order to expand its business. The new location was chosen because it offers the firm more visibility. The store offers find silver and gold pieces and specializes in Pacific Northwest native jewelry.

13280 ■ *"Sylvie Collection Offers a Feminine Perspective and Voice in Male Dominated Bridal Industry" in Benzinga.com (October 29, 2011)*
Pub: Benzinga.com
Ed: Benzinga Staff. **Description:** Bridal jewelry designer Sylvie Levine has created over 1,000 customizable styles of engagement rings and wedding bands and is reaching out to prospective new brides through a new Website, interactive social media campaign and monthly trunk show appearances.

13281 ■ *"Women Prioritize Luxury Spending" in Marketing to Women (Vol. 22, July 2009, No. 7, pp. 8)*
Pub: EPM Communications Inc.
Contact: Ira Mayer, President
E-mail: imayer@epmcom.com
Description: In 2008, women spent 7 percent less on luxury items than in the previous year, according to Unity Marketing. Some luxury items, such as facial care products, are faring better than others. Statistical data included.

STATISTICAL SOURCES

13282 ■ *The Precious and Fashion Jewelry Market*
Pub: Business Trend Analysts, Inc.
Released: 2003. **Price:** $1695.00. **Description:** Statistical report and analysis of the Trends jewelry industry, including past, present, and projected sales figures. Report also discusses key issues of interest to the industry, such as import penetration and export markets, consumer demographics and buying habits, strategies and ideas for advertising and promotions, distribution and supply, and the economics of the industry. Provides company profiles of industry leaders.

13283 ■ *RMA Annual Statement Studies*
Pub: Risk Management Association
Contact: Kevin M. Blakey, President
Released: Annual. **Price:** $175.00 2006-07 edition, $105.00. **Description:** Contains composite balance sheets and income statements for more than 360

industries, including the accounting, auditing, and bookkeeping industries. Also contains five years of comparative historical data for discerning trends. Includes 16 commonly used ratios, computed for most of the size groupings for nearly every industry.

TRADE PERIODICALS

13284 ■ *The Diamond Registry Bulletin*
Pub: Joseph Schlussel
Ed: Joseph Schlussel, Editor. **Released:** Monthly. **Description:** Supplies current data on the present and future outlook of the diamond market. Provides information concerning trends in jewelry and investment companies and actual wholesale prices by size, quality, and shape for certified and commercial diamonds. Recurring features include reviews of fashion trends, diamond sales boosters, quotes, and anecdotes.

13285 ■ *The Jewelry Appraiser*
Pub: National Association of Jewelry Appraisers
Contact: Ms. Gail Brett Levine, Executive Director
Ed: Gail Breit Leving, Editor. **Released:** Quarterly. **Price:** Included in membership. **Description:** Provides information on jewelry and gem appraising. Carries items on current appraisal practices and standards, and a wholesale price guide titled the Price Reporter. Recurring features include editorials, news of research, letters to the editor, news of new products, news of members, book reviews, a calendar of events, and columns titled News and Views, Industry News, and Association News.

13286 ■ *MJSA Benchmark*
Pub: Manufacturing Jewelers & Suppliers of America
Contact: Rich Youmans, Publisher
Ed: Tina Wojtkielo, Editor. **Released:** Monthly. **Price:** Included in membership. **Description:** Informs members of association news, as well as jewelry manufacturing industry events and issues.

13287 ■ *National Jeweler*
Pub: Nielsen Co.
Contact: Greg Farrar, President
URL(s): www.nationaljewelernetwork.com/njn/index.jsp. **Released:** Semimonthly

13288 ■ *Watch & Jewelry Review*
Pub: Golden Bell Press
Contact: Lawrence Bell, President
E-mail: larry@goldenbellpress.com
URL(s): www.goldenbellpress.com/Pages/front.html. **Released:** 10/yr. **Price:** $19.50, Individuals; $35, Two years; $60, Other countries; $115, Two years other countries.

TRADE SHOWS AND CONVENTIONS

13289 ■ *Beijing International Jewellery Fair*
Neway International Trade Fairs Ltd.
9/F, Fortis Tower
77 Gloucester Rd.
Wan Chai, China
Ph: 852 2561 5566
Fax: 852 2811 9156
Co. E-mail: info@newayfairs.com
URL: http://www.newayfairs.com
URL(s): www.newayfairs.com. **Principal Exhibits:** Jewellery, gemstones, jewellry materials, and manufacturing.

13290 ■ *International Jewelry Fair/General Merchandise Show - Fall*
Helen Brett Enterprises, Inc.
5111 Academy Dr.
Lisle, IL 60532-2171
Ph: (630)241-9865
Fax: (630)241-9870
URL: http://www.gift2jewelry.com
Frequency: Semiannual. **Audience:** Wholesale buyers. **Principal Exhibits:** Jewelry and related items.

13291 ■ *Jewelers International Showcase*
Jewelers International Showcase, Inc.
6421 Congress Ave., Ste. 105
Boca Raton, FL 33487

Fax: (561)998-0209
Co. E-mail: showdirector@jisshow.com
URL: http://www.jisshow.com
URL(s): www.jisshow.com. **Frequency:** 3/year. **Audience:** Professional jewelers, manufacturers, wholesale importers, and buyers from retail jewelry stores primarily from Florida, Latin America and Caribbean countries. **Principal Exhibits:** Fine jewelry, fashion jewelry, and related products and services to jewelry trade members. **Telecommunication Services:** jisshow@aol.com.

13292 ■ *Memphis Gift and Jewelry Show Fall*
Helen Brett Enterprises, Inc.
5111 Academy Dr.
Lisle, IL 60532-2171
Ph: (630)241-9865
Fax: (630)241-9870
URL: http://www.gift2jewelry.com
URL(s): www.gift2jewelry.com. **Frequency:** Semiannual. **Audience:** Wholesale buyers. **Principal Exhibits:** Giftware and jewelry, apparel, home decor, novelties, silk flowers, fine/costume jewelry and accessories.

13293 ■ *Mid-South Jewelry & Accessories Fair Spring*
Helen Brett Enterprises, Inc.
5111 Academy Dr.
Lisle, IL 60532-2171
Ph: (630)241-9865
Fax: (630)241-9870
URL: http://www.gift2jewelry.com
URL(s): www.gift2jewelry.com. **Frequency:** Semiannual. **Audience:** Wholesale buyers. **Principal Exhibits:** Fine/costume jewelry, apparel, leathers, silks, beaded items, home decor, novelties.

13294 ■ *New Orleans Gift and Jewelry Show Spring*
Helen Brett Enterprises, Inc.
5111 Academy Dr.
Lisle, IL 60532-2171
Ph: (630)241-9865
Fax: (630)241-9870
URL: http://www.gift2jewelry.com
URL(s): www.gift2jewelry.com. **Frequency:** Semiannual. **Audience:** Wholesale buyers. **Principal Exhibits:** Giftware and jewelry, apparel, home decor, rugs, silk plants, fine jewelry, costume jewelry, loose gemstones.

13295 ■ *Shanghai International Jewellery Fair*
Neway International Trade Fairs Ltd.
9/F, Fortis Tower
77 Gloucester Rd.
Wan Chai, China
Ph: 852 2561 5566
Fax: 852 2811 9156
Co. E-mail: info@newayfairs.com
URL: http://www.newayfairs.com
URL(s): www.newayfairs.com. **Principal Exhibits:** Jewellery, gemstones, jewellery materials and production.

FRANCHISES AND BUSINESS OPPORTUNITIES

13296 ■ *Fast-Fix Jewelry and Watch Repairs*
Jewelry Repair Enterprises, Inc.
Description: Jewelry and watch repairs. **No. of Franchise Units:** 160. **Founded:** 1984.. **Franchised:** 1987. **Equity Capital Needed:** $130,000-270,000. **Franchise Fee:** $40,000. **Training:** Yes.

13297 ■ *Hannoush Jewelers*
Hannoush Franchise Corp.
134 Capital Dr.
West Springfield, MA 01089
Ph: (413)846-4640
Fax: (413)788-7588
Description: Fine jewelry sales. **No. of Franchise Units:** 20. **No. of Company-Owned Units:** 52. **Founded:** 1980.. **Franchised:** 1995. **Equity Capital Needed:** $291,000-$717,000. **Franchise Fee:**

$20,000. **Royalty Fee:** 4%. **Training:** Offers 2 weeks at headquarters, 3 months at franchisee's location as needed with ongoing support.

LIBRARIES

13298 ■ Gemological Institute of America - Richard T. Liddicoat Gemological Library and Information Center—GIA Carlsbad Library; GIA Library.
The Robert Mouawad Campus

5345 Armada Dr.
Carlsbad, CA 92008
Ph: (760)603-4000
Free: 800-421-7250, x-4046
Fax: (760)603-4256
Co. E-mail: library@gia.edu
URL: http://www.gia.edu/research-resources/library/
   index.html
Contact: Dona Mary Dirlam, Director
Scope: Gemology, mineralogy, geology in relation to gem deposits, mining of gem deposits, jewelry his-
tory, jewelry manufacturing, lapidary (the art of cutting gems). **Services:** Library open to the public with restrictions. **Founded:** 1931. **Holdings:** 38,000 volumes; 92,500 digital assets; 1000 videos/DVDs. **Subscriptions:** 300 periodicals.

ASSOCIATIONS AND OTHER ORGANIZATIONS

13299 ■ Center on Education and Training for Employment (CETE)
Ohio State University
1900 Kenny Rd.
Columbus, OH 43210-1016
Ph: (614)292-8008
Free: 800-848-4815
Fax: (614)292-1260
Co. E-mail: kelsey.28@osu.edu
URL: http://www.cete.org
Contact: Robert Mahlman, Director
Description: Aims to increase the ability of diverse agencies, institutions, and organizations to solve educational problems relating to individual career planning, preparation, and progression. Conducts occupational analyses and staff training programs. Evaluates programs and agencies and provides technical assistance. Researches identified problems or needs. Develops databases, information systems, and occupational curricula. **Scope:** Provider of computer searches, document delivery, and reference services in the areas of technical and vocational education, adult education, training and related topics. The firms principal clients is the graduate students, government agencies, school districts and state departments. **Founded:** 1965. **Subscriptions:** 64000; 64000. **Publications:** *CenteGram* (Quarterly). **Educational Activities:** Center on Education and Training for Employment Workshop. **Seminars:** Test Construction, Columbus, Jul, 2007; ISO 10015 - Quality of Training Planning To Use The Standard, Columbus, Jun, 2007; SCID Workshop, Columbus, Apr, 2007; Decreasing the Dropout Rates in the United States.

13300 ■ National Training and Simulation Association (NTSA)
2111 Wilson Blvd., Ste. 400
Arlington, VA 22201-3061
Ph: (703)247-9471
Fax: (703)243-1659
Co. E-mail: jrobb@ndia.org
URL: http://www.trainingsystems.org
Contact: James A. Robb, President
Description: Represents the business interests of manufacturers of simulation systems, computer-based training systems, and training support systems; providers of contract training and other related training support services. Promotes the growth, development, and application of military training systems, products, and services. Seeks to contribute to the operational readiness and combat effectiveness of the armed forces of the U.S. and its allies; assist in fulfilling the training requirements of related federal agencies; enhance public education and training; increase understanding and appreciation of training systems technologies and services. Fosters communication between government and industry regarding requirements and procurement issues and policies; promotes responsibility and integrity among members. Compiles statistics; conducts research and educational programs. **Founded:** 1988. **Publications:** *NTSA Training Industry News* (Bimonthly); *NTSA Training 2012* (Biennial); *NTSA Yearbook* (Annual). **Educational Activities:** Forums for Industry (Monthly); Training and Simulation Industry (Annual). **Awards:** Modeling and Simulation Award (Annual).

REFERENCE WORKS

13301 ■ Career Information Center
Pub: Macmillan Reference USA
Contact: Frank Menchaca, Executive Vice President
E-mail: frank.menchaca@cengage.com
URL(s): www.gale.cengage.com. **Released:** Biennial; Latest edition 9th; December 2006. **Price:** $494, Individuals. **Description:** Organized into 13 occupational clusters (comprising 13 volumes and an index volume). Each volume includes a section listing accredited occupational educational and vocational institutions. A second section lists more than 700 occupational profiles and over 3,000 organizations with jobs in the field of work with which the volume is concerned. **Entries include:** For institutions--Name, address, programs and degrees offered. For organizations--Name, address. **Database includes:** Job summary chart; industry snapshots that summarize major developments; photographs; overview of the job market; job hunting information and tips. **Arrangement:** By Career Area/Industry. **Indexes:** Each volume contains a general index, and a master index to the entire series appears in a 13th volume.

13302 ■ "Home Grown" in Hawaii Business (Vol. 53, November 2007, No. 5, pp. 51)
Pub: Hawaii Business Publishing
Ed: Jolyn Okimoto Rosa. **Description:** Discusses a program that focuses on Native Hawaiian entrepreneurs and offers business training at the Kapiolani Community College; upon completion of the program, participants may apply for a loan provided by the Office of Hawaiian Affairs (OHA) to help them start their business. OHA plans to present the restructured loan program in November 2007, with aims of shortening the loan process.

13303 ■ "Mitch D'Olier" in Hawaii Business (Vol. 53, November 2007, No. 5, pp. 27)
Pub: Hawaii Business Publishing
Ed: Cathy S. Cruz-George. **Description:** Mitch D'Olier chief executive officer of Kaneohe Ranch/ Harold K.L. Castle Foundation thinks that achievement gaps are a nationwide problem and that the Knowledge is Power Program is one of the programs that focuses on achievement gaps in some communities across the US. He also provides his insights on education in Hawaii and the current shortage of teachers.

13304 ■ "Up Against the Ropes: A Professional Coach May Help" in Black Enterprise (Vol. 37, December 2006, No. 5, pp. 72)
Pub: Earl G. Graves Publishing Co. Inc.
Description: Executive coaching is now a $1 billion industry. The coaching process itself and traits to look for in a coach are discussed.

SOURCES OF SUPPLY

13305 ■ Tech Directions--Annual Buyers' Guide: A Directory of Suppliers
Prakken Publications Inc.
Contact: Vanessa Revelli, Manager
E-mail: vanessa@techdirections.com
URL(s): www.techdirections.com. **Released:** Annual; April. **Publication includes:** Directory of manufacturers and suppliers of equipment and materials to industrial and vocational/technical schools, community colleges, and universities. **Entries include:** Company name, address, phone, fax, logo, e-mail, web address, product descriptions. **Arrangement:** Classified by subject. **Indexes:** Company name.

TRADE PERIODICALS

13306 ■ FERA--Focus
Pub: FERA Inc.
Ed: John A. Seeley, Editor. **Released:** 3/year. **Price:** Free. **Description:** Discusses consulting work and research on evaluation of corporate training, human resource development programs, community-based social services, and educational programs.

13307 ■ TD Magazine
Pub: ASTD
Contact: Tony Bingham, President
E-mail: tbingham@astd.org
URL(s): www.astd.org/Publications/Magazines/TD/About-TD.aspx. **Ed:** Paula Ketter. **Released:** Monthly **Price:** $89, Members; $150, Nonmembers outside US; $300, Institutions.

13308 ■ Training Media Review
Pub: TMR Publications
Contact: William C. Ellet, Editor
E-mail: wellet@tmreview.com
Released: Bimonthly. **Price:** $229 print and online; $189 online only; $25 trial subscription. **Description:** Provides information for business trainers. Recurring features include software, video, Internet, and book reviews. **Remarks:** Also available online with searchable database of all reviews.

RESEARCH CENTERS

13309 ■ Academy for Educational Development - National Institute for Work and Learning (NIWL)
1825 Connecticut Ave. NW
Washington, DC 20009
Ph: (202)884-8184
Fax: (202)884-8422
Co. E-mail: icharner@aed.org
URL: http://www.niwl.org
Contact: Ivan Charner, Director
Founded: 1971. **Publications:** *Policy papers*; *NIWL Reports*. **Educational Activities:** Career Passport Program, to assist young people in resume preparation; NIWL Forums; Governmental Process Seminars (10/year); Teacher Preparation & Professional Development; Technical Assistance & Training; Training

workshops and consultations, for businesses and community-based operations. **Telecommunication Services:** niwl@aed.org.

13310 ■ Brandeis University - Center for Youth and Communities (CYC)

Heller Bldg., 3rd Fl., MS 035
415 S St.
Waltham, MA 02454
Ph: (781)736-4835
Free: 800-343-4705
Fax: (781)736-3729
Co. E-mail: curnan@brandeis.edu
URL: http://cyc.brandeis.edu
Contact: Prof. Susan P. Curnan, Director
Founded: 1983. **Publications:** *Anthology*; *CYD Journal* (Occasionally); *CYC Reports*. **Educational Activities:** Practitioner training (Annual), on project-based learning, case management, evaluation, nonprofit

management; Research and consultation, for multiple clients - continuous; Program Management and Evaluation. **Telecommunication Services:** cyc@brandeis.edu.

13311 ■ Florida State University - Center for Human Resource Management

821 Academic Way
Department of Management
College of Business
Tallahassee, FL 32306-1110
Ph: (850)644-7848
Fax: (850)644-7843
Co. E-mail: pperrewe@cob.fsu.edu
URL: http://www.cob.fsu.edu/man/hrcenter
Contact: Dr. Pamela Perrewe, Director
Services: Contract research; Technical assistance: to small and medium-sized businesses; Training assistance. **Founded:** 1983. **Educational Activities:**

Center for Human Resource Management Conference (Semiannual), on special personnel topics; Center for Human Resource Management Workshops, for personnel professionals to earn accreditation in their fields.

13312 ■ Human Resources Research Organization (HumRRO)

66 Canal Ctr. Plz., Ste. 700
Alexandria, VA 22314-1591
Ph: (703)549-3611
Fax: (703)549-9025
URL: http://www.humrro.org
Contact: William J. Strickland, President
Founded: 1951. **Awards:** Meredith Crawford Fellowship for Industrial and Organizational Psychology (Annual), Scholarship to graduate students in Industrial and Organizational Psychology for completing dissertations.

REFERENCE WORKS

13313 ■ *"Annapolis Seeks City Market Vendors"* in Boston Business Journal (Vol. 29, June 10, 2011, No. 5, pp. 3)
Pub: American City Business Journals Inc.
Ed: Daniel J. Sernovitz. **Description:** The city of Annapolis, Maryland is planning to revive the historical landmark Market House and it is now accepting bids from vendors until June 10, 2011. The city hopes to reopen the facility by July 2011 for a six-month period after which it will undergo renovations.

13314 ■ *"At Wine Kiosk, Show ID, Face Camera, Swipe Card and Blow"* in Pittsburgh Post-Gazette (November 28, 2010)
Pub: Pittsburgh-Post Gazette
Ed: Dennis B. Roddy. **Description:** New technology installed on wine kiosks enables sellers to abide by the law. This technology tests blood alcohol levels and warns people if they have recently used a mouthwash before testing.

13315 ■ *"Blue Cross to Put Kiosk in Mall"* in News & Observer (November 9, 2010)
Pub: News & Observer
Ed: Alan M. Wolf. **Description:** Blue Cross and Blue Shield of North Carolina has placed a kiosk in Durham's Streets of Southpoint in order to market its health insurance.

13316 ■ *"Border Boletin: UA to Take Lie-Detector Kiosk to Poland"* in Arizona Daily Star (September 14, 2010)
Pub: Arizona Daily Star
Ed: Brady McCombs. **Description:** University of Arizona's National Center for Border Security and Immigration Research will send a team to Warsaw, Poland to show border guards from 27 European Union countries the center's Avatar Kiosk. The Avatar technology is designed for use at border ports and airports to assist Customs officers detect individuals who are lying.

13317 ■ *"Boston Globe"* in Ice Cream Reporter (Vol. 21, August 20, 2008, No. 9, pp. 7)
Pub: Ice Cream Reporter
Description: Boston City Council approved an ordinance that will limit when ice cream vendors can announce their presence with music over loud speakers. The rules are simple: when the wheels stop moving, the jingles stop playing.

13318 ■ *"Cox Opens Norfolk Mall Kiosk; Wireless Service Not Ready"* in Virginian-Pilot (September 20, 2010)
Pub: Virginian-Pilot
Ed: Carolyn Shapiro. **Description:** Cox Communications opened a kiosk at MacArthur Center that will sell wireless telephone devices and plans.

13319 ■ *"Eagle's Wine Kiosk Is Area's 1st"* in Pittsburgh Post-Gazette (October 28, 2010)
Pub: Pittsburgh-Post Gazette
Ed: Bob Batz Jr. **Description:** Giant Eagle Market District store at Settlers Ridge opened the first self-serve wine kiosk in Western Pennsylvania. The kiosk will have a built-in breathalyzer panel to ensure safety.

13320 ■ *"easyhome Ltd. Discovers Employee Fraud at an Easyfinancial Kiosk Company"* in Internet Wire (October 14, 2010)
Pub: Comtex
Description: Canada's leading merchandise leasing company and provider of financial services, easyhome Ltd., reported employee fraud totaling $3.4 million that was perpetrated against the firm's easyfinancial services business.

13321 ■ *"Fire Destroys Veterans' Kiosk"* in Houston Chronicle (November 24, 2010, pp. 14)
Pub: Houston Chronicle
Description: A leaking propane heater is believed to have started a fire that destroyed a kiosk near the Vietnam Veterans Memorial in Washington DC. The kiosk, manned by volunteers from the Rolling Thunder veterans group, provide education to the public about those individuals still missing from the Vietnam War.

13322 ■ *"Floral-Design Kiosk Business in Colorado Springs Blossoming"* in Colorado Springs Business Journal (September 24, 2010)
Pub: Dolan Media Newswires
Ed: Monica Mendoza. **Description:** Profile of Shellie Greto and her mother Jackie Martin who started a wholesale flower business in their garage. The do-it-yourself floral arrangement firm started a kiosk business in supermarkets called Complete Design.

13323 ■ *"Generous Donations Fund Repairs for Benton Trail Kiosk"* in Morning Sentinel (December 22, 2010)
Pub: Morning Sentinel
Ed: Scott Monroe. **Description:** The new kiosk at the entrance to a trail off Benton Avenue was paid for through donations and community contributions after the original was destroyed by vandals. The new kiosk's material was donated by the Huhtamaki manufacturing firm.

13324 ■ *"IF Challenges Atlanta's Vending Monopoly"* in Benzinga.com (July 28, 2011)
Pub: Benzinga.com
Ed: Benzinga Staff. **Description:** A lawsuit was filed by The Institute for Justice to challenge Atlanta's unconstitutional vending monopoly on behalf of two Atlanta street vendors.

13325 ■ *"iMozi Integrates Esprida LiveControl for Advanced DVD Kiosk Hardware"* in Wireless News (December 20, 2010)
Pub: Close-Up Media Inc.
Description: Provider of self-service entertainment technology, iMozi Canada has partnered with Esprida to make its automated DVD Kiosk solutions Esprida-enabled. Esprida develops remote device management solutions and will offer enhanced capabilities and to improve customer experience for users.

13326 ■ *"Kiosk Outfit ecoATM Now Recycling Video Games"* in San Diego Union-Tribune (October 7, 2010)
Pub: San Diego Union-Tribune
Ed: Mike Freeman. **Description:** ecoATM makes automated kiosks to buy back cell phones will now include video games as part of their recycling business.

13327 ■ *"LCB Puts a Cork in Kiosk Wine Sales"* in Times Leader (December 22, 2010)
Pub: Wilkes-Barre Publishing Company
Ed: Andrew M. Seder. **Description:** The Pennsylvania Liquor Control Board closed down thirty Pronto Wine Kiosks located in supermarkets throughout the state. The Board cited mechanical and technological issues such as products not dispensing.

13328 ■ *"LCB Turning Off Wine Vending Machines"* in Pittsburgh Post-Gazette (September 20, 2011)
Pub: PG Publishing Company
Ed: Tracie Mauriello. **Description:** Grocery store shoppers will no longer be able to purchase a bottle of wine from wine kiosks in Pennsylvania.

13329 ■ *"Pet Kiosk Offers Search Options"* in Times-News (October 14, 2010)
Pub: Times-News Publishing Company
Ed: Roselee Papandrea. **Description:** Chameleon Pet Kiosk located at the Spay and Neuter Clinic of Alamance County in Burlington, North Carolina allows users to see and read about animals available for adoption at the center.

13330 ■ *"Public Media Works to Launch DVD Kiosk Operations in Toronto, Canada"* in Internet Wire (November 15, 2010)
Pub: Comtex
Description: Public Media Works Inc. along with its EntertainmentXpress Inc., have partnered with Spot Venture Distribution Inc. and Signifi Solutions Inc., both headquartered in Toronto, Canada, to manage and expand the Spot DVD movie and game kiosk business in greater Toronto and other Canadian locations.

13331 ■ *"Titan to Become New York's Largest Provider of Phone Kiosk Advertising"* in Marketing Weekly News (September 11, 2010, pp. 150)
Pub: VerticalNews
Description: Titan will acquire from Verizon 1,900 payphones at 1,300 phone kiosk locations in New York City, New York. This transaction will triple the firm's inventory of New York Phone Kiosk media to over 5,000 advertising faces. Details are included.

13332 ■ *"'Unknown' Muted Grand Prix Impact"* in Boston Business Journal (Vol. 29, September 9, 2011, No. 18, pp. 3)
Pub: American City Business Journals Inc.
Ed: Alexander Jackson. **Description:** Baltimore Grand Prix caught restaurateurs, hoteliers and street vendors in Baltimore, Maryland unprepared for the thousands of race fans who attended the inaugural

event over Labor Day weekend. The race popularity is relatively unknown to them and some felt they were not able to make as much money as they had hoped.

13333 ■ "Ventura Police Install Electronic Kiosk to Access Services" in Ventura County Star (October 28, 2010)

Pub: Ventura County Star

Description: Ventura Police Department installed a kiosk in the front lobby of its building in order to provide services to the public. The kiosk allows access to the Department's Website; to retrieve a collision report, file an abandoned vehicle report, receive a permit for an oversized vehicle, or filing a citizen's complaint; information can be obtained about alarms, programs and permits; users can pay a parking ticket and review calls for services on an interactive map.

13334 ■ "A Wireless Makes 8 Store-In-Store Kiosk Acquisitions" in Wireless News (October 16, 2010)

Pub: Close-Up Media Inc.

Description: A Wireless, a retailer for Verizon Wireless has acquired eight of Verizon's retail kiosks that are positioned in home appliance and electronics stores.

FRANCHISES AND BUSINESS OPPORTUNITIES

13335 ■ Breeze Freeze

13340 Merriman Rd.
Livonia, MI 48150
Free: 866-472-6482
Fax: (734)414-6537

Description: Frozen fruit drinks. **No. of Franchise Units:** 31. **No. of Company-Owned Units:** 303. **Founded:** 2001.. **Franchised:** 2004. **Equity Capital Needed:** $9,200-$94,300, express/kiosk option available. **Franchise Fee:** $5,000/$40,000. **Royalty Fee:** None. **Training:** Offers 1-3 days at headquarters, 1-2 days at franchisees location with ongoing support.

13336 ■ California Quivers

5284 Eastgate Mall
San Diego, CA 92121
Ph: (858)558-1300
Fax: (858)558-1200

Description: Carts serving fruit ices, hot dogs and coffee. **No. of Franchise Units:** 3. **No. of Company-Owned Units:** 10. **Founded:** 1997.. **Franchised:** 2004. **Equity Capital Needed:** $45,000-$149,300. **Franchise Fee:** $22,500. **Royalty Fee:** 6%. **Training:** Offers training 1 week at headquarters and ongoing support.

13337 ■ Cena

12501 N Hwy. 395, Ste. 3
Spokane, WA 99218

Ph: (509)448-1725
Free: 888-667-2362
Fax: (509)448-9380

Description: Meal preparation/assembly center and wine shop. **No. of Franchise Units:** 10. **No. of Company-Owned Units:** 1. **Founded:** 2004.. **Franchised:** 2005. **Equity Capital Needed:** $148,400-$205,500; express/kiosk option available. **Franchise Fee:** $30,000. **Royalty Fee:** 5%. **Training:** Provides 4 days training at headquarters, 3 days onsite and ongoing support.

13338 ■ Frankitude

21 NW Miami Ct.
Miami, FL 33128
Ph: (305)371-9875
Free: 877-275-8778

Description: Hot dogs, salads, panini, and wraps. **No. of Franchise Units:** 1. **No. of Company-Owned Units:** 1. **Founded:** 2006.. **Franchised:** 2006. **Equity Capital Needed:** $170,200-$325,000 (Express/kiosk option available). **Franchise Fee:** $25,000. **Royalty Fee:** 6%. **Training:** Offers 2 weeks training at headquarters, 1 week plus, onsite and ongoing support.

13339 ■ Indigos Fruit Smoothies

Indigos Franchising, Inc.
21551 Arbor Way
Boca Raton, FL 33433
Ph: (407)383-3872

Description: Retail smoothie/juice bar & healthy restaurant. **No. of Franchise Units:** 9. **Founded:** 2004.. **Franchised:** 2004. **Equity Capital Needed:** $89,800-$272,000. **Franchise Fee:** $25,000. **Royalty Fee:** 6%. **Financial Assistance:** Limited third party financing available. **Training:** Includes 6 days training at headquarters, 7 days at franchisee's location and ongoing support.

13340 ■ Motion Golf LLC

55 Lane Rd.
Fairfield, NJ 07004
Free: 866-585-6033

Description: Golf swing analysis, instruction, and club fitting. **No. of Company-Owned Units:** 3. **Founded:** 2006. **Franchised:** 2007. **Equity Capital Needed:** $250,000 (Express/kiosk option available). **Franchise Fee:** $79,500. **Royalty Fee:** 6%. **Training:** 1 week at franchisee's location.

13341 ■ Mr. Payroll Check Cashing

Cash America Intl.
1600 W 7th St.
Fort Worth, TX 76102
Ph: (800)322-3250

Fax: (817)333-1934
URL: http://www.cashamerica.com

Description: Operates as a financial services kiosk inside a busy retail business, such as a grocery and convenience stores. Our pre-fabricated 48 square foot kiosk is space efficient and helps retailers increase sales from check cashing customers. Franchisees may be owners of such retail businesses or can operate as subtenants. Services include check cashing, money orders, wire transfers, bill payments, pre-paid phones and ancillary services. **No. of Franchise Units:** 113. **No. of Company-Owned Units:** 6. **Founded:** 1988.. **Franchised:** 1990. **Equity Capital Needed:** $75,300-$326,500. **Franchise Fee:** $10,000. **Royalty Fee:** 10%. **Training:** Offers 3 days at headquarters with ongoing support.

13342 ■ Mr. Pickle's Sandwich Shop

670 Auburn-Folsom Rd., Ste. 106-571
Auburn, CA 95603
Ph: (916)746-7727
Fax: (916)746-7787

Description: Sandwiches, soups, and salads. **No. of Franchise Units:** 24. **Founded:** 1996. **Franchised:** 2006. **Equity Capital Needed:** $249,000 (Express/kiosk option available). **Franchise Fee:** $25,000. **Royalty Fee:** None. **Training:** 2 weeks training included at franchisee's location and ongoing support.

13343 ■ Printwell Management Inc.

1200 St. Laurent Blvd.
Ottawa, ON, Canada K1K 3B8
Ph: (613)744-2001
Fax: (613)744-6555
Co. E-mail: sales@printwell.ca
URL: http://www.printwell.ca

Description: A unique shopping mall-based business offering onsite inkjet cartridge refills, as well as the sale of a variety of inkjet and laser toner cartridges. Printwell has award-winning designed kiosks and offers turnkey operations, as well as an extensive franchisee training program. We can save our customers money and yet maintain a quality product, with an extremely high profit level. We are a popular destination for the printing needs of local businesses and mall customers. **No. of Franchise Units:** 15. **No. of Company-Owned Units:** 1. **Founded:** 2002.. **Franchised:** 2005. **Equity Capital Needed:** $110,000-$180,000. **Franchise Fee:** $25,000. **Training:** Provides 3 weeks training.

13344 ■ Smash Hit Subs

Orion Food Systems L.L.C.
2930 W Maple St.
Sioux Falls, SD 57107-0745
Ph: (800)336-1320
Free: 800-648-6227
Fax: (605)336-0141
URL: http://www.hotstufffoods.com

Description: Sub sandwiches. **No. of Franchise Units:** 1,300. **No. of Company-Owned Units:** 12. **Founded:** 1984.. **Franchised:** 1986. **Equity Capital Needed:** $25,000. **Franchise Fee:** $4,950. **Financial Assistance:** Yes. **Training:** Yes.

ASSOCIATIONS AND OTHER ORGANIZATIONS

13345 ■ American Nursery and Landscape Association (ANLA)
1200 G St. NW, Ste. 800
Washington, DC 20005
Ph: (202)789-2900
Fax: (202)789-1893
Co. E-mail: info@anla.org
URL: http://www.anla.org
Contact: Robert S. Lyons, President
Description: Vertical organization of wholesale growers; landscape firms; garden centers; mail order nurseries; suppliers. Promotes the industry and its products. Offers management and consulting services and public relations programs. Provides government representation and bank card plan for members. Maintains hall of fame. **Founded:** 1876. **Publications:** *American Nursery & Landscape Association-- Member Directory: Who's Who in the Nursery Industry* (Annual).

13346 ■ American Seed Trade Association (ASTA)
1701 Duke St., Ste. 675
Alexandria, VA 22314
Ph: (703)837-8140
Fax: (703)837-9365
Co. E-mail: info@amseed.org
URL: http://www.amseed.com
Contact: Andrew W. LaVigne, President
Description: Breeders, growers, assemblers, conditioners, wholesalers, and retailers of grain, grass, vegetable, flower, and other seed for planting purposes. **Founded:** 1883. **Publications:** *Corn and Sorghum Proceedings* (Annual); *Soybean Seed Proceedings* (Annual).

13347 ■ Association of Professional Landscape Designers (APLD)
4305 N Sixth St., Ste. A
Harrisburg, PA 17110
Ph: (717)238-9780
Fax: (717)238-9985
Co. E-mail: info@apld.org
URL: http://www.apld.org
Contact: Denise Calabrese, Executive Director
URL(s): www.apld.com. **Description:** Landscape design professionals, students; and interested others. Works to improve status and establish professional credentials for landscape designers. International and regional continuing education opportunities. Offers certification programs. **Founded:** 1989. **Educational Activities:** Association of Professional Landscape Designers Annual Conference. **Awards:** Award of Distinction; Harry Schuster Award (Annual); Award of Distinction; Harry Schuster Award; International Landscape Design Awards; Landscape Design Award - Residential Designs (Annual).

13348 ■ Independent Turf and Ornamental Distributors Association (ITODA)
174 Crestview Dr.
Bellefonte, PA 16823-8516

Ph: (717)243-7677
Free: 877-326-5995
Fax: (814)335-2452
Co. E-mail: info@itoda.org
URL: http://www.itoda.org
Contact: Patricia E. Heuser, Executive Director
Description: Wholesale suppliers of lawn and turf chemicals, fertilizers, and equipment. Represents members' interests. Conducts educational programs. Provides consulting services. Maintains speakers' bureau; compiles statistics. **Founded:** 1990. **Educational Activities:** Independent Turf and Ornamental Distributors Association Conference (Annual).

13349 ■ New York State Turf and Landscape Association (NYSTLA)
1 Prospect Ave.
White Plains, NY 10607
Ph: (914)993-9455
Fax: (914)993-9051
Co. E-mail: nystla@aol.com
URL: http://www.nystla.com
Contact: Peter Muller, President
Description: Landscaping and grounds keeping professionals. Promotes the landscaping industry. **Founded:** 1968. **Publications:** *Installation; Irrigation; Mantenimiento* (Monthly). **Educational Activities:** Professional Turf and Landscape Conference (Annual). **Awards:** NYSTLA Scholarship; Louis Squobbo Scholarship Award (Annual); Person of the Year Award (Annual).

13350 ■ North American Flowerbulb Wholesalers Association (NAFWA)
c/o Marlboro Bulb Company
2424 Hwy. 72/221 E
Greenwood, SC 29649
Ph: (864)229-1618
Fax: (864)229-5719
Co. E-mail: nafwa1@aol.com
URL: http://www.nafwa.com
Contact: Thijs Leenders, President
Description: Wholesalers and dealers of flower bulbs and related floricultural commodities. **Founded:** 1983. **Awards:** Karl Schroff Memorial Scholarship (Annual).

REFERENCE WORKS

13351 ■ *"All the Trimmings"* in Green Industry Pro (Vol. 23, March 2011, No. 3, pp. 29)
Pub: Cygnus Business Media

Ed: Gregg Wartgow. **Description:** When choosing lawn mowing equipment, it is advised to purchase commercial-grade 21-inch walk mowers rather than less expensive consumer-grade mowers. John Deere is reentering the commercial 21-inch walk behind mower market after a five-year hiatus.

13352 ■ *"Best Turnaround Stocks"* in Canadian Business (Vol. 82, Summer 2009,

No. 8, pp. 32)
Pub: Rogers Media
Ed: Calvin Leung. **Description:** Canadian companies that are believed to have the potential for the best turnaround stocks are presented. Suggested stocks include those of Migao Corporation, which is rated by most research firms as a Buy. Migao produces potash-based fertilizers for the Chinese market.

13353 ■ *"Hey, You Can't Do That"* in Green Industry Pro (Vol. 23, September 2011)
Pub: Cygnus Business Media
Ed: Rod Dickens. **Description:** Manufacturers of landscape equipment are making better use of energy resources, such as the use of fuel-injection systems instead of carburetors, lightweight materials, better lubricants, advanced battery technology, and innovative engine designs.

13354 ■ *"Precision Crop Control with Valley Irrigation/CropMetrics Partnership"* in Farm Industry News (January 6, 2011)
Pub: Penton Business Media Inc.

Description: Irrigation systems have become a precision farming tool since partnering with agronomic software systems to apply products across the field by prescription. Valley Irrigation and CropMetrics have partnered in order to variably control water, fertilizer and other crop management products through a center pivot irrigation system.

TRADE PERIODICALS

13355 ■ *Landscape Trades: Canada's Premier Horticultural Trade Publication*
Pub: Landscape Ontario Horticultural Trades Association

URL(s): www.landscapetrades.com. **Ed:** Robert Ellidge. **Released:** 9/yr (not published Feb., Aug., and Dec.). **Price:** $43.58, Individuals; $78.74, Two years; $110.24, Individuals 3 years.

FRANCHISES AND BUSINESS OPPORTUNITIES

13356 ■ Nite Time Decor Inc.
The Decor Group
PO Box 5183
Lubbock, TX 79408-5183
Free: 866-321-4077
Fax: (806)722-9627

Description: Landscape lighting products and services. **No. of Franchise Units:** 37. **Founded:** 1986.. **Franchised:** 1999. **Equity Capital Needed:** $37,500-$74,350. **Franchise Fee:** $16,900. **Royalty Fee:** 5%. **Training:** Includes 4 days training at headquarters and ongoing support.

13357 ■ Outdoor Lighting Perspectives Franchise, Inc.
2924 Emerywood Parkway, Ste. 101
Richmond, VA 23294

Ph: (800)722-4668
URL: http://www.olpfranchise.com
Description: Design and installation of landscape lighting. **No. of Franchise Units:** 70. **No. of**

Company-Owned Units: 1. **Founded:** 1995.. **Franchised:** 1998. **Equity Capital Needed:** $69,000-$102,000. **Franchise Fee:** $49,000. **Training:** 5 days of training at corporate location and 3 days within

ninety days of start-up in that city. Product & technical training at manufacturing plant shortly after start-up.

START-UP INFORMATION

13358 ■ *How to Open and Operate a Financially Successful Landscaping, Nursery or Lawn Service Business: With Companion CD-ROM*
Pub: Atlantic Publishing Company
Ed: Lynn Wasnak. **Released:** June 1, 2009. **Price:** $39.95. **Description:** Guide provides understanding of the basic concepts of starting and running a service business, focusing on the operation of a small nursery, landscaping, or lawn service or combining the three operations. It also offers tips for running the business from the home.

13359 ■ *How to Start a Home-Based Landscaping Business*
Pub: Globe Pequot Press
Ed: Owen E. Dell. **Released:** December 2005. **Price:** $18.95. **Description:** Guide to starting and running a home-based landscaping business.

13360 ■ *How to Start and Run a Home-Based Landscaping Business*
Pub: Globe Pequot Press
Ed: Owen E. Dell. **Released:** December 2005. **Price:** $18.95. **Description:** Guide to starting and running a successful home-based landscaping business, including tips for marketing on the Internet.

13361 ■ *"Some Good Earners: Preparing Prison Inmates to Start Businesses Upon Their Release" in Inc. (Vol. 31, January-February 2009, No. 1)*
Pub: Mansueto Ventures LLC
Ed: Mike Hoffman. **Description:** Prison Entrepreneurship Program (PEP) is a nonprofit organization that works with the Texas Department of Criminal Justice to teach entrepreneurship to prison inmates. Profiled is Hans Becker, owner of Armadillo Tree and Shrub in Dallas; Becker studied the PEP program while serving five years in prison and started his successful company when released.

13362 ■ *Start Your Own Lawn Care Business: Your Step-by-Step Guide to Success*
Pub: Entrepreneur Press
Ed: Eileen Figure Sandlin. **Released:** March 2007. **Price:** $17.95. **Description:** Steps for starting and running a lawn care service.

13363 ■ *Start Your Own Lawn Care or Landscaping Business*
Pub: Entrepreneur Press
Ed: Eileen Figure Sandlin. **Released:** May 2007. **Price:** $19.95 (CND). **Description:** Advice for starting a lawn care and landscaping business is given.

ASSOCIATIONS AND OTHER ORGANIZATIONS

13364 ■ **American Society of Consulting Arborists (ASCA)**
9707 Key W Ave., Ste. 100
Rockville, MD 20850
Ph: (301)947-0483
Fax: (301)990-9771
Co. E-mail: asca@mgmtsol.com
URL: http://www.asca-consultants.org
Contact: James R. Clark, President
Description: Arboriculture professionals who possess extensive technical knowledge and experience including skills in the areas of written and oral communications, consulting ethics, expert witness activities, and practice management. Allows members to provide independent diagnoses, opinions, appraisal of value, and condition evaluation on trees for clients in the legal, insurance, and development communities as well as the general public. **Founded:** 1967. **Educational Activities:** Consulting Academy (Annual). **Awards:** Chadwick Scholarship Fund (Annual).

13365 ■ **American Society of Landscape Architects (ASLA)**
636 Eye St. NW
Washington, DC 20001-3736
Ph: (202)898-2444
Free: 888-999-ASLA
Fax: (202)898-1185
Co. E-mail: info@asla.org
URL: http://www.asla.org
Contact: Susan M. Hatchell, President
Description: Professional society of landscape architects. Promotes the advancement of education and skill in the art of landscape architecture as an instrument in service to the public welfare. Seeks to strengthen existing and proposed university programs in landscape architecture. Offers counsel to new and emerging programs; encourages state registration of landscape architects. Sponsors annual educational exhibit. Offers placement service; conducts specialized education and research. **Scope:** landscape architecture, planning, design, urban growth, historic preservation, horticulture. **Founded:** 1899. **Subscriptions:** 1500 books periodicals reports. **Publications:** *Landscape Architecture: The Magazine of the American Society of Landscape Architects* (Monthly); *American Society of Landscape Architects--Members' Handbook* (Annual); *LAND; LAND; ASLA Members Handbook* (Monthly); *Landscape Architecture Magazine* (Monthly); *ASLA Members Handbook* (Annual); *Landscape Architecture Accredited Programs* (Annual); *Landscape Architecture News Digest - LAND Online* (Biweekly); *Guide to Educational Programs in Landscape Architecture* (Biennial). **Educational Activities:** American Society of Landscape Architects Meeting (Annual); American Society of Landscape Architects Annual Meeting and Expo (Annual). **Awards:** ASLA Medal; President's Medal; ASLA Council of Fellows; Honorary Member; Professional Awards; Frederick Law Olmsted Medal; Alfred B. LaGasse Medal; Design Medal; Landscape Architecture Firm Award; Community Service Award; Landmark Award; Medal of Excellence; American Society of Landscape Architects Council of Fellow Scholarships; Edith H. Henderson Scholarships; William J. Locklin Scholarships; Raymond E. Page Scholarships; Rae L. Price Scholarships; Harriet Barnhart Wimmer Scholarships; David T. Woolsey Scholarships; Alfred B. LaGasse Medal (Annual); ASLA Medal (Annual); Bradford Williams Medal (Annual); The Design Medal (Annual); Honorary Membership (Annual); Jot D. Carpenter Teaching Medal (Annual); The Landscape Architecture Firm Award (Annual); The Landscape Architecture Medal of Excellence (Annual); Olmsted Medal (Annual); President's Medal (Annual); LAF/ Class Fund AILA/YAMAGAMI/Hope Fellowships. **Telecommunication Services:** nsomerville@asla.org; email@asla.org.

13366 ■ **Association of Professional Landscape Designers (APLD)**
4305 N Sixth St., Ste. A
Harrisburg, PA 17110
Ph: (717)238-9780
Fax: (717)238-9985
Co. E-mail: info@apld.org
URL: http://www.apld.org
Contact: Denise Calabrese, Executive Director
URL(s): www.apld.com. **Description:** Landscape design professionals, students; and interested others. Works to improve status and establish professional credentials for landscape designers. International and regional continuing education opportunities. Offers certification programs. **Founded:** 1989. **Educational Activities:** Association of Professional Landscape Designers Annual Conference. **Awards:** Award of Distinction; Harry Schuster Award (Annual); Award of Distinction; Harry Schuster Award; International Landscape Design Awards; Landscape Design Award - Residential Designs (Annual).

13367 ■ **Canadian Nursery Landscape Association (CNLA)—Association Candienne des Pepinieristes et des Paysagistes**
RR No. 4, Sta. Main
7856 5th Line S
Milton, ON, Canada L9T 2X8
Ph: (905)875-1399
Free: 888-446-3499
Fax: (905)875-1840
Co. E-mail: info@canadanursery.com
URL: http://www.canadanursery.com
Contact: Victor Santacruz, Executive Director
Description: Growers, retail garden centers, lawn care and gardening services, sod growers, landscape, construction, and maintenance contractors, and other horticultural industries. Promotes expansion of the nursery and related industries. Devises standards and develops and administers tests to ensure competence in nursery production, garden supply retailing, landscape contracting, and construction and maintenance. Makes available support and services to members including discount insurance policies and merchant credit cards, educational programs, and representation before government agencies. Sponsors research; compiles statistics. **Founded:** 1922. **Publications:** *CNLA Newsbrief* (Bimonthly). **Awards:** Honourary Life Member (Periodic); President's Award (Periodic). **Telecommunication Services:** victor@canadanursery.com.

13368 ■ **Canadian Society of Landscape Architects (CSLA)—L'Association des architects paysagistes du Canada (AAPC)**
PO Box 13594
Ottawa, ON, Canada K2K 1X6

Free: 866-781-9799
Fax: (866)871-1419
Co. E-mail: info@csla.ca
URL: http://www.csla.ca
Contact: Michelle Legault, Executive Director
Description: National association of landscape architects. Represents and promotes members' interests at national and international levels; develops and supports national activities and programs implemented by members. Maintains accreditation program; makes available professional liability insurance program. **Founded:** 1934. **Publications:** *Landscapes/Paysages*. **Awards:** Awards of Excellence (Annual); Community Service Award (Annual); Lifetime Achievement Award; Presidents Award (Annual); Schwabenbauer Award; Student Awards of Merit (Annual); Teaching Award (Annual); Jules Stachiewicz Medal; Syncrude Canada Innovation Award; Awards of Excellence; Process Safety Management Award; D. G. Fisher Award; Schwabenbauer Award; Community Service Award (Annual); Bantrel Award in Design and Industrial Practice; R.S. Jane Memorial Award. **Telecommunication Services:** executive-director@csla. ca.

13369 ■ *CNLA Newsbrief*
RR No. 4, Sta. Main
7856 5th Line S
Milton, ON, Canada L9T 2X8
Ph: (905)875-1399
Free: 888-446-3499
Fax: (905)875-1840
Co. E-mail: info@canadanursery.com
URL: http://www.canadanursery.com
Contact: Victor Santacruz, Executive Director
Released: Bimonthly

13370 ■ Independent Turf and Ornamental Distributors Association (ITODA)
174 Crestview Dr.
Bellefonte, PA 16823-8516
Ph: (717)243-7677
Free: 877-326-5995
Fax: (814)335-2452
Co. E-mail: info@itoda.org
URL: http://www.itoda.org
Contact: Patricia E. Heuser, Executive Director
Description: Wholesale suppliers of lawn and turf chemicals, fertilizers, and equipment. Represents members' interests. Conducts educational programs. Provides consulting services. Maintains speakers' bureau; compiles statistics. **Founded:** 1990. **Educational Activities:** Independent Turf and Ornamental Distributors Association Conference (Annual).

13371 ■ International Society of Arboriculture (ISA)
PO Box 3129
Champaign, IL 61826-3129
Ph: (217)355-9411
Free: 888-472-8733
Fax: (217)355-9516
Co. E-mail: isa@isa-arbor.com
URL: http://www.isa-arbor.com
Contact: Colin Bashford, President
Description: Individuals engaged in commercial, municipal, and utility arboriculture; city, state, and national government employees; municipal and commercial arborists; others interested in shade tree welfare. Disseminates information on the care and preservation of shade and ornamental trees. Supports research projects at educational institutions. **Founded:** 1924. **Publications:** *Arborist News* (Bimonthly); *Arborist News Magazine* (Bimonthly); *Arboriculture & Urban Forestry* (Bimonthly); *Diseases of Trees and Shrubs*. **Educational Activities:** International Society of Arboriculture Annual Conference and Industrial Trade Show (Annual). **Awards:** Gold Leaf Award; Research Trust Funds (Annual); Alex L. Shigo Award for Excellence in Arboricultural Education.

13372 ■ Landscape Architecture Foundation (LAF)
818 18th St. NW, Ste. 810
Washington, DC 20006
Ph: (202)331-7070

Fax: (202)331-7079
Co. E-mail: bdeutsch@lafoundation.org
URL: http://www.lafoundation.org
Contact: Lucinda R. Sanders, President
Description: Serves as an education and research vehicle for the landscape architecture profession in the U.S. Combines the capabilities of landscape architects, interests of environmentalists, and needs of agencies and resource foundations. Provides for the preparation and dissemination of educational and scientific information through publications, exhibits, lectures, and seminars. Solicits and expends gifts, legacies, and grants. Established an endowment fund for professorships at colleges and universities. Sponsors California Landscape Architectural Student Scholarship Fund. Conducts a study of the profession to establish goals in terms of education, research needs, practice, and formulation of public policy. **Founded:** 1966. **Publications:** *American Landscape Report* (Quarterly). **Awards:** ASLA Council of Fellows (Annual); Dangermond Fellowship (Annual); Landscape Forms Design for People (Annual); ASLA Council of Fellows Scholarships; CLASS Fund Irrigation Scholarship Program; Paul Courtland Scholarships; Steven G. King Play Environments Scholarships; Landscape Forms Design for People Scholarships; Rain Bird Intelligent Use of Water Scholarships; Hawaii Chapter/David T. Woolsey Scholarships; Peridian International, Inc./Rae L. Price, FASLA Scholarships. **Telecommunication Services:** scholarships@ lafoundation.org.

13373 ■ *Landscapes/Paysages*
PO Box 13594
Ottawa, ON, Canada K2K 1X6
Free: 866-781-9799
Fax: (866)871-1419
Co. E-mail: info@csla.ca
URL: http://www.csla.ca
Contact: Michelle Legault, Executive Director

13374 ■ New York State Turf and Landscape Association (NYSTLA)
1 Prospect Ave.
White Plains, NY 10607
Ph: (914)993-9455
Fax: (914)993-9051
Co. E-mail: nystla@aol.com
URL: http://www.nystla.com
Contact: Peter Muller, President
Description: Landscaping and grounds keeping professionals. Promotes the landscaping industry. **Founded:** 1968. **Publications:** *Installation*; *Irrigation*; *Mantenimiento* (Monthly). **Educational Activities:** Professional Turf and Landscape Conference (Annual). **Awards:** NYSTLA Scholarship; Louis Squobbo Scholarship Award (Annual); Person of the Year Award (Annual).

13375 ■ North American Flowerbulb Wholesalers Association (NAFWA)
c/o Marlboro Bulb Company
2424 Hwy. 72/221 E
Greenwood, SC 29649
Ph: (864)229-1618
Fax: (864)229-5719
Co. E-mail: nafwa1@aol.com
URL: http://www.nafwa.com
Contact: Thijs Leenders, President
Description: Wholesalers and dealers of flower bulbs and related floricultural commodities. **Founded:** 1983. **Awards:** Karl Schroff Memorial Scholarship (Annual).

13376 ■ Outdoor Power Equipment Institute (OPEI)
341 S Patrick St.
Alexandria, VA 22314
Ph: (703)549-7600
Fax: (703)549-7604
Co. E-mail: info@opei.org
URL: http://www.opei.org
Contact: Kris Kiser, President
Description: Manufacturers of lawn mowers, garden tractors, snow throwers, utility vehicles, chainsaws, motor tillers, shredder/grinders, edger/trimmers, leaf vacuums, log splitters, stump cutters, chippers and sprayers, and major components. Compiles statistics and forecasting information; sponsors industry trade

shows; produces comprehensive consumer education materials on safety and other industry issues; hosts' annual member meeting; represents members' interests on important legislative and regulatory issues. **Founded:** 1952. **Publications:** *SmartBrief* (Weekly). **Educational Activities:** International Lawn, Garden, and Power Equipment Expo (Annual).

13377 ■ Professional Landcare Network (PLANET)
950 Herndon Pky., Ste. 450
Herndon, VA 20170-5528
Ph: (703)736-9666
Free: 800-395-2522
Fax: (703)736-9668
Co. E-mail: info@landcarenetwork.org
URL: http://www.landcarenetwork.org
Contact: Jason K. Cupp, President
Description: Landscape contractors. Works to represent, lead, and unify the interior and exterior landscape industry by working together on a national basis; addressing environmental and legislative issues; and creating increased opportunities in business. Provides forum to encourage members' profitability, personal growth, and professional advancement. **Scope:** technical, business management, training, marketing. **Founded:** 2005. **Subscriptions:** 150 books video recordings. **Publications:** *PLANET News*; *PLANET News*; *Who's Who in Landscape Contracting* (Annual); *Landscape Contractor News* (Monthly). **Educational Activities:** Executive Forum (Annual); Green Industry Conference (Annual). **Awards:** Safety Recognition Awards; Environmental Improvement Awards Program; ALCA Environmental Improvement Award (Annual). **Telecommunication Services:** webmaster@landcarenetwork.org.

13378 ■ Turf and Ornamental Communicators Association (TOCA)
120 W Main St.
New Prague, MN 56071
Ph: (952)758-6340
Fax: (952)758-5813
Co. E-mail: toca@gardnerandgardnercommunications.com
URL: http://www.toca.org
Contact: Den Gardner, Executive Director
Description: Editors, writers, photographers, public relations and advertising practitioners involved in green industry communications (turf and ornamental). Promotes communications excellence within trade and consumer media. Maintains speakers' bureau. **Founded:** 1990. **Publications:** *Turf and Ornamental Communicators Association--Membership Directory*. **Awards:** Turf and Ornamental Communicators Association Scholarship Program; Environmental Communicator of the Year (Annual); Photography/Design Award (Annual); TOCA Scholarship (Annual); Writing Award (Annual).

REFERENCE WORKS

13379 ■ *"Accelerator Welcomes First Hispanic Firms" in Business Courier (Vol. 27, August 13, 2010, No. 15, pp. 1)*
Pub: Business Courier
Ed: Lucy May. **Description:** The Minority Business Accelerator (MBA) initiative of the Cincinnati USA Regional Chamber in Ohio has included Hispanic-owned firms Best Upon Request and Vivian Llambi and Associates Inc. to its portfolio. Vivian Llambi and Associates is a design, landscape architecture and civil engineering specialist. Prior to these firms' membership, MBA was limited to black-owned companies.

13380 ■ *"Active Sales" in Green Industry Pro (Vol. 23, September 2011)*
Pub: Cygnus Business Media
Ed: Gregg Wartgow. **Description:** Craig den Hartog, owner of Emerald Magic Lawn Care located in Holtsville, New York, describes the various marketing tactics he has developed to increase sales in the current economic environment. Statistical data included.

13381 ■ *"All the Trimmings" in Green Industry Pro (Vol. 23, March 2011, No. 3, pp. 29)*
Pub: Cygnus Business Media
Ed: Gregg Wartgow. **Description:** When choosing lawn mowing equipment, it is advised to purchase

commercial-grade 21-inch walk mowers rather than less expensive consumer-grade mowers. John Deere is reentering the commercial 21-inch walk behind mower market after a five-year hiatus.

13382 ■ American Society of Consulting Arborists--Membership Directory
Pub: American Society of Consulting Arborists
URL(s): www.asca-consultants.org. **Released:** Annual; March. **Price:** Free available to members only. **Covers:** About 400 persons specializing in the growth and care of urban shade and ornamental trees; includes expert witnesses and monetary appraisals. **Entries include:** Name, address, phone, fax. **Arrangement:** Geographical. **Indexes:** Alphabetical.

13383 ■ "Be Innovative In Other Ways" in Green Industry Pro (Vol. 23, March 2011, No. 3, pp. 4)
Pub: Cygnus Business Media
Ed: Rod Dickens. **Description:** Emphasis is put on the importance of putting the customer first in order to successfully market any product or service. Six marketing ideas are presented to promote a landscaping business.

13384 ■ "Customer Retention is Proportionate to Employee Retention" in Green Industry Pro (Vol. 23, September 2011)
Pub: Cygnus Business Media
Description: Presented in a question-answer format, information is provided to help retain customers as well as keeping workers happy.

13385 ■ "Customized Before Custom Was Cool" in Green Industry Pro (July 2011)
Pub: Cygnus Business Media
Ed: Gregg Wartgow. **Description:** Profile of Turf Care Enterprises and owner Kevin Vogeler, who discusses his desire to use more natural programs using little or no chemicals in 1986. At that time, that sector represented 20 percent of his business, today it shares 80 percent.

13386 ■ "Deep in the Heart of Drought" in Green Industry Pro (Vol. 23, October 2011)
Pub: Cygnus Business Media
Ed: Gregg Wartgow. **Description:** Challenges faced by landscape contractors during the recent drought in Texas are explored. Despite these challenges, opportunity for contractors providing irrigation services has risen.

13387 ■ "Dozens 'Come Alive' in Downtown Chicago" in Green Industry Pro (July 2011)
Pub: Cygnus Business Media
Ed: Gregg Wartgow. **Description:** Highlights from the Come Alive Outside training event held in Chicago, Illinois July 14-15, 2011 are shared. Nearly 80 people representing 38 landscape companies attended the event that helps contractors review their services and find ways to sell them in new and various ways.

13388 ■ "Finding a Way to Continue Growing" in Green Industry Pro (Vol. 23, March 2011, No. 3, pp. 31)
Pub: Cygnus Business Media
Description: Profile of Brett Lemcke, VP of R.M. Landscape located in Rochester, New York. Lemcke tells how his Landscape Industry Certified credentials helped him to grow his business and beat out his competition.

13389 ■ "Five Distinct Divisions, One Collective Focus" in Green Industry Pro (Vol. 23, October 2011)
Pub: Cygnus Business Media
Ed: Gregg Wartgow. **Description:** Profile of ACLS Inc., an amalgamation of All Commercial Landscape Service (commercial maintenance), All Custom Landscape Service (design/build), Fresno Tree Service, Certified Water Consulting (irrigation), and Tractor Service (disking and flailing services on everything from one-acre lots to hundreds of acres of open land). The firm discusses its rebranding effort in order to increase sales.

13390 ■ "Forward Motion" in Green Industry Pro (July 2011)
Pub: Cygnus Business Media
Ed: Gregg Wartgow. **Description:** Several landscape contractors have joined this publication's Working Smarter Training Challenge over the last year. This process is helping them develop ways to improve work processes, boost morale, drive out waste, reduce costs, improve customer service, and be more competitive.

13391 ■ "Gain the 'Come Alive Outside' Selling Edge" in Green Industry Pro (July 2011)
Pub: Cygnus Business Media
Ed: Jim Paluch. **Description:** Marketing the 'Come Alive Outside' slogan can help landscapers to increase their market share by identifying and applying these elements to each customer as well as their workers.

13392 ■ "The Green Industry Jobs Gap" in Green Industry Pro (Vol. 23, October 2011)
Pub: Cygnus Business Media
Ed: Gregg Wartgow. **Description:** According to the U.S. Bureau of Labor Statistics, the landscaping industry employs over 829,000 workers. According to another private study, the industry would employ more if they were able to find more people interested in performing the required work.

13393 ■ "Hey, You Can't Do That" in Green Industry Pro (Vol. 23, September 2011)
Pub: Cygnus Business Media
Ed: Rod Dickens. **Description:** Manufacturers of landscape equipment are making better use of energy resources, such as the use of fuel-injection systems instead of carburetors, lightweight materials, better lubricants, advanced battery technology, and innovative engine designs.

13394 ■ "How to Dominate in Residential Maintenance" in Green Industry Pro (Vol. 23, October 2011)
Pub: Cygnus Business Media
Ed: Gregg Wartgow. **Description:** Lawn care services were ranked among the most expendable consumer expenditures, according to the National Retail Federation data accumulated in early 2011. This makes it critical for any landscape firm to target sales efforts toward higher-income households and higher-value homes.

13395 ■ "How To Turn Your Efforts Into Results" in Green Industry Pro (Vol. 23, September 2011)
Pub: Cygnus Business Media
Ed: Bob Coulter. **Description:** Working Smarter Training Challenge teaches them are able to carry out solutions directly into their organization, develop skills and drive business results in key areas by creating a culture of energized workers who are able to take ownership of their performance as well as the performance of the company as a whole.

13396 ■ "Labor of Love" in Green Industry Pro (Vol. 23, March 2011, No. 3, pp. 14)
Pub: Cygnus Business Media
Ed: Gregg Wartgow. **Description:** Profile of CLS Landscape Management in Chino, California and its owner who started the company when he was 21 years old. Kevin Davis built his landscape firm into a $20 million a year business without using any dedicated salesperson.

13397 ■ "The Price of Profitability" in Green Industry Pro (Vol. 23, March 2011, No. 3, pp. 18)
Pub: Cygnus Business Media
Ed: Tony Bass. **Description:** Profit Builder Process is used to help landscaping companies be more competitive. Landscape contractors report pricing among their largest challenges and although the economy is improving, homeowners are paying closer attention to quality and service.

13398 ■ "Rediscovering the Land of Opportunity" in Green Industry Pro (July 2011)
Pub: Cygnus Business Media
Ed: Gregg Wartgow. **Description:** Landscape contractors need to discover new strategies that will generate leads and convert those leads into sales.

13399 ■ "Take Control of Your Company's Finances" in Green Industry Pro (Vol. 23, March 2011, No. 3, pp. 24)
Pub: Cygnus Business Media
Ed: Gregg Wartgow. **Description:** Understanding that when certain leading indicators that affect the outcome of certain lagging indicators are aligned, companies will be able to take control of their firm's finances. Ways to improve the processes that drive financial performance for landscape firms are outlined.

13400 ■ "Take This Job and Love It" in Green Industry Pro (Vol. 23, October 2011)
Pub: Cygnus Business Media
Ed: Gregg Wartgow. **Description:** Details of the lawsuit filed by the Professional Landcare Network (PLANET) against the U.S. Department of Labor are explained. Challenges faced by landscape firms because of employment costs are outlined. Statistical data included.

13401 ■ "Time to Fight Back" in Green Industry Pro (Vol. 23, March 2011, No. 3, pp. 8)
Pub: Cygnus Business Media
Ed: Rod Dickens. **Description:** Lawn care operators in the United States must learn from Canada that a shift to socialism will impact their industry in a negative way. Government regulation over the application of control products regarding environmental health in Canada has been a death sentence for small lawn care businesses.

13402 ■ "Urban Tree Service" in New Hampshire Business Review (Vol. 33, March 25, 2011, No. 6, pp. 35)
Pub: Business Publications Inc.
Description: Urban Tree Service received the Professional Communications Award from the Tree Care Industry Association for excellence in marketing and communications.

13403 ■ "Way More Than Mowing" in Green Industry Pro (Vol. 23, September 2011)
Pub: Cygnus Business Media
Ed: Rod Dickens. **Description:** Shipp Shape Lawn Services located in Sylvester, Georgia now offers aeration, fertilizing and weed control, mulching, yard renovation, flowerbed maintenance, landscaping, as well as irrigation repairs and installation in order to diversify the business and stay competitive.

STATISTICAL SOURCES

13404 ■ RMA Annual Statement Studies
Pub: Risk Management Association
Contact: Kevin M. Blakey, President
Released: Annual. **Price:** $175.00 2006-07 edition, $105.00. **Description:** Contains composite balance sheets and income statements for more than 360 industries, including the accounting, auditing, and bookkeeping industries. Also contains five years of comparative historical data for discerning trends. Includes 16 commonly used ratios, computed for most of the size groupings for nearly every industry.

TRADE PERIODICALS

13405 ■ Arboriculture Consultant
Pub: American Society of Consulting Arborists
Contact: Beth W. Palys, Executive Director
Released: Quarterly. **Description:** Contains information on trees.

13406 ■ California Garden
Pub: San Diego Floral Association
Contact: Barbara Clark, President
URL(s): www.sdfloral.org/magazine.htm. **Released:** Bimonthly

13407 ■ *Country Home*
Pub: Meredith Corp.
URL(s): www.countryhome.com. **Released:** Monthly; 10/yr. **Price:** $4.95, Individuals newstand; $21.97, Two years.

13408 ■ *Fairchild Tropical Garden Views*
Pub: Fairchild Tropical Botanic Garden
Ed: Susan Knorr, Editor, sknorr@excel.net. **Released:** Quarterly. **Price:** Included in membership. **Description:** Provides information on tropical gardening. Includes news on botanical garden and horticulture, list of classes, and a calendar of events.

13409 ■ *Fuchsia Flash*
Pub: Northwest Fuchsia Society
Ed: Ken Gronert, Editor, editor@nwfuchsia.com. **Released:** Monthly. **Price:** $12; $16, out of country. **Description:** Provides information for individuals who cultivate fuchsia flowers worldwide.

13410 ■ *Garden Design*
Pub: World Publications Inc.
Contact: Dave Freygang, Chief Executive Officer
URL(s): www.gardendesign.com/index.jsp. **Ed:** Sarah Kinbar. **Released:** 8/yr. **Price:** $14.97, Individuals 7 issues; $19.97, Canada 7 issues; $32.97, Other countries 7 issues.

13411 ■ *Horticulture: The Art and Science of Smart Gardening*
Pub: FW Publications
Contact: Sara Domville, President
E-mail: sara.domville@fwpubs.com
URL(s): www.hortmag.com. **Released:** 8/yr. **Price:** $19.95, Individuals; $39.95, Canada; $39.95, Other countries.

13412 ■ *LAND*
Pub: American Society of Landscape Architects
Contact: Susan M. Hatchell, President
Ed: Susan Hines, Editor, shines@asla.org. **Released:** Biweekly, 26 issues/year. **Price:** Included in membership. **Description:** Carries news and monitors developments in landscape architecture, environmental design, and related fields. Focuses on public policy, education, and other areas affecting landscape architecture.

13413 ■ *Landscape Architect and Specifier News*
Pub: Landscape Communications Inc.
URL(s): www.landscapeonline.com/contact/contact_mag.php?pub=lasn. **Ed:** Larry Shield, George Schmok, Leslie McGuire. **Released:** Monthly

13414 ■ *Landscape Architecture: The Magazine of the American Society of Landscape Architects*
Pub: American Society of Landscape Architects
Contact: Susan M. Hatchell, President
URL(s): archives.asla.org/nonmembers/lam.html. **Ed:** Daniel Jost, Bradford McKee. **Released:** Monthly **Price:** $59, Nonmembers; $99, Other countries; $118, Two years; $198, Other countries 2 years.

13415 ■ *The Landscape Contractor: Landscape Contracting*
Pub: Illinois Landscape Contractor Association
URL(s): https://www.ilca.net/publications.aspx. **Released:** Monthly **Price:** $75, Individuals; $150, Out of state.

13416 ■ *Landscape Journal*
Pub: University of Wisconsin Press
Contact: Gwen Walker, Director
E-mail: gcwalker@wisc.edu
URL(s): uwpress.wisc.edu/journals/journals/lj.html. **Ed:** Lance Neckar, Arnold Alanen, James F. Palmer, Robert B. Riley, David Pitt. **Released:** 2/yr. **Price:** $236, Institutions and libraries; print & online; $208, Institutions and libraries; online; $75, Individuals print & online; $68, Individuals online only.

13417 ■ *Landscape Management*
Contact: Marisa Palmieri, Editor
E-mail: mpalmieri@northcoastmedia.net
URL(s): www.landscapemanagement.net/landscape/. **Ed:** Marisa Palmieri. **Released:** 12/yr. **Price:** $46, Individuals domestic; $69, Canada and Mexico; $89, Other countries.

13418 ■ *Landscape Trades: Canada's Premier Horticultural Trade Publication*
Pub: Landscape Ontario Horticultural Trades Association
URL(s): www.landscapetrades.com. **Ed:** Robert Ellidge. **Released:** 9/yr (not published Feb., Aug., and Dec.). **Price:** $43.58, Individuals; $78.74, Two years; $110.24, Individuals 3 years.

13419 ■ *Lawn & Landscape Magazine*
Pub: G.I.E. Media, MC
Contact: Chris Foster, President
E-mail: chris.foster@gie.net
URL(s): www.lawnandlandscape.com. **Ed:** Chuck Bowen. **Released:** Monthly **Price:** $15, U.S., Canada, and Mexico; $35, Individuals; $100, Other countries South America/Europe.

13420 ■ *Pro: Business Strategies for Landscape Contractors*
Pub: Cygnus Business Media
Contact: Rich Reiff, President
URL(s): www.greenindustrypros.com/magazine/pro/issue/2012/augwww.cygnusb2b.com/PropertyPub.cfm?PropertyID=571. **Released:** 9/yr.

13421 ■ *Tree City USA Bulletin*
Pub: Arbor Day Foundation
Contact: John Rosenow, President
Ed: James R. Fazio, Editor. **Released:** Bimonthly. **Price:** $3, single issue; $15 membership subscription. **Description:** Provides tree planting and care instructions and information.

13422 ■ *Virginia Native Plant Society Bulletin*
Pub: Virginia Native Plant Society
Contact: Ms. Sally Anderson, Vice President
Ed: Nancy Sorrells, Editor, lotswife@adelphia.net. **Released:** 5/year. **Price:** $30, Included in membership. **Description:** Examines the native plants of Virginia and their habitats and provides information on botany.

VIDEOCASSETTES/ AUDIOCASSETTES

13423 ■ *Garden Pond Basics*
Karol Media
Hanover Industrial Estates
375 Stewart Rd.
Wilkes Barre, PA 18773-7600
Ph: (570)822-8899
Free: 800-526-4773
Co. E-mail: sales@karolmedia.com
URL: http://www.karolmedia.com
Released: 1997. **Price:** $14.95. **Description:** Provides instruction on care and maintenance of garden ponds. **Availability:** VHS.

13424 ■ *Groundskeeping Series*
AMS Distributors, Inc.
PO Box 658
Lady Lake, FL 32158
Free: 800-424-3464
Fax: (352)750-5635
Co. E-mail: orders@vpats.com
URL: http://www.vpats.com
Released: 1986. **Description:** A series of instruction on the art of industrial groundskeeping. **Availability:** VHS; 3/4 U.

13425 ■ *Landscape Equipment Safety for the 90s*
American Nurseryman Publishing Co.
223 W Jackson Blvd., Ste. 500
Chicago, IL 60606-6904
Ph: (312)427-7339
Free: 800-621-5727
Fax: (312)427-7346
Co. E-mail: admin@amerinursery.com
URL: http://www.amerinursery.com/
Released: 1991. **Price:** $64.99. **Description:** Series of programs updating OSHA information and federal regulations for landscape equipment use. **Availability:** VHS.

13426 ■ *Landscape Tools: Use and Safety*
American Nurseryman Publishing Co.
223 W Jackson Blvd., Ste. 500
Chicago, IL 60606-6904
Ph: (312)427-7339
Free: 800-621-5727
Fax: (312)427-7346
Co. E-mail: admin@amerinursery.com
URL: http://www.amerinursery.com/
Released: 1989. **Price:** $94.99. **Description:** Demonstrates the proper use of 12 landscape tools, emphasizing safety rules. **Availability:** VHS.

13427 ■ *Master Gardener Series*
RMI Media
1365 N. Winchester St.
Olathe, KS 66061-5880
Ph: (913)768-1696
Free: 800-745-5480
Fax: (800)755-6910
Co. E-mail: actmedia@act.org
URL: http://www.actmedia.org
Released: 1987. **Description:** Provides information on gardening and landscaping. **Availability:** VHS; 3/4 U.

TRADE SHOWS AND CONVENTIONS

13428 ■ American Society of Landscape Architects Annual Meeting and Expo
American Society of Landscape Architects (ASLA)
636 Eye St. NW
Washington, DC 20001-3736
Ph: (202)898-2444
Free: 888-999-ASLA
Fax: (202)898-1185
Co. E-mail: info@asla.org
URL: http://www.asla.org
Contact: Susan M. Hatchell, President
URL(s): www.asla.org. **Price:** $270, Pre-registered, members; $465, Pre-registered, non-members; $420, Members; $615, Non-members. **Frequency:** Annual. **Audience:** Landscape architects and trade professionals. **Principal Exhibits:** Irrigation supplies, outdoor lighting, park and playground equipment, paving and ground cover, street and park furniture, landscape maintenance equipment, computer hardware and software, architectural finishing materials, construction materials, historic preservation services, surveying and mapping equipment, and related equipment, supplies, and services.

13429 ■ International Conference on Oral and Maxillofacial Surgery (ICOMS)
Kenes International
Rue de Chantepoulet 1-3
CH-1211 Geneva, Switzerland
Ph: 41 22 9080488
Fax: 41 22 9069140
Co. E-mail: info@kenes.com
URL: http://www.kenes.com
URL(s): www.icoms2011.com/. **Frequency:** Biennial. **Audience:** Medical professionals. **Principal Exhibits:** Oral and maxillofacial surgery, including diseases, injuries, and defects.

13430 ■ International Society of Arboriculture Annual Conference and Industrial Trade Show
International Society of Arboriculture (ISA)
PO Box 3129
Champaign, IL 61826-3129
Ph: (217)355-9411
Free: 888-472-8733
Fax: (217)355-9516
Co. E-mail: isa@isa-arbor.com
URL: http://www.isa-arbor.com
Contact: Colin Bashford, President
URL(s): www.isa-arbor.com. **Price:** $350, Pre-registered; $425, Onsite. **Frequency:** Annual. **Audience:** Arborists. **Principal Exhibits:** Chippers, bucket trucks, chain saws, hand tools, computer software and hardware, consulting services, and tree and lawn care products.

CONSULTANTS

13431 ■ Richard L. Baldwin, Horticultural Consultant
215 Virginia Dr.
Ventura, CA 93003
Ph: (805)643-8406
Scope: Provider of diagnosis of plant disorders and management, construction and maintenance recommendations for horticulture, including playing fields. Also offers arboriculture consultation, including hazardous conditions, evaluation of loss, and related landscape research. Services include consultation on production of ornamental plants, including turf grass and management of landscape plants. **Founded:** 1983. **Seminars:** Pruning Fruit Trees; Propagation of Fruit Trees; Diagnosing Plant Disorders; Pest Control on Ornamental Plants; Turf grass Fertilization.

13432 ■ Boone's Landscaping Nursery Corp.—Boone's Landscaping L.L.C.
736 Grathwol Dr.
Wilmington, NC 28405-1241
Ph: (936)647-2904
Fax: (936)647-1437
Co. E-mail: boone@booneslandscaping.com
URL: http://www.booneslandscaping.com
Contact: John C. Boone, Jr., President
Scope: Offers landscaping consultation with particular expertise in land scaping design. Additional expertise available in nursery design, development, and maintenance, water gardening and aquatic plants, and bonsai gardens. Licensed landscape contractor. **Founded:** 1973.

13433 ■ Erin Services Inc.
111 Travelers Way
Saint Simons Island, GA 31522-5632
Ph: (912)638-9916
Fax: (912)638-5701
Co. E-mail: dennisd@ns.technonet.com
Contact: Dennis J. Donnelly, III, President
E-mail: dennis179@yahoo.com
Scope: Offers assistance in technical proposal production, marketing, and research. Industries served: Food service, janitorial, landscaping, hospitality and lodging, parks, and recreational. **Founded:** 1990.

13434 ■ Forman & Biller Tree Expert Co.
856 N Harrison St.
Arlington, VA 22205-1229
Ph: (703)522-3141
Contact: James E. Biller, Owner
Scope: Consulting arbores providing tree care for residential and commercial properties. **Founded:** 1977.

13435 ■ Jobs In Horticulture Inc.
57 Rosedown Blvd.
Debary, FL 32713
Ph: (386)753-0996
Free: 800-428-2474
Fax: (386)753-0997
Co. E-mail: info@hortjobs.com
URL: http://www.hortjobs.com
Contact: David Shaw, Director
Scope: Career consulting and career services with emphasis on horticulture. **Founded:** 1993.

13436 ■ Western Arborists Inc.
502 W Rte. 66, Ste. 20
Glendora, CA 91740-4370
Ph: (626)963-1171
Fax: (626)963-8243
Contact: James W. Walker, President
Scope: Offers consulting on tree disease and insect problems. Also provides appraisal services covering damage or value of trees lost. **Founded:** 2002.

FRANCHISES AND BUSINESS OPPORTUNITIES

13437 ■ Birthflowers.com, Inc.
161 Swint Ave.
Milledgeville, GA 31061

Ph: (478)452-0008
Description: Landscaping and design. **No. of Company-Owned Units:** 1. **Founded:** 1995.. **Franchised:** 2005. **Equity Capital Needed:** $4,000. **Franchise Fee:** $7,000. **Financial Assistance:** Yes. **Training:** Yes.

13438 ■ Clintar Groundskeeping Services
Truserve Groundcare Inc.
70 Esna Park Dr., Unit 1
Markham, ON, Canada L3R 1E3
Ph: (905)943-9530
Free: 800-361-3542
Fax: (905)943-9529
Co. E-mail: info@clintar.com
URL: http://www.clintar.com
Description: Grounds keeping services including landscape maintenance, snow and ice control, power sweeping, light construction, tree care and irrigation maintenance. **No. of Franchise Units:** 21. **Founded:** 1973.. **Franchised:** 1984. **Equity Capital Needed:** $100,000-$125,000; $50,000-$60,000 cash. **Franchise Fee:** $40,000. **Training:** Yes.

13439 ■ The Gardener Inc.
7030 Woodbine Ave., Unit 101
Markham, ON, Canada L3R 6G2
Ph: (905)305-3000
Free: 800-970-6947
Fax: (905)305-3001
Co. E-mail: info@hirthegardener.com
URL: http://www.HireTheGardner.com
Description: The company franchises residential landscape maintenance and snow removal services. **No. of Franchise Units:** 40. **Founded:** 1994.. **Franchised:** 1994. **Equity Capital Needed:** $45,000-$50,000. **Franchise Fee:** $25,000. **Training:** 1 week in class, 1 week in field, and ongoing support.

13440 ■ IntelliTurf
PO Box 8685
Atlanta, GA 31106
Ph: (800)429-2971
Fax: (859)201-1164
Co. E-mail: franchise@intelliturf.com
URL: http://www.IntelliTurf.com
Description: Design & installation of custom, synthetic golf surfaces that look, play & feel like natural grass. The applications include, swimming pools, outdoor courts, croquet fields, soccer fields, and indoor putting surfaces. **No. of Company-Owned Units:** 1. **Founded:** 1997.. **Equity Capital Needed:** $60,000. **Franchise Fee:** $32,000. **Training:** Offers initial training at corporate headquarters in Atlanta and at franchisee's location.

13441 ■ Nite Time Decor Inc.
The Decor Group
PO Box 5183
Lubbock, TX 79408-5183
Free: 866-321-4077
Fax: (806)722-9627
Description: Landscape lighting products and services. **No. of Franchise Units:** 37. **Founded:** 1986.. **Franchised:** 1999. **Equity Capital Needed:** $37,500-$74,350. **Franchise Fee:** $16,900. **Royalty Fee:** 5%. **Training:** Includes 4 days training at headquarters and ongoing support.

13442 ■ Professional Polish, Inc
Professional Polish, Inc.
5450 E Loop 820 S
Ft. Worth, TX 76119
Ph: (817)572-7353
Free: 800-255-0488
Fax: (817)561-6193
Description: Janitorial, lawn, landscape and light building maintenance service at the local level. **No. of Franchise Units:** 28. **No. of Company-Owned Units:** 1. **Founded:** 1981.. **Franchised:** 1986. **Equity Capital Needed:** $10,000-$150,000. **Franchise Fee:** $4,500-$50,000. **Financial Assistance:** Yes. **Training:** Yes.

13443 ■ Sunshine Grounds Care
22 Coles Cres
Orangeville, ON, Canada L9W 2Z2
Ph: (647)338-9435
Free: 800-361-5296

Fax: (800)909-9515
Co. E-mail: info@sunshinebrands.ca
URL: http://www.sunshinegroundscare.com
Description: Commercial and residential property maintenance and landscape design and construction. **No. of Franchise Units:** 17. **No. of Company-Owned Units:** 1. **Founded:** 1987.. **Franchised:** 2004. **Equity Capital Needed:** $76,000-$96,000. **Franchise Fee:** $19,000. **Training:** Provides 1 week initial training and ongoing.

13444 ■ Tuff Turf Inc.
6822 W Grovers Ave.
Glendale, AZ 85308
Ph: (602)290-0499
Free: 866-431-2468
Fax: (602)548-5567
Description: Selling and installing synthetic turf. **No. of Franchise Units:** 6. **Founded:** 1998.. **Franchised:** 2002. **Equity Capital Needed:** $35,900-$65,100. **Franchise Fee:** $19,500. **Training:** Yes.

COMPUTER SYSTEMS/ SOFTWARE

13445 ■ *Advance Grower Solutions / Nursery/Greenhouse Accounting Software*
4900 SW Griffith Dr., Ste. 248
Beaverton, OR 97005
Ph: (503)646-5581
Free: 800-367-7082
Fax: (503)646-0622
URL: http://www.advgrower.com/
Price: Prices vary depending on modules needed. **Description:** Available for IBM computers and compatibles. System provides accounting and report capabilities for nursery and landscaping businesses.

LIBRARIES

13446 ■ American Horticultural Society Library
7931 E. Boulevard Dr.
Alexandria, VA 22308
Ph: (703)768-5700
Free: 800-777-7931
Fax: (703)768-8700
Co. E-mail: tunderwood@ahs.org
URL: http://www.ahs.org/
Contact: Tom Underwood, Executive Officer
Scope: Horticulture. **Services:** Copying; Library open to the public by appointment. **Holdings:** 5000 books.

13447 ■ American Society of Landscape Architects - Professional Practice Library
636 Eye St., NW
Washington, DC 20001-3736
Ph: (202)898-2444
Fax: (202)898-1185
Co. E-mail: library@asla.org
URL: http://www.asla.org/LibraryAndResearchServices.aspx
Contact: Marlene Koenig, Librarian
Scope: Landscape architecture, landscape design, sustainable design, urban planning and development, land use and design, land planning, the environment, gardens, historic preservation. **Services:** Interlibrary loan; library open to the public by appointment. **Founded:** 1899. **Holdings:** 2000 books; 1000 nonbook items. **Subscriptions:** 130 journals and other serials.

13448 ■ The Arboretum at Flagstaff - Transition Zone Horticultural Institute Library
4001 S. Woody Mountain Rd.
Flagstaff, AZ 86001-8775
Ph: (928)774-1442
Fax: (928)774-1441
Co. E-mail: lynne.nemeth@thearb.org
URL: http://www.thearb.org
Contact: Lynne Nemeth
Scope: Horticulture, forestry, botany, ecology, Colorado Plateau, environmental education, nonprofit management. **Services:** Library open to arboretum

members and researchers by appointment for reference use only. **Founded:** 1989. **Holdings:** 3000 books, 3000 images. **Subscriptions:** 5 journals and other serials.

13449 ■ Birmingham Botanical Gardens - Library

2612 Lane Park Rd.
Birmingham, AL 35223
Ph: (205)414-3920
Fax: (205)414-3922
Co. E-mail: hopel@bham.lib.al.us
URL: http://www.bbgardens.org/library.php
Contact: Hope Long, Director, Library Services
Scope: Horticulture, botany, floriculture, gardens and gardening, landscaping, flower arranging and children's books, organic gardening, insects, animals, nature crafts. **Services:** Copying; printing (black and white, color); faxing; free wifi and internet access; Library open to the public. **Founded:** 1971. **Holdings:** 6000 circulating books; 870 reference books; 450 children's books; 100 CD-ROMs; DVDs. **Subscriptions:** 60 journals and other serials. **Telecommunication Services:** thelibrary@bbgardens.org.

13450 ■ Chicago Park District - Garfield Park Conservatory

300 N. Central Park Ave.
Chicago, IL 60624-1945
Ph: (312)746-5100
Fax: (773)638-1777
URL: http://www.garfield-conservatory.org/
Contact: Mary Eysenbach, Director
Scope: Horticulture. **Services:** Library not open to the public. **Founded:** 1907. **Holdings:** 600 books. **Subscriptions:** 2 journals and other serials.

13451 ■ Cleveland Botanical Garden - Eleanor Squire Library

11030 East Blvd.
Cleveland, OH 44106
Ph: (216)721-1600
Fax: (216)721-2056
Co. E-mail: info@cbgarden.org
URL: http://www.cbgarden.org/Learn/Library.html
Contact: Gary Esmonde, Librarian
Scope: Gardening, horticulture, landscape architecture, herbs, flower arranging, botany. **Services:** Library open to the public with paid admission (members may borrow); rare books open to the public by appointment for review, research, and study. **Founded:** 1930. **Holdings:** 17,000 volumes; seed and nursery catalogs; slides; botanical prints; 1000 rare books. **Subscriptions:** 50 journals and other serials. **Telecommunication Services:** gesmonde@cbgarden.org.

13452 ■ Horticultural Society of New York Library

148 W. 37th St., 13th Fl.
New York, NY 10018-6976
Ph: (212)757-0915, x-100
Fax: (212)246-1207
Co. E-mail: kpowis@hsny.org
URL: http://www.hsny.org
Contact: Katherine Powis, Librarian
Scope: Gardening; garden design and garden history; horticulture; landscape design; botanical illustration; flower arrangement. **Services:** Library open to the public for reference use only. **Founded:** 1922. **Holdings:** 6000 books; 3500 bound periodical volumes; 75 lin.ft. of institutional archives. **Subscriptions:** 120 journals and other serials. **Telecommunication Services:** library@thehort.org.

13453 ■ Carol R. Johnson & Associates, Inc. Library

115 Broad St.
Boston, MA 02110-3032
Ph: (617)896-2500
Fax: (617)896-2340
Co. E-mail: info@crja.com
URL: http://www.crja.com
Contact: Abby Saunders, Librarian
Scope: Landscape architecture, horticulture, parks and recreation, design. **Services:** Copying; Library open to the public by appointment. **Founded:** 1980. **Holdings:** 2000 books; technical data; product literature; reports. **Subscriptions:** 170 journals and other serials.

13454 ■ Morton Arboretum - Sterling Morton Library

4100 Illinois Rte. 53
Lisle, IL 60532-1288
Ph: (630)719-2430
Fax: (630)719-7956
Co. E-mail: library@mortonarb.org
URL: http://www.mortonarb.org/sterling-morton-library.html
Contact: Rita Hassert, Manager, Collections
Scope: Botany, horticulture, dendrology, botanical art and illustration, arboriculture, landscape architecture, natural history, ecology and the environment. **Services:** Interlibrary loan; copying; SDI; library open to the public. **Founded:** 1922. **Holdings:** 28,000 volumes; 1000 nursery and seed catalogs. **Subscriptions:** 800 journals and other serials.

13455 ■ Ontario Association of Landscape Architects Library

3rd Church St., Ste. 4017
Toronto, ON, Canada M5E 1M2
Ph: (416)231-4181
Fax: (416)231-2679
Co. E-mail: oala@oala.ca
URL: http://www.oala.ca
Contact: Ronda Kellington, Administrator
Scope: Landscape architecture. **Services:** Library open to OALA members and interns only. **Founded:** 1968. **Holdings:** 250 books; 50 serials; 100 reports; archives; videos and audio tapes. **Subscriptions:** 12 journals and other serials.

13456 ■ State Botanical Garden of Georgia Library

Callaway Bldg.
University of Georgia
2450 S. Milledge Ave.
Athens, GA 30605
Ph: (706)542-1244
Co. E-mail: garden@uga.edu
URL: http://www.botgarden.uga.edu
Scope: Plants, gardening, horticulture, botany, conservation, ethnobotany, landscape design, floral crafts. **Services:** Library open to the public for reference use only. **Founded:** 1975. **Holdings:** 2000 books; 85 videotapes; CD-ROMs; archives; manuscripts. **Subscriptions:** 14 journals and other serials.

13457 ■ U.S. National Arboretum Library

3501 New York Ave., NE
Washington, DC 20002-1958
Ph: (202)245-2726
Fax: (202)245-4575
Co. E-mail: everlyr@ars.usda.gov
URL: http://www.usna.usda.gov/
Contact: Robin Everly, Librarian
Scope: Botany, taxonomy, floristics, horticulture, gardening, plant genetics and breeding. **Services:** Interlibrary loan (through National Agricultural Library only); Library open to the public by appointment for onsite research only. **Founded:** 1966. **Holdings:** 10,000 books; 500 periodical titles. **Subscriptions:** 165 journals and other serials.

13458 ■ U.S. National Park Service - Blue Ridge Parkway Archives

199 Hemphill Knob Rd.
Asheville, NC 28803-8686
Ph: (828)271-4779
Fax: (828)271-4313
URL: http://www.nps.gov/blri
Contact: Jackie Holt, Curator
Scope: Blue Ridge Parkway - history, development, design, construction, landscape, resource management. **Services:** Archives open to researchers by appointment only. **Founded:** 1990. **Holdings:** 350,000 archives.

13459 ■ University of Alberta - Devonian Botanic Garden Library

Edmonton, AB, Canada T6G 2E1
Ph: (770)987-3054, x2240

Fax: (780)987-4141
Co. E-mail: rbelland@ualberta.ca
URL: http://www.devonian.ualberta.ca
Contact: Rene Belland, Curator
Scope: Horticulture, botany, gardening, landscape design, natural history, plant diversity, conservation. **Services:** Library open to the public with restrictions. **Founded:** 1971. **Holdings:** 1000 books; reports; manuscripts; archives. **Subscriptions:** 6 journals and other serials.

13460 ■ University of Nevada, Las Vegas - Architecture Studies Library

Box 454049
4505 Maryland Pkwy.
Las Vegas, NV 89154-4049
Ph: (702)895-1959
Fax: (702)895-1975
Co. E-mail: caroline.smith@unlv.edu
URL: http://www.library.unlv.edu/arch/index.html
Contact: Caroline Smith, Director
Scope: Architecture - history, design, theory, and criticism; landscape architecture; interior design; construction; urban planning. **Services:** Interlibrary loan; copying; scanners; Library open to the public. **Founded:** 1997. **Holdings:** 25,000 volumes; 600 videos/DVDs; archives; microfiche and microfilm. **Subscriptions:** 150 journals and other serials.

RESEARCH CENTERS

13461 ■ Landscape Architecture Foundation (LAF)

818 18th St. NW, Ste. 810
Washington, DC 20006
Ph: (202)331-7070
Fax: (202)331-7079
Co. E-mail: bdeutsch@lafoundation.org
URL: http://www.lafoundation.org
Contact: Barbara Deutsch, Executive Director
Founded: 1966. **Publications:** *American Landscape Report* (Quarterly); *Land & Community Design Case Study Series* (Quarterly). **Educational Activities:** LAF Conferences; LAF Seminars, workshops. **Awards:** Scholarships, internships, grants.

13462 ■ The Nature Conservancy in Maine

14 Maine St., Ste. 401
Brunswick, ME 04011
Ph: (207)729-5181
Fax: (207)729-4118
Co. E-mail: naturemaine@tnc.org
URL: http://www.nature.org/ourinitiatives/regions/northamerica/unitedstates/maine
Contact: Mike Tetreault, Executive Director
Founded: 1956.

13463 ■ University of Guelph - Arboretum

Guelph, ON, Canada N1G 2W1
Ph: (519)824-4120
Fax: (519)763-9598
Co. E-mail: awatson@uoguelph.ca
URL: http://www.uoguelph.ca/arboretum
Contact: Prof. Alan P. Watson, Director
Services: Annual one day plant sale; Nature Interpretation Programs. **Founded:** 1970. **Publications:** *The Green Web*; *Ontario Tree Atlas*; *Seasonal Program*; *A Life Zone Approach to School Yard Naturalization*. **Educational Activities:** Horticultural and zoological adult programs; Special events and conservation-related symposia. **Telecommunication Services:** arbor@uoguelph.ca.

13464 ■ University of Pennsylvania - Morris Arboretum

100 E Northwestern Ave.
Philadelphia, PA 19118
Ph: (215)247-5777
Fax: (215)248-4439
Co. E-mail: info@morrisarboretum.org
URL: http://www.business-services.upenn.edu/arboretum
Contact: Paul W. Meyer, Director
Services: Plant clinic. **Founded:** 1933. **Publications:** *Morris Arboretum Annual report*; *Morris Arboretum Newsletter* (Quarterly). **Educational Activities:** Adult Education Courses, in horticulture and botany and opportunities for graduate research in

taxonomy, phytopathology, and landscape architecture on a 166-acre tract with a living collection of 13,000 plants representing 2,500 taxa; Community Service Program; Development Courses, for arborists; Morris Arboretum Internships; Teacher Training, for Philadelphia and suburban teachers; Workshops and Symposia.

START-UP INFORMATION

13465 ■ *How to Open and Operate a Financially Successful Landscaping, Nursery or Lawn Service Business: With Companion CD-ROM*
Pub: Atlantic Publishing Company
Ed: Lynn Wasnak. **Released:** June 1, 2009. **Price:** $39.95. **Description:** Guide provides understanding of the basic concepts of starting and running a service business, focusing on the operation of a small nursery, landscaping, or lawn service or combining the three operations. It also offers tips for running the business from the home.

13466 ■ *Start Your Own Lawn Care or Landscaping Business*
Pub: Entrepreneur Press
Ed: Eileen Figure Sandlin. **Released:** May 2007. **Price:** $19.95 (CND). **Description:** Advice for starting a lawn care and landscaping business is given.

ASSOCIATIONS AND OTHER ORGANIZATIONS

13467 ■ **Outdoor Power Equipment Institute (OPEI)**
341 S Patrick St.
Alexandria, VA 22314
Ph: (703)549-7600
Fax: (703)549-7604
Co. E-mail: info@opei.org
URL: http://www.opei.org
Contact: Kris Kiser, President
Description: Manufacturers of lawn mowers, garden tractors, snow throwers, utility vehicles, chainsaws, motor tillers, shredder/grinders, edger/trimmers, leaf vacuums, log splitters, stump cutters, chippers and sprayers, and major components. Compiles statistics and forecasting information; sponsors industry trade shows; produces comprehensive consumer education materials on safety and other industry issues; hosts' annual member meeting; represents members' interests on important legislative and regulatory issues. **Founded:** 1952. **Publications:** *SmartBrief* (Weekly). **Educational Activities:** International Lawn, Garden, and Power Equipment Expo (Annual).

REFERENCE WORKS

13468 ■ *"Active Sales"* in *Green Industry Pro (Vol. 23, September 2011)*
Pub: Cygnus Business Media
Ed: Gregg Wartgow. **Description:** Craig den Hartog, owner of Emerald Magic Lawn Care located in Holtsville, New York, describes the various marketing tactics he has developed to increase sales in the current economic environment. Statistical data included.

13469 ■ *"All the Trimmings"* in *Green Industry Pro (Vol. 23, March 2011, No. 3, pp. 29)*
Pub: Cygnus Business Media
Ed: Gregg Wartgow. **Description:** When choosing lawn mowing equipment, it is advised to purchase commercial-grade 21-inch walk mowers rather than less expensive consumer-grade mowers. John Deere is reentering the commercial 21-inch walk behind mower market after a five-year hiatus.

13470 ■ *"Be Innovative In Other Ways"* in *Green Industry Pro (Vol. 23, March 2011, No. 3, pp. 4)*
Pub: Cygnus Business Media
Ed: Rod Dickens. **Description:** Emphasis is put on the importance of putting the customer first in order to successfully market any product or service. Six marketing ideas are presented to promote a landscaping business.

13471 ■ *"Customer Retention is Proportionate to Employee Retention"* in *Green Industry Pro (Vol. 23, September 2011)*
Pub: Cygnus Business Media
Description: Presented in a question-answer format, information is provided to help retain customers as well as keeping workers happy.

13472 ■ *"Customized Before Custom Was Cool"* in *Green Industry Pro (July 2011)*
Pub: Cygnus Business Media
Ed: Gregg Wartgow. **Description:** Profile of Turf Care Enterprises and owner Kevin Vogeler, who discusses his desire to use more natural programs using little or no chemicals in 1986. At that time, that sector represented 20 percent of his business, today it shares 80 percent.

13473 ■ *"Deep in the Heart of Drought"* in *Green Industry Pro (Vol. 23, October 2011)*
Pub: Cygnus Business Media
Ed: Gregg Wartgow. **Description:** Challenges faced by landscape contractors during the recent drought in Texas are explored. Despite these challenges, opportunity for contractors providing irrigation services has risen.

13474 ■ *"Dozens 'Come Alive' in Downtown Chicago"* in *Green Industry Pro (July 2011)*
Pub: Cygnus Business Media
Ed: Gregg Wartgow. **Description:** Highlights from the Come Alive Outside training event held in Chicago, Illinois July 14-15, 2011 are shared. Nearly 80 people representing 38 landscape companies attended the event that helps contractors review their services and find ways to sell them in new and various ways.

13475 ■ *"Finding a Way to Continue Growing"* in *Green Industry Pro (Vol. 23, March 2011, No. 3, pp. 31)*
Pub: Cygnus Business Media
Description: Profile of Brett Lemcke, VP of R.M. Landscape located in Rochester, New York. Lemcke tells how his Landscape Industry Certified credentials helped him to grow his business and beat out his competition.

13476 ■ *"Five Distinct Divisions, One Collective Focus"* in *Green Industry Pro (Vol. 23, October 2011)*
Pub: Cygnus Business Media
Ed: Gregg Wartgow. **Description:** Profile of ACLS Inc., an amalgamation of All Commercial Landscape Service (commercial maintenance), All Custom Landscape Service (design/build), Fresno Tree Service, Certified Water Consulting (irrigation), and Tractor Service (disking and flailing services on everything from one-acre lots to hundreds of acres of open land). The firm discusses its rebranding effort in order to increase sales.

13477 ■ *"Forward Motion"* in *Green Industry Pro (July 2011)*
Pub: Cygnus Business Media
Ed: Gregg Wartgow. **Description:** Several landscape contractors have joined this publication's Working Smarter Training Challenge over the last year. This process is helping them develop ways to improve work processes, boost morale, drive out waste, reduce costs, improve customer service, and be more competitive.

13478 ■ *"Gain the 'Come Alive Outside' Selling Edge"* in *Green Industry Pro (July 2011)*
Pub: Cygnus Business Media
Ed: Jim Paluch. **Description:** Marketing the 'Come Alive Outside' slogan can help landscapers to increase their market share by identifying and applying these elements to each customer as well as their workers.

13479 ■ *"The Green Industry Jobs Gap"* in *Green Industry Pro (Vol. 23, October 2011)*
Pub: Cygnus Business Media
Ed: Gregg Wartgow. **Description:** According to the U.S. Bureau of Labor Statistics, the landscaping industry employs over 829,000 workers. According to another private study, the industry would employ more if they were able to find more people interested in performing the required work.

13480 ■ *"Hey, You Can't Do That"* in *Green Industry Pro (Vol. 23, September 2011)*
Pub: Cygnus Business Media
Ed: Rod Dickens. **Description:** Manufacturers of landscape equipment are making better use of energy resources, such as the use of fuel-injection systems instead of carburetors, lightweight materials, better lubricants, advanced battery technology, and innovative engine designs.

13481 ■ *"How to Dominate in Residential Maintenance"* in *Green Industry Pro (Vol. 23, October 2011)*
Pub: Cygnus Business Media
Ed: Gregg Wartgow. **Description:** Lawn care services were ranked among the most expendable consumer expenditures, according to the National Retail Federation data accumulated in early 2011. This makes it critical for any landscape firm to target sales efforts toward higher-income households and higher-value homes.

13482 ■ *"How To Turn Your Efforts Into Results" in Green Industry Pro (Vol. 23, September 2011)*
Pub: Cygnus Business Media
Ed: Bob Coulter. **Description:** Working Smarter Training Challenge teaches that leaders are able to carry out solutions directly into their organization, develop skills and drive business results in key areas by creating a culture of energized workers who are able to take ownership of their performance as well as the performance of the company as a whole.

13483 ■ *"Labor of Love" in Green Industry Pro (Vol. 23, March 2011, No. 3, pp. 14)*
Pub: Cygnus Business Media
Ed: Gregg Wartgow. **Description:** Profile of CLS Landscape Management in Chino, California and its owner who started the company when he was 21 years old. Kevin Davis built his landscape firm into a $20 million a year business without using any dedicated salesperson.

13484 ■ *"The Price of Profitability" in Green Industry Pro (Vol. 23, March 2011, No. 3, pp. 18)*
Pub: Cygnus Business Media
Ed: Tony Bass. **Description:** Profit Builder Process is used to help landscaping companies be more competitive. Landscape contractors report pricing among their largest challenges and although the economy is improving, homeowners are paying closer attention to quality and service.

13485 ■ *"Rediscovering the Land of Opportunity" in Green Industry Pro (July 2011)*
Pub: Cygnus Business Media
Ed: Gregg Wartgow. **Description:** Landscape contractors need to discover new strategies that will generate leads and convert those leads into sales.

13486 ■ *"Take Control of Your Company's Finances" in Green Industry Pro (Vol. 23, March 2011, No. 3, pp. 24)*
Pub: Cygnus Business Media
Ed: Gregg Wartgow. **Description:** Understanding that when certain leading indicators that affect the outcome of certain lagging indicators are aligned, companies will be able to take control of their firm's finances. Ways to improve the processes that drive financial performance for landscape firms are outlined.

13487 ■ *"Take This Job and Love It" in Green Industry Pro (Vol. 23, October 2011)*
Pub: Cygnus Business Media
Ed: Gregg Wartgow. **Description:** Details of the lawsuit filed by the Professional Landcare Network (PLANET) against the U.S. Department of Labor are explained. Challenges faced by landscape firms because of employment costs are outlined. Statistical data included.

13488 ■ *"Time to Fight Back" in Green Industry Pro (Vol. 23, March 2011, No. 3, pp. 8)*
Pub: Cygnus Business Media
Ed: Rod Dickens. **Description:** Lawn care operators in the United States must learn from Canada that a shift to socialism will impact their industry in a negative way. Government regulation over the application of control products regarding environmental health in Canada has been a death sentence for small lawn care businesses.

13489 ■ *"Way More Than Mowing" in Green Industry Pro (Vol. 23, September 2011)*
Pub: Cygnus Business Media
Ed: Rod Dickens. **Description:** Shipp Shape Lawn Services located in Sylvester, Georgia now offers aeration, fertilizing and weed control, mulching, yard renovation, flowerbed maintenance, landscaping, as well as irrigation repairs and installation in order to diversify the business and stay competitive.

SOURCES OF SUPPLY

13490 ■ *Yard & Garden*
Cygnus Business Media
Contact: Rich Reiff, President
URL(s): www.greenindustrypros.com/magazine/yg/ current-issuewww.cygnusb2b.com/PropertyPub.cfm-

?PropertyID=564. **Ed:** Robert Warde. **Released:** Irregular; Latest edition October 2010. **Publication includes:** Lists of about 33,000 dealers, retailers, and distributors of lawn and garden power equipment. **Entries include:** Product name, description and photograph, name and address of distributor or manufacturer. **Arrangement:** Classified by type of product.

TRADE PERIODICALS

13491 ■ *The Avant Gardener*
Pub: Horticultural Data Processors
Ed: Thomas Powell, Editor. **Released:** Monthly. **Price:** $24 year. **Description:** Contains information on such subjects as indoor and outdoor plants, edible plants, new products, methods of cultivation, breeding and growing techniques, pest control, fertilizers, and landscaping. Recurring features include several special issues per year on specific topics.

13492 ■ *Landscape Management*
Contact: Marisa Palmieri, Editor
E-mail: mpalmieri@northcoastmedia.net
URL(s): www.landscapemanagement.net/landscape/.
Ed: Marisa Palmieri. **Released:** 12/yr. **Price:** $46, Individuals domestic; $69, Canada and Mexico; $89, Other countries.

13493 ■ *Lawn & Landscape Magazine*
Pub: G.I.E. Media, MC
Contact: Chris Foster, President
E-mail: chris.foster@gie.net
URL(s): www.lawnandlandscape.com. **Ed:** Chuck Bowen. **Released:** Monthly **Price:** $15, U.S., Canada, and Mexico; $35, Individuals; $100, Other countries South America/Europe.

13494 ■ *Pro: Business Strategies for Landscape Contractors*
Pub: Cygnus Business Media
Contact: Rich Reiff, President
URL(s): www.greenindustrypros.com/magazine/pro/ issue/2012/augwww.cygnusb2b.com/PropertyPub. cfm?PropertyID=571. **Released:** 9/yr.

VIDEOCASSETTES/ AUDIOCASSETTES

13495 ■ *The Home Gardener*
RMI Media
1365 N. Winchester St.
Olathe, KS 66061-5880
Ph: (913)768-1696
Free: 800-745-5480
Fax: (800)755-6910
Co. E-mail: actmedia@act.org
URL: http://www.actmedia.com
Released: 1987. **Description:** A series that provides basic instruction in ornamental horticulture. **Availability:** VHS; 3/4 U.

13496 ■ *The Home Gardener, Revised Edition*
Coast Telecourses
11460 Warner Ave.
Fountain Valley, CA 92708-2597
Ph: (714)241-6109
Free: 800-547-4748
Fax: (714)241-6286
Co. E-mail: coastlearning@coastline.edu
URL: http://www.coastlearning.org
Released: 1976. **Description:** A series about the fundamentals of indoor and outdoor gardening, planting for patios and balconies, gardening in containers, and simple landscaping. **Availability:** VHS; 3/4 U; Q.

13497 ■ *Landscape Equipment Safety for the 90s*
American Nurseryman Publishing Co.
223 W Jackson Blvd., Ste. 500
Chicago, IL 60606-6904
Ph: (312)427-7339
Free: 800-621-5727

Fax: (312)427-7346
Co. E-mail: admin@amerinursery.com
URL: http://www.amerinursery.com/
Released: 1991. **Price:** $64.99. **Description:** Series of programs updating OSHA information and federal regulations for landscape equipment use. **Availability:** VHS.

13498 ■ *Landscape Tools: Use and Safety*
American Nurseryman Publishing Co.
223 W Jackson Blvd., Ste. 500
Chicago, IL 60606-6904
Ph: (312)427-7339
Free: 800-621-5727
Fax: (312)427-7346
Co. E-mail: admin@amerinursery.com
URL: http://www.amerinursery.com/
Released: 1989. **Price:** $94.99. **Description:** Demonstrates the proper use of 12 landscape tools, emphasizing safety rules. **Availability:** VHS.

13499 ■ *Lawn Care for the North American Gardener*
Film Ideas, Inc.
308 N. Wolf Rd.
Wheeling, IL 60090
Ph: (874)419-0255
Free: 800-475-3456
Fax: (874)419-8933
Co. E-mail: info@filmideas.com
URL: http://www.filmideas.com
Released: 1992. **Price:** $89.00. **Description:** Provides simple prescriptions that will help make your lawn green and healthy. **Availability:** VHS.

13500 ■ *Lawn and Garden*
RMI Media
1365 N. Winchester St.
Olathe, KS 66061-5880
Ph: (913)768-1696
Free: 800-745-5480
Fax: (800)755-6910
Co. E-mail: actmedia@act.org
URL: http://www.actmedia.com
Released: 1987. **Description:** This instructional series takes the viewer from basic to advanced gardening. **Availability:** VHS; 3/4 U.

13501 ■ *Lawns: Planting and Maintenance*
RMI Media
1365 N. Winchester St.
Olathe, KS 66061-5880
Ph: (913)768-1696
Free: 800-745-5480
Fax: (800)755-6910
Co. E-mail: actmedia@act.org
URL: http://www.actmedia.com
Released: 1980. **Description:** The topics of this program on how to seed a lawn and then how to maintain it include: liming and moss control, raking, thatching, mowing and trimming. **Availability:** VHS; 3/4 U; Special order formats.

TRADE SHOWS AND CONVENTIONS

13502 ■ **Builders St. Charles Home Show**
Home Builders Association of Greater St. Louis
10104 Old Olive St. Rd.
St. Louis, MO 63141
Ph: (314)994-7700
Fax: (314)432-7185
URL: http://www.stlhba.com
Contact: Patrick Sullivan, Executive Vice President
E-mail: sullivap@hbastl.com
URL(s): www.stlhomeshow.com/stcharles. **Price:** $9, Onsite adults; $4, children 6-12; children 5 and under free. **Frequency:** Annual. **Audience:** General public and construction industry. **Principal Exhibits:** Home remodeling equipment and supplies, lawn and garden equipment, swimming pools, home furnishings, model homes and kitchen and bath. **Dates and Locations:** , America's Center & Edward Jones Dome.

13503 ■ **Green Industry and Equipment Expo**
PLANET, The Professional Landcare Network
950 Herndon Parkway, Ste. 450
Herndon, VA 20170

Ph: (703)736-9666
Free: 800-395-2522
Fax: (703)736-9668
Co. E-mail: info@landcarenetwork.org
URL: http://www.landcarenetwork.org
Contact: Gerald J. Grossi, President
E-mail: jerry@arborlawn.com
URL(s): www.gie-expo.com/gieexpo/. **Frequency:** Annual. **Audience:** Lawn care professionals, landscape contractors, grounds managers. **Principal Exhibits:** Lawn care equipment, supplies, and services, including fertilizers, weed control materials, insurance information, and power equipment.

CONSULTANTS

13504 ■ All Seasons Tree Service Inc.
998 New Loudon Rd.
Latham, NY 12110
Ph: (518)783-7363
Fax: (518)783-8937
Co. E-mail: info@allseasonstree.com
URL: http://www.allseasonstree.com
Contact: Richard C. Johnson, President
E-mail: treeguy333@aol.com
Scope: Offers counsel on the development of tree care and lawn care programs for maintenance as well as on damage appraisals for trees and shrubs. **Founded:** 1976. **Seminars:** All Seasons Lawn Care Program; All Seasons Organic Lawn Care Program.

13505 ■ Richard L. Baldwin, Horticultural Consultant
215 Virginia Dr.
Ventura, CA 93003
Ph: (805)643-8406
Scope: Provider of diagnosis of plant disorders and management, construction and maintenance recommendations for horticulture, including playing fields. Also offers arboriculture consultation, including hazardous conditions, evaluation of loss, and related landscape research. Services include consultation on production of ornamental plants, including turf grass and management of landscape plants. **Founded:** 1983. **Seminars:** Pruning Fruit Trees; Propagation of Fruit Trees; Diagnosing Plant Disorders; Pest Control on Ornamental Plants; Turf grass Fertilization.

13506 ■ The Caretakers Inc.
5657 W Maple Rd.
West Bloomfield, MI 48322
Ph: (248)626-3300
Contact: Thomas Mann, President
Scope: Landscape maintenance consulting services to establish level and quality of exterior grounds maintenance for commercial, industrial, condominium and town home clients. Includes screening of prospective qualified contractors to perform various grounds maintenance services including, but not restricted to the following: lawn mowing, tree and shrub, fertilization, weed control, pruning and snow removal and control. Also assists with selection of both equipment and personnel. Industries served: Commercial and industrial, property owners, developers of high grade corporate headquarters, multitenant and single tenant commercial and industrial properties and business parks as well as government agencies. **Founded:** 2003. **Seminars:** Selection of the Right Landscape Management Contractor.

13507 ■ Dinsmore Tree & Landscape Service
113 Stoneyside Ln.
Saint Louis, MO 63132-4123
Ph: (314)991-0796
Contact: Lewis E. Dinsmore, Owner
Scope: Offers outdoor environmental consulting including plant maintenance programs, landscaping and pre-construction planning where trees involved, plant appraisal and evaluation for insurance, tax and legal implications. **Founded:** 1932.

13508 ■ Forest City Tree Protection Company Inc.
1884 S Green Rd.
South Euclid, OH 44121-4246
Ph: (216)381-1700
Free: 800-332-8733

Fax: (216)381-1894
Co. E-mail: forestcitytree@hotmail.com
URL: http://www.forestcitytree.com
Contact: Lauren S. Lanphear, President
E-mail: lauren@lanphearsupply.com
Scope: Provider of complete tree care/arboricultural services to home owners and commercial establishments. Work includes: Diagnosis, appraisals, planting recommendations, small and large tree planting, insect and disease management, fertilizing, pruning, removals, cabling and bracing. Serves private industries as well as government agencies. **Founded:** 1910. **Seminars:** Evaluating Trees and Damage to Trees, 1987; Tree Fertilization, 1987; Knots, Ropes and Rigging, 1987; Tree Appraisal, 1985; Trees, People and the Law, 1985. **Special Services:** Lanphear Supply®.

13509 ■ Forman & Biller Tree Expert Co.
856 N Harrison St.
Arlington, VA 22205-1229
Ph: (703)522-3141
Contact: James E. Biller, Owner
Scope: Consulting arbores providing tree care for residential and commercial properties. **Founded:** 1977.

13510 ■ North Haven Gardens Inc.
7700 Northaven Rd.
Dallas, TX 75230
Ph: (214)363-5316
Fax: (214)360-1555
Co. E-mail: plantquestion@nhg.com
URL: http://www.nhg.com
Contact: Jon Pinkus, Director
E-mail: jpinkus@nhg.com
Scope: Landscape architects offering the following services: Exterior landscape maintenance; interior scape and maintenance; design consultation; budgeting, cost estimates and scheduling; master plans; construction drawings, documents and specifications; bid packages; contract administration; garden decorations. Serves both public and private sectors. **Founded:** 1951. **Seminars:** Gardening 101, Jan, 2008.

13511 ■ Plantscape Inc.
3101 Liberty Ave.
Pittsburgh, PA 15201-1415
Ph: (412)281-6352
Free: 800-303-1380
Fax: (412)281-4775
Co. E-mail: info@plantescape.com
URL: http://www.plantescape.com
Contact: Carole Horowitz, President
Scope: Provider of interior and exterior landscape services to the Pittsburgh business commercial market. **Founded:** 1973.

13512 ■ Fred J. Robinson & Associates Inc.
7680 Eillie Pl.
Mentor, OH 44060-7154
Ph: (440)255-4471
Fax: (440)255-4822
Contact: Fred J. Robinson, Owner
E-mail: fjrtree@lightstream.net
Scope: Provider of information concerning trees: health, appraised value, pest management and both care and preservation. Consults with architects, landscape architects, attorneys, insurance adjusters, government agencies and engineers in addition to tree owners. **Founded:** 1989.

13513 ■ TruGreen LandCare
951 N Ridge Ave.
Lombard, IL 60148
Ph: (630)629-9660
Free: 877-526-3227
Contact: Rodney L. Bailey, President
Scope: Landscape management company providing full service grounds care programs. Also provides consulting services to clients, landscape architects, building and property managers, and developers on contract and specification development, as well as design related consultation regarding long range cost impacts of various landscape design features. Also consulting on water management programs. Industries served building property and facilities management. **Founded:** 1968.

13514 ■ Western Arborists Inc.
502 W Rte. 66, Ste. 20
Glendora, CA 91740-4370
Ph: (626)963-1171
Fax: (626)963-8243
Contact: James W. Walker, President
Scope: Offers consulting on tree disease and insect problems. Also provides appraisal services covering damage or value of trees lost. **Founded:** 2002.

13515 ■ W.S. Moore Consulting—Moore New Homeowners
1200 Brighton Ave.
Berkeley, CA 94709
Ph: (510)524-1163
Free: 800-359-3435
Fax: (510)524-8085
Co. E-mail: mooreconsult@earthlink.net
URL: http://www.moorenewhomeowners.com
Contact: Dr. Wayne S. Moore, President
URL(s): www.nurserymarketingservices.com. **Scope:** Delivers key new customers into retail nurseries and garden centers. Providing you with a professionally designed, beautiful full-color "Welcome Card" personalized and mailed to each new homeowner, with first class postage for maximum impact. Active in the marketing of horticulture and gardening-related products, including pest-control products. **Founded:** 1982. **Telecommunication Services:** info@nurserymarketingservices.com.

FRANCHISES AND BUSINESS OPPORTUNITIES

13516 ■ Clean Cut Lawn and Garden Services
24701 108th Ave.
Maple Ridge, BC, Canada V2W 1G7
Ph: (604)467-9273
Free: 866-974-7277
Fax: (604)466-2892
Co. E-mail: kelly@cleancutcanada.com
URL: http://www.cleancutcanada.com
Description: Lawn and garden service. **No. of Company-Owned Units:** 1. **Founded:** 2006.. **Franchised:** 2006. **Equity Capital Needed:** $38,500. **Franchise Fee:** $10,000. **Royalty Fee:** 5%. **Training:** Provides 5 days hands on training and ongoing support.

13517 ■ Clintar Groundskeeping Services
Truserve Groundcare Inc.
70 Esna Park Dr., Unit 1
Markham, ON, Canada L3R 1E3
Ph: (905)943-9530
Free: 800-361-3542
Fax: (905)943-9529
Co. E-mail: info@clintar.com
URL: http://www.clintar.com
Description: Grounds keeping services including landscape maintenance, snow and ice control, power sweeping, light construction, tree care and irrigation maintenance. **No. of Franchise Units:** 21. **Founded:** 1973.. **Franchised:** 1984. **Equity Capital Needed:** $100,000-$125,000; $50,000-$60,000 cash. **Franchise Fee:** $40,000. **Training:** Yes.

13518 ■ Environmental Factor Inc.
85 Chambers Dr., Unit 8
Ajax, ON, Canada L1Z 1E2
Ph: (905)686-9909
Free: 888-820-9992
Fax: (905)686-0357
Co. E-mail: info@environmentalfctor.com
URL: http://www.environmentalfactor.com
Description: Non-chemical lawn care company. **No. of Franchise Units:** 7. **No. of Company-Owned Units:** 1. **Founded:** 1991.. **Franchised:** 2001. **Equity Capital Needed:** $30,000-$40,000. **Franchise Fee:** $20,000. **Training:** Initial and ongoing one on one training.

13519 ■ Jim's Mowing Canada Inc.
1515 Pemberton Ave., Ste. 105
North Vancouver, BC, Canada V7P 2S3
Ph: (604)990-0714

Fax: (604)990-0724
Co. E-mail: info@jimsmowing.ca
URL: http://www.jimsmowing.ca
Description: Lawn and garden franchise. **No. of Franchise Units:** 2,500 plus. **Founded:** 1989.. **Equity Capital Needed:** $35,000. **Franchise Fee:** $490.00/month. **Training:** Training and ongoing support provided.

13520 ■ Lawn Doctor, Inc.
142 State Rte. 34
Holmdel, NJ 07733
Ph: (866)529-6362
Fax: (732)946-0002
Co. E-mail: franchiseinformation@lawndoctor.com
URL: http://www.lawndoctor.com
Description: Automated lawn-care service, all-natural and regular fertilizer. **No. of Franchise Units:** 460. **Founded:** 1967.. **Franchised:** 1967. **Equity Capital Needed:** $65,000-$80,000 initial investment; $27,000-$40,000 liquid capital required. **Franchise Fee:** $25,000. **Financial Assistance:** Yes. **Training:** Field and classroom intensive training program.

13521 ■ Naturalawn of America
Franchise Department
1 E Church St.
Frederick, MD 21701
Ph: (800)989-5444
Fax: (301)846-0320
Description: Franchises organic-based lawn care services. **No. of Franchise Units:** 61. **No. of Company-Owned Units:** 5. **Founded:** 1986.. **Franchised:** 1989. **Equity Capital Needed:** Ability to secure a credit line of $150,000 and have a minimum net worth of $250,000. **Franchise Fee:** $29,500. **Financial Assistance:** Yes. **Training:** No.

13522 ■ NiteLites Outdoor Lighting Franchise
NiteLites Franchise Systems, Inc.
6107 Market Ave.
Franklin, OH 45005
Ph: (513)425-5510
Free: 866-648-3548
Fax: (513)433-0242
Description: Outdoor/landscape lighting professionals. **No. of Franchise Units:** 33. **No. of Company-Owned Units:** 6. **Founded:** 1988.. **Franchised:** 2004. **Equity Capital Needed:** $75,000; minimum net worth $300,000. **Franchise Fee:** $84,000-$165,000. **Training:** Yes.

13523 ■ Nutri-Lawn
2077 Dundas St. E, Ste. 202
Mississauga, ON, Canada L4X 1M2
Ph: (416)525-4998
Free: 800-396-6096
Co. E-mail: jlavin@nutrilawn.com
URL: http://www.franchisedirectory.ca
URL(s): www.nutrilawn.com. **Description:** Ecology friendly lawn care. **No. of Franchise Units:** 2. **No. of Company-Owned Units:** 1. **Equity Capital Needed:** $80,000-$90,000 start-up investment, including franchise fee. **Franchise Fee:** $28,000. **Training:** Provides 1 week initial training, onsite for 1 week and ongoing support.

13524 ■ Scotts Lawn Service
E.G. Systems, Inc.
14111 Scottslawn Rd.
Marysville, OH 43041
Free: 800-264-8973

Fax: (937)644-7422
Description: Residential and commercial lawn care. **No. of Franchise Units:** 85. **No. of Company-Owned Units:** 86. **Founded:** 1984.. **Franchised:** 1985. **Equity Capital Needed:** $84,400-$299,500. **Franchise Fee:** $25,000-$105,000. **Royalty Fee:** 6-10%. **Financial Assistance:** Limited in-house financing available. **Training:** Offers 1 week at headquarters, 1 week at franchisee's location, annual business/operations training with ongoing training as needed.

13525 ■ Spectrum Home Services
SHS Franchising
9690 S 300 W, Ste 320 G-H
Sandy, UT 84070
Ph: (801)957-5671
Free: 800-496-5993
Fax: (801)957-5291
Co. E-mail: spectrumhomeserv@qwest.net
URL: http://www.spectrumhomeservice.com
Description: Full service senior care. Multiple profit centers such as homemaking, personal care, maintenance, yard care and relocation services increase your bottom line. **No. of Franchise Units:** 35. **Founded:** 2000.. **Franchised:** 2004. **Equity Capital Needed:** $66,380-$104,433. **Franchise Fee:** $36,000. **Training:** Includes 1 week training at headquarters and 1 week at franchisee's location with ongoing support.

13526 ■ Spring-Green Lawn Care Corp.
11909 Spaulding School Dr.
Plainfield, IL 60544
Free: 800-777-8608
Fax: (815)436-9056
URL: http://www.spring-green.com
Description: National network of lawn and tree care businesses. **No. of Franchise Units:** 126. **No. of Company-Owned Units:** 5. **Founded:** 1977.. **Franchised:** 1977. **Equity Capital Needed:** $60,000 or $125,000. **Franchise Fee:** $30,000-$40,000 or $60,000-$80,000. **Financial Assistance:** Yes. **Training:** Initial training at headquarters covering areas of marketing, operations and computer system Besides, on-going training is offered through field visits, regional meetings, professional development programs, intranet, website, telephone and newsletters.

13527 ■ Turf Logic Inc.
92 Caplan Ave. Ste. 241
Barrie, ON, Canada L4N 0Z7
Ph: (705)812-1363
Free: 866-239-4056
Fax: (705)733-0090
Co. E-mail: franchisesales@turflogic.ca
URL: http://www.turflogic.ca
Description: An opportunity to get involved in pesticide-free lawn care, the fastest growing sector of the green trades industry. With several years of professional turf experience, Turf Logic provides you with proven programs, exclusive products and high-tech equipment in a protected territory. **No. of Franchise Units:** 8. **Founded:** 2004.. **Franchised:** 2005. **Equity Capital Needed:** $50,000. **Franchise Fee:** $25,000. **Training:** Provides 2 weeks training.

13528 ■ Weed Man - USA
Turf Holdings, Inc.
1129 Wentworth St., Unit B3
Oshawa, ON, Canada L1J 8P7
Ph: (905)579-4000

Fax: (905)579-5772
URL: http://www.weed-man.com
Description: Residential lawn care services. **No. of Franchise Units:** 399. **Founded:** 1970.. **Franchised:** 1976. **Equity Capital Needed:** $65,980-$82,940. **Franchise Fee:** $20,000-$34,000. **Financial Assistance:** Yes. **Training:** Yes.

RESEARCH CENTERS

13529 ■ Kansas State University - John C. Pair Horticultural Center
1901 E 95th St. S
Haysville, KS 67060-8351
Ph: (316)788-0492
Fax: (316)788-3844
Co. E-mail: jgriffin@oznet.ksu.edu
URL: http://www.oznet.ksu.edu/rc_hefw
Contact: Dr. Jason J. Griffin, Director
Founded: 1970. **Publications:** *John C. Pair Horticultural Center Newsletter* (Semiannual). **Educational Activities:** Group tours (Periodic); Open House (Annual); Ornamental Field Day; Vegetable Twilight Tour. **Awards:** John C. Pair Horticultural Center Internships. **Telecommunication Services:** hrc@lists.oznet.ksu.edu.

13530 ■ North Carolina Department of Agriculture and Consumer Services - Sandhills Research Station (SRS)
2148 Windblow Rd.
Jackson Springs, NC 27281-9124
Ph: (910)974-4673
Fax: (910)974-4462
Co. E-mail: sandhills.resst@ncagr.gov
URL: http://www.ncagr.gov/Research/srs.htm
Contact: Jeff Chandler, Manager, Operations
Founded: 1951. **Educational Activities:** Peach Field Day; Small Fruits Field Day (Biennial), focuses on research related to strawberries, brambles and blueberries; Turfgrass Field Day (Biennial), to promote turfgrass management.

13531 ■ University of Arizona - Karsten Turfgrass Research Facility
2101 E Roger Rd.
Tucson, AZ 85719
Ph: (520)318-7142
Fax: (520)621-7186
Co. E-mail: dkopec@cals.arizona.edu
URL: http://turf.arizona.edu/karsten.htm
Services: Troubleshooting and consulting. **Founded:** 1991. **Publications:** *Annual Turfgrass and Ornamentals Research Summary*. **Educational Activities:** Turfgrass field day; Conferences, trade shows, seminars, workshops, and educational programs.

13532 ■ University of Guelph - Guelph Turfgrass Institute (GTI)
328 Victoria Rd. S
Guelph, ON, Canada N1L 0H2
Ph: (519)767-5009
Fax: (519)766-1704
Co. E-mail: robwith@uoguelph.ca
URL: http://www.guelphturfgrass.ca
Contact: Prof. Rob Witherspoon, Director
Services: Consulting: through the Institute and through Ontario Ministry of Agriculture and Food. **Founded:** 1987. **Publications:** *Annual Research Report; GTI advisor* (Biweekly). **Educational Activities:** GTI Research Field Day (Biennial), in August; Ontario Turfgrass Symposium (Annual), in February; Turf Managers Course (Annual), in February; Independent study correspondence courses; short courses, workshops and seminars. **Awards:** Monsanto Turfgrass Research Scholarship. **Telecommunication Services:** gti@uoguelph.ca.

ASSOCIATIONS AND OTHER ORGANIZATIONS

13533 ■ National Limousine Association (NLA)
49 S Maple Ave.
Marlton, NJ 08053
Ph: (856)596-3344
Free: 800-652-7007
Fax: (856)596-2145
Co. E-mail: patricia.nelson@limo.org
URL: http://www.limo.org
Contact: Ms. Patricia A. Nelson, Executive Director

URL(s): www.nlaride.com. **Description:** Limousine owners and operators; limousine manufacturers and suppliers to the industry. Seeks to: promote and advance industry professionalism and the common interests of members; increase use of chauffeured transportation in both business and public sectors. Monitors legislation and organizes lobbying activities. Sponsors seminars on safety/regulatory issues and management techniques. **Founded:** 1985. **Telecommunication Services:** info@limo.org.

REFERENCE WORKS

13534 ■ "21st Century Filling Station" in Austin Business JournalInc. (Vol. 29, December 11, 2009, No. 40, pp. 1)
Pub: American City Business Journals

Ed: Jacob Dirr. **Description:** Clean Energy Fuels Corporation announced plans for the construction of a $1 million, 17,000 square foot compressed natural gas fueling station at or near the Austin-Bergstrom International Airport (ABIA). Clean Energy Fuels hopes to encourage cab and shuttle companies in the ABIA to switch from gasoline to natural gas.

13535 ■ "Business Start-Up a Learning Experience for Young Bellingham Entrepreneur" in Bellingham Herald (July 18, 2010)
Pub: Bellingham Herald

Ed: Dave Gallagher. **Description:** Profile of 21-year-old entrepreneur, Chase Larabee, who developed an online program that helps airport fixed-based operators handle refueling, hotel and transportation reservations and other requests from private airplane pilots.

13536 ■ "Capital Metro May Soon Seek Contractor to Replace Star Tran" in Austin Business Journal (Vol. 31, June 10, 2011, No. 14, pp. 1)
Pub: American City Business Journals Inc.

Ed: Vicky Garza. **Description:** Capital Metropolitan Transportation Authority may be forced to contract out its bus services provided by StarTran Inc. as early as September 2012 following legislation approved by the Texas legislature. The bill originates in a report by the Sunset Advisory Commission. Details are included.

13537 ■ "Funkhouser Wants Region to Get On Board Light Rail" in Business Journal-Serving Metropolitan Kansas City (November 30, 2007)
Pub: American City Business Journals, Inc.

Ed: Suzanna Stagemeyer. **Description:** Mark Funhouser, Mayor of Kansas City, is planning to construct a regional multimodal public transit system. A previous light rail plan was rescinded due to logistical, financial and legal problems. Details of the light transit plans are discussed.

13538 ■ How to Start a Home-Based Senior Care Business: Check-in-Care, Transportation Services, Shopping and Cooking
Pub: Globe Pequot Press

Ed: James L. Ferry. **Released:** January 1, 2010. **Price:** $18.95. **Description:** Information is provided to start a home-based senior care business.

13539 ■ "MV Transportation Winds $133M Contract" in Black Enterprise (Vol. 38, November 2007, No. 4, pp. 30)
Pub: Earl G. Graves Publishing Co. Inc.

Ed: Marcia A. Wade. **Description:** MV Transportation won a $133 million contract to operate 139 fixed-route buses in the San Gabriel and Pomona valley areas of California.

13540 ■ "Professional Help: Cross That Off Your To-Do List" in Inc. (November 2007, pp. 89-90, 92)
Pub: Gruner & Jahr USA Publishing

Ed: Alison Stein Wellner. **Description:** Small business owners are finding that it pays to hire someone to takeover the personal tasks of daily living, including hiring a personal assistant, chauffeur, chef, stylist, pet caregiver, or concierge service.

13541 ■ "Taxis Are Set to Go Hybrid" in Philadelphia Business Journal (Vol. 30, September 16, 2011, No. 31, pp. 1)
Pub: American City Business Journals Inc.

Ed: Natalie Kostelni. **Description:** Taxis are going hybrid in several major states such as New York, California and Maryland where it is mandated, but it is yet to happen in Philadelphia, Pennsylvania with the exception of one taxi company. Freedom Taxi is awaiting Philadelphia Parking Authority's sign off.

STATISTICAL SOURCES

13542 ■ RMA Annual Statement Studies
Pub: Risk Management Association
Contact: Kevin M. Blakey, President

Released: Annual. **Price:** $175.00 2006-07 edition, $105.00. **Description:** Contains composite balance sheets and income statements for more than 360 industries, including the accounting, auditing, and bookkeeping industries. Also contains five years of comparative historical data for discerning trends. Includes 16 commonly used ratios, computed for most of the size groupings for nearly every industry.

TRADE PERIODICALS

13543 ■ In the Driver's Seat
Pub: Ontario Safety League

Ed: Terry Thompson, Editor. **Released:** Monthly. **Price:** Included in membership. **Description:** Commercial driver safety newsletter.

13544 ■ LCT
Pub: Bobit Business Media
Contact: Ty Bobit, President

URL(s): www.lctmag.com. **Ed:** Martin Romjue. **Released:** Monthly **Price:** $24, Individuals.

LIBRARIES

13545 ■ Alabama Department of Transportation - Research & Development Bureau - Research Library
1409 Coliseum Blvd.
Montgomery, AL 36110
Ph: (334)253-6940
Fax: (334)264-2042
Co. E-mail: brownje@dot.state.al.us
URL: http://www.dot.state.al.us/rdweb/Index.htm
Contact: Jeffrey W. Brown

Scope: Transportation. **Services:** Interlibrary loan; Library not open to the public. **Founded:** 1953. **Holdings:** 1000 books; 5000 reports. **Subscriptions:** 8 journals and other serials.

13546 ■ California State Department of Motor Vehicles - Licensing Operations Division - Research and Development Branch - Traffic Safety Research Library
2415 1st Ave., MS F-126
Sacramento, CA 95818
Ph: (916)657-3079
Free: 800-368-4327
Fax: (916)657-8589
Co. E-mail: dluong@dvm.ca.gov
Contact: Douglas Luong, Analyst

Scope: Automobile transportation. **Services:** Copying; library not open to the public. **Holdings:** 500 books; 10,000 bound periodical volumes; reports; manuscripts. **Subscriptions:** 20 journals and other serials.

13547 ■ ConnDOT Library and Information Center
2800 Berlin Tpke.
Newington, CT 06111-4116
Ph: (860)594-2000
Fax: (860)594-3039
Co. E-mail: drew.coleman@ct.gov
URL: http://www.ct.gov/dot/site/default.asp
Contact: Betty Ambler, Librarian

Scope: Transportation. **Services:** Interlibrary loan; copying; library open to the public by appointment. **Founded:** 1983. **Holdings:** 10,000 books; 10,000 reports; videos.

13548 ■ Kansas Department of Transportation Library—KDOT Library.
700 SW Harrison St.
Eisenhower State Office Bldg., 4th Fl. W.
Topeka, KS 66603-3745
Ph: (785)291-3854
Fax: (785)291-3717
Co. E-mail: library@ksdot.org
Contact: Marie Manthe, Librarian
Scope: Transportation. **Services:** Interlibrary loan; Library open to the public. **Founded:** 1963. **Holdings:** 3000 books; 20,000 reports; 175 CD-ROMs; 100 videos. **Subscriptions:** 100 journals and other serials.

13549 ■ Kentucky Transportation Center Library
University of Kentucky
176 Raymond Bldg.
Lexington, KY 40506-0281
Ph: (859)257-2155
Free: 800-432-0719
Fax: (859)257-1815
Co. E-mail: lwhayne@engr.uky.edu
URL: http://www.kyt2.com/
Contact: Laura Whayne, Librarian
Scope: Transportation. **Services:** Interlibrary loan; copying; Library open to the public. **Founded:** 1980. **Holdings:** 6000 books; 9000 reports; 800 videotapes. **Subscriptions:** 300 journals and other serials. **Telecommunication Services:** vbrock@engr.uky.edu.

13550 ■ Missouri Highway and Transportation Department - Division of Materials Library
105 W. Capitol Ave.
Jefferson City, MO 65102-0270
Ph: (573)751-6735
Free: 888-275 6636
Fax: (573)526-5636
Co. E-mail: michael.meyerhoff@mail.modot.state.mo.us
URL: http://www.modot.org/
Contact: Mona Scott
Scope: Transportation. **Services:** Library not open to the public. **Holdings:** Figures not available.

13551 ■ Montana Department of Transportation Library
2701 Prospect Ave.
Helena, MT 59620-1001
Ph: (406)444-6338
Free: 800-335-7592
Fax: (406)444-6204
Co. E-mail: ssillick@mt.gov
URL: http://www.mdt.mt.gov/research/unique/services.shtml
Contact: Susan Sillick
Scope: Transportation. **Services:** Interlibrary loan; copying. **Holdings:** 10,000 items; reports; CD-ROMs; video. **Subscriptions:** 10 journals and other serials. **Telecommunication Services:** mdtresearch@mt.gov.

13552 ■ New Jersey Department of Transportation Research Library
1035 Parkway Ave.
Trenton, NJ 08625-0600
Ph: (609)530-5289
Fax: (609)530-2052
Co. E-mail: library@dot.state.nj.us
URL: http://www.state.nj.us/transportation/refdata/library/
Contact: Carol Paszamant, Librarian
Scope: Transportation. **Services:** Interlibrary loan; copying; library open to the public by appointment. **Founded:** 1962. **Holdings:** 300 books; 11,000 reports. **Subscriptions:** 50 journals and other serials.

13553 ■ North Carolina Department of Transportation, Research and Development Library
PO Box 25201
Raleigh, NC 27611
Ph: (919)715-2463
Fax: (919)715-0137
Co. E-mail: rhhall@dot.state.nc.us
URL: http://www.ncdot.org/
Contact: Bob Hall
Scope: Transportation. **Services:** Interlibrary loan; copying; Library open to the public for reference use only. **Holdings:** 11,209 books; 20,021 reports; 132 videos. **Subscriptions:** 57 journals and other serials.

13554 ■ North Dakota Department of Transportation - Materials and Research Division Library
608 East Blvd.
Bismarck, ND 58505-0700
Ph: (701)328-2500
Free: 855-637-6237
Fax: (701)328-0310
Co. E-mail: gweisger@nd.gov
URL: http://www.dot.nd.gov
Contact: Gerri Weisgerber, Manager, Administration
Scope: Transportation. **Services:** Library not open to the public. **Founded:** 1970. **Holdings:** 6600 reports. **Subscriptions:** 5 journals and other serials.

13555 ■ South Carolina Department of Transportation Library
955 Park St., Rm. 110
Columbia, SC 29202
Ph: (803)737-9897
Free: 855-467-2368
Fax: (803)737-0824
Co. E-mail: adcockda@dot.state.sc.us
URL: http://www.dot.state.sc.us
Contact: Ann Adcock, Manager
Scope: Transportation, engineering, mass transit. **Services:** Interlibrary loan; transportation related research; library open to the public. **Founded:** 1998. **Holdings:** 5500 books; 90 bound periodical volumes; 1900 reports; 250 videos. **Subscriptions:** 41 journals and other serials; 10 newspapers. **Telecommunication Services:** SCDOT_contact@scdot.org.

13556 ■ Vermont Agency of Transportation, Policy and Planning Division Library
1 National Drive
c, VT 05633-0001
Ph: (802)828-3960
Fax: (802)828-3983
URL: http://www.aot.state.vt.us
Contact: Sandy Aja
Scope: Transportation. **Holdings:** Figures not available.

ASSOCIATIONS AND OTHER ORGANIZATIONS

13557 ■ **American Apparel and Footwear Association (AAFA)**
1601 N Kent St., 12 th Fl., Ste. 1200
Arlington, VA 22209
Ph: (703)524-1864
Free: 800-520-2262
Fax: (703)522-6741
Co. E-mail: info@apparelandfootwear.org
URL: http://www.apparelandfootwear.org
Contact: Kevin M. Burke, President
Description: Manufacturers of infants', children's, boys', girls', juniors', men's, and women's wearing apparel; associate members are suppliers of fabrics, equipment, accessories, and services to the apparel industry. Operates the Apparel Foundation; offers placement service through newsletter. Compiles statistics. **Founded:** 2000. **Publications:** *SoleSource: The footwear industry reservice directory* (Annual); *Technical Advisory Committee Bulletin* (Periodic); *SoleSource: The Footwear Industry Directory* (Annual); *AAFA Directory of Members and Associate Members* (Annual). **Educational Activities:** Bobbin Show (Annual); Global Leather (Annual). **Telecommunication Services:** pcarty@apparelandfootwear.org; mrust@apparelandfootwear.org; rmond@apparelandfootwear.org.

13558 ■ **Hosiery Association**
3623 Latrobe Dr., Suite 130
Charlotte, NC 28211-2117
Ph: (704)365-0913
Fax: (704)362-2056
Co. E-mail: thainfo@hosieryassociation.com
URL: http://www.hosieryassociation.com
Contact: Sally F. Kay, President
E-mail: sally.kay@hosieryassociation.com
Description: Hosiery manufacturers and suppliers. Develops standards for hosiery measurement. Sponsors annual "Celebrate Hosiery" to educate consumers on hosiery varieties. Conducts field visitations for assistance in technical areas. Compiles statistics; conducts research programs. Operates Group Purchasing Program. **Scope:** hosiery. **Publications:** *Hosiery News*; *Hosiery News* (Monthly); *THA Directory of Hosiery Mill Suppliers* (Periodic); *Hosiery News* (Monthly); *Directory of Hosiery Manufacturers, Distributors, and Suppliers* (Biennial); *NAHM's Directory of Hosiery Mill Suppliers* (Annual); *Industry Directory of Manufacturers, Marketers, Distributors, Suppliers* (Periodic); *THA Directory of Hosiery Manufacturers and Mill Suppliers* (Periodic). **Educational Activities:** International Hosiery Exposition (Quadrennial); International Hosiery Exposition.

13559 ■ **Intimate Apparel Square Club (IASC)**
326 Field Rd.
Clinton Corners, NY 12514
Ph: (845)758-5752
Fax: (845)758-2546
Co. E-mail: iasc@frontiernet.net
URL: http://thehugaward.org
Contact: Adam Masry, Secretary
Description: Members of the women's and children's intimate apparel industry. Works with other charity groups in the greater New York City area. Strives to "help those who cannot help themselves". Provides support to needy medical school students and makes contributions to children's organizations and rehabilitation clinics, primarily Rusk Institute. **Founded:** 1955. **Awards:** Al Jaffin Award (Annual).

REFERENCE WORKS

13560 ■ **"The Bottom Line" in Retail Merchandiser (Vol. 51, July-August 2011, No. 4, pp. 60)**
Pub: Phoenix Media Corporation
Description: Hanky Panky believes that comfort and style don't have to be mutually exclusive when designing their line of intimate apparel for women. The lingerie retailer was launched in 1977.

13561 ■ **"Pink Label: Victoria's Sales Secret" in Advertising Age (Vol. 79, July 7, 2008, No. 26, pp. 4)**
Pub: Crain Communications, Inc.
Ed: Natalie Zmuda. **Description:** Victoria Secret's Pink label accounted for roughly 17 percent of the retailer's total sales last year. The company is launching a Collegiate Collection which will be promoted by a campus tour program.

SOURCES OF SUPPLY

13562 ■ **Canadian Apparel Directory**
Canadian Apparel Federation
Contact: Bob Kirke, Executive Director
URL(s): www.apparel.ca. **Released:** Biennial; May/June. **Price:** $132, Members; $350, Nonmembers. **Publication includes:** Lists of Canadian industry suppliers, and manufacturers of apparel. **Entries include:** Company name, address, phone, fax, names and titles of key personnel, name and title of contact, product/service, description of company business activities. **Arrangement:** Alphabetical. **Indexes:** Trade name, product/service, geographical.

TRADE SHOWS AND CONVENTIONS

13563 ■ **Denver Apparel and Accessory Market**
Denver Merchandise Mart
451 E. 58th Ave., Ste. 4270
Denver, CO 80216-8470
Ph: (303)292-6278
Free: 800-289-6278
Fax: (303)297-8473
Co. E-mail: info@denvermart.com
URL: http://www.denvermart.com
URL(s): www.denvermart.com. **Frequency:** 5/year. **Audience:** Retailers of women's, children's, and men's apparel and accessories. **Principal Exhibits:** Women's, men's, and children's apparel and accessories. **Dates and Locations:** Merchandise Mart. **Telecommunication Services:** info@denvermart.com.

13564 ■ **Florida Fashion Focus Show**
Southern Apparel Exhibitors, Inc.
1856 Sheridan St.
Evanston, IL 60201
Ph: (847)475-1856
Free: 888-249-1377
Co. E-mail: info@saemiami.com.
URL: http://www.saemiami.com
Contact: John Harper, President
E-mail: harper@saemiami.com
URL(s): www.floridafashionfocus.com/. **Frequency:** 5/year. **Audience:** Trade buyers. **Principal Exhibits:** Ladies ready-to-wear clothing; handbags, jewelry, and accessories. Order-writing for future delivery. **Dates and Locations:** Merchandise Mart. **Telecommunication Services:** Info@FocusTradeshow.com.

13565 ■ **Women's and Children's Apparel and Accessories Mart**
Dallas Market Center Co.
2100 Stemmons Fwy.
Dallas, TX 75207
Ph: (214)655-6100
Free: 800-DAL-MKTS
Co. E-mail: lvillarreal@dmcmail.com
URL: http://www.dallasmarketcenter.com/
Audience: Apparel and accessories and home furnishings retailers. **Principal Exhibits:** Regional Merchandising Mart servicing department and specialty store buyers nationwide.

ASSOCIATIONS AND OTHER ORGANIZATIONS

13566 ■ American Beverage Licensees (ABL)
5101 River Rd., Ste. 108
Bethesda, MD 20816-1560
Ph: (301)656-1494
Free: 800-441-9894
Fax: (301)656-7539
Co. E-mail: bodnovich@ablusa.org
URL: http://www.ablusa.org
Contact: Chuck Ferrar, President
Description: Federation of associations of alcohol beverage retailers. **Founded:** 2002. **Publications:** *National Licensed Beverage Association--Members Directory.* **Educational Activities:** American Beverage Licensees Convention (Annual). **Awards:** Retailer of the Year Award (Annual); Top Shelf Award. **Telecommunication Services:** info@ablusa.org; nabr@nabronline.org.

13567 ■ National Association of Beverage Importers (NABI)
National Press Bldg.
529 14th St. NW, Ste. 1183
Washington, DC 20045
Ph: (202)393-6224
Fax: (202)393-6594
Co. E-mail: beverageimportersinfo@nabi-inc.org
URL: http://www.bevimporters.org
Contact: William T. Earle, President
Description: Represents importers of alcoholic beverages. Compiles and reports statistics from Bureau of Census and Internal Revenue sources. **Founded:** 1934. **Publications:** *Statistics and Member Letter* (Periodic).

13568 ■ National Beer Wholesalers Association (NBWA)
1101 King St., Ste. 600
Alexandria, VA 22314-2944
Ph: (703)683-4300
Free: 800-300-6417
Fax: (703)683-8965
Co. E-mail: info@nbwa.org
URL: http://www.nbwa.org
Contact: Steve Lytle, Chairman
Description: Independent wholesalers of malt beverages and affiliates of the malt beverage industry. Conducts specialized education programs. **Scope:** malt beverages. **Founded:** 1938. **Publications:** *NBWA Beer Perspectives* (Biweekly).

13569 ■ Wine and Spirits Wholesalers of America
805 15th St. NW, Ste. 430
Washington, DC 20005
Ph: (202)371-9792
Fax: (202)789-2405
Co. E-mail: juanita.duggan@wswa.org
URL: http://www.wswa.org
Contact: Craig Wolf, President
Description: Represents wholesale distributors of domestic and imported wine and distilled spirits. **Publications:** *Upfront* (Monthly); *WSWA Member Roster and Industry Directory* (Annual); *WSWA Member Roster and Industry Directory* (Annual); *Wine and Spirits Wholesalers of America--Membership Roster and Industry Directory* (Annual). **Educational Activities:** Wine and Spirits Wholesalers of America Convention and Exposition (Annual). **Telecommunication Services:** info@wswa.org.

REFERENCE WORKS

13570 ■ "Beer Stocks Rally on Anheuser, InBev Report" in Globe & Mail (February 16, 2007, pp. B3)
Pub: CTVglobemedia Publishing Inc.
Ed: Keith McArthur. **Description:** The stock prices of beer manufacturing industries have increased considerably after impressive profit reports from Anheuser Busch Cos Inc. and InBev SA. Complete analysis in this context is presented.

13571 ■ Beverage Industry--Annual Manual Issue
Pub: BNP Media
Contact: Al Reser, President
URL(s): directories.bevindustry.com/manual. **Released:** Annual; Latest edition 2010. **Publication includes:** List of over 1,700 companies supplying equipment and materials to the soft drink, beer, wine, bottled water, and juice industries; industry associations; bottling and supply franchise companies; beer importers distributors; manufacturers' representatives; soft drink distributors. **Entries include:** For suppliers--Company name, address, phone, code to indicate products. For associations--Name, address, phone, name of president; some association listings also include meeting date and location and names of other executives. For franchise companies--Name, address, phone, names and titles of executives, number of plants, number of franchised plants, products, foreign involvement. For beer importers and distributors--Name, address, phone, names and titles of key executives, brands handled. For manufacturers' representatives--Name, address, phone, names of contacts, market areas, products represented. **Database includes:** Statistics and industry surveys. **Arrangement:** State associations and supplier associations are geographical; other listings are alphabetical. **Indexes:** Trade name, product/service.

13572 ■ Beverage Marketing Directory
Pub: Beverage Marketing Corp.
Contact: Michael C. Bellas, Chief Executive Officer
E-mail: mbellas@beveragemarketing.com
URL(s): www.beveragemarketing.com/?service=publications&section=directory. **Released:** Annual; Latest edition 33rd; 2011. **Price:** $1435, Individuals softcover or in PDF format; $5495, Individuals database on CD-ROM; $5495, Canada database on CD-ROM. **Covers:** Over 25,500 beer wholesalers, wine and spirits wholesalers, soft drink bottlers and franchisors, breweries, wineries, distilleries, alcoholic beverage importers, bottled water companies; and trade associations, government agencies, micro breweries, juice, coffee, tea, milk companies, and others concerned with the beverage and bottling industries; coverage includes Canada. **Entries include:** Beverage and bottling company listings contain company name, address, phone, names of key executives, number of employees, brand names, and other information, including number of franchisees, number of delivery trucks, sales volume. Suppliers and related companies and organizations listings include similar but less detailed information. **Arrangement:** Geographical. **Indexes:** Personnel, supplier's product, company name.

13573 ■ "Black Diamond Holdings Corp. Receives SEC Approval" in Canadian Corporate News (May 16, 2007)
Pub: Comtex News Network Inc.
Description: Black Diamond Holdings, Corp., a British Columbia domiciled company and its two wholly owned subsidiaries are engaged in the bottling, importation, distribution, marketing, and brand creation of premium spirits and wines to worldwide consumers, announced that it has completed the SEC review process and has applied to list for trading in the United States on the OTC.BB.

13574 ■ "Booze Makers Battle Over Turkey Day" in Advertising Age (Vol. 78, October 29, 2007, No. 43, pp. 4)
Pub: Crain Communications, Inc.
Ed: Jeremy Mullman. **Description:** Beer and wine marketers are jockeying for position in regards to the Thanksgiving holiday.

13575 ■ "Bottoms Up!" in Entrepreneur (Vol. 36, April 2008, No. 4, pp. 128)
Pub: Entrepreneur Media, Inc.
Ed: Amanda C. Kooser. **Description:** Jill Bernheimer launched her online alcohol business Domaine547 in 2007, and encountered challenges as legal issues over the licensing and launching of the business took about seven months to finish. Domain547 features blog and forum areas. Marketing strategy that connects to the social community is one of the ways to reach out to customers.

13576 ■ "Cheap Thrills: Where to Look When You're Craving a Low-Price Wine" in Chicago Tribune (January 12, 2009)
Pub: McClatchy-Tribune Information Services
Ed: Bill Daley. **Description:** Wines priced $15 and above are being hit the hardest by the economic downturn while cheaper wines, specifically those priced between $3 and $6, are seeing a growth in sales.

13577 ■ "Day-Care Center Owner to Argue Against Liquor Store Opening Nearby" in Chicago Tribune (March 13, 2008)
Pub: McClatchy-Tribune Information Services
Ed: Matthew Walberg. **Description:** NDLC's owner feels that Greenwood Liquors should not be granted its liquor license due to the claim that the NDLC is not only a day-care center but also a school that employs state-certified teachers.

13578 ■ "Discount Beers Take Fizz Out Of Molson" in Globe & Mail (February 10, 2006, pp. B3)
Pub: CTVglobemedia Publishing Inc.
Ed: Omar El Akkad. **Description:** The reasons behind the decline in profits by 60 percent for Molson Coors Brewing Co., during fourth quarter 2005, are presented.

13579 ■ *"Executive Decision: Damn the Profit Margins, Sleeman Declares War on Buck-a-Beer Foes"* in *Globe & Mail (January 28, 2006, pp. B3)*
Pub: CTVglobemedia Publishing Inc.
Ed: Andy Hoffman. **Description:** The cost savings plans of chief executive officer John Sleeman of Sleeman Breweries Ltd. are presented.

13580 ■ *"First Venture Reports Proprietary Yeasts Further Reduce Ethyl Carbamate in Sake"* in *Canadian Corporate News (May 16, 2007)*
Pub: Comtex News Network Inc.
Description: First Ventures Technologies Corp., a biotechnology company that develops and commercializes advanced yeast products, confirmed that two of their proprietary yeasts used in the making of sake have yielded reductions in ethyl carbamate compared to previous sake brewing trials.

13581 ■ *"Grape Expectations"* in *Canadian Business (Vol. 80, March 12, 2007, No. 6, pp. 55)*
Pub: Rogers Media
Ed: Andrea Jezvovit. **Description:** The emergence of Nova Scotia as one of the leading wine-making places in Canada, in view of its favorable climate for growing grapes, is discussed.

13582 ■ *"Hike in Md.'s Alcohol Tax May Be Hard For Lawmakers to Swallow"* in *Baltimore Business Journal (Vol. 28, November 19, 2010, No. 28)*
Pub: Baltimore Business Journal
Ed: Emily Mullin. **Description:** Maryland's General Assembly has been reluctant to support a dime-per-drink increase in alcohol tax that was drafted in the 2009 bill if the tax revenue goes into a separate fund. The alcohol tax increase is considered unnecessary by some lawmakers and business leaders due to impending federal spending boosts.

13583 ■ *"Homes, Not Bars, Stay Well Tended"* in *Advertising Age (Vol. 79, January 28, 2008, No. 4, pp. 8)*
Pub: Crain Communications, Inc.
Ed: Jeremy Mullman. **Description:** Due to the downturn in the economy, consumers are drinking less at bars and restaurants; however, according to the Distilled Spirits Council of the United States, they are still purchasing expensive liquor to keep in their homes.

13584 ■ *"Imports Frothing Up Beer Market"* in *Globe & Mail (February 16, 2006, pp. B4)*
Pub: CTVglobemedia Publishing Inc.
Ed: Andy Hoffman. **Description:** The reasons behind the rise in market share of beer imports, in Canada, are presented.

13585 ■ *"Labatt to Swallow Lakeport"* in *Globe & Mail (February 2, 2007, pp. B1)*
Pub: CTVglobemedia Publishing Inc.
Ed: Keith McArthur. **Description:** The decision of Labatt Brewing Company Ltd. to acquire Lakeport Brewing Income Fund for $201.4 million is discussed.

13586 ■ *"Lawyers Cash In On Alcohol"* in *Business Journal Portland (Vol. 27, November 19, 2010, No. 38, pp. 1)*
Pub: Portland Business Journal
Ed: Andy Giegerich. **Description:** Oregon-based law firms have continued to corner big business on the state's growing alcohol industry as demand for their services increased. Lawyers, who represent wine, beer and liquor distillery interests, have seen their workload increased by 20 to 30 percent in 2009.

13587 ■ *"Leinie's Charts National Craft Beer Rollout"* in *The Business Journal-Milwaukee (Vol. 25, August 29, 2008, No. 49, pp. A1)*
Pub: American City Business Journals, Inc.
Ed: Rich Rovito. **Description:** Jacob Leinenkugel Brewing Co. is expected to complete the national rollout of its craft beer brands, while the launch of a new beer is prepared for this fall. The rollout is will likely benefit MillerCoors LLC, and will leave Alaska

as the only state without Leinenkugel beer. Other views and information on Leinenkugel's national rollout are presented.

13588 ■ *"Liquor Stores Sips on Growth Cocktail"* in *Globe & Mail (February 6, 2006, pp. B5)*
Pub: CTVglobemedia Publishing Inc.
Ed: Omar El Akkad. **Description:** The business growth plans of Liquor Stores Income Fund are presented.

13589 ■ *"Little Cheer in Holiday Forecast for Champagne"* in *Advertising Age (Vol. 88, November 17, 2008, No. 43, pp. 6)*
Pub: Crain Communications, Inc.
Ed: Jeremy Mullman. **Description:** Due to a weak economy that has forced consumers to trade down from the most expensive alcoholic beverages as well as a weak U.S. dollar that has driven already lofty Champagne prices higher, makers of the French sparkling wine are anticipating a brutally slow holiday season.

13590 ■ *"MillerCoors Needs the Quickie Mart"* in *Crain's Chicago Business (Vol. 32, November 16, 2009, No. 46, pp. 2)*
Pub: Crain Communications, Inc.
Ed: David Sterrett. **Description:** Power Marts convenience store owner Sam Odeh says that Chicago-based MillerCoors LLC has done a poor job at promoting its brand, keeping its signs up to date and stocking the shelves at his stores. He complains that the company's service has been awful and the marketing pathetic. Convenience stores accounted for more than $14 billion in beer sales in the past year.

13591 ■ *"Moet, Rivals Pour More Ad Bucks Into Bubbly"* in *Advertising Age (Vol. 88, September 3, 2007, No. 35, pp. 4)*
Pub: Crain Communications, Inc.
Ed: Jeremy Mullman. **Description:** In an attempt to revive sluggish sales, champagne companies are raising their advertising budgets, transforming themselves from light-spending seasonal players to year-round heavyweights in the advertising world.

13592 ■ *"On the Itinerary: Your Future"* in *Entrepreneur (Vol. 37, October 2009, No. 10, pp. 92)*
Pub: Entrepreneur Media, Inc.
Ed: Joel Holland. **Description:** Josh Hackler's Spanish Vines imports and distributes wines from Spain while using Spanish culture to help market the wines. The business was hatched after Hackler signed up for a study-abroad program in Spain.

13593 ■ *"The Price Is Right: What You Can Learn From the Wine Industry"* in *Advertising Age (Vol. 88, February 11, 2008, No. 6, pp. 14)*
Pub: Crain Communications, Inc.
Ed: Lenore Skenazy. **Description:** In California a wine study was conducted in which participants' brains were hooked up to an MRI so researchers could watch what was happening in both the taste centers as well as the pleasure centers; the participants were given three different wines but were told that the samples were from a variety of wines that differed radically in price; surprisingly, the differences did not affect the taste centers of the brain, however, when the participants were told that a sample was more expensive, the pleasure centers were greatly affected.

13594 ■ *"Sobering Consequences"* in *The Business Journal-Milwaukee (Vol. 25, July 11, 2008, No. 42, pp. A1)*
Pub: American City Business Journals, Inc.
Ed: Rich Rovito. **Description:** Milwaukee Mayor Tom Barrett and Wisconsin Governor Jim Doyle met with MillerCoors management in an effort to convince the company to locate its corporate headquarters in the city. The company is expected to announce its decision by mid-July 2008. It was revealed that the decision-making process is focusing on determining an optimal location for the headquarters.

13595 ■ *"A Very Good Year for Beer"* in *Entrepreneur (Vol. 37, October 2009, No. 10, pp. 18)*
Pub: Entrepreneur Media Inc.
Ed: Jennie Dorris. **Description:** Americans are shifting to craft beers, as shown by the almost 6 percent rise in craft beer sales in 2008. Mass-market domestic brand sales grew 0.6 percent while imported beer sales declined by 3.4 percent.

13596 ■ *"What'll You Have Tonight?"* in *Barron's (Vol. 88, July 4, 2008, No. 28, pp. 22)*
Pub: Dow Jones & Co., Inc.
Ed: Neil A. Martin. **Description:** Shares of Diageo could rise by 30 percent a year from June 2008 after it slipped due to U.S. sales worries. The company also benefits from the trend toward more premium alcoholic beverage brands worldwide especially in emerging markets.

13597 ■ *"Wirtz Partners With California Liquor Wholesaler To Expand Reach"* in *Chicago Tribune (December 17, 2008)*
Pub: McClatchy-Tribune Information Services
Ed: Mike Hughlett. **Description:** Young's Market Co. and Wirtz Beverage Group have tentatively agreed to a joint venture that will give both companies a larger reach in the wine and liquor distribution business.

SOURCES OF SUPPLY

13598 ■ *Beverage World--Buyers Guide Issue*
Beverage World
Contact: Lisa Adams, Director, Sales
E-mail: leoguenther@bellsouth.net
URL(s): www.beverageworld.com. **Released:** Annual; Latest edition June 2008. **Publication includes:** List of suppliers to the beverage industry. **Entries include:** Company name, address. **Arrangement:** Classified by product.

STATISTICAL SOURCES

13599 ■ *RMA Annual Statement Studies*
Pub: Risk Management Association
Contact: Kevin M. Blakey, President
Released: Annual. **Price:** $175.00 2006-07 edition, $105.00. **Description:** Contains composite balance sheets and income statements for more than 360 industries, including the accounting, auditing, and bookkeeping industries. Also contains five years of comparative historical data for discerning trends. Includes 16 commonly used ratios, computed for most of the size groupings for nearly every industry.

13600 ■ *The U.S. Liquor Market*
Business Trend Analysts, Inc. Industry Studies
Released: 2004-2005. **Price:** $1695.00. **Description:** Tracks the size and growth of the U.S. liquor market, covering all types of white and dark distilled spirits, cordials, liqueurs, cognac, brandy, and more.

TRADE PERIODICALS

13601 ■ *Beverage Dynamics: Wine, Beer & Spirits for Retail Decision Makers*
Pub: Beverage Information Group
URL(s): www.beveragedynamics.com/. **Ed:** Richard Brandes. **Released:** Bimonthly **Price:** $35, Individuals print version; $50, Canada and Mexico print version; $130, Other countries print version; $45, Individuals print & digital version; $60, Canada and Mexico print & digital version; $140, Other countries print & digital version.

13602 ■ *Beverage World*
Pub: Beverage World
Contact: Lisa Adams, Director, Sales
E-mail: leoguenther@bellsouth.net
URL(s): www.beverageworld.com. **Released:** Monthly **Price:** $99, Individuals.

13603 ■ *Modern Brewery Age*
Pub: Business Journals, Inc.
Contact: Britton Jones, President
E-mail: brittonj@busjour.com
URL(s): www.breweryage.com. **Ed:** Peter V.K. Reid. **Released:** Bimonthly **Price:** $125, Individuals.

FRANCHISES AND BUSINESS OPPORTUNITIES

13604 ■ Bevinco
505 Consumers Rd., Ste. 510
Toronto, ON, Canada M2J 4V8
Ph: (416)490-6266
Fax: (416)490-6899
Co. E-mail: info@bevinco.com
URL: http://www.bevinco.com
Description: Liquor inventory control system for bars, restaurants, hotels, clubs, etc. **No. of Franchise Units:** 250. **No. of Company-Owned Units:** 1. **Founded:** 1987.. **Franchised:** 1991. **Equity Capital Needed:** $40,000. **Franchise Fee:** $40,000. **Financial Assistance:** Yes. **Training:** 7 days corporate training in Toronto, 5-10 days regional training with state master franchise.

LIBRARIES

13605 ■ Distilled Spirits Council of the U.S. Library
1250 Eye St. NW, Ste. 400
Washington, DC 20005
Ph: (202)628-3544
Fax: (202)682-8877
URL: http://www.discus.org/
Scope: Distilled spirits industry, prohibition, temperance movement, alcoholism, liquor laws, alcohol and health/safety issues, moderate drinking, drinking customs. **Services:** Interlibrary loan; copying; library open to researchers with prior approval. **Founded:** 1974. **Holdings:** 3500 volumes; 72 VF drawers of information on subjects and organizations. **Subscriptions:** 225 journals and other serials.

ASSOCIATIONS AND OTHER ORGANIZATIONS

13606 ■ **Association of Authors' Representatives (AAR)**
676A 9th Ave., Ste. 312
New York, NY 10036
Ph: (212)840-5770
Co. E-mail: administrator@aaronline.org
URL: http://www.aaronline.org
Contact: Jody Klein, Secretary, Administration
URL(s): www.aar-online.org. **Description:** Literary and dramatic agents who market books, plays, and other literary and dramatic material. **Founded:** 1991. **Publications:** *The Literary Agent.* **Telecommunication Services:** aarinc@mindspring.com.

13607 ■ **Association of Talent Agents (ATA)**
9255 Sunset Blvd., Ste. 930
Los Angeles, CA 90069
Ph: (310)274-0628
Fax: (310)274-5063
Co. E-mail: rnoval@agentassociation.com
URL: http://www.agentassociation.com
Contact: Karen Stuart, Executive Director
Description: Talent agencies that have clients in the Screen Actors Guild, American Federation of Television and Radio Artists, Directors Guild of America, Writers Guild of America, East, and Writers Guild of America, West. Negotiates terms of franchise agreements with these guilds and maintains liaison with their representatives. Assists members with contract problems, interpretations, rulings, residual matters, and arbitrations. Employs legal counsel to prepare opinions upon request and to file briefs in arbitrations and labor commission hearings. Maintains liaison with labor commission representatives in San Francisco and Los Angeles, CA, and intervenes on behalf of individual members having special problems. Conducts seminars and symposia. **Scope:** law, arbitration, minority rights, legislative history. **Founded:** 1937. **Subscriptions:** books monographs periodicals. **Publications:** *Employment Law.* **Awards:** Distinguished Agent (Periodic).

REFERENCE WORKS

13608 ■ **International Literary Market Place: The Directory of the International Book Publishing Industry**
Pub: Information Today Inc.
Contact: Thomas H. Hogan, President
E-mail: ctuthill@infotoday.com
URL(s): www.literarymarketplace.combooks.infotoday.com. **Released:** Annual; Latest edition 2012. **Price:** $289, Individuals softbound; $260.10, Individuals first time standing order. **Covers:** Over 10,500 publishers in over 180 countries outside the United States and Canada, and about 1,499 trade and professional organizations related to publishing abroad; includes major printers, binders, typesetters, book manufacturers, book dealers, libraries, literary agencies, translators, book clubs, reference books and journals, periodicals, prizes, and international reference section. **Entries include:** For publishers--Name, address, phone, fax, telex, names and titles of key personnel, branches, type of publications, subjects, ISBN prefix. Listings for others include similar information but less detail. **Arrangement:** Classified by business activities, then geographical. **Indexes:** Company name, subject, type of publication.

TRADE PERIODICALS

13609 ■ **Fiction Writer's Guideline**
Pub: Fiction Writer's Connection
Contact: Blythe Camenson, Director
E-mail: bcamenson@aol.com
Released: Enewsletter. **Description:** Offers practical advice and support on writing and getting published. Recurring features include interviews, book reviews, and Advice From agents and editors and Writing Tips.

13610 ■ **Publishers Weekly: The International voice for Book Publishing and Bookselling**
Pub: Publishers Weekly
URL(s): www.publishersweekly.com. **Released:** Weekly **Price:** $249.99, Individuals; $299.99, Canada; $399.99, Other countries air delivery.

13611 ■ **Writer's Digest**
Pub: FW Publications
Contact: Sara Domville, President
E-mail: sara.domville@fwpubs.com
URL(s): www.writersdigest.com. **Released:** 8/yr. **Price:** $19.96, Individuals; $29.96, Canada including GST/HST; $31.96, Other countries surface delivery.

ASSOCIATIONS AND OTHER ORGANIZATIONS

13612 ■ Associated Locksmiths of America (ALOA)
3500 Easy St.
Dallas, TX 75247
Ph: (214)819-9733
Free: 800-532-2562
Fax: (214)819-9736
Co. E-mail: president@aloa.org
URL: http://www.aloa.org
Contact: Robert Mock, President
Description: Retail locksmiths; associate members are manufacturers and distributors of locks, keys, safes, and burglar alarms. Aims to educate and provide current information to individuals in the physical security industry. Maintains information and referral services for members; offers insurance and bonding programs. Holds annual five-day technical training classes and 3-day technical exhibit. Maintains museum. **Scope:** locksmithing, locks, tools, technical procedures. **Founded:** 1955. **Subscriptions:** 2000 books periodicals video recordings. **Publications:** *Associated Locksmiths of America--Membership Directory* (Annual); *Keynotes* (Monthly); *Keynotes* (Monthly). **Educational Activities:** Associated Locksmiths of America Convention (Annual); ALOA Security Expo. **Awards:** ALOA Scholarship Foundation. **Telecommunication Services:** aloa@aloa.org; media@aloa.org.

13613 ■ Lock Museum of America (LMA)
PO Box 104
Terryville, CT 06786-0104
Ph: (860)480-4408
URL: http://www.lockmuseumofamerica.org
Contact: Thomas F. Hennessy, Jr., President
Description: Locksmiths, lock collectors, lock and key manufacturers, and builders. Seeks to preserve and exhibit the colonial American craft of lock, key, and security device making. Maintains hall of fame and museum. **Founded:** 1971. **Publications:** *Newsletter and Historical Research Series* (Quarterly). **Educational Activities:** Lock Collection Show (Annual).

13614 ■ Security Hardware Distributors Association (SHDA)
105 Eastern Ave., Ste. 104
Annapolis, MD 21403
Ph: (410)940-6346
Fax: (410)263-1659
Co. E-mail: info@shda.org
URL: http://associationdatabase.com/aws/SHDA/pt/sp/Home_Page
Contact: Karen Hoffman-Kahl, President
Description: Wholesalers of locksmith supplies; associate members are manufacturers of locks and locksmith supplies. **Founded:** 1958. **Publications:**

SHDA Unlocked (Monthly). **Educational Activities:** Security Hardware Distributors Association Conference (Annual).

DIRECTORIES OF EDUCATIONAL PROGRAMS

13615 ■ *Directory of Private Accredited Career Schools and Colleges of Technology*
Pub: Accrediting Commission of Career Schools and Colleges of Technology
Contact: Michale S. McComis, Executive Director
Released: On web page. **Price:** Free. **Description:** Covers 3900 accredited post-secondary programs that provide training programs in business, trade, and technical fields, including various small business endeavors. Entries offer school name, address, phone, description of courses, job placement assistance, and requirements for admission. Arrangement is alphabetical.

REFERENCE WORKS

13616 ■ *"Eve in the Sky: A Look at Security Tech from All Angles" in Bellingtham Business Journal (October 2008, pp. 23)*
Pub: Sun News Inc.
Ed: Lance Henderson. **Description:** High tech solutions to security issues in any company are not the only things to be considered; a low-tech evaluation of a building and its security fixtures, such as door knobs, locks, doors and windows as well as lighting are important aspects to security any office.

13617 ■ *"SECO Manufacturing" in Point of Beginning (Vol. , 2008, No. , pp.)*
Pub: BNP Media
Contact: Al Reser, President
Description: Seco Manufacturing's 3015-Series lock features an all-metal tilting holder with an improved brass front locking lever for improved security for any building.

13618 ■ *"Vandal-Resistant Mortise Locks" in Building Design and Construction (Vol. 49, September 1, 2008, No. 12, pp. 78)*
Pub: Reed Business Information
Description: Stanley Security Solutions offers mortise locks with a vandal-resistant feature that includes a clutch mechanism designed to break away when excessive force is applied either by kicking or standing on the lever. Once the mortise lock breaks away it can be easily reset to its original position without sustaining damage.

TRADE PERIODICALS

13619 ■ *American Lock Collectors Association Newsletter*
Pub: American Lock Collectors Association
Ed: Robert Dix, Editor, dixlock@aol.com. **Released:** Bimonthly. **Price:** $18, U.S.; $22, Canada; $30,

elsewhere. **Description:** Provides information on the collecting, history, buying, selling, and trading of antique and unusual locks, keys, handcuffs, and locking devices. Carries announcements and reports of collector shows.

13620 ■ *Keynotes*
Pub: Associated Locksmiths of America
Contact: Robert Mock, President
URL(s): www.aloa.org/membership/index.php. **Released:** Monthly

13621 ■ *National Locksmith*
Pub: National Publishing Company Inc.
URL(s): www.thenationallocksmith.com/. **Ed:** Greg Mango. **Released:** 13/yr.

TRADE SHOWS AND CONVENTIONS

13622 ■ ALOA Security Expo
Associated Locksmiths of America (ALOA)
3500 Easy St.
Dallas, TX 75247
Ph: (214)819-9733
Free: 800-532-2562
Fax: (214)819-9736
Co. E-mail: president@aloa.org
URL: http://www.aloa.org
Contact: Robert Mock, President
URL(s): www.aloa.org. **Audience:** Retailers, wholesalers and manufacturers of physical security products. **Principal Exhibits:** Physical security products, including: locks, safes, door hardware, alarms and related products and services. **Telecommunication Services:** convention@aloa.org.

FRANCHISES AND BUSINESS OPPORTUNITIES

13623 ■ Pop-A-Lock
SystemForward America, Inc.
1018 Harding St., Ste. 101
Lafayette, LA 70503
Ph: (337)233-6211
Co. E-mail: michaelkleimeyer@systemforward.com
URL: http://www.popalock.com
Description: Mobile locksmith/car unlocking service. There is no build-out required with quick to market/revenue generation. Your employees provide our mobile tech services to commercial & residential customers, and national accounts. **No. of Franchise Units:** 220. **Founded:** 1991.. **Franchised:** 1994. **Equity Capital Needed:** $50,000 and up, based on territory population. **Franchise Fee:** $29,000. **Training:** Offers new franchisee business training, employee advanced technical training including state-of-the-art

dispatch service. Provides ongoing technical updates, public relations and marketing, business analysis, and National Accounts Support-mentor program.

LIBRARIES

13624 ■ Lock Museum of America Inc. Library
230 Main St., Rte. 6
Terryville, CT 06786-0104
Ph: (860)589-6359
Fax: (860)589-6359
Co. E-mail: thomasnsc@aol.com
URL: http://www.lockmuseum.com/
Contact: Thomas F. Hennessy, Curator
Scope: Locks, keys, ornate hardware. **Services:** Copying; Library open to the public. **Founded:** 1972. **Holdings:** 1000 books; 500 bound periodical volumes; 1200 patents; patent indexes, 1790-1977.

ASSOCIATIONS AND OTHER ORGANIZATIONS

13625 ■ Leather Apparel Association (LAA)
4705 Center Blvd., Ste. 806
Long Island City, NY 11109
Ph: (718)606-0767
Fax: (718)606-6345
Co. E-mail: info@leatherassociation.com
URL: http://www.leatherapparelassociation.com
Contact: Richard Harrow, Executive Director
Description: Manufacturers, retailers, tanners, cleaners, and other individuals involved in the leather garment industry. Seeks to increase the sales of leather clothing through public relations, consumer education, and business support services. Marketing programs focus on fashion videos, media tours, press kits, brochures, hangtags, manufacturing and cleaning guidelines, and market research. Conducts seminars. **Founded:** 1990.

13626 ■ Leather Industries of America (LIA)
3050 K St. NW, Ste. 400
Washington, DC 20007
Ph: (202)342-8497
Fax: (202)342-8583
Co. E-mail: info@leatherusa.com
URL: http://www.leatherusa.com
Description: Represents the interests of the American tanner and leather suppliers. Provides environmental, technical, education, statistical and marketing services. **Founded:** 1917. **Publications:** *Newsbreak*; *Technical Bulletin* (Periodic); *Leather Industries of America--Membership Directory & Buyer's Guide* (Annual); *Leather Industries of America's Member Directory and Buyer's Guide* (Annual); *U.S. Leather Industries Statistics* (Annual). **Educational Activities:** Asia Pacific Leather Fair (Annual); Leather Industries of America Meeting (Annual).

13627 ■ National Luggage Dealers Association (NLDA)—NLDA Associates
1817 Elmdale Ave.
Glenview, IL 60026
Ph: (847)998-6869
Fax: (847)998-6884
Co. E-mail: inquiry@nlda.com
URL: http://www.nlda.com
Description: Represents retailers of luggage, leather goods, gifts, and handbags. Buying group producing promotional materials. **Founded:** 1925. **Educational Activities:** Luggage, Gift and Travel Goods Show (Annual).

REFERENCE WORKS

13628 ■ Leather Manufacturer Directory
Pub: Shoe Trades Publishing Co.
Contact: Inta Huns, Editor
E-mail: inta@shoetrades.com
URL(s): www.shoetrades.com/directories.php. **Released:** Annual; Latest edition 2008. **Price:** $61, Individuals. **Covers:** Tanneries, leather finishers, and hide processors and their suppliers in the United States and Canada. **Entries include:** Company name, address, phone, names of executives, list of products or services and over 300 companies classified by their goods and services. **Arrangement:** Tanners and hide processors are geographical; suppliers are classified by product. **Indexes:** Tanners, classifications, hide processors.

13629 ■ "Packing Chic" in Black Enterprise (Vol. 38, February 2008, No. 7, pp. 154)
Pub: Earl G. Graves Publishing Co. Inc.
Ed: Sonai Alleyne. **Description:** Profile of Angela Theodora's leather overnight bags that offer a variety of smart compartments for the business traveler.

STATISTICAL SOURCES

13630 ■ RMA Annual Statement Studies
Pub: Risk Management Association
Contact: Kevin M. Blakey, President
Released: Annual. **Price:** $175.00 2006-07 edition, $105.00. **Description:** Contains composite balance sheets and income statements for more than 360 industries, including the accounting, auditing, and bookkeeping industries. Also contains five years of comparative historical data for discerning trends. Includes 16 commonly used ratios, computed for most of the size groupings for nearly every industry.

TRADE PERIODICALS

13631 ■ Travel Goods Showcase: Products & Trends for Travelers
Pub: Travel Goods Association
Contact: Michele Marini Pittenger, President
URL(s): www.travel-goods.org/travel-goods-showcase/index.asp. **Released:** Periodic; 5/yr.

TRADE SHOWS AND CONVENTIONS

13632 ■ Canadian Luggage, Leathergoods, Handbags and Accessories Show
Pro-Sho Inc.
298 Sheppard Ave. E.
North York, ON, Canada M2N 3B1
Ph: (416)229-2060
Fax: (416)223-2826
URL(s): www.mediaedge.ca/llhashow. **Frequency:** Annual. **Audience:** Luggage, leather goods, and handbag retailers. **Principal Exhibits:** Luggage, leather goods, handbags, and travel accessories. **Dates and Locations:** International Centre. **Telecommunication Services:** Richards@mediaedge.ca.

FRANCHISES AND BUSINESS OPPORTUNITIES

13633 ■ Leather Medic
5565 Lee St., Ste. 1
Lehigh Acres, FL 33971
Free: 888-561-0423
Fax: (239)561-5715
Co. E-mail: klife@leathermedic.com
URL: http://www.leathermedic.com
Description: Repairing and refinishing leather furniture. **No. of Franchise Units:** 35. **No. of Company-Owned Units:** 1. **Founded:** 1988.. **Equity Capital Needed:** $47,500. **Franchise Fee:** $47,500. **Financial Assistance:** Yes. **Training:** Offers 2 weeks of one-on-one training.

ASSOCIATIONS AND OTHER ORGANIZATIONS

13634 ■ American Lumber Standard Committee (ALSC)
PO Box 210
Germantown, MD 20875-0210
Ph: (301)972-1700
Fax: (301)540-8004
Co. E-mail: alsc@alsc.org
URL: http://www.alsc.org
Contact: R.K. Caron, Chairman

Description: Members appointed by the Department of Commerce to represent producers, consumers, and specifiers of softwood lumber. Establishes and maintains standards for size, grade, and other matters; elects an independent board of review to approve softwood lumber grading rules and accredit agencies that audit treating plants and accredit agencies that audit pallet, box and crate manufacturers for international trade. **Founded:** 1922.

13635 ■ American Walnut Manufacturers Association (AWMA)
1007 N 725 W
West Lafayette, IN 47906-9431
Co. E-mail: jackson@purdue.edu
URL: http://www.walnutassociation.org
Contact: Liz Jackson, Executive Director

Description: Manufacturers of hardwood veneer and lumber, especially American black walnut. Seeks to improve the sale of products made from hardwoods through advertising, promotion, sales education and product improvement; also promotes good forest management. **Scope:** wood technology, furniture design and construction, forestry production. **Founded:** 1912. **Subscriptions:** 240.

13636 ■ APA: The Engineered Wood Association
7011 S 19th St.
Tacoma, WA 98466
Ph: (253)565-6600
Fax: (253)565-7265
Co. E-mail: help@apawood.org
URL: http://www.apawood.org
Contact: Dennis J. Hardman, President

Description: Manufacturers of structural panel products, oriented strand board and composites. Conducts trade promotion through advertising, publicity, merchandising, and field promotion. Maintains quality supervision in accordance with U.S. product standards, APA performance standards, and APA trademarking. Conducts research to improve products, applications, and manufacturing techniques. Sponsors Engineered Wood Research Foundation; compiles statistics. **Scope:** structural panel products. **Founded:** 1933. **Publications:** *Engineered Wood Journal* (Semiannual); *Management Report* (Monthly); *APA--The Engineered Wood Association--Management Journal*; *APA--Membership and Product Directory: Structural Panels and Engineered Wood*

Products. **Educational Activities:** Info Fair (Annual). **Awards:** APA Safety Awards (Annual). **Telecommunication Services:** marilyn.lemoine@apawood.org.

13637 ■ Hardwood Manufacturers Association
665 Rodi Rd., Ste. 305
Pittsburgh, PA 15235
Ph: (412)244-0440
Fax: (412)244-9090
Co. E-mail: ljovanovich@hardwood.org
URL: http://www.hmamembers.org
Description: Represents manufacturers of hardwood lumber and hardwood products. Conducts national consumer promotion program. **Publications:** *HMA Link* (Monthly); *Hardwood Manufacturers Association--Membership Directory* (Annual); *Hardwood Manufacturers Association Buyers Guide.* **Educational Activities:** National Conference and Expo (Annual). **Awards:** Robert B. Hendricks/Hardwood Manufacturers Association Scholarship (Annual). **Telecommunication Services:** darleen@hardwood.org.

13638 ■ Hardwood Plywood and Veneer Association (HPVA)
1825 Michael Faraday Dr.
Reston, VA 20190
Ph: (703)435-2900
Fax: (703)435-2537
Co. E-mail: hpva@hpva.org
URL: http://www.hpva.org
Contact: Kip Hawlett, President
E-mail: khowlett@hpva.org

Description: Manufacturers and finishers of hardwood plywood; manufacturers and sales agents of veneer; suppliers of glue, machinery, and other products related to the industry; stocking distributors. Conducts laboratory testing of plywood, adhesives, finishes, flamespread, formaldehyde emissions, structural, and smoke density. Performs glue bond, flamespread, formaldehyde emissions, and structural listing services. Provides public relations, advertising, marketing, and technical services to members. Represents the industry in legislative matters and keeps members informed on tariff and trade actions. **Scope:** hardwood plywood and veneer manufacturing and uses. **Services:** Planting of hardwood trees. **Founded:** 1921. **Subscriptions:** 300. **Publications:** *Hardwood Plywood & E-News* (Semimonthly); *Hardwood Plywood; Hardwood Plywood and Veneer News* (Monthly); *Directory of Veneer Manufacturers, Veneer Sales Representatives, Veneer Importers in the United States and Canada* (Annual); *Directory of Manufacturers of Marine Hardwood Plywood* (Annual); *HPMA Testing and Inspection and Listed Products Manual* (Annual); *Where to Buy Hardwood Plywood and Veneer Directory* (Annual); *Veneer Manufacturers in the United States and Canada* (Annual); *Where to Buy Hardwood Plywood, Veneer, and Engineered Hardwood Flooring Buyers' Guide* (Annual); *Where to Buy Hardwood Plywood, Veneer, and Engineered Hardwood Flooring Membership Directory* (Annual); *Associations and Organizations of Interest to Hardwood Plywood & Veneer Manufactur-*

ers (Annual); *Magazines & Publications of Interest to Hardwood Plywood & Veneer Manufacturers* (Irregular); *Hardwood Plywood Manufacturers Association--Face Veneer Manufacturers List.* **Educational Activities:** Semiannual conventions; HPVA Workshops. **Telecommunication Services:** khowlett@hpva.org.

13639 ■ International Wood Products Association (IWPA)
4214 King St.
Alexandria, VA 22302
Ph: (703)820-6696
Fax: (703)820-8550
Co. E-mail: info@iwpawood.org
URL: http://www.iwpawood.org
Contact: Brent J. McClendon, Executive Vice President

Description: Importers, processors, manufacturers, and distributors of imported wood products; steamship companies; customs brokers, etc. Membership figure represents participants from 30 countries. Promotes acceptance and use of imported wood products; develops product standards; compiles statistics; supports good forestry management. **Founded:** 1956. **Publications:** *International Wood Products Association--Directory* (Annual); *International Wood* (Annual). **Educational Activities:** World of Wood (Annual); World of Wood (Annual). **Awards:** Aesthetic Design Excellence (Annual); Environmental Excellence (Annual); Innovative Design Excellence (Annual).

13640 ■ National Hardwood Lumber Association (NHLA)
6830 Raleigh La Grange Rd.
Memphis, TN 38134-0518
Ph: (901)377-1818
Free: 800-933-0318
Fax: (901)382-6419
Co. E-mail: info@nhla.com
URL: http://www.nhla.com
Contact: Dave Redmond, President

URL(s): www.natlhardwood.org. **Description:** United States, Canadian and International hardwood lumber and veneer manufacturers, distributors and consumers. Inspects hardwood lumber. Maintains inspection training school. Conducts management and marketing seminars for the hardwood industry. Promotes research in hardwood timber management and utilization. Promotes public awareness of the industry. **Founded:** 1898. **Publications:** *National Hardwood Lumber Association--Members* (Annual); *NHLA Newsletter, National Hardwood Lumber Association Membership Directory; Hardwood Research Bulletin; Hardwood Matters* (Monthly). **Educational Activities:** National Hardwood Lumber Association Convention (Annual). **Telecommunication Services:** info@natlhardwood.org; info@lhardwood.org; membership@nhla.com.

13641 ■ National Lumber and Building Material Dealers Association (NLBMDA)
2025 M St. NW, Ste. 800
Washington, DC 20036-3309
Ph: (202)367-1169

Free: 800-634-8645
Fax: (202)367-2169
Co. E-mail: info@dealer.org
URL: http://www.dealer.org
Contact: Cally Fromme, Chairman of the Board

Description: Represents more than 8,000 lumber and building material companies with over 400,000 employees, 20 state and regional associations and the industry's leading manufacturers and service providers. **Founded:** 1917. **Publications:** *Building Material Dealer*, *NLBMDA Advocate* (Monthly); *Nuts & Bolts*; *ProSales* (Monthly); *Cost of Doing Business* (Annual); *Forklift and You*; *Risk Management Best Practices*; *Your National Perspective* (Quarterly). **Educational Activities:** Industry Summit (Annual); Legislative Conference (Annual). **Awards:** Grassroots Award (Annual); Safety Award (Annual); Excellence in Human Resources (Annual); Member of Congress Award (Annual). **Telecommunication Services:** nlbmda@dealer.org.

13642 ■ North American Wholesale Lumber Association (NAWLA)
3601 Algonquin Rd., Ste. 400
Rolling Meadows, IL 60008
Ph: (847)870-7470
Free: 800-527-8258
Fax: (847)870-0201
Co. E-mail: info@nawla.org
URL: http://www.lumber.org
Contact: Mark Donovan, Director

Description: Wholesale distributors of lumber, wood products, and complementary products. Aids members with procedure for settling trade disputes. Provides weeklong course for wholesale lumber traders. Compiles statistics. Provides networking opportunities at regional, and annual meetings, trade show, and NAWLA Traders Market. **Founded:** 1893. **Publications:** *North American Wholesale Lumber Association--Distribution Directory* (Annual); *North American Wholesale Lumber Association--Membership Bulletin* (Monthly). **Educational Activities:** NAWLA Traders Market (Annual).

13643 ■ Northeastern Lumber Manufacturers Association (NELMA)
PO Box 87A
Cumberland, ME 04021
Ph: (207)829-6901
Fax: (207)829-4293
Co. E-mail: info@nelma.org
URL: http://www.nelma.org
Contact: Jeff Easterling, President

Description: Manufacturers of hardwood and softwood lumber and timber products in the New England states, New York, and Pennsylvania. Promotes the interests of the northeastern lumber manufacturing industry. Encourages uniformity, efficiency, and economy in the manufacture, gradation, distribution, and use of lumber and timber products. Encourages the use of lumber and timber products and the conservation and renewal of forest resources by improved forest utilization and practices. Conducts economic research on forest and other industry problems, and technical and other investigations of the properties and uses of wood. Collects and disseminates statistics and other economic information. Presents the views of the industry to other organizations, the government, and the public. Sponsors annual two-week training school for softwood lumber graders. **Founded:** 1933. **Publications:** *Dimensional Lumber*, *Eastern White Pine*; *Membership Directory* (Annual); *Northeastern Lumber Manufacturers Association--Buyers Guide and Membership Directory* (Annual); *Northeastern Lumber Manufacturers Association--Buyer's Guide and Membership Directory* (Annual); *Standard Grading Rules for Northeastern Lumber*.

13644 ■ Northwestern Lumber Association (NLA)
5905 Golden Valley Rd., No. 110
Minneapolis, MN 55422
Ph: (763)544-6822
Free: 888-544-6822
Fax: (763)595-4060
Co. E-mail: psiewert@nlassn.org
URL: http://www.nlassn.org
Contact: Paula Siewert, President

Description: Building materials dealers in Iowa, Minnesota, North Dakota, South Dakota and Wisconsin; associate members are distributors, manufacturers, and allied industries. **Founded:** 1890. **Publications:** *Building Products Connection* (Bimonthly); *Dealer Reference Manual and Buyers' Guide* (Annual); *Northwestern Scene* (Monthly). **Educational Activities:** Iowa Lumber Convention (Annual); Nebraska Lumber Dealers Convention (Annual); Northwestern Building Products Expo (Annual).

13645 ■ Southeastern Lumber Manufacturers Association (SLMA)
200 Greencastle Rd.
Tyrone, GA 30290
Ph: (770)631-6701
Fax: (770)631-6720
Co. E-mail: wendy@slma.org
URL: http://www.slma.org
Contact: Bryan Smalley, President

Description: Independent southeastern lumber manufacturers. Represents and coordinates efforts of membership to alleviate local, regional, and national problems that affect independent southeastern lumber manufacturing industry. Conducts marketing and promotional activities. **Founded:** 1962.

13646 ■ Western Building Material Association (WBMA)
909 Lakeridge Dr. SW
Olympia, WA 98502-6064
Ph: (360)943-3054
Free: 888-551-9262
Fax: (360)943-1219
Co. E-mail: casey@wbma.org
URL: http://www.wbma.org
Contact: Casey Voorhees, Executive Director

Description: Retail lumber and building material dealers in states of Alaska, Hawaii, Idaho, Montana, Oregon, and Washington. Seeks to further and protect the interests of retail lumber dealers. Services include: classes, workshops, and seminars; group insurance and pension; printing of business forms; government and legislative action; information clearinghouse; training courses for personnel. Maintains a learning resource center. Conducts educational programs. **Scope:** business, industry related. **Founded:** 1903. **Subscriptions:** 500 audiovisuals books periodicals. **Publications:** *Western Building Material Association--Management Guide* (Monthly); *Western Building Material Association--Newsletter* (Monthly); *Western News* (Monthly). **Educational Activities:** Building Products Showcase (Annual); Western Building Material Association Annual Convention (Annual). **Awards:** Distinguished Dealer of the Year (Annual).

13647 ■ Western Red Cedar Lumber Association (WRCLA)
1501-700 W. Pender St.
Pender Pl. 1, Business Bldg.
Vancouver, BC, Canada V6C 1G8
Ph: (604)684-0266
Free: 866-778-9096
Fax: (604)687-4930
Co. E-mail: wrcla@wrcla.org
URL: http://www.wrcla.org

Description: Represents producers of Western Red Cedar lumber products. Aims to help consumers understand cedar's long-term benefits and special features. Provides information on how to use cedar properly. **Founded:** 1954. **Publications:** *Where to Buy Western Red Cedar* (Annual). **Educational Activities:** Western Red Cedar Lumber Association Meeting (Annual); WRCL Cedar School (Semiannual); WRCL Cedar School (Annual).

13648 ■ Western Wood Products Association (WWPA)
522 SW 5th Ave., Ste. 500
Portland, OR 97204-2122
Ph: (503)224-3930
Fax: (503)224-3934
Co. E-mail: info@wwpa.org
URL: http://www.wwpa.org
Contact: Kevin Binam, President

Description: Represents lumber manufacturers in 12 Western states and Alaska. Delivers lumber grade inspection and quality control, technical support, product/market support and statistical services to Western sawmills. **Founded:** 1964. **Publications:** *Western Lumber Facts* (Monthly); *Export Report* (Monthly); *Injury and Illness Incidence* (Quarterly); *Western Lumber Export Buyers Guide* (Annual); *Western Wood Products Association--Buyers Manual* (Annual); *Monthly F.O.B. Price Summary, Past Sales--Coast Mills* (Monthly); *Monthly F.O.B. Price Summary, Past Sales--Inland Mills* (Monthly).

13649 ■ Where to Buy Western Red Cedar
1501-700 W. Pender St.
Pender Pl. 1, Business Bldg.
Vancouver, BC, Canada V6C 1G8
Ph: (604)684-0266
Free: 866-778-9096
Fax: (604)687-4930
Co. E-mail: wrcla@wrcla.org
URL: http://www.wrcla.org
Released: Annual **Price:** free.

REFERENCE WORKS

13650 ■ "Bad News for Canada: U.S. New-Home Starts Sink" in Globe & Mail (February 17, 2007, pp. B7)
Pub: CTVglobemedia Publishing Inc.

Ed: Tavia Grant. **Description:** The new-home construction in the United States dropped by 14.3 percent in January 2007. The sinking construction activity shows significant impact on the Canadian factories and lumber companies.

13651 ■ "Blueprint for Profit: Family-Run Lumberyard Sets Sites On Sales of $100 Million a Year" in Small Business Opportunities (Jan. 2008)
Pub: Harris Publications Inc.

Ed: Stan Roberts. **Description:** Profile of family-run lumberyard whose owner shares insight into the challenges of competing with big box operations like Home Depot and Lowe's.

13652 ■ Directory of Home Center Operators & Hardware Chains
Pub: Chain Store Guide
Contact: Lisa Patterson, President

URL(s): www.chainstoreguide.com. **Released:** Annual; Latest edition 2012. **Price:** $395, Individuals Directory; $445, Individuals online lite; $1075, Individuals online pro; $1375, Individuals online pro plus. **Covers:** 4,500 U.S. and Canadian companies which operate home centers, home center warehouses, lumber and building material outlets, specialty paint and home decorating stores, and kitchen and bath centers. Concentrates on companies with a minimum annual sales of one million dollars. **Entries include:** Company name, address, phone, fax, 6,100 personnel e-mail address, web site, Internet order processing indicator, listing type, product lines, total sales, sales percentage per customer type, total selling square footage, total stores, units by type of store operated, units made by trade name, trading areas, projected openings and remodeling, distribution center locations, buying and/or marketing group name and location, number of nurseries operated, average number of check-outs, year founded, public company indicator, parent and subsidiary company information, division and branch office locations, key personnel, and number of locations by city. **Arrangement:** Geographical. **Indexes:** Product line, alphabetical, exclusions, state.

13653 ■ "Furniture Making May Come Back--Literally" in Business North Carolina (Vol. 28, March 2008, No. 3, pp. 32)
Pub: Business North Carolina

Description: Due to the weak U.S. dollar and the fact that lumber processors never left the country, foreign furniture manufacturers are becoming interested in moving manufacturing plants to the U.S.

13654 ■ *"Goldbelt Inc.: Targeting Shareholder Development"* in Alaska Business Monthly *(Vol. 27, October 2011, No. 10, pp. 108)*
Pub: Alaska Business Publishing Company
Ed: Tracy Kalytiak. **Description:** Profile of Goldbelt Inc., the company that has changed its original focus of timber to real estate to tourism and then to government contracting opportunities.

13655 ■ *International Wood Products Association--Directory*
Pub: International Wood Products Association
Contact: Brent J. McClendon, Executive Vice President
URL(s): www.iwpawood.org. **Released:** Annual; summer. **Covers:** Includes 220 U.S. importers, overseas suppliers, and service providers to the imported wood products industry. **Entries include:** Company name, address, phone, names of executives, list of products or services, fax, e-mail addresses, URL. **Arrangement:** Classified by type of membership.

13656 ■ *"Lumber Rebounds"* in Business Journal Portland *(Vol. 26, December 11, 2009, No. 40, pp. 1)*
Pub: American City Business Journals Inc.
Ed: Erik Siemers. **Description:** Oregon's lumber industry could be boosted as wood consumption across the country is expected to increase by 11 percent or 34.5 billion board feet in 2010.

13657 ■ *"The Main Event"* in Canadian Business *(Vol. 80, November 19, 2007, No. 23, pp. 28)*
Pub: Rogers Media
Ed: Zena Olijnyk. **Description:** U.S.-based Lowe's Companies, Inc. will be opening three stores in Canada in December 2007 and another three in 2008. The housing market crisis in the U.S. is the reason behind the home improvement store's Canadian expansion. The impacts of the expansion on Canadian home care stores and on the market competition are evaluated.

13658 ■ *Merchant Magazine--Buyers Guide*
Pub: Cutler Publishing Inc.
URL(s): www.building-products.com. **Released:** Monthly **Price:** $3, U.S. per issue; $22, U.S. per year. **Publication includes:** List of over 400 suppliers of lumber and home improvement goods in 13 western states. **Entries include:** Company name and phone. **Arrangement:** Geographical.

13659 ■ *Mid-America Lumbermens Association--Buyer's Guide and Dealer Directory*
Pub: Mid-America Lumbermens Association
Contact: Robert Uhler, Manager
E-mail: ruhler@themla.com
URL(s): www.themla.com/ProductsAndServices/BuyersGuide.html. **Released:** Annual; Latest edition 2011. **Price:** $150, Nonmembers plus shipping; Free to members; $30, Members additional copies. **Covers:** Lumber and building material suppliers nationwide and retail lumber dealers in Arkansas, Kansas, Missouri, Nebraska, Oklahoma; retail associations, national building industry associations, and line yards. **Entries include:** For dealers--Company name, address, phone, names of contacts. For suppliers--Company name, address, phone, fax, toll free number, email, URL, representative's names. **Arrangement:** Alphabetical for suppliers; geographical for dealers. **Indexes:** Product, brand name, supplier, retail dealer.

13660 ■ *"Montana's Manufacturing Industry"* in Montana Business Quarterly *(Vol. 49, Spring 2011, No. 1, pp. 29)*
Pub: Bureau of Business & Economic Research
Ed: Todd A. Morgan, Charles E. Keegan III, Colin B. Sorenson. **Description:** Manufacturing remains a vital part of Montana's economy despite the recession and decline in the production of wood products. Statistical data included.

13661 ■ *National Hardwood Lumber Association--Members*
Pub: National Hardwood Lumber Association
Contact: Dave Redmond, President
URL(s): www.natlhardwood.org. **Released:** Annual; January. **Covers:** 2,000 United States, Canadian, and foreign hardwood lumber manufacturers, distributors, and consumers. **Entries include:** Company, address, headquarters location if a plant or branch office. **Arrangement:** Separate geographical sections for active, associate, and sustaining members.

13662 ■ *North American Building Material Distribution Association--Membership Directory*
Pub: North American Building Material Distribution Association
Contact: Bill Delaney, President
URL(s): www.nbmda.org. **Released:** Annual **Covers:** About 200 wholesale distributors of building products who are members, and 150 manufacturers in that field who are associate members and over 800 of their locations. **Entries include:** Company name, address, phone, fax, name of principal executive, products offered. **Arrangement:** Geographical. **Indexes:** Alphabetical.

13663 ■ *Panel World--Directory and Buyers' Guide Issue*
Pub: Hatton-Brown Publishers Inc.
Contact: Cindy Sparks, Manager
E-mail: cindy@hattonbrown.com
URL(s): www.hattonbrown.netwww.panelworldmag.com/magazine-issue/january-2011. **Ed:** Dan Shell. **Released:** Annual; Latest edition January 2011. **Covers:** List of manufacturers and suppliers of machinery, equipment, and supplies, including veneers and panels, to the woodworking industry; trade associations. **Entries include:** For companies--Name, address, phone, fax, e-mail, website address. For associations--Name, address, phone, fax, e-mail, website, annual meeting dates, key contacts. **Arrangement:** Separate geographical sections for machinery manufacturers and veneer/panel manufacturers. **Indexes:** Product, machine manufacturers.

13664 ■ *"Pulp Friction: Spin Off Mills to Boost Wood Products"* in Globe & Mail *(February 18, 2006, pp. B3)*
Pub: CTVglobemedia Publishing Inc.
Ed: Peter Kennedy. **Description:** The reasons behind the decision of chief executive officer Jim Shepherd of Canfor Corp. to sell pulp mills are presented.

13665 ■ *Where to Buy Hardwood Plywood, Veneer, and Engineered Hardwood Flooring Buyers' Guide*
Pub: Hardwood Plywood and Veneer Association
Contact: Kip Hawlett, President
E-mail: khowlett@hpva.org
URL(s): www.hpva.org. **Released:** Annual; Latest edition 2011. **Price:** Free plus $7.50 postage and handling. **Covers:** About 196 member manufacturers of veneer and hardwood plywood, prefinishers and their suppliers. Also includes wholesale stocking distributors. **Entries include:** Company name, address, phone, name and title of sales contact, list of products and services. **Arrangement:** Classified by type of manufacturer or member.

STATISTICAL SOURCES

13666 ■ *RMA Annual Statement Studies*
Pub: Risk Management Association
Contact: Kevin M. Blakey, President
Released: Annual. **Price:** $175.00 2006-07 edition, $105.00. **Description:** Contains composite balance sheets and income statements for more than 360 industries, including the accounting, auditing, and bookkeeping industries. Also contains five years of comparative historical data for discerning trends. Includes 16 commonly used ratios, computed for most of the size groupings for nearly every industry.

13667 ■ *Standard & Poor's Industry Surveys*
Pub: Standard & Poor's Corp.
Released: Annual. **Price:** $3633.00. **Description:** Two-volume book that examines the prospects for specific industries, including trucking. Also provides analyses of trends and problems, statistical tables and charts, and comparative company analyses.

TRADE PERIODICALS

13668 ■ *APA--The Engineered Wood Association--Management Journal*
Pub: APA: The Engineered Wood Association
Contact: Dennis J. Hardman, President
Ed: Jack Merry, Editor, jack.merry@apawood.org. **Released:** Semiannual. **Description:** Provides news influencing the use or acceptance of structural panels. Covers subjects including economic outlook, promotional programs and other activities of the Association, and legislative developments.

13669 ■ *Ask NELMA Newsletter*
Pub: Northeastern Lumber Manufacturers Association
Ed: Donna J. Reynolds, Editor. **Released:** Monthly. **Description:** Discusses the growth, harvesting, production, and marketing of Northeastern lumber. Includes news of federal and state activities and of business of the Association.

13670 ■ *Building Products Digest*
Pub: Cutler Publishing Inc.
URL(s): www.building-products.com/BPDSiteMap.aspx. **Released:** Monthly **Price:** $24, Individuals; $39, Two years.

13671 ■ *The Lumber Co-Operator: The Official Publication of the Northeastern Retail Lumber Association*
Pub: Northeastern Retail Lumber Association
URL(s): www.nrla.org/content.aspx?id=78. **Released:** Bimonthly **Price:** Free NRLA members on request; $40, Individuals; $50, Canada; $35, Nonmembers groups of five or more.

13672 ■ *The Merchant Magazine*
Pub: Cutler Publishing Inc.
URL(s): www.building-products.com/MMSiteMap.aspx. **Released:** Monthly **Price:** $22, Individuals; $36, Two years.

13673 ■ *Northwestern Scene*
Pub: Northwestern Lumber Association
Ed: Gary L. Smith, Editor. **Released:** Monthly. **Price:** Included in membership. **Description:** Concentrates on providing retail lumber dealers in Iowa, Minnesota, North Dakota, and South Dakota with information and news relating to the lumber industry. Also contains information of interest to distributors, manufacturers, and allied industries. Recurring features include news of members, news of research, reports of industry developments and trends, and notices of Association activities and events.

13674 ■ *Panel World*
Pub: Hatton-Brown Publishers Inc.
Contact: Cindy Sparks, Manager
E-mail: cindy@hattonbrown.com
URL(s): www.panelworldmag.com/. **Released:** Bimonthly

13675 ■ *Random Lengths Weekly Report*
Pub: Random Lengths Publications, Inc.
Contact: Jon Anderson, President
Ed: Burrle Elmore, Editor. **Released:** Weekly. **Price:** $345, U.S.; $357, Canada by mail; $289. **Description:** Covers the North American softwood markets, including lumber, plywood, oriented strand board, and related products. Includes price guides. Recurring features include a calendar of events and notices of publications available.

TRADE SHOWS AND CONVENTIONS

13676 ■ *Lumbermen's Association of Texas Convention*
Lumbermen's Association of Texas & Louisiana
1016 La Posada Dr., Ste. 150
Austin, TX 78752

Ph: (512)472-1194
Free: 800-749-5862
Fax: (512)472-7378
Co. E-mail: latadmin@lat.org
URL: http://www.lat.org
Contact: Barbara Douglas, Executive Vice President
E-mail: barbara@lat.org
URL(s): www.lat.org/125th-annual-convention. **Price:** $50, Onsite; $free, Pre-registered. **Frequency:** Annual. **Audience:** Retail lumber and building material dealers. **Principal Exhibits:** Lumber, building materials, hardware, and related products.

13677 ■ Mississippi Lumber Manufacturers Association Convention and Trade Show
Mississippi Lumber Manufacturers Association
PO Box 5241
Jackson, MS 39296-5241
Ph: (601)982-1731
Fax: (601)982-5263
Co. E-mail: sylvianapper@bellsouth.net
URL: http://www.mslumbermfg.org
Contact: Glenn Lott, President
E-mail: glott@hoodindustries.com
URL(s): www.mslumbermfg.org. **Frequency:** Annual. **Audience:** Mill members, lumber and mill producers, business related firms, wholesalers and producers in other states. **Principal Exhibits:** Lumber manufacturing equipment, supplies, and services.

13678 ■ Northwestern Building Products Expo
Northwestern Lumber Association
5905 Golden Valley Rd., Ste. 110
Minneapolis, MN 55422
Ph: (763)544-6822
Free: 888-544-6822
Fax: (763)595-4060
Co. E-mail: nlassn@nlassn.org
URL: http://www.nlassn.org
Contact: Paula Siewert, President
E-mail: psiewert@nlassn.org
Frequency: Annual. **Audience:** Retail lumber and building material dealers. **Principal Exhibits:** Any product or service that is ultimately sold or used by retail lumber and building material dealers. **Dates and Locations:** , Convention Center.

CONSULTANTS

13679 ■ Lee Resources International Inc.—Lumbersearch
210 Main St.
Greenwood, SC 29646
Ph: (864)229-0600
Free: 800-277-7888
Fax: (877)230-6329
Co. E-mail: info@leeresources.com
URL: http://www.leeresources.com
Contact: Bob Erwin, President
Scope: Consulting service assists clients in the lumber and building supply industry to improve organizational productivity. Specializes in site selection; site planning; facility design and specification; equipment requirements and procurement; personnel needs and job descriptions; inventory assortment; Proforma P and L budgets; initial capitalization requirements. **Founded:** 1987. **Publications:** "The Artichoke Factor"; "Customer Care"; "The Impact Selling System"; "Time Out"; "You Can Sell More Professionally"; "You Can Build a Better You"; "You Can Prospect More Creatively"; "You Can Manage and Motivate"; "The Secrets of Power Negotiating"; "Take

Charge of Your Life"; "Swim with the Sharks Without Being Eaten Alive"; "The Psychology of Winning"; "The Psychology of Selling"; "The Management Advantage"; "The 7 Habits of Highly Effective People"; "Even Further Up the Organization"; "Defrosting Telephone Cold Calls"; "Guide to Everyday Negotiating". **Seminars:** Developing Your Sales Process; I Dare You; Relationship Selling; Time Management; Customer Service; Protecting Your Margins; Business Development.

LIBRARIES

13680 ■ National Hardwood Lumber Association Library
6830 Raleigh-LaGrange Rd.
Memphis, TN 38134-7000
Ph: (901)377-1818
Free: 800-933-0318
Fax: (901)399-7581
Co. E-mail: m.barford@nhla.com
URL: http://www.nhla.com
Contact: Mark Barford, Executive Director
Scope: Hardwood lumber; grading rules. **Services:** Copying; library open to members of NHLA. **Founded:** 1898. **Holdings:** 2500 volumes.

13681 ■ Society of Wood Science and Technology Library
PO Box 6155
Monona, WI 53716-6155
Ph: (608)577-1342
Fax: (608)467-8979
Co. E-mail: vicki@swst.org
URL: http://www.swst.org
Contact: Dr. Todd Shupe, President
Scope: Wood and fiber science. **Services:** Library open to the public. **Founded:** 1958. **Holdings:** 30 periodicals. **Subscriptions:** 880 journals and other serials.

13682 ■ Texas Forest Service - Texas Forest Products Laboratory Library
Box 310
Lufkin, TX 75902
Ph: (936)639-8180
Co. E-mail: sshockley@tfs.tamu.edu
URL: http://texasforestservice.tamu.edu
Contact: Susan Shockley, Assistant
Scope: Wood science, forest products technology and utilization. **Services:** Copying; Library open to the public for reference use only. **Founded:** 1930. **Telecommunication Services:** webmaster@tfs.tamu.edu.

13683 ■ U.S.D.A. Forest Service - Forest Products Laboratory Library
One Gifford Pinchot Dr.
Madison, WI 53726-2398
Ph: (608)231-9491
Fax: (608)231-9311
Co. E-mail: pdl_fpl_library@fs.fed.us
URL: http://www.fpl.fs.fed.us/products/library/index.php
Contact: Julie Blankenburg, Librarian, Reference
Scope: Forest products utilization, energy from wood, paper and pulp, wood engineering, wood processing and protection, timber, wood products economics. **Services:** Interlibrary loan; copying (limited); Library open to the public. **Founded:** 1910. **Holdings:** 56,300 books and bound periodical volumes; 30,300 technical reports; 20,000 bulletins, reports, reprints;

6200 patents; 5900 microforms. **Subscriptions:** 340 journals. **Telecommunication Services:** jblankenburg@fs.fed.us.

13684 ■ Weyerhaueser Company - Archives NP-190
PO Box 9777
Federal Way, WA 98063-9777
Ph: (253)924-2345
Free: 800-525-5440
Fax: (253)924-7863
Co. E-mail: megan.moholt@weyerhaeuser.com
URL: http://www.weyerheauser.com
Contact: Megan Moholt, Archivist
Scope: Weyerhaeuser Company, forest products, logging, lumber manufacturing, pulp/paperboard, Pacific Northwest. **Services:** Archives open to the public on a limited basis with restrictions. **Founded:** 1974. **Holdings:** 3000 cubic feet and 128 lin.ft. of archival material including correspondence and office files, 1900-2008, ledgers, journals, Annual and financial reports, biographical files, speeches of company executives and personnel, company publications, minute books of the company, photographs of company facilities and operations, photographs of logging in the Northwest, films, oral history interviews, artifacts and memorabilia, maps, archives.

RESEARCH CENTERS

13685 ■ Hardwood Plywood and Veneer Association (HPVA)
1825 Michael Faraday Dr.
Reston, VA 20190
Ph: (703)435-2900
Fax: (703)435-2537
Co. E-mail: hpva@hpva.org
URL: http://www.hpva.org
Contact: Kip Hawlett, President
E-mail: khowlett@hpva.org
Description: Manufacturers and finishers of hardwood plywood; manufacturers and sales agents of veneer; suppliers of glue, machinery, and other products related to the industry; stocking distributors. Conducts laboratory testing of plywood, adhesives, finishes, flamespread, formaldehyde emissions, structural, and smoke density. Performs glue bond, flamespread, formaldehyde emissions, and structural listing services. Provides public relations, advertising, marketing, and technical services to members. Represents the industry in legislative matters and keeps members informed on tariff and trade actions. **Scope:** hardwood plywood and veneer manufacturing and uses. **Services:** Planting of hardwood trees. **Founded:** 1921. **Subscriptions:** 300. **Publications:** *Hardwood Plywood & E-News* (Semimonthly); *Hardwood Plywood*; *Hardwood Plywood and Veneer News* (Monthly); *Directory of Veneer Manufacturers, Veneer Sales Representatives, Veneer Importers in the United States and Canada* (Annual); *Directory of Manufacturers of Marine Hardwood Plywood* (Annual); *HPMA Testing and Inspection and Listed Products Manual* (Annual); *Where to Buy Hardwood Plywood and Veneer Directory* (Annual); *Veneer Manufacturers in the United States and Canada* (Annual); *Where to Buy Hardwood Plywood, Veneer, and Engineered Hardwood Flooring Buyers' Guide* (Annual); *Where to Buy Hardwood Plywood, Veneer, and Engineered Hardwood Flooring Membership Directory* (Annual); *Associations and Organizations of Interest to Hardwood Plywood & Veneer Manufacturers* (Annual); *Magazines & Publications of Interest to Hardwood Plywood & Veneer Manufacturers* (Irregular); *Hardwood Plywood Manufacturers Association--Face Veneer Manufacturers List*. **Educational Activities:** Semiannual conventions; HPVA Workshops. **Telecommunication Services:** khowlett@hpva.org.

ASSOCIATIONS AND OTHER ORGANIZATIONS

13686 ■ Aluminum Extruders Council (AEC)
1000 N Rand Rd., Ste. 214
Wauconda, IL 60084
Ph: (847)526-2010
Fax: (847)526-3993
Co. E-mail: mail@aec.org
URL: http://www.aec.org
Contact: Duncan Crowdis, Chairman
Description: Manufacturers of extruded aluminum shapes and their suppliers. Compiles statistics; provides technical assistance and develops markets. Conducts workshops for management, sales, and plant personnel. **Founded:** 1950. **Publications:** *Aluminum Extrusion*; *Buyer's Guide*; *Executive Report* (Bimonthly); *Publications Catalog*. **Educational Activities:** Management Conference (Annual).

13687 ■ American Machine Tool Distributors' Association (AMTDA)
7361 Calhoun Pl., Ste. 320
Rockville, MD 20855
Ph: (301)738-1200
Fax: (301)738-9499
Co. E-mail: info@amtda.org
URL: http://www.amtda.org
Contact: Douglas K. Woods, President
URL(s): www.amtonline.org. **Description:** Distributors and builders of manufacturing technology. Offers technical training, sales training and management. Compiles statistics. **Founded:** 1925. **Publications:** *AMTDA Directory* (Annual); *Tool Talk* (10/year); *American Machine Tool Distributors' Association--Directory of Members* (Annual); *US Machine Tool Consumption Report* (Monthly). **Educational Activities:** APEX Detroit - Advanced Productivity Exposition/Detroit (Biennial); APEX Orlando - Advanced Productivity Exposition/Orlando (Biennial); Dallas APEX - Advanced Productivity Exposition/Dallas (Biennial); Mid-Atlantic Machine Tool Show; Pacific Coast Machine Tool Expo (Annual); Twin Cities APEX - Advanced Productivity Exposition/Twin Cities (Biennial); WESTEC - Advanced Productivity Exposition (Biennial). **Telecommunication Services:** amt@amtonline.org.

13688 ■ Canadian Foundry Association (CFA)—Association des Fonderies Canadiennes
1 Nicholas St., Ste. 1500
Ottawa, ON, Canada K1N 7B7
Ph: (613)789-4894
Fax: (613)789-5957
Co. E-mail: judy@foundryassociation.ca
URL: http://www.foundryassociation.ca
Contact: Peter Clark, President
Description: Foundries. Seeks to advance the metals and forging industries. Serves as a forum for the exchange of information among members; represents members' interests before labor and industrial organizations, government agencies, and the public. **Founded:** 1975.

13689 ■ Canadian Welding Bureau (CWB)—Le Bureau Canadien de Soudage
8260 Parkhill Dr.
Milton, ON, Canada L9T 5V7
Free: 800-844-6790
Fax: (905)542-1318
Co. E-mail: info@cwbgroup.org
URL: http://eng.cwbgroup.org
Contact: Doug Luciani, President
Description: Participants include welding organizations, consumable manufacturers, welding inspectors, welders and welding educators and trainers. Seeks to ensure maintenance of high standards of practice and compliance to accepted workmanship standards in the welding profession. Provides welding certification for fabricating and manufacturing companies and manufacturers of steel building systems, welding inspection companies and metal products inspectors, and welding consumables. Conducts ISO 9000, 14000 quality training and education. Holds examinations. (Quasar Division) Provides training and education study material and software. Conducts education and training of welding personnel (Learning Centre). **Scope:** welding. **Founded:** 1947. **Subscriptions:** books periodicals. **Publications:** *CWB NET* (Periodic). **Awards:** R.M. Gooderham Bursary (Annual).

13690 ■ CWB NET
8260 Parkhill Dr.
Milton, ON, Canada L9T 5V7
Free: 800-844-6790
Fax: (905)542-1318
Co. E-mail: info@cwbgroup.org
URL: http://eng.cwbgroup.org
Contact: Doug Luciani, President
Released: Periodic **Price:** included in membership dues.

13691 ■ Fabricators and Manufacturers Association International (FMA)
833 Featherstone Rd.
Rockford, IL 61107-6301
Ph: (815)399-8775
Free: 888-394-4362
Fax: (815)484-7701
Co. E-mail: info@fmanet.org
URL: http://www.fmanet.org
Contact: Dave Barber, Chairman of the Board
URL(s): www.fmafabtech.com. **Description:** People involved in the metal forming and fabricating industry. Disseminates technological information on the fabrication of sheet, coil, tube, pipe, plate, and structural metal shapes. Conducts continuing education conferences. Maintains technical information center. **Scope:** sheet metal fabricating, stamping, roll forming, welding, coil processing, tube and pipe producing, tube and pipe fabricating. **Founded:** 1970. **Subscriptions:** 500 articles audiovisuals books periodicals. **Publications:** *Member Connections*; *Member Connections* (Bimonthly); *Practical Welding Today* (Bimonthly); *Stamping Journal* (Monthly); *American Tube Association--FMA Member Resource Directory* (Annual); *Who's Who in Metal Forming & Fabricating* (Annual); *The Fabricator: Journal of Metal Forming and Fabricating Technology* (Monthly); *Who's Who in Metal Forming and Fabricating*. **Educational Activities:** FABTECH International and The AWS Welding Show (Annual); FABTECH International Exposition and Conference Series (Annual). **Telecommunication Services:** mhoper@fmafabtech.com.

13692 ■ Precision Metalforming Association (PMA)
6363 Oak Tree Blvd.
Independence, OH 44131-2556
Ph: (216)901-8800
Fax: (216)901-9190
Co. E-mail: dsansone@pma.org
URL: http://www.metalform.com
Contact: Patrick Thompson, Chairman
Description: Represents the metalforming industry of North America; the industry that creates precision metal products using stamping, fabricating and other value-added processes. Its member companies include metal stampers, fabricators, spinners, slide formers and roll formers, as well as suppliers of equipment, materials and services to the industry. Members are located in 30 countries, with the majority found in North America; in 41 states of the United States as well as Canada and Mexico. Conducts technical and educational programs, compiles statistics, offers training systems, and provides legislative and regulatory assistance to members. **Founded:** 1942. **Publications:** *MetalForming* (Monthly); *PMA Update*. **Educational Activities:** METALFORM Exhibition (Biennial). **Awards:** A.R. Hedberg Training and Education Award (Annual); Pitcher Insurance Agency Award for Safety (Annual); R.D. Pritchard-Higgins Award for Design (Annual); Signature Technologies Process Control Award; SKD Automotive Group Award for Productivity (Annual); Higgins-Caditz Design Award; Parkview Metal Products Award for Excellence in Quality Assurance (Annual); Ulbrich Award for Competitive Excellence in Product Development.

13693 ■ Society of Manufacturing Engineers (SME)
One SME Dr.
Dearborn, MI 48121
Ph: (313)425-3000
Free: 800-733-4763
Fax: (313)425-3401
Co. E-mail: service@sme.org
URL: http://www.sme.org
Contact: Barbara M. Fossum, President
E-mail: bfossum@sme.org
Description: Professional society of manufacturing engineers, practitioners and management executives concerned with manufacturing technologies for improved productivity. Seeks to advance the science of manufacturing through the continuing education of manufacturing engineers, practitioners and management. Conducts expositions, international seminars and clinics. **Founded:** 1932. **Publications:** *Plastics Insights* (Quarterly); *Composites in Manufacturing* (Quarterly); *Journal of Manufacturing Systems* (Quarterly); *Manufacturing Engineering* (Monthly; 10/year); *SME News* (Bimonthly); *Composites in Manu-*

facturing; *Machine Vision and Robotics Industry Directory; Manufacturing Engineering* (Monthly); *Electronics Manufacturing: SME's Quarterly on Electronics Manufacturing Technology* (Quarterly); *Finishing Line: AFP/SME's Quarterly on Finishing and Coatings Technology* (Quarterly); *Vision: SME's Quarterly on Vision Technology* (Quarterly); *Directory of Composites Manufacturers, Suppliers, Consultants, and Research Organizations* (Biennial); *Manufacturing Engineering New Manufacturing Equipment Buyers Guide* (Annual); *Machine Vision and Robotics Industry Directory* (Biennial); *INTIME Manufacturing Data Bank; TMEH Knowledge Base; Vision--Show Directory Issue; Directory of Manufacturing Education Programs in Colleges, Universities, and Technical Institutes* (Updated continuously; printed on request); *Forming & Fabricating* (Monthly). **Educational Activities:** AeroDef (Annual); Finishing (Biennial); APEX Detroit - Advanced Productivity Exposition/Detroit (Biennial); APEX Orlando - Advanced Productivity Exposition/Orlando (Biennial); Automotive Finishing Conference and Exposition (Biennial); Canadian Manufacturing Technology Show 2012 (Annual); Cleveland APEX - Advanced Productivity Exposition (Biennial); Dallas APEX - Advanced Productivity Exposition/Dallas (Biennial); EASTEC - Advanced Productivity Exposition (Annual); FABTECH International and The AWS Welding Show (Annual); Micro-Manufacturing Conference & Exhibits (Annual); Midwest Machine Tool Show (Biennial); NanoManufacturing Conference & Exhibits (Annual); Orlando APEX (Biennial); SOUTH TEC - Greenville APEX (Biennial); Twin Cities APEX - Advanced Productivity Exposition/Twin Cities (Biennial); WESTEC - Advanced Productivity Exposition (Biennial). **Awards:** Award of Merit; Honorary Membership; Outstanding Young Manufacturing Engineer Award (Annual); Joseph A. Siegel Service Award (Annual); Education Award; SME Gold Medal (Annual); Eli Whitney Productivity Award; Award of Merit (Annual); Donald C. Burnham Manufacturing Management Award (Annual); Eli Whitney Productivity Award (Annual); SME Education Award (Annual); Donald C. Burnham Manufacturing Management Award; Albert M. Sargent Progress Award; Frederick W. Taylor Research Medal; SME Albert M. Sargent Progress Award (Annual); SME Frederick W. Taylor Research Medal (Annual). **Telecommunication Services:** webmaster@sme.org.

13694 ■ **Specialty Tools and Fasteners Distributors Association (STAFDA)**
PO Box 44
Elm Grove, WI 53122
Ph: (262)784-4774
Free: 800-352-2981
Fax: (262)784-5059
Co. E-mail: info@stafda.org
URL: http://www.stafda.org
Contact: Mike Kangas, President
Description: Distributors and suppliers of power tools, power-actuated tools, anchors, fastening systems, diamond drilling, and related construction equipment. Encourages legal, ethical, and friendly business relations within the industry. Collects and disseminates information pertinent to the industry; develops more effective, economical, and profitable distribution. **Founded:** 1976. **Publications:** *Specialty Tools & Fasteners Distributors Association--Membership Directory* (Annual). **Educational Activities:** Specialty Tools and Fasteners Distributors Association Convention (Annual); STAFDA Convention & Trade Show/Specialty Tools & Fasteners Distributors Association (Annual).

13695 ■ **Tooling, Manufacturing and Technologies Association (TMTA)**
PO Box 2204
Farmington Hills, MI 48333-2204
Ph: (248)488-0300
Free: 800-969-9682
Fax: (248)488-0500
Co. E-mail: rob@thetmta.com
URL: http://www.thetmta.com
Contact: Herbert Trute, Chairman
Description: Manufacturers of dies, jigs, fixtures, molds, gages, tools, special machinery, and related products; suppliers of die tryout, machining, and

experimental and designing service. **Founded:** 1933. **Publications:** *TMTA Talk* (Monthly).

13696 ■ **United States Cutting Tool Institute (USCTI)**
1300 Sumner Ave.
Cleveland, OH 44115-2851
Ph: (216)241-7333
Fax: (216)241-0105
Co. E-mail: uscti@uscti.com
URL: http://www.uscti.com
Contact: David J. Povich, President
Description: Manufacturers of rotary metal cutting tools. Objectives are to: promote the manufacture and sale of rotary metal cutting tools in the U.S. and in foreign markets; promote the standardization of sizes, dimensions, and tolerances in cooperation with the American National Standards Institute, American Society of Mechanical Engineers, and other engineering organizations; increase the use of metal cutting tools and allied products. **Founded:** 1988. **Publications:** *Drilled Holes for Tapping; Standards and Dimensions for Ground Thread Taps.*

DIRECTORIES OF EDUCATIONAL PROGRAMS

13697 ■ *Directory of Private Accredited Career Schools and Colleges of Technology*
Pub: Accrediting Commission of Career Schools and Colleges of Technology
Contact: Michale S. McComis, Executive Director
Released: On web page. **Price:** Free. **Description:** Covers 3900 accredited post-secondary programs that provide training programs in business, trade, and technical fields, including various small business endeavors. Entries offer school name, address, phone, description of courses, job placement assistance, and requirements for admission. Arrangement is alphabetical.

REFERENCE WORKS

13698 ■ *AMT--Member Product Directory*
Pub: Association for Manufacturing Technology
Contact: Douglas K. Woods, President
URL(s): www.amtonline.org/directory/AMTdirectory.cfm. **Released:** Annual; winter. **Covers:** Machine tools and related products built by members of the Association for Manufacturing Technology. **Entries include:** Company name, address, phone, telex, fax, e-mail, website, and product specifications. **Arrangement:** Product type; company name. **Indexes:** Product type (in English, French, Spanish, German, Japanese, Italian, Portuguese, Chinese).

13699 ■ *"The Consequences of Tardiness" in Modern Machine Shop (Vol. 84, August 2011, No. 3, pp. 34)*
Pub: Gardner Business Media, Inc.
Contact: Richard G. Kline, President
E-mail: rkline@gardnerweb.com
Ed: Wayne S. Chaneski. **Description:** Five point addressing motivating factors behind employees who are tardy and those who choose to be on time in the workplace are shared.

13700 ■ *"Customer Service Center Will Rise in Indian Land" in Charlotte Observer (February 4, 2007)*
Pub: Knight-Ridder/Tribune Business News
Ed: Taylor Bright. **Description:** Kennametal is building a new customer service center in Lancaster County, North Carolina. Kennametal makes metal tools and parts, specializing in metals highly resistant to heat.

13701 ■ *Cutting Tool Engineering--Superabrasives Directory Issue*
Pub: CTE Publications Inc.
Contact: Alan Rooks, Director
URL(s): www.ctemag.com. **Ed:** Don Nelson. **Released:** Annual; November. **Covers:** Nearly 400 manufacturers and distributors of industrial diamond

and superabrasive products and related equipment. **Entries include:** Company name, address, phone, key personnel. **Arrangement:** Alphabetical. **Indexes:** Product.

13702 ■ *Dun and Bradstreet's Industrial Guide: The Metalworking Directory*
Pub: Dun and Bradstreet Corp.
Contact: David J. Emery, President
URL(s): www.dnb.com. **Released:** Annual; hardcover, August; looseleaf, August. **Covers:** Over 120,000 original equipment manufacturers, metal distributors, and machine tools/metalworking machinery distributors. **Entries include:** Company name, address, phone, Dun & Bradstreet D-U-N-S number, Standard Industrial Classification (SIC) code, trade name, year established, names and titles of key personnel, number of employees, principal manufacturing processes performed, metal and non-metal products purchased, end products manufactured, plant square footage, territory serviced, import/export code. **Arrangement:** Same information arranged geographically, alphabetically, and classified by industry in separate volumes. **Indexes:** Company name (with location and primary SIC code), SIC code (with address).

13703 ■ *"Engineering Services Supplier Launches 'Robotic Renaissance" in Modern Machine Shop (Vol. 84, September 2011, No. 4, pp. 46)*
Pub: Gardner Business Media, Inc.
Contact: Richard G. Kline, President
E-mail: rkline@gardnerweb.com
Description: Profile of Applied Manufacturing Technologies (AMT) new hiring initiative that supports continuing growth in the robotics industry. AMT is located in Orion, Michigan and supplies factory automation design, engineering and process consulting services.

13704 ■ *"Evaluate Your Process and Do It Better" in Modern Machine Shop (Vol. 84, October 2011, No. 5, pp. 34)*
Pub: Gardner Business Media, Inc.
Contact: Richard G. Kline, President
E-mail: rkline@gardnerweb.com
Ed: Wayne S. Chaneski. **Description:** In order to be more competitive, many machine shops owners are continually looking at their processes and procedures in order to be more competitive.

13705 ■ *"Getting the Word Out" in Modern Machine Shop (Vol. 84, September 2011, No. 4, pp. 16)*
Pub: Gardner Business Media, Inc.
Contact: Richard G. Kline, President
E-mail: rkline@gardnerweb.com
Ed: Derek Korn. **Description:** Many times machine shops create devices to streamline their own machining processes and find these devices can be used by other shops, thus developing a marketable product. Tips for this process are outlined.

13706 ■ *"Insert Grade Coating Improves Tool Live" in Modern Machine Shop (Vol. 84, October 2011, No. 5, pp. 124)*
Pub: Gardner Business Media, Inc.
Contact: Richard G. Kline, President
E-mail: rkline@gardnerweb.com
Ed: Emily K. Tudor. **Description:** Profile of Sumitomo Electric Carbide's AC420K insert that is a CVD-coated carbide grade that features layers of TiCN and Al.sub.2 O.sub.3 for wear, chipping and heat resistance.

13707 ■ *"Lincoln Electric Installs Large Wind Tower" in Modern Machine Shop (Vol. 84, October 2011, No. 5, pp. 42)*
Pub: Gardner Business Media, Inc.
Contact: Richard G. Kline, President
E-mail: rkline@gardnerweb.com
Description: Lincoln Electric, a welding product manufacturer, constructed a 443-foot-tall wind tower at its plant in Euclid, Ohio. The tower is expected to generate as much as 10 percent of the facility's energy and save as much as $500,000 annually in energy costs.

13708 ■ *Machine Tool Reference Guide*
Pub: Machinery Dealers National Association
Contact: Terry A. Yoder, Director
URL(s): www.mdna.org. **Released:** 64 **Price:** $19.
95, Individuals; $29.95, Nonmembers. **Covers:**
Nearly 1,000 metalworking machine tool manufacturers; international coverage. **Entries include:** Company name, address, phone, fax, product/service
provided. **Database includes:** Information on mergers and sources of parts. **Arrangement:** Alphabetical. **Indexes:** Company name, type of equipment.

13709 ■ *"A Model Machine for Titanium" in
Modern Machine Shop (Vol. 84, October 2011,
No. 5, pp. 84)*
Pub: Gardner Business Media, Inc.
Contact: Richard G. Kline, President
E-mail: rkline@gardnerweb.com
Ed: Peter Zelinski. **Description:** Researchers have
developed a machine tool that controls vibration in
order to mill titanium more productively. In-depth
information on the machine tool as well as under-
standing the processes involved in milling titanium is
covered.

13710 ■ *"Pedal to the Medal" in Small
Business Opportunities (Summer 2010)*
Pub: Harris Publications Inc.
Ed: Chuck Green. **Description:** Profile of Darlene
Miller who became and partner and eventually took
over Permac Industries, a firm that specializes in
precision machine products.

13711 ■ *"Sandvik Expands Energy-Saving
Program" in Modern Machine Shop (Vol. 84,
September 2011, No. 4, pp. 48)*
Pub: Gardner Business Media, Inc.
Contact: Richard G. Kline, President
E-mail: rkline@gardnerweb.com
Description: Sandvik Coromant, based in Fair Lawn,
New Jersey, expanded its Sustainable Manufacturing
Program that originally was developed to help
Japanese-based firms reduce electricity consumption
by 15 percent after the recent earthquake that cause
loss of electrical power. The program now provides
energy reduction through the Sandvick cutting tool
technology, application techniques and productivity
increases.

13712 ■ *"Tempering Urgency Within Your
Shop" in Modern Machine Shop (Vol. 84,
October 2011, No. 5, pp. 16)*
Pub: Gardner Business Media, Inc.
Contact: Richard G. Kline, President
E-mail: rkline@gardnerweb.com
Ed: Derek Korn. **Description:** Because machine
shops operate under an environment of urgency,
patience can commingle with the pressure to produce
products efficiently and timely.

13713 ■ *"To Be or Not To Be an S
Corporation" in Modern Machine Shop (Vol.
84, September 2011, No. 4, pp. 38)*
Pub: Gardner Business Media, Inc.
Contact: Richard G. Kline, President
E-mail: rkline@gardnerweb.com
Ed: Irving L. Blackman. **Description:** The definitions
of both C corporations and S corporations are defined
to help any machine shop discover which best suits
the owner's business plan.

13714 ■ *Used Machinery Buyer's Guide*
Pub: Machinery Dealers National Association
Contact: Terry A. Yoder, Director
URL(s): www.mdna.org. **Released:** Annual; Latest
edition 2011. **Price:** Free. **Covers:** 450 member dealers in used capital equipment. **Entries include:**
Company name, address, phone, names of executives, telex number, telefax. **Arrangement:** Geographical, Alphabetical, specialty. **Indexes:** Company
name, types of equipment.

13715 ■ *"A Virtual Jog Mode for CAM" in
Modern Machine Shop (Vol. 84, November
2011, No. 6, pp. 22)*
Pub: Gardner Business Media, Inc.
Contact: Richard G. Kline, President
E-mail: rkline@gardnerweb.com
Ed: Edwin Gasparraj. **Description:** In many cases,
CAM programming required a specific, user-defined
path. Siemens PLMs Generic Motion Controller is an

alternative that defines the tool path within CAM. The
program is a virtual 'teach' mode that enables the
user to capture cutter locations by jogging machines
axes within CAM.

13716 ■ *"What Do Your ISO Procedures
Say?" in Modern Machine Shop (Vol. 84,
September 2011, No. 4, pp. 34)*
Pub: Gardner Business Media, Inc.
Contact: Richard G. Kline, President
E-mail: rkline@gardnerweb.com
Ed: Wayne S. Chaneski. **Description:** ISO 9000
certification can be time-consuming and costly, but it
is a necessary step in developing a quality manage-
ment system that meets both current and potential
customer needs.

13717 ■ *"What Is In Your Company Library?"
in Modern Machine Shop (Vol. 84, October
2011, No. 5, pp. 60)*
Pub: Gardner Business Media, Inc.
Contact: Richard G. Kline, President
E-mail: rkline@gardnerweb.com
Ed: Mike Lynch. **Description:** A good company
library in any machine shop can help keep employees
productive. Safety as well as information are critical
to complete any task in a shop.

13718 ■ *"What Makes for an Effective,
Production-Oriented VMC?" in Modern
Machine Shop (Vol. 84, November 2011, No.
6, pp. 24)*
Pub: Gardner Business Media, Inc.
Contact: Richard G. Kline, President
E-mail: rkline@gardnerweb.com
Ed: Derek Korn. **Description:** When a machine
shop's existing VMC only offers a modest spindle
performance and slow, non-cutting functions, the latest VMC technology for high-volume production that
minimizes cycle times and maximizes competitiveness could be helpful. Makino's new Production
Standard (PS) series of VMCs provides not only a
number of standard features to shrink cycle times,
but also design elements that can effectively support
a shops production elements are defined.

SOURCES OF SUPPLY

13719 ■ *Aluminum Extrusion Press Directory*
The Aluminum Association Inc.
URL(s): www.aluminum.org. **Released:** Irregular
Price: $70, Members; $135, Nonmembers. **Covers:**
Locations of 496 aluminum presses at 217 plants in
148 US companies; details on extruders, locations,
press sizes, anodizing, painting and billet casting
facilities. **Entries include:** Names of extruders and
plant addresses.

13720 ■ *Utillaje: Compendio de Maquinaria*
Utillaje Inc.
URL(s): www.utillaje.com. **Released:** Monthly **Covers:** Over 10,000 listings of manufacturing and
industrial equipment listed by over 300 sellers
throughout North, Central, and South America. Equipment includes new, used, and rebuilt machinery,
chemical/food, as well as electrical equipment. **Entries include:** Company name, location, phone
number, fax number, description of services and
products provided. **Arrangement:** Classified by
product. **Indexes:** Name, geographical.

STATISTICAL SOURCES

13721 ■ *RMA Annual Statement Studies*
Pub: Risk Management Association
Contact: Kevin M. Blakey, President
Released: Annual. **Price:** $175.00 2006-07 edition,
$105.00. **Description:** Contains composite balance
sheets and income statements for more than 360
industries, including the accounting, auditing, and
bookkeeping industries. Also contains five years of
comparative historical data for discerning trends.
Includes 16 commonly used ratios, computed for
most of the size groupings for nearly every industry.

TRADE PERIODICALS

13722 ■ *American Machinist*
Pub: Penton Media Inc.
URL(s): www.americanmachinist.com/. **Released:**
Monthly

13723 ■ *American Tool, Die & Stamping
News*
Pub: Eagle Publications Inc.
URL(s): www.ameritooldie.com. **Released:** Bimonthly
Price: $65, U.S., Canada, and Mexico; $125, Other
countries.

13724 ■ *Die Casting Engineer*
Pub: North American Die Casting Association
Contact: Daniel L. Twarog, President
URL(s): www.diecastingengineer.org. **Released:** 6/yr.
Price: $60, U.S., Canada, and Mexico; $120, U.S.,
Canada, and Mexico two years; $270, Other countries
two years; $135, Other countries; included in mem-
bership dues.

13725 ■ *The Fabricator*
Pub: The Croydon Group Ltd. Fabricators &
Manufacturers Association
URL(s): www.thefabricator.com. **Released:** Monthly

13726 ■ *Machining Science & Technology*
Pub: Taylor & Francis Group Journals
Contact: Kevin J. Bradley, President
URL(s): www.tandf.co.uk/journals/journal.as-
p?issn=1091-0344&linktype=5. **Ed:** I.S. Jawahir, Dr.
R. Stevenson. **Released:** 4/yr. **Price:** $259, Individu-
als print only; $853, Institutions online only; $948,
Institutions print & online; €752, Institutions print &
online; €677, Institutions online only; €208, Individu-
als print only.

13727 ■ *Metalforming: Serving the Precision
Metalforming Industry*
Pub: Precision Metalforming Association MetalForm-
ing Magazine
URL(s): www.metalformingmagazine.com. **Ed:** Brad
Kuvin. **Released:** Monthly **Price:** $40, Individuals
North America; $225, Other countries.

13728 ■ *Modern Casting Magazine*
Pub: American Foundry Society, Inc.
Contact: Laura Moreno, Director
E-mail: lmoreno@afsinc.org
URL(s): www.moderncasting.com/. **Released:**
Monthly **Price:** $40, Individuals; $5, Single issue;
$50, Individuals; $75, By mail.

13729 ■ *Practical Welding Today*
Pub: The Croydon Group Ltd. Fabricators &
Manufacturers Association
URL(s): www.fma-communications.com/pwt. **Re-
leased:** Bimonthly

13730 ■ *Production Technology News*
Pub: Advantage Business Media L.L.C.
Contact: George Fox, President
URL(s): www.productiontechnologynews.com. **Released:** Monthly; 9/yr. **Price:** $64, Free to qualified
subscribers; $109, U.S.; $109, Canada; $10, Individu-
als Mexico; $10, Single issue.

13731 ■ *Tooling & Production: Providing
Solutions for Metalworking Manufacturers*
Pub: Nelson Publishing Inc.
URL(s): www.manufacturingcenter.comwww.toolinga-
ndproduction.com. **Released:** Monthly **Price:** Free.

TRADE SHOWS AND
CONVENTIONS

13732 ■ METALFORM Mexico
Precision Metalforming Association
6363 Oak Tree Blvd.
Independence, OH 44131-2500
Ph: (216)901-8800

Fax: (216)901-9190
Co. E-mail: pma@pma.org
URL: http://www.metalforming.com
Contact: Robert Clay, Chief Executive Officer
E-mail: bob@pridgeonandclay.com
URL(s): www.metalforming.com. **Frequency:** Annual.
Audience: Metal stampers, and spinnings and fabricated parts industry. **Principal Exhibits:** Presses and stamping equipment, tooling and fabricating machines, management aids, and related materials. **Telecommunication Services:** pma@pma.org.

CONSULTANTS

13733 ■ **Machine Tool Sales Co. (MTSC)**
2694 Dorchester Rd.
Birmingham, MI 48009
Ph: (248)614-0063
Co. E-mail: tom@tshipley.cnchost.com
URL: http://www.tshipley.cnchost.com
Contact: Thomas E. Shipley, President
E-mail: tom@tshipley.cnchost.com

Scope: Offers complete marketing service for metal working, computer, and machine automation fields. **Founded:** 1976. **Seminars:** Precision Grinding Seminar; Radio for Industrial Advertising - What It Needs to Do; What's Wrong With Metalworking Marketing?.

LIBRARIES

13734 ■ **Erico Inc. - Information Resources Center**
34600 Solon Rd.
Solon, OH 44139
Ph: (440)248-0100
Fax: (440)248-0723
URL: http://www.erico.com/library.asp

Scope: Engineering, science and technology, materials, metals, research and development, sales, marketing, personnel. **Services:** Interlibrary loan; copying; center open to the public with restrictions.

Founded: 1989. **Holdings:** 6000 books; 2000 patents; 500 manuscripts; standards; specifications. **Subscriptions:** 100 journals and other serials; 5 newspapers.

RESEARCH CENTERS

13735 ■ **Lehigh University - Institute for Metal Forming (IMF)**
Materials Science & Engineering Department
5 E Packer Ave.
Bethlehem, PA 18015-1657
Ph: (610)758-4252
Fax: (610)758-4244
Co. E-mail: wzm2@lehigh.edu
URL: http://www.lehigh.edu/~inimf
Contact: Prof. Wojciech Z. Misiolek, Director
Founded: 1969. **Publications:** *IMF Reports.*

START-UP INFORMATION

13736 ■ *55 Surefire Food-Related Businesses: You Can Start for Under $5000*
Pub: Entrepreneur Press
Contact: Perlman Neil, President
Ed: Cheryl Kimball. **Released:** March 1, 2009. **Price:** $17.95. **Description:** Advice is given to start 55 various food-related companies and goes beyond restaurant or catering services. Home-based, retail and mail order ventures are covered, as well as food safety and standards.

13737 ■ *An Eye for Winners*
Pub: DIANE Publishing Co.
Ed: Lillian Vernon. **Released:** 1999. **Price:** $23.00.

13738 ■ *How to Start a Home-Based Mail Order Business*
Pub: Globe Pequot Press
Ed: Georganne Fiumara. **Released:** January 2005. **Price:** $17.95. **Description:** Step-by-step guide for starting and growing a home-based mail order business. Information about equipment, pricing, online marketing, are included along with worksheets and checklists for planning.

ASSOCIATIONS AND OTHER ORGANIZATIONS

13739 ■ **Catalog and Multichannel Marketing Council**
1120 Ave. of the Americas
New York, NY 10036-6700
Ph: (212)768-7277
Fax: (212)302-6714
Co. E-mail: customerservice@the-dma.org
URL: http://www.the-dma.org
Contact: Matt Blumberg, President
Description: Catalog houses, catalog printers, and list brokers; members of Direct Marketing Association. Aims to keep members abreast of legislative and legal matters concerning the industry, exchange up-to-date ideas on graphics, production, and lists and share the benefits of consumer-oriented publicity projects about catalogs in newspapers and magazines. Provides representation in Congress on legislative and postal matters. Conducts workshops. **Scope:** current state-of-the-art industry information. **Subscriptions:** 2520 books business records. **Publications:** *Current and Crossroads* (Monthly); *DMA Insider* (Quarterly). **Educational Activities:** Catalog Conference Day (Annual). **Awards:** DMA International ECHO (Annual); DMFE Corporate Leadership (Annual); DMFE Vision (Annual); DMFE Corporate Leadership; DMFE Educational Leadership; DMFE Vision.

13740 ■ **Direct Marketing Association (DMA)**
1120 Ave. of the Americas
New York, NY 10036-6700
Ph: (212)768-7277
Fax: (212)302-6714
Co. E-mail: ceo@the-dma.org
URL: http://www.the-dma.org
Contact: Linda A. Woolley, Chief Executive Officer
Description: Manufacturers, wholesalers, public utilities, retailers, mail order firms, publishers, schools, clubs, insurance companies, financial organizations, business equipment manufacturers, paper and envelope manufacturers, list brokers, compilers, managers, owners, computer service bureaus, advertising agencies, letter shops, research organizations, printers, lithographers, creators and producers of direct mail and direct response advertising. Studies consumer and business attitudes toward direct mail and related direct marketing statistics. Offers Mail Preference Service for consumers who wish to receive less mail advertising, Mail Order Action Line to help resolve difficulties with mail order purchases and Telephone Preference Service for people who wish to receive fewer telephone sales calls. Maintains hall of fame; offers placement service; compiles statistics. Sponsors several three-day Basic Direct Marketing Institutes, Advanced Direct Marketing Institutes and special interest seminars and workshops. Maintains Government Affairs office in Washington, DC. Operates Direct Marketing Educational Foundation. **Scope:** direct marketing. **Founded:** 1917. **Subscriptions:** 700 articles books periodicals. **Publications:** *The DMA Insider* (Quarterly); *Politically Direct* (Quarterly); *DMA Politically Direct.* **Awards:** DMA Hall of Fame (Annual); International ECHO Awards (Annual); International ECHO Awards; USPS Gold Mailbox Award. **Telecommunication Services:** lrc@the-dma.org.

REFERENCE WORKS

13741 ■ *Direct Marketing List Source*
Pub: Standard Rate and Data Service
Contact: Christopher Lehman, Chief Executive Officer
URL(s): www.srds.com/frontMatter/ips/directmarketing/index.html. **Released:** Annual **Price:** $788, annual unlimited single-user. **Covers:** Over 38,000 mailing lists composed of business persons and firms, general consumers, and rural and farm consumers, plus cooperative mailings, card decks, and package insert programs. Includes separate sections for new listings, mailing list brokers, compilers, managers; and suppliers of products and services to the direct mail industry (e.g., lettershops, etc.); and an international counterpart to all of the above. **Entries include:** For mailing lists--Title of list; name, address, phone of owner, manager, or broker, and name of contact; description of list, and its arrangement, maintenance, quantity, etc.; specific identification of source of list; addressing selections, method of delivery, schedules; mailing services offered; restrictions on use of list; price. For brokers and compilers--Firm name, address, phone, names of principal personnel, types of lists handled, fees and deposit mailing services offered, association memberships. **Arrangement:** Lists arranged by market classification (safety, literature and book buyers, etc.), by list name within classifications; managers, compilers, and brokers are alpha-

betical; suppliers classified by service. **Indexes:** Subject/market classification, list title/list owner.

13742 ■ *The Directory of Mail Order Catalogs*
Pub: Grey House Publishing
Contact: Richard Gottlieb, President
E-mail: rhg2@greyhouse.com
URL(s): www.greyhouse.com/marketing.htm. **Released:** Annual; Latest edition 2013. **Price:** $450, Individuals; $250, Libraries. **Covers:** Over 13,000 mail order firms and the catalogs they offer. **Entries include:** Company, address and phone for catalog orders, fax, description of merchandise offered; names of buyers, company president, marketing and production manager; size of catalog, price and frequency of catalog, availability of mailing list, number of employees, sales volume. **Arrangement:** Type of catalog or merchandise offered. **Indexes:** Company name, product, online.

13743 ■ *Mail Order in the Internet Age*
Pub: Morgan James Publishing, LLC
Ed: Ted Ciuba. **Released:** May 2004. **Price:** $19.95. **Description:** Direct response market, or mail order, for marketing and selling a product or service is discussed, with emphasis on how direct marketing compares favorably to other methods in terms of speed, ease, profitability, and affordability. Advice is given for writing ads; seminars to attend; and newsletters, mailing lists and magazines in which to subscribe.

13744 ■ *"Netflix vs. Blockbuster" in Inc. (October 2007, pp. 32)*
Pub: Gruner & Jahr USA Publishing
Description: Nexflix, the mail-order DVD rental service, is losing market share to Blockbuster, even after matching prices to that of its competitors. Entrepreneurs are asked how they would run Netflix to gain back market share.

13745 ■ *"Up, Up and Away" in Small Business Opportunities (November 2007)*
Pub: Harris Publications Inc.
Ed: Stan Roberts. **Description:** Profile of Miniature Aircraft USA, a mail order business providing kits to build flying machines priced from $500 to $2,500.

STATISTICAL SOURCES

13746 ■ *Mail Service Pharmacy Market*
MarketResearch.com
Released: 1999. **Price:** $3250.00 (Online).

13747 ■ *RMA Annual Statement Studies*
Pub: Risk Management Association
Contact: Kevin M. Blakey, President
Released: Annual. **Price:** $175.00 2006-07 edition, $105.00. **Description:** Contains composite balance sheets and income statements for more than 360 industries, including the accounting, auditing, and bookkeeping industries. Also contains five years of comparative historical data for discerning trends. Includes 16 commonly used ratios, computed for most of the size groupings for nearly every industry.

13748 ■ *Standard & Poor's Industry Surveys*
Pub: Standard & Poor's Corp.
Released: Annual. **Price:** $3633.00. **Description:** Two-volume book that examines the prospects for specific industries, including trucking. Also provides analyses of trends and problems, statistical tables and charts, and comparative company analyses.

TRADE PERIODICALS

13749 ■ *Business Mailers Review*
Pub: Sedgwick Publishing
Ed: Kate Phelan Muth, Editor, muth@erols.com. **Released:** Biweekly, 25/year. **Price:** $377, U.S. and Canada year; $392, elsewhere year. **Description:** Concerned with the monitoring of the U.S. Postal Service, private carriers, and suppliers. Offers volume mailers, traffic managers, parcel shippers, and operators of letter-shops news of current developments in the field of business mailings. Reports on new technologies and products, rate changes, metering alternatives, and relevant legislative activity. Recurring features include interviews and news of research.

13750 ■ *DM News: The Weekly Newspaper of Record for Direct Marketers*
Pub: DM News
URL(s): www.dmnews.com/. **Released:** Weekly **Price:** $148, Individuals; $198, Canada; $228, Other countries; $265, Two years; $355, Canada 2 years; $395, Other countries 2 years.

TRADE SHOWS AND CONVENTIONS

13751 ■ *Direct Marketing Association Annual Conference & Exhibition*
Direct Marketing Association
1120 Ave. of the Americas
New York, NY 10036-6700
Ph: (212)768-7277
Free: 800-255-0006

Fax: (212)302-6714
Co. E-mail: customerservice@the-dma.org
URL: http://www.the-dma.org
URL(s): www.dma11.org/index.php. **Frequency:** Annual. **Audience:** Trade professionals. **Principal Exhibits:** Printers, list brokers, envelope manufacturers, telephone marketing companies, computers and other equipment, supplies, and services for direct marketing. **Telecommunication Services:** customerservice@the-dma.org.

CONSULTANTS

13752 ■ *Leon Gelfond & Associates*
17266 Boca Club Blvd., Apt. 1606
Boca Raton, FL 33487-1279
Ph: (561)995-0865
Contact: Leon Gelfond, President
Scope: Consultants offering services in mail order, fulfillment, data processing, shipping and warehousing, printing, and book packaging. Primarily serving the publishing industry. Also has the capabilities and facilities for providing clients with a complete mail order package, from the creation to the printing and mailing of the promotion. Serves government also. **Founded:** 1986.

13753 ■ *Jeffrey Lant Associates Inc.*
50 Follen St., Ste. 507
Cambridge, MA 02138
Ph: (617)547-6372
Fax: (617)547-0061
URL: http://www.jeffreylant.com
Contact: Dr. Jeffrey L. Lant, President
E-mail: drjlant@worldprofit.com
Description: Description: Publishes technical assistance books for nonprofit organizations, consultants, independent professionals and small and home-based businesses. Offers audio cassettes, workshops and consultation services. Also publishes twice monthly Worlgram newsletter. Reaches market through commission representatives, direct mail, telephone sales and the Internet. Accepts unsolicited

manuscripts. **Scope:** Sets up businesses online, design websites and assists with marketing. **Founded:** 1979. **Publications:** "E-mail El Dorado," JLA Publications, 1998; "Web Wealth: How to Turn the World Wide Web Into a Cash Hose for Your Business. Whatever You're Selling," 1997; "Multi-Level Money," JLA Publications, 1994; "No More Cold Calls," JLA Publications, 1997; "Cash Copy"; "How to make at least $100000 a year"; "E-Money". **Seminars:** Business and personal development, including Establishing and Operating Your Successful Consulting Business; Successfully Promoting Your Small Business and Professional Practice; Succeeding in Your Mail Order Business; Successfully Raising Money for Your Nonprofit Organization from Foundations, Corporations and Individuals; Money Making Marketing; Finding the People Who Need What You're Selling and Making Sure They Buy It; Getting Corporations, Foundations, and Individuals to Give You the Money Your Nonprofit Organization Needs.

LIBRARIES

13754 ■ *Direct Marketing Association Library & Resource Center*
1120 Ave. of the Americas
New York, NY 10036-6700
Ph: (212)768-7277
Fax: (212)398-6725
Co. E-mail: lrc@the-dma.org
URL: http://www.the-dma.org
Contact: Terri L. Bartlett, Director, Library Services
Scope: Direct response advertising and marketing, including media applications (direct mail, catalog, telemarketing, print, interactive media, television), markets (business-to-business, consumer) and management basics. **Services:** Center open to nonmembers on a fee basis. **Founded:** 1946. **Holdings:** 1500 bound portfolios of direct marketing ECHO Awards campaigns. **Subscriptions:** 50 journals, magazines, and newsletters. **Telecommunication Services:** research@the-dma.org; tbartlett@the-dma.org.

START-UP INFORMATION

13755 ■ *How to Start a Home-Based Consulting Business: Define Your Specialty Build a Client Base Make Yourself Indispensable*
Pub: Globe Pequot Press
Ed: Bert Holtje. **Released:** January 10, 2010. **Price:** $18.95. **Description:** Everything needed for starting and running a successful consulting business from home.

13756 ■ *Starting and Running a Coaching Business*
Pub: How To Books
Ed: Aryanne Oade. **Released:** August 9, 2010. **Price:** $26.00. **Description:** Guide for the comprehensive, practical and personalized process of starting and running a coaching business is presented.

ASSOCIATIONS AND OTHER ORGANIZATIONS

13757 ■ **American Management Association (AMA)**
1601 Broadway
New York, NY 10019-7420
Ph: (212)586-8100
Free: 877-566-9441
Fax: (212)903-8168
Co. E-mail: customerservice@amanet.org
URL: http://www.amanet.org
Contact: Charles R. Craig, Chairman
URL(s): www.amanet.org/books. **Description:** Provides educational forums worldwide where members and their colleagues learn superior, practical business skills and explore best practices of world-class organizations through interaction with each other and expert faculty practitioners. Maintains a publishing program providing tools individuals use to extend learning beyond the classroom in a process of lifelong professional growth and development through education. **Founded:** 1923. **Publications:** *HR Focus* (Monthly); *Management Review* (Monthly); *The Take-Charge Assistant* (Monthly); *The Take-Charge Assistant*; *Organizational Dynamics: A Quarterly Review of Organizational Behavior for Management Executives*; *Small Business Reports: For Decision Makers in America's Small and Mid-Size Companies* (Monthly); *Organizational Dynamics: A Quarterly Review of Organizational Behavior for Professional Managers* (Quarterly); *AMA's Directory of Human Resource Products and Services*; *Make Your Contacts Count*. **Educational Activities:** Effective Technical Writing (Onsite); Conference for Executive Secretaries and Administrative Assistants (Annual); Conference for Executive Secretaries and Administrative Assistants (Annual). **Telecommunication Services:** membership@amanet.org; cust-serv@amanet.org.

13758 ■ **Association of Management Consulting Firms (AMCF)**
370 Lexington Ave., Ste. 2209
New York, NY 10017
Ph: (212)262-3055
Fax: (212)262-3054
Co. E-mail: info@amcf.org
URL: http://www.amcf.org
Contact: Elizabeth A. Kovacs, President
E-mail: bkovacs@amcf.org
Description: Trade association for consulting organizations that provide a broad range of managerial services to commercial, industrial, governmental, and other organizations and individuals. Seeks to unite management-consulting firms in order to develop and improve professional standards and practice in the field. Offers information and referral services on management consultants; administers public relations program. Conducts research. Monitors regulatory environment. **Scope:** Offers consulting services to management. Assists its members cope with the rapid changes affecting their practices today. Serves as a resource for information on the management of a consulting practice. Provides a forum for the exchange of ideas, helping consultants to better understand developments within the profession and to capitalize on new opportunities. Promotes knowledge exchange and professional standards for the community of management consulting firms from around the world. Serves as the voice of the industry on major issues, representing the profession before government and regulatory bodies, working to improve standards and practices and enabling firms to work smarter. **Founded:** 1929. **Publications:** *15th Annual Operating Ratios for Management Consulting Firms: A Resource for Benchmarking* (Annual). **Educational Activities:** Affinity Groups (Quarterly); Association of Management Consulting Firms Meeting (Annual); Association of Management Consulting Firms Roundtable (Quarterly). **Awards:** AMCF Richard Metzler (Annual).

13759 ■ *Electronic International Journal for Time Use Research*
c/o Dr. Kimberly Fisher, Sec.
University of Oxford
Dept. of Sociology
Manor Road Bldg.
Manor Rd.
Oxford OX1 3UQ, United Kingdom
Co. E-mail: kimberly.fisher@sociology.ox.ac.uk
URL: http://iatur.timeuse.org
Contact: Prof. Michael Bittman, President
Released: Annual

13760 ■ *Fifteenth Reunion of the International Association for Time Use Research Amsterdam*
c/o Dr. Kimberly Fisher, Sec.
University of Oxford
Dept. of Sociology
Manor Road Bldg.
Manor Rd.
Oxford OX1 3UQ, United Kingdom
Co. E-mail: kimberly.fisher@sociology.ox.ac.uk
URL: http://iatur.timeuse.org
Contact: Prof. Michael Bittman, President
Released: Periodic

13761 ■ **International Association for Time Use Research (IATUR)**
c/o Dr. Kimberly Fisher, Sec.
University of Oxford
Dept. of Sociology
Manor Road Bldg.
Manor Rd.
Oxford OX1 3UQ, United Kingdom
Co. E-mail: kimberly.fisher@sociology.ox.ac.uk
URL: http://iatur.timeuse.org
Contact: Prof. Michael Bittman, President
Description: The International Association for Time Use Research (IATUR) facilitates exchange of ideas, methodology, and data collection techniques among researchers and compilers of official statistics on the patterns of daily activities and changes in people's behaviours over time. **Scope:** time use, unpaid work, leisure time, women's work, work time, exposure, health, exercise. **Founded:** 1970. **Subscriptions:** 5200 articles periodicals books archival material monographs papers. **Publications:** *Fifteenth Reunion of the International Association for Time Use Research Amsterdam* (Periodic); *Time Use Methodology: Towards Consensus*; *Electronic International Journal for Time Use Research* (Annual).

13762 ■ **Professional and Technical Consultants Association (PATCA)**
PO Box 2261
Santa Clara, CA 95055
Ph: (408)971-5902
Free: 800-74-PATCA
Fax: (866)746-1053
Co. E-mail: info@patca.org
URL: http://www.patca.org
Contact: Larry Polyak, President
Description: Represents Independent consultants active in the support of business, industry, and government. Serves as a referral service to aid independent consultants in marketing their services as well as to assist those seeking their services. **Scope:** consulting. **Founded:** 1975. **Subscriptions:** 2. **Publications:** *PATCA Directory of Consultants* (Annual); *PATCA Survey of Rates and Business Practices* (Biennial).

13763 ■ *Time Use Methodology: Towards Consensus*
c/o Dr. Kimberly Fisher, Sec.
University of Oxford
Dept. of Sociology
Manor Road Bldg.
Manor Rd.
Oxford OX1 3UQ, United Kingdom
Co. E-mail: kimberly.fisher@sociology.ox.ac.uk
URL: http://iatur.timeuse.org
Contact: Prof. Michael Bittman, President

13764 ■ **Turnaround Management Association (TMA)**
150 S Wacker Dr., Ste. 900
Chicago, IL 60606
Ph: (312)578-6900

Fax: (312)578-8336
Co. E-mail: info@turnaround.org
URL: http://www.turnaround.org
Contact: Gregory J. Fine, Chief Executive Officer
Description: Practitioners (interim managers, consultants, corporate managers and professional advisors), academics, students, attorneys and judges, commercial lenders and legislative personnel. Promotes the image and credibility of the turnaround profession; fosters professional development and networking opportunities for turnaround executives; serves as a clearinghouse of information and research pertinent to the profession. Conducts networking forums; offers educational and credentialing programs. **Founded:** 1988. **Publications:** *Professional Fees in Bankruptcy Handbook.* **Educational Activities:** Spring Leadership Meeting (Annual). **Awards:** Turnaround of the Year (Annual).

REFERENCE WORKS

13765 ■ *"Auxis Introduces Services for Government Contracting" in Entertainment Close-Up (December 22, 2010)*
Pub: Close-Up Media
Description: Profile of Auxis Inc., a management consulting and outsourcing company has launched a new service for companies involved in or bidding for government contracts. Details of the program are provided.

13766 ■ *"Benchmark Makes Granduca Entrance" in Houston Business Journal (Vol. 40, January 8, 2010, No. 35, pp. 2)*
Pub: American City Business Journals
Ed: Jennifer Dawson. **Description:** Houston, Texas-based Interfin Company, owner of the Hotel Granduca, has tapped the services of Benchmark Hospitality International to manage the property. The hiring of Benchmark is part of Interfin's efforts to develop Granduca hotels in other markets. Statistical data included.

13767 ■ *Consultants and Consulting Organizations Directory*
Pub: Cengage Learning Inc.
Contact: Ronald Dunn, President
URL(s): www.gale.cengage.com. **Released:** Annual; New edition expected 37th; February, 2012. **Price:** $1392, Individuals. **Covers:** Over 26,000 firms, individuals, and organizations active in consulting. **Entries include:** Individual or organization name, address, phone, fax, e-mail, URL, specialties, founding date, branch offices, names and titles of key personnel, number of employees, financial data, publications, seminars and workshops. **Arrangement:** By broad subject categories. **Indexes:** Subject, geographical, organization name.

13768 ■ *D & B Consultants Directory*
Pub: Dun and Bradstreet Corp.
Contact: David J. Emery, President
URL(s): www.dnb.comwww.dnblearn.com/index.php?page=consultants-directory. **Released:** Annual; Latest edition September, 2008. **Covers:** Top 30,000 U.S. consulting firms in more than 200 areas of specialization. **Entries include:** Firm name, address, phone, sales, number of employees, year established, description of service, other locations, names and titles of key personnel, reference to parent company, D&B DUNS number, trade name, consulting activity, owned companies clientele, territory served, number of accounts, stock exchange symbol and indicator for publicly owned companies. **Arrangement:** Complete consultants profiles appear in the consultants alphabetical section. Companies are cross-referenced geographically and by activity. **Indexes:** All companies with a primary or secondary Standard Industrial Classification (SIC) code of 8748 "Business Consulting Services," as well as those companies whose type of business description includes the word "consult." All companies must have a phone number and be either a headquarters or single location.

13769 ■ *Franchise: Freedom or Fantasy*
Pub: iUniverse
Ed: Mitchell York. **Released:** June 22, 2009. **Price:** $13.95. **Description:** Successful franchisee and professional certified coach guides individuals

through the many steps involved in deciding whether or not to buy a franchise and how to do it correctly.

13770 ■ *"Leadership: The Couch in the Corner Office: Surveying the Landscape of the CEO Psyche" in Inc. (January 2008, pp. 33-34)*
Pub: Gruner & Jahr USA Publishing
Description: Profile of Leslie G. Mayer, founder of the Leadership Group, a firm that provides assistance to CEOs of firms by offering a deep understanding of the relationships, insecurities, and blind spots that can weaken strong leadership.

13771 ■ *Leading at a Higher Level*
Pub: FT Press
Ed: Ken Blanchard. **Released:** November 2006. **Price:** $26.99. **Description:** Tips, advice and techniques from a management consultant to help entrepreneurs create a vision for their company; includes information on manager-employee relationships.

13772 ■ *The Management Myth: Why the "Experts" Keep Getting It Wrong*
Pub: W.W. Norton & Company
Ed: Matthew Stewart. **Released:** August 10, 2009. **Price:** $27.95. **Description:** An insider's perspective on the management consulting industry, which reveals the high fees and incompetent consultants.

13773 ■ *The Mirror Test: How to Breathe New Life Into Your Business*
Pub: Grand Central Publishing
Ed: Jeffrey W. Hayzlett. **Released:** May 10, 2010. **Price:** $24.99. **Description:** Consultant and author, Jeffrey Hayzlett, explains why a business is not doing well and asks the questions that most business managers are afraid to ask.

13774 ■ *Professional and Technical Consultants Association--Directory of Consultants*
Pub: Professional and Technical Consultants Association
Contact: Larry Polyak, President
E-mail: lpolyak@msdus.com
URL(s): www.patca.org. **Released:** Annual; January; Latest edition 2009-2010. **Covers:** More than 350 consultants involved in computer technology, management, marketing, manufacturing, engineering, etc. **Entries include:** Individual or firm name, address, phone, specialties, degrees held. **Arrangement:** Alphabetical. **Indexes:** Specialty, geographical.

13775 ■ *The Sticking Point Solution: 9 Ways to Move Your Business from Stagnation to Stunning Growth in Tough Economic Times*
Pub: Vanguard Press
Contact: Bill Smith, Director
E-mail: bill.smith@perseusbooks.com
Ed: Jay Abraham. **Released:** May 10, 2010. **Price:** $25.95. **Description:** Renowned business consultant, Jay Abraham, reveals the nine ways even successful businesses get stuck, hit plateaus, and fail to achieve their dreams and he explains how to get unstuck and create exponential growth.

STATISTICAL SOURCES

13776 ■ *RMA Annual Statement Studies*
Pub: Risk Management Association
Contact: Kevin M. Blakey, President
Released: Annual. **Price:** $175.00 2006-07 edition, $105.00. **Description:** Contains composite balance sheets and income statements for more than 360 industries, including the accounting, auditing, and bookkeeping industries. Also contains five years of comparative historical data for discerning trends. Includes 16 commonly used ratios, computed for most of the size groupings for nearly every industry.

TRADE PERIODICALS

13777 ■ *Consultants News*
Pub: Kennedy Information Inc.
Contact: Wayne E. Cooper, President
Released: Monthly. **Price:** $349, U.S. and Canada; $399, elsewhere. **Description:** The authoritative

voice of the consulting industry, covering news, analysis, practice advice, proprietary data and opinion.

13778 ■ *Innovative Leader*
Pub: Winston J. Brill & Associates
Released: Monthly. **Price:** Free. **Description:** Serves as a resource for managers on creativity and productivity.

13779 ■ *The Journal for Quality and Participation*
Pub: American Society for Quality
Contact: Paul E. Borawski, Chief Executive Officer
URL(s): www.asq.org/pub/jqp/. **Released:** 4/yr. **Price:** $52, Members domestic, individuals; $82, Members international, individuals; $75, Members includes GST individual, Canada; $87, Nonmembers domestic, individuals; $98, Nonmembers international, individuals; $98, Nonmembers Canadian, includes GST individual.

13780 ■ *Make It A Winning Life*
Pub: Wolf Rinke Associates,Inc.
Ed: Wolf J. Rinke, Ph.D., Editor, wolfrinke@aol.com. **Released:** Bimonthly. **Price:** Free. **Description:** Features ideas and strategies to help individuals succeed faster and improve the quality of their life. Remarks: America Online, Inc.

13781 ■ *Management Report for Nonunion Organizations*
Pub: John Wiley and Sons Inc.
Ed: Sarah Magee, Editor. **Released:** Monthly. **Price:** $995, U.S.; $995, Canada and Mexico; $1067, elsewhere. **Description:** Features news on current activities; employers' responses; NLRB rulings; court cases; pending legislation; government policies; and advice and opinions from Alfred T. DeMaria, "one of the country's foremost labor lawyers" representing management. Includes information on preventive tactics on how to handle human resources and labor issues without risking unionization, a campaign workshop on what the laws and regulations mean in terms of day-to-day management, white-collar organizing, and questions and answers on common problems.

13782 ■ *Productivity Software*
Pub: Worldwide Videotex
Released: Monthly. **Price:** $150. **Description:** Provides information on computer software.

VIDEOCASSETTES/AUDIOCASSETTES

13783 ■ *Building a Profitable Consulting Practice Series*
Instructional Video
2219 C St.
Lincoln, NE 68502
Ph: (402)475-6570
Free: 800-228-0164
Fax: (402)475-6500
Co. E-mail: feedback@insvideo.com
URL: http://www.insvideo.com
Released: 19??. **Description:** Two-part business educational series by Howard Shenson offers tips on how to build a profitable consulting practice. Covers consulting opportunities, market strategies, proposal writing, contracting strategies, fee setting, disclosure, and collection techniques. **Availability:** VHS.

13784 ■ *Creativity in Management*
Video Arts, Inc.
c/o Aim Learning Group
8238-40 Lehigh
Morton Grove, IL 60053-2615
Free: 877-444-2230
Fax: (416)252-2155
Co. E-mail: service@aimlearninggroup.com
URL: http://www.aimlearninggroup.com
Released: 19??. **Price:** $149.00. **Description:** John Cleese presents the five steps for building an effective and creative work team. **Availability:** VHS.

13785 ■ *The 21st Century Manger*
Karol Media
Hanover Industrial Estates
375 Stewart Rd.
Wilkes Barre, PA 18773-7600
Ph: (570)822-8899
Free: 800-526-4773
Co. E-mail: sales@karolmedia.com
URL: http://www.karolmedia.com
Released: 1997. **Price:** $69.95. **Description:** Four-volume series discusses the new era of management. **Availability:** VHS.

CONSULTANTS

13786 ■ Advanced Benefits & Human Resources
9350-F Snowden River Pkwy., Ste. 222
Columbia, MD 21045
Ph: (410)290-9037
Fax: (410)740-2568
Co. E-mail: hrb@abhr.com
Contact: Linda Polacek, President
Scope: Provides human resource consulting to high technology businesses. Offers services in the areas of human resources, benefits, and training. Creates, maintains, or updates current human resource functions. **Founded:** 1996.

13787 ■ Advent Management International Ltd.
678 Burmont Rd., Ste. 200
Drexel Hill, PA 19026-3801
Ph: (610)506-6311
Free: 800-726-7985
Fax: (413)618-5273
Co. E-mail: donna@getresults.com
URL: http://www.getresults.com
Contact: John J. Reddish, Owner
E-mail: johnr@getresults.com
Scope: Works with leaders and members of their teams who want to become their personal best to master growth, manage change and facilitate succession. Services include: strategic, succession, operational and marketing planning; process improvement and project management, standards certification preparation, merchant banking; executive search, and management development. Primary industries served: manufacturing, professional services, IT, industrial distribution and B2B e-commerce. **Founded:** 1992. **Publications:** "Boomer Succession: A Philosophy For Letting Go"; "Strategic Fees: Planning & Pricing Your Future"; "Succession and Peace of Mind"; "Who Comes Next: Succession Issues For Business Owners"; "Finding Pockets: Buying A Business"; "Valuing The Closely Held Company: Which Way Is Best"; "How to Buy a Business"; "The Business Leader: Responsibilities"; "Responsibilities of Owners In A Smaller Business"; "Valuing The Closely Held Company: Which Way Is Best"; "The Seven Signs of Business Trouble: And What They Mean"; "How To Avoid Cash Flow Problems"; "Bankruptcies And Turnarounds". **Seminars:** How To Get More From Any Workshop.

13788 ■ Advisory Management Services Inc.
9600 E 129th St., Ste. B
Kansas City, MO 64149-1025
Ph: (816)765-9611
Fax: (816)765-7447
Contact: Hal Wood, President
Scope: A management consulting and training firm specializing in employee relations, management and staff training, organizational development, strategic planning, and continuous quality improvement. **Founded:** 1979.

13789 ■ The Alliance Management Group Inc.
38 Old Chester Rd., Ste. 300
Gladstone, NJ 07934
Ph: (908)234-2344
Fax: (908)234-0638
Co. E-mail: kathy@strategicalliance.com
URL: http://www.strategicalliance.com
Contact: Gene Slowinski, Director
E-mail: gene@strategicalliance.com
Scope: The firm enables leading companies to maximize the value of their strategic alliances, mergers and acquisitions. Offers services in partner evaluation process, a planning and negotiating program, mergers and acquisition integration, management issues, the turnaround or termination of poorly performing alliances, and a competitive strategic analysis program. **Publications:** "Effective Practices For Sourcing Innovation," Jan-Feb, 2009; "Intellectual Property Issues in Collaborative Research Agreements," Nov-Dec, 2008; "Building University Relationships in China," Sep-Oct, 2008; "Reinventing Corporate Growth: Implementing the Transformational Growth Model"; "The Strongest Link"; "Allocating Patent Rights in Collaborative Research Agreements"; "Protecting Know-how and Trade Secrets in Collaborative Research Agreements," Aug, 2006; "Sourcing External Technology for Innovation," Jun, 2006. **Special Services:** "Want, Find, Get, Manage" Model®; "Want, Find, Get, Manage" Framework®; WFGM Framework®; The Alliance Implementation Program®; WFGM Paradigm®; WFGM Model®; "Want, Find, Get, Manage" Paradigm®, Transformational Growth®; T-growth®.

13790 ■ Alliance Management International Ltd.
PO Box 470691
Cleveland, OH 44147-0691
Ph: (440)838-1922
Co. E-mail: bob@bgruss.com
Contact: Ashok Vasudevan, Director
Scope: A consulting company that helps to form national and international strategic alliances. Handles alliances between companies forming joint ventures. Staff specialized in small company-large company alliance, alliance assessment and analysis, and alliance strategic planning. **Seminars:** Joint Business Planning; Developing a Shared Vision; Current and New/Prospective Partner Assessment; Customer Service; Sales Training; Leader and Management Skills.

13791 ■ Anderson/Roethle Inc.
700 N Water St., Ste. 325
Milwaukee, WI 53202-4221
Ph: (414)276-0070
Fax: (414)276-4364
Co. E-mail: info@anderson-roethle.com
URL: http://www.anderson-roethle.com
Contact: Stanley C. Johnson, President
E-mail: scj@anderson-roethle.com
Scope: Provider of merger, acquisition and divestiture advisory services. Offers strategic planning, valuations and specialized M and A advisory services. **Founded:** 1963.

13792 ■ Apex Innovations Inc.
19951 W 162nd St.
Olathe, KS 66062
Ph: (913)254-0250
Fax: (913)254-0320
Co. E-mail: sales@apex-innovations.com
URL: http://www.apex-innovations.com
Contact: Wayne Abrams, Owner
E-mail: wayne.abrams@apex-innovations.com
Scope: A firm of business operations and technology professionals providing solutions nationwide for business needs. Provides a bridge between operations and technology for clients in manufacturing, insurance, banking and government. Offers services in business planning, assessment, education, business performance improvement, change management and the planning, and implementation management of solutions. **Founded:** 2002. **Special Services:** i-INFO. EPR™; i-INFO.WORKS™; i-INFO Classes™.

13793 ■ Associated Enterprises Ltd.
183 Pauls Ln.
Bailey, CO 80421-1122
Contact: Lawrence J. Rouse, President
Scope: General management consulting in all disciplines plus specialty in franchise and franchisee development programs. Additional specialties include economic research, analysis, and forecasting, financial management, business planning, and financing packaging, involving equity, debt, SBA 7A loans, 501 or 504 program development, and federal, state, and local program packages. Also experienced with litigation support, marketing, and audiovisual services. Serves private industries as well as government agencies. **Founded:** 1968.

13794 ■ Associated Management Services Inc. (AMSI)
8701 Georgia Ave., Ste. 705
Silver Spring, MD 20910-3713
Ph: (301)588-9694
Fax: (301)588-2113
Co. E-mail: info@amsihq.com
URL: http://www.amsihq.com
Contact: Bennett K. Holomah, President
Scope: Small business management firm offers consultation in the following areas: accounting, auditing, bookkeeping services, business advisory services and tax preparation for individuals, government agencies, and businesses and computer training and software applications. **Founded:** 1984.

13795 ■ Association of Home-Based Women Entrepreneurs (HBWE)
PO Box 31561
Saint Louis, MO 63131-1561
Ph: (314)805-9519
Fax: (314)909-8179
Co. E-mail: aschaefer@advbizsol.com
URL: http://www.hbwe.org
Contact: Louise Wiedermann, President
E-mail: lw@projektek.com
Scope: Organization dedicated to women working from home-based offices. Focuses on the needs and interests of women doing their own business. It also focuses on business-related programs and issues, networking, leads and mentoring for professional growth in a dynamic and friendly atmosphere. **Founded:** 1998. **Publications:** "Taking Your Business International"; "Dressing For Success"; "Web 2.0 The Future of the Internet"; "Assertiveness Skills for Women in Business". **Seminars:** Making Connections, Jul, 2008; One Inch Wide, One Mile Deep, Jun, 2008; Accelerating Your Business, May, 2008; Change is Good, Apr, 2008; Pyro Marketing, Jan, 2007; Twenty Five Key Steps To Maintaining A Successful Home-Based Business, Nov, 2006.

13796 ■ Aurora Management Partners Inc.
4485 Tench Rd., Ste. 340
Suwanee, GA 30024
Ph: (770)904-5209
Fax: (770)904-5226
Co. E-mail: rturcotte@auroramp.com
URL: http://www.auroramp.com
Contact: William A. Barbee, Director
E-mail: abarbee@auroramp.com
Scope: Specializes in turnaround management and reorganization consulting. Firm develop strategic initiatives, organize and analyze solutions, deal with creditor issues, review organizational structure and develop time frames for decision making. Turnaround services offered include Recovery plans and their implementation, Viability analysis, Crisis management, Financial restructuring, Corporate and organizational restructuring, Facilities rationalization, Liquidation management, Loan workout, Litigation support and Expert testimony, Contract renegotiation, Sourcing loan refinancing and Sourcing equity investment. **Founded:** 2005. **Publications:** "TMA Turnaround of the Year Award, Small Company, Honorable Mention," Nov, 2005; "Back From The Brink - Bland Farms," Progressive Farmer, Oct, 2004; "New Breed of Turnaround Managers," Catalyst Magazine, Aug, 2004; "Key Performance Drivers - Bland Farms," The Produce News, Apr, 2004; "Corporate Governance: Averting Crisis's Before They Happen," ABJ journal, Feb, 2004.

13797 ■ Bahr International Inc.
PO Box 795
Gainesville, TX 76241
Ph: (940)665-2344
Fax: (940)665-2359
Co. E-mail: info@bahrintl.com
URL: http://www.bahrintl.com
Contact: C. Charles Bahr, III, Chairman of the Board
Scope: Offers consulting in general management, corporate polices and culture, and strategic and long-range planning. Provides management audits and reports and profit improvement programs. High level strategic marketing, advertising strategy/tactics, turnaround consulting and management. **Founded:** 1978.

13798 ■ Beacon Management - Management Consultants
1000 W McNab Rd.
Pompano Beach, FL 33069
Ph: (954)782-1119
Free: 800-771-8721
Fax: (954)969-2566
Co. E-mail: md@beaconmgmt.com
URL: http://www.beaconmgmt.com
Contact: Joyce Slencak, Manager
Scope: Specializes in change management, organized workplaces, multicultural negotiations and dispute resolutions and internet based decision making. **Founded:** 1985. **Publications:** "Sun-Sentinel Article," Oct, 2012.

13799 ■ Benchmark Consulting Group Inc.—Benchmark Advisors
283 Franklin St., Ste. 400
Boston, MA 02110-3100
Ph: (617)482-7661
Fax: (617)423-2158
Contact: Walter E. Robb, III, President
E-mail: werobb35@aol.com
Scope: Provides financial and management services to companies. Helps companies grow through debt, equity sourcing and restructuring, business valuation, acquisition and divestiture, computer information systems and improved operation profitability. **Founded:** 1978.

13800 ■ BioSciCon Inc.
14905 Forest Landing Cir.
Rockville, MD 20850
Ph: (301)610-9130
Fax: (301)610-7662
Co. E-mail: info@bioscicon.com
URL: http://www.bioscicon.com
Contact: Nenad Markovic, President
Scope: Sponsoring development of the technology of the Pap test accuracy via introduction of a new bio-marker that enhances visibility of abnormal cells on Pap smears or mono-layers of cervical cells obtained in solution. Conducts clinical trials for assessment of the test efficacy and safety, manufactures research tools for conduct of trials, and markets IP to license manufacturing, marketing, sales and distribution rights of the new technology line of products. **Founded:** 1996. **Publications:** "Cervical Acid Phosphates: A Biomarker of Cervical Dysplasia and Potential Surrogate Endpoint for Colposcopy," 2004; "Enhancing Pap test with a new biological marker of cervical dysplasia," 2004; "A cytoplasmic biomarker for liquid-based Pap," The FACEB Journal Experimental Biology, 2004; "Pap test and new biomarker-based technology for enhancing visibility of abnormal cells," 2004. **Special Services:** Mark-Pap®; PreservCyt®.

13801 ■ Blankinship & Associates Inc.
322 C St.
Davis, CA 95616
Ph: (530)757-0941
Fax: (530)757-0940
Co. E-mail: blankinship@envtox.com
URL: http://www.h2osci.com
Contact: Michael Blankinship, President
E-mail: mike@envtox.com
Scope: Specializes in assisting water resource and conveyance, golf and production, protection and enhancement of natural resources. **Founded:** 2000. **Publications:** "Air Blast Sprayer Calibration and Chlorpyrifos Irrigation Study," Oct, 2007; "How Green is your golf course," Prosper Magazine, 2007. **Seminars:** CDFG Wildlands IPM Seminar, Oct, 2009.

13802 ■ C. Clint Bolte & Associates
809 Philadelphia Ave.
Chambersburg, PA 17201
Ph: (717)263-5768
Fax: (717)263-8954
Co. E-mail: clint@clintbolte.com
URL: http://www.clintbolte.com
Contact: C. Clint Bolte, Principal
E-mail: cbolte3@comcast.net
Scope: Provider of management consulting services to firms involved with the printing industry. Services include outsourcing studies, graphics supply chain

management studies, company and equipment valuations, plant layout services, litigation support, fulfillment warehouse consulting and product development services. **Founded:** 1989. **Seminars:** How to compete with the majors.

13803 ■ BPT Consulting Associates Ltd.
12 Parmenter Rd., Ste. B-6
Londonderry, NH 03053
Ph: (603)437-8484
Free: 888-278-0030
Fax: (603)434-5388
Contact: John Kuczynski, Managing Director
Scope: Provides management consulting expertise and resources to cross-industry clients with services for: Business Management consulting, People/Human Resources Transition and Training programs, and a full cadre of multi-disciplined Technology Computer experts. Virtual consultants with expertise in e-commerce, supply chain management, organizational development, and business application development consulting. **Founded:** 1991.

13804 ■ Business Improvement Architects (BIA)
33 Riderwood Dr.
Toronto, ON, Canada M2L 2X4
Ph: (416)444-8225
Free: 866-346-3242
Fax: (416)444-6743
Co. E-mail: info@bia.ca
URL: http://www.bia.ca
Contact: Michael Stanleigh, Chief Executive Officer
E-mail: mstanleigh@bia.ca
Scope: Provider of the following services: strategic planning, leadership development, innovation and project and quality management. Specialize in strategic planning, change management, leadership assessment, and development of skills. **Founded:** 1989. **Publications:** "Avoiding Pit falls to Innovation"; "Create a New Dimension of Performance with Innovation"; "The Power of Appreciation in Leadership"; "Why It Makes Sense To Have a Strategic Enterprise Office"; "Burning Rubber at the Start of Your Project"; "Accounting for Quality"; "How Pareto Charts Can Help You Improve the Quality of Business Processes"; "Managing Resistance to Change". **Seminars:** The Innovation Process. . .From Vision to Reality, San Diego, Oct, 2007; Critical Thinking, Kuala Lump or, Sep, 2007; Critical Thinking, Brunei, Sep, 2007; Delivering Project Assurance, Auckland, Jun, 2007; From Crisis to Control: A New Era in Strategic Project Management, Prague, May, 2007; What Project Leaders Need to Know to Help Them Sleep Better At Night, London, May, 2007; Innovation Process. . . .From Vision To Reality, Orlando, Apr, 2007. **Special Services:** Project Planning Tool™.

13805 ■ ByrneMRG Corp.
22 Isle of Pines Dr.
Hilton Head Island, SC 29928
Ph: (215)630-7411
Free: 888-816-8080
Co. E-mail: info@byrnemrg.com
URL: http://www.byrnemrg.com
Contact: Patrick J. Boyle, President
E-mail: pjboyle@byrnemrg.com
Scope: Specializes in management consulting, including department management, equipment evaluation and selection, project management, research and development planning; and database design and management. **Founded:** 1972. **Publications:** "Implementing Solutions to Everyday Issues". **Telecommunication Services:** pjboyle@byrnemrg.com.

13806 ■ Carelli & Associates
17 Reid Pl.
Delmar, NY 12054
Ph: (518)439-0233
Fax: (518)439-3006
Co. E-mail: truthaboutsupervision@yahoo.com
URL: http://www.carelli.com
Contact: Anne O Brien Carelli, Owner
E-mail: anneobriencarelli@yahoo.com
Scope: Provider of writing and editing services to industry and businesses, health care and educational institutions, and government agencies. Also provides program management in creating and disseminating publications and in implementing related training. As-

sists organizations in designing and implementing team-based management. Offers supervisory skills training and problem-solving work sessions for managers. Individual Consultation are provided for managers, CEOs, potential supervisors including 360 degree assessments. **Founded:** 1988. **Publications:** "The Truth About Supervision: Coaching, Teamwork, Interviewing, Appraisals, 360 degree Assessments, and Recognition". **Seminars:** Supervisory Skills Training Series; Problem-Solving Work Sessions for Managers; Effective Leadership.

13807 ■ CBIZ Inc.
6050 Oak Tree Blvd. S, Ste. 500
Cleveland, OH 44131-6951
Ph: (216)447-9000
Fax: (216)447-9007
URL: http://www.cbizinc.com
Contact: Jerome P. Grisko, President
URL(s): www.cbiz.com. **Scope:** A business consulting and tax services firm providing financial, consulting, tax and business services through seven groups: Financial management, tax advisory, construction and real estate, health-care, litigation support, capital resource and CEO outsource. **Founded:** 1996. **Publications:** "FAS 154: Changes in the Way We Report Changes," 2006; "Equity-Based Compensation: How Much Does it Really Cost Your Business," 2006; "Preventing Fraud - Tips for Nonprofit Organizations"; "Today's Workforce and Nonprofit Organizations: Meeting a Critical Need"; "IRS Highlights Top Seven Form 990 Errors". **Seminars:** Health Care - What the Future Holds; Consumer Driven Health Plans; Executive Plans; Health Savings Accounts; Healthy Wealthy and Wise; Legislative Update; Medicare Part D; Retirement Plans.

13808 ■ The Center for Organizational Excellence Inc.
15204 Omega Dr., Ste. 300
Rockville, MD 20850
Ph: (301)948-1922
Free: 877-674-3923
Fax: (301)948-2158
Co. E-mail: results@center4oe.com
URL: http://www.center4oe.com
Contact: Stephen Goodrich, President
E-mail: sgoodrich@center4oe.com
Scope: An organizational effectiveness consulting firm specializing in helping organizations achieve results through people, process, and performance. Service areas include organizational performance systems, leadership systems, customer systems, and learning systems. **Founded:** 1984.

13809 ■ Center for Personal Empowerment
102 N Main St., Ste. 1
Columbia, IL 62236-1702
Ph: (618)281-3565
Free: 888-657-1530
Fax: (618)476-7083
Co. E-mail: personalempowerment@wholenet.net
Contact: Cherri Hendrix, Owner
Scope: Private consultations and trainings to educate on how to determine which emotions, events, beliefs from the past prevent you from achieving success. Methods used include time line therapy, news linguistic programming and hypnosis. Behavior modification through NLP trainings. **Founded:** 1996. **Seminars:** NLP Practitioner Training; Hypnosis Certification Training; Lifemap Seminars.

13810 ■ Chamberlain & Cansler Inc.
2251 Perimeter Park Dr.
Atlanta, GA 30341
Ph: (770)457-5699
Contact: Charles L. Cansler, Owner
Scope: Firm specializes in strategic planning; profit enhancement; small business management; interim management; crisis management; turnarounds. **Founded:** 1986.

13811 ■ Chartered Management Co.
10 S Riverside Plz., Ste. 1800
Chicago, IL 60606

Ph: (312)214-2575
Contact: William B. Avellone, President
Scope: Operations improvement consultants. Specializes in strategic planning; feasibility studies; management audits and reports; profit enhancement; start-up businesses; mergers and acquisitions; joint ventures; divestitures; interim management; crisis management; turnarounds; business process re-engineering; venture capital; and due diligence. **Founded:** 1985.

13812 ■ Claremont Consulting Group
4525 Castle Ln.
La Canada, CA 91011-1436
Ph: (818)249-0584
Fax: (818)249-5811
Contact: Donald S. Remer, Partner
Scope: Consulting, coaching, training, and litigation support in project management, engineering management, system engineering and cost estimating. **Founded:** 1979. **Publications:** "What Every Engineer Should Know About Project Management"; "100% product-oriented work breakdown structures and their importance to system engineering". **Seminars:** Project Management, System Engineering and Cost Estimating.

13813 ■ Colmen Menard Company Inc. (CMCI)
The Woods, 994 Old Eagle School Rd., Ste. 1000
Wayne, PA 19087
Ph: (484)367-0300
Fax: (484)367-0305
Co. E-mail: cmci@colmenmenard.com
URL: http://www.colmenmenard.com
Contact: David W. Menard, President
E-mail: dmenard@colmenmenard.com
Scope: Merger and acquisition corporate finance and business advisory services for public and private companies located in North America. **Founded:** 1982. **Publications:** "Success in Selling a Troubled Company," Nov, 2002; "Savvy Dealmakers," May, 2001; "Success in Selling a Troubled Company feature article from The Technology Times bimonthly newspaper," Apr, 2002; "Truisms," M&A Today, Nov, 2000.

13814 ■ Consulting & Conciliation Service (CCS)
2219 H St., Ste. 1
Sacramento, CA 95816
Ph: (916)396-0480
Free: 888-898-9780
Fax: (916)441-2828
Co. E-mail: service@azurewings.net
Contact: Jane A. McCluskey, Principal
E-mail: service@azurewings.net
Scope: Offers consulting and conciliation services. Provides pre-mediation counseling, training and research on preparing for a peaceful society, mediation and facilitation, and preparation for shifts in structure, policy and personnel. Offers sliding scale business rates and free individual consultation. **Publications:** "Native America and Tracking Shifts in US Policy"; "Biogenesis: A Discussion of Basic Social Needs and the Significance of Hope". **Seminars:** Positive Approaches to Violence Prevention: Peace building in Schools and Communities.

13815 ■ The Consulting Exchange
1770 Mass Ave., Ste. 288
Cambridge, MA 02140
Ph: (617)576-2100
Free: 800-824-4828
Co. E-mail: gday@consultingexchange.com
Contact: Geoffrey Day, President
E-mail: gday@consultingexchange.com
Scope: A consultant referral service for management and technical consultants. Serves a local, regional and international client base. **Founded:** 1982. **Publications:** "Looking for a Consultant? Success Points for Finding the Right One," Boston Business Journal, Jun, 2001; "Getting Full Value From Consulting is in Your Hands," Mass High Tech, May, 1998; "Developing Knowledge-Based Client Relationships, The Future of Professional Services"; "The Consultant's Legal Guide"; "The Business of Consulting: The Basics and Beyond".

13816 ■ The Corlund Group L.L.C. (CG)
101 Federal St., Ste. 310
Boston, MA 02110
Ph: (617)423-9364
Fax: (617)423-9371
Co. E-mail: info@corlundgroup.com
URL: http://www.corlundgroup.com
Contact: Wilmot J. Gravenslund, Director
E-mail: wgravenslund@corlundgroup.com
Scope: Boutique firm offering services in the areas of leadership, governance, and change with a particular focus on CEO and senior executive succession planning, including assessment, development, and orchestrating succession processes with management and Boards of Directors. Also Board governance effectiveness. **Founded:** 1996. **Publications:** "Are You Rolling the Dice on CEO Succession?" Center for Healthcare Governance, 2006; "Leadership Due Diligence: The Neglected Governance Frontier," Directorship, Sep, 2001; "Leadership Due Diligence: Managing the Risks," The Corporate Board, Aug, 2001; "Succession: The need for detailed insight," Directors and Boards, 2001; "CEO Succession: Who's Doing Due Diligence?," 2001. **Telecommunication Services:** corlund@corlundgroup.com.

13817 ■ Corporate Consulting Inc.
3333 Belcaro Dr.
Denver, CO 80209-4912
Ph: (303)698-9292
Fax: (303)698-9292
Co. E-mail: corpcons@compuserve.com
Contact: Devereux C. Josephs, President
Scope: Specializes in feasibility studies, organizational development, small business management, mergers and acquisitions, joint ventures, divestitures, interim management, crisis management, turnarounds, financing, appraisals valuations and due diligence studies. **Founded:** 1983.

13818 ■ COTC Technologies Inc.—COTC-TrenzSoft
172 E Industrial Blvd.
Pueblo, CO 81007-4406
Ph: (719)547-0938
Free: 888-547-0938
Fax: (719)547-1105
Contact: Tom Renz, Chief Executive Officer
E-mail: tom@cotc-consulting.com
Scope: Provides software consulting services to organizations that require assistance with their HP3000 computer system. Provides systems analysis, programming, operations support, and system management. Also provides PC software and hardware support and consulting. Additionally provides various training for the HP3000 computer system. Industries served: healthcare, aerospace procurement, aerospace proposal activities, and HP3000 computer systems. **Founded:** 2006.

13819 ■ Crystal Clear Communications Inc.
1633 W Winslow Dr., Ste. 210
Mequon, WI 53092
Ph: (262)240-0072
Fax: (262)240-0073
Co. E-mail: contact@crystalclear1.com
URL: http://www.crystalclear1.com
Contact: Barry J. Moze, Partner
E-mail: barrymoze@crystalclearl.com
Scope: Specialize in helping executives identify impediments to success, and then develop strategies to surmount them. Serves to identify core problems, suggest appropriate business changes, work with the organization to support these changes, and help executives articulate the behavior that will uphold these changes. Specializes in strategic planning; organizational development; small business management; executive coaching. **Founded:** 1986. **Publications:** "Weakest Link"; "Aware Leadership"; "Integrity"; "When Your Plate is Full"; "Problem Solving"; "Strategic Thinking".

13820 ■ Development Resource Consultants (DRC)
PO Box 118
Rancho Cucamonga, CA 91729
Ph: (909)902-7655

Fax: (909)476-6942
Co. E-mail: drc@gotodrc.com
URL: http://www.gotodrc.com
Contact: Jerry R. Frey, Business Manager
E-mail: jfrey@gotodrc.com
Scope: Specializes in office re-organization, employee training in office organization, communication skills, sales training and career counseling. **Founded:** 1985. **Publications:** "Institute of Management Consultants Southern California Chapter," Jan, 2006.

13821 ■ Donna Cornell Enterprises Inc.—Cornell Career Center
68 N Plank Rd., Ste. 204
Newburgh, NY 12550-2122
Ph: (845)565-0088
Free: 888-769-3792
Fax: (845)565-0084
Co. E-mail: rc@cornellcareercenter.com
Contact: Donna Cornell, President
E-mail: rc@cornellcareercenter.com
Scope: Offers services in career consultant, professional search, job placement and national professional search. **Founded:** 1996. **Publications:** "The Power of the Woman Within"; "Juggling it All!"; "Journey: A Woman's Guide to Success"; "Shatter the Traditions".

13822 ■ DRI Consulting (DRIC)
2 Otter Ln.
Saint Paul, MN 55127-6436
Ph: (651)415-1400
Free: 866-276-4600
Fax: (651)415-9968
Co. E-mail: dric@dric.com
URL: http://www.dric.com
Contact: Megan Brogger, Principal
E-mail: meganbrogger@dric.com
Scope: Provides high-quality, research-based services and training in leadership, team processes, supervision, and management, and organizational development, clients with direct and substantial impact on individual and team performance and on organizational success through proven processes for selecting, developing and deploying leaders. **Founded:** 1991.

13823 ■ Dubuc Lucke & Company Inc.—Adventa Global Intermediaries
120 W 5th St.
Cincinnati, OH 45202-2713
Ph: (513)579-8330
Fax: (513)241-6669
Contact: Kenneth E. Dubuc, President
Scope: Provides consulting services in the areas of profit enhancement; small business management; mergers and acquisitions; joint ventures; divestitures; interim management; crisis management; turnarounds; appraisals; valuations; due diligence; and international trade. **Founded:** 1999.

13824 ■ The DuMond Group
5282 Princeton Ave.
Westminster, CA 92683-2753
Ph: (714)373-0610
Contact: Adrianne H. Geiger-Dumond, President
Scope: Human resources and executive search consulting firm that specializes in organizational development; small business management; employee surveys and communication; performance appraisals; and team building. **Founded:** 1992.

13825 ■ Dunelm International
437 Colebrook Ln.
Bryn Mawr, PA 19010-3216
Ph: (610)989-0144
Fax: (610)964-9524
Co. E-mail: jecdunelm@worldnet.att.net
Contact: John E. Crowther, President
E-mail: Jecdunelm@dunelm.org.uk
Scope: Firm specializes in feasibility studies; start-up businesses; interim management; crisis management; turnarounds; business process re-engineering; sales forecasting; supply chain solution and project management. **Founded:** 1988.

13826 ■ Everett & Co.
3126 S Franklin St.
Englewood, CO 80113

Ph: (303)761-7999
Fax: (303)781-8296
Contact: Robert W. Everett, Manager
Scope: Provides strategic real estate solutions and project management. **Founded:** 1993.

13827 ■ Family Business Institute Inc.—Family Business Experts
904 Steffi Ct.
Lawrenceville, GA 30044-6933
Ph: (770)952-4085
Fax: (770)432-6660
Co. E-mail: asktheexpert@family-business-experts.com
URL: http://www.family-business-experts.com
Contact: Wayne Rivers, President
Scope: Assists families in business to achieve personal, family, and organizational goals by meeting challenges that are unique to family-owned businesses. Provides coordinated and integrated assessments and solutions for family issues and needs; for company finance and for human resource and operational requirements. **Founded:** 1985. **Publications:** "Professional Intervention in the Family Owned Business"; "Building Consensus in a Family Business"; "Professionalizing Family Business Management"; "Recognizing generations - know them by their weekends"; "Succession planning tactics"; "Succession Planning Obstacles in Family Business"; "Succession: three ways to ease the transition"; "Pruning the family business tree"; "Responsibility diffusion - the most critical impediment to successfully growing any kind of business"; "Breaking Up is Hard to Do: Divorce in the Family Business".

13828 ■ FCP Consulting
500 Sutter St., Ste. 507
San Francisco, CA 94102-1114
Ph: (415)956-5558
Fax: (415)956-5722
Contact: Cox Ferrall, President
Scope: Management consulting in Business-To-Business sales. **Founded:** 1986.

13829 ■ First Strike Management Consulting Inc.—FSMC Inc.
4001 Loblolly Ave.
Little River, SC 29566-1188
Ph: (843)385-6338
Fax: (843)390-1004
Co. E-mail: info@fsmc.com
URL: http://www.fsmc.com
Contact: J. D. Lewis, Chief Executive Officer
E-mail: jd.lewis@fsmc.com
Scope: Offers proposal management and program management services. Specializes in enterprise systems, management systems, and staff augmentation. Serves the following industries: Nuclear/Fossil Power, Petro-Chemical, Aerospace and Defense, Telecommunications, Engineering and Construction, Information Technology, Golf Course Construction/Management, Utility Engineering/Construction, Civil Works, and Housing Development. **Founded:** 1991. **Publications:** "Project Management for Executives"; "Project Risk Management"; "Project Communications Management"; "Winning Proposals, Four Computer Based Training (CBT) courses"; "Principles of Program Management". **Seminars:** Preparing Winning Proposals in Response to Government RFPs.

13830 ■ Freese & Associates Inc.
PO Box 814
Chagrin Falls, OH 44022-0814
Ph: (440)564-9183
Fax: (440)564-7339
Co. E-mail: tfreese@freeseinc.com
URL: http://www.freeseinc.com
Contact: Duane L. Hile, Manager
Scope: A management consulting firm offering advice in all forms of business logistics. Consulting services are in the areas of strategic planning; network analysis, site selection, facility layout and design, outsourcing, warehousing, transportation and customer service. Typical projects include 3PL marketing surveys; third party outsourcing selection; operational audits; competitive analysis; inventory management; due diligence; and implementation project management. **Founded:** 1987. **Publications:** "Building Relationships is Key to Motivation," Distribution

Center Management, Apr, 2006; "Getting Maximum Results from Performance Reviews," WERC Sheet, Oct, 2003; "SCM: Making the Vision a Reality," Supply Chain Management Review, Oct, 2003; "Contents Under Pressure," DC Velocity, Aug, 2003; "When Considering Outsourcing, It's Really a Financial Decision," Inventory Management Report, Mar, 2003. **Seminars:** WERC/CAWS Warehousing in China Conference, Sep, 2008; CSCMP Annual Conference, Denver, Oct, 2008; Keys to Retaining and Motivating Your Associates, Dallas, Mar, 2006; The Value and Challenges of Supply Chain Management, Dubai, Feb, 2006; Best Practices in Logistics in China, Jun, 2005; Keys to Motivating Associates, Dallas, May, 2005; The Goal and the Way of International Cooperation in Logistics, Jenobuk, Apr, 2005.

13831 ■ Global Business Consultants (GBC)
200 Lake Hills Rd.
Pinehurst, NC 28374-0776
Ph: (910)295-5991
Fax: (910)295-5991
Co. E-mail: gbc@pinehurst.net
Contact: Nan S. Leaptrott, President
E-mail: nan@yourculturecoach.com
Scope: Firm specializes in human resources management; project management; software development; and international trade. Offers litigation support. **Founded:** 1987. **Publications:** "Culture to Culture: Mission Trip Do's and Don'ts," Jul, 2005; "Rules of the Game: Global Business Protocol". **Seminars:** Cross-Cultural Training.

13832 ■ Global Technology Transfer L.L.C.
1500 Dixie Hwy.
Park Hills, KY 41011-2819
Ph: (859)431-1262
Fax: (859)431-5148
Contact: Anthony Zembrodt, President
Scope: Firm specializes in product development; quality assurance; new product development; and total quality management focusing on household chemical specialties, especially air fresheners. Utilizes latest technology from global resources. Specializes in enhancement products for home and automobile. **Founded:** 1992.

13833 ■ Arnold S. Goldin & Associates Inc.
5030 Champion Blvd., Ste. G-6231
Boca Raton, FL 33496
Ph: (561)994-5810
Fax: (561)994-5860
Co. E-mail: arnold@goldin.com
URL: http://www.goldin.com
Contact: Arnold S. Goldin, Principal
E-mail: arnold@goldin.com
Scope: An accounting and management consulting firm. Serves clients worldwide. Provides management services. Handles monthly write-ups and tax returns. **Founded:** 1978.

13834 ■ Great Lakes Consulting Group Inc.
54722 Little Flower Trl.
Mishawaka, IN 46545
Ph: (574)287-4500
Fax: (574)233-2688
Contact: James E. Schrager, President
Scope: Provides consulting services in the areas of strategic planning; feasibility studies; start-up businesses; small business management; mergers and acquisitions; joint ventures; divestitures; interim management; crisis management; turnarounds; business process re-engineering; venture capital; and international trade. **Founded:** 1989.

13835 ■ Great Western Association Management Inc.
7995 E Prentice Ave., Ste. 100
Greenwood Village, CO 80111
Ph: (303)770-2220
Fax: (303)770-1614
Co. E-mail: info83@gwami.com
URL: http://www.gwami.com
Contact: Karen M. Wojdyla, President
E-mail: kwojdyla@gwami.com
Scope: Provider of clients with products and services to effectively manage existing and startup, for- and not-for-profit organizations. Clients select from a menu of services including association development

and public relations, conferences and seminars, financial management, membership communications, and governance. Expertise also includes association strategic planning, compliance, lobbying, meeting planning, fundraising, marketing and communications. Serves national, regional and state organizations. **Founded:** 1983. **Seminars:** Site selection; Creative program development; Contract negotiations; On-site conference management; Trade show management; Travel and logistics.

13836 ■ Joel Greenstein & Associates (JGA)
6212 Nethercombe Ct.
McLean, VA 22101
Ph: (703)893-1888
Co. E-mail: jgreenstein@contractmasters.com
Contact: Joel Greenstein, Principal
E-mail: jgreenstein@contractmasters.com
Scope: Provides services to minority and women-owned businesses and government agencies. Specializes in interpreting federal, agency-specific acquisition regulations and contract terms and conditions. Offers assistance with preparing technical, cost proposals and sealed bids.

13837 ■ Grimmick Consulting Services (GCS)
455 Donner Way
San Ramon, CA 94582
Ph: (925)735-1036
Fax: (925)735-1100
Co. E-mail: hank@grimmickconsulting.com
URL: http://www.grimmickconsulting.com
Contact: Henry Grimmick, President
E-mail: hank@grimmickconsulting.com
Scope: Provider of consulting services in the areas of strategic planning; organizational assessment; organizational development; leadership and management development Baldridge criteria, process improvement and balanced scorecards and team dynamics. **Founded:** 1993.

13838 ■ Hewitt Development Enterprises (HDE)
1717 N Bayshore Dr., Ste. 2154
Miami, FL 33132
Ph: (305)372-0941
Fax: (305)372-0941
Co. E-mail: info@hewittdevelopment.com
URL: http://www.hewittdevelopment.com
Contact: Robert G. Hewitt, Principal
E-mail: bob@hewittdevelopment.com
Scope: Specializes in strategic planning; profit enhancement; start-up businesses; interim management; crisis management; turnarounds; production planning; just-in-time inventory management; and project management. Serves senior management (CEOs, CFOs, division presidents, etc.) and acquirers of distressed businesses. **Founded:** 1985.

13839 ■ Hickey & Hill Inc.
1009 Oak Hill Rd., Ste. 201
Lafayette, CA 94549-3812
Ph: (925)906-5331
Contact: Edwin L. Hill, Chief Executive Officer
Scope: Firm provides management consulting services to companies in financial distress. Expertise area: Corporate restructuring and turnaround. **Founded:** 1984.

13840 ■ hightechbiz.com—Leahy & Associates Inc.
4209 Santa Monica Blvd., Ste. 201
Los Angeles, CA 90029-3027
Ph: (323)913-3355
Free: 877-648-4753
Fax: (323)913-3355
URL: http://www.hightechbiz.com
Contact: Steven L. Hayes, Principal
Scope: A full service marketing agency specializing in integrated marketing solutions. Services include: marketing surveys; positioning surveys; strategic and tactical plans; implementation plans; management consulting; product brochures; product catalogs; product packaging; product data sheets; direct mail programs; media research; competitive research; complete creative; production and film; media placement; corporate identity; in-house creative; public relations. **Founded:** 1980.

13841 ■ Holt Capital
1916 Pike Pl., Ste. 12-344
Seattle, WA 98101
Ph: (206)484-0403
Fax: (206)789-8034
Co. E-mail: info@holtcapital.com
URL: http://www.holtcapital.com
Contact: Marilyn J. Holt, Chief Executive Officer
E-mail: mjholt@holtcapital.com
Scope: Registered investment advisory firm. Services include: Debt planning, private equity, mergers, divestitures and acquisitions, transaction support services. Connects companies with capital. **Founded:** 1980. **Publications:** "Early Sales Key to Early-Stage Funding"; "Financial Transactions: Who Should Be At Your Table"; "Get the Deal Done: The Four Keys to Successful Mergers and Acquisitions"; "Is Your First Paragraph a Turn-off"; "Bubble Rubble: Bridging the Price Gap for an Early-Stage Business"; "Are You Ready For The new Economy"; "Could I Get Money or Jail Time With That The Sarbanes-Oxley Act Of 2002 gives early-stage companies More Risks". **Seminars:** Attracting Private Investors; Five Proven Ways to Finance Your Company; How to Get VC Financing; Venture Packaging; How to Finance Company Expansion.

13842 ■ Human Resource Specialties Inc.
3 Monroe Pky., Ste. 900
Lake Oswego, OR 97035
Ph: (503)697-3329
Free: 800-354-3512
Fax: (503)636-1594
Co. E-mail: info@hrspecialties.com
URL: http://www.hrspecialties.com
Contact: Sandy Henderson, President
E-mail: sandyh@hrspecialties.com
Scope: Provider of human resources assistance to organizations. Offers preparation of affirmative action plans, support documents, and adverse impact studies of personnel activities. Also offers customized consultations in small business services, diversity and discrimination, and investigations, complaints and grievances. Provides investigations, including allegations of unfair treatment, equal employment opportunity (EEO) and racial or sexual harassment. Offers customized web-based training (webinars) on a variety of HR, EEO and AAP-related topics. **Founded:** 1984.

13843 ■ I.H.R. Solutions
3333 E Bayaud Ave., Ste. 219
Denver, CO 80209
Ph: (303)588-4243
Fax: (303)978-0473
Co. E-mail: dhollands@ihrsolutions.com
Contact: Deborah Hollands, Owner
E-mail: dhollands@ihrsolutions.com
Scope: Provides joint-venture and start-up human resource consulting services as well as advice on organization development for international human capital. Industries served: high-tech and telecommunications. **Founded:** 1997.

13844 ■ IMC Consulting & Training
901 McHenry Ave., Ste. A
Modesto, CA 95350
Ph: (209)572-2271
Fax: (209)572-2862
Co. E-mail: info@imc-1.net
URL: http://www.imc-1.net
Contact: Michael J. Loschke, President
E-mail: michael@imc-1.net
Scope: Helps businesses and professionals identify, develop and market their selling proposition to increase profits. Services include B-to-B surveys, direct marketing, media relations, planning and strategy, sales management, training and leadership coaching. **Founded:** 1994. **Publications:** "Consultant Earns Advanced Certificate," Hccsc Business Review, Dec, 2004; "Adapting to Change - the New Competitive Advantage," Business Journal, Jul, 2004; "Loyalty Marketing Can Divide New Business," Jun, 2004; "Eleven Major Marketing Mistakes," Jul, 2003; "Planning to Win or Racing to Fail," Jun, 2003. **Seminars:** Negotiating High Profit Sales; How to Write Winning Proposals, Modesto Chamber of Commerce,

Oct, 2007; Winning the 2nd Half: A 6-month Plan to Score New Customers and Profits. **Telecommunication Services:** imcinfo@imc-1.net.

13845 ■ The Institute for Management Excellence
PO Box 5459
Lacey, WA 98509-5459
Ph: (360)412-0404
Co. E-mail: pwoc@itstime.com
URL: http://www.itstime.com
Contact: Michael Anthony, Director
Scope: Management consulting and training focuses on improving productivity, using practices and creative techniques. Practices based on the company's theme: It's time for new ways of doing business. Industries served: public sector, law enforcement, finance or banking, non profit, computers or high technology, education, human resources, utilities. **Founded:** 1995. **Publications:** "Income Without a Job," 2008; "The Other Side of Midnight, 2000: An Executive Guide to the Year 2000 Problem"; "Concordance to the Michael Teachings"; "Handbook of Small Business Advertising"; "The Personality Game"; "How to Market Yourself for Success". **Seminars:** The Personality Game; Power Path Seminars; Productivity Plus; Sexual Harassment and Discrimination Prevention; Worker's Comp Cost Reduction; Americans with Disabilities Act; In Search of Identify: Clarifying Corporate Culture.

13846 ■ Interminds & Federer Resources Inc.
106 E 6th St., Ste. 310
Austin, TX 78701-3659
Ph: (512)476-8800
Fax: (512)476-8811
Co. E-mail: yesyoucan@interminds.com
URL: http://www.interminds.com
Contact: Frank Federer, President
E-mail: ffederer@integra100.com
Scope: Specializes in feasibility studies; startup businesses; small business management; mergers and acquisitions; joint ventures; divestitures; interim management; crisis management; turnarounds; production planning; team building; appraisals and valuations. **Founded:** 1985. **Publications:** "Yes You Can: How To Be A Success No Matter Who You Are Or Where You're From".

13847 ■ Interpersonal Coaching & Consulting (ICC)
1516 W Lake St., Ste. 2000S
Minneapolis, MN 55408
Ph: (612)381-2494
Fax: (612)381-2493
Co. E-mail: mail@interpersonal-coaching.com
URL: http://www.interpersonal-coaching.com
Contact: Mary Belfry, Partner
Scope: Provider of coaching and consulting to businesses and organizations. Assesses the interpersonal workplace through interviews, assessment instruments and individual group settings. Experienced as a therapist for over a decade. **Publications:** "Sexual Harassment In The Workplace For Newspapers". **Seminars:** More On Relationships; Sexual harassment and discrimination issues.

13848 ■ Johnston Co.
78 Bedford St.
Lexington, MA 02420
Ph: (781)862-7595
Fax: (781)862-9066
Co. E-mail: info@johnstoncompany.com
URL: http://www.johnstoncompany.com
Contact: Claire Sehringer, Manager
Scope: Specializes in management audits and reports; start-up businesses; small business management; mergers and acquisitions; joint ventures; divestitures; interim management; crisis management; turnarounds; cost controls; financing; venture capital; controller services; financial management, strategic and advisory services. **Founded:** 1987. **Publications:** "Why are board meetings such a waste of time," Boston Business Journal, Apr, 2004.

13849 ■ Keiei Senryaku Corp.
19191 S Vermont Ave., Ste. 530
Torrance, CA 90502-1049
Ph: (310)366-3331

Free: 800-951-8780
Fax: (310)366-3330
Co. E-mail: takenakaes@earthlink.net
Contact: Kurt Miyamoto, President
Scope: Offers consulting services in the areas of strategic planning; feasibility studies; profit enhancement; organizational development; start-up businesses; mergers and acquisitions; joint ventures; divestitures; executive searches; sales management; and competitive analysis. **Founded:** 1989.

13850 ■ Koch Group Inc.
129 Fairfield Way, Ste. 219
Bloomingdale, IL 60108
Ph: (630)941-1100
Free: 800-470-7845
Fax: (630)941-3865
Co. E-mail: info@kochgroup.com
URL: http://www.kochgroup.com
Contact: Peter Koch, Manager
Scope: Provider of industrial marketing consulting services to small to mid-sized manufacturers. Primary assistance includes industrial market research and analysis, identification of potential markets, strategic planning and plan implementation, market planning, sales analysis, competitor analysis. Specializes in assisting manufacturers identify, recruit, and manage agents and reps and developing website for business promotion. **Founded:** 1967. **Seminars:** Niche Marketing; Regional Industrial Association Recruiting; Strategic Marketing for Manufacturers; Strategic Marketing; How To Identify, Screen, Interview and Select High Quality Agents; Basics of Industrial Market Research; Elements of Industrial Marketing; Trade Adjustment Assistance For Firms; Developing New Business; Selecting An Industrial Web Site Developer; Strategic Selling; Pick Your Customer; Strategic and Tactical Marketing.

13851 ■ Kostka & Company Inc.
9 Wild Rose Ct.
Cromwell, CT 06416
Ph: (860)257-1045
Contact: Peter Kostka, Managing Partner
E-mail: peterpk@gmail.com
Scope: Areas of expertise: management consulting, global technology sourcing, complex project management, SKU management and new product introduction, application development, medical point-of-sale, multi-touch user interface, made-to-order management systems and Smartphone ERP connectivity. Clients include global fortune 500 companies as well as small and medium-sized businesses and startups. **Founded:** 1994.

13852 ■ William E. Kuhn & Associates
234 Cook St.
Denver, CO 80206-5305
Ph: (303)322-8233
Fax: (303)331-9032
Co. E-mail: billkuhn1@cs.com
Contact: William E. Kuhn, Owner
E-mail: billkuhn1@cs.com
Scope: Firm specializes in strategic planning; profit enhancement; small business management; mergers and acquisitions; joint ventures; divestitures; human resources management; performance appraisals; team building; sales management; appraisals and valuations. **Founded:** 1980. **Publications:** "Creating a High-Performance Dealership," Office SOLUTIONS & Office DEALER, Jul-Aug, 2006.

13853 ■ May Toy Lukens
3226 NE 26th Ct.
Renton, WA 98056
Ph: (425)891-3226
Contact: May T. Lukens, Principal
Scope: Provides training to teach people to think of ways to improve their operations continuously by changing the way they think. Industries served: All, particularly financial. Operational analysis and training. **Founded:** 1996. **Seminars:** Seminars and workshops in maximizing resource utilization and staff potential.

13854 ■ Lupfer & Associates (L&A)
92 Glen St.
Natick, MA 01760-5646
Ph: (508)655-3950

Fax: (508)655-7826
Co. E-mail: donlupfer@aol.com
Contact: Donald Lupfer, Owner
E-mail: don.lupfer@lupferassociates.com
Scope: Assists off shore hi-tech companies in entering United States markets and specializes in channel development for all sorts of products. Perform MAR-COM support for hi-tech United States clients. **Founded:** 1988. **Publications:** "What's Next For Distribution-Feast or Famine"; "The Changing Global Marketplace"; "Making Global Distribution Work". **Seminars:** How to do Business in the United States.

13855 ■ Management Resource Partners
181 2nd Ave., Ste. 542
San Mateo, CA 94401
Ph: (650)401-5850
Fax: (650)401-5850
Contact: John C. Roberts, Owner
Scope: Firm specializes in strategic planning; small business management; mergers and acquisitions; joint ventures; divestitures; interim management; crisis management; turn around; venture capital; appraisals and valuations. **Founded:** 1981.

13856 ■ Management Strategies
1000 S Old Woodward Ave., Ste. 105
Birmingham, MI 48009
Ph: (248)258-2756
Fax: (248)258-3407
Co. E-mail: bob@hois.com
Contact: Robert E. Hoisington, President
E-mail: bob@hois.com
Scope: Firm specializes in strategic planning; feasibility studies; profit enhancement; organizational studies; start up businesses; turnarounds; business process re engineering; industrial engineering; marketing; ecommerce. **Founded:** 1985.

13857 ■ Marketing Leverage Inc.
2022 Laurel Oak Ln.
Palm City, FL 34990
Ph: (772)878-6495
Free: 800-633-1422
Fax: (772)659-8664
Co. E-mail: lkelly@marketingleverage.com
Contact: Lynn C. Kelly, President
E-mail: lkelly@marketingleverage.com
Scope: Consulting and research firm focusing on the targeting, retention and satisfaction of customers. Consulting is offered for due diligence; marketing and customer retention strategy; program design and implementation. Research services offered help clients determine service improvements that increase customer loyalty; boosting sales through better understanding buyer motivations; increasing the odds of product acceptance through new product concept testing; and improving the effectiveness of advertising, collateral, publications through audience evaluation. Clients include top financial services, insurance, health care, technology and management services organizations. **Founded:** 1987. **Publications:** "Creating Strategic Leverage"; "Exploring Corporate Strategy"; "Competitive Advantage"; "Breakpoint and Beyond "; "Competitive Strategy ". **Seminars:** Best Practices in Brainstorming; Getting Results in the Real World; Finding the Leverage in Your Customer Strategy; The Role of Communications in Building Customer Loyalty; Building a Customer Centered Relationship and Making it Pay. **Special Services:** The Marketing Leverage Win/Loss Tracking System™.

13858 ■ McCreight & Company Inc.
36 Grove St.
New Canaan, CT 06840
Ph: (203)801-5000
Fax: (866)646-8339
Co. E-mail: roc@implementstrategy.com
URL: http://www.implementstrategy.com
Contact: John A. McCreight, President
E-mail: jmc@implementstrategy.com
Scope: Assist the global clients with strategy implementation involving large scale change, including mergers, divestitures, alliances and new business launches. **Founded:** 1983. **Publications:** "The Board's Role in Strengthening M and A Success," Boardroom Briefing, 2008; "Creating the Future," Ask Magazine, 2007; "Strategy Implementation Insights,"

Mccreight and Company Inc, Oct, 2007; "Sustaining Growth," Deloitte and Ct Technology Council, Jul, 2006; "A Four Phase Approach to Succession Planning," Southern Connecticut Newspapers Inc, 2005. **Seminars:** Successful Mergers and Acquisitions-An Implementation Guide; Global 100One-Face-to-the-Customer; Implementation of Strategic Change.

13859 ■ McDonald Consulting Group Inc.
1900 W Park Dr., Ste. 280
Westborough, MA 01581
Co. E-mail: info@mcdonaldconsultinggroup.com
URL: http://www.mcdonaldconsultinggroup.com
Contact: Ron A. McDonald, President
E-mail: rmcdonald@mcdonaldconsultinggroup.com
Scope: A management consulting firm specializing in assisting insurance companies improve operations. Provides services in the areas of strategic planning; profit enhancement; organizational development; interim management; crisis management; turnarounds; business process re-engineering; benefits and compensation planning and total quality management. **Founded:** 1993. **Publications:** "Improving Customer Focus through Organizational Structure," AASCIF News; "Changing Strategies in Hard Markets," The National Underwriter; "Moving Beyond Management 101: Postgraduate Time Management for Executives," The National Underwriter; "A New Attitude: 3 Clients Improved Results Through Our Fundamental Change Process," Bests Review; "How to Organize Your Company Around Your Customers," Bests Review. **Seminars:** How to establish "expense allowable"; How to design an incentive compensation plan around a units core success measures.

13860 ■ McShane Group Inc.
2345 York Rd., Ste. 102
Timonium, MD 21093
Ph: (410)560-0077
Fax: (410)560-2718
Co. E-mail: tmcshane@mcshanegroup.com
URL: http://www.mcshanegroup.com
Contact: Thomas P. McShane, President
E-mail: tmcshane@mcshanegroup.com
Scope: Turnaround consulting and crisis management firm. Specializes in due diligence services, interim management, strategic business realignments, business sale and asset depositions and debt restructuring. Industries served: technology, financial, retail, distribution, medical, educational, manufacturing, contracting, environmental and health care. **Founded:** 1987.

13861 ■ Medical Imaging Consultants Inc. (MIC)
1037 US Highway 46, Ste. G-2
Clifton, NJ 07013-2445
Ph: (973)574-8000
Free: 800-589-5685
Fax: (973)574-8001
Co. E-mail: info@micinfo.com
URL: http://www.micinfo.com
Contact: Dr. Philip A. Femano, President
E-mail: phil@micinfo.com
Scope: Provider of professional support services for radiology management and comprehensive continuing education programs for radiologic technologists. Management services include resource-critical database logistics; customer registration in educational programs; educational program development and Category A accreditation; national agency notification (e.g., ASRT, SNM-TS) of CE credits earned; meeting planning; manpower assessment; market research; expert witness; think-tank probes and executive summaries of industry issues. **Founded:** 1991. **Seminars:** Sectional Anatomy and Imaging Strategies; CT Cross-Trainer; CT Registry Review Program; MR Cross Trainer; MRI Registry Review Program; Digital Mammography Essentials for Technologists; Radiology Trends for Technologists.

13862 ■ Medical Outcomes Management Inc.
132 Central St., Ste. 215
Foxborough, MA 02035-2422
Ph: (508)543-0050

Fax: (508)543-1919
Co. E-mail: info@mom-inc.com
Contact: Alan F. Kaul, President
E-mail: alan@mom-inc.com
Scope: Management and technology consulting firm providing a specially focused group of services such as disease management programs and pharmaco-economic studies. Services include clinical and educational projects, medical writing and editing, marketing and sales projects, disease registries, educational seminars, strategic planning projects, managed care organizations; and pharmaceutical and biotechnology companies. **Founded:** 1991. **Publications:** "Treatment of acute exacerbation's of chronic bronchitis in patients with chronic obstructive pulmonary disease: A retrospective cohort analysis logarithmically extended release vs. Azithromycin," 2003; "A retrospective analysis of cyclooxygenase-II inhibitor response patterns," 2002; "DUE criteria for use of regional urokinase infusion for deep vein thrombosis,"2002; "The formulary management system and decision-making process at Horizon Blue Cross Blue Shield of New Jersey," Pharmaco therapy, 2001. **Seminars:** Economic Modeling as a Disease Management Tool, Academy of Managed Care Pharmacy, Apr, 2005; Integrating Disease State Management and Economics, Academy of Managed Care Pharmacy, Oct, 2004; Clinical and economic outcomes in the treatment of peripheral occlusive diseases, Mar, 2003.

13863 ■ Mefford, Knutson & Associates Inc. (MK)
6437 Lyndale Ave. S, Ste. 103
Richfield, MN 55423-1465
Ph: (612)869-8011
Free: 800-831-0228
Fax: (612)869-8004
Co. E-mail: info@mkaonline.net
URL: http://www.mkaonline.net
Contact: Jeanette Mefford, Director
E-mail: jmefford@mkaonline.net
Scope: A consulting and licensed business brokerage firm specializing in start-up businesses; strategic planning; mergers and acquisitions; joint ventures; divestitures; business process re-engineering; personnel policies and procedures; market research; new product development and cost controls. **Founded:** 1990.

13864 ■ Harvey A. Meier Co. (HAM)
410 W Nevada St.
Ashland, OR 97520-1043
Ph: (509)458-3210
Fax: (541)488-7905
Co. E-mail: harvey@harveymeier.com
URL: http://www.harveymeier.com
Contact: Dr. Harvey A. Meier, President
E-mail: harvey@harveymeier.com
Scope: Provider of service to chief executive officers and board of directors. Specializes in interim management, strategic planning, financial planning and organization governance. **Publications:** "The D'Artagnan Way".

13865 ■ Midwest Computer Group L.L.C. (MCG)
6060 Franks Rd.
House Springs, MO 63051
Ph: (314)954-1222
Co. E-mail: sales@mcgcomputer.com
URL: http://www.mcgcomputer.com
Contact: Leon Sanford, Jr., President
E-mail: leonjr@mcgcomputer.com
Scope: Specializes in helping businesses create accounting, marketing and business information systems; software development and database design and management. **Founded:** 1980.

13866 ■ Miller, Hellwig Associates
150 W End Ave.
New York, NY 10023-5713
Ph: (212)799-0471
Fax: (212)877-0186
Co. E-mail: millerhelwig@earthlink.net
Contact: Ernest C. Miller, President
Scope: Consulting services in the areas of start-up businesses; small business management; employee surveys and communication; performance appraisals;

executive searches; team building; personnel policies and procedures; market research. Also involved in improving cross-cultural and multi-cultural relationships, particularly with Japanese clients. **Founded:** 1984. **Seminars:** Objectives and standards/recruiting for boards of directors.

13867 ■ R.E. Moulton Inc.
50 Doaks Ln.
Marblehead, MA 01945
Ph: (781)631-1325
Fax: (781)631-2165
Co. E-mail: mike_lee@remoultoninc.com
URL: http://www.oneamerica.com/wps/wcm/connect/REMoulton
Contact: Willard A. Knarr, Jr., President
Scope: Offers underwriting services, marketing solutions, claims administration and adjudication; policy and commission administration; and risk management solutions to clients. Supplementary service s include risk management and employee assistance. Clients include individuals, business men, employers and finance professionals. **Founded:** 1976.

13868 ■ Murray Dropkin & Associates—Dropkin Consulting
390 George St.
New Brunswick, NJ 08901
Ph: (732)828-3211
Fax: (732)828-4118
Co. E-mail: murray@dropkin.com
URL: http://www.dropkin.com
Contact: Murray Dropkin, President
E-mail: murray@dropkin.com
Scope: Specializes in feasibility studies; business management; business process re-engineering; and team building, health care and housing. **Founded:** 1969. **Publications:** "Bookkeeping for Nonprofits," Jossey Bass, 2005; "Guide to Audits of Nonprofit Organizations," PPC; "The Nonprofit Report," Warren, Gorham & Lamont; "The Budget Building Book for Nonprofits," Jossey-Bass; "The Cash Flow Management Book for Nonprofits," Jossey-Bass.

13869 ■ Navarro, Kim & Associates
529 N Charles St., Ste. 202
Baltimore, MD 21201-5043
Ph: (410)837-6317
Fax: (410)837-6294
Co. E-mail: bnavarro@sprynet.com
Contact: Beltran Navarro, Director
E-mail: bnavarro@sprynet.com
Scope: Specializes in bridging the gap between firms and non-traditional ethnic communities, especially in community development and institutional building. **Founded:** 1984.

13870 ■ New Commons
545 Pawtucket Ave., Studio 106A
Pawtucket, RI 02860
Ph: (401)351-7110
Fax: (401)351-7158
Co. E-mail: info@newcommons.com
URL: http://www.newcommons.com
Contact: Robert Leaver, Chief Executive Officer
E-mail: rleaver@newcommons.com
Scope: Builder of agile human networks to champion innovation and mobilize change; to pursue business opportunities; to custom design agile organizations and communities, to foster civic engagement. Clients include organizations on-profits, corporations, government agencies, educational institutions; networks-Trade/professional groups, IT services collaborations, service-sharing collectives; and communities- municipalities, states and statewide agencies, regional collaborations. **Founded:** 1982. **Publications:** "Plexus Imperative," Sep, 2005; "Creating 21st Century Capable Innovation Systems," Aug, 2004; "Call to Action: Building Providences Creative and Innovative Economy"; "Getting Results from Meetings"; "The Entrepreneur as Artist," Commonwealth Publications; "Leader and Agent of Change," Commonwealth Publications; "Achieving our Providence: Lessons of City-Building," Commonwealth Publications. **Seminars:** Introduction to Social Computing (Web 2.0), Jan, 2009; Every Company Counts, Jun, 2009; Facilitating for Results; Story-Making and Story-Telling. **Telecommunication Services:** inquiries@newcommons.com.

13871 ■ Nightingale Associates
7445 Setting Sun Way
Columbia, MD 21046
Ph: (410)381-4280
Fax: (410)381-4280
Co. E-mail: fredericknightingale@nightingaleassociates.net
URL: http://www.nightingaleassociates.net
Contact: Frederick C. Nightingale, Managing Director
E-mail: fredericknightingale@nightingaleAssociates.net
Scope: Management training and consulting firm offering the following skills: productivity and accomplishment; leadership skills for the experienced manager; management skills for the new manager; leadership and teambuilding; supervisory development; creative problem solving; real strategic planning; providing superior customer service; international purchasing and supply chain management; negotiation skills development and fundamentals of purchasing. **Founded:** 1984. **Seminars:** Productivity and Accomplishment Management Skills for the New Manager; Leadership and Team building; Advanced Management; Business Process Re engineering; Strategic Thinking; Creative Problem Solving; Customer Service; International Purchasing and Materials Management; Fundamentals of Purchasing; Negotiation Skills Development; Providing superior customer service; Leadership skills for the experienced manager.

13872 ■ P2C2 Group Inc.
4101 Denfeld Ave.
Kensington, MD 20895-1514
Ph: (301)942-7985
Fax: (301)942-7986
Co. E-mail: info@p2c2group.com
URL: http://www.p2c2group.com
Contact: James E. Kendrick, President
E-mail: kendrick@p2c2group.com
Scope: Works with clients on the business side of federal program and project management. Services include program/project planning and optimization; acquisition strategy and work statements; IT Capital Planning and Investment Control (CPIC); business cases - new, revisions, critiques; budget analysis - cost benefits- alternatives; CPIC, SELC, and security documentation; research, metrics, analysis, and case studies. Consulting support helping to: Define or redefine programs; strengthen portfolio management; identify alternatives for lean budgets; improve capital planning and investment; develop better plans and documentation, and evaluate performance of existing program investments. **Founded:** 1994. **Publications:** "OMB 300s Go Online," Federal Sector Report, Mar, 2007; "Using Risk-Adjusted Costs for Projects," Federal Sector Report, Feb, 2007; "Make Better Decisions Using Case Studies," Federal Sector Report, Jan, 2007; "PMO Performance Measurement & Metrics"; "Executive Sponsors for Projects"; "ABCs of the Presidential Transition"; "Financial Systems and Enterprise Portfolio Management"; "The Future of CPIC"; "Critical Factors for Program and Project Success"; "Using Risk-Adjusted Costs for Projects"; "Tactics for a Successful Year of CPIC"; "Operational Analysis Reviews"; "Successful IT Strategic Planning"; "Information Technology Investment Management". **Seminars:** Requests For Information; Pre Solicitation Marketing; Qualifications Statement Support For The Capital Planning And Investment Control (cpic) Process; How To Hire A Management Consultant And Get The Results You Expect.

13873 ■ Papa and Associates Inc.
200 Consumers Rd., Ste. 305
Toronto, ON, Canada M2J 4R4
Ph: (416)512-7272
Fax: (416)512-2016
Co. E-mail: ppapa@papa-associates.com
URL: http://www.papa-associates.com
Contact: Peter Papakostantinu, President
E-mail: ppapa@papa-associates.com
Scope: Provider of broad based management consulting services in the areas of quality assurance, environmental, health and safety and integrated management systems. **Founded:** 1989.

13874 ■ Parker Consultants Inc.
230 Mason St.
Greenwich, CT 06830-6633
Ph: (203)861-6698
Contact: Donald L. Parker, President
Scope: Firm specializes in strategic planning; organizational development; small business management; performance appraisals; executive searches; team building; and customer service audits. **Founded:** 1988.

13875 ■ Partners for Market Leadership L.L.C.
400 Galleria Pky., Ste. 1500
Atlanta, GA 30339
Ph: (770)850-1409
Free: 800-984-1110
Co. E-mail: dcarpenter@market-leadership.com
URL: http://www.market-leadership.com
Contact: Nancy Surdyka, Manager
E-mail: nsurdyka@market-leadership.com
Scope: Boutique consulting firm focused on assisting clients to develop sustainable market leadership in geographic, practice area and/or industry markets. Provides consulting on market leadership, revenue enhancement, strategic development and change facilitation. Additional services are offered to legal, accounting, valuation and financial firms. **Founded:** 1995.

13876 ■ Performance Consulting Associates Inc. (PCA)
3700 Crestwood Pky., Ste. 100
Duluth, GA 30096
Ph: (770)717-2737
Fax: (770)717-7014
Co. E-mail: info@pcaconsulting.com
URL: http://www.pcaconsulting.com
Contact: Richard A. Defazio, President
E-mail: defazio@pcaconsulting.com
Scope: Maintenance consulting and engineering firm specializing in production planning, project management, team building, and re-engineering maintenance. **Founded:** 1976. **Publications:** "Does Planning Pay," Plant Services, Nov, 2000; "Asset Reliability Coordinator," Maintenance Technology, Oct, 2000; "Know What it is You Have to Maintain," Maintenance Technology, May, 2000; "Does Maintenance Planning Pay," Maintenance Technology, Nov, 2000.; "What is Asset Management?"; "Implementing Best Business Practices".

13877 ■ Performance Consulting Group Inc.
8031 SW 35th Terr.
Miami, FL 33155-3443
Ph: (305)264-5577
Fax: (305)264-9079
Contact: Patrick J. O'Brien, President
Scope: Firm provides consulting services in the areas of strategic planning; profit enhancement; product development; and production planning. **Founded:** 1980.

13878 ■ Rose & Crangle Ltd.
117 N 4th St.
Lincoln, KS 67455
Ph: (785)524-5050
Fax: (785)524-3130
Co. E-mail: rcltd@nckcn.com
URL: http://www.roseandcrangle.com
Contact: Robert D. Crangle, President
E-mail: rcltd@nckcn.com
Scope: Provider of evaluation, planning and policy analyzes for universities, associations, foundations, governmental agencies and private companies engaged in scientific, technological or educational activities. Special expertise in the development of new institutions. Special skills in providing planning and related group facilitation workshops. **Founded:** 1984. **Publications:** "Preface to Bulgarian Integration Into Europe and NATO: Issues of Science Policy And research Evaluation Practice," Ios Press, 2006; "Allocating Limited National Resources for Fundamental Research," 2005.

13879 ■ Rothschild Strategies Unlimited L.L.C.
19 Thistle Rd.
Norwalk, CT 06851-1909

Ph: (203)846-6898
Fax: (203)847-1426
Co. E-mail: bill@strategyleader.com
URL: http://www.strategyleader.com
Contact: Stephen M. Rothschild, President
Scope: Consults with senior management and business level strategy teams to develop overall strategic direction, set priorities and creates sustainable competitive advantages and differentiators. Enables organizations to enhance their own strategic thinking and leadership skills so that they can continue to develop and implement profitable growth strategies. **Founded:** 1983. **Publications:** "Putting It All Together-a guide to strategic thinking"; "Competitive Advantage"; "Ristaker, Caretaker, Surgeon & Undertaker four faces of strategic leadership"; "The Secret to GE's Success"; "Having the Right Strategic Leader and Team".

13880 ■ David G. Schantz
29 Wood Run Cir.
Rochester, NY 14612-2271
Ph: (716)723-0760
Fax: (716)723-8724
Co. E-mail: daveschantz@yahoo.com
URL: http://www.daveschantz.freeservers.com
Contact: David G. Schantz, Manager
Scope: Provider of industrial engineering services for photofinishing labs, including amateur-wholesale, professional, commercial, school, and package. **Founded:** 1992.

13881 ■ Schneider Consulting Group Inc.
50 S Steele St., Ste. 390
Denver, CO 80209-2834
Ph: (303)320-4413
Fax: (303)320-5795
Contact: Kim Schneider Malek, Vice President
E-mail: kim@scgfambus.com
Scope: Assists family-owned and privately-held business transition to the next generation and/or to a more professionally managed company, turn around consulting for small and medium size companies. **Founded:** 1987.

13882 ■ Scott Ashby Teleselling Inc.
1102 Ben Franklin Dr., Ste. 309
Sarasota, FL 34236
Ph: (941)388-4283
Fax: (941)388-5240
URL: http://www.scottashbyteleselling.com
Contact: R. Scott Ashby, President
E-mail: rscottashby@netscape.net
Scope: Provider of consulting services and customized training programs that emphasize consultative telephone selling techniques. **Founded:** 1979. **Publications:** "How Will the Internet Affect Teleselling Programs?"; "When is Telemarketing Really Not Telemarketing?"; "The Future of Account Management Telesales". **Seminars:** Start-Up Educational, Planning and Strategy Development; Existing Program Audit, Evaluation, State-of-the-Art Best Practices Comparison, Tracking and Measurement Review, Systems and Procedures Analysis, and Optional Selling Skills; Develop New or Revised Consultative Telephone Selling; Helping Clients Build Relationship and Grow Their Business by Phone.

13883 ■ Sklar and Associates Inc.
242 Laurel Bay Dr.
Murrells Inlet, SC 29576
Ph: (843)798-0412
Fax: (843)651-3090
Co. E-mail: sklarincdc@aol.com
URL: http://www.sklarinc.com
Contact: Tim Sklar, President
Scope: Provider of consulting services for business acquisitions, business development and project finance. Provides audit oversight services to listed corporations on Sarbanes-Oxley compliance. Services include: Due diligence analyses and corporate governance. Industries served: transportation sectors, energy sector and commercial real estate industries. **Seminars:** Financial Analysis in MBA; Emerging Company Finance; Due Diligence in Business Acquisition; Business Valuation.

13884 ■ Straightline Services Inc.
11 Centre St., Ste. 10
Salem, CT 06420-3845
Ph: (860)889-7929
Fax: (860)885-1894
Co. E-mail: straitln@aol.com
Contact: Wayne J. S. France, President
Scope: Design and implementation of organizational infrastructure, business plans and troubleshooting. Emphasizes on operations with a central and field or satellite offices. Industries served: Construction, resorts, Indian tribes, academies, small-medium sized business, mostly privately held. **Founded:** 1994.

13885 ■ Trendzitions Inc.
25691 Atlantic Ocean, Ste. B13
Lake Forest, CA 92630-8842
Ph: (949)727-9100
Free: 800-266-2767
Fax: (949)727-3444
Co. E-mail: ctooker@trendzitions.com
URL: http://www.trendzitions.com
Contact: Christian Tooker, President
E-mail: ctooker@trendzitions.com
Scope: Provider of services in the areas of communications consulting, project management, construction management, and furniture procurement. Offers information on spatial uses, building codes, ADA compliance and city ordinances. Also offers budget projections. **Founded:** 1986.

13886 ■ Turnaround Inc.
3415 A St. NW
Gig Harbor, WA 98335
Ph: (253)857-6730
Fax: (253)857-6344
Co. E-mail: info@turnround-inc.com
URL: http://www.turnaround-inc.com
Contact: Miles Stover, President
E-mail: mstover@turnaround-inc.com
Scope: Provider of interim executive management assistance and management advisory to small, medium and family-owned businesses that are not meeting their goals. Services include acting as an interim executive or on-site manager. Extensive practices in arena of bankruptcy management. **Founded:** 1997. **Publications:** "How to Identify Problem and Promising Management"; "How to Tell if Your Company is a Bankruptcy Candidate"; "Signs that Your Company is in Trouble"; "The Turnaround Specialist: How to File a Petition Under 11 USC 11". **Seminars:** Competitive Intelligence Gathering.

13887 ■ ValueNomics Value Specialists
50 W San Fernando St., Ste. 600
San Jose, CA 95113
Fax: (408)200-6401
Co. E-mail: info@amllp.com
Contact: Gary E. Jones, Chief Executive Officer
Scope: Consulting is offered in the areas of financial management, process re-engineering, growth business services; governance, risk/compliance, SOX readiness and compliance, SAS 70, enterprise risk management, system security, operational and internal audit; business advisory services; valuation services; CORE assessment; contract assurance; transaction advisory services, IT solutions and litigation support services. **Founded:** 1993. **Publications:** "Dueling Appraisers: How Differences in Input and Assumptions May Control the Value," Apr, 2005; "The Business of Business Valuation and the CPA as an expert witness"; "The Business of Business Valuation," McGraw-Hill Professional Publishers Inc.

13888 ■ Via Nova Consulting
1228 Winburn Dr.
Atlanta, GA 30344
Ph: (404)761-7484
Fax: (404)762-7123
Scope: Consulting services in the areas of strategic planning; privatization; executive searches; market research; customer service audits; new product development; competitive intelligence; and Total Quality Management (TQM). **Founded:** 1994.

13889 ■ Vision Management
149 Meadows Rd.
Lafayette, NJ 07848-3120
Ph: (973)702-1116

Fax: (973)702-8311
Contact: Norman L. Naidish, President
Scope: Firm specializes in profit enhancement; strategic planning; business process reengineering; industrial engineering; facilities planning; team building; inventory management; and total quality management (TQM). **Founded:** 1984. **Publications:** "To increase profits, improve quality," Manufacturing Engineering, May, 2000.

13890 ■ Walker & Associates
255 N Madison Ave.
Pasadena, CA 91102
Ph: (626)396-9593
Fax: (626)396-9222
Co. E-mail: info@waa.bz
Contact: Rodney D. Walker, Director
E-mail: rodney@waa.bz
Scope: A management consulting firm with services that include fund development, grant writing, executive coaching, board development, diversity training, organizational assessment, organizational development, strategic planning, marketing and public relations, nonprofit start-up assistance, and workshops and training. **Publications:** "Program Evaluation"; "Grant Writing"; "Financial Management"; "Risk Management"; "Strategic Planning"; "Capacity Building". **Seminars:** Strategic Planning That Makes Sense; Fundraising Essentials; Best Practices for Executive Directors; Effective Program Evaluation That Makes Sense; Marketing Your Nonprofit; How Nonprofits Can Thrive In Turbulent Times.

13891 ■ Weich & Bilotti Inc.
600 Worcester Rd., 4th Fl.
Framingham, MA 01702
Ph: (508)663-1600
Fax: (508)663-1682
Co. E-mail: info@weich-bilotti.com
Contact: Mervyn D. Weich, Director
E-mail: mweich@weich-bilotti.com
Scope: Specializes in business plans, venture capital, computer information systems, turnaround/interim management, retail consulting, start-up process, college recruiting and IS and IT personnel. **Founded:** 1995.

13892 ■ Wheeler and Young Inc.
33 Peter St.
Markham, ON, Canada L3P 2A5
Ph: (905)471-5709
Fax: (905)471-9989
Co. E-mail: wheeler@ericwheeler.ca
URL: http://www.ericwheeler.ca
Contact: Eric S. Wheeler, Managing Partner
E-mail: ewheeler@yorku.ca
Scope: Provider of consulting services to high-tech companies on the implementation of software development processes; quality management systems (including ISO 9000 compliance) and business management systems. Offers business management and knowledge-management services to organizations. Industries served: Knowledge-based industries, including software and hardware development, medical and legal professionals, information service providers. **Founded:** 1994.

13893 ■ Zogby International
901 Broad St.
Utica, NY 13501
Ph: (315)624-0200
Free: 877-462-7655
Fax: (315)624-0210
Co. E-mail: marketing@zogby.com
URL: http://www.zogby.com
Contact: John Zogby, President
E-mail: john@zogby.com
Scope: Specializes in providing market research and analysis services. **Founded:** 1984. **Publications:** "Just who are you calling anyway"; "All of this leads to a very basic question". **Seminars:** The Research Authority, Oct, 2006; Christian Science Monitor Break fast, Oct, 2006.

13894 ■ Zolfo Cooper L.L.C.
Grace Bldg., 1114 Ave. of the Americas, 41st Fl.
New York, NY 10036
Ph: (212)561-4000

Fax: (212)213-1749
Co. E-mail: rrandall@zolfocooper.com
URL: http://www.zolfocooper.com
Contact: Mark Cervi, Director
Scope: Provider of accounting consulting services to businesses. Specializes in restructuring and turnaround consulting; interim and crisis management; performance improvement; creditor advisory; cross-border restructuring and corporate finance. **Founded:** 1985.

FRANCHISES AND BUSINESS OPPORTUNITIES

13895 ■ Belron Canada Inc.
8288 Boul. PIE-IX
Montreal, QC, Canada H1Z 3T6
Ph: (514)593-3824
Fax: (514)593-7028
URL: http://www.belroncanada.com
Description: Provides services and solutions for auto glass repair and replacement. Operates under four retail banners - Apple Auto Glass, Speedy Glass, Lebeau Vitres d'autos, DURO vitres d'autos - and conducts its wholesale activities under the Vanfax and Technicentre Plus trade names. It also offers claims management services. **No. of Franchise Units:** 150. **No. of Company-Owned Units:** 211. **Founded:** 1965. **Franchised:** 1982. **Equity Capital Needed:** $40,000-$300,000. **Franchise Fee:** $25,000.

13896 ■ Clean First Time, Inc.
8810 Commodity Cir., Ste. 7
Orlando, FL 32819
Free: 866-390-2532
Fax: (407)352-1443
Description: New home construction cleaning. **No. of Franchise Units:** 15. **No. of Company-Owned Units:** 1. **Founded:** 2003. **Franchised:** 2004. **Equity Capital Needed:** $12,000-$150,000. **Franchise Fee:** $12,000-$150,000. **Royalty Fee:** 7%. **Training:** Includes 3-5 days training at headquarters, 3-5 days at franchisee's location and ongoing support.

13897 ■ Cleaning Consultant Services Inc.
PO Box 1273
Seattle, WA 98111
Ph: (206)682-9748
Description: Support services to those who own, manage and/or supervise cleaning operations. **No. of Franchise Units:** 2. **No. of Company-Owned Units:** 3. **Founded:** 1976.. **Franchised:** 1978. **Equity Capital Needed:** $7,500. **Franchise Fee:** $2,500. **Training:** 2-3 days at out training site in Seattle, WA.

13898 ■ Manufacturing Management Associates
700 Commerce Dr., Ste. 500
Oak Brook, IL 60523
Ph: (630)575-8700
Description: Has built its reputation providing small to mid-sized manufacturing and distribution companies with the technical and advisory services they need to achieve their individual business goals. Areas of expertise include manufacturing systems and network technology, process flow (JIT), quality (TQC), cost management, human resource change management, ISO 9000 certification preparation and work cell design/factory layout. days of training in Chicago, IL. Will also assist the franchisee in sales and marketing efforts to promote the success of the franchise. Other notable benefits include potential client leads, alliances with industry experts, project management methodologies, proprietary computer software sys-

tems, reference proposals and R & D. **No. of Franchise Units:** 8. **No. of Company-Owned Units:** 1. **Founded:** 1982.. **Franchised:** 1993. **Equity Capital Needed:** $14,900-$49,450. **Franchise Fee:** $10,000. **Training:** An intensive 8 day seminar in Chicago, IL, where the franchisee will be exposed to a working office and receive extensive training in the policies of running a successful franchise. The franchisee will receive a thorough explanation of proven methodologies, as well as training in proprietary software and business systems.

13899 ■ Sandler Training
Sandler Systems Inc.
300 Red Brook Blvd., Ste. 400
Owings Mills, MD 21117
Ph: (410)653-1993
Free: 800-669-3537
Fax: (410)358-7858
Co. E-mail: info@sandler.com
URL: http://www.sandler.com
Description: No. 1 Rated Management Training Franchise by Entrepreneur Magazine 2001. The franchise offered consists of the right to operate a Sandler Sales Institute business devoted to a distinctive style of training persons in the fields of sales and sales management, management consulting, human relations, leadership development, and methods of teaching such subjects through ongoing training, seminars and workshops. **No. of Franchise Units:** 235. **Founded:** 1969. **Franchised:** 1983. **Equity Capital Needed:** $82,150-$98,750; minimum net worth $150,000. **Franchise Fee:** $68,000. **Training:** Toll-free hotline for training support, frequent initial training schools, quarterly training conferences, training and operating manuals, newsletter, promotional materials, lead generation, leader's guides.

13900 ■ Turbo Leadership Systems Ltd.
36280 NE Wilsonville Rd.
Newberg, OR 97132
Ph: (503)625-1867
Fax: (503)625-2699
Description: Management training and team building training. **No. of Company-Owned Units:** 1. **Founded:** 1985.. **Franchised:** 1995. **Equity Capital Needed:** $49,000. **Franchise Fee:** $39,000. **Training:** Yes.

COMPUTERIZED DATABASES

13901 ■ *Business & Management Practices*™
10650 Toebben Dr.
Independence, KY 41051
Free: 800-354-9706
Fax: (800)487-8488
Co. E-mail: investors@cengage.com
URL: http://www.gale.cengage.com
Contact: Ronald Dunn, President
Availability: Online: ProQuest LLC - Dialog; Cengage Learning Inc. **Type:** Full-text; Bibliographic.

LIBRARIES

13902 ■ American Society for Training and Development - Information Center
1640 King St.
Alexandria, VA 22313-2043
Ph: (703)683-8100
Free: 800-628-2783
Fax: (703)683-1523
Co. E-mail: customercare@astd.org
URL: http://www.astd.org
Scope: Human resource development - general, management, training, career development, Organization development, consulting skills. **Services:**

Library open to national members of the Society. **Founded:** 1984. **Holdings:** 3000 bound volumes. **Subscriptions:** 60 journals and other serials.

13903 ■ CMA Ontario - Member Services Centre
70 University Ave., Ste. 101
Toronto, ON, Canada M5J 2M4
Ph: (416)204-3142
Fax: (416)977-1365
Co. E-mail: msc@cma-ontario.org
Contact: Patricia Black, Manager, Member Services
Scope: Accounting, management, finance, strategy, taxation, investments. **Services:** Copying; SDI; Library not open to the public. **Founded:** 1990. **Holdings:** 2069 books; 267 videocassettes; 184 audiocassettes; 6 videodiscs. **Subscriptions:** 53 journals and other serials; 2 newspapers.

13904 ■ Hanley-Wood, LLC Library
426 S. Westgate St.
Addison, IL 60101-4546
Ph: (630)543-0870
Fax: (630)543-3112
URL: http://www.hanleywood.com
Scope: Concrete, cement, masonry, construction, home building. **Services:** Interlibrary loan; copying. **Founded:** 1971. **Holdings:** 3000 books; 120 bound periodical volumes. **Subscriptions:** 100 journals and other serials.

13905 ■ Right Management Consultants - Corporate Research Center
1818 Market St., 33rd Fl.
Philadelphia, PA 19103

13906 ■ Strategic Account Management Association - Resource Search Library
33 N. LaSalle St., Ste. 3700
Chicago, IL 60602
Ph: (312)251-3131
Fax: (312)251-3132
URL: http://www.strategicaccounts.org/search/resourcesearch.asp
Contact: Elisabeth Cornell, Director, Education
Scope: National and global account management programs, account managers, strategic account management, strategic partnering and alliances, cross-functional teams, channel conflict, supply chain management, internal selling, customer viewpoint, value-added selling, account planning, account segmentation, compensation. **Services:** Library not open to the public (numerous sample documents available to non-members, and most can be purchased). **Founded:** 1964. **Holdings:** 1500 documents, periodicals, audiocassettes, case studies, white papers, research studies, books, reports, archives, PDFs, and presentation materials. **Subscriptions:** 1 journal; 3 newsletters.

13907 ■ University of Kentucky - Business & Economics Information Center
B&E Info. Ctr., Rm. 116
335-BA Gatton College of Business & Economics
Lexington, KY 40506-0034
Ph: (859)257-8936
Fax: (859)257-1333
Co. E-mail: mrazeeq@pop.uk.edu
URL: http://www.uky.edu//Provost/academicprograms.html
Contact: Michael A. Razeeq, Librarian, Business
URL(s): gatton.uky.edu/. **Scope:** Business, economics, business management, marketing, finance, accounting. **Services:** Library open to the public for reference use only. **Founded:** 1993. **Telecommunication Services:** cber@uky.edu; klimar@pop.uky.edu; provost@email.uky.edu.

ASSOCIATIONS AND OTHER ORGANIZATIONS

13908 ■ **Manufacturers' Agents Association for the Foodservice Industry (MAFSI)**
1199 Euclid Ave.
Atlanta, GA 30307
Ph: (404)214-9474
Fax: (404)522-0132
Co. E-mail: info@mafsi.org
URL: http://www.mafsi.org
Contact: Danny Collis, President
Description: Independent manufacturers' representative firms selling equipment, furnishings, and supplies to dealers and users. Sponsors annual mini manufacturer sales meetings. Conducts specialized education programs. **Founded:** 1949. **Publications:** *Outfront* (Quarterly); *MAFSI Agent Member Directory.* **Educational Activities:** Marketing Seminar Conference (Annual). **Awards:** All-Industry Awards (Annual); Lifetime Membership Award (Annual); Market Mover Award (Annual); Pacesetter Award (Annual); Special Recognition Award (Annual); Tony Award; Bill H. Loveless Chapter of the Year Award (Annual); Jack Pressberg Memorial Scholarship Fund; Bill H. Loveless Chapter of the Year Award; Lifetime Membership Award; Market Mover Award; Special Recognition Award.

13909 ■ **Manufacturers' Agents National Association (MANA)**
16 Journey, Ste. 200
Aliso Viejo, CA 92656
Ph: (949)859-4040
Free: 877-626-2776
Fax: (949)855-2973
Co. E-mail: mana@manaonline.org
URL: http://www.manaonline.org
Contact: Bryan Shirley, President
E-mail: jmiller@manaonline.org
Description: Manufacturers' agents in all fields representing two or more manufacturers on a commission basis; associate members are manufacturers and others interested in improving the agent-principal relationship. Maintains code of ethics and rules of business and professional conduct; issues model standard form of agreement. **Founded:** 1947. **Publications:** *Agency Sales Magazine* (Monthly); *Rep-Letter; MANA Matters* (Monthly); *Manufacturers' Agents National Association - Directory of Manufacturers' Sales Agencies; Agency Sales Magazine* (Monthly); *MANA Online Directory of Manufacturers' Sales Agencies; Manufacturers' Agents National Association--Directory of Manufacturers' Sales Agencies; Agency Sales: The Marketing Magazine for Manufacturers' Agencies and Their Principals; Manufacturers' Agents National Association--Special Report* (Periodic).

13910 ■ **Manufacturers Representatives of America (MRA)**
1111 Jupiter Rd., Ste. 204D
Plano, TX 75074
Ph: (682)518-6008
Fax: (682)518-6476
Co. E-mail: assnhqtrs@aol.com
URL: http://www.mra-reps.com
Contact: Eric Rud, President
Description: Independent manufacturers' representatives handling paper and plastic disposable products and sanitary supplies. Aims to improve agent sales skills, market coverage and customer service and to establish more effective agent/principal communications. **Founded:** 1978.

13911 ■ **Manufacturers Representatives Educational Research Foundation (MRERF)**
999 S Monaco Pkwy., Ste. 200
Denver, CO 80224
Ph: (303)463-1801
Fax: (303)379-6024
Co. E-mail: certify@mrerf.org
URL: http://www.mrerf.org
Contact: Gary Brusacoram, Executive Director
Description: Sponsored by 35 national and state associations of manufacturers' representatives, distributors and manufacturers. Promotes the profession of outsourced field sales through academic research and publication; disseminates research findings on the role of manufacturers' representatives to academic institutions; provides a forum for the exchange of information. Operates professional certification program for agency owners and sales people. Also provides educational programs for manufacturers who outsource field sales. **Founded:** 1984. **Educational Activities:** Certified Professional Manufacturers' Representatives (Semiannual); Certified Sales Professional; Managing Your Manufacturer's Representative Network. **Awards:** George Hayward CPMR Champion Award (Annual).

13912 ■ **NAGMR**
c/o Jim Lewis
15038 SE Fairwood Blvd.
Renton, WA 98058-8505
Ph: (425)271-4506
Fax: (425)271-0864
Co. E-mail: jnlsales@aol.com
URL: http://nagmr.com
Contact: Ken Laner, President
Description: Consumer products brokers specializing in selling drug, health, beauty aids, and nonfood products to food chains and the same products and grocery items to the nonfood market. **Founded:** 1948. **Educational Activities:** NAGMR Convention (Annual). **Awards:** NAGMR Award of Excellence (Annual).

DIRECTORIES OF EDUCATIONAL PROGRAMS

13913 ■ *New England Manufacturers Directory*
Pub: Harris InfoSource
Contact: Dennis Abrahams, President
E-mail: dennisa@harrisinfo.com
URL(s): www.harrisinfo.comwww.harrisinfo.com/products/pdfs/Harris_PriceList_0109.pdf. **Released:** Annual; March; Latest edition 2009. **Covers:** Over 30,600 manufacturers. **Entries include:** Names and titles of key personnel, company name and address, annual sales, date of establishment, employment size, import/export involvement, sic, plant size, headquarters, phone, fax, and toll-free number. **Arrangement:** Alphabetical, geographical, SIC code, product.

13914 ■ *Scott's Directories: National Manufacturers*
Pub: Scott's Directories
Contact: Rabiya Shaikh, Manager
E-mail: rshaikh@scottsdirectories.com
URL(s): www.scottsinfo.comwww.scottsdirectories.com. **Ed:** Barbara Peard. **Released:** Annual; February; latest edition 2007 edition. **Price:** $899, Individuals CD; pinpointer; $1799, Individuals CD; profiler; $3499, Individuals CD; prospector; $849, Individuals online; pinpointer; $1699, Individuals online; profiler; $3299, Individuals online; prospector. **Covers:** 58,000 manufacturers throughout Canada. **Entries include:** Company name, address, phone, fax, telex, names and titles of key personnel, number of employees, parent or subsidiary companies, North American Standard Industrial (NAICS) code, product, export interest, and year established.

REFERENCE WORKS

13915 ■ *Manufacturers' Agents National Association--Directory of Manufacturers' Sales Agencies*
Pub: Manufacturers' Agents National Association
Contact: Bryan Shirley, President
E-mail: jmiller@manaonline.org
URL(s): www.manaonline.org. **Ed:** Helen Degli-Angeli. **Released:** Online Directory. **Covers:** 4,000 independent agents and firms representing manufacturers and other businesses in specified territories on a commission basis, including consultants and associate member firms interested in the manufacturer/agency method of marketing. **Entries include:** For manufacturers--Company name, address, phone, fax, E-mail, URL, name of contact, product. For agencies--Agency name, address, phone, fax, E-mail, URL, name of contact, warehouse facilities, territory covered, number of field sales representatives, branch office location, year established, date of joining association. **Arrangement:** Separate alphabetical sections for manufacturers and agencies. **Indexes:** Geographic, target industries.

TRADE PERIODICALS

13916 ■ *Agency Sales Magazine*
Pub: Manufacturers' Agents National Association
Contact: Bryan Shirley, President
E-mail: jmiller@manaonline.org
URL(s): www.manaonline.org/html/agency_sales_magazine.html. **Ed:** Jack Foster. **Released:** Monthly **Price:** $79, Individuals; $89, Canada; $102, Other countries.

13917 ■ *The Representative*
Pub: NAGMR Consumer Products Sales Agencies
Released: Quarterly. **Price:** Included in membership. **Description:** Contains Association, industry, and tax information for consumer product brokers who specialize in selling drug, health, and non-food

products and beauty aids to food and drug chains and mass merchandisers. Recurring features include news of members, a calendar of events.

13918 ■ *UAMR Confidential Bulletin*
Pub: United Association of Manufacturers' Representatives
Ed: Karen Mazzola, Editor. **Released:** Monthly. **Price:** Included in membership. **Description:** Covers product lines offered for representation in all fields. Provides details of the company and product, type of accounts to be serviced, and the areas open for representation. Subscription includes bulletin of lines for representatives, articles on rep business, and trade show listings.

TRADE SHOWS AND CONVENTIONS

13919 ■ National Association of General Merchandise Representatives Annual Convention

National Association of General Merchandise Representatives (NAGMR)
c/o Jim Lewis
15038 SE Fairwood Blvd.
Renton, WA 98058
Ph: (425)271-4506
Fax: (425)271-0864
URL: http://www.nagmr.com/
URL(s): www.nagmr.com. **Frequency:** Annual. **Audience:** Sales representatives and trade professionals. **Principal Exhibits:** Health and beauty aids that are sold in drug stores.

RESEARCH CENTERS

13920 ■ Manufacturers Representatives Educational Research Foundation (MRERF)
999 S Monaco Pky., No. 200
Denver, CO 80224

Ph: (303)463-1801
Fax: (303)379-6024
Co. E-mail: gary@mrerf.org
URL: http://www.mrerf.org
Contact: Gary Brusacoram, Executive Director
Founded: 1984. **Publications:** *MRERF Annual report.* **Educational Activities:** Executive Education and Certification (Annual), certified professional manufacturers' representative program held each year, involves 3 annual sessions followed by an exam process; Professional Sales Certification (Bimonthly), certified sales professional designation earned by attending professional selling seminar and taking written and verbal exam. **Awards:** George Hayward CPMR Champion Trophy, given to people who are true believers in the importance of education and certification for manufacturers. **Telecommunication Services:** certify@mrerf.org.

ASSOCIATIONS AND OTHER ORGANIZATIONS

13921 ■ American Boat Builders and Repairers Association (ABBRA)
3778 SW 30th Ave.
Fort Lauderdale, FL 33312
Ph: (954)654-7821
Fax: (954)239-2600
Co. E-mail: info@abbra.org
URL: http://www.abbra.org
Contact: Pamela Lendzion, President
Description: Boat yards, marinas, and sailmakers. Seeks to: develop and encourage high standards of service and conduct within the industry; foster and promote the common business and professional interests of members; provide a forum for the discussion of problems and the exchange of experiences and ideas. **Founded:** 1943. **Publications:** *Capstan* (Monthly). **Awards:** President's Award (Annual).

13922 ■ American Boat and Yacht Council (ABYC)
613 3rd St., Ste. 10
Annapolis, MD 21403
Ph: (410)990-4460
Fax: (410)990-4466
URL: http://www.abycinc.org
Contact: George Bellwoar, Chairman of the Board
Description: Consists of boatbuilders, boat owners, boat yards, dealerships, educational institutions, equipment and accessory manufacturers, government agencies, insurance companies, law firms, marinas, marine retailers, service technicians, surveyors and trade associations. Develops the consensus-based safety standards for the design, construction, equipage, maintenance and repair of small craft and their systems through 18 project technical committees. **Scope:** boating safety. **Founded:** 1954. **Subscriptions:** 2000. **Publications:** *American Boat and Yacht Council--News* (Quarterly); *Rules and Regulations for Recreational Boats* (Periodic); *Standards and Technical Information Reports for Small Craft* (Annual); *USCG Compliance Guidelines* (Periodic). **Awards:** ABYC Service Award (Annual).

13923 ■ Boat Owners Association of the United States (BOAT US)—BoatUS
880 S Pickett St.
Alexandria, VA 22304-4695
Ph: (703)461-4666
Free: 800-395-2628
Fax: (703)461-2847
Co. E-mail: membership@boatus.com
URL: http://www.boatus.com
Contact: Nancy Michelman, President
E-mail: NMichelman@boatus.com
Description: Represents owners or prospective owners of recreational boats. Independent, consumer service organization offering representation, benefits, and programs for boat owners. Services include: legislative and regulatory representation on issues affecting boaters' interests; marine insurance; maga-

zines; trailering club; marina discounts; long-term boat financing; boating regulations and forms service; charter and group travel services; sale and chartering exchange; marine surveyor and admiralty lawyer reference service; assistance with individual boating problems and towing reimbursement; association flag. Maintains Consumer Protection Bureau, which utilizes comprehensive consumer experience files to pursue individual complaints. **Founded:** 1966. **Publications:** *BOAT U.S. Magazine* (Bimonthly); *Equipment Catalog* (Annual); *Seaworthy* (Quarterly); *Boater's Source Directory* (Semiannual); *Seaworthy*; *Boat U.S. Trailering Magazine* (Bimonthly). **Telecommunication Services:** mail@boatus.com.

13924 ■ Inland Seas Education Association (ISEA)
100 Dame St.
Suttons Bay, MI 49682
Ph: (231)271-3077
Fax: (231)271-3088
Co. E-mail: isea@schoolship.org
URL: http://www.greatlakeseducation.org
Contact: Jay Zelenock, President
Description: Individuals concerned with the stewardship of the Great Lakes. Develops leadership, understanding, and commitment needed for long-term stewardship of the Great Lakes. Provides shipboard educational programs where people of all ages can gain first-hand training and experience in the Great Lakes ecosystem. Offers aquatic science, environmental awareness, and sail training classes. **Founded:** 1989. **Publications:** *Schoolship Log* (Quarterly).

13925 ■ International Marina Institute (IMI)
50 Water St.
Warren, RI 02885
Ph: (401)247-0314
Free: 866-367-6622
Fax: (401)247-0074
Co. E-mail: info@marinaassociation.org
URL: http://www.marinaassociation.org
Contact: Jim Frye, President
Description: Marinas and other boat storage facilities. Promotes growth and professional development among members and their employees. Gathers and disseminates business and technical information of interest to members. Conducts continuing professional education courses for marina personnel in areas including management, facilities maintenance and environmental protection. **Scope:** marina education. **Founded:** 1986. **Subscriptions:** 40 books. **Publications:** *Dock Lines* (Biweekly); *Practices and Products for Clean Marinas*. **Educational Activities:** National Marina Conference and Trade Show (Annual). **Awards:** Outstanding Achievement Award (Periodic). **Telecommunication Services:** imitraining@marinaassociation.org.

13926 ■ International Shipmasters Association (ISMA)
514 Jaycox Rd.
Avon Lake, OH 44012-2219

Ph: (440)933-4376
Co. E-mail: grskuggen@oh.rr.com
URL: http://www.shipmaster.org
Contact: Capt. Sean O'Donoughue, President
Description: Represents licensed marine officers operating on the Great Lakes. Promotes legislation to increase greater safety, health, and welfare of Great Lakes transportation and navigation. **Founded:** 1890. **Awards:** Hawsepipe Scholarship Award (Annual); Cadet Scholarship Award (Annual).

13927 ■ Marine Retailers Association of America (MRAA)
PO Box 725
Boca Grande, FL 33921
Ph: (941)964-2534
Fax: (941)531-6777
Co. E-mail: mraa@mraa.com
URL: http://www.mraa.com
Contact: David Foulkrod, Chairman of the Board
Description: Marine retail dealers, marine manufacturers and accessory distributors, and marine services. Disseminates information and promotes activities and programs for the betterment of recreational boating. Co-sponsors dealer management seminars to improve professional management skills. Maintains speakers' bureau; compiles statistics. **Founded:** 1971. **Publications:** *Bearings* (Monthly). **Awards:** Excellence in Business Award (Annual).

13928 ■ National Marine Bankers Association (NMBA)
231 S LaSalle St., Ste. 2050
Chicago, IL 60604
Ph: (312)946-6260
Co. E-mail: bmcardle@nmma.org
URL: http://www.marinebankers.org
Contact: Ms. Karen Trostle, President
E-mail: karen@sterlingacceptance.com
Description: Banks, savings institutions, and financial service firms that extend credit to consumers, retailers, and manufacturers of recreational boating equipment. Provides a forum in which lenders can exchange information on developing recreational boating loan programs. Promotes the extension of credit to recreational boating manufacturers, retailers, and consumers. Educates financial institutions on correct methods of underwriting and securing consumer loans and wholesale financing through Marine Lender Workshops. Compiles national statistics on marine financing. **Founded:** 1980. **Publications:** *Business of Pleasure Boats* (Quarterly); *Lender's Boating Handbook*; *Summary of Annual Marine Lending Survey* (Annual). **Educational Activities:** National Marine Bankers Association Conference (Annual); Marine Lending Workshop (Annual). **Awards:** William B. Otto III Marine Lending Industry Service Award (Annual).

13929 ■ National Marine Distributors Association (NMDA)
37 Pratt St.
Essex, CT 06426
Ph: (860)767-7898

Fax: (860)767-7932
Co. E-mail: executivedirector@nmdaonline.com
URL: http://www.nmdaonline.com
Contact: John Rothermel, President
Description: Wholesale distributors of marine accessories and hardware to the Pleasure Boating Industry. **Founded:** 1965. **Telecommunication Services:** info@nmdaonline.com.

13930 ■ National Marine Electronics Association (NMEA)
7 Riggs Ave.
Severna Park, MD 21146
Ph: (410)975-9425
Free: 800-808-6632
Fax: (410)975-9450
Co. E-mail: info@nmea.org
URL: http://www.nmea.org
Contact: David Gratton, Chairman
Description: Manufacturers, retail service dealers, distributors, educational institutions, and organizations associated with sales and service of marine electronics. Promotes the education and advancement of the marine electronics industry and the market which it serves. **Founded:** 1957. **Publications:** *Marine Electronics* (Bimonthly). **Awards:** NMEA Product Awards (Annual).

13931 ■ National Marine Manufacturers Association (NMMA)
231 S LaSalle, Ste. 2050
Chicago, IL 60604
Ph: (312)946-6200
Co. E-mail: tdammrich@nmma.org
URL: http://www.nmma.org
Contact: Thomas Dammrich, President
URL(s): www.discoverboating.com. **Description:** Members of Association of Marine Engine Manufacturers, National Association of Boat Manufacturers, and National Association of Marine Products and Services; manufacturers of pleasure boats, marine engines, outboard motors, and boating products. Compiles statistics and provides specialized training for designers of yachts. Sponsors consumer boat shows. **Founded:** 1905. **Educational Activities:** National Marine Manufacturers Association Conference (Annual).

13932 ■ Northwest Marine Trade Association (NMTA)
1900 N Northlake Way, No. 233
Seattle, WA 98103-9087
Ph: (206)634-0911
Fax: (206)632-0078
Co. E-mail: info@nmta.net
URL: http://www.nmta.net
Contact: George Harris, President
E-mail: george@nmta.net
Description: Sole proprietorships, firms, partnerships, or corporations engaged in the sales, service, distribution, and construction of boats, engines, and accessories; allied businesses. Seeks to further the interests of members; to promote public interest in boating; to cooperate with similar organizations; to develop local and state legislation beneficial to the industry and the boating public. Produces and sponsors boat shows; serves as legislative consultant and watchdog for the industry; conducts seminars and management and sales workshops; maintains advertising and public relations programs for the industry; commissions special studies and reports; conducts social activities. **Founded:** 1947. **Publications:** *Northwest Marine Trade Association--Membership Directory* (Annual); *Water Life* (Monthly). **Educational Activities:** Seattle Boat Show (Semiannual); Seattle Boat Show (Annual).

13933 ■ Personal Watercraft Industry Association (PWIA)
444 N Capitol St., Ste. 645
Washington, DC 20001
Ph: (202)737-9761
Fax: (202)280-6953
Co. E-mail: info@pwia.org
URL: http://www.pwia.org
Contact: Dave Dickerson, Executive Director
Description: Represents the four U.S. personal watercraft manufacturers. Works to ensure that personal watercraft (PWC) and personal watercraft

users are treated fairly when local, state, and federal government officials consider boating regulations; supports and actively advocates for reasonable regulations, strong enforcement of boating and navigation laws, and mandatory boating safety education for all PWC operators. **Founded:** 1987. **Publications:** *Riding Rules for Personal Watercraft*; *An Environmental Guide for Personal Watercraft Operators.*

DIRECTORIES OF EDUCATIONAL PROGRAMS

13934 ■ *Directory of Private Accredited Career Schools and Colleges of Technology*
Pub: Accrediting Commission of Career Schools and Colleges of Technology
Contact: Michale S. McComis, Executive Director
Released: On web page. **Price:** Free. **Description:** Covers 3900 accredited post-secondary programs that provide training programs in business, trade, and technical fields, including various small business endeavors. Entries offer school name, address, phone, description of courses, job placement assistance, and requirements for admission. Arrangement is alphabetical.

REFERENCE WORKS

13935 ■ *American Boat and Yacht Council--Membership List*
Pub: American Boat & Yacht Council Inc.
Contact: Skip Burdon, President
E-mail: sburdon@abycinc.org
URL(s): www.abycinc.org/about/memberDirectory.cfm. **Price:** Free more detailed information available to members. **Covers:** Over 4,000 marine engineers, marine underwriters, naval architects, marine surveyors, manufacturers and designers of small boats and related equipment, attorneys, boat owners, and Coast Guard, Navy, and state government personnel. **Entries include:** Name, address, phone, fax, email. **Arrangement:** Alphabetical.

13936 ■ *"Bellingham Boatbuilder Norstar Yachts Maintains Family Tradition" in Bellingham Business Journal (Vol. February 2010, pp. 12)*
Pub: Sound Publishing Inc.
Ed: Isaac Bonnell. **Description:** Profile of Norstar Yachts and brothers Gary and Steve Nordtvedt who started the company in 1994. The company recently moved its operations to a 12,000 square foot space in the Fairhaven Marine Industrial Park.

13937 ■ *"Boat Sales Sputter as Cash-Strapped Buyers Drift Away" in Puget Sound Business Journal (Vol. 29, August 15, 2008, No. 17, pp. 1)*
Pub: American City Business Journals
Ed: Greg Lamm. **Description:** Boat sales in Washington fell by 44 percent in the second quarter of 2008. The decline is attributed to the soft economy, which has given customers second thoughts on purchasing recreational water vehicles.

13938 ■ *BUC Used Boat Price Guide*
Pub: BUC International Corp.
Contact: Walter Sullivan, President
URL(s): www.buc.com/index.cfm?fuseaction=books. **Released:** Semiannual; Latest edition 103rd, 2012. **Price:** $95, Individuals volume 1; $85, Individuals volume 2; $69, Individuals volume 3; $215, Individuals three volume set; $166, Individuals two volume set. **Covers:** Current market price for about 3,500 manufacturers of outboard, inboard, outdrives, sailboats, houseboats, and custom boats as well as approximately 20 manufacturers of boat trailers. In three volumes--Volume 1 covers 1994-2003; volume 2 covers 1982-1993; volume 3 covers 1905-1981. **Entries include:** Listings for manufacturers still in business include company name, city and state, and Coast Guard identification code; defunct manufacturer listings show city in which last operated. All listings show boat and engine manufacturer's complete specifications. **Arrangement:** Alphabetical by manufacturer name. **Indexes:** Company, trade name.

13939 ■ *"Half a World Away" in Tampa Bay Business Journal (Vol. 30, December 4, 2009, No. 50, pp. 1)*
Pub: American City Business Journals
Ed: Jane Meinhardt. **Description:** Enterprise Florida has offered four trade grants for Florida's marine industry businesses to give them a chance to tap into the Middle East market at the Dubai International Boat Show on March 9 to 13, 2010. The grants pay for 50 percent of the exhibition costs for the qualifying business.

13940 ■ *Marine Products Directory*
Pub: Underwriters Laboratories
Contact: Keith E. Williams, President
URL(s): www.ul.com/global/eng/pages/corporate/contactus/orderdirectories/. **Released:** Annual; Latest edition 2010. **Price:** $40, Individuals. **Covers:** Companies that have qualified to use the UL listing mark or classification marking on or in connection with products which have been found to be in compliance with UL's requirements. Coverage includes foreign companies which manufacture for distribution in the United States. **Entries include:** Company name, city, zip code, UL file number, and type of product. **Arrangement:** Classified by type of product. There is a separate section listing a limited number of trade names or trademarks authorized to use UL certification without mention of company name. **Indexes:** Company name.

13941 ■ *National Marine Representatives Association--Directory*
Pub: National Marine Representatives Association
Contact: Norm Macleod, President
E-mail: norm@commar.com
URL(s): www.nmraonline.org/membership_directory.asp. **Released:** Annual; January. **Price:** $10, Addl. Copy; $20, Hard Copy. **Covers:** Approximately 400 independent representatives selling pleasure craft and other small boats, motors, and marine accessories. **Entries include:** Name, address, phone, fax, e-mail, manufacturers represented, territories covered, customer classifications. **Arrangement:** Alphabetical. **Indexes:** Geographical.

13942 ■ *Pacific Boating Almanac*
Pub: Prostar Publications Inc.
Contact: Melody Nicholson, Manager
URL(s): www.prostarpublications.com. **Ed:** Peter L. Griffes. **Released:** Annual; Latest edition 2006. **Price:** $26.95, Individuals. **Covers:** Over 3,000 marine facilities serving recreational boating in California, Oregon, Washington, British Columbia, Alaska, and Mexico's Baja area. **Entries include:** Name of facility, address, phone, name of owner, list of services. **Arrangement:** Geographical in four volumes: Volume 1, Pacific Northwest; volume 2, Pacific Northwest and Alaska; volume 3, Northern California the Delta; volume 4, Southern California and Baja.

13943 ■ *Portbook*
Pub: Portbook Publications Inc.
Contact: Scott Tinkler, General Manager
URL(s): www.portbook.net. **Released:** Annual; March. **Price:** $4, Individuals mail copies; Free. **Covers:** Marinas, yacht clubs, boatyards, dealers, marine supply stores, repair facilities, other services for yachtsmen; also includes provisioning information, restaurants, marine and medical emergency numbers; editions available for Annapolis, Maryland; and for Newport and Narragansett Bay, Rhode Island. **Entries include:** Company name, address, phone, products or services; keyed to map of area. **Arrangement:** Alphabetical. **Indexes:** Product/service.

13944 ■ *Quimby's Cruising Guide*
Pub: Waterways Journal Inc.
Contact: Mack Gamble, Owner
URL(s): www.waterwaysjournal.net. **Ed:** John S. Shoulberg. **Released:** Annual; latest edition 2009. **Price:** $39, Individuals plus S&H. **Covers:** Fuel stations and other harbor services for over 650 pleasure boat marinas, harbors, and clubs on the Mississippi, Monongahela, Allegheny, Ohio, Illinois, Tennessee, Cumberland, Arkansas, St. Croix, Kentucky, Muskingum, Missouri, Alabama, Black Warrior, GIWW East, Kanawha, and Apalachicola-Chattahooche-Flint Rivers, and the Tennessee/Tombigbee Waterway, GIWW

West. **Entries include:** For facilities--Store, company, or facility name, location, phone, product or service provided. For harbors--Name, owner name, address, phone, depth, description. **Arrangement:** By river name, then by river mile. **Indexes:** City name.

13945 ■ World Maritime Directory
Pub: Maritime Activity Reports Inc.
Contact: Dale L. Barnett, Manager
E-mail: barnett@marinelink.com

URL(s): www.marinelink.com. **Released:** Annual **Price:** $149, plus s/h. **Publication includes:** List of several hundred manufacturers and suppliers of products used in the design, construction, and repair of commercial and naval vessels; international coverage. **Entries include:** Company name, address, phone, fax, e-mail, URL, and products provided.

STATISTICAL SOURCES

13946 ■ RMA Annual Statement Studies
Pub: Risk Management Association
Contact: Kevin M. Blakey, President
Released: Annual. **Price:** $175.00 2006-07 edition, $105.00. **Description:** Contains composite balance sheets and income statements for more than 360 industries, including the accounting, auditing, and bookkeeping industries. Also contains five years of comparative historical data for discerning trends. Includes 16 commonly used ratios, computed for most of the size groupings for nearly every industry.

13947 ■ The U.S. Market for Pleasure Boats
Business Trend Analysts, Inc. Industry Studies
Released: 2003. **Price:** $1695.00. **Description:** This in-depth investigation of the pleasure boat industry tracks current and projected sales (to 2011) of cabin cruisers, houseboats, sailboats, runabouts, center consoles, pontoon boats, canoes, rowboats, and other pleasure craft.

TRADE PERIODICALS

13948 ■ Boating Magazine
Pub: Hachette Filipacchi Media U.S. Inc.
Contact: David Carey, President

URL(s): www.hfmus.com/hfmus/media_kits/enthusiasts/boating/about_uswww.boatingmag.com. **Released:** Monthly **Price:** $18, Two years print; $10, Individuals print; $33, Canada; $33, Other countries.

13949 ■ The duPont Registry: A Buyer's Gallery of Fine Homes
Pub: duPont Publishing Inc.
Contact: Steve Chapman, Chief Executive Officer

URL(s): www.dupontregistry.com/homes/. **Released:** Bimonthly **Price:** $29.95, Individuals; $49.95, Canada; $89.95, Other countries.

13950 ■ Inter/Port
Pub: National Marine Manufacturers Association

Ed: Dan Green, Editor, dgreen@nmma.org. **Released:** Monthly. **Description:** Provides information on boating legislation, market research, marine engineering, and other subjects of significance to pleasure-boating equipment manufacturers. Recurring features include financial news of industry firms, items on personnel.

13951 ■ Power and Motoryacht
Pub: Primedia Power & Motoryacht Magazine

URL(s): www.powerandmotoryacht.com. **Released:** Monthly **Price:** $11.97, Individuals; $19.97, Two years; $23.97, Canada; $43.97, Canada two years; $35.97, Other countries; $67.97, Two years other countries.

13952 ■ Sailing World: The Authority on Performance Sailing
Pub: Miller Sports Group L.L.C.
Contact: Robert L. Miller, President

URL(s): www.sailingworld.com/index.jsp. **Ed:** John Burnham. **Released:** 9/yr. **Price:** $14.97, Individuals; $23.97, Canada; $36.97, Other countries.

13953 ■ Soundings: The Nation's Boating Newspaper
Pub: Dominion Enterprises
Contact: Jack Ross, President
URL(s): www.soundingsonline.com. **Ed:** William Sisson. **Released:** Monthly **Price:** $24.97, Individuals; $46.97, Canada; $66.97, Other countries; $39.97, Two years; $83.97, Canada 2 years; $123.97, Other countries 2 years.

13954 ■ Soundings Trade Only: Daily News for Marine Industry Professionals
Pub: Soundings Publications L.L.C.
Contact: Peter Mitchel, Manager
URL(s): www.tradeonlytoday.com. **Ed:** Tom Hubbard. **Released:** Monthly **Price:** $9.95, Individuals print and digital; $41.95, Individuals; $73.95, Two years.

13955 ■ WoodenBoat: The Magazine for Wooden Boat Owners, Builders, and Designers
Pub: Woodenboat Publications Inc.
Contact: James Miller, President
URL(s): www.woodenboat.com. **Ed:** Matthew Murphy. **Released:** Bimonthly **Price:** $32, Individuals; $59, Two years; $85, Individuals three years; $37, Canada; $69, Canada two years; $45, Other countries.

13956 ■ Yachting: The Best of Today's Boats & Gear
Pub: Time4 Media
Contact: Thomas Beusse, President
URL(s): www.yachtingmagazine.com/. **Released:** 7/yr. **Price:** $16, Individuals; $26, Canada; $46, Other countries.

VIDEOCASSETTES/ AUDIOCASSETTES

13957 ■ Navigating with Marine Electronics: A Guide to DC
Bennett Marine Video
2321 Abbot Kinney Blvd., Top Fl.
Venice, CA 90291
Ph: (310)827-8064
Free: 800-733-8862
Fax: (310)827-8074
Co. E-mail: questions@bennettmarine.com
URL: http://www.bennettmarine.com
Contact: Michael Bennett, President
Released: 1986. **Description:** A comprehensive review of new and traditional electronic items available to boaters, including battery chargers, converters, VHF ship-to-shore radios, radio direction finders, radar, sonar, autopilots, navigation computers, radar detectors and more. **Availability:** VHS.

13958 ■ Teaching Kids How to Sail
Victory Multimedia
222 N. Sepulveda Blvd., Ste. 1306
El Segundo, CA 90245
Ph: (310)416-9140
Fax: (310)416-9839
Co. E-mail: RFVictory@juno.com
Released: 19??. **Price:** $19.95. **Description:** Presents the basics of seamanship, docking, tacking, jibbing, and man overboard rescue. **Availability:** VHS.

TRADE SHOWS AND CONVENTIONS

13959 ■ Annual Spring New Products Show
Pacific Expositions
1600 Kapiolani Blvd. 1660
Honolulu, HI 96814-3801
Ph: (808)945-3594
Fax: (808)946-6399
Co. E-mail: info@prohawaii.com
URL: http://www.hawaiibid.com
URL(s): www.springproductshow.pacificexpos.com/. **Frequency:** Annual. **Audience:** Trade professionals, buyers, and general public. **Principal Exhibits:** Boats; sport and leisure vehicles; new products and services.

13960 ■ Atlanta Boat Show
Marine Trade Association of Metro Atlanta
c/o Lanier Harbor Marina
2066 Pine Dr.
Buford, GA 30501
Ph: (770)945-2884
Fax: (770)945-0052
Co. E-mail: info@mtama.com
URL: http://www.boatatlanta.com
URL(s): www.atlantaboatshow.com. **Frequency:** Annual. **Audience:** General public. **Principal Exhibits:** Powerboats, sailboats, fishing boats, water ski boats, pontoon boats, houseboats, personal watercraft, inflatable and more. Exhibits also include marine accessories, services and a showcase on outdoor travel section featuring lodges, marinas and boating resorts. **Dates and Locations:** Georgia World Congress Center. **Telecommunication Services:** mmalone@nmma.org.

13961 ■ Cincinnati Travel, Sports, and Boat Show
Hart Productions, Inc.
322 E. Main St.
Batavia, OH 45103
Ph: (513)797-7900
Free: 877-704-8190
Fax: (513)797-1013
URL: http://www.hartproductions.com
URL(s): www.hartproductions.com. **Price:** $11, Onsite. **Frequency:** Annual. **Audience:** General public. **Principal Exhibits:** Showcasing a world of travel and recreation featuring vacation travel exhibits, boats, sporting goods, fishing and hunting equipment and seminars. **Dates and Locations:** , Dr. Albert B. Sabin Convention Center. **Telecommunication Services:** chip@hartproductions.com.

13962 ■ Detroit Boat Show
Michigan Boating Industries Association
32398 5 Mile Rd.
Livonia, MI 48154-6109
Ph: (734)261-0123
Free: 800-932-2628
Fax: (734)261-0880
Co. E-mail: boatmichigan@mbia.org
URL: http://www.mbia.org
Contact: John J. Ropp, President
E-mail: jropp@mbia.org
URL(s): www.mbia.org. **Price:** $12, adult; children ages 12 & under. **Frequency:** Annual. **Audience:** Trade professionals and general public. **Principal Exhibits:** Boats, fishing equipment, boat-related accessories, charter rentals, nautical attire, trailer and outboard motors, and personal watercraft. **Dates and Locations:** , Cobo Conference and Exhibition Center.

13963 ■ Eastern Sports & Outdoor Show
Reed Exhibitions North American Headquarters
383 Main Ave.
Norwalk, CT 06851
Ph: (203)840-4800
Fax: (203)840-5805
Co. E-mail: inquiry@reedexpo.com
URL: http://www.reedexpo.com
URL(s): www.easternsportshow.com. **Price:** $10, adult; $9, seniors; $4, children 6 - 12 years. **Frequency:** Annual. **Audience:** General public. **Principal Exhibits:** Recreational vehicles, boats, hunting and fishing equipment, clothing, and related outdoor products, resorts, SUVs, retailers and manufacturers, motorcycles, ATVs, travel and tourism. **Dates and Locations:** , Pennsylvania Farm Show Complex. **Telecommunication Services:** eseveral@reedexpo.com.

13964 ■ Fort Lauderdale International Boat Show
Marine Industries Association of South Florida
2312 S Andrews Ave.
Fort Lauderdale, FL 33316
Ph: (954)524-2733
Free: 800-294-9990

Fax: (954)524-0633
Co. E-mail: admin@miasf.org
URL: http://www.miasf.org
Contact: Kristina Hebert, President
URL(s): www.miasf.org. **Price:** $14; $4, children, ages 6-12; $4, children under 6 free. **Frequency:** Annual. **Audience:** Trade professionals and general public. **Principal Exhibits:** Boats and marine equipment, supplies, and services. **Dates and Locations:** , Bahia Mar Resort & Yachting Center & Broward County Convention Center.

13965 ■ Fort Wayne Sports, Vacation, and Boat Show

Trio Enterprises, Inc.
3624 Maxim Dr.
Fort Wayne, IN 46815
Ph: (219)483-2638
Free: 800-446-2638
Fax: (219)484-0876
URL(s): www.boatsafloat.com. **Frequency:** Annual. **Audience:** General public. **Principal Exhibits:** Recreational vehicles, boats, and travel and vacation information. **Dates and Locations:** , Allen County War Memorial Coliseum. **Telecommunication Services:** data@boatsafloat.com.

13966 ■ Kansas Sports, Boat, & Travel Show

Industrial Expositions, Inc.
1675 Larimer St., No. 700
Denver, CO 80248-0084
Ph: (303)892-6800
Free: 800-457-2434
Fax: (303)892-6322
Co. E-mail: info@iei-expos.com
URL: http://www.iei-expos.com/
URL(s): www.agievents.com/shows/display.cfm?showid=74. **Frequency:** Annual. **Audience:** General public. **Principal Exhibits:** Recreational vehicles, boats, sports equipment, and travel destination information; fishing and hunting equipment, supplies, and services. **Dates and Locations:** , Coliseum. **Telecommunication Services:** rwhitacre-prp@ks.rr.com.

13967 ■ Miami International Boat Show and Strictly Sail

National Marine Manufacturers Association
9050 Pines Blvd., No. 305
Pembroke Pines, FL 33024
Ph: (954)441-3220
Fax: (954)430-4171
URL(s): www.miamiboatshow.com. **Price:** $30, adult admission, Feb. 11; $16, adult admission, Feb. 12-Feb. 15; $6, ages 13 to 15. **Frequency:** Annual. **Audience:** Marine manufacturers, distributors, and dealers; and general public. **Principal Exhibits:** Boats (power and sail), engines and accessories, fishing and water sport accessories. **Dates and Locations:** , Convention Center.

13968 ■ Portland Boat Show

O'Loughlin Trade Shows
PO Box 80750
Portland, OR 97280
Ph: (503)246-8291
Free: 800-343-6973
Fax: (503)246-1066
Co. E-mail: info@otshows.com
URL: http://www.oloughlintradeshows.com
Price: $10. **Frequency:** Annual. **Audience:** General public. **Principal Exhibits:** Boats and motors, water sporting goods, clothing, and marine accessories.

13969 ■ Tacoma Dome Boat Show

O'Loughlin Trade Shows
PO Box 110849
Tacoma, WA 98411
Ph: (253)756-2121
Fax: (253)756-6898
Co. E-mail: infotac@otshows.com
URL: http://www.otshows.com/contact/tacoma/
URL(s): www.tacomadomeboatshow.com. **Frequency:** Annual. **Audience:** General public. **Principal Exhibits:** Boats and motors, marine electronics, and accessories. **Dates and Locations:** , Tacoma Dome.

13970 ■ Yacht and Brokerage Show

Florida Yacht Broker Association
1550 SE 17th St., Ste. 1
Fort Lauderdale, FL 33316
Ph: (954)522-9270
Co. E-mail: fyba@fyba.org
URL: http://www.fyba.org
URL(s): www.showmanagement.com. **Price:** $14, adults. **Frequency:** Annual. **Audience:** Trade and general public. **Principal Exhibits:** Yachts and the industry's leading yacht brokerage firms. **Telecommunication Services:** info@showmanagement.com.

CONSULTANTS

13971 ■ Halcrow HPA

22 Cortlandt St., 31st Fl.
New York, NY 10007
Ph: (212)608-3990
Fax: (212)566-5059
Co. E-mail: pking@halcrow.com
URL: http://www.han-padron.com
Contact: Michael Dellarocca, President
E-mail: dellaroccam@halcrow.com
Scope: A full service engineering firm specializing in projects in the marine environment. Offers a unique range of services that include such specialties as underwater inspection and maritime security. **Founded:** 1979.

13972 ■ J-U-B Engineers Inc.

250 S Beechwood Ave., Ste. 201
Boise, ID 83709-0944
Ph: (208)376-7330
Free: 888-582-2647
Fax: (208)323-9336
Co. E-mail: info@jub.com
URL: http://www.jub.com
Contact: Lee E. Cammack, President
Scope: Offers consulting engineering services in the following areas civil, structural and sanitary engineering airports, bridges, buildings, land developments, drainage, highways, irrigation, fishery facilities, marine facilities, sewerage facilities including master planning, modeling, collection system design, treatment plant planning and design, storm drainage, structures, sub divisions, water treatment supply, storm and distribution; boundary and topographic surveying by GPS methods and planning subdivisions, housing, commercial, industrial, city. Serves private clients, industries, public utilities and governmental agencies including, but not limited to municipalities, counties, state, federal, road districts, water and sewer districts. **Founded:** 1954. **Publications:** "Idaho Engineering Firm of the Year," McGraw-Hill Companies, 2005.

LIBRARIES

13973 ■ Alaska Marine Safety Education Association Library

2924 Halibut Point Rd.
Sitka, AK 99835
Ph: (907)747-3287
Fax: (907)747-3259
Co. E-mail: amsea@amsea.org
URL: http://www.amsea.org
Contact: Grant Turner, Office Manager
Scope: Marine - survival, casualty news, safety studies, casualties, safety curriculum; land survival. **Services:** Copying; library open to the public. **Founded:** 1985. **Holdings:** 200 books; 200 reports; 50 videos. **Subscriptions:** 10 journals and other serials. **Telecommunication Services:** admin@amsea.org.

13974 ■ Antique Boat Museum, Inc. - Lou Smith Library and Marion Clayton Link Archives

750 Mary St.
Clayton, NY 13624
Ph: (315)686-4104, x-225

Fax: (315)686-2775
Co. E-mail: dmiller@abm.org
URL: http://www.abm.org/collections.asp
Contact: Dan Miller, Curator
Scope: Freshwater nautical history, St. Lawrence River and Seaway history, boat building and restoration. **Services:** Copying; library open to the public with restrictions on a limited schedule (appointment suggested; research for non-members is $20 per hour). **Founded:** 1983. **Holdings:** 1500 books; 2500 periodicals (1900 to present); 4000 photographs; 100 charts and maps; 20 oral history tapes; 12 VF drawers of boat plans, parts and equipment information, engine manuals, and boat manufacturers catalogs; 7 VF drawers of clippings; historic postcard files. **Subscriptions:** 25 journals and other serials; 17 newsletters.

13975 ■ Canadian Coast Guard Library—Garde Cotiere Canadienne.

Canada Bldg.
344 Slater St., Ste. 737
Ottawa, ON, Canada K1A 0N7
Ph: (613)998-1801
Fax: (613)993-8659
Contact: Ginette Dion, Officer
Scope: Marine; marine engineering; naval architecture; ships; CCGS Data Books; ship specifications - construction; instrument manuals; ships - tests, trials. **Services:** Interlibrary loan; copying. **Holdings:** Technical reports; manuals; technical drawings; photographs; documents.

13976 ■ Chesapeake Bay Maritime Museum - Howard I. Chapelle Memorial Library

PO Box 636
St. Michaels, MD 21663
Ph: (410)745-2916
Fax: (410)745-6088
Co. E-mail: plesher@cbmm.org
URL: http://www.cbmm.org
Contact: Pete Lesher, Curator
Scope: Chesapeake Bay history and marine life; boat construction, maintenance, handling; waterfowl; voyages and travel; naval and sailing craft history; ship models; steamboat history; Maryland history; Virginia history. **Services:** Library open to the public with restrictions. **Founded:** 1968. **Holdings:** 9800 volumes; 210 lin.ft. of archives; 340 taped oral histories. **Subscriptions:** 18 journals and other serials. **Telecommunication Services:** rscofield@cbmm.org.

13977 ■ Deer Isle-Stonington Historical Society Library

416 Sunset Rd.
Deer Isle, ME 04627-0652
Ph: (207)348-6400
Co. E-mail: cwiberg@myfairpoint.net
URL: http://www.dis-historicalsociety.org
Contact: Tinker Crouch, President
Scope: Marine vessels, steamboats and yachts, early children's books and school books. **Services:** Copying; Library open to the public. **Founded:** 1959. **Holdings:** 200 books; early scrapbooks; file of clippings on local subjects; diaries; photographs; archives; microfilm.

13978 ■ The Library at the Mariners' Museum

100 Museum Dr.
Newport News, VA 23606-3759
Ph: (757)591-7782
Fax: (757)591-7310
Co. E-mail: library@marinersmuseum.org
URL: http://www.marinersmuseum.org/library
Contact: Susan Berg, Director
Scope: Shipping, shipbuilding, navigation, merchant marine, navies, exploration and travel, whaling, yachting, maritime history. **Services:** Copying; Library open to the public. **Founded:** 1930. **Holdings:** 78,000 volumes; 5000 bound periodical volumes; 600,000 photographs; 500 logbooks and journals; 60 microfilm; 5000 charts and maps; 700 newspaper clippings and journals; 1 million manuscripts; ships' papers; 10,000 plans and drawings; tapes; atlases; 1500 magazines, journals and newsletters. **Subscriptions:** 250 journals and other serials. **Telecommunication Services:** manuscripts@marinersmuseum.org.

13979 ■ Maine Maritime Academy - Nutting Memorial Library
Box C-1
Pleasant St.
Castine, ME 04420-1001
Ph: (207)326-2263
Fax: (207)326-2261
Co. E-mail: library@mma.edu
URL: http://library.mma.edu
Contact: Lauren Blanchard
Scope: Marine engineering, marine transportation, nautical science, maritime management, International business and logistics, engineering technology, power engineering, yacht operations, boat yard management, ocean studies, oceanography. **Services:** Interlibrary loan; copying; Library open to the public. **Founded:** 1941. **Holdings:** 68,213 books; 5616 maps and charts; 109,610 government documents. **Subscriptions:** 470 journals and newspapers.

13980 ■ Marine Museum at Fall River, Inc. Library
70 Water St.
Fall River, MA 02721

Ph: (508)674-3533
Fax: (508)674-3534
Co. E-mail: staff@marineuseum.org
URL: http://www.marinemuseum.org
Contact: Donna J. Futoransky, President
Scope: History of steam power-driven watercraft. **Services:** Library not open to the public. **Founded:** 1968. **Holdings:** 2000 books; 125 bound periodical volumes; 5000 photographic plates; 1000 glass slides. **Subscriptions:** 3 journals and other serials. **Telecommunication Services:** richardm@marine-museum.org.

13981 ■ Mystic Seaport Museum, Inc. - G.W. Blunt White Library
95 Greenmanville Ave.
Mystic, CT 06355
Ph: (860)572-5367
Co. E-mail: collections@mysticseaport.org
URL: http://library.mysticseaport.org
Contact: Paul J. O'Pecko, Director, Library Services
URL(s): www.mysticseaport.org. **Scope:** American maritime history, shipbuilding, vessel registration, yachting, naval architecture, fisheries. **Services:** Interlibrary loan; Library open to the public for research and reference use only. **Founded:** 1965. **Holdings:** 70,000 books; 5000 bound periodical volumes; 1200 logbooks; 2000 reels of microfilm; 9000 charts and maps; 100,000 ship plans. **Subscriptions:** 392 journals and other serials. **Telecommunication Services:** kelly.drake@mysticseaport.org.

13982 ■ Robert Weinstein Maritime Historical Collection
1851 Stearns Dr.
Los Angeles, CA 90035-4629
Ph: (213)936-0558
Fax: (213)936-1661
Contact: Robert Weinstein, Owner
Scope: Sailing ships of all countries and trades. **Services:** Library not open to the public. **Holdings:** 250,000 original and copy photographs, glass negatives, clippings, post cards.

ASSOCIATIONS AND OTHER ORGANIZATIONS

13983 ■ **American Marketing Association (AMA)**
311 S Wacker Dr., Ste. 5800
Chicago, IL 60606
Ph: (312)542-9000
Free: 800-262-1150
Fax: (312)542-9001
Co. E-mail: info@ama.org
URL: http://www.marketingpower.com
Contact: Michael Kullman, Chairperson
Description: Serves as a professional society of marketing and market research executives, sales and promotion managers, advertising specialists, academics, and others interested in marketing. Fosters research; sponsors seminars, conferences, and student marketing clubs; provides educational placement service and doctoral consortium. **Scope:** marketing, marketing research. **Founded:** 1937. **Subscriptions:** 6000 archival material books clippings monographs periodicals. **Publications:** *American Marketing Association--Proceedings* (Annual); *Journal of Marketing* (Bimonthly); *Journal of Marketing Research* (Bimonthly); *Journal of Public Policy and Marketing* (Semiannual); *Marketing Academics at AMA* (Bimonthly); *Marketing Health Service* (Quarterly); *Marketing Matters* (Biweekly). **Educational Activities:** Institute for Marketing Communications and Strategy (Annual); Summer Marketing Educator's Conference (Annual); Winter Marketing Educators Conference (Annual). **Awards:** Harold H. Maynard Award; William O'Dell Award; Charles Coolidge Parlin Award; H. Paul Root Award; Explor Award (Annual); Harold H. Maynard Award (Annual); AMA/Irwin/McGraw-Hill Distinguished Marketing Educator Award; Wayne A. Lemburg Award for Distinguished Service.

13984 ■ **Marketing Research Association (MRA)**
1156 15th St. NW, Ste. 302
Washington, DC 20005
Ph: (202)800-2545
Fax: (888)512-1050
Co. E-mail: membership@marketingresearch.org
URL: http://www.marketingresearch.org
Contact: Joe Ottaviani, President
E-mail: joe.ottaviani@burke.com
URL(s): www.mra-net.org. **Description:** Companies and individuals involved in any area of opinion and marketing research, such as data collection, research, or as an end-user. **Founded:** 1954. **Publications:** *The Connector--MRA's Membership Directory*; *MRA Blue Book Research Services Directory* (Annual); *Blue Books Research Service Directory* (Annual); *Recruiting and Facility Management Qualitative Handbook*; *Blue Book Marketing Research Services Directory* (Annual).

LEGISLATIVE ASSISTANCE

13985 ■ **Office of the Governor - Economic Development and Tourism Division -**

Economic Information Clearinghouse
PO Box 12428
Austin, TX 78711
Ph: (512)463-2000
Free: 800-888-0511
Fax: (512)463-1849
URL: http://www.governor.state.tx.us/
Description: Program attempts to ensure that each state agency awards 10 percent of all purchases of articles, supplies, commodities, materials, or services to small businesses.

DIRECTORIES OF EDUCATIONAL PROGRAMS

13986 ■ *Quirk's Marketing Research Review Data Processing and Statistical Analysis Directory Issue*
Pub: Quirk Enterprises Inc.
Contact: Alice Davies, Manager
E-mail: alice@quirks.com
URL(s): www.quirks.com. **Ed:** Joe Rydhom. **Released:** Annual; March. **Publication includes:** List of companies that provides data processing and statistical analysis services for the marketing research industry. **Entries include:** Company name, address, phone, description of product. **Arrangement:** Alphabetic.

13987 ■ *Quirk's Marketing Research Review--Directory of Customer Satisfaction Research Providers Issue*
Pub: Quirk Enterprises Inc.
Contact: Alice Davies, Manager
E-mail: alice@quirks.com
URL(s): www.quirks.com. **Ed:** Joe Rydhom. **Released:** Annual; October. **Publication includes:** List of companies that offer customer satisfaction research services for the marketing research industry. **Entries include:** Company name, address, phone, description of service.

REFERENCE WORKS

13988 ■ *"The AHA Moment" in Hispanic Business (December 2010)*
Pub: Hispanic Business
Ed: Rebecca Vallaneda. **Description:** An interview with Gisela Girard on how competitive market conditions push buttons. Girard stepped down from her 18-month position as chairwoman the Association of Hispanic Advertising Agencies. She has more than 20 years of experience in advertising and research marketing.

13989 ■ *"Bar Hopping: Your Numbers At a Glance" in Inc. (January 2008, pp. 44-45)*
Pub: Gruner & Jahr USA Publishing
Ed: Michael Fitzgerald. **Description:** Software that helps any company analyze data include Crystal Xcelsius, a program that takes data from Excel documents and turns them into animated gauges, charts and graphs; CashView, a Web-based application that tracks receivables and payables; iDashboards, a

Web-based programs that produces animated gauges, maps, pie charts and graphs; Corda Human Capital Management, that transforms stats like head count, productivity, and attrition into graphs and dials; NetSuite, a Web-based application that tracks key indicators; and Cognos Now, that gauges, dials, and graphs data.

13990 ■ *"Because Kids Need To Be Heard: Tina Wells: Buzz Marketing Group: Voorhees, New Jersey" in Inc. (Volume 32, December 2010)*
Pub: Inc. Magazine
Ed: Tamara Schweitzer. **Description:** Profile of Tina Wells, founder and CEO of Buzz Marketing Group, who writes a tween book series called Mackenzie Blue to reach young girls.

13991 ■ *Bradford's International Directory of Marketing Research Agencies*
Pub: Business Research Services Inc.
Contact: Thomas D. Johnson, President
URL(s): www.bradfordsdirectory.com. **Released:** Biennial; Latest edition 30th. **Price:** $95, Individuals in-print; $95, Individuals CD-ROM; $125, Individuals in print and CD-ROM. **Covers:** Over 2,300 marketing research agencies worldwide. Includes domestic and international demographic data and professional association contacts. **Entries include:** Company name, address, phone, name and title of contact, date founded, number of employees, description of products or services, e-mail, URL. **Arrangement:** Geographical. **Indexes:** Alphabetical by company.

13992 ■ *Business Marketing Association--Membership & Resource Directory*
Pub: Business Marketing Association
Contact: Rick Kean, Executive Director
URL(s): marketing.org/i4a/pages/index.cfm?pageid=1. **Released:** Annual; January. **Covers:** Over 4,500 member business communications professionals in fields of advertising, marketing communications, and marketing; their service and supply companies are listed in the "Marketing Resources" section. **Entries include:** For individuals--Name, title, company with which affiliated, address, phone. For companies--Name, address, phone, contact, description of products or services. **Arrangement:** Individuals are alphabetical within chapter; companies are classified by product or service. **Indexes:** Alpha, company, chapter.

13993 ■ *"Decoding Demand Opportunities" in Business Strategy Review (Vol. 21, Spring 2010, No. 1, pp. 64)*
Pub: Wiley-Blackwell
Ed: Erich Joachimsthaler, Markus Pfeiffer. **Description:** Classic marketing techniques, such as the use of focus groups or ethnographies, miss the enormous opportunities that can be leveraged once companies commit to understanding consumers in the context of life experiences.

13994 ■ *"Funny Business" in Canadian Business (Vol. 82, April 27, 2009, No. 7, pp. 27)*
Pub: Rogers Media
Ed: Rachel Pulfer. **Description:** Companies are advised to use humor in marketing to drive more

revenue. IBM Canada, for example, commissioned Second City Communications for a marketing campaign that involved humor. While IBM Canada declined to give sales or traffic figures, firm executives rank the marketing campaign as an overall success.

13995 ■ "Harley-Davidson Moves to Unconventional Marketing Plan" in Business Journal-Milwaukee (Vol. 28, November 26, 2010, No. 8, pp. A1)
Pub: Milwaukee Business Journal
Ed: Rich Rovito. **Description:** Harley Davidson Inc. hired Boulder, Colorado-based Victors & Spoils, an agency that specializes in crowdsourcing, to implement a new creative marketing model. Under the plan, Harley Davidson will draw on the ideas of its brand enthusiasts to help guide the brand's marketing direction.

13996 ■ "I Hear You're Interested In a.." in Inc. (January 2008, pp. 40-43)
Pub: Gruner & Jahr USA Publishing
Ed: Leah Hoffmann. **Description:** Four tips to help any small business generate sales leads online are examined.

13997 ■ "Ideas at Work: Sparkling Innovation" in Business Strategy Review (Vol. 21, Summer 2010, No. 2, pp. 07)
Pub: Wiley-Blackwell
Ed: Julian Birkinshaw, Peter Robbins. **Description:** GlaxoSmithKline faced a situation common to large global organizations: how to allocate marketing resources to smaller, regional brands. The company's approach to worldwide marketing that led to the development of a unique and productive network is outlined.

13998 ■ Integration Marketing: How Small Businesses Become Big Businesses and Big Businesses Become Empires
Pub: John Wiley & Sons, Inc.
Ed: Mark Joyner. **Released:** May 1, 2009. **Price:** $22.95. **Description:** Leading Internet marketing expert offers a marketing methodology to grow any business.

13999 ■ Marketing for Dummies
Pub: John Wiley & Sons Inc.
Contact: Stephen M. Smith, President
URL(s): www.wiley.com/WileyCDA/WileyTitle/productCd-047050210X.html. **Ed:** Alexander Hiam. **Released:** latest edition 3rd; Published October, 2009. **Price:** $21.99, Individuals paperback. **Publication includes:** Marketing web sites, marketing consultants, trade associations, market researchers, and other experts. **Entries include:** Individual or company name, address, phone number, web site address (where applicable). Principal content of publication is articles on marketing strategies.

14000 ■ Marketing for Entrepreneurs
Pub: FT Press
Ed: Jurgen Wolff. **Released:** December 9, 2010. **Price:** $24.99. **Description:** This text identifies marketing as the entire process of researching, creating, distributing and selling a product or service. It isn't about theory and metrics, rather it is a practical guide that starts with the basics of all marketing aspects.

14001 ■ The Markets Directory
Pub: The Markets Directory
URL(s): www.focusgroups.com/mktdsk.htmwww.marketsresearch.com, www.marketsdirectory.com. **Released:** Annual **Entries include:** Company name, address, phone, fax, contact name, line of business, facilities. **Database covers:** Over 7,000 service organizations implementing marketing research projects for marketing professionals in the U.S. and around the world.

14002 ■ "Mars Advertising's Orbit Grows as Other Ad Segments Fall" in Crain's Detroit Business (Vol. 25, June 1, 2009, No. 22, pp. 10)
Pub: Crain Communications Inc. - Detroit
Ed: Bill Shea. **Description:** An electrical fire burned at Mars Advertising's headquarters in Southfield, Michigan. The company talks about its plans for

regrouping and rebuilding. The family firm specializes in in-store marketing that targets consumers already in the buying mode.

14003 ■ "Miller's Crossroad" in Canadian Business (Vol. 83, September 14, 2010, No. 15, pp. 58)
Pub: Rogers Media Ltd.
Ed: Joe Castaldo. **Description:** Future Electronics founder and billionaire Robert Miller shares the secret of Future's unique operating model, which is based on inventory and market research. Miller attributes much of the company's success to its privately held status that enables quick movement against competitors.

14004 ■ "Network Marketing Strategies for Marketing Professionals" in Black Enterprise (Vol. 38, October 2007, No. 3, pp. 70)
Pub: Earl G. Graves Publishing Co. Inc.
Description: Network marketing programs are redefining the sales business and leveraging opportunities in the ever-expanding global, highly networked, and ultra-specialized marketplace.

14005 ■ Qualitative Research Consultants Association--Membership Directory
Pub: Qualitative Research Consultants Association
Contact: Ms. Shannon Pfarr Thompson, Executive Director
URL(s): www.qrca.org. **Released:** Annual; Spring. **Covers:** About 600 qualitative market and social researchers and consultants. **Entries include:** Company name, address, phone, name of contact, specialties, areas. **Arrangement:** Alphabetical. **Indexes:** Geographical.

14006 ■ Research Alert
Pub: EPM Communications Inc.
Contact: Ira Mayer, President
E-mail: imayer@epmcom.com
URL(s): www.epmcom.com. **Released:** Annual; latest edition 2005. **Price:** $389, Individuals. **Publication includes:** Companies and abstracts of marketing studies that analyze trends, consumer buying habits, lifestyles, and prospective markets. **Entries include:** Company name, address, phone, name and title of contact, products or services, summary of key findings. Principal content is a collection of consumer marketing studies. **Database includes:** Highlights from 20 to 40 studies in each issue. **Arrangement:** Classified by subject.

14007 ■ "Research and Markets Adds Report: Vending Machines" in Travel and Leisure Close-Up (October 20, 2011)
Pub: Close-Up Media
Description: Research and Markets has added 'Vending Machines — Global Strategic Business Report' to its lineup. The report analyzes globally installed vending machines in US million dollars by the following product types: Beverage, Food, Cigarette, and Other Products (includes personal and health care products, contraceptives, books, magazines).

14008 ■ Researching Company Financial Information
Pub: MarketResearch.com
Contact: Charlie Terry, President
E-mail: cterry@marketresearch.com
URL(s): www.marketresearch.com/vendors/viewvendor.asp?g=1&VendorID=708. **Released:** Edition V. **Price:** $59, Individuals. **Description:** Helps readers learn how to research and understand financial data from companies, as well as compile in-depth financial data on competitors in order to get a better picture of the competition. **Publication includes:** A directory of corporate financial info sources.

14009 ■ "Ric Elis/Dan Feldstein" in Charlotte Business Journal (Vol. 25, December 31, 2010, No. 41, pp. 6)
Pub: Charlotte Business Journal
Ed: Ken Elkins. **Description:** Charlotte, North Carolina-based Internet marketing firm Red Ventures has grown significantly. General Atlantic has purchased stakes in Red Ventures.

14010 ■ "The Rise of Pompei" in Retail Merchandiser (Vol. 51, September-October 2011, No. 5, pp. 13)
Pub: Phoenix Media Corporation
Description: Soho creative consulting group follows its C3 philosophy to create an invigorated brand experience that transforms customers from consumers to empowered buyers. Pompei AD is a leading creative consultancy that specializes in design and branding for retail, museum, hospitality, and other sectors.

14011 ■ "Security Alert: Data Server" in Entrepreneur (Vol. 36, February 2008, No. 2, pp. 28)
Pub: Entrepreneur Media Inc.
Ed: Amanda C. Kooser. **Description:** Michael Kogon is the founder of Definition 6, a technology consulting and interactive marking firm. He believes in the philosophy that the best way to keep sensitive data safe is not to store it. Details on the security policies of his firm are discussed.

14012 ■ "Sophistication in Research in Marketing" in Journal of Marketing (Vol. 75, July 2011, No. 4, pp. 155)
Pub: American Marketing Association
Ed: Donald R. Lehmann, Leigh McAlister, Richard Staelin. **Description:** A look at the current imbalance in the research in marketing is presented. The level of analytical rigor has risen in articles published in marketing academic journals but other desirable characteristics, such as communicability, relevance, and simplicity have been downplayed.

14013 ■ "Strength In Numbers" in Black Enterprise (Vol. 38, January 2008, No. 6, pp. 53)
Pub: Earl G. Graves Publishing Co. Inc.
Description: According to recent studies geared to advertisers, African Americans represent a demographic that drives style and consumer trends. The African American buying power is expected to increase to $1.1 trillion by 2011. Beyond Demographics helps clients identify ways to value and measure investments within the black community.

14014 ■ The Unofficial Guide to Starting a Small Business
Pub: John Wiley & Sons, Incorporated
Ed: Marcia Layton Turner. **Released:** October 2004. **Price:** $16.99. **Description:** Information and tools for starting a small business, covering the start-up process, from market research, to business plans, to marketing programs.

14015 ■ "Why You Need a New-Media 'Ringmaster" in Harvard Business Review (Vol. 88, December 2010, No. 12, pp. 78)
Pub: Harvard Business School Publishing
Ed: Patrick Spenner. **Description:** The concept of ringmaster is applied to brand marketing. This concept includes integrative thinking, lean collaboration skills, and high-speed decision cycles.

14016 ■ "Your Turn in the Spotlight" in Inc. (Volume 32, December 2010, No. 10, pp. 57)
Pub: Inc. Magazine
Ed: John Brandon. **Description:** Examples of three video blogs created by entrepreneurs to promote their businesses and products are used to show successful strategies. Wine Library TV promotes a family's wine business; SHAMA.TV offers marketing tips and company news; and Will It Blend? promotes sales of a household blender.

TRADE PERIODICALS

14017 ■ ADM Flash
Pub: Association of Directory Marketing
Contact: Neg Norton, President
Ed: Nancy Augustine, Editor, naugustine@admworks.org. **Released:** 10/year. **Price:** Free. **Description:** Features information about marketing directories.

14018 ■ Alert!
Pub: Marketing Research Association
Ed: Paul Melillo, Editor, paul.melillo@mra-net.org.
Released: Monthly. **Price:** Included in membership.
Description: Provides information about marketing industry events, trends in marketing research, management techniques, association events, and legislative activities affecting the marketing industry. Recurring features include news of research, a calendar of events, reports of meetings, news of educational opportunities, job listings, notices of publications available, business opportunities, and facilities for sale.

14019 ■ The Gauge
Pub: Delahaye Medialink
Contact: Katharine Delahaye Paine, Publisher
E-mail: kpaine@delahaye.com
Ed: William Teunis Paarlberg, Editor, wpaarlberg@aol.com. **Released:** Bimonthly. **Price:** $75. **Description:** Provides information on and evaluates marketing communications activities of companies. Recurring features include interviews, news of research, and a calendar of events.

14020 ■ Internet Marketing Report
Pub: Progressive Business Publications
Ed: Alan Field, Editor. **Released:** Semimonthly.
Price: $299, individuals. **Description:** Communicates the latest news and trends in website marketing. g.

14021 ■ Journal of Marketing Research
Pub: American Marketing Association
Contact: Lucille Pointer, President
URL(s): www.marketingpower.com/. **Ed:** Robert Meyer. **Released:** Bimonthly **Price:** $85, Individuals additional 7% GST pay for Canadian residents; $125, Institutions additional 7% GST pay for Canadian residents; $115, Other countries; $160, Institutions, other countries.

14022 ■ Larry Chase's Web Digest for Marketers (WDFM)
Pub: Chase Online Marketing Strategies,Inc
Contact: Larry Chase, Executive Editor
E-mail: larry@wdfm.com
Ed: Mary Gillen, Editor. **Released:** Weekly. **Price:** Free. **Description:** Delivers 15 short reviews of business-related websites every issue. Remarks: America Online, Inc.

14023 ■ Marketing Magazine: Canada's Weekly Newspaper of Marketing Communications
Pub: Rogers Media Publishing Marketing Media Group
URL(s): www.marketingmag.ca. **Released:** 41/yr.
Price: $95, Canada; $55, Students.

14024 ■ Marketing Management
Pub: American Marketing Association
Contact: Lucille Pointer, President
URL(s): www.marketingpower.com/. **Ed:** Gordon Wyner. **Released:** Bimonthly **Price:** $100, Individuals print only; $135, Institutions print only; $105, Canada print only; $141.75, Institutions, Canada print only; $165, Institutions, other countries print only; $135, Other countries print only.

14025 ■ Marketing News: Reporting on the Marketing Profession
Pub: American Marketing Association
Contact: Lucille Pointer, President
URL(s): www.marketingpower.com/AboutAMA/Pages/AMA%20Publications/Marketing% 20News/MarketingNews.aspx. **Ed:** Elisabeth Sullivan. **Released:** 16/yr. **Price:** $35, Members; $100, Nonmembers; $130, Institutions libraries and corporations; $3, Single issue individuals; $5, Single issue institutions; $140, Institutions, other countries extra for air delivery.

14026 ■ Marketing Research: A Magazine of Management and Applications
Pub: American Marketing Association
Contact: Lucille Pointer, President
URL(s): www.marketingpower.com/. **Ed:** Chuck Chakrapani. **Released:** Quarterly **Price:** $100, Individuals print only; $135, Institutions print only;

$105, Canada print only; $141.75, Institutions, Canada print only; $165, Institutions, other countries print only; $135, Other countries print only.

14027 ■ Research Alert
Pub: EPM Communications Inc.
Contact: Ira Mayer, President
E-mail: imayer@epmcom.com
Ed: Barbara Perrin, Editor, bperrin@epmcom.com.
Released: 24/year. **Price:** $389, individuals $369/year, U.S. and Canada; $429 elsewhere. **Description:** Summarizes the most current consumer marketing research reports. Includes complete contact, methodology, and price information.

14028 ■ SRIC-BI News
Pub: Business Intelligence Program
Ed: Judith Clay Lhamon, Editor. **Released:** Monthly.
Description: Reports research being performed in technical, market, and management areas. Analyzes early signs of potential social, political, economic, and technological change, and, relating these developments to one another, suggests possible implications for BIP's clients.

14029 ■ Survey Research
Pub: Survey Research Laboratory
Contact: Diane O'Rourke, Managing Editor
E-mail: dianeo@srl.uic.edu
Ed: Lisa Kelly-Wilson, Editor, lisakw@srl.uic.edu. **Released:** 3/year. **Price:** $15, individuals; $60 organizations; $600 patrons (up to 60 copies of each. **Description:** Contains descriptions of current survey research projects by academic and not-for-profit survey research organizations; news from survey research centers; descriptions of recent methodological publications on survey Current Research, Personnel Notes, and New Methodological Publications.

14030 ■ The Top 100 List
Pub: Luce Press Clippings
Ed: Richard Weiner, Editor. **Description:** Presents marketing information and demographics from newspapers, magazines, and other media on U.S. cities.

VIDEOCASSETTES/ AUDIOCASSETTES

14031 ■ Marketing Research
GPN Educational Media
1550 Executive Drive
Elgin, IL 60123
Ph: (402)472-2007
Free: 800-228-4630
Fax: (800)306-2330
Co. E-mail: askgpn@smarterville.com
URL: http://www.shopgpn.com
Released: 1988. **Price:** $69.95. **Description:** Looks at the format, systematic approach and the informal, casual methods of marketing research, and how companies make their marketing decisions. **Availability:** VHS.

CONSULTANTS

14032 ■ Adam Market Research Inc.
2246 University Square Mall, Ste. C
Tampa, FL 33612
Ph: (813)875-4005
Fax: (813)875-4055
Co. E-mail: adam.market.research@worldnet.att.net
Contact: Mark R. Segal, Owner
Scope: Offers a variety of market research interviewing services. **Founded:** 1985.

14033 ■ American Cut Crystal Corp.
1150 Broadway
Hewlett, NY 11557
Ph: (516)569-1300
Fax: (516)569-5656
Contact: Marvin Wolf, President
Scope: Provides a wide range of marketing research services, both to consumer and business-to-business, as well as to government agencies. Specialties include new product development, market studies, psychologically probing qualitative research and trend spotting. **Founded:** 1934.

14034 ■ Ken Berwitz Marketing Research (KBMR)
9 S Main St.
Marlboro, NJ 07746-1539
Ph: (732)780-5657
Fax: (732)780-5657
Co. E-mail: kbmr@optonline.net
Contact: Ken Berwitz, Owner
Scope: Conducts market research specializing in focus group research. Work involves both qualitative and quantitative methods. Industries served: manufacturers, communications, insurance, and advertising. **Founded:** 1980. **Publications:** "The Hopelessly Partisan Guide to American Politics: An Irreverent Look at the Private Lives of Republicans and Democrats," Select Books, Sep, 2006; "Ken Berwitz marketing research Guide".

14035 ■ Bowman R&C Projects
8613 W Richardson Rd.
Pasco, WA 99301-1611
Ph: (509)544-9520
Contact: Carol H. Bowman, President
Scope: Active in the design and analysis of primary marketing research. Industries served: Catalog, retail, direct marketing, and service-oriented businesses. **Founded:** 1987.

14036 ■ Brink & Associates Inc.
2325 N Glebe Rd.
Arlington, VA 22207
Ph: (703)312-5244
Fax: (703)312-5246
Co. E-mail: info@brinkassociates.net
URL: http://www.brinkassociates.net
Contact: Debby Brink, President
Scope: A full-service healthcare consulting company. Provides services in clinical operations, research, hospital administration, marketing, and communications. **Founded:** 1990.

14037 ■ The Browning Group
1300 Clay St., Ste. 600
Oakland, CA 94612
Ph: (510)635-3878
Fax: (510)464-8001
Co. E-mail: partners@browninggroup.com
URL: http://www.browninggroup.com
Contact: Robert B. Hessler, Director
E-mail: rhessler@browninggroup.com
Scope: Offers marketing research, strategic planning, and program implementation services for travel, hospitality, specialty retail, restaurant and food service, real estate, office products, and health services. **Founded:** 1980. **Seminars:** 21st Century Maxims; Meeting The Business Challenges of the 21st Century, 2006; Vision Marketing Workshop for marketing staff, management and senior management of client organizations; Getting to Real.

14038 ■ The Chatham Group Inc. (CG)
PO Box 780
Chatham, MA 02633
Ph: (508)945-2675
Fax: (508)945-4888
Co. E-mail: info@chathamgroup.com
URL: http://www.chathamgroup.com
Contact: Frederick T. Miller, President
E-mail: miller@chathamgroup.com
Scope: Management consulting firm specializing in the areas of strategy, competitive positioning, governance, and organizational effectiveness. The philosophy of CG is based on three tenets: information driven strategy, multi-discipline teams to assure requisite expertise, and state of the art applications of knowledge and technology. Principal industries served: advertising and public relations, arts, cultural education, health, minority entrepreneurs, philanthropy, professional firms, service, social service, and government agencies. **Founded:** 1984. **Seminars:** Board development, planning, and management.

14039 ■ Mark Clements Research Inc.
25 Barker St., Ste. 309
Mount Kisco, NY 10549
Ph: (914)241-1803

Fax: (914)241-7763
Co. E-mail: mjfharvey@aol.com
URL: http://www.markclementsresearch.com
Contact: Mark Clements, President
E-mail: mcresearch@aol.com
Scope: Marketing research consultants active in marketing management, sales and product research for magazines, manufacturers, media ad agencies and associations. Studies individually designed, quantitative or qualitative, to answer clients needs and problems. Founded: 1959.

14040 ■ Consumer Research Corp.
445 Butler Sq.
Minneapolis, MN 55403
Ph: (612)332-8741
Fax: (612)332-8617
Co. E-mail: crc@conresco.com
URL: http://www.conresco.com
Contact: David L. Frey, President
Scope: Offers comprehensive market research and planning for every phase of marketing, including strategic planning, consumer and marketing research, acquisition analysis, trade research, opinion polls, retail site location, communications research and focus groups. Serves private industries as well as government agencies. Founded: 1974.

14041 ■ The Coxe Group Inc.
1904 3rd Ave., Securities Bldg., Ste. 229
Seattle, WA 98101-1194
Ph: (206)467-4040
Fax: (206)467-4038
Co. E-mail: info@coxegroup.com
URL: http://www.coxegroup.com
Contact: Sharlene Silverman, Manager
E-mail: ssilverman@coxegroup.com
Scope: Offers counsel in organization management, marketing planning, market research, financial management, ownership transition, and mergers/acquisitions. Exclusively serves the design community, i.e. architects, engineers, planners, etc. worldwide. Founded: 1967. Publications: "Being a Real Architect Means Being a Conscientious Practitioner, Spring," 2008; "Those Without Courage Step Aside, Summer," 2008; "So You're Starting a Practice," 2007; "Practice Made Simple," 2006; "Observations From Prague," 2005; "Tips for Anticipating and Strategizing for the Next Ten Years," 2005; "Cultural Understanding the First Step to Successful Offshoring Strategy," 2005; "Sell, Acquire, Merge: Another Perspective," 2005; "Architects Advised to Get Smart About Design Competitions," 2004; "Architect's Essentials of Ownership Transition," John Wiley And Qmp; Sons Inc, 2002; "Architect's Essentials of Starting a Design Firm," John Wiley and Sons Inc, 2002; "So You're Starting a Practice". Seminars: Marketing Coordinators Clinic; Leadership Development Programs; Clinic for Marketing Professionals; Advanced Marketing Workshop; Effective Negotiations; Marketing Workshop; Project Management Workshop; Project Process Workshop; Selling Skills Clinic.

14042 ■ Creative Research International Inc. (CRII)
4950 Yonge St., Ste. 1002
North York, ON, Canada M2N 6K1
Ph: (416)250-8500
Co. E-mail: info@crii.com
Contact: Marilyn E. Sandler, President
E-mail: marilyn@crii.com
Scope: Custom research firm specializing in design, implementation, analysis and reporting of all types of public opinion, marketing and advertising research. Multi-disciplinary professional staff to handle government, commercial assignments, large or small studies, marketing models, and group interviews. Conducts syndicated studies on social values. Founded: 1995.

14043 ■ Customer Perspectives
213 W River Rd.
Hooksett, NH 03106-2628
Ph: (603)647-1300
Free: 800-277-4677

Fax: (603)647-0900
Co. E-mail: info@customerperspectives.com
URL: http://www.customerperspectives.com
Contact: Angie Deschenes, Vice President
Scope: A market research consultancy specializing in mystery shopping. Founded: 1983. Special Services: Customer Perspectives™.

14044 ■ The Fairfield Factor Inc.
30 Main St., Ste. 407
Danbury, CT 06810
Ph: (203)798-8850
Fax: (203)798-8779
Co. E-mail: mail@fairfieldfactor.com
URL: http://www.fairfieldfactor.com
Contact: Arthur Kerley, President
E-mail: artk@fairfieldfactor.com
Scope: Provider of marketing consulting and research solutions. It also deals with product designs, manufacturing, packaging, and allied support services. Founded: 1984.

14045 ■ Goldhaber Research Associates L.L.C.
1525 Amherst Manor Dr., Ste. 907
Williamsville, NY 14221
Ph: (716)689-3311
Fax: (716)689-3342
Co. E-mail: employment@goldhaber.com
URL: http://www.goldhaber.com
Contact: Dr. Gerald M. Goldhaber, President
E-mail: gmg1234@hotmail.com
Scope: Full service market research company that specializes in custom-designed market studies, public opinion research and communication research. Industries served: Business, finance, real estate development, politics entertainment arts and the legal profession. Founded: 1978. Publications: "Organizational Communication". Seminars: Design and Development of a Product Warning System.

14046 ■ Lynn Greenberg Associates (LGA)
36 Country Ridge Rd.
Scarsdale, NY 10583
Ph: (914)478-1296
Fax: (914)472-4051
Co. E-mail: lgaresearch@cs.com
URL: http://www.lynngreenberg.com
Contact: Lynn P. Greenberg, President
Scope: Marketing research firm offering strategic planning services and research involving both qualitative and quantitative methods. Experienced with focus groups, interviewing, new product development and marketing, packaging, and advertising. The children's market is a specialty. Founded: 1985. Seminars: The Art of the Immediate Debrief; What you Don't Learn in Moderating School; Report Writing Alternatives; Sharing Secrets of Success; Taking your Business to the Next Level; The New Normal Consumer: Understanding the Consumer in Uncertain Times.

14047 ■ Ilium Associates Inc.
600 108th Ave. NE, Ste. 660
Bellevue, WA 98004
Ph: (425)646-6525
Free: 800-874-6525
Fax: (425)646-6525
Co. E-mail: ilium@ilium.com
URL: http://www.ilium.com
Contact: Carolyn Perez Andersen, President
E-mail: carolyn@ilium.com
Scope: Marketing consultants active in market research and analysis, marketing planning, product and packaging design and graphics, as well as architectural design, graphics, signage, electronics. Industries served: transportation, real estate development, architecture, manufacturing, software publishing and government agencies worldwide. Founded: 1972.

14048 ■ Industrial Technology Consultants (ITC)
9650 W 51st Pl., Unit E-201
Arvada, CO 80002-4103
Ph: (303)422-3431

Fax: (303)422-5982
Co. E-mail: drlynn@iindustrialtechnologyconsultants.net
URL: http://www.industrialtechnologyconsultants.net
Contact: Dr. Lynn J. Tomjack, President
E-mail: lynnjtomjack@comcast.net
Scope: Designs; develops and utilizes specific research models which identify multi-million dollar opportunities. Models are provided for: Mergers and Acquisitions; Research and Development of New Technologies and Products; Competitor Evaluations; Market Assessments; Sales and Forecast Models and Distribution Channel Strategies. Founded: 1980. Seminars: Proprietary Marketing Intelligence Research Gathering Techniques; How to Insulate Your Organization Against Competitive Data Gathering; Industrial Expionage Techniques and Strategies; New Business Development; Competitive Marketing Intelligence; Customer Strategic Intelligence Research.

14049 ■ Irwin Broh & Associates Inc. (IB&A)
1011 E Touhy Ave., Ste. 450
Des Plaines, IL 60018
Ph: (847)297-7515
Fax: (847)297-7847
Co. E-mail: info@irwinbroh.com
URL: http://www.irwinbroh.com
Contact: David L. Waitz, President
E-mail: dwaitz@irwinbroh.com
Description: Description: Publishes market surveys on consumer goods. Reaches market through direct mail. Scope: Offers research services in market strategy, acquisition, market and customer analysis, new products, customer satisfaction, advertising, and market segmentation studies. Provides both custom and syndicated research. Industries served: sporting goods, recreation, marine, outdoor power equipment, publishing hardware, industrial products, and government in the United States. Founded: 1971.

14050 ■ Harold L. Kestenbaum P.C.—Harold L. Kestenbaum and Kick Solutions
1425 Rexcorp Plz., E Twr., 15th Fl.
Uniondale, NY 11556
Ph: (516)745-0099
Fax: (516)745-0293
Co. E-mail: hkestenbaum@farrellfritz.com
URL: http://www.franchiseatty.com
Contact: Harold L. Kestenbaum, Principal
E-mail: hkesten@worldnet.att.net
Scope: Provider of consulting services for startup and existing franchisors. Services include feasibility studies, determination of franchise format, business plan development, capital resources, manual preparation and legal services. Practices franchise law and provides marketing services as well. Serves all industries. Founded: 1977. Publications: "Four tips to starting a successful franchise".

14051 ■ Kidfacts Research—Creative Group Inc.
3331 W Big Beaver Rd.
Troy, MI 48084
Ph: (248)816-6772
Fax: (248)816-6778
Co. E-mail: kidfacts@kidfacts.com
Contact: Dana Blackwell, Principal
Scope: Market research firm specializes in qualitative research with children, teens and parents. Expertise in toys and games, food and beverages, clothing, computer software, electronic interactive media, television, entertainment and advertising research. Services include research, analysis and report presentation.

14052 ■ Maritz Inc.—Maritz
1375 N Hwy. Dr.
Fenton, MO 63026-1929
Ph: (636)827-4000
Fax: (636)827-3312
URL: http://www.maritz.com
Contact: W. Stephen Maritz, Chief Executive Officer
Scope: Offers sales and marketing services including employee recognition programs, incentive travel programs, learning programs, loyalty marketing, marketing research, meetings and events organization, sales incentives and sponsorship marketing. Industries served: consumer, industrial, medical and healthcare. Founded: 1894. Seminars: Creating a

Successful Health and Productivity Strategy, Mar, 2009; Coaching Your Sales Team to Higher Levels of Performance, Nov, 2005.

14053 ■ Mayeri Research Inc.
134 W 92nd St.
New York, NY 10025
Ph: (707)944-8585
Free: 888-282-0155
Fax: (707)581-1721
URL: http://www.internetpoll.com
Contact: Harriet Mayeri, Partner
E-mail: ray@mayeriresearch.com
Scope: Specializes in the design, execution and analysis of research us in gone-on-one computer-conducted interviewing and online interviewing via the internet and e-mail. Special Services: Internet Poll™; The Internet Poll™; EmailPoll™; The Email Poll™.

14054 ■ Musicals Tonight Inc.
2162 Broadway
New York, NY 10024
Ph: (212)362-5620
Co. E-mail: contactus@musicalstonight.org
URL: http://www.musicalstonight.org
Contact: Melvin Miller, President
Scope: A not-for-profit theatre company involved in theatrical productions for the revival of neglected musicals in a manner affordable to most audience members. Founded: 1986.

14055 ■ The Performance Group Inc.—PGI Research
233 Main St.
Mount Vernon, IN 47620-1839
Ph: (812)838-9814
Fax: (812)838-8076
Contact: Walter E. Babcock, Jr., President
E-mail: wb@pgiresearch.com
Scope: Marketing research firm. Founded: 1985.

14056 ■ Research USA Inc.
180 N Wacker Dr., Ste. 202
Chicago, IL 60606
Ph: (847)762-7850
Free: 800-863-4800
Fax: (312)658-0085
Co. E-mail: info@researchusainc.com
URL: http://www.researchusainc.com
Contact: Clarence Jackson, President
E-mail: cj@researchusainc.com
Scope: Providing customized primary research services for associations, magazines and other media, advertisers, businesses, government agencies and all other types of organizations. Founded: 1972.

14057 ■ The Spectrem Group Inc.
840 S Waukegan Rd., Ste. 211
Lake Forest, IL 60045
Ph: (312)382-8284
Fax: (312)382-8283
Co. E-mail: info@spectrem.com
URL: http://www.spectrem.com
Contact: George H. Walper, President
E-mail: gwalper@spectrem.com
Scope: Provider of strategic consulting and market research services to financial services clients sewing the affluent and retirement markets. Founded: 1990. Publications: "Affluent Market Insights," 2009; "Ultra Rich Invest Far More Aggressively Than Other Wealthy Individuals," Nov, 2007.

14058 ■ Sumerford System Seven L.L.C.—Sumerford Business Systems L.L.C.
333 Singing Quail Trl.
Haslet, TX 76052
Ph: (817)439-0928
Co. E-mail: w2@sumerford7.com
Contact: Kenneth Scott Sumerford, President
Scope: Offers marketing services especially marketing databases, market research and direct marketing and information systems for small companies. Provides off-the-shelf marketing software and develops custom software applications. Provides services in Web site creation, web page enhancement, web page design and content, e commerce, and database programming. Industries served: manufacturing,

sales and marketing organizations, real estate agents, office managers, and small business owners. Founded: 1989. Publications: "One True Friend," 2007. Special Services: Sumerford Marketing Database 1™; Sumerford Real Estate1™.

14059 ■ Technology Management Associates Inc.
1699 Wall St., Ste. 515
Mount Prospect, IL 60056
Ph: (312)984-5050
Fax: (312)984-5057
Co. E-mail: jogucwa@techmanage.com
URL: http://www.techmanage.com
Contact: Joanne F. Gucwa, President
E-mail: jogucwa@techmanage.com
Scope: Offers research and development strategic planning, high-technology business analysis, industrial marketing, sales strategy, environmental expertise, and general management consulting. Assists organizations in reaching their business goals more efficiently and more profitably. Serves entrepreneurs, governments, associations, and international management clients worldwide. Founded: 1973. Publications: "Three Indisputable Truths About Business Intelligence and The Internet"; "Beyond Customer Satisfaction"; "Keys to Creating Successful New Products"; "Increased Profitability By Building Customer Loyalty"; "Global-scale partnering and business alliances"; "10 Keys to Collecting Information"; "The Thinking Manager's Toolbox: Effective Processes for Problem Solving and Decision Making"; "My Say"; "Successful Project Management"; "Thinking Through the Privatization Option"; "Your Marketing Mindset"; "Intellectual Capital: The New Wealth of Organizations"; "Lean and Meaningful"; "Nuts!: Southwest Airlines' Crazy Recipe for Business and Personal Success"; "If Aristotle Ran General Motors: The New Soul of Business"; "Real Time: Preparing for the Age of the Never Satisfied Customer"; "Webonomics: Nine Essential Principles for Growing your Business on the World Wide Web"; "Asia Rising"; "Customer Centered Growth: Five Proven Strategies for Building Competitive Advantage"; "Cybercorp: The New Business Revolution"; "Net Gain: Expanding Markets Through Virtual Communities"; "Strategic Cost Management"; "Three Indisputable Truths About Business Intelligence and the Internet"; "Leveraging Technology To Build Customer Loyalty"; "Practical and Effective Customer Satisfaction Studies".

14060 ■ Vertex Consultants Inc.
111 Queen St. E, Ste. 501
Toronto, ON, Canada M5C 1S2
Ph: (416)968-9397
Fax: (416)920-6975
Co. E-mail: mnesbitt@vertexconsultants.com
URL: http://www.vertexconsultants.com
Contact: Mark Nesbitt, President
E-mail: mnesbitt@vertexconsultants.com
Scope: A management consultancy whose practice focus is on the intersection between strategy and implementation. Committed to helping clients identify and implement profitable change. Core services include: Assisting insetting and evolving effective strategy; assisting in the implementation of strategy throughout the organization; and research. Founded: 1993.

14061 ■ Paul A. Warner Associates Inc.
4521 PGA Blvd., Ste. 122
Palm Beach Gardens, FL 33418
Ph: (404)401-2002
Fax: (904)398-3506
Co. E-mail: john@pwarner.com
URL: http://www.pwarner.com
Contact: Paul A. Warner, President
E-mail: paul@pwarner.com
Scope: Marketing research and marketing consulting in African-American and urban culture markets. Founded: 1980. Telecommunication Services: paul@pwarner.com.

14062 ■ Young & Associates Inc.
121 E Main St.
Kent, OH 44240
Ph: (330)678-0524
Free: 800-525-9775

Fax: (330)678-6219
Co. E-mail: online@younginc.com
URL: http://www.younginc.com
Contact: Gary J. Young, Chief Executive Officer
E-mail: gyoung@younginc.com
Scope: Provider of a variety of management consulting, outsourcing, educational, and research services, including strategic planning, risk management, capital planning, mergers and acquisitions, internal audit, branching and expansion, loan review, information technology, marketing, market research, human resources planning and management, site/location feasibility studies, development of business plans, and organizational analysis and development and regulatory compliance. Specialists in small and mid-size companies. Industries served: financial institutions, manufacturers (business-to-business and consumer), banking, healthcare (hospitals and practitioners), retailers, and services. Founded: 1978. Publications: "An Avalanche of New Compliance Regulations," Oct, 2009; "Fair Lending Risk Assessment," May, 2009. Special Services: The Compliance Monitoring System™; Compliance Monitoring Update Service™; The Compliance Review Program™; Compliance Review Program Update Service™.

FRANCHISES AND BUSINESS OPPORTUNITIES

14063 ■ Fransurvey.com
Franchise Research Institute
PO Box 6385
Lincoln, NE 68506-0385
Free: 800-410-5205
Fax: (402)477-3898
Description: Complete market research services.

LIBRARIES

14064 ■ Advertising Research Foundation Information Center
432 Park Ave. S., 6th Fl.
New York, NY 10016-8013
Ph: (212)751-5656
Fax: (212)319-5265
Co. E-mail: mihui@thearf.org
URL: http://www.thearf.org
Contact: Jill Peled
Scope: Market research, advertising, research methods, media research. Services: Library open to members. Founded: 1952. Holdings: 3000 volumes; 2000 vertical files of clippings, reports, surveys. Subscriptions: 110 journals and other serials.

14065 ■ BayerDiag, a Bayer Company Library
63 North St.
Medfield, MA 02052
Ph: (508)359-3538
Fax: (508)359-3442
Co. E-mail: kathleen.mccabe.b@bayer.com
URL: http://www.bayerdiag.com/
Contact: Kathleen E. McCabe, Manager, Info Systems
Scope: Clinical medicine, market research, engineering, biotechnology, business. Services: Center not open to the public. Founded: 1978. Holdings: 3000 books; 3500 periodical volumes; 28,000 patents; 850 research reports. Subscriptions: 425 journals and other serials.

14066 ■ Business Trend Analysts Library
2171 Jericho Tpke., Ste. 200
Commack, NY 11725
Ph: (631)462-5454
Free: 800-866-4648
Fax: (631)462-1842
Co. E-mail: sales@bta-ler.com
URL: http://www.businesstrendanalysts.com
Contact: J. Marquardt, Librarian
Scope: Marketing, business, economics. Services: Library not open to the public. Founded: 1979. Holdings: 200 reports. Subscriptions: 400 journals and other serials; 8 newspapers.

14067 ■ Clapp and Mayne Library
8401 Colesville Rd., Ste. 425
Silver Spring, MD 20910-3363
Ph: (301)495-9572
URL: http://www.nbr-bd.org/nbrweb/Support/supportPage1.htm
Scope: Marketing research, economics. **Services:** Library open to the public with restrictions. **Holdings:** 4000 books; 1000 reports. **Subscriptions:** 10 journals and other serials.

14068 ■ Elrick and Lavidge Library
3 Westbrook Corporate Center, Ste. 600
Westchester, IL 60154
Ph: (708)449-5300
Fax: (708)449-4498
Contact: Theresa Litoborski, Librarian
Scope: Market research, marketing, consumer behavior, business and management, industry, statistics. **Services:** Interlibrary loan; Library not open to the public. **Founded:** 1965. **Holdings:** 300 books; 7 VF drawers of pamphlets; 2 drawers of maps; 100 directories; 283 telephone directories; census publications. **Subscriptions:** 50 journals and other serials.

14069 ■ Frankel & Company Information Center
111 E. Wacker Dr.
Chicago, IL 60601
Ph: (312)552-5197
Fax: (312)552-5424
Co. E-mail: Karen_trimberger@frankel.com
Contact: Karen Trimberger
Scope: Marketing, sales promotion. **Services:** Interlibrary loan; center open to the public by appointment. **Founded:** 1980. **Holdings:** 20 books. **Subscriptions:** 100 journals and other serials; 5 newspapers.

14070 ■ General Mills, Inc. - Business Information Center
1 General Mills Blvd.
Minneapolis, MN 55426
Ph: (763)764-5461
Co. E-mail: gail.wolfson@genmills.com
Contact: Gail Wolfson
Scope: Business, marketing, food industry. **Services:** Center not open to the public. **Founded:** 1947. **Hold**ings: 800 books; 22,000 internal marketing research reports, electronic, hardcopy and microfiche. **Subscriptions:** 180 journals and other serials; 5 newspapers.

14071 ■ IIMI Information Center
4205 K St.
Philadelphia, PA 19124
Ph: (215)537-1790
Contact: Albert C. Vara
Scope: Marketing; food research; job location; population studies; multicultural sources; area studies; African-American, Asian-American, and Hispanic writers; company personnel information. **Services:** Library not open to the public. **Founded:** 1970. **Holdings:** 2700 books; 95 bound periodical volumes; 1990 reports; manuscripts; 16 VF drawers of documents and reports; 2000 microfiche. **Subscriptions:** 54 journals and other serials; 6 newspapers.

14072 ■ Marketemps - Marketing Intelligence Center
3435 Ocean Park Blvd., Ste. 112
Santa Monica, CA 90405
Ph: (310)471-5590
Fax: (310)471-0932
Contact: Clifford S. Lightfoot, Principal
Scope: Marketing intelligence, new product development, growth industries, market trends, technology assessment, technology transfer, commercialization, trade shows. **Services:** Provides marketing outsourcing services and executive recruiting; center open to the public on fee basis. **Founded:** 1982. **Holdings:** 500 books; 200 reports and presentations, start-up businesses. **Subscriptions:** 40 journals and other serials; 5 newspapers.

14073 ■ MORPACE International Library
31700 Middlebelt Rd., Ste. 200
Farmington Hills, MI 48334-2373
Ph: (248)737-5300
Fax: (248)737-5326
Co. E-mail: information@morpace.com
URL: http://www.morpace.com
Scope: Market, automotive, and consumer research. **Services:** Library not open to the public. **Founded:** 1978. **Holdings:** 4000 proprietary reports and surveys. **Subscriptions:** 125 journals and other serials; 7 newspapers.

14074 ■ Ricerca Biosciences - Information Services
7528 Auburn Rd.
Concord, OH 44077-1000
Ph: (440)357-3300
Free: 888-742-3722
Fax: (440)354-6276
Co. E-mail: info@ricerca.com
URL: http://www.ricerca.com
Contact: R. Ian Lennox, Chief Executive Officer
Scope: Pharmaceuticals, chemistry, agriculture, business, biotechnology, engineering, management, marketing research, finance. **Services:** Library not open to the public. **Founded:** 1980. **Holdings:** 2000 books; 2500 bound periodical volumes; 3000 reels of microfilm. **Subscriptions:** 50 journals and other serials.

14075 ■ Silver Burdett & Ginn - Editorial Library
299 Jefferson Rd.
Parsippany, NJ 07054
Ph: (973)739-8000
Fax: (973)898-0114
Scope: General education, publishing, market research. **Services:** Library not open to the public. **Holdings:** 10,000 books. **Subscriptions:** 150 journals and other serials.

14076 ■ The Vineyard - Real Estate, Shopping Center & Urban Development Information Center
100 W. Shaw Ave.
Fresno, CA 93704
Ph: (209)222-0182
Contact: Richard Erganian, Director, Information Services
Scope: Real estate, shopping centers, urban and regional planning, architecture, mortgage financing, market research, landscaping. **Services:** Library open to real estate developers. **Founded:** 1956. **Holdings:** 3000 books; 500 bound periodical volumes; 2000 other cataloged items; 30 real estate transcripts; 50 shopping center development transcripts; 20 appraisal tapes and cassettes; 25 income property reports and transcripts; 150 video cassettes. **Subscriptions:** 25 journals and other serials; 5 newspapers.

ASSOCIATIONS AND OTHER ORGANIZATIONS

14077 ■ American Amateur Karate Federation (AAKF)
445 S Figueroa St., Ste. 2600
Los Angeles, CA 90071
Free: 888-939-8882
Fax: (888)939-8555
Co. E-mail: office@aakf.org
URL: http://www.aakf.org
Contact: Anne Kageyama, Director, Administration
Description: Represents karate clubs and schools representing over 20000 individuals. Serves as a national governing body for karate. Seeks to improve the physical and mental health of the public through the practice of karate; promotes public understanding of karate. Establishes competition standards such as rules, judging, and athlete qualifications. Sets ranking standards in accordance with international standards. Sanctions and conducts national competitions including the All America Karate Championship; recognizes karate practitioners. Plans and executes karate development programs. Sponsors U.S. team development camp, national summer training course, U.S. regional instructor program, championship ranking and judging programs, and examiner qualification program. **Founded:** 1961. **Publications:** *Times Newsletter* (Monthly).

14078 ■ American Kenpo Karate International (AKKI)
PO Box 768
Evanston, WY 82931
Ph: (307)789-4124
Co. E-mail: akki@allwest.net
URL: http://www.akki.com
Contact: Mr. Paul Mills, President
Description: Seeks to preserve, honor, and elevate the strength of Kenpo Karate. Sponsors competitions. Maintains educational, charitable, and research programs, children's services, and a speakers' bureau. **Founded:** 1995. **Publications:** *1st Level Club Manual; 1st Level Knife Manual; Kenpo Karate-Works; Professional Business Guide.* **Awards:** KKI Black Belt Certification.

14079 ■ Canadian Kendo Federation (CKF)—Federation Canadienne de Kendo
8013 Hunter St.
Burnaby, BC, Canada V5A 2B8
Ph: (604)420-0438
Fax: (604)420-1971
Co. E-mail: hokusa@kendo-canada.com
URL: http://kendo-canada.com
Contact: Hiro Okusa, President
Description: Kendo enthusiasts. Promotes increased interest and participation in Kendo, a Japanese form of swordsmanship. Facilitates creation of Kendo clubs; conducts educational programs; sponsors competitions. **Publications:** *Kendo Referee Handbook.*

14080 ■ International Traditional Karate Federation (ITKF)
1930 Wilshire Blvd., Ste. 503
Los Angeles, CA 90057-3603
Ph: (213)483-8262
Fax: (213)483-4060
Co. E-mail: office@itkf.org
URL: http://www.itkf.org
Description: Represents national karate federations. Provides international rules, regulations, and competition standards for traditional karate; sanctions international competitions and seminars. **Founded:** 1974.

14081 ■ *Kendo Referee Handbook*
8013 Hunter St.
Burnaby, BC, Canada V5A 2B8
Ph: (604)420-0438
Fax: (604)420-1971
Co. E-mail: hokusa@kendo-canada.com
URL: http://kendo-canada.com
Contact: Hiro Okusa, President

14082 ■ Tomiki Aikido of the Americas (TAA)
5752 S Kingston Way
Englewood, CO 80111
Ph: (303)740-7424
Co. E-mail: nettles@tomiki.org
URL: http://www.tomiki.org
Contact: Seiji Tanaka, Director
Description: Fosters international amateur sports competition. Seeks to introduce and promote the Japanese martial art Aikido by organizing training camps, exhibitions, and tournaments around the world. Promotes international and intercultural exchange, education, and understanding. **Founded:** 1990. **Publications:** *The Aikido Times* (Quarterly). **Educational Activities:** International Tournaments (Biennial); National Tournaments (Biennial); Japan Aikido Association U.S.A. International Tournaments (Biennial).

14083 ■ United States Judo Association (USJA)
PO Box 1880
Tarpon Springs, FL 34688-1880
Free: 877-411-3409
Fax: (888)276-3432
Co. E-mail: membership@usja-judo.org
URL: http://www.usja-judo.org
Contact: Katrina Davis, Executive Director
Description: Amateur judo athletes and coaches. Promotes the recreational and physical benefits of judo; advocates practice of the sport to develop sportsmanship, good citizenship, and mental well-being. Encourages public interest and participation in Judo. Seeks the advancement of amateur judo competition in the U.S. and worldwide. Maintains National Judo Hall of Fame. Sanctions local, state, and regional tournaments. Offers training and certification program for coaches and referees. **Founded:** 1954. **Publications:** *American Judo Magazine* (Quarterly). **Educational Activities:** Junior National Tournament (Annual). **Awards:** Judo Coaches of the Year (Annual); Male and Female Judo Athletes of the Year (Annual); Most Improved Male and Female Judo Athletes of the Year (Annual).

14084 ■ U.S. Taekwondo Union (USTU)
1 Olympic Plz.
Colorado Springs, CO 80909
Ph: (719)866-4632
Fax: (719)866-4642
Co. E-mail: david.askinas@usa-taekwondo.us
URL: http://www.usa-taekwondo.us
Contact: Eric Parthen, Chief Executive Officer
Description: A member of the United States Olympic Committee and the national governing body for the sport of Taekwondo. Amateur Taekwondo athletes and instructors. Promotes Taekwondo programs in the U.S. and represents the U.S. in the Olympics and World Championships and other international competitions under sanction of the World Taekwondo Federation. Offers referee and coaching certification programs; conducts seminars. Sponsors competitions; selects national Olympic Taekwondo teams. **Founded:** 1974. **Publications:** *U.S. Referee Seminar; U.S. Taekwondo Journal* (Annual); *USTU Club Newsletter* (Bimonthly). **Educational Activities:** National Championships (Semiannual); U.S. Jr. Olympic Taekwondo Championship (Annual).

14085 ■ U.S.A. Karate Federation (USAKF)
1550 Ritchie Rd.
Stow, OH 44224
Co. E-mail: usakarate@usakarate.us
URL: http://www.usakarate.org
Contact: Patrick M. Hickey, President
Description: Individuals, corporations, sports organizations, and karate clubs. Serves as a national federation for karate in the U.S. Seeks to promote karate as a sport and to advance karate performance and instruction; certifies karate instructors. Organizes competitions, selects U.S. a national karate team. Conducts classes for karate students and masters. Conducts research; compiles statistics; maintains hall of fame and speakers' bureau. **Founded:** 1986.

14086 ■ World Martial Arts Association (WMAA)
Redeemer St. John's Church
939-83rd St.
Brooklyn, NY 11228
Ph: (718)833-9039
URL: http://www.wmaa.com
Description: Persons interested in the martial arts. Purpose is to teach, promote, and grade the technical aspects of martial arts such as judo, karate, tae kwon do, kung fu, jujitsu, and aikido. **Founded:** 1979.

14087 ■ Zen-do Kai Martial Arts (ZDK)
PO Box 186
Johnstown, NY 12095
Ph: (518)762-1589
Fax: (518)762-1589
Co. E-mail: director@zdkusa.com
URL: http://www.zdkusa.com
Contact: Michael J. Campos, Director
Description: Martial art clubs. Teaches Shotokan, Shokukai, Uechi-Ryu, Pentjak-Silat, and Tae Kwon Do styles of karate. Sponsors tournaments and anti-

rape and police training seminars. Conducts demonstrations of the martial arts. Organizes martial arts sports production. Conducts instructor training programs. Provides guest instructors and seminars; maintains hall of fame and speakers' bureau; sponsors competitions. Offers children's services and charitable program. **Founded:** 1969. **Publications:** *The Warrior* (Quarterly). **Educational Activities:** Awards Banquet Weekend (Annual); Zen-do Kai Martial Arts Meeting (Annual). **Awards:** Instructor of the Year (Annual).

TRADE PERIODICALS

14088 ■ *Black Belt Magazine: World's Leading Magazine of Martial Arts*
Pub: Ohara
URL(s): www.blackbeltmag.com/. **Ed:** Jim Coleman.
Released: Monthly **Price:** $24, Individuals; $45, Two years; $36, Canada; $69, Canada two years; $48, Other countries; $93, Other countries two years.

14089 ■ *T'ai Chi: International Magazine of T'ai Chi Ch'uan*
Pub: Wayfarer Publications
Contact: Marvin Smallheiser, Publisher
URL(s): www.tai-chi.com/. **Ed:** Marvin Smalheiser.
Released: Bimonthly **Price:** $20, Individuals; $5.99, Single issue U.S.; $6.25, Single issue international; $30, Other countries; $30, Two years; $50, Other countries two years.

14090 ■ *The Warrior*
Pub: Zen-Do Kai Martial Arts Association
Ed: Michael J. Campos, Editor. **Released:** Quarterly.
Description: Reports on activities of the Association and its member clubs, Karate philosophy, and other material of interest to members. Recurring features include tournament news and announcements of special events.

14091 ■ *The World of ASP*
Pub: American Self-Protection Association
Contact: Dr. Evan S. Baltazzi, Chairman
Ed: Nellie Baltazzi, Editor, ebaltazzi@aol.com. **Released:** Quarterly. **Price:** Included in membership.
Description: Encourages the development of self-defense and physical fitness programs in YMCAs (Young Men's Christian Associations) and schools across the U.S. Highlights research conducted in the field of combative arts. Recurring features include notices of publications available, news of members, and announcements of upcoming radio, television, and group presentations.

VIDEOCASSETTES/ AUDIOCASSETTES

14092 ■ *Daito-Ryu Revelations*
Keen Media
857 Pulpit Rock Circle N.
Colorado Springs, CO 80918
Ph: (719)593-2155
Free: 800-363-5336
Fax: (719)593-2888
Co. E-mail: jim@keenmedia.com
URL: http://www.keenmedia.com
Released: 1995. **Price:** $99. **Description:** Two-part set features advanced martial arts instruction from master Seigo Okamoto. **Availability:** VHS.

14093 ■ *Daito-Ryu Secrets*
Keen Media
857 Pulpit Rock Circle N.
Colorado Springs, CO 80918
Ph: (719)593-2155
Free: 800-363-5336
Fax: (719)593-2888
Co. E-mail: jim@keenmedia.com
URL: http://www.keenmedia.com
Released: 1995. **Price:** $99. **Description:** Two-part set features martial arts instruction from master Seigo Okamoto. **Availability:** VHS.

14094 ■ *Guide to Karate-Do*
ESPN Inc.
ESPN Plz.
Bristol, CT 06010
Ph: (860)766-2000
Free: 888-549-3776
Fax: (860)766-2213
Co. E-mail: espnpr@espn.com
URL: http://espn.go.com
Contact: Steven M. Bornstein, President
Released: 19??. **Price:** $19.95. **Description:** James Coffman, 7th degree black belt champion, teaches the discipline of Okinawan Shorin-Ryu karate. **Availability:** VHS.

ASSOCIATIONS AND OTHER ORGANIZATIONS

14095 ■ American Society of Civil Engineers (ASCE) - Architectural Engineering Institute (AEI)
1801 Alexander Bell Dr.
Reston, VA 20191-4400
Ph: (703)295-6300
Free: 800-548-2723
Fax: (703)295-6222
Co. E-mail: aei@asce.org
URL: http://content.aeinstitute.org
Contact: D. Wayne Klotz, President

URL(s): www.asce.org, asce-news.asce.org, secure.asce.org/ASCEWebSite/BOOKSTORE/BookDescription.aspx?ProdId=5436. **Description:** Seeks to advance the state-of-the-art and state-of-the-practice of the building industry worldwide by facilitating effective and timely technology transfer. Provides a multidisciplinary forum for building industry professionals to examine technical, scientific and professional issues of common interest. **Founded:** 1998. **Publications:** *Civil Engineering* (Monthly); *American Society of Civil Engineers: Transactions*; *Journal of Infrastructure Systems* (Quarterly); *Journal of Architectural Engineering* (Quarterly); *Practice Periodical on Structural Design and Construction* (Quarterly); *Journal of Bridge Engineering* (Bimonthly); *Waterpower '99: Hydro's Future: Technology, Markets, and Policy*; *Engineering Approaches to Ecosystem Restoration*; *Natural Hazards Review*; *Minimum Design Loads for Buildings and Other Structures, ASCE/SEI 7-05*; *Civil Engineering-ASCE* (Monthly); *Journal of Nanomechanics and Micromechanics* (Quarterly); *Research Library*; *Civil Engineering: Engineered Design and Construction*; *Journal of Engineering Mechanics* (Monthly); *Journal of Environmental Engineering* (Monthly); *Journal of Geotechnical and Geoenvironmental Engineering* (Monthly); *Journal of Hydraulic Engineering* (Monthly); *Journal of Irrigation and Drainage Engineering* (Monthly); *Journal of Management in Engineering* (Quarterly); *Journal of Materials in Civil Engineering* (Monthly); *Journal of Performance of Constructed Facilities* (Bimonthly); *Journal of Professional Issues in Engineering Education and Practice* (Quarterly); *Journal of Structural Engineering* (Monthly); *Journal of Surveying Engineering* (Quarterly); *Journal of Transportation Engineering* (Monthly); *Journal of Urban Planning and Development* (Quarterly); *Journal of Waterway, Port, Coastal, and Ocean Engineering* (Quarterly); *ASCE News* (Monthly); *Practice Periodical on Structural Design and Construction*; *Journal of Structural Engineering*; *Journal of Infrastructure Systems*; *Journal of Water Resources Planning and Management*; *Journal of Waterway, Port, Coastal, and Ocean Engineering*; *Practice Periodical of Hazardous, Toxic, and Radioactive Waste Management*; *Journal of Computing in Civil Engineering*; *Journal of Urban Planning and Development*; *Journal of Professional Issues in Engineering Education & Practice*; *Journal of Surveying Engineering*; *ASCE News*; *Journal of Energy Engineering: The International Journal*; *Journal of*

Hydrologic Engineering (Monthly); *Natural Hazards Review* (Quarterly); *Practice Periodical of Hazardous, Toxic, and Radioactive Waste Management* (Quarterly); *Civil Engineering Database*; *Journal of Water Resources Planning and Management* (Bimonthly); *Civil Engineering Database (CEDB)*; *Leadership and Management in Engineering* (Quarterly); *ASCE Publications Information* (Bimonthly); *Emerging Technology* (Bimonthly); *Manuals and Reports on Engineering Practice* (Periodic); *Worldwide Projects* (Quarterly); *American Society of Civil Engineers--Official Register* (Annual); *Civil Engineering--Buyers' Guide Issue*; *Journal of Aerospace Engineering* (Quarterly); *Journal of Cold Regions Engineering* (Quarterly); *Journal of Computing in Civil Engineering* (Bimonthly); *Journal of Construction Engineering and Management* (Monthly); *Journal of Energy Engineering* (Quarterly); *Journal of Composites for Construction* (Bimonthly); *Leadership and Management in Engineering* (Quarterly); *International Journal of Geomechanics* (Bimonthly); *Changing Our World: True Stories of Women Engineers*; *Preparing for Design-Build Projects: A Primer for Owners, Engineers, and Contractors*. **Educational Activities:** American Society of Civil Engineers Annual Conference and Exposition (Annual); Architectural Engineering Conference Building Integration Solutions; ASCE's Pipeline Conference; Geo Congress (Annual); Structures Congress (Annual); Watershed Management Conference (Quinquenial). **Awards:** Achievement Award (Annual); Arid Lands Hydraulic Engineering Award; Presidents' Award; Presidents' Medal; State-of-the-Art of Civil Engineering Award; Award of Excellence of the Pipeline Division; Harland Bartholomew Award; Stephen D. Bechtel Pipeline Engineering Award; John O. Bickel Award; Can-Am Civil Engineering Amity Award; Honorary Membership Award (Annual); Arthur Casagrande Professional Development Award; Civil Engineering History and Heritage Award; Civil Government Award; Collingwood Prize; Construction Management Award; J. James R. Croes Medal; Hans Albert Einstein Award; Freeman Fellowship; Simon W. Freese Environmental Engineering Award and Lecture; Alfred M. Freudenthal Medal; Edmund Friedman Professional Recognition Award; Edmund Friedman Young Engineer Award for Professional Achievement; Government Civil Engineer of the Year Award; Samuel Arnold Greeley Award; Shortridge Hardesty Award; Rudolph Hering Medal; Karl Emil Hilgard Hydraulic Prize; Julian Hinds Award; Phillip R. Hoffman Award; Distinguished Member; Wesley W. Horner Award; Robert Horonjeff Award of the Air Transport Division; Ernest E. Howard Award; Walter L. Huber Civil Engineering Research Prizes; Hydraulic Structures Medal; Innovation in Civil Engineering Award; International Coastal Engineering Award; Martin S. Kapp Foundation Engineering Award; James Laurie Prize; T. Y. Lin Award; Frank M. Masters Transportation Engineering Award; Daniel W. Mead Prizes; Thomas A. Middlebrooks Award; John G. Moffat - Frank E. Nichol Harbor and Coastal Engineering Award; Moisseiff Award; Nathan M. Newmark Medal; Alfred Noble Prize; Norman Medal; Outstanding Civil Engineering Achievement Award (OCEA); John I. Parcel - Leif J. Sverdrup Civil Engineering Management Award; Peurifoy Construction Research Award; Harold R. Peyton Award for

Cold Regions Engineering; Raymond C. Reese Research Prize; Rickey Medal; Robert Ridgway Student Chapter Award; Roebling Award; Hunter Rouse Hydraulic Engineering Lecture; Thomas Fitch Rowland Prize; Wilbur S. Smith Award; J. Waldo Smith Hydraulic Fellowship; J. C. Stevens Award; Surveying and Mapping Award; Royce J. Tipton Award; Richard R. Torrens Award; Francis C. Turner Lecture; Theodore von Karman Medal; Arthur M. Wellington Prize; William H. Wisely American Civil Engineer Award; Young Government Civil Engineer of the Year Award; Younger Member Group Award; Charles Martin Duke Lifeline Earthquake Engineering Award; George Winter Award; Stephen D. Bechtel, Jr. Energy Award; Honorary Fellow; Ven Te Chow Award; Excellence in Journalism Award; Maurice A. Biot Medal; Jack E. Cermak Medal; Charles Pankow Award for Innovation; Henry L. Michel Award for Industry Advancement of Research; Citizen Engineer Award; Computing in Civil Engineering Award; Professional Practice Ethics and Leadership Award; Walter LeFevre Award; Raymond D. Mindlin Award; Walter P. Moore Jr. Award; Outstanding Projects and Leaders Awards (OPAL) (Annual); Ralph B. Peck Award; Robert H. Scanlan Medal; Harry Schnabel Jr. Award for Career Excellence in Earth Retaining Structures; H. Bolton Seed Medal; Elmer A. Sperry Award; Dennis L. Tewksbury Award; Karl Terzaghi Award; Architectural Engineering Award. **Telecommunication Services:** pnatale@asce.org; marketing@asce.org; gsd_master@asce.org; jdavis@asce.org; contacts@mercommawards.com.

14096 ■ Association of the Wall and Ceiling Industries International (AWCI)
513 W Broad St., Ste. 210
Falls Church, VA 22046
Ph: (703)538-1600
Fax: (703)534-8307
Co. E-mail: info@awci.org
URL: http://www.awci.org
Contact: Steven A. Etkin, Chief Executive Officer
Description: Acoustical tile, drywall, demountable partitions, lathing and plastering, fireproofing, light-gauge steel framing, stucco and exterior insulation finish systems contractors, suppliers and manufacturers. **Scope:** walls and ceiling information. **Founded:** 1918. **Subscriptions:** 7500 articles books periodicals video recordings. **Publications:** *Construction Dimensions Magazine* (Monthly); *Information Resources*. **Awards:** Pinnacle Award (Annual); Excellence in Construction Safety Award (Annual).

14097 ■ Brick Industry Association (BIA)
1850 Centennial Park Dr., Ste. 301
Reston, VA 20191
Ph: (703)620-0010
Fax: (703)620-3928
Co. E-mail: brickinfo@bia.org
URL: http://www.gobrick.com
Contact: J. Gregg Borchelt, President
E-mail: borchelt@bia.org

URL(s): www.bia.org. **Description:** Manufacturers and distributors of clay brick. Promotes clay brick with the goal of increasing its market share. **Scope:** engineering and ceramics pertinent to masonry construction. **Founded:** 1956. **Subscriptions:** 2000 articles books periodicals. **Publications:** *Annual Sales and Marketing Report* (Annual); *BIA News* (Monthly); *Brick in Architecture* (Quarterly); *Directory of Manufacturers* (Annual); *BIA News* (Monthly); *Brick Industry Association--Membership Directory* (Annual). **Educational Activities:** The Brick Show (Annual). **Awards:** Brick in Architecture Awards (Biennial); Brick Paving Design Awards (Biennial).

14098 ■ Building Stone Institute (BSI)
5 Riverside Dr., Bldg. 2
Chestertown, NY 12817
Ph: (518)803-4336
Free: 866-786-6313
Fax: (518)803-6313
Co. E-mail: jane@buildingstoneinstitute.org
URL: http://www.buildingstoneinstitute.org
Contact: Jane Bennett, Executive Vice President
Description: Represents natural stone quarriers, fabricators, installers, dealers, importers, expo and restorers. Serves as a clearinghouse of information for architects, contractors, and masons. Promotes the use of natural stone. **Founded:** 1919. **Publications:** *Building Stone Magazine* (Quarterly); *Stone Information Manual*; *Who's Who in the Stone Business* (Annual). **Educational Activities:** Study Tour (Annual). **Awards:** Tucker Architectural Award (Biennial); Tucker Architectural Awards Competition.

14099 ■ Ceilings and Interior Systems Construction Association (CISCA)
405 Illinois Ave., Unit 2B
St. Charles, IL 60174
Ph: (630)584-1919
Fax: (866)560-8537
Co. E-mail: cisca@cisca.org
URL: http://www.cisca.org
Contact: Shawn Burnum, President
Description: International trade association for the advancement of the interior commercial construction industry. Provides quality education, resources and a forum for communication among its members. **Founded:** 1949. **Publications:** *Ceiling Systems*. **Awards:** Construction Excellence Award (Annual).

14100 ■ Indiana Limestone Institute of America (ILIA)
1502 I St., Ste. 400
Bedford, IN 47421
Ph: (812)275-4426
Fax: (812)279-8682
Co. E-mail: todd@iliai.com
URL: http://www.iliai.com
Contact: Todd Schnatzmeyer, Executive Director
Description: Conducts promotional and technical services for the Indiana limestone industry; sponsors research; establishes standards; offers technical service in product use to architects, builders and owners. Maintains speakers' bureau; conducts specialized education. **Founded:** 1928.

14101 ■ International Institute for Lath and Plaster (IILP)
PO Box 1663
Lafayette, CA 94549
Ph: (925)283-5160
Fax: (925)283-5161
Co. E-mail: frank@lpinst.org
URL: http://www.iilp.org
Contact: Frank E. Nunes, Secretary
Description: Industry-wide federation of lathing and plastering contractors, labor organizations, and manufacturers of lathing and plastering supplies. Promotes use of lath and plaster. **Founded:** 1976.

14102 ■ International Masonry Institute (IMI)
The James Brice House
42 East St.
Annapolis, MD 21401
Ph: (410)280-1305
Free: 800-803-0295
Fax: (301)261-2855
Co. E-mail: masonryquestions@imiweb.org
URL: http://www.imiweb.org
Contact: James Boland, Co-Chairman
Description: Joint labor/management trust fund of the International Union of Bricklayers and Allied Craftworkers and union masonry contractors. Aims for the

advancement of quality masonry construction through national and regional training, promotion, advertising and labor management relations programs in the U.S. and Canada. Provides support and materials for local/regional masonry promotion groups in the U.S. and Canada, and cooperates with national groups and organizations promoting the industry. Sponsors craft training and research programs. Offers educational programs. Maintains museum. **Scope:** masonry construction, design, installation. **Founded:** 1970. **Subscriptions:** books clippings periodicals reports. **Publications:** *IMI Today* (Bimonthly). **Educational Activities:** Mason Industry Educational Conference (Annual). **Awards:** Golden Trowel Award (Periodic); Golden Trowel Awards.

14103 ■ Mason Contractors Association of America (MCAA)
1481 Merchant Dr.
Algonquin, IL 60102
Ph: (224)678-9709
Free: 800-536-2225
Fax: (224)678-9714
URL: http://www.masoncontractors.org
Contact: Jeff Buczkiewicz, Executive Director
Description: Masonry construction firms. Conducts specialized education and research programs. Compiles statistics. **Founded:** 1950. **Educational Activities:** Masonry Showcase (Annual). **Awards:** International Masonry Skills Challenge; International Excellence in Masonry Award Competition.

14104 ■ The Masonry Society (TMS)
105 S Sunset St., Ste. Q
Longmont, CO 80501-6172
Ph: (303)939-9700
Fax: (303)541-9215
Co. E-mail: info@masonrysociety.org
URL: http://www.masonrysociety.org
Contact: Phillip J. Samblanet, Executive Director
Description: Represents individuals interested in the art and science of masonry. Serves as professional, technical, and educational association dedicated to the advancement and knowledge of masonry. Gathers and disseminates technical information. **Founded:** 1977. **Publications:** *The Masonry Society Journal*; *TMS Journal*; *2011 MSJC - Masonry Building Code Requirements and Specifications for Masonry Construction* (Triennial). **Educational Activities:** The Masonry Society Meeting (Annual); North American Masonry Conference (Quadrennial). **Awards:** Fellow Member Award (Annual); Grimm Student Scholarship (Annual); Honorary Members (Annual); James L. Noland Student Scholarship (Quadrennial); John B. Scalzi Research Award (Annual); Outstanding Doctor and Masters Thesis (Annual); Outstanding Journal Paper Awards (Quadrennial); Paul Haller Structural Design Award (Triennial); President's Award (Annual); Service Award (Annual); Outstanding North American Masonry Conference Paper Awards (Quadrennial).

14105 ■ National Concrete Masonry Association (NCMA)
13750 Sunrise Valley Dr.
Herndon, VA 20171-4662
Ph: (703)713-1900
Free: 877-627-3976
Fax: (703)713-1910
Co. E-mail: rthomas@ncma.org
URL: http://www.ncma.org
Contact: Robert D. Thomas, President
Description: Manufacturers of concrete masonry units (concrete blocks), segmental retaining wall units and paving block; associate members are machinery, cement and aggregate manufacturers. Conducts testing and research on masonry units and masonry assemblies. Compiles statistics. **Scope:** concrete masonry, masonry engineering, energy conservation. **Founded:** 1918. **Subscriptions:** 4000 articles books periodicals reports. **Publications:** *CM News* (Monthly); *CM News* (Monthly); *CM News*; *National Concrete Masonry Association--Membership Directory*; *C/M News--Directory of Products and Services for the Block Industry Issue*. **Educational Activities:** Masonry Expo (Annual); The Manufactured Concrete Products Exposition (MCX) (Annual). **Awards:**

Design Awards of Excellence (Annual); Honorary Membership (Annual). **Telecommunication Services:** ncma@ncma.org.

14106 ■ Precast/Prestressed Concrete Institute (PCI)
200 W Adams St., No. 2100
Chicago, IL 60606
Ph: (312)786-0300
Fax: (312)786-0353
Co. E-mail: info@pci.org
URL: http://www.pci.org
Contact: James G. Toscas, President
E-mail: jtoscas@pci.org
Description: Manufacturers, suppliers, educators, engineers, technicians and others interested in the design and construction of prestressed concrete. Compiles statistics. Maintains 17 committees, including marketing, technical and research committees. **Founded:** 1954. **Publications:** *Journal of the Precast/Prestressed Concrete Institute* (Bimonthly); *PCI Journal: Journal of the Precast/Prestressed Concrete Institute* (Bimonthly). **Educational Activities:** PCI Annual Convention/Exhibition & National Bridge Conference (Annual). **Awards:** Martin P. Korn Award; Robert J. Lyman Award; Charles C. Zollman Award; Fellow Award; Harry H. Edwards Industry Advancement Award.

14107 ■ Tile Council of North America (TCNA)
100 Clemson Research Blvd.
Anderson, SC 29625
Ph: (864)646-8453
Fax: (864)646-2821
Co. E-mail: info@tileusa.com
URL: http://www.tileusa.com
Contact: Eric Astrachan, Executive Director
Description: Manufacturers of domestic ceramic tile for floors, walls, and related products. Promotes increase in the marketability of ceramic tile. Conducts testing program on tile and tile installation materials. Supervises international licensing program with 16 licensees. Compiles statistics. **Founded:** 1945. **Publications:** *Handbook for Ceramic Tile Installation* (Annual); *TileFlash* (Monthly); *Directory of Manufacturers of Ceramic Tile and Related Products* (Annual). **Educational Activities:** Coverings (Annual).

DIRECTORIES OF EDUCATIONAL PROGRAMS

14108 ■ *Directory of Private Accredited Career Schools and Colleges of Technology*
Pub: Accrediting Commission of Career Schools and Colleges of Technology
Contact: Michale S. McComis, Executive Director
Released: On web page. **Price:** Free. **Description:** Covers 3900 accredited post-secondary programs that provide training programs in business, trade, and technical fields, including various small business endeavors. Entries offer school name, address, phone, description of courses, job placement assistance, and requirements for admission. Arrangement is alphabetical.

REFERENCE WORKS

14109 ■ *Association of the Wall and Ceiling Industries International--Buyer's Guide*
Pub: Association of the Wall and Ceiling Industries International
URL(s): www.awci.org/buyersguidestore.awci.org/cgi-bin/awci/product?;37;. **Ed:** Laura M. Porinchak.
Released: Annual; August. **Price:** $10, Members; $20, Nonmembers. **Covers:** Manufacturers and suppliers of products and equipment used in the wall and ceiling, asbestos removal, and related industries; relevant trade associations and publishers allied with the industry; coverage includes Canada. **Entries include:** Name, address, phone; description of product or service. **Arrangement:** Alphabetical. **Indexes:** Product.

14110 ■ Brick Industry Association--Membership Directory
Pub: Brick Industry Association
Contact: J. Gregg Borchelt, President
E-mail: borchelt@bia.org
URL(s): www.gobrick.com. **Released:** Annual **Covers:** Brick distributors, brick manufacturers, and related service providers throughout the U.S. and Canada. **Entries include:** Company name, address, phone, name of principal executives, list of products or services. **Arrangement:** Alphabetical by personnel.

14111 ■ "Firms Sue Doracon to Recoup More Than $1M in Unpaid Bills" in Baltimore Business Journal (Vol. 28, July 9, 2010, No. 9, pp. 1)
Pub: Baltimore Business Journal
Ed: Scott Dance. **Description:** Concrete supplier Paul J. Rach Inc., Selective Insurance Company, and equipment leasing firm Colonial Pacific Leasing Corporation intend to sue Baltimore, Maryland-based Doracon Contracting Inc. for $1 million in unpaid bills. Doracon owed Colonial Pacific $794,000 and the equipment is still in Doracon's possession. Selective Insurance and Paul J. Rach respectively seek $132,000 and $88,000.

14112 ■ "Housing Slide Picks Up Speed" in Crain's Chicago Business (Vol. 31, April 21, 2008, No. 16, pp. 2)
Pub: Crain Communications, Inc.
Ed: Eddie Baeb. **Description:** According to Tracy Cross & Associates Inc., a real estate consultancy, sales of new homes in the Chicago area dropped 61 percent from the year-earlier period which is more bad news for homebuilders, contractors and real estate agents who are eager for an indication that market conditions are improving.

STATISTICAL SOURCES

14113 ■ RMA Annual Statement Studies
Pub: Risk Management Association
Contact: Kevin M. Blakey, President
Released: Annual. **Price:** $175.00 2006-07 edition, $105.00. **Description:** Contains composite balance sheets and income statements for more than 360 industries, including the accounting, auditing, and bookkeeping industries. Also contains five years of comparative historical data for discerning trends. Includes 16 commonly used ratios, computed for most of the size groupings for nearly every industry.

TRADE PERIODICALS

14114 ■ CM News
Pub: National Concrete Masonry Association
Contact: Robert D. Thomas, President
Ed: Heidi Lorence, Editor, hlorence@ncma.org. **Released:** Monthly. **Price:** Free. **Description:** Focuses on the manufacturing and marketing of concrete masonry products and the managment of production plants. Covers legislative and regulatory developments, production and marketing developments, and new products and services of interest to the industry. Also reports the news and activities of the Association. Recurring features include news of research, news of members, and a calendar of events.

14115 ■ Stone Magazine
Pub: Tile and Stone Inc.
URL(s): www.stonemag.com. **Ed:** Eemrson Schwart-kopf. **Released:** Monthly

14116 ■ TMS Journal
Pub: The Masonry Society
Contact: Phillip J. Samblanet, Executive Director
Ed: John Chrysler, Editor. **Released:** Annual. **Price:** $55, individuals; $60, out of area. **Description:** Presents news of the activities of this Society, devoted to the use of masonry. Contains information on codes and standards, testing, research and development, education and training, inspection, quality control, construction, and public relations.

14117 ■ Walls & Ceilings: Voice of the Industry since 1938
Pub: BNP Media
Contact: Al Reser, President
URL(s): www.wconline.com/www.bnpmedia.com/. **Released:** Monthly **Price:** Free.

VIDEOCASSETTES/ AUDIOCASSETTES

14118 ■ Basic Masonry
Bergwall Productions, Inc.
1 DIckinson Drive, Brandywine BUilding 5, Ste. 105
Chadds Ford, PA 19317
Ph: (610)361-0334
Free: 800-934-8696
Fax: (610)361-0092
URL: http://www.bergwall.com
Released: 1987. **Price:** $359.00. **Description:** The basics of masonry construction are demonstrated. Also available on a single tape at the same cost. **Availability:** VHS.

14119 ■ Masonry Block Explained
Bergwall Productions, Inc.
1 DIckinson Drive, Brandywine BUilding 5, Ste. 105
Chadds Ford, PA 19317
Ph: (610)361-0334
Free: 800-934-8696
Fax: (610)361-0092
URL: http://www.bergwall.com
Released: 1989. **Price:** $1289.00. **Description:** The function, use, and composition of masonry is examined. Also available on a single tape at the same cost. **Availability:** VHS.

TRADE SHOWS AND CONVENTIONS

14120 ■ Construction Directions
Association of the Wall and Ceiling Industries International
513 W. Broad St., Ste. 210
Falls Church, VA 22046
Ph: (703)538-1600
Fax: (703)534-8307
Co. E-mail: info@awci.org
URL: http://www.awci.org
URL(s): www.awci.org. **Frequency:** Annual. **Audience:** Contractors, architects, distributors, and suppliers in the wall and ceiling industries. **Principal Exhibits:** Construction equipment, materials, and tools. **Telecommunication Services:** info@AWCI.org.

14121 ■ MCAA's Masonry Showcase & MCAA Annual Convention
Mason Contractors Association of America
1481 Merchant Dr.
Algonquin, IL 60102
Ph: (224)678-9709
Free: 800-536-2225
Fax: (224)678-9714
Co. E-mail: info@masoncontractors.com
URL: http://www.masoncontractors.org
Contact: Mackie Bounds, President
URL(s): www.masonryshowcase.com. **Frequency:** Annual. **Audience:** Mason contractors and related industry officials. **Principal Exhibits:** Masonry equipment, supplies, and services. **Telecommunication Services:** cfaul@masoncontractors.org.

14122 ■ World of Concrete
Hanley-Wood Exhibitions
6191 N State Hwy. 161, Ste. 500
Irving, TX 75038
Ph: (972)536-6300
Fax: (972)536-6301
URL: http://www.hanley-wood.com
URL(s): www.worldofconcrete.com. **Frequency:** Annual. **Audience:** Concrete contractors, developers, architects, engineers, distributors, dealers, and precast, and ready-mix producers. **Principal Exhibits:** Equipment and services for the construction industry.

FRANCHISES AND BUSINESS OPPORTUNITIES

14123 ■ A-1 Concrete Leveling Inc.
388 S Main St., Ste. 402
Akron, OH 44311
Free: 888-675-3835
Fax: (330)253-1261
Description: Concrete leveling service. **No. of Franchise Units:** 47. **Founded:** 1992.. **Franchised:** 1993. **Equity Capital Needed:** $115,500-$145,900 total investment. **Franchise Fee:** $85,000. **Royalty Fee:** 6%. **Financial Assistance:** Limited in-house and third party financing available. **Training:** Provides 1 week at headquarters, 2 weeks of onsite and ongoing support including newsletter, meetings toll-free phone line, Internet, security/safety procedures, and field operations/evaluations.

14124 ■ Case Handyman & Remodeling Services LLC
Case Design/Remodeling Inc.
North Plz., Ste. 40
4701 Sangamore Rd.
Bethesda, MD 20816
Ph: (301)229-4600
Free: 800-426-9434
Fax: (301)229-2089
Co. E-mail: info@casehandyman.com
URL: http://www.casehandyman.com
Description: Handyman services. **No. of Franchise Units:** 57. **No. of Company-Owned Units:** 4. **Founded:** 1992. **Franchised:** 1997. **Equity Capital Needed:** $105,000-$150,000. **Franchise Fee:** $25,000. **Royalty Fee:** 4-6%. **Training:** Includes 3 weeks training at headquarters, 2 days at franchisee's location and ongoing support.

14125 ■ Concrete Raising of America
2855 South 166th St.
New Berlin, WI 53151
Ph: (800)270-0011
Fax: (262)287-5005
Description: Concrete raising, stabilizing and repair. **No. of Franchise Units:** 18. **No. of Company-Owned Units:** 3. **Founded:** 1947.. **Franchised:** 1995. **Equity Capital Needed:** $75,000 liquid; franchise fee includes training; equipment leasing available. **Franchise Fee:** Up to $25,000. **Financial Assistance:** Yes. **Training:** Yes.

14126 ■ Precision Concrete Cutting
Datigen.com, Inc.
3191 N Canyon Rd.
Provo, UT 84604
Ph: (801)830-4060
Free: 800-833-7770
Description: Trip hazard removal of sidewalks. **No. of Franchise Units:** 32. **No. of Company-Owned Units:** 5. **Founded:** 1992. **Franchised:** 2002. **Equity Capital Needed:** $140,000-$166,500. **Franchise Fee:** $65,000. **Royalty Fee:** 8%. **Financial Assistance:** Third party financing available. **Training:** Offers 1 week at headquarters and 1 week at franchisee's location with ongoing support.

14127 ■ Systems Paving Franchising Inc.
System's Paving, Inc.
1600 Dove St., Ste. 250
Newport Beach, CA 92660
Ph: (949)263-8300
Fax: (949)263-0452
Description: Offers services like marketing, sales, and installation of paving stones. **No. of Franchise Units:** 6. **No. of Company-Owned Units:** 9. **Founded:** 1992.. **Franchised:** 2001. **Equity Capital Needed:** $39,950-$120,800. **Franchise Fee:** $14,800-$17,800. **Royalty Fee:** 6%. **Training:** Offers 10-12 days at headquarters, 10 days at franchisees location, and ongoing for new employees.

LIBRARIES

14128 ■ Brick Industry Association - Library
1850 Centennial Park Dr., Ste. 301
Reston, VA 20191
Ph: (703)620-0010

Fax: (703)620-3928
Co. E-mail: brickinfo@bia.org
URL: http://www.gobrick.com
Scope: Engineering and research pertinent to masonry construction. **Services:** Library open to the public with approval from Engineering Department. **Founded:** 1934. **Holdings:** 2500 volumes. **Subscriptions:** 10 journals and other serials.

14129 ■ Foundation of the Wall & Ceiling Industry - John H. Hampshire Memorial Library
513 W. Broad St., Ste. 210
Falls Church, VA 22046
Ph: (703)538-1600
Fax: (703)534-8307
Co. E-mail: smith@awci.org
URL: http://www.awci.org/thefoundation.shtml
Contact: Don Smith, Technical Director
Scope: Construction - specifications and standards, management, and law; asbestos removal; fire standards; insulation. **Services:** Copying; Library open to the public. **Founded:** 1981. **Holdings:** 10,000 volumes; 3000 books; 500 unbound reports; manufacturers' catalogs. **Subscriptions:** 100 journals and other serials.

14130 ■ Hanley-Wood, LLC Library
426 S. Westgate St.
Addison, IL 60101-4546
Ph: (630)543-0870
Fax: (630)543-3112
URL: http://www.hanleywood.com
Scope: Concrete, cement, masonry, construction, home building. **Services:** Interlibrary loan; copying.

Founded: 1971. **Holdings:** 3000 books; 120 bound periodical volumes. **Subscriptions:** 100 journals and other serials.

14131 ■ LaFarge Canada Inc. Technical Library
6150 Royalmount Ave.
Montreal, QC, Canada H4P 2R3
Ph: (514)738-1202
Fax: (514)738-1124
Co. E-mail: library@accent.net
URL: http://www.lafargenorthamerica.com/wps/portal/
Contact: Irene M. Paulmier, Librarian
Scope: Cement; concrete; engineering; physical sciences. **Services:** Library not open to the public. **Founded:** 1988. **Holdings:** Figures not available.

14132 ■ National Concrete Masonry Association Library
13750 Sunrise Valley Dr.
Herndon, VA 20171-4662
Ph: (703)713-1900
Fax: (703)713-1910
Co. E-mail: jthompson@ncma.org
URL: http://www.ncma.org
Contact: Jason Thompson, Director, Engineering
Scope: Concrete masonry and related topics. **Services:** Library not open to the public. **Founded:** 1918. **Holdings:** 1000 volumes; 10,000 journal articles. **Subscriptions:** 40 journals and other serials; 10 newspapers.

RESEARCH CENTERS

14133 ■ National Concrete Masonry Association - Research and Development Laboratory
13750 Sunrise Valley Dr.
Herndon, VA 20171-4662
Ph: (703)713-1900
Fax: (703)713-1910
Co. E-mail: rthomas@ncma.org
URL: http://www.ncma.org/lab/Pages/default.aspx
Contact: Robert D. Thomas, President
Services: Consulting services for developmental research of new products for concrete masonry industry. **Publications:** *C/M News* (Monthly); *Engineering Bulletins* (Bimonthly).

14134 ■ University of Manitoba - W.R. McQuade Laboratory
Ag & Civil Engineering Bldg.
A250-96 Dafoe Rd.
Winnipeg, MB, Canada R3T 2N2
Ph: (204)474-8506
Fax: (204)474-7519
Co. E-mail: muftia@cc.umanitoba.ca
URL: http://www.isiscanada.com
Contact: Dr. Aftab Mufti, President
Founded: 1995. **Publications:** *Design manuals*; *Innovator Newsletter* (Biennial). **Educational Activities:** W.R. McQuade Laboratory Conference (Annual); W.R. McQuade Laboratory Workshops, seminars. **Awards:** International exchange students scholarships; W.R. McQuade Laboratory Student scholarships. **Telecommunication Services:** central@isiscanada.com.

Massage Therapist

START-UP INFORMATION

14135 ■ *Becoming a Personal Trainer for Dummies*
Pub: John Wiley and Sons, Inc.
Ed: Melyssa Michael, Linda Formichelli. **Released:** October 2004. **Price:** $19.99 (US), $25.99 (Canadian). **Description:** Legal and tax issues involved in starting and running a personal trainer firm. The book offers suggestions for incorporating massage and nutritional services.

ASSOCIATIONS AND OTHER ORGANIZATIONS

14136 ■ **American Massage Therapy Association (AMTA)**
500 Davis St., Ste. 900
Evanston, IL 60201-4695
Ph: (847)864-0123
Free: 877-905-0577
Fax: (847)864-5196
Co. E-mail: info@amtamassage.org
URL: http://www.amtamassage.org
Contact: Shelly Johnson, Executive Director
Description: Massage therapists and massage schools. Promotes standards for the profession, has a Code of Ethics, and supports chapter efforts for state regulation of massage. Sponsors National Massage Therapy Awareness Week to promote public education on the benefits of massage; offers educational literature. Supports research on the efficacy of massage. Offers free Find A Massage Therapists National locator service to help consumers and healthcare professionals find qualified, professional massage therapists. **Founded:** 1943. **Publications:** *Massage Therapy*; *Massage Therapy Journal* (Quarterly); *Sports Massage*; *Stress*; *Massage Therapy Journal* (Annual); *AMTA's Find a Massage Therapist/ Experience the Benefits of Massage*.

14137 ■ **American Organization for Bodywork Therapies of Asia (AOBTA)**
1010 Haddonfield-Berlin Rd., Ste. 408
Voorhees, NJ 08043-3514
Ph: (856)782-1616
Fax: (856)782-1653
Co. E-mail: office@aobta.org
URL: http://www.aobta.org
Contact: Wayne Mylin, President
Description: Professional Asian Bodywork Therapy (ABT) practitioners, teachers, schools and programs; interested individuals. (Asian bodywork therapy is a form of therapeutic bodywork which utilizes theories and techniques directly and derived from ancient and traditional Chinese medicine, as well as evolving forms which stem from that 'root'. ABT focuses on balancing the Qi flow in the body, utilizing many techniques.) Identifies qualified practitioners; serves as a legal entity representing members when dealing with the government, especially in terms of establishing professional status. Sets educational standards for all styles of Asian bodywork including acupressure, Tuina, Amma, Chi Nei Tsang, Nuad bo Rarn,

and Shiatsu, among others. Sponsors speakers' bureau; conducts educational programs. **Scope:** Asian bodywork therapy, business practices, history of Asian medicines, Asian medicine. **Founded:** 1989. **Subscriptions:** articles books photographs. **Publications:** *AOBTA Directory* (Annual).

14138 ■ **American Society of Hand Therapists (ASHT)**
15000 Commerce Pkwy., Ste. C
Mount Laurel, NJ 08054
Ph: (856)380-6856
Fax: (856)439-0525
Co. E-mail: asht@asht.org
URL: http://www.asht.org
Contact: Dorit H. Aaron, President
Description: Registered and licensed occupational and physical therapists specializing in hand therapy and committed to excellence and professionalism in hand rehabilitation. Works to promote research, publish information, improve treatment techniques, and standardize hand evaluation and care. Fosters education and communication between therapists in the U.S. and abroad. Compiles statistics; conducts research and education programs and continuing education seminars. **Founded:** 1977. **Publications:** *Journal of Hand Therapy* (Quarterly).

14139 ■ **Associated Bodywork and Massage Professionals (ABMP)**
25188 Genesee Trail Rd., Ste. 200
Golden, CO 80401
Ph: (303)674-8478
Free: 800-458-2267
Fax: (800)667-8260
Co. E-mail: expectmore@abmp.com
URL: http://www.abmp.com
URL(s): www.abmp.com/home/index.html. **Description:** Professional massage therapists and bodyworkers, sports massage therapists, skin care professionals, reflexologists, energy practitioners, etc.; massage therapy schools; affiliated organizations. Promotes massage and bodywork. Seeks to improve the image of massage therapy and bodywork, and to educate the public about its benefits. Fosters greater credibility and cooperation with the medical profession. Encourages ethical practices, high standards of professional conduct, and continuing education. Provides members with low-cost liability insurance coverage and product discounts. **Founded:** 1987. **Publications:** *ABMP Massage Marketplace* (Annual); *ABMP Successful Business Handbook*; *ABMP Touch Resource Guide*; *Body Sense* (Biennial); *Different Strokes* (Bimonthly); *Massage and Bodywork* (Bimonthly); *The Massage Educator* (Quarterly); *Skin Deep* (Bimonthly); *Body Sense* (Semiannual); *Massage & Bodywork: Nurturing Mind, Body & Spirit* (Bimonthly). **Educational Activities:** School Issues Forum (Annual).

14140 ■ **International Association of Infant Massage (IAIM)—International Association of Infant Massage Instructors**
PO Box 6370
Ventura, CA 93006
Ph: (805)644-8524

Fax: (805)830-1729
Co. E-mail: iaim4us@aol.com
URL: http://www.iaim.ws
Contact: Andrea M. Kelly, Chief Executive Officer
URL(s): www.iaim-us.com. **Description:** Parents, caregivers. Works to promote nurturing touch, positive interactive contact, and communication through massage. Trains and certifies individuals to teach parents and caregivers to massage their babies. **Founded:** 1986.

14141 ■ **National Association of Nurse Massage Therapists (NANMT)**
PO Box 232
West Milton, OH 45383
Ph: (937)698-4128
Free: 855-366-2668
Fax: (937)698-6153
Co. E-mail: info@nanmt.org
URL: http://www.nanmt.org
Contact: Roe Long-Wagner, Executive Director
Description: Nurses and other healthcare professionals who practice massage therapy. Promotes the integration of massage and other therapeutic forms of body work into existing healthcare practice. Promotes Nurse Massage Therapists as specialists within the nursing profession. Establishes standards of professional practice and criteria for national certification of Nurse Massage Therapists. Educates the medical community and the general public about bodywork therapies. Monitors legislation. **Founded:** 1987. **Publications:** *NANMT News* (Quarterly). **Educational Activities:** Nurse Massage Therapy for the Aging Population.

REFERENCE WORKS

14142 ■ *"Do Your Homework" in Black Enterprise (Vol. 38, November 2007, No. 4, pp. 114)*
Pub: Earl G. Graves Publishing Co. Inc.
Ed: Tennille M. Robinson. **Description:** Preschool teacher seeks advice for starting a hotel resort and day spa.

14143 ■ *"How I Did It: Jack Ma" in Inc. (January 2008, pp. 94-102)*
Pub: Gruner & Jahr USA Publishing
Ed: Rebecca Fannin. **Description:** Profile of Jack Ma, who started as a guide and interpreter for Western tourists in Hangzhou. Ma used the Internet to build Alibaba.com, China's largest business-to-business site and one of the hottest IPOs in years.

14144 ■ *"Want a Facial With That Steak?" in Charlotte Observer (February 5, 2007)*
Pub: Knight-Ridder/Tribune Business News
Ed: Jen Aronoff. **Description:** Profile of Burke Myotherapy Massage & Spa and Schell's Bistro. Lynn Shell moved her massage therapy business into a 106-year old home that had been used as a restaurant. She opened her own eatery on the first floor and offers massage therapy upstairs.

SOURCES OF SUPPLY

14145 ■ Massage: A Career at Your Fingertips
Enterprise Publishing
URL(s): www.careeratyourfingertips.com/. **Released:** Triennial; Latest edition 5th Edition. **Price:** $25.95, Individuals. **Publication includes:** Approximately 1,000 organizations involved in the massage industry, including schools, associations, massage equipment suppliers, bodywork organizations, and massage marketing companies in the United States. **Entries include:** For schools--Name, address, phone, hours of training required, number of in-class hours required, cost, financial aid availability, subjects covered, unique aspects of school or curriculum. For others--Name, address, phone, description of products/services offered. Principal content of publication is information on becoming a successful massage therapist. **Arrangement:** Schools are geographical by state, then alphabetical. Others are classified by line of business, then alphabetical. **Indexes:** Alphabetical list of schools.

TRADE PERIODICALS

14146 ■ Journal of Spiritual Bodywork
Pub: Spiritual Massage Healing Ministry
URL(s): www.healingandlaw.com/. **Released:** Quarterly

VIDEOCASSETTES/ AUDIOCASSETTES

14147 ■ Advanced Shiatsu Massage
Artistic Video
c/o Long Island School of Tai-Chi-Chuan
87 Tyler Ave.
Sound Beach, NY 11789-2639
Ph: (631)744-5999
Free: 888-982-4244
Fax: (631)744-5993
Co. E-mail: service@movementsofmagic.com
URL: http://www.movementsofmagic.com
Released: 1991. **Price:** $39.95. **Description:** Understand the techniques of fine Oriental massage after viewing this video. **Availability:** VHS.

14148 ■ Back Shiatsu for Lovers
Acupressure Institute
1533 Shattuck Ave.
Berkeley, CA 94709
Ph: (510)845-1059
Free: 800-442-2232
Fax: (510)845-1496
Co. E-mail: info@acupressure.com
URL: http://www.acupressure.com
Contact: Michael Reed Gach, Founder
Released: 19??. **Price:** $29.95. **Description:** Presents how to eroticize your partner with a full-body back massage. **Availability:** VHS.

14149 ■ Healthy Massage Series
ESPN Inc.
ESPN Plz.
Bristol, CT 06010
Ph: (860)766-2000
Free: 888-549-3776
Fax: (860)766-2213
Co. E-mail: espnpr@espn.com
URL: http://espn.go.com
Contact: Steven M. Bornstein, President
Released: 1989. **Price:** $19.95. **Description:** Three easy-to-follow educational tapes teach proper technique in both Swedish and Oriental (Accupressure) method. Part 1 covers the scalp, face, neck and chest; Part 2 covers the back; Part 3 covers the legs and feet. **Availability:** VHS.

14150 ■ Massage for Health
Video Collectibles
PO Box 385
Lewiston, NY 14092-0385
Free: 800-268-3891
Fax: (800)269-8877
Co. E-mail: info@collectablesdirect.com
URL: http://www.collectablesdirect.com
Released: 1988. **Price:** $24.95. **Description:** A step-by-step guide to Western style/Swedish massage techniques for the entire body. Fifty effective stroke techniques are demonstrated, as well as simple methods of self-massage and stress relaxation. Includes a massage handbook and bottle of professional massage oil. In HiFi Stereo. **Availability:** VHS; 8 mm.

14151 ■ Relaxing Touch: A Guide to the Healing Art of Massage Therapy
ESPN Inc.
ESPN Plz.
Bristol, CT 06010
Ph: (860)766-2000
Free: 888-549-3776
Fax: (860)766-2213
Co. E-mail: espnpr@espn.com
URL: http://espn.go.com
Contact: Steven M. Bornstein, President
Released: 1988. **Price:** $29.95. **Description:** A method of full body massage is demonstrated for the amateur. Viewers learn stress-relieving techniques for consenting adults. **Availability:** VHS.

14152 ■ Shiatsu Massage
Artistic Video
c/o Long Island School of Tai-Chi-Chuan
87 Tyler Ave.
Sound Beach, NY 11789-2639
Ph: (631)744-5999
Free: 888-982-4244

Fax: (631)744-5993
Co. E-mail: service@movementsofmagic.com
URL: http://www.movementsofmagic.com
Released: 1987. **Price:** $39.95. **Description:** A complete demonstration of a full body massage is given. **Availability:** VHS.

14153 ■ Therapeutic Massage for Sports and Fitness
Cambridge Educational
c/o Films Media Group
132 West 31st Street, 17th Floor
Ste. 124
New York, NY 10001
Free: 800-257-5126
Fax: (609)671-0266
Co. E-mail: custserve@films.com
URL: http://www.cambridgeol.com
Released: 19??. **Price:** $39.95. **Description:** Comprehensive, step-by-step instruction in all phases of deep-muscle massage. **Availability:** VHS.

FRANCHISES AND BUSINESS OPPORTUNITIES

14154 ■ Elements Therapeutic Massage
Elements Therapeutic Massage Inc.
9092 S Ridgeline Blvd., Ste. A
Highlands Ranch, CO 80129
Ph: (303)663-0880
Free: 877-663-0880
Fax: (303)663-1617
Description: Professional, affordable, therapeutic massage. **No. of Franchise Units:** 113. **Founded:** 2000.. **Franchised:** 2006. **Equity Capital Needed:** $70,000 cash; $140,387-$336,187. **Franchise Fee:** $34,000. **Financial Assistance:** Yes. **Training:** Yes.

14155 ■ Hand and Stone Massage and Facial Spa
Hand and Stone Franchise Corp.
Description: Massage therapy spas. **No. of Franchise Units:** 71. **No. of Company-Owned Units:** 2. **Founded:** 2004.. **Franchised:** 2006. **Equity Capital Needed:** $320,797-$402,522. **Franchise Fee:** $39,000. **Royalty Fee:** 5%. **Financial Assistance:** Limited third party financing available. **Training:** Offers 3 weeks at headquarters, 1 week onsite with ongoing support.

14156 ■ Massage Envy
Massage Envy Limited, LLC
Description: Therapeutic massage services. **No. of Franchise Units:** 792. **Founded:** 2001.. **Franchised:** 2003. **Equity Capital Needed:** $351-985-$568,623. **Franchise Fee:** $45,000. **Royalty Fee:** 6%. **Financial Assistance:** Limited third party financing available. **Training:** Offers 5 days at headquarters, 5 days onsite and ongoing training and support as requested.

ASSOCIATIONS AND OTHER ORGANIZATIONS

14157 ■ ADR Institute of Canada (ADR Canada)
234 Eglinton Ave. E, Ste. 405
Toronto, ON, Canada M4P 1K5
Ph: (416)487-4733
Free: 877-475-4353
Fax: (416)487-4429
Co. E-mail: admin@adrcanada.ca
URL: http://www.adrcanada.ca
Contact: Mary Anne Harnick, Executive Director
Description: Professionals providing arbitration and mediation services. Promotes the professional advancement of members; seeks to raise awareness of arbitration and services. Makes available arbitration and mediation rules and services to parties wishing to resolve disputes; works with regional affiliate institutes to set standards. Offers educational programs. **Founded:** 1974.

14158 ■ American Arbitration Association, Inc.
335 Madison Ave.
New York, NY 10017
Ph: (212)716-5800
Free: 800-778-7879
Fax: (212)716-5905
Co. E-mail: websitemail@adr.org
URL: http://www.adr.org
Contact: William K. Slate, II, President
Description: Works to achieve the resolution of disputes through the use of mediation, arbitration, democratic elections, and other voluntary methods. Provides administrative services for arbitrating, mediating, or negotiating disputes and impartial administration of elections. Maintains National Roster of Arbitrators and Mediators for referrals to parties involved in disputes. Conducts skill-building sessions to promote a more complete understanding of conflict resolution processes. **Founded:** 1926. **Publications:** *Labor Arbitration in Government* (Monthly); *New York No-Fault Arbitration Reports*; *Dispute Resolution Journal* (Quarterly); *The Punch List* (Quarterly); *Summary of Labor Arbitration Awards* (Monthly). **Awards:** Gavel Award. **Telecommunication Services:** aaauniversity@adr.org.

14159 ■ Association for Conflict Resolution (ACR)
12100 Sunset Hills Rd., Ste. 130
Reston, VA 20190
Ph: (703)234-4141
Fax: (703)435-4390
Co. E-mail: membership@acrnet.org
URL: http://www.acrnet.org
Contact: Perri E. Mayes, President
Description: Professional organization dedicated in enhancing the practice and public understanding of conflict resolution. **Founded:** 2001. **Publications:** *ACResolution* (Quarterly).

14160 ■ Center for Dispute Settlement (CDS)
1666 Connecticut Ave. NW, Ste. 525
Washington, DC 20009-1039
Ph: (202)265-9572
Fax: (202)332-3951
Co. E-mail: administrator@cdsusa.org
URL: http://www.cdsusa.org
Contact: Linda R. Singer, President
Description: Seeks to design, implement, and evaluate programs that apply mediation and other dispute resolution techniques to government, interpersonal, community, business, and institutional problems. Manages complaint center and operates service for the mediation of disputes. Offers consulting and training services. **Founded:** 1971. **Educational Activities:** Mediation for the Professional Advanced Mediation Techniques (Annual).

14161 ■ Institute for Mediation and Conflict Resolution (IMCR)—IMCR Dispute Resolution Center
384 E 149th St., Ste. 330
Bronx, NY 10455
Ph: (718)585-1190
Co. E-mail: seslate19@imcr.org
URL: http://www.imcr.org
Contact: Stephen Slate, Executive Director
Description: Agency, supported by foundation grants and contracts, to which community disputants can turn for assistance in resolving differences on a voluntary basis. Seeks to: mediate community conflicts; train people in mediation techniques and conflict resolution skills; design dispute settlement systems. Facilitates discussion on current trends in dispute resolution. **Founded:** 1969. **Publications:** *F.Y.I., Institute for Mediation and Conflict Resolution* (Quarterly). **Educational Activities:** Dispute Resolution Forum (Quarterly).

14162 ■ International Ombudsman Institute (IOI)—Institut International de l'Ombudsman
PO Box 20
1015 Vienna, Austria
Ph: 43 1 5129388
Fax: 43 1 5129388
Co. E-mail: ioi@volksanw.gv.at
URL: http://www.theioi.org
Contact: Ms. Beverly A. Wakem, President
URL(s): www.theioi.com. **Description:** Ombudsman offices, complaint handling organizations, institutions, libraries, and individuals in 74 countries. Promotes concept of ombudsmanship and supports research and educational efforts in the field. Disseminates information about ombudsmanship; participates in seminars concerning the ombudsman concept. **Founded:** 1978. **Publications:** *International Ombudsman Institute--Directory* (Annual). **Telecommunication Services:** ioi@volksanw.qv.at.

14163 ■ National Academy of Arbitrators (NAA)
1 N Main St., Ste. 412
Cortland, NY 13045
Ph: (607)756-8363
Free: 800-872-5617

Fax: (888)317-1729
Co. E-mail: naa@naarb.org
URL: http://www.naarb.org
Contact: Sarah Adler, President
Description: Labor-management arbitrators. Works to improve general understanding of the nature and use of arbitration as a means of settling labor disputes. Conducts research and educational programs. **Founded:** 1947.

14164 ■ Peace Education Foundation
1900 Biscayne Blvd.
Miami, FL 33132
Ph: (305)576-5075
Free: 800-749-8838
Fax: (305)576-3106
Co. E-mail: lloyd@peace-ed.org
URL: http://www.peace-ed.org
Contact: Lloyd Van Bylevett, President
Description: Teachers, counselors, and school administrators; clergy and laypersons; interested others. Works to educate students, parents, and teachers on creative and nonviolent methods of resolving conflict. Develops and disseminates grade-specific curricula on nonviolent conflict resolution and mediation for preschool through high school students. Maintains the Training Institute for Conflict Resolution, Mediation, and Peacemaking. Conducts workshops and seminars; maintains speakers' bureau. Sponsors contests. **Scope:** peace movement, conflict resolution, mediation. **Founded:** 1980. **Subscriptions:** 1000 articles books periodicals. **Publications:** *Prepared for Action: Responding Effectively to Crisis in Your School.* **Educational Activities:** Peacemakers Conference to Stop the Violence (Annual). **Awards:** Peace Essay (Annual).

DIRECTORIES OF EDUCATIONAL PROGRAMS

14165 ■ *Martindale-Hubbell International Dispute Resolution Directory: A Unique Guide to International ADR Professionals and Procedures*
Pub: Martindale-Hubbell Inc.
Contact: John A. Lawler, IV, President
URL(s): dispute.martindale.commartindale.com. **Released:** Annual **Price:** $250, Individuals. **Covers:** Service providers in over 90 countries of international arbitration and dispute resolution at both international levels and within the individual's national jurisdiction; Professionals and their credentials. **Entries include:** Contact information. **Database includes:** Information on the processes of dispute resolution and the rules which govern it. **Arrangement:** In three main sections.

TRADE PERIODICALS

14166 ■ *Conflict Resolution & Mediation: Journal of the Academy of Family Mediator*
Pub: Jossey-Bass Publishers
Contact: Matthew Hoover, Manager
E-mail: fwelsch@jbp.com
URL(s): www.josseybass.com/WileyCDA/WileyTitle/productCd-0787996092.html. **Ed:** Jon Jenkins, Tricia S. Jones. **Released:** Quarterly **Price:** $40, Individuals.

14167 ■ *Dispute Resolution Journal*
Pub: American Arbitration Association, Inc.
Contact: William K. Slate, II, President
URL(s): www.adr.org/sp.asp?id=29265. **Ed:** Susan Zuckerman. **Released:** Quarterly **Price:** included in membership dues; $55, /year for nonmembers.

14168 ■ *Labor Arbitration in Government*
Pub: American Arbitration Association, Inc.
Contact: William K. Slate, II, President
URL(s): www.adr.org/publicationsorder.asp. **Released:** Monthly **Price:** $142, Individuals.

14169 ■ *Ohio State Journal on Dispute Resolution*
Pub: Ohio State University Moritz College of Law
URL(s): www.osu.edu/moritzlaw.osu.edu/jdr/. **Released:** Quarterly **Price:** $50, Individuals; $60, Other countries.

CONSULTANTS

14170 ■ Consulting & Conciliation Service (CCS)
2219 H St., Ste. 1
Sacramento, CA 95816
Ph: (916)396-0480
Free: 888-898-9780
Fax: (916)441-2828
Co. E-mail: service@azurewings.net
Contact: Jane A. McCluskey, Principal
E-mail: service@azurewings.net
Scope: Offers consulting and conciliation services. Provides pre-mediation counseling, training and research on preparing for a peaceful society, mediation and facilitation, and preparation for shifts in structure, policy and personnel. Offers sliding scale business rates and free individual consultation. **Publications:** "Native America and Tracking Shifts in US Policy"; "Biogenesis: A Discussion of Basic Social Needs and the Significance of Hope". **Seminars:** Positive Approaches to Violence Prevention: Peace building in Schools and Communities.

COMPUTERIZED DATABASES

14171 ■ *Daily Labor Report® (DLR)*
1801 S Bell St.
Arlington, VA 22202
Free: 800-372-1033
Co. E-mail: customercare@bna.com
URL: http://www.bna.com
Availability: Online: Bloomberg LP-Bloomberg BNA; Thomson Reuters - Westlaw. **Type:** Full-text.

14172 ■ *Government Employee Relations Report™*
1801 S Bell St.
Arlington, VA 22202
Free: 800-372-1033
Co. E-mail: customercare@bna.com
URL: http://www.bna.com
Availability: Online: Bloomberg LP-Bloomberg BNA; Thomson Reuters - Westlaw. **Type:** Full-text.

LIBRARIES

14173 ■ American Arbitration Association - Library and Information Center on the Resolution of Disputes
1633 Broadway, Fl. 10
New York, NY 10019-6708
Ph: (212)716-5800
Fax: (212)716-5905
URL: http://www.adr.org
Scope: Arbitration, mediation, and other forms of alternative dispute resolution - general, commercial, International, labor, environmental, maritime, insur-

ance, medical and health, employment, mandatory arbitration. **Services:** Interlibrary loan (to LLAGNY members); copying; library open to the public on a fee basis (free to AAA ADR Information Package subscribers and AAA Library Services Subscribers). **Founded:** 1954. **Holdings:** 24,000 titles; arbitration awards. **Subscriptions:** 240 journals and other serials.

14174 ■ The Peace Center Library
102 W. Maple Ave.
Langhorne, PA 19047-2820
Ph: (215)750-7220
Fax: (215)750-9237
Co. E-mail: info@thepeacecenter.org
URL: http://www.thepeacecenter.org
Contact: Barbara Simmons, Executive Director
Scope: Conflict resolution, violence prevention, peacemaking, multiculturalism, mediation, parenting. **Services:** Library open by appointment. **Founded:** 1982. **Holdings:** 200 books; curricula; videos; articles relating to violence prevention, conflict resolution, mediation, parenting, cooperative games, and peace issues.

14175 ■ York University - Centre for Research in Work and Society
York Res. Tower, 6th Fl.
4700 Keele St.
Toronto, ON, Canada M3J 1P3
Ph: (416)736-5612
Fax: (416)736-5916
Co. E-mail: crws@yorku.ca
URL: http://www.yorku.ca/crws
Contact: Stephanie Ross, Director
Scope: Work and society, unions, arbitration. **Services:** Library open to students, faculty and staff; open by appointment only from May to August. **Holdings:** 500 books; journals; primary and secondary documents and sources.

RESEARCH CENTERS

14176 ■ Center for Dispute Settlement (CDS)
1666 Connecticut Ave. NW
Washington, DC 20009-1039
Ph: (202)265-9572
Fax: (202)332-3951
Co. E-mail: administrator@cdsusa.org
URL: http://www.cdsusa.org
Contact: Linda R. Singer, President
Services: Dispute Resolution Center; Mediation, Facilitation. **Founded:** 1971. **Publications:** *CDS Reports*. **Educational Activities:** Training programs in mediation and negotiation.

14177 ■ Center for Policy Research (CPR)
1570 Emerson St.
Denver, CO 80218
Ph: (303)837-1555
Fax: (303)837-1557
Co. E-mail: jspearson@centerforpolicyresearch.org
URL: http://www.centerforpolicyresearch.org
Contact: Dr. Jessica Pearson, Director
Founded: 1981. **Publications:** *Reports, papers, articles*.

14178 ■ Harvard University - Harvard Negotiation Project (HNP)
513 Pound Hall
Harvard Law School
1563 Massachusetts Ave.
Cambridge, MA 02138
Ph: (617)495-1684

Fax: (617)495-7818
Co. E-mail: jsebenius@hbs.edu
URL: http://www.pon.harvard.edu/research_projects/harvard-negotiation-project/hnp
Contact: Prof. James K. Sebenius, Director
Founded: 1979. **Educational Activities:** Negotiation Workshop (Semiannual), one-week intensive course on negotiation offered each June and November.

14179 ■ Northwestern University - Dispute Resolution Research Center (DRRC)
Jacobs Ctr. 371
J.L. Kellogg School of Management
2001 Sheridan Rd.
Evanston, IL 60208-2001
Ph: (847)491-8068
Fax: (847)467-5700
Co. E-mail: jmbrett@kellogg.northwestern.edu
URL: http://www.kellogg.northwestern.edu/research/drrc
Contact: Prof. Jeanne M. Brett, Director
Founded: 1986. **Publications:** *Teaching Materials*; *Working Paper Series*. **Educational Activities:** Negotiation teaching workshops; Practitioner workshops; Problem solving workshops; Research seminar series; DRRC Seminars, for managers and lawyers; Negotiation Teaching Certificate Program. **Awards:** Faculty research grant program. **Telecommunication Services:** drrc@kellogg.northwestern.edu.

14180 ■ Pennsylvania State University - Center for Research in Conflict and Negotiation (CRCN)
475 Business Bldg.
Smeal College of Business
University Park, PA 16802
Ph: (814)865-3822
Fax: (814)865-0123
Co. E-mail: b9g@psu.edu
URL: http://www.smeal.psu.edu/crcn
Contact: Dr. Barbara Gray, Director
Services: Consulting; Mediation programs. **Founded:** 1988. **Publications:** *CRCN Newsletter*; *Working Paper Series*. **Educational Activities:** Negotiations training for organizations (Periodic), provides team building workshops and negotiations training and training on collaborative problem solving, and collaborative leadership for public, private and NGO organizations; Practitioners' Conferences; CRCN Seminar series. **Awards:** CRCN Research assistantships. **Telecommunication Services:** crcn@smeal.psu.edu.

14181 ■ Syracuse University - Program on the Analysis and Resolution of Conflicts (PARC)
400 Eggers Hall
Maxwell School of Citizenship & Public Affairs
Syracuse, NY 13244-1020
Ph: (315)443-2367
Fax: (315)443-3818
Co. E-mail: roleary@maxwell.syr.edu
URL: http://www.maxwell.syr.edu/parc
Contact: Rosemary O'Leary, Director
Services: Outreach programs; Training and consulting services. **Founded:** 1986. **Publications:** *PARC Articles*; *PARC Newsletter*; *Occasional papers*; *Reprint series*; *Working Paper Series*. **Educational Activities:** PARC Conferences; Public forums, workshops; Summer Institute on Creative Conflict Resolution. **Telecommunication Services:** parc@maxwell.syr.edu.

Medical and Dental Instrument Manufacturing

ASSOCIATIONS AND OTHER ORGANIZATIONS

14182 ■ Advanced Medical Technology Association (AdvaMed)—AdvaMed
701 Pennsylvania Ave. NW, Ste. 800
Washington, DC 20004-2654
Ph: (202)783-8700
Fax: (202)783-8750
Co. E-mail: info@advamed.org
URL: http://www.advamed.org
Contact: Stephen J. Ubl, President
E-mail: subl@advamed.org
Description: Represents domestic (including U.S. territories and possessions) manufacturers of medical devices, diagnostic products, and healthcare information systems. Develops programs and activities on economic, technical, medical, and scientific matters affecting the industry. Gathers and disseminates information concerning the United States and international developments in legislative, regulatory, scientific or standards-making areas. Conducts scientific and educational seminars and programs. **Founded:** 1974. **Publications:** *In Brief. . .; Health Industry Manufacturers Association--Directory* (Annual); *Health Industry Manufacturers Association--Directory* (Annual); *In Brief* (Monthly); *Advanced Medical Technology Association--Directory* (Monthly).

14183 ■ Association for the Advancement of Medical Instrumentation (AAMI)
4301 N Fairfax Dr., Ste. 301
Arlington, VA 22203-1633
Ph: (703)525-4890
Free: 800-332-2264
Fax: (703)276-0793
Co. E-mail: mlogan@aami.org
URL: http://www.aami.org
Contact: Mary Logan, President
Description: Clinical engineers, biomedical equipment technicians, physicians, hospital administrators, consultants, engineers, manufacturers of medical devices, nurses, researchers and others interested in medical instrumentation. Works to improve the quality of medical care through the application, development, and management of technology. Maintains placement service. Offers certification programs for biomedical equipment technicians and clinical engineers. Produces numerous standards and recommended practices on medical devices and procedures. Offers educational programs. **Founded:** 1967. **Publications:** *Biomedical Instrumentation and Technology* (Bimonthly). **Awards:** AAMI Foundation Laufman-Greatbatch Prize; AAMI/BD Professional Achievement Award; Biomedical Instrumentation and Technology Outstanding Paper Awards; Clinical/Biomedical Engineering Achievement Award; AAMI/GE Healthcare BMET of the Year Award; AAMI Foundation/ACCE Robert L. Morris Humanitarian Award (Annual); AAMI Foundation/Laufman-Greatbatch Award (Annual); Becton Dickinson Career Achievement Award (Annual); Clinical/Biomedical Engineering Achievement Award (Annual).

14184 ■ Dental Trade Alliance (DTA)
4350 N Fairfax Dr., Ste. 220
Arlington, VA 22203-1673
Ph: (703)379-7755
Fax: (703)931-9429
Co. E-mail: info@dentaltradealliance.org
URL: http://www.dentaltradealliance.org
Contact: Gary W. Price, President
URL(s): dentaltradealliance.org. **Description:** Represents dental manufacturers, dental dealers, dental laboratories, dental market service providers and dental publications. **Founded:** 2004. **Publications:** *Dental Trade Newsletter* (Bimonthly); *Large Equipment Sales Report.* **Awards:** Distinguished Service and Chairman's Award (Annual). **Telecommunication Services:** staff@dmanews.org.

14185 ■ Health Industry Distributors Association (HIDA)
310 Montgomery St.
Alexandria, VA 22314-1516
Ph: (703)549-4432
Free: 800-549-4432
Fax: (703)549-6495
Co. E-mail: muller@hida.org
URL: http://www.hida.org
Contact: Andrea Logan, Chairman
Description: Represents distributors of medical, laboratory, surgical, and other health care equipment and supplies to hospitals, physicians, nursing homes, and industrial medical departments. Conducts sales training, management seminars, and research through the HIDA Educational Foundation. **Founded:** 1902. **Publications:** *HIDA--Membership Directory and Buyer's Guide.* **Educational Activities:** Health Industry Distributors Association Trade Show and Education Forum (Annual); Streamlining Healthcare Conference (Annual). **Awards:** Exhibit of the Year (Annual); Frank M. Rhatigan Award (Annual); Manufacturer Excellence in Service Award (Annual); Product of the Year (Annual); Repertoire/HIDA Excellence in Sales Awards (Annual); Sales Promotion of the Year (Annual); Industry Award of Distinction. **Telecommunication Services:** rowan@hida.org.

14186 ■ Hearing Industries Association (HIA)
1444 I St. NW, Ste. 700
Washington, DC 20005
Ph: (202)449-1090
Fax: (202)216-9646
Co. E-mail: mjones@bostrom.com
URL: http://www.hearing.org
Contact: Carole M. Rogin, Executive Director
Description: Companies engaged in the manufacture and/or sale of electronic hearing aids, their component parts, and related products and services on a national basis. Cooperates in and contributes toward efforts to promote the number of hearing aid users; collects trade statistics; conducts market research activities, investigations, and studies in connection with hearing and hearing aids. **Founded:** 1957.

14187 ■ Independent Medical Distributors Association (IMDA)
5204 Fairmount Ave.
Downers Grove, IL 60515

Ph: (630)655-9280
Free: 866-463-2937
Fax: (630)493-0798
Co. E-mail: imda@imda.org
URL: http://www.imda.org
Contact: Anthony Marmo, President
Description: Represents sales, marketing and distribution organizations focused on bringing innovative medical technologies to market. Employs salespeople who are technically sophisticated, and who enjoy long-standing relationships with clinicians in their territories. **Founded:** 1978. **Publications:** *IMDA Directory* (Annual); *IMDA--Update* (Monthly); *Independent Medical Distributors Association--Membership Directory* (Annual); *IMDA Update.*

DIRECTORIES OF EDUCATIONAL PROGRAMS

14188 ■ Hospital Telephone Directory: The Quick Reference Information Center of U.S. Hospitals
Pub: UNICOL Inc.
Contact: Henry A. Rose, President
URL(s): www.unicol-publishing.com. **Released:** Annual; Latest edition 2012. **Price:** $119, Individuals. **Covers:** Almost 7,000 hospitals and medical centers in the U.S. **Entries include:** name, address and telephone number. **Arrangement:** Geographical. **Indexes:** Alphabetical.

REFERENCE WORKS

14189 ■ Advanced Medical Technology Association--Directory
Pub: Advanced Medical Technology Association
Contact: Stephen J. Ubl, President
E-mail: subl@advamed.org
URL(s): www.advamed.org/membership.shtml. **Released:** Monthly **Covers:** About 1,100 member manufacturers of medical devices, diagnostic products, and health information systems and products. **Entries include:** For public site--Company name plus hyperlinks to company websites. For private member site--Company name, address, phone, name of official representative or correspondent; product or service provided, plus hyperlinks to company websites. **Arrangement:** Alphabetical.

14190 ■ Association for the Advancement of Medical Instrumentation--Membership Directory
Pub: Association for the Advancement of Medical Instrumentation
Contact: Michael J. Miller, President
URL(s): www.aami.org. **Covers:** 6,500 physicians, clinical engineers, biomedical engineers and technicians, nurses, researchers, and medical equipment manufacturers. **Entries include:** Name, title, affiliation, office address, phone, code for occupational specialization. **Arrangement:** Alphabetical. **Indexes:** Specialty, geographical, job function.

14191 ■ *"Bovie Medical Makes Electrosurgical Strike"* in *The Business Journal-Serving Greater Tampa Bay (Vol. 28, August 22, 2008, No. 35)*

Pub: American City Business Journals, Inc.

Ed: Margie Manning. **Description:** Bovie Medical Group, which manufactures electrosurgical products, is planning to sell its manufacturing plant in the Tyrone Industrial Park and to purchase the former Harland Clarke facility. The moves are expected to boost the efficiency and the development of new products. Other information on Bovie Medical Group is presented.

14192 ■ *"Ending the Ebola Death Sentence"* in *Canadian Business (Vol. 83, August 17, 2010, No. 13-14, pp. 22)*

Pub: Rogers Media Ltd.

Ed: Michael McCullough. **Description:** US Army Medical Research Institute of Infectious Diseases made a $140 million agreement with Tekmira Pharmaceuticals Corporation to develop both a drug delivery system and delivery technology for curing the Ebola virus. Tekmira's delivery technology, which has been shown to halt Ebola in laboratory animals, might be the key to finding a cure.

14193 ■ *"Ethics and the End of Life"* in *Crain's Chicago Business (Vol. 34, October 24, 2011, No. 42, pp. 31)*

Pub: Crain Communications Inc.

Ed: Lisa Bertagnoli. **Description:** Technology has enabled doctors to provide more and better methods for helping patients, however end of life issues faced by medical ethicists are discussed.

14194 ■ *"Finalist: Private Company, Less Than $100M"* in *Crain's Detroit Business (Vol. 25, June 22, 2009, No. 25)*

Pub: Crain Communications Inc. - Detroit

Ed: Sherri Begin Welch. **Description:** Profile of family-owned Guardian Alarm Company is presented. The firm has expanded to include medical monitoring and video equipment of doors and windows.

14195 ■ *"Former Synthes Officers Receive Prison Sentences"* in *Wall Street Journal Eastern Edition (November 22 , 2011, pp. B4)*

Pub: Dow Jones & Company Inc.

Ed: Peter Loftus. **Description:** Michael D. Huggins, formerly chief operating officer of medical-device maker Synthes Ltd., and Thomas B. Higgins, formerly the president of Synthes spine unit, were given prison sentences of nine months while a third executive, John J. Walsh, formerly director of regulatory and clinical affairs in the spine division, was given a five-month sentence for their involvement in the promotion of the unauthorized use of a bone cement produced by the company.

14196 ■ *"The Game of Operation"* in *Crain's Chicago Business (Vol. 31, April 28, 2008, No. 17, pp. 26)*

Pub: Crain Communications, Inc.

Ed: Samantha Stainburn. **Description:** Revenue at Medline Industries Inc., a manufacturer of medical products, has risen 12 percent a year since 1976, reaching $2.81 billion last year. Growth at the company is due to new and increasingly sophisticated operations by surgeons which brings about the need for more specialized tools.

14197 ■ *"GeckoSystems Reduces Sensor Fusion Costs Due to Elder Care Robot Trials"* in *Internet Wire (December 14, 2010)*

Pub: Comtex

Description: GeckoSystems International Corporation has been able to reduce the cost of its sensor fusion system while maintaining reliability and performance. The firm's ongoing first in-home elder care robot trials have sparked interest regarding its business model, technologies available for licensing, and joint domestic and international ventures.

14198 ■ *"Growing at the Margins"* in *Business Journal Serving Greater Tampa Bay*

(Vol. 30, November 5, 2010, No. 46, pp. 1)

Pub: Tampa Bay Business Journal

Ed: Margie Manning. **Description:** Jabil Circuit Inc. has reported an increase in revenues from its smart phones and medical devices. The company has been focusing on its core services such as making smart phone parts and medical devices.

14199 ■ *Health Devices Sourcebook*

Pub: ECRI Institute

Contact: Jeffrey C. Lerner, President

URL(s): https://www.ecri.org/Pages/default.aspx. **Released:** Annual; Latest edition 2011. **Price:** $475, Individuals. **Covers:** Over 6,800 suppliers of patient care equipment, medical and surgical instruments, implants, clinical laboratory equipment and supplies, medical and hospital disposable supplies, and testing instruments; also lists companies that service, recondition, lease, or buy and sell used equipment; coverage includes U.S. and Canada. **Entries include:** Company name, address, phone, toll-free phone, fax, toll-free fax, URL, e-mail, total sales, names of key executives and contacts, product categories handled, trade names, methods of distribution, typical pricing, annual volume. Price of directory includes custom updates upon request. **Arrangement:** Alphabetical. **Indexes:** Product listings, manufacturers' product lines, service company profiles, product categories (by number), product categories (alphabetic), product categories (by specialty), manufacturers addresses (geographic), trade names, equipment services, numerical listings, executive contacts, bioterrorism and emergency preparedness.

14200 ■ *"Heart Hospitals Analyzed"* in *Philadelphia Business Journal (Vol. 30, September 2, 2011, No. 29, pp. 1)*

Pub: American City Business Journals Inc.

Ed: John George. **Description:** Centers for Medicare and Medicaid Services (CMS) released updated data on mortality rates for heart attack patients as hospitals in Pennsylvania. Doylestown Hospital posted the lowest mortality rates with 10.9 percent, tying the fourth best in the entire nation. Other details on the CMS data are presented.

14201 ■ *"Heart Test No Boom for BG Medical"* in *Boston Business Journal (Vol. 31, June 17, 2011, No. 21, pp. 1)*

Pub: Boston Business Journal

Ed: Julie M. Donnelly. **Description:** The Galectin-3 test failed to boost stock prices of its manufacturer, BG Medicine, which has fallen to $6.06/share. The company hopes that its revenue will be boosted by widespread adoption of an automated and faster version of the test, which diagnoses for heart failure.

14202 ■ *"Hospitals Try to Buy Smarter"* in *Crain's Detroit Business (Vol. 25, June 1, 2009, No. 22, pp. M025)*

Pub: Crain Communications Inc. - Detroit

Ed: Jay Greene. **Description:** Hospitals in southeast Michigan are using bulk discount purchasing of medical and non-medical supplies through group purchasing organizations in order to cut costs.

14203 ■ *"Inventive Doctor New Venture Partner"* in *Houston Business Journal (Vol. 40, January 29, 2010, No. 38, pp. A2)*

Pub: American City Business Journals

Ed: Ford Gunter. **Description:** Dr. Billy Cohn, a surgeon from Houston, Texas has been named as venture partner for venture firm Sante Ventures LLC of Austin, Texas. Cohn will be responsible for seeing marketable developing technologies in the medical industry. The motivation for Cohn's naming as venture partner is his development of a minimally invasive therapy for end-stage renal disease.

14204 ■ *"Medical Connectors: Meeting the Demands of Reliability, Portability, Size and Cost"* in *Canadian Electronics (February 2008)*

Pub: CLB Media Inc.

Ed: Murtaza Fidaali, Ted Worroll. **Description:** Component manufacturers who serve the medical industry need to ensure component reliability in order to maintain patient safety. Because of this, connec-

tors in medical equipment are becoming more versatile. It is concluded that these manufacturers are facing challenges meeting the medical industry standards or reliability, miniaturization, portability, and cost.

14205 ■ *"Medical Market a Healthy Alternative"* in *Crain's Cleveland Business (Vol. 30, June 1, 2009, No. 21, pp. 3)*

Pub: Crain Communications, Inc.

Ed: Dan Shingler. **Description:** Manufacturing for the Medical Market: Requirements for Supply Chain Entry, was an event held in Northeast Ohio. Representatives from various health systems addressed 250 area manufacturers about their future medical supply needs.

14206 ■ *"Mentor Medical Device Maker's Partnerships Open New Opportunities"* in *Crain's Cleveland Business (Vol. 30, June 22, 2009, No. 24)*

Pub: Crain Communications, Inc.

Ed: Chuck Soder. **Description:** Frantz Medical Development Ltd. develops medical devices based on ideas from outside inventors. The company wants to manufacture the innovations at its Mentor campus.

14207 ■ *"Oakland County Hopes Auto Suppliers Can Drive Medical Industry Growth"* in *Crain's Detroit Business (March 10, 2008)*

Pub: Crain Communications, Inc.

Ed: Chad Halcom. **Description:** Oakland County officials are hoping to create further economic development for the region by pairing health care companies and medical device makers with automotive suppliers in an attempt to discover additional crossover technology.

14208 ■ *"Playing Defense"* in *Crain's Chicago Business (Vol. 31, November 10, 2008, No. 45, pp. 4)*

Pub: Crain Communications, Inc.

Ed: Monee Fields-White. **Description:** Chicago's money managers are increasingly investing in local companies such as Caterpillar Inc., a maker of construction and mining equipment, Kraft Foods Inc. and Baxter International Inc., a manufacturer of medical products, in an attempt to bolster their portfolios. These companies have a history of surviving tough economic times.

14209 ■ *"SAGE Publications Announced a Partnership with Which Medical Device"* in *Information Today (Vol. 28, November 2011, No. 10, pp. 15)*

Pub: Information Today, Inc.

Description: SAGE Publications has partnered with Which Medical Device to offer insights, tutorials, and reviews of medical devices.

14210 ■ *Scott's Canadian Dental Directory*

Pub: Business Information Group

Contact: Bruce Creighton, President

URL(s): www.businessinformationgroup.ca/dental/cnddentaldir.asp. **Released:** Biennial; Latest edition 2010. **Price:** $239, Individuals Plus Applicable Taxes + S/H; $249, Individuals Web pinpointer; $599, Individuals Web profiler; $6499, Individuals Web prospector. **Covers:** Approximately 18,000 dentists, dental suppliers, and dental laboratories and associations in Canada. **Entries include:** Name, address, phone, names and titles of key personnel, biographical data (for dentists), geographical area served. **Arrangement:** For dentists--Same information available in geographical and alphabetical sections. For others--Classified by line of business, then alphabetical.

14211 ■ *"Somanetics to Buy Back Up to $15 Million of Common Shares"* in *Crain's Detroit Business (Vol. 24, April 7, 2008, No. 14, pp. 4)*

Pub: Crain Communications, Inc.

Ed: Tom Henderson. **Description:** Somanetics Corp., a company that manufactures and markets noninvasive devices for monitoring blood oxygen levels in the brain and elsewhere in the body during surgery, plans to buy back up to $15 million worth of its common shares. Statistical data included on the company's current and past earnings and stock prices as well as its plans to increase revenue.

14212 ■ *"Sterotaxis Needs $10 Million in 60 Days" in Saint Louis Business Journal (Vol. 32, October 7, 2011, No. 6, pp. 1)*
Pub: Saint Louis Business Journal
Ed: E.B. Solomont. **Description:** Medical device firm Stereotaxis signed a loan modification deal with Silicon Valley Bank. The company suffered massive losses during second quarter 2011. Under the deal, the company waived the minimum tangible net work covenant of the original loan in exchange for reduction in its credit line.

14213 ■ *"Survey: Most Approve of Donating Used Pacemakers to Medically Underserved" in Crain's Detroit Business (Vol. 25, June 1, 2009)*
Pub: Crain Communications Inc. - Detroit
Description: According to a survey conducted by University of Michigan Cardiovascular Center, 87 percent of those with pacemakers and 71 percent of the general population would donate the device to patients in underserved nations.

14214 ■ *"UMKC, Hospital Drill Down on Deal" in The Business Journal-Serving Metropolitan Kansas City (Vol. 26, July 18, 2008, No. 45, pp. 1)*
Pub: American City Business Journals, Inc.
Ed: Rob Roberts. **Description:** University of Missouri Kansas City and Children's Mercy Hospital are negotiating the hospital's potential acquisition of the university's School of Dentistry building. The deal would transfer the 240,000-square foot dental school building to Children's Mercy. Plans for a new dental school building for the UMKC are also presented.

14215 ■ *"Zit Zapper Lands New Funding" in Houston Business Journal (Vol. 40, November 27, 2009, No. 29, pp. 1)*
Pub: American City Business Journals
Ed: Mary Ann Azevedo. **Description:** Tyrell Inc. of Houston, Texas generated $20 million in funds for making a cheaper version of its acne-removing Zeno device. The upcoming product, Zeno Mini, will be targeted to a mass market with a price tag of about $89. In 2005, the original Zeno acne treatment device could only be bought through medical offices and spas at about $225.

STATISTICAL SOURCES

14216 ■ *The Market for Dental Equipment and Supplies*
Pub: MarketResearch.com
Released: 2007. **Price:** $2495.00. **Description:** This report quantifies market trends through 2009 for all types of dental equipment for professional use. A special section of the report examines relevant trends in the two major end-use markets for professional dental products-dental offices and dental laboratories.

14217 ■ *RMA Annual Statement Studies*
Pub: Risk Management Association
Contact: Kevin M. Blakey, President
Released: Annual. **Price:** $175.00 2006-07 edition, $105.00. **Description:** Contains composite balance sheets and income statements for more than 360 industries, including the accounting, auditing, and bookkeeping industries. Also contains five years of comparative historical data for discerning trends. Includes 16 commonly used ratios, computed for most of the size groupings for nearly every industry.

14218 ■ *Standard & Poor's Industry Surveys*
Pub: Standard & Poor's Corp.
Released: Annual. **Price:** $3633.00. **Description:** Two-volume book that examines the prospects for specific industries, including trucking. Also provides analyses of trends and problems, statistical tables and charts, and comparative company analyses.

14219 ■ *Trends in Noninvasive and Minimally Invasive Medical Device Market*
Pub: MarketResearch.com
Released: 2006. **Price:** $4850.00.

TRADE PERIODICALS

14220 ■ *24x7*
Pub: Ascend Integrated Media
URL(s): www.24x7mag.com. **Ed:** Deborah Overman, Julie Kirst. **Released:** Monthly

14221 ■ *AAMI News*
Pub: Association for the Advancement of Medical Instrumentation
Ed: Steve Campbell, Editor, scampbell@aami.org.
Released: Monthly. **Price:** Included in membership; $160, nonmembers; $195, other countries. **Description:** Covers Association programs, policies, and meetings. Reports on AAMI standards program and publications in the Standards Monitor section as well as regulatory and legislative proposals or actions. Recurring features include news of educational opportunities and a calendar of events.

14222 ■ *Biomedical Instrumentation & Technology: Association for the Advancement of Medical Instrumentation*
Pub: Elsevier
URL(s): www.aami.org/publications/BIT/index.html-www.aami-bit.org/perlserv/?request=get-archive. **Released:** Bimonthly **Price:** $182, Individuals; $211, Out of country; $219, Institutions; $252, Out of country; Free to AAMI members.

14223 ■ *Biomedical Safety & Standards*
Pub: Lippincott Williams & Wilkins
Ed: Timothy Baker, Editor. **Released:** Semimonthly, 22/year. **Price:** $349.98, individuals in USA; $699.98, institutions in USA; $548.96. **Description:** Reports on biomedical safety and standards. Provides information on safety hazards, product recalls, product and facilities standards, legal actions, legislation and regulations, hospital safety, and biomedical equipment technician activities. Recurring features include news of research, book reviews, and a calendar of events.

14224 ■ *Bioscience Technology: Tools and Techniques for Life Science Researchers*
Pub: Advantage Business Media L.L.C.
Contact: George Fox, President
URL(s): www.biosciencetechnology.com/Default.aspx?CommonCount=0. **Released:** Monthly **Price:** Free.

14225 ■ *Dental Economics*
Pub: PennWell Corp.
URL(s): www.dentaleconomics.com/index.html. **Ed:** Joseph A. Blaes. **Released:** Monthly **Price:** $132, Individuals; $179, Canada and Mexico; $248, Other countries; $211, Two years; $312, Canada and Mexico; $428, Other countries two years; $65, online. **Availability:** Online: PennWell Corp. **Type:** Full-text.

14226 ■ *Dentaletter*
Pub: MPL Communications Inc.
Contact: Barrie Martland, President
E-mail: bmartland@mplcomm.com
Ed: Dr. Brian Waters, Editor. **Released:** 11/year. **Price:** $119. **Description:** Publishes news of dental research. Also covers related web sites.

14227 ■ *Devices & Diagnostics Letter*
Pub: FDA News
Ed: Nick Wakeman, Editor. **Released:** Weekly. **Price:** $1,047, U.S., Canada, and Mexico; $1,087, elsewhere. **Description:** Seeks to provide executives in the industry with information on regulatory developments regarding medical devices and in vitro diagnostic products. Reports on the Food and Drug Administration (FDA), the Health Care Financing Administration, and Congress. Discusses a variety of issues, including manufacturing practices, compliance and inspection programs, defect reporting, labeling and testing rules, and performance standards. Recurring features include news of research and reports of meetings.

14228 ■ *Healthcare Corporate Finance News*
Pub: Irving Levin Associates Inc.
Contact: Stephen M. Monroe, Managing Editor
Ed: Gretchen S. Swanson, Editor. **Released:** Monthly. **Price:** $495. **Description:** Reports on the growth strategies of managed care providers, hospi-

tals, drug companies, medical device manufacturers, and other healthcare organizations. Also reports on the latest deals in the healthcare sector, and how healthcare companies are doing on Wall Street.

14229 ■ *In Brief. . .*
Pub: Advanced Medical Technology Association
Contact: Stephen J. Ubl, President
E-mail: subl@advamed.org
Ed: John Arnold, Editor, jarnold@aduamed.org. **Released:** Semimonthly. **Description:** Covers regulatory, legislative, and standards activities related to the medical device, health care information systems, and the diagnostic products industries. Remarks: Also available via e-mail.

14230 ■ *Journal of Nuclear Cardiology: Official Journal of the American Society of Nuclear Cardiology*
Pub: Springer-Verlag New York Inc.
Contact: Ruediger Gebauer, President
URL(s): www.springer.com/medicine/cardiology/journal/12350. **Ed:** Barry L. Zaret. **Released:** Bimonthly **Price:** €405, Institutions print + online; €486, Institutions print + enhanced access.

14231 ■ *Medical Devices, Diagnostics & Instrumentation Reports - The Gray Sheet*
Pub: F-D-C Reports Inc.
Contact: Jaimie Kelley, Managing Editor
Ed: Mary Houghton, Editor. **Released:** Weekly. **Price:** $1,860. **Description:** Covers the medical device and diagnostics field, including FDA regulations; policies and congressional reform initiatives concerning pre-market approvals and 501(k) exemptions; new products; business start-ups and financial deals; international developments; and technology reimbursement. Recurring features include columns titled In Brief, Financings In Brief, Device Approvals, Recalls & FDA Seizures, and MDDI Stock Index.

14232 ■ *Medical Imaging: News, Issues, and Trends in Health Technology Management*
Contact: Debra Britton, Art Director
E-mail: dbritton@ascendmedia.com
URL(s): www.imagingeconomics.com/. **Ed:** Marianne Matthews. **Released:** Monthly **Price:** Free U.S. and Canadian residents.

14233 ■ *MEEN Diagnostic and Invasive Technology*
Pub: Reilly Publishing Co.
URL(s): www.dicardiology.net/www.itnonline.net. **Released:** Bimonthly; 9/yr. **Price:** $90, Canada and Mexico; $120, Other countries.

14234 ■ *Proofs: The Magazine of Dental Sales and Marketing*
Contact: Kevin Henry, Editor
E-mail: kevinh@pennwell.com
URL(s): www.proofs.com/index.html. **Ed:** Kevin Henry. **Released:** 5/yr. **Price:** $17, Individuals; $55, Canada and Mexico; $164, Other countries air-mailed out of country.

14235 ■ *Warning Letter Bulletin*
Pub: Washington Information Source
Contact: Kenneth Reid, Editor
Released: Biweekly. **Price:** $799. **Description:** Digests warnings issued by the U.S. Food and Drug Administration (FDA) to companies that are allegedly violating the law. Recurring features include news of research, calendar of events, reports of meetings, and book reviews.

14236 ■ *Wednesday in Washington*
Pub: American Association for Homecare
Released: Weekly, via fax, email or mail. **Price:** Included in membership. **Description:** Informs members of developments in government agencies, state legislatures, and on Capitol Hill, as well as any other pertinent information that affects the home medical equipment services and homecare industries. Remarks: Available in print, e-mail, or fax format.

TRADE SHOWS AND CONVENTIONS

14237 ■ *American Academy of Implant Dentistry Annual Meeting*
American Academy of Implant Dentistry (AAID)
211 E Chicago Ave., Ste. 750
Chicago, IL 60611

Ph: (312)335-1550
Free: 877-335-2243
Fax: (312)335-9090
Co. E-mail: info@aaid.com
URL: http://www.aaid-implant.org
Contact: Sharon Bennett, Executive Director
URL(s): www.aaid-implant.org/education/Annual_Meeting.html. Price: $75, for student; $945, for general member; $995, Non-members; $150, for life member. Frequency: Annual. Audience: Dentists. Principal Exhibits: Dental equipment, supplies, and services. Telecommunication Services: aaid@aaid-implant.org.

14238 ■ Association for the Advancement of Medical Instrumentation Annual Conference and Expo
Association for the Advancement of Medical Instrumentation—AAMI
4301 N. Fairfax Dr., Ste. 301
Arlington, VA 22203
Ph: (703)525-4890
Free: 800-332-2264
Fax: (703)276-0793
Co. E-mail: customerservice@aami.org
URL: http://www.aami.org
Contact: Mary Logan, President
URL(s): www.aami.org/ac/. Frequency: Annual. Audience: Biomedical equipment technicians, clinical engineers, hospital administrators, manufacturers, students, government personnel, nurses, equipment engineers. Principal Exhibits: Over 66 product categories of medical device technologies, products and services. Telecommunication Services: lfreeman@aami.org.

14239 ■ Chicagoland
Advanstar Communications
641 Lexington Ave., 8th Fl.
New York, NY 10022
Ph: (212)951-6600
Free: 800-346-0085
Fax: (212)951-6793
Co. E-mail: info@advanstar.com
URL: http://www.advanstar.com
Contact: Robert Krakoff, President
URL(s): www.abilitiesexpo.com. Audience: Disabled consumers, seniors, rehab and healthcare professionals, hospital personnel, special educators, dealers and representatives. Principal Exhibits: Wheelchairs, assistive technology, personal care products, support organizations, and daily living aids.

CONSULTANTS

14240 ■ John C. Palmer Associates Inc.
54 W Shore Dr.
Pennington, NJ 08534-2121
Ph: (609)737-3213
Contact: John C. Palmer, President
Scope: Provider of management consulting specializing in executive selection. Particular expertise in search assignments in the biomedical, pharmaceutical, medical device and instrumentation segments of the health care industry. Offers services in locating, selecting and evaluating candidates for middle and upper management line and staff positions.

FRANCHISES AND BUSINESS OPPORTUNITIES

14241 ■ BioPed Footcare Centres
2150 Winston Park Dr. Unit 21
Oakville, ON, Canada L6H 5V1
Ph: (905)829-0505

Fax: (905)829-5199
Co. E-mail: franchising@bioped.com
URL: http://www.bioped.com
Description: Provides aid to people of all ages requiring comfort or relief from lower limb disorders through the design and manufacture of high quality, biomechanical designed, foot support systems and footwear. No. of Franchise Units: 48. Founded: 1980.. Franchised: 1985. Equity Capital Needed: $162,000-$225,000. Franchise Fee: $29,700. Training: Yes.

14242 ■ MEDIchair Ltd.
20 Egliton Ave. W, Ste. 2100
Toronto, ON, Canada M4R 1K8
Ph: (403)204-1409
Free: 800-667-0087
Co. E-mail: development@medichair.com
URL: http://www.medichair.com
Description: MEDIchair Franchise offer sales, rentals and services of Home Medical Equipments. No. of Franchise Units: 67. No. of Company-Owned Units: 3. Founded: 1985.. Equity Capital Needed: $400,000 total investment; $200,000 start-up capital required. Franchise Fee: $50,000. Training: Initial and ongoing support provided.

COMPUTERIZED DATABASES

14243 ■ *Health Devices International Sourcebase*
5200 Butler Pke.
Plymouth Meeting, PA 19462-1298
Ph: (610)825-6000
Fax: (610)834-1275
Co. E-mail: info@ecri.org
URL: http://www.ecri.org
Contact: Jeffrey C. Lerner, President
Availability: Online: ProQuest LLC - Dialog; German Institute of Medical Documentation and Information; ECRI Institute. Type: Directory.

14244 ■ *WinMDR--Medical Device Register on Disk*
201 28th St., Ste. 100
Santa Monica, CA 90405
Ph: (310)445-4200
Fax: (310)445-4299
Co. E-mail: info@cancom.com
URL: http://www.ubmcanon.com
URL(s): www.mdrweb.com. Released: Published 2006. Entries include: Name, address, phone, fax, e-mail and Web site addresses for manufacturers and companies; current executives; company background; FDA codes and descriptions of products. Database covers: The entire 2-volume print edition of the MDR on CDROM; More than 17,600 companies and 82,000 products searchable by supplier, product category, location, keyword, or trade name.

LIBRARIES

14245 ■ Sentron Medical Inc. - Senmed Medical Ventures Library
4445 Lake Forest Dr., No. 600
Cincinnati, OH 45242-3798
Ph: (513)563-3240
Fax: (513)563-3261
URL: http://www.senmed.com/organization.htm
Contact: Rosanne Wohlwender
Scope: Biotechnology, medical devices and diagnostics, technology transfer, pharmaceuticals, venture capital, licensing. Services: Library not open to the public. Founded: 1987. Holdings: 800 books; 50 reports. Subscriptions: 100 journals and other serials; 2 newspapers.

RESEARCH CENTERS

14246 ■ ECRI Institute
5200 Butler Pke.
Plymouth Meeting, PA 19462-1298
Ph: (610)825-6000
Fax: (610)834-1275
Co. E-mail: info@ecri.org
URL: http://www.ecri.org
Contact: Jeffrey C. Lerner, President
Description: Improves the safety, performance, reliability, and cost effectiveness of health care technology through research testing, and publication of results. Provides technical consulting and accident investigation and educational programs. Functions as a worldwide information clearinghouse for health care technology assessment and hazards and deficiencies in medical devices; sponsors seminars. Provides information and technical assistance for planning, procurement and management of medical equipment. Conducts research; compiles statistics and operates speakers' bureau. Scope: Offers assistance in health care technology including, strategic planning, management consulting, assessment, evaluation, specification and acquisition of medical devices and systems, health care facilities and equipment planning, risk management, accident investigation, and forensic engineering. Additional services include health care and environmental management. Also offers expertise in medical technology assessment, medical equipment acquisition and medical equipment purchasing. Industries served: health care institutions, health care insurers and government. Services: Litigation support and expert witness services; Technical assistance in accident investigation and clinical engineering; Technical assistance to health care facilities in planning, specification, evaluation, procurement and management of medical equipment. Founded: 1955. Holdings: The computer-readable Health Devices Alerts database contains more than 400,000 records dating from 1977 to the present and is updated weekly. The computer-readable Health Devices Sourcebook database contains more than 5000 device categories and is reloaded annually. CD-ROM products are updated quarterly. Subscriptions: 36000 archival material articles audio recordings books papers reports. Publications: "Health Devices Source book". Educational Activities: Annual conference, seminars, distance learning, audio and web conferences. Seminars: Top Ten Health Technology Hazards, Vancouver, Mar, 2010; Biomedical Engineering; State of the infusion technology market; Role of smarter infusion pumps in the field of medication safety technologies; Pump evaluation and selection factors; Implementation challenges and successes; How to assess your facilities readiness and infrastructure requirements for implementation; Clinical implications and work flow impact; Maintenance of libraries and log analysis; Successful wireless implementation; Hands-on interaction with the latest devices, guided by on-site pump trainers is offered; Infection Control Risk Assessment (ICRA) for Construction Activities; Take Control: Hazard and Recall Management Strategies, Royal Oak, MI, Sep, 2006. Telecommunication Services: executiveadmins@ecri.org.

14247 ■ University of Wisconsin—Madison - Medical Instrumentation Laboratory
1550 Engineering Dr.
Madison, WI 53706
Ph: (608)263-1574
Fax: (608)265-9239
Co. E-mail: webster@engr.wisc.edu
Founded: 1970.

ASSOCIATIONS AND OTHER ORGANIZATIONS

14248 ■ American Health Information Management Association (AHIMA)
233 N Michigan Ave., 21st Fl.
Chicago, IL 60601-5809
Ph: (312)233-1100
Free: 800-335-5535
Fax: (312)233-1090
Co. E-mail: info@ahima.org
URL: http://www.ahima.org
Contact: Kathleen Frawley, President
Description: Registered record administrators; accredited record technicians with expertise in health information management, biostatistics, classification systems, and systems analysis. Sponsors Independent Study Programs in Medical Record Technology and coding. Conducts annual qualification examinations to credential medical record personnel as Registered Record Administrators (RRA), Accredited Record Technicians (ART) and Certified Coding Specialists (CCS). Maintains Foundation of Research and Education Library, Scholarships and loans. **Scope:** medical records administration, coding, management. **Founded:** 1928. **Subscriptions:** 2500. **Publications:** *Journal of AHIMA* (10/year); *Leader: AHIMA Volunteer* (Quarterly); *QA Section Connection* (Bimonthly); *Spectrum* (Quarterly); *Journal of AHIMA*; *From the Couch: Official Newsletter of the Mental Health Record Section of the American Medical Record Association* (Quarterly); *Accredited Educational Programs in Health Information Technology and Health Information Administration.* **Educational Activities:** American Health Information Management Association Meeting (Annual); AHIMA Leadership Conference (Annual); American Health Information Management Association National Convention (Annual).

14249 ■ International Claim Association (ICA)
1155 15th St. NW, Ste. 500
Washington, DC 20005
Ph: (202)452-0143
Fax: (202)530-0659
Co. E-mail: dchuba@claim.org
URL: http://www.claim.org
Contact: Marlon Nettleton, President
Description: Claim executives and administrators representing companies writing life, health, or accident insurance. Promotes efficiency, effectiveness and high standards of performance in claim administration by member companies. Provides a forum for research, education and the exchange of ideas relating to various aspects of claim administration. **Founded:** 1909. **Publications:** *ICA News* (Quarterly); *International Claim Association--Annual Report* (Annual). **Educational Activities:** International Claim Association Annual Education Conference (Annual). **Awards:** Outstanding Claim Achievement Award (Annual); Student of the Year (Annual). **Telecommunication Services:** cmurphy@claim.org.

REFERENCE WORKS

14250 ■ *"New York Collection Agency's Bribery Case Resolved" in Collections & Credit Risk (Vol. 15, August 1, 2010, No. 7, pp. 19)*
Pub: SourceMedia Inc.
Description: Criminal conviction and civil settlement in a bribery case and Medicaid scam involving H.I.S. Holdings Inc. and owner Deborah Kantor is examined.

TRADE PERIODICALS

14251 ■ *Materials Management in Health Care*
Pub: Health Forum L.L.C.
Contact: Neil Jesuele, President
E-mail: njesuel1@aha.org
URL(s): www.matmanmag.com/matmanmag_app/index.jsp. **Ed:** Bob Kehoe. **Released:** Monthly

14252 ■ *Reimbursement Advisor*
Pub: Aspen Publishers Inc.
Contact: Mark Dorman, President
Ed: Dennis Barry, Esq., Editor. **Released:** Monthly. **Price:** $485, individuals. **Description:** Provides information on health care spending and Medicare reimbursement. Deals with universal health insurance, physician payments, preventative services, and the industry's regulations.

COMPUTERIZED DATABASES

14253 ■ *HMO and Chains Directory*
25 Vintinner Rd.
Campton, NH 03223
Ph: (603)726-4800
Free: 800-729-2600
Fax: (603)726-4840
Co. E-mail: info@firstmark.com
URL: http://www.firstmark.com
Contact: Michael H. Pomerantz, President
Availability: CD-ROM: F1RSTMARK Inc. **Type:** Directory.

14254 ■ *State Health Care Regulatory Developments™*
1801 S Bell St.
Arlington, VA 22202
Free: 800-372-1033
Co. E-mail: customercare@bna.com
URL: http://www.bna.com
Availability: Online: Bloomberg LP-Bloomberg BNA; Thomson Reuters - Westlaw. **Type:** Full-text.

RESEARCH CENTERS

14255 ■ American University - National Center for Health Fitness (NCHF)
Nebraska Hall, Lower Level
4400 Massachusetts Ave. NW
Washington, DC 20016-8037
Ph: (202)885-6275
Fax: (202)885-6288
Co. E-mail: nchfaa@american.edu
URL: http://www.american.edu/cas/seth/health/research.cfm
Contact: Dr. Robert C. Karch, Executive Director
Services: Consulting. **Founded:** 1980. **Educational Activities:** Health/fitness specialist training; International Institute for Health Promotion Conference (Annual). **Awards:** Dean Meyerson Award, for Leadership in Health Promotion.

ASSOCIATIONS AND OTHER ORGANIZATIONS

14256 ■ American Association of Bioanalysts (AAB)
906 Olive St., Ste. 1200
St. Louis, MO 63101-1448
Ph: (314)241-1445
Free: 800-457-3332
Fax: (314)241-1449
URL: http://www.aab.org
Contact: LeAnn Hampton, Office Manager
Description: Professional organization of directors, owners, managers, supervisors, technologists and technicians of bioanalytical clinical laboratories devoting their efforts to clinical laboratory procedure and testing. Sponsors Proficiency Testing Service open to individuals engaged in the clinical laboratory field. Provides specialized education and representation before federal and state legislatures and regulatory agencies. **Founded:** 1956. **Publications:** *AAB Bulletin* (Quarterly); *AAB Update* (Periodic); *Andrology and Embryology Review Course Manual*; *General Knowledge for the Clinical Lab Director*; *QA Manual for POLs and Industries and Hospital Labs*. **Educational Activities:** Meeting and Educational Conference (Annual). **Awards:** Lucien Dean Hertert Memorial Award.

14257 ■ American Association for Laboratory Accreditation (A2LA)
5301 Buckeystown Pke., Ste. 350
Frederick, MD 21704-8307
Ph: (301)644-3248
Fax: (301)662-2974
Co. E-mail: info@a2la.org
URL: http://www.a2la.org
Contact: Peter Unger, President
E-mail: punger@a2la.org
Description: Represents individuals, associations, corporations, universities, laboratories, research institutes and government agencies interested in improving the quality of laboratories. Accredits testing laboratories, certifies laboratory reference materials and registers quality systems. **Founded:** 1978. **Publications:** *American Association for Laboratory Accreditation Annual Report* (Annual); *A2LA News* (Quarterly); *A2LA Today*; *A2LA Directory* (Annual); *Directory of Accredited Laboratories* (Weekly); *American Association for Laboratory Accreditation Directory of Accredited Laboratories* (Annual); *A2LA Today*. **Educational Activities:** American Association for Laboratory Accreditation Seminar.

14258 ■ American Board of Bioanalysis (ABB)
906 Olive St., Ste. 1200
St. Louis, MO 63101-1448
Ph: (314)241-1445
Fax: (314)241-1449
URL: http://www.aab.org/aab/American_Board_of_Bioanalysis.asp
Description: Certifying agency consisting of scientists, educators, and recognized authorities in the clinical laboratory field. Certifies clinical laboratory

directors at two levels depending on qualifications, including High Complexity or Moderate Complexity Clinical Laboratory Director. Also certifies Technical Consultants, two levels of supervisor (Technical and General), and Bioanalyst Laboratory Manager (BLM). **Founded:** 1968.

14259 ■ American Clinical Laboratory Association (ACLA)
1100 New York Ave. NW, Ste. 725 W
Washington, DC 20005
Ph: (202)637-9466
Fax: (202)637-2050
Co. E-mail: info@clinical-labs.org
URL: http://www.acla.com
Contact: Alan Mertz, President
Description: Corporations, partnerships, or individuals owning or controlling one or more independent clinical laboratory facilities operating for a profit and licensed under the Clinical Laboratories Improvement Act of 1967 or the Clinical Laboratories Improvement Amendment of 1988, or accredited by the Medicare program. Promotes the development of uniformly high quality laboratory testing; eliminates the present inequalities in the standards applied to different segments of the clinical laboratory market; discourages the enactment of restrictive legislative or regulatory policies that may impede the free flow of commerce or operate to the detriment of the public. Examines federal and state health care and laboratory regulatory and legislative proposals and submits comments and opinions to the appropriate agencies or legislative bodies. **Founded:** 1971. **Publications:** *Results* (Monthly).

14260 ■ American Medical Technologists (AMT)
10700 W Higgins Rd., Ste. 150
Rosemont, IL 60018
Ph: (847)823-5169
Free: 800-275-1268
Fax: (847)823-0458
Co. E-mail: membership@amt1.com
URL: http://www.amt1.com
Contact: Roxann Clifton, President
Description: Represents medical technologists, medical laboratory technicians, medical assistants, medical administrative specialists, dental assistants, office laboratory technicians, phlebotomy technicians, laboratory consultants, and allied health instructors. Provides allied health professionals with professional certification services and membership programs to enhance their professional and personal growth. Aims to issue certification credentials to medical and dental assistants, clinical laboratory personnel, laboratory consultants, and allied health instructors. **Founded:** 1939. **Publications:** *AMT Events and Continuing Education Supplement* (Quarterly); *Continuing Education Topics & Issues* (3/year). **Educational Activities:** American Medical Technologists Convention (Annual); Educational and National Meeting (Annual); Joint Educational Program and Convention. **Awards:** Order of the Golden Microscope; Technologist of the Year; Outstanding Student Award; Medallion of Merit; RMA of the Year; The Becky Award; The Silver Service Award; The Pillar Award; Exceptional Merit

(Annual); Member and Student Writing (Annual); President's Award (Annual); RMA Medallion of Merit (Annual); RMA of the Year (Annual); Technologist of the Year (Annual); Distinguished Achievement (Annual). **Telecommunication Services:** mail@amt1.com.

14261 ■ American Society for Clinical Laboratory Science (ASCLS)
1861 International Dr., Ste. 200
Tysons Corner, VA 22102
Ph: (571)748-3770
Co. E-mail: ascls@ascls.org
URL: http://www.ascls.org
Contact: Linda Smith, President
Description: Primarily clinical laboratory personnel who have an associate or baccalaureate degree and clinical training and specialists who hold at least a master's degree in one of the major fields of clinical laboratory science such as bacteriology, mycology, or biochemistry; also includes technicians, specialists, and educators with limited certificates and students enrolled in approved programs of clinical laboratory studies and military medical technology schools. Promotes and maintains high standards in clinical laboratory methods and research and advances standards of education and training of personnel. Conducts educational program of seminars and workshops. Approves programs of continuing education and maintains records on participation in continuing education programs for members. **Founded:** 1933. **Publications:** *Clinical Laboratory Science* (Quarterly). **Awards:** Member of the Year (Annual); Dorothy Morrison Undergraduate Scholarships; Gloria F. "Mike" Gilbert Memorial Trustee Award; Joseph J. Kleiner Memorial Award; Robin H. Mendelson Memorial Awards; Alpha Mu Tau Undergraduate Scholarships; Ruth M. French Graduate or Undergraduate Scholarships; ASCLS Education and Research Fund (E and R) Scholarship Program (Annual); Education Scientific Assembly Student Paper Award (Annual).

14262 ■ American Society for Clinical Pathology (ASCP)
33 W Monroe, Ste. 1600
Chicago, IL 60603
Ph: (312)541-4999
Free: 800-267-2727
Fax: (312)541-4998
Co. E-mail: info@ascp.org
URL: http://www.ascp.org
Contact: C. Bruce Alexander, President
Description: Works to promote public health and safety by the appropriate application of pathology and laboratory medicine. Provides educational programs for pathologists and laboratory professionals throughout the year, certification for laboratory professionals, and publishes scientific journals and reference textbooks. **Founded:** 1922. **Publications:** *ASCP Member News* (Monthly); *Laboratory Medicine* (Monthly); *Pathology Today* (Bimonthly); *Laboratory Medicine: An Official Publication of the American Society for Clinical Pathology* (Monthly). **Educational Activities:** College of American Pathologists and American Society of Clinical Pathologists Annual

Meeting (Annual). **Awards:** Lifetime Achievement Award; Ward Burdick Award for Distinguished Service to Clinical Pathology; Philip Levine Award for Outstanding Research; H. P. Smith Award for Distinguished Pathology Educator.

14263 ■ Annual Roster
LCD 1
Hamilton, ON, Canada L8N 3N8
Ph: (905)528-8642
Free: 800-263-8277
Fax: (905)528-4968
Co. E-mail: info@csmls.org
URL: http://www.csmls.org
Contact: Christine Nielsen, Executive Director
Released: Annual

14264 ■ Canadian Journal of Medical Laboratory Science
LCD 1
Hamilton, ON, Canada L8N 3N8
Ph: (905)528-8642
Free: 800-263-8277
Fax: (905)528-4968
Co. E-mail: info@csmls.org
URL: http://www.csmls.org
Contact: Christine Nielsen, Executive Director
Released: Bimonthly

14265 ■ Canadian Society for Medical Laboratory Science (CSMLS)—Societe Canadienne de Science de Laboratoire Medical (SCSLM)
LCD 1
Hamilton, ON, Canada L8N 3N8
Ph: (905)528-8642
Free: 800-263-8277
Fax: (905)528-4968
Co. E-mail: info@csmls.org
URL: http://www.csmls.org
Contact: Christine Nielsen, Executive Director
Description: Laboratory technologists in 20 countries. Seeks to maintain high standards of medical laboratory technology to insure effective and economical laboratory services. Promotes the interests of medical laboratory technologists. Emphasizes the importance of continuing education; sponsors courses. Communicates with government authorities concerning issues affecting members. Offers insurance program to members. Organizes national medical laboratory week annually. **Scope:** medical laboratory technology. **Founded:** 1937. **Subscriptions:** 350. **Publications:** Annual Roster (Annual); Canadian Journal of Medical Laboratory Science (Bimonthly); Catalogs of Continuing Education; Guidelines for Laboratory Safety. **Educational Activities:** Scientific Congress (Annual).

14266 ■ Catalogs of Continuing Education
LCD 1
Hamilton, ON, Canada L8N 3N8
Ph: (905)528-8642
Free: 800-263-8277
Fax: (905)528-4968
Co. E-mail: info@csmls.org
URL: http://www.csmls.org
Contact: Christine Nielsen, Executive Director

14267 ■ Clinical Laboratory Management Association (CLMA)
401 N Michigan Ave., Ste. 2200
Chicago, IL 60611
Ph: (312)321-5111
Fax: (312)673-6927
Co. E-mail: info@clma.org
URL: http://www.clma.org
Contact: Rodney W. Forsman, President
URL(s): www.meclma.com, www.clma.org/?page=Maine. **Description:** Individuals holding managerial or supervisory positions with clinical laboratories; persons engaged in education of such individuals; manufacturers or distributors of equipment or services to clinical laboratories. Objectives are: to enhance management skills and promote more efficient and productive department operations; to further exchange of professional knowledge, new technology, and colleague experience; to encourage cooperation among those engaged in management

or supervisory functions. Activities include: workshops, seminars, and expositions; dissemination of information about legislation and other topics. **Founded:** 1976. **Publications:** Vantage Point; Clinical Leadership and Management Review: CLMR (Bimonthly); Clinical Leadership Management Review (Bimonthly); Clinical Laboratory Management Association--Membership Directory (Annual). **Educational Activities:** CLMA/ASCP Annual Conference and Exhibition—ThinkLab (Annual). **Awards:** Clinical Laboratory Management Association High School Senior Scholarships; Clinical Laboratory Management Association Undergraduate Scholarships; Chapter of the Year (Annual); Educational Scholarship (Annual). **Telecommunication Services:** srobinson@clma.org.

14268 ■ Clinical and Laboratory Standards Institute (CLSI)
940 W Valley Rd., Ste. 1400
Wayne, PA 19087
Ph: (610)688-0100
Free: 877-447-1888
Fax: (610)688-0700
Co. E-mail: customerservice@clsi.org
URL: http://www.nccls.org
Contact: Mary Lou Gantzer, President
URL(s): www.clsi.org. **Description:** Government agencies, professional societies, clinical laboratories, and industrial firms with interests in medical testing. Purposes are to promote the development of national and international standards for medical testing and to provide a consensus mechanism for defining and resolving problems that influence the quality and cost of healthcare work performed. **Founded:** 1968. **Publications:** NCCLS - Update/Standards Status; Member/Volunteer Directory. **Awards:** Russell J. Eilers Memorial Award (Annual).

14269 ■ Guidelines for Laboratory Safety
LCD 1
Hamilton, ON, Canada L8N 3N8
Ph: (905)528-8642
Free: 800-263-8277
Fax: (905)528-4968
Co. E-mail: info@csmls.org
URL: http://www.csmls.org
Contact: Christine Nielsen, Executive Director

14270 ■ National Accrediting Agency for Clinical Laboratory Sciences (NAACLS)
5600 N River Rd., Ste. 720
Rosemont, IL 60018-5119
Ph: (773)714-8880
Fax: (773)714-8886
Co. E-mail: info@naacls.org
URL: http://www.naacls.org
Contact: Jerry Phipps, President
Description: Independently accredits academic programs in hospitals, colleges, and universities for the following health professional classifications: Clinical Laboratory Scientist/Medical Technologist, Clinical Laboratory Technician/Medical laboratory Technician, Cytogenetic Technologist, Histologic Technician, Histotechnologist, Pathologists' Assistant. Independently approves academic programs in hospitals and colleges for the following: Phlebotomist, Clinical Assistant. Establishes standards for quality educational programs; determines if hospitals and colleges are maintaining standards through self-study and on-site visits. Provides workshops for program officials on self-study and accreditation. **Founded:** 1973. **Publications:** NAACLS News (Quarterly); National Accrediting Agency for Clinical Laboratory Sciences--Annual Report (Annual).

DIRECTORIES OF EDUCATIONAL PROGRAMS

14271 ■ Directory of Private Accredited Career Schools and Colleges of Technology
Pub: Accrediting Commission of Career Schools and Colleges of Technology
Contact: Michale S. McComis, Executive Director
Released: On web page. **Price:** Free. **Description:** Covers 3900 accredited post-secondary programs that provide training programs in business, trade, and

technical fields, including various small business endeavors. Entries offer school name, address, phone, description of courses, job placement assistance, and requirements for admission. Arrangement is alphabetical.

REFERENCE WORKS

14272 ■ Directory of International and Regional Organizations Conducting Standards-Related Activities
Pub: National Technical Information Service U.S. Department of Commerce Technology Administration
URL(s): gsi.nist.gov/global/index.cfm/L1-5/L2-44/A-144. **Ed:** Breitenberg Maureen. **Covers:** 338 international and regional organizations which conduct standardization, certification, laboratory accreditation, and other standards-related activities. **Entries include:** Description, scope of each organization, national affiliations of members, U.S. Participants, restrictions on membership, availability of any standards in English.

14273 ■ "Ending the Ebola Death Sentence" in Canadian Business (Vol. 83, August 17, 2010, No. 13-14, pp. 22)
Pub: Rogers Media Ltd.
Ed: Michael McCullough. **Description:** US Army Medical Research Institute of Infectious Diseases made a $140 million agreement with Tekmira Pharmaceuticals Corporation to develop both a drug delivery system and delivery technology for curing the Ebola virus. Tekmira's delivery technology, which has been shown to halt Ebola in laboratory animals, might be the key to finding a cure.

14274 ■ "HER's: the Future is Free" in Benzinga.com (October 29, 2011)
Pub: Benzinga.com
Ed: Benzinga Staff. **Description:** In order to create and maintain electronic health records that connects every physician and hospital it is essential to create a reliable, easy-to-use, certified Web-based ambulatory ERH using an ad-supported model. eBay seems to be the company showing the most potential for improving services to physicians and consumers, but requires sellers to pay fees based upon sales price.

14275 ■ "mChip: Claros Diagnostics" in Inc. (Vol. 33, November 2011, No. 9, pp. 42)
Pub: Inc. Magazine
Ed: Christine Lagorio. **Description:** Harvard University researchers have developed a device called the mChip that produces accurate blood tests in about 10 minutes. Plans to apply for FDA approval for the mChip in the US should happen in 2012.

14276 ■ Medical and Health Information Directory: A Guide to Organizations, Agencies, Institutions, Programs, Publications, Services, and Other Resources Concerned with Clinical Medicine. . .
Pub: Cengage Learning Inc.
Contact: Ronald Dunn, President
URL(s): www.gale.cengage.com. **Released:** Annual; Latest edition April 2011. **Price:** $1190, Individuals set; $501, Individuals per volume. **Covers:** In volume 1, more than 33,000 medical and health oriented associations, organizations, institutions, and government agencies, including health maintenance organizations (HMOs), preferred provider organizations (PPOs), insurance companies, pharmaceutical companies, research centers, and medical and allied health schools. In Volume 2, over 20,000 medical book publishers; medical periodicals, directories, audiovisual producers and services, medical libraries and information centers, electronic resources, and health-related internet search engines. In Volume 3, more than 40,500 clinics, treatment centers, care programs, and counseling/diagnostic services for 34 subject areas. **Entries include:** Institution, service, or firm name, address, phone, fax, email and URL; many include names of key personnel and, when pertinent, descriptive annotation. Volume 3 was formerly listed separately as Health Services Direc-

tory. **Arrangement:** Classified by organization activity, service, etc. **Indexes:** Each volume has a complete alphabetical name and keyword index.

STATISTICAL SOURCES

14277 ■ *RMA Annual Statement Studies*
Pub: Risk Management Association
Contact: Kevin M. Blakey, President
Released: Annual. **Price:** $175.00 2006-07 edition, $105.00. **Description:** Contains composite balance sheets and income statements for more than 360 industries, including the accounting, auditing, and bookkeeping industries. Also contains five years of comparative historical data for discerning trends. Includes 16 commonly used ratios, computed for most of the size groupings for nearly every industry.

TRADE PERIODICALS

14278 ■ *A2LA Today*
Pub: American Association for Laboratory Accreditation
Contact: Peter Unger, President
E-mail: punger@a2la.org
Ed: Teresa Barnett, Editor. **Released:** 4/year. **Price:** Free. **Description:** Updates the latest accreditation actions. Provides information on improving the quality of test data.

14279 ■ *AAB Bulletin*
Pub: American Association of Bioanalysts
Ed: Mark S. Birenbaum, Ph.D., Editor. **Released:** Quarterly. **Price:** Included in membership. **Description:** Addresses legislative and regulatory issues and scientific developments. Contains commentary, news from other laboratory professionals, regional activities, and continuing education programs. Recurring features include interviews, news of research, a calendar of events, reports of meetings, news of educational opportunities, and job listings.

14280 ■ *AIDS Policy and Law*
Pub: LRP Publications
Contact: Kenneth Kahn, President
E-mail: kKahn@lrp.com
Ed: Frank Baran, Editor. **Released:** Biweekly, 22/year. **Price:** $497, U.S. plus $39.50 s/h. **Description:** Reports on federal, state, and local news pertaining to the Acquired Immune Deficiency Syndrome (AIDS) virus. Discusses fair employment practices, litigation, legislation, regulation, policy guidelines, case studies, and interviews. Recurring features include news of research and summaries of state and federal legislation.

14281 ■ *AIDS Research and Human Retroviruses*
Pub: Mary Ann Liebert Inc. Publishers
URL(s): www.liebertpub.com/publication.aspx?pub_id=2. **Released:** Monthly **Price:** $872, Individuals print and online; $997, Other countries print and online; $868, Individuals online only; $4911, Institutions print and online; $5696, Institutions, other countries print and online; $4169, Institutions print only; $4920, Institutions, other countries print only; $4633, Institutions online only.

14282 ■ *Bulletin of Experimental Treatments for AIDS: Bulletin of Experimental Treatments for AIDS (BETA)*
Pub: San Francisco AIDS Foundation
URL(s): www.sfaf.org/hiv-info/hot-topics/beta/. **Ed:** Reilly O'Neal, Liz Highleyman. **Released:** Biennial **Price:** Free.

14283 ■ *Laboratory Compliance Insider*
Pub: Brownstone Publishers Inc.
Contact: John M. Striker, Publisher
Ed: Kevin Lamberson, Editor. **Released:** Monthly. **Price:** $357, individuals print; $385, individuals electronic; $437, individuals. **Description:** Features information for laboratory managers on compliance with regulatory requirements set by the federal Health Care Financing Administration (HFCA). Recurring features include ready-to-use compliance plan language, billing and coding guidelines, and model forms.

14284 ■ *Laboratory Medicine: An Official Publication of the American Society for Clinical Pathology*
Pub: American Society for Clinical Pathology
Contact: C. Bruce Alexander, President
URL(s): labmed.ascpjournals.org/. **Released:** Monthly **Price:** $95, Individuals online; $120, Individuals print and online; $120, Institutions online; $145, Institutions print and online.

14285 ■ *Laboratory Product News*
Pub: Business Information Group
Contact: Bruce Creighton, President
URL(s): www.labcanada.com. **Ed:** Leslie Burt. **Released:** 7/yr. **Price:** $66, Individuals in U.S.; $36, Canada applicable taxes; $105, Other countries.

14286 ■ *Medical Laboratory Observer (MLO)*
Pub: Nelson Publishing Inc.
URL(s): www.mlo-online.com. **Ed:** Alan Lenhoff. **Released:** Monthly **Price:** Free to qualified clinical laboratory professionals.

14287 ■ *NAACLS News*
Pub: National Accrediting Agency for Clinical Laboratory Sciences
Ed: Megan Hennessy Eggert, Editor, mheggert@juno.com. **Released:** 3/year. **Price:** Included in membership; $25, nonmembers. **Description:** Provides news of the activities of the Agency as well as issues related to laboratory scientists.

14288 ■ *Translational Research: The Journal of Laboratory and Clinical Medicine*
Pub: Mosby Inc.
Contact: Brian Nairin, President
URL(s): www.elsevier.com/wps/find/journaldescription.cws_home/623309/descrip tion#descriptionwww.translationalres.com/. **Released:** Monthly **Price:** $290, Individuals; $139, Students; $383, Other countries; $196, Students, other countries; $698, Institutions; $806, Institutions, other countries.

VIDEOCASSETTES/ AUDIOCASSETTES

14289 ■ *AIDS: The Workplace and the Law*
Phoenix Learning Group
2349 Chaffee Dr.
Saint Louis, MO 63146-3306
Ph: (314)569-0211
Free: 800-221-1274
Fax: (314)569-2834
URL: http://www.phoenixlearninggroup.com
Released: 1988. **Price:** $600.00. **Description:** Dionne Warwick, in her official capacity as U.S. Ambassador of Health, hosts this look at the deadly disease and what ordinary people can do to stop its destructive spread. **Availability:** VHS; 8 mm; 3/4 U.

14290 ■ *Laboratory Technician Training*
Williams Learning Network
15400 Calhoun Dr.
Rockville, MD 20855-2762
Fax: (301)315-6880
Co. E-mail: mait@willearn.com
URL: http://www.willearn.com
Released: 19??. **Description:** Twenty-six part laboratory technician training program that offers instruction in all areas of chemical training that provides a solid understanding of chemical fundamentals as well as of laboratory equipment and procedures. Each section comes with 10 textbooks and an instructor guide. **Availability:** VHS.

TRADE SHOWS AND CONVENTIONS

14291 ■ American Association for Laboratory Animal Science Conference & Exhibits
American Association for Laboratory Animal Science (AALAS)
9190 Crestwyn Hills Dr.
Memphis, TN 38125-8538
Ph: (901)754-8620
Fax: (901)753-0046
Co. E-mail: info@aalas.org
URL: http://www.aalas.org
Contact: Ann Tourigny Turner, Associate Director
URL(s): www.aalas.org. **Frequency:** Annual. **Audience:** Research veterinarians, medical doctors, PhDs, laboratory animal technicians, and commercial animal breeders. **Principal Exhibits:** Pharmaceuticals and laboratory animal facility equipment and supplies. **Telecommunication Services:** info@aalas.org.

14292 ■ American Medical Technologists Convention
American Medical Technologists (AMT)
10700 W Higgins Rd., Ste. 150
Rosemont, IL 60018
Ph: (847)823-5169
Free: 800-275-1268
Fax: (847)823-0458
Co. E-mail: membership@amt1.com
URL: http://www.amt1.com
Contact: Roxann Clifton, President
URL(s): www.amt1.com. **Frequency:** Annual. **Audience:** Clinical laboratory technologists and directors and medical assistants. **Principal Exhibits:** Clinical laboratory books, equipment, supplies, and services.

14293 ■ CLMA/ASCP Annual Conference and Exhibition—ThinkLab
Clinical Laboratory Management Association (CLMA)
401 N Michigan Ave., Ste. 2200
Chicago, IL 60611
Ph: (312)321-5111
Fax: (312)673-6927
Co. E-mail: info@clma.org
URL: http://www.clma.org
Contact: Rodney W. Forsman, President
URL(s): clma.org. **Frequency:** Annual. **Audience:** Directors, managers, supervisors, healthcare executives and educators responsible for laboratories and clinical systems mgmt in hospitals health systems, group. **Principal Exhibits:** Laboratory devices manufacturers, laboratory information systems, coagulation homeostasis, publishers, autoimmune disease testing, bacteriology, allergy testing, chemistry systems. **Telecommunication Services:** wmetzgar@clma.org.

14294 ■ United States and Canadian Academy of Pathology Convention & Exhibits
United States and Canadian Academy of Pathology
3643 Walton Way Ext.
Augusta, GA 30909
Ph: (706)733-7550
Fax: (706)733-8033
Co. E-mail: help@uscap.org
URL: http://www.uscap.org
Contact: Gregory N. Fuller, President
URL(s): www.uscap.org. **Frequency:** Annual. **Audience:** General pathologists, veterinary pathologists, toxicologists, pediatric pathologists, osteopathic pathologists, oncologists, and immunologists. **Principal Exhibits:** Medical equipment, laboratory supplies, and medical books. **Telecommunication Services:** nancy@uscap.org.

CONSULTANTS

14295 ■ Barry Page Consulting
1304 Buckingham Rd.
Garner, NC 27529-4706
Ph: (919)779-3037
Co. E-mail: Bioservice@compuserve.com
Contact: Barry F. Page, Owner
E-mail: bfjpage@aol.com
Scope: Provides consulting for laboratory operations, product and process troubleshooting, technical file preparation, and product submissions. Expert knowledge of domestic and international standards and requirements for risk assessment, material characterization, biological evaluation, product sterilization, sterilization residuals, and the changing regulatory requirements for medical devices. On site supervision and training for laboratory operations. **Founded:** 1993.

FRANCHISES AND BUSINESS OPPORTUNITIES

14296 ■ DNA Services of America
130 Fifth Ave., 10th Fl.
New York, NY 10011-4399
Ph: (212)242-4399
Description: Own a high-demand, innovative business that serves the growing needs of Americans by offering members of your community peace of mind through evidence provided by DNA identification test results for paternity, family relationship establishment, infidelity testing and forensic DNA. **Equity Capital Needed:** $49,175-$97,100 total investment. **Training:** Offers a complete, proven business system, ongoing support, and thorough training.

COMPUTERIZED DATABASES

14297 ■ The American Hospital Directory
4350 Brownsboro Rd., Ste. 110
Louisville, KY 40207
Fax: (502)899-7738
Co. E-mail: inbox@ahd.com
URL: http://www.ahd.com
URL(s): www.ahd.com. **Price:** Free. **Entries include:** Hospital name, address, phone, fax, characteristics, financial statistics, services, accreditation status, utilization statistics, hospital web page. **Database covers:** Comparative data on hospitals in the U.S.

14298 ■ Diagnostic Imaging Centers and Chains Directory
25 Vintinner Rd.
Campton, NH 03223
Ph: (603)726-4800
Free: 800-729-2600
Fax: (603)726-4840
Co. E-mail: info@firstmark.com
URL: http://www.firstmark.com
Contact: Michael H. Pomerantz, President
Availability: CD-ROM: F1RSTMARK Inc. **Type:** Directory.

14299 ■ Health Devices International Sourcebase
5200 Butler Pke.
Plymouth Meeting, PA 19462-1298
Ph: (610)825-6000
Fax: (610)834-1275
Co. E-mail: info@ecri.org
URL: http://www.ecri.org
Contact: Jeffrey C. Lerner, President
Availability: Online: ProQuest LLC - Dialog; German Institute of Medical Documentation and Information; ECRI Institute. **Type:** Directory.

14300 ■ KINETIDEX® System
777 E Eisenhower Pky.
Ann Arbor, MI 48108
Co. E-mail: info@truvenhealth.com
URL: http://www.truvenhealth.com
Availability: Online: Truven Health Analytics Inc. **Type:** Full-text; Numeric.

14301 ■ Smoking and Health Resource Library
4770 Buford Hwy.
MS K-50
Atlanta, GA 30341
Ph: (404)639-3311
Free: 800-331-3435
Fax: (404)232-3299
Co. E-mail: tobaccoinfo@cdc.gov
URL: http://www.cdc.gov/tobacco
Availability: Online: U.S. Centers for Disease Control and Prevention - Office on Smoking and Health. **Type:** Bibliographic.

14302 ■ State Health Care Regulatory Developments™
1801 S Bell St.
Arlington, VA 22202
Free: 800-372-1033
Co. E-mail: customercare@bna.com
URL: http://www.bna.com
Availability: Online: Bloomberg LP-Bloomberg BNA; Thomson Reuters - Westlaw. **Type:** Full-text.

LIBRARIES

14303 ■ BloodCenter of Wisconsin - Benz Oil Library
PO Box 2178
Milwaukee, WI 53201-2178
Ph: (414)937-6112
Fax: (414)937-6332
Co. E-mail: marylou.rice@bcw.edu
URL: http://www.bcw.edu
Contact: Mary L. Rice, Librarian
Scope: Hematology, immunology, cell biology, clinical medicine. **Services:** Interlibrary loan; copying; library not open to the public. **Founded:** 1952. **Holdings:** 925 books; 3400 bound periodical volumes. **Subscriptions:** 100 journals and other serials; 1 newspaper. **Telecommunication Services:** bc-info@bcw.edu.

14304 ■ Canadian Society for Medical Laboratory Science Library
33 Wellington St., N.
Hamilton, ON, Canada L8R 1M7
Ph: (905)528-8642
Free: 800-263-8277
Fax: (905)528-4968
Co. E-mail: info@csmls.org
URL: http://www.csmls.org
Contact: Lucy Agro, Coordinator
Scope: Laboratory technology, laboratory standards. **Services:** Library not open to the public. **Founded:** 1980. **Holdings:** 291 standards; 125 modules.

RESEARCH CENTERS

14305 ■ American Federation for Medical Research (AFMR)
500 Cummings Ctr., Ste. 4550
Beverly, MA 01915-6534
Ph: (978)927-8330

Fax: (978)524-8890
Co. E-mail: afmr@prri.com
URL: http://www.afmr.org
Contact: Sharma S. Prabhakar, President
Description: Provides a forum for young clinical scientists (under 43); promotes and encourages original research in clinical and laboratory medicine. Offers specialized education program; maintains information services on membership status, files, and National Abstracting Processing. Annual scientific program presents sections on: Cardiovascular; Dermatology; Endocrinology; Gastroenterology; Genetics; Hematology; Immunology and Connective Tissue; Infectious Disease; Metabolism; Neoplastic Disease; Patient Care; Pulmonary; Renal and Electrolytes. **Services:** Information assistance: on membership status, files, and national abstracting processing. **Founded:** 1940. **Publications:** Journal of Investigative Medicine (Bimonthly); Journal of Investigative Medicine (Bimonthly). **Educational Activities:** Scientific programs (Annual); Specialized education programs. **Awards:** AFMR Foundation Awards; Henry Christian Awards (Annual); Junior Physician-Investigator Awards (Annual); Outstanding Investigator Awards (Annual); Henry Christian Awards; Junior Physician-Investigator Awards; Outstanding Investigator Awards.

14306 ■ Indiana University-Purdue University at Indianapolis - Center for Alzheimer's Disease and Related Disorders
550 N University Blvd., Ste. 1710
Indianapolis, IN 46202
Ph: (317)944-4000
Free: 888-944-3627
Fax: (317)274-5873
Co. E-mail: mfarlow@iupui.edu
URL: http://www.research.iu.edu/centers/cadrnd.html
Contact: Martin R. Farlow, Director
Founded: 1983.

14307 ■ Public Health Institute (PHI)
555 12th St., 10th Fl.
Oakland, CA 94607
Ph: (510)285-5500
Fax: (510)285-5501
Co. E-mail: mpittman@phi.org
URL: http://www.phi.org
Contact: Mary A. Pittman, President
Founded: 1964. **Educational Activities:** Annual California Cancer Registries Conference (Annual). **Telecommunication Services:** communications@phi.org.

14308 ■ University of California, San Francisco - Center for AIDS Prevention Studies (CAPS)
50 Beale St., Ste. 1300
San Francisco, CA 94105
Ph: (415)597-9100
Fax: (415)597-9213
Co. E-mail: steve.morin@ucsf.edu
URL: http://www.caps.ucsf.edu
Contact: Steve Morin, Director
Founded: 1986. **Publications:** Prevention Fact Sheets. **Educational Activities:** CAPS conference (Annual). **Awards:** CAPS Postdoctoral fellowships, for two-three years of training in epidemiology and public health with emphasis on AIDS prevention research; Traineeships in AIDS Prevention Studies. **Telecommunication Services:** caps.web@ucsf.edu.

START-UP INFORMATION

14309 ■ *"Hot Market Opportunity" in Small Business Opportunities (January 2011)*
Pub: Harris Publications Inc.

Description: Mobility products for seniors give this small business a $3 million lift. Profile of 101 Mobility, the nation's first full-service sales, service and installation provider of mobility and accessibility products and equipment including stair lifts, auto lifts, ramps, porch lifts, power wheelchairs and scooters as well as other medical equipment such as walkers, hospital beds and more.

ASSOCIATIONS AND OTHER ORGANIZATIONS

14310 ■ **Advanced Medical Technology Association (AdvaMed)—AdvaMed**
701 Pennsylvania Ave. NW, Ste. 800
Washington, DC 20004-2654
Ph: (202)783-8700
Fax: (202)783-8750
Co. E-mail: info@advamed.org
URL: http://www.advamed.org
Contact: Stephen J. Ubl, President
E-mail: subl@advamed.org

Description: Represents domestic (including U.S. territories and possessions) manufacturers of medical devices, diagnostic products, and healthcare information systems. Develops programs and activities on economic, technical, medical, and scientific matters affecting the industry. Gathers and disseminates information concerning the United States and international developments in legislative, regulatory, scientific or standards-making areas. Conducts scientific and educational seminars and programs. **Founded:** 1974. **Publications:** *In Brief. . .*; *Health Industry Manufacturers Association--Directory* (Annual); *Health Industry Manufacturers Association--Directory* (Annual); *In Brief* (Monthly); *Advanced Medical Technology Association--Directory* (Monthly).

14311 ■ **American Association for Homecare (AAHomecare)**
2011 Crystal Dr., Ste. 725
Arlington, VA 22202
Ph: (703)836-6263
Fax: (703)836-6730
Co. E-mail: info@aahomecare.org
URL: http://www.aahomecare.org
Contact: Joel D. Marx, Chairman

Description: Represents all elements of home care; dedicated to advancing value and practice of quality healthcare services at home. **Founded:** 2000. **Publications:** *AAHomecare Update* (Weekly); *HME Answer Book* (Quarterly). **Awards:** Industry Achievement Awards (Annual).

REFERENCE WORKS

14312 ■ *"Beaumont Outsources Purchasing as Route to Supply Cost Savings" in Crain's*

Detroit Business (Vol. 25, June 1, 2009, No. 22)
Pub: Crain Communications Inc. - Detroit
Ed: Jay Greene. **Description:** William Beaumont Hospitals in Royal Oak have begun outsourcing the purchasing of supplies in order to cut costs. So far, Beaumont is the only hospital in southeast Michigan to outsource its purchasing department. Other hospitals employ their own purchasing supply workers.

14313 ■ *Emergency Medical Services Magazine--Buyers Guide Issue: The Journal of Emergency Care, Rescue and Transportation*
Pub: Cygnus Business Media
Contact: Rich Reiff, President
URL(s): www.emsresponder.com. **Released:** Annual; September; Latest edition 2011. **Publication includes:** Lists of about 1,000 manufacturers, suppliers, and distributors of equipment and other products used in emergency medical services; coverage includes Canada. Also covers 50 emergency medical service associations, state agencies, and meetings, workshops, and other conferences of interest. **Entries include:** For companies--Company name, address, phone, fax, toll-free, E-mail address, name of principal executive, product/service. For associations--Name, address, phone, name of director, number of members, description of membership, publications, meeting time. **Arrangement:** Alphabetical. **Indexes:** Product/service.

14314 ■ *"GeckoSystems Reduces Sensor Fusion Costs Due to Elder Care Robot Trials" in Internet Wire (December 14, 2010)*
Pub: Comtex

Description: GeckoSystems International Corporation has been able to reduce the cost of its sensor fusion system while maintaining reliability and performance. The firm's ongoing first in-home elder care robot trials have sparked interest regarding its business model, technologies available for licensing, and joint domestic and international ventures.

14315 ■ *Health Devices Sourcebook*
Pub: ECRI Institute
Contact: Jeffrey C. Lerner, President
URL(s): https://www.ecri.org/Pages/default.aspx. **Released:** Annual; Latest edition 2011. **Price:** $475, Individuals. **Covers:** Over 6,800 suppliers of patient care equipment, medical and surgical instruments, implants, clinical laboratory equipment and supplies, medical and hospital disposable supplies, and testing instruments; also lists companies that service, recondition, lease, or buy and sell used equipment; coverage includes U.S. and Canada. **Entries include:** Company name, address, phone, toll-free phone, fax, toll-free fax, URL, e-mail, total sales, names of key executives and contacts, product categories handled, trade names, methods of distribution, typical pricing, annual volume. Price of directory includes custom updates upon request. **Arrangement:** Alphabetical. **Indexes:** Product listings, manufacturers' product lines, service company profiles, product categories (by number), product

categories (alphabetic), product categories (by specialty), manufacturers addresses (geographic), trade names, equipment services, numerical listings, executive contacts, bioterrorism and emergency preparedness.

14316 ■ *"HER's: the Future is Free" in Benzinga.com (October 29, 2011)*
Pub: Benzinga.com

Ed: Benzinga Staff. **Description:** In order to create and maintain electronic health records that connects every physician and hospital it is essential to create a reliable, easy-to-use, certified Web-based ambulatory ERH using an ad-supported model. eBay seems to be the company showing the most potential for improving services to physicians and consumers, but requires sellers to pay fees based upon sales price.

14317 ■ *"Hospitals Try to Buy Smarter" in Crain's Detroit Business (Vol. 25, June 1, 2009, No. 22, pp. M025)*
Pub: Crain Communications Inc. - Detroit
Ed: Jay Greene. **Description:** Hospitals in southeast Michigan are using bulk discount purchasing of medical and non-medical supplies through group purchasing organizations in order to cut costs.

14318 ■ *Medical Device Register*
Pub: Canon Communications L.L.C.
URL(s): www.mdrweb.com/. **Released:** Annual; Latest edition 2007. **Price:** $325, Individuals; $499, Individuals online. **Covers:** More than 65,000 U.S. Manufacturers of medical devices and clinical laboratory products; includes OEM manufacturers. **Entries include:** For manufacturers--Company name, address, phone, fax, telex, names and titles of key personnel, ownership, medical product sales volume, number of employees, method of distribution, medical product subsidiaries; public company listings include annual revenues and net income. **Arrangement:** Alphabetical. **Indexes:** Product (includes suppliers names, addresses, phone numbers, prices, trade names, product specifications, and advertising), manufacturer, keyword, trade name, OEM manufacturer profile.

14319 ■ *"Mentor Medical Device Maker's Partnerships Open New Opportunities" in Crain's Cleveland Business (Vol. 30, June 22, 2009, No. 24)*
Pub: Crain Communications, Inc.
Ed: Chuck Soder. **Description:** Frantz Medical Development Ltd. develops medical devices based on ideas from outside inventors. The company wants to manufacture the innovations at its Mentor campus.

14320 ■ *"Survey: Most Approve of Donating Used Pacemakers to Medically Underserved" in Crain's Detroit Business (Vol. 25, June 1, 2009)*
Pub: Crain Communications Inc. - Detroit

Description: According to a survey conducted by University of Michigan Cardiovascular Center, 87 percent of those with pacemakers and 71 percent of the general population would donate the device to patients in underserved nations.

TRADE PERIODICALS

14321 ■ *Homecare DIRECTION*
Pub: Beacon Health Corp.
Contact: Diane J. Omdahl, Editor-in-Chief
Released: Monthly. **Price:** $337. **Description:** Delivers timely regulatory information with how-to elements to apply to everyday care delivery. Equips agency patient care personnel with knowledge they need to deliver quality care and comply with medicare certification and reimbursement requirements. Offers valuable tips on interpreting medicare rules to justify care; how to create policies that reduce survey surprises, and documentation tips and examples. Recurring features include columns titled Documenting with Impact, Survey Sense, Looking for Direction, and From the Lamp Room.

14322 ■ *The League Letter*
Pub: Center for Hearing and Communication
Contact: Laurie Hanin, Executive Director
Price: Included in membership. **Description:** Reports on news and events of the The League for the Hard of Hearing. Recurring features include a calendar of events. **Remarks:** TTY available at (917)305-7999.

14323 ■ *OrthoKinetic Review*
Pub: Novicom Inc.
URL(s): www.laspineinstitute.com/OrthoKineticReview.htm. **Released:** Bimonthly **Price:** Free to U.S. residents.

14324 ■ *Physical Therapy Products*
Pub: Novicom Inc.
URL(s): www.ptproductsonline.com/. **Ed:** Frank Long. **Released:** Monthly

14325 ■ *Surgical Products*
Pub: Advantage Business Media L.L.C.
Contact: George Fox, President
URL(s): www.surgicalproductsmag.com/scripts/default.asp. **Ed:** Jon Minnick. **Released:** 10/yr. **Price:** Free.

TRADE SHOWS AND CONVENTIONS

14326 ■ American Academy of Implant Dentistry Annual Meeting
American Academy of Implant Dentistry (AAID)
211 E Chicago Ave., Ste. 750
Chicago, IL 60611
Ph: (312)335-1550
Free: 877-335-2243
Fax: (312)335-9090
Co. E-mail: info@aaid.com
URL: http://www.aaid-implant.org
Contact: Sharon Bennett, Executive Director
URL(s): www.aaid-implant.org/education/Annual_Meeting.html. **Price:** $75, for student; $945, for general member; $995, Non-members; $150, for life member. **Frequency:** Annual. **Audience:** Dentists. **Principal Exhibits:** Dental equipment, supplies, and services. **Telecommunication Services:** aaid@aaid-implant.org.

14327 ■ Chicagoland
Advanstar Communications
641 Lexington Ave., 8th Fl.
New York, NY 10022
Ph: (212)951-6600
Free: 800-346-0085
Fax: (212)951-6793
Co. E-mail: info@advantstar.com
URL: http://www.advanstar.com
Contact: Robert Krakoff, President
URL(s): www.abilitiesexpo.com. **Audience:** Disabled consumers, seniors, rehab and healthcare professionals, hospital personnel, special educators, dealers and representatives. **Principal Exhibits:** Wheelchairs, assistive technology, personal care products, support organizations, and daily living aids.

14328 ■ North Carolina Medical Society Annual Meeting
North Carolina Medical Society
PO Box 27167
Raleigh, NC 27611
Ph: (919)833-3836
Free: 800-722-1350
Fax: (919)833-2023
URL: http://www.ncmedsoc.org
Contact: Robert W. Seligson
E-mail: rseligson@ncmedsoc.org
URL(s): www.ncderm.org. **Frequency:** Annual. **Audience:** Physicians. **Principal Exhibits:** Medical equipment, supplies, and services. **Dates and Locations:** , Charlotte Marriott City Center. **Telecommunication Services:** nlowe@ncmedsoc.org.

14329 ■ Southern Medical Association Annual Scientific Assembly
Southern Medical Association
35 Lakeshore Dr.
Birmingham, AL 35209
Ph: (205)945-1840
Free: 800-423-4992
Fax: (205)945-1548
URL: http://www.sma.org
URL(s): www.sma.org. **Price:** $695, physician; $100, Members; $125, Non-members. **Frequency:** Annual. **Audience:** Doctors, students, residents, and related professionals. **Principal Exhibits:** Medical equipment and pharmaceutical products. **Telecommunication Services:** mstone@sma.org.

CONSULTANTS

14330 ■ Harry Schwartz & Associates
100 E Hartsdale Ave.
Hartsdale, NY 10530
Ph: (914)725-1642
Fax: (914)725-1134
Contact: Harry Schwartz, President
Scope: Provider of public relations and marketing assistance to many entities in the healthcare field, including physician groups, hospitals, manufacturers and sellers of pharmaceuticals and hospital supplies. **Founded:** 1979. **Publications:** "Scrip Pharmaceutical Executive"; "Physician's Management".

FRANCHISES AND BUSINESS OPPORTUNITIES

14331 ■ Relax the Back Corp.
6 Centerpoint Dr.
La Palma, CA 90623
Ph: (714)523-2980
Free: 800-222-5728
Fax: (714)523-2980
Co. E-mail: franchise@relaxtheback.com
URL: http://www.relaxtheback.com
Description: Ergonomic and back care retailers. **No. of Franchise Units:** 97. **Founded:** 1984. **Franchised:** 1989. **Equity Capital Needed:** $221,000-$371,200 total investment; $500,000 net worth; $100,000 liquid. **Franchise Fee:** $49,500. **Royalty Fee:** 2-5%. **Financial Assistance:** Third party financing available. **Training:** Provides 14 days training at headquarters, 4 days at franchisee's location, 2 days of regional training and ongoing support.

14332 ■ Sona MedSpa
Sona MedSpa Intl., Inc.
10710 Sikes Pl., Ste. 120
Charlotte, NC 28277
Ph: (615)591-5040
Fax: (615)591-5041
Co. E-mail: info@sonamedspa.com
URL: http://www.sonamedspa.com
Description: Sona offers FDA approved laser hair removal & skin rejuvenation treatments performed by trained, certified medical personnel. We provide safe, effective treatments using the most advanced technology equipment & technologies. **No. of Franchise Units:** 40. **No. of Company-Owned Units:** 5. **Founded:** 1997.. **Franchised:** 2002. **Equity Capital Needed:** $409,200-$824,900. **Franchise Fee:** $59,500. **Royalty Fee:** 7.5%. **Training:** Provides 14 days training at headquarters, 6 days at franchisee's location, regional training, web-based training, monthly webcasts and ongoing support.

COMPUTERIZED DATABASES

14333 ■ *The American Hospital Directory*
4350 Brownsboro Rd., Ste. 110
Louisville, KY 40207
Fax: (502)899-7738
Co. E-mail: inbox@ahd.com
URL: http://www.ahd.com
URL(s): www.ahd.com. **Price:** Free. **Entries include:** Hospital name, address, phone, fax, characteristics, financial statistics, services, accreditation status, utilization statistics, hospital web page. **Database covers:** Comparative data on hospitals in the U.S.

14334 ■ *Health Devices® Alerts*
5200 Butler Pke.
Plymouth Meeting, PA 19462-1298
Ph: (610)825-6000
Fax: (610)834-1275
Co. E-mail: info@ecri.org
URL: http://www.ecri.org
Contact: Jeffrey C. Lerner, President
Availability: Online: ProQuest LLC - Dialog; German Institute of Medical Documentation and Information; ECRI Institute. **Type:** Bibliographic; Full-text.

14335 ■ *Health Devices International Sourcebase*
5200 Butler Pke.
Plymouth Meeting, PA 19462-1298
Ph: (610)825-6000
Fax: (610)834-1275
Co. E-mail: info@ecri.org
URL: http://www.ecri.org
Contact: Jeffrey C. Lerner, President
Availability: Online: ProQuest LLC - Dialog; German Institute of Medical Documentation and Information; ECRI Institute. **Type:** Directory.

14336 ■ *Medical Device Register (MDR)*
11444 W Olympic Blvd.
Los Angeles, CA 90064
Ph: (310)445-4200
Fax: (310)445-4299
Co. E-mail: info@ubm.com
URL: http://www.ubmcanon.com
Availability: Online: UBM plc - UBM Canon. CD-ROM: UBM plc - UBM Canon. **Type:** Directory.

LIBRARIES

14337 ■ Association of Tongue Depressors - Library
c/o Matthew Schorr
100 E. Maple St.
Teaneck, NJ 07666
Ph: (201)387-6969
Fax: (201)387-6969
Contact: Matthew Schorr, Secretary
Scope: Health care, medical products, marketing. **Founded:** 1978. **Holdings:** 280 volumes.

14338 ■ BayerDiag, a Bayer Company Library
63 North St.
Medfield, MA 02052
Ph: (508)359-3538
Fax: (508)359-3442
Co. E-mail: kathleen.mccabe.b@bayer.com
URL: http://www.bayerdiag.com/
Contact: Kathleen E. McCabe, Manager, Info Systems
Scope: Clinical medicine, market research, engineering, biotechnology, business. **Services:** Center not open to the public. **Founded:** 1978. **Holdings:** 3000 books; 3500 periodical volumes; 28,000 patents; 850 research reports. **Subscriptions:** 425 journals and other serials.

14339 ■ ECRI Institute Library—Emergency Care Research Institute.
5200 Butler Pike
Plymouth Meeting, PA 19462
Ph: (610)825-6000

Fax: (610)834-1275
Co. E-mail: info@ecri.org
URL: http://www.ecri.org
Contact: Evelyn Kuserk, Supervisor
Scope: Medical devices, biomedical engineering, hospital safety, health services research, health technology assessment. **Services:** Interlibrary loan; Library not open to the public. **Founded:** 1969. **Holdings:** 11,000 books; 470 VF drawers of technical reports and evaluation data. **Subscriptions:** 2000 journals and other serials.

14340 ■ Harvard University - School of Medicine - The Libraries of the Massachusetts Eye and Ear Infirmary
243 Charles St.
Boston, MA 02114

Ph: (617)573-3196
Fax: (617)573-3370
Co. E-mail: judith_nims@meei.harvard.edu
URL: http://www.masseyeandear.org/about-us/ library-resources/
Contact: Chris Nims, Director, Library Services
Scope: Ophthalmology, otolaryngology. **Services:** Interlibrary loan; copying; Library blog; Library open to the public for reference use only. **Founded:** 1828. **Holdings:** 7000 volumes; 11,000 bound periodical volumes; 300 stereophotographs of diseases of the eye; 130 cubic feet of archival materials; 40 cubic feet of manuscripts; 2000 rare books. **Subscriptions:** 130 journals and other serials.

14341 ■ U.S. Food & Drug Administration - Center for Devices & Radiological Health

Library HFZ-46
10903 New Hampshire Ave.
Silver Spring, MD 20993
Ph: (301)796-7100
Free: 800-638-2041
Fax: (301)847-8149
Co. E-mail: dsmica@fda.hhs.gov
URL: http://www.fda.gov/MedicalDevices/default.htm
Contact: Harriet Albersheim, Librarian
Scope: Medical devices, artificial organs, biomedical engineering, biomaterials, radiology, radiobiology, radiation, nuclear medicine, radiological health, radiation protection, radiation hazards, emission, microwaves, ultrasonics, lasers. **Services:** Interlibrary loan; Library open to the public for reference use only. **Founded:** 1976. **Holdings:** 7000 books; periodical titles (bound and microfilm). **Subscriptions:** 700 journals and other serials.

ASSOCIATIONS AND OTHER ORGANIZATIONS

14342 ■ Association for Healthcare Documentation Integrity (AHDI)—AHDI
4230 Kiernan Ave., Ste. 130
Modesto, CA 95356
Ph: (209)527-9620
Free: 800-982-2182
Fax: (209)527-9633
Co. E-mail: ahdi@ahdionline.org
URL: http://www.ahdionline.org
Contact: Barb Marques, President
Description: Medical transcriptionists, their supervisors, teachers and students of medical transcription, owners and managers of medical transcription services, and other interested health personnel. Provides information about the profession of medical transcription and gives continuing education for medical transcriptionists. Advocates professional recognition of medical transcriptionists in county, state, and national medical societies and in health care facilities nationwide. Sponsors voluntary certification/ credentialing program. Offers updates on developments in medicine and curricula, and on new transcription methods and equipment; sponsors and encourages research in the field. Establishes guidelines for education of medical transcriptionists. **Founded:** 1978. **Publications:** *Health Data Matrix* (Bimonthly); *Vitals* (Weekly); *Health Data Matrix* (Bimonthly). **Educational Activities:** Association for Healthcare Documentation Integrity Annual Meeting (Annual). **Awards:** Chapter of the Year (Annual); CMT Key Award (Annual); Employer of the Year (Annual); Practitioner of the Year (Annual); State/Regional Association of the Year (Annual); The Marilyn Craddock Student of the Year (Annual).

REFERENCE WORKS

14343 ■ *"Help Wanted: 100 Hospitals IT Workers"* in Business Courier (Vol. 27, *October 8, 2010, No. 23, pp. 1)*
Pub: Business Courier
Ed: James Ritchie. **Description:** Hospitals in the Greater Cincinnati area are expected to hire more than 100 information technology (IT) workers to help digitize medical records. Financial incentives from the health care reform bill encouraged investments in electronic medical record systems, increasing the demand for IT workers that would help make information exchange across the healthcare system easier.

**14344 ■ *"Providers Ride First Wave of eHealth Dollars"* in Boston Business Journal (Vol. 31, June 10, 2011, No. 20, pp. 1)*
Pub: Boston Business Journal
Ed: Julie M. Donnelly. **Description:** Health care providers in Massachusetts implementing electronic medical records technology started receiving federal stimulus funds. Beth Israel Deaconess Medical Center was the first hospital to qualify for the funds.

LIBRARIES

14345 ■ American Health Information Management Association - FORE Library
233 N. Michigan Ave., 21st Fl.
Chicago, IL 60601
Ph: (312)233-1803
Fax: (312)253-7060
Co. E-mail: library.services@ahima.org
URL: http://www.ahimafoundation.org/PolicyResearch/LibraryServices.aspx
Contact: Nadine Caputo, Director, Research and Development
Scope: Medical records; codes and coding - classification of disease. **Services:** Document delivery; library not open to the public. **Founded:** 1965. **Holdings:** 1100 books. **Subscriptions:** 130 journals and other serials. **Telecommunication Services:** info@ahimafoundation.org.

14346 ■ Davenport University - Thomas F. Reed, Jr. Memorial Library
4123 W. Main St.
Kalamazoo, MI 49006
Ph: (616)382-2835
Free: 800-632-8928
Fax: (269)382-2657
Co. E-mail: kz_library@davenport.edu
URL: http://www.davenport.edu/
Contact: Judith J. Bosshart, Director
Scope: Business, data processing, administrative services, accounting, humanities, paralegal, medical records, healthcare administration, computer and information processing. **Services:** Interlibrary loan; copying; faxing; library open to the public for reference use only. **Founded:** 1981. **Holdings:** 14,200 books; 995 videotapes. **Subscriptions:** 12,000 journals and other serials; 6 newspapers. **Telecommunication Services:** judy.bosshart@davenport.edu; Library@Davenport.edu.

14347 ■ Florida A&M University - Frederick S. Humphries Science Research Center Library
401-501 Science Research Center
309 Pershing St.
Tallahassee, FL 32307
Ph: (850)599-3393
Fax: (850)599-3422
URL: http://www.famu.edu/index.cfm?a=library&p=ScienceResearch
Scope: Pharmacy, allied health, physics, computer science, environmental science, respiratory therapy, physical therapy, healthcare management, medical records administration, occupational therapy. **Services:** Interlibrary loan; copying; SDI; Library open to the public. **Founded:** 1957. **Holdings:** 5989 bound periodical volumes; 915 print and online journals; 791 microcards; 24,102 monographs. **Subscriptions:** 697 journals and other serials; 5 newspapers.

START-UP INFORMATION

14348 ■ *"Courier Service Delivers Big Profits and Top-Notch Customer Service" in Small Business Opportunities (November 2007)*
Pub: Harris Publications Inc.
Description: Profile of Relay Express, a courier franchising business started by three friends in 1986. The company focuses on customer service and calls them every 19 minutes to report on progress of a parcel until it is delivered.

ASSOCIATIONS AND OTHER ORGANIZATIONS

14349 ■ **Canadian Courier and Logistics Association (CCLA)—Association Canadienne des Enterprises de Messagerie**
660 Eglinton Ave. E, Unit 119, Box 333
Toronto, ON, Canada M4G 3K2
Ph: (416)696-9995
Free: 877-766-6604
Fax: (416)696-9993
Co. E-mail: dturnbull@canadiancourier.org
URL: http://canadiancourier.org
Contact: David Turnbull, President
Description: Courier services and shipping and delivery companies. Promotes growth and development of the shipping and delivery industries. Facilitates communication and cooperation among members; represents members' interests before trade and labor organizations, government agencies, and the public. **Founded:** 1986. **Publications:** *E-News* (Bimonthly). **Awards:** Courier Executive of the Year.

14350 ■ *E-News*
660 Eglinton Ave. E, Unit 119, Box 333
Toronto, ON, Canada M4G 3K2
Ph: (416)696-9995
Free: 877-766-6604
Fax: (416)696-9993
Co. E-mail: dturnbull@canadiancourier.org
URL: http://canadiancourier.org
Contact: David Turnbull, President
Released: Bimonthly **Price:** free for members.

14351 ■ **Messenger Courier Association of America (MCAA)**
750 National Press Bldg.
Washington, DC 20045
Ph: (202)591-2460
Fax: (202)223-9741
Co. E-mail: info@mcaa.com
URL: http://www.mcaa.com
Contact: Bob DeCaprio, Executive Director
Description: Trade organization of local and international messenger courier companies. Addresses issues facing the industry, including municipal traffic ordinances that impede industry operations. Works to establish driver pools and to develop centralized core computer service bureaus for smaller courier companies. Provides training, discount purchasing programs, and legislative and regulatory issue monitoring. Conducts educational and research programs; compiles statistics. **Founded:** 1987. **Publications:** *Who's Who in the Messenger Courier Industry* (Annual); *Messenger Courier Association of America--Network Guide and Membership Directory* (Annual). **Telecommunication Services:** bdecaprio@mcaa.com.

14352 ■ **National Association of Professional Process Servers**
PO Box 4547
Portland, OR 97208-4547
Ph: (503)222-4180
Free: 800-477-8211
Fax: (503)222-3950
Co. E-mail: administrator@napps.org
URL: http://www.napps.org
Contact: Lawrence Yellon, President
Description: Individuals and companies who serve summonses, complaints, subpoenas, and other legal documents. Goals are to: promote and upgrade the process-serving industry; establish high moral and ethical standards for the industry; monitor legislation at the state and federal level; assist in the formation and continuation of state associations representing the industry. Seeks to improve relations between process servers and members of the legal community such as attorneys, judges, clerks, and court officers. Assists with service of process in foreign countries through the Hague Service Convention; makes discount insurance programs available to members. **Scope:** laws and procedures pertaining to service of process, general material on process serving, process serving. **Subscriptions:** archival material articles audio recordings periodicals. **Publications:** *The Docket Sheet* (Bimonthly); *NAPPS Membership Directory* (Semiannual); *Membership Directory and Civil Rules Guide* (Semiannual); *NAPPS Annual Seminar Conferences.* **Awards:** Donald C. MacDonald Award (Annual).

REFERENCE WORKS

14353 ■ *The Concierge Manual: A Step-by-Step Guide to Starting Your Own Concierge Service or Lifestyle Management Company*
Pub: New Road Publishing
Ed: Katharine C. Giovanni. **Released:** September 9, 2010. **Price:** $23.00. **Description:** Answering some of the biggest questions about the logistics of running a concierge business, this guide provides all the tools necessary to create a successful concierge, lifestyle management, errand service, or personal assistant company.

14354 ■ *"Pocket Change?' in Inc. (Vol. 30, December 2008, No. 12, pp. 28)*
Pub: Mansueto Ventures LLC
Ed: Ryan McCarthy. **Description:** Owner of a chain of nine retail billiard showrooms grew his business by starting to deliver pool tables for Sears. The company, consisting of seven retail locations and two warehouses, is now for sale. Details are included.

FRANCHISES AND BUSINESS OPPORTUNITIES

14355 ■ **AIM Mail Centers**
Amailcenter Franchise Corp.
15550-D Rockfield Blvd.
Irvine, CA 92618
Ph: (949)837-4145
Free: 800-669-4246
Fax: (949)837-4537
Description: Business service center. **No. of Franchise Units:** 58. **Founded:** 1985.. **Franchised:** 1989. **Equity Capital Needed:** $138,800-$199,050l. **Franchise Fee:** $29,950. **Royalty Fee:** 5%. **Training:** Provides 10 days training at headquarters, 3 days at franchisees location, regional meetings, annual convention, and ongoing support.

14356 ■ **Fastway Couriers (Vancouver, Canada)**
1687 West Broadway Ste. 300
Vancouver, BC, Canada V6J 1X2
Ph: (604)739-2520
Free: 877-739-2520
Fax: (604)739-2560
Co. E-mail: info@fastway.ca
URL: http://www.fastway.ca
Description: Sole Regional Franchise rights for each city are awarded to only one entrepreneur who enters the business of franchising, not package distribution. Cities are then divided into territories which are awarded to Courier Franchisees who conduct the actual distribution of packages. **Founded:** 1983.. **Franchised:** 1984. **Equity Capital Needed:** Regional $200,000-$700,000; Courier $8,000 van.

14357 ■ **Parcel Plus**
International Center For Entrepreneurial Development
12715 Telge Rd.
Cypress, TX 77429
Free: 888-280-2053
Fax: (281)256-4178
Co. E-mail: ppsales@iced.net
URL: http://www.parcelplus.com
Description: Offer packaging, freight, cargo, crating and international shipping in a retail setting. **No. of Franchise Units:** 56. **No. of Company-Owned Units:** 1. **Founded:** 1986.. **Franchised:** 1988. **Equity Capital Needed:** $45,000 minimum. **Franchise Fee:** $35,000. **Financial Assistance:** Yes. **Training:** Owners attend 4 days classroom training and visit existing locations.

ASSOCIATIONS AND OTHER ORGANIZATIONS

14358 ■ National Golf Foundation (NGF)
1150 S US Hwy. 1, Ste. 401
Jupiter, FL 33477
Ph: (561)744-6006
Free: 888-275-4643
Fax: (561)744-6107
Co. E-mail: general@ngf.org
URL: http://www.ngf.org
Contact: Joseph F. Beditz, President
E-mail: jbeditz@ngf.org
Description: Golf-oriented businesses including: equipment and apparel companies; golf facilities; golf publications; golf course architects, developers and builders; companies offering specialized services to the golf industry; golf associations; teachers, coaches and instructors and other interested individuals. Serves as a market research and strategic planning organization for the golf industry and promotes public golf course development in the U.S. Provides information and consulting services for golf course planning, construction, and operation. Conducts golf course development and operations seminars including the National Institute of Golf Management. **Founded:** 1936. **Publications:** *NGF Membership Directory* (Quarterly); *The NGF's Golf Course Directory*; *The NGF's Media Directory*; *Golf Industry Report* (Quarterly); *Golf Industry Report* (Bimonthly); *Golf Course Directory*; *The NGF's Directory of Golf Retailers: Off-Course Golf Retail Stores in the U.S.*; *The NGF's Executive and Par-3 Golf Course Directory: A Viable Enterprise*; *The NGF's Golf Course Directory and Range Directory*; *The NGF's Golf Practice Range and Learning Center Directory*; *Directory of Golf: The People and Businesses in Golf* (Annual); *Golf Facilities in the U.S.* (Annual). **Educational Activities:** Golf course management schools. **Awards:** Graffis Award. **Telecommunication Services:** ngf@ngf.org; research@ngf.org.

14359 ■ Professional Putters Association (PPA)
8105 Timberlake Rd.
Lynchburg, VA 24502-2607

Ph: (434)237-7888
Co. E-mail: joe@proputters.com
URL: http://www.proputters.com
Contact: Joe Aboid, Commissioner
Description: Persons over age 18 who compete in national putting tournaments sanctioned by the Association; "Putt Putt" golf course franchise owners, managers, and suppliers. Seeks to recognize, develop, and reward the skills and abilities of America's putters. Sponsors competitions; compiles statistics; presents awards national, regional and local titles and cash prizes. Produces Putt-Putt Golf Courses Championship currently airing on ESPN Series, a television sports show of three half-hour segments. **Founded:** 1959. **Publications:** *Putt Putt World* (Biennial). **Awards:** PPA Hall of Fame Award (Annual); Sportsman of the Year (Annual).

14360 ■ United States Golf Association (USGA)
PO Box 708
Far Hills, NJ 07931
Ph: (908)234-2300
Free: 800-223-0041
Fax: (908)234-9687
Co. E-mail: membership@usga.org
URL: http://www.usga.org
Contact: James F. Vernon, President
Description: Regularly organized golf clubs and golf courses. Serves as governing body for golf in the United States. Turfgrass Visiting Service promotes scientific work in turf management. Provides data on rules, handicapping, amateur status, tournament procedure, turf maintenance, and golf balls and implements. Administers Golf House Museum, a collection of memorabilia including clubs of champions, the Moon Club, and paintings, insignia, and portraits of USGA champions. Sponsors USGA Research and Educational Fund. Conducts 13 annual national championships and research programs; sponsors teams for international competitions. **Founded:** 1894. **Publications:** *Golf Journal* (9/year); *Golf Journal: Official Publication of the United States Golf Association.* **Awards:** United States Golf Association Fellowship Program; United States Golf Association Scholarship Program; Curtis Cup; Green Section Award; Bob Jones Award; Walker Cup; Joe Dey Award; U.S. Women's Open; U.S. Senior Open; U.S. Amateur Championship; Bob Jones Award; Golf House Book Award; USGA Green Selection Award; U.S. Women's Amateur Championship.

TRADE SHOWS AND CONVENTIONS

14361 ■ FUN Expo
Reed Exhibitions North American Headquarters
383 Main Ave.
Norwalk, CT 06851
Ph: (203)840-4800
Fax: (203)840-5805
Co. E-mail: inquiry@reedexpo.com
URL: http://www.reedexpo.com
URL(s): www.funexpo.com. **Price:** $20, Pre-registered, members; $40, Pre-registered, non-members; $65, Onsite registered, members; $90, Onsite registered, non-members. **Frequency:** Annual. **Principal Exhibits:** Amusement and recreation products for family and location based entertainment centers, small amusement parks and family oriented businesses such as bowling centers, skating rinks, sports parks, miniature golf courses, golf driving ranges, family restaurants, resorts and other entertainment/recreation businesses.

FRANCHISES AND BUSINESS OPPORTUNITIES

14362 ■ Monster Mini Golf
Monster Entertainment
Description: Family entertainment center featuring glow-in-the-dark mini golf. **No. of Franchise Units:** 23. **No. of Company-Owned Units:** 1. **Founded:** 2004.. **Franchised:** 2005. **Equity Capital Needed:** $431,000-$520,000. **Franchise Fee:** $30,000. **Royalty Fee:** 7%. **Financial Assistance:** Third party financing available. **Training:** Offers 2-4 weeks at headquarters, 2 weeks onsite with ongoing support.

DIRECTORIES OF EDUCATIONAL PROGRAMS

14363 ■ *Directory of Private Accredited Career Schools and Colleges of Technology*
Pub: Accrediting Commission of Career Schools and Colleges of Technology
Contact: Michale S. McComis, Executive Director
Released: On web page. **Price:** Free. **Description:** Covers 3900 accredited post-secondary programs that provide training programs in business, trade, and technical fields, including various small business endeavors. Entries offer school name, address, phone, description of courses, job placement assistance, and requirements for admission. Arrangement is alphabetical.

REFERENCE WORKS

14364 ■ *"A Digital Makeover for the Modeling Business" in Inc. (February 2008, pp. 82-86, 88-89)*
Pub: Gruner & Jahr USA Publishing
Ed: David H. Freedman. **Description:** Ways the Ford Modeling Agency is using the online You Tube to realign its business are presented. Products to help a firm grow its presence on the Internet are included.

14365 ■ *"Fashionistas Weigh in on the Super-Thin" in Charlotte Observer (February 7, 2007)*
Pub: Knight-Ridder/Tribune Business News
Ed: Crystal Dempsey. **Description:** Council of Fashion Designers of America held a panel discussion regarding the weight and ages of models used to highlight clothing.

VIDEOCASSETTES/ AUDIOCASSETTES

14366 ■ *Modeling, Commercials, & Acting*
Educational Video Network
1401 19th St.
Huntsville, TX 77340
Ph: (936)295-5767
Free: 800-762-0060
Fax: (936)294-0233
URL: http://www.evndirect.com
Released: 19??. **Price:** $49.95. **Description:** Features interviews from TV stars, models, and Hollywood agents who offer advice on how to get started in acting and modeling, including tips on photo preparation, resume writing, and agents. **Availability:** VHS.

14367 ■ *Modeling Made Easy*
Videoactive Co.
2522 Hyperion Ave.
Los Angeles, CA 90027-3317
Ph: (323)669-8544
Free: 800-927-2949
Co. E-mail: bill@videoactive.com
URL: http://www.videoactive.com
Released: 19??. **Description:** In-depth instructional video on modeling techniques, including runway techniques for both men and women, breaking into modeling, the different types of modeling, and tips on the fashion show. Features Jill Donnellan, model, actress, and former Miss Bermuda. **Availability:** VHS.

START-UP INFORMATION

14368 ■ *Foreclosure Cleanout Business: High Profits — Low Start Up Cost*
Pub: James R. Tolliver

Ed: James Tolliver. **Released:** October 11, 2011. **Price:** $17.99. **Description:** Foreclosure cleanout business is booming. This manual teaches how to start a foreclosure firm, who to contact, what to charge, services provided and more.

ASSOCIATIONS AND OTHER ORGANIZATIONS

14369 ■ **Council of Real Estate Brokerage Managers (CRB)**
430 N Michigan Ave.
Chicago, IL 60611-4011
Ph: (312)321-4414
Free: 800-621-8738
Fax: (312)329-8882
Co. E-mail: info@crb.com
URL: http://www.crb.com
Contact: Matthew Ferrara, Chief Executive Officer

Description: Represents managers, brokers and owners, serving nearly 7,000 members through superior educational programming, products and publications. Exemplifies professional achievement and recognition in real estate brokerage management. Bestows CRB (Certified Real Estate Brokerage Manager) designation on members who have completed courses conducted by REBMC. **Founded:** 1968. **Publications:** *e-Connections Newsletter* (Monthly); *Real Estate Business Magazine* (Bimonthly). **Awards:** Hall of Leaders Award (Annual).

14370 ■ **Mortgage Bankers Association (MBA)**
1717 Rhode Island Ave. NW, Ste. 400
Washington, DC 20036
Ph: (202)557-2700
Free: 800-793-6222
Co. E-mail: membership@mortgagebankers.org
URL: http://www.mortgagebankers.org
Contact: Michael W. Young, Chairman

Description: Principal lending and investor interests in the mortgage finance field, including mortgage banking firms, commercial banks, life insurance companies, title companies, and savings and loan associations. Seeks to improve methods of originating, servicing, and marketing loans of residential and income-producing properties through industry education and cooperation with federal agencies and the Congress. Holds clinics on all aspects of the mortgage finance business. Sponsors School of Mortgage Banking, and correspondence courses and web-based training on mortgage subjects for member personnel. Collects statistics and conducts research on the industry. **Scope:** commercial and residential finance. **Founded:** 1914. **Subscriptions:** 6500 periodicals. **Publications:** *Mortgage Bankers Performance Study* (Quarterly); *National Delinquency Survey* (Quarterly); *Mortgage Banking: The Magazine of Real Estate Finance* (Monthly). **Awards:** FW Thompson Award (Annual).

14371 ■ **Mortgage Insurance Companies of America (MICA)**
727 15th St. NW, Ste. 1200, 12th Fl.
Washington, DC 20005
Ph: (202)682-2683
Fax: (202)842-9252
Co. E-mail: info@privatemi.com
URL: http://www.micanews.com
Contact: Jeff Lubar, Director
E-mail: jeff@micadc.org
URL(s): www.privatemi.com. **Description:** U.S. and Australian mortgage insurance companies united to provide a forum for discussion of industrywide standards, and for representation before Congress and federal and state regulatory agencies that reviews housing-related legislation. Compiles statistics. **Founded:** 1973. **Publications:** *PrivateMI Perspective* (Quarterly); *MICA Fact Book and Membership Directory* (Annual).

14372 ■ **National Association of Mortgage Brokers (NAMB)**
7900 Westpark Dr., Ste. T309
McLean, VA 22102
Ph: (703)342-5900
Fax: (317)575-4360
Co. E-mail: dfrommeyer@amtrust.net
URL: http://www.namb.org
Contact: Donald J. Frommeyer, President

Description: Mortgage brokers seeking to increase professionalism and to foster business relationships among members. Offers three levels of professional certification. Focuses on education and government affairs. **Founded:** 1973. **Publications:** *NAMB Certification Applicant Handbooks*. **Awards:** Broker of the Year (Annual).

14373 ■ **National Association of Professional Mortgage Women (NAPMW)**
PO Box 451718
Garland, TX 75045
Free: 800-827-3034
Fax: (469)524-5121
Co. E-mail: napmw1@aol.com
URL: http://www.napmw.org
Contact: Candace M. Smith, President

Description: Supports professional and personal development for individuals in the mortgage lending industry. Aims to maintain high standards of professional conduct and to encourage the educational advancement of women in the industry. Believes in equal recognition and professional opportunities for women. Offers professional designations through the Institute of Mortgage Lending. **Founded:** 1964. **Educational Activities:** National Association of Professional Mortgage Women Annual Convention (Annual).

14374 ■ **National Association of Real Estate Brokers (NAREB)**
9831 Greenbelt Rd.
Lanham, MD 20706
Ph: (301)552-9340
Fax: (301)552-9216
Co. E-mail: julius.cartwright@nareb.com
URL: http://www.nareb.com
Contact: Julius L. Cartwright, President
Description: Members of the real estate industry. Research, educational and certification programs include: Real Estate Management Brokers Institute; National Society of Real Estate Appraisers; Real Estate Brokerage Institute; United Developers Council. Encourages unity among those who are engaged in real estate. Promotes and maintains high standards of conduct. Protects the public against unethical, improper, or fraudulent practices connected with the real estate business. Conducts research; compiles statistics on productivity, marketing and development. Gives members license to use "Realtist" symbol. Sponsors educational seminars. Maintains Willis E. Carson Library. **Founded:** 1947. **Publications:** *Realtist Membership Directory* (Annual). **Awards:** Realtist of the Year (Annual).

14375 ■ **National Association of Review Appraisers and Mortgage Underwriters (NARA/MU)**
810 N Farrell Dr.
Palm Springs, CA 92262
Ph: (760)327-5284
Fax: (760)327-5631
Co. E-mail: support@assoc-hdqts.org
URL: http://www.naramu.org
Contact: Dr. Bill Merrell, Advisor
Description: Real estate professionals and mortgage underwriters who aid in determining value of property. Acts as umbrella group for real estate appraisers. Conducts educational seminars; maintains speakers' bureau; operates placement service. **Founded:** 1975.

REFERENCE WORKS

14376 ■ *"The 35 Year Mortgage-Built to Last Time" in Globe & Mail (March 17, 2006, pp. B1)*
Pub: CTVglobemedia Publishing Inc.

Ed: Patrick Brethour. **Description:** The 35-year mortgage has arrived in Canada. The plan will give an opportunity to the first-time buyers into the real estate market. Details of the new mortgage are analyzed.

14377 ■ *"AIG Fixed; Is Michigan Next?" in Crain's Detroit Business (Vol. 24, September 22, 2008, No. 38, pp. 1)*
Pub: Crain Communications Inc.

Ed: Jay Greene. **Description:** Michigan's economic future is examined as is the mortgage buyout plan and American International Group Inc.'s takeover by the U.S. government.

14378 ■ *"All Bubbles Must Burst" in Canadian Business (Vol. 83, August 17, 2010, No. 13-14, pp. 12)*
Pub: Rogers Media Ltd.

Ed: Matthew McClearn. **Description:** Canada's housing markets is showing signs of cooling down as home and condo sales both fell for the first time in 16 years. The Canadian government has fueled the market over an extended period through Canada Mortgage and Housing Corporation's role in insuring mortgage lenders against risk of defaults.

14379 ■ *"Antwerpen Takes on Chrysler Financial Over Foreclosure Sales"* in *Baltimore Business Journal (Vol. 28, July 30, 2010, No. 12, pp. 1)*
Pub: Baltimore Business Journal
Ed: Gary Haber. **Description:** Antwerpen Motorcars Ltd. aims to fight the scheduled foreclosure sale of real estate it leases in Baltimore County, including the showroom for its Hyundai dealership on Baltimore National Pike in Catonsville, Maryland. The company is planning to file papers in court to stop the scheduled August 11, 2010 auction sought by Chrysler Financial Services Americas LLC.

14380 ■ *"Apartment Market Down, Not Out"* in *Crain's Detroit Business (Vol. 24, October 6, 2008, No. 40, pp. 9)*
Pub: Crain Communications, Inc.
Ed: Daniel Duggan. **Description:** Detroit's apartment market is considered to have some of the strongest fundamentals of any apartment market in the country with relatively low vacancy rates and a relatively low supply of new units compared with demand. Investors continue to show interest in the buildings but the national lending market is making it difficult to invest in the city.

14381 ■ *"Asia Breathes a Sigh of Relief"* in *Business Week (September 22, 2008, No. 4100, pp. 32)*
Pub: McGraw-Hill Companies, Inc.
Ed: Bruce Einhorn; Theo Francis; Chi-Chu Tschang; Moon Ihlwan; Hiroko Tashiro. **Description:** Foreign bankers, such as those in Asia, that had been investing heavily in the United States began to worry as the housing crisis deepened and the impact on Freddie Mac and Fannie Mae became increasingly clear. Due to the government bailout, however, central banks will most likely continue to buy American debt.

14382 ■ *"Au Revoir Or Goodbye?"* in *Barron's (Vol. 88, July 14, 2008, No. 28, pp. 5)*
Pub: Dow Jones & Co., Inc.
Ed: Alan Abelson. **Description:** Former Senator Phil Gramm's opinion that the U.S. is a 'nation of whiners' as they moan about recession is another example of the disconnection between Washington and Wall Street on one hand and the real world on the other. It would be a catastrophe for most of the world if Fannie Mae and Freddie Mac were to go under and take their trillions of mortgage debt with them.

14383 ■ *"Back on Track-Or Off the Rails?"* in *Business Week (September 22, 2008, No. 4100, pp. 22)*
Pub: McGraw-Hill Companies, Inc.
Ed: Peter Coy; Tara Kalwarski. **Description:** Discusses the possible scenarios the American economy may undergo due to the takeover of Fannie Mae and Freddie Mac. Statistical data included.

14384 ■ *"Bad-Loan Bug Bites Mid-Tier Banks; More Pain, Tighter Lending Standards Ahead, CEOs Say"* in *Crain's Chicago Business (May 5, 2008)*
Pub: Crain Communications, Inc.
Ed: Steve Daniels. **Description:** Mid-sized commercial banks form the bedrock of Chicago's financial-services industry and they are now feeling the results of the credit crisis that has engulfed the nation's largest banks and brokerages. Commercial borrowers are seeing tighter terms on loans and higher interest rates while bank investors are unable to forecast lenders' earnings performance from quarter to quarter. Statistical data included.

14385 ■ *"Bad Loans Start Piling Up"* in *Crain's New York Business (Vol. 24, January 7, 2008, No. 1, pp. 2)*
Pub: Crain Communications, Inc.
Ed: Tom Fredrickson. **Description:** Problems in the subprime mortgage industry have extended to other lending activities as evidenced by bank charge-offs on bad commercial and industrial loans which have more than doubled in the third quarter.

14386 ■ *"Bailout May Force Cutbacks, Job Losses"* in *The Business Journal - Serving Phoenix and the Valley of the Sun (Vol. 29, September 26, 2008, No. 4, pp. 1)*
Pub: American City Business Journals, Inc.
Ed: Mike Sunnucks. **Description:** Economists say the proposed $700 billion bank bailout could affect Arizona businesses as banks could be forced to reduce the amount and number of loans it has thereby forcing businesses to shrink capital expenditures and then jobs. However, the plan could also stimulate the economy by taking bad loans off banks balance sheets according to another economist.

14387 ■ *"Bankruptcies Swell"* in *The Business Journal-Portland (Vol. 25, July 4, 2008, No. 17, pp. 1)*
Pub: American City Business Journals, Inc.
Ed: Andy Giegerich. **Description:** Individual and business bankruptcy filings in Portland, Oregon had increased. The rising gas and food prices, mortgage crisis and tightening lending standards are seen as causes of bankruptcies. Statistics on bankruptcy filings are also provided.

14388 ■ *"Bankruptcy Blowback"* in *Business Week (September 22, 2008, No. 4100, pp. 36)*
Pub: McGraw-Hill Companies, Inc.
Ed: Jessica Silver-Greenberg. **Description:** Changes to bankruptcy laws which were enacted in 2005 after banks and other financial institutions lobbied hard for them are now suffering the consequences of the laws which force more troubled borrowers to let their homes go into foreclosure; lenders suffer financially every time they have to take on a foreclosure and the laws in which they lobbied so hard to see enacted are now becoming a problem for these lending institutions. Details of the changes in the laws are outlined as are the affects on the consumer, the economy and the lenders.

14389 ■ *"Banks Seeing Demand for Home Equity Loans Slowing"* in *Crain's Cleveland Business (Vol. 28, December 3, 2007, No. 48, pp. 1)*
Pub: Crain Communications, Inc.
Ed: Shawn A. Turner. **Description:** Discusses the reasons for the decline in demand for home equity loans and lines of credit. Statistical data included.

14390 ■ *"Best Income Trust"* in *Canadian Business (Vol. 81, Summer 2008, No. 9, pp. 69)*
Pub: Rogers Media Ltd.
Ed: Calvin Leung. **Description:** Table showing five-year annualized growth rate and one-year stock performance of real estate investment trusts firms in Canada is presented. Calgary-based Boardwalk REIT is projected to grow the fastest among North American REITs over the next two years. Other details on the stock performance analysis are presented.

14391 ■ *"Beware the Ides of March"* in *Canadian Business (Vol. 81, April 14, 2008, No. 6, pp. 13)*
Pub: Rogers Media
Ed: Jeff Sanford. **Description:** Financial troubles of Bear Stearns in March, 2008 was part of the credit crunch that started in the summer of 2007 in the U.S. when subprime mortgages that were written for people who could barely afford the payments started defaulting. The bankruptcy protection given to 20 asset backed commercial paper trusts is being fought by the investors in these securities who could stand to lose 40 percent of their money under the agreement.

14392 ■ *"Bills Would Regulate Mortgage Loan Officers"* in *Crain's Detroit Business (Vol. 24, February 25, 2008, No. 8, pp. 9)*
Pub: Crain Communications Inc. - Detroit
Ed: Amy Lane. **Description:** New legislation in Michigan, if passed, would create a registration process for mortgage loan officers in the state in order to address the mortgage loan crisis.

14393 ■ *"BofA Will Reach the Top with Countrywide Deal"* in *Business North*

Carolina (Vol. 28, March 2008, No. 3, pp. 36)
Pub: Business North Carolina
Description: Bank of America, headquartered in Charlotte, North Carolina, will add Countrywide to its let of credits. Countrywide is the largest U.S. mortgage lender. Statistical data included.

14394 ■ *"Bottom's Up"* in *Barron's (Vol. 88, July 14, 2008, No. 28, pp. 25)*
Pub: Dow Jones & Co., Inc.
Ed: Jonathan R. Laing. **Description:** Economist Chip Case believes that home prices are nearing a bottom based on his analysis of the history of the housing market; surprisingly, in the past the housing market has rebounded after a quarter from a massive housing start drop. The drop in early stage delinquencies is another sign of the housing market's recovery.

14395 ■ *"Business Still Expected to Take Hit in 2008"* in *Business Journal-Serving Phoenix and the Valley of the Sun (December 28, 2007)*
Pub: American City Business Journals, Inc.
Ed: Chris Casacchia. **Description:** Community banks in 2008 are still projected to suffer from the repercussions of the subprime mortgage and credit crises. Meanwhile, the asset devaluation of big banks and global investment companies are higher than that of smaller banks. The third quarter and fourth quarter losses of banks such as Bear Stearns are discussed as well.

14396 ■ *Chain of Blame: How Wall Street Caused the Mortgage and Credit Crisis*
Pub: John Wiley & Sons, Inc.
Ed: Paul Muolo, Mathew Padilla. **Released:** 2009. **Price:** $27.95. **Description:** The book describes how risky loans given irresponsibly put big investment banks at the center of the subprime crisis.

14397 ■ *"Citi Ruling Could Chill SEC, Street Legal Pacts"* in *Wall Street Journal Eastern Edition (November 29, 2011, pp. C1)*
Pub: Dow Jones & Company Inc. Enterprise Media Group
Contact: Clare Hart, President
Ed: Jean Eaglesham, Chad Bray. **Description:** A $285 million settlement was reached between the Securities and Exchange Commission and Citigroup Inc. over allegations the bank misled investors over a mortgage-bond deal. Now, Judge Jed S. Rakoff has ruled against the settlement, a decision that will affect the future of such attempts to prosecute Wall Street fraud. Rakoff said that the settlement was 'neither fair, nor reasonable, nor adequate, nor in the public interest.'.

14398 ■ *"Coming Soon: Bailouts of Fannie and Freddie"* in *Barron's (Vol. 88, July 14, 2008, No. 28, pp. 14)*
Pub: Dow Jones & Co., Inc.
Ed: Jonathan R. Laing. **Description:** Assurances from the government that Fannie Mae and Freddie Mac are adequately capitalized and able to carry on their duties as guarantors or owners of over $5 trillion of U.S. home mortgages are designed to keep both entities afloat until they attempt to raise $10 billion in new equity. The government would assume any losses in a bailout and owners of the banks' papers would profit as yields drop.

14399 ■ *"Condominium Sales Fall to a Seven-Year Low"* in *Crain's Chicago Business (Vol. 31, November 10, 2008, No. 45, pp. 2)*
Pub: Crain Communications, Inc.
Ed: Alby Gallun. **Description:** Downtown Chicago condominium market is experiencing the lowest number of sales in years due to the tightening of the mortgage lending market, the Wall Street crisis and the downturn in the economy. The supply of new condos is soaring, the result of the building boom of 2005 and 2006; many developers are finding it difficult to pay off construction loans and fear foreclosure on their properties. Additional information and statistical data related to the downtown condominium market is provided.

14400 ▪ *"Contingent Offers: Weighing the Risk"* in *Crain's Chicago Business (Vol. 31, April 21, 2008, No. 16, pp. 48)*
Pub: Crain Communications, Inc.
Ed: Darci Smith. **Description:** Interview with Greer Haseman, the broker-owner of Town Square Associates, who discusses contingent offers in a challenging housing market.

14401 ▪ *"Cornered by Credit; As $1 Billion in Loans Come Due, Will Landlords Find Funds?"* in *Crain's Detroit Business (October 6, 2008)*
Pub: Crain Communications, Inc.
Ed: Daniel Duggan. **Description:** Conduit loans are used by many real estate investors and are normally issued in 7- to 10-year terms with balloon payments due at the end, requiring the full balance to be paid upon maturity. Many building owners may find their properties going into foreclosure as these loans mature next year since these loans cannot be extended like typical loans and the credit crisis along with falling property values is making it more difficult to secure new sources of funding. Possible solutions to this problem are also explored.

14402 ▪ *"Corporate Elite Show Resilience"* in *The Business Journal-Serving Greater Tampa Bay (Vol. 28, August 1, 2008, No. 32, pp. 1)*
Pub: American City Business Journals, Inc.
Ed: Margie Manning; Alexis Muellner. **Description:** Stocks of the largest public companies in Tampa Bay, Florida, outperformed the S&P 500 index by 28 percent in the first half of 2008. The escalation is attributed to the growth orientation of the companies in the area and the lack of exposure to the real estate and financial services sectors.

14403 ▪ *"Cost of Home Purchase Loans are Higher for Hispanics"* in *Hispanic Business (October 2007, pp. 88)*
Pub: Hispanic Business
Description: Home loans for Hispanics generally are offered at a higher interest rate. Statistical data included.

14404 ▪ *"Crash Pads"* in *Business Courier (Vol. 24, November 2, 2008, No. 29, pp. 1)*
Pub: American City Business Journals, Inc.
Ed: Jon Newberry. **Description:** Francisca Webster accumulated $4 million in mortgage debt in about 2 months. She filed a lawsuit against her tax preparer and her mortgage broker contending that the defendants had breached their fiduciary duties to her and made fraudulent misrepresentations to her. The other details of the case are supplied.

14405 ▪ *"The Credit Crisis Continues"* in *Barron's (Vol. 88, March 10, 2008, No. 10, pp. M12)*
Pub: Dow Jones & Company, Inc.
Ed: Randall W. Forsyth. **Description:** Short-term Treasury yields dropped to new cyclical lows in early March 2008, with the yield for the two-year Treasury note falling to 1.532 percent. Spreads of the mortgage-backed securities of Fannie Mae and Freddie Mac rose on suspicion of collapses in financing.

14406 ▪ *"Critics: Efforts to Fix Loans Won't Stop Foreclosure Wave"* in *Business First Columbus (Vol. 25, November 14, 2008, No. 12, pp. A1)*
Pub: American City Business Journals
Ed: Adrian Burns. **Description:** Efforts by U.S. banks to help homeowners pay mortgages are seen to have little if any impact on foreclosures. Banks have announced plans to identify and aid troubled borrowers. Statistical data included.

14407 ▪ *"Delinquent Properties on the Rise"* in *Business Courier (Vol. 27, June 11, 2010, No. 6, pp. 1)*
Pub: Business Courier
Ed: Dan Monk. **Description:** Reports show that Cincinnati now ranks in the U.S. Top 20 for its delinquency rate on securitized commercial real estate loans. In December 2009, the region ranked 28th out of 50 cities studied by Trepp LLC. As of May 30, 2010, more than $378 million in commercial mortgage-backed security loans were more than 60 days past due.

14408 ▪ *"Detroit Residential Market Slows; Bright Spots Emerge"* in *Crain's Detroit Business (Vol. 24, October 6, 2008, No. 40, pp. 11)*
Pub: Crain Communications, Inc.
Ed: Daniel Duggan. **Description:** Discusses the state of the residential real estate market in Detroit; although condominium projects receive the most attention, deals for single-family homes are taking place in greater numbers due to financing issues. Buyers can purchase a single family home with a 3.5 percent down payment compared to 20 percent for some condo deals because of the number of first-time homebuyer programs under the Federal Housing Administration.

14409 ▪ *"Developer Wins Bout with Bank in Roundabout Way"* in *Tampa Bay Business Journal (Vol. 30, January 29, 2010, No. 6, pp. 1)*
Pub: American City Business Journals
Ed: Janet Leiser. **Description:** Developer Donald E. Phillips of Phillips Development and Realty LLC won against the foreclosure filed by First Horizon National Corporation, which is demanding the company to fully pay its $2.9 million loan. Phillips requested that his company pay monthly mortgage and extend the loan's maturity date.

14410 ▪ *Dictionary of Real Estate Terms*
Pub: Barron's Educational Series Inc.
Contact: Alex Holtz, President
E-mail: aholtz@berronseduc.com
Ed: Jack P. Friedman, Jack C. Harris, J. Bruce Lindeman. **Released:** October 2008. **Price:** $13.99. **Description:** More than 2,500 real estate terms relating to mortgages and financing, brokerage law, architecture, rentals and leases, property insurance, and more.

14411 ▪ *"Docs Might Hold Cure for Real Estate, Banks"* in *Baltimore Business Journal (Vol. 28, November 5, 2010, No. 26, pp. 1)*
Pub: Baltimore Business Journal
Ed: Gary Haber. **Description:** Health care providers, including physicians are purchasing their office space instead of renting it as banks lower interest rates to 6 percent on mortgages for medical offices. The rise in demand offers relief to the commercial real estate market. It has also resulted in a boom in building new medical offices.

14412 ▪ *"Downtown Evens Tenant Ledger"* in *The Business Journal-Serving Metropolitan Kansas City (Vol. 26, July 11, 2008, No. 44, pp. 1)*
Pub: American City Business Journals, Inc.
Ed: Rob Roberts. **Description:** Financial services company PricewaterhouseCoopers will relocate its office from the Broadway Square building, but it will not leave downtown as it signs a long-term lease for a 27,000 square feet of space in Town Pavilion. Town Pavilion is the biggest multitenant office building in downtown. Downtown's market competitiveness is also examined.

14413 ▪ *"East-Side Real Estate Forum Detours To Grand Rapids"* in *Crain's Detroit Business (Vol. 24, October 6, 2008, No. 40, pp. 17)*
Pub: Crain Communications, Inc.
Ed: Daniel Duggan. **Description:** Tom Wackerman was elected chairman of the University of Michigan-Urban Land Institute Real Estate Forum and proposed that the annual conference be held in Grand Rapids due to the brisk economic activity he was finding there; although the idea was initially met with resistance, the plan to introduce East-siders to the West side began receiving more enthusiasm due to the revitalization of the area, which was once considered to have a bleak outlook. Many are hoping to learn the lessons of those who were able to change a negative economic climate into a positive one in which the cooperation of private business and government can work together to accomplish goals.

14414 ▪ *"Easy to be Queasy"* in *Canadian Business (Vol. 81, December 24, 2007, No. 1, pp. 25)*
Pub: Rogers Media
Ed: Jack Mintz. **Description:** Canada could be facing a slowdown in economic growth for 2008 as the country's economy depends on the U.S. economy, which is still facing recession in the subprime market. Details on Canada's economic growth, the impact of the weak U.S. dollar, increase in the unemployment rate, and decline in tax revenue are explored.

14415 ▪ *"Economy Peddles Rent In This Cycle"* in *The Business Journal-Serving Metropolitan Kansas City (Vol. 26, August 8, 2008, No. 48)*
Pub: American City Business Journals, Inc.
Ed: Ashlee Kieler. **Description:** Rental demand for apartment units in downtown Kansas City, Missouri, is increasing due to the housing crisis, lack of real estate development, and increasing popularity of the downtown area. The downtown area has 7,378 multifamily units as of June 2008, of which 4,114 are rentals. •

14416 ▪ *"Exposed?"* in *Mergers & Acquisitions: The Dealmaker's Journal (March 1, 2008)*
Pub: SourceMedia, Inc.
Ed: Jerry Abejo. **Description:** State-run pension plans' contributions are declining due to a loss of tax revenue from plummeting home values.

14417 ▪ *"Fannie and Freddie: How They'll Change"* in *Business Week (September 22, 2008, No. 4100, pp. 30)*
Pub: McGraw-Hill Companies, Inc.
Ed: Jane Sasseen. **Description:** Three possible outcomes of the fate of struggling mortgage giants Freddie Mac and Fannie Mae after the government bailout are outlined.

14418 ▪ *"FBI Initiates Fraud Inquiry Into Mortgage Lenders"* in *Miami Daily Business Review (March 26, 2008)*
Pub: ALM Media Inc.
Description: FBI has launched investigations into Countrywide Financial, the nation's largest mortgage lender, along with sixteen other firms, tied to the subprime mortgage crisis.

14419 ▪ *"Fifth Third Grapples With Account Snafu"* in *Business Courier (Vol. 24, December 7, 2008, No. 34, pp. 1)*
Pub: American City Business Journals, Inc.
Ed: Jon Newberry. **Description:** Fifth Third Bank's vendor committed an error which led to a badly damaged credit score for Brett and Karen Reloka. The couple reported the incident to the bank and are still waiting for action to be taken. A major outourced services vendor caused paid-off mortgages to be reported delinquent.

14420 ▪ *"Final Player In Big Mortgage Fraud Operation Gets Jail Time"* in *Boston Business Journal (Vol. 31, May 27, 2011, No. 18, pp. 3)*
Pub: Boston Business Journal
Ed: Galen Moore. **Description:** Real estate broker Ralp Appolon has been sentenced to 70 months in prison for wire fraud. Appolon was part of a group that falsified information about property purchase prices. A total of ten mortgage lenders have been victims of the group.

14421 ▪ *"Finger-Pointing Time"* in *Barron's (Vol. 88, March 10, 2008, No. 10, pp. 9)*
Pub: Dow Jones & Company, Inc.
Ed: Michael Santoli. **Description:** Discusses who is to blame for the financial crisis brought about by the credit crunch in the United States; the country's financial markets will eventually digest this crisis but will bottom out first before the situation improves.

14422 ▪ *"First-Time Homebuyer Credit May Add Some Momentum to Market"* in *Crain's Cleveland Business (Vol. 30, May 18, 2009, No. 20)*
Pub: Crain Communications, Inc.
Ed: Stan Bullard. **Description:** Federal tax credits for first-time homebuyers have increased the number of homes being sold. Details of the tax credit are defined.

14423 ■ *"A Flawed Yardstick for Banks"* in *Barron's* (Vol. 88, July 14, 2008, No. 28, pp. M6)
Pub: Dow Jones & Co., Inc.
Ed: Arindam Nag. **Description:** Return on equity is no longer the best measure for investors to judge banks by in a post-subprime-crises world. Investors should consider the proportion of a bank's total assets that are considered risky and look out for any write-downs of goodwill when judging a bank's financial health.

14424 ■ *The Foreclosure of America: Life Inside Countrywide Home Loans and the Selling of the American Dream*
Pub: Berkley Trade/Penguin Group USA Inc.
Ed: Adam Michaelson. **Released:** April 6, 2010. **Price:** $16.00. **Description:** An inside look at Countrywide Home Loans and the mortgage crisis.

14425 ■ *"Foreclosures Crisis Expected to Significantly Drain Wealth"* in *Black Enterprise* (Vol. 41, September 2010, No. 2, pp. 24)
Pub: Earl G. Graves Publishing Co. Inc.
Description: African American communities will lose billions in wealth because of the current foreclosure crisis. Statistical data included.

14426 ■ *"FTC Takes Aim At Foreclosure 'Rescue' Firm"* in *The Business Journal-Serving Greater Tampa Bay* (Vol. 28, September 19, 2008, No. 39)
Pub: American City Business Journals, Inc.
Ed: Michael Hinman. **Description:** United Home Savers LLP has been ordered to halt its mortgage foreclosure rescue services after the Federal Trade Commission accused it of deceptive advertising. The company is alleged to have charged customers $1,200 in exchange for unfulfilled promises to keep them in their homes.

14427 ■ *"GM's Mortgage Unit Deal Brings in $9 Billion"* in *Globe & Mail* (March 24, 2006, pp. B3)
Pub: CTVglobemedia Publishing Inc.
Ed: Shawn McCarthy. **Description:** General Motors Corp. sells General Motors Acceptance Corp.'s commercial real estate division to Kohlberg Kravis Roberts & Co. Five Mile Capital Partners LLC and Goldman Sachs Capital Partners. The reasons behind the deal are presented.

14428 ■ *"A Good Sign for Commercial Real Estate"* in *Austin Business JournalInc.* (Vol. 29, December 18, 2009, No. 41, pp. 1)
Pub: American City Business Journals
Ed: Kate Harrington. **Description:** Factors that could contribute to the reemergence of the commercial mortgage-backed securities market in Texas are discussed. These securities can potentially boost the commercial real estate market statewide as well as nationwide. Commercial mortgage-backed securities origination in 2009 is worth less that $1 billion, compared with $238 billion in 2008.

14429 ■ *"A Good Step, But There's a Long Way to Go"* in *Business Week* (September 22, 2008, No. 4100, pp. 10)
Pub: McGraw-Hill Companies, Inc.
Ed: James C. Cooper. **Description:** Despite the historic action by the U.S. government to nationalize the mortgage giants Freddie Mac and Fannie Mae, rising unemployment rates may prove to be an even bigger roadblock to bringing back the economy from its downward spiral. The takeover is meant to restore confidence in the credit markets and help with the mortgage crisis but the rising rate in unemployment may make many households unable to take advantage of any benefits which arise from the bailout. Statistical data included.

14430 ■ *Grow Your Money: 101 Easy Tips to Plan, Save and Invest*
Pub: HarperBusiness
Ed: Jonathan D. Pond. **Released:** December 2007. **Price:** $26.95. **Description:** In what should be required reading for anyone entering the work world,

the author offers helpful investment and financial definitions, debt-management strategies, retirement and home ownerships considerations and more.

14431 ■ *"Hank Paulson On the Housing Bailout and What's Ahead"* in *Business Week* (September 22, 2008, No. 4100, pp. 19)
Pub: McGraw-Hill Companies, Inc.
Ed: Maria Bartiromo. **Description:** Interview with Treasury Secretary Henry Paulson in which he discusses the bailout of Fannie Mae and Freddie Mac as well as the potential impact on the American economy and foreign interests and investments in the country. Paulson has faith that the government's actions will help to stabilize the housing market.

14432 ■ *"Hastily Enacted Regulation Will Not Cure Economic Crisis"* in *Crain's Chicago Business* (Vol. 31, May 5, 2008, No. 18, pp. 18)
Pub: Crain Communications, Inc.
Ed: Stephen P. D'Arcy. **Description:** Policymakers are looking for ways to respond to what is possibly the greatest financial crisis of a generation due to the collapse of the housing market, the credit crisis and the volatility of Wall Street.

14433 ■ *"Hollander 95 Project Getting Bigger"* in *Boston Business Journal* (Vol. 29, September 23, 2011, No. 20, pp. 1)
Pub: American City Business Journals Inc.
Ed: Gary Haber. **Description:** Hollander 95 Business Park is in for a huge change as its new owners plan a $50 million expansion which calls for building as many as eight more buildings or a total of more than 500,000 square feed. FRP Development bought the site for $4.35 million at a foreclosure sale in July 2010 and is now seeking city approval for an Industrial Planned Unit Development designation.

14434 ■ *"Home Builder, Four Others, Face Sentencing"* in *Business Courier* (Vol. 27, November 26, 2010, No. 30, pp. 1)
Pub: Business Courier
Ed: Jon Newberry. **Description:** Home builder Bernie Kurlemann was convicted on November 10, 2010 on six felony counts and faces up to 65 years in prison due to his part in a 2006 Warren County mortgage fraud scheme. Four other business people have pleaded guilty to related charges, and all are awaiting sentencing in early 2011.

14435 ■ *"Home Prices Sag"* in *Crain's Chicago Business* (Vol. 31, April 28, 2008, No. 17, pp. 3)
Pub: Crain Communications, Inc.
Ed: Alby Gallun. **Description:** Since the slump in the housing market is continuing with no sign of recovery, Chicago-area home prices are poised for an even steeper drop this year. In 2007, the region's home prices fell nearly 5 percent and according to a forecast by Fiserv Inc., they will decline 8.1 percent this year and another 2.2 percent in 2009. Statistical data included.

14436 ■ *"Home Sweet Home"* in *Canadian Business* (Vol. 79, October 9, 2006, No. 20, pp. 22)
Pub: Rogers Media
Ed: Peter Shawn Taylor. **Description:** Changes being made in the management of mortgage insurance business in Canada are critically analyzed.

14437 ■ *"Homeownership: Still the American Dream?"* in *Gallup Management Journal* (May 5, 2011)
Pub: Gallup
Description: The mortgage finance system is broken. Housing prices continue to fall. Foreclosures are expected to increase in the coming months. However, Gallup's chief economist does not believe this is the end of the American dream of owning one's own home.

14438 ■ *"Hotel Woes Reflect Area Struggle"* in *Business Journal Serving Greater Tampa Bay* (Vol. 30, December 3, 2010, No. 50, pp. 1)
Pub: Tampa Bay Business Journal
Ed: Mark Holan. **Description:** Quality Inn and Suites in East Tampa, Florida has struggled against the sluggish economy but remained open to guests despite

facing a foreclosure. The hotel project is the center of East Tampa's redevelopment plans and public officials defend the $650,000 investment in public amenities near the building.

14439 ■ *"Housing Hedge"* in *Canadian Business* (Vol. 79, July 17, 2006, No. 14-15, pp. 66)
Pub: Rogers Media
Ed: Jeff Sanford. **Description:** The idea of starting a hedge scheme for housing is presented using the advent of pension schemes as an example to follow.

14440 ■ *"Housing Slide Picks Up Speed"* in *Crain's Chicago Business* (Vol. 31, April 21, 2008, No. 16, pp. 2)
Pub: Crain Communications, Inc.
Ed: Eddie Baeb. **Description:** According to Tracy Cross & Associates Inc., a real estate consultancy, sales of new homes in the Chicago area dropped 61 percent from the year-earlier period which is more bad news for homebuilders, contractors and real estate agents who are eager for an indication that market conditions are improving.

14441 ■ *"How About Trying a Foreclosure Tax?"* in *Crain's Detroit Business* (Vol. 24, January 28, 2008, No. 4, pp. 9)
Pub: Crain Communications Inc. - Detroit
Ed: Mark Goodell. **Description:** According to a recent study, local communities could see a $100 million decrease in property tax revenues, and the state could lose as much as $12 million in lower sales tax proceeds. Experts discuss options for Michigan's government to institute a foreclosure tax.

14442 ■ *How to Start, Operate and Market a Freelance Notary Signing Agent Business*
Pub: Gom Publishing, LLC
Ed: Victoria Ring. **Released:** September 2004. **Price:** $8.18. **Description:** Due to the changes in the 2001 Uniform Commercial Code allowing notary public agents to serve as a witness to mortgage loan closings (eliminating the 2-witness requirement under the old code), notaries are working directly for mortgage, title and signing companies as mobile notaries.

14443 ■ *"Hunter and the Hunted"* in *Canadian Business* (Vol. 81, Summer 2008, No. 9, pp. 12)
Pub: Rogers Media Ltd.
Ed: Thomas Watson. **Description:** Brian Hunter, a partner in oil and gas engineering firm Montane Resources, invested his life savings in Vancouver-based Canacord Capital Corp. Details of the asset-backed commercial paper fiasco and Hunter's use of Facebook to encourage other investors to participate in his claim against the mortgage company are presented.

14444 ■ *"In Control: Tips For Navigating a Buyer's Market"* in *Black Enterprise* (Vol. 38, December 2007, No. 5, pp. 64)
Pub: Earl G. Graves Publishing Co. Inc.
Ed: Erinn R. Johnson. **Description:** Tips are given to help would-be home buyers. The importance of finding a good real estate agent is stressed.

14445 ■ *"Independence's Day Keeps on Getting Brighter"* in *Business Courier* (Vol. 27, June 11, 2010, No. 6, pp. 1)
Pub: Business Courier
Ed: Lucy May. **Description:** Reports show that residential and commercial development continues in Independence, Kentucky despite the recession, with a 144-unit apartment complex under construction. The city recorded 152 new-home closings in 2009, or 25 percent of all new homes closed in Boone, Campbell, and Kenton counties.

14446 ■ *"The Influencers"* in *Entrepreneur* (Vol. 36, March 2008, No. 3, pp. 66)
Pub: Entrepreneur Media Inc.
Ed: Andrea Cooper. **Description:** Among the 25 people, events, and trends that will influence business in 2008 are: the 2008 U.S. presidential elections, climate change, China, weakening U.S. dollar, mortgage crisis, generational shift, Bill Drayton, and Bill Gates. Other 2008 influencers are presented.

14447 ■ *"It Could Be Worse"* in *Barron's (Vol. 89, July 27, 2009, No. 30, pp. 5)*
Pub: Dow Jones & Co., Inc.
Ed: Alan Abelson. **Description:** Media sources are being fooled by corporate America who is peddling an economic recovery rather than reality as shown by the report of a rise in existing home sales which boosted the stock market even if it was a seasonal phenomenon. The phrase 'things could be worse' sums up the reigning investment philosophy in the U.S. and this has been stirring up the market.

14448 ■ *"Latest Volley Tries to Press Port Group"* in *Business Courier (Vol. 26, November 20, 2009, No. 30, pp. 1)*
Pub: American City Business Journals, Inc.
Ed: Dan Monk. **Description:** Subcontractors filed a new legal argument to force the Port of Greater Cincinnati Development Authority to pursue default claim against Bank of America. The bank issued letters of credit to guarantee bond payments in addition to holding the mortgage of the Kenwood Towne Place. Details of the claim are discussed.

14449 ■ *"Laugh or Cry?"* in *Barron's (Vol. 88, March 24, 2008, No. 12, pp. 7)*
Pub: Dow Jones & Company, Inc.
Ed: Alan Abelson. **Description:** Discusses the American economy which is just starting to feel the effect of the credit and housing crises. JPMorgan Chase purchased Bear Stearns for $2 a share, much lower than its share price of $60, while quasi-government entities Fannie Mae and Freddie Mac are starting to run into trouble.

14450 ■ *"Law Firms See Improvement in Financing Climate"* in *Sacramento Business Journal (Vol. 28, October 14, 2011, No. 33, pp. 1)*
Pub: Sacramento Business Journal
Ed: Kathy Robertson. **Description:** Sacramento, California-based Weintraub Genshlea Chediak Law Corporation has helped close 26 financing deals worth more than $1.6 billion in 2010, providing indication of improvement in Sacramento's economy. Lawyers have taken advantage of low interest rates to make refinancing agreements and help clients get new funds.

14451 ■ *"Lean on Me"* in *Entrepreneur (Vol. 36, February 2008, No. 2, pp. 40)*
Pub: Entrepreneur Media Inc.
Ed: Farnoosh Torabi. **Description:** Investing in tax liens is booming with the growth in the number of homeowners missing property tax payments. Details on how to bid for and when to redeem tax liens are outlined.

14452 ■ *"Leaning Tower"* in *Business Courier (Vol. 27, June 4, 2010, No. 5, pp. 1)*
Pub: Business Courier
Ed: Jon Newberry. **Description:** New York-based developer Armand Lasky, owner of Tower Place Mall in downtown Cincinnati, Ohio has sued Birmingham, Alabama-based Regions Bank to prevent the bank's foreclosure on the property. Regions Bank claims Lasky was in default on an $18 million loan agreement. Details on the mall's leasing plan is also discussed.

14453 ■ *"Lehman's Hail Mary Pass"* in *Business Week (September 22, 2008, No. 4100, pp. 28)*
Pub: McGraw-Hill Companies, Inc.
Ed: Matthew Goldstein; David Henry; Ben Levison. **Description:** Overview of Lehman Brothers' CEO Richard Fuld's plan to keep the firm afloat and end the stock's plunge downward; Fuld's strategy calls for selling off a piece of the firm's investment management business.

14454 ■ *"Lenders Get Boost from Low Rates"* in *Saint Louis Business Journal (Vol. 32, September 9, 2011, No. 2, pp. 1)*
Pub: Saint Louis Business Journal
Ed: Greg Edwards. **Description:** St. Louis, Missouri-based lenders have benefitted from record low mortgage interest rates. Housing loan applications have increased in view of the development.

14455 ■ *"Local Commercial Real Estate Foreclosures Continue to Rise"* in *Baltimore Business Journal (Vol. 28, October 1, 2010, No. 21, pp. 1)*
Pub: Baltimore Business Journal
Ed: Daniel J. Sernovitz. **Description:** Foreclosures of commercial real estate across the Greater Baltimore area have continued to rise. The region is now host to about $2 billion worth of commercial properties that carry a maturing debt or have been foreclosed. Commercial real estate owners are unable to finance their debts because banks have become stricter in passing out loans.

14456 ■ *"Lotus Starts Slowly, Dodges Subprime Woes"* in *Crain's Detroit Business (Vol. 24, April 14, 2008, No. 15, pp. 3)*
Pub: Crain Communications, Inc.
Ed: Tom Henderson. **Description:** Discusses Lotus Bancorp Inc. and their business plan, which although is not right on target due to the subprime mortgage meltdown, is in a much better position than its competitors due to the quality of their loans.

14457 ■ *"A Matter of Perspective"* in *Business Journal-Portland (Vol. 24, November 2, 2007, No. 35, pp. 1)*
Pub: American City Business Journals, Inc.
Ed: Andy Giegerich. **Description:** Oregon Governor Ted Kulongoski assembled the Mortgage Lending Work Group, made up of members of the mortgage industry and consumer groups, to recommend possible bills for the Oregon Senate and House to consider. How its members try to balance philosophical differences in mortgage lending rules is discussed.

14458 ■ *"Mequon Plan On Tracks, Bucks Housing Trend"* in *The Business Journal-Milwaukee (Vol. 25, September 26, 2008, No. 53, pp. A1)*
Pub: American City Business Journals, Inc.
Ed: Pete Millard. **Description:** Insight Development Group plans to build condominium units and single-family homes despite the residential market downturn. The Orchard Glen project, a planned development in Mequon, is a $22 million project which will include 38 condos and 12 single-family homes. Details of the project are provided.

14459 ■ *"More Questions Face Huntington"* in *Business First-Columbus (December 7, 2007, pp. A3)*
Pub: American City Business Journals, Inc.
Ed: Adrian Burns. **Description:** Marty Adams' abrupt resignation has lead to speculation that he was dismissed by the bank in relation to the unexpected run-in with the subprime mortgage fiasco. Analysis predict Columbus-based Huntington Bancshares Inc. might be targeted for acquisition. Details on the company's revenues and shares of stock prices are presented.

14460 ■ Mortgage Industry Directory
Pub: Thomson Financial
URL(s): www.nationalmortgagenews.com. **Ed:** Paul Muolo. **Released:** Annual; latest edition 14th, 2008. **Price:** $529, Individuals. **Covers:** Approximately 700 mortgage industry leaders, profiles, and 700 top bank, S&L and credit union mortgage holders, including industry rankings. **Entries include:** Organization name, address, phone plus complete data on all aspects of the mortgage industry.

14461 ■ *"Mortgage Mess Continues To Trigger Bids To Ease Crisis"* in *Business First-Columbus (December 14, 2007, pp. A1)*
Pub: American City Business Journals, Inc.
Ed: Adrian Burns. **Description:** Measures to prevent foreclosures in Ohio are presented. On December 6, 2007, the Bush Administration started a national incentive that will establish a streamlined process for modifying loans. Some have questioned the proposal, since it is expected the plan will only help about 90,000 of the 1.8 million borrowers. According to Ohio Treasurer, Richard Cordray, one of the state's objectives is to calm the markets on Wall Street.

14462 ■ *"Mortgage Mess: How To Determine Your Exposure To the Subprime Crisis"* in *Black Enterprise (Vol. 38, November 2007, No. 4, pp. 46)*
Pub: Earl G. Graves Publishing Co. Inc.
Ed: Ilana Polyak. **Description:** Stocks and mutual funds have experienced declines because of the subprime crisis. Morningstar's Website can help investors research firms in which they have invested; if a fund is named high yield or high income or in the financial services sector, investments will have greater exposure to the mess.

14463 ■ *"Mortgage Securities Drop Hits Home"* in *The Business Journal-Serving Metropolitan Kansas City (Vol. 27, October 17, 2008, No. 5)*
Pub: American City Business Journals, Inc.
Ed: Rob Roberts. **Description:** Sale of commercial mortgage-backed securities (CMBS) in Kansas City, Missouri have declined. The area may avoid layoffs if the United States government succeeds in stabilizing the economy. Major CMBS players in the area include Midland Loan Services Inc. and KeyBank Real Estate Capital.

14464 ■ *"Mortgages Going Under"* in *Black Enterprise (Vol. 41, December 2010, No. 5, pp. 20)*
Pub: Earl G. Graves Publishing Co. Inc.
Description: Nearly one-fifth of the country's homeowners are underwater in their mortgages, which means they owe more on their home than the home's worth. Statistical data included.

14465 ■ *"Myths of Deleveraging"* in *Barron's (Vol. 90, August 23, 2010, No. 34, pp. M14)*
Pub: Barron's Editorial & Corporate Headquarters
Ed: Gene Epstein. **Description:** The opposite is true against reports about deleveraging or the decrease in credit since inflation-adjusted-investment factories and equipment rose 7.8 percent in the first quarter of 2010. On consumer deleveraging, sales of homes through credit is weak but there is a trend towards more realistic homeownership and consumer spending on durable goods rose 8.8 percent.

14466 ■ *"Neighborhood Watch"* in *Baltimore Business Journal (Vol. 28, July 23, 2010, No. 11, pp. 1)*
Pub: Baltimore Business Journal
Ed: Daniel J. Sernovitz. **Description:** Maryland government and housing leaders are set to spend $100 million in federal funding to stem the increase in foreclosures in the area. The federal funding is seen as inadequate to resolve the problem of foreclosures.

14467 ■ *"New Century's Fall Has a New Culprit"* in *Barron's (Vol. 88, March 31, 2008, No. 13, pp 20)*
Pub: Dow Jones & Company, Inc.
Ed: Jonathan R. Laing. **Description:** Court examiner Michael Missal reports that New Century Financial's auditor contributed to New Century's demise by its negligence in permitting improper and imprudent practices related to New Century's accounting processes. New Century's bankruptcy filing is considered the start of the subprime-mortgage crisis.

14468 ■ *"New Rule Rankles In Jersey"* in *Philadelphia Business Journal (Vol. 30, September 16, 2011, No. 31, pp. 1)*
Pub: American City Business Journals Inc.
Ed: Jeff Blumenthal. **Description:** A new rule in New Jersey which taxes out-of-state companies that conduct business in the state earned the ire of several banks, mortgage lenders and credit card companies and prompted opponents to threaten to file lawsuits. The new rule is an amendment to New Jersey Division of Taxation's corporate business tax regulation and is retroactive to 2002. Details are given.

14469 ■ *"The Next Government Bailout?"* in *Barron's (Vol. 88, March 10, 2008, No. 10, pp. 21)*
Pub: Dow Jones & Company, Inc.
Ed: Jonathan Laing. **Description:** Fannie Mae may need a government bailout as it faces huge hits

brought about by the effects of the housing crisis. The shares of the government-sponsored enterprise have dropped 65 percent since the housing crisis began.

14470 ■ *"Nightmare on Wall Street" in Canadian Business (Vol. 80, November 19, 2007, No. 23, pp. 33)*
Pub: Rogers Media
Ed: Thomas Watson. **Description:** Merrill Lynch Stanley O'Neal resigned after the company experienced a $2.2 billion loss in third quarter 2007. Citigroup's Charles Prince will also be leaving due to the crisis involving subprime mortgages and collaterized debt obligations. Forecasts for the stock market are supplied.

14471 ■ *"Nine Sectors to Watch: Gold" in Canadian Business (Vol. 81, December 24, 2007, No. 1, pp. 53)*
Pub: Rogers Media
Ed: John Gray. **Description:** Turmoil in the financial markets, triggered by the meltdown in subprime mortgages, has pushed the price of gold to more than $840 an ounce in November 2007. Details on investor interest in gold and prediction on price trends in trade are discussed.

14472 ■ *"Number of Mechanic's Liens Triple Since 2005" in The Business Journal - Serving Phoenix and the Valley of the Sun (Vol. 28, August 22, 2008, No. 51, pp. 1)*
Pub: American City Business Journals, Inc.
Ed: Jan Buchholtz. **Description:** Experts are blaming the mortgage and banking industries for the tripling of mechanic's liens that were filed in Arizona from 2005 through August 6, 2008. The rise in mechanic's liens is believed to indicate stress in the real estate community. Other views and information on the rise of mechanic's liens filed in Arizona are presented.

14473 ■ *"October 2009: Recovery Plods Along" in Hispanic Business (October 2009, pp. 10-11)*
Pub: Hispanic Business
Ed: Dr. Juan Solana. **Description:** Economist reports on a possible economic recovery which will not be allowed to rely on a strong domestic demand in order to sustain it. Consumers, looking to counterbalance years of leverage financing based on unrealistic, ever-increasing home and portfolio valuations, are saving rather than spending money.

14474 ■ *"Office Market May Turn Down" in Crain's New York Business (Vol. 24, January 14, 2008, No. 2, pp. 26)*
Pub: Crain Communications, Inc.
Description: Although still dominated by Wall Street, the downturn in the economy is raising fears that the continuing fallout from the subprime mortgage crisis could result in layoffs that will derail the office market.

14475 ■ *"OK, Bring in the Lawyers" in Crain's Chicago Business (Vol. 31, November 17, 2008, No. 46, pp. 26)*
Pub: Crain Communications, Inc.
Ed: Daniel Rome Levine. **Description:** Bankruptcy attorneys are finding the economic and credit crisis a benefit for their businesses due to the high number of business owners and mortgage holders that are need of their services. One Chicago firm is handling ten times the number of cases they did the previous year and of that about 80 percent of their new clients are related to the real estate sector.

14476 ■ *"Optimism Index" in Black Enterprise (Vol. 41, September 2010, No. 2, pp. 24)*
Pub: Earl G. Graves Publishing Co. Inc.
Description: According to a Pew Research Center report, 81 percent of African Americans expect to improve their finances in 2011. Blacks have carried a disproportionate share of job losses and housing foreclosures in the recession that began in 2007.

14477 ■ *"Past Due: $289 Million in Loans" in Saint Louis Business Journal (Vol. 32, September 23, 2011, No. 4, pp. 1)*
Pub: Saint Louis Business Journal
Ed: Evans Binns. **Description:** New York-based Trepp LLC research found about $289 million in local commercial mortgage-backed securities loans on 20

properties delinquent in payments by 30 days or more as of August 31, 2011. The report also placed the delinquency rate for St. Louis at that time at 9.64 percent.

14478 ■ *"Paying for the Recession: Rebalancing Economic Growth" in Montana Business Quarterly (Vol. 49, Spring 2011, No. 1, pp. 2)*
Pub: Bureau of Business & Economic Research
Ed: Patrick M. Barkey. **Description:** Four key issues required to address in order to rebalance economic growth in America are examined. They include: savings rates, global trade imbalances, government budgets and most importantly, housing price correction.

14479 ■ *"A Place in the Sun" in Canadian Business (Vol. 81, July 22, 2008, No. 12-13, pp. 56)*
Pub: Rogers Media Ltd.
Description: Experts believe that it is the best time for Canadians to own a retirement home in the U.S., where real estate prices are up to 50 percent below their peak. Other views concerning the economic conditions occurring in the United States, as well as on the implications for Canadians planning to invest in the country are presented.

14480 ■ *"Private Equity Firms Shopping Valley For Deals" in The Business Journal - Serving Phoenix and the Valley of the Sun (Vol. 29, September 19, 2008, No. 3, pp. 1)*
Pub: American City Business Journals, Inc.
Ed: Mike Sunnucks. **Description:** Private equity firms from California, Boston, New York, and overseas are expected to invest in growth-oriented real estate markets that include Phoenix. Real estate experts revealed that privately held investment and acquisition firms are looking to invest in real estate markets hit by the housing crisis. Views and information on private equity firms' real estate investments are presented.

14481 ■ *"Race, Not Income, Played Role in Subprime Loans" in Black Enterprise (Vol. 40, July 2010, No. 12, pp. 26)*
Pub: Earl G. Graves Publishing Co. Inc.
Ed: Deborah Creighton Skinner. **Description:** African Americans were 80 percent more likely than whites to receive a subprime loan and were almost 20 percent more likely to go into foreclosure, according to a study done by the National Community Reinvestment Coalition. Statistical data included.

14482 ■ *"Ready for a Rally?" in The Economist (Vol. 390, January 3, 2009, No. 8612, pp. 54)*
Pub: The Economist Newspaper Inc.
Description: Analysts predict that the recession could end by 2010. The current economic crisis is presented in detail.

14483 ■ *"Real Estate Defaults Top $300M" in Business Courier (Vol. 26, January 15, 2010, No. 39, pp. 1)*
Pub: American City Business Journals, Inc.
Ed: Dan Monk. **Description:** Cincinnati commercial real estate owners defaulting in securitized loans reached $306 million at the end of 2009. The trend has lifted the region's default rate to nearly 9 percent. National average for commercial real estate default is examined.

14484 ■ *"Real Estate Vets Take Times In Stride" in The Business Journal-Serving Metropolitan Kansas City (Vol. 26, July 25, 2008, No. 46)*
Pub: American City Business Journals, Inc.
Ed: Rob Roberts. **Description:** Kansas City, Missouri's real estate industry veterans like Allen Block believe that the challenges faced by the industry in the 1980s, when the Federal Reserve Board controlled the money supply to slow down inflation, were worse than the challenges faced today. Other views, trends and information on the real estate industry of the city, are presented.

14485 ■ *"Real Estate Woes Mount for State's Smaller Banks" in Boston Business Journal (Vol. 27, November 30, 2007, No. 44, pp. 1)*
Pub: American City Business Journals Inc.
Ed: Craig M. Douglas. **Description:** Massachusetts banking industry is facing a steep increase on loan defaults such as in home mortgages and condominium projects, contrary to public belief that the local industry is safe from the real estate meltdown. The dollar value of local banks' nonperforming loans doubled in 2007, and is rising statewide. Other banking issues in the state are discussed.

14486 ■ *"Red Tape Ties Detroit Housing Rehab Plan" in Crain's Detroit Business (Vol. 24, September 22, 2008, No. 38, pp. 1)*
Pub: Crain Communications Inc.
Ed: Ryan Beene. **Description:** Venture-capital firm Wilherst Oxford LLC is a Florida-based company that has purchased 300 inner-city homes which were in foreclosure in Detroit. Wilherst Oxford is asking the city to forgive the existing tax and utility liens so the firm can utilize the money for home improvements. The city, however, is reluctant but has stated that they are willing to negotiate.

14487 ■ *"Regulation Papered Over" in Charlotte Business Journal (Vol. 25, November 5, 2010, No. 33, pp.)*
Pub: Charlotte Business Journal
Ed: Adam O'Daniel. **Description:** County courts in North Carolina are having challenges coping with its oversight and regulation duties as it becomes too busy with foreclosure cases. Clerks in some county courts have presided over foreclosure hearings because of the flooding of foreclosure cases.

14488 ■ *"Revitalizing Real Estate: Couple Sails Through Sea of Housing Woes" in Black Enterprise (Vol. 38, February 2008, No. 7, pp. 50)*
Pub: Earl G. Graves Publishing Co. Inc.
Ed: Ayana Dixon. **Description:** Owner, Christopher Gablin and Regina Mincey-Garlin offer a broad range of real estate-related services to clients in order to not only survive, but thrive in today's market.

14489 ■ *"Rogue's Gallery" in Canadian Business (Vol. 81, November 10, 2008, No. 19, pp. 44)*
Pub: Rogers Media Ltd.
Ed: Rachel Pulfer. **Description:** Laissez-faire capitalism or poor oversight of Fannie Mae and Freddie Mac are causes for the financial crisis in the U.S., depending or Democrat or Republican viewpoint. Events leading up to the 2008 financial crisis are covered.

14490 ■ *"Rules Will Tighten, Bankers are Told: House Panel Chairman Expects More Regulation" in Charlotte Observer (February 6, 2007)*
Pub: Knight-Ridder/Tribune Business News
Ed: Binyamin Appelbaum. **Description:** House Financial Services Committee will impose more federal regulation on banks offering mortgages.

14491 ■ *"Servicers Back National Effort" in Business First-Columbus (October 19, 2007, pp. A1)*
Pub: American City Business Journals, Inc.
Ed: Adrian Burns. **Description:** Ohio is having difficulty convincing mortgage companies to sign a compact containing guidelines when working with troubled borrowers. Many of Ohio's mortgage companies are supporting a national initiative to respond to the mortgage crisis instead.

14492 ■ *"A Shallow Pool" in Canadian Business (Vol. 81, Summer 2008, No. 9, pp. 44)*
Pub: Rogers Media Ltd.
Ed: Joe Castaldo. **Description:** Bank of Canada projected in its 'Monetary Policy Report' a growth rate of 1.4 percent in 2008 and does not expect the economy to fully recover until mid-2010. The Canadian stock market has been recovering although slowly with just a 1.6 percent gain by April 30. Other details on the Canadian equity market are presented.

14493 ■ *"'Short Sales,' A Sign of Housing Troubles, Start Popping Up"* in *The Business Review Albany (Vol. 35, April 11, 2008, No. 1, pp. 1)*
Pub: The Business Review
Ed: Michael DeMasi. **Description:** Discusses the number of short sales, where homeowners ask banks to forgive part of their mortgages to sell the properties, which is starting to increase in the Albany, New York area. Real estate agents in the area are taking up crash courses in short selling.

14494 ■ *"Six Leading Economists on What to Expect in the Year Ahead: Derek Holt; Housing"* in *Canadian Business (December 24, 2007)*
Pub: Rogers Media
Ed: Derek Holt. **Description:** The Canadian subprime mortgage market could take a different turn from that of the U.S. as laws governing Canada's mortgage market indirectly limit the probability of a slowdown. Details on how Canada avoided the slowdown in the housing market and forecasts of new homes for 2008 are discussed.

14495 ■ *"A Slice of Danish; Fixing Finance"* in *The Economist (Vol. 390, January 3, 2009, No. 8612, pp. 55)*
Pub: The Economist Newspaper Inc.
Description: Denmark's mortgage-holders and the county's lending system is presented.

14496 ■ *"S.O.S. Sorting Out Subprime"* in *Black Enterprise (Vol. 38, November 2007, No. 4, pp. 76)*
Pub: Earl G. Graves Publishing Co. Inc.
Ed: Trevor Delaney. **Description:** Subprime distress in the housing market is discussed and the impact it has put on investors.

14497 ■ *"State Barks At Servicers Over Reluctance To Back Compact"* in *Business First-Columbus (2007, pp.)*
Pub: American City Business Journals, Inc.
Ed: Adrian Burns. **Description:** State of Ohio asked members of the mortgage industry to back a compact as a way to prevent foreclosures. Mortgage services denied the state's request. Other measures to help borrowers avoid foreclosure are investigated.

14498 ■ *"State Targets Credit Fixers"* in *Business Journal-Portland (Vol. 24, October 12, 2007, No. 33, pp. 1)*
Pub: American City Business Journals, Inc.
Ed: Andy Giegerich, Justin Matlick. **Description:** Number of companies that offer quick fix to consumers is growing; the State of Oregon is considering rules to target them. A group working on a study in the state's mortgage lending regulations could craft bills to be examined for legislative session in February 2008.

14499 ■ *"Struggling Community Banks Find Little Help In Wall Street Bailout"* in *Crain's Detroit Business (Vol. 24, September 29, 2008)*
Pub: Crain Communications Inc.
Ed: Tom Henderson. **Description:** Both public and private Michigan bands have been hit hard by poorly performing loan portfolios and although their problems were not caused by high-risk securities but by a longtime statewide recession and a housing slump, these community banks have little hope of seeing any of the bailout money that has been allotted for the larger institutions.

14500 ■ *"Stuck With Two Mortgages; The Nightmare When Buyers Upgrade"* in *Crain's Chicago Business (Vol. 31, April 21, 2008, No. 16)*
Pub: Crain Communications, Inc.
Ed: Darci Smith. **Description:** Discusses the problem a number of people are facing due to the slump in the housing market: being stuck with two mortgages when they move because their former homes have not sold. Many thought they could afford to move to a larger home, anticipating significant equity apprecia-

tion that did not occur; now they are left with lowering their price and competing with the host of new developments.

14501 ■ *"Subprime Hits Huntington"* in *Business First-Columbus (November 23, 2007, pp. A1)*
Pub: American City Business Journals, Inc.
Ed: Adrian Burns. **Description:** Huntington Bancshares Inc. picked up a $1.5 billion exposure to the country's subprime mortgage mess. It caused the bank to set aside $450 million to cover increases in loan losses. When Huntington acquired Sky Financial, it absorbed a 17-year relationship Sky had with Franklin Credit Corporation, which is a subprime lender and servicer.

14502 ■ *"Subprime Lenders Under Fire: Does the NAACP Have a Viable Case?"* in *Black Enterprise (Vol. 38, October 2007, No. 3, pp. 31)*
Pub: Earl G. Graves Publishing Co. Inc.
Ed: Trevor Delaney. **Description:** NAACP filed a lawsuit charging a number of mortgage lenders with 'institutionalized systematic racism'. Lenders named in the suit include Accredited Home Lenders, Ameriquest Mortgage Company, BNC Mortgage, Citigroup, Encore Credit, First Franklin Financial Corporation, Fremont Investment and Loan, HSBC Finance Corporation, Long Beach Mortgage Company, Option One Mortgage Corporation, Washington Mutual Inc., and WMC Mortgage Corporation. Details of the lawsuit are included.

14503 ■ *"Subprime Problems Loom"* in *The Business Journal-Portland (Vol. 25, August 29, 2008, No. 25, pp. 1)*
Pub: American City Business Journals, Inc.
Ed: Wendy Culverwell. **Description:** Over half of subprime mortgages in Portland are resetting by the end of 2008, which will cause more problems to the local real estate market. The inventory of unsold homes has also been increasing for over a year. Forecasts for the Portland housing market in relation to mortgage resets are supplied.

14504 ■ *"Sunwest Vies To Stave Off Bankruptcy"* in *The Business Journal-Portland (Vol. 25, August 15, 2008, No. 23, pp. 1)*
Pub: American City Business Journals, Inc.
Ed: Robin J. Moody. **Description:** Sunwest Management Inc. is teetering on the edge of bankruptcy as creditors start foreclosure on nine of their properties. This could potentially displace residents of the assisted living operator. Sunwest is trying to sell smaller packages of properties to get a $100 million bridge loan to maintain operations.

14505 ■ *"Survival Guide: There Can Be an Upside to Managing a Downturn"* in *Canadian Business (Vol. 81, November 10, 2008, No. 19, pp. 54)*
Pub: Rogers Media Ltd.
Ed: Sharda Prashad. **Description:** Canada-based Foxy is already limiting its exposure to retailers who could be a credit problem in case of recession. Retirement Life Communities is entering into fixed-rate and fixed-term loans for them to have sufficient financing to grow. Business owners need to realize that customers want more for less.

14506 ■ *"Tampa Bay's CMBS Exposure Looms Large"* in *Tampa Bay Business Journal (Vol. 30, December 4, 2009, No. 50, pp. 1)*
Pub: American City Business Journals
Ed: Margie Manning. **Description:** Tampa, Florida's metropolitan statistical area have listed 50 to 601 commercial mortgage-backed securities loans as delinquent with a total delinquent loan balance of $439 million. The total was 9.7 percent of the $4.5 billion loans outstanding and was higher than the delinquency rate in New York and Los Angeles.

14507 ■ *"The Trillion Dollar Meltdown: Easy Money, High Rollers, and the Great Credit Crash"*
Pub: Public Affairs
Ed: Charles R. Morris. **Released:** 2009. **Price:** $22.95. **Description:** Former banker believes that Wall Street and the financial community have too much

power in America. He estimates that writedowns and defaults of residential mortgages, commercial mortgages, junk bonds, leveraged loans, credit cards, and complex securitized bonds could reach $1 trillion.

14508 ■ *"Try, Try Again"* in *Baltimore Business Journal (Vol. 28, August 20, 2010, No. 15, pp. 1)*
Pub: Baltimore Business Journal
Ed: Gary Haber. **Description:** Customers' refinancing of mortgages has boosted Baltimore, Maryland mortgage banking business. The housing decline has resulted in a decrease in the number of people looking for new mortgages.

14509 ■ *"Unions Pony Up $1 Million for McBride Stimulus"* in *Saint Louis Business Journal (Vol. 31, July 29, 2011, No. 49, pp. 1)*
Pub: Saint Louis Business Journal
Ed: Evan Binns. **Description:** Carpenters District Council of Greater St. Louis and International Brotherhood of Electrical Workers Local 1 were among the nine unions that agreed to split the cost of nearly $1 million in incentives for homebuyers who purchase homes in McBride communities. McBride & Son has spent over $100,000 to promote the incentive program.

14510 ■ *"U.S. Economy's Underlying Strengths Limit Recession Threat"* in *Hispanic Business (Vol. 30, April 2008, No. 4, pp. 14)*
Pub: Hispanic Business
Ed: Dr. Juan B. Solana. **Description:** Large and small businesses as well as consumers and policymakers are attempting to identify the areas of risk and loss created by the economic crisis; analysts are now estimating that U.S. mortgage losses could reach the $380 to $400 billion mark. Also discusses the falling of wages and the rising of unemployment. Statistical data included.

14511 ■ *"Valenti: Roots of Financial Crisis Go Back to 1998"* in *Crain's Detroit Business (Vol. 24, October 6, 2008, No. 40, pp. 25)*
Pub: Crain Communications, Inc.
Ed: Tom Henderson; Nathan Skid. **Description:** Interview with Sam Valenti III who is the chairman and CEO of Valenti Capital L.L.C., a wealth-management firm; Valenti discusses in detail the history that led up to the current economic crisis as well as his prediction for the future of the country.

14512 ■ *"What's Ahead for Fannie and Fred?"* in *Barron's (Vol. 90, August 30, 2010, No. 35, pp. 26)*
Pub: Barron's Editorial & Corporate Headquarters
Ed: Jonathan R. Laing. **Description:** A meeting presided by Treasury Secretary Timothy Geithner discussed the future of Fannie Mae and Freddie Mac. The two government sponsored enterprises were mismanaged and reforming these two agencies is critical.

14513 ■ *"Where Are the Vultures?"* in *Mergers & Acquisitions: The Dealmaker's Journal (March 1, 2008)*
Pub: SourceMedia, Inc.
Ed: Ken MacFadyen. **Description:** Although the real estate market is distressed, not many acquisitions are being made by distress private equity investors; this is due, in part, to the difficulty in assessing real estate industry firms since it is a sector which is so localized.

14514 ■ *"Where to Stash Your Cash"* in *Barron's (Vol. 88, March 17, 2008, No. 11, pp. 41)*
Pub: Dow Jones & Company, Inc.
Ed: Mike Hogan. **Description:** Investors are putting their money in money-market mutual funds seeking fractionally better yields and a safe haven from the uncertainties that was brought about by subprime lending. These funds, however, are hovering near 3.20 percent which is less than the 4 percent inflation rate.

14515 ▪ *"The Worst Lies Ahead for Wall Street; More Losses Certain" in Crain's New York Business (Vol. 24, January 21, 2008, No. 3, pp. 1)*
Pub: Crain Communications, Inc.
Ed: Aaron Elstein. **Description:** Due to the weakening economy, many financial institutions will face further massive losses forcing them to borrow more at higher interest rates and dragging down their earnings for years to come. The effects on commercial real estate and credit card loans are also discussed as well as the trend to investing in Asia and the Middle East.

14516 ▪ *"You Better Shop Around: Four Steps to Getting the Best Deal On a Home Loan" in Black Enterprise (Vol. 40, July 2010, No. 12, pp. 78)*
Pub: Earl G. Graves Publishing Co. Inc.
Ed: Tara-Nicholle Nelson. **Description:** Four steps to help anyone seeking a mortgage for a home purchase are listed.

14517 ▪ *"Your Exposure to Bear Stearns" in Barron's (Vol. 88, March 17, 2008, No. 11, pp. 45)*
Pub: Dow Jones & Company, Inc.
Ed: Tom Sullivan; Jack Willoughby. **Description:** Bear Stearns makes up 5.5 percent of Pioneer Independence's portfolio, 1.4 percent of Vanguard Windsor II's portfolio, 1.2 percent of Legg Mason Value Trust, about 1 percent of Van Kampen Equity & Income, and 0.79 percent of Putnam Fund for Growth & Income. Ginnie Mae securities are now trading at 1.78 percentage points over treasuries due to the mortgage crises.

TRADE PERIODICALS

14518 ▪ *Commercial Mortgage Alert*
Pub: Harrison Scott Publications Inc.
Contact: Andrew Albert, Publisher
E-mail: tferris@hspnews.com
Ed: Thomas J. Ferris, Editor. **Released:** 48/year. **Price:** $2,797, U.S., Canada and elsewhere. **Description:** Covers the commercial mortgage market. Recurring features include a calendar of events and a column titled The Grapevine. Remarks: Available via email in PDF format. Sold with the CMBS Database.

14519 ▪ *Inside MBS & ABS*
Pub: Inside Mortgage Finance Publications Inc.
Contact: John Bancroft, Managing Editor
E-mail: jbancroft@imfpubs.com
Released: Weekly, 48 times/year. **Price:** $1,997, individuals. **Description:** Covers the mortgage-related securities market and secondary mortgage market, including regulatory and market developments. Also covers ABS and CMBS markets. Recurring features include interviews, news of research, and exclusive market statistics.

14520 ▪ *Inside Mortgage Finance*
Pub: Inside Mortgage Finance Publications Inc.
Contact: John Bancroft, Managing Editor
E-mail: jbancroft@imfpubs.com
Released: Weekly, 48 times/year. **Price:** $1,097, individuals. **Description:** Contains coverage and analysis of market trends and developments affecting the residential (primary) mortgage market. Includes extensive data on mortgage originations and servicing as well as secondary market activity.

14521 ▪ *Mortgage Banking Magazine: The Magazine of Real Estate Finance*
Pub: Mortgage Bankers Association of America
URL(s): www.mortgagebankingmagazine.com. **Ed:** Lesley Hall. **Released:** Monthly **Price:** $65, Members; $75, Nonmembers; $90, Other countries.

14522 ▪ *Mortgage Technology*
Pub: SourceMedia Inc.
Contact: Douglas J. Manoni, Chief Executive Officer
E-mail: doug.manoni@sourcemedia.com
URL(s): www.nationalmortgagenews.com/technology/. **Released:** Monthly **Price:** $88, U.S.; $108, Canada; $108, Other countries.

14523 ▪ *National Mortgage News*
Pub: SourceMedia Inc.
Contact: Douglas J. Manoni, Chief Executive Officer
E-mail: doug.manoni@sourcemedia.com
URL(s): www.nationalmortgagenews.com. **Ed:** Mark Fogarty, Bonnie Sinnock. **Released:** Weekly

VIDEOCASSETTES/AUDIOCASSETTES

14524 ▪ *Financial Business Services*
Morris Video
12881 Knott St.
Garden Grove, CA 92841
Ph: (310)533-4800
Fax: (310)320-3171
Released: 1983. **Price:** $24.95. **Description:** Money management careers are explored, including investment counselors, securities brokers, trust officers and mortgage underwriters. **Availability:** VHS.

TRADE SHOWS AND CONVENTIONS

14525 ▪ **The Bond Market Association - Fixed Income Summit Expo on E-Commerce & Technology**
Flagg Management, Inc.
353 Lexington Ave.
New York, NY 10016
Ph: (212)286-0333
Fax: (212)286-0086
Co. E-mail: flaggmgmt@msn.com
URL: http://www.flaggmgmt.com
URL(s): www.sifma.org. **Frequency:** Annual. **Audience:** Bond Market Association members, government bond officers, fixed income brokers and dealers. **Principal Exhibits:** Online services, Internet systems, fixed-income trading and executions systems, real-time systems, Internet and other new products and solutions; online trading and execution systems; bond market services; online research and global markets information. **Telecommunication Services:** sweiss@bondmarkets.com.

14526 ▪ **National Association of Review Appraisers and Mortgage Underwriters Convention - National Conference & Expo**
National Association of Review Appraisers and Mortgage Underwriters
1224 N Nokomis NE
Alexandria, MN 56308-5072
Ph: (320)763-6870
Fax: (320)763-9290
URL: http://iami.org/nara
URL(s): www.naramu.org/. **Price:** $485, Preregistered; $385, Pre-registered, non-members guests for social events only. **Frequency:** Annual. **Audience:** Appraisers, mortgage loan officers, review appraisers, and other trade professionals. **Principal Exhibits:** Real estate-related information and services. **Telecommunication Services:** info@naramu.org.

CONSULTANTS

14527 ▪ **M. S. Franks & Company Inc.**
11 La Cuesta Rd.
Orinda, CA 94563
Ph: (925)254-1469
Co. E-mail: msf@msfranksco.com
URL: http://www.msfranksco.com
Contact: Richard F. Kijewski, Manager
Scope: Offers services in cash management, check processing, general ledger, financial reporting, loan processing, international, branch operations and merger integrations. Specializes in operations design to financial service companies with a focus on impact analysis, user requirements, work flow analysis and design, project communications, development of training programs and material, project management. **Founded:** 1990. **Seminars:** Facilitating Great Meetings; Creating Great Project Documentation; Producing Great Meeting Notes.

14528 ▪ **Hilbren Consulting Services Inc.**
287 Valencia Dr.
Monroe Township, NJ 08831
Ph: (732)545-7913
Fax: (732)220-8188
Co. E-mail: info@hilbren.com
URL: http://www.hilbren.com
Contact: Gary L. Tinkel, President
E-mail: gtinkel@hilbren.com
Scope: Provider of the commercial banking and brokerage industries with expertise in designing and implementing financial systems. Backgrounds include foreign exchange, funds transfer, offshore loans, money markets and Euro dollar systems working with both front and back office operations. Also provide a full range of professional services including project management, feasibility studies, systems analysis, programming and support. **Founded:** 1983. **Telecommunication Services:** gtinkel@hilbren.com.

14529 ▪ **James Quinn Agency Inc.**
513 W Park Ave.
Greenwood, MS 38930-2945
Ph: (662)453-3269
Fax: (662)453-3269
Co. E-mail: amadeus8@bellsouth.net
Contact: Nancy Candy, Manager
E-mail: njcandy@microsped.com
Scope: Offers a wide range of real estate appraisal and brokerage services involving residential, commercial, industrial and agricultural properties. Also provides investment analysis and feasibility studies. Serves attorneys, accountants, banks, mortgage lenders, trustees for estates and individual investors on land development, financing and valuation matters. Available for expert witness testimony.

FRANCHISES AND BUSINESS OPPORTUNITIES

14530 ▪ **Centum Financial Group Inc.**
1199 West Pender St., Ste. 700
Vancouver, BC, Canada V6E 2R1
Ph: (604)257-3946
Free: 888-257-3940
Fax: (604)257-3940
URL: http://www.centum.ca
Description: Mortgage broker firms. **No. of Franchise Units:** 260. **No. of Company-Owned Units:** 1. **Founded:** 2002.. **Franchised:** 2002. **Equity Capital Needed:** Minimal to $10,000. **Franchise Fee:** Contact for more information. **Training:** Yes.

14531 ▪ **Realty Direct**
Realty Direct Franchise Corp.
44075 Pipeline Plz., Ste. 320
Ashburn, VA 20147
Ph: (703)327-2428
Free: 800-359-5220
Fax: (703)852-3508
Co. E-mail: franchise@realtydirect.com
URL: http://www.realtydirect.com
Description: Full service discount residential brokerage company. Our model provides for a quick start-up in a local market. Our quality program and streamlined operations provide our franchisees with the tools they need to provide residential brokerage services to their clients. Our discount service approach, full-service quality, and our technology focus set us apart from other discount brokerages. **No. of Franchise Units:** 10. **Founded:** 2001.. **Franchised:** 2004. **Equity Capital Needed:** $39,600-$67,700. **Franchise Fee:** $19,900. **Royalty Fee:** 6%. **Training:** Provides 4 days training at headquarters, 1 day of onsite training and ongoing support.

COMPUTERIZED DATABASES

14532 ▪ *ABA Banking Journal*
345 Hudson St., 12th Fl.
New York, NY 10014
Ph: (212)620-7200

Free: 800-895-4389
URL: http://www.simmonsboardman.com
Contact: Arthur J. McGinnis, Jr., President
E-mail: amcginnis@sbpub.com
Availability: Online: LexisNexis Group; Simmons-Boardman Publishing Corp.; Intuit Inc. - Intuit Financial Services. **Type:** Full-text.

14533 ■ American Banker Financial Publications
1 State St. Plz., 27th Fl.
New York, NY 10004
Ph: (212)803-8200
Free: 800-221-1809
Fax: (212)843-9600
Co. E-mail: custserv@AmericanBanker.com
URL: http://www.americanbanker.com
Availability: Online: ProQuest LLC - Dialog. **Type:** Full-text.

14534 ■ Barron's Online
1 World Financial Ctr.
200 Liberty St.
New York, NY 10281
Ph: (212)416-2000
Fax: (212)416-4348
Co. E-mail: info@dowjones.com
URL: http://www.dowjones.com
Availability: Online: Dow Jones & Company Inc. **Type:** Full-text; Numeric; Statistical.

14535 ■ BlockDATA®
3 Times Sq.
New York, NY 10036

Ph: (646)223-4000
Co. E-mail: salesinquires@thomsonreuters.com
URL: http://thomsonreuters.com/products_services/financial
Availability: Online: Thomson Reuters - Financial Unit. **Type:** Full-text; Numeric.

14536 ■ Business Wire
44 Montgomery St., 39th Fl.
San Francisco, CA 94104
Ph: (415)986-4422
Free: 800-227-0845
Fax: (415)788-5335
Co. E-mail: SF_sales_group@bizwire.com
URL: http://www.businesswire.com
Availability: Online: ProQuest LLC - Dialog; Dow Jones & Company Inc.; Mzinga Inc.; LexisNexis Group; Bloomberg L.P. **Type:** Full-text.

14537 ■ CANNEX
1200 Bay St., Ste. 1001
Toronto, ON, Canada M5R 2A5
Ph: (416)926-0882
Free: 800-387-1269
Fax: (416)926-0706
Co. E-mail: cannex@cannex.com
URL: http://www.cannex.com
Availability: Online: CANNEX Financial Exchanges Ltd. **Type:** Numeric.

14538 ■ Mortgage Delinquency Rates
60 E 42nd St.
New York, NY 10165
Ph: (212)986-9300

Fax: (212)986-5857
Co. E-mail: data@haver.com
URL: http://www.haver.com
Availability: Online: Haver Analytics - HaverSelect. **Type:** Numeric.

14539 ■ Securities Law Daily™
1801 S Bell St.
Arlington, VA 22202
Free: 800-372-1033
Co. E-mail: customercare@bna.com
URL: http://www.bna.com
Availability: Online: Bloomberg LP-Bloomberg BNA; Thomson Reuters - Westlaw. **Type:** Full-text.

14540 ■ U.S. Banker Online
1 State St. Plz., 27th Fl.
New York, NY 10004
Ph: (212)803-8200
Free: 800-221-1809
Co. E-mail: custserv@sourcemedia.com
URL: http://www.sourcemedia.com
Availability: Online: Investcorp International Inc. - SourceMedia Inc. **Type:** Full-text.

14541 ■ U.S. Weekly Statistics
60 E 42nd St.
New York, NY 10165
Ph: (212)986-9300
Fax: (212)986-5857
Co. E-mail: data@haver.com
URL: http://www.haver.com
Availability: Online: Haver Analytics - HaverSelect. **Type:** Statistical; Numeric.

ASSOCIATIONS AND OTHER ORGANIZATIONS

14542 ■ American Motorcyclist Association (AMA)
13515 Yarmouth Dr.
Pickerington, OH 43147
Ph: (614)856-1900
Free: 800-262-5646
Fax: (614)856-1920
URL: http://www.americanmotorcyclist.com
Contact: Rober Rasor, President
Description: Represents motorcycle enthusiasts. Acts as a rulemaking body for motorcycle competition. Promotes highway safety. Maintains museum and hall of fame. **Founded:** 1924. **Publications:** *American Motorcyclist: Journal of the American Motorcyclist Assn* (Monthly); *American Motorcycle Association--Action* (Bimonthly); *Cycle Connection: Motorcyclings' Yellow Pages* (Annual). **Educational Activities:** Long Beach International Motorcycle Show (Annual). **Awards:** AMA Hazel Kolb Brighter Image Award; Daytona 200.

14543 ■ Motorcycle Industry Council (MIC)
2 Jenner St., Ste. 150
Irvine, CA 92618-3806
Ph: (949)727-4211
Fax: (949)727-3313
Co. E-mail: ciannello@mic.org
URL: http://www.mic.org
Description: Manufacturers and distributors of motorcycles and allied industries. Maintains liaison with state and federal governments. Operates collection of research documents, federal and state government documents, and trade publications. Compiles statistics. **Founded:** 1914. **Publications:** *Motorcycle Statistical Annual* (Annual). **Educational Activities:** Dealernews International Powersports Dealer Expo (Annual).

REFERENCE WORKS

14544 ■ *Achieving Planned Innovation: A Proven System for Creating Successful New Products and Services*
Pub: Simon and Schuster
Ed: Frank R. Bacon. **Released:** August 2007. **Price:** $16.95. **Description:** Planned innovation is a disciplined and practical step-by-step sequence of procedures for reaching the intended destination point: successful products. This easy-to-read book explains the system along with an action-oriented program for continuous success in new-product innovations. Five steps outlined include: a disciplined reasoning process; lasting market orientation; proper selection criteria that reflect both strategic and tactical business objectives and goals along with dynamic matching of resources to present and future opportunities, and positive and negative requirements before making major expenditures; and proper organizational staffing. The author explains what to do and evaluating the potential of any new product or service, ranging from ventures in retail distribution to the manufac-

ture of goods as diverse as bicycles, motorcycles, aerospace communication and navigation equipment, small business computers, food packaging, and medical products.

14545 ■ *"Harley-Davidson Moves to Unconventional Marketing Plan" in Business Journal-Milwaukee (Vol. 28, November 26, 2010, No. 8, pp. A1)*
Pub: Milwaukee Business Journal
Ed: Rich Rovito. **Description:** Harley Davidson Inc. hired Boulder, Colorado-based Victors & Spoils, an agency that specializes in crowdsourcing, to implement a new creative marketing model. Under the plan, Harley Davidson will draw on the ideas of its brand enthusiasts to help guide the brand's marketing direction.

14546 ■ *"Local Shops' Wares Sound Good To Boomers Needing Some Fun" in Crain's Cleveland Business (Vol. 30, May 18, 2009, No. 20, pp. 5)*
Pub: Crain Communications, Inc.
Ed: Dan Shingler. **Description:** Dr. Z Amplification, who makes amplifiers for guitars and SuperTrapp Performance Exhausts, producer of tunable exhausts for motorcycles, are seeing increased sales as baby boomers look to add enjoyment to their lives.

14547 ■ *"MANAfest Provides Reps with Tools for the Future" in Agency Sales Magazine (Vol. 39, September-October 2009, No. 9, pp. 36)*
Pub: MANA
Ed: Jack Foster. **Description:** Former Harley Davidson director of communications Ken Schmidt was the keynote speaker at the MANAfest conference; he discussed how the company delivered itself from bankruptcy. Selling Power magazine publisher Gerhard Gschwandtner also made a presentation; he believes that there will be opportunities for sales people involved in relationship selling.

14548 ■ *"A New Way to Arrive in Style" in Inc. (Vol. 33, September 2011, No. 7, pp. 54)*
Pub: Inc. Magazine
Ed: Matthew Rist. **Description:** EagleRider is a franchise offering various two-wheeled rentals, including BMWs and Harley-Davidsons at more than 100 locations worldwide.

14549 ■ *"Wowing Her Customers" in Women In Business (Vol. 61, August-September 2009, No. 4, pp. 34)*
Pub: American Business Women's Association
Ed: Kathleen Leighton. **Description:** Gail Worth, together with her brother, bought her parents' Harley-Davidson motorcycle dealership in Grandview, Missouri. She eventually had the dealership to herself when her brother broke out of the partnership. Gail says she is comfortable in a man's world kind of business and has expanded the business with a 10-acre site.

STATISTICAL SOURCES

14550 ■ *RMA Annual Statement Studies*
Pub: Risk Management Association
Contact: Kevin M. Blakey, President
Released: Annual. **Price:** $175.00 2006-07 edition, $105.00. **Description:** Contains composite balance

sheets and income statements for more than 360 industries, including the accounting, auditing, and bookkeeping industries. Also contains five years of comparative historical data for discerning trends. Includes 16 commonly used ratios, computed for most of the size groupings for nearly every industry.

TRADE PERIODICALS

14551 ■ *American Motorcyclist: Journal of the American Motorcyclist Assn*
Pub: American Motorcyclist Association
Contact: Rober Rasor, President
URL(s): www.americanmotorcyclist.com/asp/magazine/. **Released:** Monthly **Price:** $15, Nonmembers.

14552 ■ *Cycle News*
Pub: CN Publishing
URL(s): www.cyclenews.com. **Ed:** Henny Ray Abrams, Paul Carruthers. **Released:** Weekly **Price:** $45, Individuals include online; $150, Other countries include online; $80, Two years include online; $29.95, Individuals online edition only.

14553 ■ *Cycle World*
Pub: Hachette Filipacchi Media U.S. Inc.
Contact: David Carey, President
URL(s): www.cycleworld.com/. **Released:** Monthly **Price:** $12, Individuals; $35, Other countries.

14554 ■ *Dealernews: The Voice Of The Powersports Industry*
Pub: Advanstar Communications Inc.
Contact: Mr. Joseph Loggia, Chief Executive Officer
E-mail: jloggia@advanstar.com
URL(s): www.dealernews.com. **Released:** Monthly

14555 ■ *The Motorcyclist's Post: Voice of Northeast Motorcycle Riders*
Pub: The Motorcyclist's Post
URL(s): www.motorcyclistpost.com. **Ed:** Leo Castell. **Released:** Monthly **Price:** $25, Individuals; $45, Two years.

TRADE SHOWS AND CONVENTIONS

14556 ■ Minneapolis International Motorcycle Show
Advanstar Communications
641 Lexington Ave., 8th Fl.
New York, NY 10022
Ph: (212)951-6600
Free: 800-346-0085
Fax: (212)951-6793
Co. E-mail: info@advanstar.com
URL: http://www.advanstar.com
Contact: Robert Krakoff, President
URL(s): www.motorcycleshows.com. **Audience:** Public: Motorcycle, watercraft and ATV enthusiasts. **Principal Exhibits:** A marketplace where manufactur-

ers and retailers can display and sell their products such as motorcycles, all-terrain vehicles (ATV), scooters, watercraft, apparel, parts and accessories.

14557 ■ Seattle International Motorcycle Show
Toyota Trucks
1901 South Western Ave.
Dept. WC11
Torrance, CA 90501
Ph: (310)618-4000
Fax: (310)618-7800
URL(s): www.motorcycleshows.com/. **Audience:** Motorcycle, watercraft and ATV enthusiasts. **Principal Exhibits:** A marketplace where manufacturers and retailers can display and sell their products such as motorcycles, all-terrain vehicles (ATV), scooters, watercraft, apparel, parts and accessories.

14558 ■ Southern California International Motorcycle Show
Advanstar Communications
641 Lexington Ave., 8th Fl.
New York, NY 10022

Ph: (212)951-6600
Free: 800-346-0085
Fax: (212)951-6793
Co. E-mail: info@advantstar.com
URL: http://www.advanstar.com
Contact: Robert Krakoff, President
URL(s): www.motorcycleshows.com. **Audience:** Public: Motorcycle, watercraft, and ATV enthusiasts. **Principal Exhibits:** A marketplace where manufacturers and retailers can display and sell their products such as motorcycles, all-terrain vehicles (ATV), scooters watercraft, apparel, parts and accessories.

LIBRARIES

14559 ■ Antique Automobile Club of America - AACA Library & Research Center, Inc.
501 W. Governor Rd.
Hershey, PA 17033

Ph: (717)534-2082
Fax: (717)534-9101
Co. E-mail: critter@aacalibrary.org
URL: http://www.aacalibrary.org
Contact: Steven L. Moskowitz, Executive Director
Scope: Automobiles, automotive history, automobile restoration, commercial vehicles, trucks, motorcycles. **Services:** Copying; library open to the public. **Founded:** 1977. **Holdings:** 6000 books; 300 bound periodical volumes; 400,000 pieces of sales literature, owners and shop manuals; 70 reels of microfilm; 3000 microfiche; 15 drawers of blueprints; paint chips; photographs; sheet music; memorabilia; maps; postcards; 40,000 periodicals. **Subscriptions:** 220 journals and other serials.

ASSOCIATIONS AND OTHER ORGANIZATIONS

14560 ■ *Cinescope*
1235 Bay St., Ste. 400
Toronto, ON, Canada M5R 3K4
Ph: (416)969-7057
Fax: (416)969-8916
Co. E-mail: mptac.ca@ca.inter.net
URL: http://www.mptac.ca
Contact: Adina Lebo, Executive Director
Released: Monthly

14561 ■ **Independent Film and Television Alliance (IFTA)**
10850 Wilshire Blvd., 9th Fl.
Los Angeles, CA 90024-4321
Ph: (310)446-1000
Fax: (310)446-1600
Co. E-mail: rburt@ifta-online.org
URL: http://www.ifta-online.org
Contact: Paul Hertzberg, Chairman
Description: Trade association for the worldwide independent film and television industry. Contributes to negotiations with foreign producer associations; develops standardized theatrical, TV and video contracts for international distribution. Established and maintains the IFTA International Arbitration Tribunal, a system through which prominent entertainment attorneys throughout the world assist members and consenting clients in reaching equitable and binding agreements. Facilitates the formulation of policies, standardized private practices and language contracts and the exchange of information and experience among members. Produces the American Film Market (AFM), the largest international motion picture trade event in the world. **Founded:** 1980. **Awards:** AFMA Honors (Annual).

14562 ■ **Motion Picture Association of America (MPAA)**
15301 Ventura Blvd., Bldg. E
Sherman Oaks, CA 91403
Ph: (818)995-6600
Fax: (818)285-4403
Co. E-mail: contactus@mpaa.org
URL: http://www.mpaa.org
Contact: A. Robert Pisano, President
Description: Represents principal producers and distributors of motion pictures in the U.S. Serves as an advocate of the American motion picture, home video, and television industries; activities also include preserving and protecting the rights of copyright owners; fighting censorship and restrictive attacks on First Amendment rights of motion picture, television, and home video producers; and directing anti-piracy programs to protect U.S. films, television programming, and home video throughout the U.S. **Founded:** 1922.

14563 ■ **Motion Picture Theatre Associations of Canada (MPTAC)—Federation des Associations de proprietaires de cinemas du Canada**
1235 Bay St., Ste. 400
Toronto, ON, Canada M5R 3K4

Ph: (416)969-7057
Fax: (416)969-8916
Co. E-mail: mptac.ca@ca.inter.net
URL: http://www.mptac.ca
Contact: Adina Lebo, Executive Director
Description: Cinema associations. Promotes a business climate beneficial to members. Functions as a trade association for exhibitors in the motion picture industry. Conducts research; sponsors competitions; compiles industry statistics. **Founded:** 1969. **Publications:** *Cinescope* (Monthly). **Educational Activities:** Show Canada (Annual). **Awards:** ShowCanada Showmanship Awards; Show Canada Showmanship Awards (Periodic).

14564 ■ **National Association of Theatre Owners (NATO)**
750 1st St. NE, Ste. 1130
Washington, DC 20002
Ph: (202)962-0054
Fax: (202)962-0370
Co. E-mail: nato@natodc.com
URL: http://www.natoonline.org
Contact: S. David Passman, III, Chairman
Description: Owners, operators and executives of motion picture theaters. Provides services to assist theater owners in successfully operating their theaters including monitoring legislative and technological advancements; compiles statistics. **Founded:** 1948. **Publications:** *Encyclopedia of Exhibition* (Annual). **Educational Activities:** Show East (Annual); Show West (Annual). **Awards:** NATO Awards; NATO Stars of the Year (Annual).

REFERENCE WORKS

14565 ■ *"AMC Scouts Downtown for New HQ"* in Business Journal-Serving Metropolitan Kansas City (Vol. 26, October 19, 2007, No. 6, pp. 1)
Pub: American City Business Journals, Inc.
Ed: Jim Davis. **Description:** AMC Entertainment Inc. is seeking a new 100,000 square foot office in downtown Kansas City. The new headquarters is expected to bring additional employment and revenue to the city. AMC's stay on Main Street since 2002 is discussed.

14566 ■ *"Are Movie Theaters Doomed?"* in Business Horizons (November-December 2007, pp. 491)
Pub: Elsevier Technology Publications
Ed: Jon Silver, John McDonnell. **Description:** Theater operators must embrace new technologies and more diverse target markets if they are to stem the decline in theatergoers. Movie theaters remain highly vulnerable to trends in the home entertainment industry.

14567 ■ *"Calling An Audible"* in The Business Journal-Milwaukee (Vol. 25, August 1, 2008, No. 45, pp. A1)
Pub: American City Business Journals, Inc.
Ed: David Dedge. **Description:** Tough economic conditions are forcing entertainment businesses in Milwaukee, Wisconsin, to try new business strategies

to keep attracting customers. These strategies include keeping prices steady despite increasing costs and new sales promotions.

14568 ■ *"Deltona to Get First Movie Theater, Shopping Center"* in Orlando Business Journal (Vol. 26, December 4, 2009, No. 26, pp. 1)
Pub: American City Business Journals
Ed: Anjali Fluker. **Description:** Epic Theaters Inc. revealed plans to build a new 900,000 square foot retail center anchored by a 12-screen movie theater in the city of Deltona in Volusia County, Florida by 2010. The project, dubbed Deltona Village, would provide the city with its first movie theater and shopping center.

14569 ■ *"EX3D to Launch In-Theater Vending Machines for Stylish RealD 3D Glasses"* in Entertainment Close-Up (August 16, 2011)
Pub: Close-Up Media
Description: Marchon3d has partnered with Cinemark and UltraStar Cinemas to install vending machines selling Marchon3D's line of patented, curved RealD 3D compatible eyeglasses.

14570 ■ *"Feldman Pushing Past 'Pain' of Cost Overruns, Delays at Colonie Center"* in Business Review, Albany New York (November 9, 2007)
Pub: American City Business Journals, Inc.
Ed: Michael DeMasi. **Description:** Details of major improvements at Colonie Center are presented. The total cost for these projects increased by $15 million, and the construction of the nearly ten-story theater in the mall is experiencing delays. According to Larry Feldman, chairman of Feldman Mall Properties, which owns a minority stake in the mall, the cost overruns have pushed the company's renovation costs to around $85 million.

14571 ■ **Film Journal International--Equipment, Concessions & Services Guide**
Contact: Kevin Lally, Executive Editor
E-mail: kevin.lally@nielsen.com
URL(s): directories.vnuemedia.com/fjiguides/equipment. **Ed:** Robert Sunshine. **Released:** Annual; Latest edition 2008. **Publication includes:** Lists of about 300 manufacturers and suppliers of equipment, products, and services for the theatrical motion picture and concession industries; more than 20 film processors, and over 200 dealers and distributors of equipment and supplies. **Entries include:** Company name, address, phone, names and titles of key personnel, products or services. **Arrangement:** Separate alphabetical sections for manufacturers and processors; dealers are geographical. **Indexes:** Product/service.

14572 ■ *"Ghouls, Goblins, and Harry Potter: Cashing In On Halloween"* in Inc. (Vol. 33, October 2011, No. 8, pp. 24)
Pub: Inc. Magazine
Ed: Darren Dahl. **Description:** Costume Craze, an online costume retailer reports $13.2 million in sales

last year. Originally the family business started out as a software company called StaticAdvantage, but switched gears.

14573 ■ *Motion Picture TV and Theatre Directory*

Pub: Motion Picture Enterprises Publications Inc. **URL(s):** www.mpe.net. **Released:** Semiannual; spring and fall. **Price:** $22.53, Individuals each, within New York; $20.79, Individuals each, outside New York. **Covers:** Companies providing products and services to the motion picture and television industries. All listings are paid. **Entries include:** Company name, address, phone. **Arrangement:** Classified by product or service. **Indexes:** Alphabetical.

14574 ■ *The Pixar Touch: The Making of a Company*

Pub: Pantheon Books
Ed: David A. Price. **Released:** 2009. **Price:** $27.95. **Description:** Profile of how Pixar's founders turned their computer-animated films into a successful movie studio.

14575 ■ *"Sneak Preview: Alamo Revamp" in Austin Business JournalInc. (Vol. 28, December 12, 2008, No. 39, pp. 1)*

Pub: American City Business Journals
Ed: Sandra Zaragoza. **Description:** Austin, Texas-based Alamo Drafthouse Cinemas is planning to build a new Circle C Ranch. The new theater will showcase digital projectors and the latest sound systems to show 3-D movies. The company is in lease negotiations with developer Stratus Properties Inc.

14576 ■ *"Stars Shine Downtown" in The Business Journal-Serving Metropolitan Kansas City (Vol. 26, August 29, 2008, No. 51, pp. 1)*

Pub: American City Business Journals, Inc.
Ed: Rob Roberts. **Description:** Movie chain AMC Entertainment Inc. renews its lease for 97,000 square feet of space at Ten Main Center. HNTB Federal Services Corp., meanwhile, is to take up 42,000 square feet at an office building located at 120 W. 12th St. The leases' impacts on downtown office market are examined.

14577 ■ *Theatre Directory*

Pub: Theatre Communications Group
Contact: Dafina McMillan, Director
E-mail: dmcmillan@tcg.org
URL(s): www.tcg.org. **Released:** Annual; Latest edition 2007-2008. **Price:** $14.95, Individuals each. **Covers:** Approximately 450 not-for-profit profession theatres, and over 100 arts resource organizations. **Entries include:** For theatres--company name, address, business and box office phone and fax numbers, name and title of 3 primary staff members, e-mail and web addresses, season, union contracts and special interests. For resource organizations--company name, address, business phone and fax numbers, name and title of contact, e-mail and web addresses, and a brief description of the organization. **Arrangement:** Classified by activity or service. **Indexes:** Special interest, personnel, theatre by state.

STATISTICAL SOURCES

14578 ■ *RMA Annual Statement Studies*

Pub: Risk Management Association
Contact: Kevin M. Blakey, President
Released: Annual. **Price:** $175.00 2006-07 edition, $105.00. **Description:** Contains composite balance sheets and income statements for more than 360 industries, including the accounting, auditing, and bookkeeping industries. Also contains five years of comparative historical data for discerning trends. Includes 16 commonly used ratios, computed for most of the size groupings for nearly every industry.

TRADE PERIODICALS

14579 ■ *Boxoffice Magazine: The Business Magazine of The Global Motion Picture Industry*

Pub: Media Enterprises L.P.
Contact: Morris Schlozman, Editor
URL(s): www.boxoffice.com. **Ed:** Amy Nicholson. **Released:** Monthly **Price:** $59.95, Individuals; $74.95, Canada; $135, Other countries.

14580 ■ *Film Comment*

Pub: Film Society of Lincoln Center
URL(s): www.filmcomment.com. **Ed:** Gavin Smith. **Released:** Bimonthly **Price:** $29.95, Individuals; $35.95, Institutions and libraries; $40, Canada and Mexico; $45, Institutions, Canada and Mexico libraries; $60, Other countries; $70, Institutions, other countries libraries.

14581 ■ *Film Journal International*

Pub: Pubsun Corp.
URL(s): www.filmjournal.com. **Released:** Monthly **Price:** $65, Individuals; $100, Two years.

VIDEOCASSETTES/ AUDIOCASSETTES

14582 ■ *Inside Business Today*

GPN Educational Media
1550 Executive Drive
Elgin, IL 60123
Ph: (402)472-2007
Free: 800-228-4630
Fax: (800)306-2330
Co. E-mail: askgpn@smarterville.com
URL: http://www.shopgpn.com
Released: 1989. **Description:** Leaders in business and industry tell their success stories in this extensive series. **Availability:** VHS; 3/4 U.

CONSULTANTS

14583 ■ Stage Equipment and Lighting Inc.

12250 NE 13th Ct.
Miami, FL 33161-6518
Ph: (305)891-2010
Fax: (305)893-2828
Co. E-mail: ike@seal-fla.com
URL: http://www.seal-fla.com
Contact: Vivian Gill, President
Scope: Offers creative services for presentations, staging, and lighting, including systems designs, installation supervision, seminars for personnel, theatrical equipment maintenance and lighting for all forms of presentations and presentation facilities, theaters, television, film, audiovisuals, meetings, and product presentations. **Founded:** 1967. **Publications:** "Lighting&Sound America".

FRANCHISES AND BUSINESS OPPORTUNITIES

14584 ■ Actor's Garage

152 Ryder Rd.
Manhasset, NY 11030
Ph: (516)627-7211
Fax: (516)627-7230
Description: Children's acting schools. **No. of Franchise Units:** 3. **No. of Company-Owned Units:** 13. **Founded:** 2004.. **Franchised:** 2006. **Equity Capital Needed:** $30,600-$31,700. **Franchise Fee:** $24,000. **Royalty Fee:** 9%. **Training:** Provides 5 days at headquarters with ongoing support.

14585 ■ Kidstage

PO Box 1072
Appleton, WI 54912
Ph: (877)415-5115
Description: Drama classes and performance opportunities. **No. of Franchise Units:** 14. **No. of Company-Owned Units:** 3. **Founded:** 1996.. **Franchised:** 2003. **Equity Capital Needed:** $14,000. **Franchise Fee:** $12,500. **Financial Assistance:** Yes. **Training:** Yes.

LIBRARIES

14586 ■ Academy of Motion Picture Arts and Sciences - Margaret Herrick Library

Fairbanks Center for Motion Picture Studies
333 S. La Cienega Blvd.
Beverly Hills, CA 90211
Ph: (310)247-3020

Fax: (310)859-9619
Co. E-mail: lmehr@oscars.org
URL: http://www.oscars.org/library/index.html
Contact: Linda Harris Mehr, Director
URL(s): www.oscars.org. **Scope:** Motion picture history, biography, and production. **Services:** Copying; photographic reproduction; Library open to the public for reference use only; special collections open to the public by appointment. **Founded:** 1928. **Holdings:** 32,000 books; 3117 periodical titles; 1875 VF drawers of clippings on film productions, individuals, general subject, festivals, awards, Academy history; 80,000 scripts; 10 million photographs; 42,000 posters. **Subscriptions:** 152 journals and other serials; 3 newspapers; 79 online titles.

14587 ■ John E. Allen, Inc. - Motion Picture Archives

PO Box 452
Newfoundland, PA 18445
Ph: (570)676-4152
Fax: (570)676-9194
Co. E-mail: jeainc@gmail.com
URL: http://www.allenarchive.com/wordpress/
Contact: Beverley Allen, Archivist
Scope: Motion pictures, 1896-1980s; general coverage with wide subject base, actuality and dramatic. **Services:** Copying; archives open to the public by appointment on fee basis. **Founded:** 1961. **Holdings:** 25 million feet of 35mm and 16mm film.

14588 ■ American Film Institute - Louis B. Mayer Library

2021 N. Western Ave.
Box 27999
Los Angeles, CA 90027-1657
Ph: (323)856-7654
Fax: (323)856-7803
Co. E-mail: library@afi.com
URL: http://www.afi.com/about/library.aspx
Contact: Caroline Sisneros, Librarian
Scope: Moving pictures, television, video, cable, satellite. **Services:** Copying; indexing (microfiche); library open to the public. **Founded:** 1969. **Holdings:** 14,000 books; 900 bound periodical volumes; 6000 motion picture and television scripts; 44 oral history transcripts; 535 seminar transcripts; 600 seminar audiotapes; 75 reels of microfilm. **Subscriptions:** 100 journals and other serials (approximately); 5 newspapers.

14589 ■ Hollywood Film Archive Library

8391 Beverly Blvd. PMB 321
Hollywood, CA 90048
Ph: (323)655-4968
Co. E-mail: cabaret66@aol.com
URL: http://hfarchive.com
Contact: D. Richard Baer, Director
Scope: Motion pictures, television, video. **Services:** Library open to the public by appointment only. **Founded:** 1972. **Holdings:** 2400 volumes; 6000 motion picture stills; Monthly Film Bulletin, 1934 to present; Motion Picture Exhibitor, 1931-1972; Motion Picture Herald, 1944-1960; Boxoffice, 1960 to present.

14590 ■ Motion Picture Association of America Library

15301 Ventura Blvd., Bldg. E
Sherman Oaks, CA 91403-5885
Ph: (818)995-6600
Fax: (818)285-4403
URL: http://www.mpaa.org
Scope: Theatrical motion pictures - history, finance, censorship, content. **Services:** Library available to qualified persons for consultation by mail or telephone. **Founded:** 1946. **Holdings:** 3000 volumes. **Subscriptions:** 20 journals and other serials.

14591 ■ University of Southern California - Cinematic Arts Library

Doheny Memorial Library, Ground Fl.
3550 Trousdale Pkwy.
Los Angeles, CA 90089-0185

Ph: (213)740-3994

Co. E-mail: shanson@usc.edu

URL: http://www.usc.edu/libraries/locations/cinema_
tv/

Contact: Stephen Hanson, Director

Scope: Motion pictures, television, radio. **Services:** Interlibrary loan (limited); copying; Library open to the public for reference use only. **Founded:** 1964. **Holdings:** 22,000 volumes; 250 reels of microfilm; 427 cartridges of videotape of David Wolper productions, 1962-1972; teleplay collection; screenplay collection; 1700 reels and cartridges of audiotape; 1200 soundtracks and original cast recordings. **Subscriptions:** 220 journals and other serials. **Telecommunication Services:** garciamy@usc.edu.

RESEARCH CENTERS

14592 ■ Theatre Historical Society of America (THSA)
York Theatre Bldg., 2nd Fl.
152 N York St.
Elmhurst, IL 60126-2806

Ph: (630)782-1800

Fax: (630)782-1802

Co. E-mail: thrhistsoc@aol.com

URL: http://www.historictheatres.org

Contact: Karen Colizzi Noonan, President

Services: Research assistance to both members and nonmembers. **Founded:** 1969. **Publications:** *Marquee* (Quarterly). **Educational Activities:** Annual convention and theater tour. **Awards:** Jeffery Weiss Memorial Writing Competition.

ASSOCIATIONS AND OTHER ORGANIZATIONS

14593 ■ American Moving and Storage Association (AMSA)
1611 Duke St.
Alexandria, VA 22314-3406
Ph: (703)683-7410
Free: 888-849-2672
Fax: (703)683-7527
Co. E-mail: amconf@amconf.org
URL: http://www.promover.org
Contact: Linda Bauer Darr, President
Description: Local, intrastate, interstate, and international movers who transport household goods, office and institutional equipment, and high-value products. Sponsors Household Goods Dispute Settlement Program which handles consumer complaints between consumers and interstate moving companies. **Founded:** 1936. **Publications:** *AMSA Direction* (Monthly); *Government Traffic News* (Monthly); *The Moving World* (Biweekly); *Scale Directory* (Biennial); *Direction* (Monthly); *Moving World: The American Moving and Storage Association* (Semimonthly); *Direction*; *AMSA Membership Directory* (Annual); *National Moving and Storage Association--Membership Directory and Buyer's Guide* (Annual); *M & S Times* (Biweekly); *Directory of Repair Shops for Furniture and Appliances*; *Transportation Fact Book* (Annual). **Educational Activities:** GSA Household Goods and Freight Conference (Semiannual); Management Conference and Trade Show (Annual). **Awards:** Safety Awards (Annual); Super Driver Awards (Annual).

REFERENCE WORKS

14594 ■ "For His Bigness of Heart: Larry O'Toole: Gentle Giant Moving, Somerville, Massachusetts" in Inc. (Volume 32, December 2010)
Pub: Inc. Magazine
Description: Profile of Larry O'Toole, owners of Gentle Giant Moving Company, where his company charges more, but in return consumers receive a higher quality service.

14595 ■ "KXAN Seeks Larger Studio, Office Space" in Austin Business Journal (Vol. 31, May 27, 2011, No. 12, pp. A1)
Pub: American City Business Journals Inc.
Ed: Cody Lyon. **Description:** Austin NBC affiliate KXAN Television is opting to sell its property north of downtown and relocate to another site. The station is now inspecting possible sites to house its broadcasting facility and employees totaling as many as 200 people. Estimated cost of the construction of the studios and offices is $13 million plus another million in moving the equipment.

STATISTICAL SOURCES

14596 ■ *RMA Annual Statement Studies*
Pub: Risk Management Association
Contact: Kevin M. Blakey, President
Released: Annual. **Price:** $175.00 2006-07 edition, $105.00. **Description:** Contains composite balance sheets and income statements for more than 360 industries, including the accounting, auditing, and bookkeeping industries. Also contains five years of comparative historical data for discerning trends. Includes 16 commonly used ratios, computed for most of the size groupings for nearly every industry.

FRANCHISES AND BUSINESS OPPORTUNITIES

14597 ■ Craters & Freighters
Craters & Freighters Franchise Co.
331 Corporate Cir., No. J
Golden, CO 80401
Free: 800-949-9931
Fax: (303)399-8190
Co. E-mail: franchise@CratersAndFreighters.com
URL: http://www.CratersAndFreighters.com
Description: As "speciality freight handlers," the Company serves an up-scale market on art galleries, museums, estate liquidators, interior decorators and a host of other clients to fulfill their specialized needs in moving a multitude of large, delicate and valuable freight shipments. **No. of Franchise Units:** 65. **Founded:** 1990.. **Franchised:** 1991. **Equity Capital Needed:** $88,00-$140,000. **Franchise Fee:** $15,000-$35,000. **Royalty Fee:** 5%. **Training:** Offers training at headquarters 10 days, 2-3 days at franchisee's location, 2 days annual convention with ongoing support.

14598 ■ Mobile Attic Franchising Company
Mobile Attic, Inc.
246 Larkin Rd.
Elba, AL 36323
Ph: (334)897-1346
Free: 866-874-8474
Fax: (334)897-1349
Description: Portable self-storage. **No. of Franchise Units:** 40. **No. of Company-Owned Units:** 4.

Founded: 2000.. **Franchised:** 2004. **Equity Capital Needed:** $250,000+. **Financial Assistance:** Yes. **Training:** Yes.

14599 ■ Moving Solutions Franchise LLC
115 W Eagle Rd.
Havertown, PA 19083
Ph: (610)853-2600
Fax: (610)853-2600
Description: Move management and relocation services. **No. of Franchise Units:** 6. **No. of Company-Owned Units:** 1. **Founded:** 1996.. **Franchised:** 2005. **Equity Capital Needed:** $29,300-$40,700. **Franchise Fee:** $9,000-$29,000. **Royalty Fee:** 4%. **Training:** Available at headquarters for 10 days and ongoing support.

14600 ■ Two Men and a Truck
Two Men and a Truck Intl., Inc.
3400 Belle Chase Way
Lansing, MI 48911
Ph: (517)394-7210
Fax: (517)394-7432
Co. E-mail: shirleyk@twomenandatruck.com
URL: http://www.twomenandatruck.com
Description: One of the largest local-moving franchises in the U.S. High-growth unique profitable market niche. No experience necessary. Strong and steady year-round market, regardless of economy. Nationally recognized name and logo. Industry-wide leadership position with a proven operating system of success. Award winning advertising and marketing support. Franchisee Advisory Council - TEAM, rated in Entrepreneur Magazine top 500. Excellent opportunity for women and men. **No. of Franchise Units:** 225. **Founded:** 1985.. **Franchised:** 1989. **Equity Capital Needed:** $158,000-$430,910. **Franchise Fee:** $45,000. **Training:** Training at Stick Men University: marketing, moving logistics, employee issues, computerized franchise management system "Movers Who Care" and more. Ongoing support: unlimited consulting, onsite visits, monthly training, advanced training, custom ads, annual convention and much more.

14601 ■ Two Men and a Truck Canada
245 Yorkland Blvd., Ste. 100
Toronto, ON, Canada M2J 4W9
Ph: (416)646-0486
Fax: (416)490-1456
Co. E-mail: franchise@twomenandatruck.ca
URL: http://www.twomenandatruck.ca
Description: Moving service. **No. of Franchise Units:** 20. **No. of Company-Owned Units:** 2. **Founded:** 2005.. **Franchised:** 2005. **Equity Capital Needed:** $177,500-$406,910. **Franchise Fee:** $35,000. **Training:** Provides 3 weeks training.

ASSOCIATIONS AND OTHER ORGANIZATIONS

14602 ■ American String Teachers Association (ASTA)
4155 Chain Bridge Rd.
Fairfax, VA 22030
Ph: (703)279-2113
Fax: (703)279-2114
Co. E-mail: asta@astaweb.com
URL: http://www.astaweb.com
Contact: Donna Sizemore Hale, Executive Director
Description: Promotes excellence in string and orchestra teaching and playing, together with the National School Orchestra Association. Pursues its mission through: an open sharing of ideas; benefits, services, and activities responsive to the needs of all members; development of strong state leadership and chapters; enhancing the image and visibility of string teaching and study; advocacy for string education; and an inclusive community of string teachers and players. **Founded:** 1946. **Publications:** *American String Teacher* (Quarterly); *ASTA eNews* (Monthly). **Educational Activities:** ASTA National Conference; ASTA with NSOA (Annual). **Awards:** Artist-Teacher Award (Annual); Elizabeth A.H. Green School Educator Award.

14603 ■ Association for Technology in Music Instruction (ATMI)
312 E Pine St.
Missoula, MT 59802
Ph: (406)721-1152
Fax: (406)721-9419
Co. E-mail: jimf@soundtree.com
URL: http://www.atmionline.org
Contact: James Frankel, President
URL(s): atmionline.org/. **Description:** University professors, public school teachers, music industry professionals, and research laboratory personnel. Seeks to increase public awareness of computer-based music systems. Provides a forum for publishing research; facilitates the exchange of information among users of computers in music instruction; aids music teachers in implementing computer-based systems in music education. Serves as a research clearinghouse in the field. **Founded:** 1975. **Publications:** *ATMI Music Technology Directory* (Annual); *Technology Directory* (Annual); *Technology Directory* (Annual); *ATMI International Newsletter.* **Educational Activities:** Association for Technology in Music Instruction Conference (Annual). **Telecommunication Services:** atmi@music.org.

14604 ■ Canadian Federation of Music Teachers' Associations (CFMTA)—Federation Canadienne des Professeurs de Musique
c/o Bernadette Bullock, Sec.-Treas.
302-550 Berkshire Dr.
London, ON, Canada N6J 3S2
Ph: (519)471-6051
Fax: (519)471-9126
Co. E-mail: admin@cfmta.org
URL: http://www.cfmta.org
Contact: Bernadette Bullock, Secretary Treasurer
Description: Private music teachers. Promotes music education in Canada. Organizes performances

and competitions. Sponsors Canada Music Week and Young Artists' series. **Founded:** 1935. **Publications:** *The Canadian Music Teacher* (3/year); *The Canadian Music Teacher: Canada Music Week Edition* (Annual). **Awards:** Bill Andrews Award (Annual); Memorial Pedagogy Award (Biennial); Canada Music Week Music Writing Awards (Annual).

14605 ■ The Canadian Music Teacher
c/o Bernadette Bullock, Sec.-Treas.
302-550 Berkshire Dr.
London, ON, Canada N6J 3S2
Ph: (519)471-6051
Fax: (519)471-9126
Co. E-mail: admin@cfmta.org
URL: http://www.cfmta.org
Contact: Bernadette Bullock, Secretary
Released: 3/year

14606 ■ The Canadian Music Teacher: Canada Music Week Edition
c/o Bernadette Bullock, Sec.-Treas.
302-550 Berkshire Dr.
London, ON, Canada N6J 3S2
Ph: (519)471-6051
Fax: (519)471-9126
Co. E-mail: admin@cfmta.org
URL: http://www.cfmta.org
Contact: Bernadette Bullock, Secretary
Released: Annual

14607 ■ Canadian University Music Society (CUMS)—Societe de Musique des Universites Canadiennes (SMUC)
10 Morrow Ave., Ste. 202
Toronto, ON, Canada M6R 2J1
Ph: (416)538-1650
Fax: (416)489-1713
Co. E-mail: membership@cums-smuc.ca
URL: http://www.cums-smuc.ca
Contact: Mary Ingraham, President
Description: Represents university music schools and professors, graduate students, and independent scholars. **Founded:** 1964. **Publications:** *Intersections* (Semiannual). **Awards:** George Proctor Prize (Annual).

14608 ■ International Association for Jazz Education (IAJE)
PO Box 70213
San Diego, CA 92167-1213
Ph: (619)223-2069
Co. E-mail: mail@apassion4jazz.net
URL: http://www.apassion4jazz.net/iaje.html
Description: Music teachers from grade school through college, professional musicians, and others; students from junior high through college; libraries; individuals from the music industry. Fosters and promotes understanding, appreciation, and artistic performance of jazz music; disseminates educational and professional news. Encourages the adoption of curricula that will explore contemporary composition, arrangement, and improvisation; cooperation with all organizations dedicated to the development of musi-

cal culture in America. Maintains hall of fame. **Founded:** 1968. **Educational Activities:** International Association for Jazz Education Workshop (Periodic).

14609 ■ International Computer Music Association (ICMA)
1819 Polk St., Ste. 330
San Francisco, CA 94109
Fax: (734)878-3031
Co. E-mail: icma@umich.edu
URL: http://www.computermusic.org
Contact: Tae Hong Park, President
Description: Composers, computer software and hardware developers, researchers and musicians. Works to advance individuals and institutions involved in the technical, creative and performance aspects of computer music. Provides networking opportunities; sponsors research and projects; holds competitions. **Scope:** computer music. **Founded:** 1974. **Subscriptions:** archival material articles. **Awards:** Best Presentation Award; Eric Siday Musical Creativity Award (Annual); International Computer Music Commission Awards (Annual); Best Presentation Award; International Computer Music Commission Awards; Swets & Zeitlinger Distinguished Paper Award (Annual); Eric Siday Musical Creativity Award; Swets and Zeitlinger Distinguished Paper Award.

14610 ■ Intersections
10 Morrow Ave., Ste. 202
Toronto, ON, Canada M6R 2J1
Ph: (416)538-1650
Fax: (416)489-1713
Co. E-mail: membership@cums-smuc.ca
URL: http://www.cums-smuc.ca
Contact: Mary Ingraham, President
Released: Semiannual **Price:** C$40, /year.

14611 ■ Organization of American Kodaly Educators (OAKE)
10951 Pico Blvd., Ste. 405
Los Angeles, CA 90064-2191
Ph: (310)441-3555
Fax: (310)441-3577
Co. E-mail: info@oake.org
URL: http://www.oake.org
Contact: Paul Baumann, President
Description: Represents music educators, students, organizations, schools, and libraries interested in the Kodaly concept of music education. Zoltan Kodaly (1882-1967), Hungarian composer and educator, originated a concept of music education that seeks to develop the sensibilities, intellectual facilities, and skills of children, with the intention of creating a musically educated public. Objectives are: to encourage communication and cooperation among Kodaly educators; to encourage musical and human growth; to provide a forum for comment on the impact of the Kodaly concept; to recognize, identify, and convey the multicultural musical heritage of American society; to contribute to and encourage the aesthetic education of the child. Conducts clinics and other small unit activities. **Scope:** music education. **Founded:** 1973. **Subscriptions:** 31 archival material. **Publications:** *Kodaly Concept of Music Education; Kodaly Envoy*

(Quarterly); *Kodaly Envoy*; *Sourwood Mountain*; *OAKE Research Collection Vol. 1*; *The Owl Sings*; *Who Was Kodaly: OAKE Monograph No. 1*. **Educational Activities:** Organization of American Kodaly Educators Conference (Annual).

14612 ■ MENC: The National Association for Music Education (MENC)
1806 Robert Fulton Dr.
Reston, VA 20191
Ph: (703)860-4000
Free: 800-336-3768
Fax: (703)860-1531
Co. E-mail: michaelb@nafme.org
URL: http://musiced.nafme.org
Contact: Michael A. Butera, Executive Director
Description: Comprised of music educators, administrators, supervisors, consultants, and music education majors in colleges. Publishes materials for music educators, presents conferences, compiles statistics. **Founded:** 1907. **Publications:** *Music Educators Journal* (Bimonthly); *Teaching Music* (Bimonthly); *Music Educators Journal*; *Teaching Music*; *General Music Today*; *Update: Applications of Research in Music Education* (Semiannual); *Journal of Music Teacher Education* (Semiannual); *Journal of Research in Music Education* (Quarterly); *Journal of Music Teacher Education* (Semiannual); *Journal of Research in Music Education* (Quarterly). **Awards:** FAME Awards (Annual). **Telecommunication Services:** mbrserv@menc2.org.

14613 ■ Music Publishers' Association of the United States (MPA)
243 5th Ave., Ste. 236
New York, NY 10016
Ph: (212)327-4044
Co. E-mail: admin@mpa.org
URL: http://www.mpa.org
Contact: Lauren Keiser, President
Description: Publishers of music intended for educational and concert purposes. Promotes trade and commerce; encourages understanding of and compliance with copyright laws to protect musical works against piracy and infringement. **Founded:** 1895. **Awards:** Paul Revere Awards for Graphic Excellence (Annual).

14614 ■ Music Teachers National Association (MTNA)
441 Vine St., Ste. 3100
Cincinnati, OH 45202-2811
Ph: (513)421-1420
Free: 888-512-5278
Fax: (513)421-2503
URL: http://www.mtna.org
Contact: Dr. Gary L. Ingle, Chief Executive Officer
Description: Professional society of independent and collegiate music teachers committed to furthering the art of music through programs that encourage and support teaching, performance, composition, and scholarly research. **Founded:** 1876. **Publications:** *American Music Teacher* (Bimonthly); *Directory of Nationally Certified Teachers* (Annual); *The American Music Teacher--Directory of Local Associations and Student Chapters Issue*. **Educational Activities:** MTNA National Conference (Annual). **Awards:** Junior Performance Competition; Student Composition Competition; Senior Performance Competitions; Chamber Music Performance Competition; Distinguished Composer of the Year (Annual); Shepherd Distinguished Composer of the Year Award.

14615 ■ NAMM - The International Music Products Association
5790 Armada Dr.
Carlsbad, CA 92008-4608
Ph: (760)438-8001
Free: 800-767-6266
Fax: (760)438-7327
Co. E-mail: info@namm.org
URL: http://www.namm.org
Contact: Joe Lamond, President
URL(s): www.namm.org. **Description:** Retailers of musical instruments and allied products, manufacturers, distributors, jobbers, wholesalers and publishers of print music. Holds several professional development seminars in various locations around the country and 2 major trade shows. **Scope:** statistics,

retailing, professional development. **Founded:** 1901. **Subscriptions:** books video recordings. **Publications:** *Playback* (Bimonthly); *NAMM PlayBack*. **Educational Activities:** The NAMM Show (Annual); The NAMM Show (Annual); NAMM - Summer Session (Annual). **Awards:** William R. Gard Memorial Scholarship (Annual). **Telecommunication Services:** info@namm.com.

14616 ■ National Association of School Music Dealers (NASMD)
14070 Proton Rd., Ste. 100
Dallas, TX 75244-3601
Ph: (972)233-9107
Fax: (972)490-4219
Co. E-mail: office@nasmd.com
URL: http://www.nasmd.com
Contact: Joel Menchey, President
Description: Retail music stores and companies engaged in sales, service and repair of band and orchestra instruments to elementary and secondary schools and colleges. **Founded:** 1962. **Publications:** *NASMD Newsletter* (Quarterly).

14617 ■ National Association of Schools of Music (NASM)
11250 Roger Bacon Dr., Ste. 21
Reston, VA 20190-5248
Ph: (703)437-0700
Fax: (703)437-6312
Co. E-mail: info@arts-accredit.org
URL: http://nasm.arts-accredit.org
Contact: Daniel P. Sher, President
Description: Serves as an accrediting agency for music educational programs. Compiles statistics. **Founded:** 1924. **Publications:** *National Association of Schools of Music--Directory* (Annual).

14618 ■ National Association for the Study and Performance of African-American Music (NASPAAM)
c/o Martha Cistrunk Brown, Treas.
809 E Gladwick St.
Carson, CA 90746-3818
Co. E-mail: webmaster@naspaam.org
URL: http://www.naspaam.org
Contact: Charles E. Hicks, President
Description: Fosters the creation, study, and promotion of black-derived music in education. Seeks to heighten public awareness of the problems faced by black music educators and students and to increase public understanding of those problems. Provides a forum for the discussion of concerns. Coordinates and disseminates materials concerning black-derived music in order to assist music teachers in teaching black music and students. Encourages blacks to aspire to leadership positions and to demand inclusion in the development and presentation of Music Educators National Conference activities, including participation in MENC's regional conferences. Sponsors collegiate and high school gospel choir competitions. Compiles list of music, books, and related music materials by blacks. **Founded:** 1972. **Publications:** *Con Brio* (Quarterly). **Educational Activities:** National Association for the Study and Performance of African-American Music Conference (Biennial).

14619 ■ National Association of Teachers of Singing (NATS)
9957 Moorings Dr., Ste. 401
Jacksonville, FL 32257
Ph: (904)992-9101
Fax: (904)262-2587
Co. E-mail: info@nats.org
URL: http://www.nats.org
Contact: Allen Henderson, Executive Director
Description: Serves as a professional society of teachers of singing. Encourages the highest standards of the vocal art and of ethical principles in the teaching of singing. Promotes vocal education and research at all levels, both for the enrichment of the general public and for the professional advancement of the talented. **Founded:** 1944. **Publications:** *Journal of Singing* (5/year); *National Association of Teachers of Singing--Membership Directory*. **Awards:** NATS Art Song Composition Award (Annual); NATS Artist Awards Competition (Biennial).

REFERENCE WORKS

14620 ■ *American Musicological Society--Directory*
Pub: American Musicological Society Inc.
URL(s): www.theams.us/. **Released:** Annual; February. **Covers:** About 5,000 members and subscribers to the society's Journal. **Entries include:** Name, address, phone, fax, and e-mail. **Arrangement:** Members are alphabetical; subscribers are geographical.

14621 ■ *Directory of Festivals, Schools and Workshops*
Pub: Chamber Music America
Contact: Margaret M. Lioi, Chief Executive Officer
URL(s): www.chamber-music.org. **Ed:** Leonard Levine. **Released:** Annual; Latest edition 2011. **Covers:** over 150 chamber music workshops and schools for students, young professionals, and adult amateurs; international listings. **Entries include:** Name, location or address, description of program and participants sought, procedure for auditions, type of accommodations and recreational facilities, dates, age requirements, and fees as of spring 2000. **Arrangement:** Geographical. **Indexes:** Alphabetical by state, alphabetical by program.

14622 ■ *Directory of Nationally Certified Teachers*
Pub: Music Teachers National Association
Contact: Dr. Gary L. Ingle, Chief Executive Officer
URL(s): www.mtna.org/home.htm. **Released:** Annual; April. **Covers:** 4,300 nationally certified music teachers, searchable by instrument or type of education. **Entries include:** Teacher name, address, phone, specialty. **Arrangement:** Geographical.

14623 ■ *Instrumentalist--Buyer's Guide Issue*
Pub: Instrumentalist Co.
Contact: John Hiess, Manager
URL(s): www.theinstrumentalist.com. **Released:** Annual; July. **Publication includes:** List of about 460 companies associated with the music business. **Entries include:** Name and address. Paid listings include additional data. **Arrangement:** Classified by product or service. **Indexes:** Product/service.

14624 ■ *Instrumentalist--Directory of Summer Music Camps, Clinics, and Workshops Issue*
Pub: Instrumentalist Co.
Contact: John Hiess, Manager
URL(s): www.theinstrumentalist.com. **Released:** Annual; Latest edition 2009. **Price:** $2.50. **Publication includes:** List of nearly 250 summer music camps, clinics, and workshops in the United States; limited Canadian and foreign coverage. **Entries include:** Camp name, location, name of director, opening and closing dates, tuition fees, courses offered. **Arrangement:** Geographical.

14625 ■ *National Association of Schools of Music--Directory*
Pub: National Association of Schools of Music
Contact: Daniel P. Sher, President
URL(s): nasm.arts-accredit.org. **Released:** Annual **Price:** $20, Individuals. **Covers:** Approximately 630 college and university departments of music and music conservatories accredited by the association. **Entries include:** School name, address, type of membership, description of music program, name of chief administrator, phone, degree or other study programs offered in music. **Arrangement:** Alphabetical.

14626 ■ *National Opera Association--Membership Directory: Opera Journal*
Pub: National Opera Association
Contact: Elizabeth Kirkpatrick Vrenios, President
E-mail: evrenios@netzero.com
URL(s): www.noa.org. **Released:** Semiannual **Covers:** About 675 music and singing teachers, singers, directors, and about 300 schools, colleges, and organizations interested in opera; international coverage. **Entries include:** Name, address, phone, activity or occupation. **Arrangement:** Alphabetical within membership divisions. **Indexes:** Geographical.

14627 ■ *"Sound Fundamentals" in Hispanic Business (September 2007, pp. 12, 14, 16)*
Pub: Hispanic Business
Ed: Michael T. Mena. **Description:** Profile of Ozomatli, a Los Angeles-based multicultural, multi-ethnic musical group that has topped Billboard's Latin Pop chart without relying on record sales. Members explain how they run the group like a small business.

SOURCES OF SUPPLY

14628 ■ *Music Trades--Purchaser's Guide to the Music Industry Issue*
Music Trades Corp.
Contact: Dennis Houlihan, President
URL(s): www.musictrades.com. **Ed:** Brian T. Majeski. **Released:** Annual; Latest edition 2010; New edition expected 2012. **Price:** $16, Individuals per year. **Publication includes:** List of 3,000 musical instrument manufacturers and wholesalers, publishers of sheet music, and manufacturers of musical accessories; international coverage. **Entries include:** Company name, address, phone, names of executives, trade and brand names, products or services. **Arrangement:** Alphabetical.

TRADE PERIODICALS

14629 ■ *Accordionists and Teachers Guild--Bulletin*
Pub: Accordionists and Teachers Guild, International
Contact: Joan Sommers, President
Ed: Julia Cortinas, Editor, jcortina@uiuc.edu. **Released:** 4/year. **Price:** Included in membership. **Description:** Focuses on accordion teaching and performing. Carries items on concerts, recitals, new music, conventions, and the activities of the Guild and its members.

14630 ■ *Acoustic Guitar Magazine*
Pub: Acoustic Guitar
URL(s): www.acousticguitar.com. **Released:** 8/yr. **Price:** $29.95, Individuals.

14631 ■ *American Music Teacher*
Pub: Music Teachers National Association
Contact: Dr. Gary L. Ingle, Chief Executive Officer
URL(s): www.mtna.org/publications/american-music-teacher/. **Released:** Bimonthly **Price:** $6, Single issue domestic; $30, Nonmembers; $40, Other countries; $24, Libraries; $7, Single issue international.

14632 ■ *American Suzuki Journal*
Pub: Suzuki Association of Americas
URL(s): suzukiassociation.org/journal/. **Ed:** Robert F. Bennett. **Released:** Quarterly **Price:** $56, Members and Canada; $39, U.S. and Canada associate.

14633 ■ *AMS Newsletter*
Pub: American Musicological Society Inc.
Ed: Kristen Lavoie, Editor. **Released:** Semiannual, in February and August. **Price:** Included in membership. **Description:** Serves members of this Association, which is a constituent member of the American Council of Learned Societies. Reports on committee and chapter activities and on items of general interest to musicologists. Recurring features include news of research, fellowships, grants, awards, and significant musical publications.

14634 ■ *ATMI International Newsletter*
Pub: Association for Technology in Music Instruction
Contact: James Frankel, President
Released: Quarterly. **Price:** Included in membership. **Description:** Discusses computer-based education in music, music synthesis, and music instruction and music classroom management using computers. Reports calls for information and new products of interest to members. Recurring features include book reviews, news of research, and a calendar of events.

14635 ■ *British Journal of Music Education*
Pub: Cambridge University Press
Contact: Richard Ziemacki, President
E-mail: rziemacki@cambridge.org
URL(s): www.cambridge.org/journals/journal_catalogue.asp?mnemonic=BME. **Ed:** Karen Burland, Dr. Pamela Burnard, Gary Spruce. **Released:** 3/yr.

Price: £171, Institutions online & print; £155, Institutions online; $30, Single issue article; $294, Institutions online & print; $264, Institutions online.

14636 ■ *Clavier*
Pub: Instrumentalist Co.
Contact: John Hiess, Manager
URL(s): www.instrumentalistmagazine.com/current-mags/clavcurrent.htm. **Released:** Monthly; 10/yr except June and August. **Price:** $17, Individuals; $25, Two years; $9, Students; $32, Individuals 3 years.

14637 ■ *Contemporary A Cappella News*
Pub: Contemporary A Cappella Society of America
Ed: Amy Malkoff, Editor. **Price:** Free. **Description:** Internet newsletter addressing various types and styles of a cappella music worldwide. Recurring features include interviews, a calendar of events, job listings, recording and concert reviews, and notices of publications available.

14638 ■ *Down Beat: Jazz, Blues & Beyond*
Pub: Maher Publications Inc.
Contact: James Petrillo, President
URL(s): www.downbeat.com. **Released:** Monthly **Price:** $48.99, Two years; $26.99, Individuals; $48.99, Other countries; $92.99, Other countries two years; $37.99, Canada; $70.99, Canada two years.

14639 ■ *Journal of Music Teacher Education*
Pub: MENC: The National Association for Music Education
Contact: Michael A. Butera, Executive Director
URL(s): jmt.sagepub.com/. **Ed:** Janice Killian. **Released:** Semiannual **Price:** £36, Institutions e-access.

14640 ■ *Journal of Research in Music Education*
Pub: MENC: The National Association for Music Education
Contact: Michael A. Butera, Executive Director
URL(s): jrm.sagepub.com/. **Ed:** Wendy L. Sims. **Released:** Quarterly **Price:** £93, Institutions print & e-access; £84, Institutions e-access; £91, Institutions print only.

14641 ■ *Kodaly Envoy*
Pub: Organization of American Kodaly Educators
Contact: Paul Baumann, President
Ed: Kim Vitray, Editor, kvitray@sbcglobal.net. **Released:** Quarterly. **Price:** Included in membership. **Description:** Promotes the use of Kodaly music education, a teaching approach founded by Hungarian composer, teacher, and ethnomusicologist, Zoltan Kodaly (1882-1967). The Kodaly approach is for general and choral music education. Recurring features include book reviews, news of members, a calendar of events, news of research, and feature articles.

14642 ■ *Kodaly Society of Canada, Alla Breve*
Pub: Kodaly Society of Canada
URL(s): www.kodalysocietyofcanada.ca/. **Ed:** Moira Szabo, Maureen MacDougall. **Released:** Semiannual

14643 ■ *MASTA notes*
Pub: American String Teachers Association with National School Orchestra Association--Michigan Chapter
Ed: Molly Rebeck, Editor, momokay@home.com. **Released:** Quarterly. **Price:** Included in membership. **Description:** Reports on news, events, programs, and workshops for members of the Michigan chapter of the American String Teachers Association. Recurring features include a calendar of events.

14644 ■ *Music Educators Journal*
Pub: MENC: The National Association for Music Education
Contact: Michael A. Butera, Executive Director
URL(s): www.sagepub.com/journalsProdDesc.nav?ct_p=subscribe&prodId=Journal2 01900. **Ed:** Patrick Freer. **Released:** 4/yr. **Price:** $173, Institutions print & E-access; $156, Institutions E-access; $170, Institutions print only.

14645 ■ *Music Trades*
Pub: Music Trades Corp.
Contact: Dennis Houlihan, President
URL(s): www.musictrades.com/. **Ed:** Brian T. Majeski. **Released:** Monthly **Price:** $45, Individuals foreign; $23, Two years domestic; $16, Individuals domestic.

14646 ■ *Percussion News*
Pub: Percussive Arts Society
Contact: Lisa Rogers, President
Ed: Rick Mattingly, Editor, rick@pas.org. **Released:** 6/year. **Price:** Included in membership. **Description:** Provides membership activity news and includes classified advertisements and industry news.

14647 ■ *Tri-M News*
Pub: TRI-M Music Honor Society
Contact: Michael A. Butera, Chief Executive Officer
Released: Semiannual. **Price:** Included in membership. **Description:** Publishes news of chapter events and projects and scholarship information. Announces individual awards as well as chapter activities, new and reactivated chapters, and member achievements.

VIDEOCASSETTES/ AUDIOCASSETTES

14648 ■ *Flute for Beginners*
Calprod Pro Film/Video Production, Inc.
730 S. Central Ave., Ste. 209
Glendale, CA 91204
Ph: (818)548-8822
Fax: (818)548-4499
Co. E-mail: info@profilmvideo.com
URL: http://www.profilmvideo.com
Released: 19??. **Price:** $19.95. **Description:** Introductory lessons cover posture, notes, hand positions, reading music, breathing, playing the instrument, and more. **Availability:** VHS.

14649 ■ *Piano for Quitters*
Leslie T. McClure
PO Box 1223
Pebble Beach, CA 93953
Ph: (831)656-0553
Fax: (831)656-0555
Co. E-mail: leslie@411videoinfo.com
URL: http://www.411videoinfo.com
Released: 1998. **Price:** $29.95. **Description:** Mark Almond provides instruction for those who have previously tried to learn piano-playing. **Availability:** VHS.

14650 ■ *Play Guitar Overnight—Rock*
Cambridge Educational
c/o Films Media Group
132 West 31st Street, 17th Floor
Ste. 124
New York, NY 10001
Free: 800-257-5126
Fax: (609)671-0266
Co. E-mail: custserve@films.com
URL: http://www.cambridgeol.com
Released: 19??. **Description:** Introductory lessons focus on style and soloing techniques. Also includes simple to use songbook and practice audio tape. **Availability:** VHS.

14651 ■ *Trombone for Beginners*
Calprod Pro Film/Video Production, Inc.
730 S. Central Ave., Ste. 209
Glendale, CA 91204
Ph: (818)548-8822
Fax: (818)548-4499
Co. E-mail: info@profilmvideo.com
URL: http://www.profilmvideo.com
Released: 19??. **Price:** $19.95. **Description:** Introductory lessons cover posture, notes, hand positions, reading music, breathing, playing the instrument, and more. **Availability:** VHS.

14652 ■ *Trumpet for Beginners*
Calprod Pro Film/Video Production, Inc.
730 S. Central Ave., Ste. 209
Glendale, CA 91204
Ph: (818)548-8822

Fax: (818)548-4499
Co. E-mail: info@profilmvideo.com
URL: http://www.profilmvideo.com
Released: 19??. **Price:** $19.95. **Description:** Introductory lessons cover posture, notes, hand positions, reading music, breathing, playing the instrument, and more. **Availability:** VHS.

14653 ■ *Tuba for Beginners*
Calprod Pro Film/Video Production, Inc.
730 S. Central Ave., Ste. 209
Glendale, CA 91204
Ph: (818)548-8822
Fax: (818)548-4499
Co. E-mail: info@profilmvideo.com
URL: http://www.profilmvideo.com
Released: 19??. **Price:** $19.95. **Description:** Introductory lessons cover posture, notes, hand positions, reading music, breathing, playing the instrument, and more. **Availability:** VHS.

14654 ■ *Viola for Beginners*
Calprod Pro Film/Video Production, Inc.
730 S. Central Ave., Ste. 209
Glendale, CA 91204
Ph: (818)548-8822
Fax: (818)548-4499
Co. E-mail: info@profilmvideo.com
URL: http://www.profilmvideo.com
Released: 19??. **Price:** $19.95. **Description:** Introductory lessons cover posture, notes, hand positions, reading music, breathing, playing the instrument, and more. **Availability:** VHS.

14655 ■ *Violin for Beginners*
Calprod Pro Film/Video Production, Inc.
730 S. Central Ave., Ste. 209
Glendale, CA 91204
Ph: (818)548-8822
Fax: (818)548-4499
Co. E-mail: info@profilmvideo.com
URL: http://www.profilmvideo.com
Released: 19??. **Price:** $19.95. **Description:** Introductory lessons cover posture, notes, hand positions, reading music, breathing, playing the instrument, and more. **Availability:** VHS.

14656 ■ *Vladimir Ashkenazy*
Tapeworm Video Distributors
25876 The Old Road #141
Stevenson Ranch, CA 91381
Ph: (661)257-4904
Fax: (661)257-4820
Co. E-mail: sales@tapeworm.com
URL: http://www.tapeworm.com
Released: 1996. **Price:** $19.95. **Description:** Documents the life and career of the pianist and conductor. Also provides excerpts of his tour in Russia, Switzerland, Sweden, and Germany. **Availability:** VHS.

TRADE SHOWS AND CONVENTIONS

14657 ■ American Choral Directors Association National Conference
American Choral Directors Association
545 Couch Dr.
Oklahoma City, OK 73102-2207
Ph: (405)232-8161
Fax: (405)232-8162
Co. E-mail: acda@acdaonline.org
URL: http://www.acdaonline.org
Contact: Dr. Tim Sharp, Executive Director
URL(s): acdaonline.org. **Frequency:** Biennial. **Audience:** Choral directors. **Principal Exhibits:** Choral music and supplies.

14658 ■ American Harp Society National Conference
American Harp Society
c/o Ashanti Pretlow
3416 Primm Ln.
Birmingham, AL 35216
Ph: (205)795-7130

Fax: (205)823-2760
Co. E-mail: execsecretary@harpsociety.org
URL: http://www.harpsociety.org
Contact: Delaine Fedson, President
E-mail: president@harpsociety.org
URL(s): www.harpsociety.org. **Frequency:** Annual. **Audience:** Professional and amateur harpists and students. **Principal Exhibits:** Harps and related materials.

14659 ■ College Music Society National Conference
College Music Society (CMS)
312 E Pine St.
Missoula, MT 59802
Ph: (406)721-9616
Fax: (406)721-9419
Co. E-mail: cms@music.org
URL: http://www.music.org
Contact: David Brian Williams, President
E-mail: davew_cms@me.com
URL(s): www.music.org. **Frequency:** Annual. **Audience:** Publishers, record companies, related trade professionals, college and university music faculty. **Principal Exhibits:** Music publishers, instrument manufacturers, music retailers, non-profit associations, music hardware and software manufacturers.

14660 ■ European Congress on Psychiatry
Kenes International
Rue de Chantepoulet 1-3
CH-1211 Geneva, Switzerland
Ph: 41 22 9080488
Fax: 41 22 9069140
Co. E-mail: info@kenes.com
URL: http://www.kenes.com
URL(s): www2.kenes.com/epa/Pages/Home.aspx. **Frequency:** Annual. **Audience:** Medical professionals. **Principal Exhibits:** Psychiatry and neuropsychiatry.

14661 ■ The Midwest Clinic An International Band and Orchestra Conference
The Midwest Clinic
1111 E Touhy, Ste. 250
Des Plaines, IL 60018
Ph: (847)424-4163
Fax: (773)321-1509
Co. E-mail: info@midwestclinic.org
URL: http://www.midwestclinic.org
Contact: Richard Crain, President
URL(s): www.midwestclinic.com. **Price:** $110, for director, administrator, and spouse; $50, for college students; $20, elementary, junior high school, and high school students. **Frequency:** Annual. **Audience:** Trade professionals. **Principal Exhibits:** Music instruments and publications, supplies, and services, universities, military organizations, fund raisers, music publishers. **Dates and Locations:** , McCormick Place. **Telecommunication Services:** info@midwestclinic.org.

14662 ■ NAfME National In-Service Conference
National Association for Music Education (NAfME)
1806 Robert Fulton Dr.
Reston, VA 20191
Ph: (703)860-4000
Free: 800-336-3768
Fax: (703)860-1531
Co. E-mail: michaelb@nafme.org
URL: http://www.nafme.org/
Contact: Michael A. Butera, Executive Director
E-mail: michaelb@nafme.org
URL(s): musiced.nafme.org/events/. **Frequency:** Biennial. **Audience:** Music educators teaching in public and private schools and colleges. **Principal Exhibits:** Music education equipment, supplies, and services. **Telecommunication Services:** lisat@nafme.org.

14663 ■ New York State School Music Association Winter Conference
New York State School Music Association
718 Plain Rd.
Westbury, NY 11590-5931
Free: 888-NYSSMA1

Fax: (516)997-1700
Co. E-mail: executive@nyssma.org
URL: http://www.nyssma.org
Contact: Steven E. Schopp, Executive Director
E-mail: Executive@nyssma.org
URL(s): www.nyssma.org. **Price:** $145, Pre-registered; $185. **Frequency:** Annual. **Audience:** Music teachers and general public. **Principal Exhibits:** Music publishers, musical instruments, fund-raising materials, and educational materials. **Dates and Locations:** Concord Hotel.

14664 ■ Texas Music Educators Association Clinic/Convention
Texas Music Educators Association
PO Box 140465
Austin, TX 78714-0465
Ph: (512)452-0710
Free: 888-318-TMEA
Fax: (512)451-9213
URL: http://www.tmea.org
Contact: Robert Floyd, Executive Director
E-mail: rfloyd@tmea.org
URL(s): tmea.org. **Price:** $50, active member; $15, retired. **Frequency:** Annual. **Audience:** Music teachers. **Principal Exhibits:** Music publishers, uniform/gowns, recruitment, photographers, software. **Dates and Locations:** , Convention Center.

FRANCHISES AND BUSINESS OPPORTUNITIES

14665 ■ Arcadia Academy of Music
661 Chrislea Rd., Unit 7
Woodbridge, ON, Canada L4L 8A3
Ph: (905)850-3701
Fax: (905)850-8489
URL: http://www.arcadiamusicacademy.com
Description: Music school. **No. of Franchise Units:** 9. **No. of Company-Owned Units:** 1. **Founded:** 1984.. **Franchised:** 1998. **Equity Capital Needed:** $60,000 and up leasehold/equipment. **Franchise Fee:** $20,000. **Training:** Yes.

COMPUTERIZED DATABASES

14666 ■ *Jazz Greats from Louis Armstrong to Duke Ellington*
1601 N Sepulveda Blvd., Ste. 374
Manhattan Beach, CA 90267
Ph: (310)406-1803
Fax: (310)406-0833
Co. E-mail: contact@tdcinteractive.com
URL: http://www.tdcinteractive.net
Availability: CD-ROM: Technology Dynamics Corp. - TDC Interactive. **Type:** Full-text.

LIBRARIES

14667 ■ American Conservatory of Music - Robert R. McCormick Memorial Library
252 Wildwood Rd.
Hammond, IN 46324
Ph: (219)931-6000
Co. E-mail: registrar@americanconservatory.edu
URL: http://www.americanconservatory.edu/library.html
Contact: Mary Ellen Newsom, Registrar
Scope: Music - piano, organ, strings, woodwinds, percussion, brass, opera, lieder, classical guitar, jazz. **Services:** Copying; library not open to the public. **Founded:** 1962. **Holdings:** 15,628 books and music scores; 563 bound periodical volumes; 276 dissertations; 2784 discs; 584 audio and video tapes.

14668 ■ American Music Center Collection at the New York Public Library for the Performing Arts
Dorothy and Lewis B. Cullman Center
40 Lincoln Center Plaza
New York, NY 10023-7498
Ph: (212)870-1630

Fax: (212)366-5265
Co. E-mail: performingarts@nypl.org
URL: http://www.amc.net
Contact: Jacqueline Z. Davis, Executive Director
URL(s): www.nypl.org/locations/lpa. **Scope:** Works of contemporary American composers. **Services:** Interlibrary loan; library open to the public on a limited schedule (call for appointment). **Founded:** 1939. **Holdings:** 50,000 published and unpublished scores; 15,000 recordings; 8000 tapes; 7000 files of composers' biographies; 4000 CDs; posters; photographs.

14669 ■ Bagaduce Music Lending Library

5 Music Library Ln.
Blue Hill, ME 04614
Ph: (207)374-5454
Fax: (207)374-2733
Co. E-mail: library@bagaducemusic.org
URL: http://www.bagaducemusic.org/
Contact: Martina Herries, Executive Director
Scope: Printed music - choral, keyboard, instrumental, popular and classical vocals. **Services:** Library open to the public. **Founded:** 1983. **Holdings:** 215,000 pieces of sheet music, scores, collections, and anthologies. **Subscriptions:** 2 journals and other serials. **Telecommunication Services:** martina@bagaducemusic.org.

14670 ■ Baylor University - Crouch Fine Arts Library—CFAL.

1 Bear Pl., No. 97148
Waco, TX 76798
Ph: (254)710-2164
Fax: (254)710-3116
Co. E-mail: sha_towers@baylor.edu
URL: http://www.baylor.edu/lib/FineArts
Contact: Sha Towers, Librarian, Art Librarian, Music
Scope: Musicology, music theory, church music, instrumental and orchestral music, historical sets (collected), music education, vocal music, monuments of music, visual arts architecture. **Services:** Library open to the public. **Founded:** 1929. **Holdings:** 50,000 books; 4300 bound periodical volumes; 650 microforms; 75,000 musical items; 23,000 phonograph records; 17,000 compact disc recordings; 5000 videocassettes, 500 DVDs, and 200 laser discs; 6300 audiocassettes. **Subscriptions:** 200 journals and other serials. **Telecommunication Services:** james_floyd@baylor.edu.

14671 ■ Berklee College of Music - Stan Getz Library

1140 Boylston St.
Boston, MA 02115
Ph: (617)747-2258
Free: 866-237-5533
Fax: (617)247-6878
Co. E-mail: pengle@berklee.edu
URL: http://library.berklee.edu
Contact: Paul Engle, Director, Library Services
Scope: Core music, jazz, core humanities, commercial music. **Services:** Interlibrary loan; Library open to the public with restrictions. **Founded:** 1945. **Holdings:** 24,837 books; 19,573 scores; 27,500 sound recordings; 3315 videos. **Subscriptions:** 215 journals and other serials.

14672 ■ John Brown University - Music Library

2000 W. University St.
Siloam Springs, AR 72761
Ph: (479)524-7266
Co. E-mail: twubbena@jbu.edu
URL: http://www.jbu.edu/music/facilities/
Contact: Mrs. Terri R. Wubbena, Chairperson
Scope: Music. **Services:** Library open to the public. **Holdings:** 1000 music scores; 2400 music sound recordings on LPs and CDs.

14673 ■ Brown University - Orwig Music Library

Box A
One Young Orchard Ave.
Providence, RI 02912

Ph: (401)863-3759
Co. E-mail: orwig@brown.edu
URL: http://dl.lib.brown.edu/libweb/about/orwig/
Contact: Ned Quist, Librarian, Music
Scope: Music. **Services:** Interlibrary loan; Library open to persons affiliated with Brown University. **Founded:** 1988. **Holdings:** 21,000 books; 43,000 sound recordings; 24,000 scores; 1100 videos. **Subscriptions:** 150 periodicals. **Telecommunication Services:** edwin_quist@brown.edu; sheila_hogg@brown.edu.

14674 ■ California University of Pennsylvania - Louis L. Manderino Library - Special Collections

250 University Ave., Rm. 435
California, PA 15419
Ph: (724)938-5926
Fax: (724)938-5901
Co. E-mail: pokol@calu.edu
URL: http://library.calu.edu
Contact: Alber Pokol, Archivist Librarian, Special Collections
Scope: Rare books, art, music. **Services:** Interlibrary loan; Library open to the public by appointment.

14675 ■ Cambridge Public Library - Audio-Visual Department

449 Broadway
Cambridge, MA 02138
Ph: (617)349-4040
Fax: (617)349-4026
URL: http://www.cambridgema.gov/cpl/Services/Collections/AudioVisual.aspx
Contact: Susan Flannery, Director, Library Services
Scope: Music - piano, jazz. **Services:** Interlibrary loan; Wi-Fi; library open to the public. **Holdings:** 5000 books, bound periodicals, music scores; 75 full orchestral scores; 15,724 sound recordings; 500 videocassettes; 8000 music CDs; 12,000 DVDs.

14676 ■ Catholic University of America - Music Library

101 Ward Hall
620 Michigan Ave., NE
Washington, DC 20064
Ph: (202)319-5424
Fax: (202)319-4735
Co. E-mail: saylor@cua.edu
URL: http://libraries.cua.edu/music
Contact: Maurice Saylor, Librarian
Scope: Musicology, music education, performance. **Services:** Interlibrary loan; copying; Library open to the public with restrictions. **Founded:** 1952. **Holdings:** 25,000 books and score; 4605 bound periodical volumes; 12,917 pieces of music; 16,256 sound recordings; 6000 CDs; 309 LDs; 15,000 long-playing records; 300 DVDs; 300 laser video discs. **Subscriptions:** 150 journals. **Telecommunication Services:** barham@cua.edu.

14677 ■ Chapman University - Albert Schweitzer Institute Library

1 University Dr.
Orange, CA 92866
Ph: (714)997-6636
Fax: (714)532-6078
Co. E-mail: meyer@chapman.edu
URL: http://www.chapman.edu
Contact: Marvin Meyer, Librarian
Scope: Albert Schweitzer's life and works. **Services:** Interlibrary loan. **Holdings:** Books.

14678 ■ Chicago Public Library - Visual & Performing Arts Division - Music Information Center

Harold Washington Library Center
400 S. State St., 8th Fl.
Chicago, IL 60605
Ph: (312)747-4850
URL: http://www.chipublib.org/branch/details/library/harold-washington/p/Vpa
Contact: Brian Bannon, Commissioner
Scope: History and theory of music, biographies of musicians and composers, music education, opera, musical comedy, sacred music, popular music, discography, music business, musical instruments, vocal and instrumental pedagogy, music therapy, folk

music, composition and orchestration, arranging. **Services:** Interlibrary loan; copying; listening/viewing Center; practice rooms; music chamber; Center open to the public. **Founded:** 1915. **Holdings:** 49,800 books; 8025 bound periodical volumes; 67,000 bound volumes of music; 30,000 pieces of music; 15 VF drawers of pamphlets and clippings; 6102 microfiche of music; 2220 reels of microfilm of periodicals; 169,000 phonograph records, compact discs, audiocassettes; 3900 music videos; 334 laserdiscs; 4250 photographs; 51,957 uncatalogued scores. **Subscriptions:** 561 journals and other serials.

14679 ■ Cleveland Institute of Music - Robinson Music Library

11021 East Blvd.
Cleveland, OH 44106
Ph: (216)795-3114
Fax: (216)707-4505
Co. E-mail: jean.toombs@case.edu
URL: http://www.cim.edu/library/
Contact: Jean S. Toombs, Director, Library Services
Scope: Music - performance materials, scores, analytical works, bibliographies, biographies. **Services:** Interlibrary loan; copying; Internet access; library open to staff and students only. **Founded:** 1920. **Holdings:** 53,000 books and scores; 23,500 audio/visual materials. **Subscriptions:** 110 journals and other serials; 2 newspapers. **Telecommunication Services:** bonnie.houser@case.edu.

14680 ■ Concord Free Public Library - Music Collection

129 Main St.
Concord, MA 01742
Ph: (978)318-3377
Fax: (508)371-6244
URL: http://www.concordlibrary.org
Contact: Kerry Cronin, Director, Library Services
Scope: Music. **Services:** Interlibrary loan; Wi-Fi; library open to the public for reference use only. **Holdings:** 1500 books and bound periodical volumes; 375 music scores; 4450 sound recordings.

14681 ■ Conservatoire de Musique de Quebec - Bibliotheque

270 rue St. Amable
Quebec, QC, Canada G1R 5G1
Ph: (418)643-2190
Fax: (418)644-9658
Co. E-mail: cmq_bib@conservatoire.gouv.qc.ca
URL: http://www.conservatoire.gouv.qc.ca/quebec/index.asp
Contact: Pierre Plante, Librarian, Music
Scope: Classical music, orchestral music. **Services:** Library open to the public for reference use only. **Founded:** 1944. **Holdings:** 65,000 books. **Subscriptions:** 33 journals and other serials; 1 newspaper.

14682 ■ Curtis Institute of Music - Milton L. Rock Resource Center

1720 Locust St.
Philadelphia, PA 19103
Ph: (215)717-3147
Co. E-mail: michelle.oswell@curtis.edu
URL: http://www.curtis.edu/about-curtis/facilities/rock-resource-center
Contact: Elizabeth Walker, Director, Library Services
Scope: Music orchestral, chamber, solo instrumental, vocal. **Services:** Interlibrary loan; Library open to the public by appointment only. **Founded:** 1925. **Holdings:** 9797 books; 55,255 scores; 858 LPs; 2996 audio tapes; 682 videotapes; 486 videodiscs; 1231 DVDs; 17,617 compact discs; 5368 microfiche; 72 reels of microfilm. **Subscriptions:** 70 journals and other serials. **Telecommunication Services:** helene.vanrossum@curtis.edu.

14683 ■ Edinboro University - Baron-Forness Library - Special Collections

200 Tartan Rd., 7th Fl.
Edinboro, PA 16444
Ph: (814)732-2415

Fax: (814)732-2883
Co. E-mail: obringer@edinboro.edu
URL: http://www.edinboro.edu/departments/library/
archives/page_one.dot
Contact: Prof. David Obringer

Scope: Music, art, education, Pennsylvania history, Civil War regimental history, rare books. **Services:** Interlibrary loan; tutoring; Library open to the public with restrictions. **Founded:** 1860. **Holdings:** 3000 volumes; prints.

14684 ■ Grinnell College - Burling Library - Listening Room
1111 Sixth Ave.
Grinnell, IA 50112-1690
Ph: (641)269-3365
Fax: (641)269-4283
Co. E-mail: jonesran@grinnell.edu
URL: http://www.grinnell.edu/library/collections/listen-ingroom
Contact: Randye Jones, Supervisor

Scope: Music, arts, humanities, sciences. **Services:** Library open to the public with restrictions (public may use items in-house, unless space is needed by students or faculty). **Founded:** 1846. **Holdings:** 25,000 cataloged titles in compact disc, LP record, cassette tape, and videocassettes formats; 6000 cataloged titles in DVD and VHS formats.

14685 ■ Hardin-Simmons University - Smith Music Library
Caldwell Hall
2200 Hickory
Box 16195
Abilene, TX 79689
Ph: (915)670-1565
Co. E-mail: james.floyd@hsutx.edu
URL: http://www.hsutx.edu/library
Contact: James Floyd, Librarian, Music

URL(s): www.hsutx.edu/HSUDirectory.php. **Scope:** Music. **Services:** Interlibrary loan. **Holdings:** Scores; collected works of various composers; recordings; basic music books; listening equipment.

14686 ■ Hartford Conservatory - Carolyn B. Taylor Library
834 Asylum Ave.
Hartford, CT 06105
Ph: (860)246-2588
Fax: (860)249-6330
Co. E-mail: mhuntington@hartfordconservatory.org
URL: http://www.hartfordconservatory.org
Contact: Marilynn Huntington

Scope: Music (classical and jazz), dance, theater. **Services:** Interlibrary loan; Library open to the public for reference use only. **Founded:** 1890. **Holdings:** 1600 books and bound periodical volumes; 5114 music scores; 400 pieces of sheet music; 4800 sound recordings; 130 compact discs. **Subscriptions:** 10 journals and other serials.

14687 ■ Interlochen Center for the Arts - Frederick and Elizabeth Ludwig Fennell Music Library
4000 S. M-137 Hwy.
Interlochen, MI 49643
Ph: (231)276-7230
Co. E-mail: admission@interlochen.org
URL: http://www.interlochen.org
Contact: Sandra Besselsen, Director, Library Services

Scope: Music. **Services:** Copying; Library open to the public for reference use only. **Holdings:** 8175 orchestra titles; 6525 band titles; 4675 choir titles; 985 jazz band titles; 37,725 solo and small ensemble titles; 10,275 recordings; 6565 study score titles. **Telecommunication Services:** besselsens@interlochen.org.

14688 ■ Lawrence University - Seeley G. Mudd Library - Music Collections
113 S. Lawe St.
Appleton, WI 54911

Ph: (920)832-6750
Co. E-mail: antoinette.powell@lawrence.edu
URL: http://www.lawrence.edu/library/music/collection.shtml
Contact: Erin Dix, Archivist

Scope: Music - instrumental solo, chamber works, orchestral, piano, vocal, classical, jazz, Western art, world music, musical theater, opera. **Services:** Interlibrary loan. **Holdings:** 14,000 scores; 1500 LPs; 10,000 compact discs; 8000 books on music; 400 music videotapes. **Subscriptions:** 160 journals and other serials. **Telecommunication Services:** reference@lawrence.edu.

14689 ■ Lenox Library Association - Music Department
18 Main St.
Lenox, MA 01240
Ph: (413)637-0197
Co. E-mail: alafave@lenoxlib.org
URL: http://lenoxlib.org
Contact: Amy Lafave, Librarian, Reference Specialist, Music Collections

Scope: Music. **Services:** Interlibrary loan; copying; library open to the public. **Founded:** 1940. **Holdings:** 1300 books and bound periodical volumes; 850 music scores; 950 music parts; 60 librettos; 5700 sound recordings; 4000 CD-ROM; 1800 musical scores; 400 LPs; 300 audiocassettes; 250 videocassettes. **Subscriptions:** 5 journals and other serials.

14690 ■ Weill-Lenya Research Center—Kurt Weill Foundation.
7 E 20th St.
New York, NY 10003
Ph: (212)505-5240
Fax: (212)353-9663
Co. E-mail: wlrc@kwf.org
URL: http://www.kwf.org/kwf/foundation/weill-lenya-research-center
Contact: Dave Stein, Archivist

Scope: Life and work of composer Kurt Weill and Lotte Lenya, musicology, music theory, theater history, 20th-century culture, Weimar Republic culture, women's studies, Jewish studies, emigre studies. **Services:** Information referral. **Founded:** 1983. **Holdings:** Books; printed music; music manuscripts; scripts; correspondence; audio and video recordings; films; programs; photographs; posters; press clippings; business records; personal papers. **Subscriptions:** 1 journal. **Publications:** *Guide to the Weill-Lenya Research Center*; *Kurt Weill Newsletter* (Semiannual). **Awards:** Research and travel grants. **Telecommunication Services:** dstein@kwf.org.

14691 ■ Library of Congress - Music Division
101 Independence Ave., SE
James Madison Memorial Bldg., Rm. LM 113
Washington, DC 20540-4710
Ph: (202)707-5507
Fax: (202)707-0621
URL: http://www.loc.gov/rr/perform

Scope: Music and music literature, dance, and theater of the world, emphasizing Western civilization, American music, opera and librettos, and chamber music; music organizations; literature about music in various languages (excepting Hebraic and Asiatic). **Services:** Interlibrary loan (limited); listening facilities in the Performing Arts Reading Room. **Founded:** 1896. **Holdings:** 20.5 million items; manuscripts, scores, correspondence, and personal papers of musicians; printed books and music; microforms. **Subscriptions:** 1000 journals.

14692 ■ Longy School of Music - Bakalar Music Library
27 Garden St.
Cambridge, MA 02138
Ph: (617)876-0956, x1540
Co. E-mail: roy.rudolph@longy.edu
URL: http://www.longy.edu/library_bakalar/library_hours.htm
Contact: Roy Rudolph, Director, Library Services

Scope: Music - piano, string chamber, general. **Services:** Interlibrary loan; copying; library open to the public for reference use only with letter from a music librarian. **Founded:** 1915. **Holdings:** 4300 books; 11,000 music scores; 9000 sound recordings; 150

videos and DVDs. **Subscriptions:** 30 journals and other serials. **Telecommunication Services:** catherine.klenov@longy.edu.

14693 ■ Manhattan School of Music - Peter Jay Sharp Library
120 Claremont Ave.
New York, NY 10027
Ph: (212)749-2802
Fax: (212)749-5471
Co. E-mail: library@msmnyc.edu
URL: http://www.msmnyc.edu/About-MSM/Campus/Libraries
Contact: Peter Caleb, Director, Library Services

Scope: Music. **Services:** Interlibrary loan; copying; library open to the public by appointment or via METRO card. **Founded:** 1925. **Holdings:** 18,000 books; 20,000 CDs; 9000 LPs; 2500 DVDs; 50,000 music scores. **Subscriptions:** 107 paper journals. **Telecommunication Services:** pcaleb@msmnyc.edu.

14694 ■ Mannes College The New School for Music - Harry Scherman Music Library
150 W. 85th St.
New York, NY 10024
Ph: (212)580-0210, x4803
Co. E-mail: scarcele@newschool.edu
URL: http://library.newschool.edu/scherman
Contact: Ed Scarcelle, Director

Scope: Music. **Services:** Interlibrary loan; copying; library open to the public for reference use only upon application for specific materials. **Founded:** 1954. **Holdings:** 8529 books; 31,298 scores; 9000 phonograph records; 2000 compact discs; 152 videocassettes; 300 video recordings. **Subscriptions:** 74 journals and other serials. **Telecommunication Services:** reference@newschool.edu.

14695 ■ Mount Holyoke College Library - Music and Dance Library
50 College St.
South Hadley, MA 01075-6404
Ph: (413)538-6261
Co. E-mail: kmehl@mtholyoke.edu
URL: http://www.mtholyoke.edu
Contact: Karen Mehl, Manager, Circulation

Scope: Music, dance. **Services:** Interlibrary loan; copying; Library open to the public for reference use only. **Holdings:** 4600 books and bound periodical volumes; 6948 music scores. **Telecommunication Services:** libcirc@mtholyoke.edu.

14696 ■ New England Conservatory of Music - Harriet M. Spaulding Library
33 Gainsborough St.
Boston, MA 02115
Ph: (617)585-1250
Fax: (617)585-1245
Co. E-mail: jean.morrow@necmusic.edu
URL: http://necmusic.edu/study-nec/libraries/spaulding-library
Contact: Jean A. Morrow, Director, Library Services

Scope: Music and music literature. **Services:** Interlibrary loan; copying; Library open to the public for reference use only. **Founded:** 1867. **Holdings:** 85,000 books and scores; 55,000 sound recordings; 1000 video recordings; 250 theses; 500 reels of microfilm; publications and documents on Boston musical life and history of the conservatory. **Subscriptions:** 300 journals and other serials. **Telecommunication Services:** patrick.maxfield@necmusic.edu.

14697 ■ Nipawin School Division - Education Resource Centre
Box 2044
Nipawin, SK, Canada S0E 1E0
Ph: (306)862-4616
Fax: (306)862-9733
Co. E-mail: verda.hoppe-nsd@saskschools.ca
Contact: Verda Hoppe, Library Technician

Scope: Music, special education. **Services:** Interlibrary loan. **Founded:** 1950. **Holdings:** 10,000 books; 1500 videotapes; 1000 recordings. **Subscriptions:** 10 journals and other serials.

14698 ■ Ohio Wesleyan University - Kinnison Music Library
Sanborn Hall, Rm. 005
Delaware, OH 43105
Ph: (740)368-3715
Co. E-mail: paszabo@owu.edu
URL: http://library.owu.edu/libmusic.htm
Contact: Peter Szabo, Librarian, Music
Scope: Music. **Services:** Interlibrary loan; copying; Library open to the public. **Holdings:** 15,000 items - 6000 books; 1184 bound periodical volumes; 1500 CD-ROMs; 4500 LPs. **Subscriptions:** 34 journals and other serials.

14699 ■ Orchestras Canada Resource Centre—Orchestres Canada.
425 Adelaide St. W., Ste. 700
Toronto, ON, Canada M5V 3C1
Ph: (416)366-8834
Fax: (416)366-1780
Co. E-mail: info@oc.ca
URL: http://orchestrascanada.org/resources/
Contact: Katherine Carleton, Executive Director
Scope: Music, arts education, orchestral training. **Services:** Library not open to the public. **Founded:** 1972. **Holdings:** Available to members only; Books; reports.

14700 ■ Percussive Arts Society Library
110 W. Washington St., Ste. A
Indianapolis, IN 46204
Ph: (317)974-4488
Fax: (317)974-4499
Co. E-mail: percarts@pas.org
URL: http://www.pas.org
Contact: Otice Sircy, Curator Librarian
Scope: Percussion instruments and music reference. **Services:** Library open to the public for reference use only. **Founded:** 1961. **Holdings:** 5000 archival materials; manuscripts. **Subscriptions:** 50 journals and other serials. **Telecommunication Services:** museum@pas.org.

14701 ■ Portland Public Library - Art/Audiovisual Department
5 Monument Sq.
Portland, ME 04101
Ph: (207)871-1725
Fax: (207)871-1714
Co. E-mail: audiovisual@portland.lib.me.us
URL: http://www.portlandlibrary.com
Contact: Stephen J. Podgajny, Executive Director
Scope: Music. **Services:** Interlibrary loan; copying; Library open to the public. **Holdings:** 2500 books and bound periodical volumes; 7 file drawers of sheet music; 9500 sound recordings; 3600 videocassettes. **Subscriptions:** 16 journals and other serials. **Telecommunication Services:** podgajny@portland.lib.me.us; reference@portland.lib.me.us.

14702 ■ St. Norbert Arts Centre Archives
PO Box 175
Winnipeg, MB, Canada R3V 1L6
Ph: (204)269-0564
Fax: (204)261-1927
Co. E-mail: snac@snac.mb.ca
URL: http://www.snac.mb.ca
Contact: Louise May, Director
Scope: Art - visual art, music, theater, and dance. **Services:** Archives open to the public. **Founded:** 1996. **Holdings:** Graphic materials; textual records.

14703 ■ San Francisco Conservatory of Music Library
50 Oak St.
San Francisco, CA 94102
Ph: (415)503-6253
Co. E-mail: library@sfcm.edu
URL: http://www.sfcm.edu/library.aspx
Contact: Kevin McLaughlin, Librarian
Scope: Music. **Services:** Interlibrary loan; copying; library open to the public by appointment for reference use only. **Founded:** 1967. **Holdings:** 16,500 books; 50,000 musical scores; 75 bound periodical volumes; 2250 tapes; 16,500 phonograph records and CDs. **Subscriptions:** 77 journals and other serials. **Telecommunication Services:** kmclaughlin@sfcm.edu.

14704 ■ San Francisco Public Library - Bernard Osher Foundation - Art, Music & Recreation Center
100 Larkin St., 4th Fl.
San Francisco, CA 94102
Ph: (415)557-4525
Fax: (415)557-4524
Co. E-mail: info@sfpl.org
URL: http://www.sfpl.org
Contact: Mark Hall, Manager
URL(s): sfpl.org/index.php?pg=0200001401. **Scope:** Arts - visual, graphic; sports and recreation; photography; architecture; arts and crafts; performing arts; music - orchestral, chamber, opera, popular, folk, jazz. **Services:** Center open to the public. **Holdings:** Books; serials; scores. **Telecommunication Services:** artmusicrec@sfpl.org.

14705 ■ Settlement Music School - Blanche Wolf Kohn Library
416 Queen St.
Philadelphia, PA 19147
Ph: (215)320-2600
Fax: (215)551-0483
URL: http://www.smsmusic.org
Contact: Jean Peoples
Scope: Music. **Services:** Library open to students, faculty, staff, alumni, and record musicians. **Founded:** 1957. **Holdings:** 10,000 record albums; books; 10,000 scores; 100,000 pieces of classical sheet music.

14706 ■ State University of New York at Buffalo - Music Library
112 Baird Hall, 1st Fl.
Buffalo, NY 14260-4750
Ph: (716)645-2923
Fax: (716)645-3906
Co. E-mail: musique@buffalo.edu
URL: http://library.buffalo.edu/music/
Contact: Nancy Nuzzo, Director
Scope: Music - history, theory, performance; jazz history; new music; computer composition. **Services:** Interlibrary loan; copying; Library open to the public. **Founded:** 1970. **Holdings:** 41,000 books; 24,000 bound periodical volumes; 93,000 scores and parts; 44,000 sound recordings; 8000 microforms; 2100 slides; 5000 photographs; 1000 videos. **Subscriptions:** 1400 journals and other serials. **Telecommunication Services:** nuzzo@buffalo.edu.

14707 ■ Sweet Briar College - Junius P. Fishburn Music Library
134 Chapel Rd.
Sweet Briar, VA 24595
Ph: (434)381-6138
Fax: (434)381-6173
Co. E-mail: jgjaffe@sbc.edu
URL: http://library.sbc.edu
Contact: John Jaffe, Director
Scope: Music. **Services:** Interlibrary loan; library open to the public. **Holdings:** 12,000 items.

14708 ■ Temple University - Esther Boyer College of Music - New School Institute - Alice Tully Library
1715 N. Broad St., Rock Hall Rm. 102
Philadelphia, PA 19101
Ph: (215)204-6950
Fax: (215)204-5528
URL: http://library.temple.edu/about/libraries/tully.jsp?bhcp=1
Contact: Millie Bai, Supervisor
URL(s): www.temple.edu. **Scope:** Music, music literature. **Services:** Library not open to the public. **Founded:** 1965. **Holdings:** 400 books; 5000 scores; 200 recordings; archival materials of the Curtis String Quartet.

14709 ■ Tiger Hills Arts Association - Music Resource Library
103 Broadway St.
Holland, MB, Canada R0G 0X0
Ph: (204)526-2063

Fax: (204)526-2105
Co. E-mail: thaa@mymts.net
URL: http://www.tigerhillsarts.com/
Contact: Catheryn Pedersen, Executive Director
Scope: Music - vocal, guitar, recorder; arts; music teaching. **Services:** Copying; library open to the public. **Holdings:** Figures not available.

14710 ■ Toronto Reference Library - Performing Arts Centre
789 Yonge St., 5th Fl.
Toronto, ON, Canada M4W 2G8
Ph: (416)393-7131
Fax: (416)393-7147
Co. E-mail: mmilne@torontopubliclibrary.ca
Contact: Mary Shantz, Manager
Scope: Music, dance, film, theatre. **Services:** Library open to the public. **Founded:** 1915. **Holdings:** 17,000 LPs; 12,000 CDs; 47,000 music scores; 11,000 photographs; 4000 original stage drawings; prints; engravings; Canadian theatre and concert programs; clippings; archival materials; Canadian sheet music; microfiche; microfilm. **Subscriptions:** 150 journals and other serials.

14711 ■ U.S. Armed Forces School of Music Reference Library
1420 Gator Blvd.
Virginia Beach, VA 23521-2617
Ph: (757)462-7511
Fax: (757)464-7294
Co. E-mail: gysgt-jon.fishman@cnet.navy.mil
URL: http://www.bands.army.mil/organizations/pages/default.asp?unit=ASOM&p=leaders
Contact: Jon Fishman, Sergeant
Scope: Music - analysis, conducting, composition, counterpoint, harmony, theory, instruments; jazz; military music. **Services:** Library open to the public with restrictions. **Founded:** 1942. **Holdings:** 5200 books; 2600 scores; 7000 phonograph records; 765 compact discs; 110 song books; 1900 reel-to-reel tapes; 467 cassette tapes; 350 archives. **Subscriptions:** 30 journals and other serials.

14712 ■ University of California, Los Angeles - Music Library
1102 Schoenberg Music Bldg.
Box 951490
Los Angeles, CA 90095-1490
Ph: (310)825-4882
Fax: (310)206-7322
URL: http://www2.library.ucla.edu/libraries/Music/index.cfm
Contact: Kevin Mulroy, Director
Scope: Music, musicology, ethnomusicology, music education. **Services:** Interlibrary loan; copying; Library open to the public. **Founded:** 1942. **Holdings:** 182,816 volumes (books & scores); 6476 reels of microfilm; 18,454 microfiche; 67,500 sound recordings (CD and LP); 950 video recordings (disc and cassette). **Subscriptions:** 1267 journals and other serials.

14713 ■ University of Cincinnati - College Conservatory of Music - Gorno Memorial Music Library
600 Carl Blegen Library
Cincinnati, OH 45221-0152
Ph: (513)556-1970
Fax: (513)556-3777
Co. E-mail: mark.palkovic@uc.edu
URL: http://www.libraries.uc.edu/libraries/ccm/index.html
Contact: Mark Palkovic, Director, Library Services
Scope: Music performance, history, and theory; musicology; dance; theater arts; music education. **Services:** Interlibrary loan; copying; Library open to the public for reference use only. **Founded:** 1949. **Holdings:** 40,500 bound volumes; 74,000 scores; 57,000 sound recordings; 6000 microforms; 3000 media materials. **Subscriptions:** 550 journals and other serials. **Telecommunication Services:** paul.cauthen@uc.edu.

14714 ■ University of Nevada, Las Vegas - Music Library
Beam Music Center
4505 S. Maryland Pkwy.
Las Vegas, NV 89154
Ph: (702)895-2541
Co. E-mail: music.library@unlv.edu
URL: http://www.unlv.edu
Contact: Cheryl Taranto, Librarian, Music
URL(s): www.library.unlv.edu/music. **Scope:** Music. **Services:** Interlibrary loan; copying; document delivery; Library open to the public. **Holdings:** 35,000 volumes; 11,000 recordings (compact discs, LPs, audiocassettes); 1200 videos; 9000 books. **Subscriptions:** 156 journals and other serials. **Telecommunication Services:** cheryl.taranto@unlv.edu.

14715 ■ University of North Carolina at Greensboro - Special Collections & Rare Books, Jackson Library - Cello Music Collections
222B Jackson Library
Greensboro, NC 27402-6170
Ph: (336)334-5246
Fax: (336)334-5399
Co. E-mail: bill_finley@uncg.edu
URL: http://library.uncg.edu/info/depts/scua/collections/cello
Contact: William K. Finley
Scope: Luigi Silva, Elizabeth Cowling, Rudolf Matz, Maurice Eisenberg, Janos Scholz; history and teaching of the cello. **Services:** Copying (limited); collection open to the public for research. **Holdings:** 300 books, including 20 bound periodical volumes and 80 bound volumes of chamber music; 240 boxes of manuscripts and printed scores, representing 4300 indexed items; 100 boxes of archival materials, including photographs, teaching notes, and correspondence.

14716 ■ University of North Carolina School of the Arts - Semans Library
UNC School of the Arts
1533 S. Main St.
Winston-Salem, NC 27127
Ph: (336)770-3270
Fax: (336)770-3271
Co. E-mail: rebeccab@uncsa.edu
URL: http://www.uncsa.edu/library
Contact: Christia Thomason
Scope: Music, art and design, theater, film, dance, humanities. **Services:** Interlibrary loan; Library open to the public. **Founded:** 1965. **Holdings:** 111,000 books; 9000 bound periodical volumes; 50,000 music scores; 45,000 sound recordings; 5200 DVDs and videos. **Subscriptions:** 470 journals and other serials; 25 newspapers.

14717 ■ University of Redlands - Armacost Library - Special Collections
1200 E. Colton Ave.
Redlands, CA 92373-0999
Ph: (909)748-8022
Co. E-mail: les_canterbury@redlands.edu
URL: http://www.redlands.edu/library/index.aspx
Contact: Les Canterbury, Librarian
Scope: Music, literature, religion, East Asia. **Services:** Interlibrary loan; copying; library open to the public with restrictions. **Founded:** 1907. **Holdings:** 208,503 book; 314,219 microforms; 168,228 documents. **Subscriptions:** 18,953 journals and other serials.

14718 ■ Vandercook College of Music - Harry Ruppel Memorial Library
3140 S. Federal St.
Chicago, IL 60616-3731
Ph: (312)225-6288, x-301
Fax: (312)225-5211
Co. E-mail: rdeland@vandercook.edu
URL: http://www.vandercook.edu/library
Contact: Rob DeLand, Librarian
Scope: Music and music education, education. **Services:** Interlibrary loan; listening facilities; library open to alumni and associates of Vandercook College and one neighboring institution (Illinois Institute of Technology identification necessary). **Founded:** 1967. **Holdings:** 14,653; volumes; 7166 books; 3461 sound recordings; 381 videotapes; 43 CD-ROMs; 2183 scores; 987 archives. **Subscriptions:** 84 journals and other serials.

14719 ■ Andy Warhol Museum - Archives Study Center
117 Sandusky St.
Pittsburgh, PA 15212-5890
Ph: (412)237-8300
Fax: (412)237-8340
Co. E-mail: wrbicanm@warhol.org
URL: http://www.warhol.org/collections/archives.html
Contact: Matt Wrbican, Archivist
Scope: Andy Warhol, pop art movement, journalism, rock music, celebrity culture, fashion. **Services:** Archives is open to researchers by appointment. **Founded:** 1994. **Holdings:** Business records; scrapbooks; photographs; audiocassettes; videotapes; published materials; books; art work; clothing; posters; correspondence; personal objects; 4000 audio tapes. **Telecommunication Services:** information@warhol.org.

14720 ■ Western Connecticut State University - Ruth A. Haas Library
Midtown Campus
181 White St.
Danbury, CT 06810
Ph: (203)837-9100
Fax: (203)837-9108
Co. E-mail: oharae@wcsu.edu
URL: http://library.wcsu.edu
Contact: Brian Stevens
Scope: Music. **Services:** Interlibrary loan; Library open to the public for reference use only. **Founded:** 1903. **Holdings:** 175,000 volumes; 359 bound periodical volumes; 4712 music scores; 3084 sound recordings; 8 reels of microfilm; 8700 media titles. **Subscriptions:** 23 journals and other serials.

14721 ■ Westminster Choir College - Rider University - Talbott Library
101 Walnut Ln.
Princeton, NJ 08540
Ph: (609)921-7100
Fax: (609)497-0243
Co. E-mail: chyun@rider.edu
URL: http://www.rider.edu/academics/libraries/talbott
Contact: Julia Telonidis
Scope: Music - choral, vocal, keyboard, sacred. **Services:** Interlibrary loan (fee); copying; library open to the public with fee for circulation for area residents. **Founded:** 1926. **Holdings:** 67,000 books; 29,000 scores; 23,000 sound and video recordings; college archives; 5400 choral music titles; 80,000 choral music reference. **Subscriptions:** 170 journals and other serials. **Telecommunication Services:** rterrio@rider.edu.

RESEARCH CENTERS

14722 ■ American Institute of Musical Studies (AIMS)
28 E 69th St.
Kansas City, MO 64113-2512
Ph: (816)268-3657
Co. E-mail: aimsgraz@gmail.net
URL: http://www.aimsgraz.com
Contact: Thomas King, Director
Description: Institute that sponsors The AIMS Graz Experience in Graz, Austria, which includes the Summer Vocal Institute, and the AIMS Festival Orchestra. Launches advanced young singers, pianists and instrumentalists on a professional career by providing experience and emphasizing audition training. Faculty, comprised of over 60 internationally known professional musicians, conducts hands-on training programs. **Scope:** vocal and orchestral works. **Founded:** 1969. **Publications:** *The AIMSer Newsletter.* **Educational Activities:** Hands-on training programs. **Awards:** Meistersinger Competition (Annual). **Telecommunication Services:** aimsgraz@gmail.com.

14723 ■ Council for Research in Music Education (CRME)
University of Illinois at Urbana-Champaign
Urbana, IL 61801
Ph: (217)244-0626
Fax: (866)244-0626
Co. E-mail: crme@illinois.edu
URL: http://bcrme.press.illinois.edu
Contact: Martin Bergee, Manager
URL(s): www.crme.illinois.edu. **Description:** International organization of authors who contribute articles to the Bulletin of the Council for Research in Music Education. Aims to promote scholarly research in music education. **Founded:** 1963. **Publications:** *Bulletin of the Council for Research in Music Education* (Quarterly); *Bulletin of the Council for Research in Music Education* (Quarterly). **Awards:** Outstanding Dissertation Award. **Telecommunication Services:** tinahapp@illinois.edu.

14724 ■ Florida State University - Center for Music Research (CMR)
College of Music - KMU 218
Tallahassee, FL 32306-1180
Ph: (850)644-5787
Fax: (850)644-2033
Co. E-mail: jgeringer@fsu.edu
URL: http://www.music.fsu.edu/Music-Research-Centers/Center-for-Music-Research
Contact: Prof. John M. Geringer, Director
Founded: 1980. **Educational Activities:** CMR Seminars; CMR Workshops.

14725 ■ Rutgers University - Institute of Jazz Studies (IJS)
John Cotton Dana Library
185 University Ave.
Newark, NJ 07102
Ph: (973)353-5595
Fax: (973)353-5944
Co. E-mail: dmorgens@andromeda.rutgers.edu
URL: http://newarkwww.rutgers.edu/IJS
Contact: Dan Morgenstern, Director
Founded: 1952. **Publications:** *Annual Review of Jazz Studies* (Periodic); *Studies in Jazz Monograph Series.* **Educational Activities:** IJS Conferences; Jazz from the Archives (Weekly), weekly radio program on WBGO-FM Newark; Research Roundtable (Monthly); IJS Seminars (Occasionally). **Awards:** Morroe Berger - Benny Carter Jazz Research Fund (Annual), assists students and scholars in pursuing jazz research projects.

ASSOCIATIONS AND OTHER ORGANIZATIONS

14726 ■ American School Band Directors' Association (ASBDA)
PO Box 696
Guttenberg, IA 52052-0696
Ph: (563)252-2500
Co. E-mail: asbda@alpinecom.net
URL: http://www.asbda.com
Contact: Kevin Beaber, President

Description: Persons actively engaged in teaching instrumental music at the elementary, junior high or senior high school level; affiliates are persons no longer engaged in active teaching; associates are commercial firms dealing in products used by members. Seeks to improve instruction of instrumental music in the schools, the equipment used in instrumental music, music materials and methods, audiovisual aids, and acoustics of musical instruments used in school instructional programs. **Founded:** 1953. **Publications:** *ASBDA Directory and Handbook* (Annual). **Awards:** Austin Harding Award (Annual); Edwin Franko Goldman Award (Annual); Outstanding State Chair Award (Annual).

14727 ■ Early Music America (EMA)
2366 Eastlake Ave. E, No. 429
Seattle, WA 98102
Ph: (206)720-6270
Free: 888-722-5288
Fax: (206)720-6290
Co. E-mail: info@earlymusic.org
URL: http://www.earlymusic.org
Contact: Robert Johnson, President

Description: Serves and strengthens the early music community in North America. Compiles statistics. Conducts educational programs. **Scope:** historical performance in North America. **Founded:** 1985. **Subscriptions:** 300 books. **Publications:** *Early Music America* (Quarterly); *Early Music America--Directory of Members* (Annual); *EMA Electronic Bulletin* (Quarterly); *Early Music America magazine* (Quarterly). **Educational Activities:** Early Music America Conference (Annual). **Awards:** Barbara Thornton Memorial Scholarship (Annual); Early Music Outreach Award (Annual); Howard Mayer Brown Award (Annual); Thomas Binkley Award (Annual); Early Music Outreach Award; Howard Mayer Brown Award; Thomas Binkley Award.

14728 ■ MIAC E-News
505 Consumers Rd., Ste. 807
Toronto, ON, Canada M2J 4V8
Ph: (416)490-1871
Free: 877-490-6422
Fax: (416)490-0369
Co. E-mail: barbara@miac.net
URL: http://www.miac.net
Contact: Barbara Cole, Executive Director
Released: Monthly

14729 ■ Music Industries Association of Canada (MIAC)—Association Canadiene Des Industries De La Musique
505 Consumers Rd., Ste. 807
Toronto, ON, Canada M2J 4V8
Ph: (416)490-1871
Free: 877-490-6422
Fax: (416)490-0369
Co. E-mail: barbara@miac.net
URL: http://www.miac.net
Contact: Barbara Cole, Executive Director

Description: Manufacturers, distributors, and retailers of musical instruments, accessories, sound reinforcement products, and published music. Promotes and represents members' interests. **Founded:** 1972. **Publications:** *MIAC E-News* (Monthly). **Educational Activities:** PAL Showcase (Annual); Music Industries Association of Canada Tradeshow (Annual). **Awards:** MIAC Scholarship (Annual).

14730 ■ National Association of School Music Dealers (NASMD)
14070 Proton Rd., Ste. 100
Dallas, TX 75244-3601
Ph: (972)233-9107
Fax: (972)490-4219
Co. E-mail: office@nasmd.com
URL: http://www.nasmd.com
Contact: Joel Menchey, President

Description: Retail music stores and companies engaged in sales, service and repair of band and orchestra instruments to elementary and secondary schools and colleges. **Founded:** 1962. **Publications:** *NASMD Newsletter* (Quarterly).

REFERENCE WORKS

14731 ■ "AllHipHop.com's Founders Thought a Weeklong Event Would Raise the Company" in Inc. (February 2008, pp. 48-51)
Pub: Gruner & Jahr USA Publishing

Ed: Kermit Pattison. **Description:** Co-founders Greg Watkins and Chuck Creekmur, planned a weeklong festival to promote their company, AllHipHop.com; the event nearly ruined the firm. The online firm provides news about hip hop artists and the industry and is updated daily.

14732 ■ The Big Payback: The History of the Business of Hip-Hop
Pub: New American Library/Penguin Group
Ed: Dan Charnas. **Price:** $24.95. **Description:** The complete history of hip-hop music is presented, by following the money and the relationship between artist and merchant. In its promise of economic security and creative control for black artist-entrepreneurs, it is the culmination of dreams of black nationalists and civil rights leaders.

14733 ■ "The Book On Indigo" in Canadian Business (Vol. 81, July 22, 2008, No. 12-13, pp. 29)
Pub: Rogers Media Ltd.
Ed: Thomas Watson. **Description:** Indigo Books & Music Inc. reported record sales of $922 million resulting in a record net profit of $52.8 million for the 2008 fiscal year ended March 29, 2008. Earnings per share were $2.13, greater than Standard & Poor's expected $1.70 per share. Additional information concerning Indigo Books is presented.

14734 ■ "Handleman Liquidation Leaves Questions For Shareholders" in Crain's Detroit Business (Vol. 24, October 6, 2008, No. 40, pp. 4)
Pub: Crain Communications, Inc.

Ed: Nancy Kaffer. **Description:** Discusses Handleman Co., a Troy-based music distribution company, and their plan of liquidation and dissolution as well as how shareholders will be affected by the company's plan. Handleman filed its plan to liquidate and dissolve assets with the Securities and Exchange Commission in mid-August, following several quarters of dismal earnings.

14735 ■ How to Market and Sell Your Art, Music, Photographs, and Handmade Crafts Online
Pub: Atlantic Publishing Group, Inc.

Ed: Lee Rowley. **Released:** May 2008. **Price:** $24.95. **Description:** The book provides all the basics for starting and running an online store selling arts, crafts, photography or music. There are more than 300 Websites listed to help anyone market and promote their arts and/or crafts online.

14736 ■ Music Trades--Purchaser's Guide to the Music Industry Issue
Pub: Music Trades Corp.
Contact: Dennis Houlihan, President
URL(s): www.musictrades.com. **Ed:** Brian T. Majeski. **Released:** Annual; Latest edition 2010; New edition expected 2012. **Price:** $16, Individuals per year. **Publication includes:** List of 3,000 musical instrument manufacturers and wholesalers, publishers of sheet music, and manufacturers of musical accessories; international coverage. **Entries include:** Company name, address, phone, names of executives, trade and brand names, products or services. **Arrangement:** Alphabetical.

14737 ■ "Sound Fundamentals" in Hispanic Business (September 2007, pp. 12, 14, 16)
Pub: Hispanic Business

Ed: Michael T. Mena. **Description:** Profile of Ozomatli, a Los Angeles-based multicultural, multi-ethnic musical group that has topped Billboard's Latin Pop chart without relying on record sales. Members explain how they run the group like a small business.

14738 ■ "Universal Music Sues Grooveshark's Parent" in Wall Street Journal Eastern Edition (November 22 , 2011, pp. B5)
Pub: Dow Jones & Company Inc.

Ed: Ethan Smith. **Description:** Escape Media Group Inc., the parent company of online-music service Grooveshark, and seven of its executives have been sued by Universal Music Group, which alleges patent infringement involving its sound recordings. The executives are alleged to have uploaded thousands of songs onto Grooveshark.

14739 ■ "Welcome to Babesland" in Women In Business (Vol. 62, June 2010, No. 2, pp. 33)
Pub: American Business Women's Association
Ed: Leigh Elmore. **Description:** Music group, Four Bitchin' Babes will be performing at the 2010 American Business Women's Association's National Women's Leadership Conference. The group has been in the industry for 20 years and has released nine albums. The Four Bitchin' Babes consist of Sally Fingerett, Nancy Moran, Deirdre Flint, and Debi Smith.

STATISTICAL SOURCES

14740 ■ The Market for Musical Instruments
Pub: Business Trend Analysts, Inc.
Released: 2002-2003. **Price:** $1695.00.

14741 ■ RMA Annual Statement Studies
Pub: Risk Management Association
Contact: Kevin M. Blakey, President
Released: Annual. **Price:** $175.00 2006-07 edition, $105.00. **Description:** Contains composite balance sheets and income statements for more than 360 industries, including the accounting, auditing, and bookkeeping industries. Also contains five years of comparative historical data for discerning trends. Includes 16 commonly used ratios, computed for most of the size groupings for nearly every industry.

14742 ■ Standard & Poor's Industry Surveys
Pub: Standard & Poor's Corp.
Released: Annual. **Price:** $3633.00. **Description:** Two-volume book that examines the prospects for specific industries, including trucking. Also provides analyses of trends and problems, statistical tables and charts, and comparative company analyses.

TRADE PERIODICALS

14743 ■ Acoustic Guitar Magazine
Pub: Acoustic Guitar
URL(s): www.acousticguitar.com. **Released:** 8/yr. **Price:** $29.95, Individuals.

14744 ■ American Music
Contact: Neil Lerner, Editor
E-mail: nelerner@davidson.edu
URL(s): www.press.uillinois.edu/journals/am.html. **Ed:** Neil Lerner, Norma Coates, Mark Perry. **Released:** Quarterly **Price:** $47, Individuals print or online; $52, Individuals print + online; $99, Institutions print or online; $109, Institutions print + online; $25, Students online.

14745 ■ Down Beat: Jazz, Blues & Beyond
Pub: Maher Publications Inc.
Contact: James Petrillo, President
URL(s): www.downbeat.com. **Released:** Monthly **Price:** $48.99, Two years; $26.99, Individuals; $48.99, Other countries; $92.99, Other countries two years; $37.99, Canada; $70.99, Canada two years.

14746 ■ Harmonica Happenings
Pub: Society for the Preservation and Advancement of the Harmonica
Contact: Doug Tate, President
E-mail: dougtate@istal.com
Ed: George Davis, Editor, gdavis9@ix.netcom.com. **Released:** Quarterly. **Description:** Promotes appreciation for harmonica music. Contains material of interest to harmonica players, with profiles of and interviews with musicians, instructional material, and news notes. Recurring features include letters to the editor, editorials on professional harmonicists.

14747 ■ ITG Journal
Pub: International Trumpet Guild
Contact: David C. Jones, Treasurer
Released: 4/year. **Price:** Included in membership. **Description:** Carries news of interest to trumpet players, teachers, and students. Contains book reviews, record reviews, and listings of new publications and recordings, and occasionally includes sheet music and CD recordings. Also carries articles on trumpet pedagogy, players of note, musical analysis, and historical instruments.

14748 ■ MASTA notes
Pub: American String Teachers Association with National School Orchestra Association--Michigan Chapter
Ed: Molly Rebeck, Editor, momokay@home.com. **Released:** Quarterly. **Price:** Included in membership. **Description:** Reports on news, events, programs, and workshops for members of the Michigan chapter of the American String Teachers Association. Recurring features include a calendar of events.

14749 ■ Music Inc.: For Progresive Music Retailers
Pub: Maher Publications Inc.
Contact: James Petrillo, President
URL(s): www.musicincmag.com/magazine.html. **Released:** 11/yr. **Price:** $17, Individuals.

14750 ■ Music Trades
Pub: Music Trades Corp.
Contact: Dennis Houlihan, President
URL(s): www.musictrades.com/. **Ed:** Brian T. Majeski. **Released:** Monthly **Price:** $45, Individuals foreign; $23, Two years domestic; $16, Individuals domestic.

14751 ■ NAMM PlayBack
Pub: NAMM - The International Music Products Association
Contact: Joe Lamond, President
Released: Bimonthly. **Price:** Included in membership. **Description:** Published to keep member retailers and manufacturers of musical instruments apprised of industry news and Association trade shows. Also publicizes the Association's educational services and membership benefits. Recurring features include a calendar of events, reports of meetings, and notices of publications available.

14752 ■ Premiere Guitar
Pub: Gearhead Communications, LLC
URL(s): www.premierguitar.com/Main/Default.aspx. **Released:** Monthly **Price:** $24.95, Individuals + 1 issue free; $39.95, Two years + 3 issues free.

14753 ■ Sheet Music Magazine
Pub: Piano Today
URL(s): www.sheetmusicmagazine.com/. **Released:** Quarterly **Price:** $47.44, Two years; $24.97, Individuals.

VIDEOCASSETTES/ AUDIOCASSETTES

14754 ■ Vladimir Ashkenazy
Tapeworm Video Distributors
25876 The Old Road #141
Stevenson Ranch, CA 91381
Ph: (661)257-4904
Fax: (661)257-4820
Co. E-mail: sales@tapeworm.com
URL: http://www.tapeworm.com
Released: 1996. **Price:** $19.95. **Description:** Documents the life and career of the pianist and conductor. Also provides excerpts of his tour in Russia, Switzerland, Sweden, and Germany. **Availability:** VHS.

TRADE SHOWS AND CONVENTIONS

14755 ■ American Choral Directors Association National Conference
American Choral Directors Association
545 Couch Dr.
Oklahoma City, OK 73102-2207
Ph: (405)232-8161
Fax: (405)232-8162
Co. E-mail: acda@acdaonline.org
URL: http://www.acdaonline.org
Contact: Dr. Tim Sharp, Executive Director
URL(s): acdaonline.org. **Frequency:** Biennial. **Audience:** Choral directors. **Principal Exhibits:** Choral music and supplies.

14756 ■ College Music Society National Conference
College Music Society (CMS)
312 E Pine St.
Missoula, MT 59802
Ph: (406)721-9616
Fax: (406)721-9419
Co. E-mail: cms@music.org
URL: http://www.music.org
Contact: David Brian Williams, President
E-mail: davew_cms@me.com
URL(s): www.music.org. **Frequency:** Annual. **Audience:** Publishers, record companies, related trade professionals, college and university music faculty. **Principal Exhibits:** Music publishers, instrument manufacturers, music retailers, non-profit associations, music hardware and software manufacturers.

14757 ■ European Congress on Psychiatry
Kenes International
Rue de Chantepoulet 1-3
CH-1211 Geneva, Switzerland
Ph: 41 22 9080488
Fax: 41 22 9069140
Co. E-mail: info@kenes.com
URL: http://www.kenes.com
URL(s): www2.kenes.com/epa/Pages/Home.aspx. **Frequency:** Annual. **Audience:** Medical professionals. **Principal Exhibits:** Psychiatry and neuropsychiatry.

14758 ■ NAfME National In-Service Conference
National Association for Music Education (NAfME)
1806 Robert Fulton Dr.
Reston, VA 20191
Ph: (703)860-4000
Free: 800-336-3768
Fax: (703)860-1531
Co. E-mail: michaelb@nafme.org
URL: http://www.nafme.org/
Contact: Michael A. Butera, Executive Director
E-mail: michaelb@nafme.org
URL(s): musiced.nafme.org/events/. **Frequency:** Biennial. **Audience:** Music educators teaching in public and private schools and colleges. **Principal Exhibits:** Music education equipment, supplies, and services. **Telecommunication Services:** lisat@nafme.org.

14759 ■ The NAMM Show
NAMM - The International Music Products Association
5790 Armada Dr.
Carlsbad, CA 92008-4608
Ph: (760)438-8001
Free: 800-767-6266
Fax: (760)438-7327
Co. E-mail: info@namm.org
URL: http://www.namm.org
Contact: Joe Lamond, President
URL(s): www.namm.org/thenammshow/2012. **Frequency:** Annual. **Audience:** Retail music merchants; manufacturers of musical instruments and accessories; manufacturers of acoustical equipment; sheet music publishers. **Principal Exhibits:** Musical instruments and accessories, acoustical equipment, and sheet music publications.

14760 ■ New York State School Music Association Winter Conference
New York State School Music Association
718 Plain Rd.
Westbury, NY 11590-5931
Free: 888-NYSSMA1
Fax: (516)997-1700
Co. E-mail: executive@nyssma.org
URL: http://www.nyssma.org
Contact: Steven E. Schopp, Executive Director
E-mail: Executive@nyssma.org
URL(s): www.nyssma.org. **Price:** $145, Preregistered; $185. **Frequency:** Annual. **Audience:** Music teachers and general public. **Principal Exhibits:** Music publishers, musical instruments, fundraising materials, and educational materials. **Dates and Locations:** Concord Hotel.

14761 ■ Texas Music Educators Association Clinic/Convention
Texas Music Educators Association
PO Box 140465
Austin, TX 78714-0465
Ph: (512)452-0710
Free: 888-318-TMEA
Fax: (512)451-9213
URL: http://www.tmea.org
Contact: Robert Floyd, Executive Director
E-mail: rfloyd@tmea.org
URL(s): tmea.org. **Price:** $50, active member; $15, retired. **Frequency:** Annual. **Audience:** Music teachers. **Principal Exhibits:** Music publishers, uniform/ gowns, recruitment, photographers, software. **Dates and Locations:** , Convention Center.

CONSULTANTS

14762 ■ Jess Barker, Document Research/ Retrieval L.L.C.
209A S Macoupin St.
Gillespie, IL 62033-1605
Ph: (217)839-3219
Free: 888-316-3773
Fax: (877)522-7537
Co. E-mail: documentretrieval@frontiernet.net
URL: http://www.documentresearch.biz
Contact: James Barker, Principal
Scope: A full service title search company that provides Title Reports to investors who are interested in making offers on properties. **Founded:** 1993.

FRANCHISES AND BUSINESS OPPORTUNITIES

14763 ■ Music Go Round
Winmark Corp.
605 Hwy. 169 N, Ste. 400
Minneapolis, MN 55441-6536
Ph: (763)520-8500
Free: 800-433-2540
Fax: (763)520-8410
Co. E-mail: winmark.information@winmarkcorporation.com
URL: http://www.winmarkcorporation.com
Description: Sales of new, used, and consignment musical instruments. **No. of Franchise Units:** 34. **Founded:** 1986.. **Franchised:** 1994. **Equity Capital Needed:** $253,450-$325,200; approximately 30% cash requirement. **Franchise Fee:** $25,000. **Training:** Training program includes product acquisition, inventory management, retail store operations, employee management, and ongoing support.

LIBRARIES

14764 ■ Alberta Band Association - Music Lending Library
10612-124 St., Ste. 206
Edmonton, AB, Canada T5N 1S4
Ph: (780)488-2263
Free: 877-687-4239
Fax: (780)488-4132
URL: http://albertabandassociation.com/library.php
Contact: Neil Corlett, Managing Director
Scope: Music. **Services:** Library not open to the public. **Holdings:** Concert band titles, scores, methods, and recordings.

14765 ■ Bagaduce Music Lending Library
5 Music Library Ln.
Blue Hill, ME 04614
Ph: (207)374-5454
Fax: (207)374-2733
Co. E-mail: library@bagaducemusic.org
URL: http://www.bagaducemusic.org/
Contact: Martina Herries, Executive Director
Scope: Printed music - choral, keyboard, instrumental, popular and classical vocals. **Services:** Library open to the public. **Founded:** 1983. **Holdings:** 215,000 pieces of sheet music, scores, collections, and anthologies. **Subscriptions:** 2 journals and other serials. **Telecommunication Services:** martina@ bagaducemusic.org.

14766 ■ John Brown University - Music Library
2000 W. University St.
Siloam Springs, AR 72761
Ph: (479)524-7266
Co. E-mail: twubbena@jbu.edu
URL: http://www.jbu.edu/music/facilities/
Contact: Mrs. Terri R. Wubbena, Chairperson
Scope: Music. **Services:** Library open to the public. **Holdings:** 1000 music scores; 2400 music sound recordings on LPs and CDs.

14767 ■ California University of Pennsylvania - Louis L. Manderino Library - Special Collections
250 University Ave., Rm. 435
California, PA 15419
Ph: (724)938-5926
Fax: (724)938-5901
Co. E-mail: pokol@calu.edu
URL: http://library.calu.edu
Contact: Alber Pokol, Archivist Librarian, Special Collections
Scope: Rare books, art, music. **Services:** Interlibrary loan; Library open to the public by appointment.

14768 ■ Chicago Public Library - Visual & Performing Arts Division - Music Information Center
Harold Washington Library Center
400 S. State St., 8th Fl.
Chicago, IL 60605
Ph: (312)747-4850
URL: http://www.chipublib.org/branch/details/library/ harold-washington/p/Vpa
Contact: Brian Bannon, Commissioner
Scope: History and theory of music, biographies of musicians and composers, music education, opera, musical comedy, sacred music, popular music, discography, music business, musical instruments, vocal and instrumental pedagogy, music therapy, folk music, composition and orchestration, arranging. **Services:** Interlibrary loan; copying; listening/viewing Center; practice rooms; music chamber; Center open to the public. **Founded:** 1915. **Holdings:** 49,800 books; 8025 bound periodical volumes; 67,000 bound volumes of music; 30,000 pieces of music; 15 VF drawers of pamphlets and clippings; 6102 microfiche of music; 2220 reels of microfilm of periodicals; 169,000 phonograph records, compact discs, audiocassettes; 3900 music videos; 334 laserdiscs; 4250 photographs; 51,957 uncatalogued scores. **Subscriptions:** 561 journals and other serials.

14769 ■ Conservatoire de Musique de Quebec - Bibliotheque
270 rue St. Amable
Quebec, QC, Canada G1R 5G1
Ph: (418)643-2190
Fax: (418)644-9658
Co. E-mail: cmq_bib@conservatoire.gouv.qc.ca
URL: http://www.conservatoire.gouv.qc.ca/quebec/ index.asp
Contact: Pierre Plante, Librarian, Music
Scope: Classical music, orchestral music. **Services:** Library open to the public for reference use only. **Founded:** 1944. **Holdings:** 65,000 books. **Subscriptions:** 33 journals and other serials; 1 newspaper.

14770 ■ Edinboro University - Baron-Forness Library - Special Collections
200 Tartan Rd., 7th Fl.
Edinboro, PA 16444
Ph: (814)732-2415
Fax: (814)732-2883
Co. E-mail: obringer@edinboro.edu
URL: http://www.edinboro.edu/departments/library/ archives/page_one.dot
Contact: Prof. David Obringer
Scope: Music, art, education, Pennsylvania history, Civil War regimental history, rare books. **Services:** Interlibrary loan; tutoring; Library open to the public with restrictions. **Founded:** 1860. **Holdings:** 3000 volumes; prints.

14771 ■ Grinnell College - Burling Library - Listening Room
1111 Sixth Ave.
Grinnell, IA 50112-1690
Ph: (641)269-3365
Fax: (641)269-4283
Co. E-mail: jonesran@grinnell.edu
URL: http://www.grinnell.edu/library/collections/listeningroom
Contact: Randye Jones, Supervisor
Scope: Music, arts, humanities, sciences. **Services:** Library open to the public with restrictions (public may use items in-house, unless space is needed by students or faculty). **Founded:** 1846. **Holdings:** 25,000 cataloged titles in compact disc, LP record, cassette tape, and videocassettes formats; 6000 cataloged titles in DVD and VHS formats.

14772 ■ Hardin-Simmons University - Smith Music Library
Caldwell Hall
2200 Hickory
Box 16195
Abilene, TX 79689
Ph: (915)670-1565
Co. E-mail: james.floyd@hsutx.edu
URL: http://www.hsutx.edu/library
Contact: James Floyd, Librarian, Music
URL(s): www.hsutx.edu/HSUDirectory.php. **Scope:** Music. **Services:** Interlibrary loan. **Holdings:** Scores; collected works of various composers; recordings; basic music books; listening equipment.

14773 ■ Lawrence University - Seeley G. Mudd Library - Music Collections
113 S. Lawe St.
Appleton, WI 54911
Ph: (920)832-6750
Co. E-mail: antoinette.powell@lawrence.edu
URL: http://www.lawrence.edu/library/music/collection.shtml
Contact: Erin Dix, Archivist
Scope: Music - instrumental solo, chamber works, orchestral, piano, vocal, classical, jazz, Western art, world music, musical theater, opera. **Services:** Interlibrary loan. **Holdings:** 14,000 scores; 1500 LPs; 10,000 compact discs; 8000 books on music; 400 music videotapes. **Subscriptions:** 160 journals and other serials. **Telecommunication Services:** reference@lawrence.edu.

14774 ■ Weill-Lenya Research Center—Kurt Weill Foundation.
7 E 20th St.
New York, NY 10003
Ph: (212)505-5240
Fax: (212)353-9663
Co. E-mail: wlrc@kwf.org
URL: http://www.kwf.org/kwf/foundation/weill-lenya-research-center
Contact: Dave Stein, Archivist
Scope: Life and work of composer Kurt Weill and Lotte Lenya, musicology, music theory, theater history, 20th-century culture, Weimar Republic culture, women's studies, Jewish studies, emigre studies. **Services:** Information referral. **Founded:** 1983. **Holdings:** Books; printed music; music manuscripts; scripts; correspondence; audio and video recordings; films; programs; photographs; posters; press clippings; business records; personal papers. **Subscriptions:** 1 journal. **Publications:** Guide to the Weill-Lenya Research Center; Kurt Weill Newsletter (Semiannual). **Awards:** Research and travel grants. **Telecommunication Services:** dstein@kwf.org.

14775 ■ Nipawin School Division - Education Resource Centre
Box 2044
Nipawin, SK, Canada S0E 1E0
Ph: (306)862-4616
Fax: (306)862-9733
Co. E-mail: verda.hoppe-nsd@saskschools.ca
Contact: Verda Hoppe, Library Technician
Scope: Music, special education. **Services:** Interlibrary loan. **Founded:** 1950. **Holdings:** 10,000 books; 1500 videotapes; 1000 recordings. **Subscriptions:** 10 journals and other serials.

14776 ■ Ohio Wesleyan University - Kinnison Music Library
Sanborn Hall, Rm. 005
Delaware, OH 43105
Ph: (740)368-3715
Co. E-mail: paszabo@owu.edu
URL: http://library.owu.edu/libmusic.htm
Contact: Peter Szabo, Librarian, Music
Scope: Music. **Services:** Interlibrary loan; copying; Library open to the public. **Holdings:** 15,000 items - 6000 books; 1184 bound periodical volumes; 1500 CD-ROMs; 4500 LPs. **Subscriptions:** 34 journals and other serials.

14777 ■ St. Norbert Arts Centre Archives
PO Box 175
Winnipeg, MB, Canada R3V 1L6
Ph: (204)269-0564
Fax: (204)261-1927
Co. E-mail: snac@snac.mb.ca
URL: http://www.snac.mb.ca
Contact: Louise May, Director
Scope: Art - visual art, music, theater, and dance. **Services:** Archives open to the public. **Founded:** 1996. **Holdings:** Graphic materials; textual records.

14778 ■ San Francisco Public Library - Bernard Osher Foundation - Art, Music & Recreation Center
100 Larkin St., 4th Fl.
San Francisco, CA 94102
Ph: (415)557-4525
Fax: (415)557-4524
Co. E-mail: info@sfpl.org
URL: http://www.sfpl.org
Contact: Mark Hall, Manager
URL(s): sfpl.org/index.php?pg=0200001401. **Scope:** Arts - visual, graphic; sports and recreation; photogra-phy; architecture; arts and crafts; performing arts; music - orchestral, chamber, opera, popular, folk, jazz. **Services:** Center open to the public. **Holdings:** Books; serials; scores. **Telecommunication Services:** artmusicrec@sfpl.org.

14779 ■ Sweet Briar College - Junius P. Fishburn Music Library
134 Chapel Rd.
Sweet Briar, VA 24595
Ph: (434)381-6138
Fax: (434)381-6173
Co. E-mail: jgjaffe@sbc.edu
URL: http://library.sbc.edu
Contact: John Jaffe, Director
Scope: Music. **Services:** Interlibrary loan; library open to the public. **Holdings:** 12,000 items.

14780 ■ University of Nevada, Las Vegas - Music Library
Beam Music Center
4505 S. Maryland Pkwy.
Las Vegas, NV 89154
Ph: (702)895-2541
Co. E-mail: music.library@unlv.edu
URL: http://www.unlv.edu
Contact: Cheryl Taranto, Librarian, Music
URL(s): www.library.unlv.edu/music. **Scope:** Music. **Services:** Interlibrary loan; copying; document delivery; Library open to the public. **Holdings:** 35,000 volumes; 11,000 recordings (compact discs, LPs, au-diocassettes); 1200 videos; 9000 books. **Subscriptions:** 156 journals and other serials. **Telecommunication Services:** cheryl.taranto@unlv.edu.

14781 ■ University of North Carolina School of the Arts - Semans Library
UNC School of the Arts
1533 S. Main St.
Winston-Salem, NC 27127
Ph: (336)770-3270
Fax: (336)770-3271
Co. E-mail: rebeccab@uncsa.edu
URL: http://www.uncsa.edu/library
Contact: Christia Thomason
Scope: Music, art and design, theater, film, dance, humanities. **Services:** Interlibrary loan; Library open to the public. **Founded:** 1965. **Holdings:** 111,000 books; 9000 bound periodical volumes; 50,000 music scores; 45,000 sound recordings; 5200 DVDs and videos. **Subscriptions:** 470 journals and other serials; 25 newspapers.

14782 ■ Andy Warhol Museum - Archives Study Center
117 Sandusky St.
Pittsburgh, PA 15212-5890
Ph: (412)237-8300
Fax: (412)237-8340
Co. E-mail: wrbicanm@warhol.org
URL: http://www.warhol.org/collections/archives.html
Contact: Matt Wrbican, Archivist
Scope: Andy Warhol, pop art movement, journalism, rock music, celebrity culture, fashion. **Services:** Archives is open to researchers by appointment. **Founded:** 1994. **Holdings:** Business records; scrap-books; photographs; audiocassettes; videotapes; published materials; books; art work; clothing; post-ers; correspondence; personal objects; 4000 audio tapes. **Telecommunication Services:** information@warhol.org.

ASSOCIATIONS AND OTHER ORGANIZATIONS

14783 ■ American Institute of Organbuilders (AIO)
PO Box 35306
Canton, OH 44735
Ph: (330)806-9011
Co. E-mail: robert_sullivan@pipeorgan.org
URL: http://www.pipeorgan.org
Contact: Fredrick W. Bahr, President
Description: Professional builders and service technicians of pipe organs. Advances the art of pipe organ building by encouraging discussion, inquiry, and research; furthers knowledge regarding pipe organ building through lectures and the exchange of information. Conducts examinations and small-group training seminars. **Founded:** 1974. **Publications:** *AIO Service Manual; Apprenticeship and Training Policy Manual; Journal of American Organbuilding* (Quarterly); *Membership List* (Annual). **Educational Activities:** American Institute of Organbuilders Convention (Annual). **Awards:** AIO Scholarship (Annual).

14784 ■ American Musical Instrument Society (AMIS)
c/o Joanne Kopp, Treas.
1106 Garden St.
Hoboken, NJ 07030
Ph: (201)656-0107
Co. E-mail: j2kopp@aol.com
URL: http://www.amis.org
Contact: Albert R. Rice, President
Description: Individuals, museums, and other institutions interested in all aspects of musical instruments. Disseminates information on all types of instruments (both Western and non-Western) through demonstrations, papers, slides, and meetings. **Founded:** 1971. **Educational Activities:** American Musical Instrument Society Meeting (Annual). **Awards:** Nicolas Bessaraboff Prize; Frances Densmore Prize; Curt Sachs Award; Curt Sachs (Annual); Frances Densmore Prize (Biennial); Nicholas Bessaraboff Prize (Biennial); William E. Gribbon Memorial Award for Student Travel (Annual).

14785 ■ Associated Pipe Organ Builders of America (APOBA)
PO Box 155
Chicago Ridge, IL 60415
Ph: (660)747-3066
Free: 800-473-5270
URL: http://www.apoba.com
Description: Manufacturers of pipe organs and pipe organ parts. Aims to expand and perfect the art of pipe organ building in the U.S. Sponsors educational programs and speakers' bureau. Compiles marketing statistics. **Founded:** 1941. **Publications:** *Success Stories: Five Pipe Organ Projects Summarized.*

14786 ■ International Association of Piano Builders and Technicians (IAPBT)
1584-2 402, Mi Gwan Bldg.
Seocho-Dong, Seocho-Gu
Seoul, South Korea

Ph: 82 2 7322211
Fax: 82 2 5217979
Co. E-mail: oripia@nate.com
URL: http://www.iapbt.com
Contact: Kerry Cooper, Vice President
Description: Works as worldwide association of piano service organizations and individuals. Seeks to form and maintain a worldwide fellowship of piano technicians and rebuilders. Provides a means of exchange of technical information and related subjects and for cooperation in scientific research to improve the quality of pianos. Exchange of information is on a voluntary basis. **Founded:** 1979.

14787 ■ National Association of Professional Band Instrument Repair Technicians (NAPBIRT)
PO Box 51
Normal, IL 61761
Ph: (309)452-4257
Fax: (309)452-4825
Co. E-mail: napbirt@napbirt.org
URL: http://www.napbirt.org
Description: Aims to offer continuing education in the field of band instrument repair. Promotes technical integrity in the craft. Conducts self-evaluation programs, local parts and services exchange programs, and problem solution services. Surveys tools and procedures to improve work quality. Serves as liaison between manufacturers/suppliers and technicians by providing a technical audience for the introduction and evaluation of new products and policies. Has established a code of ethics. Provides placement service. Holds hands-on training sessions per year. **Scope:** construction, repair, restoration of band instruments. **Founded:** 1976. **Subscriptions:** 500 archival material articles audiovisuals books periodicals video recordings.

14788 ■ Piano Manufacturers Association International (PMAI)
14070 Proton Rd., Ste. 100, LB9
Dallas, TX 75244
Ph: (972)233-9107
Fax: (972)490-4219
Co. E-mail: mad@madcrouch.com
URL: http://www.pianonet.com
Description: Manufacturers of pianos and parts suppliers. Compiles monthly unit shipment and dollar volume reports. Supports National Piano Foundation. **Founded:** 1881. **Educational Activities:** Piano Manufacturers Association International Tradeshow (Annual).

14789 ■ Piano Technicians Guild (PTG)
4444 Forest Ave.
Kansas City, KS 66106-3750
Ph: (913)432-9975
Fax: (913)432-9986
Co. E-mail: ptg@ptg.org
URL: http://www.ptg.org
Contact: Ms. Barbara J. Cassaday, Executive Director
Description: Piano tuners and technicians. Conducts technical institutes at conventions, seminars and local chapter meetings. Promotes public education in

piano care; maintains liaison with piano manufacturers and teachers. Maintains hall of fame. **Scope:** all aspects of the piano and piano history. **Founded:** 1958. **Subscriptions:** 352 articles books periodicals video recordings. **Publications:** *Piano Technicians Journal* (Monthly). **Educational Activities:** Piano Technicians Guild Convention (Annual); Piano Technicians Guild Annual Convention (Annual). **Awards:** Golden Hammer Award; Hall of Fame; Member of Note.

DIRECTORIES OF EDUCATIONAL PROGRAMS

14790 ■ *Directory of Private Accredited Career Schools and Colleges of Technology*
Pub: Accrediting Commission of Career Schools and Colleges of Technology
Contact: Michale S. McComis, Executive Director
Released: On web page. **Price:** Free. **Description:** Covers 3900 accredited post-secondary programs that provide training programs in business, trade, and technical fields, including various small business endeavors. Entries offer school name, address, phone, description of courses, job placement assistance, and requirements for admission. Arrangement is alphabetical.

TRADE PERIODICALS

14791 ■ *Acoustic Guitar Magazine*
Pub: Acoustic Guitar
URL(s): www.acousticguitar.com. **Released:** 8/yr. **Price:** $29.95, Individuals.

14792 ■ *Premiere Guitar*
Pub: Gearhead Communications, LLC
URL(s): www.premierguitar.com/Main/Default.aspx. **Released:** Monthly **Price:** $24.95, Individuals + 1 issue free; $39.95, Two years + 3 issues free.

TRADE SHOWS AND CONVENTIONS

14793 ■ The Midwest Clinic An International Band and Orchestra Conference
The Midwest Clinic
1111 E Touhy, Ste. 250
Des Plaines, IL 60018
Ph: (847)424-4163
Fax: (773)321-1509
Co. E-mail: info@midwestclinic.org
URL: http://www.midwestclinic.org
Contact: Richard Crain, President
URL(s): www.midwestclinic.com. **Price:** $110, for director, administrator, and spouse; $50, for college students; $20, elementary, junior high school, and high school students. **Frequency:** Annual. **Audience:** Trade professionals. **Principal Exhibits:** Music instruments and publications, supplies, and services,

universities, military organizations, fund raisers, music publishers. **Dates and Locations:** , McCormick Place. **Telecommunication Services:** info@ midwestclinic.org.

RESEARCH CENTERS

14794 ■ University of Hartford - Acoustics Laboratory
College of Engineering, Technology & Architecture
200 Bloomfield Ave.
West Hartford, CT 06117
Ph: (860)768-4792
Free: 800-766-4024
Co. E-mail: celmer@hartford.edu
URL: http://uhaweb.hartford.edu/celmer/lab.htm
Contact: Dr. Robert D. Celmer, Director

ASSOCIATIONS AND OTHER ORGANIZATIONS

14795 ■ **Professional Beauty Association (NMC) - Nail Manufacturers Council (NMC)**
15825 N 71st St., Ste. 100
Scottsdale, AZ 85254
Ph: (480)281-0424
Free: 800-468-2274
Fax: (480)905-0708
Co. E-mail: info@probeauty.org
URL: http://www.probeauty.org/about/committees/nmc
Contact: Bruce Selan, Chairman

Description: Division of American Beauty Association. Nail product manufacturers and marketers. Promotes unity within the nail product industry. Works to: elevate safety standards; maintain high ethical standards in advertising; increase public awareness of nail care. Lobbies the government concerning issues that affect the industry. Acts as a forum for the exchange of information. Maintains safety guidelines. **Founded:** 1989.

DIRECTORIES OF EDUCATIONAL PROGRAMS

14796 ■ *Directory of Private Accredited Career Schools and Colleges of Technology*
Pub: Accrediting Commission of Career Schools and Colleges of Technology
Contact: Michale S. McComis, Executive Director
Released: On web page. **Price:** Free. **Description:** Covers 3900 accredited post-secondary programs that provide training programs in business, trade, and technical fields, including various small business endeavors. Entries offer school name, address, phone, description of courses, job placement assistance, and requirements for admission. Arrangement is alphabetical.

REFERENCE WORKS

14797 ■ *"Every Little Bit Helps" in Black Enterprise (Vol. 38, November 2007, No. 4, pp. 102)*
Pub: Earl G. Graves Publishing Co. Inc.
Ed: Tennille M. Robinson. **Description:** After a career in the cosmetics industry, Tricialee Riley is marketing and advertising her new venture, the Polish Bar, a salon offering manicures, pedicures, makeup application, and waxing.

CONSULTANTS

14798 ■ **Contempo Nails—Diane Day Designs**
108 W Avenida Gaviota
San Clemente, CA 92672
Ph: (949)498-7060
Fax: (949)498-3962
Contact: Diane Day, President
Scope: Provider of consulting on all aspects of sculptured acrylic nail application and care; use of acrylic nails and nail products to improve hand appearance, enhance self-image and self-confidence, prevent nail biting and other hand-related nervous disorders. **Founded:** 1984.

FRANCHISES AND BUSINESS OPPORTUNITIES

14799 ■ **Atir Natural Nail Care Clinic**
1301 Jamestown Rd., Ste. 101
Williamsburg, VA 23185
Ph: (757)258-0696
Fax: (757)258-8999
Description: Natural manicures & pedicures. **No. of Franchise Units:** 6. **No. of Company-Owned Units:** 2. **Founded:** 2004.. **Franchised:** 2004. **Equity Capital Needed:** $200,000-$288,000. **Franchise Fee:** $34,000. **Royalty Fee:** 6%. **Training:** Offers 7 days at headquarters, 3 days at franchisees location with ongoing support.

ASSOCIATIONS AND OTHER ORGANIZATIONS

14800 ■ Au Pair in America (APIA)
9 W Broad St., River Plz.
Stamford, CT 06902
Ph: (203)399-5000
Free: 800-928-7247
Fax: (203)399-5592
Co. E-mail: aupair.info@aifs.org
URL: http://www.aupairinamerica.com
Contact: Ruth Ferry, Director
URL(s): www.aifs.org. **Description:** A program of the American Institute for Foreign Study, Inc. International youth exchange program organized to promote cross-cultural understanding and cooperation between American families and Western European young adults by providing the opportunity for young people overseas to learn about American culture and family life while living in the U.S. Arranges for foreigners between the ages of 18 and 26 to reside in the U.S. for a year while caring for the children of a host family; participants serve as an "au pair," or equal person, in the host family's household. Has developed a reciprocal program which allows young Americans to travel to Europe. **Founded:** 1986.

14801 ■ International Nanny Association (INA)
PO Box 1299
Hyannis, MA 02601
Ph: (713)526-2670
Free: 888-878-1477
Fax: (508)638-6462
Co. E-mail: info@nanny.org
URL: http://www.nanny.org
Contact: Wendy Sachs, Co-President
Description: An educational association for nannies and those who educate, place, employ, and support professional in-home child care. Membership is open to those who are directly involved with the in-home child care profession, including nannies, nanny employers, nanny placement agency owners (and staff), nanny educators, and providers of special services related to the nanny profession. **Founded:** 1985. **Publications:** *A Nanny for Your Family*; *INAVision* (Quarterly); *Recommended Practices for Nannies*; *Annual Directory of Nanny Training Programs, Nanny Placement Agencies and Special Services* (Annual); *Directory of Nanny Training Programs, Placement Agencies and Special Services* (Annual); *So You Want to Be a Nanny*; *Beyond Peanut Butter and Jelly*. **Educational Activities:** International Nanny Association Conference (Annual); International Nanny Association Conference (Annual). **Awards:** Nanny of the Year (Annual).

DIRECTORIES OF EDUCATIONAL PROGRAMS

14802 ■ *Directory of Private Accredited Career Schools and Colleges of Technology*
Pub: Accrediting Commission of Career Schools and Colleges of Technology
Contact: Michale S. McComis, Executive Director
Released: On web page. **Price:** Free. **Description:** Covers 3900 accredited post-secondary programs that provide training programs in business, trade, and technical fields, including various small business endeavors. Entries offer school name, address, phone, description of courses, job placement assistance, and requirements for admission. Arrangement is alphabetical.

REFERENCE WORKS

14803 ■ *"Domestic Workers Organize!' in WorkingUSA (Vol. 11, December 2008, No. 4, pp. 413)*
Pub: Blackwell Publishers Ltd.
Ed: Eileen Boris, Premilla Nadasen. **Description:** History of domestic workers in the U.S. is examined. The article challenges the long-standing assumption that these, primarily women of color cleaners, nannies, and elder care providers are unable to organize and assesses the possibilities and limitations of recent organizing efforts. The nature of the occupation, its location in the home, the isolated character of the work, informal arrangements with employers, and exclusions from labor law protection, has fostered community-based, social movement organizing to build coalitions, reform legislation and draw public attention to the plight of domestic workers.

VIDEOCASSETTES/ AUDIOCASSETTES

14804 ■ *Day Care Grows Up*
Films for the Humanities & Sciences
132 West 31st Street
New York, NY 10001
Ph: (609)671-1000
Free: 800-257-5126
Fax: (609)671-0266
Co. E-mail: custserv@films.com
URL: http://www.films.com
Released: 1991. **Price:** $159.00. **Description:** Discusses the new attitudes and measures being taken to increase the quality of childcare in the U.S. **Availability:** VHS.

FRANCHISES AND BUSINESS OPPORTUNITIES

14805 ■ A+ Nannies Inc.
6730 E McDowell Rd., Ste. 133
Scottsdale, AZ 85257
Ph: (480)690-7558
Fax: (888)202-7738
Description: Nanny referral service. **No. of Franchise Units:** 2. **No. of Company-Owned Units:** 3. **Founded:** 2001.. **Franchised:** 2007. **Equity Capital Needed:** $39,250-$53,000. **Franchise Fee:** $28,000. **Royalty Fee:** 6%. **Financial Assistance:** Limited in-house financing available. **Training:** Offers 4 days training at headquarters and ongoing support.

14806 ■ Absolute Best Care Nanny Agency
Absolute Best Care Franchising LLC
274 Madison Ave.
New York, NY 10016
Ph: (212)481-5705
Fax: (212)481-5706
Description: Placement agency for nannies, baby nurses, housekeepers and sitters. **No. of Franchise Units:** 5. **No. of Company-Owned Units:** 2. **Founded:** 2002.. **Franchised:** 2006. **Equity Capital Needed:** $66,990-$74,240. **Franchise Fee:** $49,900. **Royalty Fee:** 8.5%. **Training:** Offers 1 week at headquarters and 1 week onsite with ongoing support.

14807 ■ Nanny Poppinz Corporate, Inc.
121 Delmar Ave.
Fort Myers Beach, FL 33931
Ph: (954)775-6017
Fax: (954)752-6708
Description: Nanny agency franchise. **No. of Franchise Units:** 3. **No. of Company-Owned Units:** 2. **Founded:** 1999.. **Franchised:** 2004. **Equity Capital Needed:** $65,000-$107,000. **Franchise Fee:** $35,000. **Training:** Yes.

START-UP INFORMATION

14808 ■ *"Best In Show" in Pet Product News (Vol. 64, November 2010, No. 11, pp. 20)*
Pub: BowTie Inc.
Ed: Lizett Bond. **Description:** Cherrybrook Premium Pet Supplies offers an expanded array of quality holistic products and is staffed by people who possess wide knowledge of these products. Aside from receiving the Outstanding Holistic Approach award, Cherrybrook has opened three stores in New Jersey. How a holistic approach to service kept customers coming back is discussed.

ASSOCIATIONS AND OTHER ORGANIZATIONS

14809 ■ **Acupuncture Foundation of Canada Institute (AFCI)—Institute de la Fondation D'Acupuncture du Canada**
2131 Lawrence Ave. E, Ste. 204
Scarborough, ON, Canada M1R 5G4
Ph: (416)752-3988
Fax: (416)752-4398
Co. E-mail: afciweb@afcinstitute.com
URL: http://www.afcinstitute.com
Contact: Mac Mierzejewski, President
Description: Promotes acupuncture's legitimate place in health care by initiating and supporting research in acupuncture. **Founded:** 1995. **Educational Activities:** Acupuncture Foundation of Canada Institute Board meeting. **Awards:** Clifford G. Woolfe Award.

14810 ■ **Alexander Technique International (ATI)**
1692 Massachusetts Ave., 3rd Fl.
Cambridge, MA 02138
Ph: (617)497-5151
Free: 888-668-8996
Fax: (617)497-2615
Co. E-mail: alexandertechnique@verizon.net
URL: http://www.ati-net.com
Contact: Jen Fries, Administrative Assistant
Description: Worldwide organization of Alexander technique teachers, students and supporters of the technique, created to promote and advance the work discovered by F.M. Alexander. Alexander Technique can improve health by overcoming harmful habits that cause stress and pain which often restrict physical and mental capabilities. **Founded:** 1992. **Publications:** *E-Communique; The ExChange.*

14811 ■ **American Reflexology Certification Board (ARCB)**
PO Box 141553
Grand Rapids, MI 49514
Ph: (303)933-6921
Fax: (303)904-0460
Co. E-mail: info@arcb.net
URL: http://www.arcb.net
Contact: Michael Rainone, President
Description: Works to protect the public; promotes advancement of field through recognition of competent reflexologists meeting national standards;

provides National Board Certified Reflexologist certification. **Founded:** 1992. **Publications:** *Reflexology Today* (Semiannual).

14812 ■ **American Reiki Master Association (ARMA)**
PO Box 130
Lake City, FL 32056-0130
Ph: (904)755-9638
Co. E-mail: american_reiki@yahoo.com
URL: http://members.atlantic.net/~arma
Contact: Cheri L. Robertson, President
Description: Promotes the Reiki therapy technique as a method of natural healing; offers training and certification.

14813 ■ **International Society for the Study of Ghosts and Apparitions (ISSGA)—Headquarters for Ghost Investigations**
Penthouse N
29 Washington Sq. W
New York, NY 10011-9180
Co. E-mail: theghostpost@yahoo.com
URL: http://www.phantasm.mynetcologne.de/issga.html
Contact: Dr. Jeanne Keyes Youngson, President
Description: Professional ghost hunters; individuals interested in ghosts and apparitions. Provides information on ghosts, apparitions, and other phenomena. Sponsors private tours in Greenwich Village, NY, led by the president of the society. Compiles statistics; conducts research. **Founded:** 1985.

14814 ■ **Reflexology Association of America (RAA)**
PO Box 714
Chepachet, RI 02814
Ph: (980)234-0159
Fax: (401)568-6449
Co. E-mail: inforaa@reflexology-usa.org
URL: http://www.reflexology-usa.org
Contact: Ms. Alison Gingras, President
Description: Promotes and supports reflexology ("the systematic, manual stimulation of the reflex maps located on the feet, hands and outer ears that resemble the shape of the human body"). **Founded:** 1995. **Publications:** *Reflexology Across America* (Quarterly); *State Leadership Training Manual; Guidelines to Setting up a Reflexology Association; How do Reflexologists Earn a Living; State Organizational Development Guidelines.*

REFERENCE WORKS

14815 ■ *The Secrets of Spiritual Marketing: A Complete Guide for Natural Therapists*
Pub: O Books
Ed: Lawrence Ellyard. **Released:** November 1, 2009. **Price:** $24.95. **Description:** Strategies for marketing and advertising a natural therapy business are examined.

STATISTICAL SOURCES

14816 ■ *The U.S. Market for Vitamin, Minerals, and Herbal Supplements*
Pub: Business Trend Analysts, Inc.
Released: 2002. **Price:** $2495.00. **Description:** Tracks historical, current, and projected sales trends (to 2006) for all types of nutritional supplements, on a product-by-product basis.

TRADE PERIODICALS

14817 ■ *Aquarian Alternatives*
Pub: Aquarian Research Foundation
Ed: Art Rosenblum, Editor, artr@juno.com. **Released:** Varies. **Description:** Concerned with alternative lifestyles, new-age and positive future information, and related subjects arising from 'a concern for peace and love in the world.' Recurring features include book reviews, a calendar of events, and news of research.

14818 ■ *Body Soul Magazine: The Journal for Holistic Living*
Pub: Martha Stewart Living Omnimedia Inc.
Contact: Wenda Harris Millard, President
URL(s): www.marthastewart.com/. **Released:** 8/yr. **Price:** $20, Individuals.

14819 ■ *Geocosmic Magazine*
Pub: National Council for GeoCosmic Research
Contact: Liane Thomas Wade, Executive Secretary
URL(s): www.geocosmic.org. **Ed:** Leigh Westin. **Released:** Semiannual **Price:** $10, Individuals depending on size.

14820 ■ *Journal of Spiritual Bodywork*
Pub: Spiritual Massage Healing Ministry
URL(s): www.healingandlaw.com/. **Released:** Quarterly

14821 ■ *Light Lines*
Pub: L/L Research
Ed: Jim McCarty, Editor, jim@llresearch.org. **Released:** Quarterly, 4/year (spring, summer, winter, and fall). **Price:** Free. **Description:** Provides news of interest regarding metaphysical evolution.

14822 ■ *Revelations of Awareness*
Pub: Cosmic Awareness Communications
Ed: Avaton, Editor, avaton@aol.com. **Released:** Monthly. **Price:** Included in membership. **Description:** Consists of a series of questions submitted by readers which are answered through channelings from a force describing itself as Cosmic Awareness or 'Universal Mind'. Offers deeply spiritual, yet practical and current information that can be applied to the daily life of the reader on such topics as holistic health, philosophy, and unsolved mysteries. Recurring features include letters to the editor, news of research, book reviews, notices of publications available, reports of meetings, and a calendar of events. Exposes UFO and New World Order conspiracies.

14823 ■ *SCP Journal*
Pub: SCP Journal
URL(s): www.scp-inc.org/. **Ed:** Tal Brooke. **Released:** Quarterly **Price:** $25, Individuals; $35, Out of country.

14824 ■ *Soaring Spirit: Tools & Teachings to Create Your Own Reality*
Pub: Office for History of Science and Technology
Contact: Richard Sutphen, President
URL(s): www.dicksutphen.com/html/soaring_spirit_online.html. **Ed:** Dick Sutphen. **Released:** Biennial

14825 ■ *Triangles*
Pub: Lucis Trust
Released: Quarterly. **Price:** Free. **Description:** Contains articles regarding the Triangles Network of Light, a service activity for men and women of goodwill who believe in the power of thought. Concerned with the principles of brotherhood, the one humanity, and with the global community preparing for the New Age and the Reappearance of the Christ. Reports on organizations and movements of interest to Network members. Recurring features include editorials and news from Network units.

VIDEOCASSETTES/ AUDIOCASSETTES

14826 ■ *Caroline Myss' The Energetics of Healing*
PBS Home Video
Catalog Fulfillment Center
Charlotte, NC 28275-1089
Ph: (800)531-4727
Free: 800-645-4PBS
Co. E-mail: info@pbs.org
URL: http://www.pbs.org
Released: 1998. **Price:** $49.95. **Description:** Dr. Caroline Myss takes you on a guided tour of your energy anatomy, a vast network that determines how your body functions and heals. Three hours on two videocassettes. **Availability:** VHS.

TRADE SHOWS AND CONVENTIONS

14827 ■ Great San Francisco Crystal Fair
Pacific Crystal Guild
PO Box 1371
Sausalito, CA 94966

Ph: (415)383-7837
Co. E-mail: jerry@crystalfair.com
URL: http://www.crystalfair.com
URL(s): www.crystalfair.com. **Frequency:** 3/year. **Audience:** Mineralologists, geologists, collectors, new agers, and general public. **Principal Exhibits:** Gems, minerals, jewelry, and metaphysical healing tools. **Dates and Locations:** Ft. Mason Conference Center. **Telecommunication Services:** sfxtl@earthlink.net.

14828 ■ Toronto Psychic Expo
Impact Event Management
Newcastle upon Tyne
Box 65060
Toronto, ON, Canada M4K 3Z2
Ph: (416)461-5306
Fax: (416)461-8460
URL: http://www.impact-events.co.uk
URL(s): www.esp888.com. **Price:** $10, Onsite. **Frequency:** and mid-October. **Audience:** General public. **Principal Exhibits:** Psych, tarot astrology readings and information, including occult books, computerized fortune telling, holistic health information and supplies, and mind awareness information. **Telecommunication Services:** impactevent@sympatico.ca.

LIBRARIES

14829 ■ As-You-Like-It Library—Seattle Metaphysical Library.
2200 NW Market St., L-05
Seattle, WA 98107
Ph: (206)329-1794
Co. E-mail: contact@seattlemetaphysicallibrary.org
URL: http://www.seattlemetaphysicallibrary.org
Contact: Margaret Bartley, Executive Director
Scope: Alternative and complementary health, spirituality, metaphysics, astrology, psychology, alchemy, occult and secret societies, unidentified flying objects, consciousness expansion, world religions and lineage teachings, future science, ancient civilizations, parapsychology, unexplained phenomena, self-help, feminist, Goddess and gender studies, conspiratorial political history, cryptozoology, meditation, yoga, Hindu studies, Chinese philosophy, Ancient Near East, alternative science, magic, Manly P. Hall, spiritual communities (EST, Course in Miracles, Scientology, Divine Life, Rajneesh). **Services:** Copying;

Library open to the public. **Founded:** 1961. **Holdings:** 13,000 books; 200 cassette tapes; 400 video tapes; DVDs; Newspaper reference topics; magazines.

14830 ■ Astrological Research Library of Canada
240 Crestwood Rd.
Thurnhill, ON, Canada L4J 1A9
Ph: (905)889-0793
Scope: Astrology, astronomy, metaphysical systems, divinatory sciences, myth and magic, healing, parapsychology. **Services:** Library open to the public by appointment. **Founded:** 1973. **Holdings:** 12,000 books; 5000 bound periodical volumes; 2000 slides and charts. **Subscriptions:** 12 journals and other serials.

14831 ■ Bastyr University Library
14500 Juanita Dr., NE
Kenmore, WA 98028
Ph: (425)602-3020
Fax: (425)602-3188
Co. E-mail: library@bastyr.edu
URL: http://www.bastyr.edu/student-life/library
Contact: Jane D. Saxton, Director, Library Services
Scope: Complementary and alternative medicine, acupuncture and traditional Chinese medicine, naturopathic medicine, nutrition, health psychology, exercise science, primary care medicine, homeopathy, midwifery, herbal science, botanical medicine. **Services:** Interlibrary loan; copying; Library open to the public for reference use only. **Founded:** 1980. **Holdings:** 19,000 books; 4000 CD/audiocassettes; 800 DVD/videocassettes; online databases. **Subscriptions:** 250 journals and other serials.

14832 ■ Geisinger Medical Center - Community Health Library
100 N. Academy Ave.
Danville, PA 17822-4401
Ph: (570)271-5638
Fax: (570)271-5635
Co. E-mail: chrl@geisinger.edu
URL: http://www.geisinger.edu
Contact: Patricia A Ulmer, Librarian
Scope: General medicine, nutrition, alternative and complementary medicine, pediatrics, cancer, AIDS. **Services:** Interlibrary loan. **Founded:** 1996. **Holdings:** 860 books; 200 audio/visual materials. **Subscriptions:** 14 journals and other serials.

START-UP INFORMATION

14833 ■ *"David Maus Debuting New Dealership"* in *Orlando Business Journal (Vol. 26, February 5, 2010, No. 36, pp. 1)*
Pub: American City Business Journals
Ed: Anjali Fluker. **Description:** Automotive dealers David Maus Automotive Group and Van Tuyl Automotive Investment Group will launch David Maus Chevrolet in Sanford, Florida in fall 2010. The 12-acre site of the Chevy dealership will be located adjacent to the David Maus Toyota dealership. The new store is expected to generate nearly 125 new jobs.

ASSOCIATIONS AND OTHER ORGANIZATIONS

14834 ■ **1953-54 Buick Skylark Club**
51 Statesville Quarry Rd.
Lafayette, NJ 07848
Ph: (973)383-6035
Fax: (973)383-6035
Co. E-mail: buick5354@aol.com
URL: http://www.skylarkclub.org
Contact: JoAnne DePeppo, Corresponding Secretary
Description: Owners and admirers of Buick Skylark automobiles built in 1953 and 1954. Promotes preservation and maintenance of classic Buicks. Serves as a clearinghouse on 1953 and 1954 Buick Skylarks; facilitates communication and good fellowship among members. **Founded:** 1978.

14835 ■ **American Automotive Leasing Association (AALA)**
675 N Washington St., Ste. 410
Alexandria, VA 22314-1939
Ph: (703)548-0777
Fax: (703)548-1925
Co. E-mail: sederholm@aalafleet.com
URL: http://www.aalafleet.com
Contact: Mike Pitcher, President
Description: Represents the commercial automotive fleet leasing and management industry. **Founded:** 1955.

14836 ■ **American International Automobile Dealers Association (AIADA)**
211 N Union St., Ste. 300
Alexandria, VA 22314
Ph: (703)519-7800
Free: 800-462-4232
Fax: (703)519-7810
Co. E-mail: membership@aiada.org
URL: http://www.aiada.org
Contact: Ray Mungenast, Chairman
Description: Trade association for America's international nameplate automobile dealerships and their employees who sell and service automobiles manufactured in the U.S. and abroad. Works to preserve a free market for international automobiles in the U.S. and is dedicated to increasing public awareness of the benefits the industry provides. **Founded:** 1970. **Publications:** *AIADA's Showroom* (9/year); *AIADA News / Auto Dealer*. **Educational Activities:**

American-International Automotive Congress (Annual). **Awards:** David H. Gezon Lifetime Achievement Award (Annual). **Telecommunication Services:** goaiada@aiada.org.

14837 ■ **Canadian Automobile Dealers Association (CADA)—Corporation des associations de detaillants d'automobiles**
85 Renfrew Dr.
Markham, ON, Canada L3R 0N9
Ph: (905)940-4959
Free: 800-463-5289
Fax: (905)940-6870
Co. E-mail: mail@cada.ca
URL: http://www.cada.ca
Contact: Alex Baum, Chairman
Description: Automobile dealers. Seeks to advance the automotive and automotive services industries. Facilitates communication and cooperation among members; represents members' interests before industrial organizations and government agencies. **Founded:** 1941. **Publications:** *Newsline* (Monthly). **Awards:** Business in Automotive Management Scholarship (Annual).

14838 ■ **Ford Motor Minority Dealers Association (FMMDA)**
16000 W 9 Mile Rd., Ste. 603
Southfield, MI 48075
Ph: (248)557-2500
Free: 800-247-0293
Fax: (248)557-2882
Co. E-mail: fmmdafacts@aol.com
URL: http://www.fmmda.org
Contact: Dr. A.V. Fleming, Chief Executive Officer
Description: Minority-owned car dealerships. Promotes professional standards of minority dealerships. Strives to increase the number of minority dealerships. **Founded:** 1980. **Educational Activities:** Ford Motor Minority Dealers Association Competition (Annual).

14839 ■ **National Association of Fleet Resale Dealers (NAFRD)**
2521 Brown Blvd.
Arlington, TX 76006
Ph: (817)649-5858
Fax: (817)649-5866
Co. E-mail: jd@niada.com
URL: http://www.nafrd.com
Contact: Mitch Pomerantz, President
Description: Used car wholesalers dealing exclusively with large fleets. Encourages members to employ effective marketing methods and to conduct businesses soundly and ethically. Seeks a favorable public image of wholesale used cars and the used car industry. Serves as a forum for exchange of ideas and information; monitors legislation. **Founded:** 1984. **Publications:** *Inside Tracks* (Quarterly); *NAFRD Resource Guide* (Annual).

14840 ■ **National Association of Minority Automobile Dealers (NAMAD)**
9475 Lottsford Rd., Ste. 150
Largo, MD 20774
Ph: (301)306-1614

Fax: (301)306-1493
Co. E-mail: damon.lester@namad.org
URL: http://www.namad.org
Contact: Damon Lester, President
Description: Automobile dealers. Acts as liaison between membership, the federal government, the community, and industry representatives; seeks to better the business conditions of its members on an ongoing basis. Serves as a confidential spokesperson for dealers. Offers business analysis, financial counseling, and short- and long-term management planning. Conducts research programs; compiles statistics. **Founded:** 1980. **Publications:** *NAMAD Newsletter*.

14841 ■ **National Auto Auction Association (NAAA)**
5320 Spectrum Dr., Ste. D
Frederick, MD 21703
Ph: (301)696-0400
Fax: (301)631-1359
Co. E-mail: naaa@naaa.com
URL: http://www.naaa.com
Contact: Charlotte Pyle, President
Description: Owners/operators of wholesale automobile and truck auctions; associate members are car and truck manufacturers, insurers of checks and titles, car and truck rental companies, publishers of auto price guide books, and others connected with the industry. Maintains hall of fame. **Founded:** 1948. **Publications:** *National Auto Auction Association--Membership Directory* (Annual); *On the Block* (Quarterly). **Educational Activities:** Convention and Equipment and Services Exposition (Annual); National Auto Auction Association Annual Convention and Equipments and Services Exposition (Annual). **Awards:** Hall of Fame (Annual).

14842 ■ **National Automobile Dealers Association (NADA)**
8400 Westpark Dr.
McLean, VA 22102
Ph: (703)821-7000
Free: 800-252-6232
Fax: (703)821-7234
Co. E-mail: nadainfo@nada.org
URL: http://www.nada.org
Contact: Peter K. Welch, President
Description: Franchised new car and truck dealers. Provides representation for franchised new car and truck dealers in the areas of government, industry, and public affairs. Offers management services and retirement and insurance programs to member dealers. Maintains National Automobile Dealers Charitable Foundation. **Founded:** 1917. **Publications:** *AutoExec* (Monthly); *DEAC Report* (Quarterly); *NADA Headlines* (Daily); *NADA Appraisal Guides*; *NADA's AutoExec Magazine: Official Publication of the National Automobile Dealers Association* (Monthly); *Automotive Executive--Dealer Business Guide Issue*. **Educational Activities:** National Automobile Dealers Association Convention (Annual); American Truck Dealers Convention & Exposition (Annual); NADA Convention and Exposition (Annual).

14843 ■ National Independent Automobile Dealers Association (NIADA)
2521 Brown Blvd.
Arlington, TX 76006
Ph: (817)640-3838
Free: 800-682-3837
Fax: (817)649-5866
Co. E-mail: mike@niada.com
URL: http://www.niada.com
Contact: Don Fincher, President
Description: Individuals, companies, or corporations licensed by their states as dealers to buy and sell used motor vehicles; associate members are businesses related to or associated with the buying or selling of motor vehicles. Gathers and disseminates information relative to the used car industry; represents used car dealers before regulatory and legislative bodies; provides educational and other programs to help used car dealers understand their responsibilities; works for the betterment of the automobile industry. Works closely with local and state independent automobile dealers' associations and others concerning dealers and the public. Maintains code of fair dealing for members. Conducts seminars, meetings, and professional training programs. Maintains speakers' bureau, services for children, and charitable programs. Sponsors competitions; compiles statistics. **Founded:** 1946. **Publications:** *Dealer Connection* (Quarterly); *Used Car Dealer* (Monthly); *Used Car Dealer* (Monthly); *Used Car Dealer, Used Car Industry Report* (Annual); *Used Car Dealer Magazine* (Monthly). **Educational Activities:** National Independent Automobile Dealers Association Convention (Annual); National Independent Automobile Dealers Association Convention (Annual); National Independent Automobile Dealers Association Convention & Expo (Annual). **Awards:** National Quality Dealer Award; Ring of Honor; Eagle Award; Crystal Eagle Award; Crystal Eagle Award (Biennial); Eagle Award (Annual); National Quality Dealer Award (Annual); Ring of Honor (Annual); Scholarship Award (Annual); State Executive of the Year (Annual); Eagle Award (Annual); National Quality Dealer Award (Annual); Ring of Honor (Annual).

14844 ■ Newsline
85 Renfrew Dr.
Markham, ON, Canada L3R 0N9
Ph: (905)940-4959
Free: 800-463-5289
Fax: (905)940-6870
Co. E-mail: mail@cada.ca
URL: http://www.cada.ca
Contact: Alex Baum, Chairman
Released: Monthly **Price:** free for members.

14845 ■ Used Truck Association (UTA)
325 Country Club Dr., Ste. A
Stockbridge, GA 30281
Free: 877-438-7882
Co. E-mail: contact@uta.org
URL: http://www.uta.org
Contact: Rick Clark, President
Description: Truck dealerships with substantial used truck sales; truck manufacturers. Promotes professionalism among members; works to elevate the image of the used truck sales business. Monitors federal regulatory developments affecting used truck sales; conducts lobbying activities. **Founded:** 1988. **Educational Activities:** Sales and Employee Training Seminar (Semiannual). **Awards:** Marvin F. Gordon Lifetime Achievement Award (Annual).

REFERENCE WORKS

14846 ■ *"$3 Million in Repairs Prep Cobo for Auto Show"* **in Crain's Detroit Business (Vol. 26, January 4, 2010, No. 1, pp. 1)**
Pub: Crain Communications Inc.

Ed: Nancy Kaffer. **Description:** Overview of the six projects priced roughly at $3 million which were needed in order to host the North American International Auto Show; show organizers stated that the work was absolutely necessary to keep the show in the city of Detroit.

14847 ■ *"The 490 Made Chevy a Bargain Player"* **in Automotive News (Vol. 86, October 31, 2011, No. 6488, pp. S22)**
Pub: Crain Communications Inc.

Ed: David Phillips. **Description:** The first Chevrolet with the 490 engine was sold in 1913, but it was too expensive for masses. In 1914 the carmaker launched a lower-priced H-series of cars competitively priced. Nameplates such as Corvette, Bel Air, Camaro and Silverado have defined Chevrolet through the years.

14848 ■ *"1914 Proved to Be Key Year for Chevy"* **in Automotive News (Vol. 86, October 31, 2011, No. 6488, pp. S18)**
Pub: Crain Communications Inc.

Ed: Jamie Lareau. **Description:** Chevy Bow Tie emblem was born in 1914, creating the brand's image that has carried through to current days.

14849 ■ *"2011 FinOvation Awards"* **in Farm Industry News (January 19, 2011)**
Pub: Penton Business Media Inc.

Ed: Jodie Wehrspann. **Description:** The 2011 FinOvation Award winners are announced, covering new products that growers need for corn and soybean crops. Winners range from small turbines and a fuel-efficient pickup to a Class 10 combine and drought-tolerant hybrids.

14850 ■ *"A123-Fisker Deal May Mean 540 Jobs"* **in Crain's Detroit Business (Vol. 26, January 18, 2010, No. 3, pp. 4)**
Pub: Crain Communications Inc.

Ed: Dustin Walsh. **Description:** Manufacturing plants in Livonia and Romulus may be hiring up to 540 skilled workers due to a contract that was won by A123 Systems Inc. that will result in the company supplying lithium-ion batteries to Fisker Automotive Inc. to be used in their Karma plug-in hybrid electric vehicle.

14851 ■ *"Ad Firms Stew Over Lost Car Biz; Diversifying Business Is Uphill Battle"* **in Crain's Detroit Business (Vol. 23, July 30, 2007, No. 31)**
Pub: Crain Communications, Inc.

Ed: Jean Halliday. **Description:** Struggling Detroit automakers are breaking their tradition of loyalty and moving their advertising accounts to agencies in Los Angeles, San Francisco, and Boston; This has Detroit's advertising community very worried.

14852 ■ *"Antwerpen Takes on Chrysler Financial Over Foreclosure Sales"* **in Baltimore Business Journal (Vol. 28, July 30, 2010, No. 12, pp. 1)**
Pub: Baltimore Business Journal

Ed: Gary Haber. **Description:** Antwerpen Motorcars Ltd. aims to fight the scheduled foreclosure sale of real estate it leases in Baltimore County, including the showroom for its Hyundai dealership on Baltimore National Pike in Catonsville, Maryland. The company is planning to file papers in court to stop the scheduled August 11, 2010 auction sought by Chrysler Financial Services Americas LLC.

14853 ■ *"Auction Company Grows with Much Smaller Sites"* **in Automotive News (Vol. 86, October 31, 2011, No. 6488, pp. 23)**
Pub: Crain Communications Inc.

Ed: Arlena Sawyers. **Description:** Auction Broadcasting Company has launched auction sites and is expanding into new areas. The family-owned business will provide auctions half the size traditionally used. The firm reports that 40 percent of the General Motors factory-owned vehicles sold on consignment were purchased by online buyers, up 30 percent over 2010.

14854 ■ *"Auto Bankruptcies Could Weaken Defense"* **in Crain's Detroit Business (Vol. 25, June 8, 2009, No. 23, pp. 1)**
Pub: Crain Communications Inc. - Detroit

Ed: Chad Halcom. **Description:** Bankruptcy and supplier consolidation of General Motors Corporation and Chrysler LLC could interfere with the supply chains of some defense contractors, particularly makers of trucks and smaller vehicles.

14855 ■ *"Auto Show Aims to Electrify"* **in Crain's Detroit Business (Vol. 26, January 11, 2010, No. 2, pp. 1)**
Pub: Crain Communications, Inc.

Ed: Ryan Beene. **Description:** Overview of the North American International Auto show include sixteen production and concept vehicles including eight from the Detroit 3. High-tech battery suppliers as well as hybrid and electric vehicles will highlight the show.

14856 ■ *"Auto Show Taps Moms"* **in Marketing to Women (Vol. 21, April 2008, No. 4, pp. 3)**
Pub: EPM Communications Inc.
Contact: Ira Mayer, President
E-mail: imayer@epmcom.com

Description: Teamed with Mother Proof, an online site which features automotive content aimed at moms, the Chicago Auto Show will present a full day of programming with the emphasis on mom.

14857 ■ *"Autoline Goes West"* **in Michigan Vue (Vol. 13, July-August 2008, No. 4, pp. 6)**
Pub: Entrepreneur Media Inc.

Ed: Dave Gibbons. **Description:** Profile of Blue Sky Productions, a Detroit-based production company that produces the nationally syndicated television series 'Autoline', which traditionally probes inside the Detroit auto industry; the company recently decided to shoot in Southern California, an area that now has an immense auto industry but has been virtually ignored by the media. Blue Sky originally slated four shows but ended up producing eleven due to the immense amount of material they discovered concerning the state of California's auto market.

14858 ■ *"Automotive Trouble"* **in Canadian Business (Vol. 82, April 27, 2009, No. 7, pp. 11)**
Pub: Rogers Media

Ed: Thomas Watson. **Description:** The likely effects of a possible bailout of the U.S. automotive industry are examined. Some experts believe that a bailout will be good for the automotive industry and on the U.S. economy. Others argue however, that the nationalization may have a negative impact on the industry and on the economy.

14859 ■ *"Bankruptcies"* **in Crain's Detroit Business (Vol. 24, October 6, 2008, No. 40, pp. 26)**
Pub: Crain Communications, Inc.

Description: Current businesses that have filed for Chapter 7 or 11 protection in U.S. Bankruptcy Court include an auto dealership, a gun range and a grocery service.

14860 ■ *"Battered U.S. Auto Makers in Grip of Deeper Sales Slump"* **in Globe & Mail (April 4, 2007, pp. B1)**
Pub: CTVglobemedia Publishing Inc.

Ed: Greg Keenan. **Description:** The fall in Canadian sales and market share of Ford Motor Co., General Motors Corp. and Chrysler Group is discussed.

14861 ■ *"Because He Is Always On the Accelerator: Jay Rogers: Local Motors, Chandler, Arizona"* **in Inc. (Volume 32, December 2010, No. 10)**
Pub: Inc. Magazine

Description: Profile of Jay Rogers, founder of Local Motors, who manufactures cars, including the Phoenix Rally Fighter made from lightweight composites rather than steel.

14862 ■ *"Black On Black Business: Moorehead Buys Hank Aaron's Toyota Dealership"* **in Black Enterprise (Vol. 38, February 2008, No. 7, pp. 28)**
Pub: Earl G. Graves Publishing Co. Inc.

Ed: Brenda Porter. **Description:** In a move to expand his automotive business, Thomas A. Moorehead, CEO of BMW/MINI of Sterling, Georgia bought Hank Aaron's Toyota automobile dealership in McDonough, Georgia. Moorehead stated that he will call the new store Toyota of McDonough.

14863 ■ *"BMW Makes Bet on Carbon Maker"* in Wall Street Journal Eastern Edition (November 19 , 2011, pp. B3)

Pub: Dow Jones & Company Inc.

Ed: Christoph Rauwald. **Description:** Eight months ago, Volkswagen AG acquired a 10 percent holding in carbon-fiber maker SGL Carbon SE. Its rival BMW AG is catching up by acquiring 15.2 percent stake in SGL as it seeks alliances like the rest of the industry in order to share industrial costs of new product development.

14864 ■ *"BMW Revs Up for a Rebound"* in Barron's (Vol. 89, July 13, 2009, No. 28, pp. M7)

Pub: Dow Jones & Co., Inc.

Ed: Jonathan Buck. **Description:** Investors may like BMW's stocks because the company has maintained its balance sheet strength and has an impressive production line of new models that should boost sales in the next few years. The company's sales are also gaining traction, although their vehicle delivery was down 1.7 percent year on year on June 2009, this was still the best monthly sales figure for 2009.

14865 ■ *"Bob Johnson Opens Car Dealership: Plans To Provide a Bridge To Create More Minority Owners"* in Black Enterprise (December 2007)

Pub: Earl G. Graves Publishing Co. Inc.

Ed: Wendy Isom, Jeff Fortson. **Description:** Robert L. Johnson, founder of RLJ Companies and majority owner of RLJ-McLarty Automotive Landers Automotive Partnership which carries Chrysler, Dodge, Ford, Jeep, Scion, and Toyota vehicles has a plan to create opportunity for minority car dealers.

14866 ■ *"Brand Police Keep the Lines Distinct at GM"* in Automotive News (Vol. 86, October 31, 2011, No. 6488, pp. 3)

Pub: Crain Communications Inc.

Ed: Mike Colias. **Description:** Joel Ewanick, marketing chief at General Motors, is working to keep General Motor's four brands distinct within their brands.

14867 ■ *"Buick Prices Verano Below Rival Luxury Compacts"* in Automotive News (Vol. 86, October 31, 2011, No. 6488, pp. 10)

Pub: Crain Communications Inc.

Ed: Mike Colias. **Description:** General Motors's Verano will compete with other luxury compacts such as the Lexus IS 250 and the Acura TSX, but will be prices significantly lower coming in with a starting price of $23,470, about $6,000 to $10,000 less than those competitors.

14868 ■ *"Burning Issues: Four of Today's Hottest Energy Topics"* in Canadian Business (Vol. 83, August 17, 2010, No. 13-14, pp. 45)

Pub: Rogers Media Ltd.

Description: A look at four issues dominating Canada's energy industry is presented. These issues are lack of transmission capacity and difficulty in transferring power across provincial boundaries, the management of intermittency of renewable generation, techniques that would clean up the Alberta's oil sands, and the impending massive use of electric cars in North America.

14869 ■ *Buyology: Truth and Lies About Why We Buy*

Pub: Doubleday, a Division of Random House

Ed: Martin Lindstrom. **Released:** 2009. **Price:** $24.95. **Description:** Marketers study brain scans to determine how consumers rate Nokia, Coke, and Ford products.

14870 ■ *"Can a Brazilian SUV Take On the Jeep Wrangler?"* in Business Week (September 22, 2008, No. 4100, pp. 50)

Pub: McGraw-Hill Companies, Inc.

Ed: Helen Walters. **Description:** Profile of the Brazilian company TAC as well as the flourishing Brazilian car market; TAC has launched a new urban vehicle, the Stark, which has won prizes for innovation; the company uses local technology and manufacturing expertise.

14871 ■ *"Canadian Vehicle Sales Accelerate in April, but U.S. Goes on Bumpy Ride"* in Globe & Mail (May 2, 2007, pp. B7)

Pub: CTVglobemedia Publishing Inc.

Ed: Greg Keenan. **Description:** The increase in Canadian vehicle sales to 169,280 in April 2007, but decline in their sales in the United States due to slump in housing sector are discussed.

14872 ■ *"Car Dealer Closings: Immoral, Slow-Death"* in Crain's Detroit Business (Vol. 25, June 8, 2009, No. 23)

Pub: Crain Communications Inc. - Detroit

Ed: Daniel Duggan. **Description:** Colleen McDonald discusses the closing of her two Chrysler dealerships located in Taylor and Livonia, Michigan, along with her Farmington Hills store, Holiday Chevrolet.

14873 ■ *"Car Dealers Shift Gears to Survive"* in Puget Sound Business Journal (Vol. 29, November 14, 2008, No. 30, pp. 1)

Pub: American City Business Journals

Ed: Gregg Lamm. **Description:** Washington-based automobile dealers are offering incentives such as repairs, parts and used cars in order to supplement the decline in new car sales.

14874 ■ *"Car Trouble"* in Canadian Business (Vol. 80, October 22, 2007, No. 21, pp. 27)

Pub: Rogers Media

Ed: Thomas Watson. **Description:** Contract between General Motors Corporation and the United Auto Workers Union has created a competitive arm for the U.S. Big Three automakers. Data on the market and production data of car companies are presented.

14875 ■ *"CarBiz Inc. Speaking At NABD"* in Canadian Corporate News (May 14, 2007)

Pub: Comtex News Network Inc.

Description: CarBiz Inc., a leading provider of software, consulting, and training solutions to the United States' automotive industry, had two of its executive officers speak at the National Alliance of Buy Here - Pay Here Dealers (NABD), a conference that draws over 2,000 dealers, service providers, and experts from across the United States.

14876 ■ *"CarTango Lauches Site for Women"* in Marketing to Women (Vol. 21, April 2008, No. 4, pp. 5)

Pub: EPM Communications Inc.

Contact: Ira Mayer, President

E-mail: imayer@epmcom.com

Description: CarTango.com is an Internet site that seeks to overcome what women say are dismissive or pushy salespeople by allowing the shoppers the chance to decide what they want before inviting dealers to compete for their business.

14877 ■ *"CAW Hopes to Beat Xstrata Deadline"* in Globe & Mail (January 30, 2007, pp. B3)

Pub: CTVglobemedia Publishing Inc.

Ed: Andy Hoffman. **Description:** The decision of Canadian Auto Workers to strike work at Xstrata PLC over wage increase is discussed.

14878 ■ *"Charged Up for Sales"* in Charlotte Business Journal (Vol. 25, October 15, 2010, No. 30, pp. 1)

Pub: Charlotte Business Journal

Ed: Susan Stabley. **Description:** Li-Ion Motors Corporation is set to expand its production lines of electric cars in Sacramento, California. The plan is seen to create up to 600 jobs. The company's total investment is seen to reach $500 million.

14879 ■ *"Chinese Fund Loans $33.5 Million to Prestolite"* in Crain's Detroit Business (Vol. 26, January 18, 2010, No. 3, pp. 1)

Pub: Crain Communications Inc.

Ed: Ryan Beene. **Description:** Prestolite Electric Inc., a distributor of alternators and starter motors for commercial and heavy-duty vehicles, looked to China for fresh capital in order to fund new product launches.

14880 ■ *"Combat Mission: Rebuffed, BAE Systems Fights Army Contract Decision"* in Business Courier (Vol. 26, September 25, 2009)

Pub: American City Business Journals, Inc.

Ed: Jon Newberry. **Description:** BAE Systems filed a complaint with the US Government Accountability Office after the US Army issued an order to BAE's competitor for armoured trucks which is potentially worth over $3 billion. Hundreds of jobs in Butler County, Ohio hinge on the success of the contract protest.

14881 ■ *"Consumers Like Green, But Not Mandates"* in Business Journal-Milwaukee (Vol. 28, December 10, 2010, No. 10, pp. A1)

Pub: Milwaukee Business Journal

Ed: Sean Ryan. **Description:** Milwaukee, Wisconsin consumers are willing to spend more on green energy, a survey has revealed. Respondents also said they will pay more for efficient cars and appliances. Support for public incentives for homeowners and businesses that reduce energy use has also increased.

14882 ■ *"Courting Canadian Customers Confounds Car Dealers"* in Business First Buffalo (November 9, 2007, pp. 1)

Pub: American City Business Journals, Inc.

Ed: James Fink. **Description:** Strength of the Canadian dollar has led to an influx of potential customers for the Western New York automobile industry, but franchising restrictions and licensing as well as insurance issues have limited the potential of having larger sales figures. Border and trade issues that affect the car industry in WNY are also discussed.

14883 ■ *"Dealer Gets a Lift with Acquisitions at Year's End"* in Crain's Detroit Business (Vol. 26, January 11, 2010, No. 2, pp. 3)

Pub: Crain Communications, Inc.

Ed: Ryan Beene. **Description:** Alta Equipment Co., a forklift dealer, closed 2009 with a string of acquisitions expecting to double the firm's employee headcount and triple its annual revenue. Alta Lift Truck Services, Inc., as the company was known before the acquisitions, was founded in 1984 as Michigan's dealer for forklift manufacturer Yale Materials Handling Corp.

14884 ■ *"Dealers Fight To Steer Course"* in The Business Journal-Serving Metropolitan Kansas City (Vol. 27, November 7, 2008, No. 9, pp. 1)

Pub: American City Business Journals, Inc.

Ed: Steve Vockrodt. **Description:** One local automobile dealer says that their sales are down by 30 to 40 percent and that car financing is now in the low 60 percentile from 85 to 88 percent. The National Automobile Dealers Association says that 700 dealerships are likely to be lost for 2008.

14885 ■ *"Dealers Trying Not to Fold"* in Business First Columbus (Vol. 25, December 5, 2008, No. 15, pp. A1)

Pub: American City Business Journals

Ed: Dan Eaton. **Description:** Increase in the number of automobile dealer closures in Ohio is seen to impact the state's economy. The trend of consolidation is forecasted to adversely affect employment and sales. Statistical data included.

14886 ■ *"Despite Gloom, Auto Sales Saw Gains in 2005"* in Globe & Mail (January 5, 2006, pp. B1)

Pub: CTVglobemedia Publishing Inc.

Ed: Greg Keenan. **Description:** An overview of positve automotive sales in Canada, for 2005, is presented.

14887 ■ *"Detroit 3's Fall Would Be a Big One in Ohio"* in Business First Columbus (Vol. 25, November 28, 2008, No. 14, pp. A1)

Pub: American City Business Journals

Ed: Dan Eaton. **Description:** Ohio's economy will suffer huge negative effects in the event of a failure of one or more of the automotive companies, General

Motors Corporation, Ford Motor Company, or Chrysler LLC. The state is home to 97,900 jobs in the automotive industry and is a vital link to the industry's supply network.

14888 ■ *"The Doomsday Scenario" in Conde Nast Portfolio (Vol. 2, June 2008, No. 6, pp. 91)*
Pub: Conde Nast Publications
Contact: David Carey, President

Ed: Jeffrey Rothfeder. **Description:** Detroit and the U.S. auto industry are discussed as well as the ramifications of the demise of this manufacturing base. Similarities and differences between the downfall of the U.S. steel business and the impact it had on Pittsburg, Pennsylvania is also discussed.

14889 ■ *"Everyone Has a Story Inspired by Chevrolet" in Automotive News (Vol. 86, October 31, 2011, No. 6488, pp. S003)*
Pub: Crain Communications Inc.

Ed: Keith E. Crain. **Description:** Besides being a great ad slogan, 'Baseball, Hot Dogs, Apple Pie and Chevrolet', the brand conjures up memories for most everyone in our society. Louis Chevrolet had a reputation as a race car driver and lent his name to the car that has endured for 100 years.

14890 ■ *"Extra Rehab Time Boosts M-B's Off-Lease Profits" in Automotive News (Vol. 86, October 31, 2011, No. 6488, pp. 22)*
Pub: Crain Communications Inc.

Ed: Arlena Sawyers. **Description:** Mercedes-Benz Financial Services USA is holding on to off-lease vehicles in order to recondition them and the move is boosting profits for the company.

14891 ■ *"Fair Play? China Cheats, Carney Talks and Rankin Walks; Here's the Latest" in Canadian Business (Vol. 81, March 17, 2008, No. 4)*
Pub: Rogers Media

Description: Discusses the World Trade Organization which says that China is breaking trade rules by taxing imports of auto parts at the same rate as foreign-made finished cars. Mark Carney first speech as the governor of the Bank of Canada made economists suspect a rate cut on overnight loans. Andre Rankin was ordered by the Ontario Securities Commission to pay $250,000 in investigation costs.

14892 ■ *"Fighting Detroit" in Baltimore Business Journal (Vol. 27, January 22, 2010, No. 38, pp. 1)*
Pub: American City Business Journals

Ed: Daniel J. Sernovitz. **Description:** Baltimore, Maryland-based car dealers could retrieve their franchises from car manufacturers, Chrysler LLC and General Motors Corporation, through a forced arbitration. A provision in a federal budget mandates the arbitration. The revoking of franchises has been attributed to the car manufacturers' filing of bankruptcy protection.

14893 ■ *"Finalist: Private Company, $100M-$1B" in Crain's Detroit Business (Vol. 25, June 22, 2009, No. 25)*
Pub: Crain Communications Inc. - Detroit

Ed: Chad Halcom. **Description:** Profile of U.S. Far-athane Corporation, the Sterling Heights, Michigan-based automotive plastic components maker. The company's CFO discusses ways they are coping with the cutbacks at major automobile factories.

14894 ■ *"Florin Car Dealers Drive Plan" in Sacramento Business Journal (Vol. 25, August 22, 2008, No. 25, pp. 1)*
Pub: American City Business Journals, Inc.

Ed: Melanie Turner. **Description:** Automobile dealers in Sacramento, California are working with the city and the business district in planning for future redevelopment in Florin Road. The move stemmed from pressure from the Elk Grove Auto Mall, high fuel prices and the credit crunch. The area has suffered business closures recently.

14895 ■ *"Former Chrysler Dealers Build New Business Model" in Crain's Detroit Business (Vol. 25, June 22, 2009, No. 25, pp. 3)*
Pub: Crain Communications Inc. - Detroit

Ed: Daniel Duggan. **Description:** Joe Ricci is one of 14 Detroit area dealerships whose franchises have been terminated. Ricci and other Chrysler dealers in the area are starting new businesses or switching to new franchises.= Ricci's All American Buyer's Service will be located in Dearborn and will sell only used cars.

14896 ■ *"Former Football Pro Closes Doors of Car Dealership" in Black Enterprise (Vol. 38, March 2008, No. 8, pp. 28)*
Pub: Earl G. Graves Publishing Co. Inc.

Ed: Brenda Porter. **Description:** Aenease Williams automobile dealerships closed their doors in Louisiana due to low sales. Williams, a former NFL safety retired in 2005. According to an expert, the image of the Lincoln as a luxury brand has been diminished.

14897 ■ *"Former Schaefer and Strohminger Dealerships to Hit Auction Block" in Baltimore Business Journal (Vol. 28, September 10, 2010)*
Pub: Baltimore Business Journal

Ed: Gary Haber. **Description:** Maryland's real estate developers have a chance to vie for almost 11 acres of prime Baltimore County real estate that are on the auction block. The five properties were once home to Schaefer and Strohminger car dealerships and were located in the county's busiest areas. Other potential uses for the properties are also discussed.

14898 ■ *"From American Icon to Global Juggernaut" in Automotive News (Vol. 86, October 31, 2011, No. 6488, pp. S003)*
Pub: Crain Communications Inc.

Ed: Peter Brown. **Description:** Chevrolet celebrates its 100th Anniversary. The brand revolutionized its market with affordable cars that bring technology to the masses. Chevys have been sold in 140 countries and the company is responding to a broader market.

14899 ■ *"Fuel for Thought" in Canadian Business (Vol. 81, April 14, 2008, No. 6, pp. 18)*
Pub: Rogers Media

Ed: John Gray. **Description:** Discusses a web poll of 133 CEOs and other business leaders that shows that they predict oil prices to increase to US $113 per barrel over the 2008 to 2010 timeframe. Most of the respondents did not favor cutting gas taxes but this group wants the government to cut taxes on fuel-efficient vehicles and increase subsidies to local transit systems.

14900 ■ *"Full Speed Ahead: How to Get the Most Out of Your Company Vehicles" in Entrepreneur (Vol. 37, October 2009, No. 10, pp. 78)*
Pub: Entrepreneur Media, Inc.

Ed: Jill Amadio. **Description:** Methods of saving costs on purchasing and maintaining vehicles are described. Tips include shopping online, choosing hybrid vehicles, and choosing cars with incentives and lower insurance costs.

14901 ■ *"Future Autoworkers will Need Broader Skills" in Crain's Detroit Business (Vol. 25, June 8, 2009, No. 23, pp. 13)*
Pub: Crain Communications Inc. - Detroit

Ed: Ryan Beene. **Description:** Auto industry observers report that new workers in the industry will need advanced skills and educational backgrounds in engineering and technical fields because jobs in the factories will become more technology-based and multidisciplinary.

14902 ■ *"General Motors Can't Kick Incentives-But They Work" in Advertising Age (Vol. 79, July 7, 2008, No. 26, pp. 3)*
Pub: Crain Communications, Inc.

Ed: Jean Halliday. **Description:** General Motors Corp. was able to maintain their market share just as Toyota Motor Corp. was beginning to pass the manufacturer; GM lured in customers with a sales incentive that they heavily advertised and subse-

quently helped build demand; investors, however, were not impressed and GM shares were hammered to their lowest point in 50 years after analysts speculated the company might go bankrupt.

14903 ■ *"GM-Chrysler Merger Could Cull Dealerships From Coast to Coast" in Globe & Mail (February 20, 2007, pp. B17)*
Pub: CTVglobemedia Publishing Inc.

Ed: Greg Keenan. **Description:** General Motors Corp. is planning to acquire Chrysler Group. The challenges before the possible merger are presented.

14904 ■ *"GM-Chrysler Merger: Just a Bigger Mess?" in Globe & Mail (February 17, 2007, pp. B3)*
Pub: CTVglobemedia Publishing Inc.

Ed: Barrie McKenna; Greg Keenan. **Description:** The General Motors Corp. is negotiating talks to acquire DaimlerChrysler AG's Chrysler Group. The five reasons for the possible merger of the companies are presented.

14905 ■ *"GM Flexes Muscles With New Camaro Concept" in Globe & Mail (January 10, 2006, pp. B15)*
Pub: CTVglobemedia Publishing Inc.

Ed: Greg Keenan. **Description:** General Motors Corp., has displayed the new concept car Chevrolet Camaro, at the North American International Auto Show in Detroit. The features of this automobile manufactured at the company's assembly plant in Quebec are discussed.

14906 ■ *"GM Is On the Road Again" in Canadian Business (Vol. 83, September 14, 2010, No. 15, pp. 14)*
Pub: Rogers Media Ltd.

Ed: Thomas Watson. **Description:** Former General Motors CEO Rick Wagoner has been credited for single-handedly putting the automaker back on track before he was forced to resign and GM was restructured by the government. GM earned $2.19 billion the first half of 2010 after losing more than $80 billion in the three years leading up to its failure. GM's comeback is discussed.

14907 ■ *"GM Releases 2010 Product Guide, Ends Production of Medium-Duty Trucks" in Contractor (Vol. 56, July 2009, No. 7, pp. 5)*
Pub: Penton Media, Inc.

Ed: Candace Roulo. **Description:** General Motors will cease production of the Chevrolet Kodiak and GMC Topkick by July 31, 2009. Their 2010 Product Guide for the U.S. still has four remaining brands including the Buick, Cadillac, Chevrolet, and GMC.

14908 ■ *"GM's Decision to Boot Dealer Prompts Sale" in Baltimore Business Journal (Vol. 27, November 6, 2009, No. 26, pp. 1)*
Pub: American City Business Journals

Ed: Daniel J. Sernovitz. **Description:** General Motors Corporation's (GM) decision to strip Baltimore's Anderson Automotive Group Inc. of its GM franchise has prompted the owner, Bruce Mortimer, to close the automotive dealership and sell the land to a developer. The new project could make way for new homes, a shopping center and supermarket.

14909 ■ *"GM's Volt Woes Cast Shadow on E-Cars" in Wall Street Journal Eastern Edition (November 28, 2011, pp. B1)*
Pub: Dow Jones & Company Inc. Enterprise Media Group
Contact: Clare Hart, President

Ed: Sharon Terlep. **Description:** The future of electric cars is darkened with the government investigation by the National Highway Traffic Safety Administration into General Motor Company's Chevy Volt after two instances of the car's battery packs catching fire during crash tests conducted by the Agency.

14910 ■ *"Greening the Auto Industry" in Business Journal-Serving Phoenix & the Valley of the Sun (Vol. 30, July 23, 2010, No. 46, pp. 1)*
Pub: Phoenix Business Journal

Ed: Patrick O'Grady. **Description:** Thermo Fluids Inc. has been recycling used oil products since 1993 and could become Arizona's first home for oil filter recycling after retrofitting its Phoenix facility to include a compaction machine. The new service could help establish Thermo Fluids as a recycling hub for nearby states.

14911 ■ *"Have I Got a Deal For You"* in *Canadian Business (Vol. 83, October 12, 2010, No. 17, pp. 65)*
Pub: Rogers Media Ltd.

Ed: Bryan Borzykowski. **Description:** U.S. automobile market currently has more than three players, providing investors with a number of investment options. The sector is still mired in uncertainty, but people believe that these companies can only grow from this point forward. However, investors should use due diligence before jumping into the market.

14912 ■ *"High-Yield Turns Into Road Kill"* in *Barron's (Vol. 88, July 7, 2008, No. 27, pp. M7)*
Pub: Dow Jones & Co., Inc.

Ed: Emily Barrett. **Description:** High-yield bonds have returned to the brink of collapse after profits have recovered from the shock brought about by the collapse of Bear Stearns. The high-yield bond market could decline again due to weakness in the automotive sector, particularly in Ford and General Motors.

14913 ■ *"Hispantelligence Report"* in *Hispanic Business (July-August 2007, pp. 18)*
Pub: Hispanic Business

Description: Presentation of the Hispanic Business Stock Index shows the current value of fifteen Hispanic companies from January 3 through July 6, 2007. Results of a survey covering Hispanic household spending on new automobiles are also included. Statistical data included.

14914 ■ *"How Much Profit is Enough?"* in *Automotive News (Vol. 86, October 31, 2011, No. 6488, pp. 12)*
Pub: Crain Communications Inc.

Ed: Keith Crain. **Description:** Workers at the big three automobile companies are unhappy about the issues of class wealth, like the high compensations offered to CEOs.

14915 ■ *"Hyannis Mercedes Franchise Sold"* in *Cape Cod Times (December 2, 2010)*
Pub: Cape Cod Times

Ed: Sarah Shemkus. **Description:** Trans-Atlantic Motors franchise has been sold to Mercedes-Benz of Westwood.

14916 ■ *"Hyundai Enters Minivan Market"* in *Globe & Mail (February 15, 2006, pp. B7)*
Pub: CTVglobemedia Publishing Inc.

Ed: Greg Keenan. **Description:** The reasons behind the launch of minivan by Hyundai Auto Canada Inc. are presented.

14917 ■ *"Hyundai's Hitting Its Stride"* in *Barron's (Vol. 89, July 20, 2009, No. 29, pp. M7)*
Pub: Dow Jones & Co., Inc.

Ed: Assif Shameen. **Description:** Hyundai Motors has kept growing by producing better products, enabling it to increase its sales and market share despite the weaker automotive market. The shares of Hyundai and Kia are poised to rise due to their improved finances.

14918 ■ *"Impressive Numbers: Companies Experience Substantial Increases in Dollars, Employment"* in *Hispanic Business (July-August 2007)*
Pub: Hispanic Business

Ed: Derek Reveron. **Description:** Profiles of five fastest growing Hispanic companies reporting increases in revenue and employment include Brightstar, distributor of wireless products; Greenway Ford Inc., a car dealership; Fred Loya Insurance, auto insurance carrier; and Group O, packaging company; and Diverse Staffing, Inc., an employment and staffing firm.

14919 ■ *"Japan-Brand Shortages Will Linger Into '12"* in *Automotive News (Vol. 86, October 31, 2011, No. 6488, pp. 1)*
Pub: Crain Communications Inc.

Ed: Amy Wilson, Mark Rechtin. **Description:** Floods in Thailand and the tsunami in Japan have caused shortages of Japanese-brand vehicle parts. These shortages are expected to linger into 2012.

14920 ■ *"J.C. Watts First Black John Deere Dealer"* in *Black Enterprise (Vol. 37, November 2006, No. 4, pp. 36)*
Pub: Earl G. Graves Publishing Co. Inc.

Ed: Kiara Ashanti. **Description:** Profile of former Congressman J.C. Watts Jr., a man who grew up in rural America and is the first African American to own a John Deere Dealership.

14921 ■ *"KC Plants Downshift"* in *The Business Journal-Serving Metropolitan Kansas City (Vol. 27, November 7, 2008, No. 9, pp. 1)*
Pub: American City Business Journals, Inc.

Ed: James Dornbrook. **Description:** Discusses Ford Motor Co. and General Motors' factories in the region; Ford Motor Co. removed the second shift on the F-150 line at the Kansas City Assembly Plant but added a shift to the production of the Ford Escape and Mercury Mariner in an attempt to avoid layoffs. One spokesman for General Motors, however, states that they cannot guarantee that they won't make any production cuts or layoffs in the future.

14922 ■ *"LatinWorks Cozies Up to Chevy in Detroit"* in *Austin Business Journal (Vol. 31, August 12, 2011, No. 23, pp. A1)*
Pub: American City Business Journals Inc.

Ed: Sandra Zaragoza. **Description:** Hispanic marketing agency LatinWorks opened an office in Detroit to better serve its client Chevrolet and to potentially secure more contracts from its parent company General Motors, whose offices are located nearby.

14923 ■ *"The Lithium Deficit"* in *Canadian Business (Vol. 82, April 27, 2009, No. 7, pp. 17)*
Pub: Rogers Media

Ed: Joe Castaldo. **Description:** Experts are concerned that there may not be enough lithium available to support the expected rise in demand for the natural resource. Lithium is used in lithium ion batteries, the standard power source for electric and hybrid vehicles. Experts believe that the demand for lithium can only be measured once the technology is out in the market.

14924 ■ *"Local Auto Suppliers Upbeat as Detroit 3's Prospects Trend Up"* in *Crain's Cleveland Business (Vol. 30, June 8, 2009, No. 22, pp. 1)*
Pub: Crain Communications, Inc.

Ed: Dan Shingler. **Description:** According to the Center for Automotive Research located in Ann Arbor, Michigan, if Detroit automakers can hold their market share, they will end up producing more vehicles as the market recovers.

14925 ■ *"Local Dealers Fear Shortages in Car Supply"* in *Boston Business Journal (Vol. 29, May 13, 2011, No. 1, pp. 1)*
Pub: American City Business Journals Inc.

Ed: Scott Dance. **Description:** The earthquake and tsunami in Japan are seen to impact the automobile dealers in Baltimore, Maryland. Automobile supply in the area is seen to decrease dramatically during the summer sales season. Shortage of transmission parts and paint colors is also forecasted.

14926 ■ *"Local Green Technology on Display"* in *Crain's Detroit Business (Vol. 26, January 18, 2010, No. 3, pp. 1)*
Pub: Crain Communications Inc.

Ed: Ryan Beene. **Description:** Detroit's 2010 North American International Auto Show put the newest, most innovative green technologies on display showing that the Southeast Michigan automobile industry is gaining traction with its burgeoning e-vehicle infrastructure. Think, a Norwegian electric city-car

manufacturer is eyeing sites in Southeast Michigan in which to locate its corporate headquarters and technical center for its North American branch.

14927 ■ *"A Look At Three Gas-Less Cars"* in *Hispanic Business (Vol. 30, September 2008, No. 9, pp. 90)*
Pub: Hispanic Business, Inc.

Ed: Daniel Soussa. **Description:** Three major car manufacturers, Chevrolet, BMW, and Honda, are giving market leader Toyota competition for the next generation of eco-friendly car. The latest and most advanced of the gasoline-less cars designed by the three firms, namely, the Chevrolet Volt, BMW's Hydrogen 7, and the Honda FCX Clarity, are reviewed.

14928 ■ *"Luxe Men Are In Style"* in *Brandweek (Vol. 49, April 21, 2008, No. 16, pp. 12)*
Pub: VNU Business Media, Inc.

Description: According to a recent survey by Unity Marketing, among 1,300 luxury shoppers found that men spent an average of $2,401 on fashion items over a three-month period which is nearly $1,000 more than women. Men also spring for more luxury items such as vehicles and memberships to exclusive clubs.

14929 ■ *"McIntosh Family Sells Car Dealership"* in *Black Enterprise (Vol. 38, December 2007, No. 5)*
Pub: Earl G. Graves Publishing Co. Inc.

Ed: Brenda Porter. **Description:** Seattle's McIntosh family sold its Kirkland Chrysler Jeep dealership to private equity firm Cerberus Capital Management. Details of the deal are given.

14930 ■ *"Mercury (1939-2010)"* in *Canadian Business (Vol. 83, June 15, 2010, No. 10, pp. 27)*
Pub: Rogers Media Ltd.

Ed: Steve Maich. **Description:** Ford's Mercury brand of cars began in 1939 and it was designed by Ford to attract a wealthier clientele. Mercury was mentioned in a 1949 song by K.C. Douglas and was driven in the movie, 'Rebel Without a Cause'. However, the brand was too expensive for the mass market and not exclusive enough through the years, so Ford Motor Company decided to discontinue the brand in 2010.

14931 ■ *"The New Frontier"* in *Crain's Detroit Business (Vol. 26, January 18, 2010, No. 3, pp. S025)*
Pub: Crain Communications Inc.

Ed: Richard Truett; Bradford Wernle. **Description:** Due to the changing consumer preference resulting from new fuel-efficiency standards, concern about climate change and higher gasoline prices, Detroit car designers are beginning to shift focus onto smaller vehicles.

14932 ■ *"New Life for Porsche's VW Dreams"* in *Barron's (Vol. 89, July 6, 2009, No. 27, pp. 9)*
Pub: Dow Jones & Co., Inc.

Ed: Vito J. Racanelli. **Description:** Porsche and Volkswagen moved closer to a merger after the Qatar Investment Authority offered to take a stake in Porsche. The QIA could take up to a 30 percent stake in Porsche and purchase all Volkswagen calls for up to $6 billion.

14933 ■ *"Next Generation Audi TT Hits Canadian Streets"* in *Canadian Corporate News (May 16, 2007)*
Pub: Comtex News Network Inc.

Description: Audi Canada prepares for the launch of the highly anticipated 2008 Audi TT, recipient of the 2007 World Car Design of the Year due to its contemporary look, powerful engine, and innovative technology, with a multiple touch-point marketing campaign.

14934 ■ *"Nine Sectors to Watch: Automotive"* in *Canadian Business (Vol. 81, December 24, 2007, No. 1, pp. 47)*
Pub: Rogers Media

Ed: Thomas Watson. **Description:** Forecasts on the Canadian automotive sector for 2008 are presented. Details on contract concessions made by American unions, the industry's Big Three (General Motors, Chrysler, and Ford) operations in Canada, and Canadian Auto Workers demand for higher wages are also discussed.

14935 ■ "Nissan Unveils Family Concept Car" in Marketing to Women (Vol. 21, February 2008, No. 2, pp. 3)
Pub: EPM Communications Inc.
Contact: Ira Mayer, President
E-mail: imayer@epmcom.com
Description: Nissan displayed its latest design for the ultimate family vehicle at the 2008 North American International Auto Show in Detroit. The Nissan Forum targets families with older children.

14936 ■ "No End to the Nightmare; America's Car Industry" in The Economist (Vol. 390, January 3, 2009, No. 8612, pp. 46)
Pub: The Economist Newspaper Inc.
Description: Detroit's struggling auto industry and the government loan package is discussed as well as the United Auto Worker union, which is loathed by Senate Republicans.

14937 ■ "No Frills - And No Dodge" in Crain's Detroit Business (Vol. 24, September 22, 2008, No. 38, pp. 3)
Pub: Crain Communications Inc.
Ed: Bradford Wernie. **Description:** Chrysler LLC is in the middle of a business plan known as Project Genesis, a five-year strategy in which the company will reduce the dealer count by combining its Jeep, Chrysler and Dodge brands under one rooftop wherever possible. Not every dealer will be able to arrange this deal because of the investment required to expand stores in which have low-overhead; many of these stores feel that low-overhead structures are more likely to survive difficult times than the larger stores in which the Genesis consolidation plan intends to implement.

14938 ■ "O'Reilly Will Soup Up KC Warehouse" in The Business Journal-Serving Metropolitan Kansas City (Vol. 26, August 15, 2008, No. 49)
Pub: American City Business Journals, Inc.
Ed: Rob Roberts. **Description:** O'Reilly Automotive Inc. plans to construct a 215,000-square foot warehouse in Kansas City. The move is expected to triple the size of the company's distribution center. Other views and information on the planned warehouse construction, are presented.

14939 ■ "Pain Ahead as Profit Pressure Increases" in Crain's Chicago Business (Vol. 31, May 5, 2008, No. 18, pp. 4)
Pub: Crain Communications, Inc.
Ed: Daniel Rome Levine. **Description:** Interview with David Klaskin, the chairman and chief investment officer at Oak Ridge Investments LLC, who discusses the outlook for the economy and corporate earnings, particularly in the housing and auto industries, the impact of economic stimulus checks, the weakness of the dollar and recommendations of stocks that individual investors may find helpful.

14940 ■ "Penske Opens Its First Smart Car Dealership In Bloomfield Hills" in Crain's Detroit Business (Vol. 24, January 21, 2008, No. 3)
Pub: Crain Communications Inc. - Detroit
Ed: Sheena Harrison. **Description:** Information about Penske Automotive Group's Smart Car addition to its dealership lineup. Smart Car pricing starts at $11,590, with more than 30,000 individuals reserving vehicles.

14941 ■ "Porsche Raises VW Stake, Makes Bid for Firm" in Globe & Mail (March 26, 2007, pp. B5)
Pub: CTVglobemedia Publishing Inc.
Ed: Chad Thomas. Jeremy Van Logan. **Description:** Automobile giant Porsche AG has increased its stake in Volkswagen AG to $54 billion recently. The company is planning a merger by claiming 30% stake under German law.

14942 ■ "Providing Expertise Required to Develop Microsystems" in Canadian Electronics (Vol. 23, February 2008, No. 1, pp. 6)
Pub: CLB Media Inc.
Ed: Ian McWalter. **Description:** CMC Microsystems, formerly Canadian Microelectronics Corporation, is focused on empowering microelectronics and Microsystems research in Canada. Microsystems offers the basis for innovations in the fields of science, environment, technology, automotives, energy, aerospace and communications technology. CMC's strategy in developing Microsystems in Canada is described.

14943 ■ "Put It In Drive" in Entrepreneur (Vol. 36, April 2008, No. 4, pp. 31)
Pub: Entrepreneur Media, Inc.
Ed: Jill Amadio. **Description:** Commercial vehicle models for 2008 are presented. These new models are more user- and environment-friendly. Features and prices of car models and tips to consider before purchasing are presented.

14944 ■ "Realities May Blur Vision" in The Business Journal-Serving Metropolitan Kansas City (Vol. 27, September 19, 2008, No. 1, pp. 1)
Pub: American City Business Journals, Inc.
Ed: Rob Roberts. **Description:** Vision Metcalf is a study by Kansas City that depicts how Metcalf Avenue could look like if redeveloped. Redevelopment plans for the Metcalf corridor include a 20-story mixed-use building on a vacant car dealership. The challenges that the redevelopment plans will face are also analyzed.

14945 ■ "Reply! Grows at Unprecedented Rate, Rips Beta Off Its Marketplace" in Marketing Weekly News (September 19, 2009, pp. 149)
Pub: Investment Weekly News
Description: Profile of Reply.com, a leader in locally-targeted Internet marketing, announced significant growth in terms of revenue, enhanced features and services and new categories since launching its beta Reply! Marketplace platform. Even in the face of an economic downturn, the company has posted over 50 percent revenue growth in the Real Estate and Automotive categories.

14946 ■ "Ron Carpenter" in Crain's Cleveland Business (Vol. 30, June 29, 2009, No. 25, pp. 12)
Pub: Crain Communications, Inc.
Ed: Dan Shingler. **Description:** Profile of Ron Carpenter, owner of Production Tool Company located in Twinsburg, Ohio. Carpenter was forced to lay off half of his staff of 14 workers after the auto business tanked. He believes it was the single most difficult decision he had to make as a manager.

14947 ■ "Ross: There's Still Money In the Auto Industry" in Crain's Detroit Business (Vol. 24, January 28, 2008, No. 4, pp. 12)
Pub: Crain Communications Inc. - Detroit
Ed: Brent Snavely. **Description:** Wilbur Ross, chairman and CEO of WL Ross and Company LLC, a private equity firm, predicts U.S. vehicle sales will fall by about 750,000 in 2008, but continues to look for supplier bargains.

14948 ■ "Sellers Shift Gears" in Crain's Detroit Business (Vol. 25, June 22, 2009, No. 25, pp. 3)
Pub: Crain Communications Inc. - Detroit
Description: Of the 14 new car Chrysler dealerships in the Detroit area who had franchises terminated, Joe Ricci of Dearborn will sell used cars at his new business called All American Buyer's Service; Lochmoor Automotive Group in Detroit will focus on Mahindra & Mahindra trucks; Mt. Clemens Dodge, Clinton Township is also selling Mahindra & Mahindra trucks; and Monicatti Chrysler Jeep, Sterling Heights, will offer service along with selling used cars.

14949 ■ "Selling Michigan; R&D Pushed as Reason For Chinese To Locate In State" in

Crain's Detroit Business (Vol. 24, January 14, 2008)
Pub: Crain Communications Inc. - Detroit
Ed: Marti Benedetti. **Description:** Southeast Michigan Economic Development organizations are working to develop relationships with Chinese manufacturers so they will locate their automotive research and development operations in the state.

14950 ■ "Slimmer Interiros Make Small Cars Seem Big" in Automotive News (Vol. 86, October 31, 2011, No. 6488, pp. 16)
Pub: Crain Communications Inc.
Ed: David Sedgwick. **Description:** Cost-conscious buyers want luxury car amenities in their smaller vehicles, so automakers are rethinking interiors. Style, efficiency and value could be the next trend in vehicles.

14951 ■ "Small is the New Big in Autos" in Globe & Mail (February 16, 2006, pp. B3)
Pub: CTVglobemedia Publishing Inc.
Ed: Greg Keenan. **Description:** The reasons behind the introduction of subcompact cars by companies such as Ford Motor Co. are presented. The automobiles were unveiled at Canadian International Auto Show in Toronto.

14952 ■ "Smart Car Sales Take Big Hit in Recession" in Business Journal-Milwaukee (Vol. 28, December 10, 2010, No. 10, pp. A1)
Pub: Milwaukee Business Journal
Ed: Stacey Vogel Davis. **Description:** Sales of smart cars in Milwaukee declined in 2010. Smart Center Milwaukee sold only 52 new cars through October 2010. Increased competition is seen as a reason for the decline in sales.

14953 ■ "Solidarity UAW Forever" in Crain's Detroit Business (Vol. 25, June 1, 2009, No. 22, pp. M001)
Pub: Crain Communications Inc. - Detroit
Ed: Ryan Beene. **Description:** United Auto Workers union has made it difficult for certain businesses to move to Michigan. Discussion is made about the issues involved and changes that need to be made in the way labor and management do business.

14954 ■ "The Solution" in Entrepreneur (Vol. 37, October 2009, No. 10, pp. 71)
Pub: Entrepreneur Media, Inc.
Ed: Jennifer Wang. **Description:** Ford's 2010 Transit Connect is a compact commercial van developed specifically for small business owners. The compact van offers an integrated in-dash computer system providing a cellular broadband connection.

14955 ■ "Speed Reader" in Crain's Chicago Business (Vol. 30, February 2007, No. 6, pp. 58)
Pub: Crain Communications, Inc.
Ed: Laura Bianchi. **Description:** Interview with Paul Tamraz, president and CEO of Motor Werkes, which carries luxury vehicle lines like BMW, Porsche, and Mercedes-Benz. Tamraz discusses the importance of keeping up to speed with not only U.S. business but what is happening around the world.

14956 ■ "Steering Toward Profitability" in Black Enterprise (Vol. 41, December 2010, No. 5, pp. 72)
Pub: Earl G. Graves Publishing Co. Inc.
Ed: Alan Hughes. **Description:** Systems Electro Coating LLC had to make quick adjustments when auto manufacturers were in a slump. The minority father-daughter team discuss their strategies during the auto industry collapse.

14957 ■ "Stimulus 'Loser' Won't Build Plant in Mass." in Boston Business Journal (Vol. 30, November 5, 2010, No. 41, pp. 1)
Pub: Boston Business Journal
Ed: Kyle Alspach. **Description:** Boston-Power Inc. no longer plans to build an electric vehicle battery plant in Massachusetts after it failed to obtain stimulus funds from the federal government. The company is instead looking to build a lithium-ion battery plant in China and possibly Europe.

14958 ■ *"Stock Car Racing" in Canadian Business (Vol. 81, September 15, 2008, No. 14-15, pp. 29)*

Pub: Rogers Media Ltd.

Ed: Thomas Watson. **Description:** Some analysts predict a Chapter 11-style tune-up making GM and Ford a speculative turnaround stock. However, the price of oil could make or break the shares of the Big Three U.S. automobile manufacturers and if oil goes up too high then a speculative stock to watch is an electric car company called Zenn Motor Co.

14959 ■ *"Suppliers May Follow Fiat" in Crain's Detroit Business (Vol. 25, June 15, 2009, No. 24, pp. 1)*

Pub: Crain Communications Inc. - Detroit

Ed: Ryan Beene. **Description:** Italian suppliers to Fiat SpA are looking toward Detroit after the formation of Chrysler Group LLC, the Chrysler-Fiat partnership created from Chrysler's bankruptcy. The Italian American Alliance for Business and Technology is aware of two Italy-based powertrain component suppliers that are considering a move to Detroit.

14960 ■ *"The 'Supply Side' of the Auto Industry" in Montly Labor Review (Vol. 133, September 2010, No. 9, pp. 72)*

Pub: Bureau of Labor Statistics

Description: Restructuring and geographic change in the automobile industry is discussed.

14961 ■ *"The Tata Way" in Business Strategy Review (Vol. 21, Summer 2010, No. 2, pp. 14)*

Pub: Wiley-Blackwell

Description: Tata Motors is one of the world's most talked-about companies. Its new ultra-low-cost Nano car is being heralded as the people's car. Vice chairman, Ravi Kant, talks about India and its emerging markets.

14962 ■ *"There's More Upside in Germany" in Barron's (Vol. 90, September 6, 2010, No. 36, pp. M7)*

Pub: Barron's Editorial & Corporate Headquarters

Ed: Jonathan Buck. **Description:** Germany's stocks have gone up since the beginning of 2010, and investors can still benefit. These stocks will benefit from Germany's stellar economic performance and the relative weakness of the Euro. The prospects of the shares of Daimler and Hochtief are discussed.

14963 ■ *"This Just In" in Crain's Detroit Business (Vol. 25, June 1, 2009, No. 22, pp. 1)*

Pub: Crain Communications Inc. - Detroit

Description: Three veterans of the auto industry have partnered to create, Revitalizing Michigan, a nonprofit dedicated to help manufacturers improve their processes. The firm is seeking federal, state and private grants to fund the mission.

14964 ■ *"Toyota Marks Record Profit Sales" in Globe & Mail (February 7, 2007, pp. B10)*

Pub: CTVglobemedia Publishing Inc.

Ed: Martin Fackler. **Description:** The record quarterly sales and earnings reported by Japanese automaker Toyota Motor Corp. are discussed. The company sold 2.16 million vehicles during the quarter while registering 426.8 billion yen in profits.

14965 ■ *"Trillium Turmoil" in Canadian Business (Vol. 81, December 8, 2008, No. 21, pp. 16)*

Pub: Rogers Media Ltd.

Ed: Jeff Sanford. **Description:** Ontario's manufacturing success in the past was believed to have been built by the 1965 Canada-U.S. automotive pact and by advantages such as low-cost energy. The loss of these advantages along with the challenging economic times has hurt Ontario's manufacturing industry.

14966 ■ *"Uncle Volodya's Flagging Christmas Spirit; Russia" in The Economist (Vol. 390, January 3, 2009, No. 8612, pp. 22)*

Pub: The Economist Newspaper Inc.

Description: Overview of Russia's struggling economy as well as unpopular government decisions such as raising import duties on used foreign vehicles so as to protect Russian carmakers.

14967 ■ *Why GM Matters: Inside the Race to Transform an American Icon*

Pub: Walker & Company

Ed: William J. Holstein. **Released:** 2009. **Price:** $26.00. **Description:** A timely examination of General Motors Corporation and the problems it is facing.

14968 ■ *"With Traffic Jam in Super Bowl, Can Any Auto Brand Really Win?" in Advertising Age (Vol. 81, December 6, 2010, No. 43, pp. 1)*

Pub: Crain Communications Inc.

Ed: Rupal Parekh, Brian Steinberg. **Description:** Car marketers are doubling down for Super Bowl XLV in Arlington, Texas and asking their ad agencies to craft commercials unique enough to break through the clutter and to capture viewers' attention.

14969 ■ *"Worry No. 1 at Auto Show" in Crain's Detroit Business (Vol. 24, January 21, 2008, No. 3, pp. 1)*

Pub: Crain Communications Inc. - Detroit

Ed: Brent Snavely. **Description:** Recession fears clouded activity at the 2008 Annual North American International Auto Show. Automakers are expecting to see a drop in sales due to slow holiday retail spending as well as fallout from the subprime lending crisis.

14970 ■ *"Xstrata and CAW Get Tentative Deal" in Globe & Mail (February 2, 2007, pp. B3)*

Pub: CTVglobemedia Publishing Inc.

Ed: Andy Hoffman. **Description:** The agreement between Xstrata PLC and Canadian Auto Workers union over wage hike is discussed.

14971 ■ *"ZF Revving Up Jobs, Growth" in Business Courier (Vol. 26, November 6, 2009, No. 28, pp. 1)*

Pub: American City Business Journals, Inc.

Ed: Jon Newberry. **Description:** Proposed $96 million expansion of German-owned automotive supplier ZF Steering systems LLC is anticipated to generate 299 jobs in Boone County, Kentucky. ZF might invest $90 million in equipment, while the rest will go to building and improvements.

STATISTICAL SOURCES

14972 ■ *RMA Annual Statement Studies*

Pub: Risk Management Association

Contact: Kevin M. Blakey, President

Released: Annual. **Price:** $175.00 2006-07 edition, $105.00. **Description:** Contains composite balance sheets and income statements for more than 360 industries, including the accounting, auditing, and bookkeeping industries. Also contains five years of comparative historical data for discerning trends. Includes 16 commonly used ratios, computed for most of the size groupings for nearly every industry.

14973 ■ *Standard & Poor's Industry Surveys*

Pub: Standard & Poor's Corp.

Released: Annual. **Price:** $3633.00. **Description:** Two-volume book that examines the prospects for specific industries, including trucking. Also provides analyses of trends and problems, statistical tables and charts, and comparative company analyses.

TRADE PERIODICALS

14974 ■ *AIADA News / Auto Dealer*

Pub: American International Automobile Dealers Association

Contact: Ray Mungenast, Chairman

Ed: Lori McMahon, Editor. **Released:** Monthly. **Description:** Offers international auto dealers current news on the issues impacting the business.

14975 ■ *Automotive Industries*

Pub: Reed Business Information

Contact: Tad Smith, Chief Executive Officer

URL(s): www.ai-online.com/. **Ed:** Ed Richardson. **Released:** Monthly **Price:** $88, Individuals in North America; $168, Other countries airmail.

14976 ■ *Automotive News*

Pub: Crain Communications Inc.

URL(s): www.autonews.com. **Released:** Weekly **Price:** $159, Individuals print and digital online; $99, Individuals digital/online; $199, Individuals data center only; $24.95, Individuals 1 month, website access only; $14.95, Individuals 1 week, website access only.

14977 ■ *AutoWeek*

Pub: Crain Communications Inc.

URL(s): www.autoweek.com. **Ed:** Dutch Mandel. **Released:** Weekly **Price:** $29.95, Individuals 26 issues; $49.95, Two years.

14978 ■ *Car and Driver*

Pub: Hachette Filipacchi Media U.S. Inc.

Contact: David Carey, President

URL(s): www.caranddriver.com. **Released:** Monthly **Price:** $10, Individuals; $15, Two years.

14979 ■ *FDA Newsletter*

Pub: Ford Dealers Alliance

Released: Bimonthly. **Price:** Included in membership. **Description:** Covers factory-dealer relations focusing on factory encroachment on dealer equity in their own franchise. Discusses fleet subsidies, sales agreements, terminations, add points, warranty administration, and product distribution. Examines individual dealer problems. Recurring features include letters to the editor, news of research, book reviews, reports of meetings, and interviews.

14980 ■ *Hemmings Motor News: World's Largest Collector--Car Marketplace Since 1954*

Pub: Hemmings Motor News

Contact: Ray Gillotte, Manager

URL(s): www.hemmings.com/subscribe/current_issue.html?publication=HMN. **Released:** Quarterly **Price:** $56.14, Canada 4th class; $108.52, Canada 2 years, 4th class; $94.24, Canada priority mail; $184.71, Canada priority mail, 2 years; $31.95, Individuals 4th class; $60.95, Two years 4th class; $86.95, Individuals priority mail; $169.95, Two years priority mail; $163.95, By mail Asia, Africa, Australia or New Zealand; $118.95, By mail Central America.

14981 ■ *Motor Trend: The World's Automotive Authority*

Pub: PRIMEDIA Los Angeles

URL(s): www.motortrend.com/. **Released:** Monthly **Price:** $10, Individuals; $18, Two years; $22, Canada; $42, Canada 2 years; $34, Other countries; $66, Other countries 2 years.

14982 ■ *Road & Track*

Pub: Hachette Filipacchi Media U.S. Inc.

Contact: David Carey, President

URL(s): www.roadandtrack.com. **Released:** Monthly **Price:** $12, Individuals; $19.95, Two years; $40, Other countries.

14983 ■ *Used Car Dealer*

Pub: National Independent Automobile Dealers Association

Contact: Don Fincher, President

URL(s): usedcardealer.epubxpress.com/. **Released:** Monthly **Price:** $80, Nonmembers.

14984 ■ *Vehicle Leasing Today*

Pub: National Vehicle Leasing Association

Contact: Ben Carfrae, President

URL(s): www.vehicleleasingtoday.com/. **Ed:** Chris Brown. **Released:** Bimonthly; Quarterly **Price:** $39, Individuals per year; included in membership dues; $39, /year for nonmembers.

14985 ■ *Ward's Auto World*

Pub: Ward's Communications

Contact: David E. Zoia, Director

E-mail: dzoia@wardsauto.com

URL(s): wardsauto.com/about/waw/. **Released:** Monthly **Price:** $69, Individuals U.S.A and Mexico; $85, Canada; $104, Other countries.

VIDEOCASSETTES/ AUDIOCASSETTES

14986 ■ *Auto Buyer Alert*
Tapeworm Video Distributors
25876 The Old Road #141
Stevenson Ranch, CA 91381
Ph: (661)257-4904
Fax: (661)257-4820
Co. E-mail: sales@tapeworm.com
URL: http://www.tapeworm.com
Released: 1996. **Price:** $14.95. **Description:** Presents car buying tips on when to buy, how to make trade-ins, financing, and more. **Availability:** VHS.

14987 ■ *Get the Upper Hand*
Tapeworm Video Distributors
25876 The Old Road #141
Stevenson Ranch, CA 91381
Ph: (661)257-4904
Fax: (661)257-4820
Co. E-mail: sales@tapeworm.com
URL: http://www.tapeworm.com
Released: 19??. **Price:** $19.95. **Description:** Presents a guideline for buying and leasing a new or used vehicle. **Availability:** VHS.

14988 ■ *The Insider's Guide to Buying and Leasing Automobiles*
Tapeworm Video Distributors
25876 The Old Road #141
Stevenson Ranch, CA 91381
Ph: (661)257-4904
Fax: (661)257-4820
Co. E-mail: sales@tapeworm.com
URL: http://www.tapeworm.com
Released: 1997. **Price:** $19.95. **Description:** Discusses how to save on new car purchases, tricks of the trade, and lease language. **Availability:** VHS.

TRADE SHOWS AND CONVENTIONS

14989 ■ Great American Trucking Show (GATS)
Sellers Expositions
222 Pearl St., Ste. 300
New Albany, IN 47150
Ph: (812)949-9200
Free: 800-558-8767
Fax: (812)949-9600
URL: http://www.sellersexpo.com
Contact: Warren Sellers, Chief Executive Officer
E-mail: wss315@aol.com
URL(s): www.gatsonline.com. **Audience:** Truck owners and operators, exempt haulers, company drivers and truck drivers for hire, aftermarket parts purchasers, purchasing agents, mechanics, fleet owner. **Principal Exhibits:** Trucks and related equipment, supplies, and services.

14990 ■ New England International Auto Show
Paragon Group, Inc.
197 1st Ave., Ste. 150
Needham, MA 02494
Ph: (781)237-5533
Free: 800-258-8912
Fax: (781)237-0407
URL: http://www.paragonexpo.com
URL(s): www.paragonexpo.com/index.php/NE-General/. **Frequency:** Annual. **Audience:** General public. **Principal Exhibits:** New model domestic, import, and specialty cars and light trucks, and accessories. **Dates and Locations:** , Bayside Exposition Center. **Telecommunication Services:** prose@paragonexpo.com.

14991 ■ North American International Auto Show
North American International Auto Show
1900 W. Big Beaver Rd., Ste. 100
Troy, MI 48084
Ph: (248)643-0250

Fax: (248)647-0784
Co. E-mail: naiasmail@dada.orr
URL: http://www.naias.com
URL(s): www.naias.com/. **Price:** $12, adult ticket; $6, senior citizen ticket; $6, children 7-12. **Frequency:** Annual. **Audience:** General public and trade; automotive analysts, executives, media. **Principal Exhibits:** New automobiles and trucks, concept cars, manufacturer-related displays. **Dates and Locations:** , Cobo Conference Center.

14992 ■ San Diego International Auto Show
Liberty Productions
8170 Adams Drive
Hummelstown, PA 17036
Ph: (717)566-6100
Fax: (717)566-7868
URL: http://www.autoshowusa.com
URL(s): www.sdautoshow.com. **Frequency:** Annual. **Audience:** General public. **Principal Exhibits:** Equipment, supplies, and services.

14993 ■ Service Specialists Association Annual Convention
Service Specialists Association
c/o Wade & Partners
160 Symphony Way
Elgin, IL 60120
Ph: (330)725-7160
Free: 800-763-5717
Fax: (330)722-5638
Co. E-mail: trucksvc@aol.com
URL: http://www.truckservice.org
URL(s): truckservice.org. **Frequency:** Annual. **Audience:** Trade-Heavy Duty Aftermarket. **Principal Exhibits:** Exhibits related to truck repair operations, rebuilding departments, individuals who have maintained shop equipment such as hydraulic press or heat treating furnace.

14994 ■ West Virginia International Auto Show
West Virginia Automobile & Truck Dealers Association
1618 Kanawha Blvd. E.
Charleston, WV 25327
Ph: (304)343-4158
Fax: (304)343-8474
URL: http://www.wvcar.com/
URL(s): www.motortrendautoshows.com/charwv/generalinfo.jsp. **Price:** $7, adults; $5, senior citizens; $4, children 7-12. **Frequency:** Annual. **Audience:** Car enthusiasts. **Principal Exhibits:** Hundreds of new model domestic and imported automobiles.

CONSULTANTS

14995 ■ ASC Retail Consulting
10 Iverness Center Pky., Ste. 320
Birmingham, AL 35242
Ph: (205)995-5300
Free: 800-633-4767
Fax: (205)995-5360
Co. E-mail: martincic@hoffman.ds.adp.com
URL: http://www.ascconsulting.com
Contact: Mark Martincic, Director
E-mail: martincic@hoffman.ds.adp.com
Scope: Offers management consulting for auto dealers, distributors and manufacturers specializing in service, parts and body shop departments. Industries served automotive retail, wholesale and manufacturers. **Founded:** 1971. **Publications:** "Competitive and Profitable"; "Controlling Service Expense". **Special Services:** Applied Service Management; Extended Service Performance; Process Reengineering; Applied Body Shop Management; Customized Solutions.

FRANCHISES AND BUSINESS OPPORTUNITIES

14996 ■ J.D. Byrider
J.D. Byrider Systems, Inc.
12802 Hamilton Crossing Blvd.
Carmel, IN 46032
Ph: (317)249-3000
Free: 800-947-4532

Fax: (317)249-3001
Description: Used car sales and finance. **No. of Franchise Units:** 123. **No. of Company-Owned Units:** 12. **Founded:** 1989. **No. of Company-Owned Units:** 12. **Founded:** 1989. **Franchised:** 1989. **Equity Capital Needed:** $267,550-$1,933,000. **Franchise Fee:** $35,000-$50,000. **Financial Assistance:** Yes. **Training:** Yes.

14997 ■ Rent 'N Drive
Rent 'n Drive Franchising LLC
1440 Plumridge Rd.
Lincoln, NE 68527
Ph: (402)467-4994
Fax: (402)466-3819
Description: Used car, van, and truck rentals. **No. of Franchise Units:** 1. **No. of Company-Owned Units:** 1. **Founded:** 1990.. **Franchised:** 1996. **Equity Capital Needed:** $83,000-$189,000, depending on fleet size. **Franchise Fee:** $7,500. **Training:** Yes.

14998 ■ Thrifty Car Sales Inc.
5310 E 31st St., CIMS 1130
Tulsa, OK 74135
Free: 877-289-2583
Fax: (918)669-2654
URL: http://www.thriftycarsales.com
Description: Deals with car sales. **No. of Franchise Units:** 51. **Founded:** 1998.. **Franchised:** 1998. **Equity Capital Needed:** $765,000-$4,000,000. **Franchise Fee:** $35,000. **Royalty Fee:** $110/vehicle. **Training:** Available at headquarters, with ongoing support.

COMPUTERIZED DATABASES

14999 ■ *Automotive News*
1155 Gratiot Ave.
Detroit, MI 48207
Ph: (313)446-6000
Free: 800-678-2427
Fax: (313)446-1616
Co. E-mail: info@crain.com
URL: http://www.crain.com
Availability: Online: ProQuest Co.; LexisNexis Group; Crain Communications Inc. **Type:** Full-text.

15000 ■ *AutoSite Pro*
18872 MacArthur Blvd., Ste. 200
Irvine, CA 92612
Ph: (949)225-4500
Fax: (949)225-4557
Co. E-mail: consumercare@autobytel.com
URL: http://www.autobytel.com
Contact: Jeffrey Coats, President
Availability: Online: Autobytel Inc. **Type:** Full-text; Numeric; Directory.

15001 ■ *Highway Vehicles Safety Database*
400 Commonwealth Dr.
Warrendale, PA 15096-0001
Ph: (724)776-4841
Free: 877-606-7323
Fax: (724)776-0790
Co. E-mail: CustomerService@sae.org
URL: http://www.sae.org
Availability: Online: SAE International. CD-ROM: SAE International. **Type:** Bibliographic.

15002 ■ *Tire Business*
1155 Gratiot Ave.
Detroit, MI 48207
Ph: (313)446-6000
Free: 800-678-2427
Fax: (313)446-1616
Co. E-mail: info@crain.com
URL: http://www.crain.com
Availability: Online: Crain Communications Inc. **Type:** Full-text; Numeric.

COMPUTER SYSTEMS/ SOFTWARE

15003 ■ *Black Book, Inc.*
PO Box 758
Gainesville, GA 30503
Ph: (770)532-4111
Free: 800-554-1026

Fax: (800)357-3444

URL: http://www.blackbookusa.com

Description: Available for IBM computers and MS-DOS compatibles. System provides including cost and retail, options, and finance and lease payments. pricing information on cars and light trucks, including cost and retail, options, and finance and lease payments.

15004 ■ F & I Billing System

1632 Denniston Ave.

Pittsburgh, PA 15217-1458

Ph: (412)421-4446

Fax: (412)421-4446

URL: http://americansystemscorp.com/

Price: Contact American Systems for pricing. **Description:** Available for all personal computers. Program for automobile dealers. Calculates monthly payments and prints retail delivery forms.

LIBRARIES

15005 ■ American Automobile Association Research Library—AAA Research Library.

1000 AAA Dr.

Heathrow, FL 32746-5060

Ph: (407)444-7965

Fax: (407)444-7759

Co. E-mail: rinesta@aaasouth.com

URL: http://www.aaasouth.com

Contact: Renaldo Inesta, Division Manager

Scope: Travel guide books; market studies; highway and traffic safety; driver education; automobiles - history, statistics, insurance. **Services:** Interlibrary loan; Library open to researchers with permission. **Founded:** 1955. **Holdings:** 10,000 books; 20 VF drawers of pamphlets; reports. **Subscriptions:** 100 journals and other serials.

15006 ■ Crain Communications Information Center

1155 Gratiot Ave.

Detroit, MI 48207

Ph: (313)446-0367

Fax: (313)259-3319

Co. E-mail: detinfo@crain.com

URL: http://www.crain.com

Contact: Corinne M. Young, Manager

Scope: Automotive; company information. **Services:** Copying; Library not open to the public. **Founded:** 1972. **Holdings:** 2000 books; 1000 bound periodical volumes; 300 reports; archival items; microfiche; microfilm. **Subscriptions:** 52 journals and other serials; 13 newspapers.

15007 ■ NAFA Fleet Management Association - FleetED

125 Village Blvd., Ste. 200

Princeton, NJ 08540

Ph: (609)720-0882

Fax: (609)452-8004

Co. E-mail: info@nafa.org

URL: http://www.nafa.org

Contact: Kimla Beasley, Manager, Product Development

Scope: Automotive fleet management, leasing, automotive safety programs, alternative fuels, fleet industry laws and regulations. **Services:** Interlibrary loan; copying; library open to the public by appointment. **Founded:** 1992. **Holdings:** 8000 records, including books, articles, reports, and webinars. **Subscriptions:** 45 journals and other serials.

15008 ■ UAW-Daimler Chrysler - Technology Training Center - Resource Library

2500 E. Nine Mile Rd.

Warren, MI 48091

Free: 800-683-8840

Fax: (313)369-6111

Co. E-mail: vking@ucntc.org

URL: http://www.uaw-chrysler.com/training/ttc.cfm

Contact: Virdell King, Assistant Director

URL(s): www.uaw-chrysler.com/resources/libraries.cfm. **Scope:** Automobile industry and skilled trades. **Services:** Interlibrary loan; copying; Library not open to the public. **Founded:** 1996. **Holdings:** 2000 books; reports; standards; manuals. **Subscriptions:** 80 journals and other serials; 7 newspapers.

ASSOCIATIONS AND OTHER ORGANIZATIONS

15009 ■ **Specialized Information Publishers Association (SIPA)**
8229 Boone Blvd., Ste. 260
Vienna, VA 22182
Ph: (703)992-9339
Free: 800-356-9302
Fax: (703)992-7512
Co. E-mail: kfritz@sipaonline.com
URL: http://sipaonline.com
Contact: Wayne Cooper, President
URL(s): www.newsletters.org/. **Description:** Represents firms that publish for-profit, subscription-based newsletters and specialized information products and suppliers of goods and services to the newsletter publishing industry. Aims to further the professional, economic, and organizational interest of members and their employees. Plans include: conducting research and preparing reports; representing members before federal agencies and monitoring legislation; holding seminars and workshops for members. **Scope:** newsletter publishing. **Founded:** 1977. **Subscriptions:** books periodicals. **Publications:** *Hotline* (Biweekly); *Specialized Information Publishers Association--SIPA Membership Directory & Buyer's Guide* (Annual); *Directory of Members and Industry Suppliers*; *How To Launch A Newsletter*; *Newsletter Publishers' Guidebook*; *The Ultimate Guide to Newsletter Publishing*. **Educational Activities:** International Newsletter and Specialized-Information Conference (Annual); Reality Marketing (Annual); International Newsletter Conference (Annual); Specialized Information Publishers Association Annual International Conference (Annual). **Awards:** Newsletter Journalism Awards (Annual); Editorial Awards. **Telecommunication Services:** sipa@sipaonline.com.

EDUCATIONAL PROGRAMS

15010 ■ **Creating Successful Newsletters**
EEI Communications
8945 Guilford Rd., Ste. 145
Columbia, MD 21046
Ph: (410)309-8200
Free: 888-253-2762
Fax: (410)630-3980
Co. E-mail: train@eeicom.com
URL: http://www.eeicom.com/eei-training-services
Price: $745.00. **Description:** Covers development of audience profile, understanding publishing goals, writing and editing skills, and publication design. **Dates and Locations:** Alexandria, VA.

15011 ■ **Writing News (Onsite)**
EEI Communications
8945 Guilford Rd., Ste. 145
Columbia, MD 21046
Ph: (410)309-8200
Free: 888-253-2762

Fax: (410)630-3980
Co. E-mail: train@eeicom.com
URL: http://www.eeicom.com/eei-training-services
Price: $797.00. **Description:** Covers current techniques for newsletter and news periodical writing, including using more compelling reporting techniques; avoiding common grammar and punctuation errors in condensed writing; formulating dynamic leads and conclusions; understanding and using tone to convey news appropriately; using spoken and printed quotations correctly; checking statistics and logical generalizations; and finding resources for research and story ideas. **Dates and Locations:** Silver Spring, MD; and Alexandria, VA.

DIRECTORIES OF EDUCATIONAL PROGRAMS

15012 ■ *Directory of Private Accredited Career Schools and Colleges of Technology*
Pub: Accrediting Commission of Career Schools and Colleges of Technology
Contact: Michale S. McComis, Executive Director
Released: On web page. **Price:** Free. **Description:** Covers 3900 accredited post-secondary programs that provide training programs in business, trade, and technical fields, including various small business endeavors. Entries offer school name, address, phone, description of courses, job placement assistance, and requirements for admission. Arrangement is alphabetical.

REFERENCE WORKS

15013 ■ *Oxbridge Directory of Newsletters*
Pub: Oxbridge Communications Inc.
Contact: Patricia Hagood, President
URL(s): www.oxbridge.com/ODNCluster/theODN.asp. **Released:** Annual; Latest edition 2011. **Price:** $995, Individuals print version; $1195, Individuals CD-ROM single user; $1995, Individuals print and CD-ROM. **Covers:** Approximately 15,000 newsletters in the U.S. and Canada. **Entries include:** Publication name, publisher name, address, phone; names of editor and other key personnel; description of contents and types of material used, year founded, frequency, advertising and subscription rates, print method, page size, number of pages. **Arrangement:** Classified by subject. **Indexes:** Title, geographical, publisher.

15014 ■ *Standard Periodical Directory*
Pub: Oxbridge Communications Inc.
Contact: Patricia Hagood, President
URL(s): www.oxbridge.com. **Ed:** Deborah Striplin. **Released:** Annual; Latest edition January 2011. **Price:** $1995, Individuals print version; $1995, Single issue CD-ROM single user; $2995, Individuals print and CD-ROM. **Covers:** 63,000 magazines, journals, newsletters, directories, house organs, association publications, etc. , in the United States and Canada. **Entries include:** Publication current and former title; publisher name, address, phone; names and titles of key personnel; circulation and advertising rates;

description of contents; ISSN, year founded, frequency; subscription rates, print method, page size, number of pages. **Arrangement:** Classified by subject. **Indexes:** Subject, title.

15015 ■ *Ulrich's Periodicals Directory: International Periodicals Information Since 1932*
Pub: R.R. Bowker L.L.C.
URL(s): www.ulrichsweb.com/ulrichsweb/faqs.asp. **Released:** Annual; Latest edition 2010. **Price:** $1260, Individuals Hardcover, 4 volumes. **Covers:** Nearly 200,000 current periodicals and newspapers published worldwide. **Entries include:** In main list-- Publication title; Dewey Decimal Classification number, Library of Congress Classification Number (where applicable), CODEN designation (for sci-tech serials), British Library Document Supply Centre shelfmark number, country code, ISSN; subtitle, language(s) of text, year first published, frequency, subscription prices, sponsoring organization, publishing company name, address, phone, fax, e-mail and website addresses, editor and publisher names; regular features (reviews, advertising, abstracts, bibliographies, trade literature, etc.), indexes, circulation, format, brief description of content; availability of microforms and reprints; whether refereed; CD-ROM availability with vendor name; online availability with service name; services that index or abstract the periodical, with years covered; advertising rates and contact; right and permissions contact name and phone; availability through document deliver. **Arrangement:** Main listing is classified by subject; U.S. general daily and weekly newspapers are listed in a separate volume; lists of cessations, online services, and CD-ROM vendors are alphabetical. **Indexes:** Cessations, subjects, title (including variant, former, and ceased titles), ISSN, periodicals available on CD-ROM, online periodical title, refereed serial, and international organization publication title.

TRADE PERIODICALS

15016 ■ *How To Be Your Own Publisher Update*
Pub: Bibliotheca Press
Ed: A. Doyle, Editor. **Released:** Annual. **Price:** $12.95, U.S.; $15.95, Canada; $19.95, other countries. **Description:** Acts as a reference for self publishers. Distributed by Prosperity & Profits Unlimited Distribution Services, PO Box 416, Denver, CO, 80201.

15017 ■ *Independent Publisher Online: The Voice of The Independent Publishing Industry*
Pub: Jenkins Group Inc.
Contact: James J. Kalajian, President
E-mail: jjk@bookpublishing.com
URL(s): www.independentpublisher.com/. **Released:** Monthly **Price:** Free.

15018 ■ *Newsletter Communications*
Pub: The Newsletter Factory
Contact: Tondra Bowen, President
Released: Quarterly. **Description:** Provides news and information to help professionals use newsletters for effective communications. Scope includes creat-

ing, enhancing, and/or improving newsletters of varying types, sizes, and purposes. Also spotlights design, editorial, and production topics.

15019 ■ *The Newsletter on Newsletters*
Pub: Newsletter on Newsletters
Contact: Roger C. Parker, Chairman of the Board
Released: 22/year. **Price:** $275, U.S. and Canada; $295, elsewhere. **Description:** Informs readers about all aspects of the newsletter and specialized information industry. Profiles new newsletters and publishers, reports on mergers and acquisitions in the industry, offers advice on marketing, editing, design, management, and online publishing and marketing.

15020 ■ *Oregon Publisher*
Pub: Oregon Newspaper Publishers Association
Contact: LeRoy Yorgason, Publisher
E-mail: leroy@orenews.com
Ed: David Merrill, Editor, dmerrill@orenews.com. **Released:** Every other month. **Price:** Included in membership. **Description:** Covers journalism and publishing topics.

15021 ■ *Publishing Executive: Creative, Production and Work Flow at Digital Speed*
Pub: North American Publishing Co.
Contact: Ned S. Borowsky, President
URL(s): www.napco.comwww.pubexec.com. **Ed:** Brian Howard. **Released:** 10/yr.

CONSULTANTS

15022 ■ Editorial Code and Data Inc. (ECDI)
814 Wolverine Dr., Ste. 2
Walled Lake, MI 48390
Ph: (248)926-5187
Fax: (248)926-6047
Co. E-mail: monique.magee@gmail.com
URL: http://www.marketsize.com
Contact: Monique D. Magee, President
E-mail: monique@marketsize.com
Scope: Provider of data and computer services primarily to the publishing industry, with specialization in statistical data drawn from government sources. Services include data acquisition, analysis, formatting, and typesetting, archiving of computer data on CD-ROM, custom data display, search, and printing software, information brokering services, and related services such as design, writing, and data processing design. Industries served: publishing, in-house printing, non-profit organizations, government agencies, utilities, and manufacturing. **Founded:** 1990. **Publications:** "Market Share Reporter"; "Encyclopedia of Products & Industries"; "Economic Indicators Handbook"; "American Salaries and Wages Survey"; "Dun and Bradstreet & Gale: Industrial Handbook"; "Reference American Cost of Living Survey".

15023 ■ Heidelberg Graphics (HG)
2 Stansbury Ct.
Chico, CA 95928
Ph: (530)342-6582
Fax: (530)342-6582
Co. E-mail: service@heidelberggraphics.com
URL: http://www.heidelberggraphics.com
Contact: Jennifer Rowe, Manager
Description: Description: Publishes books on fiction, poetry, biography and history. Reaches market through Internet, direct mail, reviews and listings and wholesalers and distributors. Does not accept unsolicited manuscripts. **Scope:** Offers services including scans, disc conversions, layouts, editing and printing for books, catalogs and magazines. Provides the codes on paper, disk, film, embedded in designs, or in variable labeling and personalized printing. Serves private industries as well as government agencies. **Founded:** 1972. **Publications:** "Chronicles of the Clandestine Knights: Hyacinth Blue," 2003; "A Book of Thoughts II," 2001; "Historic Shot Glasses: The pre-Prohibition," 1992; "After the War," 1981; "Phantasm," 1980.

15024 ■ Moseley Associates Inc.
6 Bart Bull Rd.
Middletown, NY 10941
Ph: (845)673-5955
Co. E-mail: pwadams@consultmoseley.com
URL: http://www.consultmoseley.com
Contact: Peter W. Adams, President
E-mail: pwadams@consultmoseley.com
Scope: Provider of management consulting services. It is also engaged in appraisals of books, magazines, and learning materials. **Founded:** 1971. **Publications:** "Is This the End of Publishing? As We Know It," Jun, 2007; "US School Publishing," Apr, 2001; "A Century of Progress," Jun, 2006; "Technology in Publishing: A Century of Progress," Against the Grain, May, 2001; "Why I Don't Read Electronic Journals: An Iconoclast Speaks Out," Sep, 1997; "Post-Traumatic Shock Syndrome, Or, Surviving the Merger," Jun, 2009; "Familiar and Unfamiliar Quotations," Apr, 2009.

15025 ■ Stillman H. Publishers Inc.
21405 Woodchuck Ln.
Boca Raton, FL 33428
Ph: (561)482-6343
Contact: Herbert Stillman, President
Scope: Offers consulting services in the following areas: management, start ups, profit maximization, world wide negotiating, interim management, corporate debt resolution. **Founded:** 1984.

FRANCHISES AND BUSINESS OPPORTUNITIES

15026 ■ Coffee News
Coffee News USA, Inc.
120 Linden St.
Bangor, ME 04402-8444

Ph: (207)941-0860
Fax: (207)941-1050
Co. E-mail: bill@coffeenews.com
URL: http://www.coffeenewsusa.com
Description: Weekly publication for distribution in coffee shops and restaurants. **No. of Franchise Units:** 1,005. **Founded:** 1988. **Franchised:** 1995. **Equity Capital Needed:** $6,000 per franchise, plus a one-time training fee of $2,500 for first franchise. **Franchise Fee:** $8,500. **Training:** Quarterly training sessions, open to all franchisees and personal mentor program.

15027 ■ Disciple's Directory, Inc.
PO Box 100
Wilmington, MA 01887
Ph: (800)696-2344
Fax: (978)657-5411
Description: Church telephone directories. **No. of Franchise Units:** 6. **No. of Company-Owned Units:** 2. **Founded:** 1984. **Franchised:** 1998. **Equity Capital Needed:** $7,500. **Franchise Fee:** $7,500. **Financial Assistance:** Yes. **Training:** Yes.

15028 ■ My City Daily
9333 N Meridian St., Ste. 115
Indianapolis, IN 46260
Ph: (317)571-1525
Description: Local daily newsletter. **No. of Franchise Units:** 3. **No. of Company-Owned Units:** 1. **Founded:** 2006. **Franchised:** 2006. **Equity Capital Needed:** $74,200. **Franchise Fee:** $22,900. **Royalty Fee:** None. **Training:** Provides 4 days training at headquarters, 3 days at franchisee's location and ongoing support.

COMPUTERIZED DATABASES

15029 ■ *Daily Brief Services*
5 Alfred St.
Oxford OX1 4EH, United Kingdom
Ph: 1865 261600
Fax: 1865 242018
URL: http://www.oxan.com
Availability: Online: Oxford Analytica Ltd. **Type:** Full-text.

15030 ■ *Oxbridge Directory of Newsletters*
186 5th Ave.
New York, NY 10010
Ph: (212)741-0231
Free: 800-955-0231
Fax: (212)633-2938
Co. E-mail: info@oxbridge.com
URL: http://www.oxbridge.com
Contact: Patricia Hagood, President
Availability: CD-ROM: Oxbridge Communications Inc. **Type:** Directory.

Novelty Items Business

ASSOCIATIONS AND OTHER ORGANIZATIONS

15031 ■ Toy Industry Association (TIA)
1115 Broadway, Ste. 400
New York, NY 10010
Ph: (212)675-1141
Free: 888-884-TOYS
Fax: (212)633-1429
Co. E-mail: info@toyassociation.org
URL: http://www.toyassociation.org
Contact: Soren Torp Laursen, Chairman
URL(s): www.toy-tia.org. **Description:** Provides business services to U.S. manufacturers and importers of toys. Manages American International Toy Fair; represents the industry before Federal, State and Local government on issues of importance; provides legal and legislative counsel; conducts educational programs; compiles industry statistics. **Founded:** 1916. **Publications:** ToyInfo.org; American International Toy Fair Official Directory (Annual); Toy Challenges and Opportunities (Annual); The Official American International Toy Fair Directory (Annual). **Educational Activities:** Toy Fair '13 (Annual); American International Toy Fair (Annual). **Awards:** Toy of the Year (Annual).

SOURCES OF SUPPLY

15032 ■ Souvenirs, Gifts & Novelties Magazine--Buyer's Guide Issue
Kane Communications Inc.
Contact: Scott Borowsky, Editor
E-mail: scborowsky@kanec.com
URL(s): www.sgnmag.com. **Released:** 8/year. **Price:** $40, U.S. (one year); $50, Individuals (one year), foreign and Canadian rate. **Publication includes:** List of 1,000 manufacturers, wholesalers, and importers of souvenirs, gifts, apparel, toys, jewelry novelty, and candle items. **Entries include:** Company name, address, phone, products, whether firm is manufacturer, wholesaler, or importer. **Arrangement:** Classified by product. **Indexes:** Alphabetical.

TRADE PERIODICALS

15033 ■ The Toy Book
Pub: Adventure Publishing Group Inc.
URL(s): www.adventurepublishinggroup.com/ap-toy-book.html. **Released:** Monthly **Price:** $48, Individuals; $200, Other countries airmail only; $80, Two years; $56, Canada and Mexico; $100, Individuals 3 years.

VIDEOCASSETTES/AUDIOCASSETTES

15034 ■ Gift and Bazaar Projects, Part 2
RMI Media
1365 N. Winchester St.
Olathe, KS 66061-5880
Ph: (913)768-1696
Free: 800-745-5480
Fax: (800)755-6910
Co. E-mail: actmedia@act.org
URL: http://www.actmedia.com
Released: 1981. **Description:** Lee Maher shows how to make fun items and novelties, including kitchen witches, woven fabric baskets, decorated kitchen brooms and other imaginative creations. **Availability:** VHS; 3/4 U; Special order formats.

TRADE SHOWS AND CONVENTIONS

15035 ■ Boston Gift Show
Urban Expositions
1395 S. Marietta Pkwy., Bldg. 400, Ste. 210
Marietta, GA 30067
Ph: (678)285-3976
Free: 800-318-2238
URL(s): www.bostongiftshow.com/. **Frequency:** Annual. **Audience:** Specialty and department store retailers, importer/export firms, distributors, gift shops, mail-order/catalog, houses and boutique. **Principal Exhibits:** Stationery, gourmet products and foods, toys, general gifts, floral items, decorative and personal accessories, souvenirs, jewelry, traditional and contemporary crafts, and tabletop items. Features Handmade and Made in New England sections. **Dates and Locations:** Bayside Expo Center.

15036 ■ International Association of Fairs and Expositions Trade Show
International Association of Fairs and Expositions (IAFE)
3043 E. Cairo St.
Springfield, MO 65802
Ph: (417)862-5771
Free: 800-516-0313
Fax: (417)862-0156
Co. E-mail: iafe@fairsandexpos.com
URL: http://www.fairsandexpos.com
Contact: Jim Tucker, Chief Executive Officer
E-mail: jimt@fairsandexpos.com
URL(s): www.fairsandexpos.com. **Frequency:** Annual. **Audience:** Fair managers, staffs, and board members; carnival owners and staffs; concessionaires; talent and other agencies related to the fair industry. **Principal Exhibits:** Talent agencies, concessionaires, novelties, amusement devices, insurance, ribbons, plaques, attractions, and equipment. Products and services for the fair industry. **Dates and Locations:** , Hilton Hotel. **Telecommunication Services:** iafe@fairsandexpos.com.

FRANCHISES AND BUSINESS OPPORTUNITIES

15037 ■ Precious Prints Baby Art, Inc.
20 Stonepath Cres.
Stittsville, ON, Canada K2S 1S4
Ph: (613)599-7999
Free: 866-907-7999
Co. E-mail: info@preciousprints.ca
URL: http://www.preciousprints.ca
Description: Precious Prints Baby Art creates lasting memories for new parents and grandparents in a unique and wonderful way. Precious Prints are three dimensional impressions of baby's and children's hands and feet in all their tiny perfection. We are offering turn-key franchises; perfect for a stay-at-home parent, or retired couple. **No. of Franchise Units:** 2. **No. of Company-Owned Units:** 1. **Founded:** 2004. **Franchised:** 2007. **Equity Capital Needed:** $15,500. **Training:** 3 days mandatory training in Ottawa.

15038 ■ Watch It! Inc.
10544B-82 Ave.
Edmonton, AB, Canada T6E 2A4
Ph: (780)435-2824
Free: 877-404-2824
Fax: (780)434-5039
Co. E-mail: partner@watchit.ca
URL: http://www.watchit.ca
Description: Watch It! Is a cool and funky retail boutique that offers a wide selection of premium brand name watches, sunglasses and accessories. With its trademarked names, a consistent look and feel across stores, low start-up costs and operating procedures that are polished and efficient, purchasing a Watch It franchise is a sensible investment. **No. of Franchise Units:** 17. **No. of Company-Owned Units:** 7. **Founded:** 1999.. **Franchised:** 2004. **Equity Capital Needed:** $200,000-$400,000. **Franchise Fee:** $25,000. **Training:** Yes.

LIBRARIES

15039 ■ Haystack Mountain School of Crafts Library
PO Box 518
Deer Isle, ME 04627-0518
Ph: (207)348-2306
Fax: (207)348-2307
Co. E-mail: haystack@haystack-mtn.org
URL: http://www.haystack-mtn.org/
Contact: Lissa Hunter, President
Scope: Fine arts, ceramics, weaving, glassblowing, flat glass, jewelry, surface and textile design, wood, blacksmithing, printmaking, papermaking, weaving. **Services:** Library open to the public on a limited basis. **Holdings:** 1000 books. **Subscriptions:** 20 journals and other serials.

15040 ■ Museum of Contemporary Craft Library
724 NW Davis St.
Portland, OR 97209
Ph: (503)223-2654
Fax: (503)223-0190
Co. E-mail: info@museumofcontemporarycraft.org
URL: http://www.museumofcontemporarycraft.org/
Contact: Linda Brower, Treasurer
Scope: Ceramics and pottery, weaving and textiles, Pacific Northwest craftsmen, contemporary designers, metalwork and jewelry, contemporary glass, sculpture, woodworking, architecture. **Services:**

Library open during Museum hours. **Founded:** 1937. **Holdings:** 420 books; 74 bound and 125 unbound periodical volumes. **Telecommunication Services:** nnathan@museumofcontemporarycraft.org.

START-UP INFORMATION

15041 ■ *"Bond Hill Cinema Site To See New Life" in Business Courier (Vol. 27, October 29, 2010, No. 26, pp. 1)*
Pub: Business Courier
Ed: Dan Monk. **Description:** Avondale, Ohio's Corinthian Baptist Church will redevelop the 30-acre former Showcase Cinema property to a mixed-use site that could feature a college, senior home, and retail. Corinthian Baptist, which is one of the largest African-American churches in the region, is also planning to relocate the church.

15042 ■ *How to Start a Home-Based Senior Care Business: Develop a Winning Business Plan*
Pub: Globe Pequot Press
Ed: James L. Ferry. **Released:** January 10, 2010. **Price:** $18.95. **Description:** Everything needed to know in order to start and run a profitable, ethical, and satisfying senior care business from your home. Information covers writing a good business plan, marketing services to families, creating a fee structure, and developing a network of trusted caregivers and service providers.

ASSOCIATIONS AND OTHER ORGANIZATIONS

15043 ■ **American College of Health Care Administrators (ACHCA)**
1321 Duke St., Ste. 400
Alexandria, VA 22314
Ph: (202)536-5120
Free: 888-882-2422
Fax: (866)874-1585
Co. E-mail: mgrachek@achca.org
URL: http://www.achca.org
Contact: Marianna Kern Grachek, President
Description: Persons actively engaged in the administration of long-term care facilities, such as nursing homes, retirement communities, assisted living facilities, and sub-acute care programs. Administers professional certification programs for assisted living, sub-acute and nursing home administrators. Works to elevate the standards in the field and to develop and promote a code of ethics and standards of education and training. Seeks to inform allied professions and the public that good administration of long-term care facilities calls for special formal academic training and experience. Encourages research in all aspects of geriatrics, the chronically ill, and administration. Maintains placement service. Holds special education programs; facilitates networking among administrators. **Scope:** long-term care administration, geriatrics, gerontology. **Founded:** 1962. **Subscriptions:** 500 books papers periodicals. **Publications:** *ACHCA E-News* (Biweekly); *Balance: The Source for Administrators in Long-Term Health Care*; *Continuum*. **Educational Activities:** Winter Marketplace (Annual); ACHCA Annual Winter Marketplace (Annual); American College of Health Care Administrators (Annual). **Awards:** Distinguished

Administrator Award (Annual); Education Award (Annual); Journalism Award (Annual); New Administrator Award (Annual); Richard L. Thorpe Fellowship (Annual); Abbott Nutrition Award for Distinguished Service to ACHCA (Annual); Phillip McConnell Student Scholarship Fund (Annual). **Telecommunication Services:** mtn@achca.org; meetings@achca.org; info@achca.org.

15044 ■ **American Health Care Association (AHCA)**
1201 L St. NW
Washington, DC 20005
Ph: (202)842-4444
Free: 800-321-0343
Fax: (202)842-3860
Co. E-mail: hr@ahca.org
URL: http://www.ahcancal.org/Pages/Default.aspx
Contact: Mark Parkinson, President
Description: Federation of state associations of long-term health care facilities. Promotes standards for professionals in long-term health care delivery and quality care for patients and residents in a safe environment. Focuses on issues of availability, quality, affordability, and fair payment. Operates as liaison with governmental agencies, Congress, and professional associations. Compiles statistics. **Scope:** long-term care, nursing facilities, assisted living, subacute care. **Services:** Interlibrary loan; copying; Library open to the public with restrictions by appointment. **Founded:** 1949. **Holdings:** 5000 volumes. **Subscriptions:** audiovisuals books clippings monographs periodicals; 100 journals and other serials. **Publications:** *Caring for Someone with Alzheimer's*; *Tips on Visiting Friends and Relatives*; *Family Questions: The First Thirty Days*; *Making the Transition to Nursing Facility Life*; *Paying for Long Term Care*; *Glossary of Terms*; *Advice for Families*; *Coping with the Transition*; *Capitol Connection*; *NCAL Focus*; *AHCA Notes* (Monthly); *American Health Care Association: Provider*; *Choosing a Nursing Home*; *Having Your Say: Advance Directives*; *Understanding Long Term Care Insurance*; *NCAL Connections*; *Assessing Your Needs: Consumer Guides to Nursing and Assisted Living Facilities*; *Living in a Nursing Home: Myths and Realities*; *Moving Into an Assisted Living Residence: Making a Successful Transition*; *Advance Preparation: Having the Conversation About Long Term Care*; *Talking To Your Loved Ones About Their Care*; *Provider: For Long Term Care Professionals* (Monthly); *Provider--LTC Buyers' Guide Issue* (Annual); *Choosing An Assisted Living Residence: A Consumer's Guide*; *Assisted Living State Regulatory Review*; *Resident Assistant Newsletter*. **Educational Activities:** American Health Care Association Annual Convention and Exposition (Annual). **Awards:** Adult Volunteer of the Year; Group Volunteer of the Year; AHCA/NCAL Quality Award (Annual); James Durante Nurse Scholarship (Annual); Young Adult Volunteer of the Year Award. **Telecommunication Services:** webmaster@ahca.org.

15045 ■ **American Hospital Association (AHA)**
155 N Wacker Dr.
Chicago, IL 60606

Ph: (312)422-3000
Free: 800-242-2626
Fax: (312)422-4796
Co. E-mail: rich@aha.org
URL: http://www.aha.org
Contact: Richard Umbdenstock, President
E-mail: rwade@aha.org
URL(s): www.aha.org/research/rc/index.shtml, americanhospitalassociation.com, www.aha.org/aha/. **Description:** Represents health care provider organizations. Seeks to advance the health of individuals and communities. Leads, represents, and serves health care provider organizations that are accountable to the community and committed to health improvement. **Scope:** Administration, planning, and financing of healthcare facilities; administrative aspects of medical, nursing, paramedical, and prepayment fields. **Services:** Interlibrary loan (fee); copying; center open to the public for reference use only (access fee for non-members). **Founded:** 1898. **Holdings:** Advocacy reports, news articles, regulatory information, products and services.; 66,000 volumes. **Subscriptions:** ; 100 journals and other serials. **Publications:** *Coding Clinic for ICD-9-CM*; *Healthcare QuickDisc*; *Guide to the Health Care Field* (Annual); *Hospital Statistics* (Annual); *Hospitals and Health Networks* (Monthly); *American Hospital Association--Ambulatory Outreach*; *AHA News Now* (Daily); *AHA Guide to the Health Care Field* (Annual); *AHA Integrated Delivery Network Directory: U.S. Health Care Systems, Networks, and Alliances*; *AHA Directory of Health Care Professionals*; *Directory of Planning and Design Professionals for Health Facilities* (Annual); *American Hospital Association--Guide to the Health Care Field* (Annual). **Awards:** Hospital Awards for Volunteer Excellence; Award of Honor; Distinguished Service Award; Honorary Life Membership; Justin Ford Kimball Innovators Award; Board of Trustees Award; Federal Health Care Executive Special Achievement Award. **Telecommunication Services:** rwade@aha.org; storeservice@aha.org; hbaumann@aha.org; rc@aha.org.

15046 ■ **American Medical Directors Association (AMDA)**
11000 Broken Land Pkwy., Ste. 400
Columbia, MD 21044
Ph: (410)740-9743
Free: 800-876-2632
Fax: (410)740-4572
Co. E-mail: info@amda.com
URL: http://www.amda.com
Contact: Lorraine Tarnove, Executive Director
Description: Physicians providing care in long-term facilities including nursing homes. Sponsors continuing medical education in geriatrics and medical administration. Promotes improved long-term care. **Scope:** long-term care and geriatrics, medical administration. **Founded:** 1975. **Subscriptions:** archival material audiovisuals books clippings periodicals. **Publications:** *Caring for the Ages* (Monthly); *JAMDA* (9/year); *State Network News* (Quarterly). **Educational Activities:** AMDA Long Term Care Medicine (Annual).

15047 ■ **American Seniors Housing Association (ASHA)**
5225 Wisconsin Ave. NW, Ste. 502
Washington, DC 20015

Ph: (202)237-0900
Fax: (202)237-1616
URL: http://www.seniorshousing.org
Contact: William D. Pettit, Chairman
Description: Members are engaged in all aspects of the development and operation of housing for older adults, including construction, finance, and management of the housing. Represents the interests of firms participating in seniors housing and has played an integral role in seniors housing advocacy. Focuses on long-term care policy, state regulations, and other issues concerned with this topic. **Founded:** 1991. **Publications:** *The Seniors Housing Construction Trends Report*; *Seniors Housing Legal Notes*; *Seniors Housing Research Notes*; *Seniors Housing Statistical Handbook*; *Seniors Housing Update*. **Educational Activities:** American Seniors Housing Association Board meeting; American Seniors Housing Association Meeting (Annual).

15048 ■ Assisted Living Federation of America (ALFA)
1650 King St., Ste. 602
Alexandria, VA 22314-2747
Ph: (703)894-1805
Fax: (703)894-1831
Co. E-mail: rgrimes@alfa.org
URL: http://www.alfa.org
Contact: Richard Grimes, President
Description: Providers of assisted living, state associations of providers, and others interested or involved in the industry. Promotes the interests of the assisted living industry and works to enhance the quality of life for the population it serves. Provides a forum for assisted living providers to unite, exchange information, and interact. Encourages the development of high standards for the industry. Promotes the concept of assisted living facilities with public and private agencies and other professionals. Works to educate providers and the public and increase national awareness of assisted living. Sponsors speakers' bureau, conferences, educational opportunities, trade show, research & training products. **Founded:** 1990. **Publications:** *ALFA Alert* (Weekly); *Assisted Living Executive* (9/year); *Guide to Choosing an Assisted Living Residence*; *ALFA Executive Portfolio: Inside the Minds of the Leaders in Assisted Living and Senior Housing*. **Awards:** Hero Awards (Annual); Pioneer Award (Annual); Best of Home Architectural Design Award (Annual).

15049 ■ Association of Jewish Aging Services
316 Pennsylvania Ave. SE, Ste. 402
Washington, DC 20003-1172
Ph: (202)543-7500
Fax: (202)543-4090
Co. E-mail: info@ajas.org
URL: http://www.ajas.org
Contact: Martin Goetz, Chairman
Description: Represents charitable Jewish homes and nursing homes; retirement and housing units; independent and assisted living, geriatric hospitals, and special facilities for Jewish aged and chronically ill. Conducts institutes and conferences; undertakes legislative activities; compiles statistics. Conducts studies and maintains demographic and other information on Jewish aging. Publishes journals and periodicals on aging. **Publications:** *Journal on Jewish Aging* (Semiannual); *Directory of Jewish Homes and Housing for the Aged in the United States and Canada* (Biennial). **Awards:** Jewish Programming Award; Trustee of the Year Award; Professional Award; Award of Honor (Annual); Humanitarian Award (Annual); Jewish Programming Award (Annual); Mentor of the Year (Annual); Professional Award (Annual); Trustee of the Year (Annual); Young Executive Award (Annual); Dr. Herbert Shore Award of Honor.

15050 ■ Beverly Foundation (BF)
1120 Pennsylvania St. NE
Albuquerque, NM 87110
Ph: (505)222-0620
Co. E-mail: info@beverlyfoundation.org
URL: http://www.beverlyfoundation.org
Contact: Don Pearson, Chairman
Description: Aims to enhance the quality of life and care until the last moment of life, thus bettering the well being of older adults, their caregivers, and their

families. Engages in research, education and demonstration. Addresses special concerns through programs such as: mobility and transportation within the community; service delivery and care support within institutional and home settings; life enrichment of the body, mind, and spirit for those who live independently and in institutions. Provides technical and informational assistance to professionals, caregivers, and families. Influences other organizations and groups through communication, collaboration, and limited financial support to program partners. Funds activities through efficient use of its own resources and the contributions of others. **Founded:** 1979. **Awards:** STAR Award for Excellence (Annual).

15051 ■ Center for the Study of Aging of Albany (CSA)—International Association of Physical Activity
c/o HarrisCom Group
676 Huron Ave., Ste. 53
Cambridge, MA 02138
Ph: (617)576-0906
Co. E-mail: harrison@comcast.net
URL: http://www.centerforthestudyofaging.org
Contact: Anita M. Harris, Founder
URL(s): harriscom.com. **Description:** Participants include behavioral scientists, educators, gerontologists, physicians, and other health professionals. Promotes education, research, and training; provides leadership in the field of health and fitness for older people. Includes: programs for volunteers and professionals in aging, gerontology, geriatrics, wellness, physical fitness, and mental health; consultant services include adult day care, nutrition, physical and mental fitness, nursing home, housing, and retirement; speakers' bureau. Develops national and international conferences on health, fitness, and prevention. Provides expert assistance in research, institutional and community program development, planning, and organization; offers consultation addressing the development of library resource centers and collections of books on aging. Conducts seminars and offers information and referral services. **Founded:** 1957.

15052 ■ Foundation Aiding the Elderly (FATE)
PO Box 254849
Sacramento, CA 95865-4849
Ph: (916)481-8558
Free: 877-481-8558
Fax: (916)481-2239
Co. E-mail: caroleh@4fate.org
URL: http://www.4fate.org
Contact: Carole Herman, President
Description: Assists the public with relatives and friends in long-term care nursing homes. Provides awareness of the existence of, and potential for, abuse, neglect, and lack of dignity of the elderly in nursing homes. Initiates action to make improvements. Raises funds to bring about nursing home reform. Offers referrals for senior issues and advocates for legislation. **Founded:** 1982.

15053 ■ Health Industry Distributors Association (HIDA)
310 Montgomery St.
Alexandria, VA 22314-1516
Ph: (703)549-4432
Free: 800-549-4432
Fax: (703)549-6495
Co. E-mail: muller@hida.org
URL: http://www.hida.org
Contact: Andrea Logan, Chairman
Description: Represents distributors of medical, laboratory, surgical, and other health care equipment and supplies to hospitals, physicians, nursing homes, and industrial medical departments. Conducts sales training, management seminars, and research through the HIDA Educational Foundation. **Founded:** 1902. **Publications:** *HIDA--Membership Directory and Buyer's Guide*. **Educational Activities:** Health Industry Distributors Association Trade Show and Education Forum (Annual); Streamlining Healthcare Conference (Annual). **Awards:** Exhibit of the Year (Annual); Frank M. Rhatigan Award (Annual); Manufacturer Excellence in Service Award (Annual); Product of the Year (Annual); Repertoire/HIDA Excel-

lence in Sales Awards (Annual); Sales Promotion of the Year (Annual); Industry Award of Distinction. **Telecommunication Services:** rowan@hida.org.

15054 ■ LeadingAge
2519 Connecticut Ave. NW
Washington, DC 20008-1520
Ph: (202)783-2242
Fax: (202)783-2255
Co. E-mail: info@leadingage.org
URL: http://www.leadingage.org
Contact: William L. Minnix, Jr., President
Description: Works to advance the vision of healthy, affordable and ethical aging services for America. Represents 5,600 mission-driven, not-for-profit nursing homes, continuing care retirement communities, assisted living and senior housing facilities, and community service organizations throughout the U.S. **Founded:** 1961. **Publications:** *Aging Services: The Not-for-Profit Difference*; *FutureAge* (Bimonthly); *HCBS Report* (Monthly); *Savings and Solutions* (Bimonthly); *The Consumer's Directory of Continuing Care Retirement Communities*; *American Association of Homes for the Aging--Directory of Consulting Firms*; *American Association of Homes and Services for the Aging--Directory of Members* (Biennial). **Educational Activities:** Future of Aging Services (Semiannual); American Association of Homes and Services for the Aging Convention (Annual). **Awards:** Award of Honor; Chair's Citation; Innovation of the Year Awards; Hobart Jackson Cultural Diversity Award; Meritorious Service Award; Trustee of the Year Award; Distinguished Service Award; Community Service Award; Award of Honor (Annual); Dr. Herbert Shore Outstanding Mentor Award (Annual); Excellence in Leadership Award (Annual); Hobart Jackson Cultural Diversity Award (Annual).

15055 ■ National Association of Boards of Examiners of Long Term Care Administrators (NAB)
1444 I St. NW, No. 700
Washington, DC 20005-6542
Ph: (202)712-9040
Co. E-mail: nab@nabweb.org
URL: http://www.nabweb.org
Contact: Randy Lindner, President
Description: State boards responsible for licensing nursing homes administrators. Produces exam to test the competence of nursing home administrators; operates continuing education review service; disseminates information and educational materials on nursing home administration. **Founded:** 1972. **Publications:** *NAB/AIT Preceptor's Domains of Practice Internship Manual*; *NAB Study Guide: How To Prepare For the Nursing Home Administrators Examination*; *RC/AL AIT Preceptor's Domains of Practice Internship Manual*; *RC/AL Study Guide: How to Prepare for the Residential Care/Assisted Living Administrators Examination*. **Educational Activities:** Mid-Year Meeting (Annual).

15056 ■ National Association of Directors of Nursing Administration in Long Term Care (NADONA/LTC)
Reed Hartman Tower
11353 Reed Hartman Hwy., Ste. 210
Cincinnati, OH 45241
Ph: (513)791-3679
Free: 800-222-0539
Fax: (513)791-3699
Co. E-mail: rarnicar@comcast.net
URL: http://www.nadona.org
Contact: Robin Arnicar, President
Description: Directors, assistant directors, and former directors of nursing in long term care. Aims are: to create and establish an acceptable ethical standard for practices in long term care nursing administration and to promote and encourage research in the profession; to develop and provide a consistent program of education and certification for the positions of director, associate director, and assistant director; to promote a positive image of the long-term health care industry. Encourages members to share concerns and experiences; sponsors research programs. Advocates legislation pertaining to the practice of professional nursing. Maintains speakers' bureau. **Scope:** long term care, clinical nursing.

Founded: 1986. **Subscriptions:** 1150. **Awards:** Above and Beyond (Annual); Caring (Annual); Nursing Administrator of the Year (Annual); Upward Bound (Annual).

15057 ■ National Association of Professional Geriatric Care Managers (NAPGCM)
3275 W Ina Rd., Ste. 130
Tucson, AZ 85741-2198
Ph: (520)881-8008
Fax: (520)325-7925
Co. E-mail: kboothroyd@napgcm.org
URL: http://www.caremanager.org
Contact: Kaaren Boothroyd, Executive Director
E-mail: kboothroyd@napgcm.org
Description: Promotes quality services and care for elderly citizens. Provides referral service and distributes information to individuals interested in geriatric care management. Maintains referral network. **Founded:** 1986. **Publications:** *GCM Journal* (Quarterly); *Inside GCM* (Quarterly); *National Association of Professional Geriatric Care Managers-- Membership Directory*. **Educational Activities:** National Association of Professional Geriatric Care Managers Conference (Annual). **Awards:** Adell Elkind Award (Annual).

15058 ■ National Association of State United for Aging and Disabilities (NASUAD)
1201 15th St. NW, Ste. 350
Washington, DC 20005
Ph: (202)898-2578
Fax: (202)898-2583
Co. E-mail: info@nasuad.org
URL: http://www.nasuad.org
Contact: Lance Robertson, President
Description: Public interest organization that provides information, technical assistance, and professional development support to State Units on Aging. (A state unit is an agency of state government designated by the governor and state legislature to administer the Older Americans Act and to serve as a focal point for all matters relating to older people.) Serves as organized channel for officially designated state leadership in aging to exchange information and mutual experiences, and to join together for appropriate action on behalf of the elderly. Services include: information on federal policy and program developments in aging; training and technical assistance on a wide range of program and management issues; liaison with organizations representing the public and private sectors. **Founded:** 1964.

15059 ■ National Citizens' Coalition for Nursing Home Reform (NCCNHR)
1828 L St. NW, Ste. 801
Washington, DC 20036
Ph: (202)332-2275
Fax: (202)332-2949
Co. E-mail: info@nccnhr.org
Contact: Norma Harrison Atteberry, President
E-mail: normahatt@aol.com
Description: National, state and local consumer/ citizen groups and individuals seeking nursing home and board and care reform. Seeks to provide a consumer voice at the national, state, and local levels in the development and implementation of the long-term care system. Provides a platform through which groups can keep informed of current movements for change and can make their views known. Conducts seminars and training programs and utilizes a speakers' bureau consisting of advocates from around the country. Serves as a clearinghouse for information on nursing home and board care issues, and publishes consumer books and pamphlets. Maintains speakers' bureau; conducts research and advocacy programs. **Founded:** 1975. **Publications:** *Avoiding Physical Restraint Use: New Standards in Care*; *Nursing Home Staffing: A Guide for Residents, Families, Friends, and Caregivers*; *Piecing Together Quality Long-Term Care: A Consumer's Guide to Choices and Advocacy*; *Quality Care Advocate* (Quarterly); *Where Do I Go From Here A Guide for Nursing Home Residents, Families, and Friends a Consulting on Attorney*; *Nursing Homes: Getting Good Care There* (Bimonthly).

15060 ■ National Institute on Community-Based Long-Term Care (NICLC)
National Council on Aging
1901 L St. NW, 4th Fl.
Washington, DC 20036
Ph: (202)479-1200
Fax: (202)479-0735
Co. E-mail: cha@ncoa.org
URL: http://www.ncoa.org/strengthening-community-organizations
Description: Serves as a unit of the National Council on Aging. Seeks to promote a comprehensive long-term care system that will integrate home-and community-based services, enabling older adults to live in their own homes as long as it is medically, socially, and economically feasible. Serves as information clearinghouse for long-term care professionals. Advocates public policies that support home and community-based services. Maintains speakers' bureau; offers educational sessions; compiles statistics. **Founded:** 1984. **Publications:** *NCOA Networks* (Bimonthly); *NICLC Perspective on Aging* (Periodic); *Care Management Standards*. **Awards:** Claude Pepper Award for Excellence in Community-Based Long-Term Care (Annual).

15061 ■ New England Gerontological Association (NEGA)
1 Cutts Rd.
Durham, NH 03824
Ph: (603)868-5757
Co. E-mail: info@negaonline.org
URL: http://www.negaonline.org
Contact: Dr. Eugene E. Tillock, Executive Director
Description: Promotes the study of the aging process. Conducts educational programs in aging, health service administration and long-term care administration. Computer Assisted Home Study Programs for CEU credits are made available. **Scope:** aging, long-term care. **Founded:** 1958. **Subscriptions:** 500 books periodicals.

REFERENCE WORKS

15062 ■ "$20M Aimed at Affordable Los Angeles Seniors Housing" in Commercial Property News (March 17, 2008)
Pub: Nielsen Company
Description: Grand Plaza Apartments in Los Angeles, California will be renovated in order to maintain housing for over 400 low-income seniors. Details of plans are included.

15063 ■ "Advancing the Ball" in Inside Healthcare (Vol. 6, December 2010, No. 7, pp. 31)
Pub: RedCoat Publishing Inc.
Ed: Michelle McNickle. **Description:** Profile of Medicalodges an elder-care specialty company that provides both patient care and technology development. President and CEO of the firm believes that hiring good employees is key to growth for any small business.

15064 ■ "Analysts Not Too Sad Over Gemunder" in Business Courier (Vol. 27, August 6, 2010, No. 14, pp. 1)
Pub: Business Courier
Ed: James Ritchie. **Description:** Analysts and investors do not understand why Omnicare chief executive officer (CEO) Joel Gemunder suddenly retired after nearly thirty years with the Covington, Kentucky company. They believe that new leadership might invigorate the firm, which provides pharmacy and related services to the long-term care industry.

15065 ■ "Chemed's Vitas Aims to Acquire" in Business Courier (Vol. 27, July 9, 2010, No. 10, pp. 1)
Pub: Business Courier
Ed: James Ritchie. **Description:** Chemed Corporation's Vitas Healthcare Corporation is looking for smaller nonprofit hospices as it looks to become more streamlined in a tougher reimbursement environment. CFO David Williams syas they want to acquire these hospices as fast as they can integrate them.

15066 ■ "Connecting the Dots Between Wellness and Elder Care" in Benefits and Compensation Digest (Vol. 47, August 2010, No. 8, pp. 18)
Pub: International Foundation of Employee Benefit Plans
Contact: Richard Lyall, President
Ed: Sandra Timmermann. **Description:** Employees caring for aged and infirm parents deal with time and financial issues and other stresses. The connection between health status of caregivers and employers' health care costs could be aided by linking programs and benefits with wellness and caregiving.

15067 ■ "Domestic Workers Organize!" in WorkingUSA (Vol. 11, December 2008, No. 4, pp. 413)
Pub: Blackwell Publishers Ltd.
Ed: Eileen Boris, Premilla Nadasen. **Description:** History of domestic workers in the U.S. is examined. The article challenges the long-standing assumption that these, primarily women of color cleaners, nannies, and elder care providers are unable to organize and assesses the possibilities and limitations of recent organizing efforts. The nature of the occupation, its location in the home, the isolated character of the work, informal arrangements with employers, and exclusions from labor law protection, has fostered community-based, social movement organizing to build coalitions, reform legislation and draw public attention to the plight of domestic workers.

15068 ■ "Elder Care Costs Surge" in National Underwriter Life & Health (Vol. 114, November 8, 2020, No. 21, pp. 25)
Pub: Summit Business Media
Ed: Trevor Thomas. **Description:** Nursing home and assisted living rates rose from 2009 to 2010, according to MetLife Mature Market Institute. Statistical data included.

15069 ■ "Elder Care, Rx Drugs Reforms Top Zoeller's Agenda" in Times (December 21, 2010)
Pub: The Times
Ed: Sarah Tompkins. **Description:** Indiana Attorney General Greg Zoeller is hoping to develop a program in the state that will help regulate care for the elderly; freeze medical licenses for doctors involved in criminal investigations; address illegal drug use; and to establish a program to help individuals dispose of old prescription medications easily at pharmacies.

15070 ■ "Elder-Care Seminar to Teach Ways to Avoid Falls" in Virginian-Pilot (November 25, 2010)
Pub: Virginian-Pilot
Ed: Amy Jeter. **Description:** ResCare HomeCare, a home health services firm, offers free seminars on helping to make residences safer for seniors prone to falling.

15071 ■ "EVMS Gets Grant to Train Providers for Elder Care" in Virginian-Pilot (October 29, 2010)
Pub: Virginian-Pilot
Ed: Elizabeth Simpson. **Description:** Eastern Virginia Medical School received a federal grant to train health providers in elder care. Details of the program are provided.

15072 ■ "Face Issues if Elder Care, Unemployment Collide" in Atlanta Journal-Constitution (December 26, 2010, pp. G1)
Pub: Atlanta Journal-Constitution
Ed: Amy Lindgren. **Description:** More issues arise during holiday for families with older members requiring care, including the issue of employment for those doing the caregiving.

15073 ■ "GeckoSystems Reduces Sensor Fusion Costs Due to Elder Care Robot Trials" in Internet Wire (December 14, 2010)
Pub: Comtex
Description: GeckoSystems International Corporation has been able to reduce the cost of its sensor fusion system while maintaining reliability and performance. The firm's ongoing first in-home elder care

robot trials have sparked interest regarding its business model, technologies available for licensing, and joint domestic and international ventures.

15074 ■ *"New Elder Care Center to Focus on Residents with Failing Memories" in Tulsa World (November 30, 2010)*
Pub: World Publishing

Ed: Robert Evatt. **Description:** People with Alzheimer's disease and other mental disorders require specialized care. Constant Care Management Company runs 'memory care' centers designed for the elderly with such conditions.

15075 ■ *"Novi Eyed for $11 Million, 100-Bed Medilodge" in Crain's Detroit Business (Vol. 25, June 1, 2009, No. 22, pp. M032)*
Pub: Crain Communications Inc. - Detroit

Description: Novi, Michigan is one of the cities being considered for construction of a new 110-bed skilled nursing facility. Details of the project are included.

15076 ■ *"Nursing Home Group Put on the Block" in Globe & Mail (February 23, 2006, pp. B1)*
Pub: CTVglobemedia Publishing Inc.

Ed: Elizabeth Church. **Description:** The reasons behind the decision of Exetendicare Inc. to go for sale are presented.

15077 ■ *"Priority: Business For Sale" in Inc. (January 2008, pp. 28)*
Pub: Gruner & Jahr USA Publishing

Ed: Elaine Appleton Grant. **Description:** Profile of an employment agency providing registered nurses to hospitals and nursing homes. The company began as an temporary placement agency for IT professionals and is now for sale at the asking price of $4.2 million.

15078 ■ *Provider--LTC Buyers' Guide Issue*
Pub: American Health Care Association
Contact: Mark Parkinson, President

URL(s): www.providermagazine.com. **Released:** Annual; August; latest edition 2008. **Price:** $48, in U.S.; $61, in Canada and North America; $85, foreign; Included in membership. **Publication includes:** List of several hundred manufacturers and suppliers of products and services to the long-term care industry. **Entries include:** Company name, address, phone, products or services. **Arrangement:** Classified by product or service. **Indexes:** Product/service.

15079 ■ *"Renewed Vision" in Hawaii Business (Vol. 54, August 2008, No. 2, pp. 49)*
Pub: Hawaii Business Publishing

Ed: Jason Ubay. **Description:** Saint Francis Healthcare System of Hawaii, ranked 81 in Hawaii's top 250 companies for 2008, has been rebranding to focus on senior community healthcare and sold some of its operations, which explains the decline in gross sales from $219.5M in 2006 to $122.7M in 2007. The system's senior services and home hospice service expansion are provided.

15080 ■ *"Silver Dollars" in Small Business Opportunities (September 2008)*
Pub: Entrepreneur Media Inc.

Description: Profile of Always Best Care Senior Services, a franchise created by Michael Newman, which offers non-medical In-Home Care, Personal Emergency Response Systems, and Assisted Living Placement Services to seniors; the company offers franchisees the opportunity to fill what is oftentimes a void for the seniors and their families in the community.

15081 ■ *"Small Is Best, Says Housing Officials" in Business First Buffalo (November 16, 2007, pp. 1)*
Pub: American City Business Journals, Inc.

Ed: Tracey Drury. **Description:** Nonprofit organizations in some parts of the U.S. are moving senior citizens from larger institutions into smaller housing. The benefits of smaller housing for the elderly are evaluated.

15082 ■ *"They've Fallen, But They Can Get Up" in Barron's (Vol. 88, March 10, 2008, No. 10, pp. 43)*
Pub: Dow Jones & Company, Inc.

Ed: Kopin Tan. **Description:** Shares of senior housing companies present buying opportunities to investors because of their low prices. Companies such as Brookdale Senior Living are not as dependent on housing prices but have suffered declines in share prices.

15083 ■ *"Trisun Healthcare Eager to Add Centers" in Austin Business JournalInc. (Vol. 28, August 22, 2008, No. 23, pp. 1)*
Pub: American City Business Journals

Ed: Kate Harrington. **Description:** Austin-based nursing and rehabilitation centers operator Trisun Healthcare plans to build more facilities as part of a growth strategy that can expand beyond Texas. Trisun has 16 facilities along the corridor from San Antonio to Temple, and projects to have three more in Texas in 2008.

15084 ■ *"VA Seeking Bidders for Ft. Howard" in Baltimore Business Journal (Vol. 28, June 25, 2010, No. 7, pp. 1)*
Pub: Baltimore Business Journal

Ed: Daniel J. Sernovitz. **Description:** The Veterans Affairs Maryland Health Care Systems has requested proposals from developers to build a retirement community at Fort Howard in Baltimore County. The historic site, which has about 36 mostly vacant buildings, could become the home to hundreds of war veterans. Details of the proposed development are discussed.

STATISTICAL SOURCES

15085 ■ *RMA Annual Statement Studies*
Pub: Risk Management Association
Contact: Kevin M. Blakey, President

Released: Annual. **Price:** $175.00 2006-07 edition, $105.00. **Description:** Contains composite balance sheets and income statements for more than 360 industries, including the accounting, auditing, and bookkeeping industries. Also contains five years of comparative historical data for discerning trends. Includes 16 commonly used ratios, computed for most of the size groupings for nearly every industry.

15086 ■ *Standard & Poor's Industry Surveys*
Pub: Standard & Poor's Corp.

Released: Annual. **Price:** $3633.00. **Description:** Two-volume book that examines the prospects for specific industries, including trucking. Also provides analyses of trends and problems, statistical tables and charts, and comparative company analyses.

TRADE PERIODICALS

15087 ■ *Abbeyfield Houses Society of Canada Newsletter*
Pub: Abbeyfield Houses Society of Canada

Ed: Robert McMullan, Editor. **Released:** Quarterly. **Description:** Reports on news of Abbeyfield Houses Society of Canada, a provider of care and companionship for the elderly. Also features articles related to aging, housing, and lifestyle in Canada and internationally. Recurring features include letters to the editor, and columns titled News of Local Societies and Bits 'n Bites.

15088 ■ *Abstracts in Social Gerontology: Current Literature on Aging*
Pub: EBSCO Publishing
Contact: Tim Collins, President
E-mail: tcollins@ebscohost.com

URL(s): www.ebscohost.com/academic/abstracts-in-social-gerontology. **Released:** Quarterly **Price:** $685, Institutions print only; $179, Individuals print only; $189, Institutions single print issue; $58, Individuals single print issue.

15089 ■ *AHCA Notes*
Pub: American Health Care Association
Contact: Mark Parkinson, President

Ed: Nathan Childs, Editor, nchilds@ahca.org. **Released:** Monthly; Monthly, 12/year. **Price:** Included in membership.; included in membership dues; Included

in membership. **Description:** Presents information on nursing homes, assisted living, and residential care facilities. Covers legislation on prescription drug prices, nurse assistant training, certification enforcement, Medicare/Medicaid and long term care requirements, and legal activities.

15090 ■ *The Capsule Newsletter*
Pub: Children of Aging Parents
Contact: Lenore Sherman, Executive Director

Ed: Lorraine Sailor, Editor. **Released:** Bimonthly. **Price:** Included in membership; Free; $100. **Description:** Contains articles and informational notices on the concerns and issues of elderly persons and those who care for them. Provides organizations, resources, and services to help caregivers of elderly.

15091 ■ *Clinical Gerontologist: The Journal of Aging and Mental Health*
Pub: Routledge Journals Taylor & Francis Group

URL(s): www.tandf.co.uk/journals/WCLI. **Ed:** Dolores Gallagher-Thompson, Larry W. Thompson. **Released:** Quarterly **Price:** $140, Individuals online; $156, Individuals print + online; $970, Institutions online only; $1078, Institutions print + online.

15092 ■ *Contemporary Long Term Care*
Pub: Leisure Publications Inc.
Contact: Nancy Field, President

URL(s): www.cltcmag.com. **Released:** Monthly; 11/yr. **Price:** $80, Individuals; $95, Canada and Mexico; $130, Two years; $129, Other countries.

15093 ■ *Elderly Health Services Letter*
Pub: Health Resources Publishing
Contact: Beth-Ann Kerber, Managing Editor

Released: Monthly. **Price:** $147, individuals. **Description:** Predicts future trends in hospital based health care services for the elderly.

15094 ■ *Housing for Seniors Report*
Pub: CD Publications

Ed: Marcella Kogan, Editor. **Released:** Monthly. **Price:** $297/year. **Description:** Provides news and practical suggestions concerning the production, management, marketing and other business aspects of housing for the elderly. Coverage includes nursing homes, apartment projects, and retirement communities; also government-operated programs. Recurring features include news of research.

15095 ■ *Long Term Care: Published for the Canadian Long Term care community*
Pub: Ontario Long Term Care Association

URL(s): www.oltca.com/en/mag/index.html. **Released:** Quarterly **Price:** $15, Canada; $27, Canada two years; $21, Individuals; $33, Two years; $4.95, Single issue.

15096 ■ *Physical Medicine and Rehabilitation Clinics of North America*
Pub: Elsevier

URL(s): www.elsevier.com/wps/find/journaldescription.cws_home/623372/descrip tion#description. **Ed:** Prof. George H. Kraft. **Released:** Quarterly **Price:** $575, Institutions, other countries; $373, Other countries; $189, Students, other countries; $441, Institutions; $132, Students; $302, Canada; $248, Individuals; $575, Institutions, Canada.

15097 ■ *Quality Care Advocate*
Pub: The National Consumer Voice for Quality Long-Term Care

Released: Bimonthly. **Price:** Included in membership; $45, nonmembers. **Description:** Reports on current efforts at federal, state, and local levels to achieve better quality nursing homes and other long-term care facilities in the U.S. Discusses current legislation and regulations, summarizes current litigation proceedings and past court cases related to long term care, and evaluates the effectiveness of various direct advocacy campaigns. Recurring features include news of research and notices of publications available.

15098 ■ *Topics in Geriatric Rehabilitation (TGR)*
Pub: Lippincott Williams & Wilkins

URL(s): www.lww.com/webapp/wcs/stores/servlet/product__11851_-1_9012052_Prod -08827524. **Ed:** Carole B. Lewis. **Released:** Quarterly **Price:** $105.

49, Individuals; $395.49, Institutions; $197.73, Other countries; $536.73, Institutions, other countries; $74. 49, Individuals in-training.

VIDEOCASSETTES/ AUDIOCASSETTES

15099 ■ *Activities of Daily Living*
AJN Video Library/Lippincott Williams & Wilkins
American Journal of Nursing
345 Hudson St., 16th Fl.
New York, NY 10014
Ph: (212)886-1200
Free: 800-256-4045
Fax: (212)886-1276
Co. E-mail: info@nursingcenter.com
URL: http://www.nursingcenter.com

Released: 19??. **Price:** $285.00. **Description:** Part of the Functional Assessment of the Elderly nursing training series. Teaches methods on assessing an elderly client's functions as changed by age and pathophysiology and how to use assessment data to plan appropriate nursing interventions. Contains information on activities of daily life, including eating, ambulating, toileting, grooming, climbing stairs, shopping, keeping house, interacting with others, and traveling. Also discusses how the cardiovascular, respiratory, neuromuscular, gastrointestinal, and genitourinary systems affect daily functions. Includes study guide. Approved for CE credit. **Availability:** VHS.

15100 ■ *Activities of Daily Living*
University of Maryland
Video Press
100 N. Greene St., Ste. 300
Baltimore, MD 21201-1082
Ph: (410)706-5497
Free: 800-328-7450
Fax: (410)706-8471
Co. E-mail: videopressmail@som.umaryland.edu
URL: http://www.videopress.org

Released: 19??. **Price:** $200.00. **Description:** Part of the Restorative Care Series. Details the activities of daily living in the nursing home environment. Covers bed activities, wheelchair abilities, ambulation, elevation activities, and self-care. **Availability:** VHS.

15101 ■ *Advance Directives and the Elderly: Making Decisions about Treatment Limitations*
University of Maryland
Video Press
100 N. Greene St., Ste. 300
Baltimore, MD 21201-1082
Ph: (410)706-5497
Free: 800-328-7450
Fax: (410)706-8471
Co. E-mail: videopressmail@som.umaryland.edu
URL: http://www.videopress.org

Released: 19??. **Price:** $150.00. **Description:** Discusses with three nursing home residents their wishes to limit treatment. Covers artificial feeding, CPR, and use of antibiotics. **Availability:** VHS.

15102 ■ *Agitation, Aggression and Violence*
University of Maryland
Video Press
100 N. Greene St., Ste. 300
Baltimore, MD 21201-1082
Ph: (410)706-5497
Free: 800-328-7450
Fax: (410)706-8471
Co. E-mail: videopressmail@som.umaryland.edu
URL: http://www.videopress.org

Released: 19??. **Price:** $150.00. **Description:** Part of the Nursing Home Mental Health Series. Details verbal and physical aggression in the nursing home, outlining an approach that stresses proper assessment, early recognition, specific interventions, and avoidance of future episodes. **Availability:** VHS.

15103 ■ *Alleviating Stress Associated with Nursing Home Admission*
University of Maryland
Video Press
100 N. Greene St., Ste. 300
Baltimore, MD 21201-1082
Ph: (410)706-5497
Free: 800-328-7450
Fax: (410)706-8471
Co. E-mail: videopressmail@som.umaryland.edu
URL: http://www.videopress.org

Released: 19??. **Price:** $300.00. **Description:** Examines the anxiety and stress patients and their families face when admission into a nursing home is necessary. Three residents discuss their fears and anxieties prior to being admitted into the nursing home and how they have adjusted their lives. Emphasis is placed on how staff can ease the transition. **Availability:** VHS.

15104 ■ *The Business of Caring*
Victoria International Corp.
1 Harts Cove, PO Box 14
New Castle, NH 03854
Ph: (603)436-1067
Fax: (603)433-4204
URL: http://www.victoriainternationalcorp.com

Released: 1987. **Description:** A series of programs for nursing professionals about patient care, consideration and relation to the family. Each program has nine episodes. **Availability:** VHS; 3/4 U.

15105 ■ *Comprehensive Care of Elderly*
Lippincott Williams & Wilkins
Department of Audiovisual Media
530 Walnut St.
Philadelphia, PA 19106
Ph: (215)521-8300
Free: 800-638-3030
Fax: (215)521-8902
Co. E-mail: info@lww.com
URL: http://www.lww.com

Released: 1986. **Description:** A nurse-training series for the care of elderly patients. **Availability:** VHS; 3/4 U.

15106 ■ *Coping and Home Safety Tips for Caregivers of the Elderly*
Jefferson Area Board for Aging (JABA)
674 Hillsdale Dr., Ste. 9
Charlottesville, VA 22901
Ph: (434)817-5222
Fax: (434)817-5230
Co. E-mail: jabacares@gmail.com
URL: http://www.jabacares.org
Contact: Gordon Walker, Chief Executive Officer

Released: 1989. **Price:** $89.95. **Description:** Designed for family caregivers and home care workers, this videotape demonstrates ways in which to help older people with chronic physical and mental dysfunction in their daily activities. Includes a manual. **Availability:** VHS.

15107 ■ *Foundations in Long-Term Care*
University of Maryland
Video Press
100 N. Greene St., Ste. 300
Baltimore, MD 21201-1082
Ph: (410)706-5497
Free: 800-328-7450
Fax: (410)706-8471
Co. E-mail: videopressmail@som.umaryland.edu
URL: http://www.videopress.org

Released: 19??. **Price:** $1000.00. **Description:** Module 1 of the Elder-Core Training Modules series. Contains four sessions: One East—Portrait of a Nursing Home; Understanding Your Elderly Patient; Caring for Disordered Behavior in the Nursing Home; and Working with Families in Long-Term Care. **Availability:** VHS.

TRADE SHOWS AND CONVENTIONS

15108 ■ American Association of Homes and Services for the Aging Convention
LeadingAge
2519 Connecticut Ave. NW
Washington, DC 20008-1520
Ph: (202)783-2242
Fax: (202)783-2255
Co. E-mail: info@leadingage.org
URL: http://www.leadingage.org
Contact: William L. Minnix, Jr., President

URL(s): www2.aahsa.org. **Frequency:** Annual. **Audience:** Professionals, administrators, and invited guests. **Principal Exhibits:** Equipment, supplies, and services for housing and long-term care facilities for the aged. **Telecommunication Services:** mraynor@ aahsa.com.

15109 ■ American Health Care Association Annual Convention and Exposition
American Health Care Association (AHCA)
1201 L St. NW
Washington, DC 20005
Ph: (202)842-4444
Free: 800-321-0343
Fax: (202)842-3860
Co. E-mail: hr@ahca.org
URL: http://www.ahcancal.org/Pages/Default.aspx
Contact: Mark Parkinson, President

URL(s): www.ahca.org. **Frequency:** Annual. **Audience:** Long-term care and nursing home owners and administrators. **Principal Exhibits:** Supplies for the long-term healthcare industry.

15110 ■ Senior Housing South
Merchandise Mart Properties Inc.
222 Merchandise Mart, Ste. 470
Chicago, IL 60654
Ph: (312)527-4141
Free: 800-677-6278
URL: http://www.merchandisemart.com

URL(s): www.seniorhousingshows.com. **Frequency:** Annual. **Principal Exhibits:** Equipment, supplies, and services for the planning, building, design and management of long-term care facilities.

CONSULTANTS

15111 ■ Sarah G. Burger
3403 Woodley Rd. NW
Washington, DC 20016-5030
Ph: (202)966-3025
Co. E-mail: sgburger@rcu.com
Contact: Sarah G. Burger, President
E-mail: sgburger@rcu.com

Scope: Nursing consultant in management and supervision of long-term patient care facilities. Works with individuals and families making decisions about the combination of services needed for long-term care in the community or in institutions. **Founded:** 1976. **Seminars:** Chemical and Physical Restraint Reduction; Working with the Minimum DataSet.

15112 ■ Diversified Health Resources Inc.
875 N Michigan Ave., Ste. 3250
Chicago, IL 60611-1901
Ph: (312)266-0466
Fax: (312)266-0715
Contact: Andrea R. Rozran, President

Scope: Offers health care consulting for hospitals, nursing homes including homes for the aged, and other health related facilities and companies. Specializes in planning and marketing. Also conducts executive searches for top level health care administrative positions. Serves private industries as well as government agencies. **Founded:** 1979. **Publications:** "City Finance".

15113 ■ Charlotte Eliopoulos Considine, PhD—Charlotte Eliopoulos & Associates
11104 Glen Arm Rd.
Glen Arm, MD 21057
Ph: (410)668-7055
Free: 800-690-1150
Fax: (410)668-7718
Contact: Charlotte Elipoulos, Owner

Scope: Offers holistic-focused consultation and educational programs to long-term care facilities and geriatric care agencies. Services include workshop presentation, assistance in integrating alternative complementary therapies, and planning and development of new programs. Industries served: long-term care facilities, assisted living, and hospitals. **Founded:** 1978. **Publications:** "Gerontological Nursing, 5th edition," Lippincott, 2001; "Nursing Administration Manual for LTCF, 5th edition," Health Education Network, 2001; "Manual of Gerontologic Nursing," Mosby, 1995; "Integrating Alternative and Conventional Care: Holistic Care of Chronic Conditions," Mosby; "Relationship of Faith and Healing". **Seminars:** Alternative therapies in LTC, Holistic Chronic Care Nursing, Gerontological Nursing Update; LTC Clinical and Managerial Updates; Geriatric Care.

15114 ■ Nutrition Entrepreneurs
9212 Delphi Rd. SW
Olympia, WA 98512
Ph: (360)956-1367
Free: 800-861-9406
Fax: (360)956-1367
Co. E-mail: nedpg@aol.com
URL: http://www.nedpg.org
Contact: Vanessa Cavallaro, Director
Scope: Serves as the clearinghouse for nutrition entrepreneurs throughout the U.S. and Canada. Members provide consultation to a variety of clients which include consumers, medical clinics, physician's offices, outpatient departments of hospitals, restaurants, corporations, long-term care facilities, television, radio-television-print media, supermarkets, and food companies. In addition, many members produce and market nutrition related products. Industries served: Acute and long term health care settings, all forms of media, consumer and professional education, corporate wellness, entrepreneurial production and marketing of products for consumers and/or professionals. **Founded:** 1977. **Publications:** "Time is Money: Finding Balance in Your Life," 2007; "The Future is Now: Focusing Your Vision," 2007; "Financial Planning 101," 2006; "Marketing Your Private Practice for Dietitians"; "Drawing the Line on Calories, Carbs, and Fat"; "Is Your Personality Type Making You Fat?". **Seminars:** Public Policy Workshop, 2009; Thriving in a Virtual Business Landscape: FNCE 2007; NE Teleconferences 2007.

15115 ■ Professional Healthcare Associates Inc.
422 Morris Ave., Ste. 1
Long Branch, NJ 07740
Ph: (732)229-4545
Free: 800-634-2498
Fax: (732)229-9647
Co. E-mail: czagury@vistapubl.com
Contact: Carolyn S. Zagury, President
E-mail: czagury@vistapubl.com
Scope: Offers health care consulting services in the areas of geriatric service development; grant funding research, development and application preparation; and system development and strategic planning for nursing. Additional work in education and training for health care professionals in management training, clinical areas, and writing skills. Other services include manuscript development, editing, publishing and marketing of books, journals and articles related to health care, human services and women's issues. Industries served: health care, long term care, human services, and municipal government agencies. **Founded:** 1991. **Publications:** "Nurse Entrepreneur Building the Bridge of Opportunity".

15116 ■ Helen Tredway
1638 Rd. W
RR 1
Neosho Rapids, KS 66864-8700
Ph: (620)343-3637
Scope: Nursing consultant to nursing homes. Offers services in service education. **Founded:** 1982. **Seminars:** Meeting the Needs of the Nursing Home Nurse; Adult Day Care.

FRANCHISES AND BUSINESS OPPORTUNITIES

15117 ■ Age Advantage Home Care Franchising Inc.
1810 Gillespie Way, Ste. 105
El Cajon, CA 92020
Ph: (619)433-0141

Fax: (619)858-2317
Description: In-home senior care. **No. of Franchise Units:** 6. **No. of Company-Owned Units:** 1. **Founded:** 1998.. **Franchised:** 2006. **Equity Capital Needed:** $44,830-$128,000. **Franchise Fee:** $20,000-60,000. **Royalty Fee:** 5%. **Financial Assistance:** Limited third party financing available.

15118 ■ Home Instead Inc.
13330 California St., Ste. 200
Omaha, NE 68154-5241
Ph: (888)484-5759
Free: 888-484-5759
Fax: (402)498-5757
Co. E-mail: info@homeinstead.com
URL: http://www.homeinstead.com
Contact: Paul Hogan, President
Description: Non-medical companionship and homecare services for elderly people. **No. of Franchise Units:** 587. **No. of Company-Owned Units:** 1. **Founded:** 1994. **Franchised:** 1995. **Equity Capital Needed:** $55,000-$70,000. **Franchise Fee:** $39,000. **Financial Assistance:** No. **Training:** Yes. **Telecommunication Services:** pcampbell@homeinstead.com.

COMPUTERIZED DATABASES

15119 ■ *Consumer InSite<svs>*
610 Opperman Dr.
Eagen, MN 55122
Free: 800-477-4300
Co. E-mail: gale.contentlicensing@cengage.com
URL: http://www.insite2.gale.com
Availability: Online: Cengage Learning Inc. - Gale - InSite2. **Type:** Full-text.

15120 ■ *Health & Wellness InSite<svs>*
610 Opperman Dr.
Eagen, MN 55122
Free: 800-477-4300
Co. E-mail: gale.contentlicensing@cengage.com
URL: http://www.insite2.gale.com
Availability: Online: Cengage Learning Inc. - Gale - InSite2. **Type:** Full-text.

15121 ■ *State Health Care Regulatory Developments™*
1801 S Bell St.
Arlington, VA 22202
Free: 800-372-1033
Co. E-mail: customercare@bna.com
URL: http://www.bna.com
Availability: Online: Bloomberg LP-Bloomberg BNA; Thomson Reuters - Westlaw. **Type:** Full-text.

LIBRARIES

15122 ■ American College of Health Care Administrators - ACHCA Information Center
1321 Duke St., Ste. 400
Alexandria, VA 22314
Ph: (202)536-5120
Fax: (866)874-1585
Co. E-mail: mgrachek@achca.org
URL: http://www.achca.org
Scope: Long-term care, gerontology. **Services:** Center open to ACHCA members only. **Founded:** 1991. **Holdings:** 100 books; governmental statistical reports. **Subscriptions:** 125 journals and other serials.

15123 ■ Anderson Area Medical Center Library
800 N. Fant St.
Anderson, SC 29621
Ph: (864)261-1253
Fax: (864)261-1552
URL: http://www.anmedhealth.org
Contact: Beth Addis
Scope: Medicine, nursing. **Services:** Interlibrary loan. **Holdings:** 750 books. **Subscriptions:** 125 journals and other serials; 2 newspapers.

15124 ■ Clemson University - College of Health, Education & Human Development Learning Resource Center
203 Edwards Hall Clemson
Box 340744
Clemson, SC 29634
Ph: (864)656-5477
Fax: (864)656-1688
Co. E-mail: marches@clemson.edu
URL: http://www.clemson.edu/centers-institutes/clrc/index.html
Contact: Michelle Marchesse, Director
Scope: Nursing, health. **Services:** Photocopying. **Holdings:** 250 books; 400 videotapes; 30 software.

15125 ■ Evangelical Lutheran Good Samaritan Society - Resource Library
PO Box 5038
Sioux Falls, SD 57117-5038
Ph: 605-362-3271
Co. E-mail: cnelson2@good-sam.com
URL: http://www.good-sam.com/
Contact: Crystal Gering Nelson, Coordinator
Scope: Nursing home care. **Holdings:** 760 videos; 553 books; 48 cassettes; 223 DVDs; 6 CDs; 5 kits. **Subscriptions:** 16 journals and other serials.

15126 ■ Genesis Medical Center - Illini Campus - Perlmutter Library of the Health Sciences
855 Illini Dr., Ste. 102
Silvis, IL 61282
Ph: (309)792-4360
Fax: (309)792-4362
Co. E-mail: tharpb@genesishealth.com
URL: http://www.genesishealth.com/facilities/illini/index/
Contact: Barb Tharp, Librarian
Scope: Clinical medicine, healthcare management, nursing. **Services:** Interlibrary loan; literature searches; PUBMED training; library open to the public. **Founded:** 1980. **Holdings:** 1600 books; 500 video recordings. **Subscriptions:** 225 journals and other serials.

15127 ■ Lexington Medical Center - LMC Health Library
2720 Sunset Blvd.
West Columbia, SC 29169
Ph: (803)791-2000
Fax: (803)791-2623
Co. E-mail: librarian@lexhealth.org
URL: http://www.lexmed.com/about/community-involvement/health-library.aspx
Scope: Medical science, psychology, nutrition, childcare, sports medicine, health care law, general health. **Holdings:** 1000 books; 500 audiocassettes; 200 journals.

15128 ■ Mercy Medical Center - Health Sciences Library
2700 Stewart Pkwy.
Roseburg, OR 97470
Ph: (541)677-2144
Fax: (541)677-4391
Co. E-mail: mercycommunityrelations@chiwest.com
URL: http://www.mercyrose.org
Scope: Medicine, nursing, patient education, allied health. **Services:** Interlibrary loan; copying; library open to the public. **Founded:** 1975. **Holdings:** 250 books; 50 bound periodical volumes. **Subscriptions:** 25 journals and other serials.

15129 ■ Mid-Columbia Medical Center - Planetree Health Resource Center
1700 E. 19th St.
The Dalles, OR 97058
Ph: (541)296-8444
Fax: (541)296-7600
Co. E-mail: library@mcmc.net
URL: http://www.mcmc.net/planetreeresources
Scope: Consumer health, medicine, cancer, complementary therapies, smoking cessation, violence prevention and conflict resolution. **Services:** Interlibrary loan; copying; Library open to the public.

Founded: 1992. **Holdings:** 3600 books; 981 clipping files; 350 audio/visual items; teaching tools. **Subscriptions:** 53 journals and other serials; 2 newspapers.

15130 ■ Millcreek Community Hospital/ LECOM Medical Library
5515 Peach St.
Erie, PA 16509
Ph: (814)868-8217
Fax: (814)868-8249
Co. E-mail: rschnick@lecom.edu
URL: http://www.millcreekcommunityhospital.com
Contact: Robert Schnick, Director, Library Services
Scope: Family practice, orthopedic surgery, internal medicine, osteopathic medicine, obstetrics, gynecology. **Services:** Interlibrary loan; photocopying; information consultation; library not open to the public. **Holdings:** 550 books; 9000 periodical back issues. **Subscriptions:** 110 journals and other serials. **Telecommunication Services:** ferraro@lecom. edu; dwelch@lecom.edu; jlin@mch1.org .

15131 ■ Princeton Community Hospital Library
122 12th St.
Princeton, WV 24740-1369
Ph: (304)487-7246
Fax: (304)487-2161
Co. E-mail: mperdue@pchonline.org
URL: http://www.pchonline.org
Contact: Wayne B. Griffith, Chief Executive Officer
Scope: Medicine, nursing, and allied health sciences. **Services:** Library open to the public. **Founded:** 1972. **Holdings:** 400 books. **Subscriptions:** 12 journals and other serials.

15132 ■ Reedsburg Area Medical Center Medical Library
2000 N. Dewey Ave.
Reedsburg, WI 53959
Ph: (608)768-6275
Fax: (608)524-2104
URL: http://www.ramchealth.com
Contact: Jeff Steel, Chairman
Scope: Family practice, nursing, surgery. **Services:** Interlibrary loan; computer access for research; copying; library open to the public. **Founded:** 1980. **Holdings:** 120 books. **Subscriptions:** 20 journals and other serials.

15133 ■ Southwest Health Center Medical Library
1400 East Side Rd.
Platteville, WI 53818
Ph: (608)348-2331
Fax: (608)342-5011
Co. E-mail: library@southwesthealth.org
URL: http://www.southwesthealth.org/index.php
Contact: Medicine, nursing, and allied health sciences.
Scope: Medicine, nursing, and allied health sciences. **Services:** Interlibrary loan; copying; library open to the public. **Founded:** 1975. **Holdings:** 500 books. **Subscriptions:** 80 journals and other serials.

15134 ■ Toronto Rehabilitation Institute Library
University Centre
550 University Ave.
Toronto, ON, Canada M5G 2A2
Ph: (416)597-3422, x3050
Fax: (416)591-6515
Co. E-mail: winterbottom.marcia@torontorehab.on.ca
URL: http://www.torontorehab.com/Education---Learning/Library-Services.aspx
Contact: Doreen Millman-Wilson, Director, Library Services
Scope: Gerontology, acquired brain injury, stroke rehabilitation, long-term care, complex continuing care, spinal cord injury. **Services:** Interlibrary loan; copying; document delivery; literature searches; library open to the public for reference use only. **Founded:** 1978. **Holdings:** 4200 books; 1500 bound periodical volumes; 200 videotapes. **Subscriptions:** 120 journals and other serials. **Telecommunication Services:** libraryall@torontorehab.on.ca.

15135 ■ United Way 2-1-1 - Information & Referral Service
PO Box 7548
Madison, WI 53707-7548
Ph: (608)246-4350
Fax: (608)246-4367
Co. E-mail: sandye@uwdc.org
URL: http://www.unitedwaydanecounty.org
Contact: Sandy Erickson, Director
Scope: Geriatrics, medical care. **Services:** Community resource telephone line providing information and referral services for Dane County. **Founded:** 1982.

15136 ■ University of South Florida - College of Medicine - Suncoast Gerontology Center - The Eastern Star Library on Alzheimer's Disease
4001 E. Fletcher Ave.
Tampa, FL 33613
Ph: (813)974-4355
Free: 800-633-4563
Fax: (813)974-4251
Co. E-mail: jardila@hsc.usf.edu
URL: http://hsc.usf.edu/suncoast/alzheimer/index.html
Contact: Jill Ardila, Coordinator
Scope: Alzheimer's disease, aging, caregiving, long-term care, mental health, dementia. **Services:** Interlibrary loan; copying; SDI; Library open to the public for reference use only. **Founded:** 1985. **Holdings:** 800 books; 450 reports; 50 archival materials; 25 videocassettes. **Subscriptions:** 6 journals and other serials.

15137 ■ UPMC Braddock Health Sciences Library
400 Holland Ave.
Braddock, PA 15104
Ph: (412)784-4238
Fax: (412)351-5602
Co. E-mail: haughaj@msx.upmc.edu
URL: http://braddock.upmc.com/
Contact: Amy Haugh, Director
Scope: Clinical medicine, clinical psychiatry, clinical nursing, clinical geriatrics. **Services:** Interlibrary loan; copying; SDI; library open to the public with restrictions. **Founded:** 1961. **Holdings:** 500 books; 1000 bound periodical volumes; 34 microfiche titles. **Subscriptions:** 80 journals and other serials.

15138 ■ Virginia Commonwealth University - Virginia Center on Aging - Information Resources Center
730 E. Broad St.
Theatre Row Building
Richmond, VA 23219
Ph: (804)828-1525
Fax: (804)828-7905
Co. E-mail: eansello@vcu.edu
URL: http://www.sahp.vcu.edu/vcoa
Contact: Dr. Edward F. Ansello, Director
Scope: Gerontology, mental health, sociology and the politics of aging, geriatrics, family relationships, long-term care, lifelong learning. **Services:** Library open to the public with restrictions (audio/visual materials available to Virginia residents only). **Founded:** 1978. **Holdings:** 1500 books; 4 archives; 120 AV items. **Subscriptions:** 6 journals and other serials.

15139 ■ Western Illinois Area Agency on Aging - Greta J. Brook Elderly Living and Learning Facility—Elderly Living and Learning Facility (ELLF).
729 34th Ave.
Rock Island, IL 61201
Ph: (309)793-6800
Free: 800-322-1051
Fax: (309)793-6807
Co. E-mail: firststopforseniors@wiaaa.org
URL: http://www.wiaaa.org
Contact: Barbara Eskildsen, Executive Director
Scope: Gerontology, Senior Housing, Family Caregiving, Medicare, Medicaid, Social Security, Retirement Planning, Intergenerational Programs, Program Development. **Services:** Interlibrary loan; Senior Computer Center open to those fifty years of age or

older; facility open to the public. **Founded:** 1988. **Holdings:** 1108 books; 260 videotapes; 130 audio/ visual materials; 35 DVDs and CDs. **Subscriptions:** 2 journals and other serials, 12 periodicals. **Telecommunication Services:** jblaser@wiaaa.org.

RESEARCH CENTERS

15140 ■ Center for Health Care Strategies (CHCS)
200 American Metro Blvd., Ste. 119
Hamilton, NJ 08619
Ph: (609)528-8400
Fax: (609)586-3679
Co. E-mail: ssomers@chcs.org
URL: http://www.chcs.org
Contact: Stephen A. Somers, President
Founded: 1995. **Publications:** *Case studies* (Monthly); *CHCS Fact sheets* (Monthly); *Policy and issue briefs* (Monthly); *CHCS Reports* (Monthly); *Resource papers* (Monthly); *Technical assistance tools* (Monthly). **Telecommunication Services:** mail@ chcs.org.

15141 ■ Center for the Study of Aging, Inc. (CSA)
706 Madison Ave.
Albany, NY 12208-3604
Ph: (518)465-6927
Fax: (518)462-1339
Co. E-mail: csa@centerforthestudyofaging.org
URL: http://www.centerforthestudyofaging.org
Contact: Sara Harris, Executive Director
Services: Consulting; Information and referral services, education and training, and fitness programming. **Founded:** 1957. **Publications:** *Lifelong Health and Fitness Newsletter* (Quarterly). **Educational Activities:** International Conferences on Physical Activity, Aging, Sports, and Prevention of Illness and Maintenance of Well-being. **Awards:** Outstanding Leadership and Research in Physical Activity and Aging Award, presented at International Conference. **Telecommunication Services:** iapaas@aol.com.

15142 ■ Research Institute on Aging
6105 Montrose Rd.
Rockville, MD 20852-4881
Ph: (301)770-8449
Fax: (301)770-8455
Co. E-mail: cohen-mansfield@hebrew-home.org
URL: http://www.researchinstituteonaging.org
Contact: Jiska Cohen-Mansfield, Director
Founded: 1984. **Publications:** *Monograph series*; *Papers in professional journals*. **Educational Activities:** Hurwitz Lecture Series.

15143 ■ Sherbrooke University - Research Centre on Aging—Sherbrooke University - Centre de Recherche sur le Vieillissement (CDRV)
1036, rue Belvédère Sud
Sherbrooke, QC, Canada J1H 4C4
Ph: (819)829-7131
Fax: (819)829-7141
Co. E-mail: communication@cdrv.ca
URL: http://www.csss-iugs.ca/cdrv/index.php?L=en
Contact: Prof. Michel Tousignant, Director
Founded: 1988. **Educational Activities:** Lunch time scientific conferences, every 2 weeks, Sept.-May; Research Day (Annual). **Awards:** Research Centre on Aging Grants.

15144 ■ University of Arizona - Arizona Center on Aging (ACOA)
1821 E Elm St.
Tucson, AZ 85719-4324
Ph: (520)626-5800
Fax: (520)626-5801
Co. E-mail: mfain@aging.arizona.edu
URL: http://aging.medicine.arizona.edu
Contact: Dr. Mindy Fain, Director
Founded: 1980. **Publications:** *ACOA Monographs*; *ACOA Papers*. **Educational Activities:** Caregiver and Alzheimer's training.

15145 ■ University of Massachusetts at Boston - Gerontology Institute
Wheatley Bldg., 3rd Fl., Rm. 124A
100 Morrissey Blvd.
Boston, MA 02125-3393
Ph: (617)287-7300

Fax: (617)287-7080
Co. E-mail: ellen.bruce@umb.edu
URL: http://www.geront.umb.edu
Contact: Ellen Bruce, Director
Founded: 1984. **Publications:** *Journal of Aging & Social Policy* (Quarterly). **Educational Activities:**
Osher Life Long Learning Institute (Daily), lifelong learning program for people aged 50 and over, which offers non-credit courses, lectures, social events, and trips; Seminars, conferences, special events and forums, open to the public. **Telecommunication Services:** gerontology@umb.edu.

START-UP INFORMATION

15146 ■ *Becoming a Personal Trainer for Dummies*
Pub: John Wiley and Sons, Inc.
Ed: Melyssa Michael, Linda Formichelli. **Released:** October 2004. **Price:** $19.99 (US), $25.99 (Canadian). **Description:** Legal and tax issues involved in starting and running a personal trainer firm. The book offers suggestions for incorporating massage and nutritional services.

ASSOCIATIONS AND OTHER ORGANIZATIONS

15147 ■ Academy of Nutrition and Dietetics (AND)
120 S Riverside Plaza, Ste. 2000
Chicago, IL 60606
Ph: (312)899-0040
Free: 800-877-1600
Fax: (312)899-4873
Co. E-mail: sales@eatright.org
URL: http://www.eatright.org
Contact: Judith C. Rodriguez, President
Description: Represents food and nutrition professionals. Promotes nutrition, health and well-being. **Scope:** foods, nutrition, dietetics practice. **Founded:** 1917. **Subscriptions:** 3000 audiovisuals books periodicals. **Publications:** *Directory of Dietetics Programs* (Annual); *Journal of the American Dietetic Association* (Monthly); *Directory of Registered Dietitians*; *Directory of Consulting Dietitians in Private Practice*; *Find a Nutrition Professional Consumer Search*; *Directory of Columbus Registered Dietitians*; *Dieting for Dummies, 2nd Edition*; *The Healthy Beef Cookbook*; *365 Days of Healthy Eating from the American Dietetic*; *International Dietetics and Nutrition Terminology Reference Manual: Standardized Language for the Nutrition Care Process, 3rd Edition.* **Educational Activities:** Food and Nutrition Conference and Expo (Annual); Food & Nutrition Conference & Expo (Annual). **Telecommunication Services:** foundation@eatright.org.

15148 ■ American Association of Nutritional Consultants (AANC)
220 Parker St.
Warsaw, IN 46580
Ph: (574)269-6165
Free: 888-828-2262
Co. E-mail: registrar@aanc.net
URL: http://www.aanc.net
Description: Professional nutritional consultants. Seeks to create a forum for exchange of nutritional information. Offers benefits such as car rental and laboratory discounts. **Founded:** 1980. **Publications:** *American Association of Nutritional Consultants Brochure*.

15149 ■ American Nutrition Association (ANA)
PO Box 262
Western Springs, IL 60558

Ph: (708)246-3663
Co. E-mail: contact@americannutritionassociation.org
URL: http://www.americannutritionassociation.org
Description: Aims to promote optimal health through nutrition and wellness education. Performs at the cutting edge of science-based nutrition, educating both laypeople and professionals about the health benefits of nutrition and wellness. Hosts hundreds of expert nutrition presentations in Chicago from such luminaries in the healthcare field as Nobel Laureate Linus Pauling. Engages in numerous other nutrition outreach programs, such as: over 30 years of quarterly Nutrition Digest Children's nutrition programs in local schools. **Founded:** 1972. **Publications:** *Nutrition Digest*.

15150 ■ Canadian Foundation for Dietetic Research (CFDR)—Fondation Canadienne de la Recherche en Dietetique
480 University Ave., Ste. 604
Toronto, ON, Canada M5G 1V2
Ph: (519)267-0755
Fax: (416)596-0603
Co. E-mail: isla.horvath@cfdr.ca
URL: http://www.cfdr.ca/index.aspx
Contact: Isla Horvath, Executive Director
Description: Dietitians and other individuals with an interest in nutrition. Seeks to advance dietetic research. Provides support and assistance to nutrition research projects. Conducts educational programs. **Founded:** 1991. **Publications:** *Keeping In Touch* (3/year). **Awards:** Research Awards (Annual); Regular Research Grants.

15151 ■ Canadian Health Food Association (CHFA)—Association Canadienne des Aliements de Sante
235 Yorkland Blvd., Ste. 302
Toronto, ON, Canada M2J 4Y8
Ph: (416)497-6939
Free: 800-661-4510
Fax: (416)497-3214
Co. E-mail: info@chfa.ca
URL: http://www.chfa.ca
Contact: Matthew James, Chairman
Description: Represents producers and distributors of health foods. Seeks to advance the health food industries. Facilitates communication and cooperation among members; represents the commercial and regulatory interests of the health food industries; sponsors educational and promotional programs. **Founded:** 1964. **Publications:** *The Natural Voice* (5/year).

15152 ■ *Canadian Journal of Dietetic Practice and Research*
480 University Ave., Ste. 604
Toronto, ON, Canada M5G 1V2
Ph: (416)596-0857
Fax: (416)596-0603
Co. E-mail: centralinfo@dietitians.ca
URL: http://www.dietitians.ca
Contact: Marsha Sharp, Chief Executive Officer
Released: Quarterly **Price:** C$85, /year in Canada (print only); C$100, /year in U.S. (print only); $135, /year in other countries (print only).

15153 ■ Canadian Nutrition Society (CNS)—Societe Canadienne de Nutrition (SCN)
310-2175 Sheppard Ave. E
Toronto, ON, Canada M2J 1W8
Ph: (416)491-7188
Free: 888-414-7188
Fax: (416)491-1670
Co. E-mail: info@cns-scn.ca
URL: http://www.cns-scn.ca
Contact: Katherine Gray-Donald, President
Description: Dieticians and other scientists and health care professionals with an interest in nutrition. Seeks to advance the study and practice of the nutritional sciences. Serves as a forum for the exchange of information among members; sponsors research and educational programs. **Founded:** 1957. **Awards:** New Scientist Award for Outstanding Research.

15154 ■ Dietary Managers Association (DMA)
406 Surrey Woods Dr.
St. Charles, IL 60174
Ph: (630)587-6336
Free: 800-323-1908
Fax: (630)587-6308
Co. E-mail: info@dmaonline.org
URL: http://www.dmaonline.org
Contact: Ricky Clark, Chairman of the Board
URL(s): www.anfponline.org. **Description:** Dietary managers united to maintain a high level of competency and quality in dietary departments through continuing education. Provides educational programs and placement service. **Scope:** food, nutrition management, food services, recipe, health, associations. **Founded:** 1960. **Subscriptions:** 74 books. **Publications:** *Dietary Manager* (Bimonthly); *DMA Master Track Human Resource*; *DMA Master Track Operations Management*; *Dietary Manager Magazine* (Monthly); *ANFP Publications Catalog*; *Accounting and Finance Fundamentals*; *Alzheimer's Disease*; *Managing Foodservice Operations*; *Diet Therapy for the Dietary Manager.* **Educational Activities:** Dietary Managers Association Meeting and Expo (Annual); 2013 National Leadership Conference; ANFP Regional Meeting. **Awards:** State Achievement Award (Annual). **Telecommunication Services:** info@anfponline.org.

15155 ■ Dietetics in Health Care Communities (DHCC)
c/o Marla Carlson, Exec. Dir.
2219 Cardinal Dr.
Waterloo, IA 50701
Ph: (319)235-0991
Fax: (319)235-7224
Co. E-mail: dhccdpg@mchsi.com
URL: http://www.dhccdpg.org
Contact: Barbara Wakeen, Chairperson
Description: A special interest group of the American Dietetic Association. Dietitians employed in extended care facilities, nursing homes, homecare, and a variety of food service operations. Disseminates information; assists in solving their problems in the field. Conducts workshops; offers networking op-

portunities for professionals. **Founded:** 1975. **Publications:** *The Consultant Dietitian* (Quarterly); *Inservice Manual.* **Educational Activities:** Dietetics in Health Care Communities Meeting (Annual). **Awards:** Best Practice Award (Quarterly); CDHCF Circle Award (Annual); CDHCF Distinguished Member Award (Annual); CDHCF Horizon Award (Annual); CDHCF Scholarship Award (Annual); Gaynold Jenson Educational Stipend (Annual); Ross Leadership Award (Annual); DHCC Board Scholarships; Gaynold Jensen Education Stipends; Best Practice Award; Circle Award; Distinguished Member Award; Chair's Scholarship; Ross Leadership Award; Up and Coming Member of the Year Award; Gaynold Jenson Educational Stipend. **Telecommunication Services:** carlsonmom@mchsi.com.

15156 ■ Dietitians of Canada (DC)—Les Dietetistes du Canada
480 University Ave., Ste. 604
Toronto, ON, Canada M5G 1V2
Ph: (416)596-0857
Fax: (416)596-0603
Co. E-mail: centralinfo@dietitians.ca
URL: http://www.dietitians.ca
Contact: Marsha Sharp, Chief Executive Officer
Description: Leads and supports members to promote health and well being through expertise in food and nutrition. **Founded:** 1935. **Publications:** *Canadian Journal of Dietetic Practice and Research* (Quarterly); *Canadian Journal of Dietetic Practice and Research* (Quarterly).

15157 ■ International Union of Nutritional Sciences (IUNS)
c/o Dr. Suzanne Murphy, Treas.
University of Hawaii
Cancer Research Center of Hawaii
1236 Lauhala St., Ste. 407
Honolulu, HI 96813
Ph: (808)564-5861
Fax: (808)564-2982
Co. E-mail: suzanne@crch.hawaii.edu
URL: http://www.iuns.org
Contact: Prof. Rekia Belahsen, Secretary General
Description: Promotes advancement in nutrition science, research and development through international cooperation at the global level. Encourages communication and collaboration among nutrition scientists as well as to disseminate information in nutritional sciences through modern communication technology. **Founded:** 1946. **Educational Activities:** International Congress of Nutrition (Quadrennial). **Awards:** IUNS Award (Quadrennial); IUNS Fellow (Quadrennial).

15158 ■ *Keeping In Touch*
480 University Ave., Ste. 604
Toronto, ON, Canada M5G 1V2
Ph: (519)267-0755
Fax: (416)596-0603
Co. E-mail: isla.horvath@cfdr.ca
URL: http://www.cfdr.ca/index.aspx
Contact: Isla Horvath, Executive Director
Released: 3/year

15159 ■ National Eating Disorder Information Centre (NEDIC)
200 Elizabeth St., ES 7-421
Toronto, ON, Canada M5G 2C4
Ph: (416)340-4156
Free: 866-633-4220
Fax: (416)340-4736
Co. E-mail: nedic@uhn.on.ca
URL: http://www.nedic.ca
Contact: Merryl Bear, Director
Description: Provides information and resources on causes, symptoms of, and therapeutic and health care treatments for eating disorders and the preoccupation with food and weight. Aims to raise awareness on eating disorders through conducting lectures and workshops. **Scope:** eating disorders. **Founded:** 1985. **Subscriptions:** books video recordings articles periodicals. **Educational Activities:** Eating Disorder Awareness Week (Annual).

15160 ■ National Food Service Management Institute (NFSMI)
University of Mississippi
6 Jeanette Philips Dr.
PO Drawer 188
University, MS 38677-0188
Ph: (662)915-7658
Free: 800-321-3054
Fax: (800)321-3061
Co. E-mail: nfsmi@olemiss.edu
URL: http://www.nfsmi.org
Contact: Dr. Katie Wilson, Executive Director
Description: Seeks to be the leader in providing education, research, and resources to promote excellence in child nutrition programs. Provides information, conducts applied research, and offers training and education opportunities using appropriate technology. **Scope:** school food service, child nutrition program, computer-based instructional program, food safety, nutrition education, food service management, recipe, health promotion, applied research, customer service, procurement, financial management. **Founded:** 1989. **Subscriptions:** 3000 archival material audiovisuals books clippings photographs reports. **Publications:** *NFSMI Newsletters*; *Resource guide*; *Insight* (Quarterly); *Resource Guide*; *Update* (Semiannual); *Mealtime Memo for Child Care* (Bimonthly). **Educational Activities:** NFSMI Workshops; National Food Service Management Institute Convention. **Telecommunication Services:** helpdesk@nfsmi.org.

15161 ■ *The Natural Voice*
235 Yorkland Blvd., Ste. 302
Toronto, ON, Canada M2J 4Y8
Ph: (416)497-6939
Free: 800-661-4510
Fax: (416)497-3214
Co. E-mail: info@chfa.ca
URL: http://www.chfa.ca
Contact: Matthew James, Chairman
Released: 5/year

REFERENCE WORKS

15162 ■ *Everything is Possible: Life and Business Lessons from a Self-Made Billionaire and the Founder of Slim-Fast*
Pub: Newmarket Press
Ed: S. Daniel Abraham. **Released:** February 10, 2010. **Price:** $24.95. **Description:** A profile of the founder of Slim-Fast nutritional diet drink used to help people lose weight.

15163 ■ *"Experts Strive to Educate on Proper Pet Diets"* in Pet Product News (Vol. 64, November 2010, No. 11, pp. 40)
Pub: BowTie Inc.
Ed; John Hustace Walker. **Description:** Pet supply manufacturers have been bundling small mammal food and treats with educational sources to help retailers avoid customer misinformation. This action has been motivated by the customer's quest to seek proper nutritional advice for their small mammal pets.

15164 ■ *"Food as Nature Intended"* in Pet Product News (Vol. 64, November 2010, No. 11, pp. 30)
Pub: BowTie Inc.
Ed: Nikki Moustaki. **Description:** Dog owners have been extending their health-consciousness to their pets by seeking natural products that will address their pets' raw food diet. Retailers response to this trend are outlined.

15165 ■ *"In the Raw: Karyn Calabrese Brings Healthy Dining to a New Sophisticated Level"* in Black Enterprise (Vol. 41, September 2010)
Pub: Earl G. Graves Publishing Co. Inc.
Ed: Sonia Alleyne. **Description:** Profile of Karyn Calabrese whose businesses are based in Chicago, Illinois. Calabrese has launched a complete line of products (vitamins and beauty items), services (spa, chiropractic, and acupuncture treatments), and restaurants to bring health dining and lifestyles to a better level.

15166 ■ *"Kubicki Juggles Lineup at Vianda"* in Business Courier (Vol. 26, December 11, 2009, No. 33, pp. 1)
Pub: American City Business Journals, Inc.
Ed: Dan Monk. **Description:** Cincinnati real estate developer Chuck Kubicki replaced the management team of Vianda LLC and cancelled contracts with two vendors that caused a surge of customer complaints. Vianda is a direct-response marketing firm that sells and distributes dietary supplements for wellness and sexual performance.

15167 ■ *"Making It Work"* in Pet Product News (Vol. 64, December 2010, No. 12, pp. S8)
Pub: BowTie Inc.
Ed: Kerri Chladnicek. **Description:** How focusing on service and flexibility allowed New Jersey-based pet supply store B.C. Woof to achieve success is discussed. B.C. Woof began as a pet-sitting business which eventually concentrated on natural foods. Aside from conducting a do-it-yourself approach in food formulation for customers, B.C. Woof has also been guiding customers on nutrients they need for their pets.

15168 ■ *"Must Work for Food"* in Pet Product News (Vol. 64, November 2010, No. 11, pp. 24)
Pub: BowTie Inc.
Ed: Wendy Bedwell-Wilson. **Description:** Pet supply retailers can benefit from stocking foods and treats that address obesity, which according to the American Veterinary Medical Association, has become the most prevalent nutritional disorder in dogs. With the rise in dog obesity, products like work-for-their food toys have been sought by dog owners.

15169 ■ *"No-Shed Dogs Lead the Way to Big Growth"* in Business Courier (Vol. 26, January 8, 2010, No. 38, pp. 1)
Pub: American City Business Journals, Inc.
Ed: Lucy May. **Description:** Ed Lukacevic of Grant County, Kentucky is developing Dinovite, a dietary supplement that minimizes shedding and scratching in dogs. Statistical data included.

15170 ■ *"Supplements Mix Nutrition With Convenience"* in Pet Product News (Vol. 64, November 2010, No. 11, pp. 44)
Pub: BowTie Inc.
Ed: Karen Shugart. **Description:** Pet supply manufacturers have been making supplements and enhanced foods that improve mineral consumption, boost bone density, and sharpen appetite in herps. Customers seem to enjoy the convenience as particular herps demands are being addressed by these offerings. Features of other supplements and enhanced foods for herps are described.

15171 ■ *"Sustaining Health"* in Pet Product News (Vol. 64, November 2010, No. 11, pp. 28)
Pub: BowTie Inc.
Ed: Angela Pham. **Description:** How pet supply retailers have responded to dog owners' interest in health supplements and their ingredients is discussed. Dog owners are showing interest in the ingredients inside the supplements and are reading labels. Retailers must now prove the beneficial effects of these ingredients in order to make the sale.

TRADE PERIODICALS

15172 ■ *American Journal of Clinical Nutrition*
Pub: American Society for Nutrition
Contact: John Courtney, Executive Officer
URL(s): www.nutrition.org/publications/the-american-journal-of-clinical-nutr ition/. **Released:** Monthly **Price:** $555, Institutions print and online U.S.; $515, Institutions online U.S.; $215, Individuals print and online U.S.; $180, Individuals online U.S.; $585, Institutions, Canada and Mexico print and online; $515, Institutions, Canada and Mexico online only; $610, Other countries print and online; $515, Other countries online only.

15173 ■ Better Nutrition Magazine
Pub: Active Interest Media
Contact: Efrem Zimbalist, President
URL(s): www.betternutrition.comwww.aimmedia.com/
bn.html. Ed: Nicole Brechka. Released: Monthly

15174 ■ Eating Well Magazine: The Magazine of Food & Health
Pub: Eating Well Inc.
Contact: Michael Balzano, Director
E-mail: michael@eatingwell.com
URL(s): www.eatingwell.com/. Ed: Nicci Micco, James M. Lawrence, Jessie Price. Released: Bi-monthly Price: $14.97, Individuals; $24.97, Canada; $34.97, Other countries.

15175 ■ Journal of Culinary Science & Technology
Pub: Taylor & Francis Group Ltd.
Contact: William Germanno, Manager
E-mail: williamgermano@gmail.com
URL(s): www.tandfonline.com/toc/wcsc20/current. Ed: John M. Antun, Joseph A. Hegarty. Released: Quarterly Price: $84, Individuals online; $92, Individuals print & online; $276, Institutions online; $306, Institutions print & online.

15176 ■ Journal of Nutrition
Pub: American Society for Nutrition
Contact: John Courtney, Executive Officer
URL(s): www.nutrition.org/publications/the-journal-of-nutrition/. Ed: Catharine A. Ross. Released: Monthly Price: $700, Institutions online only; domestic & foreign; $775, Institutions print + online; $830, Institutions, other countries print + online; $215, Individuals print + online; $265, Other countries print + online; $180, Individuals online only; domestic & foreign.

15177 ■ No Salt Week-The Newsletter
Pub: Prosperity & Profits Unlimited, Distribution Services
Ed: A. Doyle, Editor. Released: Annual. Price: $2, U.S.; $3, Canada; $4, elsewhere. Description: Presents possibilities for herb and spice blends that contain no added salt. Also contains ideas for cooking and much more.

15178 ■ Nutrition Reviews
Pub: International Life Sciences Institute Subscription Office
URL(s): www.ilsi.org/Pages/NutritionReviews.aspxwww.wiley.com/bw/submit.asp?ref=0029-6643. Released: Monthly Price: $237, Individuals print + online; $467, Institutions print + online; $405, Institutions online; €230, Individuals European, print + online; £375, Institutions European, print + online; €326, Institutions European, online; £154, Other countries print + online; $576, Institutions, other countries print + online; $501, Institutions, other countries online.

15179 ■ Nutrition Today
Pub: Lippincott Williams & Wilkins
Contact: Rich Wohl, Executive Vice President
URL(s): journals.lww.com/nutritiontodayonline/pages/default.aspx. Ed: Johanna Dwyer. Released: Bi-monthly Price: $94, Individuals; $325, Institutions; $56, Individuals in-training; $189, Other countries; $445, Institutions, other countries.

15180 ■ The Tan Sheet
Pub: F-D-C Reports Inc.
Contact: Jaimie Kelley, Managing Editor
Ed: Christopher Walker, Editor. Released: Weekly, 50/year. Price: $2,020, U.S. print and web. Description: Provides 'in-depth coverage of nonprescription pharmaceuticals and dietary supplement/nutritionals.' Topics include congressional hearings and legislation, business and marketing news, FDA recalls and seizures, regular listing of product trademarks, and activities of FTC, CPSC, and FDA.

15181 ■ Topics in Clinical Nutrition (TICN)
Pub: Lippincott Williams & Wilkins
URL(s): www.lww.com/webapp/wcs/stores/servlet/product__11851_-1_9012052_Prod -08835691. Ed: Judith A. Gilbride. Released: Quarterly Price: $98.99, Individuals; $354.49, Institutions; $197.73, Other countries; $453.73, Institutions, other countries; $60.99, Individuals in-training.

VIDEOCASSETTES/AUDIOCASSETTES

15182 ■ Chow! A Nutrition Curriculum
Sunburst Digital Inc.
1550 Executive Dr.
Elgin, IL 60123-9311
Free: 800-321-7511
Fax: (914)747-4109
Co. E-mail: service@sunburst.com
URL: http://www.sunburst.com
Contact: Dan Figurski, President
Released: 1998. Price: $99.95. Description: Educates middle school viewers about the importance of a healthy diet. Includes teacher's guide. Availability: VHS.

15183 ■ Diet and Cancer
Discovery Education
One Discovery Pl.
Silver Spring, MD 20910
Ph: (847)328-6700
Free: 800-323-9084
Fax: (847)328-6706
URL: http://www.discoveryeducation.com
Released: 1988. Price: $295.00. Description: The latest research on the relationship between diet and cancer is reviewed and viewers are instructed on how they may change their eating habits to reduce the risk of cancer. Availability: VHS; 3/4 U.

15184 ■ The Diet Maze
RMI Media
1365 N. Winchester St.
Olathe, KS 66061-5880
Ph: (913)768-1696
Free: 800-745-5480
Fax: (800)755-6910
Co. E-mail: actmedia@act.org
URL: http://www.actmedia.com
Released: 1987. Description: Doctors and nutritionists rate various diets and discuss the role of family and overweight camps in helping dieters. Availability: VHS; 3/4 U.

15185 ■ 8 Weeks to Optimum Health
Tapeworm Video Distributors
25876 The Old Road #141
Stevenson Ranch, CA 91381
Ph: (661)257-4904
Fax: (661)257-4820
Co. E-mail: sales@tapeworm.com
URL: http://www.tapeworm.com
Released: 1996. Price: $19.95. Description: Dr. Andrew Weil discusses his easy to follow program of exercise, diet, vitamins and meditation drawn from medical techniques from around the world. Availability: VHS.

15186 ■ Nutrition for Better Health
Encyclopedia Britannica
331 N. LaSalle St.
Chicago, IL 60654
Ph: (312)347-7159
Free: 800-323-1229
Fax: (312)294-2104
URL: http://www.britannica.com
Released: 1984. Price: $99.00. Description: Profiles good health through proper nutrition. Contains information on how overeating can hurt the body and how to avoid obesity, osteoporosis, hypertension, and heart disease. Availability: VHS; 3/4 U; SVS.

15187 ■ Nutrition: Eat and Be Healthy
Milner-Fenwick, Inc.
119 Lakefront Dr.
Hunt Valley, MD 21030-2216
Free: 800-432-8433
Fax: (410)252-6316
Co. E-mail: patiented@milner-fenwick.com
URL: http://www.milner-fenwick.com
Released: 1994. Price: $250.00. Description: Introduces the USDA food-guide pyramid and provides suggestions for preparing meals that meet nutritional guidelines. Availability: VHS.

15188 ■ Nutrition Facts: The New Food Label with Supermarket Savvy's Leni Reed
Family Experiences Productions, Inc.
PO Box 5879
Austin, TX 78763-5879
Ph: (512)494-0338
Fax: (512)494-0340
Co. E-mail: todd@fepi.com
URL: http://www.fepi.com
Released: 1994. Price: $39.95. Description: Registered dietitian Leni Reed explains components of standardized food labels and their relationship to daily nutritional needs. Availability: VHS.

15189 ■ Nutrition for Wellness
AJN Video Library/Lippincott Williams & Wilkins
American Journal of Nursing
345 Hudson St., 16th Fl.
New York, NY 10014
Ph: (212)886-1200
Free: 800-256-4045
Fax: (212)886-1276
Co. E-mail: info@nursingcenter.com
URL: http://www.nursingcenter.com
Released: 19??. Price: $250.00. Description: Part of the Lifestyles for Wellness Series. Features a clinical nutritionist who explains what a nutrient is, making it clear why good nutrition is so important to good health. She offers tips on how to choose the right and proper amounts of foods from the four food groups and also discusses food quality and developing new habits for wellness. Availability: VHS.

15190 ■ Nutrition for You
Educational Activities, Inc.
PO Box 87
Baldwin, NY 11510
Free: 800-797-3223
Fax: (516)623-9282
URL: http://www.edact.com
Released: 19??. Price: $79.00. Description: Outlines the effects that nutrition has on the body, emphasizing the importance of good nutrition. Covers how proteins, carbohydrates, vitamins, minerals, and water affect the diet. Also contains information about anorexia and bulimia, nutritional importance of limiting fat, salt, and sugar intake, and adequate fiber intake. Includes teacher's guide, interactive video masters, and reproducible masters. Availability: VHS.

15191 ■ Nutritional Assessment of the Elderly
AJN Video Library/Lippincott Williams & Wilkins
American Journal of Nursing
345 Hudson St., 16th Fl.
New York, NY 10014
Ph: (212)886-1200
Free: 800-256-4045
Fax: (212)886-1276
Co. E-mail: info@nursingcenter.com
URL: http://www.nursingcenter.com
Released: 19??. Price: $285.00. Description: Discusses the effects of human aging on nutritional assessment, enabling the health provider to identify the need for nutritional intervention much quicker. Provides information on the importance of a thorough history, normal physiological aging, socioeconomic status, acute and chronic illness, genetics, accessibility of care, climate, and individual nutritional habits. Demonstrates different measuring methods, including anthropometric, biochemical, hematologic, immune functions, oral, polypharmacy, psychosocial factors, and functional status. Includes study guide. Availability: VHS.

15192 ■ Shopping for Health
Family Experiences Productions, Inc.
PO Box 5879
Austin, TX 78763-5879
Ph: (512)494-0338
Fax: (512)494-0340
Co. E-mail: todd@fepi.com
URL: http://www.fepi.com
Released: 1997. Description: Four-volume series on women's nutrition and health issues. Availability: VHS.

TRADE SHOWS AND CONVENTIONS

15193 ■ California Dietetic Association Meeting

California Dietetic Association
7740 Manchester Ave., Ste. 102
Playa Del Rey, CA 90293-8499
Ph: (310)822-0177
Fax: (310)823-0264
Co. E-mail: patsmith@dietitian.org
URL: http://www.dietitian.org
Contact: Nicole Quartuccio, President
E-mail: president@dietitian.org
Frequency: Annual. **Audience:** Nutrition and dietetic professionals. **Principal Exhibits:** Food and nutrition services.

15194 ■ Soho Expo

National Nutritional Foods Association, Southeast Region
5309 Lime St.
New Port Richey, FL 34652
Ph: (727)846-0320
Fax: (727)848-7654
Co. E-mail: senpa@southeastnpa.org
URL: http://www.nnfase.org
Contact: Carylene Reed, Executive Director
E-mail: creed@nnfase-soho.org
URL(s): www.southeastnpa.org. **Frequency:** Annual. **Audience:** Industry - owners/staff natural/health food stores. **Principal Exhibits:** Nutritional foods and related equipment, supplies, and services.

CONSULTANTS

15195 ■ Center for Lifestyle Enhancement - Columbia Medical Center of Plano

3901 W 15th St.
Plano, TX 75075
Ph: (972)596-6800
Fax: (972)519-1299
Co. E-mail: mcp.cle@hcahealthcare.com
URL: http://www.medicalcenterofplano.com
Contact: Harvey Fishero, President
Scope: Provides professional health counseling in the areas of general nutrition for weight management, eating disorders, diabetic education, cholesterol reduction and adolescent weight management. Offers work site health promotion and preventive services. Also coordinates speaker's bureau, cooking classes and physician referrals. Industries served: education, insurance, healthcare, retail or wholesale, data processing and manufacturing throughout Texas. **Founded:** 1975. **Seminars:** Rx Diet and Exercise; Smoking Cessation; Stress Management; Health Fairs; Fitness Screenings; Body Composition; Nutrition Analysis; Exercise Classes; Prenatal Nutrition; SHAPEDOWN; Successfully Managing Diabetes; Gourmet Foods for Your Heart; The Aging Heart; Heart Smart Saturday featuring Day of Dance; Weight-Loss Management Seminars; The Right Stroke for Men; Peripheral Artery Disease Screening; Menstruation: The Cycle Begins; Boot Camp for New Dads; Grand parenting 101: Caring for Kids Today; Teddy Bear Camp; New Baby Day Camp; Safe Sitter Baby-Sitting Class.

15196 ■ Krumkill Stables

460 Krumkill Rd.
Albany, NY 12203
Ph: (518)482-8704
Fax: (518)482-7672
Co. E-mail: diet_farm@yahoo.com
URL: http://www.krumkillstables.com
Contact: Jean M. Bigaouette, Owner
E-mail: diet_farm@yahoo.com
Scope: Full service facility offering care for horses. Other services include taking riding lessons, organizing summer camps and offering trial rides.

15197 ■ Debra F. Latimer Nutrition and Diabetes Associates L.L.C.

6300 W Loop S, Ste. 333
Bellaire, TX 77401
Ph: (713)795-0876

Fax: (713)432-7989
Co. E-mail: dfl.nutrition@sbcglobal.net
URL: http://www.debraflatimer.com
Contact: Debra F. Latimer, Owner
E-mail: dfl.nutrition@sbcglobal.net
Scope: Provider of medical nutrition therapy on individual and group bases. Plans and conducts corporate wellness programs. Consultant to service and food manufacturing industries, as well as government agencies. Specializes in diabetes and renal education and management, weight management and compulsive eating disorders. **Founded:** 1981. **Seminars:** Diabetes-Self Management and Training Program, Houston, Jul, 2007; Preventive and Treatment Plans for Cardiac Care; Pre and Post-natal Nutrition; Pre-menstrual Syndrome; Eating for the Health of It; Weight Management and Wellness Program; Supermarket Nutrition Tours; Diabetes education and training. The Diabetes-Self Management and Education Program.

15198 ■ Margaret L. Mikkola

435 Central St.
Acton, MA 01720
Ph: (978)264-9040
Fax: (978)264-9040
Co. E-mail: mmikkola@verizon.net
Contact: Jeanette Norden, Manager
Scope: Nutrition consultant provides expertise for individuals and groups regarding food/health related issues. **Founded:** 1982.

15199 ■ NRH Nutrition Consultants Inc.

334 Hollywood Ave.
Little Neck, NY 11363
Ph: (718)229-0606
Fax: (718)631-4336
Co. E-mail: foodscount@aol.com
URL: http://www.thenutritionexperts.com
Contact: Karen J. Nolan, Manager
Scope: Registered dietitians and nutritionists providing services as translators of nutrition concepts and information. Serves private industries as well as government agencies. **Founded:** 1975. **Publications:** "The Fat Counter"; "The Complete Food Counter"; "The Healthy Whole foods Counter"; "The Cholesterol Counter"; "The Calorie Counter"; "The Diabetes, Carbohydrate and Calorie Counter"; "The Most Complete Food Counter"; "The Complete Food Counter"; "The Fat Counter"; "The Ultimate Carbohydrate Counter"; "The Vitamin and Mineral Food Counter"; "The Protein Counter"; "The Healthy Heart Food Counter"; "The Eating Out Food Counter"; "The Fat Attack Plan"; "Get Skinny the Smart Way: Your Personalized Weight Attack Plan".

15200 ■ R.D. Network Inc.

PO Box 375
Lafayette Hill, PA 19444
Ph: (215)482-4461
Free: 877-482-4991
Fax: (215)836-0378
Co. E-mail: info@rdnetwork.com
URL: http://www.rdnetwork.com
Contact: Leslie Grant, Owner
Scope: Dietitians, diet technicians, and certified dietary managers available nationwide and worldwide through an international registry for consulting positions to wellness and employee education programs, drug or alcohol rehabilitation, hospital, LTC, nutrition and labeling communications, nutrition consultation, weight control classes, healthcare staff supplementation, media and program development, and all nutrition and food-related needs. Expert witness and speakers bureau also available. Industries served: healthcare, food industry, food service, restaurateurs, supermarkets, pharmaceutical companies, home health agencies, insurance companies, HMOs, and government agencies. **Founded:** 1983. **Seminars:** Labour/Staffing; Outsourcing; Healthy Dining Etiquette for Executives and Sales Staff Diet and Wellness; Cardiovascular Nutrition; Starting a Nutrition Consulting Practice; AIDS and Diet Therapy; Nutrition Care for Your Parents in Their Elder Years; Increase Your Energy-Increase Your Sales.

15201 ■ VitaFlo Consultant

7707 Paragon Rd., Ste. 105
Centerville, OH 45459-4041

Ph: (937)436-1985
Co. E-mail: vitaflo@vitaflousa.com
URL: http://vitaflousa.com
Contact: Monica A. Cengia, President
E-mail: monica.cengia@vitaflo.co.uk
Scope: Registered dietitian offers nutritional assessments and consultations. Also provides individualized nutrition counseling, wellness programs, nutrition education programs, long-term health-care counseling, and media presentations. Industries served: long-term health-care, hospitals, universities, private businesses, health clubs/spas, physicians' offices, food industry, radio, television, and newspaper. **Founded:** 1985. **Seminars:** Fresh Start for Healthy Lifestyle Changes in 2007.

FRANCHISES AND BUSINESS OPPORTUNITIES

15202 ■ The Dentist Choice, Inc.

Choice Corporation, Inc.
33971 Selva Rd., Ste. 200
Dana Point, CA 92629
Free: 888-757-1333
Fax: (949)443-2074
Description: Dental health services. **No. of Franchise Units:** 120. **No. of Company-Owned Units:** 1. **Founded:** 1994.. **Franchised:** 1994. **Equity Capital Needed:** $60,000. **Franchise Fee:** $45,000. **Financial Assistance:** Yes. **Training:** Provides 1 week at headquarters and ongoing support.

15203 ■ Discount Sport Nutrition

Discount Sport Nutrition Franchising, L.P.
7324 Gaston Ave., Ste. 124-422
Dallas, TX 75214
Ph: (972)489-7925
Fax: (214)292-8619
Co. E-mail: franchising@sportsupplements.com
URL: http://www.sportsupplements.com
Description: Nutritional sport supplements retail store. **No. of Franchise Units:** 6. **Founded:** 1996.. **Franchised:** 2000. **Equity Capital Needed:** $92,774-$185,344. **Franchise Fee:** $25,000. **Financial Assistance:** Yes. **Training:** 3 phase hands on training program located at current stores, as well as your location. Provides assistance with site location, leases, layout design, suppliers, advertising, marketing, and ongoing assistance.

15204 ■ GNC Holdings Inc. (GNC)—GNC Corp.

GNC Franchising, Inc.
300 Sixth Ave.
Pittsburgh, PA 15222
Ph: (412)3388-2503
Free: 800-766-7099
Fax: (412)402-7105
Co. E-mail: livewell@gncfranchising.com
URL: http://www.gncfranchising.com
Contact: Joseph Fortunato, President
Description: Retailer of vitamins, minerals, herbs and sports nutrition supplements. GNC is the provider of products & information for personal health enhancement. **No. of Franchise Units:** 2,014. **No. of Company-Owned Units:** 3,799. **Founded:** 1989. **Franchised:** 1988. **Equity Capital Needed:** $132,681-$182,031. **Franchise Fee:** $40,000. **Training:** Training and support provided.

15205 ■ Griswold Special Care

Griswold Special Care, Inc.
717 Bethlehem Pike, Ste. 300
Erdenheim, PA 19073
Ph: (215)402-0200
Fax: (215)402-0202
URL: http://www.griswoldspecialcare.com
Description: Non-medical homecare. **No. of Franchise Units:** 191. **No. of Company-Owned Units:** 9. **Founded:** 1982.. **Franchised:** 1984. **Equity Capital Needed:** $84,725-$107,700. **Franchise Fee:** $41,900. **Royalty Fee:** 3-4%. **Financial Assistance:** Third party financing available. **Training:** Provides 7 days at corporate headquarters, annual visit to franchisee's location, additional as needed and ongoing support.

15206 ■ The Hungry Heart
Hungry Heart Franchise, LLC
28202 Cabot Rd., Ste. 300
Laguna Niguel, CA 92677
Free: 877-486-4797
Fax: (714)280-9755
Description: A caring approach to out of control eating. **No. of Franchise Units:** 5. **No. of Company-Owned Units:** 1. **Founded:** 1996.. **Franchised:** 2006. **Equity Capital Needed:** $43,000-$57,000. **Franchise Fee:** $24,500. **Training:** Yes.

COMPUTERIZED DATABASES

15207 ■ *Health & Wellness InSite<svs>*
610 Opperman Dr.
Eagen, MN 55122
Free: 800-477-4300
Co. E-mail: gale.contentlicensing@cengage.com
URL: http://www.insite2.gale.com
Availability: Online: Cengage Learning Inc. - Gale - InSite2. **Type:** Full-text.

LIBRARIES

15208 ■ Abbott Laboratories, Ross Products Division Resource Center
625 Cleveland Ave.
Columbus, OH 43215-1724
Free: 800-227-5767
Co. E-mail: rosswebmaster@abbott.com
URL: http://abbottnutrition.com
Scope: Nutrition, food technology, business, analytical chemistry. **Services:** Current Awareness. **Founded:** 1949. **Holdings:** 3500 books; 6000 bound periodical volumes. **Subscriptions:** 350 journals and other serials.

15209 ■ American Dietetic Association - Knowledge Center
120 S. Riverside Plaza, Ste. 20000
Chicago, IL 60606-6995
Ph: (312)877-1600, x4864
Free: 800-877-1600
Fax: (312)899-4739
Co. E-mail: knowledge@eatright.org
URL: http://www.eatright.org/
Scope: Nutrition, dietetics, food service. **Services:** Interlibrary loan; copying; Library open to the public by appointment. **Founded:** 1990. **Holdings:** 3000 books. **Subscriptions:** 60 journals and other serials; 4 newspapers.

15210 ■ American Institute for Biosocial and Medical Research, Inc. - Library—AIBMR Life Sciences, Inc. - Library.
4117 S. Meridian
Puyallup, WA 98373
Ph: (253)286-2888
Fax: (253)286-2451
Co. E-mail: aibmrinfo@aibmr.com
URL: http://www.aibmr.com
Contact: Alexander Schauss
Scope: Behavioral science - eating disorders, abnormal behavior, learning disabilities, behavior disorders; mental illness; biochemistry; environmental health; nutrition; psychology; sociology; criminology; medicine; organic chemistry; botanical pharmacognosy; photobiology; neurology; toxicology. **Services:** Library not open to the public. **Founded:** 1978. **Holdings:** 10,330 books; 350 periodicals; 60,000 reference papers. **Subscriptions:** 303 journals and other serials; 3 newspapers.

15211 ■ Bastyr University Library
14500 Juanita Dr., NE
Kenmore, WA 98028
Ph: (425)602-3020
Fax: (425)602-3188
Co. E-mail: library@bastyr.edu
URL: http://www.bastyr.edu/student-life/library
Contact: Jane D. Saxton, Director, Library Services
Scope: Complementary and alternative medicine, acupuncture and traditional Chinese medicine, naturopathic medicine, nutrition, health psychology, exercise science, primary care medicine, homeopathy, midwifery, herbal science, botanical medicine.

Services: Interlibrary loan; copying; Library open to the public for reference use only. **Founded:** 1980. **Holdings:** 19,000 books; 4000 CD/audiocassettes; 800 DVD/videocassettes; online databases. **Subscriptions:** 250 journals and other serials.

15212 ■ Beech-Nut Nutrition Corporation Library
100 Hero Dr.
Amsterdam, NY 12010
Free: 800-233-2468
Fax: (518)673-3259
URL: http://www.beechnut.com
Scope: Nutrition, pediatrics, food chemistry. **Services:** Library not open to the public. **Holdings:** 1000 books. **Subscriptions:** 31 journals and other serials.

15213 ■ California Culinary Academy Library
350 Rhode Island St.
San Francisco, CA 94103
Ph: (415)771-3500
Free: 888-897-3222
Co. E-mail: bgk@baychef.com
URL: http://www.chefs.edu/San-Francisco
Scope: Culinary arts, nutrition, restaurant and hospitality industry. **Services:** Library open to the public by special appointment only. **Founded:** 1989. **Holdings:** 3500 books. **Subscriptions:** 90 journals and other serials.

15214 ■ Campbell Soup Company Research Information Center
1 Campbell Pl.
Camden, NJ 09103-1799
Ph: (856)342-4800
Free: 800-257-8443
Fax: (856)342-3878
URL: http://www.campbellsoup.com
Contact: Denise Morrison, President
Scope: Food technology, biochemistry, microbiology, nutrition. **Services:** Interlibrary loan; Library not open to the public. **Founded:** 1941. **Holdings:** 5000 books; 2200 bound periodical volumes; 3500 patents. **Subscriptions:** 250 journals and other serials.

15215 ■ Cleveland Health Sciences Library
Sch. of Medicine, Robbins Bldg.
2210 Circle Dr.
Cleveland, OH 44106-4914
Ph: (216)368-4540
Co. E-mail: virginia.saha@case.edu
URL: http://www.case.edu/chsl/library/index.html
Contact: Virginia G. Saha, Director
Scope: Medicine, dentistry, nursing, biology, nutrition. **Services:** Interlibrary loan; copying; SDI; scanning and digitization; Library open to the public for reference use only. **Founded:** 1965. **Holdings:** 430,000 books and journal volumes; 3752 microfiche; 1000 lin.ft. of archives; 500 CD-ROMs; 2634 audio/visual programs; 51,433 slides. **Subscriptions:** 14,642 journals and other serials (91 print, 14,551 electronic). **Telecommunication Services:** kathleen.blazar@case.edu.

15216 ■ Dairy Management Inc. Information Resources
10255 W. Higgins Rd., Ste. 900
Rosemont, IL 60018-5616
Free: 800-853-2479
URL: http://www.dairyinfo.com
Contact: Ronald Stoner, Director
Scope: Dairy products, food, nutrition. **Services:** Interlibrary loan; technical background information; library not open to the public. **Founded:** 1956. **Holdings:** 3000 books. **Subscriptions:** 300 journals and other serials.

15217 ■ Geisinger Medical Center - Community Health Library
100 N. Academy Ave.
Danville, PA 17822-4401
Ph: (570)271-5638
Fax: (570)271-5635
Co. E-mail: chrl@geisinger.edu
URL: http://www.geisinger.edu
Contact: Patricia A Ulmer, Librarian
Scope: General medicine, nutrition, alternative and complementary medicine, pediatrics, cancer, AIDS. **Services:** Interlibrary loan. **Founded:** 1996. **Holdings:** 860 books; 200 audio/visual materials. **Subscriptions:** 14 journals and other serials.

15218 ■ General Mills, Inc. - Betty Crocker Kitchens Library
PO Box 9452
Minneapolis, MN 55440
Free: 800-446-1898
Fax: (763)764-8330
URL: http://www.bettycrocker.com
URL(s): www.generalmills.com. **Scope:** Cookery. **Services:** Center not open to the public. **Holdings:** 9000 books. **Subscriptions:** 81 journals and other serials.

15219 ■ The Gottesman Libraries at Teachers College
Columbia University
525 W. 120th St.
Box 69
New York, NY 10027
Ph: (212)678-3494
Fax: (212)678-3092
URL: http://library.tc.columbia.edu
Contact: Jennifer Whitten Govan, Director, Collections
Scope: Education, psychology, health sciences, nutrition, nursing, communications, computing, technology, speech and language pathology, audiology. **Services:** Interlibrary loan; copying; consultations; eReserves; bibliographic instruction; course-specific instruction; library open to the public with METRO cards. **Founded:** 1887. **Holdings:** 500,000 monograph and serial volumes; 224,227 microforms; 6679 nonprint materials; 3694 cubic feet of manuscript material; 93,639 photographs; 8361 titles in microform; 5251 computer files; sound recordings; 65 cartographic; 2345 graphic; 1488 audio; 2781 film and video. **Subscriptions:** 2104 journals and other serials.

15220 ■ Kellogg Company - Kellogg Information Center
2 Hamblin Ave., E.
Battle Creek, MI 49016-3423
Ph: (269)961-6917
Free: 800-962-1413
Fax: (269)565-1227
Co. E-mail: liz.scalia@kellogg.com
URL: http://www.kelloggs.com
Contact: Liz Scalia
Scope: Food science and nutrition. **Services:** Document delivery (for Kellogg employees); center not open to the public. **Holdings:** 3000 books. **Subscriptions:** 115 journals and other serials.

15221 ■ Kraft Foods, Inc. - Technical Information Center
801 Waukegan Rd.
Glenview, IL 60025
Ph: (847)646-3509
Fax: (847)646-5150
URL: http://www.kraft.com
Scope: Food technology, dairy science, nutrition, microbiology, packaging. **Services:** Library not open to the public. **Founded:** 1938. **Holdings:** 8600 books; 800 bound periodical volumes; 8600 reels of microfilm; 42,000 research reports. **Subscriptions:** 325 journals and other serials.

15222 ■ Lemmen-Holton Cancer Pavilion Library
145 Michigan, NE
Grand Rapids, MI 49503
Ph: (616)486-5700
URL: http://www.spectrumhealth.org/lhcp
Scope: Cancer. **Services:** Library open to the public. **Holdings:** Pamphlets.

15223 ■ National College of Natural Medicine Library
049 SW Porter St.
Portland, OR 97201-4848
Ph: (503)552-1542
Fax: (503)219-1547
Co. E-mail: circulation@ncnm.edu
URL: http://www.ncnm.edu/library/
Contact: Steve Dehner
Scope: Naturopathy, homeopathy, nutrition, physiotherapy, botanical medicine, Chinese medicine, acupuncture, clinical and basic sciences. **Services:**

Interlibrary loan; copying; library open to the public with restrictions. **Founded:** 1956. **Holdings:** 14,000 books, videos, and audiotapes; 1000 bound periodical volumes. **Subscriptions:** 140 journals and other serials. **Telecommunication Services:** rseverson@ncnm.edu.

15224 ■ National Eating Disorder Information Centre
ES 7-421
200 Elizabeth St.
Toronto, ON, Canada M5G 2C4
Ph: (416)340-4156
Free: 866-633-4220
Fax: (416)340-4736
Co. E-mail: nedic@uhn.on.ca
URL: http://www.nedic.ca
Contact: Merryl Bear, Director
Scope: Eating disorders, food preoccupation, weight preoccupation, support groups. **Services:** Centre open to the public. **Founded:** 1985. **Holdings:** 50 books. **Subscriptions:** 250 journals and other serials.

15225 ■ New York Public Library - Mid-Manhattan Library - General Reference and Advisory Services/Health Information Center
455 5th Ave. at 40th St.
New York, NY 10016
Ph: (212)340-0863
URL: http://www.nypl.org/locations/mid-manhattan-library
Contact: Theresa Myrhol, Librarian
URL(s): legacy.www.nypl.org/branch/collections/hic. html. **Scope:** Consumer, health medicine, nursing, allied health. **Services:** Copying; Library open to the public. **Founded:** 1996. **Holdings:** 22,000 books and videocassettes; 4 VF of pamphlets. **Subscriptions:** 278 journals and other serials.

15226 ■ PepsiCo - The Information Center
617 W. Main St.
Barrington, IL 60010
Ph: (847)304-2064
Fax: (847)304-2062
Co. E-mail: sharon.lazzara@pepsico.com
URL: http://www.pepsico.com
Contact: Sharon Lazzara, Analyst
Scope: Food, nutrition, exercise physiology, beverages. **Services:** Interlibrary loan; copying (limited). **Founded:** 1956. **Holdings:** 3000 books. **Subscriptions:** 200 journals and other serials.

15227 ■ Price-Pottenger Nutrition Foundation Library—Health and Healing Wisdom; PPNF.
7890 Broadway
Lemon Grove, CA 91945
Ph: (619)462-7600
Free: 800-366-3748
Fax: (619)433-3136
Co. E-mail: info@ppnf.org
URL: http://www.ppnf.org
Contact: Edward Bennett, President
Scope: Nutrition, preventative medicine, health, natural farming and gardening, pesticides, fluoride, mercury, dental health, natural farming and gardening, natural pet care, traditional/historic diets, primitive diets, holistic medicine. **Services:** Copying; library open to members only for reference use. **Founded:** 1952. **Holdings:** Journals and other serials; 10,000 volumes; 18,000 film positives; 6000 glass lantern slides; scientific reprints; video and audio tapes; reports; archives. **Telecommunication Services:** jack@ppnf.org; joan@ppnf.org.

15228 ■ Tufts University - Hirsh Health Sciences Library
145 Harrison Ave.
Boston, MA 02111
Ph: (617)636-6705
Fax: (617)636-4039
Co. E-mail: eric.albright@tufts.edu
URL: http://www.library.tufts.edu/hsl/index.html
Contact: Eric D. Albright, Director
Scope: Medicine, dentistry, veterinary medicine, nutrition. **Services:** Interlibrary loan; copying; online databases searching; SDI; Library open to the public

by subscription. **Founded:** 1900. **Holdings:** 47,227 books; 160,127 bound periodical volumes; 581 audiotapes; 292 slide titles; reels of microfilm; microcards; 255 videotapes; phonograph records; video discs. **Subscriptions:** 921 journals and other serials; 19,000 electronic journals and other serials. **Telecommunication Services:** hhsl@tufts.edu.

15229 ■ U.S.D.A. Agricultural Research Service - Western Regional Research Center Library
800 Buchanan St.
Albany, CA 94710
Ph: (510)559-5603
Fax: (510)559-5766
Co. E-mail: howard.zhang@ars.usda.gov
URL: http://www.ars.usda.gov/AboutUs/AboutUs. htm?modecode=53-25-00-00
Contact: Howard Q. Zhang, Director
Scope: Cereals, fruits and vegetables, field and industrial crops, food technology, chemistry, nutrition. **Founded:** 1940. **Holdings:** Figures not available. **Telecommunication Services:** michael.cooley@ars. usda.gov.

15230 ■ U.S.D.A. National Agricultural Library - Food and Nutrition Information Center
10301 Baltimore Ave., Rm. 108
Beltsville, MD 20705-2351
Ph: (301)504-5414
Fax: (301)504-6409
Co. E-mail: shirley.evans@ars.usda.gov
URL: http://fnic.nal.usda.gov
Contact: Shirley King Evans
Scope: Human nutrition education, nutrition resources for USDA food and nutrition programs. **Services:** Interlibrary loan; Center open to the public with restricted lending. **Founded:** 1971. **Holdings:** 50,000 books; VF drawers. **Subscriptions:** 200 journals and other serials.

15231 ■ U.S. Food & Drug Administration osciences Library - CFSAN Branch Library—FDA.
5100 Paint Branch Pkwy.
HFS-678
College Park, MD 20740
Ph: (301)436-2163
Fax: (301)436-2653
Co. E-mail: cfsanlib@fda.hhs.gov
Contact: Lee S. Bernstein, Manager
Scope: Chemistry, analytical chemistry, toxicology, food technology, nutrition, medicine, biology, cosmetics. **Services:** Interlibrary loan; Library open to the public. **Founded:** 1961. **Holdings:** 1000 books; 500 reports, documents, pamphlets; 16,000 cartridges of microfilm. **Subscriptions:** 100 journals and other serials.

15232 ■ University of California, Berkeley - Marian Koshland Bioscience and Natural Resources Library
2101 Valley Life Sciences Bldg., No. 6500
Berkeley, CA 94720-6500
Ph: (510)642-2531
Fax: (510)642-8217
Co. E-mail: bweil@library.berkeley.edu
URL: http://www.lib.berkeley.edu/BIOS
Contact: Beth Weil, Librarian
Scope: Agriculture, anatomy, botany, cell biology, environmental sciences, molecular biology, biology, nutrition, pest management, physiology, forestry, entomology, paleontology. **Services:** Interlibrary loan (through General Library); copying; Library open to the public for reference use with restricted circulation; printing; scanning. **Founded:** 1930. **Holdings:** 542,000 volumes; 50,633 pamphlets and reprints; 1543 reels of microfilm; 24,005 microfiche. **Subscriptions:** 5000 journals and other serials; 10,000 e-journals. **Telecommunication Services:** nkobzina@library.berkeley.edu.

15233 ■ University of Hawaii - John A. Burns School of Medicine - Health Sciences Library
651 Ilalo St., MEB
Honolulu, HI 96813
Ph: (808)692-0810

Fax: (808)692-1244
Co. E-mail: hslinfo@hawaii.edu
URL: http://www.hawaii.edu/hslib
Contact: Virginia Tanji, Director, Library Services
Scope: Public health, health services planning and administration, quantitative health sciences, health education, clinical medicine. **Services:** Interlibrary loan; copying; document delivery; Library open to the public. **Founded:** 1968. **Holdings:** 12,000 books; 1200 bound periodical volumes. **Subscriptions:** 70 journals and other serials. **Telecommunication Services:** tanji@hawaii.edu.

15234 ■ University of Nebraska--Lincoln - C.Y. Thompson Library
38th and Holdrege Sts., East Campus
Lincoln, NE 68583-0717
Ph: (402)472-4401
Fax: (402)472-7005
Co. E-mail: cytmail@unlnotes.unl.edu
URL: http://libraries.unl.edu/cyt
Contact: Rebecca Bernthal, Liaison
Scope: Agriculture, natural resources, home economics, textiles, wildlife conservation, human development, family therapy, nutrition, food science, applied sciences, speech pathology, audiology, special education, dentistry, dental hygiene, oral surgery. **Services:** Interlibrary loan; copying; Library open to the public. **Founded:** 1964. **Holdings:** 187,399 books; 181,237 bound periodical volumes; 49,116 microforms. **Subscriptions:** 14,789 journals and other serials; 3 newspapers. **Telecommunication Services:** rbernthal1@unl.edu.

RESEARCH CENTERS

15235 ■ Center for Medical Consumers (CMC)
239 Thompson St.
New York, NY 10012
Ph: (212)674-7105
Fax: (212)674-7100
Co. E-mail: centerformedicalconsumers@gmail.com
URL: http://medicalconsumers.org
Contact: Arthur Aaron Levin, President
Description: Serves as an advocacy group on health and medical information at the state and local legislative level. **Scope:** medicine, health. **Founded:** 1976. **Subscriptions:** articles. **Publications:** *HealthFacts* (Monthly). **Telecommunication Services:** medconsumers@earthlink.net.

15236 ■ Columbia University - Institute of Human Nutrition (IHN)
College of Physicians & Surgeons, Ste. 1512
Presbyterian Hospital
630 W 168th St.
New York, NY 10032
Ph: (212)305-4808
Fax: (212)305-3079
Co. E-mail: nutrition@mail.cumc.columbia.edu
URL: http://www.cumc.columbia.edu/ihn
Contact: Richard J. Deckelbaum, Director
Founded: 1954.

15237 ■ Ohio State University - Food Industries Center (FIC)
Howlett Hall, Ste. 140
2001 Fyffe Rd.
Columbus, OH 43210-1007
Ph: (614)292-7004
Free: 800-752-2751
Fax: (614)688-5459
Co. E-mail: alvarez.23@osu.edu
URL: http://foodindustries.osu.edu
Contact: Dr. Valente B. Alvarez, Director
Founded: 1980. **Publications:** *FIC Annual Reports*; *FIC Bulletins*; *Newsletter Quarterly* (Quarterly). **Educational Activities:** FIC Seminars; Better Process Control School. **Telecommunication Services:** osufic@osu.edu.

15238 ■ University of Florida - Center for Nutritional Sciences
201 Food Science & Human Nutrition Bldg.
Gainesville, FL 32611
Ph: (352)392-2133

Fax: (352)392-1008
Co. E-mail: cousins@ufl.edu
URL: http://nutritionalsciences.centers.ufl.edu/default.
  aspx
Contact: Dr. Robert J. Cousins, Director
Founded: 1987. **Educational Activities:** Graduate
Program; Center for Nutritional Sciences Seminars

(Periodic), on nutrition; Center for Nutritional Sciences Graduate Research Assistantships.

**15239 ■ University of Texas Southwestern
Medical Center at Dallas - Center for Human
Nutrition**
5323 Harry Hines Blvd.
Dallas, TX 75390-9052

Ph: (214)648-2890
Fax: (214)648-8955
Co. E-mail: nutrition@utsouthwestern.edu
URL: http://www.utsouthwestern.edu/utsw/cda/
  dept27712/files/40245.html
Contact: Prof. Scott M. Grundy, Director

ASSOCIATIONS AND OTHER ORGANIZATIONS

15240 ■ Business and Institutional Furniture Manufacturer's Association (BIFMA International)
678 Front Ave. NW, Ste. 150
Grand Rapids, MI 49504-5368
Ph: (616)285-3963
Fax: (616)285-3765
Co. E-mail: email@bifma.org
URL: http://www.bifma.org
Contact: Stan Askren, President
Description: Organized group of furniture manufacturers and suppliers addressing issues of common concern to the contract furnishings industry. Works to develop, expand, and promote work environments that enhance the productivity and comfort of customers. **Founded:** 1973. **Publications:** *The Download, BIFMA International* (Quarterly). **Educational Activities:** Leadership Conference (Annual).

15241 ■ International Interior Design Association (IIDA)
222 Merchandise Mart, Ste. 567
Chicago, IL 60654
Ph: (312)467-1950
Free: 888-799-4432
Fax: (312)467-0779
Co. E-mail: iidahq@iida.org
URL: http://www.iida.org
Contact: Peter Conant, President
Description: Represents professional interior designers, including designers of commercial, healthcare, hospitality, government, retail, residential facilities; educators; researchers; representatives of allied manufacturing sources. Conducts research, student programs and continuing education programs for members. Has developed a code of ethics for the professional design membership. **Founded:** 1994. **Publications:** GRAction.

15242 ■ MTM Association for Standards and Research—Methods Time Measurements Association for Standards and Research
1111 E Touhy Ave.
Des Plaines, IL 60018
Ph: (847)299-1111
Fax: (847)299-3509
Co. E-mail: webmaster@mtm.org
URL: http://www.mtm.org
Description: Persons interested in the fields of industrial engineering, industrial psychology, and human engineering. Conducts research at accredited institutions on human motion (the physical movement of body and limb), with emphasis on examining: internal velocity, acceleration, tension, and control characteristics of a given motion under several conditions; external regularities of given groups of motion as they vary under several conditions of performance; the proper use of motion information in measuring, controlling, and improving manual activities. Also studies ergonomics and the effects of workplace environment on productivity. Provides information on fatigue, optimum methods of performance, the effect of practice on motion performance, and the use of motion information for determining allowances and predicting total performance time. Has developed computer programs for the application of Methods Time Measurement (MTM) and MTM-based work measurement systems. Conducts training courses and testing for certification of practitioners and instructors in all Association MTM Systems. Develops and makes available specialized productivity management services. **Founded:** 1951.

REFERENCE WORKS

15243 ■ "Bridging the Ingenuity Gap" in Canadian Business (Vol. 79, November 6, 2006, No. 22, pp. 12)
Pub: Rogers Media
Ed: Rachel Pulfer. **Description:** The views of Patrick Whitney, director of Illinois Institute of Technology's Institute of design, on globalization and business design methods are presented.

15244 ■ "Colores Origenes: Martha Kruse" in Advertising Age (Vol. 77, November 13, 2006, No. 46, pp. S12)
Pub: Crain Communications, Inc.
Ed: Laurel Wentz. **Description:** Home Depot has created a range of Latin paint colors called Colores Origenes; the new line was originally intended to launch only at locations with heavily Hispanic patrons but the company decided to make the line available at all of their stores.

15245 ■ "Fabulous New Office Furniture: Ways to Revamp Your Workspace" in Inc. (Vol. 33, September 2011, No. 7, pp. 51)
Pub: Inc. Magazine
Ed: Nadine Heintz. **Description:** Various new looks to revamp any office space are highlighted including a table lamp by designer Peter Stathis for Joby.

15246 ■ "Inside the Googleplex" in Canadian Business (Vol. 79, November 6, 2006, No. 22, pp. 59)
Pub: Rogers Media
Ed: Christina Campbell. **Description:** The views of Clive Wilkinson, a designer, on relationship between interior design and employee's productivity are presented.

15247 ■ "Intel Joins Movement to Turn Cube Farms Into Wide-Open Spaces" in Sacramento Business Journal (Vol. 28, May 27, 2011, No. 13, pp. 1)
Pub: Sacramento Business Journal
Ed: Melanie Turner. **Description:** Intel Corporation has remodeled its facility in Folsom, California. The renovation has required some workers to give up their cubicles. Comments from executives are included.

15248 ■ "Let Your Stuff Tell a Story: How to Edit Your Accessories to Showcase Your Personality" in Charlotte Observer (February 8, 2007)
Pub: Knight-Ridder/Tribune Business News
Ed: Nancy Brachey. **Description:** Tips to accessorize any home or office are presented; eliminating clutter is stressed.

15249 ■ "Make a Resolution: ADA Training" in HRMagazine (Vol. 54, January 2009, No. 1, pp. 81)
Pub: Society for Human Resource Management
Contact: Henry G. Jackson, President
E-mail: hjackson@shrm.org
Ed: Victoria Zellers. **Description:** Americans with Disabilities Act (ADA) Amendments Act took effect January 1, 2009. The ADA Amendments Act means that more applicants and employees are eligible for reasonable accommodations and that employers need to develop a new ADA compliance strategy.

15250 ■ "Procter Gambles on Wallpaper; Putting Paint On a Roll" in Advertising Age (Vol. 77, September 18, 2006, No. 38, pp. 4)
Pub: Crain Communications, Inc.
Ed: Jack Neff. **Description:** Procter & Gamble Co. has launched a new line of textured paints that are already applied to a wallpaper-like roll that can be hung without paste or wallpaper tools.

15251 ■ "Shore Total Office Liquidates Massive Supply of Bank Furniture and Used Furniture" in Internet Wire (June 21, 2010)
Pub: Comtex
Description: Shore Total Office, located in San Diego, California, is liquidating quality bank furniture and used furniture to customers hoping to outfit their facilities with stylish new furnishings. Shore Total Office is a leading supplier of high quality office furniture and designs.

TRADE PERIODICALS

15252 ■ Human Factors and Ergonomics Society Bulletin
Pub: Human Factors and Ergonomics Society
Contact: Waldemar Karwowski, President
Released: Monthly. **Description:** Recurring features include letters to the editor, news of research, a calendar of events, reports of meetings, news of educational opportunities, job listings, and notices of publications available.

15253 ■ IE News: Ergonomics
Pub: Institute of Industrial Engineers
Contact: Don H. Greene, Chief Executive Officer
Ed: Wendy Kavanagh, Editor. **Released:** Quarterly. **Price:** Included in membership. **Description:** Focuses on ergonomics (human factors) in the work place, the development of ergonomic standards, and case studies. Recurring features include a calendar of events, reports of meetings, and columns titled Message from the Director, Academic Roundup: Update, and Message from the Editor.

15254 ■ *Interior Design*

Pub: Reed Business Information
Contact: Jeff Greisch, President
URL(s): www.interiordesign.net/. **Released:** 15/yr.
Price: $59.95, Individuals; $87, Canada; $187, Other countries.

15255 ■ *Today's Facility Manager: The Facility Decision Maker's Source for Products and Services*

Pub: Group C Communications Inc.
Contact: Lyle Connor, Manager
E-mail: lconnor@groupc.com
URL(s): todaysfacilitymanager.com. **Ed:** Heidi Schwartz. **Released:** Monthly **Price:** Free.

CONSULTANTS

15256 ■ Building Design Service

350 Kresge Ln., Ste. B
Sparks, NV 89431-6435
Ph: (775)356-7870
Contact: Brian A. Beecher, Owner
Scope: Building design consultants with additional expertise in mine plant and facility design, structural and miscellaneous steel detailing and construction estimating. **Founded:** 1965.

15257 ■ Carmichael Associates

4255 Auburn St.
Wichita, KS 67220
Ph: (316)681-1535
Fax: (316)681-1548
Co. E-mail: joewmc@aol.com
Contact: Joe William Carmichael, President
E-mail: joewmc@aol.com
Scope: Architectural consultant active in legal assistance, library design, church design, health care projects, nursing homes, clinics, apartments, governmental buildings, renovations and remodeling work, residential and commercial, heavy truck maintenance and operations design, and small college buildings and planning. **Founded:** 1958.

15258 ■ Cassway/Albert Ltd.

1528 Walnut St., Ste. 1100
Philadelphia, PA 19102
Ph: (215)545-4900
Fax: (215)545-8222
Co. E-mail: cal@icdc.com
Contact: Robert L. Cassway, President
Scope: Consultants in architecture, landscape architecture, urban planning, interior design, and space planning. **Founded:** 1963.

15259 ■ Hewitt Architects

101 Stewart St., Ste. 200
Seattle, WA 98101
Ph: (206)624-8154
Fax: (206)626-0541
Co. E-mail: information@hewittseattle.com
URL: http://www.hewittseattle.com
Contact: Kevin J. Ryden, Manager
E-mail: ryden@hewittarchitects.com
Scope: Multi-disciplinary firm with architecture, design and landscape architecture expertise specializing in new construction and renovation of administrative, waterfront, transportation facilities, urban residential and mixed-use complexes; master plan development for urban centers, village concepts, destination resorts, office parks/campuses, shopping facilities and transportation/multi-modal facilities. **Founded:** 1975.

15260 ■ The Hezner Corp.

678 Broadway St., Ste. 100
Libertyville, IL 60048-2324
Ph: (847)918-3800
Fax: (847)549-7633
Co. E-mail: info@hezner.com
URL: http://www.hezner.biz
Contact: Kurt E. Hezner, President
E-mail: kurth@hezner.biz
Scope: Architectural design and internal layout design of financial institutions-banks, savings and loan associations, credit unions, and commercial facilities. Recommends practical procedures and practices, site plans and floor plans. Serves private

industries as well as government, particularly the United States. **Founded:** 1932. **Telecommunication Services:** info@hezner.biz.

15261 ■ HLW International L.L.P.

115 Fifth Ave., 5th Fl.
New York, NY 10003-1004
Ph: (212)353-4600
Fax: (212)353-4666
Co. E-mail: jgering@hlw.com
URL: http://www.hlw.com
Contact: Leevi Kiil, Chief Executive Officer
E-mail: lkiil@hlw.com
Scope: Provider of comprehensive services for many diverse projects located throughout the United States and the world, including architecture, engineering, planning, interior design, and consulting. As part of its expanding practice, offers a series of next-generation services, which provide clients with expertise outside the realm of traditional disciplines: workplace management, strategic facilities planning and design/build. **Founded:** 1885. **Publications:** "Interior Design". **Seminars:** Rehabilitation of Office Facilities; R&D Facilities Costs and Cost Analysis; Renovation of R&D Buildings and Labs; Trends and New Developments for Medical Research Facilities; New Technologies for R&D Building Systems; New Labs for Pharmaceutical, Biotechnology, Medical Device and Personal Care Products. **Special Services:** Workplace ED/GE.

15262 ■ Marconi Designs

985 University Ave., Ste. 22
Los Gatos, CA 95032-0115
Ph: (408)807-8330
Fax: (408)841-7234
Co. E-mail: patricia@marconidesigns.com
URL: http://www.wahlichusa.com/design
Contact: Patricia A. Wahli, Owner
E-mail: patricia@marconidesigns.com
Scope: Provider of interior design, space planning and facility design for commercial office buildings of any size. Renovation, remodel and reconfiguration of personnel workspaces and existing buildings the firms specialties. Tenant improvements for new and existing office space also handled. Industries served electronics, medical, banking industries and government agencies in California, state-wide, with emphasis on San Francisco Bay Area. **Founded:** 1981. **Telecommunication Services:** patty.wahli@gmail.com.

15263 ■ Michaels Associates Design Consultants Inc.

14809 N 73rd St.
Scottsdale, AZ 85260-3113
Ph: (480)998-7476
Fax: (480)998-9390
Co. E-mail: madinc@vsnl.com
Contact: Andrea Arthur Michaels, President
E-mail: andrea@madcap.nu
Scope: Twenty year specialization in all areas of library (public, academic, corporate and national) programming and planning, including needs assessments and interior and graphic design. Michaels Associates expertise also includes ADA audits, furniture and product design for offices, lighting and graphic design. **Founded:** 1975. **Publications:** "Forum III: Physical Spaces for the E-ssential Library," 2003; "Library facility Planning"; "Library Administration & Management"; "Enhance Security With Effective Interior Planning and Design"; "Designing for Technology in Todays Libraries". **Seminars:** Library Environments: Changing to Fit New Technologies and Services, Dowling College, Long Island, NY, Nov, 2004; Reconfiguration Strategies Library Space for the E-Library, Information Futures Institute, San Francisco, CA, Sep, 2004; Creative Learning Seminars; Library Interior Planning & Design; Accessible, Healthy, Imaginative Spaces: Old & New; Fresh Looks for Library Interiors; The Future is Now: Library Planning &Design for the 21st Century; ADA Furnishings Response for Today's Libraries; Lighting & Libraries; Library Planning Based on New Functional Space Guidelines; Crime Prevention through Environmental Design.

15264 ■ Site Design Group Ltd.

888 S Michigan Ave., Ste. 1000
Chicago, IL 60605
Ph: (312)427-7240
Fax: (312)427-7241
Co. E-mail: ecwong@site-design.com
URL: http://www.site-design.com
Contact: Michelle M. Inouye, Manager
E-mail: mminouye@site-design.com
Scope: An architectural/engineering consulting firm with experience in food facilities design; interior design; landscape planning and plant/office layout and design. Serves a wide variety of industries and government agencies. **Founded:** 1986. **Publications:** "Wilderness Experiences inspire Urban design," Apr, 2004; "A Cultural Revolution: In Chicago's Chinatown, carving a public space out of an urban wasteland," Landscape Architecture, Jul, 2002; "Chinatown returns to center stage," Chicago Tribune, Jan, 2002; "An el of a tour," Chicago Magazine, Dec, 2000; "Chinatown cheers new park on river," Chicago Sun-Times, Sep, 1999; "Gateway to a greener China town," Chicago Sun-Times, Aug, 1998; "When does home remodeling become big rehab," News Chicago, Sep, 1987.

15265 ■ Alfred Swenson Pao-Chi Chang Architects—Swenson Alfred Pao-Chi Chang Architects

11 E Adams St.
Chicago, IL 60603
Ph: (312)431-1720
Fax: (312)431-1721
URL: http://www.swensonchangcasina.com
Contact: Alfred Swenson, Partner
E-mail: alfred_swenson@swensonchangcasina.com
Scope: Expertise and is internationally recognized in providing architectural theory and conceptual design for small, mid-rise, high-rise and ultra-tall buildings, offer traditional architectural services. **Founded:** 1973.

15266 ■ Vinod H. Dholakia-Architect P.C.

107-16 Jamaica Ave.
Richmond Hill, NY 11418-2239
Ph: (718)805-6790
Fax: (718)805-6790
URL: http://www.vinod-architect.com
Contact: Vinod H Dholakia, Owner
Scope: Architect and interior designer of residential, commercial stores, offices and restaurants and industrial buildings and spaces including zoning analysis and code compliance, space planning, lighting design, graphic design and furniture and furnishings selections. Active in new and renovation conversion projects. Industries served home owners, businesses, real estate investors and developers, retail corporations and government agencies. **Founded:** 1986.

15267 ■ Walsh Bishop Associates (WBA)

900 N 3rd St.
Minneapolis, MN 55401
Ph: (612)338-8799
Free: 888-871-5615
Fax: (612)337-5785
Co. E-mail: info@walshbishop.com
URL: http://www.walshbishop.com
Contact: Dennis F. Walsh, Chief Executive Officer
E-mail: dennis.walsh@walshbishop.com
Scope: Provider of customer solutions through architecture, interior design and facility management services. Those services include, master planning, landscape design, strategic facility planning, tenant services, programming, project management and food service design. Walsh Bishop is a 50-person firm located in downtown Minneapolis specializing in the areas of corporate, industrial, commercial, hospitality, entertainment, and housing projects locally and nationally. **Founded:** 1984. **Publications:** "We are proud to announce the completion and opening of the Swinomish Casino & Lodge," Apl, 2012; "We are extremely pleased to announce the topping off of the Swinomish Lodge and Casino," Aug, 2011; "Walsh Bishop aids Marquette Plaza in attaining LEED Platinum certification," 2011; "Duke Realty LEED Certified Norman Pointe II," 2010; "RBC

Wealth Management Seattle WA Two full floors totaling 30, 462 square feet," 2010. **Telecommunication Services:** marketing@walshbishop.com.

FRANCHISES AND BUSINESS OPPORTUNITIES

15268 ■ California Closet Company
1000 4th St., Ste. 800
San Rafael, CA 94901
Ph: (415)256-8500
Free: 800-241-3222
Fax: (415)256-8501
Co. E-mail: franchising@calclosets.com
URL: http://www.californiaclosets.com

Description: Custom closet design, manufacture, and installation. **No. of Franchise Units:** 88. **Founded:** 1978.. **Franchised:** 1982. **Equity Capital Needed:** $127,500-$377,000 total investment. **Franchise Fee:** $40,000. **Royalty Fee:** 6%. **Financial Assistance:** Third party financing available. **Train-**ing: Includes training at headquarters, franchisee's location and ongoing support.

COMPUTERIZED DATABASES

15269 ■ *Art Index™*
10 Estes St.
Ipswich, MA 01938-2106
Ph: (978)356-6500
Free: 800-653-2726
Fax: (978)356-6565
Co. E-mail: information@ebscohost.com
URL: http://www.ebscohost.com
Contact: Tim Collins, President
E-mail: tcollins@ebscohost.com
Availability: Online: EBSCO Publishing. **Type:** Bibliographic.

LIBRARIES

15270 ■ Tech-U-Fit Corporation Library
400 Madison St., No. 210
Alexandria, VA 22314
Ph: (703)549-0512
Fax: (703)548-0780
Contact: John Molino
Scope: Engineering, psychology, human factors engineering, ergonomics. **Holdings:** 200 volumes.

RESEARCH CENTERS

15271 ■ Western Michigan University - Human Performance Institute (HPI)
Department of Industrial & Manufacturing Engineering
College of Engineering & Applied Sciences
4601 Campus Dr.
Kalamazoo, MI 49008-5336
Ph: (269)276-3360
Co. E-mail: tycho.fredericks@wmich.edu
URL: http://www.wmich.edu/ime/facilities/hpi.html
Contact: Dr. Tycho Fredericks, Director
Services: In-house presentations and ergonomic audits. **Educational Activities:** Public workshops.

ASSOCIATIONS AND OTHER ORGANIZATIONS

15272 ■ Business Technology Association (BTA)
12411 Wornall Rd., Ste. 200
Kansas City, MO 64145
Ph: (816)941-3100
Free: 800-325-7219
Fax: (816)941-4838
Co. E-mail: info@bta.org
URL: http://www.bta.org
Contact: Tom Ouellette, President
Description: Dealers and resellers of office equipment and networking products and services. Offers 60 seminars on management, service, technology, and business systems. Conducts research, provides business-supporting services and benefits, including insurance, and legal counsel. **Founded:** 1926. **Publications:** *BTA Membership Directory* (Annual); *Business Owner* (Bimonthly). **Awards:** Channel Choice Awards; Manufacturer/Supplier Award; Reseller of the Year; Channel Choice Award (Annual); Manufacturer/Supplier Award (Annual); Reseller of the Year (Annual).

15273 ■ Information Technology Industry Council (ITI)
1101 K St. NW, Ste. 610
Washington, DC 20005
Ph: (202)737-8888
Fax: (202)638-4922
Co. E-mail: info@itic.org
URL: http://www.itic.org
Contact: Dean Garfield, President
Description: Represents manufacturers of information technology products. Serves as secretariat and technology for ANSI-accredited standards committee x3 information technology group. Conducts public policy programs; compiles industry statistics. **Founded:** 1916. **Publications:** *Washington Letter* (Biweekly). **Awards:** Public Policy Award (Annual). **Telecommunication Services:** rdawson@itic.org.

15274 ■ ISDA - Association of Storage and Retrieval Professionals
750 Holiday Dr., Bldg. 9, Ste. 500
Pittsburgh, PA 15220
Free: 877-921-3501
Fax: (412)921-3525
Co. E-mail: elborne@isdanet.net
URL: http://www.isdanet.net
Description: Independent dealers of office filing systems and microfilm equipment. Aims to promote the development of the filing systems industry, and to maintain a high standard of ethics among members. Distributes information, encourages better business methods, and promotes the services of members to consumers. Sponsors dealer management and sales training programs. **Founded:** 1973.

15275 ■ Print Services and Distribution Association (PSDA)
401 N Michigan Ave., Ste. 2200
Chicago, IL 60611
Free: 800-230-0175
Fax: (312)673-6880
Co. E-mail: psda@psda.org
URL: http://www.psda.org
Contact: Robert O'Connell, President
Description: Independent distributors, manufacturers and suppliers to the forms, business printing and document management industries. Sponsors educational and channel marketing programs. Compiles statistics. **Scope:** business printing, document management, home study courses. **Founded:** 1947. **Subscriptions:** articles books periodicals. **Publications:** *PERF Print Report* (Quarterly); *Print Solutions Weekly* (Weekly); *Who's Who Among Business Printing Independents* (Annual); *Print Solutions: Award-Winning Coverage of the Printing Industry* (Monthly); *Who's Who in the Business Printing and Document Management Industry* (Annual); *Print Solutions--Buyers' Guide Issue* (Annual). **Awards:** Manufacturer Member of the Year; Member of the Year; President's Award; Manufacturer Award (Annual); Member of the Year (Annual); Presidents' Award (Annual); Print Excellence and Knowledge Awards (Annual).

15276 ■ School and Office Products Network
3131 Elbee Rd.
Dayton, OH 45439
Ph: (937)610-3333
Co. E-mail: stevej@shopa.org
URL: http://www.schoolandofficenetwork.org
Contact: Dee Dee Hunt, Secretary
Description: Manufacturers, wholesaler and service merchandisers, importers, retailers, commercial/contract stationers, manufacturers' representatives, and associated individuals. Promotes the advancement of the school, office, and home office product industry through an annual trade show, research initiations and other benefits and services. **Founded:** 1991. **Awards:** Life Member Recognition (Annual).

REFERENCE WORKS

15277 ■ "Bringing Charities More Bang for Their Buck" in Crain's Chicago Business (Vol. 34, May 23, 2011, No. 21, pp. 31)
Pub: Crain Communications Inc.
Ed: Lisa Bertagnoli. **Description:** Marcy-Newberry Association connects charities with manufacturers in order to use excess items such as clothing, janitorial and office supplies.

15278 ■ "Firm Stays In the 'Family'; After Owner's Death, Employees Buy Company" in Crain's Detroit Business (Vol. 24, January 28, 2008)
Pub: Crain Communications Inc. - Detroit
Ed: Chad Halcom. **Description:** Sterling Office Systems Inc., distributor of photocopiers and other office machines was purchased from the owner's family after his demise. The new owners would like to hit $1.75 million in sales their first year.

15279 ■ "A Labelmaker with Style" in Inc. (Vol. 33, October 2011, No. 8, pp. 48)
Pub: Inc. Magazine
Ed: John Brandon. **Description:** Epson's first labelmaker, the LabelWorks LW-400 offers many design

options and has a full QWERTY keyboard that allows users to create and print labels in various sizes.

15280 ■ *Orion Blue Book--Copier*
Pub: Orion Research Corp.
Contact: Pati Hendricks, Manager
E-mail: pati@bluebook.com
URL(s): www.usedprice.com. **Released:** Annual; Latest edition 2007. **Price:** $130, Individuals hardbound or CD. **Publication includes:** List of manufacturers of copiers and other office equipment. **Entries include:** Company name, address, phone. Principal content of publication is a listing of 3,091 office equipment products with the original retail value, value paid to customer on trade-in when in mint condition, and average value paid to customer on trade-in. **Arrangement:** Alphabetical.

15281 ■ "Staples Advantage Receives NJPA National Contract for Janitorial Supplies" in Professional Services Close-Up (April 22, 2011)
Pub: Close-Up Media
Description: Staples Advantage, the business-to-business division of Staples Inc. was awarded a contract for janitorial supplies to members of the National Joint Powers Alliance (NJPA). NJPA is a member-owned buying cooperative serving public and private schools, state and local governments, and nonprofit organizations.

STATISTICAL SOURCES

15282 ■ *The American Demand for Office Furniture and Anticipated Trends*
Pub: AKTRIN Furniture Research
Ed: Stephan Wille. **Released:** 2008. **Price:** $785.00 (paper).

15283 ■ *Office Furniture Market*
Business Trend Analysts
Released: 2008. **Price:** $3000.00. **Description:** Offers statistical analysis of the office furniture trade, including sales data and past performance, projections to the year 2000, labor trends in white-collar occupations, new product and design innovations, methods for janitorial supplies, construction and remodeling trends, pricing, industry economic structure, and strategies for advertising and promotions. Profiles of major companies in the industry are also included.

15284 ■ *RMA Annual Statement Studies*
Pub: Risk Management Association
Contact: Kevin M. Blakey, President
Released: Annual. **Price:** $175.00 2006-07 edition, $105.00. **Description:** Contains composite balance sheets and income statements for more than 360 industries, including the accounting, auditing, and bookkeeping industries. Also contains five years of comparative historical data for discerning trends. Includes 16 commonly used ratios, computed for most of the size groupings for nearly every industry.

FRANCHISES AND BUSINESS OPPORTUNITIES

15285 ■ California Closet Company
1000 4th St., Ste. 800
San Rafael, CA 94901

Ph: (415)256-8500
Free: 800-241-3222
Fax: (415)256-8501
Co. E-mail: franchising@calclosets.com
URL: http://www.californiaclosets.com
Description: Custom closet design, manufacture, and installation. **No. of Franchise Units:** 88. **Founded:** 1978.. **Franchised:** 1982. **Equity Capital Needed:** $127,500-$377,000 total investment. **Franchise Fee:** $40,000. **Royalty Fee:** 6%. **Financial Assistance:** Third party financing available. **Training:** Includes training at headquarters, franchisee's location and ongoing support.

15286 ■ Island Ink-Jet Systems Inc.
244 4th St.
Courtney, BC, Canada V9N 1G6
Ph: (877)446-5538
Co. E-mail: franchise@islandinkjet.com
URL: http://www.islandinkjet.com
Description: Inkjet refill mall location and area service centers. **No. of Franchise Units:** 250. **Founded:** 1995.. **Franchised:** 1977. **Equity Capital**

Needed: Minimum $50,000; total investment $100,000 plus. **Franchise Fee:** $29,000. **Training:** Yes.

15287 ■ PostNet Canada
1819 Wazee St.
Denver, CO 80202
Ph: (800)338-7401
Fax: (303)771-7133
Co. E-mail: info@postnethq.com
URL: http://www.postnetfranchise.com
Description: Offers an array of high demand services and products, tailored to meet the needs of small business owners and today's busy consumer. We like to think of PostNet as an entrepreneur's store, helping the small office, home office and small business owners get what they need, when they need it. At the same time, PostNet caters to the general consumer, offering a host of products and services to help them complete their personal business needs quickly and efficiently. **No. of Franchise Units:** 19. **Founded:** 2004. **Franchised:** 2004. **Equity Capital**

Needed: $175,000 investment required; $60,000 start-up capital required. **Franchise Fee:** $35,000. **Training:** Provides 7 days training full-time.

15288 ■ Proforma Inc.
8800 E Pleasant Valley Rd.
Independence, OH 44131
Ph: (216)520-8400
Free: 800-825-1525
Fax: (216)520-8474
Co. E-mail: franchise@proforma.com
URL: http://www.proforma.com
Contact: Greg Muzzillo, Owner
URL(s): www.connectwithperforma.com. **Description:** Franchises business service operations that handle business forms, commercial printing, computer supplies, office supplies, and computers. **No. of Franchise Units:** 723. **Founded:** 1978. **Franchised:** 1986. **Equity Capital Needed:** $19,500. **Franchise Fee:** $19,500. **Training:** 1 week franchise training at headquarters, local development agent support, ongoing classroom and regional training. Local and national campaigns. Regional meetings and annual national conventions.

START-UP INFORMATION

15289 ■ *Complete Idiot's Guide to Starting an Ebay Business*
Pub: Penguin Books USA Inc.
Ed: Barbara Weltman, Malcolm Katt. **Released:** February 2008. **Price:** $19.95 (US), $29.00 (Canadian). **Description:** Guide for starting an eBay business includes information on products to sell, how to price merchandise, and details for working with services like PayPal, and how to organize fulfillment services.

15290 ■ *Design and Launch an Online Travel Business in a Week*
Pub: Entrepreneur Press
Contact: Perlman Neil, President
Ed: Charlene Davis. **Released:** May 1, 2009. **Price:** $17.95. **Description:** Guide providing techniques and professional advice for starting an online travel business. Tips are given to build a Website, find qualified providers and to set up a payment system.

15291 ■ *Design and Launch Your Online Boutique in a Week*
Pub: Entrepreneur Press
Ed: Melissa Campanelli. **Released:** June 26, 2008. **Price:** $17.95. **Description:** Tips for starting an online boutique in a short amount of time are given. The books shows how to build the online boutique with designer goods or your own product, ways to create eye-catching content, online tools to handle payments and accept orders, marketing and advertising techniques, and customer service.

15292 ■ *eBay Business the Smart Way*
Pub: AMACOM
Ed: Joseph T. Sinclair. **Released:** June 6, 2007. **Price:** $17.95. **Description:** eBay commands ninety percent of all online auction business. Computer and software expert and online entrepreneur shares information to help online sellers get started and move merchandise on eBay. Tips include the best ways to build credibility, find products to sell, manage inventory, create a storefront Website, and more.

15293 ■ *EBay Business Start-up Kit: 100s of Live Links to All the Information and Tools You Need*
Pub: NOLO
Ed: Richard Stim. **Released:** July 2008. **Price:** $24.99. **Description:** Interactive kit that connects user directly to EBay is presented.

15294 ■ *EBay Income: How ANYONE of Any Age, Location, and/or Background Can Build a Highly Profitable Online Business with eBay*
Pub: Atlantic Publishing Company
Released: December 1, 2010. **Price:** $24.95. **Description:** A complete overview of eBay is given and guides any small company through the entire process of creating the auction and auction strategies, photography, writing copy, text and formatting, multiple sales, programming tricks, PayPal, accounting, creating marketing, merchandising, managing email lists, advertising plans, taxes and sales tax, best time to list items and for how long, sniping programs, international customers, opening a storefront, electronic commerce, buy-it now pricing, keywords, Google marketing and eBay secrets.

15295 ■ *How to Open and Operate a Financially Successful Bookstore on Amazon and Other Web Sites: With Companion CD-ROM*
Pub: Atlantic Publishing Company
Released: December 1, 2010. **Price:** $39.95. **Description:** This book was written for every used book aficionado and bookstore owner who currently wants to take advantage of the massive collection of online resources available to start and run your own online bookstore business.

15296 ■ *How to Use the Internet to Advertise, Promote, and Market Your Business or Web Site: With Little or No Money*
Pub: Atlantic Publishing Company
Released: December 1, 2010. **Price:** $24.95. **Description:** Information is given to help build, promote, and make money from your Website or brick and mortar store using the Internet, with minimal costs.

15297 ■ *"Online Fortunes" in Small Business Opportunities (Fall 2008)*
Pub: Entrepreneur Media Inc.
Description: Fifty hot, e-commerce enterprises for the aspiring entrepreneur to consider are featured; virtual assistants, marketing services, party planning, travel services, researching, web design and development, importing as well as creating an online store are among the businesses featured.

15298 ■ *"Power Up" in Entrepreneur (Vol. 35, November 2007, No. 11, pp. 140)*
Pub: Entrepreneur Media Inc.
Ed: Amanda C. Kooser. **Description:** PowerSeller is a status in the Internet company eBay, wherein sellers average at least $1,000 in sales per month for three consecutive months. There are five tiers in the PowerSeller status, which ranges from Bronze to Titanium. Launching startups at eBay can help entrepreneurs pick up a wide customer base, but getting and maintaining PowerSeller status is a challenge.

15299 ■ *Selling Online: Canada's Bestselling Guide to Becoming a Successful E-Commerce Merchant*
Pub: John Wiley and Sons Canada Ltd.
Ed: Jim Carroll; Rick Broadhead. **Released:** September 6, 2002. **Description:** Helps individuals build online retail enterprises; this updated version includes current tools, information and success strategies, how to launch an online storefront, security, marketing strategies, and mistakes to avoid.

15300 ■ *Start Your Own Business on eBay, 2nd Edition*
Pub: Entrepreneur Press
Ed: Jacquelyn Lynn. **Released:** May 2007. **Price:** $19.95. **Description:** Tips for starring a new online business on eBay are shared.

15301 ■ *Start Your Own Net Services Business*
Pub: Entrepreneur Press
Contact: Perlman Neil, President
Released: February 1, 2009. **Price:** $17.95. **Description:** Web design, search engine marketing, new-media online, and blogging, are currently the four most popular web services available. This book provides information to start a net service business.

15302 ■ *Starting an Ebay Business for Canadians for Dummies*
Pub: John Wiley & Sons, Incorporated
Ed: Marsha Collier; Bill Summers. **Released:** February 2007. **Price:** $35.99. **Description:** Tips for turning a hobby into a successful online eBay company.

15303 ■ *"Tee Off Online" in Black Enterprise (Vol. 37, January 2007, No. 6, pp. 52)*
Pub: Earl G. Graves Publishing Co. Inc.
Ed: James C. Johnson. **Description:** The E-Com Resource Center is one of many resources that are available for those interested in starting an e-commerce business. One of the first steps is to create a business plan, of which there are free samples available at BPlans.com.

15304 ■ *"Virtual Playground" in Entrepreneur (Vol. 36, March 2008, No. 3, pp. 112)*
Pub: Entrepreneur Media Inc.
Ed: Amanda C. Kooser. **Description:** The growing number of children visiting virtual worlds provides opportunity for entrepreneurs to start online businesses catering to this market. Entrepreneurs need to be aware of the Children's Online Privacy Protection Act with regard to collecting children's information. Details of other things to know about with reference to these businesses are examined.

ASSOCIATIONS AND OTHER ORGANIZATIONS

15305 ■ Internet Society (ISOC)—ISOC
1775 Wiehle Ave., Ste. 201
Reston, VA 20190-5158
Ph: (703)439-2120
Fax: (703)326-9881
Co. E-mail: isoc@isoc.org
URL: http://www.isoc.org
Contact: Lynn St. Amour, President
URL(s): www.isoc.org/isoc/contact.shtml. **Description:** Technologists, developers, educators, researchers, government representatives, and business people. Seeks to ensure global cooperation and coordination for the Internet and related internetworking technologies and applications. Supports the development and dissemination of standards for the Internet. Promotes the growth of Internet architecture and Internet-related education and research. Encourages assistance to technologically developing countries in implementing local Internet infrastructures. **Founded:** 1992. **Publications:** *ISOC Forum* (Monthly); *IETF Journal*; *ISP Column*. **Educational Activities:** Internet Society Conference (Annual); Symposium on Network and Distributed System

Security (Annual). **Awards:** Internet Society Fellowships to the IETF; Jonathan B. Postel Memorial Service Award (Annual).

REFERENCE WORKS

15306 ■ *"Analyzing the Analytics"* in *Entrepreneur (Vol. 37, October 2009, No. 10, pp. 42)*
Pub: Entrepreneur Media, Inc.
Ed: Mikal E. Belicove. **Description:** Startups can maximize Web analytics by using them to monitor traffic sources and identify obstacles to converting them into targeted behaviors . Startups should set trackable Web site goals and continuously track traffic and conversion rates.

15307 ■ *"Attract More Online Customers: Make Your Website Work Harder for You"* in *Black Enterprise (Vol. 37, November 2006, No. 4, pp. 66)*
Pub: Earl G. Graves Publishing Co. Inc.
Description: Having an impressive presence on the Internet has become crucial. Detailed advice on making your website serve your business in the best way possible is included.

15308 ■ *"Babynut.com to Shut Down"* in *Bellingham Business Journal (Vol. February 2010, pp. 3)*
Pub: Sound Publishing Inc.
Description: Saralee Sky and Jerry Kilgore, owners of Babynut.com will close their online store. The site offered a free online and email newsletter to help mothers through pregnancy and the first three years of their child's life. Products being sold at clearance prices include organic and natural maternity and nursing clothing, baby and toddler clothes, books on pregnancy, and more.

15309 ■ *"Best Buy's CEO On Learning to Love Social Media"* in *Harvard Business Review (Vol. 88, December 2010, No. 12, pp. 43)*
Pub: Harvard Business School Publishing
Ed: Brian J. Dunn. **Description:** Effective utilization of online social networks to enhance brand identity, connect with consumers, and address bad publicity scenarios is examined.

15310 ■ *"Boom and Bust in the Book Biz"* in *Canadian Business (Vol. 83, August 17, 2010, No. 13-14, pp. 16)*
Pub: Rogers Media Ltd.
Ed: Jordan Timm. **Description:** Electronic book marketplace is booming with Amazon.com's e-book sales for the Kindle e-reader exceeding the hardcover sales. Kobo Inc. has registered early success with its Kobo e-reader and has partnered with Hong Kong telecom giant on an e-book store.

15311 ■ *"Bottoms Up!"* in *Entrepreneur (Vol. 36, April 2008, No. 4, pp. 128)*
Pub: Entrepreneur Media, Inc.
Ed: Amanda C. Kooser. **Description:** Jill Bernheimer launched her online alcohol business Domaine547 in 2007, and encountered challenges as legal issues over the licensing and launching of the business took about seven months to finish. Domain547 features blog and forum areas. Marketing strategy that connects to the social community is one of the ways to reach out to customers.

15312 ■ *"Brite-Strike Tactical Launches New Internet Marketing Initiatives"* in *Internet Wire (September 15, 2009)*
Pub: Comtex News Network, Inc.
Description: Brite-Strike Tactical Illumination Products, Inc. has enlisted the expertise of Internet marketing guru Thomas J. McCarthy to help revamp the company's Internet campaign. An outline of the Internet marketing strategy is provided.

15313 ■ *Building Buzz to Beat the Big Boys*
Pub: Greenwood Publishing Group, Inc.
Ed: Steve O'Leary; Kim Sheehan. **Released:** March 30, 2008. **Price:** $39.95. **Description:** Seventy to eighty percent of small retail stores fail within the first five years of opening due to competition from big-box

retailers and online stores. Service providers and small retailers should capitalize on the fact that they are local and can connect on a personal level with customers in a way the big stores cannot. Word of mouth marketing methods are very critical to any small retail or service company. This book is designed to help any small business compete against large competitors.

15314 ■ *"Business Forecast: Stormy and Successful"* in *Women In Business (Vol. 62, June 2010, No. 2, pp. 12)*
Pub: American Business Women's Association
Ed: Kathleen Leighton. **Description:** Stormy Simon, vice president of customer service at Overstock.com is a self-made career woman who started out as a temporary employee in the company in 2001. She was not able to attend college because she had two sons to care for after her divorce. Simon got involved in advertising and media buying and shares her love for business.

15315 ■ *The Complete Guide to Google Adwords: Secrets, Techniques, and Strategies You Can Learn to Make Millions*
Pub: Atlantic Publishing Company
Released: December 1, 2010. **Price:** $24.95. **Description:** Google AdWords, when it launched in 2002 signaled a fundamental shift in what the Internet was for so many individuals and companies. Learning and understanding how Google AdWords operates and how it can be optimized for maximum exposure, boosting click through rates, conversions, placement, and selection of the right keywords, can be the key to a successful online business.

15316 ■ *"A Counter Offer"* in *Inc. (February 2008, pp.)*
Pub: Gruner & Jahr USA Publishing
Ed: Elaine Appleton Grant. **Description:** Online retailer offering a line of kitchen and home products has upgraded its Website in order to make the business more attractive to possible buyers of the company. The firm is asking $9.9 million and reported gross revenue of $12.7 in 2007. The owner suggests that a buyer add product lines geared towards more rooms of the home than currently offer on the retail site.

15317 ■ *"Cyber Thanksgiving Online Shopping a Growing Tradition"* in *Marketing Weekly News (December 12, 2009, pp. 137)*
Pub: Investment Weekly News
Description: According to e-commerce analysts, Thanksgiving day is becoming increasingly important to retailers in terms of online sales. Internet marketers are realizing that consumers are already searching for Black Friday sales and if they find deals on the products they are looking for, they are highly likely to make their purchase on Thanksgiving day instead of waiting.

15318 ■ *"Cyberwise"* in *Black Enterprise (Vol. 41, September 2010, No. 2, pp. 49)*
Pub: Earl G. Graves Publishing Co. Inc.
Ed: Marcia Wade Talbert. **Description:** Advice is given to assist in selling an online store called theupscalegaragesale.com. A listing of business brokers specializing in the sale of Internet businesses is included.

15319 ■ *"Dear Customer: Managing E-Mail Campaigns"* in *Inc. (March 2008, pp. 58-59)*
Pub: Gruner & Jahr USA Publishing
Ed: Ryan Underwood. **Description:** Internet services that help firms manage their online business including email marketing, to manage subscriber lists, comply with spam regulations, monitor bouncebacks, and track potential customers are profiled. Constant Contact, MobileStorm Stun, Campaign Monitor, Pop Commerce, Emma, and StrongMail E-mail Server are among software and services highlighted.

15320 ■ *"Dots Sings To New Tune With Its Radio Station"* in *Crain's Cleveland Business (Vol. 30, June 15, 2009, No. 23, pp. 7)*
Pub: Crain Communications, Inc.
Description: Dots LLC, a women's clothing retailer, has launched an online radio station on its Website. The station plays the in-store music to customers while they are shopping online.

15321 ■ *The Ebay Seller's Tax and Legal Answer Book*
Pub: AMACOM
Ed: Cliff Ennico. **Released:** April 30, 2007. **Price:** $19.95. **Description:** Helps sellers using Ebay to file taxes properly, while saving money.

15322 ■ *Ebay the Smart Way: Selling, Burying, and Profiting on the Web's Number One Auction Site*
Pub: AMACOM
Ed: Joseph T. Sinclair. **Released:** May 2007. **Price:** $17.95. **Description:** Resource to help individuals sell, buy and profit using the Internet auction site Ebay.

15323 ■ *The Facebook Era: Tapping Online Social Networks to Build Better Products, Reach New Audiences, and Sell More Stuff*
Pub: Prentice Hall
Ed: Clara Shih. **Price:** $24.99. **Description:** The '90s were about the World Wide Web of information and the power of linking Web pages. Today it's about the World Wide Web of people and the power of the social graph. Online social networks are fundamentally changing the way we live, work, and interact. They offer businesses immense opportunities to transform customer relationships for profit: opportunities that touch virtually every business function, from sales and marketing to recruiting, collaboration to executive decision-making, product development to innovation.

15324 ■ *"Full Speed Ahead: How to Get the Most Out of Your Company Vehicles"* in *Entrepreneur (Vol. 37, October 2009, No. 10, pp. 78)*
Pub: Entrepreneur Media, Inc.
Ed: Jill Amadio. **Description:** Methods of saving costs on purchasing and maintaining vehicles are described. Tips include shopping online, choosing hybrid vehicles, and choosing cars with incentives and lower insurance costs.

15325 ■ *"Get Sold On eBay"* in *Entrepreneur (Vol. 36, March 2008, No. 3, pp. 94)*
Pub: Entrepreneur Media Inc.
Ed: Marcia Layton Turner. **Description:** Entrepreneurs are increasingly using eBay to sell products. Some tips to start selling products through eBay include: starting with used items, developing a niche to sell specific products, and researching product pricing. Other tips with regard to starting an eBay business are covered.

15326 ■ *"Google Book Search Tosses Magazines Into the Mix"* in *Information Today (Vol. 26, February 2009, No. 2, pp. 31)*
Pub: Information Today, Inc.
Description: Google Book Search expanded services to include magazines..

15327 ■ *"The Greening of Lunch"* in *Entrepreneur (Vol. 37, October 2009, No. 10, pp. 44)*
Pub: Entrepreneur Media, Inc.
Ed: Deborah Song. **Description:** Kids Konserve is a self-funded online business selling reusable and recycled lunch kits for kids. The company also aims to increase awareness about waste reduction.

15328 ■ *How to Market and Sell Your Art, Music, Photographs, and Handmade Crafts Online*
Pub: Atlantic Publishing Group, Inc.
Ed: Lee Rowley. **Released:** May 2008. **Price:** $24.95. **Description:** The book provides all the basics for starting and running an online store selling arts, crafts, photography or music. There are more than 300 Websites listed to help anyone market and promote their arts and/or crafts online.

15329 ■ *"Inside an Online Bazaar"* in *Entrepreneur (Vol. 37, September 2009, No. 9, pp. 38)*
Pub: Entrepreneur Media Inc.
Ed: Kara Ohngren. **Description:** Etsy.com is a website that provides a marketplace for handmade products. The site has attracted more than 250,000 sellers since its launch in 2005. Site features and services are also supplied.

15330 ■ *Internet Industry Almanac: The Complete Guide to the Ever-Changing Internet Industry*

Pub: Computer Industry Almanac Inc.

Contact: Dr. Egil Juliussen, President

E-mail: ej@c-i-a.com

URL(s): www.c-i-a.com. **Price:** $50, Individuals paperback; $60, Individuals hardcover. **Publication includes:** Lists of Internet companies; Internet publications; Internet research and testing companies; Internet conferences; Internet people; Internet resource directory; Internet publishers; Internet associations and organizations; and Internet conference companies. Principal content of publication is information about the Internet industry, including a definition of the Internet, employment data, Internet humor, salary information, Internet market forecasts, and technology forecasts. **Arrangement:** By industry.

15331 ■ *"It's a Hit" in Entrepreneur (Vol. 36, March 2008, No. 3, pp. 110)*

Pub: Entrepreneur Media Inc.

Ed: John Jantsch. **Description:** Entrepreneurs use the Web to market business and keeping relevant content in the Website is important to address questions from customers. Other considerations in marketing businesses online include: interacting with site visitors, using Web applications for project collaboration and file storage, and encouraging customers to post reviews.

15332 ■ *"It's a New Game: Killerspin Pushes Table Tennis to Extreme Heights" in Black Enterprise (Vol. 37, October 2006, No. 3, pp. 73)*

Pub: Earl G. Graves Publishing Co. Inc.

Ed: Bridget McCrea. **Description:** Profile of Robert Blackwell and his company Killerspin L.L.C., which is popularizing the sport of table tennis. Killerspin has hit $1 million in revenues due to product sales primarily generated through the company's website, magazines, DVDs, and event ticket sales.

15333 ■ *"Jo-Ann Fabric and Craft Stores Joins ArtFire.com to Offer Free Online Craft Marketplace" in Internet Wire (January 26, 2010)*

Pub: Comtex News Network, Inc.

Description: Jo-Ann Fabric and Craft Stores has entered into a partnership with ArtFire.com which will provide sewers and crafters all the tools they need in order to make and sell their products from an online venue.

15334 ■ *"Last Founder Standing" in Conde Nast Portfolio (Vol. 2, June 2008, No. 6, pp. 124)*

Pub: Conde Nast Publications

Contact: David Carey, President

Ed: Kevin Maney. **Description:** Interview with Amazon CEO Jeff Bezos in which he discusses the economy, the company's new distribution center and the hiring of employees for it, e-books, and the overall vision for the future of the firm.

15335 ■ *"A Life of Spice" in Entrepreneur (Vol. 37, September 2009, No. 9, pp. 46)*

Pub: Entrepreneur Media, Inc.

Ed: Jason Daley. **Description:** Matt and Bryan Walls have successfully grown their Atlanta, Georgia-based Snorg Tees T-shirt company. The company has expanded its product offering and redesigned its Website to be more user-friendly. The company has registered between $5 and 10 million in 2008.

15336 ■ *"Luxe Hotels on a Budget" in Inc. (Volume 32, December 2010, No. 10, pp. 60)*

Pub: Inc. Magazine

Ed: Adam Baer. **Description:** Off & Away Website allows users to vie for discounted hotel rooms at more than 100 luxury properties. To compete, uses buy $1 bids and each time an individual bids the price of the room goes up by 10 cents.

15337 ■ *"Navigate to Better Direct Response Messaging Through Search Marketing" in DM*

News (Vol. 32, January 18, 2010, No. 2, pp. 26)

Pub: Haymarket Media, Inc.

Ed: Mark Simon. **Description:** Important lessons to apply when utilizing Internet marketing schemes include telling your customers you have what they want to buy, provide them with discounts or ways to save additional money and drive them to a customized destination like an Online store.

15338 ■ *"The Next Dimension" in Entrepreneur (Vol. 35, November 2007, No. 11, pp. 62)*

Pub: Entrepreneur Media Inc.

Ed: Heather Clancy. **Description:** Entrepreneurs can make use of virtual worlds like Second Life to promote their products or services. Details and cautions on the use of virtual worlds are discussed.

15339 ■ *"The One Thing You Must Get Right When Building a Brand" in Harvard Business Review (Vol. 88, December 2010, No. 12, pp. 80)*

Pub: Harvard Business School Publishing

Ed: Patrick Barwise, Sean Meehan. **Description:** Four uses for new media include: communicating a clearly defined customer promise, creating trust via delivering on the promise, regularly improving on the promise, and innovating past what is familiar.

15340 ■ *"Online Reverse Auctions: Common Myths Versus Evolving Reality" in Business Horizons (September-October 2007, pp. 373)*

Pub: Elsevier Technology Publications

Ed: Tobias Schoenherr, Vincent A. Mabert. **Description:** Common misconceptions about online reverse auctions are examined based on the data obtained from 30 case study companies. Strategies for maintaining a good buyer-supplier relationship and implications for firms and supply managers are presented.

15341 ■ *"Online Security Crackdown: Scanning Service Oversees Site Security at David's Bridal" in (Vol. 84, July 2008, No. 7, pp. 46)*

Pub: Chain Store Age

Ed: Samantha Murphy. **Description:** Online retailers are beefing up security on their Websites. Cyber thieves use retail systems in order to gain entry to consumer data. David's Bridal operates over 275 bridal showrooms in the U.S. and has a one-stop wedding resource for new brides planning weddings.

15342 ■ *"Optimize.ca Supplies Free Online Financial Advice" in Entertainment Close-Up (October 9, 2010)*

Pub: Close-Up Media Inc.

Description: Optimize.ca provides free online financial advice, focusing on instant savings for their mutual funds and other banking products while improving rates of return and overall financial health.

15343 ■ *The Power of Social Networking: Using the Whuffie Factor to Build Your Business*

Pub: Crown Business Books

Ed: Tara Hunt. **Released:** May 4, 2010. **Price:** $15.00. **Description:** This book shows how any small business can harness its power by increasing whuffie, the store of social capital that is the currency of the digital world. Blogs and social networks such as Facebook and Twitter are used to help grow any small firm.

15344 ■ *"Retail Franchises to Start Now" in Entrepreneur (Vol. 37, August 2009, No. 8, pp. 88)*

Pub: Entrepreneur Media, Inc.

Ed: Tracy Stapp. **Description:** Listing of retail franchises is presented and is categorized based on their products sold. The total cost of the franchise and the website are also included as well as additional statistical data.

15345 ■ *"Ric Elis/Dan Feldstein" in Charlotte Business Journal (Vol. 25, December 31,*

2010, No. 41, pp. 6)

Pub: Charlotte Business Journal

Ed: Ken Elkins. **Description:** Charlotte, North Carolina-based Internet marketing firm Red Ventures has grown significantly. General Atlantic has purchased stakes in Red Ventures.

15346 ■ *"Search and Discover New Opportunities" in DM News (Vol. 31, December 14, 2009, No. 29, pp. 13)*

Pub: Haymarket Media, Inc.

Ed: Chantal Tode. **Description:** Although other digital strategies are gaining traction in Internet marketing, search marketing continues to dominate this advertising forum. Companies like American Greetings, which markets e-card brands online, are utilizing social networking sites and affiliates to generate a higher demand for their products.

15347 ■ *"Shipping 2.0" in Entrepreneur (Vol. 36, April 2008, No. 4, pp. 54)*

Pub: Entrepreneur Media, Inc.

Ed: Heather Clancy. **Description:** Doggypads.com contacted with Web 2.0 service provider Shipwire to handle its warehouse concerns. The service works by paying a rent to Shipwire and they will store the client's items. The client's customers can continue to order from the client's website and Shipwire will take care of delivery. Doggypads was able to save up on costs by using Shipwire.

15348 ■ *"Tell Us What You Really Think Collecting Customer Feedback" in Inc. (Vol. 30, December 2008, No. 12, pp. 52)*

Pub: Mansueto Ventures LLC

Ed: Ryan Underwood. **Description:** According to a recent survey, nearly 77 percent of online shoppers review consumer-generated reviews of products before making a purchase.

15349 ■ *"Things Really Clicking for Macy's Online" in Business Courier (Vol. 24, November 30, 2008, No. 33, pp. 1)*

Pub: American City Business Journals, Inc.

Ed: Lisa Biank Fasig. **Description:** Retailer Macy's online division Macys.com are projecting sales at $1billion in 2007, compared to $620 million in 2006. Macy's new online features and products and the growth of online retail sector are also discussed.

15350 ■ *Titanium EBay: A Tactical Guide to Becoming a Millionaire PowerSeller*

Pub: Penguin Group Incorporated

Ed: Skip McGrath. **Released:** June 2006. **Price:** $24.95. **Description:** Advice is given to help anyone selling items on eBay to become a Power Seller, an award presented based on monthly gross merchandise sales.

15351 ■ *"Traffic's Up: Website's Down Preventing Costly Crashes" in Inc. (March 2008, pp. 55-56)*

Pub: Gruner & Jahr USA Publishing

Ed: Darren Dahl. **Description:** Grid Web hosting protects a small company's Website when a sudden burst of Internet traffic hits enabling it to continue rather than be crippled. Options can vary in cost from $4 to $1,000 monthly and include using a shared server, grid server, virtual private server, or a dedicated server. The article explains each option.

15352 ■ *"Understanding Persuasive Online Sales Messages from eBay Auctions" in Business Communication Quarterly (December 2007, pp. 482)*

Pub: SAGE Publications USA

Contact: Blaise R. Simqu, President

Ed: Barbara Jo White, Daniel Clapper, Rita Noel, Jenny Fortier, Pierre Grabolosa. **Description:** eBay product listings were studied to determine the requirements of persuasive sales writing. Potential sellers should use the proper keywords and make an authentic description with authentic photographs of the item being auctioned.

15353 ■ *"Uptick in Clicks: Nordstrom's Online Sales Surging" in Puget Sound Business Journal (Vol. 29, August 22, 2008,*

No. 18, pp. 1)
Pub: American City Business Journals

Ed: Gregg Lamm. **Description:** Nordstrom Inc.'s online division grew its sales by 15 percent in the second quarter of 2008, compared to 2007's 4.3 percent in overall decline. The company expects their online net sales to reach $700 million in 2008 capturing eight percent of overall sales.

15354 ■ *"Web Sight: Do You See What I See?" in Entrepreneur (Vol. 35, October 2007, No. 10, pp. 58)*
Pub: Entrepreneur Media Inc.

Ed: Heather Clancy. **Description:** Owners of Trunkt, a boutique in New York that showcases independent designs, have created a new style of Website called Trunkt.org. The Website allows buyers to select the products they want to see and designers can choose anytime which of their items will be displayed on the site. An explanation of the strategy that helped bring Trunkt closer to its clients is presented.

15355 ■ *"White Cat Media Tells You Where to Get a Bargain. Now It's Shopping for $1.5 Million" in Inc. (March 2008, pp. 48)*
Pub: Gruner & Jahr USA Publishing

Ed: Athena Schindelheim. **Description:** Profile of White Cat Media which runs two shopping Websites: SheFinds.com for fashion and beauty items, and MomFinds.com for mothers. The New York City firm reported revenues for 2007 at $400,000 and is looking for funding capital in the amount of $1.7 million.

15356 ■ *"Women Clicking to Earn Virtual Dollars" in Sales and Marketing Management (November 11, 2009)*
Pub: Nielsen Business Media, Inc.

Ed: Stacy Straczynski. **Description:** According to a new report from Internet marketing firm Q Interactive, women are increasingly playing social media games where they are able to click on an ad or sign up for a promotion to earn virtual currency. Research is showing that this kind of marketing may be a potent tool, especially for e-commerce and online stores.

15357 ■ *"Women Workers Spend Lunchtime on Fridays Shopping Online" in Marketing to Women (Vol. 23, November 2010, No. 11, pp. 8)*
Pub: EPM Communications Inc.
Contact: Ira Mayer, President
E-mail: imayer@epmcom.com

Description: Forty percent of women shop online during work hours, particularly on Fridays. The largest number of women make these purchases during their lunch break. Demographics are included.

15358 ■ *"You Are What They Click" in Entrepreneur (Vol. 37, July 2009, No. 7, pp. 43)*
Pub: Entrepreneur Media, Inc.

Ed: Mikal Belicove. **Description:** Hiring the right website design firm is the first stage in building an online business, and this involves various factors such as price, technical expertise, and talent. Writing a request for proposal (RFP) detailing the website's details, which include purpose, budget and audience, is the first step the process. Other tips in finding the right web designer are given.

15359 ■ *"Young Entrepreneur Gets Some Recognition and Some Help for College" in Philadelphia Inquirer (August 30, 2010)*
Pub: Philadelphia Inquirer

Ed: Susan Snyder. **Description:** Profile of Zachary Gosling, age 18, who launched an online auction Website from his bedroom, using advertising and sponsorship funds rather than charging fees to users.

TRADE PERIODICALS

15360 ■ *Online: The Leading Magazine for Information Professionals*
Pub: Online, A Division of Information Today Inc.

URL(s): www.infotoday.com/online/default.shtml. **Ed:** Marydee Ojala. **Released:** Bimonthly **Price:** $124.95, Individuals; $235, Two years; $141, Canada and Mexico; $167, Other countries.

15361 ■ *Spotlights*
Pub: Internet/Media Strategies Inc.
Released: Weekly. **Description:** Analyzes business opportunities on the Internet and other technologies.

FRANCHISES AND BUSINESS OPPORTUNITIES

15362 ■ TheYardSale.com
10700 Montgomery Rd., Ste. 300
Cincinnati, OH 45242
Free: 800-291-0771
Fax: (513)563-2691
Description: Selling items on Ebay for others. **Franchised:** 2005. **Equity Capital Needed:** $10,000. **Franchise Fee:** $15,900 1st, $11,900 2nd. **Training:** Yes.

LIBRARIES

15363 ■ Alabama A & M University - J.F. Drake Memorial Learning Resources Center—Alabama Agricultural and Mechanical University.
4900 Meridian St.
Normal, AL 35762
Ph: (256)372-4747
Fax: (256)372-5764
URL: http://www.aamu.edu/administrativeoffices/
library/pages/about-the-library.aspx
Contact: Sadie Davis, Specialist, Circulation
Scope: Education, business and economics, agriculture, the sciences, computer science, literature. **Services:** Interlibrary loan; copying; media services; Center open to the public (courtesy card must be purchased for check out of materials by persons not enrolled at the university or at one of the cooperating institutions). **Founded:** 1904. **Holdings:** 236,147 books; 25,517 bound periodical volumes; 5044 AV programs; 20,869 periodicals on microfilm; 1053 college catalogs; various telephone directories; 16,166 ERIC microfiche; 141,376 government documents; Wall Street Journal on microfiche (11,643). **Subscriptions:** 1657 journals and other serials; 93 newspapers; 359 microfilm subscriptions.

START-UP INFORMATION

15364 ■ *"Franchises with an Eye on Chicago"*
in Crain's Chicago Business (Vol. 34, March
14, 2011, No. 11, pp. 20)
Pub: Crain Communications Inc.
Description: Profiles of franchise companies seeking franchisees for the Chicago area include: Extreme Pita, a sandwich shop; Hand and Stone, offering massage, facial and waxing services; Molly Maid, home-cleaning service; Primrose Schools, private accredited schools for children 6 months to 6 hears and after-school programs; Protect Painters, residential and light-commercial painting contractor; and Wingstop, a restaurant offering chicken wings in nine flavors, fries and side dishes.

15365 ■ *How to Start a Faux Painting or*
Mural Business, Second Edition
Pub: Allworth Press
Ed: Rebecca Pittman. **Released:** October 1, 2010.
Price: $24.95. **Description:** Updated and expanded to cover better ways to advertise, innovative supplies (such as Venetian plasters and stained cements), unique bidding and studio setups required for new plasters and varnishes.

ASSOCIATIONS AND OTHER ORGANIZATIONS

15366 ■ **American Coatings Association (ACA)**
1500 Rhode Island Ave. NW
Washington, DC 20005
Ph: (202)462-6272
Fax: (202)462-8549
Co. E-mail: npca@paint.org
URL: http://www.paint.org
Contact: J. Andrew Doyle, President
Description: Manufacturers of paints and chemical coatings; suppliers of raw materials and equipment. Conducts: statistical surveys; research, government, and public relations programs. Provides management information programs and management and technician development programs. Compiles statistics. **Founded:** 1933. **Publications:** *Paint & Coatings Buyers Guide; Insider News; Member Services Directory; Technical Bulletin; Trademark Directory* (Periodic); *Trademark Directory* (Irregular). **Awards:** George Baugh Heckel Award (Annual); Industry Achievement Award; Industry Statesman Awards; George Baugh Heckel Award. **Telecommunication Services:** members@paint.org.

15367 ■ **Wallcoverings Association (WA)**
401 N Michigan Ave., Ste. 2200
Chicago, IL 60611
Ph: (312)321-5166
Fax: (312)673-6928
Co. E-mail: wallcoverings@sba.com
URL: http://www.wallcoverings.org
Contact: Justin P. Allman Award, President
Description: Manufacturers, converters, distributors and suppliers in the wallcoverings industry. **Founded:** 1920. **Publications:** *Wallcoverings Association--*
Directory of Members (Annual). **Awards:** Allman Award (Annual). **Telecommunication Services:** info@wallcoverings.org.

DIRECTORIES OF EDUCATIONAL PROGRAMS

15368 ■ *Rauch Guide to the U.S. Paint*
Industry
Pub: Grey House Publishing
Contact: Richard Gottlieb, President
E-mail: rhg2@greyhouse.com
URL(s): www.greyhouse.com/rauch_pnt.htm. **Released:** latest edition 6th; published August, 2010.
Price: $595, Individuals softcover. **Covers:** Approximately 800 industry manufacturers with sales estimates, products, mergers and acquisitions, divestitures, and other information for the 400 largest companies. **Entries include:** Company name, address, description of products and services, branch office and location, financial date, number of employees.

REFERENCE WORKS

15369 ■ *"Contractors Must be Lead Certified*
by April 2010" in Contractor (Vol. 57,
February 2010, No. 2, pp. 3)
Pub: Penton Media, Inc.
Description: Contractors should be trained and certified to comply with the U.S. Environmental Protection Agency's Lead Renovation, Repair, and Painting regulation if they work on housing built before 1978 by April 2010. Contractors with previous lead abatement training must be trained and certified under this new program.

15370 ■ *Decorating Registry*
Pub: Paint and Decorating Retailers Association
Contact: Jeff Baggaley, President
URL(s): www.pdra.org/registrywww.pdra.org/magazines/faux_finisher_magazine. **Released:** Annual; July. **Publication includes:** List of about 1,500 manufacturers, manufacturers' representatives, distributors, and suppliers of decorating merchandise; a comprehensive trademark and brand name directory; associations, societies, and trade shows related to the home decorating industry. **Entries include:** For companies and manufacturer representatives-- Firm name, address, phone, fax, name and title of contact, trademark, brand names. For associations-- Name, address, phone, statement of purpose or description of service, key personnel, trade shows sponsored with dates and locations. Principal content of publication is decorative products (coatings, wallcoverings, window treatments, flooring, sundries). **Arrangement:** Alphabetical. **Indexes:** Brand and trade name.

15371 ■ *Directory of Home Center Operators*
& Hardware Chains
Pub: Chain Store Guide
Contact: Lisa Patterson, President
URL(s): www.chainstoreguide.com. **Released:** Annual; Latest edition 2012. **Price:** $395, Individuals Directory; $445, Individuals online lite; $1075,
Individuals online pro; $1375, Individuals online pro plus. **Covers:** 4,500 U.S. and Canadian companies which operate home centers, home center warehouses, lumber and building material outlets, specialty paint and home decorating stores, and kitchen and bath centers. Concentrates on companies with a minimum annual sales of one million dollars. **Entries include:** Company name, address, phone, fax, 6,100 personnel e-mail address, web site, Internet order processing indicator, listing type, product lines, total sales, sales percentage per customer type, total selling square footage, total stores, units by type of store operated, units made by trade name, trading areas, projected openings and remodeling, distribution center locations, buying and/or marketing group name and location, number of nurseries operated, average number of check-outs, year founded, public company indicator, parent and subsidiary company information, division and branch office locations, key personnel, and number of locations by city. **Arrangement:** Geographical. **Indexes:** Product line, alphabetical, exclusions, state.

15372 ■ *"Local Dealers Fear Shortages in Car*
Supply" in Boston Business Journal (Vol. 29,
May 13, 2011, No. 1, pp. 1)
Pub: American City Business Journals Inc.
Ed: Scott Dance. **Description:** The earthquake and tsunami in Japan are seen to impact the automobile dealers in Baltimore, Maryland. Automobile supply in the area is seen to decrease dramatically during the summer sales season. Shortage of transmission parts and paint colors is also forecasted.

15373 ■ *"Retail Woes: The Shoe Doesn't Fit*
for Gerald Loftin's Stock Picks" in Black
Enterprise (Vol. 38, July 2008, No. 12, pp. 40)
Pub: Earl G. Graves Publishing Co. Inc.
Ed: Steve Garmhausen. **Description:** Each of the three stocks that Gerald Loftin picked in May 2007 have lost money; DSW, the designer shoe retailer, fell by 63.7 percent; paint and coatings retailer Sherwin-Williams Co. fell by 7.2 percent; and Verizon Communications Inc. fell by 1.4 percent. Statistical data included.

15374 ■ *"Synthetic Drywall Rots Mechanical*
Parts" in Contractor (Vol. 56, December 2009,
No. 12, pp. 50)
Pub: Penton Media, Inc.
Ed: Bob Mader. **Description:** Chinese-made synthetic drywalls have been found to corrode mechanical and electrical products in homes. Drywalls always contain a certain amount of sulfur. The hydrogen sulfide gas component of synthetic drywalls causes copper and silver sulfide corrosion.

15375 ■ *"Why Women Blog and What They*
Read" in Marketing to Women (Vol. 22, July
2009, No. 7, pp. 8)
Pub: EPM Communications Inc.
Contact: Ira Mayer, President
E-mail: imayer@epmcom.com
Description: Listing of topics that are visited the most by female Internet users. Statistical data included.

SOURCES OF SUPPLY

15376 ■ *Gold Book: Directory of the Wallcovering Industry*
Paint and Decorating Retailers Association
Contact: Jeff Baggaley, President
URL(s): www.pdra.org. **Released:** Annual; Latest edition 2007. **Price:** $15, Individuals per copy. **Covers:** Companies that manufacture/distribute wallcovering collections and related products. Ie. Window treatments, stencils. **Entries include:** Name, address, phone, name and title of contact, subsidiary and branch names and locations, product/services provided, collection characteristics (vinyl, pre-pasted, strippable, scrubbable), expiration dates, distributor information for U.S., Canada, and Puerto Rico. **Arrangement:** Alphabetical. **Indexes:** Product/service.

STATISTICAL SOURCES

15377 ■ *Outlook for the Paints and Coatings Industry*
Pub: Business Trend Analysts, Inc.
Released: 2007-2008. **Price:** $2495.00. **Description:** This comprehensive report quantifies current and projected sales (through 2015) of architectural coatings, OEM product finishes, special-purpose coatings, and miscellaneous allied paint products.

15378 ■ *Paints and Coatings*
Business Trend Analysts, Inc. Industry Studies
Released: 1998. **Price:** $1495.00. **Description:** Profiles the paints and coatings market, covering interior and exterior trade paints, solvent and water-based paints, varnishes, stains, lacquers, OEM product finishes, powder coatings, and paint thinners and removers. Includes projections to the year 2001 on a product-by-product basis. Provides information on the paint retailing industry, distribution, pricing, and advertising. Also contains profiles of major manufacturers.

15379 ■ *RMA Annual Statement Studies*
Pub: Risk Management Association
Contact: Kevin M. Blakey, President
Released: Annual. **Price:** $175.00 2006-07 edition, $105.00. **Description:** Contains composite balance sheets and income statements for more than 360 industries, including the accounting, auditing, and bookkeeping industries. Also contains five years of comparative historical data for discerning trends. Includes 16 commonly used ratios, computed for most of the size groupings for nearly every industry.

TRADE PERIODICALS

15380 ■ *Paint & Decorating Retailer Magazine*
Pub: Paint and Decorating Retailers Association
Contact: Jeff Baggaley, President
URL(s): www.pdra.org/pdr_magazine. **Released:** Monthly

LIBRARIES

15381 ■ Sherwin-Williams Automotive Finishes Corporation Library
4440 Warrensville Center Rd.
Warrensville Heights, OH 44128-2837
Free: 800-798-5872
URL: http://www.sherwin-automotive.com
Contact: Elizabeth Rinz, Manager
Scope: Paint, polymers, pigments, coatings. **Services:** Interlibrary loan. **Founded:** 1957.

Painting Contractor

START-UP INFORMATION

15382 ■ *"Franchises with an Eye on Chicago" in Crain's Chicago Business (Vol. 34, March 14, 2011, No. 11, pp. 20)*
Pub: Crain Communications Inc.
Description: Profiles of franchise companies seeking franchisees for the Chicago area include: Extreme Pita, a sandwich shop; Hand and Stone, offering massage, facial and waxing services; Molly Maid, home-cleaning service; Primrose Schools, private accredited schools for children 6 months to 6 hears and after-school programs; Protect Painters, residential and light-commercial painting contractor; and Wingstop, a restaurant offering chicken wings in nine flavors, fries and side dishes.

15383 ■ *How to Start a Faux Painting or Mural Business, Second Edition*
Pub: Allworth Press
Ed: Rebecca Pittman. **Released:** October 1, 2010. **Price:** $24.95. **Description:** Updated and expanded to cover better ways to advertise, innovative supplies (such as Venetian plasters and stained cements), unique bidding and studio setups required for new plasters and varnishes.

ASSOCIATIONS AND OTHER ORGANIZATIONS

15384 ■ **American Coatings Association (ACA)**
1500 Rhode Island Ave. NW
Washington, DC 20005
Ph: (202)462-6272
Fax: (202)462-8549
Co. E-mail: npca@paint.org
URL: http://www.paint.org
Contact: J. Andrew Doyle, President
Description: Manufacturers of paints and chemical coatings; suppliers of raw materials and equipment. Conducts: statistical surveys; research, government, and public relations programs. Provides management information programs and management and technician development programs. Compiles statistics. **Founded:** 1933. **Publications:** *Paint & Coatings Buyers Guide*; *Insider News*; *Member Services Directory*; *Technical Bulletin*; *Trademark Directory* (Periodic); *Trademark Directory* (Irregular). **Awards:** George Baugh Heckel Award (Annual); Industry Achievement Award; Industry Statesman Awards; George Baugh Heckel Award. **Telecommunication Services:** members@paint.org.

15385 ■ **American Subcontractors Association (ASA)**
1004 Duke St.
Alexandria, VA 22314-3588
Ph: (703)684-3450
Free: 888-374-3133
Fax: (703)836-3482
Co. E-mail: asaoffice@asa-hq.com
URL: http://www.asaonline.org
Contact: Colette Nelson, Executive Vice President
Description: Construction subcontractors of trades and specialties such as foundations, concrete, masonry, steel, mechanical, drywall, electrical, painting, plastering, roofing and acoustical. Formed to deal with issues common to subcontractors. Works with other segments of the construction industry in promoting ethical practices, beneficial legislation and education of construction subcontractors and suppliers. Manages the Foundation of the American Subcontractors Association (FASA). **Founded:** 1966. **Publications:** *ASA Today*; *Action ASA* (Monthly); *The Contractor's Compass* (Quarterly). **Telecommunication Services:** asaoffice-hq@aol.com.

15386 ■ **National Guild of Professional Paperhangers (NGPP)**
136 S Keowee St.
Dayton, OH 45402
Ph: (937)222-6477
Free: 800-254-6477
Fax: (937)222-5794
Co. E-mail: ngpp@ngpp.org
URL: http://www.ngpp.org
Contact: Cyndi Green, President
Description: Paperhangers united to promote use of wallcoverings; upgrade the skills of paperhangers and the quality of materials; foster unity among members; encourage good business practices and ethics in the industry. Conducts charitable programs. Sponsors educational programs. **Scope:** wallcovering installation. **Founded:** 1973. **Subscriptions:** 110. **Publications:** *American Painting Contractor*; *Jobsite*; *Paint Pro*. **Educational Activities:** National Guild of Professional Paperhangers Meeting (Annual); National Paperhangers Forum (Annual). **Awards:** Golden Shears Award; Guy Cooper Golden Plumbline Award; Sam Kovnat Award; Skip Lowe Award; Bob Isenberger Paperhanger Member of the Year (Annual).

15387 ■ **Paint and Decorating Retailers Association (PDRA)**
1401 Triad Center Dr.
St. Peters, MO 63376-7353
Ph: (636)326-2636
Free: 800-737-0107
Fax: (636)229-4750
Co. E-mail: info@pdra.org
URL: http://www.pdra.org
Contact: Jeff Baggaley, President
Description: Serves as a trade association of locally-owned paint and decorating stores in the U.S., Canada and around the world. Offers professional advice, personal service and quality products for every paint, wall covering, window treatment and floor covering project. **Founded:** 1947. **Publications:** *Paint and Decorating Retailer*; *Paint & Decorating Retailer Magazine* (Monthly); *PDRA Decorating Registry* (Annual); *PDRA Gold Book* (Annual); *PDRA Paint and Decorating Retailer* (Monthly); *Gold Book* (Annual); *Decorating Registry* (Annual); *Decorating Retailer--Directory of the Wallcoverings Industry Issue* (Annual); *Gold Book: Directory of the Wallcovering Industry* (Annual). **Educational Activities:** Paint and Decorating Show (Annual). **Telecommunication Services:** dan@lloydspaint.com.

15388 ■ **Painting and Decorating Contractors of America (PDCA)**
1801 Park 270 Dr.
St. Louis, MO 63146-4020
Ph: (314)514-7322
Free: 800-332-7322
Fax: (314)890-2068
Co. E-mail: rbright@pdca.org
URL: http://www.pdca.org
Contact: Dave Ayala, President
Description: Painting and wall covering contractors. Operates educational and charitable programs. Compiles statistics. **Founded:** 1884. **Publications:** *Hazardous Waste Handbook*; *Painting and Wallcovering Contractor* (Bimonthly); *PDCA Directory* (Annual); *Painting and Wallcovering Contractor--PDCA Roster* (Annual). **Awards:** Humanitarian Award; Safety Awards (Annual); A.E. Robert Friedman Scholarships (Annual); "Picture It Painted Professionally" Awards; Al Quilici Outstanding Member Award; L.E. Travis, Jr. PDCA Craftsman of the Year Award (Annual); Picture It Painted Professionally Award (Annual). **Telecommunication Services:** rgreene@pdca.org; emcdermott@pdca.org.

15389 ■ **Wallcoverings Association (WA)**
401 N Michigan Ave., Ste. 2200
Chicago, IL 60611
Ph: (312)321-5166
Fax: (312)673-6928
Co. E-mail: wallcoverings@sba.com
URL: http://www.wallcoverings.org
Contact: Justin P. Allman Award, President
Description: Manufacturers, converters, distributors and suppliers in the wallcoverings industry. **Founded:** 1920. **Publications:** *Wallcoverings Association--Directory of Members* (Annual). **Awards:** Allman Award (Annual). **Telecommunication Services:** info@wallcoverings.org.

DIRECTORIES OF EDUCATIONAL PROGRAMS

15390 ■ *Directory of Private Accredited Career Schools and Colleges of Technology*
Pub: Accrediting Commission of Career Schools and Colleges of Technology
Contact: Michale S. McComis, Executive Director
Released: On web page. **Price:** Free. **Description:** Covers 3900 accredited post-secondary programs that provide training programs in business, trade, and technical fields, including various small business endeavors. Entries offer school name, address, phone, description of courses, job placement assistance, and requirements for admission. Arrangement is alphabetical.

REFERENCE WORKS

15391 ■ *American Painting Contractor--Buyers' Guide*
Pub: Briefings Media Group
Contact: Alan M. Douglas, President
E-mail: adouglas@douglaspublications.com
URL(s): www.paintmag.com. **Released:** Annual; Latest edition 2011. **Publication includes:** List of more

than 600 manufacturers of products, tools, and equipment for the paint and wallcoverings application industry. **Entries include:** Name, address, phone, fax, e-mail, URL, and contact name; some listings include logo and products. **Arrangement:** Alphabetical by product. **Indexes:** Product.

15392 ■ *"Colores Origenes: Martha Kruse" in Advertising Age (Vol. 77, November 13, 2006, No. 46, pp. S12)*

Pub: Crain Communications, Inc.

Ed: Laurel Wentz. **Description:** Home Depot has created a range of Latin paint colors called Colores Origenes; the new line was originally intended to launch only at locations with heavily Hispanic patrons but the company decided to make the line available at all of their stores.

15393 ■ *"Contractors Must be Lead Certified by April 2010" in Contractor (Vol. 57, February 2010, No. 2, pp. 3)*

Pub: Penton Media, Inc.

Description: Contractors should be trained and certified to comply with the U.S. Environmental Protection Agency's Lead Renovation, Repair, and Painting regulation if they work on housing built before 1978 by April 2010. Contractors with previous lead abatement training must be trained and certified under this new program.

15394 ■ *"Local Dealers Fear Shortages in Car Supply" in Boston Business Journal (Vol. 29, May 13, 2011, No. 1, pp. 1)*

Pub: American City Business Journals Inc.

Ed: Scott Dance. **Description:** The earthquake and tsunami in Japan are seen to impact the automobile dealers in Baltimore, Maryland. Automobile supply in the area is seen to decrease dramatically during the summer sales season. Shortage of transmission parts and paint colors is also forecasted.

15395 ■ *Painting and Wallcovering Contractor--PDCA Roster*

Pub: Painting and Decorating Contractors of America

Contact: Dave Ayala, President

URL(s): www.pdca.org. **Released:** Annual; August. **Publication includes:** Roster of about 3,500 member contractors engaged in painting, decorating, drywall, wallcovering, and special coatings application. **Entries include:** Company name, address, phone, fax, name of principal executive. **Arrangement:** By geographic council or chapter.

15396 ■ *"Procter Gambles on Wallpaper; Putting Paint On a Roll" in Advertising Age (Vol. 77, September 18, 2006, No. 38, pp. 4)*

Pub: Crain Communications, Inc.

Ed: Jack Neff. **Description:** Procter & Gamble Co. has launched a new line of textured paints that are already applied to a wallpaper-like roll that can be hung without paste or wallpaper tools.

15397 ■ *"Software Solutions Increase Productivity" in Contractor (Vol. 57, February 2010, No. 2, pp. 26)*

Pub: Penton Media, Inc.

Ed: William Feldman; Patti Feldman. **Description:** Singletouch is a real-time data capture solution for mechanical and other contractors that work in jobs that require materials and workload tracking. Contractors get information on extreme weather and sudden changes in the cost of materials. The OptimumHVAC optimization software by Optimum Energy is designed to optimize energy savings in commercial buildings.

15398 ■ *"Synthetic Drywall Rots Mechanical Parts" in Contractor (Vol. 56, December 2009, No. 12, pp. 50)*

Pub: Penton Media, Inc.

Ed: Bob Mader. **Description:** Chinese-made synthetic drywalls have been found to corrode mechanical and electrical products in homes. Drywalls always

contain a certain amount of sulfur. The hydrogen sulfide gas component of synthetic drywalls causes copper and silver sulfide corrosion.

15399 ■ *"Troubled Project In Court" in The Business Journal-Portland (Vol. 25, July 25, 2008, No. 20, pp. 1)*

Pub: American City Business Journals, Inc.

Ed: Wendy Culverwell. **Description:** Views and information on Salpare Bay's Hayden Island project, as well as on financing problems and cases associated with the project, are presented. Construction of luxurious waterside condominiums stopped last fall, after the discovery of financing problems and subcontractors and other parties started filing claims and counterclaims.

SOURCES OF SUPPLY

15400 ■ *Decorating Registry*

Paint and Decorating Retailers Association

Contact: Jeff Baggaley, President

URL(s): www.pdra.org/registrywww.pdra.org/magazines/faux_finisher_magazine. **Released:** Annual; July. **Publication includes:** List of about 1,500 manufacturers, manufacturers' representatives, distributors, and suppliers of decorating merchandise; a comprehensive trademark and brand name directory; associations, societies, and trade shows related to the home decorating industry. **Entries include:** For companies and manufacturer representatives-- Firm name, address, phone, fax, name and title of contact, trademark, brand names. For associations-- Name, address, phone, statement of purpose or description of service, key personnel, trade shows sponsored with dates and locations. Principal content of publication is decorative products (coatings, wallcoverings, window treatments, flooring, sundries). **Arrangement:** Alphabetical. **Indexes:** Brand and trade name.

STATISTICAL SOURCES

15401 ■ *RMA Annual Statement Studies*

Pub: Risk Management Association

Contact: Kevin M. Blakey, President

Released: Annual. **Price:** $175.00 2006-07 edition, $105.00. **Description:** Contains composite balance sheets and income statements for more than 360 industries, including the accounting, auditing, and bookkeeping industries. Also contains five years of comparative historical data for discerning trends. Includes 16 commonly used ratios, computed for most of the size groupings for nearly every industry.

CONSULTANTS

15402 ■ Historic Exterior Paint Colors Consulting—Historic House Colors

3661 Waldenwood Dr.

Ann Arbor, MI 48105

Ph: (734)668-0298

Co. E-mail: robs@umich.edu

URL: http://www.historichousecolors.com

Contact: Robert Schweitzer, Owner

E-mail: robs@umich.edu

Scope: Provider of exterior paint color consulting services. Provides services for historic, contemporary, new, commercial and residential services; museums. **Publications:** "Proof that Paint Color Lends Detail," Arts and Crafts Homes, 2006; "Bungalow Colors-Exteriors," Gibbs-Smith Publishers, 2002; "Color Scheming," Design NJ, 2002; "Colonial Revival Homes," Victorian Homes, Feb, 2003; "America's Favorite Homes"; "Color a New World," 60s Ranch Color Makeover, Romantic Homes, Aug, 2001; "How Shall I Paint my House," American Bungalow, 1999; "Color Concepts and Bungalow Basics," Cottages & Bungalows.

FRANCHISES AND BUSINESS OPPORTUNITIES

15403 ■ Certapro Painters

The Franchise Company

150 Green Tree Rd.

Oaks, PA 19456

Free: 800-689-7494

Fax: (610)650-9997

Description: Residential and commercial painting franchise. **No. of Franchise Units:** 325. **Founded:** 1992.. **Franchised:** 1992. **Equity Capital Needed:** $129,000-$156,000. **Franchise Fee:** $50,000. **Training:** 2 weeks of training prior to start-up; quarterly training in field. Advance training is also provided.

15404 ■ Color World Housepainting Inc.

420 W Olentangy St., No. B

Powell, OH 43065

Ph: (614)581-1652

Free: 877-724-6877

Fax: (614)861-7751

Description: Residential & commercial painting. **No. of Franchise Units:** 2. **No. of Company-Owned Units:** 6. **Founded:** 1997.. **Franchised:** 2007. **Equity Capital Needed:** $25,000-$110,000. **Franchise Fee:** $25,000. **Royalty Fee:** 5%. **Training:** Includes 2 weeks training.

15405 ■ Hester Painting & Decorating

Hester Decorating

7340 N Monticello Ave.

Skokie, IL 60076

Free: 877-437-8371

Fax: (847)677-5139

Co. E-mail: info@hesterdecorating.com

URL: http://www.hesterfranchising.com

Description: Painting and faux finishing company. No painting experience is needed. Based on 39 years experience, the Hester Painting & Decorating franchise program provides training program, estimating software, professional marketing system, and exclusive faux finish showroom. **No. of Company-Owned Units:** 2. **Founded:** 1968.. **Franchised:** 2007. **Franchise Fee:** $50,000. **Training:** Provides 9 days management training at headquarters covering award winning business systems along with over 3 weeks of hands on training for your staff at training facility and at your new showroom. You will learn approximately 30 faux and decorative finishing techniques.

15406 ■ The Painting Pros

1624-C Cross Beam Dr.

Charlotte, NC 28217

Ph: (704)424-5555

Fax: (704)424-1111

Description: Residential and commercial painting contractor. **No. of Franchise Units:** 7. **No. of Company-Owned Units:** 5. **Founded:** 2003.. **Franchised:** 2006. **Franchise Fee:** $15,000-$50,000. **Training:** Yes.

15407 ■ Protect Painters

Service Brands International

Description: Painting service. **No. of Franchise Units:** 37. **Founded:** 1995.. **Franchised:** 1995. **Equity Capital Needed:** $100,000 total investment. **Franchise Fee:** $14,900. **Training:** 8-10 days hands-on training courses. Ongoing support includes marketing, sales, weekly analysis of marketing and production, weekly teleconferences, workshops, personal visits and regional meetings.

LIBRARIES

15408 ■ Sherwin-Williams Automotive Finishes Corporation Library

4440 Warrensville Center Rd.

Warrensville Heights, OH 44128-2837

Free: 800-798-5872

URL: http://www.sherwin-automotive.com

Contact: Elizabeth Rinz, Manager

Scope: Paint, polymers, pigments, coatings. **Services:** Interlibrary loan. **Founded:** 1957.

START-UP INFORMATION

15409 ■ *"Fun And Easy Gold Mines" in Small Business Opportunities (Fall 2008)*
Pub: Entrepreneur Media Inc.

Description: Twenty-five businesses that cater to the booming children's market are profiled; day care services, party planning, special events video-making, tutoring, personalized children's toys and products and other services geared toward the kids market are included.

ASSOCIATIONS AND OTHER ORGANIZATIONS

15410 ■ **Clowns of America International (COAI)**
PO Box 1171
Englewood, FL 34295-1171
Ph: (941)474-4351
Free: 877-816-6941
URL: http://www.coai.org
Contact: Pamela Bacher, President

Description: Professional and amateur clowns, magicians, puppeteers, jugglers, and others who present a humorous program for the circus, radio, television, stage, and screen; friends of clowns and persons interested in clowning as a profession or hobby. Includes activities such as: training sessions, and entertaining in parades and shows. Provides entertainment for charitable organizations and events. Promotes first week of August as National Clown Week. **Founded:** 1968. **Publications:** *The New Calliope* (Bimonthly). **Awards:** Best of the Press Award; Charlie Award; Clown of the Year; Best of the Press Award (Annual); Charlie Award (Annual); Clown of the Year (Annual); Lifetime Achievement Award (Annual).

REFERENCE WORKS

15411 ■ *"Green It Like You Mean It" in Special Events Magazine (Vol. 28, February 1, 2009, No. 2)*
Pub: Special Events Magazine

Ed: Christine Landry. **Description:** Eco-friendly party planners offer advice for planning and hosting green parties or events. Tips include information for using recycled paper products, organic food and drinks. The Eco Nouveau Fashion Show held by Serene Star Productions reused old garments to create new fashions as well as art pieces from discarded doors and window frames for the show; eco-friendly treats and gift bags were highlighted at the event.

15412 ■ *"Holiday Parties to Take a Hit in Hard Times" in Philadelphia Business Journal (Vol. 28, November 6, 2009, No. 38, pp. 1)*
Pub: American City Business Journals

Ed: Peter van Allen. **Description:** Companies are cutting expenses in view of the economic downturn and are changing the way holiday parties will be held.

Sixty-two percent of firms will still hold parties in 2009, but last minute decisions about reduced-cost parties are being made.

15413 ■ *"How I Did It: Laurel Touby Mediabistro" in Inc. (March 2008, pp. 124-126)*
Pub: Gruner & Jahr USA Publishing

Ed: Eric Schine. **Description:** Profile of Laurel Touby and her business plan; Touby started Mediabistro as a series of parties that turned into an influential job listing and training Website for journalists. Last year she sold it for $23 million.

15414 ■ *"Party Animals" in Business Review, Albany New York (Vol. 34, November 16, 2007, No. 33, pp. 1)*
Pub: American City Business Journals, Inc.

Ed: Donna Abbott Viahos. **Description:** Total Events LLC, an event planning firm founded by Richard Carrier, generated sales from $13,000 to $1.5 million in eight years. Fine Affairs Inc. generates more than a million of revenues a year. Both companies provide party planning, organizing and decorating, wedding, galas, bar mitzvahs and other event planning.

TRADE PERIODICALS

15415 ■ *Balloons & Parties Magazine*
Pub: PartiLife Publications

URL(s): www.balloonsandparties.com. **Released:** Quarterly **Price:** $16.95, Two years; $9.95, Individuals.

15416 ■ *Linking Ring*
Pub: International Brotherhood of Magicians

URL(s): www.magician.org/portal/en/node/367. **Released:** Monthly

15417 ■ *Magic: The Independent Magazine for Magicians*
Pub: Stagewrite Publishing Inc.

URL(s): www.magicmagazine.com/. **Ed:** Stan Allen. **Released:** Monthly **Price:** $54, Individuals; $103, Two years; $74, Canada; $82, Individuals Mexico; $143, Two years for Canada; $159, Two years for Mexico; $89, Out of country airmail.

VIDEOCASSETTES/ AUDIOCASSETTES

15418 ■ *Magic: The Sleeveless Way*
Silver Mine Video Inc.
31316 Via Colinas, Ste. 104
Westlake Village, CA 91362-6715
Ph: (818)707-0300
Fax: (818)707-1606
Co. E-mail: quksil@aol.com
URL: http://www.quicksilverrecords.zoomshare.com
Contact: Howard L. Silver, President

Released: 1985. **Price:** $29.95. **Description:** A detailed demonstration of how to perform magic tricks with common household items. **Availability:** VHS.

FRANCHISES AND BUSINESS OPPORTUNITIES

15419 ■ **Complete Music**
7877 L St.
Omaha, NE 68127
Ph: (402)339-0001
Fax: (402)898-1777

Description: Mobile entertainment service. Entertainment for special events. Franchise owners hire and train a staff of DJs to perform at these events. **No. of Franchise Units:** 170. **No. of Company-Owned Units:** 2. **Founded:** 1974. **Franchised:** 1981. **Equity Capital Needed:** $15,000-$35,000. **Franchise Fee:** $18,000-$35,500. **Financial Assistance:** Yes. **Training:** 10 days at corporate office, covering day-to-day operations, including marketing, training of staff, hiring procedures, etc. Additional 4 day onsite provided.

15420 ■ **Cool Daddy's**
4188 Roswell Rd.
Atlanta, GA 30342
Ph: (404)352-9996
Fax: (404)352-9106

Description: Frozen drink party rentals & entertainment. **No. of Franchise Units:** 1. **No. of Company-Owned Units:** 1. **Founded:** 2000. **Franchised:** 2005. **Equity Capital Needed:** $105,000-$187,500. **Franchise Fee:** $25,000. **Royalty Fee:** 6%. **Training:** Provides 2 weeks at headquarters. 1 week at franchisee's location, with ongoing support.

15421 ■ **Grove Recreations, Inc.**
1207 Hillside Dr. N
N Myrtle Beach, SC 29582
Ph: (843)249-2118
Fax: (849)249-2118

Description: Recreation and entertainment service. **No. of Franchise Units:** 37. **No. of Company-Owned Units:** 4. **Founded:** 1977.. **Equity Capital Needed:** $200,000-$450,000. **Financial Assistance:** Yes. **Training:** Yes.

15422 ■ **The Party Image**
Pampered Girls, Inc.
2007 Oakview Dr.
Round Rock, TX 78681
Ph: (512)218-9390
Fax: (512)218-9970

Description: Spa atmosphere parties for young girls. **No. of Company-Owned Units:** 3. **Founded:** 2005.. **Franchised:** 2006. **Equity Capital Needed:** $46,000-$80,000. **Franchise Fee:** $20,000. **Royalty Fee:** 6%. **Financial Assistance:** Limited third party financing available. **Training:** Available 4 days at headquarter with ongoing support.

15423 ■ **Party Land**
5215 Militia Hill Rd.
Plymouth Meeting, PA 19462
Ph: (610)941-6200
Free: 800-778-9563

Fax: (610)941-6301
Co. E-mail: jbarry@partyland.com
URL: http://www.partyland.com
Description: Retail party supply stores. **No. of Franchise Units:** 43. **Founded:** 1986.. **Franchised:** 1988. **Equity Capital Needed:** $150,000 -$297,000. **Franchise Fee:** $35,000. **Royalty Fee:** 5%. **Training:** 1 week training.

RESEARCH CENTERS

15424 ■ **International Clown Hall of Fame Museum and Research Center, Inc. (ICHOF)**
640 S 84th St., Ste. 526
West Allis, WI 53214
Ph: (414)290-0105

Fax: (414)290-0106
Co. E-mail: contact@theclownmuseum.org
URL: http://www.theclownmuseum.org
Founded: 1986. **Publications:** *ICHOF Newsletter* (Quarterly). **Educational Activities:** Workshops, seminars, special events, and live performances. **Telecommunication Services:** ttendeavors@aol.com.

START-UP INFORMATION

15425 ■ *"Fun And Easy Gold Mines"* in *Small Business Opportunities* (Fall 2008)
Pub: Entrepreneur Media Inc.
Description: Twenty-five businesses that cater to the booming children's market are profiled; day care services, party planning, special events video-making, tutoring, personalized children's toys and products and other services geared toward the kids market are included.

ASSOCIATIONS AND OTHER ORGANIZATIONS

15426 ■ **National Association of Casino Party Operators (NACPO)**
PO Box 5626
South San Francisco, CA 94083
Free: 888-922-0777
Co. E-mail: info@casinoparties.com
URL: http://www.nactpo.com
Contact: Mike Miller, Director
Description: Casino party operators, party planners, party rental shop owners, theme party and special events operators, and others involved in casino party rental business. Strives to strengthen the casino and theme party industry and advance the industry into more geographical markets. Promotes members' interests. **Founded:** 1992.

REFERENCE WORKS

15427 ■ *"2011 Summer Wedding and Party Tips and Must Have's"* in *Benzinga.com* (June 17, 2011)
Pub: Benzinga.com
Ed: Benzinga Staff. **Description:** Tips for hosting garden parties and get-togethers, but focusing on wedding receptions are provided.

15428 ■ *"Green It Like You Mean It"* in *Special Events Magazine* (Vol. 28, February 1, 2009, No. 2)
Pub: Special Events Magazine
Ed: Christine Landry. **Description:** Eco-friendly party planners offer advice for planning and hosting green parties or events. Tips include information for using recycled paper products, organic food and drinks. The Eco Nouveau Fashion Show held by Serene Star Productions reused old garments to create new fashions as well as art pieces from discarded doors and window frames for the show; eco-friendly treats and gift bags were highlighted at the event.

15429 ■ *"Holiday Bloom: Event Designer Collin Abraham Heightens Glamour With Florals"* in *Black Enterprise* (Vol. 41, November 2010, No. 4)
Pub: Earl G. Graves Publishing Co. Inc.
Ed: Sean Drakes. **Description:** Profile of Collin Abraham, who works out of his Harlem boutique to arrange unique floral pieces to complement the social gatherings and main events he plans for his clients.

15430 ■ *"Holiday Parties to Take a Hit in Hard Times"* in *Philadelphia Business Journal* (Vol. 28, November 6, 2009, No. 38, pp. 1)
Pub: American City Business Journals
Ed: Peter van Allen. **Description:** Companies are cutting expenses in view of the economic downturn and are changing the way holiday parties will be held. Sixty-two percent of firms will still hold parties in 2009, but last minute decisions about reduced-cost parties are being made.

15431 ■ *"Holy Wasabi! Sushi Not Just For Parents Anymore"* in *Chicago Tribune* (March 13, 2008)
Pub: McClatchy-Tribune Information Services
Ed: Christopher Borrelli. **Description:** Wicker Park cooking school, The Kid's Table, specializes in cooking classes for pre-teens; Elena Marre who owns the school was surprised when she was asked to plan a children's party in which she would teach a course in sushi making. More and more adolescents and small children are eating sushi.

15432 ■ *"How I Did It: Laurel Touby Mediabistro"* in *Inc.* (March 2008, pp. 124-126)
Pub: Gruner & Jahr USA Publishing
Ed: Eric Schine. **Description:** Profile of Laurel Touby and her business plan; Touby started Mediabistro as a series of parties that turned into an influential job listing and training Website for journalists. Last year she sold it for $23 million.

15433 ■ *"Interbrand's Creative Recruiting"* in *Business Courier* (Vol. 27, November 12, 2010, No. 28, pp. 1)
Pub: Business Courier
Ed: Dan Monk. **Description:** Global brand consulting firm Interbrand uses a creative recruitment agency to attract new employees into the company. Interbrand uses themed parties to attract prospective employees. The 'Alice In Wonderland' tea party for example, allowed the company to hire five new employees.

15434 ■ *"On Your Marks, American Airlines, Now Vote!"* in *Benzinga.com* (, 2011)
Pub: Benzinga.com
Ed: Benzinga Staff. **Description:** Wedding planner, Aviva Samuels, owner of Kiss the Planner boutique wedding and event planning agency in Florida, says that winning this contest would help her increase her knowledge base and provide in-depth, personal experience offering more destination wedding destinations.

15435 ■ *"Party Animals"* in *Business Review, Albany New York* (Vol. 34, November 16, 2007, No. 33, pp. 1)
Pub: American City Business Journals, Inc.
Ed: Donna Abbott Viahos. **Description:** Total Events LLC, an event planning firm founded by Richard Carrier, generated sales from $13,000 to $1.5 million in eight years. Fine Affairs Inc. generates more than a million of revenues a year. Both companies provide party planning, organizing and decorating, wedding, galas, bar mitzvahs and other event planning.

15436 ■ *"Plan Your Wedding with Cleveland Airport Marriott's Certified Event Planners"* in *Benzinga.com* (February 2, 2011)
Pub: Benzinga.com
Ed: Benzinga Staff. **Description:** Cleveland's Airport Marriott makes wedding planning easy with its venue spaces and a full team of wedding planners.

15437 ■ *Tent Rental Directory: Ideabook*
Pub: Industrial Fabrics Association International
Contact: Stephen M. Warner, Chief Executive Officer
E-mail: smwarner@ifai.com
URL(s): tentexperts.org. **Released:** Annual; May. **Covers:** Over 200 manufacturing and rental firms of party, fair, and commercial tents; international coverage. **Entries include:** Company name, address, phone, name of contact, product or service provided. **Arrangement:** Geographical.

15438 ■ *"Velvet Ice Cream"* in *Ice Cream Reporter* (Vol. 23, November 20, 2010, No. 12, pp. 7)
Pub: Ice Cream Reporter
Description: Velvet Ice Cream will open its Ye Olde Mill for private corporate parties around the holidays. Their facility can accommodate groups ranging from 30 to 125 individuals. The historic site houses the company headquarters, an ice cream museum, and a restaurant.

TRADE PERIODICALS

15439 ■ *The Polar Bear ROARS*
Pub: Polar Bear Alumni Association
Ed: Leeann Faust, Editor, lfaust@columbus.rr.com. **Released:** Quarterly. **Price:** Included in membership; $8 /year. **Description:** Provides news of current events regarding reunion information, memories of alumni, history of school and articles about alumni and faculty. Recurring features include reports of reunions.

15440 ■ *Singles in the Suburbs Newsletter*
Pub: Singles in the Suburbs Inc.
Contact: James Mackey, President
Ed: Sarah Regan, Editor. **Released:** Monthly. **Price:** $30, individuals. **Description:** Lists events that the club will be holding in the next calendar month. The events are planned to provide a low-pressure, casual way for singles to meet and socialize.

FRANCHISES AND BUSINESS OPPORTUNITIES

15441 ■ **Plan Ahead Events**
United Franchise Group
2121 Vista Pky.
West Palm Beach, FL 33411
Ph: (800)466-2812
Fax: (561)478-4340
URL: http://www.planaheadevents.com
Description: Event planning. **No. of Franchise Units:** 75. **Founded:** 2007. **Franchised:** 2007. **Equity Capital Needed:** $38,855-$70,245. **Franchise**

Fee: $32,500. **Royalty Fee:** $300+/month. **Financial Assistance:** Limited third party financing available. **Training:** Provides 1 week at headquarters, 1 week at franchisee's location and ongoing support.

ASSOCIATIONS AND OTHER ORGANIZATIONS

15442 ■ **National Pawnbrokers Association (NPA)**
PO Box 508
Keller, TX 76244
Ph: (817)337-8830
Fax: (817)337-8875
Co. E-mail: info@nationalpawnbrokers.org
URL: http://www.nationalpawnbrokers.org
Contact: Dana Meinecke, Executive Director
Description: Pawnbrokers and interested others. Seeks to educate and inform the public on the pawnbroking industry. Provides continuing education on technological changes. **Founded:** 1989. **Publications:** *National Pawnbroker* (Quarterly); *Pawnbroker News* (Periodic); *Buyers Guide* (Periodic). **Educational Activities:** National Pawnbrokers Association Conference (Annual); National Pawnbrokers Association Convention (Annual).

REFERENCE WORKS

15443 ■ *"B-N Pawn Shop Auctions Off Jimmy Hoffa's Rifle" in Pantagraph (September 14, 2010)*
Pub: The Pantagraph

Ed: Ryan Denham. **Description:** Midwest Exchange pawn shop located in IAA Drive in Bloomington, Illinois auctioned a rifle once belonging to Jimmy Hoffa.

15444 ■ *"Boyd's Pawn Shop Looks More Like a Mini-Mall With Plenty For Sale" in The Hawk Eye (January 2, 2011)*
Pub: McClatchy-Tribune Information Services

Ed: Rex L. Troute. **Description:** Profile of Brian Boyd, aka 'the king of pawn' and his shop located in West Burlington, Iowa. Boyd also operates a redemption center at the rear of his shop and collects nearly 42 million cans and bottles annually.

15445 ■ *"BRIEF: Montana Street Pawn Shop Closing Doors" in Montana Standard (November 6, 2010)*
Pub: Montana Standard

Ed: John Grant Emeigh. **Description:** First National Pawn located in Butte, Montana will close its doors after losing its lease. Co-owner Pat Evenson reported the lease situation coupled with the economy prompted the decision to close.

15446 ■ *"Detroit Pawn Shop to be Reality TV Venue" in UPI NewsTrack (July 10, 2010)*
Pub: United Press International-USA

Description: TruTV will present a new series called 'Hardcore Pawn' to compete with the History Channel's successful show 'Pawn Stars'. The show will feature American Jewelry and Loan in Detroit, Michigan and its owner Les Gold, who runs the store with his wife and children.

15447 ■ *"Family Feud: Pawn Shop Empire Stalls with Transition to Second Generation" in Billings Gazette (December 19, 2010)*
Pub: Billings Gazette

Ed: Jan Falstad. **Description:** Profile of Ben L. Brown Sr. and his pawn shop located in Billings, Montana is presented. Brown discusses his plan to transition his business to his children.

15448 ■ *"Gold Still Has That Glitter" in Barron's (Vol. 89, July 20, 2009, No. 29, pp. M8)*
Pub: Dow Jones & Co., Inc.

Ed: Allen Sykora. **Description:** Gold prices appear to be ready for an increase starting in the fall of 2009 due to an increase in demand. The price of the August 2009 gold contract fell to as low as $904.08 an ounce before recovering to $937.50.

15449 ■ *"Pawn Shop Plan Snubbed by Citizen Group" in North County Times (October 14, 2010)*
Pub: North County Times

Ed: Ray Huard. **Description:** A citizens advisory group is against the opening of an upscale pawn shop in downtown Oceanside, California. The group contends that a pawn shop does not fit the plans for revitalizing the area.

15450 ■ *"Waco Pawn Shop Owners Say Reality Isn't Much Like 'Pawn Stars' TV Show" in Waco Tribune-Herald (August 15, 2010)*
Pub: Waco Tribune-Herald

Ed: Mike Copeland. **Description:** Area pawn shop owners report that the television show on cable TV does not represent the true life operations of a pawn shop. The Las Vegas shop represented on TV boasts 30 employees and 21 on-call experts, which is not the case in reality.

ASSOCIATIONS AND OTHER ORGANIZATIONS

15451 ■ American Payroll Association (APA)
660 N Main Ave., Ste. 100
San Antonio, TX 78205-1217
Ph: (210)226-4600
Free: 800-398-8681
Fax: (210)226-4027
Co. E-mail: info@americanpayroll.org
URL: http://www.americanpayroll.org
Contact: Kathleen Menda, President
Description: Payroll employees. Works to increase members' skills and professionalism through education and mutual support. Represents the interest of members before legislative bodies. Conducts training courses. Operates speakers' bureau; conducts educational programs. Administers the certified payroll professional program of recognition. **Scope:** Offers expertise in comprehensive payroll and accounts payable training programs, certification, research and education. **Founded:** 1982. **Publications:** "The Payroll Source"; "Federal Payroll Non-Tax Laws and Regulations"; "APA's Guide to Federal and State Garnishment Laws"; "Payroll Practice Fundamentals"; "APA's Guide to Federal and State Wage and Hour Laws"; "APA's Guide to Local Payroll Taxes"; "APA's Guide to State Payroll Laws"; "The Guide to Successful Direct Deposit or The Guide to Successful Electronic Payments"; "Your Paycheck"; "Survey of Salaries and the Payroll Profession"; "The Payroll Source". **Educational Activities:** American Payroll Association Annual Congress (Annual); American Payroll Association Congress (Annual); Educational Institutions Payroll Conference (Annual); Implementing Payroll Best Practices (Annual). **Awards:** Donald W. Sharper Education Grant (Annual). **Seminars:** Standard Foundation of Payroll Administration; Implementing Payroll Best Practices; Payroll System Selection and Implementation; Accounts Payable or Disbursements Preparing for Year-End and 2009; Canadian Payrolls Preparing for Year-End and 2009; Government/Public Sector Preparing for Year-End and 2009; Payroll Issues For Multi-State Employers. **Telecommunication Services:** apa@americanpayroll.org.

15452 ■ Canadian Payroll Association (CPA)—Association canadienne de la paie
250 Bloor St. E, Ste. 1600
Toronto, ON, Canada M4W 1E6
Ph: (416)487-3380
Free: 800-387-4693
Fax: (416)487-3384
Co. E-mail: membership@payroll.ca
URL: http://www.payroll.ca
Contact: Patrick Culhane, President
Description: Represents the payroll community in Canada; offers education programs, advocacy efforts, products and services to help members enhance and adapt payroll operations, meet new legislative requirements, address changing workplace needs and take advantage of emerging technologies. **Scope:** payroll, finance, employment standards, accounting, monetary, fiscal legislation. **Founded:**

1978. **Subscriptions:** archival material books clippings periodicals. **Publications:** *CPA E-Source* (Bimonthly); *Dialogue Magazine* (Bimonthly). **Awards:** The Board of Directors Award (Annual); The CPA Partner Award; The Diana Ferguson Award (Annual); Board of Directors Award; Certification Achievement Award; CPA Partner Award; Diana Ferguson Award.

15453 ■ CPA E-Source
250 Bloor St. E, Ste. 1600
Toronto, ON, Canada M4W 1E6
Ph: (416)487-3380
Free: 800-387-4693
Fax: (416)487-3384
Co. E-mail: membership@payroll.ca
URL: http://www.payroll.ca
Contact: Patrick Culhane, President
Released: Bimonthly

15454 ■ Dialogue Magazine
250 Bloor St. E, Ste. 1600
Toronto, ON, Canada M4W 1E6
Ph: (416)487-3380
Free: 800-387-4693
Fax: (416)487-3384
Co. E-mail: membership@payroll.ca
URL: http://www.payroll.ca
Contact: Patrick Culhane, President
Released: Bimonthly **Price:** C$95, /year.

REFERENCE WORKS

15455 ■ "DHS Finalizes Rules Allowing Electronic I-9s" in HR Specialist (Vol. 8, September 2010, No. 9, pp. 5)
Pub: Capitol Information Group Inc.
Description: U.S. Department of Homeland Security issued regulations that give employers more flexibility to electronically sing and store I-9 employee verification forms.

15456 ■ Employer Legal Forms Simplified
Pub: Nova Publishing Company
Ed: Daniel Sitarz. **Released:** August 2007. **Price:** $24.95. **Description:** Business reference containing the following forms needed to handle employees in any small business environment: application, notice, confidentiality, absence, federal employer forms and notices, and many payroll forms. All forms are included on a CD that comes in both PDF and text formats. Adobe Acrobat Reader software is also included on the CD. The forms are valid in all fifty states and Washington, DC.

15457 ■ "May I Handle That For You?" in Inc. (March 2008, pp. 40, 42)
Pub: Gruner & Jahr USA Publishing
Ed: Taylor Mallory. **Description:** According to a recent survey, 53 percent of all companies outsource a portion of their human resources responsibilities. Ceridian, Administaff, Taleo, KnowledgeBank, and CheckPoint HR are among the companies profiled.

15458 ■ "More Businesses Will Shift Health Costs to Workers" in Business Review, Albany New York (Vol. 34, November 16, 2007, No. 33, pp. 1)
Pub: American City Business Journals, Inc.
Ed: Barbara Pinckney. **Description:** Survey conducted by consulting firm Benetech Inc. showed that sixty percent of employers are planning to increase payroll deductions to pay for health insurance premiums. More than ninety percent of the employers prefer HMO plans, followed by Preferred Provider Organizations. Other details of the survey are discussed.

15459 ■ "Privacy Concern: Are 'Group' Time Sheets Legal?" in HR Specialist (Vol. 8, September 2010, No. 9, pp. 4)
Pub: Capitol Information Group Inc.
Description: Under the Fair Labor Standards Act (FLSA) employers are required to maintain and preserve payroll or other records, including the number of hours worked, but it does not prescribe a particular order or form in which these records must be kept.

15460 ■ QuickBooks X for Dummies
Pub: John Wiley & Sons, Incorporated
Ed: Stephen L. Nelson. **Released:** November 2006. **Price:** $21.99. **Description:** Key features of QuickBooks software for small business are introduced. Invoicing and credit memos, recoding sales receipts, accounting, budgeting, taxes, payroll, financial reports, job estimating, billing, tracking, data backup, are among the features.

15461 ■ "What to Pay Your Top Team" in Inc. (March 2008, pp. 108-112, 114)
Pub: Gruner & Jahr USA Publishing
Ed: Jennifer Gill. **Description:** In-depth examination to help business owners decide if they paying their executives properly. A guide to executive salaries at private companies is presented. Statistical data included.

TRADE PERIODICALS

15462 ■ Keep Up to Date on Payroll
Pub: Progressive Business Publications
Ed: Ken Thorne, Editor, thorne@pbp.com. **Released:** Semimonthly. **Price:** $230, individuals. **Description:** Presents the latest on federal and state tax laws and unemployment insurance. Recurring features include interviews, a calendar of events, news of educational opportunities, and columns titled Law and Reg Update, Real Problems/Real Solutions, and Sharpen Your Judgment.

15463 ■ Payroll Legal Alert
Pub: Alexander Hamilton Institute Inc.
Ed: Alice Gilman, ESQ, Editor. **Released:** Monthly. **Price:** $99. **Description:** Covers aspects of payroll operations, including key tax and benefits laws, regulations, rulings, and cases. Includes new trends in tax law, ideas on benefits, wage and hour traps, and unemployment issues.

15464 ■ Payroll Manager's Letter
Pub: Aspen Publishers, Inc.
Contact: Robert Becker, President
Released: Semimonthly. **Price:** $325, individuals.
Description: Provides information payroll professionals require to comply with IRS, SSA, and other government regulations. Includes reports on court cases and their impact on payroll, relevant technology updates, and innovations in the payroll field. Recurring features include interviews and annual updates on Forms W-2 and W-4, tax rates, and per diems.

FRANCHISES AND BUSINESS OPPORTUNITIES

15465 ■ Universal Payroll Company
290 Main St., Ste. 300
Alpharetta, GA 30009
Ph: (770)778-6148
Fax: (770)421-8171
Description: Full service payroll company.

COMPUTER SYSTEMS/ SOFTWARE

15466 ■ Aatrix Top Pay
2100 Library Cir.
Grand Forks, ND 58201
Ph: (701)746-6017
Free: 800-426-0854
Fax: (701)787-0594
URL: http://www.aatrix.com
Price: Contact Aatrix. **Description:** Handles payroll calculations and tax deductions for both salaried and hourly employees.

15467 ■ ABS Payroll System
315 Littleton Rd.
Chelmsford, MA 01824
Ph: (978)250-9600
Free: 800-356-4034
Fax: (978)250-8027
Co. E-mail: sales@abs-software.com
URL: http://www.abs-software.com
Description: Available for Windows XP, 2000, NT, ME, 98, or 95 platforms. Payroll and management system including an employee database driving payroll processing. System provides audit reports, and user-defined earnings and deduction categories.

15468 ■ ACCESS Payroll / Warren Computer Center
1945 Mitchell Ave.
Waterloo, IA 50702
Ph: (319)232-9504
Free: 800-553-0002
Fax: (319)232-8903
Co. E-mail: warren@warrencomputer.com
URL: http://www.warrencomputer.com
Contact: John Warren, President
Description: Available for IBM computers and MS-DOS compatibles. Payroll package featuring employee, company, and governmental reporting information and a master record for each employee.

15469 ■ Comprehensive Integrated Payroll System: CHIPS / Donald R. Frey and Company, Inc.
40 N Grand Ave., Ste. 303
Ft. Thomas, KY 41075
Ph: (859)441-6566
Free: 800-659-3739
Fax: (859)441-7152
Co. E-mail: drfrey@drfrey.com
URL: http://www.drfrey.com
Description: CHIPS (CompreHensive Integrated Payroll System) is designed to provide the special functional and reporting capabilities required for fund based accounting operations.

15470 ■ CompuSystems, Inc.
1 Science Ct.
Columbia, SC 29203-9344
Ph: (803)735-7700
Free: 800-800-6472
Fax: (800)800-8355
URL: http://www.misyshealth.com
Description: Available for MS-DOS compatibles. System maintaining employee records, and printing checks, check register, monthly reports, quarterly reports, annual reports, W-2 forms, and 1099 forms.

15471 ■ Custom Payroll
10020 Fontana
Overland Park, KS 66207
Ph: (913)381-9118
Fax: (913)381-9118
URL: http://www.datasmithpayroll.com
Price: Contact Datasmith product cost. **Description:** Contact Datasmith product cost.

15472 ■ DacEasy Payroll / Sage Software SB, Inc.
1505 Pavilion Place
Norcross, GA 30093
Ph: (770)724-4000
Free: 800-322-3279
Fax: (972)713-6331
Co. E-mail: dachelp@daceasy.com
URL: http://www.daceasy.com/
Price: Contact DacEasy for Pricing.

15473 ■ Open Systems Payroll System
4301 Dean Lakes Blvd.
Shakopee, MN 55379
Ph: (952)403-5700
Free: 800-328-2276
Fax: (952)496-2495
Co. E-mail: info@osas.com
URL: http://www.osas.com
Description: Available for CP/M, MP/M environments. System designed for meeting government reporting requirements for hourly and salaried employees. Features check processing, withholding and department reporting, payroll processing, and labor expense distribution and reporting by department.

15474 ■ Ultimate Payroll
2100 Library Cir.
Grand Forks, ND 58201
Ph: (701)746-6017
Free: 800-426-0854

Fax: (701)746-4393
URL: http://www.aatrix.com
Contact: Steve Lunseth, President
Price: Contact Aatrix. **Description:** Available for Apple Macintosh computers. Features payroll functions as well as restaurant tips reporting, unlimited pay rates, piecework, and deductions. Also prints information on federal forms, and tracks check amounts, sick, vacation, and holiday pay.

LIBRARIES

15475 ■ Ernst & Young Library
875 E. Wisconsin Ave.
Milwaukee, WI 53202
Ph: (414)273-5900
URL: http://www.ey.com
Scope: Taxation, tax law, accounting, auditing. **Services:** Performs searches on fee basis for clients only. **Holdings:** 1200 books. **Subscriptions:** 35 journals and other serials.

15476 ■ International Public Management Association for Human Resources - HR Center
1617 Duke St.
Alexandria, VA 22314
Ph: (703)549-7100
Fax: (703)684-0948
Co. E-mail: nreichenberg@ipma-hr.org
URL: http://www.ipma-hr.org
Contact: Neil E. Reichenberg, Executive Director
Scope: Public sector human resource management - classification, job analysis, policies and procedures, personnel, separation and retirement; wage and salary administration; employee relations; benefits; test development; total quality management. **Services:** Center not open to the public. **Founded:** 1973. **Holdings:** 500 volumes. **Subscriptions:** 12 newsletters.

15477 ■ Mercer Information Research Centre—Mercer Human Resource Consulting - Information Research Centre.
161 Bay St.
Toronto, ON, Canada M5J 2S5
Ph: (416)868-2005
Fax: (416)868-7171
Co. E-mail: jo-anne.weiler@mercer.com
Contact: Jo-Anne Weiler, Manager
Scope: Employee benefits, pensions, human resources consulting, financial planning, strategic planning, salary administration, executive compensation, group insurance benefits. **Services:** Interlibrary loan. **Founded:** 1974. **Holdings:** 2500 books; 450 subject files; company financial reports. **Subscriptions:** 180 journals and other serials; 3 newspapers.

RESEARCH CENTERS

15478 ■ University of Waterloo - Centre for Accounting Research and Education (CARE)
School of Accounting & Finance
200 University Ave. W
Waterloo, ON, Canada N2L 3G1
Ph: (519)888-4567
Fax: (519)888-7562
Co. E-mail: jbarnett@uwaterloo.ca
URL: http://accounting.uwaterloo.ca/research/care. html
Contact: James (Jim) Barnett, Director
Founded: 1981. **Publications:** *CARE Working Papers* (Occasionally).

ASSOCIATIONS AND OTHER ORGANIZATIONS

15479 ■ Alliance of Area Business Publications (AABP)
1970 E Grand Ave., Ste. 330
El Segundo, CA 90245
Ph: (310)364-0193
Fax: (310)364-0196
Co. E-mail: info@bizpubs.org
URL: http://www.bizpubs.org
Contact: Mark Singletary, President
E-mail: mark.singletary@nopg.com

Description: Local area business publications. Encourages high journalistic standards among area business publications. Acts as a forum for the exchange of ideas and information, especially on common issues such as editorial excellence, postal regulations, government regulations, and advertising. Compiles statistics of business patterns in markets of members and engages in cooperative member market research. **Founded:** 1979. **Publications:** *Alliance of Area Business Publications--Membership Directory* (Annual); *Association of Area Business Publications--Directory* (Annual). **Educational Activities:** Editorial and Design Awards Banquet (Annual); Editorial and Design Awards Banquet (Annual). **Awards:** Editorial and Design Award (Annual).

15480 ■ American Business Media (ABM)
675 3rd Ave., 7th Fl.
New York, NY 10017-5704
Ph: (212)661-6360
Fax: (212)370-0736
Co. E-mail: info@abmmail.com
URL: http://www.americanbusinessmedia.com
Contact: Clark Pettit, President

Description: Represents global business-to-business information providers. Members include producers of print and online magazines, newsletters and databases, as well as trade shows, conferences, seminars and other ancillary media. Exists to advance the common interests of business-to-business media organizations. Focuses on governmental affairs, promotion of the industry, best practices, and ethical standards. Its 200 plus member companies represent upwards of 1200 print publications, 1350 websites, and 850 trade shows, serving 181 industries and reaching 90 million readers. **Founded:** 1906. **Publications:** *Business Media Matters* (Monthly); *E-News* (Weekly). **Educational Activities:** American Business Media Conference (Annual); Top Management Meeting (Annual). **Awards:** Circulation Career Award; Creative Hall of Fame; G.D. Crain Award (Annual); HR Executive of the Year (Annual); McAllister Fellowships (Annual); Media Kit Awards; Neal Awards (Annual); Reed Business Information Outstanding Intern Award (Annual); Reed Exhibitions Event Award; Thomas W. Tully Award; Timothy White Award for Editorial Integrity (Annual); Nielsen Corporate Achievement Award for Creative Excellence in Business Advertising.

15481 ■ American Court and Commercial Newspapers (ACCN)
c/o Public Notice Resource Center
PO Box 5337
Arlington, VA 22205
Ph: (703)237-9806
Fax: (703)237-9808
Co. E-mail: info@pnrc.net
URL: http://www.pnrc.net
Contact: Mark W.C. Stodder, President

Description: Newspapers of general circulation devoted to lawyers and courts, financial and real estate professionals, contractors, and business interests. Functions as an advertising medium for business and legal vendors, marketers, advertising agencies, and related businesses. Operates speakers' bureau; conducts research reports. Compiles statistics. **Founded:** 1930.

15482 ■ American Society of Magazine Editors (ASME)
810 7th Ave., 24th Fl.
New York, NY 10019
Ph: (212)872-3700
Fax: (212)906-0128
Co. E-mail: asme@magazine.org
URL: http://www.magazine.org/asme
Contact: Lucy Danziger, President

Description: Represents magazine editors. Sponsors annual editorial internship program for college juniors and the National Magazine Awards. **Founded:** 1963. **Awards:** National Magazine Awards; Lifetime Achievement (Annual); Magazine Editor's Hall of Fame (Annual); National Magazine Award (Annual).

15483 ■ American Society of Media Photographers Inc. (Society of Magazine Photographers)
150 N 2nd St.
Philadelphia, PA 19106-1912
Ph: (215)451-2767
Fax: (215)451-0880
Co. E-mail: info@asmp.org
URL: http://www.asmp.org
Contact: Eugene Mopsik, Executive Director
E-mail: mopsik@asmp.org

Description: Professional society of freelance photographers. Works to evolve trade practices for photographers in communications fields. Provides business information to photographers and their potential clients; promotes ethics and rights of members. Holds educational programs and seminars. Compiles statistics. **Founded:** 1944. **Publications:** *ASMP Bulletin* (Quarterly); *ASMP Bulletin*; *American Society of Media Photographers--Membership Directory*.

15484 ■ Association of Alternative Newsweeklies (AAN)
1156 15th St. NW, Ste. 905
Washington, DC 20005
Ph: (202)289-8484
Fax: (202)289-2004
Co. E-mail: web@aaan.org
URL: http://www.altweeklies.com
Contact: Fran Zankowski, President

Description: Members include Village Voice, L.A. Weekly, Chicago Reader and Washington City Paper. Provides members with information and communication relevant to the business of publishing an alternative newspaper. Holds annual convention. Compiles financial standards report, publishes monthly newsletter and administers annual editorial awards contest. **Scope:** member publications. **Founded:** 1978. **Subscriptions:** clippings periodicals. **Publications:** *Association of Alternative Newsweeklies--Directory*. **Awards:** Alternative Newsweekly Awards (Annual); Diversity Internship Grant (Semiannual). **Telecommunication Services:** web@aan.org.

15485 ■ Audit Bureau of Circulations (ABC)
48 W Seegers Rd.
Arlington Heights, IL 60005-3913
Ph: (224)366-6939
Fax: (224)366-6949
Co. E-mail: service@accessabc.com
URL: http://www.accessabc.com
Contact: Michael J. Lavery, President

Description: Represents advertisers, advertising agencies, and publishers of daily and weekly newspapers, farm publications, consumer magazines, and business publications in the United States and Canada. Issues standardized statements on the circulation of publisher members; verifies the figures shown in these statements by auditors' examination of publishers' records; disseminates circulation data. Provides academic associate support; conducts forums and seminars. **Founded:** 1914. **Publications:** *Canadian Circulation of U.S. Magazines* (Annual); *County Penetration Reports* (Semiannual); *FAS-FAX Reports* (Semiannual); *Periodical Statement Library* (Semiannual); *ABC Audit Report and Publisher's Statements* (Annual). **Educational Activities:** Newspaper Association of America Annual Connecticut (Annual).

15486 ■ *Baker's Journal*
c/o Trish Torrance, Exec. Dir.
2100 Banbury Crescent
Oakville, ON, Canada L6H 5P6
Ph: (905)844-6822
Co. E-mail: torrance@cbp.ca
URL: http://www.cbp.ca
Contact: Trish Torrance, Executive Director

15487 ■ Book and Periodical Council (BPC)
192 Spadina Ave., Ste. 107
Toronto, ON, Canada M5T 2C2
Ph: (416)975-9366
Fax: (416)975-1839
Co. E-mail: info@thebpc.ca
URL: http://www.thebpc.ca
Contact: Anne McClelland, Executive Director

Description: Associations representing writers, editors, and publishers of books and periodicals and manufacturers, distributors, and sellers and lenders of printed materials. Promotes improved market conditions for Canadian publications and seeks to insure availability of a representative range of Canadian books and periodicals. Works to strengthen book and periodical distribution systems; supports development of new and existing Canadian-owned publishing companies; serves as a forum for discussion of industry issues. **Founded:** 1975.

15488 ■ *CAJ Media*
Box 280
Brantford, ON, Canada N3T 5M8
Ph: (613)526-8061
Fax: (613)521-3904
Co. E-mail: canadianjour@magma.ca
URL: http://www.caj.ca
Contact: John Dickins, Executive Director
Released: 3/year **Price:** C$14.98, /year.

15489 ■ Canadian Association of Journalists (CAJ)—L'Association Canadienne des Journalistes
Box 280
Brantford, ON, Canada N3T 5M8
Ph: (613)526-8061
Fax: (613)521-3904
Co. E-mail: canadianjour@magma.ca
URL: http://www.caj.ca
Contact: John Dickins, Executive Director
Description: Professional organization representing the interests of journalists in Canada. Promotes high professional standards. Disseminates information. **Founded:** 1978. **Publications:** *CAJ Media* (3/year); *Directory of Canadian Journalists.* **Awards:** Code of Silence Award; Awards for Investigative Journalism; Code of Silence Award (Annual); Investigative Journalist Award (Annual).

15490 ■ Canadian Business Press (CBP)
c/o Trish Torrance, Exec. Dir.
2100 Banbury Crescent
Oakville, ON, Canada L6H 5P6
Ph: (905)844-6822
Co. E-mail: torrance@cbp.ca
URL: http://www.cbp.ca
Contact: Trish Torrance, Executive Director
Description: Business publishers. Promotes the business press as a communications medium and source of information on Canadian business, industry, professions, and government. Works to improve standards among members; represents members' interests before government agencies; facilitates communication among members. Gathers and disseminates information; makes available technical assistance to members; serves as arbitrator in conflicts involving members. Sponsors competitions. **Founded:** 1920. **Publications:** *Baker's Journal*; *Canadian Contractor*; *Computing Canada* (Biweekly); *Marketing* (Weekly); *Wings* (Semimonthly). **Awards:** Kenneth R. Wilson Awards; Kenneth R. Wilson Awards (Annual).

15491 ■ Canadian Circulation Management Association (CCMA)—Association Canadienne de Gerance de Tirage
100 Belliveau Beach Rd.
Pointe du Chene, NB, Canada E4P 3W6
Ph: (506)859-8600
Co. E-mail: dorman@nbnet.nb.ca
URL: http://www.ccmanet.ca
Contact: Dave Dorman, Secretary Treasurer
Description: Circulation managers employed by publishing companies. Promotes professional development of members; seeks to advance the publishing industry. Facilitates exchange of information among members; conducts educational programs.

15492 ■ Canadian Community Newspapers Association (CCNA)
890 Yonge St., Ste. 200
Toronto, ON, Canada M4W 3P4
Ph: (416)923-3567
Free: 877-305-2262
Fax: (416)923-7206
Co. E-mail: info@newspaperscanada.ca
URL: http://www.communitynews.ca
Contact: John Hinds, Chief Executive Officer
Description: Community newspapers. Promotes growth and development of small newspapers. Represents the interests of community newspapers before labor and industrial organizations, government

agencies, and the public. Conducts educational and promotional activities. **Founded:** 1919. **Publications:** *The Publisher* (10/year). **Awards:** Better Newspapers Competition (Annual).

15493 ■ *Canadian Contractor*
c/o Trish Torrance, Exec. Dir.
2100 Banbury Crescent
Oakville, ON, Canada L6H 5P6
Ph: (905)844-6822
Co. E-mail: torrance@cbp.ca
URL: http://www.cbp.ca
Contact: Trish Torrance, Executive Director

15494 ■ Canadian Copyright Institute (CCI)
192 Spadina Ave., Ste. 107
Toronto, ON, Canada M5T 2C2
Ph: (416)975-1756
Fax: (416)975-1839
Co. E-mail: info@thecci.ca
URL: http://www.canadiancopyrightinstitute.ca
Contact: Anne McClelland, Administrator
Description: Creators, producers, and distributors of copyrighted works. Encourages a more complete understanding of copyright laws among members and the public. Consults with government and judicial bodies regarding reform of copyright laws. Conducts and sponsors research on copyright laws worldwide. Works with organizations pursuing similar goals to improve copyright legislation and enforcement. **Founded:** 1965. **Publications:** *Copyright Reform Legislation Reporting Service* (Periodic).

15495 ■ Canadian Newspaper Association (CNA)—Association Canadienne des Journaux
890 Yonge St., Ste. 200
Toronto, ON, Canada M4W 3P4
Ph: (416)923-3567
Free: 877-305-2262
Fax: (416)923-7206
Co. E-mail: info@newspaperscanada.ca
URL: http://www.newspaperscanada.ca
Contact: Peter Kvarnstrom, Chairman
Description: Daily newspapers. Promotes the growth and ongoing vitality of printed news media. Represents members' interests before government agencies, labor and industrial organizations, and the public. **Founded:** 1996. **Publications:** *CNA Members' Bulletin* (Periodic). **Awards:** Edward Goff Penny Memorial Prizes (Annual); National Newspaper Awards (Annual); National Newspaper Awards.

15496 ■ Canadian University Press (CUP)
920 Yonge St., Ste. 503
Toronto, ON, Canada M4W 3C7
Ph: (416)962-2287
Free: 866-250-5595
Fax: (416)966-3699
Co. E-mail: president@cup.ca
URL: http://www.cup.ca
Contact: Sam Brooks, President
Description: Student newspapers. Serves as a communication and support network for members; promotes exchange of news and features among members; seeks to develop journalistic skills among Canadian students; provides mechanism for sharing of national advertising by members. Encourages cultural diversity in Canadian student media. Conducts political action caucuses. **Founded:** 1938. **Publications:** *House Organ* (Monthly); *This Week and More* (Weekly).

15497 ■ City and Regional Magazine Association (CRMA)
1970 E Grand Ave., Ste. 330
El Segundo, CA 90245
Ph: (310)364-0193
Fax: (310)364-0196
Co. E-mail: administrator@list.citymag.org
URL: http://www.citymag.org
Contact: C. James Dowden, Executive Director
Description: City and regional consumer-oriented magazines; related businesses involved in printing, advertising, and circulation. Strives to gain presence in the marketplace and command an increased following among national advertisers. Serves as a channel of communication between city and regional consumer magazines and coordinates research

projects. Distributes information; creates press materials. Compiles statistics. **Founded:** 1978. **Educational Activities:** City and Regional Magazine Association Seminar (Semiannual). **Awards:** National City and Regional Magazine Awards (Annual); National City and Regional Magazine Awards.

15498 ■ *CNA Members' Bulletin*
890 Yonge St., Ste. 200
Toronto, ON, Canada M4W 3P4
Ph: (416)923-3567
Free: 877-305-2262
Fax: (416)923-7206
Co. E-mail: info@newspaperscanada.ca
URL: http://www.newspaperscanada.ca
Contact: Peter Kvarnstrom, Chairman
Released: Periodic **Price:** included in membership dues.

15499 ■ *Computing Canada*
c/o Trish Torrance, Exec. Dir.
2100 Banbury Crescent
Oakville, ON, Canada L6H 5P6
Ph: (905)844-6822
Co. E-mail: torrance@cbp.ca
URL: http://www.cbp.ca
Contact: Trish Torrance, Executive Director
Released: Biweekly

15500 ■ *Copyright Reform Legislation Reporting Service*
192 Spadina Ave., Ste. 107
Toronto, ON, Canada M5T 2C2
Ph: (416)975-1756
Fax: (416)975-1839
Co. E-mail: info@thecci.ca
URL: http://www.canadiancopyrightinstitute.ca
Contact: Anne McClelland, Administrator
Released: Periodic **Price:** C$650, /year for members; C$750, /year for nonmembers.

15501 ■ *House Organ*
920 Yonge St., Ste. 503
Toronto, ON, Canada M4W 3C7
Ph: (416)962-2287
Free: 866-250-5595
Fax: (416)966-3699
Co. E-mail: president@cup.ca
URL: http://www.cup.ca
Contact: Sam Brooks, President
Released: Monthly

15502 ■ *The Inside Edge*
460 Sarsons Rd.
Kelowna, BC, Canada V1W 1C2
Ph: (250)764-2143
Fax: (250)764-2145
Co. E-mail: nasja@shaw.ca
URL: http://www.nasja.org
Contact: Phil Johnson, President
Released: Quinquenial **Price:** included in membership dues; $52, for nonmembers.

15503 ■ International Newsmedia Marketing Association (INMA)
PO Box 740186
Dallas, TX 75374
Ph: (214)373-9111
Fax: (214)373-9112
Co. E-mail: megan.deleon@inma.org
URL: http://www.inma.org
Contact: Ravi Dhariwal, President
Description: Represents individuals engaged in marketing, circulation, research, and public relations of newspapers. Conducts conferences; holds newspaper executives marketing and strategic planning seminars. **Founded:** 1930. **Educational Activities:** World Congress (Annual). **Awards:** Silver Shovel (Annual); INMA Awards; Silver Shovel Award.

15504 ■ Magazines Canada (CMPA)—Association/L'Association des editeurs de magazines canadiens
425 Adelaide St. W, Ste. 700
Toronto, ON, Canada M5V 3C1
Ph: (416)504-0274

Fax: (416)504-0437
Co. E-mail: cmpainfo@cmpa.ca
URL: http://www.magazinescanada.ca
Contact: Mark Jamison, Chief Executive Officer
E-mail: mjamison@magazinescanada.ca
Description: Magazine publishers. Promotes growth of magazine circulation and advancement of the publishing industries. Represents members' interests before government agencies and provides support and assistance to magazine publishers. **Scope:** A professional magazine industry association, representing more than 300 consumer titles of all scope and size. The member-driven, not-for-profit organization serves Canadian magazines through advocacy and special initiatives, and offers extensive member services including small magazine direct-to-retail distribution, nationally delivered professional development, communications, marketing, and advertising services. **Founded:** 1973. **Publications:** "Kenya: Healing the Nation," Apr, 2008; "Finding a good fit with a new recruit". **Awards:** Outstanding Volunteer; Volunteer of the Year; Outstanding Volunteer (Annual); Volunteer of the Year (Annual). **Seminars:** You built it but do they come?; The Naked Truth About Magazines; Powerhouse Websites: On a Budget. **Telecommunication Services:** info@magazinescanada.com; info@magazinescanada.ca; adinfo@magazinescanada.ca.

15505 ■ Marketing
c/o Trish Torrance, Exec. Dir.
2100 Banbury Crescent
Oakville, ON, Canada L6H 5P6
Ph: (905)844-6822
Co. E-mail: torrance@cbp.ca
URL: http://www.cbp.ca
Contact: Trish Torrance, Executive Director
Released: Weekly

15506 ■ MPA - The Association of Magazine Media
810 7th Ave., 24th Fl.
New York, NY 10019
Ph: (212)872-3700
Fax: (212)888-4217
Co. E-mail: mpa@magazine.org
URL: http://www.magazine.org
Contact: Nina Link, President
Description: Publishers of more than 1000 consumer and other magazines issued not less than four times a year. Activities include: Advertising Marketing Department to promote magazines as an advertising medium; Washington office to report on federal legislation and postal rates and regulations; Consumer Marketing Department to provide information services and assistance to members in all areas of circulation marketing. Conducts member surveys on magazine finance, paper usage, and compensation. Administers Publishers Information Bureau and Media Credit Association. **Scope:** magazine publishing. **Founded:** 1919. **Subscriptions:** periodicals. **Publications:** MPA Washington Newsletter; Newsletter of International Publishing. **Educational Activities:** American Magazine Conference (Annual). **Awards:** Kelly Awards; Lifetime Achievement Awards.

15507 ■ NASJA Directory
460 Sarsons Rd.
Kelowna, BC, Canada V1W 1C2
Ph: (250)764-2143
Fax: (250)764-2145
Co. E-mail: nasja@shaw.ca
URL: http://www.nasja.org
Contact: Phil Johnson, President
Released: Annual

15508 ■ National Association of Hispanic Publications (NAHP)
529 14th St. NW, Ste. 1126
Washington, DC 20045
Ph: (202)662-7250
Co. E-mail: mgomez@nahp.org
URL: http://www.nahp.org
Contact: Amy Hinojosa, Executive Director
Description: Newspapers, magazines, and other periodicals published in Spanish (or bilingually in English and Spanish) in the United States. Promotes adherence to high standards of ethical and professional standards by members; advocates continuing

professional development of Hispanic journalists and publishers. Provides technical assistance to members in areas including writing and editing skills, circulation and distribution methods, attracting advertisers, obtaining financing, design and layout, and graphic arts. Conducts public service programs including voter registration drives. **Scope:** Hispanic scholarship. **Founded:** 1982. **Subscriptions:** books. **Publications:** The Hispanic Press (Quarterly). **Educational Activities:** National Association of Hispanic Publications Convention (Annual). **Awards:** Amigo Awards (Annual); Corporate Recognition Awards (Annual); Hispanic Print Awards (Annual).

15509 ■ North American Snowsports Journalists Association (NASJA)
460 Sarsons Rd.
Kelowna, BC, Canada V1W 1C2
Ph: (250)764-2143
Fax: (250)764-2145
Co. E-mail: nasja@shaw.ca
URL: http://www.nasja.org
Contact: Phil Johnson, President
Description: Newspaper, magazine, book, television, radio writers and broadcasters, and photographers who report on skiing and other snow sports. Covers skiing and other snow sports. **Founded:** 1963. **Publications:** The Inside Edge (Quinquenial); NASJA Directory (Annual). **Awards:** Lifetime Achievement Award; Carson White Golden Quill Award (Annual); Harold Hirsch Award (Annual); Lifetime Achievement Award (Annual); Outstanding Competitor Award (Annual); Carson White Golden Quill Award; Harold S. Hirsch Award for Column Writing; Harold S. Hirsch Award for Excellence in Broadcasting; Harold S. Hirsch Award for Excellence in Snow Sports Photography; Paul Robbins Outstanding Competitor Award.

15510 ■ Periodical and Book Association of America (PBAA)
481 8th Ave., Ste. 526
New York, NY 10001
Ph: (212)563-6502
Fax: (212)563-4098
Co. E-mail: lisawscott@hotmail.com
URL: http://www.pbaa.net
Contact: Lisa W. Scott, Executive Director
Description: Magazine and paperback publishers concerned with single copy or newsstand sales. Carries out concerted action in areas of publishing, production, and sales. **Founded:** 1965. **Awards:** Publishing Leader of the Year (Annual).

15511 ■ Printing Industries of America (PIA)
200 Deer Run Rd.
Sewickley, PA 15143-2324
Ph: (412)741-6860
Free: 800-910-4283
Fax: (412)741-2311
Co. E-mail: printing@printing.org
URL: http://www.printing.org
Contact: Michael Makin, President
Description: Commercial printing firms (lithography, letterpress, gravure, platemakers, typographic houses); allied firms in the graphic arts. Provides extensive management services for member companies, including government relations, industry research and statistical information, technology information and assistance, and management education and publications. Compiles statistical and economic data, including annual ratio study that provides a benchmark for printers to compare profits as a basis for improving individual member company and industry profits. Provides reporting system on provisions, rates, and other matters relating to union contracts in effect throughout the industry. Sponsors annual Premier Print Awards Competition. **Founded:** 1999. **Publications:** Printing Industries of America Ratios; Sales and Marketing Success. **Educational Activities:** President's Conference (Annual). **Awards:** Naomi Berber Memorial Award; Education Awards of Excellence; InterTech Technology Awards; Robert F. Reed Technology Medal; William D. Schaeffer Environmental Award; Frederick D. Kagy Education Award of Excellence. **Telecommunication Services:** egleeson@printing.org; gain@printing.org.

15512 ■ The Publisher
890 Yonge St., Ste. 200
Toronto, ON, Canada M4W 3P4
Ph: (416)923-3567
Free: 877-305-2262
Fax: (416)923-7206
Co. E-mail: info@newspaperscanada.ca
URL: http://www.communitynews.ca
Contact: John Hinds, Chief Executive Officer
Ed: Maureen de Jong. **Released:** 10/year; 10/year.
Price: $25; included in membership dues.

15513 ■ Publishers Information Bureau (PIB)
810 7th Ave., 24th Fl.
New York, NY 10019
Ph: (212)872-3700
Co. E-mail: weadie@magazine.org
URL: http://www.magazine.org
Contact: Wayne Eadie, President
Description: Measures the amount and type of advertising in magazines and reports this information monthly through printed and electronic formats; service prepared by TNSMI/Competitive Media Reporting (contracting agent). **Founded:** 1945.

15514 ■ Society of Publication Designers (SPD)
27 Union Sq. W, Ste. 207
New York, NY 10003
Ph: (212)223-3332
Fax: (212)223-5880
Co. E-mail: mail@spd.org
URL: http://www.spd.org
Contact: Josh Klenert, President
Description: Represents art directors, designers, editors, photographers and illustrators with the responsibility of layout and design of consumer, business and professional publications and newspapers. Holds speakers' luncheons and auctions. **Founded:** 1965. **Publications:** GRIDS (Quarterly); Solid Gold. **Awards:** Herb Lubalin; Magazine of the Year Award (Annual); Herb Lubalin Award.

15515 ■ This Week and More
920 Yonge St., Ste. 503
Toronto, ON, Canada M4W 3C7
Ph: (416)962-2287
Free: 866-250-5595
Fax: (416)966-3699
Co. E-mail: president@cup.ca
URL: http://www.cup.ca
Contact: Sam Brooks, President
Released: Weekly

15516 ■ Wings
c/o Trish Torrance, Exec. Dir.
2100 Banbury Crescent
Oakville, ON, Canada L6H 5P6
Ph: (905)844-6822
Co. E-mail: torrance@cbp.ca
URL: http://www.cbp.ca
Contact: Trish Torrance, Executive Director
Released: Semimonthly

REFERENCE WORKS

15517 ■ "Advertising May Take a Big Hit in Southwest/AirTran Merger" in Baltimore Business Journal (Vol. 28, October 1, 2010, No. 21, pp. 1)
Pub: Baltimore Business Journal
Ed: Gary Haber. **Description:** Advertising on television stations and the publishing industry in Baltimore could drop as a result of the merger between rival discount airlines Southwest Airlines and AirTran Airways. Southwest is among the top advertisers in the U.S., spending $126 million in 2009. No local jobs are expected to be affected because neither airline uses a local advertising firm.

15518 ■ "Analyst Questions CanWest Papers' Viability" in Globe & Mail (January 14, 2006, pp. B3)
Pub: CTVglobemedia Publishing Inc.
Ed: Grant Robertson. **Description:** The opinions of analyst Tim Casey of BMO Nesbitt Burns Inc. over the prospects of two newspapers Dose and National Post of CanWest Global Communications Corp., which planned cost restructuring efforts, are presented.

15519 ■ *"Best Value Stocks" in Canadian Business (Vol. 82, Summer 2009, No. 8, pp. 30)*
Pub: Rogers Media
Ed: Calvin Leung. Description: Canadian companies that are believed to have the best value stocks are suggested. Suggestions include publishing firm Glacier Media, which has reported a four-fold growth in sales in the last three years. While publishers like Glacier Media face challenges such as declining circulation, the firm's industry diversification is expected to help it weather the economic downturn.

15520 ■ *"Calista Sells Rural Newspapers" in Alaska Business Monthly (Vol. 27, October 2011, No. 10, pp. 8)*
Pub: Alaska Business Publishing Company
Ed: Nancy Pounds. Description: Calista sold its six newspapers, a magazine, shoppers and its printing house. Details of the sales are given.

15521 ■ *"Canadians Love Their Magazines" in MarketingMagazine (Vol. 115, September 27, 2010, No. 13, pp. 42)*
Pub: Rogers Publishing Ltd.
Description: Market data covering magazine published or consumed in Canada is presented.

15522 ■ *"A Class Act" in Hawaii Business (Vol. 53, March 2008, No. 9, pp. 25)*
Pub: Hawaii Business Publishing
Ed: Cathy S. Cruz-George. Description: UBoost is a startup company that offers online content for the educational magazine 'Weekly Reader'. The website features quizzes and allows users to accumulate points and redeem rewards afterward. Other details about the company are discussed.

15523 ■ *"Community Newspapers" in MarketingMagazine (Vol. 115, September 27, 2010, No. 13, pp. 38)*
Pub: Rogers Publishing Ltd.
Description: Market data for the newspaper industry in Canada is presented.

15524 ■ *"Copyright Clearance Center (CCC) Partnered with cSubs" in Information Today (Vol. 28, November 2011, No. 10, pp. 14)*
Pub: Information Today, Inc.
Description: Copyright Clearance Center (CCC) partnered with cSubs to integrate CCC's point-of-content licensing solution RightsLink Basic directly into cSubs workflow. The partnership will allow cSubs' customers a user-friendly process for obtaining permissions. Csubs is a corporate subscription management service for books, newspapers, and econtent.

15525 ■ *"Crain's Makes Ad Sales, Custom Marketing Appointments" in Crain's Chicago Business (Vol. 34, October 24, 2011, No. 42, pp. 13)*
Pub: Crain Communications Inc.
Description: Crain's Chicago Business announced key appointments in its sales department: David Denor has been named first director of custom marketing services and Kate Van Etten will succeed Denor as advertising director.

15526 ■ *"Crain's Nabs 15 Press Club Awards" in Crain's Cleveland Business (Vol. 30, June 29, 2009, No. 25, pp. 6)*
Pub: Crain Communications, Inc.
Description: Crain's Cleveland Business was honored with 15 awards at the Ohio Excellence in Journalism competition conducted by the Press Club of Cleveland.

15527 ■ *"Daily Newspapers" in MarketingMagazine (Vol. 115, September 27, 2010, No. 13, pp. 32)*
Pub: Rogers Publishing Ltd.
Description: Market data covering the newspaper industry in Canada is examined.

15528 ■ *Directory of Small Press--Magazine Editors and Publishers*
Pub: Dustbooks
Contact: Len Fulton, Publisher
E-mail: lenfulton@dustbooks.com
URL(s): www.dustbooks.com/de.htm. Ed: Len Fulton. Released: Annual; Latest edition 42nd; 2011-

2012. Price: $49.95, Individuals online; $21, Individuals CD-ROM. Covers: About 7,500 publishers and editors. Entries include: Individual name, title of press or magazine, address and phone number. Arrangement: Alphabetical.

15529 ■ *"EBSCO Adds New Features to EBSCOhost Content Viewer" in Information Today (Vol. 26, February 2009, No. 2, pp. 31)*
Pub: Information Today, Inc.
Description: EBSCOhost Content Viewer historical digital archive collection provides a visual overview of a displayed document, highlighting search keywords on the page as well as providing a document map that shows the number of times a given keyword is mentioned in a periodical, monograph, article, or other document. For periodical content, the viewer lets users browse multiple issues in a volume without leaving the interface; features include zoom and pan technology similar to online maps.

15530 ■ *The Facebook Effect: The Inside Story of the Company That Is Connecting the World*
Pub: Simon & Shuster
Ed: David Kirkpatrick. Released: June 8, 2010. Price: $26.00. Description: There's never been a Website like Facebook: more than 350 million people have accounts, and if the growth rate continues, by 2013 every Internet user worldwide will have his or her own page. No one's had more access to the inner workings of the phenomenon than Kirkpatrick, a senior tech writer at Fortune magazine. Written with the full cooperation of founder Mark Zuckerberg, the book follows the company from its genesis in a Harvard dorm room through its successes over Friendster and MySpace, the expansion of the user base, and Zuckerberg's refusal to sell.

15531 ■ *"FCC Adopts New Media Ownership Rules" in Black Enterprise (Vol. 38, March 2008, No. 8, pp. 26)*
Pub: Earl G. Graves Publishing Co. Inc.
Ed: Joyce Jones. Description: Federal Communications Commission approved a ruling that lifts a ban on newspaper and/or broadcast cross ownership. Because of declining sales in newspaper advertising and readership the ban will allow companies to share local news gathering costs across multiple media platforms.

15532 ■ *Freelancing for Journalists*
Pub: Routledge
Ed: Diana Harris. Released: January 1, 2010. Price: $110.00. Description: Comprehensive guide showing the specific skills required for those wishing to freelance in newspapers, magazines, radio, television, and as online journalists.

15533 ■ *Gale Directory of Publications and Broadcast Media*
Pub: Cengage Learning Inc.
Contact: Ronald Dunn, President
URL(s): www.gale.cengage.com. Released: Annual; Latest edition April 2011. Price: $1297, Individuals. Covers: Approximately 57,000 publications and broadcasting stations, including newspapers, magazines, journals, radio stations, television stations, radio/television/cable networks, syndicates and cable systems in the U.S. and Canada. Newsletters and directories are excluded. Entries include: For publications--Title, publishing and editorial addresses, phone, fax, description, names of editor, publisher, and advertising manager, base advertising rate, page specifications, subscription rate, circulation, frequency, ISSN, former names, additional contacts. For broadcast media--Call letters or cable system name, address, phone, fax, format, networks, owner, date founded, former call letters, operating hours, names and titles of key personnel, local programming, wattage, ad rates, additional contacts. Database includes: Appendices with maps and statistical tables, city descriptions, state descriptions with statistics, broadcast and cable networks, news and features syndicates. Arrangement: Geographical. Indexes: Title; radio station format; publisher; geographic market; lists of agricultural, college, foreign language, Jewish, fraternal, black, women's, Hispanic, religious, general circulation, and trade and

technical publications (by subject and/or geographical as needed); daily newspaper; daily periodical; free circulation newspaper; and shopping guides (each geographical); list of feature editors at daily newspapers with 50,000 or more circulation.

15534 ■ *"Galvanizing the Scientific Community" in Information Today (Vol. 26, February 2009, No. 2, pp. 20)*
Pub: Information Today, Inc.
Ed: Barbara Brynko. Description: Profile of John Haynes, newly appointed vice president of publishing for the American Institute of Physics; the Institute consists of ten organizations specializing in STM publishing as well as providing publishing services for over 170 science and engineering journals.

15535 ■ *"Google Book Search Tosses Magazines Into the Mix" in Information Today (Vol. 26, February 2009, No. 2, pp. 31)*
Pub: Information Today, Inc.
Description: Google Book Search expanded services to include magazines..

15536 ■ *"Growth of Free Dailies Dropping" in Globe & Mail (March 24, 2007, pp. B7)*
Pub: CTVglobemedia Publishing Inc.
Ed: Grant Robertson. Description: The decrease in the readership of free newspapers in Canada, in view of growing preference for online news, is discussed.

15537 ■ *"Health Care Leads Sectors Attracting Capital" in Hispanic Business (March 2008, pp. 14-16, 18)*
Pub: Hispanic Business
Ed: Scott Williams. Description: U. S. Hispanic healthcare, media, and food were the key industries in the U.S. gaining investors in 2007.

15538 ■ *"Help for Job Seekers" in Crain's Detroit Business (Vol. 26, January 4, 2010, No. 1, pp. 14)*
Pub: Crain Communications Inc.
Description: CareerWorks is weekly paper targeting readers who are in a career transition or are looking for new employment.

15539 ■ *How to Get Rich*
Pub: Ebury Press
Ed: Felix Dennis. Released: 2008. Price: $25.95. Description: Publisher of Maxim, The Week, and Stuff magazines, discusses the mistakes he made running his companies. He didn't understand that people who buy computer gaming magazines wanted a free game with each copy, as one of his rivals was offering. And he laments not diversifying into television and exploiting the Internet.

15540 ■ *"Ideas at Work: Total Communicator" in Business Strategy Review (Vol. 21, Autumn 2010, No. 3, pp. 10)*
Pub: Blackwell Publishers Ltd.
Ed: Stuart Crainer. Description: Vittorio Colao has been chief executive of Vodafone Group for two years. He brings to the company special experience as CEO of RCS MediaGroup in Milan, which publishes newspapers, magazines and books in Italy, Spain and France. Prior to RCS, he held other positions within Vodafone. Colao shares his views on business, the global economy and leading Vodafone.

15541 ■ *"Ideas at Work: Total Communicator" in Business Strategy Review (Vol. 21, Autumn 2010, No. 3, pp. 10)*
Pub: Wiley-Blackwell
Ed: Stuart Crainer. Description: Vittorio Colao has been chief executive of Vodafone Group for two years. He brings to the company some special experience: from 2004-2006 he was CEO of RCS Media-Group in Milan, which publishes newspapers, magazines and books in Italy, Spain and France. Colao shares his views on business, the global economy and leading Vodafone.

15542 ■ *"In Print and Online" in Marketing to Women (Vol. 22, August 2009, No. 8, pp. 3)*
Pub: EPM Communications Inc.
Contact: Ira Mayer, President
E-mail: imayer@epmcom.com
Description: Seventeen magazine is unifying its print and Online editions with complementary content, a strategy that seems to be working as every aspect of Seventeen drives the reader to another component.

15543 ■ *"Integral USA Magazine Sponsors Eco-Fashion in the Park" in Entertainment Close-Up (September 2, 2011)*
Pub: Close-Up Media
Description: Integral Magazine sponsored Eco-Fashion in the Park, a fashion show for the fashion conscious. Eleven independent designers will show their eco-friendly fashions at the event.

15544 ■ *International Directory of Little Magazines and Small Presses*
Pub: Dustbooks
Contact: Len Fulton, Publisher
E-mail: lenfulton@dustbooks.com
URL(s): www.dustbooks.com/d.htm. **Ed:** Len Fulton. **Released:** Annual; Latest edition 47th; 2011-2012. **Price:** $65, Individuals CD-ROM (3 directories); $49.95, Individuals online; $30, Individuals CD-ROM. **Covers:** Over 4,000 small, independent magazines, presses, and papers. **Entries include:** Name, address, size, circulation, frequency, price, type of material used, number of issues or books published annually, and other pertinent data. **Arrangement:** Alphabetical. **Indexes:** Subject, regional.

15545 ■ *"It's a New Game: Killerspin Pushes Table Tennis to Extreme Heights" in Black Enterprise (Vol. 37, October 2006, No. 3, pp. 73)*
Pub: Earl G. Graves Publishing Co. Inc.
Ed: Bridget McCrea. **Description:** Profile of Robert Blackwell and his company Killerspin L.L.C., which is popularizing the sport of table tennis. Killerspin has hit $1 million in revenues due to product sales primarily generated through the company's website, magazines, DVDs, and event ticket sales.

15546 ■ *"Joe Wikert, General Manager, O'Reilly Technology Exchange" in Information Today (Vol. 26, February 2009, No. 2, pp. 21)*
Pub: Information Today, Inc.
Ed: Jamie Babbitt. **Description:** Joe Wikert, general manager of O'Reilly Technology Exchange discusses his plans to develop a free content model that will evolve with future needs. O'Reilly's major competitor is Google. Wikert plans to expand the firm's publishing program to include print, online, and in-person products and services.

15547 ■ *"Johnson Publishing Expands: Moving Into Television and Internet To Extend Brand" in Black Enterprise (October 2007)*
Pub: Earl G. Graves Publishing Co. Inc.
Ed: Tamara E. Holmes. **Description:** Johnson Publishing Company has followed the lives of black families in both Ebony and Jet magazines. The media firm has expanded its coverage by developing entertainment content for television, the Internet and other digital arenas.

15548 ■ *"Knight Sold as Industry Struggles" in Globe & Mail (March 14, 2006, pp. D1)*
Pub: CTVglobemedia Publishing Inc.
Ed: Christopher Rowland. **Description:** McClatchy Co. said it would buy Knight Ridder Inc. for $4.5 billion, which is a newspaper giant in United States. The details of McClatchy acquisition plans for Knight Ridder news syndicate are analyzed.

15549 ■ *"Lessons From My Father" in Crain's Chicago Business (Vol. 31, November 10, 2008, No. 45, pp. 28)*
Pub: Crain Communications, Inc.
Ed: Rance Crain. **Description:** Rance Crain discusses his father, G.D. Crain Jr., who founded Crain Communications Inc. during the Great Depression. Advice is given for sustaining a business, even one that seems to be failing, during tough economic times.

15550 ■ *Library and Book Trade Almanac*
Pub: Information Today Inc.
Contact: Thomas H. Hogan, President
E-mail: ctuthill@infotoday.com
URL(s): books.infotoday.com. **Released:** Annual; Latest edition 57th; June 2012. **Price:** $249, Individuals hardbound; plus $17 shipping and handling charges; $224.10, Individuals first time standing

order. **Publication includes:** Lists of accredited library schools; scholarships for education in library science; library organizations; library statistics; publishing and bookselling organizations. **Entries include:** Directory listings give name of institution, address, phone, fax, name of officer or contact, publications; scholarship listings include requirements, value of grant, contact name. Principal content is articles and special reports on topics of interest to those in library/information science and publishers; international reports; annual reports from federal agencies and libraries and from national associations; information on legislation, funding, etc. **Database includes:** Lists of notable books, best-sellers, literary prize winners; library and trade statistics; calendar of events. **Arrangement:** Topical. **Indexes:** Organization; subject.

15551 ■ *"Life's Work: Ben Bradlee" in Harvard Business Review (Vol. 88, September 2010, No. 9, pp. 128)*
Pub: Harvard Business School Publishing
Ed: Alison Beard. **Description:** Newspaper publisher Ben Bradlee discusses factors that lead to success, including visible supervisors, enthusiasm, appropriate expansion, and the importance of truth in reporting.

15552 ■ *"Media Giant Remakes Itself: Job Cuts Signal Journal Sentinel's Focus on New Products" in Business Journal-Milwaukee (Oct. 12, 2007)*
Pub: American City Business Journals, Inc.
Ed: Rich Kirchen. **Description:** Milwaukee Journal Sentinel is reducing its workforce by offering separation pay, and is willing to consider layoffs if the separation program fails. The downsizing is a result of lowered revenue, which was caused by the decline in printed news demand and increase in online competition. Strategies that the Journal Sentinel are employing, such as developing new products, to increase revenue are presented.

15553 ■ *"Media Industry Collection Agency Completes Acquisition" in Collections & Credit Risk (Vol. 15, December 1, 2010, No. 11, pp. 22)*
Pub: SourceMedia Inc.
Description: Media Receivable Management Inc. (MRM) will take over the collection operations at Borden, Jones & Mitchell, in Miami, Florida. MRM clients are basically magazine and electronic media publishers.

15554 ■ *Media, Organizations and Identity*
Pub: Palgrave Macmillan
Ed: Lilie Chouliaraki, Mette Morsing. **Released:** January 19, 2010. **Price:** $90.00. **Description:** The mass media, press and television are a essential in the formation of corporate identity and the promotion of business image and reputation. This book offers a new perspective into the interrelationships between media and organizations over three dimensions: media as business, media in business and business in the media.

15555 ■ *"Media Wars" in Canadian Business (Vol. 83, August 17, 2010, No. 13-14, pp. 32)*
Pub: Rogers Media Ltd.
Ed: Thomas Watson. **Description:** Canada's newspaper industry has changed considerably with The Glove, under Philip Crawley, positioned as corporate Canada's newspaper of record. However, the National Post under Paul Godfrey is making a comeback by re-launching it as the flagship of a national chain of so-called digital first news organizations.

15556 ■ *Mississippi News Media Directory*
Pub: News Media Directories
Contact: Brian Highberger, Publisher
URL(s): www.newsmediadirectories.net/product-p/07msnmd.htm. **Released:** Annual; Latest edition 2011-2012. **Price:** $45, Individuals; $65, Individuals CD; $85, Individuals Combo-Directory and CD. **Covers:** Newspapers, periodicals, radio and television broadcasting stations, and press services operating in Mississippi. **Entries include:** Publisher or company name, address, phone, names and titles of key

personnel, publication title, call letters, hours of operation, and frequency. **Arrangement:** Classified by type of media. **Indexes:** Title, call letters, county index.

15557 ■ *"Moms Are Still Shopping" in Marketing to Women (Vol. 21, February 2008, No. 2, pp. 1)*
Pub: EPM Communications Inc.
Contact: Ira Mayer, President
E-mail: imayer@epmcom.com
Description: According to a monthly poll by Parenting Magazine, although the economic signs worsen many moms are still shopping. Statistical data included.

15558 ■ *"Murdock Lifer Mans Main Street Journal" in Advertising Age (Vol. 79, July 7, 2008, No. 26, pp. 1)*
Pub: Crain Communications, Inc.
Ed: Nat Ives. **Description:** Profile of Les Hinton, the U.K. executive who was chosen by Rupert Murdoch to run Dow Jones and The Wall Street Journal; Hinton discusses The Wall Street Journal's unique spot in American business which has helped it survive a dwindling newspaper industry.

15559 ■ *"New Beginnings for VIBE" in Black Enterprise (Vol. 37, November 2006, No. 4, pp. 34)*
Pub: Earl G. Graves Publishing Co. Inc.
Ed: Mashaun D. Simon. **Description:** Danyel Smith replaced Mimi Valdes as editor-in-chief of VIBE magazine after the Wicks Group, private equity firm focused on selected segments of the media, communications, and information industries, purchased the magazine.

15560 ■ *"New Sony HD Ads Tout Digital" in Brandweek (Vol. 49, April 21, 2008, No. 16, pp. 5)*
Pub: VNU Business Media, Inc.
Description: Looking to promote Sony Electronics' digital imaging products, the company has launched another campaign effort known as HDNA, a play on the words high-definition and DNA; originally Sony focused the HDNA campaign on their televisions, the new ads will include still and video cameras as well and marketing efforts will consist of advertising in print, Online, television spots and publicity at various venues across the country.

15561 ■ *"Paper Tigers" in Conde Nast Portfolio (Vol. 2, June 2008, No. 6, pp. 84)*
Pub: Conde Nast Publications
Contact: David Carey, President
Ed: Roger Lowenstein. **Description:** Newspapers are losing their advertisers and readers and circulation today is equal to that of 1950, a time when the U.S. population was half its present size.

15562 ■ *"PD Targeting Audience Growth with Web Initiatives" in Crain's Cleveland Business (Vol. 30, June 29, 2009, No. 25, pp. 1)*
Pub: Crain Communications, Inc.
Ed: Kathy Ames Carr. **Description:** Plain Dealer's publisher C.Z. Egger has his news organization focusing on online offerings in order to build circulation of its newspaper. The 167-year-old paper boasts 1,305,203 readers in print and online weekly.

15563 ■ *"People; E-Commerce, Online Games, Mobile Apps" in Advertising Age (Vol. 80, October 19, 2009, No. 35, pp. 14)*
Pub: Crain's Communications
Ed: Nat Ives. **Description:** Profile of People Magazine and the ways in which the publisher is moving its magazine forward by exploring new concepts in a time of declining newsstand sales and advertising pages; among the strategies are e-commerce such as the brand People Style Watch in which consumers are able highlight clothing and jewelry and then connect to retailers' sites and a channel on Taxi TV, the network of video-touch screens in New Your City taxis.

15564 ■ *"People; E-Commerce, Online Games, Mobile Apps: This Isn't Your Mom's People"* in *Advertising Age (Vol. 80, October 19, 2009, No. 35)*
Pub: Crain's Communications
Ed: Nat Ives. **Description:** Profile of People Magazine and the ways in which the publisher is moving its magazine forward by exploring new concepts in a time of declining newsstand sales and advertising pages; among the strategies are e-commerce such as the brand People Style Watch in which consumers are able highlight clothing and jewelry and then connect to retailers' sites and a channel on Taxi TV, the network of video-touch screens in New Your City taxis.

15565 ■ *"Playboy to Target Lucrative India Market With No-Nudes Version"* in *Globe & Mail (January 2, 2006, pp. B2)*
Pub: CTVglobemedia Publishing Inc.
Ed: Anand Giridharadas. **Description:** The planning of Chicago based Playboy Enterprises Inc. to target lucrative India market with no nudes version, in order to increase its market shares is discussed.

15566 ■ *"Printing Company Edwards Brothers Grapples With a Shrinking Market"* in *Crain's Detroit Business (Vol. 26, Jan. 4, 2010)*
Pub: Crain Communications Inc.
Ed: Bill Shea. **Description:** Overview of the publishing industry, which has seen a huge decline in revenue; Edwards Brothers, Inc., a family printing business that was founded 117 years ago is struggling due to a variety of factors, many of which are explored.

15567 ■ *"Pro Teams Shift Ad Budgets; Naming Rights Deals Near $1 Billion"* in *Brandweek (Vol. 49, April 21, 2008, No. 16, pp. 18)*
Pub: VNU Business Media, Inc.
Ed: Barry Janoff. **Description:** More and more professional sports marketers are spending less of their advertising budgets on traditional media outlets such as television, print and radio; the growing trend in sports marketing is in utilizing new media venues such as the Internet in which innovative means are used to encourage interaction with fans.

15568 ■ *"Publishing Technology Introduces IngentaConnect Mobile"* in *Information Today (Vol. 26, February 2009, No. 2, pp. 33)*
Pub: Information Today, Inc.
Description: College undergraduates will find Publishing Technology's newest publisher product, IngentaConnect Mobile helpful. The product allows users to read articles and abstracts on mobile devices. According to a recent study, 73 percent of young adults with wireless hand-held devices use them to access non-voice data on any given day.

15569 ■ *"Reducing the Book's Carbon Footprint"* in *American Printer (Vol. 128, July 1, 2011, No. 7)*
Pub: Penton Media Inc.
Description: Green Press Initiative's Book Industry Environmental Council is working to achieve a 20 percent reduction in the book industry's carbon footprint by 2020. The Council is made up of publishers, printers, paper suppliers, and non-governmental organizations.

15570 ■ *"Renren Partners With Recruit to Launch Social Wedding Services"* in *Benzinga.com (June 7, 2011)*
Pub: Benzinga.com
Ed: Benzinga Staff. **Description:** Renren Inc. and Recruit Company Ltd. partnered to build a wedding social media catering to engaged couples and newlyweds in China. The platform will integrate online wedding related social content and offline media such as magazine and wedding exhibitions.

15571 ■ *Standard Periodical Directory*
Pub: Oxbridge Communications Inc.
Contact: Patricia Hagood, President
URL(s): www.oxbridge.com. Ed: Deborah Striplin.
Released: Annual; Latest edition January 2011.
Price: $1995, Individuals print version; $1995, Single

issue CD-ROM single user; $2995, Individuals print and CD-ROM. **Covers:** 63,000 magazines, journals, newsletters, directories, house organs, association publications, etc. , in the United States and Canada. **Entries include:** Publication current and former title; publisher name, address, phone; names and titles of key personnel; circulation and advertising rates; description of contents; ISSN, year founded, frequency; subscription rates, print method, page size, number of pages. **Arrangement:** Classified by subject. **Indexes:** Subject, title.

15572 ■ *"Storytelling Star of Show for Scripps"* in *Business Courier (Vol. 26, November 13, 2009, No. 29, pp. 1)*
Pub: American City Business Journals, Inc.
Ed: Dan Monk. **Description:** Rich Boehne, CEO Of the EW Scripps Company in Cincinnati has authorized a new training program in storytelling for employees at Scripps' 10 television stations. He believes that the training will improve the quality of broadcasting content. His plans to improve quality of newspaper content are also discussed.

15573 ■ *"Study: New Moms Build A Lot of Brand Buzz"* in *Brandweek (Vol. 49, April 21, 2008, No. 16, pp. 7)*
Pub: VNU Business Media, Inc.
Description: According to a new survey which sampled 1,721 pregnant women and new moms, this demographic is having 109 word-of-mouth conversations per week concerning products, services and brands. Two-thirds of these conversations directly involve brand recommendations. The Internet is driving these word-of-mouth, or W-O-M, conversations among this segment, beating out magazines, television and other forms of media.

15574 ■ *"The Superfluous Position"* in *Entrepreneur (Vol. 37, July 2009, No. 7, pp. 62)*
Pub: Entrepreneur Media, Inc.
Description: Profile of an anonymous editor at a multimedia company that publishes tourism guides who shares his experiences in dealing with an officemate who was promoted as creative manager of content. Everyone was irritated by this person, who would constantly do something to justify his new title. The biggest problem was the fact that this person didn't have a clear job description.

15575 ■ *"Survey: More Buyers Expect to Spend Less in Most Media"* in *Advertising Age (Vol. 79, July 7, 2008, No. 26, pp. 3)*
Pub: Crain Communications, Inc.
Ed: Megan McIlroy. **Description:** Marketers are decreasing their budgets for advertising in television, radio, newspaper and outdoor due to the economic downturn. Statistical data concerning advertising agencies and marketers included.

15576 ■ *"Swedes Swoop In To Save Time4"* in *Advertising Age (Vol. 78, January 29, 2007, No. 5, pp. 4)*
Pub: Crain Communications, Inc.
Ed: Nat Ives. **Description:** Overview of Stockholm's Bonnier Group, a family-owned publisher that is looking to expand its U.S. presence; Bonnier recently acquired a number of Time Inc. magazines.

15577 ■ *"To JM On Its 75th Anniversary"* in *Journal of Marketing (Vol. 75, July 2011, No. 4, pp. 129)*
Pub: American Marketing Association
Ed: Ruth M. Bolton. **Description:** How the Journal of Marketing influenced the marketing science and practice is presented. The Marketing Science Institute's 50th anniversary coincides with the journal's 75th anniversary and both have collaborated to tackle important marketing issues identified in MSI's priorities. The mind-set of managers worldwide was also influenced by ideas in the journal's articles.

15578 ■ *"Transform Your Life"* in *Black Enterprise (Vol. 37, January 2007, No. 6, pp. 14)*
Pub: Earl G. Graves Publishing Co. Inc.
Description: Through the magazine, television and radio programs, events, and the website, the various platforms of Black Enterprise will provide the tools necessary to achieve success in business ventures, career aspirations, and personal goals.

15579 ■ *"A Turn in the South"* in *The Economist (Vol. 390, January 3, 2009, No. 8612, pp. 34)*
Pub: The Economist Newspaper Inc.
Description: Overview of Charleston, South Carolina, a region that lost its navy base in 1996, which had had provided work for more than 22,000 people; the city developed a plan called Noisette in order to redevelop the area and today the economy is healthier and more diversified than it was a decade ago. Charleston was described as among the best cities for doing business by Inc. Magazine and seems to be handling the downturn of the economy fairly well. Statistical data regarding growth, business and population is included.

15580 ■ *Ulrich's Periodicals Directory: International Periodicals Information Since 1932*
Pub: R.R. Bowker L.L.C.
URL(s): www.ulrichsweb.com/ulrichsweb/faqs.asp.
Released: Annual; Latest edition 2010. **Price:** $1260, Individuals Hardcover, 4 volumes. **Covers:** Nearly 200,000 current periodicals and newspapers published worldwide. **Entries include:** In main list-- Publication title; Dewey Decimal Classification number, Library of Congress Classification Number (where applicable), CODEN designation (for sci-tech serials), British Library Document Supply Centre shelfmark number, country code, ISSN; subtitle, language(s) of text, year first published, frequency, subscription prices, sponsoring organization, publishing company name, address, phone, fax, e-mail and website addresses, editor and publisher names; regular features (reviews, advertising, abstracts, bibliographies, trade literature, etc.), indexes, circulation, format, brief description of content; availability of microforms and reprints; whether refereed; CD-ROM availability with vendor name; online availability with service name; services that index or abstract the periodical, with years covered; advertising rates and contact; right and permissions contact name and phone; availability through document deliver. **Arrangement:** Main listing is classified by subject; U.S. general daily and weekly newspapers are listed in a separate volume; lists of cessations, online services, and CD-ROM vendors are alphabetical. **Indexes:** Cessations, subjects, title (including variant, former, and ceased titles), ISSN, periodicals available on CD-ROM, online periodical title, refereed serial, and international organization publication title.

15581 ■ *The Weather Channel*
Pub: Harvard Business School Press
Ed: Frank Batten with Jeffrey L. Cruikshank. **Released:** 2002. **Price:** $29.95. **Description:** Frank Batten illustrates the power of a resourceful growth strategy along with details the journey he successfully took his small, private newspaper into the cable industry.

15582 ■ *"Welch's Uses Taste Strips in Ads"* in *Marketing to Women (Vol. 21, April 2008, No. 4, pp. 3)*
Pub: EPM Communications Inc.
Contact: Ira Mayer, President
E-mail: imayer@epmcom.com
Description: Welch's is positioning its 139-year-old brand in a new and inventive way with a new marketing campaign in which print ads will feature a tamper-evident flavor pouch that contains a dissolving taste strip flavored with Welch's grape juice.

STATISTICAL SOURCES

15583 ■ *RMA Annual Statement Studies*
Pub: Risk Management Association
Contact: Kevin M. Blakey, President
Released: Annual. **Price:** $175.00 2006-07 edition, $105.00. **Description:** Contains composite balance sheets and income statements for more than 360 industries, including the accounting, auditing, and bookkeeping industries. Also contains five years of comparative historical data for discerning trends. Includes 16 commonly used ratios, computed for most of the size groupings for nearly every industry.

TRADE PERIODICALS

15584 ■ Canastota Bee-Journal
Pub: Eagle Newspapers
Contact: Thomas Lanctot, President
URL(s): cnylink.com/aboutcny/. **Released:** Weekly
(Wed.) **Price:** $28, Individuals in-state (NY); $45,
Two years in-state (NY); $60, Individuals 3 years; in-
state (NY); $33, Out of state out-of-state; $60, Out of
state 2 years; out-of-state; $79, Out of state 3 years;
out-of-state; $28, Out of country; $46, Out of country
2 years; $63, Out of country; $23, Individuals senior
rate in-county.

**15585 ■ ENT: The Independent Newspaper
for Windows NT Enterprise Computing**
Pub: 101 Communications
Contact: Neil Vitale, President
URL(s): entmag.com/aboutus/aboutent.asp?editorial-
sid=17. **Released:** 18/yr. **Price:** Free U.S.; $54.95,
Canada and Mexico; $64.95, Other countries.

15586 ■ Granville Sentinel
Pub: Gannett Co.
Released: Weekly

15587 ■ Hamilton/Morrisville Tribune
Pub: Eagle Newspapers
Contact: Thomas Lanctot, President
URL(s): cnylink.com/aboutcny/. **Released:** Weekly
(Wed.) **Price:** $25, Individuals in-state, one year; $30,
Individuals out-of-state, one year; $28, Individuals in-
state outside Ononandoga and Madison Counties;
$23, Individuals senior in-county, one year; $19,
Individuals college, one year; $99, Individuals outside
the U.S., one year; $15, Individuals Syracuse parent,
one year; $10, Individuals prime for senior citizens,
one year.

**15588 ■ How To Be Your Own Publisher
Update**
Pub: Bibliotheca Press
Ed: A. Doyle, Editor. **Released:** Annual. **Price:** $12.
95, U.S.; $15.95, Canada; $19.95, other countries.
Description: Acts as a reference for self publishers.
Distributed by Prosperity & Profits Unlimited Distribu-
tion Services, PO Box 416, Denver, CO, 80201.

**15589 ■ Independent Publisher Online: The
Voice of The Independent Publishing Industry**
Pub: Jenkins Group Inc.
Contact: James J. Kalajian, President
E-mail: jjk@bookpublishing.com
URL(s): www.independentpublisher.com/. **Released:**
Monthly **Price:** Free.

15590 ■ La Jolla Village News
Pub: San Diego Community Newspaper Group
URL(s): www.sdnews.com/pages/home?site=ljvn.
Ed: Kendra Hartmann. **Released:** Semiannual;
weekly on web.

**15591 ■ Publishing Executive: Creative,
Production and Work Flow at Digital Speed**
Pub: North American Publishing Co.
Contact: Ned S. Borowsky, President
URL(s): www.napco.comwww.pubexec.com. **Ed:**
Brian Howard. **Released:** 10/yr.

15592 ■ Redlands Daily Facts
Pub: Donrey Media Group
URL(s): www.redlandsdailyfacts.com. **Released:**
Daily (eve.) and Sun. (morn.) **Price:** $38, Individuals
home delivery.

15593 ■ Wireless Week
Pub: Wireless Week
Contact: Monica Allewen,
URL(s): www.wirelessweek.com. **Released:** Weekly
Price: Free.

TRADE SHOWS AND CONVENTIONS

15594 ■ Folio Show
Cowles Event Management
11 River Bend Dr. South
Stamford, CT 06907
Ph: (203)358-3751
URL(s): www.folioshow.com. **Frequency:** 3/year. **Audience:** Magazine and book publishing trades. **Principal Exhibits:** Publishing supplies, paper, printing
equipment, color separators, fulfillment houses, lists,
and related equipment, supplies, and services to the
magazine and book publishing trades. **Telecommunication Services:** registration@primediabusi-
ness.com.

CONSULTANTS

**15595 ■ Capell & Associates—Capell's
Circulation Report**
601 Central Ave.
Barnegat Light, NJ 08006
Ph: (202)572-8774
Fax: (609)494-7369
Co. E-mail: contact@capellandassociates.com
URL: http://www.capellandassociates.com
Contact: E. Daniel Capell, President
E-mail: dan_capell@att.net
Scope: Specialized consulting firm focused on direct
marketing, magazine publishing and circulation.
Consulting services include due diligence, circulation
audits, benchmarking and list rental analysis.
Founded: 1982. **Seminars:** Circulation for the Non-
Circulator.

15596 ■ J. S. Eliezer Associates Inc. (JSEA)
300 Atlantic St., 7th Fl.
Stamford, CT 06901-3513
Ph: (203)658-1300
Fax: (203)658-1301
Contact: Judah S. Eliezer, President
E-mail: jeliezer@jseliezer.com
Scope: Management and market research consultants offering design and implementation of manufacturing strategy, feasibility analysis and systems
analysis, as well as management information systems
and prepress systems; manufacturing proposals
analysis, negotiations and contracts; paper purchasing strategy and contract negotiations; catalog
distribution effectiveness analysis. Serves the publishing and catalog industries. **Founded:** 1964.

15597 ■ Heidelberg Graphics (HG)
2 Stansbury Ct.
Chico, CA 95928
Ph: (530)342-6582
Fax: (530)342-6582
Co. E-mail: service@heidelberggraphics.com
URL: http://www.heidelberggraphics.com
Contact: Jennifer Rowe, Manager
Description: Description: Publishes books on fiction,
poetry, biography and history. Reaches market
through Internet, direct mail, reviews and listings and
wholesalers and distributors. Does not accept unsolicited manuscripts. **Scope:** Offers services including
scans, disc conversions, layouts, editing and printing
for books, catalogs and magazines. Provides the
codes on paper, disk, film, embedded in designs, or
in variable labeling and personalized printing. Serves
private industries as well as government agencies.
Founded: 1972. **Publications:** "Chronicles of the
Clandestine Knights: Hyacinth Blue," 2003; "A Book
of Thoughts II," 2001; "Historic Shot Glasses: The
pre-Prohibition," 1992; "After the War," 1981; "Phantasm," 1980.

15598 ■ Moseley Associates Inc.
6 Bart Bull Rd.
Middletown, NY 10941
Ph: (845)673-5955
Co. E-mail: pwadams@consultmoseley.com
URL: http://www.consultmoseley.com
Contact: Peter W. Adams, President
E-mail: pwadams@consultmoseley.com
Scope: Provider of management consulting services.
It is also engaged in appraisals of books, magazines,
and learning materials. **Founded:** 1971. **Publica-
tions:** "Is This the End of Publishing? As We Know
It," Jun, 2007; "US School Publishing," Apr, 2001; "A
Century of Progress," Jun, 2006; "Technology in
Publishing: A Century of Progress," Against the Grain,
May, 2001; "Why I Don't Read Electronic Journals:
An Iconoclast Speaks Out," Sep, 1997; "Post-
Traumatic Shock Syndrome, Or, Surviving the
Merger," Jun, 2009; "Familiar and Unfamiliar Quota-
tions," Apr, 2009.

15599 ■ James Peter Associates Inc.
PO Box 772
Tenafly, NJ 07670
Ph: (201)568-0760
Fax: (201)568-2959
Contact: Herbert F. Holtje, Principal
E-mail: bholtje@attmail.com
Scope: Consults with publishers and industry on
such projects for total book production from concep-
tion through writing, design and illustration to camera-
ready copy, video tapes and programmed instruction.
Also works with businesses and non-profit organiza-
tions to develop books and periodical publications.
Founded: 1971.

FRANCHISES AND BUSINESS OPPORTUNITIES

**15600 ■ AroundAbout Community Magazines
Inc.**
2449 Towne Lake Pkwy., 2449 Towne Pkwy.
Woodstock, GA 30189
Ph: (770)516-7105
Fax: (770)516-4809
URL: http://www.aroundaboutlocalmedia.com
Description: Direct-mail community magazine. **No.
of Franchise Units:** 6. **No. of Company-Owned
Units:** 3. **Founded:** 1996.. **Franchised:** 2003. **Equity
Capital Needed:** $49,151-$69,797 total investment;
$250,000 net worth, $100,000 cash liquidity. **Fran-
chise Fee:** $37,500. **Royalty Fee:** 6%. **Training:**
Provides 2 weeks at headquarters, 1 week onsite
with ongoing support.

15601 ■ The Bingo Bugle Newspaper
Frontier Publications, Inc.
PO Box 527
Vashon, WA 98070
Ph: (206)463-5656
Fax: (206)463-5630
Description: Sell franchises for the Bingo Bugle
Newspaper nationally. The Bingo Bugle is a monthly
publication for bingo players. desktop publishing,
typesetting and paste-up, bookkeeping and billing,
distribution and multiple-edition advertising. **No. of
Franchise Units:** 46. **Founded:** 1980.. **Franchised:**
1980. **Equity Capital Needed:** $9,070-$15,020.
Franchise Fee: $5,000. **Royalty Fee:** 8%. **Training:**
Available 2 days at franchisee's location, headquarters or regional location and onging support.

15602 ■ EasyChair Media LLC
800 Third St.
Windsor, CO 80550-5424
Free: 800-741-6308
Fax: (800)438-2150
Description: Regional & city publications. **No. of
Franchise Units:** 1. **No. of Company-Owned Units:**
5. **Founded:** 2000.. **Franchised:** 2002. **Equity
Capital Needed:** $32,700-$36,700. **Franchise Fee:**
$10,000-$20,000. **Royalty Fee:** None. **Training:** Of-
fers 2-3 days at headquarters, 2-3 weeks at franchi-
sees location with ongoing support.

15603 ■ Homes & Land
Endurance Business Media
1830 E Park Ave.
Tallahassee, FL 32310
Free: 800-458-9250
Fax: (850)575-9567
Co. E-mail: franchise@homesandland.com
URL: http://www.homesandland.com
Description: Network of more than 250 magazines,
publishing approximately 60 million magazines cover-
ing thousands of communities across the U.S. and
Canada. **No. of Franchise Units:** 260. **No. of
Company-Owned Units:** 29. **Founded:** 1973.. **Fran-
chised:** 1984. **Equity Capital Needed:** Minimum
$50,000 liquid assets; $150,000 net worth. **Franchise
Fee:** $27,000. **Training:** 1 week of classroom train-
ing at corporate office, and continued support with
workshops, toll-free number, marketing materials and
more.

15604 ■ TheHomeMag
1732 SE 47th Ter.
Cape Coral, FL 33904
Ph: (239)549-6960
Fax: (239)549-1212
Co. E-mail: southwestfl@thehomemag.com
URL: http://thehomemag.com
URL(s): southwestfl.thehomemag.com. **Description:**
Home improvement magazine. **No. of Franchise
Units:** 17. **No. of Company-Owned Units:** 5.
Founded: 2002. **Franchised:** 2006. **Equity Capital
Needed:** $108,575-$135,575. **Franchise Fee:**
$19,000-$34,000. **Royalty Fee:** 5.5%. **Training:** Offers 1 week training at headquarters and at franchisee's location upon request.

COMPUTERIZED DATABASES

15605 ■ *Daily Brief Services*
5 Alfred St.
Oxford OX1 4EH, United Kingdom
Ph: 1865 261600
Fax: 1865 242018
URL: http://www.oxan.com
Availability: Online: Oxford Analytica Ltd. **Type:** Full-text.

15606 ■ *Ethnic NewsWatch: A History*™
789 E Eisenhower Pky.
Ann Arbor, MI 48106-1346
Ph: (734)761-4700

Free: 800-760-2455
Co. E-mail: info@proquest.com
URL: http://www.proquest.com/en-US/products/
   brands/pl_ch.shtml
Availability: Online: ProQuest LLC - Chadwyck-Healey. **Type:** Full-text; Directory.

15607 ■ *NewsFile Collection*
4501 Tamiami Trl. N, Ste. 316
Naples, FL 34103
Ph: (802)875-2910
Free: 800-762-8182
Fax: (802)875-2904
Co. E-mail: sales@newsbank.com
URL: http://www.newsbank.com
Availability: Online: NewsBank Inc. **Type:** Full-text.

LIBRARIES

15608 ■ Hanley-Wood, LLC Library
426 S. Westgate St.
Addison, IL 60101-4546
Ph: (630)543-0870
Fax: (630)543-3112
URL: http://www.hanleywood.com
Scope: Concrete, cement, masonry, construction,
home building. **Services:** Interlibrary loan; copying.
Founded: 1971. **Holdings:** 3000 books; 120 bound
periodical volumes. **Subscriptions:** 100 journals and
other serials.

**15609 ■ Magazine Publishers of America
Information Center**
810 Seventh Ave., 24th Fl.
New York, NY 10019
Ph: (212)872-3745
Fax: (212)888-4217
Co. E-mail: infocenter@magazine.org
URL: http://www.magazine.org
Contact: Sandy Jimenez, Director, Information
   Services
Scope: Magazine publishing and advertising. **Services:** Open only to MPA members, advertisers, and
agencies by appointment. **Founded:** 1919. **Holdings:** Books; magazine publishers research reports;
circulation reports; magazine advertising expenditures
statistics; 400 vertical files of information on markets
and media. **Subscriptions:** 150 journals and other
serials. **Telecommunication Services:** mpa@
magazine.org.

**15610 ■ Reader's Digest Association -
Editorial Research Library**
1 Reader Digest Rd.
Pleasantville, NY 10570
Free: 800-310-2181
Co. E-mail: letters@rd.com
URL: http://www.rd.com
Contact: Ann DiCesare, Librarian
Scope: General reference, current news, Reader's
Digest. **Services:** Interlibrary loan (limited); libraries
not open to the public. **Founded:** 1938. **Holdings:**
10,000 books; archival materials. **Subscriptions:**
350 journals and other serials; 20 newspapers.

REFERENCE WORKS

15611 ■ *How to Start a Home-Based Senior Care Business: Check-in-Care, Transportation Services, Shopping and Cooking*
Pub: Globe Pequot Press
Ed: James L. Ferry. **Released:** January 1, 2010. **Price:** $18.95. **Description:** Information is provided to start a home-based senior care business.

15612 ■ *"Professional Help: Cross That Off Your To-Do List" in Inc. (November 2007, pp. 89-90, 92)*
Pub: Gruner & Jahr USA Publishing
Ed: Alison Stein Wellner. **Description:** Small business owners are finding that it pays to hire someone to takeover the personal tasks of daily living, including hiring a personal assistant, chauffeur, chef, stylist, pet caregiver, or concierge service.

15613 ■ *"Q&A With Devin Ringling: Franchise's Services Go Beyond Elder Care" in Gazette (October 2, 2010)*
Pub: The Gazette
Ed: Bill Radford. **Description:** Profile of franchise, Interim HealthCare, in Colorado Springs, Colorado; the company offers home care services that include wound care and specialized feedings to shopping and light housekeeping. It also runs a medical staffing company that provides nurses, therapists and other health care workers to hospitals, prisons, schools and other facilities.

TRADE PERIODICALS

15614 ■ *Fulton Pennysaver*
Pub: Scotsman Community Publications
URL(s): www.scotsmanonline.com. **Released:** Weekly (Mon.)

FRANCHISES AND BUSINESS OPPORTUNITIES

15615 ■ Foot Solutions, Inc.
Foot Solutions, Inc.
2359 Windy Hill Rd., Ste. 400
Marietta, GA 30067
Ph: (770)955-0099
Free: 866-338-2597
Fax: (770)953-6270
Description: Personalized and custom designed products. **No. of Franchise Units:** 190. **No. of Company-Owned Units:** 1. **Founded:** 2000.. **Franchised:** 2000. **Equity Capital Needed:** $40,000 start-up retail store front, mobile unit $25,000. **Franchise Fee:** $32,500 retail/$29,500 mobile. **Training:** Yes.

15616 ■ Instant Imprints
Instant Imprints Franchising, Inc.
5897 Oberlin Dr., Ste. 200
San Diego, CA 92121
Ph: (858)642-4848
Free: 800-542-3437
Fax: (858)453-6513
Description: Offers Personalized shopping services. **No. of Franchise Units:** 60. **No. of Company-Owned Units:** 1. **Founded:** 1992.. **Franchised:** 2002. **Equity Capital Needed:** $50,000-$60,000 liquid; $193,000 total cost. **Franchise Fee:** $29,500. **Training:** Yes.

15617 ■ Interiors by Decorating Den
8659 Commerce Dr.
Easton, MD 21601
Ph: (800)332-3367
Fax: (410)820-5131
Co. E-mail: decden@decoratingden.com
URL: http://www.decoratingden.com
Description: Interiors by Decorating is one of the oldest, international, shop-at-home interior decorating franchises in the world. Our company-trained interior decorators bring 1000's of samples including window coverings, wall coverings, floor coverings, furniture and accessories to their customer's home in our uniquely equipped ColorVan. Special business features include: home-based, marketing systems, business systems, training, support, and complete sampling. **No. of Franchise Units:** 501. **Founded:** 1969. **Franchised:** 1970. **Equity Capital Needed:** $25,000. **Franchise Fee:** $29,900. **Training:** Training combines classroom work, home study, meetings, seminars and on-the-job experience including working with an experienced interior decorator. Secondary, advanced and graduate certification training continue throughout the franchise owner's career with Interiors by Decorating Den.

Pest Control Service

START-UP INFORMATION

15618 ■ *"Monsanto Acquires Targeted-Pest Control Technology Start-Up; Terms Not Disclosed"* in Benzinga.com (, 2011)
Pub: Benzinga.com
Ed: Benzinga Staff. **Description:** Monsanto Company acquired Beelogics, a firm that researches and develops biological tools that control pests and diseases. Research includes a product that will help protect bee health.

15619 ■ *"New Businesses"* in Arkansas Business (Vol. 28, June 27, 2011, No. 26, pp. 35)
Pub: Arkansas Business Publishing Group
Ed: Nathan Vandiver. **Description:** Profile of United Pest Control the new business co-owned by Roddy McCaskill Jr., Graham Smith, Chuck Collins and Scott Hurley. The firm focuses on education and the use of nontoxic chemicals.

15620 ■ *"Termite Trouble"* in Arkansas Business (Vol. 28, March 28, 2011, No. 13, pp. 5)
Pub: Arkansas Business Publishing Group
Description: Thomas Pest Control of Little Rock, Arkansas has had liens placed against it by the Internal Revenue Service. The owner's daughter took over the business after her father passed away and is trying to rectify the situation.

ASSOCIATIONS AND OTHER ORGANIZATIONS

15621 ■ **Association of Applied IPM Ecologists (AAIE)**
PO Box 1119
Coarsegold, CA 93614
Ph: (559)761-1064
Co. E-mail: director@aaie.net
URL: http://www.aaie.net
Contact: Bill Rothfuss, Executive Director
Description: Professional agricultural pest management consultants, entomologists, and field personnel. Promotes the implementation of integrated pest management in agricultural and urban environments. Provides a forum for the exchange of technical information on pest control. Offers placement service. **Founded:** 1967. **Awards:** Member of the Year (Annual); Outstanding Achievement (Annual).

15622 ■ **National Pest Management Association International (NPMA)**
10460 N St.
Fairfax, VA 22030
Ph: (703)352-6762
Free: 800-678-6722
Fax: (703)352-3031
Co. E-mail: npma@pestworld.org
URL: http://www.pestworld.org
Contact: Mr. Robert F. Lederer, Executive Vice President
URL(s): www.npmapestworld.org. **Description:** Represents firms engaged in control of insects, rodents, birds, and other pests, in or around struc-

tures, through use of insecticides, rodenticides, miticides, fumigants, and non-chemical methods. Provides advisory services on control procedures, new products, and safety and business administration practices. Promotes June as National Pest Control Month. Sponsors research, periodic technical and management seminars. **Founded:** 1933. **Publications:** *Pest Gazette* (Quarterly); *National Pest Control Association--Technical Release* (Monthly); *National Pest Management Association--Series of Management Reports* (Periodic). **Educational Activities:** PestWorld (Annual). **Awards:** Committee of the Year Award (Annual).

15623 ■ **Responsible Industry for a Sound Environment (RISE)—RISE**
1156 15th St. NW, Ste. 400
Washington, DC 20005
Ph: (202)872-3860
Fax: (202)355-1467
Co. E-mail: kreardon@pestfacts.org
URL: http://www.pestfacts.org
Contact: Angela B. Jamison, President
Description: Manufacturers, formulators, distributors, and representatives of the specialty pesticides industry. Promotes the environmental, health, and safety benefits of the proper use of specialty pesticides. **Founded:** 1991.

REFERENCE WORKS

15624 ■ *"Ag Officials Employ Preventive Pest Control"* in Yakima Herald-Republic (June 24, 2011)
Pub: Yakima Herald-Republic
Ed: Ross Courtney. **Description:** Washington State Department of Agriculture is placing vineyard traps for the European grapevine moth, an invasive species whose larvae eat grape buds and fruit clusters, thus exposing the vines to diseases that could destroy them.

15625 ■ *"Autumn Rat Control Essential for Poultry Units"* in Poultry World (Vol. 165, September 2011, No. 9, pp. 32)
Pub: Reed Business Information Inc.
Description: Dr. Alan Buckle discusses the use of rodenticides control, focusing on poultry units.

15626 ■ *"Bedbugs Are Here, But Help Is At Hand"* in Register-Guard (June 26, 2011)
Pub: The Register-Guard
Ed: Diane Dietz. **Description:** A survey conducted by the National Pest Control Association found that 95 percent of its 7,000 members have treated buildings for bed bugs. That number is up 25 percent from 2000.

15627 ■ *"Bountiful Exterminator Indicted for Unlawful Pesticide Use"* in Standard-Examiner (February 3, 2011)
Pub: Standard-Examiner
Contact: Bart Wade, Director
E-mail: bwade@standard.net
Ed: Bryon Saxton. **Description:** Bugman Pest and Lawn Inc. indicted Coleman Nocks and his business,

Bugman Pest and Lawn Inc. for three counts of unlawful use of the pesticide Fumitoxin, resulting in the death of two little girls.

15628 ■ *Crop Protection Handbook*
Pub: Meister Publishing Co.
Contact: Gary T. Fitzgerald, Chief Executive Officer
E-mail: gtfitzgerald@meistermedia.com
URL(s): www.meistermedia.com. **Released:** Annual; Latest edition 2013. **Price:** $189, Individuals print & CD; $89, Individuals print/CD, discounted price. **Covers:** Manufacturers and suppliers of fertilizers, pesticides, and related equipment and services used in agribusiness. **Entries include:** Company name, address, phone, fax numbers, e-mail address, trade and brand names, product information. **Database includes:** Dictionaries of fertilizers, pesticides, biocontrols, and enhanced seed, regulatory file, environmental and safety section, and buyer's guide. **Arrangement:** Alphabetical.

15629 ■ *"Don't Let the Bed Bugs Bite"* in Yuma Sun (April 22, 2011)
Pub: The Yuma Sun
Ed: Mara Knaub. **Description:** Bug specialists note that bed bugs are returning. Exterminators say that eliminating these pests can be costly. Most bed bugs are picked up while traveling.

15630 ■ *"Faulkner Pest Service Has Been Providing Quality Pest Control Solutions for 23 Years"* in OfficialSpin (September 30, 2011)
Pub: SPIN
Description: Profile of Faulkner Pest Service, which has been providing pest control services in Amarillo for twenty-three years.

15631 ■ *"Hearing Damage Leads to Settlement"* in Register-Guard (August 13, 2011)
Pub: The Register-Guard
Ed: Karen McCowan. **Description:** Cynergy Pest Control lost a court battle when a rural Cottage Grove man was granted a $37,000 settlement after his hearing was damaged by the pest control companies method to eradicate gophers, using blasts in his neighbor's yard.

15632 ■ *"Suncoast Pest Control Introduces New Website"* in Entertainment Close-Up (March 16, 2011)
Pub: Close-Up Media
Description: Florida pest control company, Suncoast Pest Control, launched a new Website to better serve their customers. The new Website will allow users to reach local Florida pest control professionals 24 hours a day.

15633 ■ *"US Hygiene Adds Bed Bug Fix to Its Line of Highly Effective Cleaning and Pest Control Products"* in Benzinga.com (October 29, 2011)
Pub: Benzinga.com
Ed: Benzinga Staff. **Description:** US Hygiene LLC introduced its newest product called Bed Bug Fix, which is a naturally-derived, nontoxic insecticide that

kills a multitude of bugs including bed bugs and dust mites. The product is safe to use around children, plants and pets.

STATISTICAL SOURCES

15634 ■ RMA Annual Statement Studies
Pub: Risk Management Association
Contact: Kevin M. Blakey, President
Released: Annual. **Price:** $175.00 2006-07 edition, $105.00. **Description:** Contains composite balance sheets and income statements for more than 360 industries, including the accounting, auditing, and bookkeeping industries. Also contains five years of comparative historical data for discerning trends. Includes 16 commonly used ratios, computed for most of the size groupings for nearly every industry.

TRADE PERIODICALS

15635 ■ Biological Control
Pub: Academic Press
Contact: Peter S. H. Bolman, President
URL(s): www.elsevier.com/wps/find/journaldescription.cws_home/622791/descrip tion#description. **Ed:** D. Te Beest, J. Brodeur, J.H. Hoffmann. **Released:** 9/yr. **Price:** €472, Individuals for European countries and Iran; $49200, Individuals for Japan; $366, Individuals all countries except Europe, Japan, and Iran; €1103, Institutions for European countries and Iran; $115300, Institutions; $858, Institutions for all countries except Europe, Japan and Iran; €150, Students for European countries and Iran; $15600, Students; $131, Students for all countries except Europe, Japan and Iran.

15636 ■ Common Sense Pest Control Quarterly
Pub: Bio-Integral Resource Center
Contact: William Quarles, Managing Editor
Released: 4/year. **Price:** $30, individuals U.S. and Canada; $50, institutions U.S. and Canada; $40. **Description:** Presents information regarding least-toxic pest management in layperson's terms. Evaluates alternative strategies for many pest problems still being treated exclusively with pesticides. Discusses such concerns as least-toxic management of pests on indoor plants, pests that damage paper, controlling fleas and ticks on pets, and garden pants, pests that damage paper, controlling fleas and ticks on pets, and garden pests. Recurring features include letters to the editor, interviews, news of research, book reviews, and notices of.

15637 ■ The IPM Practitioner
Pub: Bio-Integral Resource Center
Contact: William Quarles, Managing Editor
Released: 10/year. **Price:** Included in membership; $35, individuals; $60 business and institution;. **Description:** Supports the Center in its efforts to publish information on all aspects of environmentally-sound pest control. Investigates the least-toxic methods of controlling pests in agriculture, urban landscapes and structures, greenhouse and general horticulture, forestry, medical/veterinary, range, and other settings. Recurring features include letters to the editor, interviews, news of research, reports of meetings, news of educational opportunities and job listings, notices and reviews of publications available, and a calendar of events. Contains yearly listings of products.

15638 ■ Pest Control Technology
Pub: G.I.E. Media, MC
Contact: Chris Foster, President
E-mail: chris.foster@gie.net
URL(s): www.pctonline.com. **Ed:** Jodi Dorsch. **Released:** Monthly **Price:** $35, Individuals print and digital; $45, Canada and Mexico print and digital; $88, Other countries print and digital.

15639 ■ Pest Management Professional: Solution for your Business
Pub: Advanstar Communications Inc.
Contact: Mr. Joseph Loggia, Chief Executive Officer
E-mail: jloggia@advanstar.com
URL(s): www.mypmp.net. **Released:** Monthly **Price:** $45, U.S.; $69, Canada and Mexico; $106, Other countries.

15640 ■ Pesticide Biochemistry and Physiology
Pub: Elsevier Science B.V.
URL(s): www.elsevier.com/wps/find/journaldescription.cws_home/622930/descri ption#description. **Ed:** J.M. Clark. **Released:** 9/yr. **Price:** $1583.20, Institutions online; $652, Individuals print; $1583, Institutions print.

15641 ■ Pesticide & Toxic Chemical News
Pub: CRC Press
Contact: Emmitt Dages, President
Ed: Jeffrey Winograd, Editor, jwinograd@crcpress.com. **Released:** Daily. **Price:** $887. **Description:** Provides news and analysis of chemical regulatory and legislative developments. Covers Environmental Protection Agency and other national and international organization activities and research.

15642 ■ Tri-Ology
Pub: Florida Department of Agriculture and Consumer Services, Division of Plant Industry
URL(s): doacs.state.fl.us/pi/enpp/triology.html. **Released:** Monthly

VIDEOCASSETTES/ AUDIOCASSETTES

15643 ■ Rat
Vanguard International Cinema, Inc.
359 SOuth Hewitt St., Ste. 535
Los Angeles, CA 90013
Ph: (949)258-2000
Free: 800-218-7888
Fax: (213)599-7260
Co. E-mail: info@vanguardcinema.com
URL: http://www.vanguardcinema.com
Released: 1997. **Price:** $19.98. **Description:** Documentary uses humor and horror to reveal the struggle of man against rats in New York City. **Availability:** VHS.

TRADE SHOWS AND CONVENTIONS

15644 ■ Florida Pest Management Association Convention and Exposition
Florida Pest Management Association
6150 Metrowest Boulevard, Ste. 302
Orlando, FL 32835
Ph: (407)293-8627
Free: 800-426-4829
Fax: (407)292-0918
Co. E-mail: info@flpma.org
URL: http://www.flpma.org
Contact: Allen Fugler, Executive Director
URL(s): www.fpca.org. **Frequency:** Annual. **Audience:** Pest control operators and companies. **Principal Exhibits:** Equipment, services, and supplies for the chemical industry.

CONSULTANTS

15645 ■ Pest Pros Inc.—Data Associates
10086 1st St.
Plainfield, WI 54966
Ph: (715)335-4046
Fax: (715)335-4746
Co. E-mail: pestpros@uniontel.net
URL: http://www.pestprosinc.com
Contact: Randy M. Van Haren, President
Scope: Offers agricultural consulting involving fertility and pesticide recommendations, soil microbe assay and contract research. **Founded:** 1984. **Telecommunication Services:** pestpros@wrc.coop.

FRANCHISES AND BUSINESS OPPORTUNITIES

15646 ■ Critter Control
Critter Franchise
9435 E Cherry Bend Rd.
Traverse City, MI 49684

Free: 800-Cri-tter
Description: Animal & wildlife control services. **No. of Franchise Units:** 109. **No. of Company-Owned Units:** 1. **Founded:** 1983.. **Franchised:** 1987. **Equity Capital Needed:** $12,750-$80,500 total investment. **Franchise Fee:** $5,000-$47,000. **Royalty Fee:** 7%. **Financial Assistance:** Limited in-house financing available. **Training:** Available 1 week at headquarters, franchisees' locations and annual conferences with ongoing support.

15647 ■ Mosquito Squad
2924 Emerywood Pkwy., Ste. 101
Richmond, VA 23294
Free: 800-722-4668
Description: Pest control for residential and commercial. **No. of Franchise Units:** 27. **Equity Capital Needed:** $32,000-$58,000. **Franchise Fee:** $17,500. **Training:** Yes.

15648 ■ MosquitoNix
12655 N Central Expy., Ste. 425
Dallas, TX 75243
Ph: (972)934-3131
Fax: (972)934-1055
Description: Pest-control misting system. **No. of Franchise Units:** 8. **No. of Company-Owned Units:** 2. **Founded:** 2003.. **Franchised:** 2004. **Equity Capital Needed:** $130,000-$213,000. **Franchise Fee:** $25,000-$55,000. **Royalty Fee:** 5%. **Training:** Offers 5 days at headquarters and ongoing support.

15649 ■ Terminix Termite & Pest Control
3635 Knight Rd., Ste. 7
Memphis, TN 38118
Ph: (901)363-1132
Free: 800-441-5390
Fax: (901)363-8541
URL: http://www.terminix.com
Description: Commercial, industrial and residential pest control and termite protection. **No. of Franchise Units:** 137. **No. of Company-Owned Units:** 329. **Founded:** 1927.. **Franchised:** 1927. **Equity Capital Needed:** $24,700-$85,300. **Franchise Fee:** $25,000-$50,000. **Royalty Fee:** 7-10%. **Financial Assistance:** In-house financial assistance with franchise fee. **Training:** 1 week at headquarters, in-field training and ongoing self-tutorial.

15650 ■ Truly Nolen
Truly Nolen of America, Inc.
3636 East Speedway
Tucson, AZ 85716
Ph: (520)322-4055
Free: 800-458-3664
Fax: (520)322-4010
Co. E-mail: truly@truly.com
URL: http://trullyfranchise.com
Description: Environmentally friendly pest and insect control. **No. of Franchise Units:** 13. **No. of Company-Owned Units:** 65. **Founded:** 1938.. **Franchised:** 1996. **Equity Capital Needed:** varies. **Franchise Fee:** $10,000-$45,000. **Financial Assistance:** Yes. **Training:** Yes.

COMPUTERIZED DATABASES

15651 ■ Integrated Pest Management Reviews
Van Godewijckstraat 30
NL-3311 GX Dordrecht, Netherlands
Ph: 78 657 6000
Fax: 78 657 6555
URL: http://www.springer.com
Availability: Online: Springer Science + Business Media BV. **Type:** Full-text; Properties.

15652 ■ National Pesticide Information Retrieval System (NPIRS)
1435 Win Hentschel Blvd., Ste. 207
West Lafayette, IN 47906
Ph: (765)494-6616

Fax: (765)494-9727
Co. E-mail: info@ceris.purdue.edu
URL: http://ceris.purdue.edu
Availability: Online: Wolters Kluwer Health - Ovid; Purdue University - Entomology Department - Center for Environmental and Regulatory Information Systems. CD-ROM: Wolters Kluwer Health - Ovid. **Type:** Full-text; Numeric.

LIBRARIES

15653 ■ California Department of Pesticide Regulation Library
1001 I St.
Sacramento, CA 95812-4015
Ph: (916)445-4038
Fax: (916)324-1719
Co. E-mail: ckawamoto@cdpr.ca.gov
URL: http://apps.cdpr.ca.gov/ereglib
Scope: Pesticides. **Services:** Library not open to the public. **Founded:** 1981. **Holdings:** 81,900 volumes. **Subscriptions:** 150 journals and other serials.

15654 ■ Rachel Carson Council Library
PO Box 10779
Silver Spring, MD 20914
Ph: (301)593-7507
Fax: (301)587-3863
Co. E-mail: rccouncil@aol.com
URL: http://www.rachelcarsoncouncil.org
Contact: Dr. Diana Post, Executive Director
Scope: Pesticides, toxic substances, government regulation, pest management programs, alternatives to toxic chemical pesticides. **Services:** Copying (limited); Library open to the public by appointment. **Founded:** 1965. **Holdings:** 2000 books; 1500 documents and unbound reports; 50 drawers of specialized files; Environmental Protection Agency Pesticide Product Information and Registry of Toxic Effects of Chemical Substances materials on microfiche. **Subscriptions:** 85 journals and other serials.

15655 ■ National Pest Management Association Library
10460 North St.
Fairfax, VA 22030
Ph: (703)352-6762
Fax: (703)352-3031
Co. E-mail: npmateam@vaultcommunications.com
URL: http://www.pestworld.org
Contact: Greg Baumann, Vice President, Technical Services
Scope: Entomology, pest control. **Services:** Library not open to the public. **Founded:** 1938. **Holdings:** 2000 volumes. **Subscriptions:** 10 journals and other serials. **Telecommunication Services:** info@pestworld.org.

15656 ■ U.S. Environmental Protection Agency - Andrew W. Breidenbach Environmental Research Center Library
26 W. Martin Luther King Dr.
Cincinnati, OH 45268
Ph: (513)569-7703

Fax: (513)569-7709
Co. E-mail: garza.david@epa.gov
URL: http://www.epa.gov/libraries/awberc.html
Contact: David Garza, Librarian
Scope: Water - pollution, quality, research; hazardous waste; chemistry; environmental studies; biotechnology. **Services:** Interlibrary loan; copying. **Founded:** 1971. **Holdings:** 25,000 books; 200,000 reports on microfiche; 6000 documents. **Subscriptions:** 700 journals and other serials. **Telecommunication Services:** ci_awberc_library@epamail.epa.gov.

15657 ■ U.S. Environmental Protection Agency - National Enforcement Investigations Center Environmental Forensics Library—NEIC Library.
Bldg. 25, E2, Denver Federal Ctr.
Denver, CO 80225
Ph: (303)462-9353
Fax: (303)462-9354
Co. E-mail: neic-library@epamail.epa.gov
URL: http://www.epa.gov/libraries/neic.html
Contact: Jannie Morgan, Officer
Scope: Environmental law, water quality, industrial and agricultural pollution abatement practices, air and water pollution, hazardous wastes, chemistry. **Services:** Interlibrary loan (OCLC=EOB); copying; library open to the public by appointment. **Founded:** 1972. **Holdings:** 7300 volumes; 760,000 microforms; EPA technical reports; R&D reports; conference documents. **Subscriptions:** 100 journals and other serials.

RESEARCH CENTERS

15658 ■ Bio-Integral Resource Center (BIRC)
PO Box 7414
Berkeley, CA 94707
Ph: (510)524-2567
Fax: (510)524-1758
Co. E-mail: birc@igc.org
URL: http://www.birc.org
Contact: William Quarles, Executive Director
Services: Consulting service. **Founded:** 1978. **Publications:** Common Sense Pest Control Quarterly (Quarterly); IPM Practitioner (10/year). **Educational Activities:** Training courses and lectures, on integrated pest management.

15659 ■ Cornell University - Cornell Cooperative Extension - New York State Integrated Pest Management Program
NYSAES
630 W N St.
Geneva, NY 14456
Ph: (315)787-2208
Fax: (315)787-2360
Co. E-mail: dar11@cornell.edu
URL: http://www.nysipm.cornell.edu
Contact: Prof. Donald A. Rutz, Director
Publications: New York State Integrated Pest Management Program Annual report; New York State Integrated Pest Management Program Articles; New York State Integrated Pest Management Program Brochures; Cornell Urban IPM News (Quarterly); IPM

Today (Monthly); New York State Integrated Pest Management Program Manuals. **Telecommunication Services:** nysipm@cornell.edu.

15660 ■ Kerr Center for Sustainable Agriculture, Inc. (KCSA)
PO Box 588
Poteau, OK 74953
Ph: (918)647-9123
Fax: (918)647-8712
Co. E-mail: mailbox@kerrcenter.com
URL: http://www.kerrcenter.com
Contact: James E. (Jim) Horne, President
Services: Field days and ranch tours; Speakers. **Founded:** 1986. **Publications:** Kerr Center Newsletter. **Educational Activities:** KCSA Conferences; KCSA Workshops and seminars. **Awards:** Oklahoma producer grant program.

15661 ■ Ohio State University - Laboratory for Pest Control Application Technology (LPCAT)
Ohio Agriculture Research & Development Ctr.
1680 Madison Ave.
Wooster, OH 44691
Ph: (330)263-3931
Fax: (330)263-3686
Co. E-mail: downer.2@osu.edu
URL: http://www.oardc.ohio-state.edu/lpcat
Contact: Dr. Roger A. Downer, Director
Founded: 1981. **Educational Activities:** Seminars and professional meetings.

15662 ■ Purdue University - Center for Urban and Industrial Pest Management
Department of Entomology
901 W State St.
West Lafayette, IN 47907
Ph: (765)494-4564
Fax: (765)494-0535
Co. E-mail: gbennett@purdue.edu
URL: http://extension.entm.purdue.edu/urban/home.html
Contact: Dr. Gary Bennett, Coordinator
Founded: 1990. **Educational Activities:** Conferences, workshops, seminars, and correspondence courses; Undergraduate and graduate degree programs in urban and industrial pest management in conjunction with the School of Agriculture at the Universe.

15663 ■ University of Florida - Institute of Food and Agricultural Sciences - Florida Medical Entomology Laboratory (FMEL)
200 9th St. SE
Vero Beach, FL 32962
Ph: (772)778-7200
Co. E-mail: wjt@ufl.edu
URL: http://fmel.ifas.ufl.edu
Contact: Walter J. Tabachnick, Director
Services: State Organizations and Districts Assistance. **Founded:** 1956. **Educational Activities:** International Symposium (Biennial), on Host Regulated Developmental Mechanisms in vector Anthropods; FMEL Training, for students, in medical entomology.

START-UP INFORMATION

15664 ■ *101 Best Businesses for Pet Lovers*
Pub: Sourcebooks, Inc.
Contact: Len Vlahos, President
E-mail: dominique@sourcebooks.com
Ed: Nicholas Nigro. **Released:** September 2007.
Price: $18.95. **Description:** Advice for any individual wishing to start a business providing goods and services to pet lovers.

15665 ■ *"Groomers Eye Profit Growth Through Services" in Pet Product News (Vol. 64, December 2010, No. 12, pp. 26)*
Pub: BowTie Inc.
Ed: Kathleen M. Mangan. **Description:** Pet groomers can successfully offer add-on services by taking into account insider customer knowledge, store image, and financial analysis in the decision-making process. Many pet groomers have decided to add services such as spa treatments and training due to a slump in the bathing and grooming business. How some pet groomers gained profitability through add-on services is explored.

15666 ■ *"Keeping Customers Satisfied" in Pet Product News (Vol. 64, December 2010, No. 12, pp. 10)*
Pub: BowTie Inc.
Ed: Devon McPhee. **Description:** Windsor, California-based Debbie's Pet Boutique, recipient of Pet Product News International's Outstanding Customer Service Award, has been dedicated to combining topnotch grooming services with a robust retail selection. These features might gain return customers for Debbie's Pet Boutique.

15667 ■ *Pet Care Business*
Pub: Globe Pequot Press
Ed: Kathy Salzberg. **Released:** March 2006. **Price:** $18.95. **Description:** Guide for starting and running a pet care business such as professional groomer, dog walker, pet sitter, or obedience training; issues regarding zoning, insurance, and health are discussed.

15668 ■ *"Succeed With the Right Equipment" in Pet Product News (Vol. 64, November 2010, No. 11, pp. 42)*
Pub: BowTie Inc.
Ed: Sandi Cain. **Description:** Grooming shop owners have been focusing on obtaining ergonomic, durable, and efficient products such as restraints, tables, and tubs. These products enhance the way grooming tasks are conducted. Ways pet supply manufacturers have responded to this trend are examined.

ASSOCIATIONS AND OTHER ORGANIZATIONS

15669 ■ **National Association of Professional Pet Sitters (NAPPS)**
15000 Commerce Pkwy., Ste. C
Mount Laurel, NJ 08054
Ph: (856)439-0324
Fax: (856)439-0525
Co. E-mail: napps@petsitters.org
URL: http://www.petsitters.org
Contact: John D'Ariano, President
Description: Owners or employees of pet-sitting services; professionals or businesses in related fields. Promotes professional and ethical standards in pet sitting and fosters cooperation among members of the pet-care industry. Serves as a network for the exchange of ideas and information on pet sitting and current industry practices. Disseminates information educating the pet-owning public on the advantages of leaving pets in a home environment and how to choose a reliable sitter. **Scope:** pet-sitting. **Founded:** 1989. **Educational Activities:** National Association of Professional Pet Sitters - NAPPS Annual Conference & Small Business Forum (Annual). **Awards:** Pet Sitters Hall of Fame (Annual).

15670 ■ **National Dog Groomers Association of America (NDGAA)**
PO Box 101
Clark, PA 16113-0101
Ph: (724)962-2711
Fax: (724)962-1919
Co. E-mail: ndga@nationaldoggroomers.com
URL: http://www.nationaldoggroomers.com
Contact: Jeffrey L. Reynolds, Executive Director
Description: Dog groomers and supply distributors organized to upgrade the profession. Conducts state and local workshops; sponsors competitions and certification testing. Makes groomer referrals. **Founded:** 1969.

15671 ■ **Pet Care Services Association**
2670 Academy Blvd.
Colorado Springs, CO 80917
Ph: (719)667-1600
Free: 877-570-7788
Fax: (719)667-0116
Co. E-mail: membership@petcareservices.org
URL: http://www.petcareservices.org
Contact: Joan Saunders, Chief Executive Officer
Description: Persons or firms that board pets; kennel suppliers; others interested in the facility boarding kennel industry. Seeks to upgrade the industry through accreditation educational programs, seminars and conventions. Provides insurance resources for members and supplies pet care information to the public. Promotes code of ethics and accreditation program for recognition and training of superior kennel operators. Compiles boarding facility statistics. **Scope:** how to select a boarding kennel, pet services. **Founded:** 1977. **Subscriptions:** periodicals. **Publications:** *Pet Service Journal* (Bimonthly); *All About Dog Daycare*. **Educational Activities:** Pet Care Services Association Convention (Annual). **Awards:** Golden Scoop Award (Annual).

15672 ■ **Pet Industry Joint Advisory Council (PIJAC)**
1140 19th St. NW, Ste. 300
Washington, DC 20036
Ph: (202)452-1525
Free: 800-553-7387
Fax: (202)452-1516
Co. E-mail: info@pijac.org
URL: http://www.pijac.org
Contact: Michael F. Canning, Jr., President
Description: Pet retailers, manufacturers and distributors; companion animal suppliers; pet industry trade associations. Works to monitor federal and state regulations and legislation affecting the industry. Sponsors research projects and industry-related educational programs. **Founded:** 1971. **Publications:** *Our Pets, Our Health*; *PetLetter* (Periodic); *Tips on Travel With Your Pets*.

DIRECTORIES OF EDUCATIONAL PROGRAMS

15673 ■ *Directory of Private Accredited Career Schools and Colleges of Technology*
Pub: Accrediting Commission of Career Schools and Colleges of Technology
Contact: Michale S. McComis, Executive Director
Released: On web page. **Price:** Free. **Description:** Covers 3900 accredited post-secondary programs that provide training programs in business, trade, and technical fields, including various small business endeavors. Entries offer school name, address, phone, description of courses, job placement assistance, and requirements for admission. Arrangement is alphabetical.

REFERENCE WORKS

15674 ■ *"Bark Up The Right Tree" in Small Business Opportunities (Winter 2009)*
Pub: Entrepreneur Press
Contact: Perlman Neil, President
Description: Profile of Central Bark, a daycare company catering to pets that offers franchise opportunities and is expanding rapidly despite the economic downturn; the company's growth strategy is also discussed.

TRADE PERIODICALS

15675 ■ *Pet Services Journal*
Pub: The Pet Care Services Association
Contact: Angela Ashmore, Coordinator, Member Services
Ed: Tracy Sellars, Editor, tracy@abka.com. **Released:** Bimonthly. **Price:** Included in membership. **Description:** Publishes articles related to the pet services industry and the Association. Contains information on animal health and kennel and grooming shop operation. Carries regional and national news on new products and programs, and kennel and shop profiles. Recurring features include editorials, news of research, letters to the editor, news of members, and columns titled From the Director's Desk, Message from the President.

TRADE SHOWS AND CONVENTIONS

15676 ■ **Super Zoo**
World Wide Pet Industry Association, Inc.
135 W. Lemon Ave.
Monrovia, CA 91016

Ph: (626)447-2222
Free: 800-999-7295
Fax: (626)447-8350
Co. E-mail: info@wwpsa.com
URL: http://www.wwpsa.com
Contact: Ruth Jeffers, Chairman
URL(s): www.superzoo.org/. **Frequency:** Annual. **Audience:** Pet retailers, grooming shops, kennels, and veterinary clinic owners and other trade professionals. **Principal Exhibits:** Pet care foods, equipment, products and services. **Dates and Locations:** , Convention Center.

FRANCHISES AND BUSINESS OPPORTUNITIES

15677 ■ Aussie Pet Mobile Inc.
95 Argonaut, Ste. 115
Aliso Viejo, CA 92656
Ph: (949)234-0680
Fax: (949)234-0688
Co. E-mail: corp@aussiepetmobile.com
URL: http://www.aussiepetmobile.com
Description: Mobile pet grooming service. **No. of Franchise Units:** 335. **No. of Company-Owned Units:** 8. **Founded:** 1996.. **Franchised:** 1996. **Equity Capital Needed:** $65,000-$140,000. **Franchise Fee:** $29,000 core territory, $20,000 additional territory. **Training:** Yes.

15678 ■ Camp Bow Wow
D.O.G. Development, LLC
1877 Broadway, Ste. 101
Boulder, CO 80302
Ph: (720)259-2250
Fax: (866)821-0412
Co. E-mail: CC@campbowwowusa.com
URL: http://www.campbowwow.tv
Description: We provide doggy day camp, as well as overnight boarding for travelers. We utilize consistent start-up and operations systems that keep the franchise locations similar in look and customer experience. We oversee the growth of the company in a thoughtful, strategic manner that allows franchises to be successful in each location. **No. of Franchise Units:** 200. **No. of Company-Owned Units:** 1. **Founded:** 2000.. **Franchised:** 2002. **Equity Capital Needed:** Cash investment $80,000 liquid; $300,000-$600,000 total investment; minimum net worth $100,000. **Franchise Fee:** $50,000. **Training:** Yes.

15679 ■ Canine Campus
3116 Karen Pl.
Colorado Springs, CO 80907
Ph: (719)448-9600
Fax: (719)448-0496
Description: Day care, boarding, grooming & training services for dogs. **No. of Company-Owned Units:** 1. **Founded:** 1999.. **Franchised:** 2004. **Equity Capital Needed:** $71,500-$182,300. **Franchise Fee:** $30,000. **Royalty Fee:** 4%. **Training:** Offers 7 days training at headquarters, 7 days at franchisee's location and ongoing support.

15680 ■ Dogtopia
4920 Wyaconda Rd.
North Bethesda, MD 20852
Free: 888-364-8674
Fax: (240)514-0214
URL: http://www.dogdaycare.com
Description: Dog day care, boarding, and spa services. **No. of Franchise Units:** 22. **No. of Company-Owned Units:** 3. **Founded:** 2001.. **Franchised:** 2004. **Equity Capital Needed:** $243,100-$458,500. **Franchise Fee:** $40,000. **Royalty Fee:** 7%. **Financial Assistance:** Limited third party financing available. **Training:** Available 2-4 weeks at headquarters, 5 days at franchisee's location, and onging support.

15681 ■ Groomer On The Go
44 E Beaver Creek Rd., Unit 4
Richmond Hill, ON, Canada L4B 1G8
Ph: (905)707-7440
Free: 877-476-6655
Fax: (905)889-1680
Co. E-mail: info@groomeronthego.com
URL: http://www.groomeronthego.com
Description: Groomer On The Go is a low cost with high profit potential mobile pet grooming franchise that taps into Canada's $3 billion booming pet industry. Delivering quality pet grooming with the ultimate in convenience for the owner and the one-on-one attention for the pet. No grooming experience required. **No. of Franchise Units:** 2. **Founded:** 2005.. **Franchised:** 2005. **Equity Capital Needed:** $50,000. **Franchise Fee:** $24,995. **Training:** Provides 3 weeks comprehensive training.

15682 ■ Happy Tails Dog Spa
Happy to Be Here, Inc.
8528-F Tyco Rd.
Vienna, VA 22182
Ph: (703)821-1777
Fax: (703)821-1778
Description: Luxury dog daycare and boarding services. **No. of Franchise Units:** 6. **No. of Company-Owned Units:** 2. **Founded:** 2002.. **Franchised:** 2005. **Equity Capital Needed:** $50,000 cash available; $120,000-$200,000 total investment. **Franchise Fee:** $35,000. **Training:** Yes.

15683 ■ Kennelwood Pet Resorts
1875 Lackland Hill Pky.
St. Louis, MO 63146
Ph: (314)446-1000
Free: 877-447-4173
Fax: (314)446-1001
Co. E-mail: franchise@kennelwood.com
URL: http://www.kennelwood.com
Description: Provides pets a safe & healthy vacation & lots of fun and attention. All resorts are full-service facilities offering a wide variety of services, including all suite pet accommodations, grooming, personalized play time. **No. of Company-Owned Units:** 6. **Founded:** 1974.. **Franchised:** 2007. **Equity Capital Needed:** $250,000. **Franchise Fee:** $55,000. **Training:** As part of our system, you will have the assistance & support of the entire franchisor organiza-

tion, with access to our trained team, our established trademarks & operating systems, & full selection of tools & services designed to get you started & keep your business running efficiently.

15684 ■ Laund-UR-Mutt
Pet Pioneers, Inc.
12512-B W. Ken Caryl Ave.
Littleton, CO 80127
Ph: (303)470-1540
Description: Self-service dog grooming.● **No. of Franchise Units:** 3. **Founded:** 1992.. **Franchised:** 1994. **Equity Capital Needed:** $150,000. **Franchise Fee:** $25,000. **Royalty Fee:** 5%/month. **Training:** Offers 1 week at headquarters, 1 week at franchisee's location and ongoing support.

15685 ■ Pet Supplies 'Plus'
22710 Haggerty Rd.
Farmington Hills, MI 48335
Ph: (248)374-1900
Fax: (248)374-7900
Description: Discount pet food and supplies. **No. of Franchise Units:** 164. **No. of Company-Owned Units:** 94. **Founded:** 1988.. **Franchised:** 1990. **Equity Capital Needed:** $623,300-$1,401,000. **Franchise Fee:** $40,000. **Royalty Fee:** $3,000 /month. **Training:** Provides 4 weeks training at headquarters.

15686 ■ Preppy Pet
Preppy Pet Franchises
57 West Michigan St.
Orlando, FL 32806
Ph: (407)420-1060
Free: 877-377-9738
Fax: (407)420-1068
Description: Overnight dog boarding and day care. **No. of Franchise Units:** 17. **No. of Company-Owned Units:** 1. **Founded:** 2003.. **Franchised:** 2006. **Equity Capital Needed:** $127,750. **Franchise Fee:** $34,500. **Financial Assistance:** Yes. **Training:** Yes.

15687 ■ Ryan's Pet Food
Ryan's Pet Food, Inc.
70 Don Caster Rd.
Thornhille, ON, Canada L3T 1L3
Ph: (905)771-9227
Fax: (905)795-8903
Description: Specialty pet foods and products. **No. of Franchise Units:** 14. **No. of Company-Owned Units:** 24. **Founded:** 1979.. **Franchised:** 1993. **Equity Capital Needed:** $95,000 inclusive; opening inventory, initial fee, leaseholds and working capital. **Franchise Fee:** $25,000. **Training:** Yes.

15688 ■ U-Wash Doggie
Total Pet Inc.
23013 Soledad Canyon Rd.
Santa Clarita, CA 91350
Ph: (818)846-9600
Fax: (661)297-2029
Description: Self and full service pet grooming. **No. of Franchise Units:** 1. **No. of Company-Owned Units:** 5. **Founded:** 1992.. **Franchised:** 1997. **Equity Capital Needed:** $98,000. **Franchise Fee:** $15,000. **Training:** Yes.

START-UP INFORMATION

15689 ■ *101 Best Businesses for Pet Lovers*
Pub: Sourcebooks, Inc.
Contact: Len Vlahos, President
E-mail: dominique@sourcebooks.com
Ed: Nicholas Nigro. **Released:** September 2007.
Price: $18.95. **Description:** Advice for any individual wishing to start a business providing goods and services to pet lovers.

15690 ■ *"Biz Pays Tribute: Franchise Helps Owners Grieve and Honor Their Beloved Pets" in Small Business Opportunities (November 2007)*
Pub: Harris Publications Inc.

Description: Paws and Remember is a franchise company that provides pet cremation and memorial products while assisting veterinary clinics and other pet specialists to help clients when they lose a pet.

REFERENCE WORKS

15691 ■ *Minding Your Dog Business: A Practical Guide to Business Success for Dog Professionals*
Pub: Dogwise Publishing
Ed: Veronica Boutelle, Rikke Jorgensen. **Released:** June 1, 2010. **Price:** $19.95. **Description:** Setting up and running a successful dog-related business is an achievement in itself, but the real test is to build success and growth for the long haul.

ASSOCIATIONS AND OTHER ORGANIZATIONS

15692 ■ National Association of Dog Obedience Instructors (NADOI)
PO Box 1439
Socorro, NM 87801
Ph: (505)850-5957
URL: http://www.nadoi.org
Contact: Helen Cariotis, President
Description: Dog obedience instructors who have met certain standards as established by the association. Promotes improved dog obedience instruction. Endorses instructors; serves as a network for communication among members. Maintains speakers' bureau. **Founded:** 1965. **Publications:** *FORWARD* (Quarterly); *NADOI News* (Bimonthly).

DIRECTORIES OF EDUCATIONAL PROGRAMS

15693 ■ *Directory of Private Accredited Career Schools and Colleges of Technology*
Pub: Accrediting Commission of Career Schools and Colleges of Technology
Contact: Michale S. McComis, Executive Director
Released: On web page. **Price:** Free. **Description:** Covers 3900 accredited post-secondary programs that provide training programs in business, trade, and technical fields, including various small business endeavors. Entries offer school name, address, phone, description of courses, job placement assistance, and requirements for admission. Arrangement is alphabetical.

REFERENCE WORKS

15694 ■ *Minding Your Dog Business: A Practical Guide to Business Success for Dog Professionals*
Pub: Dogwise Publishing
Ed: Veronica Boutelle, Rikke Jorgensen. **Released:** June 1, 2010. **Price:** $19.95. **Description:** Setting up and running a successful dog-related business is an achievement in itself, but the real test is to build success and growth for the long haul.

TRADE PERIODICALS

15695 ■ *Miniature Donkey Talk: The Talk of the Donkey World*
Pub: Pheasant Meadow Farm
URL(s): www.qis.net/~minidonk/mdt.htmwww.web-donkeys.com/index.php. **Ed:** Bonnie Gross. **Released:** Bimonthly **Price:** $40, By mail 1st class; $75, Two years mailed 1st class.

15696 ■ *Your Dog*
Pub: Tufts University
Contact: Linda Ross, Editor-in-Chief
Ed: Gloria Parkinson, Editor. **Released:** Monthly. **Price:** $20, individuals. **Description:** Publishes medi-

cal and behavioral advice and tips on dogs by veterinarians. Recurring features include columns titled My Dog and Chewing It Over.

VIDEOCASSETTES/ AUDIOCASSETTES

15697 ■ *Advanced Training for Your Retriever*
Stoney-Wolf Productions, Inc.
130 West Columbia Ct.
Chaska, MN 55318
Ph: (952)556-0075
Free: 800-237-7583
Fax: (952)361-4217
Co. E-mail: stoneywolf@montana.com
URL: http://www.stoneywolf.com
Released: 1993. **Price:** $19.95. **Description:** Professional dog trainer and hunting guide Mike Mathiot provides continued training for retrievers. In this installment he covers steadying, decoys, blind retrieves, pattern work, cover, and distance. Contains actual hunting footage. **Availability:** VHS.

15698 ■ *Ask Dr. Jim about Dogs*
Tapeworm Video Distributors
25876 The Old Road #141
Stevenson Ranch, CA 91381
Ph: (661)257-4904
Fax: (661)257-4820
Co. E-mail: sales@tapeworm.com
URL: http://www.tapeworm.com
Released: 1994. **Price:** $19.95. **Description:** Veterinarian Jim Humphries discusses crate training puppies and adult dogs, spay and neutering, lyme disease, pet health insurance, overweight pets, and more. **Availability:** VHS.

15699 ■ *Beginning Training for Your Retriever*
Stoney-Wolf Productions, Inc.
130 West Columbia Ct.
Chaska, MN 55318
Ph: (952)556-0075
Free: 800-237-7583
Fax: (952)361-4217
Co. E-mail: stoneywolf@montana.com
URL: http://www.stoneywolf.com
Released: 1993. **Price:** $19.95. **Description:** Mike Mathiot, professional dog trainer and hunting guide, illustrates techniques for training your hunting dog including obedience, voice and whistle commands, and water retrieving. **Availability:** VHS.

15700 ■ *Caring for Your Dog*
CinemaNow
4553 Glencoe Ave., Ste. 200
Marina Del Rey, CA 90292
Co. E-mail: sales@cinemanow.com
URL: http://www.cinemanow.com
Released: 1987. **Price:** $29.95. **Description:** Canine experts offer advice on dealing with dogs, from health care to achieving emotional stability. **Availability:** VHS.

15701 ■ *Cats and Dogs*
PBS Home Video
Catalog Fulfillment Center
Charlotte, NC 28275-1089
Ph: (800)531-4727
Free: 800-645-4PBS
Co. E-mail: info@pbs.org
URL: http://www.pbs.org
Released: 1985. **Description:** This series explores all aspects of human-pet relationships, with tips on pet care, visits to feline and canine clinics, grooming, obedience and nutrition. **Availability:** VHS; 3/4 U.

15702 ■ *Dog Care*
Karol Media
Hanover Industrial Estates
375 Stewart Rd.
Wilkes Barre, PA 18773-7600
Ph: (570)822-8899
Free: 800-526-4773
Co. E-mail: sales@karolmedia.com
URL: http://www.karolmedia.com
Released: 1987. **Price:** $9.95. **Description:** Pet authority Dr. Michael Fox offers this complete guide to dog care, from selecting and training a puppy to grooming and massaging a grown canine. **Availability:** VHS.

15703 ■ *The Mentally Sound Dog*
Tapeworm Video Distributors
25876 The Old Road #141
Stevenson Ranch, CA 91381
Ph: (661)257-4904
Fax: (661)257-4820
Co. E-mail: sales@tapeworm.com
URL: http://www.tapeworm.com
Released: 19??. **Description:** Explains how to shape, train, and change canine behavior. **Availability:** VHS.

15704 ■ *Raising Your Dog with the Monks of New Skete*
PBS Home Video
Catalog Fulfillment Center
Charlotte, NC 28275-1089
Ph: (800)531-4727
Free: 800-645-4PBS
Co. E-mail: info@pbs.org
URL: http://www.pbs.org
Released: 1998. **Price:** $64.95. **Description:** The Monks of New Skete present a unique view of the bond between dogs and humans and how this relationship can be used in the successful training of a puppy to bring out the best sides of both dog and human. Two hours and 53 minutes on three videocassettes. **Availability:** VHS.

15705 ■ *Secret of Training Dogs*
Video Collectibles
PO Box 385
Lewiston, NY 14092-0385
Free: 800-268-3891

Fax: (800)269-8877
Co. E-mail: info@collectablesdirect.com
URL: http://www.collectablesdirect.com
Released: 19??. **Price:** $24.95. **Description:** Video features the top ten fundamentals of dog training proven through solid research. **Availability:** VHS.

15706 ■ *Training Dogs the Barbara Woodhouse Way*
Video Collectibles
PO Box 385
Lewiston, NY 14092-0385
Free: 800-268-3891
Fax: (800)269-8877
Co. E-mail: info@collectablesdirect.com
URL: http://www.collectablesdirect.com
Released: 19??. **Price:** $39.95. **Description:** From the BBC series starring Barbara Woodhouse, practical, step-by-step training procedures for your dog (and you). **Availability:** VHS.

15707 ■ *Training the Family Dog*
CinemaNow
4553 Glencoe Ave., Ste. 200
Marina Del Rey, CA 90292
Co. E-mail: sales@cinemanow.com
URL: http://www.cinemanow.com
Released: 198?. **Price:** $19.99. **Description:** Keep that hound in check with this instructional video. **Availability:** VHS.

FRANCHISES AND BUSINESS OPPORTUNITIES

15708 ■ Bark Busters
PO Box 2558
Garibaldi Highlands, BC, Canada V0N 1T0
Ph: (604)815-0905
Free: 866-418-4584
Fax: (604)815-1808
Co. E-mail: franchise.inquiries@barkbusters.ca
URL: http://www.barkbusters.ca
Description: Dog training company. **No. of Franchise Units:** 30. **Founded:** 1989.. **Franchised:** 1994. **Equity Capital Needed:** $55,000-$65,000. **Franchise Fee:** $33,000. **Training:** Provides 23 days training.

15709 ■ Bark Busters Home Dog Training
Dingo Inc.
250 W Lehow Ave., Ste. B
Englewood, CO 80110
Free: 877-300-2275
Fax: (720)283-2819
URL: http://www.barkbusters.com
Description: In-home dog training. **No. of Franchise Units:** 218. **No. of Company-Owned Units:** 2. **Founded:** 1989.. **Franchised:** 1994. **Equity Capital Needed:** $50,600-$97,100 total investment; $100,000-$250,000 net worth; $10,000-$39,000 cash liquidity. **Franchise Fee:** $20,000-$37,500. **Royalty Fee:** 8%. **Financial Assistance:** Third party financing available. **Training:** Offers a minimum 120 hours at headquarters with ongoing support.

15710 ■ Canine Dimensions
Davidson and Michaels LLC
PO Box 1192
Marlton, NJ 08053
Ph: (813)935-5087
Fax: (813)425-5799
Description: Dog training. **No. of Franchise Units:** 1. **No. of Company-Owned Units:** 1. **Founded:** 2007.. **Franchised:** 2007. **Equity Capital Needed:** $44,050-$50,050. **Franchise Fee:** $22,500. **Training:** Yes.

15711 ■ Ryan's Pet Food
Ryan's Pet Food, Inc.
70 Don Caster Rd.
Thornhille, ON, Canada L3T 1L3
Ph: (905)771-9227
Fax: (905)795-8903
Description: Specialty pet foods and products. **No. of Franchise Units:** 14. **No. of Company-Owned Units:** 24. **Founded:** 1979.. **Franchised:** 1993. **Equity Capital Needed:** $95,000 inclusive; opening inventory, initial fee, leaseholds and working capital. **Franchise Fee:** $25,000. **Training:** Yes.

LIBRARIES

15712 ■ American Kennel Club Library
260 Madison Ave., 4th Fl.
New York, NY 10016
Ph: (212)696-8234
Fax: (212)696-8252
Co. E-mail: jxc@akc.org
URL: http://www.akc.org/about/library/index.cfm
Contact: Barbara Kolk, Librarian
Scope: Dogs - breeds, training, health, literature, art. **Services:** Copying; Library open to the public by appointment. **Founded:** 1934. **Holdings:** 18,000 volumes; VF drawers of clippings; videocassettes; fine art collection; 5 dissertations. **Subscriptions:** 300 journals and other serials.

15713 ■ National Animal Control Association - Research Library
101 N Church St.
Olathe, KS 66061
Ph: (913)768-1319
Fax: (913)768-1378
Co. E-mail: naca@nacanet.org
URL: http://www.nacanet.org
Contact: John Mays, Executive Director
Scope: Animal control, bites and attacks, rabies, euthanasia, humane education, officer training. **Services:** Copying; library open to the public. **Founded:** 1978. **Holdings:** 85 books; 50 bound periodical volumes; 10,000 reports; videocassettes. **Subscriptions:** 15 journals and other serials; 1 newspaper.

15714 ■ U.S. Dept. of Defense - Central Repository for Military Working Dog Records Archives
DOD Dog Center
Lackland AFB, TX 78236-5000
Ph: (512)671-3402
Scope: Military working dogs - training, working assignments, veterinary records.

Pet Shop

START-UP INFORMATION

15715 ■ *101 Best Businesses for Pet Lovers*
Pub: Sourcebooks, Inc.
Contact: Len Vlahos, President
E-mail: dominique@sourcebooks.com
Ed: Nicholas Nigro. **Released:** September 2007.
Price: $18.95. **Description:** Advice for any individual wishing to start a business providing goods and services to pet lovers.

15716 ■ *"Big Bucks In Pet-ty Cash" in Small Business Opportunities (Fall 2008)*
Pub: Entrepreneur Media Inc.
Description: Twenty-five ways in which to start a business that caters to pets by either creating a product or a service that pet owners desire are profiled.

15717 ■ *"Birdcage Optimization" in Pet Product News (Vol. 64, November 2010, No. 11, pp. 54)*
Pub: BowTie Inc.
Description: Manufacturers have been emphasizing size, security, quality construction, stylish design, and quick cleaning when guiding consumers on making birdcage options. Selecting a birdcage is gaining importance considering that cage purchases have become the highest expense associated with owning a bird. Other avian habitat trends are also examined.

15718 ■ *"Capture New Markets" in Pet Product News (Vol. 64, December 2010, No. 12, pp. 12)*
Pub: BowTie Inc.
Ed: Ethan Mizer. **Description:** Flea and tick treatments are among the product categories that can be offered in order to clinch new markets. With the help of manufacturers, pet store retailers are encouraged to educate themselves about these products considering that capturing markets involves variations in customer perceptions. Retailers would then be deemed as resources and sources for these products.

15719 ■ *"Come Together" in Pet Product News (Vol. 64, December 2010, No. 12, pp. 28)*
Pub: BowTie Inc.
Ed: Lizett Bond. **Description:** Pet supply retailers have posted improved sales and improved customer service by bundling their offerings. Bundling pertains to grouping related items such as collars and leashes into a single unit for marketing purposes. Aside from providing convenience and enhanced product information to customers, bundling has facilitated more efficient purchases.

15720 ■ *"Experts Strive to Educate on Proper Pet Diets" in Pet Product News (Vol. 64, November 2010, No. 11, pp. 40)*
Pub: BowTie Inc.
Ed: John Hustace Walker. **Description:** Pet supply manufacturers have been bundling small mammal food and treats with educational sources to help retailers avoid customer misinformation. This action has been motivated by the customer's quest to seek proper nutritional advice for their small mammal pets.

15721 ■ *"Fed May Ban Amphibian Trade" in Pet Product News (Vol. 64, November 2010, No. 11, pp. 13)*
Pub: BowTie Inc.
Description: U.S. Fish and Wildlife Service is seeking public input on a petition submitted by the conservation activist group Defenders of Wildlife. The petition involves possible classification of chytrid fungus-infected amphibians and amphibian eggs as 'injurious wildlife' under the Lacey Act. Interstate trading or importation of injurious wildlife into the U.S. is not allowed.

15722 ■ *"Food as Nature Intended" in Pet Product News (Vol. 64, November 2010, No. 11, pp. 30)*
Pub: BowTie Inc.
Ed: Nikki Moustaki. **Description:** Dog owners have been extending their health-consciousness to their pets by seeking natural products that will address their pets' raw food diet. Retailers response to this trend are outlined.

15723 ■ *"Helping Customers Fight Pet Waste" in Pet Product News (Vol. 64, November 2010, No. 11, pp. 52)*
Pub: BowTie Inc.
Ed: Sandy Robins. **Description:** Pet cleaning products manufacturers have been enjoying high sales figures by paying attention to changing pet ownership trends and environmental awareness. Meanwhile, the inclusion of user-friendly features in these products has also been boosted by the social role of pets and the media attention to pet waste. How manufacturers have been responding to this demand is explored.

15724 ■ *"Making It Work" in Pet Product News (Vol. 64, December 2010, No. 12, pp. S8)*
Pub: BowTie Inc.
Ed: Kerri Chladnicek. **Description:** How focusing on service and flexibility allowed New Jersey-based pet supply store B.C. Woof to achieve success is discussed. B.C. Woof began as a pet-sitting business which eventually concentrated on natural foods. Aside from conducting a do-it-yourself approach in food formulation for customers, B.C. Woof has also been guiding customers on nutrients they need for their pets.

15725 ■ *"Must Work for Food" in Pet Product News (Vol. 64, November 2010, No. 11, pp. 24)*
Pub: BowTie Inc.
Ed: Wendy Bedwell-Wilson. **Description:** Pet supply retailers can benefit from stocking foods and treats that address obesity, which according to the American Veterinary Medical Association, has become the most prevalent nutritional disorder in dogs. With the rise in dog obesity, products like work-for-their food toys have been sought by dog owners.

15726 ■ *"Nestle Acquires Waggin' Train Dog Treat Company" in Pet Product News (Vol. 64, November 2010, No. 11, pp. 7)*
Pub: BowTie Inc.
Description: Vevey, Switzerland-based Nestle has acquired South Carolina-based dog treat firm Waggin' Train LLC from private equity firm VMG Partners

in September 2010. Waggin' Train LLC, which will be operated as a wholly owned subsidiary, is expected to fill a gap in Nestle's dog treat product portfolio.

15727 ■ *"North American Pet Health Insurance Market Poised for Growth" in Pet Product News (Vol. 64, December 2010, No. 12, pp. 4)*
Pub: BowTie Inc.
Ed: David Lummis. **Description:** The pet health insurance market is expected to further grow after posting about $350 million in sales in 2009, a gain of more than $40 million. Pet insurance firms have offered strategies such as product humanization in response to this growth forecast. Meanwhile, pet insurance shoppers have been provided more by insurance firms with wider choices.

15728 ■ *"Online Pet Medication Store Supports Free Vaccinations for Cats" in Internet Wire (August 31, 2010)*
Pub: Comtex
Description: Pethealth Inc., The Petango Store will help to support The Humane Society of Tampa Bay's efforts by offering free feline vaccinations for the cat's entire lifetime that is adopted between September 1, 2010 and February 28, 2010. The cat must be one year or older at time of adoption.

15729 ■ *"Perfecting Customer Services" in Pet Product News (Vol. 64, November 2010, No. 11, pp. 18)*
Pub: BowTie Inc.
Description: Pet supply retailers are encouraged to emphasize customer experience and sales representatives' knowledge of the store's product offerings to foster repeat business. Employee protocols could be implemented to improve customer interaction. Other guidelines on developing a pet supply retail environment that advances repeat business are presented.

15730 ■ *"Pet Food Bank 'Shares the Love" in Pet Product News (Vol. 64, December 2010, No. 12, pp. 6)*
Pub: BowTie Inc.
Description: Winston-Salem, North Carolina-based nonprofit Share the Love Pet Food Bank has donated 60,000 pounds of pet food since its establishment in 2009. It has been linking pet food manufacturers and rescue groups to supply unsold pet food to needy animals. The nonprofit intends to reach out to more animal welfare groups by building more warehouses.

15731 ■ *"Promotions Create a Path to Better Profit" in Pet Product News (Vol. 64, December 2010, No. 12, pp. 1)*
Pub: BowTie Inc.
Ed: Joan Hustace Walker. **Description:** Pet store retailers can boost small mammal sales by launching creative marketing and promotions such as social networking and adoption days.

15732 ■ *"Rest Easy, Retailers" in Pet Product News (Vol. 64, December 2010, No. 12, pp. S1)*
Pub: BowTie Inc.
Ed: Wendy Bedwell-Wilson. **Description:** Pointers on how retailers can market all-natural beds and bed-

ding products for pets are provided. The demand for these pet beds and bedding products has been increasing as customers become aware of the benefits of natural rest and relaxation products.

15733 ■ "Roundtable: Functional Foods and Treats" in Pet Product News (Vol. 64, December 2010, No. 12, pp. S1)

Pub: BowTie Inc.

Description: Executives and business owners from the pet supplies industries deliberate on the role of functional foods in the retail sector. Functional foods pertain to foods with specified health benefits. Insight into marketing functional foods and convincing pet owners to make the transition to these products is examined.

15734 ■ "Smarts Drive Sales" in Pet Product News (Vol. 64, December 2010, No. 12, pp. 1)

Pub: BowTie Inc.

Ed: Karen Shugart. **Description:** Retailers could make smart decisions by deciding how to best attract customers into their stores or resolving whether to nurture in-store or buy herps (reptiles) from suppliers. Paying attention to these smart decisions could help boost customer interest in herps and address customer demands.

15735 ■ "Solutions for the Frustrating Feline" in Pet Product News (Vol. 64, November 2010, No. 11, pp. 46)

Pub: BowTie Inc.

Ed: Lori Luechtefeld. **Description:** Products that can help customers deal with problematic cat behaviors, such as out-of-the-box urination and scratching are described. Information on such products including litter box deodorants and disposable scratchers is provided. Feline territorial behaviors can also be addressed by pheromone products that can calm hyperactive cats.

15736 ■ "Supplements Mix Nutrition With Convenience" in Pet Product News (Vol. 64, November 2010, No. 11, pp. 44)

Pub: BowTie Inc.

Ed: Karen Shugart. **Description:** Pet supply manufacturers have been making supplements and enhanced foods that improve mineral consumption, boost bone density, and sharpen appetite in herps. Customers seem to enjoy the convenience as particular herps demands are being addressed by these offerings. Features of other supplements and enhanced foods for herps are described.

15737 ■ "Sustaining Health" in Pet Product News (Vol. 64, November 2010, No. 11, pp. 28)

Pub: BowTie Inc.

Ed: Angela Pham. **Description:** How pet supply retailers have responded to dog owners' interest in health supplements and their ingredients is discussed. Dog owners are showing interest in the ingredients inside the supplements and are reading labels. Retailers must now prove the beneficial effects of these ingredients in order to make the sale.

15738 ■ "Tapping the 'Well' in Wellness" in Pet Product News (Vol. 64, November 2010, No. 11, pp. 1)

Pub: BowTie Inc.

Ed: Wendy-Bedwell Wilson. **Description:** Healthy food and treats are among the leading wellness products being sought by customers from specialty retailers to keep their pets healthy. With this demand for pet wellness products, retailers suggest making sure that staff know key ingredients to emphasize to customers. Other insights into this trend and ways to engage customers are discussed.

15739 ■ "Teachable Moments: Worth Every Penny" in Pet Product News (Vol. 64, December 2010, No. 12, pp. 34)

Pub: BowTie Inc.

Ed: Cheryl Reeves. **Description:** Pet bird retailers can attain both outreach to customers and enhanced profitability by staging educational events such as the annual Parrot Palooza event of Burlington, New Jersey-based Bird Paradise. Aside from attracting a global audience, Parrot Palooza features seminars, workshops, classes, and bird-related contests.

15740 ■ "To Be Seen Is to Be Successful" in Pet Product News (Vol. 64, December 2010, No. 12, pp. 12)

Pub: BowTie Inc.

Ed: David Arvin. **Description:** Guidelines on how pet business retailers can boost customer visibility are described considering that complacency could hamper retailers' efforts to effectively market their businesses. To enhance customer base and stand out from competing businesses, being different, strategic, creative, and differentiated is emphasized.

15741 ■ "Tradeshow Attendance Incentives Add Up" in Pet Product News (Vol. 64, December 2010, No. 12, pp. 14)

Pub: BowTie Inc.

Ed: Mark E. Battersby. **Description:** Pointers on how pet specialty retailers can claim business travel tax and income tax deductions for expenses paid or incurred in participation at tradeshows, conventions, and meetings are presented. Incentives in form of these deductions could allow pet specialty retailers to gain business benefits, aside from the education and enjoyment involved with the travel.

15742 ■ "Young Adult, Childless May Help Fuel Post-Recession Rebound" in Pet Product News (Vol. 64, November 2010, No. 11, pp. 4)

Pub: BowTie Inc.

Description: Pet industry retailers and marketers are encouraged to tap into the young adult and childless couple sectors to boost consumer traffic and sales to pre-recession levels. Among young adult owners, pet ownership increased from 40 percent in 2003 to 49 percent in 2009. Meanwhile, the childless couple sector represented 63 percent of all dog/cat owners in 2009.

ASSOCIATIONS AND OTHER ORGANIZATIONS

15743 ■ American Pet Products Association (APPA)

255 Glenville Rd.
Greenwich, CT 06831
Ph: (203)532-0000
Free: 800-452-1225
Fax: (203)532-0551
Co. E-mail: memberservices@americanpetproducts.
org
URL: http://www.americanpetproducts.org/default.asp
Contact: Roger Morgan, Chairman

Description: U.S. Manufacturers and importers of pet products. Provides public relations program to promote pet ownership and pet care. Sponsors the association's annual National Pet Products Trade Show; publishes the National Pet Owner's Survey, the association's research study in the pet industry. **Founded:** 1958. **Awards:** APPMA Jules Schwimmer Scholarship Program (Annual); New Product and Point-of-Purchase Award (Annual); New Product Showcase Awards.

15744 ■ Pet Food Institute (PFI)

2025 M St. NW, Ste. 800
Washington, DC 20036-2422
Ph: (202)367-1120
Fax: (202)367-2120
Co. E-mail: info@petfoodinstitute.org
URL: http://www.petfoodinstitute.org
Contact: Duane Ekedahl, President

Description: Represents the manufacturers of 97% of the commercial pet food produced in the United States. Serves as the voice of the industry before legislative and regulatory bodies at both the federal and state levels. **Founded:** 1958. **Educational Activities:** Suppliers Mart (Annual).

15745 ■ Pet Industry Distributors Association (PIDA)

2105 Laurel Bush Rd., Ste. 200
Bel Air, MD 21015-5200
Ph: (443)640-1060

Fax: (443)640-1031
Co. E-mail: pida@kingmgmt.org
URL: http://www.pida.org
Contact: Fred Schober, Chairman

Description: Strives to enhance the well-being of the pet product wholesaler-distributor. Promotes partnerships between suppliers and customers. Fosters the human-companion animal bond. **Founded:** 1968. **Publications:** PIDA Bulletin (Bimonthly); Roster (Annual). **Educational Activities:** Pet Industry Distributors Association Conference (Annual); Global Pet Expo (Annual). **Awards:** Lifetime Achievement Award (Periodic); Performance Benchmarking Awards Program (Annual).

15746 ■ Pet Industry Joint Advisory Council (PIJAC)

1140 19th St. NW, Ste. 300
Washington, DC 20036
Ph: (202)452-1525
Free: 800-553-7387
Fax: (202)452-1516
Co. E-mail: info@pijac.org
URL: http://www.pijac.org
Contact: Michael F. Canning, Jr., President

Description: Pet retailers, manufacturers and distributors; companion animal suppliers; pet industry trade associations. Works to monitor federal and state regulations and legislation affecting the industry. Sponsors research projects and industry-related educational programs. **Founded:** 1971. **Publications:** Our Pets, Our Health; PetLetter (Periodic); Tips on Travel With Your Pets.

15747 ■ World Pet Association (WPA)

135 W Lemon Ave.
Monrovia, CA 91016-2809
Ph: (626)447-2222
Free: 800-999-7295
Fax: (626)447-8350
Co. E-mail: info@wpamail.org
URL: http://www.worldpetassociation.org/files/homepage/index.html
Contact: Ruth Jeffers, Chairman of the Board

Description: Manufacturers, retailers and distributors of pet food and services and of avian, aquarium and companion animal care products, equipment and services. Seeks to advance the economic interests of members; promotes responsible pet ownership. Conducts trade shows, certificate training courses and seminars for pet shop retailers, grooming establishments and veterinary clinics. **Founded:** 1951. **Educational Activities:** Super Zoo (Annual).

REFERENCE WORKS

15748 ■ "AAAFCO Unveils Pet Food Resource" in Feedstuffs (Vol. 83, August 29, 2011, No. 35, pp. 15)

Pub: Miller Publishing Company

Description: The Association of American Feed Control Officials has launched a Website called The Business of Pet Food, which will address frequently asked questions about U.S. regulatory requirements for pet food. The site serves as an initial reference for anyone wishing to start a pet food business because it provides information and guidance.

15749 ■ "Add Aquatics to Boost Business" in Pet Product News (Vol. 64, December 2010, No. 12, pp. 20)

Pub: BowTie Inc.

Ed: David Lass. **Description:** Pet stores are encouraged to add aquatics departments to increase profitability through repeat sales. This goal can be realized by sourcing, displaying, and maintaining high quality live fish. Other tips regarding the challenges associated with setting up an aquatics department are presented.

15750 ■ "Aquatic Medications Engender Good Health" in Pet Product News (Vol. 64, November 2010, No. 11, pp. 47)

Pub: BowTie Inc.

Ed: Madelaine Heleine. **Description:** Pet supply manufacturers and retailers have been exerting consumer education and preparedness efforts to help aquarium hobbyists in tackling ornamental fish disease problems. Aquarium hobbyists have been also assisted in choosing products that facilitate aquarium maintenance before disease attacks their pet fish.

15751 ■ "Best In Show" in Pet Product News (Vol. 64, November 2010, No. 11, pp. 20)
Pub: BowTie Inc.

Ed: Lizett Bond. **Description:** Cherrybrook Premium Pet Supplies offers an expanded array of quality holistic products and is staffed by people who possess wide knowledge of these products. Aside from receiving the Outstanding Holistic Approach award, Cherrybrook has opened three stores in New Jersey. How a holistic approach to service kept customers coming back is discussed.

15752 ■ "Bits 'n' Pieces: Shelter Gives Out Pet Food to Keep Animals At Home" in Columbian (January 19, 2009)
Pub: The Columbian

Ed: Elisa Williams. **Description:** Lend a Paw program gives surplus food to pet owners in need; since August 2008 they distributed over 7,000 pounds of dry and wet food to shelters and pet owners.

15753 ■ "Breaking the Mold" in Entrepreneur (Vol. 37, September 2009, No. 9, pp. 87)
Pub: Entrepreneur Media, Inc.

Ed: Tracy Stapp. **Description:** Profiles of top franchise businesses in the United States are presented. Hey Buddy! Pet Supply Vending Co. offers pet supply vending machines. Home Health Mates, on the other hand, provides professional medical care at home.

15754 ■ "Canine Cuisine: Tips for a Healthful Diet" in Seattle Times (September 13, 2008, pp. D9)
Pub: Associated Press

Description: The American Kennel Club recommends feeding dogs food with balanced essential nutrients, including proteins, carbohydrates, fats, vitamins, minerals, and water; types of food, feeding practices and what not to feed a dog is discussed.

15755 ■ "Elanco Challenges Bayer's Advantage, K9 Advantix Ad Claims" in Pet Product News (Vol. 64, November 2010, No. 11, pp. 11)
Pub: BowTie Inc.

Description: Elanco Animal Health has disputed Bayer Animal Health's print and Web advertising claims involving its flea, tick, and mosquito control products Advantage and K9 Advantix. The National Advertising Division of the Council of Better Business Bureaus recommended the discontinuation of ads, while Bayer Animal Health reiterated its commitment to self-regulation.

15756 ■ "Foods for Thought" in Pet Product News (Vol. 64, December 2010, No. 12, pp. 16)
Pub: BowTie Inc.

Ed: Maddy Heleine. **Description:** Manufacturers have been focused at developing species-specific fish foods due to consumer tendency to assess the benefits of the food they feed their fish. As retailers stock species-specific fish foods, manufacturers have provided in-store items and strategies to assist in efficiently selling these food products. Trends in fish food packaging and ingredients are also discussed.

15757 ■ "Fromm Family Foods Converts Old Feed Mill Into Factory for Gourmet Pet Food" in Wisconsin State Journal (August 3, 2011)
Pub: Capital Newspapers

Ed: Barry Adams. **Description:** Fromm Family Foods, a gourmet cat and dog food company spent $10 million to convert an old feed mill into a pet food manufacturing facility. The owner forecasts doubling or tripling its production of 600 tons of feed per week in about five years.

15758 ■ "Give This Pooch a Home" in Advertising Age (Vol. 78, August 13, 2007, No. 32, pp. 4)
Pub: Crain Communications, Inc.

Ed: Kimberly D. Williams. **Description:** Overview of FlexPetz, a pet-sharing program that targets customers that live in metropolitan areas and travel frequently, who want to have a dog but cannot care for one on a full time basis.

15759 ■ "High Growth Reported for the Natural Supermarket Pet Department Close-Up" in Canadian Corporate News (October 20, 2008)
Pub: Comtex News Network Inc.

Description: Leading natural supermarket chains have been outperforming mainstream grocers by carrying natural and organic pet products. Statistical data included.

15760 ■ "Howl-o-ween" in Decatur Daily (October 25, 2011)
Pub: Decatur Daily

Ed: Catherine Godbey. **Description:** Animal Friends Humane Society provides free pet food and cat litter to Meals on Wheels clients.

15761 ■ "Importers Share Safety Liability" in Feedstuffs (Vol. 80, January 21, 2008, No. 3, pp. 19)
Pub: Miller Publishing Company, Inc.

Description: Pet food and toys containing lead paint are among products from China being recalled due to safety concerns. American Society for Quality's list of measures that outsourcing companies can take to help ensure safer products being imported to the U.S.

15762 ■ "In the Wake of Pet-Food Crisis, Iams Sales Plummet Nearly 17 Percent" in Advertising Age (Vol. 78, May 14, 2007, No. 18, pp. 3)
Pub: Crain Communications, Inc.

Ed: Jack Neff. **Description:** Although the massive U.S. pet-food recall impacted more than 100 brands, Procter & Gamble Co.'s Iams lost more sales and market share than any other industry player. According to Information Resources Inc. data, the brand's sales dropped 16.5 percent in the eight-week period ended April 22. Many analysts feel that the company could have handled the crisis in a better manner.

15763 ■ "Keeping Customers Satisfied" in Pet Product News (Vol. 64, December 2010, No. 12, pp. 10)
Pub: BowTie Inc.

Ed: Devon McPhee. **Description:** Windsor, California-based Debbie's Pet Boutique, recipient of Pet Product News International's Outstanding Customer Service Award, has been dedicated to combining topnotch grooming services with a robust retail selection. These features might gain return customers for Debbie's Pet Boutique.

15764 ■ "Marketer Bets Big on U.S.'s Growing Canine Obsession" in Advertising Age (Vol. 79, April 14, 2008, No. 15, pp. 14)
Pub: Crain Communications, Inc.

Ed: Emily Bryson York. **Description:** Overview of FreshPet, a New Jersey company that began marketing two brands of refrigerated dog food-Deli Fresh and FreshPet Select-which are made from fresh ingredients such as beef, rice and carrots. The company projects continued success due to the amount of money consumers spend on their pets as well as fears derived from the 2007 recalls that inspired consumers to look for smaller, independent manufacturers that are less likely to source ingredients from China.

15765 ■ "Melamine Analytical Methods Released" in Feedstuffs (Vol. 80, October 6, 2008, No. 41, pp. 2)
Pub: Miller Publishing Company

Description: Romer Labs has released new validations for its AgraQuant Melamine enzyme-linked immunosorbent assay. The test kit screens for melamine in feed and diary products, including pet foods, milk and milk powder. Melamine by itself is nontoxic in low doses, but when combined with cyanuric acid it can cause fatal kidney stones. The Chinese dairy industry is in the midst of a huge melamine crisis; melamine-contaminated dairy and food products from China have been found in more than 20 countries.

15766 ■ "Menu Foods Seeks Answers in Death of Ten Pets" in Globe & Mail (March 19,

2007, pp. B2)
Pub: CTVglobemedia Publishing Inc.

Ed: Thomas M. Burton. **Description:** The failure of Menu Foods Inc. to ascertain the cause of ten deaths of house pets, which were fed its food products, prompting the government to recall the products from the market, is discussed.

15767 ■ Minding Your Dog Business: A Practical Guide to Business Success for Dog Professionals
Pub: Dogwise Publishing

Ed: Veronica Boutelle, Rikke Jorgensen. **Released:** June 1, 2010. **Price:** $19.95. **Description:** Setting up and running a successful dog-related business is an achievement in itself, but the real test is to build success and growth for the long haul.

15768 ■ "New Recipes Added to IAMS Naturals Pet Food Line" in MMR (Vol. 28, August 1, 2011, No. 11, pp. 17)
Pub: Racher Press Inc.

Description: Procter & Gamble Company's IAMS brand has created a new pet food line called IAMS Naturals for pet owners wishing to feed their pets natural, wholesome food. IAMS Sensitive Naturals has ocean fish and its first ingredient for dogs with sensitivities. IAMS Simple & Natural features chicken with no fillers.

15769 ■ "Options Abound in Winter Wares" in Pet Product News (Vol. 64, November 2010, No. 11, pp. 1)
Pub: BowTie Inc.

Ed: Maggie M. Shein. **Description:** Pet supply manufacturers emphasize creating top-notch construction and functional design in creating winter clothing for pets. Meanwhile, retailers and pet owners seek human-inspired style, quality, and versatility for pets' winter clothing. How retailers generate successful sales of pets' winter clothing outside of traditional brand marketing is also examined.

15770 ■ "Organic Dog Treats" in Veterinary Economics (Vol. 49, November 2008, No. 11, pp. 52)
Pub: Advanstar Communications Inc.

Contact: Mr. Joseph Loggia, Chief Executive Officer
E-mail: jloggia@advanstar.com

Description: Wet Noses all-natural dog treats come in six flavors: dogranola, pumpkin, sweet potato curry, apples and carrots, cheddar, and peanut butter and molasses. The treats are made without animal by-products, added chemicals, preservatives, corn, soy or wheat.

15771 ■ "P&G's Iams Finds Itself in a Pet-Food Dogfight" in Advertising Age (Vol. 78, March 5, 2007, No. 10, pp. 6)
Pub: Crain Communications, Inc.

Ed: Jack Neff. **Description:** Proctor & Gamble Co.'s Iams has been slow to embrace the trend toward foods for pets that appear fit for human consumption. Competitors such as Nestle Purina have made big gains with its colorful premium Beneful brand and dry nuggets that look like chunks of vegetables and meat. Statistical data included.

15772 ■ "Paws That Refresh" in Prepared Foods (Vol. 177, August 2008, No. 8, pp. 35)
Pub: BNP Media

Description: Wellness Pet Food is offering enhanced dog foods to meet the dietary needs of both large and small dots.

15773 ■ Pet Age--Sourcebook Issue
Pub: H.H. Backer Associates Inc.

Contact: Patty Backer, President
E-mail: pbacker@hhbacker.com

URL(s): www.petage.com. **Released:** Annual; December; latest edition 2007. **Publication includes:** Lists of manufacturers and distributors of pet food, equipment, and accessories; companion animal suppliers, including livestock wholesalers and brokers; manufacturers' representatives; and trade associations. **Entries include:** For manufacturers--Company name, address, phone, fax, e-mail, URL, name of principal executive, date established, brokers, and wholesalers--Company name, address, phone, fax, e-mail, URL, name of principal executive, date established, principal activity, products by type, modes of sale or distribution, size of sales staff, geographical area served. For associations--Organization name, address, phone, chief officers, purposes and activities, annual meeting date, dues, types of membership, number of members, publications. **Arrangement:** Distributors are geographical; others are alphabetical within separate sections. **Indexes:** Brand name, livestock, product.

15774 ■ "Pet-Food Crisis a Boon to Organic Players" in Advertising Age (Vol. 78, April 9, 2007, No. 15, pp. 3)
Pub: Crain Communications, Inc.

Ed: Jack Neff. **Description:** In the wake of the pet-food recall crisis, the natural-and-organic segment of the market is gaining recognition and sales; one such manufacturer, Blue Buffalo, has not only seen huge sale increases but also has witnessed a 50-60 percent increase in traffic to the brand's website which has led to the decision to move up the timetable for the brand's first national ad campaign.

15775 ■ "Pet-Food Industry Too Slow" in Advertising Age (Vol. 78, March 26, 2007, No. 13, pp. 29)
Pub: Crain Communications, Inc.

Description: Many crisis-communications experts believe that the pet-food industry mishandled the problem by waiting almost a month to recall the 60 million 'wet-food' products after numerous consumer complaints. Experts site that the first 24 to 49 hours are the most important in dealing with a crisis of this nature.

15776 ■ "Pet Treats Recalled in Widening Salmonella Scare" in Seattle Times (January 2009, pp. A2)
Pub: Associated Press

Ed: Ricardo Alonso-Zaldivar. **Description:** PetSmart recalled seven varieties of its Grreat Choice dog biscuits due to contaminated dog biscuits. Dogs rarely get salmonella illness, but owners can pick up the bacteria when feeding pets.

15777 ■ "PetSmart: A Barking Buy" in Barron's (Vol. 89, July 6, 2009, No. 27, pp. 15)
Pub: Dow Jones & Co., Inc.

Ed: Jay Palmer. **Description:** Shares of PetSmart could climb from $21.70 to about $28 due to the company's improving profits, cash flow, and product portfolio. The company's shares are trading at 14 times projected 2010 earnings of $1.64 a share.

15778 ■ "The Progressive Pet Shop: Showcasing Strays" in Animals' Agenda (March-April 1993, pp. 34)
Pub: Animal Rights Network Inc.

Ed: Athena Rhiannon Schaffer. **Description:** Brothers Pets stopped selling cats and dogs in order to donate kennel space to the Aspen Hill, Maryland animal shelter. The events leading to this small business decision and its success are presented.

15779 ■ "Secaucus-Based Freshpet is Barking Up the Right Tree" in Record (September 8, 2011)
Pub: North Jersey Media Group

Ed: Rebecca Olles. **Description:** Freshpet produces a variety of nutritious, refrigerated pet foods and treats for cats and dogs. The firm introduced five new recipes and treats to its grain-free line called Vital line. The Vital line mimics the ancestral diets of dogs and cats.

15780 ■ "Shipping 2.0" in Entrepreneur (Vol. 36, April 2008, No. 4, pp. 54)
Pub: Entrepreneur Media, Inc.

Ed: Heather Clancy. **Description:** Doggypads.com contacted with Web 2.0 service provider Shipwire to handle its warehouse concerns. The service works by paying a rent to Shipwire and they will store the client's items. The client's customers can continue to order from the client's website and Shipwire will take care of delivery. Doggypads was able to save up on costs by using Shipwire.

15781 ■ "To Catch Up, Colgate May Ratchet Up Its Ad Spending" in Advertising Age (Vol. 81, December 6, 2010, No. 43, pp. 1)
Pub: Crain Communications, Inc.

Ed: Jack Neff. **Description:** Colgate-Palmolive Company has been losing market share in the categories of toothpaste, deodorant, body wash, dish soap and pet food.

15782 ■ "Want to Unleash the Next Best Seller? Think Like a Dog" in Advertising Age (Vol. 79, March 10, 2008, No. 10, pp. 14)
Pub: Crain Communications, Inc.

Ed: Lenore Skenazy. **Description:** Cott Corp. has launched a new product, fortified water for pets, in flavors ranging from peanut butter to parsley to spearmint.

15783 ■ "Wegmans Uses Database for Recall" in Supermarket News (Vol. 56, September 22, 2008, No. 38)
Pub: Penton Business Media, Inc.

Ed: Carol Angrisani. **Description:** Wegmans used data obtained through its loyalty card that, in turn, sent automated telephone calls to every customer who had purchased tainted pet food when Mars Petcare recalled dog food products.

15784 ■ "What's Next, Pup Tents in Bryant Park?" in Advertising Age (Vol. 78, January 29, 2007, No. 5, pp. 4)
Pub: Crain Communications, Inc.

Ed: Stephanie Thompson. **Description:** Designers such as Ralph Lauren, Juicy Couture, Burberry and Kiehl's have been expanding their businesses with new clothing lines for pets. Packaged Facts, a division of MarketResearch.com, predicts that pet expenditures will continue to grow in the years to come.

STATISTICAL SOURCES

15785 ■ The Pet Food Market
Pub: Rector Press, Ltd.
Contact: Lewis Sckolnick, President
Released: 2009. **Price:** Contact Rector Press.

15786 ■ The U.S. Market for Pet Supplies and Pet Care Products, 5th Edition
Pub: MarketResearch.com

Released: 2003. **Price:** $2250.00. **Description:** by Packaged Facts. Analyzes the dynamics of the pet supplies and accessories market. Covers a wide range of pets, but concentrates on dogs, cats, birds, and fish. Pinpoints the major factors impacting market growth. Includes sales projections to 1996; leading marketers; the competitive situation; new-product development; distribution channels, including distributors and rack jobbers; the retail level, including independent pet shops, supermarkets, drug chains, military exchanges, veterinarian offices, discount stores, and warehouse clubs; and consumer usage, including data on pet ownership.

TRADE PERIODICALS

15787 ■ Dog World: Active Dogs, Active People
Pub: Bowtie, Inc. Fancy Publications Pet Product News Magazine

URL(s): www.dogchannel.com/dog-magazines/dog-world/default.aspx. **Ed:** Maureen Kochan. **Released:** Monthly **Price:** $15, Individuals; $27, Other countries.

15788 ■ PIDA Bulletin
Pub: Pet Industry Distributors Association

Ed: Mary Ann O'Brian, Editor. **Released:** Bimonthly. **Price:** Included in membership. **Description:** Deals with the pet industry, including companion animals, pet products manufacturers, assistance dogs, and animal welfare. Recurring features include news of research, a calendar of events, reports of meetings, news of educational opportunities, and notices of publications available.

15789 ■ Reptiles
Pub: Bowtie, Inc. Fancy Publications Pet Product News Magazine
URL(s): www.reptilechannel.com/rmrc_portal.aspx.
Ed: Russ Case. **Released:** Monthly **Price:** $14.99, Individuals print; $26.99, Other countries.

VIDEOCASSETTES/ AUDIOCASSETTES

15790 ■ Ask Dr. Jim about Cats
Tapeworm Video Distributors
25876 The Old Road #141
Stevenson Ranch, CA 91381
Ph: (661)257-4904
Fax: (661)257-4820
Co. E-mail: sales@tapeworm.com
URL: http://www.tapeworm.com
Released: 1994. **Price:** $19.95. **Description:** Veterinarian Jim Humphries discusses how to chose a cat, nutrition and obesity, vaccinations, behavior problems, human allergies, and more. **Availability:** VHS.

15791 ■ Ask Dr. Jim about Dogs
Tapeworm Video Distributors
25876 The Old Road #141
Stevenson Ranch, CA 91381
Ph: (661)257-4904
Fax: (661)257-4820
Co. E-mail: sales@tapeworm.com
URL: http://www.tapeworm.com
Released: 1994. **Price:** $19.95. **Description:** Veterinarian Jim Humphries discusses crate training puppies and adult dogs, spay and neutering, lyme disease, pet health insurance, overweight pets, and more. **Availability:** VHS.

15792 ■ Escape
Tapeworm Video Distributors
25876 The Old Road #141
Stevenson Ranch, CA 91381
Ph: (661)257-4904
Fax: (661)257-4820
Co. E-mail: sales@tapeworm.com
URL: http://www.tapeworm.com
Released: 1996. **Price:** $19.95. **Description:** Explains basic camping methods such as packing for the trip, finding the perfect campsite, building a fire, safeguarding food, and more. **Availability:** VHS.

15793 ■ Freshwater Aquarium Basics
Karol Media
Hanover Industrial Estates
375 Stewart Rd.
Wilkes Barre, PA 18773-7600
Ph: (570)822-8899
Free: 800-526-4773
Co. E-mail: sales@karolmedia.com
URL: http://www.karolmedia.com
Released: 1997. **Price:** $14.95. **Description:** Provides instruction on the care and maintenance of aquariums. **Availability:** VHS.

15794 ■ Raising Your Dog with the Monks of New Skete
PBS Home Video
Catalog Fulfillment Center
Charlotte, NC 28275-1089
Ph: (800)531-4727
Free: 800-645-4PBS
Co. E-mail: info@pbs.org
URL: http://www.pbs.org
Released: 1998. **Price:** $64.95. **Description:** The Monks of New Skete present a unique view of the bond between dogs and humans and how this relationship can be used in the successful training of a puppy to bring out the best sides of both dog and human. Two hours and 53 minutes on three videocassettes. **Availability:** VHS.

15795 ■ Show off Your Dog-Grooming Basics
Tapeworm Video Distributors
25876 The Old Road #141
Stevenson Ranch, CA 91381
Ph: (661)257-4904

Fax: (661)257-4820
Co. E-mail: sales@tapeworm.com
URL: http://www.tapeworm.com
Released: 1997. **Price:** $19.95. **Description:** Breeder/exhibitor Ena Lane demonstrates grooming techniques such as proper brushing methods, bathing, blow drying, ironing, trimming, and the top knot. **Availability:** VHS.

15796 ■ *Understanding Cats*
PBS Home Video
Catalog Fulfillment Center
Charlotte, NC 28275-1089
Ph: (800)531-4727
Free: 800-645-4PBS
Co. E-mail: info@pbs.org
URL: http://www.pbs.org
Released: 1998. **Price:** $19.98. **Description:** Cat expert Roger Tabor examines why cats behave the way they do. Covers both understanding and caring for cats. **Availability:** VHS.

TRADE SHOWS AND CONVENTIONS

15797 ■ Pet Industry Christmas Trade Show
H.H. Backer Associates Inc.
18 S. Michigan Ave., No. 1100
Chicago, IL 60603
Ph: (312)578-1818
Fax: (312)578-1819
Co. E-mail: hhbacker@hhbacker.com
URL: http://www.hhbacker.com
Contact: Patty Backer, President
E-mail: pbacker@hhbacker.com
URL(s): www.hhbacker.com/ChristmasTradeshow. asp. **Price:** $10, Pre-registered onsite. **Frequency:** Annual. **Audience:** Pet store owners, managers, gift stores. **Principal Exhibits:** Pet supplies, gift products, lawn and garden products. **Telecommunication Services:** hhbacker@hhbacker.com.

15798 ■ Super Zoo
World Wide Pet Industry Association, Inc.
135 W. Lemon Ave.
Monrovia, CA 91016
Ph: (626)447-2222
Free: 800-999-7295
Fax: (626)447-8350
Co. E-mail: info@wwpsa.com
URL: http://www.wwpsa.com
Contact: Ruth Jeffers, Chairman
URL(s): www.superzoo.org/. **Frequency:** Annual. **Audience:** Pet retailers, grooming shops, kennels, and veterinary clinic owners and other trade professionals. **Principal Exhibits:** Pet care foods, equipment, products and services. **Dates and Locations:** , Convention Center.

FRANCHISES AND BUSINESS OPPORTUNITIES

15799 ■ Global Pet Foods
Franchise Bancorp, Inc.
294 Walker Dr., Ste. 2
Brampton, ON, Canada L6T 4Z2

Ph: (905)790-9023
Free: 866-463-4124
Co. E-mail: franchises@franchisebancorp.com
URL: http://www.globalpetfoods.com
Description: Pet food store specializing in natural and wholesome pet foods with a full range of pet care accessories. We offer unprecedented support to all of our franchise owners while encouraging them to personalize their business for their market. **No. of Franchise Units:** 150. **No. of Company-Owned Units:** 3. **Founded:** 1976.. **Franchised:** 1976. **Equity Capital Needed:** $160,000-$220,000. **Franchise Fee:** $30,000. **Training:** Yes.

15800 ■ Multi-Menu
1700 boul. St-Elzear W, Ste. 105
Laval, QC, Canada H7L 3N2
Ph: (450)682-5056
Free: 877-462-0056
Fax: (450)682-5054
Co. E-mail: communication@multimenue.ca
URL: http://www.multimenu.ca/franchise.
    asp?lang=en
Description: Pet food and accessories franchise and free home delivery of exclusive products. **No. of Franchise Units:** 130. **Founded:** 1996.. **Franchised:** 1997. **Equity Capital Needed:** Up to $14,000 start-up capital required; $12,000 investment required. **Franchise Fee:** $7,000. **Training:** Ongoing support and training.

15801 ■ Pet Supplies 'Plus'
22710 Haggerty Rd.
Farmington Hills, MI 48335
Ph: (248)374-1900
Fax: (248)374-7900
Description: Discount pet food and supplies. **No. of Franchise Units:** 164. **No. of Company-Owned Units:** 94. **Founded:** 1988.. **Franchised:** 1990. **Equity Capital Needed:** $623,300-$1,401,000. **Franchise Fee:** $40,000. **Royalty Fee:** $3,000 /month. **Training:** Provides 4 weeks training at headquarters.

15802 ■ Petland
Petland, Inc.
250 Riverside St.
Chillicothe, OH 45601
Ph: (800)221-5935
Fax: (740)775-2575
Co. E-mail: franchise@petland.com
URL: http://www.petland.com
Description: Retailing of pets for hobbies and ownership. **No. of Franchise Units:** 194. **No. of Company-Owned Units:** 5. **Founded:** 1967.. **Franchised:** 1971. **Equity Capital Needed:** $95,000 liquid; $200,000 net worth. **Franchise Fee:** $30,000. **Training:** 5 weeks of training, including 1 week of onsite training. Training comprised of classroom, hands-on in corporate training store, 1 week in new store prior to opening and 1 week of post-opening training. Video and audio training tapes and comprehensive operating manuals Bi-annual franchise meetings, monthly marketing guides.

15803 ■ Pets Are Inn
Pets Are Inn, Inc.
5100 Edina Industrial Blvd., Ste. 208
Minneapolis, MN 55439

Ph: (952)944-8298
Free: 866-343-0086
Description: Pet boarding service without kennels or cages. **No. of Franchise Units:** 19. **Founded:** 1982. **Franchised:** 1986. **Equity Capital Needed:** $49,950-$75,150. **Franchise Fee:** $35,000. **Royalty Fee:** 5-10%. **Training:** Provides 5 days at headquarters, 1 day at franchisee's location, weekly, monthly & quarterly "checkups" at owner's location.

15804 ■ Ruffin's Pet Centres Inc.
109 Industrial Ct.
Dunnville, ON, Canada N1A 2X5
Ph: (905)774-7079
Fax: (905)774-1096
Co. E-mail: franchise@ruffinspet.com
URL: http://www.ruffinspet.com
Description: Offers a combination of a traditional pet shop with the convenience of a pet food store. **No. of Franchise Units:** 10. **No. of Company-Owned Units:** 1. **Founded:** 1981.. **Franchised:** 1987. **Equity Capital Needed:** $85,000-$125,000; $40,000 start-up capital required. **Franchise Fee:** $20,000. **Training:** As required.

15805 ■ Ryan's Pet Food
Ryan's Pet Food, Inc.
70 Don Caster Rd.
Thornhill, ON, Canada L3T 1L3
Ph: (905)771-9227
Fax: (905)795-8903
Description: Specialty pet foods and products. **No. of Franchise Units:** 14. **No. of Company-Owned Units:** 24. **Founded:** 1979.. **Franchised:** 1993. **Equity Capital Needed:** $95,000 inclusive; opening inventory, initial fee, leaseholds and working capital. **Franchise Fee:** $25,000. **Training:** Yes.

15806 ■ Wild Bird Center
Wild Bird Centers of America, Inc.
7370 MacArthur Blvd.
Glen Echo, MD 20812
Ph: (301)229-9585
Free: 800-WIL-BIRD
Fax: (301)320-6154
Description: Franchises "one-stop" bird seed and supply stores. **No. of Franchise Units:** 50. **Founded:** 1985.. **Franchised:** 1990. **Equity Capital Needed:** $129,125-$198,350. **Franchise Fee:** 5.5% of gross sales. **Training:** Yes.

15807 ■ Wild Birds Unlimited Inc.
11711 N College Ave., Ste. 146
Carmel, IN 46032-5601
Ph: (888)730-7108
Free: 888-302-2473
Fax: (317)208-4050
Co. E-mail: webmaster@wbu.com
URL: http://www.wbu.com
Contact: Jim Carpenter, President
Description: Retail outlets for birdseed, bird feeders and gift items. **No. of Franchise Units:** 275. **Founded:** 1981. **Franchised:** 1983. **Equity Capital Needed:** $25,000-$35,000 cash; $93,121-$147,936 total investment. **Franchise Fee:** $18,000. **Training:** Training available 6 days at headquarters, 2 days at franchisee's location, 5 days at annual meeting and ongoing support.

START-UP INFORMATION

15808 ■ *101 Best Businesses for Pet Lovers*
Pub: Sourcebooks, Inc.
Contact: Len Vlahos, President
E-mail: dominique@sourcebooks.com
Ed: Nicholas Nigro. **Released:** September 2007.
Price: $18.95. **Description:** Advice for any individual wishing to start a business providing goods and services to pet lovers.

15809 ■ *Pet Care Business*
Pub: Globe Pequot Press
Ed: Kathy Salzberg. **Released:** March 2006. **Price:** $18.95. **Description:** Guide for starting and running a pet care business such as professional groomer, dog walker, pet sitter, or obedience training; issues regarding zoning, insurance, and health are discussed.

15810 ■ *"Pet Project Pays Off" in Small Business Opportunities (March 2011)*
Pub: Harris Publications Inc.
Ed: Vicki Gerson. **Description:** Pet sitting goes big time, reporting $40 million annually for Camp Bow Wow. Pet-oriented businesses are recession-proof because of Americans love for pampering their canines.

ASSOCIATIONS AND OTHER ORGANIZATIONS

15811 ■ National Association of Professional Pet Sitters (NAPPS)
15000 Commerce Pkwy., Ste. C
Mount Laurel, NJ 08054
Ph: (856)439-0324
Fax: (856)439-0525
Co. E-mail: napps@petsitters.org
URL: http://www.petsitters.org
Contact: John D'Ariano, President
Description: Owners or employees of pet-sitting services; professionals or businesses in related fields. Promotes professional and ethical standards in pet sitting and fosters cooperation among members of the pet-care industry. Serves as a network for the exchange of ideas and information on pet sitting and current industry practices. Disseminates information educating the pet-owning public on the advantages of leaving pets in a home environment and how to choose a reliable sitter. **Scope:** pet-sitting. **Founded:** 1989. **Educational Activities:** National Association of Professional Pet Sitters - NAPPS Annual Conference & Small Business Forum (Annual). **Awards:** Pet Sitters Hall of Fame (Annual).

15812 ■ Pet Care Services Association
2670 Academy Blvd.
Colorado Springs, CO 80917
Ph: (719)667-1600
Free: 877-570-7788
Fax: (719)667-0116
Co. E-mail: membership@petcareservices.org
URL: http://www.petcareservices.org
Contact: Joan Saunders, Chief Executive Officer
Description: Persons or firms that board pets; kennel suppliers; others interested in the facility boarding kennel industry. Seeks to upgrade the industry through accreditation educational programs, seminars and conventions. Provides insurance resources for members and supplies pet care information to the public. Promotes code of ethics and accreditation program for recognition and training of superior kennel operators. Compiles boarding facility statistics. **Scope:** how to select a boarding kennel, pet services. **Founded:** 1977. **Subscriptions:** periodicals. **Publications:** *Pet Service Journal* (Bimonthly); *All About Dog Daycare.* **Educational Activities:** Pet Care Services Association Convention (Annual). **Awards:** Golden Scoop Award (Annual).

15813 ■ Pet Care Trust (PCT)
2105 Laurel Bush Blvd., Ste. 200
Bel Air, MD 21015
Ph: (443)640-1060
Fax: (443)640-1086
Co. E-mail: info@petsintheclassroom.org
URL: http://www.petsintheclassroom.org
Contact: Brent Weinmann, President
Description: Promotes public understanding regarding the value of and the right to enjoy companion animals; enhances society's knowledge about companion animals through research and education; promotes professionalism among members of the companion animal community. Compiles statistics. Provides animals in the classroom teacher education workshops. **Founded:** 1990. **Awards:** Sue J. Busch Companion Award (Annual).

15814 ■ Pet Sitters International (PSI)
201 E King St.
King, NC 27021
Ph: (336)983-9222
Fax: (336)983-5266
Co. E-mail: info@petsit.com
URL: http://www.petsit.com
Contact: Patti J. Moran, President
Description: Represents professional pet sitters. Serves as an educational organization for professional pet sitters and advocates of at-home pet care. Promotes, recognizes and supports excellence in pet sitting. Provides a forum of communication for members who share a common vision of excellence in at-home pet care. **Scope:** pet sitting. **Founded:** 1994. **Subscriptions:** clippings periodicals. **Publications:** *Pet Owner's World* (Annual); *The World of Professional Pet Sitting* (Bimonthly). **Educational Activities:** Quest for Excellence (Annual); Quest for Excellence (Annual). **Awards:** Pet Sitter of the Year (Annual); PSIs "First Canine" Award (Annual).

REFERENCE WORKS

15815 ■ *"Bark Up The Right Tree" in Small Business Opportunities (Winter 2009)*
Pub: Entrepreneur Press
Contact: Perlman Neil, President
Description: Profile of Central Bark, a daycare company catering to pets that offers franchise opportunities and is expanding rapidly despite the economic downturn; the company's growth strategy is also discussed.

15816 ■ *"Making It Work" in Pet Product News (Vol. 64, December 2010, No. 12, pp. S8)*
Pub: BowTie Inc.
Ed: Kerri Chladnicek. **Description:** How focusing on service and flexibility allowed New Jersey-based pet supply store B.C. Woof to achieve success is discussed. B.C. Woof began as a pet-sitting business which eventually concentrated on natural foods. Aside from conducting a do-it-yourself approach in food formulation for customers, B.C. Woof has also been guiding customers on nutrients they need for their pets.

15817 ■ *Minding Your Dog Business: A Practical Guide to Business Success for Dog Professionals*
Pub: Dogwise Publishing
Ed: Veronica Boutelle, Rikke Jorgensen. **Released:** June 1, 2010. **Price:** $19.95. **Description:** Setting up and running a successful dog-related business is an achievement in itself, but the real test is to build success and growth for the long haul.

15818 ■ *"Professional Help: Cross That Off Your To-Do List" in Inc. (November 2007, pp. 89-90, 92)*
Pub: Gruner & Jahr USA Publishing
Ed: Alison Stein Wellner. **Description:** Small business owners are finding that it pays to hire someone to takeover the personal tasks of daily living, including hiring a personal assistant, chauffeur, chef, stylist, pet caregiver, or concierge service.

TRADE PERIODICALS

15819 ■ *The Voice: Medical Case Management - Physical Rehabilitation Newspaper*
Pub: The Voice of Florida
URL(s): www.voicepaper.com/. **Ed:** Ray Brasted. **Released:** Monthly **Price:** $25, Individuals.

FRANCHISES AND BUSINESS OPPORTUNITIES

15820 ■ Central Bark Doggy Day Care
BVI, Inc.
3699 N Dixie Hwy.
Oakland Park, FL 33334
Free: 866-799-2275
Fax: (954)568-3669
Description: Canine care facility. **No. of Franchise Units:** 25. **Founded:** 1997.. **Franchised:** 2004. **Equity Capital Needed:** $60,000 plus, $250,000-$380,000 investment. **Franchise Fee:** $40,000. **Training:** Yes.

15821 ■ In Home Pet Services Inc.
88-25 247th St.
Bellerose, NY 11426
Ph: (718)347-7387
Co. E-mail: info@inhomepetservices.com
URL: http://www.inhomepetservices.com
Description: Pet sitting & dog walking services. **No. of Franchise Units:** 6. **No. of Company-Owned Units:** 1. **Founded:** 2001.. **Franchised:** 2005. **Equity Capital Needed:** $7,200-$31,100. **Franchise Fee:** $6,000. **Royalty Fee:** 5%. **Training:** Includes 1 week training at headquarters.

15822 ■ Pet-Tenders
Pet-Tenders International, Inc.
PO Box 23622
San Diego, CA 92193
Ph: (619)298-3033
Description: In-home pet and house sitting service. **No. of Franchise Units:** 4. **No. of Company-Owned Units:** 1. **Founded:** 1983.. **Franchised:** 1990. **Equity Capital Needed:** $2,000-$5,400. **Franchise Fee:** $8,500. **Financial Assistance:** Yes. **Training:** Yes.

15823 ■ Preppy Pet
Preppy Pet Franchises
57 West Michigan St.
Orlando, FL 32806
Ph: (407)420-1060
Free: 877-377-9738
Fax: (407)420-1068
Description: Overnight dog boarding and day care. **No. of Franchise Units:** 17. **No. of Company-Owned Units:** 1. **Founded:** 2003.. **Franchised:** 2006. **Equity Capital Needed:** $127,750. **Franchise Fee:** $34,500. **Financial Assistance:** Yes. **Training:** Yes.

ASSOCIATIONS AND OTHER ORGANIZATIONS

15824 ■ International Imaging Industry Association (I3A)
c/o Virtual, Inc.
401 Edgewater Pl., Ste. 600
Wakefield, MA 01880
Ph: (914)285-4933
Fax: (914)645-1443
Co. E-mail: i3ainfo@i3a.org
URL: http://www.i3a.org
Contact: Lisa A. Walker, President
Description: Develops and promotes the adoption of open industry standards, addressing environmental issues and providing a voice for the industry that will benefit all users. Promotes environment, health and safety concerns; works with various government agencies including the EPA, TSA, and WTO to ensure the best interests of the imaging industry are represented. **Founded:** 1946. **Publications:** *13A Eye on Imaging* (Bimonthly); *13A Eye on Standards* (Bimonthly). **Awards:** Achievement Award (Annual); Leadership Award (Annual); Safety Excellence Award (Annual).

15825 ■ Professional School Photographers of America
3000 Picture Pl.
Jackson, MI 49201
Ph: (517)788-8100
Free: 800-762-9287
Fax: (517)788-8371
Co. E-mail: pma_trade_exhibits@pmai.org
URL: http://www.pmai.org
Contact: Allen Showalter, President
Description: Retailers of photo and video equipment, film, and supplies; firms developing and printing film. Maintains hall of fame. Compiles statistics; conducts research and educational programs. **Scope:** photo finishing, retailing. **Founded:** 1924. **Subscriptions:** 200 periodicals. **Publications:** *Photo Marketing*; *PMA Magazine: Connecting the Imaging Communities* (Monthly); *Cost of Doing Business Survey*; *NAPET News* (Bimonthly); *Photo Marketing Association International--Newsline* (Semimonthly); *Photo Marketing Magazine* (Monthly); *Sales Counter* (Monthly); *Specialty Lab Update* (Monthly); *Who's Who in Photographic Management* (Annual); *Who's Who in Photographic Management* (Annual); *School Photographer*. **Educational Activities:** PMA Europe (Biennial); PMAI Imaging Conference & Mini-Trade Show (Annual); Photo Marketing Association International Annual Convention and Trade Show (PMA) (Annual).

REFERENCE WORKS

15826 ■ "Interactive Stores a Big Part of Borders' Turnaround Plan" in Crain's Detroit Business (Vol. 24, February 18, 2008, No. 7, pp. 4)
Pub: Crain Communications Inc. - Detroit
Description: Borders Group Inc. is using digital technology and interactive media as a part of the firm's turnaround plan. The digital store will allow shoppers to create CDs, download audio books, publish their own works, print photos and search family genealogy.

15827 ■ "Kodak Cuts Deep in Effort to Change Focus" in Globe & Mail (February 9, 2007, pp. B8)
Pub: CTVglobemedia Publishing Inc.
Ed: Gillian Wee. **Description:** Eastman Kodak Co., the world's largest photography company, is eliminating 5,000 more jobs than the originally planned 28,000 jobs. The job cuts are being driven by the sale of Kodak's health-imaging unit.

STATISTICAL SOURCES

15828 ■ RMA Annual Statement Studies
Pub: Risk Management Association
Contact: Kevin M. Blakey, President
Released: Annual. **Price:** $175.00 2006-07 edition, $105.00. **Description:** Contains composite balance sheets and income statements for more than 360 industries, including the accounting, auditing, and bookkeeping industries. Also contains five years of comparative historical data for discerning trends. Includes 16 commonly used ratios, computed for most of the size groupings for nearly every industry.

TRADE PERIODICALS

15829 ■ Master Guide
Pub: Apex Publications Inc.
URL(s): www.photolife.com/. **Released:** Annual
Price: $27, Individuals 6 issues; $50, Two years.

15830 ■ Professional Photographer: the official magazine of Professional Photographers of America
Pub: Professional Photographers of America
Contact: Tim Walden, President
URL(s): www.ppa.com/ppmag/. **Released:** Monthly
Price: $19.95, Individuals print (U.S.); $35.95, Individuals print (Canada).

LIBRARIES

15831 ■ International Center of Photography Library
1114 Ave. of the Americas
New York, NY 10036
Ph: (212)857-0004
Fax: (212)857-0091
Co. E-mail: library@icp.org
Contact: Deirdre Donohue, Librarian
Scope: Photography, critical writing on photography. **Services:** Copying; Center open to the public by appointment. **Founded:** 1975. **Holdings:** 15,000 books and unbound volumes of photography periodicals and journals; 2500 vertical files on photographers and photo subjects with biographical data from primary materials; critical essays. **Subscriptions:** 75 journals and other serials.

15832 ■ Polaroid Corporation - Research Library
750 Main St.
Cambridge, MA 02139
Ph: (617)386-8245
Fax: (617)386-8241
Co. E-mail: poppenj@polaroid.com
Contact: James Poppenhouse, Department Manager
Scope: Photography, chemistry, physics, engineering, mathematics, social sciences, general business. **Services:** Interlibrary loan; copying; Library open to the public for reference use only with approval of the department manager or the library administrator. **Founded:** 1948. **Holdings:** 30,000 books; 9000 bound periodical volumes; standards, government documents, translations, scientific papers, technical reports; CD-ROMs. **Subscriptions:** 900 journals and other serials; 5 newspapers.

START-UP INFORMATION

15833 ■ *In Fashion: From Runway to Retail, Everything You Need to Know to Break Into the Fashion Industry*
Pub: Crown Business Books
Ed: Annemarie Iverson. **Released:** August 10, 2010.
Price: $16.99. **Description:** Whether your dream is to photograph models, outfit celebrities, design fashions, this book provides details into every aspect for working in the fashion industry.

ASSOCIATIONS AND OTHER ORGANIZATIONS

15834 ■ **American Photographic Artists (APA)**
PO Box 725146
Atlanta, GA 31139
Free: 888-272-6264
Co. E-mail: ceo@apanational.com
URL: http://www.apanational.com
Contact: Theresa Raffetto, President
Description: Enhances dialogue among professional photographers and their clients. Suggests standards and business practices to improve the quality of professional photography; and acts as a forum for discussion of problems and solutions. Conducts discussion groups. **Founded:** 1981. **Publications:** *1999 APA National Photographer's Survey Report.*

15835 ■ **American Photographic Artists Guild (APAG)**
2269 N 400 Rd.
Eudora, KS 66025
Ph: (785)883-4166
Co. E-mail: hancock69@peoplepc.com
URL: http://apag.net
Description: Photographic color artists, retouchers, airbrush artists, color correctors, laboratory technicians, receptionists and professional photographers working in the photography business. Encourages a better understanding between the photographer and the color artist and retoucher. Conducts educational programs on all types of work on color and black and white photographs (including industrial and commercial). **Founded:** 1966.

15836 ■ **American Society of Media Photographers Inc. (Society of Magazine Photographers)**
150 N 2nd St.
Philadelphia, PA 19106-1912
Ph: (215)451-2767
Fax: (215)451-0880
Co. E-mail: info@asmp.org
URL: http://www.asmp.org
Contact: Eugene Mopsik, Executive Director
E-mail: mopsik@asmp.org
Description: Professional society of freelance photographers. Works to evolve trade practices for photographers in communications fields. Provides business information to photographers and their potential clients; promotes ethics and rights of members. Holds educational programs and seminars. Compiles statistics. **Founded:** 1944. **Publications:** *ASMP Bulletin* (Quarterly); *ASMP Bulletin*; *American Society of Media Photographers--Membership Directory.*

15837 ■ **American Society of Photographers (ASP)**
3120 N Argonne Dr.
Milwaukee, WI 53222
Ph: (414)871-6600
Co. E-mail: jonallyn@aol.com
URL: http://www.asofp.com
Contact: Kathryn Meek, President
Description: Photographers who have earned the degrees of Master of Photography, Photographic Craftsman, and Photographic Specialist through the Professional Photographers of America. Sponsors annual traveling exhibit of Masters' photographs and annual National Student Competition and Exhibit. **Founded:** 1937. **Awards:** Service Award (Annual).

15838 ■ **Canadian Association of Photographers and Illustrators in Communications (CAPIC)—Association Canadienne de Photographes et Illustrateurs de Publicite**
720 Spadina Ave., Ste. 202
Toronto, ON, Canada M5S 2T9
Ph: (416)462-3677
Free: 888-252-2742
Fax: (416)929-5256
Co. E-mail: administrator@capic.org
URL: http://www.capic.org
Contact: Andre Cornellier, Chairman
Description: Photographers and illustrators employed in communications. Promotes professional and artistic advancement of members. Represents members' interests before industrial organizations; formulates standards of ethics and practice for members. **Founded:** 1978.

15839 ■ **Photographic Society of America (PSA)**
3000 United Founders Blvd., Ste. 103
Oklahoma City, OK 73112-4294
Ph: (405)843-1437
Free: 855-772-4636
Fax: (405)843-1438
Co. E-mail: hq@psa-photo.org
URL: http://www.psa-photo.org
Contact: John Davis, President
URL(s): psa-photo.org/. **Description:** Camera clubs; amateur, advanced amateur photographers. Sponsors competitions. Conducts slide and print contests, provides instruction slide sets, slide analysis, print portfolios, and other technical services. **Founded:** 1934. **Publications:** *PSA Journal* (Monthly).

15840 ■ **Pictorial Photographers of America (PPA)**
147-10 41st Ave.
Flushing, NY 11355-1266
Co. E-mail: info@ppa-photoclub.org
URL: http://www.ppa-photoclub.org
Contact: Kathryn Buck, President
Description: Amateur and professional photographers. Aids members in perfecting their photographic techniques. Sponsors individual print and slide analysis, exhibitions, and field trips. **Founded:** 1916. **Educational Activities:** Pictorial Photographers of America Dinner (Annual). **Telecommunication Services:** blsspks@aol.com.

15841 ■ **Professional Photographers of America (PPA)**
229 Peachtree St. NE, Ste. 2200
Atlanta, GA 30303-1608
Ph: (404)522-8600
Free: 800-786-6277
Fax: (404)614-6406
Co. E-mail: csc@ppa.com
URL: http://www.ppa.com
Contact: Tim Walden, President
URL(s): www.ppw.org. **Description:** Strives to create a global perspective that promotes business, creativity and excellence. Aims to be the leader in the dissemination of knowledge in the areas of professional business practices and creative image-making and to define and maintain the industry's standards of excellence. Represents portrait, wedding, commercial, industrial and specialized photographers. Sponsors PPA International School of Professional Photography. Maintains speakers' bureau. **Founded:** 1880. **Publications:** *Directory of Professional Photography* (Annual); *PP of A Today* (Monthly); *Professional Photographer* (Monthly); *Professional Photographer: the official magazine of Professional Photographers of America* (Monthly); *Who's Who in Professional Imaging* (Annual). **Awards:** Master Artists; Master Electronic Imaging Degree.

15842 ■ **Professional Women Photographers (PWP)**
119 W 72nd St., No. 223
New York, NY 10023
Co. E-mail: info@pwponline.org
URL: http://www.pwponline.org
Contact: Beth Portnoi Shaw, President
Description: Women professional photographers; other interested individuals. Supports and promotes the work of women photographers through the sharing of ideas, resources, and experience. Provides educational forums to encourage artistic growth and photographic development. Stimulates public interest and support for the art of photography. **Founded:** 1975. **Publications:** *PWP Newsletter* (10/year). **Awards:** High School Student Awards for Photography (Annual).

15843 ■ **San Francisco Camerawork**
1011 Market St., 2nd Fl.
San Francisco, CA 94103
Ph: (415)487-1011
Fax: (415)512-7109
Co. E-mail: info@sfcamerawork.org
URL: http://www.sfcamerawork.org
Contact: Stephen Vance, President
Description: Represents nationally recognized artists' organization whose purpose is to stimulate dialogue, encourage inquiry, and communicate ideas about contemporary photography and related media through a variety of artistic and professional programs. **Scope:** photography, art theory. **Founded:**

1974. **Subscriptions:** 3500 articles books monographs periodicals. **Publications:** *Camerawork: A Journal of Photographic Arts* (Semiannual).

REFERENCE WORKS

15844 ■ *The Accidental Millionaire: How to Succeed in Life Without Really Trying*
Pub: BenBella Books
Contact: Glen Yeffeth, President
Ed: Gary Fong. **Released:** January 1, 2010. **Price:** $11.99 (GBP). **Description:** Gary Fong shares his memoirs about growing up in poverty in Los Angeles. Fong discusses how he revolutionized wedding photography and invented photography aids.

15845 ■ *American Society of Media Photographers--Membership Directory*
Pub: American Society of Media Photographers Inc.
Contact: Eugene Mopsik, Executive Director
E-mail: mopsik@asmp.org
URL(s): www.asmp.org/tips. **Covers:** 5,000 professional photographers for publications. **Entries include:** Name, address, phone, fax, e-mail address, specialty.

15846 ■ *"Boxing, Tech Giants Team to Help Teens" in Hispanic Business (January-February 2009, pp. 44)*
Pub: Hispanic Business
Ed: Daniel Soussa. **Description:** Microsoft and Oscar de la Hoya are providing teens a head start for careers in the sciences by offering a competition in the categories of photography, short films or Web-based games.

15847 ■ *"CPI Corporation Acquires Assets of Bella Pictures" in Benzinga.com (January 28, 2011)*
Pub: Benzinga.com
Ed: Benzinga Staff. **Description:** CPI Corporation acquired assets of Bella Pictures Inc., a leading provider of branded wedding photography services. Details of the acquisition are explained.

15848 ■ *Films and Videos on Photography*
Pub: A and C Black Publishers Ltd.
Contact: Jonathan Glasspool, Director
URL(s): www.artfilm.org. **Ed:** Nadine Covert. **Price:** $15, Individuals. **Covers:** Films and videos dealing with photography. **Entries include:** Title, length, whether in color or black-and-white, format, release date, country in which produced, language, name of director, names of producing agency and distributors, synopsis, series note, review citations, and awards; distributors' name and address given in a separate list. **Arrangement:** Alphabetical. **Indexes:** Distributor.

15849 ■ *How to Market and Sell Your Art, Music, Photographs, and Handmade Crafts Online*
Pub: Atlantic Publishing Group, Inc.
Ed: Lee Rowley. **Released:** May 2008. **Price:** $24.95. **Description:** The book provides all the basics for starting and running an online store selling arts, crafts, photography or music. There are more than 300 Websites listed to help anyone market and promote their arts and/or crafts online.

SOURCES OF SUPPLY

15850 ■ *PhotoSource Book: The Stock Photographer Directory*
PhotoSource International
Contact: Rohn Engh, Director
URL(s): www.photosource.com. **Released:** Bimonthly; and weekly. **Covers:** Magazine and book publishers, public relations firms, advertising and government agencies currently soliciting photographs for publication; 6-12 listings per issue. **Entries include:** Company name, name of contact, address, phone, project title, and nature of photos sought. **Indexes:** CD-ROM editors.

TRADE PERIODICALS

15851 ■ *Applied Arts Magazine*
Pub: Applied Arts Inc.
URL(s): www.appliedartsmag.com/about_us.php. **Ed:** Peter Giffen. **Released:** 6/yr. **Price:** C$60, Individu-

als; C$100, Two years; $75, U.S. and other countries; $150, Two years U.S. & other countries.

15852 ■ *ICG Magazine*
Pub: International Cinematographers Guild
URL(s): icgmagazine.com. **Released:** Monthly

15853 ■ *Master Guide*
Pub: Apex Publications Inc.
URL(s): www.photolife.com/. **Released:** Annual **Price:** $27, Individuals 6 issues; $50, Two years.

15854 ■ *The Photo Review*
Pub: The Photo Review
URL(s): www.photoreview.org. **Ed:** Stephen Perloff. **Released:** Quarterly **Price:** $45, Individuals; $80, Two years; $60, Canada and Mexico; $65, Other countries; $110, Canada and Mexico 2 years.

15855 ■ *PhotoDaily*
Pub: PhotoSource International
Ed: Deb Koehler, Editor, eds@photosource.com. **Released:** Daily, at 2:00p.m. **Price:** $35/Month; $375/ Year. **Description:** Announces current photograph needs of book and magazine publishers, corporations, government, and advertising agencies. Provides specific information on deadlines and prices. Remarks: Available only via facsimile or e-mail.

15856 ■ *PhotoStock Notes/Plus*
Pub: PhotoSource International
Released: Monthly. **Price:** $95, individuals /month; $21.99, two years. **Description:** Provides information for stock photographers and suggests equipment and materials for photobuyers. Recurring features include news of educational opportunities, a calendar of events, and book reviews.

15857 ■ *PhotoStockNotes*
Pub: PhotoSource International
Contact: Angela Dober, Managing Editor
Released: Monthly. **Price:** $35 /year; $3.50, two years /monthly. **Description:** Features information on marketing of and trends involved with stock photos for such publications as textbooks, magazines, and encyclopedias.

15858 ■ *Professional Photographer: the official magazine of Professional Photographers of America*
Pub: Professional Photographers of America
Contact: Tim Walden, President
URL(s): www.ppa.com/ppmag/. **Released:** Monthly **Price:** $19.95, Individuals print (U.S.); $35.95, Individuals print (Canada).

15859 ■ *PSA Journal*
Pub: Photographic Society of America
Contact: John Davis, President
URL(s): psa-photo.org/psa-journal/. **Ed:** Donna Brennan. **Released:** Monthly

15860 ■ *The Rangefinder*
Pub: The Rangefinder Publishing Company Inc.
URL(s): www.rangefindermag.com. **Ed:** Bill Hurter. **Released:** Monthly **Price:** $18, Individuals.

15861 ■ *School Photographer*
Pub: Professional School Photographers of America
Contact: Allen Showalter, President
Released: Enewsletter. **Price:** Included in membership. **Description:** Provides news and information on school photography. Recurring features include news of market research, a calendar of events, and news of educational opportunities.

15862 ■ *Shutterbug*
Pub: Source Interlink Media L.L.C.
URL(s): www.shutterbug.com. **Released:** Monthly **Price:** $17.95, Individuals; $32.95, Two years; $29.95, Canada; $41.95, Other countries.

15863 ■ *Wedding Photography Monthly*
Pub: Wedding & Portrait Photographers International
Ed: Bill Hurter, Editor, bill_tr@earthlink.net. **Released:** Monthly. **Price:** Included in membership. **Description:** Features current topics and new techniques in professional wedding photography. Recurring features include spotlights of individual members and columns titled Legal Issues, New Products, and WPI Convention Updates.

VIDEOCASSETTES/ AUDIOCASSETTES

15864 ■ *ART/New York, Vol. 11*
ART/new york
Inner-Tube Video
138 Prince St.
New York, NY 10012
Ph: (212)966-7446
Fax: (845)265-4302
Co. E-mail: artny@bestweb.net
URL: http://www.artnewyork.org
Released: 1982. **Description:** This tape covers photography exhibitions, including exhibits and interviews with Hans Namuth, Cindy Sherman, Robert Rauschenberg. Foreign language versions can be made available. **Availability:** VHS; 3/4 U.

15865 ■ *The Classroom Collection, Vol. 2: Basic Daylight Exposure and Equivalent Exposures*
Crystal Productions
1812 Johns Dr.
Box 2159
Glenview, IL 60025-6519
Ph: (847)657-8144
Free: 800-255-8629
Fax: (847)657-8149
Co. E-mail: custserv@crystalproductions.com
URL: http://www.crystalproductions.com
Released: 19??. **Price:** $24.95. **Description:** Part of a six-volume teaching aid for photography education, explains the concept of basic daylight exposure and alternative camera settings. **Availability:** VHS.

15866 ■ *The Classroom Collection, Vol. 3: Metering and Exposure Controls*
Crystal Productions
1812 Johns Dr.
Box 2159
Glenview, IL 60025-6519
Ph: (847)657-8144
Free: 800-255-8629
Fax: (847)657-8149
Co. E-mail: custserv@crystalproductions.com
URL: http://www.crystalproductions.com
Released: 19??. **Price:** $24.95. **Description:** Part of a six-volume teaching aid for photography education, explains the function of a camera meter and how to determine the correct exposure according to the film being used. **Availability:** VHS.

15867 ■ *The Classroom Collection, Vol. 4: Advanced Camera Techniques*
Crystal Productions
1812 Johns Dr.
Box 2159
Glenview, IL 60025-6519
Ph: (847)657-8144
Free: 800-255-8629
Fax: (847)657-8149
Co. E-mail: custserv@crystalproductions.com
URL: http://www.crystalproductions.com
Released: 19??. **Price:** $24.95. **Description:** Part of a six-volume teaching aid for photography education, explains a variety of lenses and camera support devices. **Availability:** VHS.

15868 ■ *The Classroom Collection, Vol. 5: Black and White Techniques*
Crystal Productions
1812 Johns Dr.
Box 2159
Glenview, IL 60025-6519
Ph: (847)657-8144
Free: 800-255-8629
Fax: (847)657-8149
Co. E-mail: custserv@crystalproductions.com
URL: http://www.crystalproductions.com
Released: 19??. **Price:** $24.95. **Description:** Part of a six-volume teaching aid for photography education, explains black and white techniques including papers, filters, and enlargers. **Availability:** VHS.

15869 ■ *The Classroom Collection, Vol. 6: Careers in Photography*
Crystal Productions
1812 Johns Dr.
Box 2159
Glenview, IL 60025-6519
Ph: (847)657-8144
Free: 800-255-8629
Fax: (847)657-8149
Co. E-mail: custserv@crystalproductions.com
URL: http://www.crystalproductions.com
Released: 19??. **Price:** $24.95. **Description:** Part of a six-volume teaching aid for photography education, explores career possibilities in the field of photography. **Availability:** VHS.

15870 ■ *Focus on Photography*
Encyclopedia Britannica
331 N. LaSalle St.
Chicago, IL 60654
Ph: (312)347-7159
Free: 800-323-1229
Fax: (312)294-2104
URL: http://www.britannica.com
Released: 1986. **Price:** $69.00. **Description:** Illustrates camera function and film development procedures, and profiles the history of photography. **Availability:** VHS; 3/4 U; SVS.

15871 ■ *Photography 101*
Crystal Productions
1812 Johns Dr.
Box 2159
Glenview, IL 60025-6519
Ph: (847)657-8144
Free: 800-255-8629
Fax: (847)657-8149
Co. E-mail: custserv@crystalproductions.com
URL: http://www.crystalproductions.com
Released: 19??. **Price:** $39.95. **Description:** Teaching aid for photography education includes four programs: people, landscapes, animals, and travel. **Availability:** VHS.

TRADE SHOWS AND CONVENTIONS

15872 ■ Mid-East States Regional Print Competition and Exhibition and Trade Show
Professional Photographers of Ohio
37 W. Broad St., Ste. 480
Columbus, OH 43215
Ph: (614)228-6703
Fax: (614)241-2215
Co. E-mail: carol@ppofohio.org
URL: http://www.ppofohio.org
URL(s): www.ppofohio.org. **Price:** $181, Pre-registered. **Frequency:** Annual. **Audience:** Professional photographers and photographic labs and studios. **Principal Exhibits:** Photographic equipment, supplies, and services; to include office equipment, computers and phone systems. **Dates and Locations:** Ohio Center. **Telecommunication Services:** ppofoh@ol.com.

CONSULTANTS

15873 ■ Carlson Communications Corp.
276 W Main St., Ste. 200
Northborough, MA 01532
Ph: (508)393-9922
Free: 877-393-9922
Fax: (508)393-2118
Co. E-mail: info@carlcomm.com
URL: http://www.carlcomm.com
Contact: Peter Rowlyk, Director
Scope: Offers consulting programs in photo journalism. Will help photographers and reporters develop a better eye, a creative approach, and an enthusiastic attitude and realize the importance of entering national, state and local photography competitions. Serves the private sector and government agencies. If your newsroom lacks direction and motivation, choose the proven winner, Carlson Communications. It is also a full-service marketing communications company specializing in marketing residential and commercial real estate. offers a full range of marketing communications services, from strategic planning to complete creative design and production services, from project launch to sell-out. **Founded:** 1989.

15874 ■ F/22 Press
85 Lake St.
Englewood, NJ 07631-4910
Ph: (201)568-6250
Contact: Robert Martin, Manager
Scope: Offers expertise in the fields of personal computer applications, photography, publications and writing, and public relations. Serves private industries as well as government agencies. **Founded:** 1978. **Special Services:** DARKSTAR; TIMESTAR.

15875 ■ PhotoSource International (PSI)
Pine Lake Farm, 1910 35th Rd.
Osceola, WI 54020-5602
Ph: (715)248-3800
Free: 800-624-0266
Fax: (715)248-7394
Co. E-mail: info@photosource.com
URL: http://www.photosource.com
Contact: Rohn Engh, Director
Scope: Offers counsel in the general field of public relations including brochure development, self-promotion, seminars, and audio-visual presentations. Particular expertise in advising photo editors and photo illustrators on photo acquisition, and on advising photographers on placing or selling their pictures. **Founded:** 1976. **Publications:** "PhotoSourceBOOK"; "PhotoLETTER"; "PhotoStockNOTES"; "PhotoDAILY"; "PhotoStockNotes/Plus". **Seminars:** How to Sell Your Stock Photos. **Special Services:** PhotoSourceBANK; PhotoSourceFOLIO.

FRANCHISES AND BUSINESS OPPORTUNITIES

15876 ■ A Day to Cherish Wedding Videos
10174 S Memorial Dr.
South Jordan, UT 84095
Ph: (801)253-2450
Description: Wedding and special occasion videos. **No. of Franchise Units:** 2. **No. of Company-Owned Units:** 1. **Founded:** 2004.. **Franchised:** 2004. **Equity Capital Needed:** $33,400-$39,400 total investment. **Franchise Fee:** $17,500. **Royalty Fee:** 6%. **Training:** Provides 6 days at headquarters and 2 days at franchisee's location with ongoing support.

15877 ■ EagleShotz
6834 Grand Marina Cir.
Gainesville, GA 30506
Ph: (888)553-2453
Co. E-mail: info@eagleshotz.com
URL: http://www.eagleshotz.com
Description: Event photography specializing in corporate, charity and celebrity golf events. **No. of Franchise Units:** 4. **Founded:** 2006.. **Franchised:** 2007. **Equity Capital Needed:** $34,950. **Franchise Fee:** $34,950. **Royalty Fee:** 6%. **Training:** Offered at franchisee's location 24 hours with ongoing support.

15878 ■ Kids At Heart Photography
1631 S Olden Ave.
Hamilton, NJ 08610
Ph: (800)438-0083
Fax: (609)888-3993
Description: School & sports photography. **No. of Franchise Units:** 6. **No. of Company-Owned Units:** 5. **Founded:** 1992.. **Franchised:** 2006. **Equity Capital Needed:** $50,000-$75,000. **Franchise Fee:** $35,000. **Training:** Yes.

15879 ■ Portraitefx Franchising Corp.
2600 E Southlake Blvd., Ste. 120-369
Southlake, TX 76092
Ph: (214)295-5249
Free: 800-765-7561
Co. E-mail: CDoyle@portraitefx.com
URL: http://www.portraitefx.com
Description: Digital photography services for schools, day cares, sports, families and more. **No. of Franchise Units:** 65. **No. of Company-Owned Units:** 3. **Founded:** 2006.. **Franchised:** 2006. **Equity**

Capital Needed: $25,000-$35,000. **Franchise Fee:** $20,000. **Financial Assistance:** Yes. **Training:** In-house and on location training included.

15880 ■ Print Three Franchising Corp.
8400 Jane St. Bldg. D, Ste. 300
Concord, ON, Canada L4K 4L8
Ph: (905)669-8895
Free: 800-335-5918
Fax: (905)669-0712
URL: http://www.printthree.com
Description: Business service franchise focusing on the increasing demand for digital imaging. Franchise offers complete digital reproduction, design, finishing and fulfillment. The only print franchise having a fully integrated web-based ordering system. Provides total imaging solutions for the corporate community. **No. of Franchise Units:** 51. **Founded:** 1970.. **Franchised:** 1981. **Equity Capital Needed:** $200,000. **Franchise Fee:** $70,000. **Training:** Yes.

15881 ■ TSS Photography
B & H Products, Inc.
2150 Boggs Rd., Ste. 200
Duluth, GA 30096
Ph: (678)740-0800
Free: 800-321-9127
Fax: (678)740-0808
Co. E-mail: frandev@office.sports-section.com
URL: http://www.Sports-Section.com
Description: Youth and sports photography. **No. of Franchise Units:** 210. **No. of Company-Owned Units:** 1. **Founded:** 1983.. **Franchised:** 1984. **Equity Capital Needed:** $30,250-$75,150. **Franchise Fee:** $18,700-$39,700. **Financial Assistance:** Limited third party financing available. **Training:** Available 3 days at headquarters, 5 days at franchisee's location with ongoing support.

COMPUTERIZED DATABASES

15882 ■ *Earthshots®*
300 Jeanette Dr.
Tappahannock, VA 22560-2070
Ph: (804)443-9000
Free: 800-800-8560
Fax: (804)443-3632
URL: http://www.digiwis.com
Availability: CD-ROM: Digital Wisdom Inc. **Type:** Image.

15883 ■ *Photography Collections Online*
George Eastman House
900 East Ave.
Rochester, NY 14607
Ph: (585)271-3361
Fax: (585)271-3970
URL: http://www.eastmanhouse.org
Availability: Online: George Eastman House International Museum of Photography and Film. **Type:** Directory; Bibliographic.

LIBRARIES

15884 ■ Art Institute of Philadelphia Library
1610 Chestnut St.
Philadelphia, PA 19103
Ph: (215)405-6402
Co. E-mail: rschachter@aii.edu
URL: http://www.artinstitutes.edu/philadelphia
Contact: Ruth Schachter, Director
URL(s): www.artinstitutes.edu/philadelphia/student-life/library.aspx. **Scope:** Visual communications, interior design, industrial design, animation, fashion marketing, fashion design, visual merchandising, photography, website design, multimedia. **Services:** Interlibrary loan; copying; library not open to the public (circulation services provided for students and faculty). **Founded:** 1974. **Holdings:** 31,000 volumes; 2000 videocassettes; audiocassettes. **Subscriptions:** 180 print subscriptions and other serials.

15885 ■ Brooks Institute - Library
27 E. Cota St.
Santa Barbara, CA 93101
Ph: (805)690-7627

Fax: (805)564-1475

URL: http://www.brooks.edu/Student-Life/Library

Scope: Photography. **Services:** Copying; Library open to the public for reference use only. **Founded:** 1973. **Holdings:** 6953 books; 25,000 unbound periodicals; 2500 pamphlets; 200 videotapes. **Subscriptions:** 92 journals and other serials.

15886 ■ Canadian Museum of Contemporary Photography - Research Resources—Musee Canadien de la Photographie Contemporaine.

380 Sussex Dr.

Ottawa, ON, Canada K1N 9N4

Ph: (613)990-1985

Fax: (613)993-4385

Co. E-mail: mwadding@gallery.ca

URL: http://cmcp.gallery.ca/en/index.php

Contact: Murray Waddington, Section Chief

Scope: Canadian photography - contemporary, historical. **Services:** CMCP; access to holdings through the Library of the National Gallery of Canada. **Founded:** 1990. **Holdings:** 4000 books.

15887 ■ Canadian Society of Scientific Photography Library—Societe Canadienne de la Photographie Scientifique.

330 Dixon Rd., No. 1401

Etobicoke, ON, Canada M9R 1S9

Ph: (416)247-5640

Contact: J.D. Dunn, Executive Director

Scope: Scientific photography. **Services:** Library open to the public by appointment. **Founded:** 1995. **Holdings:** 3000 books; films; slides; videotapes.

15888 ■ Drury University - F.W. Olin Library - Art & Architecture Slide Library

900 N. Benton Ave.

Springfield, MO 65802

Ph: (417)873-7337

Fax: (417)873-7432

Co. E-mail: jtygart@drury.edu

URL: http://library.drury.edu/services-info/collections/slide-library/

Contact: Jacqueline Tygart, Curator

Scope: Architecture, art, photography, textiles, ceramics. **Services:** Library open to the public. **Holdings:** 60,000 35mm slides.

15889 ■ Ringling College of Art and Design - Verman Kimbrough Memorial Library

2700 N. Tamiami Trail

Sarasota, FL 34234

Ph: (941)359-7587

Free: 800-255-7695

Fax: (941)359-7632

Co. E-mail: library@ringling.edu

URL: http://www.ringling.edu

Contact: Kathleen List, Director, Library Services

Scope: Art history, interior design, graphic design, computer animation, photography, architecture, fine arts, decorative arts, illustration. **Services:** Interlibrary loan; copying; library open to artists and researchers. **Founded:** 1932. **Holdings:** 49,000 books; 110,000 art slides; 34 16mm films; 3000 videocassettes and DVDs. **Subscriptions:** 320 journals and other serials. **Telecommunication Services:** klist@ringling.edu.

15890 ■ San Francisco Public Library - Bernard Osher Foundation - Art, Music & Recreation Center

100 Larkin St., 4th Fl.

San Francisco, CA 94102

Ph: (415)557-4525

Fax: (415)557-4524

Co. E-mail: info@sfpl.org

URL: http://www.sfpl.org

Contact: Mark Hall, Manager

URL(s): sfpl.org/index.php?pg=0200001401. **Scope:** Arts - visual, graphic; sports and recreation; photography; architecture; arts and crafts; performing arts; music - orchestral, chamber, opera, popular, folk, jazz. **Services:** Center open to the public. **Holdings:** Books; serials; scores. **Telecommunication Services:** artmusicrec@sfpl.org.

15891 ■ School of Visual Arts - Visual Arts Library

380 2nd Ave., 22nd St., 2nd Fl.

New York, NY 10010-3994

Ph: (212)592-2660

Fax: (212)592-2655

Co. E-mail: rlobe@sva.edu

URL: http://www.schoolofvisualarts.edu/sr/index.jsp?sid0=258&sid1=290

Contact: Robert Lobe, Director, Library Services

Scope: Fine arts, graphic design, advertising, photography, film, computer graphics, humanities. **Services:** Copying; Library open to students, faculty, staff, and alumni (METRO passes honored). **Founded:** 1961. **Holdings:** 70,000 books and bound periodical volumes; 2000 pamphlets; 270,000 pictures; 152,000 slides. **Subscriptions:** 300 journals and other serials.

15892 ■ SF Camerawork Reference Library

1011 Market St., 2nd Fl.

San Francisco, CA 94103

Ph: (415)487-1011

Co. E-mail: info@sfcamerawork.org

URL: http://www.sfcamerawork.org

Scope: Photography, contemporary art, art theory and criticism. **Services:** Library open for the refer-

ence use of students, educators, scholars, and visitors. **Founded:** 1974. **Holdings:** 3500 volumes; 700 bound periodical volumes.

15893 ■ Smithsonian Institution - Smithsonian American Art Museum - National Portrait Gallery Library

750 9th St. NW, Ste. 2100

Washington, DC 20013-7012

Ph: (202)633-8230

Co. E-mail: littsd@si.edu

URL: http://www.sil.si.edu/libraries/aapg

Contact: Douglas Litts, Director

Scope: American painting, sculpture, graphic arts, biography, history, photography; portraiture; contemporary art. **Services:** Interlibrary loan; copying; Library open to the public for reference use only. **Founded:** 1937. **Holdings:** 180,000 books; exhibitions catalogs; catalogues raisonnes; serials; dissertations; artists' books; ephemeral materials; auction catalogs; scrapbooks; microforms; CD-ROMs.

15894 ■ Springfield Art Museum - Art Reference Library

1111 E. Brookside Dr.

Springfield, MO 65807

Ph: (417)837-5700

Fax: (417)837-5704

Co. E-mail: artmuseum@springfieldmo.gov

URL: http://www.springfieldmo.gov/art/

Contact: Jerry Berger, Director

Scope: Art history, painting, sculpture, graphics, decorative arts, photography. **Services:** Library open to the public. **Founded:** 1937. **Holdings:** 8000 volumes; periodicals; catalogs; AV materials. **Subscriptions:** 65 journals and other serials.

15895 ■ Walker Art Center - Staff Reference Library

1750 Hennepin Ave.

Vineland Pl.

Minneapolis, MN 55403

Ph: (612)375-7680

Co. E-mail: rosemary.furtak@walkerart.org

URL: http://www.walkerart.org

Contact: Rosemary Furtak, Librarian

Scope: Contemporary art, art history, architecture, design, film, artists' books, graphics, photography, painting, sculpture. **Services:** Copying; internet searches; reference services; library open to the public by appointment. **Founded:** 1950. **Holdings:** 35,000 books; 550 bound periodical volumes; vertical files. **Subscriptions:** 140 journals. **Telecommunication Services:** info@walkerart.org.

ASSOCIATIONS AND OTHER ORGANIZATIONS

15896 ■ **Photographic Society of America (PSA)**
3000 United Founders Blvd., Ste. 103
Oklahoma City, OK 73112-4294
Ph: (405)843-1437
Free: 855-772-4636
Fax: (405)843-1438
Co. E-mail: hq@psa-photo.org
URL: http://www.psa-photo.org
Contact: John Davis, President
URL(s): psa-photo.org/. **Description:** Camera clubs; amateur, advanced amateur photographers. Sponsors competitions. Conducts slide and print contests, provides instruction slide sets, slide analysis, print portfolios, and other technical services. **Founded:** 1934. **Publications:** *PSA Journal* (Monthly).

15897 ■ **Professional Photographers of America (PPA)**
229 Peachtree St. NE, Ste. 2200
Atlanta, GA 30303-1608
Ph: (404)522-8600
Free: 800-786-6277
Fax: (404)614-6406
Co. E-mail: csc@ppa.com
URL: http://www.ppa.com
Contact: Tim Walden, President
URL(s): www.ppw.org. **Description:** Strives to create a global perspective that promotes business, creativity and excellence. Aims to be the leader in the dissemination of knowledge in the areas of professional business practices and creative image-making and to define and maintain the industry's standards of excellence. Represents portrait, wedding, commercial, industrial and specialized photographers. Sponsors PPA International School of Professional Photography. Maintains speakers' bureau. **Founded:** 1880. **Publications:** *Directory of Professional Photography* (Annual); *PP of A Today* (Monthly); *Professional Photographer* (Monthly); *Professional Photographer: the official magazine of Professional Photographers of America* (Monthly); *Who's Who in Professional Imaging* (Annual). **Awards:** Master Artists; Master Electronic Imaging Degree.

15898 ■ **Professional School Photographers Association International (PSPA)**
PMA - The Worldwide Communit of Imaging Associations
2282 Springport Rd., Ste. F
Jackson, MI 49202
Ph: (517)788-8100
Fax: (517)788-8371
Co. E-mail: m.bell@bellphoto.com
URL: http://www.pmai.org/pspa
Contact: Mark Schoenrock, Director
Description: A section of the Photo Marketing Association International. Firms engaged in the photographing and/or processing of school photographs. Purposes are: to encourage the exchange of production ideas and economies; to cooperate in the overall promotion of photography; to work for better relations and understanding with schools; to act as a group in making manufacturers of sensitized goods and photographic equipment aware of the specialized needs of school photography; to maintain a close watch on any legislation that may affect school photography; to promote career possibilities and personnel training and recruitment for school photography; to foster the well-being of the member firms by providing some of the advantages of a large-scale operation. **Founded:** 1951.

15899 ■ **San Francisco Camerawork**
1011 Market St., 2nd Fl.
San Francisco, CA 94103
Ph: (415)487-1011
Fax: (415)512-7109
Co. E-mail: info@sfcamerawork.org
URL: http://www.sfcamerawork.org
Contact: Stephen Vance, President
Description: Represents nationally recognized artists' organization whose purpose is to stimulate dialogue, encourage inquiry, and communicate ideas about contemporary photography and related media through a variety of artistic and professional programs. **Scope:** photography, art theory. **Founded:** 1974. **Subscriptions:** 3500 articles books monographs periodicals. **Publications:** *Camerawork: A Journal of Photographic Arts* (Semiannual).

15900 ■ **Wedding and Portrait Photographers International (WPPI)**
c/o Nielsen Expositions
6255 Sunset Blvd., 19th Fl.
Los Angeles, CA 90028-7420
Ph: (323)817-3500
URL: http://www.wppionline.com/index.shtml
Contact: Steven Sheanin, President
URL(s): www.wppionline.com. **Description:** Represents wedding portrait and digital photographers and photographers employed at general photography studios. Promotes high artistic and technical standards in wedding photography. Serves as a forum for the exchange of technical knowledge and experience; makes available the expertise of top professionals in the field of photographic arts and technology, advertising, sales promotion, marketing, public relations, accounting, business management, tax, and profit planning. Members are offered the opportunity to purchase special products and services. **Founded:** 1973. **Publications:** *Rangefinder*; *Wedding Photographer* (Monthly); *WPPI Photography Monthly* (Monthly); *Marketing and Technical Manual* (Quarterly). **Educational Activities:** Wedding and Portrait Photographers International Competition (Semiannual); Wedding and Portrait Photographers International Convention (Semiannual). **Awards:** Accolade Program (Semiannual); Print Competitions (Annual); Awards of Excellence.

DIRECTORIES OF EDUCATIONAL PROGRAMS

15901 ■ **Directory of Private Accredited Career Schools and Colleges of Technology**
Pub: Accrediting Commission of Career Schools and Colleges of Technology
Contact: Michale S. McComis, Executive Director
Released: On web page. **Price:** Free. **Description:** Covers 3900 accredited post-secondary programs that provide training programs in business, trade, and technical fields, including various small business endeavors. Entries offer school name, address, phone, description of courses, job placement assistance, and requirements for admission. Arrangement is alphabetical.

REFERENCE WORKS

15902 ■ **The Accidental Millionaire: How to Succeed in Life Without Really Trying**
Pub: BenBella Books
Contact: Glen Yeffeth, President
Ed: Gary Fong. **Released:** January 1, 2010. **Price:** $11.99 (GBP). **Description:** Gary Fong shares his memoirs about growing up in poverty in Los Angeles. Fong discusses how he revolutionized wedding photography and invented photography aids.

15903 ■ **"CPI Corporation Acquires Assets of Bella Pictures" in Benzinga.com (January 28, 2011)**
Pub: Benzinga.com
Ed: Benzinga Staff. **Description:** CPI Corporation acquired assets of Bella Pictures Inc., a leading provider of branded wedding photography services. Details of the acquisition are explained.

15904 ■ **How to Market and Sell Your Art, Music, Photographs, and Handmade Crafts Online**
Pub: Atlantic Publishing Group, Inc.
Ed: Lee Rowley. **Released:** May 2008. **Price:** $24. 95. **Description:** The book provides all the basics for starting and running an online store selling arts, crafts, photography or music. There are more than 300 Websites listed to help anyone market and promote their arts and/or crafts online.

STATISTICAL SOURCES

15905 ■ **RMA Annual Statement Studies**
Pub: Risk Management Association
Contact: Kevin M. Blakey, President
Released: Annual. **Price:** $175.00 2006-07 edition, $105.00. **Description:** Contains composite balance sheets and income statements for more than 360 industries, including the accounting, auditing, and bookkeeping industries. Also contains five years of comparative historical data for discerning trends. Includes 16 commonly used ratios, computed for most of the size groupings for nearly every industry.

TRADE PERIODICALS

15906 ■ **ASMP Bulletin**
Pub: American Society of Media Photographers Inc.
Contact: Eugene Mopsik, Executive Director
E-mail: mopsik@asmp.org
Ed: Peter Skinner, Editor, skinner@asmp.org. **Released:** Quarterly, 10/year. **Price:** Included in membership. **Description:** Features articles on profes-

sional photography, copyright laws, and photographic techniques. Recurring features include interviews and news of research. For ASMP members only.

15907 ■ *Light and Shade*
Pub: Pictorial Photographers of America
Ed: Sylvia Mavis, Editor. **Released:** Monthly. **Price:** Included in membership. **Description:** Designed to help amateur and professional photographers perfect their photographic techniques. Carries how-to articles and information on photography equipment. Recurring features include organizational news, announcements of educational opportunities, and book reviews.

15908 ■ *Photo Techniques*
Pub: Preston Publications
Contact: S. Tinsley Preston, III, President
URL(s): www.phototechmag.com. **Ed:** Wendy Erickson. **Released:** Bimonthly **Price:** $29.99, Individuals; $39.99, Two years.

15909 ■ *PhotoDaily*
Pub: PhotoSource International
Ed: Deb Koehler, Editor, eds@photosource.com. **Released:** Daily, at 2:00p.m. **Price:** $35/Month; $375/Year. **Description:** Announces current photograph needs of book and magazine publishers, corporations, government, and advertising agencies. Provides specific information on deadlines and prices. Remarks: Available only via facsimile or e-mail.

15910 ■ *The Polar Bear ROARS*
Pub: Polar Bear Alumni Association
Ed: Leeann Faust, Editor, lfaust@columbus.rr.com. **Released:** Quarterly. **Price:** Included in membership; $8 /year. **Description:** Provides news of current events regarding reunion information, memories of alumni, history of school and articles about alumni and faculty. Recurring features include reports of reunions.

15911 ■ *Popular Photography and Imaging*
Pub: Hachette Filipacchi Media U.S. Inc.
Contact: David Carey, President
URL(s): www.popphoto.com. **Ed:** John Owens. **Released:** Monthly **Price:** $24, Two years; $14, Individuals.

15912 ■ *Professional Photographer: the official magazine of Professional Photographers of America*
Pub: Professional Photographers of America
Contact: Tim Walden, President
URL(s): www.ppa.com/ppmag/. **Released:** Monthly **Price:** $19.95, Individuals print (U.S.); $35.95, Individuals print (Canada).

15913 ■ *PSA Journal*
Pub: Photographic Society of America
Contact: John Davis, President
URL(s): psa-photo.org/psa-journal/. **Ed:** Donna Brennan. **Released:** Monthly

15914 ■ *The Rangefinder*
Pub: The Rangefinder Publishing Company Inc.
URL(s): www.rangefindermag.com. **Ed:** Bill Hurter. **Released:** Monthly **Price:** $18, Individuals.

15915 ■ *School Photographer*
Pub: Professional School Photographers of America
Contact: Allen Showalter, President
Released: Enewsletter. **Price:** Included in membership. **Description:** Provides news and information on school photography. Recurring features include news of market research, a calendar of events, and news of educational opportunities.

15916 ■ *Shutterbug*
Pub: Source Interlink Media L.L.C.
URL(s): www.shutterbug.com. **Released:** Monthly **Price:** $17.95, Individuals; $32.95, Two years; $29.95, Canada; $41.95, Other countries.

15917 ■ *Wedding Photography Monthly*
Pub: Wedding & Portrait Photographers International
Ed: Bill Hurter, Editor, bill_tr@earthlink.net. **Released:** Monthly. **Price:** Included in membership. **Description:** Features current topics and new techniques in professional wedding photography. Recur-

ring features include spotlights of individual members and columns titled Legal Issues, New Products, and WPI Convention Updates.

VIDEOCASSETTES/ AUDIOCASSETTES

15918 ■ *Focus on Photography*
Encyclopedia Britannica
331 N. LaSalle St.
Chicago, IL 60654
Ph: (312)347-7159
Free: 800-323-1229
Fax: (312)294-2104
URL: http://www.britannica.com
Released: 1986. **Price:** $69.00. **Description:** Illustrates camera function and film development procedures, and profiles the history of photography. **Availability:** VHS; 3/4 U; SVS.

15919 ■ *Photography*
Crystal Productions
1812 Johns Dr.
Box 2159
Glenview, IL 60025-6519
Ph: (847)657-8144
Free: 800-255-8629
Fax: (847)657-8149
Co. E-mail: custserv@crystalproductions.com
URL: http://www.crystalproductions.com
Released: 1991. **Price:** $59.95. **Description:** A two-part course in single-lens reflex camera use, including the mechanics of the camera, special effects for color and black & white film, and methods for developing and printing pictures. **Availability:** VHS.

FRANCHISES AND BUSINESS OPPORTUNITIES

15920 ■ Glamour Shots Licensing Inc.
1300 Metropolitan Ave.
Oklahoma City, OK 73108
Ph: (405)947-8747
Free: 800-336-4550
Fax: (405)951-7343
Description: High fashion photography studio. **No. of Franchise Units:** 100. **No. of Company-Owned Units:** 2. **Founded:** 1988.. **Franchised:** 1992. **Equity Capital Needed:** $25,000 cash, plus financial investment, ranging from $38,500-$86,000. **Franchise Fee:** $20,000 U.S. **Financial Assistance:** Yes. **Training:** Yes.

15921 ■ Images 4 Kids
12200 Ford Rd., Ste. 108
Dallas, TX 75234
Ph: (855)783-4000
URL: http://www.images4kids.com
Description: Portraits of kids. **No. of Franchise Units:** 67. **Founded:** 1983.. **Franchised:** 2004. **Equity Capital Needed:** $53,600-$77,100. **Franchise Fee:** $29,900. **Royalty Fee:** None. **Financial Assistance:** Limited third party financing available. **Training:** Provides 4 days training at corporate headquarters.

15922 ■ Lil' Angels Photography
6831 Crumpler Blvd., Ste. 101
Olive Branch, MS 38654
Ph: (662)890-9103
Free: 800-358-9101
Fax: (662)890-9104
URL: http://www.angelus.com
Description: Photo studio with professional studio equipments and techniques. **No. of Franchise Units:** 72. **Founded:** 1996.. **Franchised:** 1998. **Equity Capital Needed:** $46,700-$51,200. **Franchise Fee:** $35,000. **Royalty Fee:** Varies. **Training:** 6 days provided at corporate headquarters, 2 days of onsite, and regional and annual convention included.

15923 ■ Lil'Pals Pet Photography
6831 Crumpler Blvd., Ste. 101
Olive Branch, MS 38654
Ph: (901)682-9566
Free: 800-358-9101

Fax: (901)682-2018
Description: Pet photography. **No. of Franchise Units:** 8. **Founded:** 2004.. **Franchised:** 2005. **Equity Capital Needed:** $50,000-$102,000. **Franchise Fee:** $10,000. **Training:** Yes.

15924 ■ PoGoPix Studios
4916 139th Ave. SE, Unit 218
Calgary, AB, Canada T2Z 0G4
Ph: (403)269-6790
Fax: (403)263-0849
Co. E-mail: southtrail@pogopix.ca
URL: http://www.pogopixstudios.com
Description: Children's photography. **Founded:** 2000. **Franchised:** 2005.

15925 ■ TSS Photography
B & H Products, Inc.
2150 Boggs Rd., Ste. 200
Duluth, GA 30096
Ph: (678)740-0800
Free: 800-321-9127
Fax: (678)740-0808
Co. E-mail: frandev@office.sports-section.com
URL: http://www.Sports-Section.com
Description: Youth and sports photography. **No. of Franchise Units:** 210. **No. of Company-Owned Units:** 1. **Founded:** 1983.. **Franchised:** 1984. **Equity Capital Needed:** $30,250-$75,150. **Franchise Fee:** $18,700-$39,700. **Financial Assistance:** Limited third party financing available. **Training:** Available 3 days at headquarters, 5 days at franchisee's location with ongoing support.

COMPUTERIZED DATABASES

15926 ■ *Earthshots®*
300 Jeanette Dr.
Tappahannock, VA 22560-2070
Ph: (804)443-9000
Free: 800-800-8560
Fax: (804)443-3632
URL: http://www.digiwis.com
Availability: CD-ROM: Digital Wisdom Inc. **Type:** Image.

LIBRARIES

15927 ■ Brooks Institute - Library
27 E. Cota St.
Santa Barbara, CA 93101
Ph: (805)690-7627
Fax: (805)564-1475
URL: http://www.brooks.edu/Student-Life/Library
Scope: Photography. **Services:** Copying; Library open to the public for reference use only. **Founded:** 1973. **Holdings:** 6953 books; 25,000 unbound periodicals; 2500 pamphlets; 200 videotapes. **Subscriptions:** 92 journals and other serials.

15928 ■ George Eastman House - International Museum of Photography & Film - Richard and Ronay Menschel Library
900 East Ave.
Rochester, NY 14607
Ph: (585)271-3361, x-313
Fax: (585)271-3970
URL: http://www.eastmanhouse.org/collections/ library.php
Contact: Rachel Stuhlman, Curator Librarian
Scope: Photography and cinematography - history, science, aesthetics. **Services:** Interlibrary loan; copying; mail reference; Library open to the public by appointment. **Founded:** 1949. **Holdings:** 59,000 books; 15,000 bound periodical volumes; 25 VF drawers of history of photography and current activities; letters and manuscripts; microfilm; microfiche. **Subscriptions:** 316 journals and other serials.

15929 ■ International Center of Photography Library
1114 Ave. of the Americas
New York, NY 10036
Ph: (212)857-0004

Fax: (212)857-0091
Co. E-mail: library@icp.org
Contact: Deirdre Donohue, Librarian

Scope: Photography, critical writing on photography. **Services:** Copying; Center open to the public by appointment. **Founded:** 1975. **Holdings:** 15,000 books and unbound volumes of photography periodicals and journals; 2500 vertical files on photographers and photo subjects with biographical data from

primary materials; critical essays. **Subscriptions:** 75 journals and other serials.

15930 ■ University of Arizona - Center for Creative Photography Library
1030 N. Olive Rd.
Tucson, AZ 85721-0103
Ph: (520)621-7968
Fax: (520)621-9444
Co. E-mail: diazj@u.library.arizona.edu
URL: http://ccp.library.arizona.edu/index.html

Contact: Bob Diaz, Librarian, Art

Scope: Photography. **Services:** Interlibrary loan; copying; Center open to the public. **Founded:** 1975. **Holdings:** 26,000 titles including several thousand rare books; 3000 bound periodical volumes; 600 reels of microfilm; 40 feet of biographical files; 600 oral history videotapes. **Subscriptions:** 100 journals and other serials. **Telecommunication Services:** info@ccp.library.arizona.edu.

START-UP INFORMATION

15931 ■ *Becoming a Personal Trainer for Dummies*
Pub: John Wiley and Sons, Inc.
Ed: Melyssa Michael, Linda Formichelli. **Released:** October 2004. **Price:** $19.99 (US), $25.99 (Canadian). **Description:** Legal and tax issues involved in starting and running a personal trainer firm. The book offers suggestions for incorporating massage and nutritional services.

15932 ■ *"Former Boxer Fits Into New Business Role" in Houston Business Journal (Vol. 40, January 8, 2010, No. 35, pp. 1)*
Pub: American City Business Journals
Ed: Greg Barr. **Description:** Lou Savarese explains how the lessons he learned as a professional boxer help him to manage his new business venture, a gym called Savarese Fight Gym. Customers who desire to learn boxing and to stay fit like a boxer comprise the fitness center's target market.

15933 ■ *"Land Swap Key to Ending Royal Oak Project Impasse" in Crain's Detroit Business (Vol. 25, June 8, 2009, No. 23, pp. 20)*
Pub: Crain Communications Inc. - Detroit
Ed: Chad Halcom. **Description:** Details of the new construction of the LA Fitness health club near Woodward and Washington Avenues in Royal Oak, Michigan are discussed.

15934 ■ *"Pump Up the Profits" in Small Business Opportunities (Summer 2010)*
Pub: Harris Publications Inc.
Description: New fitness franchise offers customized personal training at bargain rates. Profile of Alan Katz, president of EduFit, a concept that allows small groups of people to workout with customized training is provided.

15935 ■ *"Riches In Recreation" in Small Business Opportunities (March 2011)*
Pub: Harris Publications Inc.
Description: Making money is child's play thanks to new gym concept that makes parents and franchisors happy. Profile of Great Play, the franchised children's gym is provided.

ASSOCIATIONS AND OTHER ORGANIZATIONS

15936 ■ **American Alliance for Health, Physical Education, Recreation and Dance (AAHPERD)**
1900 Association Dr.
Reston, VA 20191-1598
Ph: (703)476-3400
Free: 800-213-7193
Fax: (703)476-9527
Co. E-mail: membership@aahperd.org
URL: http://www.aahperd.org
Contact: Ang Chen, President
Description: Students and educators in physical education, dance, health, athletics, safety education,

recreation, and outdoor education. Works to improve its fields of education at all levels through such services as consultation, periodicals and special publications, leadership development, determination of standards, and research. Sponsors placement service. **Founded:** 1885. **Publications:** *Health Education* (Bimonthly); *Journal of Health Education* (Bimonthly); *Strategies: A Journal for Physical and Sport Educators* (Bimonthly); *Research Quarterly for Exercise and Sport* (Quarterly); *AAHPERD Update*; *Dance Directory--Programs of Professional Preparation in American Colleges and Universities* (Biennial); *Journal of Physical Education, Recreation & Dance* (Monthly); *American Journal of Health Education*; *The International Electronic Journal of Health Education* (Annual); *Directory of Professional Preparation Programs in Recreation, Parks, and Related Areas*; *AAHPERD Update* (Bimonthly); *AAHPERD UpdatePLUS*. **Educational Activities:** American Alliance for Health, Physical Education, Recreation, and Dance - National Conference and Exposition (Annual). **Awards:** Ruth Abernathy Presidential Scholarships; Anderson Award; Charles D. Henry Award; Honor Award; Luther Halsey Gulick Medal; Mabel Lee Award; R. Tait McKenzie Award; William G. Anderson Award; Luther Halsey Gulick Medal; Charles D. Henry Award; Honor Award; Mabel Lee Award; R. Tait McKenzie Award. **Telecommunication Services:** info@aahperd.org; research@aahperd.org.

15937 ■ **American Council on Exercise**
4851 Paramont Dr.
San Diego, CA 92123
Ph: (858)576-6500
Free: 888-825-3636
Fax: (858)576-6564
Co. E-mail: pubs@acefitness.org
URL: http://www.acefitness.org
Contact: Scott Goudeseune, President
Description: Promotes the benefits of physical activity and protects consumers against unsafe and ineffective fitness products and instruction. Sponsors university-based exercise science research and testing that targets fitness products and trends. Sets standards for fitness professionals. **Scope:** exercise, fitness, sports medicine, nutrition. **Subscriptions:** 500 audiovisuals books clippings periodicals. **Publications:** *ACE FitnessMatters* (Bimonthly); *ACE Certified News* (Bimonthly); *ACE Fitness Matters* (Bimonthly). **Awards:** Joe Q. Bryant American Council on Exercise Educational Scholarships; William J. Merriman American Council on Exercise Educational Scholarships; William Shannon American Council on Exercise Certification Scholarships; Joe Q. Bryant American Council on Exercise Educational Scholarship (Annual); William J. Merriman American Council on Exercise Educational Scholarship (Annual); William Shannon American Council on Exercise Educational Scholarship (Annual).

15938 ■ **American Running Association**
4405 E West Hwy., Ste. 405
Bethesda, MD 20814-4535
Ph: (301)913-9517
Free: 800-776-2732

Fax: (301)913-9520
Co. E-mail: run@americanrunning.org
URL: http://www.americanrunning.org
Contact: Jeffrey T. Harbison, President
E-mail: jharbison@springfieldmontco.org
Description: Represents individual runners, exercise enthusiasts, and sports medicine professionals. Promotes running and other aerobic activities; fosters the preventive maintenance concept in health preservation. Serves as a repository for data on running and fitness. Reports on research in exercise physiology and in techniques of increasing total human performance and maintaining physical fitness. Maintains speakers' bureau. Conducts educational programs and charitable activities. **Founded:** 1968. **Publications:** *Running and FitNews* (Bimonthly). **Educational Activities:** American Running Association Meeting.

15939 ■ **American Sports Builders Association (ASBA)**
8480 Baltimore National Pike, No. 307
Ellicott City, MD 21043
Ph: (410)730-9595
Free: 866-501-2722
Fax: (410)730-8833
Co. E-mail: info@sportsbuilders.org
URL: http://sportsbuilders.org
Contact: Mark Brogan, Chairman
Description: Contractors who install running tracks, synthetic turf fields, tennis courts and indoor sports surfaces; manufacturers who supply basic materials for construction; accessory suppliers, designers, architects, and consultants of facilities. Provides guidelines for tennis court construction, running track construction, fencing, synthetic turf field construction and lighting. Offers certification and awards programs. **Founded:** 1965. **Publications:** *Tennis and Track Construction Guidelines* (Periodic); *Buyers Guide for Tennis Court Construction* (Periodic); *Running Tracks: A Construction and Maintenance Manual* (Semiannual). **Awards:** Outstanding Indoor Tennis Facility Award (Annual); Outstanding Outdoor Tennis Facility Award (Annual); Outstanding Track/Facility Award (Annual); Outstanding Residential Tennis Court/Facility Award (Annual).

15940 ■ **Aquatic Exercise Association (AEA)—World Aquatic Coalition, Inc.**
PO Box 1609
Nokomis, FL 34274-1609
Ph: (941)486-8600
Free: 888-232-9283
Fax: (941)486-8820
Co. E-mail: info@aeawave.com
URL: http://www.aeawave.com
Contact: Julie See, President
Description: Aquatic fitness instructors and therapists, pool and club owners, recreation departments, and manufacturers of pool products and services. Fosters members' professional development; serves as a resource center for services and products related to the aquatic fitness and therapy industries. Compiles and disseminates information through educational events and networking opportunities; offers certification to aquatic exercise instructors.

Conducts educational programs. **Founded:** 1984. **Publications:** *AKWA Magazine* (Bimonthly); *Aquatic Therapy and Fitness Research Journal* (Semiannual). **Educational Activities:** International Aquatic Fitness Conference (Annual). **Awards:** Global Award for Aquatic Fitness (Annual).

15941 ■ *Avante*
301-2197 Riverside Dr.
Ottawa, ON, Canada K1H 7X3
Ph: (613)523-1348
Free: 800-663-8708
Fax: (613)523-1206
Co. E-mail: info@phecanada.ca
URL: http://www.phecanada.ca
Contact: Laurissa Kenworthy, Manager
E-mail: laurissa@phecanada.ca
Released: 3/year **Price:** C$100, /year for institutions; C$65, /year for individuals.

15942 ■ Canadian Fitness and Lifestyle Research Institute (CFLRI)—Institut Canadien de la Recherche sur la Condition Physique et le Mode de Vie
201-185 Somerset St. W
Ottawa, ON, Canada K2P 0J2
Ph: (613)233-5528
Fax: (613)233-5536
Co. E-mail: info@cflri.ca
URL: http://www.cflri.ca
Description: Conducts research on physical activities in Canada and distributes information about physical activity. **Founded:** 1980. **Publications:** *The Research File* (Quarterly; 3/year); *Physical Activity Monitor* (Annual).

15943 ■ *Congress Report*
2875 Bates Rd.
Montreal, QC, Canada H3S 1B7
Ph: (514)731-3783
Fax: (514)731-9026
Co. E-mail: info@ifbb.com
URL: http://www.ifbb.com
Contact: Dr. Rafael Santonja, President
Released: Annual **Price:** free.

15944 ■ Exercise Safety Association (ESA)
PO Box 547916
Orlando, FL 32854-7916
Ph: (407)246-5090
Co. E-mail: askesa@aol.com
URL: http://www.exercisesafety.com
Contact: Sharon Foy, Director
Description: Fitness instructors, personal trainers, health spas, YMCAs, community recreation departments, and hospital wellness programs. Purposes are: to improve the qualifications of exercise instructors; to train instructors to develop safe exercise programs that will help people avoid injury while exercising; to prepare instructors for national certification. Offers training in aerobics and exercise and on the physiological aspects of exercise. Conducts exercise safety and research programs. Sponsors charitable program; maintains speakers' bureau. Offers instructor placement services. **Founded:** 1978. **Publications:** *ESA Member Directory* (Annual); *Exercise Safety Association Newsletter* (Bimonthly). **Awards:** STAR Certification.

15945 ■ *Flex*
2875 Bates Rd.
Montreal, QC, Canada H3S 1B7
Ph: (514)731-3783
Fax: (514)731-9026
Co. E-mail: info@ifbb.com
URL: http://www.ifbb.com
Contact: Dr. Rafael Santonja, President
Released: Monthly

15946 ■ IDEA Health and Fitness Association
10455 Pacific Center Ct.
San Diego, CA 92121
Ph: (858)535-8979
Free: 800-999-4332

Fax: (858)535-8234
Co. E-mail: contact@ideafit.com
URL: http://www.ideafit.com
Contact: Kathie Davis, Executive Director
Description: Provides continuing education for fitness professionals including; fitness instructors, personal trainers, program directors, and club/studio owners. Offers workshops for continuing education credits. **Founded:** 1982. **Publications:** *IDEA Fitness Journal*; *IDEA Health & Fitness Source* (10/year); *IDEA Personal Trainer* (10/year); *Trainer Success* (5/year). **Educational Activities:** IDEA Personal Trainer (Annual); IDEA World Fitness and Personal Trainer Convention (Annual). **Awards:** IDEA Fitness Instructor of the Year (Annual); IDEA Program Director of the Year (Annual); Fitness Inspiration Award; Fitness Instructor of the Year; IDEA Personal Trainer of the Year Award (Annual); Personal Trainer of the Year; Program Director of the Year.

15947 ■ *In Touch*
301-2197 Riverside Dr.
Ottawa, ON, Canada K1H 7X3
Ph: (613)523-1348
Free: 800-663-8708
Fax: (613)523-1206
Co. E-mail: info@phecanada.ca
URL: http://www.phecanada.ca
Contact: Laurissa Kenworthy, Manager
E-mail: laurissa@phecanada.ca
Released: 3/year

15948 ■ International Federation of Body Building and Fitness (IFBB)—Federation Internationale des Culturistes
2875 Bates Rd.
Montreal, QC, Canada H3S 1B7
Ph: (514)731-3783
Fax: (514)731-9026
Co. E-mail: info@ifbb.com
URL: http://www.ifbb.com
Contact: Dr. Rafael Santonja, President
Description: National federations of bodybuilding enthusiasts united to promote better health and fitness through bodybuilding, physical culture, proper nutrition, and weight training. Conducts and compiles research dealing with physical culture, bodybuilding, weight training, nutrition, sports injuries, and sports medicine. Compiles statistics on the results of competitions and evaluates judges' accuracy. Sanctions amateur, professional, and open world and continental bodybuilding competitions for men and women. Sponsors the Mr./Ms. Olympia contests and the World Amateur Men's and Women's Championships. Establishes rules and appoints qualified judges. Plans to establish hall of fame. **Founded:** 1946. **Publications:** *Congress Report* (Annual); *Flex* (Monthly); *Scientific Athletic Reports* (Periodic). **Awards:** Special Medals for Fitness Achievement (Periodic).

15949 ■ International Health, Racquet and Sportsclub Association (IHRSA)
Seaport Ctr.
70 Fargo St.
Boston, MA 02210
Ph: (617)951-0055
Free: 800-228-4772
Fax: (617)951-0056
Co. E-mail: info@ihrsa.org
URL: http://www.ihrsa.org
Contact: Joe Moore, President
Description: Health, racquet, and sport clubs; racquet sports manufacturers and suppliers. Promotes the continued growth of the health, racquet, and sports club industry in 70 countries. Aids member clubs in making educated business decisions. Sets standards for club management; offers group purchasing program. Organizes management training seminars. Compiles statistics; disseminates information. Conducts market research and educational programs; conducts sponsored membership promotion programs. Provides government relations and public relations services. **Scope:** government relations, club operations. **Founded:** 1981. **Publications:** *Profiles of Success*; *Club Business Interna-*

tional (Monthly). **Educational Activities:** International Health, Racquet and Sportsclub Association Convention (Annual).

15950 ■ International Physical Fitness Association (IPFA)
415 W Court St.
Flint, MI 48503
Ph: (810)239-2166
Free: 877-520-IPFA
Fax: (810)239-9390
Co. E-mail: contact@ipfa.us
URL: http://www.ipfa.us
Contact: Jerry Kahn, President
Description: Physical fitness centers. Facilitates the transfer of individual memberships from one member club to another. **Founded:** 1960. **Publications:** *IPFA Roster* (Annual).

15951 ■ National Federation of Professional Trainers (NFPT)
PO Box 4579
Lafayette, IN 47903-4579
Free: 800-729-6378
Fax: (765)471-7369
Co. E-mail: info@nfpt.com
URL: http://www.nfpt.com
Contact: Ron Clark, President
Description: Offers affordable, convenient, comprehensive, and applicable information to those seeking personal fitness trainer certification. Offers organizational certification credentials for consumer recognition of competence; provides certified affiliates with ongoing education; establishes a network of support, and provides professional products and services to trainers and consumers; and facilitates and encourages the exchange of ideas, knowledge, business experiences, and financial opportunities between all fitness administrators internationally. Offers educational programs. **Founded:** 1988.

15952 ■ *Physical Activity Monitor*
201-185 Somerset St. W
Ottawa, ON, Canada K2P 0J2
Ph: (613)233-5528
Fax: (613)233-5536
Co. E-mail: info@cflri.ca
URL: http://www.cflri.ca
Released: Annual **Price:** C$50, each.

15953 ■ Physical and Health Education Canada (PHE Canada)—Education physique et sante Canada
301-2197 Riverside Dr.
Ottawa, ON, Canada K1H 7X3
Ph: (613)523-1348
Free: 800-663-8708
Fax: (613)523-1206
Co. E-mail: info@phecanada.ca
URL: http://www.phecanada.ca
Contact: Laurissa Kenworthy, Manager
E-mail: laurissa@phecanada.ca
Description: National professional organization with charitable status. Professionals in the field of health, physical education, and related disciplines. Promotes the long-term health benefits of health and active lifestyles. Seeks to facilitate the professional development of members and teachers, teacher education in the education field. Collaborates with international, national, provincial, and local organizations to devise, implement, and monitor health and physical education programs. Advocates for enhanced social and physical environments supporting physically active and healthy lives. Sponsors continuing professional education and training programs; conducts research; develops resources. Manages school based fundraising programs. **Founded:** 1933. **Publications:** *Avante* (3/year); *In Touch* (3/year); *Physical and Health Education Journal* (Quarterly); *Avante* (Triennial). **Awards:** Recognition Award Program (RAP); North American Society Fellowship (Periodic); PHE Canada Health Educator Award (Annual); Physical Education Teaching Excellence Award (Periodic); School Recognition Award (Annual); Student Award (Annual); Dr. Andy Anderson Young Professional Award (Annual); R. Tait McKenzie Honour Award (Periodic).

15954 ■ *Physical and Health Education Journal*
301-2197 Riverside Dr.
Ottawa, ON, Canada K1H 7X3
Ph: (613)523-1348
Free: 800-663-8708
Fax: (613)523-1206
Co. E-mail: info@phecanada.ca
URL: http://www.phecanada.ca
Contact: Laurissa Kenworthy, Manager
E-mail: laurissa@phecanada.ca
Released: Quarterly

15955 ■ *The Research File*
201-185 Somerset St. W
Ottawa, ON, Canada K2P 0J2
Ph: (613)233-5528
Fax: (613)233-5536
Co. E-mail: info@cflri.ca
URL: http://www.cflri.ca
Contact: Christine Cameron, President (Acting)
Released: Quarterly; 3/year **Price:** C$25, /copy; free online.

15956 ■ *Scientific Athletic Reports*
2875 Bates Rd.
Montreal, QC, Canada H3S 1B7
Ph: (514)731-3783
Fax: (514)731-9026
Co. E-mail: info@ifbb.com
URL: http://www.ifbb.com
Contact: Dr. Rafael Santonja, President
Released: Periodic

15957 ■ United States Competitive Aerobics Federation (USCAF)
8033 Sunset Blvd., No. 920
Los Angeles, CA 90046
Ph: (323)850-3777
Fax: (323)850-7795
Co. E-mail: nacusa@aol.com
URL: http://www.sportaerobics-nac.com
Description: Governs and organizes sports fitness and aerobic competitions for youth and adults. Seeks to maintain high standards and consistency in the sport. Conducts educational programs. **Founded:** 1989.

15958 ■ United States Racquetball Association (USAR)—USA Racquetball
1685 W Uintah St.
Colorado Springs, CO 80904-2969
Ph: (719)635-5396
Fax: (719)635-0685
Co. E-mail: jhiser@usra.org
URL: http://www.usra.org
Contact: Cheryl Kirk, President
Description: Represents racquetball players and enthusiasts. Promotes racquetball as a sport; organizes racquetball to be a self-governing sport of, by, and for the players; encourages building of facilities for the sport; conducts racquetball events including annual national and international tournaments. Maintains hall of fame, junior player programs, and charitable programs. **Founded:** 1969. **Publications:** *Racquetball Magazine* (Bimonthly). **Educational Activities:** United States Racquetball Association Competition (Annual); High Performance Camp (Annual). **Awards:** Athletes (Annual); Hall of Fame (Annual); Racquetball Hall of Fame; Joe Sobek Outstanding Contribution Award; John Halverson Fair Play Award.

15959 ■ United States Water Fitness Association
PO Box 243279
Boynton Beach, FL 33424-3279
Ph: (561)732-9908
Fax: (561)732-0950
Co. E-mail: uswfa@aol.com
URL: http://www.uswfa.com
Contact: John R. Spannuth, President
Description: Promotes aquatics, including water fitness, through activities such as water aerobics, water walking, water running, and deep water exercise. Awards certification for water fitness instructors, program coordinators, and aquatic directors. Helps to identify and establish trends in water fitness and

aquatics. Sponsors National Water Fitness Week, National Water Walking Week, and National and World Water Fitness competitions. Encourages research. Promotes aquatics throughout the country by educating aquatic professionals on the organization and administration of aquatic programming. Maintains speakers' bureau; compiles statistics. **Publications:** *National Aquatics Newsletter* (Quarterly). **Educational Activities:** International Aquatics Conference (Annual). **Awards:** Who's Who in Aquatic Leadership in the USA (Annual).

REFERENCE WORKS

15960 ■ *Athletic Business--Buyers Guide Issue*
Pub: Athletic Business Publications Inc.
URL(s): www.athleticbusiness.com/buyers_guide.
Released: Annual; Latest edition 2011. **Price:** Free.
Publication includes: Listings of about 2,000 manufacturers and suppliers of athletic equipment, trainers' supplies, conditioning and testing equipment, building and facility equipment, sports surfaces, aquatic components, and outdoor recreation equipment; related trade associations and consultants and other professionals in the field. **Entries include:** Name, address, phone, fax, e-mail address. **Arrangement:** Separate alphabetical sections for manufacturers and suppliers, associations, and professionals. **Indexes:** Product, advertiser name.

15961 ■ *"Because 10 Million Zumba Lovers Can't Be Wrong" in Inc. (Volume 32, December 2010, No. 10, pp. 106)*
Pub: Inc. Magazine
Ed: Christine Lagorio. **Description:** Profile of partners, Alberto Perez, Alberto Perlman, and Alberto Aghion, founders of Zumba, a form of dance used for fitness.

15962 ■ *"'Biggest Loser' Adds Bit of Muscle to Local Economy" in Crain's Detroit Business (Vol. 26, January 4, 2010, No. 1, pp. 1)*
Pub: Crain Communications Inc.
Ed: Chad Halcom. **Description:** NBC's weight-loss reality show, 'The Biggest Loser' has helped the local economy and generated a new crop of local startup businesses due to past contestants that were from the Detroit area.

15963 ■ *"Carving a Niche" in Hawaii Business (Vol. 53, November 2007, No. 5, pp. 58)*
Pub: Hawaii Business Publishing
Ed: Kyle Galdeira. **Description:** Stephanie Lay created Extreme Surf Fitness which is a program that promotes natural performance enhancement and rehabilitation of surfers using core and balance exercises. Lay's goal is to become a full time coach for a big surf brand and tour the world with the team.

15964 ■ *"Corporate Training" in Hawaii Business (Vol. 53, October 2007, No. 4, pp. 46)*
Pub: Hawaii Business Publishing
Ed: Cathy S. Cruz-George. **Description:** Kalani Pa, Mike Hann, and Li Si Yang are three of the fitness trainers who have worked with some of the participants at the Hawaii's Fittest CEO contest. Pa has trained Group Pacific Inc.'s Chip Doyle while Hann was Sharon Serene's trainer. Their insights on the profession of being a fitness trainer, and on working with executives are given.

15965 ■ *"Elements For Success" in Small Business Opportunities (November 2008)*
Pub: Entrepreneur Press
Contact: Perlman Neil, President
Description: Profile of Elements, a physical fitness club that approach a healthy lifestyle for women, which includes the components of body, beauty and mind; the network of upscale, boutique style health clubs differ from other providers in its 'balanced lifestyle' approach to a healthy lifestyle. This unique niche is gaining in popularity despite the faltering economy.

15966 ■ *"Fiscally Fit" in Entrepreneur (Vol. 37, October 2009, No. 10, pp. 130)*
Pub: Entrepreneur Media, Inc.
Ed: Jason Daley. **Description:** Landrie Peterman, owner of an Anytime Fitness franchise in Oregon, describes how she turned her business around. The franchise, located in an industrial park, saw growth after six months with the help of corporate clients.

15967 ■ *"Fitness Made Fun" in Playthings (Vol. 106, September 1, 2008, No. 8, pp. 12)*
Pub: Reed Business Information
Contact: Jeff Greisch, President
Ed: Karyn M. Peterson. **Description:** Nintendo Wii has developed the Wii Fit game that allows gamers to engage in over forty physical activities through its Balance Board accessory, an engineered platform that senses weight and shifts in movement and balance. It also offers virtual trainers to talk participants through the activities and keeps track of the progress of multiple users.

15968 ■ *"Fitter from Twitter" in Boston Business Journal (Vol. 30, December 17, 2010, No. 47, pp. 1)*
Pub: Boston Business Journal
Ed: Lisa van der Pool. **Description:** Small businesses are increasing their use of the Twitter microblogging platform to attract and retain customers. Lisa Johnson, who owns Modern Pilates studios, managed to raise awareness of her personal brand nationally through the social media platform.

15969 ■ *"From Fat to Fit" in Canadian Business (Vol. 79, September 25, 2006, No. 19, pp. 100)*
Pub: Rogers Media
Ed: Graham Scott. **Description:** The increase in physical fitness clubs across Canada is discussed.

15970 ■ *"Get Fit On a Dine: Resolve To Be Healthy-and-Wealthy-This New Year" in Black Enterprise (Vol. 38, January 2008, No. 6, pp. 86)*
Pub: Earl G. Graves Publishing Co. Inc.
Ed: Angela P. Moore-Thorpe. **Description:** According to International Health, Racquet, and Sportsclub Association, nearly 43 million people are members of health clubs in the U.S. Corporate wellness programs as well as laws and your rights as a club member are explained.

15971 ■ *"Getting in Shape" in Crain's Cleveland Business (Vol. 28, December 3, 2007, No. 48, pp. 13)*
Pub: Crain Communications, Inc.
Ed: Chrissy Kadleck. **Description:** According to the Medical Fitness Association, the number of medically integrated health and fitness centers has grown from 79 centers in 1985 to 875 in 2006. Summa Wellness Institute, the 65,000-square-foot health-and-fitness facility which opened next to Summa Health Systems's outpatient medical center is discussed.

15972 ■ *"How I Did It: Mel Zuckerman" in Inc. (December 2007, pp. 140-142)*
Pub: Gruner & Jahr USA Publishing
Ed: Daniel McGinn. **Description:** Profile of Mel Zuckerman, who tells how transformed his life as a middle-aged, overweight homebuilder to a healthy addition to the fitness and spa industry with his posh Canyon Ranch retreats.

15973 ■ *"In It For the Long Run" in Business Journal-Serving Phoenix & the Valley of the Sun (Vol. 30, August 20, 2010, No. 50, pp. 1)*
Pub: Phoenix Business Journal
Ed: Angela Gonzales. **Description:** Cancer survivor Helene Neville has finished a record-breaking 2,520-mile run in 93 days and then celebrated her 50th birthday despite being diagnosed with Hodgkins' lymphoma in 1991. Neveille, who is also a Phoenix area registered nurse, made stops along the way to promote her book, 'Nurses in Shape'. Neville also discusses how she fought her cancer through running.

15974 ■ *"Insider" in Canadian Business (Vol. 80, Winter 2007, No. 24, pp.)*
Pub: Rogers Media
Ed: Zena Olijnyk. **Description:** Lululemon Athletica started in 1998 after Dennis Wilson takes a yoga class and notices a demand from women for breathable clothes. The company opened their first outlet in Vancouver in November 2000 then opened their first U.S. store in 2003 until finally going public July 27, 2007 where its stocks doubled in value within days of trading.

15975 ■ *"Kenosha 'Lifestyle Center' Delayed" in The Business Journal-Milwaukee (Vol. 25, August 8, 2008, No. 46, pp. A1)*
Pub: American City Business Journals, Inc.
Ed: Rich Kirchen. **Description:** Quality Centers of Orlando, Florida has postponed construction plans for the Kenosha Town Center in Kenosha County, Wisconsin to 2009 due to the economic downturn and lending concerns. The $200-million, 750,000-square-foot retail and residential center will be located near the corner of Wisconsin Highway 50 and I-94.

15976 ■ *"Nautilus Fights For Its Life" in Business Journal-Portland (Vol. 24, November 23, 2007, No. 38, pp. 1)*
Pub: American City Business Journals, Inc.
Ed: Matthew Kish. **Description:** Shareholders meeting will determine whether four members at Nautilus Inc. will be ousted and control given to New York firm Sherborne Investors LP. The decision on December 18, 2007 is crucial since the investor's record is varied. For some it has significantly increased shares, while others have ended in near-bankruptcy stages.

15977 ■ *"Our Gadget of the Week: Balancing Act" in Barron's (Vol. 88, March 31, 2008, No. 13, pp. 40)*
Pub: Dow Jones & Company, Inc.
Ed: Naureen S. Malik. **Description:** Wii Fit gives users the experience of a virtual personal trainer and workouts that become progressively harder. The device turns the typical fitness regimes into fun exercises and users can choose workouts in four categories including yoga, balance, strength-training and, low impact aerobics.

15978 ■ *"Ritz Kapalua Sells 93 Suites for $176M to Fund Renovation" in Commercial Property News (March 17, 2008)*
Pub: Nielsen Company
Description: Ritz-Carlton, Kapalua in Lahaina, Hawaii sold ninety-three of its units in order to fund renovations of 463 rooms and suites along with construction of a new spa and fitness center, new and expanded restaurants and pools and an environmental education center for children.

15979 ■ *"Shape Up! Jamal Williams Develops KIDFIT App to Combat Childhood Obesity" in Black Enterprise (Vol. 41, August 2010, No. 1, pp. 62)*
Pub: Earl G. Graves Publishing Co. Inc.
Ed: Sonya A. Donaldson. **Description:** Profile of Jamal Williams who developed KIDFIT, an app that helps to combat childhood obesity by offering 150 various exercises for children, with an emphasis on training, conditioning, coordination, and flexibility.

15980 ■ *"The Spirit of a Man: Kedar Massenburg's Intoxicating Style of Conducting Business" in Black Enterprise (Vol. 38, March 2008)*
Pub: Earl G. Graves Publishing Co. Inc.
Ed: Sonia Alleyne. **Description:** Profile of Kedar Massenburg, personal trainer at The Gym in Montvale, New Jersey. Massenburg also operates an independent record label and management company as well as Kedar Beverages LLC founded in 2005. His latest venture is winemaking.

15981 ■ *"Taxing Position: Yoga Studios Hit for Back Sales Tax" in Puget Sound Business Journal (Vol. 29, August 29, 2008, No. 19, pp. 1)*
Pub: American City Business Journals
Ed: Deirdre Gregg. **Description:** Several yoga studies were audited and told they owe several years worth of back taxes. A spokesman from the Washing-

ton Department of Revenue stated the yoga studies should be collecting the tax in general and that yoga classes given for the purpose of physical fitness are taxable.

STATISTICAL SOURCES

15982 ■ *The Market for Physical Fitness Equipment*
Pub: MarketResearch.com
Released: 1999. **Price:** $3250.00 (paper). **Description:** This report on the physical fitness and exercise equipment industry provides the latest information available for aerobic riders, aerobic step platforms/benches, elliptical trainers (cross trainers), free weights, home gyms, rowing machines, stationary exercise bicycles and many more.

15983 ■ *RMA Annual Statement Studies*
Pub: Risk Management Association
Contact: Kevin M. Blakey, President
Released: Annual. **Price:** $175.00 2006-07 edition, $105.00. **Description:** Contains composite balance sheets and income statements for more than 360 industries, including the accounting, auditing, and bookkeeping industries. Also contains five years of comparative historical data for discerning trends. Includes 16 commonly used ratios, computed for most of the size groupings for nearly every industry.

TRADE PERIODICALS

15984 ■ *American Fitness*
Pub: American Fitness
Contact: Linda D. Pfeffer, President
URL(s): www.americanfitness.com. **Ed:** Meg Jordan. **Released:** Bimonthly **Price:** $27, Individuals; $49, Canada and Mexico; $72, Other countries.

15985 ■ *IDEA Personal Trainer*
Pub: IDEA Inc.
URL(s): www.ideafit.com/idea-personal-trainer. **Ed:** Nicholas Drake. **Released:** Monthly; 10/yr.

15986 ■ *Men's Fitness: Your Guide to Healthy Living*
Pub: American Media, Inc.
URL(s): www.mensfitness.com. **Released:** Monthly; 10/yr. **Price:** $15, Two years; $24.97, Canada.

15987 ■ *Muscle & Fitness: The Super Fitness & Vigorous Health @ Any Age*
Pub: American Media, Inc.
URL(s): www.muscleandfitness.com/. **Released:** Monthly **Price:** $39.97, Individuals; $56.97, Canada; $71.97, Other countries.

15988 ■ *Muscular Development*
Pub: Advanced Research Press Inc.
URL(s): www.musculardevelopment.com/. **Released:** Monthly **Price:** $49.97, Individuals; $79.97, Two years.

15989 ■ *NSCA Bulletin*
Pub: National Strength and Conditioning Association
Contact: Steve Fleck, President
Ed: Lori Marker, Editor. **Released:** Bimonthly, 6/year. **Price:** Included in membership. **Description:** Tracks Association activities. Recurring features include interviews, a calendar of events, reports of meetings, news of educational opportunities, job listings, book reviews, and notices of publications available.

15990 ■ *Shape*
Pub: American Media, Inc.
URL(s): www.shape.com. **Released:** Monthly **Price:** $17.97, Individuals print; $32.97, Canada; $46.97, Other countries; $29.97, Individuals digital & print.

VIDEOCASSETTES/ AUDIOCASSETTES

15991 ■ *Acu-Yoga for Flexibility*
Acupressure Institute
1533 Shattuck Ave.
Berkeley, CA 94709
Ph: (510)845-1059
Free: 800-442-2232

Fax: (510)845-1496
Co. E-mail: info@acupressure.com
URL: http://www.acupressure.com
Contact: Michael Reed Gach, Founder
Released: 19??. **Price:** $29.95. **Description:** Demonstrates stretches for the lower, middle and upper back, pelvis and legs. **Availability:** VHS.

15992 ■ *The Ballet Workout II*
Princeton Book Co. Publishers
614 Rte. 130
Hightstown, NJ 08520
Ph: (609)426-0602
Free: 800-220-7149
Fax: (609)426-1344
Co. E-mail: pbc@dancehorizons.com
URL: http://www.dancehorizons.com
Released: 1993. **Price:** $19.95. **Description:** Melissa Lowe's follow-up the the Ballet Workout, provides the viewer with two new workouts that address the goal of achieving a lithe, supple body, an improves carriage, and the look and grace of a professional dancer. **Availability:** VHS.

15993 ■ *Beginning Bodybuilding*
Victory Multimedia
222 N. Sepulveda Blvd., Ste. 1306
El Segundo, CA 90245
Ph: (310)416-9140
Fax: (310)416-9839
Co. E-mail: RFVictory@juno.com
Released: 19??. **Price:** $9.98. **Description:** Demonstrates exercises that best target muscle stimulation and common errors to avoid. **Availability:** VHS.

15994 ■ *Beyond Protection*
Tapeworm Video Distributors
25876 The Old Road #141
Stevenson Ranch, CA 91381
Ph: (661)257-4904
Fax: (661)257-4820
Co. E-mail: sales@tapeworm.com
URL: http://www.tapeworm.com
Released: 1996. **Price:** $19.95. **Description:** Personal trainer, kinesiologist and martial artist Vanessa Friedman conducts an aerobic workout mixed with self defense techniques. **Availability:** VHS.

15995 ■ *Chi Kung the Healing Workout*
Bayview Entertainment
107 Pink St.
Hackensack, NJ 07601
Ph: (201)488-6110
Fax: (201)488-6112
Co. E-mail: sales@bayviewent.com
URL: http://www.bayviewentertainment.com
Released: 1996. **Description:** Presents gentle, easy to learn movements that aid in keeping the body fit. **Availability:** DVD.

15996 ■ *Dancing a Miracle*
Leslie T. McClure
PO Box 1223
Pebble Beach, CA 93953
Ph: (831)656-0553
Fax: (831)656-0555
Co. E-mail: leslie@411videoinfo.com
URL: http://www.411videoinfo.com
Released: 1997. **Price:** $19.95. **Description:** Dr. Irene Lamberti presents a workout program for the body and spirit. **Availability:** VHS.

15997 ■ *Dyna-Gym*
Princeton Book Co. Publishers
614 Rte. 130
Hightstown, NJ 08520
Ph: (609)426-0602
Free: 800-220-7149
Fax: (609)426-1344
Co. E-mail: pbc@dancehorizons.com
URL: http://www.dancehorizons.com
Released: 1992. **Price:** $24.95. **Description:** Describes an adjustable, body-shaping, resistance workout for women and men with musical accompaniment. A complete shaping workout that is a safe and gentle alternative to weights. **Availability:** VHS.

15998 ■ Exercise Ball Workout
Artistic Video
c/o Long Island School of Tai-Chi-Chuan
87 Tyler Ave.
Sound Beach, NY 11789-2639
Ph: (631)744-5999
Free: 888-982-4244
Fax: (631)744-5993
Co. E-mail: service@movementsofmagic.com
URL: http://www.movementsofmagic.com
Released: 1997. **Price:** $29.95. **Description:** Presents a unique workout to tone abs, hips, legs, arms and chest. **Availability:** VHS.

15999 ■ Forever Fit
Tapeworm Video Distributors
25876 The Old Road #141
Stevenson Ranch, CA 91381
Ph: (661)257-4904
Fax: (661)257-4820
Co. E-mail: sales@tapeworm.com
URL: http://www.tapeworm.com
Released: 1997. **Price:** $24.95. **Description:** Certified Fitness Instructor Loura White leads an exercise regimen for seniors. **Availability:** VHS.

16000 ■ Gentle Fitness
Tapeworm Video Distributors
25876 The Old Road #141
Stevenson Ranch, CA 91381
Ph: (661)257-4904
Fax: (661)257-4820
Co. E-mail: sales@tapeworm.com
URL: http://www.tapeworm.com
Released: 1994. **Price:** $19.95. **Description:** Catherine MacRae guides viewers through six routines of gentle exercise intended to relieve arthritis, poor circulation, and inactivity. **Availability:** VHS.

16001 ■ Geri-Fit: The First Workout with Weights for Older Adults
Tapeworm Video Distributors
25876 The Old Road #141
Stevenson Ranch, CA 91381
Ph: (661)257-4904
Fax: (661)257-4820
Co. E-mail: sales@tapeworm.com
URL: http://www.tapeworm.com
Released: 19??. **Price:** $19.95. **Description:** Provides instruction for improving strength, flexibility, balance, and arthritic conditions. **Availability:** VHS.

16002 ■ Lean Teen
Tapeworm Video Distributors
25876 The Old Road #141
Stevenson Ranch, CA 91381
Ph: (661)257-4904
Fax: (661)257-4820
Co. E-mail: sales@tapeworm.com
URL: http://www.tapeworm.com
Released: 19??. **Price:** $12.95. **Description:** Provides teenagers with information on fitness. **Availability:** VHS.

16003 ■ Madonna Grimes Cardio Sculpt
Tapeworm Video Distributors
25876 The Old Road #141
Stevenson Ranch, CA 91381
Ph: (661)257-4904
Fax: (661)257-4820
Co. E-mail: sales@tapeworm.com
URL: http://www.tapeworm.com
Released: 1997. **Price:** $19.95. **Description:** Ms. Fitness Champion conducts cardiovascular conditioning and light resistance weight work with isometric muscle training. **Availability:** VHS.

16004 ■ Madonna Grimes Hip Hop Dance Workout
Tapeworm Video Distributors
25876 The Old Road #141
Stevenson Ranch, CA 91381
Ph: (661)257-4904

Fax: (661)257-4820
Co. E-mail: sales@tapeworm.com
URL: http://www.tapeworm.com
Released: 1997. **Price:** $19.95. **Description:** Ms. Fitness Champion conducts an aerobic program designed for all levels. **Availability:** VHS.

16005 ■ Native Spirit
Leslie T. McClure
PO Box 1223
Pebble Beach, CA 93953
Ph: (831)656-0553
Fax: (831)656-0555
Co. E-mail: leslie@411videoinfo.com
URL: http://www.411videoinfo.com
Released: 1997. **Price:** $19.95. **Description:** Dr. Irene Lamberti presents a workout program for the body and spirit. **Availability:** VHS.

16006 ■ Nautilus Aerobics Plus: High Impact Aerobics
Karol Media
Hanover Industrial Estates
375 Stewart Rd.
Wilkes Barre, PA 18773-7600
Ph: (570)822-8899
Free: 800-526-4773
Co. E-mail: sales@karolmedia.com
URL: http://www.karolmedia.com
Released: 1990. **Price:** $9.95. **Description:** High-energy, high-calorie burning workout for those already familiar with aerobics. **Availability:** VHS.

16007 ■ Nautilus Aerobics Plus: Low Impact Aerobics
Karol Media
Hanover Industrial Estates
375 Stewart Rd.
Wilkes Barre, PA 18773-7600
Ph: (570)822-8899
Free: 800-526-4773
Co. E-mail: sales@karolmedia.com
URL: http://www.karolmedia.com
Released: 1990. **Price:** $9.95. **Description:** Nautilus aerobic fitness tape. Fat-burning tape (keep it on simmer) is low intensity. **Availability:** VHS.

16008 ■ Nike HealthWalking Training System
Karol Media
Hanover Industrial Estates
375 Stewart Rd.
Wilkes Barre, PA 18773-7600
Ph: (570)822-8899
Free: 800-526-4773
Co. E-mail: sales@karolmedia.com
URL: http://www.karolmedia.com
Released: 1988. **Price:** $29.95. **Description:** After developing a walking program that offers an exciting combination of both mental and physical fitness, Nike offers this video designed to train anyone looking for a walking system that produces maximum results. Two audio cassettes and a study guide are optional assets that can be purchased with this video. **Availability:** VHS.

16009 ■ Pre- and Post-Natal Fitness
Leslie T. McClure
PO Box 1223
Pebble Beach, CA 93953
Ph: (831)656-0553
Fax: (831)656-0555
Co. E-mail: leslie@411videoinfo.com
URL: http://www.411videoinfo.com
Released: 1997. **Price:** $24.95. **Description:** Presents a low-impact fitness program adapted from Imperial Russian ballet toning techniques. **Availability:** VHS.

16010 ■ Pumping Iron After Fifty
Tapeworm Video Distributors
25876 The Old Road #141
Stevenson Ranch, CA 91381
Ph: (661)257-4904
Fax: (661)257-4820
Co. E-mail: sales@tapeworm.com
URL: http://www.tapeworm.com
Released: 19??. **Description:** Presents easy weight training exercises for seniors. **Availability:** VHS.

16011 ■ Yoga to Go with Misty Carey Volume 2: Strength
Santa Monica Yoga
1640 Ocean Park Blvd.
Santa Monica, CA 90405
Ph: (310)396-4040
Fax: (310)392-7404
Co. E-mail: contact@santamonicayoga.com
URL: http://www.santamonicayoga.com
Released: 1997. **Price:** $29.95. **Description:** Presents exercises and techniques to build strength, balance and flexibility. **Availability:** VHS.

16012 ■ Yoga to Go with Misty Carey Volume 3: Health
Santa Monica Yoga
1640 Ocean Park Blvd.
Santa Monica, CA 90405
Ph: (310)396-4040
Fax: (310)392-7404
Co. E-mail: contact@santamonicayoga.com
URL: http://www.santamonicayoga.com
Released: 1997. **Price:** $29.95. **Description:** Presents exercises and techniques to stimulate and balance the immune system. **Availability:** VHS.

CONSULTANTS

16013 ■ Health Fitness Dynamics Inc.—HFD Spa
1012 N Ocean Blvd., Ste. 103
Pompano Beach, FL 33062
Ph: (954)942-0049
Fax: (954)941-0854
Co. E-mail: hfd@hfdspa.com
URL: http://www.hfdspa.com
Contact: Patricia A. Monteson, Owner Founder
E-mail: pattymonteson@hfdspa.com
Scope: Offers spa consulting services in the following areas: program development, facility planning, feasibility and market studies, staffing requirements, product and equipment selection, coordinating of support departments, systems of operation, personnel, and on-going management. Industries served: hospitality, hotels and resorts, and health spas. **Founded:** 1983. **Publications:** "Spa News & Views: If The Spa Will Not Help Sell Rooms, Do Not Add A Spa," Spa Management, Mar, 2006; "Thinking of Jumping on the Spa Bandwagon Look Before You Leap"; "Spa Savvy-Best Practices for Hiring, Training & Retaining Your Staff". **Seminars:** Management Workshop; Managing a Revenue Generating Spa within a Resort; The Health Spa - Another Marketable and Complementary Dimension of a Resort; Planning and Managing a Health Spa in a Resort.

FRANCHISES AND BUSINESS OPPORTUNITIES

16014 ■ American Ramp Systems
Gordon Industries
202 W 1st St.
South Boston, MA 02127
Free: 800-649-5215
Fax: (617)268-3701
Co. E-mail: info@americanramp.com
URL: http://www.americanramp.com
Description: Sales and rentals of accessibility ramps. **No. of Franchise Units:** 43. **No. of Company-Owned Units:** 1. **Founded:** 1970.. **Franchised:** 2002. **Equity Capital Needed:** $125,410-$207,180. **Franchise Fee:** $49,250-$98,500. **Royalty Fee:** 12%. **Financial Assistance:** Third party financing available. **Training:** Provides 1 week at headquarters with ongoing support.

16015 ■ Anytime Fitness
12181 Margo Ave., S
Hastings, MN 55033
Ph: (800)704-5004
Fax: (651)438-5099
Description: Anytime Fitness focuses on health, nutrition and senior care services. **No. of Franchise Units:** 1,620. **No. of Company-Owned Units:** 16. **Founded:** 2001.. **Franchised:** 2002. **Equity Capital Needed:** $56,299-$353,900 total investment. **Fran-

chise Fee: $20,999-$26,999. **Royalty Fee:** $499/month. **Financial Assistance:** Third party financing available. **Training:** Provides 3 days minimum at headquarters and 3 days minimum onsite with ongoing support.

16016 ■ Baby Boot Camp
665 S Orange Ave., Ste. 7
Sarasota, FL 34236
Ph: (941)953-5000
Free: 888-990-2229
Fax: (941)953-5002
URL: http://www.babybootcamp.com

Description: Pre and postnatal fitness. **No. of Franchise Units:** 142. **No. of Company-Owned Units:** 1. **Founded:** 2001.. **Franchised:** 2005. **Equity Capital Needed:** $4,490-$10,300. **Franchise Fee:** $3,700-$5,700. **Royalty Fee:** $115-$340/month. **Financial Assistance:** In-house financial assistance available with franchisee fee. **Training:** Available 2 days at headquarters, by phone and online with ongoing support.

16017 ■ Butterfly Life
2404 San Ramon Valley Blvd., Ste. 200
San Ramon, CA 94583
Free: 800-290-2977
Fax: (925)743-8820

Description: Women's healthy living & fitness center. **No. of Franchise Units:** 100. **Founded:** 2003. **Franchised:** 2003. **Equity Capital Needed:** $63,990-$139,500. **Franchise Fee:** $29,500. **Royalty Fee:** $1,000/month. **Training:** Offers 1 week at headquarters, 3 days at franchisee's location, annual conferences, phone and onsite assistance as needed.

16018 ■ CKO Kickboxing
900 Madison St.
Hoboken, NJ 07030
Ph: (201)963-7774
Fax: (201)963-6177
URL: http://www.ckokickboxing.com

Description: Kickboxing classes. **No. of Franchise Units:** 19. **No. of Company-Owned Units:** 3. **Founded:** 1997.. **Franchised:** 2007. **Equity Capital Needed:** $102,937-$358,597. **Franchise Fee:** $25,000. **Royalty Fee:** 7%. **Training:** Consists of intensive training in the following areas: class structure and size, pre-opening and set-up, marketing, operations and customer service with ongoing mentoring and support.

16019 ■ Club 50 Fitness
9410 Prototype Dr., Ste. 18
Reno, NV 89521
Ph: (206)337-8658
Free: 877-425-8250
Fax: (775)201-1180
Co. E-mail: info@club50fitness.com
URL: http://www.club50fitness.com

Description: 30 minute circuit training that incorporates fitness and nutrition into a unique and fun format designed exclusively for men and women age 50 and up. Provides a complete package for all franchisees including equipment, training, support, pre-produced television, radio and print ads, and public relations support. **No. of Franchise Units:** 13. **No. of Company-Owned Units:** 1. **Founded:** 2003.. **Franchised:** 2005. **Equity Capital Needed:** $50,000-$80,000. **Franchise Fee:** $24,900, including equipment. **Training:** Start-up, onsite and offsite with continued ongoing support.

16020 ■ CoachMeFit
2433 Oak Valley Dr., Ste. 500
Ann Arbor, MI 48103
Ph: (734)477-9450
Fax: (734)477-9427
URL: http://www.coachmefit.com

Description: Personal fitness training. **No. of Franchise Units:** 1. **No. of Company-Owned Units:** 3. **Founded:** 2001.. **Franchised:** 2007. **Equity Capital Needed:** $106,700-$261,500. **Franchise Fee:** $12,500. **Royalty Fee:** 5%. **Financial Assistance:** Limited third party financing available. **Training:** 3-5 days at headquarters.

16021 ■ Contours Express
Contours Express, LLC
156 Imperial Way
Nicholasville, KY 40356
Ph: (859)885-6441
Free: 877-227-2282
Fax: (859)241-2234
Co. E-mail: info@contoursexpress.com
URL: http://www.contoursexpress.com

Description: Women's only fitness and weight loss studio. **No. of Franchise Units:** 600. **Founded:** 1998. **Franchised:** 1998. **Equity Capital Needed:** $75,000 net worth. **Franchise Fee:** $18,000. **Financial Assistance:** Yes. **Training:** Site selection, lease negotiation, 3-4 day onsite training at location, and club layout assistance.

16022 ■ Fit Zone For Women
4341 S Westnedge Ave., Ste 1103
Kalamazoo, MI 49008
Ph: (269)226-9564
Fax: (269)226-9566

Description: Full service fitness center for women. **No. of Franchise Units:** 25. **No. of Company-Owned Units:** 2. **Founded:** 2004.. **Franchised:** 2006. **Equity Capital Needed:** $100,100-$150,500. **Franchise Fee:** $25,000. **Royalty Fee:** Varies. **Training:** Provides 7 days at headquarters and 3 days onsite and ongoing support.

16023 ■ Fitwize 4 Kids Inc.
384 Bel Marin Keys Blvd., Ste. 210
Novato, CA 94949
Ph: (415)883-1798
Fax: (415)883-1825

Description: Healthy lifestyle center for kids. **No. of Franchise Units:** 14. **No. of Company-Owned Units:** 1. **Founded:** 2004.. **Franchised:** 2005. **Equity Capital Needed:** $125,000. **Franchise Fee:** $39,000. **Royalty Fee:** $495/month.

16024 ■ Fun Bus USA, Inc. - 'Fitness Fun on Wheels'
32 Timothy Ln.
Tinton Falls, NJ 07724
Ph: (732)578-1287
Fax: (732)530-8287

Description: Mobile fun fitness program. **No. of Franchise Units:** 36. **Founded:** 2001.. **Franchised:** 2003. **Equity Capital Needed:** $85,000. **Franchise Fee:** $32,500. **Financial Assistance:** Yes. **Training:** Yes.

16025 ■ Gold's Gym
Gold's Gym International Inc.
125 E John Carpenter Fwy., Ste. 1300
Irving, TX 75062-2366
Ph: (214)296-5062
Fax: (214)296-5000
URL: http://www.goldsgym.com

Description: Offers health, and nutrition services. **No. of Franchise Units:** 700. **No. of Company-Owned Units:** 65. **Founded:** 1965.. **Equity Capital Needed:** $895,500-$3,800,000. **Franchise Fee:** $25,000 initial fee. **Financial Assistance:** Yes. **Training:** Yes.

16026 ■ The HIT Center
9446 Philips Hwy., Ste. 3
Jacksonville, FL 32256
Ph: (904)475-9600
Co. E-mail: info@thehitcenters.com
URL: http://www.thehitcenters.com

Description: Athletic development, weight loss, and fitness center. **No. of Franchise Units:** 11. **Founded:** 2000. **Franchised:** 2003. **Equity Capital Needed:** $500,000. **Franchise Fee:** $40,000. **Royalty Fee:** 5%. **Training:** Training includes 4 weeks training at headquarters, 1 week at franchisee's location and as needed.

16027 ■ IM=X Pilates Studio
The Xercize Studio, LLC
265 Madison Ave., 2nd Fl.
New York, NY 10016
Free: 877-748-3249

Fax: (714)281-8009
Co. E-mail: franchise@xercizestudio.com
URL: http://www.imxpilatesstudio.com

Description: For 10 years, IM=X has been in the business of pilates certification, developing patented equipment, and helping customers grow pilates programs. We now offer the IM=X Pilates Studio franchise as an innovative, elite fitness program plus business operations, marketing, and educational support to prospective franchise owners. Success experienced by clubs offering IM=X Pilates is now available to meet current market demands for this challenging program. **No. of Company-Owned Units:** 1. **Founded:** 2003.. **Franchised:** 2003. **Equity Capital Needed:** Full model $75,000-$160,000; express model $15,000-$30,000. **Franchise Fee:** $15,000-$22,000. **Financial Assistance:** 30-V, FRA handbook. **Training:** Operations Manual and Training course prepare you to grow and operate your own studio or studio chain. Every year we will train and certify up to 12 of your staff in the Basic And Advanced IM=X Pilates program.

16028 ■ J.W. Tumbles
312 S Cedros, Ste. 329
Solana Beach, CA 92075
Ph: (858)794-0484
Fax: (858)794-0398

Description: Children's gym for fitness & fun. **No. of Franchise Units:** 33. **No. of Company-Owned Units:** 1. **Founded:** 1994.. **Franchised:** 2004. **Equity Capital Needed:** $138,600-$215,600. **Franchise Fee:** $42,850. **Training:** Yes.

16029 ■ La Boxing Franchise Corp.
2915 Tech Center Dr.
Santa Ana, CA 92705
Free: 866-522-6946
Fax: (714)668-9231
Co. E-mail: franchise@laboxing.com
URL: http://www.laboxing.com

Description: The business you will conduct as an LA Boxing Franchise is a membership physical fitness system consisting of unique boxing and kickboxing training regiment, utilizing a system and products that are proprietary to the company. We authorize our franchisees to offer memberships to promote boxing fitness training and instruction programs utilizing a professional ring, weight room, and other equipment with unique construction and design features. No experience necessary. **No. of Franchise Units:** 116. **Founded:** 1992.. **Franchised:** 2004. **Equity Capital Needed:** $174,900-$185,750. **Franchise Fee:** $25,000. **Training:** 5 days of initial training at corporate training facilities, and 1 day onsite. Initial training includes instruction in owner/operator responsibilities, instructor training, equipment, membership sales, administration, operations, product and services sales and marketing.

16030 ■ Lady of America Franchise Corporation
Lady of America, Inc.
500 E Broward Blvd., Ste. 1650
Ft. Lauderdale, FL 33394
Ph: (954)644-7827
Free: 800-833-5239
Fax: (954)527-5436

Description: Franchises ladies-only fitness centers. **No. of Franchise Units:** 211. **No. of Company-Owned Units:** 5. **Founded:** 1984.. **Franchised:** 1989. **Equity Capital Needed:** $192,700-$454,600. **Franchise Fee:** $30,000. **Royalty Fee:** 8%. **Training:** Yes.

16031 ■ Lucille Roberts Fitness Express
Women's Fitness Franchising, LLC

Description: Women's fitness & weight-loss center. **No. of Franchise Units:** 5. **No. of Company-Owned Units:** 47. **Founded:** 1970. **Franchised:** 2005. **Equity Capital Needed:** $271,850-$402,400. **Franchise Fee:** $25,000. **Royalty Fee:** 6%. **Financial Assistance:** Third party financing available. **Training:** Offers 1 week at headquarters with ongoing support.

16032 ■ McGruff Safe Kids Total Identification System
Arfmann Marketing, LLC
35246 US Hwy. 19 N
Palm Harbor, FL 34684

Ph: (727)725-9674
Free: 888-209-4218
Fax: (727)725-9740
Co. E-mail: neil@mcgruff-tid.com
URL: http://www.mcgruff-tid.com
Description: Digital child identification safety system. **No. of Franchise Units:** 31. **Founded:** 2003.. **Franchised:** 2003. **Equity Capital Needed:** An additional $3,000-$5,000. **Franchise Fee:** $30,000. **Training:** Offers 3 days of training.

16033 ■ Monart School of The Arts

Monart Franchise Corp.
2340 Powell St., Ste. 397
Emeryville, CA 94608
Ph: (310)390-0386
Free: 877-MON-ART1
Fax: (310)391-4355
Description: Children's school of the arts. **No. of Franchise Units:** 27. **Founded:** 1981. **Franchised:** 2004. **Equity Capital Needed:** $65,000-$75,000. **Franchise Fee:** $15,000. **Royalty Fee:** 8%. **Training:** Yes.

16034 ■ My Gym Children's Fitness Center

My Gym Enterprises
15300 Ventura Blvd., Ste. 414
Sherman Oaks, CA 91403
Ph: (818)907-6966
Free: 800-469-4967
Fax: (818)907-0735
URL: http://www.my-gym.com
Description: My Gym Children's Fitness Centers help youngsters 3 mos. - 9 yrs. develop physically, cognitively and emotionally. Structured, age-appropriate weekly classes incorporate music, dance, relays, games, special rides, gymnastics, sports and original activities. Our unique, award-winning My Gym Program, non competitive atmosphere and ideal student/teacher ratio build confidence and self-esteem. Kids just love the state-of-the-art facility w/ its My Gym custom-made equipment. **No. of Franchise Units:** 200. **No. of Company-Owned Units:** 5. **Founded:** 1983. **Franchised:** 1995. **Equity Capital Needed:** $25,000-$55,000. **Franchise Fee:** $40,000-55,000. **Training:** 21 day training course-Ref. manuals and videos-Complete bus. operating systems-Detailed class curricula-Full handholding process thru Grand Opening and 1st session-Exceptional ongoing support w/ onsite visits, written materials, phone calls-Program innovations-Promotions-My Gym National and Regional Seminars.

16035 ■ Nexgym

1430 E Southlake Blvd., Ste. 110
Southlake, TX 76092
Ph: (888)696-8444
Fax: (636)412-9300
Description: Children's interactive fitness program. **No. of Franchise Units:** 1. **No. of Company-Owned Units:** 1. **Founded:** 2005. **Franchised:** 2006. **Equity Capital Needed:** $213,000-$397,000. **Franchise Fee:** $30,000. **Royalty Fee:** 6%. **Training:** Includes 2 weeks training at headquarters, 1 week at franchisee's location and ongoing support.

16036 ■ One 2 One Bodyscapes

1197 Walnut St.
Newton, MA 02461
Ph: (617)796-8808
Description: One on one personal training center. **Founded:** 1997.. **Franchised:** 2006. **Equity Capital Needed:** $135,900-$195,900. **Franchise Fee:** $30,000. **Training:** Yes.

16037 ■ Oogles N Googles

9640 N Augusta Dr.
Carmel, IN 46032
Ph: (317)228-9177
Fax: (317)228-9178
Description: Birthday parties, and preschool enrichment. **No. of Franchise Units:** 10. **Founded:** 2001.. **Franchised:** 2003. **Equity Capital Needed:** $33,400-$40,700. **Franchise Fee:** $19,900. **Royalty Fee:** 7%. **Training:** Available at headquarters for 10 days.

16038 ■ Platoon Fitness

899 Penn St.
Bryn Mawr, PA 19010
Free: 888-752-8666
Fax: (610)581-7174
Description: Outdoor fitness and personal training centers. **No. of Company-Owned Units:** 5. **Founded:** 1999. **Franchised:** 2006. **Equity Capital Needed:** $2,500. **Franchise Fee:** $5,000. **Training:** Offers 2 weeks training at headquarters, 2 months onsite, additional training 5 times a year at franchisee's location, and ongoing support.

16039 ■ Retro Fitness

Retro Fitness, LLC
Description: Fitness center. **No. of Franchise Units:** 75. **No. of Company-Owned Units:** 4. **Founded:** 2002.. **Franchised:** 2006. **Equity Capital Needed:** $861,250-$1,522,499. **Franchise Fee:** $69,000. **Royalty Fee:** 5%. **Financial Assistance:** Third party financing available. **Training:** Provides 8 days training at headquarters, 8 days at franchisee's location and ongoing support.

16040 ■ SMASHMOUTH

2378 Boston Rd., Ste. 522
Wilbraham, MA 01095
Ph: (413)242-1111
URL: http://www.smashmouthbrand.com
Description: SMASHMOUTH is fitness "formatter" and your "one-stop" fitness source. We have taken over 30 formats & brought them together under the umbrella of one brand. Our "Pure Fitness" and "Personal Enhancement" categories encompass dozens of different formats for coed, women, men, seniors and kids. **Founded:** 2005.. **Equity Capital Needed:** Varies, depending on format. **Training:** Yes.

16041 ■ Snap Fitness Inc.

2411 Galpin Ct., Ste. 110
Chanhassen, MN 55317
Ph: (952)474-5422
Free: 877-474-542
Fax: (952)426-7161
Co. E-mail: inquiries@snapfitness.com
URL: http://www.snapfitness.com
Description: 24-hour fitness center. **No. of Franchise Units:** 1,023. **No. of Company-Owned Units:** 80. **No. of Operating Units:** 1183. **Founded:** 2003.. **Franchised:** 2004. **Equity Capital Needed:** $68,618-$376,700. **Franchise Fee:** $15,000. **Royalty Fee:** $449/month. **Financial Assistance:** Limited in-house financial assistance available. **Training:** Provides 2 days at headquarters with ongoing support.

16042 ■ Sportball Systems Inc.

39 Glen Cameron Rd., Unit 8
Thornhill, ON, Canada L3T 1P1
Ph: (905)882-4473
Free: 877-678-5437
Fax: (905)882-8453
Co. E-mail: franchise@sportball.ca
URL: http://www.sportball.ca
Description: Sportball provides unique, non-competitive sports programs, camps and birthday parties for children 16 months to 8 years. Children learn the concepts and skills required for hockey, baseball, basketball, soccer, volleyball, tennis and golf. **No. of Franchise Units:** 193. **No. of Company-Owned Units:** 215. **Founded:** 1995. **Franchised:** 2005. **Equity Capital Needed:** $30,000 (min). **Franchise Fee:** $20,000. **Training:** Yes.

16043 ■ Survivor Bootcamp

11087 Barnston View Rd.
Pitt Meadows, BC, Canada V3Y 2W8
Ph: (604)357-3179
Free: 877-266-8267
Fax: (604)460-7194
Co. E-mail: seana@survivorbootcamp.com
URL: http://www.survivorbootcamp.com
URL(s): www.survivorfitness.com. **Description:** Indoor/Outdoor Fitness Training for EveryBody! Get Motivated for 1 hour a day / 3-5 days a week / 4 weeks What sets us apart from other fitness companies? We motivate clients in small classes with personal training attention. We are all about total body conditioning for accelerated results for all fitness levels. Our program is designed to encourage

personal improvement and goal achievement in a supportive group setting. Participants are encouraged to compete only against themselves. **No. of Franchise Units:** 47. **No. of Company-Owned Units:** 2. **Founded:** 2004.. **Franchised:** 2006. **Equity Capital Needed:** $8,000 investment required; $2,000 start-up capital. **Franchise Fee:** $5,000. **Training:** Provides 1 week training in Vancouver.

16044 ■ Time For Fitness LLC

667 Waterview Cove
Eagan, MN 55123
Ph: (612)703-6151
Fax: (952)345-8870
Description: Health club for baby boomers and seniors. **Founded:** 2004.. **Franchised:** 2005. **Equity Capital Needed:** $58,000-$68,000. **Franchise Fee:** $30,000. **Royalty Fee:** 5%. **Training:** Provides 6 days training at headquarters and ongoing support.

16045 ■ Twist Sport Conditioning Centers

1225 East Keith Rd., Ste. 12
North Vancouver, BC, Canada V7J 1J3
Ph: (604)904-6556
Fax: (604)904-6558
Co. E-mail: franchise@sportconditioning.ca
URL: http://www.twistconditioning.com
Description: Specializes in performance enhancement through sport-specific conditioning. **No. of Franchise Units:** 5. **No. of Company-Owned Units:** 1. **Founded:** 1999.. **Franchised:** 2006. **Equity Capital Needed:** $300,000-$400,000 investment required; $100,000 start-up capital required. **Franchise Fee:** $40,000.

COMPUTERIZED DATABASES

16046 ■ *The Physician & Sportsmedicine*

149 5th Ave., 10th Fl.
New York, NY 10010
Ph: (212)812-8420
Free: 800-519-3692
Fax: (212)228-1308
Co. E-mail: info@vendomegrp.com
URL: http://www.vendomegrp.com
Availability: Online: Vendome Group L.L.C. **Type:** Full-text.

16047 ■ *Smoking and Health Resource Library*

4770 Buford Hwy.
MS K-50
Atlanta, GA 30341
Ph: (404)639-3311
Free: 800-331-3435
Fax: (404)232-3299
Co. E-mail: tobaccoinfo@cdc.gov
URL: http://www.cdc.gov/tobacco
Availability: Online: U.S. Centers for Disease Control and Prevention - Office on Smoking and Health. **Type:** Bibliographic.

16048 ■ *SportDiscus™*

10 Estes St.
Ipswich, MA 01938-2106
Ph: (978)356-6500
Free: 800-653-2726
Fax: (978)356-6565
Co. E-mail: information@ebscohost.com
URL: http://www.ebscohost.com
Contact: Tim Collins, President
E-mail: tcollins@ebscohost.com
Availability: Online: EBSCO Publishing; Wolters Kluwer Health - Ovid. CD-ROM: Wolters Kluwer Health - Ovid. **Type:** Bibliographic.

LIBRARIES

16049 ■ Indiana University - Health, Physical Education & Recreation Library

HPER Bldg. 029
1025 E. 7th St.
Bloomington, IN 47405
Ph: (812)855-4420

Fax: (812)855-6778
Co. E-mail: jiliu@indiana.edu
URL: http://www.libraries.iub.edu/index.php-
?pageId=83
Contact: Jian Liu, Director
Scope: Physical education, recreation and park administration, health and safety, coaching, adapted physical education and therapeutic recreation, sports medicine and psychology. **Services:** Interlibrary loan; copying; Library open to the public. **Founded:** 1978. **Holdings:** 25,274 volumes; 10,871 microforms. **Subscriptions:** 250 journals and other serials. **Telecommunication Services:** libhper@indiana.edu.

16050 ■ Lemmen-Holton Cancer Pavilion Library
145 Michigan, NE
Grand Rapids, MI 49503
Ph: (616)486-5700
URL: http://www.spectrumhealth.org/lhcp
Scope: Cancer. **Services:** Library open to the public. **Holdings:** Pamphlets.

16051 ■ Springfield College - Babson Library - Special Collections
263 Alden St.
Springfield, MA 01109-3797
Ph: (413)748-3315
Free: 800-730-5279
Fax: (413)748-3631
Co. E-mail: libraryref@spfldcol.edu
URL: http://www.spfldcol.edu/library
Contact: Rachael Naismith
Scope: Recreation, physical education and training. **Services:** Interlibrary loan; copying; faxing; collections open to the public with permission. **Founded:** 1885. **Holdings:** 145,700 books; 25,000 bound periodical volumes; 3000 archives; 735,000 microfiche; 12,900 microfilm; 2960 videocassettes; 5000 phone cards. **Subscriptions:** 820 journals and other serials; 10 newspapers. **Telecommunication Services:** jmonseau@spfldcol.edu.

16052 ■ State University of New York College at Cortland Memorial Library
81 Prospect Terrace
Cortland, NY 13045
Ph: (607)753-2525
Fax: (607)753-5669
Co. E-mail: library@cortland.edu
URL: http://www2.cortland.edu/library
Contact: Gail Wood, Director, Library Services
Scope: Education, recreation, physical education, health education. **Services:** Interlibrary loan; copying; SDI; Library open to the public with restrictions. **Founded:** 1868. **Holdings:** 371,692 books; 45,403 bound periodical volumes; 844,207 microforms; 4104 audio/visual programs; 50 VF drawers; 9800 pamphlets; 89 online databases. **Subscriptions:** 526 journals; 3 newspapers; 36 electronic databases. **Telecommunication Services:** woodg@cortland.edu.

16053 ■ Tuality Health Information Resource Center
335 SE 8th Ave.
Hillsboro, OR 97123-9019
Ph: (503)681-1702
Co. E-mail: tuality.library@tuality.org
URL: http://www.tuality.org
Scope: Health, fitness, nutrition, diseases, support groups. **Services:** Interlibrary loan; copying; library open to the public. **Founded:** 1988. **Holdings:** 800 books; 3000 pamphlets; 90 anatomical models and charts; 450 videotapes. **Subscriptions:** 24 journals and other serials.

16054 ■ Universite de Montreal - Bibliotheque de Kinesiologie
Universite de Montreal
C.P. 6128, succursale Centre-ville
Montreal, QC, Canada H3C 3J7
Ph: (514)343-6765
Fax: (514)343-2181
Co. E-mail: denis.arvisais@umontreal.ca
URL: http://www.bib.umontreal.ca/SA/kinesio.htm
Contact: Sylvie Desbiens, Librarian
Scope: Physical education, sports medicine, exercise, physiology and training. **Services:** Interlibrary loan; copying; Library open to the public with restrictions. **Founded:** 1966. **Holdings:** 11,908 books; 9349 bound periodical volumes; 24,028 microforms; 1982 reports; 310 AV programs. **Subscriptions:** 819 journals and other serials.

16055 ■ University of Illinois at Urbana-Champaign - Applied Health Sciences Library
Main Library, Rm. 146
1408 W. Gregory Dr.
Urbana, IL 61801
Ph: (217)333-3615
Fax: (217)333-8384
Co. E-mail: mballen@uiuc.edu
URL: http://www.library.illinois.edu/ahs/
Contact: Mary Beth Allen
Scope: Kinesiology and exercise science, sports medicine, psychology, sociology, history of sport, rehabilitation education, counseling, speech and hearing science, community health, public health, gerontology, aging. **Services:** Interlibrary loan. **Founded:** 1949. **Holdings:** 20,00 books; 1407 theses; 6 VF drawers of pamphlets; 10,536 microcards; 30,000 microfiche; 19,000 microform publications. **Subscriptions:** 300 journals and other serials. **Telecommunication Services:** gregory2@uiuc.edu.

16056 ■ University of North Carolina at Greensboro - Special Collections & Rare Books, Jackson Library - History of Physical Education and Dance Collection
222B Jackson Library
Greensboro, NC 27402-6170
Ph: (336)334-5246
Free: 888-245-0180

Fax: (336)334-5399
Co. E-mail: carolyn_shankle@uncg.edu
URL: http://library.uncg.edu/info/depts/scua
Contact: Carolyn Shankle, Specialist, Collections
Scope: Physical activity, training, theory; gymnastics; dance history. **Services:** Wi-Fi access; collection open to the public for research. **Holdings:** 1800 books and pamphlets. **Telecommunication Services:** bill_finley@uncg.edu; scua@uncg.edu.

RESEARCH CENTERS

16057 ■ Canadian Fitness and Lifestyle Research Institute (CFLRI)—Institut Canadien de la Recherche sur la Condition Physique et le mode de vie (ICRCP)
201-185 Somerset St. W
Ottawa, ON, Canada K2P 0J2
Ph: (613)233-5528
Fax: (613)233-5536
Co. E-mail: info@cflri.ca
URL: http://www.cflri.ca
Contact: Christine Cameron, President (Acting)
Founded: 1985. **Publications:** The Research File (Quarterly; 3/year).

16058 ■ Cooper Institute (CI)
12330 Preston Rd.
Dallas, TX 75230
Ph: (972)341-3200
Free: 800-635-7050
Fax: (972)341-3227
Co. E-mail: courses@cooperinst.org
URL: http://www.cooperinstitute.org
Contact: Susan Campbell, President
Description: Promotes understanding of the relationship between living habits and health. Provides leadership in enhancing the physical and emotional well-being of individuals. Promotes participation in aerobics. Seeks to increase the quality and quantity of fitness programs within major institutions. Conducts innovative studies on health and living habits and methods of facilitating changes in living habits; promotes the awareness and skills needed to develop a positive life-style. Sponsors workshops and seminars; conducts weekly training course and certification testing of fitness leaders in education, government, human services and corporate sectors. **Services:** Assistance for public and private organizations in the implementation of wellness programs for employees; Fitnessgram: a computerized fitness report card for children. **Founded:** 1970. **Publications:** Providing Dietary Guidance Course; Steps to Better Health; The Walking Handbook; Aerobics Center Longitudinal Study; Fitness After 50. **Telecommunication Services:** studies@cooperinst.org.

ASSOCIATIONS AND OTHER ORGANIZATIONS

16059 ▪ Acupuncture Foundation of Canada Institute (AFCI)—Institute de la Fondation D'Acupuncture du Canada
2131 Lawrence Ave. E, Ste. 204
Scarborough, ON, Canada M1R 5G4
Ph: (416)752-3988
Fax: (416)752-4398
Co. E-mail: afciweb@afcinstitute.com
URL: http://www.afcinstitute.com
Contact: Mac Mierzejewski, President
Description: Promotes acupuncture's legitimate place in health care by initiating and supporting research in acupuncture. **Founded:** 1995. **Educational Activities:** Acupuncture Foundation of Canada Institute Board meeting. **Awards:** Clifford G. Woolfe Award.

16060 ▪ American Alternative Medical Association (AAMA)
2200 Market St., Ste. 803
Galveston, TX 77550-1530
Ph: (409)621-2600
Free: 888-764-2237
Fax: (775)703-5334
Co. E-mail: office@joinaama.com
URL: http://www.joinaama.com
Contact: Donald A. Rosenthal, Executive Director
Description: Fosters unity among "grassroots practitioners" and those with advanced academic credentials. Educates the public that good health can be obtained without the use of drugs. Encourages improved public awareness of the benefits of alternative health care. **Founded:** 1990.

16061 ▪ American Physical Therapy Association (APTA)
1111 N Fairfax St.
Alexandria, VA 22314-1488
Ph: (703)684-2782
Free: 800-999-2782
Fax: (703)706-8536
Co. E-mail: memberservices@apta.org
URL: http://www.apta.org
Contact: R. Scott Ward, President
E-mail: scottward@apta.org
Description: Professional organization of physical therapists and physical therapist assistants and students. Fosters the development and improvement of physical therapy service, education, and research; evaluates the organization and administration of curricula; directs the maintenance of standards and promotes scientific research. Acts as an accrediting body for educational programs in physical therapy. Establishes standards. Offers advisory and consultation services to schools of physical therapy and facilities offering physical therapy services; provides placement services at conference. **Scope:** physical therapy, rehabilitation. **Founded:** 1921. **Subscriptions:** archival material books periodicals. **Publications:** *PT in Motion* (Monthly); *Physical Therapy* (Monthly); *PT Bulletin Online* (Weekly); *PT Magazine*

(Monthly); *Physical Therapy Reimbursement News*; *Clinical Management: The Magazine of the American Physical Therapy Association* (Bimonthly). **Educational Activities:** Combined Sections Meeting (Annual); American Physical Therapy Association Annual Conference (Annual). **Awards:** APTA Minority Scholarships - Physical Therapist Students; Lucy Blair Service Award; Chattanooga Research Award; Honorary Member; Mary McMillan Lecture Award; Minority Initiatives Award; Jack Walker Award; Catherine Worthingham Fellows Award; APTA Minority Scholarships - Faculty Development Scholarships; APTA Minority Scholarships - Physical Therapist Assistant Students; Dorothy E. Baethke - Eleanor J. Carlin Award for Excellence in Academic Teaching; Dorothy Briggs Memorial Scientific Inquiry Award; Signe Brunnstrom Award for Excellence in Clinical Teaching; Jules M. Rothstein Golden Pen Award for Scientific Writing; Henry O. and Florence P. Kendall Practice Award; Eugene Michels New Investigator Award; Margaret L. Moore Award for Outstanding New Academic Faculty Member; Marian Williams Award for Research in Physical Therapy; Helen J. Hislop Award for Outstanding Contributions to Professional Literature.

16062 ▪ American Physical Therapy Association, Orthopaedic Section
2920 E Ave. S, Ste. 200
La Crosse, WI 54601
Ph: (608)788-3982
Free: 800-444-3982
Fax: (608)788-3965
Co. E-mail: tdeflorian@orthopt.org
URL: http://www.orthopt.org
Contact: Terri DeFlorian, Executive Director
Description: Orthopaedic physical therapists and physical therapist assistants who belong to the American Physical Therapy Association; physical therapy educators and students. Supports the continued growth of the physical therapy profession through education and research; promotes development of a standard certification procedure for the field. Seeks to assure the quality of physical therapy curricula at both the undergraduate and postgraduate levels. Facilitates communication among orthopedic physical therapists and other health care professionals. Gathers and disseminates information on the care of musculoskeletal disorders. Provides access to a network of orthopaedic study groups. **Founded:** 1974. **Publications:** *Orthopaedic Physical Therapy Practice* (Quarterly); *Journal of Orthopaedic and Sports Physical Therapy* (Monthly). **Awards:** James A. Gould Excellence in Teaching Orthopaedic Physical Therapy Award (Annual); Outstanding PT & PTA Student Award (Annual); Paris Distinguished Service Award (Annual).

16063 ▪ American Physical Therapy Association, Private Practice Section (PPS)
1055 N Fairfax St., Ste. 100
Alexandria, VA 22314
Ph: (703)299-2410
Fax: (703)299-2411
Co. E-mail: privatepracticesection@apta.org
URL: http://www.ppsapta.org
Contact: Laurie Kendall-Ellis, Executive Director
Description: Physical therapists who are members of the American Physical Therapy Association and

who are in private practice. Purposes are: to provide physical therapists with information on establishing and managing a private practice; to promote high standards of private practice physical therapy; to represent private practitioners before governmental and professional agencies; to disseminate information relating to private practice. Monitors federal and state legislation. Holds forums and seminars. **Founded:** 1956. **Publications:** *IMPACT* (Monthly); *Hire for Fit*; *Private Practice Section Membership Directory*; *Safeguarding Your Practice: The Corporate Compliance Manual* (Annual); *Twenty Questions About Private Practice*; *Private Practice Physical Therapy: The How-To Manual*; *Understanding Computers in Healthcare: A Guidebook for Rehabilitation Professionals*; *The Valuation of a Physical Therapy Practice*. **Awards:** Practice Award; Section Achievement Award; Robert G. Dicus Award; Friends of Private Practice Award; Robert G. Dicus Award.

16064 ▪ Canadian Academy of Sport Medicine (CASM)—L' Academie Canadienne de Medecine du Sport
180 Elgin St., Ste. 1400
Ottawa, ON, Canada K2P 2K3
Ph: (613)748-5851
Free: 877-585-2394
Fax: (613)231-3739
Co. E-mail: bfalardeau@casm-acms.org
URL: http://www.casm-acms.org
Contact: Dawn Haworth, Executive Director
Description: Physicians committed to excellence in the practice of medicine as it applies to all aspects of physical activity. Seeks to be a leader in advancing the art and science of sport medicine, including health promotion and disease prevention, for the benefit of all Canadians through programs of education, research, and service. **Founded:** 1970. **Publications:** *Clinical Journal of Sport Medicine* (Quarterly).

16065 ▪ Canadian Association of Physical Medicine and Rehabilitation (CAPM&R)
774 Echo Dr.
Ottawa, ON, Canada K1S 5N8
Ph: (613)707-0483
Fax: (613)707-0480
Co. E-mail: info@capmr.ca
URL: http://www.capmr.ca
Contact: Dr. Jeff Blackmer, President
Description: Aims to provide and maintain a national professional forum and network for the exchange of information and opinion. Contributes to the advancement of the specialty of physical medicine and rehabilitation. Seeks to provide rehabilitation within the health care of Canadians. **Founded:** 1952. **Publications:** *CAPM&R Newsletter* (3/year). **Awards:** Visitor Professorship; Research Fellowship Award (Annual); Resident Essay Contest (Annual); Resident Research Contest (Annual); Visitor Professorship (Annual); Medical Student Essay Award; Resident Essay Contest; Resident Research Contest; Canadian Medical Student Essay Award (Annual).

16066 ▪ Canadian Athletic Therapists Association (CATA)—Association Canadienne

des Therapeutes du Sport
1040 7th Ave. SW, Ste. 402
Calgary, AB, Canada T2P 3G9
Ph: (403)509-2282
Fax: (403)509-2280
Co. E-mail: info@athletictherapy.org
URL: http://www.athletictherapy.org
Contact: Ms. Helena De Fazio, Administrative Assistant

Description: Athletic therapists and other individuals engaged in the practice of sports medicine. Promotes advancement of the study and practice of sports medicine and athletic therapy; seeks to enhance the professional status of members. Encourages adoption of healthy and active lifestyles. Facilitates communication among members. Develops standards of conduct and practice. Delivers sports medical services to grass roots sports organizations throughout Canada. Conducts educational programs; maintains hall of fame. **Founded:** 1965. **Awards:** Human Kinetics Writing Awards; Distinguished Athletic Therapy Educator Award; Larry Ashley Award; Special Recognition Award; Merit Award; CATA Writing Award (Annual); Distinguished Athletic Therapy Educator Award (Annual); Larry Ashley Award (Annual); Special Recognition Award (Annual).

16067 ■ CAPM&R Newsletter
774 Echo Dr.
Ottawa, ON, Canada K1S 5N8
Ph: (613)707-0483
Fax: (613)707-0480
Co. E-mail: info@capmr.ca
URL: http://www.capmr.ca
Contact: Dr. Jeff Blackmer, President
Released: 3/year

16068 ■ Clinical Journal of Sport Medicine
180 Elgin St., Ste. 1400
Ottawa, ON, Canada K2P 2K3
Ph: (613)748-5851
Free: 877-585-2394
Fax: (613)231-3739
Co. E-mail: bfalardeau@casm-acms.org
URL: http://www.casm-acms.org
Contact: Dawn Haworth, Executive Director
Released: Quarterly

16069 ■ Foundation for Physical Therapy (FPT)
c/o American Physical Therapy Association
1111 N Fairfax St.
Alexandria, VA 22314-1488
Ph: (703)684-2782
Free: 800-875-1378
Fax: (703)706-8587
Co. E-mail: info@foundation4pt.org
URL: http://foundation4pt.org
Contact: Barbara Malm, Executive Director
Description: Supports the physical therapy profession's research needs by funding scientific and clinically-relevant physical therapy research. **Founded:** 1979. **Awards:** Charles M Magistro Distinguished Service Award (Annual); Spirit of Philanthropy Award (Annual); Robert C. Bartlett Innovation in Fundraising Award (Annual).

16070 ■ Institute for Traditional Medicine and Preventive Health Care (ITM)
2017 SE Hawthorne Blvd.
Portland, OR 97214
Ph: (503)233-4907
Fax: (503)233-1017
Co. E-mail: itm@itmonline.org
URL: http://www.itmonline.org
Contact: Subhuti Dharmananda, Director
Description: Helps people seeking traditional medicine knowledge and services by clarifying the nature of traditional medicine and demonstrating how it can be utilized in the modern setting. Provides educational materials and articles on traditional medicine and related topics. Conducts background research in traditional medicine including journal searches in China and computer searches in the US. Provides especially designed herbal formulations for use in clinics and practitioners who read institutes literature. **Founded:** 1979. **Publications:** A Bag of Pearls; Internet Journal of the Institute for Traditional Medicine.

16071 ■ National Ayurvedic Medical Association (NAMA)
620 Cabrillo Ave.
Santa Cruz, CA 95065
Free: 800-669-8914
Co. E-mail: info@ayurveda-nama.org
URL: http://www.ayurveda-nama.org
Contact: Ms. Hilary Garivaltis, President
Description: Represents the interests of the Ayurvedic profession. Aims to preserve, protect, improve, and promote the philosophy, knowledge, science and practice of Ayurveda. Maintains the professional competency and licensing of Ayurveda through enhancement of knowledge, practice and application of Ayurvedic profession. Encourages the public to appreciate and accept Ayurveda. **Founded:** 2000. **Educational Activities:** Ayurveda: Healing People, Healing Communities (Annual).

16072 ■ Rehab Review
201 Consumers Rd., Ste. 302
Toronto, ON, Canada M2J 4G8
Ph: (416)494-4700
Free: 888-876-9992
Fax: (416)494-9139
Co. E-mail: info@vracanada.com
URL: http://vracanada.com
Contact: Kathy Regan, Executive Director
Released: Quarterly **Price:** included in membership dues; C$50, /year for nonmembers.

16073 ■ Rehabilitation Journal
201 Consumers Rd., Ste. 302
Toronto, ON, Canada M2J 4G8
Ph: (416)494-4700
Free: 888-876-9992
Fax: (416)494-9139
Co. E-mail: info@vracanada.com
URL: http://vracanada.com
Contact: Kathy Regan, Executive Director
Released: Quarterly **Price:** included in membership dues.

16074 ■ Sound Healers Association (SHA)
PO Box 2240
Boulder, CO 80306
Ph: (303)443-8181
Free: 800-246-9764
Fax: (303)443-6023
Co. E-mail: info@soundhealersassociation.org
URL: http://www.soundhealersassociation.org
Contact: Jonathan Goldman, Director
URL(s): www.healingsounds.com. **Description:** Promotes research and awareness for the use of sound and music as therapeutic and transformational modalities for healing. **Founded:** 1982. **Educational Activities:** Concerts; Healing Sounds Seminars. **Telecommunication Services:** soundheals@aol.com.

16075 ■ Vocational Rehabilitation Association of Canada (VRA Canada)
201 Consumers Rd., Ste. 302
Toronto, ON, Canada M2J 4G8
Ph: (416)494-4700
Free: 888-876-9992
Fax: (416)494-9139
Co. E-mail: info@vracanada.com
URL: http://vracanada.com
Contact: Kathy Regan, Executive Director
Description: Professional association for people working in the field of rehabilitation. Promotes excellence in rehabilitation education, training, and practice. Formulates and enforces Code of Ethics. Facilitates communication to its members and stakeholders. Responsible for professional development, promotion of the Canadian Certified Rehabilitation Counsellor (CCRC), Certified Vocational Evaluator (CVE), and the granting of the Registered Rehabilitation Professional (RRP) designation to qualified members. **Founded:** 1970. **Publications:** Rehab Review (Quarterly); Rehabilitation Journal (Quarterly). **Awards:** Canadian Association of Rehabilitation Professionals Fellowship Award (Annual).

REFERENCE WORKS

16076 ■ "Kenosha 'Lifestyle Center' Delayed" in The Business Journal-Milwaukee (Vol. 25, August 8, 2008, No. 46, pp. A1)
Pub: American City Business Journals, Inc.
Ed: Rich Kirchen. **Description:** Quality Centers of Orlando, Florida has postponed construction plans for the Kenosha Town Center in Kenosha County, Wisconsin to 2009 due to the economic downturn and lending concerns. The $200-million, 750,000-square-foot retail and residential center will be located near the corner of Wisconsin Highway 50 and I-94.

16077 ■ "On Their Own" in Crain's Cleveland Business (Vol. 28, November 12, 2007, No. 45, pp. 19)
Pub: Crain Communications, Inc.
Ed: Eileen Beal. **Description:** Discusses the reasons more physicians with entrepreneurial spirit are opening their own practices as well the added challenges and responsibilities that comes with owning one's own practice.

16078 ■ "Q&A With Devin Ringling: Franchise's Services Go Beyond Elder Care" in Gazette (October 2, 2010)
Pub: The Gazette
Ed: Bill Radford. **Description:** Profile of franchise, Interim HealthCare, in Colorado Springs, Colorado; the company offers home care services that include wound care and specialized feedings to shopping and light housekeeping. It also runs a medical staffing company that provides nurses, therapists and other health care workers to hospitals, prisons, schools and other facilities.

TRADE PERIODICALS

16079 ■ Pediatric Physical Therapy: Official Journal of the Section on Pediatrics of the American Physical Therapy Association
Pub: Lippincott Williams & Wilkins
Contact: Rich Wohl, Executive Vice President
URL(s): journals.lww.com/pedpt/pages/default.aspx.
Ed: Ann F. VanSant. **Released:** Quarterly **Price:** $175, Individuals; $380, Institutions; $125, Individuals in-training; $282, Other countries; $487, Institutions, other countries.

16080 ■ Physical Medicine and Rehabilitation Clinics of North America
Pub: Elsevier
URL(s): www.elsevier.com/wps/find/journaldescription.cws_home/623372/descrip tion#description. **Ed:** Prof. George H. Kraft. **Released:** Quarterly **Price:** $575, Institutions, other countries; $373, Other countries; $189, Students, other countries; $441, Institutions, $132, Students; $302, Canada; $248, Individuals; $575, Institutions, Canada.

16081 ■ Physical & Occupational Therapy in Geriatrics: Current Trends in Geriatric Rehabilitation
Pub: Informa Healthcare
URL(s): informahealthcare.com/pog. **Ed:** Ellen Dunleavey Taira. **Released:** Quarterly **Price:** £560, Institutions; $995, Institutions; €740, Institutions.

16082 ■ Physical and Occupational Therapy in Pediatrics: A Quarterly Journal of Developmental Therapy
Pub: Informa Healthcare
URL(s): informahealthcare.com/loi/pop. **Ed:** Robert J. Palisano, Doreen Bartlett. **Released:** Quarterly **Price:** $1020, Institutions; €755, Institutions; £570, Institutions.

16083 ■ Physical Therapy
Pub: American Physical Therapy Association
Contact: R. Scott Ward, President
E-mail: scottward@apta.org
URL(s): ptjournal.apta.org. **Released:** Monthly **Price:** included in membership dues; $99, /year for individuals; $139, /year for institutions.

16084 ■ *Physical Therapy Products*
Pub: Novicom Inc.
URL(s): www.ptproductsonline.com/. **Ed:** Frank
Long. **Released:** Monthly

**16085 ■ *Physical Therapy Reimbursement
News***
Pub: American Physical Therapy Association
Contact: R. Scott Ward, President
E-mail: scottward@apta.org
Ed: Debra Lansey, Editor, debralansey@apta.org.
Released: Bimonthly. **Price:** $79, members; $110,
nonmembers. **Description:** Tracks reimbursement
trends in the medical field of physical therapy.

16086 ■ *PT in Motion*
Pub: American Physical Therapy Association
Contact: R. Scott Ward, President
E-mail: scottward@apta.org
URL(s): www.apta.org/PTinMotion. **Ed:** Eric Ries,
Donald Tepper. **Released:** Monthly **Price:** $119,
Institutions non-members; $139, Institutions, other
countries non-members.

TRADE SHOWS AND CONVENTIONS

**16087 ■ American Academy of Physical
Medicine and Rehabilitation Annual Assembly**
American Academy of Physical Medicine and
   Rehabilitation (AAPM&R)
9700 W Bryn Mawr Ave., Ste. 200
Rosemont, IL 60018-5706
Ph: (847)737-6000
Fax: (847)737-6001
Co. E-mail: info@aapmr.org
URL: http://www.aapmr.org
Contact: David L. Bagnall, President
URL(s): www.aapmr.org. **Price:** $475, Pre-registered,
members; $525, Onsite registered, members; $590,
Pre-registered, non-members; $640, Onsite regis-
tered, non-members. **Frequency:** Annual. **Audience:**
Physicians specializing in physical medicine and
rehabilitation. **Principal Exhibits:** Pharmaceuticals,
electrodiagnostic equipment, wheelchairs, and
related equipment, supplies, and services.

**16088 ■ American Physical Therapy
Association Annual Conference**
American Physical Therapy Association (APTA)
1111 N Fairfax St.
Alexandria, VA 22314-1488
Ph: (703)684-2782
Free: 800-999-2782
Fax: (703)706-8536
Co. E-mail: memberservices@apta.org
URL: http://www.apta.org
Contact: R. Scott Ward, President
E-mail: scottward@apta.org
URL(s): www.apta.org/annualconference. **Fre-
quency:** Annual. **Audience:** Physical therapists,
physical therapists assistants, and allied health
professionals. **Principal Exhibits:** Physical therapy
products, equipment, and services.

**16089 ■ National Association of
Rehabilitation Professionals in the Private
Sector Annual Conference**
International Association of Rehabilitation Profes-
   sionals (IARP)
1926 Waukegan Rd., Ste. 1
Glenview, IL 60025
Ph: (847)657-6964
Free: 888-427-7722
Fax: (847)657-6963
URL: http://www.rehabpro.org
Contact: Carl Wangman, Executive Director
Frequency: Annual. **Audience:** Medical and voca-
tional rehabilitation providers, insurance industry
representatives, and medical rehabilitation equipment
manufacturers. **Principal Exhibits:** Medical and
vocational rehabilitation products, facilities, and case
management companies.

**16090 ■ Texas Physical Therapy Association
Annual Conference**
Texas Physical Therapy Association
900 Congress Ave., Ste. 410
Austin, TX 78701
Ph: (512)477-1818
Fax: (512)477-1434
Co. E-mail: orlando@tpta.org
URL: http://www.tpta.org
URL(s): www.tpta.org. **Frequency:** Annual. **Audi-
ence:** Physical therapists, physical theapists as-
sistants, and physical therapy students. **Principal
Exhibits:** Physical therapy recruiters, equipment,
supplies, books, and services.

CONSULTANTS

16091 ■ T. L. Coward
112 Kenwood St.
Belmont, NC 28012-3119
Ph: (704)825-1904
Fax: (704)825-1905
Contact: Thaddeus L. Coward, Owner
Scope: Professional practice management consult-
ant serving physicians, dentists, and other health
care professionals. **Founded:** 1983.

16092 ■ Pathways To Wellness
617 Everhart Rd.
Corpus Christi, TX 78411
Ph: (361)985-9642
Fax: (361)949-4627
Co. E-mail: path2wellness@earthlink.net
URL: http://www.path2wellness.com
Contact: Evy Coppola, Owner
Scope: Offer natural holistic health counseling, yoga
and hatha yoga classes, teachers training and
cookery classes for individuals and companies.
Health counseling includes nutritional guidance, kinesiology, iridology, reflexology, energy healing, massage therapy, herbal and vitamin therapy, creative
visualization and meditation. Provides supplements
which bring about the same effects as that of natural
sunshine. **Founded:** 1988. **Seminars:** Is It You Holding You Back?; The Balancing Act. . .Career. . . Family. . .and Self; Learning the Art of Friendly Persua-
sion; Stop Accepting What You Are Getting and Start
Asking for What You Want!; Introduction to Natural
Health and Healthy Living; Learn Why One Size Approaches to the Answers on Health Do Not Work;
Introduction to Yoga. What is it? Who can do it? What
can it do for you.

16093 ■ Cedric Prange Associates Inc.
11120 Fort St.
Omaha, NE 68164-2118
Ph: (402)493-1888
Fax: (402)493-1007
Contact: Cedric Prange, President
Scope: Provider of consulting services in management, financial and tax planning for physicians,
dentists, and health-related businesses. **Founded:**
1970. **Publications:** "Money Magazines Tax Pre-
parer," Mar, 1997.

COMPUTERIZED DATABASES

16094 ■ *AbleData*
8630 Fenton St., Ste. 930
Silver Spring, MD 20910
Ph: (301)608-8998
Free: 800-227-0216
Fax: (301)608-8958
Co. E-mail: abledata@macrointernational.com
URL: http://www.abledata.com
Availability: Online: U.S. National Institute on Dis-
ability and Rehabilitation Research - AbleData. **Type:**
Directory.

LIBRARIES

**16095 ■ American Physical Therapy
Association Information Resources**
1111 N. Fairfax St.
Alexandria, VA 22314-1488
Ph: (703)706-8534

Free: 800-999-2782
Fax: (703)706-8536
Co. E-mail: inforesources@apta.org
URL: http://www.apta.org
Contact: Gini Blodgett Birchett, Director, Information
   Services
Scope: Physical therapy, rehabilitation. **Services:**
Library available to researchers by appointment only.
Founded: 1921. **Holdings:** 3000 books; photo-
graphs; reports; dissertations; oral histories; confer-
ence proceedings; Annual reports; board of directors
meeting minutes; House of Delegates minutes. **Sub-
scriptions:** 200 journals and other serials. **Telecom-
munication Services:** memberservices@apta.org.

**16096 ■ Community Therapy Services Inc.
Library**
201-1555 St. James
Winnipeg, MB, Canada R3H 1B5
Ph: (204)949-0533
Fax: (204)942-1428
Co. E-mail: cts@ctsinc.mb.ca
URL: http://www.ctsinc.mb.ca
Contact: Irwin Corobow, Executive Director
Scope: Physiotherapy, occupational therapy, speech
language, pathology. **Services:** Interlibrary loan;
library accepts phone inquiries. **Founded:** 1980.
Holdings: 200 books; 50 videocassettes. **Subscrip-
tions:** 5 journals and other serials. **Telecommunica-
tion Services:** icorobow@ctsinc.mb.ca.

**16097 ■ Florida A&M University - Frederick
S. Humphries Science Research Center
Library**
401-501 Science Research Center
309 Pershing St.
Tallahassee, FL 32307
Ph: (850)599-3393
Fax: (850)599-3422
URL: http://www.famu.edu/index.
   cfm?a=library&p=ScienceResearch
Scope: Pharmacy, allied health, physics, computer
science, environmental science, respiratory therapy,
physical therapy, healthcare management, medical
records administration, occupational therapy. **Services:** Interlibrary loan; copying; SDI; Library open to
the public. **Founded:** 1957. **Holdings:** 5989 bound
periodical volumes; 915 print and online journals; 791
microcards; 24,102 monographs. **Subscriptions:**
697 journals and other serials; 5 newspapers.

**16098 ■ Texas Woman's University - F.W. and
Bessie Dye Memorial Library**
5500 Southwestern Medical Ave.
Dallas, TX 75235
Ph: (214)689-6580
Fax: (214)689-6583
Co. E-mail: eoliphant@twu.edu
URL: http://www.twu.edu/library
Contact: Eula Oliphant, Coordinator
Scope: Nursing, healthcare administration. **Services:**
Interlibrary loan; copying; library open to the public
for reference use only. **Founded:** 1966. **Holdings:**
15,872 books; 40,000 books (for all TWU locations);
5400 bound periodical volumes; 225 bound theses,
dissertations, and professional papers. **Subscrip-
tions:** 72 print journals and other serials.

**16099 ■ University of South Dakota -
Christian P. Lommen Health Sciences Library**
University of South Dakota School of Medicine
414 E. Clark St.
Vermillion, SD 57069-2307
Ph: (605)677-5348
Fax: (605)677-5124
Co. E-mail: dhulkone@usd.edu
URL: http://www.usd.edu/library/
Contact: David A. Hulkonen, Director
Scope: Anatomy, physiology, pharmacology, microbi-
ology, pathology, biochemistry, nursing, dental
hygiene, medical technology, physical therapy, oc-
cupational therapy, physician assistant, clinical
medicine, social work. **Services:** Interlibrary loan;
copying; SDI; consultation services for hospitals;
Library open to the public. **Founded:** 1907. **Holdings:** 35,000 books; 60,000 bound periodical vol-

umes; 300 AV programs. **Subscriptions:** 1000 journals and other serials. **Telecommunication Services:** webmed@usd.edu.

RESEARCH CENTERS

16100 ■ Ball State University - Human Performance Laboratory (HPL)
2000 W University Ave.
Muncie, IN 47306
Ph: (765)285-1158
Fax: (765)285-8596
Co. E-mail: hpl@bsu.edu
URL: http://cms.bsu.edu/Academics/CentersandInsti-tutes/HPL.aspx
Contact: Scott Trappe, Director
Founded: 1965. **Educational Activities:** Adult Fitness Program. **Awards:** Graduate assistantships and doctoral fellowships. **Telecommunication Services:** strappe@bsu.edu.

16101 ■ Boston Biomedical Research Institute (BBRI)
64 Grove St.
Watertown, MA 02472
Ph: (617)658-7806
Fax: (617)972-1759
Co. E-mail: emersonc@bbri.org
URL: http://www.bbri.org
Contact: Charles P. Emerson, Jr., Director
Founded: 1968. **Publications:** *Messenger Newsletter* (Semiannual). **Educational Activities:** International Meetings and Symposia; BBRI Seminars (Weekly).

16102 ■ Boston University - Neuromuscular Research Center (NMRC)
19 Deerfield St., 4th Fl.
Boston, MA 02215
Ph: (617)353-9757
Fax: (617)353-5737
Co. E-mail: cjd@bu.edu
URL: http://www.bu.edu/nmrc
Contact: Prof. Carlo J. De Luca, Director
Founded: 1984. **Publications:** *Annual Activity Report.* **Educational Activities:** NMRC Seminar Series.

16103 ■ Boston University - Neuromuscular Research Center - Muscle Fatigue Laboratory
19 Deerfield St., 4th Fl.
Boston, MA 02215
Ph: (617)358-0718
Fax: (617)353-5737
Co. E-mail: sroy@bu.edu
URL: http://www.bu.edu/nmrc/labs/mfl
Contact: Prof. Serge Roy, Supervisor
Founded: 1999.

16104 ■ Bridgewater State College - Human Performance Lab
325 Plymouth St., Rm. 230
Bridgewater, MA 02325
Ph: (508)531-2064
Fax: (508)531-4064
Co. E-mail: rhaslam@bridgew.edu
Contact: Dr. Robert W. Haslam, Director
Services: Provides standards for police and fire fighter fitness. **Founded:** 1975. **Educational Activities:** M.S. and B.S. programs in exercise science.

16105 ■ Brigham Young University - Human Performance Research Center (HPRC)
116 Richards Bldg.
Provo, UT 84602
Ph: (801)422-6651
Fax: (801)422-0555
Co. E-mail: gary_mack@byu.edu
URL: http://hprc.byu.edu
Contact: Dr. Gary Mack, Director
Founded: 1967.

16106 ■ Case Western Reserve University - Skeletal Research Center (SRC)
Millis Science Ctr., Rm. 118
Department of Biology
2080 Adelbert Rd.
Cleveland, OH 44106-7080
Ph: (216)368-3562

Fax: (216)368-4077
Co. E-mail: aic@cwru.edu
URL: http://www.case.edu/artsci/biol/skeletal
Contact: Prof. Arnold I. Caplan, Director
Services: Medical services: through the Musculoskeletal Institute. **Founded:** 1986. **Educational Activities:** Graduate degree programs; Sponsors weekly, monthly, and annual conferences.

16107 ■ Cleveland FES Center (FESC)—VA National Rehabilitation Research and Development Center for Functional Electrical Stimulation
11000 Cedar Ave., Ste. 230
Cleveland, OH 44106-3052
Ph: (216)231-3257
Fax: (216)231-3258
Co. E-mail: cdudek@fescenter.org
URL: http://fescenter.org/index.php
Contact: P. Hunter Peckham, Executive Director
Services: Consulting. **Founded:** 1988. **Publications:** *FESC Newsletter* (Quarterly). **Educational Activities:** Neural prosthesis seminars (Monthly), presentations focusing on all aspects of FES research from leading researchers throughout the world. Open to all students, researchers, and professionals. **Awards:** FESC Fellowships.

16108 ■ Colorado State University - Human Performance Clinical/Research Laboratory (HPCRL)
Department of Health & Exercise Science
Fort Collins, CO 80523-1582
Ph: (970)491-3847
Fax: (970)491-7677
Co. E-mail: israel@cahs.colostate.edu
URL: http://hes.cahs.colostate.edu/ResearchLabs/
Contact: Dr. Richard Gay Israel, Executive Director
Services: Stress testing: to the community. **Founded:** 2000.

16109 ■ Georgia Institute of Technology - Center for Assistive Technology and Environmental Access (CATEA)
College of Architecture
490 10th St. NW
Atlanta, GA 30332-0156
Ph: (404)894-4960
Free: 800-726-9119
Fax: (404)894-9320
Co. E-mail: jon.sanford@coa.gatech.edu
URL: http://www.catea.gatech.edu
Contact: Jon Sanford, Director
Founded: 1980. **Publications:** *CATEA Newsletter* (Quarterly). **Educational Activities:** Continuing education classes; Webinars; CATEA Workshops. **Telecommunication Services:** catea@coa.gatech. edu.

16110 ■ National Institute for Fitness and Sport (NIFS)
250 University Blvd.
Indianapolis, IN 46202
Ph: (317)274-3432
Fax: (317)274-7408
Co. E-mail: mroberts@nifs.org
URL: http://www.nifs.org
Contact: Melanie Roberts, Director
Founded: 1985. **Publications:** *NIF Source* (Bi-monthly). **Educational Activities:** Seminars, workshops, and classes; Health/fitness conferences and programs. **Awards:** NIFS Paid Internships.

16111 ■ National Institute for Rehabilitation Engineering (NIRE)
PO Box T
Hewitt, NJ 07421
Ph: (973)853-6585
Free: 800-736-2216
Fax: (928)832-2894
Co. E-mail: nire@theoffice.net
URL: http://www.angelfire.com/nj/nire2
Contact: Tom Schwanda, President
Services: Information services for special or personalized inquiries; User-training and placement: for physically disabled individuals. **Founded:** 1967.

16112 ■ Rehabilitation Institute of Chicago - Sensory Motor Performance Program (SMPP)
345 E Superior, Ste. 1396
Chicago, IL 60611-2654
Ph: (312)238-3381
Fax: (312)238-2208
Co. E-mail: w-rymer@northwestern.edu
URL: http://www.ric.org/research/centers/smpp/index. aspx
Contact: Dr. W. Zev Rymer, Director
Founded: 1954.

16113 ■ Rehabilitation Institute of Michigan (RIM)
261 Mack Ave.
Detroit, MI 48201
Ph: (313)745-1203
Fax: (313)745-1163
URL: http://www.rimrehab.org/
Contact: William H. Restum, President
Services: Inpatient and outpatient medical and rehabilitation services: in rheumatology, internal medicine, cardiology, orthopedic surgery, urology, psychiatry, neuropsychology, rehabilitation psychology, rehabilitation nursing, and occupational, speech and language, and physical. **Founded:** 1951. **Publications:** *RIM Research report* (Annual); *Thinking Cap.* **Educational Activities:** Clinical and research training for medical rehabilitation professionals; Del Harder Research Conference (Annual); RIM Meetings, on rehabilitation clinical interventions and research. **Awards:** Del Harder Research Awards (Annual).

16114 ■ University of Calgary - Human Performance Laboratory (HPL)
Faculty of Kinesiology
2500 University Dr. NW
Calgary, AB, Canada T2N 1N4
Ph: (403)220-6472
Fax: (403)284-3553
Co. E-mail: nigg@ucalgary.ca
URL: http://www.ucalgary.ca/hpl
Contact: Prof. Benno M. Nigg, Director
Services: High performance team testing and sport surface/shoe testing. **Founded:** 1981. **Publications:** *HPL Annual report.* **Educational Activities:** Congress (Periodic).

16115 ■ University of Delaware - Human Performance Laboratory
Department of Health, Nutrition & Exercise Sciences
Newark, DE 19716
Ph: (302)831-2265
Fax: (302)831-2828
Co. E-mail: provost@udel.edu
URL: http://www.udel.edu/HNES/OpenHouse/An-nouncement.htm
Contact: Michelle Provost-Craig, Director
Awards: Graduate teaching and research assistantships. **Telecommunication Services:** sjhall@udel. edu.

16116 ■ University of Florida - Center for Exercise Science (CES)
Department of Applied Physiology & Kinesiology, Rm. 100, FLG
Gainesville, FL 32611
Ph: (352)392-0584
Fax: (352)392-5262
Co. E-mail: spowers@hhp.ufl.edu
URL: http://www.hhp.ufl.edu/apk/ces/ces.php
Contact: Scott Powers, Director
Founded: 1979. **Publications:** *Journal of Cardiopulmonary Rehabilitation.* **Educational Activities:** CES Symposium (Biennial).

16117 ■ University of Miami - Laboratory of Clinical and Applied Physiology
Max Orovitz Laboratories
Coral Gables, FL 33124-8065
Ph: (305)284-3024

Fax: (305)284-5168
Co. E-mail: aperry@miami.edu
URL: http://www.education.miami.edu/Program/
  Programs.asp?Program_ID=38
Contact: Dr. Arlette Perry, Director
Services: Clinical evaluations for specialty populations: including diabetics, the elderly, the obese, and athletes; Laboratory services. **Founded:** 1984. **Educational Activities:** Graduate and postdoctoral instruction and extensive laboratory training (Monthly). **Awards:** Laboratory of Clinical and Applied Physiology Graduate assistantships; Laboratory of Clinical and Applied Physiology Grants.

16118 ■ University of Texas at Arlington - Human Performance Institute (HPI)
PO Box 19180
Arlington, TX 76019-0180
Ph: (817)273-2335
Co. E-mail: gvk@hpi.uta.edu
URL: http://www-ee.uta.edu/hpi/
Contact: George V. Kondraske, Director

Services: Assistive device services to rehabilitation providers; Cooperative research program with outside organizations enabling them to obtain a replica of the instrumented measurement system. **Founded:** 1983. **Publications:** *HPI Newsletter* (Semiannual); *Progress Report* (Annual). **Educational Activities:** Workshops focusing on human performance measurement and rehabilitation technology.

16119 ■ University of Utah - Human Performance Research Laboratory
202 HPER N Bldg.
College of Health
Salt Lake City, UT 84112
Ph: (801)585-1451
Co. E-mail: kerry.m.jacques@hsc.utah.edu
URL: http://www.health.utah.edu/ess/clinics/
  performance.html
Contact: Kerry Jacques, Director

Services: Peak Academy: an applied sport science service for the University and surrounding community. **Founded:** 1972.

16120 ■ University of Vermont - McClure Musculoskeletal Research Center
Robert T. Stafford Hall, 4th Fl.
95 Carrigan Dr.
Burlington, VT 05405-1746
Ph: (802)656-4257
Fax: (802)656-4247
Co. E-mail: bruce.beynnon@uvm.edu
URL: http://www.med.uvm.edu/ortho/TB1+BL+I+C.
  asp?SiteAreaID=1113
Contact: Bruce D. Beynnon, Director, Research

Services: Research and development consultation: to industry, business, government, and public agencies. **Educational Activities:** In-service training, to rehabilitation professionals; McClure Musculoskeletal Research Center Workshops, for service providers in rehabilitation engineering techniques.

ASSOCIATIONS AND OTHER ORGANIZATIONS

16121 ■ **National Frozen Pizza Institute (NFPI)**
2000 Corporate Ridge, Ste. 1000
McLean, VA 22102
Ph: (703)821-0770
Fax: (703)821-1350
URL: http://nfpi.affi.org
Contact: Joseph Pacinelli, President
Description: Aims to advance the interests of the frozen pizza industry. Monitors federal regulatory agency activities affecting frozen pizza processors and serves as an information resource for the trade and general public about the nutrition, value and convenience of frozen pizza and pizza products. **Founded:** 1975.

REFERENCE WORKS

16122 ■ **"All Fired Up!" in Small Business Opportunities (November 2008)**
Pub: Entrepreneur Media Inc.

Ed: Stan Roberts. **Description:** Profile of Brixx Wood Fired Pizza, which has launched a franchising program due to the amount of interest the company's founders received over the years; franchisees do not need experience in the food industry or pizza restaurant service business in order to open a franchise of their own because all franchisees receive comprehensive training in which they are educated on all of the necessary tools to effectively run the business.

16123 ■ **"A Bigger Slice; Buscemi's Adds Licensees, Profits" in Crain's Detroit Business (Vol. 23, October 15, 2007, No. 42, pp. 3)**
Pub: Crain Communications Inc. - Detroit

Ed: Brent Snavely. **Description:** Six new licensees have opened under the Original Buscemi's Inc. The firm was founded in 1958 and expects to open nine more restaurants by the end of 2008.

16124 ■ **"Doyle: Domino's New Pizza Seasoned with Straight Talk" in Crain's Detroit Business (Vol. 26, January 11, 2010, No. 2, pp. 1)**
Pub: Crain Communications Inc.

Ed: Nathan Skid. **Description:** Interview with J. Patrick Doyle, the CEO of Domino's Pizza, Inc.; the company has launched a new marketing campaign that focuses on its bold new vision.

16125 ■ **"Eatery Honored for Top Alaska Pizza" in Alaska Business Monthly (Vol. 27, October 2011, No. 10, pp. 10)**
Pub: Alaska Business Publishing Company

Ed: Nancy Pounds. **Description:** Capri Pizza of Anchorage, Alaska was honored in Food Network magazine's, '50 States, 50 Pizzas'. Capri's salmon pizza won the prize for the restaurant.

16126 ■ **"For the Seasoned Buyer" in Inc. (Vol. 30, November 2008, No. 11, pp. 32)**
Pub: Mansueto Ventures LLC

Ed: Darren Dahl. **Description:** Dominick Fimiano shares his plans to sell his ten-year-old business that manufactures and sells frozen pizza dough and crusts as well as a variety of topped pizzas. Products are purchased by schools, hospitals, bowling alleys and amusement parks. The business sale includes the buyer's taking on Fimiano's son the firm's most senior employee.

16127 ■ **"Invasion of the New York Pizza" in Charlotte Observer (February 5, 2007)**
Pub: Knight-Ridder/Tribune Business News

Ed: Leigh Dyer. **Description:** Dozens of new pizza restaurants are cropping up in the Charlotte, North Carolina area, a result of New Yorker transplants.

16128 ■ **"Local Firm Snaps up 91 Area Pizza Huts" in Orlando Business Journal (Vol. 26, January 8, 2010, No. 32, pp. 1)**
Pub: American City Business Journals

Ed: Alexis Muellner, Anjali Fluker. **Description:** Orlando, Florida-based CFL Pizza LLC bought the 91 Orlando-area Pizza Hut restaurants for $35 million from parent company Yum! Brands Inc. CFL Pizza plans to distribute parts of the business to Central Florida vendors and the first business up for grabs is the advertising budget.

16129 ■ **"Ohio Franchise Buys 21 Jacksonville Area Papa John's" in Florida Times-Union (December 20, 2010)**
Pub: Florida Times-Union

Ed: Mark Basch. **Description:** Ohio-based Papa John's pizza franchise acquired 21 of the restaurants in Duval, Clay and St. Johns counties in Jacksonville, Florida.

16130 ■ **"Personal Pizza Goes Franchise Route" in Atlanta Journal-Constitution (December 22, 2010)**
Pub: Atlanta Journal-Constitution

Ed: Bob Townsend. **Description:** Your Pie, developer of the personal-size pizza franchise concept is profiled.

16131 ■ **Pizza Today--Pizza Industry Buyer's Guide Issue**
Pub: National Association of Pizza Operators
URL(s): www.pizzatoday.com. **Released:** Monthly; Latest edition 2010. **Publication includes:** List of over 3,000 manufacturers and suppliers of products, equipment, and services to the pizza industry. **Entries include:** Company name, address, phone, fax, product/service, branch locations. **Arrangement:** Alphabetical. **Indexes:** Product/service.

TRADE PERIODICALS

16132 ■ **Canadian Pizza Magazine**
Pub: Annex Publishing & Printing Inc.

URL(s): www.canadianpizzamag.comwww.annex-web.com/. **Ed:** Laura Aiken. **Released:** 8/yr. **Price:** $18, Canada.

TRADE SHOWS AND CONVENTIONS

16133 ■ **Pizza Expo**
Macfadden Protech, LLC
908 S. 8th St., Ste. 200
Louisville, KY 40203
Ph: (502)736-9500
Fax: (502)736-9502
URL: http://www.pizzaexpo.com
URL(s): www.pizzaexpo.com. **Frequency:** Annual. **Audience:** Pizza shop operators and owners from franchises, independent shops, and chains. **Principal Exhibits:** Food and equipment for the pizza industry. **Dates and Locations:** Convention Center.

CONSULTANTS

16134 ■ **Erin Services Inc.**
111 Travelers Way
Saint Simons Island, GA 31522-5632
Ph: (912)638-9916
Fax: (912)638-5701
Co. E-mail: dennisd@ns.technonet.com
Contact: Dennis J. Donnelly, III, President
E-mail: dennis179@yahoo.com
Scope: Offers assistance in technical proposal production, marketing, and research. Industries served: Food service, janitorial, landscaping, hospitality and lodging, parks, and recreational. **Founded:** 1990.

16135 ■ **Riedel Marketing Group (RMG)**
5327 E Pinchot Ave.
Phoenix, AZ 85018-2963
Ph: (602)840-4948
Fax: (602)840-4928
Co. E-mail: ajr@4rmg.com
URL: http://www.4rmg.com
Contact: Timothy D. Riedel, President
Scope: The house wares and food service industry strategic marketing planning experts. Help manufacturers of house wares and food products solve marketing problems and identify and exploit marketing opportunities. Provides a full-range of strategic marketing planning services including development of marketing strategy, development of fact-based sales presentations, category management, definition of market opportunities and new product development exclusively to the house wares and food service industries. **Founded:** 1991. **Publications:** "Your Key Consumer: Her Take on the International Home & Housewares Show," Mar, 2008; "What's Hot, What's Not: The Consumer Speaks," Mar, 2006; "HIPsters SPEAK: What We Love to Buy and Why," Apr, 2005; "Influentials: Who They Are and Why You Should Care," Jun, 2004; "The Seven Secrets to Selling More Housewares," Jan, 2003. **Seminars:** Consumers Speak: What We Love to Buy and Why, What Do Those Consumers Think; The Seven Secrets to Selling More House wares. **Special Services:** Home Trend Influentials Panel.

FRANCHISES AND BUSINESS OPPORTUNITIES

16136 ■ Azpco Arizona Pizza Co.
Azpco Arizona Pizza Co., Inc.
370 SE 15th Ave.
Pompano Beach, FL 33060
Ph: (954)942-9424
Fax: (954)783-5177
Description: Pizza restaurant. **No. of Franchise Units:** 10. **No. of Company-Owned Units:** 1. **Founded:** 1996.. **Franchised:** 2003. **Equity Capital Needed:** $400,000-$865,000. **Franchise Fee:** $35,000. **Financial Assistance:** Yes. **Training:** Yes.

16137 ■ Bellacino's Pizza & Grinders Inc.
10096 Shaver Rd.
Portage, MI 49024
Free: 877-379-0700
Fax: (269)329-0930
Description: Oven baked grinders and pizza. **No. of Franchise Units:** 68. **Founded:** 1993.. **Franchised:** 1995. **Equity Capital Needed:** $279,000-$422,190. **Franchise Fee:** $30,000. **Royalty Fee:** 3%. **Training:** Provides 14 days at headquarters, 10 days on-site with ongoing support.

16138 ■ The Boston's Gourmet Pizza
Boston Pizza International
1501 LBJ Fwy., Ste. 450
Dallas, TX 75234
Ph: (972)484-9022
Free: 800-277-8721
Fax: (972)484-7630
Description: Casual restaurant specializing in pizza. **No. of Franchise Units:** 389. **No. of Company-Owned Units:** 4. **Founded:** 1963.. **Franchised:** 1968. **Equity Capital Needed:** $1,165,000-$350,000-$2,838,000. **Franchise Fee:** $50,000 U.S. **Training:** Yes.

16139 ■ Breadeaux Pizza
Breadeaux Pisa Inc.
PO Box 6158
St. Joseph, MO 64506
Ph: (800)835-6534
Fax: (816)364-3739
Description: Fast pizza operation. **No. of Franchise Units:** 95. **No. of Company-Owned Units:** 3. **Founded:** 1985.. **Franchised:** 1985. **Equity Capital Needed:** $69,500-$310,000. **Franchise Fee:** $15,000/15 years. **Training:** Yes.

16140 ■ Buck's Pizza
Buck's Pizza Fran. Corp. Inc.
PO Box 405
DuBois, PA 15801
Ph: (814)371-3076
Free: 800-310-8848
Co. E-mail: lance@buckspizza.com
URL: http://www.buckspizza.com
Description: Pizza carry-out and delivery. **No. of Franchise Units:** 70. **Founded:** 1994.. **Franchised:** 1994. **Equity Capital Needed:** $163,450-$341,400. **Franchise Fee:** $20,000. **Training:** Provides onsite training at opening.

16141 ■ Chicken Delight
395 Berry St.
Winnipeg, MB, Canada R3J 1N6
Ph: (204)885-7570
Fax: (204)831-6176
URL: http://www.franchisedirectory.ca
Description: Pressure-fried chicken and fresh-dough pizza, plus other tasty selections. **No. of Franchise Units:** 26. **No. of Company-Owned Units:** 11. **Founded:** 1952.. **Franchised:** 1952. **Equity Capital Needed:** $75,000 minimum cash liquidity; $275,000-$600,000 total investment range. **Franchise Fee:** $20,000. **Royalty Fee:** 5%. **Training:** Offers an intensive 4 week, in-field training program at our corporate stores.

16142 ■ CiCi's Pizza
CiCi Enterprises, Inc.
1080 W Bethel Rd.
Coppell, TX 75019
Ph: (972)745-4200

Fax: (469)675-6405
Description: Pizza, pasta, salad bar and dessert on an all-you-can-eat lunch and dinner buffet. Also offers a value-priced take-out menu. **No. of Franchise Units:** 578. **No. of Company-Owned Units:** 13. **Founded:** 1985.. **Franchised:** 1988. **Equity Capital Needed:** $461,343-$714,912. **Franchise Fee:** $30,000. **Training:** Yes.

16143 ■ Dolly's Pizza
Dolly's Pizza Franchising, Inc.
1097 Union Lake Rd., Ste. B
White Lake, MI 48386
Ph: (248)360-6440
Fax: (248)360-7020
Description: Offers pizza, subs, and salads. **No. of Franchise Units:** 28. **No. of Company-Owned Units:** 2 . **Founded:** 1966.. **Franchised:** 1994. **Equity Capital Needed:** $120,000-$160,000 total; approximately $30,000 cash. **Franchise Fee:** $17,500. **Training:** Yes.

16144 ■ Domino's Pizza
Canada's Pizza Delivery Corp.
PO Box 430
Leamington, ON, Canada N8H 4K5
Ph: (519)326-5280
Co. E-mail: customersfirst@dominoscanada.ca
URL: http://www.dominos.ca
Description: Domino's Pizza is an outdoor delivery of pizza throughout Canada. Delivers superior quality pizzas, chicken wings, soft drinks etc. **No. of Franchise Units:** 265. **No. of Company-Owned Units:** 20. **Founded:** 1983. **Equity Capital Needed:** $200,000-$300,000; $80,000 minimum in unemcumbered cash. **Franchise Fee:** $25,000. **Royalty Fee:** 5.5% (gross sales less takes and discounts). **Training:** Required to successfully complete an initial 6 week training program in a designated training center with ongoing support.

16145 ■ East of Chicago Pizza Co.
121 W High St.
Lima, OH 45801
Ph: (419)225-7116
Fax: (419)225-7138
Description: Pizza, sandwiches, and pasta carry-out and delivery. **No. of Franchise Units:** 105. **No. of Company-Owned Units:** 5. **Founded:** 1990.. **Franchised:** 1991. **Equity Capital Needed:** $130,000-$250,000, store type. **Franchise Fee:** $20,000. **Training:** Yes.

16146 ■ Famous Famiglia
Famiglia - DeBartolo, LLC
199 Main St., 8th Fl.
White Plains, NY 10601
Ph: (914)328-4444
Fax: (914)328-4479
Description: Pizza, pasta, salads, and sandwiches. **No. of Franchise Units:** 98. **No. of Company-Owned Units:** 5. **Founded:** 1986.. **Franchised:** 2002. **Equity Capital Needed:** $350,000-$500,000. **Franchise Fee:** $25,000-$35,000. **Royalty Fee:** 6%. **Training:** Yes.

16147 ■ Figaro's Pizza
Figaro's Italian Pizza, Inc.
1500 Liberty St., SE
Salem, OR 97302
Ph: (503)371-9318
Free: 888-344-2767
Fax: (503)363-5364
Description: Pizza restaurant. **No. of Franchise Units:** 68. **Founded:** 1981.. **Franchised:** 1986. **Equity Capital Needed:** $150,000 liquid. **Franchise Fee:** $35,000 1st; $10,000 2nd; $5,000 additional. **Training:** 18 days in-store and classroom training.

16148 ■ Flying Wedge Pizza Co.
4088 Cambie St., Ste. 202
Vancouver, BC, Canada V5Z 2X8
Ph: (604)681-1288

Fax: (604)681-1258
Co. E-mail: franchise@flyingwedge.com
URL: http://www.flyingwedge.com
Description: Take out, sit down, delivery gourmet pizza. **No. of Franchise Units:** 14. **No. of Company-Owned Units:** 5. **Founded:** 1989.. **Franchised:** 1999. **Equity Capital Needed:** $95,000-$130,000. **Franchise Fee:** $35,000. **Training:** Provides 6 weeks training.

16149 ■ Fox's Pizza Den, Inc.
Fox's Pizza Den, Inc.
4425 WM Penn Hwy.
Murrysville, PA 15668
Ph: (800)899-3697
Fax: (724)325-5479
Co. E-mail: foxs@alltel.net
URL: http://www.foxspizza.com
Description: A complete pizza and sandwich operation, offering both fresh dough and shell pizza. Six different size pizzas, plus a large variety of sandwiches and Fox's famous Wedgies (a sandwich made on a pizza shell). May expand menu as desired. May choose a sit-down store or a take-out and delivery. Has a commissary to service all franchise needs. **No. of Franchise Units:** 330. **Founded:** 1971. **Franchised:** 1974. **Equity Capital Needed:** $110,000-$140,000. **Franchise Fee:** $10,000. **Training:** Yes.

16150 ■ Garlic Jim's Famous Gourmet Pizza
802 134th St. SW, Ste. 130
Everett, WA 98204
Ph: (425)918-1900
Fax: (425)918-1700
URL: http://www.garlicjims.com
Description: Gourmet pizza. **No. of Franchise Units:** 50. **No. of Company-Owned Units:** 4. **Founded:** 2004.. **Franchised:** 2003. **Equity Capital Needed:** $170,600-$347,300. **Franchise Fee:** $10,000-$20,000. **Royalty Fee:** 5.5%. **Financial Assistance:** Yes. **Training:** Initial and ongoing training.

16151 ■ Godfather's Pizza, Inc.
2808 N 108th St.
Omaha, NE 68164
Ph: (402)391-1452
Fax: (402)255-2699
Description: Pizza restaurant serving 2 types of pizza crust, salads, beverages and sandwiches. **No. of Franchise Units:** 609. **No. of Company-Owned Units:** 39. **Founded:** 1973.. **Franchised:** 1974. **Equity Capital Needed:** Net worth of $200,000, excluding personal property; $100,000 cash or liquid assets. **Franchise Fee:** 5% of weekly gross. **Training:** Yes.

16152 ■ Greco Pizza Donair
Grinner's Food Systems Limited
105 Walker St.
Truro, NS, Canada B2N 5G9
Ph: (902)893-4141
Description: Home-delivery chain of pizza, donair and oven-sub sandwiches in Atlantic Canada. Specializes in fast, free delivery. **No. of Franchise Units:** 101. **No. of Company-Owned Units:** 2. **Founded:** 1977.. **Franchised:** 1977. **Equity Capital Needed:** $40,000 total investment; $140,000-$180,000 Canadian. **Franchise Fee:** $15,000 Canadian. **Training:** Yes.

16153 ■ Happy Joes, Inc.
2705 Happy Joe Dr.
Bettendorf, IA 52722
Ph: (319)332-8811
Description: Family style pizza and ice cream parlor. **No. of Franchise Units:** 58. **No. of Company-Owned Units:** 1. **Founded:** 1972.. **Franchised:** 1973. **Equity Capital Needed:** $79,700-$1,019,000, depending on full-service or delivery only. **Franchise Fee:** $1,500-$20,000. **Training:** Yes.

16154 ■ Hungry Howie's Pizza, Inc.
Hungry Howie's Pizza and Subs, Inc.
30300 Stephenson Hwy., Ste. 200
Madison Heights, MI 48071
Ph: (248)414-3300
Free: 800-624-8122

Fax: (248)414-3301
Co. E-mail: franchiseinfo@hungryhowies.com
URL: http://www.hungryhowies.com
Description: Menu features flavored crust pizzas in 8 varieties, subs, fresh salads and Fruzza dessert pizzas. **No. of Franchise Units:** 575. **Founded:** 1973.. **Franchised:** 1982. **Equity Capital Needed:** $70,000 cash, $150,000 net worth; $161,100-$403,000 total investment. **Franchise Fee:** $20,000 first/$15,000. **Training:** Comprehensive classroom and in-store training program. Field supervision provided for site selection, construction, lease negotiations, store layout, and store opening.

16155 ■ Italo's Pizza Shop, Inc.
3560 Middlebranch Rd., NE
Canton, OH 44705
Ph: (330)455-7443
Description: A carry-out operation with limited dining, specializing in pizza, chicken, pasta and other Italian dishes. Delivery is optional to franchisee. Stresses quality, quantity, personal service and value. **No. of Franchise Units:** 11. **No. of Company-Owned Units:** 2. **Founded:** 1966.. **Franchised:** 1975. **Equity Capital Needed:** $75,000-$150,000, depending upon options chosen. **Franchise Fee:** $20,000. **Training:** An intensive 3 weeks of training at corporate headquarters is provided, with additional assistance, if necessary, at the franchisee's location.

16156 ■ Jerry's Subs and Pizza
Jerry's Systems, Inc.
15942 Shady Grove Rd.
Gaithersburg, MD 20877
Free: 800-990-9176
Fax: (301)948-3508
Description: Fresh-dough pizza and stuffed submarine sandwiches, served in upscale retail outlets, featuring take-out service and self-service dining. **No. of Franchise Units:** 135. **No. of Company-Owned Units:** 3. **Founded:** 1954.. **Franchised:** 1981. **Equity Capital Needed:** $250,000-$350,000. **Franchise Fee:** $25,000. **Royalty Fee:** 6%. **Financial Assistance:** Limited third party financing available. **Training:** Available 5 weeks at headquarters.

16157 ■ Jet City Pizza
Jet City Pizza Franchise Systems, Inc.
13450 NE 177th Pl.
Woodinville, WA 98072
Ph: (425)402-9673
Fax: (425)488-8919
Co. E-mail: jimw@jetcitypizza.com
URL: http://www.jetcitypizza.com
Description: Gourmet pizza delivery/carry-out. A simple hands on operation that offers only the finest ingredients with a mix of 85% delivery & 15% carry-out. Our trademark slogan is "Finally Gourmet Pizza Delivered.". **No. of Franchise Units:** 8. **No. of Company-Owned Units:** 3. **Founded:** 1994.. **Franchised:** 1996. **Equity Capital Needed:** $175,000-$325,000. **Franchise Fee:** $15,000. **Training:** Offers 5 week training program that consists of in-store operations at one of our corporate locations and classroom business seminars at headquarters.

16158 ■ Ledo Pizza Systems, Inc.
2001 Tidewater Colony Way, Ste. 203
Annapolis, MD 21401
Ph: (410)721-6887
Fax: (410)571-8395
Description: Full service Italian restaurant. **No. of Franchise Units:** 82. **Founded:** 1955.. **Franchised:** 1988. **Franchise Fee:** $30,000. **Training:** Yes.

16159 ■ Little Caesars Pizza
Illitch Holdings
Fox Office Ctr.
2211 Woodward Ave.
Detroit, MI 48201
Ph: (313)471-6469
Free: 800-553-5776
Fax: (313)471-6345
Co. E-mail: usdevelopment@Icecorp.com
URL: http://www.littlecaesars.com
Description: Carry-out and delivery pizza chain. **No. of Franchise Units:** 3,000+. **Founded:** 1959.. **Franchised:** 1962. **Equity Capital Needed:** $194,250-

$622,500. **Franchise Fee:** $20,000. **Training:** Training school is 6 weeks in duration and covers every aspect of the business. Provides continuing ongoing classes.

16160 ■ Marco's Pizza
Marco's Franchising, LLC
Description: Offers pizza, hot sub sandwiches and cheese bread for carry-out and delivery. Has grown steadily to over 65 stores in Ohio, Michigan and Indiana. Built its business on a strong foundation of excellent quality products, superb customer service and great value. Representative to help the franchisee and consult with him/her on any necessary matters. **No. of Franchise Units:** 282. **Founded:** 1978.. **Franchised:** 1979. **Equity Capital Needed:** $179,000-$310,000 total; equity capital, $75,000-$100,000. **Franchise Fee:** $25,000. **Financial Assistance:** Yes. **Training:** Trained in each and every aspect of the system, including marketing, advertising and administration. Approximately 6 weeks in duration, 2 of which are held at the corporate training center. Prior food service or related experience is required.

16161 ■ Mazzio's Italian Eatery
Mazzio's Corp.
4441 S 72nd E Ave.
Tulsa, OK 74145-4692
Ph: (918)663-8880
Free: 800-827-1910
Description: Up-scale pizza restaurants. **No. of Franchise Units:** 114. **No. of Company-Owned Units:** 61. **Founded:** 1961.. **Franchised:** 1979. **Equity Capital Needed:** $400,000. **Franchise Fee:** $20,000. **Training:** Yes.

16162 ■ Me-n-Ed's Pizzerias
Pizza World Supreme
6729 N Palm Ave., Ste. 200
Fresno, CA 93704
Ph: (559)432-0399
Free: 888-636-3373
Fax: (559)432-0398
Description: Pizzeria. **No. of Franchise Units:** 6. **No. of Company-Owned Units:** 52. **Founded:** 1958. **Franchised:** 1958. **Equity Capital Needed:** $175,000-$486,000. **Franchise Fee:** $25,000. **Royalty Fee:** 5%. **Training:** Training provided at headquarters, franchisee's location and ongoing support.

16163 ■ New Orleans Pizza Canada, Inc.
404 James St. S
St. Marys, ON, Canada N4X 1C7
Ph: (519)349-2380
Fax: (519)349-2288
Co. E-mail: lsantolini@chairmansbrands.com
URL: http://www.neworleanspizza.ca
Description: Specializing in pizza and submarines. **No. of Franchise Units:** 67. **No. of Company-Owned Units:** 9. **Founded:** 1978.. **Franchised:** 1978. **Equity Capital Needed:** $40,000-$50,000. **Franchise Fee:** $10,000. **Training:** Yes.

16164 ■ NYPD Pizza
NYPD Pizza Development, LLC
2589 S Hiawassee Rd.
Orlando, FL 32835
Ph: (407)872-6973
Fax: (407)296-4463
Co. E-mail: franchisenypd@aol.com
URL: http://www.nypdpizza.net
Description: Upscale pizzeria with authentic hand tossed New York style pizza. The NYPD Pizza restaurants are themed with great admiration for the police forces worldwide, memorabilia of New York and its rich history. NYPD Pizza offers 3 types of franchises, the Sub Station, the Metro Unit, and the Precinct. **No. of Franchise Units:** 11. **No. of Company-Owned Units:** 2. **Founded:** 1996.. **Franchised:** 2004. **Equity Capital Needed:** $125,000. **Franchise Fee:** $30,000. **Training:** Training program is mandatory for franchise owner, management team and the pie cooks. First hand experience where the franchisee learns what it takes to operate a franchise. The training and support includes opening to closing, advertising and marketing, and ordering.

16165 ■ Old Chicago Pizza
Rock Bottom Restaurants, Inc.
248 Centennial Pky.
Louisville, CO 80027
Ph: (303)664-4200
Fax: (303)664-4007
Description: Pizza restaurant with a large high energy bar. **No. of Franchise Units:** 22. **No. of Company-Owned Units:** 58. **Founded:** 1976.. **Equity Capital Needed:** $3,000,000 net worth; $750,000 available for investment. **Franchise Fee:** $15,000 area $40,000 fee. **Training:** Yes.

16166 ■ OOC Inc.
OOC Inc.
1062 Folsom St.
San Francisco, CA 94103
Ph: (415)760-2199
Free: 866-695-5595
Fax: (415)701-9100
Contact: Todd Parent, President
Description: Pizzeria. **No. of Franchise Units:** 32. **No. of Company-Owned Units:** 9. **Founded:** 1994. **Franchised:** 2000. **Equity Capital Needed:** $184,000-$392,000. **Franchise Fee:** $30,000. **Royalty Fee:** 4%. **Financial Assistance:** Limited third party financing available. **Training:** Provides 4 weeks at headquarters, 2 weeks at franchisee's location and ongoing support. **Telecommunication Services:** jimmy@extremepizza.com.

16167 ■ Panago Pizza Inc.
33149 Mill Lake Rd.
Abbotsford, BC, Canada V2S 2A4
Ph: (604)859-6621
Free: 877-731-0310
Fax: (905)690-3392
Co. E-mail: development@panago.com
URL: http://www.panagofranchise.com
Description: With over 150 locations and sales in excess of 100 million, Panago has built a reputation as Canada's premiere delivery takeout pizza franchise. Our chef-created pizza originals and fresh salads have proven to be the perfect response to today's evolving consumer, satisfying their expanding culinary tastes, demand for convenience, and focus on quality. With industry-leading innovations and a consumer experience that sets us apart, Panago is rapidly expanding into new markets. **No. of Franchise Units:** 180. **No. of Company-Owned Units:** 4. **Founded:** 1986. **Franchised:** 1986. **Equity Capital Needed:** $325,000-$400,000 required investment. **Franchise Fee:** $25,000. **Training:** 6 week intensive training program complemented with ongoing operational support.

16168 ■ Panzerotto Pizza Ltd.
246 Parliament St.
Toronto, ON, Canada M5A 3A4
Ph: (416)362-5555
Fax: (416)362-8217
Co. E-mail: joeschiavone@rogers.com
URL: http://www.panzerottopizza.com
Description: Pizza restaurant. **No. of Franchise Units:** 30. **No. of Company-Owned Units:** 3. **Founded:** 1976.. **Franchised:** 1978. **Equity Capital Needed:** $95,000-$150,000 total investment; $15,000 minimum cash liquidity. **Franchise Fee:** $20,000. **Training:** Franchisee will receive professional training prior to opening. Our store liaison support group is always available to serve you with store operations questions, equipment and local promotion ideas. Our Call centre staff is there for you on customer service issues and delivery zone inquires.

16169 ■ Papa Gino's Pizzeria
Papa Gino's Inc.
600 Providence Hwy.
Dedham, MA 02026-6804
Ph: (781)461-1200
Free: 800-727-2446
Fax: (781)326-7552
Co. E-mail: HR@papaginos.com
URL: http://www.papaginos.com
Description: Pizza, dine in & takeout. **No. of Company-Owned Units:** 160. **Founded:** 1968.. **Franchised:** 2006. **Equity Capital Needed:** $175,000 liquid capital; $500,000 net worth. **Franchise Fee:** $20,000. **Training:** Yes.

16170 ■ Papa John's International, Inc.
2002 Papa John's Blvd.
Louisville, KY 40229
Fax: (502)261-4324
Co. E-mail: Franchise_Opportunities@PapaJohns. com
URL: http://www.PapaJohns.com
Description: Pizza franchise. **No. of Franchise Units:** 3,060. **No. of Company-Owned Units:** 601. **Founded:** 1984.. **Franchised:** 1986. **Equity Capital Needed:** Visit website for requirements & fee information. **Franchise Fee:** $25,000. **Training:** Provides initial management training program and offers ongoing assistance regarding operations, marketing, real estate, and development, food and equipment supply.

16171 ■ Papa Murphy's Take'N'Bake Pizza
8000 NE Pky. Dr.
Vancouver, WA 98662
Ph: (800)257-7272
Co. E-mail: franchise@papamurphys.com
URL: http://www.papamurphys.com
Description: Papa Murphy's is great pizza made from top-quality ingredients. Letting customers bake it themselves is smart business. Put the two together and you get one of the largest, fastest growing concepts of Take'N'Bake Pizza franchises in the world. **No. of Franchise Units:** 1,300. **No. of Company-Owned Units:** 33. **Founded:** 1981. **Franchised:** 1982. **Equity Capital Needed:** $250,000 net worth; $80,000 liquid assets. **Franchise Fee:** $25,000. **Financial Assistance:** None. **Training:** Offers extensive training for new franchise owners, including in-store skill training and structured classroom training at our headquarters.

16172 ■ Papa's Pizza To-Go, Inc.
4465 Commerce Dr., Ste. 101
Buford, GA 30518
Ph: (770)614-6676
Fax: (770)614-9095
URL: http://papaspizzatogo.com
Description: Pizzeria. **No. of Franchise Units:** 60. **No. of Company-Owned Units:** 9. **Founded:** 1986.. **Franchised:** 1990. **Equity Capital Needed:** $138,950-$386,800. **Franchise Fee:** $9,500-$12,500. **Royalty Fee:** 5%. **Training:** Yes.

16173 ■ Paul Revere's Pizza
1570 42nd St. NE, Ste. 4
Cedar Rapids, IA 52402
Ph: (319)395-9113
Fax: (319)395-9115
Description: Pizza delivery, take-out and sit-down. **No. of Franchise Units:** 15. **Founded:** 1975.. **Franchised:** 1982. **Equity Capital Needed:** $92,400-$202,500, includes $25,000-$90,000 working capital. **Franchise Fee:** $5,000-$15,000. **Training:** Yes.

16174 ■ Pizza Depot
2 Automatic Rd., Unit 122
Brampton, ON, Canada L6S 6K8
Ph: (905)458-9711
Fax: (905)458-8644
Co. E-mail: info@pizzadepot.ca
URL: http://www.pizzadepot.ca
Description: Pizzeria. **No. of Franchise Units:** 28. **No. of Company-Owned Units:** 3. **Founded:** 2000.. **Franchised:** 2002. **Equity Capital Needed:** $197,000-$210,000 investment required; $100,000 start-up capital required. **Franchise Fee:** $20,000. **Training:** Yes.

16175 ■ Pizza Factory, Inc.
49430 Rd. 426
Oakhurst, CA 93644
Ph: (559)683-3377
Free: 800-654-4840
Fax: (559)683-6879
URL: http://www.pizzafactory.com
Description: Family-oriented pizza restaurant, serving pizza, pasta, sandwiches and salad bar. Specializing in communities of 15,000 or less. **No. of Franchise Units:** 108. **No. of Company-Owned Units:** 1. **Founded:** 1979.. **Franchised:** 1985. **Equity Capital Needed:** $137,500-$426,000. **Franchise Fee:** $20,000. **Royalty Fee:** 5%. **Training:** Offers 325 hours training.

16176 ■ Pizza Fusion
2200 W Cypress Creek Rd., Ste 1
Fort Lauderdale, FL 33309
Ph: (954)449-7244
Fax: (954)449-4957
Description: Organic pizza, sandwiches, and salads. **No. of Franchise Units:** 12. **Founded:** 2006. **Franchised:** 2007. **Equity Capital Needed:** $328,000-$571,000. **Franchise Fee:** $30,000. **Financial Assistance:** Yes. **Training:** Yes.

16177 ■ Pizza Inn, Inc.
3551 Plano Pky.
The Colony, TX 75056
Ph: (800)284-3466
Fax: (469)574-4407
Description: Express, delivery/carry out, buffet. **No. of Franchise Units:** 307. **No. of Company-Owned Units:** 4. **Founded:** 1961.. **Franchised:** 1963. **Equity Capital Needed:** $30,000-$150,000. **Franchise Fee:** $5,000-$25,000. **Training:** Yes.

16178 ■ Pizza Nova Take Out Ltd.
2247 Midland Ave.
Toronto, ON, Canada M1P 4R1
Ph: (416)439-0051
Fax: (416)299-3558
URL: http://www.pizzanova.com
Description: Pizza delivery. **No. of Franchise Units:** 125. **No. of Company-Owned Units:** 1. **Founded:** 1963.. **Franchised:** 1967. **Equity Capital Needed:** $290,000-$310,000. **Franchise Fee:** $20,000. **Training:** Yes.

16179 ■ Pizza Patron Inc.
10999 Petal St., Ste. 200
Dallas, TX 75238
Ph: (972)613-8000
Fax: (972)613-8014
Co. E-mail: guillermo@pizzapatron.com
URL: http://www.pizzapatron.com
Description: Pizzeria. **No. of Franchise Units:** 86. **No. of Company-Owned Units:** 6. **Founded:** 1986.. **Equity Capital Needed:** $150,000 net worth and $50,000 investment equity per location to be developed. **Franchise Fee:** $20,000 1st store. **Training:** A comprehensive hands-on training program, onsite, at our company store and concludes with a 4 day "owner simulation" where you run our company store as if it were your own and ongoing support.

16180 ■ The Pizza Pipeline
The Pizza Pipeline
418 W Sharp Ave.
Spokane, WA 99201
Ph: (509)326-1977
Free: 800-509-1977
Fax: (509)326-3017
URL: http://www.pizzapipeline.com
Description: Pizza delivery. **No. of Franchise Units:** 9. **No. of Company-Owned Units:** 7. **Founded:** 1988. **Franchised:** 1990. **Equity Capital Needed:** None. **Franchise Fee:** $18,000. **Training:** Includes 4-6 weeks training at corporate headquarters, 2 weeks at franchisee's location and ongoing support.

16181 ■ Pizza Pit
SB Acquisitions, LLC
433 Grand Canyon Dr., Ste. 204
Madison, WI 53719
Ph: (608)833-3030
Fax: (608)602-9081
Description: Free home delivery and carry-out of handcrafted pizzas, specialty sandwiches, pasta and salads. Units are adaptable to inside seating. Single and multiple-unit programs are available. Merged business concepts with family fun centers, bowling centers and convenience stores. Profit planning available. **No. of Franchise Units:** 18. **Founded:** 1969.. **Franchised:** 1982. **Equity Capital Needed:** Range $128,280-$242,640. **Franchise Fee:** $17,500. **Training:** Yes.

16182 ■ Pizza Pizza
500 Kipling Ave.
Toronto, ON, Canada M8Z 5E5
Ph: (416)967-1010
Free: 800-263-5556

Fax: (416)967-9865
Co. E-mail: dmason@pizzapizza.ca
URL: http://www.pizzapizza.ca
Description: Take-out and delivery stores with a menu that includes pizza, salads, wings, subs and Italian dinners. Recently began an international expansion program, with the first Restaurant opening in Costa Rica. **No. of Franchise Units:** 363. **No. of Company-Owned Units:** 16. **Founded:** 1967.. **Franchised:** 1974. **Equity Capital Needed:** $100,000-$200,000. **Franchise Fee:** $30,000. **Training:** Offers 8 weeks training and ongoing support.

16183 ■ Pizza Schimizza
Schmizza International, Inc.
1500 Liberty St. SE, Ste. 160
Salem, OR 97302
Ph: (503)371-9318
Fax: (503)363-5364
Description: Gourmet New York style pizza. **No. of Franchise Units:** 24. **Founded:** 1993.. **Franchised:** 2001. **Equity Capital Needed:** $150,000 liquid. **Franchise Fee:** $35,000 1st; $10,000 2nd; $5,000 additional. **Training:** Yes.

16184 ■ Pizzaville, Inc.
741 Rowntree Dairy Rd., Unit 1
Woodbridge, ON, Canada L4L 5T9
Ph: (905)850-0070
Fax: (905)850-0339
URL: http://www.pizzaville.ca/franchise
Description: Operating as Pizzaville, Pizza Panzerotto. Regionally based Southern Ontario Italian pizza and panzerotto take out and delivery chain. **No. of Franchise Units:** 69. **No. of Company-Owned Units:** 1. **Founded:** 1963.. **Franchised:** 1979. **Equity Capital Needed:** $100,000-$125,000 start-up capital required; $275,000-$325,000 investment required. **Franchise Fee:** $25,000. **Training:** Yes.

16185 ■ Pizzeria Valdiano
Ligman Franchise group
1315 S Industrial Pky., Ste. 1101
Lake Mary, FL 32746
Ph: (813)935-5087
Fax: (813)425-5799
Description: Pizzeria. **No. of Franchise Units:** 1. **No. of Company-Owned Units:** 1. **Founded:** 2006.. **Franchised:** 2007. **Equity Capital Needed:** $276,000-$394,000. **Franchise Fee:** $27,500. **Training:** Yes.

16186 ■ Pizzicato Gourmet Pizza
2523 SE 9th Ave.
Portland, OR 97202
Ph: (503)274-0375
Fax: (503)274-0473
Description: Upscale gourmet pizza & salads. **No. of Franchise Units:** 1. **No. of Company-Owned Units:** 16. **Founded:** 1989.. **Franchised:** 2004. **Equity Capital Needed:** $200,000-$400,000. **Franchise Fee:** 25,000. **Training:** Yes.

16187 ■ Rocky Rococo Pizza & Pasta
Rococo Franchise Corp.
P.O. Box 207
Oconomowoc, WI 53066
Ph: (262)569-5580
Fax: (262)569-5591
Description: Quick service pizza. **No. of Company-Owned Units:** 17. **Founded:** 1974.. **Franchised:** 1995. **Franchise Fee:** $25,000. **Training:** Yes.

16188 ■ Rotelli Pizza & Pasta Inc.
9045 La Fontana Blvd.
Boca Raton, FL 33434
Ph: (561)826-0900
Description: Pizza and pasta restaurant. **No. of Franchise Units:** 31. **Founded:** 1999. **Franchised:** 1999. **Equity Capital Needed:** $300,000-$674,000. **Franchise Fee:** $25,000. **Royalty Fee:** 6%. **Training:** Provides a total of 6 weeks training between headquarters and franchisee's location and ongoing support.

16189 ■ San Francisco Oven
1845 E Sunshine St.
Springfield, MO 65804
Ph: (703)549-5332

Fax: (703)549-0740

Description: Made to order pizza, sandwiches and soup. **No. of Company-Owned Units:** 1. **Founded:** 2001.. **Franchised:** 2002. **Equity Capital Needed:** $150,000-$350,000. **Franchise Fee:** $25,000. **Training:** Yes.

16190 ■ Sanfratello's Pizza

Sanfratello's Franchise Systems LLC
127 W Main St.
Glenwood, IL 60425
Ph: (877)70P-IZZA
Free: 877-707-4992
Fax: (219)924-2450
URL: http://www.sanfratellos.com

Description: Family pizzeria specializing in thin crust & pan pizza offering traditional pasta dishes, BBQ ribs, hot & cold sandwiches, an assortment of salads, appetizers and more. Currently offering "Full service" franchises (Dine-in, Pick-up & Delivery services) with a Beer & Wine minimum or full bar service. Also offering a "Pick-up & Delivery only" franchise option. **No. of Franchise Units:** 1. **No. of Company-Owned Units:** 4. **Founded:** 1969.. **Franchised:** 2006. **Equity Capital Needed:** $300,850-$763,500. **Franchise Fee:** $17,500-$25,000. **Training:** Provides a 3 week training program, pre-opening support, opening support with staff and ongoing support.

16191 ■ Sarpino's Pizzeria Canada Ltd.

Sarpino's World LTD
1133 Regent St., Ste. 203
Fredericton, NB, Canada E3B 3Z2
Ph: (506)462-9270
Fax: (506)451-8692
Co. E-mail: rbuckingham@nb.aibn.com
URL: http://www.sarpinos.com

Description: Pizzeria. **No. of Franchise Units:** 9. **No. of Company-Owned Units:** 1. **Founded:** 2001.. **Franchised:** 2002. **Equity Capital Needed:** $195,000-$235,000. **Franchise Fee:** $25,000. **Training:** Provides 2 weeks training.

16192 ■ Snappy Tomato Pizza

Deters Co.
6111 Burgundy Hill Dr., Unit A
Burlington, KY 41005
Free: 888-463-7627
Fax: (859)525-4686

Description: A delivery, dine-in and carry-out pizzeria that makes the highest-quality pizza available. Menu features hoagies, salads and award-winning 'Ranch Pizza.'. **No. of Franchise Units:** 68. **No. of**

Company-Owned Units: 4. **Founded:** 1978.. **Franchised:** 1982. **Equity Capital Needed:** $94,000-$250,000, depending on site selection and equipment. **Franchise Fee:** $15,000. **Training:** Training program covers every aspect of the business, including actual time in stores getting hands-on experience.

16193 ■ Straw Hat Pizza

18 Crow Canyon Ct., Ste. 270
San Ramon, CA 94583
Ph: (925)837-3400

Description: Family Pizza restaurant. **No. of Franchise Units:** 81. **Founded:** 1959.. **Franchised:** 1987. **Equity Capital Needed:** $129,400-$256,500 (totaling up to $436,500). **Franchise Fee:** $25,000-$45,000. **Financial Assistance:** Yes. **Training:** Yes.

16194 ■ Stuft Pizza, Stuft Pizza Bar & Grill, Stuft Pizza Pronto

Stuft Pizza Franchise Corp.
50855 Washington St., Ste. 210
La Quinta, CA 92253
Ph: (949)361-2522
Fax: (949)361-2501

Description: Stuft pizza, pasta, salads, and microbrewery. **No. of Franchise Units:** 18. **No. of Company-Owned Units:** 2. **Founded:** 1976.. **Franchised:** 1986. **Equity Capital Needed:** $100,000 and up. **Franchise Fee:** $25,000. **Training:** Yes.

16195 ■ Villa Enterprises

25 Washington St.
Morristown, NJ 07960
Ph: (973)285-4800
Fax: (973)401-0121

Description: Quick service pizza & Italian restaurant. **No. of Franchise Units:** 150. **No. of Company-Owned Units:** 150. **Founded:** 1964.. **Franchised:** 1999. **Equity Capital Needed:** 100,100 liquid; $300,000 net worth. **Franchise Fee:** $25,000. **Training:** Yes.

16196 ■ Vocelli Pizza

1005 South Bee St.
Pittsburgh, PA 15220
Ph: (412)919-2100
Fax: (412)937-9200
Co. E-mail: lmolnar@cocellipizza.com

Description: Pizza, subs, wings; delivery or carry-out. **No. of Franchise Units:** 102. **No. of Company-Owned Units:** 3. **Founded:** 1969.. **Franchised:** 1988. **Equity Capital Needed:** $168,000-$538,000.

Franchise Fee: $20,000. **Royalty Fee:** 5%. **Financial Assistance:** Limited third party financing available. **Training:** Yes.

16197 ■ We Toss'em, They're Awesome Pizza Factory

Pizza Factory Inc.
49430 Rd. 426
Oakhurst, CA 93644
Ph: (559)683-3377
Free: 800-654-4840
Fax: (559)683-6879

Description: Pizzeria. **No. of Franchise Units:** 110. **Founded:** 1979.. **Franchised:** 1985. **Equity Capital Needed:** $137,000-$426,000. **Franchise Fee:** Full, Mid, Express $20,000. **Training:** Yes.

16198 ■ Whata Lotta Pizza

7011 Warner Ave., Unit M
Huntington Beach, CA 92647
Ph: (714)848-6148
Free: 888-425-6882
Fax: (714)849-2029
Co. E-mail: info@whatalottapizza.com
URL: http://www.4alotta.com

Description: Restaurant franchise. **No. of Franchise Units:** 50. **No. of Company-Owned Units:** 8. **Founded:** 1992.. **Franchised:** 2005. **Equity Capital Needed:** $90,000-$208,500. **Franchise Fee:** $25,000. **Training:** Yes.

16199 ■ Z Pizza

19712 MacArthur Blvd. Ste. 210
Irvine, CA 92612
Ph: (949)222-5600
Free: 800-230-5761
Fax: (949)721-4053
Co. E-mail: zpizzadan@aol.com
URL: http://www.zpizza.com

Description: They serve delicious gourmet-style pizza, pasta and sandwiches. **No. of Franchise Units:** 81. **No. of Company-Owned Units:** 1. **Founded:** 1986.. **Franchised:** 1999. **Equity Capital Needed:** $253,500-$352,500. **Franchise Fee:** $30,000. **Royalty Fee:** 6%. **Training:** 4 weeks at headquarters, 2 weeks at franchisee's location, and ongoing support.

16200 ■ Zoo Pizza

3273 N Shepard
Milwaukee, WI 53211

Description: Pizzeria. **No. of Company-Owned Units:** 1. **Founded:** 1994.. **Equity Capital Needed:** $300,000-$400,000. **Franchise Fee:** $89,000. **Training:** No.

TRADE PERIODICALS

16201 ■ PLANET News
Pub: Professional Landcare Network
Contact: Jason K. Cupp, President
Ed: Kathy Wemhoff, Editor, kathywemhoff@alca.org.
Released: Monthly. **Price:** Included in membership.
Description: Serves specialists interested in the design, installation, and maintenance of interior and exterior landscapes, with emphasis on artistic and healthful results. Carries technical information and tips on subjects such as pricing work to make money. Recurring features include news of research, book reviews, award winning landscapes, and a calendar of events.

TRADE SHOWS AND CONVENTIONS

16202 ■ Nursery/Landscape Expo
Texas Nursery & Landscape Association
7730 S. IH-35
Austin, TX 78745-6698
Ph: (512)280-5182
Free: 800-880-0343
Fax: (512)280-3012
Co. E-mail: info@tnlaonline.org
URL: http://www.txnla.org
URL(s): www.txnla.org. **Frequency:** Annual. **Audience:** Nursery, landscape and related trades professionals. **Principal Exhibits:** Plant materials including foliage, bedding plants, trees, palms; allied products including machinery, equipment and supplies for horticulture and landscape industry. **Dates and Locations:** , Convention Center.

16203 ■ OFA Short Course
Ohio Florists Association
2130 Stella Ct., Ste. 200
Columbus, OH 43215-1033
Ph: (614)487-1117
Fax: (614)487-1216
Co. E-mail: ofa@ofa.org
URL: http://www.ofa.org
Contact: Mike McCabe, Executive Director
E-mail: mike@mccabesflowers.com
URL(s): www.ofa.org. **Frequency:** Annual. **Audience:** Growers, retailers, garden centers, and other trade professionals. **Principal Exhibits:** Exhibits for the greenhouse grower and related industries. **Dates and Locations:** , Convention Center.

16204 ■ The World's Showcase of Horticulture
Southern Nursery Association
894 Liberty Farm Rd.
Oak Grove, GA 22443-5200
Ph: (804)224-9352
Co. E-mail: mail@sna.org
URL: http://www.sna.org
Contact: Danny Summers, Executive Vice President
E-mail: danny@mail.sna.org
URL(s): www.sna.org. **Frequency:** Annual. **Audience:** Wholesale and retail nursery professionals and landscapers. **Principal Exhibits:** Nursery products, including plants, chemicals, machinery and equipment, soil and soil supplements, and plant containers. **Dates and Locations:** , Georgia World Congress Center. **Telecommunication Services:** mail@sna.org.

CONSULTANTS

16205 ■ Foliage Service by Concepts—Concepts in Green
10310 NE Skidmore St.
Portland, OR 97294-3387
Ph: (503)234-3459
Fax: (503)256-0472
Co. E-mail: info@foliage-services.com
URL: http://www.foliage-services.com
Contact: Angela Lucente, Sales Executive
Scope: A professional interior plant sales and maintenance company dedicated to the design, placement, care and sales of interior plants with services to include all aspects of the interior scape business. Works closely with architects and designers to provide the proper plant species for various office and building environments. **Founded:** 1968.

FRANCHISES AND BUSINESS OPPORTUNITIES

16206 ■ Foliage Design Systems
Foliage Design Systems Franchise Co., Inc.
7048 Narcoossee Rd.
Orlando, FL 32822
Ph: (800)933-7351
Fax: (407)245-7533
Description: Provides the sale, lease and short-term rental of live, artificial and preserved interior foliage and decorative containers. Related products include seasonal decorative items. Designs, installs and maintains interior foliage in office buildings, hotels, residences, and restaurants. **No. of Franchise Units:** 37. **No. of Company-Owned Units:** 3. **Founded:** 1971.. **Franchised:** 1980. **Equity Capital Needed:** $49,400-$144,000, includes initial franchise fee. **Franchise Fee:** $25,000-$100,000. **Training:** followed by onsite training covering all facets of business from plant care and plant identification to sales and marketing to office procedures. Complete operations manuals provided.

RESEARCH CENTERS

16207 ■ Ohio State University - C. Wayne Ellett Plant and Pest Diagnostic Clinic (CWEPPDC)
8995 E Main St., Bldg. 23
Reynoldsburg, OH 43068-3399
Ph: (614)292-5006
Fax: (614)466-9754
Co. E-mail: ppdc@cfaes.osu.edu
URL: http://ppdc.osu.edu
Services: Diagnosis of plant problems, plant diseases, insects, weeds. **Founded:** 1985.

16208 ■ University of British Columbia - Botanical Garden
6804 SW Marine Dr.
Vancouver, BC, Canada V6T 1Z4
Ph: (604)822-3928
Fax: (604)822-2016
Co. E-mail: sean.graham@ubc.ca
URL: http://www.botanicalgarden.ubc.ca
Contact: Prof. Sean Graham, Director, Research
Services: Develops Professional Training Programs: for the British Columbia nursery industry; Plant Information and Identification Services. **Founded:** 1916. **Publications:** Davidsonia. **Educational Activities:** Educational Programs, for the community; Botanical Garden Workshops and conferences (Occasionally). **Telecommunication Services:** botg@interchange.ubc.ca.

ASSOCIATIONS AND OTHER ORGANIZATIONS

16209 ■ American Society of Plumbing Engineers (ASPE)
2980 S River Rd.
Des Plaines, IL 60018
Ph: (847)296-0002
Fax: (847)296-2963
Co. E-mail: info@aspe.org
URL: http://aspe.org
Contact: Jim Kendzel, Executive Director

URL(s): www.aspe.org. **Description:** Represents engineers and designers involved in the design and specification of plumbing systems; manufacturers, governmental officials, and contractors related to the industry may become members on a limited basis. Seeks to resolve professional problems in plumbing engineering; advocates greater cooperation among members and plumbing officials, contractors, laborers, and the public. Code committees examine regulatory codes pertaining to the industry and submit proposed revisions to code writing authorities to simplify, standardize, and modernize all codes. Sponsors American Society of Plumbing Engineers Research Foundation; operates certification program. **Founded:** 1964. **Publications:** *Data Book* (Annual). **Educational Activities:** Convention and Engineered Plumbing Exposition (Biennial); Technical Symposium (Biennial); American Society of Plumbing Engineers Convention (Biennial). **Awards:** Alfred Steele Engineering Scholarship (Annual); ASPE Honor Roll of Employers (Biennial); ASPE Industry Award (Biennial); George W. Runkle Award of Merit (Biennial).

16210 ■ American Society of Sanitary Engineering (ASSE)
901 Canterbury Rd., Ste. A
Westlake, OH 44145
Ph: (440)835-3040
Fax: (440)835-3488
Co. E-mail: info@asse-plumbing.org
URL: http://www.asse-plumbing.org
Contact: Donald R. Summers, Jr., President

Description: Plumbing officials, sanitary engineers, plumbers, plumbing contractors, building officials, architects, engineers, designing engineers, physicians, and others interested in health. Conducts research on plumbing and sanitation, and develops performance standards for components of the plumbing system. Sponsors disease research program and other studies of water-borne epidemics. **Scope:** backflow, medical gas, graywater legionnaires. **Founded:** 1906. **Subscriptions:** articles books periodicals. **Awards:** Henry B. Davis Award (Annual); Henry B. Davis Award; Fellowship Award; Dewey R. Dedrick, Jr. Award.

16211 ■ American Supply Association (ASA)
1200 N Arlington Heights Rd., Ste. 150
Itasca, IL 60143
Ph: (630)467-0000

Fax: (630)467-0001
Co. E-mail: info@asa.net
URL: http://www.asa.net
Contact: Scott Weaver, President

Description: Represents wholesale, distributors, and manufacturers of plumbing and heating, cooling, pipes, valves, and fittings. Compiles statistics on operating costs and makes occasional studies of compensation, fringe benefits, wages, and salaries. Conducts research studies and forecasting surveys. Offers group insurance. Maintains management institutes, home study courses under the ASA Education Foundation and Endowment program, provides technology and produces a CD-ROM and internet catalogue of manufacturers. **Founded:** 1969. **Publications:** *American Supply Association Operating Performance Report*; *American Supply Association-- Membership Directory: Resource Guide* (Annual); *American Supply Association--Membership Directory* (Annual); *ASA News* (Bimonthly); *Report of Operating Performance* (Annual). **Educational Activities:** American Supply Association Conference (Biennial); North American Exposition (Biennial); NEX - North American Exposition (Biennial).

16212 ■ Association of Independent Manufacturers'/Representatives (AIM/R)
16 A Journey, Ste. 200
Aliso Viejo, CA 92656
Ph: (949)859-2884
Free: 866-729-0975
Fax: (949)855-2973
Co. E-mail: info@aimr.net
URL: http://www.aimr.net
Contact: Mike Parham, Chairman

Description: Manufacturers' representative companies in the plumbing-heating-cooling-piping industry promoting the use of independent sales representatives. Conducts educational programs and establishes a code of ethics between members and customers. **Founded:** 1972. **Publications:** *AIM/R News and Views* (Quarterly). **Awards:** National Manufacturer of the Year (Annual); National Wholesaler of the Year (Annual).

16213 ■ National Association of Plumbing, Heating, Cooling Contractors (PHCC)
180 S Washington St.
Falls Church, VA 22046
Ph: (703)237-8100
Free: 800-533-7694
Fax: (703)237-7442
URL: http://www.phccweb.org
Contact: Keith Bienvenu, President

Description: Federation of state and local associations of plumbing, heating, and cooling contractors. Seeks to advance sanitation, encourage sanitary laws, and generally improve the plumbing, heating, ventilating, and air conditioning industries. Conducts apprenticeship training programs, workshops, seminars, political action committee, educational and research programs. **Founded:** 1883. **Publications:** *Who's Who in the Plumbing-Heating-Cooling Contracting Business* (Annual). **Awards:** Chapter Excellence Award (Annual).

16214 ■ Plumbing & Drainage Institute (PDI)
800 Turnpike St., Ste. 300
45 Bristol Dr.
North Andover, MA 01845
Ph: (978)557-0720
Free: 800-589-8956
Fax: (978)557-0721
Co. E-mail: pdi@pdionline.org
URL: http://www.pdionline.org
Contact: Rand Ackroyd, Executive Director

Description: Represents manufacturers of engineered plumbing and drainage products. Promotes the advancement of engineered plumbing products through publicity, public relations, research and standardization of plumbing requirements. Works on codes and standards for plumbing drainage products. **Founded:** 1928.

16215 ■ Plumbing Manufacturers Institute (PMI)
1921 Rohlwing Rd., Unit G
Rolling Meadows, IL 60008
Ph: (847)481-5500
Fax: (847)481-5501
Co. E-mail: bhiggens@pmihome.org
URL: http://www.pmihome.org
Contact: Barbara C. Higgens, Executive Director

Description: Manufacturers of plumbing products. **Founded:** 1956.

DIRECTORIES OF EDUCATIONAL PROGRAMS

16216 ■ *Directory of Private Accredited Career Schools and Colleges of Technology*
Pub: Accrediting Commission of Career Schools and Colleges of Technology
Contact: Michale S. McComis, Executive Director

Released: On web page. **Price:** Free. **Description:** Covers 3900 accredited post-secondary programs that provide training programs in business, trade, and technical fields, including various small business endeavors. Entries offer school name, address, phone, description of courses, job placement assistance, and requirements for admission. Arrangement is alphabetical.

REFERENCE WORKS

16217 ■ *"Advances in Pump Technology - Part Two"* in Contractor (Vol. 57, February 2010, No. 2, pp. 22)
Pub: Penton Media, Inc.

Ed: Mark Eatherton. **Description:** Chinese and Japanese companies have come up with refrigerant based heat pump products that are air based which will significantly lower the installed cost of heat pump based systems. Some of these newer models have variable speed, soft start compressors and have the ability to perform high-efficiency heat pump operation on a modulating basis.

16218 ▪ *"Be Proactive - Closely Review Contracts"* in *Contractor (Vol. 56, July 2009, No. 7, pp. 19)*
Pub: Penton Media, Inc.
Ed: Al Schwartz. **Description:** Contract disputes can make subcontractors suffer big financial losses or even cause a new subcontractor to fail. Subcontractors should scour the plans and specifications for any references to work that might remotely come under their scope and to cross out any line in the contract that does not accurately reflect the work that they agreed to.

16219 ▪ *"Be Safe: CSE Requires a Series of Steps"* in *Contractor (Vol. 56, October 2009, No. 10, pp. 40)*
Pub: Penton Media, Inc.
Ed: Dave Yates. **Description:** Confined Space Entry claims 91 lives each year and plumbers can prevent this by following several steps starting with the use of a four-gas analyzer which costs $1,262. It measures oxygen levels, as well as combustible gases, carbon monoxide, and hydrogen sulfide.

16220 ▪ *"BIM and You: Know Its Benefits and Risks"* in *Contractor (Vol. 57, January 2010, No. 1, pp. 46)*
Pub: Penton Media, Inc.
Ed: Susan Linden McGreevy. **Description:** Building Information Modeling is intended to be 'collaborative' and this could raise legal issues if a contractor sends an electronic bid and it is filtered out. Other legal issues that mechanical contractors need to consider before using this technology are discussed.

16221 ▪ *"A Burning Issue: Lives Are at Stake Every Day"* in *Contractor (Vol. 56, October 2009, No. 10, pp. 29)*
Pub: Penton Media, Inc.
Ed: Julius A. Ballanco; Stanley Wolfson. **Description:** American Society of Plumbing Engineers has been accused of being biased for supporting rules that require residential fire sprinklers although the society's members will not receive any benefit from their installation. The organization trains and certifies plumbing engineers who design life-saving fire protection systems.

16222 ▪ *"The Business End of Staying in Business"* in *Contractor (Vol. 56, September 2009, No. 9, pp. 51)*
Pub: Penton Media, Inc.
Ed: Al Schwartz. **Description:** Advice on how to manage a new plumbing business in the United States are offered. The transition from being a workman to an employer is seen as one that accompanies a steep learning curve. The importance of managing cash flow is also highlighted.

16223 ▪ *"A Call for Common Sense with WaterSense"* in *Contractor (Vol. 56, July 2009, No. 7, pp. 42)*
Pub: Penton Media, Inc.
Ed: Dave Yates. **Description:** Instillation of a shower that is supposed to protect bathers from being scalded is presented. Plumbers should be aware that the WaterSense shower heads still have a 50/50 chance of scalding their users.

16224 ▪ *"Charlotte Pipe Launches Satirical Campaign"* in *Contractor (Vol. 57, January 2010, No. 1, pp. 6)*
Pub: Penton Media, Inc.
Description: Charlotte Pipe and Foundry Co. launched an advertising campaign that uses social media and humor to make a point about how it can be nearly impossible to determine if imported cast iron pipes and fittings meet the same quality standards as what is made in the U.S. The campaign features 'pipe whisperers' and also spoofs pipe sniffing dogs.

16225 ▪ *"Chicago Botanic Garden Builds Green Research Facility"* in *Contractor (Vol. 56, December 2009, No. 12, pp. 5)*
Pub: Penton Media, Inc.
Ed: Candace Roulo. **Description:** Chicago Botanic Garden has built a laboratory and research facility in Illinois. The facility is set to receive a United States

Green Building Council LEED Gold certification. The building features a solar photovoltaic array, radiant flooring and water-conserving plumbing products.

16226 ▪ *"Climate Right Systems Provides Pre-Assembled Equipment Packages"* in *Contractor (Vol. 56, July 2009, No. 7, pp. 1)*
Pub: Penton Media, Inc.
Description: Climate Right Systems offers completely engineered, assembled, and tested equipment packages for hydronic heating and cooling. This package does away with the need to custom fabricate on-site and lets mechanical and plumbing contractors expand their offerings without added overhead and risk.

16227 ▪ *"Commercial Water Efficiency Initiatives Announced"* in *Contractor (Vol. 56, November 2009, No. 11, pp. 5)*
Pub: Penton Media, Inc.
Ed: Robert P. Mader. **Description:** Plumbing engineers John Koeller and Bill Gauley are developing a testing protocol for commercial toilets. The team said commercial toilets should have a higher level of flush performance than residential toilets for certification. The Environmental Protection Agency's WaterSense program wants to expand the program into the commercial/institutional sector.

16228 ▪ *"Contractors Can't Do It Alone, PHCC's Pfeffer Says"* in *Contractor (Vol. 56, October 2009, No. 10, pp. 3)*
Pub: Penton Media, Inc.
Ed: Robert P. Mader. **Description:** President Herbert 'Skip' Pfeffer of the Plumbing-Heating-Cooling Contractors National Association says lobbying and education are the services that the association offers that a contractor cannot do individually. Pfeffer says the dues for the association are set up in a manner that allows members to pay monthly.

16229 ▪ *"Contractors Fret Over Credit, People, Government"* in *Contractor (Vol. 57, February 2010, No. 2, pp. 7)*
Pub: Penton Media, Inc.
Ed: Robert P. Mader. **Description:** Telephone interviews with 22 plumbing and HVAC contractors reveal that only two had sales increases for 2009 and that overall, contractors were down anywhere from seven to 25 percent. In the repair/service market, the residential sector was holding its own but the commercial portion was lagging behind.

16230 ▪ *"Contractors Should Expand Their Services"* in *Contractor (Vol. 56, July 2009, No. 7, pp. 34)*
Pub: Penton Media, Inc.
Ed: Steven Scandaliato. **Description:** All single family homes will be required to have fire sprinkler systems installed when the 2009 International Residential Code arrives. This presents an opportunity for plumbing contractors and they can be competitively priced against a fire protection contractor if they train their workforce to install sprinklers.

16231 ▪ *"Corporate Park Retrofits for Water Savings"* in *Contractor (Vol. 56, October 2009, No. 10, pp. 5)*
Pub: Penton Media, Inc.
Description: Merrit Corporate Park in Norwalk, Connecticut has been interested in improving building efficiency and one of their buildings has been retrofitted with water-efficient plumbing systems which will allow them to save as much as two million gallons of water. ADP Service Corp. helped the park upgrade their plumbing system.

16232 ▪ *"CSE: Contractors Are Always Responsible"* in *Contractor (Vol. 56, November 2009, No. 11, pp. 34)*
Pub: Penton Media, Inc.
Ed: Dave Yates. **Description:** Plumbing contractors should purchase a long snorkel hose, a tripod with manual-crank hoist, and a sump pump in order to prevent accidents associated with Confined Space Entry. Liability issues surrounding confined space entry prevention and accidents are discussed.

16233 ▪ *"The Customer Is Right Even If He's Wrong"* in *Contractor (Vol. 57, February 2010, No. 2, pp. 12)*
Pub: Penton Media, Inc.
Ed: Al Schwarz. **Description:** Mechanical contractors should note that customers will make a judgment based upon the impression that they form on their first meeting. Contractors can maintain a professional image by washing their trucks and having the personnel dress uniformly. Contractors have every right to demand that employees clean up and make a better impression on customers.

16234 ▪ *Directory of Listed Plumbing Products*
Pub: IAPMO
Contact: Dan Daniels, President
URL(s): www.iapmo.org/Pages/splash.aspx. **Released:** Bimonthly **Price:** $118, Members per year. **Covers:** About 1,500 manufacturers of approximately 10,000 plumbing products and appliances. **Entries include:** Manufacturer name, address, product name, model number, product description. **Arrangement:** Alphabetical. **Indexes:** Manufacturer, product.

16235 ▪ *"Do the Right Thing"* in *Contractor (Vol. 56, December 2009, No. 12, pp. 16)*
Pub: Penton Media, Inc.
Ed: Robert P. Mader. **Description:** Applewood Plumbing, Heating and Electric has won Contractor magazine's 2009 Contractor of the Year Award. The company has ranked eighth among more than 300 service companies in the United States. A brief history of the company is also provided.

16236 ▪ *"DOE Proposes New Water Heater Efficiency Standards"* in *Contractor (Vol. 57, January 2010, No. 1, pp. 3)*
Pub: Penton Media, Inc.
Ed: Robert P. Mader. **Description:** U.S. Department of Energy is proposing higher efficiency standards for gas and electric water heaters which will not take effect until 2015. The proposal calls for gas-fired storage water heaters less than 60 gallons to have an Energy Factor of 0.675 and those larger than 60 gallons to have an Energy Factor of 0.717.

16237 ▪ *"EPA 'Finalizes' WaterSense for Homes"* in *Contractor (Vol. 57, January 2010, No. 1, pp. 70)*
Pub: Penton Media, Inc.
Ed: Bob Mader. **Description:** U.S. Environmental Protection Agency released its 'final' version of the WaterSense for Homes standard. The standard's provisions that affect plumbing contractors includes the specification that everything has to be leak tested and final service pressure cannot exceed 60 psi.

16238 ▪ *"Expect Action on Health Care and the Economy"* in *Contractor (Vol. 57, January 2010, No. 1, pp. 30)*
Pub: Penton Media, Inc.
Ed: Kevin Schwalb. **Description:** The Plumbing-Heating-Cooling Contractors National Association is working to solidify its standing in the public policy arena as the legislative agenda will focus on health care reform, estate tax and immigration reform, all of which will impact the industries.

16239 ▪ *"Federal Buildings to Achieve Zero-Net Energy by 2030"* in *Contractor (Vol. 56, December 2009, No. 12, pp. 5)*
Pub: Penton Media, Inc.
Ed: Candace Roulo. **Description:** United States president Barack Obama has issued sustainable goals for federal buildings. Federal agencies are also required to increase energy efficiency, conserve water and support sustainable communities. Obama has also announced a $3.4 billion investment in a smart energy creed.

16240 ▪ *"Get Online Quick in the Office Or in the Field"* in *Contractor (Vol. 56, October 2009, No. 10, pp. 47)*
Pub: Penton Media, Inc.
Ed: William Feldman; Patti Feldman. **Description:** Contractors can set up a web site in minutes using the www.1and1.com website. Verizon's Novatel MIFI

2372 HSPA personal hotspot device lets contractors go online in the field. The StarTech scalable business management system helps contractors manage daily operations.

16241 ■ *"Got to be Smarter than the Average Bear" in Contractor (Vol. 56, September 2009, No. 9, pp. 82)*
Pub: Penton Media, Inc.
Ed: Bob Mader. **Description:** International Association of Plumbing and Mechanical Officials Green Technical Committee has debated the need for contractors to have certifications in installing green plumbing. Some have argued that qualifications would discourage homeowners from improving their properties. Comments from executives are also included.

16242 ■ *"How to Improve Your Mobile Marketing" in Contractor (Vol. 56, October 2009, No. 10, pp. 54)*
Pub: Penton Media, Inc.
Ed: Matt Michel. **Description:** Plumbers can improve their mobile advertising by making their logos as large as possible and positioning their logo on top of the truck so people can see it over traffic. They should also make the phone numbers small because people only take note of these when the truck is parked.

16243 ■ *"IAPMO GTC Debates Supplement" in Contractor (Vol. 56, September 2009, No. 9, pp. 3)*
Pub: Penton Media, Inc.
Ed: Robert P. Mader. **Description:** Green Technical Committee of the International Association of Plumbing and Mechanical Officials is developing a Green Plumbing and Mechanical Supplement. The supplement provides for installation of systems by licensed contractors and installers. Comments from officials are also presented.

16244 ■ *"IAPMO GTC Finalizes Green Supplement" in Contractor (Vol. 57, January 2010, No. 1, pp. 1)*
Pub: Penton Media, Inc.
Description: International Association of Plumbing and Mechanical Officials' Green Technical Committee finalized the Green Plumbing & Mechanical Code Supplement. The supplement was created to provide a set of provisions that encourage sustainable practices and work towards the design and construction of plumbing and mechanical systems.

16245 ■ *"IAPMO GTC Votes to Limit Showers to 2.0-GPM" in Contractor (Vol. 56, September 2009, No. 9, pp. 1)*
Pub: Penton Media, Inc.
Ed: Robert P. Mader. **Description:** Green Technical Committee of the International Association of Plumbing and Mechanical Officials has voted to limit showers to 2.0 GPM. It is also developing a Green Plumbing and Mechanical Supplement. Comments from executives are also supplied.

16246 ■ *"It's New or Improved, But Does It Work?" in Contractor (Vol. 57, January 2010, No. 1, pp. 22)*
Pub: Penton Media, Inc.
Ed: Al Schwartz. **Description:** There is a place for skepticism in the HVAC and plumbing industry as not all new products that are specified may not always perform. The tradesman has the responsibility of integrating new technology into the field.

16247 ■ *"Kohler Building Earns LEED Silver Certification" in Contractor (Vol. 56, September 2009, No. 9, pp. 12)*
Pub: Penton Media, Inc.
Description: United States Green Building Council has awarded Kohler Co. with the Silver Leadership in Energy and Environmental Design Status. The award has highlighted the company's work to transform its building into a more environmentally efficient structure. A description of the facility is also provided.

16248 ■ *"LA Passes HET Ordinance, California Greens Code" in Contractor (Vol. 56, September 2009, No. 9, pp. 1)*
Pub: Penton Media, Inc.
Ed: Candace Ruolo. **Description:** Los Angeles City Council has passed a Water Efficiency Requirements ordinance. The law mandates lower low-flow plumb-

ing requirements for plumbing fixtures installed in new buildings and retrofits. Under the ordinance, a toilet's maximum flush volume may not exceed 1.28-gpf.

16249 ■ *"Lead-Free Products must Meet Requirements" in Contractor (Vol. 56, September 2009, No. 9, pp. 30)*
Pub: Penton Media, Inc.
Ed: Robert Gottermeier. **Description:** United States Environmental Protection Agency's adoption of the Safe Drinking Water Act is aimed at lowering lead extraction levels from plumbing products. Manufacturers have since deleaded brass and bronze potable water products. Meanwhile, California and Vermont have passed a law limiting lead content for potable water conveying plumbing products.

16250 ■ *"Major Advances in Heat Pump Technology" in Contractor (Vol. 57, January 2010, No. 1, pp. 42)*
Pub: Penton Media, Inc.
Ed: Mark Eatherton. **Description:** Tax credits make ground-source heat pump technology more economically feasible. Suggestions on how to choose the right ground-source heat pump technology to install in a house are discussed.

16251 ■ *"Minnesota State Park Building Exemplifies Sustainability" in Contractor (Vol. 56, November 2009, No. 11, pp. 5)*
Pub: Penton Media, Inc.
Ed: Candace Roulo. **Description:** Camden State Park's newly remodeled information/office building in Lynd, Minnesota features a 10 kw wind turbine which is capable of offsetting most of the facility's electricity and a geothermal heat pump system. The heat pump is a 4-ton vertical closed-loop ground source heat pump by ClimateMaster.

16252 ■ *"More Than 1,000 Attend Second WaterSmart" in Contractor (Vol. 56, November 2009, No. 11, pp. 3)*
Pub: Penton Media, Inc.
Description: Over 1,000 plumbing and water conservation professionals attended the second WaterSmart Innovations Conference and Exposition in Las Vegas. Plumbing industry personalities made presentations during the conference and several innovative products were displayed at the trade show.

16253 ■ *"A Necessary Balancing Act: Bookkeeping" in Contractor (Vol. 56, November 2009, No. 11, pp. 22)*
Pub: Penton Media, Inc.
Ed: Al Schwartz. **Description:** Pros and cons of getting a bookkeeper or a certified public accountant for the subcontractor are discussed. A bookkeeper can help a subcontractor get new accounting software up and running while an accountant will more than likely keep after the books at regular intervals throughout the year.

16254 ■ *"Online Training Requires Tools, Accessories" in Contractor (Vol. 56, September 2009, No. 9, pp. 67)*
Pub: Penton Media, Inc.
Ed: Larry Drake. **Description:** Importance of the right equipment and tools to members of the United States plumbing industry undergoing online training is discussed. Portable devices such as Blackberrys and I-phones could be used for online training. The use of headphones makes listening easier for the trainee.

16255 ■ *"Papal Permit Trumps the Plumbing Codes" in Contractor (Vol. 57, February 2010, No. 2, pp. 20)*
Pub: Penton Media, Inc.
Ed: Dave Yates. **Description:** Despite the plumbing code, a plumbing contractor was able to convince the inspector to approve his application to install a sacristy sink which drains into the ground instead of the sewer system. Details of the church's system are presented.

16256 ■ *"PHCC Convention, Show Gets High Marks" in Contractor (Vol. 56, December 2009, No. 12, pp. 1)*
Pub: Penton Media, Inc.
Ed: Robert P. Mader. **Description:** Plumbing-Heating-Cooling Contractors National Association has held its first convention and trade show in New

Orleans, Louisiana. Attendees were treated to a variety of seminars and exhibitors during the event. Comments from event organizers are also given.

16257 ■ *Plumbing Engineer--Product Directory Issue: Engineered Plumbing Systems Directory*
Pub: Trend Publishing
URL(s): www.thewholesaler.com. **Released:** Monthly; 12 times a year. **Price:** $50, Individuals one year. **Covers:** Over 400 plumbing products from approximately 250 manufacturers. **Entries include:** Company name, phone, fax, website, and e-mail; name of engineering contact with the firm. **Database includes:** List of American Society of Plumbing Engineers (ASPE) national officers, industry associations.

16258 ■ *"Plumbing, Heating Products Shine at Greenbuild" in Contractor (Vol. 57, January 2010, No. 1, pp. 3)*
Pub: Penton Media, Inc.
Ed: Robert P. Mader. **Description:** Among the many exhibitors at Greenbuild 2009 was T&S Brass which showcased their low-flow pre-rinse spray valves and Watts Water Technologies which showed off their hot water recirculating system. Aquatherm and Acorn Engineering were also at the show.

16259 ■ *"Plumbing, Heating Products Shine at Greenbuild Expo" in Contractor (Vol. 56, December 2009, No. 12, pp. 1)*
Pub: Penton Media, Inc.
Ed: Robert P. Mader. **Description:** Greenbuild Show held in Phoenix, Arizona has showcased the latest in plumbing and heating products. Zurn displayed its EcoVantage line of fixtures and valves during the event. Meanwhile, Sloan Valve offered its washdown 1-pint/flush Alphine urinal.

16260 ■ *"PMA Launches Online Education Program" in Contractor (Vol. 56, October 2009, No. 10, pp. 8)*
Pub: Penton Media, Inc.
Description: Plumbing & Mechanical Association of Georgia launched an online program that covers technical and business management that will help contractors run their businesses. Future courses will include math for plumbers, graywater systems, and recession-proofing your business.

16261 ■ *"Portland Home Is First in U.S. to Use Variable Speed 'Inverter' Technology" in Contractor (Vol. 56, December 2009, No. 12, pp. 5)*
Pub: Penton Media, Inc.
Description: Daikin Altherma heat pump with inverter drive has been installed in a Portland, Oregon home. The heat pump provides a high coefficient of performance while delivering hydronic and domestic hot water functionality. Other product features and dimensions are also supplied.

16262 ■ *"Pre-Certified LEED Hotel Prototype Reduces Energy Use, Conserves Water" in Contractor (Vol. 57, January 2010, No. 1, pp. 3)*
Pub: Penton Media, Inc.
Ed: Candace Roulo. **Description:** Marriott International Inc.'s LEED pre-certified prototype hotel will reduce a hotel's energy and water consumption by 25 percent and save owners approximately $100,000. Their Courtyard Settler's Ridge in Pittsburgh will be the first hotel built based on the prototype.

16263 ■ *"Proposal Ruffles Builders" in Austin Business JournalInc. (Vol. 29, November 20, 2009, No. 37, pp. 1)*
Pub: American City Business Journals
Ed: Jacob Dirr. **Description:** A proposal that requires heating, ventilation and cooling equipment checking for a new commercial building having an area of at least 10,000 square feet might cost 25 cents to 50 cents per square foot for the owners. This may lead to higher housing costs. Both the Building and Fire Code Board of Appeals and the Mechanical Plumbing and Solar Board have recommended the plan.

16264 ■ *"Public Bathroom Pressure Woes Resolved"* in Contractor (Vol. 56, September 2009, No. 9, pp. 44)
Pub: Penton Media, Inc.
Ed: Dave Yates. **Description:** Design and construction of a public bathroom's plumbing system in the United States are discussed. Installed plumbing fixtures with flush valves would not function properly. The installation of Grundfos SQE variable-speed pumps has resolved problems with the bathroom's water pressure.

16265 ■ *"Put Power in Your Direct Mail Campaigns"* in Contractor (Vol. 56, September 2009, No. 9, pp. 64)
Pub: Penton Media, Inc.
Ed: Matt Michel. **Description:** Advice on how members of the United States plumbing industry should manage direct mail marketing campaigns are offered. Determining the purpose of a campaign is recommended. Focusing on a single message, product or service is also encouraged.

16266 ■ *"Rehab Center Slashes Energy Bills By Going Tankless"* in Contractor (Vol. 56, December 2009, No. 12, pp. 3)
Pub: Penton Media, Inc.
Description: Melburne Health and Rehabilitation Center in Florida has reduced its energy bills by installing a tankless hot water system. Sun Plumbing was selected to install the system. The system was installed on a mechanical room that housed the old tank-type heaters.

16267 ■ *"Route Optimization Impacts the Bottom Line"* in Contractor (Vol. 56, November 2009, No. 11, pp. 48)
Pub: Penton Media, Inc.
Ed: Dave Beaudry. **Description:** Plumbing and HVAC businesses can save a significant amount of money from route optimization. The process begins with gathering information on a fleet and a routing software tool can determine the effectiveness of current route configurations and identify preferable route plans.

16268 ■ *"Selling a Job When There's Buyer's Remorse"* in Contractor (Vol. 56, December 2009, No. 12, pp. 37)
Pub: Penton Media, Inc.
Ed: H. Kent Craig. **Description:** Advice on how contractors should manage low-profit jobs in the United States are presented. Efforts should be made to try and find at least one quality field foreman or superintendent. Contractors should also try to respectfully renegotiate the terms of the job.

16269 ■ *"Software Solutions Increase Productivity"* in Contractor (Vol. 57, February 2010, No. 2, pp. 26)
Pub: Penton Media, Inc.
Ed: William Feldman; Patti Feldman. **Description:** Singletouch is a real-time data capture solution for mechanical and other contractors that work in jobs that require materials and workload tracking. Contractors get information on extreme weather and sudden changes in the cost of materials. The OptimumHVAC optimization software by Optimum Energy is designed to optimize energy savings in commercial buildings.

16270 ■ *"Solar Choices"* in Contractor (Vol. 56, October 2009, No. 10, pp. 32)
Pub: Penton Media, Inc.
Ed: Tom Scheel. **Description:** Price, performance, and ease of installation of a flat plate versus an evacuated tube collector for a plumbing and heating job are compared. The better choice with regards to weight, aesthetics, efficiency in warm or cool climates, year round load, and space heating is discussed.

16271 ■ *"Solar Hot Water Sales Are Hot, Hot, Hot"* in Contractor (Vol. 56, December 2009, No. 12, pp. 22)
Pub: Penton Media, Inc.
Ed: Dave Yates. **Description:** Plumbing contractors in the United States can benefit from the increased sales of solar thermal water systems. Licensed

plumbers have the base knowledge on the risks associated from heating and storing water. Safety issues associated with solar water heaters are also included.

16272 ■ *"Sprinkler Advocates Beat Builders Again"* in Contractor (Vol. 56, November 2009, No. 11, pp. 58)
Pub: Penton Media, Inc.
Ed: Bob Mader. **Description:** Proponents of residential fire sprinklers were able to fend off the attempt by the National Association of Home Builders to do away with mandated fire sprinklers on the International Residential Code by the International Code Council (ICC). The ICC's vote on the issue is good news for fire sprinkler contractors and plumbing contractors.

16273 ■ *"Three Steps to Follow when Job Hunting"* in Contractor (Vol. 56, September 2009, No. 9, pp. 62)
Pub: Penton Media, Inc.
Ed: H. Kent Craig. **Description:** Advice on how project managers in the United States plumbing industry should look for jobs in view of the economic crisis. Job seekers should consider relocating to places where there are an abundance of project management jobs. Resumes should also be revised to make an applicant stand out.

16274 ■ *"Tips to Improve Your Direct Mail Results"* in Contractor (Vol. 57, January 2010, No. 1, pp. 55)
Pub: Penton Media, Inc.
Ed: Matt Michel. **Description:** Plumbers can improve their direct mail efforts by buying quality lists and writing good headlines. The mail should also tell a story and urge its readers to action.

16275 ■ *"Tracking Your Fleet Can Increase Bottom Line"* in Contractor (Vol. 56, November 2009, No. 11, pp. 26)
Pub: Penton Media, Inc.
Ed: Candace Roulo. **Description:** GPS fleet management system can help boost a contractor's profits, employee productivity, and efficiency. These are available as a handheld device or a cell phone that employees carry around or as a piece of hardware installed in a vehicle. These lets managers track assets and communicate with employees about jobs.

16276 ■ *"Trade Craft: Take Pride in Your Trade, Demand Excellence"* in Contractor (Vol. 56, October 2009, No. 10, pp. 24)
Pub: Penton Media, Inc.
Ed: Al Schwartz. **Description:** There is a need for teaching, developing, and encouraging trade craft. An apprentice plumber is not only versed in the mechanical aspects of the trade but he also has a working knowledge of algebra, trigonometry, chemistry, and thermal dynamics. Contractors should be demanding on their personnel regarding their trade craft and should only keep and train the very best people they can hire.

16277 ■ *"Use Social Media to Enhance Brand, Business"* in Contractor (Vol. 56, December 2009, No. 12, pp. 14)
Pub: Penton Media, Inc.
Ed: Elton Rivas. **Description:** Advice on how plumbing contractors should use online social networks to increase sales is presented including such issues as clearly defining goals and target audience. An additional advantage to this medium is that advertisements can easily be shared with other users.

16278 ■ *"Water Conservation Helps GC's Building Attain LEED Gold Status"* in Contractor (Vol. 56, September 2009, No. 9, pp. 5)
Pub: Penton Media, Inc.
Description: Green contractor Marshall Erdman has built a new office building using green design. The facility is seen to become a prime Leadership in Energy and Environmental Design (LEED) building model. Details of the building's design and features are also provided.

16279 ■ *"Water Efficiency Bill Move Through Congress"* in Contractor (Vol. 56, July 2009, No. 7, pp. 20)
Pub: Penton Media, Inc.
Ed: Kevin Schwalb. **Description:** National Association, a plumbing-heating-cooling contractor, was instrumental in drafting the Water Advanced Technologies for Efficient Resource Use Act of 2009 and they are also backing the Water Accountability Tax Efficiency Reinvestment Act. The first bill promotes WaterSense-labeled products while the other promotes water conservation through tax credits.

16280 ■ *"Web-Based Solutions Streamline Operations"* in Contractor (Vol. 56, December 2009, No. 12, pp. 28)
Pub: Penton Media, Inc.
Ed: William Feldman; Patti Feldman. **Description:** Sage Project Lifecycle Management is a Web-based service platform for plumbing and HVAC contractors. It enables effective workflow and document management. Projectmates, on the other hand, is a Web-based enterprise-wide solution for managing both commercial plumbing and HVAC projects.

16281 ■ *The Wholesaler--Directory of Manufacturers Representatives Issue*
Pub: Trend Publishing
URL(s): www.plumbingengineer.comwww.thewholesaler.com. **Released:** Annual; Latest edition 2009. **Price:** $50, Individuals hardcopy or CD-ROM. **Publication includes:** 2,000 manufacturers' representatives handling plumbing, heating, piping, air conditioning, and refrigeration products. **Entries include:** Representative's name or firm name, address, phone, fax, territory, and lines carried. **Arrangement:** Geographical by territory (Central States, North Pacific, etc.).

16282 ■ *The Wholesaler--'The Wholesaling 100' Issue*
Pub: TMB Publishing Inc.
Contact: Mark Bruno, Director
URL(s): www.plumbingengineer.com. **Released:** Annual; July. **Price:** $50, Individuals print or CD-ROM. **Publication includes:** Ranks 100 leading wholesalers of plumbing, heating, air conditioning, refrigeration equipment, and industrial pipe, valves and fittings. **Entries include:** Company name, address, phone, fax, names and titles of key personnel, number of employees, business breakdown (percentage). **Arrangement:** Ranked by sales.

16283 ■ *"WQA Develops Certification Program"* in Contractor (Vol. 57, January 2010, No. 1, pp. 56)
Pub: Penton Media, Inc.
Description: Water Quality Association is now offering a new certification program for companies that may be affected by California's law that prohibits any products intended to convey or dispense water for human consumption that is not lead-free. All pipe or plumbing fixtures must be certified by a third party certification body.

SOURCES OF SUPPLY

16284 ■ *American Supply Association--Membership Directory: Resource Guide*
American Supply Association
Contact: Scott Weaver, President
URL(s): www.asa.net/Membership/MemberDirectory/tabid/65/Default.aspx. **Released:** Annual **Price:** $25, Members; $299, Nonmembers; $1125, Individuals electronic; $225, Nonmembers diskette; $145, Members print and diskette; $265, Nonmembers print and diskette. **Covers:** 4,000 member wholesalers handling plumbing, heating, and cooling materials and supplies. **Entries include:** Company name, address, phone, names of executives, list of products or services, fax numbers, email and website. **Arrangement:** Geographical and alphabetical. **Indexes:** Special interest divisions.

STATISTICAL SOURCES

16285 ■ *RMA Annual Statement Studies*
Pub: Risk Management Association
Contact: Kevin M. Blakey, President
Released: Annual. **Price:** $175.00 2006-07 edition, $105.00. **Description:** Contains composite balance

sheets and income statements for more than 360 industries, including the accounting, auditing, and bookkeeping industries. Also contains five years of comparative historical data for discerning trends. Includes 16 commonly used ratios, computed for most of the size groupings for nearly every industry.

TRADE PERIODICALS

16286 ■ *Heating-Plumbing-Air Conditioning Magazine (HPAC)*
Pub: Business Information Group
Contact: Bruce Creighton, President
URL(s): www.hpacmag.com. **Ed:** Kerry Turner. **Released:** 7/yr.

16287 ■ *Indiana Contractor: Air Conditioning, Heating, Plumbing, Refrigeration, Sheet Metal*
Pub: Indiana Association of Plumbing, Heating, Cooling Contractors
URL(s): www.iaphcc.com/Membership/IndianaContractorMagazine/tabid/75/Default. **Released:** Quarterly

16288 ■ *MCAA Reporter*
Pub: Mechanical Contractors Association of America Inc.
Contact: Stephanie Mills, Managing Editor
Ed: Adrienne Breedlove, Editor. **Released:** Monthly, except in February and August. **Price:** Included in membership; $50, nonmembers. **Description:** Covers labor issues and government affairs as they affect mechanical contractors in the plumbing, pipefitting, air conditioning, refrigeration, fire protection, and high-purity piping industries. Recurring features include reports on the activities of the Association and notices of pertinent seminars and meetings.

16289 ■ *Plumbing Engineer*
Pub: TMB Publishing Inc.
Contact: Mark Bruno, Director
URL(s): www.plumbingengineer.com/. **Released:** Monthly

TRADE SHOWS AND CONVENTIONS

16290 ■ CMX - CIPHEX National Tradeshow and Learning Forum
Canadian Institute of Plumbing & Heating
295 The W. Mall, Ste. 330
Toronto, ON, Canada M9C 4Z4
Ph: (416)695-0447
Free: 800-639-0450
Fax: (416)695-0450
Co. E-mail: info@ciph.com
URL: http://www.ciph.com
URL(s): www.cmxciphexshow.com. **Price:** $7, Preregistered; $14, Onsite. **Frequency:** Biennial. **Audience:** Contractors, wholesalers, consulting engineers, building managers, and chemical specifiers. **Principal Exhibits:** Heating, air-conditioning, refrigeration, ventilation, and mechanical plumbing equipment. **Dates and Locations:** , Metro Toronto Convention Centre. **Telecommunication Services:** cmxciphex@salshow.com.

16291 ■ North Carolina Association of Plumbing, Heating, and Cooling Contractors Annual Trade Show
North Carolina Association of Plumbing, Heating, and Cooling Contractors
5540 McNeely Dr., Ste. 202
Raleigh, NC 27612
Ph: (919)532-0522
Fax: (919)532-0523
URL: http://www.ncaphcc.org
Contact: Jim Pendergrass, Executive Director
E-mail: jim@phccnc.org
URL(s): www.phccnc.org. **Price:** $30, Members; $50, Non-members. **Frequency:** Annual. **Audience:** Plumbing, heating, and cooling contractors; architects; engineers; and general public. **Principal Exhibits:** Plumbing, heating, and cooling equipment, supplies, and services.

CONSULTANTS

16292 ■ GHT Ltd.
1010 N Glebe Rd., Ste. 200
Arlington, VA 22201-4749
Ph: (703)243-1200
Fax: (703)276-1376
Co. E-mail: ght@ghtltd.com
URL: http://www.ghtltd.com
Contact: Robert M. Menuet, Principal
E-mail: rmenuet@ghtltd.com
Scope: Provider of design services in mechanical engineering. Offers telecommunications and security engineering services. Provides life safety engineering services and utilities planning services. Provides estimates of life expectancy and replacement or upgrade costs for mechanical and electrical equipment and systems. **Founded:** 1965. **Publications:** "Critical spaces keep the pace of business humming," May, 2004; "To avoid staticlater, hire right telecom consultant," Oct, 2007. **Special Services:** LEED®.

16293 ■ Greacen Consulting Engineers Inc.
919 Old Hwy. 8 NW, Ste. 200
Saint Paul, MN 55112
Ph: (651)633-1318
Fax: (651)633-1885
Contact: Ed Greacen, Principal
Scope: Specializes in plumbing, heating, ventilating, air conditioning and project management. Designs domestic water and water treatment systems, fire protection, fuel and gas piping, humidification and de-humidification systems, variable air volume (VAV), fan-powered VAV, and retrofit systems for Indoor Air Quality (IAQ). **Founded:** 1999.

16294 ■ Lundquist, Killeen, Potvin and Bender Inc.—LKPB Engineers Inc.
1935 W County Road B2, Ste. 300
Saint Paul, MN 55113-2722
Ph: (651)633-1223
Fax: (651)633-1355
Co. E-mail: nbart@lkpb.com
URL: http://www.lkpb.com
Contact: Allen V. Theisen, Manager
Scope: Provider of services in heating, ventilation, plumbing, piping, refrigeration, air conditioning, fire protection, lighting design and fixture selection, communications, electrical power distribution, security, life safety system design, energy conservation analysis, design and implementation. **Founded:** 1969.

16295 ■ Stueven Engineering Consultants
140 W 3rd Ave.
Escondido, CA 92025
Ph: (760)735-8577
Fax: (760)735-8578
Co. E-mail: sb@stueven-engineering.com
URL: http://www.stueven-engineering.com
Contact: Harold J. Stueven, President
E-mail: hjs@stueven-engineering.com
Scope: Provider of services in professional engineering, planning, design, and construction support services for mechanical and plumbing systems. **Founded:** 1994.

FRANCHISES AND BUSINESS OPPORTUNITIES

16296 ■ Ace DuraFlo Systems LLC
1370 Reynolds Ave., Ste. 112
Irvine, CA 92614
Free: 888-775-0220
Fax: (949)263-8771
Description: Pipe restoration services. **No. of Franchise Units:** 33. **No. of Company-Owned Units:** 5. **Founded:** 1997.. **Franchised:** 2001. **Equity Capital Needed:** $36,190-$410,100. **Franchise Fee:** $21,900-$34,900. **Royalty Fee:** 6-8%. **Financial Assistance:** Limited third party financing available. **Training:** Provides 1 week at headquarters, 2 weeks at franchisee's location with ongoing support.

16297 ■ American Leak Detection
888 Research Dr., Ste. 100
Palm Springs, CA 92262

Ph: (760)320-9991
Free: 800-755-6697
Fax: (760)320-1288
Description: Detection of water or sewer leaks under concrete slabs of homes, pools, spas, fountains, commercial buildings, etc., with electronic equipment manufactured by the company. **No. of Franchise Units:** 316. **No. of Company-Owned Units:** 15. **Founded:** 1974.. **Franchised:** 1984. **Equity Capital Needed:** $76,755-$259,550. **Franchise Fee:** $29,500-$120,000. **Royalty Fee:** 6-10%. **Training:** Provides 6-12 weeks at headquarters, 1 week at franchisee's location with ongoing support.

16298 ■ Canadian Pool Players Association
1000 Lake Saint Louis Blvd., Ste. 325
Lake Saint Louis, MO 63367
Ph: (636)625-8611
Fax: (636)625-2975
URL: http://www.poolplayers.ca
Description: Oversees and provides ongoing support to recreational pool league operators. **No. of Franchise Units:** 17. **Founded:** 1989.. **Franchised:** 1989. **Franchise Fee:** $5,000. **Training:** Provides 7 days training.

16299 ■ Handyman Connection
Mamar, Inc.
10250 Alliance Rd., Ste.100
Cincinnati, OH 45242
Ph: (513)771-3003
Free: 800-466-5530
Fax: (513)771-6439
Co. E-mail: soaks@handymanconnection.com
URL: http://www.handymanconnection.com
Description: Small to medium home repairs and remodeling. **No. of Franchise Units:** 160. **No. of Company-Owned Units:** 1. **Founded:** 1990.. **Franchised:** 1993. **Equity Capital Needed:** $90,000-$125,000. **Franchise Fee:** $25,000-$40,000. **Training:** 2 weeks at corporate training center and 1 week grand opening onsite.

16300 ■ Mr. Rooter Plumbing
1010 N University Parks Dr.
Waco, TX 76707
Ph: (800)298-6855
Free: 800-298-6855
Fax: (254)759-5863
Co. E-mail: sam.thurman@mrrooter.com
URL: http://www.mrrooterfranchise.ca
Description: Complete residential and commercial plumbing service company. **No. of Franchise Units:** 16. **Founded:** 1970.. **Franchised:** 1974. **Equity Capital Needed:** $27,000 investment required; $50,000 start-up capital required. **Franchise Fee:** $27,000, per 100,000 population. **Training:** Initial, onsite, intranet and ongoing support.

16301 ■ Potty Doctor Plumbing Service
Potty Doctor Franchise Systems Inc.
424 No. Dixie Hwy.
Lake Worth, FL 33460
Ph: (561)582-0334
Free: 888-377-6889
Co. E-mail: sales@pottydoctor.com
Description: Residential plumbing services. **No. of Franchise Units:** 3. **Founded:** 1943.. **Franchised:** 1997. **Equity Capital Needed:** $5,000-$37,000, depends on existing business conversion or new start-up. **Franchise Fee:** $15,000. **Training:** Yes.

LIBRARIES

16302 ■ Intertek Testing Services - Warnock Hersey Library
1500 Brigantine Dr.
Coquitlam, BC, Canada V3K 7C1
Ph: (604)520-3321
Fax: (604)524-9186
Co. E-mail: lawrence.gibson@intertek.com
URL: http://www.intertek.com/
Scope: Building codes, electrical codes, plumbing codes, standards. **Services:** Library open to potential clients at librarian's discretion. **Holdings:** Standards; codes; handbooks; manuals; directories. **Subscriptions:** 20 journals and other serials.

16303 ■ New England Wholesalers Association - Lending Library
111 Centre St., Ste. A
Middleboro, MA 02346-2273
Ph: (508)533-3335
Fax: (508)533-3337
Co. E-mail: newa@newa.org
Contact: Alayne Bradley

Scope: Plumbing, heating, air conditioning, industrial pipe, wholesale distribution. **Services:** Library open to the public with restrictions (deposit required). **Founded:** 1932. **Holdings:** 300 surveys and reports, training manuals, management and sales texts. **Subscriptions:** 5 journals and other serials.

ASSOCIATIONS AND OTHER ORGANIZATIONS

16304 ■ Porcelain Enamel Institute (PEI)
PO Box 920220
Norcross, GA 30010
Ph: (770)676-9366
Fax: (770)409-7280
URL: http://www.porcelainenamel.com
Contact: Mike Horton, Chairman
Description: Trade association of the porcelain enamel industry. Manufacturers of major appliances, sanitary ware, architectural porcelain enamel, signs, and other porcelain enamel products; suppliers to the industry such as producers of steel, aluminum, and porcelain enamel frit; chemical companies. Conducts market development and promotion programs, develops test methods for evaluation of porcelain enamel properties, and maintains weather resistance testing sites jointly with the National Bureau of Standards. Serves as information clearinghouse. **Scope:** porcelain enameling and coatings. **Founded:** 1930. **Subscriptions:** 100 books. **Publications:** *First Firing* (Bimonthly); *Technical Forum* (Annual). **Educational Activities:** Porcelain Enamel Institute Meeting (Annual); Technical Forum (Annual). **Awards:** Long-Oliver Distinguished Service Award (Annual).

FRANCHISES AND BUSINESS OPPORTUNITIES

16305 ■ BMR Bathmaster Reglazing Ltd.
1600 Industrial Rd., Unit B7
Cambridge, ON, Canada N3H 4W5
Ph: (519)653-8823
Free: 877-767-2336
Fax: (888)789-0947
Co. E-mail: info@bathmaster.com
URL: http://www.bathmaster.com
Description: BathMaster offers top quality, cost-effective bathtub re-glazing, bathtub liners & wall installation services This in-home service, saving customers up to 75% of replacement cost. BathMaster excels in completing project sin a single day,

transforming customer's bathroom into an environment they will be proud of. BathMaster's innovative products and system support gives our franchisees the markets advantage necessary for success and growth. **No. of Franchise Units:** 16. **No. of Company-Owned Units:** 2. **Founded:** 1989. **Franchised:** 1994. **Equity Capital Needed:** $45,000-$80,000. **Franchise Fee:** $25,000. **Training:** 10 day training and full support.

16306 ■ Kott Koatings, Inc.
27161 Burbank St.
Foothill Ranch, CA 92610
Free: 800-452-6161
Fax: (714)770-5101
Description: A porcelain, fiberglass, and bathtub reglazing business opportunity. **No. of Franchise Units:** 400. **No. of Company-Owned Units:** 1. **Founded:** 1953.. **Equity Capital Needed:** $2,200. **Franchise Fee:** $16,900-$20,995. **Financial Assistance:** Yes. **Training:** Yes.

16307 ■ Perma-Glaze, Inc. Multi-Surface Restoration
1638 S Research Loop Rd., Ste. 160
Tucson, AZ 85710
Ph: (800)332-7397
Fax: (520)296-4393
Co. E-mail: permaglaze@permaglaze.com
URL: http://www.permaglaze.com
Description: Restoration and refinishing of bathroom and kitchen fixtures, such as bathtubs, sinks and ceramic tiles. Materials to be refinished include porcelain, fiberglass, acrylic, cultured marble, Formica, kitchen appliances, shower enclosures and most building materials. Services include chip repair, fiberglass and acrylic repairs, restoration and reglazing of fixtures. franchisees return from Tucson. **No. of Franchise Units:** 100. **No. of Company-Owned Units:** 2. **Founded:** 1978.. **Franchised:** 1981. **Equity Capital Needed:** Approximately $2,500. **Franchise Fee:** 29,500. **Financial Assistance:** Yes. **Training:** Training includes 5-10 day technical, hands-on training and all tools and equipment.

16308 ■ PremierGarage
PremierGarage Systems, Inc.
21405 N 15th Ln., Ste. 100
Phoenix, AZ 85027

Ph: (480)483-3030
Free: 866-483-GARA
Fax: (480)483-7895
Co. E-mail: dealer@PremierGarage.com
URL: http://www.PremierGarage.com
Description: Offers premium quality Garage Floor Coatings, Cabinetry and Organizers for residential applications. **No. of Franchise Units:** 74. **No. of Company-Owned Units:** 1. **Founded:** 1999.. **Franchised:** 2002. **Equity Capital Needed:** $76,200-$429,500. **Franchise Fee:** $7,500-150,000. **Training:** Yes.

16309 ■ Re-Bath, LLC
421 W Alameda Dr.
Tempe, AZ 85282
Ph: (480)844-1575
Fax: (480)833-7199
Description: Custom-manufactured, high-impact acrylic bathtub liners, wall systems and shower liners designed to go over existing bathtubs, ceramic tile walls and shower bases. **No. of Franchise Units:** 225. **Founded:** 1979.. **Franchised:** 1991. **Equity Capital Needed:** $3,500-$89,000. **Franchise Fee:** $6,000-$40,000. **Financial Assistance:** Yes. **Training:** Phases of installation, operations, sales and marketing. Both classroom and hands-on training.

16310 ■ Surface Specialists
Surface Specialists Systems, Inc.
621-B Stallings Rd.
Matthews, NC 28104
Ph: (704)821-3380
Free: 866-239-8707
Fax: (704)821-2097
Co. E-mail: amy@surfacespecialists.com
URL: http://www.surfacespecialists.com
Description: Offers services like repair and refinish of acrylic spas, porcelain tubs and sinks. **No. of Franchise Units:** 43. **Founded:** 1980.. **Franchised:** 1981. **Equity Capital Needed:** $25,000-$40,000. **Franchise Fee:** $21,000. **Financial Assistance:** Yes. **Training:** Provides 15 days hands-on training, annual convention, and 24/7 direct access to company president.

REFERENCE WORKS

16311 ■ *"Butane Heated Pressure Washer Offers Diverse Cleaning Options" in Product News Network (March 8, 2011)*
Pub: Product News Network

Description: Profile of the Super Max (TM) 6000B power sprayer the can clean with cold or heated water and wet steam. Daimer Industries, provider of janitorial supplies, announced the availability of the machine that offers a variety of cleaning options for a range of applications.

FRANCHISES AND BUSINESS OPPORTUNITIES

16312 ■ **Sparkle Wash**
Sparkle International, Inc.
7599 First Pl.
Bedford, OH 44146
Ph: (800)321-0770

Fax: (216)464-8869
Description: Offers mobile pressure cleaning and restoration service. **No. of Franchise Units:** 172. **No. of Company-Owned Units:** 1. **Founded:** 1965.. **Franchised:** 1967. **Equity Capital Needed:** Approximately $50,000. **Franchise Fee:** Minimum $25,000. **Financial Assistance:** 30-V, FRA handbook. **Training:** 5 day initial program at headquarters, includes classroom, shop, and in-field training on the franchisees own equipment. An optional 6th day of in-field experience is available at no added charge. Sparkle Wash sends a qualified trainer to work with the franchisee for 3 Days at his location.

16313 ■ **Window Gang**
Window Gang Ventures Corp.
405 Arendell St.
Morehead City, NC 28557
Ph: (252)726-1463
Free: 800-849-2308
Fax: (252)726-2837
Co. E-mail: tim@windowgang.com
URL: http://www.windowgang.com
Description: Residential window washing, gutter cleaning, and power washing. **No. of Franchise**

Units: 210. **Founded:** 1986.. **Franchised:** 1996. **Equity Capital Needed:** $50,000. **Franchise Fee:** $25,000. **Training:** Up to 14 days of training in both the corporate location and in your territory that includes successful technical, sales, marketing, and business procedures. Provides non-stop customer leads.

16314 ■ **Window Genie**
FOR Franchising, LLC
800 E Ross Ave.
Cincinnati, OH 45207
Free: 800-700-0022
URL: http://www.windowgenie.com

Description: Window cleaning service. **No. of Franchise Units:** 146. **Founded:** 1994.. **Franchised:** 1998. **Equity Capital Needed:** $60,700-$128,600. **Franchise Fee:** $19,500-$57,000. **Royalty Fee:** 7%. **Financial Assistance:** Limited third party financing available. **Training:** Offers 5 days at headquarters, 5 days at franchisees location with ongoing support.

TRADE PERIODICALS

16315 ■ *Communications Daily*
Pub: Warren Communications News Inc.
Contact: Daniel Warren, President
E-mail: dwarren@warren-news.com

Released: Daily, 5/wk. **Price:** $3,695. **Description:** Covers telephone and data communications, broadcasting, cable TV, teleconferencing, satellite communications, electronic publishing, and emerging technologies. Recurring features include personnel updates, obituaries, statistics, trade show news, and news of research.

16316 ■ *State Telephone Regulation Report*
Pub: Warren Communications News Inc.
Contact: Daniel Warren, President
E-mail: dwarren@warren-news.com

Released: Biweekly. **Price:** $745 Print; $725 Electronic. **Description:** Examines state telephone regulatory issues and decisions. Covers major state-level telephone lawsuits and court action, providing complete citations of lawsuits and decisions. Reports on new tariffed services and the restructuring of existing rates or services, including hybrid local rates that combine flat rates with measured services, discount programs for intrastate toll calls, lifeline services, and custom calling features.

TRADE SHOWS AND CONVENTIONS

16317 ■ **National Telecommunications Cooperative Association Annual Meeting & Expo**
National Telecommunications Cooperative Association
4121 Wilson Blvd., Ste. 1000
Arlington, VA 22203
Ph: (703)351-2000
Fax: (703)351-2001
URL: http://www.ntca.org
Contact: Shirley A. Bloomfield, Chief Executive Officer
E-mail: sbloomfield@ntca.org
URL(s): www.ntca.org. **Price:** $295, Pre-registered, members; $320, Onsite registered, members; $450, Pre-registered, non-members; $475, Onsite registered, non-members. **Frequency:** Annual. **Audience:** Managers, Board of Directors & Employees of Telephone Companies. **Principal Exhibits:** Equipment, supplies, and services for the telecommunications industry.

RESEARCH CENTERS

16318 ■ **National Regulatory Research Institute (NRRI)**
8730 Georgia Ave., No. 201
Silver Spring, MD 20910
Ph: (301)588-5385
Co. E-mail: shempling@nrri.org
URL: http://www.nrri.org
Contact: Scott Hempling, Executive Director
Services: International regulatory assistance. **Founded:** 1976. **Publications:** *Director's Monthly*

Essays on Regulatory Quality. **Educational Activities:** NRRI Conferences and workshops, for state regulatory commissions and their staff members; Fundamentals of Electricity Law Seminar (Annual). **Telecommunication Services:** nrri.admin@nrri.org.

16319 ■ **Telecommunications Research and Action Center (TRAC)**
PO Box 27279
Washington, DC 20005
Ph: (202)263-2950
Fax: (202)263-2962
Co. E-mail: trac@trac.org
URL: http://www.trac.org
Contact: Rev. Robert Chase, Director

Description: Offers computerized long distance telephone analysis for cost comparison for long distance companies. **Founded:** 1983. **Publications:** *Tele-Tip*; *Long Distance Residential and Business Rates* (Biennial). **Telecommunication Services:** johnb@trac.org.

16320 ■ **University of Nebraska—Omaha - Center for Management of Information Technology (CMIT)**
College of Information Science & Technology
Peter Kiewit Institute
Omaha, NE 68182-0459
Ph: (402)554-3182
Fax: (402)554-3400
Co. E-mail: izigurs@mail.unomaha.edu
URL: http://cmit.unomaha.edu
Founded: 1989.

ASSOCIATIONS AND OTHER ORGANIZATIONS

16321 ■ Print Council of America (PCA)
The Art Institute of Chicago
Dept. of Drawings and Prints
111 S Michigan Ave.
Chicago, IL 60603
Ph: (312)857-7162
Co. E-mail: mtedeschi@artic.edu
URL: http://www.printcouncil.org
Contact: Dr. Martha Tedeschi, President
Description: Museum professionals. Fosters the study and appreciation of new and old prints, drawings, and photographs; stimulates discussion. Sponsors educational programs and research publications; offers placement services. **Founded:** 1956. **Publications:** *Guidelines for The Lending of Works of Art on Paper.*

16322 ■ Professional Picture Framers Association (PPFA)
3000 Picture Pl.
Jackson, MI 49201
Ph: (517)788-8100
Free: 800-762-9287
Fax: (517)788-8371
Co. E-mail: ppfa@ppfa.com
URL: http://www.ppfa.com
Contact: Fran Gray, President
E-mail: roneyframe@aol.com
Description: Individuals, firms, or corporations engaged in the picture framing and fine art businesses (art dealers, manufacturers, wholesalers, importers, and publishers). Provides guidance and service in developing quality craftsmanship in the art of picture framing. Sponsors certification program and national consumer marketing program. Provides education and trade show programming. Offers business and insurance services and products. Researches and disseminates information concerning technical and service problems. Maintains hall of fame and bookstore; compiles statistics. **Founded:** 1971. **Publications:** *Who's Who in Picture Framing & Fine Art* (Annual). **Awards:** Innovation Award (Annual); Leadership Award (Annual); Service Award (Annual); International Print Framing Competition.

REFERENCE WORKS

16323 ■ *"P/Kaufmann Sells Bennettsville" in Home Textiles Today (Vol. 31, May 24, 2011, No. 13, pp. 6)*
Pub: Reed Business Information
Contact: Jeff Greisch, President
Description: Decorative Screen Printers purchased the printing and finishing facility of P/Kaufmann in Bennettsville, South Carolina. However, the firm will continue its focus on its core business, a vat printing facility for home furnishings fabrics.

16324 ■ *Printworld Directory of Contemporary Prints and Prices*
Pub: Printworld International Inc.
Contact: Selma Smith, Owner
URL(s): www.printworlddirectory.com. **Released:** Irregular; Latest edition 14th; 2013. **Price:** $359,

Individuals regular price; $259, Individuals discount price. **Publication includes:** Biographical data on 5,000 international artists in contemporary printmaking; thousands of galleries who handle prints and hundreds of print publishers, and 600,000 print/price listings. **Entries include:** For artists--Name, address, personal and educational data, major exhibits, collections, publishers, printers, galleries, awards, teaching positions and documentation of prints. For galleries and publishers--Name, address. **Database includes:** Documentation on approximately 600,000 prints which have appeared in limited editions of no more than 500 and have a retail value of $100-1,000,000, and approximately 500 photos of recent & vintage prints. **Arrangement:** Alphabetical. **Indexes:** Artist name, printer/print workshop, publisher, gallery, art appraiser.

16325 ■ *"Retail News: Children's Boutique Relocates to Conway" in Sun News (June 4, 2010)*
Pub: The Sun News
Description: Little Angel's Children's Boutique and Big Oak Frame Shop have moved to downtown locations in Conway, South Carolina. Little Angel's will sell children's clothing and accessories, shoes and gifts, while the frame shop will offer custom framing along with the sale of stationary, invitations and local prints.

TRADE PERIODICALS

16326 ■ *Picture Framing Magazine: Online*
Pub: Hobby Publications Inc.
URL(s): www.pictureframingmagazine.com. **Released:** 13/yr. **Price:** $20, Individuals; $30, Two years; $40, Canada and Mexico; $70, Canada and Mexico 2 years; $60, Other countries; $110, Other countries 2 years.

FRANCHISES AND BUSINESS OPPORTUNITIES

16327 ■ Big Picture Framing
Big Picture Franchising, LLC
60 Needham St.
Newton, MA 02461
Free: 800-315-0024
Fax: (617)552-5032
URL: http://www.bigpictureframing.com
Description: Picture framing store that is reshaping the custom picture framing industry through great design, low prices, fast turnaround and unparalleled customer guarantees. Our proprietary "Framing While-You-Wait" process meets the needs of today's busy lifestyles. Our superior training, deep commitment to ongoing support and our complete turn-key package will ensure your success. **No. of Franchise Units:** 4. **No. of Company-Owned Units:** 10. **Founded:** 2000. **Franchised:** 2003. **Equity Capital Needed:** $121,000-$151,000. **Franchise Fee:** $25,000. **Training:** Offers a comprehensive 2 1/2 week training program that provides you with everything you need to know to operate a store, including

store operations, framing, sales and design, marketing and advertising, purchasing, hiring and business management.

16328 ■ Deck the Walls
Franchise Concepts, Inc.
101 S Hanley Rd., No. 1280
St. Louis, MO 63105
Free: 800-543-3325
Co. E-mail: franinfo@FClbiz.com
URL: http://www.deckthewalls.com
Description: Art and custom framing retail stores located in regional malls. **No. of Franchise Units:** 49. **Founded:** 1979.. **Franchised:** 1981. **Equity Capital Needed:** $250,000. **Franchise Fee:** $30,000. **Training:** Classroom and in-store training prepare franchisees for all aspects of business, including custom framing. Support includes: site, lease, construction aid; national buying power; vendor network and national marketing.

16329 ■ Fastframe USA
1200 Lawrence Dr., Ste. 300
Newbury Park, CA 91320
Ph: (800)333-3225
Fax: (805)498-8983
URL: http://www.fastframe.com
Description: Custom picture framing franchise. Provide high quality custom framing and art sales in both the retail and commercial markets. Offers a turn-key package from site selection to final store build out. **No. of Franchise Units:** 215. **No. of Company-Owned Units:** 9. **Founded:** 1986.. **Franchised:** 1987. **Equity Capital Needed:** $93,500-$131,000. **Franchise Fee:** $25,000. **Financial Assistance:** Yes. **Training:** Provides 2 weeks of training at the corporate training center. Topics include in store operations, marketing and advertising, framing, business management, and the FAST system. Ongoing field support and 1 week on site training.

16330 ■ Framing & Art Centre
3524 Mainway
Burlington, ON, Canada L7M 1A8
Ph: (905)332-6116
Free: 800-563-7263
Fax: (800)565-5755
Co. E-mail: dgateman@bellnet.ca
URL: http://www.framingartcentre.com
Description: The franchise provides a business for people who are creative at work and good at art and decoration. **No. of Franchise Units:** 36. **Founded:** 1974.. **Franchised:** 1977. **Equity Capital Needed:** $118,000-$179,400. **Franchise Fee:** $30,000. **Training:** Yes.

16331 ■ The Great Frame Up, Inc.
Franchise Concepts, Inc.
221 First Executive Ave.
St. Peters, MO 63376
Ph: (800)543-3325
Free: 886-719-8200

Fax: (877)832-6694
Co. E-mail: anance@fcibiz.com
URL: http://www.greatframeup.com
Description: Do-it-yourself and custom framing retail stores. **No. of Franchise Units:** 114. **Founded:** 1971.. **Franchised:** 1975. **Equity Capital Needed:** $200,000. **Franchise Fee:** $30,000. **Financial Assistance:** Yes. **Training:** 2 weeks classroom and in-

store training including custom framing, covering all aspects of framing, as well as hands-on training in an actual store situation. Workshops and a toll-free number to the training center are provided for ongoing education.

16332 ■ Marad Fine Art International
66 Glenbrook Rd., Ste. 3327
Stamford, CT 06902

Ph: (203)912-8402

Description: Artwork supplies business. **No. of Franchise Units:** 3. **No. of Company-Owned Units:** 1. **Founded:** 1938.. **Franchised:** 2000. **Equity Capital Needed:** $49,000-$70,000. **Franchise Fee:** $39,000. **Training:** Yes.

START-UP INFORMATION

16333 ■ "Revel in Riches!" in Small Business Opportunities (May 2008)
Pub: Harris Publications Inc.
Description: Profile of Proforma, a business-to-business franchise firm providing print and promotional products.

16334 ■ "Visual Appeal" in Small Business Opportunities (Fall 2007)
Pub: Harris Publications Inc.
Ed: Michael L. Corne. **Description:** Profile of Jim Huffman, who launched his new Video Business Card Distributorship. The business cards allow companies and individuals to put personal video messages on their cards explaining the benefits of doing business with them. The cards take prospective customers to Websites and even provide a printable document for brochures or special offers.

ASSOCIATIONS AND OTHER ORGANIZATIONS

16335 ■ Amalgamated Printers' Association (APA)
c/o Phillip Driscoll, Sec.
135 E Church St.
Clinton, MI 49236
Co. E-mail: phil@phillipdriscoll.com
URL: http://www.apa-letterpress.com
Contact: Jim Daggs, President
Description: Active printers interested in furthering of the art and craft of printing. Encourages excellence of printing content, design and techniques among members. Sponsors competitions. **Scope:** personal correspondence, printing, bibliographies of printers, typefounders, type designers, graphic arts personalities. **Founded:** 1958. **Subscriptions:** 600 archival material. **Publications:** *Membership List* (Annual).

16336 ■ American Institute of Graphic Arts (AIGA)
164 5th Ave.
New York, NY 10010-5901
Ph: (212)807-1990
Fax: (212)807-1799
Co. E-mail: grefe@aiga.org
URL: http://www.aiga.org
Contact: Doug Powell, President
Description: Graphic designers, art directors, illustrators and packaging designers. Sponsors exhibits and projects in the public interest. Sponsors traveling exhibitions. Operates gallery. Maintains library of design books and periodicals; offers slide archives. **Founded:** 1914. **Publications:** *365: AIGA Year in Design 24* (Annual). **Educational Activities:** AIGA Design Conference (Biennial). **Awards:** Gold Medal (Annual); Corporate Leadership Award; AIGA Medal; 50 Books/50 Covers Competition.

16337 ■ Digital Printing and Imaging Association (DPI)
c/o Specialty Graphic Imaging Association
10015 Main St.
Fairfax, VA 22031-3489
Ph: (703)385-1335
Free: 888-385-3588
Fax: (703)273-0456
Co. E-mail: sgia@sgia.org
URL: http://www.sgia.org
Contact: Michael E. Robertson, President
Description: Electronic printing, pre-press companies, commercial printers, service bureaus, photo labs, reprographic companies, and printer suppliers, and educational institutions. Works to advance the electronic imaging field by promoting the use of digital printing devices, responding to industry needs and concerns, and improving the industry's ability to serve its market and customers. Conducts educational programs. **Founded:** 1992. **Publications:** *RIP* (Quarterly). **Awards:** Andre Schellenberg Award (Annual); Product of the Year (Annual); Vision Award (Annual).

16338 ■ Flexographic Technical Association (FTA)
3920 Veterans Memorial Hwy., Ste. 9
Bohemia, NY 11716
Ph: (631)737-6020
Fax: (631)737-6813
Co. E-mail: memberinfo@flexography.org
URL: http://www.flexography.org
Contact: Mark Cisternino, President
E-mail: markc@flexography.org
URL(s): www.ftastore.com. **Description:** Firms engaged in printing by flexographic process suppliers to the industry; end users. Seeks to advance the art and science of flexographic printing and assist and recommend developments in flexography. Conducts educational activities including seminars and regional workshops for production, supervisory, and management personnel, and annual technical forum. Markets textbooks and audiovisual material for in-plant training. Sponsors the Foundation of Flexographic Technical Association. Maintains hall of fame, speakers' bureau, advisory service, and 13 committees. **Founded:** 1958. **Publications:** *FLEXO* (Monthly); *SourceBook* (Annual). **Educational Activities:** Flexographic Technical Association Meeting (Annual); Flexographic Technical Association Forum (Annual). **Awards:** Authors' Award (Annual); Environmental Excellence Award (Annual); Excellence in Flexography (Annual); Flexography Scholarships (Annual); FIRST Operator Certification Scholarships; Graphic Design Award (Annual); Hall of Fame (Annual); Presidents' Award (Annual); Technical Innovation Award (Annual).

16339 ■ Graphic Arts Employers of America (GAE)
c/o Printing Industries of America/Graphic Arts Technical Foundation
200 Deer Run Rd.
Sewickley, PA 15143
Ph: (412)741-6860

Free: 800-910-4283
Fax: (412)741-2311
Co. E-mail: jkyger@piagatf.org
URL: http://www.gain.net
Contact: Jim Kyger, Director, Human Resources
Description: Serves as a division of Printing Industries of America. Represents graphic communications, imaging, and printing companies who have at least some unionization or are interested in keeping informed on industrial relations issues. Assists management in functioning at optimal efficiency in a unionized environment. Compiles statistics and assists companies that deal with the major printing unions in the U.S. and Canada. Compiles statistics. **Founded:** 1891. **Educational Activities:** Graphic Arts Employers of America Seminar (Periodic).

16340 ■ IDEAlliance - International Digital Enterprise Alliance
1421 Prince St., Ste. 230
Alexandria, VA 22314-2805
Ph: (703)837-1070
Fax: (703)837-1072
Co. E-mail: dsteinhardt@idealliance.org
URL: http://www.idealliance.org
Contact: Chip Harding, Chairman
Description: Works to advance user-driven, cross-industry solutions for all publishing and content-related processes by developing standards fostering business alliances and identifying best practices. **Founded:** 1966.

16341 ■ International Association of Printing House Craftsmen (IAPHC)
PO Box 2549
Maple Grove, MN 55311-7549
Ph: (763)560-1620
Free: 800-466-4274
Fax: (763)560-1350
Co. E-mail: headquarters@iaphc.org
URL: http://www.iaphc.org
Contact: Kevin P. Keane, President
Description: Individuals world-wide employed or interested in any facet of the graphic arts. Conducts field trips; maintains speakers' bureau; sponsors educational programs. Sponsors International Printing Week and International Gallery of Superb Printing. **Founded:** 1919. **Publications:** *TMN: Graphics Industry News* (Monthly). **Awards:** Craftsman of the Year (Annual); Gallery of Superb Printing Awards (Annual).

16342 ■ International Publishing Management Association (IPMA)
105 S Jefferson, Ste. B-4
Kearney, MO 64060
Ph: (816)902-4762
Fax: (816)902-4766
Co. E-mail: ipmainfo@ipma.org
URL: http://www.ipma.org
Contact: Rob Lingard, President
Description: Managers of in-house corporate publishing or distribution activities. Offers continuing education courses and certification programs. Conducts research, surveys, and studies on industrial and technological trends. Maintains bookstore.

Scope: management, in-house publishing technology. **Founded:** 1964. **Subscriptions:** audiovisuals books periodicals. **Publications:** *Inside Edge*; *IPMA Bookstore*; *IPMA International Directory* (Annual); *In-House Salary and Compensation Survey* (Biennial). **Awards:** James M. Brahney Scholarship; Management Award; In-Print Award; In-House Promotional Excellence Award (Annual); James M. Brahney Scholarship (Annual); Management Award (Annual); Outstanding Contributor Award (Annual); Vision Award (Annual); In-House Promotional Excellence Award; IPMA Mail Center of the Year (Annual).

16343 ■ IPA - Association of Graphic Solutions Providers
7200 France Ave. S, Ste. 223
Edina, MN 55435
Ph: (952)896-1908
Free: 800-255-8141
Fax: (952)896-0181
Co. E-mail: info@ipa.org
URL: http://www.ipa.org
Contact: Steven Bonoff, President
Description: Provides management and technical resources that help companies build, manage and enhance an integrated graphics workflow, from creative to output. **Founded:** 1897. **Publications:** *IPA Bulletin* (Bimonthly); *IPA News* (Monthly); *SWOP 10th Edition*. **Educational Activities:** Business Development (Annual); Technical Seminar (Annual). **Awards:** Holzinger Award.

16344 ■ National Association of Litho Clubs (NALC)
3268 N 147th Ln.
Goodyear, AZ 85395
Ph: (734)475-9145
Co. E-mail: clubnalc@gmail.com
URL: http://www.graphicarts.org
Contact: Bill Wearne, President
Description: Federation of technicians and supervisors for lithograph plants. Provides a forum for sharing industry information and technology. Offers educational presentations and seminars. **Founded:** 1945. **Awards:** Elmer G. Voigt Award (Annual); Hadronics/NALC Club of the Year (Annual); NALC Litho Member of the Year (Annual); Presidential Award (Annual); Rae Goss Management Training Scholarship (Annual); Toby Morgan Scholarship (Annual); NALC/Tom McGill Outstanding Member of the Year (Annual). **Telecommunication Services:** saxelrood@att.net.

16345 ■ National Association of Printing Ink Manufacturers (NAPIM)
581 Main St., Ste. 520
Woodbridge, NJ 07095-1144
Ph: (732)855-1525
Fax: (732)855-1838
Co. E-mail: napim@napim.org
URL: http://www.napim.org
Contact: Brad Bergey, Executive Director
Description: Represents printing ink manufacturers and suppliers. Sponsors National Printing Ink Research Institute. **Founded:** 1914. **Awards:** Ault Award (Annual); Ault Award; Printing Ink Pioneer Award.

16346 ■ National Association for Printing Leadership (NAPL)
1 Meadowlands Plz., Ste. 1511
East Rutherford, NJ 07073
Ph: (201)634-9600
Free: 800-642-6275
Fax: (201)634-0324
Co. E-mail: jtruncale@napl.org
URL: http://www.napl.org
Contact: Joseph P. Truncale, President
Description: Represents commercial printers and suppliers to the commercial printing industry. Enables those in the industry to operate their businesses for maximum profitability. Offers following management products and services: sales and marketing, customer service, financial, human resources, operations and economic. Maintains Management Institute, which conducts Executive Certification Program. Compiles extensive economic statistics. **Scope:** A not-for-profit graphic arts trade association dedicated to providing a full range of management and educational services.

Provides on-site consulting services on a wide range of topics including: Business issues, cost-studies, environmental areas, human resource concerns and sales and marketing issues. **Founded:** 1933. **Publications:** "Csr Training"; "Customer Needs"; "Customer Service Management"; "Customer Service Strategies"; "NAPL Business Review"; "NAPL White Papers"; "Economic Edge"; "Journal of Graphic Communications Management"; "Management Institute Review"; "Marketing Action Planner"; "Sales Focus"; "Tech Trends". **Awards:** Industry Award (Annual); Management Plus Award (Annual); Technical Leadership Award (Annual); Walter E. Soderstrom Award. **Telecommunication Services:** naplmemberservice@napl.org.

16347 ■ National Association of Quick Printers (NAQP)
2250 E Devon Ave., Ste. 245
Des Plaines, IL 60018
Ph: (847)298-8680
Free: 800-234-0040
Fax: (847)298-8705
Co. E-mail: info@naqp.com
URL: http://www.naqp.com
Description: Independent printers and printing franchise businesses; industry suppliers. Seeks to bring recognition, improved quality, and increased profits to the entire quick printing field. Provides services to members; works to advance the collective interests of the printing industries at the national and international levels. **Scope:** technical manuals. **Founded:** 1975.

16348 ■ NPES: Association for Suppliers of Printing, Publishing and Converting Technologies
1899 Preston White Dr.
Reston, VA 20191
Ph: (703)264-7200
Fax: (703)620-0994
Co. E-mail: npes@npes.org
URL: http://www.npes.org
Contact: Ralph J. Nappi, President
E-mail: rnappi@npes.org
Description: Companies engaged in the manufacture and distribution of equipment, systems, software and/or supplies used in the printing, publishing and converting industries. Represents members before federal agencies and allied trade groups. Funds programs at educational institutions to train graphic arts personnel. Organizes a monthly industry statistical program that compiles and distributes data on orders and shipments. **Founded:** 1933. **Publications:** *Guide to Audio Visual Materials and Public Speakers in the Printing and Publishing Technologies Industry* (Annual); *Directory of International Suppliers of Printing, Publishing and Converting Technologies* (Annual); *Vanguard* (Semiannual); *Directory of International Suppliers of Printing, Publishing, and Converting Technologies* (Annual). **Educational Activities:** GRAPH EXPO (Annual); Graphic Arts - Charlotte Show (Annual). **Awards:** Harold W. Gegenheimer Awards for Industry Service (Annual); Harold W. Gegenheimer Awards for Industry Service, Individual and Corporate (Annual).

16349 ■ Printing Brokerage/Buyers Association International (PB/BA)—PBBA International Inc.
1530 Locust St., Mezanine 124
Philadelphia, PA 19102
Ph: (215)821-6581
Free: 877-585-7141
Fax: (215)359-1577
Co. E-mail: contactus@pbba.org
URL: http://www.pbba.org
Contact: Vincent Mallardi, President
E-mail: vince@pbba.org
Description: Printing buyers/brokers/distributors, printers, typographers, binders, envelope and book manufacturers, packagers, color separation houses, pre-press service organizations, and related companies in the graphic arts industry. Promotes understanding, cooperation, and interaction among members while obtaining the highest standard of professionalism in the graphic arts industry. Gathers information on current technology in the graphic com-

munications industry. Sponsors seminars for members to learn how to work with buyers, brokers and printers; also conducts technical and management seminars. Maintains referral service; compiles statistics. Conducts charitable programs. **Scope:** Printing and publishing marketing and corporate development specialists, whose services include start ups, joint ventures, acquisitions, mergers, contract negotiation, international trade, seminars, workshops, facilities planning, and cost reduction programs. Serves private industries as well as government agencies. **Founded:** 1985. **Subscriptions:** 500 books. **Publications:** "Hot Markets for 2007-2008," Jan, 2005. **Awards:** Printing Broker of the Year (Annual); Vendor of the Year (Annual). **Seminars:** How to Sell Printing Effectively; Sales Compensation and Management; How to Buy Printing Effectively; Hot Markets; International Priority Commerce. **Special Services:** Findprint®; Salesort®.

16350 ■ Printing Industries of America (PIA)
200 Deer Run Rd.
Sewickley, PA 15143-2324
Ph: (412)741-6860
Free: 800-910-4283
Fax: (412)741-2311
Co. E-mail: printing@printing.org
URL: http://www.printing.org
Contact: Michael Makin, President
Description: Commercial printing firms (lithography, letterpress, gravure, platemakers, typographic houses); allied firms in the graphic arts. Provides extensive management services for member companies, including government relations, industry research and statistical information, technology information and assistance, and management education and publications. Compiles statistical and economic data, including annual ratio study that provides a benchmark for printers to compare profits as a basis for improving individual member company and industry profits. Provides reporting system on provisions, rates, and other matters relating to union contracts in effect throughout the industry. Sponsors annual Premier Print Awards Competition. **Founded:** 1999. **Publications:** *Printing Industries of America Ratios*; *Sales and Marketing Success*. **Educational Activities:** President's Conference (Annual). **Awards:** Naomi Berber Memorial Award; Education Awards of Excellence; InterTech Technology Award; Robert F. Reed Technology Medal; William D. Schaeffer Environmental Award; Frederick D. Kagy Education Award of Excellence. **Telecommunication Services:** egleeson@printing.org; gain@printing.org.

16351 ■ Specialty Graphic Imaging Association (SGIA)
10015 Main St.
Fairfax, VA 22031-3489
Ph: (703)330-5600
Free: 888-385-3588
Fax: (703)330-5357
Co. E-mail: sgia@sgia.org
URL: http://www.sgia.org
Contact: Gordon Brown, Chairman
Description: Printers who use screen printing and/or digital printing; associate members are suppliers and manufacturers; educational institutions. Provides training and information on technical, managerial, governmental, safety, and research issues. Conducts safety, environmental, and print quality recognition programs. Compiles statistics; conducts research programs. **Scope:** screen printing, digital printing, pad printing, embroidery, sublimation, technology-related. **Founded:** 1948. **Subscriptions:** 1000 articles books periodicals. **Publications:** *Operating Rate Survey* (Biennial); *SGIA Journal* (Quarterly); *SGIA News* (Monthly); *Who's Who in SGIA* (Annual); *Who's Who in SGIA* (Annual); *Guide to Digital Garment Decoration*. **Educational Activities:** Specialty Graphic Imaging Association Convention (Annual); Safety and Environmental Conference (Annual); SGIA/DPI Conference (Annual). **Awards:** Certificate of Appreciation Award (Annual); Certificate of Merit (Annual); Distinguished Service Award (Annual); Golden Image Award (Annual); Key Award (Annual); Magnus Award (Annual); Mentor Award (Annual); Outstanding Service Award (Annual); Parmele Award (Annual); Safety Recognition Award (Annual); Swormstedt Award (Annual).

16352 ■ **Specialty Graphic Imaging Association (SPTF) - Screen Printing Technical Foundation (SPTF)**
10015 Main St.
Fairfax, VA 22031
Ph: (703)385-1335
Co. E-mail: sptf@sgia.org
URL: http://www.sgia.org/sptf
Description: Participants include corporations, institutions, and individuals interested in screen-printing. Advances the screen-printing industry. Conducts technical research and hands-on training programs to address production problems and processes. Sponsors educational programs and prepares educational materials. **Founded:** 1986.

DIRECTORIES OF EDUCATIONAL PROGRAMS

16353 ■ *Directory of Private Accredited Career Schools and Colleges of Technology*
Pub: Accrediting Commission of Career Schools and Colleges of Technology
Contact: Michale S. McComis, Executive Director
Released: On web page. **Price:** Free. **Description:** Covers 3900 accredited post-secondary programs that provide training programs in business, trade, and technical fields, including various small business endeavors. Entries offer school name, address, phone, description of courses, job placement assistance, and requirements for admission. Arrangement is alphabetical.

REFERENCE WORKS

16354 ■ *"Agfa: M-Press Leopard Debuts"* in *American Printer (Vol. 128, June 1, 2011, No. 6)*
Pub: Penton Media Inc.
Description: M-Press Leopard is a new version of the machine that offers advanced ink jet technology at a lower price point. Agfa Graphics introduced the new version that allows for new applications that require more manual handling.

16355 ■ *"Avanti Hosts Users Conference"* in *American Printer (Vol. 128, July 1, 2011, No. 7)*
Pub: Penton Media Inc.
Description: Avanti Computer Systems Ltd. hosted its 19th annual users conference in Washington DC. In-plant and commercial printers were in attendance.

16356 ■ *"Avoid a Tablet Generation Gap"* in *American Printer (Vol. 128, July 1, 2011, No. 7)*
Pub: Penton Media Inc.
Description: Individuals between the ages of 18-34 are the only generation that is more likely to own a laptop computer or netbook insead of a desktop computer. Statistical data included.

16357 ■ *"Bankruptcies"* in *Crain's Detroit Business (Vol. 24, September 29, 2008, No. 39, pp. 4)*
Pub: Crain Communications Inc.
Description: Current list of business that filed for Chapter 7 or 11 protection in U.S. Bankruptcy Court in Detroit include manufacturers, real estate companies, a printing company and a specialized staffing company.

16358 ■ *"Boston Printer Celebrates 60th Anniversary"* in *American Printer (Vol. 128, August 1, 2011, No. 8)*
Pub: Penton Media Inc.
Description: Shawmut printing is celebrating its 60th anniversary. The family business plans to increase efficiency through automation, monitoring job progress online from start to finish.

16359 ■ *"Business is Unbelievable"* in *American Printer (Vol. 128, August 1, 2011, No. 8)*
Pub: Penton Media Inc.
Ed: Katherine O'Brien. **Description:** Most commercial printers have seen an increase in business over the last year.

16360 ■ *"Calista Sells Rural Newspapers"* in *Alaska Business Monthly (Vol. 27, October 2011, No. 10, pp. 8)*
Pub: Alaska Business Publishing Company
Ed: Nancy Pounds. **Description:** Calista sold its six newspapers, a magazine, shoppers and its printing house. Details of the sales are given.

16361 ■ *"Challenges Await Quad in Going Public"* in *Milwaukee Business Journal (Vol. 27, January 29, 2010, No. 18, pp. A1)*
Pub: American City Business Journals
Ed: Rich Rovito. **Description:** Sussex, Wisconsin-based Quad/Graphics Inc.'s impending acquisition of rival Canadian World Color Press Inc. will transform it into a publicly held entity for the first time. Quad has operated as a private company for nearly 40 years and will need to adjust to changes, such as the way management shares information with Quad/Graphics' employees. Details of the merger are included.

16362 ■ *"ContiTech Celebrates 100 Years"* in *American Printer (Vol. 128, July 1, 2011, No. 7)*
Pub: Penton Media Inc.
Description: ContiTech celebrated 100 years in business. The firm started in 1911 after developing the first elastic printing blanket. Other milestones for the firm include its manufacturing process for compressible printing blankets, the Conti-Air brand and climate-neutral printing blankets.

16363 ■ *"Crouser Offers UV Coating Price Report"* in *American Printer (Vol. 128, June 1, 2011, No. 6)*
Pub: Penton Media Inc.
Description: Crouser and Associates will offer the 'Pricing Off-Line UV Coating' report that provides background information on all three types of protective printing coatings and price guidance. The report will also offer comparisons of four popular types of offline equipment.

16364 ■ *"Customer OKs on Press"* in *American Printer (Vol. 128, August 1, 2011, No. 8)*
Pub: Penton Media Inc.
Description: Printers discuss the value of having customers meet at the plant in order to okay print colors for projects.

16365 ■ *"Design Center Shows Quality of Digital Paper"* in *American Printer (Vol. 128, June 1, 2011, No. 6)*
Pub: Penton Media Inc.
Description: Digital Design Centers allows printers to customize marketing tools in order to promote their own digital printing capabilities.

16366 ■ *"Digital Printing Walks the Plank"* in *American Printer (Vol. 128, August 1, 2011, No. 8)*
Pub: Penton Media Inc.
Description: Digital print manufacturing is discussed.

16367 ■ *"Feeding the Elephants While Searching for Greener Pastures"* in *American Printer (Vol. 128, July 1, 2011, No. 7)*
Pub: Penton Media Inc.
Ed: Bob Rosen. **Description:** Three steps to help printers to build a new business while facing the challenges to the existing business are outlined.

16368 ■ *"First U.S. :M-Press Tiger with Inline Screen Printing"* in *American Printer (Vol. 128, June 1, 2011, No. 6)*
Pub: Penton Media Inc.
Description: Graphic Tech located in California bought :M-Press Tiger, the first in North America with an inline screen printing unit.

16369 ■ *"Flint Group Raises Prices"* in *American Printer (Vol. 128, August 1, 2011, No. 8)*
Pub: Penton Media Inc.
Description: Due to the rising cost for raw materials, Flint Group is raising their prices for inks and coatings in North American.

16370 ■ *"Four Exhibition Considerations"* in *American Printer (Vol. 128, August 1, 2011, No. 8)*
Pub: Penton Media Inc.
Description: Four questions to ask at the Graph Expo will help printers improve their own business.

16371 ■ *"Fujifilm Invites Printers to Take the 'Onset Challenge"* in *American Printer (Vol. 128, August 1, 2011, No. 8)*
Pub: Penton Media Inc.
Description: Fujifilm North American Corporation's Graphic Systems Division offers a new five-step product selection and return-on-investment calculator for the Onset family of wide-format printers.

16372 ■ *"Guide to Carbon Footprinting"* in *American Printer (Vol. 128, June 1, 2011, No. 6)*
Pub: Penton Media Inc.
Description: PrintCity Alliance published its new report, 'Carbon Footprint & Energy Reduction for Graphic Industry Value Chain.' The report aims to help improve the environmental performance of printers, converters, publishers, brand owners and their suppliers.

16373 ■ *"How to Save Money on Ink"* in *American Printer (Vol. 128, July 1, 2011, No. 7)*
Pub: Penton Media Inc.
Description: Tips are shared to help graphic arts and printing companies save money on raw materials. Factors to consider once the type of ink is decided are also outlined.

16374 ■ *"Improving the USPS"* in *American Printer (Vol. 128, July 1, 2011, No. 7)*
Pub: Penton Media Inc.
Description: National Postal Forum held in San Diego, California May 1-4, 2011 hosted 4,000 attendees. Highlights of the event are provided.

16375 ■ *"Industry Events 2011"* in *American Printer (Vol. 128, August 1, 2011, No. 8)*
Pub: Penton Media Inc.
Description: Listing of events of interest to graphic arts and printing businesses in presented.

16376 ■ *"Industry/Events 2011"* in *American Printer (Vol. 128, July 1, 2011, No. 7)*
Pub: Penton Media Inc.
Description: PMA, the Worldwide Community of Imaging Association launched its new CliQ with how-to tips, product reviews and monthly photo contests. PMA formed a partnership with the Consumer Electronics Association to make changes to this year's annual convention.

16377 ■ *"Interchangeable or Irreplaceable?"* in *American Printer (Vol. 128, August 1, 2011, No. 8)*
Pub: Penton Media Inc.
Description: Creating and maintaining customers is important for all graphic design and printing companies. Tips are shared to help maintain good customer satisfaction and repeat business.

16378 ■ *"IPEX Moves to London Venue"* in *American Printer (Vol. 128, July 1, 2011, No. 7)*
Pub: Penton Media Inc.
Description: IPES 2014 is being relocated to London's ExCeL International Exhibition and Conference Centre from March 26 to April 2, 2014.

16379 ■ *"JDF Integration: 3 Key Tips"* in *American Printer (Vol. 128, August 1, 2011, No. 8)*
Pub: Penton Media Inc.
Description: Three tips for implementing cross-vendor integrations are outlined.

16380 ■ *"KBA, Graphic Art System Partner on Cold Foil"* in *American Printer (Vol. 128, June 1, 2011, No. 6)*
Pub: Penton Media Inc.
Description: KBA North America has partnered with Graphic Art System to retrofit and equip presses with cold foil machines.

16381 ■ *"Kodak Offers Cloud-Based Operating Option"* in American Printer (Vol. 128, June 1, 2011, No. 6)
Pub: Penton Media Inc.
Description: Kodak partnered with VMware to offer its first Virtual Operating Environment option for Kodak Unified Workflow Solutions. The new feature enables cost savings, increased efficiency and failover protection.

16382 ■ *"Metallics Education"* in American Printer (Vol. 128, June 1, 2011, No. 6)
Pub: Penton Media Inc.
Description: Guide 'Curious About Print: Your Guide to the World of Curious Metallics' provides hints and tips to help printers maximize selection and reproduction, advice on working with metallic and UV inks, and recommendations for gaining quantity without sacrificing quality.

16383 ■ *"MFSA Officially Endorses Five-Day USPS Delivery"* in American Printer (Vol. 128, August 1, 2011, No. 8)
Pub: Penton Media Inc.
Description: Board of Directors of the Mailing and Fulfillment Service Association (MFSA) voted to support the US Postal Service's move to five-day delivery service.

16384 ■ *"New Approach to Mechanical Binding"* in American Printer (Vol. 128, July 1, 2011, No. 7)
Pub: Penton Media Inc.
Description: EcoBinder coil binding system from Kugler-Womako eliminates traditional plastic combs or wire spiral with the use of 22-mm wide printable paper rings.

16385 ■ *"OCE Boosts JetStream Productivity"* in American Printer (Vol. 128, August 1, 2011, No. 8)
Pub: Penton Media Inc.
Description: New Oce JetStream 1400 and 3000 digital full-color inkjet presses are profiled. The new models promise higher speed to grow print volume.

16386 ■ *"One World"* in American Printer (Vol. 128, August 1, 2011, No. 8)
Pub: Penton Media Inc.
Description: Graph Expo will highlight entrepreneurs focused on the connection between content, technology and business models.

16387 ■ *"P/Kaufmann Sells Bennettsville"* in Home Textiles Today (Vol. 31, May 24, 2011, No. 13, pp. 6)
Pub: Reed Business Information
Contact: Jeff Greisch, President
Description: Decorative Screen Printers purchased the printing and finishing facility of P/Kaufmann in Bennettsville, South Carolina. However, the firm will continue its focus on its core business, a vat printing facility for home furnishings fabrics.

16388 ■ *"Paper a la Carte"* in American Printer (Vol. 128, June 1, 2011, No. 6)
Pub: Penton Media Inc.
Description: Blurb, the online publishing platform, launched ProLine which features Mohawk Superfine and Mohawk proPhoto papers. ProLine papers offer two finishes: Pearl Photo and Uncoated.

16389 ■ *"Paper Choices Made Simple"* in American Printer (Vol. 128, June 1, 2011, No. 6)
Pub: Penton Media Inc.
Description: Choices, a new initiative by Boise, provides professional guidance to help customers and consumers make informed, effective choices for using paper.

16390 ■ *"Paper Replaces PVC for Gift Cards"* in American Printer (Vol. 128, June 1, 2011, No. 6)
Pub: Penton Media Inc.
Description: Monadnock Envi Card Stock replaces paper for gift cards, loyalty cards, membership cards, hotel keys and durable signage. This renewable wood fiber alternative to PVC card materials comes from Monadock Paper Mills.

16391 ■ *"Please Pass the Mayo"* in Crain's Chicago Business (Vol. 31, April 28, 2008, No. 17, pp. 32)
Pub: Crain Communications, Inc.
Ed: Samantha Stainburn. **Description:** Fort Dearborn Co. has come a long way since it started as on one-press print shop; the family-owned company was struggling to keep up with the technology of making consumer product labels for curvy bottles of products like V8 V-Fusion juice and in 2006 sold off to Genstar Capital LLC which has pushed for acquisitions; last year, Fort Derborn bought its biggest competitor, Renaissance Mark Inc., doubling its size and adding spirit and wine makers to its client roster.

16392 ■ *"Prices Continue to Rise"* in American Printer (Vol. 128, June 1, 2011, No. 6)
Pub: Penton Media Inc.
Description: Prices were increased by both Flint Group and Ashland Performance Materials by 7-10 percent and 5-15 percent respectively.

16393 ■ *"Printers to the Trade"* in American Printer (Vol. 128, July 1, 2011, No. 7)
Pub: Penton Media Inc.
Description: Wholesale printing is discussed. Two wholesale printers share insight into their success, from business philosophies in general to practices that build strong relationships.

16394 ■ Printing Impressions--Top 500 Printers Issue
Pub: North American Publishing Co.
Contact: Ned S. Borowsky, President
URL(s): www.piworld.com/. **Ed:** Erik Cagle, Julie Greenbaum. **Released:** Annual; December. **Price:** Free. **Publication includes:** List of the leading 500 commercial, financial, directory, publication, check, book, business form, packaging, and specialty printers. **Entries include:** Company name, city and state, sales, name of president or chief executive officer, number of press units, number of employees, coded list of printing specialties (periodicals, commercial, specialty, etc.), whether publicly or privately owned. **Arrangement:** Ranked by annual sales.

16395 ■ *"QR Codes: OK, I Get It Now"* in American Printer (Vol. 128, July 1, 2011, No. 7)
Pub: Penton Media Inc.
Description: QR Code technology is discussed. It is up to the user to enter the proper QR Code.

16396 ■ *"Reducing the Book's Carbon Footpring"* in American Printer (Vol. 128, July 1, 2011, No. 7)
Pub: Penton Media Inc.
Description: Green Press Initiative's Book Industry Environmental Council is working to achieve a 20 percent reduction in the book industry's carbon footprint by 2020. The Council is made up of publishers, printers, paper suppliers, and non-governmental organizations.

16397 ■ *"Root, Root, Root for the P.A. Hutchison Co."* in American Printer (Vol. 128, August 1, 2011, No. 8)
Pub: Penton Media Inc.
Description: The P.A. Hutchison Company celebrate 100 years in the printing business. President and CEO Chris Hutchison presented awards to employees, however employees also presented awards to Chris and his father as Employer of the Century.

16398 ■ *"Sappi Awards Gold NA Printers of the Year Winners"* in American Printer (Vol. 128, July 1, 2011, No. 7)
Pub: Penton Media Inc.
Description: Sappi Fine Paper North America honored ten gold winners of its 14th North American Printers of the Year awards. Each gold winning printer will receive $20,000 to support marketing and brand initiatives.

16399 ■ *"Seeing the Light"* in American Printer (Vol. 128, July 1, 2011, No. 7)
Pub: Penton Media Inc.
Description: Four printing demos on sheetfed, digital, label and pad printing equipment were highlighted at the Fifth UV Days held in Stuttgart, Germany in May 2011.

16400 ■ *"Seven Tips for Continuous Improvement"* in American Printer (Vol. 128, July 1, 2011, No. 7)
Pub: Penton Media Inc.
Description: Seven tips are given to help any graphic arts or printing company improve by integrating lean manufacturing into operations.

16401 ■ *"Something Old and Something New"* in American Printer (Vol. 128, August 1, 2011, No. 8)
Pub: Penton Media Inc.
Description: Trade journalists and industry analysts were invited to Fujifilm North America Corporation's Hanover Park, Illinois facility to view it's sheetfed inkjet press. The JPress 720 is the first and only of its kind in the world.

16402 ■ *"Successful First Year for Twin Rivers"* in American Printer (Vol. 128, June 1, 2011, No. 6)
Pub: Penton Media Inc.
Description: Profile of Twin Rivers located in Maine. The firm manufactured 380,000 tons of free sheet and hybrid-groundwood papers in its first year.

16403 ■ *"Sudden Shift Leaves Wells Vendor Scrambling"* in Charlotte Business Journal (Vol. 25, July 9, 2010, No. 16, pp. 1)
Pub: Charlotte Business Journal
Ed: Adam O'Daniel. **Description:** Rubber stamps vendor Carolina Marking Devices is facing a 30 percent drop in business after banking firm Wells Fargo & Company decided to buy its rubber stamps from another vendor. Carolina Marking Devices had provided rubber to First Union Corporation and its successor Wachovia Corporation, which was eventually acquired by Wells Fargo. Other reactions from Carolina Marking Device owners are given.

16404 ■ *"Sunriver Venture Hits Snag"* in The Business Journal-Portland (Vol. 25, August 1, 2008, No. 21, pp. 1)
Pub: American City Business Journals, Inc.
Ed: Robin J. Moody. **Description:** Portland, Oregon based-Sunwest Management Inc. has divided its Sunriver resort community to make way for a redevelopment plan. Sunwest owner Jon Harder and three partners formed SilverStar Destinations LLC to broker the purchase and redevelopment of the property. Details and description of the redevelopment project are also presented.

16405 ■ *"Ted Stahl: Executive Chairman"* in Inside Business (Vol. 13, September-October 2011, No. 5, pp. NC6)
Pub: Great Lakes Publishing Co.
Ed: Miranda S. Miller. **Description:** Profile of Ted Stahl, who started working in his family's business when he was ten years old is presented. The firm makes dies for numbers and letters used on team uniforms. Another of the family firms manufactures stock and custom heat-printing products, equipment and supplies. It also educates customers on ways to decorate garments with heat printing products and offers graphics and software for customers to create their own artwork.

16406 ■ *"Tic-Tac-Show"* in American Printer (Vol. 128, August 1, 2011, No. 8)
Pub: Penton Media Inc.
Description: Graph Expo has become the US print industry's main event. There will be as many as 500 exhibitors at this year's event and the Graphic Arts Show Company lists over 30 co-located events as well as 53 new sessions in the seminar program's 28 education categories.

16407 ■ *"Transcontinental to Exchange Assets with Quad/Graphics"* in American Printer (Vol. 128, August 1, 2011, No. 8)
Pub: Penton Media Inc.
Description: Transcontinental Inc. and Quad/Graphics Inc. entered into an agreement where Transcontinental will indirectly acquire all shares of Quad Graphics Canada Inc.

16408 ■ *"Try a Little Social Media" in American Printer (Vol. 128, June 1, 2011, No. 6)*
Pub: Penton Media Inc.

Description: Social media helps keep Ussery Printing on customers radar. Jim David, VP of marketing for the firm, states that 350 people following them on Facebook are from the local area.

16409 ■ *"Turning Green Ink to Black" in The Business Journal-Serving Metropolitan Kansas City (Vol. 26, August 8, 2008, No. 48, pp. 1)*
Pub: American City Business Journals, Inc.

Ed: James Dornbrook. **Description:** InkCycle has introduced grenk, a line of environmentally-friendly printer toner and ink cartridges. The cartridges are collected and recycled after use by the company, which separates them into their metal, cardboard, and plastic components.

16410 ■ *"Use Ink Presets to Minimize Makeready" in American Printer (Vol. 128, July 1, 2011, No. 7)*
Pub: Penton Media Inc.

Description: Automatic registration systems enable most printers to be in register very quickly after press startup. If the paper, ink and press time wasted during makeready can be reduced, these savings will flow directly to the bottom line. Ink presetting as an economical solution to set color quickly is a trend that continues to gain momentum.

16411 ■ *"UV Suppliers Form Strategic Alliance" in American Printer (Vol. 128, June 1, 2011, No. 6)*
Pub: Penton Media Inc.

Description: British ultra-violent curing systems developer Integration Technology Ltd. formed a strategic alliance with UV technology provider IST Metz GmbH of Germany in order to offer a complete line of UV solutions for the printing industry.

16412 ■ *"Web to Print" in American Printer (Vol. 128, August 1, 2011, No. 8)*
Pub: Penton Media Inc.

Description: Jerry Kennelly, CEO and founder of Tweak.com believes that Web-to-Design is middleware with no content. His firm offers an easy to use interface that flows right into the printer's workflow with no additional costs.

STATISTICAL SOURCES

16413 ■ *RMA Annual Statement Studies*
Pub: Risk Management Association
Contact: Kevin M. Blakey, President

Released: Annual. **Price:** $175.00 2006-07 edition, $105.00. **Description:** Contains composite balance sheets and income statements for more than 360 industries, including the accounting, auditing, and bookkeeping industries. Also contains five years of comparative historical data for discerning trends. Includes 16 commonly used ratios, computed for most of the size groupings for nearly every industry.

TRADE PERIODICALS

16414 ■ *American Printer: The Graphic Arts Managers Magazine*
Pub: Penton
Contact: Raymond E. Maloney, President

URL(s): www.americanprinter.com. **Ed:** Katherine O'Brien. **Released:** Monthly **Price:** $85, Individuals; $97, Other countries; $380, Individuals 5 years; $398, Other countries 5 years.

16415 ■ *Economic Edge*
Pub: National Association for Printing Leadership
Released: Quarterly. **Price:** Included in membership. **Description:** Provides current economic data for the printing industry. Also covers sales growth projections, capital spending, and employment.

16416 ■ *FLEXO: Converting Technology*
Pub: Foundation of Flexographic Technical Association
Contact: Mark Cisternino, President
E-mail: markc@flexography.org

URL(s): www.flexography.org/flexo/index.cfm. **Released:** Monthly **Price:** $55, U.S., Canada, and Mexico; $76, Other countries; $30, Individuals; $92, Two years; $125, Individuals 3 years.

16417 ■ *Guild of Book Workers Newsletter*
Pub: Guild of Book Workers Inc.
Contact: Andrew Huot, President
E-mail: vicepresident@guildofbookworkers.allmail.net

Ed: Margaret Johnson, Editor. **Released:** Bimonthly, Every 2 months. **Price:** Included in membership. **Description:** Covers issues in book arts, binding, book conservation, calligraphy, and printing. Recurring features include letters to the editor, interviews, news of research, a calendar of events, reports of meetings, news of educational opportunities, job listings, book reviews, and notices of publications available.

16418 ■ *Imaging News: Guide*
Contact: Arthur S. Diamond, Editor

URL(s): www.imagingnews.com/imagingnews.html. **Ed:** Arthur S. Diamond. **Released:** Monthly **Price:** $175, Individuals.

16419 ■ *Printer's Ink*
Pub: Thomson-Shore Inc.
Contact: Kevin Spall, President

Ed: Todd Gaffner, Editor, toddg@tshore.com. **Released:** Quarterly. **Price:** Free. **Description:** Provides information on developments in printing and binding and other tenets of book manufacturing. Includes a feature article, company news, information on printing prices, and a column titled Trivia.

16420 ■ *Printing Impressions: America's Most Influential and Widely Read Publication for Commercial Printers*
Pub: North American Publishing Co.
Contact: Ned S. Borowsky, President

URL(s): www.napco.comwww.piworld.com. **Released:** Monthly **Price:** Free.

16421 ■ *Quick Printing: The Information Source for Commercial Copyshops & Printshops*
Pub: Cygnus Business Media
Contact: Rich Reiff, President

URL(s): www.myprintresource.com/magazinewww.cygnusb2b.com/PropertyPub.cfm?PropertyID=158. **Ed:** Karen Lowery Hall. **Released:** Monthly **Price:** Free.

16422 ■ *Sales and Marketing Success*
Pub: Printing Industries of America
Contact: Michael Makin, President

Released: Quarterly. **Description:** Provides management information to graphic arts companies for marketing products and improving sales techniques.

16423 ■ *Signs of the Times & Screen Printing en Espanol*
Pub: ST Media Group International Inc.
Contact: Tedd Swormstedt, President

URL(s): www.stmediagroup.com/index.php3?d=pubs&p=ssen. **Ed:** Nancy Bottoms. **Released:** Bimonthly

VIDEOCASSETTES/ AUDIOCASSETTES

16424 ■ *Controlling Waste in Web Offset Printing*
Printing Industries of America (PIA)
200 Deer Run Rd.
Sewickley, PA 15143-2324
Ph: (412)741-6860
Free: 800-910-4283

Fax: (412)741-2311
Co. E-mail: printing@printing.org
URL: http://www.printing.org
Contact: Michael Makin, President

Released: 1988. **Price:** $420.00. **Description:** Proven ways of decreasing waste and increasing efficiency in the printing business are demonstrated. **Availability:** VHS.

16425 ■ *The Web Offset Press*
Printing Industries of America (PIA)
200 Deer Run Rd.
Sewickley, PA 15143-2324
Ph: (412)741-6860
Free: 800-910-4283
Fax: (412)741-2311
Co. E-mail: printing@printing.org
URL: http://www.printing.org
Contact: Michael Makin, President

Released: 1987. **Description:** An overview of the web offset for the printer, differentiating between sheetfed and webfed presses, and other details. **Availability:** VHS.

TRADE SHOWS AND CONVENTIONS

16426 ■ *Graphics of the Americas*
Printing Association of Florida, Inc.
6275 Hazeltine National Dr.
Orlando, FL 32822
Ph: (407)240-8009
Free: 800-749-4855
Fax: (407)240-8333
Co. E-mail: agaither@pafgraf.org
URL: http://www.pafgraf.org

URL(s): www.graphicsoftheamericas.com. **Frequency:** Annual. **Audience:** Graphics arts trade. **Principal Exhibits:** Graphic arts and specialty printing equipment, supplies, and services. **Dates and Locations:** , Convention Center. **Telecommunication Services:** spatt@pafgraf.org.

16427 ■ *ON DEMAND Digital Printing & Publishing Strategy Conference and Exposition*
Advanstar Communications
641 Lexington Ave., 8th Fl.
New York, NY 10022
Ph: (212)951-6600
Free: 800-346-0085
Fax: (212)951-6793
Co. E-mail: info@advantstar.com
URL: http://www.advanstar.com
Contact: Robert Krakoff, President

URL(s): www.ondemandexpo.com. **Frequency:** Annual. **Audience:** Corporate executives, print providers, government users. **Principal Exhibits:** Addresses the digitalization of workflow in the printing and publishing marketplace. **Telecommunication Services:** sfrank@advanstar.com.

16428 ■ *Print Ontario*
IAPHC, Inc.
IAPHC Corporate HQ
Maple Grove, MN 55311-7549
Co. E-mail: headquarters@iaphc.org
URL: http://www.iaphc.org

URL(s): www.printontario.com. **Price:** $7, Pre-registered; $15, Onsite. **Frequency:** Biennial. **Audience:** Small and mid-size commercial printers, instant printers, implant shops, brokers and forms distributors. **Principal Exhibits:** Press manufactures, bindery equipment, high speed photocopiers, color copiers, paper manufactures, ink manufactures, trade business, manufactures, trade labels. **Dates and Locations:** , Exhibition Place.

CONSULTANTS

16429 ■ *C. Clint Bolte & Associates*
809 Philadelphia Ave.
Chambersburg, PA 17201
Ph: (717)263-5768

Fax: (717)263-8954
Co. E-mail: clint@clintbolte.com
URL: http://www.clintbolte.com
Contact: C. Clint Bolte, Principal
E-mail: cbolte3@comcast.net
Scope: Provider of management consulting services to firms involved with the printing industry. Services include outsourcing studies, graphics supply chain management studies, company and equipment valuations, plant layout services, litigation support, fulfillment warehouse consulting and product development services. **Founded:** 1989. **Seminars:** How to compete with the majors.

16430 ■ J. S. Eliezer Associates Inc. (JSEA)
300 Atlantic St., 7th Fl.
Stamford, CT 06901-3513
Ph: (203)658-1300
Fax: (203)658-1301
Contact: Judah S. Eliezer, President
E-mail: jeliezer@jseliezer.com
Scope: Management and market research consultants offering design and implementation of manufacturing strategy, feasibility analysis and systems analysis, as well as management information systems and prepress systems; manufacturing proposals analysis, negotiations and contracts; paper purchasing strategy and contract negotiations; catalog distribution effectiveness analysis. Serves the publishing and catalog industries. **Founded:** 1964.

FRANCHISES AND BUSINESS OPPORTUNITIES

16431 ■ AlphaGraphics, Inc.
268 S State St., Ste. 300
Salt Lake City, UT 84117
Ph: (801)595-7259
Fax: (801)533-7959
Co. E-mail: opportunity@alphagraphics.com
URL: http://www.alphagraphics.com
Description: Print-related and digital publishing services which include high-speed duplication, single and multi-color printing, desktop design and publishing, custom presentation materials and an international satellite computer network that transmits camera-ready text and graphics in minutes to any AlphaGraphics store worldwide. **No. of Franchise Units:** 273. **Founded:** 1970.. **Franchised:** 1980. **Equity Capital Needed:** $150,000 liquid of $700,000 net worth. **Franchise Fee:** $40,000. **Training:** 4 weeks new franchisee training, 1 week in-store training and advanced franchisee training.

16432 ■ Babies 'N' Bells Inc.
4489 Mira Vista Dr.
Frisco, TX 75034
Free: 888-318-2229
Fax: (469)384-0138
Description: Custom invitations, announcements and thank-you notes. **No. of Franchise Units:** 56. **No. of Company-Owned Units:** 44. **Founded:** 1996.. **Franchised:** 1997. **Equity Capital Needed:** $16,700-$28,900 total investment; $15,000 net worth, $15,000 cash liquidity. **Franchise Fee:** $9,000. **Royalty Fee:** 8%. **Financial Assistance:** Limited in-house financing available. **Training:** Offers 1 week at headquarters with ongoing support.

16433 ■ Cartridge Express
20 Charles St., Ste. B
Northvale, NJ 07647
Ph: (877)887-5495
Fax: (877)568-2578
Description: Cartridge refilling. **No. of Franchise Units:** 2. **No. of Company-Owned Units:** 1. **Founded:** 2004.. **Franchised:** 2005. **Equity Capital Needed:** $25,000. **Franchise Fee:** $10,000 (1st 10 free). **Training:** Yes.

16434 ■ Cartridge World
3106 N U.S. Hwy. 12
Spring Grove, IL 60081
Ph: (888)997-3345

Fax: (815)675-6321
Co. E-mail: burt@cartridgeworld.com
URL: http://www.cartridgeworldusa.com
Description: Provides cartridge refilling service. **No. of Franchise Units:** 1,700. **Founded:** 1997.. **Franchised:** 1998. **Equity Capital Needed:** $120,100-$184,600. **Franchise Fee:** $30,000. **Training:** An intensive 2 week training course.

16435 ■ Disciple's Directory, Inc.
PO Box 100
Wilmington, MA 01887
Ph: (800)696-2344
Fax: (978)657-5411
Description: Church telephone directories. **No. of Franchise Units:** 6. **No. of Company-Owned Units:** 2. **Founded:** 1984.. **Franchised:** 1998. **Equity Capital Needed:** $7,500. **Franchise Fee:** $7,500. **Financial Assistance:** Yes. **Training:** Yes.

16436 ■ Kwik Kopy Business Centers
Kwik Kopy Business Centers, Inc. Kwik Kopy Business Centers
12715 Telge Rd.
Cypress, TX 77429
Free: 888-638-8722
Fax: (281)256-4178
Co. E-mail: franchisedevelopment@iced.net
URL: http://www.iced.net
Description: Offers business advertisement aids and printing and copying services. **No. of Franchise Units:** 16. **No. of Company-Owned Units:** 1. **Founded:** 2001.. **Franchised:** 2001. **Equity Capital Needed:** $65,000 liquid capital; $250,000 net worth. **Franchise Fee:** $35,000. **Financial Assistance:** Yes. **Training:** Owners attend classroom and field training, as well as ongoing training through workshops and conferences.

16437 ■ Kwik-Kopy Printing Canada
1550 16th Ave., Bldg. D, Unit 4
Richmond Hill, ON, Canada L4B 3K9
Ph: (416)798-7007
Free: 800-387-9725
Fax: (905)780-0575
Co. E-mail: duncanmacpherson@kwikkopy.ca
URL: http://www.kwikkopyprintingfranchise.ca
Description: Offers printing, photocopying, design, fax and related reproduction services. **No. of Franchise Units:** 62. **Founded:** 1979.. **Franchised:** 1979. **Equity Capital Needed:** $130,000-$208,000. **Franchise Fee:** $29,500. **Training:** Offers 36 days of training.

16438 ■ Mini Cities Inc.
28439 Great Bend Pl.
Westly Chapel, FL 33543
Free: 800-576-2180
URL: http://www.minicities.com
Description: Local online & print directory. **No. of Franchise Units:** 4. **No. of Company-Owned Units:** 57. **Founded:** 2005.. **Franchised:** 2007. **Equity Capital Needed:** $15,675-$20,700. **Franchise Fee:** $9,500. **Royalty Fee:** 30%. **Financial Assistance:** Financing available for franchise fee.

16439 ■ Minuteman Press
Minuteman Press International
61 Executive Blvd.
Farmingdale, NY 11735
Ph: (631)249-1370
Free: 800-645-3006
Co. E-mail: info@MPIHQ.com
URL: http://www.minuteman-press.com
Description: Full service printing and graphics centers offering a complete range of services from graphic design to multi-color capabilities, primarily geared to the business/commercial community. Typically a 5 day - Monday thru Friday - business. No experience necessary. **No. of Franchise Units:** 950. **Founded:** 1973.. **Franchised:** 1975. **Equity Capital Needed:** $35,000-$50,000 deposits and working capital. **Franchise Fee:** Call for more info. **Financial Assistance:** Yes. **Training:** Training program and over 24 regional support offices providing ongoing, in-store training and assistance in the management, technical and marketing aspects of your business. Computerized management and pricing programs are made available to all franchisees.

16440 ■ Minuteman Press International
61 Executive Blvd.
Farmingdale, NY 11735
Ph: (631)249-1370
Free: 800-645-3006
Fax: (631)249-5618
Co. E-mail: info@mpihq.com
URL: http://www.minutemanpress.com
Description: Full-service printing and graphics centers offering a complete range of services from graphic design to multi-color capabilities, primarily geared to the business/commercial community. Five-day, Monday thru Friday business. Award-winning training program/27 regional support offices providing ongoing, in-store training and assistance in management, technical and marketing aspects. Computerized management and pricing programs available. **No. of Franchise Units:** 75. **Founded:** 1973.. **Franchised:** 1975. **Equity Capital Needed:** $100,000-$150,000 total investment. **Franchise Fee:** $45,500. **Training:** Provides 2 weeks plus additional ononsite training.

16441 ■ Pip Printing and Document Services
26722 Plz. Dr., Ste. 200
Mission Viejo, CA 92691
Ph: (800)894-7498
Fax: (800)747-0679
URL: http://www.pip.com
Description: Offers complete range of business including multi-color printing, high-volume copying, desktop publishing, layout, design and finishing on newsletters, brochures, bound presentations, business stationery and forms. **No. of Franchise Units:** 285. **Founded:** 1965.. **Franchised:** 1968. **Equity Capital Needed:** Minimum cash investment $83,000 living expenses; Total investment $232,850-$465,840. **Franchise Fee:** $20,000. **Financial Assistance:** Yes. **Training:** 2 1/2 weeks of training at PIP University and field visit within the first six months of operation.

16442 ■ Postal Connections of America
Templar Franchise Company
275 E. Douglas Ave., Ste. 115
El Cajon, CA 92020
Ph: (619)294-7550
Free: 800-767-8257
Fax: (619)294-4550
Co. E-mail: info@postalconnections.com
URL: http://www.postalconnections.com.
Description: Postal Connections stores offer packaging, shipping, mail receiving & forwarding, copies, printing, scanning & storage of digital documents, eBay auction support, office & packing supplies, crate & freight shipping and more. **No. of Franchise Units:** 99. **Founded:** 1985.. **Franchised:** 1996. **Equity Capital Needed:** $119,000-$153,900, average initial investment. **Franchise Fee:** $23,900. **Financial Assistance:** Yes. **Training:** Extensive training prior to & after opening. Franchisee's receive 5 days live action training in a regional training store, Unique Act video training program & 4 days onsite.

16443 ■ Print Three Franchising Corp.
8400 Jane St. Bldg. D, Ste. 300
Concord, ON, Canada L4K 4L8
Ph: (905)669-8895
Free: 800-335-5918
Fax: (905)669-0712
URL: http://www.printthree.com
Description: Business service franchise focusing on the increasing demand for digital imaging. Franchise offers complete digital reproduction, design, finishing and fulfillment. The only print franchise having a fully integrated web-based ordering system. Provides total imaging solutions for the corporate community. **No. of Franchise Units:** 51. **Founded:** 1970.. **Franchised:** 1981. **Equity Capital Needed:** $200,000. **Franchise Fee:** $70,000. **Training:** Yes.

16444 ■ RWorld Franchise Canada Inc.
6154 5th Line
Tottenham, ON, Canada L0G 1W0
Ph: (905)936-9346
Free: 800-307-3719

Fax: (905)936-9382
Co. E-mail: doug@rworld.ca
URL: http://www.rworld.ca
Description: RWorld is a unique and comparatively low start-up cost franchise, in the highly profitable printer cartridge industry. We offer choices: store in store or leading edge mobile concept. Our model is regional master micro plants, eliminating the need for each individual franchisee to waste precious resources remanufacturing cartridges! It allows for consistency in product and the franchise investor concentrates on promoting and growing their business. **No. of Franchise Units:** 4. **No. of Company-Owned Units:** 1. **Founded:** 2002.. **Franchised:** 2002. **Equity Capital Needed:** $40,000-$60,000. **Franchise Fee:** $20,000. **Training:** Full training and support.

16445 ■ Sir Speedy Inc.—Sir Speedy
26722 Plz. Dr.
Mission Viejo, CA 92691-6390
Ph: (949)348-5000
Free: 800-747-7733
Fax: (949)348-5066
Co. E-mail: markting@sirspeedy.com
URL: http://www.sirspeedy.com
Contact: Rich Lowe, President
Description: Franchisor of printing, copying, graphic design and digital networking centers. **No. of Franchise Units:** 237. **Founded:** 1968. **Franchised:** 1968. **Equity Capital Needed:** $221,040-$271,040; net worth $450,000. **Franchise Fee:** $25,000. **Royalty Fee:** 4-6%. **Training:** Available at headquarters 2 weeks, 2 weeks at franchisee's location, at regional meeings 1-3 days, and ongoing support.

16446 ■ The UPS Store
1115 North Service Rd.W, Unit 1
Oakville, ON, Canada L6M 2V9
Ph: (905)338-9754

Free: 800-661-6232
Fax: (905)338-7491
Co. E-mail: development@theupsstore.ca
URL: http://www.theupsstore.ca
Description: Offering one-stop convenience for small business: digital print and photocopies (colour & B/W), document finishing, worldwide courier services, packaging services & supplies, fax services, computer rental, WIFI and mail receiving services. **No. of Franchise Units:** 350. **Founded:** 1990.. **Equity Capital Needed:** $146,150-$179,550. **Franchise Fee:** $35,000.

LIBRARIES

16447 ■ Carnegie-Mellon University - University Libraries - Special Collections
Hunt Library
4909 Frew St.
Pittsburgh, PA 15213-3890
Ph: (412)268-2444
Fax: (412)268-6945
Co. E-mail: mj0g@andrew.cmu.edu
URL: http://www.library.cmu.edu
Contact: Mary Kay Johnsen, Librarian, Special Collections
Scope: History of printing, 19th-century English literature, landmark books of science. **Services:** Library open to the public. **Founded:** 1960. **Holdings:** 12,000 books. **Telecommunication Services:** UL-huntref@andrew.cmu.edu.

16448 ■ Flint Ink - Information Resource Center
4600 Arrowhead Dr.
Ann Arbor, MI 48105
Ph: (734)622-6000

Fax: (734)622-6362
URL: http://www.flintgrp.com/index.html
Scope: Printing inks, inkjet inks, pigments, polymers, coatings, solvents, resins. **Services:** Research; SDI; Library not open to the public. **Holdings:** 2100 books; 27 titles on microfiche; 350 audiocassettes and videocassettes. **Subscriptions:** 90 journals and other serials; 5 newspapers.

16449 ■ Graphic Communications World Library
PO Box 1126
Port Orchard, WA 98366
Ph: (360)769-5417
Fax: (360)769-5622
URL: http://www.quoinpublishing.com
Contact: William Esler, President
Scope: Printing and graphic communications technology. **Services:** Library open to subscribers. **Founded:** 1968. **Holdings:** Figures not available. **Subscriptions:** 150 journals and other serials.

RESEARCH CENTERS

16450 ■ Gravure Association of America (GAA)
PO Box 25617
Rochester, NY 14625
Ph: (201)523-6042
Fax: (201)523-6048
Co. E-mail: bmartin@gaa.org
URL: http://www.gaa.org
Contact: Bill Martin, President
Founded: 1947. **Publications:** *Gravure* (Quarterly). **Educational Activities:** GAA Conferences and seminars; GAA Annual Convention, in April. **Awards:** GAA Grants and scholarships. **Telecommunication Services:** gaa@gaa.org.

START-UP INFORMATION

16451 ■ How to Open and Operate a Financially Successful Private Investigation Business: With Companion CD-ROM
Pub: Atlantic Publishing Company
Released: December 1, 2010. **Price:** $39.95. **Description:** With a massive upside and potential for growth the private investigation sector is growing. The book will teach everything needed to know about working in the private investigation field, starting with the basics of what you can expect and what preconceptions that may just be Hollywood. Information is given to help choose a niche of investigation and hot to start thinking in the abstract, questioning everything but recognizing facts for what they are, as well as the differences between a private investigator and a police officer.

ASSOCIATIONS AND OTHER ORGANIZATIONS

16452 ■ Council of International Investigators (CII)
2150 N 107th St., Ste. 205
Seattle, WA 98133-9009
Ph: (206)361-8869
Free: 888-759-8884
Fax: (206)367-8777
Co. E-mail: office@cii2.org
URL: http://www.cii2.org
Contact: Roy Whitehouse, Chairman
Description: Represents licensed and accredited professional private investigators and detectives in 28 countries. Conducts seminars on investigation, security work, criminology and lie detection. **Founded:** 1955. **Publications:** *International Councilor* (Bimonthly). **Awards:** International Investigator of the Year (Annual); Malcolm W. Thomson Memorial Medal (Annual); Meritorious Service Award (Annual).

16453 ■ International Foundation for Protection Officers (IFPO)
PO Box 771329
Naples, FL 34107-1329
Ph: (239)430-0534
Fax: (239)430-0533
Co. E-mail: adminifpo@earthlink.net
URL: http://www.ifpo.org
Contact: Sandi Davies, Executive Director
Description: Seeks to provide for the education, training, and certification of protection officers worldwide. Maintains and improves standards of excellence and establish ethical standards within the industry. Improves the public perception of protection officers. Interacts with colleges, universities, and other post-secondary educational institutions to facilitate education and certification; conducts research. Maintains Certified Protections Officer program, that provides professional designation and consists of training in patrols, report writing, crime scenes, interviewing, investigations, public relations, stress management, physical security, VIP protection, and first aid. **Founded:** 1988. **Publications:** *Business Crime Prevention; Protection Officer News* (Quarterly); *Protection Officer Survival; Careers in Security--2nd Edition; Protection Officer Guidebook.*

16454 ■ ION Inc.—Investigators Anywhere Resource Line
4548 Jones Rd.
Oak Harbor, WA 98277
Ph: (360)279-8343
Free: 800-338-3463
Fax: (480)730-8103
Co. E-mail: webreq@ioninc.com
URL: http://www.ioninc.com
Contact: Leroy E. Cook, President
URL(s): www.investigatorsanywhere.com. **Description:** Private investigators, insurance claims investigators, information vendors, and journalists. Provides international referral service for hiring. **Scope:** Offers a referral and screening service known as the Investigators; Provides services for human resources and risk management departments. Industries served: legal, insurance, corporate security, quality control, human resources and government. **Founded:** 1987. **Publications:** "Email Dangers And Pitfalls To Be Aware Of"; "Will Private Investigation Survive?"; "Amazing Feats and Gadgets"; "A License to Learn"; "Being A Professional PI"; "Brain Surgery by Appointment"; "Clients: Who and What are they?"; "Investigators Investigating Investigators"; "Stan Comstock's Million Dollar Investigative Service"; "Celebrating Investigation"; "Bizarre Job Description for a Private Investigator"; "Sales and the Art of Private Investigation"; "Telephone Technique"; "The K.I.S.S. Online Glossary"; "The Truth About Your Sleuth"; "The Real HP Culprits"; "Private Investigation and the Good Life". **Educational Activities:** ION Retreat (Periodic).

16455 ■ National Association of Investigative Specialists (NAIS)
PO Box 82148
Austin, TX 78708
Ph: (512)719-3595
Fax: (512)719-3594
Co. E-mail: rthomas007@aol.com
URL: http://www.pimall.com/nais/dir.menu.html
Contact: Ralph D. Thomas, Director
URL(s): www.pimall.com/nais. **Description:** Private investigators, automobile repossessors, bounty hunters, and law enforcement officers. Promotes professionalism and provides for information exchange among private investigators. Lobbies for investigative regulations. Offers training programs and issues certificates of completion. Sponsors charitable programs; compiles statistics; maintains speakers' bureau and placement service. Operates Investigators' Hall of Fame of Private Investigators. Offers seminars on cassette tape. **Founded:** 1984. **Publications:** *Physical Surveillance Training Manual* (Annual); *PI Bites; PI Daily* (Daily); *Private Investigator's Catalog* (Bimonthly); *Private Investigator's Connection* (Bimonthly); *Investigator's Information Access Directory* (Annual); *How to Find Anyone Anywhere: Secret Sources and Techniques for Locating Missing Persons* (Annual); *Investigator's International All-in-One Directory* (Annual). **Educational Activities:** PI Super Conference (Annual). **Telecommunication Services:** joseph@cibir.net.

16456 ■ National Association of Legal Investigators (NALI)
235 N Pine St.
Lansing, MI 48933-1021
Ph: (517)702-9835
Free: 866-520-6254
Fax: (517)372-1501
Co. E-mail: trcox@lonewolfgroup.com
URL: http://www.nalionline.org
Contact: Terry R. Cox, Director
Description: Legal investigators, both independent and law firm staff, who specialize in investigation of personal injury matters for the plaintiff and criminal defense. Promotes professionalization of the legal investigator, accomplished by seminars and a professional certification program. Provides nationwide network of contact among members. Compiles statistics. **Founded:** 1967. **Awards:** Editor/Publisher Award (Annual); Editor-Publisher Award.

16457 ■ National Association of Professional Background Screeners (NAPBS)
12100 Sunset Hills Rd., Ste. 130
Reston, VA 20190
Ph: (703)234-4066
Free: 888-686-2727
Fax: (703)435-4390
Co. E-mail: info@napbs.com
URL: http://www.napbs.com
Contact: Carol Wynne, Executive Director
Description: Represents the interests of companies offering employment and background screening. Promotes ethical business practices. Fosters awareness of issues related to consumer protection and privacy rights. Maintains the standard of the background screening industry. **Founded:** 2003. **Educational Activities:** National Association of Professional Background Screeners Meeting (Annual).

16458 ■ National Council of Investigation and Security Services (NCISS)
7501 Sparrows Point Blvd.
Baltimore, MD 21219-1927
Free: 800-445-8408
Fax: (410)388-9746
Co. E-mail: nciss@comcast.net
URL: http://www.nciss.org
Contact: Maria Landry, President
Description: Monitors national and state legislative and regulatory activities. Develops and encourages the practice of high standards of personal and professional conduct. Acquires, preserves, and disseminates data and valuable information; promotes the purpose of investigation and guard companies. Provides information about state legislation and regulatory activities that could have an impact on a particular firm or on the industry in general; acts as spokesman for the industry before legislative and regulatory bodies at both federal and state levels. **Founded:** 1975. **Publications:** *NCISS Report* (Quarterly). **Awards:** Wayne Wonder Award (Annual); John J. Duffy Award (Annual).

16459 ■ Nine Lives Associates (NLA)
Executive Protection Institute
16 Penn Pl., Ste. 1570
New York, NY 10001
Ph: (212)268-4555
Fax: (212)563-4783
Co. E-mail: info@personalprotection.com
URL: http://www.personalprotection.com/nla.cfm
Contact: Dr. Jerry Heying, President
Description: Law enforcement, correctional, military, and security professionals who have been granted Personal Protection Specialist Certification through completion of the protective services program offered by the Executive Protection Institute; conducts research; EPI programs emphasize personal survival skills and techniques for the protection of others. Provides professional recognition for qualified individuals engaged in executive protection assignments. Maintains placement service. Operates speakers' bureau; compiles statistics. **Scope:** law enforcement and security subjects. **Founded:** 1978. **Subscriptions:** 1000. **Educational Activities:** Nine Lives Associates Conference (Annual). **Awards:** N.L.A. Achievement Award (Annual).

16460 ■ Society of Professional Investigators (SPI)
c/o David Roberts, Treas.
PO Box 1087
Bellmore, NY 11710
Ph: (646)584-9081
Fax: (212)349-0338
URL: http://spionline.info
Contact: Bruce Sackman, President
Description: Persons with at least 5 years' investigative experience for an official federal, state, or local government agency or for a quasi-official agency formed for law enforcement or related activities. Seeks to advance knowledge of the science and technology of professional investigation, law enforcement, and police science; maintains high standards and ethics; promotes efficiency of investigators in the services they perform. **Scope:** law enforcement. **Founded:** 1955. **Subscriptions:** books. **Publications:** SPI Newsletter (8/year). **Awards:** Irwin R. Rutman Award (Annual).

DIRECTORIES OF EDUCATIONAL PROGRAMS

16461 ■ Directory of Private Accredited Career Schools and Colleges of Technology
Pub: Accrediting Commission of Career Schools and Colleges of Technology
Contact: Michale S. McComis, Executive Director
Released: On web page. **Price:** Free. **Description:** Covers 3900 accredited post-secondary programs that provide training programs in business, trade, and technical fields, including various small business endeavors. Entries offer school name, address, phone, description of courses, job placement assistance, and requirements for admission. Arrangement is alphabetical.

REFERENCE WORKS

16462 ■ American Polygraph Association--Member Directory
Pub: American Polygraph Association
Contact: Pam Shaw, President
URL(s): www.polygraph.org. **Ed:** Stuart Senter. **Price:** $125, Individuals; $150, Other countries. **Covers:** Approximately 2,500 member individuals and companies involved the polygraph field. **Arrangement:** Geographical.

16463 ■ Nine Lives Associates--Membership Directory
Pub: Executive Protection Institute
Contact: Dr. H. H. A. Cooper, President
URL(s): www.personalprotection.com. **Ed:** Dr. Richard W. Kobetz. **Released:** Annual; March. **Covers:** 2,000 individuals certified as personal protection specialists through completion of a training program. **Entries include:** Specialist name and title, address, phone, company name. **Arrangement:** Classified by class completed.

STATISTICAL SOURCES

16464 ■ RMA Annual Statement Studies
Pub: Risk Management Association
Contact: Kevin M. Blakey, President
Released: Annual. **Price:** $175.00 2006-07 edition, $105.00. **Description:** Contains composite balance sheets and income statements for more than 360 industries, including the accounting, auditing, and bookkeeping industries. Also contains five years of comparative historical data for discerning trends. Includes 16 commonly used ratios, computed for most of the size groupings for nearly every industry.

TRADE PERIODICALS

16465 ■ American Polygraph Association Newsletter
Pub: American Polygraph Association
Contact: Pam Shaw, President
Ed: Donald J. Krapohl, Editor, dkrapohl@aol.com. **Released:** Bimonthly. **Price:** $80, nonmembers in U.S.; $100, elsewhere. **Description:** Reviews developments in polygraph techniques and instruments, police and private uses of the polygraph, and pertinent law and legislation. Covers activities of state, regional, and foreign polygraph associations. Recurring features include news of research, case studies, editorials, and notices of upcoming seminars.

16466 ■ Criminal Justice Magazine
Pub: American Bar Association
Contact: Carolyn Lamm, President
URL(s): www.abanet.org/crimjust/cjmag/home.html. **Ed:** MaryAnn Dadisman. **Released:** Quarterly **Price:** $48, Individuals non-member U.S.; $57, Individuals non-member outside U.S.; $15.95, Individuals + shipping and handling.

16467 ■ Polygraph Update
Pub: Lafayette Instrument Company Inc.
Contact: Roger McClellan, President
E-mail: rbmc@lafayetteinstrument.com
Ed: Christopher Fausett, Editor. **Released:** Annual. **Price:** Free. **Description:** Provides information on research studies, new products, and usage opportunities of polygraph machines.

TRADE SHOWS AND CONVENTIONS

16468 ■ ISC Chicago
Reed Exhibitions North American Headquarters
383 Main Ave.
Norwalk, CT 06851
Ph: (203)840-4800
Fax: (203)840-5805
Co. E-mail: inquiry@reedexpo.com
URL: http://www.reedexpo.com
URL(s): isc.reedexpo.com. **Frequency:** Biennial. **Audience:** Security equipment dealers and installers, corporate, industrial and institutional security managers and directors. **Principal Exhibits:** Residential, commercial, industrial and institutional security equipment, systems and services. **Telecommunication Services:** inquiry@isc.reedexpo.com.

CONSULTANTS

16469 ■ Lenow International Inc.
1503 Union Ave., Ste. 210
Memphis, TN 38173
Ph: (901)726-0735
Fax: (901)725-4079
URL: http://www.lenowinternational.com
Contact: Nate Lenow, Jr., President
E-mail: nate@lenowinternational.com
Scope: Acts as a consultant for investigative strategies to resolve civil or criminal investigations. Conducts surveys or evaluations to prevent crime directed toward business, in particular crime involving fraudulent activity. Recommends security procedures or equipment to aid loss prevention by business. Available to serve as expert witness in forensic security and fraud examination. Referral source for investigative agencies. Industries served: Corporate

security departments, private investigative agencies, small business, and government agencies. **Founded:** 1977. **Publications:** "Competitive Intelligence," Law Enforcement Quarterly. **Seminars:** Automate your reports with software, Tennessee Association of Investigators, May, 2000; Use of Computer as an Investigative Tool; Criminal Investigation.

16470 ■ National Training Center of Polygraph Science
200 W 57th St., Ste. 1400
New York, NY 10019-3211
Ph: (212)755-5241
Free: 800-643-6597
Fax: (973)838-8661
Contact: Richard O. Arther, Director
Scope: Provides polygraph training and conducts pre employment seminars. Industries served: law enforcement and business firms of all types, as well as government agencies. **Founded:** 1958.

16471 ■ Navigator Research Group Inc.
310 Blount St., Ste. 221
Tallahassee, FL 32317
Ph: (850)878-5437
Free: 866-620-4636
Fax: (850)878-1131
Co. E-mail: info@navigatorresearchgroup.com
URL: http://www.navigatorresearchgroup.com
Contact: Lorena N. Ratcliff, Manager
Scope: Licensed company that conducts person and background checks. Industries served include private investigators, insurance companies and adjustors, law firms and other corporations. The firm serves the state of Florida, but has a network of correspondents nationwide and access to various databases which provides coverage across the country, private investigation agency specializing in locating missing. **Founded:** 1986. **Telecommunication Services:** support@navigatorresearchgroup.com; orders@navigatorresearchgroup.com.

FRANCHISES AND BUSINESS OPPORTUNITIES

16472 ■ Case In Point
PO Box 1286
Londonderry, NH 03053-1286
Free: 800-370-2116
Fax: (800)397-2963
Description: Investigation services. **No. of Franchise Units:** 2. **No. of Company-Owned Units:** 4. **Founded:** 1992.. **Franchised:** 2002. **Equity Capital Needed:** $40,000. **Franchise Fee:** $10,000. **Royalty Fee:** 6%. **Training:** Offers 2 weeks at headquarters, 1 week at franchisees location and ongoing support.

16473 ■ L & W Investigations, Inc.
Lyons & Wolivar Co.
3140 Red Hill Ave., Ste. 270
Costa Mesa, CA 92627
Ph: (714)979-0707
Fax: (714)979-0708
Description: Private investigations, specializing in all types of insurance fraud. **No. of Franchise Units:** 35. **No. of Company-Owned Units:** 3. **Equity Capital Needed:** $75,000. **Franchise Fee:** $70,000-$200,000. **Financial Assistance:** Yes. **Training:** Yes.

LIBRARIES

16474 ■ National Training Center of Polygraph Science Library
200 W. 57th St., Ste. 1400
New York, NY 10019-3211
Ph: (212)755-5241
Fax: (212)755-5242
Contact: Richard O. Arther, School Administrator
Scope: Polygraphs, lie detection, interrogation. **Services:** Library not open to the public. **Founded:** 1958. **Holdings:** 800 books.

16475 ■ Thomas Investigative Publications Library
PO Box 82148
Austin, TX 78708
Ph: (512)719-3595

Fax: (512)719-3594
Co. E-mail: rthomas007@aol.com
URL: http://www.pimall.com/nais
Contact: Ralph Thomas, President
Scope: Private investigations, bail enforcement, information brokering, law enforcement. **Services:** Library open to the public. **Founded:** 1986. **Holdings:** 200 books. **Telecommunication Services:** naisbiz@aol.com.

RESEARCH CENTERS

16476 ■ Michigan State University - American Polygraph Association Credibility Assessment Research Center
560 Baker Hall
East Lansing, MI 48824
Ph: (803)751-9196
Fax: (803)751-9178
Co. E-mail: horvath@msu.edu
Contact: Dr. Frank Horvath, Director
Founded: 1982.

ASSOCIATIONS AND OTHER ORGANIZATIONS

16477 ■ Private Label Manufacturers Association (PLMA)
630 3rd Ave.
New York, NY 10017
Ph: (212)972-3131
Fax: (212)983-1382
Co. E-mail: info@plma.com
URL: http://plma.com
Contact: Mr. Brian Sharoff, President

URL(s): www.plma.com. **Description:** Membership consists of manufacturers, brokers, suppliers, and consultants. Educates consumers on the quality and value of private label or store brand products; promotes private label industry. Compiles statistics; conducts research programs for members. **Founded:** 1979. **Publications:** *PLMA Scanner* (Quarterly). **Educational Activities:** Domestic Trade Show (Annual); International Trade Show (Annual); Private Label Trade Show. **Awards:** Salute to Excellence.

REFERENCE WORKS

16478 ■ Private Label Directory
Pub: E.W. Williams Publications Co.
Contact: Andrew Williams, President
E-mail: awilliams@ewwpi.com

URL(s): www.williamspublications.comwww.pldirectory.com. **Released:** Annual; July. **Price:** $75, U.S. and Canada; $125, Elsewhere; $75, Canada. **Covers:** Over 1,400 suppliers of food, health and beauty care, household supplies, general merchandise and service and supplies, with private and generic labels; international coverage. **Entries include:** Company name, address, phone, fax, e-mail, internet, names and titles of key personnel, products. **Arrangement:** Alphabetical. **Indexes:** Product, geographical.

TRADE PERIODICALS

16479 ■ Min's b2b
Pub: Phillips Business Information Inc. Access Intelligence L.L.C.
Contact: Heather Farley, President
E-mail: hfarley@accessintel.com

Ed: Jeremy Greenfield, Editor. **Released:** Biweekly. **Description:** Provides news on business relations and strategies and tactics to increase online publishing and new media business.

FRANCHISES AND BUSINESS OPPORTUNITIES

16480 ■ Cap-It International Inc.
4954 275th St.
Langley, BC, Canada V4W 0A3
Ph: (604)857-1211
Fax: (604)857-1255
URL: http://www.cap-it.com
Description: Franchise offers retailing and installation of canopies and accessories for light trucks, sport utility vehicles, vans and cars. **No. of Franchise Units:** 22. **Founded:** 1973.. **Franchised:** 1990. **Equity Capital Needed:** $150,00 and up. **Franchise Fee:** $49,000. **Training:** Provides 6 weeks of training.

16481 ■ Cash Converters Canada
275 Renfrew Dr., Unit 104
Markham, ON, Canada L3R 0N9
Ph: (905)480-2400
URL: http://www.cashconverters.ca
Description: Buying and selling of quality second-hand goods, which include jewelry, televisions, stereos, tools, electrical goods etc. are made possible by this international retailer. **No. of Franchise Units:** 13. **No. of Company-Owned Units:** 64. **Founded:** 1995.. **Franchised:** 1989. **Equity Capital Needed:** $160,000-$300,000. **Franchise Fee:** $35,000. **Training:** Initial and ongong training.

START-UP INFORMATION

16482 ■ *How to Start a Home-Based Professional Organizing Business*
Pub: Globe Pequot Press
Ed: Dawn Noble. **Released:** March 2007. **Price:** $18.95. **Description:** Tips for starting a home-based professional organizing business are presented.

REFERENCE WORKS

16483 ■ *"6 Worth the Price Fix-Ups" in Realtor Magazine (Vol. 44, April-May 2011, No. 44, pp. 23)*
Pub: Realtor Magazine
Description: Advice on how realtors could increase a home's resale value through do-it-yourself projects is given. Removal of personal items and clutter is recommended, along with rearrangement of furniture. A clutter consultant could also be used.

16484 ■ *"How to Declutter Your Life Closet Cleanup: Putting a Lid on Clutter" in Atlanta Journal-Constitution (May 1, 2011)*
Pub: Atlanta Journal-Constitution
Ed: Felicia Feaster. **Description:** The annual Closets and Home Organization Convention and Expo spotlights new products and services designed to help people get organized at home or the workplace. The organization sector is holding steady despite the recession and is expected to expand into garage organization.

16485 ■ *"Impressive Numbers: Companies Experience Substantial Increases in Dollars, Employment" in Hispanic Business (July-August 2007)*
Pub: Hispanic Business
Ed: Derek Reveron. **Description:** Profiles of five fastest growing Hispanic companies reporting increases in revenue and employment include Brightstar, distributor of wireless products; Greenway Ford Inc., a car dealership; Fred Loya Insurance, auto insurance carrier; and Group O, packaging company; and Diverse Staffing, Inc., an employment and staffing firm.

16486 ■ *"Integrating Business Core Knowledge through Upper Division Report Composition" in Business Communication Quarterly (December 2007)*
Pub: SAGE Publications USA
Contact: Blaise R. Simqu, President
Ed: Joy Roach, Daniel Tracy, Kay Durden. **Description:** An assignment that integrates subjects and encourages the use of business communication report-writing skills is presented. This assignment is designed to complement business school curricula and help develop critical thinking and organizational skills.

16487 ■ *"Make It Easier On Yourself" in Women In Business (Vol. 63, Fall 2011, No. 3, pp. 28)*
Pub: American Business Women's Association
Ed: Maureen Sullivan. **Description:** Getting and staying organized helps avoid wasting time on deciding which priorities to address first. Taking help and avoiding hoarding are examples of how to become organized. The use of technology for organizing priorities is also explained.

16488 ■ *"Monday Organizer: Clean and De-Clutter in 15 Minutes" in Tulsa World (June 13, 2011)*
Pub: McClatchy Company
Ed: Kim Brown. **Description:** New weekly series highlights practical tips and helpful ideas to simply life by taking 15 minutes to de-clutter your home or office. Paper clutter can be eliminated in 15 minutes by gathering up newspapers and magazines to recycle; sort mail as soon as you receive it and throw away any junk mail at that time. If watching TV, use commercial time to accomplish small tasks.

16489 ■ *"StorageByMail Lets Customers Ship Away Their Clutter" in Inc. (Vol. 33, April 2011, No. 3, pp. 92)*
Pub: Inc. Magazine
Ed: Issie Lapowsky. **Description:** StorageByMail allows people to put items into storage by mailing them to the company. The firm charges a monthly fee, customers describe contents of each box, and ship to the Jersey City facility using a preprinted label. StorageByMail pays the $25 shipment charge.

FRANCHISES AND BUSINESS OPPORTUNITIES

16490 ■ California Closet Company
1000 4th St., Ste. 800
San Rafael, CA 94901
Ph: (415)256-8500
Free: 800-241-3222
Fax: (415)256-8501
Co. E-mail: franchising@calclosets.com
URL: http://www.californiaclosets.com
Description: Custom closet design, manufacture, and installation. **No. of Franchise Units:** 88. **Founded:** 1978.. **Franchised:** 1982. **Equity Capital Needed:** $127,500-$377,000 total investment. **Franchise Fee:** $40,000. **Royalty Fee:** 6%. **Financial Assistance:** Third party financing available. **Training:** Includes training at headquarters, franchisee's location and ongoing support.

16491 ■ Closet Factory
12800 S Broadway
Los Angeles, CA 90061
Ph: (310)715-1000
Fax: (310)516-8065
Description: Design, sell, manufacture, and install custom closets. **No. of Franchise Units:** 82. **No. of Company-Owned Units:** 4. **Founded:** 1983.. **Franchised:** 1986. **Equity Capital Needed:** Total investment approximately $325,000-$400,000, franchise fee included; Liquidity $100,000 plus. **Franchise Fee:** $64,500. **Financial Assistance:** Yes. **Training:** Yes.

16492 ■ Closets by Design Franchising
11145 Knott Ave., Ste. A
Cypress, CA 90630
Ph: (714)890-5860
Free: 800-377-5737
Fax: (714)901-0424
URL: http://www.closets-by-design.com
Description: Closets by design franchising custom closets, garage organizers, entertainment centers and shelving for home, offices and garages. **No. of Franchise Units:** 30. **No. of Company-Owned Units:** 6. **Founded:** 1982.. **Franchised:** 1998. **Equity Capital Needed:** $124,900-$278,400. **Franchise Fee:** $36,900. **Royalty Fee:** 6%. **Financial Assistance:** Limited third party financing available. **Training:** Provides 3 weeks at headquarters, and additional 3 weeks at franchisee's location.

16493 ■ Closets & Storage Concepts
1000 White Horse Rd., Ste. 404
Voorhees, NJ 08043
Ph: (856)627-5700
Fax: (856)627-7447
Description: Custom closet and storage systems. **No. of Franchise Units:** 10. **No. of Company-Owned Units:** 3. **Founded:** 1987.. **Franchised:** 2000. **Equity Capital Needed:** $10,000-$200,000. **Franchise Fee:** $5,000-$38,500. **Financial Assistance:** Yes. **Training:** Yes.

16494 ■ Floorguard
340 Marshall Ave., Unit 101
Aurora, IL 60506
Ph: (813)935-5087
Free: 888-694-2724
Fax: (813)425-5799
Co. E-mail: info@floorguard.com
Description: Garage flooring and storage systems. **No. of Franchise Units:** 1. **No. of Company-Owned Units:** 1. **Founded:** 1988.. **Franchised:** 2006. **Equity Capital Needed:** $162,000-$234,000. **Franchise Fee:** $40,000. **Training:** Yes.

16495 ■ Garagetek
5 Aerial Way, Ste. 200
Syosset, NY 11791
Ph: (516)621-4300
Fax: (516)992-8600
Co. E-mail: SBarrett@GarageTek.com
URL: http://www.GarageTek.com
Description: Franchise of construction, remodeling, bath and closet services. **No. of Franchise Units:** 55. **No. of Company-Owned Units:** 2. **Founded:** 2000.. **Franchised:** 2001. **Equity Capital Needed:** $250,000. **Franchise Fee:** $50,000. **Training:** Provides 2 weeks at corporate and ongoing field support.

16496 ■ Granite Transformations
RockSolid Granit USA Inc.
10360 USA Today Way
Miramar, FL 33025
Ph: (954)435-5538
Free: 866-685-5300
Fax: (954)435-5579
Co. E-mail: info@granittransformations.com
URL: http://www.granitetransformations.com
Description: Construction, remodeling, and bath and closets services. **No. of Franchise Units:** 79. **No. of Company-Owned Units:** 1. **Founded:** 2001.. **Fran-**

chised: 2001. **Equity Capital Needed:** $127,000-$350,000. **Franchise Fee:** $25,000-$75,000. **Training:** Training program consists of operations, installations, and sales training. Each training module is supported with training material. Training facility is an actual working location allowing trainees to evaluate, test, and see results. Grand opening supported by sales manager onsite and ongoing support.

16497 ■ HouseWall Garage System
8100 W 30th Ct.
Hialeah, FL 33018
Ph: (305)817-9881
Fax: (305)826-1882

Description: Garage organization systems. **No. of Franchise Units:** 7. **No. of Company-Owned Units:** 1. **Founded:** 2002.. **Franchised:** 2006. **Equity Capital Needed:** $136,000-$168,000. **Franchise Fee:** $15,000. **Royalty Fee:** 6-5.5%. **Training:** Offers 1 week at headquarters and ongoing support.

16498 ■ Kwik Kloset
607A Old Stouffville Rd.
Uxbridge, ON, Canada L9P 1R4
Ph: (905)852-2108
Fax: (866)973-8510
Co. E-mail: franchiseinfo@kwikkloset.com
URL: http://www.kwikkloset.com

Description: Kwik Kloset has an exciting new approach to the burgeoning home organization business. Bringing together our lowoverhead business model, an innovative mobile closet installation vehicle, and our one point of contact "Spaceman" concept, only Kwik Kloset can offer very cost-effective, same-day closet design and installation services. Kwik Kloset has signed a "Sell, furnish & install" contract with The Home Depot Canada, and is now active in 45 stores. Kwik Kloset is seeking both owner/operator franchisees, and larger area master franchisees across Canada, the USA and possibly international. **No. of Franchise Units:** 8. **No. of Company-Owned Units:** 2. **Founded:** 2003.. **Franchised:** 2005. **Equity Capital Needed:** $100,000 investment required' $25,000 start-up capital. **Franchise Fee:** $75,000. **Training:** Spaceman Training Program includes sales, design, and installation.

16499 ■ Parties By Terrye Inc.
12115 Long Lake Dr.
Owings Mills, MD 21117
Ph: (410)581-1080
Fax: (410)902-7171

Description: Event planning for social & corporate events. **No. of Company-Owned Units:** 1. **Founded:** 1983.. **Franchised:** 2006. **Equity Capital Needed:** $14,500-$59,300. **Franchise Fee:** $20,000. **Training:** Yes.

Property Management

START-UP INFORMATION

16500 ■ *"Rehab Will Turn Hospital Into Incubator"* in *The Business Journal-Serving Metropolitan Kansas City* (Vol. 26, September 12, 2008)

Pub: American City Business Journals, Inc.

Ed: Rob Roberts. **Description:** Independence Regional Health Center will be purchased by CEAH Realtors and be converted into the Independence Regional Entrepreneurial Center, a business incubator that will house startups and other tenants. Other details about the planned entrepreneurial center are provided.

ASSOCIATIONS AND OTHER ORGANIZATIONS

16501 ■ **Institute of Real Estate Management (IREM)**
430 N Michigan Ave.
Chicago, IL 60611
Ph: (312)329-6000
Free: 800-837-0706
Fax: (800)338-4736
Co. E-mail: custserv@irem.org
URL: http://www.irem.org
Contact: James A. Evans, President

Description: Professional organization of real property and asset managers. Awards professional designation Certified Property Manager (CPM) to qualifying individuals, Accredited Management Organization (AMO) to qualifying management firms and also awards Accredited Residential Manager (ARM) accreditation to qualifying individuals who are primarily residential site managers. Monitors legislation affecting real estate management. Offers management courses and seminars; conducts research and educational programs, publishes books and reports; maintains formal code of ethics; compiles statistics; maintains employment Website for real estate management industry. **Founded:** 1933. **Publications:** *Apartment Building Income-Expense Analysis*. **Educational Activities:** Leadership and Legislative Summit (Annual). **Awards:** Academy of Authors; Diversity Outreach Scholarship; Donald M. Furbush Scholarship (Annual); J. Wallace Paletou Award (Annual); Lloyd D. Hanford Sr. Distinguished Faculty Award; Louise L. and Y. T. Lum Award; Paul H. Rittle, Sr. Scholarship; Lloyd D. Hanford Sr. Distinguished Faculty Award (Annual); Louise L. and Y.T. Lum Award (Annual); Paul H. Rittle Sr. Memorial Scholarship Award (Quarterly); George M. Brooker Collegiate Scholarships for Minorities; Donald M. Furbush Professional Development Grants; Paul H. Rittle Sr. Professional Development Grants.

16502 ■ **International Facility Management Association (IFMA)**
1 E Greenway Plz., Ste. 1100
Houston, TX 77046-0104
Ph: (713)623-4362

Fax: (713)623-6124
Co. E-mail: ifma@ifma.org
URL: http://www.ifma.org
Contact: Kathy O. Roper, Chairwoman

Description: Facility managers worldwide representing all types of organizations including banks, insurance companies, hospitals, colleges and universities, utility companies, electronic equipment manufacturers, petroleum companies, museums, auditoriums and federal, state, provincial and local governments. Purposes are to enhance the professional goals of persons involved or interested in the field of facility management (the planning, designing and managing of workplaces); to cultivate cooperation, foster understanding and create interest among firms, individuals and other associations and professions as they may affect facility management; to engage in the interchange of views regarding legislation, regulation and procedures that affect facility management. Offers job placement assistance; sponsors academic research; certifies facility managers; compiles statistics; sells books. Conducts educational and research programs. **Scope:** facility management, workplace management, real estate, ergonomics, outsourcing, telecommuting. **Founded:** 1980. **Subscriptions:** 500 books periodicals. **Publications:** *Annual Conference Proceedings* (Annual); *Operations and Maintenance Benchmarks Survey*. **Educational Activities:** World Workplace (Periodic); World Workplace - Europe (Annual). **Awards:** Chapter of the Year Award; Council of the Year Award; IFMA Award of Excellence (Annual); IFMA Fellows; Chapter Award for Excellence in Membership Marketing; Chapter Award for Excellence in Newsletter Publishing; Student Chapter of the Year Award.

16503 ■ **National Property Management Association (NPMA)**
28100 US Hwy. 19 N, Ste. 400
Clearwater, FL 33761
Ph: (727)736-3788
Fax: (727)736-6707
Co. E-mail: hq@npma.org
URL: http://www.npma.org
Contact: Jefferson Lab, President

Description: Aims to build leadership by educating, training and promoting standards of competency and ethical behavior in the asset management of personal property. Serves property professionals throughout the United States; members represent companies and organizations in both the public and private sectors, including scientific laboratories, universities, hospitals, public school systems, and local, state and federal government agencies. **Scope:** asset and government property management. **Founded:** 1970. **Subscriptions:** 6 archival material articles books papers periodicals reports. **Publications:** *NPMA Survey; Property Manual*. **Awards:** Chapter of the Year (Annual); Federal Property Person of the Year (Annual); Jack Griffiths Property Person of the Year.

16504 ■ **Property Management Association (PMA)**
7508 Wisconsin Ave., 4th Fl.
Bethesda, MD 20814
Ph: (301)657-9200

Fax: (301)907-9326
Co. E-mail: info@pma-dc.org
URL: http://www.pma-dc.org
Contact: Zakiya Kainu, President

Description: Property management professionals who own and operate multifamily residential, commercial, retail, industrial and other income-producing properties and firms that provide goods and services used in real property management. Works to enhance the interests and welfare of property owners, managers, supervisory employees and contractors involved in the management of multifamily residential and commercial property. Provides education and a forum for exchange of ideas on efficient methods of operation and progressive policies of management. **Founded:** 1952. **Publications:** *Property Management Association--Bulletin* (Monthly).

16505 ■ **Vacation Rental Managers Association (VRMA)**
9100 Purdue Rd., Ste. 200
Indianapolis, IN 46268
Ph: (317)454-8315
Fax: (317)454-8316
Co. E-mail: vrma@vrma.com
URL: http://www.vrma.com
Contact: Steve Ingram, Executive Director

Description: Companies that rent and manage vacation properties, resorts, townhomes and condominiums on a short-term basis. Promotes the interests of the vacation rental industry to the public. **Founded:** 1985.

REFERENCE WORKS

16506 ■ *"1Q Office Vacancies Mainly Up; Class A Space Bucks Trend, Falls"* in *Crain's Detroit Business* (Vol. 24, April 14, 2008, No. 15)

Pub: Crain Communications, Inc.

Ed: Daniel Duggan. **Description:** Although more office space became vacant in the first quarter, Class A space went in the opposite direction with several local businesses are moving from less-desirable to more desirable areas.

16507 ■ *"Affordable Again"* in *The Business Journal-Serving Greater Tampa Bay* (Vol. 28, July 18, 2008, No. 30, pp. 1)

Pub: American City Business Journals, Inc.

Ed: Janet Leiser. **Description:** Rental rates for office space in the Tampa Bay area has dropped to $21.68 a foot, after demand for the second quarter of 2008 has remained low. Commercial real estate experts say that the industry can easily rebound from what is believed to be the weakest demand in 20 years. Other views, information and statistics on real estate demand and prices in Tampa Bay are, are presented.

16508 ■ *"Apartment Ambitions"* in *The Business Journal-Portland* (Vol. 25, August 8, 2008, No. 22, pp. 1)

Pub: American City Business Journals, Inc.

Ed: Wendy Culverwell. **Description:** Unico Properties LLC's Asa FlatsLofts is one of the first of eight high-end apartment projects planned for Portland which will add a total of 2,130 new units to the Pearl District, South Waterfront, and downtown Portland. These apartments charge costs more than $1,600 or more per month over the average rent.

16509 ■ *"Apartment Market Down, Not Out"* **in Crain's Detroit Business (Vol. 24, October 6, 2008, No. 40, pp. 9)**
Pub: Crain Communications, Inc.
Ed: Daniel Duggan. **Description:** Detroit's apartment market is considered to have some of the strongest fundamentals of any apartment market in the country with relatively low vacancy rates and a relatively low supply of new units compared with demand. Investors continue to show interest in the buildings but the national lending market is making it difficult to invest in the city.

16510 ■ *"Aquila HQ Hits the Market"* **in The Business Journal-Serving Metropolitan Kansas City (Vol. 26, July 25, 2008, No. 46, pp. 1)**
Pub: American City Business Journals, Inc.
Ed: Rob Roberts. **Description:** Commercial real estate experts believe that Aquila Inc.'s former headquarters will be hard to rent out. The historic value of the building, being Kansas City's first skyscraper, is not expected to add value to the price of the rent. Other views and information on the building, as well as on Aquila, are presented.

16511 ■ *"Bangles, BMWs Elbow Out Delis and Discount Shops"* **in Crain's New York Business (Vol. 24, January 14, 2008, No. 2, pp. 35)**
Pub: Crain Communications, Inc.
Ed: Wendy Davis. **Description:** Lured by a growing number of affluent residents and high-earning professionals, a number of upscale retailers have opened locations downtown which is driving up rents and forcing out longtime independent merchants.

16512 ■ *"Battelle Given Keys to Group"* **in Business First-Columbus (October 12, 2007, pp. 1)**
Pub: American City Business Journals, Inc.
Ed: Kevin Kemper. **Description:** Battelle Memorial Institute has been contracted by Compete Columbus to manage the organization's daily operations. Compete Columbus was formerly managed by a single executive, David Powell, who resigned in September 2006. Profile of Compete Columbus is included.

16513 ■ *"Block Plans Office Park Along K-10 Corridor"* **in The Business Journal-Serving Metropolitan Kansas City (Vol. 27, October 3, 2008)**
Pub: American City Business Journals, Inc.
Ed: Rob Roberts. **Description:** Kansas City, Missouri-based Block and Co. is planning to build four office buildings at the corner of College Boulevard and Ridgeview Road in Olathe. Features of the planned development are provided. Comments from executives are also presented.

16514 ■ *"Briarcliff Office Building Fills Up Fast"* **in The Business Journal-Serving Metropolitan Kansas City (Vol. 26, Sept. 5, 2008, pp. 1)**
Pub: American City Business Journals, Inc.
Ed: Rob Roberts. **Description:** Prior to its opening the Hilltop Office Building in Kansas City Missouri has attained 80 percent occupancy. FCStone Group Inc.'s plan to move to the building has boosted the facility's occupancy. Description and dimensions of the office building are also provided.

16515 ■ *"Channelside On the Blocks"* **in The Business Journal-Serving Greater Tampa Bay (Vol. 28, August 29, 2008, No. 36, pp. 1)**
Pub: American City Business Journals, Inc.
Ed: Michael Hinman. **Description:** In a bankruptcy auction for The Place, one of the more visible condominium projects at Channelside, the lowest bid is just below $73 a square foot. KeyBank National Association, the Key Developers Group LLC's lender,

leads the auction planned for October 15, 2008. The reason behind the low minimum bid required to participate in the said action is discussed.

16516 ■ *"Children's Hospital to Build in New Berlin"* **in The Business Journal-Milwaukee (Vol. 25, August 1, 2008, No. 45, pp. A1)**
Pub: American City Business Journals, Inc.
Ed: Corrinne Hess. **Description:** Children's Hospital of Wisconsin plans a clinic in the 35-acre medical office park in New Berlin, Wisconsin, owned by Froedtert Memorial Lutheran Hospital and Medical College of Wisconsin Real Estate Ventures LLC. The hospital will be the first major tenant in the park, to be built by Irgens Development Partners LLC.

16517 ■ *"Condominium Sales Fall to a Seven-Year Low"* **in Crain's Chicago Business (Vol. 31, November 10, 2008, No. 45, pp. 2)**
Pub: Crain Communications, Inc.
Ed: Alby Gallun. **Description:** Downtown Chicago condominium market is experiencing the lowest number of sales in years due to the tightening of the mortgage lending market, the Wall Street crisis and the downturn in the economy. The supply of new condos is soaring, the result of the building boom of 2005 and 2006; many developers are finding it difficult to pay off construction loans and fear foreclosure on their properties. Additional information and statistical data related to the downtown condominium market is provided.

16518 ■ *"A Conversation With; Ron Gatner, Jones Lang LaSalle"* **in Crain's Detroit Business (Vol. 24, October 6, 2008, No. 40, pp. 9)**
Description: Interview with Ron Gatner who is a corporate real estate adviser with the real estate company Jones Lang LaSalle as well as the company's executive vice president and part of the tenant advisory team; Gatner speaks about the impact that the Wall Street crisis is having on the commercial real estate market in Detroit.

16519 ■ *"Cool on Chicago Office Properties"* **in Crain's Chicago Business (Vol. 31, March 31, 2008, No. 13, pp. 16)**
Pub: Crain Communications, Inc.
Ed: Eddie Baeb. **Description:** Investors predict values on Chicago office buildings to drop 1.3 percent over the next year.

16520 ■ *"Cornered by Credit; As $1 Billion in Loans Come Due, Will Landlords Find Funds?"* **in Crain's Detroit Business (October 6, 2008)**
Pub: Crain Communications, Inc.
Ed: Daniel Duggan. **Description:** Conduit loans are used by many real estate investors and are normally issued in 7- to 10-year terms with balloon payments due at the end, requiring the full balance to be paid upon maturity. Many building owners may find their properties going into foreclosure as these loans mature next year since these loans cannot be extended like typical loans and the credit crisis along with falling property values is making it more difficult to secure new sources of funding. Possible solutions to this problem are also explored.

16521 ■ *"Detroit Residential Market Slows; Bright Spots Emerge"* **in Crain's Detroit Business (Vol. 24, October 6, 2008, No. 40, pp. 11)**
Pub: Crain Communications, Inc.
Ed: Daniel Duggan. **Description:** Discusses the state of the residential real estate market in Detroit; although condominium projects receive the most attention, deals for single-family homes are taking place in greater numbers due to financing issues. Buyers can purchase a single family home with a 3.5 percent down payment compared to 20 percent for some condo deals because of the number of first-time homebuyer programs under the Federal Housing Administration.

16522 ■ *"Downtown Evens Tenant Ledger"* **in The Business Journal-Serving Metropolitan**

Kansas City (Vol. 26, July 11, 2008, No. 44, pp. 1)
Pub: American City Business Journals, Inc.
Ed: Rob Roberts. **Description:** Financial services company PricewaterhouseCoopers will relocate its office from the Broadway Square building, but it will not leave downtown as it signs a long-term lease for a 27,000 square feet of space in Town Pavilion. Town Pavilion is the biggest multitenant office building in downtown. Downtown's market competitiveness is also examined.

16523 ■ *"East-Side Real Estate Forum Detours To Grand Rapids"* **in Crain's Detroit Business (Vol. 24, October 6, 2008, No. 40, pp. 17)**
Pub: Crain Communications, Inc.
Ed: Daniel Duggan. **Description:** Tom Wackerman was elected chairman of the University of Michigan-Urban Land Institute Real Estate Forum and proposed that the annual conference be held in Grand Rapids due to the brisk economic activity he was finding there; although the idea was initially met with resistance, the plan to introduce East-siders to the West side began receiving more enthusiasm due to the revitalization of the area, which was once considered to have a bleak outlook. Many are hoping to learn the lessons of those who were able to change a negative economic climate into a positive one in which the cooperation of private business and government can work together to accomplish goals.

16524 ■ *"Economy Peddles Rent In This Cycle"* **in The Business Journal-Serving Metropolitan Kansas City (Vol. 26, August 8, 2008, No. 48)**
Pub: American City Business Journals, Inc.
Ed: Ashlee Kieler. **Description:** Rental demand for apartment units in downtown Kansas City, Missouri, is increasing due to the housing crisis, lack of real estate development, and increasing popularity of the downtown area. The downtown area has 7,378 multifamily units as of June 2008, of which 4,114 are rentals.

16525 ■ *"Eminent Domain Fight Looks Imminent"* **in The Business Journal-Serving Metropolitan Kansas City (Vol. 26, August 1, 2008, No. 47)**
Pub: American City Business Journals, Inc.
Ed: Rob Roberts. **Description:** Views and information on the proposed constitutional amendments that will limit the use of eminent domain in Missouri, are presented. The proposals are expected to largely ban the taking of private property for private development. It may be included in a November 4,2008 statewide vote for approval.

16526 ■ *"For Sale: Old Florida Panache"* **in The Business Journal-Serving Greater Tampa Bay (Vol. 28, July 4, 2008, No. 28, pp. 1)**
Pub: American City Business Journals, Inc.
Ed: Jane Meinhardt. **Description:** Linger Lodge, owned by real estate investor and developer Martin Kaplan and Senator Michael Bennett, is now on the market for a sealed bid process facilitated by Levin & Associates. The business partners bought the riverfront property for about $3 million in 2005. Other details on the sale of the property are presented.

16527 ■ *"Grand Letdown"* **in The Business Journal-Milwaukee (Vol. 25, September 12, 2008, No. 51, pp. A1)**
Pub: American City Business Journals, Inc.
Ed: Rich Kirchen. **Description:** Overview of retail trade in Milwaukee, Wisconsin is presented. It has been observed that vacancies in storefronts both east and west of the Milwaukee River have increased, and the Shops of Grand Avenue has yet to attract new retailers or shoppers. The completion of the Marquette Interchange is also discussed.

16528 ■ *"Home Sprinklers Blocked in Texas, Long Beach, California"* **in Contractor (Vol. 56, July 2009, No. 7, pp. 1)**
Pub: Penton Media, Inc.
Ed: Robert P. Mader. **Description:** Long Beach, California has exempted older residential high rises and large apartment complexes from a rule to install

fire sprinkler systems. Texas has also prohibited municipalities from enacting residential sprinkler ordinances.

16529 ■ "ICC Works on Prescriptive Green Construction Code" in Contractor (Vol. 56, October 2009, No. 10, pp. 1)
Pub: Penton Media, Inc.

Ed: Robert P. Mader. **Description:** International Code Council launched an initiative to create a green construction code that focuses on existing commercial buildings. The initiative's timeline will include public meetings leading up to a final draft that will be available in 2010.

16530 ■ "Industrial Vacancies Hit High; Economic Downturn Taking Toll on Area's Demand for Space" in Crain's Chicago Business (Apr. 21, 2008)
Pub: Crain Communications, Inc.

Ed: Alby Gallun. **Description:** Hitting its highest level in four years in the first quarter is the Chicago-area industrial vacancy rate, a sign that the slumping economy is depressing demand for warehouse and manufacturing space.

16531 ■ "The Kitchen is Closed; Eateries Forced Out by Soaring Rents, Declining Revenues" in Crain's New York Business (January 21, 2008)
Pub: Crain Communications, Inc.

Ed: Lisa Fickenscher. **Description:** Many restaurants have already closed in the area and experts expect many more will follow due to skyrocketing rents and declining revenues.

16532 ■ "Local Industrial Vacancies Climb" in Crain's Chicago Business (Vol. 31, November 17, 2008, No. 46, pp. 18)
Pub: Crain Communications, Inc.

Ed: Eddie Baeb. **Description:** Demand for local industrial real estate has declined dramatically as companies that use warehouse and factory space struggle to survive in an ailing economy. According to a report by Colliers Bennett & Kahnweiler Inc., a commercial real estate brokerage, the regional vacancy rate has risen to 9.86 percent in the third quarter, the fourth straight increase and the highest in the past 14 years.

16533 ■ "Look Before You Lease" in Women Entrepreneur (February 3, 2009)
Pub: Entrepreneur Media Inc.

Ed: Nina L. Kaufman. **Description:** Top issues to consider before leasing an office space are discussed including: additional charges that may be expected on top of the basic rental price; determining both short- and long-term goals; the cost of improvements to the space; the cost of upkeep; and the conditions of the lease.

16534 ■ "Mandel Site Favored For UWM Hall" in The Business Journal-Milwaukee (Vol. 25, September 19, 2008, No. 52, pp. A1)
Pub: American City Business Journals, Inc.

Description: University of Wisconsin-Milwaukee student residence hall's leading location is a site pushed by Mandel Group Inc. Real estate sources say that the developer's proposal offers the best opportunity for business development and the least conflict with nearby neighborhoods. Plans for the Mandel site are presented.

16535 ■ "Mequon Plan On Tracks, Bucks Housing Trend" in The Business Journal-Milwaukee (Vol. 25, September 26, 2008, No. 53, pp. A1)
Pub: American City Business Journals, Inc.

Ed: Pete Millard. **Description:** Insight Development Group plans to build condominium units and single-family homes despite the residential market downturn. The Orchard Glen project, a planned development in Mequon, is a $22 million project which will include 38 condos and 12 single-family homes. Details of the project are provided.

16536 ■ "Midtown Tampa Bay Taking Shape" in The Business Journal-Serving Greater

Tampa Bay (Vol. 28, September 12, 2008, No. 38, pp. 1)
Pub: American City Business Journals, Inc.

Ed: Janet Leiser. **Description:** Midtown Tampa Bay's 610,000 square foot shopping and entertainment center is being planned in Florida and is to replace the Tampa Bay One project proposed years earlier. The retail center is to be developed by Bromley Cos. and Opus South Corp. and is expected to have five buildings. Other details about the plan are discussed.

16537 ■ "Millions Needed To Finish First Place" in The Business Journal-Milwaukee (Vol. 25, August 15, 2008, No. 47, pp. A1)
Pub: American City Business Journals, Inc.

Ed: Rich Kirchen. **Description:** First Place on the River condominium project in Milwaukee, Wisconsin, needs $18.2 million before it can be completed. A total of $6.8 million have already been spent since the project went into receivership on 31 January 2008.

16538 ■ "More Offices Planned For Percheron Square" in The Business Journal-Milwaukee (Vol. 25, August 22, 2008, No. 48, pp. A1)
Pub: American City Business Journals, Inc.

Ed: Pete Millard. **Description:** More office projects are under way at Percheron Square. Ryan Cos. US Inc., for example, plans to build over 200,000 square feet of office space at the area. Details of new office projects in Wisconsin are presented.

16539 ■ "A New Mix of Tenants Settles In" in Crain's New York Business (Vol. 24, January 14, 2008, No. 2, pp. 26)
Pub: Crain Communications, Inc.

Ed: Andrew Marks. **Description:** More and more nonfinancial firms are relocating downtown due to the new retailers and restaurants that are reshaping the look and feel of lower Manhattan.

16540 ■ "N.Y. Group Top Bidder for Last Duke Sites" in Crain's Cleveland Business (Vol. 28, November 19, 2007, No. 46, pp. 1)
Pub: Crain Communications, Inc.

Ed: Stan Bullard. **Description:** Overview of the possible portfolio sale of Duke Realty Corp.'s last Northeast Ohio properties, 14 office buildings in Independence, Seven Hills and North Olmsted, believed to be purchased by a real estate investor group led by Nightingale Properties LLC of New York.

16541 ■ "Part-Time Office Space" in Hawaii Business (Vol. 53, December 2007, No. 6, pp. 132)
Pub: Hawaii Business Publishing

Ed: Ashley Hamershock. **Description:** My Office is one of the companies that are renting space office not only by the month, but by the hour. Such setup is beneficial to small businesses that do not need a whole office all to themselves, and are interested in cutting the cost of office space rental. The prices of office space in Hawaii are mentioned.

16542 ■ "A Place to Call Home" in Business Courier (Vol. 24, March 7, 2008, No. 48, pp. 1)
Pub: American City Business Journals, Inc.

Ed: Lucy May. **Description:** Discusses a new type of housing for Cincinnati's chronically homeless that will be developed by the Over-the-Rhine Community Housing Network and the Cincinnati Center City Development Corp. Advocates believe that it is the missing link in the community's efforts to eradicate homelessness. The details of the project are also presented.

16543 ■ "Population Growing Faster Than Retail, Service Sector" in Crain's New York Business (Vol. 24, January 14, 2008, No. 2, pp. 30)
Pub: Crain Communications, Inc.

Ed: Andrew Marks. **Description:** Downtown Manhattan is seeing more residential development; however, as more families call the area home the need for more retail and services is becoming evident.

16544 ■ Property Management Association--Directory
Pub: Property Management Association

URL(s): www.pma-dc.org. **Released:** Annual; spring. **Price:** $50, Nonmembers. **Covers:** Over 539 property managers and 336 related supplier firms. **Entries include:** For property managers--Name, firm name, address, phone, fax, specialty. For supplier firms--Company name, name of contact, address, phone, fax. **Arrangement:** Each list is alphabetical. **Indexes:** Supplier product/service.

16545 ■ "Protect Your Assets" in Black Enterprise (Vol. 38, January 2008, No. 6, pp. 38)
Pub: Earl G. Graves Publishing Co. Inc.

Ed: Trevor Delaney. **Description:** Owner of rental properties seeks advice for incorporating versus getting an LLC for the business.

16546 ■ "Real Estate Vets Take Times In Stride" in The Business Journal-Serving Metropolitan Kansas City (Vol. 26, July 25, 2008, No. 46)
Pub: American City Business Journals, Inc.

Ed: Rob Roberts. **Description:** Kansas City, Missouri's real estate industry veterans like Allen Block believe that the challenges faced by the industry in the 1980s, when the Federal Reserve Board controlled the money supply to slow down inflation, were worse than the challenges faced today. Other views, trends and information on the real estate industry of the city, are presented.

16547 ■ "Realities May Blur Vision" in The Business Journal-Serving Metropolitan Kansas City (Vol. 27, September 19, 2008, No. 1, pp. 1)
Pub: American City Business Journals, Inc.

Ed: Rob Roberts. **Description:** Vision Metcalf is a study by Kansas City that depicts how Metcalf Avenue could look like if redeveloped. Redevelopment plans for the Metcalf corridor include a 20-story mixed-use building on a vacant car dealership. The challenges that the redevelopment plans will face are also analyzed.

16548 ■ "Red Tape Ties Detroit Housing Rehab Plan" in Crain's Detroit Business (Vol. 24, September 22, 2008, No. 38, pp. 1)
Pub: Crain Communications Inc.

Ed: Ryan Beene. **Description:** Venture-capital firm Wilherst Oxford LLC is a Florida-based company that has purchased 300 inner-city homes which were in foreclosure in Detroit. Wilherst Oxford is asking the city to forgive the existing tax and utility liens so the firm can utilize the money for home improvements. The city, however, is reluctant but has stated that they are willing to negotiate.

16549 ■ "A Renewal in Rentals" in Barron's (Vol. 88, March 17, 2008, No. 11, pp. 17)
Pub: Dow Jones & Company, Inc.

Description: Discusses the projected entry of the estimated 82 million echo-boomers into the rentals market and the influx of immigrants and displaced homeowners which could turn apartments into lucrative investments again. While apartment-building completions rose slowly since 2003, demand is expected to increase steeply until 2015.

16550 ■ "Rental Demand Boosts Revenue for Sun Communities Inc." in Crain's Detroit Business (Vol. 24, March 24, 2008, No. 12, pp. 4)
Pub: Crain Communications, Inc.

Ed: Daniel Duggan. **Description:** Despite the decline in sales of manufactured homes, demand for rental units and rent-to-own programs have brought Sun Communities Inc. increased revenue. The real estate investment trust, based in Southfield, owns, operates, finances and develops manufactured home communities in the Midwest and Southeast. Statistical data included.

16551 ■ "A Second Chance to Make a Living" in The Business Journal-Milwaukee (Vol. 25, September 19, 2008, No. 52, pp. A1)
Pub: American City Business Journals, Inc.

Description: Unemployed workers and baby boomers are driving interest in purchasing small businesses. BizBuySell general manager Mike Handelsman reveals that the supply of small businesses for sale is decreasing due to the increased demand. The trends in the small business market are analyzed.

16552 ■ *"Silverdome Bidders Bring New Proposals" in Crain's Detroit Business (Vol. 24, March 17, 2008, No. 11, pp. 23)*
Pub: Crain Communications, Inc.

Ed: Daniel Duggan. **Description:** Discusses the seven plans which have been proposed as part of the third round of bidding for the Pontiac Silverdome; proposals range from Global Baseball Inc., a baseball league that would pit a team from every country against one another, to an Indian casino, a musical 'hall of fame', a convention center, a horse track, a hotel and an indoor water park.

16553 ■ *"Sixty-Acre Vision for North Suburbs" in Business Courier (Vol. 24, April 4, 2008, No. 52, pp. 1)*
Pub: American City Business Journals, Inc.

Ed: Laura Baverman. **Description:** Al Neyer Inc. plans for a mixed-use development at the 60-acre site it has recently purchased. The mixed-use project could cost up to $100 million, and will include medical offices, residential buildings, and corporate offices. Details of Al Neyer's plans for the site are given.

16554 ■ *"Soured Relationship Plays Out in Courts" in The Business Journal-Serving Greater Tampa Bay (Vol. 28, September 19, 2008, No. 39)*
Pub: American City Business Journals, Inc.

Ed: Janet Leiser. **Description:** Heirs of developer Julian Hawthorne Lifset won a court battle to end a 50-year lease with Specialty Restaurants Corp. in Rocky Point. The decision opens the Tampa Bay prime waterfront property for new development.

16555 ■ *"Stars Shine Downtown" in The Business Journal-Serving Metropolitan Kansas City (Vol. 26, August 29, 2008, No. 51, pp. 1)*
Pub: American City Business Journals, Inc.

Ed: Rob Roberts. **Description:** Movie chain AMC Entertainment Inc. renews its lease for 97,000 square feet of space at Ten Main Center. HNTB Federal Services Corp., meanwhile, is to take up 42,000 square feet at an office building located at 120 W. 12th St. The leases' impacts on downtown office market are examined.

16556 ■ *"Subprime Problems Loom" in The Business Journal-Portland (Vol. 25, August 29, 2008, No. 25, pp. 1)*
Pub: American City Business Journals, Inc.

Ed: Wendy Culverwell. **Description:** Over half of subprime mortgages in Portland are resetting by the end of 2008, which will cause more problems to the local real estate market. The inventory of unsold homes has also been increasing for over a year. Forecasts for the Portland housing market in relation to mortgage resets are supplied.

16557 ■ *"Troy Complex has New Brand, New Leases" in Crain's Detroit Business (Vol. 24, April 14, 2008, No. 15, pp. 32)*
Pub: Crain Communications Inc.

Ed: Daniel Duggan. **Description:** Discusses the re-branding of the 1.2 million-square-foot collection of office buildings in Troy purchased by New York-based Emmes Co. The firm has also pledged more than $6 million in upgrades, hired a new leasing company and completed 67,000 square feet of leasing with another 100,000 in negotiations.

TRADE PERIODICALS

16558 ■ *Journal of Property Management*
Pub: Institute of Real Estate Management
Contact: Ronald Goss, President

URL(s): www.irem.org/sechome.cfm?sec=JPM. **Released:** Bimonthly **Price:** $72.32, Canada; $62.95, Individuals; $115.50, Two years; $110.99, Other countries airmail; $169.10, Individuals 3 years.

TRADE SHOWS AND CONVENTIONS

16559 ■ Apartment Association of Metro Denver Seminar and Trade Show
Apartment Association of Metro Denver
3773 Cherry Creek N. Dr., Ste. 1001
Denver, CO 80209
Ph: (303)329-3300
Fax: (303)329-0403
URL: http://www.aamdhq.org
Contact: Betty Knecht, Executive Vice President
E-mail: betty@aamdhq.org

URL(s): www.aamdhq.org. **Price:** $40, Non-members; $20, Members. **Frequency:** Annual. **Audience:** Trade professionals. **Principal Exhibits:** Apartment management equipment, supplies, and services.

16560 ■ Building Owners and Managers Association International Annual Convention and The Office Building Show
Building Owners and Managers Association International
1101 15th St., N.W., Ste. 800
Washington, DC 20005
Ph: (202)408-2662
Fax: (202)682-5934
Co. E-mail: meetings@boma.org
URL: http://www.bomaconvention.org

URL(s): www.boma.org. **Frequency:** Annual. **Audience:** Owners and managers of office buildings, developers, brokers, and real estate professionals. **Principal Exhibits:** Products, supplies and equipment for the office building industry, including architectural and building hardware, asbestos abatement, building automation, carpeting, control systems, doors, elevators and elevator maintenance, electrical and lighting, environmental services, financial services, fire protection, flooring and floor machines, hazardous waste removal, interior design, landscaping, locks, paper products, parking, pest control, plumbing and fixtures, recycling, renovation and restoration, roofing, security, signage, water treatment, windows. **Telecommunication Services:** info@boma.org.

16561 ■ Columbus Apartment Association Education Conference and Trade Expo
Columbus Apartment Association
1225 Dublin Rd.
Columbus, OH 43215
Ph: (614)488-2115
Fax: (614)488-8526
Co. E-mail: caa@caahq.com
URL: http://www.caahq.com

URL(s): www.columbusapts.org. **Frequency:** Annual. **Audience:** Apartment owners, investors, managers, leasing and maintenance personnel. **Principal Exhibits:** Products and services for the apartment industry. **Dates and Locations:** State Fairgrounds. **Telecommunication Services:** sgladman@columbusapts. org.

CONSULTANTS

16562 ■ Beer-Wells Real Estate Services Inc.
11311 N Central Expy., Ste. 100
Dallas, TX 75243
Ph: (214)750-5600
Fax: (214)750-5603
Co. E-mail: mbtbwt@aol.com
URL: http://www.beerwells.com
Contact: William K. Wells, President
E-mail: bwells@beerwells.com
Scope: Offers professional counseling on asset management, property management, appraisal, property tax reduction, sales, leasing, investing, work-out, problem solving and all areas related to leasing, sales and marketing of commercial real estate. Serves private industries as well as government agencies. **Founded:** 1952.

16563 ■ Crown Management Inc.
4233 Roanoke Rd., Ste. 200
Kansas City, MO 64111-4142
Ph: (816)756-1084

Fax: (816)756-1188
Contact: Robert W. Haas, President
Scope: Real estate firm which advises clients regarding the planning, development and management of office buildings, commercial and multi-family properties, and conventional and FHA programs. Services include appraisals, brokerage and property management. **Founded:** 1981.

16564 ■ Garrity & Associates
9200 Middlebelt Rd., Ste. 734
Livonia, MI 48150-4046
Ph: (734)261-7020
Contact: Stephen Garrity, Principal
Scope: Property management consultants offer assistance full service management and leasing relating to commercial, multiple and industrial real estate. Industries served: real estate, government agencies, and institutions. **Founded:** 1990. **Seminars:** New Business Start Up.

16565 ■ Gates, Hudson & Associates Inc.—GHA Inc.
3020 Hamaker Ct., Ste. 301
Fairfax, VA 22031
Ph: (703)876-9590
Fax: (703)876-0304
Co. E-mail: contact@gateshudson.com
URL: http://www.gateshudson.com
Contact: Patricia J. M. Blackburn, President
E-mail: ce-hudson@gateshudson.com
Scope: Property management consulting firm expertise in financial services; utility management; facility services and information systems. **Founded:** 1980. **Publications:** "A British Invasion," Jul, 2009. **Telecommunication Services:** vannese@gateshudson. com.

16566 ■ GFA Management Inc.
7550 S Meridian St., Ste. A
Indianapolis, IN 46247
Ph: (317)346-7156
Free: 877-633-4764
Fax: (317)346-7158
Co. E-mail: gfa7156@aol.com
Contact: George Allen, President
E-mail: gallen@manufactured-housing.net
Scope: Firm offers real estate management consulting, specializing in manufactured home communities. Industries served: manufactured housing, and real estate. **Founded:** 1981. **Publications:** "Chapbook of Business and Management Wisdom," PMN Publishing, 2002; "Manufactured Home Community Management," PMN Publishing, 2001; "How to Find, Buy, Manage and Sell a Manufactured Home Community as an Investment," J. Wiley and Sons, 1996; "Development, Marketing and Operation of Manufactured Home Communities," J. Wiley and Co., 1994. **Seminars:** Land Development; Property Management; Sales and Marketing; Manufactured Housing Manager Certification Training and Designation.

16567 ■ Hanford-Freund & Co.
47 Kearny St.
San Francisco, CA 94108
Ph: (415)981-5780
Free: 800-972-5968
Fax: (415)296-0725
Co. E-mail: info@hanfordfreund.com
URL: http://www.hanfordfreund.com
Contact: J. Timothy Falvey, President
E-mail: tfalvey@hanfordfreund.com
Scope: Specializing in advisory service to clients in real estate investments and financial service, including equity and Marketing, asset management, valuation of real property. evaluation of current assets. Management analysis of problem properties and problem ventures. Workouts of major real estate projects. **Founded:** 1930.

16568 ■ Hastings Co.
8414 Braes Meadow Dr.
Houston, TX 77071-1112
Ph: (713)774-4091

Fax: (713)785-0553
Contact: Edmund S. Hastings, President
Scope: Property development consultants offering technical, administrative, and business management services. Specializes in small business development worldwide. Serves private industries as well as government agencies. **Founded:** 1948.

16569 ■ Investors' Property Services
27042 Towne Centre Dr., Ste. 250
Foothill Ranch, CA 92610
Ph: (949)900-6160
Free: 800-247-4044
Fax: (949)900-6601
Co. E-mail: info@investorshq.com
URL: http://www.investorshq.com
Contact: Robert C. Warren, III, President
E-mail: bob@investorshq.com
Scope: Property management consultants offer expertise in third party management and on due diligence property analyses and inspections, market evaluations for office buildings, medical buildings, hotels, motels, shopping centers, apartments, and industrial properties. Also serve as receiver during fore closure examiner in bankruptcy, operating forecasts, budgets and variance analyses. Industries served financial institutions, legal profession, medical, banks, insurance companies, trustees, REITs, pensions and partnerships. **Founded:** 1980.

16570 ■ Renal Center
12 Chelsea Ct.
Hillsdale, NJ 07642-1227
Ph: (201)664-4451
Fax: (201)664-1267
Contact: Christopher N. Carson, Principal
Scope: Construction Consulting, Construction Management, Building Management Consulting, Provide Expert Witness Testimony in Dispute Matters. Arbitrator for Alternate Dispute Resolution cases. **Founded:** 1984.

FRANCHISES AND BUSINESS OPPORTUNITIES

16571 ■ Parker Finch Management
209 E Baseline Rd., Ste. E208
Tempe, AZ 85283

Ph: (877)508-1974
Fax: (480)907-1141
Description: Property management services for condos & home owners associations. **No. of Franchise Units:** 8. **No. of Company-Owned Units:** 1. **Founded:** 1993.. **Franchised:** 2006. **Equity Capital Needed:** $65,000-$105,000. **Franchise Fee:** $30,000. **Royalty Fee:** 3%. **Training:** 2 weeks training provided at headquarters and ongoing support.

COMPUTERIZED DATABASES

16572 ■ *ABI/INFORM®*
789 E Eisenhower Pkwy.
Ann Arbor, MI 48106-1346
Ph: (734)761-4700
Free: 800-521-0600
Co. E-mail: info@il.proquest.com
URL: http://www.il.proquest.com
Contact: Matt Dunie, President
Availability: Online: ProQuest Co.; ProQuest LLC-Dialog; ProQuest LLC - Dialog; LexisNexis Group; STN International; Wolters Kluwer Health - Ovid.
Type: Full-text; Bibliographic; Image.

LIBRARIES

16573 ■ California Department of Housing and Community Development - Housing Resource Center
1800 3rd St.
Sacramento, CA 94252-2053
Ph: (916)445-4782
Fax: (916)327-2643
Co. E-mail: jtochterman@hcd.ca.gov
URL: http://www.hcd.ca.gov/hpd/biblio.html
Contact: Linn Warren, Director
Scope: Housing, planning, community development, redevelopment, land use. **Services:** Center open to the public with restrictions. **Founded:** 1987. **Holdings:** 4000 reports. **Subscriptions:** 175 journals.

16574 ■ Housing Association of Delaware Valley Library
1528 Walnut St., Ste. 1000
Philadelphia, PA 19102

Ph: (215)545-6010
Fax: (215)790-9132
Co. E-mail: info@hadv.org
URL: http://www.hadv.org
Scope: Housing, urban development, city/regional planning, zoning, law, local government. **Services:** Copying; Library open to the public. **Founded:** 1909. **Holdings:** 1000 books; 2000 pamphlets. **Subscriptions:** 50 journals and other serials; 8 newspapers. **Telecommunication Services:** tony.lewis@hadv.org.

16575 ■ U.S. Dept. of Housing and Urban Development - Southeast/Caribbean Library
Five Points Plaza Bldg.
40 Marietta St., NW
Atlanta, GA 30303-2812
Ph: (404)331-5001
Co. E-mail: sue.h.barron@hud.gov
URL: http://www.hud.gov/local/index.
    cfm?state=ga&topic=library
Contact: Sue H. Barron, Director
Scope: Housing, planning, urban development, economic analysis, law, statistics. **Services:** Library open to the public for reference use only. **Founded:** 1968. **Holdings:** 17,000 books; 87 bound periodical volumes; Federal Register, 1967 to present (microfilm); 12 VF drawers. **Telecommunication Services:** answers@hud.gov.

16576 ■ Steven Winter Associates, Inc. Library
61 Washington St.
Norwalk, CT 06854
Ph: (203)857-0200
Fax: (203)852-0741
Co. E-mail: swa@swinter.com
URL: http://www.swinter.com
Contact: Helki Roundtree, Director, Library Services
Scope: Housing technology, energy conservation, engineering, construction technology, LEED consulting. **Services:** Library not open to the public. **Founded:** 1972. **Holdings:** 2008 books; 1200 bound periodical volumes; 700 microfiche. **Subscriptions:** 356 journals and other serials. **Telecommunication Services:** hroundtree@swinter.com.

ASSOCIATIONS AND OTHER ORGANIZATIONS

16577 ■ Agricultural Relations Council (ARC)
PO Box 156
New Prague, MN 56071
Ph: (952)758-5811
Fax: (952)758-5813
Co. E-mail: arc@gardnerandgardnercommunications.com
URL: http://www.agrelationscouncil.org
Contact: Mr. Den Gardner, Executive Director
Description: Professional society of agricultural public relations executives employed by private business firms, associations, publications, and government agencies. Operates placement service. **Founded:** 1953. **Publications:** *Agricultural Relations Council--Directory of Members* (Annual); *ARClight* (Quarterly). **Educational Activities:** Agricultural Relations Council Conference (Annual). **Awards:** Golden ARC Award (Annual).

16578 ■ Canadian Public Relations Society (CPRS)—Societe Canadienne des Relations Publiques
4195 Dundas St. W, Ste. 346
Toronto, ON, Canada M8X 1Y4
Ph: (416)239-7034
Fax: (416)239-1076
Co. E-mail: admin@cprs.ca
URL: http://www.cprs.ca
Contact: Ms. Karen Dalton, Executive Director
Description: Public relations professionals. Seeks to advance the practice of public relations; promotes ongoing professional development of members. Serves as a forum for the exchange of information among members; sponsors research and educational programs. **Founded:** 1948. **Educational Activities:** Canadian Public Relations Society Conference (Annual). **Awards:** Awards of Excellence; Philip A. Novikoff Memorial Award; Award of Attainment; Shield of Public Service; Outstanding Achievement Award; Lamp of Service; CPRS Lectern; Student Award of Excellence; Major Awards (Annual); Torchia Scholarship in Public Relations (Annual); Don Rennie Memorial Award for Excellence in Government Public Relations; Emery LeBlanc Membership Achievement Award.

16579 ■ Public Relations Society of America (PRSA)
33 Maiden Ln., 11th Fl.
New York, NY 10038-5150
Ph: (212)460-1400
Fax: (212)995-0757
Co. E-mail: william.murray@prsa.org
URL: http://www.prsa.org
Contact: William Murray, President
Description: Professional society of public relations practitioners in business and industry, counseling firms, government, associations, hospitals, schools, and nonprofit organizations. Conducts professional development programs. Maintains a Professional Resource Center. Offers accreditation program.

Scope: Public relations firm specializes in counseling firms and training programs. **Founded:** 1947. **Subscriptions:** 1000 archival material. **Publications:** "Tactics"; "Professional Development". **Educational Activities:** Public Relations Society of America Conference & Expo (Annual). **Awards:** PR Professional of the Year; Gold Anvil Award; Outstanding Educator Award; Bronze Anvil Awards; Silver Anvil Awards; Bronze Anvil Awards (Annual); Gold Anvil Award (Annual); Outstanding Educator Award (Annual); Paul M. Lund Public Service Award (Annual); Silver Anvil Awards (Annual); Paul M. Lund Public Service Award; MacEachern Chief Executive Officer Award. **Seminars:** PR Boot Camp: Key Concepts and Techniques of Effective Public Relations, New York, Dec, 2009. **Telecommunication Services:** ppc@prsa.org; hq@prsa.org; info@prsany.org.

16580 ■ Public Relations Student Society of America (PRSSA)
33 Maiden Ln., 11th Fl.
New York, NY 10038-5150
Ph: (212)460-1474
Fax: (212)995-0757
Co. E-mail: prssa@prsa.org
URL: http://www.prssa.org
Contact: Lauren Gray, President
Description: Professionally oriented student association organized to cultivate a favorable and mutually advantageous relationship between students and professional public relations practitioners. Fosters understanding of public relations theories and procedures; encourages students to adhere to high ideals and principles of public relations. **Founded:** 1967. **Awards:** National Gold Key Award (Annual); Betsy Plank/PRSSA Scholarships; PRSSA Multicultural Affairs Scholarships; Gary Yoshimura Scholarships; Stephen D. Pisinski Memorial Scholarships.

DIRECTORIES OF EDUCATIONAL PROGRAMS

16581 ■ *Who's Who in the Media and Communications*
Pub: Marquis Who's Who L.L.C.
Contact: James A. Finkelstein, President
URL(s): www.marquiswhoswho.com. **Covers:** More than 18,500 professionals in print journalism, broadcasting, publishing, television, public relations, advertising, radio, telecommunications, interactive multimedia, and education. **Entries include:** Biographical data.

REFERENCE WORKS

16582 ■ *"1914 Proved to Be Key Year for Chevy"* in Automotive News (Vol. 86, October 31, 2011, No. 6488, pp. S18)
Pub: Crain Communications Inc.
Ed: Jamie Lareau. **Description:** Chevy Bow Tie emblem was born in 1914, creating the brand's image that has carried through to current days.

16583 ■ *"Another California Firm On Way"* in Austin Business Journal (Vol. 31, May 6, 2011, No. 9, pp. 1)
Pub: American City Business Journals Inc.
Ed: Christopher Calnan. **Description:** Main Street Hub Inc. is planning to build a facility in Austin, Texas. The company helps businesses manage their online reputations. Main Street has selected Aquila Commercial LLC as its real estate broker.

16584 ■ *Birthing the Elephant: The Woman's Go-for-It! Guide to Overcoming the Big Challenges of Launching a Business*
Pub: Celestial Arts Publishing Co.
Contact: Patricia Kelly, Manager
Ed: Karin Abarbanel; Bruce Freeman. **Released:** March 2008. **Price:** $15.95. **Description:** Advice for women entrepreneurs is given. The book explores the emotional challenges faced by women starting businesses, along with advice for reshaping image. This handbook helps women survive and succeed in business.

16585 ■ *"Brand Imaging"* in Small Business Opportunities (November 2010)
Pub: Harris Publications Inc.
Ed: Karen Harnesk. **Description:** Design and branding pro shares strategies and tips to help guide any small business' image development.

16586 ■ *"The Buck Stops Here"* in Canadian Business (Vol. 81, November 10, 2008, No. 19, pp. 25)
Pub: Rogers Media Ltd.
Ed: Sarka Halas. **Description:** Reputation strategist Leslie Gaines-Ross says that minimizing the damage followed by the identification of what went wrong are the first steps that companies need to take when trying to salvage their reputation. Gaines-Ross states that it is up to the CEO to ensure the company's speedy recovery and they need to be at the forefront of the process.

16587 ■ *"Deskside Story: As the Latest Buzzword Suggests, PR Firms Are Happy To Drop By"* in Inc. (December 2007, pp. 70, 73)
Pub: Gruner & Jahr USA Publishing
Ed: Nitasha Tiku. **Description:** Setting up a meeting between a company's CEO and a journalist is known as deskside and is becoming popular again whereby a publicist offers clients deskside visits, briefings and alerts to help promote public relations for a company.

16588 ■ *"Empowered"* in Harvard Business Review (Vol. 88, July-August 2010, No. 7-8, pp. 94)
Pub: Harvard Business School Publishing
Ed: Josh Bernoff, Ted Schadler. **Description:** HERO concept (highly empowered and resourceful operative) which builds a connection between employees, managers, and IT is outlined. The resultant additional experience and knowledge gained by employees improves customer relationship management.

16589 ■ *"Hopkins' Security, Reputation Face Challenges in Wake of Slaying" in Baltimore Business Journal (Vol. 28, August 6, 2010, No. 13)*

Pub: Baltimore Business Journal

Ed: Gary Haber. **Description:** The slaying of Johns Hopkins University researcher Stephen Pitcairn has not tarnished the reputation of the elite school in Baltimore, Maryland among students. Maintaining Hopkins' reputation is important since it is Baltimore's largest employer with nearly 32,000 workers. Insights on the impact of the slaying among the Hopkins' community are also given.

16590 ■ *If You Have to Cry, Go Outside: And Other Things Your Mother Never Told You*

Pub: HarperOne

Ed: Kelly Cutrone. **Released:** February 2, 2010. **Price:** $22.99. **Description:** Women's mentor advices on how to make it in one of the most competitive industries in the world, fashion. She has kicked people out of fashion shows, forced some of reality television's shiny start to fire their friends, and built her own company which is one of the most powerful public relations firms in the fashion business.

16591 ■ *"Increasing Building Work at Ryan Cos." in Crain's Chicago Business (Vol. 34, May 23, 2011, No. 21, pp. 6)*

Pub: Crain Communications Inc.

Ed: Eddie Baeb. **Description:** Profile of Tim Hennelly, who is working to make Ryan Company known as a pure builder rather than a developer-builder.

16592 ■ *"It's Time to Take Full Responsibility" in Harvard Business Review (Vol. 88, October 2010, No. 10, pp. 42)*

Pub: Harvard Business School Publishing

Ed: Rosabeth Moss Kanter. **Description:** A case for corporate responsibility is cited, focusing on long-term impact and the effects of public accountability.

16593 ■ *Media, Organizations and Identity*

Pub: Palgrave Macmillan

Ed: Lilie Chouliaraki, Mette Morsing. **Released:** January 19, 2010. **Price:** $90.00. **Description:** The mass media, press and television are a essential in the formation of corporate identity and the promotion of business image and reputation. This book offers a new perspective into the interrelationships between media and organizations over three dimensions: media as business, media in business and business in the media.

16594 ■ *O'Dwyer's Directory of Public Relations Firms*

Pub: J.R. O'Dwyer Company Inc.

URL(s): www.odwyerpr.com. **Ed:** Kevin McCauley. **Released:** Annual; Latest edition 2012. **Price:** $95, Individuals. **Covers:** Over 1,600 public relations firms; international coverage. **Entries include:** Firm name, address, phone, principal executives, branch and overseas offices, billings, date founded, and 7,750 clients are cross-indexed. **Database includes:** List of top 50 public relations firms. **Arrangement:** Geographical by country. **Indexes:** Specialty (beauty and fashions, finance/investor, etc.), geographical, client.

16595 ■ *"Optima Public Relations Gains Partners" in Alaska Business Monthly (Vol. 27, October 2011, No. 11, pp. 10)*

Pub: Alaska Business Publishing Company

Ed: Nancy Pounds. **Description:** OPrima Public Relations has partnered with Gogerty Marriott of Seattle and Seattle Design Group.

16596 ■ *Public Relations Tactics--Member Services Directory--The Blue Book: The PRSA Membership Networking Issue*

Pub: Public Relations Society of America

Contact: William Murray, President

URL(s): www.prsa.orgauth.iweb.prsa.org/xmembernet/main/directory.cfm. **Released:** Annual; latest edition 2007. **Covers:** PRSA members--headquaters, staff contacts, and chapter, section, and district information. **Entries include:** Name, professional af-

filiation and title, address, phone, membership rank. **Arrangement:** Alphabetical. **Indexes:** Geographical, organizational.

16597 ■ *"Reputation Warfare" in Harvard Business Review (Vol. 88, December 2010, No. 12, pp. 70)*

Pub: Harvard Business School Publishing

Ed: Leslie Gaines-Ross. **Description:** Steps are presented for addressing attacks on corporate public image. These include responding promptly, avoiding disproportionate displays of force, empowering employees to present the firm's position, and stockpiling credentials to bolster credence.

16598 ■ *"Timberland's CEO On Standing Up to 65,000 Angry Activists" in Harvard Business Review (Vol. 88, September 2010, No. 9, pp. 39)*

Pub: Harvard Business School Publishing

Ed: Jeff Swartz. **Description:** Timberland Company avoided a potential boycott by taking a two-way approach. It addressed a supplier issue that posed a threat to the environment, and launched an email campaign to keep Greenpeace activists informed of the development of a new supplier agreement.

16599 ■ *"To Be Seen Is to Be Successful" in Pet Product News (Vol. 64, December 2010, No. 12, pp. 12)*

Pub: BowTie Inc.

Ed: David Arvin. **Description:** Guidelines on how pet business retailers can boost customer visibility are described considering that complacency could hamper retailers' efforts to effectively market their businesses. To enhance customer base and stand out from competing businesses, being different, strategic, creative, and differentiated is emphasized.

16600 ■ *"Vanity Plates" in Canadian Business (Vol. 82, April 27, 2009, No. 7, pp. 26)*

Pub: Rogers Media

Ed: Andy Holloway. **Description:** Politicians in the U.S. called for the review of firms that availed of the bailout money but are under deals for naming rights of sports stadiums. Angus Reid's Corporate Reputation and Sponsorship Index found for example, that there is little correlation between sponsoring arenas on having a better brand image. It is suggested that firms who enter these deals build closer to people's homes.

16601 ■ *"Voice: Rebuilding Trust" in Business Strategy Review (Vol. 21, Summer 2010, No. 2, pp. 79)*

Pub: Wiley-Blackwell

Ed: David De Cremer. **Description:** The financial world's attempts to rebuild trust are charted. Three steps to jump-start that process are outlined.

16602 ■ *"We Had to Won the Mistakes" in Harvard Business Review (Vol. 88, July-August 2010, No. 7-8, pp. 108)*

Pub: Harvard Business School Publishing

Ed: Adi Ignatius. **Description:** Interview with Howard Schultz, CEO of Starbucks, covers topics that include investment in retraining, the impact of competition, premium quality, authenticity, customer services, strategy development, work-and-life issues, and international presence.

16603 ■ *When the Headline Is You: An Insider's Guide to Handling the Media*

Pub: Jossey-Bass

Ed: Jeff Ansell, Jeff Lesson. **Price:** $29.95. **Description:** How-to guide for executives and other professionals whose high-visibility requires frequent interviews with the media. Tested techniques, tools, and insights for how to respond to all types of media in tough situation are provided. The books also reveals the lessons learned and the pitfalls to avoid by referencing actual news stores from around the world and provides exercises for readers who wish to sharpen their media-handling skills.

TRADE PERIODICALS

16604 ■ *Bulldog Reporter Business Media / Media Pro*

Pub: Infocom Group

Contact: Stephen Beale, Editor

E-mail: sbeale@infocomgroup.com

Ed: Megan Caluza, Editor, mcaluza@infocomgroup. com. **Released:** Semimonthly. **Price:** $649. **Descrip-**

tion: Covers U.S. news media for public relations professionals. Recurring features include interviews, media contact lists, and media personnel changes.

16605 ■ *The Counselor*

Pub: The Counselor

Ed: Steve Erickson, Editor. **Released:** 6/year. **Description:** Reports on membership news and other public relations topics.

16606 ■ *The Gauge*

Pub: Delahaye Medialink

Contact: Katharine Delahaye Paine, Publisher

E-mail: kpaine@delahaye.com

Ed: William Teunis Paarlberg, Editor, wpaarlberg@aol.com. **Released:** Bimonthly. **Price:** $75. **Description:** Provides information on and evaluates marketing communications activities of companies. Recurring features include interviews, news of research, and a calendar of events.

16607 ■ *Lifestyle Media-Relations Reporter / Media Pro*

Pub: Infocom Group

Ed: Meghan Collins, Editor. **Released:** Semimonthly. **Price:** $439. **Description:** Covers lifestyle/consumer media for public relations professionals. Recurring features include interviews.

16608 ■ *Public Relations Review: A Global Journal of Research and Comment*   ●

Pub: Elsevier Science Inc.

Contact: Derk Haank, President

URL(s): www.elsevier.com/wps/find/journaldescription.cws_home/620188/descri ption#description. **Released:** 5/yr. **Price:** $321, Individuals and institution; online; $190, Individuals print; $643, Institutions print.

16609 ■ *Public Relations Tactics*

Pub: Public Relations Society of America

Contact: William Murray, President

URL(s): www.prsa.org/publications/tactics/index.html. **Released:** Monthly **Price:** $100, Individuals; $110, Canada; $120, Other countries; $24, Students non-PRSSA members.

16610 ■ *The Publicity Hound*

Pub: Joan Stewart

Contact: Joan Stewart, Publisher

E-mail: jstewart@publicityhound.com

Released: Weekly. **Price:** Free internet service. **Description:** Provides techniques and strategies on self-promotion and inexpensive publicity. Recurring features include letters to the editor, interviews, news of research, book reviews, news of educational opportunities, notices of publications available, and columns titled Advice From Media People, Seasonal Story Ideas, Resource Page, Success Stories, and Media Insider Secrets. Does not report public relations agency staff changes.

VIDEOCASSETTES/ AUDIOCASSETTES

16611 ■ *Building a Profitable Consulting Practice Series*

Instructional Video

2219 C St.

Lincoln, NE 68502

Ph: (402)475-6570

Free: 800-228-0164

Fax: (402)475-6500

Co. E-mail: feedback@insvideo.com

URL: http://www.insvideo.com

Released: 19??. **Description:** Two-part business educational series by Howard Shenson offers tips on how to build a profitable consulting practice. Covers consulting opportunities, market strategies, proposal writing, contracting strategies, fee setting, disclosure, and collection techniques. **Availability:** VHS.

CONSULTANTS

16612 ■ Sol Abrams Public Relations Counsel & Marketing Consultants

331 Webster Dr.

New Milford, NJ 07646

Ph: (201)262-4111

Fax: (201)262-7669
Contact: Sol Abrams, Owner
E-mail: solbabrams@aol.com
Scope: Independent consulting provides publicity, public relations and marketing counsel and services to management of private and public enterprises. Also serves as public relations consultants to other public relations consulting firms, advertising agencies and marketing companies. Provides expert witness services involving public relations. Also lectures, trains, teaches, and conducts seminars in public relations and marketing. Industries served: Corporate management, businesses large and small including real estate, construction, entertainment, food, fashion, fundraising, automotive, aviation, franchising, government agencies, and nonprofit organizations. **Founded:** 1962. **Seminars:** How to Select a Public Relations Firm; Publicity and Promotion for Small Business Owner; Expose Yourself - Don't Be a Secret Agent -Increase Your Sales, Incomes, Images, Publicity, Profits and Prestige via Professional Public Relations.

16613 ■ Ashland Group L.P.
11550 Fuqua St., Ste. 560
Houston, TX 77034
Ph: (281)484-1700
Free: 800-684-2246
Fax: (281)484-1822
URL: http://www.ashlandgroup.com
Contact: Randy Casey, Managing Partner
E-mail: rcasey@ashlandgroup.com
Scope: Government and political affairs agency that specializes in government relations, advocacy communications, media relations, campaign management and government contract lobbying. Offers creative and innovative tax issues. **Founded:** 1990. **Publications:** "State Tax Guide," Jan, 2009; "State Tax Guide," Jan, 2007.

16614 ■ Campaign Solutions
117 N St. Asaph St.
Alexandria, VA 22314
Ph: (703)684-3435
Fax: (703)684-3758
Co. E-mail: info@campaignsolutions.com
URL: http://www.campaignsolutions.com
Contact: Timothy Nurnberger, Principal
Scope: Republican campaign consultants. Brings a breadth and depth of knowledge and experience not found in any other republican voter contact and communications firm. **Founded:** 1998. **Seminars:** Absolutely Interactive e-marketing Solution.

16615 ■ Coyne Associates
4010 E Lake St.
Minneapolis, MN 55406-2201
Ph: (612)724-1188
Fax: (612)722-1379
Contact: John T. Coyne, Chief Executive Officer
Scope: A marketing and public relations consulting firm that specializes in assisting architectural, engineering, and contractor/developer firms. Services include: marketing plains and audits, strategic planning, corporate identity, turnarounds, and sales training. **Founded:** 2008.

16616 ■ The Da Vinci Group
18512 Bear Creek Terr.
Leesburg, VA 20176
Ph: (703)669-5862
Fax: (703)669-5863
Co. E-mail: dvg@aol.com
URL: http://www.davincigroup.org
Contact: Mark R. Smith, President
E-mail: dvg@aol.com
Scope: A full service consulting firm. Capabilities include government relations, public affairs, public relations, and corporate development.

16617 ■ Democracy Data & Communications L.L.C.
44 Canal Center Plz., Ste. 200
Alexandria, VA 22314-1542
Ph: (703)684-9690
Fax: (703)683-9626
Contact: Jim Gianiny, President
Scope: Provides grassroots technology solutions and online database management. **Founded:** 1996.

16618 ■ Donna Cornell Enterprises Inc.—Cornell Career Center
68 N Plank Rd., Ste. 204
Newburgh, NY 12550-2122
Ph: (845)565-0088
Free: 888-769-3792
Fax: (845)565-0084
Co. E-mail: rc@cornellcareercenter.com
Contact: Donna Cornell, President
E-mail: rc@cornellcareercenter.com
Scope: Offers services in career consultant, professional search, job placement and national professional search. **Founded:** 1996. **Publications:** "The Power of the Woman Within"; "Juggling it All!"; "Journey: A Woman's Guide to Success"; "Shatter the Traditions".

16619 ■ Fletcher & Rowley Inc.—FRR Media
1720 West End, Ste. 630
Nashville, TN 37203
Ph: (615)329-9559
Fax: (615)329-9633
Co. E-mail: info@frcr.biz
URL: http://www.frrmedia.com
Contact: John Rowley, President
E-mail: rowley@frrmedia.com
Scope: Media consulting includes conceptualization, writing, directing and production supervision of television and radio spots, media market surveys, time-buying and placement, theme and message development, categorical media budgets and paid media plans, coordination of campaign communications. **Founded:** 1989. **Seminars:** Campaigns and Elections Magazine Campaign.

16620 ■ The Harwood Institute for Public Innovation
4915 St. Elmo Ave., Ste. 402
Bethesda, MD 20814
Ph: (301)656-3669
Fax: (301)656-0533
Co. E-mail: thi@theharwoodinstitute.org
URL: http://www.theharwoodinstitute.org
Contact: Richard C. Harwood, President
E-mail: jrichards@theharwoodinstitute.org
Scope: Works to understand the essence of society's complex challenges and understands how to create effective action. **Founded:** 1988. **Publications:** "Hope Unraveled: The People's Retreat and Our Way Back," Kettering Foundation Press; "Public Engagement and School Facilities Conversation Workbook," 2004; "Telling Stories of Self-Trust and Hope: A Tool for Engaging Youth in Community Change," 2003; "Making it Real: How to Make Civic Engagement a Public Sensibility," 2003; "New Political Covenant: America's Aspirations for Political Conduct," 2002; "Public Engagement and Small Schools Conversation Guide," 2002; "Creating A New Story: Flint's Struggle to Move Forward," 2001. **Seminars:** Devotion: Declaring Our Intentions in Public Life; Creating A New Public Story; Originating Civic Faith and Self-Trust in America; Moving From a Flat World to a Round World in Public Life; The Public Realm: Where America Must Address Its Concerns.

16621 ■ The Hathaway Group Inc.
1010 Pendleton St.
Alexandria, VA 22314-1837
Ph: (703)837-1818
Fax: (703)837-1822
Contact: Timothy Hathaway, President
E-mail: trh@thehathawaygroup.com
Scope: Political consultant whose services includes voter and databases, network design and administration, web site creation, maintenance and hosting, and fax broadcasting. **Founded:** 1997.

16622 ■ Matson & Associates (M&A)
7831 Western Ct. SE
Olympia, WA 98501-6839
Ph: (360)956-9694
Fax: (360)754-8114
Co. E-mail: support@olywa.net
URL: http://www.matsonassociates.com
Contact: Mike Matson, Owner
E-mail: mmatson@matsonassociates.com
Scope: Consulting in the areas of: strategic planning, issue management, needs analysis, political action, campaign consulting, campaign management, fund

raising and custom-designed education and recruitment programs. **Founded:** 1985. **Seminars:** Politics. . .A Cost of Doing Business; Political Action Committee Development; Coalition Building; Keystone Conference; Activist/Advocate Training.

16623 ■ The Media Guys Inc.
7436 E Stetson Dr., Ste. 290
Scottsdale, AZ 85251
Ph: (480)784-4890
Free: 866-784-4890
Fax: (480)784-4999
Co. E-mail: info@mediaguys.tv
Contact: Bob Grossfeld, President
Scope: A strategic communications firm specializing in public affairs and issues management. Expertise in social marketing, strategic communications and political campaigns. **Founded:** 1992.

16624 ■ Midwest Computer Group L.L.C. (MCG)
6060 Franks Rd.
House Springs, MO 63051
Ph: (314)954-1222
Co. E-mail: sales@mcgcomputer.com
URL: http://www.mcgcomputer.com
Contact: Leon Sanford, Jr., President
E-mail: leonjr@mcgcomputer.com
Scope: Specializes in helping businesses create accounting, marketing and business information systems; software development and database design and management. **Founded:** 1980.

16625 ■ R.E. Moulton Inc.
50 Doaks Ln.
Marblehead, MA 01945
Ph: (781)631-1325
Fax: (781)631-2165
Co. E-mail: mike_lee@remoultoninc.com
URL: http://www.oneamerica.com/wps/wcm/connect/ REMoulton
Contact: Willard A. Knarr, Jr., President
Scope: Offers underwriting services, marketing solutions, claims administration and adjudication; policy and commission administration; and risk management solutions to clients. Supplementary service s include risk management and employee assistance. Clients include individuals, business men, employers and finance professionals. **Founded:** 1976.

16626 ■ ReCourses Inc.
6101 Stillmeadow Dr.
Nashville, TN 37211-6518
Ph: (615)831-2277
Free: 888-476-5884
Fax: (615)831-2212
Co. E-mail: info@recourses.com
URL: http://www.recourses.com
Contact: Julie Warren, Manager
Scope: A management consulting firm that works exclusively with small service providers in the communications industry, including public relations firms, advertising agencies, interactive companies and design studios. Services include Total Business Review, a complete examination of your business starting with an on site examination or discussion, followed by written recommendations and then supplemented with six months of implementation guidance. Areas reviewed include positioning, marketing, management, personnel, structure, finance, retirement, technology and specific growth issues. **Founded:** 1994. **Publications:** "Managing (Right) for the First Time"; "Financial Management of a Marketing Firm". **Seminars:** 10th Annual New Business Summit , Jan, 2013; Event - TEDx Nashville: Success from the Inside Out--Alignment & Engagement , Apr, 20163; Event - AIGA Brand Academy (Emory Executive Education @ Goizueta Business School) , Apr, 2013; Measuring Economic Performance: Measuring and Enhancing Performance in a Marketing Firm, Dec, 2012; Managing Client Relationships: Being Indispensable, Growing the Account, Making Money, Nov, 2012; The Business of Design Oct, 2012; Getting a Good Start in Your Creative Career, Nov, 2011; Research and Insights, Nov, 2011; Managing Client Relationships; Research and Strategy; Financial Management: Measuring and Enhancing Performance in a Marketing Firm, Sep, 2009; Building and Leading a Staff: The When, How, and What

of Growth and Culture, Sep, 2009; Doing Effective Work: Adding Significance to the Strategic Portion of Your Work for Clients, Sep, 2009; Resourcing the Creative Process: Managing Pricing, Deadlines, Budgets, Quality, and Capacity, Apr, 2009. **Special Services:** ReCourses®.

16627 ■ Guy Rodgers & Associates Inc.
748 Montebello Cir.
Chesapeake, VA 23322-7257
Ph: (757)686-0088
Co. E-mail: graa@acninc.net
Contact: Guy Rodgers, Owner
E-mail: graa@pinn.net
Scope: Legislative and campaign consulting, grass-roots and coalition development, fund raising, and political training. **Founded:** 1994.

16628 ■ The Rothschild Image
13900 Tahiti Way, Ste. 308
Marina del Rey, CA 90292
Ph: (310)574-6018
Co. E-mail: info@rothschildimage.com
URL: http://www.rothschildimage.com
Contact: Ashley Rothschild, President
E-mail: ashley@rothschildimage.com
Scope: Image consultant offering advice through group exercises, lectures, wardrobe, and hair and makeup makeovers on how to discover the key components of a winning image. Specializes in designing the images of power brokers, politicians, and entrepreneurs, as well as clients at the start of their careers. **Publications:** "Is There an O'Neal Family Curse? - ABC News," Feb, 2007; "Can an Image Consultant Help You Dress for Success? - Wall Street Journal," Feb, 2006; "Reality Check - Paris Hilton & Amber Moore," Jan, 2004; "Britney's Mystery Man - Britney Spears," Dec, 2003; "People who need to redo their image," Jun, 2003; "Reshaping an Image," Jun, 2003; "Dress to Impress the World International Business Fashion," Apr, 2003. **Seminars:** S.T. A.R.POWER: A Professional Image Consultant Training Program; Learn How to Have More Success, Power and Romance in Your Life.

16629 ■ Smith, Dawson & Andrews
1150 Connecticut Ave. NW, Ste. 1025
Washington, DC 20036
Ph: (202)835-0740
Free: 866-482-2395
Fax: (202)775-8526
Co. E-mail: jims@sda-inc.com
URL: http://www.sda-inc.com
Contact: James P. Smith, President
Scope: A government relations/public affairs firm specializing in public policy, communications, legislative strategy and business development. **Founded:** 1981.

16630 ■ Stelle & Associates Inc.
4137 S 87th E Ave.
Tulsa, OK 74145
Ph: (918)425-4277
Fax: (918)622-2206
Co. E-mail: scott@stelleassociates.com
URL: http://www.stelleassociates.com
Contact: J. Scott Stelle, President
E-mail: scott@stelleassociates.com
Scope: Consulting consortium which allows highly qualified and experienced specialists an opportunity to function singly or in conjunction with others on projects of any size or duration. Has developed several levels of environmental due diligence to fulfill the need of clients in the most cost effective manner. **Founded:** 1991.

16631 ■ Stevens, Reed, Curcio and Potholm
201 N Union St., Ste. 200
Alexandria, VA 22314
Ph: (703)683-8326
Fax: (703)683-8826
Co. E-mail: pcurcio@srcpmedia.com
URL: http://www.srcpmedia.com
Contact: Betsy Vonderheid, Director
Scope: Republican media consulting firm that specializes in media production, public opinion research, direct mail design, opposition research and political strategy. **Founded:** 1993.

16632 ■ The Tarrance Group
201 N Union St., Ste. 410
Alexandria, VA 22314
Ph: (703)684-6688
Fax: (703)836-8256
Co. E-mail: tarrance@tarrance.com
URL: http://www.tarrance.com
Contact: Laura Osuna, Director
Scope: Specializes in research and international polling. Services include: political polling/political campaign consulting, corporate affairs, reputation management, issue advocacy, national political and environment research. **Founded:** 1977.

16633 ■ Triad Strategies L.L.C.
116 Pine St.
Harrisburg, PA 17101
Ph: (717)238-2970
URL: http://www.triadstrategies.com
Contact: Roy J. Wells, President
E-mail: rwells@triadstrategies.com
Scope: Government relations firm. Services include legislative and regulatory monitoring, legislative and executive branch lobbying, independent and quasi-public agency lobbying, issue research, issue management, grassroots organizing, public relations, strategic planning, and network marketing. **Founded:** 2002.

LIBRARIES

16634 ■ Burson-Marsteller Knowledge Center
230 Park Ave. S.
New York, NY 10003
Ph: (212)614-4000
Fax: (212)598-5581
Co. E-mail: tony.telloni@bm.com
URL: http://www.burson-marsteller.com/default.aspx
Contact: Tony Telloni, Manager
Scope: Advertising, public relations, marketing research. **Services:** Interlibrary loan; library open to clients and librarians; copying. **Founded:** 1955. **Holdings:** 1000 books. **Subscriptions:** 100 journals and other serials. **Telecommunication Services:** contactbm@bm.com.

16635 ■ University of Illinois at Urbana-Champaign - Communications Library
1st Fl. Gregory Hall, Rm. 122
810 S. Wright St.
Urbana, IL 61801
Ph: (217)333-2216
Fax: (217)333-2214
Co. E-mail: l-romero@illinois.edu
URL: http://www.library.illinois.edu/cmx/
Contact: Lisa Romero, Librarian
Scope: Advertising, broadcasting, journalism, magazines, newspapers, public relations, communication theory, mass communications, media studies. **Services:** Interlibrary loan; Library open to the public with permit from Main Library. **Founded:** 1933. **Holdings:** 16,000 books; 5 million advertisements; 400 videos. **Subscriptions:** 267 journals and other serials; 27 newspapers. **Telecommunication Services:** comlibrarian@library.illinois.edu.

16636 ■ University of Missouri--Columbia - Frank Lee Martin Memorial Journalism Library
102 Donald W. Reynolds Journalism Institute
Columbia, MO 65211
Ph: (573)882-7502
Fax: (573)884-4963
Co. E-mail: carnerd@missouri.edu
URL: http://mulibraries.missouri.edu/Journalism/
Contact: Dorothy Carner, Director, Library Services
Scope: Advertising, marketing, broadcasting, journalism, magazines, news writing and management, newspaper publishing, photojournalism, public relations, semantics, typography, graphic design, linotype, mass communication, International journalism, history. **Services:** Interlibrary loan; copying; computer access for research use; reference services; library open to the public with restrictions. **Founded:** 1908. **Holdings:** 50,000 books; 9000 bound periodical volumes. **Subscriptions:** 300 journals and newspapers. **Telecommunication Services:** jlib@missouri.edu.

ASSOCIATIONS AND OTHER ORGANIZATIONS

16637 ■ Affiliated Warehouse Companies (AWC)
PO Box 295
Hazlet, NJ 07730-0295
Ph: (732)739-2323
Fax: (732)739-4154
Co. E-mail: sales@awco.com
URL: http://www.awco.com
Description: Represents franchised public merchandise warehouse companies united for national sales work, advertising, and public relations. Assists in gathering rates and data pertaining to warehousing and distribution. Offers free consultation services to industry. Maintains placement service; compiles statistics. **Founded:** 1953.

16638 ■ American Chain of Warehouses (ACWI)
156 Flamingo Dr.
Beecher, IL 60401
Ph: (708)946-9792
Fax: (708)946-9793
Co. E-mail: bjurus@acwi.org
URL: http://www.acwi.org
Contact: William L. Jurus, Vice President of Sales and Marketing Vice President, Sales and Marketing
Description: Represents commercial warehouses. Provides national sales representation. Disseminates information. **Founded:** 1911. **Publications:** *American Chain of Warehouses--Membership Directory* (Annual).

16639 ■ American Society of Transportation and Logistics (AST&L)
PO Box 3363
Warrenton, VA 20188
Ph: (202)580-7270
Fax: (202)962-3939
Co. E-mail: info@astl.org
URL: http://www.astl.org
Contact: Mike Segal, Chairman
Description: Persons engaged in transportation, traffic, logistics, or physical distribution management. Works to establish standards of knowledge, technical training, experience, conduct, and ethics, and to encourage high standards of education and technical training requisite for the proper performance of traffic, transportation, logistics, and physical distribution management. Conducts extensive educational programs. **Founded:** 1946. **Publications:** *Transportation Journal* (Quarterly). **Awards:** Honorary Distinguished Logistics Professional (Annual). **Telecommunication Services:** astl@nitl.org.

16640 ■ International Association of Refrigerated Warehouses (IARW)
1500 King St., Ste. 201
Alexandria, VA 22314
Ph: (703)373-4300

Fax: (703)373-4301
Co. E-mail: email@gcca.org
URL: http://www.iarw.org
Contact: J. William Hudson, President
Description: Public refrigerated warehouses storing all types of perishable foods and other perishable products; associate members are industry suppliers. **Founded:** 1891. **Publications:** *Cold Facts* (Bimonthly); *Crisis Management Manual* (Periodic); *Directory of Public Refrigerated Warehouses* (Annual); *Maintenance and Modernization Manual*. **Educational Activities:** International Association of Refrigerated Warehouses Convention (Annual).

16641 ■ International Warehouse Logistics Association (IWLA)
2800 S River Rd., Ste. 260
Des Plaines, IL 60018-6003
Ph: (847)813-4699
Free: 800-525-0165
Fax: (847)813-0115
Co. E-mail: email@iwla.com
URL: http://www.iwla.com
Contact: Arthur Barrett, Chairman
Description: Fosters and promotes the growth and success of public and contract warehousing and related logistics services. Serves as the unified voice of the global outsourced warehouse logistics industry, representing 3PLs (third party logistics providers), 4PLs (fourth party logistics providers), public and contract warehouse logistics companies and their suppliers, setting standards, legal frameworks and best practices for the warehousing logistics industry for 110 years. Members of the Association receive services including legal assistance, marketing assistance and group buying programs. Owns its own insurance company (passing cost savings to members), holds an annual convention each year, and produces educational programs. **Founded:** 1891. **Publications:** *This Week at IWLA* (Weekly).

16642 ■ Order Fulfillment Council - Material Handling Industry of America
8720 Red Oak Blvd., Ste. 201
Charlotte, NC 28217-3992
Ph: (704)676-1190
Fax: (704)676-1199
URL: http://www.mhia.org/industrygroups/ofc
Contact: Larry E. Strayhorn, Executive Chairman of the Board
Description: Trade associations comprising storage industries. Compiles statistics; sponsors research and educational programs. **Founded:** 1986. **Publications:** *Storage and Handling Idea Book*. **Awards:** Material Handling Education Foundation Annual Scholarship (Annual).

16643 ■ Recreational Vehicle Aftermarket Association (RVAA)
1833 Centre Point Cir., Ste. 123
Naperville, IL 60563-4848
Ph: (630)596-9004

Fax: (630)544-5055
Co. E-mail: info@rvaahq.org
URL: http://www.rvaahq.com
Contact: Aaron Engberg, President
Description: Distributors, suppliers, and manufacturer's agents in the RV aftermarket industry. **Founded:** 1969. **Educational Activities:** Executive Conference (Annual). **Awards:** Agent of the Year (Annual); Best of the Year (Annual); Catalog of the Year (Annual); Suppliers of the Year (Annual).

16644 ■ Self Storage Association (SSA)
1901 N Beauregard St., Ste. 450
Alexandria, VA 22311
Ph: (703)575-8000
Free: 888-735-3784
Fax: (703)575-8901
Co. E-mail: info@selfstorage.org
URL: http://www.selfstorage.org
Contact: Patrick Reilly, Director
Description: Represents owners and operators of self-storage facilities. Improves the quality of management, customer service, facilities; promotes public management, marketing, security and related topics. Lobbies for state legislation protecting and recognizing self-storage owners and operators. **Scope:** self storage. **Founded:** 1975. **Subscriptions:** 1000 archival material audiovisuals books periodicals. **Publications:** *SSA Globe Magazine* (Monthly).

16645 ■ SOLE - The International Society of Logistics (SOLE)
8100 Professional Pl., Ste. 111
Hyattsville, MD 20785-2229
Ph: (301)459-8446
Fax: (301)459-1522
Co. E-mail: solehq@erols.com
URL: http://www.sole.org
Contact: Mr. Timothy H. Overstreet, President
Description: Represents corporate and individual management and technical practitioners in the field of logistics, including scientists, engineers, educators, managers, and other specialists in commerce, aerospace, and other industries, government, and the military. (Logistics is the art and science of management engineering and technical activities concerned with requirements, and designing, supplying, and maintaining resources to support objectives, plans, and operations.) Covers every logistics specialty, including reliability, maintainability, systems and equipment maintenance, maintenance support equipment, human factors, training and training equipment, spare parts, overhaul and repair, handbooks, field site activation and operation, field engineering, facilities, packaging, supply chain management, materials handling, and transportation. Sponsors on-line job referral service; conducts specialized education programs. **Founded:** 1966. **Publications:** *Logistics Spectrum* (Quarterly); *Annual International Conference and Exposition Proceedings* (Annual); *SOLE-The International Society of Logistics--Membership Directory* (Annual). **Educational Activities:** International Logistics Congress (Periodic); District 02 Professional Development Forum (Annual); SOLE Annual International Logistics Conference and Exhibition (Annual). **Awards:** Fel-

low; Field Awards; Founders Medal; Armitage Medal (Periodic); Eccles Medal (Periodic); Fellow (Periodic); Field Awards (Annual); Founders Medal (Periodic); Young Logistician Award (Annual); President's Award for Merit; Jack L. Williams Space Logistics Medal; Young Logistician Award; Doctoral Dissertation Award/Scholarships (Annual); Jack H. Williams Space Logistics Medal (Periodic); Logistics in the Community Award (Periodic); Morris L. Grumbine Award for Service (Periodic); Presidents Award for Merit (Annual); Prize Papers - Logistics Spectrum and Annual Symposium Proceedings Award (Annual).

16646 ■ Warehousing Education and Research Council (WERC)
1100 Jorie Blvd., Ste. 170
Oak Brook, IL 60523-4413
Ph: (630)990-0001
Fax: (630)990-0256
Co. E-mail: wercoffice@werc.org
URL: http://www.werc.org
Contact: Michael J. Mikitka, Chief Executive Officer
Description: Represents distribution and warehousing professionals who lead, direct, and manage the efficient flow of information, materials, and finished goods throughout the supply chain. Provides practical ways that can be apply to improve service and reduce costs. **Scope:** warehousing, distribution. **Founded:** 1977. **Subscriptions:** 25 books reports. **Educational Activities:** Warehousing Education and Research Council Annual Conference; Warehousing Education and Research Council Conference (Annual).

REFERENCE WORKS

16647 ■ Allied Distribution, Inc.--Membership Directory
Pub: Allied Distribution Inc.
URL(s): www.warehousenetwork.com. **Released:** Biennial **Covers:** About 60 member public warehouses in the United States, Canada and Mexico. **Entries include:** Company name, address, phone, principal executives, financial data, and list of services. **Arrangement:** Geographical. **Indexes:** Alphabetical, geographical.

16648 ■ American Chain of Warehouses--Membership Directory
Pub: American Chain of Warehouses
Contact: William L. Jurus, Vice President of Sales and Marketing
URL(s): www.acwi.org. **Released:** Annual; April. **Covers:** About 45 member public warehouses in the U.S. **Entries include:** Company name, address, names of executives, facilities, capital, types of storage, floor space, insured contents rate. **Arrangement:** Geographical.

16649 ■ Associated Warehouses--Directory of Services
Pub: Associated Warehouses Inc.
URL(s): www.awilogistics.com. **Released:** Annual; August. **Price:** Free. **Covers:** 50 members. **Entries include:** Warehouse name, address, phone, telex, executives' names, and descriptive information (railroad siding and service data, storage area available, insurance rates, financial references, and facilities). **Arrangement:** Geographical. **Indexes:** Geographical and warehouse name.

16650 ■ "Cold-Storage Cargo Facility a Late Bloomer" in Houston Business Journal (Vol. 40, August 28, 2009, No. 16, pp. 1A)
Pub: American City Business Journals
Ed: Jennifer Dawson. **Description:** Trammell Crow Company leased half of the 61,000 square foot IAH International Air Cargo Centre II to Tradewinds Cargo Handling. The facility, located at George Bush Intercontinental Airport, is intended to be a destination of fresh flowers and food from Latin America.

16651 ■ "Company Hopes To Pack Profits With Self-Storage" in Crain's Detroit Business (Vol. 24, February 18, 2008, No. 7, pp. 15)
Pub: Crain Communications Inc. - Detroit
Ed: Daniel Duggan. **Description:** Storage Opportunity Partners has purchased a vacant building to convert into a self-storage facility.

16652 ■ International Warehouse Logistics Association--Roster of Members
Pub: International Warehouse Logistics Association
Contact: Joel Anderson, President
E-mail: janderson@iwla.com
URL(s): www.iwla.com/members/roster.aspx. **Released:** Annual **Covers:** 550 warehouses, general storage facilities and distribution centers for non-refrigerated products in the US, Canada, Panama, Mexico, Venezuela, Puerto Rico, Dominican Republic and Costa Rica. **Arrangement:** Geographical.

16653 ■ Leonard's Guide National Warehouse and Distribution Directory
Pub: G.R. Leonard & Co.
Contact: David Ercolani, Manager
URL(s): www.leonardsguide.com. **Released:** Latest edition 2011. **Price:** $175, Individuals print. **Covers:** Approximately 4,000 warehouses in the U.S. and Canada. **Entries include:** Name, address, phone, storage areas, facilities, truck dock capacity, rail siding, geographical area served, products handled, services offered, year established, number of employees, distribution service, insurance and general information. **Arrangement:** Geographical by state. **Indexes:** Geographical by ZIP code, alphabetical, categorical.

16654 ■ "Merchants Association Working on Deal for Large Wholesale Warehouse" in Austin Business JournalInc. (September 19, 2008)
Pub: American City Business Journals
Ed: Jean Kwon. **Description:** Greater Austin Merchants Association planning to buy a former Dell Outlet Factory in Austin, Texas and convert it into a warehouse for convenience stores and gas stations.

16655 ■ "Substantial Deal Expected to Create Jobs, Help Industrial Market" in Tampa Bay Business Journal (Vol. 30, January 8, 2010, No. 3)
Pub: American City Business Journals
Ed: Janet Leiser. **Description:** Food distribution firm Gordon Food Service (GFS) is on the brink of purchasing Albertson's million-square-foot warehouse along with 158 acres of space. The deal between GFS and Albertson's could expand GFS' presence in west Central Florida. A history of GFS' growth is included.

STATISTICAL SOURCES

16656 ■ RMA Annual Statement Studies
Pub: Risk Management Association
Contact: Kevin M. Blakey, President
Released: Annual. **Price:** $175.00 2006-07 edition, $105.00. **Description:** Contains composite balance sheets and income statements for more than 360 industries, including the accounting, auditing, and bookkeeping industries. Also contains five years of comparative historical data for discerning trends. Includes 16 commonly used ratios, computed for most of the size groupings for nearly every industry.

TRADE PERIODICALS

16657 ■ Self-Storage Now!
Pub: Mini-Storage Messenger
Contact: Dan Sommer, Vice President, Communications
Ed: Darin Barney, Editor. **Released:** Bimonthly, 4/year. **Price:** Free. **Description:** Written to help mini-storage management personnel increase profits through marketing tips, business advice, new products, space rental sales techniques, and the sale of products and services to tenants.

TRADE SHOWS AND CONVENTIONS

16658 ■ Self Storage Association Conference and Tradeshow
Self Storage Association
1900 N. Beauregard St., Ste. 110
Alexandria, VA 22311

Ph: (703)575-8000
Free: 888-735-3784
Fax: (703)575-8901
Co. E-mail: ssa@selfstorage.org
URL: http://www.selfstorage.org
Contact: Michael Riva, Chairman of the Board
URL(s): www.selfstorage.org. **Frequency:** Semiannual. **Audience:** Traders, buyers, and association members. **Principal Exhibits:** Equipment, supplies, and services designed for and pertinent to construction, maintenance, and operation of self storage facilities. Meal functions held in exhibit hall. **Telecommunication Services:** jclisham@ctselfstor.com.

CONSULTANTS

16659 ■ K.B. Ackerman Co. (KBA)—Ken Ackerman's Warehousing Forum
2041 Riverside Dr., Ste. 204
Columbus, OH 43221
Ph: (614)488-3165
Fax: (614)488-9243
Co. E-mail: ken@warehousing-forum.com
URL: http://www.warehousingforum.com
Contact: Kenneth B. Ackerman, President
E-mail: ken@warehousing-forum.com
Scope: Consultant on warehousing and logistics management. Also serves as expert witness in litigation and labor arbitration matters. **Founded:** 1981. **Publications:** "Warehousing Tips"; "Lean Warehousing"; "Fundamentals of Supply Chain Management"; "Auditing Warehouse Performance"; "Warehousing Tips"; "Warehousing Fundamentals"; "Words of Warehousing 2". **Seminars:** Family Business-Perpetuating Success; Best Practices In Warehouse Management; Quality and Leadership in the Warehouse; Improving Warehouse Performance; Warehousing as a Competitive Weapon; Lean Warehousing.

16660 ■ M.W. Burke & Associates Inc.
185 Front St., Ste. 207
Danville, CA 94526
Ph: (925)838-9070
Fax: (925)838-4695
Co. E-mail: mwburke@aol.com
Contact: Maurice W. Burke, President
Scope: Provider of engineering and management consulting services to manufacturing, distribution and service oriented firms. Specializes in industrial engineering, distribution and warehousing, manpower analysis and scheduling systems, site selection, plant layout, material handling systems, cost reduction and methods improvement, equipment selection and replacement, inventory management, administrative systems, manufacturing systems, and packaging. **Founded:** 1976.

16661 ■ KEOGH Consulting Inc.
10217 Brecksville Rd.
Brecksville, OH 44141
Ph: (440)526-2002
Fax: (440)526-9466
Co. E-mail: information@keogh1.com
URL: http://www.keogh1.com
Contact: Ravi Madala, President
Scope: A professional supply chain logistics consulting firm offering a full range of facility planning, design, and management consulting services for companies involved in manufacturing, warehousing, and distribution. Specializes in integrated supply chain solutions, focusing on logistics network and supply chain strategy, operations planning and assessment, and software selection, integration, configuration and implementation. **Founded:** 1983. **Publications:** "Operations & Fulfillment - Work WITH me"; "Supply Chain Optimization101"; "Don't Waste Your Space!"; "Finding Hidden Productivity"; "Product Slotting The Secret to Increased Productivity"; "New Equipment Digest". **Seminars:** Keys to DC Automation Excellence, Oct, 2008; Keys to Operations and Integration Success, Sep, 2008.

16662 ■ Raymond Nelson Distribution Consultants
247 S Gate Ln.
Southport, CT 06890-1465

Ph: (203)319-7479
Contact: Raymond A. Nelson, Owner
Scope: Offers consulting services in advanced warehousing, distribution, materials handling, inventory control and management and transportation systems. **Founded:** 1969. **Seminars:** Order Picking, Packing, and Warehousing; Controlling the Costs of Physical Distribution; Modernizing and Mechanizing Warehousing Operations; Computerizing Warehouse Operations; Logistic Management.

16663 ■ Trainor & Associates
5720 Robin Hop Ln.
Memphis, TN 38134
Ph: (901)373-8940
Fax: (901)377-0111
Co. E-mail: bobt@gotrainor.com
URL: http://www.gotrainor.com
Contact: Robert P. Trainor, President
E-mail: rpt3@prodigy.net

Scope: Provider of industrial engineering services to include work process analysis. Industries served: Food, machining, assembly, engine rebuild for automotive and locomotive, metal fabrication, packaging, manufacturing, warehousing, and distribution. **Founded:** 1986. **Publications:** "You Want it When?," Memphis Business Journal; "Walking the Assembly Line," The Daily News, May, 2006. **Seminars:** Cost Control for Work Measurement Process Improvements, Kaizen Event; Managers and Supervisors.

16664 ■ Wesley-Kind Associates Inc.
200 Old Country Road, Ste. 364
Mineola, NY 11501-4235
Ph: (516)747-3434
Fax: (516)248-2728
Contact: Daniel A. Kind, Executive Director
Scope: Material handling and distribution consultants offering advice on plant and warehouse layouts and operating systems for the movement, storage and control of materials and products. Expertise includes materials and production management, advanced handling/storage systems, packaging and unitizing systems, capacity, productivity and customer service audits, order filling systems, data processing control systems, transportation systems, site location analysis, facilities planning, and implementation. Industries served: manufacturing, distribution and retail corporations and state and U.S. Government agencies. **Founded:** 1974. **Publications:** "How to Reengineer the Storage Function," Penton Publishing, 1995.

COMPUTER SYSTEMS/ SOFTWARE

16665 ■ *RealEasyBooks, Inc.* / *RPMW*
PO Box 133
Alamo, CA 94507
Ph: (925)280-7769
Fax: (831)855-9033
Co. E-mail: support@rpmw.com
URL: http://www.rpmw.com

Price: $100.00-$1650.00. **Description:** Available for IBM computers and compatibles. System maintains records of monthly income and expenses from properties such as mini-storage units.

RESEARCH CENTERS

16666 ■ Warehousing Education and Research Council (WERC)
1100 Jorie Blvd., Ste. 170
Oak Brook, IL 60523-4413
Ph: (630)990-0001
Fax: (630)990-0256
Co. E-mail: wercoffice@werc.org
URL: http://www.werc.org
Contact: Michael J. Mikitka, Chief Executive Officer

Founded: 1977. **Telecommunication Services:** mmikitka@werc.org.

ASSOCIATIONS AND OTHER ORGANIZATIONS

16667 ■ Automotive Oil Change Association (AOCA)
1701 N Greenville Ave., Ste. 404
Richardson, TX 75081
Ph: (972)458-9468
Free: 800-331-0329
Fax: (972)458-9539
Co. E-mail: pawirth@cox.net
URL: http://www.aoca.org
Contact: Pat Wirth, President
Description: Owners and operators of oil change shops. Works to solve problems and advance interests of members. Offers group insurance and credit card program. Compiles statistics; disseminates information, employee training programs. **Founded:** 1987. **Publications:** *Oil Changing Times* (Bimonthly). **Educational Activities:** Fast Lube Expo (Annual); Fast Lube Expo (Annual). **Awards:** Member of the Year (Annual).

REFERENCE WORKS

16668 ■ *"Banking on Twitter"* in Baltimore Business Journal (Vol. 27, February 6, 2010, No. 40, pp. 1)
Pub: American City Business Journals
Ed: Gary Haber. **Description:** Ways that banks are using Twitter, Facebook and other social networking sites to provide customer services is discussed. First Mariner Bank is one of those banks that are finding the social media platform as a great way to reach customers. Privacy issues regarding this marketing trend are examined.

16669 ■ *"Thomas Morley; President, The Lube Stop Inc., 37' in Crain's Cleveland Business (Vol. 28, November 19, 2007, No. 46, pp. F-12)
Pub: Crain Communications, Inc.
Ed: David Bennett. **Description:** Profile of Thomas Morley, president of The Lube Stop Inc., who is dedicated to promoting the company's strong environmental record as an effective way to differentiate Lube Stop from its competition. Since Mr. Morley came to the company in 2004, Lube Stop has increased sales by 10 percent and has boosted its operating profits by 30 percent.

TRADE PERIODICALS

16670 ■ *O & A Marketing News*
Pub: KAL Publications Inc.
Contact: Linda Squeo, Manager
URL(s): www.kalpub.com/OANews/oa.html. **Ed:** Kathy Laderman. **Released:** 7/yr. **Price:** $20, Individuals; $35, Two years.

FRANCHISES AND BUSINESS OPPORTUNITIES

16671 ■ All Tune and Lube
ATL International, Inc.
8334 Veterans Hwy.
Millersville, MD 21108
Ph: (410)987-1011
Free: 800-935-8863
Fax: (410)987-4827
Co. E-mail: alltune@erols.com
URL: http://www.alltuneandlube.com
Description: Automotive servicing. "One stop" total car care, including tune-ups, brakes, exhaust, engine replacement and more. **No. of Franchise Units:** 300. **Founded:** 1986.. **Franchised:** 1986. **Equity Capital Needed:** $35,000+. **Franchise Fee:** $32,000. **Financial Assistance:** Yes. **Training:** All Tune and Lube provides extensive training at headquarters and in the individual center locations. Provides 1 week of center management training and operational support.

16672 ■ Econo Lube N' Tune
128 S Tryon St., Ste. 900
Charlotte, NC 28202
Ph: (800)275-5200
Description: Auto service, lube, tune and brakes. **No. of Franchise Units:** 173. **No. of Company-Owned Units:** 95. **Founded:** 1973.. **Franchised:** 1978. **Franchise Fee:** $39,500. **Financial Assistance:** Yes. **Training:** Yes.

16673 ■ Equipro Inc.
W180 N11691 River Ln., Ste. A
Germantown, WI 53022
Ph: (262)257-4100
Free: 866-378-4776
Fax: (262)257-4105
Co. E-mail: info@equiproservice.com
URL: http://www.equiproservice.com
Description: Nationwide network of franchised service centers. A full service solution for the light construction industry. **No. of Franchise Units:** 11. **No. of Company-Owned Units:** 2. **Founded:** 2003.. **Franchised:** 2005. **Equity Capital Needed:** $151,100-$345,400. **Franchise Fee:** $20,000-$30,000. **Royalty Fee:** 7.5%. **Training:** Provides 1 week at headquarters, 1 week onsite, 9 weeks technical training by product manufacturers, and ongoing support.

16674 ■ Express Oil Change
1880 Southpark Dr.
Birmingham, AL 35244
Ph: (205)397-1148
Fax: (205)940-6025
Description: Fast automotive service and minor automotive repair. **No. of Franchise Units:** 109. **No. of Company-Owned Units:** 76. **Founded:** 1979. **Franchised:** 1979. **Equity Capital Needed:** $300,000. **Franchise Fee:** $35,000. **Training:** Provides 8 to 10 weeks of training for franchisee and/or key operator and 2 weeks training for franchisee's store crew.

16675 ■ Fresh Coat
Franchise Dept.
10700 Montgomery Rd., Ste. 300
Cincinnati, OH 45242
Ph: (866)708-9355
Fax: (513)563-2691
Co. E-mail: inquiry@freshcoatpainters.com
URL: http://www.freshcoatpainters.com
Description: Homeowners spend millions of dollars everyday on painting kitchens, family rooms, every room in the house. Fresh coat has captured a niche in the multi-billion dollar industry. As a franchisee, you build your business through proven marketing, expertise and a system exclusive to Fresh Coat. This business is about building an organization and managing people; not doing the work yourself. **No. of Franchise Units:** 60. **Founded:** 2004.. **Franchised:** 2005. **Equity Capital Needed:** $38,850-$63,850. **Franchise Fee:** $31,900. **Financial Assistance:** Yes. **Training:** A complete turnkey operation. Training program provides tools needed to operate a successful and profitable business, including getting the business, payroll, computer training, market knowledge, recruitment, operations, scheduling and bidding.

16676 ■ Grease Monkey International
7450 East Progress Pl.
Greenwood Village, CO 80111
Ph: (800)364-0352
Fax: (303)308-5906
Co. E-mail: franchiseinfo@greasemonkeyintl.com
Description: Provides quick, convenient vehicle maintenance services. Offers quick oil change and lubrication services. **No. of Franchise Units:** 242. **No. of Company-Owned Units:** 2. **Founded:** 1978.. **Franchised:** 1979. **Equity Capital Needed:** $250,000 liquidity; $500,000 net worth. **Franchise Fee:** $30,000. **Training:** Training is provided at corporate headquarters and onsite. Franchisor also assists with site selection and construction.

16677 ■ Jiffy Lube Canada
1101 Blair Rd.
Burlington, ON, Canada L7M 1T3
Free: 800-327-9532
Co. E-mail: jiffy-lube-development@shell.com
URL: http://www.jiffylube.com
Description: Fast oil change and preventative maintenance services. **No. of Franchise Units:** 45. **Founded:** 1979.. **Franchised:** 1979. **Equity Capital Needed:** $187,000-$400,000. **Franchise Fee:** $25,000. **Training:** Initial and ongoing training provided.

16678 ■ Jiffy Lube Intl., Inc.
Pennzoil Quaker State Co.
PO Box 4427
Houston, TX 77210-4427
Free: 800-327-9532
Fax: (713)546-8762
Description: Quick oil change and preventative maintenance. **No. of Franchise Units:** 1,931. **Founded:** 1979.. **Franchised:** 1979. **Equity Capital Needed:** $196,500-$304,000. **Franchise Fee:** $0-$7,500. **Royalty Fee:** 3%. **Financial Assistance:** Limited third party financing available. **Training:** Provides 2-4 weeks training at headquarters, followed with onsite with ongoing support.

16679 ■ Lubepro's International, Inc.
1740 S Bell School Rd.
Cherry Valley, IL 61016
Ph: (815)332-9200
Fax: (815)332-9355
Description: LubePros service centers provides fast-service oil changes, lubrication, replacement of certain filters and fluids and certain related courtesy services for motor vehicles. **No. of Franchise Units:** 19. **No. of Company-Owned Units:** 15. **Equity Capital Needed:** $223,000 initial investment, not including land, building, improvements; $400,000 net worth, $150,000 liquid. **Franchise Fee:** $32,500. **Training:** Offers 10 days of marketing management, operational, and advertising support services are provided.

16680 ■ Oil Butler International, Corp.
1599 Rte. 22 W
Union, NJ 07083
Ph: (908)687-3283
Fax: (908)687-7617
Description: Provides oil change service. **No. of Franchise Units:** 100. **No. of Company-Owned Units:** 1. **Founded:** 1987.. **Franchised:** 1991. **Equity Capital Needed:** $25,000-$34,000. **Franchise Fee:** $15,000. **Training:** Yes.

16681 ■ Oil Can Henry's
OCH International, Inc.
19150 SW 90th Ave.
Tualatin, OR 97062
Ph: (503)243-6311

Free: 800-765-6244
Description: Fast oil, lube and fluid franchises. **No. of Franchise Units:** 59. **No. of Company-Owned Units:** 29. **Founded:** 1978.. **Franchised:** 1989. **Equity Capital Needed:** $237,900 cash; $300,000 total investment. **Franchise Fee:** $25,000. **Royalty Fee:** 5.5%. **Training:** Available 5-6 weeks at headquarters, 10+ days at franchisee's location and onging support.

16682 ■ Precision Tune Auto Care, Inc.
Precision Auto Care, Inc.
748 Miller Dr. SE
Leesburg, VA 20175
Ph: (703)777-9095
Free: 800-438-8863
Fax: (703)669-1539
URL: http://www.precision-tune.com
Description: Auto care, quick lube. **No. of Franchise Units:** 400. **No. of Company-Owned Units:** 5. **Founded:** 1975.. **Franchised:** 1978. **Equity Capital Needed:** $100,000 or more. **Franchise Fee:** $25,000. **Financial Assistance:** Yes. **Training:** Yes.

16683 ■ Valvoline Instant Oil Change
Ashland Inc.
3499 Blazer Pky.
Lexington, KY 40509
Ph: (859)357-7303
Free: 800-622-6846
Fax: (859)357-6919
Co. E-mail: jjtaylor@ashland.com
URL: http://www.viocfranchise.com
Description: Automobile oil change service. **No. of Franchise Units:** 612. **No. of Company-Owned**

Units: 300. **Founded:** 1986.. **Franchised:** 1988. **Equity Capital Needed:** $800,000-$1,000,000 liquid assets/$1,000,000 net worth. **Franchise Fee:** $30,000. **Financial Assistance:** Yes. **Training:** Yes.

16684 ■ Victory Lane Quick Oil Change
405 Little Lake Dr.
Ann Arbor, MI 48103
Ph: (734)996-1196
Fax: (734)996-4912
Description: Quick oil and lube service. **No. of Franchise Units:** 41. **No. of Company-Owned Units:** 5. **Founded:** 1980.. **Franchised:** 1986. **Equity Capital Needed:** $100,000-$350,000 net worth. **Franchise Fee:** $30,000. **Financial Assistance:** Yes. **Training:** Yes.

COMPUTERIZED DATABASES

16685 ■ *International Petroleum Encyclopedia*
1421 S Sheridan Rd.
Tulsa, OK 74112
Ph: (918)835-3161
Free: 800-331-4463
Fax: (918)831-9497
Co. E-mail: headquarters@pennwell.com
URL: http://www.pennwell.com
Availability: CD-ROM: PennWell Corp. **Type:** Full-text; Statistical.

ASSOCIATIONS AND OTHER ORGANIZATIONS

16686 ■ Alliance of Canadian Cinema, Television and Radio Artists (ACTRA)
625 Church St., 3rd Fl.
Toronto, ON, Canada M4Y 2G1
Ph: (416)489-1311
Free: 800-387-3516
Fax: (416)489-8076
Co. E-mail: national@actra.ca
URL: http://www.actra.ca
Contact: Ferne Downey, President
Description: Performing artists in the television, radio, film, and other recorded media. Seeks to obtain equitable compensation and safe working conditions for members. Represents members in negotiations with employers; monitors workplace conditions in the film and broadcasting industries. **Founded:** 1943. **Publications:** *InterACTRA News* (Quarterly).

16687 ■ Associated Press Broadcast (APB)
AP Broadcast News Center
1100 13th St., Ste. 700
Washington, DC 20005
Ph: (202)641-9921
Free: 800-342-5127
Co. E-mail: lperryman@ap.org
URL: http://www.apbroadcast.com
Contact: Mary Junck, Chairwoman
Description: Broadcast stations in the United States that are members of the Associated Press. Advances journalism through radio and television. Cooperates with the AP in order to make available accurate and impartial news. Serves as a liaison between radio and television stations that are members of the AP and representatives of those stations. **Founded:** 1941. **Awards:** APB National Awards (Annual).

16688 ■ Broadcast Cable Credit Association (BCCA)
550 W Frontage Rd., Ste. 3600
Northfield, IL 60093
Ph: (847)881-8757
Fax: (847)784-8059
Co. E-mail: info@bccacredit.com
URL: http://www.bccacredit.com
Contact: Richard Taub
Description: Enables members to efficiently manage credit risk and increase profitability. Provides industry specific credit reports on individual agencies, advertisers, or buying services (local or national). **Founded:** 1961. **Publications:** *BCCA Credit Handbook* (Annual); *Credit and Collection Survey*; *Update* (Monthly); *The Financial Manager for the Media Professional/Credit Topics* (Bimonthly). **Educational Activities:** Broadcast Cable Credit Association Conference (Annual); Distance Learning (Monthly). **Awards:** Lifetime Achievement (Annual).

16689 ■ Canadian Association of Broadcasters (CAB)—Association Canadienne des Radiodiffuseurs (ACR)
PO Box 627, Sta. B
Ottawa, ON, Canada K1P 5S2
Ph: (613)233-4035
Fax: (613)233-6961
Co. E-mail: cab@cab-acr.ca
URL: http://www.cab-acr.ca
Contact: Mr. Elmer Hildebrand, Chairman
Description: Collective voice of the majority of Canada's private radio and television stations, networks, and specialty services. Develops industry-wide strategic plans, works to improve the financial health of the industry, and promotes private broadcasting's role as Canada's leading programmer and local service provider. **Founded:** 1926. **Awards:** Gold Ribbon Award for Broadcast Excellence (Annual); Hall of Fame (Annual); BBM Canada Scholarships; Ruth Hancock Scholarships; Gold Ribbon for Community Service (Radio); Gold Ribbon for Promotion of Musical Canadian Talent (Radio); Gold Ribbon Award for Broadcast Excellence; Gold Ribbon for Community Service (Television); Gold Ribbon for Community Service (Specialty/Pay/PPV); Gold Ribbon for Outstanding Community Service by an Individual Broadcaster; Gold Ribbon Award for News, Documentary, and Information Programming (Annual). **Telecommunication Services:** cab@cab-acr.org.

16690 ■ Canadian Disc Jockey Association (CDJA)
1008 Manchester Rd.
London, ON, Canada N6H 5J1
Ph: (519)287-3600
Free: 877-472-0653
Fax: (519)472-0242
Co. E-mail: chairperson@cdja.ca
URL: http://www.cdja.ca
Contact: Darryl Thompson, Chairman of the Board
Description: Disc jockeys and others promote excellence in service through education, information, networking, and support. Promotes professional development among members. Facilitates exchange of information among members; represents members' interests. **Founded:** 1976. **Publications:** *CUED-UP Street*; *DJ Pulse* (Quarterly). **Awards:** National President's Award; National President's Award (Annual).

16691 ■ Country Radio Broadcasters (CRB)
819 18th Ave. S
Nashville, TN 37203
Ph: (615)327-4487
Fax: (615)329-4492
Co. E-mail: bill@crb.org
URL: http://www.crb.org
Contact: Bill Mayne, Executive Director
Description: Seeks to advance and promote the study of the science of broadcasting through the mutual exchange of ideas by conducting seminars and workshops, as well as providing scholarships to broadcasting students. **Founded:** 1970. **Educational Activities:** Country Radio Broadcasters Seminar; Country Radio Seminar & Show (Annual). **Awards:** Artist Humanitarian Award (Annual); Career Achievement Award (Annual); Country Music DJ Hall of Fame (Annual); Country Radio Hall of Fame (Annual); President's Award (Annual); Radio Humanitarian Award (Annual); Tom Rivers Humanitarian Award (Annual); Artist Humanitarian Award; Career Achieve-ment Award; Country Music DJ Hall of Fame; Country Radio Hall of Fame; President's Award; Radio Humanitarian Award.

16692 ■ *CUED-UP Street*
1008 Manchester Rd.
London, ON, Canada N6H 5J1
Ph: (519)287-3600
Free: 877-472-0653
Fax: (519)472-0242
Co. E-mail: chairperson@cdja.ca
URL: http://www.cdja.ca
Contact: Darryl Thompson, Chairman of the Board

16693 ■ *DJ Pulse*
1008 Manchester Rd.
London, ON, Canada N6H 5J1
Ph: (519)287-3600
Free: 877-472-0653
Fax: (519)472-0242
Co. E-mail: chairperson@cdja.ca
URL: http://www.cdja.ca
Contact: Darryl Thompson, Chairman of the Board
Released: Quarterly **Price:** included in membership dues.

16694 ■ *InterACTRA News*
625 Church St., 3rd Fl.
Toronto, ON, Canada M4Y 2G1
Ph: (416)489-1311
Free: 800-387-3516
Fax: (416)489-8076
Co. E-mail: national@actra.ca
URL: http://www.actra.ca
Contact: Ferne Downey, President
Released: Quarterly

16695 ■ *InteRadio*
705 Bourget St., Ste. 100
Montreal, QC, Canada H4C 2M6
Ph: (514)982-0351
Fax: (514)849-7129
Co. E-mail: secretariat@si.amarc.org
URL: http://www.amarc.org
Contact: Marcelo Solervicens, Secretary General
Released: Periodic

16696 ■ International Radio and Television Society Foundation (IRTS)
1697 Broadway, 10th Fl.
New York, NY 10019
Ph: (212)867-6650
Fax: (212)867-6653
URL: http://irtsfoundation.org
Contact: Joyce M. Tudryn, President
URL(s): www.irts.org. **Description:** Individuals interested in management, sales, or executive production in the radio, television, and cable industries and their allied fields. Seeks to educate members through seminars. Conducts summer internships for college students majoring in communications. **Founded:** 1939. **Publications:** *International Radio and Television Society Newsletter*; *International Radio and Television Society Foundation--Roster Yearbook* (Annual); *International Radio and Television Society Foundation--Roster Yearbook* (Annual).

Educational Activities: International Radio and Television Society Foundation Luncheon. **Awards:** Barry Sherman Fellowship (Annual); Coltrin Case Study Award (Annual); IRTS Foundation Award (Annual); IRTS Gold Medal (Annual); IRTS Stanton Fellow Award (Annual); Foundation Award; Gold Medal Award; International Radio and Television Society Foundation Summer Fellowships Program; Coltrin Professor of the Year (Annual); Stephen K. Nenno Inspirational Fellow Award (Annual).

16697 ■ National Association of Broadcasters (NAB)
1771 N St. NW
Washington, DC 20036
Ph: (202)429-5300
Fax: (202)429-4199
Co. E-mail: nab@nab.org
URL: http://www.nab.org
Contact: Steven W. Newberry, Chairman of the Board

Description: Serves as the voice for the nation's radio and television broadcasters. Advances the interests of members in federal government, industry and public affairs; improves the quality and profitability of broadcasting; encourages content and technology innovation; and spotlights the important and unique ways stations serve their communities. Delivers value to its members through advocacy, education and innovation. Relies on the grassroots strength of its television and radio members and state broadcast associations. Helps broadcasters seize opportunities in the digital age. Offers broadcasters a variety of programs to help them grow in their careers, promote diversity in the workplace and strengthen their businesses. **Scope:** broadcasting. **Founded:** 1922. **Subscriptions:** archival material books clippings monographs periodicals. **Awards:** Crystal Awards (Annual); Distinguished Service Award (Annual); Engineering Achievement in Radio Award (Annual); Engineering Achievement in Television Award (Annual); Mal Beville Award (Annual); Marconi Radio Award (Annual); National Radio Award (Annual); Service to America Awards (Annual); Engineering Achievement Awards; Marconi Radio Awards; Hugh Malcolm Beville, Jr. Award; Spirit of Broadcasting Award; International Broadcasting Excellence Award; Wally Jorgenson Award.

16698 ■ National Federation of Community Broadcasters (NFCB)
1970 Broadway, Ste. 1000
Oakland, CA 94612
Ph: (510)451-8200
Fax: (510)451-8208
Co. E-mail: comments@nfcb.org
URL: http://www.nfcb.org
Contact: Sue Matters, Chairwoman

Description: Independent, community-licensed radio and radio production organizations. Fosters the development of public policy at the legislative, regulatory and administrative levels; aids the growth of community-oriented radio stations and advances the public interest in mass communications; seeks an equitable distribution of federal funds appropriated for noncommercial broadcasting and develops support for community-oriented broadcast projects; facilitates the exchange of program materials, information and technical expertise; assists in the organization and expansion of new and innovative broadcast stations throughout the U.S. Provides services and consultation. **Founded:** 1975. **Publications:** Community Radio News (Monthly); The NFCB Public Radio Legal Handbook: A Guide to FCC Rules and Regulations; NFCB's Guide to Underwriting for Public Radio; Audiocraft: Tools and Techniques of Audio Production (Monthly); Starting an LPFM Station. **Educational Activities:** Community Radio Conference (Annual). **Awards:** Bader Award (Annual); Volunteer of the Year (Annual).

16699 ■ North American Broadcasters Association (NABA)
Canadian Broadcasting Ctre.
25 John St. W, Ste. 6C300
Toronto, ON, Canada M5V 3G7
Ph: (416)598-9877
Fax: (416)598-9774
Co. E-mail: contact@nabanet.com
URL: http://www.nabanet.com/nabaweb
Contact: Robert Briskman, President

Description: Network broadcasters in North America concerned with international matters that affect broadcasting. Seeks to identify, study and provide solutions to international questions concerning broadcasting. Creates opportunities for North American broadcasters to share information, identify common interests and reach on issues of an international nature. Works with other international broadcasters' associations and unions toward gaining an effective voice in international circles on matters that affect broadcasting. Organizes international conferences in conjunction with other broadcasting associations. **Founded:** 1972. **Educational Activities:** North American Broadcasters Association Meeting (Annual). **Awards:** NABA International Achievement Award; NABA International Achievement Award (Annual).

16700 ■ Radio Advertising Bureau (RAB)
1320 Greenway Dr., Ste. 500
Irving, TX 75038-2587
Ph: (212)681-7214
Free: 800-232-3131
Co. E-mail: efarber@rab.com
URL: http://www.rab.com
Contact: Erica Farber, President

Description: Includes radio stations, radio networks, station sales representatives, and allied industry services, such as producers, research firms, schools, and consultants. Calls on advertisers and agencies to promote the sale of radio time as an advertising medium. Sponsors program to increase professionalism of radio salespeople, awarding Certified Radio Marketing Consultant designation to those who pass examination. Sponsors regional marketing conferences. Conducts extensive research program into all phases of radio sales. Issues reports on use of radio by national, regional, and local advertisers. Speaks before conventions and groups to explain benefits of radio advertising. Sponsors Radio Creative Fund. Compiles statistics. **Scope:** advertising, retailing, demographics, marketing. **Founded:** 1951. **Subscriptions:** 500 archival material books clippings periodicals. **Publications:** Radio Co-op Sources (Annual); Guide to Competitive Media (Biennial); RAB Media Fact Book (Annual). **Educational Activities:** Managing Sales Conference (Annual). **Awards:** Radio Mercury Awards; Radio-Mercury Award (Annual).

16701 ■ Radio-Television News Directors' Association (RTNDA)
2175 Sheppard Ave. E, Ste. 310
Toronto, ON, Canada M2J 1W8
Ph: (416)756-2213
Free: 877-257-8632
Fax: (416)491-1670
Co. E-mail: info@rtndacanada.com
URL: http://www.rtndacanada.com
Contact: Ian Koenigsfest, President

Description: Radio and television news executives and personnel. Promotes the professional development of broadcast journalists in Canada. Sponsors national scholarship program. **Founded:** 1962. **Awards:** Lifetime Achievement Award (Annual); President's Fellowship (Annual); RTNDA National Awards (Annual); RTNDA National Awards.

16702 ■ World Association of Community Radio Broadcasters (AMARC)—Asociacion Mondial de Radios Communautarias
705 Bourget St., Ste. 100
Montreal, QC, Canada H4C 2M6
Ph: (514)982-0351
Fax: (514)849-7129
Co. E-mail: secretariat@si.amarc.org
URL: http://www.amarc.org
Contact: Marcelo Solervicens, Secretary General

Description: Supports and promotes the work of community radio broadcasters worldwide. Provides technical support for members, and fosters communication between members. Seeks to contribute to free expression worldwide; works to combat censorship based on social or political viewpoints. **Scope:**

communication, radio, development. **Founded:** 1983. **Publications:** InteRadio (Periodic). **Educational Activities:** World Association of Community Radio Broadcasters Conference (Quadrennial). **Awards:** Solidarity Prize (Quadrennial).

REFERENCE WORKS

16703 ■ "Abacast, Citadel Strike Radio Ad Deal" in Business Journal Portland (Vol. 27, December 31, 2010, No. 44, pp. 3)
Pub: Portland Business Journal
Ed: Erik Siemers. **Description:** Software firm Abacast Inc. has partnered with Citadel Media to aid the latter's advertising sales. Citadel provides radio networks and syndicated programs to 4,200 affiliate stations.

16704 ■ "ACTRA Phones It In" in Canadian Business (Vol. 80, January 15, 2007, No. 2, pp. 8)
Pub: Rogers Media
Ed: Denis Seguin. **Description:** The strike held by the members of the ACTRA or Canadian Cinema, Television and Radio Artists from January 8 2007, due to the contract dispute with the trade association representing Canadian producers, is discussed.

16705 ■ Bacon's Radio/TV/Cable Directory, Volume 1
Pub: Cision US Inc.
Contact: Joe Bernardo, President
URL(s): us.cision.com. **Released:** Annual; Latest edition 2012. **Price:** $650, Individuals. **Covers:** over 13,500 radio and television stations, including college radio and public television stations, and cable companies. **Entries include:** For radio and television stations--Call letters, address, phone, names and titles of key personnel, programs, times broadcast, name of contact, network affiliation, frequency or channel number, target audience data. For cable companies--Name, address, phone, description of activities. **Arrangement:** Geographical.

16706 ■ Broadcast Engineering--Equipment Reference Manual
Pub: Penton
Contact: Raymond E. Maloney, President
URL(s): www.broadcastengineering.comwww.penton.com/Profile/BroadcastEngineering.aspx. **Released:** Annual; fall. **Publication includes:** List of more than 1,400 manufacturers and distributors of communications equipment for radio, television, and recording applications. **Entries include:** For manufacturers--Company name, address. For distributors and dealers--Company name, address, phone, product or service provided, geographic area covered. **Database includes:** Specifications for major brands of professional broadcast hardware. **Arrangement:** Manufacturers are alphabetical; dealers and distributors are geographical. **Indexes:** Product/service.

16707 ■ Broadcasting & Cable Yearbook: A Broadcasting and R.R. Bowker Publication
Pub: R.R. Bowker L.L.C.
URL(s): www.bowker.com. **Released:** Annual; latest edition 2010. **Price:** $395, Individuals softbound. **Covers:** Over 17,000 television and radio stations in the United States, its territories, and Canada; cable MSOs and their individual systems; television and radio networks, broadcast and cable group owners, station representatives, satellite networks and services, film companies, advertising agencies, government agencies, trade associations, schools, and suppliers of professional and technical services, including books, serials, and videos; communications lawyers. **Entries include:** Company name, address, phone, fax, names of executives. Station listings include broadcast power, other operating details. **Arrangement:** Stations and systems are geographical, others are alphabetical. **Indexes:** Alphabetical.

16708 ■ "The Buzz About HD Radio" in Black Enterprise (Vol. 37, February 2007, No. 7, pp. 58)
Pub: Earl G. Graves Publishing Co. Inc.
Ed: James C. Johnson. **Description:** HD radio broadcasting will send CD quality sound and extra information to more radio stations using the same amount of bandwidth.

16709 ■ *"Dear Diary, Arbitron is Dumping You" in Business Courier (Vol. 26, September 25, 2009, No. 22, pp. 1)*
Pub: American City Business Journals, Inc.
Ed: Dan Monk. **Description:** Arbitron Inc. is replacing hand-written ratings diaries with Portable People Meters or electronic sensors that measure local radio audiences. The technology counts all exposure to radio and stations; those that penetrate the workplace will see success, while the more 'niche' oriented formats will have a more difficult time.

16710 ■ *"Dots Sings To New Tune With Its Radio Station" in Crain's Cleveland Business (Vol. 30, June 15, 2009, No. 23, pp. 7)*
Pub: Crain Communications, Inc.
Description: Dots LLC, a women's clothing retailer, has launched an online radio station on its Website. The station plays the in-store music to customers while they are shopping online.

16711 ■ *"Dramatic Results: Making Opera (Yes, Opera) Seem Young and Hip" in Inc. (October 2007, pp. 61-62)*
Pub: Gruner & Jahr USA Publishing
Description: Profile of Peter Gelb, who turned New York's Metropolitan Opera into one of the most media-savvy organizations in the country, using a multifaceted marketing strategy through the media. Gelb used streaming audio and simulcasts on satellite radio and movie theaters to promote a message that opera is hip.

16712 ■ *"A Family's Fortune" in Canadian Business (Vol. 80, Winter 2007, No. 24, pp. 103)*
Pub: Rogers Media
Ed: Graham F. Scott. **Description:** James Richardson started as a tailor before moving into the grain business because his clients paid him in sacks of wheat and barley. The James Richardson and Sons Ltd. entered the radio business in 1927 but later sold it off in 1951.

16713 ■ *"Far Out: Satellite Radio Finds New Way to Tally Listeners" in Globe & Mail (March 14, 2007, pp. B14)*
Pub: CTVglobemedia Publishing Inc.
Ed: Grant Robertson. **Description:** The marketing strategy adopted by satellite radio broadcasting firm XM Satellite Radio Inc. in Canada for increasing its subscriber based is discussed.

16714 ■ *Freelancing for Journalists*
Pub: Routledge
Ed: Diana Harris. **Released:** January 1, 2010. **Price:** $110.00. **Description:** Comprehensive guide showing the specific skills required for those wishing to freelance in newspapers, magazines, radio, television, and as online journalists.

16715 ■ *Investing in Radio Market Report*
Pub: BIA Financial Network Inc.
Contact: Thomas J. Buono, Chief Executive Officer
E-mail: tbuono@bia.com
URL(s): www.bia.com. **Released:** Annual; Latest edition 2011. **Price:** $1375, Individuals; $2700, Individuals quarterly set; $3185, Individuals full financial set. **Covers:** U.S. Radio industry markets and inclusive stations. **Entries include:** For stations--Call letters, technical attributes, format, estimated revenues, owner, last acquisition date and price, ratings for eight books. **Database includes:** Market data, including revenues, demographics, and economic indicators. **Arrangement:** Numerical by market rank size. **Indexes:** Market name, station call letters, city of license.

16716 ■ *"It Could Be Worse" in Barron's (Vol. 89, July 27, 2009, No. 30, pp. 5)*
Pub: Dow Jones & Co., Inc.
Ed: Alan Abelson. **Description:** Media sources are being fooled by corporate America who is peddling an economic recovery rather than reality as shown by the report of a rise in existing home sales which boosted the stock market even if it was a seasonal phenomenon. The phrase 'things could be worse' sums up the reigning investment philosophy in the U.S. and this has been stirring up the market.

16717 ■ *"Making Visitors Out Of Listeners" in Hawaii Business (Vol. 54, July 2008, No. 1, pp. 18)*
Pub: Hawaii Business Publishing
Ed: Casey Chin. **Description:** Japanese workers are subscribing to the Official Hawaii Podcast in iTunes, which offers a free 20-minute, Japanese-language audio content on different topics, such as dining reviews and music from local artists. The concept is a way to attract Japanese travelers to come to Hawaii.

16718 ■ *"Marketing: You Are On the Air: Radio and TV Producers Are Looking For Shows Starring Smart CEOs" in Inc. (December 2007, pp. 67-69)*
Pub: Gruner & Jahr USA Publishing
Ed: Sarah Goldstein. **Description:** Many successful entrepreneurs are being hired to host television and radio shows in order to share business expertise.

16719 ■ *Matthews Media Directory*
Pub: Marketwire
URL(s): www.cdn-news.comwww.marketwire.com. **Released:** Semiannual; Latest edition 50th. **Covers:** Daily newspapers, radio and television stations, trade magazines, networks and newswires and press galleries in Canada.

16720 ■ *Media, Organizations and Identity*
Pub: Palgrave Macmillan
Ed: Lilie Chouliaraki, Mette Morsing. **Released:** January 19, 2010. **Price:** $90.00. **Description:** The mass media, press and television are a essential in the formation of corporate identity and the promotion of business image and reputation. This book offers a new perspective into the interrelationships between media and organizations over three dimensions: media as business, media in business and business in the media.

16721 ■ *Mississippi News Media Directory*
Pub: News Media Directories
Contact: Brian Highberger, Publisher
URL(s): www.newsmediadirectories.net/product-p/07msnmd.htm. **Released:** Annual; Latest edition 2011-2012. **Price:** $45, Individuals; $65, Individuals CD; $85, Individuals Combo-Directory and CD. **Covers:** Newspapers, periodicals, radio and television broadcasting stations, and press services operating in Mississippi. **Entries include:** Publisher or company name, address, phone, names and titles of key personnel, publication title, call letters, hours of operation, and frequency. **Arrangement:** Classified by type of media. **Indexes:** Title, call letters, county index.

16722 ■ *"New King Top the Charts" in The Business Journal-Portland (Vol. 25, August 8, 2008, No. 22, pp. 1)*
Pub: American City Business Journals, Inc.
Ed: Andy Giegerich. **Description:** Spanish-language KRYP-FM station's spring 2008 ratings soared to 6.4 from 2.8 for the previous year. The station timing is flawless given the fact that one of every three new Portland-area residents between 2002 and 2007 were Latino.

16723 ■ *"Online Radio That's Cool, Addictive, Free, and Just Maybe A Lasting Business" in Inc. (October 2007, pp. 100-106, 108)*
Pub: Gruner & Jahr USA Publishing
Ed: Stephanie Clifford. **Description:** Profile of the Internet radio company, Pandora, whose founder, Tim Westergren discusses his business plans to fruition. The station has over eight million loyal listeners, advertisers and a database of 500,000 songs.

16724 ■ *"Out of This World: Noah Samara and WorldSpace" in Black Enterprise (November 2007)*
Pub: Earl G. Graves Publishing Co. Inc.
Ed: Anthony Calypso. **Description:** Profile of Noah Samara, CEO of WorldSpace Inc. who raised $1 billion to help create the technological architecture for satellite radio.

16725 ■ *"Pro Teams Shift Ad Budgets; Naming Rights Deals Near $1 Billion" in Brandweek (Vol. 49, April 21, 2008, No. 16, pp. 18)*
Pub: VNU Business Media, Inc.
Ed: Barry Janoff. **Description:** More and more professional sports marketers are spending less of their advertising budgets on traditional media outlets such as television, print and radio; the growing trend in sports marketing is in utilizing new media venues such as the Internet in which innovative means are used to encourage interaction with fans.

16726 ■ *"Radio" in MarketingMagazine (Vol. 115, September 27, 2010, No. 13, pp. 24)*
Pub: Rogers Publishing Ltd.
Description: Market data in the radio broadcasting industry in Canada is outlined.

16727 ■ *"Radio Feels Heat from IPod Generation" in Globe & Mail (March 16, 2006, pp. B1)*
Pub: CTVglobemedia Publishing Inc.
Ed: Simon Tuck; Grant Robertson. **Description:** Conventional radio stations are losing the younger generation listeners to new technology such as MP3 players, satellite radio and music-playing cell phones. The report of Canadian Association of Broadcasters (CAB) is detailed.

16728 ■ *"Radio Roots Run Deep" in The Business Journal-Milwaukee (Vol. 25, July 4, 2008, No. 41, pp. A1)*
Pub: American City Business Journals, Inc.
Ed: Rich Kirchen. **Description:** Profile of Steve Palec, a real estate broker at CB Richard Ellis, also works as a radio host for shows 'Rock & Roll Roots' and 'Legends of Rock'. Palec shares that real estate is still his top priority, even with his radio gig. Palec's career as a broker and as a radio host is discussed.

16729 ■ *"Reds Hit Ratings Homer" in Business Courier (Vol. 27, July 30, 2010, No. 13, pp. 1)*
Pub: Business Courier
Ed: Steve Watkins, James Ourand. **Description:** Cincinnati Reds fans have tuned in to their TVs and radios as their team made a hottest start to a season. The Reds TV ratings have increased 49 percent during the first six months of 2010 and continued to rise while the Reds' games broadcast on WLW-AM reported the highest average audience share per game of any Major League Baseball team.

16730 ■ *"Regent's Signal, Once Powerful, Fading From Local Scene" in Business Courier (Vol. 27, June 4, 2010, No. 5, pp. 1)*
Pub: Business Courier
Ed: Dan Monk. **Description:** Los Angeles, California-based Oaktree Capital Management bought former Regent Communications Inc. from Chapter 11 bankruptcy and transformed it into Townsquare Media Inc., a privately held firm. Regent's corporate presence has faded fast in Cincinnati, Ohio as its operations wind down. Insights on Regent's failed business model are also given.

16731 ■ *"Research Reports: How Analysts Size Up Companies" in Barron's (Vol. 90, August 23, 2010, No. 34, pp. M13)*
Pub: Barron's Editorial & Corporate Headquarters
Description: Shares of Sirius XM Radio, Target and Deere and Company received an eBuyE rating, while shares of Research in Motion got an eNeutralE rating.

16732 ■ *"Satellite Wars" in Canadian Business (Vol. 79, October 23, 2006, No. 21, pp. 35)*
Pub: Rogers Media
Ed: Andy Holloway. **Description:** The strategies used by Sirius Canada Inc. and XM Canada, two major satellite radio companies to acquire more number of suscribers, are discussed.

16733 ■ *"Survey: More Buyers Expect to Spend Less in Most Media" in Advertising*

Age (Vol. 79, July 7, 2008, No. 26, pp. 3)
Pub: Crain Communications, Inc.
Ed: Megan McIlroy. **Description:** Marketers are decreasing their budgets for advertising in television, radio, newspaper and outdoor due to the economic downturn. Statistical data concerning advertising agencies and marketers included.

16734 ■ *"Transform Your Life" in Black Enterprise (Vol. 37, January 2007, No. 6, pp. 14)*
Pub: Earl G. Graves Publishing Co. Inc.
Description: Through the magazine, television and radio programs, events, and the website, the various platforms of Black Enterprise will provide the tools necessary to achieve success in business ventures, career aspirations, and personal goals.

16735 ■ *"Wendy Turner; Vice-President and General Manager, Vocalo.org" in Crain's Chicago Business (Vol. 31, May 5, 2008, No. 18, pp. 22)*
Pub: Crain Communications, Inc.
Ed: Kevin McKeough. **Description:** Profile of Wendy Turner who is a leader at Vocalo, a combination of talk radio and Web site, where listeners can set up profile pages similar to those on Facebook.

16736 ■ *"XM Burning Through Cash to Catch Sirius" in Globe & Mail (April 17, 2007, pp. B5)*
Pub: CTVglobemedia Publishing Inc.
Ed: Grant Robertson. **Description:** The effort of XM Satellite Radio Holdings Inc. to spend about $45 million to increase sale of its radio in Canada is discussed.

16737 ■ *"XM Mulls Betting the Bank in Competitive Game of Subscriber Growth" in Globe & Mail (March 18, 2006, pp. B3)*
Pub: CTVglobemedia Publishing Inc.
Ed: Grant Robertson. **Description:** Canadian Satellite Radio Inc., XM Canada, president and Chief Operating Officer Stephen Tapp feel that establishing a profile in satellite radio to attract subscribers is a very big challenge. His views on the Canadian radio market are detailed.

16738 ■ *"XM and Sirius Satellite Radio Face Up to Their Losses and Decide to Get Hitched" in Globe & Mail (February 20, 2007, pp. B17)*
Pub: CTVglobemedia Publishing Inc.
Ed: Grant Robertson. **Description:** XM Satellite Radio and Sirius Satellite Radio are planning to merge operations, after years of losses. The possible merger could create a $13 billion company.

SOURCES OF SUPPLY

16739 ■ *BIA's Radio Yearbook*
BIA Financial Network Inc.
Contact: Thomas J. Buono, Chief Executive Officer
E-mail: tbuono@bia.com
URL(s): www.bia.com. **Released:** Annual; Latest edition 2012. **Price:** $240, Individuals. **Covers:** U.S. Radio stations, radio equipment manufacturers, and related service providers and trade associations. **Entries include:** For radio stations--Call letters, address; general manager and owner names and phones; technical attributes, last acquisition date and price, Arbitron ratings. For others--Name, address, phone, name and title of contact. **Database includes:** Annual market data, including radio revenue, demographics, economic indicators, and listening trends. **Arrangement:** Classified by market. **Indexes:** Market rank, call letter, city of license/Arbitron market, group owner (alphabetical and geographical), broker/lender (geographical).

TRADE PERIODICALS

16740 ■ *Communicator: The Magazine for Electronic Journalists*
Pub: Radio-Television News Directors Association
Contact: Jane Nassiri, Executive Director
E-mail: janen@rtdna.org
URL(s): www.rtdna.org/pages/commindex.php. **Released:** Monthly **Price:** $125, Other countries; $75, Individuals domestic; $8.50, Single issue.

16741 ■ *Community Radio News*
Pub: National Federation of Community Broadcasters
Ed: Evona Balcziunas, Editor. **Released:** Monthly. **Price:** Included in membership; $75 University Libraries. **Description:** Serves as a medium of communication for independent, community-licensed radio stations. Contains brief articles and news items on such topics as public broadcasting and programming, legislative developments, activities of the Federal Communications Commission, and local stations. Recurring features include notices of grants and awards, job openings, and a calendar of events/conferences for noncommercial broadcasters.

16742 ■ *Feedback*
Pub: Broadcast Education Association
Contact: Heather Birks, Executive Director
E-mail: hbirks@nab.org
URL(s): www.beaweb.org/feedback.html. **Ed:** Joe Misiewicz. **Released:** Quarterly

16743 ■ *FMedia!*
Pub: FM Atlas Publishing
Contact: Carol J. Elving, Director
Ed: Bruce F. Elving, Ph.D., Editor. **Released:** Monthly. **Price:** $75 for broadcasters; $26 for individuals. **Description:** Lists information on the facilities and formats of FM radio, including new station grants and applications. Also provides official and unofficial news and comments, as well as FM Dxing and FM reception concerns. Recurring features include letters to the editor, news of research, job listings, and notices of publications available.

16744 ■ *Radio World*
Pub: IMAS Publishing Inc.
URL(s): www.rwonline.com/. **Released:** Biweekly **Price:** $39.95, Individuals; $75, Two years; $99, Other countries; $198, Other countries 2 years.

16745 ■ *TelevisionWeek*
Pub: Crain Communications Inc.
URL(s): www.tvweek.com/. **Released:** Weekly **Price:** $119, Individuals; $171, Canada incl. GST; $309, Other countries airmail.

VIDEOCASSETTES/ AUDIOCASSETTES

16746 ■ *Career Insights*
RMI Media
1365 N. Winchester St.
Olathe, KS 66061-5880
Ph: (913)768-1696
Free: 800-745-5480
Fax: (800)755-6910
Co. E-mail: actmedia@act.org
URL: http://www.actmedia.com
Released: 1987. **Description:** Describes 50 occupations, including skill requirements and interviews with people employed in these fields. **Availability:** VHS; 3/4 U.

TRADE SHOWS AND CONVENTIONS

16747 ■ **Radio-Television News Directors Association International Conference & Exhibition**
Radio-Television News Directors Association
529 14th St., N.W., Ste. 425
Washington, DC 20045
Ph: (202)659-6510
Free: 800-807-8632
Fax: (202)223-4007
Co. E-mail: rtnda@rtnda.org
URL: http://www.rtnda.org
Contact: Jane Nassiri, Executive Director
E-mail: janen@rtdna.org
URL(s): www.rtnda.org. **Frequency:** Annual. **Audience:** Professionals from the television, radio and cable industries, along with representatives from government, publications and special interest groups. **Principal Exhibits:** Equipment, supplies, and services for the radio and television news industries, including cameras, recorders, weather equipment, computers, and software.

CONSULTANTS

16748 ■ **A & A Research**
690 Sunset Blvd.
Kalispell, MT 59901-3641
Ph: (406)752-7857
Fax: (406)752-0194
Contact: Judith Doonan, President
Scope: Offers marketing research services, specializing in newspaper readership and advertising studies. Also specializes in audience research and programming studies for radio and television stations, minority broadcasting, new business and retail marketing research, and advertising consulting and research. Also prepares public opinion polls. Serves private industries as well as government agencies. **Founded:** 1978. **Seminars:** Three R's of Advertising; Precision Advertising; Audience Research Workshop; Use of Research in Radio Programming.

16749 ■ **Baker Scott & Co.**
1259 Rte. 46
Parsippany, NJ 07054
Ph: (973)263-3355
Fax: (973)263-9255
Co. E-mail: exec.search@bakerscott.com
URL: http://www.bakerscott.com
Contact: Judith Bouer, President
E-mail: judy@bakerscott.com
Scope: Consulting services include executive recruiting, employment attitude surveys, and screening organization plans. Industries served: telecommunication, cable TV, broadcasting entertainment, and financial institutions. The firm is integrated horizontally across functional discipline such as accounting, administration, call center, data processing, engineering, finance, general operations, marketing and technical and plant operations. **Founded:** 1979. **Seminars:** Offers seminar programs on interview techniques, management skills, and customer service.

16750 ■ **The Benchmark Co.—Benchmark Market Research**
907 S Congress Ave., Ste. 7
Austin, TX 78704
Ph: (512)707-7500
Free: 800-688-7010
Fax: (512)707-7757
Co. E-mail: thebenc@earthlink.net
URL: http://www.thebenchmarkcompany.net
Contact: Dr. Robert E. Balon, Chief Executive Officer
E-mail: rob@diningoutwithrobbalon.com
Scope: Full service consultants to the communications industry, specializing in radio and television. Also serves newspapers and ad agencies with extensive market research. **Founded:** 1987. **Publications:** "Radio in the 90S; Audience, Promotion and Marketing Strategies". **Seminars:** The Rules of the Ratings Game Seminar.

16751 ■ **D.E.M. Allen & Associates Ltd.**
130 Cree Cres.
Winnipeg, MB, Canada R3J 3W1
Ph: (204)889-9202
Fax: (204)831-6650
Co. E-mail: gneilson@dema.mb.ca
URL: http://www.dema.mb.ca
Contact: G. R. Henke, President
E-mail: ghenke@dema.mb.ca
URL(s): www.dema.ca. **Scope:** Telecommunications consultants, experienced in AM, FM and television broadcasting, CATV systems, LF/HF, VHF/UHF and microwave systems and satellite earth stations; RF measurements and evaluations related to SCADA; LMCS in the millimeters portion of the spectrum as well as the 2.5Ghz MDS/MMDS field; electromagnetic compatibility and electromagnetic immunity including non-ionizing radiation evaluation and measurement. Services include planning, design, supervision and adjustment of broadcast transmitting facilities, including specifications, tender evaluation, preparation of reports, technical briefs for Federal Regulatory bodies, evaluation and measurements associated with

RF propagation and electromagnetic energy throughout the radio frequency spectrum. Industries served: Broadcast, communications and national defense agencies. **Founded:** 1964. **Telecommunication Services:** ghenke@dema.mb.ca.

16752 ■ DeMers Programming Media Consultants
204 Exton Commons
Exton, PA 19341
Ph: (610)363-2636
Fax: (610)363-2198
Co. E-mail: info@demersprogramming.com
URL: http://www.demersprogramming.com
Contact: Alex Demers, President
E-mail: alex@demersprogramming.com

Scope: Programming and marketing consultants offering advice for broadcasters and broadcast related businesses. Services include: music and format controls, strategic planning, talent coaching and acquisition, research and promotional planning. Serves private and government sectors. **Founded:** 1986. **Publications:** "12 Steps To A One Share - Uncovering The Clutter," Feb, 2005; "Get Your Mind Out Of The Clutter - DeMers Dispatch Winter '05"; "See Spot Run...Over The Golden Goose"; "Radio's Attention Deficit Disorder"; "Program The Seller"; "At Issue: Staying Creative"; "Take A Hard Look At Your Special Programming"; "A Fresh Coat Of Paint"; "Guerrilla Radio". **Seminars:** Diary Keepers Plus Research; Marketing, Merchandising and Money.

16753 ■ Donna Halper & Associates
550 Adams St., Ste. 3-365
Quincy, MA 02169
Ph: (617)786-0666
Co. E-mail: dlh@donnahalper.com
URL: http://www.donnahalper.com
Contact: Donna L. Halper, President
E-mail: dlh@donnahalper.com

Scope: Offers staff training; market research; positioning studies and music software. Expertise in helping radio station owners to choose the right format. Also expertise in news and public affairs programming. Industries served primarily radio both professional and college but has also served nonprofit service organizations and has trained numerous women and minority staff for management positions. 23 years of experience. **Founded:** 1980. **Publications:** "Invisible Stars: A Social History of Women in America Broadcasting".; "Icons of Talk". **Seminars:** Improving Communication at Your Station; Dealing with Diversity; a Media History of Your Market (custom designed and researched for your station and your city). **Special Services:** Music rotation software for radio stations.

16754 ■ Elder Engineering Inc.
35 Auckland Ln.
King City, ON, Canada L7B 1C1
Ph: (905)833-5141
Fax: (905)833-2101
Co. E-mail: eldeng@sympatico.ca
Contact: Stuart K. Hahn, Manager

Scope: Expertise regarding communications and broadcast transmitting systems encompasses feasibility study, frequency search, site selection, propagation tests, and protection analysis. Experienced with antenna design, contour predictions, equipment specification, technical brief, bid selection, tuning, testing, certification and proof of performance for newer improved transmitting facilities in LF to UHF bands; design studies for broadband multi station AM, FM, TV or DRB antenna and transmission systems at a common site, point-to-point STL, microwave distant learning, MDS, or teleconferencing systems. Industries served: radio, television, broadcasters and applicants, power utilities, government agencies, radio communications licensees, and manufacturers. **Founded:** 1961.

16755 ■ Engineering Harmonics Inc.
29A Leslie St.
Toronto, ON, Canada M4M 3C3
Ph: (416)465-3378

Fax: (416)465-9037
Co. E-mail: 2012-info@engineeringharmonics.com
URL: http://www.engineeringharmonics.com
Contact: Philip Giddings, President
E-mail: pgiddings@engineeringharmonies.com

Scope: Specializing in audio, audio and video, control, and communication based systems. **Founded:** 1988. **Publications:** "Designing Sound for Frank Gehry's Vision"; "Precis of WDCH PSVC System"; "PSVC Design Challenges at WDCH"; "Power and Ground Update"; "Noise Reduction Systems"; "Mandating the House Audio System," Overture Hall; "Betting on Legends," Nov, 2008; "Examining our Roots, Defining our Future," Dec, 2008; "Walking The Hall: A Guide to Tuning a Loudspeaker System," Nov, 2007; "National Ballet School," Nov, 2007; "The Puzzle of PA for a Hall-in-the-Round," Aug, 2007; "A House for All Seasons," Aug, 2006; "Hooray for LA," Jan, 2004; "A Kodak Moment," Apr, 2002.

16756 ■ Financial Solutions Inc.
309 W Jefferson St.
La Grange, KY 40031
Ph: (502)225-9900
Free: 877-952-9766
Fax: (502)225-9997
Co. E-mail: robin@lawsonfinancial.net
URL: http://www.lawsonfinancial.net
Contact: Robin H. Lawson, Owner
E-mail: robin@lawsonfinancial.net

Scope: Offers financial brokerage services to the broadcasting industry in the Midwest United States. **Founded:** 1993. **Publications:** "Eighty percent of Americans agree they would benefit from having basic financial education and information," 2009; "Finra Investor Education Survey, 2007"; "How Are Mutual Funds Taxed". **Seminars:** Long Term Care, Estate Planning, Retirement, Financial Management.

16757 ■ Forsyth Consulting
9 Laurier Ave.
Toronto, ON, Canada M4X 1S2
Ph: (416)964-0812
Fax: (416)964-1304
Co. E-mail: ajforsyth9@rogers.com
Contact: Andrew J. Forsyth, President
E-mail: ajforsyth9@rogers.com

Scope: Specialized in regulatory affairs applicable to radio, television, cable, and satellite. Provides CRTC applications and interventions, compliance strategies and analysis, strategic planning and market positioning, creative programming, management sales, talent and formative development, acquisitions, benefit package strategies, and broadcast property sale representation. Industries served: Broadcasting. **Founded:** 1989.

16758 ■ Hartech Inc.
6882 S Prince Cir.
Littleton, CO 80120-3538
Ph: (303)794-0196
Fax: (303)794-0196
Co. E-mail: jhart@chicagogsb.edu
URL: http://www.hartechinc.com
Contact: James W. Hart, President
E-mail: jhart@du.edu

Scope: Specializes in radio system design including communications needs assessments, system designs, coverage modeling, profiling, path determinations and reliabilities, interference studies, specification generation, economic analysis and cost estimates, field engineering, system acceptance requirements assurance, expert witnessing. Also specialized in hazardous radiation calculations and measurements. Industries served: two-way radio, microwave radio, broadcasters private and government. **Founded:** 1971. **Publications:** "Understanding Wireless Communications in Public Safety, a Guidebook to Technology, Issues, Planning, and Management"; "Tri-State Tackles Coverage in Challenging Terrain," Radio Resource Magazine, Jul, 1999.

16759 ■ Radiotechniques Engineering Corp.
402 10th Ave.
Haddon Heights, NJ 08035-0367
Ph: (856)546-8008

Fax: (856)546-1841
Co. E-mail: sales@radiotechniques.com
URL: http://www.radiotechniques.com
Contact: Edward Ted Schober, President
E-mail: ted@radiotechniques.com

Scope: Provider of design, FCC allocation engineering and field engineering services for broadcast, private and common carrier radio clients. Particular emphasis is on optimized broadcast systems using directional antennas and service area improvement through engineering measures. Offers RF-oriented product-design services in the fields of digital and analog modulation systems, transmitters, battery powered receivers and computer control systems. Specializes in RF instrumentation and antennas. **Founded:** 1979. **Special Services:** Point Manager™; Palm Pilot™; Treo™.

16760 ■ Sellmeyer Engineering
2 Pecan Grove Cir.
Lucas, TX 75002
Ph: (972)542-2056
Fax: (972)636-5940
Co. E-mail: jack@sellmeyereng.com
URL: http://www.sellmeyereng.com
Contact: Jack S. Sellmeyer, President
E-mail: jack@sellmeyereng.com

Scope: Broadcast and communications engineering consultants. Offer services in FCC applications, transmitter plant design, construction supervision, broadcast studio facilities planning and construction, AM directional antenna design and adjustment and measurements. **Founded:** 1980.

16761 ■ Strategic Computer Solutions Inc.
2625 Shefman Terr., Ste. 200
Ann Arbor, MI 48105-3441
Ph: (248)888-0666
Free: 866-727-7276
Fax: (248)888-0665
Co. E-mail: info@stratcom.com
URL: http://www.stratcom.com
Contact: Leeron Kopelman, President
E-mail: lk@stratcom.com

Scope: Computer technology consultants specializing in notebooks, Pcs, Unix systems, networking, custom turnkey programming, database development, web hosting and development. Industries served medical, dental, legal, property management, marinas, unions, radio stations, and other businesses function as your ITMIS department. **Founded:** 1987. **Telecommunication Services:** sales@stratcom.com. **Special Services:** gloEMR™.

COMPUTERIZED DATABASES

16762 ■ RAB.com
1320 Greenway Dr., Ste. 500
Irving, TX 75038
Ph: (972)753-6822
Free: 800-232-3131
Fax: (972)753-6727
Co. E-mail: jhaley@rab.com
URL: http://www.rab.com

Availability: Online: Radio Advertising Bureau. **Type:** Directory.

LIBRARIES

16763 ■ Canadian Broadcasting Corporation - Reference Library/Image Research Library
PO Box 500, Sta. A
Toronto, ON, Canada M5W 1E6
Ph: (416)205-3241
Free: 866-306-4636
Co. E-mail: stillphoto@cbc.ca
URL: http://www.cbc.ca/designlibrary/index.html
Contact: Linda Barnett, Librarian

Scope: Radio and television broadcasting, Canadiana, current affairs, drama, design. **Services:** Interlibrary loan; copying; Library open to the public for research on CBC or broadcasting in Canada. **Founded:** 1946. **Holdings:** 27,000 books; 8000 files of newspaper clippings. **Subscriptions:** 200 journals and other serials; 13 newspapers. **Telecommunication Services:** imageresearchlibrary@cbc.ca.

16764 ■ CBS News Reference Library
51 W. 52nd St.
New York, NY 10019
Ph: (212)975-4321
URL: http://www.cbsnews.com
Contact: Laura B. Kapnick, Director
Scope: Radio, television, biography, current events, government, politics. **Founded:** 1940. **Holdings:** 38,000 books; 2500 bound periodical volumes; 15,000 clippings files; 7700 reels of microfilm; 50,000 microfiche. **Subscriptions:** 270 journals and other serials; 10 newspapers.

16765 ■ Library of Congress - Motion Picture, Broadcasting & Recorded Sound Division
James Madison Memorial Bldg., LM 336
101 Independence Ave., SE
Washington, DC 20540-4690
Ph: (202)707-8572
Fax: (202)707-2371
Co. E-mail: mpref@loc.gov
URL: http://www.loc.gov/rr/mopic
Contact: Gregory Lukow, Section Chief
URL(s): www.loc.gov/rr/record. **Scope:** All genres and formats of moving images and sound recordings, ranging from the earliest motion pictures registered for copyright (1894-1912), the earliest sound recordings on both cylinder and disc, along with recordings of radio broadcasts beginning in the late 1920s to current feature films, television programs, documentaries, educational films and videos, with an emphasis on American productions; current popular, folk, jazz, opera, and classical music recorded on compact disc. **Services:** Collections open to the public with restrictions. **Holdings:** 3000 books, bound volumes of early periodicals, and vertical files; 300,000 film items; 350,000 television items; 3 million sound recordings preserved on cylinders, discs, tapes, wires, Dictaphone belts, music box discs, and piano rolls. **Subscriptions:** 150 journals and other serials.

16766 ■ National Association of Broadcasters - Information Resource Center—IRC.
1771 N St., NW
Washington, DC 20036
Ph: (202)429-5490
Fax: (202)429-4199
Co. E-mail: irc@nab.org
URL: http://www.nab.org
Contact: Steven Mitchel, Librarian, Reference
Scope: Radio and television broadcasting and allied subjects. **Services:** Special Library open to members and others by special request. **Founded:** 1946. **Holdings:** 8000 volumes. **Subscriptions:** 200 journals and other serials. **Telecommunication Services:** nab@nab.org.

16767 ■ National Public Radio Broadcast Library—NPR Broadcast Library.
635 Massachusetts Ave. NW, Ste. 1
Washington, DC 20001
Ph: (202)513-2060

Fax: (202)513-3329
Co. E-mail: rrobinson@npr.org
URL: http://www.npr.org
Contact: Robert Robinson, Senior Librarian
Scope: News and current events, drama, music. **Services:** Collection open to the public by appointment. **Founded:** 1971. **Holdings:** 100,000 audiotapes; 10,000 phonograph records and compact discs; CD-ROMs. **Subscriptions:** 6 journals and other serials.

16768 ■ NBC Universal Information Resource Center
30 Rockefeller Plaza
Room 470S
New York, NY 10112
Ph: (212)664-5307
Fax: (212)664-7842
Co. E-mail: debra.levinson@nbcuni.com
Contact: Debra Levinson, Director, Information Services
Scope: Broadcasting, politics and government, current events, business, economics, marketing, advertising. **Services:** Library open to NBCU and General Electric employees, and to other librarians by appointment. **Founded:** 1930. **Holdings:** 5000 books; 650 bound periodical volumes; 8800 reels of microfilm. **Subscriptions:** 150 journals and other serials; 16 newspapers.

16769 ■ North American Radio Archives Library
33888 The Farm Rd.
Wildomar, CA 92595
Ph: (951)244-5242
URL: http://wildomar.californiapath.com/c-850139.htm
Contact: Janis DeMoss, Executive Officer
Scope: Radio - drama, comedy, entertainment, news, documentary; radio programming. **Services:** Library open to members of NARA who may borrow its material. **Founded:** 1973. **Holdings:** 200 books; 100,000 radio programs, 1926-1965, on tape; slides of radio personalities; radio scripts and magazines; reproduced articles on radio. **Subscriptions:** 300 journals and other serials.

16770 ■ North American Radio Archives - Tape and Printed Materials Libraries
4741 E. Grant St.
Fresno, CA 93702
Ph: (209)456-2020
Co. E-mail: archives@bostonradio.org
URL: http://www.bostonradio.org/essays/narba.html
Contact: Scott Jones, Librarian, Film and Video
Scope: Radio - history, programming, broadcasting, scripts, publications; television broadcasting; film. **Services:** Libraries open to members only and researchers by written request. **Founded:** 1973. **Holdings:** 800 books; 5000 reel-to-reel tapes; 250 scripts; 300 slides; 400 magazines; 300 reprints of articles; 15,000 cassettes; 6000 television shows. **Subscriptions:** 400 journals and other serials.

16771 ■ The Paley Center for Media - Research Services
25 W. 52nd St.
New York, NY 10019
Ph: (212)621-6600
Fax: (212)621-6632
URL: http://www.paleycenter.org
Contact: Pat Mitchell, President
Scope: Television (except technical aspects) and radio. **Services:** Reference inquiries from the public accepted by mail or fax only; telephone reference service available for museum members at contributing level and above. **Founded:** 1975. **Holdings:** 2600 books. **Subscriptions:** 60 journals and other serials; 7 newspapers.

16772 ■ Radio Advertising Bureau - Marketing Information Center
1320 Greenway Dr., Ste. 500
Irving, TX 75038
Ph: (516)753-6782
Free: 800-232-3131
Fax: (212)753-6727
Co. E-mail: arainey@rab.com
URL: http://www.rab.com/
Contact: Daniel Moores, Analyst
Scope: Radio, advertising and marketing, consumer markets, demographics, competitive media, leading advertisers, retailing. **Services:** Interlibrary loan (limited); copying; center open to the public by special permission. **Founded:** 1951. **Holdings:** 600 volumes; 70 VF drawers of clippings. **Subscriptions:** 152 journals and other serials. **Telecommunication Services:** dmoores@rab.com.

16773 ■ Temple University - Temple University Libraries - Blitman Resource Center
334 Annenberg Hall
Main Campus
Philadelphia, PA 19122-6080

16774 ■ University of Maryland, College Park Libraries - Hornbake Library - Library of American Broadcasting
3210 Hornbake Library
College Park, MD 20742
Ph: (301)405-9160
Fax: (301)314-2634
Co. E-mail: labcast@umd.edu
URL: http://www.lib.umd.edu/special
Contact: Chuck Howell, Curator
Scope: Radio and television broadcasting history. **Services:** Copying; Library open to the public. **Founded:** 1972. **Holdings:** 8700 books; 250 periodical titles; 320 VF drawers and boxes of archives, clippings, research studies, scripts, scrapbooks, documents, and correspondence; 1000 oral histories, including interviews with prominent broadcasters; 5445 audiotapes; 25,000 photographs; 1500 subject files; 6000 pamphlets. **Subscriptions:** 240 journals and other serials. **Telecommunication Services:** chuckh@umd.edu.

ASSOCIATIONS AND OTHER ORGANIZATIONS

16775 ■ **American Association of Radon Scientists and Technologists (AARST)**
PO Box 2109
Fletcher, NC 28732
Free: 866-772-2778
Fax: (828)890-8071
Co. E-mail: office@aarst.org
URL: http://www.aarst.org/home.html
Contact: Peter Hendrick, Executive Director

Description: Scientists and tradespeople engaged in radon gas testing and remediation and advocacy on behalf of radon lung cancer victims. Works for policy changes at local, state and federal level to implement the 1988 Indoor Radon Abatement Act. Seeks to improve members' skills and effectiveness; conducts international educational and research programs; maintains speakers' bureau; compiles statistics. **Founded:** 1986. **Publications:** *Radon Reporter*

(Quarterly); *Annual Proceedings International Radon Symposium* (Annual). **Educational Activities:** International Radon Symposium (Annual).

FRANCHISES AND BUSINESS OPPORTUNITIES

16776 ■ **Professional House Doctors Inc.**
1406 E 14th St.
Des Moines, IA 50316
Ph: (515)265-6667
Free: 800-288-7437
Fax: (515)278-2070
Description: Providers of environmental and building science services to residential and commercial clients. Services include radon testing and mitigation, building inspections, indoor air quality analysis, asbestos and lead analysis, energy analysis and consultation, structural moisture analysis, healthy house investigations, environmental do-it-yourself test kits and much more. **No. of Franchise Units:** 7. **No. of Company-Owned Units:** 1. **Founded:** 1982..

Franchised: 1991. **Equity Capital Needed:** $15,000-$30,000. **Franchise Fee:** $9,800. **Royalty Fee:** 6%. **Training:** Offers 2 weeks at headquarters and ongoing support.

LIBRARIES

16777 ■ **Radiation Safety Institute of Canada Library**
165 Avenue Rd., Ste. 300
Toronto, ON, Canada M5R 3S4
Ph: (416)650-9090
Free: 800-263-5803
Fax: (416)650-9920
Co. E-mail: info@radiationsafety.ca
URL: http://www.radiationsafety.ca
Contact: George Polak, Manager, Marketing and Sales

Scope: Radiation, radiation safety, radon, radiation/health, radioactive waste, nuclear power. **Services:** Copying; library open to the public. **Founded:** 1980. **Holdings:** Books; reports; clipping file.

START-UP INFORMATION

16778 ■ *"No Place Like Home"* in Small Business Opportunities (Winter 2010)
Pub: Harris Publications Inc.
Description: Five reasons to start a home-staging business in any economy are listed. Home staging is listed as the top emerging career on Website, Careerbuilder.com.

ASSOCIATIONS AND OTHER ORGANIZATIONS

16779 ■ American Land Title Association (ALTA)
1828 L St. NW, Ste. 705
Washington, DC 20036
Ph: (202)296-3671
Free: 800-787-ALTA
Fax: (202)223-5843
Co. E-mail: service@alta.org
URL: http://www.alta.org
Contact: Christopher Abbinante, President
Description: Represents the abstracters, title insurance companies, and attorneys specializing in real property law. **Founded:** 1907. **Publications:** *Title News* (Monthly); *Title News.* **Educational Activities:** Federal Conference (Annual); Federal Conference (Annual).

16780 ■ American Real Estate Society (ARES)
c/o Diane Quarles, Membership Services Mgr.
Clemson, SC 29634-1343
Ph: (864)656-1373
Fax: (864)656-3748
Co. E-mail: equarle@exchange.clemson.edu
URL: http://www.aresnet.org
Contact: Mr. John E. Williams, President
Description: College and university professors; high-level practicing professionals involved in real estate finance, investment, development, valuation, marketing, consulting, management, education, and law; and institutions. Acts as a forum for the exchange of information and research on applied business and individual decision-making within real estate finance, real estate market analysis, investment, valuation, development, and other areas related to real estate in the private sector. Operates ARES Case Clearinghouse, which makes available copies of instructional cases pertinent to real estate practice. Conducts educational programs for real estate professionals. **Founded:** 1985. **Publications:** *ARES Newsletter* (Semiannual); *Journal of Housing Research*; *Journal of Real Estate Literature* (Semiannual); *Journal of Real Estate Portfolio Management* (Quarterly); *The Journal of Real Estate Research* (Bimonthly); *Journal of Real Estate Practice and Education* (Annual); *Journal of Real Estate Literature* (Semiannual); *Journal of Real Estate Research*; *Journal of Real Estate Portfolio Management* (Quarterly); *Journal of Real Estate Practice and Education.* **Educational Activities:**

American Real Estate Society Meeting (Annual). **Awards:** James A. Graaskamp Award (Annual). **Telecommunication Services:** equarle@clemson.edu.

16781 ■ Canadian Real Estate Association (CREA)—L'Association canadienne de l'immeuble
200 Catherine St., 6th Fl.
Ottawa, ON, Canada K2P 2K9
Ph: (613)237-7111
Free: 800-842-2732
Fax: (613)234-2567
Co. E-mail: info@crea.ca
URL: http://www.crea.ca
Contact: Wayne Moen, President
Description: Real estate professionals. Seeks the professional advancement of members and to increase the profitability of the real estate industry. Advocates public policies favorable to the sale of real estate and protective of property and ownership rights; conducts educational programs; compiles statistics. **Scope:** real estate. **Founded:** 1943. **Subscriptions:** archival material books periodicals.

16782 ■ Counselors of Real Estate (CRE)
430 N Michigan Ave.
Chicago, IL 60611-4089
Ph: (312)329-8427
Fax: (312)329-8881
Co. E-mail: info@cre.org
URL: http://www.cre.org
Contact: Mary Walker Fleischmann, President
Description: Professional society of individuals with extensive experience in all phases of real estate who provide a counseling service. Members are entitled to use the Professional Designation CRE (Counselor of Real Estate). Conducts educational programs during three national meetings. **Founded:** 1953. **Publications:** *Real Estate Issues*; *Real Estate Issues*; *CRE Member Directory* (Annual); *Real Estate Issues* (3/year); *Counselors Real Estate--Membership Directory* (Annual). **Awards:** James Felt Creative Counseling Award (Annual); William S. Ballard Award (Annual); James D. Landauer/John R. White Award (Annual). **Telecommunication Services:** cre@interaccess.com.

16783 ■ FIABCI-U.S.A.
1961 Wilson Blvd., Ste. 306
Arlington, VA 22201
Ph: (703)524-4279
Fax: (703)991-6256
Co. E-mail: info@fiabci-usa.com
URL: http://www.fiabci-usa.com
Contact: Sharon K. Young, President
Description: Brings together nearly 1,000,000 members in 57 countries; members represent all specializations in real estate, including brokerage, development, counseling, management, appraisal and financing. Conducts discussion among members in global real estate trends, emerging markets, case studies of international real estate transactions and refer business to each other. **Founded:** 1956. **Publications:** *FIABCI Press* (5/year). **Awards:** Prix d'Excellence Award (Annual).

16784 ■ Institute of Real Estate Management (IREM)
430 N Michigan Ave.
Chicago, IL 60611
Ph: (312)329-6000
Free: 800-837-0706
Fax: (800)338-4736
Co. E-mail: custserv@irem.org
URL: http://www.irem.org
Contact: James A. Evans, President
Description: Professional organization of real property and asset managers. Awards professional designation Certified Property Manager (CPM) to qualifying individuals, Accredited Management Organization (AMO) to qualifying management firms and also awards Accredited Residential Manager (ARM) accreditation to qualifying individuals who are primarily residential site managers. Monitors legislation affecting real estate management. Offers management courses and seminars; conducts research and educational programs, publishes books and reports; maintains formal code of ethics; compiles statistics; maintains employment Website for real estate management industry. **Founded:** 1933. **Publications:** *Apartment Building Income-Expense Analysis.* **Educational Activities:** Leadership and Legislative Summit (Annual). **Awards:** Academy of Authors; Diversity Outreach Scholarship; Donald M. Furbush Scholarship (Annual); J. Wallace Paletou Award (Annual); Lloyd D. Hanford Sr. Distinguished Faculty Award; Louise L. and Y. T. Lum Award; Paul H. Rittle, Sr. Scholarship; Lloyd D. Hanford Sr. Distinguished Faculty Award (Annual); Louise L. and Y.T. Lum Award (Annual); Paul H. Rittle Sr. Memorial Scholarship Award (Quarterly); George M. Brooker Collegiate Scholarships for Minorities; Donald M. Furbush Professional Development Grants; Paul H. Rittle Sr. Professional Development Grants.

16785 ■ Mortgage Bankers Association (MBA)
1717 Rhode Island Ave. NW, Ste. 400
Washington, DC 20036
Ph: (202)557-2700
Free: 800-793-6222
Co. E-mail: membership@mortgagebankers.org
URL: http://www.mortgagebankers.org
Contact: Michael W. Young, Chairman
Description: Principal lending and investor interests in the mortgage finance field, including mortgage banking firms, commercial banks, life insurance companies, title companies, and savings and loan associations. Seeks to improve methods of originating, servicing, and marketing loans of residential and income-producing properties through industry education and cooperation with federal agencies and the Congress. Holds clinics on all aspects of the mortgage finance business. Sponsors School of Mortgage Banking, and correspondence courses and web-based training on mortgage subjects for member personnel. Collects statistics and conducts research on the industry. **Scope:** commercial and residential finance. **Founded:** 1914. **Subscriptions:** 6500 periodicals. **Publications:** *Mortgage Bankers Performance Study* (Quarterly); *National Delinquency Sur-*

vey (Quarterly); *Mortgage Banking: The Magazine of Real Estate Finance* (Monthly). **Awards:** FW Thompson Award (Annual).

16786 ■ National Association of Real Estate Brokers (NAREB)
9831 Greenbelt Rd.
Lanham, MD 20706
Ph: (301)552-9340
Fax: (301)552-9216
Co. E-mail: julius.cartwright@nareb.com
URL: http://www.nareb.com
Contact: Julius L. Cartwright, President
Description: Members of the real estate industry. Research, educational and certification programs include: Real Estate Management Brokers Institute; National Society of Real Estate Appraisers; Real Estate Brokerage Institute; United Developers Council. Encourages unity among those who are engaged in real estate. Promotes and maintains high standards of conduct. Protects the public against unethical, improper, or fraudulent practices connected with the real estate business. Conducts research; compiles statistics on productivity, marketing and development. Gives members license to use "Realtist" symbol. Sponsors educational seminars. Maintains Willis E. Carson Library. **Founded:** 1947. **Publications:** *Realtist Membership Directory* (Annual). **Awards:** Realtist of the Year (Annual).

16787 ■ National Association of Realtors (NAR)
430 N Michigan Ave.
Chicago, IL 60611
Ph: (312)329-8495
Free: 800-441-5263
Fax: (312)329-8633
Co. E-mail: rli@realtors.org
URL: http://www.realtor.org
Contact: Thomas M. Stevens, President
URL(s): www.realtormag.com, www.realtor.com. **Description:** Federation of 54 state and territory associations and 1,860 local real estate boards whose members are real estate brokers and agents; terms are registered by the association in the U.S. Patent and Trademark Office and in the states. Promotes education, high professional standards and modern techniques in specialized real estate work such as brokerage, appraisal, property management, land development, industrial real estate, farm brokerage and counseling. Conducts research programs. **Scope:** real estate. **Founded:** 1908. **Publications:** *REALTORS Land Institute*; *Realtor Magazine*; *NAR Real Estate Outlook* (Monthly); *Real Estate Today: Official Publication of the National Association of Realtors*; *Existing-Home Sales*; *Realtor Magazine: The Business tool for Real Estate Professionals* (Monthly). **Awards:** Distinguished Service Award. **Telecommunication Services:** infocentral@realtors.org; nar-pubs@realtors.org.

16788 ■ National Association of Review Appraisers and Mortgage Underwriters (NARA/MU)
810 N Farrell Dr.
Palm Springs, CA 92262
Ph: (760)327-5284
Fax: (760)327-5631
Co. E-mail: support@assoc-hdqts.org
URL: http://www.naramu.org
Contact: Dr. Bill Merrell, Advisor
Description: Real estate professionals and mortgage underwriters who aid in determining value of property. Acts as umbrella group for real estate appraisers. Conducts educational seminars; maintains speakers' bureau; operates placement service. **Founded:** 1975.

16789 ■ National Council of Exchangors (NCE)
8255 Las Vegas Blvd. S, Ste. No. 1202
Las Vegas, NV 89123
Ph: (702)475-5331
Co. E-mail: nce@ncexchangors.com
URL: http://www.ncexchangors.com
Contact: Bill Pitts, President
Description: Real estate professionals who possess specialized training in the fields of real estate exchanging, real estate tax law, investment analysis, client counseling, and equity marketing. Promotes

educational programs. Provides a forum for member exchanges. **Founded:** 1977. **Publications:** *NCE News* (Periodic). **Educational Activities:** Marketing Conference (Semiannual).

16790 ■ Real Property Association of Canada (REALpac)—Association des biens Immobiliers du Canada
One University Ave., Ste. 1410
Toronto, ON, Canada M5J 2P1
Ph: (416)642-2700
Free: 855-732-5722
Fax: (416)642-2727
Co. E-mail: info@realpac.ca
URL: http://www.realpac.ca
Contact: Paul Morse, Chief Executive Officer
Description: Real estate and development companies and related businesses. Promotes growth in the real estate development and related industries. Serves as a forum for discussion of issues facing the industry; represents members' interests before the public. **Founded:** 1971.

16791 ■ Realtors Land Institute
430 N Michigan Ave.
Chicago, IL 60611
Ph: (800)441-5263
Free: 800-441-LAND
Fax: (312)329-8633
Co. E-mail: rli@realtors.org
URL: http://www.rliland.com
Contact: Ray Brownfield, President
E-mail: rbrownfield@johngreeneland.com
Description: Real estate brokers and salespersons selling, managing, appraising, or developing all types of land. Maintains educational programs for real estate brokers; promotes competence and accredits members. Sponsors courses for realtors and others seeking professional excellence on Land Brokerage, Agricultural Land Brokerage, Exchanging Properties, Estate Planning, Subdivision Development and Financial Analysis of Land Investment. **Publications:** *Realtors Land Institute Newsletter*.

16792 ■ Women's Council of Realtors (WCR)
430 N Michigan Ave.
Chicago, IL 60611
Ph: (312)329-8481
Free: 800-245-8512
Fax: (312)329-3290
Co. E-mail: wcr@wcr.org
URL: http://www.wcr.org
Contact: Bobbie Nelson, President
Description: Women and men real estate brokers and salespeople. Provides opportunity for real estate professionals to participate at local, state, and national levels. Makes programs available for personal and career growth. Offers courses in leadership training, referral and relocation business. Members may earn the Leadership Training Graduate (LTG) designation. **Founded:** 1938. **Publications:** *Women's Council of Realtors--Referral Roster* (Annual). **Awards:** Pinnacle Awards (Annual).

DIRECTORIES OF EDUCATIONAL PROGRAMS

16793 ■ *Directory of Private Accredited Career Schools and Colleges of Technology*
Pub: Accrediting Commission of Career Schools and Colleges of Technology
Contact: Michale S. McComis, Executive Director
Released: On web page. **Price:** Free. **Description:** Covers 3900 accredited post-secondary programs that provide training programs in business, trade, and technical fields, including various small business endeavors. Entries offer school name, address, phone, description of courses, job placement assistance, and requirements for admission. Arrangement is alphabetical.

REFERENCE WORKS

16794 ■ *"$1M Home Sales Spike"* in *Business Courier* (Vol. 27, December 3, 2010, No. 31, pp. 1)
Pub: Business Courier
Ed: Tom Demeropolis. **Description:** Cincinnati Area Board of Realtors reported the increase of sales of

multi-million dollar Tri-State homes in 2010, particularly in Indian Hill where sales surged nearly 60 percent. Sales of homes of $1 million and above are up 21 percent through November in Hamilton County with 58 homes sales.

16795 ■ *"1Q Office Vacancies Mainly Up; Class A Space Bucks Trend, Falls"* in *Crain's Detroit Business* (Vol. 24, April 14, 2008, No. 15)
Pub: Crain Communications, Inc.
Ed: Daniel Duggan. **Description:** Although more office space became vacant in the first quarter, Class A space went in the opposite direction with several local businesses are moving from less-desirable to more desirable areas.

16796 ■ *"3CDC Investing $8 Million To Put New Life Into Old Homes"* in *Globe & Mail* (February 28, 2006, pp. B1)
Pub: CTVglobemedia Publishing Inc.
Ed: Lucy May. **Description:** The Cincinnati Center City Development Corp. has bought more than 100 empty buildings and many around Washington Park in Over-the-Rhine. Its new project, called 3CDC, is to revitalize the historic neighborhood in the Washington Park area near Music Hall.

16797 ■ *"6 Worth the Price Fix-Ups"* in *Realtor Magazine* (Vol. 44, April-May 2011, No. 44, pp. 23)
Pub: Realtor Magazine
Description: Advice on how realtors could increase a home's resale value through do-it-yourself projects is given. Removal of personal items and clutter is recommended, along with rearrangement of furniture. A clutter consultant could also be used.

16798 ■ *"A 16-Year Housing Slump? It Could Happen"* in *Barron's* (Vol. 88, March 17, 2008, No. 11, pp. 27)
Pub: Dow Jones & Company, Inc.
Ed: Gene Epstein. **Description:** Housing remains a good protection against inflation but over very long periods. Inflation-adjusted stock prices did even better but have greater volatility. Commodities, on the other hand, underperformed both housing and stocks as inflation hedges. House prices tend to rise faster than the consumer price index is because land is inherently limited.

16799 ■ *"The 35 Year Mortgage-Built to Last Time"* in *Globe & Mail* (March 17, 2006, pp. B1)
Pub: CTVglobemedia Publishing Inc.
Ed: Patrick Brethour. **Description:** The 35-year mortgage has arrived in Canada. The plan will give an opportunity to the first-time buyers into the real estate market. Details of the new mortgage are analyzed.

16800 ■ *"$100 Million in Projects Jeopardized"* in *Business Courier* (Vol. 24, March 28, 2008, No. 51, pp. 1)
Pub: American City Business Journals, Inc.
Ed: Dan Monk. **Description:** Ohio's historic preservation tax credit program may be reinstated after some companies planned to sue over its stoppage. The Ohio Department of Development said the program was halted because it exceeded the allocated budget for the credit. $34 million in credits are at stake for more than two dozen local projects if the program is reinstated.

16801 ■ *"217 Homes Planned for Former Crystal Cream Site"* in *Sacramento Business Journal* (Vol. 25, August 8, 2008, No. 23, pp. 1)
Pub: American City Business Journals, Inc.
Ed: Michael Shaw. **Description:** MetroNova Development LLC plans to develop housing at the former Crystal Cream & Butter Co. site near downtown Sacramento. The developer expects to sell the new loft houses for about $300,000 without public subsidies. Views and other information on the planned development project, is presented.

16802 ■ *"2009 Real Estate in Review: Median Prices Drop, Sales Up"* in Bellingham Business Journal (Vol. February 2010, pp. 15)
Pub: Sound Publishing Inc.
Ed: Isaac Bonnell. **Description:** Bellingham and Whatcom County, Washington saw a rise in home sales in 2008. Single family home sales were up 3.3 percent in Bellingham and 0.5 percent for the entire county. Statistical data included.

16803 ■ *"2010 Book of Lists"* in Austin Business JournalInc. (Vol. 29, December 25, 2009, No. 42, pp. 1)
Pub: American City Business Journals
Description: Rankings of companies and organizations within the business services, finance, healthcare, hospitality and travel, insurance, marketing and media, professional services, real estate, education and technology industries in Austin, Texas are presented. Rankings are based on sales, business size, and other statistics.

16804 ■ *"2010 Book of Lists"* in Business Courier (Vol. 26, December 26, 2009, No. 36, pp. 1)
Pub: American City Business Journals, Inc.
Description: Rankings of companies and organizations within the business services, education, finance, health care, hospitality and tourism, real estate, and technology industries in the Cincinnati, Ohio-Northern Kentucky area are presented. Rankings are based on sales, business size, or other statistics.

16805 ■ *"2010 Book of Lists"* in Tampa Bay Business Journal (Vol. 30, December 22, 2009, No. 53, pp. 1)
Pub: American City Business Journals
Description: Rankings of companies and organizations within the human resources, banking and finance, business services, healthcare, real estate, technology, hospitality and travel, and education industries in the Greater Tampa Bay area are presented. Rankings are based on sales, business size, and more.

16806 ■ *"Affordable Again"* in The Business Journal-Serving Greater Tampa Bay (Vol. 28, July 18, 2008, No. 30, pp. 1)
Pub: American City Business Journals, Inc.
Ed: Janet Leiser. **Description:** Rental rates for office space in the Tampa Bay area has dropped to $21.68 a foot, after demand for the second quarter of 2008 has remained low. Commercial real estate experts say that the industry can easily rebound from what is believed to be the weakest demand in 20 years. Other views, information and statistics on real estate demand and prices in Tampa Bay are, are presented.

16807 ■ *"Affordable Housing on the Rise"* in Philadelphia Business Journal (Vol. 28, October 23, 2009, No. 36, pp. 1)
Pub: American City Business Journals
Ed: Natalie Kostelni. **Description:** Philadelphia, Pennsylvania led an affordable housing boom with more than 800 new affordable housing units in the works in spite of the recession. The converging of developers and federal stimulus money has driven the sudden increase with the launching of several projects across the city.

16808 ■ *"Agricultural Community Implements Green Technologies, Building Team"* in Contractor (Vol. 56, September 2009, No. 9, pp. 5)
Pub: Penton Media, Inc.
Ed: Candace Ruolo. **Description:** John DeWald and Associates has initiated a residential development project which uses green technologies in Illinois. The community features a community center, organic farm and recreational trails. Comments from executives are also provided.

16809 ■ *"AIC To Buy $350M of Real Estate"* in Austin Business JournalInc. (Vol. 28, November 14, 2008, No. 35, pp. 1)
Pub: American City Business Journals
Ed: Kate Harrington. **Description:** Austin-based AIC Ventures LP is planning to buy $350 million worth of commercial real estate. The company's move will double its acquisitions. It is also planning to acquire 30 assets for its eight fun in 2009 from middle-market companies.

16810 ■ *"All Bubbles Must Burst"* in Canadian Business (Vol. 83, August 17, 2010, No. 13-14, pp. 12)
Pub: Rogers Media Ltd.
Ed: Matthew McClearn. **Description:** Canada's housing markets is showing signs of cooling down as home and condo sales both fell for the first time in 16 years. The Canadian government has fueled the market over an extended period through Canada Mortgage and Housing Corporation's role in insuring mortgage lenders against risk of defaults.

16811 ■ *"All-Star Advice 2010"* in Black Enterprise (Vol. 41, October 2010, No. 3, pp. 97)
Pub: Earl G. Graves Publishing Co. Inc.
Ed: Renita Burns, Sheiresa Ngo, Marcia Wade Talbert. **Description:** Financial experts share tips on real estate, investing, taxes, insurance and debt management.

16812 ■ *"Allen Tate Expanding to Research Triangle Park: Firm Expects Raleigh Market to Grow Faster"* in Charlotte Observer (January 31, 2007)
Pub: Knight-Ridder/Tribune Business News
Ed: Doug Smith; Dudley Price. **Description:** Allen Tate Realtors expanded its operations to the Research Triangle area. The firm is predicting a strong market and growth in Charlotte, North Carolina.

16813 ■ *"Another California Firm On Way"* in Austin Business Journal (Vol. 31, May 6, 2011, No. 9, pp. 1)
Pub: American City Business Journals Inc.
Ed: Christopher Calnan. **Description:** Main Street Hub Inc. is planning to build a facility in Austin, Texas. The company helps businesses manage their online reputations. Main Street has selected Aquila Commercial LLC as its real estate broker.

16814 ■ *"Another Man's Pain"* in Canadian Business (Vol. 80, October 22, 2007, No. 21, pp. 33)
Pub: Rogers Media
Ed: Andy Holloway. **Description:** U.S. financial collapse can have a positive impact on Canadian investors. Graphs on the total number of home foreclosures in the U.S. from January to August 2007, as well as foreclosure market by type, are presented.

16815 ■ *"Antwerpen Takes on Chrysler Financial Over Foreclosure Sales"* in Baltimore Business Journal (Vol. 28, July 30, 2010, No. 12, pp. 1)
Pub: Baltimore Business Journal
Ed: Gary Haber. **Description:** Antwerpen Motorcars Ltd. aims to fight the scheduled foreclosure sale of real estate it leases in Baltimore County, including the showroom for its Hyundai dealership on Baltimore National Pike in Catonsville, Maryland. The company is planning to file papers in court to stop the scheduled August 11, 2010 auction sought by Chrysler Financial Services Americas LLC.

16816 ■ *"Apartment Ambitions"* in The Business Journal-Portland (Vol. 25, August 8, 2008, No. 22, pp. 1)
Pub: American City Business Journals, Inc.
Ed: Wendy Culverwell. **Description:** Unico Properties LLC's Asa FlatsLofts is one of the first of eight high-end apartment projects planned for Portland which will add a total of 2,130 new units to the Pearl District, South Waterfront, and downtown Portland. These apartments charge costs more than $1,600 or more per month over the average rent.

16817 ■ *"Apartment Market Down, Not Out"* in Crain's Detroit Business (Vol. 24, October 6, 2008, No. 40, pp. 9)
Pub: Crain Communications, Inc.
Ed: Daniel Duggan. **Description:** Detroit's apartment market is considered to have some of the strongest fundamentals of any apartment market in the country with relatively low vacancy rates and a relatively low supply of new units compared with demand. Investors continue to show interest in the buildings but the national lending market is making it difficult to invest in the city.

16818 ■ *"Apartment Tower in River North Fetches More Than $90 Million"* in Crain's Chicago Business (Vol. 34, October 24, 2011, No. 42, pp. 17)
Pub: Crain Communications Inc.
Ed: Alby Gallun. **Description:** Apartment tower in River North was sold for over $90 million to a Texas pension fund adviser. Details are included.

16819 ■ *"Aquila HQ Hits the Market"* in The Business Journal-Serving Metropolitan Kansas City (Vol. 26, July 25, 2008, No. 46, pp. 1)
Pub: American City Business Journals, Inc.
Ed: Rob Roberts. **Description:** Commercial real estate experts believe that Aquila Inc.'s former headquarters will be hard to rent out. The historic value of the building, being Kansas City's first skyscraper, is not expected to add value to the price of the rent. Other views and information on the building, as well as on Aquila, are presented.

16820 ■ *"Ask Inc."* in Inc. (December 2007, pp. 83-84)
Pub: Gruner & Jahr USA Publishing
Ed: Ari Weinzweig. **Description:** Questions regarding knowledge management in the case of a retiring CFO, issues involved in opening a satellite office for a New York realtor, and information for hiring a multicultural workforce are all discussed.

16821 ■ *"Athletes Face Wins and Losses After Pro Sport"* in The Business Journal - Serving Phoenix and the Valley of the Sun (Vol. 29, September 19, 2008, No. 3, pp. 1)
Pub: American City Business Journals, Inc.
Ed: Chris Casacchia. **Description:** Professional athletes like hockey star Jeremy Roenick start businesses, while others like Joel Adamson work to boost local communities. Former athletes were found to be particularly interested with real estate businesses. Other views and information on former athletes and their life after sports are presented.

16822 ■ *"Au Revoir Or Goodbye?"* in Barron's (Vol. 88, July 14, 2008, No. 28, pp. 5)
Pub: Dow Jones & Co., Inc.
Ed: Alan Abelson. **Description:** Former Senator Phil Gramm's opinion that the U.S. is a 'nation of whiners' as they moan about recession is another example of the disconnection between Washington and Wall Street on one hand and the real world on the other. It would be a catastrophe for most of the world if Fannie Mae and Freddie Mac were to go under and take their trillions of mortgage debt with them.

16823 ■ *"Austin Homes are Overpriced, Study Says"* in Austin Business JournalInc. (Vol. 29, January 1, 2010, No. 43, pp. 1)
Pub: American City Business Journals
Ed: Kate Harrington. **Description:** Study by Forbes.com shows that Austin-Round Rock metropolitan statistical area ranked 10th on the list of cities with the most over-priced homes. For instance, the average price for a single-family home pegged at $188,000.

16824 ■ *"Back on Track-Or Off the Rails?"* in Business Week (September 22, 2008, No. 4100, pp. 22)
Pub: McGraw-Hill Companies, Inc.
Ed: Peter Coy; Tara Kalwarski. **Description:** Discusses the possible scenarios the American economy may undergo due to the takeover of Fannie Mae and Freddie Mac. Statistical data included.

16825 ■ *"Bangles, BMWs Elbow Out Delis and Discount Shops"* in Crain's New York Business (Vol. 24, January 14, 2008, No. 2, pp. 35)
Pub: Crain Communications, Inc.
Ed: Wendy Davis. **Description:** Lured by a growing number of affluent residents and high-earning professionals, a number of upscale retailers have opened locations downtown which is driving up rents and forcing out longtime independent merchants.

**16826 ■ "Bankruptcies Shoot Up 68 Percent"
in Sacramento Business Journal (Vol. 25,
July 18, 2008, No. 20, pp. 1)**
Pub: American City Business Journals, Inc.
Ed: Kathy Robertson. **Description:** Personal bankruptcy in the Sacramento area rose by 88 percent for
the first half of 2008 while business bankruptcies rose
by 50 percent for the same period. The numbers of
consumer bankruptcy reflects the effect of high debt,
rising mortgage costs, and declining home values on
U.S. households.

**16827 ■ "Best Income Trust" in Canadian
Business (Vol. 81, Summer 2008, No. 9, pp.
69)**
Pub: Rogers Media Ltd.
Ed: Calvin Leung. **Description:** Table showing five-
year annualized growth rate and one-year stock
performance of real estate investment trusts firms in
Canada is presented. Calgary-based Boardwalk REIT
is projected to grow the fastest among North American REITs over the next two years. Other details on
the stock performance analysis are presented.

**16828 ■ "Bill Kaneko" in Hawaii Business
(Vol. 53, December 2007, No. 6, pp. 32)**
Pub: Hawaii Business Publishing
Ed: David K. Choo. **Description:** Hawaii Institute for
Public Affairs chief executive officer and president Bill
Kaneko believes that the Hawaiian economy is boom-
ing, however, he also asserts that the economy is too
focused on tourism and real estate. Kaneko has also
realized the that the will of the people is strong while
he was helping with the Hawaiian 2050 Sustainability
Plan. The difficulties of making a sustainable Hawaii
are discussed.

**16829 ■ "Bills Would Regulate Mortgage
Loan Officers" in Crain's Detroit Business
(Vol. 24, February 25, 2008, No. 8, pp. 9)**
Pub: Crain Communications Inc. - Detroit
Ed: Amy Lane. **Description:** New legislation in
Michigan, if passed, would create a registration
process for mortgage loan officers in the state in
order to address the mortgage loan crisis.

**16830 ■ "Block Plans Office Park Along K-10
Corridor" in The Business Journal-Serving
Metropolitan Kansas City (Vol. 27, October 3,
2008)**
Pub: American City Business Journals, Inc.
Ed: Rob Roberts. **Description:** Kansas City,
Missouri-based Block and Co. is planning to build
four office buildings at the corner of College Boulevard and Ridgeview Road in Olathe. Features of the
planned development are provided. Comments from
executives are also presented.

**16831 ■ "Block Pulls Plug On Riverside Deal"
in The Business Journal-Serving Metropolitan
Kansas City (Vol. 27, October 10, 2008, No. 4)**
Pub: American City Business Journals, Inc.
Ed: Rob Roberts. **Description:** Real estate developer
Ken Block has backed out from a $300 million
Riverside industrial project. Block says he has
already invested $1 million of his own money into the
deal. Details regarding the project are given.

**16832 ■ "Bond OK Could Bring Back the
Housing Battle?" in Charlotte Business
Journal (Vol. 25, November 5, 2010, No. 33,
pp. 1)**
Pub: Charlotte Business Journal
Ed: Susan Stabley. **Description:** The approval of the
$15 million housing bond in Charlotte, North Carolina
could bring back the debates on housing in the
region. Protesters have opposed affordable housing
developments that were proposed in the area since
2008. Other information on the recently approved
housing bond and on other real estate issues in North
Carolina is presented.

**16833 ■ "Book of Lists 2010" in Philadelphia
Business Journal (Vol. 28, December 25,
2009, No. 45, pp. 1)**
Pub: American City Business Journals
Description: Rankings of companies and organizations within the banking, biotechnology, economic
development, healthcare, hospitality, law and ac-

counting, marketing and media, real estate, and
technology industries in the Philadelphia, Pennsylvania area are presented. Rankings are based on sales,
business size, and more.

**16834 ■ "Boston Hedge Fund Pours Money
Into Real Estate Projects" in Charlotte
Business Journal (Vol. 25, December 3, 2010,
No. 37, pp. 1)**
Pub: Charlotte Business Journal
Ed: Will Boye. **Description:** Boston-based hedge
fund Baupost Group has been financing real estate
project in Charlotte, North Carolina including more
than 80 acres just north of uptown. Aside from
purchasing the $23.8 million note for the Rosewood
Condominiums from Regions Financial Corporation,
the Baupost Group is also negotiating with Regions
to buy the $93.9 million debt of the EipCentre real
estate project.

**16835 ■ "Bottom's Up" in Barron's (Vol. 88,
July 14, 2008, No. 28, pp. 25)**
Pub: Dow Jones & Co., Inc.
Ed: Jonathan R. Laing. **Description:** Economist Chip
Case believes that home prices are nearing a bottom
based on his analysis of the history of the housing
market; surprisingly, in the past the housing market
has rebounded after a quarter from a massive housing start drop. The drop in early stage delinquencies
is another sign of the housing market's recovery.

**16836 ■ "A Bright Spot: Industrial Space in
Demand Again" in Sacramento Business
Journal (Vol. 28, October 21, 2011, No. 34, pp.
1)**
Pub: Sacramento Business Journal
Ed: Michael Shaw. **Description:** Sacramento, California's industrial sites have been eyed by potential tenants who are actively seeking space larger than
50,000 square feet.

**16837 ■ "Brokerages Seek a Foothold in
Local Real Estate Market" in Charlotte
Business Journal (Vol. 25, October 15, 2010,
No. 30, pp. 1)**
Pub: Charlotte Business Journal
Ed: Will Boye. **Description:** Charlotte, North Carolina
has become an attractive destination for out-of-town
brokerage firms. Colliers International has signed an
affiliate deal with Anthony and Company to set up
shop in Charlotte. Grubb and Ellis Company, on the
other hand, is planning to open an office in the city.

**16838 ■ "Builder Comes Back Home" in
Houston Business Journal (Vol. 40,
September 18, 2009, No. 19, pp. 1A)**
Pub: American City Business Journals
Ed: Allison Wollam. **Description:** Jason Hammonds,
who has been previously involved in the local home
building market in Texas, has launched a new home
building company called J. Kyle Homes. The new
company has chosen Cinco Ranch, a neo-traditional
styled neighborhood in Katy, Texas to build its first
housing community.

**16839 ■ "Builder's Bankruptcy Fans Fears" in
Crain's Cleveland Business (Vol. 28, October
22, 2007, No. 42, pp. 1)**
Pub: Crain Communications, Inc.
Ed: Stan Bullard. **Description:** Whitlatch & Co.,
Northeast Ohio's largest builder by unit volume in the
early 1990s, has filed for Chapter 11 bankruptcy. This
is causing builders and others in the real estate
industry to wonder how long and severe the housing
slump will be and which companies will survive.

**16840 ■ "Builder's Comeback Highlights
Uptick in Demand for New Homes" in Boston
Business Journal (Vol. 29, June 3, 2011, No.
4, pp. 1)**
Pub: American City Business Journals Inc.
Ed: Gary Haber. **Description:** The return of builder
Michael Canock after a series of credit crisis and the
funding for his new projects are discussed in light of
the recent upsurge in the home-building industry in
the Baltimore area. New single-family homes num-
bered 318 in first quarter 2011 which is a 20 percent
increase from first quarter 2010.

**16841 ■ "Buy Now?" in Hawaii Business (Vol.
53, March 2008, No. 9, pp. 32)**
Pub: Hawaii Business Publishing
Ed: David K. Choo. **Description:** Discusses the
Honolulu Board of REALTORS which said that the
last two months of 2007 saw double-digit housing
sales drop, with December figures showing 30.6
percent and 22.9 percent decline in sales of single-
family homes and condominiums, respectively.
Forecasts on Hawaii's real estate market for 2008
are discussed.

**16842 ■ "Buyers' Market" in Baltimore
Business Journal (Vol. 27, November 20,
2009, No. 28, pp. 1)**
Pub: American City Business Journals
Ed: Daniel J. Sernovitz. **Description:** Some business owners in Maryland are removing their leases
and purchasing buildings due to the lower costs of
real estate. This trend has enabled small business
owners to avoid rent hikes, while setting equity into
their companies. The pros and cons of owning buildings and how business owners assess their return on
investment are examined.

**16843 ■ "Calendar" in Crain's Detroit
Business (Vol. 24, October 6, 2008, No. 40,
pp. 22)**
Pub: Crain Communications, Inc.
Description: Listing of events in the Detroit area
include conferences addressing entrepreneurialism,
economic development, manufacturing, marketing,
the housing crisis and women business ownership.

**16844 ■ "Canadian Vehicle Sales Accelerate
in April, but U.S. Goes on Bumpy Ride" in
Globe & Mail (May 2, 2007, pp. B7)**
Pub: CTVglobemedia Publishing Inc.
Ed: Greg Keenan. **Description:** The increase in
Canadian vehicle sales to 169,280 in April 2007, but
decline in their sales in the United States due to
slump in housing sector are discussed.

**16845 ■ "C&W Gets Green Star" in Crain's
New York Business (Vol. 24, January 7, 2008,
No. 1, pp. 25)**
Pub: Crain Communications, Inc.
Ed: Theresa Agovino. **Description:** Cushman &
Wakefield Inc. has hired Eleni Reed as director of
sustainability strategies; the real estate firm wants to
ensure that the 500 million square feet of office space
it manages around the globe meets environmental
standards.

**16846 ■ "Cedar Fair to Solicit Bids for
Geauga Lake" in Crain's Cleveland Business
(Vol. 28, October 8, 2007, No. 40, pp. 1)**
Pub: Crain Communications, Inc.
Ed: Stan Bullard. **Description:** Cedar Fair Entertain-
ment Co. plans to seek sealed bids for the redevelop-
ment of nearly 540 acres of their amusement park
site in southwest Geauga County and northwest
Portage County.

**16847 ■ "Channelside On the Blocks" in The
Business Journal-Serving Greater Tampa Bay
(Vol. 28, August 29, 2008, No. 36, pp. 1)**
Pub: American City Business Journals, Inc.
Ed: Michael Hinman. **Description:** In a bankruptcy
auction for The Place, one of the more visible
condominium projects at Channelside, the lowest bid
is just below $73 a square foot. KeyBank National
Association, the Key Developers Group LLC's lender,
leads the auction planned for October 15, 2008. The
reason behind the low minimum bid required to
participate in the said action is discussed.

**16848 ■ "Children's Hospital to Build in New
Berlin" in The Business Journal-Milwaukee
(Vol. 25, August 1, 2008, No. 45, pp. A1)**
Pub: American City Business Journals, Inc.
Ed: Corrinne Hess. **Description:** Children's Hospital
of Wisconsin plans a clinic in the 35-acre medical office park in New Berlin, Wisconsin, owned by Froedtert Memorial Lutheran Hospital and Medical College
of Wisconsin Real Estate Ventures LLC. The hospital
will be the first major tenant in the park, to be built by
Irgens Development Partners LLC.

16849 ■ *"City Sets Yamhill Makeover"* in *The Business Journal-Portland (Vol. 25, July 4, 2008, No. 17, pp. 1)*

Pub: American City Business Journals, Inc.

Ed: Andy Giegerich. **Description:** City government is scheduled to redevelop Peterson's property on Yamhill Street in Portland. The redevelopment is seen as a way to better developing commercial properties in the area. Problems associated with the project, which include cost and developer selection, are also discussed.

16850 ■ *"Coherent Laying Off 144 As It Prepares To Shut Auburn Plant"* in *Sacramento Business Journal (Vol. 25, August 1, 2008, No. 22, pp. 1)*

Pub: American City Business Journals, Inc.

Ed: Melanie Turner. **Description:** Sacramento, California-based Coherent Inc. is planning to lay off 144 workers at its Auburn facility. Coherent has been cutting payroll and its real estate holdings. Statistics on the company's earnings are also provided.

16851 ■ *"Colliers Shifts Its Brokerage Home"* in *Charlotte Business Journal (Vol. 25, November 5, 2010, No. 33, pp. 1)*

Pub: Charlotte Business Journal

Ed: Will Boye. **Description:** Colliers International signed a long-term affiliate agreement with commercial real estate firm Clarus Properties, in a move that would allow Colliers to resume business in Charlotte, North Carolina. Colliers also hired well known brokers Brad Grow and Brent Royall.

16852 ■ *"Columbia's JPB Raising $175M to Acquire Companies, Real Estate"* in *Boston Business Journal (Vol. 29, May 27, 2011, No. 3, pp. 1)*

Pub: American City Business Journals Inc.

Ed: Gary Haber. **Description:** JPB Enterprises is preparing to raise $175 million in its goal of acquiring companies and real estate that are major names in America. The $75 million will be raised for a buyout fund that will target wide range of industries while the $100 million will be used for land investment projects in the Florida Panhandle. Baltimore firms are expected to benefit from this deal.

16853 ■ *"Coming Soon: Bailouts of Fannie and Freddie"* in *Barron's (Vol. 88, July 14, 2008, No. 28, pp. 14)*

Pub: Dow Jones & Co., Inc.

Ed: Jonathan R. Laing. **Description:** Assurances from the government that Fannie Mae and Freddie Mac are adequately capitalized and able to carry on their duties as guarantors or owners of over $5 trillion of U.S. home mortgages are designed to keep both entities afloat until they attempt to raise $10 billion in new equity. The government would assume any losses in a bailout and owners of the banks' papers would profit as yields drop.

16854 ■ *"Con-Way Project Back in High Gear"* in *Business Journal Portland (Vol. 27, November 5, 2010, No. 36, pp. 1)*

Pub: Portland Business Journal

Ed: Wendy Culverwell. **Description:** Trucking firm Con-Way Inc. intends to sell parcels of land from a property comprising 16 blocks and 20 prime acres west of the Pearl District in Portland, Oregon. In 2009, Con-Way abandoned plans to sell the property. As Con-Way reclaims control over design and usage of the property, it also expressed willingness to cooperate with a master developer on a related real estate project.

16855 ■ *"Condo Markdown"* in *Boston Business Journal (Vol. 27, November 30, 2007, No. 44, pp. 1)*

Pub: American City Business Journals Inc.

Ed: Michelle Hillman. **Description:** Boston real estate market is softening, and condominium developers such as Beacon Communities LLC are sending out various incentives like markdowns and unit upgrades. Developers have also held auctions and even offered brand new cars to lure buyers. Other perks being offered by various Boston developers are discussed.

16856 ■ *"Condominium Sales Fall to a Seven-Year Low"* in *Crain's Chicago Business (Vol. 31, November 10, 2008, No. 45, pp. 2)*

Pub: Crain Communications, Inc.

Ed: Alby Gallun. **Description:** Downtown Chicago condominium market is experiencing the lowest number of sales in years due to the tightening of the mortgage lending market, the Wall Street crisis and the downturn in the economy. The supply of new condos is soaring, the result of the building boom of 2005 and 2006; many developers are finding it difficult to pay off construction loans and fear foreclosure on their properties. Additional information and statistical data related to the downtown condominium market is provided.

16857 ■ *"Contingent Offers: Weighing the Risk"* in *Crain's Chicago Business (Vol. 31, April 21, 2008, No. 16, pp. 48)*

Pub: Crain Communications, Inc.

Ed: Darci Smith. **Description:** Interview with Greer Haseman, the broker-owner of Town Square Associates, who discusses contingent offers in a challenging housing market.

16858 ■ *"A Conversation with; Renea Butler, Real Estate One Inc."* in *Crain's Detroit Business (Vol. 25, June 8, 2009, No. 23, pp. 12)*

Pub: Crain Communications Inc. - Detroit

Ed: Ryan Beene. **Description:** Renea Butler, vice president of administration and human resources for Real Estate One Inc. in Southfield as well as vice president for public relations for the Human Resource Association of Greater Detroit, talks about how the economy has affected human resource services.

16859 ■ *"A Conversation With; Ron Gatner, Jones Lang LaSalle"* in *Crain's Detroit Business (Vol. 24, October 6, 2008, No. 40, pp. 9)*

Pub: Crain Communications, Inc.

Description: Interview with Ron Gatner who is a corporate real estate adviser with the real estate company Jones Lang LaSalle as well as the company's executive vice president and part of the tenant advisory team; Gatner speaks about the impact that the Wall Street crisis is having on the commercial real estate market in Detroit.

16860 ■ *"Cool on Chicago Office Properties"* in *Crain's Chicago Business (Vol. 31, March 31, 2008, No. 13, pp. 16)*

Pub: Crain Communications, Inc.

Ed: Eddie Baeb. **Description:** Investors predict values on Chicago office buildings to drop 1.3 percent over the next year.

16861 ■ *"Cornered by Credit; As $1 Billion in Loans Come Due, Will Landlords Find Funds?"* in *Crain's Detroit Business (October 6, 2008)*

Pub: Crain Communications, Inc.

Ed: Daniel Duggan. **Description:** Conduit loans are used by many real estate investors and are normally issued in 7- to 10-year terms with balloon payments due at the end, requiring the full balance to be paid upon maturity. Many building owners may find their properties going into foreclosure as these loans mature next year since these loans cannot be extended like typical loans and the credit crisis along with falling property values is making it more difficult to secure new sources of funding. Possible solutions to this problem are also explored.

16862 ■ *"Corporex in Battle With Hedge Fund"* in *Business Courier (Vol. 24, December 21, 2008, No. 36, pp. 1)*

Pub: American City Business Journals, Inc.

Ed: Jon Newberry. **Description:** Discusses a breach of contract complaint that was filed by Apollo Real Estate Advisors against Corporex Companies Inc. but Corporex said that the lawsuit was intended to counter an arbitration complaint filed by Corporex against Apollo, which seeks $11 million in termination fees. The issue is in relation to the acquisition of Eagle Hospitality by Apollo earlier in 2007.

16863 ■ *"Cost of Home Purchase Loans are Higher for Hispanics"* in *Hispanic Business (October 2007, pp. 88)*

Pub: Hispanic Business

Description: Home loans for Hispanics generally are offered at a higher interest rate. Statistical data included.

16864 ■ *"Creativity is Essential in Sagging Relocation Market"* in *Crain's Cleveland Business (Vol. 28, November 5, 2007, No. 44, pp. 19)*

Pub: Crain Communications, Inc.

Ed: Christine Gordillo. **Description:** Since Northeast Ohio was headquarters to a number of Fortune 500 companies, residential real estate builders and brokers could count on corporate relocation clients for a steady stream of business. Today, corporations have become more cautious when relocating talent due to the costs involved which has forced industry experts to be more patient and more creative in the ways they attract out-of-town buyers who are likely to be a sure sell.

16865 ■ *"Credit-Market Crisis Batters Origen Financial's Bottom Line"* in *Crain's Detroit Business (Vol. 24, March 31, 2008, No. 13, pp. 4)*

Pub: Crain Communications, Inc.

Description: Overview of the effect the credit-market crisis has had on Origen Financial Inc., a company that underwrites and services loans for manufactured housing. CEO Ronald Klein didn't think Origen would be affected by the collapse due to its sound operations but the company's share price dropped considerably causing its auditors to warn that the company's existence could be in jeopardy.

16866 ■ *"Critics: Efforts to Fix Loans Won't Stop Foreclosure Wave"* in *Business First Columbus (Vol. 25, November 14, 2008, No. 12, pp. A1)*

Pub: American City Business Journals

Ed: Adrian Burns. **Description:** Efforts by U.S. banks to help homeowners pay mortgages are seen to have little if any impact on foreclosures. Banks have announced plans to identify and aid troubled borrowers. Statistical data included.

16867 ■ Crittenden Directory of Real Estate Financing

Pub: Crittenden Research Inc.

Contact: Alan Crittenden, Manager

URL(s): www.crittendenonline.com/index.php/directories/. **Released:** Semiannual; updated by weekly newsletter. **Price:** $967, Individuals print; $387, Individuals online. **Covers:** Over 300 major lenders, investors, and joint ventures engaged in commercial and residential real estate financing and investing. **Entries include:** Company name, nickname, total assets, typical rate, real estate investment portfolio value, production totals (broken down by type of investment), maximum and minimum loan/investment amounts; preferred types of loans, interest rates, fees, and related data; names, addresses, phone numbers of contacts, pension fund name. **Arrangement:** Geographical (by principal area of lending activity). **Indexes:** Type of real estate, company name, project type.

16868 ■ Crittenden's Real Estate Buyers Directory

Pub: Crittenden Research Inc.

Contact: Alan Crittenden, Manager

URL(s): www.crittendenonline.com. **Released:** Semiannual; updated/supplemented weekly by "Real Estate Buyers Newsletter". **Price:** $967, Individuals CD-ROM version; $967, Individuals paper version. **Covers:** Over 400 real estate buyers, including private investors, banks, pension funds, real estate investment trusts (REITs), foreign investors, and life insurance companies. **Entries include:** Organization name, contact name, title, address, and phone; type of property purchased, geographic territory covered, previous year's estimated purchases, minimum and maximum purchase amount. **Arrangement:** Alphabetical. **Indexes:** Annual and quarterly indexes.

16869 ▪ *"The Debt Mountain in Mid-Collapse"* in Canadian Business (Vol. 83, October 12, 2010, No. 17, pp. 28)
Pub: Rogers Media Ltd.
Ed: Michael McCullough. **Description:** A growing real estate market has made Intrawest ULC's Whistler-Blackcomb resort a model for a booming industry for years. However, resorts are now required to manage themselves better because of the recession. Some mountains are also trimming the cost of labor and cutting peripheral services.

16870 ▪ *"Detroit Residential Market Slows; Bright Spots Emerge"* in Crain's Detroit Business (Vol. 24, October 6, 2008, No. 40, pp. 11)
Pub: Crain Communications, Inc.
Ed: Daniel Duggan. **Description:** Discusses the state of the residential real estate market in Detroit; although condominium projects receive the most attention, deals for single-family homes are taking place in greater numbers due to financing issues. Buyers can purchase a single family home with a 3.5 percent down payment compared to 20 percent for some condo deals because of the number of first-time homebuyer programs under the Federal Housing Administration.

16871 ▪ *"Developer Backs Out of Major Bastrop Project"* in Austin Business JournalInc. (Vol. 28, December 19, 2008, No. 40, pp. 1)
Pub: American City Business Journals
Ed: Kate Harrington. **Description:** Weingarten Realty Investors, a Houston, Texas-based real estate company, has backed out of its contract on more than 1 million square feet of retail space at the County Road 304 and State Highway 71 corner in Bastrop, Texas, according to landowner Tom Brundage. Analysts say that the Bastrop area is not ready for big retail projects.

16872 ▪ *"Developer Banks On East Submarket, Slowdown Not a Hinderance"* in The Business Journal-Serving Greater Tampa Bay (August 1, 2008)
Pub: American City Business Journals, Inc.
Ed: Janet Leiser. **Description:** CLW Industrial Group and Cobalt Industrial REIT II have teamed up to develop a 14-acre area in northeast Hillsborough County, Florida. The $15 million industrial park project includes the 175,000-square-foot New Tampa Commerce Center, scheduled for completion in the first quarter of 2009.

16873 ▪ *"Developer Tries to Bring Homes to Buda"* in Austin Business JournalInc. (Vol. 28, December 26, 2008, No. 41, pp. 1)
Pub: American City Business Journals
Ed: Kate Harrington. **Description:** Real estate developer Jeremiah Venture LP is planning a residential, single-family development on about 600 acres near Buda, Texas. The company also plans to construct a membrane waste treatment plant, and has applied to do land application. However, several groups have come forward to ask for more information on the application due to concerns about soil density.

16874 ▪ *"Developer Wins Bout with Bank in Roundabout Way"* in Tampa Bay Business Journal (Vol. 30, January 29, 2010, No. 6, pp. 1)
Pub: American City Business Journals
Ed: Janet Leiser. **Description:** Developer Donald E. Phillips of Phillips Development and Realty LLC won against the foreclosure filed by First Horizon National Corporation, which is demanding the company to fully pay its $2.9 million loan. Phillips requested that his company pay monthly mortgage and extend the loan's maturity date.

16875 ▪ *"Developers Give Big to Mayor's Bid"* in Boston Business Journal (Vol. 29, August 26, 2011, No. 16, pp. 1)
Pub: American City Business Journals Inc.
Ed: Scott Dance. **Description:** Mayor Stephanie Rawlings-Blake received thousands of dollars in her political campaign from companies of real estate developers who are vying to build key development projects in Baltimore, Maryland. Rawlings-Blake created a major fundraising advantage over other mayoral candidates with the help of those contributions.

16876 ▪ *"Developers Give City Dwellings a Modern Spin"* in Crain's Cleveland Business (Vol. 28, November 5, 2007, No. 44, pp. 18)
Pub: Crain Communications, Inc.
Description: Cleveland is increasingly becoming a canvas for fresh, cutting-edge design due to several recent projects, some at prominent sites.

16877 ▪ *"Developers Poised to Pull Trigers"* in Boston Business Journal (Vol. 30, November 12, 2010, No. 42, pp. 1)
Pub: Boston Business Journal
Ed: Craig M. Douglas. **Description:** Large residential projects are expected to break ground in Boston, Massachusetts in 2011, as real estate developers expect growth for the industry. Real estate experts expect more than 2,000 rental units to be available by 2011. Information on key real estate projects in Boston is presented.

16878 ▪ *Dictionary of Real Estate Terms*
Pub: Barron's Educational Series Inc.
Contact: Alex Holtz, President
E-mail: aholtz@berronseduc.com
Ed: Jack P. Friedman, Jack C. Harris, J. Bruce Lindeman. **Released:** October 2008. **Price:** $13.99. **Description:** More than 2,500 real estate terms relating to mortgages and financing, brokerage law, architecture, rentals and leases, property insurance, and more.

16879 ▪ *"Docs Might Hold Cure for Real Estate, Banks"* in Baltimore Business Journal (Vol. 28, November 5, 2010, No. 26, pp. 1)
Pub: Baltimore Business Journal
Ed: Gary Haber. **Description:** Health care providers, including physicians are purchasing their office space instead of renting it as banks lower interest rates to 6 percent on mortgages for medical offices. The rise in demand offers relief to the commercial real estate market. It has also resulted in a boom in building new medical offices.

16880 ▪ *"Downtown Evens Tenant Ledger"* in The Business Journal-Serving Metropolitan Kansas City (Vol. 26, July 11, 2008, No. 44, pp. 1)
Pub: American City Business Journals, Inc.
Ed: Rob Roberts. **Description:** Financial services company PricewaterhouseCoopers will relocate its office from the Broadway Square building, but it will not leave downtown as it signs a long-term lease for a 27,000 square feet of space in Town Pavilion. Town Pavilion is the biggest multitenant office building in downtown. Downtown's market competitiveness is also examined.

16881 ▪ *"Drawn to York County: Less-Expensive Homes, Good Schools Attract Charlotteans"* in Charlotte Observer (February 4, 2007)
Pub: Knight-Ridder/Tribune Business News
Ed: Taylor Bright. **Description:** York County, North Carolina offers low-priced homes and good schools, making it attractive to workers and small business.

16882 ▪ *"East-Side Real Estate Forum Detours To Grand Rapids"* in Crain's Detroit Business (Vol. 24, October 6, 2008, No. 40, pp. 17)
Pub: Crain Communications, Inc.
Ed: Daniel Duggan. **Description:** Tom Wackerman was elected chairman of the University of Michigan-Urban Land Institute Real Estate Forum and proposed that the annual conference be held in Grand Rapids due to the brisk economic activity he was finding there; although the idea was initially met with resistance, the plan to introduce East-siders to the West side began receiving more enthusiasm due to the revitalization of the area, which was once considered to have a bleak outlook. Many are hoping to learn the lessons of those who were able to change a negative economic climate into a positive one in which the cooperation of private business and government can work together to accomplish goals.

16883 ▪ *"Economy Hammers Local Builders"* in Business Courier (Vol. 24, February 8, 2008, No. 44, pp. 1)
Pub: American City Business Journals, Inc.
Ed: Laura Baverman. **Description:** Home builders in Cincinnati, Ohio, have lower revenue and smaller workforces as a result of the housing crisis and economic slowdown. Only four out of the top 25 home builders registered revenue gains, average revenue for 2007 is down 21 percent from 2006 levels, and employment declined by 37 percent from 2006.

16884 ▪ *"Economy Peddles Rent In This Cycle"* in The Business Journal-Serving Metropolitan Kansas City (Vol. 26, August 8, 2008, No. 48)
Pub: American City Business Journals, Inc.
Ed: Ashlee Kieler. **Description:** Rental demand for apartment units in downtown Kansas City, Missouri, is increasing due to the housing crisis, lack of real estate development, and increasing popularity of the downtown area. The downtown area has 7,378 multifamily units as of June 2008, of which 4,114 are rentals.

16885 ▪ *"Editor's Note"* in Canadian Business (Vol. 81, March 17, 2008, No. 4, pp. 7)
Pub: Rogers Media
Ed: Joe Chidley. **Description:** Canadian Consolidated government expenditures increased by an average of 4.5 percent annually from 2003 to 2007. Health care, housing, and the environment were some of the areas which experienced higher spending. However, government spending in labor, employment, and immigration dropped 6.6 percent.

16886 ▪ *"Eminent Domain Fight Looks Imminent"* in The Business Journal-Serving Metropolitan Kansas City (Vol. 26, August 1, 2008, No. 47)
Pub: American City Business Journals, Inc.
Ed: Rob Roberts. **Description:** Views and information on the proposed constitutional amendments that will limit the use of eminent domain in Missouri, are presented. The proposals are expected to largely ban the taking of private property for private development. It may be included in a November 4,2008 statewide vote for approval.

16887 ▪ *"Energy Efficiency Ordinance Softened"* in Austin Business JournalInc. (Vol. 28, October 3, 2008, No. 29)
Pub: American City Business Journals
Ed: Jean Kwon. **Description:** City of Austin has eliminated mandatory energy efficiency upgrades to single-family housing as a condition for selling or renting homes or buildings. The new law proposes that an energy performance audit be conducted on single-family homes before being sold and the results of the audit disclosed to perspectives buyers.

16888 ▪ *"Everyone Out of the Pool"* in Barron's (Vol. 89, July 20, 2009, No. 29, pp. 18)
Pub: Dow Jones & Co., Inc.
Ed: Sandra Ward. **Description:** Shares of Pool Corp. could drop as continued weakness in the housing market weakens the market for swimming pool equipment. The company's shares are trading at $18.29, about 20 times projected 2009 earnings of $0.91 a share.

16889 ▪ *Everything You Need to Know to Sell By Owner*
Pub: FSBO Publishing
Ed: Karen Varnas; Roy Wysack. **Released:** February 2007. **Price:** $19.95. **Description:** Provides the knowledge and strategies required to sell real estate in today's market.

16890 ▪ *"Evidence Growing of Commercial Real Estate"* in Boston Business Journal (Vol. 27, October 5, 2007, No. 36, pp. 1)
Pub: American City Business Journals Inc.
Ed: Michelle Hillman. **Description:** Commercial real estate industry in Boston, Massachusetts is experiencing a downturn in the number of sales transac-

tions. A table on the commercial real estate's value of transactions for the first three quarters from 2004 to 2007 is presented.

16891 ▪ *"Exposed?" in Mergers & Acquisitions: The Dealmaker's Journal (March 1, 2008)*
Pub: SourceMedia, Inc.

Ed: Jerry Abejo. **Description:** State-run pension plans' contributions are declining due to a loss of tax revenue from plummeting home values.

16892 ▪ *"Eyes to the Sky" in Canadian Business (Vol. 80, March 26, 2007, No. 7, pp. 33)*
Pub: Rogers Media

Ed: Joe Castaldo. **Description:** The growth and prices of condominium market in the Canada are analyzed.

16893 ▪ *"Fifth Third Spinoff" in Business Courier (Vol. 27, July 16, 2010, No. 11, pp. 1)*
Pub: Business Courier

Ed: Dan Monk, Steve Watkins. **Description:** Electronic-funds transfer company Fifth Third Solutions (FTPS), a spinoff of Fifth Third Bancorp, is seeking as much as 200,000 square feet of new office space in Ohio. The bank's sale of 51 percent ownership stake to Boston-based Advent International Corporation has paved the way for the growth of FTPS. How real estate brokers' plans have responded to FTPS' growth mode is discussed.

16894 ▪ *"Final Player In Big Mortgage Fraud Operation Gets Jail Time" in Boston Business Journal (Vol. 31, May 27, 2011, No. 18, pp. 3)*
Pub: Boston Business Journal

Ed: Galen Moore. **Description:** Real estate broker Ralp Appolon has been sentenced to 70 months in prison for wire fraud. Appolon was part of a group that falsified information about property purchase prices. A total of ten mortgage lenders have become victims of the group.

16895 ▪ *"Final State Budget Is a Mixed Bag of Key Industries" in The Business Journal - Serving Phoenix and the Valley of the Sun (Vol. 28, July 4, 2008, No. 44, pp. 3)*
Pub: American City Business Journals, Inc.

Ed: Mike Sunnucks; Patrick O'Grady. **Description:** Approved by Governor Janet Napolitano and passed by the Arizona Legislature, the $9.9 billion state budget is beneficial to some industries in the business community. The tax cap for on Arizona Lottery has been removed which is beneficial to the industry, while the solar energy industry and real estate developers stand to lose from the spending bill. Other details of the finance budget are presented.

16896 ▪ *"First-Time Homebuyer Credit May Add Some Momentum to Market" in Crain's Cleveland Business (Vol. 30, May 18, 2009, No. 20)*
Pub: Crain Communications, Inc.

Ed: Stan Bullard. **Description:** Federal tax credits for first-time homebuyers have increased the number of homes being sold. Details of the tax credit are defined.

16897 ▪ *"Five Low-Cost Home Based Startups" in Women Entrepreneur (December 16, 2008)*
Pub: Entrepreneur Media Inc.

Ed: Lesley Spencer Pyle. **Description:** During tough economic times, small businesses have an advantage over large companies because they can adjust to economic conditions more easily and without having to go through corporate red tape that can slow the implementation process. A budding entrepreneur may find success by taking inventory of his or her skills, experience, expertise and passions and utilizing those qualities to start a business. Five low-cost home-based startups are profiled. These include starting an online store, a virtual assistant service, web designer, sales representative and a home staging counselor.

16898 ▪ *FLIP: How to Find, Fix, and Sell Houses for Profit*
Pub: McGraw-Hill Companies Inc.
Contact: Deven Sharma, President

Ed: Rick Villani; Clay Davis. **Released:** December 19, 2006. **Price:** $21.95. **Description:** Advice is given to help find, fix and sell houses for profit.

16899 ▪ *"Florin Car Dealers Drive Plan" in Sacramento Business Journal (Vol. 25, August 22, 2008, No. 25, pp. 25)*
Pub: American City Business Journals, Inc.

Ed: Melanie Turner. **Description:** Automobile dealers in Sacramento, California are working with the city and the business district in planning for future redevelopment in Florin Road. The move stemmed from pressure from the Elk Grove Auto Mall, high fuel prices and the credit crunch. The area has suffered business closures recently.

16900 ▪ *"Fogg Planning Twinsburg Warehouse Project" in Crain's Cleveland Business (Vol. 28, November 26, 2007, No. 47, pp. 6)*
Pub: Crain Communications, Inc.

Ed: Stan Bullard. **Description:** Discusses such projects as the proposed 205,000-square-foot distribution center in the works by Ray Fogg Corporate Properties LLC as well as other industrial real estate developments that are looking to target tenants that need larger spaces.

16901 ▪ *"For $150 Million Mall, Failure to Launch" in Business Courier (Vol. 24, January 25, 2008, No. 42, pp. 1)*
Pub: American City Business Journals, Inc.

Ed: Lisa Biank Fasig. **Description:** Blue Ash-based Bear Creek Capital and Chattanooga, Tennessee-based CBL & Associates Properties had abandoned their plan to build a mixed-use project in South Lebanon. The construction of the proposed $475 million open-air mall was cancelled when real estate developer CBL failed to secure retailers.

16902 ▪ *"For Developer, a Boulevard of Golden Dreams" in Globe & Mail (February 10, 2007, pp. B3)*
Pub: CTVglobemedia Publishing Inc.

Ed: Elizabeth Church. **Description:** A profile of Ian Gillespie, president of Westbank Projects Corp., including his achievements in the real estate industry which are presented.

16903 ▪ *The Foreclosure of America: Life Inside Countrywide Home Loans and the Selling of the American Dream*
Pub: Berkley Trade/Penguin Group USA Inc.

Ed: Adam Michaelson. **Released:** April 6, 2010. **Price:** $16.00. **Description:** An inside look at Countrywide Home Loans and the mortgage crisis.

16904 ▪ *"Foreclosures Crisis Expected to Significantly Drain Wealth" in Black Enterprise (Vol. 41, September 2010, No. 2, pp. 24)*
Pub: Earl G. Graves Publishing Co. Inc.

Description: African American communities will lose billions in wealth because of the current foreclosure crisis. Statistical data included.

16905 ▪ *"Former Mayor Driving $500 Million Real Estate Equity Fund" in The Business Journal - Serving Phoenix and the Valley of the Sun (Vol. 28, August 15, 2008, No. 50, pp. 1)*
Pub: American City Business Journals, Inc.

Ed: Jan Buchholz. **Description:** Paul John, the former mayor of Phoenix, is establishing a $500 million real estate asset management fund. The fund is dubbed Southwest Next Capital Management and has attracted three local partners, namely Joseph Meyer, Jay Michalowski, and James Mullany, who all have background in finance and construction.

16906 ▪ *"Former Schaefer and Strohminger Dealerships to Hit Auction Block" in Baltimore Business Journal (Vol. 28,*

September 10, 2010)
Pub: Baltimore Business Journal

Ed: Gary Haber. **Description:** Maryland's real estate developers have a chance to vie for almost 11 acres of prime Baltimore County real estate that are on the auction block. The five properties were once home to Schaefer and Strohminger car dealerships and were located in the county's busiest areas. Other potential uses for the properties are also discussed.

16907 ▪ *"From Bikes to Building" in Austin Business JournalInc. (Vol. 29, October 30, 2009, No. 34, pp. 1)*
Pub: American City Business Journals

Ed: Kate Harrington. **Description:** Tour de France champion Lance Armstrong, Bill Stapleton his long-time agent, and business manager Bart Knaggs have formed a privately held real estate investment company CSE Realty Parters in Austin, Texas. They see tremendous opportunity in the commercial real estate market in the area.

16908 ▪ *"The Furniture Company Wanted to Sell Him Its Buildings-And Close Down. Should He Buy the Company, Too?" in Inc. (November 2007)*
Pub: Gruner & Jahr USA Publishing

Ed: Alex Salkever. **Description:** Rick Detkowski, real estate investor, discusses his decision to purchase the furniture company housed in the buildings he was interested in buying. The property would have cost him between $500,000 to $1 million, he was able to purchase the property and business with its entire inventory of furniture, vehicles, and machinery for $1.8 million.

16909 ▪ *"Gables Unveils Plan for Downtown Tower" in Austin Business JournalInc. (Vol. 28, August 8, 2008, No. 21, pp. A1)*
Pub: American City Business Journals

Ed: Jean Kwon. **Description:** Gables Residential plans to develop a residential tower with 220 units and 15,000 square feet of retail and commercial spaces in the Warehouse District in Ohio. The development is expected to start in late 2009 and be completed in 18 to 24 months.

16910 ▪ *"Gail Lissner; Vice-President, Appraisal Research Counselors" in Crain's Chicago Business (Vol. 31, May 5, 2008, No. 18, pp. 28)*
Pub: Crain Communications, Inc.

Ed: Phuong Ly. **Description:** Profile of Gail Lissner who is the vice-president of the Appraisal Research Counselors, a company that puts out the quarterly 'Residential Benchmark Report,' in which Ms. Lissner co-authors and is considered a must-read in the industry. Ms. Lissner has risen to become one of the most sought-after experts on the Chicago market considering real estate.

16911 ▪ *"Generation Y Driving Portland Multifamily Market" in Daily Journal of Commerce, Portland (October 29, 2010)*
Pub: Dolan Media Newswires

Ed: Nick Bjork. **Description:** Generation Y, young adults between the ages of 18-30, are interested in multifamily residents in the Portland, Oregon area. Developers in the area, particularly North Portland, have recognized this trend and are looking into multifamily investments.

16912 ▪ *"Ghazi Insists Downtown Project Still On" in The Business Journal-Milwaukee (Vol. 25, August 1, 2008, No. 45, pp. A1)*
Pub: American City Business Journals, Inc.

Ed: Rich Kirchen. **Description:** Afshin Ghazi remains confident that his $200 million Catalyst project in downtown Milwaukee, Wisconsin, will push through despite financial disputes delaying his EpiCentre project in Charlotte, North Carolina. He added that the Catalyst is on schedule for groundbreaking in the spring of 2009.

16913 ▪ *"GL Homes Buys 1,000 Acres in Former Agricultural Reserve" in Miami Daily*

Business Review (March 26, 2008)
Pub: ALM Media Inc.

Ed: Polyana da Costa. **Description:** One of the nation's largest home builders, GL Homes, purchased over 1,000 acres of agricultural land in Southern Palm Beach County, Florida. Plans for 554 residential units are detailed.

16914 ■ *"Glendale Pumping $29 Million Into Redevelopment" in The Business Journal - Serving Phoenix and the Valley of the Sun (Vol. 28, August 1, 2008, No. 48, pp. 1)*
Pub: American City Business Journals, Inc.

Ed: Mike Sunnucks. **Description:** Glendale City is planning to invest $29 million to improve city infrastructure like roadways and water and sewer lines over the next five years. Glendale's city council is also planning to hold a workshop on the redevelopment projects in September 2008. Other views and information on the redevelopment project, are presented.

16915 ■ *"GMREB/Analysis of the Resale Market-First Quarter 2007: Year Off to a Great Start" in Canadian Corporate News (May 14, 2007)*
Pub: Comtex News Network Inc.

Description: According to statistics gathered by the Greater Montreal Real Estate Board (GMREB), the Montreal census metropolitan area (CMA) resale market was vigorous in the first quarter of 2007 yielding 10 percent more existing homes being than the first quarter of 2006.

16916 ■ *"GM's Mortgage Unit Deal Brings in $9 Billion" in Globe & Mail (March 24, 2006, pp. B3)*
Pub: CTVglobemedia Publishing Inc.

Ed: Shawn McCarthy. **Description:** General Motors Corp. sells General Motors Acceptance Corp.'s commercial real estate division to Kohlberg Kravis Roberts & Co. Five Mile Capital Partners LLC and Goldman Sachs Capital Partners. The reasons behind the deal are presented.

16917 ■ *"Goldbelt Inc.: Targeting Shareholder Development" in Alaska Business Monthly (Vol. 27, October 2011, No. 10, pp. 108)*
Pub: Alaska Business Publishing Company

Ed: Tracy Kalytiak. **Description:** Profile of Goldbelt Inc., the company that has changed its original focus of timber to real estate to tourism and then to government contracting opportunities.

16918 ■ *"A Good Sign for Commercial Real Estate" in Austin Business JournalInc. (Vol. 29, December 18, 2009, No. 41, pp. 1)*
Pub: American City Business Journals

Ed: Kate Harrington. **Description:** Factors that could contribute to the reemergence of the commercial mortgage-backed securities market in Texas are discussed. These securities can potentially boost the commercial real estate market statewide as well as nationwide. Commercial mortgage-backed securities origination in 2009 is worth less that $1 billion, compared with $238 billion in 2008.

16919 ■ *"Green Housing for the Rest of Us" in Inc. (November 2007, pp. 128-129)*
Pub: Gruner & Jahr USA Publishing

Ed: Nitasha Tiku. **Description:** Profile of Full Spectrum NY, real estate developer firm, offering residences at the Kalahari, a green high-rise with state-of-the-art features at a reasonable price.

16920 ■ *"Grin and Bear It" in Canadian Business (Vol. 81, March 3, 2008, No. 3, pp. 53)*
Pub: Rogers Media

Ed: Jeff Sanford. **Description:** Discusses the United States economic downturn, caused by the credit market crisis, which is expected to affect the Canadian economy, as Canada depend on the U.S. for 80 percent of its exports. Economist David Rosenberg thinks that in 2008, housing prices will decline by 15 percent and gross domestic product growth will slow to 0.8 percent. Other forecasts for Canadian economy are given.

16921 ■ *"Groundbreaking 2.0" in Philadelphia Business Journal (Vol. 30, September 23, 2011, No. 32, pp. 1)*
Pub: American City Business Journals Inc.

Ed: Natalie Kostelni. **Description:** University Place Associates, the developer of 2.0 University Place in West Philadelphia, Pennsylvania, will break ground on a five-story, 97,000-square-foot office building in December 2011. The decision follows the Citizenship and Immigration Services signing of a 15-year lease as anchor tenant.

16922 ■ *"Growth in Fits and Starts" in Canadian Business (Vol. 83, July 20, 2010, No. 11-12, pp. 18)*
Pub: Rogers Media Ltd.

Ed: James Cowan. **Description:** US home sales and manufacturing indicators have dropped and fears of a double-dip recession are widespread. However, a chief economist says that this is endemic to what can be seen after a recession caused by a financial crisis. In Canada, consumer optimism is rising and anxiety over losing one's job is waning.

16923 ■ *"Hank Paulson On the Housing Bailout and What's Ahead" in Business Week (September 22, 2008, No. 4100, pp. 19)*
Pub: McGraw-Hill Companies, Inc.

Ed: Maria Bartiromo. **Description:** Interview with Treasury Secretary Henry Paulson in which he discusses the bailout of Fannie Mae and Freddie Mac as well as the potential impact on the American economy and foreign interests and investments in the country. Paulson has faith that the government's actions will help to stabilize the housing market.

16924 ■ *"Hastily Enacted Regulation Will Not Cure Economic Crisis" in Crain's Chicago Business (Vol. 31, May 5, 2008, No. 18, pp. 18)*
Pub: Crain Communications, Inc.

Ed: Stephen P. D'Arcy. **Description:** Policymakers are looking for ways to respond to what is possibly the greatest financial crisis of a generation due to the collapse of the housing market, the credit crisis and the volatility of Wall Street.

16925 ■ *"High-End Blunders" in Crain's Chicago Business (Vol. 31, April 21, 2008, No. 16, pp. 54)*
Pub: Crain Communications, Inc.

Ed: Laura Bianchi. **Description:** Discusses some of the biggest errors sellers make that keep their homes from selling including: pricing too high; expecting to recoup the cost of very high-end amenities and decor; avant-garde decorating; owners that hover when the house is being shown; stripping the home of top-quality light fixtures and hardware and replacing them with inferior versions with the assumption that the new buyer will come in with their own decorator and redo it; and poorly maintained properties.

16926 ■ *"His Place in the Sun" in Canadian Business (Vol. 79, October 23, 2006, No. 21, pp. 77)*
Pub: Rogers Media

Ed: Zena Olijnyk. **Description:** The business interests of Canadian real estate developer Derek Elliott in the Dominican Republic, is discussed.

16927 ■ *"A Home of Her Own" in Hawaii Business (Vol. 53, October 2007, No. 4, pp. 51)*
Pub: Hawaii Business Publishing

Ed: Maria Torres-Kitamura. **Description:** It was observed that the number of single women in Hawaii purchasing their own home has increased, as that in the whole United States where the percentage has increased from 14 percent in 1995 to 22 percent in 2006. However, First Hawaiian Bank's Wendy Lum thinks that the trend will not continue in Hawaii due to lending restrictions. The factors that women consider in buying a home of their own are presented.

16928 ■ *"Home Prices Sag" in Crain's Chicago Business (Vol. 31, April 28, 2008, No. 17, pp. 3)*
Pub: Crain Communications, Inc.

Ed: Alby Gallun. **Description:** Since the slump in the housing market is continuing with no sign of recovery, Chicago-area home prices are poised for an even

steeper drop this year. In 2007, the region's home prices fell nearly 5 percent and according to a forecast by Fiserv Inc., they will decline 8.1 percent this year and another 2.2 percent in 2009. Statistical data included.

16929 ■ *Home Staging for Dummies*
Pub: John Wiley and Sons, Inc.

Ed: Christine Rae; Janice Saunders Maresh. **Released:** May 2008. **Price:** $19.99. **Description:** Guide shows how to make improvements room by room in order to generate a higher profit on home sales. The book offers tips to clear clutter and show the home's best features, inspire curb appeal, and how to depersonalize and neutralize every room.

16930 ■ *"Homeownership: Still the American Dream?" in Gallup Management Journal (May 5, 2011)*
Pub: Gallup

Description: The mortgage finance system is broken. Housing prices continue to fall. Foreclosures are expected to increase in the coming months. However, Gallup's chief economist does not believe this is the end of the American dream of owning one's own home.

16931 ■ *"A Home's Identity in Black and White" in Crain's Chicago Business (Vol. 31, April 21, 2008, No. 16, pp. 35)*
Pub: Crain Communications, Inc.

Ed: Lisa Bertagnoli. **Description:** Real estate agents are finding that showing customers a written floor plan is a trend that is growing since many buyers feel that Online virtual tours distort a room. Although floor plans cost up to $500 to have drawn up, they clearly show potential buyers the exact dimensions of rooms and how they connect.

16932 ■ *"Homes Stall As Owners Resist Major Price Cuts" in Crain's Chicago Business (Vol. 31, April 21, 2008, No. 16, pp. 38)*
Pub: Crain Communications, Inc.

Ed: Kevin Davis. **Description:** Discusses the high-end housing market and the owners who are resisting major price cuts as well as the buyers who look at long market times as a sign that something is wrong with the property.

16933 ■ *"Homing In On the Future" in Black Enterprise (Vol. 38, October 2007, No. 3, pp. 61)*
Pub: Earl G. Graves Publishing Co. Inc.

Ed: Sean Drakes. **Description:** More and more people are wanting new homes wired automated systems that integrate multiple home devices such as computers, audio/visual entertainment, security, communications, utilities, and lighting and environmental controls.

16934 ■ *"House Prices Cooling Off, With Alberta Gearing Down" in Globe & Mail (February 9, 2007, pp. B4)*
Pub: CTVglobemedia Publishing Inc.

Ed: Tavia Grant. **Description:** The house prices in Alberta, which are experiencing a torrid pace in price growth, are steady in the first month of 2007. The easing in house prices may show impact on inflation.

16935 ■ *The Housing Boom and Bust*
Pub: Basic Books

Ed: Thomas Sowell. **Price:** $24.95. **Description:** An explanation of the economics and politics of the housing boom and its collapse.

16936 ■ *"Housing Market Dinged, But Not Done In, By Nationwide Slump" in Business Review, Albany New York (Vol. 34, December 21, 2007)*
Pub: American City Business Journals, Inc.

Ed: Michael DeMasi. **Description:** Kirsten Keefe, a staff attorney of the Empire Justice Center, is questioning the validity of statistics that represent the number of home foreclosures in New York.

16937 ▪ *"Housing Markets Still Struggling"* in *Montana Business Quarterly (Vol. 49, Spring 2011, No. 1, pp. 17)*
Pub: Bureau of Business & Economic Research
Ed: Scott Rickard. **Description:** Montana's economic conditions are a bit better than national averages. Data ranked by state, year-over-year price change, and total price peak is presented, along with statistical data for the entire nation.

16938 ▪ *"Housing Slide Picks Up Speed"* in *Crain's Chicago Business (Vol. 31, April 21, 2008, No. 16, pp. 2)*
Pub: Crain Communications, Inc.
Ed: Eddie Baeb. **Description:** According to Tracy Cross & Associates Inc., a real estate consultancy, sales of new homes in the Chicago area dropped 61 percent from the year-earlier period which is more bad news for homebuilders, contractors and real estate agents who are eager for an indication that market conditions are improving.

16939 ▪ *How to Open and Operate a Financially Successful Redesign, Redecorating, and Home Staging Business: With Companion CD-ROM*
Pub: Atlantic Publishing Group, Inc.
Ed: Mary Larsen; Teri B. Clark. **Released:** January 2008. **Price:** $39.95 paperback. **Description:** Questions are asked to help individuals determine if they should launch their own redesign or real estate staging firm.

16940 ▪ *"Illinois Farmland Tops $11,000 Per Acre"* in *Farm Industry News (June 27, 2011)*
Pub: Penton Business Media Inc.
Ed: Karen McMahon. **Description:** Farmland property in Illinois continues to grow in value, selling for $11,000 per acre. Statistical data included.

16941 ▪ *"In Control: Tips For Navigating a Buyer's Market"* in *Black Enterprise (Vol. 38, December 2007, No. 5, pp. 64)*
Pub: Earl G. Graves Publishing Co. Inc.
Ed: Erinn R. Johnson. **Description:** Tips are given to help would-be home buyers. The importance of finding a good real estate agent is stressed.

16942 ▪ *"In Sickness and In Wealth Management"* in *Hispanic Business (Vol. 30, March 2008, No. 3, pp. 28)*
Pub: Hispanic Business
Ed: Rick Munarriz. **Description:** Discusses the investment and wealth management firms owned and operated by Hispanics. There are only a handful of these firms owned by Hispanics, as most of them prefer capital preservation by investing in hard assets like cash and real estate than in capital appreciation.

16943 ▪ *"Incentives Debate Rages On Unabated"* in *The Business Journal-Serving Metropolitan Kansas City (Vol. 26, September 5, 2008, No. 52)*
Pub: American City Business Journals, Inc.
Ed: Rob Roberts. **Description:** Debate on the new economic development and incentives policy adopted by the Kansas City Council is still on. The city's Planned Industrial Expansion Authority has rejected a standard property tax abatement proposal. The real estate development community has opposed the rejection of proposed the tax incentives policy.

16944 ▪ *"Independence's Day Keeps on Getting Brighter"* in *Business Courier (Vol. 27, June 11, 2010, No. 6, pp. 1)*
Pub: Business Courier
Ed: Lucy May. **Description:** Reports show that residential and commercial development continues in Independence, Kentucky despite the recession, with a 144-unit apartment complex under construction. The city recorded 152 new-home closings in 2009, or 25 percent of all new homes closed in Boone, Campbell, and Kenton counties.

16945 ▪ *"Industrial RE Market Shows Signs of Health"* in *Business Courier (Vol. 27, August 20, 2010, No. 16, pp. 1)*
Pub: Business Courier
Ed: Jon Newberry. **Description:** Cincinnati, Ohio's industrial real estate sector has experienced growth during the first half of 2010. The industry has seen a large net loss of occupied space in 2009.

16946 ▪ *"Industrial Vacancies Hit High; Economic Downturn Taking Toll on Area's Demand for Space"* in *Crain's Chicago Business (Apr. 21, 2008)*
Pub: Crain Communications, Inc.
Ed: Alby Gallun. **Description:** Hitting its highest level in four years in the first quarter is the Chicago-area industrial vacancy rate, a sign that the slumping economy is depressing demand for warehouse and manufacturing space.

16947 ▪ *"Insider"* in *Canadian Business (Vol. 81, March 31, 2008, No. 5, pp. 76)*
Pub: Rogers Media
Ed: John Gray. **Description:** Discusses a comparison of an average Canadian family's finances in 1990 with the data from 2007. The average family in 2007 has over $80,000 in debt compared to just under $52,000 in 1990. However, Canadians have also been accumulating solid assets such as homes and stocks. This means that Canadian debt load has fallen from 22 percent in 1990 to 20 percent in 2007 when taken as a percentage of total net worth.

16948 ▪ *"Insurer Buys Foundation's Uptown HQ"* in *Charlotte Business Journal (Vol. 25, December 17, 2010, No. 39, pp. 1)*
Pub: Charlotte Business Journal
Ed: Will Boye. **Description:** Charlotte, North Carolina-based Synergy Coverage Solutions has purchased the three-story building owned by Foundations For the Carolinas for slightly more than $3 million. Synergy plans to relocate its operation in the uptown building by August 2011.

16949 ▪ *Internet Resources and Services for International Real Estate Information*
Pub: Greenwood Press
Contact: Wayne Smith, President
URL(s): www.abc-clio.com. **Price:** $82.95, Individuals Paperback; £57.95, Individuals Sterling price. **Covers:** Internet sources related to international real estate, finance, and investment.

16950 ▪ *"Inventory Glut"* in *Business Courier (Vol. 24, March 28, 2008, No. 51, pp. 1)*
Pub: American City Business Journals, Inc.
Ed: Laura Baverman. **Description:** Indian Hill and the downtown area have the highest monthly absorption rate for housing on a list of 42 Greater Cincinnati and Northern Kentucky neighborhoods. The two neighborhoods have 19 and 27 months of housing inventory respectively, which means home sellers need to either lower their prices or be very patient.

16951 ▪ *"Investors Sue Jackson Properties for Fraud, Breach of Contract"* in *The Business Journal - Serving Phoenix and the Valley of the Sun (Vol. 28, July 18, 2008, No. 46, pp. 1)*
Pub: American City Business Journals, Inc.
Ed: Jan Buchholz. **Description:** Investors sued Jackson Properties EVB Inc. and Jackson Properties EVB LLC for fraud and breach of contract over a botched housing development deal. The investors also filed a complaint before the Arizona Corporation Commission. The investors stand to lose $8 million from the halted development deal.

16952 ▪ *"Is this a Buying Opportunity?"* in *Canadian Business (Vol. 82, April 27, 2009, No. 7, pp. 46)*
Pub: Rogers Media
Ed: Andy Holloway. **Description:** Home prices in Canada are down by as much as 14.2 percent in 2009 compared to prices in 2008, making homes more affordable now. Some housing experts believe that homes are still good investments as prices of rent and properties always recover. Meanwhile, a survey found that Canadians under 35 plan to buy a home within two years.

16953 ▪ *"It Could Be Worse"* in *Barron's (Vol. 89, July 27, 2009, No. 30, pp. 5)*
Pub: Dow Jones & Co., Inc.
Ed: Alan Abelson. **Description:** Media sources are being fooled by corporate America who is peddling an economic recovery rather than reality as shown by the report of a rise in existing home sales which

boosted the stock market even if it was a seasonal phenomenon. The phrase 'things could be worse' sums up the reigning investment philosophy in the U.S. and this has been stirring up the market.

16954 ▪ *"Kimball Hill Files for Chapter 11"* in *Crain's Chicago Business (Vol. 31, April 28, 2008, No. 17, pp. 12)*
Pub: Crain Communications, Inc.
Description: Homebuilder Kimball Hill filed for Chapter 11 bankruptcy protection after months of negotiations with lenders. The firm plans to continue operations as it restructures its debt.

16955 ▪ *"The Kitchen is Closed; Eateries Forced Out by Soaring Rents, Declining Revenues"* in *Crain's New York Business (January 21, 2008)*
Pub: Crain Communications, Inc.
Ed: Lisa Fickenscher. **Description:** Many restaurants have already closed in the area and experts expect many more will follow due to skyrocketing rents and declining revenues.

16956 ▪ *"Kubicki Juggles Lineup at Vianda"* in *Business Courier (Vol. 26, December 11, 2009, No. 33, pp. 1)*
Pub: American City Business Journals, Inc.
Ed: Dan Monk. **Description:** Cincinnati real estate developer Chuck Kubicki replaced the management team of Vianda LLC and cancelled contracts with two vendors that caused a surge of customer complaints. Vianda is a direct-response marketing firm that sells and distributes dietary supplements for wellness and sexual performance.

16957 ▪ *"Land on Boardwalk"* in *Canadian Business (Vol. 82, April 27, 2009, No. 7, pp. 19)*
Pub: Rogers Media
Ed: Calvin Leung. **Description:** Boardwalk REIT remains as one of the most attractive real estate investment trusts in Canada, with 73 percent of analysts rating the firm a Buy. Analyst Neil Downey believes that good management, as well as a good business model, makes Boardwalk a good investment. Downey is concerned however, that a worsening of Alberta's economy could significantly impact Boardwalk.

16958 ▪ *"Large Homes can be Energy Efficient Too"* in *Contractor (Vol. 56, October 2009, No. 10, pp. 5)*
Pub: Penton Media, Inc.
Ed: Candace Roulo. **Description:** Eco Estate at Briggs Chaney subdivision in Silver Spring, Maryland has model houses that use sustainable technologies and products and the homes that will be built on the subdivision will feature some of the technologies featured on the model home. The energy efficient HVAC system of the model homes are discussed.

16959 ▪ *"Laugh or Cry?"* in *Barron's (Vol. 88, March 24, 2008, No. 12, pp. 7)*
Pub: Dow Jones & Company, Inc.
Ed: Alan Abelson. **Description:** Discusses the American economy which is just starting to feel the effect of the credit and housing crises. JPMorgan Chase purchased Bear Stearns for $2 a share, much lower than its share price of $60, while quasi-government entities Fannie Mae and Freddie Mac are starting to run into trouble.

16960 ▪ *"Local Commercial Real Estate Foreclosures Continue to Rise"* in *Baltimore Business Journal (Vol. 28, October 1, 2010, No. 21, pp. 1)*
Pub: Baltimore Business Journal
Ed: Daniel J. Sernovitz. **Description:** Foreclosures of commercial real estate across the Greater Baltimore area have continued to rise. The region is now host to about $2 billion worth of commercial properties that carry a maturing debt or have been foreclosed. Commercial real estate owners are unable to finance their debts because banks have become stricter in passing out loans.

16961 ■ *"Local Industrial Vacancies Climb"* in *Crain's Chicago Business (Vol. 31, November 17, 2008, No. 46, pp. 18)*
Pub: Crain Communications, Inc.
Ed: Eddie Baeb. **Description:** Demand for local industrial real estate has declined dramatically as companies that use warehouse and factory space struggle to survive in an ailing economy. According to a report by Colliers Bennett & Kahnweiler Inc., a commercial real estate brokerage, the regional vacancy rate has risen to 9.86 percent in the third quarter, the fourth straight increase and the highest in the past 14 years.

16962 ■ *"Lytle Place Listing Seen as Bellweather"* in *Business Courier (Vol. 27, December 3, 2010, No. 31, pp. 1)*
Pub: Business Courier
Ed: Dan Monk. **Description:** Denver, Colorado-based Apartment Investment and Management Company (AIMCO) has offered the 25-story One Lytle Place Apartments for sale through CB Richard Ellis for the third time in three years. The potential sale could define the recovery for Cincinnati, Ohio's struggling apartment industry.

16963 ■ *"The Main Event"* in *Canadian Business (Vol. 80, November 19, 2007, No. 23, pp. 28)*
Pub: Rogers Media
Ed: Zena Olijnyk. **Description:** U.S.-based Lowe's Companies, Inc. will be opening three stores in Canada in December 2007 and another three in 2008. The housing market crisis in the U.S. is the reason behind the home improvement store's Canadian expansion. The impacts of the expansion on Canadian home care stores and on the market competition are evaluated.

16964 ■ *"Major Tech Employers Pulling Out"* in *Sacramento Business Journal (Vol. 25, August 1, 2008, No. 22, pp. 1)*
Pub: American City Business Journals, Inc.
Ed: Celia Lamb. **Description:** Biotechnology company Affymetrix Inc. is planning to close its West Sacramento, California plant and lay off 110 employees. The company said it will expand a corporate restructuring plan. Affymetrix also plans to lease out or sell its building at Riverside Parkway.

16965 ■ *"Mandel Site Favored For UWM Hall"* in *The Business Journal-Milwaukee (Vol. 25, September 19, 2008, No. 52, pp. A1)*
Pub: American City Business Journals, Inc.
Description: University of Wisconsin-Milwaukee student residence hall's leading location is a site pushed by Mandel Group Inc. Real estate sources say that the developer's proposal offers the best opportunity for business development and the least conflict with nearby neighborhoods. Plans for the Mandel site are presented.

16966 ■ *"Mann to Lead Builders"* in *Charlotte Observer (January 31, 2007)*
Pub: Knight-Ridder/Tribune Business News
Ed: Allen Norwood. **Description:** Elliot Mann of Standard Pacific Homes was sworn in as president of Home Builders Association of Charlotte, North Carolina.

16967 ■ *"Market Gamble"* in *Business Journal-Serving Phoenix and the Valley of the Sun (Vol. 5, October 5, 2007, No. 28, pp. 1)*
Pub: American City Business Journals, Inc.
Ed: Mike Padgett. **Description:** AI-BSR LLC, an Israeli group believes the housing market will regain its strength within three years. The group plans to build its $385 million project, called One Phoenix. The condominiums start at $500,000, with units ranging from 800 to 2,000 square feet.

16968 ■ *"Market for Retail Space Flat, but Recovery Still Uncertain"* in *Sacramento Business Journal (Vol. 28, August 26, 2011, No. 26, pp. 1)*
Pub: Sacramento Business Journal
Ed: Kelly Johnson. **Description:** The retail market in the Sacramento, California region remains challenged with the stock market volatility being the latest of its

hurdles. The overall vacancy was 13.1 percent as of mid-2011, but retail real estate professionals express hopes that the worst is behind. A list and description of the region's winners and losers in retail vacancies is provided.

16969 ■ *"Market Swings Intensify Yearning for Bonds"* in *Globe & Mail (March 9, 2007, pp. B9)*
Pub: CTVglobemedia Publishing Inc.
Ed: Keith Damsell. **Description:** The rise in demand for proper fixed-income bonds in Canada as a result of uncertainties in the equity market is discussed. Some big Canadian fixed-income funds are presented.

16970 ■ *"A Matter of Perspective"* in *Business Journal-Portland (Vol. 24, November 2, 2007, No. 35, pp. 1)*
Pub: American City Business Journals, Inc.
Ed: Andy Giegerich. **Description:** Oregon Governor Ted Kulongoski assembled the Mortgage Lending Work Group, made up of members of the mortgage industry and consumer groups, to recommend possible bills for the Oregon Senate and House to consider. How its members try to balance philosophical differences in mortgage lending rules is discussed.

16971 ■ *"Medical Office Developers To Merge November 1"* in *The Business Journal - Serving Phoenix and the Valley of the Sun (Vol. 29, September 26, 2008, No. 4, pp. 1)*
Pub: American City Business Journals, Inc.
Ed: Angela Gonzales. **Description:** Ensemble Real Estate Services LLC and DevMan Co. will merge effective November 1, 2008 and will call the firm Ensemble DevMan of Arizona after the merger. The two companies will combine their resources and expertise on planned projects that include the Phoenix Children's Hospital's Specialty Clinic and Banner Ironwood Medical Office Building.

16972 ■ *"Mequon Plan On Tracks, Bucks Housing Trend"* in *The Business Journal-Milwaukee (Vol. 25, September 26, 2008, No. 53, pp. A1)*
Pub: American City Business Journals, Inc.
Ed: Pete Millard. **Description:** Insight Development Group plans to build condominium units and single-family homes despite the residential market downturn. The Orchard Glen project, a planned development in Mequon, is a $22 million project which will include 38 condos and 12 single-family homes. Details of the project are provided.

16973 ■ *"Millions Needed To Finish First Place"* in *The Business Journal-Milwaukee (Vol. 25, August 15, 2008, No. 47, pp. A1)*
Pub: American City Business Journals, Inc.
Ed: Rich Kirchen. **Description:** First Place on the River condominium project in Milwaukee, Wisconsin, needs $18.2 million before it can be completed. A total of $6.8 million have already been spent since the project went into receivership on 31 January 2008.

16974 ■ *"Minnesota Farms' Net Worth Grows 10 Percent Each Year for 15 Years"* in *Farm Industry News (August 22, 2011)*
Pub: Penton Business Media Inc.
Ed: Dale Nordquist. **Description:** The average value of farms in Minnesota is growing at a fast pace. Total assets per farm have increased by more than $1.1 million over the past 15 years. Statistical data included.

16975 ■ *"A Model Development"* in *Crain's Cleveland Business (Vol. 28, October 1, 2007, No. 39, pp. 12)*
Pub: Crain Communications, Inc.
Description: Profile a Forest City Enterprises Inc., a firm that is developing a project in New Mexico called Mesa del Sol. The Albuquerque development is being seen as the vanguard of master-planned communities with its high-tech economic development center which is expected to become the site of 60,000 jobs, 38,000 homes and a town center.

16976 ■ *"Modular Home Center Opens in Arcadia"* in *Charlotte Observer (February 1, 2007)*
Pub: Knight-Ridder/Tribune Business News
Ed: John Lawhorne. **Description:** Arcadia Home Center features modular homes constructed on a steel frame; regulations regarding the manufacture and moving of these homes are included.

16977 ■ *"More Contractors Unpaid"* in *Puget Sound Business Journal (Vol. 29, October 3, 2008, No. 24, pp. 1)*
Pub: American City Business Journals
Ed: Brad Berton. **Description:** An 80 percent rise in the filing of mechanics' liens was reported in Seattle, Washington. It is believed that financial problems are spreading to construction companies and contractors as home sales slide and builders default on construction loans. Delinquencies of single-family construction homes has increased.

16978 ■ *"More Offices Planned For Percheron Square"* in *The Business Journal-Milwaukee (Vol. 25, August 22, 2008, No. 48, pp. A1)*
Pub: American City Business Journals, Inc.
Ed: Pete Millard. **Description:** More office projects are under way at Percheron Square. Ryan Cos. US Inc., for example, plans to build over 200,000 square feet of office space at the area. Details of new office projects in Wisconsin are presented.

16979 ■ *"Mortgage Mess: How To Determine Your Exposure To the Subprime Crisis"* in *Black Enterprise (Vol. 38, November 2007, No. 4, pp. 46)*
Pub: Earl G. Graves Publishing Co. Inc.
Ed: Ilana Polyak. **Description:** Stocks and mutual funds have experienced declines because of the subprime crisis. Morningstar's Website can help investors research firms in which they have invested; if a fund is named high yield or high income or in the financial services sector, investments will have greater exposure to the mess.

16980 ■ *"Mortgage Securities Drop Hits Home"* in *The Business Journal-Serving Metropolitan Kansas City (Vol. 27, October 17, 2008, No. 5)*
Pub: American City Business Journals, Inc.
Ed: Rob Roberts. **Description:** Sale of commercial mortgage-backed securities (CMBS) in Kansas City, Missouri have declined. The area may avoid layoffs if the United States government succeeds in stabilizing the economy. Major CMBS players in the area include Midland Loan Services Inc. and KeyBank Real Estate Capital.

16981 ■ *"Move Over - Or Out"* in *Puget Sound Business Journal (Vol. 29, November 28, 2008, No. 32, pp. 1)*
Pub: American City Business Journals
Ed: Kirsten Grind. **Description:** Real estate agents in the state of Washington are either moving to smaller real estate firms or quitting the industry due to the weak housing market. Lesser-known firms are experiencing an influx of experienced real estate agents, while 2,800 agents in the state have left the industry.

16982 ■ *"Myths of Deleveraging"* in *Barron's (Vol. 90, August 23, 2010, No. 34, pp. M14)*
Pub: Barron's Editorial & Corporate Headquarters
Ed: Gene Epstein. **Description:** The opposite is true against reports about deleveraging or the decrease in credit since inflation-adjusted-investment factories and equipment rose 7.8 percent in the first quarter of 2010. On consumer deleveraging, sales of homes through credit is weak but there is a trend towards more realistic homeownership and consumer spending on durable goods rose 8.8 percent.

16983 ■ *"The Neighborhood Watch"* in *Hawaii Business (Vol. 53, March 2008, No. 9, pp. 36)*
Pub: Hawaii Business Publishing
Ed: David K. Choo. **Description:** OahuRe.com offers information on Hawaii real estate market, with spreadsheets and comparative market analysis page, which shows properties that are active, sold, or in

escrow. Other details about OahuRe.com are discussed. A list of other top real estate websites in Hawaii and in the U.S. in general is provided.

16984 ■ *"Neighborhood Watch" in Baltimore Business Journal (Vol. 28, July 23, 2010, No. 11, pp. 1)*
Pub: Baltimore Business Journal

Ed: Daniel J. Sernovitz. **Description:** Maryland government and housing leaders are set to spend $100 million in federal funding to stem the increase in foreclosures in the area. The federal funding is seen as inadequate to resolve the problem of foreclosures.

16985 ■ *"New-Home Sales Grab a Foothold With Q2 Boost" in Sacramento Business Journal (Vol. 25, July 11, 2008, No. 19, pp. 1)*
Pub: American City Business Journals, Inc.

Ed: Michael Shaw. **Description:** Statistics show that homebuilders in Sacramento, California experienced an increase in new-home sales during the second quarter of 2008. It was also reported that builders moved more homes without slashing prices significantly. Barry Grant, president of KB Home's Sacramento division, believes that the improvement is caused by the stability in the supply of resale homes.

16986 ■ *"A New Mix of Tenants Settles In" in Crain's New York Business (Vol. 24, January 14, 2008, No. 2, pp. 26)*
Pub: Crain Communications, Inc.

Ed: Andrew Marks. **Description:** More and more nonfinancial firms are relocating downtown due to the new retailers and restaurants that are reshaping the look and feel of lower Manhattan.

16987 ■ *"New York City-Based New Street Realty Advisors has Secured a New Flagship for David's Bridal" in Chain Store Age (August 2008)*
Pub: Chain Store Age

Description: New York City-based New Street Realty Advisors secured a new flagship store for David's Bridal in the Chelsea district of Manhattan. David's Bridal will occupy 12,800 square feet on two floors in a retail condominium development.

16988 ■ *"The Next Government Bailout?" in Barron's (Vol. 88, March 10, 2008, No. 10, pp. 21)*
Pub: Dow Jones & Company, Inc.

Ed: Jonathan Laing. **Description:** Fannie Mae may need a government bailout as it faces huge hits brought about by the effects of the housing crisis. The shares of the government-sponsored enterprise have dropped 65 percent since the housing crisis began.

16989 ■ *"The Next Real Estate Boom" in Canadian Business (Vol. 80, March 26, 2007, No. 7, pp. 25)*
Pub: Rogers Media

Ed: Erik Heinrich. **Description:** The better places to invest in Canadian real estate market are presented. The future price performance of the industry is analyzed.

16990 ■ *"N.H. Near the LEED in Green Space" in New Hampshire Business Review (Vol. 33, March 25, 2011, No. 6, pp. 30)*
Pub: Business Publications Inc.

Description: New Hamphire's architects, contractors and suppliers are among the leaders with LEED-certified space per capita.

16991 ■ *"No Wild Highs Means No Wild Lows" in Business Courier (Vol. 24, January 18, 2008, No. 41, pp. 1)*
Pub: American City Business Journals, Inc.

Ed: Laura Baverman. **Description:** Discusses a PMI Group report which revealed that the Greater Cincinnati area is in the lowest risk category for home value declines. The report forecast that the chance that housing prices in the area will fall below their current status by the year 2010 is less than 5 percent. Housing price forecasts for other areas are also provided.

16992 ■ *"Not In My Backyard" in Entrepreneur (Vol. 36, May 2008, No. 5, pp. 42)*
Pub: Entrepreneur Media, Inc.

Ed: Farnoosh Torabi. **Description:** More investors are turning to overseas real estate investments as the U.S. market sees a slowdown. Analysts say that risk-averse investors opt for funds with record of strong returns and U.S. real estate investment trusts that partner with foreign businesses for transparency purposes. Other details about foreign real estate investments are discussed.

16993 ■ *"Number of Mechanic's Liens Triple Since 2005" in The Business Journal - Serving Phoenix and the Valley of the Sun (Vol. 28, August 22, 2008, No. 51, pp. 1)*
Pub: American City Business Journals, Inc.

Ed: Jan Buchholtz. **Description:** Experts are blaming the mortgage and banking industries for the tripling of mechanic's liens that were filed in Arizona from 2005 through August 6, 2008. The rise in mechanic's liens is believed to indicate stress in the real estate community. Other views and information on the rise of mechanic's liens filed in Arizona are presented.

16994 ■ *"N.Y. Group Top Bidder for Last Duke Sites" in Crain's Cleveland Business (Vol. 28, November 19, 2007, No. 46, pp. 1)*
Pub: Crain Communications, Inc.

Ed: Stan Bullard. **Description:** Overview of the possible portfolio sale of Duke Realty Corp.'s last Northeast Ohio properties, 14 office buildings in Independence, Seven Hills and North Olmsted, believed to be purchased by a real estate investor group led by Nightingale Properties LLC of New York.

16995 ■ *"October 2009: Recovery Plods Along" in Hispanic Business (October 2009, pp. 10-11)*
Pub: Hispanic Business

Ed: Dr. Juan Solana. **Description:** Economist reports on a possible economic recovery which will not be allowed to rely on a strong domestic demand in order to sustain it. Consumers, looking to counterbalance years of leverage financing based on unrealistic, ever-increasing home and portfolio valuations, are saving rather than spending money.

16996 ■ *"Office Leasing Gains Ground" in Sacramento Business Journal (Vol. 25, July 18, 2008, No. 20, pp. 1)*
Pub: American City Business Journals, Inc.

Ed: Michael Shaw. **Description:** There were at least 84,000 square feet leased to companies in the Sacramento area in the three months prior to August 2008. This development is good news considering that overall vacant leases were around 247,000 square feet for the previous quarter.

16997 ■ *"OK, Bring in the Lawyers" in Crain's Chicago Business (Vol. 31, November 17, 2008, No. 46, pp. 26)*
Pub: Crain Communications, Inc.

Ed: Daniel Rome Levine. **Description:** Bankruptcy attorneys are finding the economic and credit crisis a benefit for their businesses due to the high number of business owners and mortgage holders that are need of their services. One Chicago firm is handling ten times the number of cases they did the previous year and of that about 80 percent of their new clients are related to the real estate sector.

16998 ■ *"Old Ford Plant to Sign New Tenants" in Business Courier (Vol. 27, August 13, 2010, No. 15, pp. 1)*
Pub: Business Courier

Ed: Dan Monk. **Description:** Ohio Realty Advisors LLC, a company handling the marketing of the 1.9 million-square-foot former Ford Batavia plant is on the brink of landing one distribution and three manufacturing firms as tenants. These tenants are slated to occupy about 20 percent of the facility and generate as many as 250 jobs in Ohio.

16999 ■ *"Optimism Index" in Black Enterprise (Vol. 41, September 2010, No. 2, pp. 24)*
Pub: Earl G. Graves Publishing Co. Inc.

Description: According to a Pew Research Center report, 81 percent of African Americans expect to

improve their finances in 2011. Blacks have carried a disproportionate share of job losses and housing foreclosures in the recession that began in 2007.

17000 ■ *"Ottawa's Real Estate Targets Exceed Market Appraisals" in Globe & Mail (March 19, 2007, pp. B1)*
Pub: CTVglobemedia Publishing Inc.

Ed: Danier Leblanc. **Description:** The growth in the real estate market in Ottawa and the huge revenue the government is expecting from sale of nine buildings as part of its lease back plan is discussed.

17001 ■ *"Outlook 2007" in Canadian Business (Vol. 80, December 25, 2006, No. 1, pp.)*
Pub: Rogers Media

Ed: David Wolf. **Description:** Economists' 2007 forecast on global economy, particularly about Canada's housing and labor market among other sectors, is discussed.

17002 ■ *"Outside Investors Hot On Detroit Commercial Real Estate" in Crain's Detroit Business (Vol. 24, January 28, 2008, No. 4, pp. 25)*
Pub: Crain Communications Inc. - Detroit

Ed: Daniel Duggan. **Description:** An overview of out-of-town investors seeking to purchase commercial real estate in Michigan is presented. Statistical data included.

17003 ■ *"Pain Ahead as Profit Pressure Increases" in Crain's Chicago Business (Vol. 31, May 5, 2008, No. 18, pp. 4)*
Pub: Crain Communications, Inc.

Ed: Daniel Rome Levine. **Description:** Interview with David Klaskin, the chairman and chief investment officer at Oak Ridge Investments LLC, who discusses the outlook for the economy and corporate earnings, particularly in the housing and auto industries, the impact of economic stimulus checks, the weakness of the dollar and recommendations of stocks that individual investors may find helpful.

17004 ■ *"The Paper Shredder" in Business Courier (Vol. 26, September 11, 2009, No. 20, pp. 1)*
Pub: American City Business Journals, Inc.

Ed: Dan Monk. **Description:** DotLoop Company, owned by entrepreneur Austin Allison, is developing the DotLoop software, which eliminates paperwork in the processing of real estate contracts. The software allows realtors to take control of the negotiation process and is adaptable to the rules of different US states.

17005 ■ *"Part-Time Office Space" in Hawaii Business (Vol. 53, December 2007, No. 6, pp. 132)*
Pub: Hawaii Business Publishing

Ed: Ashley Hamershock. **Description:** My Office is one of the companies that are renting space office not only by the month, but by the hour. Such setup is beneficial to small businesses that do not need a whole office all to themselves, and are interested in cutting the cost of office space rental. The prices of office space in Hawaii are mentioned.

17006 ■ *"Pat Modica" in Crain's Cleveland Business (Vol. 30, June 29, 2009, No. 25, pp. 15)*
Pub: Crain Communications, Inc.

Ed: Stan Bullard. **Description:** Profile of Pat Modica, real estate agent with Howard Hanna. Ms. Modica states that in her 29 years as a residential real estate agent, she has never seen a market like the present one. She discusses home sales and activity for the area.

17007 ■ *"Pavilions Poised for Image Overhaul" in The Business Journal - Serving Phoenix and the Valley of the Sun (Vol. 28, August 22, 2008)*
Pub: American City Business Journals, Inc.

Ed: Jan Buchholz. **Description:** DeRitto Partners Inc. is expected to push through with plans for a major renovation of the 1.1 million-square foot Scottsdale Pavilions in Scottsdale, Arizona. An aggressive marketing campaign is planned to be included in the renovation, which aims to address high vacancy rates and competition. Views and information on the planned renovation are presented.

17008 ■ *"Paying for the Recession: Rebalancing Economic Growth" in Montana Business Quarterly (Vol. 49, Spring 2011, No. 1, pp. 2)*
Pub: Bureau of Business & Economic Research
Ed: Patrick M. Barkey. **Description:** Four key issues required to address in order to rebalance economic growth in America are examined. They include: savings rates, global trade imbalances, government budgets and most importantly, housing price correction.

17009 ■ *The Peebles Principles: Insights from an Entrepreneur's Life of Business Success, Making Deals, and Creating a Fortune from Scratch*
Pub: John Wiley and Sons Inc.
Ed: R. Donahue Peebles. **Released:** April 2007. **Price:** $29.99. **Description:** Successful entrepreneur shares his business experience. Peebles went from CEO of the nation's largest Black-owned real estate development firm to founding his own firm.

17010 ■ *Peggy's Corner: The Art of Staging*
Pub: Eaton-Moghannam Publishing
Ed: Peggy Selinger-Eaton; Gayla Moghannam. **Released:** June 2005. **Description:** Techniques to enhance the value of any home are given. Seven principles of staging a home for sale include making a great first impression, maximizing space and eliminating clutter, using lighting for open spacious feeling, de-emphasize flaws, make the home appealing to buyers with varied tastes, creating warmth, and modernizing the home.

17011 ■ *"A Perfect Predator: Brookfield Asset Management Isn't Brash" in Canadian Business (Vol. 83, July 20, 2010, No. 11-12, pp. 50)*
Pub: Rogers Media Ltd.
Ed: Joanna Pachner. **Description:** Brookfield Asset Management CEO Bruce Flatt manages $108 billion worth of real estate and the company has become one of the world's biggest prime real estate owners since he became leader. Flatt says their goal is to earn a 12-15 percent compound annual return per share and that they would shrink in size if it meant reaching that goal.

17012 ■ *"Peter Gilgan" in Canadian Business (Vol. 82, April 27, 2009, No. 7, pp. 58)*
Pub: Rogers Media
Ed: Calvin Leung. **Description:** Mattamy Homes Ltd. president and chief executive officer Peter Gilgan believes that their business model of building communities in an organized way brings advantages to the firm and for their customers. He also believes in adopting their product prices to new market realities. Gilgan considers the approvals regime in Ontario his biggest challenge in the last 20 years.

17013 ■ *"Phillips Edison Launches $1.8B Retail REIT" in Business Courier (Vol. 27, October 15, 2010, No. 24, pp. 1)*
Pub: Business Courier
Ed: Dan Monk. **Description:** Retail center operator Phillips Edison & Company is organizing a real estate investment trust (REIT) to raise $1.8 billion to finance the planned purchase of 150 grocery-centered shopping centers around the U.S. The offering would be Phillips largest. Phillips Edison employesss 174 workers and operates 250 shopping centers nationwide.

17014 ■ *"A Place to Call Home" in Business Courier (Vol. 24, March 7, 2008, No. 48, pp. 1)*
Pub: American City Business Journals, Inc.
Ed: Lucy May. **Description:** Discusses a new type of housing for Cincinnati's chronically homeless that will be developed by the Over-the-Rhine Community Housing Network and the Cincinnati Center City Development Corp. Advocates believe that it is the missing link in the community's efforts to eradicate homelessness. The details of the project are also presented.

17015 ■ *"A Place in the Sun" in Canadian Business (Vol. 81, July 22, 2008, No. 12-13, pp. 56)*
Pub: Rogers Media Ltd.
Description: Experts believe that it is the best time for Canadians to own a retirement home in the U.S., where real estate prices are up to 50 percent below their peak. Other views concerning the economic conditions occurring in the United States, as well as on the implications for Canadians planning to invest in the country are presented.

17016 ■ *"Placer Land Sells for $12 Million" in Sacramento Business Journal (Vol. 25, July 25, 2008, No. 21, pp. 1)*
Pub: American City Business Journals, Inc.
Ed: Michael Shaw; Celia Lamb. **Description:** Reynen & Bardis Communities Inc., a Sacramento, California-based homebuilder, has purchased the Antonio Mountain Ranch in Placer County, California shortly before the property's scheduled foreclosure on June 27, 2008. Placer County Recorder's data show that the purchase price of the 808-acre wetland-rich property is $12 million.

17017 ■ *"Population Growing Faster Than Retail, Service Sector" in Crain's New York Business (Vol. 24, January 14, 2008, No. 2, pp. 30)*
Pub: Crain Communications, Inc.
Ed: Andrew Marks. **Description:** Downtown Manhattan is seeing more residential development; however, as more families call the area home the need for more retail and services is becoming evident.

17018 ■ *"'Pre-Sale' for Planned Could Mich Tower" in Crain's Chicago Business (Vol. 31, March 24, 2008, No. 12, pp. 14)*
Pub: Crain Communications, Inc.
Ed: Eddie Baeb. **Description:** Condominium developer William Warman is planning to build a mixed-use tower at 300 North Michigan Avenue which would include a hotel, retail space, apartments and a parking garage. Mr. Warman is looking for investors to buy part or all of the space in order to make it easier to land financing.

17019 ■ *"Price War: Managerial Salaries Are Beating the National Average, But Maybe Not for Long" in Canadian Business (March 31, 2008)*
Pub: Rogers Media
Ed: Megan Harman. **Description:** Real average hourly earnings of managers increase by 20 percent in ten years as companies increase wages to avoid the risk of losing key managers to the competition and in preparation for the retirement of baby boomers. Tough market conditions affect management more since their incentives are tied to individual and corporate performance.

17020 ■ *"Priced-Out Tenants Flocking to Class B" in Boston Business Journal (Vol. 27, October 19, 2007, No. 38, pp. 1)*
Pub: American City Business Journals Inc.
Ed: Michelle Hillman. **Description:** Tenants who usually rent top-tier office buildings are migrating to building that are not as expensive. The shift from Class A to Class B buildings is influenced by the high rental cost of the flashy office towers.

17021 ■ *"Prince of the City" in Canadian Business (Vol. 80, November 19, 2007, No. 23, pp. 62)*
Pub: Rogers Media
Ed: Rachel Pulfer. **Description:** Robert Fung and the Salilent Group aim to revive the poverty-stricken communities in Vancouver by transforming the city's old buildings into designer condominiums using city incentives. Fung and his partners have increased property values in the most unlikely neighborhoods by creating luxury real estate. Fung's recommendations on Vancouver's real estate development are given.

17022 ■ *"Private Equity Firms Shopping Valley For Deals" in The Business Journal - Serving Phoenix and the Valley of the Sun*

(Vol. 29, September 19, 2008, No. 3, pp. 1)
Pub: American City Business Journals, Inc.
Ed: Mike Sunnucks. **Description:** Private equity firms from California, Boston, New York, and overseas are expected to invest in growth-oriented real estate markets that include Phoenix. Real estate experts revealed that privately held investment and acquisition firms are looking to invest in real estate markets hit by the housing crisis. Views and information on private equity firms' real estate investments are presented.

17023 ■ *"Proposal Ruffles Builders" in Austin Business JournalInc. (Vol. 29, November 20, 2009, No. 37, pp. 1)*
Pub: American City Business Journals
Ed: Jacob Dirr. **Description:** A proposal that requires heating, ventilation and cooling equipment checking for a new commercial building having an area of at least 10,000 square feet might cost 25 cents to 50 cents per square foot for the owners. This may lead to higher housing costs. Both the Building and Fire Code Board of Appeals and the Mechanical Plumbing and Solar Board have recommended the plan.

17024 ■ *"Proposed Accounting Changes Could Complicate Tenant's Leases" in Baltimore Business Journal (Vol. 28, July 2, 2010, No. 8, pp. 1)*
Pub: Baltimore Business Journal
Ed: Daniel J. Sernovitz. **Description:** The Financial Accounting Standards Board has proposed that companies must indicate the value of real estate leases as assets and liabilities on balance sheets instead of expenses. The proposals could cause some companies to document millions of dollars in charges on their books or find difficulty in getting loans.

17025 ■ *"Proposed Law Would Stop REIS Bid for Annexation by Livonia" in Crain's Detroit Business (Vol. 24, March 10, 2008, No. 10, pp. 2)*
Pub: Crain Communications, Inc.
Ed: Chad Halcom. **Description:** REIS Northville L.L. C., a joint venture made up of Real Estate Interests Group Inc. and Schostak Bros. & Co., has proposed an $800 million project called Highwood at the former Northville Psychiatric Hospital site but has been stalled due to a disagreement with Northville Township on several terms including: the amount of retail at the site and the paying for cleanup of environmental and medical waste.

17026 ■ *"Proposed Triangle Redo in Motion" in Crain's Cleveland Business (Vol. 28, October 15, 2007, No. 41, pp. 1)*
Pub: Crain Communications, Inc.
Ed: Stan Bullard. **Description:** Zaremba Homes and MRN Ltd. are partnering to redevelop the so-called Triangle section of University Circle. The proposed project will include a total of 434 new rental and for-sale residential suites and as much as 227,000 square feet of retail and restaurant space.

17027 ■ *"Pulte May Be Bouncing Back From Stock-Price Doldrums" in Crain's Detroit Business (Vol. 23, October 8, 2007, No. 41, pp. 4)*
Pub: Crain Communications Inc. - Detroit
Ed: Daniel Duggan. **Description:** Pulte Homes saw a jump in its stocks due to Citigroup's analysts rating Pulte and other builders higher due to strong balance sheets.

17028 ■ *"Radio Roots Run Deep" in The Business Journal-Milwaukee (Vol. 25, July 4, 2008, No. 41, pp. A1)*
Pub: American City Business Journals, Inc.
Ed: Rich Kirchen. **Description:** Profile of Steve Palec, a real estate broker at CB Richard Ellis, also works as a radio host for shows 'Rock & Roll Roots' and 'Legends of Rock'. Palec shares that real estate is still his top priority, even with his radio gig. Palec's career as a broker and as a radio host is discussed.

17029 ■ *"Real Estate Ambitions" in Black Enterprise (Vol. 37, January 2007, No. 6, pp. 101)*
Pub: Earl G. Graves Publishing Co. Inc.
Description: National Real Estate Investors Association is a nonprofit trade association for both advanced

as well as novice real estate investors that offers information on builders to contractors to banks. When looking to become a real estate investor utilize this organization, talk to various investors like the president of your local chapter, let people know your aspirations, and see if you can find a partner who has experience in the field. Resources included.

17030 ■ "Real Estate Defaults Top $300M' in Business Courier (Vol. 26, January 15, 2010, No. 39, pp. 1)
Pub: American City Business Journals, Inc.

Ed: Dan Monk. **Description:** Cincinnati commercial real estate owners defaulting in securitized loans reached $306 million at the end of 2009. The trend has lifted the region's default rate to nearly 9 percent. National average for commercial real estate default is examined.

17031 ■ "Real Estate Funds Swell Past $350M' in Business Journal Portland (Vol. 27, December 31, 2010, No. 44, pp. 1)
Pub: Portland Business Journal

Ed: Wendy Culverwell. **Description:** Oregon-based real estate funds have raised around half of the $735 million that was raised by local companies. Investors have been purchasing distressed properties. Commercial real estate prices have declined since 2007.

17032 ■ Real Estate Loopholes: Secrets of Successful Real Estate Investing
Pub: Warner Books, Incorporated

Ed: Diane Kennedy, Garrett Sutton, Robert T. Kiyosaki. **Released:** April 2003. **Description:** Knowledge, planning, and building a team of advisor and mentors is key to successful real estate investments.

17033 ■ "Real Estate Market Still in a Slump" in Montana Business Quarterly (Vol. 49, Summer 2011, No. 2, pp. 15)
Pub: Bureau of Business & Economic Research

Ed: Patrick M. Barkey. **Description:** Montana's housing market is still in decline with no sign of improving in the near future. Statistical data included.

17034 ■ The Real Estate Recipe: Make Millions by Buying Small Apartment Properties in Your Spare Time
Pub: DNA Press

Ed: Brian K. Friedman. **Released:** September 2004. **Price:** $29.95. **Description:** Guide for anyone interested in property investments; the book provides information for choosing an apartment property and answers questions in a chronological workbook format. The author shares his own experiences in apartment investing and shares the entire process of analyzing and buying an apartment property using a hypothetical ten-unit complex. Sample worksheets, checklists, and tables are provided to help readers maintain their own records.

17035 ■ "Real Estate Vets Take Times In Stride" in The Business Journal-Serving Metropolitan Kansas City (Vol. 26, July 25, 2008, No. 46)
Pub: American City Business Journals, Inc.

Ed: Rob Roberts. **Description:** Kansas City, Missouri's real estate industry veterans like Allen Block believe that the challenges faced by the industry in the 1980s, when the Federal Reserve Board controlled the money supply to slow down inflation, were worse than the challenges faced today. Other views, trends and information on the real estate industry of the city, are presented.

17036 ■ "Real Estate Wheeling and Dealing Picks Up" in Business Journal Portland (Vol. 27, October 29, 2010, No. 35, pp. 1)
Pub: Portland Business Journal

Ed: Wendy Culverwell. **Description:** LoopNet has listed 33 prominent commercial real estate properties for sale in Portland, Oregon's real estate market. However, reasons for the sales rush are not totally clear, but speculations point to the end of the Bush tax cuts in 2010 that prompted real estate investors to close the deals and avoid the increase in capital gains taxes.

17037 ■ "Real Estate Woes Mount for State's Smaller Banks" in Boston Business Journal (Vol. 27, November 30, 2007, No. 44, pp. 1)
Pub: American City Business Journals Inc.

Ed: Craig M. Douglas. **Description:** Massachusetts banking industry is facing a steep increase on loan defaults such as in home mortgages and condominium projects, contrary to public belief that the local industry is safe from the real estate meltdown. The dollar value of local banks' nonperforming loans doubled in 2007, and is rising statewide. Other banking issues in the state are discussed.

17038 ■ "Real Estate's New Reality" in Entrepreneur (Vol. 37, July 2009, No. 7, pp. 32)
Pub: Entrepreneur Media, Inc.

Ed: Rosalind Resnick. **Description:** Investing in real estate is still an advisable move, as long as investors are prepared to hold on to the property and there is a rent roll to provide a decent return on investment. Among the key considerations when investing in real estate is the property's expenses and cash flow. Other suggestions for future real estate investors are given.

17039 ■ "Real Opportunities: Don't Let Mortgage Mayhem Steer You Away From Sound Investments" in Black Enterprise (December 2007)
Pub: Earl G. Graves Publishing Co. Inc.

Ed: James A. Anderson. **Description:** Real estate investment trusts (REITs) that operate office buildings, industrial parks, shopping malls, hotels, hospitals, or other commercial properties may be a sound investment, despite the mortgage crisis facing the U.S. financial sector.

17040 ■ "Realities May Blur Vision" in The Business Journal-Serving Metropolitan Kansas City (Vol. 27, September 19, 2008, No. 1, pp. 1)
Pub: American City Business Journals, Inc.

Ed: Rob Roberts. **Description:** Vision Metcalf is a study by Kansas City that depicts how Metcalf Avenue could look like if redeveloped. Redevelopment plans for the Metcalf corridor include a 20-story mixed-use building on a vacant car dealership. The challenges that the redevelopment plans will face are also analyzed.

17041 ■ "Realtors Signing Out" in The Business Journal-Serving Metropolitan Kansas City (Vol. 27, November 21, 2008, No. 11, pp. 1)
Pub: American City Business Journals, Inc.

Ed: Rob Roberts. **Description:** The Kansas City Regional Association of Realtors has lost 1,000 of its members due to the downturn in the housing market. Applications for realtor licenses have dropped by 159 percent. Changes in Missouri's licensing requirements are seen as additional reasons for the declines.

17042 ■ "Recovery on Tap for 2010?" in Orlando Business Journal (Vol. 26, January 1, 2010, No. 31, pp. 1)
Pub: American City Business Journals

Ed: Melanie Stawicki Azam, Richard Bilbao, Christopher Boyd, Anjali Fluker. **Description:** Economic forecasts for Central Florida's leading business sectors in 2010 are presented. These sectors include housing, film and TV, sports business, law, restaurants, aviation, tourism and hospitality, banking and finance, commercial real estate, retail, health care, insurance, higher education, and manufacturing. According to some local executives, Central Florida's economy will slowly recover in 2010.

17043 ■ "Red Tape Ties Detroit Housing Rehab Plan" in Crain's Detroit Business (Vol. 24, September 22, 2008, No. 38, pp. 1)
Pub: Crain Communications Inc.

Ed: Ryan Beene. **Description:** Venture-capital firm Wilherst Oxford LLC is a Florida-based company that has purchased 300 inner-city homes which were in foreclosure in Detroit. Wilherst Oxford is asking the city to forgive the existing tax and utility liens so the

firm can utilize the money for home improvements. The city, however, is reluctant but has stated that they are willing to negotiate.

17044 ■ "Refi Requests Soar, But New Rules May Mean Fewer Closings" in The Business Review Albany (Vol. 35, April 4, 2008, No. 53, pp. 1)
Pub: The Business Review

Ed: Barbara Pinckney. **Description:** National refinancing applications grew by 82 percent in the week that ended March 21, 2008, due to the depressed real estate market and lower interest rates. Refinancing applicants, however, may be surprised with new rules on loan applications such as the required credit score of at least 720 in avoiding payment of extra fees. The developments in application standards for home loans are also examined.

17045 ■ "The REIT Stuff' in Canadian Business (Vol. 80, March 26, 2007, No. 7, pp. 72)
Pub: Rogers Media

Description: The stock performance of various real estate investment trusts in Canada is analyzed.

17046 ■ "REIT's Decry Foreign Limits on Investment" in Globe & Mail (March 29, 2007, pp. B4)
Pub: CTVglobemedia Publishing Inc.

Ed: Elizabeth Church. **Description:** The planned legislation by Canadian government for regulation foreign investments by real estate investment trusts is discussed.

17047 ■ "A Renewal in Rentals" in Barron's (Vol. 88, March 17, 2008, No. 11, pp. 17)
Pub: Dow Jones & Company, Inc.

Description: Discusses the projected entry of the estimated 82 million echo-boomers into the rentals market and the influx of immigrants and displaced homeowners which could turn apartments into lucrative investments again. While apartment-building completions rose slowly since 2003, demand is expected to increase steeply until 2015.

17048 ■ "Rental Demand Boosts Revenue for Sun Communities Inc." in Crain's Detroit Business (Vol. 24, March 24, 2008, No. 12, pp. 4)
Pub: Crain Communications, Inc.

Ed: Daniel Duggan. **Description:** Despite the decline in sales of manufactured homes, demand for rental units and rent-to-own programs have brought Sun Communities Inc. increased revenue. The real estate investment trust, based in Southfield, owns, operates, finances and develops manufactured home communities in the Midwest and Southeast. Statistical data included.

17049 ■ "Reply! Grows at Unprecedented Rate, Rips Beta Off Its Marketplace" in Marketing Weekly News (September 19, 2009, pp. 149)
Pub: Investment Weekly News

Description: Profile of Reply.com, a leader in locally-targeted Internet marketing, announced significant growth in terms of revenue, enhanced features and services and new categories since launching its beta Reply! Marketplace platform. Even in the face of an economic downturn, the company has posted over 50 percent revenue growth in the Real Estate and Automotive categories.

17050 ■ "Restoring Grandeur" in Business Courier (Vol. 26, December 4, 2009, No. 32, pp. 1)
Pub: American City Business Journals, Inc.

Ed: Dan Monk. **Description:** Eagle Realty Group intends to spend more than $10 to restore the historic 12-story Phelps apartment building in Lytle Park in Cincinnati. Its president, Mario San Marco, expressed the need to invest in the building in order to maintain operations. The building could be restored into a hotel catering to executives and consultants.

17051 ■ "Retail Center Pitched" in Business Courier (Vol. 27, June 18, 2010, No. 7, pp. 1)
Pub: Business Courier

Ed: Dan Monk. **Description:** Jeffrey R. Anderson Real Estate Inc.'s plan for a retail center in Butler

County, Ohio could have three department stores in the 1.1 million-square-foot property. An outdoor sports retailer is also part of the plans.

17052 ■ *"Revitalizing Real Estate: Couple Sails Through Sea of Housing Woes" in Black Enterprise (Vol. 38, February 2008, No. 7, pp. 50)*

Pub: Earl G. Graves Publishing Co. Inc.

Ed: Ayana Dixon. **Description:** Owner, Christopher Gablin and Regina Mincey-Garlin offer a broad range of real estate-related services to clients in order to not only survive, but thrive in today's market.

17053 ■ *"The Right Time for REITs" in Barron's (Vol. 88, July 14, 2008, No. 28, pp. 32)*

Pub: Dow Jones & Co., Inc.

Ed: Mike Hogan. **Description:** Discusses the downturn in U.S. real estate investment trusts so these are worth considering for investment. Several Websites that are useful for learning about real estate investment trusts for investment purposes are presented.

17054 ■ *"A Rise in Rental Units" in Philadelphia Business Journal (Vol. 30, October 7, 2011, No. 34, pp. 1)*

Pub: American City Business Journals Inc.

Ed: Natalie Kostelni. **Description:** Housing developers have been stepping up the construction of new apartment complexes throughout the suburbs of Pennsylvania in order to capture growing demand for rental properties. BPG Properties Ltd. has nearly 1,000 new apartments under construction.

17055 ■ *"Sales at Furniture Showrooms Sink" in Puget Sound Business Journal (Vol. 29, October 10, 2008, No. 25, pp. 1)*

Pub: American City Business Journals

Ed: Greg Lamm. **Description:** Furniture showrooms are seeing a drop in sales due to the bad economy. Buyer demand has also fallen because of the slumping real estate market.

17056 ■ *"Scaled-Down Phoenix Condos Emerge as DNA" in The Business Journal - Serving Phoenix and the Valley of the Sun (Vol. 28, July 11, 2008, No. 45, pp. 1)*

Pub: American City Business Journals, Inc.

Ed: Yvonne Zusel. **Description:** Pointe of View Developments and Belleview Communities have scaled back their Copper Pointe Condominiums project in downtown Phoenix, Arizona. The scaled-back project has also changed its name into Downtown's Newest Address Condominiums and will cost $42 million.

17057 ■ *"Sellers Face Excess Land Dilemma" in Crain's Cleveland Business (Vol. 28, November 12, 2007, No. 45, pp. 1)*

Pub: Crain Communications, Inc.

Ed: Stan Bullard. **Description:** Overview on the way in which the housing slump is effecting builders, land developers and lot prices. Statistical data included.

17058 ■ *"'Short Sales,' A Sign of Housing Troubles, Start Popping Up" in The Business Review Albany (Vol. 35, April 11, 2008, No. 1, pp. 1)*

Pub: The Business Review

Ed: Michael DeMasi. **Description:** Discusses the number of short sales, where homeowners ask banks to forgive part of their mortgages to sell the properties, which is starting to increase in the Albany, New York area. Real estate agents in the area are taking up crash courses in short selling.

17059 ■ *"Sitting, Sitting, Sitting-Snapshots of Homes that Just Won't Sell" in Crain's Chicago Business (Vol. 31, April 21, 2008, No. 16)*

Pub: Crain Communications, Inc.

Ed: Kevin Davis. **Description:** Listing of five Chicago-area homes that have been on the market for an extended length of time; also includes the original asking price, current asking price, special features and the biggest challenge of each home.

17060 ■ *"Six Leading Economists on What to Expect in the Year Ahead: Derek Holt; Housing" in Canadian Business (December 24, 2007)*

Pub: Rogers Media

Ed: Derek Holt. **Description:** The Canadian subprime mortgage market could take a different turn from that of the U.S. as laws governing Canada's mortgage market indirectly limit the probability of a slowdown. Details on how Canada avoided the slowdown in the housing market and forecasts of new homes for 2008 are discussed.

17061 ■ *"Small Changes Can Mean Big Energy Savings" in Crain's Cleveland Business (Vol. 28, November 5, 2007, No. 44, pp. 21)*

Pub: Crain Communications, Inc.

Ed: Harriet Tramer. **Description:** Many Northeast Ohio businesses are taking their cues from the residential real estate market to draw and capitalize on interest in energy efficiency and is regularly taken into account by local architects.

17062 ■ *"S.O.S. Sorting Out Subprime" in Black Enterprise (Vol. 38, November 2007, No. 4, pp. 76)*

Pub: Earl G. Graves Publishing Co. Inc.

Ed: Trevor Delaney. **Description:** Subprime distress in the housing market is discussed and the impact it has put on investors.

17063 ■ *"South Loop Site Lands a Buyer" in Crain's Chicago Business (Vol. 31, March 24, 2008, No. 12, pp. 1)*

Pub: Crain Communications, Inc.

Ed: Alby Gallun. **Description:** Russland Capital Group, a little-known condominium developer from Skokie, recently purchased a 6.5-acre riverside property in the site known as Franklin Point for $40 million.

17064 ■ *"Staging a Martini-and-GQ Lifestyle; Faux Possessions Play to Buyer's Aspirations" in Crain's Chicago Business (April 21, 2008)*

Pub: Crain Communications, Inc.

Ed: Kevin Davis. **Description:** Due to the competition of the slumping housing market, home stagers are becoming more prominent and are using creative ways to make an impression beyond de-cluttering, painting and cleaning by using accents such as casually placed magazines, candles and table settings.

17065 ■ *"State Printing Plant on the Move" in Sacramento Business Journal (Vol. 25, August 29, 2008, No. 26, pp. 1)*

Pub: American City Business Journals, Inc.

Ed: Michael Shaw; Celia Lamb. **Description:** California is planning to replace its printing plant on Richards Boulevard and 7th Street with a newly built or leased facility in the Sacramento area. It was revealed that the project will meet the state's standards for new buildings. It is believed that the new site will require 15 acres or more depending on requirements.

17066 ■ *"State Wants to Add Escape Clause to Leases" in Sacramento Business Journal (Vol. 28, October 14, 2011, No. 33, pp. 1)*

Pub: Sacramento Business Journal

Ed: Michael Shaw. **Description:** California Governor Jerry Brown's administration has decided to add escape clauses to new lease agreements, which created new worry for building owners and brokers in Sacramento, California. Real estate brokers believe the appropriation of funds clauses have been making the lenders nervous and would result in less competition.

17067 ■ *"Still Looking Good" in Canadian Business (Vol. 80, March 26, 2007, No. 7, pp. 29)*

Pub: Rogers Media

Ed: Andy Holloway. **Description:** The real estate prices in various parts of Canada are analyzed. The future growth potential of the industry is forecasted.

17068 ■ *"Stuck With Two Mortgages; The Nightmare When Buyers Upgrade" in Crain's Chicago Business (Vol. 31, April 21, 2008, No. 16)*

Pub: Crain Communications, Inc.

Ed: Darci Smith. **Description:** Discusses the problem a number of people are facing due to the slump in the housing market: being stuck with two mortgages when they move because their former homes have not sold. Many thought they could afford to move to a larger home, anticipating significant equity appreciation that did not occur; now they are left with lowering their price and competing with the host of new developments.

17069 ■ *"Subprime Problems Loom" in The Business Journal-Portland (Vol. 25, August 29, 2008, No. 25, pp. 1)*

Pub: American City Business Journals, Inc.

Ed: Wendy Culverwell. **Description:** Over half of subprime mortgages in Portland are resetting by the end of 2008, which will cause more problems to the local real estate market. The inventory of unsold homes has also been increasing for over a year. Forecasts for the Portland housing market in relation to mortgage resets are supplied.

17070 ■ *"Survey: Apartment Rents Continue to Climb as Home Market Slows" in Business Review, Albany New York (November 23, 2007)*

Pub: American City Business Journals, Inc.

Ed: Michael DeMasi. **Description:** Survey by Sunrise Management and Consulting shows that asking rents for apartments in the Capital Region increased for the thirteenth consecutive time. The survey, which was conducted between August and October 2007, also showed that Albany County, New York had the highest average asking rent, followed by Rensselaer County, Saratoga County, and Schenectady County.

17071 ■ *"Survey Says Commercial Real Estate Headed for Turbulence" in Commercial Property News (March 17, 2008)*

Pub: Nielsen Company

Description: Commercial real estate sector is declining due to the sluggish U.S. economy. According to a recent survey, national office, retail and hospitality markets are also on the decline.

17072 ■ *"A Survival Guide for Crazy Times" in Canadian Business (Vol. 81, March 3, 2008, No. 3, pp. 61)*

Pub: Rogers Media

Ed: David Wolf. **Description:** Investors should ensure that their portfolios are positioned defensively more than the average as the U.S. and Canadian markets face turbulent times. They should not assume that U.S. residential property is a good place to invest only because prices have dropped and the Canadian dollar is showing strength. Other tips that investors can use during unstable periods are supplied.

17073 ■ *"Tampa Condo Conversion Sells for $14.8 Million Less" in The Business Journal-Serving Greater Tampa Bay (Vol. 28, September 5, 2008)*

Pub: American City Business Journals, Inc.

Ed: Janet Leiser. **Description:** Former apartment complex Village Oaks at Tampa, which was converted to condominiums, has been sold to Tennessee-based real estate investment trust Mid-America Apartment Communities Inc. for $21.2 million in August 2008. The amount was $14.2 million less than what developer Radco Management LLC paid for in 2005.

17074 ■ *"Tax Abatement Changes Seen as Home Run for Cleveland Condo Market" in Crain's Cleveland Business (Vol. 30, June 15, 2009, No. 23)*

Pub: Crain Communications, Inc.

Ed: Jay Miller. **Description:** Condominium ownership became a bit more affordable for Cleveland residents since changes in both state and local tax abatement policy changes. The tax credits are examined.

17075 ■ *"Tax Credit Crunch" in Miami Daily Business Review (March 26, 2008)*
Pub: ALM Media Inc.
Ed: Paula Iuspa-Abbott. **Description:** Uncertainty is growing over the future of the low-income housing project in South Florida and the tax credit program that helps fuel the projects.

17076 ■ *"That Empty Feeling" in Crain's Cleveland Business (Vol. 28, October 15, 2007, No. 41, pp. 1)*
Pub: Crain Communications, Inc.
Ed: Stan Bullard. **Description:** Townhouses, cluster homes and condominiums lured both buyers and builders for most of this decade but now that market is suffering to an even greater degree than the single-family home market. Statistical data included.

17077 ■ *"They've Fallen, But They Can Get Up" in Barron's (Vol. 88, March 10, 2008, No. 10, pp. 43)*
Pub: Dow Jones & Company, Inc.
Ed: Kopin Tan. **Description:** Shares of senior housing companies present buying opportunities to investors because of their low prices. Companies such as Brookdale Senior Living are not as dependent on housing prices but have suffered declines in share prices.

17078 ■ *"Threat of New Office Space Records Rent Hikes" in Globe & Mail (March 21, 2007, pp. B4)*
Pub: CTVglobemedia Publishing Inc.
Ed: Elizabeth Church. **Description:** The increasing commercial rent prices in the Toronto region amid the high office building construction market are discussed.

17079 ■ *"Tom Gaglardi" in Canadian Business (Vol. 82, April 27, 2009, No. 7, pp. 56)*
Pub: Rogers Media
Ed: Calvin Leung. **Description:** Northland Properties Corporation president Tom Gaglardi believes that their business model of keeping much of operations in-house allows the firm to crate assets at a lesser price while commanding higher margins than their competitors. He believes that it is an ideal time to invest in the hospitality industry because of opportunities to purchase properties at low prices.

17080 ■ *"Top 10 Retirement Mistakes and How to Avoid Them" in Canadian Business (Vol. 83, July 20, 2010, No. 11-12, pp. 39)*
Pub: Rogers Media Ltd.
Ed: Jacqueline Nelson, Angelina Chapin. **Description:** Some of the top retirement mistakes is relying on selling one's house to find a retirement. Other mistakes are paying too much for investments and planning to work in retirement since no one can be sure that they will be healthy enough to accomplish this. Suggestions to avoid these pitfalls are discussed.

17081 ■ *"Top Twenty Wealthiest Landowners" in Hawaii Business (Vol. 53, November 2007, No. 5, pp. 34)*
Pub: Hawaii Business Publishing
Description: Provided is a table of the wealthiest landowners in Hawaii. Their assessed value, total acres owned, prominent holdings, other notable holdings and years of presence in Hawaii are also provided. Statistical data included.

17082 ■ *"Tough Sell: Senior Projects Hustle to Keep Buyers" in Puget Sound Business Journal (Vol. 29, November 21, 2008, No. 31, pp.)*
Pub: American City Business Journals
Ed: Heidi Dietrich. **Description:** Plans to move to retirement communities are being postponed by seniors in Washington's Puget Sound area due to difficulty selling their current homes in the slow economy. Retirement communities are trying to lure clients by offering new finance programs and sales plans.

17083 ■ *"Troy Complex has New Brand, New Leases" in Crain's Detroit Business (Vol. 24, April 14, 2008, No. 15, pp. 32)*
Pub: Crain Communications Inc.
Ed: Daniel Duggan. **Description:** Discusses the re-branding of the 1.2 million-square-foot collection of office buildings in Troy purchased by New York-based Emmes Co. The firm has also pledged more than $6 million in upgrades, hired a new leasing company and completed 67,000 square feet of leasing with another 100,000 in negotiations.

17084 ■ *"Try, Try Again" in Baltimore Business Journal (Vol. 28, August 20, 2010, No. 15, pp. 1)*
Pub: Baltimore Business Journal
Ed: Gary Haber. **Description:** Customers' refinancing of mortgages has boosted Baltimore, Maryland mortgage banking business. The housing decline has resulted in a decrease in the number of people looking for new mortgages.

17085 ■ *Use What You've Got*
Pub: Portfolio Publishing
Ed: Barbara Corcoran, Bruce Littlefield. **Released:** 2003. **Price:** $24.95. **Description:** Founder and chairman of New York's premier real estate company, the Corcoran Group, shares her successes in the real estate industry. The book offers tips and pointers to salespeople, entrepreneurs and business people alike. Corcoran explains how she went from waiting tables and borrowed $1,000 from a boyfriend to build her real estate company into the industry's powerhouse.

17086 ■ *"Valenti: Roots of Financial Crisis Go Back to 1998" in Crain's Detroit Business (Vol. 24, October 6, 2008, No. 40, pp. 25)*
Pub: Crain Communications, Inc.
Ed: Tom Henderson; Nathan Skid. **Description:** Interview with Sam Valenti III who is the chairman and CEO of Valenti Capital L.L.C., a wealth-management firm; Valenti discusses in detail the history that led up to the current economic crisis as well as his prediction for the future of the country.

17087 ■ *"Vision for Camden in Better Focus" in Philadelphia Business Journal (Vol. 30, September 30, 2011, No. 33, pp. 1)*
Pub: American City Business Journals Inc.
Ed: Natalie Kostelni. **Description:** More than $500 million worth of projects aimed at redeveloping the downtown and waterfront areas of Camden, New Jersey are being planned. These include the construction of residential, commercial, and education buildings.

17088 ■ *"Wannabe Buyers Take Their Own Sweet Time" in Crain's Chicago Business (Vol. 31, April 21, 2008, No. 16, pp. 50)*
Pub: Crain Communications, Inc.
Ed: Lisa Bertagnoli. **Description:** Although all factors are in place for a robust real-estate market in the Chicago area: low interest rates, plenty of inventory and the region's relatively strong employment, buyers are taking their time and doing more research in order to see how bad the economy will get.

17089 ■ *"Was Mandating Solar Power Water Heaters For New Homes Good Policy?" in Hawaii Business (Vol. 54, August 2008, No. 2, pp. 28)*
Pub: Hawaii Business Publishing
Description: Senator Gary L. Kooser of District 7 Kauai-Niihau believes that the mandating of energy-efficient water heaters for new single-family homes starting in 2010 will help cut Hawaii's oil consumption. Ron Richmond of the Hawaii Solar Energy Association says that the content of SB 644 has negative consequences as it allows for choice of energy and not just solar, and it also eliminates tax credits for new homebuyers.

17090 ■ *"What Homes Do Retirees Want?" in Canadian Business (Vol. 79, July 17, 2006, No. 14-15, pp.)*
Pub: Rogers Media
Ed: Joe Cataldo. **Description:** The obstacles and challenges faced by homebuilders in Canada as well as the approach adopted by them to appeal to the mature homebuilders segment, is discussed.

17091 ■ *"What's Ahead for Fannie and Fred?" in Barron's (Vol. 90, August 30, 2010, No. 35, pp. 26)*
Pub: Barron's Editorial & Corporate Headquarters
Ed: Jonathan R. Laing. **Description:** A meeting presided by Treasury Secretary Timothy Geithner discussed the future of Fannie Mae and Freddie Mac. The two government sponsored enterprises were mismanaged and reforming these two agencies is critical.

17092 ■ *"When Anything (And Everything) Goes" in Globe & Mail (January 12, 2007, pp. B4)*
Pub: CTVglobemedia Publishing Inc.
Ed: Elizabeth Church. **Description:** The forecast on acquisition of different real estate firms is presented.

17093 ■ *"Where Are the Vultures?" in Mergers & Acquisitions: The Dealmaker's Journal (March 1, 2008)*
Pub: SourceMedia, Inc.
Ed: Ken MacFadyen. **Description:** Although the real estate market is distressed, not many acquisitions are being made by distress private equity investors; this is due, in part, to the difficulty in assessing real estate industry firms since it is a sector which is so localized.

17094 ■ *"Will Home Buyers Pay for Green Features?" in Contractor (Vol. 56, October 2009, No. 10, pp. 70)*
Pub: Penton Media, Inc.
Ed: Bob Mader. **Description:** National Association of Home Builders commissioned a survey which shows that homeowners are interested in green as long as they do no have to pay much for it. The association did not allow a board member to read the survey which raises questions about how the questions were phrased and how the sample was selected.

17095 ■ *"With Building Plans in Flux, County Could Sell Key Site" in Crain's Cleveland Business (Vol. 28, October 8, 2007, No. 40, pp. 1)*
Pub: Crain Communications, Inc.
Ed: Jay Miller. **Description:** Due to such issues as financial and administrative problems, Cuyahoga County commissioners have pushed back the construction timeline for a planned county administration center and are saying that they are considering selling the site in downtown Cleveland to developers who would erect a new office building that another large tenant could occupy.

17096 ■ *"Working It Out! How a Young Executive Overcomes Obstacles on the Job" in Black Enterprise (Vol. 37, January 2007, No. 6, pp. 55)*
Pub: Earl G. Graves Publishing Co. Inc.
Ed: Laura Egodigwe. **Description:** Interview with Susan Chapman, Global Head of Operations for Citigroup Realty Services, in which she discusses issues such as the important skills necessary for overcoming obstacles in the workplace.

17097 ■ *The Working Man and Woman's Guide to Becoming a Millionaire*
Pub: Prentiss Publishing
Ed: Al Herron. **Released:** November 2006. **Description:** President and CEO of a Century 21 office in Dallas, Texas shares insight into financial security and commitment to community.

17098 ■ *"You Better Shop Around: Four Steps to Getting the Best Deal On a Home Loan" in Black Enterprise (Vol. 40, July 2010, No. 12, pp. 78)*
Pub: Earl G. Graves Publishing Co. Inc.
Ed: Tara-Nicholle Nelson. **Description:** Four steps to help anyone seeking a mortgage for a home purchase are listed.

17099 ■ *"You Won't Go Broke Filling Up On These Stocks" in Barron's (Vol. 88, July 14, 2008, No. 28, pp. 38)*
Pub: Dow Jones & Co., Inc.
Ed: Assif Shameen. **Description:** Due to high economic growth, pro-business policies and a consumption boom, the Middle East is a good place to

look for equities. The best ways in which to gain exposure to this market include investing in the real estate industry and telecommunications markets as well as large banks that serve corporations and consumers.

17100 ■ *Your First Year in Real Estate: Making the Transition from Total Novice to Successful Professional*
Pub: Crown Business Books
Ed: Dirk Zeller. **Released:** $August 3, 2010. **Price:** $20.00. **Description:** Zeller helps new realtors to select the right company, develop mentor and client relationships, using the Internet and social networking to stay ahead of competition, to set and reach career goals, to stay current in the market, and more.

17101 ■ *"Your Place: Housing Developers Try to Read Generation Y" in Philadelphia Inquirer (December 2, 2010)*
Pub: Philadelphia Media Network Inc.
Ed: Al Heavens. **Description:** Results of a survey conducted with Generation Y individuals are examined, focusing on housing developments and whether this particular generation prefers suburban or rural lifestyles. Generation Y encompasses people ages 18 to 32 years old. Statistical data included.

17102 ■ *Your Successful Real Estate Career, 5h Edition*
Pub: American Management Association
Contact: Charles R. Craig, Chairman
Ed: Kenneth W. Edwards. **Released:** 2006. **Price:** $18.95.

SOURCES OF SUPPLY

17103 ■ *Real Estate Software Directory and Catalog*
Z-Law Software Inc.
Contact: Gary L. Sherman, President
URL(s): www.z-law.com. **Released:** Semiannual; January and July. **Price:** Free. **Publication includes:** Listings of producers of real estate related software programs and ordering information. Principal content of publication is product name, description, specifications, requirements. **Database includes:** Applications for landlords, realtors, investors, property managers, lenders, contractors, attorneys, developers, and appraisers. **Arrangement:** Classified by product/service. **Indexes:** Product/service; subject.

STATISTICAL SOURCES

17104 ■ *RMA Annual Statement Studies*
Pub: Risk Management Association
Contact: Kevin M. Blakey, President
Released: Annual. **Price:** $175.00 2006-07 edition, $105.00. **Description:** Contains composite balance sheets and income statements for more than 360 industries, including the accounting, auditing, and bookkeeping industries. Also contains five years of comparative historical data for discerning trends. Includes 16 commonly used ratios, computed for most of the size groupings for nearly every industry.

17105 ■ *Standard & Poor's Industry Surveys*
Pub: Standard & Poor's Corp.
Released: Annual. **Price:** $3633.00. **Description:** Two-volume book that examines the prospects for specific industries, including trucking. Also provides analyses of trends and problems, statistical tables and charts, and comparative company analyses.

TRADE PERIODICALS

17106 ■ *The CF Apartment Reporter*
Pub: Clayton-Fillmore Ltd.
Contact: Howard Treibitz, President
URL(s): www.clayfil.com. **Released:** Bimonthly **Price:** $199, Individuals 4.00 per city.

17107 ■ *Commercial Investment Real Estate*
Pub: CCIM Institute
Contact: Tim Hatlestad, President
E-mail: tim@investaz.com
URL(s): www.ccim.org/cire-magazinewww.ccim.com. **Released:** Bimonthly **Price:** $45, Individuals; $55, Canada and Mexico.

17108 ■ *CONNECTIONS*
Pub: Women's Council of Realtors
Contact: Dianna Dearen, Editor
Ed: Dianna Dearen, Editor, ddearen@wcr.org. **Released:** 8/year. **Description:** Carries articles on personal and career growth topics relating to women in real estate. Includes council news.

17109 ■ *The duPont Registry: A Buyer's Gallery of Fine Boats*
Pub: duPont Publishing Inc.
Contact: Steve Chapman, Chief Executive Officer
URL(s): www.dupontregistry.com/boats/. **Released:** Monthly **Price:** $15.95, Individuals; $25.95, Canada; $45.95, Other countries.

17110 ■ *First Tuesday*
Pub: Realty Publications Inc.
URL(s): www.firsttuesdayonline.com/. **Released:** Monthly

17111 ■ *Homes Magazine*
Pub: Reflector Publishing
URL(s): www.reflector.com. **Released:** Monthly

17112 ■ *The Institutional Real Estate Letter*
Pub: Institutional Real Estate Inc.
Contact: Nyia Dohrmann, President
E-mail: n.dohrmann@irei.com
URL(s): www.irei.com/web/do/pub/publication/view?id=4. **Ed:** Geoffrey Dohrmann. **Released:** Monthly **Price:** $2495, Individuals.

17113 ■ *Journal of Property Management*
Pub: Institute of Real Estate Management
Contact: Ronald Goss, President
URL(s): www.irem.org/sechome.cfm?sec=JPM. **Released:** Bimonthly **Price:** $72.32, Canada; $62.95, Individuals; $115.50, Two years; $110.99, Other countries airmail; $169.10, Individuals 3 years.

17114 ■ *National Delinquency Survey*
Pub: Mortgage Bankers Association
Ed: Douglas G. Duncan, Editor, Laura_Armstrong@mbaa.org. **Released:** Quarterly. **Price:** $250, members; $450, nonmembers. **Description:** Carries information on residential mortgage delinquency and foreclosure rates at national, regional, and state levels. Reports delinquency rates by length of time and type of loan.

17115 ■ *National Property Law Digests*
Pub: Strafford Publications Inc.
Contact: Richard M. Ossoff, President
E-mail: richardossoff@straffordpub.com
Released: Monthly. **Price:** $827, individuals plus $48.50 s/h. **Description:** Digest of the most significant property law cases in the U.S. court system. Cases are screened and selected to provide concise, comprehensive coverage of the latest issues concerning real property law.

17116 ■ *National Real Estate Investor*
Pub: Penton
Contact: Raymond E. Maloney, President
URL(s): www.nreionline.com. **Released:** Monthly

17117 ■ *The Practical Real Estate Lawyer*
Pub: American Law Institute-American Bar Association Continuing Professional Education
URL(s): www.ali-aba.org/index.cfm?fuseaction=publications.periodical&pub=PRE L. **Released:** Bimonthly **Price:** $75, Individuals print only; $55, Individuals online only; $99, Individuals print and online; $129, Two years print only; $89, Two years online only; $169, Two years print and online.

17118 ■ *Professional Report*
Pub: Society of Industrial and Office Realtors
Contact: Geoffrey Kreusser, President
Ed: Linda P. Nasvaderani, Editor, lnasvaderani@mail.sior.com. **Released:** Quarterly, QRT. **Price:** $35, members Included in membership; $45/year for nonmembers, U.S.; $55. **Description:** Dedicated to corporate real estate brokerage, development, and management. Recurring features include news of members and the Society, news of educational programs sponsored by the Society, book reviews, news of research, and statistics.

17119 ■ *Real Estate Broker's Insider*
Pub: Alexander Communications Group Inc.
Contact: Margaret DeWitt, Publisher
E-mail: mklein@brokersinsider.com
Ed: Jeff Ostrowski, Editor. **Released:** Semimonthly, 2/month. **Price:** $247. **Description:** Provides residential agency broker/owners with actionable news and information on managing their businesses for greater profitability.

17120 ■ *Real Estate Forum: America's Premier Business Real Estate Magazine*
Pub: Incisive Media
Contact: Lee Feldman, Manager
E-mail: lee.feldman@incisivemedia.com
URL(s): www.incisivemediarealestategroup.com/?page_id=1452. **Ed:** Sule Aygoren Carranza. **Released:** Monthly **Price:** $129.95, Individuals; $245, Two years; $275, Other countries; $400, Two years other countries.

17121 ■ *Real Estate Law Report*
Pub: Research Institute of America
Contact: Peter Warwick, President
Ed: Alvin Arnold, Editor. **Released:** 12/year. **Price:** $513.96. **Description:** Contains digests of recent real estate law cases with expert commentary.

17122 ■ *Real Estate Weekly*
Pub: Hagedorn Communications
URL(s): www.rew-online.com/. **Released:** Weekly **Price:** $49, Individuals.

17123 ■ *Realtor Magazine: The Business tool for Real Estate Professionals*
Pub: National Association of Realtors
Contact: Thomas M. Stevens, President
URL(s): www.realtor.org/RMODaily.nsf/pages/aboutusintro?OpenDocument. **Released:** Monthly **Price:** $56, Individuals; $83, Canada; $103, Other countries.

17124 ■ *Realtors Land Institute Newsletter*
Pub: Realtors Land Institute
Contact: Ray Brownfield, President
E-mail: rbrownfield@johngreeneland.com
Ed: Belinda Carter, Editor, belindarli@aol.com. **Released:** 6/year. **Description:** Contains articles of interest to realtors dealing with farm and land real estate. Recurring features include news of the Institute and tax information.

17125 ■ *The Residential Specialist*
Pub: Council of Residential Specialists
Contact: Nina Cottrell, Chief Executive Officer
E-mail: ncottrell@crs.com
URL(s): www.crs.com/Resources/166. **Ed:** Michael Fenner. **Released:** Bimonthly **Price:** $29.95, Nonmembers; $54.95, Two years.

VIDEOCASSETTES/ AUDIOCASSETTES

17126 ■ *Inside Business Today*
GPN Educational Media
1550 Executive Drive
Elgin, IL 60123
Ph: (402)472-2007
Free: 800-228-4630
Fax: (800)306-2330
Co. E-mail: askgpn@smarterville.com
URL: http://www.shopgpn.com

Released: 1989. **Description:** Leaders in business and industry tell their success stories in this extensive series. **Availability:** VHS; 3/4 U.

CONSULTANTS

17127 ■ **Lehrer Financial and Economic Advisory Services**
5555 Del Monte Dr., Ste. 802
Houston, TX 77056-4100
Ph: (713)626-8184
Free: 866-275-4958

Fax: (713)964-0444
Co. E-mail: drken@lehecoserv.com
URL: http://www.lehecoserv.com
Contact: Dr. Kenneth Eugene Lehrer, Managing Director
E-mail: drken@lehecoserv.com
Scope: Provider of real estate finance, economic damages, non public business valuations, institutional loan presentations, market and feasibility analysis, fairness opinions, investment and portfolio analysis, business plans in corporate finance and expert witness for court testimony. Acts a san economic consulting group, capable of fulfilling the complete economic or financial needs of corporations, banks, attorneys, insurance companies, pension funds, medical groups and other investment organizations. **Founded:** 1982.

17128 ■ Real Resources
27 Indian Hill Rd.
Medfield, MA 02052-2908
Ph: (508)359-6780
Fax: (508)359-6780
Co. E-mail: sharonloewe@comcast.net
Contact: Sharon Loewenthal, Principal
E-mail: sharonloewe@comcast.net
Scope: Consulting in areas of housing development, including site acquisition, market research, feasibility analysis, fiscal impact studies, zoning, mortgage underwriting, grant procurement, preparation, project and construction management, residential rent-up and marketing plans, retail and commercial leasing, small business plans and tax syndication analysis. Consulting in areas of housing development, including site acquisition, market research, feasibility analysis, fiscal impact studies, zoning, mortgage underwriting, grant procurement, preparation, project and construction management, residential rent-up and marketing plans, retail and commercial leasing, small business plans, and tax syndication analysis. **Founded:** 1985.

17129 ■ White, Hutchinson, Leisure & Learning Group
4036 Baltimore Ave.
Kansas City, MO 64111-2257
Ph: (816)931-1040
Fax: (816)756-5058
Co. E-mail: info@whitehutchinson.com
URL: http://www.whitehutchinson.com
Contact: Randy White, Chief Executive Officer
E-mail: randy@whitehutchinson.com
Scope: Provider of real estate development services. It offers feasibility studies, concept development, design and project management, and financing solutions. **Founded:** 1987. **Publications:** "Twenty Ways to Become More Family Friendly," Ialei Fun Extra, Feb, 2002; "The Importance of Food to Location-Based Leisure," Sep, 2001; "Guest Sacrifice: A Sure Trip to Prison Or a Path to Profitability," Entertainment Management, Aug, 2000; "Beyond Androcentrism: How to Design Lbls to Please Guests (Women & Children) Instead of Owners and Architects," Entertainment Management, Jun, 2000; "Child's Play: More Complicated Than it Looks," Entertainment Management, Feb, 2000; "How Can I Finance My Leisure Project?"; "The Feasibility Study: The Foundation for Success"; "New Luxury: Rich Design is No Longer Optional". **Seminars:** Renovation and Construction of Outdoor Play Environments Using Nature As The Play Element, Oct 2002; "Designing and Renovating Outdoor Play Spaces Using Nature As Part Of The Play Element, Nov, 2002.

FRANCHISES AND BUSINESS OPPORTUNITIES

17130 ■ Advance Realty
Advance Realty Inc.
8640 Ridgleys Choice Dr., Lower level
Baltimore, MD 21236
Ph: (410)529-9111
Free: 888-925-0004
Fax: (410)529-9119
Co. E-mail: info@advancerealtyusa.com
URL: http://www.advancerealtyusa.com
Description: Full service discount experts, Advance Realty offers a one-of-a-kind first to market franchise

opportunity in select territories throughout the U.S. benefit from an industry leading turnkey franchise offering, including its unique 'quick-start' start-up package and 1-on-1 ongoing support. Franchisees receive support in areas of business development, site selection/build-out, recruitment and operations with streamlined technology. **No. of Franchise Units:** 17. **Equity Capital Needed:** $50,000-$100,000. **Franchise Fee:** $17,500. **Training:** Up to 5 days corporate based training and 2 days minimum onsite training and ongoing support.

17131 ■ Assist-2-Sell
1610 Meadow Wood Ln.
Reno, NV 89502
Ph: (775)688-6060
Free: 800-528-7816
Fax: (775)688-6069
Description: Discount real estate brokerage. **No. of Franchise Units:** 300. **Founded:** 1987.. **Franchised:** 1993. **Equity Capital Needed:** $29,000-$34,000, including franchise fee. **Franchise Fee:** $9,995. **Training:** Yes.

17132 ■ Benham REO Group
8410 Pit Stop Ct.
Concord, NC 28027
Ph: (704)788-4603
Fax: (704)788-4604
URL: http://benhamreo.com
Description: Foreclosed property sales. **No. of Franchise Units:** 84. **No. of Company-Owned Units:** 2. **Founded:** 2004.. **Franchised:** 2007. **Equity Capital Needed:** $11,800-$31,750. **Franchise Fee:** $6,500-$9,500. **Royalty Fee:** $195/transaction. **Financial Assistance:** Financial assistamce with franchise fee available. **Training:** 1 week training provided at headquarters and ongoing support.

17133 ■ Better Homes Realty, Inc.
1777 Botelho Dr., Ste. 390
Walnut Creek, CA 94596
Free: 800-642-4428
Fax: (925)988-2270
Description: Principally engaged in franchising real estate sales offices. **No. of Franchise Units:** 42. **Founded:** 1964.. **Franchised:** 1975. **Equity Capital Needed:** $61,500. **Franchise Fee:** $9,950. **Royalty Fee:** Varies. **Training:** Yes.

17134 ■ The BrickKicker
RonLen Enterprises Inc.
849 N Ellsworth St.
Naperville, IL 60563
Free: 888-339-5425
Fax: (630)420-2270
Co. E-mail: linda@brickkicker.com
URL: http://www.brickkicker.com
Description: Building inspection service. **No. of Franchise Units:** 152. **Founded:** 1989.. **Franchised:** 1995. **Equity Capital Needed:** $15,000-$40,000. **Franchise Fee:** $9,000-$40,000. **Financial Assistance:** Yes. **Training:** Yes.

17135 ■ Century 21 Canada Limited Partnership
1199 W Pender St., Ste. 700
Vancouver, BC, Canada V6E 2R1
Ph: (604)606-2100
Fax: (604)606-2125
URL: http://www.century21canada.ca
Description: The franchise offers real estate services. **No. of Franchise Units:** 400. **Founded:** 1976.. **Franchised:** 1976. **Equity Capital Needed:** $50,000-$100,000. **Franchise Fee:** $10,500-$21,000. **Training:** Yes.

17136 ■ Commission Express
Commission Express National
8306 Professional Hill Dr.
Fairfax, VA 22031
Ph: (703)560-5500
Fax: (703)560-5502
Co. E-mail: manager@commissionexpress.com
URL: http://www.commissionexpress.com
Description: Buy real estate agent commissions. **No. of Franchise Units:** 74. **No. of Company-Owned Units:** 1. **Founded:** 1992.. **Franchised:**

1996. **Equity Capital Needed:** $94,300-$213,500. **Franchise Fee:** $20,000-$80,000. **Training:** Provides 1 week at Fairfax, VA and annual conference.

17137 ■ Flat Rate Realty
123 Christel Oaks Dr.
Scotts Valley, CA 95066
Ph: (831)426-3800
Fax: (800)413-1496
Co. E-mail: flatratereality@gmail.com
URL: http://www.flatraterealityfranchise.com
Description: "The Premier Discount Real Estate Franchise." Brings to a community a new look and new business model to sell real estate. Offers small overhead, more profits. A state of the art business plan that uses the new technology, charging a fee for service. **No. of Franchise Units:** 26. **No. of Company-Owned Units:** 4. **Founded:** 2004.. **Franchised:** 2006. **Equity Capital Needed:** $21,000-$43,000. **Franchise Fee:** $5,000. **Royalty Fee:** $500/month. **Financial Assistance:** Yes. **Training:** Initial training, start up support, consultation and communication.

17138 ■ Help-U-Sell Real Estate
Realty Information Systems, Inc.
3121 Michelson Dr., Ste. 150
Irvine, CA 92612
Free: 800-366-1177
Fax: (949)788-1360
Co. E-mail: info@helpusell.com
URL: http://www.helpusell.com
Description: Offers full-service real estate brokerage franchises. **No. of Franchise Units:** 94. **Founded:** 1976. **Franchised:** 1976. **Equity Capital Needed:** $43,750-$136,750 depending on marketplace costs, franchise fee subject to change. **Franchise Fee:** $17,750. **Royalty Fee:** 6%. **Financial Assistance:** Limited in-house and third party financing available. **Training:** Offers 4 days at headquarters, at franchisee's location, 8 weeks by phone, retreats, regional meetings, convention, Help-U-Sell University and ongoing support.

17139 ■ Homes 4Sale By Owner Network
5761 Eagle Trace Dr.
Sylvania, OH 43560
Ph: (619)328-5988
Free: 877-615-5177
Fax: (619)749-3922
Description: Full service real estate marketing. **No. of Franchise Units:** 3. **No. of Company-Owned Units:** 1. **Founded:** 2002.. **Franchised:** 2006. **Equity Capital Needed:** $25,000-$35,000. **Franchise Fee:** $19,500. **Training:** Yes.

17140 ■ Me, MyHome, And I
For Sale By Owner Group Ltd.
19785 W 12 Mile Rd., Ste. 52
Southfield, MI 48075
Ph: (313)629-3325
Description: For sale by owner assistance. **Founded:** 2006.. **Franchised:** 2006. **Equity Capital Needed:** $100,000. **Franchise Fee:** $20,000. **Training:** Yes.

17141 ■ Picket Fence Preview
Picket Fence Franchising Corp.
One Kennedy Dr.
South Burlington, VT 05403
Ph: (802)660-3167
Free: 800-201-0338
Description: For sale by owner magazine. **No. of Franchise Units:** 5. **No. of Company-Owned Units:** 1. **Founded:** 1993.. **Franchised:** 1994. **Equity Capital Needed:** $20,000-$35,000. **Franchise Fee:** $10,000. **Training:** Yes.

17142 ■ PropertyGuys.com Inc.
1133 St. George Blvd., Ste. 50
Moncton, NB, Canada E1E 4E1
Ph: (506)860-3433
Free: 866-666-9744
Fax: (506)857-2630
Co. E-mail: franchiseleads@propertyguys.com
URL: http://www.propertyguysfranchise.com
Description: The franchise aims at establishing a national network of local business professionals, which will develop a national database of "For sale

by owner listings.". **No. of Franchise Units:** 118. **Founded:** 1998.. **Franchised:** 2002. **Equity Capital Needed:** $50,000-$100,000 investment required; $100,000 start-up capital required. **Franchise Fee:** $40,000-$75,000. **Training:** Offers 5 days at PropertyGuys University.

17143 ■ Re/Max LLC
RE/MAX International, Inc.
PO Box 3907
Englewood, CO 80155-3907
Ph: (303)770-5531
Free: 800-525-7452
URL: http://www.remax.com
Description: International real estate franchise network. **No. of Franchise Units:** 3,207. **No. of Company-Owned Units:** 24. **Founded:** 1973.. **Franchised:** 1976. **Equity Capital Needed:** $35,000-$194,000. **Franchise Fee:** $12,500-$28,000. **Royalty Fee:** Varies. **Financial Assistance:** Third party financing available and in-house assistance available with franchise fee. **Training:** Provides 5 days training at headquarters, annual conference, online training and ongoing support.

17144 ■ Realty Executives International
Realty Executives
7600 N 16th St., Ste. 100
Phoenix, AZ 85020
Ph: (602)957-0747
Free: 800-252-3366
Description: Real estate franchise. **No. of Franchise Units:** 569. **Founded:** 1965.. **Franchised:** 1987. **Equity Capital Needed:** $15,000-$75,000. **Franchise Fee:** $5,000-$25,000. **Training:** Yes.

17145 ■ Remerica Real Estate
41017 Ann Arbor Rd.
Plymouth, MI 48170
Ph: (734)459-4500
Free: 800-REM-ERIC
Fax: (734)459-1566
Co. E-mail: info@remerica.com
URL: http://www.remerica.com
Contact: Jim Preston, Manager
Description: Real estate franchise. **No. of Franchise Units:** 40. **Founded:** 1989.. **Franchised:** 1991. **Equity Capital Needed:** $50,000-$500,000. **Franchise Fee:** $10,000. **Publications:** *Remerica Real Estate.* **Training:** Yes.

17146 ■ United Capital Mortgage Assistance, L.L.C.
1300 Mercantile Ln., Ste. 124
Largo, MD 20774
Ph: (301)386-8803
Free: 800-474-1407
Fax: (301)386-8804
Description: Homeowner foreclosure service. **No. of Company-Owned Units:** 1. **Founded:** 1996.. **Franchised:** 1998. **Equity Capital Needed:** $18,500-$27,000, includes franchise fee. **Franchise Fee:** $9,995, including training. **Training:** Yes.

17147 ■ Weichert Real Estate Affiliates Inc.
225 Littleton Rd.
Morris Plains, NJ 07950
Ph: (973)359-8377
Fax: (973)292-1428
URL: http://www.weichert.com
Description: They serve as real estate brokerage. **No. of Franchise Units:** 233. **No. of Company-Owned Units:** 146. **Founded:** 1969.. **Franchised:** 2000. **Equity Capital Needed:** $50,000-$346,700. **Franchise Fee:** $25,000. **Royalty Fee:** 6%. **Training:** Offers 4 days at corporate headquarters, onsite and annual conference, quarterly workshops, and ongoing support.

COMPUTERIZED DATABASES

17148 ■ The National Registry
1401 H St. NW, Ste. 760
Washington, DC 20005
Ph: (202)289-2735

Fax: (202)289-4101
URL: http://www.asc.gov
Availability: Online: Federal Financial Institutions Examination Council - Appraisal Subcommittee. **Type:** Directory.

17149 ■ New Residential Construction Index
4600 Silver Hill Rd.
Washington, DC 20233-0001
Ph: (301)457-4100
Free: 800-923-8282
Fax: (301)457-4714
Co. E-mail: webmaster@census.gov
URL: http://www.census.gov
Availability: Online: U.S. Census Bureau. **Type:** Statistical.

17150 ■ New Residential Sales
4600 Silver Hill Rd.
Washington, DC 20233-0001
Ph: (301)457-4100
Free: 800-923-8282
Fax: (301)457-4714
Co. E-mail: webmaster@census.gov
URL: http://www.census.gov
Availability: Online: U.S. Census Bureau. **Type:** Statistical.

COMPUTER SYSTEMS/ SOFTWARE

17151 ■ Real Estate Analyzer
7852 Ivanhoe Ave.
La Jolla, CA 92037
Ph: (858)454-0121
Fax: (858)454-7559
Co. E-mail: support@howardsoft.com
URL: http://www.howardsoft.com
Price: $395. **Description:** Available for Apple II and IBM computers and compatibles. System provides financial analysis for property investment purposes.

LIBRARIES

17152 ■ Baker Botts, L.L.P. Law Library
1299 Pennsylvania Ave., NW
Washington, DC 20004
Ph: (202)639-7700
Fax: (202)639-7890
URL: http://www.bakerbotts.com
Scope: Law - banking, corporate, International, public utilities, real estate, taxation, environmental, intellectual property. **Services:** Interlibrary loan; copying; library open to the public by appointment with restrictions. **Founded:** 1986. **Holdings:** 22,000 volumes; microforms; videocassettes; audiocassettes; CD-ROM. **Subscriptions:** 125 journals and other serials.

17153 ■ Buset & Partners Library
1121 Barton St.
Thunder Bay, ON, Canada P7B 5N3
Ph: (807)623-2500
Free: 866-532-8738
Fax: (807)622-7808
Co. E-mail: cenns@buset-partners.com
URL: http://www.buset-partners.com
Contact: Carolyn Enns, Librarian
Scope: Law - real estate, labor, corporate, commercial, family, personal injury, insurance; civil litigation, wills and estates, employment, municipal, environmental. **Services:** Library not open to the public. **Holdings:** 2100 books; 1 bound periodical volumes. **Subscriptions:** 7 journals and other serials; 3 newspapers. **Telecommunication Services:** law@buset-partners.com.

17154 ■ Landauer Realty Group Information Center
2 Science Rd.
Glenwood, IL 60425-1586
Ph: (708)755-7000
Free: 800-323-8830

Fax: (708)755-7016
Co. E-mail: custserv@landauer.com
URL: http://www.landauer.com
Contact: Catherine A. Heyward, Director, Library Services
Scope: Real estate, finance, marketing, land use, development, property acquisition and management. **Services:** Center not open to the public. **Founded:** 1974. **Holdings:** 375 books; 100 VF drawers of reports; 16,000 clippings, offerings, brochures, statistical data; 125 VF drawers of research materials; U.S. maps; Annual reports; 1960, 1970, 1980 census publications; government documents. **Subscriptions:** 200 journals and other serials.

17155 ■ National Association of Realtors - Information Central
430 N. Michigan Ave.
Chicago, IL 60611-4087
Ph: (312)329-8200
Free: 800-874-6500
Fax: (312)329-5960
Co. E-mail: infocentral@realtors.org
URL: http://www.realtor.org
Contact: John Krukoff
Scope: Real estate, architecture, city planning, association management. **Services:** Library open to the public by appointment on fee basis. **Founded:** 1923. **Holdings:** 15,000 volumes. **Subscriptions:** 700 journals and other serials.

17156 ■ Polsinelli Shalton Welte Suelthaus PC Law Library
700 W. 47th St., Ste. 1000
Kansas City, MO 64112
Ph: (816)753-1000
Fax: (816)753-1536
Co. E-mail: bfullerton@pswlaw.com
URL: http://www.pswlaw.com/
Contact: Karin L. Weaver
Scope: Law - tax, bankruptcy, real estate; litigation; product liability. **Services:** Interlibrary loan; copying; SDI; Library open to clients only. **Holdings:** 15,000 books. **Subscriptions:** 1500 journals and other serials; 10 newspapers.

17157 ■ Protape, Inc. Library
1540 Broadway
New York, NY 10036
Contact: Richard Sobelsohn
Scope: Accounting, law, real estate, English, math, insurance, travel, taxation, stock broker, medical billing, claims adjusting, private investigation, paralegal. **Services:** Library not open to the public. **Founded:** 1970. **Holdings:** 25,000 books; 250 bound periodical volumes. **Subscriptions:** 65 journals and other serials; 20 newspapers.

17158 ■ Toronto Real Estate Board Library
1400 Don Mills Rd.
Don Mills, ON, Canada M3B 3N1
Ph: (416)443-8100
URL: http://www.torontorealestateboard.com
Scope: Real estate. **Services:** Library open to the public by appointment; copying. **Founded:** 1986. **Holdings:** 3000 books; 120 serials; 500 reports; 120 audio- and videocassettes, and reel-to-reel tapes. **Subscriptions:** 100 journals and other serials.

RESEARCH CENTERS

17159 ■ Ohio State University - Center for Real Estate Education and Research
606 Fisher Hall
Fisher College of Business
2100 Neil Ave.
Columbus, OH 43210-1144
Ph: (614)292-2109
Fax: (614)292-2418
Co. E-mail: realestate@osu.edu
URL: http://fisher.osu.edu/centers/real-estate
Contact: Dr. Ken Gold, Director
Founded: 1976. **Educational Activities:** Assists in the development of educational programs in real estate offered by the University; Center for Real Estate Education and Research Conferences (Occasionally); Seminars and colloquia. **Telecommunication Services:** gold_54@fisher.osu.edu.

ASSOCIATIONS AND OTHER ORGANIZATIONS

17160 ■ **International Real Estate Institute (IREI)**
PO Box 879
Palm Springs, CA 92263
Ph: (760)327-5284
Free: 877-743-6799
Fax: (760)327-5631
Co. E-mail: support@assoc-hdqts.org
URL: http://irei-assoc.org
Contact: Snehal Jardosh, Consultant
Description: Professionals in 120 countries specializing in the development, finance, investment and valuation of real estate. Conducts educational seminars and regional programs; operates speakers' bureau and placement service. Compiles statistics, consults United Nations on property issues. **Founded:** 1975. **Educational Activities:** World Real Estate Congress (Annual); World Real Estate Congress (Annual).

17161 ■ **Investment Management Consultants Association (IMCA)**
5619 DTC Pkwy., Ste. 500
Greenwood Village, CO 80111
Ph: (303)770-3377
Fax: (303)770-1812
Co. E-mail: imca@imca.org
URL: http://www.imca.org
Contact: Sean Walters, Chief Executive Officer
Description: Consultants, money managers, and others in the investment management consultant business. Seeks to increase public awareness of investment management consultants, provide educational programs to members, and encourage high business standards. Operates consulting industry certification program. Maintains a legislative network with state and federal legislative information affecting the industry. **Founded:** 1985. **Publications:** *Essentials of Investment Consulting*; *The Facts About Investing*; *The Monitor* (Bimonthly); *Wealth Management Course*; *The Journal of Investment Consulting* (Semiannual). **Educational Activities:** Investment Management Consultants Association Conference (Annual); Fall Investment Management Expo (Annual); Regional Consultants Conferences (Quarterly). **Awards:** IMCA Journalism Award (Annual); The Richard J. Davis Ethics Award (Annual); Stephen L. Kessler Writing Award (Annual).

17162 ■ **National Apartment Association (NAA)**
4300 Wilson Blvd., Ste. 400
Arlington, VA 22203
Ph: (703)518-6141
Fax: (703)248-9440
Co. E-mail: webmaster@naahq.org
URL: http://www.naahq.org
Contact: Jerry Wilkinson, Chairman of the Board
Description: Federation of 155 state and local associations of industry professionals engaged in all aspects of the multifamily housing industry, including owners, builders, investors, developers, managers, and allied service representatives. Provides education and certification for property management executives, on-site property managers, maintenance personnel, property supervisors, and leasing agents. Offers a nationwide legislative network concerned with governmental decisions at the federal, state, and local levels. **Founded:** 1939.

17163 ■ **National Association of Real Estate Companies (NAREC)**
216 W Jackson Blvd., Ste. 625
Chicago, IL 60606
Ph: (312)263-1755
Fax: (312)750-1203
Co. E-mail: info@narec.org
URL: http://www.narec.org
Contact: Michael Heiken, President
Description: Individuals associated with companies involved in the financial management of real estate development companies. Purpose: Seeks to formulate positions and inform members on current accounting and financial reporting issues relating to real estate companies and to voice these positions to appropriate accounting rule-making bodies. Cooperates with such bodies in order to establish accounting and financial guidelines; provides a forum for members dealing with issues faced in managing the financial affairs of real estate companies such as financial reporting, financial management, tax planning, and information technology. **Founded:** 1977. **Publications:** *National Association of Real Estate Companies--Membership Directory* (Quarterly). **Educational Activities:** National Association of Real Estate Companies Meeting (Annual).

17164 ■ **National Association of Real Estate Investment Trusts (NAREIT)**
1875 I St. NW, Ste. 600
Washington, DC 20006-5413
Ph: (202)739-9400
Free: 800-3NA-REIT
Fax: (202)739-9401
Co. E-mail: baiken@nareit.com
URL: http://www.reit.com
Contact: Donald C. Wood, Chairman
Description: Real estate investment trusts; corporations, partnerships, or individuals (other than trusts) that manage multiple-owned real estate, or that have a business or professional interest in real estate trusts, associations, corporations and funds. Compiles statistics. **Founded:** 1960. **Publications:** *NAREIT Quick Member Guide* (Annual). **Educational Activities:** Institutional Investor Forum (Annual); Law and Accounting Conference (Annual).

17165 ■ **National Association of Realtors (NAR)**
430 N Michigan Ave.
Chicago, IL 60611
Ph: (312)329-8495
Free: 800-441-5263
Fax: (312)329-8633
Co. E-mail: rli@realtors.org
URL: http://www.realtor.org
Contact: Thomas M. Stevens, President
URL(s): www.realtormag.com, www.realtor.com. **Description:** Federation of 54 state and territory associations and 1,860 local real estate boards whose members are real estate brokers and agents; terms are registered by the association in the U.S. Patent and Trademark Office and in the states. Promotes education, high professional standards and modern techniques in specialized real estate work such as brokerage, appraisal, property management, land development, industrial real estate, farm brokerage and counseling. Conducts research programs. **Scope:** real estate. **Founded:** 1908. **Publications:** *REALTORS Land Institute*; *Realtor Magazine*; *NAR Real Estate Outlook* (Monthly); *Real Estate Today: Official Publication of the National Association of Realtors*; *Existing-Home Sales*; *Realtor Magazine: The Business tool for Real Estate Professionals* (Monthly). **Awards:** Distinguished Service Award. **Telecommunication Services:** infocentral@realtors.org; nar-pubs@realtors.org.

17166 ■ **Real Property Association of Canada (REALpac)—Association des biens Immobiliers du Canada**
One University Ave., Ste. 1410
Toronto, ON, Canada M5J 2P1
Ph: (416)642-2700
Free: 855-732-5722
Fax: (416)642-2727
Co. E-mail: info@realpac.ca
URL: http://www.realpac.ca
Contact: Paul Morse, Chief Executive Officer
Description: Real estate and development companies and related businesses. Promotes growth in the real estate development and related industries. Serves as a forum for discussion of issues facing the industry; represents members' interests before the public. **Founded:** 1971.

DIRECTORIES OF EDUCATIONAL PROGRAMS

17167 ■ *Directory of Real Estate Development & Related Education Programs*
Pub: Urban Land Institute
URL(s): www.uli.org. **Ed:** Gayle Berens. **Released:** Biennial; latest edition 11th, 2008. **Price:** $19.95, Members; $24.95, Nonmembers. **Covers:** over 60 real estate development education programs currently being offered at colleges and universities. **Entries include:** College or university name, address, list of faculty members, curriculum, tuition, length of program, degrees offered, financial aid information, job placement services, international programs, e-mail addresses. **Indexes:** Faculty, Programs by degree type, Programs by geographical.

REFERENCE WORKS

17168 ■ *"$1M Home Sales Spike" in Business Courier (Vol. 27, December 3, 2010, No. 31, pp. 1)*
Pub: Business Courier
Ed: Tom Demeropolis. **Description:** Cincinnati Area Board of Realtors reported the increase of sales of multi-million dollar Tri-State homes in 2010, particu-

larly in Indian Hill where sales surged nearly 60 percent. Sales of homes of $1 million and above are up 21 percent through November in Hamilton County with 58 homes sales.

17169 ■ *"1Q Office Vacancies Mainly Up; Class A Space Bucks Trend, Falls" in Crain's Detroit Business (Vol. 24, April 14, 2008, No. 15)*

Pub: Crain Communications, Inc.

Ed: Daniel Duggan. **Description:** Although more office space became vacant in the first quarter, Class A space went in the opposite direction with several local businesses are moving from less-desirable to more desirable areas.

17170 ■ *"3CDC Investing $8 Million To Put New Life Into Old Homes" in Globe & Mail (February 28, 2006, pp. B1)*

Pub: CTVglobemedia Publishing Inc.

Ed: Lucy May. **Description:** The Cincinnati Center City Development Corp. has bought more than 100 empty buildings and many around Washington Park in Over-the-Rhine. Its new project, called 3CDC, is to revitalize the historic neighborhood in the Washington Park area near Music Hall.

17171 ■ *"13D Filings: Investors Report to the SEC" in Barron's (Vol. 88, July 4, 2008, No. 28, pp. M10)*

Pub: Dow Jones & Co., Inc.

Description: Robino Stortini Holdings will seek control of Investors Capital Holdings either alone or with members of the company's management. Discovery Group I will withhold its votes at the nomination of directors for TESSCO Technologies while JMB Capital Partners Master Fund plans to nominate a slate of candidates to the board of Maguire Properties.

17172 ■ *"A 16-Year Housing Slump? It Could Happen" in Barron's (Vol. 88, March 17, 2008, No. 11, pp. 27)*

Pub: Dow Jones & Company, Inc.

Ed: Gene Epstein. **Description:** Housing remains a good protection against inflation but over very long periods. Inflation-adjusted stock prices did even better but have greater volatility. Commodities, on the other hand, underperformed both housing and stocks as inflation hedges. House prices tend to rise faster than the consumer price index is because land is inherently limited.

17173 ■ *"The 35 Year Mortgage-Built to Last Time" in Globe & Mail (March 17, 2006, pp. B1)*

Pub: CTVglobemedia Publishing Inc.

Ed: Patrick Brethour. **Description:** The 35-year mortgage has arrived in Canada. The plan will give an opportunity to the first-time buyers into the real estate market. Details of the new mortgage are analyzed.

17174 ■ *"$50 Million Project for West Chester" in Business Courier (Vol. 24, December 14, 2008, No. 35, pp. 1)*

Pub: American City Business Journals, Inc.

Ed: Laura Baverman. **Description:** Commercial developer Scott Street Partners is planning to invest $50 million for the development of a site south of the Streets of West Chester retail center. The 31-acre project will generate 1,200 jobs, and will bring in offices, restaurants and a hotel. The development plans and the features of the site are discussed as well.

17175 ■ *"$100 Million Complex To Be Built..On a Bridge" in Business Courier (Vol. 27, November 12, 2010, No. 28, pp. 1)*

Pub: Business Courier

Ed: Lucy May. **Description:** A development firm closed a deal with the Newport Southbank Bridge Company for a $100M entertainment complex that will be built on tope of the Purple People Bridge. The proposed project will cover 150,000 square feet with attractions such as restaurants, a boutique hotel, and pubs.

17176 ■ *"$100 Million in Projects Jeopardized" in Business Courier (Vol. 24, March 28, 2008, No. 51, pp. 1)*

Pub: American City Business Journals, Inc.

Ed: Dan Monk. **Description:** Ohio's historic preservation tax credit program may be reinstated after some companies planned to sue over its stoppage. The Ohio Department of Development said the program was halted because it exceeded the allocated budget for the credit. $34 million in credits are at stake for more than two dozen local projects if the program is reinstated.

17177 ■ *"217 Homes Planned for Former Crystal Cream Site" in Sacramento Business Journal (Vol. 25, August 8, 2008, No. 23, pp. 1)*

Pub: American City Business Journals, Inc.

Ed: Michael Shaw. **Description:** MetroNova Development LLC plans to develop housing at the former Crystal Cream & Butter Co. site near downtown Sacramento. The developer expects to sell the new loft houses for about $300,000 without public subsidies. Views and other information on the planned development project, is presented.

17178 ■ *"2009 Real Estate in Review: Median Prices Drop, Sales Up" in Bellingham Business Journal (Vol. February 2010, pp. 15)*

Pub: Sound Publishing Inc.

Ed: Isaac Bonnell. **Description:** Bellingham and Whatcom County, Washington saw a rise in home sales in 2008. Single family home sales were up 3.3 percent in Bellingham and 0.5 percent for the entire county. Statistical data included.

17179 ■ *"2010 Book of Lists" in Austin Business JournalInc. (Vol. 29, December 25, 2009, No. 42, pp. 1)*

Pub: American City Business Journals

Description: Rankings of companies and organizations within the business services, finance, healthcare, hospitality and travel, insurance, marketing and media, professional services, real estate, education and technology industries in Austin, Texas are presented. Rankings are based on sales, business size, and other statistics.

17180 ■ *"2010 Book of Lists" in Business Courier (Vol. 26, December 26, 2009, No. 36, pp. 1)*

Pub: American City Business Journals, Inc.

Description: Rankings of companies and organizations within the business services, education, finance, health care, hospitality and tourism, real estate, and technology industries in the Cincinnati, Ohio-Northern Kentucky area are presented. Rankings are based on sales, business size, or other statistics.

17181 ■ *"2010 Book of Lists" in Tampa Bay Business Journal (Vol. 30, December 22, 2009, No. 53, pp. 1)*

Pub: American City Business Journals

Description: Rankings of companies and organizations within the human resources, banking and finance, business services, healthcare, real estate, technology, hospitality and travel, and education industries in the Greater Tampa Bay area are presented. Rankings are based on sales, business size, and more.

17182 ■ *"ABM Janitorial Services Receives Service Excellence Award from Jones Lang LaSalle" in Investment Weekly News (July 16, 2011, pp. 75)*

Pub: NewsRX

Description: ABM Janitorial Services was awarded the 2010 Jones Lang LaSalle Distinction award in the category of Service Excellence. LaSalle is a leading financial and professional services firm that specializes in real estate services and investment management. The program recognizes supplier partners who play a vital role in LaSalle's aim to provide the highest quality of services, value and innovation to clients.

17183 ■ *"Affordable Again" in The Business Journal-Serving Greater Tampa Bay (Vol. 28,*

July 18, 2008, No. 30, pp. 1)

Pub: American City Business Journals, Inc.

Ed: Janet Leiser. **Description:** Rental rates for office space in the Tampa Bay area has dropped to $21.68 a foot, after demand for the second quarter of 2008 has remained low. Commercial real estate experts say that the industry can easily rebound from what is believed to be the weakest demand in 20 years. Other views, information and statistics on real estate demand and prices in Tampa Bay are, are presented.

17184 ■ *"Agricultural Community Implements Green Technologies, Building Team" in Contractor (Vol. 56, September 2009, No. 9, pp. 5)*

Pub: Penton Media, Inc.

Ed: Candace Ruolo. **Description:** John DeWald and Associates has initiated a residential development project which uses green technologies in Illinois. The community features a community center, organic farm and recreational trails. Comments from executives are also provided.

17185 ■ *"AIC To Buy $350M of Real Estate" in Austin Business JournalInc. (Vol. 28, November 14, 2008, No. 35, pp. 1)*

Pub: American City Business Journals

Ed: Kate Harrington. **Description:** Austin-based AIC Ventures LP is planning to buy $350 million worth of commercial real estate. The company's move will double its acquisitions. It is also planning to acquire 30 assets for its eight fun in 2009 from middle-market companies.

17186 ■ *"All About The Benjamins" in Canadian Business (Vol. 81, September 29, 2008, No. 16, pp. 92)*

Pub: Rogers Media Ltd.

Ed: David Baines. **Description:** Discusses real estate developer Royal Indian Raj International Corp., a company that planned to build a $3 billion 'smart city' near the Bangalore airport; to this day nothing has ever been built. The company was incorporated in 1999 by Manoj C. Benjamin one investor, Bill Zack, has been sued by the developer for libel due to his website that calls the company a scam. Benjamin has had a previous case of fraud issued against him as well as a string of liabilities and lawsuits.

17187 ■ *"All Bubbles Must Burst" in Canadian Business (Vol. 83, August 17, 2010, No. 13-14, pp. 12)*

Pub: Rogers Media Ltd.

Ed: Matthew McClearn. **Description:** Canada's housing markets is showing signs of cooling down as home and condo sales both fell for the first time in 16 years. The Canadian government has fueled the market over an extended period through Canada Mortgage and Housing Corporation's role in insuring mortgage lenders against risk of defaults.

17188 ■ *"All-Star Advice 2010" in Black Enterprise (Vol. 41, October 2010, No. 3, pp. 97)*

Pub: Earl G. Graves Publishing Co. Inc.

Ed: Renita Burns, Sheiresa Ngo, Marcia Wade Talbert. **Description:** Financial experts share tips on real estate, investing, taxes, insurance and debt management.

17189 ■ *"Allen Tate Expanding to Research Triangle Park: Firm Expects Raleigh Market to Grow Faster" in Charlotte Observer (January 31, 2007)*

Pub: Knight-Ridder/Tribune Business News

Ed: Doug Smith; Dudley Price. **Description:** Allen Tate Realtors expanded its operations to the Research Triangle area. The firm is predicting a strong market and growth in Charlotte, North Carolina.

17190 ■ *"Another California Firm On Way" in Austin Business Journal (Vol. 31, May 6, 2011, No. 9, pp. 1)*

Pub: American City Business Journals Inc.

Ed: Christopher Calnan. **Description:** Main Street Hub Inc. is planning to build a facility in Austin, Texas. The company helps businesses manage their online reputations. Main Street has selected Aquila Commercial LLC as its real estate broker.

17191 ■ *"Another Man's Pain"* in *Canadian Business* (Vol. 80, October 22, 2007, No. 21, pp. 33)

Pub: Rogers Media

Ed: Andy Holloway. **Description:** U.S. financial collapse can have a positive impact on Canadian investors. Graphs on the total number of home foreclosures in the U.S. from January to August 2007, as well as foreclosure market by type, are presented.

17192 ■ *"Antwerpen Takes on Chrysler Financial Over Foreclosure Sales"* in *Baltimore Business Journal* (Vol. 28, July 30, 2010, No. 12, pp. 1)

Pub: Baltimore Business Journal

Ed: Gary Haber. **Description:** Antwerpen Motorcars Ltd. aims to fight the scheduled foreclosure sale of real estate it leases in Baltimore County, including the showroom for its Hyundai dealership on Baltimore National Pike in Catonsville, Maryland. The company is planning to file papers in court to stop the scheduled August 11, 2010 auction sought by Chrysler Financial Services Americas LLC.

17193 ■ *"Apartment Ambitions"* in *The Business Journal-Portland* (Vol. 25, August 8, 2008, No. 22, pp. 1)

Pub: American City Business Journals, Inc.

Ed: Wendy Culverwell. **Description:** Unico Properties LLC's Asa FlatsLofts is one of the first of eight high-end apartment projects planned for Portland which will add a total of 2,130 new units to the Pearl District, South Waterfront, and downtown Portland. These apartments charge costs more than $1,600 or more per month over the average rent.

17194 ■ *"Apartment Market Down, Not Out"* in *Crain's Detroit Business* (Vol. 24, October 6, 2008, No. 40, pp. 9)

Pub: Crain Communications, Inc.

Ed: Daniel Duggan. **Description:** Detroit's apartment market is considered to have some of the strongest fundamentals of any apartment market in the country with relatively low vacancy rates and a relatively low supply of new units compared with demand. Investors continue to show interest in the buildings but the national lending market is making it difficult to invest in the city.

17195 ■ *"Apartment Tower in River North Fetches More Than $90 Million"* in *Crain's Chicago Business* (Vol. 34, October 24, 2011, No. 42, pp. 17)

Pub: Crain Communications Inc.

Ed: Alby Gallun. **Description:** Apartment tower in River North was sold for over $90 million to a Texas pension fund adviser. Details are included.

17196 ■ *"Aquila HQ Hits the Market"* in *The Business Journal-Serving Metropolitan Kansas City* (Vol. 26, July 25, 2008, No. 46, pp. 1)

Pub: American City Business Journals, Inc.

Ed: Rob Roberts. **Description:** Commercial real estate experts believe that Aquila Inc.'s former headquarters will be hard to rent out. The historic value of the building, being Kansas City's first skyscraper, is not expected to add value to the price of the rent. Other views and information on the building, as well as on Aquila, are presented.

17197 ■ *"Are We There Yet?"* in *Business Courier* (Vol. 24, April 4, 2008, No. 52, pp. 1)

Pub: American City Business Journals, Inc.

Ed: Lucy May; Dan Monk. **Description:** Groundbreaking for The Banks project happened in April 2, 2008, however, the future of the development remains uncertain due to some unresolved issues such as financing. Developers Harold A. Dawson Co. and Carter still have to pass final financing documents to Hamilton County and Cincinnati. The issue of financial commitment for the central riverfront project is examined.

17198 ■ *"The Asian Decade"* in *Hawaii Business* (Vol. 53, January 2008, No. 7, pp. 19)

Pub: Hawaii Business Publishing

Ed: Cathy S. Cruz-George. **Description:** Chaney Brooks, a Hawaiian real estate company, has affiliated with commercial real estate network NAI Global.

The NAI partnership will improve Hawaii's international business, particularly its Asian investments. Hawaii's diverse workforce is evaluated, with regards to being an asset for international businesses.

17199 ■ *"Ask Inc."* in *Inc.* (December 2007, pp. 83-84)

Pub: Gruner & Jahr USA Publishing

Ed: Ari Weinzweig. **Description:** Questions regarding knowledge management in the case of a retiring CFO, issues involved in opening a satellite office for a New York realtor, and information for hiring a multicultural workforce are all discussed.

17200 ■ *"Athletes Face Wins and Losses After Pro Sport"* in *The Business Journal - Serving Phoenix and the Valley of the Sun* (Vol. 29, September 19, 2008, No. 3, pp. 1)

Pub: American City Business Journals, Inc.

Ed: Chris Casacchia. **Description:** Professional athletes like hockey star Jeremy Roenick start businesses, while others like Joel Adamson work to boost local communities. Former athletes were found to be particularly interested with real estate businesses. Other views and information on former athletes and their life after sports are presented.

17201 ■ *"Athletes' Performance Building $10 Million Facility In ASU Park"* in *The Business Journal - Serving Phoenix and the Valley of the Sun* (Vol. 28, August 8, 2008, No. 49, pp. 1)

Pub: American City Business Journals, Inc.

Ed: Jan Buchholz. **Description:** Athletes' Performance's planned facility at Arizona State University is scheduled to begin in November 2008 and expected to be completed by September 2009. The new building will almost double the company's training space as it will expand from around 19,000 square feet to 35,000 square feet.

17202 ■ *"Austin Homes are Overpriced, Study Says"* in *Austin Business JournalInc.* (Vol. 29, January 1, 2010, No. 43, pp. 1)

Pub: American City Business Journals

Ed: Kate Harrington. **Description:** Study by Forbes.com shows that Austin-Round Rock metropolitan statistical area ranked 10th on the list of cities with the most over-priced homes. For instance, the average price for a single-family home pegged at $188,000.

17203 ■ *"Bangles, BMWs Elbow Out Delis and Discount Shops"* in *Crain's New York Business* (Vol. 24, January 14, 2008, No. 2, pp. 35)

Pub: Crain Communications, Inc.

Ed: Wendy Davis. **Description:** Lured by a growing number of affluent residents and high-earning professionals, a number of upscale retailers have opened locations downtown which is driving up rents and forcing out longtime independent merchants.

17204 ■ *"Bankruptcies Shoot Up 68 Percent"* in *Sacramento Business Journal* (Vol. 25, July 18, 2008, No. 20, pp. 1)

Pub: American City Business Journals, Inc.

Ed: Kathy Robertson. **Description:** Personal bankruptcy in the Sacramento area rose by 88 percent for the first half of 2008 while business bankruptcies rose by 50 percent for the same period. The numbers of consumer bankruptcy reflects the effect of high debt, rising mortgage costs, and declining home values on U.S. households.

17205 ■ *"Before Signing a Lease"* in *Business Owner* (Vol. 35, September-October 2011, No. 5, pp. 14)

Pub: DL Perkins Company

Description: The following terms are essential to investigate before renewing or negotiating a lease for a small business: Term, Neighbors, Actual Usable Space, Gross or Net, Tenant Improvements, Renewal Option, Purchase Option, Cancelation Option, Sublease or Assignment, Security Deposit, Code Restrictions and Zoning, Parking, Relief and Lease Agreement.

17206 ■ *"Best Income Trust"* in *Canadian Business* (Vol. 81, Summer 2008, No. 9, pp. 69)

Pub: Rogers Media Ltd.

Ed: Calvin Leung. **Description:** Table showing five-year annualized growth rate and one-year stock performance of real estate investment trusts firms in Canada is presented. Calgary-based Boardwalk REIT is projected to grow the fastest among North American REITs over the next two years. Other details on the stock performance analysis are presented.

17207 ■ *"Bigger TIF Makes Development Inroads"* in *The Business Journal-Serving Metropolitan Kansas City* (Vol. 26, July 11, 2008, No. 44)

Pub: American City Business Journals, Inc.

Ed: Rob Roberts. **Description:** On July 9, 2008 the Tax Increment Financing Commission voted to expand a TIF district to Tiffany Springs Road. The plan for the TIF district close to Kansas City International Airport is to include a-half mile of the road. The impacts of the expansion on construction projects and on the road network are analyzed.

17208 ■ *"Biggest UM Landlords"* in *Crain's Detroit Business* (Vol. 25, June 15, 2009, No. 24, pp. 1)

Pub: Crain Communications Inc. - Detroit

Description: University of Michigan will purchase the two million-square-foot Pfizer campus in June 2009. The university is the largest occupier of commercial real estate off campus in and around Ann Arbor, Michigan.

17209 ■ *"Bill Kaneko"* in *Hawaii Business* (Vol. 53, December 2007, No. 6, pp. 32)

Pub: Hawaii Business Publishing

Ed: David K. Choo. **Description:** Hawaii Institute for Public Affairs chief executive officer and president Bill Kaneko believes that the Hawaiian economy is booming, however, he also asserts that the economy is too focused on tourism and real estate. Kaneko has also realized the that the will of the people is strong while he was helping with the Hawaiian 2050 Sustainability Plan. The difficulties of making a sustainable Hawaii are discussed.

17210 ■ *"Bills Would Regulate Mortgage Loan Officers"* in *Crain's Detroit Business* (Vol. 24, February 25, 2008, No. 8, pp. 9)

Pub: Crain Communications Inc. - Detroit

Ed: Amy Lane. **Description:** New legislation in Michigan, if passed, would create a registration process for mortgage loan officers in the state in order to address the mortgage loan crisis.

17211 ■ *"Block Plans Office Park Along K-10 Corridor"* in *The Business Journal-Serving Metropolitan Kansas City* (Vol. 27, October 3, 2008)

Pub: American City Business Journals, Inc.

Ed: Rob Roberts. **Description:** Kansas City, Missouri-based Block and Co. is planning to build four office buildings at the corner of College Boulevard and Ridgeview Road in Olathe. Features of the planned development are provided. Comments from executives are also presented.

17212 ■ *"Block Pulls Plug On Riverside Deal"* in *The Business Journal-Serving Metropolitan Kansas City* (Vol. 27, October 10, 2008, No. 4)

Pub: American City Business Journals, Inc.

Ed: Rob Roberts. **Description:** Real estate developer Ken Block has backed out from a $300 million Riverside industrial project. Block says he has already invested $1 million of his own money into the deal. Details regarding the project are given.

17213 ■ *"Bond OK Could Bring Back the Housing Battle?"* in *Charlotte Business Journal* (Vol. 25, November 5, 2010, No. 33, pp. 1)

Pub: Charlotte Business Journal

Ed: Susan Stabley. **Description:** The approval of the $15 million housing bond in Charlotte, North Carolina could bring back the debates on housing in the region. Protesters have opposed affordable housing developments that were proposed in the area since

2008. Other information on the recently approved housing bond and on other real estate issues in North Carolina is presented.

17214 ■ *"Book of Lists 2010"* in *Philadelphia Business Journal (Vol. 28, December 25, 2009, No. 45, pp. 1)*
Pub: American City Business Journals

Description: Rankings of companies and organizations within the banking, biotechnology, economic development, healthcare, hospitality, law and accounting, marketing and media, real estate, and technology industries in the Philadelphia, Pennsylvania area are presented. Rankings are based on sales, business size, and more.

17215 ■ *"Boston Hedge Fund Pours Money Into Real Estate Projects"* in *Charlotte Business Journal (Vol. 25, December 3, 2010, No. 37, pp. 1)*
Pub: Charlotte Business Journal

Ed: Will Boye. **Description:** Boston-based hedge fund Baupost Group has been financing real estate project in Charlotte, North Carolina including more than 80 acres just north of uptown. Aside from purchasing the $23.8 million note for the Rosewood Condominiums from Regions Financial Corporation, the Baupost Group is also negotiating with Regions to buy the $93.9 million debt of the EipCentre real estate project.

17216 ■ *"Bottom's Up"* in *Barron's (Vol. 88, July 14, 2008, No. 28, pp. 25)*
Pub: Dow Jones & Co., Inc.

Ed: Jonathan R. Laing. **Description:** Economist Chip Case believes that home prices are nearing a bottom based on his analysis of the history of the housing market; surprisingly, in the past the housing market has rebounded after a quarter from a massive housing start drop. The drop in early stage delinquencies is another sign of the housing market's recovery.

17217 ■ *"Briarcliff Office Building Fills Up Fast"* in *The Business Journal-Serving Metropolitan Kansas City (Vol. 26, Sept. 5, 2008, pp. 1)*
Pub: American City Business Journals, Inc.

Ed: Rob Roberts. **Description:** Prior to its opening the Hilltop Office Building in Kansas City Missouri has attained 80 percent occupancy. FCStone Group Inc.'s plan to move to the building has boosted the facility's occupancy. Description and dimensions of the office building are also provided.

17218 ■ *"A Bright Spot: Industrial Space in Demand Again"* in *Sacramento Business Journal (Vol. 28, October 21, 2011, No. 34, pp. 1)*
Pub: Sacramento Business Journal

Ed: Michael Shaw. **Description:** Sacramento, California's industrial sites have been eyed by potential tenants who are actively seeking space larger than 50,000 square feet.

17219 ■ *"Brokerages Seek a Foothold in Local Real Estate Market"* in *Charlotte Business Journal (Vol. 25, October 15, 2010, No. 30, pp. 1)*
Pub: Charlotte Business Journal

Ed: Will Boye. **Description:** Charlotte, North Carolina has become an attractive destination for out-of-town brokerage firms. Colliers International has signed an affiliate deal with Anthony and Company to set up shop in Charlotte. Grubb and Ellis Company, on the other hand, is planning to open an office in the city.

17220 ■ *"Builder's Bankruptcy Fans Fears"* in *Crain's Cleveland Business (Vol. 28, October 22, 2007, No. 42, pp. 1)*
Pub: Crain Communications, Inc.

Ed: Stan Bullard. **Description:** Whitlatch & Co., Northeast Ohio's largest builder by unit volume in the early 1990s, has filed for Chapter 11 bankruptcy. This is causing builders and others in the real estate industry to wonder how long and severe the housing slump will be and which companies will survive.

17221 ■ *"Building Portfolios for a World of 2.5 Percent Gains"* in *Barron's (Vol. 88, July 7, 2008, No. 27, pp. L9)*
Pub: Dow Jones & Co., Inc.

Ed: Karen Hube. **Description:** Interview with Harold Evenski whom is a financial planner running a fee-only planning practice; he continues to caution investors against pursuing short-term gains and focusing on long-term trends. He advises investors against investing in commodity and real estate stocks and is concerned about the possible effects of high inflation.

17222 ■ *"Burritos New Bag for Shopping Developer"* in *Houston Business Journal (Vol. 40, December 4, 2009, No. 30, pp. 4A)*
Pub: American City Business Journals

Ed: Allison Wollam. **Description:** Houston, Texas-based Rob Johnson is the newest franchisee for Bullritos and plans to open eight area locations to market the quick-casual burrito concept. The former shopping center developer was looking for a new business sector after selling off his shopping center holdings.

17223 ■ *"Business Owners Lien Trinity Project"* in *The Business Journal-Serving Greater Tampa Bay (Vol. 28, July 25, 2008, No. 31, pp. 1)*
Pub: American City Business Journals, Inc.

Ed: Janet Leiser. **Description:** The Internal Revenue Service is trying to collect $2.9 million from the developer of the Trinity Town Center, William Plaines, due to the delays in the project. This is in addition to a $5.2 million lien by the project's subcontractors.

17224 ■ *"Buy Now?"* in *Hawaii Business (Vol. 53, March 2008, No. 9, pp. 32)*
Pub: Hawaii Business Publishing

Ed: David K. Choo. **Description:** Discusses the Honolulu Board of REALTORS which said that the last two months of 2007 saw double-digit housing sales drop, with December figures showing 30.6 percent and 22.9 percent decline in sales of single-family homes and condominiums, respectively. Forecasts on Hawaii's real estate market for 2008 are discussed.

17225 ■ *"Buyers' Market"* in *Baltimore Business Journal (Vol. 27, November 20, 2009, No. 28, pp. 1)*
Pub: American City Business Journals

Ed: Daniel J. Sernovitz. **Description:** Some business owners in Maryland are removing their leases and purchasing buildings due to the lower costs of real estate. This trend has enabled small business owners to avoid rent hikes, while setting equity into their companies. The pros and cons of owning buildings and how business owners assess their return on investment are examined.

17226 ■ *"Cal-ISO Plans $125 Million Facility"* in *Sacramento Business Journal (Vol. 25, August 1, 2008, No. 22, pp. 1)*
Pub: American City Business Journals, Inc.

Ed: Celia Lamb; Michael Shaw. **Description:** Sacramento, California-based nonprofit organization California Independent System Operator (ISO) is planning to build a new headquarters in Folsom. The new building would double its current leased space to 227,000 square feet. The ISO will seek tax-exempt bond financing for the project.

17227 ■ *"Calendar"* in *Crain's Detroit Business (Vol. 24, October 6, 2008, No. 40, pp. 22)*
Pub: Crain Communications, Inc.

Description: Listing of events in the Detroit area include conferences addressing entrepreneurialism, economic development, manufacturing, marketing, the housing crisis and women business ownership.

17228 ■ *"Can Avenue be Fashionable Again? Livernois Merchants, City Want Revival"* in *Crain's Detroit Business (March 10, 2008)*
Pub: Crain Communications, Inc.

Ed: Nancy Kaffer. **Description:** Once a busy retail district, the Avenue of Fashion, a Livernois Avenue strip between Six Mile and Eight Mile roads, is facing a community business effort being backed by city support whose aim is to restore the area to its former glory.

17229 ■ *"Canadian Vehicle Sales Accelerate in April, but U.S. Goes on Bumpy Ride"* in *Globe & Mail (May 2, 2007, pp. B7)*
Pub: CTVglobemedia Publishing Inc.

Ed: Greg Keenan. **Description:** The increase in Canadian vehicle sales to 169,280 in April 2007, but decline in their sales in the United States due to slump in housing sector are discussed.

17230 ■ *"Casino Minority Spend: $80 Million"* in *Business Courier (Vol. 27, August 20, 2010, No. 16, pp. 1)*
Pub: Business Courier

Ed: Lucy May. **Description:** Real estate developers are planning to invest $80 million to build the Harrah's casino project in Cincinnati, Ohio. Rock Ventures LLC is seeking a 20 percent inclusion rate in the project.

17231 ■ *"Cedar Fair to Solicit Bids for Geauga Lake"* in *Crain's Cleveland Business (Vol. 28, October 8, 2007, No. 40, pp. 1)*
Pub: Crain Communications, Inc.

Ed: Stan Bullard. **Description:** Cedar Fair Entertainment Co. plans to seek sealed bids for the redevelopment of nearly 540 acres of their amusement park site in southwest Geauga County and northwest Portage County.

17232 ■ *"Centerpoint Funding In Limbo"* in *The Business Journal - Serving Phoenix and the Valley of the Sun (Vol. 28, August 1, 2008, No. 48)*
Pub: American City Business Journals, Inc.

Ed: Jan Buchholz. **Description:** Avenue Communities LLC has threatened to file a case against Mortgages Ltd. over the finance of the Centerpoint development project in Tempe, Arizona. Avenue Communities want Mortgages Ltd. to file a motion with the U.S. Bankruptcy Court so that it can secure financing for the project. Other views and information on the finance of Centerpoint, are presented.

17233 ■ *"Channelside On the Blocks"* in *The Business Journal-Serving Greater Tampa Bay (Vol. 28, August 29, 2008, No. 36, pp. 1)*
Pub: American City Business Journals, Inc.

Ed: Michael Hinman. **Description:** In a bankruptcy auction for The Place, one of the more visible condominium projects at Channelside, the lowest bid is just below $73 a square foot. KeyBank National Association, the Key Developers Group LLC's lender, leads the auction planned for October 15, 2008. The reason behind the low minimum bid required to participate in the said action is discussed.

17234 ■ *"Children's Hospital to Build in New Berlin"* in *The Business Journal-Milwaukee (Vol. 25, August 1, 2008, No. 45, pp. A1)*
Pub: American City Business Journals, Inc.

Ed: Corrinne Hess. **Description:** Children's Hospital of Wisconsin plans a clinic in the 35-acre medical office park in New Berlin, Wisconsin, owned by Froedtert Memorial Lutheran Hospital and Medical College of Wisconsin Real Estate Ventures LLC. The hospital will be the first major tenant in the park, to be built by Irgens Development Partners LLC.

17235 ■ *"City Sets Yamhill Makeover"* in *The Business Journal-Portland (Vol. 25, July 4, 2008, No. 17, pp. 1)*
Pub: American City Business Journals, Inc.

Ed: Andy Giegerich. **Description:** City government is scheduled to redevelop Peterson's property on Yamhill Street in Portland. The redevelopment is seen as a way to better developing commercial properties in the area. Problems associated with the project, which include cost and developer selection, are also discussed.

17236 ■ *"CityLink Project On Hold"* in *Business Courier (Vol. 24, November 9, 2008, No. 30, pp. 3)*
Pub: American City Business Journals, Inc.

Ed: Dan Monk. **Description:** Developers of the CityLink project have indicated that it will be at least a year before they start the planned social services mall at 800 Bank West End. According to Tim Senff, Citylink CEO, the company wants to build bridges before constructing the buildings. The project's critics are still considering whether to appeal a court ruling regarding the facility's compliance with the city's zoning code.

17237 ■ *"Clock Ticking for Hotel Berry"* in *Sacramento Business Journal (Vol. 25, July 25, 2008, No. 21, pp. 1)*
Pub: American City Business Journals, Inc.
Ed: Michael Shaw. **Description:** Federal tax credits worth $13.6 million have been awarded to boost the renovation project for the aging Hotel Berry in downtown Sacramento, California. The owners of the hotel have five months before the expiration of the tax credits to raise the remaining funding for the $20 million renovation.

17238 ■ *"Coherent Laying Off 144 As It Prepares To Shut Auburn Plant"* in *Sacramento Business Journal (Vol. 25, August 1, 2008, No. 22, pp. 1)*
Pub: American City Business Journals, Inc.
Ed: Melanie Turner. **Description:** Sacramento, California-based Coherent Inc. is planning to lay off 144 workers at its Auburn facility. Coherent has been cutting payroll and its real estate holdings. Statistics on the company's earnings are also provided.

17239 ■ *"Colliers Shifts Its Brokerage Home"* in *Charlotte Business Journal (Vol. 25, November 5, 2010, No. 33, pp. 1)*
Pub: Charlotte Business Journal
Ed: Will Boye. **Description:** Colliers International signed a long-term affiliate agreement with commercial real estate firm Clarus Properties, in a move that would allow Colliers to resume business in Charlotte, North Carolina. Colliers also hired well known brokers Brad Grow and Brent Royall.

17240 ■ *"Columbia Sale Narrowed To Two Developers"* in *The Business Journal-Milwaukee (Vol. 25, July 18, 2008, No. 43, pp. A1)*
Pub: American City Business Journals, Inc.
Ed: Corrinne Hess. **Description:** Officials of Columbia St. Mary's Inc plan to pick one of two real-estate developers who will buy the 8-acre property of the Columbia Hospital which the company will move away from when their new hospital has been constructed. The hospital on Newport Ave. has been on the market since 2001.

17241 ■ *"Columbia's JPB Raising $175M to Acquire Companies, Real Estate"* in *Boston Business Journal (Vol. 29, May 27, 2011, No. 3, pp. 1)*
Pub: American City Business Journals Inc.
Ed: Gary Haber. **Description:** JPB Enterprises is preparing to raise $175 million in its goal of acquiring companies and real estate that are major names in America. The $75 million will be raised for a buyout fund that will target wide range of industries while the $100 million will be used for land investment projects in the Florida Panhandle. Baltimore firms are expected to benefit from this deal.

17242 ■ *"Commercial Builders Take It on the Chin"* in *Crain's Chicago Business (Vol. 31, April 28, 2008, No. 17, pp. 16)*
Pub: Crain Communications, Inc.
Ed: Alby Gallun. **Description:** Although the health care development sector has seen growth, the rest of Chicago's local commercial building industry has seen steep declines in the first quarter of this year. According to McGraw-Hill Construction, Chicago-area non-residential construction starts totaled $731 million in the quarter, a 60 percent drop from the year-earlier period. Volume in the retail, office and hotel markets fell by nearly 70 percent.

17243 ■ *"Con-Way Project Back in High Gear"* in *Business Journal Portland (Vol. 27, November 5, 2010, No. 36, pp. 1)*
Pub: Portland Business Journal
Ed: Wendy Culverwell. **Description:** Trucking firm Con-Way Inc. intends to sell parcels of land from a property comprising 16 blocks and 20 prime acres west of the Pearl District in Portland, Oregon. In 2009, Con-Way abandoned plans to sell the property.

As Con-Way reclaims control over design and usage of the property, it also expressed willingness to cooperate with a master developer on a related real estate project.

17244 ■ *"Condo Markdown"* in *Boston Business Journal (Vol. 27, November 30, 2007, No. 44, pp. 1)*
Pub: American City Business Journals Inc.
Ed: Michelle Hillman. **Description:** Boston real estate market is softening, and condominium developers such as Beacon Communities LLC are sending out various incentives like markdowns and unit upgrades. Developers have also held auctions and even offered brand new cars to lure buyers. Other perks being offered by various Boston developers are discussed.

17245 ■ *"Condominium Sales Fall to a Seven-Year Low"* in *Crain's Chicago Business (Vol. 31, November 10, 2008, No. 45, pp. 2)*
Pub: Crain Communications, Inc.
Ed: Alby Gallun. **Description:** Downtown Chicago condominium market is experiencing the lowest number of sales in years due to the tightening of the mortgage lending market, the Wall Street crisis and the downturn in the economy. The supply of new condos is soaring, the result of the building boom of 2005 and 2006; many developers are finding it difficult to pay off construction loans and fear foreclosure on their properties. Additional information and statistical data related to the downtown condominium market is provided.

17246 ■ *"Contingent Offers: Weighing the Risk"* in *Crain's Chicago Business (Vol. 31, April 21, 2008, No. 16, pp. 48)*
Pub: Crain Communications, Inc.
Ed: Darci Smith. **Description:** Interview with Greer Haseman, the broker-owner of Town Square Associates, who discusses contingent offers in a challenging housing market.

17247 ■ *"A Conversation with; Renea Butler, Real Estate One Inc."* in *Crain's Detroit Business (Vol. 25, June 8, 2009, No. 23, pp. 12)*
Pub: Crain Communications Inc. - Detroit
Ed: Ryan Beene. **Description:** Renea Butler, vice president of administration and human resources for Real Estate One Inc. in Southfield as well as vice president for public relations for the Human Resource Association of Greater Detroit, talks about how the economy has affected human resource services.

17248 ■ *"A Conversation With; Ron Gatner, Jones Lang LaSalle"* in *Crain's Detroit Business (Vol. 24, October 6, 2008, No. 40, pp. 9)*
Pub: Crain Communications, Inc.
Description: Interview with Ron Gatner who is a corporate real estate adviser with the real estate company Jones Lang LaSalle as well as the company's executive vice president and part of the tenant advisory team; Gatner speaks about the impact that the Wall Street crisis is having on the commercial real estate market in Detroit.

17249 ■ *"Cool on Chicago Office Properties"* in *Crain's Chicago Business (Vol. 31, March 31, 2008, No. 13, pp. 16)*
Pub: Crain Communications, Inc.
Ed: Eddie Baeb. **Description:** Investors predict values on Chicago office buildings to drop 1.3 percent over the next year.

17250 ■ *"Cornered by Credit; As $1 Billion in Loans Come Due, Will Landlords Find Funds?"* in *Crain's Detroit Business (October 6, 2008)*
Pub: Crain Communications, Inc.
Ed: Daniel Duggan. **Description:** Conduit loans are used by many real estate investors and are normally issued in 7- to 10-year terms with balloon payments due at the end, requiring the full balance to be paid upon maturity. Many building owners may find their properties going into foreclosure as these loans mature next year since these loans cannot be extended like typical loans and the credit crisis along

with falling property values is making it more difficult to secure new sources of funding. Possible solutions to this problem are also explored.

17251 ■ *"Corporate Elite Show Resilience"* in *The Business Journal-Serving Greater Tampa Bay (Vol. 28, August 1, 2008, No. 32, pp. 1)*
Pub: American City Business Journals, Inc.
Ed: Margie Manning; Alexis Muellner. **Description:** Stocks of the largest public companies in Tampa Bay, Florida, outperformed the S&P 500 index by 28 percent in the first half of 2008. The escalation is attributed to the growth orientation of the companies in the area and the lack of exposure to the real estate and financial services sectors.

17252 ■ *"Corus Eases Off Ailing Condo Market; Office Developers Get Majority of 1Q Loans"* in *Crain's Chicago Business (April 28, 2008)*
Pub: Crain Communications, Inc.
Ed: H. Lee Murphy. **Description:** Corus Bankshares Inc., a specialist in lending for the condominium high-rise construction market, is diversifying its portfolio by making loans to office developers and expects to be investing in hotels through the rest of the year. Corus' $7.57 billion loan portfolio is also discussed in detail as well as the company's earnings and share price. Statistical data included.

17253 ■ *"Councilman May Revive Labor Bill"* in *Baltimore Business Journal (Vol. 28, August 13, 2010, No. 14, pp. 1)*
Pub: Baltimore Business Journal
Ed: Daniel J. Sernovitz. **Description:** Baltimore, Maryland Councilman Bill Henry has started reviving controversial legislation that would force developers and contractors to give preference to union labor. The legislation requires contractors to give preference to city workers in order to lower Baltimore's unemployment rate.

17254 ■ *"Creativity is Essential in Sagging Relocation Market"* in *Crain's Cleveland Business (Vol. 28, November 5, 2007, No. 44, pp. 19)*
Pub: Crain Communications, Inc.
Ed: Christine Gordillo. **Description:** Since Northeast Ohio was headquarters to a number of Fortune 500 companies, residential real estate builders and brokers could count on corporate relocation clients for a steady stream of business. Today, corporations have become more cautious when relocating talent due to the costs involved which has forced industry experts to be more patient and more creative in the ways they attract out-of-town buyers who are likely to be a sure sell.

17255 ■ *"The Debt Mountain in Mid-Collapse"* in *Canadian Business (Vol. 83, October 12, 2010, No. 17, pp. 28)*
Pub: Rogers Media Ltd.
Ed: Michael McCullough. **Description:** A growing real estate market has made Intrawest ULC's Whistler-Blackcomb resort a model for a booming industry for years. However, resorts are now required to manage themselves better because of the recession. Some mountains are also trimming the cost of labor and cutting peripheral services.

17256 ■ *"Delinquent Properties on the Rise"* in *Business Courier (Vol. 27, June 11, 2010, No. 6, pp. 1)*
Pub: Business Courier
Ed: Dan Monk. **Description:** Reports show that Cincinnati now ranks in the U.S. Top 20 for its delinquency rate on securitized commercial real estate loans. In December 2009, the region ranked 28th out of 50 cities studied by Trepp LLC. As of May 30, 2010, more than $378 million in commercial mortgage-backed security loans were more than 60 days past due.

17257 ■ *"Detroit Residential Market Slows; Bright Spots Emerge"* in *Crain's Detroit Business (Vol. 24, October 6, 2008, No. 40, pp. 11)*
Pub: Crain Communications, Inc.
Ed: Daniel Duggan. **Description:** Discusses the state of the residential real estate market in Detroit; although condominium projects receive the most at-

tention, deals for single-family homes are taking place in greater numbers due to financing issues. Buyers can purchase a single family home with a 3.5 percent down payment compared to 20 percent for some condo deals because of the number of first-time homebuyer programs under the Federal Housing Administration.

17258 ■ "Developer Backs Out of Major Bastrop Project" in Austin Business JournalInc. (Vol. 28, December 19, 2008, No. 40, pp. 1)

Pub: American City Business Journals

Ed: Kate Harrington. **Description:** Weingarten Realty Investors, a Houston, Texas-based real estate company, has backed out of its contract on more than 1 million square feet of retail space at the County Road 304 and State Highway 71 corner in Bastrop, Texas, according to landowner Tom Brundage. Analysts say that the Bastrop area is not ready for big retail projects.

17259 ■ "Developer Banks On East Submarket, Slowdown Not a Hinderance" in The Business Journal-Serving Greater Tampa Bay (August 1, 2008)

Pub: American City Business Journals, Inc.

Ed: Janet Leiser. **Description:** CLW Industrial Group and Cobalt Industrial REIT II have teamed up to develop a 14-acre area in northeast Hillsborough County, Florida. The $15 million industrial park project includes the 175,000-square-foot New Tampa Commerce Center, scheduled for completion in the first quarter of 2009.

17260 ■ "Developer Tries to Bring Homes to Buda" in Austin Business JournalInc. (Vol. 28, December 26, 2008, No. 41, pp. 1)

Pub: American City Business Journals

Ed: Kate Harrington. **Description:** Real estate developer Jeremiah Venture LP is planning a residential, single-family development on about 600 acres near Buda, Texas. The company also plans to construct a membrane waste treatment plant, and has applied to do land application. However, several groups have come forward to ask for more information on the application due to concerns about soil density.

17261 ■ "Developer Wins Bout with Bank in Roundabout Way" in Tampa Bay Business Journal (Vol. 30, January 29, 2010, No. 6, pp. 1)

Pub: American City Business Journals

Ed: Janet Leiser. **Description:** Developer Donald E. Phillips of Phillips Development and Realty LLC won against the foreclosure filed by First Horizon National Corporation, which is demanding the company to fully pay its $2.9 million loan. Phillips requested that his company pay monthly mortgage and extend the loan's maturity date.

17262 ■ "Developers Await Hotel" in The Business Journal-Portland (Vol. 25, July 11, 2008, No. 18, pp. 1)

Pub: American City Business Journals, Inc.

Ed: Wendy Culverwell. **Description:** Developers are eager to start the construction of a new hotel at the Oregon Convention Center in Portland, Oregon as hey say that the project will help boost the convention center neighborhood. The project, called The Westin Portland at the Convention Center, is partly handled by Ashforth Pacific Inc.

17263 ■ "Developers Compete for APG Project" in Baltimore Business Journal (Vol. 27, October 16, 2009, No. 23, pp. 1)

Pub: American City Business Journals

Ed: Daniel J. Sernovitz. **Description:** Corporate Office Properties Trust has lost the case in Delaware bankruptcy court to prevent rival St. John Properties Inc. from going ahead with its plans to develop the 400 acres at Aberdeen Proving Ground (APG) in Maryland. Both developers have competed for the right to develop the two million square foot business park in APG.

17264 ■ "Developers Give Big to Mayor's Bid" in Boston Business Journal (Vol. 29, August 26, 2011, No. 16, pp. 1)

Pub: American City Business Journals Inc.

Ed: Scott Dance. **Description:** Mayor Stephanie Rawlings-Blake received thousands of dollars in her political campaign from companies of real estate developers who are vying to build key development projects in Baltimore, Maryland. Rawlings-Blake created a major fundraising advantage over other mayoral candidates with the help of those contributions.

17265 ■ "Developers Give City Dwellings a Modern Spin" in Crain's Cleveland Business (Vol. 28, November 5, 2007, No. 44, pp. 18)

Pub: Crain Communications, Inc.

Description: Cleveland is increasingly becoming a canvas for fresh, cutting-edge design due to several recent projects, some at prominent sites.

17266 ■ "Developers Poised to Pull Trigers" in Boston Business Journal (Vol. 30, November 12, 2010, No. 42, pp. 1)

Pub: Boston Business Journal

Ed: Craig M. Douglas. **Description:** Large residential projects are expected to break ground in Boston, Massachusetts in 2011, as real estate developers expect growth for the industry. Real estate experts expect more than 2,000 rental units to be available by 2011. Information on key real estate projects in Boston is presented.

17267 ■ "Developers Vie for UWM Dorm" in The Business Journal-Milwaukee (Vol. 25, July 11, 2008, No. 42, pp. A1)

Pub: American City Business Journals, Inc.

Ed: Rich Kirchen. **Description:** Eight developers are competing to build a 500- to 700-student residence hall for the University of Wisconsin-Milwaukee. The residence hall will probably be developed within two miles of the main campus. It was revealed that the university's real estate foundation will select the successful bidder on July 25, 2008, and construction will begin by January 2009.

17268 ■ Dictionary of Real Estate Terms

Pub: Barron's Educational Series Inc.

Contact: Alex Holtz, President

E-mail: aholtz@berronseduc.com

Ed: Jack P. Friedman, Jack C. Harris, J. Bruce Lindeman. **Released:** October 2008. **Price:** $13.99. **Description:** More than 2,500 real estate terms relating to mortgages and financing, brokerage law, architecture, rentals and leases, property insurance, and more.

17269 ■ "Docs Might Hold Cure for Real Estate, Banks" in Baltimore Business Journal (Vol. 28, November 5, 2010, No. 26, pp. 1)

Pub: Baltimore Business Journal

Ed: Gary Haber. **Description:** Health care providers, including physicians are purchasing their office space instead of renting it as banks lower interest rates to 6 percent on mortgages for medical offices. The rise in demand offers relief to the commercial real estate market. It has also resulted in a boom in building new medical offices.

17270 ■ "Downtown Evens Tenant Ledger" in The Business Journal-Serving Metropolitan Kansas City (Vol. 26, July 11, 2008, No. 44, pp. 1)

Pub: American City Business Journals, Inc.

Ed: Rob Roberts. **Description:** Financial services company PricewaterhouseCoopers will relocate its office from the Broadway Square building, but it will not leave downtown as it signs a long-term lease for a 27,000 square feet of space in Town Pavilion. Town Pavilion is the biggest multitenant office building in downtown. Downtown's market competitiveness is also examined.

17271 ■ "Downtown Retail Site Sold to ATCO" in Austin Business JournalInc. (Vol. 29, November 20, 2009, No. 37, pp. 1)

Pub: American City Business Journals

Ed: Kate Harrington. **Description:** New York-based real estate company ATCO Advisory Services purchased a 13,700 square foot retail space in Austin,

Texas from 360 Condominiums. The selection of the retail space, named the Shops at 360 has been attributed to the local tenant mix and its location in downtown Austin. Meanwhile, ATCO may continue investing in the area in the near future.

17272 ■ "Drawn to York County: Less-Expensive Homes, Good Schools Attract Charlotteans" in Charlotte Observer (February 4, 2007)

Pub: Knight-Ridder/Tribune Business News

Ed: Taylor Bright. **Description:** York County, North Carolina offers low-priced homes and good schools, making it attractive to workers and small business.

17273 ■ "East-Side Real Estate Forum Detours To Grand Rapids" in Crain's Detroit Business (Vol. 24, October 6, 2008, No. 40, pp. 17)

Pub: Crain Communications, Inc.

Ed: Daniel Duggan. **Description:** Tom Wackerman was elected chairman of the University of Michigan-Urban Land Institute Real Estate Forum and proposed that the annual conference be held in Grand Rapids due to the brisk economic activity he was finding there; although the idea was initially met with resistance, the plan to introduce East-siders to the West side began receiving more enthusiasm due to the revitalization of the area, which was once considered to have a bleak outlook. Many are hoping to learn the lessons of those who were able to change a negative economic climate into a positive one in which the cooperation of private business and government can work together to accomplish goals.

17274 ■ "Economy Hammers Local Builders" in Business Courier (Vol. 24, February 8, 2008, No. 44, pp. 1)

Pub: American City Business Journals, Inc.

Ed: Laura Baverman. **Description:** Home builders in Cincinnati, Ohio, have lower revenue and smaller workforces as a result of the housing crisis and economic slowdown. Only four out of the top 25 home builders registered revenue gains, average revenue for 2007 is down 21 percent from 2006 levels, and employment declined by 37 percent from 2006.

17275 ■ "Economy Peddles Rent In This Cycle" in The Business Journal-Serving Metropolitan Kansas City (Vol. 26, August 8, 2008, No. 48)

Pub: American City Business Journals, Inc.

Ed: Ashlee Kieler. **Description:** Rental demand for apartment units in downtown Kansas City, Missouri, is increasing due to the housing crisis, lack of real estate development, and increasing popularity of the downtown area. The downtown area has 7,378 multifamily units as of June 2008, of which 4,114 are rentals.

17276 ■ "Elevated Status" in Business Courier (Vol. 24, March 21, 2008, No. 50, pp. 1)

Pub: American City Business Journals, Inc.

Ed: James Ritchie. **Description:** Overview of Tri-Health Inc.'s growth is presented. Currently, the company's revenue is estimated to be around $1 billion. Since 2004, the company was able to build patient towers, an outpatient facility in Lebanon, and was able to acquire the Group Health Associates physician practice. TriHealth recently hired 500 nurses in order to meet its needs.

17277 ■ "Embassy Suites Signs On: Dulski Building Developer Lands Anchor Tenant" in Business First Buffalo (October 26, 2007, pp. 1)

Pub: American City Business Journals, Inc.

Ed: James Fink. **Description:** Embassy Suites will open a 150-room hotel at the former Dulski Federal Office Building in Buffalo, New York. Bringing in Embassy Suite to the building is hoped to increase the interest of tenants at the building which is being renovated by Uniland Development Company and Acquest Development Company.

17278 ■ "Eminent Domain Fight Looks Imminent" in The Business Journal-Serving Metropolitan Kansas City (Vol. 26, August 1,

2008, No. 47)
Pub: American City Business Journals, Inc.
Ed: Rob Roberts. **Description:** Views and information on the proposed constitutional amendments that will limit the use of eminent domain in Missouri, are presented. The proposals are expected to largely ban the taking of private property for private development. It may be included in a November 4,2008 statewide vote for approval.

17279 ■ *"Empty Office Blues" in Business Journal Portland (Vol. 26, December 4, 2009, No. 39, pp. 1)*
Pub: American City Business Journals Inc.
Ed: Wendy Culverwell. **Description:** Portland's office vacancy rates could reach almost 15 percent by the end of 2010 due to job reductions and mergers.

17280 ■ *"Everett Dowling" in Hawaii Business (Vol. 54, August 2008, No. 2, pp. 32)*
Pub: Hawaii Business Publishing
Ed: Jason Ubay. **Description:** Real estate developer Everett Dowling, president of Dowling Company Inc., talks about the company's sustainable management and services. The company's office has been retrofitted to earn a Leadership in Energy and Environmental Design (LEED) certification. Dowling believes that real estate development can be part of the sustainable solution.

17281 ■ *"Everyone Out of the Pool" in Barron's (Vol. 89, July 20, 2009, No. 29, pp. 18)*
Pub: Dow Jones & Co., Inc.
Ed: Sandra Ward. **Description:** Shares of Pool Corp. could drop as continued weakness in the housing market weakens the market for swimming pool equipment. The company's shares are trading at $18.29, about 20 times projected 2009 earnings of $0.91 a share.

17282 ■ *Everything You Need to Know to Sell By Owner*
Pub: FSBO Publishing
Ed: Karen Varnas; Roy Wysack. **Released:** February 2007. **Price:** $19.95. **Description:** Provides the knowledge and strategies required to sell real estate in today's market.

17283 ■ *"Evidence Growing of Commercial Real Estate" in Boston Business Journal (Vol. 27, October 5, 2007, No. 36, pp. 1)*
Pub: American City Business Journals Inc.
Ed: Michelle Hillman. **Description:** Commercial real estate industry in Boston, Massachusetts is experiencing a downturn in the number of sales transactions. A table on the commercial real estate's value of transactions for the first three quarters from 2004 to 2007 is presented.

17284 ■ *"Exxon Mobil Campus 'Clearly Happening" in Houston Business Journal (Vol. 40, January 15, 2010, No. 36, pp. 1)*
Pub: American City Business Journals
Ed: Jennifer Dawson. **Description:** Oil and gas company Exxon Mobil intends to relocate its employees from Houston, Texas and Fairfax, Virginia into a 400-acre site near the town of Spring, Texas. Meanwhile, Exxon Mobil has refused to disclose further details of the relocation plan. Insights from real estate professionals on this relocation plan are examined.

17285 ■ *"Eyes to the Sky" in Canadian Business (Vol. 80, March 26, 2007, No. 7, pp. 33)*
Pub: Rogers Media
Ed: Joe Castaldo. **Description:** The growth and prices of condominium market in the Canada are analyzed.

17286 ■ *"Fifth Third Spinoff" in Business Courier (Vol. 27, July 16, 2010, No. 11, pp. 1)*
Pub: Business Courier
Ed: Dan Monk, Steve Watkins. **Description:** Electronic-funds transfer company Fifth Third Solutions (FTPS), a spinoff of Fifth Third Bancorp, is seeking as much as 200,000 square feet of new office space in Ohio. The bank's sale of 51 percent ownership stake to Boston-based Advent International

Corporation has paved the way for the growth of FTPS. How real estate brokers' plans have responded to FTPS' growth mode is discussed.

17287 ■ *"The Final Piece; Lowe's to Fill Last Big Parcel Near Great Lakes Crossing" in Crain's Detroit Business (March 10, 2008)*
Pub: Crain Communications, Inc.
Ed: Daniel Duggan. **Description:** Silverman Development Co. is developing a Lowe's home-improvement store on the last major retail parcel near the intersection of I-75 and Joslyn Road, an area which was once desolate but is now home to several restaurants and other retail facilities.

17288 ■ *"Final Player In Big Mortgage Fraud Operation Gets Jail Time" in Boston Business Journal (Vol. 31, May 27, 2011, No. 18, pp. 3)*
Pub: Boston Business Journal
Ed: Galen Moore. **Description:** Real estate broker Ralp Appolon has been sentenced to 70 months in prison for wire fraud. Appolon was part of a group that falsified information about property purchase prices. A total of ten mortgage lenders have become victims of the group.

17289 ■ *"Final State Budget Is a Mixed Bag of Key Industries" in The Business Journal - Serving Phoenix and the Valley of the Sun (Vol. 28, July 4, 2008, No. 44, pp. 3)*
Pub: American City Business Journals, Inc.
Ed: Mike Sunnucks; Patrick O'Grady. **Description:** Approved by Governor Janet Napolitano and passed by the Arizona Legislature, the $9.9 billion state budget is beneficial to some industries in the business community. The tax cap for on Arizona Lottery has been removed which is beneficial to the industry, while the solar energy industry and real estate developers stand to lose from the spending bill. Other details of the finance budget are presented.

17290 ■ *"Financing for NNSA Plant Is a Work in Progress" in The Business Journal-Serving Metropolitan Kansas City (October 24, 2008)*
Pub: American City Business Journals, Inc.
Ed: Rob Roberts. **Description:** The Kansas City Council approved a development plan for a $500 million nuclear weapons parts plant in south Kansas City. The US Congress approved a $59 million annual lease payment to the plant's developer. Financing for the construction of the plant remains in question as the plant's developers have to shoulder construction costs.

17291 ■ *"Finding Room for Financing" in The Business Journal-Serving Metropolitan Kansas City (Vol. 26, August 1, 2008, No. 47, pp. 1)*
Pub: American City Business Journals, Inc.
Ed: Rob Roberts. **Description:** Kansas City officials are expecting to receive financing recommendations for a new 1,000-room convention headquarters hotel. The $300-million project could be financed either through private ownership with public subsidies, or through public ownership with tax-exempt bond financing. Other views and information on the project and its expected economic impact, are presented.

17292 ■ *"First-Time Homebuyer Credit May Add Some Momentum to Market" in Crain's Cleveland Business (Vol. 30, May 18, 2009, No. 20)*
Pub: Crain Communications, Inc.
Ed: Stan Bullard. **Description:** Federal tax credits for first-time homebuyers have increased the number of homes being sold. Details of the tax credit are defined.

17293 ■ *FLIP: How to Find, Fix, and Sell Houses for Profit*
Pub: McGraw-Hill Companies Inc.
Contact: Deven Sharma, President
Ed: Rick Villani; Clay Davis. **Released:** December 19, 2006. **Price:** $21.95. **Description:** Advice is given to help find, fix and sell houses for profit.

17294 ■ *"Florin Car Dealers Drive Plan" in Sacramento Business Journal (Vol. 25, August 22, 2008, No. 25, pp. 1)*
Pub: American City Business Journals, Inc.
Ed: Melanie Turner. **Description:** Automobile dealers in Sacramento, California are working with the city and the business district in planning for future redevelopment in Florin Road. The move stemmed from pressure from the Elk Grove Auto Mall, high fuel prices and the credit crunch. The area has suffered business closures recently.

17295 ■ *"Fogg Planning Twinsburg Warehouse Project" in Crain's Cleveland Business (Vol. 28, November 26, 2007, No. 47, pp. 6)*
Pub: Crain Communications, Inc.
Ed: Stan Bullard. **Description:** Discusses such projects as the proposed 205,000-square-foot distribution center in the works by Ray Fogg Corporate Properties LLC as well as other industrial real estate developments that are looking to target tenants that need larger spaces.

17296 ■ *"For $150 Million Mall, Failure to Launch" in Business Courier (Vol. 24, January 25, 2008, No. 42, pp. 1)*
Pub: American City Business Journals, Inc.
Ed: Lisa Biank Fasig. **Description:** Blue Ash-based Bear Creek Capital and Chattanooga, Tennessee-based CBL & Associates Properties had abandoned their plan to build a mixed-use project in South Lebanon. The construction of the proposed $475 million open-air mall was cancelled when real estate developer CBL failed to secure retailers.

17297 ■ *"For Developer, a Boulevard of Golden Dreams" in Globe & Mail (February 10, 2007, pp. B3)*
Pub: CTVglobemedia Publishing Inc.
Ed: Elizabeth Church. **Description:** A profile of Ian Gillespie, president of Westbank Projects Corp., including his achievements in the real estate industry which are presented.

17298 ■ *"For Kenwood, Cavalry Could Be Close" in Business Courier (Vol. 26, October 2, 2009, No. 23, pp. 1)*
Pub: American City Business Journals, Inc.
Ed: Dan Monk. **Description:** New York-based Black-Rock Inc. is believed to be participating in the settlement liens at Kenwood Towne Place, a mixed-use development site in Cincinnati, Ohio. BlackRock may play a key role as an advisor or investor representative to an unnamed investors.

17299 ■ *"For Sale: Old Florida Panache" in The Business Journal-Serving Greater Tampa Bay (Vol. 28, July 4, 2008, No. 28, pp. 1)*
Pub: American City Business Journals, Inc.
Ed: Jane Meinhardt. **Description:** Linger Lodge, owned by real estate investor and developer Martin Kaplan and Senator Michael Bennett, is now on the market for a sealed bid process facilitated by Levin & Associates. The business partners bought the riverfront property for about $3 million in 2005. Other details on the sale of the property are presented.

17300 ■ *The Foreclosure of America: Life Inside Countrywide Home Loans and the Selling of the American Dream*
Pub: Berkley Trade/Penguin Group USA Inc.
Ed: Adam Michaelson. **Released:** April 6, 2010. **Price:** $16.00. **Description:** An inside look at Countrywide Home Loans and the mortgage crisis.

17301 ■ *"Foreclosures Crisis Expected to Significantly Drain Wealth" in Black Enterprise (Vol. 41, September 2010, No. 2, pp. 24)*
Pub: Earl G. Graves Publishing Co. Inc.
Description: African American communities will lose billions in wealth because of the current foreclosure crisis. Statistical data included.

17302 ■ *"Former Mayor Driving $500 Million Real Estate Equity Fund" in The Business Journal - Serving Phoenix and the Valley of*

the Sun (Vol. 28, August 15, 2008, No. 50, pp. 1)
Pub: American City Business Journals, Inc.
Ed: Jan Buchholz. **Description:** Paul John, the former mayor of Phoenix, is establishing a $500 million real estate asset management fund. The fund is dubbed Southwest Next Capital Management and has attracted three local partners, namely Joseph Meyer, Jay Michalowski, and James Mullany, who all have background in finance and construction.

17303 ■ *"Former Schaefer and Strohminger Dealerships to Hit Auction Block" in Baltimore Business Journal (Vol. 28, September 10, 2010)*
Pub: Baltimore Business Journal
Ed: Gary Haber. **Description:** Maryland's real estate developers have a chance to vie for almost 11 acres of prime Baltimore County real estate that are on the auction block. The five properties were once home to Schaefer and Strohminger car dealerships and were located in the county's busiest areas. Other potential uses for the properties are also discussed.

17304 ■ *"From Bikes to Building" in Austin Business JournalInc. (Vol. 29, October 30, 2009, No. 34, pp. 1)*
Pub: American City Business Journals
Ed: Kate Harrington. **Description:** Tour de France champion Lance Armstrong, Bill Stapleton his long-time agent, and business manager Bart Knaggs have formed a privately held real estate investment company CSE Realty Parters in Austin, Texas. They see tremendous opportunity in the commercial real estate market in the area.

17305 ■ *"The Furniture Company Wanted to Sell Him Its Buildings-And Close Down. Should He Buy the Company, Too?" in Inc. (November 2007)*
Pub: Gruner & Jahr USA Publishing
Ed: Alex Salkever. **Description:** Rick Detkowski, real estate investor, discusses his decision to purchase the furniture company housed in the buildings he was interested in buying. The property would have cost him between $500,000 to $1 million, he was able to purchase the property and business with its entire inventory of furniture, vehicles, and machinery for $1.8 million.

17306 ■ *"Gables Unveils Plan for Downtown Tower" in Austin Business JournalInc. (Vol. 28, August 8, 2008, No. 21, pp. A1)*
Pub: American City Business Journals
Ed: Jean Kwon. **Description:** Gables Residential plans to develop a residential tower with 220 units and 15,000 square feet of retail and commercial spaces in the Warehouse District in Ohio. The development is expected to start in late 2009 and be completed in 18 to 24 months.

17307 ■ *"Gail Lissner; Vice-President, Appraisal Research Counselors" in Crain's Chicago Business (Vol. 31, May 5, 2008, No. 18, pp. 28)*
Pub: Crain Communications, Inc.
Ed: Phuong Ly. **Description:** Profile of Gail Lissner who is the vice-president of the Appraisal Research Counselors, a company that puts out the quarterly 'Residential Benchmark Report,' in which Ms. Lissner co-authors and is considered a must-read in the industry. Ms. Lissner has risen to become one of the most sought-after experts on the Chicago market considering real estate.

17308 ■ *"Gateway Delays Start" in The Business Journal-Serving Metropolitan Kansas City (Vol. 27, October 31, 2008, No. 8, pp. 1)*
Pub: American City Business Journals, Inc.
Ed: Rob Roberts. **Description:** Economic problems caused, in part, by the Wall Street crisis has resulted in the setback of a proposed mixed-use redevelopment project, The Gateway. The $307 million project, which includes the Kansas Aquarium, will be delayed due to financing problems. Details of the project are given.

17309 ■ *"Generation Y Driving Portland Multifamily Market" in Daily Journal of Commerce, Portland (October 29, 2010)*
Pub: Dolan Media Newswires
Ed: Nick Bjork. **Description:** Generation Y, young adults between the ages of 18-30, are interested in multifamily residents in the Portland, Oregon area. Developers in the area, particularly North Portland, have recognized this trend and are looking into multifamily investments.

17310 ■ *"Ghazi Insists Downtown Project Still On" in The Business Journal-Milwaukee (Vol. 25, August 1, 2008, No. 45, pp. A1)*
Pub: American City Business Journals, Inc.
Ed: Rich Kirchen. **Description:** Afshin Ghazi remains confident that his $200 million Catalyst project in downtown Milwaukee, Wisconsin, will push through despite financial disputes delaying his EpiCentre project in Charlotte, North Carolina. He added that the Catalyst is on schedule for groundbreaking in the spring of 2009.

17311 ■ *"GL Homes Buys 1,000 Acres in Former Agricultural Reserve" in Miami Daily Business Review (March 26, 2008)*
Pub: ALM Media Inc.
Ed: Polyana da Costa. **Description:** One of the nation's largest home builders, GL Homes, purchased over 1,000 acres of agricultural land in Southern Palm Beach County, Florida. Plans for 554 residential units are detailed.

17312 ■ *"Glendale Pumping $29 Million Into Redevelopment" in The Business Journal - Serving Phoenix and the Valley of the Sun (Vol. 28, August 1, 2008, No. 48, pp. 1)*
Pub: American City Business Journals, Inc.
Ed: Mike Sunnucks. **Description:** Glendale City is planning to invest $29 million to improve city infrastructure like roadways and water and sewer lines over the next five years. Glendale's city council is also planning to hold a workshop on the redevelopment projects in September 2008. Other views and information on the redevelopment project, are presented.

17313 ■ *"GMREB/Analysis of the Resale Market-First Quarter 2007: Year Off to a Great Start" in Canadian Corporate News (May 14, 2007)*
Pub: Comtex News Network Inc.
Description: According to statistics gathered by the Greater Montreal Real Estate Board (GMREB), the Montreal census metropolitan area (CMA) resale market was vigorous in the first quarter of 2007 yielding 10 percent more existing homes being than the first quarter of 2006.

17314 ■ *"GM's Decision to Boot Dealer Prompts Sale" in Baltimore Business Journal (Vol. 27, November 6, 2009, No. 26, pp. 1)*
Pub: American City Business Journals
Ed: Daniel J. Sernovitz. **Description:** General Motors Corporation's (GM) decision to strip Baltimore's Anderson Automotive Group Inc. of its GM franchise has prompted the owner, Bruce Mortimer, to close the automotive dealership and sell the land to a developer. The new project could make way for new homes, a shopping center and supermarket.

17315 ■ *"GM's Mortgage Unit Deal Brings in $9 Billion" in Globe & Mail (March 24, 2006, pp. B3)*
Pub: CTVglobemedia Publishing Inc.
Ed: Shawn McCarthy. **Description:** General Motors Corp. sells General Motors Acceptance Corp.'s commercial real estate division to Kohlberg Kravis Roberts & Co. Five Mile Capital Partners LLC and Goldman Sachs Capital Partners. The reasons behind the deal are presented.

17316 ■ *"Goldbelt Inc.: Targeting Shareholder Development" in Alaska Business Monthly (Vol. 27, October 2011, No. 10, pp. 108)*
Pub: Alaska Business Publishing Company
Ed: Tracy Kalytiak. **Description:** Profile of Goldbelt Inc., the company that has changed its original focus of timber to real estate to tourism and then to government contracting opportunities.

17317 ■ *"A Good Sign for Commercial Real Estate" in Austin Business JournalInc. (Vol. 29, December 18, 2009, No. 41, pp. 1)*
Pub: American City Business Journals
Ed: Kate Harrington. **Description:** Factors that could contribute to the reemergence of the commercial mortgage-backed securities market in Texas are discussed. These securities can potentially boost the commercial real estate market statewide as well as nationwide. Commercial mortgage-backed securities origination in 2009 is worth less that $1 billion, compared with $238 billion in 2008.

17318 ■ *"Green Housing for the Rest of Us" in Inc. (November 2007, pp. 128-129)*
Pub: Gruner & Jahr USA Publishing
Ed: Nitasha Tiku. **Description:** Profile of Full Spectrum NY, real estate developer firm, offering residences at the Kalahari, a green high-rise with state-of-the-art features at a reasonable price.

17319 ■ *"Grin and Bear It" in Canadian Business (Vol. 81, March 3, 2008, No. 3, pp. 53)*
Pub: Rogers Media
Ed: Jeff Sanford. **Description:** Discusses the United States economic downturn, caused by the credit market crisis, which is expected to affect the Canadian economy, as Canada depend on the U.S. for 80 percent of its exports. Economist David Rosenberg thinks that in 2008, housing prices will decline by 15 percent and gross domestic product growth will slow to 0.8 percent. Other forecasts for Canadian economy are given.

17320 ■ *"Groundbreaking 2.0" in Philadelphia Business Journal (Vol. 30, September 23, 2011, No. 32, pp. 1)*
Pub: American City Business Journals Inc.
Ed: Natalie Kostelni. **Description:** University Place Associates, the developer of 2.0 University Place in West Philadelphia, Pennsylvania, will break ground on a five-story, 97,000-square-foot office building in December 2011. The decision follows the Citizenship and Immigration Services signing of a 15-year lease as anchor tenant.

17321 ■ *"Growth in Fits and Starts" in Canadian Business (Vol. 83, July 20, 2010, No. 11-12, pp. 18)*
Pub: Rogers Media Ltd.
Ed: James Cowan. **Description:** US home sales and manufacturing indicators have dropped and fears of a double-dip recession are widespread. However, a chief economist says that this is endemic to what can be seen after a recession caused by a financial crisis. In Canada, consumer optimism is rising and anxiety over losing one's job is waning.

17322 ■ *"Hard Times for Hard Money" in Sacramento Business Journal (Vol. 25, July 18, 2008, No. 20, pp. 1)*
Pub: American City Business Journals, Inc.
Ed: Michael Shaw. **Description:** Three private lenders who supplied $1 million sued VLD Realty, its associated companies and owners Volodymyr and Leonid Dubinsky accusing them of default after a plan to build two subdivisions fell through. Investigators are finding that borrowers and lenders ignored most rules on private investments on real estate.

17323 ■ *"Hastily Enacted Regulation Will Not Cure Economic Crisis" in Crain's Chicago Business (Vol. 31, May 5, 2008, No. 18, pp. 18)*
Pub: Crain Communications, Inc.
Ed: Stephen P. D'Arcy. **Description:** Policymakers are looking for ways to respond to what is possibly the greatest financial crisis of a generation due to the collapse of the housing market, the credit crisis and the volatility of Wall Street.

17324 ■ *"High-End Blunders" in Crain's Chicago Business (Vol. 31, April 21, 2008, No. 16, pp. 54)*
Pub: Crain Communications, Inc.
Ed: Laura Bianchi. **Description:** Discusses some of the biggest errors sellers make that keep their homes from selling including: pricing too high; expecting to

recoup the cost of very high-end amenities and decor; avant-garde decorating; owners that hover when the house is being shown; stripping the home of top-quality light fixtures and hardware and replacing them with inferior versions with the assumption that the new buyer will come in with their own decorator and redo it; and poorly maintained properties.

17325 ■ *"His Place in the Sun" in Canadian Business (Vol. 79, October 23, 2006, No. 21, pp. 77)*
Pub: Rogers Media

Ed: Zena Olijnyk. **Description:** The business interests of Canadian real estate developer Derek Elliott in the Dominican Republic, is discussed.

17326 ■ *"Historic Glenview Homes Could Be Torn Down" in Chicago Tribune (September 25, 2008)*
Pub: McClatchy-Tribune Information Services

Ed: Courtney Flynn. **Description:** Leaders of the Glenview New Church would like to see a buyer emerge who would move and restore two historic homes sitting on the church's property. If a buyer does not come forward the church plans to demolish the homes to make room for condominiums and the expansion of their school.

17327 ■ *"HOK Sport May Build Own Practice" in The Business Journal-Serving Metropolitan Kansas City (Vol. 26, August 29, 2008, No. 51, pp. 1)*
Pub: American City Business Journals, Inc.

Ed: Rob Roberts. **Description:** HOK Sport Venue Event is considering a spin-off from its parent company, HOK Group Inc. HOK Sport spokeswoman Gina Leo confirms that the firm is exploring structures, including a management buyout. Some of HOK Sport Venue Event's Minnesota projects are discussed.

17328 ■ *"Hollander 95 Project Getting Bigger" in Boston Business Journal (Vol. 29, September 23, 2011, No. 20, pp. 1)*
Pub: American City Business Journals Inc.

Ed: Gary Haber. **Description:** Hollander 95 Business Park is in for a huge change as its new owners plan a $50 million expansion which calls for building as many as eight more buildings or a total of more than 500,000 square feed. FRP Development bought the site for $4.35 million at a foreclosure sale in July 2010 and is now seeking city approval for an Industrial Planned Unit Development designation.

17329 ■ *"Home Prices Sag" in Crain's Chicago Business (Vol. 31, April 28, 2008, No. 17, pp. 3)*
Pub: Crain Communications, Inc.

Ed: Alby Gallun. **Description:** Since the slump in the housing market is continuing with no sign of recovery, Chicago-area home prices are poised for an even steeper drop this year. In 2007, the region's home prices fell nearly 5 percent and according to a forecast by Fiserv Inc., they will decline 8.1 percent this year and another 2.2 percent in 2009. Statistical data included.

17330 ■ *Home Staging for Dummies*
Pub: John Wiley and Sons, Inc.

Ed: Christine Rae; Janice Saunders Maresh. **Released:** May 2008. **Price:** $19.99. **Description:** Guide shows how to make improvements room by room in order to generate a higher profit on home sales. The book offers tips to clear clutter and show the home's best features, inspire curb appeal, and how to depersonalize and neutralize every room.

17331 ■ *"Homes Stall As Owners Resist Major Price Cuts" in Crain's Chicago Business (Vol. 31, April 21, 2008, No. 16, pp. 38)*
Pub: Crain Communications, Inc.

Ed: Kevin Davis. **Description:** Discusses the high-end housing market and the owners who are resisting major price cuts as well as the buyers who look at long market times as a sign that something is wrong with the property.

17332 ■ *"House Prices Cooling Off, With Alberta Gearing Down" in Globe & Mail (February 9, 2007, pp. B4)*
Pub: CTVglobemedia Publishing Inc.

Ed: Tavia Grant. **Description:** The house prices in Alberta, which are experiencing a torrid pace in price growth, are steady in the first month of 2007. The easing in house prices may show impact on inflation.

17333 ■ *The Housing Boom and Bust*
Pub: Basic Books

Ed: Thomas Sowell. **Price:** $24.95. **Description:** An explanation of the economics and politics of the housing boom and its collapse.

17334 ■ *"Housing Market Dinged, But Not Done In, By Nationwide Slump" in Business Review, Albany New York (Vol. 34, December 21, 2007)*
Pub: American City Business Journals, Inc.

Ed: Michael DeMasi. **Description:** Kirsten Keefe, a staff attorney of the Empire Justice Center, is questioning the validity of statistics that represent the number of home foreclosures in New York.

17335 ■ *"Housing Markets Still Struggling" in Montana Business Quarterly (Vol. 49, Spring 2011, No. 1, pp. 17)*
Pub: Bureau of Business & Economic Research

Ed: Scott Rickard. **Description:** Montana's economic conditions are a bit better than national averages. Data ranked by state, year-over-year price change, and total price peak is presented, along with statistical data for the entire nation.

17336 ■ *"Housing Slide Picks Up Speed" in Crain's Chicago Business (Vol. 31, April 21, 2008, No. 16, pp. 2)*
Pub: Crain Communications, Inc.

Ed: Eddie Baeb. **Description:** According to Tracy Cross & Associates Inc., a real estate consultancy, sales of new homes in the Chicago area dropped 61 percent from the year-earlier period which is more bad news for homebuilders, contractors and real estate agents who are eager for an indication that market conditions are improving.

17337 ■ *How to Open and Operate a Financially Successful Redesign, Redecorating, and Home Staging Business: With Companion CD-ROM*
Pub: Atlantic Publishing Group, Inc.

Ed: Mary Larsen; Teri B. Clark. **Released:** January 2008. **Price:** $39.95 paperback. **Description:** Questions are asked to help individuals determine if they should launch their own redesign or real estate staging firm.

17338 ■ *"ICC Works on Prescriptive Green Construction Code" in Contractor (Vol. 56, October 2009, No. 10, pp. 1)*
Pub: Penton Media, Inc.

Ed: Robert P. Mader. **Description:** International Code Council launched an initiative to create a green construction code that focuses on existing commercial buildings. The initiative's timeline will include public meetings leading up to a final draft that will be available in 2010.

17339 ■ *"Illinois Farmland Tops $11,000 Per Acre" in Farm Industry News (June 27, 2011)*
Pub: Penton Business Media Inc.

Ed: Karen McMahon. **Description:** Farmland property in Illinois continues to grow in value, selling for $11,000 per acre. Statistical data included.

17340 ■ *"IMRA's Ultrafast Lasers Bring Precision, profits; Ann Arbor Company Eyes Expansion" in Crain's Detroit Business (March 10, 2008)*
Pub: Crain Communications, Inc.

Ed: Tom Henderson. **Description:** IMRA America Inc. plans to expand its headquarters and has applied for permits to build a fourth building that will house research and development facilities and allow the company more room for manufacturing; the company plans to add about 20 more employees that would include research scientists, manufacturing and assembly workers, engineers and salespeople. The

growth is due mainly to a new technology of ultrafast fiber lasers that reduce side effects for those getting eye surgeries and help manufacturers of computer chips to reduce their size and cost.

17341 ■ *"In Control: Tips For Navigating a Buyer's Market" in Black Enterprise (Vol. 38, December 2007, No. 5, pp. 64)*
Pub: Earl G. Graves Publishing Co. Inc.

Ed: Erinn R. Johnson. **Description:** Tips are given to help would-be home buyers. The importance of finding a good real estate agent is stressed.

17342 ■ *"Incentives Debate Rages On Unabated" in The Business Journal-Serving Metropolitan Kansas City (Vol. 26, September 5, 2008, No. 52)*
Pub: American City Business Journals, Inc.

Ed: Rob Roberts. **Description:** Debate on the new economic development and incentives policy adopted by the Kansas City Council is still on. The city's Planned Industrial Expansion Authority has rejected a standard property tax abatement proposal. The real estate development community has opposed the rejection of proposed the tax incentives policy.

17343 ■ *"Incubator Cooking Up Expansion Plans" in Business First Columbus (Vol. 25, December 5, 2008, No. 15, pp.)*
Pub: American City Business Journals

Ed: Kevin Kemper. **Description:** United States-based Science and Technology Campus Corporation is planning to build additional office space in Columbus, Ohio. The site is designed to accommodate three large tenants. Comment from company executives are presented.

17344 ■ *"Independence's Day Keeps on Getting Brighter" in Business Courier (Vol. 27, June 11, 2010, No. 6, pp. 1)*
Pub: Business Courier

Ed: Lucy May. **Description:** Reports show that residential and commercial development continues in Independence, Kentucky despite the recession, with a 144-unit apartment complex under construction. The city recorded 152 new-home closings in 2009, or 25 percent of all new homes closed in Boone, Campbell, and Kenton counties.

17345 ■ *"Industrial RE Market Shows Signs of Health" in Business Courier (Vol. 27, August 20, 2010, No. 16, pp. 1)*
Pub: Business Courier

Ed: Jon Newberry. **Description:** Cincinnati, Ohio's industrial real estate sector has experienced growth during the first half of 2010. The industry has seen a large net loss of occupied space in 2009.

17346 ■ *"Industrial Vacancies Hit High; Economic Downturn Taking Toll on Area's Demand for Space" in Crain's Chicago Business (Apr. 21, 2008)*
Pub: Crain Communications, Inc.

Ed: Alby Gallun. **Description:** Hitting its highest level in four years in the first quarter is the Chicago-area industrial vacancy rate, a sign that the slumping economy is depressing demand for warehouse and manufacturing space.

17347 ■ *"Inflation Woes: Secure Your Portfolio Against Rising Prices" in Black Enterprise (Vol. 37, January 2007, No. 6, pp. 40)*
Pub: Earl G. Graves Publishing Co. Inc.

Ed: Donald Jay Korn. **Description:** Inflation has a huge impact on investing and it is important to take the steady increase on cost into account when looking at your financial goals and investing in your future. Statistical data included.

17348 ■ *"Inventory Glut" in Business Courier (Vol. 24, March 28, 2008, No. 51, pp. 1)*
Pub: American City Business Journals, Inc.

Ed: Laura Baverman. **Description:** Indian Hill and the downtown area have the highest monthly absorption rate for housing on a list of 42 Greater Cincinnati and Northern Kentucky neighborhoods. The two neighborhoods have 19 and 27 months of housing inventory respectively, which means home sellers need to either lower their prices or be very patient.

17349 ■ *"Investors Eye Old Buildings" in Business Journal-Portland (Vol. 24, October 19, 2007, No. 34, pp. 1)*
Pub: American City Business Journals, Inc.
Ed: Wendy Culverwell. **Description:** Office vacancy rates in downtown Portland has dipped to around five percent, causing brokers and investors to search for older buildings in the Class B and Class C categories where the rent is also cheaper. Some notable older and cheaper buildings will be renovated for use.

17350 ■ *"Investors Sue Jackson Properties for Fraud, Breach of Contract" in The Business Journal - Serving Phoenix and the Valley of the Sun (Vol. 28, July 18, 2008, No. 46, pp. 1)*
Pub: American City Business Journals, Inc.
Ed: Jan Buchholz. **Description:** Investors sued Jackson Properties EVB Inc. and Jackson Properties EVB LLC for fraud and breach of contract over a botched housing development deal. The investors also filed a complaint before the Arizona Corporation Commission. The investors stand to lose $8 million from the halted development deal.

17351 ■ *"Is this a Buying Opportunity?" in Canadian Business (Vol. 82, April 27, 2009, No. 7, pp. 46)*
Pub: Rogers Media
Ed: Andy Holloway. **Description:** Home prices in Canada are down by as much as 14.2 percent in 2009 compared to prices in 2008, making homes more affordable now. Some housing experts believe that homes are still good investments as prices of rent and properties always recover. Meanwhile, a survey found that Canadians under 35 plan to buy a home within two years.

17352 ■ *"Jennifer Hernandez Helps Developers Transform Contaminated Properties" in Hispanic Business (Vol. 30, April 2008, No. 4, pp. 32)*
Pub: Hispanic Business
Ed: Hildy Medina. **Description:** Jennifer Hernandez is a partner and head of the law firm of Holland & Knight's environmental practice which specializes in the restoration of polluted land where former industrial and commercial buildings once stood, known as brownfields. Brownfield redevelopment can be lucrative but costly due to the cleaning up of contaminated land and challenging because of federal and state environmental laws.

17353 ■ *"Karen Case; President of Commercial Real Estate Lending, Privatebancorp Inc." in Crain's Chicago Business (May 5, 2008)*
Pub: Crain Communications, Inc.
Ed: Dee Gill. **Description:** Profile of Karen Case who was hired by PrivateBancorp Inc. to turn its minor share of the city's commercial real estate lending market into a major one.

17354 ■ *"KC Presents Healthy Market for Medical REIT" in Business Journal-Serving Metropolitan Kansas City (Vol. 26, November 30, 2007)*
Pub: American City Business Journals, Inc.
Ed: Rob Roberts. **Description:** Medical Properties Trust, the only real estate investment trust that specializes in buying hospitals, is planning to invest in Kansas City due to its fast growing hospital market. The company owns 29 properties nationwide and is still planning to increase its portfolio.

17355 ■ *"Kenosha 'Lifestyle Center' Delayed" in The Business Journal-Milwaukee (Vol. 25, August 8, 2008, No. 46, pp. A1)*
Pub: American City Business Journals, Inc.
Ed: Rich Kirchen. **Description:** Quality Centers of Orlando, Florida has postponed construction plans for the Kenosha Town Center in Kenosha County, Wisconsin to 2009 due to the economic downturn

and lending concerns. The $200-million, 750,000-square-foot retail and residential center will be located near the corner of Wisconsin Highway 50 and I-94.

17356 ■ *"Kent Officials Seek Further KSU, City Unity" in Crain's Cleveland Business (Vol. 28, December 3, 2007, No. 48, pp. 3)*
Pub: Crain Communications, Inc.
Ed: Jay Miller. **Description:** Kent State University and Portage County are searching for a developer who will use a three-acre parcel to bring new life to the city's sagging downtown and create an area that will better link the town and the Kent State campus. The project will include a hotel and conference center as well as retail and restaurant space.

17357 ■ *"Kimball Hill Files for Chapter 11" in Crain's Chicago Business (Vol. 31, April 28, 2008, No. 17, pp. 12)*
Pub: Crain Communications, Inc.
Description: Homebuilder Kimball Hill filed for Chapter 11 bankruptcy protection after months of negotiations with lenders. The firm plans to continue operations as it restructures its debt.

17358 ■ *"The Kitchen is Closed; Eateries Forced Out by Soaring Rents, Declining Revenues" in Crain's New York Business (January 21, 2008)*
Pub: Crain Communications, Inc.
Ed: Lisa Fickenscher. **Description:** Many restaurants have already closed in the area and experts expect many more will follow due to skyrocketing rents and declining revenues.

17359 ■ *"Kubicki Juggles Lineup at Vianda" in Business Courier (Vol. 26, December 11, 2009, No. 33, pp. 1)*
Pub: American City Business Journals, Inc.
Ed: Dan Monk. **Description:** Cincinnati real estate developer Chuck Kubicki replaced the management team of Vianda LLC and cancelled contracts with two vendors that caused a surge of customer complaints. Vianda is a direct-response marketing firm that sells and distributes dietary supplements for wellness and sexual performance.

17360 ■ *"KXAN Seeks Larger Studio, Office Space" in Austin Business Journal (Vol. 31, May 27, 2011, No. 12, pp. A1)*
Pub: American City Business Journals Inc.
Ed: Cody Lyon. **Description:** Austin NBC affiliate KXAN Television is opting to sell its property north of downtown and relocate to another site. The station is now inspecting possible sites to house its broadcasting facility and employees totaling as many as 200 people. Estimated cost of the construction of the studios and offices is $13 million plus another million in moving the equipment.

17361 ■ *"Land Agent Taken Over" in Farmer's Weekly (March 28, 2008, No. 320)*
Pub: Reed Business Information
Contact: Jeff Greisch, President
Description: Property business Smiths Gore will take over Cluttons' rural division, one of the oldest names in land agency. Cluttons said it had decided to sell its rural business as part of a strategic repositioning that would refocus the business on commercial, residential and overseas opportunities.

17362 ■ *"Land on Boardwalk" in Canadian Business (Vol. 82, April 27, 2009, No. 7, pp. 19)*
Pub: Rogers Media
Ed: Calvin Leung. **Description:** Boardwalk REIT remains as one of the most attractive real estate investment trusts in Canada, with 73 percent of analysts rating the firm a Buy. Analyst Neil Downey believes that good management, as well as a good business model, makes Boardwalk a good investment. Downey is concerned however, that a worsening of Alberta's economy could significantly impact Boardwalk.

17363 ■ *"Landlord Puts 7 Tops Locations On Market" in Business First Buffalo (November*

16, 2007, pp. 1)
Pub: American City Business Journals, Inc.
Ed: James Fink. **Description:** New York-based Benesen Capital Partners LLC has put its 388,000-square-foot property up for sale. Seven Tops Grocery Markets have two to nine years remaining on their lease contracts.

17364 ■ *"Laugh or Cry?" in Barron's (Vol. 88, March 24, 2008, No. 12, pp. 7)*
Pub: Dow Jones & Company, Inc.
Ed: Alan Abelson. **Description:** Discusses the American economy which is just starting to feel the effect of the credit and housing crises. JPMorgan Chase purchased Bear Stearns for $2 a share, much lower than its share price of $60, while quasi-government entities Fannie Mae and Freddie Mac are starting to run into trouble.

17365 ■ *Law for the Small and Growing Business*
Pub: Jordans Publishing Limited
Ed: P. Bohm. **Released:** February 2007. **Price:** $59.98. **Description:** Legal and regulatory issues facing small businesses, including employment law, health and safety, commercial property, company law and finance are covered.

17366 ■ *"Leaning Tower" in Business Courier (Vol. 27, June 4, 2010, No. 5, pp. 1)*
Pub: Business Courier
Ed: Jon Newberry. **Description:** New York-based developer Armand Lasky, owner of Tower Place Mall in downtown Cincinnati, Ohio has sued Birmingham, Alabama-based Regions Bank to prevent the bank's foreclosure on the property. Regions Bank claims Lasky was in default on an $18 million loan agreement. Details on the mall's leasing plan is also discussed.

17367 ■ *"Leasing Midway; Look for Higher Parking Fees, More Retail Under Private Airport Operator" in Crain's Chicago Business (May 5, 2008)*
Pub: Crain Communications, Inc.
Ed: Paul Merrion. **Description:** According to experts, bids for the first privatization of a major U.S. airport could run as high as $3.5 billion. Information-gathering and negotiations will soon get under way with some or all of the six major international investor groups that recently expressed interest in running Midway.

17368 ■ *"Legacy Hotels Looks for a Buyer" in Globe & Mail (March 2, 2007, pp. B3)*
Pub: CTVglobemedia Publishing Inc.
Ed: Elizabeth Church. **Description:** Legacy Hotels Real Estate Investment Trust, which has a portfolio of 25 properties, plans to sell its businesses. The shares of the real estate investment trust climbed $13.21, as the sales news was delivered.

17369 ■ *"Legislature Passes Increased Tax Credit for Urban Brownfield Projects" in Crain's Detroit Business (Vol. 24, March 31, 2008, No. 13)*
Pub: Crain Communications, Inc.
Ed: Amy Lane. **Description:** Discusses the bill passed by the Legislature that creates a tax credit of up to 20 percent for projects in urban development areas.

17370 ■ *"Lenders" in The Business Journal - Serving Phoenix and the Valley of the Sun (Vol. 28, July 25, 2008, No. 47, pp. 1)*
Pub: American City Business Journals, Inc.
Ed: Jan Buchholz. **Description:** Private equity lender Investor Mortgage Holdings Inc. has continued growing despite the crisis surrounding the real estate and financial industries and has accumulated a $700 million loan portfolio. Private lending has become increasingly important in financing real estate deals as commercial credit has dried up.

17371 ■ *"Local Commercial Real Estate Foreclosures Continue to Rise" in Baltimore Business Journal (Vol. 28, October 1, 2010,*

No. 21, pp. 1)
Pub: Baltimore Business Journal
Ed: Daniel J. Sernovitz. **Description:** Foreclosures of commercial real estate across the Greater Baltimore area have continued to rise. The region is now host to about $2 billion worth of commercial properties that carry a maturing debt or have been foreclosed. Commercial real estate owners are unable to finance their debts because banks have become stricter in passing out loans.

17372 ■ *"Local Industrial Vacancies Climb" in Crain's Chicago Business (Vol. 31, November 17, 2008, No. 46, pp. 18)*
Pub: Crain Communications, Inc.
Ed: Eddie Baeb. **Description:** Demand for local industrial real estate has declined dramatically as companies that use warehouse and factory space struggle to survive in an ailing economy. According to a report by Colliers Bennett & Kahnweiler Inc., a commercial real estate brokerage, the regional vacancy rate has risen to 9.86 percent in the third quarter, the fourth straight increase and the highest in the past 14 years.

17373 ■ *"Lytle Place Listing Seen as Bellwether" in Business Courier (Vol. 27, December 3, 2010, No. 31, pp. 1)*
Pub: Business Courier
Ed: Dan Monk. **Description:** Denver, Colorado-based Apartment Investment and Management Company (AIMCO) has offered the 25-story One Lytle Place Apartments for sale through CB Richard Ellis for the third time in three years. The potential sale could define the recovery for Cincinnati, Ohio's struggling apartment industry.

17374 ■ *"Major Renovation Planned for Southridge" in Business Journal-Milwaukee (Vol. 28, November 12, 2010, No. 6, pp. A1)*
Pub: Milwaukee Business Journal
Ed: Stacy Vogel Davis. **Description:** Simon Property Group plans to invest more than $20 million in upgrading and renovating Southridge Mall in Milwaukee County, Wisconsin. The project, which is partially financed by a $10 million grant from the Village of Greendale, could boost the property's value by $52.5 million.

17375 ■ *"Major Tech Employers Pulling Out" in Sacramento Business Journal (Vol. 25, August 1, 2008, No. 22, pp. 1)*
Pub: American City Business Journals, Inc.
Ed: Celia Lamb. **Description:** Biotechnology company Affymetrix Inc. is planning to close its West Sacramento, California plant and lay off 110 employees. The company said it will expand a corporate restructuring plan. Affymetrix also plans to lease out or sell its building at Riverside Parkway.

17376 ■ *"Making the Cut; Osprey Takes Undervalued Courses to the Leader Board" in Crain's Detroit Business (Vol. 24, April 7, 2008, No. 14)*
Pub: Crain Communications, Inc.
Ed: Jason Deegan. **Description:** Profile of Osprey Management Co., a diverse real estate company that continues to expand its golf portfolio through the company's recreation division; although many developers are getting out of the field due to Michigan's sluggish golf industry, Osprey has found success by purchasing properties in turmoil for more affordable prices.

17377 ■ *"Mandel Site Favored For UWM Hall" in The Business Journal-Milwaukee (Vol. 25, September 19, 2008, No. 52, pp. A1)*
Pub: American City Business Journals, Inc.
Description: University of Wisconsin-Milwaukee student residence hall's leading location is a site pushed by Mandel Group Inc. Real estate sources say that the developer's proposal offers the best opportunity for business development and the least conflict with nearby neighborhoods. Plans for the Mandel site are presented.

17378 ■ *"Mann to Lead Builders" in Charlotte Observer (January 31, 2007)*
Pub: Knight-Ridder/Tribune Business News
Ed: Allen Norwood. **Description:** Elliot Mann of Standard Pacific Homes was sworn in as president of Home Builders Association of Charlotte, North Carolina.

17379 ■ *"Marine Act Amendments Gain Parliamentary Approval" in Canadian Sailings (July 7, 2008)*
Pub: UBM Global Trade
Contact: Leonard J. Corallo, President
Ed: Alex Binkley. **Description:** Changes to the Canada Marine Act provides better borrowing deals as well as an ability to tap into federal infrastructure funding for environmental protection measures, security improvements and other site enhancements.

17380 ■ *"Market Gamble" in Business Journal-Serving Phoenix and the Valley of the Sun (Vol. 5, October 5, 2007, No. 28, pp. 1)*
Pub: American City Business Journals, Inc.
Ed: Mike Padgett. **Description:** AI-BSR LLC, an Israeli group believes the housing market will regain its strength within three years. The group plans to build its $385 million project, called One Phoenix. The condominiums start at $500,000, with units ranging from 800 to 2,000 square feet.

17381 ■ *"Market for Retail Space Flat, but Recovery Still Uncertain" in Sacramento Business Journal (Vol. 28, August 26, 2011, No. 26, pp. 1)*
Pub: Sacramento Business Journal
Ed: Kelly Johnson. **Description:** The retail market in the Sacramento, California region remains challenged with the stock market volatility being the latest of its hurdles. The overall vacancy was 13.1 percent as of mid-2011, but retail real estate professionals express hopes that the worst is behind. A list and description of the region's winners and losers in retail vacancies is provided.

17382 ■ *"Market Swings Intensify Yearning for Bonds" in Globe & Mail (March 9, 2007, pp. B9)*
Pub: CTVglobemedia Publishing Inc.
Ed: Keith Damsell. **Description:** The rise in demand for proper fixed-income bonds in Canada as a result of uncertainties in the equity market is discussed. Some big Canadian fixed-income funds are presented.

17383 ■ *"Mason Fashions Its Future" in Business Courier (Vol. 24, December 7, 2008, No. 34, pp. 1)*
Pub: American City Business Journals, Inc.
Ed: Laura Baverman. **Description:** Economic Development Director Michele Blair contracted Cincinnati-based Jack Rouse & Associates to tap the remaining undeveloped land in Mason. The real estate firm is set to develop the 2,000 acres of undeveloped land.

17384 ■ *"A Matter of Perspective" in Business Journal-Portland (Vol. 24, November 2, 2007, No. 35, pp. 1)*
Pub: American City Business Journals, Inc.
Ed: Andy Giegerich. **Description:** Oregon Governor Ted Kulongoski assembled the Mortgage Lending Work Group, made up of members of the mortgage industry and consumer groups, to recommend possible bills for the Oregon Senate and House to consider. How its members try to balance philosophical differences in mortgage lending rules is discussed.

17385 ■ *"McDonald's Founders Fund $80 Million Project" in The Business Journal - Serving Phoenix and the Valley of the Sun (Vol. 28, September 12, 2008, No. 53, pp. 1)*
Pub: American City Business Journals, Inc.
Ed: Jan Buchholz. **Description:** Construction will begin in early 2009 on an $80 million Ray and Joan Kroc Community Center in Phoenix, Arizona. It will be located adjacent to the Salvation Army, which received a $1.9 billion contribution from Joan Kroc after her death in 2003. This fund will be divided to construct 30 community centers across the country.

17386 ■ *"Medical Office Developers To Merge November 1" in The Business Journal - Serving Phoenix and the Valley of the Sun (Vol. 29, September 26, 2008, No. 4, pp. 1)*
Pub: American City Business Journals, Inc.
Ed: Angela Gonzales. **Description:** Ensemble Real Estate Services LLC and DevMan Co. will merge effective November 1, 2008 and will call the firm Ensemble DevMan of Arizona after the merger. The two companies will combine their resources and expertise on planned projects that include the Phoenix Children's Hospital's Specialty Clinic and Banner Ironwood Medical Office Building.

17387 ■ *"Mequon Plan On Tracks, Bucks Housing Trend" in The Business Journal-Milwaukee (Vol. 25, September 26, 2008, No. 53, pp. A1)*
Pub: American City Business Journals, Inc.
Ed: Pete Millard. **Description:** Insight Development Group plans to build condominium units and single-family homes despite the residential market downturn. The Orchard Glen project, a planned development in Mequon, is a $22 million project which will include 38 condos and 12 single-family homes. Details of the project are provided.

17388 ■ *"Midtown Tampa Bay Taking Shape" in The Business Journal-Serving Greater Tampa Bay (Vol. 28, September 12, 2008, No. 38, pp. 1)*
Pub: American City Business Journals, Inc.
Ed: Janet Leiser. **Description:** Midtown Tampa Bay's 610,000 square foot shopping and entertainment center is being planned in Florida and is to replace the Tampa Bay One project proposed years earlier. The retail center is to be developed by Bromley Cos. and Opus South Corp. and is expected to have five buildings. Other details about the plan are discussed.

17389 ■ *"Millions Needed To Finish First Place" in The Business Journal-Milwaukee (Vol. 25, August 15, 2008, No. 47, pp. A1)*
Pub: American City Business Journals, Inc.
Ed: Rich Kirchen. **Description:** First Place on the River condominium project in Milwaukee, Wisconsin, needs $18.2 million before it can be completed. A total of $6.8 million have already been spent since the project went into receivership on 31 January 2008.

17390 ■ *"Minnesota Farms' Net Worth Grows 10 Percent Each Year for 15 Years" in Farm Industry News (August 22, 2011)*
Pub: Penton Business Media Inc.
Ed: Dale Nordquist. **Description:** The average value of farms in Minnesota is growing at a fast pace. Total assets per farm have increased by more than $1.1 million over the past 15 years. Statistical data included.

17391 ■ *"A Model Development" in Crain's Cleveland Business (Vol. 28, October 1, 2007, No. 39, pp. 12)*
Pub: Crain Communications, Inc.
Description: Profile a Forest City Enterprises Inc., a firm that is developing a project in New Mexico called Mesa del Sol. The Albuquerque development is being seen as the vanguard of master-planned communities which with its high-tech economic development center which is expected to become the site of 60,000 jobs, 38,000 homes and a town center.

17392 ■ *"The Money Train: How Public Projects Shape Our Economic Future" in Hawaii Business (Vol. 54, September 2008, No. 3, pp. 31)*
Pub: Hawaii Business Publishing
Ed: Jason Ubay. **Description:** Public projects impact the construction industry as such projects create jobs and new infrastructure that can lead to private developments. Details on the government contracts and construction projects in Hawaii and their rising costs and impact on the state's economy are discussed.

17393 ■ *"More Offices Planned For Percheron Square" in The Business Journal-Milwaukee (Vol. 25, August 22, 2008, No. 48, pp. A1)*
Pub: American City Business Journals, Inc.
Ed: Pete Millard. **Description:** More office projects are under way at Percheron Square. Ryan Cos. US Inc., for example, plans to build over 200,000 square feet of office space at the area. Details of new office projects in Wisconsin are presented.

17394 ■ *"Mortgage Mess: How To Determine Your Exposure To the Subprime Crisis"* in *Black Enterprise (Vol. 38, November 2007, No. 4, pp. 46)*
Pub: Earl G. Graves Publishing Co. Inc.
Ed: Ilana Polyak. **Description:** Stocks and mutual funds have experienced declines because of the subprime crisis. Morningstar's Website can help investors research firms in which they have invested; if a fund is named high yield or high income or in the financial services sector, investments will have greater exposure to the mess.

17395 ■ *"Mortgage Securities Drop Hits Home"* in *The Business Journal-Serving Metropolitan Kansas City (Vol. 27, October 17, 2008, No. 5)*
Pub: American City Business Journals, Inc.
Ed: Rob Roberts. **Description:** Sale of commercial mortgage-backed securities (CMBS) in Kansas City, Missouri have declined. The area may avoid layoffs if the United States government succeeds in stabilizing the economy. Major CMBS players in the area include Midland Loan Services Inc. and KeyBank Real Estate Capital.

17396 ■ *"Mortgages Going Under"* in *Black Enterprise (Vol. 41, December 2010, No. 5, pp. 20)*
Pub: Earl G. Graves Publishing Co. Inc.
Description: Nearly one-fifth of the country's home-owners are underwater in their mortgages, which means they owe more on their home than the home's worth. Statistical data included.

17397 ■ *"Museum Center to Exhibit New Look"* in *Business Courier (Vol. 24, February 22, 2008, No. 46, pp. 1)*
Pub: American City Business Journals, Inc.
Ed: Dan Monk. **Description:** Discusses a $120 million renovation is being planned for the Cincinnati Museum Center complex at Union Terminal. The project aims to build a 14-acre park and office spaces in the area. Details of the Museum Center's renovation plans are given.

17398 ■ *"The Neighborhood Watch"* in *Hawaii Business (Vol. 53, March 2008, No. 9, pp. 36)*
Pub: Hawaii Business Publishing
Ed: David K. Choo. **Description:** OahuRe.com offers information on Hawaii real estate market, with spreadsheets and comparative market analysis page, which shows properties that are active, sold, or in escrow. Other details about OahuRe.com are discussed. A list of other top real estate websites in Hawaii and in the U.S. in general is provided.

17399 ■ *"Neighborhood Watch"* in *Baltimore Business Journal (Vol. 28, July 23, 2010, No. 11, pp. 1)*
Pub: Baltimore Business Journal
Ed: Daniel J. Sernovitz. **Description:** Maryland government and housing leaders are set to spend $100 million in federal funding to stem the increase in foreclosures in the area. The federal funding is seen as inadequate to resolve the problem of foreclosures.

17400 ■ *"New-Home Sales Grab a Foothold With Q2 Boost"* in *Sacramento Business Journal (Vol. 25, July 11, 2008, No. 19, pp. 1)*
Pub: American City Business Journals, Inc.
Ed: Michael Shaw. **Description:** Statistics show that homebuilders in Sacramento, California experienced an increase in new-home sales during the second quarter of 2008. It was also reported that builders moved more homes without slashing prices significantly. Barry Grant, president of KB Home's Sacramento division, believes that the improvement is caused by the stability in the supply of resale homes.

17401 ■ *"A New Mix of Tenants Settles In"* in *Crain's New York Business (Vol. 24, January 14, 2008, No. 2, pp. 26)*
Pub: Crain Communications, Inc.
Ed: Andrew Marks. **Description:** More and more nonfinancial firms are relocating downtown due to the new retailers and restaurants that are reshaping the look and feel of lower Manhattan.

17402 ■ *"New York City-Based New Street Realty Advisors has Secured a New Flagship for David's Bridal"* in *Chain Store Age (August 2008)*
Pub: Chain Store Age
Description: New York City-based New Street Realty Advisors secured a new flagship store for David's Bridal in the Chelsea district of Manhattan. David's Bridal will occupy 12,800 square feet on two floors in a retail condominium development.

17403 ■ *"New York Firm Secures Sheffield, Amherst Centers for $26 Million"* in *Crain's Cleveland Business (Vol. 28, December 3, 2007, No. 48)*
Pub: Crain Communications, Inc.
Ed: Stan Bullard. **Description:** Silverman Realty Group completed a $26 million transaction which made it the new owner of the Sheffield Crossing and Amherst Marketplace shopping centers in Lorain County.

17404 ■ *"The Next Government Bailout?"* in *Barron's (Vol. 88, March 10, 2008, No. 10, pp. 21)*
Pub: Dow Jones & Company, Inc.
Ed: Jonathan Laing. **Description:** Fannie Mae may need a government bailout as it faces huge hits brought about by the effects of the housing crisis. The shares of the government-sponsored enterprise have dropped 65 percent since the housing crisis began.

17405 ■ *"The Next Real Estate Boom"* in *Canadian Business (Vol. 80, March 26, 2007, No. 7, pp. 25)*
Pub: Rogers Media
Ed: Erik Heinrich. **Description:** The better places to invest in Canadian real estate market are presented. The future price performance of the industry is analyzed.

17406 ■ *"N.H. Near the LEED in Green Space"* in *New Hampshire Business Review (Vol. 33, March 25, 2011, No. 6, pp. 30)*
Pub: Business Publications Inc.
Description: New Hamphire's architects, contractors and suppliers are among the leaders with LEED-certified space per capita.

17407 ■ *"No Wild Highs Means No Wild Lows"* in *Business Courier (Vol. 24, January 18, 2008, No. 41, pp. 1)*
Pub: American City Business Journals, Inc.
Ed: Laura Baverman. **Description:** Discusses a PMI Group report which revealed that the Greater Cincinnati area is in the lowest risk category for home value declines. The report forecast that the chance that housing prices in the area will fall below their current status by the year 2010 is less than 5 percent. Housing price forecasts for other areas are also provided.

17408 ■ *"Not Enough To Go Around"* in *The Business Journal-Milwaukee (Vol. 25, August 15, 2008, No. 47, pp. A1)*
Pub: American City Business Journals, Inc.
Ed: David Doege. **Description:** Most of the creditors of bankrupt real estate developer Scott Fergus are likely to remain unpaid as he only has an estimated $30,000 available for paying debts. Creditors, as of the 13 August 2008 deadline for filing claims, have filed a total of $79.1 million in claims.

17409 ■ *"Not In My Backyard"* in *Entrepreneur (Vol. 36, May 2008, No. 5, pp. 42)*
Pub: Entrepreneur Media, Inc.
Ed: Farnoosh Torabi. **Description:** More investors are turning to overseas real estate investments as the U.S. market sees a slowdown. Analysts say that risk-averse investors opt for funds with record of strong returns and U.S. real estate investment trusts that partner with foreign businesses for transparency purposes. Other details about foreign real estate investments are discussed.

17410 ■ *"Number of Mechanic's Liens Triple Since 2005"* in *The Business Journal - Serving Phoenix and the Valley of the Sun (Vol. 28, August 22, 2008, No. 51, pp. 1)*
Pub: American City Business Journals, Inc.
Ed: Jan Buchholtz. **Description:** Experts are blaming the mortgage and banking industries for the tripling of mechanic's liens that were filed in Arizona from 2005 through August 6, 2008. The rise in mechanic's liens is believed to indicate stress in the real estate community. Other views and information on the rise of mechanic's liens filed in Arizona are presented.

17411 ■ *"N.Y. Group Top Bidder for Last Duke Sites"* in *Crain's Cleveland Business (Vol. 28, November 19, 2007, No. 46, pp. 1)*
Pub: Crain Communications, Inc.
Ed: Stan Bullard. **Description:** Overview of the possible portfolio sale of Duke Realty Corp.'s last Northeast Ohio properties, 14 office buildings in Independence, Seven Hills and North Olmsted, believed to be purchased by a real estate investor group led by Nightingale Properties LLC of New York.

17412 ■ *"October 2009: Recovery Plods Along"* in *Hispanic Business (October 2009, pp. 10-11)*
Pub: Hispanic Business
Ed: Dr. Juan Solana. **Description:** Economist reports on a possible economic recovery which will not be allowed to rely on a strong domestic demand in order to sustain it. Consumers, looking to counterbalance years of leverage financing based on unrealistic, ever-increasing home and portfolio valuations, are saving rather than spending money.

17413 ■ *"Office Leasing Gains Ground"* in *Sacramento Business Journal (Vol. 25, July 18, 2008, No. 20, pp. 1)*
Pub: American City Business Journals, Inc.
Ed: Michael Shaw. **Description:** There were at least 84,000 square feet leased to companies in the Sacramento area in the three months prior to August 2008. This development is good news considering that overall vacant leases were around 247,000 square feet for the previous quarter.

17414 ■ *"Office Market May Turn Down"* in *Crain's New York Business (Vol. 24, January 14, 2008, No. 2, pp. 26)*
Pub: Crain Communications, Inc.
Description: Although still dominated by Wall Street, the downturn in the economy is raising fears that the continuing fallout from the subprime mortgage crisis could result in layoffs that will derail the office market.

17415 ■ *"Ohio's Reputation Lags Its Business Ranking"* in *Business Courier (Vol. 24, November 23, 2008, No. 32, pp. 1)*
Pub: American City Business Journals, Inc.
Ed: Jon Newberry. **Description:** Site Selection magazine's annual ranking of the top states for new business facilities has ranked Ohio and Kentucky in seventh and eight place respectively, but an opinion survey of real estate executives had placed Ohio much lower at 14. The survey asked 6,000 executives if Ohio's conditions were best for new building projects.

17416 ■ *"Old Ford Plant to Sign New Tenants"* in *Business Courier (Vol. 27, August 13, 2010, No. 15, pp. 1)*
Pub: Business Courier
Ed: Dan Monk. **Description:** Ohio Realty Advisors LLC, a company handling the marketing of the 1.9 million-square-foot former Ford Batavia plant is on the brink of landing one distribution and three manufacturing firms as tenants. These tenants are slated to occupy about 20 percent of the facility and generate as many as 250 jobs in Ohio.

17417 ■ *"O'Reilly Will Soup Up KC Warehouse"* in *The Business Journal-Serving Metropolitan Kansas City (Vol. 26, August 15, 2008, No. 49)*
Pub: American City Business Journals, Inc.
Ed: Rob Roberts. **Description:** O'Reilly Automotive Inc. plans to construct a 215,000-square foot warehouse in Kansas City. The move is expected to triple

the size of the company's distribution center. Other views and information on the planned warehouse construction, are presented.

17418 ■ *"Ottawa's Real Estate Targets Exceed Market Appraisals" in Globe & Mail (March 19, 2007, pp. B1)*
Pub: CTVglobemedia Publishing Inc.
Ed: Danier Leblanc. **Description:** The growth in the real estate market in Ottawa and the huge revenue the government is expecting from sale of nine buildings as part of its lease back plan is discussed.

17419 ■ *"Out With the Old? City Officials Investigating Options for New Hopkins Hotel" in Crain's Cleveland Business (October 22, 2007)*
Pub: Crain Communications, Inc.
Ed: Jay Miller. **Description:** Cleveland officials have begun talks that could lead to a new hotel which would replace the aging, nine-story Sheraton Cleveland Hopkins Hotel at Cleveland Hopkins International Airport.

17420 ■ *"Outlook 2007" in Canadian Business (Vol. 80, December 25, 2006, No. 1, pp.)*
Pub: Rogers Media
Ed: David Wolf. **Description:** Economists' 2007 forecast on global economy, particularly about Canada's housing and labor market among other sectors, is discussed.

17421 ■ *"Outside Investors Hot On Detroit Commercial Real Estate" in Crain's Detroit Business (Vol. 24, January 28, 2008, No. 4, pp. 25)*
Pub: Crain Communications Inc. - Detroit
Ed: Daniel Duggan. **Description:** An overview of out-of-town investors seeking to purchase commercial real estate in Michigan is presented. Statistical data included.

17422 ■ *"Pain Ahead as Profit Pressure Increases" in Crain's Chicago Business (Vol. 31, May 5, 2008, No. 18, pp. 4)*
Pub: Crain Communications, Inc.
Ed: Daniel Rome Levine. **Description:** Interview with David Klaskin, the chairman and chief investment officer at Oak Ridge Investments LLC, who discusses the outlook for the economy and corporate earnings, particularly in the housing and auto industries, the impact of economic stimulus checks, the weakness of the dollar and recommendations of stocks that individual investors may find helpful.

17423 ■ *"The Paper Shredder" in Business Courier (Vol. 26, September 11, 2009, No. 20, pp. 1)*
Pub: American City Business Journals, Inc.
Ed: Dan Monk. **Description:** DotLoop Company, owned by entrepreneur Austin Allison, is developing the DotLoop software, which eliminates paperwork in the processing of real estate contracts. The software allows realtors to take control of the negotiation process and is adaptable to the rules of different US states.

17424 ■ *"Part-Time Office Space" in Hawaii Business (Vol. 53, December 2007, No. 6, pp. 132)*
Pub: Hawaii Business Publishing
Ed: Ashley Hamershock. **Description:** My Office is one of the companies that are renting space office not only by the month, but by the hour. Such setup is beneficial to small businesses that do not need a whole office all to themselves, and are interested in cutting the cost of office space rental. The prices of office space in Hawaii are mentioned.

17425 ■ *"Past Promises Haunt Project" in The Business Journal-Portland (Vol. 25, August 1, 2008, No. 21, pp. 1)*
Pub: American City Business Journals, Inc.
Ed: Aliza Earnshaw. **Description:** Oregon University System and Oregon Health and Science University will face the state Legislature to defend their request for a $250 million in state bonds to fund a life-sciences collaborative research building. The project

is meant to help grow the Oregon bioscience industry. Comments from industry observers and legislators are also presented.

17426 ■ *"Pat Modica" in Crain's Cleveland Business (Vol. 30, June 29, 2009, No. 25, pp. 15)*
Pub: Crain Communications, Inc.
Ed: Stan Bullard. **Description:** Profile of Pat Modica, real estate agent with Howard Hanna. Ms. Modica states that in her 29 years as a residential real estate agent, she has never seen a market like the present one. She discusses home sales and activity for the area.

17427 ■ *"Pavilions Poised for Image Overhaul" in The Business Journal - Serving Phoenix and the Valley of the Sun (Vol. 28, August 22, 2008)*
Pub: American City Business Journals, Inc.
Ed: Jan Buchholz. **Description:** DeRitto Partners Inc. is expected to push through with plans for a major renovation of the 1.1 million-square foot Scottsdale Pavilions in Scottsdale, Arizona. An aggressive marketing campaign is planned to be included in the renovation, which aims to address high vacancy rates and competition. Views and information on the planned renovation are presented.

17428 ■ *"Paying for the Recession: Rebalancing Economic Growth" in Montana Business Quarterly (Vol. 49, Spring 2011, No. 1, pp. 2)*
Pub: Bureau of Business & Economic Research
Ed: Patrick M. Barkey. **Description:** Four key issues required to address in order to rebalance economic growth in America are examined. They include: savings rates, global trade imbalances, government budgets and most importantly, housing price correction.

17429 ■ *The Peebles Principles: Insights from an Entrepreneur's Life of Business Success, Making Deals, and Creating a Fortune from Scratch*
Pub: John Wiley and Sons Inc.
Ed: R. Donahue Peebles. **Released:** April 2007. **Price:** $29.99. **Description:** Successful entrepreneur shares his business experience. Peebles went from CEO of the nation's largest Black-owned real estate development firm to founding his own firm.

17430 ■ *Peggy's Corner: The Art of Staging*
Pub: Eaton-Moghannam Publishing
Ed: Peggy Selinger-Eaton; Gayla Moghannam. **Released:** June 2005. **Description:** Techniques to enhance the value of any home are given. Seven principles of staging a home for sale include making a great first impression, maximizing space and eliminating clutter, using lighting for open spacious feeling, de-emphasize flaws, make the home appealing to buyers with varied tastes, creating warmth, and modernizing the home.

17431 ■ *"A Perfect Predator: Brookfield Asset Management Isn't Brash" in Canadian Business (Vol. 83, July 20, 2010, No. 11-12, pp. 50)*
Pub: Rogers Media Ltd.
Ed: Joanna Pachner. **Description:** Brookfield Asset Management CEO Bruce Flatt manages $108 billion worth of real estate and the company has become one of the world's biggest prime real estate owners since he became leader. Flatt says their goal is to earn a 12-15 percent compound annual return per share and that they would shrink in size if it meant reaching that goal.

17432 ■ *"Peter Bynoe Trades Up" in Black Enterprise (Vol. 38, July 2008, No. 12, pp. 30)*
Pub: Earl G. Graves Publishing Co. Inc.
Ed: Alexis McCombs. **Description:** Chicago-based Loop Capital Markets L.L.C. has named Peter Bynoe managing director of corporate finance. Bynoe was previously a senior partner at the law firm DLA Piper U.S. L.L.P., where he worked on stadium deals.

17433 ■ *"Peter Gilgan" in Canadian Business (Vol. 82, April 27, 2009, No. 7, pp. 58)*
Pub: Rogers Media
Ed: Calvin Leung. **Description:** Mattamy Homes Ltd. president and chief executive officer Peter Gilgan believes that their business model of building communities in an organized way brings advantages to the firm and for their customers. He also believes in adopting their product prices to new market realities. Gilgan considers the approvals regime in Ontario his biggest challenge in the last 20 years.

17434 ■ *"Phillips Edison Launches $1.8B Retail REIT" in Business Courier (Vol. 27, October 15, 2010, No. 24, pp. 1)*
Pub: Business Courier
Ed: Dan Monk. **Description:** Retail center operator Phillips Edison & Company is organizing a real estate investment trust (REIT) to raise $1.8 billion to finance the planned purchase of 150 grocery-centered shopping centers around the U.S. The offering would be Phillips largest. Phillips Edison employesss 174 workers and operates 250 shopping centers nationwide.

17435 ■ *"A Place to Call Home" in Business Courier (Vol. 24, March 7, 2008, No. 48, pp. 1)*
Pub: American City Business Journals, Inc.
Ed: Lucy May. **Description:** Discusses a new type of housing for Cincinnati's chronically homeless that will be developed by the Over-the-Rhine Community Housing Network and the Cincinnati Center City Development Corp. Advocates believe that it is the missing link in the community's efforts to eradicate homelessness. The details of the project are also presented.

17436 ■ *"A Place in the Sun" in Canadian Business (Vol. 81, July 22, 2008, No. 12-13, pp. 56)*
Pub: Rogers Media Ltd.
Description: Experts believe that it is the best time for Canadians to own a retirement home in the U.S., where real estate prices are up to 50 percent below their peak. Other views concerning the economic conditions occurring in the United States, as well as on the implications for Canadians planning to invest in the country are presented.

17437 ■ *"Placer Land Sells for $12 Million" in Sacramento Business Journal (Vol. 25, July 25, 2008, No. 21, pp. 1)*
Pub: American City Business Journals, Inc.
Ed: Michael Shaw; Celia Lamb. **Description:** Reynen & Bardis Communities Inc., a Sacramento, California-based homebuilder, has purchased the Antonio Mountain Ranch in Placer County, California shortly before the property's scheduled foreclosure on June 27, 2008. Placer County Recorder's data show that the purchase price of the 808-acre wetland-rich property is $12 million.

17438 ■ *"Population Growing Faster Than Retail, Service Sector" in Crain's New York Business (Vol. 24, January 14, 2008, No. 2, pp. 30)*
Pub: Crain Communications, Inc.
Ed: Andrew Marks. **Description:** Downtown Manhattan is seeing more residential development; however, as more families call the area home the need for more retail and services is becoming evident.

17439 ■ *"Portland's Hilton For Sale" in Business Journal Portland (Vol. 27, October 22, 2010, No. 34, pp. 1)*
Pub: Portland Business Journal
Ed: Wendy Culverwell. **Description:** Hilton Portland & Executive Tower, Portland's biggest hotel, is being sold by Cornerstone Real Estate Advisers LLC. Cornerstone hopes to close the deal for the 782-room complex by the end of 2010. Cornerstone contracted Jones Lang LaSalle to manage the sale, but terms to the deal are not available.

17440 ■ *"The Power of Fun" in Canadian Business (Vol. 79, November 6, 2006, No. 22, pp. 58)*
Pub: Rogers Media
Ed: Zena Olijnyk. **Description:** The creative efforts of Phillippe Starck in designing condos are analyzed.

17441 ■ *"'Pre-Sale' for Planned Could Mich Tower"* in Crain's Chicago Business (Vol. 31, March 24, 2008, No. 12, pp. 14)
Pub: Crain Communications, Inc.
Ed: Eddie Baeb. **Description:** Condominium developer William Warman is planning to build a mixed-use tower at 300 North Michigan Avenue which would include a hotel, retail space, apartments and a parking garage. Mr. Warman is looking for investors to buy part or all of the space in order to make it easier to land financing.

17442 ■ *"Priced-Out Tenants Flocking to Class B"* in Boston Business Journal (Vol. 27, October 19, 2007, No. 38, pp. 1)
Pub: American City Business Journals Inc.
Ed: Michelle Hillman. **Description:** Tenants who usually rent top-tier office buildings are migrating to building that are not as expensive. The shift from Class A to Class B buildings is influenced by the high rental cost of the flashy office towers.

17443 ■ *"Prime Site Lands Retirement Center"* in Business Courier (Vol. 24, November 2, 2008, No. 29, pp. 1)
Pub: American City Business Journals, Inc.
Ed: Laura Baverman. **Description:** Erickson Retirement Communities plans to build a $220 milllion campus on 65 acres of land between Evendale and Glendale. The project will depend on votes casted by village councils in Evendale and Glendale, expected to take place in December 2007. Both areas must sign on and alter zoning rules before the development can proceed.

17444 ■ *"Prince of the City"* in Canadian Business (Vol. 80, November 19, 2007, No. 23, pp. 62)
Pub: Rogers Media
Ed: Rachel Pulfer. **Description:** Robert Fung and the Salilent Group aim to revive the poverty-stricken communities in Vancouver by transforming the city's old buildings into designer condominiums using city incentives. Fung and his partners have increased property values in the most unlikely neighborhoods by creating luxury real estate. Fung's recommendations on Vancouver's real estate development are given.

17445 ■ *"Private Equity Firms Focus on Failing Banks"* in Baltimore Business Journal (Vol. 28, July 16, 2010, No. 10, pp. 1)
Pub: Baltimore Business Journal
Ed: Gary Haber. **Description:** Four deals in which assets of failed banks were acquired by private equity firms have been approved by the Federal Deposit Insurance Corporation in the past couple of years. Bay Bank FSK, for example, purchased Bay National Bank's assets in July 2010. Forecasts on more private equity acquisitions in the community banking industry are given.

17446 ■ *"Private Equity Firms Shopping Valley For Deals"* in The Business Journal - Serving Phoenix and the Valley of the Sun (Vol. 29, September 19, 2008, No. 3, pp. 1)
Pub: American City Business Journals, Inc.
Ed: Mike Sunnucks. **Description:** Private equity firms from California, Boston, New York, and overseas are expected to invest in growth-oriented real estate markets that include Phoenix. Real estate experts revealed that privately held investment and acquisition firms are looking to invest in real estate markets hit by the housing crisis. Views and information on private equity firms' real estate investments are presented.

17447 ■ *"Proposal Ruffles Builders"* in Austin Business JournalInc. (Vol. 29, November 20, 2009, No. 37, pp. 1)
Pub: American City Business Journals
Ed: Jacob Dirr. **Description:** A proposal that requires heating, ventilation and cooling equipment checking for a new commercial building having an area of at least 10,000 square feet might cost 25 cents to 50 cents per square foot for the owners. This may lead to higher housing costs. Both the Building and Fire Code Board of Appeals and the Mechanical Plumbing and Solar Board have recommended the plan.

17448 ■ *"Proposed Law Would Stop REIS Bid for Annexation by Livonia"* in Crain's Detroit Business (Vol. 24, March 10, 2008, No. 10, pp. 2)
Pub: Crain Communications, Inc.
Ed: Chad Halcom. **Description:** REIS Northville L.L. C., a joint venture made up of Real Estate Interests Group Inc. and Schostak Bros. & Co., has proposed an $800 million project called Highwood at the former Northville Psychiatric Hospital site but has been stalled due to a disagreement with Northville Township on several terms including: the amount of retail at the site and the paying for cleanup of environmental and medical waste.

17449 ■ *"Proposed Triangle Redo in Motion"* in Crain's Cleveland Business (Vol. 28, October 15, 2007, No. 41, pp. 1)
Pub: Crain Communications, Inc.
Ed: Stan Bullard. **Description:** Zaremba Homes and MRN Ltd. are partnering to redevelop the so-called Triangle section of University Circle. The proposed project will include a total of 434 new rental and for-sale residential suites and as much as 227,000 square feet of retail and restaurant space.

17450 ■ *"Protect Your Assets"* in Black Enterprise (Vol. 38, January 2008, No. 6, pp. 38)
Pub: Earl G. Graves Publishing Co. Inc.
Ed: Trevor Delaney. **Description:** Owner of rental properties seeks advice for incorporating versus getting an LLC for the business.

17451 ■ *"PSU Launches $90 Million Project"* in The Business Journal-Portland (Vol. 25, July 18, 2008, No. 19, pp. 1)
Pub: American City Business Journals, Inc.
Ed: Aliza Earnshaw. **Description:** Portland State University (PSU) has launched a $90-million project for a new business school building, which is to be located at Southwest Market and Southwest Park. The business school is expected to move in to its new 130,000-suqare-foot building by 2013. PSU business school needs to raise $30 million for the project.

17452 ■ *"Pulte May Be Bouncing Back From Stock-Price Doldrums"* in Crain's Detroit Business (Vol. 23, October 8, 2007, No. 41, pp. 4)
Pub: Crain Communications Inc. - Detroit
Ed: Daniel Duggan. **Description:** Pulte Homes saw a jump in its stocks due to Citigroup's analysts rating Pulte and other builders higher due to strong balance sheets.

17453 ■ *"Quarreling Parties Keep Schenectady Redevelopment Plan In Limbo"* in The Business Review Albany (Vol. 35, April 4, 2008, No. 53)
Pub: The Business Review
Ed: Michael DeMasi. **Description:** First National Bank of Scotia chairman Louis H. Buhrmaster opposes the Erie Boulevard design project. as it could negatively affect access to the bank. Buhrmaster, aslo a vice president for Schenectady Industrial Corp, prohibits environmental assessment at the former American Locomotive property. The issues affecting the progress of the planned redevelopment at Schenectady are analyzed.

17454 ■ *"Radio Roots Run Deep"* in The Business Journal-Milwaukee (Vol. 25, July 4, 2008, No. 41, pp. A1)
Pub: American City Business Journals, Inc.
Ed: Rich Kirchen. **Description:** Profile of Steve Palec, a real estate broker at CB Richard Ellis, also works as a radio host for shows 'Rock & Roll Roots' and 'Legends of Rock'. Palec shares that real estate is still his top priority, even with his radio gig. Palec's career as a broker and as a radio host is discussed.

17455 ■ *"Real Estate Ambitions"* in Black Enterprise (Vol. 37, January 2007, No. 6, pp. 101)
Pub: Earl G. Graves Publishing Co. Inc.
Description: National Real Estate Investors Association is a nonprofit trade association for both advanced as well as novice real estate investors that offers information on builders to contractors to banks. When looking to become a real estate investor utilize this organization, talk to various investors like the president of your local chapter, let people know your aspirations, and see if you can find a partner who has experience in the field. Resources included.

17456 ■ *"Real Estate Defaults Top $300M"* in Business Courier (Vol. 26, January 15, 2010, No. 39, pp. 1)
Pub: American City Business Journals, Inc.
Ed: Dan Monk. **Description:** Cincinnati commercial real estate owners defaulting in securitized loans reached $306 million at the end of 2009. The trend has lifted the region's default rate to nearly 9 percent. National average for commercial real estate default is examined.

17457 ■ *"Real Estate Funds Swell Past $350M"* in Business Journal Portland (Vol. 27, December 31, 2010, No. 44, pp. 1)
Pub: Portland Business Journal
Ed: Wendy Culverwell. **Description:** Oregon-based real estate funds have raised around half of the $735 million that was raised by local companies. Investors have been purchasing distressed properties. Commercial real estate prices have declined since 2007.

17458 ■ *Real Estate Loopholes: Secrets of Successful Real Estate Investing*
Pub: Warner Books, Incorporated
Ed: Diane Kennedy, Garrett Sutton, Robert T. Kiyosaki. **Released:** April 2003. **Description:** Knowledge, planning, and building a team of advisor and mentors is key to successful real estate investments.

17459 ■ *"Real Estate Market Still in a Slump"* in Montana Business Quarterly (Vol. 49, Summer 2011, No. 2, pp. 15)
Pub: Bureau of Business & Economic Research
Ed: Patrick M. Barkey. **Description:** Montana's housing market is still in decline with no sign of improving in the near future. Statistical data included.

17460 ■ *The Real Estate Recipe: Make Millions by Buying Small Apartment Properties in Your Spare Time*
Pub: DNA Press
Ed: Brian K. Friedman. **Released:** September 2004. **Price:** $29.95. **Description:** Guide for anyone interested in property investments; the book provides information for choosing an apartment property and answers questions in a chronological workbook format. The author shares his own experiences in apartment investing and shares the entire process of analyzing and buying an apartment property using a hypothetical ten-unit complex. Sample worksheets, checklists, and tables are provided to help readers maintain their own records.

17461 ■ *"Real Estate Vets Take Times In Stride"* in The Business Journal-Serving Metropolitan Kansas City (Vol. 26, July 25, 2008, No. 46)
Pub: American City Business Journals, Inc.
Ed: Rob Roberts. **Description:** Kansas City, Missouri's real estate industry veterans like Allen Block believe that the challenges faced by the industry in the 1980s, when the Federal Reserve Board controlled the money supply to slow down inflation, were worse than the challenges faced today. Other views, trends and information on the real estate industry of the city, are presented.

17462 ■ *"Real Estate Wheeling and Dealing Picks Up"* in Business Journal Portland (Vol. 27, October 29, 2010, No. 35, pp. 1)
Pub: Portland Business Journal
Ed: Wendy Culverwell. **Description:** LoopNet has listed 33 prominent commercial properties for sale in Portland, Oregon's real estate market. However, reasons for the sales rush are not totally clear, but speculations point to the end of the Bush tax cuts in 2010 that prompted real estate investors to close the deals and avoid the increase in capital gains taxes.

17463 ■ *"Real Estate Woes Mount for State's Smaller Banks"* in Boston Business Journal

(Vol. 27, November 30, 2007, No. 44, pp. 1)
Pub: American City Business Journals Inc.
Ed: Craig M. Douglas. **Description:** Massachusetts banking industry is facing a steep increase on loan defaults such as in home mortgages and condominium projects, contrary to public belief that the local industry is safe from the real estate meltdown. The dollar value of local banks' nonperforming loans doubled in 2007, and is rising statewide. Other banking issues in the state are discussed.

17464 ■ *"Real Estate's New Reality" in Entrepreneur (Vol. 37, July 2009, No. 7, pp. 32)*
Pub: Entrepreneur Media, Inc.
Ed: Rosalind Resnick. **Description:** Investing in real estate is still an advisable move, as long as investors are prepared to hold on to the property and there is a rent roll to provide a decent return on investment. Among the key considerations when investing in real estate is the property's expenses and cash flow. Other suggestions for future real estate investors are given.

17465 ■ *"Real Opportunities: Don't Let Mortgage Mayhem Steer You Away From Sound Investments" in Black Enterprise (December 2007)*
Pub: Earl G. Graves Publishing Co. Inc.
Ed: James A. Anderson. **Description:** Real estate investment trusts (REITs) that operate office buildings, industrial parks, shopping malls, hotels, hospitals, or other commercial properties may be a sound investment, despite the mortgage crisis facing the U.S. financial sector.

17466 ■ *"Realities May Blur Vision" in The Business Journal-Serving Metropolitan Kansas City (Vol. 27, September 19, 2008, No. 1, pp. 1)*
Pub: American City Business Journals, Inc.
Ed: Rob Roberts. **Description:** Vision Metcalf is a study by Kansas City that depicts how Metcalf Avenue could look like if redeveloped. Redevelopment plans for the Metcalf corridor include a 20-story mixed-use building on a vacant car dealership. The challenges that the redevelopment plans will face are also analyzed.

17467 ■ *"Recovery on Tap for 2010?" in Orlando Business Journal (Vol. 26, January 1, 2010, No. 31, pp. 1)*
Pub: American City Business Journals
Ed: Melanie Stawicki Azam, Richard Bilbao, Christopher Boyd, Anjali Fluker. **Description:** Economic forecasts for Central Florida's leading business sectors in 2010 are presented. These sectors include housing, film and TV, sports business, law, restaurants, aviation, tourism and hospitality, banking and finance, commercial real estate, retail, health care, insurance, higher education, and manufacturing. According to some local executives, Central Florida's economy will slowly recover in 2010.

17468 ■ *"Red Tape Ties Detroit Housing Rehab Plan" in Crain's Detroit Business (Vol. 24, September 22, 2008, No. 38, pp. 1)*
Pub: Crain Communications Inc.
Ed: Ryan Beene. **Description:** Venture-capital firm Wilherst Oxford LLC is a Florida-based company that has purchased 300 inner-city homes which were in foreclosure in Detroit. Wilherst Oxford is asking the city to forgive the existing tax and utility liens so the firm can utilize the money for home improvements. The city, however, is reluctant but has stated that they are willing to negotiate.

17469 ■ *"The REIT Stuff" in Canadian Business (Vol. 80, March 26, 2007, No. 7, pp. 72)*
Pub: Rogers Media
Description: The stock performance of various real estate investment trusts in Canada is analyzed.

17470 ■ *"REIT's Decry Foreign Limits on Investment" in Globe & Mail (March 29, 2007, pp. B4)*
Pub: CTVglobemedia Publishing Inc.
Ed: Elizabeth Church. **Description:** The planned legislation by Canadian government for regulation foreign investments by real estate investment trusts is discussed.

17471 ■ *"A Renewal in Rentals" in Barron's (Vol. 88, March 17, 2008, No. 11, pp. 17)*
Pub: Dow Jones & Company, Inc.
Description: Discusses the projected entry of the estimated 82 million echo-boomers into the rentals market and the influx of immigrants and displaced homeowners which could turn apartments into lucrative investments again. While apartment-building completions rose slowly since 2003, demand is expected to increase steeply until 2015.

17472 ■ *"Rental Demand Boosts Revenue for Sun Communities Inc." in Crain's Detroit Business (Vol. 24, March 24, 2008, No. 12, pp. 4)*
Pub: Crain Communications, Inc.
Ed: Daniel Duggan. **Description:** Despite the decline in sales of manufactured homes, demand for rental units and rent-to-own programs have brought Sun Communities Inc. increased revenue. The real estate investment trust, based in Southfield, owns, operates, finances and develops manufactured home communities in the Midwest and Southeast. Statistical data included.

17473 ■ *"Reply! Grows at Unprecedented Rate, Rips Beta Off Its Marketplace" in Marketing Weekly News (September 19, 2009, pp. 149)*
Pub: Investment Weekly News
Description: Profile of Reply.com, a leader in locally-targeted Internet marketing, announced significant growth in terms of revenue, enhanced features and services and new categories since launching its beta Reply! Marketplace platform. Even in the face of an economic downturn, the company has posted over 50 percent revenue growth in the Real Estate and Automotive categories.

17474 ■ *"Restoring Grandeur" in Business Courier (Vol. 26, December 4, 2009, No. 32, pp. 1)*
Pub: American City Business Journals, Inc.
Ed: Dan Monk. **Description:** Eagle Realty Group intends to spend more than $10 to restore the historic 12-story Phelps apartment building in Lytle Park in Cincinnati. Its president, Mario San Marco, expressed the need to invest in the building in order to maintain operations. The building could be restored into a hotel catering to executives and consultants.

17475 ■ *"Retail Center Pitched" in Business Courier (Vol. 27, June 18, 2010, No. 7, pp. 1)*
Pub: Business Courier
Ed: Dan Monk. **Description:** Jeffrey R. Anderson Real Estate Inc.'s plan for a retail center in Butler County, Ohio could have three department stores in the 1.1 million-square-foot property. An outdoor sports retailer is also part of the plans.

17476 ■ *"Retail Center Planned for Canton Site" in Boston Business Journal (Vol. 29, May 20, 2011, No. 2, pp. 1)*
Pub: American City Business Journals Inc.
Ed: Daniel J. Sernovitz. **Description:** A real estate development team is planning to build a shopping center at Canton Crossing in Baltimore, Maryland and is near closing the deal with ExxonMobil Corporation who owns the waterfront site.

17477 ■ *"Retail Slump Deflates Local Development" in Business Courier (Vol. 24, February 29, 2008, No. 47, pp. 1)*
Pub: American City Business Journals, Inc.
Ed: Lisa Biank Fasig. **Description:** 2007 sales of the retail industry are the slowest since the year 2003, driving retail stores to reconsider their expansion plans for 2008. A number of retail projects have been delayed, cancelled or altered, including Newport Pavilion, Rivers Crossing, Wal-Mart Supercenters, Legacy Place and Millworks. The impacts of retail slowdown on development projects are analyzed further.

17478 ■ *"Revitalizing Real Estate: Couple Sails Through Sea of Housing Woes" in Black*

Enterprise (Vol. 38, February 2008, No. 7, pp. 50)
Pub: Earl G. Graves Publishing Co. Inc.
Ed: Ayana Dixon. **Description:** Owner, Christopher Gablin and Regina Mincey-Garlin offer a broad range of real estate-related services to clients in order to not only survive, but thrive in today's market.

17479 ■ *"Rise in Occupancy Rate Fuels Area Hotel Building Boom" in Crain's Detroit Business (Vol. 24, March 10, 2008, No. 10, pp. 14)*
Pub: Crain Communications, Inc.
Ed: Jonathan Eppley. **Description:** Due to a rise in the region's yearly occupancy rate, a number of new hotel construction and renovation projects are slated for the Detroit area.

17480 ■ *"A Rise in Rental Units" in Philadelphia Business Journal (Vol. 30, October 7, 2011, No. 34, pp. 1)*
Pub: American City Business Journals Inc.
Ed: Natalie Kostelni. **Description:** Housing developers have been stepping up the construction of new apartment complexes throughout the suburbs of Pennsylvania in order to capture growing demand for rental properties. BPG Properties Ltd. has nearly 1,000 new apartments under construction.

17481 ■ *"Roger Rechler Played Major Role in Long Island's Evolution" in Commercial Property News (March 17, 2008)*
Pub: Nielsen Company
Description: Profile of Roger Rechler, real estate developer on Long Island, New York, is presented. Rechler, who died in March 2008, was instrumental in the development, ownership and operations of the largest commercial real estate portfolio on Long Island.

17482 ■ *"Roy MacDowell Jr." in Boston Business Journal (Vol. 31, June 10, 2011, No. 20, pp. 1)*
Pub: Boston Business Journal
Ed: Craig M. Douglas. **Description:** Real estate developer Roy MacDowell is selling his Boston, Massachusetts estate. The asking price for the property is $21.8 million. MacDowell recently suffered setbacks in his finances.

17483 ■ *"Sale of Solo Cup Plant Pending" in Boston Business Journal (Vol. 29, June 17, 2011, No. 6, pp. 1)*
Pub: American City Business Journals Inc.
Ed: Daniel J. Sernovitz. **Description:** Baltimore developers Vanguard Equities Inc. and Greenberg Gibbons Commercial have contracted to buy the Solo Cup Company facility in Owing Mills and are now considering several plans for the property. Sale should be completed by September 2011 but no proposed sale terms are disclosed.

17484 ■ *"Sandi Jackson; Alderman, 7th Ward, City of Chicago" in Crain's Chicago Business (Vol. 31, May 5, 2008, No. 18, pp. 31)*
Pub: Crain Communications, Inc.
Ed: Sarah A. Klein. **Description:** Profile of Sandi Jackson who is an alderman of the 7th ward of the city of Chicago and is addressing issues such as poverty and crime as well as counting on a plan to develop the former USX Corp. steel mill to revitalize the area's economic climate.

17485 ■ *"Scaled-Down Phoenix Condos Emerge as DNA" in The Business Journal - Serving Phoenix and the Valley of the Sun (Vol. 28, July 11, 2008, No. 45, pp. 1)*
Pub: American City Business Journals, Inc.
Ed: Yvonne Zusel. **Description:** Pointe of View Developments and Belleview Communities have scaled back their Copper Pointe Condominiums project in downtown Phoenix, Arizona. The scaled-back project has also changed its name into Downtown's Newest Address Condominiums and will cost $42 million.

17486 ■ *"Search Engine: GE Looks Around"* **in Business Courier (Vol. 24, March 7, 2008, No. 48, pp. 1)**
Pub: American City Business Journals, Inc.
Ed: Laura Baverman. **Description:** GE Aviation, an aircraft engine company, could move about 1,500 Tri-employees to its new office in West Chester, Liberty Township, Northern Kentucky, as its leases are set to expire in 2009 and 2010. The company revealed that developers are prompting the firm to send out a request-for-proposal to choose development companies in 2008.

17487 ■ *"Seeing Green in Going Green"* **in The Business Journal-Serving Greater Tampa Bay (Vol. 28, July 4, 2008, No. 28, pp. 1)**
Pub: American City Business Journals, Inc.
Ed: Janet Leiser. **Description:** Atlanta, Georgia-based developer IDI Corp. is pushing for Leadership in Energy and Environmental Design certification for the warehouse that is currently under construction at Madison Business Center along Port Sutton and U.S. 41. The industrial building is the first in Tampa Bay to seek certification for LEED as set by the U.S. Green Building Council.

17488 ■ *"Sellers Face Excess Land Dilemma"* **in Crain's Cleveland Business (Vol. 28, November 12, 2007, No. 45, pp. 1)**
Pub: Crain Communications, Inc.
Ed: Stan Bullard. **Description:** Overview on the way in which the housing slump is effecting builders, land developers and lot prices. Statistical data included.

17489 ■ *"Silverdome Bidders Bring New Proposals"* **in Crain's Detroit Business (Vol. 24, March 17, 2008, No. 11, pp. 23)**
Pub: Crain Communications, Inc.
Ed: Daniel Duggan. **Description:** Discusses the seven plans which have been proposed as part of the third round of bidding for the Pontiac Silverdome; proposals range from Global Baseball Inc., a baseball league that would pit a team from every country against one another, to an Indian casino, a musical 'hall of fame', a convention center, a horse track, a hotel and an indoor water park.

17490 ■ *"Sitting, Sitting, Sitting-Snapshots of Homes that Just Won't Sell"* **in Crain's Chicago Business (Vol. 31, April 21, 2008, No. 16)**
Pub: Crain Communications, Inc.
Ed: Kevin Davis. **Description:** Listing of five Chicago-area homes that have been on the market for an extended length of time; also includes the original asking price, current asking price, special features and the biggest challenge of each home.

17491 ■ *"Six Leading Economists on What to Expect in the Year Ahead: Derek Holt; Housing"* **in Canadian Business (December 24, 2007)**
Pub: Rogers Media
Ed: Derek Holt. **Description:** The Canadian subprime mortgage market could take a different turn from that of the U.S. as laws governing Canada's mortgage market indirectly limit the probability of a slowdown. Details on how Canada avoided the slowdown in the housing market and forecasts of new homes for 2008 are discussed.

17492 ■ *"Sixty-Acre Vision for North Suburbs"* **in Business Courier (Vol. 24, April 4, 2008, No. 52, pp. 1)**
Pub: American City Business Journals, Inc.
Ed: Laura Baverman. **Description:** Al Neyer Inc. plans for a mixed-use development at the 60-acre site it has recently purchased. The mixed-use project could cost up to $100 million, and will include medical offices, residential buildings, and corporate offices. Details of Al Neyer's plans for the site are given.

17493 ■ *"Small Changes Can Mean Big Energy Savings"* **in Crain's Cleveland Business (Vol. 28, November 5, 2007, No. 44, pp. 21)**
Pub: Crain Communications, Inc.
Ed: Harriet Tramer. **Description:** Many Northeast Ohio businesses are taking their cues from the

residential real estate market to draw and capitalize on interest in energy efficiency and is regularly taken into account by local architects.

17494 ■ *"Sneak Preview: Alamo Revamp"* **in Austin Business JournalInc. (Vol. 28, December 12, 2008, No. 39, pp. 1)**
Pub: American City Business Journals
Ed: Sandra Zaragoza. **Description:** Austin, Texas-based Alamo Drafthouse Cinemas is planning to build a new Circle C Ranch. The new theater will showcase digital projectors and the latest sound systems to show 3-D movies. The company is in lease negotiations with developer Stratus Properties Inc.

17495 ■ *"S.O.S. Sorting Out Subprime"* **in Black Enterprise (Vol. 38, November 2007, No. 4, pp. 76)**
Pub: Earl G. Graves Publishing Co. Inc.
Ed: Trevor Delaney. **Description:** Subprime distress in the housing market is discussed and the impact it has put on investors.

17496 ■ *"Soured Relationship Plays Out in Courts"* **in The Business Journal-Serving Greater Tampa Bay (Vol. 28, September 19, 2008, No. 39)**
Pub: American City Business Journals, Inc.
Ed: Janet Leiser. **Description:** Heirs of developer Julian Hawthorne Lifset won a court battle to end a 50-year lease with Specialty Restaurants Corp. in Rocky Point. The decision opens the Tampa Bay prime waterfront property for new development.

17497 ■ *"South Loop Site Lands a Buyer"* **in Crain's Chicago Business (Vol. 31, March 24, 2008, No. 12, pp. 1)**
Pub: Crain Communications, Inc.
Ed: Alby Gallun. **Description:** Russland Capital Group, a little-known condominium developer from Skokie, recently purchased a 6.5-acre riverside property in the site known as Franklin Point for $40 million.

17498 ■ *"Stadium Developers Seek a Win With the State"* **in The Business Journal-Serving Metropolitan Kansas City (Vol. 26, August 22, 2008)**
Pub: American City Business Journals, Inc.
Ed: Rob Roberts. **Description:** Three Trails Redevelopment LLC is hoping to win $30 million in state tax credits from the Missouri Development Finance Board for the construction of an 18,500-seat Wizards stadium. The project is contingent on state tax incentives and the company remains optimistic about their goal.

17499 ■ *"Staging a Martini-and-GQ Lifestyle; Faux Possessions Play to Buyer's Aspirations"* **in Crain's Chicago Business (April 21, 2008)**
Pub: Crain Communications, Inc.
Ed: Kevin Davis. **Description:** Due to the competition of the slumping housing market, home stagers are becoming more prominent and are using creative ways to make an impression beyond de-cluttering, painting and cleaning by using accents such as casually placed magazines, candles and table settings.

17500 ■ *"State Center Lease Deal High for Md."* **in Baltimore Business Journal (Vol. 28, August 6, 2010, No. 13, pp. 1)**
Pub: Baltimore Business Journal
Ed: Daniel J. Sernovitz. **Description:** The proposed $1.5 billion State Center development project in Midtown Baltimore might cause the State of Maryland to pay the most expensive rental rates in the city. The state will have to pay an effective rental rate of $34 per square foot, including expenses, on the leasing. Other details of the redevelopment project are discussed.

17501 ■ *"State Printing Plant on the Move"* **in Sacramento Business Journal (Vol. 25, August 29, 2008, No. 26, pp. 1)**
Pub: American City Business Journals, Inc.
Ed: Michael Shaw; Celia Lamb. **Description:** California is planning to replace its printing plant on Richards Boulevard and 7th Street with a newly built or

leased facility in the Sacramento area. It was revealed that the project will meet the state's standards for new buildings. It is believed that the new site will require 15 acres or more depending on requirements.

17502 ■ *"State Wants to Add Escape Clause to Leases"* **in Sacramento Business Journal (Vol. 28, October 14, 2011, No. 33, pp. 1)**
Pub: Sacramento Business Journal
Ed: Michael Shaw. **Description:** California Governor Jerry Brown's administration has decided to add escape clauses to new lease agreements, which created new worry for building owners and brokers in Sacramento, California. Real estate brokers believe the appropriation of funds clauses have been making the lenders nervous and would result in less competition.

17503 ■ *"Still Looking Good"* **in Canadian Business (Vol. 80, March 26, 2007, No. 7, pp. 29)**
Pub: Rogers Media
Ed: Andy Holloway. **Description:** The real estate prices in various parts of Canada are analyzed. The future growth potential of the industry is forecasted.

17504 ■ *"Stuck With Two Mortgages; The Nightmare When Buyers Upgrade"* **in Crain's Chicago Business (Vol. 31, April 21, 2008, No. 16)**
Pub: Crain Communications, Inc.
Ed: Darci Smith. **Description:** Discusses the problem a number of people are facing due to the slump in the housing market: being stuck with two mortgages when they move because their former homes have not sold. Many thought they could afford to move to a larger home, anticipating significant equity appreciation that did not occur; now they are left with lowering their price and competing with the host of new developments.

17505 ■ *"Sundt, DPR Score $470 Million Biotech Project"* **in The Business Journal - Serving Phoenix and the Valley of the Sun (Vol. 29, September 19, 2008, No. 3, pp. 1)**
Pub: American City Business Journals, Inc.
Ed: Jan Buchholz. **Description:** Sundt Inc. and DPR Construction Inc. were awarded the winning joint-venture contract to develop the second phase of the Arizona Biomedical Collaborative on the Phoenix Biomedical Campus. Both firms declined to comment, but an employee of the Arizona Board of Regents confirmed that the firms won the bidding. Views and information on the development project are presented.

17506 ■ *"Sunriver Venture Hits Snag"* **in The Business Journal-Portland (Vol. 25, August 1, 2008, No. 21, pp. 1)**
Pub: American City Business Journals, Inc.
Ed: Robin J. Moody. **Description:** Portland, Oregon based-Sunwest Management Inc. has divided its Sunriver resort community to make way for a redevelopment plan. Sunwest owner Jon Harder and three partners formed SilverStar Destinations LLC to broker the purchase and redevelopment of the property. Details and description of the redevelopment project are also presented.

17507 ■ *"Sunwest Vies To Stave Off Bankruptcy"* **in The Business Journal-Portland (Vol. 25, August 15, 2008, No. 23, pp. 1)**
Pub: American City Business Journals, Inc.
Ed: Robin J. Moody. **Description:** Sunwest Management Inc. is teetering on the edge of bankruptcy as creditors start foreclosure on nine of their properties. This could potentially displace residents of the assisted living operator. Sunwest is trying to sell smaller packages of properties to get a $100 million bridge loan to maintain operations.

17508 ■ *"Survey: Apartment Rents Continue to Climb as Home Market Slows"* **in Business Review, Albany New York (November 23, 2007)**
Pub: American City Business Journals, Inc.
Ed: Michael DeMasi. **Description:** Survey by Sunrise Management and Consulting shows that asking rents for apartments in the Capital Region increased for

the thirteenth consecutive time. The survey, which was conducted between August and October 2007, also showed that Albany County, New York had the highest average asking rent, followed by Rensselaer County, Saratoga County, and Schenectady County.

17509 ■ *"Survey Says Commercial Real Estate Headed for Turbulence"* in *Commercial Property News (March 17, 2008)*
Pub: Nielsen Company
Description: Commercial real estate sector is declining due to the sluggish U.S. economy. According to a recent survey, national office, retail and hospitality markets are also on the decline.

17510 ■ *"Swope: Breakup Won't Delay Job"* in *The Business Journal-Serving Metropolitan Kansas City (Vol. 26, August 22, 2008, No. 50, pp. 1)*
Pub: American City Business Journals, Inc.
Ed: Rob Roberts. **Description:** Swope Community Builders said that the Kansas City Redevelopment Project will not be delayed by the breakup of their partnership with Sherman Associates Inc. Swopes will be the sole master developer of the project.

17511 ■ *"Tampa Condo Conversion Sells for $14.8 Million Less"* in *The Business Journal-Serving Greater Tampa Bay (Vol. 28, September 5, 2008)*
Pub: American City Business Journals, Inc.
Ed: Janet Leiser. **Description:** Former apartment complex Village Oaks at Tampa, which was converted to condominiums, has been sold to Tennessee-based real estate investment trust Mid-America Apartment Communities Inc. for $21.2 million in August 2008. The amount was $14.2 million less than what developer Radco Management LLC paid for in 2005.

17512 ■ *"Tax Abatement Changes Seen as Home Run for Cleveland Condo Market"* in *Crain's Cleveland Business (Vol. 30, June 15, 2009, No. 23)*
Pub: Crain Communications, Inc.
Ed: Jay Miller. **Description:** Condominium ownership became a bit more affordable for Cleveland residents since changes in both state and local tax abatement policy changes. The tax credits are examined.

17513 ■ *"Taxpayers' Banks Share Even Higher"* in *Business Courier (Vol. 24, October 26, 2008, No. 28, pp. 1)*
Pub: American City Business Journals, Inc.
Ed: Dan Monk; Lucy May. **Description:** Banks Working Group originally announced that it needs $106 million in public funds to build the Banks riverfront development but then declared it needs $45 million more from Cincinnati and Hamilton County after it approved a deal for the project. It would not be easy for the city and the county to come up with the money but many decision-makers think it's worth it.

17514 ■ *"That Empty Feeling"* in *Crain's Cleveland Business (Vol. 28, October 15, 2007, No. 41, pp. 1)*
Pub: Crain Communications, Inc.
Ed: Stan Bullard. **Description:** Townhouses, cluster homes and condominiums lured both buyers and builders for most of this decade but now that market is suffering to an even greater degree than the single-family home market. Statistical data included.

17515 ■ *"Threat of New Office Space Records Rent Hikes"* in *Globe & Mail (March 21, 2007, pp. B4)*
Pub: CTVglobemedia Publishing Inc.
Ed: Elizabeth Church. **Description:** The increasing commercial rent prices in the Toronto region amid the high office building construction market are discussed.

17516 ■ *"Three Trails Blazes Tax Credit Deal"* in *The Business Journal-Serving Metropolitan Kansas City (Vol. 27, November 7, 2008, No. 9)*
Pub: American City Business Journals, Inc.
Ed: Rob Roberts. **Description:** Three Trails Redevelopment LLC plans to redevelop the Bannister Mall area. The Missouri Development Finance Board is

expected to approve $30 million in tax credits for the project. A verbal agreement on the terms and conditions has already been reached according to the agency's executive director.

17517 ■ *"TMC Development Closes $1.1 Million Real Estate Purchase"* in *Internet Wire (September 17, 2009)*
Pub: Comtex News Network, Inc.
Description: TMC Development announced the closing of a $1.1 million real estate purchase for Mansa, LLC dba Kwikee Mart, a Napa-based convenience store; TMC helped the company secure a Small Business Administration 504 loan in order to purchase the acquisition of a 3,464 square foot building. SBA created the 504 loan program to provide financing for growing small and medium-sized businesses.

17518 ■ *"Tom Gaglardi"* in *Canadian Business (Vol. 82, April 27, 2009, No. 7, pp. 56)*
Pub: Rogers Media
Ed: Calvin Leung. **Description:** Northland Properties Corporation president Tom Gaglardi believes that their business model of keeping much of operations in-house allows the firm to crate assets at a lesser price while commanding higher margins than their competitors. He believes that it is an ideal time to invest in the hospitality industry because of opportunities to purchase properties at low prices.

17519 ■ *"Top Twenty Wealthiest Landowners"* in *Hawaii Business (Vol. 53, November 2007, No. 5, pp. 34)*
Pub: Hawaii Business Publishing
Description: Provided is a table of the wealthiest landowners in Hawaii. Their assessed value, total acres owned, prominent holdings, other notable holdings and years of presence in Hawaii are also provided. Statistical data included.

17520 ■ *"Tough Sell: Senior Projects Hustle to Keep Buyers"* in *Puget Sound Business Journal (Vol. 29, November 21, 2008, No. 31, pp.)*
Pub: American City Business Journals
Ed: Heidi Dietrich. **Description:** Plans to move to retirement communities are being postponed by seniors in Washington's Puget Sound area due to difficulty selling their current homes in the slow economy. Retirement communities are trying to lure clients by offering new finance programs and sales plans.

17521 ■ *"Tripped by Trump?"* in *The Business Journal-Serving Greater Tampa Bay (Vol. 28, July 25, 2008, No. 31, pp. 1)*
Pub: American City Business Journals, Inc.
Ed: Michael Hinman. **Description:** Jean Shahnasarian, a buyer of the Trump Tower Tampa, filed cases against Donald Trump, The Trump Organization Inc., and Trump Tower Tampa for giving misleading information about Trump's involvement in the project. She wants a return of her $278,000 deposit and does not want to take part in the sale of the project.

17522 ■ *"Troubled Project In Court"* in *The Business Journal-Portland (Vol. 25, July 25, 2008, No. 20, pp. 1)*
Pub: American City Business Journals, Inc.
Ed: Wendy Culverwell. **Description:** Views and information on Salpare Bay's Hayden Island project, as well as on financing problems and cases associated with the project, are presented. Construction of luxurious waterside condominiums stopped last fall, after the discovery of financing problems and subcontractors and other parties started filing claims and counterclaims.

17523 ■ *"Troy Complex has New Brand, New Leases"* in *Crain's Detroit Business (Vol. 24, April 14, 2008, No. 15, pp. 32)*
Pub: Crain Communications Inc.
Ed: Daniel Duggan. **Description:** Discusses the re-branding of the 1.2 million-square-foot collection of office buildings in Troy purchased by New York-based Emmes Co. The firm has also pledged more than $6

million in upgrades, hired a new leasing company and completed 67,000 square feet of leasing with another 100,000 in negotiations.

17524 ■ *"UMKC, Hospital Drill Down on Deal"* in *The Business Journal-Serving Metropolitan Kansas City (Vol. 26, July 18, 2008, No. 45, pp. 1)*
Pub: American City Business Journals, Inc.
Ed: Rob Roberts. **Description:** University of Missouri Kansas City and Children's Mercy Hospital are negotiating the hospital's potential acquisition of the university's School of Dentistry building. The deal would transfer the 240,000-square foot dental school building to Children's Mercy. Plans for a new dental school building for the UMKC are also presented.

17525 ■ *"Unwanted News for Hospitals"* in *Business Courier (Vol. 24, October 26, 2008, No. 28, pp. 1)*
Pub: American City Business Journals, Inc.
Description: Christ and St. Luke Hospital might be sharing responsibility costs on the $207 million hospital being built by Health Alliance, the group they are parting with. Christ and St. Lu ke hospitals will be paying $60 million and $25 miilion for partial liability res pectively because the plans for the said project were already underway before they decided to withdraw. Christ Hospital is involved in a whistleblower case that might cause $424 million in liability across the group.

17526 ■ *Use What You've Got*
Pub: Portfolio Publishing
Ed: Barbara Corcoran, Bruce Littlefield. **Released:** 2003. **Price:** $24.95. **Description:** Founder and chairman of New York's premier real estate company, the Corcoran Group, shares her successes in the real estate industry. The book offers tips and pointers to salespeople, entrepreneurs and business people alike. Corcoran explains how she went from waiting tables and borrowed $1,000 from a boyfriend to build her real estate company into the industry's powerhouse.

17527 ■ *"Vernon Revamp"* in *Business Courier (Vol. 26, October 9, 2009, No. 24, pp. 1)*
Pub: American City Business Journals, Inc.
Ed: Dan Monk. **Description:** Al Neyer Inc. will redevelop the Vernon Manor Hotel as an office building for the Cincinnati Children's Hospital Medical Center. The project will cost $35 million and would generate a new investment vehicle for black investors who plan to raise $2.7 million in private offerings to claim majority ownership of the property after its renovations.

17528 ■ *"Vision for Camden in Better Focus"* in *Philadelphia Business Journal (Vol. 30, September 30, 2011, No. 33, pp. 1)*
Pub: American City Business Journals Inc.
Ed: Natalie Kostelni. **Description:** More than $500 million worth of projects aimed at redeveloping the downtown and waterfront areas of Camden, New Jersey are being planned. These include the construction of residential, commercial, and education buildings.

17529 ■ *"Wannabe Buyers Take Their Own Sweet Time"* in *Crain's Chicago Business (Vol. 31, April 21, 2008, No. 16, pp. 50)*
Pub: Crain Communications, Inc.
Ed: Lisa Bertagnoli. **Description:** Although all factors are in place for a robust real-estate market in the Chicago area: low interest rates, plenty of inventory and the region's relatively strong employment, buyers are taking their time and doing more research in order to see how bad the economy will get.

17530 ■ *"Wary Investors Turn to a Different Market for Strong Returns"* in *Boston Business Journal (Vol. 29, September 2, 2011, No. 17, pp. 1)*
Pub: American City Business Journals Inc.
Ed: Daniel J. Sernovitz. **Description:** Maryland-based investors have been choosing to put their money in the supermarket business. Retail property sales have increased during the second quarter of 2011.

17531 ■ *"Was Mandating Solar Power Water Heaters For New Homes Good Policy?" in Hawaii Business (Vol. 54, August 2008, No. 2, pp. 28)*
Pub: Hawaii Business Publishing

Description: Senator Gary L. Kooser of District 7 Kauai-Niihau believes that the mandating of energy-efficient water heaters for new single-family homes starting in 2010 will help cut Hawaii's oil consumption. Ron Richmond of the Hawaii Solar Energy Association says that the content of SB 644 has negative consequences as it allows for choice of energy and not just solar, and it also eliminates tax credits for new homebuyers.

17532 ■ *"Watershed Solution" in Business Courier (Vol. 24, December 14, 2008, No. 35, pp. 1)*
Pub: American City Business Journals, Inc.

Ed: Dan Monk. **Description:** Discusses the Metropolitan Sewer District of Greater Cincinnati which is planning to spend around $128 million for its 20-year green-infrastructure improvement projects. Part of the project involves construction of green roofs, rain gardens and restored wetlands to manage water overflows.

17533 ■ *"Waugh Chapel to Expand" in Baltimore Business Journal (Vol. 28, August 27, 2010, No. 16, pp. 1)*
Pub: Baltimore Business Journal

Ed: Daniel J. Sernovitz. **Description:** Developer Greenberg Gibbons Corporation has broken ground on a $275 million, 1.2 million-square-foot addition to its Village at the Waugh Chapel mixed-use complex. Aside from creating 2,600 permanent jobs, the addition, named Village South, is expected to lure Target and Wegmans Food Markets to Crofton, Maryland. Funding for this project is discussed.

17534 ■ *"Weyerhaeuser's REIT Decision Shouldn't Scare Investors Away" in Barron's (Vol. 88, June 30, 2008, No. 26, pp. 18)*
Pub: Dow Jones & Co., Inc.

Ed: Christopher Williams. **Description:** Weyerhaeuser Co.'s management said that a conversion to a real estate investment trust was not likely in 2009 since the move is not tax-efficient as of the moment and would overload its non-timber assets with debt. The company's shares have fallen by 19.5 percent. However, the company remains an asset-rich outfit and its activist shareholder is pushing for change.

17535 ■ *"What Happens in Vegas Could Happen in Baltimore, Too" in Boston Business Journal (Vol. 29, June 17, 2011, No. 6, pp. 1)*
Pub: American City Business Journals Inc.

Ed: Daniel J. Sernovitz. **Description:** At least 36 companies expressed their interest in developing a casino in South Baltimore following the state commission's announcement for bids. Developers have until July 28, 2011 to submit their proposals. Baltimore's strong economy is the major factor for the interest, yet the fact that blackjack and poker are outlawed in Maryland could be a drawback.

17536 ■ *"What Homes Do Retirees Want?" in Canadian Business (Vol. 79, July 17, 2006, No. 14-15, pp.)*
Pub: Rogers Media

Ed: Joe Cataldo. **Description:** The obstacles and challenges faced by homebuilders in Canada as well as the approach adopted by them to appeal to the mature homebuilders segment, is discussed.

17537 ■ *"What Players in the Midmarket Are Talking About" in Mergers & Acquisitions: The Dealmaker's Journal (March 1, 2008)*
Pub: SourceMedia, Inc.

Description: Sports Properties Acquisition Corp. went public at the end of January; according to the company's prospectus, it is not limiting its focus to just teams, it is also considering deals for stadium construction companies, sports leagues, facilities, sports-related advertising and licensing of products, in addition to other related segments.

17538 ■ *"What's Ahead for Fannie and Fred?" in Barron's (Vol. 90, August 30, 2010, No. 35, pp. 26)*
Pub: Barron's Editorial & Corporate Headquarters

Ed: Jonathan R. Laing. **Description:** A meeting presided by Treasury Secretary Timothy Geithner discussed the future of Fannie Mae and Freddie Mac. The two government sponsored enterprises were mismanaged and reforming these two agencies is critical.

17539 ■ *"When Anything (And Everything) Goes" in Globe & Mail (January 12, 2007, pp. B4)*
Pub: CTVglobemedia Publishing Inc.

Ed: Elizabeth Church. **Description:** The forecast on acquisition of different real estate firms is presented.

17540 ■ *"Where Are the Vultures?" in Mergers & Acquisitions: The Dealmaker's Journal (March 1, 2008)*
Pub: SourceMedia, Inc.

Ed: Ken MacFadyen. **Description:** Although the real estate market is distressed, not many acquisitions are being made by distress private equity investors; this is due, in part, to the difficulty in assessing real estate industry firms since it is a sector which is so localized.

17541 ■ *"With Building Plans in Flux, County Could Sell Key Site" in Crain's Cleveland Business (Vol. 28, October 8, 2007, No. 40, pp. 1)*
Pub: Crain Communications, Inc.

Ed: Jay Miller. **Description:** Due to such issues as financial and administrative problems, Cuyahoga County commissioners have pushed back the construction timeline for a planned county administration center and are saying that they are considering selling the site in downtown Cleveland to developers who would erect a new office building that another large tenant could occupy.

17542 ■ *"Wobbling Economy" in The Business Journal-Serving Metropolitan Kansas City (Vol. 27, September 26, 2008, No. 2, pp. 1)*
Pub: American City Business Journals, Inc.

Ed: Rob Roberts. **Description:** Real estate developers in Kansas City Metropolitan Area are worried of the possible impacts of the crisis at Wall Street. They expect tightening of the credit market, which will result in difficulty of financing their projects. The potential effects of the Wall Street crisis are examined further.

17543 ■ *"Working It Out! How a Young Executive Overcomes Obstacles on the Job" in Black Enterprise (Vol. 37, January 2007, No. 6, pp. 55)*
Pub: Earl G. Graves Publishing Co. Inc.

Ed: Laura Egodigwe. **Description:** Interview with Susan Chapman, Global Head of Operations for Citigroup Realty Services, in which she discusses issues such as the important skills necessary for overcoming obstacles in the workplace.

17544 ■ *The Working Man and Woman's Guide to Becoming a Millionaire*
Pub: Prentiss Publishing

Ed: Al Herron. **Released:** November 2006. **Description:** President and CEO of a Century 21 office in Dallas, Texas shares insight into financial security and commitment to community.

17545 ■ *"The Worst Lies Ahead for Wall Street; More Losses Certain" in Crain's New York Business (Vol. 24, January 21, 2008, No. 3, pp. 1)*
Pub: Crain Communications, Inc.

Ed: Aaron Elstein. **Description:** Due to the weakening economy, many financial institutions will face further massive losses forcing them to borrow more at higher interest rates and dragging down their earnings for years to come. The effects on commercial real estate and credit card loans are also discussed as well as the trend to investing in Asia and the Middle East.

17546 ■ *"Yamasaki Lays Off Last of U.S. Workers, to Vacate World Headquarters in Troy" in Crain's Detroit Business (Jan. 11, 2010)*
Pub: Crain Communications Inc.

Ed: Chad Halcom. **Description:** Overview of the impact on the local economy resulting from the closing of Yamasaki Associates, Inc.'s world headquarters located in Troy. The architectural firm notified the last of its employees that they would, indeed be laid off effective December 31.

17547 ■ *"Yamasaki Lays Off Last of U.S. Workers, to Vacate World Headquarters in Troy" in Crain's Detroit Business (Vol. 26, January 11, 2010)*
Pub: Crain Communications, Inc.

Ed: Chad Halcom. **Description:** Overview of the impact on the local economy resulting from the closing of Yamasaki Associates, Inc.'s world headquarters located in Troy. The architectural firm notified the last of its employees that they would, indeed be laid off effective December 31.

17548 ■ *"You Won't Go Broke Filling Up On These Stocks" in Barron's (Vol. 88, July 14, 2008, No. 28, pp. 38)*
Pub: Dow Jones & Co., Inc.

Ed: Assif Shameen. **Description:** Due to high economic growth, pro-business policies and a consumption boom, the Middle East is a good place to look for equities. The best ways in which to gain exposure to this market include investing in the real estate industry and telecommunications markets as well as large banks that serve corporations and consumers.

17549 ■ *Your First Year in Real Estate: Making the Transition from Total Novice to Successful Professional*
Pub: Crown Business Books

Ed: Dirk Zeller. **Released:** $August 3, 2010. **Price:** $20.00. **Description:** Zeller helps new realtors to select the right company, develop mentor and client relationships, using the Internet and social networking to stay ahead of competition, to set and reach career goals, to stay current in the market, and more.

17550 ■ *"Your Place: Housing Developers Try to Read Generation Y" in Philadelphia Inquirer (December 2, 2010)*
Pub: Philadelphia Media Network Inc.

Ed: Al Heavens. **Description:** Results of a survey conducted with Generation Y individuals are examined, focusing on housing developments and whether this particular generation prefers suburban or rural lifestyles. Generation Y encompasses people ages 18 to 32 years old. Statistical data included.

17551 ■ *Your Successful Real Estate Career, 5h Edition*
Pub: American Management Association
Contact: Charles R. Craig, Chairman

Ed: Kenneth W. Edwards. **Released:** 2006. **Price:** $18.95.

TRADE PERIODICALS

17552 ■ *Business Opportunities Journal*
Pub: Business Service Corp.

URL(s): www.boj.com. **Ed:** Mark Adkins. **Released:** Monthly

17553 ■ *California Real Estate Journal*
Pub: Daily Journal Corp.
Contact: Gerald L. Salzman, President

URL(s): www.dailyjournal.com/www.carealestatejournal.com/. **Released:** Weekly **Price:** $124, Individuals; $41, Individuals first time subscriber for 6 months.

17554 ■ *The CF Apartment Reporter*
Pub: Clayton-Fillmore Ltd.
Contact: Howard Treibitz, President

URL(s): www.clayfil.com. **Released:** Bimonthly **Price:** $199, Individuals 4.00 per city.

17555 ■ Commercial Investment Real Estate
Pub: CCIM Institute
Contact: Tim Hatlestad, President
E-mail: tim@investaz.com
URL(s): www.ccim.com/cire-magazinewww.ccim.
com. **Released:** Bimonthly **Price:** $45, Individuals;
$55, Canada and Mexico.

17556 ■ Corporate Real Estate Executive
Pub: CoreNet Global
Contact: Angela Cain, Chief Executive Officer
Ed: Kathleen B. Dempsey. **Released:** 9/year.

**17557 ■ Daily Commerce: Serving the
Southern California Real Estate Investor**
Pub: Daily Journal Corp.
Contact: Gerald L. Salzman, President
URL(s): www.dailyjournal.com. **Ed:** David Houston.
Released: Daily (eve.) **Price:** $264, Individuals;
$191, Individuals 6 months.

17558 ■ The Daily Record
Pub: The Daily Record Corp.
URL(s): www.dailyrecord.com. **Released:** Daily
Price: $13.48, Individuals daily; $7.57, Individuals
weekends; $5.61, Individuals Sundays only.

**17559 ■ Entertainment and Specialty
Projects**
Pub: TKO/Real Estate Advisory Group Inc.
Ed: Ann O'Neal, Editor, ann@specialtyretail.net. **Released:** Monthly. **Price:** $249. **Description:** Covers
various aspects of entertainment and specialty retailing, real estate, and downtown redevelopment.
Recurring features include letters to the editor,
interviews, news of research, a calendar of events,
book reviews, news of educational opportunities, job
listings, and notices of publications available.

17560 ■ First Tuesday
Pub: Realty Publications Inc.
URL(s): www.firsttuesdayonline.com/. **Released:**
Monthly

17561 ■ The Institutional Real Estate Letter
Pub: Institutional Real Estate Inc.
Contact: Nyia Dohrmann, President
E-mail: n.dohrmann@irei.com
URL(s): www.irei.com/web/do/pub/publication/vie-
w?id=4. **Ed:** Geoffrey Dohrmann. **Released:** Monthly
Price: $2495, Individuals.

**17562 ■ Montana Land Magazine: Features
Properties for Sale in Montana and
Surrounding States**
Pub: Lee Enterprises Inc.
Contact: Mary E. Junck, President
URL(s): www.montanalandmagazine.com. **Released:**
Quarterly **Price:** $30, Individuals; $60, Out of country.

17563 ■ National Property Law Digests
Pub: Strafford Publications Inc.
Contact: Richard M. Ossoff, President
E-mail: richardossoff@straffordpub.com
Released: Monthly. **Price:** $827, individuals plus
$48.50 s/h. **Description:** Digest of the most signifi-
cant property law cases in the U.S. court system.
Cases are screened and selected to provide concise,
comprehensive coverage of the latest issues concern-
ing real property law.

17564 ■ National Real Estate Investor
Pub: Penton
Contact: Raymond E. Maloney, President
URL(s): www.nreionline.com. **Released:** Monthly

17565 ■ New England Real Estate Journal
Pub: East Coast Publications
Contact: Thomas Murray, Chief Executive Officer
URL(s): www.rejournal.com/ne/homeNE.aspx. **Re-
leased:** Weekly (Fri.) **Price:** $139, Individuals.

17566 ■ New York Real Estate Journal
Pub: East Coast Publications
Contact: Thomas Murray, Chief Executive Officer
URL(s): nyrej.com/. **Released:** Weekly (Fri.) **Price:**
$99, Individuals.

17567 ■ Professional Report
Pub: Society of Industrial and Office Realtors
Contact: Geoffrey Kreusser, President
URL(s): www.siordata.com/publications/profrept.html.
Released: Quarterly **Price:** $25, Members; $75,
Nonmembers non-members within U.S.; $80, Non-
members outside U.S.

17568 ■ Real Estate Broker's Insider
Pub: Alexander Communications Group Inc.
Contact: Margaret DeWitt, Publisher
E-mail: mklein@brokersinsider.com
Ed: Jeff Ostrowski, Editor. **Released:** Semimonthly,
2/month. **Price:** $247. **Description:** Provides residen-
tial agency broker/owners with actionable news and
information on managing their businesses for greater
profitability.

**17569 ■ Realtor Magazine: The Business tool
for Real Estate Professionals**
Pub: National Association of Realtors
Contact: Thomas M. Stevens, President
URL(s): www.realtor.org/RMODaily.nsf/pages/abou-
tusintro?OpenDocument. **Released:** Monthly **Price:**
$56, Individuals; $83, Canada; $103, Other countries.

17570 ■ The Residential Specialist
Pub: Council of Residential Specialists
Contact: Nina Cottrell, Chief Executive Officer
E-mail: ncottrell@crs.com
URL(s): www.crs.com/Resources/166. **Ed:** Michael
Fenner. **Released:** Bimonthly **Price:** $29.95, Non-
members; $54.95, Two years.

17571 ■ Retail Traffic
Pub: Penton
Contact: Raymond E. Maloney, President
URL(s): retailtrafficmag.com/. **Released:** Monthly

17572 ■ SNL REIT Weekly
Pub: SNL Financial L.C.
Released: Weekly. **Description:** Communicates by
fax the previous week's activity involving REITs.
Includes comprehensive articles on current industry
trends, condensed news stories, recent capital offerings and the latest market information.

VIDEOCASSETTES/
AUDIOCASSETTES

17573 ■ Basic Real Estate Investing
Blockbuster L.L.C.
3000 N Redbud Blvd.
McKinney, TX 75069
Ph: (972)683-8000
Free: 800-733-1939
Fax: (214)854-3271
Co. E-mail: corporate.communications@blockbuster.
com
URL: http://www.blockbuster.com
Contact: Mark Gerstein, President
Released: 19??. **Price:** $19.95. **Description:** Chuck
Baker, a seasoned Real Estate professional, gives
his sage advice on Real Estate as an investment.
Availability: VHS.

**17574 ■ Commercial Real Estate Loan
Documentation Program**
Executive Enterprises
Videotape Division
2 Shaw's Cove, Ste. 205
New London, CT 06320-4675
Ph: (860)701-5900
Free: 800-831-8333
Fax: (860)701-5909
Co. E-mail: info@eeiconferences.com
URL: http://www.eeiconferences.com
Released: 1986. **Description:** A training program for
financiers regarding the entitled transaction and its
necessary documentation. **Availability:** VHS.

**17575 ■ Purchase and Sale of Commercial
Real Estate**
American Bar Association (ABA)
321 N Clark St.
Chicago, IL 60654-7598
Ph: (312)988-5522
Free: 800-285-2221

Fax: (312)988-5177
Co. E-mail: service@americanbar.org
URL: http://www.americanbar.org
Contact: Carolyn Lamm, President
Released: 1988. **Price:** $295.00. **Description:** This
is a step by step look at the legal issues of com-
mercial land transactions. **Availability:** VHS; 3/4 U.

17576 ■ Real Estate Financing
American Bar Association (ABA)
321 N Clark St.
Chicago, IL 60654-7598
Ph: (312)988-5522
Free: 800-285-2221
Fax: (312)988-5177
Co. E-mail: service@americanbar.org
URL: http://www.americanbar.org
Contact: Carolyn Lamm, President
Released: 1987. **Price:** $295.00. **Description:** An
overview is provided of the ways that the finances
behind a real estate deal can be structured. **Avail-
ability:** VHS; 3/4 U.

**17577 ■ Tax and Financial Planning for Real
Estate**
SmartPros Ltd.
12 Skyline Dr.
Hawthorne, NY 10532-2133
Ph: (914)345-2620
Co. E-mail: admin@smartpros.com
URL: http://www.smartpros.com
Contact: Jack Fingerhut, President
Released: 1990. **Description:** The step-by-step
process of buying real estate, its taxation and
financial aspects is presented. **Availability:** VHS; 3/4
U.

CONSULTANTS

17578 ■ Arnheim & Neely Inc.
425 N Craig St., Ste. 100
Pittsburgh, PA 15213
Ph: (412)391-1900
Fax: (412)316-0090
URL: http://www.arnheimandneely.com
Contact: Edward F. Zehfuss, President
E-mail: ezehfuss@nauticom.net
Scope: Real estate firm which advises clients on of-
fice building and apartment building operation. Also
performs market studies, eminent domain testimony,
land assemblages, apartment building due diligence,
energy efficiency studies and recommendations and
successful conversion counseling. **Founded:** 1943.

17579 ■ Boston Consulting Group Inc. (BCG)
1 Exchange Pl., 31st Fl.
Boston, MA 02109-2803
Ph: (617)973-1200
Fax: (617)973-1339
URL: http://www.bcg.com
Contact: Stephen J. Zaleski, President
Scope: An international consulting group active in
the general field of management, corporate strategy,
and organization development. Clients are primarily
multinational corporations from all industries.
Founded: 1963. **Publications:** "Innovation 2006,"
Jul, 2006; "Measuring Innovation 2006," Jul, 2006;
"How the Worlds Top Performers Managed Profitable
Growth," Mar, 2006. **Seminars:** Building energy ef-
ficiency with local media.

17580 ■ Bowes & Co.
789 Sherman St., Ste. 590
Denver, CO 80203-3529
Ph: (303)297-0400
Fax: (303)297-2314
Co. E-mail: bowes@bowesandco.com
URL: http://www.bowesandco.com
Contact: Peter D. Bowes, President
E-mail: pbowes@bowesandco.com
Scope: Specializes in appraisal and counseling
regarding land, commercial, special purpose, recre-
ational, environmentally impacted and other invest-
ment real estate. **Founded:** 1950. **Publications:** "In-
fill Sites are Being Filled at Lowry Stapleton Fitzsi-
mons," Colorado Real Estate Journal, Jun, 2007;
"Fitzsimons Stapleton Lowry Redevelopment Beat
Goes On," Colorado Real Estate Journal, Sep, 2006;

"Appraisers Better Market Stats But Continued Uncertainty Exists," Colorado Real Estate Journal, Feb, 2006; "No Credit," Colorado Chapter Appraiser News, Jan, 2006; "Downtown Lots Happening," Colorado Real Estate Journal, Nov, 2005; "Redevelopment is Big Market Segment," Colorado Real Estate Journal, Oct, 2001.

17581 ■ Cantey & Company Inc.
3300 Harrison Rd.
Columbia, SC 29204
Ph: (803)256-7150
Fax: (803)256-4632
Co. E-mail: billy@cantey.com
URL: http://www.cantey.com
Contact: William C. Cantey, Jr., President
E-mail: billy@cantey.com
Scope: Offers residential, commercial, and investment real estate. As an independent counselor, analyzes various real estate situations, either proposed or existing, for individuals and for institutions. Clients include investors, home buyers, and sellers, developers, syndicates, bank trust departments, attorneys, and corporate Realtors. Services also used in conjunction with the client's planning team of attorneys, accountants, and tax advisers. **Founded:** 1977.

17582 ■ Cantrell, Harris & Associates (CHA)—CHA Consulting
2001 Union St., Ste. 106
San Francisco, CA 94123-4120
Ph: (415)956-6000
Fax: (415)440-7672
Co. E-mail: cantrellharris@cantrellharris.com
URL: http://www.cantrellharris.com
Contact: Ronald A. Harris, President
E-mail: ron@cantrellharris.com
Scope: Provider of real estate consulting services which include value enhancement, property or asset management, investment analysis and due diligence, strategy and disposition of real property, development coordination, complete feasibility studies, market studies and projections, independent reporting to joint ventures, litigation support, location analysis and site selection and investment partnerships. Industries served: real estate. **Founded:** 1986. **Publications:** "Leasing and Management of Office Buildings, Institute of Real Estate Management"; "The Office Building From Concept to Investment Reality, Counselors of Real Estate". **Telecommunication Services:** charealty@cantrellharris.com. **Special Services:** CPM®; CRE®.

17583 ■ Capmark Financial Group Inc.
601 Montgomery St., Ste. 1500
San Francisco, CA 94104-1010
Ph: (415)835-2000
Fax: (415)391-2949
URL: http://www.capmark.com
Contact: Jay N. Levine, President
Scope: Provides financial services to investors in commercial real estate-related assets. Also deals with lending and mortgage banking; investments and funds management and servicing.

17584 ■ Coldwell Banker Commercial United Realty Services
8044 Hosbrook Rd., Ste. 475
Cincinnati, OH 45236
Ph: (513)241-1100
Fax: (513)241-4170
Co. E-mail: support@cbcurs.com
Contact: Walter C. Daniels, President
E-mail: wdaniels@coldwellbanker.com
Scope: Real estate services company maintains a brokerage in commercial, industrial, office, retail, land, and residential properties. Provides sales, leasing, appraising, consulting, investments, and property management services. Serves private industries as well as government agencies. **Founded:** 1925.

17585 ■ Colliers International
50 Milk St., 20th Fl.
Boston, MA 02109-5011
Ph: (617)722-0221
Free: 800-393-1206

Fax: (617)722-0224
Co. E-mail: contact@colliers.com
URL: http://www.colliers.com
Contact: Ryan Kratz, President
Scope: Advises clients regarding commercial and industrial development properties, suburban acreage, retail centers, office buildings, warehouses, manufacturing facilities, and deepwater-oriented industrial sites. Serves companies, government agencies, and individuals in Texas and the Gulf Coast area. **Founded:** 1957.

17586 ■ Consulting, Appraisals & Studies Ltd.
111 W Jackson Blvd.
Chicago, IL 60604
Ph: (312)939-7775
Contact: Alfred K. Eckersberg, President
Scope: Real estate and planning consultants offering economic market analyses, feasibility studies, appraisals, development and investment evaluations, fiscal impact reviews and counseling for private and public sector clients. Projects have involved housing, retail shopping and services, industrial, office, hotels and motels, recreational, institutional and public facilities. Other services include demographic surveys and social and economic impacts, with specialized expertise in rehab and redevelopment, historical preservation and urban planning and zoning. Industries served: Business, financial, real estate, developers and government agencies in the U.S. and Canada. **Founded:** 1981.

17587 ■ Continental Appraisal Co.
1111 Schrock Rd., Ste. 202
Columbus, OH 43229-1155
Ph: (614)436-0200
Fax: (614)221-9362
Co. E-mail: jmgarvin@sbcglobal.net
Contact: John M. Garvin, Jr., President
E-mail: jmgarvin@sbcglobal.net
Scope: Provider of counseling and appraisal services regarding real estate investment properties. Includes portfolio analysis, tax reviews, investment projects, and market studies on commercial, multi family, and industrial property. Specializes in private investors, trust advisors, financial institutions, corporate owners, pension funds and government agencies. **Founded:** 1962.

17588 ■ Crosswhite Property Advisors
6 Beacon St., Ste. 215
Boston, MA 02108
Ph: (617)742-6061
Fax: (617)742-6162
Co. E-mail: jcbowman@post.harvard.edu
Contact: John C. Bowman, III, President
Scope: Firm provides consulting services in real estate investment analysis, valuation, development feasibility, project management, and permitting. Also experienced in the development of affordable housing involving substantial rehabilitation and historic preservation. **Founded:** 1988.

17589 ■ Fitzgerald Valuation Services Inc.
2 Jericho Plz., Ste. 104, 1st Fl., Wing B
Jericho, NY 11753-1658
Ph: (516)822-2700
Fax: (516)822-2702
Co. E-mail: fairvalu@optonline.net
Contact: Michael F. Fitzgerald, President
E-mail: fairvalu@optonline.net
Scope: Real estate firm offering investment analysis and valuation reports including feasibility studies in the development, financing or acquisition of real estate properties. Industries served banking, real estate, finance and insurance. **Founded:** 1994.

17590 ■ Fredericton Appraisal Associates Ltd.—ARA Fredericton Appraisal Associates Ltd.
102-3 Main St.
Fredericton, NB, Canada E3A 9N6
Ph: (506)458-9533

Fax: (506)458-1334
Co. E-mail: fappraisals@ara.ca
URL: http://www.frederictonappraisals.ca
Contact: Peter E. Atkinson, Principal
E-mail: patkinson@ara.ca
Scope: Real estate appraisal and counseling specialists with expertise in market analyses, site selection, real estate investment analysis, etc. Serving private and public corporations, governments, legal firms, accounting firms, banks, lending institutions, and individuals, Market Studies / Rental Analysis, Arbitration and Expert Testimony, Property Review for Mortgage Renewals. **Founded:** 1973.

17591 ■ Goldman Associates Inc. (GA)
1014 Bridge Rd.
Charleston, WV 25314
Ph: (304)343-5695
Free: 800-598-6112
Fax: (304)343-5694
URL: http://www.goldmanassociates.org
Contact: Jay Goldman, President
E-mail: jgoldman@goldmanassociates.org
Scope: Real estate consultant with specialized expertise in commercial, industrial and investment properties. Services include the purchase and sale of properties for corporate, institutional and individual clients. **Founded:** 1964.

17592 ■ Paul Hornsby & Co.
2100 Kramer Ln., Ste. 550
Austin, TX 78758
Ph: (512)477-6311
Free: 888-584-2065
Fax: (512)477-1793
Co. E-mail: phornsby@paulhornsbyandco.com
URL: http://www.paulhornsbyandco.com
Contact: Paul Hornsby, President
E-mail: phornsby@paulhornsbyandco.com
Scope: Provider of real estate counseling and appraisal services, investment analysis and feasibility studies, site selection, and land use studies. Serves private industries as well as government agencies. Specializes in litigation support and counseling. **Founded:** 1998. **Publications:** "Real Estate Appraisal Issues and Ethics Eminent Domain for Attorneys Central Texas Commercial Property Exchange ," 2007; "Contemporary Appraisal Issues," 2007; "Capitalization Theory & Techniques Chartered Financial Analysts," 2007; "Material and Substantial Impairment of Access CLE International," 2003; Fee Simple Versus Leased Fee Valuation: "A Study of Appraisal Models," 2001; "Regulatory Takings International Right of Way Association," 2000; "The Schmidt Opinion From the Appraisers Perspective Office of the Attorney General," 1993; "Asbestos Abatement and Lead Paint: Effects on Real Estate Value," 1992; "The Endangered Species Act and Its Impact on Property Value Texas Savings and Loan League," 1989; "Valuation Theory Real Estate Symposium," 1984. **Seminars:** Fee Simple Estate - How Many Sticks in the Bundle- Ad Valorem Taxation, 2008. **Telecommunication Services:** info@paulhornsbyandco.com.

17593 ■ William Latimore Associates
240 Forest Ave., Ste. 403
Chattanooga, TN 37405
Ph: (423)267-9044
Contact: Dr. William S. Latimore, Jr., President
E-mail: latimore@mindspring.com
Scope: Offers expertise in investment real estate, industrial or special purpose property. Also provides feasibility and related studies, and valuation services.

17594 ■ Leland Speakes & Associates
103 S Court St., Ste. 100
Cleveland, MS 38732
Ph: (662)843-2751
Fax: (662)843-3091
Co. E-mail: speakes@tecinfo.com
URL: http://www.lelandspeakes.com
Contact: Leland Speakes, III, President
Scope: Advises clients regarding real estate development and financing, estate tax problems, feasibility studies and investment analysis. Also performs real estate appraisals and offers brokerage services for residential, commercial, industrial and agricultural properties. **Founded:** 1956.

17595 ■ Merritt & Harris Inc.
90 John St., Ste. 503
New York, NY 10038
Ph: (212)697-3188
Fax: (212)687-2859
URL: http://www.merrittandharris.com
Contact: Manny P. Kratsios, President
E-mail: mkratsios@mharrisinc.com
Scope: The firm provides independent and objective third-party consulting services to the real estate lending and investment community. **Founded:** 1937. **Publications:** "M and H Observations"; "Formula 1 Texas Style," 2011; "Spring Cost Corner," 2011; "The Construction Consultant's Role on the Workout Team," 2011; "What's New In Green for 2011?," 2011; "Taylor Made in New Jersey," 2010. **Seminars:** Preclosing Project Analysis for Construction Loans; Construction Monitoring for Lenders; Workout Seminar; Engineering Due Diligence; Basic Construction for Lenders and Investors; Analyzing the Development Team.

17596 ■ Robert W. Neill Companies
204 E Washington St.
Carrollton, MS 38917-0264
Ph: (662)237-6969
Free: 800-856-6122
Fax: (662)237-4402
Co. E-mail: rwneill@rwneill.com
Contact: Robert W. Neill, Jr., Chief Executive Officer
E-mail: rob@rwneill.com
Scope: Business consultants offering multiple services including: real estate, brokerage, auction, and consulting in the areas of commercial, industrial, and investment real estate including apartments, shopping centers, hotels, motels, net leases, and office buildings; business services such as brokerage and consulting for mergers and acquisitions of small-to-medium-sized companies; health care and social services namely, brokerage and consulting for health care businesses and properties including nursing homes, hospitals, home health care, retirement housing and specialty fields; financial services including brokerage and consulting in the areas of capital, mortgage and financing sources; sale of mortgages and portfolios; and related matters. **Founded:** 1976.

17597 ■ Normandale Associates Inc.
1105 Terminal Way, Ste. 202
Reno, NV 89502-2162
Ph: (775)747-0606
Fax: (775)747-4886
Co. E-mail: normandaleassoc@aol.com
Contact: James N. Verhey, President
Scope: Facility development and project management firm offering the following services for expansions, consolidations and re-locations: strategic real estate site selection studies; property documentation and valuation; buyer/tenant representation; furniture and equipment inventories; procurement, installation coordination; signage and art; planning and installation; move/relocation management; excess property disposition. Serves private corporations, health systems, hospitals and clinics, as well as government agencies. **Founded:** 1975. **Publications:** "Project Success Management: The Owners Perspective"; "The Art & Science of Project Management". **Seminars:** Planning and Managing Corporate/Governments/Healthcare Institution Re-locations.

17598 ■ M. C. O'Brien Inc.
4718 Ave. N
Brooklyn, NY 11234-3523
Ph: (718)252-9191
Fax: (718)252-4864
Co. E-mail: info@mcobrien.com
URL: http://www.mcobrien.com
Contact: William P. O'Brien, President
E-mail: wobrien@mcobrien.com
Scope: Offers commercial and industrial real estate investment analysis with expertise in financing, selling, leasing and appraising. **Founded:** 1909. **Publications:** "M.C. O'Brien Brokers 27, 115 SF Lease in Marine Park," Mar, 2012; "O'Brien Brokers 40, 000 s/f Industrial Lease," Jun, 2011; "M.C. O'Brien Launches New Website," Mar, 2011; "O'Brien Brokers 23, 700 s/f Lease to Shindler Fish Co.," Feb, 2011.

17599 ■ PKF Consulting Corp.
50 California St., 19th Fl.
San Francisco, CA 94111
Ph: (415)788-3102
Free: 800-633-4931
Fax: (415)433-7844
Co. E-mail: thomas.callahan@pkfc.com
URL: http://www.pkfc.com
Contact: Thomas E. Callahan, Chief Executive Officer
E-mail: thomas.callahan@pkfc.com
Scope: Consulting firm of management consultants, industry specialists, and appraisers who provide a full range of services to the hospitality, real-estate, and tourism industries. **Founded:** 1992. **Publications:** "Bench CLUSTER"; "Bench MARKET"; "Hotel Outlook Forecast"; "Trends in the Hotel Industry"; "Hotel Horizons"; "Clubs In Town and Country"; "Southern California Lodging Forecast".

17600 ■ Schostak Brothers and Company Inc.—Schostak BrosSchostak Brothers;
17800 Laurel Park Dr. N, Ste. 200C
Livonia, MI 48152-3985
Ph: (248)262-1000
Fax: (248)262-1814
Co. E-mail: watson@schostak.com
URL: http://www.schostak.com
Contact: Bill Angott, President
E-mail: ncadotte@kingventure.com
Scope: Real estate firm which performs feasibility and market studies, as well as valuations for industrial, commercial, and investment property. **Founded:** 1922.

17601 ■ Stephen M. Segal Inc.
1545 Lamberton Rd.
Trenton, NJ 08611
Ph: (609)394-7557
Fax: (609)394-6894
Co. E-mail: info@segalinc.com
URL: http://www.segalinc.com
Contact: Chuck Segal, President
E-mail: chuck@chucksegal.com
Scope: Provider of counseling on all areas of real estate including marketing of industrial, commercial, office, and investment properties; land acquisition; financing; market and feasibility studies; site selection and analysis; and property management. Also offers complete appraisal services for sale, lease, or acquisition, investment analyses, real estate tax assessments, and eminent domain matters. Serves industry, financial institutions, individuals, attorneys, government agencies, and utilities. **Founded:** 1968.

17602 ■ Stevenson Real Estate Group Ltd.
200 - 260 St. Mary Ave.
Winnipeg, MB, Canada R3C 1W3
Ph: (204)956-1901
Fax: (204)957-7976
Co. E-mail: info@stevenson.mb.ca
URL: http://www.stevenson.mb.ca
Contact: Patrick Hamilton, President
E-mail: phamilton@stevenson.mb.ca
Scope: Real estate consulting firm providing advice and appraisal services regarding investment, commercial and industrial properties for individuals, government, and industry. Acts on behalf of clients in all areas of real estate investment. Industries served: Commercial real estate sales and leasing, commercial appraisals, and property management. **Founded:** 1901. **Publications:** "National survey finds Winnipeg office space in big demand"; "Destination Winnipeg-Economic Highlights".

17603 ■ J. Ed Turner Real Estate—J Ed Turner Co.
301 Humble Ave., Ste. 145
Hattiesburg, MS 39401
Ph: (601)268-7900
Fax: (601)268-7972
Contact: James E. Turner, Jr., President
Scope: Advises clients regarding the use, sale, purchase, lease and financing of investment, commercial, industrial and residential property. Specializes in pine timberland and cattle ranches. Also provides appraisal and property management services. **Founded:** 1946.

17604 ■ West Virginia Commercial L.L.C.—NAI McCabe-Henley
305 Washington St. W
Charleston, WV 25302
Ph: (304)347-7500
Fax: (304)342-2252
URL: http://www.wv-commercial.com
Contact: Steven W. Jordan, Manager
E-mail: sjordan@mccabehenley.com
Scope: Offers commercial and investment real estate consulting that includes investment analysis, location analysis, site acquisition, development services, and tenant representation. Additional consulting services available in property and asset management, joint ventures and real estate syndications. Serves private industries as well as government agencies. **Founded:** 1980. **Publications:** "Times West Virginian Published," Jun, 2007; "The Charleston Gazette," Dec, 2004; "Views and Visions," Nov, 2004; "WASHINGTON POST," Sep, 2004.

17605 ■ C B Richard Ellis Whittier Partners (CBRE)
33 Arch St., 28th Fl.
Boston, MA 02110
Ph: (617)912-7000
Fax: (617)912-7001
Co. E-mail: info@cbre.com
URL: http://www.cbre.com/default.htm
Contact: Robert Blain, President
E-mail: Rob.Blain@cbre.com.hk
Scope: Specializes in real estate analysis of income-producing commercial and residential property. Services include feasibility, development and redevelopment programs for new or existing buildings; investment property analysis; tax equalization studies; and management program analysis. Serves real estate developers, corporate owners, investment trusts, banks, institutional investors, and private individuals. **Founded:** 1906. **Publications:** "Nonprofits on the Run," Oct, 2007; "Developing a Strategic Real Estate Plan," Jul, 2007; "The ABCs of Office Leasing for Associations," 2006; "Multi-Housing Monitor," 2004; "Don't Let The Numbers Fool You," Nov, 2003. **Seminars:** Real estate challenges faced by new companies, UCSD School of Medicine Lecture Facility, Apr, 2009; Advanced Managerial Strategies Seminar; Dimensional Management Training Seminar.

FRANCHISES AND BUSINESS OPPORTUNITIES

17606 ■ Charlwood International Corporation
1199 West Pender St., Ste. 900
Vancouver, BC, Canada V6E 2R1
Ph: (604)718-2600
Fax: (604)718-2678
Co. E-mail: ugarycharlwood@uniglobe.com
URL: http://www.ugarycharlwood.com
Description: Comprised of well-known global brands such as Uniglobe Travel International, Century 21 Canada and Centum Financial Group. Uniglobe Travel provides travel services to small and mid-sized corporate accounts in 30 countries worldwide. Century 21 Canada started operations in 1975 and has grown into 6,600 offices in 41 countries. Centum Financial Group is a network of independently operated mortgage broker firms accessing rates from over 30 financial lenders. **No. of Franchise Units:** 644. **Founded:** 1975.. **Franchised:** 1975. **Equity Capital Needed:** Varies. **Franchise Fee:** Varies. **Training:** Yes.

17607 ■ HomeVestors of America, Inc.
6500 Greenville Ave., Ste. 400
Dallas, TX 75206
Ph: (800)704-6992
Fax: (972)761-9022
Co. E-mail: FranchiseInquiry@homevestors.com
URL: http://www.uglyhouses.com
Description: Real estate investors specializing in buying and selling undervalued houses. **No. of Franchise Units:** 225. **Founded:** 1989.. **Franchised:** 1996. **Equity Capital Needed:** $41,300. **Franchise**

Fee: $12,000. **Training:** 2 weeks initial training in Dallas, TX, annual convention, bi-annual advanced training; and year-round support.

17608 ■ Royal LePage Real Estate Services
39 Wynford Dr.
North York, ON, Canada M3C 3K5
Ph: (416)510-5827
Fax: (416)510-5856
URL: http://www.royallepage.ca
Description: Offers leading-edge technology, training, products and services to its franchisees to compete effectively in the real estate industry. **No. of Franchise Units:** 600. **No. of Company-Owned Units:** 15. **Founded:** 1913.. **Franchised:** 1995. **Franchise Fee:** Varies. **Training:** Yes.

COMPUTERIZED DATABASES

17609 ■ *Banking Information Source™*
789 E Eisenhower Pkwy.
Ann Arbor, MI 48106-1346
Ph: (734)761-4700
Free: 800-521-0600
Co. E-mail: info@il.proquest.com
URL: http://www.il.proquest.com
Contact: Matt Dunie, President
Availability: Online: ProQuest Co.; ProQuest LLC - Dialog; ProQuest LLC - Dialog; LexisNexis Group.
Type: Bibliographic; Full-text.

17610 ■ *The National Registry*
1401 H St. NW, Ste. 760
Washington, DC 20005
Ph: (202)289-2735
Fax: (202)289-4101
URL: http://www.asc.gov
Availability: Online: Federal Financial Institutions Examination Council - Appraisal Subcommittee.
Type: Directory.

17611 ■ *New Residential Construction Index*
4600 Silver Hill Rd.
Washington, DC 20233-0001
Ph: (301)457-4100
Free: 800-923-8282
Fax: (301)457-4714
Co. E-mail: webmaster@census.gov
URL: http://www.census.gov
Availability: Online: U.S. Census Bureau. **Type:** Statistical.

17612 ■ *New Residential Sales*
4600 Silver Hill Rd.
Washington, DC 20233-0001
Ph: (301)457-4100
Free: 800-923-8282
Fax: (301)457-4714
Co. E-mail: webmaster@census.gov
URL: http://www.census.gov
Availability: Online: U.S. Census Bureau. **Type:** Statistical.

LIBRARIES

17613 ■ Building Owners and Managers Association International Library—BOMA.
1101 15th St., NW, Ste. 800
Washington, DC 20005
Ph: (202)408-2662
Fax: (202)371-0181
Co. E-mail: info@boma.org
URL: http://www.boma.org
Contact: Henry H. Chamberlain, President
Scope: Owning, managing, developing, and investing in commercial office buildings. **Services:** Library not open to the public. **Founded:** 1907. **Holdings:** 1500 volumes. **Subscriptions:** 25 journals and other serials; 2 newspapers.

17614 ■ Buset & Partners Library
1121 Barton St.
Thunder Bay, ON, Canada P7B 5N3
Ph: (807)623-2500
Free: 866-532-8738

Fax: (807)622-7808
Co. E-mail: cenns@buset-partners.com
URL: http://www.buset-partners.com
Contact: Carolyn Enns, Librarian
Scope: Law - real estate, labor, corporate, commercial, family, personal injury, insurance; civil litigation, wills and estates, employment, municipal, environmental. **Services:** Library not open to the public. **Holdings:** 2100 books; 1 bound periodical volumes. **Subscriptions:** 7 journals and other serials; 3 newspapers. **Telecommunication Services:** law@buset-partners.com.

17615 ■ Landauer Realty Group Information Center
2 Science Rd.
Glenwood, IL 60425-1586
Ph: (708)755-7000
Free: 800-323-8830
Fax: (708)755-7016
Co. E-mail: custserv@landauer.com
URL: http://www.landauer.com
Contact: Catherine A. Heyward, Director, Library Services
Scope: Real estate, finance, marketing, land use, development, property acquisition and management. **Services:** Center not open to the public. **Founded:** 1974. **Holdings:** 375 books; 100 VF drawers of reports; 16,000 clippings, offerings, brochures, statistical data; 125 VF drawers of research materials; U.S. maps; Annual reports; 1960, 1970, 1980 census publications; government documents. **Subscriptions:** 200 journals and other serials.

17616 ■ Polsinelli Shalton Welte Suelthaus PC Law Library
700 W. 47th St., Ste. 1000
Kansas City, MO 64112
Ph: (816)753-1000
Fax: (816)753-1536
Co. E-mail: bfullerton@pswlaw.com
URL: http://www.pswlaw.com/
Contact: Karin L. Weaver
Scope: Law - tax, bankruptcy, real estate; litigation; product liability. **Services:** Interlibrary loan; copying; SDI; Library open to clients only. **Holdings:** 15,000 books. **Subscriptions:** 1500 journals and other serials; 10 newspapers.

RESEARCH CENTERS

17617 ■ Indiana University Bloomington - Benecki Center for Real Estate Studies (BCRES)
Kelley School of Business
1309 E 10th St., Ste. 746
Bloomington, IN 47405-1701
Ph: (812)855-7794
Fax: (812)855-9006
Co. E-mail: cres@indiana.edu
URL: http://www.kelley.iu.edu/bcres
Contact: Jeffrey D. Fisher, Director
Founded: 1985. **Educational Activities:** BCRES Annual Conference; Faculty/graduate student research seminar (Periodic); Special Meetings, for sponsors.

17618 ■ Massachusetts Institute of Technology - Center for Real Estate (CRE)
Bldg. W31-310
77 Massachusetts Ave.
Cambridge, MA 02139-4307
Ph: (617)253-4373
Fax: (617)258-6991
Co. E-mail: mit-cre@mit.edu
URL: http://web.mit.edu/cre
Contact: Prof. David Geltner, Director, Research
Founded: 1984. **Publications:** *CRE Working Papers*. **Educational Activities:** Industry members (Semiannual); Executive education programs; M.S. in real estate development; Seminars and professional development courses. **Awards:** CRE Fellowship program.

17619 ■ Northwestern University - Guthrie Center for Real Estate Research
Kellogg School
2001 Sheridan Rd., Rm. 6214
Evanston, IL 60208
Ph: (847)491-3564
Fax: (847)467-6459
Co. E-mail: tsm@kellogg.northwestern.edu
URL: http://www.kellogg.northwestern.edu/realestate
Contact: Therese J. McGuire, Director
Founded: 1987. **Publications:** *Guthrie Center for Real Estate Research Newsletter* (Annual). **Educational Activities:** Conferences, panel discussions and executive speakers luncheon series, for industry leaders, faculty, real estate alumni, student clubs.

17620 ■ Real Estate Research Institute (RERI)
100 Pearl St., 13th Fl.
Hartford, CT 06103
Ph: (860)692-6341
Fax: (860)692-6351
Co. E-mail: reri@reri.org
URL: http://www.reri.org
Contact: Tony Ciochetti, President
Founded: 1966.

17621 ■ St. Cloud State University - Minnesota Real Estate Research Center
Herberger College of Business
720 4th Ave. S
Saint Cloud, MN 56301-4498
Ph: (320)308-3074
Fax: (320)308-3986
Co. E-mail: moon@stcloudstate.edu
Contact: Dr. Steven Mooney, Director
Founded: 1980. **Publications:** *Real Estate Report Series*. **Educational Activities:** Distinguished Lecturer Series; Professional seminars. **Awards:** Minnesota Real Estate Research Center Paid internships; Minnesota Real Estate Research Center Scholarships (Annual); Undergraduate scholarships for real estate majors.

17622 ■ Southern Methodist University - Center for Research in Real Estate and Land Use Economics
Fincher Bldg.
Dallas, TX 75275
Ph: (214)768-3548
Fax: (214)768-4099
Co. E-mail: wbruegge@cox.smu.edu
URL: http://www.cox.smu.edu/centers/realestate
Contact: Prof. William B. Brueggeman, Director
Publications: *Occasional Paper Series*; *Working Paper Series*. **Educational Activities:** Semiannual Executive Seminars.

17623 ■ Texas A&M University - Real Estate Center
2115 TAMU
1700 Research Pky., Ste. 200
College Station, TX 77843
Ph: (979)845-2031
Fax: (979)845-0460
Co. E-mail: gmaler@mays.tamu.edu
URL: http://www.recenter.tamu.edu
Contact: Gary Maler, Director
Founded: 1971. **Publications:** *Special Reports*; *Real Estate Center Technical Reports*; *Tierra Grande* (Quarterly); *English/Spanish Glossary of Real Estate Terms*. **Educational Activities:** Educational seminars; Annual Legal Seminar on Ad Valorem Taxation; Annual Texas Land Market Outlook Conference; Conferences for real estate professionals, educators, and the general public, throughout the year.

17624 ■ University of Florida - Bergstrom Center for Real Estate Studies
Warrington College of Business Administration
Gainesville, FL 32611-7168
Ph: (352)273-1827

Fax: (352)392-0301
Co. E-mail: tim.becker@warrington.ufl.edu
URL: http://warrington.ufl.edu/fire/realestate
Contact: Prof. Wayne Archer, Executive Director
E-mail: wayne.archer@cba.ufl.edu
Founded: 1964. **Publications:** *Survey of Emerging Market Conditions* (Quarterly). **Educational Activities:** Alfred Ring Distinguished Speaker Series (Quarterly); Appraisal seminars and professional education; Bergstrom Center for Real Estate Studies Conferences (Semiannual); Bergstrom Center for Real Estate Studies Lectures; Undergraduate and graduate instruction and research training on real estate problems and urban analyses; Regional meetings (Bimonthly). **Awards:** Adjunct faculty stipends; Graduate student assistantships; Bergstrom Center for Real Estate Studies Paid internships, totaling about $32,000; Bergstrom Center for Real Estate Studies Research grants; Bergstrom Center for Real Estate Studies Scholarships, totaling approximately $85,000.

17625 ■ University of Illinois at Urbana-Champaign - Office of Real Estate Research
140A Wohlers Hall
1206 S Sixth St.
Champaign, IL 61820
Ph: (217)333-2278
Fax: (217)244-3102
Co. E-mail: orer@uiuc.edu
URL: http://www.business.uiuc.edu/orer/
Contact: Prof. Roger E. Cannaday, Director (Acting)
Founded: 1980. **Educational Activities:** Office of Real Estate Research Lecture Series. **Awards:** CCIM Scholarship (Annual); Eisenberg Scholarship (Annual); Morgan L. Fitch Scholarship (Annual); SIOR Scholarship (Annual). **Telecommunication Services:** rcannada@illinois.edu.

17626 ■ University of Kentucky - Center for Real Estate Studies (CRES)
Gatton College of Business & Economics
Lexington, KY 40506-0034

Ph: (859)257-7726
Co. E-mail: ambrose@uky.edu
Contact: Brent W. Ambrose, Director
Founded: 1974. **Publications:** *Booklets*; *CRES Newsletter*; *CRES Papers*. **Educational Activities:** Educational and Market Outlook Seminars.

17627 ■ University of Nevada, Las Vegas - Lied Institute for Real Estate Studies
College of Business
4505 Maryland Pky., Box 456025
Las Vegas, NV 89154-6025
Ph: (702)895-4492
Fax: (702)895-4650
Co. E-mail: nasser.daneshvary@unlv.edu
URL: http://www.liedinstitute.com
Contact: Nasser Daneshvary, Executive Director (Acting)
Founded: 1991. **Publications:** *Annual Real Estate White Paper*; *Nevada Law and Reference Guide*; *Reserve Fund Guidelines for Common Interest Communities*. **Educational Activities:** Commercial Real Estate Certification (10/year); Executive Education (Monthly), includes BOMA series, online mortgage lending training; Lied Online Mortgage Training (Daily); Mentor Program (Weekly), matches business leaders with students; Roundtables (Annual); Real Estate and Business Society (Monthly), student organization. **Awards:** Lieder Award (Annual); Lied Institute for Real Estate Studies Internships; Real estate scholarships. **Telecommunication Services:** june.jackson@unlv.edu.

17628 ■ University of Pennsylvania - Samuel Zell and Robert Lurie Real Estate Center at Wharton
Steinberg Hall-Dietrich Hall, Ste. 1400
Wharton School
3620 Locust Walk
Philadelphia, PA 19104-6302
Ph: (215)898-9687

Fax: (215)573-2220
Co. E-mail: frostr@wharton.upenn.edu
URL: http://realestate.wharton.upenn.edu
Contact: Joseph Gyourko, Director
Founded: 1983. **Publications:** *Wharton Real Estate Center Newsletter*; *Wharton Real Estate Review*. **Educational Activities:** Public conferences (Periodic); Seminars, lectures; Semiannual meeting for real estate industry professionals and scholars. **Awards:** American Society of Real Estate Counselors Award; Andrew Murphy Fellowship in Real Estate; Benjamin Franklin Kahn/WRIT Real Estate Award; Boyd T. Barnard Real Estate Award; Institute of Real Estate Management Award; Jerome Freedman Memorial Award in Real Estate; Jimmy Goettee Award for Entrepreneurial Excellence; William Mack Award; William Zucker Award; Herbert K. Brown Scholarship Foundation; Herbert Z. Gold Scholarship; ICSC Educational Foundation Scholarship; Martin Bucksbaum Memorial Fellowship; Robert E. Linneman Memorial Fellowship; SIOR Fellowship. **Telecommunication Services:** wrec@wharton.upenn.edu.

17629 ■ University of South Carolina at Columbia - South Carolina Real Estate Center
Darla Moore School of Business
Columbia, SC 29208
Ph: (803)777-1512
Fax: (803)777-9344
Co. E-mail: wharrison@moore.sc.edu
URL: http://www.moore.sc.edu/facultyandresearch/researchcenters/sccenterforrealestate.a spx
Services: Media interviews. **Founded:** 1973. **Publications:** *South Carolina Real Estate Center Newsletter* (Semiannual). **Educational Activities:** South Carolina Real Estate Center Conference (Annual), in February; South Carolina Real Estate Center Seminars. **Telecommunication Services:** realestate@moore.sc.edu.

ASSOCIATIONS AND OTHER ORGANIZATIONS

17630 ■ Audio Engineering Society Inc. (AES)
60 E 42nd St., Rm. 2520
New York, NY 10165-2520
Ph: (212)661-8528
Free: 800-541-7299
Fax: (212)682-0477
Co. E-mail: hq@aes.org
URL: http://www.aes.org
Contact: Bob Moses, Executive Director
Description: Engineers, administrators, and technicians who design or operate recording and reproducing equipment for radio, television, motion picture, and recording studios, or who produce, install, and operate disc, magnetic tape, and sound amplifying equipment; educators who use recording in teaching, or who teach acoustics, electronics, and other sciences basic to the recording and reproducing of sound; administrators, sales engineers, and technicians in the sound industry and related fields. Operates educational and research foundation. **Founded:** 1948. **Publications:** *Journal of the Audio Engineering Society* (Monthly); *Audio Engineering Society-- Directory of Educational Programs*; *Journal of the Audio Engineering Society: Audio/Acoustics/Applications* (10/year); *Journal of the Audio Engineering Society*. **Educational Activities:** Audio Engineering Society Convention (Semiannual). **Awards:** Publications Award; Bronze Medal Award; Board of Governors Award; Gold Medal Award; Silver Medal Award; Audio Engineering Society Educational Foundation Scholarships.

17631 ■ Canadian Academy of Recording Arts and Sciences (CARAS)
345 Adelaide St. W, 2nd Fl.
Toronto, ON, Canada M5V 1R5
Ph: (416)485-3135
Free: 888-440-5866
Fax: (416)485-4978
Co. E-mail: membership@carasonline.ca
URL: http://www.carasonline.ca
Contact: Melanie Berry, President
Description: Individuals actively working within the Canadian music industry. Promotes advancement in the field of recording and related disciplines. Conducts educational and charitable programs; maintains hall of fame. **Founded:** 1975. **Awards:** Juno Awards; Juno Awards (Annual).

17632 ■ Canadian Independent Music Association (CIMA)
30 St. Patrick St., 2nd Fl.
Toronto, ON, Canada M5T 3A3
Ph: (416)485-3152
Co. E-mail: stuart@cimamusic.ca
URL: http://cimamusic.ca
Contact: Stuart Johnston, President
Description: Works to secure a strong and economically stable Canadian independent music and sound recording industry. **Founded:** 1975.

17633 ■ Content Delivery and Storage Association (CDSA)
39 N Bayles Ave.
Port Washington, NY 11050
Ph: (516)767-6720
Fax: (516)883-5793
Co. E-mail: mporter@cdsaonline.org.org
URL: http://www.cdsaonline.org
Contact: Martin Porter, Executive Director
Description: Serves as the advocate for the growth and development of all recording media and as a forum for the exchange of information regarding global trends and innovations. Provides members an opportunity to join forces and be a strong industry voice allowing them to grow and expand their business. Encompasses all facets of the recording media. **Founded:** 1970. **Publications:** *Mediaware* (9/year).

17634 ■ Music Canada—L'association de l'industrie canadienne de L'enregistrement
85 Mowat Ave.
Toronto, ON, Canada M6K 3E3
Ph: (416)967-7272
Fax: (416)967-9415
Co. E-mail: info@musiccanada.com
URL: http://www.musiccanada.com
Contact: Graham Henderson, President
Description: Record companies and manufacturers. Promotes high standards of ethics and practice in the recording industry. Represents members' interests. **Founded:** 1964. **Awards:** Gold and Platinum Awards; Gold and Platinum Awards.

17635 ■ National Academy of Recording Arts and Sciences (NARAS)—The Recording Academy
3402 Pico Blvd.
Santa Monica, CA 90405
Ph: (310)392-3777
Fax: (310)399-3090
URL: http://www.grammy.com
Contact: Jimmy Jam, Chairman
Description: Musicians, producers and other recording professionals. Dedicated to improving the cultural environment and quality of life for music and its makers. The Recording Academy is internationally known for the Grammy Awards and is responsible for numerous groundbreaking outreach, professional development, cultural enrichment, education and human service programs. **Founded:** 1957. **Publications:** *Grammy Magazine* (Periodic); *The Grammy Winners Book* (Annual); *Program Book* (Annual). **Educational Activities:** The Grammy Awards (Annual). **Awards:** The Grammy Award (Annual); Hall of Fame Award.

17636 ■ National Association of Recording Merchandisers (NARM)
9 Eves Dr., Ste. 120
Marlton, NJ 08053
Ph: (856)596-2221
Fax: (856)596-3268
Co. E-mail: donio@narm.com
URL: http://www.narm.com
Contact: Rachelle Friedman, Chairman
Description: Serves the music and other prerecorded entertainment software industry as a forum for insight and dialogue; members include retailers, wholesalers, distributors, entertainment software suppliers, and suppliers of related products and services. **Scope:** merchandising, loss prevention, classical music, EDI. **Founded:** 1958. **Publications:** *NARM Convention Official Guide* (Annual); *NARM News Bits* (Monthly); *NARM Research Briefs* (Monthly); *NARM Membership Directory and Buyer's Guide* (Annual). **Educational Activities:** Insights and Sounds (Annual). **Awards:** Marketing Awards; Harry Chapin Memorial Humanitarian Award; Presidential Award for Sustained Executive Achievement.

17637 ■ Society of Professional Audio Recording Services (SPARS)
441 W 53rd St.
New York, NY 10019
Ph: (212)765-7500
Fax: (212)765-7450
Co. E-mail: info@spars.com
URL: http://www.spars.com
Contact: Kirk Imamura, President
Description: Recording and video studio owners; suppliers, manufacturers, producers, engineers, and recording service users involved with audio commercial facilities. Works to improve every phase of business operations and to provide members with the opportunity to play an effective role in shaping the future of their industry. Acts as a forum for the industry; maintains a high technical cultural standard; addresses interested parties on issues confronting the industry's present and future equipment needs. Analyzes, evaluates, and comments upon the use of professional audio equipment; fosters the dissemination of information concerning techniques of studio management and technical innovation; conducts educational activities. Assists in the development of projects, undertakings, and studies related to the industry; considers and deals with intratrade problems; attempts to reform abuses and inculcate principles of justice and equity in the audio recording industry. **Founded:** 1979.

DIRECTORIES OF EDUCATIONAL PROGRAMS

17638 ■ *Directory of Private Accredited Career Schools and Colleges of Technology*
Pub: Accrediting Commission of Career Schools and Colleges of Technology
Contact: Michale S. McComis, Executive Director
Released: On web page. **Price:** Free. **Description:** Covers 3900 accredited post-secondary programs that provide training programs in business, trade, and technical fields, including various small business endeavors. Entries offer school name, address, phone, description of courses, job placement assistance, and requirements for admission. Arrangement is alphabetical.

REFERENCE WORKS

17639 ■ *The Big Payback: The History of the Business of Hip-Hop*
Pub: New American Library/Penguin Group
Ed: Dan Charnas. **Price:** $24.95. **Description:** The complete history of hip-hop music is presented, by

following the money and the relationship between artist and merchant. In its promise of economic security and creative control for black artist-entrepreneurs, it is the culmination of dreams of black nationalists and civil rights leaders.

17640 ■ *Here Come the Regulars: How to Run a Record Label on a Shoestring Budget*
Pub: Faber & Faber, Inc.
Ed: Ian Anderson. **Released:** October 1, 2009. **Price:** $15.00. **Description:** Author, Ian Anderson launched his own successful record label, Afternoon Records when he was 18 years old. Anderson shares insight into starting a record label, focusing on label image, budget, blogging, potential artists, as well as legal aspects.

17641 ■ *The Rhythm of Success: How an Immigrant Produced His Own American Dream*
Pub: Penguin Group USA Inc.
Ed: Emilio Estefan. **Released:** January 10, 2010. **Price:** $24.95. **Description:** Emilio Estafan, husband to singer Gloria Estefan and founder of the Latin pop legend Miami Sound Machine, is the classic example of the American dream. He shares his guiding principles that entrepreneurs need to start and grow a business.

17642 ■ *"Scoring Music" in Canadian Business (Vol. 81, December 8, 2008, No. 21, pp. S3)*
Pub: Rogers Media Ltd.
Ed: Jay Somerset. **Description:** Boyd Devereaux, who plays with the Toronto Maple Leafs, collaborates with musicians through his record label Elevation Records. Devereaux won a Stanley Cup with the Detroit Red Wings in 2002 and has released five limited edition discs through Elevation records.

17643 ■ *"Sound Fundamentals" in Hispanic Business (September 2007, pp. 12, 14, 16)*
Pub: Hispanic Business
Ed: Michael T. Mena. **Description:** Profile of Ozomatli, a Los Angeles-based multicultural, multi-ethnic musical group that has topped Billboard's Latin Pop chart without relying on record sales. Members explain how they run the group like a small business.

17644 ■ *"Welcome to Babesland" in Women In Business (Vol. 62, June 2010, No. 2, pp. 33)*
Pub: American Business Women's Association
Ed: Leigh Elmore. **Description:** Music group, Four Bitchin' Babes will be performing at the 2010 American Business Women's Association's National Women's Leadership Conference. The group has been in the industry for 20 years and has released nine albums. The Four Bitchin' Babes consist of Sally Fingerett, Nancy Moran, Deirdre Flint, and Debi Smith.

17645 ■ *"When the Longtime Star Fades" in Harvard Business Review (Vol. 88, September 2010, No. 9, pp. 117)*
Pub: Harvard Business School Publishing
Ed: Jimmy Guterman. **Description:** A fictitious aging employee scenario is presented, with contributors offering advice. The scenarios focuses on an older employee's match with a rapidly changing industry; suggestions include consolidating a niche business around the employee, and also engaging the older employee in solving the productivity issue.

SOURCES OF SUPPLY

17646 ■ *Broadcast Engineering--Equipment Reference Manual*
Penton
Contact: Raymond E. Maloney, President
URL(s): www.broadcastengineering.comwww.penton.com/Profile/BroadcastEngineering.aspx. **Released:** Annual; fall. **Publication includes:** List of more than 1,400 manufacturers and distributors of communications equipment for radio, television, and recording applications. **Entries include:** For manufacturers--Company name, address. For distributors and dealers--Company name, address, phone, product or service provided, geographic area covered. **Database includes:** Specifications for major brands of professional broadcast hardware.

Arrangement: Manufacturers are alphabetical; dealers and distributors are geographical. **Indexes:** Product/service.

TRADE PERIODICALS

17647 ■ *etracks Newsletter*
Pub: Society of Professional Audio Recording Services
Released: Periodic. **Price:** Included in membership. **Description:** Examines technical developments in audio equipment and techniques of audio studio management. Discusses industry issues and trends. Recurring features include reports on Society programs, services, and activities. **Remarks:** Available only via e-mail, or on website.

17648 ■ *Journal of the Audio Engineering Society*
Pub: Audio Engineering Society Inc.
Contact: Bob Moses, Executive Director
URL(s): www.aes.org/journal. **Ed:** John Vanderkooy. **Released:** Monthly; except Jan., Feb. and July, Aug. when it is published Bimonthly. **Price:** $50, Members; $280, Nonmembers print; $525, Nonmembers online; $695, Nonmembers print and online.

17649 ■ *Pro Sound News*
Pub: NewBay Media, LLC
URL(s): www.prosoundnews.com/. **Ed:** Frank Wells. **Released:** Monthly **Price:** Free.

17650 ■ *Sound & Video Contractor: The International Management & Engineering Journal for Systems Contractors & Consultants*
Pub: NewBay Media, LLC
URL(s): svconline.com/. **Ed:** Cynthia Wisehart. **Released:** Monthly

TRADE SHOWS AND CONVENTIONS

17651 ■ *The NAMM Show*
NAMM - The International Music Products Association
5790 Armada Dr.
Carlsbad, CA 92008-4608
Ph: (760)438-8001
Free: 800-767-6266
Fax: (760)438-7327
Co. E-mail: info@namm.org
URL: http://www.namm.org
Contact: Joe Lamond, President
URL(s): www.namm.org/thenammshow/2012. **Frequency:** Annual. **Audience:** Retail music merchants; manufacturers of musical instruments and accessories; manufacturers of acoustical equipment; sheet music publishers. **Principal Exhibits:** Musical instruments and accessories, acoustical equipment, and sheet music publications.

17652 ■ *NAMM - Summer Session*
NAMM - The International Music Products Association
5790 Armada Dr.
Carlsbad, CA 92008-4608
Ph: (760)438-8001
Free: 800-767-6266
Fax: (760)438-7327
Co. E-mail: info@namm.org
URL: http://www.namm.org
Contact: Joe Lamond, President
URL(s): www.namm.org/summer/2010. **Frequency:** Annual. **Audience:** All attendees must be owners or employees of companies in the music-products industry, either retailers or suppliers-closed trade show. **Principal Exhibits:** Musical instruments and accessories, acoustical equipment, and sheet music publications. **Telecommunication Services:** tradeshow@namm.com.

CONSULTANTS

17653 ■ *Jess Barker, Document Research/ Retrieval L.L.C.*
209A S Macoupin St.
Gillespie, IL 62033-1605

Ph: (217)839-3219
Free: 888-316-3773
Fax: (877)522-7537
Co. E-mail: documentretrieval@frontiernet.net
URL: http://www.documentresearch.biz
Contact: James Barker, Principal
Scope: A full service title search company that provides Title Reports to investors who are interested in making offers on properties. **Founded:** 1993.

17654 ■ *Engineering Harmonics Inc.*
29A Leslie St.
Toronto, ON, Canada M4M 3C3
Ph: (416)465-3378
Fax: (416)465-9037
Co. E-mail: 2012-info@engineeringharmonics.com
URL: http://www.engineeringharmonics.com
Contact: Philip Giddings, President
E-mail: pgiddings@engineeringharmonies.com
Scope: Specializing in audio, audio and video, control, and communication based systems. **Founded:** 1988. **Publications:** "Designing Sound for Frank Gehry's Vision"; "Precis of WDCH PSVC System"; "PSVC Design Challenges at WDCH"; "Power and Ground Update"; "Noise Reduction Systems"; "Mandating the House Audio System," Overture Hall; "Betting on Legends," Nov, 2008; "Examining our Roots, Defining our Future," Dec, 2008; "Walking The Hall: A Guide to Tuning a Loudspeaker System," Nov, 2007; "National Ballet School," Nov, 2007; "The Puzzle of PA for a Hall-in-the-Round," Aug, 2007; "A House for All Seasons," Aug, 2006; "Hooray for LA," Jan, 2004; "A Kodak Moment," Apr, 2002.

17655 ■ *Lougheed Resource Group Inc. (LRG)*
17608 Deer Isle Cir.
Winter Garden, FL 34787
Ph: (407)654-1212
Fax: (407)654-5419
Co. E-mail: info@lrgconstruction.com
URL: http://www.lrgconstruction.com
Contact: Karen Lougheed, Owner
E-mail: karen@lrgmanagement.com
Scope: Construction consultants specializing in project strategies, scope preparation, contract negotiation, project management, document and code evaluation, peer reviews, scheduling/estimates, dispute resolution, and forensic analysis expert testimony. **Founded:** 1987.

17656 ■ *Triad Studios*
4572 150th Ave. NE
Redmond, WA 98052
Ph: (425)881-9322
Fax: (425)881-3645
Co. E-mail: info@triadstudios.com
Contact: Jeff Crookall, Manager
E-mail: jcrookall@triadstudios.com
Scope: Firm has expertise in recording studio design, acoustics, and sound issues. The firm serves the music industry in the Northwest. **Founded:** 1982.

LIBRARIES

17657 ■ *Bowling Green State University - Music Library and Sound Recordings Archives*
Wm. T. Jerome Library, 3rd Fl.
Bowling Green, OH 43403
Ph: (419)372-2307
Fax: (419)372-7996
Co. E-mail: mlsra@bgsu.edu
URL: http://www.bgsu.edu/colleges/library/music
Contact: Susannah Cleveland, Librarian
Scope: Popular music, recording industry, classical music. **Services:** Library open to the public with restrictions; researchers should contact Library prior to making extended visit. **Founded:** 1967. **Holdings:** 60,000 books and scores; 1700 bound periodical volumes; 16,000 pieces of popular sheet music; 6 drawers of popular music posters. **Subscriptions:** 200 journals and other serials. **Telecommunication Services:** clevels@bgsu.edu.

17658 ■ Delaware State Museums Division of Historical and Cultural Affairs - Johnson Victrola Museum
Museum Sq.
375 S. New St.
Dover, DE 19901
Ph: (302)744-5055
Co. E-mail: nena.todd@state.de.us
URL: http://history.delaware.gov/museums/jvm/jvm_
  main.shtml
Contact: Nena Todd, Site Manager
Scope: Sound recording industry, Victor Talking Machine Company. **Services:** Copying; library open

to the public for reference and by appointment only. **Founded:** 1967. **Holdings:** Books; reference materials; advertisement; manuscripts; patents.

17659 ■ Recording Industry Association of America Reference Library
1025 F St. NW, 10th Fl.
Washington, DC 20004
Ph: (202)775-0101
Fax: (202)775-7253
URL: http://www.riaa.com
Contact: Mitch Bainwol, Chief Executive Officer
Scope: Audio and video recording industry, trade association that represents the U.S. recording industry.

Services: Library not open to the public. **Founded:** 1952. **Holdings:** Books; magazines; clippings; other reference materials; CDs; cassettes. **Subscriptions:** 50 journals and other serials; 6 newspapers.

ASSOCIATIONS AND OTHER ORGANIZATIONS

17660 ■ BlueRibbon Coalition (BRC)
4555 Burley Dr., Ste. A
Pocatello, ID 83202-1945
Ph: (208)237-1008
Free: 800-BLUE-RIB
Fax: (208)237-9424
Co. E-mail: brmem@sharetrails.org
URL: http://www.sharetrails.org
Contact: Joni Mogstad, President
Description: Represents individuals, organizations and businesses involved in off highway recreation such as snowmobiling, motorcycle trail riding, mountain biking, ATVing, hiking, horseback riding, 4x4ing, rock hounding and boating. Seeks to preserve access for off highway recreation; promotes conservation of natural resources; encourages cooperation among members and government land managers. **Founded:** 1987. **Publications:** *BlueRibbon Magazine* (Monthly). **Educational Activities:** BlueRibbon Coalition Board meeting (Semiannual).

17661 ■ Canadian Recreational Vehicle Association (CRVA)—Association Canadienne du Vehicule Recreatif
110 Freelton Rd.
Freelton, ON, Canada L0R 1K0
Ph: (905)659-8802
Fax: (905)659-9900
URL: http://dev.crva.ca
Description: Suppliers (122) and manufacturers (49) of recreational vehicles. Represents the interests of the industry before consumers and government agencies; provides for information exchange. Collects statistics; sponsors educational programs; presents awards. Ensures a continuity of professional standards beneficial to the RV industry and ultimately to the interest of the consumer. **Founded:** 1975.

17662 ■ Recreation Vehicle Dealers Association of America (RVDA)
3930 University Dr.
Fairfax, VA 22030-2515
Ph: (703)591-7130
Free: 888-687-7832
Fax: (703)359-0152
Co. E-mail: info@rvda.org
URL: http://www.rvda.org
Contact: Phil Ingrassia, President
Description: Firms that have as their principal business the retail sale of recreation vehicles (commonly known as travel trailers, camping trailers, truck campers, and motor homes) and who maintain a permanent business establishment oPEN for business and service on what they sell year-round. Provides information and liaison on government regulation of safety, trade, warranty, and franchising; fosters improved dealer-manufacturer relations; encourages communications among dealers and state and local RV associations. Offers education programs and training, advertising, sales, and service information. Provides public relations and publicity among the RV dealers and the rest of the industry, the public, and

the government; works to improve standards of service to the consumer; sponsors local retail RV shows and dealer seminars. Supports improved availability and quality of campgrounds. Maintains speakers' bureau; compiles statistics; sponsors educational programs. Maintains the Recreation Vehicle Rental Association and Recreation Vehicle Aftermarket Division to help improve the professional quality of rental and service businesses. **Founded:** 1970. **Publications:** *RV Executive Today* (Monthly); *RV Technician Magazine* (Quarterly). **Educational Activities:** RV Dealers International Convention/Expo (Annual). **Awards:** Top Quality Dealer of the Year Award (Annual).

17663 ■ Recreation Vehicle Industry Association (RVIA)
1896 Preston White Dr.
Reston, VA 20191
Ph: (703)620-6003
Free: 800-336-0154
Fax: (703)620-5071
Co. E-mail: rvia@rvia.org
URL: http://www.rvia.org
Contact: Derald Bontrager, President
Description: Recreation vehicle manufacturers, manufacturers' representatives, and suppliers of accessories and equipment used by manufacturers. Seeks to provide a unified recreation vehicle organization for manufacturers and component parts suppliers of motor homes, travel trailers, fifth wheel trailers, horse trailer conversions, sport-utility trailers, truck campers and folding camping trailers. Promotes and represents the growth and concerns of the industry to federal and state government departments, the media, and the public. Collects shipment statistics, technical data, and consumer and media information. Monitors industry compliance with safety standards and the activities of federal and state governments that affect the RV industry. Provides legal and public relations services. Sponsors market research. **Founded:** 1963. **Publications:** *Recreation Vehicle Industry Association--Industry Profile Report* (Annual); *Recreation Vehicle Market Report* (Monthly); *Survey of RV Financing* (Annual); *RVIA Today* (Quarterly); *Recreation Vehicle Industry Association--Membership Directory and Industry Buyer's Guide* (Annual). **Educational Activities:** The National RV Trade Show (Annual). **Awards:** Distinguished Achievement in RV Standards Award (Annual); Distinguished Service to the RV Industry Award (Annual); National Service Award (Periodic); National Legislative Award; National Service Award; RV Automotive Achievement Award; National Scholastic Award; Special Award; National Education Service Award; Spirit of America Award; Distinguished Achievement in RV Journalism Award; Distinguished Achievement in RV Standards Award; Distinguished Service to the RV Industry Award. **Telecommunication Services:** dstuebing@rvia.org.

17664 ■ Recreation Vehicle Rental Association (RVRA)
3930 University Dr.
Fairfax, VA 22030-2515
Ph: (703)591-7130

Fax: (703)359-0152
Co. E-mail: info@rvda.org
URL: http://www.rvra.org
Description: Dealers involved in the rental of recreation vehicles such as folding trailers, travel trailers, and motor homes. Works to improve the professionalism of the RV rental dealer through educational programs and promote the use of rentals by disseminating information. Compiles statistics; conducts seminars. **Founded:** 1982.

REFERENCE WORKS

17665 ■ *"Business For Sale: Your Cold Calling?' in Inc. (December 2007, pp. 34)*
Pub: Gruner & Jahr USA Publishing
Ed: Elaine Appleton Grant. **Description:** Profile of a recreational outfitting company in northern New England with an asking price of $6.185 million, with gross revenue of $9.4 million in 2007.

17666 ■ *Recreation Vehicle Industry Association--Membership Directory and Industry Buyer's Guide*
Pub: Recreation Vehicle Industry Association
Contact: Derald Bontrager, President
URL(s): www.rvia.org. **Ed:** Karen Mason. **Released:** Annual; February; latest edition 2009. **Covers:** Approximately 500 member recreation vehicle manufacturers, component parts suppliers, and associate firms; RV-related state and regional associations. **Entries include:** For businesses--Company name, address, phone, fax, name of contact, subsidiary and branch names and locations, product provided. For associations--Association name, address, phone. **Arrangement:** Separate sections for manufacturers, suppliers, finance firms, associate firms, manufacturers reps, and related associations. **Indexes:** Product/service, geographical, company name and brand names.

17667 ■ *RV Business--RV Industry Directory Issue*
Pub: TL Enterprises Inc. Affinity Group Inc.
Contact: Rebecca Zuniga, Manager
E-mail: rzuniga@affinitygroup.com
URL(s): https://tledir.magserv.com/cgi-bin/subscribe. **Released:** Annual; Latest edition 2010. **Price:** $19.95, Individuals 1-4 copies; $14.95, Individuals 5 or more copies. **Publication includes:** About 250 recreational vehicle manufacturers, 700 suppliers, and 600 distributors, wholesalers, manufacturers' representatives, and others in the industry; limited international coverage. **Entries include:** For manufacturers--Company name, address, phone, fax, names of key personnel, location of branch plants, types of vehicles made, brand names. For suppliers, and distributors--Company name, address, phone, fax, names of key personnel, products. For representatives--Company name, address, phone, fax, names and titles of key personnel, companies represented. **Arrangement:** Classified by line of business or type of service. **Indexes:** Company name, brand names for manufacturers, supplier products.

17668 ■ *The RVDA Membership Directory and Resource Guide*
Pub: Recreation Vehicle Dealers Association of North America
URL(s): www.rvda.org. **Released:** Annual; Latest edition 2008. **Price:** Free. **Covers:** Over 900 retail sales firms handling travel trailers, camping trailers, truck campers, and motor homes in the United States and Canada that are open for business twelve months of the year. **Entries include:** Company name, address, phone, and owner's or manager's name. **Arrangement:** Alphabetical. **Indexes:** Geographical, membership status.

STATISTICAL SOURCES

17669 ■ *The Market Outlook for Leisure and Recreational Vehicles*
Business Trend Analysts, Inc. Industry Studies
Released: 2005 -2006. **Price:** $1295.00. **Description:** Since the last decline in the value of manufacturers' sales of recreational vehicles (RVs) in 2001, this market has exhibited positive-sometimes almost overwhelming-growth.

17670 ■ *RMA Annual Statement Studies*
Pub: Risk Management Association
Contact: Kevin M. Blakey, President
Released: Annual. **Price:** $175.00 2006-07 edition, $105.00. **Description:** Contains composite balance sheets and income statements for more than 360 industries, including the accounting, auditing, and bookkeeping industries. Also contains five years of comparative historical data for discerning trends. Includes 16 commonly used ratios, computed for most of the size groupings for nearly every industry.

TRADE PERIODICALS

17671 ■ *Escapees Magazine*
Pub: Escapees, Inc.
Contact: Janice Lasko
Released: Bimonthly. **Description:** Provides members with the opportunity to exchange ideas and information on traveling in recreational vehicles. Carries hints for modifying vehicles for full-time living, saving and earning money, and keeping in touch with others. Recurring features include technical advice, travel in Mexico and abroad, housekeeping hints, where to find free and inexpensive parking, book reviews, announcements of rallies and other events, and information about the Escapee support network and RV Park system.

17672 ■ *ISTVS Newsletter*
Pub: International Society for Terrain-Vehicle Systems
Ed: Dvoralai Wulfsohn, Editor, dw@kvl.dk. **Released:** 2-3/year. **Description:** Concerned with off-road vehicle research. Recurring features include news of the Society and a calendar of events.

17673 ■ *RV Business (Recreational Vehicle)*
Pub: TL Enterprises Inc. Affinity Group Inc.
Contact: Rebecca Zuniga, Manager
E-mail: rzuniga@affinitygroup.com
URL(s): www.rvbusiness.com. **Ed:** Bruce Hampson, Dave Barbulesco. **Released:** Monthly **Price:** Free.

17674 ■ *Trailer Life: America's No. 1 RV Magazine*
Pub: TL Enterprises Inc. Affinity Group Inc.
Contact: Rebecca Zuniga, Manager
E-mail: rzuniga@affinitygroup.com
URL(s): www.trailerlife.com. **Released:** Monthly **Price:** $15.97, Individuals print; $27.97, Two years print; $27.97, Canada print; $51.97, Canada print; 2 years.

17675 ■ *Woodall's Northeast Outdoors*
Pub: Woodall Publications Corp.
Contact: Mellissa Robinson, Manager
E-mail: mrobinson@affinityroup.com
URL(s): www.woodalls.biz/output.cfm?id=1017811.
Released: Bimonthly **Price:** $20, Individuals.

17676 ■ *Woodall's Southern RV: The RVers Guide to Family Camping in the Southeast*
Pub: Woodall Publications Corp.
Contact: Mellissa Robinson, Manager
E-mail: mrobinson@affinityroup.com
URL(s): www.woodalls.com/regpubs/southern. **Ed:** Brent Peterson. **Released:** Bimonthly **Price:** $20, Individuals retail price.

TRADE SHOWS AND CONVENTIONS

17677 ■ *Annual Rockford RV, Camping and Travel Show*
International Sport Show Producers Association (ISSPA)
PO Box 480084
Denver, CO 80248-0084
Ph: (303)892-6800
Free: 800-457-2434
Fax: (303)892-6322
Co. E-mail: dseymour@iei-expos.com
URL: http://www.sportshow.org
Contact: Jeff Haughton, President
URL(s): www.showtimeproduction.net/rvshow/. **Frequency:** Annual. **Principal Exhibits:** RVs, camping and travel. **Telecommunication Services:** brenda@showtimeproduction.net.

17678 ■ *Eastern Sports & Outdoor Show*
Reed Exhibitions North American Headquarters
383 Main Ave.
Norwalk, CT 06851
Ph: (203)840-4800
Fax: (203)840-5805
Co. E-mail: inquiry@reedexpo.com
URL: http://www.reedexpo.com
URL(s): www.easternsportshow.com. **Price:** $10, adult; $9, seniors; $4, children 6 - 12 years. **Frequency:** Annual. **Audience:** General public. **Principal Exhibits:** Recreational vehicles, boats, hunting and fishing equipment, clothing, and related outdoor products, resorts, SUVs, retailers and manufacturers, motorcycles, ATVs, travel and tourism. **Dates and Locations:** , Pennsylvania Farm Show Complex. **Telecommunication Services:** eseveral@reedexpo.com.

17679 ■ *Fort Wayne Sports, Vacation, and Boat Show*
Trio Enterprises, Inc.
3624 Maxim Dr.
Fort Wayne, IN 46815
Ph: (219)483-2638
Free: 800-446-2638
Fax: (219)484-0876
URL(s): www.boatsafloat.com. **Frequency:** Annual. **Audience:** General public. **Principal Exhibits:** Recreational vehicles, boats, and travel and vacation information. **Dates and Locations:** , Allen County War Memorial Coliseum. **Telecommunication Services:** data@boatsafloat.com.

17680 ■ *Idaho Sportsmen's Show*
Idaho Gun Owners Association
URL(s): www.spectraproductions.com. **Frequency:** Annual. **Audience:** General public. **Principal Exhibits:** Recreational vehicles and sporting goods, including fishing, hunting, and camping equipment and supplies. **Dates and Locations:** , Western Idaho Fairgrounds. **Telecommunication Services:** david@spectraproductions.com.

17681 ■ *Kansas Sports, Boat, & Travel Show*
Industrial Expositions, Inc.
1675 Larimer St., No. 700
Denver, CO 80248-0084
Ph: (303)892-6800
Free: 800-457-2434
Fax: (303)892-6322
Co. E-mail: info@iei-expos.com
URL: http://www.iei-expos.com/
URL(s): www.agievents.com/shows/display.cfm?showid=74. **Frequency:** Annual. **Audience:** General public. **Principal Exhibits:** Recreational vehicles, boats, sports equipment, and travel destination information; fishing and hunting equipment, supplies, and services. **Dates and Locations:** , Coliseum. **Telecommunication Services:** rwhitacre-prp@ks.rr.com.

17682 ■ *Maryland RV Show*
Maryland Recreational Vehicle Dealers Association, Inc.
729 MD Rt. 3 N.
Gambrills, MD 21054
Ph: (410)987-6300
Fax: (410)987-6300
Co. E-mail: info@mdrv.com
URL: http://www.mdrv.com
URL(s): www.mdrv.com. **Price:** $8, children under 12 free. **Frequency:** Semiannual. **Audience:** General public. **Principal Exhibits:** Recreational vehicles and accessories; campground displays. **Dates and Locations:** , State Fairgrounds. **Telecommunication Services:** info@mdrv.com.

17683 ■ *The National RV Trade Show*
Recreation Vehicle Industry Association (RVIA)
1896 Preston White Dr.
Reston, VA 20191
Ph: (703)620-6003
Free: 800-336-0154
Fax: (703)620-5071
Co. E-mail: rvia@rvia.org
URL: http://www.rvia.org
Contact: Derald Bontrager, President
URL(s): www.rvia.org. **Frequency:** Annual. **Audience:** RV dealers, warehouse distributors, accessory/part store personnel, and campground representatives. **Principal Exhibits:** Recreational vehicles, component parts, services, and accessories. **Dates and Locations:** , Kentucky Fair & Expo Center.

17684 ■ *Tacoma RV Show*
O'Loughlin Trade Shows
PO Box 110849
Tacoma, WA 98411
Ph: (253)756-2121
Fax: (253)756-6898
Co. E-mail: infotac@otshows.com
URL: http://www.otshows.com/contact/tacoma/
URL(s): otshows.com/shows/trv/. **Price:** $10, Onsite adults; $8, Onsite seniors; children under 12 years old. **Frequency:** Annual. **Audience:** General public. **Principal Exhibits:** Recreational vehicles, motor homes, and related accessories. **Dates and Locations:** , Tacoma Dome.

ASSOCIATIONS AND OTHER ORGANIZATIONS

17685 ■ *Canada EarthSaver*
349 W. Georgia St.
Vancouver, BC, Canada V6B 3W2
Ph: (604)731-5885
Fax: (604)731-5805
Co. E-mail: office@earthsave.bc.ca
URL: http://www.earthsave.bc.ca
Contact: Dave Steele, President
Released: Bimonthly

17686 ■ Canadian Association of Recycling Industries (CARI)—Association Canadienne des Industries du Recyclage (ACIR)
682 Monarch Ave., Unit 1
Ajax, ON, Canada L1S 4S2
Ph: (905)426-9313
Fax: (905)426-9314
Co. E-mail: donna.turner-cari@on.aibn.com
URL: http://www.cari-acir.org
Description: Companies engaged in the recycling of used materials and products. Seeks to advance the recycling industries; promotes reuse of products containing nonrenewable resources. Represents members' interests; conducts promotional and advocacy activities. **Founded:** 1941. **Publications:** *The Pulse* (Monthly).

17687 ■ Canadian Environmental Network (CEN)—Reseau canadien de l'environment (RCEN)
39 McArthur Ave., Level 1-1
Ottawa, ON, Canada K1L 8L7
Ph: (613)728-9810
Fax: (613)728-2963
Co. E-mail: info@cen-rce.org
URL: http://www.cen-rce.org
Contact: Maggie Paquet, Chairman
Description: Environmental organizations. Seeks to advance the projects and activities of members. Promotes ecologically sustainable development. Serves as a clearinghouse on environmental issues; provides support and assistance to members. **Founded:** 1988. **Publications:** *Canadian Environmental Network News* (Annual). **Awards:** Caucus Achievement Award.

17688 ■ *Canadian Environmental Network News*
39 McArthur Ave., Level 1-1
Ottawa, ON, Canada K1L 8L7
Ph: (613)728-9810
Fax: (613)728-2963
Co. E-mail: info@cen-rce.org
URL: http://www.cen-rce.org
Contact: Maggie Paquet, Chairman
Released: Annual

17689 ■ *Connector*
PO Box 23
Bluffton, AB, Canada T0C 0M0
Ph: (403)843-6563
Fax: (403)843-4156
Co. E-mail: info@recycle.ab.ca
URL: http://www.recycle.ab.ca
Contact: Jason London, Director
Released: Quarterly **Price:** free.

17690 ■ EarthSave Canada
349 W. Georgia St.
Vancouver, BC, Canada V6B 3W2
Ph: (604)731-5885
Fax: (604)731-5805
Co. E-mail: office@earthsave.bc.ca
URL: http://www.earthsave.bc.ca
Contact: Dave Steele, President
URL(s): www.earthsave.ca. **Description:** Seeks to increase the awareness of the health, ethical, and environmental impacts of food choices. Promotes transition to a plant-based diet for optimum health, environmental sustainability, and compassion. **Publications:** *Canada EarthSaver* (Bimonthly); *Earthsave Canada--Vegetarian Directory.* **Educational Activities:** Taste of Health (Annual).

17691 ■ *Enviro Business Guide*
PO Box 23
Bluffton, AB, Canada T0C 0M0
Ph: (403)843-6563
Fax: (403)843-4156
Co. E-mail: info@recycle.ab.ca
URL: http://www.recycle.ab.ca
Contact: Jason London, Director

17692 ■ *For R Information*
127 Wyndham St. N, Ste. 100
Guelph, ON, Canada N1H 4E9
Ph: (519)823-1990
Fax: (519)823-0084
Co. E-mail: mwa@municipalwaste.ca
URL: http://www.municipalwaste.ca
Contact: Sue McCrae, Chairman
Released: Quarterly

17693 ■ Institute of Scrap Recycling Industries (ISRI)
1615 L St. NW, Ste. 600
Washington, DC 20036-5610
Ph: (202)662-8500
Fax: (202)626-0900
Co. E-mail: robinwiener@isri.org
URL: http://www.isri.org
Contact: Robin K. Wiener, President
E-mail: rwh@audubonmet.com
Description: Represents processors, brokers, and consumers engaged in the recycling of ferrous, nonferrous, paper, plastics, glass, textiles, rubber and electronics scrap. Conducts specialized education and research programs. **Founded:** 1987. **Publications:** *ISRI Focus*; *Scrap Magazine* (Bimonthly); *Scrap* (Bimonthly); *Institute of Scrap Recycling Industries Directory of Members* (Annual); *Institute of Scrap Recycling Industries--Membership Directory* (Annual). **Telecommunication Services:** isri@isri. org.

17694 ■ Municipal Waste Association (MWA)
127 Wyndham St. N, Ste. 100
Guelph, ON, Canada N1H 4E9
Ph: (519)823-1990
Fax: (519)823-0084
Co. E-mail: mwa@municipalwaste.ca
URL: http://www.municipalwaste.ca
Contact: Sue McCrae, Chairman
Description: Municipal waste management professionals. Promotes more effective and environmentally sustainable removal of solid wastes. Facilitates sharing of municipal waste management, reduction, recycling, and reuse information and facilities. Conducts continuing professional education courses for members; operates job hotline; represents members' interests before government agencies and the public. Sponsors research; compiles statistics. **Founded:** 1987. **Publications:** *For R Information* (Quarterly). **Awards:** Promotion and Education Awards.

17695 ■ *The Pulse*
682 Monarch Ave., Unit 1
Ajax, ON, Canada L1S 4S2
Ph: (905)426-9313
Fax: (905)426-9314
Co. E-mail: donna.turner-cari@on.aibn.com
URL: http://www.cari-acir.org
Released: Monthly

17696 ■ Recycling Council of Alberta (RCA)
PO Box 23
Bluffton, AB, Canada T0C 0M0
Ph: (403)843-6563
Fax: (403)843-4156
Co. E-mail: info@recycle.ab.ca
URL: http://www.recycle.ab.ca
Contact: Jason London, Director
Description: Promotes and facilitates waste reduction, recycling and resource conservation in the province of Alberta. **Founded:** 1987. **Publications:** *Connector* (Quarterly); *Enviro Business Guide.* **Awards:** Rs of Excellence Awards; R's of Excellence (Annual).

17697 ■ Saskatchewan Environmental Society (SES)
Box 1372
Saskatoon, SK, Canada S7K 3N9
Ph: (306)665-1915
Fax: (306)665-2128
Co. E-mail: info@environmentalsociety.ca
URL: http://www.environmentalsociety.ca
Contact: Allyson Brady, Executive Director
Description: Seeks to support and encourage the creation of a global community in which all needs are met in sustainable ways. **Founded:** 1970. **Publications:** *SES Newsletter* (Bimonthly).

17698 ■ *SES Newsletter*
Box 1372
Saskatoon, SK, Canada S7K 3N9
Ph: (306)665-1915

Fax: (306)665-2128
Co. E-mail: info@environmentalsociety.ca
URL: http://www.environmentalsociety.ca
Contact: Allyson Brady, Executive Director
Released: Bimonthly **Price:** C$40, /subscription.

17699 ■ Society Promoting Environmental Conservation (SPEC)
2060-B Pine St.
Vancouver, BC, Canada V6J 4P8
Ph: (604)736-7732
Fax: (604)736-7115
Co. E-mail: admin@spec.bc.ca
URL: http://www.spec.bc.ca
Contact: Tara Moreau, President
Description: Promotes environmental research, advocacy, and education. **Founded:** 1969. **Publications:** *SPECTRUM* (Quarterly).

17700 ■ *SPECTRUM*
2060-B Pine St.
Vancouver, BC, Canada V6J 4P8
Ph: (604)736-7732
Fax: (604)736-7115
Co. E-mail: admin@spec.bc.ca
URL: http://www.spec.bc.ca
Contact: Tara Moreau, President
Released: Quarterly **Price:** free.

17701 ■ Steel Recycling Institute (SRI)
680 Andersen Dr.
Pittsburgh, PA 15220-2700
Ph: (412)922-2772
Free: 800-876-7274
Fax: (412)922-3213
Co. E-mail: sri@recycle-steel.org
URL: http://www.recycle-steel.org
Contact: James Woods, Director, Public Relations
Description: Educates the solid waste management industry, government, business and the consumer about the economic and environmental benefits of recycling steel.

17702 ■ U.S. Composting Council (USCC)
One Comac Loop 14B1
Ronkonkoma, NY 11779
Ph: (301)897-2715
Fax: (301)530-5072
Co. E-mail: uscc@compostingcouncil.org
URL: http://www.compostingcouncil.org
Contact: Dr. Stuart Buckner, Executive Director
Description: Supports the recycling of all organic materials in the waste stream, including compostable materials from solid waste, wastewater, and agriculture that are not otherwise recycled. (Composting is a way of naturally recycling organic wastes and converting them into beneficial products that are safe to the public and the environment.) Works to improve public and market acceptance of composting processes and products; defines compost product standards; ensures that composting products are defined as "recycled" in federal, state, and local regulations and legislation; removes procedural and regulatory barriers; provides product classification and quality control for product liability and controlled use issues; and serves as an information clearinghouse. Maintains speakers' bureau; compiles statistics; and conducts research and educational programs. **Scope:** composting issues. **Founded:** 1990. **Subscriptions:** books clippings monographs periodicals video recordings. **Publications:** *Compost Facility Operating Guide*; *U.S. Composting Council--Membership Directory*; *Field Guide to Compost Use*; *Landscape Architecture Specifications for Compost Utilization.* **Awards:** Clean Water Award; Composter of the Year Award (Annual); H. Clark Gregory Award (Annual); Hi Kellogg Award (Annual); Jerome Goldstein Lifetime Achievement Award; Rufus Chaney Award (Annual).

17703 ■ *Walk Softly*
302 Hawkins St.
Whitehorse, YT, Canada Y1A 1X6
Ph: (867)668-5678

Fax: (867)668-6637
Co. E-mail: ycs@ycs.yk.ca
URL: http://www.yukonconservation.org
Contact: Mary Whitley, President
Released: Quarterly **Price:** included in membership dues.

17704 ■ Yukon Conservation Society (YCS)
302 Hawkins St.
Whitehorse, YT, Canada Y1A 1X6
Ph: (867)668-5678
Fax: (867)668-6637
Co. E-mail: ycs@ycs.yk.ca
URL: http://www.yukonconservation.org
Contact: Mary Whitley, President
Description: Seeks to protect Canada's natural environment; particularly that of the Yukon region. Encourages the conservation of Yukon wilderness, wildlife and natural resources. **Founded:** 1968. **Publications:** *Walk Softly* (Quarterly). **Awards:** Ted Parnell Scholarship (Annual).

REFERENCE WORKS

17705 ■ *"Austin Energy May Build $2.3B Biomass Plant"* in Austin Business JournalInc. (Vol. 28, July 25, 2008, No. 19, pp. A1)
Pub: American City Business Journals
Ed: Kate Harrington. **Description:** An approval from the Austin City Council is being sought by Austin Energy for a 20-year supply contract with Nacogdoches Power LLC to build a $2.3 billion biomass plant in East Texas. The 100-megawatt biomass plant, which is to run on waste wood, will have Austin Energy as its sole buyer.

17706 ■ *"Battling Back from Betrayal"* in Harvard Business Review (Vol. 88, December 2010, No. 12, pp. 130)
Pub: Harvard Business School Publishing
Ed: Daniel McGinn. **Description:** Stephen Greer's scrap metal firm, Hartwell Pacific, lost several million dollars due to a lack of efficient and appropriate inventory audits, accounting procedures, and new-hire reference checks for his foreign operations. Greer believes that balancing growth with control is a key component of success.

17707 ■ *"Boyd's Pawn Shop Looks More Like a Mini-Mall With Plenty For Sale"* in The Hawk Eye (January 2, 2011)
Pub: McClatchy-Tribune Information Services
Ed: Rex L. Troute. **Description:** Profile of Brian Boyd, aka 'the king of pawn' and his shop located in West Burlington, Iowa. Boyd also operates a redemption center at the rear of his shop and collects nearly 42 million cans and bottles annually.

17708 ■ *The Complete Idiot's Guide to Starting and Running a Thrift Store*
Pub: Alpha Publishing House
Ed: Ravel Buckley, Carol Costa. **Released:** January 5, 2010. **Price:** $18.95. **Description:** Thrift stores saw a 35 percent increase in sales during the falling economy in 2008. Despite the low startup costs, launching and running a thrift store is complicated. Two experts cover the entire process, including setting up a store on a nonprofit basis, choosing a location, funding, donations for saleable items, recruiting and managing staff, sorting items, pricing, and recycling donations.

17709 ■ *"Developer Tries to Bring Homes to Buda"* in Austin Business JournalInc. (Vol. 28, December 26, 2008, No. 41, pp. 1)
Pub: American City Business Journals
Ed: Kate Harrington. **Description:** Real estate developer Jeremiah Venture LP is planning a residential, single-family development on about 600 acres near Buda, Texas. The company also plans to construct a membrane waste treatment plant, and has applied to do land application. However, several groups have come forward to ask for more information on the application due to concerns about soil density.

17710 ■ *"Electronics Recycler Poised to Grow"* in Austin Business Journal (Vol. 31, July 22, 2011, No. 20, pp. A1)
Pub: American City Business Journals Inc.
Ed: Cody Lyon. **Description:** Electronic Recycling and Trading Inc. has leased 138,000 square feet of space in North Austin, Texas. The company requires more space for bigger equipment.

17711 ■ *The Green Guide for Business: The Ultimate Environment for Businesses of All Sizes*
Pub: Profile Books Limited
Ed: Roger East, Hannah Bullock, Chris Goodall. **Released:** May 10, 2010. **Description:** Everyone wants to go green these days, but for small businesses that's easier said than done. How do you measure a company's carbon footprint? Are dryers or hand towels more eco-friendly? Recycled paper or FSC-certified? All these questions and more are explored.

17712 ■ *"Greening the Auto Industry"* in Business Journal-Serving Phoenix & the Valley of the Sun (Vol. 30, July 23, 2010, No. 46, pp. 1)
Pub: Phoenix Business Journal
Ed: Patrick O'Grady. **Description:** Thermo Fluids Inc. has been recycling used oil products since 1993 and could become Arizona's first home for oil filter recycling after retrofitting its Phoenix facility to include a compaction machine. The new service could help establish Thermo Fluids as a recycling hub for nearby states.

17713 ■ *Greening Your Small Business: How to Improve Your Bottom Line, Grow Your Brand, Satisfy Your Customers and Save the Planet*
Pub: Prentice Hall Press
Contact: Dame Marjorie M. Scardino, Chief Executive Officer
Ed: Jennifer Kaplan. **Released:** November 3, 2009. **Price:** $19.95. **Description:** A definitive resource for anyone who wants their small business to be cutting-edge, competitive, profitable, and eco-conscious. Stories from small business owners address every aspect of going green, from basics such as recycling waste, energy efficiency, and reducing information technology footprint, to more in-depth concerns such as green marketing and communications, green business travel, and green employee benefits.

17714 ■ *Institute of Scrap Recycling Industries--Membership Directory*
Pub: Institute of Scrap Recycling Industries
Contact: Robin K. Wiener, President
E-mail: rwh@audubonmet.com
URL(s): www.isri.org. **Released:** Annual; August. **Covers:** Member processors, brokers, and consumers of scrap ferrous and nonferrous metals, paper, glass, plastics, rubber, and textiles; suppliers to the industry. **Entries include:** Company name, address, phone, contact name, product or service provided. **Arrangement:** Information is arranged geographically, by firm name and by individual name in separate sections.

17715 ■ *"Kiosk Outfit ecoATM Now Recycling Video Games"* in San Diego Union-Tribune (October 7, 2010)
Pub: San Diego Union-Tribune
Ed: Mike Freeman. **Description:** ecoATM makes automated kiosks to buy back cell phones will now include video games as part of their recycling business.

17716 ■ *"Recycling 202: How to Take Your Recycling Practices to the Next Level"* in Black Enterprise (Vol. 41, September 2010, No. 2, pp. 38)
Pub: Earl G. Graves Publishing Co. Inc.
Ed: Tamara E. Holmes. **Description:** Consumer Electronics Association and other organizations, manufacturers and retailers list ways to recycle all household items.

17717 ■ *Recycling and Waste Management Guide to the Internet*
Pub: Government Institutes
Contact: Judith Rothman, Director
URL(s): www.govinstpress.com. **Price:** $72, Individuals. **Covers:** More than 350 web sites, discussion lists, and news groups on the internet covering waste management and recycling issues. **Entries include:** Site name, address, subject, site summary, contact name and e-mail. **Arrangement:** Alphabetical. **Indexes:** Subject.

17718 ■ *"Shifting Gears" in Business Journal-Serving Phoenix & the Valley of the Sun (Vol. 31, November 12, 2010, No. 10, pp. 1)*
Pub: Phoenix Business Journal
Ed: Patrick O'Grady. **Description:** Automotive parts recyclers in Arizona are benefiting from the challenging national economic conditions as well as from the green movement. Recyclers revealed that customers prefer recycled parts more because they are cheaper and are more environmentally friendly. Other information about the automotive parts recycling industry is presented.

17719 ■ *"Survey: Most Approve of Donating Used Pacemakers to Medically Underserved" in Crain's Detroit Business (Vol. 25, June 1, 2009)*
Pub: Crain Communications Inc. - Detroit
Description: According to a survey conducted by University of Michigan Cardiovascular Center, 87 percent of those with pacemakers and 71 percent of the general population would donate the device to patients in underserved nations.

17720 ■ *"Unilever to Sustainably Source All Paper and Board Packaging" in Ice Cream Reporter (Vol. 23, July 20, 2010, No. 8, pp. 1)*
Pub: Ice Cream Reporter
Description: Unilever, a leader in the frozen dessert market, has developed a new sustainable paper and board packaging sourcing policy that will reduce environmental impact by working with suppliers to source 75 percent of paper and board packaging from sustainably managed forests or from recycled material. Unilever is parent company to Breyers, Haagen-Dazs, Klondike, Popsicle and other ice cream brands.

17721 ■ *"A Whiff of TV Reality" in Houston Business Journal (Vol. 40, January 22, 2010, No. 37, pp. A1)*
Pub: American City Business Journals
Ed: Christine Hall. **Description:** Houston, Texas-based Waste Management Inc.'s president and chief operation officer, Larry O'Donnell shares some of his experience as CBS Television Network reality show 'Undercover Boss' participant. O'Donnell believes the show was a great way to show the customers how tough their jobs are and reveals that the most difficult job was being a sorter at the recycling center.

17722 ■ *"Xerox Diverts Waste from Landfills" in Canadian Electronics (Vol. 23, February 2008, No. 1, pp. 1)*
Pub: CLB Media Inc.
Description: Xerox Corporation revealed that it was able to divert more than two billion pounds of electronic waste from landfills through waste-free initiatives. The company's program, which was launched in 1991, covers waste avoidance in imaging supplies and parts reuse. Environmental priorities are also integrated into manufacturing operations.

STATISTICAL SOURCES

17723 ■ *Standard & Poor's Industry Surveys*
Pub: Standard & Poor's Corp.
Released: Annual. **Price:** $3633.00. **Description:** Two-volume book that examines the prospects for specific industries, including trucking. Also provides analyses of trends and problems, statistical tables and charts, and comparative company analyses.

TRADE PERIODICALS

17724 ■ *Composting News*
Pub: McEntee Media Corp.
Ed: Ken McEntee, Editor, ken@recycle.cc. **Released:** Monthly. **Price:** $83, individuals; $93, Canada and

Mexico; $105, other countries. **Description:** Covers news and trends in the composting industry. Also reports on compost product prices. Recurring features include letters to the editor, interviews, news of research, a calendar of events, reports of meetings, and notices of publications available.

17725 ■ *Environmental Quality Management*
Pub: John Wiley & Sons Inc.
Contact: Stephen M. Smith, President
URL(s): onlinelibrary.wiley.com/journal/10.1002/(-ISSN)1520-6483. **Ed:** Ginger Griffin. **Released:** Quarterly **Price:** $775, Individuals print only; $1129, U.S., Canada, and Mexico institutional, print only; $1153, Institutions, other countries print only.

17726 ■ *Plastic Recycling Update*
Pub: Resource Recycling
Contact: Dan Forester, Director
E-mail: dan@resource-recycling.com
Ed: Jerry Powell, Editor, editor@resource-recycling.com. **Released:** Monthly. **Price:** $58, individuals. **Description:** Markets newsletter that covers all aspects of plastic waste recovery.

17727 ■ *Re-News*
Pub: Recycling Council of Ontario
Contact: Jo-Anne St. Godard, Executive Director
Ed: John Hanson, Editor, john@rco.on.ca. **Released:** Monthly. **Price:** Included in membership. **Description:** Promotes recycling and waste reduction through an examination of social, economic, and environmental trends in current and developing markets, technologies, and government initiatives. Covers local, regional, federal, and international programs. Recurring features include a calendar of events.

17728 ■ *Recycling Today*
Pub: G.I.E. Media, MC
Contact: Chris Foster, President
E-mail: chris.foster@gie.net
URL(s): www.recyclingtoday.com. **Released:** Monthly

17729 ■ *Remgro Recycling Equipment Marketing News*
Pub: Bruce Mooney Associates Inc.
Ed: Bruce C. Mooney, Editor. **Released:** Annual. **Price:** Free. **Description:** Promotes the sale of equipment and systems for processing household recyclables and solicits inquiries for the company's processing products. Lists prices.

17730 ■ *Resource Recycling: North America's Recycling and Composting Journal*
Pub: Resource Recycling
Contact: Dan Forester, Director
E-mail: dan@resource-recycling.com
URL(s): www.resource-recycling.com/. **Released:** Monthly **Price:** $52, Individuals.

17731 ■ *Scrap*
Pub: Institute of Scrap Recycling Industries
Contact: Robin K. Wiener, President
E-mail: rwh@audubonmet.com
URL(s): www.scrap.org. **Ed:** Rachel H. Pollack. **Released:** Bimonthly **Price:** $44, Individuals companies; $40, Libraries government & non-profit organizations; $52, Canada and Mexico first class; $139, Other countries; $73, Two years companies; $66, Libraries govt. & non profit organizations, 2 years; $86, Canada and Mexico 2 years; $230, Other countries airmail 2 years.

17732 ■ *Waste Recovery Report*
Pub: ICON Inc.
Released: Monthly. **Price:** $60, U.S. and Canada; $75, elsewhere. **Description:** Contains news of the recycling, waste-to-energy, and other resource recovery fields. Supplies news on legislative and regulatory changes, new facilities and technologies, and environmental concerns. Recurring features include news of research, reports of meetings, notices of publications available, and a calendar of events.

TRADE SHOWS AND CONVENTIONS

17733 ■ **GLOBE - International Environmental Industry Trade Fair and Conference**
GLOBE Foundation of Canada
World Trade Ctr.
999 Canada Pl., Ste. 578
Vancouver, BC, Canada V6C 3E1
Ph: (604)695-5001
Free: 800-274-6097
Fax: (604)695-5019
Co. E-mail: info@globe.ca
URL: http://www.globe.ca
URL(s): www.globe.ca. **Price:** $35, Pre-registered; $1050, Onsite. **Frequency:** Biennial. **Audience:** Trade professionals. **Principal Exhibits:** Environmental equipment, supplies, and services. **Dates and Locations:** , Trade & Convention Centre. **Telecommunication Services:** info@globeseries.com.

FRANCHISES AND BUSINESS OPPORTUNITIES

17734 ■ **Expense Reduction Consulting**
Expense Reduction Consulting, Inc.
27902 Meadow Dr., No. 130
Evergreen, CO 80439
Free: 877-255-2511
Fax: (954)255-7786
Co. E-mail: vic@ercinc.com
URL: http://www.ercfranchise.com
Description: ERC Franchises employ a finely tuned methodology that has helped companies minimize indirect costs. This methodology along with proprietary web based tools and Knowledge Base, assist franchisees in increasing their client's bottom lines by decreasing their indirect costs. **No. of Franchise Units:** 25. **Founded:** 1993. **Franchised:** 2005. **Equity Capital Needed:** $73,360-$82,210. **Franchise Fee:** $45,000. **Training:** 5 days at ERC University coupled with a 1 year long sales training program and ongoing support is provided as long as you are an ERC franchisee.

17735 ■ **Ink Solution & Postal**
9524 Hebron Commerce Dr.
Charlotte, NC 28273
Free: 866-482-4657
Fax: (704)523-8720
Description: Inkjet & toner cartridge recycling/postal services. **No. of Franchise Units:** 19. **Founded:** 2001. **Franchised:** 2007. **Equity Capital Needed:** $118,000. **Franchise Fee:** $29,000. **Royalty Fee:** 4%. **Training:** Provides 1 week training at headquarters, 1 week at franchisee's location, 1 week at corporate store and ongoing support.

17736 ■ **Shred-It**
Shred-It
2794 S Sheridan Way
Oakville, ON, Canada L6J 7T4
Ph: (905)829-2794
Free: 877-637-4733
Fax: (905)829-1999
URL: http://www.securit.com
Description: Mobile paper shredding and recycling operation, serving medical, financial, government and large and small business. Offers onsite shredding and recycling of shredded material. **No. of Franchise Units:** 53. **No. of Company-Owned Units:** 65. **Founded:** 1988.. **Franchised:** 1992. **Equity Capital Needed:** $300,000-$500,000 net worth required. **Franchise Fee:** $75,000. **Training:** 1 week in the field at time of opening. Provides 8 manuals on all aspects of the business.

LIBRARIES

17737 ■ **California Department of Conservation - Division of Recycling - Resource Center**
801 K St.
MS-18-58
Sacramento, CA 95814-3530

Ph: (916)323-3836
Free: 800-RECYCLE
Fax: (916)324-1224
Co. E-mail: doriis@calrecycle.ca.gov
URL: http://www.consrv.ca.gov
Contact: Patti Holmes, Director, Library Services
URL(s): www.calrecycle.ca.gov/BevContainer/ DORIIS/. **Scope:** Recycling, waste reduction, resource conservation. **Services:** Copying; library open to the public with restrictions. **Founded:** 1989. **Holdings:** 300 books; 400 reports; 277 videocassettes. **Subscriptions:** 93 journals and other serials.

17738 ■ California Integrated Waste Management Board Library
1001 I St.
Sacramento, CA 95812-4025
Ph: (916)341-6198
Fax: (916)319-7239
Co. E-mail: michael.vanbaaren@calrecycle.ca.gov
URL: http://www.calrecycle.ca.gov
Contact: Michael VanBaaren, Analyst
Scope: Waste management, recycling, source reduction, landfill technology. **Services:** Interlibrary loan; copying; library open to the public for reference use only. **Founded:** 1992. **Holdings:** 8000 books; reports; manuscripts; patents; archives; microfiche. **Subscriptions:** 117 journals and other serials; 2 newspapers.

17739 ■ Institute for Local Self-Reliance
2001 S. St., NW, Ste. 570
Washington, DC 20009
Ph: (202)898-1610
Fax: (202)332-0463
Co. E-mail: info@ilsr.org
URL: http://www.ilsr.org
Contact: Neil Seldman, President
Scope: Recycling and waste utilization, energy, alternative energy sources, cities and neighborhoods, ecology and environment, local economic development, materials policy, economic development, sustainable communities. **Founded:** 1974.

17740 ■ Long Island Lighting Company Resource Center
131 Hoffman Ln.
Central Islip, NY 11722
Ph: (516)436-4003

Fax: (516)436-4036
Contact: Carolyn Jaskot, Specialist
Scope: Energy, electricity, public utilities, business management. **Services:** Library not open to the public. **Founded:** 1986. **Holdings:** 1570 books; 100 periodical titles; videocassettes; audiocassettes. **Subscriptions:** 30 journals and other serials; 2 newspapers.

17741 ■ Pennsylvania Environmental Council Library
1315 Walnut St., Ste. 532
Philadelphia, PA 19107
Ph: (215)545-4570
Free: 800-322-9214
Fax: (215)545-4594
URL: http://www.pecpa.org
Contact: Paul King, President
Scope: Solid waste and energy issues, water issues, air pollution, transportation, growth management, land use, industrial sites reuse, mediation, population. **Services:** Copying; faxing; library open to the public by appointment. **Founded:** 1970. **Holdings:** 400 books; 100 reports; 40 videotapes; 10 slide shows. **Subscriptions:** 200 journals and other serials.

RESEARCH CENTERS

17742 ■ Brown University - Center for Environmental Studies (CES)
135 Angell St., Box 1943
Providence, RI 02912
Ph: (401)863-3449
Fax: (401)863-3503
Co. E-mail: j_timmons_roberts@brown.edu
URL: http://envstudies.brown.edu
Contact: Prof. J. Timmons Roberts, Director
Founded: 1978. **Educational Activities:** Lectures and seminars; Project 20/20 (Weekly), promotes the use of high-efficiency lighting in low-income households in Providence; Science and policy-related courses; Sustainability Consulting Partnership (Weekly), creates professional development opportunities for Brown University students to apply their interdisciplinary backgrounds to business sustainability topics; CES Tours, by appointment; The Brown is Green Campus Environmental Stewardship Initiative; Farm Fresh Rhode Island (Weekly), devel-

ops local food system that values the environment, health and quality of life of Rhode Island farmers and eaters, links local farmers and buyers.

17743 ■ Cornell University - Cornell Waste Management Institute (CWMI)
Bradfield Hall
Department of Crop & Soil Sciences
Ithaca, NY 14853
Ph: (607)255-1187
Fax: (607)255-2644
Co. E-mail: cwmi@cornell.edu
URL: http://cwmi.css.cornell.edu
Contact: Prof. Murray B. McBride, Director
Services: Technical assistance: to communities, including a series of audio-visual and print resources addressing waste disposal, land use, and water contamination problems. **Founded:** 1987. **Publications:** *CWMI Fact sheets*; *CWMI Training manuals*; *Videos*. **Telecommunication Services:** mbm7@cornell.edu.

17744 ■ Earthworm, Inc.
35 Medford St.
Somerville, MA 02143
Ph: (617)628-1844
Fax: (617)628-2773
Co. E-mail: info@earthwormrecycling.org
URL: http://www.earthwormrecycling.org
Founded: 1970. **Publications:** *Earthworm Recycling Guide*.

17745 ■ Ecology Action Centre (EAC)—Centre d'Action Écologique
2705 Fern Ln.
Halifax, NS, Canada B3K 4L3
Ph: (902)429-2202
Fax: (902)405-3716
Co. E-mail: info@ecologyaction.ca
URL: http://www.ecologyaction.ca
Contact: Maggy Burns, Director
Services: Briefs preparation and research: on ocean habitat and biodiversity. **Founded:** 1971. **Publications:** *Between the Issues Newsletter* (Bimonthly). **Educational Activities:** Diverse volunteer opportunities; Educational workshops, on environmental and science topics; Environment and Development Group Meetings (Monthly).

ASSOCIATIONS AND OTHER ORGANIZATIONS

17746 ■ American Rental Association (ARA)
1900 19th St.
Moline, IL 61265-4179
Ph: (309)764-2475
Free: 800-334-2177
Fax: (309)764-1533
URL: http://www.ararental.org
Contact: Ted Cook, President
Description: Firms engaged in the rental of event and party equipment, tools, machinery, and other products; includes independent, franchised, and chain store operators. Associates are suppliers of equipment, merchandise, and other items. Seeks to foster better business methods; promote study of economic trends in the rental industry. **Scope:** management, products, training. **Founded:** 1956. **Subscriptions:** video recordings. **Publications:** *Rental Management*; *RM's Management Source Book* (Annual); *Cost of Doing Business Report*; *ARA Rental Management* (Monthly); *Rental Management: Official Magazine of the American Rental Association* (Monthly); *Who's Who in the Party Equipment Rental Industry*; *Rental Management--Who's Who in the Rental Industry Issue: Who's Who in the Rental Industry* (Annual). **Educational Activities:** The Rental Show (Annual); The Rental Show (Annual); American Rental Association Annual Convention and Rental Trade Show (Annual). **Awards:** Distinguished Service Award (Annual); Meritorious Service Award (Annual); Outstanding Leadership Award (Annual); Regional Person of the Year (Annual); Rental E-Web Image Award (Annual); Rental Hall of Fame (Annual); Special Service Award (Annual); Distinguished Service Award; Meritorious Service Award; Outstanding Leadership Award; Regional Person of the Year Award; Rental Hall of Fame; Special Service Award.

17747 ■ Association of Progressive Rental Organizations (APRO)
1504 Robin Hood Trl.
Austin, TX 78703
Ph: (512)794-0095
Free: 800-204-2776
Fax: (512)794-0097
Co. E-mail: rmay@rtohq.org
URL: http://www.rtohq.org
Contact: Shelley Martinek, Director
E-mail: smartinek@aprovision.org
Description: Represents dealer and industry suppliers. Serves rental dealers in the home appliance, furniture, and consumer electronics industry who market their products with a rental-purchase plan. Purposes are to: foster trade and commerce; collect and disseminate information; represent members before legislative committees, government bureaus, and other bodies in matters affecting the industry. Encourages competition among members and increased use of industry services; establishes advertising standards to prevent misleading and false advertising; considers and deals with common problems of management, including those involving production, distribution, employment, and financial functions within the rental industry. Sponsors workshops and seminars in accounting, sales, customer satisfaction and relations, personnel, inventory management, management development, and legal issues; makes available training materials. Conducts government relations program; compiles statistics. **Founded:** 1980. **Publications:** *RTOHQ: The Magazine* (Bimonthly); *Rental-To-Own Almanac* (Annual); *APRO Rental Viewpoint Online* (Biweekly); *RTO Today* (Weekly); *RTOHQ: The Magazine* (Bimonthly); *RTO Almanac* (Annual). **Educational Activities:** Convention/Buying Show (Annual); Association of Progressive Rental Organizations Annual Convention and Trade Show (APRO) (Annual). **Awards:** Buddy Awards (Annual).

17748 ■ Equipment Leasing and Finance Association (ELFA)
1825 K St. NW, Ste. 900
Washington, DC 20006
Ph: (202)238-3400
Fax: (202)238-3401
Co. E-mail: wsutton@elfaonline.org
URL: http://www.elfaonline.org
Contact: William G. Sutton, President
URL(s): www.elfaonline.org/DomainChg.cfm. **Description:** Individuals, companies, divisions, or subsidiaries whose principal activity is the leasing of equipment to other commercial users. Includes companies that function or operate in the capacity of brokers and that do not write leases on their own forms, as well as bank-related lessors. Promotes understanding of problems involved in equipment leasing; works to advance the interests of members so they may better serve the public. Compiles statistics. **Founded:** 1961. **Publications:** *Who's Who in Equipment Leasing*. **Educational Activities:** Equipment Leasing and Finance Association Meeting (Annual). **Telecommunication Services:** rscoggins@elfaonline.org.

17749 ■ International Furniture Rental Association (IFRA)
c/o Alston & Bird LLP
950 F St., NW, 10th Fl.
Washington, DC 20004
Ph: (202)239-3818
Fax: (202)654-4818
Co. E-mail: info@ifra.org
URL: http://www.ifra.org
Contact: Bill Anaya, Executive Director
Description: Companies whose major business is the leasing and rental of home furnishings and accessories; suppliers of products and services to these companies are associate members. Dedicated in upholding ethical standards of the furniture rental industry and providing quality products and service. Conducts industry exposition and statistical surveys. Promotes industry through nationwide consumer education program. Works to safeguard against adverse legislation and regulation. **Founded:** 1967. **Publications:** *Furniture Rental Association of America--Newsletter* (Bimonthly).

REFERENCE WORKS

17750 ■ "$550 Cash Rent on 330 Acres in Iowa" in Farm Industry News (November 30, 2011)
Pub: Penton Business Media Inc.
Ed: Karen McMahon. **Description:** A farmer in Iowa accepted a bid for $550/acre for his 330-acre farm for one year. The next closest bid was $350/acre. This rent will amount to more than the farmer paid for all of his land in the 1960s and 1970s. High rents are not alarming because of the high profitability farmers are currently receiving from crops.

17751 ■ "The 2011 Rental Readers' Choice Award Winners" in Rental Product News (Vol. 33, October 2011)
Pub: Cygnus Business Media
Ed: Jenny Lescohier. **Description:** Rental Product News conducted a survey asking readers what they considered to be the best product in their rental industry. A listing of winners is provided.

17752 ■ "AF Expands in New Green Building in Gothenburg" in Ecology,Environment & Conservation Business (September 24, 2011, pp. 2)
Pub: HighBeam Research
Description: AF signed a ten-year tenancy contract with Skanska for the premises of its new green building in Gothenburg, Sweden. AF offers qualified services and solutions for industrial processes, infrastructure projects and the development of products and IT systems.

17753 ■ "Antwerpen Takes on Chrysler Financial Over Foreclosure Sales" in Baltimore Business Journal (Vol. 28, July 30, 2010, No. 12, pp. 1)
Pub: Baltimore Business Journal
Ed: Gary Haber. **Description:** Antwerpen Motorcars Ltd. aims to fight the scheduled foreclosure sale of real estate it leases in Baltimore County, including the showroom for its Hyundai dealership on Baltimore National Pike in Catonsville, Maryland. The company is planning to file papers in court to stop the scheduled August 11, 2010 auction sought by Chrysler Financial Services Americas LLC.

17754 ■ "Apartment Tower in River North Fetches More Than $90 Million" in Crain's Chicago Business (Vol. 34, October 24, 2011, No. 42, pp. 17)
Pub: Crain Communications Inc.
Ed: Alby Gallun. **Description:** Apartment tower in River North was sold for over $90 million to a Texas pension fund adviser. Details are included.

17755 ■ "Asterand Eyes Jump to Ann Arbor; TechTown Tenant" in Crain's Detroit Business (Vol. 25, June 22, 2009)
Pub: Crain Communications Inc. - Detroit
Ed: Tom Henderson. **Description:** Asterand PLC is considering a move to Ann Arbor from its current location as anchor tenant at TechTown, an incubator and

technology park associated with Wayne State University. The university believes the Ann Arbor location's rent is too expensive for the tissue bank company.

17756 ■ *"BancVue to Expand"* in *Austin Business JournalInc. (Vol. 29, November 27, 2009, No. 38, pp. 1)*
Pub: American City Business Journals
Ed: Kate Harrington. **Description:** Significant growth of BancVue in the past six years has prompted the company to look for a site that could increase its office space from 25,000 square feet to 65,000 square feet. BancVue offers bank and credit union software solutions and is planning to lease or buy a property in Austin, Texas.

17757 ■ *"Banks Could Greet Tenants in One Year"* in *Business Courier (Vol. 26, October 16, 2009, No. 25, pp. 1)*
Pub: American City Business Journals, Inc.
Ed: Lucy May. **Description:** The Banks project's initial phase is expected to start in 60 days, which may mean that the project's first tenant could move in by the end of 2010 or beginning of 2011. Carter, an Atlanta-based firm has partnered with Dawson Company in this riverfront development. The first phase will include 80,000 square feet of retail and 300 apartments.

17758 ■ *"Before Signing a Lease"* in *Business Owner (Vol. 35, September-October 2011, No. 5, pp. 14)*
Pub: DL Perkins Company
Description: The following terms are essential to investigate before renewing or negotiating a lease for a small business: Term, Neighbors, Actual Usable Space, Gross or Net, Tenant Improvements, Renewal Option, Purchase Option, Cancelation Option, Sublease or Assignment, Security Deposit, Code Restrictions and Zoning, Parking, Relief and Lease Agreement.

17759 ■ *"Beware of Bad Blade Rentals"* in *Rental Product News (Vol. 33, June 2011)*
Pub: Cygnus Business Media
Ed: Jenny Lescohier. **Description:** Blade rentals, despite their return on investment, can result in lost revenue because if handled incorrectly customers can injure themselves.

17760 ■ *"Beware of E15"* in *Rental Product News (Vol. 33, October 2011)*
Pub: Cygnus Business Media
Ed: Curt Bennink. **Description:** Environmental Protection Agency (EPA) set a new regulation that grants partial waivers to allow gasoline containing up to 15 percent ethanol (E15) to be introduced into commerce for use in model year 2001 and newer light-duty motor vehicles, subject to certain conditions.

17761 ■ *"Biggest UM Landlords"* in *Crain's Detroit Business (Vol. 25, June 15, 2009, No. 24, pp. 1)*
Pub: Crain Communications Inc. - Detroit
Description: University of Michigan will purchase the two million-square-foot Pfizer campus in June 2009. The university is the largest occupier of commercial real estate off campus in and around Ann Arbor, Michigan.

17762 ■ *"BRIEF: Montana Street Pawn Shop Closing Doors"* in *Montana Standard (November 6, 2010)*
Pub: Montana Standard
Ed: John Grant Emeigh. **Description:** First National Pawn located in Butte, Montana will close its doors after losing its lease. Co-owner Pat Evenson reported the lease situation coupled with the economy prompted the decision to close.

17763 ■ *"Buyers' Market"* in *Baltimore Business Journal (Vol. 27, November 20, 2009, No. 28, pp. 1)*
Pub: American City Business Journals
Ed: Daniel J. Sernovitz. **Description:** Some business owners in Maryland are removing their leases and purchasing buildings due to the lower costs of real estate. This trend has enabled small business owners to avoid rent hikes, while setting equity into

their companies. The pros and cons of owning buildings and how business owners assess their return on investment are examined.

17764 ■ *"Cash Rents Reach Sky-High Levels"* in *Farm Industry News (November 23, 2011)*
Pub: Penton Business Media Inc.
Ed: Karen McMahon. **Description:** Strong commodity prices are driving land values creating a hot rental market for farm land. Highest rents occur when farmers compete head-to-head for land.

17765 ■ *"Cold-Storage Cargo Facility a Late Bloomer"* in *Houston Business Journal (Vol. 40, August 28, 2009, No. 16, pp. 1A)*
Pub: American City Business Journals
Ed: Jennifer Dawson. **Description:** Trammell Crow Company leased half of the 61,000 square foot IAH International Air Cargo Centre II to Tradewinds Cargo Handling. The facility, located at George Bush Intercontinental Airport, is intended to be a destination of fresh flowers and food from Latin America.

17766 ■ *The Commonsense Way to Build Wealth: One Entrepreneur Shares His Secrets*
Pub: Griffin Publishing Group
Ed: Jack Chou. **Released:** September 2004. **Price:** $19.95. **Description:** Entrepreneurial tips to accumulate wealth, select the proper business or franchise, choose and manage rental property, and how to negotiate a good lease.

17767 ■ *"Cupcake Maker Grabs Outpost"* in *Crain's New York Business (Vol. 27, August 15, 2011, No. 33, pp. 16)*
Pub: Crain Communications, Inc.
Ed: Jermaine Taylor. **Description:** Family-owned miniature cupcake maker, Baked by Melissa, singed a ten-year lease, expanding their stores to five. The business was started three years ago by advertising executive Melissa Bushell.

17768 ■ *"Customer Preferences Control Skid Steer Choices"* in *Rental Product News (Vol. 33, June 2011)*
Pub: Cygnus Business Media
Ed: Jenny Lescohier. **Description:** Understanding the types of controls available on skid steer equipment is essential. The article provides a comprehensive guide to using and maintaining skid steers for rental agencies.

17769 ■ *"Delta Looks at Downtown Departure"* in *Business Courier (Vol. 27, October 1, 2010, No. 22, pp. 1)*
Pub: Business Courier
Ed: Dan Monk. **Description:** Delta Air Lines Inc. has been looking for a smaller office for its reservations center in downtown Cincinnati, Ohio. Delta has informed the city of its plan to seek proposals on office space alternatives in advance of the 2011 lease expiration. Insights on the current employment status at the reservations center are also given.

17770 ■ *"Developers Poised to Pull Trigers"* in *Boston Business Journal (Vol. 30, November 12, 2010, No. 42, pp. 1)*
Pub: Boston Business Journal
Ed: Craig M. Douglas. **Description:** Large residential projects are expected to break ground in Boston, Massachusetts in 2011, as real estate developers expect growth for the industry. Real estate experts expect more than 2,000 rental units to be available by 2011. Information on key real estate projects in Boston is presented.

17771 ■ *Dictionary of Real Estate Terms*
Pub: Barron's Educational Series Inc.
Contact: Alex Holtz, President
E-mail: aholtz@barronseduc.com
Ed: Jack P. Friedman, Jack C. Harris, J. Bruce Lindeman. **Released:** October 2008. **Price:** $13.99. **Description:** More than 2,500 real estate terms relating to mortgages and financing, brokerage law, architecture, rentals and leases, property insurance, and more.

17772 ■ *"The Display Group Is Super-Sized"* in *Michigan Vue (Vol. 13, July-August 2008, No. 4, pp. 34)*
Pub: Entrepreneur Media Inc.
Description: Profile of the Display Group, located in downtown Detroit, this company provides custom designed mobile marketing displays as well as special event production services for trade show displays. The rental house and design service is also beginning to see more business due to the film initiative, which provides incentives for films that are shooting in Michigan.

17773 ■ *"Do You Need to Reinvent Your Managers?"* in *Rental Product News (Vol. 33, June 2011)*
Pub: Cygnus Business Media
Ed: Dick Detmer. **Description:** Rental business owners need to assess their management and be sure they perform as true leaders of the organization.

17774 ■ *"Docs Might Hold Cure for Real Estate, Banks"* in *Baltimore Business Journal (Vol. 28, November 5, 2010, No. 26, pp. 1)*
Pub: Baltimore Business Journal
Ed: Gary Haber. **Description:** Health care providers, including physicians are purchasing their office space instead of renting it as banks lower interest rates to 6 percent on mortgages for medical offices. The rise in demand offers relief to the commercial real estate market. It has also resulted in a boom in building new medical offices.

17775 ■ *"Doctors Buy In to Medical Timeshares"* in *Houston Business Journal (Vol. 40, December 11, 2009, No. 31, pp. 1)*
Pub: American City Business Journals
Ed: Mary Ann Azevedo. **Description:** Memorial Hermann Hospital System has leased to doctors three examination rooms and medical office space in the Memorial Hermann Medical Plaza in line with its new timeshare concept. The concept was designed to bring primary care physicians to its Texas Medical Center campus.

17776 ■ *"easyhome Ltd. Discovers Employee Fraud at an Easyfinancial Kiosk Company"* in *Internet Wire (October 14, 2010)*
Pub: Comtex
Description: Canada's leading merchandise leasing company and provider of financial services, easyhome Ltd., reported employee fraud totaling $3.4 million that was perpetrated against the firm's easyfinancial services business.

17777 ■ *"Empty Office Blues"* in *Business Journal Portland (Vol. 26, December 4, 2009, No. 39, pp. 1)*
Pub: American City Business Journals Inc.
Ed: Wendy Culverwell. **Description:** Portland's office vacancy rates could reach almost 15 percent by the end of 2010 due to job reductions and mergers.

17778 ■ *"Ethnic Businesses Ending Vacancies"* in *Business First-Columbus (Vol. 26, August 20, 2010, No. 51, pp. 1)*
Pub: Business First
Ed: Carrie Ghose. **Description:** The Morse Road commercial corridor in Columbus, Ohio has several immigrant-owned businesses that were recognized as instrumental in preventing widespread vacancies when the Northland Mall closed in 2002. The ethnic stores have created a diverse destination that attracted traffic and more businesses.

17779 ■ *"Extra Rehab Time Boosts M-B's Off-Lease Profits"* in *Automotive News (Vol. 86, October 31, 2011, No. 6488, pp. 22)*
Pub: Crain Communications Inc.
Ed: Arlena Sawyers. **Description:** Mercedes-Benz Financial Services USA is holding on to off-lease vehicles in order to recondition them and the move is boosting profits for the company.

17780 ■ *"Firms Sue Doracon to Recoup More Than $1M in Unpaid Bills"* in *Baltimore Business Journal (Vol. 28, July 9, 2010, No. 9, pp. 1)*
Pub: Baltimore Business Journal
Ed: Scott Dance. **Description:** Concrete supplier Paul J. Rach Inc., Selective Insurance Company, and equipment leasing firm Colonial Pacific Leasing

Corporation intend to sue Baltimore, Maryland-based Doracon Contracting Inc. for $1 million in unpaid bills. Doracon owed Colonial Pacific $794,000 and the equipment is still in Doracon's possession. Selective Insurance and Paul J. Rach respectively seek $132,000 and $88,000.

17781 ■ *"Formaspace Finds a Bigger Home"* in Austin Business JournalInc. (Vol. 29, December 4, 2009, No. 39, pp. 1)
Pub: American City Business Journals

Ed: Kate Harrington. **Description:** Formaspace Technical Furniture has signed a lease for 56,700 square feet in Harris Ridge Business Center at Northeast Austin, Texas, which represents one of the area's largest leases for 2009. The new lease enables Formaspace to hire new employees, invest in new equipment, and take advantage of a taxing designation created for manufacturers.

17782 ■ *"Furniture Chain Moving to Harford"* in Baltimore Business Journal (Vol. 27, January 22, 2010, No. 38, pp. 1)
Pub: American City Business Journals

Ed: David J. Sernovitz. **Description:** Manchester, Connecticut-based Bob's Discount Furniture signed a lease for 672,000 square feet of space in Harford County, Maryland. The site will become the discount furniture retailer's distribution center in mid-Atlantic US. As many as 200 jobs could be generated when the center opens.

17783 ■ *"Generation Y Driving Portland Multifamily Market"* in Daily Journal of Commerce, Portland (October 29, 2010)
Pub: Dolan Media Newswires

Ed: Nick Bjork. **Description:** Generation Y, young adults between the ages of 18-30, are interested in multifamily residents in the Portland, Oregon area. Developers in the area, particularly North Portland, have recognized this trend and are looking into multifamily investments.

17784 ■ *"Go Back to Basics to Maximize Skid Steer ROI"* in Rental Product News (Vol. 33, October 2011)
Pub: Cygnus Business Media

Ed: Jenny Lescohier. **Description:** There are two types of rental customers in the market for skid steers: the small contractor or weekend warrior who rents for a day or a week and the longer-term rental going to large contractor firms.

17785 ■ *"Groundbreaking 2.0"* in Philadelphia Business Journal (Vol. 30, September 23, 2011, No. 32, pp. 1)
Pub: American City Business Journals Inc.

Ed: Natalie Kostelni. **Description:** University Place Associates, the developer of 2.0 University Place in West Philadelphia, Pennsylvania, will break ground on a five-story, 97,000-square-foot office building in December 2011. The decision follows the Citizenship and Immigration Services signing of a 15-year lease as anchor tenant.

17786 ■ *"Higher Thread Count for Metropole"* in Business Courier (Vol. 26, September 25, 2009, No. 22, pp. 1)
Pub: American City Business Journals, Inc.

Ed: Lisa Biank Fasig, Lucy May. **Description:** Cincinnati Center City Development Corporation is under contract to buy the 225-unit apartment building called Metropole Apartments and 21c Museum Hotel is the lead candidate for the space. Advocates of some residents of the low-income rental complex complain that this move could leave them homeless.

17787 ■ *"How Fast Can This Thing Go Anyway?"* in Inc. (March 2008, pp. 94-101)
Pub: Gruner & Jahr USA Publishing

Ed: Stephanie Clifford. **Description:** Founder of Zip-car, an auto rental company, tell how he brought a new CEO into the company to boost revenue. The new CEO instituted a seven-step strategy to increase business.

17788 ■ *"Independence's Day Keeps on Getting Brighter"* in Business Courier (Vol.

27, June 11, 2010, No. 6, pp. 1)
Pub: Business Courier

Ed: Lucy May. **Description:** Reports show that residential and commercial development continues in Independence, Kentucky despite the recession, with a 144-unit apartment complex under construction. The city recorded 152 new-home closings in 2009, or 25 percent of all new homes closed in Boone, Campbell, and Kenton counties.

17789 ■ *"Industrial RE Market Shows Signs of Health"* in Business Courier (Vol. 27, August 20, 2010, No. 16, pp. 1)
Pub: Business Courier

Ed: Jon Newberry. **Description:** Cincinnati, Ohio's industrial real estate sector has experienced growth during the first half of 2010. The industry has seen a large net loss of occupied space in 2009.

17790 ■ *"Investors Eye Old Buildings"* in Business Journal-Portland (Vol. 24, October 19, 2007, No. 34, pp. 1)
Pub: American City Business Journals, Inc.

Ed: Wendy Culverwell. **Description:** Office vacancy rates in downtown Portland has dipped to around five percent, causing brokers and investors to search for older buildings in the Class B and Class C categories where the rent is also cheaper. Some notable older and cheaper buildings will be renovated for use.

17791 ■ *"Is this a Buying Opportunity?"* in Canadian Business (Vol. 82, April 27, 2009, No. 7, pp. 46)
Pub: Rogers Media

Ed: Andy Holloway. **Description:** Home prices in Canada are down by as much as 14.2 percent in 2009 compared to prices in 2008, making homes more affordable now. Some housing experts believe that homes are still good investments as prices of rent and properties always recover. Meanwhile, a survey found that Canadians under 35 plan to buy a home within two years.

17792 ■ *"Is It Time for a Change?"* in Rental Product News (Vol. 33, October 2011)
Pub: Cygnus Business Media

Ed: Jenny Lescohier. **Description:** Management software for running a rental business is examined.

17793 ■ *"Joint Venture Plans Bronzeville Project"* in Business Journal-Milwaukee (Vol. 25, October 5, 2007, No. 1, pp. A1)
Pub: American City Business Journals, Inc.

Ed: Rich Kirchen. **Description:** Proposal for construction of an apartment building and possible expansion of Northtown Mall in Milwaukee, Wisconsin is being planned by developers in the city's Bronzeville area. The project for rehabilitating the existing mall and building of a 50-unit apartment would amount to about $12.5 million.

17794 ■ *"Leaning Tower"* in Business Courier (Vol. 27, June 4, 2010, No. 5, pp. 1)
Pub: Business Courier

Ed: Jon Newberry. **Description:** New York-based developer Armand Lasky, owner of Tower Place Mall in downtown Cincinnati, Ohio has sued Birmingham, Alabama-based Regions Bank to prevent the bank's foreclosure on the property. Regions Bank claims Lasky was in default on an $18 million loan agreement. Details on the mall's leasing plan is also discussed.

17795 ■ *"Lytle Place Listing Seen as Bellwether"* in Business Courier (Vol. 27, December 3, 2010, No. 31, pp. 1)
Pub: Business Courier

Ed: Dan Monk. **Description:** Denver, Colorado-based Apartment Investment and Management Company (AIMCO) has offered the 25-story One Lytle Place Apartments for sale through CB Richard Ellis for the third time in three years. The potential sale could define the recovery for Cincinnati, Ohio's struggling apartment industry.

17796 ■ *"Market for Retail Space Flat, but Recovery Still Uncertain"* in Sacramento Business Journal (Vol. 28, August 26, 2011,

No. 26, pp. 1)
Pub: Sacramento Business Journal

Ed: Kelly Johnson. **Description:** The retail market in the Sacramento, California region remains challenged with the stock market volatility being the latest of its hurdles. The overall vacancy was 13.1 percent as of mid-2011, but retail real estate professionals express hopes that the worst is behind. A list and description of the region's winners and losers in retail vacancies is provided.

17797 ■ *"A New Way to Arrive in Style"* in Inc. (Vol. 33, September 2011, No. 7, pp. 54)
Pub: Inc. Magazine

Ed: Matthew Rist. **Description:** EagleRider is a franchise offering various two-wheeled rentals, including BMWs and Harley-Davidsons at more than 100 locations worldwide.

17798 ■ *"Nothing But Green Skies"* in Inc. (November 2007, pp. 115-120)
Pub: Gruner & Jahr USA Publishing

Ed: Alison Stein Wellner. **Description:** Profile of Enterprise Rent-A-Car, one of the largest family-owned businesses in the U.S. Andy Taylor, CEO, discusses the company's talks about the idea of offering carbon off-sets for a few years.

17799 ■ *"Old Ford Plant to Sign New Tenants"* in Business Courier (Vol. 27, August 13, 2010, No. 15, pp. 1)
Pub: Business Courier

Ed: Dan Monk. **Description:** Ohio Realty Advisors LLC, a company handling the marketing of the 1.9 million-square-foot former Ford Batavia plant is on the brink of landing one distribution and three manufacturing firms as tenants. These tenants are slated to occupy about 20 percent of the facility and generate as many as 250 jobs in Ohio.

17800 ■ *"The Perks of Going Public"* in Austin Business Journal (Vol. 31, July 15, 2011, No. 19, pp. A17)
Pub: American City Business Journals Inc.

Ed: Christopher Calnan. **Description:** HomeAway Inc. launched a $216 million initial public offering. Austin Ventures has generated more than $32 million from the IPO.

17801 ■ *"Plans for $160M Condo Resort in Wisconsin Dells Moves Forward"* in Commercial Property News (March 18, 2008)
Pub: Nielsen Company

Description: Plans for the Grand Cambrian Resort in the Wisconsin Dells is discussed. The luxury condominium resort will include condos, townhomes, and condo-hotel style residences, two water parts, meeting space and indoor entertainment space, as well as a spa, four restaurants and retail offerings.

17802 ■ *"Priced-Out Tenants Flocking to Class B"* in Boston Business Journal (Vol. 27, October 19, 2007, No. 38, pp. 1)
Pub: American City Business Journals Inc.

Ed: Michelle Hillman. **Description:** Tenants who usually rent top-tier office buildings are migrating to building that are not as expensive. The shift from Class A to Class B buildings is influenced by the high rental cost of the flashy office towers.

17803 ■ *"Proposed Accounting Changes Could Complicate Tenant's Leases"* in Baltimore Business Journal (Vol. 28, July 2, 2010, No. 8, pp. 1)
Pub: Baltimore Business Journal

Ed: Daniel J. Sernovitz. **Description:** The Financial Accounting Standards Board has proposed that companies must indicate the value of real estate leases as assets and liabilities on balance sheets instead of expenses. The proposals could cause some companies to document millions of dollars in charges on their books or find difficulty in getting loans.

17804 ■ *"Protect Your Assets"* in Black Enterprise (Vol. 38, January 2008, No. 6, pp. 38)
Pub: Earl G. Graves Publishing Co. Inc.

Ed: Trevor Delaney. **Description:** Owner of rental properties seeks advice for incorporating versus getting an LLC for the business.

17805 ■ "Questions to Ask Your Customers Before They Rent a Generator" in Rental Product News (Vol. 33, October 2011)
Pub: Cygnus Business Media
Ed: Jenny Lescohier. **Description:** According to a national strategic account manager at Kohler Rental Power, the most important factors when choosing a generator include volts, amps and phase. Understanding the relationship between these three electrical values will help rent the power equipment to customers.

17806 ■ "Rent Check" in Boston Business Journal (Vol. 31, July 29, 2011, No. 27, pp. 1)
Pub: Boston Business Journal
Ed: Lisa van der Pool. **Description:** Merchants at Newbury Street in Boston, Massachusetts are concerned with the annual increase of already inflated rents that prevent many small businesses from expanding.

17807 ■ Rental Management--Who's Who in the Rental Industry Issue: Who's Who in the Rental Industry
Pub: American Rental Association
Contact: Ted Cook, President
URL(s): www.rentalmanagementmag.com/aboutrm. html. **Ed:** Brian Alm. **Released:** Annual; July. **Price:** $25, Individuals member price; $75, Individuals non-member price. **Publication includes:** Lists of about 8,500 member rental companies, branch locations, services, and suppliers to the rental industry in the United States, limited international coverage; also lists association officers, other associations in the industry, and ARA state and local groups. **Entries include:** For rental firms--Company name, address, phone, key personnel and kind of rental service provided (construction, general tool, health, party). For suppliers--Company name, address, phone, products or service. For associations--Organization name, contact name, address, phone. For officers--Name, company, address, phone; listings for present officers include first name of spouse; listings for past presidents show the year(s) of tenure. **Arrangement:** Rental firms are listed geographically; associations are by country or state; current officers are hierarchical, past officers are listed alphabetically, past presidents are chronological; suppliers are alphabetical. **Indexes:** Personal name.

17808 ■ "Renters' Review - Secret Shoppers Strike Again" in Rental Product News (Vol. 33, June 2011)
Pub: Cygnus Business Media
Description: Staff of Rental Product News set out to rent various items from three different rental sources in order to evaluate the rental experience from the eyes of the average customer.

17809 ■ "Restaurateurs Follow High-End Apartments Into Kendall Square" in Boston Business Journal (Vol. 31, July 22, 2011, No. 26, pp. 3)
Pub: Boston Business Journal
Ed: Lisa van der Pool. **Description:** Kendall Square in Cambridge, Massachusetts is attracting restaurants, 16 of which have opened since 2009. The influx of restaurants is being driven by lower commercial rents.

17810 ■ "Restoring Grandeur" in Business Courier (Vol. 26, December 4, 2009, No. 32, pp. 1)
Pub: American City Business Journals, Inc.
Ed: Dan Monk. **Description:** Eagle Realty Group intends to spend more than $10 to restore the historic 12-story Phelps apartment building in Lytle Park in Cincinnati. Its president, Mario San Marco, expressed the need to invest in the building in order to maintain operations. The building could be restored into a hotel catering to executives and consultants.

17811 ■ "A Rise in Rental Units" in Philadelphia Business Journal (Vol. 30, October 7, 2011, No. 34, pp. 1)
Pub: American City Business Journals Inc.
Ed: Natalie Kostelni. **Description:** Housing developers have been stepping up the construction of new apartment complexes throughout the suburbs of Pennsylvania in order to capture growing demand for rental properties. BPG Properties Ltd. has nearly 1,000 new apartments under construction.

17812 ■ "Sales Tax Proposed to Revive KRM" in Business Journal-Milwaukee (Vol. 25, October 26, 2007, No. 4, pp. A1)
Pub: American City Business Journals, Inc.
Ed: Rich Kirchen. **Description:** City and county officials are proposing a $13 increase in rental car fees to finance the Kenosha-Racine-Milwaukee line. The Alliance of Cities proposed sales tax are backed by Milwaukee-area business groups, however it failed to generate support from the public.

17813 ■ "Shedding Light on Innovation" in Rental Product News (Vol. 33, June 2011)
Pub: Cygnus Business Media
Ed: Rod Dickens. **Description:** Light tower manufacturers have introduced numerous new products that feature alternative power sources, LED lighting and a second generation of performance and value.

17814 ■ "State Center Lease Deal High for Md." in Baltimore Business Journal (Vol. 28, August 6, 2010, No. 13, pp. 1)
Pub: Baltimore Business Journal
Ed: Daniel J. Sernovitz. **Description:** The proposed $1.5 billion State Center development project in Midtown Baltimore might cause the State of Maryland to pay the most expensive rental rates in the city. The state will have to pay an effective rental rate of $34 per square foot, including expenses, on the leasing. Other details of the redevelopment project are discussed.

17815 ■ "State Wants to Add Escape Clause to Leases" in Sacramento Business Journal (Vol. 28, October 14, 2011, No. 33, pp. 1)
Pub: Sacramento Business Journal
Ed: Michael Shaw. **Description:** California Governor Jerry Brown's administration has decided to add escape clauses to new lease agreements, which created new worry for building owners and brokers in Sacramento, California. Real estate brokers believe the appropriation of funds clauses have been making the lenders nervous and would result in less competition.

17816 ■ "Survey: Apartment Rents Continue to Climb as Home Market Slows" in Business Review, Albany New York (November 23, 2007)
Pub: American City Business Journals, Inc.
Ed: Michael DeMasi. **Description:** Survey by Sunrise Management and Consulting shows that asking rents for apartments in the Capital Region increased for the thirteenth consecutive time. The survey, which was conducted between August and October 2007, also showed that Albany County, New York had the highest average asking rent, followed by Rensselaer County, Saratoga County, and Schenectady County.

17817 ■ "Survey Says Commercial Real Estate Headed for Turbulence" in Commercial Property News (March 17, 2008)
Pub: Nielsen Company
Description: Commercial real estate sector is declining due to the sluggish U.S. economy. According to a recent survey, national office, retail and hospitality markets are also on the decline.

17818 ■ "Take the Right Approach to Concrete Polishing Rentals" in Rental Product News (Vol. 33, June 2011)
Pub: Cygnus Business Media
Ed: Jenny Lescohier. **Description:** A recent trend in flooring is concrete polishing for a practical, beautiful and sustainable way to decorate homes and businesses. Things to keep in mind when assessing the value of adding concrete polishing equipment to an existing rental store are evaluated.

17819 ■ "Tulsa-Based Dollar Thrifty Adds Franchises" in Journal Record (December 7, 2010)
Pub: Dolan Media Newswires
Ed: D. Ray Tuttle. **Description:** Dollar Thrifty Automotive Group Inc. opened 31 franchise locations in 2010 as part of its expansion plan in the U.S.

17820 ■ "UC May Expand into Old Ford Plant" in Business Courier (Vol. 26, December 25, 2009, No. 35, pp. 1)
Pub: American City Business Journals, Inc.
Ed: Dan Monk. **Description:** Developer Stuart Lichter is planning to acquire University of Cincinnati (UC) as a tenant at a two-story office building on a 132-acre site where a vacant Ford transmission plant is located. Details of the transaction are outlined.

17821 ■ "Welcome Back" in Canadian Business (Vol. 82, April 27, 2009, No. 7, pp. 25)
Pub: Rogers Media
Ed: Sarka Halas. **Description:** Some Canadian companies such as Gennum Corporation have taken advantage of corporate sale-leasebacks to raise money at a time when credit is hard to acquire. Corporate sale-leasebacks allow companies to sell their property assets while remaining as tenants of the building. Sale-leasebacks allow firms to increase capital while avoiding the disruptions that may result with moving.

17822 ■ "Where the Loans Are" in Boston Business Journal (Vol. 30, October 22, 2010, No. 39, pp. 1)
Pub: Boston Business Journal
Ed: Craig M. Douglas. **Description:** Massachusetts-based community banks have been investing in multi-family apartment projects. Lending has decline during the first half of 2010. A $264 million increase in multifamily loans has also been observed.

STATISTICAL SOURCES

17823 ■ RMA Annual Statement Studies
Pub: Risk Management Association
Contact: Kevin M. Blakey, President
Released: Annual. **Price:** $175.00 2006-07 edition, $105.00. **Description:** Contains composite balance sheets and income statements for more than 360 industries, including the accounting, auditing, and bookkeeping industries. Also contains five years of comparative historical data for discerning trends. Includes 16 commonly used ratios, computed for most of the size groupings for nearly every industry.

TRADE PERIODICALS   •

17824 ■ Heavy Equipment Guide
Pub: Baum Publications Ltd.
URL(s): heg.baumpub.com/. **Released:** 10/yr. **Price:** Free.

17825 ■ Rental Management: Official Magazine of the American Rental Association
Pub: American Rental Association
Contact: Ted Cook, President
URL(s): www.rentalmanagementmag.comwww.ara-rental.org/MyARA/ARAPublications.aspx. **Ed:** Wayne Walley. **Released:** Monthly **Price:** $85, Individuals.

17826 ■ Rental Product News
Pub: Cygnus Business Media
Contact: Rich Reiff, President
URL(s): www.forconstructionpros.com/magazine/rpn-www.forconstructionpros.com/cover/Rental-Product-News/6FCP, www.cygnusb2b.com/PropertyPub.cfm-?PropertyID=113, www.cygnusb2b.com. **Released:** Annual; 10/yr. **Publication includes:** List of about 400 manufacturers of trailers, loaders and backhoes, service maintenance and shop equipment, home-owner tools and supplies, and other rental equipment. **Entries include:** Product name, description, and photograph; name and address of manufacturer. **Arrangement:** Classified by type of product.

TRADE SHOWS AND CONVENTIONS

17827 ■ American Rental Association Annual Convention and Rental Trade Show
American Rental Association (ARA)
1900 19th St.
Moline, IL 61265-4179
Ph: (309)764-2475

Free: 800-334-2177
Fax: (309)764-1533
URL: http://www.ararental.org
Contact: Ted Cook, President
URL(s): www.ararental.org. **Frequency:** Annual. **Audience:** Owners and managers of rental equipment stores. **Principal Exhibits:** Equipment for rental, including party, construction, industrial, and do-it-yourself equipment.

17828 ■ Association of Progressive Rental Organizations Annual Convention and Trade Show (APRO)
Association of Progressive Rental Organizations (APRO)
1504 Robin Hood Trl.
Austin, TX 78703
Ph: (512)794-0095
Free: 800-204-2776
Fax: (512)794-0097
Co. E-mail: rmay@rtohq.org
URL: http://www.rtohq.org
Contact: Shelley Martinek, Director
E-mail: smartinek@aprovision.org
URL(s): www.rtohq.org/. **Frequency:** Annual. **Audience:** Rental-purchase store owners, managers, and suppliers. **Principal Exhibits:** Products of interest to rent-to-own dealers, such as audio products, computers, home appliances, home furniture, video products, jewelry, advertising, electronics, fabric protection, marketing, promotional services, and related equipment, supplies, and services. **Telecommunication Services:** smartinek@aprovision.org.

FRANCHISES AND BUSINESS OPPORTUNITIES

17829 ■ Abrakadoodle Remarkable Art Education
Abrakadoodle, Inc.
1800 Robert Fulton Dr., Ste. 205
Reston, VA 20191
Ph: (703)860-6570
Fax: (703)860-6574
Co. E-mail: info@abrakadoodle.com
URL: http://www.abrakadoodle.com
Description: Arts education program. **No. of Franchise Units:** 70. **No. of Company-Owned Units:** 2. **Founded:** 2002.. **Franchised:** 2004. **Equity Capital Needed:** $100,000 net worth. **Franchise Fee:** $29,900-$36,900. **Training:** Provides 5 days at headquarters with ongoing support.

17830 ■ Affiliated Car Rental LC
105 Hwy. 36
Eatontown, NJ 07724
Free: 800-367-5159
Fax: (732)290-8305
Description: Vehicle rentals. **No. of Franchise Units:** 254. **Founded:** 1987.. **Franchised:** 1987. **Equity Capital Needed:** $44,980-$71,800. **Franchise Fee:** $5,000-$11,600. **Royalty Fee:** Varies. **Financial Assistance:** Limited third party financing available. **Training:** Provides 2 days at headquarters, 2 days onsite with ongoing support.

17831 ■ Colortyme
Colortyme, Inc.
5501 Headquarters Dr.
Plano, TX 75024
Ph: (972)403-4900
Fax: (972)403-4923
Description: Provides a specialized inventory of rental products, such as televisions, audio-video equipment, appliances, furniture, jewelry, papers and computers. **No. of Franchise Units:** 195. **Founded:** 1979. **Franchised:** 1982. **Equity Capital Needed:** $229,575-$357,500. **Franchise Fee:** $20,000. **Royalty Fee:** 4%. **Financial Assistance:** In-house financial assistance available. **Training:** Provides 2 weeks at headquarters, 2-4 weeks at franchisee's location, and ongoing support.

17832 ■ Cool Daddy's
4188 Roswell Rd.
Atlanta, GA 30342
Ph: (404)352-9996

Fax: (404)352-9106
Description: Frozen drink party rentals & entertainment. **No. of Franchise Units:** 1. **No. of Company-Owned Units:** 1. **Founded:** 2000. **Franchised:** 2005. **Equity Capital Needed:** $105,000-$187,500. **Franchise Fee:** $25,000. **Royalty Fee:** 6%. **Training:** Provides 2 weeks at headquarters. 1 week at franchisee's location, with ongoing support.

17833 ■ Dollar Thrifty Automotive Group Canada Inc.
6050 Indian Line
Mississauga, ON, Canada L4V 1G5
Ph: (905)671-7858
Free: 800-667-5925
Fax: (905)612-1893
URL: http://www.thrifty.com/Franchise/14860.aspx
Description: Daily, weekly, monthly rental of all passenger vehicles and light trucks. **No. of Franchise Units:** 66. **No. of Company-Owned Units:** 54. **Founded:** 1985.. **Franchised:** 1985. **Equity Capital Needed:** $150,000 start-up capital required; $50,000-$300,000 investment required. **Franchise Fee:** $5,000-$50,000. **Training:** Yes.

17834 ■ Grand Rental Station
True Value Specialty Co., LLC
8600 W Bryn Mawr Ave.
Chicago, IL 60631-3505
Ph: (773)695-5000
URL: http://www.grandrental.com
Description: Industry leading store design, cooperative supply of rental and sale products. General rental store. Grand Rental Station/Taylor Rental Centers is the largest general rental store in the USA. **No. of Franchise Units:** 475. **Founded:** 1910.. **Franchised:** 1985. **Equity Capital Needed:** $250,000-$325,000. **Franchise Fee:** $1,500. **Royalty Fee:** 1.2%. **Training:** Offers 1 week of training program at company headquarters.

17835 ■ Joe Loue Tout Rent All Inc.
28 Vanier
Chateauguay, QC, Canada J6J 3W8
Ph: (450)692-6268
Free: 800-361-2020
Fax: (450)692-2848
Co. E-mail: mrjoe@videotron.ca
URL: http://www.joelouetout.ca
Description: Tool and equipment rental centre, offering full line of services from procurement of specific legalized stationary, rental inventory of tools, equipment and recreational vehicles. **No. of Franchise Units:** 80. **Founded:** 1982.. **Franchised:** 1982. **Equity Capital Needed:** $40,000-$400,000. **Franchise Fee:** $20,000. **Training:** Yes.

17836 ■ Nation-Wide General Rental Centers Inc.
5510 Hwy. 9 N
Alpharetta, GA 30004
Ph: (770)664-7765
Free: 800-227-1643
Fax: (770)664-0052
Co. E-mail: office@nation-widerental.com
URL: http://www.nation-widerental.com
Contact: Ike Goodvin, President
Description: Complete line for contractor, home owner and party. **No. of Franchise Units:** 412. **Founded:** 1976. **Equity Capital Needed:** $65,000-$80,000 cash investment; complete turn-key package from $135,000-$225,000. **Franchise Fee:** None. **Royalty Fee:** None. **Training:** Training provided when you need it; before you open; at an established general rental center with ongoing support.

17837 ■ Party Central
True Value Specialty Company, LLC
203 Jandus Rd.
Cary, IL 60013-2861
Free: 800-833-3004
Description: Rental store. **No. of Franchise Units:** 475. **Founded:** 1910.. **Franchised:** 1985. **Equity Capital Needed:** $250,000-$325,000. **Franchise Fee:** $1,500. **Training:** Yes.

17838 ■ Priceless Rent-A-Car
Bundy American Corp.
105 Main St.
Laurel, MD 20707
Ph: (240)581-1359
Fax: (240)581-1385
Description: Automobiles is the main area of interest and offers rentals. **No. of Franchise Units:** 50. **Founded:** 1996.. **Franchised:** 1996. **Equity Capital Needed:** $134,600-$636,500. **Franchise Fee:** $8,000. **Training:** Yes.

17839 ■ Rent-A-Tire Canada, Inc.
16 Victoria St. N
Kitchener, ON, Canada N2H 6S2
Ph: (519)578-3800
Fax: (519)578-2822
Co. E-mail: info@rentatirecanada.com
URL: http://www.rentatirecanada.com
Description: Specialists in tire, custom wheel and automotive accessories. Offering the 'affordable alternative' of rent-to-own purchases. **No. of Company-Owned Units:** 1. **Founded:** 2000.. **Franchised:** 2002.

17840 ■ Rent A Wreck
7710 5th St. SE, Ste. 204
Calgary, AB, Canada T2H 2L9
Ph: (403)259-6666
Free: 800-668-8591
Fax: (403)259-6776
Co. E-mail: info@rent-a-wreck.ca
URL: http://www.rent-a-wreck.ca
Description: The franchise specializes in renting high-quality, clean and dependable used vehicles at reasonable price. Strong brand awareness, international name recognition, national reservation network, national and regional marketing initiative, training, ongoing support and used car sales program are provided. **No. of Franchise Units:** 64. **Founded:** 1976.. **Franchised:** 1977. **Equity Capital Needed:** $80,000-$120,000 start-up capital required; $120,000 investment required. **Franchise Fee:** $20,000-$35,000. **Training:** Full classroom and ongoing training provided.

17841 ■ Rent 'N Drive
Rent 'n Drive Franchising LLC
1440 Plumridge Rd.
Lincoln, NE 68527
Ph: (402)467-4994
Fax: (402)466-3819
Description: Used car, van, and truck rentals. **No. of Franchise Units:** 1. **No. of Company-Owned Units:** 1. **Founded:** 1990.. **Franchised:** 1996. **Equity Capital Needed:** $83,000-$189,000, depending on fleet size. **Franchise Fee:** $7,500. **Training:** Yes.

17842 ■ Scooter Planet
2620 Regatta Dr., Ste. 102
Las Vegas, NV 89128
Ph: (702)869-0099
Fax: (702)446-6071
Description: Recreational equipment rental franchise. **No. of Franchise Units:** 1. **Founded:** 2004.. **Franchised:** 2004. **Equity Capital Needed:** $75,000 estimated. **Franchise Fee:** $29,500. **Training:** Yes.

17843 ■ Taylor Rental
TruServ Specialty Co., LLC
203 Jandus Rd.
Cary, IL 60013-2861
Free: 800-833-3004
Co. E-mail: pagee@truserv.com
URL: http://www.taylorrental.com
Description: A 100% member-owned Co-Operative, offering the Rental Industry's most complete Rental Franchise. Full line general rental stores offering tools as well as party, event, and contractor equipment to the homeowner and professional contractor. Grand Rental Station/Taylor Rental/Party Central offer the benefits of national name recognition, strong purchasing power, modern store design and effective advertising programs. New and existing business opportunities available. **No. of Franchise Units:** 475. **Founded:** 1910. **Franchised:** 1985. **Equity Capital Needed:** $250,000-$325,000. **Franchise Fee:** $1,500. **Training:** Yes.

17844 ■ U-Save Car & Truck Rental
Franchise Services of North America, Inc.
4780 I-55 N, Ste. 300
Jackson, MS 39211
Ph: (601)713-4333
Free: 800-438-2300
Fax: (601)982-9850
Co. E-mail: info@usave.net
URL: http://www.usave.net
Description: Auto rental. **No. of Franchise Units:** 169. **Founded:** 1979.. **Franchised:** 1979. **Equity**

Capital Needed: $300,000 net worth; $60,000 liquid. **Franchise Fee:** $20,000. **Financial Assistance:** Yes. **Training:** Initial training program focuses on management, marketing, and operational techniques.

17845 ■ Wheel Fun Rentals
Freetime Inc.
4526 Telephone Rd., Ste. 202
Ventura, CA 93004
Ph: (805)650-7770

Fax: (805)650-7771
Description: Bicycle and specialty products rental. **No. of Franchise Units:** 93. **No. of Company-Owned Units:** 13. **Founded:** 1987.. **Franchised:** 2000. **Equity Capital Needed:** $46,000-$230,000. **Franchise Fee:** $12,500-$25,000. **Royalty Fee:** 6%. **Financial Assistance:** Limited third party financing available. **Training:** Offers 7 days training headquarters, at franchisee's location and ongoing as needed. **Telecommunication Services:** franchise@Wheel-FunRentals.com.

START-UP INFORMATION

17846 ■ 55 Surefire Food-Related Businesses: You Can Start for Under $5000
Pub: Entrepreneur Press
Contact: Perlman Neil, President
Ed: Cheryl Kimball. **Released:** March 1, 2009. **Price:** $17.95. **Description:** Advice is given to start 55 various food-related companies and goes beyond restaurant or catering services. Home-based, retail and mail order ventures are covered, as well as food safety and standards.

17847 ■ "Ahead of the Pack" in Small Business Opportunities (Fall 2010)
Pub: Harris Publications Inc.
Description: Profile of an organic fast-food business that is carving out a niche that is gaining favor. Elevation Burger is a unique concept offering healthier burgers in sustainable buildings.

17848 ■ "'Crazy' Or Not, Restaurateurs Are Finding Ways to Open New Eateries" in Baltimore Business Journal (Vol. 28, October 8, 2010)
Pub: Baltimore Business Journal
Ed: Joanna Sullivan. **Description:** New restaurants have been opening in Maryland. However, 515 restaurants have closed down due to the economic crisis. Comments from restaurateurs are also provided.

17849 ■ Culinary Careers: How to Get Your Dream Job in Food with Advice from Top Culinary Professionals
Pub: Crown Business Books
Ed: Rick Smilow, Anne E. McBride. **Released:** May 4, 2010. **Price:** $16.99. **Description:** Top culinary experts offer advice for working in or owning a food service firm.

17850 ■ "Franchises with an Eye on Chicago" in Crain's Chicago Business (Vol. 34, March 14, 2011, No. 11, pp. 20)
Pub: Crain Communications Inc.
Description: Profiles of franchise companies seeking franchisees for the Chicago area include: Extreme Pita, a sandwich shop; Hand and Stone, offering massage, facial and waxing services; Molly Maid, home-cleaning service; Primrose Schools, private accredited schools for children 6 months to 6 hears and after-school programs; Protect Painters, residential and light-commercial painting contractor; and Wingstop, a restaurant offering chicken wings in nine flavors, fries and side dishes.

17851 ■ "Jean-Rober's 'oui" in Business Courier (Vol. 27, August 6, 2010, No. 14, pp. 1)
Pub: Business Courier
Ed: Dan Monk. **Description:** Jean-Robert de Cavel will open his new restaurant in Cincinnati, Ohio. The culinary arts program at Cincinnati State Technical and Community College offered him $100,000 to be

its 'chef in residence'. He was able to energize students, boost enrollment, and increase the stature of the culinary program.

17852 ■ "Proven Success Pays Off" in Small Business Opportunities (January 2011)
Pub: Harris Publications Inc.
Description: Industry pioneers of the fast-casual restaurant launch new venture with sales of $43 million. Profile of Newk's Express Cafe and its founders is included.

17853 ■ Small Business Desk Reference
Pub: Penguin Books USA Inc.
Ed: Gene Marks. **Released:** December 2004. **Description:** Comprehensive guide for starting or running a successful small business, focusing on buying a business or franchise, writing a business plan, financial management, accounting, legal issues, human resources management, operations, marketing, sales, customer service, taxes, insurance, and ethics. Information for launching a restaurant, property management firm, retail outlet, consulting firm, and service business is included.

17854 ■ Start and Run a Delicatessen: Small Business Starters Series
Pub: How To Books
Ed: Deborah Penrith. **Released:** November 9, 2010. **Price:** $30.00. **Description:** Information for starting and running a successful delicatessen is provided. Insight is offered into selecting a location, researching the market, writing a business plan and more.

17855 ■ Start Small, Finish Big
Pub: Business Plus/Warner Business Books
Ed: Fred DeLuca with John P. Hayes. **Released:** April 2009. **Price:** $16.95. **Description:** Fred DeLuca is profiled; after founding the multi-billion dollar chain of Subway sandwich restaurants, DeLuca is committed to helping microentrepreneurs, people who start successful small businesses with less than $1,000.

17856 ■ "Thirsty Lion on the Prowl" in Business Journal Portland (Vol. 27, November 5, 2010, No. 36, pp. 1)
Pub: Portland Business Journal
Ed: Wendy Culverwell. **Description:** Concept Entertainment Inc.'s impending launch of the Thirsty Lion Pub and Grill at the Washington Square in downtown Portland, Oregon is part of its West Coast expansion plan. A discussion of the planning involved in realizing Thirsty Lion is discussed, along with pub offerings that are expected to be enjoyed by customers.

ASSOCIATIONS AND OTHER ORGANIZATIONS

17857 ■ Association of Food Industries (AFI)
3301 Rte. 66, Ste. 205, Bldg. C
Neptune, NJ 07753
Ph: (732)922-3008
Fax: (732)922-3590
Co. E-mail: info@afius.org
URL: http://www.afius.org
Contact: Andy Gellert, Chairman
Description: Food processors, importers, and import agents nationally; food brokers in the New York

metropolitan market and overseas food exporters. Maintains arbitration tribunal, government relations, and information services. **Founded:** 1906. **Publications:** Standard Import Contract.

17858 ■ Beverage Network (BN)
44 Pleasant St., Ste. 110
Watertown, MA 02472
Ph: (617)231-8800
Fax: (617)812-7740
Co. E-mail: jcraven@bevnet.com
URL: http://www.bevnet.com
Contact: John Craven, Chief Executive Officer
Description: Beverage distributors dealing primarily in "new wave specialty non-alcoholic" products and some specialty food items. Serves as a forum for the exchange of information among members. Assists members in identifying new products. **Founded:** 1986.

17859 ■ Broker Management Council (BMC)
PO Box 150229
Arlington, TX 76015
Ph: (682)518-6008
Fax: (682)518-6476
Co. E-mail: assnhqtrs@aol.com
URL: http://www.bmcsales.com
Contact: Pamela L. Bess, Executive Director
Description: Foodservice sales and marketing companies specializing in institutional and restaurant food and allied products. Aims to: facilitate communication and exchange of management information; increase efficiency and reduce the cost of doing business; promote a favorable image of brokers in order to enhance their acceptance. Compiles statistics; conducts specialized education program. **Founded:** 1980. **Educational Activities:** FEDA (Monthly).

17860 ■ Canadian Foodservice Industry Operations Report
316 Bloor St. W
Toronto, ON, Canada M5S 1W5
Ph: (416)923-8416
Free: 800-387-5649
Fax: (416)923-1450
Co. E-mail: info@crfa.ca
URL: http://www.crfa.ca
Contact: Garth Whyte, President
Released: Biennial

17861 ■ Canadian Restaurant and Foodservices Association (CRFA)—Association Canadienne des Restaurateurs et des Services Alimentaires
316 Bloor St. W
Toronto, ON, Canada M5S 1W5
Ph: (416)923-8416
Free: 800-387-5649
Fax: (416)923-1450
Co. E-mail: info@crfa.ca
URL: http://www.crfa.ca
Contact: Garth Whyte, President
Description: Restaurant and food service corporations, hotels, caterers, and food service suppliers and educators. Seeks to create a favorable business

environment for members. Represents members' interests before government; conducts trade research. Makes available group buying programs and other services to members; owns and operates three industry trade shows. **Scope:** hospitality industries. **Founded:** 1944. **Subscriptions:** books periodicals. **Publications:** *Foodservice Facts* (Annual); *Legislation Guide* (Quarterly); *Canadian Foodservice Industry Operations Report* (Biennial); *CRFA National Hospitality News.* **Educational Activities:** Canadian Food and Beverage Show (Annual); ApEx; Canadian International Food and Beverage Show (Annual).

17862 ■ Commercial Food Equipment Service Association (CFESA)
2216 W Meadowview Rd., Ste. 100
Greensboro, NC 27407
Ph: (336)346-4700
Fax: (336)346-4745
Co. E-mail: cstrickland@cfesa.com
URL: http://www.cfesa.com
Contact: Joe Pierce, President
Description: Represents firms that repair food preparation equipment used by restaurants, hotels, and institutions. Provides training and education for members and their employees. **Scope:** technical training. **Founded:** 1963. **Subscriptions:** audiovisuals. **Publications:** *Commercial Food Equipment Service Association Directory* (Annual); *Commercial Food Equipment Service Association--Directory* (Annual); *On Target* (Bimonthly). **Educational Activities:** Commercial Food Equipment Service Association Conference (Semiannual).

17863 ■ Foodservice Equipment Distributors Association (FEDA)
2250 Point Blvd., Ste. 200
Elgin, IL 60123-7887
Ph: (224)293-6500
Free: 800-677-9605
Fax: (224)293-6505
Co. E-mail: feda@feda.com
URL: http://www.feda.com
Contact: Brad Wasserstrom, President
Description: Distributors of foodservice equipment, such as ovens, ranges, dishwashing machines, china, utensils, and cutlery for hotels, restaurants, and institutions. Conducts specialized education programs. **Founded:** 1933. **Publications:** *FEDA News and Views* (Bimonthly); *FEDA News and Views* (Bimonthly). **Awards:** Sam Anoff Lifetime Achievement Award (Periodic); Sam Anoff President's Award (Periodic); FEDA President Dealer-Based Distribution Award (Periodic).

17864 ■ Foodservice Facts
316 Bloor St. W
Toronto, ON, Canada M5S 1W5
Ph: (416)923-8416
Free: 800-387-5649
Fax: (416)923-1450
Co. E-mail: info@crfa.ca
URL: http://www.crfa.ca
Contact: Garth Whyte, President
Released: Annual

17865 ■ International Foodservice Manufacturers Association (IFMA)
2 Prudential Plz.
180 N Stetson Ave., Ste. 4400
Chicago, IL 60601
Ph: (312)540-4400
Fax: (312)540-4401
Co. E-mail: ifma@ifmaworld.com
URL: http://www.ifmaworld.com
Contact: Michael J. Licata, President
Description: Represents food, equipment and supply manufacturers in the foodservice industry, as well as related marketing service organizations, foodservice trade publications, distributors and brokers. Aims to shape the future of foodservice by creating an environment for positive change and actionable solutions benefiting manufacturers and their foodservice channel partners. **Founded:** 1952. **Publications:** *IFMA World* (9/year); *International Foodservice Manufacturers Association: Membership Directory*; *International Foodservice Manufacturers Association--Membership Directory* (Annual); *Encyclopedia of the Foodservice Industry* (Irregular). **Edu-**

cational Activities: Chain Operators Exchange (Annual). **Awards:** Gold Plate Award (Annual); Silver Plate Award (Annual).

17866 ■ Legislation Guide
316 Bloor St. W
Toronto, ON, Canada M5S 1W5
Ph: (416)923-8416
Free: 800-387-5649
Fax: (416)923-1450
Co. E-mail: info@crfa.ca
URL: http://www.crfa.ca
Contact: Garth Whyte, President
Released: Quarterly

17867 ■ National Barbecue Association (NBBQA)
455 S Fourth St., Ste. 650
Louisville, KY 40202
Free: 888-909-2121
Fax: (502)589-3602
Co. E-mail: nbbqa@hqtrs.com
URL: http://www.nbbqa.org
Contact: Kell Phelps, President
Description: Industry professionals and barbecue enthusiasts including restaurants, caterers, specialty equipment retailers, grill manufacturers and distributors, smoker manufacturers and distributors, food product suppliers and distributors, sauces and spice distributors, backyard hobbyists. **Founded:** 1991. **Publications:** *National Barbecue News* (Monthly); *NBBQA Barbecue Buyers' Guide* (Annual). **Awards:** Award of Excellence and People's Choice (Annual).

17868 ■ National Black McDonald's Operators Association (NBMOA)
PO Box 820668
South Florida, FL 33082-0668
Ph: (954)389-4487
Fax: (954)349-5408
Co. E-mail: nbmoa1@aol.com
URL: http://www.nbmoa.org
Contact: Rita Mack, Chief Executive Officer
Description: Black owners of McDonald's restaurants. Provides a forum for the exchange of ideas on the improvement of community relations and on the operation and management of restaurants. Seeks to build and improve the McDonald's restaurant image throughout the community. Sponsors training seminars on marketing, better sales practices, labor relations and profit sharing. Conducts charitable programs. **Founded:** 1972.

17869 ■ National Council of Chain Restaurants (NCCR)
325 7th St. NW, Ste. 1100
Washington, DC 20004
Ph: (202)783-7971
Free: 800-673-4692
Fax: (202)737-2849
Co. E-mail: info@nrf.com
URL: http://www.nccr.net
Contact: Rob Green, Executive Director
Description: Represents chain restaurant companies. Works to advance sound public policy that best serves the interests of restaurant businesses and the millions of people they employ. **Founded:** 1965. **Educational Activities:** Membership, Tax Forum and Food Safety (Quarterly).

17870 ■ National Restaurant Association Educational Foundation (NRAEF)
175 W Jackson Blvd., Ste. 1500
Chicago, IL 60604-2814
Ph: (312)715-1010
Free: 800-765-2122
Fax: (312)583-9841
Co. E-mail: info@restaurant.org
URL: http://www.nraef.org
Contact: Mary M. Adolf, President
E-mail: madolf@nraef.org
Description: Serves as an educational foundation supported by the National Restaurant Association and all segments of the foodservice industry including restaurateurs, foodservice companies, food and equipment manufacturers, distributors and trade associations. Advances the professional standards of the industry through education and research. Offers video training programs, management courses and

careers information. Conducts research and maintains hall of fame. **Founded:** 1987. **Publications:** *Foodservice/Hospitality College Directory* (Irregular); *Directory of Computer Hardware and Software for the Food Service Industry.* **Awards:** College of Diplomates Award; Al Schuman Ecolab Undergraduate Entrepreneurial Scholarships; Thad and Alice Eure Ambassador of Hospitality Award. **Telecommunication Services:** lmckee@nraef.org; scholars@nraef.org.

17871 ■ National Restaurant Association - Multi-Unit Architects, Engineers and Construction Officers Executive Study Group (MAECO)
2055 L Str., NW
Washington, DC 20036
Ph: (202)973-3678
Free: 800-424-5156
Fax: (202)331-2429
URL: http://www.restaurant.org/education/study-groups/maeco
Contact: Dawn Sweeney, President
Description: Professional architects, engineers, and construction officers from member companies of the National Restaurant Association who are involved in the construction and equipping of food service and hospitality facilities. Provides a forum for the sharing of common goals, concerns, ideas, and problems.

17872 ■ North American Association of Food Equipment Manufacturers (NAFEM)
161 N Clark St., Ste. 2020
Chicago, IL 60601
Ph: (312)821-0201
Fax: (312)821-0202
Co. E-mail: info@nafem.org
URL: http://www.nafem.org
Contact: Thomas R. Campion, President
Description: Represents manufacturers of commercial food service equipment and supplies for restaurant, hotel, and institutional use. Conducts certification program. **Founded:** 1948. **Publications:** *NAFEM for Operators* (Quarterly); *NAFEM in Print* (Quarterly). **Educational Activities:** North American Association of Food Equipment Manufacturers Tradeshow (Biennial). **Awards:** Doctorate of Foodservice (Annual); President's Award; William W. Carpenter Award; Doctorate of Food Service Medallion.

17873 ■ Society for Foodservice Management (SFM)
455 S 4th St., Ste. 650
Louisville, KY 40202-2554
Ph: (502)574-9931
Fax: (502)589-3602
Co. E-mail: sfm@hqtrs.com
URL: http://www.sfm-online.org
Contact: Barbara Kane, President
Description: Operates or maintains food service and vending facilities in businesses and industrial plants, or supply food products, equipment, or other essential industry services. Serves the needs and interests of onsite employee food service executives and management. Provides an opportunity for the exchange of experiences and opinions through study, discussion, and publications; develops greater efficiency and more economical methods of providing high-quality food and service at a reasonable cost; assists members in solving specific operating and management problems; keeps pace with the rapidly changing conditions of the employee food service segment of the industry. Develops and encourages the practice of high standards and professional conduct among management and executive personnel; provides job placement and management personnel recruiting service; sends representative to the U.S. Air Force Hennessey Award Team, which selects the Air Force base having the most superior food service. **Founded:** 1979. **Publications:** *Journal of Foodservice Systems* (Quarterly).

DIRECTORIES OF EDUCATIONAL PROGRAMS

17874 ■ Directory of Private Accredited Career Schools and Colleges of Technology
Pub: Accrediting Commission of Career Schools and Colleges of Technology
Contact: Michale S. McComis, Executive Director
Released: On web page. **Price:** Free. **Description:** Covers 3900 accredited post-secondary programs

that provide training programs in business, trade, and technical fields, including various small business endeavors. Entries offer school name, address, phone, description of courses, job placement assistance, and requirements for admission. Arrangement is alphabetical.

REFERENCE WORKS

17875 ■ *"$50 Million Project for West Chester"* in *Business Courier (Vol. 24, December 14, 2008, No. 35, pp. 1)*
Pub: American City Business Journals, Inc.
Ed: Laura Baverman. **Description:** Commercial developer Scott Street Partners is planning to invest $50 million for the development of a site south of the Streets of West Chester retail center. The 31-acre project will generate 1,200 jobs, and will bring in offices, restaurants and a hotel. The development plans and the features of the site are discussed as well.

17876 ■ *"$100 Million Complex To Be Built..On a Bridge"* in *Business Courier (Vol. 27, November 12, 2010, No. 28, pp. 1)*
Pub: Business Courier
Ed: Lucy May. **Description:** A development firm closed a deal with the Newport Southbank Bridge Company for a $100M entertainment complex that will be built on tope of the Purple People Bridge. The proposed project will cover 150,000 square feet with attractions such as restaurants, a boutique hotel, and pubs.

17877 ■ *"2010 Book of Lists"* in *Austin Business JournalInc. (Vol. 29, December 25, 2009, No. 42, pp. 1)*
Pub: American City Business Journals
Description: Rankings of companies and organizations within the business services, finance, healthcare, hospitality and travel, insurance, marketing and media, professional services, real estate, education and technology industries in Austin, Texas are presented. Rankings are based on sales, business size, and other statistics.

17878 ■ *"2010 Book of Lists"* in *Tampa Bay Business Journal (Vol. 30, December 22, 2009, No. 53, pp. 1)*
Pub: American City Business Journals
Description: Rankings of companies and organizations within the human resources, banking and finance, business services, healthcare, real estate, technology, hospitality and travel, and education industries in the Greater Tampa Bay area are presented. Rankings are based on sales, business size, and more.

17879 ■ *"Airmall Mulls I-95 Travel Plazas Bid"* in *Boston Business Journal (Vol. 29, September 2, 2011, No. 17, pp. 3)*
Pub: American City Business Journals Inc.
Ed: Alexander Jackson. **Description:** Airmall USA is planning to move its food courts from the Baltimore/Washington International Thurgood Marshall Airport to the new travel plazas on Interstate 95. The plazas are up for bid.

17880 ■ *"All Fired Up!"* in *Small Business Opportunities (November 2008)*
Pub: Entrepreneur Media Inc.
Ed: Stan Roberts. **Description:** Profile of Brixx Wood Fired Pizza, which has launched a franchising program due to the amount of interest the company's founders received over the years; franchisees do not need experience in the food industry or pizza restaurant service business in order to open a franchise of their own because all franchisees receive comprehensive training in which they are educated on all of the necessary tools to effectively run the business.

17881 ■ *"Anja Carroll; Media Director-McDonald's USA"* in *Advertising Age (Vol. 79, November 17, 2008, No. 34, pp. 6)*
Pub: Crain Communications, Inc.
Ed: Emily Bryson York. **Description:** Profile of Anja Carroll who is the media director for McDonald's USA and has the challenge of choosing the right mix of media for the corporation.

17882 ■ *"Aramark Rolls Out Ballpark Food Truck"* in *Nation's Restaurant News (Vol. 45, August 8, 2011, No. 16, pp. 4)*
Pub: Penton Media Inc.
Contact: John French, President
Ed: Ron Ruggless. **Description:** Aramark installed its first ballpark food truck serving Asian-inspired noodle bowls at the outfield concourse at Coors Field in Colorado.

17883 ■ *"Are You Looking for an Environmentally Friendly Dry Cleaner?"* in *Inc. (Vol. 30, December 2008, No. 12, pp. 34)*
Pub: Mansueto Ventures LLC
Ed: Shivani Vora. **Description:** Greenopia rates the greenness of 52 various kinds of businesses, including restaurants, nail salons, dry cleaners, and clothing stores. The guidebooks are sold through various retailers including Barnes & Noble and Amazon.com.

17884 ■ *"Bars, Restaurants to Offer Prix Fixe Menus, Space to Race Patrons"* in *Boston Business Journal (Vol. 29, July 22, 2011, No. 11, pp. 1)*
Pub: American City Business Journals Inc.
Ed: Alexander Jackson. **Description:** Restaurants and bar owners in Baltimore, Maryland have changed the way they do business as the Baltimore Grand Prix approaches. Owners have gone so far as to offering new services or renting out their entire restaurants to companies for the three-day event in September.

17885 ■ *"Baskin-Robbins Tests New Upscale Concept"* in *Ice Cream Reporter (Vol. 21, September 20, 2008, No. 10, pp. 1)*
Pub: Ice Cream Reporter
Description: Baskin-Robbins is opening its new upscale store, Cafe 31 in an effort to invigorate its brand. The shop will serve fondues, cakes and other treats prepared by an in-store chef.

17886 ■ *"Beyond Grits: The Many Varieties of Southern Cuisine"* in *Women In Business (Vol. 62, June 2010, No. 2, pp. 14)*
Pub: American Business Women's Association
Ed: Debbie Gold. **Description:** Southern cuisine is believed to be associated with grits, but the cuisine is not always with grits and offers varieties from Europe, Native American and African cooking. Southern cuisine varieties include soul food, Creole food, Cajun food and Low Country food. Examples are provided.

17887 ■ *"A Bigger Slice; Buscemi's Adds Licensees, Profits"* in *Crain's Detroit Business (Vol. 23, October 15, 2007, No. 42, pp. 3)*
Pub: Crain Communications Inc. - Detroit
Ed: Brent Snavely. **Description:** Six new licensees have opened under the Original Buscemi's Inc. The firm was founded in 1958 and expects to open nine more restaurants by the end of 2008.

17888 ■ *"BK Franchisees Lose Sleep Over Late-Night Rule"* in *Advertising Age (Vol. 79, August 11, 2008, No. 31, pp. 1)*
Pub: Crain Communications, Inc.
Ed: Emily Bryson York. **Description:** Burger King's corporate headquarters mandates that franchisees remain open until at least 2 a.m. Three Miami operators have filed a lawsuit that alleges the extended hours can be dangerous, do not make money and overtax the workforce.

17889 ■ *"BK Menu Gives Casual Dining Reason to Worry"* in *Advertising Age (Vol. 79, November 17, 2008, No. 43, pp. 12)*
Pub: Crain Communications, Inc.
Ed: Emily Bryson York. **Description:** Burger King is beginning to compete with such casual dining restaurants as Applebees and the Cheesecake Factory with new premium menu items, including thicker burgers and ribs; statistical data regarding the casual dining segment which continues to fall and Burger King, whose sales continue to rise is included.

17890 ■ *"Blue Tractor Barbeque and Brewery, Cafe Havana"* in *Crain's Detroit Business (Vol. 23, October 1, 2007, No. 40, pp. 15)*
Pub: Crain Communications Inc. - Detroit
Ed: Daniel Duggan. **Description:** Two restaurants are converted from a Buddhist Temple to become the most unique spaces in Ann Arbor, Michigan.

17891 ■ *"Book of Lists 2010"* in *Philadelphia Business Journal (Vol. 28, December 25, 2009, No. 45, pp. 1)*
Pub: American City Business Journals
Description: Rankings of companies and organizations within the banking, biotechnology, economic development, healthcare, hospitality, law and accounting, marketing and media, real estate, and technology industries in the Philadelphia, Pennsylvania area are presented. Rankings are based on sales, business size, and more.

17892 ■ *"Burger Heirs' Long-Bottled Fight Plays Out"* in *Business Courier (Vol. 24, January 11, 2008, No. 40, pp. 1)*
Pub: American City Business Journals, Inc.
Ed: Dan Monk. **Description:** Discussion of an heir to the Burger Brewing Co. Michael Cundall who has filed for permission to pursue efforts to question the legality of a 1984 transaction in which the Cundall family sold its share of the Central Investment Corp. (CIC). The court ruled that Cundall may continue fighting for his claim that his uncle, John Koons, breached fiduciary duties by pressuring the family to sell its CIC stake. Details of the court rulings are given.

17893 ■ *"Burger Market Sizzling with Newcomers"* in *Boston Business Journal (Vol. 29, June 10, 2011, No. 5, pp. 1)*
Pub: American City Business Journals Inc.
Ed: Ryan Sharrow. **Description:** The burger trend in Maryland is on the rise with burger joints either opening up or expanding into several branches. Startup costs for this kind of business range between $250,000 to $400,000. With a growth rate of roughly 17 percent in 2009, this so-called better burger segment of the burger categories is expected to dominate the market for quite some time.

17894 ■ *"Burritos New Bag for Shopping Developer"* in *Houston Business Journal (Vol. 40, December 4, 2009, No. 30, pp. 4A)*
Pub: American City Business Journals
Ed: Allison Wollam. **Description:** Houston, Texas-based Rob Johnson is the newest franchisee for Bullritos and plans to open eight area locations to market the quick-casual burrito concept. The former shopping center developer was looking for a new business sector after selling off his shopping center holdings.

17895 ■ *"Choice Bits"* in *Crain's Cleveland Business (Vol. 30, June 29, 2009, No. 25, pp. 19)*
Pub: Crain Communications, Inc.
Description: Ross Farro, Cleveland area restaurateur who was featured in the New York Times story about casual dining chains competing over lunch traffic through pricing.

17896 ■ *"Chuy's Gears Up to Serve Atlants, Other Untapped Cities"* in *Austin Business Journal (Vol. 31, June 17, 2011, No. 15, pp. 1)*
Pub: American City Business Journals Inc.
Ed: Cody Lyon. **Description:** Chuy's Holdings Inc. plans to expand into the Southeastern United States, particularly in Atlanta, Georgia. The restaurant, which secured $67.5 million in debt financing in May 2011, added 20 stores in five years and plans to open eight locations in 2011.

17897 ■ *"City Board Tweaks Internet Cafe Ordinance"* in *Ocala Star-Banner (July 19, 2011)*
Pub: Ocala Star-Banner
Ed: Susan Latham Carr. **Description:** Ocala Planning and Zoning Commission revised the proposed draft of the Internet Cafe ordinance by eliminating the cap on number of locations allowed, but keeping fees and number of devices the same.

17898 ■ *"City Hopes Casino Will Be $333M Jackpot"* in *Business First Buffalo (October 5, 2007, pp. 1)*
Pub: American City Business Journals, Inc.
Ed: James Fink. **Description:** Construction of the $333 million Seneca Buffalo Creek Casino, which includes a hotel, spa and restaurants, is schedule to begin in October 2007. The 5,000 square-foot casino is expected to generate revenue and provide 1,000 jobs for the City of Buffalo, New York.

17899 ■ *"Cluster Truck Events Updates on Curbside Dining Sweeps in Las Vegas"* in *Food & Beverage Close-Up (November 4, 2011)*
Pub: Close-Up Media
Description: Gourmet food trucks will provide mobile dining for attendees of the South Point Gourmet Food Truck Fest held in Las Vegas, Nevada November 5, 2011.

17900 ■ *"Come One, Come All"* in *Black Enterprise (Vol. 38, October 2007, No. 3, pp. 58)*
Pub: Earl G. Graves Publishing Co. Inc.
Ed: Tennille M. Robinson. **Description:** Ways to market a restaurant are cited.

17901 ■ *"Competitive Restaurant Scene Lures Buyers to Saratoga Springs"* in *Business Review, Albany New York (Vol. 34, October 26, 2007)*
Pub: American City Business Journals, Inc.
Ed: Robin K. Cooper. **Description:** Restaurant industry in Saratoga Springs, New York, a competitive market, with the city having 102 licensed restaurants and 28,499 residents in 2006. Buyers tend to acquire restaurants in Saratoga Springs, New York due to its good market condition. Examples of restaurant acquisitions in Saratoga Springs are given.

17902 ■ *Council on Hotel, Restaurant and Institutional Education--Member Directory and Resource Guide*
Pub: International Council on Hotel, Restaurant, and Institutional Education
Contact: Susan Fournier, President
E-mail: susan.fournier@ritz.edu
URL(s): www.chrie.org. **Released:** Biennial; March of even years. **Covers:** Over 2,000 educational programs and institutions in the hotel, restaurant, and tourism industry. **Entries include:** Name, address, phone, fax. **Arrangement:** Alphabetical. **Indexes:** Geographical, membership category.

17903 ■ *"Counter Service"* in *Nation's Restaurant News (Vol. 45, September 26, 2011, No. 20, pp. 8)*
Pub: Penton Media Inc.
Contact: John French, President
Description: As food trucks continue their momentum, a study was conducted showing how many consumer would visit a food truck. Nearly two thirds of 18-44 year olds would likely visit a food truck, while individuals over the age of 65 only 38 percent would eat from a food truck.

17904 ■ *"Counting Crabs: Supply Dips, Putting Crimp on Memorial Day Feast"* in *Boston Business Journal (Vol. 29, June 3, 2011, No. 4, pp. 1)*
Pub: American City Business Journals Inc.
Ed: Scott Dance. **Description:** Restaurateurs in Baltimore City experienced low supply of crabs this Memorial Day 2011 owing to the early season and the fact that many small crabbers took time off during the weekend. Sales were cut in half compared with previous Memorial Day weekends and prices rose to as much as $185 to $200 per box of crabs. Normal supply is expected, though, as summer pushes on.

17905 ■ *"Credit Crunch Takes Bite Out Of McDonald's"* in *Advertising Age (Vol. 79, September 29, 2008, No. 36, pp. 1)*
Pub: Crain Communications, Inc.
Ed: Emily Bryson York. **Description:** McDonald's will delay its launch of coffee bars inside its restaurants due to the banking crisis which has prompted Bank of America to halt loans to the franchise chains.

17906 ■ *"Culture, Community and Chicken Fingers"* in *Entrepreneur (Vol. 37, July 2009, No. 7, pp. 96)*
Pub: Entrepreneur Media, Inc.
Ed: Jason Daley. **Description:** Raising Cane's Chicken Fingers founder Todd Graves shares his experiences in running the company - from getting funding to plans for company. Graves believes that the company wants franchisees to live and breathe the brand, and that the key to its success is doing one thing and doing it right. Cane's Pillar Program, a financial support program for franchisees, is also discussed.

17907 ■ *"Deals Still Get Done at Drake's Coq d'Or"* in *Crain's Chicago Business (Vol. 31, November 17, 2008, No. 46, pp. 35)*
Pub: Crain Communications, Inc.
Ed: Shia Kapos. **Description:** Chicago's infamous Coq d'Or, a restaurant and lounge located at the Drake Hotel, is still a favorite establishment for noted executives but the eatery is now trying to cater to younger professionals through marketing and offering new beverages that appeal to that demographic. Many find it the perfect environment in which to close deals, relax or network.

17908 ■ *Directory of Chain Restaurant Operators*
Pub: Chain Store Guide
Contact: Lisa Patterson, President
URL(s): www.chainstoreguide.com. **Released:** Annual; Latest edition 2012. **Price:** $425, Individuals Directory; $495, Individuals online lite; $1175, Individuals online pro; $695, Individuals online lite plus; $1475, Individuals online pro plus. **Covers:** 7,560 chain restaurant and chain hotel operators, nontraditional foodservice operators and food service management operators who operate 2 or more food service locations. **Entries include:** 37,460 chain restaurant buyers, chefs, executives--company name, address, phone and fax numbers; 23,935 personal e-mail and web addresses; type of business; listing type; total annual sales; food service sales; system wide sales; percent of sales of alcohol; percent of sales from Internet; alcohol types served; total units; company owned units; units franchised to and from; trade names; co-branded names and numbers; food service management location types; trading areas; foreign trading areas; units by primary menu types and type of foodservice; self distributing and catering services indicators; franchise affiliations names and locations; primary distributors names and locations; parent and subsidiary company names and locations; regional; divisional; and branch office locations; distribution centers locations; year founded; public company indicator; key personnel with titles. For chain hotel operators--includes number of restaurants in hotels. For food service management operators--includes number of food service management accounts and total number of locations served. **Arrangement:** Geographical. **Indexes:** Alphabetical, type of food service, menu type, franchisee, food service management, state, exclusions.

17909 ■ *"Don's Pomeroy House a Strongsville Staple"* in *Crain's Cleveland Business (Vol. 30, June 1, 2009, No. 21, pp. 12)*
Pub: Crain Communications, Inc.
Ed: Kathy Ames Carr. **Description:** Profile of Don's Pomeroy House, an upscale restaurant inside a 162-year-old brick mansion. The building is listed on the National Register of Historic Places and features a main restaurant, pub and outdoor patio.

17910 ■ *"Drought Takes Toll on Farmers, Restaurants"* in *Saint Louis Business Journal (Vol. 31, August 12, 2011, No. 51, pp. 1)*
Pub: Saint Louis Business Journal
Ed: E.B. Solomont. **Description:** The drought in St. Louis, Missouri has adversely impacted farmers and restaurants in the areas. Diners can expect to lose some ingredients from their menus.

17911 ■ *"Dunnellon Welcomes Internet Cafe Jobs"* in *Ocala Star-Banner (August 18, 2011)*
Pub: Ocala Star-Banner
Ed: Fred Hiers. **Description:** Despite the fact that a few Internet cafes offering patrons to win cash and are facing legal challenges, the city's planning commission would welcome the cafes in order to provide more jobs for its residents.

17912 ■ *"Eat, Drink and Be a Success"* in *Entrepreneur (Vol. 37, August 2009, No. 8, pp. 70)*
Pub: Entrepreneur Media, Inc.
Ed: Joel Holland. **Description:** Profile of Fritz Brogan, who is a full time student but also runs a successful bar and restaurant named Gin & Tonic and Kitchen. The bar was built with their target audience in mind which happens to be Brogan's college friends.

17913 ■ *"Eat Up!"* in *Entrepreneur (Vol. 36, April 2008, No. 4, pp. 104)*
Pub: Entrepreneur Media, Inc.
Ed: Tracy Stapp. **Description:** Provides a list of the top restaurant franchises. The restaurant franchises presented are picked out from the 2008 Franchise 500 ranking and are listed according to category.

17914 ■ *"Entrepreneurship: As Cool As It Gets"* in *Canadian Business (Vol. 80, January 29, 2007, No. 3, pp. 10)*
Pub: Rogers Media
Ed: Norman de Bono. **Description:** The proposed construction of a restaurant with ice in Dubai by the Canadian firm Iceculture Inc. for the Sharaf Group is discussed. The growth of the clientele of Iceculture Inc. is described.

17915 ■ *Everything I Know About Business I Learned at McDonald's: The 7 Leadership Principles that Drive Break Out Success*
Pub: The McGraw-Hill Companies
Ed: Paul Facella. **Released:** 2009. **Price:** $24.95.
Description: McDonald's management philosophy is as simple as its menu, but don't underestimate the effectiveness of founder Ray Kroc's business plan.

17916 ■ *"Explosive Growth: Wings Over To Triple In Size By 2010"* in *Small Business Opportunities (Fall 2007)*
Pub: Harris Publications Inc.
Ed: Michael L. Corne. **Description:** Profile of Wings Over, a franchised chain of restaurants offering chicken wings in 22 flavors; all items are cooked to order.

17917 ■ *"A Failed Promise: A Dream Job Gone..or Just Delayed?"* in *Restaurant Business (Vol. 107, September 2008, No. 9, pp. 34)*
Pub: Ideal Media
Ed: Patricia Cobe, Joan M. Lang, Dana Tanyeri. **Description:** Profile of Jeremy Lycanwas, executive chef who taught at the California Culinary Academy. Lycanwas tells of accepting a position as executive chef from his mentor, and later started his own restaurant.

17918 ■ *"Fair Exchange"* in *Food and Drink (Winter 2010, pp. 84)*
Pub: Schofield Media Group
Ed: Don Mardak. **Description:** Bartering can assist firms in the food and beverage industry to attract new customers, maximize resources, and reduce cash expenses.

17919 ■ *"The Final Piece; Lowe's to Fill Last Big Parcel Near Great Lakes Crossing"* in *Crain's Detroit Business (March 10, 2008)*
Pub: Crain Communications, Inc.
Ed: Daniel Duggan. **Description:** Silverman Development Co. is developing a Lowe's home-improvement store on the last major retail parcel near the intersection of I-75 and Joslyn Road, an area which was once desolate but is now home to several restaurants and other retail facilities.

17920 ■ *"Food-Truck Learnings Travel Indoors"* in *Nation's Restaurant News (Vol. 45, June 27, 2011, No. 13, pp. 3)*
Pub: Penton Media Inc.
Contact: John French, President
Ed: Lisa Jennings. **Description:** Challenges faced by owners of food truck businesses are discussed. Ways a food truck can be used to promote a restaurant's menu are covered.

17921 ■ *"For Staying True: Bobby Flam: Jumbo's Restaurant, Miami"* in Inc. *(Volume 32, December 2010, No. 10, pp. 102)*
Pub: Inc. Magazine
Ed: Leigh Buchanan. **Description:** Profile of Bobby Flam, owner of Jumbo's Restaurant in Miami, Florida.

17922 ■ *"Former NFL Player Tackles a New Restaurant Concept"* in Inc. *(Vol. 33, September 2011, No. 7, pp. 32)*
Pub: Inc. Magazine
Ed: Nadine Heintz. **Description:** Matt Chatham, former NFL player, launched SkyCrepers, a chain of fast-serve crepe shops with his wife Erin. Chatham entered Babson College's MBA program after retiring from football.

17923 ■ *"Franchisees Lose Battle Against BK"* in Advertising Age *(Vol. 79, June 2, 2008, No. 22, pp. 46)*
Pub: Crain Communications, Inc.
Ed: Emily Bryson York. **Description:** Burger King has had continuing litigation with former franchisees from New York, Luan and Elizabeth Sadik, who claim that Burger King's double cheeseburger, along with additional problems, created the environment for their eventual insolvency. Burger King has since terminated its test of selling the double cheeseburger for $1, although the company declined to comment on the reason for this decision.

17924 ■ *"Fries With That?"* in Canadian Business *(Vol. 81, September 29, 2008, No. 16, pp. 33)*
Pub: Rogers Media Ltd.
Ed: Calvin Leung. **Description:** Profile of Toronto-based New York Fries, which has four stores in South Korea, is planning to expand further as well as into Hong Kong and Macau; the company also has a licensee in the United Arab Emirates whom is also planning to expand.

17925 ■ *"Game On at Jordan's New Spot"* in Crain's Chicago Business *(Vol. 34, October 24, 2011, No. 42, pp. 34)*
Pub: Crain Communications Inc.
Ed: Laura Bianchi. **Description:** Michael Jordan partnered with Cornerstone Restaurant Group to launch Michael Jordan's Steakhouse in Chicago. Details are included.

17926 ■ *"Hard Rock on Pike"* in Puget Sound Business Journal *(Vol. 29, September 5, 2008, No. 20, pp. 1)*
Pub: American City Business Journals
Ed: Jeanne Lang Jones. **Description:** A branch of the Hard Rock Cafe is opening in 2009 in the Liberty Building on Pike Street in downtown Seattle, Washington. The location is being renovated as a green building; the restaurant and concert venue will seat 300 patrons and has a rooftop deck and memorabilia shop.

17927 ■ *"Health Care Leads Sectors Attracting Capital"* in Hispanic Business *(Vol. 30, March 2008, No. 3, pp. 14)*
Pub: Hispanic Business
Ed: Scott Williams. **Description:** Discusses the capital gains of Hispanic-owned companies and other Hispanic leaders in the investment and retail fields in the year 2007. Sectors like health care, media, food and technology saw a healthy flow of capital due to successful mergers, acquisitions and increased private equity investments.

17928 ■ *"Here's the Deal"* in Crain's Cleveland Business *(Vol. 30, June 15, 2009, No. 23, pp. 14)*
Pub: Crain Communications, Inc.
Description: Incentives being offered by hotels, restaurants, golf courses and major chains in order to promote bookings for meetings or conferences in the Cleveland area are listed.

17929 ■ *"Holy Wasabi! Sushi Not Just For Parents Anymore"* in Chicago Tribune *(March 13, 2008)*
Pub: McClatchy-Tribune Information Services
Ed: Christopher Borrelli. **Description:** Wicker Park cooking school, The Kid's Table, specializes in cooking classes for pre-teens; Elena Marre who owns the

school was surprised when she was asked to plan a children's party in which she would teach a course in sushi making. More and more adolescents and small children are eating sushi.

17930 ■ *"Homes, Not Bars, Stay Well Tended"* in Advertising Age *(Vol. 79, January 28, 2008, No. 4, pp. 8)*
Pub: Crain Communications, Inc.
Ed: Jeremy Mullman. **Description:** Due to the downturn in the economy, consumers are drinking less at bars and restaurants; however, according to the Distilled Spirits Council of the United States, they are still purchasing expensive liquor to keep in their homes.

17931 ■ *"How I Did It: George Naddaff: From Spit 'n' Shine Boy To Boston Chicken and Beyond"* in Inc. *(February 2008, pp. 98-101)*
Pub: Gruner & Jahr USA Publishing
Ed: Leigh Buchanan. **Description:** Profile of George Naddaff, founder of Boston Chicken as well as numerous other business ventures.

17932 ■ *"Hyde Park Hungry for Expansion at Cap"* in Business First-Columbus *(October 12, 2007, pp. A1)*
Pub: American City Business Journals, Inc.
Ed: Dan Eaton. **Description:** The Cap, an area developed for the retail and restaurant industry, is experiencing major changes such as Hyde Park Restaurant System's planned expansion, and the expected departure of other tenants. The expansion of Hyde Park will lead to the relocation of Schakolad Chocolate Factory.

17933 ■ *In-N-Out Burger: A Behind-the-Counter Look at the Fast-Food Chain That Breaks All the Rules*
Pub: HarperCollins Publishers
Ed: Stacy Perman. **Released:** April 2009. **Price:** $24.99. **Description:** Business analysis of the factors that helped In-N-Out Burgers, a family owned burger chain in California, along with a history of its founding family, the Synders.

17934 ■ *"In the Raw: Karyn Calabrese Brings Healthy Dining to a New Sophisticated Level"* in Black Enterprise *(Vol. 41, September 2010)*
Pub: Earl G. Graves Publishing Co. Inc.
Ed: Sonia Alleyne. **Description:** Profile of Karyn Calabrese whose businesses are based in Chicago, Illinois. Calabrese has launched a complete line of products (vitamins and beauty items), services (spa, chiropractic, and acupuncture treatments), and restaurants to bring health dining and lifestyles to a better level.

17935 ■ *"Inn at Saratoga Owners Buy Caribbean Hotel"* in Business Review, Albany New York *(Vol. 34, November 2, 2007, No. 31, pp. 3)*
Pub: American City Business Journals, Inc.
Ed: Robin K. Cooper. **Description:** Bob Israel, owner of the Inn at Saratoga in Saratoga Springs, New York, made a $3 million to $4 million acquisition of the 22-room Mafolie Hotel and Restaurant in the Island of St. Thomas in the Caribbean. This is Israel's first real estate venture out of Saratoga Springs.

17936 ■ *"Internet Cafe Logging in to Chardon Plaza?"* in News-Herald *(July 16, 2011)*
Pub: Journal Register Ohio
Ed: Betsy Scott. **Description:** Pearl's High Rollers Inc. applied for an Internet sweepstakes cafe license that would reside in a vacant space in Chardon Plaza. City officials have created regulations for such businesses and Pearl's applied for a license and is awaiting approval.

17937 ■ *"Internet Cafe 'Sweepstakes' Expanding in Arkansas"* in Arkansas Business *(Vol. 28, September 5, 2011, No. 36, pp. 1)*
Pub: Arkansas Business Publishing Group
Ed: Mark Friedman. **Description:** Despite the fact that video games resembling casino games in Lucky's Business Center in Little Rock, representatives of the Internet cafe insist they are not offering

gambling but a type of sweepstakes promotion and that business model is thriving. Lucky's, Cancun Cyber Cafe & Business Center Inc., and Wild Rides Business Center & Internet Cafe has opened in the area in the last few weeks.

17938 ■ *"Invasion of the New York Pizza"* in Charlotte Observer *(February 5, 2007)*
Pub: Knight-Ridder/Tribune Business News
Ed: Leigh Dyer. **Description:** Dozens of new pizza restaurants are cropping up in the Charlotte, North Carolina area, a result of New Yorker transplants.

17939 ■ *"It Sure Beats Pizza: San Francisco Company Delivers Gourmet Lunches to Businesses"* in Inc. *(Vol. 33, November 2011, No. 9, pp. 30)*
Pub: Inc. Magazine
Ed: Bobbie Gossage. **Description:** Gastronaut caters daily meals to local companies. The firm was started by two former chefs at Google and employs 24 people to deliver buffet-style meals to eight businesses, with lunches costing $16 to $18 per serving.

17940 ■ *"It's all Kosher at Downtown Eatery/ Bakery"* in AZ Daily Star *(July 10, 2008)*
Pub: Arizona Daily Star
Ed: Valerie Vinyard. **Description:** Rabbi James Botwright and partner Wayne Anderson are profiled. Details of how the partners opened their bakery and eatery in Tucson, Arizona. Botwright, who attended culinary school in San Francisco, learned much from his grandfather who was a pastry chef.

17941 ■ *"The Kitchen is Closed; Eateries Forced Out by Soaring Rents, Declining Revenues"* in Crain's New York Business *(January 21, 2008)*
Pub: Crain Communications, Inc.
Ed: Lisa Fickenscher. **Description:** Many restaurants have already closed in the area and experts expect many more will follow due to skyrocketing rents and declining revenues.

17942 ■ *"Learn New Ideas from Experienced Menu Makers"* in Nation's Restaurant News *(Vol. 45, June 27, 2011, No. 13, pp. 82)*
Pub: Penton Media Inc.
Contact: John French, President
Ed: Nancy Kruse. **Description:** National Restaurant Association Restaurant, Hotel-Motel Show featured the Food Truck Spot, a firm committed to all aspects of mobile catering, foodtruck manufacturers, leasers of fully equipped truck and a food-truck franchising group.

17943 ■ *Lessons in Service From Charlie Trotter*
Pub: Celestial Arts Publishing Co.
Contact: Patricia Kelly, Manager
Ed: Edmund Lawler. **Released:** March 2004. **Price:** $24.95. **Description:** Chef Charlie Trotter, owner of a restaurant, shares insight into managing any business successfully.

17944 ■ *"Looking To Hire Young? Be Careful"* in Boston Business Journal *(Vol. 30, November 19, 2010, No. 43, pp. 1)*
Pub: Boston Business Journal
Ed: Lisa van der Pool. **Description:** The Massachusetts Commission Against Discrimination (MCAD) has been using undercover job applicants to expose discrimination. Cabot's Ice Cream and Restaurant has been accused of denying older workers equal employment opportunities. MCAD has discovered unfair hiring practices such as hiring high school and college students.

17945 ■ *"Losing the Top Job - And Winning It Back"* in Harvard Business Review *(Vol. 88, October 2010, No. 10, pp. 136)*
Pub: Harvard Business School Publishing
Ed: Alison Beard. **Description:** Michael Mack chronicles the changes in perspectives that occurred when he was fired from Garden Fresh, a restaurant firm he co-owned. Once again at the company helm, he is now more receptive to outside input and acknowledges the importance of work-life balance.

17946 ■ *"Lux Coffees, Breads Push Chains to React"* in *Advertising Age (Vol. 77, June 26, 2006, No. 26, pp. S14)*

Pub: Crain Communications, Inc.

Ed: Kate MacArthur. **Description:** Fast-food giants such as McDonald's, Burger King, Dunkin' Donuts and Subway have adjusted their menus in order to become more competitive with gourmet coffee shops and bakeries like Panera Bread and Starbucks which have taken a large share in the market. Statistical data included.

17947 ■ *"MBA Project Turns on Tastebuds"* in *The Business Journal - Serving Phoenix and the Valley of the Sun (Vol. 28, August 15, 2008, No. 50)*

Pub: American City Business Journals, Inc.

Ed: Angela Gonzales. **Description:** Amol Khade, Venkat Nallapati and Govind Arora, master of businesss administration graduates from Thunderbird School of Global Management, have opened an Indian restaurant, called The Daba, in Tempe, Arizona. The Indian name of the restaurant means 'a place for travelers to stop for rest and food'. Franchise plans for the restaurant are discussed.

17948 ■ *"McD's Dollar-Menu Fixation Sparks Revolt"* in *Advertising Age (Vol. 79, June 2, 2008, No. 22, pp. 1)*

Pub: Crain Communications, Inc.

Ed: Emily Bryson York. **Description:** McDonald's franchisees say that low-cost dollar-menu offerings are impacting their bottom line and many have discontinued the dollar-menu altogether due to rising commodity costs, an increase in minimum wage and consumers trading down to the lower-price items.

17949 ■ *"McD's Picks a Soda Fight; Takes on 7-Eleven With $1 Pop as Economy Softens"* in *Crain's Chicago Business (April 14, 2008)*

Pub: Crain Communications, Inc.

Ed: David Sterrett. **Description:** McDonald's Corp. is urging franchise owners to slash prices on large soft drinks to one dollar this summer to win customers from convenience store chains like 7-Eleven.

17950 ■ *"McD's Tries to Slake Consumer Thirst for Wider Choice of Drinks"* in *Advertising Age (Vol. 79, June 9, 2008, No. 23, pp. 1)*

Pub: Crain Communications, Inc.

Ed: Natalie Zmuda; Emily Bryson York. **Description:** McDonald's is testing the sale of canned and bottled drinks in about 150 locations in an attempt to offer more options to consumers who are going elsewhere for their beverage choices.

17951 ■ *"McD's Warms Up For Olympics Performance"* in *Advertising Age (Vol. 79, July 7, 2008, No. 26, pp. 8)*

Pub: Crain Communications, Inc.

Description: Overview of McDonald's marketing plans for the company's sponsorship of the Olympics which includes a website, an alternate-reality game, names featured on U.S. athletes and on-the-ground activities.

17952 ■ *"Menchie's Tops Restaurant Business' Future 50 List"* in *Ice Cream Reporter (Vol. 23, August 20, 2010, No. 9, pp. 4)*

Pub: Ice Cream Reporter

Description: Menchie's, frozen yogurt shop, announced it placed first in the Restaurant Business Magazine's Future 50, ranking the franchise the fastest-growing in the food industry.

17953 ■ *"More SouthPark Shopping"* in *Charlotte Business Journal (Vol. 25, July 16, 2010, No. 17, pp. 1)*

Pub: Charlotte Business Journal

Ed: Will Boye. **Description:** Charlotte, North Carolina-based Bissel Companies has announced plans to expand its retail presence at the Siskey and Sharon properties in SouthPark. Bissel Companies has requested a rezoning to a mixed-use development classification so that it can utilize the entire ground floor of the Siskey building for restaurant and retail uses.

17954 ■ *My Life From Scratch: A Sweet Journey of Starting Over, One Cake at a Time*

Pub: Broadway Books

Contact: David Drake, Manager

E-mail: ddrake@randomhouse.com

Released: June 8, 2010. **Price:** $14.00. **Description:** Lively account of Old World recipes, Bullock-Prado, a former Hollywood film developer and sister to actress Sandra Bullock, recounts the joys and heartbreak of running her own patisserie in Montpelier, Vermont. Having fled Los Angeles with her husband, Ray for the simpler pleasures of a small town near the Green Mountains, she opened her own bake shop, Gesine Confectionary in 2004, mostly on the fame of the macaroons she refashioned from her German mother's favorite almond treat, mandelhoernchen (and the casual mention of her sister in an interview). Her memoir follows one day in a busy baker's life, from waking at 3 a.m. to prepare the batter and bake her croissants, scones, and sticky buns, before opening her shop at 7 a.m., through the hectic lunch, and 3 p.m. tea time.

17955 ■ *"New CEO For Friendly's"* in *Ice Cream Reporter (Vol. 23, September 20, 2010, No. 10, pp. 1)*

Pub: Ice Cream Reporter

Description: Friendly Ice Cream Corporation named Harsha V. Agadi as new chief executive officer. Agadi has 24 years experience in food service, most recently serving as CEO of Church's Chicken.

17956 ■ *"A New Flavor for Second Street: Lamberts Chef Backs New Restaurant"* in *Austin Business JournalInc. (Vol. 28, January 2, 2009)*

Pub: American City Business Journals

Ed: Sandra Zaragoza. **Description:** Chef Larry McGuire has teamed up with the Icon Group to develop the La Condesa restaurant and the Malverde lounge in the Second Street district. The La Condesa restaurant will be a Mexico City-inspired restaurant, while the Malverde lounge atop the La Condesa will host DJs and live music.

17957 ■ *"A New Mix of Tenants Settles In"* in *Crain's New York Business (Vol. 24, January 14, 2008, No. 2, pp. 26)*

Pub: Crain Communications, Inc.

Ed: Andrew Marks. **Description:** More and more nonfinancial firms are relocating downtown due to the new retailers and restaurants that are reshaping the look and feel of lower Manhattan.

17958 ■ *"New Technology, Growing Fan Base Fuel Truck Trend"* in *Nation's Restaurant News (Vol. 45, June 13, 2001, No. 12, pp. 16)*

Pub: Penton Media Inc.

Contact: John French, President

Ed: Ron Ruggless. **Description:** Food trucks drove more interest at this year's National Restaurant Association Restaurant Hotel-Motel Show in Chicago. The trend continues to show long-term growth.

17959 ■ *"Nighttime Shuttle to Connect Detroit, Ferndale, Royal Oak"* in *Crain's Detroit Business (Vol. 24, October 6, 2008, No. 40, pp. 24)*

Pub: Crain Communications, Inc.

Ed: Nancy Kaffer. **Description:** With hopes of bridging the social gap between the cities and suburbs, Chris Ramos has launched The Night Move, a new shuttle service that will ferry passengers between Royal Oak, Ferndale and downtown Detroit. The cost for a round trip ticket is $12.

17960 ■ *"Nurturing Talent for Tomorrow"* in *Restaurants and Institutions (Vol. 118, September 15, 2008, No. 14, pp. 90)*

Pub: Reed Business Information

Contact: Jeff Greisch, President

Description: Hormel Foods Corporation and The Culinary Institute of America (CIA) have teamed to develop The Culinary Enrichment and Innovation Program that supports future culinary leaders by providing creative and competitive staff development. Sixteen students attend four three-day sessions at

the CIA's campus in Hyde Park, New York; sessions include classroom teaching, one-on-one interaction with leading culinarians, and hands-on kitchen time.

17961 ■ *"Ohio Franchise Buys 21 Jacksonville Area Papa John's"* in *Florida Times-Union (December 20, 2010)*

Pub: Florida Times-Union

Ed: Mark Basch. **Description:** Ohio-based Papa John's pizza franchise acquired 21 of the restaurants in Duval, Clay and St. Johns counties in Jacksonville, Florida.

17962 ■ *"Old Friends Make Old Buildings Successful Restaurants"* in *Crain's Detroit Business (Vol. 24, February 4, 2008, No. 5, pp. 14)*

Pub: Crain Communications Inc. - Detroit

Ed: Brent Snavely. **Description:** Profiles of Jon Carlson and Gregory Lobdell, founders of ten new restaurants in Ann Arbor, Royal Oak, and Traverse City, Michigan, and their plans to add four more in the near future.

17963 ■ *"On the Green: Sheila Johnson Adds $35 Million Golf Resort To Her Expanding Portfolio"* in *Black Enterprise (January 2008)*

Pub: Earl G. Graves Publishing Co. Inc.

Ed: Donna M. Owens. **Description:** Profile of Sheila Johnson, CEO of Salamander Hospitality LLC, made history when she purchased the Innisbrook Resort and Golf Club, making her the first African American woman to own this type of property. The resort includes four championship golf courses, six swimming pools, four restaurants, eleven tennis courts, three conference halls, and a nature preserve.

17964 ■ *"Ordering Pizza Hut From Your Facebook Page?"* in *Advertising Age (Vol. 79, November 10, 2008, No. 42, pp. 50)*

Pub: Crain Communications, Inc.

Ed: Emily Bryson York. **Description:** Fast-food chains are experimenting with delivery/takeout services via social networks such as Facebook and iPhone applications. This also allows the chains to build valuable databases of their customers.

17965 ■ *The Pampered Chef*

Pub: Doubleday Broadway Publishing Group

Ed: Doris Christopher. **Price:** $24.95.

17966 ■ *"Paying the Price"* in *Baltimore Business Journal (Vol. 28, July 9, 2010, No. 9, pp. 1)*

Pub: Baltimore Business Journal

Ed: Emily Mullin. **Description:** Crab prices have never been higher in Baltimore, Maryland and businesses have been led to count on strengthening demand for seafood. For instance, the average price for a dozen large crabs has increased by 5 percent to $58.90. How restaurants have responded to the increase in prices is discussed, along with factors that might have caused the harvest of smaller crabs.

17967 ■ *"Pepsi Co. Breaches the Walls of Coke Fortress McDonald's"* in *Globe & Mail (March 13, 2007, pp. B1)*

Pub: CTVglobemedia Publishing Inc.

Ed: Keith McArthur. **Description:** Soft drinks giant Pepsi Co. has entered an agreement with fast food chain McDonald's for offering its products in outlets across Canada. Earlier Coca-Cola Co. used to offer its exclusive products in these outlets.

17968 ■ *"Personal Pizza Goes Franchise Route"* in *Atlanta Journal-Constitution (December 22, 2010)*

Pub: Atlanta Journal-Constitution

Ed: Bob Townsend. **Description:** Your Pie, developer of the personal-size pizza franchise concept is profiled.

17969 ■ *"A Piece of the Action"* in *Black Enterprise (Vol. 38, January 2008, No. 6, pp. 42)*

Pub: Earl G. Graves Publishing Co. Inc.

Ed: Alan Hughes. **Description:** Andre Williams, owner of Kaze Sushi restaurant, offered generous incentive plan-equity in the business in order to acquire Chef Kaze Chan and Chef Hari Chan. Williams' entrepreneurial pursuits are discussed.

17970 ■ *"Plan B Saloon Opened New Year's Eve"* in *Bellingham Business Journal (Vol. February 2010, pp. 7)*
Pub: Sound Publishing Inc.
Description: Plan B Saloon, located in Bellingham, Washington, opened New Year's Eve 2010. The bar/restaurant will feature classic American food consisting of sandwiches and burgers and will host local musicians on Friday and Saturday nights.

17971 ■ *"Plans for $160M Condo Resort in Wisconsin Dells Moves Forward"* in *Commercial Property News (March 18, 2008)*
Pub: Nielsen Company
Description: Plans for the Grand Cambrian Resort in the Wisconsin Dells is discussed. The luxury condominium resort will include condos, townhomes, and condo-hotel style residences, two water parts, meeting space and indoor entertainment space, as well as a spa, four restaurants and retail offerings.

17972 ■ *"Proposed Triangle Redo in Motion"* in *Crain's Cleveland Business (Vol. 28, October 15, 2007, No. 41, pp. 1)*
Pub: Crain Communications, Inc.
Ed: Stan Bullard. **Description:** Zaremba Homes and MRN Ltd. are partnering to redevelop the so-called Triangle section of University Circle. The proposed project will include a total of 434 new rental and for-sale residential suites and as much as 227,000 square feet of retail and restaurant space.

17973 ■ *"Quiznos Franchisees Walloped by Recession"* in *Advertising Age (Vol. 79, October 20, 2008, No. 39, pp. 3)*
Pub: Crain Communications, Inc.
Ed: Emily Bryson York. **Description:** While the recession has taken a toll on the entire restaurant industry, a number of Quiznos franchisees claim to have been disproportionately affected due to lackluster marketing, higher-than-average commodity costs, competition with Subway and a premium-pricing structure that is incompatible with a tight economy.

17974 ■ *"Ready, Aim, (Cool) Fire"* in *Saint Louis Business Journal (Vol. 32, September 2, 2011, No. 1, pp. 1)*
Pub: Saint Louis Business Journal
Ed: E.B. Solomont. **Description:** Coolfire Originals' CEO Jeff Keane is co-producing 'Welcome Sweetie Pie's' with Los Angeles, California-based Pilgrims Films and Television Films for the Oprah Winfrey Network. The reality show focuses on restaurant owner Robbie Montgomery of Sweetie Pie's in St. Louis, Missouri.

17975 ■ *"Ready for the Back Burner"* in *Barron's (Vol. 88, March 17, 2008, No. 11, pp. 47)*
Pub: Dow Jones & Company, Inc.
Ed: Vito J. Racanelli. **Description:** McDonald's has promised to return $15 billion to $17 billion to shareholders in 2007-2009 but headwinds are rising for the company. December, 2007 same-store sales were flat and the company's traffic growth in the U.S. is slowing. Its shares are likely to trade in tandem with the market until recession fears recede.

17976 ■ *"A Recipe for Change"* in *Canadian Business (Vol. 80, October 22, 2007, No. 21, pp. 25)*
Pub: Rogers Media
Ed: Erin Pooley. **Description:** Market conditions have changed and customers around the world are demanding low-fat alternatives. Labor costs have risen and so did the price of foodstuffs. The impacts of this on fast food restaurants as well as the measures they have taken to cope with the new demands are discussed.

17977 ■ *"Recipe for Disaster?"* in *Sacramento Business Journal (Vol. 25, July 4, 2008, No. 18, pp. 1)*
Pub: American City Business Journals, Inc.
Ed: Mark Anderson. **Description:** Restaurateurs are challenged with balancing rising operating costs and what customers are willing to pay for their services. Flour prices in 2008 have increased by 46 percent from April 2007. Other views on the situation, as well

as trends, forecasts and statistics on sales, outlook on economic conditions, consumer price index, and the typical split of restaurant revenue, are presented.

17978 ■ *"Recovery on Tap for 2010?"* in *Orlando Business Journal (Vol. 26, January 1, 2010, No. 31, pp. 1)*
Pub: American City Business Journals
Ed: Melanie Stawicki Azam, Richard Bilbao, Christopher Boyd, Anjali Fluker. **Description:** Economic forecasts for Central Florida's leading business sectors in 2010 are presented. These sectors include housing, film and TV, sports business, law, restaurants, aviation, tourism and hospitality, banking and finance, commercial real estate, retail, health care, insurance, higher education, and manufacturing. According to some local executives, Central Florida's economy will slowly recover in 2010.

17979 ■ *"Reinventing the Cheeseburger"* in *Inc. (November 2007, pp. 124-125)*
Pub: Gruner & Jahr USA Publishing
Ed: Chris Lydgate. **Description:** Profile of Burgerville's Tom Mears, who turned his drive-through burger restaurant green.

17980 ■ *"Report: McD's Pepsi Score Best With Young Hispanics"* in *Brandweek (Vol. 49, April 21, 2008, No. 16, pp. 8)*
Pub: VNU Business Media, Inc.
Ed: Della de Lafuente. **Description:** According to a new report, in order to reach Hispanic Gen Yers, marketing strategists need to understand this demographic's 'bi-dentity,' something which has proved an elusive task to many marketers. Another trend is the emergence of Latinas who have careers, as opposed to just jobs. There is an opportunity to tap this new, young and empowered female market with innovative messaging. Statistical data included.

17981 ■ *The Restaurant Manager's Handbook: How to Set Up, Operate, and Manage a Financially Successful Food Service Operation*
Pub: Atlantic Publishing Company
Released: September 25, 2007. **Price:** $79.95. **Description:** Insight is offered on running a successful food service business. Nine new chapters detail restaurant layout, new equipment, principles for creating a safer work environment, and new effective techniques to interview, hire, train, and manage employees.

17982 ■ *Restaurant Marketing for Owners and Managers*
Pub: John Wiley & Sons, Incorporated
Ed: Patti J. Shock, John T. Bowen, John M. Stefanelli. **Released:** October 2003. **Price:** $30.00. **Description:** Tools for combining marketing theory to practice in a restaurant business are covered.

17983 ■ *"Restaurants Dish Up Meal Deals To Attract Customers"* in *Crain's Detroit Business (Vol. 24, October 6, 2008, No. 40, pp. 1)*
Pub: Crain Communications, Inc.
Ed: Nathan Skid. **Description:** Restaurateurs are devising many creative and rewarding incentives to get customers to frequent their establishments during this economic crisis. Innovative ways in which even higher-end establishments are drawing in business are discussed.

17984 ■ *"Restaurants Rewrite Menu to Get Financing"* in *Saint Louis Business Journal (Vol. 31, August 19, 2011, No. 52, pp. 1)*
Pub: Saint Louis Business Journal
Ed: Peter Solomont. **Description:** St. Louis, Missouri-based restaurants are finding new ways to secure financing. The weak economy has made it difficult for restaurants to secure bank financing.

17985 ■ *"Restaurants Slammed by Economy"* in *Business Courier (Vol. 24, April 4, 2008, No. 52, pp. 1)*
Pub: American City Business Journals, Inc.
Ed: Lisa Biank Fasig. **Description:** Restaurants in Cincinnati are closing some of their stores due to growing costs of fuel, eggs and meat. The establishments are also affected by lower consumer spending

that was brought on by unemployment, higher grocery prices and foreclosures. The economic problems in Cincinnati are also compared to those in other cities.

17986 ■ *"Restaurants Stewing Over Food Prices"* in *The Business Journal-Milwaukee (Vol. 25, August 22, 2008, No. 48, pp. A1)*
Pub: American City Business Journals, Inc.
Ed: David Doege. **Description:** Many restaurant operators in the Milwaukee area are changing their menus, increasing prices and decreasing workers' hours amid the soaring prices of commodities. The prices of some staples have risen by over 50 percent since 2006. The impacts of the continued rise in food prices are examined further.

17987 ■ *"Restaurateurs Follow High-End Apartments Into Kendall Square"* in *Boston Business Journal (Vol. 31, July 22, 2011, No. 26, pp. 3)*
Pub: Boston Business Journal
Ed: Lisa van der Pool. **Description:** Kendall Square in Cambridge, Massachusetts is attracting restaurants, 16 of which have opened since 2009. The influx of restaurants is being driven by lower commercial rents.

17988 ■ *"Ritz Kapalua Sells 93 Suites for $176M to Fund Renovation"* in *Commercial Property News (March 17, 2008)*
Pub: Nielsen Company
Description: Ritz-Carlton, Kapalua in Lahaina, Hawaii sold ninety-three of its units in order to fund renovations of 463 rooms and suites along with construction of a new spa and fitness center, new and expanded restaurants and pools and an environmental education center for children.

17989 ■ *"Salad Creations To Open 2nd Location"* in *Crain's Detroit Business (Vol. 24, March 3, 2008, No. 9, pp. 26)*
Pub: Crain Communications Inc. - Detroit
Ed: Brent Snavely. **Description:** Salad Creations, a franchise restaurant that allows customers to create their own salads and also offers soups and sandwiches; Salad Creations plans to open a total of five locations by the end of 2008.

17990 ■ *"Seasonal Franchises"* in *Franchising World (Vol. 42, August 2010, No. 8, pp. 50)*
Pub: International Franchise Association
Ed: Jennifer Lemcke. **Description:** Seasonal franchises, such as tax businesses can be slow during the summer months. Restaurants are slow during the months of January and February. The various challenges faced by seasonal franchises are examined.

17991 ■ *Setting the Table*
Pub: HarperCollins Publishers Inc.
Ed: Danny Meyer. **Price:** $29.95. **Description:** Renowned restauranteur profiles his success in the hospitality business.

17992 ■ *"Seward Restaurant Garners Accolades"* in *Alaska Business Monthly (Vol. 27, October 2011, No. 10, pp. 9)*
Pub: Alaska Business Publishing Company
Ed: Nancy Pounds. **Description:** Resurrection Road House of Seward, Alaska won the Wine Spectator's Aware of Excellence in 2011. The award honors restaurants that handle at least 100 gourmet wines that are skillfully paired with the cuisine.

17993 ■ *"Social Networkers for Hire"* in *Black Enterprise (Vol. 40, December 2009, No. 5, pp. 56)*
Pub: Earl G. Graves Publishing Co., Inc.
Ed: Brittany Hutson. **Description:** Companies are utilizing social networking sites in order to market their brand and personally connect with consumers and are increasingly looking to social media specialists to help with this task. Aliya S. King is one such web strategist, working for ICED Media by managing their Twitter, Facebook, YouTube and Flickr accounts for one of their publicly traded restaurant clients.

17994 ■ *"Soured Relationship Plays Out in Courts"* in The Business Journal-Serving Greater Tampa Bay (Vol. 28, September 19, 2008, No. 39)

Pub: American City Business Journals, Inc.

Ed: Janet Leiser. **Description:** Heirs of developer Julian Hawthorne Lifset won a court battle to end a 50-year lease with Specialty Restaurants Corp. in Rocky Point. The decision opens the Tampa Bay prime waterfront property for new development.

17995 ■ *"Speakers Address Authenticity, R&D Evolution"* in Nation's Restaurant News (Vol. 45, October 24, 2011, No. 32, pp. 32)

Pub: Penton Media, Inc.

Contact: John French, President

Ed: Bret Thorn. **Description:** Culinary trends are discussed, along with an examination of the food truck trend and how this small sector is creating a great influence on food and communication with customers and delivery expectations.

17996 ■ *"Startup to Serve Bar Scene"* in Austin Business JournalInc. (Vol. 29, December 18, 2009, No. 41, pp. 1)

Pub: American City Business Journals

Ed: Christopher Calnan. **Description:** Startup ATX Innovation Inc. of Austin, Texas has developed a test version of TabbedOut, a Web-based tool that would facilitate mobile phone-based restaurant and bar bill payment. TabbedOut has been tested by six businesses in Austin and will be available to restaurant and bar owners for free. Income would be generated by ATX through a 99-cent convenience charge per transaction.

17997 ■ *"Sweet Tea; Neil Golden"* in Advertising Age (Vol. 79, November 17, 2008, No. 43, pp. 4)

Pub: Crain Communications, Inc.

Ed: Emily Bryson York. **Description:** McDonald's launch of iced coffee and sweat tea, which were promoted via price cuts over the summer, helped to boost sales at the fast-food chain.

17998 ■ *"Taco Bell; David Ovens"* in Advertising Age (Vol. 79, November 17, 2008, No. 43, pp. S2)

Pub: Crain Communications, Inc.

Ed: Emily Bryson York. **Description:** Due to the addition of new products such as a low-calorie, low-fat Fresco menu; a fruity iced beverage; and a value initiative, Taco Bell now accounts for half of Yum Brands' profits. The chain has also benefited from a new chief marketing officer, David Ovens, who oversees ad support.

17999 ■ *"Taking a Pounding; Recession Fears Weigh Down Steakhouse Operator Morton's"* in Crain's Chicago Business (March 31, 2008)

Pub: Crain Communications, Inc.

Ed: Monee Fields-White. **Description:** Morton's Restaurant Group Inc. has seen a 50 percent drop in shares in the past six months due to the economy and cutbacks in corporate expense accounts; business customers provide the restaurant about 80 percent of its revenue.

18000 ■ *"Tap Into Food Truck Trend to Rev Up Sales, Build Buzz"* in Nation's Restaurant News (Vol. 45, February 7, 2011, No. 3, pp. 18)

Pub: Penton Media, Inc.

Ed: Brian Sacks. **Description:** Food truck trend is growing, particularly in New York City, Philadelphia, Washington DC, and Los Angeles, California. Man entrepreneurs are using a mobile food component to market their food before opening a restaurant.

18001 ■ *"This Week: McD's Eyes Ad Plan, Shifts Breakfast Biz"* in Crain's Chicago Business (Vol. 30, February 2007, No. 6, pp. 1)

Pub: Crain Communications, Inc.

Ed: Kate MacArthur. **Description:** McDonald's is moving its national breakfast ad account from DDB Chicago to Arnold Worldwide of Boston and Moroch

of Dallas in an attempt to change its marketing strategy. It is also doing a study to keep abreast of consumer trends.

18002 ■ *"Tim Hortons Aims for Breakfast Breakout"* in Globe & Mail (February 13, 2006, pp. B3)

Pub: CTVglobemedia Publishing Inc.

Ed: Andy Hoffman. **Description:** Fast food chain Tim Hortons will be launching its new breakfast menu with more combinations that include bacons, eggs and coffee. Tim Horton is subsidiary of Wendy's International Inc and has 290 outlets in America.

18003 ■ *"TiVo, Domino's Team to Offer Pizza Ordering by DVR"* in Advertising Age (Vol. 79, November 17, 2008, No. 43, pp. 48)

Pub: Crain Communications, Inc.

Ed: Brian Steinberg. **Description:** Domino's Pizza and TiVo are teaming up to make it possible for customers to order from the restaurant straight from their DVR. The companies see that this kind of interactive television and consumer experience will only serve to generate more sales as the customer can be exposed to a fuller range of menu selections and will not have to interrupt their viewing, while workers can spend more time making the product.

18004 ■ *"To Live and Thrive in L.A."* in Canadian Business (Vol. 81, October 13, 2008, No. 17, pp. 78)

Pub: Rogers Media Ltd.

Ed: Rachel Pulfer. **Description:** Toronto entrepreneur Shereen Arazm thrived in Los Angeles, California as the queen of nightlife. Arazm holds or has held ownership stakes in bars, nightspots and restaurants that include the Geisha House, Concorde, Shag, Parc and Central, and Terroni L.A.

18005 ■ *"Top Coffee Has Concord Ties"* in Charlotte Observer (February 7, 2007)

Pub: Knight-Ridder/Tribune Business News

Ed: Adam Bell. **Description:** McDonald's highly rated premium coffee is supplied by Concord's S&D Coffee, one of three McDonald's coffee suppliers. The blend outranked Starbucks and Dunkin' Donuts coffee by Consumer Reports.

18006 ■ *"Travel Tears"* in Crain's Chicago Business (Vol. 31, November 17, 2008, No. 46, pp. 3)

Pub: Crain Communications, Inc.

Ed: Bob Tita. **Description:** Hotels, restaurants and conventions are seeing a decline in profits due to corporate travel cutbacks and the sagging economy. City and state revenues derived from taxes on tourism-related industries are also suffering.

18007 ■ *"Truffled Ahead: Farms for Rare Delicacy Gain Ground In State"* in Puget Sound Business Journal (Vol. 29, December 26, 2008, No. 36)

Pub: American City Business Journals

Ed: Steve Wilhelm. **Description:** Twenty farmers in Washington started small plots for truffles, which are irregular fungi growing around tree roots and are considered restaurant delicacies. These truffles could generate $35,000 per acre, although they need a decade to mature.

18008 ■ *"Union, Uneven But Imaginative, Works"* in Crain's Chicago Business (Vol. 34, September 12, 2011, No. 37, pp. 30)

Pub: Crain Communications Inc.

Ed: Alison Neumer Lara. **Description:** Japanese restaurant, Union Sushi & Barbecue Bar opened in Chicago this year. Union is a hip and urban place for business and leisure diners.

18009 ■ *"'Unknown' Muted Grand Prix Impact"* in Boston Business Journal (Vol. 29, September 9, 2011, No. 18, pp. 3)

Pub: American City Business Journals Inc.

Ed: Alexander Jackson. **Description:** Baltimore Grand Prix caught restaurateurs, hoteliers and street vendors in Baltimore, Maryland unprepared for the thousands of race fans who attended the inaugural event over Labor Day weekend. The race popularity is relatively unknown to them and some felt they were not able to make as much money as they had hoped.

18010 ■ *"Velvet Ice Cream"* in Ice Cream Reporter (Vol. 23, November 20, 2010, No. 12, pp. 7)

Pub: Ice Cream Reporter

Description: Velvet Ice Cream will open its Ye Olde Mill for private corporate parties around the holidays. Their facility can accommodate groups ranging from 30 to 125 individuals. The historic site houses the company headquarters, an ice cream museum, and a restaurant.

18011 ■ *"Waite, Cancer Survivor, Readies Sch'dy 'Big House' after Long Delay"* in Business Review, Albany New York (October 26, 2007)

Pub: American City Business Journals, Inc.

Ed: Michael DeMasi. **Description:** Stephen Waite, owner of Big House Brewing Company, will be opening its new nightclub called Big House Underground. The nightclub is part of a $3.25 million project Waite started in 2005, which was delayed due to his battle with tonsil cancer. Details of turning the building into a restaurant, bar and nightclub are provided.

18012 ■ *"Want a Facial With That Steak?"* in Charlotte Observer (February 5, 2007)

Pub: Knight-Ridder/Tribune Business News

Ed: Jen Aronoff. **Description:** Profile of Burke Myotherapy Massage & Spa and Schell's Bistro. Lynn Shell moved her massage therapy business into a 106-year old home that had been used as a restaurant. She opened her own eatery on the first floor and offers massage therapy upstairs.

18013 ■ *"What'll You Have Tonight?"* in Barron's (Vol. 88, July 4, 2008, No. 28, pp. 22)

Pub: Dow Jones & Co., Inc.

Ed: Neil A. Martin. **Description:** Shares of Diageo could rise by 30 percent a year from June 2008 after it slipped due to U.S. sales worries. The company also benefits from the trend toward more premium alcoholic beverage brands worldwide especially in emerging markets.

18014 ■ *"What's Cooking?"* in Entrepreneur (Vol. 36, April 2008, No. 4, pp. 98)

Pub: Entrepreneur Media, Inc.

Ed: Eileen Figure Sandlin. **Description:** Unique and unusual restaurants have the potential to attract customers and provide them with fresh menu options. Outlining goals, strategies and details on proposed concept and target market can also help in restaurant planning. Other tips on how to plan launching your own restaurant are provided.

18015 ■ *"While Competitors Shut Doors, Subway Is Still Growing"* in Advertising Age (Vol. 79, July 21, 2008, No. 28, pp. 4)

Pub: Crain Communications, Inc.

Ed: Emily Bryson York. **Description:** Subway, the largest fast-food chain, with 22,000 U.S. locations, is adding 800 this year, despite the economic downturn that has caused competitors such as Starbucks to close stores and McDonald's to focus its expansion abroad.

18016 ■ *"Whopper; Russ Klein"* in Advertising Age (Vol. 79, November 17, 2008, No. 43, pp. S10)

Pub: Crain Communications, Inc.

Ed: Emily Bryson York. **Description:** Burger King has seen a double digit increase in the sales of its Whopper hamburger despite the economic recession that has hit many in the restaurant industry particularly hard. For most of the spring, U.S. same-store-sales gains beat McDonald's.

SOURCES OF SUPPLY

18017 ■ *Directory of Foodservice Distributors*

Chain Store Guide

Contact: Lisa Patterson, President

URL(s): www.chainstoreguide.com. **Released:** Annual; Latest edition 2012. **Price:** $425, Individuals Directory; $495, Individuals online lite; $1175, Individuals online pro; $1475, Individuals online pro plus. **Covers:** About 4,700 companies in the United States and Canada with at least $500,000 in sales to foodservice companies. Included companies must distribute more than one product line and obtain no more than 95% of its total sales volume from self-manufactured merchandise. **Entries include:** Company name, address, phone and fax numbers, e-mail and web addresses; Internet order processing indicator and sales percentage; total sales; foodservice and wholesale sales; product lines; total units served; foodservice accounts served; trading areas; distribution center locations; markets served; buying/marketing group name and location; subsidiaries names and locations; divisional, regional and branch office locations; year founded; public company indicator; key personnel with titles; 21,700 foodservice distribution contacts; 9,642 Name, address, phone, fax. **Arrangement:** Geographical. **Indexes:** Product lines, alphabetical, exclusions.

STATISTICAL SOURCES

18018 ■ *Fast Food and Multi-Unit Restaurant Business*
Pub: Business Trend Analysts, Inc.
Released: 2006-2007. **Price:** $3795.00. **Description:** Profiles the fast food industry, covering hamburger, hot dog, roast beef, chicken, and pizza outlets; seafood restaurant chains; and Mexican restaurant chains. Provides information on demographics, sales, promotional spending, and new products and menu expansion. Also contains profiles of leading marketers.

18019 ■ *RMA Annual Statement Studies*
Pub: Risk Management Association
Contact: Kevin M. Blakey, President
Released: Annual. **Price:** $175.00 2006-07 edition, $105.00. **Description:** Contains composite balance sheets and income statements for more than 360 industries, including the accounting, auditing, and bookkeeping industries. Also contains five years of comparative historical data for discerning trends. Includes 16 commonly used ratios, computed for most of the size groupings for nearly every industry.

18020 ■ *Standard & Poor's Industry Surveys*
Pub: Standard & Poor's Corp.
Released: Annual. **Price:** $3633.00. **Description:** Two-volume book that examines the prospects for specific industries, including trucking. Also provides analyses of trends and problems, statistical tables and charts, and comparative company analyses.

TRADE PERIODICALS

18021 ■ *ConcepTrac*
Pub: Technomic Information Services
Ed: Eric Giandelone, Editor, egiandelone@technomic.com. **Released:** Monthly. **Price:** $395, individuals. **Description:** Provides news on chain restaurant development. Includes information on decor, atmosphere, service styles, cooking preparation methods, and unit economics.

18022 ■ *Cooking for Profit*
Pub: CP Publishing Inc.
Contact: Craig Culver, President
URL(s): www.cookingforprofit.com/home.html. **Released:** Monthly **Price:** $30, Individuals; $55, Two years; $52, Canada; $98, Canada 2 years; $85, Other countries; $160, Other countries 2 years.

18023 ■ *Cornell Hoospitality Quarterly*
Pub: Cornell University School of Hotel Administration
URL(s): cqx.sagepub.com. **Ed:** J. Bruce Tracey. **Released:** Quarterly **Price:** £311, Institutions combined print and electronic access; £305, Institutions print only; £98, Individuals print & online; £32, Single issue.

18024 ■ *CRFA National Hospitality News*
Pub: Canadian Restaurant and Foodservices Association
Contact: Garth Whyte, President
Ed: David Harris, Editor. **Released:** 5/year. **Price:** Included in membership. **Description:** Informs members of association activities and industry concerns, including labor shortages, sales tax reform, and government issues. Recurring features include

news of research, reports of meetings, notices of publications available, statistics, and the columns titled National Infostats, The Personnel File, and Focus on Ottawa. **Remarks:** Reprints articles in French.

18025 ■ *Fancy Food & Culinary Products*
Pub: Talcott Communication Corp.
URL(s): www.fancyfoodmagazine.comwww.talcott.com/contact.htm. **Ed:** Erika Flynn. **Released:** Monthly **Price:** $26, Individuals; $37, Two years; $47, Canada 3 years; $32, Canada; $60, Other countries.

18026 ■ *The Food & Beverage Journal*
Pub: Journal Publications Inc.
URL(s): www.fbworld.com. **Ed:** Ellen Walsh, Jason Barlow. **Released:** Bimonthly **Price:** $30, Individuals; $40, Two years.

18027 ■ *Hospitality Design*
Pub: Nielsen Co.
Contact: Greg Farrar, President
URL(s): www.hdmag.com. **Released:** 10/yr. **Price:** $79, Individuals; $94, Canada; $139, Other countries by airmail.

18028 ■ *HOTELS: The Magazine of the Worldwide Hotel Industry*
Pub: Marketing & Technology Group Inc.
Contact: Mark Lefens, President
E-mail: mlefens@meatingplace.com
URL(s): www.hotelsmag.com/. **Released:** Monthly **Price:** Free.

18029 ■ *Journal of Foodservice Business Research*
Pub: Routledge Journals Taylor & Francis Group
URL(s): www.tandfonline.com/toc/wfbr20/current. **Ed:** David A. Cranage. **Released:** Quarterly **Price:** $96, Individuals online only; $103, Individuals print + online; $339, Institutions online only; $376, Institutions print + online.

18030 ■ *The National Culinary Review: Official Magazine of the American Culinary Federation*
Contact: Kay Orde, Editor
E-mail: korde@acfchefs.net
URL(s): www.acfchefs.org/Content/NavigationMenu2/About/Media/Publications/de fault.htm. **Ed:** Kay Orde. **Released:** Monthly **Price:** $60, Individuals; $200, Other countries.

18031 ■ *Pastry Art & Design*
Pub: Haymarket Group Ltd.
URL(s): www.pastryartanddesign.com/. **Ed:** Tish Boyle. **Released:** Bimonthly **Price:** $50, Individuals; $100, Two years; $60, Canada; $120, Canada for two years; $60, Other countries; $120, Other countries for two years.

18032 ■ *Restaurant Hospitality: Ideas for Full Service Restaurants*
Pub: Penton Media Inc.
URL(s): restaurant-hospitality.comwww.penton.com. **Released:** Monthly **Price:** Free.

18033 ■ *TECHNOMIC Foodservice Digest*
Pub: Technomic Information Services
Ed: Jan Sneesby, Editor, jsneesby@technomic.com. **Released:** Monthly. **Price:** $295, individuals. **Description:** Contains abstracted citations from 100 publications on business developments in the foodservice industry. Recurring features include a column titled As I See It on forces and factors shaping the industry.

VIDEOCASSETTES/ AUDIOCASSETTES

18034 ■ *Food Services*
RMI Media
1365 N. Winchester St.
Olathe, KS 66061-5880
Ph: (913)768-1696
Free: 800-745-5480

Fax: (800)755-6910
Co. E-mail: actmedia@act.org
URL: http://www.actmedia.com
Released: 1987. **Description:** Methods of food preparation and equipment maintenance used in the food industry are discussed. **Availability:** VHS; 3/4 U.

18035 ■ *Inside Business Today*
GPN Educational Media
1550 Executive Drive
Elgin, IL 60123
Ph: (402)472-2007
Free: 800-228-4630
Fax: (800)306-2330
Co. E-mail: askgpn@smarterville.com
URL: http://www.shopgpn.com
Released: 1989. **Description:** Leaders in business and industry tell their success stories in this extensive series. **Availability:** VHS; 3/4 U.

18036 ■ *The Key to Cleanliness*
Film Library/National Safety Council California Chapter
4553 Glencoe Ave., Ste. 150
Marina Del Rey, CA 90292
Ph: (310)827-9781
Free: 800-421-9585
Fax: (310)827-9861
Co. E-mail: California@nsc.org
URL: http://www.nsc.org/nsc_near_you/FindYourLocalChapter/Pages/California.aspx
Released: 198?. **Description:** This is an explanation of what food poisoning is and how to avoid it through sanitary work habits like taking that extra moment. **Availability:** VHS; 3/4 U.

TRADE SHOWS AND CONVENTIONS

18037 ■ **Annual Hotel, Motel, and Restaurant Supply Show of the Southeast**
Leisure Time Unlimited, Inc.
708 Main St.
Myrtle Beach, SC 29577
Ph: (843)448-9483
Free: 800-261-5591
Fax: (843)626-1513
Co. E-mail: ltushows@sc.rr.com
URL: http://www.leisuretimeunlimited.com/
Contact: Brooke P. Baker, Show Manager
E-mail: dickensshow@sc.rr.com
URL(s): www.hmrsss.com. **Frequency:** Annual. **Audience:** Hospitality industry, managers, and buyers. **Principal Exhibits:** Carpeting, furniture, coffee makers, produce companies, wine and beer and food companies, and services to motels, hotels, and restaurants. **Dates and Locations:** , Convention Center. **Telecommunication Services:** hmrss@sc.rr.com.

18038 ■ **ApEx**
Canadian Restaurant and Foodservices Association (CRFA)
316 Bloor St. W
Toronto, ON, Canada M5S 1W5
Ph: (416)923-8416
Free: 800-387-5649
Fax: (416)923-1450
Co. E-mail: info@crfa.ca
URL: http://www.crfa.ca
Contact: Garth Whyte, President
URL(s): www.crfa.ca/tradeshows/apex. **Audience:** Trade. **Principal Exhibits:** Products and services for the restaurant and hospitality industry, as well as institutions, convenience stores, delis and bakeries. **Telecommunication Services:** escanlan@crfa.ca.

18039 ■ **IH/M & RS - International Hotel/Motel & Restaurant Show**
American Hotel and Lodging Association (American Hotel & Motel Association)
1201 New York Ave. NW, Ste. 600
Washington, DC 20005-3931
Ph: (202)289-3100
Free: 800-752-4567

Fax: (202)289-3199
Co. E-mail: informationcenter@ahla.com
URL: http://www.ahla.com
Contact: Joseph A. McInerney, President
E-mail: joe@ahla.com
URL(s): www.ihmrs.com. **Frequency:** Annual. **Audience:** Representatives from mass feeding, lodging, and healthcare industries. **Principal Exhibits:** Products and services for lodging and food serving properties, including: technology, uniforms, linens and bedding, tabletop accessories, guest amenities and services, food and beverages, cleaning maintenance, food service equipment and supplies, franchising information, finance and management furnishings and fixtures, fitness equipment, and leisure and entertainment services. **Dates and Locations:** , Jacob K. Javits Convention Center. **Telecommunication Services:** ihmrs@glmshows.com.

18040 ■ International Restaurant & Foodservice Show of New York
Reed Exhibitions North American Headquarters
383 Main Ave.
Norwalk, CT 06851
Ph: (203)840-4800
Fax: (203)840-5805
Co. E-mail: inquiry@reedexpo.com
URL: http://www.reedexpo.com
URL(s): www.internationalrestaurantny.com/. **Frequency:** Annual. **Principal Exhibits:** Equipment, supplies, and services for the food products, foodservice, restaurant, and institutional food service industries. **Dates and Locations:** , Jacob K. Javits Convention Center.

18041 ■ Michigan Restaurant Show
Michigan Restaurant Association (MRA)
c/o Robert A. Gifford, Pres./CEO
225 W Washtenaw St.
Lansing, MI 48933-1506
Ph: (517)482-5244
Free: 800-968-9668
Fax: (517)482-7663
Co. E-mail: rgifford@mramail.org
URL: http://www.michiganrestaurant.org
Contact: Robert A. Gifford, President
URL(s): www.michiganrestaurant.org. **Price:** $5, Preregistered restaurant non-member (per attendee). **Frequency:** Annual. **Audience:** Food service industry professionals. **Principal Exhibits:** Equipment, supplies, and services for the food service industry.

18042 ■ Mid-America Restaurant Softserve and Pizza Show
Ohio Restaurant Association
1525 Bethel Rd. Ste. 301
Columbus, OH 43220
Ph: (614)442-3535
Free: 800-282-9049
Fax: (614)442-3550
Co. E-mail: info@ohiorestaurant.org
URL: http://www.ohiorestaurant.org
Contact: Rick Cassara, Chairman of the Board
URL(s): www.ohiorestaurant.org. **Price:** $15, Preregistered; $10, Onsite. **Frequency:** Annual. **Audience:** Restaurant owner, managers, institutions, country clubs. **Principal Exhibits:** Food distributors, manufacturers, equipment, beverages. **Dates and Locations:** Greater Columbus Convention Center.

18043 ■ National Prepared Food Festival
National Prepared Food Association
Frequency: Annual. **Audience:** Foodservice professionals, chefs, and restaurant owners. **Principal Exhibits:** Manufacturers of frozen, prepared, and refrigerated foods. **Dates and Locations:** , Meadowlands Sports Complex.

18044 ■ Nightclub & Bar/Beverage Retailer/ Food and Beverage Convention & Tradeshow
Oxford Publishing Inc.
307 W Jackson Ave.
Oxford, MS 38655-2154
Free: 800-247-3881

Fax: (662)236-5541
Co. E-mail: info@oxpub.com
URL: http://www.nightclub.com
URL(s): www.nightclub.com. **Frequency:** Semiannual. **Audience:** Owners and managers of bars, clubs, and restaurants; corporate executives and food/beverage managers of hotels, resorts, state buyers, retailers. **Principal Exhibits:** Equipment, supplies, and services for nightclubs, restaurants, bars, hotels, casinos, and retailers of alcoholic beverages.

18045 ■ Ottawa Wine and Food Show
Player Expositions International
255 Clemow Ave.
Ottawa, ON, Canada K1S 2B5
Ph: (613)567-6408
Fax: (613)567-2718
URL: http://www.playerexpo.com
URL(s): www.playerexpo.com. **Frequency:** Annual. **Audience:** Restaurant, hotels, clubs, catering-fine food stores, specialty food stores, wine clubs, and the general public. **Principal Exhibits:** Fine wines and foods, and beer from around the world. **Dates and Locations:** Congress Centre. **Telecommunication Services:** wineshow@playerexpo.com.

18046 ■ West Ex: The Rocky Mountain Regional Hospitality Exposition
Colorado Restaurant Association
430 E. 7th Ave.
Denver, CO 80203
Ph: (303)830-2972
Free: 800-522-2972
Fax: (303)830-2973
Co. E-mail: info@coloradorestaurant.com
URL: http://www.coloradorestaurant.com
Contact: Pete Meersman, President
E-mail: meersman@coloradorestaurant.com
URL(s): www.coloradorestaurant.com. **Frequency:** Annual. **Audience:** Food service and restaurant industry personnel. **Principal Exhibits:** Food service and lodging products, equipment, and services.

CONSULTANTS

18047 ■ Beer Associates
782 Hampton Rd.
Woodmere, NY 11598
Ph: (516)593-2270
Fax: (516)593-8735
Co. E-mail: beerconsul@aol.com
URL: http://www.beerassociates.com
Contact: Ira B. Beer, Owner
Scope: Provider of management and planning services. It serves banking and financial organizations, general business and industry groups, and municipal and government agencies. **Founded:** 1976. **Seminars:** Integrating Food Service Facilities Plans into Engineering Documents; Specifications: Key to a Successful Project.

18048 ■ Cini-Little International Inc.
20251 Century Blvd., Ste. 375
Germantown, MD 20874
Ph: (301)528-9700
Fax: (301)528-9711
Co. E-mail: info@cinilittle.com
URL: http://www.cinilittle.com
Contact: James H. Little, Chief Executive Officer
E-mail: jlittle@cinilittle.com
Scope: Offers a full range of independent management and design consulting services in all aspects of food service to industries such as hospitality, business, and health care. Services include feasibility studies and/or operations analyses, food service programs and concepts, operational training programs and manuals, food service contractor selection, contract documents, review of contractor submittal and site inspections. Offers consulting in materials management, materials handling, vertical horizontal transport elevator escalator moving sidewalks to all segments of the construction, hospitality, health-care and related industries. **Founded:** 1968.

18049 ■ Clevenger Associates
11803 101st Avenue Ct. E, Ste. 203
Puyallup, WA 98373-3473
Ph: (253)841-7811

Fax: (253)841-7435
Co. E-mail: info@clevengerassoc.com
URL: http://www.clevengerassoc.com
Contact: Anthony A. Clevenger, President
E-mail: tony@clevengerassoc.com
Scope: Offers food service and laundry/valet design and consulting. Will design new and remodeled space; specify equipment, and follow-up to ensure quality and likeness to specifications. Industries served: hotels, restaurants, clubhouses, health care, educational, institutional corrections, convention centers, business and industry. **Founded:** 1974.

18050 ■ Peter Cooke Associates
1480 Endicott Terr.
Teaneck, NJ 07666
Ph: (201)837-1686
Fax: (201)837-8301
Contact: Peter Cooke, President
Scope: Provides food service facility design. **Founded:** 1981.

18051 ■ Erin Services Inc.
111 Travelers Way
Saint Simons Island, GA 31522-5632
Ph: (912)638-9916
Fax: (912)638-5701
Co. E-mail: dennisd@ns.technonet.com
Contact: Dennis J. Donnelly, III, President
E-mail: dennis179@yahoo.com
Scope: Offers assistance in technical proposal production, marketing, and research. Industries served: Food service, janitorial, landscaping, hospitality and lodging, parks, and recreational. **Founded:** 1990.

18052 ■ Jeff Fetter Associates
181 Hitchcock Rd.
Salinas, CA 93908-9451
Ph: (831)455-0410
Contact: Sandra Fetter, President
Scope: Food service facilities engineering and design consultant. Industries served: Food service and hospitality. **Founded:** 1988.

18053 ■ GEC Consultants Inc.
4604 Birchwood Ave.
Skokie, IL 60076-3835
Ph: (847)674-6310
Fax: (847)674-3946
Co. E-mail: experts@gecconsultants.com
URL: http://www.gecconsultants.com
Contact: Lloyd M. Gordon, President
E-mail: legal@gecconsultants.com
Scope: Consulting in all areas of bar and restaurant operations. Restaurant manager development appraises existing locations or sites. Studies the feasibility of projects. Develop new concepts. Assist in expanding, existing food operations, marketing, expert witness (legal) for hospitality/restaurant industry. **Founded:** 1963. **Publications:** "How You Can Fight Back to Minimize This Recession!"; "New Thoughts On Leases"; "The Use of Job Analysis to Actually Reduce Payroll Costs"; "Do You Need a Feasibility Study?"; "Combat Negative Hospitality"; "How To Run A Successful Night club"; "Are Capitalists In Your Cabinet?"; "Marketing For The 21st Century"; "Profitability In The Banquet Industry"; "Starting a Restaurant, Bar or Catering Business"; "How To Find And Retain Suitable Employees"; "26 Things To Do To Plan A Restaurant"; "Wall Fabric or Paint: Decor Magic It's Your Call"; "The Art of Cafe Ambiance"; "Why You Need A Consultant". **Telecommunication Services:** legal@gecconsultants.com.

18054 ■ George Hawkins & Associates
3849 Amber Way Cir. SW
Roanoke, VA 24018
Ph: (540)774-8547
Fax: (540)774-2192
Co. E-mail: ghawkins@infi.net
Contact: George K. Hawkins, President
E-mail: ghawkins@infi.net
Scope: Offers food service facilities and management consulting expertise. Industries served: Food service. **Founded:** 1985.

18055 ■ Hostline
School of Hotel Administration Library
Cornell University
Ithaca, NY 14853-6902
Ph: (607)255-9393
Fax: (607)255-0021
Co. E-mail: hostline@cornell.edu
URL: http://www.nestlelib.cornell.edu/hostline
Contact: Mihoko Hosoi, Manager
Scope: Provider of reference service for the hospitality industry in the areas such as hotel management, franchising and management contracts, tourism and travel, and food and beverage management. **Telecommunication Services:** hotelref@cornell.edu.

18056 ■ The Hysen Group
41740 6 Mile Rd., Ste. 103
Northville, MI 48167
Ph: (248)347-0700
Free: 800-347-0687
Fax: (248)347-0660
Co. E-mail: consult@hysengroup.com
URL: http://www.hysengroup.com
Contact: P. Paul Hysen, Principal
E-mail: paul@hysengroup.com
Scope: Provider of design, engineering and management consulting activities relating to all types of food service facilities. **Founded:** 1972.

18057 ■ Isaksen Foodservice Consultants Inc.
11228 Georgia Ave.
Silver Spring, MD 20902-2712
Ph: (301)933-2100
Fax: (301)933-2101
Co. E-mail: isaksen@erols.com
Contact: Ron Isaksen, Manager
Scope: Consultants to architects, developers, and owners regarding layout and design of food service equipment for health care, elder care, country clubs, bakeries, hotels, hospitals, restaurants, nursing homes, schools, prisons and other institutions, as well as government agencies. Also space planning, lighting and acoustic design, laundry layout and design and food service area construction and installation supervision services. **Founded:** 1982. **Publications:** "Contemporary Long Term Care," Oct, 1997; "Pantries Take on Non-Institutional Look"; "Hospitality Profiles," Nov, 1994; "Interview: Ron Isak sen of Isak sen Food services Strategies"; "Food service Equipment and Supplies Specialist," Sep, 1991; "Winning Kitchens Show Their Metal"; "Food service Equipment and Supplies Specialist," Jun, 1991; "Isak sen, Others Devote Time to Charity," Restaurants and Institutions, Feb, 1991; "Nothing Fishy About Proper Seafood Refrigeration," Food service Equipment and Supplies Specialist, Oct, 1990; "Seven Great Kitchen Design Ideas". **Seminars:** Recipe for Success: New Concepts in Nutrition for the Aging; Integration of Food Delivery Systems with Decentralized Cluster Concepts.

18058 ■ JKM Associates
3545 S Ocean Blvd., Apt. 406
Palm Beach, FL 33480
Ph: (561)586-8859
Fax: (561)588-1219
Contact: James K. Maragos, Principal
Scope: Firm provides and conducts food service management advisory services including operating procedures and systems. Also offers services in food service design and litigation support. Industries served: restaurants, schools and colleges, industrial food service, and hospitals. **Founded:** 1976.

18059 ■ Neumeier Consulting Inc.
601 Academy Ave.
Owings Mills, MD 21117-1301
Ph: (410)902-0464
Free: 800-827-5715
Fax: (410)902-5890
Co. E-mail: miken@comcast.net
Contact: Michael A. Neumeier, President
E-mail: miken@comcast.net
Scope: Specializes in the design and management of retirement accounts. Offers retirement planning courses for adults of any age. **Founded:** 1983. **Seminars:** Retirement Planning Today®.

18060 ■ Nisonger Associates Inc.
202 Elm St.
Milford, OH 45150-1185
Ph: (513)248-1441
Fax: (513)248-1445
Co. E-mail: info@nisongerassoc.com
URL: http://www.nisongerassoc.com
Contact: Harry T. Nisonger, Principal
E-mail: nisongerai@aol.com
Scope: Food service consultants offering management and design services to the food service, lodging, health care, and leisure time industries, as well as to schools, private clubs and other institutions, and government agencies. Not only will the firm evaluate and prescribe, but it will take the project through the implementation process. Services include financial planning, menu development, facilities design, operations assessment, programming, systems studies, corporate valuations, contract and lease negotiations, consumer surveys, market and feasibility studies, prototype planning, and expert witness services. Construction division formed to provide clients with design or build services for fast track projects with cost efficiencies. **Founded:** 1980.

18061 ■ Progressive Sales
Roosevelt Ave., Ste. 1163, Puerto Nueva
San Juan, PR 00920
Ph: (787)782-7474
Fax: (787)793-6479
Co. E-mail: account@@progressivesales.net
URL: http://www.progressivesales.net
Contact: Carlos Berdeguer, President
E-mail: berdeguer@progressivesales.net
Scope: Provider of a full range of consulting services to all types of food service facilities including design and specifications. Industries served: restaurants, hospitals, cafeterias, and government agencies. **Founded:** 1958. **Seminars:** Designing Food Service Facilities. **Telecommunication Services:** sales@progressivesales.net; info@progressivesales.net.

18062 ■ R.D. Network Inc.
PO Box 375
Lafayette Hill, PA 19444
Ph: (215)482-4461
Free: 877-482-4991
Fax: (215)836-0378
Co. E-mail: info@rdnetwork.com
URL: http://www.rdnetwork.com
Contact: Leslie Grant, Owner
Scope: Dietitians, diet technicians, and certified dietary managers available nationwide and worldwide through an international registry for consulting positions to wellness and employee education programs, drug or alcohol rehabilitation, hospital, LTC, nutrition and labeling communications, nutrition consultation, weight control classes, healthcare staff supplementation, media and program development, and all nutrition and food-related needs. Expert witness and speakers bureau also available. Industries served: healthcare, food industry, food service, restaurateurs, supermarkets, pharmaceutical companies, home health agencies, insurance companies, HMOs, and government agencies. **Founded:** 1983. **Seminars:** Labour/Staffing; Outsourcing; Healthy Dining Etiquette for Executives and Sales Staff Diet and Wellness; Cardiovascular Nutrition; Starting a Nutrition Consulting Practice; AIDS and Diet Therapy; Nutrition Care for Your Parents in Their Elder Years; Increase Your Energy-Increase Your Sales.

18063 ■ Riedel Marketing Group (RMG)
5327 E Pinchot Ave.
Phoenix, AZ 85018-2963
Ph: (602)840-4948
Fax: (602)840-4928
Co. E-mail: ajr@4rmg.com
URL: http://www.4rmg.com
Contact: Timothy D. Riedel, President
Scope: The house wares and food service industry strategic marketing planning experts. Help manufacturers of house wares and food products solve marketing problems and identify and exploit marketing opportunities. Provides a full-range of strategic marketing planning services including development of marketing strategy, development of fact-based sales presentations, category management, definition

of market opportunities and new product development exclusively to the house wares and food service industries. **Founded:** 1991. **Publications:** "Your Key Consumer: Her Take on the International Home & Housewares Show," Mar, 2008; "What's Hot, What's Not: The Consumer Speaks," Mar, 2006; "HIPsters SPEAK: What We Love to Buy and Why," Apr, 2005; "Influentials: Who They Are and Why You Should Care," Jun, 2004; "The Seven Secrets to Selling More Housewares," Jan, 2003. **Seminars:** Consumers Speak: What We Love to Buy and Why, What Do Those Consumers Think; The Seven Secrets to Selling More House wares. **Special Services:** Home Trend Influentials Panel.

FRANCHISES AND BUSINESS OPPORTUNITIES

18064 ■ 5 & Diner
5 & Diner Of North America, LLC
24 Main St.
Maynard, MA 01754
Ph: (480)962-7104
Fax: (480)962-0159

Description: 1950's diner. **No. of Franchise Units:** 16. **No. of Company-Owned Units:** 2. **Founded:** 1989. **Franchised:** 1989. **Equity Capital Needed:** Stand alone /in-line-net worth $500,000, food court net-worth $100,000. **Franchise Fee:** $25,000 or $35,000. **Training:** Yes.

18065 ■ A&W Food Services of Canada Inc.
171 W Esplanade, Ste. 300
North Vancouver, BC, Canada V7M 3K9
Ph: (604)988-2141
Fax: (604)988-5531
Co. E-mail: awfranchise@aw.ca
URL: http://www.awfranchise.com

Description: A quick service hamburger chain in Canada with 600 restaurants. The annual sales in 2007 were $658 million. The main products include Burger Family, A&W Root Beer, fresh Onion Rings and Chubby Chicken. **No. of Franchise Units:** 749. **No. of Company-Owned Units:** 10. **Founded:** 1956.. **Franchised:** 1957. **Equity Capital Needed:** Approximately $400,000, single unit. **Franchise Fee:** $55,000 for 20 year term. **Training:** Provides 4-6 weeks of in-store training and ongoing support.

18066 ■ ABC Country Restaurants Inc.
15373 Fraser Hwy., Ste. 202
Surrey, BC, Canada V3R 3P3
Ph: (604)583-2919
Fax: (604)583-8488
Co. E-mail: info@abcCountry.ca
URL: http://www.abcCountry.ca

Description: The restaurants offer fresh food, such as Smokehouse Barbeque, roast beef dinners, focaccia Stacker sandwiches, fresh pies and desserts. Complimentary liquor, wine and beer are also served. **No. of Franchise Units:** 27. **No. of Company-Owned Units:** 3. **Founded:** 1972.. **Franchised:** 1976. **Equity Capital Needed:** $600,000. **Franchise Fee:** $50,000. **Training:** Provides 4-6 weeks before and ongoing support.

18067 ■ Amato's
312 St. John St.
Portland, ME 04102
Ph: (207)828-5981
Fax: (207)761-0977

Description: Italian take out pizza, pasta, and sandwiches. **No. of Franchise Units:** 30. **No. of Company-Owned Units:** 12. **Founded:** 1902.. **Franchised:** 2002. **Equity Capital Needed:** $75,000 liquid, investment range $380,000-$500,000. **Franchise Fee:** $25,000 full scale, $15,000 xpress. **Training:** Yes.

18068 ■ A & W Restaurants, Inc.
Yum! Brands Inc.
1900 Colonel Sanders Ln.
Louisville, KY 40213-1914

Ph: (800)544-5774
Co. E-mail: info@yum.com
URL: http://www.yum.com
Description: Restaurants, serving hamburgers, hot dogs and root beer. **No. of Franchise Units:** 322. **Founded:** 1919.. **Franchised:** 1925. **Equity Capital Needed:** $912,000-$1,623,500. **Franchise Fee:** $20,000. **Royalty Fee:** 5%. **Training:** Provides 2 weeks training and ongoing support.

18069 ■ Andrew Smash
Smash International, Inc.
PO Box 12233
Eugene, OR 97440
Ph: (541)465-9088
Fax: (541)465-9088
Description: Meatless burger and smoothie restaurant. **No. of Company-Owned Units:** 1. **Founded:** 1995.. **Franchised:** 1998. **Equity Capital Needed:** $100,000-$175,000. **Franchise Fee:** $10,000-$20,000. **Training:** Yes.

18070 ■ Applebee's Neighborhood Grill & Bar
Applebee's International, Inc.
11201 Renner Blvd.
Lenexa, KS 66207
Ph: (913)967-4000
Description: Restaurant. **No. of Franchise Units:** 1,014. **No. of Company-Owned Units:** 234. **Founded:** 1980.. **Franchised:** 1983. **Equity Capital Needed:** Net worth in excess of $3,000,000; $300,000-$500,000 in liquidity. **Franchise Fee:** $35,000 U.S.; $40,000 International. **Training:** Yes.

18071 ■ Arby's
Triarc Restaurant Group
1155 Perimeter Ctr. W, Ste. 700
Atlanta, GA 30338
Ph: (800)487-2729
Fax: (954)351-5222
Description: Fast-food restaurant, specializing in roast beef sandwiches, chicken, and subs. **No. of Franchise Units:** 2,351. **No. of Company-Owned Units:** 1,127. **No. of Operating Units:** 3,577. **Founded:** 1964.. **Franchised:** 1965. **Equity Capital Needed:** $357,500-$2,404,500. **Franchise Fee:** $37,500. **Royalty Fee:** 4%. **Financial Assistance:** Third party financing available. **Training:** Provides 5 days at certified training restaurant and ongoing on-site support.

18072 ■ Asian Chao/Maki of Japan/Chao Cajun
385 Commerce Way
Longwood, FL 32750
Ph: (407)830-5338
Fax: (407)830-7258
Description: Asian fast food. **No. of Franchise Units:** 20. **No. of Company-Owned Units:** 45. **Founded:** 1991.. **Franchised:** 2001. **Equity Capital Needed:** $330,000-$475,000. **Franchise Fee:** $30,000. **Royalty Fee:** 6%. **Training:** Provides 2 weeks training at headquarters, 2 weeks onsite and ongoing support.

18073 ■ Austin Grill
750 E St., NW
Washington, DC 20004
Ph: (202)393-3776
Co. E-mail: info@austingrill.com
URL: http://www.austingrill.com
Description: Tex-Mex restaurant. **No. of Company-Owned Units:** 7. **Founded:** 1988.. **Franchised:** 2007. **Equity Capital Needed:** $882,000-$2,800,000. **Franchise Fee:** $50,000. **Royalty Fee:** 5%. **Training:** Available for 10 days at headquarters, 10 days at franchisee's location, at opening, at an existing location, and ongoing support.

18074 ■ Back Yard Burgers Inc.
500 Church St., Ste. 200
Nashville, TN 37219
Ph: (901)367-0888
Fax: (901)367-0999
Description: Quick-service restaurant offering hamburgers, chicken and desserts. **No. of Franchise Units:** 138. **No. of Company-Owned Units:** 43. **Founded:** 1986. **Franchised:** 1988. **Equity Capital**

Needed: $1,000,000-$2,000,000 total investment; $750,000 net worth, $500,000 cash liquidity. **Franchise Fee:** $25,000. **Royalty Fee:** 4%. **Training:** Provides 6 weeks at headquarters, 2 weeks at franchisee's location with ongoing support.

18075 ■ Baja Sol Tortilla Grill
2922 Upper 55th St.
Inver Grove Heights, MN 55076
Ph: (612)280-1467
Fax: (952)944-2001
Description: Fresh Mexican food. **No. of Franchise Units:** 10. **No. of Company-Owned Units:** 4. **Founded:** 1995.. **Franchised:** 1995. **Equity Capital Needed:** $186,000-$400,000 total investment; $500,000 net worth, $100,000 cash liquidity. **Franchise Fee:** $30,000. **Royalty Fee:** 5%. **Training:** Provides 4 weeks at headquarters with ongoing support.

18076 ■ Bandana's Bar-B-Q
16141 Swingley Ridge Rd., Ste., 205
Chesterfield, MO 63017
Ph: (636)537-8200
Fax: (636)537-8004
Description: Barbecue restaurant. **No. of Franchise Units:** 5. **No. of Company-Owned Units:** 26. **Founded:** 1996.. **Franchised:** 2004. **Equity Capital Needed:** $385,200-$1,122,500 total investment. **Franchise Fee:** $40,000. **Royalty Fee:** 5%. **Training:** Provides 5 weeks at headquarters, 10 days on-site with ongoing support.

18077 ■ Bar-B-Cutie
5120 Virginia Way, Ste. B-23
Brentwood, TN 37027
Ph: (615)372-0707
Fax: (615)372-0705
Co. E-mail: inquiry@bar-b-cutie.com
URL: http://www.bar-b-cutie.com
Description: Barbecue restaurant. **No. of Franchise Units:** 11. **No. of Company-Owned Units:** 2. **Founded:** 1950.. **Franchised:** 2003. **Equity Capital Needed:** $329,500-$450,000 total investment; $500,000 net worth, $200,000 cash liquidity. **Franchise Fee:** $25,000. **Royalty Fee:** 5%. **Financial Assistance:** Third party financing available. **Training:** Provides 3 weeks at headquarters, 1 week on-site with ongoing support.

18078 ■ Beef O'Bradys Family Sports Pubs
Family Sports Concepts Inc.
5510 LaSalle St., Ste. 200
Tampa, FL 33607
Ph: (813)226-2333
Fax: (813)200-3305
Description: Family sports restaurant. **No. of Franchise Units:** 213. **No. of Company-Owned Units:** 7. **Founded:** 1985.. **Franchised:** 1988. **Equity Capital Needed:** $125,000 cash; $164,500-$662,500 total investment. **Franchise Fee:** $35,000 **Financial Assistance:** Yes. **Training:** 8 week training at headquarters included with 2 weeks onsite and ongoing support.

18079 ■ Benihana
Benihana Inc.
8685 NW 53rd Terr.
Miami, FL 33166
Ph: (305)593-0770
Fax: (305)592-6371
URL: http://www.benihana.com
Description: Food and service. a restaurant for a period of 12-16 weeks until properly trained in general restaurant management and food preparation. **No. of Franchise Units:** 30. **No. of Company-Owned Units:** 60. **Founded:** 1964.. **Franchised:** 1970. **Equity Capital Needed:** Minimum $2,000,000. **Franchise Fee:** $40,000-$50,000. **Training:** Yes.

18080 ■ Big Apple Bagels
BAB, Inc.
500 Lake Cook Rd., Ste. 475
Deerfield, IL 60015
Ph: (847)948-7520

Fax: (847)405-8140
Co. E-mail: tcervini@babcorp.com
URL: http://www.babcorp.com
Description: A bakery style cafe featuring our three brands, made from scratch daily Big Apple Bagels and My Favorite Muffin, and freshly roasted Brewster's Coffee. Product offering includes made to order gourmet sandwiches, salads, soups, and espresso beverages. **No. of Franchise Units:** 102. **Founded:** 1992. **Franchised:** 1993. **Equity Capital Needed:** $252,300-$374,800. **Franchise Fee:** $25,000. **Training:** Extensive training covers all aspects of operations and management, combines hands-on experience at our corporate store training facility with classroom presentations by management and key note vendors.

18081 ■ Big Boy Family Restaurant
Big Boy Restaurants International L.L.C.
4199 Marcy
Warren, MI 48091
Ph: (586)755-8113
Fax: (586)757-4737
Description: Full-service family restaurant, featuring in-store bakery, breakfast, dinner, soup, salad and fruit bar. **No. of Franchise Units:** 112. **No. of Company-Owned Units:** 20. **Founded:** 1936.. **Franchised:** 1952. **Equity Capital Needed:** $750,000. **Franchise Fee:** $40,000. **Training:** Yes.

18082 ■ Blenz Coffee
535 Thurlow St., Ste. 300
Vancouver, BC, Canada V6E 3L2
Ph: (604)682-2995
Fax: (604)684-2542
Description: Coffee beverages and coffee beans. **No. of Franchise Units:** 25. **No. of Company-Owned Units:** 2. **Founded:** 1990.. **Franchised:** 1992. **Equity Capital Needed:** $30,000-$70,000 plus equity. **Training:** Yes.

18083 ■ Blimpie Subs & Salads
Blimpie International, Inc.
9311 E Via De Ventura
Scottsdale, AZ 85258
Ph: (480)362-4800
Free: 866-452-4252
Fax: (480)505-0910
Co. E-mail: info@blimpie.com
URL: http://www.blimpie.com
Description: National quick-service restaurant, serving fresh-sliced submarine sandwiches and salads. **No. of Franchise Units:** 733. **No. of Company-Owned Units:** 6. **Founded:** 1964.. **Franchised:** 1970. **Equity Capital Needed:** $136,150-$385,050. **Franchise Fee:** $18,000. **Royalty Fee:** 6%. **Financial Assistance:** Limited third party financing available. **Training:** Training includes 1 week at headquarters, 2 weeks onsite and ongoing support.

18084 ■ Boardwalk Fresh Burgers & Fries
Branded Concepts, Inc.
9220 Rumsey Rd., Ste. 101
Columbia, MD 21045
Ph: (410)715-0500
Fax: (410)715-0711
Description: Fast Food. **No. of Franchise Units:** 16. **Founded:** 1981.. **Franchised:** 2008. **Equity Capital Needed:** $174,500-$626,000. **Franchise Fee:** $30,000. **Royalty Fee:** 6%. **Financial Assistance:** Third party financing available. **Training:** Yes.

18085 ■ Bojangles' Chicken 'n Biscuits
Bojangles Restaurants Inc.
9432 Southern Pine Blvd.
Charlotte 28273
Ph: (704)527-2675
Fax: (704)523-6803
Co. E-mail: contact@bojangles.com
URL: http://www.bojangles.com
Description: Fast-service chicken and biscuits restaurant. **No. of Franchise Units:** 310. **No. of Company-Owned Units:** 201. **Founded:** 1977. **Franchised:** 1979. **Equity Capital Needed:** $500,000 liquid assets; $1,000,000 net worth. **Franchise Fee:** $25,000. **Training:** Offers an 5 week training program at as well as a one week training program at Bojangles University.

18086 ■ Boneheads Grilled Fish & Piri Piri Chicken
Raving Brands
2349 Peachtree Rd.
Atlanta, GA 30305
Ph: (404)351-3500
Co. E-mail: salesleads@ravingbrands.com
URL: http://www.eatboneheads.com
Description: A culinary experience where people seeking fresh, flavorful food in a relaxed environment can indulge in fire-grilled fish seasoned with Boneheads signature spices and chicken dishes marinated with Piri Piri sauces. From the sumptuous Mahi Mahi to the fiery-skewered shrimp, Boneheads pays homage to the Piri Piri pepper, a South African spice with serious sauce-making capabilities. **No. of Franchise Units:** 35. **No. of Company-Owned Units:** 1. **Founded:** 2005.. **Franchised:** 2005. **Equity Capital Needed:** $500,000 net worth; $150,000 liquid. **Franchise Fee:** $25,000. **Training:** Raving Brands University classroom and onsite training provided.

18087 ■ Boston Pizza International Inc.
610-5600 Parkwood Way
Richmond, BC, Canada V6V 2M2
Ph: (604)270-1108
Fax: (604)270-4553
Co. E-mail: Franchising@bostonpizza.com
URL: http://www.bostonpizza.com/en/franchising
Description: The franchise promotes casual dining, restaurant, and sports bar concept. **No. of Franchise Units:** 340. **No. of Company-Owned Units:** 3. **Founded:** 1964.. **Franchised:** 1968. **Equity Capital Needed:** $600,000-$800,000. **Franchise Fee:** $60,000. **Training:** Offers 7 weeks training.

18088 ■ The Boston's Gourmet Pizza
Boston Pizza International
1501 LBJ Fwy., Ste. 450
Dallas, TX 75234
Ph: (972)484-9022
Free: 800-277-8721
Fax: (972)484-7630
Description: Casual restaurant specializing in pizza. **No. of Franchise Units:** 389. **No. of Company-Owned Units:** 4. **Founded:** 1963.. **Franchised:** 1968. **Equity Capital Needed:** $1,165,000-$350,000-$2,838,000. **Franchise Fee:** $50,000 U.S. **Training:** Yes.

18089 ■ Buffalo Philly's - Wings, Cheesesteaks N' More
Buffalo Philly's Franchising, LLC
1812 Efty Ct.
Woodbridge, VA 22191
Ph: (703)490-3428
Fax: (703)490-3427
Description: A fast casual concept wings and cheesesteaks. **No. of Franchise Units:** 5. **No. of Company-Owned Units:** 1. **Founded:** 2000.. **Franchised:** 2004. **Equity Capital Needed:** $200,000-$300,000. **Franchise Fee:** $18,000. **Training:** Yes.

18090 ■ Buffalo Wild Wings Grill & Bar
Buffalo Wild Wings International, Inc.
5500 Wayzata Blvd., Ste. 1600
Minneapolis, MN 55416
Ph: (800)499-9586
Fax: (952)593-9787
Description: Sports theme, family, wings and 12 sauces. **No. of Franchise Units:** 504. **No. of Company-Owned Units:** 325. **Founded:** 1982.. **Franchised:** 1991. **Equity Capital Needed:** $1,371,700-$3,150,700 total investment. **Franchise Fee:** $40,000. **Royalty Fee:** 5%. **Training:** Offers 7 weeks training at certified training restaurant.

18091 ■ Buffalo Wings & Rings
Buffalo Wings & Rings, LLC
564 Old State Rte. 74
Cincinnati, OH 45244
Ph: (513)831-9464
Fax: (513)831-9463
Description: Casual dining featuring wings. **No. of Franchise Units:** 43. **No. of Company-Owned Units:** 2. **Founded:** 1986.. **Franchised:** 1988. **Equity Capital Needed:** $998,500-$2,722,500. **Franchise Fee:** $35,000. **Royalty Fee:** 5%. **Training:** Yes.

18092 ■ Burger King Corp.
5505 Blue Lagoon Dr.
Miami, FL 33126-2029
Ph: (305)378-7579
Free: 866-394-2493
Fax: (305)378-7721
URL: http://www.bk.com
Contact: Nish Kankiwala, President
Description: Highly-recognized fast food hamburger restaurant. Worldwide brand with over 6,800 points of distribution. New, lower cost facility design and flexible ownership guidelines continue to make an attractive franchise investment. **No. of Franchise Units:** 10,144. **No. of Company-Owned Units:** 1,079. **Founded:** 1954. **Franchised:** 1961. **Equity Capital Needed:** $1,500,000 net worth, plus $500,000 in liquid assets. **Franchise Fee:** $40,000. **Training:** Yes.

18093 ■ Cafe Fondue Franchise Systems Inc.
281 W 80th Pl.
Merrillville, IN 46410
Ph: (219)793-1511
Fax: (219)793-1511
Description: Fondue - specialty restaurant. **No. of Company-Owned Units:** 1. **Founded:** 1998.. **Franchised:** 2003. **Equity Capital Needed:** $136,000-$307,000. **Franchise Fee:** $35,000. **Royalty Fee:** 4%. **Training:** Provides 2 weeks training at headquarters and 2 weeks onsite.

18094 ■ Carl's Jr.
CKE Restaurants, Inc.
6307 Carpinteria Ave., Ste. A
Carpinteria, CA 93013
Ph: (805)745-7842
Free: 866-253-7655
Fax: (714)780-6320
Description: Quick service restaurant. **No. of Franchise Units:** 712. **No. of Company-Owned Units:** 399. **Founded:** 1945.. **Equity Capital Needed:** Minimum $300,000 liquid; $1,000,000 net worth; $300,000 liquid per restaurant, 3 restaurant minimum. **Franchise Fee:** $35,000. **Training:** Yes.

18095 ■ Casey's Grill & Bar
10 Kingsbridge Garden Cir., Ste. 600
Mississauga, ON, Canada L5R 3K6
Ph: (905)568-0000
Free: 800-361-3111
Fax: (905)568-0080
Co. E-mail: Franchising@primerestaurants.com
URL: http://www.caseysbarandgrill.com
Description: Casual dining restaurant that offers 'grilled' food such as AAA steak house burgers and AAA steaks, and fresh cut fries. **No. of Franchise Units:** 29. **No. of Company-Owned Units:** 1. **Founded:** 1979.. **Franchised:** 1982. **Equity Capital Needed:** $520,000-$640,000 startup capital; $1,300,000-$1,600,000 investment required. **Franchise Fee:** $50,000. **Training:** Yes.

18096 ■ Casino Tony Goes Restaurant
15 Anderson St.
Trenton, NJ 08611
Ph: (609)213-2984
Description: Quick-service Italian restaurant specializing in Italian hot dogs. **No. of Franchise Units:** 2. **No. of Company-Owned Units:** 1. **Founded:** 1935.. **Franchised:** 2005. **Equity Capital Needed:** $386,100-$591,800. **Franchise Fee:** $30,000. **Royalty Fee:** 6%. **Training:** Offers 2 weeks at headquarters with ongoing support.

18097 ■ Central Park Restaurants
Central Park of America, Inc.
5751 Uptain Rd., Ste. 210
Chattanooga, TN 37411-5672
Ph: (423)855-0991
Fax: (423)899-5923
Description: Drive-thru hamburger restaurant. **No. of Franchise Units:** 25. **Founded:** 1982.. **Franchised:** 1988. **Equity Capital Needed:** $300,000-$550,000. **Franchise Fee:** $20,000. **Training:** Consists of a minimum of 5 weeks at Central Park's Training Center in Chattanooga, Tennessee or at a training site designated by Central Park. Central Park also provides ongong support.

18098 ■ The Cereal Bowl
13941 SW 112th St.
Miami, FL 33128
Ph: (305)428-2695
Fax: (305)662-2695
Description: Cereal cafe. **No. of Franchise Units:** 23. **No. of Company-Owned Units:** 1. **Founded:** 2005.. **Franchised:** 2007. **Equity Capital Needed:** $186,000-$341,000. **Franchise Fee:** $25,000. **Training:** Yes.

18099 ■ Charley's Grilled Subs
Gosh Enterprises, Inc.
2500 Farmers Dr., Ste. 140
Columbus, OH 43235-5706
Ph: (614)923-4700
Free: 877-278-2798
Fax: (614)923-4701
Co. E-mail: dmoore@charleys.com
URL: http://www.charleys.com
Description: Features freshly grilled steak and chicken subs, fresh-cut fries and old-fashioned fresh squeezed lemonade. **No. of Franchise Units:** 361. **No. of Company-Owned Units:** 43. **Founded:** 1986.. **Franchised:** 1991. **Equity Capital Needed:** $83,095-$406,504 total investment; $100,000 liquid. **Franchise Fee:** $24,500. **Royalty Fee:** 6%. **Financial Assistance:** Limited third party financing available. **Training:** Available at headquarters for 5 weeks, 7 days at franchisee's location, and ongoing support.

18100 ■ Charo Chicken Systems, Inc.
1077 Pacific Coast Hwy.
Seal Beach, CA 90740
Ph: (714)960-2348
Description: Flame-broiled chicken, salads, and sides. **No. of Franchise Units:** 20. **No. of Company-Owned Units:** 4. **Founded:** 1985.. **Franchised:** 1998. **Equity Capital Needed:** $400,000. **Franchise Fee:** $25,000. **Financial Assistance:** Yes. **Training:** Yes.

18101 ■ Checkers / Ralley's
Checkers Drive-In Restaurants Inc.
4300 W Cypress St., Ste. 600
Tampa, FL 33607
Ph: (813)283-7000
Free: 800-800-8072
Fax: (813)283-7208
Co. E-mail: fumiat@checkers.com
URL: http://www.checkers.com
Description: Restaurants offering burgers, fish and chicken sandwiches, hot dogs, fries, and soft drinks. **No. of Franchise Units:** 507. **No. of Company-Owned Units:** 323. **Founded:** 1985.. **Franchised:** 1985. **Equity Capital Needed:** $750,000 net worth, $250,000 liquid. **Franchise Fee:** $40,000. **Training:** 4-6 weeks initial training and ongoing support.

18102 ■ Cheeburger Cheeburger Restaurants, Inc.
15951 McGregor Blvd., Ste. 316
Ft. Myers, FL 33908
Free: 800-487-6211
URL: http://www.cheeburger.com
Description: Family restaurant. **No. of Franchise Units:** 68. **No. of Company-Owned Units:** 2. **Founded:** 1986.. **Franchised:** 1986. **Equity Capital Needed:** Go to Cheeburger.com. **Franchise Fee:** $35,000, $27,500, $22,000. **Training:** Yes.

18103 ■ Chester's International, LLC
3500 Colonnade Pky., Ste. 325
Birmingham, AL 35243
Ph: (800)288-1555
Fax: (205)298-0332
Co. E-mail: franchising@chestersinternational.com
URL: http://www.chestersinternational.com
Description: Offers consumers a high-quality chicken product, cooked with a unique taste and style. The company's secret is a breading recipe and process that has been successful for more than 30 years. Chester's uses only real chicken that is specially marinated and offers double breaded bone-in, tenders and potato wedges, as well as sandwiches, wraps, salads and breakfast. **No. of Franchise Units:** 22. **No. of Company-Owned Units:** 1. **Founded:** 1952. **Franchised:** 2004. **Equity Capital Needed:**

$105,857-$407,000 total investment; $50,000-$100,000 liquid. **Franchise Fee:** $15,000-$20,000. **Financial Assistance:** Yes. **Training:** Offers turn-key supply, marketing support and ongoing operations support. Franchisee's benefit from Chester's University, where employees participate in a hands-on, 5 day training program in a high-tech classroom and in-store settings, plus onsite training and grand opening support.

18104 ■ Chicken Connection Franchise Corp.
International Restaurant Management Group
4104 Aurora St.
Coral Gables, FL 33146-1416
Ph: (305)476-1611
Fax: (305)476-9622

Description: Variety of chicken items. **No. of Company-Owned Units:** 7. **Founded:** 1997.. **Franchised:** 1998. **Equity Capital Needed:** $240,500-$424,500. **Franchise Fee:** $30,000. **Financial Assistance:** Yes. **Training:** Yes.

18105 ■ Chicken Delight
395 Berry St.
Winnipeg, MB, Canada R3J 1N6
Ph: (204)885-7570
Fax: (204)831-6176
URL: http://www.franchisedirectory.ca

Description: Pressure-fried chicken and fresh-dough pizza, plus other tasty selections. **No. of Franchise Units:** 26. **No. of Company-Owned Units:** 11. **Founded:** 1952.. **Franchised:** 1952. **Equity Capital Needed:** $75,000 minimum cash liquidity; $275,000-$600,000 total investment range. **Franchise Fee:** $20,000. **Royalty Fee:** 5%. **Training:** Offers an intensive 4 week, in-field training program at our corporate stores.

18106 ■ Church's Chicken
Friedman Fleischer & Lowe LLC
980 Hammond Dr., Bldg. 2, Ste. 1100
Atlanta, GA 30328
Ph: (800)639-3495
Fax: (770)512-3924

Description: Fast-food chicken restaurant specializing in Southern-style dishes. **No. of Franchise Units:** 1,423. **No. of Company-Owned Units:** 254. **Founded:** 1952.. **Franchised:** 1972. **Equity Capital Needed:** $1,500,000 investment; $650,000 must be liquid; must develop a minimum of 3 units. **Franchise Fee:** $15,000. **Training:** Offers 4 weeks Management in Training conducted in operating restaurants. Ongoing operational support, advice, and new product training.

18107 ■ CiCi's Pizza
CiCi Enterprises, Inc.
1080 W Bethel Rd.
Coppell, TX 75019
Ph: (972)745-4200
Fax: (469)675-6405

Description: Pizza, pasta, salad bar and dessert on an all-you-can-eat lunch and dinner buffet. Also offers a value-priced take-out menu. **No. of Franchise Units:** 578. **No. of Company-Owned Units:** 13. **Founded:** 1985.. **Franchised:** 1988. **Equity Capital Needed:** $461,343-$714,912. **Franchise Fee:** $30,000. **Training:** Yes.

18108 ■ City Wok
City Wok, LLC
73744 Hwy. 11, No. 3
Palm Beach, CA 92260
Ph: (760)346-7764
Free: 800-563-8592

Description: Authentic Chinese cuisine. **No. of Franchise Units:** 1. **No. of Company-Owned Units:** 4. **Founded:** 1990.. **Franchised:** 2004. **Equity Capital Needed:** $243,400-$568,500. **Franchise Fee:** $30,000. **Royalty Fee:** 5%. **Training:** Yes.

18109 ■ Cora Breakfast and Lunch
2798 Thamesgate Dr., Unit 2
Mississauga, ON, Canada 4LT 4E8
Ph: (905)673-2672

Fax: (905)673-8271
Co. E-mail: franchising@chezcora.com
URL: http://www.chezcora.com

Description: Cora offers original breakfast platters in Canada. **No. of Franchise Units:** 129. **No. of Company-Owned Units:** 3. **Founded:** 1987.. **Franchised:** 1994. **Equity Capital Needed:** $600,000-$850,000. **Franchise Fee:** $45,000. **Training:** Provides 4-6 week training program consisting of theoretical and practical training.

18110 ■ Corn Dog Factory
Corn Dog Factory Intl.
442 N Main St., Ste. 100
Bountiful, UT 84010
Ph: (801)298-1900

Description: The franchise offers restaurant, drive-in, carryout and delivery facilities. **No. of Franchise Units:** 15. **Founded:** 1974.. **Franchised:** 2001. **Equity Capital Needed:** $90,000 and up. **Franchise Fee:** $10,000/co-brand opt. **Training:** Yes.

18111 ■ The Counter
8571 Higuera St.
Culver City, CA 90232
Ph: (310)559-3355
Fax: (310)559-3356
URL: http://www.thecounterburger.com

Description: Build-your-own-burger restaurant. **No. of Franchise Units:** 28. **No. of Company-Owned Units:** 3. **Founded:** 2003.. **Franchised:** 2005. **Equity Capital Needed:** $770,000-$2,549,000. **Franchise Fee:** $50,000. **Royalty Fee:** 6%. **Training:** Offers 2 weeks at headquarters, 2 weeks at franchisee's location and ongoing support.

18112 ■ Country Kitchen International
Kitchens Investment Group, Inc.
1289 Deming Way, Ste. 212
Madison, WI 53717
Ph: (608)833-9633
Fax: (608)826-9080

Description: Family restaurant. **No. of Franchise Units:** 127. **No. of Company-Owned Units:** 21. **Founded:** 1939.. **Franchised:** 1939. **Equity Capital Needed:** $350,000. **Franchise Fee:** $40,000. **Training:** Yes.

18113 ■ Cousins Subs
Cousins Subs Systems, Inc.
N83 W13400 Leon Rd.
Menomonee Falls, WI 53051
Ph: (262)253-7700
Fax: (262)253-7710
Co. E-mail: betterfranchise@cousinssubs.com
URL: http://www.cousinssubs.com

Description: Submarine sandwich operation, with over 20 years of expertise. Volume-oriented, fast-service concept in an upscale, in-line, strip or free-standing location, some with drive-up windows. Franchising opportunities available for single, multi-unit and area developer franchisees, seminars and training classes. A corporate area representative meets with each franchise location management 3 times per month to maintain communications and assist in problem solving. **No. of Franchise Units:** 141. **No. of Company-Owned Units:** 16. **Founded:** 1972.. **Franchised:** 1985. **Equity Capital Needed:** $80,000 cash, $106,700-$288,300 total investment. **Franchise Fee:** $25,000. **Training:** Includes a store building seminar for site selection, lease negotiation and construction 30 days of hands-on training, plus 10 days of opening assistance and training. National and local store marketing support.

18114 ■ Crepemaker
Oui Du Crepes, Inc.
14365 SW 142nd St.
Miami, FL 33186
Ph: (305)233-1113

Description: Casual fast food. **No. of Franchise Units:** 16. **No. of Company-Owned Units:** 3. **Founded:** 1992.. **Franchised:** 2001. **Equity Capital Needed:** $110,000-$315,000. **Franchise Fee:** 25,000. **Training:** Yes.

18115 ■ D'Angelo Grilled Sandwiches
Papa Gino's Inc.
600 Providence Hwy.
Dedham, MA 02026-6804
Ph: (781)461-1200
Free: 800-727-2446
Fax: (781)326-7552
Co. E-mail: HR@papaginos.com
URL: http://www.papaginos.com

Description: Fast casual restaurant. **No. of Franchise Units:** 51. **No. of Company-Owned Units:** 139. **Founded:** 1967.. **Franchised:** 1988. **Equity Capital Needed:** $127,000 liquid capital; $400,000 net worth. **Franchise Fee:** $20,000. **Training:** Yes.

18116 ■ De Dutch Pannekoek House Restaurants
8481 162nd St., Unit 108
Surrey, BC, Canada V4N 1B4
Ph: (604)543-3101
Fax: (604)543-3107
Co. E-mail: dedutch@dedutch.com
URL: http://www.dedutch.com

Description: De Dutch Pannekoek is a casual dining restaurant specializing in breakfast, lunch and brunch. The restaurant offers a unique menu with equally attractive timings. **No. of Franchise Units:** 18. **No. of Company-Owned Units:** 5. **Founded:** 1975.. **Franchised:** 1979. **Equity Capital Needed:** $350,000-$750,000. **Franchise Fee:** $42,500, includes training fee. **Training:** Provides 7 weeks at corporate training unit in Vancouver and an additional 2-3 weeks at new location.

18117 ■ Denny's, Inc.
Franchise Development
203 E Main St.
Spartanburg, SC 29319
Ph: (800)304-0222
Fax: (864)597-7708
Co. E-mail: franchisedevelopment@dennys.com
URL: http://www.dennys.com

Description: Full-service family restaurant - 24-hour operation. **No. of Franchise Units:** 1,515. **No. of Company-Owned Units:** 174. **Founded:** 1953.. **Franchised:** 1963. **Equity Capital Needed:** $1,000,000 net worth; $350,000 liquid assets. **Franchise Fee:** $40,000. **Training:** Yes.

18118 ■ Dickey's Barbecue Pit
Dickey's Barbecue Restaurants, Inc.
4514 Cole Ave., Ste. 1100
Dallas, TX 75205
Ph: (972)248-9899
Fax: (972)248-8667
Co. E-mail: rdickeyjr@dickeys.com
URL: http://www.rickeys.com

Description: Dickey's uses the latest in barbeque technology along with several proprietary concepts and recipes. Tasty, fresh food served in a fast casual dining approach featuring slowly smoked tender meat, a hot variety of veggies, cold crisp salads, desserts and soft-serve ice cream. **No. of Franchise Units:** 250. **No. of Company-Owned Units:** 8. **Founded:** 1941. **Franchised:** 1994. **Equity Capital Needed:** $50,000-$75,000 liquid capital and another $50,000 in assets. **Franchise Fee:** $15,000. **Training:** Official training site where new franchisee's and managers spend 2 weeks learning about operations, marketing and accounting.

18119 ■ DineEquity Inc.
450 N Brand Blvd.
Glendale, CA 91203-2347
Ph: (818)240-6055
Free: 888-774-4467
Fax: (818)637-4730
URL: http://www.ihop.com
Contact: Julia A. Stewart, President
E-mail: julia.stewart@ihop.com

Description: Full-service family restaurant, serving breakfast, lunch, dinner, snacks and desserts, including a variety of pancake specialties and featuring the cook's Daily Special. Wine and beer are served in some locations. **No. of Franchise Units:** 1,502. **No. of Company-Owned Units:** 11. **Founded:** 1976.. **Franchised:** 1958. **Equity Capital Needed:**

$500,000 liquid; $1,500,000 net worth. **Franchise Fee:** $50,000 single/$40,000 multi. **Financial Assistance:** No. **Training:** Yes.

18120 ■ The Dogout
PO Box 4567
Oceanside, CA 92052
Free: 800-794-0117
Co. E-mail: info@thedogout.com
URL: http://www.thedogout.com
Description: Restaurants and food delivery services. **No. of Franchise Units:** 7. **No. of Company-Owned Units:** 1. **Founded:** 2002.. **Franchised:** 2002. **Equity Capital Needed:** $200,000-$400,000. **Franchise Fee:** $25,000. **Training:** Training includes information system & financial management; market analysis and location selection; image development; opening assistance and operational assistance.

18121 ■ East Side Mario's
Prime Restaurant Group Inc.
10 Kingsbridge Garden Cir., Ste. 600
Mississauga, ON, Canada L5R 3K6
Ph: (905)568-0000
Free: 800-361-3111
Fax: (905)568-0080
Co. E-mail: franchising@primerestaurants.com
URL: http://www.eastsidemarios.com
Description: Offers good food in an exuberant atmosphere with an American Italian setting. Serves foods like Linguine Chicken Tettrazini and Peppercorn Steak Sandwich. **No. of Franchise Units:** 95. **No. of Company-Owned Units:** 1. **Founded:** 1979.. **Franchised:** 1989. **Equity Capital Needed:** $520,000-$640,000 start-up capital; $1,300,000-$1,600,000 investment required. **Franchise Fee:** $50,000. **Training:** Yes.

18122 ■ Edo Japan
4838 32nd St. SE
Calgary, AB, Canada T2B 2S6
Ph: (888)336-9888
Fax: (403)215-8801
Co. E-mail: edo@edojapan.com
URL: http://www.edojapan.com
Description: The original teppan/teriyaki-style, fast-food outlet that places emphasis on nutrition, high-quality food and the availability of vegetarian-style dishes. All menu items are prepared fresh, in full view of the customers. The teppan-style menu brings customers back again and again. Has a highly successful, very profitable, fast-food concept. There are 90 restaurants in US and Canada. **No. of Franchise Units:** 100. **No. of Company-Owned Units:** 4. **Founded:** 1977. **Franchised:** 1981. **Equity Capital Needed:** $285,000-$500,000 investment required. **Franchise Fee:** $30,000-$35,000. **Training:** Provides 5 weeks of training.

18123 ■ El Pollo Loco
El Pollo Loco Inc.
3535 Harbor Blvd., Ste. 100
Costa Mesa, CA 92626-1494
Ph: (714)599-5000
Free: 877-375-4968
Fax: (206)728-1500
Co. E-mail: contact@elpolloloco.com
URL: http://www.elpolloloco.com
Description: Restaurants specializing in Mexican-style broiled chicken. **No. of Franchise Units:** 235. **No. of Company-Owned Units:** 168. **No. of Operating Units:** 403. **Founded:** 1975.. **Franchised:** 1980. **Equity Capital Needed:** $427,850-$802,350. **Franchise Fee:** $40,000. **Royalty Fee:** 4%. **Training:** Available at headquarters 6 weeks, 2 weeks onsite with ongoing support.

18124 ■ Empress Chili
10592 Taconic Terr.
Cincinnati, OH 45215
Ph: (513)771-1441
Description: Fast food restaurant. **No. of Franchise Units:** 18. **Founded:** 1992.. **Franchised:** 1960. **Equity Capital Needed:** $65,000. **Franchise Fee:** $6,000. **Training:** Yes.

18125 ■ The Extreme Pita
2187 Dunwin Dr.
Mississauga, ON, Canada L5L 1X2

Ph: (905)820-7887
Free: 888-729-7482
Fax: (905)820-8448
URL: http://www.extremepita.com
Description: Food industry, providing fast, healthy food with exceptional quality and service. **No. of Franchise Units:** 227. **No. of Company-Owned Units:** 2. **Founded:** 1997.. **Franchised:** 1999. **Equity Capital Needed:** $181,500-$308,000 (/-); start-up capital varies. **Franchise Fee:** $20,000. **Training:** At least 6 weeks of training.

18126 ■ Famous Sam's, Inc.
16012 Metcalf Ave., Ste. 1
Overland Park, KS 66085
Ph: (913)239-0266
Free: 888-866-8808
Fax: (913)239-9768
Description: Entertainment restaurant and sports bar. **No. of Franchise Units:** 29. **Founded:** 1979.. **Franchised:** 1989. **Equity Capital Needed:** $586,000-$1,200,000. **Franchise Fee:** $30,000. **Royalty Fee:** 5%. **Training:** Offers 2 weeks at headquarters and ongoing support.

18127 ■ Farmer Boys
Farmer Boys Food, Inc.
3452 University Ave.
Riverside, CA 92501
Ph: (909)275-9900
Fax: (909)275-9930
Description: Restaurants and food delivery services. **No. of Franchise Units:** 48. **No. of Company-Owned Units:** 17. **Founded:** 1981.. **Franchised:** 1997. **Equity Capital Needed:** $515,375-$795,505. **Franchise Fee:** $40,000. **Royalty Fee:** 5%. **Financial Assistance:** Limited third party financing available. **Training:** Yes. **Telecommunication Services:** franchising@farmerboys.com.

18128 ■ Fazoli's Restaurants
Fazoli's Franchising Systems, LLC
2470 Palumbo Dr.
Lexington, KY 40509
Ph: (859)825-6259
Fax: (859)268-2263
Description: Italian food - fast. Walk-up, take-out and drive-thru operation with approximately 100 seats. **No. of Franchise Units:** 96. **No. of Company-Owned Units:** 126. **Founded:** 1990.. **Franchised:** 1991. **Equity Capital Needed:** $250,000 liquid; $750,000 total investment capability. **Franchise Fee:** $30,000. **Training:** Yes.

18129 ■ The Firkin Group of Pubs
Firkin Pub International, Inc.
20 Steelcase Rd. W, No. 1C
Markham, ON, Canada L3R 1B2
Ph: (905)305-9792
Fax: (905)305-9719
Co. E-mail: larry@firkinpubs.com
URL: http://www.firkinpubs.com
Description: Restaurants and food delivery services. **No. of Franchise Units:** 21. **No. of Company-Owned Units:** 11. **Founded:** 1987.. **Franchised:** 1999. **Equity Capital Needed:** $350,000. **Franchise Fee:** $30,000. **Training:** Training provided at headquarters and ongoing support.

18130 ■ Five Guys
10440 Furnace Rd., Ste. 205
Lorton, VA 22079
Ph: (703)339-9500
Description: Fresh made burgers and fries. **No. of Franchise Units:** 415. **No. of Company-Owned Units:** 62. **Founded:** 1997.. **Franchised:** 2002. **Equity Capital Needed:** $300,000-$550,000; $30,000 dev. Fee/store. **Franchise Fee:** $25,000. **Training:** Yes.

18131 ■ The Flame Broiler, Inc.
3525 Hyland Ave., Ste. 270
Costa Mesa, CA 92626
Ph: (714)424-0223

Fax: (714)424-0225
Description: Chicken bowl specialist. **No. of Franchise Units:** 105. **No. of Company-Owned Units:** 3. **Founded:** 1995.. **Franchised:** 1999. **Equity Capital Needed:** $213,400-$337,800. **Franchise Fee:** $25,000. **Training:** Yes.

18132 ■ Flamers Charbroiled
F.C.I. Food Group
500 S 3rd St.
Jacksonville Beach, FL 32250
Ph: (904)241-3737
Fax: (904)241-1301
Description: Gourmet hamburgers and chicken. **No. of Franchise Units:** 78. **No. of Company-Owned Units:** 6. **Founded:** 1987. **Franchised:** 1987. **Equity Capital Needed:** $164,000-$263,500. **Franchise Fee:** $30,000. **Training:** Yes.

18133 ■ Flying Biscuit
Raving Brands
1718 Peachtree St. NW, Ste. 1070
Atlanta, GA 30309
Ph: (404)351-3500
URL: http://www.flyingbiscuit.com
Description: Open for breakfast, lunch and dinner. Menu features a variety of healthy and hearty dishes. **No. of Franchise Units:** 3. **No. of Company-Owned Units:** 2. **Founded:** 1993.. **Franchised:** 2005. **Equity Capital Needed:** $750,000 net worth; $200,000 liquid. **Franchise Fee:** $25,000. **Training:** Raving Brands University classroom and onsite training provided.

18134 ■ Fox and Fiddle Corporation
44 Upjohn Rd.
Toronto, ON, Canada M3B 2W1
Ph: (416)385-7705
Fax: (416)385-1718
URL: http://www.foxandfiddle.com
Description: The franchise offers a perfect mix of high quality food and meal preparation, great entertainment, bar genius and friendly fun atmosphere. **No. of Franchise Units:** 18. **No. of Company-Owned Units:** 2. **Founded:** 1981.. **Franchised:** 1999. **Equity Capital Needed:** $500,000-$1,000,000. **Franchise Fee:** $40,000. **Training:** Yes.

18135 ■ Fresh City
Fresh City Franchising, LLC
145 Rosemary St., Ste. F
Needham, MA 02494
Ph: (781)453-0200
Fax: (781)453-8686
Description: Fresh, fast, and casual. **No. of Franchise Units:** 4. **No. of Company-Owned Units:** 9. **Founded:** 1997.. **Franchised:** 2002. **Equity Capital Needed:** $1,750,000. **Franchise Fee:** $30,000. **Training:** Yes.

18136 ■ Friendly's Restaurants Franchise LLC
Friendly Ice Cream Corp.
1855 Boston Rd.
Wilbraham, MA 01095
Ph: (413)543-2400
Free: 800-576-8088
Fax: (413)543-2820
Description: Full service restaurant with ice cream treats. **No. of Franchise Units:** 239. **No. of Company-Owned Units:** 253. **Founded:** 1935.. **Franchised:** 1997. **Equity Capital Needed:** $147,600-$1,979,350. **Franchise Fee:** $15,000-$35,000. **Royalty Fee:** 4%. **Financial Assistance:** Limited third party financing available. **Training:** Provides 12 weeks training and ongoing support.

18137 ■ Frisch's Restaurants, Inc.
Elias Brothers
2800 Gilbert Ave.
Cincinnati, OH 45206
Ph: (513)559-5304
Description: Family restaurant with drive-thru. **No. of Franchise Units:** 39. **No. of Company-Owned Units:** 103. **Founded:** 1947.. **Franchised:** 1953. **Equity Capital Needed:** $1,000,000-$150,000 liquid. **Franchise Fee:** $30,000. **Training:** Yes.

18138 ■ Fuddruckers, Inc.
Magic Restaurants
5700 Mopac Expy. S, Ste. C300
Austin, TX 78749
Ph: (512)275-0421
Fax: (512)275-0670
Description: Upscale restaurant that serves fresh ground beef patties from on-premises butcher shop and freshly baked buns from on-premises bakery. Breast of chicken, fish fillet, hot dogs, salads, fries, onion rings, fresh cookies, brownies, pies, milk shakes and beverages with unlimited refills are also available. **No. of Franchise Units:** 99. **No. of Company-Owned Units:** 113. **Founded:** 1980.. **Franchised:** 1983. **Equity Capital Needed:** $740,000-$1,500,000 total investment; $1,500,000 net worth, $550,000 cash liquidity. **Franchise Fee:** $50,000. **Royalty Fee:** 5%. **Training:** Provides 6 week training program with ongoing support.

18139 ■ Genghis Grill - The Mongolian Stir Fry
Genghis Grill Franchise Concepts, LP
The Centre Bldg. 7
4099 McEwen, Ste. 305
Dallas, TX 75244
Ph: (214)774-4240
Free: 888-GEN-GHIS
Fax: (214)774-4243
Description: Full service restaurant and bar. **No. of Franchise Units:** 49. **No. of Company-Owned Units:** 45. **Franchised:** 2001. **Equity Capital Needed:** $315,000-$740,000. **Franchise Fee:** $30,000. **Royalty Fee:** 5%. **Financial Assistance:** Third party financing available. **Training:** Yes.

18140 ■ Golden Chick
Golden Franchising Corp.
1131 Rockingham Dr., Ste. 250
Richardson, TX 75080
Ph: (972)831-0911
Fax: (972)831-0401
Description: Quick service chicken restaurant. **No. of Franchise Units:** 94. **No. of Company-Owned Units:** 6. **Founded:** 1967.. **Franchised:** 1972. **Equity Capital Needed:** $150,000. **Franchise Fee:** $25,000. **Training:** Yes.

18141 ■ Golden Corral Buffet & Grill
Investors Management Corp.
5151 Glenwood Ave.
Raleigh, NC 27612
Ph: (919)881-4479
Free: 800-284-5673
Fax: (919)881-5252
Co. E-mail: abagwell@goldencorral.net
URL: http://www.goldencorralfranchise.com
Description: Family Style restaurant specializing in steaks, chicken, and seafood. **No. of Franchise Units:** 376. **No. of Company-Owned Units:** 103. **Founded:** 1973.. **Franchised:** 1986. **Equity Capital Needed:** $2,500,000 net worth; $500,000 liquid. **Franchise Fee:** $50,000. **Training:** Offers 2 weeks training at headquartes, 8 weeks at company training location and ongoing support.

18142 ■ Golden Griddle Family Restaurants
Golden Griddle Corporation
305 Milner Ave., Ste. 900
Toronto, ON, Canada M1B 3V4
Ph: (416)609-2200
Fax: (416)609-2207
Co. E-mail: jmoyer@goldengriddlecorp.com
URL: http://www.goldengriddlecorp.com
Description: A family food franchise serving breakfast, dining and meals for all occasions. **No. of Franchise Units:** 22. **No. of Company-Owned Units:** 3. **Founded:** 1964.. **Franchised:** 1976. **Equity Capital Needed:** $100,000-$500,000; $40,000 start-up capital required. **Franchise Fee:** $25,000. **Training:** 4-6 weeks training and ongoing support included.

18143 ■ Grampa's Catfish House
1020 Airport Rd.
Hot Springs, AR 71913-4616
Ph: (501)767-2299

Fax: (501)834-3611
Description: Catfish, seafood & Southern foods. **No. of Franchise Units:** 2. **No. of Company-Owned Units:** 2. **Founded:** 1970. **Franchised:** 2005. **Equity Capital Needed:** $121,000-$234,000. **Franchise Fee:** $25,000. **Royalty Fee:** $300/week. **Training:** Includes 2 weeks training at headquarters, 2 weeks at franchisee's location and ongoing support.

18144 ■ Grandy's,
Souper Brands, Inc.
4004 Belt Line Rd., Ste. 160
Addison, TX 75001
Ph: (972)434-9225
Fax: (972)434-9244
Description: Quick service restaurant. **No. of Franchise Units:** 65. **No. of Company-Owned Units:** 5. **Founded:** 1973.. **Franchised:** 1977. **Equity Capital Needed:** $150,000 capital; $350,000 net worth. **Franchise Fee:** $29,500. **Training:** Yes.

18145 ■ The Great Canadian Bagel Ltd
1270 Central Pkwy. W, Ste. 303
Mississauga, ON, Canada L5C 4P4
Ph: (905)566-1903
Fax: (905)566-1402
URL: http://www.greatcanadianbagel.com
Description: Alternative to fast foods. The Great Canadian Bagel (TGCB) is a healthy way to enjoy a sandwich, snack or meals. TGCB is aggressively pursuing non-production/nontraditional locations: office buildings, malls, hospitals, etc. **No. of Franchise Units:** 47. **No. of Company-Owned Units:** 3. **Founded:** 1993.. **Franchised:** 1994. **Equity Capital Needed:** $250,000 investment required; $125,000 start-up capital required. **Franchise Fee:** $20,000. **Training:** 3 weeks and ongoing support provided.

18146 ■ The Great Steak & Potato Co.
Nicar Franchising Inc.
9311 E Via De Ventura
Scottsdale, AZ 85258
Ph: (480)362-4800
Fax: (480)505-0910
Co. E-mail: franchiseinfo@thegreatsteak.com
URL: http://www.kahalacorp.com
Description: Specializing in cheese steaks, grilled sandwiches, fries, and fresh squeezed lemonade offers the flexibility of operating as inline mall units, in mall food courts, airports, strip centers and freestanding units. **No. of Franchise Units:** 122. **No. of Company-Owned Units:** 1. **No. of Operating Units:** 135. **Founded:** 1985.. **Franchised:** 1986. **Equity Capital Needed:** $146,150-$554,750. **Franchise Fee:** $30,000. **Royalty Fee:** 6%. **Financial Assistance:** Limited third party financing available. **Training:** Offers 2 week training program at headquarters, onsite training the first 2 weeks, and ongoing support at existing locations as needed.

18147 ■ Great Wraps!
4 Executive Park E, Ste. 315
Atlanta, GA 30329
Ph: (404)248-9900
Fax: (404)248-0180
Description: Fast-food franchisor operating in major regional mall food courts. Serves hot, grilled, pita-wrapped sandwiches with beef and lamb, steak and cheese, fresh vegetables and strips of chicken breast, plus fresh salads, such as Greek and Caesar, fries and soft drinks. **No. of Franchise Units:** 98. **No. of Company-Owned Units:** 1. **Founded:** 1978.. **Franchised:** 1983. **Equity Capital Needed:** $225,000-$350,000 total investment; $70,000 liquid. **Franchise Fee:** $22,500. **Training:** Yes.

18148 ■ Hamburger Mary's Bar & Grille
Hamburger Mary's International, LLC
8288 Santa Monica Blvd.
West Hollywood, CA 90046
Ph: (949)729-8000
Free: 888-834-6279
Fax: (949)675-9979
Description: Full service bar and restaurants. **No. of Franchise Units:** 14. **No. of Company-Owned Units:** 1. **Founded:** 1972. **Franchised:** 1998. **Equity Capital Needed:** Purchase price, liquor license and

improvements; approximately $225,000-$1,250,000. **Franchise Fee:** $50,000. **Royalty Fee:** 5%/month. **Training:** Yes.

18149 ■ Hardee's
CKE Restaurants, Inc.
100 N Broadway, Ste. 1200
St. Louis, MO 63102
Free: 866-253-7655
Description: Fast-food restaurants featuring hamburgers and related products. Hands-on and classroom training are provided. Managerial assistance is offered. **No. of Franchise Units:** 1,227. **No. of Company-Owned Units:** 469. **Founded:** 1961. **Franchised:** 1962. **Equity Capital Needed:** $1,085,000-$1,583,500. **Franchise Fee:** $35,000. **Royalty Fee:** 4%. **Financial Assistance:** Limited third party financing available. **Training:** Provides training at franchisee's location, 8 weeks management training, and at grand opening with ongoing support.

18150 ■ Harvey's
Cara Operations Limited
199 Four Valley Dr.
Vaughan, ON, Canada L4K 0B8
Ph: (905)760-2244
Free: 888-854-4402
Fax: (866)230-9355
Co. E-mail: Franchising@cara.com
URL: http://www.harveys.ca
Description: New traditional, free standing restaurants serving excellent charbroiled hamburger. **No. of Franchise Units:** 231. **No. of Company-Owned Units:** 19. **Founded:** 1959.. **Franchised:** 1962. **Equity Capital Needed:** $550,000-$950,000 total investment; $200,000-$350,000 start-up capital required. **Franchise Fee:** $25,000. **Training:** Provides 10 weeks of training.

18151 ■ Hero Certified Burgers
78 Signet Dr., Ste. 201
Toronto, ON, Canada M9L 1T2
Ph: (416)740-2304
Fax: (416)740-5398
Co. E-mail: franchise@heroburgers.com
URL: http://www.heroburgers.com
Description: Our goal is to deliver the best tasting food and the highest quality service in a clean environment for a fair price. Our commitment to quality ensures that all our burgers are from natural free-range beef and hormone-free and antibiotic-free, cooked medium-well. **No. of Franchise Units:** 40. **Founded:** 2003.. **Franchised:** 2003. **Equity Capital Needed:** $125,000 start-up capital; $250,000-$280,000 investment required. **Franchise Fee:** $125,000. **Training:** Provides 4 weeks training.

18152 ■ The Honeybaked Ham Co. and Cafe
The HBH Franchise Co. LLC
3875 Mansell Rd.
Alpharetta, GA 30022
Ph: (678)966-3254
Free: 866-968-7424
Fax: (678)966-3134
URL: http://www.honeybakedonline.com
Description: Specialty retailer of high quality spiral-sliced hams and turkeys. **No. of Franchise Units:** 183. **No. of Company-Owned Units:** 280. **Founded:** 1957.. **Franchised:** 1998. **Equity Capital Needed:** $350,000 net worth with $100,000 available as equity contribution. **Franchise Fee:** $30,000. **Training:** Comprehensive 14 day program at corporate training store.

18153 ■ Hooters of America, Inc.
1815 The Exchange
Atlanta, GA 30339
Ph: (770)951-2040
Fax: (770)933-9464
Description: Business of restaurant and food delivery services. **No. of Franchise Units:** 210. **No. of Company-Owned Units:** 90. **Founded:** 1985.. **Franchised:** 1988. **Equity Capital Needed:** $800,000. **Franchise Fee:** $75,000. **Training:** Yes.

18154 ■ Howard Johnson

Wyndham Hotel Group
22 Sylvan Way
Parsippany, NJ 07054
Free: 888-222-7484
Description: Licensor of Howard Johnson guest lodging facilities. **No. of Franchise Units:** 500+. **Founded:** 1954.. **Franchised:** 1954. **Equity Capital Needed:** Varies depending upon project. **Franchise Fee:** $10,000 minimum; $100/room. **Training:** Yes.

18155 ■ Huddle House

Huddle House, Inc.
5901-B Peachtree Dunwoody Rd., Ste. 450
Atlanta, GA 30328
Ph: (770)325-1300
Free: 800-868-5700
Fax: (770)394-1970
Co. E-mail: franchiseinfo@huddlehouse.com
URL: http://www.huddlehouse.com
Description: Twenty-four hour fastfood restaurants featuring breakfast items, steaks, sandwiches, and seafood. **No. of Franchise Units:** 400. **No. of Company-Owned Units:** 13. **Founded:** 1964.. **Franchised:** 1966. **Equity Capital Needed:** $100,000 cash; $200,000-$750,000 total investment; $25,000 franchising fee. **Franchise Fee:** $25,000. **Training:** 7 week performance-based program covering all aspects of operations. Ongoing support in operations and field support.

18156 ■ Hudson's Grill of America, Inc.

16970 Dallas Pky., Ste. 402
Dallas, TX 75248
Ph: (972)931-9237
Fax: (972)931-1326
Description: Offers a limited bar-and-grill type menu in a casual family dining atmosphere. Lunch and dinner are featured with a full-service bar available. **No. of Franchise Units:** 17. **No. of Company-Owned Units:** 2. **Founded:** 1985.. **Franchised:** 1985. **Equity Capital Needed:** $125,000 start-up cash; $500,000 total investment required. **Franchise Fee:** $25,000. **Financial Assistance:** Yes. **Training:** Yes.

18157 ■ HuHot Mongolian Grill

223 E Main St.
Missoula, MT 59802
Ph: (406)251-4303
Fax: (406)327-1232
URL: http://www.huhot.com
Description: Mongolian grill restaurant. **No. of Franchise Units:** 38. **No. of Company-Owned Units:** 6. **Founded:** 1999.. **Franchised:** 2002. **Equity Capital Needed:** $777,000-$977,000. **Franchise Fee:** $35,000. **Royalty Fee:** 5%. **Financial Assistance:** Third party financing available. **Training:** Provides 3 weeks training at headquarters and ongoing support.

18158 ■ Humpty's Restaurants International Inc.

2505 Macleod Trl. S
Calgary, AB, Canada T2G 5J4
Ph: (403)269-4675
Fax: (403)266-1973
Co. E-mail: info@humptys.com
URL: http://www.humptys.com
Description: Full-service family restaurant open 24 hours a day. Stir fry to gourmet burgers available along with award-winning breakfast menu. **No. of Franchise Units:** 47. **No. of Company-Owned Units:** 3. **Founded:** 1977.. **Franchised:** 1986. **Equity Capital Needed:** $495,000-$695,000. **Franchise Fee:** $25,000. **Training:** Provides 7 weeks of training.

18159 ■ Indigo Joe's Sports Pub & Restaurant

Neighborhood Sports Pub Concepts, Inc.
23412 Moulton Pky., Ste. 131
Laguna Hills, CA 92653
Free: 888-303-5637
Fax: (949)457-3541
Description: Neighborhood sports pub and restaurant. **No. of Franchise Units:** 36. **No. of Company-Owned Units:** 1. **Founded:** 1994.. **Franchised:** 2003. **Equity Capital Needed:** $300,000 liquid. **Franchise Fee:** $30,000. **Training:** Yes.

18160 ■ Izzo's Illegal Burrito

422 Pinewold Dr.
Houston, TX 77056
Ph: (713)965-8108
Fax: (225)706-7001
Description: Fast-casual Mexican food. **No. of Franchise Units:** 2. **No. of Company-Owned Units:** 4. **Founded:** 2001.. **Franchised:** 2006. **Equity Capital Needed:** $544,500-$859,100. **Franchise Fee:** $40,000. **Royalty Fee:** 5%. **Training:** Includes 12 days training at headquarters, 7 days onsite and ongoing support.

18161 ■ Jerry's Subs and Pizza

Jerry's Systems, Inc.
15942 Shady Grove Rd.
Gaithersburg, MD 20877
Free: 800-990-9176
Fax: (301)948-3508
Description: Fresh-dough pizza and stuffed submarine sandwiches, served in upscale retail outlets, featuring take-out service and self-service dining. **No. of Franchise Units:** 135. **No. of Company-Owned Units:** 3. **Founded:** 1954.. **Franchised:** 1981. **Equity Capital Needed:** $250,000-$350,000. **Franchise Fee:** $25,000. **Royalty Fee:** 6%. **Financial Assistance:** Limited third party financing available. **Training:** Available 5 weeks at headquarters.

18162 ■ Joey's Only Seafood Restaurant

514-42 Ave., SE
Calgary, AB, Canada T2G 1Y6
Ph: (403)243-4584
Free: 800-661-2123
Fax: (403)243-8989
Co. E-mail: rob@joeysonly.ca
URL: http://www.joeys.ca
Description: Full-service mid-casual family style seafood restaurant. **No. of Franchise Units:** 100. **No. of Company-Owned Units:** 3. **Founded:** 1985.. **Franchised:** 1992. **Equity Capital Needed:** $80,000 minimum Streetside; $180,000 minimum Full Service. **Franchise Fee:** $25,000. **Training:** Offers 5 week training program.

18163 ■ Johnny Rockets Group Inc.

20 Enterprise., Ste. 300
Aliso Viejo, CA 92656
Ph: (949)643-6100
Free: 866-209-9523
Fax: (949)643-6200
Co. E-mail: franchisesales@johnnyrockets.com
URL: http://www.johnnyrockets.com
Description: Hamburger malt shop. **No. of Franchise Units:** 199. **No. of Company-Owned Units:** 26. **Founded:** 1986.. **Franchised:** 1987. **Equity Capital Needed:** $545,525-$986,575. **Franchise Fee:** $49,000. **Royalty Fee:** 5%. **Training:** Offers 4 weeks at certified training store with ongoing support.

18164 ■ Jugo Juice

416 Meridian Rd. SE, Ste. A8
Calgary, AB, Canada T2A 1X2
Ph: (403)207-5850
Free: 877-377-5846
Fax: (403)207-5875
Co. E-mail: contact@jugojuice.com
URL: http://www.jugojuice.com
Description: Offers premiere made to order smoothies and juices supplemented with signature food items such as wraps and salads. **No. of Franchise Units:** 142. **Founded:** 1998.. **Franchised:** 2002. **Equity Capital Needed:** $80,000-$350,000. **Franchise Fee:** $25,000. **Training:** Yes.

18165 ■ Just Fresh Franchise Systems Inc.

Just Fresh Enterprises, Inc.
8040 Arrowridge Rd.
Charlotte, NC 28273
Ph: (704)992-1818
Fax: (704)992-5699
Co. E-mail: info@justfresh.com
URL: http://www.justfresh.com
Description: Fast-casual restaurant franchise. Just Fresh capitalizes on the multiple trends of juice, gourmet coffee, bagels and premium quality, made-to-order sandwiches, salads, pizza and soup. **No. of Franchise Units:** 7. **No. of Company-Owned Units:** 7. **Founded:** 1993.. **Franchised:** 2004. **Equity**

Capital Needed: $500,000-$675,000. **Franchise Fee:** $25,000. **Royalty Fee:** 5%. **Training:** Provides 3 weeks training at headquarters and ongoing support.

18166 ■ Keg Restaurants Ltd.

10100 Shellbridge Way
Richmond, BC, Canada V6X 2W7
Ph: (604)276-0242
Fax: (604)276-2681
Co. E-mail: thekeg@kegrestaurants.com
URL: http://www.kegsteakhouse.com
Description: Steakhouse restaurant leader. **No. of Franchise Units:** 54. **No. of Company-Owned Units:** 33. **No. of Operating Units:** 100. **Founded:** 1971.. **Franchised:** 1974. **Equity Capital Needed:** $3,000,000-$4,500,000. **Franchise Fee:** $50,000. **Training:** Provides 2 weeks training.

18167 ■ Kelly's Cajun Grill Franchise Corp.

4104 Aurora St.
Coral Gables, FL 33146-1416
Ph: (305)476-1611
Fax: (305)476-9622
Description: Cajun restaurant. **No. of Franchise Units:** 74. **No. of Company-Owned Units:** 40. **Founded:** 1991.. **Franchised:** 1996. **Equity Capital Needed:** $250,000-$500,000. **Franchise Fee:** $30,000. **Training:** Yes.

18168 ■ KFC Canada

Yum! Restaurants International Company, Canada
101 Exchange Ave.
Vaughan, ON, Canada L4K 5R6
Ph: (416)664-5200
Free: 800-268-5435
Fax: (416)739-0118
Co. E-mail: franchisecanada@yum.com
URL: http://www.yumfranchises.ca
Description: Chicken restaurants selling both on and off-the-bone chicken products with fries and salads. **No. of Franchise Units:** 670. **Founded:** 1954.. **Equity Capital Needed:** $400,000-$1,200,000. **Franchise Fee:** $46,900 U.S. funds. **Training:** Yes.

18169 ■ The Krystal Co.

One Union Sq.
Chattanooga, TN 37402
Free: 800-458-5912
Fax: (423)757-1550
Co. E-mail: jschmidt@krystalco.com
URL: http://www.krystal.com
Description: Fast food hamburger concept, offering proven, destination-oriented products. Restaurants are open 24 hours. **No. of Franchise Units:** 185. **No. of Company-Owned Units:** 246. **Founded:** 1932.. **Franchised:** 1990. **Equity Capital Needed:** $525,000-$625,000 per restaurant. **Franchise Fee:** $32,500. **Training:** Provide in the restaurant training, computer training at home office. Also, provides area directors in the field to assist with business.

18170 ■ La Salsa

CKE Restaurants, Inc.
6307 Carpinteria Ave., Ste. A
Carpinteria, CA 93103
Ph: (805)745-7842
Free: 866-253-7655
Fax: (714)780-6320
Description: Fast and casual dining. **No. of Franchise Units:** 41. **No. of Company-Owned Units:** 54. **Founded:** 1979.. **Franchised:** 1989. **Equity Capital Needed:** Minimum of $200,000 liquid and $800,000 net worth per store w/3 store commitment. **Franchise Fee:** First-third $20,000. **Training:** Yes.

18171 ■ Le Muffin Plus

2464 Jean-Talon East
Montreal, QC, Canada H2E 1W2
Ph: (514)281-2067
Fax: (514)281-6405
Co. E-mail: info@cafedepot.ca
URL: http://www.muffinplus.com
Description: Specializing in healthy sandwiches, salads, muffins, and hot meals. **No. of Franchise Units:** 21. **No. of Company-Owned Units:** 2. **Founded:** 1984.. **Equity Capital Needed:** $100,000 start-up capital required; $150,000 investment required. **Franchise Fee:** $25,000. **Training:** Yes.

18172 ■ The Lion And Rose Pub
The Lion and Rose Franchise, Ltd.
PO Box 27313
San Antonio, TX 78227
Ph: (210)798-5301
Co. E-mail: franchise@thelionandrose.com
URL: http://www.thelionandrose.com
Description: Offers an opportunity to own and oper-
ate your own business. Currently looking for qualified
franchise owner/operators in Texas and the near
southwest U.S. **No. of Company-Owned Units:** 5.
Founded: 2004.. **Franchised:** 2006. **Equity Capital
Needed:** $337,000-$1,172,500 estimated start-up
costs, excluding liquor license cost or real estate
costs. **Franchise Fee:** $50,000. **Royalty Fee:** 5%.
Training: Access to operations manuals, unique
recipes, operational systems, vendor relations and
training materials with ongoing support from team of
managers and staff.

18173 ■ The Little Dooey Barbeque & Blues
16930 W Catawba Ave., Ste. 102
Cornelius, NC 28031
Ph: (704)895-2512
Fax: (704)895-2432
Description: Barbecue restaurant. **No. of Franchise
Units:** 1. **No. of Company-Owned Units:** 3.
Founded: 1985.. **Franchised:** 2004. **Equity Capital
Needed:** $928,000-$1,600,000. **Franchise Fee:**
$35,000. **Royalty Fee:** 5%. **Training:** Available 4
weeks at headquarters, 2 weeks at franchisee's loca-
tion and ongoing support.

18174 ■ Long John Silver's
Yum! Brands Inc.
1900 Colonel Sanders Ln.
Louisville, KY 40213-1914
Ph: (800)544-5774
Co. E-mail: info@yum.com
URL: http://www.yum.com
Description: Seafood chain in the fish and seafood
segment. Offers a menu of fish, seafood and chicken.
Eat-in, take-out and drive-thru. **No. of Franchise
Units:** 542. **No. of Company-Owned Units:** 760.
Founded: 1969.. **Franchised:** 1970. **Equity Capital
Needed:** Minimum net worth $400,000; Minimum
liquidity $200,000. **Franchise Fee:** $20,000 domestic.
Training: Yes.

18175 ■ Mama Fu's Asian House
Mama Fu's Franchise Group, Inc.
512 E. Riverside Dr., Ste. 250
Austin, TX 78704
Ph: (515)949-3211
Fax: (800)905-2147
Description: Pan-Asian food. **No. of Franchise
Units:** 6. **No. of Company-Owned Units:** 6.
Founded: 2002.. **Franchised:** 2003. **Equity Capital
Needed:** $150,000 liquid; $1,000,000 net worth.
Franchise Fee: $28,000/Multi unit. **Training:** Yes.

**18176 ■ Manchu Wok Inc. (Markham,
Canada)**
85 Citizen Ct., Unit 9
Markham, ON, Canada L6G 1A8
Ph: (954)427-2163
Free: 800-361-8864
Fax: (954)427-2337
Description: Oriental quick-service restaurant chains
in Canada. Operates in food courts of large regional
malls. **No. of Franchise Units:** 61. **No. of Company-
Owned Units:** 14. **Founded:** 1980.. **Franchised:**
1990. **Equity Capital Needed:** $248,000-$512,000.
Franchise Fee: $30,000. **Training:** 3 weeks real
estate, marketing, field support, and product develop-
ment included.

18177 ■ Mancino's, Samuel Italian Eatery
Nu-Ventures Inc.
1324 W Milham
Portage, MI 49024
Ph: (269)226-4400
Free: 888-432-8379
Fax: (269)226-4466
Description: Franchise of restaurants and food
delivery services of food. **No. of Franchise Units:**
38. **Founded:** 1959.. **Franchised:** 1994. **Equity
Capital Needed:** $200,000-$250,000. **Franchise
Fee:** $30,000. **Training:** Yes.

**18178 ■ Mandarin Restaurant Franchise
Corp.**
8 Clipper Ct.
Brampton, ON, Canada L6W 4T9
Ph: (905)451-4100
Fax: (905)456-3411
URL: http://www.mandarinrestaurant.com
Description: Mandarin is known for fresh and quality
food, buffet restaurant serving Chinese and Canadian
food and a-lacarte and take-out. **No. of Franchise
Units:** 20. **No. of Company-Owned Units:** 1.
Founded: 1979.. **Franchised:** 1993. **Equity Capital
Needed:** $3,000,000. **Franchise Fee:** 10% of total
construction cost. **Training:** 1-3 years and ongoing
support provided.

18179 ■ Mary Browns Inc.
250 Shield's Ct., Ste. 7
Markham, ON, Canada L3R 9W7
Ph: (905)513-0044
Fax: (905)513-0050
URL: http://www.marybrowns.com
Description: Committed in serving high quality and
innovative food items. Serves white meat chicken
filet sandwiches, mini nuggets unique to Mary
Brown's, chicken fingers, salads and our famous
hand-cut taters, all cooked in 100% canola oil. **No. of
Franchise Units:** 80. **No. of Company-Owned
Units:** 4. **Founded:** 1969. **Franchised:** 1969. **Equity
Capital Needed:** $100,000 plus investment required;
$100,000 Plus start-up capital requied. **Franchise
Fee:** $25,000. **Training:** Offers 3 weeks initial train-
ing and ongoing support.

18180 ■ McDonald's Corp.
Kroc Dr.
Oak Brook, IL 60521
Ph: (630)623-6196
Description: Food-service retailer, with restaurants
in 70 countries. 85% of franchises in the U.S. are
locally-owned and operated support. **No. of Franchise Units:** 22,591. **No. of Company-Owned
Units:** 8,180. **Founded:** 1955. **Franchised:** 1955.
Equity Capital Needed: Minimum $175,000 non-
borrowed personal resources. **Franchise Fee:**
$45,000. **Training:** Franchisees required to partici-
pate in a training and evaluation program which may,
on a part-time basis, take 2 years or longer to
complete.

**18181 ■ McDonald's Restaurants of Canada
Ltd.**
1 McDonald's Pl.
Toronto, ON, Canada M3C 3L4
Ph: (416)443-1000
Fax: (416)446-3420
Co. E-mail: mcdfranon@ca.mcd.com
URL: http://www.mcdonalds.ca/franchising
Description: McDonald's, the quick service restau-
rant provides quality service, cleanliness and value.
No. of Franchise Units: 1,136. **No. of Company-
Owned Units:** 297. **Founded:** 1967. **Franchised:**
1968. **Equity Capital Needed:** $500,000, unencum-
bered funds. **Franchise Fee:** $45,000. **Training:** Of-
fers 1-2 years training.

18182 ■ McGhin's Southern Pit Bar-B-Que
2964 N Expy.
Griffin, GA 30223
Ph: (770)229-5887
Fax: (770)229-5838
URL: http://www.southernpitbbq.com
Description: Barbecue restaurant. **No. of Franchise
Units:** 1. **No. of Company-Owned Units:** 1.
Founded: 1984. **Franchised:** 2006. **Equity Capital
Needed:** $288,000-$800,000. **Franchise Fee:**
$30,000. **Royalty Fee:** $500/week. **Training:** Pro-
vides 3 weeks training at headquarters, 1 week at
franchisee's location, and ongoing support.

18183 ■ Melting Pot Restaurants Inc.
8810 Twin Lakes Blvd.
Tampa, FL 33614-1767
Ph: (813)881-0055
Free: 800-783-0867

Fax: (813)889-9361
URL: http://www.meltingpot.com
Contact: Bob Johnston, President
Description: Offers a unique opportunity to stand
apart from the competition. Select the franchise
system that offers a unique concept, coupled with
training, education and outstanding support. **No. of
Franchise Units:** 138. **No. of Company-Owned
Units:** 4. **Founded:** 1975. **Franchised:** 1984. **Equity
Capital Needed:** $325,000-$400,000 liquid,
$886,695-$1,544,695 or more total investment. **Franchise Fee:** $45,000. **Training:** Franchisees and their
managers pay their own costs of lodging, meals and
transportation during training.

18184 ■ Mexicali Rosa's
PO Box 145
Moncton, NB, Canada E1C 8R9
Ph: (613)839-0324
Free: 877-477-3950
Fax: (613)839-0591
Co. E-mail: info@mexicalrosas.com
URL: http://www.mexicalrosas.com
Description: Authentic, California-style Mexican
Restaurants with a large emphasis on Fun, Flavour
and Integrity. Our menu features Canada's best na-
chos, hand-rolled enchiladas and tamales, sizzling
fajitas, chimichangas and Award-winning Chilis and
Margaritias. **No. of Franchise Units:** 16. **Founded:**
1977. **Franchised:** 1986. **Equity Capital Needed:**
$250,000-$800,000. **Franchise Fee:** $25,000. **Train-
ing:** Assistance with site selection, restaurant design
and construction with ongoing operational, advertising, and central purchasing support.

18185 ■ Mister Bar-B-Que
Smokey P., Inc.
1134 Grove Dr.
Rockledge, FL 32955
Ph: (321)639-0038
Free: 888-766-5399
Fax: (321)639-4318
Description: Freshly prepared barbecued meats,
fish, and burgers. **No. of Franchise Units:** 1.
Founded: 1988.. **Franchised:** 1997. **Equity Capital
Needed:** $160,000. **Franchise Fee:** $15,000. **Train-
ing:** Yes.

18186 ■ Moe's Southwest Grill
Focus Brands, Inc.
200 Glenridge Point Pky., Ste. 200
Atlanta, GA 30342
Ph: (404)255-3250
Fax: (404)255-4978
URL: http://www.carvel.com
Description: Fresh-Mex quick-service restaurant.
No. of Franchise Units: 463. **No. of Company-
Owned Units:** 4. **Founded:** 2000. **Franchised:**
2001. **Equity Capital Needed:** $450,615-$768,843.
Franchise Fee: $30,000. **Royalty Fee:** 5%. **Finan-
cial Assistance:** Third party financing available.
Training: 2 weeks at corporate headquarters, 1 week
onsite, and ongoing support included.

18187 ■ Moe's Southwest Grill
3443 Fairview St.
Burlington, ON, Canada L7N 2R4
Ph: (647)204-0877
Co. E-mail: ssilver@truenorthbrands.com
URL: http://www.moes.com
Description: Fast, casual restaurant specializing in
burritos, tacos, quesadillas, and salads. **No. of
Franchise Units:** 3. **No. of Company-Owned Units:**
1. **Founded:** 2006. **Franchised:** 2006. **Equity
Capital Needed:** $300,000-$500,000; Express/kiosk
option available. **Franchise Fee:** $25,000. **Royalty
Fee:** 5%. **Training:** Includes 2 weeks initial training
at headquarters, 1 week at franchisee's location and
ongoing support.

18188 ■ Montana Mike's Steakhouse
Stockade Franchising, LP
2908 N Plum St.
Hutchinson, KS 67502-8400
Ph: (620)669-9372

Fax: (620)669-0531
Description: Casual dining full service steakhouse. **No. of Franchise Units:** 21. **Founded:** 1998.. **Franchised:** 1998. **Equity Capital Needed:** $1,000,000 net worth; $250,000 liquid assets. **Franchise Fee:** $20,000. **Training:** Yes.

18189 ■ Mr. Goodcents Subs & Pastas
Mr. Goodcents Franchise Systems, Inc.
8997 Commerce Dr.
DeSoto, KS 66018
Ph: (913)583-8400
Free: 800-648-2368
Fax: (913)583-3500
Co. E-mail: frandev@mrgoodcents.com
URL: http://www.mrgoodcents.com
Description: Quick service restaurant serving lunch and dinner featuring submarine sandwiches with fresh meat and cheese on bread. **No. of Franchise Units:** 100. **No. of Company-Owned Units:** 1. **Founded:** 1989.. **Franchised:** 1990. **Equity Capital Needed:** $75,000. **Franchise Fee:** $20,000. **Training:** 30 days of comprehensive in-house training.

18190 ■ Mr. Greek Mediterranean Grill
Mr. Greek Mediterranean Grill
44 Upjohn Rd
Toronto, ON, Canada M3B 2W1
Ph: (416)444-3266
Free: 888-674-7355
Fax: (416)444-3484
Co. E-mail: Vicki.raios@mrgreek.com
URL: http://www.mrgreek.com
Description: Full service restaurant, take out, food court. **Founded:** 1988.. **Training:** Offers 10 weeks training with ongoing support.

18191 ■ Mr. Greek Rxpress
Mr. Greek Mediterranean Grill
44 Upjohn Rd
Toronto, ON, Canada M3B 2W1
Ph: (416)444-3266
Free: 888-674-7355
Fax: (416)444-3484
Co. E-mail: Vicki.raios@mrgreek.com
URL: http://www.mrgreek.com
Description: Mr. Greek Express is a quick-service restaurant concept with a limited menu of the most popular specialty dishes of the Mr. Greek Mediterranean Grill franchise, as well as some dishes available only at the Mr. Greek Express locations. The Express units are counter-service restaurants offering seating and take-out and, where possible, drive-through facilities. Great Food, Served Fast. The Mr. Greek Express is an outstanding business opportunity for highly motivated, customer-oriented individuals who have the desire to succeed. **No. of Franchise Units:** 18. **No. of Company-Owned Units:** 2. **Founded:** 1988.. **Franchised:** 1993. **Equity Capital Needed:** $160,000 start-up capital required; $350,000-$500,000 capital required. **Franchise Fee:** $35,000. **Training:** Offers 10 weeks training and ongoing support.

18192 ■ Mr. Hero Restaurants
Restaurant Developers Corp.
7010 Engle Rd., Ste. 100
Middleburg Heights, OH 44130
Free: 888-860-5082
Description: Specialty sandwiches & fast food. **No. of Franchise Units:** 103. **No. of Company-Owned Units:** 7. **Founded:** 1965.. **Franchised:** 1970. **Equity Capital Needed:** $113,000-$305,000. **Franchise Fee:** $18,000. **Royalty Fee:** 5.5%. **Training:** Offers 4 weeks at headquarters, 1 week at franchisees location with ongoing support.

18193 ■ Mr. SUB
2 East Beaver Creek Rd., Bldg.1
Richmond Hill, ON, Canada I4B 2N3
Ph: (905)764-7066
Free: 800-668-7827
Fax: (905)764-8426
Co. E-mail: info@mtgroup.com
URL: http://www.mtygroup.com
Description: Submarine restaurants serving fresh food like subs, wraps, soups, salads and a variety of beverages. **No. of Franchise Units:** 322. **Founded:**

1968.. **Franchised:** 1971. **Equity Capital Needed:** $175,000-$500,000 investment required. **Franchise Fee:** $25,000. **Training:** Yes.

18194 ■ Mucho Burrito
2187 Dunwin Dr.
Mississauga, ON, Canada L5L 1X2
Ph: (905)820-7887
Free: 888-729-7482
Fax: (905)820-8448
URL: http://www.muchoburrito.com
Description: Restaurant. **No. of Franchise Units:** 50. **Founded:** 2006.. **Franchised:** 2006. **Equity Capital Needed:** Start-up capital varies; $212,800$547,100+/- investment required. **Franchise Fee:** $25,000. **Training:** At least 4 (four) to 5 1/2 weeks training.

18195 ■ Nando's Flame Grilled Chicken
13931 Sparwood Pl., Unit 130
Richmond, BC, Canada V6V 1X2
Ph: (604)303-0881
Fax: (604)303-0882
Co. E-mail: askus@nandoscanada.com
URL: http://www.nandoscanada.com
Description: Dining restaurant specialist in flame grilled chicken, expanded across the world. **No. of Franchise Units:** 28. **No. of Company-Owned Units:** 1. **Founded:** 1994.. **Franchised:** 1999. **Equity Capital Needed:** $700,000. **Franchise Fee:** $35,000. **Training:** Provides full training.

18196 ■ Nathan's
Nathan's Famous Systems, Inc.
1 Jericho Plz.
Jericho, NY 11753
Ph: (516)338-8500
Fax: (516)338-7220
Description: Offers a large variety of menu items, all-beef frankfurters and fresh-cut French fries in a contemporary atmosphere. Offers 8 different prototypes, ranging from countertop modular to free-standing restaurants. **No. of Franchise Units:** 297. **No. of Company-Owned Units:** 6. **Founded:** 1916.. **Franchised:** 1989. **Equity Capital Needed:** $50,000-$200,000 liquid. **Franchise Fee:** $30,000-$37,500. **Training:** Yes.

18197 ■ New England Hot Dog Company, LLC
100 Commings Ctr., Ste. 231G
Beverly, MA 01907
Ph: (978)922-5105
Fax: (978)922-0750
Description: Gourmet hot dog and ice cream restaurant. **No. of Company-Owned Units:** 1. **Founded:** 2004.. **Franchised:** 2005. **Equity Capital Needed:** $135,000-$250,000. **Franchise Fee:** $30,000. **Royalty Fee:** 6%. **Financial Assistance:** Limited third party financing available. **Training:** Available at headquarters for 2 weeks followed by 4 weeks at franchisees location and ongoing support.

18198 ■ Nothing But Noodles
9383 E. Bahia Suite 100
Scottsdale, AZ 85260
Ph: (480)513-7008
Fax: (480)513-7989
Description: Noodles, pasta, and salads. **No. of Franchise Units:** 33. **No. of Company-Owned Units:** 1. **Founded:** 2001.. **Franchised:** 2002. **Equity Capital Needed:** $352,400-$441,800. **Franchise Fee:** $25,000. **Royalty Fee:** 6%.

18199 ■ O'Charley's Restaurants
O'Charley's Inc.
3038 Sidco Dr.
Nashville, TN 37204-4506
Ph: (615)256-8500
Fax: (615)782-5043
Co. E-mail: info@ocharleys.com
URL: http://www.ocharleys.com
Description: Casual dining, with emphasis on cuisine and service. **No. of Franchise Units:** 7. **No. of Company-Owned Units:** 230. **Founded:** 1973.. **Franchised:** 2002. **Equity Capital Needed:** $3,000,000 net worth. **Franchise Fee:** $50,000. **Training:** Yes.

18200 ■ Off the Grill Franchising, LLC
1728 General George Patton Dr., Ste. 200
Brentwood, TN 37027
Ph: (615)370-0700
Fax: (615)371-1405
Description: Carry out and delivery; steaks, burgers, and chicken. **No. of Franchise Units:** 13. **No. of Company-Owned Units:** 2. **Founded:** 1999.. **Franchised:** 1999. **Equity Capital Needed:** $250,000. **Franchise Fee:** $25,000. **Training:** Yes.

18201 ■ Orange Julius Canada Limited
5045 S Service Rd., Ste. 3000
Burlington, ON, Canada L7R 3Y3
Ph: (905)637-4741
Fax: (905)681-3623
URL: http://www.orangejulius.com
Description: Snack and drink franchise of North America easily accessible for pedestrians. **No. of Franchise Units:** 56. **Founded:** 1930.. **Franchised:** 1940. **Equity Capital Needed:** $100,000 plus. **Franchise Fee:** $30,000. **Training:** Yes.

18202 ■ Otter's Chicken Tenders
1110 Gilmore Ave.
Nashville, TN 37204
Ph: (615)832-7501
Fax: (615)523-1489
Description: Chicken tenders. **No. of Company-Owned Units:** 2. **Founded:** 2003.. **Franchised:** 2006. **Equity Capital Needed:** $291,500-$429,000. **Franchise Fee:** $30,000. **Royalty Fee:** 5%. **Training:** Includes 4-6 weeks training at headquarters, 1 week onsite and ongoing support.

18203 ■ Panchero's Mexican Grill
Panchero's Franchise Corp.
2475 Coral Ct., Ste. B
Coralville, IA 52241
Ph: (319)545-6565
Free: 888-MEX-BEST
Fax: (319)545-6570
Description: Mexican food. **No. of Franchise Units:** 29. **No. of Company-Owned Units:** 21. **Founded:** 1992.. **Franchised:** 2004. **Equity Capital Needed:** Net worth $750,000; liquid $250,000. **Franchise Fee:** $30,000. **Training:** Yes.

18204 ■ The Pantry Restaurants
1812 152 St., Ste. 203
Surrey, BC, Canada V4A 4N5
Ph: (604)536-4111
Fax: (604)536-4103
URL: http://www.RAMMP.net
Description: Pantry Hospitality Corp. is a restaurant, which focuses mainly on prime rib, certified angus beef steaks, with an assortment of seafood and pasta dishes. **No. of Franchise Units:** 15. **No. of Company-Owned Units:** 1. **Founded:** 1975.. **Franchised:** 1977. **Equity Capital Needed:** $500,000-$700,000. **Franchise Fee:** $50,000. **Training:** 6 weeks and ongoing support provided.

18205 ■ Pepe's Inc.
Pepe's, Inc.
1325 W 15th St.
Chicago, IL 60608
Ph: (312)733-2500
Contact: Robert Ptak, President
Description: Full-service Mexican restaurant franchise, featuring a full range of Mexican items, including beer, wine and liquor. **No. of Franchise Units:** 50. **Founded:** 1967. **Franchised:** 1967. **Equity Capital Needed:** $75,000-$200,000. **Franchise Fee:** $15,000. **Training:** Yes.

18206 ■ The Perfect Pita
The Perfect Pita, LLC
3193 S Stafford St.
Arlington, VA 22206
Free: 866-856-PITA
Fax: (703)549-0740
Description: Homemade Mediterranean carryout restaurant. **No. of Company-Owned Units:** 3. **Founded:** 1994.. **Franchised:** 2004. **Equity Capital Needed:** $162,000-$423,000. **Franchise Fee:** $15,000. **Training:** Yes.

18207 ■ Perkins Restaurant & Bakery

The Restaurant Co.
6075 Poplar Ave., Ste. 800
Memphis, TN 38119
Ph: (901)766-6400
Free: 800-877-7375
Fax: (901)766-6482
Description: Full-service, family-style restaurants offering breakfast, lunch and dinner entrees. More than half of the restaurants feature signature bakery. **No. of Franchise Units:** 300. **No. of Company-Owned Units:** 163. **Founded:** 1958.. **Franchised:** 1958. **Equity Capital Needed:** $500,000 liquid; $1,500,000 net. **Franchise Fee:** $20,000. **Training:** Yes.

18208 ■ The Philly Connection

Franchise Junction, LLC
Description: Fast-food franchise, specializing in Philly cheese steaks, hoagies and salads. **No. of Franchise Units:** 130. **No. of Company-Owned Units:** 1. **Founded:** 1984.. **Franchised:** 1987. **Equity Capital Needed:** $154,000-$261,500. **Franchise Fee:** $18,500. **Royalty Fee:** 6%. **Financial Assistance:** Limited third party financing available. **Training:** Provides 80 hours at training facility and ongoing support.

18209 ■ Pizza Delight

774 Main St., Ste. 400
Moncton, NB, Canada E1C 9Y3
Ph: (506)853-0990
Fax: (506)853-4131
URL: http://www.pizzadelight.com
Description: Family restaurants, specialists in pizza, pasta, salads and rotisserie chicken with delivery services too. **No. of Franchise Units:** 96. **Founded:** 1968.. **Franchised:** 1969. **Equity Capital Needed:** $100,000-$150,000 unencumbered equity. **Franchise Fee:** $15,000-$30,000. **Training:** Offers 3-4 weeks of training.

18210 ■ Pizza Hut Canada

Yum! Restaurants International Company, Canada
101 Exchange Ave.
Vaughan, ON, Canada L4K 5R6
Ph: (416)664-5200
Free: 800-268-5435
Fax: (416)739-0118
Co. E-mail: franchisecanada@yum.com
URL: http://www.yumfranchises.ca
Description: Restaurant specialized in pan pizza, thin crust pizza, pastas, garlic bread and salads. **No. of Franchise Units:** 323. **Founded:** 1958.. **Equity Capital Needed:** Delto - $350,000-$490,000 investment required. **Franchise Fee:** $23,450 U.S. Funds. **Training:** Yes.

18211 ■ Pizza Ranch, Inc.

204 19th St. SE
Orange City, IA 51041
Ph: (712)707-8800
Free: 800-321-3401
Fax: (712)707-8825
Description: Pizza and chicken restaurant. **No. of Franchise Units:** 166. **No. of Company-Owned Units:** 1. **Founded:** 1981.. **Franchised:** 1984. **Equity Capital Needed:** $660,000-$1,691,000. **Franchise Fee:** $30,000. **Training:** Yes.

18212 ■ Pluckers Wing Bar

MD Pluckers Franchising L.P.
811 Barton Springs Rd., Ste. 520
Austin, TX 78704
Ph: (512)236-9110
Fax: (512)236-9113
Description: Chicken wings, hamburgers, cheesesteaks and more. **No. of Franchise Units:** 2. **No. of Company-Owned Units:** 1. **Founded:** 1995.. **Franchised:** 2000. **Equity Capital Needed:** $70,000-$225,000. **Franchise Fee:** $18,000. **Training:** Yes.

18213 ■ Popeyes Chicken & Biscuits

AFC Enterprises Inc.
5555 Glendridge Connector NE, Ste. 300
Atlanta, GA 30342

Ph: (404)459-4450
URL: http://www.afce.com
Description: Fast-food chicken restaurant specializing in cajun-style dishes. Serves authentic red beans and rice, spicy chicken, mashed potatoes and gravy and many other cajun-style side dishes. **No. of Franchise Units:** 1,533. **No. of Company-Owned Units:** 37. **No. of Operating Units:** 1,612. **Founded:** 1972.. **Franchised:** 1976. **Equity Capital Needed:** $292,300-$442,100 total investment; $500,000 net worth, $250,000 liquid cash. **Franchise Fee:** $30,000. **Royalty Fee:** 5%. **Financial Assistance:** Third party financing available. **Training:** Popeyes Operations Management Training (OMT) Program must be attended by up to four management employees prior to the opening of a restaurant. The OMT Program covers an extensive range of subjects related to the operation of a restaurant. This 6 week program indoctrinates employee of job station areas and restaurant administration management, application of job skills and techniques, and classroom materials needed in the management of a restaurant.

18214 ■ Port of Subs

Port-of-Subs Inc.
5365 Mae Anne Ave, Ste. A-29
Reno, NV 89523-1841
Ph: (775)747-0555
Free: 800-245-0245
Fax: (775)747-1510
Co. E-mail: jwallace@portofsubs.com
URL: http://www.portofsubs.com
Description: Submarine sandwich franchise, featuring unique front-line method of preparing specialty sandwiches, soups, salads and party platters. Bread is baked fresh daily on premises. **No. of Franchise Units:** 115. **No. of Company-Owned Units:** 25. **Founded:** 1972.. **Franchised:** 1985. **Equity Capital Needed:** $80,000 liquid assets, $250,000 net worth. **Franchise Fee:** $20,000. **Training:** Offers 2 weeks of training, plus 2 weeks in the franchisee's unit during initial opening.

18215 ■ Prime Restaurants of Canada Inc.

Prime Restaurant Group Inc.
10 Kingsbridge Garden Cir., Ste. 600
Mississauga, ON, Canada L5R 3K6
Ph: (905)568-0000
Free: 800-361-3111
Fax: (905)568-0080
Co. E-mail: franchising@primerestaurants.com
URL: http://www.primerestaurants.com
Description: The pub has achieved "total value" by "raising the bar" in terms of food quality, service entertainment and decor. **No. of Franchise Units:** 147. **No. of Company-Owned Units:** 7. **Founded:** 1980.. **Franchised:** 1982. **Equity Capital Needed:** $300,000-$640,000 start-up; $750,000-$1,600,000 total investment. **Franchise Fee:** $40,000-$50,000.

18216 ■ Qdoba Mexican Grill

Qdoba Restaurant Corp.
4865 Ward Rd., Ste. 500
Wheat Ridge, CO 80033
Ph: (720)898-2300
Fax: (720)898-2396
Description: Specialist in Mexican food. **No. of Franchise Units:** 490. **No. of Company-Owned Units:** 147. **Founded:** 1995.. **Franchised:** 1997. **Equity Capital Needed:** $2,000,000 net worth; $500,000 liquid. **Franchise Fee:** $30,000. **Training:** Yes.

18217 ■ Quizno's Subs

The Quizno's Corp.
1001 17th St., Ste. 175
Denver, CO 80202-2212
Ph: (720)359-3300
Free: 800-335-4782
Description: Italian deli theme, specializing in subs, soups, salads and pasta. **No. of Franchise Units:** 2,772. **No. of Company-Owned Units:** 62. **Founded:** 1981.. **Franchised:** 1991. **Equity Capital Needed:** $157,547-$217,527, estimated initial investment for new store. **Franchise Fee:** $5,000-$12,500. **Financial Assistance:** Yes. **Training:** Twenty two day training program includes classroom and in-store training. Grand opening and initial onsite assistance.

18218 ■ Rally's Hamburgers

Checkers Drive-In Restaurants Inc.
4300 W Cypress St., Ste. 600
Tampa, FL 33607
Ph: (813)283-7000
Free: 800-800-8072
Fax: (813)283-7208
Co. E-mail: fumiat@checkers.com
URL: http://www.checkers.com
Description: Double drive-thru burgers, fries, and cola. **No. of Franchise Units:** 378. **No. of Company-Owned Units:** 98. **Founded:** 1985.. **Franchised:** 1986. **Equity Capital Needed:** $472,100-$644,100 (excludes land). **Franchise Fee:** $30,000. **Financial Assistance:** Yes. **Training:** Yes.

18219 ■ Ranch 1 Grilled Chicken

9311 E Via De Ventura
Scottsdale, AZ 85258
Ph: (866)452-4252
Description: Grilled & fried chicken quick service restaurant. **No. of Franchise Units:** 15. **Founded:** 1991. **Franchised:** 1993. **Equity Capital Needed:** $148,400-$518,300. **Franchise Fee:** $30,000. **Royalty Fee:** 6%. **Financial Assistance:** Limited third party financing available. **Training:** Provides 1 week training at headquarters, 2 weeks at franchisee's location, and ongoing support.

18220 ■ Rice King

Rice King Foods, Inc.
8396 Vickers St., Ste. 205
San Diego, CA 92111
Ph: (858)505-8677
Free: 800-418-4421
Fax: (858)505-8668
Description: Asian fast food restaurant. **No. of Franchise Units:** 35. **No. of Company-Owned Units:** 3. **Founded:** 1982.. **Franchised:** 1996. **Equity Capital Needed:** $174,000-$382,000. **Franchise Fee:** $13,000. **Financial Assistance:** Yes. **Training:** Yes.

18221 ■ Ricky's All Day Grill

1901 Rosser Ave., Ste. 401
Burnaby, BC, Canada V5C 6S3
Ph: (604)637-7272
Free: 888-597-7272
Fax: (604)637-8874
Co. E-mail: franchising@rickysr.com
URL: http://www.rickysfranchise.com
Description: Offers awesome, affordable meals for breakfast, lunch and dinner. **No. of Franchise Units:** 65. **No. of Company-Owned Units:** 4. **Founded:** 1960.. **Franchised:** 1978. **Equity Capital Needed:** $650,000-$950,000 investment required; $350,000 start-up capital required. **Franchise Fee:** $45,000. **Training:** Complete hands-on-training and strong support.

18222 ■ Rockin'Baja Lobster

Rockin'Baja Lobster, LLC
19712 MacArthurs Blvd., Ste. 210
Irvine, CA 92612
Ph: (949)719-3800
Free: 877-762-2252
Fax: (949)721-4053
Description: Baja cantina and grill. **No. of Company-Owned Units:** 40. **Founded:** 1992.. **Franchised:** 2003. **Equity Capital Needed:** $240,400-$1,200,000. **Franchise Fee:** $30,000. **Royalty Fee:** 5%. **Training:** Provides 2 weeks training at headquarters and ongoing support.

18223 ■ Rockwell's Grill & Bar

1812 152nd St., Ste. 203
Surrey, BC, Canada V4A 4N5
Ph: (604)536-4111
Fax: (604)536-4103
URL: http://www.RAMP.net
Description: Casual full service dining. **No. of Franchise Units:** 3. **Founded:** 2001.. **Franchised:** 2001. **Equity Capital Needed:** $900,000-$1,200,000. **Franchise Fee:** $50,000. **Training:** Provides 6 weeks training and ongoing support.

18224 ■ Rollerz

Kahala Corp.
9311 E Via De Ventura
Scottsdale, AZ 85258
Ph: (480)362-4800
Free: 800-438-2590
Fax: (480)443-1972
Description: Fast foods restaurant that offers delivery service too. **No. of Franchise Units:** 7. **Founded:** 1999.. **Franchised:** 1999. **Equity Capital Needed:** $143,400-$441,300. **Franchise Fee:** $30,000. **Royalty Fee:** 6%. **Financial Assistance:** Limited third party financing available. **Training:** Provides 1 week at headquarters, 2 weeks at franchisee's location and ongoing support.

18225 ■ Ronzio Pizza

Ronzio Management, Inc.
111 John St.
Lincoln, RI 02865
Ph: (401)334-9750
Fax: (401)312-0378
Description: Pizza & sub shops. **No. of Franchise Units:** 21. **Founded:** 1986.. **Franchised:** 1992. **Equity Capital Needed:** $250,000 net worth; $136,500-$207,500 total investment. **Franchise Fee:** $15,000. **Training:** Yes.

18226 ■ Roy Rogers Restaurants

Roy Rogers Franchise Company, LLC
321 Ballenger Center Dr., Ste. 201
Fredrick, MD 21703
Ph: (301)695-8563
Fax: (301)695-5066
Description: Quick service restaurant. **No. of Franchise Units:** 36. **No. of Company-Owned Units:** 17. **Founded:** 1968.. **Franchised:** 2003. **Equity Capital Needed:** $915,250-$1,472,250. **Franchise Fee:** $30,000. **Training:** Yes.

18227 ■ St. Louis Bar and Grill

St. Louis Franchise Limited
2040 Yonge St., Ste. 200B
Toronto, ON, Canada M4S 1Z9
Ph: (416)485-1094
Free: 866-674-0606
Fax: (416)480-1512
Co. E-mail: kathy@stlouisfranchise.com
URL: http://www.stlouiswings.com
Description: 20 year history in the bar and restaurant industry in owner-operated locations. **No. of Franchise Units:** 34. **No. of Company-Owned Units:** 2. **Founded:** 1992.. **Franchised:** 2002. **Equity Capital Needed:** 400,000-$600,000 investment required; $250,000 minimum. **Franchise Fee:** $40,000. **Training:** Yes.

18228 ■ Salad Creations

Lett-Us Franchise, LLC
4171 W Hillsboro Blvd., Ste. 4
Coconut Creek, FL 33073
Ph: (954)590-2467
Fax: (954)590-2484
URL: http://www.saladcreations.net
Description: 'Fresh is fabulous!' at Salad Creations, a growing franchise offering selections that fit the needs & wants of educated consumers in an exciting, welcoming environment. Consumers are always seeking healthful alternatives to traditional fast food. Along with our menu of healthful & tasty choices, we invite our guests to create meals with the assistance of enthusiastic & service focused 'salad chefs.'. **No. of Franchise Units:** 81. **No. of Company-Owned Units:** 1. **Founded:** 2002.. **Franchised:** 2003. **Equity Capital Needed:** $75,000-$225,000. **Franchise Fee:** $25,000. **Training:** Yes.

18229 ■ Saladworks LLC

Eight Tower Bridge
161 Washington St., Ste. 300
Conshohocken, PA 19428
Ph: (610)825-3080
Fax: (610)825-3280
Description: Restaurant franchise, meeting the drive-in, carryout and delivery requirements of the customers. **No. of Franchise Units:** 100. **No. of Company-Owned Units:** 4. **Founded:** 1986.. **Franchised:** 1991. **Equity Capital Needed:** $350,000

liquid, $1,000,000 net worth; $381,150-$698,400 estimated investment per location. **Franchise Fee:** $35,000. **Financial Assistance:** Yes. **Training:** Yes.

18230 ■ Salsarita's Fresh Cantina

Salsarita's Inc.
2908 Oak Lake Blvd., Ste. 205
Charlotte, NC 28208
Ph: (704)540-9447
Fax: (704)540-9448
Description: Fresh Mexican in a cantina atmosphere. **No. of Franchise Units:** 16. **Founded:** 2000.. **Franchised:** 2000. **Equity Capital Needed:** $125,000 liquid; $350,000 net worth. **Franchise Fee:** $20,000. **Training:** Yes.

18231 ■ Sammy J. Peppers Restaurant & Lounge

1075 Lougheed Hwy.
Coquitlam, BC, Canada V3K 6N5
Ph: (604)524-1422
Fax: (604)525-0745
Co. E-mail: eat@sammyjs.ca
URL: http://www.sammyjs.ca
Description: We offer an extensive, unique and bold menu with an upbeat and energetic atmosphere in our restaurants. Peppers and spices are very dominant in our menu offerings. We are a casual family restaurant with an entertainment lounge area. We currently have 5 locations in BC. Franchise opportunities are available throughout BC and Alberta. We are also seeking sites in the USA. **No. of Company-Owned Units:** 5. **Founded:** 1996.. **Franchised:** 2004. **Equity Capital Needed:** $750,000-$1,500,000. **Franchise Fee:** $50,000. **Training:** Offers 4-6 weeks training in Vancouver, BC.

18232 ■ Sawmill Prime Rib & Steak House

4810 Calgary Trl. South, 2nd Fl.
Edmonton, AB, Canada T6H 5H5
Ph: (780)463-4499
Fax: (780)463-3183
URL: http://www.sawmillrestaurant.com
Description: Offers fine dining and formal service in a comfortable atmosphere. Serving only "AAA" Alberta Beef, an extensive salad shrimp and oyster bar, as well as an array of seafood, chicken, bison and lamb. Adjoining pub/patio has lighter menu. **No. of Franchise Units:** 4. **No. of Company-Owned Units:** 2. **Founded:** 1976.. **Franchised:** 2004. **Equity Capital Needed:** $1,500,000. **Franchise Fee:** $50,000. **Training:** Yes.

18233 ■ Sbarro The Italian Eatery

401 Broadhollow Rd.
Melville, NY 11747
Ph: (631)715-4148
Free: 800-456-4837
Fax: (516)715-4193
Co. E-mail: franchise@sbarro.com
URL: http://www.sbarro.com
Description: Italian eateries. **No. of Company-Owned Units:** 280. **Founded:** 1959.. **Franchised:** 1977. **Equity Capital Needed:** $250,000-$850,000 liquid capital over $150,000, additional in high cost areas. **Franchise Fee:** $15,000-45,000. **Royalty Fee:** 7%. **Training:** Yes.

18234 ■ Scores Rotisserie & Ribs

8250 Decarie Blvd., Ste. 310
Montreal, QC, Canada H4P 2P5
Ph: (514)341-5544
Free: 866-341-9782
Fax: (514)341-5635
URL: http://www.scores.ca
Description: Casual dining concept featuring Rotisserie Chicken, BBQ Ribs and an "ALL YOU CAN EAT" salad and soup bar. **No. of Franchise Units:** 42. **Founded:** 1995.. **Franchised:** 1996. **Equity Capital Needed:** $700,000-$950,000 investment required; $280,000-$450,000 start-up capital required. **Franchise Fee:** $60,000, includes training. **Training:** Provides 8 weeks training.

18235 ■ Seattle Sutton's Franchise Corp.

611 E Stevenson Rd.
Ottawa, IL 61350
Ph: (888)795-6135

Fax: (815)795-3493
Description: Manufacturing freshly prepared healthy meals. **No. of Franchise Units:** 5. **No. of Company-Owned Units:** 1. **Founded:** 1996. **Equity Capital Needed:** $5,000,000 franchise kitchen; $500,000 distributorship. **Franchise Fee:** $35,000. **Training:** Yes.

18236 ■ Select Sandwich Co.

Select Food Services, Ltd.
155 Gordon Baker Rd., Ste. 214
Toronto, ON, Canada M2H 3N5
Ph: (416)391-1244
Free: 866-567-5648
Fax: (416)391-5244
URL: http://www.selectsandwich.com
Description: An established brand leader operating quick-service gourmet sandwich restaurants. Now expanding nationally. **No. of Franchise Units:** 23. **Founded:** 1979.. **Franchised:** 1980. **Equity Capital Needed:** $125,000-$150,000 start-up capital required; $250,000-$300,000 investment required. **Franchise Fee:** $25,000. **Training:** Offers 6 weeks training.

18237 ■ Shakey's Pizza & Buffet

Shakey's USA, Inc.
2200 W Valley Blvd.
Alhambra, CA 91803
Ph: (626)576-0616
Free: 888-444-6686
Fax: (626)284-6870
URL: http://www.shakeys.com
Description: The franchise offers food service, well-known for a variety of pizza. **No. of Franchise Units:** 35. **No. of Company-Owned Units:** 25. **Equity Capital Needed:** $500,000 liquid per unit. **Franchise Fee:** $35,000. **Training:** Yes.

18238 ■ Shane's Rib Shack

Petrus Brands
1425 Ellsworth Industrial Blvd. NW, Ste. 38
Atlanta, GA 30318
Ph: (404)856-4320
Fax: (404)856-4334
URL: http://www.shanesribshack.com
Description: Fast casual concept specializes in choice cut pork BBQ, baby back ribs, crispy chicken tenders, homemade side items and made from scratch peach cobbler. **No. of Franchise Units:** 64. **No. of Company-Owned Units:** 2. **Founded:** 2002. **Franchised:** 2005. **Equity Capital Needed:** $500,000 net worth; $150,000 liquid. **Franchise Fee:** $30,000. **Training:** Raving Brands University classroom and onsite training provided. From register operation to food preparation, from hiring staff to accounting procedures, you'll improve your management skills, setup your back office and develop airtight sales and marketing plan.

18239 ■ Shoeless Joe's Limited

8555 Jane St., Unit 201
Vaughan, ON, Canada L4K 5N9
Ph: (905)760-1295
Fax: (905)760-1296
Co. E-mail: franchising@shoelessjoes.ca
URL: http://www.shoelessjoes.ca
Description: The franchise offers restaurant and bar service with a North American sports theme. **No. of Franchise Units:** 34. **No. of Company-Owned Units:** 2. **Founded:** 1985.. **Franchised:** 1987. **Equity Capital Needed:** $350,000-$450,000 start-up capital required; $650,000-$950,000 total investment. **Franchise Fee:** $45,000. **Training:** Provides 8 weeks training and ongoing support.

18240 ■ Silver Mine Subs

8010 S County Rd. 5, Unit 203
Fort Collins, CO 80528
Ph: (970)266-2600
Fax: (970)267-3538
Description: Is a food franchise with restaurant, drive-in, carryout and delivery facilities. **No. of Franchise Units:** 20. **No. of Company-Owned Units:** 1. **Founded:** 1996. **Franchised:** 2002. **Equity Capital Needed:** $212,850-$321,350. **Franchise Fee:** $12,500-$20,000. **Training:** Yes.

18241 ■ Sizzler USA Franchise, Inc.
Sizzler USA Inc.
6101 W Centinga Ave., Ste. 300
Culver City, CA 90230
Ph: (310)846-8750
Fax: (310)848-8794
Description: Casual restaurant dining. **No. of Franchise Units:** 170. **Founded:** 1958.. **Franchised:** 1963. **Equity Capital Needed:** $1,300,000-$2,500,000 total investment. **Training:** Yes.

18242 ■ Smitty's
Smitty's Canada Ltd.
501 18th Ave. SW, Ste. 600
Calgary, AB, Canada T2S 0C7
Ph: (403)229-3838
Fax: (403)229-3899
Co. E-mail: franchiseinquiry@smittys.ca
Description: Restaurants providing a full menu, which comprises breakfast, lunch, and dinner items. Even though experts in pancakes, waffles, and eggs, Smitty's franchises offers sandwiches and burgers and include liquor service during hours. **No. of Franchise Units:** 100. **No. of Company-Owned Units:** 5. **Founded:** 1960. **Franchised:** 1960. **Equity Capital Needed:** $150,000 cash. **Franchise Fee:** $35,000 plus GST. **Training:** Yes.

18243 ■ Sonic Drive In Restaurants
Sonic Corp.
300 Johnny Bench Dr.
Oklahoma City, OK 73104
Ph: (405)225-5000
Free: 800-569-6656
Fax: (405)225-5963
Description: Drive-in fast-food restaurant offering hamburgers, hot dogs, French fries and onion rings. **No. of Franchise Units:** 3,005. **No. of Company-Owned Units:** 438. **Founded:** 1954.. **Franchised:** 1959. **Equity Capital Needed:** $1,112,300-$3,002,700. **Franchise Fee:** $45,000. **Royalty Fee:** 2-5%. **Financial Assistance:** Third party financing available. **Training:** Provides 1 week training at headquarters, 11 weeks onsite, 1 day to 1 week additional training with ongoing support.

18244 ■ Soul Fixins' Restaurant
Soul Fixins Franchise Corp. LLC
225 W 28th St.
New York, NY 10001
Ph: (212)736-1345
Description: Soul food restaurant. **No. of Franchise Units:** 1. **Founded:** 1993.. **Franchised:** 2004. **Equity Capital Needed:** $274,000-$524,000. **Franchise Fee:** $30,000. **Royalty Fee:** 5%. **Training:** Includes training at headquarters, franchisee's location and ongoing.

18245 ■ The Steak Escape
Escape Enterprises, Ltd.
222 Neilston St.
Columbus, OH 43215
Ph: (614)224-0300
Fax: (614)224-6460
Description: Specialty restaurant for grilled sandwiches, salads, freshly cut French fries. **No. of Franchise Units:** 101. **No. of Company-Owned Units:** 8. **Founded:** 1982.. **Franchised:** 1983. **Equity Capital Needed:** Grill: $350,000 net worth, $100,000 cash; Express: $175,000 net worth $50,000 cash. **Franchise Fee:** $15,000-$25,000. **Training:** Yes.

18246 ■ Steak N Shake
The Steak N Shake Co.
36 S Pennsylvania, Ste. 500
Indianapolis, IN 46204
Ph: (317)633-4100
Fax: (317)655-7317
Description: A restaurant offering quick-seared steak burgers, thin French fries, genuine chili and hand dipped milk shakes. Offers drive-thru and take-out service, in an environment reminiscent of the 50's. **No. of Franchise Units:** 79. **No. of Company-Owned Units:** 414. **Founded:** 1934. **Franchised:** 1939. **Equity Capital Needed:** $1,500,000 net worth; $500,000 liquid. **Franchise Fee:** $40,000 classic; $25,000 signature. **Training:** Provides on-the-job training program, utilizing personal instructions, training videos and workbooks.

18247 ■ Steak-Out Charbroiled Delivery
Steak-Out Franchising, Inc.
3091 Governors Lake Dr., Ste. 500
Norcross, GA 30071
Ph: (678)533-6000
Free: 877-878-3257
Fax: (678)291-0222
Co. E-mail: jmccord@steakout.com
URL: http://www.steakout.com
Description: Full meal delivery chain featuring charbroiled steaks, chicken, seafood, burgers, chef salads & deserts. Steak-Out serves the busy office worker that doesn't have time to go for lunch & the on-the-go family that needs a wholesome meal when there is no time to cook. Steak-Out features delivery, carry-out & catering. **No. of Franchise Units:** 42. **No. of Company-Owned Units:** 2. **Founded:** 1986.. **Franchised:** 1987. **Equity Capital Needed:** $100,000 liquid / $400,000 net worth. **Franchise Fee:** $30,000. **Financial Assistance:** Yes. **Training:** Training is 4 weeks in the store and at headquarters for 3 to 4 management employees. Complete support in site finding, store opening, marketing and ongoing.

18248 ■ Strings Italian Cafe/Strings Italian Express
Strings Franchises Inc.
11344 Coloma Rd., Ste. 545
Gold River, CA 95670
Ph: (916)635-3990
Fax: (916)631-9775
Description: It is a franchise of Italian restaurants. **No. of Franchise Units:** 15. **No. of Company-Owned Units:** 3. **Founded:** 1987.. **Franchised:** 1989. **Equity Capital Needed:** $159,500-$385,700. **Franchise Fee:** $37,500. **Training:** Yes.

18249 ■ Suki Hana & Chicken Connection
International Restaurant Management Group
4104 Aurora St.
Coral Gables, FL 33146-1416
Ph: (305)476-1611
Fax: (305)476-9622
Description: A restaurant providing Japanese-style food. **No. of Franchise Units:** 6. **No. of Company-Owned Units:** 16. **Founded:** 1989.. **Franchised:** 1998. **Equity Capital Needed:** $240,500-$507,000. **Franchise Fee:** $30,000. **Training:** Yes.

18250 ■ Sunset Grill
5100 Erin Mills Town Centre
Mississauga, ON, Canada L5M 5A7
Ph: (905)286-5833
Fax: (905)829-1142
Co. E-mail: info@sunsetgrill.ca
URL: http://www.sunsetgrill.ca
Description: Sunset Grill, Famous all-day Breakfast. Toronto's favorite breakfast restaurant franchising a one-shift breakfast concept. **No. of Franchise Units:** 85. **No. of Company-Owned Units:** 5. **Founded:** 1985. **Franchised:** 2003. **Equity Capital Needed:** $150,000-$200,000 start-up capital; $450,000 investment required. **Franchise Fee:** $50,000. **Training:** Offers training before and after opening.

18251 ■ Supper Thyme USA
Supper Thyme USA Franchise Services
7102 S 141st St.
Omaha, NE 68137
Ph: (402)933-4521
Fax: (402)614-5900
Description: Homemade meal preparation service. **No. of Franchise Units:** 31. **Founded:** 2003.. **Franchised:** 2004. **Equity Capital Needed:** $130,900-$238,500. **Franchise Fee:** $35,000. **Training:** Yes.

18252 ■ Sweet Peppers Deli
Sweet peppers Franchise Systems, LLC
PO Box 1368
Columbus, OH 39703
Ph: (662)327-6982
Free: 888-222-9550
Fax: (662)327-1672
Description: Fast casual, deli-style restaurant. **No. of Franchise Units:** 14. **No. of Company-Owned Units:** 5. **Founded:** 1984. **Franchised:** 2002. **Equity Capital Needed:** $200,000. **Franchise Fee:** $25,000. **Training:** Yes.

18253 ■ Taco Bell Canada
Tricon Global Restaurants Inc., Canada
101 Exchange Ave.
Vaughan, ON, Canada L4K 5R6
Ph: (416)664-5200
Free: 800-268-5435
Fax: (416)739-0118
Co. E-mail: franchisecanada@yum.com
URL: http://www.yumfranchises.com
Description: Offers quick-service Mexican-style food specializing in tacos, burritos, nachos and fries. **No. of Franchise Units:** 56. **Founded:** 1962.. **Franchised:** 1996. **Equity Capital Needed:** $400,000-$1,200,000. **Franchise Fee:** $46,900 U.S. **Training:** Offers 12 weeks minimum.

18254 ■ Taco Del Mar
Taco Del Mar franchising Corp.
6830 NE Bothell Way Ste. C-492
Kenmore, WA 98028
Ph: (206)624-7060
Fax: (206)624-7065
Description: Fast casual Mexican restaurant. **No. of Franchise Units:** 276. **No. of Company-Owned Units:** 1. **Founded:** 1992.. **Franchised:** 1995. **Equity Capital Needed:** $148,000-$294,000. **Franchise Fee:** $23,000. **Training:** Yes.

18255 ■ Taco John's International, Inc.
808 West 20th St.
Cheyenne, WY 82001
Ph: (307)635-0101
Fax: (307)772-0369
Description: A fast-food chain offering Mexican food. **No. of Franchise Units:** 419. **No. of Company-Owned Units:** 9. **Founded:** 1969.. **Franchised:** 1969. **Equity Capital Needed:** $150,000 liquid; $400,000 net worth. **Franchise Fee:** $22,500. **Training:** Yes.

18256 ■ The Taco Maker
PO Box 362888
San Juan, PR 00936-2888
Ph: (787)273-3160
Description: Fresh made Mexican fast food. **No. of Franchise Units:** 134. **No. of Company-Owned Units:** 4. **Founded:** 1978. **Equity Capital Needed:** Capability of financing $70,000-$255,000. **Franchise Fee:** $30,000-$35,000. **Royalty Fee:** 5%. **Training:** Yes.

18257 ■ Taco Mayo
Taco Mayo Franchise Systems, Inc.
10405 Greenbriar Pl.
Oklahoma City, OK 73159
Ph: (405)691-8226
Description: Quick service Tex-Mex restaurant. **No. of Franchise Units:** 76. **No. of Company-Owned Units:** 16. **Founded:** 1978.. **Franchised:** 1980. **Equity Capital Needed:** $100,000-$120,000, includes franchise fee. **Franchise Fee:** $15,000. **Training:** Yes.

18258 ■ Taco Palace
814 E Hwy. 60
Monett, MO 65708
Ph: (573)216-1739
Description: Mexican fast food. **No. of Franchise Units:** 8. **No. of Company-Owned Units:** 2. **Founded:** 1985. **Franchised:** 1997. **Equity Capital Needed:** $99,000-$139,000. **Franchise Fee:** $33,950. **Royalty Fee:** 0-4%. **Training:** Provides unlimited training at headquarters, 10 days at franchisee's location, and ongoing support.

18259 ■ Taco Time Canada Inc.
MTY TIKI Ming Enterprises
7156 Fisher St., SE
Calgary, AB, Canada T2H 0W5
Ph: (403)543-3490
Free: 800-471-5722
Fax: (403)543-3499
Co. E-mail: snickerson@tacotimecanada.com
URL: http://www.tacotimecanada.com
Description: Offers fast food in a friendly environment. **No. of Franchise Units:** 419. **No. of Company-Owned Units:** 3. **Founded:** 1978.. **Fran-**

chised: 1978. **Equity Capital Needed:** $200,000-$500,000. **Franchise Fee:** $30,000. **Training:** Offers 2 weeks at corporate plus onsite at opening.

18260 ■ TacoTime
Taco Time International, Inc.
9311 E Via De Ventura
Scottsdale, AZ 85258
Ph: (480)362-4800
Free: 800-547-8907
URL: http://www.tacotime.com
Description: A restaurant specializing in Mexican food. **No. of Franchise Units:** 153. **No. of Company-Owned Units:** 11. **No. of Operating Units:** 286. **Founded:** 1959.. **Franchised:** 1961. **Equity Capital Needed:** $323,400-$1,339,550. **Franchise Fee:** $30,000. **Royalty Fee:** 6%. **Financial Assistance:** Limited third party financing available. **Training:** Provides 2-4 weeks training at headquarters and ongoing support.

18261 ■ Teriyaki Experience
Made in Japan Japanese Restaurants
7420 E Mary Sharon Dr.
Scottsdale, AZ 85266
Ph: (905)337-7777
Fax: (905)337-0331
Co. E-mail: info@teriyakiexperience.com
URL: http://www.teriyakiexperience.com
Description: A fast food franchise serving in food courts of shopping centres and airports. **No. of Franchise Units:** 135. **Founded:** 1986.. **Franchised:** 1986. **Equity Capital Needed:** $180,000-$329,000 single store. **Franchise Fee:** $25,000. **Training:** Yes.

18262 ■ Teriyaki Stix
4833 N Edgewood Dr.
Provo, UT 84604
Ph: (801)224-6502
Free: 800-653-4581
Co. E-mail: franchise@hogiyogi.com
URL: http://www.hogiyogi.com
Description: Japanese fast food restaurant. **No. of Franchise Units:** 54. **No. of Company-Owned Units:** 1. **Founded:** 1995.. **Franchised:** 1998. **Equity Capital Needed:** $135,200-$452,500. **Franchise Fee:** $25,000-$30,000. **Royalty Fee:** 6%. **Training:** Provides 8 days of training at headquarters.

18263 ■ Tony Roma's, Famous for Ribs
Roma Corp. USA
1700 Alma Dr., Ste. 400
Plano, TX 75075
Ph: (214)343-7800
Free: 214-343-7840
Description: Casual restaurant, specializing in ribs. **No. of Franchise Units:** 141. **No. of Company-Owned Units:** 36. **Founded:** 1972.. **Franchised:** 1974. **Equity Capital Needed:** $350,000 liquid, per unit; $750,000 total. **Franchise Fee:** $50,000. **Training:** Yes.

18264 ■ Topper's Pizza
551 Bryne Drive, Unit N
Barrie, ON, Canada L4N 9Y3
Ph: (705)735-2127
Free: 877-558-5581
Fax: (705)735-4821
Co. E-mail: franchiseinfo@toppers.ca
URL: http://www.toppers.ca
Description: Delivers great tasting pizzas at a competitive price. **No. of Franchise Units:** 29. **No. of Company-Owned Units:** 6. **Founded:** 1982.. **Franchised:** 1984. **Equity Capital Needed:** $50,000-$100,000 start-up capital required. **Franchise Fee:** $25,000. **Training:** Offers 4-6 of training weeks.

18265 ■ Triple O's
1126 SE Marine Dr.
Vancouver, BC, Canada V5X 2V7
Ph: (604)321-6631
Fax: (604)325-1499
Co. E-mail: franchise-info@whitespot.ca
URL: http://www.tripleos.com
Description: White Spot Limited has developed a unique and proven "fast casual" concept. The Triple O's concept offers what many other quick service restaurant don't - high quality, unique tasting food made fresh, just for you. No one can beat Triple O's

taste - award-winning Triple "O" burger, fresh-cut fries and classic shakes. **No. of Franchise Units:** 48. **No. of Company-Owned Units:** 4. **Founded:** 1928. **Equity Capital Needed:** $500,000-$1,500,000 total investment. **Franchise Fee:** $40,000.

18266 ■ Tropik Sun Fruit & Nut
Diversifoods Inc.
899 Lakewood Dr.
Lakeforest, IL 60045
Ph: (847)968-4415
Description: "Fun Munchies," gifts, drinks and popcorn. **No. of Franchise Units:** 90. **No. of Company-Owned Units:** 4. **Founded:** 1980.. **Franchised:** 1980. **Equity Capital Needed:** $35,000-$50,000 liquid. **Franchise Fee:** $20,000. **Training:** Yes.

18267 ■ Tubby's Sub Shops, Inc.
30551 Edison Dr.
Roseville, MI 48066
Ph: (586)293-5099
Fax: (586)293-5088
Description: Specialty submarine sandwich shop, featuring grilled sandwiches, soups, salads and ice cream. **No. of Franchise Units:** 75. **No. of Company-Owned Units:** 2. **Founded:** 1968.. **Franchised:** 1978. **Equity Capital Needed:** $500,000 net worth; $75,000 cash/assets convertible to cash. **Franchise Fee:** $5,000-$13,000 (varies by type of store). **Training:** Classroom sessions where very facet of your business is covered. Additional onsite assistance is given just prior to opening and during your first few weeks of operation.

18268 ■ Turtle Jack's Grillhouse Restaurant Inc.
Tortoise Restaurant Group Inc.
3370 S Service Rd., Ste. 201
Burlington, ON, Canada L7N 3M6
Ph: (905)332-6833
Fax: (905)332-0456
Co. E-mail: info@tortoise.ca
URL: http://www.tortoise.ca
Description: Tortoise Restaurant Group Inc., is a Management group that owns and operates concepts under the name of Turtle Jack's. Offers consistent execution of a simple philosophy including high quality food, enthusiastic service in a clean and comfortable environment has been key to the company's success. **No. of Franchise Units:** 7. **No. of Company-Owned Units:** 5. **Founded:** 1992. **Equity Capital Needed:** $600,000. **Franchise Fee:** $50,000. **Training:** Offers 12 weeks of training.

18269 ■ Tuscano's Italian Style Subs
Noble Roman's Inc.
1 Virginia Ave., Ste. 800
Indianapolis, IN 46204
Ph: (317)634-3377
Free: 800-585-0669
Description: Subs - cold or grilled. **No. of Franchise Units:** 60. **No. of Company-Owned Units:** 6. **Founded:** 2003.. **Franchised:** 2003. **Equity Capital Needed:** $20,000-$175,000. **Franchise Fee:** $6,000-$15,000. **Training:** Yes.

18270 ■ Urban Kitchen
155 Gordon Baker Rd., Ste. 214
Toronto, ON, Canada M2H 3NP
Ph: (416)391-1244
Free: 866-567-5648
Fax: (416)391-5244
URL: http://www.urbankitchen.com
Description: Restaurant. **No. of Franchise Units:** 4. **No. of Company-Owned Units:** 1. **Founded:** 2007.. **Franchised:** 2007. **Equity Capital Needed:** $150,000-$250,000 start-up capital required; $300,000-$500,000 investment required. **Franchise Fee:** $25,000. **Training:** Provides 6 weeks training.

18271 ■ Villa Enterprises
25 Washington St.
Morristown, NJ 07960
Ph: (973)285-4800

Fax: (973)401-0121
Description: Quick service pizza & Italian restaurant. **No. of Franchise Units:** 150. **No. of Company-Owned Units:** 150. **Founded:** 1964.. **Franchised:** 1999. **Equity Capital Needed:** 100,100 liquid; $300,000 net worth. **Franchise Fee:** $25,000. **Training:** Yes.

18272 ■ Virginia Barbeque
Virginia Barbeque Franchise Co.
1814 Country Rd.
Beaverdam, VA 23105
Free: 800-429-9965
Description: Quick service "Genuine Southern" barbeque. **No. of Franchise Units:** 14. **No. of Company-Owned Units:** 2. **Founded:** 2000. **Franchised:** 2004. **Equity Capital Needed:** $81,500-$221,500. **Franchise Fee:** $25,000. **Royalty Fee:** 6%. **Training:** Provides 2 weeks at headquarters and 1 week at franchisee's location.

18273 ■ We Toss'em, They're Awesome Pizza Factory
Pizza Factory Inc.
49430 Rd. 426
Oakhurst, CA 93644
Ph: (559)683-3377
Free: 800-654-4840
Fax: (559)683-6879
Description: Pizzeria. **No. of Franchise Units:** 110. **Founded:** 1979.. **Franchised:** 1985. **Equity Capital Needed:** $137,000-$426,000. **Franchise Fee:** Full, Mid, Express $20,000. **Training:** Yes.

18274 ■ Wendy's Restaurants of Canada Inc.
240 Wyecroft Rd.
Oakville, ON, Canada L6K 2G7
Ph: (905)849-7685
Fax: (905)849-5545
Co. E-mail: jane_dann@wendys.com
URL: http://www.wendys.com
Description: Wendy's Restaurant supplies quality hamburgers, including, chicken sandwiches and nuggets, garden sensations salads, French fries, soft drinks, baked potatoes, chili, kids' meals and a fresh dairy dessert. **No. of Franchise Units:** 231. **No. of Company-Owned Units:** 138. **Founded:** 1969.. **Franchised:** 1972. **Equity Capital Needed:** $1,300,000+/-. **Franchise Fee:** $35,000. **Training:** Initial 16-26 weeks of training provided.

18275 ■ Western Sizzlin Corp.
416 S Jefferson St., Ste. 600
Roanoke, VA 24011-2009
Free: 800-247-8325
Fax: (877)329-6300
Co. E-mail: contactus@western-sizzlin.com
URL: http://www.western-sizzlin.com
Contact: Sardan Biglan, President
Description: Family style steak house, buffet and bakery. **No. of Franchise Units:** 142. **No. of Company-Owned Units:** 6. **Founded:** 1962. **Franchised:** 1966. **Equity Capital Needed:** $861,000-$2,660,000. **Franchise Fee:** $30,000. **Training:** Yes.

18276 ■ Wetzel's Pretzels
Wetzel's Pretzels, LLC
35 Hugus Alley, Ste. 300
Pasadena, CA 91103
Ph: (626)432-6900
Fax: (626)432-6904
Description: Pretzels. **No. of Franchise Units:** 253. **No. of Company-Owned Units:** 11. **Founded:** 1994.. **Franchised:** 1996. **Equity Capital Needed:** $156,300-$369,950. **Franchise Fee:** $35,000. **Royalty Fee:** 7%. **Training:** Offers 2 weeks at headquarters, 4 days at franchisee's location and ongoing support.

18277 ■ Whata Lotta Pizza
7011 Warner Ave., Unit M
Huntington Beach, CA 92647
Ph: (714)848-6148
Free: 888-425-6882

Fax: (714)849-2029
Co. E-mail: info@whatalottapizza.com
URL: http://www.4alotta.com
Description: Restaurant franchise. **No. of Franchise Units:** 50. **No. of Company-Owned Units:** 8. **Founded:** 1992.. **Franchised:** 2005. **Equity Capital Needed:** $90,000-$208,500. **Franchise Fee:** $25,000. **Training:** Yes.

18278 ■ White Spot Restaurants
1126 SE Marine Dr.
Vancouver, BC, Canada V5X 2V7
Ph: (604)321-6631
Fax: (604)325-1499
Co. E-mail: franchise-info@whitespot.ca
URL: http://www.whitespot.ca
Description: The franchise is a family restaurant and offers site and design assistance, extensive training and ongoing support and marketing expertise. **No. of Franchise Units:** 41. **No. of Company-Owned Units:** 25. **Founded:** 1928.. **Equity Capital Needed:** $750,000-$2,500,000. **Franchise Fee:** $75,000. **Training:** Offers 3-10 weeks of training, and assistance with staff and management.

18279 ■ Wienerschnitzel/Tastee-Freez
Galardi Group, Inc.
7700 Irvine Center Dr., Ste. 550
Irvine, CA 92618
Ph: (949)892-2619
Free: 800-764-9353
Fax: (949)892-2615
Co. E-mail: KPeters@GalardiGroup.com
URL: http://www.tastee-freez.com
Description: Fast food, including soft-serve ice cream and desserts. Plans available for free-standing building/food court/seasonal stores considered. **No. of Franchise Units:** 370. **Founded:** 1950.. **Franchised:** 1950. **Equity Capital Needed:** $150,000-$250,000 liquid; $1,200,000 total investment. **Franchise Fee:** $32,000. **Financial Assistance:** Yes. **Training:** Consists of 2 weeks at the corporate office - total operation and business training given.

18280 ■ Wimpy's Diner Inc.
3559 St. Clair Ave., E
Scarborough, ON, Canada M1K 1L6
Ph: (416)269-4679
Free: 888-594-6797
Fax: (416)269-8484
Co. E-mail: info@wimpysdiner.ca
URL: http://www.whimpysdiner.net
Description: Full menu Diner Style Restaurant chain with a nostalgic 50's and 60's atmosphere, serving Famous burgers, Home style breakfast, Lunch, Dinner specials and other entrees. **No. of Franchise Units:** 44. **Founded:** 1988. **Franchised:** 1992. **Equity Capital Needed:** $200,000. **Franchise Fee:** $20,000. **Training:** Provides 4-8 weeks training.

18281 ■ Wing Zone
WZ Franchise Corp.
900 Circle 75 Pkwy., Ste. 930
Atlanta, GA 30339
Ph: (404)875-5045
Free: 877-333-WING
Fax: (404)875-6631
Description: Take-Out and delivery buffalo wings. **No. of Franchise Units:** 28. **No. of Company-Owned Units:** 6. **Founded:** 1991. **Franchised:** 1999. **Equity Capital Needed:** $29,000-$189,000. **Franchise Fee:** $25,000. **Royalty Fee:** 5%. **Financial Assistance:** Yes. **Training:** Yes.

18282 ■ Winger's Grill & Bar
Winger's Franchising, Inc.
404 East 4500 S, Ste. A12
Salt Lake City, UT 84107
Ph: (801)261-3700
Fax: (801)261-1615
Description: Casual dining for smaller markets. **No. of Franchise Units:** 30. **No. of Company-Owned Units:** 9. **Founded:** 1993.. **Franchised:** 1997. **Equity Capital Needed:** $250,000 per unit. **Franchise Fee:** $30,000. **Training:** Yes.

18283 ■ Wings to Go
Wings to Go, Inc.
846 Ritchie Hwy., Ste. 1B
Severna Park, MD 21146
Free: 800-552-9464
Fax: (870)932-1795
Description: Retail restaurants, specializing in authentic buffalo-style chicken wings. **No. of Franchise Units:** 58. **Founded:** 1985.. **Franchised:** 1989. **Equity Capital Needed:** $219,500-$354,500. **Franchise Fee:** $20,000. **Training:** Yes.

18284 ■ Wingstop
Wingstop Restaurants, Inc.
1101 E Arapaho Rd., Ste. 150
Richardson, TX 75081
Ph: (972)686-6500
Fax: (972)686-6502
Co. E-mail: info@wingstop.com
URL: http://www.wingstop.com
Description: Non-vegetarian restaurant famous for buffalo-style chicken wings throughout southern United States. **No. of Franchise Units:** 475. **No. of Company-Owned Units:** 24. **Founded:** 1994.. **Franchised:** 1997. **Equity Capital Needed:** Minimum net worth: $400,000, $200,000 must be liquid; $263,550-$616,946 total investment. **Franchise Fee:** $20,000. **Financial Assistance:** Yes. **Training:** Yes.

18285 ■ Woody's Bar-B-Q
4745 Sutton Park Ct., Ste. 301
Jacksonville, FL 32224
Ph: (904)992-0556
Fax: (904)992-0551
URL: http://www.woodys.com
Description: Restaurant featuring smoked pork, beef, turkey, chicken, and barbecued ribs. **No. of Franchise Units:** 40. **No. of Company-Owned Units:** 1. **Founded:** 1980.. **Franchised:** 1989. **Equity Capital Needed:** $200,000-$300,000. **Franchise Fee:** $35,000. **Financial Assistance:** Third party financing available. **Training:** Required to attend and successfully complete Woody's 6 week franchise training program. Store opening provided by Corporate Training Team for 6 days prior to the opening date and 4 days after and ongoing operational support through field service representatives.

18286 ■ WOW Cafe & Wingery
WOW Cafe & Wingery Franchise Account L.L.C.
109 New Camellia Blvd., Ste. 200
Covington, LA 70433
Ph: (985)792-5776
Fax: (985)792-1201
Co. E-mail: information@wingery.com
URL: http://www.wowcafe.com
Description: All American Cafe. **No. of Franchise Units:** 66. **Founded:** 2001. **Franchised:** 2002. **Equity Capital Needed:** $234,400-$754,500. **Franchise Fee:** $15,000-$35,000. **Royalty Fee:** 5%. **Financial Assistance:** Third party financing available. **Training:** Provides 15 days training at headquarters, 14 days at franchisee's location and ongoing support.

18287 ■ Yaya's Flame Broiled Chicken
CSC, Inc.
521 S Dort Hwy.
Flint, MI 48503
Ph: (810)235-6550
Free: 800-754-1242
Fax: (810)235-5210
Description: Flame-broiled chicken, marinated with Yaya's special blend of herbs and spices. Side dishes include baked beans, mashed potatoes, rice pilaf, coleslaw and potato salad. No fried or frozen products. We specialize in flavor and nutrition. **No. of Franchise Units:** 10. **No. of Company-Owned Units:** 7. **Founded:** 1986. **Franchised:** 1988. **Equity Capital Needed:** $300,000-$400,000. **Franchise Fee:** $15,000. **Training:** Yes.

18288 ■ Yeung's Lotus Express Franchise Corp.
4104 Aurora St.
Coral Gables, FL 33146-1416
Ph: (305)476-1611

Fax: (305)476-9622
Description: Chinese food restaurant. **No. of Franchise Units:** 22. **No. of Company-Owned Units:** 19. **Founded:** 1987.. **Franchised:** 1998. **Equity Capital Needed:** $250,000-$500,000. **Franchise Fee:** $30,000. **Training:** Yes.

18289 ■ Yogurt & Such Cafe
Yogurt & Such Franchise Systems, Inc.
438 Woodbury Rd.
Plainview, NY 11803
Ph: (516)783-2655
Description: A foods - restaurant franchise offering drive-in, carryout and delivery services. **No. of Franchise Units:** 6. **No. of Company-Owned Units:** 3. **Founded:** 1982.. **Franchised:** 1989. **Equity Capital Needed:** $95,000-$150,000 cash required. **Franchise Fee:** $25,000. **Training:** Yes.

18290 ■ Yum! Restaurants International Company (Ontario, Canada)
101 Exchange Ave.
Vaughan, ON, Canada L4K 5R6
Ph: (416)664-5200
Free: 800-268-5435
Fax: (416)739-0118
Co. E-mail: franchisecanada@yum.com
URL: http://www.yumfranchises.ca
Description: One of the world's largest restaurant chain with 30,000 units and $30 billion annual sales. Our franchises include Pizza Hut Canada, KFC-Canada, and Taco Bell of Canada. **No. of Franchise Units:** 1,190. **Equity Capital Needed:** $400,000-$1,200,000. **Franchise Fee:** $46,900 U.S. funds. **Training:** Yes.

18291 ■ Zoo Pizza
3273 N Shepard
Milwaukee, WI 53211
Description: Pizzeria. **No. of Company-Owned Units:** 1. **Founded:** 1994.. **Equity Capital Needed:** $300,000-$400,000. **Franchise Fee:** $89,000. **Training:** No.

18292 ■ ZOUP!
Zoup! Systems LLC
28290 Franklin Rd.
Southfield, MI 48034
Ph: (248)663-1111
Free: 800-940-9687
Fax: (248)663-9880
Co. E-mail: franchise@zoup.com
URL: http://www.zoupfranchise.com
Description: Quick, casual soup restaurant. **No. of Franchise Units:** 38. **No. of Company-Owned Units:** 3. **Founded:** 1997.. **Franchised:** 2003. **Equity Capital Needed:** $327,500-$563,000. **Franchise Fee:** $39,000. **Royalty Fee:** 6%. **Financial Assistance:** Third party financing available. **Training:** Offers 3 weeks at headquarters, 1 week onsite and ongoing support.

18293 ■ Zyng Asian Grill
2801 rue de Centre, Ste. 111
Montreal, QC, Canada H3K 3C4
Ph: (514)939-8808
Fax: (514)227-5302
URL: http://www.zyng.com
Description: Offers new full-service restaurant concept with noodle-based soups and grilled meals-in-bowls. Menu includes beer and wine, with table service and jazz music. **No. of Franchise Units:** 3. **Founded:** 1998.. **Franchised:** 1999. **Equity Capital Needed:** $300,000-$500,000 investment required; $150,000 start-up capital required. **Franchise Fee:** $25,000. **Training:** Provides 4 weeks and ongoing support.

COMPUTER SYSTEMS/ SOFTWARE

18294 ■ Bottom Line Service System
6528 E 101st St., Ste. 430
PMB 145
Tulsa, OK 74133
Ph: (530)573-0777

Fax: (530)573-0772
Co. E-mail: sales@blss.com
URL: http://www.bottom-line-software.com
Price: $495 single user version; $2595 network version. **Description:** The Bottom Line Service System is a Windows based service management system designed specifically to meet the needs of customer service businesses. HVAC, Refrigeration, Plumbing, Electrical and Mechanical service and installation companies use our system with great deal of success.

18295 ■ *PayMaster Hospitality*
501 Church St., NE, Ste. 306
Vienna, VA 22180
Ph: (703)281-7486
Fax: (703)281-3461
URL: http://www.paymaster-pro.com/
Price: Computer Aid for pricing.

18296 ■ *Restaurant Financial Management System*
233 Rock Rd., No. 113
Glen Rock, NJ 07452
Ph: (201)670-9084
Free: 800-999-1159
Fax: (201)444-4595
Co. E-mail: bobrapp@compuserve.com
URL: http://www.rappind.com
Price: $495.00. **Description:** Available for IBM computers and MS-DOS compatibles. Restaurant accounting system including payroll, accounts payable, general ledger and menu costing, tip allocation, and sales entry by category.

LIBRARIES

18297 ■ American Beverage Association Information Center
1101 16th St., NW
Washington, DC 20036
Ph: (202)463-6732
Fax: (202)659-5349
Co. E-mail: info@ameribev.org
URL: http://www.ameribev.org/
Contact: Susan K. Neely, President
Scope: Beverage industry. **Services:** Library open to the public for reference use only. **Founded:** 1919. **Holdings:** 500 books, articles, papers, and historical materials. **Subscriptions:** 115 journals and other serials.

18298 ■ American Institute of Food Distribution, Inc. - Information and Research Center—The Food Institute.
1 Broadway Plaza, 2nd Fl.
Elmwood Park, NJ 07407
Ph: (201)791-5570
Fax: (201)791-5222
Co. E-mail: jkastrinsky@foodinstitute.com
URL: http://www.foodinstitute.com/
Contact: Brian Todd, President
Scope: Food industry. **Services:** Center open to the public on fee basis. **Founded:** 1928. **Subscriptions:** 400 journals and other serials. **Publications:** *Food Business Mergers and Acquisitions.* **Telecommunication Services:** food1@foodinstitute.com.

18299 ■ California Culinary Academy Library
350 Rhode Island St.
San Francisco, CA 94103
Ph: (415)771-3500
Free: 888-897-3222
Co. E-mail: bgk@baychef.com
URL: http://www.chefs.edu/San-Francisco
Scope: Culinary arts, nutrition, restaurant and hospitality industry. **Services:** Library open to the public by special appointment only. **Founded:** 1989. **Holdings:** 3500 books. **Subscriptions:** 90 journals and other serials.

18300 ■ Canadian Restaurant & Foodservices Association Resource Centre
316 Bloor St., W.
Toronto, ON, Canada M5S 1W5
Ph: (416)923-8416
Free: 800-387-5649
Fax: (416)923-1450
Co. E-mail: info@crfa.ca
URL: http://www.crfa.ca/research/
Contact: Prasanthi Vasanthakumar, Communications Specialist
Scope: Food service, quantity cooking, legislation, administration, management, statistics, training, customer attitude surveys. **Services:** Copying; center open to the public on fee basis. **Founded:** 1972. **Holdings:** 1000 books. **Subscriptions:** 100 journals and other serials. **Telecommunication Services:** research@crfa.ca.

18301 ■ City College of San Francisco - Department - Culinary Arts and Hospitality Studies Alice Statler Library
50 Phelan Ave.
Statler Wing, Rm. 10
San Francisco, CA 94112
Ph: (415)239-3460
Co. E-mail: aniosi@ccsf.edu
URL: http://www.ccsf.edu/NEW/en/library/about-library/library-locations/statler.html
Contact: Andrea Niosi, Librarian
Scope: Public hospitality industries - hotels, motels, restaurants, catering services, cookery and nutrition; tourism; beverages. **Services:** Copying; Wi-Fi; library open to the public for reference use only. **Founded:** 1964. **Holdings:** 10,000 books; 3500 pamphlets; 900 menus; videotapes; archives. **Subscriptions:** 80 journals and other serials. **Telecommunication Services:** astatler@ccsf.edu.

18302 ■ Cornell University - The Nestle Library
G80 Statler Hall
School of Hotel Administration
Ithaca, NY 14853-6901
Ph: (607)255-3673
Fax: (607)255-0021
Co. E-mail: hotelref@cornell.edu
URL: http://www.hotelschool.cornell.edu/research/library/
Contact: Donald Schnedeker, Director
Scope: Hotel, motel, and restaurant management, administration, accounting, quantity cookery, food facilities engineering, sanitation, advertising, sales promotion, public relations, marketing, hospitality law,

franchising, real estate, tourist industry, resort development. **Services:** Interlibrary loan; Library open to the public by appointment on a fee basis. **Founded:** 1922. **Holdings:** 37,000 volumes; 17,000 microforms; 500 computer files; 1000 reels of microfilm; 16,500 microfiche; 1500 videos. **Subscriptions:** 500 serials; 12 newspapers. **Telecommunication Services:** dws2@cornell.edu.

18303 ■ Culinary Institute of America - Conrad N. Hilton Library
1946 Campus Dr.
Hyde Park, NY 12538-1499
Ph: (845)452-9600
URL: http://www.ciachef.edu/newyork/library/
URL(s): library.culinary.edu/. **Scope:** Cookery, food service, restaurant management, hospitality. **Services:** Interlibrary loan; copying; Library open to the public by appointment. **Founded:** 1972. **Holdings:** 86,000 volumes; 30,000 menus; 4500 DVDs and videos. **Subscriptions:** 280 journals and other serials.

18304 ■ National Restaurant Association Information Services and Library
2055 L St., NW
Washington, DC 20036-4957
Ph: (202)331-5900
Free: 800-424-5156
Fax: (202)331-2429
URL: http://www.restaurant.org
Contact: Kathleen Walton, Manager
Scope: Foodservice industry, restaurants, cookery. **Services:** Library open to non-members and students for a fee (fee-based services available to non-members). **Founded:** 1976. **Holdings:** 5000 books; 2000 subject clipping files. **Subscriptions:** 150 journals and other serials.

18305 ■ Noble and Associates Library
2155 W. Chesterfield Blvd.
Springfield, MO 65807
Ph: (417)875-5000
Co. E-mail: julie.tumy@noble.net
URL: http://www.noble.net
Contact: Julie Tumy, President
Scope: Food, food service, advertising, construction, agriculture. **Services:** Interlibrary loan; copying; SDI; Library not open to the public. **Holdings:** 500 books; 1000 reports. **Subscriptions:** 300 journals and other serials; 5 newspapers.

18306 ■ Prince Edward Island Food Technology Centre - Information Services
PO Box 2000
Charlottetown, PE, Canada C1A 7N8
Ph: (902)368-5548
Fax: (902)368-5548
Co. E-mail: peiftc@gov.pe.ca
URL: http://www.biofoodtech.ca/
Contact: Kathy MacEwen, Library Technician
Scope: Agriculture, food, technology, food research. **Services:** Interlibrary loan; library open to the public by permission only. **Founded:** 1987. **Holdings:** 200 books; 9 bound periodical volumes. **Subscriptions:** 38 journals and other serials. **Telecommunication Services:** ftcweb@gov.pe.ca; kmmacewe@gov.pe.ca.

START-UP INFORMATION

18307 ■ *"Home Work" in Black Enterprise (Vol. 37, October 2006, No. 3, pp. 78)*
Pub: Earl G. Graves Publishing Co. Inc.
Ed: James C. Johnson. **Description:** Information on starting a resume-writing service is profiled.

ASSOCIATIONS AND OTHER ORGANIZATIONS

18308 ■ **Professional Association of Resume Writers and Career Coaches (PARW/CC)**
1388 Brightwaters Blvd. NE
St. Petersburg, FL 33704
Ph: (727)821-2274
Free: 800-822-7279
Fax: (727)894-1277
Co. E-mail: parwhq@aol.com
URL: http://www.parw.com
Contact: Frank Fox, Executive Director
Description: Represents the interests of professional resume writers, employment interview trainers, and career coaches. Acts as a clearinghouse for information on career topics. Provides educational programs. Offers certification for Certified Professional Resume Writers (CPRW) and for Certified Employment Interview Professionals (CEIP). **Founded:** 1990. **Publications:** *The Spotlight* (Monthly). **Awards:** Certified Professional Resume Writer.

REFERENCE WORKS

18309 ■ *"'Resume Mining' Services Can Save Time, Money" in HR Specialist (Vol. 8, September 2010, No. 9, pp. 7)*
Pub: Capitol Information Group Inc.
Description: Low-cost resume mining services can help human resource departments save time and money by searching online resume databases for candidates matching specific job qualifications.

18310 ■ *"Tracking Your Fleet Can Increase Bottom Line" in Contractor (Vol. 56, November 2009, No. 11, pp. 26)*
Pub: Penton Media, Inc.
Ed: Candace Roulo. **Description:** GPS fleet management system can help boost a contractor's profits, employee productivity, and efficiency. These are available as a handheld device or a cell phone that employees carry around or as a piece of hardware installed in a vehicle. These lets managers track assets and communicate with employees about jobs.

ASSOCIATIONS AND OTHER ORGANIZATIONS

18311 ■ American Subcontractors Association (ASA)
1004 Duke St.
Alexandria, VA 22314-3588
Ph: (703)684-3450
Free: 888-374-3133
Fax: (703)836-3482
Co. E-mail: asaoffice@asa-hq.com
URL: http://www.asaonline.com
Contact: Colette Nelson, Executive Vice President
Description: Construction subcontractors of trades and specialties such as foundations, concrete, masonry, steel, mechanical, drywall, electrical, painting, plastering, roofing and acoustical. Formed to deal with issues common to subcontractors. Works with other segments of the construction industry in promoting ethical practices, beneficial legislation and education of construction subcontractors and suppliers. Manages the Foundation of the American Subcontractors Association (FASA). **Founded:** 1966. **Publications:** *ASA Today; Action ASA* (Monthly); *The Contractor's Compass* (Quarterly). **Telecommunication Services:** asaoffice-hq@aol.com.

18312 ■ Asphalt Roofing Manufacturers Association (ARMA)
Public Information Department
750 National Press Bldg.
529 14th St. NW
Washington, DC 20045
Ph: (202)591-2450
Fax: (202)591-2445
Co. E-mail: info@asphaltroofing.org
URL: http://asphaltroofing.org
Contact: D. Greg Perkins, President
URL(s): www.asphaltroofing.org. **Description:** Manufacturers of asphalt shingles, rollgoods, built-up roofing systems (BUR) and modified bitumen roofing systems. Compiles statistics. **Founded:** 1915. **Publications:** *ARMA eNewsletter* (Semiannual); *Asphalt Roofing Manufacturers Association Newsletter; Guide to Preparing Build-Up Roofing Specifications* (Irregular); *Publication and Audio Visual Directory* (Biennial).

18313 ■ Canadian Roofing Contractors Association (CRCA)—Association Canadienne des Entrepreneurs en Couverture
2430 Don Reid Dr., Ste. 100
Ottawa, ON, Canada K1H 1E1
Ph: (613)232-6724
Free: 800-461-2722
Fax: (613)232-2893
Co. E-mail: crca@on.aibn.com
URL: http://www.roofingcanada.com
Contact: John E. Hill, Executive Director
Description: Roofing contractors. Seeks to advance the building industries. Facilitates communication and cooperation among members; represents members' interests before labor and industrial organizations, government agencies, and the public. **Founded:** 1959. **Publications:** *Roofing Canada* (Semiannual).

18314 ■ National Roofing Contractors Association (NRCA)
10255 W Higgins Rd., Ste. 600
Rosemont, IL 60018-5607
Ph: (847)299-9070
Free: 800-323-9545
Fax: (847)299-1183
URL: http://www.nrca.net
Contact: Bruce McCrory, President
Description: Roofing, roof deck, and waterproofing contractors and industry-related associate members. Assists members to successfully satisfy their customers through technical support, testing and research, education, marketing, government relations, and consultation. **Founded:** 1886. **Publications:** *Professional Roofing* (Monthly). **Educational Activities:** International Roofing Expo (Annual). **Awards:** Melvin Kruger Endowed Scholarship Program.

18315 ■ National Roofing Foundation (NRF)
c/o The Roofing Industry Alliance for Progress
10255 W Higgins Rd., Ste. 600
Rosemont, IL 60018-5607
Ph: (847)299-9070
Fax: (847)493-7959
Co. E-mail: bjudson@roofingindustryalliance.net
URL: http://www.nrca.net/rp/related/nrf
Contact: Geoff Craft, President
Description: Sponsors programs and projects that support the highest-quality programs for roofing contractors, ensures timely and forward-thinking industry responses to major economic and technological issues, and enhances the long-term viability and attractiveness of the roofing industry. **Founded:** 1970. **Awards:** National Roofing Scholarships (Annual); Roofing Industry Scholarship (Annual); William C. Cullen Research Fellowship (Annual).

18316 ■ Roof Coatings Manufacturers Association (RCMA)
750 National Press Bldg.
529 14th St. NW
Washington, DC 20045
Ph: (202)591-2452
Fax: (202)223-9741
Co. E-mail: questions@roofcoatings.org
URL: http://www.roofcoatings.org
Contact: Reed Hitchcock, Executive Director
Description: Corporations involved in the manufacture and distribution of cold-process protective roof coatings. Represents manufacturers and suppliers; conducts market research on the size, volume, and number of roof coating companies in the U.S.; provides financial management surveys, business studies, industry statistics, and technical information. Sponsors educational and training seminars. **Founded:** 1983. **Publications:** *Roof Coatings Manufacturers Association Membership Directory* (Annual). **Awards:** Martin Davis Award (Annual).

18317 ■ Roof Consultants Institute (RCI)
1500 Sunday Dr., Ste. 204
Raleigh, NC 27607
Ph: (919)859-0742
Free: 800-828-1902
Fax: (919)859-1328
Co. E-mail: jbirdsong@rci-online.org
URL: http://www.rci-online.org
Contact: James R. Birdsong, Chief Executive Officer
Description: Individuals organized to promote the field of roof consultation. (Roof consultants are individuals that provide advice to architects, engineers, and building owners on the latest and most appropriate technology in the roofing industry.) Maintains certification program; conducts research in roofing technology. **Founded:** 1983. **Publications:** *International Directory of Roofing Professionals; RCItems* (Monthly). **Educational Activities:** Roof Consultants Institute International Convention and Trade Show (Annual). **Awards:** H.W. Busching Memorial Scholarship; Michael DeFrancesco Award (Annual); Richard M. Horowitz Memorial Award (Annual); William C. Correll Award (Annual).

18318 ■ *Roofing Canada*
2430 Don Reid Dr., Ste. 100
Ottawa, ON, Canada K1H 1E1
Ph: (613)232-6724
Free: 800-461-2722
Fax: (613)232-2893
Co. E-mail: crca@on.aibn.com
URL: http://www.roofingcanada.com
Contact: John E. Hill, Executive Director
Released: Semiannual

18319 ■ Tile Roofing Institute (TRI)
35 E Wacker Dr., Ste. 850
Chicago, IL 60601
Ph: (312)670-4177
Fax: (312)644-8557
Co. E-mail: info@tileroofing.org
URL: http://www.tileroofing.org
Contact: Kevin Burlingame, Chairman
Description: Manufacturers and suppliers of clay and concrete roofing tiles; cement companies; mineral pigment producers; and others furnishing equipment and materials for manufacturing roof tiles. Promotes the use of "firesafe" roof construction, especially clay and concrete tile roofs; educates the architectural, design, and construction industries regarding the advantages of tile roofs; presents to the home-owning public the advantages and economies of tile roofs. Conducts international programs for architects, builders, building inspectors, and roofing contractors; provides sound/slide presentations, speakers, mailers, and specifications relating to tile roof construction. **Founded:** 1971.

REFERENCE WORKS

18320 ■ *ENR--Top 600 Specialty Contractors Issue*
Pub: McGraw-Hill Inc.
Contact: Henry Hirschberg, President
URL(s): enr.construction.com/toplists/SpecialtyContractors/001-100.asp. **Released:** Annual; latest edi-

tion 2010. **Price:** $82, Individuals yearly subscription. **Publication includes:** Lists of the 600 largest U.S. Specialty subcontractors with sub-lists of top firms in mechanical contracting (50 firms), electrical (50), excavation-foundation (20), steel erection (20), roofing (20), sheet metal (20), demolition-wrecking (20), glazing curtain wall (20), masonry (20), concrete (20), utilities (20), painting (20), wall/ceiling (20), and asbestos abatement (20). **Entries include:** Company name, headquarters location, total value of contracts received in preceding year and of foreign contracts, construction specialties, rank. **Arrangement:** By revenue.

18321 ■ *"For Putting Down Roots in Business: Amy Norquist: Greensulate, New York City" in Inc. (Volume 32, December 2010, No. 10, pp. 106)*
Pub: Inc. Magazine
Ed: Christine Lagorio. **Description:** Profile of Amy Norquist who left her position at an environmental nonprofit organization to found Greensulate. Her firm insulates rooftops with lavender, native grasses and succulents called sedum in order to eliminate carbon from the atmosphere.

18322 ■ *"Housing Slide Picks Up Speed' in Crain's Chicago Business (Vol. 31, April 21, 2008, No. 16, pp. 2)*
Pub: Crain Communications, Inc.
Ed: Eddie Baeb. **Description:** According to Tracy Cross & Associates Inc., a real estate consultancy, sales of new homes in the Chicago area dropped 61 percent from the year-earlier period which is more bad news for homebuilders, contractors and real estate agents who are eager for an indication that market conditions are improving.

18323 ■ *National Roofing Contractors Association--Membership Directory*
Pub: National Roofing Contractors Association
Contact: Tom Shanahan, Director
E-mail: tshanahan@nrca.net
URL(s): www.nrca.net. **Released:** Annual; July. **Covers:** 5,000 contractors applying all types of commercial and residential roofing; 600 associate member manufacturers, suppliers, and distributors; 300 foreign members; and 100 institutions and related industries. **Entries include:** Company name, address, phone, and names of voting representatives. **Arrangement:** Alphabetical. **Indexes:** Geographical, voting representative, Alphabetical, member product guide.

18324 ■ *Roofing Contractor--Single Ply Systems Index Issue*
Pub: BNP Media
Contact: Al Reser, President
URL(s): www.roofingcontractor.com. **Ed:** Chris King. **Released:** Annual; February, 2005. **Publication includes:** List of manufacturers of single ply roofing products. **Entries include:** Company name, address, phone, products. **Arrangement:** Classified by product.

18325 ■ *Steep-Slope Roofing Materials Guide*
Pub: National Roofing Contractors Association
Contact: Tom Shanahan, Director
E-mail: tshanahan@nrca.net
URL(s): shop.nrca.netwww.nrca.net/rp/pubstore/details.aspx?id=445. **Released:** Biennial; January; Latest edition 2007-2008. **Price:** $95, Members;

$175, Nonmembers. **Covers:** Over 49 manufacturers of approximately 382 products used for steep residential roofs; coverage includes Canada. **Entries include:** Product name, description, specifications and applications, manufacturer name, address, phone, fax, telex, name and title of contact, geographical area served. **Arrangement:** Classified by product type. **Indexes:** Product/service, company name.

STATISTICAL SOURCES

18326 ■ *Market for Roofing and Siding*
Business Trend Analysts, Inc. Leading Edge Reports
Released: 2001-2002. **Price:** $2495.00. **Description:** Examines national and regional markets for roofing and siding, for both new installations and replacements/additions. Current and projected demand is also quantified by material type.

18327 ■ *RMA Annual Statement Studies*
Pub: Risk Management Association
Contact: Kevin M. Blakey, President
Released: Annual. **Price:** $175.00 2006-07 edition, $105.00. **Description:** Contains composite balance sheets and income statements for more than 360 industries, including the accounting, auditing, and bookkeeping industries. Also contains five years of comparative historical data for discerning trends. Includes 16 commonly used ratios, computed for most of the size groupings for nearly every industry.

TRADE PERIODICALS

18328 ■ *Professional Roofing*
Pub: National Roofing Contractors Association
Contact: Tom Shanahan, Director
E-mail: tshanahan@nrca.net
URL(s): www.professionalroofing.net/. **Ed:** Ambika Puniani Bailey. **Released:** Monthly **Price:** Free.

TRADE SHOWS AND CONVENTIONS

18329 ■ *Southeast Roofing and Sheet Metal Spectacular Trade Exposition*
Florida Roofing, Sheet Metal, and Air Conditioning Contractors Association FRSA
4111, Metric Dr., Ste. 6
Winter Park, FL 32792
Ph: (407)671-3772
Fax: (407)679-0010
Co. E-mail: frsa@floridaroof.com
URL: http://www.floridaroof.com
URL(s): www.floridaroof.com. **Frequency:** Annual. **Audience:** Roofing, and sheet metal, contractors, architects, specifiers, and building officials. **Principal Exhibits:** Roofing and sheet metal supplies, products and services. **Telecommunication Services:** lisapate@floridaroof.com.

CONSULTANTS

18330 ■ *A/R/C Associates Inc.*
601 N Fern Creek Ave., Ste. 100
Orlando, FL 32803-4899
Ph: (407)896-7875

Fax: (407)898-6043
Co. E-mail: info@arc-arc.com
URL: http://www.arc-arc.com
Contact: Donald G. Dorner, President
Scope: Architectural firm with specialized capacities in roof consulting and construction technology. Services include: Facility evaluation reports, construction document preparation, bidding and negotiation, construction contract observation and contract administration; roof consulting-roof investigation and analysis, roof inspection and maintenance scheduling, roof litigation and expert testimony, and historical roof preservation and restoration. **Founded:** 1982.

18331 ■ *Roofing Materials Science & Technology*
9037 Monte Mar Dr.
Los Angeles, CA 90035-4235
Ph: (310)559-6090
Fax: (310)559-6090
Co. E-mail: rmstlaaly@aol.com
URL: http://www.roofsandroofing.com
Contact: Dr. Heshmat O. Laaly, President
E-mail: rmstlaaly@aol.com
Scope: Offers roofing and waterproofing inspection and diagnostics. Presents seminars and consultation on state of the art roofing and waterproofing technology, tailored to individual needs and held on premises. Provides litigation expert testimony and maintains comprehensive roofing library, documentation center, and materials showroom. Developed and patented photovoltaic single ply roofing membrane which provides free electricity for household. Industries served: Commercial and institutional roofing, residential roofing and waterproofing, information dissemination on construction materials. **Founded:** 1984. **Publications:** "The Science and Technology of Traditional and Modern Roofing Systems," 1992. **Seminars:** State of the Art in Roofing Technology.

FRANCHISES AND BUSINESS OPPORTUNITIES

18332 ■ *Jet-Black World's Most Beautiful Driveway's & Parking Lots*
Jet-Black International
990 Lone Oak Rd., Ste. 142
Eagan, MN 55121
Ph: (888)538-2525
Fax: (651)379-9559
Description: Asphalt and concrete maintenance. **No. of Franchise Units:** 102. **No. of Company-Owned Units:** 3. **Founded:** 1987.. **Franchised:** 1993. **Equity Capital Needed:** $65,000-$105,000. **Franchise Fee:** $20,000. **Training:** Yes.

LIBRARIES

18333 ■ *Construction Consultants Library*
4600 College Blvd., Ste. 104
Overland Park, KS 66211-1606
Ph: (913)491-8626
Free: 800-533-8626
Fax: (913)491-9469
Co. E-mail: callahanmt@cclcc.com
URL: http://www.cclcc.com
Contact: Michael T. Callahan, President
Scope: Construction, waterproofing, facility asset management, roofing, concrete. **Services:** Library open to the public with restrictions. **Founded:** 1974. **Holdings:** 500 books. **Subscriptions:** 6 journals and other serials. **Telecommunication Services:** rhoadesrw@cclcc.com.

ASSOCIATIONS AND OTHER ORGANIZATIONS

18334 ■ Canadian Broadcast Distribution Association (CBDA)—Association Canadienne de Distribution de Radiodiffusion (ACDR)
2233 Argentina Rd., Ste. 100
Mississauga, ON, Canada L5N 2X7
Ph: (905)826-3451
Fax: (905)826-4873
Co. E-mail: info@cbda.ca
URL: http://cbda.ca
Contact: Don Braden, Executive Director
Description: Users of satellite telecommunications services. Seeks to advance the satellite communications industries. Serves as a forum for the exchange of information among members; represents members' commercial and regulatory interests. **Educational Activities:** Canadian Broadcast Distribution Association Conference (Annual).

18335 ■ Electronics Technicians Association International (ETA)
5 Depot St.
Greencastle, IN 46135-8024
Ph: (765)653-8262
Free: 800-288-3824
Fax: (765)653-4287
Co. E-mail: eta@eta-i.org
URL: http://www.eta-i.org
Contact: Stephen Fleeman, Vice Chairman
Description: Skilled electronics technicians. Provides placement service; offers certification examinations for electronics technicians and satellite, fiber optics, and data cabling installers. Compiles wage and manpower statistics. Administers FCC Commercial License examinations and certification of computer network systems technicians and web and internet specialists. **Scope:** technical, business training, employment, customer relations. **Founded:** 1978. **Subscriptions:** 300 audiovisuals monographs video recordings. **Publications:** *The High-Tech News* (Bimonthly). **Educational Activities:** Service Retail Convention (Annual); Electronics Technicians Association International Workshop (Annual). **Awards:** Technician of the Year; Educator of the Year (Annual); President's Award (Annual); Technician of the Year (Annual).

REFERENCE WORKS

18336 ■ *Broadcasting & Cable Yearbook: A Broadcasting and R.R. Bowker Publication*
Pub: R.R. Bowker L.L.C.
URL(s): www.bowker.com. **Released:** Annual; latest edition 2010. **Price:** $395, Individuals softbound. **Covers:** Over 17,000 television and radio stations in the United States, its territories, and Canada; cable MSOs and their individual systems; television and radio networks, broadcast and cable group owners, station representatives, satellite networks and services, film companies, advertising agencies, government agencies, trade associations, schools,

and suppliers of professional and technical services, including books, serials, and videos; communications lawyers. **Entries include:** Company name, address, phone, fax, names of executives. Station listings include broadcast power, other operating details. **Arrangement:** Stations and systems are geographical, others are alphabetical. **Indexes:** Alphabetical.

18337 ■ *Directory of Computer & Consumer Electronics Retailers*
Pub: Chain Store Guide
Contact: Lisa Patterson, President
URL(s): www.csgis.com/csgis-frontend. **Released:** Annual; Published June, 2008. **Covers:** 4,500 U.S. and Canadian companies operating almost 61,000 stores with at least $500,000 in computer sales, $1 million in consumer electronics, or other included product line sales. Almost 800 distributors, each also with $500,000 in sales of these product lines, are also included. **Entries include:** Company name, address, phone and fax numbers, web and e-mail addresses; Internet order processing indicator; type of business; product lines; computer brands; network software; operating systems; total sales; consumer electronic sales; computer product sales; sales percentage by product group; sales percentage by customer type; services provided; total stores; units by trade name; trading areas; distribution center locations; projected openings and remodelings; private label credit care indicator; number of agents/resellers; wireless reseller name and location; franchise group headquarters name and location; buying group name; mail order catalog indicator; export indicator; average number of checkouts; year founded; public company indicator; parent company name and location; subsidiaries names and locations; divisional office locations; key personnel with titles. **Arrangement:** Geographical, separate sections for retailers and distributors. **Indexes:** Product lines, alphabetical, computer brand, exclusions.

18338 ■ *"Give Me Liberty With DirecTV" in Barron's (Vol. 89, July 13, 2009, No. 28, pp. M5)*
Pub: Dow Jones & Co., Inc.
Ed: Fleming Meeks. **Description:** Shares of Liberty Entertainment look cheap at $25.14 and the same goes for DirecTV at $23.19. A merger between the two companies was announced and the deal will likely close by September 2009. Barclays Capital has a target of $30 for Liberty Media and $32 for DirecTV.

18339 ■ *Telecommunications Directory*
Pub: Cengage Learning Inc.
Contact: Ronald Dunn, President
URL(s): www.gale.cengage.comhttp://www.gale.cengage.com/servlet/BrowseSeriesServlet?region=9&imprint=000&cf=es&titleCode=CSSG&edition=.
Released: Annual; Latest edition 23rd; April, 2012. **Price:** $993, Individuals. **Covers:** Two volumes-North America and International, Cover approximately 6,000 national and international voice and data communications networks, electronic mail services, teleconferencing facilities and services, facsimile services, Internet access providers, videotex and teletext operations, transactional services, local area

networks, audiotex services, microwave systems/networkers, satellite facilities, and others involved in telecommunications, including related consultants, advertisers/marketers; associations, regulatory bodies, and publishers. **Entries include:** Company or organization name, address, phone, fax, year established, name and title of contact, executive officers and board of directors, function or type of service; geographical area served; NAICS and SIC codes; number of employees; general description, including telecommunications-related activities; product/service; specific applications; means of access and equipment required; publications; intended market and availability; pricing; stock exchanges traded and ticker symbols; financial figures. **Database includes:** Extensive glossary of terms, acronyms, and concepts. **Arrangement:** Alphabetical by company name; within geographic region. **Indexes:** Name of firm/acronym, personal name, geographical (with name, address, phone, and director), and function/type of service (with name, address, phone). Indexes are cumulative. **Availability:** Online: Cengage Learning Inc. **Type:** Directory.

TRADE PERIODICALS

18340 ■ *The Orbiter*
Pub: Society of Satellite Professionals International
Contact: Dick Tauber, Director
Ed: Linda Thornberg, Editor. **Released:** 6/year. **Price:** Included in membership. **Description:** Covers member and chapter activities, developments in commercial satellite communications technology and applications, and activities of corporate sponsors. Recurring features include a calendar of events, reports of meetings, and columns titled Letter from the President and Corporate Corner.

18341 ■ *Ottawa Letter*
Pub: CCH Canadian Ltd.
Contact: Ian Rhind, President
Released: Biweekly. **Price:** $920. **Description:** Reports on current events and topics of Canada, such as free trade, human rights, employment, and defense. Also provides statistics, lending, and foreign exchange rates.

18342 ■ *Satellite News*
Pub: Phillips Business Information Inc. Access Intelligence L.L.C.
Contact: Heather Farley, President
E-mail: hfarley@accessintel.com
Ed: Paul Dykewicz, Editor, pdykewicz@pbimedia.com. **Released:** 50/year. **Price:** $1,197. **Description:** Provides business insights and analysis into the commercial satellite industry including new satellite applications, developing technologies, and unfolding partnerships. Recurring features include columns titled Satellite Spotlight, DBS News, Satellite News, Newsmaker Interiews, Satellite Circuit, and Satellite News Financial Ticker.

18343 ■ *Wireless Satellite & Broadcasting*
Pub: Information Gatekeepers Inc.
Ed: Tony Carmona, Editor. **Released:** Monthly. **Price:** $695, U.S. and Canada; $745, elsewhere. **Descrip-**

tion: Covers developments in technology, business activity, and regulation for the statellite and broadcasting telecommunications industry.

18344 ■ *Worldwide Videotex Update*
Pub: Worldwide Videotex
Released: Monthly. **Price:** $165, U.S. and Canada; $180, elsewhere outside North America; $25, single. **Description:** Reports on electronic mail, online services, satellite communication, videotex, teleconferencing, teletext, and other television related technologies. Focuses on information of interest to marketers.

VIDEOCASSETTES/ AUDIOCASSETTES

18345 ■ *Financial Aspects*
SatNews Publishers
14788 Wolfgang Rd.
Truckee, CA 96161
Ph: (707)939-9306
Free: 888-436-8889
Fax: (707)939-9235
Co. E-mail: design@satnews.com
URL: http://www.satnews.com
Contact: Hartley Lesser, Director
E-mail: hartley@satnews.com
Released: 1992. **Price:** $495.00. **Description:** Covers various financial aspects of satellite communications services, including typical fees, risk management, and future supply and demand. Part of the "Satellite Training Series.". **Availability:** VHS.

18346 ■ *Satellite & Antenna Technology Basics*
SatNews Publishers
14788 Wolfgang Rd.
Truckee, CA 96161
Ph: (707)939-9306
Free: 888-436-8889
Fax: (707)939-9235
Co. E-mail: design@satnews.com
URL: http://www.satnews.com
Contact: Hartley Lesser, Director
E-mail: hartley@satnews.com
Released: 1992. **Price:** $595.00. **Description:** The technological aspects of satellites and antennas are covered, including information on frequency bands, scrambling, television standards, and channel capacity. Part of the "Satellite Training Series.". **Availability:** VHS.

18347 ■ *Satellite Fundamentals*
SatNews Publishers
14788 Wolfgang Rd.
Truckee, CA 96161
Ph: (707)939-9306
Free: 888-436-8889
Fax: (707)939-9235
Co. E-mail: design@satnews.com
URL: http://www.satnews.com
Contact: Hartley Lesser, Director
E-mail: hartley@satnews.com
Released: 1992. **Price:** $595.00. **Description:** Pelton and Baylin discuss various aspects of satellites, including launching, satellite orbits, the environment of space, and how satellites function. Part of the "Satellite Training Series.". **Availability:** VHS.

18348 ■ *Satellite Training Series*
SatNews Publishers
14788 Wolfgang Rd.
Truckee, CA 96161
Ph: (707)939-9306
Free: 888-436-8889
Fax: (707)939-9235
Co. E-mail: design@satnews.com
URL: http://www.satnews.com
Contact: Hartley Lesser, Director
E-mail: hartley@satnews.com
Released: 1992. **Description:** A series of instructional tapes that gives a complete training program on every aspect of the satellite industry. Appropriate for non-technical persons in the satellite communications industry. Tapes are available individually. **Availability:** VHS.

18349 ■ *The World Satellite Marketplace*
SatNews Publishers
14788 Wolfgang Rd.
Truckee, CA 96161
Ph: (707)939-9306
Free: 888-436-8889
Fax: (707)939-9235
Co. E-mail: design@satnews.com
URL: http://www.satnews.com
Contact: Hartley Lesser, Director
E-mail: hartley@satnews.com
Released: 1992. **Price:** $595.00. **Description:** Discusses the world marketplace for various satellite services, including fixed satellite services, mobile satellite services, and radio determining services. Part of the "Satellite Training Series.". **Availability:** VHS.

CONSULTANTS

18350 ■ AMC Networks Inc.—Rainbow Programming HoldingsRainbow Media Enterprises;
11 Penn Plaza
New York, NY 10001-2006
Ph: (212)324-8500
URL: http://www.amcnetworks.com
Contact: Arlene Manos, President
Scope: Telecommunications consultants. Offers services in network operations facilities; satellite services, including teleport, down-linking, local channel, microwave and transponder services and production services. **Founded:** 1980.

18351 ■ W & J Partnership
PO Box 2499
Castro Valley, CA 94546-0499
Ph: (510)583-7751
Fax: (510)583-7645
Co. E-mail: jemorgan@wjpartnership.com
URL: http://www.wjpartnership.com
Contact: Judith E. Morgan, Partner
E-mail: jemorgan@wjpartnership.com
Scope: Management and technical consulting in complex network design, operations, administration, maintenance and products for large enterprises, carriers and service providers (wire-line and wireless) and governments, especially VoIP, security; R and D for vendors. Review product plans and investment opportunities. Software and hardware: Architectures, design, development and testing for manufacturers. No work for vendors and business at the same time. **Founded:** 1982. **Telecommunication Services:** wamorgan@wjpartnership.com.

LIBRARIES

18352 ■ Intelsat Library
3400 International Dr., NW
Box 40
Washington, DC 20008
Ph: (202)944-6800
Fax: (202)944-7898
URL: http://www.intelsat.com/index.asp
Scope: Satellite communication, network infrastructure, telecommunication services. **Services:** Interlibrary loan; Library not open to the public. **Founded:** 1979. **Holdings:** 9000 books; 750 bound periodical volumes; technical reports; e-books. **Subscriptions:** 325 journals and other serials.

ASSOCIATIONS AND OTHER ORGANIZATIONS

18353 ■ **Specialty Graphic Imaging Association (SGIA)**
10015 Main St.
Fairfax, VA 22031-3489
Ph: (703)330-5600
Free: 888-385-3588
Fax: (703)330-5357
Co. E-mail: sgia@sgia.org
URL: http://www.sgia.org
Contact: Gordon Brown, Chairman
Description: Printers who use screen printing and/or digital printing; associate members are suppliers and manufacturers; educational institutions. Provides training and information on technical, managerial, governmental, safety, and research issues. Conducts safety, environmental, and print quality recognition programs. Compiles statistics; conducts research programs. **Scope:** screen printing, digital printing, pad printing, embroidery, sublimation, technology-related. **Founded:** 1948. **Subscriptions:** 1000 articles books periodicals. **Publications:** *Operating Rate Survey* (Biennial); *SGIA Journal* (Quarterly); *SGIA News* (Monthly); *Who's Who in SGIA* (Annual); *Who's Who in SGIA* (Annual); *Guide to Digital Garment Decoration.* **Educational Activities:** Specialty Graphic Imaging Association Convention (Annual); Safety and Environmental Conference (Annual); SGIA/DPI Conference (Annual). **Awards:** Certificate of Appreciation Award (Annual); Certificate of Merit (Annual); Distinguished Service Award (Annual); Golden Image Award (Annual); Key Award (Annual); Magnus Award (Annual); Mentor Award (Annual); Outstanding Service Award (Annual); Parmele Award (Annual); Safety Recognition Award (Annual); Swormstedt Award (Annual).

18354 ■ **Specialty Graphic Imaging Association (SPTF) - Screen Printing Technical Foundation (SPTF)**
10015 Main St.
Fairfax, VA 22031
Ph: (703)385-1335
Co. E-mail: sptf@sgia.org
URL: http://www.sgia.org/sptf
Description: Participants include corporations, institutions, and individuals interested in screen-printing. Advances the screen-printing industry. Conducts technical research and hands-on training programs to address production problems and processes. Sponsors educational programs and prepares educational materials. **Founded:** 1986.

REFERENCE WORKS

18355 ■ *"A Life of Spice" in Entrepreneur (Vol. 37, September 2009, No. 9, pp. 46)*
Pub: Entrepreneur Media, Inc.
Ed: Jason Daley. **Description:** Matt and Bryan Walls have successfully grown their Atlanta, Georgia-based Snorg Tees T-shirt company. The company has expanded its product offering and redesigned its Website to be more user-friendly. The company has registered between $5 and 10 million in 2008.

18356 ■ *Screen Printing--Buyer's Guide Issue*
Pub: ST Media Group International Inc.
Contact: Tedd Swormstedt, President
URL(s): www.stpubs.comwww.stmediagroup.com/index.php3?d=pubs&p=sp. **Ed:** Gail Flower. **Released:** Annual; July. **Publication includes:** List of about 500 manufacturers and distributors of products and equipment used in the screen printing industry. **Entries include:** Company name, address, phone; branch office locations, phone number, name of sales contact, product lines, geographic area served. **Database includes:** Calendar of trade events; lists of industry associations, colleges and universities, reference guides. **Arrangement:** Alphabetical. **Indexes:** Product, trade name, fax number, editorial reference.

18357 ■ *Who's Who in SGIA*
Pub: Specialty Graphic Imaging Association
Contact: Gordon Brown, Chairman
URL(s): www.sgia.org. **Released:** Annual; August. **Covers:** About 3,800 screen printers and graphic imaging companies, suppliers of screen printing equipment and graphic imaging materials, and investors in the Screen Printing Technical Foundation; international coverage. **Entries include:** Company name, address, phone, fax, e-mail, name of contact, products or services. **Arrangement:** Classified by type of business, then geographical. **Indexes:** Alphabetical by company, within state or country.

SOURCES OF SUPPLY

18358 ■ *Screen Printing--Distributor/Dealer Directory Section*
ST Media Group International Inc.
Contact: Tedd Swormstedt, President
URL(s): www.stmediagroup.comwww.stmediagroup.com/index.php3?d=pubs&p=sp. **Released:** Monthly Price: $5, per issue; $42, per year. **Publication includes:** Listings of over 135 dealers and distributors of screen printing equipment, materials, and services. **Entries include:** Company name, address, phone, fax, name and title of contact, geographical area served, and product/service. **Arrangement:** Geographical.

TRADE PERIODICALS

18359 ■ *Screen Printing*
Pub: ST Media Group International Inc.
Contact: Tedd Swormstedt, President
URL(s): www.stmediagroup.com/index.php3?d=pubs&p=sp. **Ed:** Gregory Sharpless. **Released:** Monthly

VIDEOCASSETTES/AUDIOCASSETTES

18360 ■ *Basic Screen Printing*
Crystal Productions
1812 Johns Dr.
Box 2159
Glenview, IL 60025-6519
Ph: (847)657-8144
Free: 800-255-8629
Fax: (847)657-8149
Co. E-mail: custserv@crystalproductions.com
URL: http://www.crystalproductions.com
Released: 19??. **Price:** $39.95. **Description:** Teaching aid for art education introduces screen printing on paper and fabric. **Availability:** VHS.

18361 ■ *Photo Screen Printing*
Crystal Productions
1812 Johns Dr.
Box 2159
Glenview, IL 60025-6519
Ph: (847)657-8144
Free: 800-255-8629
Fax: (847)657-8149
Co. E-mail: custserv@crystalproductions.com
URL: http://www.crystalproductions.com
Released: 19??. **Price:** $39.95. **Description:** Artist Alex Wood presents the photo emulsion process, including color separation, registration, and exposure, in this teaching aid for art education. **Availability:** VHS.

18362 ■ *Printing*
Morris Video
12881 Knott St.
Garden Grove, CA 92841
Ph: (310)533-4800
Fax: (310)320-3171
Released: 1978. **Price:** $24.95. **Description:** Many aspects of the printing industry are featured. **Availability:** VHS.

18363 ■ *Printing Basics for Non-Printers 1: An Abridged Guide to Printing Fundamentals*
Cambridge Educational
c/o Films Media Group
132 West 31st Street, 17th Floor
Ste. 124
New York, NY 10001
Free: 800-257-5126
Fax: (609)671-0266
Co. E-mail: custserve@films.com
URL: http://www.cambridgeol.com
Released: 19??. **Price:** $39.95. **Description:** Explains how to save money and get your ideas across when dealing with designers and production artists. **Availability:** VHS.

TRADE SHOWS AND CONVENTIONS

18364 ■ **The Imprinted Sportswear Show, Atlantic City**
Nielsen Business Media
770 Broadway
New York, NY 10003-9595

Ph: (646)654-4500
Co. E-mail: bmcomm@nielsen.com
URL: http://www.nielsenbusinessmedia.com/
URL(s): www.issshows.com/atlantic_city/. **Price:** $99, Non-members full seminar, advanced registration; $225, Onsite full seminar. **Frequency:** Annual. **Audience:** Trade only. **Principal Exhibits:** Trade show source for the imprinted sportswear/textile screen printing/embroidery industry; t-shirts, preprints, and other apparel; design software; screen printing supplies and equipment; transfers, lettering embroidery equipment and supplies.

FRANCHISES AND BUSINESS OPPORTUNITIES

18365 ■ Bad Ass Coffee Co.
166 W 2700 South
Salt Lake City, UT 84115
Ph: (801)463-1966
Free: 888-422-3277
Fax: (801)463-2606
Description: Coffee and logo wear. **No. of Franchise Units:** 43. **Founded:** 1991.. **Franchised:** 1998. **Equity Capital Needed:** $227,000-$326,000 total

investment; $100,000 cash liquidity. **Franchise Fee:** $35,000. **Royalty Fee:** 6%. **Financial Assistance:** Third party financing available. **Training:** Provides 2 weeks at headquarters, onsite if requested with ongoing support.

18366 ■ Printwear Xpress
Printwear Xpress Franchise Corp.
1819 Wazee St.
Denver, CO 80202
Ph: (303)771-7100
Free: 888-241-0337
Fax: (303)771-7133
Co. E-mail: info@printwearxpress.com
URL: http://www.printwearxpress.com
Description: Printwear Xpress (PWX) combines shopping experience, technology & customer service to deliver a highly competitive business model. PWX stores are modern, attractive & well merchandised to help customers select the right product for their needs. Production is showcased to illustrate the capabilities of the business & customer service is second to none. PWX stores are located in neighborhood strip centers & don't require an anchor tenant. **No. of Company-Owned Units:** 1. **Founded:** 2007.. **Franchised:** 2007. **Equity Capital Needed:**

$148,200-$169,600. **Franchise Fee:** $29,900. **Royalty Fee:** 5%. **Financial Assistance:** Limited third party financing available. **Training:** Offers 1 week classroom in Denver and 1 week onsite during opening, as well as vendor training.

RESEARCH CENTERS

18367 ■ Western Michigan University - Paper and Imaging
Department of Paper Engineering, Chemical
  Engineering, & Imaging
A-217 Parkview Campus
Kalamazoo, MI 49008
Ph: (269)276-3500
Fax: (269)276-3501
Co. E-mail: said.abubakr@wmich.edu
Contact: Said Abubakr, Chairman
Founded: 1958. **Educational Activities:** Barrier coating symposium; Flexo Day; Gravure Day; Litho Day; Paper coating course; Advisory Board Meetings; Industrial seminars include courses on coated paper manufacture, paper coating advances, fundamentals of papermaking, paper recycling, de-inking, specialty coatings and laminations, and printing. **Awards:** Paper and Imaging Scholarships.

START-UP INFORMATION

18368 ■ *"Macomb County, OU Eye Business Incubator" in Crain's Detroit Business (Vol. 24, February 11, 2008, No. 6, pp. 1)*
Pub: Crain Communications Inc. - Detroit
Ed: Chad Halcom. **Description:** Officials in Macomb County, Michigan are discussing plans to create a defense-themed business incubator in the county. Macomb County was awarded $282,000 in federal budget appropriation for the project.

18369 ■ *"Secure Fortune: New Twist In Security: The Marketplace Is Going Digital" in Small Business Opportunities (November 2007)*
Pub: Harris Publications Inc.
Description: Profile of EYESthere, providing digital video security franchise opportunities.

18370 ■ *"Secure Future" in Small Business Opportunities (November 2010)*
Pub: Harris Publications Inc.
Ed: Stan Roberts. **Description:** Fed up with the corporate world, this first-time business owner sells security equipment over the phone. Last year, sales hit $4 million. Profile of the founder of SmartWatch Security & Sound, Madelaine Lock is included.

18371 ■ *"Securing a Fortune" in Small Business Opportunities (Fall 2010)*
Pub: Harris Publications Inc.
Description: Profile of Whelan Security based in Saint Louis and is a private security company operating in 17 states. The family owned business started as a safety patrol unit.

ASSOCIATIONS AND OTHER ORGANIZATIONS

18372 ■ ASIS International—American Society for Industrial Security
1625 Prince St.
Alexandria, VA 22314-2818
Ph: (703)519-6200
Fax: (703)519-6299
Co. E-mail: asis@asisonline.org
URL: http://www.asisonline.org
Contact: Eduard J. Emde, President
Scope: security and asset protection. **Purpose:** Security professionals responsible for loss prevention, asset protection and security for businesses, government, or public organizations and institutions. Sponsors educational programs on security principles (basic through advanced levels) and current security issues. Administers professional certification programs (CPP, PCI, PSP). Offers networking opportunities to professionals; provides an online service for employment and resumes, publishes books, directories, and other resources. **Founded:** 1955. **Publications:** *ASIS Security Industry Buyers Guide* (Annual); *Dynamics* (Bimonthly); *Security Journal* (Quarterly); *Security Management* (Monthly); *ASIS Security Industry Buyers Guide* (Annual); *ASIS International--*

Annual Membership Directory (Annual). **Educational Activities:** ASIS International Conference (Annual); ASIS International Annual Seminar and Exhibits (Annual); American Society for Industrial Security Seminar (Annual). **Awards:** ASIS Foundation Chapter Matching Scholarships; Allan J. Cross, CPP, Award (Annual); Chapter Matching Scholarship (Annual).

18373 ■ Canadian Fire Alarm Association (CFAA)—Association Canadienne D'Alarme Incendie
85 Citizen Ct., Unit 5
Markham, ON, Canada L6G 1A8
Ph: (905)944-0030
Free: 800-529-0552
Fax: (905)479-3639
Co. E-mail: admin@cfaa.ca
URL: http://www.cfaa.ca
Contact: Allen Hess, President
Description: Promotes improved fire safety through use of fire alarms. Facilitates communication and cooperation among members; represents members' commercial and regulatory interests; sponsors research and educational programs. **Founded:** 1973.

18374 ■ Canadian Security Association (CANASA)—L'Association Canadienne de la Securite
50 Acadia Ave., Ste. 201
Markham, ON, Canada L3R 0B3
Ph: (905)513-0622
Free: 800-538-9919
Fax: (905)513-0624
Co. E-mail: staff@canasa.org
URL: http://www.canasa.org
Contact: Donald Budden, President
Description: Alarm and security equipment manufacturers, installers, monitors, and private security guard services. Seeks to advance the industry and enhance the professionalism of members. Serves as a clearinghouse on security systems and services; acts a unified voice representing the national electronic security industry. Conducts lobbying activities; sponsors continuing professional development programs for members; sets standards of practice and ethics for the security systems and services industries. **Scope:** security systems, training. **Founded:** 1977. **Subscriptions:** audio recordings books clippings periodicals video recordings. **Publications:** *English/French EFlash* (Monthly). **Awards:** R.A. Henderson Award; R.A. Henderson Award (Annual).

18375 ■ Electronic Privacy Information Center (EPIC)
1718 Connecticut Ave. NW, Ste. 200
Washington, DC 20009
Ph: (202)483-1140
Fax: (202)483-1248
Co. E-mail: epic-info@epic.org
URL: http://www.epic.org
Contact: Marc Rotenberg, President
Description: Interested individuals. Advocates for electronic privacy, free expression, public voice. Sponsors educational and research programs; compiles statistics; conducts litigation. **Founded:**

1994. **Publications:** *EPIC Alert* (Biweekly). **Educational Activities:** Technologies of Surveillance (Semiannual).

18376 ■ Electronic Security Association (ESA)
6333 N State Hwy. 161, Ste. 350
Irving, TX 75038-2228
Ph: (972)807-6800
Free: 888-447-1689
Fax: (972)807-6883
URL: http://www.esaweb.org
Contact: Dom D'Ascoli, President
Description: Represents electronic safety, security and systems professionals. **Founded:** 1948. **Publications:** *National Burglar and Fire Alarm Association--Membership Directory* (Annual). **Educational Activities:** Leadership Summit (Annual). **Awards:** Sara E. Jackson Award; Morris F. Weinstock Memorial Award (Annual); Sara Jackson Award (Annual); Morris F. Weinstock Person of the Year.

18377 ■ *English/French EFlash*
50 Acadia Ave., Ste. 201
Markham, ON, Canada L3R 0B3
Ph: (905)513-0622
Free: 800-538-9919
Fax: (905)513-0624
Co. E-mail: staff@canasa.org
URL: http://www.canasa.org
Contact: Donald Budden, President
Released: Monthly

18378 ■ International Association of Professional Security Consultants (IAPSC)
575 Market St., Ste. 2125
San Francisco, CA 94105
Ph: (415)536-0288
Fax: (415)764-4915
Co. E-mail: iapsc@iapsc.org
URL: http://www.iapsc.org
Contact: Richard Grassie, President
Description: Security management, technical, training and forensic consultants. Promotes understanding and cooperation among members and industries or individuals requiring such services. Seeks to enhance members' knowledge through seminars, training programs and educational materials. Works to foster public awareness of the security consulting industry; serves as a clearinghouse for consultants' requirements. Maintains code of conduct, ethics and professional standards. Offers consultant referral service; operates speakers' bureau. **Founded:** 1984. **Publications:** *IAPSC News* (Quarterly); *IAPSC Consultants Directory* (Annual). **Educational Activities:** International Association of Professional Security Consultants Convention (Annual); How to Succeed as a Professional Security Consultant. **Awards:** Charles A. Sennewald Distinguished Service Accolade (Annual).

18379 ■ International Security Management Association (ISMA)
PO Box 623
Buffalo, IA 52728
Ph: (563)381-4008

Fax: (563)381-4283
Co. E-mail: isma3@aol.com
URL: http://www.isma.com
Contact: Alan Orlob, President
Description: Senior security executives of multinational business firms and chief executive officers of full service security services companies. Aims to assist senior security executives in coordinating and exchanging information about security management and to establish high business and professional standards. **Founded:** 1983.

18380 ■ Jewelers' Security Alliance (JSA)
6 E 45th St.
New York, NY 10017
Ph: (212)687-0328
Free: 800-537-0067
Fax: (212)808-9168
Co. E-mail: jsa2@jewelerssecurity.org
URL: http://www.jewelerssecurity.org
Contact: John J. Kennedy, President
Description: Advocates for crime prevention in the jewelry industry. Provides crime information and assistance to the jewelry industry and law enforcement. **Founded:** 1883. **Publications:** *JSA Manual of Jewelry Security* (Biennial); *Annual Report on Crime Against the Jewelry Industry in U.S.* (Annual). **Educational Activities:** Security Seminar and Expo for Retail Jewelry Chains (Annual). **Awards:** Gold and Silver Shield Awards (Annual).

18381 ■ National Association of Security Companies (NASCO)
444 N Capitol St. NW, Ste. 345
Washington, DC 20001
Ph: (202)347-3257
Fax: (202)393-7006
Co. E-mail: information@nasco.org
URL: http://www.nasco.org
Contact: Jim McNulty, Chairman
Description: Major security guard companies. Monitors legislation affecting the industry. **Founded:** 1972. **Awards:** Colonel Edgar B. Watson Award (Annual).

18382 ■ National Council of Investigation and Security Services (NCISS)
7501 Sparrows Point Blvd.
Baltimore, MD 21219-1927
Free: 800-445-8408
Fax: (410)388-9746
Co. E-mail: nciss@comcast.net
URL: http://www.nciss.org
Contact: Maria Landry, President
Description: Monitors national and state legislative and regulatory activities. Develops and encourages the practice of high standards of personal and professional conduct. Acquires, preserves, and disseminates data and valuable information; promotes the purpose of investigation and guard companies. Provides information about state legislation and regulatory activities that could have an impact on a particular firm or on the industry in general; acts as spokesman for the industry before legislative and regulatory bodies at both federal and state levels. **Founded:** 1975. **Publications:** *NCISS Report* (Quarterly). **Awards:** Wayne Wonder Award (Annual); John J. Duffy Award (Annual).

18383 ■ Nine Lives Associates (NLA)
Executive Protection Institute
16 Penn Pl., Ste. 1570
New York, NY 10001
Ph: (212)268-4555
Fax: (212)563-4783
Co. E-mail: info@personalprotection.com
URL: http://www.personalprotection.com/nla.cfm
Contact: Dr. Jerry Heying, President
Description: Law enforcement, correctional, military, and security professionals who have been granted Personal Protection Specialist Certification through completion of the protective services program offered by the Executive Protection Institute; conducts research; EPI programs emphasize personal survival skills and techniques for the protection of others. Provides professional recognition for qualified individuals engaged in executive protection assignments. Maintains placement service. Operates speakers' bureau; compiles statistics. **Scope:** law enforcement and security subjects. **Founded:** 1978. **Subscrip-**

tions: 1000. **Educational Activities:** Nine Lives Associates Conference (Annual). **Awards:** N.L.A. Achievement Award (Annual).

18384 ■ Security Industry Association (SIA)
635 Slaters Ln., Ste. 110
Alexandria, VA 22314-1108
Ph: (703)683-2075
Free: 866-817-8888
Fax: (703)683-2469
Co. E-mail: info@siaonline.org
URL: http://www.siaonline.org
Contact: Jay Hauhn, Chairman
Description: Security equipment manufacturers and distributors. Seeks for the advancement of companies in the security products industry. Promotes the export of American security products. Conducts research programs, educational programs, technical seminars, communications with related industries and other activities. Maintains speakers' bureau; compiles statistics. **Scope:** security. **Founded:** 1969. **Subscriptions:** 100. **Awards:** George R. Lippert Memorial Award; George R. Lippert (Annual); Gold Circle (Annual); New Product Showcase (Semiannual).

DIRECTORIES OF EDUCATIONAL PROGRAMS

18385 ■ *Directory of Private Accredited Career Schools and Colleges of Technology*
Pub: Accrediting Commission of Career Schools and Colleges of Technology
Contact: Michale S. McComis, Executive Director
Released: On web page. **Price:** Free. **Description:** Covers 3900 accredited post-secondary programs that provide training programs in business, trade, and technical fields, including various small business endeavors. Entries offer school name, address, phone, description of courses, job placement assistance, and requirements for admission. Arrangement is alphabetical.

REFERENCE WORKS

18386 ■ *"Actiontec and Verizon Team Up for a Smarter Home" in Ecology,Environment & Conservation Business (November 5, 2011, pp. 3)*
Pub: HighBeam Research
Description: Verizon is implementing Actiontec Electronics' SG200 Service Gateway as a basic component of its Home Monitoring and Control service. This new smart home service allows customers to remotely check their homes, control locks and appliances, view home-energy use and more using a smartphone, PC, or FiOS TV.

18387 ■ *"Altegrity Acquires John D. Cohen, Inc." in (November 19, 2009, pp. 14)*
Pub: Investment Weekly News
Description: John D. Cohen, Inc., a contract provider of national security policy guidance and counsel to the federal government, was acquired by Altegrity, Inc., a global screening and security solutions provider; the company will become part of US Investigations Services, LLC and operate under the auspices of Altegrity's new business, Altegrity Security Consulting.

18388 ■ *"American Chemistry Council Launches Flagship Blog" in Ecology,Environment & Conservation Business (October 29, 2011, pp. 5)*
Pub: HighBeam Research
Description: American Chemistry Council (ACC) launched its blog, American Chemistry Matters, where interactive space allows bloggers to respond to news coverage and to discuss policy issues and their impact on innovation, competitiveness, job creation and safety.

18389 ■ *"AMT's Partner Program Enables New Security Business Models" in Internet Wire (August 12, 2010)*
Pub: Comtex
Description: AMT, technical provider of physical access control Software as a Service (Saas) solutions,

has developed a new Partner Program that allows partners to outsource any technical abilities lacking to AMT with no upfront fees.

18390 ■ *"And The Winner Is.." in Canadian Business (Vol. 81, March 3, 2008, No. 3, pp. 21)*
Pub: Rogers Media
Ed: Joe Castaldo. **Description:** Thirty out of 141 Canadian chief executive officers think that Hilary Clinton would be best for U.S.-Canada relations if elected as U.S. president. Findings also revealed that 60 respondents believe that presidential candidate John McCain would be best on handling issues of international military-security. Views on the candidates' performance and their ability to deal with the declining U.S. economy as well as international trade issues are also given.

18391 ■ *ASIS International--Annual Membership Directory*
Pub: ASIS International
Contact: Eduard J. Emde, President
URL(s): www.asisonline.org. **Released:** Annual; May/June. **Covers:** 37,000 member management specialists in the private and public sectors who formulate security policy and direct security programs to prevent terrorism, document piracy, industrial espionage, counterfeiting, insurance fraud, arson, employee theft, white-collar crime, computer crime, organized crime, etc. **Entries include:** Member name, title, address, phone, company affiliation. **Arrangement:** Alphabetical. **Indexes:** Geographical, affiliated organization/company, personal name.

18392 ■ *"At Wine Kiosk, Show ID, Face Camera, Swipe Card and Blow" in Pittsburgh Post-Gazette (November 28, 2010)*
Pub: Pittsburgh-Post Gazette
Ed: Dennis B. Roddy. **Description:** New technology installed on wine kiosks enables sellers to abide by the law. This technology tests blood alcohol levels and warns people if they have recently used a mouthwash before testing.

18393 ■ *"Auto Bankruptcies Could Weaken Defense" in Crain's Detroit Business (Vol. 25, June 8, 2009, No. 23, pp. 1)*
Pub: Crain Communications Inc. - Detroit
Ed: Chad Halcom. **Description:** Bankruptcy and supplier consolidation of General Motors Corporation and Chrysler LLC could interfere with the supply chains of some defense contractors, particularly makers of trucks and smaller vehicles.

18394 ■ *"AVG Introduces Security Software Suite for SMBs 551179" in eWeek (October 12, 2010)*
Pub: Ziff Davis Enterprise
Description: AVG Technologies is offering its AVG Internet Security 2011 Business Edition and AVG Anti-Virus Business Edition designed to give Internet-active SMB owners protection. The system protects online transactions and email communications as well as sensitive customer data and AVG Anti-Virus 2011 Business edition offers real-time protection against the latest online threats.

18395 ■ *"Behind the Scenes: Companies At the Heart of Everyday Life" in Inc. (February 2008, pp. 26-27)*
Pub: Gruner & Jahr USA Publishing
Ed: Athena Schindelheim. **Description:** Profiles of companies providing services to airports, making the environment safer and more efficient, as well as more comfortable for passengers and workers. Centerpoint Manufacturing provides garbage bins that can safely contain explosions producing thousands of pounds of pressure; Infax, whose software displays arrival and departure information on 19-foot-wide screens; Lavi Industries, whose products include security barricades, hostess stands, and salad-bar sneeze guards; and SATech maker of rubber flooring that helps ease discomfort for workers having to stand for long periods of time.

18396 ■ *"Blues at the Toy Fair: Industry Reeling From Recalls, Lower Sales Volumes"*

in Crain's New York Business (February 18, 2008)

Pub: Crain Communications Inc.

Ed: Elisabeth Cordova. Description: Over 1,500 toy developers and vendors will attend the American International Toy Fair, expected to be low-key due to recent recalls of toys not meeting American safety standards. Toy retailers and manufacturers, as well as the Chinese government, are promoting product testing to prevent toxic metals in toys.

18397 ■ *"Border Boletin: UA to Take Lie-Detector Kiosk to Poland" in Arizona Daily Star (September 14, 2010)*

Pub: Arizona Daily Star

Ed: Brady McCombs. Description: University of Arizona's National Center for Border Security and Immigration Research will send a team to Warsaw, Poland to show border guards from 27 European Union countries the center's Avatar Kiosk. The Avatar technology is designed for use at border ports and airports to assist Customs officers detect individuals who are lying.

18398 ■ *"Bracing for Impact" in Playthings (Vol. 106, September 1, 2008, No. 8, pp. 15)*

Pub: Reed Business Information

Contact: Jeff Greisch, President

Ed: J. Tol Broome Jr. Description: A good risk management plan for any company consists of making correct decisions in the following six key areas: operational, reputation, regulatory, legal, liquidity, and disaster.

18399 ■ *"Building Targeted for Marriott in Violation" in Business Journal-Milwaukee (Vol. 28, December 24, 2010, No. 12, pp. A1)*

Pub: Milwaukee Business Journal

Ed: Sean Ryan. Description: Milwaukee, Wisconsin's Department of Neighborhood Services has ordered structural improvements and safeguards for the Pioneer Building after three violations from structural failures were found. Pioneer was among the five buildings wanted by Jackson Street Management LLC to demolish for the new Marriott Hotel.

18400 ■ *"Businesses Still on the Mend" in Boston Business Journal (Vol. 29, September 9, 2011, No. 18, pp. 1)*

Pub: American City Business Journals Inc.

Ed: Scott Dance. Description: The 9/11 terrorist attacks have caused many companies in the US to dramatically shift course in response to changes in the economy. The concern that the cost of being unprepared for future disasters could be larger has remained among many companies.

18401 ■ *"Buyer's Guide: Room for Improvement" in Entrepreneur (Vol. 35, October 2007, No. 10, pp. 62)*

Pub: Entrepreneur Media Inc.

Ed: Amanda C. Kooser. Description: Buyers guide for wireless routers is presented. Price, features and availability of the Belkin N1 Vision, Buffalo Wireless-N Nfinit Router, D-Link Xtreme Gigabit Router DIR 655, Linksys Wireless-N Gigabit Security Router, Netgear RangeMax Next Wireless-N Router and Zyxel NBG-460N are provided.

18402 ■ *"Cents and Sensibility" in Playthings (Vol. 107, January 1, 2009, No. 1, pp. 19)*

Pub: Reed Business Information

Contact: Jeff Greisch, President

Ed: Pamela Brill. Description: Recent concerns over safety, phthalate and lead paint and other toxic materials, as well as consumers going green, are issues discussed by toy manufacturers. Doll manufacturers also face increase labor and material costs and are working to design dolls that girls will love.

18403 ■ *"CMS Products and Avecto Team for Business Security Product Solutions" in Wireless News (November 11, 2009)*

Pub: Close-Up Media

Description: CMS Products, a provider of data security, backup, content management and disaster recovery, has agreed on a strategic partnership with Avect, a provider in least privilege management. The partnership will allow the companies to bundle their products.

18404 ■ *"Comcast Launches New Home Security Service, Developed in Portland" in The Oregonian (June 7, 2011)*

Pub: McClatchy-Tribune Regional News

Ed: Mike Rogoway. Description: Comcast introduced its new high-end home security system that provides 24-hour monitoring and control of homes and utilities, along with Web and mobile access.

18405 ■ *"Consumer Trust in E-Commerce Web Sites: a Meta-Study" in ACM Computing Surveys (Vol. 43, Fall 2011, No. 3, pp. 14)*

Pub: Association for Computing Machinery

Ed: Patricia Beatty, Ian Reay, Scott Dick, James Miller. Description: Trust is at once an elusive, imprecise concept, and a critical attribute that must be engineered into e-commerce systems. Engineering trust is examined.

18406 ■ *"Contingency Planning and Disaster Recovery: A Small Business Guide*

Pub: John Wiley & Sons, Incorporated

Ed: Donna R. Childs, Stefan Dietrich. Released: October 2002. Description: Four keys issues to help a business plan for disasters include: preparation, response, recovery, and sample IT solutions in order to secure property and confidential data files and covers the six types of disasters: human errors, equipment failures, third-party failures, environmental hazards, fires and other structural catastrophes, and terrorism and sabotage.

18407 ■ *"Contractors Scramble for Jobs" in Business Journal Portland (Vol. 26, December 18, 2009, No. 41, pp. 1)*

Pub: American City Business Journals Inc.

Ed: Andy Giegerich. Description: Contractors in Portland area are expected to bid for capital construction projects that will be funded by municipalities in the said area. Contracts for companies that work on materials handling, road improvement, and public safety structure projects will be issued.

18408 ■ *"Corporate Radar: Tracking the Forces That Are Shaping Your Business*

Pub: Amacom

Ed: Karl Albrecht. Released: December 2008. Price: $24.95. Description: Ways for a business to assess the forces operating in the external environment that can affect the business and solutions to protect from outside threats.

18409 ■ *"Council Power Shift Could Benefit Business" in Business Courier (Vol. 26, November 6, 2009, No. 28, pp. 1)*

Pub: American City Business Journals, Inc.

Ed: Lucy May. Description: A majority in the Cincinnati City Council, which is comprised of reelected members, might be created by Charlie Winburn's impending return to the council. It would be empowered to decide on public safety, stock options taxes, and environmental justice. How the presumed majority would affect the city's economic progress is discussed.

18410 ■ *"Credit Card Crackdown" in Business Journal-Portland (Vol. 24, November 23, 2007, No. 38, pp. 1)*

Pub: American City Business Journals, Inc.

Ed: Andy Giegerich. Description: Oregon's U.S. Senator Ron Wyden is sponsoring Credit Card Safety Act of 2007, a bill that requires credit card companies to reduce the jargon of credit card agreements and require the Federal Reserve Board to launch a public education campaign among credit card users. The legislation will also impose a rating system for credit card contracts with five being the safest for consumers to use.

18411 ■ *"Data Security is No. 1 Compliance Concern" in HRMagazine (Vol. 53, October 2008, No. 10, pp. 32)*

Pub: Society for Human Resource Management

Contact: Henry G. Jackson, President

E-mail: hjackson@shrm.org

Ed: Aliah D. Wright. Description: Electronic data protection and data privacy are the leading ethics and compliance issues faced by companies today.

18412 ■ *"Dealing With Dangers Abroad" in Financial Executive (Vol. 23, December 2007, No. 10, pp. 32)*

Pub: Financial Executives International

Ed: Jeffrey Marshall. Description: Clear processes and responsibilities for risk management for all companies going global are essential. U.S. toy manufacturer, Matel was put into crisis mode after its Chinese-made toys were recalled due to the use of lead-based paint or tiny magnets in its products.

18413 ■ *"Defense Budge Ax May Not Come Down So Hard On the Region" in Baltimore Business Journal (Vol. 28, August 20, 2010, No. 15, pp. 1)*

Pub: Baltimore Business Journal

Ed: Daniel J. Sernovitz. Description: U.S. Defense Secretary Robert M. Gates' planned budget cuts are having little effect on Maryland's defense industry. Gates will reduce spending on intelligence service contracts by 10 percent.

18414 ■ *"Despite Hot Toys, Holiday Sales Predicted To Be Ho-Ho-Hum" in Drug Store News (Vol. 29, November 12, 2007, No. 14, pp. 78)*

Pub: Drug Store News

Ed: Doug Desjardins. Description: Summer toy recalls have retailers worried about holiday sales in 2007. Mattel was heavily impacted from the recall of millions of toys manufactured in China.

18415 ■ *Doing Business Anywhere: The Essential Guide to Going Global*

Pub: John Wiley and Sons, Inc.

Ed: Tom Travis. Released: 2007. Price: $24.95. Description: Plans are given for new or existing businesses to organize, plan, operate and execute a business on a global basis. Trade agreements, brand protection and patents, ethics, security as well as cultural issues are among the issues addressed.

18416 ■ *"Eagle's Wine Kiosk Is Area's 1st" in Pittsburgh Post-Gazette (October 28, 2010)*

Pub: Pittsburgh-Post Gazette

Ed: Bob Batz Jr. Description: Giant Eagle Market District store at Settlers Ridge opened the first self-serve wine kiosk in Western Pennsylvania. The kiosk will have a built-in breathalyzer panel to ensure safety.

18417 ■ *Electronic Commerce*

Pub: Course Technology

Ed: Gary Schneider, Bryant Chrzan, Charles McCormick. Released: May 1, 2010. Price: $117.95. Description: E-commerce can open the door to more opportunities than ever before for small business. Packed with real-world examples and cases, the book delivers comprehensive coverage of emerging online technologies and trends and their influence on the electronic marketplace. It details how the landscape of online commerce is evolving, reflecting changes in the economy and how business and society are responding to those changes. Balancing technological issues with the strategic business aspects of successful e-commerce, the new edition includes expanded coverage of international issues, social networking, mobile commerce, Web 2.0 technologies, and updates on spam, phishing, and identity theft.

18418 ■ *Electronic Commerce: Technical, Business, and Legal Issues*

Pub: Prentice Hall PTR

Ed: Oktay Dogramaci; Aryya Gangopadhyay; Yelena Yesha; Nabil R. Adam. Released: August 1998. Description: Provides insight into the goals of using the Internet to grow a business in the areas of networking and telecommunication, security, and storage and retrieval; business areas such as marketing, procurement and purchasing, billing and payment, and supply chain management; and legal aspects such as privacy, intellectual property, taxation, contractual and legal settlements.

18419 ■ *"Encouraging Study in Critical Languages" in Occupational Outlook*

Quarterly (Vol. 55, Summer 2011, No. 2, pp. 23)
Pub: U.S. Bureau of Labor Statistics
Description: Proficiency in particular foreign languages is vital to the defense, diplomacy, and security of the United States. Several federal programs provide scholarships and other funding to encourage high school and college students to learn languages of the Middle East, China, and Russia.

18420 ■ *"Enforcer In Fantasyland" in Crain's New York Business (Vol. 24, February 25, 2008, No. 8, pp. 10)*
Pub: Crain Communications Inc.
Ed: Hilary Potkewitz. **Description:** Patent law, particularly in the toy and game industry, is recession-proof according to Barry Negrin, partner at Pryor Cashman. Negrin co-founded his patent practice group. Despite massive recalls of toys and the concern over toxic toys, legal measures are in place in this industry.

18421 ■ *"EOTech Product Improves Holographic Gun Sights" in Crain's Detroit Business (Vol. 24, February 4, 2008, No. 5, pp. 9)*
Pub: Crain Communications Inc. - Detroit
Description: L-3 Communications EOTech Inc. procured new business contracts to fulfill military and law enforcement's demand for improved holographic sites used on handheld weapons.

18422 ■ *"Eve in the Sky: A Look at Security Tech from All Angles" in Bellingtham Business Journal (October 2008, pp. 23)*
Pub: Sun News Inc.
Ed: Lance Henderson. **Description:** High tech solutions to security issues in any company are not the only things to be considered; a low-tech evaluation of a building and its security fixtures, such as door knobs, locks, doors and windows as well as lighting are important aspects to security any office.

18423 ■ *"Familiar Fun" in Crain's Cleveland Business (Vol. 28, October 22, 2007, No. 42, pp. 3)*
Pub: Crain Communications Inc.
Ed: John Booth. **Description:** Marketing for the 2007 holiday season has toy retailers focusing on American-made products because of recent recalls of toys produced in China that do not meet U.S. safety standards.

18424 ■ *"Finalist: Private Company, Less Than $100M" in Crain's Detroit Business (Vol. 25, June 22, 2009, No. 25)*
Pub: Crain Communications Inc. - Detroit
Ed: Sherri Begin Welch. **Description:** Profile of family-owned Guardian Alarm Company is presented. The firm has expanded to include medical monitoring and video equipment of doors and windows.

18425 ■ *"Fly Phishing" in Canadian Business (Vol. 80, October 22, 2007, No. 21, pp. 42)*
Pub: Rogers Media
Ed: Andy Holloway. **Description:** Symantec Corporation's report shows consumers and companies have effectively installed network defenses that prevent unwanted access. Phishing packages are readily available and are widely used. Other details of the Internet Security Threat Report are presented.

18426 ■ *"The Fort" in Hawaii Business (Vol. 53, November 2007, No. 5, pp. 19)*
Pub: Hawaii Business Publishing
Ed: Jason Ubay. **Description:** DRFortress' flagship data center The Fort located at Honolulu's Airport Industrial Park provides companies a place to store their servers in an ultra-secure environment. Anything stored in here that requires power has a back up and in case of an outage generators can supply power up to 80 hrs. The Fort caters to major carriers and Internet service providers.

18427 ■ *"Freeing the Wheels of Commerce" in Hispanic Business (July-August 2007, pp. 50, 52, 54)*
Pub: Hispanic Business
Ed: Keith Rosenblum. **Description:** SecureOrigins, a border-based partnership with high-tech innovators is working to move goods faster, more efficiently, and securely.

18428 ■ *"Frost and Sullivan" in Investment Weekly News (December 19, 2009, pp. 150)*
Pub: Investment Weekly News
Description: Demand for video analytics solutions concerning security and business intelligence is growing, especially in such regions as the Middle East, Europe and Africa. Significant advancements in the field of intelligent analysis of video hold promising opportunities in security applications.

18429 ■ *"General Clark Stresses Ethanols Role In National Security At Ag Connect" in Farm Industry News (January 11, 2011)*
Pub: Penton Business Media Inc.
Description: General Clark stressed the role of ethanols in national security at the AgConnect.

18430 ■ *"GM's Volt Woes Cast Shadow on E-Cars" in Wall Street Journal Eastern Edition (November 28, 2011, pp. B1)*
Pub: Dow Jones & Company Inc. Enterprise Media Group
Contact: Clare Hart, President
Ed: Sharon Terlep. **Description:** The future of electric cars is darkened with the government investigation by the National Highway Traffic Safety Administration into General Motor Company's Chevy Volt after two instances of the car's battery packs catching fire during crash tests conducted by the Agency.

18431 ■ *"Government Says Self-Regulation of Online Privacy is Coming Up Short" in Advertising Age (Vol. 81, December 6, 2010, No. 43, pp. 1)*
Pub: Crain Communications, Inc.
Ed: Edmund Lee. **Description:** U.S. Federal Trade Commission and the Department of Commerce are concerned about the current state of digital privacy and stated that self-regulation has not been sufficient to date.

18432 ■ *"A Hacker in India Hijacked His Website Design and Was Making Good Money Selling It" in Inc. (December 2007, pp. 77-78, 80)*
Pub: Gruner & Jahr USA Publishing
Ed: Darren Dahl. **Description:** John Anton, owner of an online custom T-shirt business and how a company in India was selling software Website templates identical to his firm's Website.

18433 ■ *"Homing In On the Future" in Black Enterprise (Vol. 38, October 2007, No. 3, pp. 61)*
Pub: Earl G. Graves Publishing Co. Inc.
Ed: Sean Drakes. **Description:** More and more people are wanting new homes wired automated systems that integrate multiple home devices such as computers, audio/visual entertainment, security, communications, utilities, and lighting and environmental controls.

18434 ■ *"Hopkins' Security, Reputation Face Challenges in Wake of Slaying" in Baltimore Business Journal (Vol. 28, August 6, 2010, No. 13)*
Pub: Baltimore Business Journal
Ed: Gary Haber. **Description:** The slaying of Johns Hopkins University researcher Stephen Pitcairn has not tarnished the reputation of the elite school in Baltimore, Maryland among students. Maintaining Hopkins' reputation is important since it is Baltimore's largest employer with nearly 32,000 workers. Insights on the impact of the slaying among the Hopkins' community are also given.

18435 ■ *"How Business Intelligence Can Affect Bottomline" in Canadian Electronics (Vol. 23, February 2008, No. 1, pp. 6)*
Pub: CLB Media Inc.
Ed: Mark Borkowski. **Description:** Business intelligence has an important role in delivering the right information in a secured manner. However, coping with data volume, cost, workload, time, availability and compliance have been a problem for business intelligence projects. Ways to avoid problems in business intelligence projects and examples of business intelligence applications are provided.

18436 ■ *"How Foreigners Could Disrupt U.S. Markets" in Barron's (Vol. 90, September 13, 2010, No. 37, pp. 30)*
Pub: Barron's Editorial & Corporate Headquarters
Ed: Jim McTague. **Description:** An informal meeting by the House Homeland Security Panel concluded that U.S. stock exchanges and related trading routes can be the subject of attacks from rogue overseas traders. A drop in funding for the U.S. Department of Defense is discussed.

18437 ■ *"iControl Networks Powers Comcast's XFINITY (Reg) Home Security Service" in Benzinga.com (June 9, 2011)*
Pub: Benzinga.com
Ed: Benzinga Staff. **Description:** Comcast's XFINITY Home Security Service is powered by iControl Networks' OpenHome (TM) software platform. The service provides intrusion and fire protection along with interactive features such as home monitoring, home management, and energy management services with Web and mobile access.

18438 ■ *"Identity Crisis: The Battle For Your Data" in Canadian Business (Vol. 81, March 17, 2008, No. 4, pp. 12)*
Pub: Rogers Media
Description: Nigel Brown explains that businesses must protect their data through encryption and tightening up access to data. Brown also points out that banks and merchants bear most of the costs for identity fraud and leaves individuals with a lot of pain and heartache in clearing their name.

18439 ■ *"Identity Thieves Hit a New Low" in Information Today (Vol. 26, February 2009, No. 2, pp. 1)*
Pub: Information Today, Inc.
Ed: Phillip Britt. **Description:** Identity thieves are opening credit lines after reading obituaries. Actual identity theft cases are examined.

18440 ■ *"Importers Share Safety Liability" in Feedstuffs (Vol. 80, January 21, 2008, No. 3, pp. 19)*
Pub: Miller Publishing Company, Inc.
Description: Pet food and toys containing lead paint are among products from China being recalled due to safety concerns. American Society for Quality's list of measures that outsourcing companies can take to help ensure safer products being imported to the U.S.

18441 ■ *"In the Mobikey of Life" in Canadian Business (Vol. 81, July 21, 2008, No. 11, pp. 42)*
Pub: Rogers Media Ltd.
Ed: John Gray. **Description:** Toronto-based Route1 has created a data security software system that allows employees to access files and programs stored in the head office without permanently transferring data to the actual computer being used. Mobikey technology is useful in protecting laptops of chief executive officers, which contain confidential financial and customer data.

18442 ■ *"Intel to Buy McAfee Security Business for 768B" in eWeek (August 19, 2010)*
Pub: Ziff Davis Enterprise
Description: Intel will acquire security giant McAfee for approximately $7.68 billion, whereby McAfee would become a wholly owned subsidiary of Intel and would report to Intel's Software and Services Group.

18443 ■ *"Kids, Computers and the Social Networking Evolution" in Canadian Business (Vol. 81, October 27, 2008, No. 18, pp. 93)*
Pub: Rogers Media Ltd.
Ed: Penny Milton. **Description:** Social networking was found to help educate students in countries like the U.S., Canada and Mexico. Schools that embrace social networking teach students how to use computers safely and responsibility in order to counter threats to children on the Internet.

18444 ■ *"Local Company Seeks Patent For Armored Trucks" in Crain's Detroit Business*

(Vol. 24, February 4, 2008, No. 5, pp. 10)
Pub: Crain Communications Inc. - Detroit
Description: Profile of James LeBlanc Sr., mechanical engineer and defense contractor, discusses his eleven utility patents pending for a set of vehicles and subsystems that would work as countermeasures to explosively formed projectiles.

18445 ■ *"Macho Men" in Canadian Business (Vol. 81, November 10, 2008, No. 19, pp. 23)*
Pub: Rogers Media Ltd.
Ed: Sharda Prashad. **Description:** Professors Robin Ely and Debra Meyerson found that oil rigs decreased accidents and increased productivity when they focused on improving safety and admitting errors rather than on a worker's individual strength. Professor Jennifer Berdahl shows there is pressure for men to be seen as masculine at work, which makes them avoid doing 'feminine' things such as parental leaves.

18446 ■ *"Making Factory Tours Count" in Playthings (Vol. 107, January 1, 2009, No. 1, pp. 14)*
Pub: Reed Business Information
Contact: Jeff Greisch, President
Ed: Malcolm Denniss. **Description:** The importance of touring an overseas toy supplier's manufacturing facility is stressed. Strategies for general factory visits are outlined in order to determine safety-related quality assurance issues in production.

18447 ■ *"Melamine Analytical Methods Released" in Feedstuffs (Vol. 80, October 6, 2008, No. 41, pp. 2)*
Pub: Miller Publishing Company
Description: Romer Labs has released new validations for its AgraQuant Melamine enzyme-linked immunosorbent assay. The test kit screens for melamine in feed and diary products, including pet foods, milk and milk powder. Melamine by itself is nontoxic in low doses, but when combined with cyanuric acid it can cause fatal kidney stones. The Chinese dairy industry is in the midst of a huge melamine crisis; melamine-contaminated dairy and food products from China have been found in more than 20 countries.

18448 ■ *"Microsoft Releases Office Security Updates" in Mac World (Vol. 27, November 2010, No. 11, pp. 66)*
Pub: Mac Publishing
Ed: David Dahlquist. **Description:** Office for Mac and Mac Business Unit are Microsoft's pair of security- and stability-enhancing updates for Office 2008 and Office 2004. The software will improve the stability and compatibility and fixes vulnerabilities that would allow attackers to overwrite Mac's memory with malicious code.

18449 ■ *"Mimosa Systems Gains 150,000 New NearPoint Users" in Information Today (Vol. 26, February 2009, No. 2, pp. 31)*
Pub: Information Today, Inc.
Description: Mimosa System's NearPoint archive solution features email and file archiving, e-discovery, archive virtualization, and disaster recovery capabilities.

18450 ■ *"Mobile Security for Business V5" in SC Magazine (Vol. 20, August 2009, No. 8, pp. 55)*
Pub: Haymarket Media, Inc.
Description: Review of F-Secure's Mobile Security for Business v5 which offers protection for business smartphones that can be centralized for protection monitoring by IT administrators.

18451 ■ *"Nampa Police Department: Electronic Systems Just One Tool in Business Security Toolbox" in Idaho Business Review (October 29, 2010)*
Pub: Dolan Media Newswires
Ed: Brad Carlson. **Description:** Police departments and private security firms can help small businesses with hard security and business consultants can assist with internal audit security and fraud prevention.

18452 ■ *"New Wave of Business Security Products Ushers in the Kaspersky Anti-Malware Protection System" in Internet Wire (October 26, 2010)*
Pub: Comtex
Description: Kaspersky Anti-Malware System provides anti-malware protection that requires minimal in-house resources for small businesses. The system offers a full range of tightly integrated end-to-end protection solutions, ensuring unified protection across an entire network, from endpoint and mobile device protection to file server, mail server, network storage and gateway protection. It provides flexible centralized management, immediate threat visibility and a level of responsiveness not seen in other anti-malware approaches.

18453 ■ *"New Ways To Think About Data Loss: Data Loss Is Costly and Painful" in Franchising World (Vol. 42, August 2010, No. 8, pp. 21)*
Pub: International Franchise Association
Ed: Ken Colburn. **Description:** Information for maintaining data securely for franchised organizations, including smart phones, tablets, copiers, computers and more is given.

18454 ■ *Nine Lives Associates--Membership Directory*
Pub: Executive Protection Institute
Contact: Dr. H. H. A. Cooper, President
URL(s): www.personalprotection.com. **Ed:** Dr. Richard W. Kobetz. **Released:** Annual; March. **Covers:** 2,000 individuals certified as personal protection specialists through completion of a training program. **Entries include:** Specialist name and title, address, phone, company name. **Arrangement:** Classified by class completed.

18455 ■ *"No Lines, No Waiting" in The Business Journal-Serving Greater Tampa Bay (Vol. 28, August 15, 2008, No. 34, pp. 1)*
Pub: American City Business Journals, Inc.
Ed: Jane Meinhardt. **Description:** Voda LLC, which was founded to commercialize developments by David Fries, develops outdoor sensor networks used for environmental monitoring by markets like research, the security industry, and the government. Fries already licensed 12 technologies for clients for about $130,000 per technology. Other information on Voda LLC is presented.

18456 ■ *"Not In Our Backyard" in Canadian Business (Vol. 80, October 22, 2007, No. 21, pp. 76)*
Pub: Rogers Media
Ed: Anrew Nikiforuk. **Description:** Alberta Energy and Utilities Board's proposed construction of electric transmission line has let to protests by landowners. The electric utility was also accused of spying on ordinary citizens and violating impartiality rules. Details of the case between Lavesta Area Group and the Board are discussed.

18457 ■ *"Now Entering A Secure Area" in Women Entrepreneur (January 14, 2009)*
Pub: Entrepreneur Media Inc.
Ed: Aliza Sherman. **Description:** Despite the fact that the field of government intelligence and security is dominated by males, many women entrepreneurs are finding opportunities for their products and services in homeland security. Profiles of several women who have found such opportunities are included.

18458 ■ *"Obama Plan May Boost Maryland Cyber Security" in Boston Business Journal (Vol. 29, May 20, 2011, No. 2, pp. 1)*
Pub: American City Business Journals Inc.
Ed: Scott Dance. **Description:** May 12, 2011 outline of the cyber security policies of President Obama may improve the cyber security industry in Maryland as the state is home to large defense and intelligence activities. Details of the proposed policies are discusses as well as their advantages to companies that deal in developing cyber security plans for other companies.

18459 ■ *"Online Security Crackdown: Scanning Service Oversees Site Security at David's Bridal" in (Vol. 84, July 2008, No. 7, pp. 46)*
Pub: Chain Store Age
Ed: Samantha Murphy. **Description:** Online retailers are beefing up security on their Websites. Cyber thieves use retail systems in order to gain entry to consumer data. David's Bridal operates over 275 bridal showrooms in the U.S. and has a one-stop wedding resource for new brides planning weddings.

18460 ■ *"Oracle and Tauri Group Honored by Homeland Security and Defense Business Council" in Wireless News (December 15, 2009)*
Pub: Close-Up Media
Description: Selected as members of the year by the Homeland Security and Defense Business Council were Oracle, a software company that has provided thought leadership and strategic insights as well as The Tauri Group, an analytical consultancy, that has demonstrated a unique understanding of the role of small business and its vital contribution to the success of the country's security.

18461 ■ *"Out Front and Strong" in WorkingUSA (Vol. 11, December 2008, No. 4, pp. 477)*
Pub: Blackwell Publishers Ltd.
Ed: Jessica Wilkerson. **Description:** History of the Tennessee Committee on Occupational Safety and Health that formed in East Tennessee in 1979 is explored. The article addresses how local women contributed to the organization at the grassroots.

18462 ■ *"Panda Security for Business 4.05" in SC Magazine (Vol. 21, July 2010, No. 7, pp. 50)*
Pub: Haymarket Media Inc.
Description: Profile of Panda Security for Business, software offering endpoint security protection for computer desktops and servers is presented.

18463 ■ *"PC Connection Acquires Cloud Software Provider" in New Hampshire Business Review (Vol. 33, March 25, 2011, No. 6, pp. 8)*
Pub: Business Publications Inc.
Description: Merrimack-based PC Connection Inc. acquired ValCom Technology, a provider of cloud-based IT service management software. Details of the deal are included.

18464 ■ *"Prevent Identity Theft: Simple Steps To Protect Yourself Against Identity Theft" in Small Business Opportunities (January 2008)*
Pub: Harris Publications Inc.
Ed: Frank W. Abagnale. **Description:** Expert shares tips to help individuals and businesses protect themselves from identity theft.

18465 ■ *"Protection One Introduces Home and Business Security iPhone App" in Wireless News (November 13, 2009)*
Pub: Close-Up Media
Description: Protection One, Inc., a provider of security systems to business and residential customers, has developed an application that allows users to access their security panels and receive real-time updates from their iPhone or iPod touch devices.

18466 ■ *"The Quality Revolution" in Canadian Business (Vol. 81, November 10, 2008, No. 19, pp. 128)*
Pub: Rogers Media Ltd.
Ed: Andrew Nikiforuk. **Description:** John Volpe believes that the pursuit of quantity of food choices leads to tasteless meals, expanding waistlines, and food poisoning and stresses emphasis on food quality and food security.

18467 ■ *"Ready for the Worst? How to Disaster-Proof Your Business" in Inc. (Vol. 33, September 2011, No. 7, pp. 38)*
Pub: Inc. Magazine
Ed: J.J. McCorvey, Dave Smith. **Description:** Twelve products to and services designed to help small businesses run smoothly in the event of a disaster are outlined.

18468 ■ *"Remote Control: Working From Wherever"* in Inc. (February 2008, pp. 46-47)
Pub: Gruner & Jahr USA Publishing
Ed: Ryan Underwood. **Description:** New technology allows workers to perform tasks from anywhere via the Internet. Profiles of products to help connect to your office from afar include, LogMein Pro, a Web-based service that allowsaccess to a computer from anywhere; Xdrive, an online service that allows users to store and swap files; Basecamp, a Web-based tools that works like a secure version of MySpace; MojoPac Freedom, is software that allows users to copy their computer's desktop to a removable hard drive and plug into any PC; WatchGuard Firebox X Core e-Series UTM Bundle, hardware that blocks hackers and viruses while allowing employees to work remotely; TightVNC, a free open-source software that lets you control another computer via the Internet.

18469 ■ *"Rep. Loretta Sanchez Holds a Hearing on Small Business Cyber Security"* in Political/Congressional Transcript Wire (July 29, 2010)
Pub: CQ Roll Call
Description: U.S. House Committee on Armed Services, Subcommittee on Terrorism, Unconventional Threats and Capabilities held a hearing on small business cyber security innovation.

18470 ■ *"Research and Market Adds Report: Endpoint Security for Business"* in Wireless News (October 26, 2009)
Pub: Close-Up Media
Description: Summarizes Research and Markets Adds Report: Endpoint Security for Business: Desktops, Laptops & Mobile Devices 2009-2014; highlights include a detailed analysis of where the industry is at present and forecasts regarding how it will develop over the next five years.

18471 ■ *"Retailers Report 'Shrinkage' of Inventory on the Rise"* in Arkansas Business (Vol. 26, September 28, 2009, No. 39, pp. 17)
Pub: Journal Publishing Inc.
Ed: Mark Friedman. **Description:** According to a National Retail Security Survey report released last June, retailers across the country have lost about $36.5 billion in shrinkage, most of it at the hands of employees and shoplifters alike. Statistical data included.

18472 ■ *"Safety Managers Need to Be Safety Experts"* in Indoor Comfort Marketing (Vol. 70, May 2011, No. 5, pp. 10)
Pub: Industry Publications Inc.
Ed: Mike Hodge. **Description:** It is imperative to have a good safety manager in place for all heating and cooling firms.

18473 ■ *"Sales Communications in a Mobile World"* in Business Communication Quarterly (December 2007, pp. 492)
Pub: SAGE Publications USA
Contact: Blaise R. Simqu, President
Ed: Daniel T. Norris. **Description:** Salespeople can take advantage of the latest mobile technologies while maintaining a personal touch with clients and customers through innovation, formality in interactions, client interactions, and protection and security of mobile data.

18474 ■ *"Scanning the Field"* in Business Courier (Vol. 26, January 8, 2010, No. 38, pp. 1)
Pub: American City Business Journals, Inc.
Ed: Jon Newberry. **Description:** Anti-terror detection systems developer Valley Force Composite Technologies Inc. of Kentucky plans to enter the market with its high-resolution ODIN and Thor-LVX screening systems. These systems are expected to meet the increasing demand for airport security equipment.

18475 ■ *"SECO Manufacturing"* in Point of Beginning (Vol. , 2008, No. , pp.)
Pub: BNP Media
Contact: Al Reser, President
Description: Seco Manufacturing's 3015-Series lock features an all-metal tilting holder with an improved brass front locking lever for improved security for any building.

18476 ■ *"Security Alert: Data Server"* in Entrepreneur (Vol. 36, February 2008, No. 2, pp. 28)
Pub: Entrepreneur Media Inc.
Ed: Amanda C. Kooser. **Description:** Michael Kogon is the founder of Definition 6, a technology consulting and interactive marking firm. He believes in the philosophy that the best way to keep sensitive data safe is not to store it. Details on the security policies of his firm are discussed.

18477 ■ *"A Security Risk?'* in Canadian Business (Vol. 80, October 22, 2007, No. 21, pp. 36)
Pub: Rogers Media
Ed: Joe Castaldo. **Description:** Garda World Security Corporation declared a C$1.5 million loss in the second quarter of 2007. The company's securities have been falling since June and hit a 52-week low of $15.90 in September. Details of the physical and cash-handling firm's strategy to integrate its acquisitions are discussed.

18478 ■ *"Selling Online: Canada's Bestselling Guide to Becoming a Successful E-Commerce Merchant*
Pub: John Wiley and Sons Canada Ltd.
Ed: Jim Carroll; Rick Broadhead. **Released:** September 6, 2002. **Description:** Helps individuals build online retail enterprises; this updated version includes current tools, information and success strategies, how to launch an online storefront, security, marketing strategies, and mistakes to avoid.

18479 ■ *"Selling Your Company"* in Inc. (March 2008, pp. 78)
Pub: Gruner & Jahr USA Publishing
Ed: Myra Goodman. **Description:** Owner of a safety consulting company seeks advice for selling the firm.

18480 ■ *"Sign of Progress"* in Playthings (Vol. 106, October 1, 2008, No. 9, pp. 4)
Pub: Reed Business Information
Contact: Jeff Greisch, President
Ed: Cliff Annicelli. **Description:** The ramifications of the toy recalls in 2007 are discussed. Mandates for lead-free toys and other safety issues are having an impact on the American toy industry.

18481 ■ *"Some Atlantic Beach Leaders Leery About Convenience Store Safety Measure"* in Florida Times-Union (November 3, 2010)
Pub: Florida Times-Union
Ed: Drew Dixon. **Description:** Jacksonville, Florida authorities are proposing a new ordinance that would require convenience stores to upgrade safety measures to protect store workers and customers from robbery and other crimes.

18482 ■ *"STAR TEC Incubator's Latest Resident Shows Promise"* in The Business Journal-Serving Greater Tampa Bay (August 8, 2008)
Pub: American City Business Journals, Inc.
Ed: Jane Meinhardt. **Description:** Field Forensics Inc., a resident of the STAR Technology Enterprise Center, has grown after being admitted into the business accelerator. The producer of defense and security devices and equipment has doubled 2007 sales as of 2008.

18483 ■ *"State Democrats Push for Changes to Plant Security Law"* in Chemical Week (Vol. 172, July 19, 2010, No. 17, pp. 8)
Pub: Access Intelligence L.L.C.
Contact: Donald Pazour, President
Ed: Kara Sissell. **Description:** Legislation has been introduced to revise the existing U.S. Chemical Facility Anti-Terrorism Standards (CFATS) that would include a requirement for facilities to use inherently safer technology (IST). The bill would eliminate the current law's exemption of water treatment plants and certain port facilities and preserve the states' authority to establish stronger security standards.

18484 ■ *"A Survey of DHT Security Techniques"* in ACM Computing Surveys (Vol. 43, Summer 2011, No. 2, pp. 8)
Pub: Association for Computing Machinery
Ed: Guido Urdaneta, Guillaume Pierre, Maarten Van Steen. **Description:** Peer-to-peer networks based on distributed hash tables (DHTs) have received considerable attention since their introduction in 2001. Unfortunately, DHT-based systems have been shown to be difficult to protect against security attacks. An overview of techniques reported in literature for making DHT-based systems resistant to the three most important attacks that can be launched by malicious nodes participating in the DHT is given: the Sybil attack, the Eclipse attack, and routing and storage attacks.

18485 ■ *Surviving in the Security Alarm Business*
Pub: Butterworth-Heinemann
Ed: Lou Sepulveda. **Released:** 1998. **Price:** $19.95.

18486 ■ *"Symantic Completes Acquisition of VeriSign's Security Business"* in Internet Wire (August 9, 2010)
Pub: Comtex
Description: Symantec Corporation acquired VeriSign's identity and authentication business, which includes Secure Sockets Layer (SSL) and Code Signing Certificate Services, the Managed Public Key Infrastructure (MPKI) Services, the VeriSign Trust Seal, the VeriSign Identity Protection (VIP) Authentication Service and the VIP Fraud Protection Service (FDS). The agreement also included a majority stake in VeriSign Japan.

18487 ■ *"Taking a Chance"* in Baltimore Business Journal (Vol. 28, July 16, 2010, No. 10, pp. 1)
Pub: Baltimore Business Journal
Ed: Scott Dance. **Description:** North Avenue in Baltimore, Maryland is considered a rough neighborhood due to the dangers of prostitution and drug dealing. However, some entrepreneurs have taken the risk of building their businesses on North Avenue as revitalization efforts grow. One of the challenges for businesses in rough neighborhoods is bringing customers to their stores or offices.

18488 ■ *"Taking the Steps Into the Clouds"* in New Hampshire Business Review (Vol. 33, March 25, 2011, No. 6, pp. 19)
Pub: Business Publications Inc.
Ed: Tim Wessels. **Description:** Cloud services include Internet and Web security, spam filtering, message archiving, work group collaboration, IT asset management, help desk and disaster recovery backup.

18489 ■ *"Tauri Group Partner Joining Homeland Security and Defense"* in Wireless News (December 15, 2009)
Pub: Close-Up Media
Description: Managing partner Cosmo DiMaggio III of the Tauri Group, a provider of analytic consulting for homeland security, defense and space clients, has been elected to the Board of Directors at Homeland Security and Defense Business Council.

18490 ■ *"Tech Data Launches Unified Communications and Network Security Specialized Business Units"* in Wireless News (October 22,2009)
Pub: Close-Up Media
Description: Responding to the growing demand for unified communications and network security, Tech Data announced the formation of two new Specialized Business Units.

18491 ■ *"Tech Investing: March's Long Road"* in Canadian Business (Vol. 80, January 29, 2007, No. 3, pp. 67)
Pub: Rogers Media
Ed: Calvin Leung. **Description:** The efforts of March Networks, a manufacturer of digital surveillance equipment, from the decline in the price of its shares at the beginning of the year 2007 are described.

18492 ■ *"Technology Protects Lottery"* in Arkansas Business (Vol. 26, September 28, 2009, No. 39, pp. 1)
Pub: Journal Publishing Inc.
Ed: George Waldon. **Description:** Arkansas Lottery Commission was initially criticized for what was seen as a major breach in security protocol by revealing the exact location of 26 million lottery tickets during a publicity stunt in which the media was invited to the

main distribution center; however, due to the high-tech security that has been implemented the tickets are worthless until their status is changed after passing through multiple security scans.

18493 ■ "Tektronix Buys Arbor Networks for Security Business" in eWeek (August 9, 2010)
Pub: Ziff Davis Enterprise

Description: Tektronix Communications, provider of communications test and network intelligence solutions will acquire Arbor Networks. The deal will help Tektronix build a brand in security. Details of the transaction are included.

18494 ■ "This Year's Model" in Playthings (Vol. 107, January 1, 2009, No. 1, pp. 23)
Pub: Reed Business Information
Contact: Jeff Greisch, President

Ed: Karyn M. Peterson. **Description:** Toy manufacturers, as well as retailers, address the need to exceed safety and quality demands by consumers when developing new toys and games for children.

18495 ■ "Thomas and His Washington Friends" in CFO (Vol. 23, October 2007, No. 10, pp. 18)
Pub: CFO Publishing Corporation

Ed: Alix Stuart. **Description:** Reliance on Chinese suppliers to America's toymakers may become quite costly as Congress considers legislation that would increase fines to as high as $50 million for companies selling tainted products. The legislation would also require independent mandatory testing for makers of products for children.

18496 ■ "The Total Cost of Ignorance: Avoiding Top Tech Mistakes" in Black Enterprise (Vol. 38, October 2007, No. 3, pp. 64)
Pub: Earl G. Graves Publishing Co. Inc.

Ed: Alwin A.D. Jones. **Description:** Cost of data loss for any small business can be devastating; lack of security is another mistake companies make when it comes to technology.

18497 ■ "Tougher Securities Rules on the Way" in Globe & Mail (February 21, 2007, pp. B1)
Pub: CTVglobemedia Publishing Inc.

Ed: Janet McFarland. **Description:** The Canadian Securities Administration will implement new regulation for the securities industry by early next year. Securities companies will now have to register its employee details and earnings according to this new rule.

18498 ■ "Toy Scares Drive Business" in Boston Business Journal (Vol. 27, November 23, 2007, No. 43, pp. 1)
Pub: American City Business Journals, Inc.

Ed: Joan Goodchild. **Description:** Several Boston businesses have tapped into the lead content scare in toys and other products manufactured in China. ConRoy Corporation LLC launched Toy Recall Alert!, an online tool to alert consumers about new recalls while Hybrivet Systems introduced screening test kit, LeadCheck. Other new products pertaining to toy safety are discussed.

18499 ■ "Toy Story" in Forbes (Vol. 180, October 15, 2007, No. 8, pp. 102)
Pub: Forbes Inc.

Description: Three voluntary recalls of Chinese-made toys were announced by American toymakers, sending Mattel stocks plummeting.

18500 ■ "Toy Story: U.S.-Made a Hot Seller" in Crain's Detroit Business (Vol. 23, December 17, 2007, No. 51, pp. 3)
Pub: Crain Communications Inc. - Detroit

Ed: Chad Halcom. **Description:** American Plastic Toys, located in Walled Lake, Michigan reports all its toys are made in the U.S. and have passed all U.S. safety standards. Revenue for American Plastic Toys reached nearly $33 million in 2005, and the company expects to exceed that because of recent toy safety recalls of products produced in China.

18501 ■ "Tragedies Add Demand for Inspiron's Alert System" in Crain's Cleveland Business (Vol. 28, October 29, 2007, No. 43, pp. 5)
Pub: Crain Communications, Inc.

Ed: Chuck Soder. **Description:** Inspiron Logistics Corp. has seen huge growth over the past months for its Wireless Emergency Notification System which colleges and universities have rushed to buy since the April 16 shootings at Virginia Tech. The company now makes more than half of its revenue by selling the systems to colleges whereas previous to the shootings the academic market accounted for just 20 percent of the company's sales.

18502 ■ "Twitter Hack: Made in Japan? User Says Attack Showed Security Flaw" in Houston Chronicle (September 24, 2010, pp. 3)
Pub: Houston Chronicle

Ed: Tomoko A. Hosaka. **Description:** Details of the attack on Twitter caused by a Japanese computer hacker are revealed.

18503 ■ "Unbound ID Raises $2 Million" in Austin Business JournalInc. (Vol. 28, December 12, 2008, No. 39, pp. 1)
Pub: American City Business Journals

Ed: Christopher Calnan. **Description:** Austin, Texas-based Unbound ID Corporation has secured $2 million in funding from venture capital firm Silverton Partners. The company has developed identity management software for network directories. The market for identity management technology is expected to grow to more than $12.3 billion by 2014.

18504 ■ "U.S. Enters BlackBerry Dispute Compromise Sought Over Security Issues" in Houston Chronicle (August 6, 2010)
Pub: Houston Chronicle

Ed: Matthew Lee. **Description:** U.S. State Department is working for a compromise with Research in Motion, manufacturer of the BlackBerry, over security issues. The Canadian company makes the smartphones and foreign governments believe they pose a security risk.

18505 ■ "Vandal-Resistant Mortise Locks" in Building Design and Construction (Vol. 49, September 1, 2008, No. 12, pp. 78)
Pub: Reed Business Information

Description: Stanley Security Solutions offers mortise locks with a vandal-resistant feature that includes a clutch mechanism designed to break away when excessive force is applied either by kicking or standing on the lever. Once the mortise lock breaks away it can be easily reset to its original position without sustaining damage.

18506 ■ "VeriFone Announces Global Security Solutions Business" in Marketing Weekly News (October 3, 2009)
Pub: Investment Weekly News

Description: Focused on delivering innovative security solutions, VeriFone Holdings, Inc. announced the formation of its Global Security Solutions Business Unit, including VeriShield Protect, an end-to-end encryption to protect cardholder data throughout the merchant and processor systems. The business will focus on consulting, sales and implementation of these new products in order to help retailers and processors protect customer data.

18507 ■ "Video Surveillance Enters Digital Era, Makes Giant Strides" in Arkansas Business (Vol. 26, September 28, 2009, No. 39, pp. 1)
Pub: Journal Publishing Inc.

Ed: Jamie Walden. **Description:** Arkansas business owners are finding that the newest technology in video surveillance is leading to swift apprehension of thieves due to the high-quality digital imagery now being captured on surveillance equipment. Motion detection software for these systems is enhancing the capabilities of these systems and providing opportunities for businesses that would normally have problems integrating these systems.

18508 ■ "Watchful Eye: Entrepreneur Protects Clients and His Bottom Line" in Black Enterprise (Vol. 38, March 2008, No. 8, pp. 46)
Pub: Earl G. Graves Publishing Co. Inc.

Ed: Tennille M. Robinson. **Description:** Profile of Elijah Shaw, founder of Icon Services Corporation, a full service security and investigative service; Shaw shares his plans to protect clients while growing his business.

18509 ■ "Wegmans Uses Database for Recall" in Supermarket News (Vol. 56, September 22, 2008, No. 38)
Pub: Penton Business Media, Inc.

Ed: Carol Angrisani. **Description:** Wegmans used data obtained through its loyalty card that, in turn, sent automated telephone calls to every customer who had purchased tainted pet food when Mars Pet-care recalled dog food products.

18510 ■ "What the Future Holds for Consumers" in Black Enterprise (Vol. 41, August 2010, No. 1, pp. 47)
Pub: Earl G. Graves Publishing Co. Inc.

Ed: Sheiresa Ngo. **Description:** The way people purchase goods and service has changed with technology. With an increased focus on security (as well as privacy and fairness) the U.S. Congress began regulating the credit card industry with the Fair Credit Reporting Act of 1970 and the Credit Card Accountability, Responsibility, and Disclosure (CARD) Act of 2009.

18511 ■ "Who Gets the Last Laugh?" in Barron's (Vol. 88, March 31, 2008, No. 13, pp. 17)
Pub: Dow Jones & Company, Inc.

Ed: Leslie P. Norton. **Description:** Nord/LB will take a charge of 82.5 million euros to cover potential losses apparently related to Vatas' refusal to take the shares of Remote MDx Inc. after buying the shares. Remote MDx's main product is an ankle bracelet to monitor criminals; the firm has lost over half of its market cap due to the Nord/LB troubles and questions about its revenues.

18512 ■ "Windstream Expands Business Service Into Monroe" in Marketing Weekly News (January 23, 2010, pp. 77)
Pub: Investment Weekly News

Description: Windstream Corp. announces the expansion of its data and voice services into Monroe, N.C., which will give local businesses a new choice for advanced communication services and network security.

STATISTICAL SOURCES

18513 ■ RMA Annual Statement Studies
Pub: Risk Management Association
Contact: Kevin M. Blakey, President
Released: Annual. **Price:** $175.00 2006-07 edition, $105.00. **Description:** Contains composite balance sheets and income statements for more than 360 industries, including the accounting, auditing, and bookkeeping industries. Also contains five years of comparative historical data for discerning trends. Includes 16 commonly used ratios, computed for most of the size groupings for nearly every industry.

TRADE PERIODICALS

18514 ■ Newsline
Pub: National Burglar and Fire Alarm Association
Ed: Amanda Johnston, Editor. **Released:** 6/year. **Price:** Included in membership. **Description:** Provides news on the security industry, including marketing tips for small businesses and false alarm prevention ideas. Recurring features include interviews, a calendar of events, reports of meetings, news of educational opportunities, book reviews, and notices of publications available.

18515 ■ Police & Security News
Pub: Days Communications
Contact: Dean Seavers, President
URL(s): policeandsecuritynews.com. **Released:** Bimonthly **Price:** $18, By mail; $75, Other countries mail.

18516 ■ *Security: For Buyers of Security Products, Systems, and Services*
Pub: BNP Media
Contact: Al Reser, President
URL(s): www.securitymagazine.com. **Ed:** Bill Zalud.
Released: Monthly **Price:** Free.

18517 ■ *Security Management*
Pub: ASIS International
Contact: Eduard J. Emde, President
URL(s): www.securitymanagement.com/. **Released:**
Monthly **Price:** Free to members; $115, Nonmembers; $115, Out of country; $48, /year.

18518 ■ *Security Sales & Integration*
Pub: Bobit Business Media
Contact: Ty Bobit, President
URL(s): www.securitysales.com. **Released:** Monthly
Price: Free. **Telecommunication Services:** Email:
info@securitysales.com .

VIDEOCASSETTES/ AUDIOCASSETTES

18519 ■ *Executive Protection Video Catalog*
Gun Video
4585 Murphy Canyon Rd.
San Diego, CA 92123
Ph: (858)569-4000
Free: 800-942-8273
Fax: (858)569-0505
Co. E-mail: info2@gunvideo.com
URL: http://www.gunvideo.com
Released: 19??. **Price:** $29.95. **Description:** A discussion of various high-tech security devices, including instructions on their use. Includes information on where they can be bought. **Availability:** VHS.

TRADE SHOWS AND CONVENTIONS

18520 ■ *ISC Chicago*
Reed Exhibitions North American Headquarters
383 Main Ave.
Norwalk, CT 06851
Ph: (203)840-4800
Fax: (203)840-5805
Co. E-mail: inquiry@reedexpo.com
URL: http://www.reedexpo.com
URL(s): isc.reedexpo.com. **Frequency:** Biennial. **Audience:** Security equipment dealers and installers, corporate, industrial and institutional security managers and directors. **Principal Exhibits:** Residential, commercial, industrial and institutional security equipment, systems and services. **Telecommunication Services:** inquiry@isc.reedexpo.com.

CONSULTANTS

18521 ■ *Lenow International Inc.*
1503 Union Ave., Ste. 210
Memphis, TN 38173

Ph: (901)726-0735
Fax: (901)725-4079
URL: http://www.lenowinternational.com
Contact: Nate Lenow, Jr., President
E-mail: nate@lenowinternational.com
Scope: Acts as a consultant for investigative strategies to resolve civil or criminal investigations. Conducts surveys or evaluations to prevent crime directed toward business, in particular crime involving fraudulent activity. Recommends security procedures or equipment to aid loss prevention by business. Available to serve as expert witness in forensic security and fraud examination. Referral source for investigative agencies. Industries served: Corporate security departments, private investigative agencies, small business, and government agencies. **Founded:** 1977. **Publications:** "Competitive Intelligence," Law Enforcement Quarterly. **Seminars:** Automate your reports with software, Tennessee Association of Investigators, May, 2000; Use of Computer as an Investigative Tool; Criminal Investigation.

FRANCHISES AND BUSINESS OPPORTUNITIES

18522 ■ *Direct Link*
10700 Montgomery Rd., Ste. 300
Cincinnati, OH 45242
Free: 800-216-4196
Fax: (513)563-2691
Co. E-mail: inquiry@homehelpers.cc
URL: http://www.HomeHelpers.cc
Description: In-home emergency monitoring system for seniors. **No. of Franchise Units:** 440. **Founded:** 1997.. **Franchised:** 1997. **Equity Capital Needed:** $21,100-$30,800. **Franchise Fee:** $18,900. **Financial Assistance:** Yes. **Training:** Yes.

18523 ■ *EYESthere*
EYESthere Franchise Inc.
10725 SW Barbur Blvd.
Portland, OR 97219
Ph: (503)726-3937
Co. E-mail: info@eyesthere.com
URL: http://www.eyesthere.com
URL(s): www.eyestheredfw.com. **Description:** Custom designs solutions that protect and empower businesses with live and recorded video. Franchises help protect our customer's premises, property, people and transactions and empower the owners, employees and customers with EYESthere unique Digital Video solutions. **No. of Company-Owned Units:** 5. **Founded:** 2006.. **Franchised:** 2007. **Equity Capital Needed:** $190,000-$310,000. **Franchise Fee:** $45,000. **Royalty Fee:** 6-10%. **Training:** Provides 2 weeks at headquarters, 2 weeks at franchisee's location and ongoing support.

18524 ■ *MonitorClosely.com*
Monitor Closely.com, LLC
901 King St., Ste. 101
Alexandria, VA 45242

Free: 800-797-7505
Description: Digital surveillance systems. **No. of Franchise Units:** 117. **Founded:** 2006.. **Franchised:** 2006. **Equity Capital Needed:** $45,000-$60,000. **Franchise Fee:** $39,500. **Royalty Fee:** 8%. **Training:** Provides 4 days training at headquarters and ongoing support.

18525 ■ *SHIELD Security Systems*
Shield Development, Ltd.
5170 Genesee St.
Bowmansville, NY 14026
Ph: (716)681-6677
Fax: (716)636-8819
Co. E-mail: franchise@SHIELDsecurity.net
URL: http://www.SHIELDsecurity.net
Description: Sales and installation of burglar and fire alarm systems. **No. of Franchise Units:** 26. **No. of Company-Owned Units:** 3. **Founded:** 1976.. **Franchised:** 2000. **Equity Capital Needed:** $74,275-$125,550. **Franchise Fee:** $40,000. **Training:** Yes.

18526 ■ *Signature Alert Security*
746 E Winchester St., Ste. 110
Salt Lake City, UT 84107
Ph: (801)743-0101
Free: 800-957-1030
Fax: (801)743-0808
Description: Sales, installation, and monitoring of security systems. **No. of Franchise Units:** 36. **No. of Company-Owned Units:** 3. **Founded:** 1999.. **Franchised:** 2003. **Equity Capital Needed:** $42,950-$50,500. **Franchise Fee:** $21,000. **Royalty Fee:** $2/customer/month. **Financial Assistance:** Limited in-house assistance available. **Training:** Includes 5 days training at corporate headquarters, 2 days at franchisee's location and ongoing support.

18527 ■ *Sonitrol Corp.*
Automated Security Holdings
1000 Westlakes Dr., Ste. 150
Berwyn, PA 19312
Ph: (610)725-9706
Fax: (610)725-9707
Description: Franchises auto intrusion alarm systems. **No. of Franchise Units:** 178. **No. of Company-Owned Units:** 57. **Founded:** 1964. **Franchised:** 1965. **Equity Capital Needed:** $245,000-$500,000. **Franchise Fee:** $25,000-$55,000. **Royalty Fee:** 4.5%. **Training:** Includes training at headquarters, franchisee's location and ongoing.

RESEARCH CENTERS

18528 ■ *University of Louisville - National Crime Prevention Institute (NCPI)*
206 Mccandless Hall
Louisville, KY 40292
Ph: (502)852-8577
Free: 800-334-8635
Fax: (502)852-0335
Co. E-mail: marianna.perry@louisville.edu
URL: http://louisville.edu/ncpi/
Contact: Marianna Perry, Director
Services: Crime Prevention Information Center. **Founded:** 1971.

START-UP INFORMATION

18529 ■ How to Start a Home-Based Event Planning Business
Pub: Globe Pequot Press
Ed: Jill Moran. **Released:** July 2007. **Price:** $18.95.
Description: Guide to starting and growing a business planning events from a home-based firm.

ASSOCIATIONS AND OTHER ORGANIZATIONS

18530 ■ Canadian Society of Professional Event Planners (CanSPEP)
312 Oakwood Ct.
Newmarket, ON, Canada L3Y 3C8
Ph: (905)868-8008
Free: 866-467-2299
Fax: (905)895-1630
Co. E-mail: info@canspep.ca
URL: http://canspep.ca
Contact: Rita Plaskett, President
Description: Provides a forum for entrepreneurs in the meetings, conferences and event planning profession to meet, share ideas, gain new and valuable information about the industry and work together to form a strong presence in the marketplace. Promotes professionalism and builds awareness of independent meeting planning industry to the target markets. **Founded:** 1996. **Publications:** *The Independent* (Quarterly).

18531 ■ Connected International Meeting Professionals Association (CIMPA)
9200 Bayard Pl.
Fairfax, VA 22032
Ph: (512)684-0889
Fax: (267)390-5193
Co. E-mail: susan@cimpa.org
URL: http://www.cimpa.org
Contact: Andrea Sigler, President
Description: Meeting planners, incentive organizers, travel agents, tour operators, and seminar organizers in 42 countries. Works to improve the skills of professional conference and convention planners. Serves as a clearinghouse of information on new travel destinations and planning technologies, techniques, and strategies. Facilitates exchange of information among Internet professionals. Produces a television program on travel and meetings. Conducts educational courses and awards Certified Internet Meeting Professional designation. Conducts research programs and placement service. Sponsors training courses on the Internet. **Scope:** A meeting planning organization offering counsel in the following areas: technology in conference planning, management services for international meetings and conventions, certification programs in effective meeting organization, educational programs and curriculum development for all types of industries and e-commerce. **Founded:** 1982. **Publications:** "Mice International"; "How Meeting Planners are Using Technology In Their Jobs"; "Internet Tools for Meeting Planners & Event Organizers"; "Getting Along With Others: Gut

Instincts"; "How to Sell to Meeting Planners"; "Meeting Checklists"; "How to Organize International Meetings". **Educational Activities:** International Technology Meetings and Incentives Conference (Annual). **Awards:** Tech-Savvy Hotels Award (Annual). **Seminars:** How to Sell to Meeting Planners; How to Be a Convention Planner; Career Opportunities in Conference Management; MAKING CONNECTIONS. **Telecommunication Services:** cimpa@cimpa.org; info@cimpa.org.

18532 ■ The Independent
312 Oakwood Ct.
Newmarket, ON, Canada L3Y 3C8
Ph: (905)868-8008
Free: 866-467-2299
Fax: (905)895-1630
Co. E-mail: info@canspep.ca
URL: http://canspep.ca
Contact: Rita Plaskett, President
Released: Quarterly

18533 ■ International Association of Speakers Bureaus (IASB)
3933 S McClintock Dr., Ste. 505
Tempe, AZ 85282
Ph: (480)839-1423
Fax: (480)603-4141
Co. E-mail: info@iasbweb.org
URL: http://www.iasbweb.org
Contact: Holli Catchpole, President
Description: Maintains speakers' bureau representing 15 countries. Focuses on continuing education for its members, promotes awareness among meeting planners and raises the bar on accepted practices in the speakers' bureau industry. **Founded:** 1986.

18534 ■ National Speakers Association (NSA)
1500 S Priest Dr.
Tempe, AZ 85281
Ph: (480)968-2552
Fax: (480)968-0911
Co. E-mail: information@nsaspeaker.org
URL: http://www.nsaspeaker.org
Contact: Kristin Arnold, President
Description: Professional speakers. Works to increase public awareness of the speaking profession, advance the integrity and visibility of professional speakers, and provide a learning and communication vehicle to professional speakers. Sponsors workshops, conventions, and labs. **Scope:** An association for experts who speak professionally. Members include experts in a variety of industries and disciplines, who reach audiences as trainers, educators, humorists, motivators, consultants and authors. Provides resources and education designed to enhance the business skills and platform performance of professional speakers. **Founded:** 1972. **Publications:** *Voices of Experience* (10/year); *Who's Who in Professional Speaking: The Meeting Planner's Guide* (Annual); *Who's Who in Professional Speaking: The Meeting Planner's Guide* (Annual). **Awards:** Certified Speaking Professional; Cavett Award; Council of Peers Award of Excellence - Speaker Hall of Fame (Annual); Council of Peers Award for Excellence/Speaker Hall of Fame.

EDUCATIONAL PROGRAMS

18535 ■ Design for Presentations
EEI Communications
8945 Guilford Rd., Ste. 145
Columbia, MD 21046
Ph: (410)309-8200
Free: 888-253-2762
Fax: (410)630-3980
Co. E-mail: train@eeicom.com
URL: http://www.eeicom.com/eei-training-services
Price: $745.00. **Description:** Seminar for professionals with experience using Microsoft PowerPoint, but minimal formal design training. Covers enhancing presentation design; creating more effective grids and graphs; using color and typeface effectively, and how to avoid ten design disasters. **Dates and Locations:** Silver Spring, MD; Alexandria, VA; Hunt Valley, MD; and Columbia, MD.

REFERENCE WORKS

18536 ■ "The Art and Business of Motivation Speaking: Your Guide" in Inc. (Volume 32, December 2010, No. 10, pp. 124)
Pub: Inc. Magazine
Ed: Leigh Buchanan. **Description:** Profile of Josh Shipp that discusses his career as a motivational speaker.

18537 ■ "BBB Hires Marketing Firm to Attract More Businesses" in Baltimore Business Journal (Vol. 27, January 1, 2010, No. 35, pp. 1)
Pub: American City Business Journals
Ed: Julekha Dash. **Description:** Better Business Bureau (BBB) of Greater Maryland hired Bystry Carson & Associates Ltd. to assist in its rebranding efforts in order to entice more businesses. Bystry Carson will promote BBB's new mission at lectures, seminars, and networking events, as well as educate businesses about the agency through blogs and Twitter. BBB's services are also outlined.

18538 ■ "Calendar" in Crain's Detroit Business (Vol. 24, March 10, 2008, No. 10, pp. 21)
Pub: Crain Communications, Inc.
Description: Listing of events in the Detroit area include conferences addressing entrepreneurialism, economic development, and women business ownership.

18539 ■ "Calendar" in Crain's Detroit Business (Vol. 24, March 17, 2008, No. 11, pp. 20)
Pub: Crain Communications, Inc.
Description: Listing of events in the Detroit area include conferences addressing entrepreneurialism, economic development, and women business ownership.

18540 ■ *"Calendar" in Crain's Detroit Business (Vol. 24, March 24, 2008, No. 12, pp. 25)*
Pub: Crain Communications, Inc.
Description: Listing of events in the Detroit area include conferences addressing entrepreneurialism, economic development, and women business ownership.

18541 ■ *"Calendar" in Crain's Detroit Business (Vol. 24, March 31, 2008, No. 13, pp. 1)*
Pub: Crain Communications, Inc.
Description: Listing of events in the Detroit area include conferences addressing entrepreneurialism, economic development, and minority business ownership.

18542 ■ *"Calendar" in Crain's Detroit Business (Vol. 24, April 7, 2008, No. 14, pp. 27)*
Pub: Crain Communications, Inc.
Description: Listing of events in the Detroit area include conferences addressing entrepreneurialism, economic development, and minority business ownership.

18543 ■ *"Calendar" in Crain's Detroit Business (Vol. 24, April 14, 2008, No. 15, pp. 25)*
Pub: Crain Communications Inc.
Description: Listing of events in the Detroit area include conferences addressing entrepreneurialism, economic development, and ways in which to develop environmentally friendly buildings.

18544 ■ *"Calendar" in Crain's Detroit Business (Vol. 24, September 22, 2008, No. 38, pp. 17)*
Pub: Crain Communications Inc.
Description: Listing of events in the Detroit area include conferences addressing entrepreneurialism, economic development, and women business ownership.

18545 ■ *"Calendar" in Crain's Detroit Business (Vol. 24, October 6, 2008, No. 40, pp. 22)*
Pub: Crain Communications, Inc.
Description: Listing of events in the Detroit area include conferences addressing entrepreneurialism, economic development, manufacturing, marketing, the housing crisis and women business ownership.

18546 ■ *"The Center of Success: Author Explores How Confidence Can Take You Further" in Black Enterprise (Vol. 38, March 2008, No. 8)*
Pub: Earl G. Graves Publishing Co. Inc.
Ed: Ayana Dixon. **Description:** Motivational speaker and author, Valorie Burton, provides a 50-question confidence quotient assessment to help business owners and managers develop confidence in order to obtain goals.

18547 ■ *"Chamber Offers Seminar on Web Design" in Charlotte Observer (February 6, 2007)*
Pub: Knight-Ridder/Tribune Business News
Ed: Joe DePriest. **Description:** Belmont Chamber of Commerce and Gaston College Small Business Center will offer seminars on online Web design.

18548 ■ *"Conference Calendar" in Marketing to Women (Vol. 21, April 2008, No. 4, pp. 7)*
Pub: EPM Communications Inc.
Contact: Ira Mayer, President
E-mail: imayer@epmcom.com
Description: Listing of current conferences and events concerning women, marketing and business.

18549 ■ *"Conference Calendar" in Marketing to Women (Vol. 21, March 2008, No. 3, pp. 7)*
Pub: EPM Communications Inc.
Contact: Ira Mayer, President
E-mail: imayer@epmcom.com
Description: Listing of current conferences and events aimed at women entrepreneurs and leaders.

18550 ■ *"Conference Calendar" in Marketing to Women (Vol. 21, February 2008, No. 2, pp. 1)*
Pub: EPM Communications Inc.
Contact: Ira Mayer, President
E-mail: imayer@epmcom.com
Description: Listing of current conferences and events concerning women, marketing and business.

18551 ■ *"Convention Calendar" in Black Enterprise (Vol. 37, February 2007, No. 7, pp. 68)*
Pub: Earl G. Graves Publishing Co. Inc.
Description: Listing of conventions and trade show of interest to minority and women business leaders.

18552 ■ *"Datebook" in Crain's Chicago Business (Vol. 31, March 24, 2008, No. 12, pp. 18)*
Pub: Crain Communications, Inc.
Description: Listing of events in the Detroit area include conferences addressing entrepreneurialism, economic development, secrets of getting hired, and women business ownership.

18553 ■ *"Datebook" in Crain's Chicago Business (Vol. 31, March 31, 2008, No. 13, pp. 1)*
Pub: Crain Communications, Inc.
Description: Listing of events in the Detroit area include conferences addressing entrepreneurialism, economic development, secrets of getting hired, and women business ownership.

18554 ■ *"Datebook" in Crain's Chicago Business (Vol. 31, April 28, 2008, No. 17, pp. 18)*
Pub: Crain Communications, Inc.
Description: Listing of events in the Detroit area include conferences addressing entrepreneurialism, economic development, and women business ownership.

18555 ■ *"Economy Forcing Meeting Planners to Think Fast" in Crain's Cleveland Business (Vol. 30, June 15, 2009, No. 23, pp. 15)*
Pub: Crain Communications, Inc.
Ed: Amy Ann Stoessel. **Description:** Meeting planners are working hard to meet lower corporate budgets when planning events.

18556 ■ *From Entrepreneur to Infopreneur: Make Money with Books, E-Books, and Other Information Products*
Pub: John Wiley & Sons, Incorporated
Ed: Stephanie Chandler. **Released:** November 2006. **Price:** $19.95. **Description:** Infopreneurs sell information online in the forms of books, e-books, special reports, audio and video products, seminars, and more.

18557 ■ *"Here's the Deal" in Crain's Cleveland Business (Vol. 30, June 15, 2009, No. 23, pp. 14)*
Pub: Crain Communications, Inc.
Description: Incentives being offered by hotels, restaurants, golf courses and major chains in order to promote bookings for meetings or conferences in the Cleveland area are listed.

18558 ■ *"The Jobs Man" in Business Courier (Vol. 26, December 25, 2009, No. 35, pp. 1)*
Pub: American City Business Journals, Inc.
Ed: Lucy May. **Description:** Entrepreneur Bob Messer, a volunteer for Jobs Plus Employment Network in Cincinnati's Over-the-Rhine neighborhood, regularly conducts a seminar that aims to help attendees prepare for employment. Jobs Plus founder Burr Robinson asked Messer to create the seminar in order to help unemployed jobseekers. So far, the program has helped 144 individuals with full time jobs in 2009.

18559 ■ *"Not Enough Room" in Austin Business JournalInc. (Vol. 29, November 13, 2009, No. 36, pp. A1)*
Pub: American City Business Journals
Ed: Jacob Dirr. **Description:** Hotel and convention business in downtown Austin, Texas lost nearly $5.3 million when Dell Inc. relocated its annual convention

to Las Vegas. However, lack of capital caused the postponement of various hotel projects which need to be finished in order to attract well-attended conventions. Makeover projects on Austin's Waller Creek and Sixth Street are discussed.

18560 ■ *"Not Your Father's Whiteboard" in Inc. (Vol. 33, November 2011, No. 9, pp. 50)*
Pub: Inc. Magazine
Ed: Adam Baer. **Description:** Sharp's new interactive whiteboard is really a 70-inch touch screen monitor with software for importing presentations from any Windows 7 computer.

18561 ■ *"On Beyond Powerpoint: Presentations Get a Wake-Up Call" in Inc. (November 2007, pp. 58-59)*
Pub: Gruner & Jahr USA Publishing
Ed: Michael Fitzgerald. **Description:** New software that allows business presentations to be shared online are profiled, including ProfCast, audio podcasts for sales, marketing, and training; SmartDraw2008, software that creates professional graphics; Dimdim, an open-Web conferencing tool; Empressr, a hosted Web service for creating, managing, and sharing multimedia presentations; Zentation, a free tool that allows users to watch slides and a videos of presenter; Spresent, a Web-based presentation tool for remote offices or conference calls.

18562 ■ *"People/Calendar" in Brandweek (Vol. 49, April 21, 2008, No. 16, pp. 30)*
Pub: VNU Business Media, Inc.
Description: Listing of current conferences, tradeshows and events concerning the marketing industry.

18563 ■ *"Polite Conversation" in Mergers & Acquisitions: The Dealmaker's Journal (March 1, 2008)*
Pub: SourceMedia, Inc.
Description: In January, industry leaders and dealmakers met at Davos to discuss topics ranging from the possibility of a recession to what lies ahead in the deal market.

18564 ■ *"Prepping for the Unpredictable" in Crain's Cleveland Business (Vol. 30, June 15, 2009, No. 23, pp. 16)*
Pub: Crain Communications, Inc.
Ed: Joel Hammond. **Description:** Michael Ferrara, event planner and designer for Executive Caterers discusses the many events he has planned.

18565 ■ *"Save the Date" in Mergers & Acquisitions: The Dealmaker's Journal (March 1, 2008)*
Pub: SourceMedia, Inc.
Description: Listing of conferences and forums that deal with business and investing, particularly with mergers and acquisitions. Includes dates, locations and Internet addresses.

18566 ■ *"Speak Better: Five Tips for Polished Presentations" in Women Entrepreneur (September 19, 2008)*
Pub: Entrepreneur Media Inc.
Ed: Suzannah Baum. **Description:** Successful entrepreneurs agree that exemplary public speaking skills are among the core techniques needed to propel their business forward. A well-delivered presentation can result in securing a new distribution channel, gaining new customers, locking into a new referral stream or receiving extra funding.

18567 ■ *"Tic-Tac-Show" in American Printer (Vol. 128, August 1, 2011, No. 8)*
Pub: Penton Media Inc.
Description: Graph Expo has become the US print industry's main event. There will be as many as 500 exhibitors at this year's event and the Graphic Arts Show Company lists over 30 co-located events as well as 53 new sessions in the seminar program's 28 education categories.

18568 ■ *"Tired of PowerPoint? Try This Instead" in Harvard Business Review (Vol. 88, September 2010, No. 9, pp. 30)*
Pub: Harvard Business School Publishing
Ed: Daniel McGinn, Stephanie Crowley. **Description:** Usefulness of graphic recording, also known as storyboarding or visual facilitation, during client meetings is illustrated.

18569 ■ *"Tourism Bureau Seeks Hotel Tax Hike" in Baltimore Business Journal (Vol. 27, December 18, 2009, No. 32, pp. 1)*
Pub: American City Business Journals
Ed: Rachel Bernstein. **Description:** Baltimore, Maryland's tourism agency, Visit Baltimore, has proposed a new hotel tax that could produce $2 million annually for its marketing budget, fund improvements to the city's 30-year-old convention center and help it compete for World Cup soccer games. Baltimore hotel leaders discuss the new tax.

18570 ■ *"The Weeks Ahead" in Crain's New York Business (Vol. 24, January 7, 2008, No. 1, pp. 26)*
Pub: Crain Communications, Inc.
Description: Listing of events in the Detroit area include conferences addressing entrepreneurialism, economic development, and women business ownership.

18571 ■ *"The Weeks Ahead" in Crain's New York Business (Vol. 24, January 14, 2008, No. 2, pp. 20)*
Pub: Crain Communications, Inc.
Description: Listing of events in the Detroit area include conferences addressing entrepreneurialism, economic development, and women business ownership.

TRADE PERIODICALS

18572 ■ *Tips*
Pub: Toastmasters International
Contact: Gary Schmidt, President
Ed: Suzanne Frey, Editor. **Released:** Bimonthly. **Price:** Included in membership. **Description:** Contains leadership tips, organization, and club programming suggestions. Recurring features include a calendar of events and news of speech competitions and awards.

18573 ■ *The Toastmaster*
Pub: Toastmasters International
Contact: Gary Schmidt, President
URL(s): www.toastmasters.org/ToastmastersMagazine/currentissue.aspx. **Released:** Monthly

VIDEOCASSETTES/ AUDIOCASSETTES

18574 ■ *Delivering Successful Presentations*
American Management Association (AMA)
1601 Broadway
New York, NY 10019-7420
Ph: (212)586-8100
Free: 877-566-9441
Fax: (212)903-8168
Co. E-mail: customerservice@amanet.org
URL: http://www.amanet.org
Contact: Charles R. Craig, Chairman
Released: 19??. **Price:** $215.00. **Description:** Presents techniques on how to become a successful presenter. **Availability:** VHS.

18575 ■ *Making Effective Presentations*
AJN Video Library/Lippincott Williams & Wilkins
American Journal of Nursing
345 Hudson St., 16th Fl.
New York, NY 10014
Ph: (212)886-1200
Free: 800-256-4045
Fax: (212)886-1276
Co. E-mail: info@nursingcenter.com
URL: http://www.nursingcenter.com
Released: 19??. **Price:** $285.00. **Description:** Offers vignettes that demonstrate do's and don'ts in making stronger, more compelling presentations. Furnishes step-by-step instruction on how to prepare, deliver, and wrap up an effective presentation. Also provides helpful hints on planning and rehearsing, speaking from an outline, using audiovisuals, and fine-tuning. Includes study guide. **Availability:** VHS.

CONSULTANTS

18576 ■ **National Speakers Association (NSA)**
1500 S Priest Dr.
Tempe, AZ 85281
Ph: (480)968-2552
Fax: (480)968-0911
Co. E-mail: information@nsaspeaker.org
URL: http://www.nsaspeaker.org
Contact: Kristin Arnold, President
Description: Professional speakers. Works to increase public awareness of the speaking profession, advance the integrity and visibility of professional speakers, and provide a learning and communication vehicle to professional speakers. Sponsors workshops, conventions, and labs. **Scope:** An association for experts who speak professionally. Members include experts in a variety of industries and disciplines, who reach audiences as trainers, educators, humorists, motivators, consultants and authors. Provides resources and education designed to enhance the business skills and platform performance of professional speakers. **Founded:** 1972. **Publications:** *Voices of Experience* (10/year); *Who's Who in Professional Speaking: The Meeting Planner's Guide* (Annual); *Who's Who in Professional Speaking: The Meeting Planner's Guide* (Annual). **Awards:** Certified Speaking Professional; Cavett Award; Council of Peers Award of Excellence - Speaker Hall of Fame (Annual); Council of Peers Award for Excellence/Speaker Hall of Fame.

START-UP INFORMATION

18577 ■ *"Pump Up the Profits: Teaching Small Biz How to Handle Fuel and Reduce Costs!"* in *Small Business Opportunities* (March 2008)
Pub: Harris Publications Inc.
Description: Profile of 4Refuel, a company that delivers diesel and biodiesel fuel to customers individual fuelings.

18578 ■ *"Rev Up Your Engine"* in *Small Business Opportunities* (Fall 2010)
Pub: Harris Publications Inc.
Description: Industry giant Meineke is adding franchisees whose average sales top $500,000 annually. Profile of Meineke is also included.

ASSOCIATIONS AND OTHER ORGANIZATIONS

18579 ■ **Automotive Service Association (ASA)**
PO Box 929
Bedford, TX 76095-0929
Ph: (817)283-6205
Free: 800-272-7467
Fax: (817)685-0225
Co. E-mail: asainfo@asashop.org
URL: http://www.asashop.org
Contact: Ron Pyle, President
Description: Automotive service businesses including body, paint, and trim shops, engine rebuilders, radiator shops, brake and wheel alignment services, transmission shops, tune-up services, and air conditioning services; associate members are manufacturers and wholesalers of automotive parts, and the trade press. Represents independent business owners and managers before private agencies and national and state legislative bodies. Promotes confidence between consumer and the automotive service industry, safety inspection of motor vehicles, and better highways. **Founded:** 1951. **Publications:** *AutoInc.* (Monthly). **Educational Activities:** Congress of Automotive Repair and Service (Annual); International Autobody Congress and Exposition (Annual); International Autobody Congress and Exposition - NACE (Annual).

18580 ■ **Canadian Automotive Repair and Service Council (CARS)—Service d'Entretien et de Reparation Automobiles du Canada**
102-6 Gurdwara Rd.
Ottawa, ON, Canada K2E 8A3
Ph: (613)798-0500
Free: 888-224-3834
Fax: (613)798-9963
Co. E-mail: information@carscouncil.ca
URL: http://www.cars-council.ca
Contact: Jennifer Steeves, Executive Director
Description: Seeks to advance the automotive service industry. Facilitates communication and cooperation among members; represents members' interests before industrial organizations, government agencies, organizations, and the public. **Founded:** 1988.

18581 ■ **Gasoline and Automotive Service Dealers Association (GASDA)**
372 Doughty Blvd., Ste. 2C
Inwood, NY 11096
Ph: (516)371-6201
Co. E-mail: gasda@nysassrs.com
URL: http://www.nysassrs.com/affiliates/gasda.aspx
Contact: Ralph Bombardiere, Executive Director
Description: Owners/operators or dealers of service stations or automotive repair facilities; interested individuals. Aims to educate, inform and help increase professionalism of members and of the industry. Offers periodic technical training clinics and other educational programs including advanced automotive technical training, prepaid group legal services plan and group health insurance and liaison with government agencies. Informs members of political and legislative action or changes affecting their industry. **Founded:** 1931.

18582 ■ **Inter-Industry Conference on Auto Collision Repair—I-CAR**
5125 Trillium Blvd.
Hoffman Estates, IL 60192
Ph: (847)590-1198
Free: 800-422-7872
Fax: (847)590-1215
URL: http://www.i-car.com
Contact: Elise Quadrozzi, Chairperson
Description: Automobile manufacturers, collision repair shops, insurance companies, tool, equipment and supply manufacturers, vocational institutions and related industrial organizations such as auto dismantlers and recyclers, appraisers and technical publishers. Works to improve the quality, safety and efficiency of collision repair, especially on newly manufactured fuel-efficient automobiles, through education in the collision repair and insurance industries. Serves as a forum providing for communication among insurance claims representatives, body shop owners and managers and interested individuals. Conducts classes to improve skills of repair technicians, insurance claims personnel and other interested individuals. Offers courses on unibody repair, refinishing, plastic repair, electronics, steering and suspension and advanced vehicle systems; also conducts collision repair research. Offers welding qualification test through its Welding Qualification Program. **Founded:** 1979. **Publications:** *Communications*; *I-CAR E-newsletter* (Biweekly). **Awards:** Achievement Award (Annual); Founder's Award (Annual); Regional Instructor of the Year Award (Annual).

18583 ■ **International Midas Dealers Association (IMDA)**
4831 Las Virgenes Rd., Ste. 159
Calabasas, CA 91302
Free: 888-916-4111
Fax: (800)443-2143
Co. E-mail: david@franchiselegalsupport.com
URL: http://www.imdaonline.org
Contact: John Inyart, President
Description: Midas auto service shop franchisees. **Founded:** 1971. **Publications:** *IMDA Today*.

18584 ■ **National Auto Body Council (NABC)**
7044 S 13th St.
Oak Creek, WI 53154
Free: 888-667-7433
Fax: (414)768-8001
Co. E-mail: info@autobodycouncil.org
URL: http://www.autobodycouncil.org
Contact: Stacy Bartnik, President
Description: Members from the collision repair industry. Seeks to promote pride in professionalism and increase consumer confidence. **Founded:** 1994. **Awards:** Pride Awards (Annual). **Telecommunication Services:** stacybartnik@carstar.com.

18585 ■ **National Automotive Radiator Service Association (NARSA)**
c/o Carol Opiela, Administrator
Eurofins Global Central Lab.
14100 Park Meadow Dr., Ste. 110
Chantilly, VA 20151
Ph: (703)480-2532
Fax: (703)480-2670
Co. E-mail: carolopiela@eurofins.com
URL: http://www.narsa.net
Contact: Wayne Juchno, Executive Director
Description: Represents operators of automotive radiator and air conditioning repair shops and cooling system service businesses as well as manufacturers and suppliers for the trade. Maintains hall of fame. **Founded:** 1954. **Publications:** *Cooling Journal* (Monthly); *NARSA Service Reports* (Bimonthly). **Educational Activities:** National Automotive Radiator Service Association Convention (Annual).

18586 ■ **National Institute for Automotive Service Excellence (ASE)—Auto Service Excellence**
101 Blue Seal Dr. SE, Ste. 101
Leesburg, VA 20175
Ph: (703)669-6600
Free: 888-273-8378
Fax: (703)669-6123
Co. E-mail: asehelp@ase.com
URL: http://www.ase.com
Contact: Tim Zilke, President
Description: Governed by a 40-member board of directors selected from all sectors of the automotive service industry and from education, government, and consumer groups. Encourages and promotes the highest standards of automotive service in the public interest. Conducts continuing research to determine the best methods for training automotive technicians; encourages the development of effective training programs. Tests and certifies the competence of automobile, medium/heavy truck, collision repair, school bus and engine machinist technicians as well as parts specialists. **Founded:** 1972. **Publications:**

ASE Catalogs of Tests (Annual); *ASE Certification Test Registration Booklet* (Semiannual). **Awards:** Top Scoring Technician Awards (Annual).

18587 ■ New York State Association of Service Stations and Repair Shops (NYSASSRS)
6 Walker Way
Albany, NY 12205
Ph: (518)452-4367
Fax: (518)452-1955
Co. E-mail: state@nysassrs.com
URL: http://www.nysassrs.com
Contact: Ralph Bombardiere, Executive Director
Description: Service station dealers united for: passage of national, state, and local legislation supportive of the service station dealer; promotion of fraternity and unity among dealers in New York State and throughout the country; achievement of the highest standards of service and safety for the motoring public. Conducts trade exhibits and seminars in automotive mechanics. **Founded:** 1967. **Publications:** *Service Station News* (Quarterly). **Awards:** Certificate of Achievement (Annual).

18588 ■ SAE International (SAE)
400 Commonwealth Dr.
Warrendale, PA 15096-0001
Ph: (724)776-4841
Free: 877-606-7323
Fax: (724)776-0790
Co. E-mail: customerservice@sae.org
URL: http://www.sae.org
Contact: Frank O. Klegon, President
Description: Collects and disseminates information on mobility technology. Fosters information exchange among the worldwide automotive and aerospace communities. Conducts educational programs. **Scope:** automotive and aerospace engineering. **Founded:** 1905. **Subscriptions:** 50000. **Publications:** *Aerospace Engineering* (11/year; Monthly); *SAE International Automotive Engineering* (Monthly); *Bosch Handbook* (Annual). **Educational Activities:** Fuels and Lubricants Meeting and Exposition (Annual); Offhighway and Powerplant Congress (Annual).

18589 ■ Service Station Dealers of America/ National Coalition of Petroleum Retailers and Allied Trades (SSDA-AT)
1532 Pointer Ridge Pl., Ste. E
Bowie, MD 20716
Ph: (301)390-4405
Fax: (301)390-3161
Co. E-mail: pfiore@wmda.net
URL: http://www.ssda-at.org
Contact: Peter S. Kischak, President
Description: Service station operators and affiliated state and local associations. Works for the betterment of its members as a voice on Capitol Hill, with federal regulators, with the media, in the courts and with suppliers. **Founded:** 1947. **Awards:** Friend of the Industry (Annual); Golden Nozzle (Annual); Hall of Fame (Annual); Friend of the Industry; Golden Nozzle; Hall of Fame.

18590 ■ Society of Collision Repair Specialists (SCRS)
PO Box 909
Prosser, WA 99350
Ph: (302)423-3537
Free: 877-841-0660
Fax: (877)851-0660
Co. E-mail: info@scrs.com
URL: http://www.scrs.com
Contact: Aaron Clark, Chairman
Description: Businesses; associations; individual owners and managers of auto collision repair shops, suppliers, insurance and educational associates. Distributes management and technical information; maintains industry standards; works to promote professionalism within the industry. **Founded:** 1982. **Educational Activities:** Society of Collision Repair Specialists Seminar; Society of Collision Repair Specialists Seminar. **Awards:** Affiliate Association Award; Collision Industry Individual Service Award;

Humanitarian Award; Industry Achievement Award (Annual); Lifetime Achievement Award (Annual); Collision Industry Non-Individual Service Award.

18591 ■ Society of Independent Gasoline Marketers of America (SIGMA)
3930 Pender Dr., Ste. 340
Fairfax, VA 22030
Ph: (703)709-7000
Fax: (703)709-7007
Co. E-mail: sigma@sigma.org
URL: http://www.sigma.org
Contact: Frank P. Greinke, President
Description: Represents chain gasoline marketers, wholesale and retail. Works to inform members of current governmental and legislative activities; represents the marketers' interests before government and legislative and regulatory agencies; and provides statistical data on industry. **Founded:** 1958. **Publications:** *Statistical Report* (Annual); *Society of Independent Gasoline Marketers Membership Directory* (Annual); *Society of Independent Gasoline Marketers of America--Weekly Report* (Weekly). **Educational Activities:** Winter Management Conference (Annual). **Awards:** Distinguished Marketer Award (Annual); Distinguished Statesman Award (Annual).

18592 ■ Truck-Frame and Axle Repair Association (TARA)
c/o Ken Dias
364 W 12th St.
Erie, PA 16501
Free: 877-735-1687
Fax: (877)735-1688
Co. E-mail: leafspg@aol.com
URL: http://www.taraassociation.com
Contact: Paul Jones, President
Description: Owners and operators of heavy-duty truck repair facilities and their mechanics; allied and associate members are manufacturers of heavy-duty trucks and repair equipment, engineers, trade press and insurance firms. Seeks to help members share skills and technical knowledge and keep abreast of new developments and technology to better serve customers in areas of minimum downtime, cost and maximum efficiency. Conducts studies and surveys regarding safety, fuel conservation and heavy-duty truck maintenance and repairs. Has formed TARA's Young Executives to help make young people at members' repair facilities more proficient in normal business functions and to ensure the future of the Association. **Founded:** 1966. **Publications:** *Truck-Frame and Axle Repair Association--Membership Directory* (Annual).

DIRECTORIES OF EDUCATIONAL PROGRAMS

18593 ■ *Directory of Private Accredited Career Schools and Colleges of Technology*
Pub: Accrediting Commission of Career Schools and Colleges of Technology
Contact: Michale S. McComis, Executive Director
Released: On web page. **Price:** Free. **Description:** Covers 3900 accredited post-secondary programs that provide training programs in business, trade, and technical fields, including various small business endeavors. Entries offer school name, address, phone, description of courses, job placement assistance, and requirements for admission. Arrangement is alphabetical.

REFERENCE WORKS

18594 ■ *"21st Century Filling Station"* in *Austin Business JournalInc.* (Vol. 29, December 11, 2009, No. 40, pp. 1)
Pub: American City Business Journals
Ed: Jacob Dirr. **Description:** Clean Energy Fuels Corporation announced plans for the construction of a $1 million, 17,000 square foot compressed natural gas fueling station at or near the Austin-Bergstrom International Airport (ABIA). Clean Energy Fuels hopes to encourage cab and shuttle companies in the ABIA to switch from gasoline to natural gas.

18595 ■ *"Auto Repair Business Owner Sentenced"* in *Ventura County Star* (November 20, 2010)
Pub: Ventura County Star
Ed: Raul Hernandez. **Description:** Oxnard, California auto repair business owner was sentenced to jail for grand theft and falsification of smog certificate information.

18596 ■ *"Bill Lee's Auto Repair Business Chugs Along Despite Life's Obstacles"* in *Bradenton Herald* (August 22, 2010)
Pub: Bradenton Herald
Ed: Grace Gagliano. **Description:** Profile of Bill Lee's Professional Automotive Services located in Bradenton, Florida. The auto repair business was opened 26 years ago and provides repair for an assortment of fleet vehicles, including truck repair.

18597 ■ *"Casey's Buys Second Marion Convenience Store"* in *Gazette* (December 14, 2010)
Pub: Gazette
Ed: Dave DeWitte. **Description:** Casey's General Stores Inc. has acquired a Short Stop convenience store on Marion's west side in Iowa. The new store includes a car and truck wash.

18598 ■ *"Convenience Store Owners Will Request New Zoning Once More"* in *Daily Republic* (November 1, 2010)
Pub: McClatchy Tribune Information Services
Ed: Tom Lawrence. **Description:** Zoning change has been requested for a proposed convenience store in Mitchell, South Dakota. Details are included.

18599 ■ *"Fees Fueling Frustration for Region's Gas Retailers"* in *Business First Buffalo* (December 7, 2007, pp. 1)
Pub: American City Business Journals, Inc.
Ed: David Bertola. **Description:** Credit card fees are a major cause of concern to gas retailers along with higher gasoline prices. Statistical details included.

18600 ■ *"Fix-It Career: Jobs in Repair"* in *Occupational Outlook Quarterly* (Vol. 54, Fall 2010, No. 3, pp. 26)
Pub: U.S. Bureau of Labor Statistics
Ed: Elka Maria Torpey. **Description:** Auto mechanics and HVAC technician occupations require repair skills. Advantages for individuals with proper skills are outlined.

18601 ■ *"Hy-Vee Plans Expansion, Convenience Store in Cedar Rapids"* in *Gazette* (November 26, 2010)
Pub: Gazette
Ed: George Ford. **Description:** Hy-Vee Inc. is awaiting approval to expand its supermarket in Cedar Rapids, Iowa. Hy-Vee is a food and drug store chain will construct a convenience store and gas station on the site.

18602 ■ *"Kroger Forges Ahead with Fuel Centers"* in *Business Courier* (Vol. 26, December 25, 2009, No. 35, pp. 1)
Pub: American City Business Journals, Inc.
Ed: Jon Newberry. **Description:** Cincinnati-based grocery chain Kroger Company plans to construct more fuel centers near supermarkets and food stores despite declining profit margins in gasoline sales. Statistical data included.

18603 ■ *"Merchants Association Working on Deal for Large Wholesale Warehouse"* in *Austin Business JournalInc.* (September 19, 2008)
Pub: American City Business Journals
Ed: Jean Kwon. **Description:** Greater Austin Merchants Association planning to buy a former Dell Outlet Factory in Austin, Texas and convert it into a warehouse for convenience stores and gas stations.

18604 ■ *"OSHA Proposes Historic Safety Penalty on BP"* in *Workforce Management* (Vol. 88, November 16, 2009, No. 12, pp. 8)
Pub: Crain Communications Inc.
Ed: Mark Schoeff Jr. **Description:** Labor Secretary Hilda Solis has warned that she aims to toughen the enforcement of workplace laws; OSHA, the Oc-

cupational Safety and Health Administration, an agency within the Department of Labor, is penalizing BP Products North America Inc. for their failure to improve workplace safety.

18605 ■ "Sellers Shift Gears" in Crain's Detroit Business (Vol. 25, June 22, 2009, No. 25, pp. 3)
Pub: Crain Communications Inc. - Detroit
Description: Of the 14 new car Chrysler dealerships in the Detroit area who had franchises terminated, Joe Ricci of Dearborn will sell used cars at his new business called All American Buyer's Service; Lochmoor Automotive Group in Detroit will focus on Mahindra & Mahindra trucks; Mt. Clemens Dodge, Clinton Township is also selling Mahindra & Mahindra trucks; and Monicatti Chrysler Jeep, Sterling Heights, will offer service along with selling used cars.

18606 ■ "Service With a Smile..And Comfy Chairs" in Crain's Chicago Business (Vol. 31, April 28, 2008, No. 17, pp. 46)
Pub: Crain Communications, Inc.
Ed: Phuong Ly. **Description:** O'Hare Auto Group has improved the experience of waiting for service on one's vehicle by offering wireless Internet, comfortable chairs and plasma TVs. The company also has long service hours, running from 6 a.m. to midnight Monday through Thursday so customers don't have to take time off work.

18607 ■ "Some Atlantic Beach Leaders Leery About Convenience Store Safety Measure" in Florida Times-Union (November 3, 2010)
Pub: Florida Times-Union
Ed: Drew Dixon. **Description:** Jacksonville, Florida authorities are proposing a new ordinance that would require convenience stores to upgrade safety measures to protect store workers and customers from robbery and other crimes.

18608 ■ "Thomas Morley; President, The Lube Stop Inc., 37' in Crain's Cleveland Business (Vol. 28, November 19, 2007, No. 46, pp. F-12)
Pub: Crain Communications, Inc.
Ed: David Bennett. **Description:** Profile of Thomas Morley, president of The Lube Stop Inc., who is dedicated to promoting the company's strong environmental record as an effective way to differentiate Lube Stop from its competition. Since Mr. Morley came to the company in 2004, Lube Stop has increased sales by 10 percent and has boosted its operating profits by 30 percent.

18609 ■ Undercar Digest--Buyer's Guide Issue: The Sourcebook
Pub: MD Publications Inc.
URL(s): www.mdpublications.com/md/mdproducts. htm.undercardigest.com. **Ed:** James R. Wilder. **Released:** Annual; Latest edition 2013. **Price:** $10, Individuals. **Publication includes:** List of automotive aftermarket manufacturers and suppliers of mufflers, exhaust pipes, brakes, chassis, steering, suspension, driveline, shop equipment and tools, and other products. **Entries include:** Company name, address, phone, fax, name and title of contact, products. **Arrangement:** Alphabetical. **Indexes:** Product, warehouse distributors, franchise headquarters.

STATISTICAL SOURCES

18610 ■ RMA Annual Statement Studies
Pub: Risk Management Association
Contact: Kevin M. Blakey, President
Released: Annual. **Price:** $175.00 2006-07 edition, $105.00. **Description:** Contains composite balance sheets and income statements for more than 360 industries, including the accounting, auditing, and bookkeeping industries. Also contains five years of comparative historical data for discerning trends. Includes 16 commonly used ratios, computed for most of the size groupings for nearly every industry.

TRADE PERIODICALS

18611 ■ The Blue Seal
Pub: National Institute for Automotive Service Excellence
Ed: Martin Lawson, Editor. **Released:** Quarterly. **Description:** Covers news of the Institute's efforts to

certify auto, medium/heavy truck, engine machinists, collision repair technicians, and parts specialists. Discusses industry trends, vehicle repair tips, and training information, and highlights activities of ASE-certified technicians.

18612 ■ BodyShop Business: The Magazine that Delivers the Collision Repair Industry
Pub: Babcox
URL(s): www.bodyshopbusiness.comwww.babcox. com/site/our-brands/bodyshop-business. **Ed:** Jason Stahl. **Released:** Monthly

18613 ■ Cooling Journal
Pub: NARSA
Contact: Tom Bremble, Director
URL(s): narsa.org/publication/cooling-journal/. **Released:** Monthly **Price:** $65, Individuals; $130, Other countries; $97, Canada.

18614 ■ Engine Builder: Serving Engine Builders and Rebuilders since 1964
Pub: Babcox
URL(s): www.enginebuildermag.comwww.babcox. com/site/our-brands/engine-builder. **Ed:** Doug Kaufman. **Released:** Monthly

18615 ■ Franchise Focus
Pub: International Midas Dealers Association
Ed: Jennifer Gentry, Editor, jennifer@robstan.com. **Released:** Bimonthly. **Price:** Included in membership. **Description:** Informs member Midas franchisees of activities performed on their behalf by the Association. Reports on all negotiations between the Association and Midas International, including updates on Association committees, which meet with Midas officials on a regular basis. Recurring features include reports of meetings and conventions and a calendar of events.

18616 ■ Gasoline and Automotive Service Dealers Association--Bulletin
Pub: Gasoline and Automotive Service Dealers Association
Released: Monthly. **Price:** Included in membership. **Description:** Reports on industry news, laws, and regulations affecting service station operators in New York. Updates Association news and provides general tips on operation. Recurring features include news of research, news of educational opportunities and Association programs, reports of meetings, and a calendar of events.

18617 ■ Motor Age: The Journal for Professional Automotive Repair
Pub: Adams Business Media/Green Media
Contact: Mark Adams, Chief Executive Officer
URL(s): www.motorage.com. **Released:** Monthly **Price:** $49, Individuals; $75, Two years; $90, Other countries.

18618 ■ Motor Magazine
Pub: Motor Information Systems
Contact: Marian Maasshoff, Director
E-mail: mmaasshoff@motor.com
URL(s): www.motor.com. **Released:** Monthly **Price:** Free in U.S.; $60, Other countries surface mail; $120, Other countries airmail; $96, Two years other countries; surface mail; $216, Two years other countries; airmail.

18619 ■ NARSA National Newsletter
Pub: National Automotive Radiator Service Association
Ed: Mike Dwyer, Editor, mdwyer@narsa.org. **Released:** 24/year. **Price:** Included in membership. **Description:** Covers issues of interest to radiator service station operators and others in the auto repair industry. Recurring features include news of conferences and a calendar of events.

18620 ■ Professional Tool & Equipment News: The Independent Tool Authority
Pub: Cygnus Business Media
Contact: Rich Reiff, President
URL(s): www.vehicleservicepros.com/magazine/pten/issue/2012/sep. **Released:** 9/yr. **Price:** $33, Individuals; $60, Two years; $49, Canada and Mexico; $93, Canada and Mexico two years; $71, Out of country; $137, Out of country two years; $10, Single issue.

18621 ■ Restoration
Pub: International Society for Vehicle Preservation
URL(s): www.aztexcorp.com/root/isvp.html. **Released:** Semiannual **Price:** $20, Members; $3, Single issue.

18622 ■ SHOPtalk / Engine Professional
Pub: Automotive Engine Rebuilders Association
Ed: Maria Hoeppner, Editor, mariahoeppner@charter. net. **Released:** Monthly. **Price:** Free. **Description:** Recurring features include interviews, news of research, a calendar of events, reports of meetings, news of educational opportunities, and notices of publications available.

18623 ■ Skinned Knuckles: A Journal of Car Restoration
Pub: SK Publications
URL(s): skinnedknuckles.net/pages/index.htm. **Released:** Monthly **Price:** $26, Individuals; $49, Two years; $3.25, Single issue; $40, Canada; $77, Canada 2 years; $43, Individuals in Australia; $83, Two years in Australia; $45, Individuals in Europe; $87, Two years in Europe; $47, Other countries.

18624 ■ Truck Parts & Service
Pub: Kona Communications Inc.
URL(s): www.truckpartsandservice.com/. **Ed:** Derek Smith. **Released:** Monthly **Price:** $50, Individuals.

18625 ■ Undercar Digest
Pub: MD Publications Inc.
URL(s): www.undercardigest.com/. **Ed:** Jim Wilder, Gary Sifford. **Released:** Monthly **Price:** $49, Individuals.

18626 ■ Underhood Service
Pub: Babcox
URL(s): www.underhoodservice.comwww.babcox. com/site/our-brands/underhood-service. **Ed:** Edward Sunkin. **Released:** Monthly

VIDEOCASSETTES/AUDIOCASSETTES

18627 ■ Anti-Lock Brake Systems Explained
Bergwall Productions, Inc.
1 DIckinson Drive, Brandywine BUilding 5, Ste. 105
Chadds Ford, PA 19317
Ph: (610)361-0334
Free: 800-934-8696
Fax: (610)361-0092
URL: http://www.bergwall.com
Released: 1989. **Price:** $369.00. **Description:** The operation and repair of anti-lock brake systems are examined for the benefit of auto mechanics. This series is also available as a single tape for the same cost. **Availability:** VHS.

18628 ■ Basic Electricity for Auto Mechanics
Bergwall Productions, Inc.
1 DIckinson Drive, Brandywine BUilding 5, Ste. 105
Chadds Ford, PA 19317
Ph: (610)361-0334
Free: 800-934-8696
Fax: (610)361-0092
URL: http://www.bergwall.com
Released: 1989. **Price:** $359.00. **Description:** Electrical basics are explained, with special emphasis on their importance to the auto mechanic. The series is also available on one tape for the same cost. **Availability:** VHS.

18629 ■ Distributorless Ignition
Bergwall Productions, Inc.
1 DIckinson Drive, Brandywine BUilding 5, Ste. 105
Chadds Ford, PA 19317
Ph: (610)361-0334
Free: 800-934-8696
Fax: (610)361-0092
URL: http://www.bergwall.com
Released: 1988. **Price:** $369.00. **Description:** Various types of electronic ignition systems are examined from a mechanic's point of view. This series is also available as a single tape at the same cost. **Availability:** VHS.

18630 ▪ *Safety in the Auto Shop*
Bergwall Productions, Inc.
1 DIckinson Drive, Brandywine BUilding 5, Ste. 105
Chadds Ford, PA 19317
Ph: (610)361-0334
Free: 800-934-8696
Fax: (610)361-0092
URL: http://www.bergwall.com
Released: 1985. **Price:** $299.00. **Description:** This safety program shows how to be accident free in a body shop. **Availability:** VHS.

18631 ▪ *Small Engines*
Bergwall Productions, Inc.
1 DIckinson Drive, Brandywine BUilding 5, Ste. 105
Chadds Ford, PA 19317
Ph: (610)361-0334
Free: 800-934-8696
Fax: (610)361-0092
URL: http://www.bergwall.com
Released: 1989. **Price:** $399.00. **Description:** Small engine construction and repair are explained for the benefit of auto mechanics. Also available as one tape at the same cost. **Availability:** VHS.

18632 ▪ *Vehicle Maintenance*
RMI Media
1365 N. Winchester St.
Olathe, KS 66061-5880
Ph: (913)768-1696
Free: 800-745-5480
Fax: (800)755-6910
Co. E-mail: actmedia@act.org
URL: http://www.actmedia.com
Released: 1989. **Price:** $89.00. **Description:** Another series on the subject of fixing car engines is offered. **Availability:** VHS; 3/4 U.

TRADE SHOWS AND CONVENTIONS

18633 ▪ National Automotive Radiator Service Association Annual Trade Show and Convention
National Automotive Radiator Service Association
PO Box 97
East Greenville, PA 18041
Ph: (215)541-4500
Fax: (215)679-4977
URL(s): www.narsa.org. **Frequency:** Annual. **Audience:** Trade professionals. **Principal Exhibits:** Manufacturers in the automotive cooling industry.

FRANCHISES AND BUSINESS OPPORTUNITIES

18634 ▪ AAMCO Transmissions, Inc.
American Driveline, Inc.
201 Gibraltar Rd.
Horsham, PA 19044
Ph: (267)464-1690
Free: 800-523-0402
Fax: (215)956-0340
Co. E-mail: franchise@aamco.com
URL: http://www.aamco.com
Description: Chain of transmission service centers, specializing in all types of automobile transmission and related repairs. The company philosophy is to continue to increase its competitive advantage and market share through technical expertise and customer satisfaction. AAMCO provides a complete A to Z training course at its corporate headquarters. No automotive experience is needed. Operational, technical and sales support is provided on an ongoing basis. **No. of Franchise Units:** 895. **Founded:** 1963.. **Franchised:** 1963. **Equity Capital Needed:** Total investment $232,500-$299,700, cash start-up $65,000. **Franchise Fee:** $39,500. **Financial Assistance:** Yes. **Training:** Offers 3 weeks training at home office, plus in field support.

18635 ▪ All Night Auto
3872 Rochester Rd.
Troy, MI 48083
Ph: (248)619-9020
Free: 877-877-6444

Fax: (248)619-0596
Description: Full service automotive repair shop. **No. of Franchise Units:** 4. **No. of Company-Owned Units:** 1. **Founded:** 1994.. **Franchised:** 1999. **Equity Capital Needed:** $100,000 minimum. **Franchise Fee:** $25,000. **Training:** Provides 3-4 weeks of training.

18636 ▪ All Tune and Lube
ATL International, Inc.
8334 Veterans Hwy.
Millersville, MD 21108
Ph: (410)987-1011
Free: 800-935-8863
Fax: (410)987-4827
Co. E-mail: alltune@erols.com
URL: http://www.alltuneandlube.com
Description: Automotive servicing. "One stop" total car care, including tune-ups, brakes, exhaust, engine replacement and more. **No. of Franchise Units:** 300. **Founded:** 1986.. **Franchised:** 1986. **Equity Capital Needed:** $35,000+. **Franchise Fee:** $32,000. **Financial Assistance:** Yes. **Training:** All Tune and Lube provides extensive training at headquarters and in the individual center locations. Provides 1 week of center management training and operational support.

18637 ▪ Automotive Maintenance Solutions
Sheldrick Inc.
1404 7th Ave.
Hendersonville, NC 28792
Ph: (828)696-9611
Fax: (828)693-0823
Description: Auto service and repair shop. **No. of Franchise Units:** 1. **No. of Company-Owned Units:** 1. **Founded:** 1962.. **Franchised:** 2002. **Franchise Fee:** $25,000. **Training:** Yes.

18638 ▪ Big O Tires
TBC Retail Group
Description: Retail tire and under-car service centers. **No. of Franchise Units:** 392. **No. of Company-Owned Units:** 64. **Founded:** 1962.. **Franchised:** 1982. **Equity Capital Needed:** $100,000 minimum liquidity; $300,000 minimum net worth. **Franchise Fee:** 0-$30,000. **Financial Assistance:** Yes. **Training:** 7-week training program, including classroom and hands-on application in a fully operational retail training store and ongoing support through regional schools, seminars, and clinics.

18639 ▪ Brake Masters
Brake Masters Systems, Inc.
6179 E Broadway Blvd.
Tucson, AZ 85711
Ph: (520)631-7200
Free: 877-524-7541
Fax: (866)459-8731
Description: Brake repair and lubrication services. **No. of Franchise Units:** 42. **No. of Company-Owned Units:** 52. **Founded:** 1983.. **Franchised:** 1994. **Equity Capital Needed:** Cash $75,000-$150,000; Total investment $175,000-$650,000. **Franchise Fee:** $22,950. **Financial Assistance:** Yes. **Training:** Training includes classroom instruction, as well as several weeks of on the job training in stores.

18640 ▪ Car-X Associates Corp.
7150 Granite Cir.
Toledo, OH 43617
Ph: (419)865-6900
Free: 800-359-2359
Co. E-mail: dmaltzman@carx.com
URL: http://www.carx.com
Description: Automobile maintenance and repair, including exhaust systems, brakes and suspension systems. **No. of Franchise Units:** 159. **No. of Company-Owned Units:** 7. **Founded:** 1971.. **Franchised:** 1973. **Equity Capital Needed:** $100,000 minimum cash required. **Franchise Fee:** $25,000. **Financial Assistance:** Yes. **Training:** Initial training for 3 weeks, plus 2 weeks at new shop at opening. Ongoing support and training programs.

18641 ▪ ColorAll Technologies
ColorAll Technologies Intl., Inc.
1520 N Powerline Rd.
Pompano Beach, FL 33069

Ph: (954)969-1599
Free: 877-412-6567
Fax: (954)969-1679
Description: Onsite auto appearance & repair management. **No. of Franchise Units:** 75. **Founded:** 1990.. **Franchised:** 1998. **Equity Capital Needed:** $100,000. **Franchise Fee:** $75,000, includes equipment. **Training:** Yes.

18642 ▪ Dent Clinic Canada 2000, Inc.
54 Deerfield Manor SE
Calgary, AB, Canada T2J 6Z4
Ph: (403)819-2705
Free: 888-722-3368
Fax: (403)910-0458
URL: http://www.dentclinic.com
Description: Dent clinic deals with paint less dent repair and other auto body services. **No. of Franchise Units:** 8. **No. of Company-Owned Units:** 1. **Founded:** 1993.. **Franchised:** 1996. **Equity Capital Needed:** $140,000 total investment requird; $150,000 start-up capital required. **Franchise Fee:** $25,000. **Training:** Yes.

18643 ▪ Dent Doctor
11301 W Markham St.
Little Rock, AR 72211
Ph: (501)224-0500
Fax: (501)224-0507
Description: Paint less dent removal services for both wholesale and retail vehicle owners. Dent Doctor franchisees operate from both mobile and fixed locations. Dent Doctor franchisees remove minor dents, door dings and nail damage from vehicles with a special process that requires no painting for a fraction of the costs and time to repair it in the body shop. **No. of Franchise Units:** 20. **No. of Company-Owned Units:** 2. **Founded:** 1986.. **Franchised:** 1990. **Equity Capital Needed:** $80,000. **Franchise Fee:** $13,900-$23,900. **Financial Assistance:** Yes. **Training:** An intensive 8 week training program is required to learn the Dent Doctor painless dent removal system. Dent Doctor also offers ongoing refresher training.

18644 ▪ Dr. Vinyl & Associates, Ltd.
201 NW Victoria Dr.
Lee's Summit, MO 64086
Ph: (800)531-6600
Fax: (816)525-6333
Description: Mobile repair, reconditioning and aftermarket sales and services to auto dealers and other commercial accounts, such as vinyl, leather, velour, fabric, bumper, windshield, plastic and paint less dent repair, application of striping, body moldings, deck racks, graphics, gold plating, etc. **No. of Franchise Units:** 253. **No. of Company-Owned Units:** 2. **Founded:** 1972.. **Franchised:** 1981. **Equity Capital Needed:** $55,000-$85,000. **Franchise Fee:** $38,950. **Financial Assistance:** Yes. **Training:** (Missouri for combined classroom and field training and 4-5 days in franchisees territory). Training also available for franchisees employees or sub-contractors.

18645 ▪ The Doctor's Touch
PO Box 770
Lee's Summit, MO 64064
Ph: (801)525-6060
Free: 800-531-6600
Fax: (816)525-6333
Description: Automotive exterior repair services. **Founded:** 2005.. **Franchised:** 2007. **Equity Capital Needed:** $56,300-$85,950. **Franchise Fee:** $38,950. **Royalty Fee:** 7%. **Training:** Provides 3 weeks training at headquarters and ongoing support.

18646 ▪ Econo Lube N' Tune
128 S Tryon St., Ste. 900
Charlotte, NC 28202
Ph: (800)275-5200
Description: Auto service, lube, tune and brakes. **No. of Franchise Units:** 173. **No. of Company-Owned Units:** 95. **Founded:** 1973.. **Franchised:** 1978. **Franchise Fee:** $39,500. **Financial Assistance:** Yes. **Training:** Yes.

18647 ■ Honest-1 Auto Care, Inc.

H-1 Auto Care, LLC
Description: Automotive maintenance and repair.
No. of Franchise Units: 26. **Founded:** 2003.. **Franchised:** 2003. **Equity Capital Needed:** $90,000 liquid; $350,000 net worth; total investment $174,200-$292,200. **Franchise Fee:** $30,000. **Financial Assistance:** Yes. **Training:** Yes.

18648 ■ Lee Myles Transmissions & Autocare

Lee Myles Associates Corp.
847 Fern Avenue
Reading, PA 19607
Ph: (610)370-6900
Free: 800-533-6953
Description: Automotive transmission service and repair. **No. of Franchise Units:** 70. **Founded:** 1947.. **Franchised:** 1964. **Equity Capital Needed:** $75,000 cash on total investment of $135,000-$210,000. **Franchise Fee:** $30,000. **Financial Assistance:** Yes. **Training:** Offers 2 week training program in the classroom and onsite followed up with continuous support.

18649 ■ Lentz USA Service Centers

Lentz USA Franchise Corp.
1001 Riverview Dr.
Kalamazoo, MI 49001
Ph: (269)342-2200
Free: 800-354-2131
Fax: (269)342-9461
Description: Automotive under car repair facility. Lentz USA is a specialty shop, concentrating on exhaust, brakes and suspension services. It is a middle-end to high-end service store with 10,000 associated warranty locations nationwide. **No. of Franchise Units:** 23. **No. of Company-Owned Units:** 11. **Founded:** 1983.. **Franchised:** 1989. **Equity Capital Needed:** $50,000 liquid assets. **Franchise Fee:** $20,000. **Financial Assistance:** Yes. **Training:** Yes.

18650 ■ Maaco Franchising, Inc.

Maaco Enterprises Inc.
610 Freedom Business Ctr., Ste. 200
King of Prussia, PA 19406
Ph: (610)265-6606
Free: 800-521-6282
Fax: (610)337-6154
Co. E-mail: info@maaco.com
URL: http://www.maaco.com
Description: Maaco Auto Painting & Bodyworks Centers are complete production auto paint and body repair centers. No prior automotive experience necessary. **No. of Franchise Units:** 459. **Founded:** 1972.. **Franchised:** 1972. **Equity Capital Needed:** $90,000 minimum cash required. **Franchise Fee:** $40,000. **Financial Assistance:** Yes. **Training:** 4 weeks formal training at corporate headquarters, continuing operational support thereafter. Assistance in financing, site selection and installation of equipment.

18651 ■ The Master Mechanic

3250 Ridgeway Dr., Unit 1
Mississauga, ON, Canada L5L 5Y6
Ph: (905)820-2552
Fax: (905)820-2558
Co. E-mail: hugh@mastermechanic.ca
URL: http://www.mastermechanic.ca
Description: Full-service automotive repair garages to the retail market. Professional service for imported and domestic cars and vans. Specializing in general repairs, tune-ups, alignments, engine performance and drive ability. franchisees. Onsite assistance by franchisor. **No. of Franchise Units:** 39. **Founded:** 1985.. **Franchised:** 1985. **Equity Capital Needed:** $175,000-$225,000. **Franchise Fee:** $25,000. **Training:** Procedures and technical training are conducted onsite and at existing locations and head office. Management training courses provided by specialists in management and automotive servicing. Business training by franchisor accountants.

18652 ■ Meineke Car Care Centers, Inc.

Meineke Discount Muffler Shops, Inc.
128 S Tyron St., Ste. 900
Charlotte, NC 28202
Free: 800-275-5200
Fax: (704)372-4826
Co. E-mail: franchise.info@meineke.com
URL: http://www.ownameineke.com
Description: Meineke Discount Muffler Shops, Inc. offers fast, courteous service in the merchandising of automotive exhaust systems, brakes, shock absorbers, struts, C.V. joints and oil changes. Unique inventory control and group purchasing power enables Meineke to adhere to a 'Discount Concept' and deliver quality service. No mechanical skills required. **No. of Franchise Units:** 941. **Founded:** 1972. **Franchised:** 1972. **Equity Capital Needed:** $60,000-$75,000 personal investment. **Franchise Fee:** $30,000. **Financial Assistance:** Yes. **Training:** 4 weeks training at the Meineke University Campus in Charlotte, NC. In addition, Meineke provides Continuous field supervision and group operational meetings. is open, franchisees receive ongoing sales analysis and operational analysis, including personnel, facility, service and sales review. Dealers also receive customer service assistance in the form of counseling and mediation assistance.

18653 ■ Merlin 200,000 Mile Shops

Merlin's Franchising, Inc.
3815 E Main St., Ste. D
St. Charles, IL 60174
Ph: (630)513-8207
Free: 800-652-9900
Fax: (630)513-1388
Co. E-mail: twilliams@merlins.com
URL: http://www.merlins.com
Description: Merlin is an upscale 'under-car' service chain with one of the highest average sales per shop statistics in its industry. Its marketing strategies are rooted in building long-term customer relationships. Merlin offers a special equity assistance program to 'proven' industry veterans. Industry experience is not always necessary. Candidates must have significant experience in managing employees & serving customers. Merlin is expanding in IL, IN, MI, GA, TX & WI. **No. of Franchise Units:** 40. **No. of Company-Owned Units:** 14. **Founded:** 1975. **Franchised:** 1975. **Equity Capital Needed:** Minimum cash investment of $50,000; $225,000-$275,000 total investment. **Franchise Fee:** $30,000. **Financial Assistance:** Conventional & SBA, as well as hybrid financing options. Special equity assistance for candidates who have industry experience, are bilingual or are current Merlin employees. **Training:** 6 week management training program at training center and selected company-operated shops. Each franchisee receives a minimum of four visits/year by field personnel as well as manuals, ongoing electronic and printed communications, ongoing training, employee recruitment programs, etc.

18654 ■ Midas Inc.—Midas-Intnl

1300 Arlington Heights Rd.
Itasca, IL 60143
Ph: (800)365-0007
Fax: (630)438-3700
Contact: Alan D. Feldman, President
URL(s): www.midasinc.com. **Description:** Provider of automotive service, including brakes, exhaust, steering/suspension services, as well as batteries, climate control and maintenance services. Midas gives you the name people know, the product people want, and the warranty people trust. If you have business management experience, a dedication to customer service and the desire to take on the challenge of single or multiple unit ownership, contact us now. **No. of Franchise Units:** 2,249. **No. of Company-Owned Units:** 80. **Founded:** 1956. **Franchised:** 1956. **Equity Capital Needed:** $50,000 cash; $200,000 net worth, $150,000-$400,000 total investment range. **Franchise Fee:** $30,000. **Financial Assistance:** Third parties, select incentive programs may be available from Midas. **Training:** Onsite participation with certified technicians, shop managers and owners. 2 week training program at Midas Institute of Technology in Palatine, IL. We want to share with you the best of what we've learned before you even open your bays for business.

18655 ■ Mighty Distributing System of America

MDSA, LLC
650 Engineering Dr.
Norcross, GA 30092
Ph: (770)448-3900
Free: 800-829-3900
Fax: (770)446-8627
URL(s): www.mightyfranchise.com. **Description:** Wholesale suppliers of automotive parts for the automotive industry. **No. of Franchise Units:** 106. **No. of Company-Owned Units:** 6. **Founded:** 1963.. **Franchised:** 1970. **Equity Capital Needed:** $138,100-$266,900. **Franchise Fee:** $10,500-$35,000. **Royalty Fee:** 5%. **Training:** Offers 4-5 days at headquarters, 5-10 days at franchisee's location with ongoing support.

18656 ■ Milex Complete Auto Care

Moran Industries Inc.
4444 W 147th St.
Midlothian, IL 60445-2524
Ph: (708)389-5922
Free: 800-377-9247
Fax: (708)389-9882
Co. E-mail: garygoodgear@moranindustries.com
URL: http://www.moranindustries.com
Description: Auto service center. **No. of Franchise Units:** 30. **Founded:** 1967.. **Franchised:** 1967. **Equity Capital Needed:** $60,000 cash; $144,150-$189,225 total investment. **Franchise Fee:** $30,000. **Financial Assistance:** Yes. **Training:** Yes.

18657 ■ Mister Transmission International Limited

9675 Yonge St., 2nd Fl.
Richmond Hill, ON, Canada L4C 1V7
Ph: (905)884-1511
Free: 800-373-8432
Fax: (905)884-4727
Co. E-mail: info@mistertransmission.com
URL: http://www.mistertransmission.com
Description: Mister Transmission offers transmission repair services in Canada. **No. of Franchise Units:** 70. **Founded:** 1963.. **Franchised:** 1969. **Equity Capital Needed:** $120,000-$150,000. **Franchise Fee:** $35,000. **Training:** Yes.

18658 ■ Mr. Lube (Delta, Canada)

725 Eaton Way, Ste. 110
Delta, BC, Canada V3M 6S5
Ph: (905)828-0909
Free: 877-258-0858
Fax: (905)568-4242
Co. E-mail: franchising@mrlube.com
URL: http://www.mrlube.com
Description: Service station that provides maintenance services and automotive lubrication. **No. of Franchise Units:** 120. **Founded:** 1976.. **Equity Capital Needed:** $800,000-$1,500,000; $400,000-$600,000 start-up capital required. **Franchise Fee:** $50,000. **Training:** 3 months training.

18659 ■ Mr. Transmission/Transmission USA

Moran Industries, Inc.
4444 W 147th St.
St. Midlothian, IL 60445
Ph: (708)389-5922
Free: 800-581-8468
Fax: (708)389-9882
Description: Transmission repair and services. **No. of Franchise Units:** 102. **No. of Company-Owned Units:** 1. **Founded:** 1956.. **Franchised:** 1976. **Equity Capital Needed:** $165,281-$211,835. **Franchise Fee:** $30,000. **Royalty Fee:** 7%. **Financial Assistance:** Limited third party financing available. **Training:** Offers 2 weeks at headquarters, 3 weeks at franchisee's location, 1 week operations visit at location when open with ongoing support.

18660 ■ Precision Tune Auto Care, Inc.

Precision Auto Care, Inc.
748 Miller Dr. SE
Leesburg, VA 20175
Ph: (703)777-9095
Free: 800-438-8863
Fax: (703)669-1539
URL: http://www.precision-tune.com
Description: Auto care, quick lube. **No. of Franchise Units:** 400. **No. of Company-Owned Units:** 5. **Founded:** 1975.. **Franchised:** 1978. **Equity Capital Needed:** $100,000 or more. **Franchise Fee:** $25,000. **Financial Assistance:** Yes. **Training:** Yes.

18661 ■ Speedy Transmission Centers

Autotech Franchise Systems Inc.
235 NE 6th Ave., Ste. H
Delray Beach, FL 33483
Ph: (561)274-0445
Free: 800-336-0310
Fax: (561)274-6456
Co. E-mail: speedytrans@mindspring.com
URL: http://www.speedytransmission.com
Description: Provides repair, replacement and servicing of components to the automotive drive train, including transmission repair, both automatic and standard. **No. of Franchise Units:** 16. **Founded:** 1983.. **Franchised:** 1983. **Equity Capital Needed:** Cash investment $40,000; approximate total investment $100,000. **Franchise Fee:** $19,500. **Financial Assistance:** Yes. **Training:** Franchisee attends a 3 week training course in either Atlanta, GA or Boca Raton, FL. Included in this period is 1 week of classroom operational training. Training can vary depending on the background and experience of the franchisee. Ongoing management training classes are provided by the franchisor in local areas.

18662 ■ Sprayglo Auto Refinishing & Body Repair

Sprayglo USA Inc.
340 Smith Street
Clayton, GA 30525
Ph: (877)677-7294
Fax: (877)677-7294
Co. E-mail: info@sprayglo.com
URL: http://www.sprayglo.com
Description: Automotive painting and body repair. **No. of Franchise Units:** 8. **No. of Company-Owned Units:** 13. **Founded:** 1986.. **Franchised:** 1995. **Equity Capital Needed:** $216,800-$296,000. **Franchise Fee:** $20,000. **Royalty Fee:** 6%. **Training:** 30 days at training facilities, and 2 weeks at site location. All paint, materials, and equipment available from franchisor.

18663 ■ Tilden Your Total Car Care Centers

Tilden Associates
300 Hempstead Tpke., Ste. 110
West Hempstead, NY 11552
Ph: (516)746-7911
Free: 800-845-3367
Fax: (516)746-1288
Description: Offers maintenance and repair services for automobiles. **No. of Franchise Units:** 41. **Founded:** 1923. **Franchised:** 1996. **Equity Capital Needed:** $155,433-$200,133. **Franchise Fee:** $29,900. **Royalty Fee:** 6%. **Financial Assistance:** Limited third party financing available. **Training:** Offers 2 weeks at headquarters, 1 week at franchisee's location and ongoing as needed.

18664 ■ Transmission Depot

2006 Hwy 7, Unit 3
Concord, ON, Canada L4K 1W6
Ph: (416)800-3191
Free: 866-785-7118
Fax: (416)783-4902
Co. E-mail: rkeene@transmissiondepot.ca
URL: http://www.transmissiondepot.ca
Description: Offers transmission repair to both wholesale and retail clients. **No. of Franchise Units:** 8. **No. of Company-Owned Units:** 1. **Founded:**

1995.. **Franchised:** 2000. **Equity Capital Needed:** $65,000. **Franchise Fee:** $25,000. **Training:** Yes.

18665 ■ Tuffy Auto Service Centers

Tuffy Associates Corp.
7150 Granite Cir.
Toledo, OH 43617
Ph: (419)865-6900
Free: 800-228-8339
Fax: (419)865-7343
Co. E-mail: jacobs@tuffy.com
URL: http://www.tuffy.com
Description: complete automotive repair franchise. **No. of Franchise Units:** 200. **No. of Company-Owned Units:** 23. **Founded:** 1970.. **Franchised:** 1971. **Equity Capital Needed:** $100,000 of liquid capital. **Franchise Fee:** $25,000. **Financial Assistance:** Yes. **Training:** 3 weeks initial training and ongoing support.

18666 ■ Tunex Automotive Specialists

Tunex Complete Car Care
Franchise Sales Dept.
12608 S 125 W, Ste. C
Draper, UT 84020
Ph: (801)676-8882
Free: 800-448-8639
Fax: (801)676-8887
Co. E-mail: info@tunex.com
URL: http://www.tunex.com
Description: Offers diagnostic services and repairs of engine related systems. **No. of Franchise Units:** 30. **No. of Company-Owned Units:** 1. **Founded:** 1974.. **Franchised:** 1995. **Equity Capital Needed:** $150,000-$235,000 total investment required, 30% liquid. **Franchise Fee:** $25,000. **Financial Assistance:** Yes. **Training:** 2 weeks initial training and 1 week during start-up of franchisee's business.

18667 ■ Valvoline Instant Oil Change

Ashland Inc.
3499 Blazer Pky.
Lexington, KY 40509
Ph: (859)357-7303
Free: 800-622-6846
Fax: (859)357-6919
Co. E-mail: jjtaylor@ashland.com
URL: http://www.viocfranchise.com
Description: Automobile oil change service. **No. of Franchise Units:** 612. **No. of Company-Owned Units:** 300. **Founded:** 1986.. **Franchised:** 1988. **Equity Capital Needed:** $800,000-$1,000,000 liquid assets/$1,000,000 net worth. **Franchise Fee:** $30,000. **Financial Assistance:** Yes. **Training:** Yes.

18668 ■ Ziebart

Ziebart International Corp.
1290 E Maple Rd.
Troy 48083-2817
Ph: (248)588-4100
Fax: (248)588-2513
Co. E-mail: info@ziebart.com
URL: http://www.ziebart.com
Description: Automotive application of detailing-accessories and protection services. **No. of Franchise Units:** 400. **No. of Company-Owned Units:**

14. **Founded:** 1954.. **Franchised:** 1962. **Equity Capital Needed:** $100,000-$250,000. **Franchise Fee:** $25,000. **Financial Assistance:** Yes. **Training:** Yes.

COMPUTERIZED DATABASES

18669 ■ *Audatex Collision Estimating Database*

15030 Ave. of Science, Ste. 100
San Diego, CA 92128
Ph: (858)946-1900
Free: 800-366-4237
Fax: (858)946-1073
Co. E-mail: SRCusomerService@audatex.com
URL: http://www.audatex.com
Availability: Online: Solera Holdings Inc. - Audatex North America Inc. **Type:** Software.

18670 ■ *International Petroleum Encyclopedia*

1421 S Sheridan Rd.
Tulsa, OK 74112
Ph: (918)835-3161
Free: 800-331-4463
Fax: (918)831-9497
Co. E-mail: headquarters@pennwell.com
URL: http://www.pennwell.com
Availability: CD-ROM: PennWell Corp. **Type:** Full-text; Statistical.

LIBRARIES

18671 ■ Automotive Service Association Library

8190 Precinct Line Rd.
Colleyville, TX 76034-7675
Ph: (817)514-2900
Free: 800-272-7467
Fax: (817)514-0770
Co. E-mail: asainfo@asashop.org
URL: http://www.asashop.org
Contact: Ron Pyle, President
Scope: Automotive repair. **Services:** Library open to the public for reference use only. **Founded:** 1951. **Holdings:** 130 video recordings; 8000 reports and industry related articles. **Subscriptions:** 50 journals and other serials.

18672 ■ Western Maryland Public Libraries - Regional Library

100 S. Potomac St.
Hagerstown, MD 21740
Ph: (301)739-3250
Fax: (301)739-5839
Co. E-mail: jthompson@washcolibrary.org
URL: http://www.westmdlib.info
Contact: Joe Thompson, Associate Director
Scope: Small business; antiques and collectibles; Civil Service and vocational tests; small scale farming. **Services:** Interlibrary loan; copying; library open to the public with restrictions. **Founded:** 1968. **Holdings:** 62,000 books; 2500 audiovisuals. **Subscriptions:** 3 newspapers.